THE ELEVENTH MENTAL
MEASUREMENTS YEARBOOK

EARLIER PUBLICATIONS IN THIS SERIES

THE ELEVENTH MENTAL MEASUREMENTS YEARBOOK

JACK J. KRAMER AND JANE CLOSE CONOLEY

Editors

LINDA L. MURPHY

Managing Editor

The Buros Institute of Mental Measurements
The University of Nebraska-Lincoln
Lincoln, Nebraska

1992
Distributed by The University of Nebraska Press

Note to Users

TABLE OF CONTENTS

INTRODUCTION

The publication of *The Eleventh Mental Measurements Yearbook* (*11th MMY*) continues the historic mission of the Buros Institute of Mental Measurements to provide test users with descriptive information, references, and critical reviews of commercially published English-language tests. Criteria for inclusion of a test in the *11th MMY* are that the test be new or revised since last reviewed in the *MMY* series. Descriptive information about the contents and use of the newest Buros Institute of Mental Measurements publication is provided below.

THE ELEVENTH MENTAL MEASUREMENTS YEARBOOK

The *11th MMY* contains reviews of tests that are new or significantly revised since the publication of the *10th MMY* in 1989. We have included reviews of tests that were available before our production deadline of January 1992. Reviews, descriptions, and references associated with older tests can be located in other Buros publications such as previous *MMY*s and *Tests in Print III*.

The contents of the *11th MMY* include: (a) a bibliography of 477 commercially available tests, new or revised, published as separates for use with English-speaking subjects; (b) 703 critical test reviews by well-qualified professional people who were selected by the editors on the basis of their expertise in measurement and, often, the content of the test being reviewed; (c) bibliographies of references for specific tests related to the construction, validity, or use of the tests in various settings; (d) a test title index with appropriate cross-references; (e) a classified subject index; (f) a publishers directory and index, including addresses and test listings by publisher; (g) a name index including the names of all authors of tests, reviews, or references; (h) an index of acronyms for easy reference when a test acronym, not the full title, is known; and (i) a score index to refer readers to tests featuring particular kinds of scores that are of interest to them.

The volume is organized like an encyclopedia, with tests being ordered alphabetically by title. If the title of a test is known, the reader can locate the test immediately without having to consult the Index of Titles.

The page headings reflect the encyclopedic organization. The page heading of the left-hand page cites the number and title of the first test listed on that page, and the page heading of the right-hand page cites the number and title of the last test listed on that page. All numbers presented in the various indexes are test numbers, not page numbers. Page numbers are important only for the Table of Contents and are indicated at the bottom of each page.

TESTS AND REVIEWS

The *11th MMY* contains descriptive information on 477 tests as well as 703 test reviews by 412 different authors. The reviewed tests have generated 3,221 references in the professional literature and reviewers have supplied 1,161 additional references in their reviews.

Table 1 presents statistics on the number and percentage of tests in each of 18 major classifications. A new category, Behavior Assessment, has been added since the publication of the *10th MMY*.

One area, Foreign Languages, had no tests included in the *11th MMY*.

TABLE 1
TESTS BY MAJOR CLASSIFICATIONS

Classification	Number	Percentage
Personality	135	28.3
Vocations	84	17.6
Developmental	33	6.9
English	32	6.7
Education	29	6.1
Miscellaneous	29	6.1
Achievement	22	4.6
Intelligence and Scholastic Aptitude	22	4.6
Reading	21	4.4
Speech and Hearing	20	4.2
Mathematics	14	2.9
Neuropsychological	14	2.9
Behavior Assessment	10	2.1
Sensory-Motor	6	1.3
Science	2	.4
Social Studies	2	.4
Fine Arts	1	.2
Multi-Aptitude Batteries	1	.2
Total	**477**	**100.0**

Table 2 provides the percentages of new and revised or supplemented tests according to major classifications. Overall, almost three-fourths of the tests included in the *11th MMY* are new and have not been listed in a previous *MMY*. The Index of Titles can be consulted to determine if a test is new or revised.

TABLE 2
NEW AND REVISED OR SUPPLEMENTED TESTS BY MAJOR CLASSIFICATIONS

Classification	Number of Tests	Percentage New	Revised
Achievement	22	40.9	59.1
Behavior Assessment	10	80.0	20.0
Developmental	33	93.9	6.1
Education	29	75.9	24.1
English	32	56.3	43.7
Fine Arts	1	100.0	.0
Intelligence and Scholastic Aptitude	22	36.4	63.6
Mathematics	14	57.1	42.9
Miscellaneous	29	86.2	13.8
Multi-Aptitude Batteries	1	100.0	.0
Neuropsychological	14	85.7	14.3
Personality	135	79.3	20.7
Reading	21	76.2	23.8
Science	2	100.0	.0
Sensory-Motor	6	66.7	33.3
Social Studies	2	50.0	50.0
Speech and Hearing	20	80.0	20.0
Vocations	84	77.4	22.6
Total	**477**	**74.2**	**25.8**

Our goal is to include all English language, commercially published tests that are new or revised. No minimal standards exist and inclusion of a test in the *MMY* does not mean that a test has met any standard of "goodness." We attempt to gather all tests, good and bad alike. We select our reviewers carefully and let well-informed readers decide for themselves about the quality of the tests.

Table 3 presents statistics on the review coverage for the various classifications. The *11th MMY* contains 703 reviews spread across 411 tests. Over 85% of the tests included in the *11th MMY* are reviewed, with more than 60% of the tests having two reviews.

TABLE 3
TESTS REVIEWS IN THE 11TH MMY

Classification	Number of Reviews	Number of Tests Reviewed	Percentage of Tests 1 or More Reviews	2 or More Reviews
Achievement	39	21	95.5	81.8
Behavior Assessment	18	10	100.0	80.0
Developmental	58	33	100.0	75.8
Education	45	25	86.2	69.0
English	49	29	90.6	62.5
Fine Arts	0	0	.0	.0
Intelligence and Scholastic Aptitude	35	20	90.9	68.2
Mathematics	28	14	100.0	100.0
Miscellaneous	43	24	82.8	65.5
Multi-Aptitude Batteries	2	1	100.0	100.0
Neuropsychological	23	14	100.0	64.3
Personality	201	121	88.9	60.7
Reading	36	19	90.5	81.0
Science	0	0	.0	.0
Sensory-Motor	10	5	83.3	83.3
Social Studies	4	2	100.0	100.0
Speech and Hearing	29	19	95.0	50.0
Vocations	83	55	65.5	33.3
Total	**703**	**412**	**86.2**	**61.4**

Because there are too many new and revised tests to permit all to be reviewed, some tests have had to be given priority over others. The highest priority has been given to tests sold commercially in the United States. Some tests have not been reviewed because (a) they were published too late to meet our production schedule; (b) competent reviewers could not be located; (c) persons who agreed to review did not meet their commitment; or (d) reviews were rejected as not meeting minimum *MMY* standards.

The selection of reviewers was done with great care. The objective was to secure measurement and subject specialists who represent a variety of different viewpoints. It was also important to find individuals who would write critical reviews competently, judiciously, and fairly. Reviewers were identified by means of extensive searches of the professional literature, attendance at professional meetings, recommendations from leaders in various professional fields, previous performance on earlier reviews, and through what might best be described as general professional knowledge. Perusal of reviews in this volume will also reveal that reviewers work in and represent a cross-section of the places in society in which tests are taught and used: universities, public schools, business, community agencies, private practice, and beyond. These reviewers represent an outstanding array of professional talent, and their contributions are obviously of primary importance in making this *Yearbook* a valuable resource.

Readers of test reviews in the *11th MMY* are encouraged to exercise an active, analytical, and evaluative perspective in reading the reviews. Just as one would evaluate a test, the reader should evaluate critically the reviewer's comments about the test. The reviewers selected are outstanding professionals in their respective fields, but it is inevitable that their reviews also reflect their individual learning histories. The *Mental Measurements Yearbooks* are intended to stimulate critical thinking about the selection of the best available test for a given purpose, not the passive acceptance of reviewer judgment. Active, evaluative reading is the key to the most effective use of the professional expertise offered in each of the reviews.

REVIEWS OF COMPUTER-BASED TEST INTERPRETATIVE SYSTEMS

There has been a dramatic increase in the number and type of computer-based-test-interpretative systems (CBTI). We had considered publishing a separate volume to track the quality of such systems. Our hopes to do so were frustrated, however, by the difficulty we encountered in accessing from the publishers the test programs and more importantly the algorithms in use by the computer-based systems.

Several reviews were accomplished before we abandoned the project as an endeavor separate from the *MMY*. These reviews are included in this volume. We are deliberating about our future involvement with CBTI, but are very grateful to the authors who completed reviews of various systems.

REFERENCES

This *Yearbook* lists a total of 4,382 references related to the development, psychometric quality, and use of specific tests. This figure may be slightly inflated because a reference involving more than one test may be listed under each of the tests in question, or because of overlap between the "Test References" section and the "Reviewer's References" section for a given test. The "Reviewer's References" section groups the reviewer's references in one convenient listing for easy identification and use by the reader. Of the total of 4,382 references, 3,221 are included under "Test References" and 1,161 are included under "Reviewer's References."

All references listed under "Test References" have been selected by Buros Institute staff searching through hundreds of professional journals. Because of the great proliferation of tests in recent years, it was decided to increase test and review coverage but to limit the increase in references by not including theses and dissertations. There is ample justification for this in that the findings from theses and dissertations, if worthwhile, usually find their way into the journal literature.

As has been traditional with Buros Institute publications, all references are listed chronologically and then alphabetically by author within year. The format for references in journals is author, year, title, journal, volume, and page numbers; for books it is author, year, title, place of publication, and publisher. A large number of additional references are listed in *Tests in Print III*, which was published in 1983.

Table 4 presents all tests in this *Yearbook* that generated more than 10 references. Within the table the tests are also rank-ordered according to number of references. This table refers only to those references listed under "Test References." The references are valuable as additions to our cumulative knowledge about specific tests, particularly as supplements to inhouse studies, and are also a useful resource for further research.

TABLE 4
NUMBER OF REFERENCES FOR MOST FREQUENTLY CITED TESTS

Name of Test	Number of References
Minnesota Multiphasic Personality Inventory-2	637
Beck Depression Inventory [Revised Edition]	286
Child Behavior Checklist	216
Wechsler Memory Scale—Revised	166
Peabody Individual Achievement Test—Revised	125
Wechsler Preschool and Primary Scale of Intelligence—Revised	118
California Psychological Inventory, Revised Edition	108
Luria-Nebraska Neuropsychological Battery: Forms I and II	105
[Bender-Gestalt Test]	92
Tennessee Self-Concept Scale [Revised]	89
Conners' Rating Scales	83
Revised Behavior Problem Checklist	80
Gates-MacGinitie Reading Test, Third Edition	78
Stanford Achievement Test, Eighth Edition	78
Millon Clinical Multiaxial Inventory—II	74
Comprehensive Tests of Basic Skills, Fourth Edition	70
Children's Depression Inventory	63
Shipley Institute of Living Scale	56
Otis-Lennon School Ability Test, Sixth Edition	48
SRA Achievement Series, Forms 1 and 2, and Survey of Basic Skills, Forms P and Q	46
Neale Analysis of Reading Ability, Revised British Edition	41
Defining Issues Test	34
FACES III	26
KeyMath Revised: A Diagnostic Inventory of Essential Mathematics	26
Iowa Tests of Basic Skills, Form J	24
Global Assessment Scale	22
Test of Language Development-2 Primary	20
Dyadic Adjustment Scale	17

TABLE 4 CONT'D.

NUMBER OF REFERENCES FOR MOST FREQUENTLY CITED TESTS

Name of Test	Number of References
Jr.-Sr. High School Personality Questionnaire	17
Ways of Coping Questionnaire, Research Edition	16
Mathematics Anxiety Rating Scale	15
Beck Hopelessness Scale	13
Student Developmental Task and Lifestyle Inventory	13
Arizona Articulation Proficiency Scale, Second Edition	12
Whitaker Index of Schizophrenic Thinking	12
The Problem Solving Inventory	11
Dimensions of Self-Concept	10
Wonderlic Personnel Test	10

INDEXES

As mentioned earlier, the *11th MMY* includes six indexes invaluable as aids to effective use: (*a*) Index of Titles, (*b*) Index of Acronyms, (*c*) Classified Subject Index, (*d*) Publishers Directory and Index, (*e*) Index of Names, and (*f*) Score Index. Additional comment on these indexes will be presented below.

Index of Titles. Because the organization of the *11th MMY* is encyclopedic in nature, with the tests ordered alphabetically by title throughout the volume, the test title index does not have to be consulted to find a test for which the title is known. However, the title index has some features that make it useful beyond its function as a complete title listing. First, it includes cross-reference information useful for tests with superseded or alternative titles or tests commonly (and sometimes inaccurately) known by multiple titles. Second, it identifies tests that are new or revised. It is important to keep in mind that the numbers in this index, like those for all *MMY* indexes, are test numbers and not page numbers.

Index of Acronyms. Some tests seem to be better known by their acronyms than by their full titles. The Index of Acronyms can help in these instances; it refers the reader to the full title of the test and to the relevant descriptive information and reviews.

Classified Subject Index. The Classified Subject Index classifies all tests listed in the *11th MMY* into 18 major categories: Achievement, Behavior Assessment, Developmental, Education, English, Fine Arts, Intelligence and Scholastic Aptitude, Mathematics, Miscellaneous, Multi-Aptitude Batteries, Neuropsychological, Personality, Reading, Science, Sensory-Motor, Social Studies, Speech and Hearing, and Vocations. Each test entry includes test title, population for which the test is intended, and test number. The Classified Subject Index is of great help to readers who seek a listing of tests in given subject areas. The Classified Subject Index represents a starting point for readers who know their area of interest but do not know how to further focus that interest in order to identify the best test(s) for their particular purposes.

Publishers Directory and Index. The Publishers Directory and Index includes the names and addresses of the publishers of all tests included in the *11th MMY* plus a listing of test numbers for each individual publisher. This index can be particularly useful in obtaining addresses for specimen sets or catalogs after the test reviews have been read and evaluated. It can also be useful when a reader knows the publisher of a certain test but is uncertain about the test title, or when a reader is interested in the range of tests published by a given publisher.

Index of Names. The Index of Names provides a comprehensive list of names, indicating authorship of a test, test review, or reference.

Score Index. The Score Index is an index to all scores generated by the tests in the *11th MMY*. Test titles are sometimes misleading or ambiguous, and test content may be difficult to define with precision. But test scores represent operational definitions of the variables the test author is trying to measure, and as such they often define test purpose and content more adequately than other descriptive information. A search for a particular test is most often a search for a test that measures some specific variables. Test scores and their associated labels can often be the best definitions of the variables of interest. It is, in fact, a detailed subject index based on the most critical operational features of any test—the scores and their associated labels.

HOW TO USE THIS YEARBOOK

A reference work like *The Eleventh Mental Measurements Yearbook* can be of far greater benefit to a reader if a little time is taken to become familiar with what it has to offer and how one might most effectively use it to obtain the information wanted. The first step in this process is to read the Introduction to the *11th MMY* in its entirety. The second step is to become familiar with the six indexes and particularly with the instructions preceding each index listing. The third step is to make actual use of the book by looking up needed information. This third step is simple if one keeps in mind the following possibilities:

1. If you know the title of the test, use the alphabetical page headings to go directly to the test entry.

2. If you do not know, cannot find, or are unsure of the title of a test, consult the Index of Titles for possible variants of the title or consult the appropriate subject area of the Classified Subject Index for other possible leads or for similar or related tests in the same area. (Other uses for both of these indexes were described earlier.)

3. If you know the author of a test but not the title or publisher, consult the Index of Names and look up the author's titles until you find the test you want.

4. If you know the test publisher but not the title or author, consult the Publishers Directory and Index and look up the publisher's titles until you find the test you want.

5. If you are looking for a test that yields a particular kind of score, but have no knowledge of which test that might be, look up the score in the Score Index and locate the test or tests that include the score variable of interest.

6. Once you have found the test or tests you are looking for, read the descriptive entries for these tests carefully so that you can take advantage of the information provided. A description of the information provided in these test entries will be presented later in this section.

7. Read the test reviews carefully and analytically, as described earlier in this Introduction. The information and evaluation contained in these reviews are meant to assist test consumers in making well-informed decisions about the choice and applications of tests.

8. Once you have read the descriptive information and test reviews, you may want to order a specimen set for a particular test so that you can examine it firsthand. The Publishers Directory and Index has the address information needed to obtain specimen sets or catalogs.

Making Effective Use of the Test Entries. The test entries include extensive information. For each test, descriptive information is presented in the following order:

a) TITLES. Test titles are printed in boldface type. Secondary or series titles are set off from main titles by a colon.

b) PURPOSE. For each test we have included a brief, clear statement describing the purpose of the test. Often these statements are quotations from the test manual.

c) POPULATION. This is a description of the groups for which the test is intended. The grade, chronological age, semester range, or employment category is usually given. "Grades 1.5–2.5, 2–3, 4–12, 13–17" means that there are four test booklets: a booklet for the middle of first grade through the middle of the second grade, a booklet for the beginning of the second grade through the end of third grade, a booklet for grades 4 through 12 inclusive, and a booklet for undergraduate and graduate students in colleges and universities.

d) PUBLICATION DATE. The inclusive range of publication dates for the various forms, accessories, and editions of a test is reported.

e) ACRONYM. When a test is often referred to by an acronym, the acronym is given in the test entry immediately following the publication date.

f) SCORES. The number of part scores is presented along with their titles or descriptions of what they are intended to represent or measure.

g) ADMINISTRATION. Individual or group administration is indicated. A test is considered a group test unless it may be administered *only* individually.

h) FORMS, PARTS, AND LEVELS. All available forms, parts, and levels are listed.

i) MANUAL. Notation is made if no manual is available. All other manual information is included under Price Data.

j) RESTRICTED DISTRIBUTION. This is noted only for tests that are put on a special market by the publisher. Educational and psychological restrictions are not noted (unless a special training course is required for use).

k) PRICE DATA. Price information is reported for test packages (usually 20 to 35 tests), answer sheets, all other accessories, and specimen sets. The statement "$17.50 per 35 tests" means that all accessories are included unless otherwise indicated by the reporting of separate prices for accessories. The statement also means 35 tests of one level, one edition, or one part unless stated otherwise. Because test prices can change very quickly, the year that the listed test prices were obtained is also given. Foreign currency is assigned the appropriate symbol. When prices are given in foreign dollars, a qualifying symbol is added (e.g., A$16.50 refers to 16 dollars and 50 cents in Australian currency). Along with cost, the publication date and number of pages on which print occurs is reported for manuals and technical reports (e.g., '85, 102 pages). All types of machine-scorable answer sheets available for use with a specific test are also reported in the descriptive entry. Scoring and reporting services provided by publishers are reported along with information on costs. In a few cases, special computerized scoring and interpretation services are given in separate entries immediately following the test.

l) FOREIGN LANGUAGE AND OTHER SPECIAL EDITIONS. This section concerns foreign language editions published by the same publisher who sells the English edition. It also indicates special editions (e.g., Braille, large type) available from the same or a different publisher.

m) TIME. The number of minutes of actual working time allowed examinees and the approximate length of time needed for administering a test are reported whenever obtainable. The latter figure is always enclosed in parentheses. Thus, "50(60) minutes" indicates that the examinees are allowed 50 minutes of working time and that a total of 60 minutes is needed to administer the test. A time of "40–50 minutes" indicates an untimed test that takes approximately 45 minutes to administer, or—in a few instances—a test so timed that working time and administration time are very difficult to disentangle. When the time necessary to administer a test is not reported or suggested in the test materials but has been obtained through correspondence with the test publisher or author, the time is enclosed in brackets.

n) COMMENTS. Some entries contain special

notations, such as: "for research use only"; "revision of the ABC Test"; "tests administered monthly at centers throughout the United States"; "subtests available as separates"; and "verbal creativity." A statement such as "verbal creativity" is intended to further describe what the test claims to measure. Some of the test entries include factual statements that imply criticism of the test, such as "1980 test identical with test copyrighted 1970."

o) AUTHOR. For most tests, all authors are reported. In the case of tests that appear in a new form each year, only authors of the most recent forms are listed. Names are reported exactly as printed on test booklets. Names of editors generally are not reported.

p) PUBLISHER. The name of the publisher or distributor is reported for each test. Foreign publishers are identified by listing the country in brackets immediately following the name of the publisher. The Publishers Directory and Index must be consulted for a publisher's address.

q) FOREIGN ADAPTATIONS. Revisions and adaptations of tests for foreign use are listed in a separate paragraph following the original edition.

r) SUBLISTINGS. Levels, editions, subtests, or parts of a test available in separate booklets are sometimes presented as sublistings with titles set in small capitals. Sub-sublistings are indented and titles are set in italic type.

s) CROSS REFERENCES. For tests that have been listed previously in a Buros Institute publication, a test entry includes—if relevant—a final paragraph containing a cross reference to the reviews, excerpts, and references for that test in those volumes. In the cross references, "T3:467" refers to test 467 in *Tests in Print III*, "8:1023" refers to test 1023 in *The Eighth Mental Measurements Yearbook*, "T2:144" refers to test 144 in *Tests in Print II*, "7:637" refers to test 637 in *The Seventh Mental Measurements Yearbook*, "P:262" refers to test 262 in *Personality Tests and Reviews I*, "2:1427" refers to test 1427 in *The 1940 Yearbook*, and "1:1110" refers to test 1110 in *The 1938 Yearbook*. In the case of batteries and programs, the paragraph also includes cross references—from the battery to the separately listed subtests and vice versa—to entries in this volume and to entries and reviews in earlier *Yearbooks*. Test numbers not preceded by a colon refer to tests in this *Yearbook*; for example, "see 45" refers to test 45 in this *Yearbook*.

If a reader finds something in a test description that is not understood, the descriptive material presented above can be referred to again and can often help to clarify the matter.

ACKNOWLEDGEMENTS

The publication of the *11th Mental Measurements Yearbook* could not have been accomplished without the contributions of many individuals. The editors acknowledge gratefully the talent, expertise, and dedication of all those who have assisted in the publication process.

Special thanks belong to Drs. Jill Harker, Michael Kavan, and James Impara who served as contributing editors to the *11th MMY*. We could not have completed the volume without their dedicated contributions. Their special insights into tests and measurements strengthened our review process significantly.

Linda Murphy, Managing Editor, is steadfast in her constant effort, knowledge, editorial skill, and cheerful attitude. She makes our job as editors easier than we could have imagined. Nor would the publication of this volume be possible without the efforts of Gary Anderson, Editorial Assistant, Rosemary Sieck, Word Processing Specialist, and Arlie Prokop, Editorial Assistant during the early stages of preparation. As always, their efforts go far beyond that required as part of normal job responsibilities. We are also pleased to acknowledge the continuous assistance available from the Director of the Buros Institute, Dr. Barbara Plake. Her enthusiasm for our work, visionary leadership, and skill in building a cohesive team effort are important to us all. The sense of accomplishment and pride we feel with the publication of the *11th MMY* is shared by our entire staff and our heartfelt thank you is extended to the individuals mentioned above.

Our gratitude is also extended to the many reviewers who have prepared test reviews for the Buros Institute. Their willingness to take time from busy professional schedules to share their expertise in the form of thoughtful test reviews is appreciated. *The Mental Measurements Yearbook* would not exist were it not for their efforts.

Many graduate students have contributed to the publication of this volume. Their efforts have included reviewing test catalogs, fact checking reviews, looking for test references, and innumerable other tasks. We thank Janet Allison, Carol Berigan, Dennison Bhola, Mike Bonner, Molly Geil, Haeok Kim, Maria Potenza, Mark Shriver, Richard Sonnenberg, Richard Taffe, Tracy Thorndike-Christ, Lori Wennstedt, and Kris Yates for their assistance.

Appreciation is also extended to our National and Departmental Advisory Committees for their willingness to assist in the operation of the Buros Institute. During the period in which this volume was prepared the National Advisory Committee has included Luella Buros, Stephen Elliott, William Mehrens, Lawrence Rudner, Douglas Whitney, and Frank Womer.

During the production of the *11th MMY* a tragic event robbed the measurement community of one of its brilliant members. T. Anne Cleary, formerly a member of our advisory panel, was killed at the University of Iowa in 1991. We miss her and add a special acknowledgment of her influence on the development of the Institute.

The Buros Institute is part of the Department of Educational Psychology of the University of Nebraska-Lincoln and we have benefitted from the many departmental colleagues who have contributed to our Departmental Advisory Committee including Collie Conoley, Terry Gutkin, Gregg Schraw, Gargi Sodowsky, and Steven Wise. Collie deserves some special recognition for his efforts in regard to the reviews of CBTI products that are included in this volume. We are also grateful for the contribution of the University of Nebraska Press, which provides expert consultation and serves as distributor of the *MMY* series.

This volume would have taken much longer to produce were it not for the efforts of Dave Spanel, Tim Myers, and their colleagues at the UNL Computing Resource Center. We thank them for their assistance in organizing our information for printing.

Our thanks also go to Ken Tornvall and his staff at Port City Press, Inc. for their care and pride in the composition, printing, and binding of this and previous volumes. Their willingness to meet impossible deadlines is much appreciated.

Luella Buros maintains an inspiring interest in and involvement with the Buros Institute. We are constantly motivated by her unflagging commitment to the work begun by Oscar Buros over a half century ago.

Finally, none of what we accomplish as editors would be as meaningful without the support of our families. Thanks Jeannie, Jamie, Jessica, Collie, Brian, Colleen, and Collin.

SUMMARY

The *MMY* series is a valuable resource for people interested in studying or using testing. Once the process of using the series is understood, a reader can gain rapid access to a wealth of information. Our hope is that with the publication of the *11th MMY*, test authors and publishers will consider carefully the comments made by the reviewers and continue to refine and perfect their assessment products.

Tests and Reviews

[1]

Abuse Risk Inventory for Women, Experimental Edition.

Purpose: To identify women who are current victims of abuse or who are at risk for abuse by their male intimate partners or ex-partners.

Population: Women seeking medical or mental health services.

Publication Date: 1989.

Acronym: ARI.

Scores: Total score only.

Administration: Group and individual.

Price Data, 1990: $8 per 25 test booklets; $2 per scoring key; $12 per manual (23 pages); $15 per specimen set (includes manual, test booklet, scoring key).

Time: (10–15) minutes.

Comments: Test booklet title is Interpersonal Relationship Survey; self-administered.

Author: Bonnie L. Yegidis.

Publisher: Consulting Psychologists Press, Inc.

Review of the Abuse Risk Inventory for Women, Experimental Edition by CYNTHIA A. ROHR-BECK, Associate Professor of Psychology, The George Washington University, Washington, DC:

The Abuse Risk Inventory for Women (ARI) was developed to "identify women who are current victims of abuse or are at risk of abuse by their male intimate partners or ex-partners." In this case, "abuse" refers to physical assault that is likely to cause injury. The author notes that abused women may seek treatment for depression, anxiety, etc., rather than for problems with abuse. Thus, the ARI was designed to serve as a screening instrument for potentially abused women receiving medical care from health care providers or social service agencies.

The scale provides an alternative to direct questions, based on the assumption that some women may not respond truthfully or may misinterpret what the clinician means by abuse; however, the manual does not cite any studies that provide empirical evidence for this assumption. However, at least several items on the ARI appear to be obvious questions about abuse. Yet, the ARI does not attempt to detect if respondents may be lying, being overly defensive, or providing socially desirable responses. Thus, it is not clear why women would respond to this measure in a more open way than they would to direct questions about abuse. This would be an important empirical question to investigate in order to show the usefulness of the ARI.

The ARI items were not derived from a unified theoretical base; rather, they were developed based on a review of the literature examining psychosocial correlates of spouse abuse. They appear to reflect factors such as economic stress, sexual dissatisfaction, past history of physical aggression in the relationship, and substance use by the spouse. The manual does not specify how these domains were selected, or how and why specific items from particular domains were generated. Point-biserial correlations of each item with the criterion (physical abuse in the past) are not provided; therefore, the usefulness of each item is unclear. Because many ARI items appear to overlap with items on other measures of different constructs (e.g., measures of conflict resolution and marital satisfaction), the uniqueness of the ARI is not clear at this time.

The one-page ARI is entitled "Interpersonal Relationship Survey." The first 15 items focus on the husband/partner and the remaining 10 items are questions about the couple. The scale could be self-administered, given a certain level of reading ability (not specified in the manual). The ARI is simple enough to allow supervised nonprofessionals to administer it and could be easily scored by hand (a scoring key is provided). Each item is answered on a 4-point scale (*Rarely or Never, Sometimes, Often,* and *Always*). Total scores range from 25 to 100; however, the author's assumption of an interval-level scale could be questioned. According to the manual, a score above the cutoff point of 50 suggests that the respondent may be in an abusive situation or be at risk for abuse.

On the reverse side of the ARI is a brief, demographic questionnaire that also contains four questions (with a *yes-no* format) that ask whether the respondent has ever been physically, emotionally, or sexually assaulted by a male partner or other male relative. These questions are designed for future research purposes.

The test is accompanied by a brief, 23-page manual that presents the current reliability and validity status of the ARI. A strength of the manual is the extent to which the author cautions about inappropriate use of the ARI because its psychometric properties are still under investigation.

Initial analyses of a 34-item ARI resulted in a 31-item preliminary version, which was later cut to a final version of 25 items. Although an initial factor analysis suggested the possibility of a two-factor structure, the author notes that these factors are only tentative and recommends that users interpret only the ARI total score.

Reliability information is available only for internal consistency; test-retest reliability is still needed to establish the stability of the inventory over time. The final version of the ARI has shown an alpha reliability of .88 for a combined sample of abused women (in spouse abuse shelters) and a comparison group, whereas the internal consistency reliability was slightly lower (.73) for a group of nonvictimized college women.

A major concern with the scale is the limited amount of validity information available to date. With reference to the scale's construct validity, it is not clear how individual items that reflect specific correlates of spouse abuse were selected. The preliminary version of the ARI showed concurrent validity when it successfully discriminated a group of abused women from a comparison group, classifying approximately 88% of the cases correctly. Several studies have examined the concurrent validity of the final ARI version. In these studies, the question about physical abuse on the demographic questionnaire has frequently been the criterion for determining whether or not the client has been abused. According to the manual, about 78% of

subjects seeking marital/relationship counseling from family service agencies were correctly classified in one study. In contrast, about 44% of abused participants with higher SES did not score above the cutoff score. No evidence of predictive validity is presented for the ARI; therefore, it should not be used to predict future abuse.

In summary, the ARI still lacks critical psychometric data. Given its potential for misuse, its clinical utility is tenuous. Although the manual clearly states that the ARI may be valid only for moderate to lower SES populations (and only for *physical* spouse abuse), researchers and clinicians might use the ARI with substantially different populations. Given this limitation, ARI items might be more useful incorporated in a structured interview procedure, especially for those clients who are reluctant to discuss abuse. The test author suggests using the ARI to obtain additional information for marital counseling or for evaluating treatment programs designed to reduce physical abuse, while noting that no validity evidence exists for these uses at this time.

Review of the Abuse Risk Inventory for Women, Experimental Edition by JANICE G. WILLIAMS, Assistant Professor of Psychology, Clemson University, Clemson, SC:

The Abuse Risk Inventory for Women (ARI) is intended as a screening device for detection of current or potential abuse from a male partner or husband. Because women may be reluctant to admit abuse, the 25 questionnaire items are drawn from the literature on those characteristics associated with abuse. For this reason, the scale is not high in face validity. Two items ask the respondent about being slapped or shoved by her partner. Other items assess characteristics of the male partner (drug use and frustrations with work) and characteristics of the relationship (response to financial problems and strategies for coping with conflict). These characteristics are consistent with those reported in the literature to be associated with abuse (Williams, 1987). The response format is a 4-point Likert scale, ranging from *Rarely or Never* to *Always*. The reverse side of the questionnaire is a research instrument that requests the respondent to provide sociodemographic information and any history of abuse for both the respondent and the male partner.

TEST DEVELOPMENT AND NORMS. The manual presents information on the rationale for item development and selection. Although the final scale consists of 25 items, the manual provides data on preliminary versions of the scale, which included more items. Very little in the way of normative data are given, other than some means and standard deviations for groups used for item selection and estimation of reliability and validity. The standard error of measurement is reported, along with instructions for establishing confidence intervals for individual scores.

RELIABILITY. The scale was constructed as a unidimensional measure. One coefficient alpha (.88) is presented for a sample of 193 women; however, this sample was used for both item selection and estimation of reliability, so that it may overestimate the internal consistency of the scale. An additional study with college students produced a more moderate (.73) coefficient alpha. An exploratory factor analysis of the preliminary version is also described. This analysis suggested that there may be two underlying factors for the ARI: (a) Communication and Conflict Resolution Skills and (b) Intimacy.

VALIDITY. Preliminary studies suggested that a cutoff score of 50 maximized correct classifications of respondents. Validity studies reported in the manual showed that the ARI correctly classified 56% to 94% of women. The higher percentages are found in studies where subjects were known to be battered or were seeking family counseling services. The low figure was obtained in a study of employees of a service agency. The base rate of self-reported abuse was quite low among the employees; it is likely that the high rate of misclassification is simply attributable to the low incidence of abuse in the population. Although the manual suggests caution in using only the ARI to decide that a woman has experienced abuse, it does not discuss the different costs of false positive and false negative outcomes with the cutoff score.

STRENGTHS. The ARI is inexpensive, brief, and easy to administer and score. The indirect nature of the measure may enable determination of possible abuse early in intervention, when direct questions about abuse might be too threatening. Because the scale exhibits low face validity, respondents may be less inclined to give socially desirable answers. The manual provides clear, cautious instructions for the use of the scale. There is some indication that the scale is reliable and valid enough to be used to generate hypotheses about individuals in clinical settings, which can be further tested by other means. Researchers may also find the scale useful for assessing characteristics that are associated with abusive relationships.

WEAKNESSES. Both the results of the validity studies and the manual indicate that the ARI may be useful only with low-income women or populations with an increased likelihood of abuse. This limitation is probably a reflection of the inherent difficulty of correctly detecting any low-frequency phenomenon. It is unclear why the items assess characteristics of the partner rather than characteristics of the respondent, such as physical health, accidents (Follingstad, Brennan, Hause, Polek, & Rutledge, 1991), or perceived dependence on the

relationship (Williams, 1987). Placing the research instrument on the reverse side of the inventory could pose a problem in some instances because respondents who read the research items would likely be sensitized to the purpose of the measure. Additionally, the manual does not specify the required reading level for respondents, which may be of concern for the targeted population. Because there are few data available on the ARI, the relationship between scores on the ARI and other potentially relevant constructs, such as social desirability, is unknown.

SUMMARY. The ARI is a new self-report instrument designed to measure indirectly the experience of abuse or women who are at risk for abuse. As an experimental measure, the ARI may be useful in clinical settings for identifying potential abuse problems. Any hypotheses generated on the basis of ARI scores should certainly be verified with other measures. Preliminary estimates of reliability and validity are encouraging, but additional data would be helpful. It appears the ARI will be most useful in populations where the incidence of abuse is likely to be relatively high.

REVIEWER'S REFERENCES

Williams, J. H. (1987). *Psychology of women: Behavior in a biosocial context* (3rd ed.). New York, Norton.

Follingstad, D. R., Brennan, A. F., Hause, E. S., Polek, D. S., & Rutledge, L. L. (1991). Factors moderating physical and psychological symptoms of battered women. *Journal of Family Violence, 6*, 81-95.

[2]
ACER Word Knowledge Test.

Purpose: Constructed to assess verbal skills and general reasoning ability.

Population: Australian years 9–11.

Publication Dates: 1984–90.

Scores: Total score only.

Administration: Group.

Editions, 2: E, F.

Restricted Distribution: Distribution of Form E restricted to personnel use.

Price Data, 1990: $1.95 per reusable test booklet; $3.50 per 10 answer sheets; $3 per scoring stencil; $15 per manual ('90, 44 pages); $20.30 per specimen set (specify Form E or F).

Time: 10(20) minutes.

Comments: Replacement for the ACER Adult Form B.

Author: Marion M. de Lemos.

Publisher: Australian Council for Educational Research Ltd. [Australia].

Review of the ACER Word Knowledge Test by J. DOUGLAS AYERS, Professor Emeritus, University of Victoria, Victoria, B. C., Canada:

The ACER Word Knowledge Test (WKT), Forms E and F, 1990 edition, is more a revision than a new edition, being based on a pool of 350 items selected from the 1960, Form B, WKT and several very old forms of the ACER Silent Reading Tests. It is a highly speeded (10 minute), 72-item, five-choice synonyms test without context.

The WKT was standardized in 1986 at the same time as the ACER Test of Reasoning Ability (TRA) and the restandardization of the Standard Progressive Matrices (SPM). The sample was quite small varying from 188 grade 11 students for Form F to 242 students in grade 9 for Form E. Although the number of cases appears small, the two-stage sampling procedure by school and student, with schools selected on a probability proportional to size and state school population, was excellent and does not require samples as large as when all students in a class are used. More standardizations should be conducted in this fashion.

The tests have nine practice items, variously referred to as examples, questions, and problems, with clear directions and excellent format and color. The author is to be commended for meeting the cautions required by the *Standards for Educational and Psychological Testing* (AERA, APA, & NCME, 1985) in interpreting test results and for the comprehensive reporting of the standardization study. The results are related not only to the other two tests being standardized at the same time, namely the ACER Test of Reasoning Ability (TRA) and Standard Progressive Matrices (SPM), but also to socioeconomic data such as language background and father's occupation and to teacher's ratings for English, mathematics, and scholastic ability.

The author states that word knowledge tests have been found to correlate highly with other measures of verbal skills and general reasoning ability. The WKT is to be used primarily as a screening test in selection testing programs when administered with other general reasoning ability or specific aptitude tests. It is claimed that word knowledge tests have proved useful in selecting applicants for various trade courses that require a minimum level of language ability. However, with Form B of the WKT being used since 1960, it is surprising that there is no evidence to support its effectiveness as a screening instrument.

In support of the author's premise that the WKT is not only a verbal measure but also a measure of general reasoning ability, she refers to Cattell and quotes Jensen. Later, the author attempts to use correlation data to support this position. During the standardization it was found that correlations between the Test of Reasoning Ability and the WKT averaged .70 for the three grade groups. On this basis, the author claims the WKT provides a valid indication of verbal skill and verbal reasoning ability. With only 50% of the variance accounted for, such a claim is at best tenuous. Moreover, one might just as well claim that the TRA is a valid measure of verbal skills because it correlates with the WKT.

Before tryout, there was apparently very little selection or revision and no new items were written. This test then was a project of the Australian Council for Educational Research rather than an authored test. Tryout data indicated problems in obtaining point biserials above .20 for most of the difficult items. This is somewhat surprising with very homogeneous vocabulary items. As the key words did not have any context, perhaps many of the difficult items did not really have a clearly best answer.

Speed tests have pretty well disappeared, especially in areas where power is more important than speed as in vocabulary testing. Moreover, the standardization study showed that when the WKT was administered after either the TRA or the SPM there was a significant practice effect, and particularly when the prior test was timed rather than untimed. Such a finding has serious implications regarding the usefulness of the WKT as a screening instrument.

Overall, the test development was adequate, the standardization and associated studies exemplary, and the manual complete. The main criticisms are with the claims of what the test measures and with its effectiveness for selecting students for educational programs, either secondary or post-secondary. The onus is on the publisher to prove its effectiveness and also to show that it is a better predictor than achievement measures, such as reading comprehension and mathematics. If a test is to be used for selection purposes norming is not nearly as important as establishing cutoff points for various types of programs and determining the degree to which the test results give valid selection information useful in each of the programs.

REVIEWER'S REFERENCE

American Educational Research Association, American Psychological Association, & National Council on Measurement in Education. (1985). *Standards for educational and psychological testing.* Washington, DC: American Psychological Association, Inc.

Review of the ACER Word Knowledge Test by WILLIAM R. MERZ, SR., *Professor and Coordinator, School Psychology Training Program, California State University, Sacramento, Sacramento, CA:*

The ACER Word Knowledge Test is a group-administered, 72-item test with two parallel forms, designed to replace the ACER Word Knowledge Test Adult, Form B (ACER, 1960). Testing time is 10 minutes. The two forms include items from the ACER Word Knowledge Test Adult, Form B and word knowledge subtests of earlier silent reading tests. According to de Lemos (1990) the test measures acquired knowledge or crystallized intelligence (Cattell, 1963). It correlates with measures of general intelligence and is a reliable indicator of verbal skills and general reasoning ability. However, cautious interpretation of the scores for non-English-speaking individuals and those with severely deprived language backgrounds is advised.

The historical antecedents of this test go back to 1933. The ACER Word Knowledge Test Adult, Form B was devised for personnel selection and training in business and industry. Development of the present form began in 1981 and was completed with publication in 1990. Item trials were conducted with 600 apprenticeship applicants, who were 15–20 years old. Norming was accomplished with more than 1,200 secondary students in school years 9–11. Of course, at these age levels with the difference between Australian and United States education systems, the designation of grade (years) must be converted to an American context for use in the United States. Along with the ACER Test of Reasoning Ability (de Lemos, 1990) and the Standard Progressive Matrices (de Lemos, 1989), the two forms were administered concurrently to norm samples of 642 and 623 individuals respectively. Evidence of the reliability of performance is presented with KR-21 quotients ranging from .91–.94. Evidence of validity of generalization from scores is presented in two forms. Criterion-related evidence includes correlations with the timed and untimed administrations of the Standard Progressive Matrices and of the Reasoning Ability Test. Coefficients for the timed version of the Standard Progressive Matrices range from .39–.49; for the untimed version, from .28–.38; and for the Reasoning Abilities Test, from .68–.82.

Construct-related evidence of the validity of test scores is presented in studies of differences between the genders, among languages spoken in the home, and among language backgrounds of parents. Along with these is the effect of order of presentation. Conclusions drawn indicate that differences in order of presentation reflect practice effect due to familiarization with test taking. The author found no significant differences between performances of the two genders, although females tended to score slightly higher. Weighted means were used to compensate for the disproportionate numbers by gender. There were, as one might expect, significant differences between those speaking other languages in the home and those speaking English only. There were also significant differences found between the various language backgrounds of parents, with those students whose parents spoke another language consistently scoring lower than those students whose parents spoke English only. Additionally, a significant difference also occurred for socioeconomic status, which was derived from the father's occupation. The magnitude of differences in these studies is small, two raw score points in some cases. The practical significance of these differences may be questioned even though they do reach statistical significance.

The scores derived are converted to percentile ranks, stanines, and standard scores with means of 100 and a standard deviation of 15. The standardization sample for each form exceeds 600 individuals. Unfortunately, comparison among subgroups is hampered by the disproportion within subsets. Norms are presented by grade level with approximately 200 individuals for each of them.

The test is well constructed. Evidence indicates that scores derived from test performance reflect valid generalizations to measures of reasoning ability. Evidence for reliable interpretation of scores is presented as interitem coefficients. This raises a question about consistency over time. The numbers in the standardization sample are smaller than desirable so that norms for the genders, the language groups, and the socioeconomic classes could not be constructed. The disproportionate numbers within subsets affect generalization for evidence of validity, as well. Norms are presented for each of the grade levels, but even these numbers are relatively small. Their representativeness for selection and training groups is not discussed and may be open to question.

A larger problem is the domain to which the scores are generalized. The manual states that scores are related to acquired knowledge, crystallized intelligence, reasoning ability, and word knowledge. Generalizing to word knowledge is reasonable. Evidence for generalizing to reasoning ability is presented. Unfortunately, generalizing to the broader concepts of acquired knowledge or crystallized intelligence rests more on belief than on evidence. Although there is a large body of evidence relating vocabulary or word knowledge to general knowledge and intelligence, correlations presented in the manual for both forms and the Standard Progressive Matrices are so small in magnitude that generalizations to the construct, and crystallized intelligence, can be questioned. The correlations with the Reasoning Abilities Test are of a much higher magnitude than with the Progressive Matrices. The question is whether or not the Reasoning Abilities Test measures crystallized intelligence. Evidence relating performance on this test to acquired knowledge is thin, too. There is no evidence presented for a relationship between the Word Knowledge Test and acquired knowledge beyond the correlation with the Test of Reasoning Abilities. Does that test assess acquired knowledge?

Whether or not this test can be used effectively or successfully with American students is an open question. Norms are derived on individuals in the Australian education system at School Years (grades) 9, 10, and 11. How representative this is of adolescents and young adults in the United States must be seriously considered. Although various language groups are compared, systematic differences between Australian and American students do exist. There is no way to compare the performance of those of Mexican American or Afro-American descent to what is presented in the norm groups. For American groups, validity studies must be replicated with appropriate subgroups.

The ACER Word Knowledge Test, Forms E and F is well constructed. Evidence for reliable, valid generalizations from test scores to word knowledge is presented. However, how well the test measures general intelligence, acquired knowledge, and crystallized intelligence remains unanswered. For use as a word knowledge test in the United States, norms for American populations should be derived. Validity studies must be replicated to demonstrate that generalizations could be made from scores of American youth to the domains of interest. A clear domain definition would have to be made, as well, because the three constructs—acquired knowledge, general intelligence, and crystallized intelligence— are not sufficiently specified, and the rationale for selection of words included in the test is not presented beyond the statement that older word knowledge tests were used. In addition, if this test were to be used for personnel selection, job relatedness of word knowledge should be established.

The ACER Word Knowledge Test, Forms E and F is not recommended for use in the United States unless it is renormed on a representative American sample. It is not recommended for use in personnel selection until the specific domain, word knowledge, has been defined, the job relatedness of word knowledge has been established, and appropriate norms have been developed. For use in training, acceptable criteria and/or applicable norms would have to be established, as well.

REVIEWER'S REFERENCES

The Australian Council for Educational Research. (1960). ACER Word Knowledge Test, Adult Form B. Victoria, Australia: Author.
Cattell, R. B. (1963). Theory of fluid and crystallized intelligence: A critical experiment. *Journal of Educational Psychology, 54*, 1-22.
de Lemos, M. M. (1989). *Standard Progressive Matrices: Australian manual.* Victoria, Australia: The Australian Council for Educational Research.
de Lemos, M. M. (1990). ACER Test of Reasoning Ability. Victoria, Australia: The Australian Council for Educational Research.

[3]
Achievement Identification Measure— Teacher Observation.

Purpose: Identify underachievers.
Population: "Students in all grades."
Publication Date: 1988.
Acronym: AIM-TO.
Scores: 5 dimension scores: Competition, Responsibility, Achievement Communication, Independence/Dependence, Respect/Dominance.
Administration: Individual.
Price Data, 1990: $85 per set of 30 test booklets/answer sheets (scoring by publisher included).
Time: (20) minutes.
Comments: Ratings by teacher.
Author: Sylvia B. Rimm.

Publisher: Educational Assessment Service, Inc.

Review of the Achievement Identification Measure— Teacher Observation by WILLIAM P. ERCHUL, Associate Professor of Psychology and Director of the School Psychology Program, North Carolina State University, Raleigh, NC:

OVERVIEW. The Achievement Identification Measure—Teacher Observation (AIM-TO) is a teacher inventory designed to distinguish under-achieving students from achieving students. The inventory is based on Dr. Sylvia B. Rimm's clinical experiences in dealing with underachieving children and adolescents in their home and school environments. Rimm believes that once a student's characteristics relative to underachievement are identified through the use of the AIM-TO, preventive and/or remedial efforts can begin. It should be noted the manual does not present a definition of the construct of underachievement; given the multifaceted nature of underachievement (cf. Thorndike, 1963), this is an unfortunate omission.

The AIM-TO consists of 50 statements that describe student ($n = 47$) and parent ($n = 3$) behaviors and attitudes (e.g., "This student seems bored with school"). For each statement, the teacher-respondent selects one of five ratings: *No, To a small extent, Average, More than average,* or *Definitely.* Some may find it difficult to use this rating scale, which places absolute, criterion-referenced judgments (e.g., *No*) and norm-referenced judgments (e.g., *Average*) along the same continuum. Respondents mark their answers in a two-page booklet that is later forwarded to the Educational Assessment Service, Inc. for computer scoring. Although it is to the author's credit that computer scoring is provided, users may have to wait up to a month to receive their results.

Six scores result from the AIM-TO. These are an overall achiever characteristics score and five dimension (i.e., subscale) scores: Competition, Responsibility, Achievement Communication, Independence/Dependence, and Respect/Dominance.

NORMS AND SCORE INTERPRETATION. The current norms for the AIM-TO are based on a poorly characterized sample of "over 500 school-aged children" (Manual, p. 5) drawn from rural, urban, and suburban areas located in unspecified but diverse geographical areas in the United States. No information is offered regarding the socioeconomic status, ethnic origin, special education labels, etc., of subjects contained in the sample. It seems doubtful the current sample is representative of any group relevant to the interpretation of the AIM-TO. Although Rimm acknowledges that norming the inventory is an ongoing process, the failure to report sample means, standard deviations, and standard errors of measurement even at this point in the AIM-TO's early development represents a serious oversight. The gravity of this situation becomes more apparent when the author provides interpretations of scores based on bands of Normal Curve Equivalent (NCE) scores. For example, students whose AIM-TO NCE scores fall below the 40th percentile are "high risks for underachievement" (Manual, p. 5), and those falling between the 40th and 60th percentile "probably are having some problems related to school achievement already" (Manual, p. 5). In the absence of data supporting the establishment of these critical score levels, the author's interpretations are best regarded as conjectural.

RELIABILITY. Alpha reliability coefficients of .96 for an elementary school form and .97 for a secondary school form of the AIM-TO indicate that the inventory is internally consistent. No test-retest reliability data are reported. This deficit is very surprising in light of the fact Rimm proposes that the AIM-TO be used in pre-post comparisons. These data should be compiled. At present, there are no data available to support the reliability of any of the five subscales.

VALIDITY. The manual briefly presents two studies documenting the construct and criterion-related validity of the overall achiever characteristics score. Together, the studies offer preliminary evidence of the AIM-TO's validity. Although the five separate dimensions are described in considerable detail in the manual, there are no data offered to support their validity. Given the high alpha reliability coefficients for the overall achiever characteristics score, it seems unlikely there are really five underlying dimensions. It appears that a next logical step would be to perform a series of factor analyses to determine empirically: (a) whether or not all five specified dimensions Rimm proposes are defensible, and (b) which items load on which dimension.

CONCLUSION. Given the AIM-TO's present developmental state, one must seriously question the practical value of this teacher inventory. Few educational professionals I know would be willing to wait up to one month for a computer-generated report that presents the possibility that a particular student is underachieving. Although information obtained from the five subscales may be interesting, no data currently support their reliability or validity. Within the public schools today, there are certainly faster and equally valid methods of determining the presence and extent of underachievement, not the least of which are teacher observations and professional judgment. The conduct of additional reliability and validity studies, further development of norms, and establishment of a stronger link between the assessment the AIM-TO provides and subsequent psychoeducational intervention, may improve the AIM-TO's usefulness as a screening instrument for school-aged children.

REVIEWER'S REFERENCE

Thorndike, R. L. (1963). *The concepts of over- and under-achievement.* New York: Teachers College Press.

Review of the Achievement Identification Measure— Teacher Observation by GEOFFREY F. SCHULTZ, Associate Professor of Educational Psychology and Special Education, Indiana University-Northwest, Gary, IN:

The Achievement Identification Measure— Teacher Observation (AIM-TO) is an observational rating scale described in the user manual as "a teacher report of achievement characteristics for school-aged children." Additionally, this instrument is reported to be able to "distinguish achieving students from underachievers." At the same time, a supplementary text entitled *Underachievement Syndrome: Causes and Cures* (Rimm, 1986), identifying specific teacher or psychological strategies for remediating underachievement, is available through the author of the test and her publishing company. The test is attractively packaged and the educational problem with which the instrument deals is of special importance to those professionals working with children. There are a number of technological and methodological questions, however, that raise serious concerns about reliability of the instrument and its valid use.

ADMINISTRATION AND SCORING. Ratings of the student's achievement behavior are derived by the classroom teacher using 50 descriptive items. The items are contained in a two-page booklet and are constructed using a 5-point Likert scale ranging from (5) *definitely* to (1) *no*. Total time for rating the student may be as little as 10 minutes if the teacher knows the student very well. Scores are reported in terms of an overall achievement characteristic score and five subscale or dimension scores. The dimension scores are in the areas of: Competition, Responsibility, Achievement Communication, Independence/Dependence, and Respect/Dominance.

Actual scoring of the AIM-TO is done through a scoring service provided by the author/publisher of the test. Percentile rankings and Normal Curve Equivalents (NCE) are the formats used in reporting results. There is no charge for the scoring service with the cost being included in the purchase of each test protocol.

NORMS. Apparently the AIM-TO is normed on a population of "over 500 school-aged children." There is no description of this sample other than that it is representative of rural, urban, and suburban students from different geographical areas of the country. Given the size of the sample, this claim of adequate standardization is questionable. It is very unlikely that significant numbers of students were present in the total sample to represent adequately the age, ability, socioeconomic, multicultural, and geographical differences necessary to be considered a normative group of school-age students from kindergarten through high school. Because this instrument is marketed as appropriate for use with the entire school-age population, the user's manual minimally needs to include documentation and information regarding sample characteristics and statistical norms (especially by age) in order for results to be interpretable.

RELIABILITY. As presented, the reporting of the reliability of the AIM-TO is unacceptable. No meaningful information is given about reliability of the test. Two high alpha reliability coefficients are reported in the manual for elementary ($r = .96$) and secondary ($r = .97$) students. These coefficients deserve further study and elaboration if users are to understand the validity and reliability of the five dimensions purported to be represented in the test. The author/publisher must also establish some level of interrater reliability given that scores are based on evaluations by school professionals.

VALIDITY. Construct validity is based on information gathered by the author during developmental history interviews with parents of underachieving children. The collective result of these consultations resulted in the identification of two "factors" believed important in discriminating between achievers and underachievers: (a) ability to compete and (b) "attention addiction" (i.e., need for attention). Although these factors appear to provide a reasonable operational construct to begin defining and differentiating achievers from underachievers, no cited documentation of empirical validation via factor analysis or cluster analysis is reported. At the same time, no indication is given as to how the five subscales were identified nor was any rationale given for assigning items to each subscale. Additionally, no evidence is presented to indicate the instrument was subjected to field testing, item-analysis, or item revision. In short, very serious questions are raised as to how the AIM-TO was constructed—especially regarding the five subscales.

Evidence of criterion-related validity was established by comparing teacher AIM-TO scores with same-teacher ratings of student achievement. No empirical documentation or clear rationale for use of this validation process is given. Correlation coefficients for grades 1–3 ($r = .72$), grades 4–6 ($r = .83$), grades 7–9 ($r = .83$), and grades 10–12 ($r = .71$) are presented. These relationships of AIM-TO scores and actual student underachievement appear important only in that they confirm that information about a student's achievement can be just as easily obtained by asking the student's teacher—certainly a less expensive alternative to using the AIM-TO. A more convincing and ambitious validation process of this type might include correlating AIM-TO scores with discrepancy scores between learning ability measures (e.g., IQ scores) and standardized achievement tests. Although differences between learning ability and achievement must be interpreted with caution, large discrepancies are considered to be a valid indicator that a student is underachieving.

Questions about the content validity of the test can also be raised. On scanning the individual items of the AIM-TO, the reviewer is struck by the fact that, in spite of the author's claim to be an objective measure of behavioral characteristics related to school-age achievement, a high percentage of items do not deal directly with behavior, or more specifically, with objective classroom observations related to academic learning. Many items typically deal with rater inferences about motivation, affect states, and the perceived quality of the interpersonal relationship with peers and the teacher. The test manual would perhaps more accurately describe the AIM-TO as a teacher evaluation measure of psychosocial and motivational development.

SUMMARY. The ease and relatively short time that it takes to administer the AIM-TO presents a tempting instrument for evaluating and classifying students with learning problems. However, the apparent lack of attention to basic scaling procedures, the lack of documentation of empirical development, the problems cited with regard to standardization and interpretation of results, and the apparent casualness in reporting information regarding technical adequacy, all suggest that the AIM-TO cannot be recommended for use where decisions regarding school-age children and adolescents are to be made.

It should be pointed out that the author/publisher does claim, via supplementary materials made available to the reviewer, that factor analysis and related item selection procedures were employed in the construction of the test. Other than a very brief mention, however, no actual source or documentation describing these important validation procedures is given. Moreover, the author/publisher claim of proper empirical development is made with regard to an earlier published and longer version of an instrument of a different name. In short, if the empirical validation process of the currently available version of the AIM-TO has been completed, clear documentation of this necessary work needs to be included in the user manual.

Because of the clear-cut need for reliable and valid instruments in identification and classification of students with learning and achievement problems, it is hoped that the AIM-TO will be upgraded into a new, more rigorously developed, version. If so, it is the reviewer's opinion that the AIM-TO could become an appropriate screening tool for identifying significant personality and motivational traits related to learning problems and academic underachievement in students.

REVIEWER'S REFERENCE

Rimm, S. B. (1986). *Underachievement syndrome: Causes and cures.* Watertown, WI: Apple Publishing Company.

[4]

ACT Proficiency Examination in Microbiology.

Purpose: "To give adult learners the opportunity to earn college credit for knowledge gained outside the classroom and to provide institutions with an objective basis for awarding such credit" in microbiology.

Population: College and adults.

Publication Dates: 1984–86.

Scores: Total score only.

Administration: Group.

Price Data, 1987: 1986 examination fee: $40 (includes reporting of score to the candidate and one college).

Time: 180(190) minutes.

Comments: Administered 6 times annually (February, March, May, June, October, November) at centers established by the publisher.

Authors: Developed by the faculty of The University of the State of New York.

Publisher: American College Testing Program.

Cross References: For information on the entire ACT Proficiency Examination Program, see 9:45 (1 reference).

[5]

An Adaptation of the Wechsler Preschool and Primary Scale of Intelligence for Deaf Children.

Purpose: To predict "overall academic achievement" for hearing-impaired children.

Population: Hearing-impaired children ages 4 to 6-6.

Publication Date: 1982.

Scores, 6: Animal House, Picture Completion, Mazes, Geometric Design, Block Design, Performance IQ.

Administration: Individual.

Price Data, 1986: $35 per complete kit including manual, Animal House sample 1 pad, Animal House sample 2 card, Picture Completion pad, Mazes sample pads, 3 Block Design cards, 6 two-dimensional blocks, 14 Animal House circles, wax colors, and pointer.

Time: Administration time not reported.

Comments: Adaptation of performance scales of WPPSI (9:1356).

Authors: Steven Ray and Stephen Mark Ulissi.

Publisher: Steven Ray Publishing. [In-print status unknown; no response from publisher after 1989—Ed.]

Review of An Adaptation of the Wechsler Preschool and Primary Scale of Intelligence for Deaf Children by ARTHUR B. SILVERSTEIN, *Professor of Psychiatry, University of California, Los Angeles, CA:*

Ray and Ulissi developed their Adaptation of the Wechsler Preschool and Primary Scale of Intelligence for Deaf Children by modifying the instructions for the five Performance subtests of the Wechsler Preschool and Primary Scale of Intelligence (WPPSI) and adding supplemental items for four of those subtests (all but Geometric Design). The scoring of the subtests is unchanged, and the raw scores are converted to scaled scores, and the sum of scaled scores to a Performance IQ, in the usual way. The first step in developing the Adaptation was to analyze Wechsler's original instructions for language difficulty and simplify them where possible. They were then reviewed by hearing-impaired adults skilled in sign language and were revised as necessary. Finally, the revisions were piloted with hearing-impaired children and further changes were made in those instances where the children experienced difficulties or confusion. Supplemental (practice) items were constructed that were similar, but not identical, to Wechsler's original items in an attempt to insure that even children with very limited linguistic competence would comprehend the various tasks.

Twenty-four psychologists who worked primarily with hearing-impaired individuals administered the Adaptation to a sample of 120 children chosen according to the following criteria: (*a*) age between 4 and 6 1/2 years, (*b*) prelingually deaf (congenital or exogenous) with a minimum of 70 db pure tone average loss in the better ear, and (*c*) no other obvious handicaps except for corrected vision. Only routine or preliminary evaluations, as opposed to special referrals, were allowed. The authors of the Adaptation maintain that the demographic characteristics of their sample closely approximate those of the WPPSI standardization sample, but there are notable differences in race and parental occupation and education. As compared with the hearing-impaired population at large, the sample also had a somewhat higher percentage of children with at least one hearing-impaired parent.

The composition of the sample in terms of the mode of communication used for administering the Adaptation was as follows: 85% total communication, 11% oral, and 4% other. It is therefore curious that the authors are critical of an earlier study in which the WISC-R Performance Scale was standardized for hearing-impaired children because in that study the method of administering the test was permitted to vary. As Ray and Ulissi themselves suggest, the heterogeneity of the hearing-impaired population precludes complete uniformity in the method of administering any test, and that includes their Adaptation.

A series of *t* tests was carried out to compare the scores of the hearing-impaired sample with those of the WPPSI standardization sample. Although the means of the hearing-impaired children were higher in every case, the only difference significant at the .01 level was on Geometric Design, although the difference on the Performance IQ reached the .02 level. A repeated measures analysis of variance of the sample's scores on the five subtests yielded a significant overall difference, and Scheffe's test (which I applied) showed the mean on Geometric Design was significantly higher than the mean on the other four subtests combined. Separate repeated

9

measures analyses of the scores of children with at least one hearing-impaired parent and those with two hearing parents showed generally higher means, except for Block Design, and a relatively flat profile for the former group. No other analyses of the data are reported in the manual.

Ray and Ulissi conclude that, in general, their findings support the idea that hearing-impaired children do not differ significantly from hearing children on the WPPSI Performance Scale; more specifically, that when factors related to test administration such as the child's comprehension of the tasks are controlled, hearing-impaired children, on the average, score very nearly the same as their hearing peers. They go far beyond their data, however, when they state that if the tasks are clear to the hearing-impaired child, the WPPSI provides an adequate estimate of his or her cognitive functioning. The scores may be very nearly the same, but do they have the same meaning? At this point, data on the reliability and validity of scores obtained through the use of the Adaptation are totally lacking, and it would be unwise to assume, because of the general similarity of the scores, that everything we have learned about the WPPSI applies equally to the Adaptation.

Although the authors of the Adaptation may have claimed too much for it, the value of their contribution should not be minimized. The degree of standardization they have introduced into the administration of the WPPSI Performance Scale is a very positive achievement, for without the Adaptation or something very much like it, psychologists would surely improvise their own idiosyncratic modifications in an effort to arrive at meaningful scores for young hearing-impaired children. The Adaptation can be used to advantage either by the relatively few psychologists who are skilled signers, or when an interpreter is employed because the examiner's ability to communicate with hearing-impaired children is more limited. But now that the WPPSI has been revised, is it not time for an Adaptation of the WPPSI-R?

Review of An Adaptation of the Wechsler Preschool and Primary Scale of Intelligence for Deaf Children by E. W. TESTUT, Associate Professor of Audiology, Department of Speech Pathology/Audiology, Ithaca College, Ithaca, NY:

The Adaptation of the Wechsler Preschool and Primary Scale of Intelligence for Deaf Children (the Adaptation) was developed to provide a means for assessing the intelligence of hearing-impaired youngsters aged 4 to 6$\frac{1}{2}$ years. According to the authors, the Adaptation also can be used with language-delayed or deficient children possessing normal hearing for whom a nonverbal assessment might yield more meaningful results than a verbal assessment. The Adaptation was accomplished by taking

an existing, widely accepted form of evaluation, the Wechsler Preschool and Primary Scale of Intelligence (WPPSI), and reducing the complexity of its instructions to be more easily understood by hearing-impaired children. Specifically, the WPPSI instructions were simplified and can be conveyed by sign language with no loss in their intended meaning. Also, additional pretest items, similar in purpose to the original WPPSI test items, were developed to familiarize children with the nature of the examination process.

The Adaptation of the WPPSI has much to offer. The instructions for administering the Adaptation are succinct, easily followed, and should be of assistance to both experts and novices with the severely hearing impaired. Additionally, adapting the WPPSI as opposed to other nonverbal tests of intelligence offers its own advantages. The WPPSI is widely used with hearing-impaired children and its results have been demonstrated to relate well to their academic performance (Blair, 1986). The development of alternative instructional modes specifically for use with the hearing impaired (or other populations possessing communication problems) combined with the selection of a popular, widely used evaluative instrument, such as the WPPSI, allows for direct comparison with normal hearing, normally communicating youngsters. This would be helpful for those professionals involved in the determination of appropriate educational placement, especially when less specialized educational placement options are being considered.

A limitation of the Adaptation is the norming groups. *T*-test and ANOVA analyses of WPPSI scores were obtained on 120 hearing-impaired children evaluated by 24 psychologists from 20 states and found to be comparable to the original Wechsler (1967) findings. Although attempts were made by the authors to replicate the norming group characteristics of the original Wechsler sample, some discrepancies exist. For example, the Adaptation's norm group has proportionally more females and African-Americans than found in the general population or among the severely hearing-impaired population. There are also a greater proportion of children from southern and western geographic regions of the United States than were represented in the original norm groups or are represented in the current U.S. Census. Users of the Adaptation should be aware of these limitations.

Another concern is the authors' argument against separate norms for deaf children and their suggestion that the Adaptation is usable with normal hearing children possessing deficient language ability or with hearing-impaired children not possessing sign language skills. Although the Adaptation may prove useful with these populations, these points were not directly supported by the statistical evaluation of the Adaptation. In fact, the available norms may not even be reflective of the hearing-impaired population, in toto, as the authors restricted their sampling to those children with hearing losses in excess of 70 db and possessing no other handicapping conditions other than corrected vision. The presence of additional handicapping conditions is thought to be much greater in the hearing-impaired population than in the general population (Blair, 1986) and severe hearing impairments account for only a portion of the total hearing-impaired population. Also, the locations of the professionals involved in the sampling of the hearing-impaired children suggest a preponderance of residential and/or specialized schools for the deaf. Such settings represent limited samples compared to the total number of educational placement options available to severely hearing-impaired children. The Adaptation's norms may be based on children who are more seriously handicapped than is typical for children from the broad array of educational sites. This, combined with the potentially biased demographic characteristics mentioned earlier, weakens the authors' argument against separate deaf norms. Further development and research may be necessary before the Adaptation's usefulness with all of its targeted populations is established.

Finally, although the instructions were designed around sign language, "sign language" is not a homogenous form of communication practiced by the severely hearing-impaired population, but instead is an umbrella term encompassing many unique forms of manual communication (e.g., American Sign Language, Signed English, Signing Exact English, Seeing Essential English, and Linguistics of Visual English, to identify but a few varieties). Differing sign language forms might be similar to that employed in the development of the Adaptation, but the potential effects of using differing sign language dialects were not considered in the evaluation of the Adaptation.

In summary, An Adaptation of the Wechsler Preschool and Primary Scale of Intelligence for Deaf Children provides a viable means for assessing severely hearing-impaired youngsters aged 4 to $6^1/_2$ years. The altering of a popular evaluative instrument, widely used with both normal hearing and hearing-impaired youngsters, alike, by making the instructions more easily understood by young severely hearing-impaired children should prove of benefit to those working with this group.

REVIEWER'S REFERENCE

Blair, J. C. (1986). Services needed. In F. S. Berg, J. C. Blair, S. H. Viehweg, & A. Wilson-Vlotman (Eds.), *Educational Audiology for the Hard of Hearing Child* (pp. 25-35). New York: Grune and Stratton, Inc.

[6]

Adaptive Behavior: Street Survival Skills Questionnaire.

Purpose: "To assess fundamental community living and prevocational skills of mentally disabled adolescents and adults."

Population: Ages 9.5 and over.

Publication Dates: 1979–83.

Acronym: SSSQ.

Scores, 10: Basic Concepts, Functional Signs, Tools, Domestics, Health and Safety, Public Services, Time, Monetary, Measurements, Total.

Administration: Individual.

Price Data, 1988: $210 per complete kit including 9 picture volumes ('79, 50 pages each), 50 scoring forms, 50 planning charts, Curriculum Guide ('82, 272 pages), and manual ('83, 95 pages); $13.75 per 50 scoring forms; $8.50 per 50 planning charts; $25 per Curriculum Guide; $18.25 per manual; $225 per computer software offered by publisher.

Time: [45] minutes.

Authors: Dan Linkenhoker and Lawrence McCarron.

Publisher: McCarron-Dial Systems.

Review of the Adaptive Behavior: Street Survival Skills Questionnaire by THOMAS G. HARING, *Associate Professor in Special Education, University of California, Santa Barbara, CA:*

The Street Survival Skills Questionnaire (SSSQ) is designed to assess the level of adaptive behavior of adults and youth with mild to moderate mental retardation. The test consists of nine subscales: Basic Concepts (e.g., color recognition and prepositional concepts such as "in front" and "inside"); Functional Signs (i.e., recognition of street signs and signs needed for basic safety in the community and in residences); Tools (e.g., receptive discrimination of the names of tools and identifying what tools are needed for simple household repairs); Domestic Management (e.g., recognition of household appliances, cooking utensils, foods, and correspondence between clothing care recommendation on labels and settings on washers and dryers); Health, First Aid, and Safety (e.g., recognition of safe and unsafe household conditions, and the correct way to lift heavy boxes); Public Services (e.g., recognition of emergency telephone numbers, who to call if your electricity goes off, and recognizing prices from a printed menu); Time (ranging from telling time to the hour through calendar skills); Money (coin and currency recognition, coin and currency equivalencies, making change, and adding purchase prices); and Measurement (reading thermometers, recognizing that when the temperature is very low, you need to wear a heavy coat, recognizing the normal body temperature of a person, recognizing liquid measures, and measuring the length of screws).

The physical layout of the test materials is excellent. Each subscale is packaged in a separate booklet that streamlines the administration of individual subscales. In addition, the item format is standardized across the subscales and is easy to administer. The format consists of four pictures for each item. The tester reads a question (e.g., "Which one must be put in the refrigerator as soon as you bring it home from the store?") and the subject looks at four line drawings or photographs and indicates the correct answer (in this example, the four pictures were realistic line drawings of a box of "Domino" granulated sugar, a six pack of "Sprite," a gallon of "Meadow Gold" milk, and a can of "Green Giant" asparagus spears). In addition to the test itself being well packaged, the answer forms are well designed and allow the plotting of an adaptive behavior profile across the nine subscales. Finally, the SSSQ includes a "Master Planning Chart," which consists of a 9 x 24 grid giving the skill assessed for each item from each subscale. Using this grid, the tester can identify rapidly which items were scored correctly and incorrectly. This summary would be very valuable in report writing and in planning curriculum recommendations.

The SSSQ differs from most commonly used adaptive behavior scales (e.g., the Vineland Adaptive Behavior Scales, Sparrow, Balla, & Cicchetti, 1984 [10:381]; or the AAMD Adaptive Behavior Scales, Public School Version, Lambert, Windmiller, Cole, & Figueroa, 1975 [9:3]) in that the SSSQ is administered as a test directly to the client, rather than being based on self-report, interviews with primary caretakers, or direct observations of behavior in natural environments. Basing the SSSQ on direct responses to items creates some substantial advantages in comparison to other adaptive behavior scales based on report or observation:

1. Direct observation requires extensive contact over multiple environmental contexts to yield reliable data.

2. Verbal reports can be biased by the degree of familiarity of the informant with the client. It is frequently difficult to assess the accuracy of data gathered from informants. If an informant does not know a client's level of performance on a given skill, direct observation (which is obviously time consuming) is necessary.

3. Reports by informants about the skill levels of a client can be biased by the degree of opportunity to demonstrate or observe a skill within a particular setting. Frequently, persons with mental retardation demonstrate skills in one setting (e.g., the home) but not other settings (e.g., a classroom). This is due to two major factors: problems in generalization, and organizational characteristics in some environments that prevent opportunities to display or practice a skill. Thus, basing test results on one informant, the most typical approach, can be expected to produce variance in reliability that is controlled by the characteristics of the setting as well as familiarity with the person being assessed.

4. As the authors of the SSSQ point out, the wording of criteria for scoring of interview-based questionnaires is, at times, vague. The SSSQ is an instrument with greater reliability than interview-based instruments.

However, a direct testing format also has inherent limitations that are evident in the SSSQ. The decision to develop the SSSQ as a direct test of knowledge pertinent to adaptive behavior, while enhancing reliability, entails an inherent trade-off in validity:

1. Because the test is based on recognition of printed stimuli, some critically important areas of adaptive behavior cannot be assessed. For example, communication skills, social interaction skills, use of leisure time, hygiene, job performance, social responsibility, clothing selection and dressing, and maladaptive behaviors are frequently included as critical components to the construct of adaptive behavior. Many of these items would be difficult or impossible to assess within a picture recognition format.

2. Requiring direct responses to test items lowers the number of adaptive behavior domains that can be sampled in a time-efficient manner. Because the SSSQ is a test rather than a description of more general skill levels, a more comprehensive sampling of skills that comprise the broader construct of adaptive behavior is not possible.

3. A major advantage of interview formats is that information is gathered which reflects an individual's responding under natural cues, environmental conditions, and consequences. Within a direct testing format with simulated materials (i.e., pictures of objects), the ability of a person to demonstrate that skill in vivo is not known.

4. The interview process itself, which is frequently conducted with a parent, primary caretaker, or teacher, can be a valuable means in generating discussions on future objectives for intervention.

5. Many students with more moderate to severe handicaps and with more limited communication ability can display skills under natural conditions, yet have great difficulty with standardized test formats. Tests requiring responding to simulated materials can substantially underestimate the ability levels of students with more severe handicaps.

Does the enhancement of reliability inherent in the SSSQ outweigh the lowering of content and construct validity inherent within the direct-testing format? If the test user is primarily interested in reliable estimates within the skill areas assessed by the SSSQ's nine subscales, then the answer is clear: The SSSQ is a reliable means to assess these skill areas. However, if a more comprehensive picture of a client's overall adaptation to the natural environment is required, the SSSQ is more limited. Given the need and mandate within current laws for fuller evaluations beyond any one test score, the use of the SSSQ would appear to offer a justifiable adjunctive method of assessment when combined with results of other more omnibus tests.

Technical Evaluation.

ITEM SELECTION. The initial item pool for the development of the SSSQ was derived from five content selection procedures: (*a*) prior adaptive behavior scales were reviewed for content, (*b*) a research review was completed that examined the predictive validity of various domains of adaptive behavior, (*c*) results of factor analytic studies with other tests of adaptive behavior were reviewed to identify the number of dimensions (i.e., types of subscales) to be included, (*d*) interviews with staff professionals were conducted, and (*e*) the skills identified from the procedures above were analyzed to determine which skills could be assessed within the multiple-choice pictorial format. The 216 items on the SSSQ were then tested through a series of investigations and field testings.

NORMATIVE DATA. Two groups were tested to produce the norms for the SSSQ. A group of 400 developmentally disabled adolescents and adults from five sheltered workshops and community employment programs in five states participated in the first group. The mean age of the group was 25 years (range 15 to 55 years) and the mean IQ score of the group was 58 (range 28 to 80). In addition, 200 adolescents from secondary programs were assessed. The mean IQ of the high school group was 97 (range 80 to 121). This group was assessed to provide a standard of comparison for normal young adults about to enter competitive employment who have a high probability of successful adaption to the community. The inclusion of both sets of norms is a valuable addition. The manual also reviews pertinent test results that summarize the norm group across a diverse range of measures. A shortcoming of the norming procedures is a lack of analysis or descriptions of participation by ethnic, linguistic, and racial minorities.

RELIABILITY. Test-retest reliability was calculated over a 1-month interval. The test-retest reliability ($N = 60$) was impressive: .99, with a range of .87 to .95 for the subtests. The Kuder-Richardson 20 was used to assess internal consistency. The internal consistency of the entire test was .97 with subtest scores ranging between .68 and .96. The manual also provides an analysis of the standard error of measurement for each subtest and the total score. Overall, the SSSQ offers an unusually high degree of reliability with a concomitant low standard error of measurement.

CONTENT VALIDITY. The content validity of the SSSQ is based on the procedures used to identify items. As reviewed above, a major limitation of the SSSQ was the selection of items that could be assessed within a multiple-choice format. This decision limits the content validity of the SSSQ.

Each item included on the SSSQ was analyzed in terms of item difficulty, item discrimination, item-to-total correlation, and distractor analysis. The final version of the SSSQ was developed using quantitative criteria developed for each of these statistical tests (e.g., items with a discrimination level of less than .20 were eliminated or rewritten). A detailed review giving item difficulty, item discrimination, and item-to-total correlation is provided for each item across each subscale.

CONSTRUCT VALIDITY. The construct validity of the SSSQ was assessed through analysis of the intercorrelation of subtests, factor analysis, correlation with intelligence scores, and reading ability. The correlations between the subtests ranged from .32 to .78 with a mean of .55. This indicates that approximately 30% of the variance is common between the subtests and 70% is unique to each subtest. This provides evidence that the assessment of performance across the nine distinct subscales is valid; that is, each scale assesses a relatively specific skill, yet at the same time, the skills intercorrelate with the abstract ability of adaptive behavior. The factor analysis indicated that one factor was sufficient to interpret the data. Factor loadings ranged from .65 to .90 on this factor. These findings are a strong indication the subtests are assessing a highly correlated cluster of responses.

The SSSQ correlates significantly with Peabody Picture Vocabulary Test IQ (Dunn, 1965), ($r = .64$) and with the Communication subscale of the Progress Assessment Chart (PAC; Gunzberg, 1963), mean correlation across subscales = .65. Thus, the adaptive behavior factor measured by the SSSQ appears related to communication skills and verbal intelligence.

CONCURRENT VALIDITY. The concurrent validity of the SSSQ was assessed by examining the correlations between the SSSQ and the San Francisco Vocational Competency Scale (SFVCS; Levine & Elzey, 1968) and the Progress Assessment Chart. The total correlation between the SSSQ and the SFVCS was .60 (range on subscales between .35 and .69). The PAC is an inventory of 120 skills that fall into four areas: Self-Help, Communication, Socialization, and Occupation. As reviewed above, the SSSQ correlated most strongly with the Communication subscale. No subscale of the SSSQ correlated significantly with the PAC subscales of Self-Help, Socialization, or Occupation.

PREDICTIVE VALIDITY. The manual for the SSSQ includes a section on predictive validity that explores the relationship between the use of the SSSQ both singly and in combination with other measures to predict successful placement in day activity and vocational placements. The authors rank the range of available programs for persons with disabilities along a continuum from least normalized to most normalized: daycare programs, work activity centers, "lower" and "upper" sheltered workshops, transitional programs, and community employment programs. The conceptual model developed by the authors indicates that adaptive behavior scores can be used in a predictive fashion to determine placement into programs along this continuum. This logic, that test performance can be used to determine and predict subsequent training opportunities and degrees of normalized services and community interaction, has been criticized on both ethical and procedural bases (e.g., Gould, 1981). At least one major professional organization, the Association for Persons with Severe Handicaps (TASH), questions the continued maintenance of restrictive placements that are based on the assessed ability levels of people with disabilities (Meyer, Peck, & Brown, 1991). The philosophic position advanced by TASH is that opportunities for competitive employment and more normalized community residential placements are rights for all people. The burden of proof is on careproviders and agencies to adapt existing normalized community environments and vocational opportunities through providing progressively higher degrees of support services. From this alternative perspective, the continuum is conceptualized as the degree of support and training needed to maintain all clients in the most normalized environments.

SUMMARY. The technical development of the SSSQ is impressive. The degree of reliability achieved is quite high for instruments of this type. In addition, the degree of technical sophistication in item selection procedures ranks this instrument among the top of currently available assessments of adaptive behavior. Although the reliability is impressive, the validity of the test is constrained on an a priori basis because of the use of the multiple-choice format with pictorial stimuli. Skills that are central to a more comprehensive assessment of adaptive behavior such as independence in self-help and socialization are not assessed with the SSSQ. The test is recommended as an adjunctive assessment of the nine skills areas covered. In addition, the test would appear to be quite useful in planning instruction in specific reference to the items assessed within the nine subscales. Its use in determining placements is not well supported, as the placement model outlined in the manual does not correspond to current best practices.

REVIEWER'S REFERENCES

Gunzburg, H. C. (1963). *Progress Assessment Chart of Social and Personal Development manual*. Bristol, IN: Aux Chandelles.
Dunn, L. M. (1965). *Peabody Picture Vocabulary Test manual*. Circle Pines, MN: American Guidance Service.
Levine, S., & Elzey, F. (1968). San Francisco Vocational Competency Scale. New York: The Psychological Corporation.
Lambert, N., Windmiller, M., Cole, L., & Figueroa, R. (1975). Adaptive Behavior Scale: Public School Version. Washington, DC: American Association of Mental Deficiency.
Gould, S. J. (1981). *The mismeasure of man*. New York: W. W. Norton & Co.

Sparrow, S. S., Balla, D. A., & Cicchetti, D. V. (1984). Vineland Adaptive Behavior Scales. Circle Pines, MN: American Guidance Service.
Meyer, L., Peck, C. A., & Brown, L. (1991). *Critical issues in the lives of people with severe disabilities*. Baltimore: P. H. Brookes Pub. Co.

[7]
ADD-H Comprehensive Teacher's Rating Scale.

Purpose: "Intended for diagnosing and monitoring the behavior of the child who manifests a deficit in attention in the classroom or is unusually active or restless."
Population: Grades K–5.
Publication Dates: 1986–88.
Acronym: ACTeRS.
Scores, 4: Attention, Hyperactivity, Social Skills, Oppositional.
Administration: Individual.
Editions, 2: Paper-and-pencil, microcomputer.
Price Data, 1989: $48 per examiner's kit including manual ('88, 16 pages) and rating/profile forms; $40 per 100 rating/profile forms; $75 per microcomputer edition; $8 per introductory kit.
Time: Administration time not reported.
Comments: Ratings by teachers; IBM-PC necessary for administration of microcomputer edition.
Authors: Rina K. Ullmann, Esther K. Sleator, and Robert L. Sprague.
Publisher: MetriTech, Inc.

TEST REFERENCES

1. Aman, M. G., Mitchell, E. A., & Turbott, S. H. (1987). The effects of essential fatty acid supplementation by Efamol in hyperactive children. *Journal of Abnormal Child Psychology, 15*, 75-90.
2. Douglas, V. I., Barr, R. G., Amin, K., O'Neill, M. E., & Britton, B. G. (1988). Dosage effects and individual responsivity to methylphenidate in attention deficit disorder. *Journal of Child Psychology and Psychiatry and Allied Disciplines, 29*, 453-475.

Review of the ADD-H Comprehensive Teacher's Rating Scale by ELLEN H. BACON, Assistant Professor of Human Services, Western Carolina University, Cullowhee, NC:

The ADD-H Comprehensive Teacher's Rating Scale (ACTeRS) is a teacher rating scale designed to collect information on a child's behavior in school. It is recommended for clinicians such as physicians, psychologists, or school personnel who evaluate students for Attention Deficit Disorders with Hyperactivity (ADD-H) or monitor the effects of treatments on behavior. The scale was developed for use with students in grades K–5 who have attention problems in the classroom. The authors state the scale is also useful in screening learning disabled students from ADD-H children (manual, p. 7; Ullmann, 1985).

The rating scale comes in two forms, a microcomputer form and a paper-and-pencil form. The paper-and-pencil edition is a simple rating sheet with 24 items and two profile charts, one for boys and one for girls. The items describe classroom behavior in four categories: Attention, Social Skills, Hyperactivity, and Oppositional. Teachers are asked to rate the items on a 5-point scale ranging from *almost never* to *almost always*. In rating the items, teachers are asked to compare the child's behavior with that of his or her classmates.

Rating scale items are short phrases describing general school-related behaviors rather than specific observable behaviors. Some of the items concerning nonverbal communication and citing of general rules are particularly difficult to interpret. The 5-point scale offers no guidance for ranking the student other than two extremes. One problem with having undefined ratings is that a teacher may interpret the midpoint rankings as average behavior. However, if students received midpoint rankings on each item, they would have percentile scores in the well-below-average or problem range. A format which offers specific behavioral descriptions indicating either frequency or extent of behavior for each rank would be more helpful.

SCORING. Scoring of the ACTeRS is simple with points assigned according to the teacher's rating and then added for four subscale scores under the four categories. Using the profile attached to the rating scale, the scorer can find the student's percentile according to the student's sex. Percentile scores for all grades, K–5, were combined, according to the authors, because there were no consistent developmental differences (manual, p. 5).

INTERPRETATION. The authors recommend that any child receiving a ranking at or below the 10th percentile on the Attention subscale be diagnosed as Attention-Deficit Disordered (ADD). Children who score above the 10th but below the 25th percentile on the Attention scale should be considered ADD if other subscales and indicators confirm the observations (manual, p. 7). It is important to note this subscale has only six items that describe school behaviors such as following instructions and working appropriately on assigned tasks. A student might exhibit these inattentive behaviors for a variety of reasons not consistent with a diagnosis of ADD.

Guidelines for interpreting other subscale scores are not given except to note that any subscale scores below the 25th percentile should be considered indicative of a major deficit. The manual does not present any justification for these percentile markers nor does it present means, standard deviations, or standard error of measurement at these cutoff levels (see American Educational Research Association, American Psychological Association, & National Council on Measurement in Education, 1985).

DEVELOPMENT AND NORMING. The test was developed from a 43-item behavioral scale with the final 24 items chosen through use of a factor analysis procedure. The manual does not adequately explain the norming procedure or the normative sample. No information is provided about the region of the country used, race, SES, the selection procedure, or the date of the norms. Without this information, a user would not know whether the test or the derived

scores were appropriate for any particular child (Salvia & Ysseldyke, 1988).

RELIABILITY. One of the most important criteria for a rating scale, especially one that is to be used in evaluating and labeling a child, is that there is high interrater reliability with correlations at the .80 level or higher for screening purposes and at the .90 level or higher for educational decisions as placement (Salvia & Ysseldyke, 1988, p. 129). The authors report interrater reliability information for 124 children indicating correlations of .61 on Attention, .73 on Hyperactivity, .51 on Social Skills, and .59 on Oppositional. No information is provided on the population or the teachers used in determining reliability. The manual also provides test-retest reliability which is more acceptable ranging from .78 to .82. These data indicate the scale is more consistent when the same person uses the test. However, the manual again does not describe the sample used to obtain the correlations, the means, or standard deviations (AERA, APA, & NCME, 1985).

VALIDITY. The manual presents several studies as indications of the validity of the rating scale. One study showed that mean scores for learning disabled students were significantly higher than those of students labeled ADD-H (Ullmann, 1985). On the basis of this the authors state the ACTeRS offers a "reasonably accurate screening device" for school systems. However, the guidelines given for interpretation of the profile are too vague to make it useful as a screening device. Only one subscale, Attention, has a percentile score that indicates a diagnosis of ADD. No information is given on scores or profiles characteristic of LD, ADD, or ADD-H children.

Two studies are reported on the use of the ACTeRS in monitoring the behavior of ADD and ADD-H students (Ullmann & Sleator, 1985; Ullmann & Sleator, 1986). Scores on two of the subscales, Attention and Hyperactivity, improved as students were placed on increased medication. According to this research, the ACTeRS could be useful for monitoring individual progress of a child with one consistent rater.

In summary, the scale attempts to provide help in evaluating children with ADD but at this time there is not adequate reliability, validity, or information on interpreting the profile to justify its use in a diagnostic or decision-making procedure. The scale could be helpful in monitoring progress of students with attention problems if the same rater consistently used the scale. However, there is not adequate information on the normative sample to know what type of populations are represented in the percentile scores.

REVIEWER'S REFERENCES

American Educational Research Association, American Psychological Association, & National Council on Measurement in Education. (1985).

Standards for educational and psychological testing. Washington, DC: American Psychological Association, Inc.

Ullmann, R. K. (1985). ACTeRS useful in screening learning disabled from attention deficit disordered (ADD-H) children. *Psychopharmacology Bulletin, 21,* 339-344.

Ullmann, R. K., & Sleator, E. K. (1985). Attention deficit disorder children with or without hyperactivity. *Clinical Pediatrics, 24,* 547-551.

Ullmann, R. K., & Sleator, E. K. (1986). Responders, nonresponders, and placebo responders among children with attention deficit disorder. *Clinical Pediatrics, 25,* 594-599.

Salvia, J., & Ysseldyke, J. E. (1988). *Assessment in special and remedial education* (4th ed.). Boston: Houghton Mifflin Co.

Review of the ADD-H Comprehensive Teacher's Rating Scale by AYRES G. D'COSTA, *Associate Professor of Education, The Ohio State University, Columbus, OH:*

The ADD-H Comprehensive Teacher's Rating Scale (ACTeRS) is a simple 24-item instrument, using a 5-point frequency rating scale, that describes classroom behavior on four factors: Attention, Hyperactivity, Social Skills, and Oppositional. Interpretation is based on percentiles with separate norms for boys and girls.

It is claimed that the ACTeRS discriminates between children with Attention-Deficit Disorders with Hyperactivity (ADD-H) and children with Learning Disorders (LD). The ACTeRS can also help physicians to determine "which children are reasonable candidates for therapeutic intervention," and to monitor the progress of ADD-H children on medication.

According to the manual, the initial pool of 12 items came from an attention/hyperactivity study of 891 children by Needleman et al. (1979). The remainder of the initial pool of 43 items were taken from a study by Pekarik, Prinz, Liebert, Weintraub, and Neale (1976) that attempted to differentiate hyperactive children from normal but overactive children. These 43 items were then administered to a norm group of 1,339 children across several elementary grade levels.

The administration, scoring, and interpretation of the instrument is handled by the teacher. The teacher completes the frequency ratings on the 24 items, which are conveniently arranged by scale. The scale scores are obtained by adding the ratings for each scale. Circling these raw scores on a preprinted gender-specific profile report, the teacher is able to read off the percentile rank of the student on each of the four scales. The critical diagnosis of Attention-Deficit Disorder (ADD) is based on achieving a percentile rank of 10 or below on the Attention scale. No empirical justification is provided for the use of this cutoff or any of the other cutoffs. Other milestones are reached at the 25th, 40th, and 50th percentiles. It is stated that, in general, a score at or below the 25th percentile is indicative of some deficit. Above the 50th percentile there is no problem. Clearly, such a norm-referenced approach merits a more careful discussion, selection, and description of the norm sample. Also, there is

need to validate that these percentile-based cutoffs are indeed significant for clinical purposes, even though the authors provide the usual caveat that these are not rigid cutoffs.

The reliability for the four scales is remarkably good (internal consistency measures are in the high .90s), given the small number of items per scale. Each scale has from five to seven items. The items for each scale were selected on the basis of factor analysis.

Another clear strength of this instrument lies in the fact that the items for the four scales were selected on the basis of previous experience and research; and the initial judgmental scales were confirmed by factor analysis. The only disturbing aspect is that in arriving at a 24-item final instrument, "items loading .33 or higher into more than one factor were considered factor complex and were eliminated." It is likely that this process may have eliminated some items that were initially judged important representatives of the four domains, thus sacrificing content validity for scale differentiation.

There is no reported attempt to assess how well each scale has been represented by the selected items. In other words, there is no discussion of the content validity of the instrument. A few other types of validity investigations are reported in the manual and published in the literature. Of special interest is the study differentiating an ADD-H group from an LD group. Differences are reported in terms of the mean percentiles achieved in the four scales. Although the differences do make clinical sense, it would have been more convincing had a MANOVA been conducted, followed by discriminant and classification analysis. Other validity research studies are needed, especially if the purported purposes of the instrument are to be justified. How sensitive is the instrument to behavioral changes effected by therapeutic interventions? A good guess is that the paucity of items in each scale may render the instrument lacking in sensitivity for this particular purpose. How can one be assured that if behavioral changes do indeed show up, these are not due to rater bias or due to increasing familiarity with the instrument, especially one with so few items.

The ACTeRS is also available in a microcomputer PC version, which permits the accumulation of results on a floppy disk, presumably for future use in generating norms or other research. Thoughtfully, the data files are password protected, thus recognizing their confidential nature.

This reviewer recommends the use of the ACTeRS and urges additional validity research.

REVIEWER'S REFERENCES

Pekarik, E. G., Prinz, R. J., Liebert, D. E., Weintraub, S., & Neale, J. M. (1976). The pupil evaluation inventory: A sociometric technique for assessing children's social behavior. *Journal of Abnormal Child Psychology, 4,* 83-97.

Needleman, H. L., Gunnoe, C., Leviton, A., Reed, R., Peresie, H., Maher, C., & Barrett, P. (1979). Deficits in psychologic and classroom performance of children with elevated dentive lead levels. *New England Journal of Medicine, 300*, 689-695.

[8]

Adolescent and Adult Psychoeducational Profile.

Purpose: Assesses skills of moderately to severely retarded and autistic individuals.
Population: Adolescents and adults with moderate to severe mental retardation or autism.
Publication Date: 1988.
Acronym: AAPEP.
Scores: 3 scales (Direct Observation, Home, School/Work); 6 scores for each: Vocational Skills, Independent Functioning, Leisure Skills, Vocational Behavior, Functional Communication, Interpersonal Behavior.
Administration: Individual.
Price Data, 1989: $29 per manual (119 pages); price data for testing kit available from Residential Services, Inc., Day Program, P.O. Box 487, Carrboro, NC 27510.
Time: (60–90) minutes per scale.
Comments: Title on manual is Individualized Assessment and Treatment for Autistic and Developmentally Disabled Children, Volume IV; other materials (e.g., ball, magazines, playing cards) necessary for test administration may be supplied by examiner or purchased from Residential Services, Inc.
Authors: Gary Mesibov, Eric Schopler, Bruce Schaffer, and Rhoda Landrus.
Publisher: PRO-ED, Inc.

Review of the Adolescent and Adult Psychoeducational Profile by LENA R. GADDIS, Assistant Professor of Educational Psychology, Northern Arizona University, Flagstaff, AZ:

The goal of the Adolescent and Adult Psychoeducational Profile (AAPEP) is to "provide an evaluation of a client's current and potential skills in those areas which are most important for successful, semi-independent functioning in the home and the community" (manual, p. 3). The target population consists of moderately to severely retarded autistic and nonautistic individuals. The profile consists of three scales, which are actually parallel forms that contain the same items, thus allowing for multisource, multisetting assessment.

The Direct Observation Scale involves administering items to the client in a prescribed order, although the order can be altered to accommodate the specific client. The manual adequately describes how to administer the items. The instructions require a minimal use of language, which is a definite asset considering that many clients in the target population probably have language deficits. Data for the remaining scales (Home and School/Work) are obtained via interviews with appropriate caretakers in the representative settings. The manual offers few guidelines for conducting these interviews. Each scale reportedly yields six scores. The three scales are integrated for use in the formulation of Individualized Education Plans

(IEPs) for adolescents or Individualized Habilitation Plans (IHPs) for adults.

The direct assessment procedures outlined by the AAPEP add a needed dimension to the evaluation process of such individuals; many measures used with these populations are checklists or are traditional measures of intelligence, which do not lend themselves to IEP/IHP development. Unfortunately, little has been done in the way of development of supporting research for this measure. With the exception of a reported interscorer reliability (86% agreement for 15 subjects) and some indication that it is perceived as "helpful" in formulating IEPs/IHPs, the AAPEP does not meet the minimum standards for evidence of reliability and validity recommended for psychological and educational tests.

No norms are presented and, in fact, there is little indication that the test was ever administered outside the 15 subjects assessed for the single reliability study performed. The term *score*, as used by the authors, appears to this reviewer to be a misnomer; what the so called scores appear to provide is merely a summary of items passed or failed or skills that are emerging. Although the authors claim that each scale yields six scores, no evidence is provided to suggest that the scores represent six truly independent entities. The manual fails to provide any information about scale development or item selection, standardization, or even theoretical rationale for test content. Also unclear are the qualifications of the evaluators used in the reliability study reported. The term *trained clinicians* could refer to a vast array of professionals.

In summary, the AAPEP appears to have potential to add a direct assessment component that allows for multisetting evaluation. At this time, however, there is little to recommend its use due to the fact that few of the attributes that characterize a technically sound test are known about the AAPEP. If the consumer is in need of a norm-referenced measure, they will be better served by traditional adaptive behavior or vocational assessment devices. Professionals experienced in evaluating the AAPEP target populations may find it a convenient way to summarize and use information from various sources to formulate recommendations for IEPs/IHPs.

Review of the Adolescent and Adult Psychoeducational Profile by J. JEFFREY GRILL, Associate Professor of Special Education, Carroll College, Helena, MT:

The Adolescent and Adult Psychoeducational Profile (AAPEP) is intended for use with autistic adolescents and adults who function in the moderately to severely retarded range. The stated purpose of the AAPEP is to evaluate a client's readiness for placement in sheltered employment settings and community-based group homes.

The AAPEP includes three scales: Direct Observation, Home, and Work/School. Each scale consists of subscales for six functional skills areas: Vocational Skills, Independent Functioning, Leisure Skills, Vocational Behavior, Functional Communication, and Interpersonal Behavior. Each functional skills area subscale includes eight items, for a total of 144. The Direct Observation scale includes an additional four "higher-level" items in each functional skills area subscale "for clients functioning at a slightly higher level on any of the function areas assessed by this instrument" (manual, p. 10).

The Direct Observation scale is administered to a client by a therapist in a clinical setting. The other scales rely on responses provided by persons most directly responsible for the client in their respective settings. The Direct Observation scale requires use of a set of materials (e.g., signs, nuts, bolts, pencils, erasers, sorting boxes) typically available in sheltered employment settings. These may be ordered separately or may be assembled on-site (with full instructions for such assembly provided in an appendix). Included in the manual is a set of Score Forms and Profile Sheets which may be photocopied. Administration time for the Direct Observation scale is estimated at $1^1/_2$ hours, but may vary according to the examinee's abilities. Administration times for the other scales are estimated at 1 hour.

The authors characterize the AAPEP as a criterion-referenced test, and, for most items on the Direct Observation scale, this is an accurate description. But the other two scales are questionnaires, not tests. Scoring is simple and direct, with each item scored as *Passing*, *Emerging*, or *Failing*. Criteria for each score category are clearly stated for each item. Special emphasis is given to those items scored as *Emerging* because this score category suggests that a client demonstrates some, but not all skills necessary for a *Passing* score. Items scored as *Emerging* are viewed as particularly important for planning instruction.

Although AAPEP items, especially those in the Direct Observation scale, should be presented in the order given in the manual, this order may be varied if necessary. The Direct Observation scale would benefit from such a reordering. First, several items on the Vocational Behavior, Functional Communication, and Interpersonal Behavior subscales are not administered items, per se, because they involve observing behaviors and scoring them at various times during the assessment. Second, for the Leisure Skills area, a series of items of varying durations is administered to the client in a sequence that seems highly unnatural. For example, the client is required to throw velcro-covered balls at a velcro-covered dart board, then to play dominoes, to play cards, to play catch, to shoot baskets, to sew, and finally to read a magazine or catalogue. These items would be more

appropriately interspersed throughout the Direct Observation scale at times of transition from one set of items to the next, rather than being grouped in a lengthy sequence. For this entire scale, a more appropriate arrangement would include one set of items to be administered in a more natural order, and a separate checklist of behaviors to be observed during administration.

After all the scales have been administered and scored, the results (i.e., numbers of items scored as *Passing* and numbers scored as *Emerging*) are transferred to the Scores Profile. These results are averaged to yield two new profiles, one for the functional skills areas averaged across the three scales, and one for the three scales averaged across the six functional skills areas. Such averaging seems superfluous for a criterion-referenced instrument, especially when the Scores Profile provides the same information.

Overall, the AAPEP appears to be what it claims, although the term *Psychoeducational* in its title is somewhat misleading. All items seem entirely appropriate to the authors' stated purposes, and the use of multiple sources of information is likewise appropriate. Further, scoring categories and criteria are stated with complete clarity.

Unfortunately, little evidence is offered to support any aspect of validity (save face validity) or reliability, and no information is provided to explain how the individual items were selected. Indeed, the choice of eight items for each of the functional skills areas on each of the three scales seems completely arbitrary and intended to yield neat, symmetrical, easily compared profiles. On norm-referenced tests, subscale profiles are common, often useful, and not dependent on having equal numbers of items in each subscale. But, such scaling is artificial and misleading on a criterion-referenced instrument. Although using this profile is simple, involving counting the numbers of items scored as *Passing* and *Emerging* and shading the same numbers of boxes on the profile forms, the boxes shaded do not necessarily correspond to the specific items scored as *Passing* or *Emerging*. The structure of the AAPEP implies that items have been presented in order of increasing difficulty or importance, yet no item analysis data is presented to support this implication. The absence of information on item selection renders the AAPEP virtually useless.

Reliability data are scant, consisting of one table supported by two narrative paragraphs, all based on percentages of agreement on individual item scorings. Although such interrater agreement data are necessary for an instrument of this sort, data presented by the authors reflect results derived from assessments of only 15 clients and using just two raters for each assessment. Such a limited sample is hardly adequate to justify the authors' claim that the instrument's reliability "is quite satisfactory" (manual, p. 5). Oddly, no evidence of the AAPEP's internal consistency is offered, even though each of the three scales assesses skills in six identically labelled categories. Surely, to justify the claim that the AAPEP assesses comparable skills across three settings, some evidence of internal consistency is needed.

The authors' discussion of validity focuses on ratings of the usefulness of recommendations derived from the AAPEP as compared to those derived from either Individualized Education Plans or Habilitation Plans (IEPs or IHPs, respectively), for 30 autistic, moderately or severely handicapped clients matched on age and IQ with 30 nonautistic, similarly handicapped clients. Although much is said to explain how a study of these ratings was accomplished, nothing in the discussion focuses on the validity of the instrument itself. A second attempt at validation involved asking home or work supervisors of the clients in the original study to rate their satisfaction with the accuracy, recommendations, and other aspects of the AAPEP. Those who responded (37 of 60) rated their satisfaction as high. Such testimonial evidence does not support the AAPEP's validity.

In summary, the AAPEP appears to assess important functional skills areas of autistic adolescents and adults who are being considered for placement in sheltered employment or community-based group homes. However, the lack of information on item selection and validation, and the grossly inadequate evidence provided to support the instrument's reliability and validity substantially limit the AAPEP's usefulness for the decision-making and instructional planning purposes its authors intended.

[9]
Adult Basic Learning Examination, Second Edition.

Purpose: "Designed to measure the educational achievement of adults who may or may not have completed twelve years of schooling . . . also useful in evaluating efforts to raise the educational level of these adults."
Population: Adults with less than 12 years of formal schooling.
Publication Dates: 1986–87.
Acronym: ABLE.
Administration: Group.
Levels, 3: 1, 2, 3 and screening test (SelectABLE).
Forms, 2: E, F (equivalent forms).
Price Data, 1988: $23 per examination kit containing test booklets and directions for administration for 1 form of each of the 3 levels, hand-scorable answer sheet, Ready Score™ Answer Sheet and group record for Level 2, and SelectABLE Ready Score™ Answer Sheet; $15 per handbook of instructional techniques and materials ('86, 67 pages); $15 per norms booklet (specify level); $5 per Reading Supplement; ABLE Computer Scoring™ software program also available for local computer scoring.

Authors: Bjorn Karlsen and Eric F. Gardner.
Publisher: The Psychological Corporation.
a) SELECTABLE.
Purpose: A screening test to determine which level of ABLE is most suitable for use with a particular individual.
Price Data: $26 per 25 Ready Score™ Answer Sheets; $23 per 50 hand-scorable test sheets; $13 per scoring key; $5 per SelectABLE Handbook ('86, 15 pages).
Time: (15) minutes.
b) LEVEL 1.
Population: Adults with 1–4 years of formal education.
Scores, 5: Vocabulary, Reading Comprehension, Spelling, Number Operations, Problem Solving.
Price Data: $33 per 25 hand-scorable test booklets and directions for administering including group record (specify Form E or F); $28 per scoring key (specify Form E or F); $8 per directions for administering ('86, 38 pages).
Time: (130–165) minutes.
c) LEVEL 2.
Population: Adults with 5–8 years of formal education.
Scores: Same as *b* plus Language.
Price Data: $33 per 25 hand-scorable or reusable test booklets (specify Form E or F); $28 per scoring key (specify Form E or F); $27 per 25 Ready Score™ Answer Sheets (specify Form E or F); $23 per 50 hand-scorable answer sheets and 2 group records; $8 per directions for administering Levels 2 and 3.
Time: (175–215) minutes.
d) LEVEL 3.
Population: Adults with 9–12 years of formal schooling who may or may not have completed 12 years of schooling.
Scores: Same as *c*.
Price Data: Same as *c*.
Time: Same as *c*.
Cross References: See also T3:121 (6 references), 8:2 (4 references), and T2:3 (3 references); for a review by A. N. Hieronymus of the earlier edition and excerpted reviews by Edward B. Fry and James W. Hall of Levels 1 and 2 of the earlier edition, see 7:3.

TEST REFERENCES

1. Minskoff, E. H., Hawks, R., Steidle, E. F., & Hoffmann, F. J. (1989). A homogeneous group of persons with learning disabilities: Adults with severe learning disabilities in vocational rehabilitation. *Journal of Learning Disabilities, 22,* 521-528.

Review of the Adult Basic Learning Examination, Second Edition by ANNE R. FITZPATRICK, Manager of Applied Research, CTB Macmillan/McGraw-Hill, Monterey, CA:

This second edition of the Adult Basic Learning Examination (ABLE) has many qualities not present in the first edition. Language mechanics and usage are assessed in the second and third levels of the new edition. The objectives assessed by all subtests are described in detail. The norms groups consist of comprehensive samples of distinct reference groups. Finally, a Handbook of Instructional Techniques and Materials and a Reading Supplement will help teachers of adults plan effective instruction. All tests, manuals, and ancillary materials are well written and easy to use, and the test items appear suitably adult-oriented in content.

SELECTABLE. This multiple-choice locator test has 30 items that measure verbal concepts and 15 items that measure numerical concepts. Once an examinee's total score has been calculated, a table of cut-scores is used to decide what level of ABLE to administer. No evidence of how accurately examinees are placed using these cut-scores is provided. Also not explained is why an examinee's total score is calculated rather than separate verbal and numerical scores, so that an examinee's verbal and quantitative skill levels could be differentiated.

ABLE TEST CONTENT. At Level 1, the Vocabulary and Spelling subtests are entirely dictated so that reading skills are not taxed. The items in the Problem Solving subtest are read aloud by the examiner, although they are also printed in the test booklets.

The term "auditory comprehension" best describes what is measured by the Level 1 Vocabulary subtest, because examinees must listen to a sentence and then choose from three alternatives the word that best completes the sentence. The Vocabulary subtests at Levels 2 and 3 are not dictated.

The Reading Comprehension subtest at Level 1 requires examinees to read signs, short passages presented in a modified cloze format, and short passages followed by questions. At Levels 2 and 3 the reading material consists of passages of an educational nature and letters, forms, instructions, and notices of the kind that adults may confront in everyday life. At all levels there are items designed to assess inference skills, although these items are not particularly challenging. In Form E of Level 2, for example, only 4 of the 24 inference items had p-values less than .50 for the ABE/GED and prison norms groups combined. The Reading subtest is among the easiest at each level.

In contrast, the mathematics subtests appear relatively difficult. For example, the average adult in each ABE/GED norms group answered only about half of the Problem Solving items correctly. Among the most difficult items at Levels 2 and 3 were those that involved ratios, percents, travel rates, and geometric formulae.

The Spelling and Language subtests at Levels 2 and 3 require examinees to identify the correct or incorrect versions of words or phrases. They appear to be suitable in content and difficulty.

ABLE NORMS. Adult reference-group norms expressed in terms of percentile ranks, stanines, and normal curve equivalents accompany each level of ABLE. At Levels 1 and 2, the norming program involved two reference groups, adults in ABE/GED programs and adults in prison education

programs. At Level 3, the norming program also involved adults in vocational/technical high school programs.

Grade equivalents (GEs) and scale scores are also given. These scores were developed when the Stanford Achievement Test (SAT) series was normed with public and nonpublic school students in 1981 and 1982. ABLE was linked to these score scales through a 1984 equating study. A discussion of the meaning of the GEs provided in each ABLE norms booklet aptly notes limits that should be applied when interpreting adults' performance in terms of a GE score scale that was developed using students' performance.

The adults comprising the reference groups for each test level are described in terms of their sex, age, race, and geographic location. Each adult was assigned to an ABLE level in light of the last grade completed by the adult in school. Because this variable of last grade completed was central in process of defining the reference groups for each level of ABLE, data should have been provided to describe the last grades completed by the members of each reference group. Such data would allow users of ABLE to better determine the similarity between each reference group and the adults they are testing.

ABLE RELIABILITY AND VALIDITY. The internal consistency estimates of reliability (KR-21s) that were reported seem reasonable, generally ranging between the low .80s and low .90s. Given that one stated use of ABLE is to evaluate educational programs for adults, test-retest reliabilities and/or alternate forms reliabilities also should have been reported.

The evidence of validity that is reported consists of intercorrelations among the ABLE subtests and correlations between ABLE and the Stanford Achievement Test series. Although these correlational findings are quite respectable, it is important to note the version of ABLE used in the correlational studies was one of the experimental forms from which the items for the published version of ABLE were selected. Therefore, the correlational evidence must be interpreted with caution, because it does not directly pertain to the published ABLE forms.

It is stated that the content of the items in ABLE were reviewed for possible ethnic and/or sex bias, although the characteristics of the reviewers are not specified. A more serious omission is that no data analyses were conducted to assess ethnic or sex bias in responses to these items.

SUMMARY COMMENTS. ABLE and the Tests of Adult Basic Education (TABE; 446) are the two preeminent batteries available to assess adults' educational achievement. Both batteries are professionally developed and of high quality. To choose between them, users should evaluate each measure in terms of how well its content matches their curricular and/or assessment objectives. For adults who wish to earn a high school equivalency certificate, the TABE may be preferable because estimates of their scores on the Tests of General Educational Development (GED) can be derived from TABE scale scores using a conversion table that is provided.

Review of the Adult Basic Learning Examination, Second Edition by ROBERT T. WILLIAMS, Professor, School of Occupational and Educational Studies, Colorado State University, Fort Collins, CO:

The second edition of this battery is a high quality, professional publication. The test booklets, directions for administering and scoring the tests, norms booklets, supplemental materials, and handbook of instructional techniques and materials are all well developed and organized, readable, attractive, and useful. SelectABLE is a useful addition to the three-level ABLE of the previous edition.

SelectABLE is a 45-item, untimed (estimated time needed is 15 minutes) screening test for placing examinees at the appropriate ABLE level. Item development, analysis, and selection are clearly and completely described. Procedures for administering, scoring, and interpreting SelectABLE are clear and meaningful. Tables are simple and easy to read. SelectABLE is a useful screening device, especially when limited educational information about the examinees is available.

There are no time limits for any subtest at any level; there are suggested time guidelines. Therefore, the ABLE is a power test that allows examinees to demonstrate their abilities without time constraints. For Level 1, examinees mark in the test booklet; for Levels 2 and 3, answer sheets are used. Following is a discussion of the subtests of ABLE, Levels 1, 2, and 3.

VOCABULARY. The examinee is to recognize the meaning of words encountered in everyday situations (16 words), in the natural and physical sciences (8 words), and in the social sciences (8 words). The examinee chooses the word or group of words that best completes each sentence. For Level 1, the sentence and the options are read to the examinee. The examinee marks the answer booklet. For Levels 2 and 3, the examples are read to the examinee, then the examinee reads and answers the 32 items.

This task is appropriate in adult content; it should be noted that nouns dominate the words. Having few items to represent a wide range of grade equivalent scores causes difficulties, as discussed below.

READING COMPREHENSION. At Level 1 (40 items) the examinee gets information from simple signs (9 items), completes sentences within short reading passages using the cloze technique (18 items), and reads and comprehends advertisements and short reading passages (13 items). In each item, the examinee selects the word or phrase that best completes the sentence. Levels 2 and 3 (48 items) evaluate functional reading, printed material that is typically encountered in everyday life (24 items), and educational reading, material found in informational pieces and content area textbooks (24 items). Both literal (24 items) and inferential (24 items) comprehension are evaluated. After reading the information, the examinee is to select from four alternatives the response that best completes a statement or answers a question.

This subtest has items of adult content in an appropriate format. The cloze technique recognizes the metacognitive and metalinguistic aspects of reading comprehension.

SPELLING. At Level 1, 30 items are dictated to the examinee who writes the word in the test booklet. At Level 2, for 30 items of four words each, the examinee is to select the misspelled word. At Level 3 (30 items), 6 items have four phrases each (each phrase has an underlined word) and the examinee is to select the misspelled word; 24 items have four words each and the examinee is to select the misspelled word. This reviewer questions the construct validity of this subtest at Levels 2 and 3. The ability to identify a misspelled word is not a measure of spelling ability; such a skill is proofreading and should be identified as such. Level 1 measures spelling ability; Levels 2 and 3 do not.

LANGUAGE. At Levels 2 and 3 only (30 items at each level), the examinee selects the correct punctuation (11 items) and capitalization (7 items) for complete sentences. For 12 items the examinee selects the word or group of words that provide the grammatical completion of a sentence.

These items are appropriate to assess the mechanics of written language. There is no assessment of the examinee's production of written or oral expressive language. Users will want to recognize the limits of this language assessment.

NUMBER OPERATIONS. At Level 1 (20 items), concepts of number items (5 items) are dictated to the examinee, and computation items (15 items) are completed by the examinee. All responses are written in the test booklet. At Level 2 (36 items, 7 concepts of number and 29 computation) and 3 (40 items, 7 concepts of number and 33 computation), the examinee selects the correct solution to a problem from five alternatives, one of which is sometimes "NG" or not given.

At Level 1, some of the first five items seem difficult; the examinee is required to "write thirty-two thousand, forty-five in numerals" and to write 1,257 in words. Other items at this level and items in the other levels seem appropriate.

PROBLEM SOLVING. At Level 1, the 20 items and the four alternative answers, one of which is often

"NG" or not given, are read to the examinee, who responds in the answer booklet. At Level 2 (30 items) and Level 3 (40 items), problems are solved by the examinee and answers are selected from five alternatives, one of which is sometimes "NG" or not given.

The items seem appropriate in difficulty and adult in content.

The authors present users with detailed guidance in understanding the types of scores generated by ABLE. There is a clear, usable discussion of content-referenced scores and norm-referenced scores. Tables of scores are well labeled, clear, and easy to read. There are enlightening, useful tables of the objectives and *p*-values (percentage of the combined group sample answering the item correctly) given for each subtest at each level.

Test-item tryout and standardization was completed using 3,471 adults involved in 132 adult basic education and high school equivalency programs in school, community, and prison settings, and vocational-technical school settings for Level 3, in 41 states. Demographic data of the participating adults suggest that characteristics of sex and race are not proportionally represented by the sample. Age and geographic region are more balanced. The user is encouraged to be aware of the demographics of the research sample and to consider the characteristics of their examinees when selecting a norm table. The authors recommend the development of local norms.

Norms for ABLE are not discussed adequately. The final forms of the ABLE were "equated to the experimental forms" described by the authors. The authors state, "Percentile rank and stanine norms for each level of ABLE, based on the performance of the adult groups taking each level, were developed for the final test forms as an outcome of the equating process." No further discussion of the norms is offered. Users are directed to the publisher for a more detailed description of this equating process. All normative data, reliability, and validity information seem to be based upon the 3,471 subjects drawn from adults involved in 132 community, school, and prison adult basic education and high school equivalency programs or joint vocational-technical high school programs in 41 states. These sample sizes are: at Level 1, ABE/GED $N = 291$; Prison Group $N = 565$; at Level 2, ABE/GED $N = 436$; Prison Group $N = 472$; and at Level 3, ABE/GED $N = 474$; Prison Group $N = 515$; Vocational-Technical Group $N = 718$.

Reliability was determined using Kuder-Richardson Formula 21. For Level 1, Forms E and F, all subtests are reliable ($>.80$) for the ABE/GED population; for the prison population, Vocabulary, Number Operations, and Problem Solving have questionable reliability ($<.80$), although Reading and Spelling are reliable; for the combined group, all subtests are reliable except Form E, Number Operations and Problem Solving, and Form F, Problem Solving. For Level 2, Forms E and F, all subtests of both forms are reliable for all groups except for Vocabulary (both forms) for the prison group (.79). For Level 3, Forms E and F, all subtests are reliable for all groups except for Vocabulary (Form E) for the ABE/GED group (.78). Note that these reliabilities approach an acceptable reliability of .80.

All subtests for all levels, except for Spelling, Level 1, have a range of PK (pre-kindergarten) to PHS (post-high school). Few items in a subtest and such a wide range of scores cause wide differences in grade level equivalents from a change of a few raw score points. For example, in the Vocabulary subtest, a range of raw score points from 11 to 20 yields a difference in grade equivalence scores of 2.3 at Level 1, 2.9 at Level 2, and 4.2 at Level 3. In the Problem Solving subtest, the raw score range from 11 to 20 yields a difference in grade equivalence scores of 6.9 at Level 1, 3.2 at Level 2, and 3.1 at Level 3.

Not all subtests or all levels are as significantly influenced as these examples. The user is encouraged to examine each subtest at each level for each sample to determine the impact on their examinees' performances. Further, all subtests have a standard error of measurement of at least 2 raw score points. Users will want to be aware of these facts when interpreting scores.

There is a discussion of the validity of each level of ABLE. Objectives measured by each level are stated and related to specific items, allowing users to evaluate content validity easily. This reviewer's opinion is that the content validity is good, except for Spelling in Levels 2 and 3, as noted above. Intercorrelations among the subtests of experimental forms are as follows: for Level 1, $\leq.68$; for Level 2, $\leq.71$; and for Level 3, $\leq.71$. This suggests each subtest is measuring separate elements of skill or knowledge. ABLE was equated to the Stanford Achievement Test series. The correlations were: for Level 1, .69 or less; for Level 2, .68 to .81; and for Level 3, about .80. One wonders why the Stanford Achievement Test might not be used instead of ABLE Level 3. Perhaps the adult content of ABLE Level 3 argues for its use with the population for whom ABLE is intended.

ABLE is a useful, efficient assessment of the educational level of adults with limited education. This edition follows in the tradition established by the earlier edition. SelectABLE, a screening device for placement in the correct level of ABLE, is a useful addition. The lack of specific information about the norm development is disappointing. The problem of having a few test items represent a wide range of grade level equivalents persists. Select-ABLE and ABLE are useful tools for their intended purposes. Consumers are encouraged to use them with the test limitations in mind.

[10]

Adult Growth Examination.

Purpose: "For use in the assessment of individual adult aging."
Population: Ages 19–71.
Publication Dates: 1981–86.
Acronym: AGE.
Scores, 4: Near Vision, Hearing Loss, Systolic Blood Pressure, Body Age.
Administration: Individual.
Price Data, 1987: $14 per test manual ('86, 70 pages including score sheet).
Time: (10–15) minutes.
Comments: Other test materials (e.g., portable electronic blood pressure monitor, portable audiometric monitor, portable visual near point indicator) must be provided locally.
Author: Robert F. Morgan.
Publisher: Robert F. Morgan.

Review of the Adult Growth Examination by CAMERON J. CAMP, *Professor of Psychology, and* CAROLYN TRIAY, *Department of Psychology, University of New Orleans, New Orleans, LA:*

The Adult Growth Examination (AGE) requires 10–15 minutes to administer and is designed for the assessment of individual adult aging. The author states, "A test of individual bodily aging may be used for information, enjoyment, self awareness, research, and social change." Specifically, the test is designed to measure the "body age" of adults from age 19–71 by measuring an individual's near point of vision (NPV), hearing loss (HL), and systolic blood pressure (SBP). (A portable electronic blood pressure monitor, portable audiometer monitor, and portable visual near point indicator must be provided locally.) The individual's body age in years is then computed by comparing raw scores of these three measures to normative body-age scores provided in conversion tables (separate tables are given for men and women). In normative samples, birth age is within 10 years of body age in two out of every three persons tested, body age was more than 10 years older than birth age in one out of six persons, and body age was more than 10 years younger than birth age in one out of six persons tested. The AGE is described as "the most valid (and only) indicator of relative bodily aging in standardized test form available." The author states the test can ultimately be used to predict life expectancy, and "In theory, AGE should be a better survival predictor for an individual than insurance company actuarial tables."

RELIABILITY. Test-retest reliabilities for the overall AGE and the three subtests were computed for 50 male volunteer Nova Scotians. Reported reliabili-

ty for the AGE was .88, with subtest reliabilities of .93 (NPV), .92 (HL), and .75 (SBP).

TEST STANDARDIZATION. Subtests were standardized by Morgan and his colleagues in Hawaii, New York, and Nova Scotia from 1966 to 1972.

NORMATIVE DATA. Normative data for men and women are described as being derived from studies conducted primarily in the 1960s. The latest referenced data set is from 1972, though the author claims these data remain valid for normative purposes.

VALIDITY. Validity for AGE scores was determined by computing correlations between these scores and chronological age for 107 Nova Scotians (56 females and 51 males). AGE total scores correlated with chronological age ($r = .8$ using product-moment coefficients) for both genders. Correlations between subtest scores and chronological age ranged from .57 to .69 for raw scores, and from .67 to .78 for body-age scores.

From this same sample, correlations between subtest scores and AGE total scores ranged from .64 to .84 for raw scores, and from .74 to .85 for body-age scores. In addition, subtest intercorrelations ranged from .43 to .47 for raw scores, and from .52 to .63 for body-age scores. The standard error of the AGE scores estimated in years of chronological age was 9.3 years for AGE total score, and ranged from 8.1 years to 14.3 years for the subtests.

The AGE can be critiqued on two levels. The first level involves the general manner in which subtest scores are gathered and interpreted. An obvious problem is the possibility of variation introduced by different examiners using different brands of testing equipment. In addition, there will be varying levels of expertise in administration and scoring of the subtests if, as the author states, the AGE will be administered by "any intelligent adult" after "sufficient supervised practice."

The norms for creating body age out of subtest raw scores are dated. In addition, they might not be appropriate for some purposes. As the author notes, local norms may need to be developed. In addition, the norms and body-age conversion data reach only to age 71. Given the rapid increase in the "old-old" segment of our population, the AGE will be of limited utility for the study of aging. Finally, data for body-age declines across decades are presented in some detail for a variety of measures separately for men (in Table 1 of the test manual) and women (in Table 2). However, the data in the two tables are identical in every feature, representing either redundancy or missing data for one of the genders.

A second level of criticism involves problems for specific subtest measures. These will be described below.

MEASUREMENT OF BLOOD PRESSURE. The AGE instructions do not take into account several factors that can affect accuracy of SBP readings. The arm used to measure blood pressure should not be restricted by clothing and should be slightly flexed at the elbow, with brachial artery approximately at heart level and forearm flat on a table. Nothing should be held in either arm, and legs should not be crossed (Schein, 1987). The inflatable bag encased in the cuff should be about 20% wider than the diameter of the arm and long enough to encircle the arm; thin and obese persons will require different cuff sizes. Irregular rhythms also produce variations in systolic pressure that can reduce reliability of measurements (Bates & Hoekelman, 1974). The test author's admonition that examiners acquire "highly practiced familiarity with test materials" does not seem to go far enough in dealing with these potential confounds.

MEASUREMENT OF HEARING LOSS. The abbreviated hearing loss measure used in the AGE differs from standard methods of measurement (Newby, 1979). For example, the AGE tests the right ear first, whereas it is advisable to test the better ear first. This allows the examiner to plan on masking the better ear if the difference in sensitivity between the ears is so great that the better ear will participate in the test of the poorer ear. Testing begins at 50db, which might be uncomfortably loud for some examinees, rather than beginning at a lower reading and then increasing the dbs. In addition, the AGE uses only a descending method of obtaining threshold, rather than a series of ascending and descending sweeps.

MEASUREMENT OF VISION. Although each ear is tested in the hearing loss subtest, eyes are not tested individually in the NPV subtest.

SUMMARY. The AGE is designed to measure body age by assessing measures of near point vision, systolic blood pressure, and hearing loss in individuals aged 19–71. These raw scores are then converted into body-age scores using tables based on normative data for individuals of different ages, thus allowing individuals to determine if their abilities are at, above, or below levels that might be expected for someone of their age. Supposedly, the AGE score could also be used to detect the influence of life style changes or interventions, as well as to make predictions regarding individual longevity.

The lack of standardized testing equipment and training could severely compromise the reliability and validity of the AGE. The very simplicity of the instructions assures that the sophistication necessary to measure complex physical phenomena may not be achieved by testers. Normative data may be inappropriate or outdated. The writing style of the test manual at times is quite colloquial (e.g., Comfort "left England for sunny California"; "correlational analysis of age-sensitive factors remains in high gear"; etc.). Reviews of the test presented in appendices often include newspaper articles written by reporters rather than reviews in professional journals. Finally, by ignoring factors such as individual personality and coping variables, social support systems, and so on, the AGE becomes severely limited in its ability to measure constructs such as survivability or functional age.

In short, the AGE highlights the need to develop reliable and valid measures of body age and related constructs, as well as how very far the testing community still has to evolve before such goals are achieved.

REVIEWER'S REFERENCES

Bates, B., & Hoekelman, R. A. (1974). *A guide to physical examination* (pp. 138-141). Philadelphia: Lippincott.

Newby, H. A. (1979). *Audiology* (4th ed.) (pp. 117-124). Englewood Cliffs, NJ: Prentice-Hall.

Schein, J. (1987). Monitoring your blood pressure at home. *Consumers' Research Magazine, 70* (Part 3), 31-34.

Review of the Adult Growth Examination by JACLYN B. SPITZER, *Chief, Audiology and Speech Pathology, Veterans Administration Medical Center, West Haven, CT, and Associate Clinical Professor, Department of Surgery (Otolaryngology), Yale University School of Medicine, New Haven, CT, and GAIL M. SULLIVAN, Chief, Geriatric Medicine, and Associate Chief of Staff for Education, Veterans Administration Medical Center, Newington, CT, and Assistant Professor of Medicine, University of Connecticut, Farmington, CT:*

The manual begins with the statement, "You do not have to be a psychologist or a physician to give the Adult Growth Examination (AGE)." The author apparently intended to provide guidelines for screening several different aspects of physiology. Unfortunately, the guidelines provided contain numerous inaccuracies that could result in serious failures to detect health problems. The flaws relate to both the methods described and the validation of the test.

For example, the methodologic guidelines given for hearing examination conform to no published screening methods for the geriatric patient or any other target clinical population. The technique described should not be applied, as the intensity levels suggested far exceed any definition of hearing impairment in professional usage and also bear no semblance to levels shown to correlate to hearing handicap (e.g., see Weinstein, 1986). Furthermore, if a person or group was interested in providing hearing screening with minimal audiologic training, there are alternative methods that can be provided with greater accuracy than the one described. Specifically, the AudioScope by Welsh-Allen can be used routinely by nursing or health care professionals where an audiologist or otologist is not available. Similar methodologic criticisms can be made of vision and blood pressure screening as outlined in the AGE manual.

The validation, both face and construct, of this test is absent. As a clinician, it makes no sense at all that these "scores" (Systolic BP ≤ 160, Near Vision, and Hearing) have much to do with biological aging, chronological aging, or *survival*. Patients can survive very well with congenital hearing and visual deficits and with systolic hypertension. No sensible geriatrician would accept the unsubstantiated assertion, by the author, that these scores have any relationship to the immensely complex, and poorly understood, process of physiologic aging.

No acceptable validation data are provided. Dr. Morgan quotes 1884 and 1932 (not very recent!) data as proof that presbyopic patients die at younger ages (p. 21). These data clearly were not stratified by what we now know are major risk factors for decreased survival (e.g., heart disease, lung disease, renal failure, functional class). No validation for the "scoring" of the test (p. 9) is given at all. The statement that a systolic blood pressure of 160 mm Hg (p. 10) is "definite hypertension" is grossly inaccurate. We do not know, although there are clinical trials to study this underway (e.g., SHEP study; Black, Brand, Greenlick, et al., 1987), the import of elevations of systolic blood pressure in different age groups and sexes. In fact, most studies show no significance whatsoever for an elevated systolic blood pressure in adult females, unless it is extremely high.

The statement that this test has been "field" tested with "apparent success" (p. 28) is not adequate validation data. Indeed, there is currently no accepted "gold standard" for "biological" age, aside from chronological age; the author certainly does not attempt to put forth his own description of a gold standard (p. 32).

At various points, the author appears to suggest the score can be used to predict chronological age (p. 35), predict survival (pp. 21, 35), or perhaps spur an individual to "reverse" his aging process (p. 10), for unclear reasons and/or benefit.

In summary, the reviewers seriously question both the intent and the execution of the manual for this examination. We believe it can have serious negative consequences in failing to identify health problems that may require treatment and rehabilitation. It is irresponsible to suggest individuals should focus on the test results and even perhaps try to improve them. Great harm may result from focusing on these probably irrelevant parameters to the exclusion of well-documented risk factors for determination of function and health: diastolic blood pressure, functional class, cholesterol level, smoking, and weight, to name just a few.

REVIEWER'S REFERENCES

Weinstein, B. (1986). Validity of a screening protocol for identifying elderly people with hearing problems. *Asha, 28*, 41-45.

Black, B. M., Brand, R. J., Greenlick, M., et al. (1987). Compliance to treatment for hypertension in elderly patients: The SHEP Pilot Study. *Journal of Gerontology, 42* (5), 552-557.

[11]
The Affective Perception Inventory/College Level.

Purpose: Focuses on the academic dimension of self-perceptions, measuring the self as a person, a student, against the school settings, and exploring the feelings about the self relative to specific subject areas.
Population: Postsecondary school students.
Publication Dates: 1975–89.
Acronym: API.
Scores: 10 scales: Self Concept, Student Self, English Perceptions, Mathematics, Science, Social Studies, Business, Arts, Humanities, Campus Perceptions.
Administration: Group.
Price Data, 1988: $.30 per single scale; $4 per booklet of 10 scales; $8 per College Level manual ('85, 83 pages); $15 per composite test manual (information on all levels, '89, 22 pages).
Time: (45–60) minutes.
Comments: Ratings by self and others; fourth of 4 levels; highest level and most recent addition to the Affective Perception Inventory (9:59).
Authors: Anthony T. Soares and Louise M. Soares.
Publisher: SOARES Associates.
Cross References: For reviews by Rosa A. Hagin and Gerald R. Smith of the first three levels, see 9:59.

Review of The Affective Perception Inventory/College Level by JOHN R. HESTER, Associate Professor of Psychology, Francis Marion College, Florence, SC:

The Affective Perception Inventory/College Level (API/CL) attempts to assess self-perception in relation to specific academic areas, and at the same time seeks to measure both a general and student self-concept. To accomplish these goals the API/CL uses a multitrait/multimethod approach, whereby the instrument assesses each student with 10 scales (multitrait) completed by the student, a peer, and a teacher (multimethod). Such a multimethod approach seeks to measure and contrast differing perceptions of each student. The College Level is similar to previously developed levels of the API (Primary Grades 1–3, Intermediate 4–8, Advanced 9–12), requiring on each item a forced choice from among four descriptors along a continuum between a pair of dichotomous phrases (i.e., "enjoys math—does not enjoy math"). Student, peer, and teacher ratings on each of the 10 scales are all completed using the same items. The College Level scales are similar to previous API scales, with the exception of Humanities substituted for Physical Education and the addition of a Business Scale. The authors cite research as the primary purpose of the instrument, but also present the API/CL as an applied tool to measure the perceptions of individual students. The manual cautions users against using measured self-perceptions to categorize individuals.

Information concerning the authors' clustering model of self-concept, as well as technical data for earlier levels of the test and the College Level, are all included in the same manual. Unfortunately, at times the manual is unclear as to which level of the test it is referring, and as a result the manual has the appearance of having been pieced together over the years. The outcome is a manual that is at times confusing and very difficult to use. Users are cautioned that norms and technical information for the Business Scale are currently available only in a supplement to the test manual.

Administration instructions in both the scale booklet and the manual are rather straightforward and clear. Simple scoring directions are provided, with numeric values attached to ratings, and an algebraic sum computed for each of the 10 scales. A table is provided for converting raw scores on each scale to a stanine. As always, stanines represent a band of scores, with more specific information lost. The manual states that both a total score and subscale scores (for seven scales) can be computed, but no norms are provided for these scores. The purported advantage of having three ratings for an individual is diminished by the fact that no guidelines are included to assist in interpreting the significance of any discrepancy among scores.

An inadequate description is provided as to how items were developed for the API/CL. The norms for the test are based upon 450 college students who are broken down by sex, but no information is provided as to race, year in school, major, grades, or how the subjects were chosen. The normative sample consists of one group of 100 students from an urban, private university and 350 from a rural, public university. No other data concerning the two academic institutions are provided. It is unlikely that using students from only two universities provides a representative sample.

Reliability in terms of internal consistency (method of computation undefined) for the API/CL is .91 for self-ratings, .83 for peers, and .69 for teachers. No internal consistency data are provided for the 10 individual scales. Test-retest reliability coefficients, based on an 8-week interval, vary from a low of .69 on Campus Perceptions to a high of .94 for Mathematics. Reliability coefficients for Arts (.77), English (.76), Humanities (.73), Social Studies (.72), and Campus Perceptions (.69) are, at best, adequate. No SEMs are provided to aid in interpreting individual scores. Reliability studies reported in the manual have no information as to the number of subjects included or other demographic information.

Convergent validity was assessed through comparisons among the three raters (self, peers, and teachers). Moderate correlations were obtained, but no information was provided as to the number of raters in each group or how they were chosen; nor were there correlations among raters for individual scales. The manual did not report any validity

studies comparing the API/CL to external criteria. Note should be made that Byrne and Shavelson (1986) in using the Advanced Level of the API found significant correlations of .56 to .86 between portions of the API (Student, Self, English, Mathematics) and portions of the Self Description Questionnaire III and the Self-Concept of Ability Scale. Intercorrelations of nine API/CL scales as presented in the API manual were moderate; however, no factor analysis was provided.

In summary, the authors of the API/CL conceived of a cluster of academic self-concepts that are to some degree dependent on experiences in different academic situations. Unfortunately, minimal information is provided as to item selection, and guidelines to interpret scores are generally lacking. The normative group seems limited and only generally described. While the test appears to have adequate reliability, inadequate information is provided about reliability studies to draw firm conclusions. External criterion validity studies are notably lacking. Normative, reliability, and validity data presented in the manual are generally confusing and incomplete. It should be noted that more extensive data for the other levels of the test are presented in the manual. In short, the API/CL cannot be recommended for applied/clinical uses. Rather, the test is best considered a research tool.

REVIEWER'S REFERENCE

Byrne, B., & Shavelson, R. (1986). On the structure of adolescent self-concept. *Journal of Educational Psychology, 78,* 474-481.

Review of The Affective Perception Inventory/College Level by MICHAEL J. SUBKOVIAK, Professor of Educational Psychology, University of Wisconsin-Madison, Madison, WI:

The College Level of The Affective Perception Inventory (API) is an extension of forms of this instrument designed for use in primary and secondary schools. The inventory consists of 10 scales composed of items measuring self-concept relative to specific subject areas (English, Mathematics, etc.) or other aspects of student life. Items employ a semantic differential format in which dichotomous traits (e.g., strong vs. weak) are positioned on either side of four ordered categories scored -2, -1, +1, +2. A raw score is calculated for each scale by summing these values across items; the raw score is then converted to a stanine, indicating the strength of an individual's self-concept in a given subject area as compared to a norm group. In addition, self-ratings can be compared for congruence to peer or instructor ratings derived from equivalent forms completed by others.

The authors recommend that the API be used primarily for research purposes, which is a responsible position to adopt in light of limited information provided in the manual regarding its technical characteristics. One would hope that the API would not be used for admission, course placement, or other purposes for which it has not been validated. In its current stage of development, the API/College Level cannot and should not be recommended for general use.

RELIABILITY. Test-retest correlations, with an 8-week interval between testings, are reported for each scale of the API. The Self Concept (.88), Student Self (.85), Mathematics (.94), and Science (.90) scales have acceptable test-retest reliabilities. However, the reliabilities of the other scales range between .69 and .76 and are substandard for a commercial instrument.

Internal consistency estimates are also reported for self-ratings (.91), peer ratings (.83), and instructor ratings (.69). Although the manual does not explain how these coefficients were derived, apparently they are Rulon (1939) split-half reliabilities for composite scores obtained by summing ratings across all items and subscales. The results suggest that self-ratings are consistent, while those for instructors are substandard.

VALIDITY. The information provided in the manual pertaining to validity is also sparse. A matrix of intercorrelations among self, peer, and instructor ratings is reported—apparently for ratings on the Self Concept subscale, but the manual is not clear on this point. In any event, self-peer ratings correlated .59 and self-instructor ratings correlated .49, which suggests that self ratings are at least moderately correlated with the perceptions of others. Peer-instructor ratings correlated a relatively low .36.

A second matrix provides information about intercorrelations among all subscales for self ratings. About half of these intercorrelations are relatively low (.20–.38), while the other half are moderate to high (.40–.71). These mixed results suggest that some, but not all, subscales of the API are independent of each other. The need for factor analysis of API subscales to identify independent dimensions of self-concept has been noted by others. Such analysis might suggest combining highly correlated subscales like Science and Mathematics (.71), which appear to be measuring much the same trait, thereby reducing the number of subscales to be administered.

A table of "construct validity" coefficients for the various subscales is also reported in the manual, but the table is not explained or discussed. Apparently these coefficients are based on judgments of experts regarding the appropriateness of items on a particular subscale of the API. However, it is difficult to evaluate the results, given the dearth of information provided about the analysis.

NORMS. The tables for converting raw scores to stanine equivalents are based on administration of the API to 450 students at two universities. The representativeness of this reference group ought to be questioned by potential users of the API. The self-perceptions of this restricted group may differ in certain respects from those of college students in other settings.

The manual provides cryptic information about the norm group of 450 students. About 75% are from a public/rural university and 25% are from a private/urban university. About 48% are female and 52% are male. Separate norm tables are *not* provided for various subgroups, although there are obvious differences in perceptions, for instance, between females and males on the Mathematics and Science subscales.

The Affective Perception Inventory/College Level is at best an "experimental model" about which little is known. Information on the reliability is mixed—some subscales are reliable and others are not. Evidence of validity is extremely limited—Self Concept ratings are moderately correlated with peer and instructor ratings. Norm groups are restricted to two universities. The manual is cryptic in many respects. As such, the API cannot be recommended for general use, and its use for research purposes should be carefully considered.

REVIEWER'S REFERENCE

Rulon, P. J. (1939). A simplified procedure for determining the reliability for a test by split halves. *Harvard Educational Review, 9*, 99-103.

[12]
The Alcadd Test, Revised Edition.

Purpose: "Designed to: a) provide an objective measurement of alcoholic addiction that could identify individuals whose behavior and personality structure indicated that they were alcoholic addicts or had serious alcoholic problems; b) identify specific areas of maladjustment in alcoholics to facilitate therapeutic and rehabilitation activities; and c) obtain better insight into the psychodynamics of alcoholic addiction."
Population: Adults.
Publication Dates: 1949–88.
Scores, 6: Regularity of Drinking, Preference for Drinking over Other Activities, Lack of Controlled Drinking, Rationalization of Drinking, Excessive Emotionality, Total.
Administration: Individual or group.
Editions, 2: Paper-and-pencil, microcomputer.
Price Data, 1989: $35 per complete kit including 25 AutoScore test booklets and manual ('88, 24 pages); $22.50 per 25 AutoScore test booklets; $12.70 per manual; $185 per microcomputer edition (IBM) including diskette (tests up to 25) and user's guide.
Time: (5–15) minutes.
Comments: Self-administered.
Authors: Morse P. Manson, Lisa A. Melchior, and G. J. Huba.
Publisher: Western Psychological Services.
Cross References: See T3:152 (3 references), T2:1098 (1 reference), and P:7 (3 references); for a review by Dugal Campbell, see 6:60 (6 references); for reviews by Charles H. Honzik and Albert L. Hunsicker, see 4:30.

TEST REFERENCES

1. Elkins, R. L. (1980). Covert sensitization treatment of alcoholism: Contributions of successful conditioning to subsequent abstinence maintenance. *Addictive Behaviors*, 5, 67-89.

Review of The Alcadd Test, Revised Edition by WILLIAM L. CURLETTE, *Professor of Educational Foundations, Georgia State University, Atlanta, GA:*

According to the revised edition of The Alcadd Test manual (1988), the purposes of The Alcadd Test are threefold: namely, to "provide an objective measurement of alcoholic addiction," to "identify specific areas of maladjustment," and to "obtain better insight into the psychodynamics of alcoholic addiction." These objectives are accomplished by having respondents answer yes or no to 65 items resulting in scores on the following five subscales: Regularity of Drinking (12 items), Preference for Drinking Over Other Activities (11 items), Lack of Controlled Drinking (20 items), Rationalization of Drinking (20 items), and Excessive Emotionality (20 items). The test and the manual are produced with an attractive format.

The original Alcadd Manual (1965, 1978) provided by Western Psychological Services consisted of only two pages and one-paragraph descriptions of validity, reliability, and administration. Thus, the revised manual with 19 pages of text and 4 additional pages for test form and profile form samples represents a substantial revision.

Previous reviewers of the test (Campbell, 6:60; Hunsicker, 4:30) have commented on the lack of a theoretical support for the dimensions used in the test. The revised manual reports a factor analysis of the five Alcadd subscales; hence, providing through empirical research some basis for the total score. Ultimately, however, the meaningfulness and usefulness of the subscales come from the studies employing the Alcadd. The revised manual reports a number of studies.

As the previous reviews of the Alcadd and the test manual indicate, scores on the test could be influenced by the response set of social desirability. This occurs because the responses to the items are obvious if a person desires to fake a nonalcoholic response. Furthermore, there is no social desirability subscale to measure faking on the test. The manual suggests the MMPI validity scales or the Social Desirability Scale by Crowne and Marlowe (1960) may be used in conjunction with the Alcadd if there is concern about faking. The discussion of this issue in the test manual is brought to a close by stating that the use of the Alcadd in voluntary treatment settings should not be a problem.

Based on information in the previous manual, scoring has improved with the new revision. Previously, scoring was done by hand using a template (or sheet next to the person's responses). Now scoring is done on a form having carbon paper underneath the sheet on which the examinee takes the test. The carbon paper eliminates one step in the hand-scoring process. Also included in the test booklet are profile sheets that convert raw scores to centiles and *T*-scores, and the probability of being an alcoholic. In addition, the manual states that a microcomputer disk (IBM $5^1/_4$ inch or $3^1/_2$ inch) is available to administer, score, and print a report (two pages long) for The Alcadd Test.

Two key aspects for using any test are the amount of time required to administer the test and its reading level. On both accounts the Alcadd appears very good. The test manual reports that it requires between 5 and 15 minutes to take the 65 items in the test. Although there are many readability formulas and approaches, there are several ways to obtain a quick estimate of the grade level for reading. The Flesch-Kincaid, as calculated by the RightWriter computer program for the first 99 words and the last 101 words of the Alcadd, was 3.0. Using the SMOG index on the same selections, the reading was at the 4.7 grade level. Thus, reading level appears low enough to be used with most populations. The manual also suggests it is appropriate to read the items to examinees.

Two bothersome technical aspects are overlapping items between subscales and 40-year-old norms. A technical aspect of the test, which may be a limitation for the use of the test in research, is the assignment of some items to more than one subscale (although many tests do this). In fact, there are 23 items that are scored on more than one subscale. Even though it may reduce test-taking time, the effect of overlapping items between subscales is to induce spurious correlation between subscales. This means the correlation between subscales sharing items may be artificially inflated unless statistical adjustments are made. Whether due to overlapping items or not, the intercorrelation (.81) between two subscales (Rationalization of Drinking and Excessive Emotionality) seems high, if only from the perspective that subscales on a test battery are typically created to measure distinct attributes and, thus, would not be expected to correlate highly.

The norms shown in a sample 1988 score report in the test manual are based on a 1949 sample. Subsequent research on norms by Dunlop is reported in the manual; however, the results do not appear to provide direct support for the 1949 norms. More recent norms are needed for score interpretation.

There is a lack of information in the test manual on topics considered necessary (primary standards) in the *Standards for Educational and Psychological Testing* (AERA, APA, & NCME, 1985). Missing from the manual are standard errors of measurement, reliabilities for the subscales, and cultural fairness research information.

A unique aspect of the test is translating an examinee's total test score into the probability of being an alcoholic. Interestingly, for both males and females in any preassigned risk group, a total raw score of exactly 22 or higher yields a .99 probability of being in the alcoholic group. This observation might be helpful as a benchmark for quickly interpreting test scores.

On a PsychALERT and PsychINFO computer literature search run during Fall 1989, two citations (not listed in the test manual) (Ramsay, 1979; Zeh, 1985) were found. Ramsay (1979) administered the Alcadd, the MMPI, and the 16PF to patients suffering from alcoholism. Zeh (1985) compared scores on the Michigan Alcoholism Screening Test, the MacAndrew Alcoholism Scale, and the Alcadd in a sample of 80 incarcerated male adolescent felons. An Educational Resources Information Center (ERIC) literature search on Alcadd using SilverPlatter V1.5 for 1/83 to 6/89 did not provide any citations.

In conclusion, the concerns of previous reviewers regarding the lack of control of social desirability and the potential to fake scores on the Alcadd still limit the use of the Alcadd. Disregarding this concern, the Alcadd does approach all three of its objectives. Additional work is needed, however, to bring the Alcadd manual into closer agreement with basic test standards.

REVIEWER'S REFERENCES

Crowne, D. P., & Marlowe, D. A. (1960). A new scale of social desirability independent of psychopathology. *Journal of Consulting Psychology, 24,* 349-354.

Ramsay, S. A. (1979). Statistical information on three personality measures used with alcoholics. National Institute for Personnel Research, Johannesburg, South Africa (Afrikaans Abstract).

American Educational Research Association, American Psychological Association, & National Council on Measurement in Education. (1985). *Standards for educational and psychological testing.* Washington, DC: American Psychological Association, Inc.

Zeh, R. S. (1985). Alcoholism and incarcerated adolescent males: Knowledge and testing (Doctoral Dissertation, The University of Akron, 1985). *Dissertation Abstracts International, 45,* 3593A. (ISSN: 04194209)

Review of The Alcadd Test, Revised Edition by PAUL RETZLAFF, *Assistant Professor of Psychology, University of Northern Colorado, Greeley, CO:*

This 65-item (60 items scored) inventory of obvious yes/no alcohol-related behaviors purports to "identify" alcoholics. Its scoring results in a total score and five subscales: Regularity of Drinking, Preference for Drinking over Other Activities, Lack of Controlled Drinking, Rationalization of Drinking, and Excessive Emotionality. It was originally developed in 1949 and remains substantially unchanged in its 1988 revision.

It is brief and easy to administer, score, and determine sophisticated hit rate statistics. The new Autoscore multipart test forms and scoring sheets are particularly noteworthy. Finally, the adoption of positive and negative predictive power statistics is found in few other tests.

There are a number of problems with the test, however. First, all items, norms, and hit rates are from the original 1949 development. The test was developed via empirical group separation at an item level. The problem with this is that empirical group separation results in poorer operating characteristics than domain theory test construction. Further, in the last 40 years it is very likely that different items would be better and that "alcoholics" as a group may have changed. This is particularly true in light of the relatively low N employed in the original study—282 split four ways, male-female and alcoholic-nonalcoholic. The reliability and validity statistics are also disturbing. Although the test as a whole has an internal consistency of .92 and .96, there are no reliabilities for the five subscales reported in the manual. There is also a problem with the independence of the five subscales. They were subjectively derived and as such have no empirical basis. Further, the manual attempts to put a positive face on their very high intercorrelations by saying this proves high internal consistency. Finally, although the test as a whole has been examined for validity indices, there are no validity estimates reported for any of the five subscales.

The most positive aspects of the test are the hit rate statistics integrated into the scoring process. The test publisher is applauded for adopting the operating characteristics of positive and negative predictive powers. The reliance on the 1949 norms, however, greatly reduces the validity of these data.

In summary, The Alcadd Test is substantively unchanged from 1949 and as such is limited by its construction, norms, and other developments. A better test is probably the Alcohol Use Inventory (AUI) (Horn, Wanberg, & Foster, 1987). Its subscales were empirically derived, have high reliabilities, and add additional dimensions. The most recent revision of the AUI has added scales, items, and norms. Although longer than the Alcadd, it is a far superior test.

REVIEWER'S REFERENCE

Horn, J. L., Wanberg, K. W., & Foster, F. M. (1986). Alcohol Use Inventory. Minneapolis, MN: National Computer Systems.

[13]

American High School Mathematics Examination.

Purpose: "To identify, through friendly competition, students with an interest and a talent for mathematical problem solving."

Population: High school students competing for individual and school awards.

Publication Dates: 1950–88.

Acronym: AHSME.

Scores: Total score only.

Administration: Group.

Price Data, 1989: $15 per school registration fee; $.60 per exam (specify English or Spanish); $4 per 10 solutions pamphlets; $.50 per specimen set of prior year exams (specify year and English or Spanish); price data available from publisher for additional study aids and supplementary materials.

Foreign Language and Special Editions: Spanish, braille, and large-print editions available.

Time: 90(100) minutes.

Comments: Test administered annually in February or March at participating secondary schools.

Authors: Sponsored jointly by the Mathematical Association of America, Society of Actuaries, Mu Alpha Theta, National Council of Teachers of Mathematics, Casualty Actuarial Society, American Statistical Association, and American Mathematical Association of Two-Year Colleges.

Publisher: Mathematical Association of America; American Mathematical Society.

Cross References: For a review by Thomas P. Hogan, see 8:252 (1 reference); see also T2:598 (3 references).

Review of the American High School Mathematics Examination by CAMILLA PERSSON BENBOW, Professor of Psychology, Iowa State University, Ames, IA:

The Mathematical Association of America's (MAA) Committee on the American Mathematics Competitions writes and administers each year a sequence of four challenging mathematics examinations: The American Junior High School Mathematics Examination (AJHSME; 15), the American High School Mathematics Examination (AHSME), the American Invitational Mathematics Examination (AIME; 14), and the USA Mathematical Olympiad (USAMO; 228). All tests, except the first, serve as screening devices for the U.S. International Mathematical Olympiad (IMO) team. Students who achieve a predetermined cutoff score on the AHSME (i.e., 100) are invited to take the AIME, a 3-hour, 15-question, short-answer test, administered 3 weeks after the AHSME. The top 50 to 75 students on the AIME are invited to take the USAMO, a 3½-hour, five-question, "essay" examination. The eight top scorers on the USAMO are honored in Washington, DC, and the top 20 to 25 students are invited to a training session for the IMO. The top students emerging from the training session are then selected to participate in the IMO as representatives of the United States.

The AHSME is the very first test students take as part of this long screening process for the IMO. It serves as a filter. A secondary objective of the AHSME, however, is to identify, through friendly competition, students with an interest and a talent for mathematical problem solving. Approximately 380,000 students in the U.S. and Canada each year take the AHSME in February or early March. Unofficially participating are several thousand students in schools in other countries.

The AHSME comprises 30 multiple-choice questions to be solved in 90 minutes. (Arrangements can be made for visually handicapped students and for Spanish-speaking students.) The items on the test are based on noncalculus mathematics and are of varying difficulties. The problems are rather clever and ingenious. They appear to tap problem-solving or mathematical reasoning ability rather than emphasize the application of learned facts and knowledge. To do well on the examination, however, students must have mastered all of precalculus mathematics. For such talented students, the AHSME should be challenging and stimulating.

Given that the test has been administered for 40 years and that the American Mathematics Competitions, of which the AHSME is a part, are sponsored by such distinguished associations as the Mathematical Association of America, the American Statistical Association, and the National Council of Teachers of Mathematics, I was surprised to find no reliability or validity data. Presumably a new test is devised each year. Nonetheless, pilot testing of the examination must have taken place. Internal reliability estimates could be computed from such data. Moreover, retest data or testing students with examinations from several years, as well as results from past testings, could have provided reliability and validity data. Including results of an item analysis along with the answers would have been most useful. In addition, we are not informed how the items that comprise the test are selected or written. What are the criteria? What is the purpose of the items? Given the important screening function the AHSME serves and its expressed use to identify talented mathematical problem solvers, the lack of technical information is difficult to overlook.

Nonetheless, the AHSME should be an educationally stimulating experience for our nation's mathematically talented students. The Committee on The American Mathematics Competitions should be commended for providing this opportunity.

Review of the American High School Mathematics Examination by RANDY W. KAMPHAUS, Associate Professor of Educational Psychology, The University of Georgia, Athens, GA:

According to the publishers, the American High School Mathematics Examination (AHSME) exists for the following purpose: "The purpose of the AHSME is to identify, through friendly competition, students with an interest and a talent for mathematical problem solving." The examination consists of 30 multiple-choice items and takes 90 minutes to administer.

The AHSME student test booklet has a number of design flaws. One is first struck by the amount of superfluous information included in the test booklet. It includes various insignias of the organizations that sponsor the examination, a great deal of information about the program in general, and information on how to order copies of publications associated with the testing program. The test book is also a rather nonstandard small size. Consequently, students work on a page of mathematics problems that is considerably smaller than they typically encounter. The typeface used in the examination booklet is very small and "busy." The organization of the multiple-choice distractors varies from item to item. As such, the student has to expend cognitive resources to search actively for a place to mark an answer to individual items. In some cases the distractors are aligned horizontally, in others vertically, and in yet others are in two different horizontal lines. As is mentioned on the front of the test booklet, the figures are not necessarily drawn to scale. Not only are the figures not drawn to scale, but in some cases they are not completely clear. There is also no space available in the test booklet for students to use in working through their answers. While they are allowed to use scratch paper, it still seems the items are too closely spaced. All in all, the AHSME test booklet is extremely poorly designed for use by high-school-age pupils.

The psychometric properties of the AHSME are unknown. They were not included with the information sent with the test. There is no information or evidence that the 30 items included are placed in appropriate difficulty order. There is no distractor analysis indicating relative quality of the individual items. There is no evidence regarding reliability or validity. The criterion for a passing score has no obvious evidence of empirical support.

Many publishers have long ago eliminated corrections for guessing because of their controversial nature and lack of proven effectiveness. Yet, the AHSME continues to use a correction for guessing. The scoring rules are given as follows: "You will receive 5 points for each correct answer, 0 points for each incorrect answer, and 2 points for each problem left *unanswered*."

The 2 points for an unanswered question is essentially a correction for guessing because if a child guesses incorrectly he/she would receive 0 points for the item, whereas if the child does not guess he/she would receive 2 points. Unless the AHSME has some empirical data to support the use of a correction for guessing, which I doubt is readily available, it should be eliminated.

In summary, the AHSME is in many ways an unknown entity. Its psychometric properties are either not available or not published. Hence, crucial psychometric information cannot be evaluated to determine the quality of the exam. The AHSME does not seem even minimally adequate, as it has an exceedingly poorly designed response booklet. Unless psychometric information is forthcoming on the AHSME, it is difficult to have any faith in the quality of this instrument in order to meet its stated purpose—to select mathematically precocious youth.

American Invitational Mathematics Examination.

Purpose: "Provides challenge and recognition to high school students in the United States and Canada who have exceptional mathematical ability."
Population: American and Canadian high school students.
Publication Dates: 1983–88.
Acronym: AIME.
Scores: Total score only.
Administration: Group.
Manual: No manual.
Price Data, 1989: $1 per practice examination set including past exam (specify year desired, 1983–present) and solution pamphlet; other price data available from publisher.
Time: 180 minutes.
Comments: Administered annually, 3 weeks after the American High School Mathematics Examination (13), to students attaining a predetermined cutoff score on the AHSME.
Authors: Sponsored jointly by the Mathematical Association of America, Society of Actuaries, Mu Alpha Theta, National Council of Teachers of Mathematics, Casualty Actuarial Society, American Statistical Association, and American Mathematical Association of Two Year Colleges.
Publisher: Mathematical Association of America; American Mathematical Society.

Review of the American Invitational Mathematics Examination by ROBERT W. LISSITZ, Professor of Education and Psychology and Chairperson, Department of Measurement, Statistics, and Evaluation, University of Maryland, College Park, MD:

This test is one in a series having to do with national and international competitions in mathematics. The Mathematical Association of America Committee on Mathematics Competitions writes and administers four mathematics examinations: The American Junior High School Mathematics Examination (15), the American High School Mathematics Examination (13), the American Invitational Mathematics Examination, and the U.S.A. Mathematical Olympiad (228). In addition to test construction and administration, they also claim to oversee U.S. participation in the International Mathematical Olympiad.

The American Invitational Mathematics Examination (AIME) is described as a 3-hour, 15-question, short-answer examination and that is consistent with the sample examination made available to the reviewer. The test is taken by students who passed a predetermined cutoff on the American High School Mathematics Examination. No description of this cutoff or the process used to determine it is provided, other than to say that the AIME is a "challenge" to students with "exceptional mathematical ability." The results of the testing are to recognize highly able students from the United

States and Canada and to select those with ability to participate in further competitions. Again, how this is done is not specified in the material provided.

One of the difficulties with writing this review is the almost total lack of information. The one-page (two sides) information sheet supplements an 11-page pamphlet (10 pages are a presentation of how to answer the sample test questions and one page is a listing of the organizations and persons involved in organizing the effort) and a sample test form, both from 1986. There are no norms, reliability, validity, item analysis, table of specifications, or almost any other information that is supposed to be a part of any serious testing effort. Despite the lack of appropriate information, this is a serious testing effort in the sense that it is important to the children involved and very important to the prestige of the United States and Canada. It is strongly recommended that a manual be prepared for this test that would summarize in one place the most important testing information.

The instructions to the test do indicate that scoring is simply the number correct, with no partial credit or correction for guessing. It would be interesting to know if there are formal rules for setting the cutoff for this test, what the distribution of scores is, and the reliability of the 15 items. It would also be interesting to see if the test serves to select those students who would do best at the next level of competition (i.e., validity evidence). At least one other mathematics talent search effort in the United States uses the mathematics score of the Scholastic Aptitude Test, and it would be interesting to see how the two efforts differ in selecting students. The test booklet is pleasing to look at, although the answers are to be placed on a computer card and it was unavailable for examination. Procedures for verifying the uniqueness and accuracy of the answer key are also unspecified.

In summary, this effort is a very important one and may be done well. The evidence provided does not support a feeling of confidence nor does it necessarily raise any alarms. Attention to the design of the test and to gathering evidence about the test is an important next step for the relevant mathematics committees.

Review of the American Invitational Mathematics Examination by CLAUDIA R. WRIGHT, Assistant Professor of Educational Psychology, California State University, Long Beach, CA:

The American Invitational Mathematics Examination (AIME) has been prepared by the Mathematical Association of America (MAA) Committee on the American Mathematics Competitions (CAMC) and is used to select those students who demonstrate exceptional ability in mathematics for competition in the U.S.A. Mathematical Olympiad (USAMO) invitational examination (which is the precursor of the International Mathematical Olympiad).

The AIME is administered annually 3 weeks after the American High School Mathematics Examination (AHSME) to those high school students in the United States and Canada who attain a predetermined cutoff score on the AHSME and who accept the invitation to participate in this competition. Requiring 3 hours for administration, the AIME consists of 15 short-answer items that can be solved using precalculus mathematics. The test is normally administered by the staff at the school attended by the examinees. A total score is obtained based upon the number of correct responses achieved by the student. Depending upon the test item, more than one solution may be possible (e.g., algebraic vs. geometric; computational vs. conceptual; or, elementary vs. advanced). No partial credit is awarded and there is no penalty for wrong answers. The use of scratch paper, a ruler, a compass, and erasers is encouraged; however, no calculators or slide rules are allowed during testing.

A test packet that includes the test booklet, a computer card for recording answers, and the AIME Solutions Pamphlet is provided for students and teachers. The Solutions Pamphlet has been designed to provide clear explanations and illustrations of correct answers and, in some instances, expanded explanations are offered detailing alternative methods that may be employed to arrive at appropriate solutions. Additional practice materials are available upon request for a modest fee.

No reports of normative or descriptive data were cited and no detailed psychometric information pertaining to the reliability and validity of the AIME was provided or referenced in any of the test materials made available by the sponsors of the examination. In a search of the literature, no validity-related investigations or behavioral (e.g., student attitude) studies were found that employed AIME scores as a variable.

It is likely that those students who are tested represent a homogeneous scoring group in mathematics. Consequently, validity estimates associated with the AIME may be quite low. However, to establish psychometric properties of the test, including factorial or construct validity as well as concurrent and predictive validities, a more heterogeneous group could be sampled. To further this type of investigation, any number of variables could be employed from scores provided by standardized achievement tests in mathematics, performance scores from other competitive mathematics examinations, and/or indicators of academic success. In addition, the establishment of the reliability of the instrument, based upon a more heterogeneous group of students, would be relatively straightforward. Any number of approaches would be appropriate including internal-consistency estimates and parallel forms (assuming that the new tests that are prepared each year can be shown to be nearly equivalent— once again, this task would be relatively easy to accomplish as, at this writing, there are approximately eight or nine versions of the test, with new versions added each year).

Overall, the AIME appears to have been a thoughtfully and expertly constructed test designed to challenge our most precocious mathematicians and logicians. It would seem that a carefully directed study targeting the psychometric properties of this series of tests could provide the empirical evidence necessary to support the selection process for which the test was developed and to confirm what appears to be a conceptually strong instrument. In addition, a thorough psychometric treatment of the test could provide those investigators in the areas of critical thinking and mathematics as well as those interested in related curriculum development with much needed insights and tools for improving instruction in these areas.

[15]
American Junior High School Mathematics Examination.

Purpose: "To increase interest in mathematics and to develop problem solving ability through a friendly competition."

Population: American and Canadian students in Grade 8 or below.

Publication Dates: 1985–88.

Acronym: AJHSME.

Scores: Total score only.

Administration: Group.

Price Data, 1988: $10 per school registration fee; $10 per 25 exam booklets.

Special Edition: Braille and large-print editions available.

Time: 40 minutes.

Comments: Test administered annually in December at participating schools.

Authors: Sponsored jointly by the Mathematical Association of America, Society of Actuaries, Mu Alpha Theta, National Council of Teachers of Mathematics, Casualty Actuarial Society, American Statistical Association, and American Mathematical Association of Two Year Colleges.

Publisher: Mathematical Association of America; American Mathematical Society.

Review of the American Junior High School Mathematics Examination by JOHN M. ENGER, Professor of Education, Arkansas State University, State University, AR:

Undoubtedly spurred by the success of the American High School Mathematics Examination (AHSME; 13), seven mathematical societies in 1985 introduced the American Junior High School Mathematics Examination (AJHSME). These sponsors are: the Mathematical Association of Amer-

ica, the Society of Actuaries, Mu Alpha Theta, the National Council of Teachers of Mathematics, the Casualty Actuarial Society, the American Statistical Association, and the American Association of Two-Year Colleges. The purpose of the AJHSME is to increase interest in mathematics and to develop problem-solving ability through a friendly competition.

This test consists of 25 multiple-choice items which cover a wide range of topics taught in junior high school (grades 7 and 8) mathematics. Because it is a competitive exam that will identify the clearly superior junior high school math students, most of the items are quite difficult. A content analysis of the AJHSME suggests that most of the items deal with number concepts. There are some items on area, ratio/proportion, graphing, and spatial concepts.

The test and solutions manual from one administration provides the student and teacher with a description of the format and type of problems to be expected on the next administration. Most junior high school mathematics teachers who administer the AJHSME will receive only this information about the test.

The schools receive a series of certificates with the AJHSME. A gold certificate is awarded to the student recording the highest test score, a silver certificate for second, and a bronze-colored certificate for third. A white certificate, which can be copied, is included for other students participating in the examination. Exceptional mathematics achievement, as measured by the test, can be recognized and rewarded with these certificates.

Because the AJHSME will be quite difficult for the majority of junior high school students, the mathematics teacher should forewarn students prior to taking the exam. The AJHSME is markedly more difficult than current nationally standardized achievement test batteries. Standardized achievement test batteries are not intended to discriminate as well as the AJHSME at higher levels of achievement. Junior high school personnel might encourage students to take the AJHSME to demonstrate particularly high levels of mathematics achievement as a motivational strategy.

The AJHSME is administered in December. No calculators are permitted in taking the exam. There is no correction for guessing in scoring the exam, thus the student should attempt to answer every item. Security in administration of the examination is stressed by having the principal verify the seal of the examination packet was not broken prior to one-half hour before the administration of the examination.

As noted in an earlier *MMY* review (8:252) of the high school mathematics examination (the AHSME), a limitation of the junior high school mathematics examination (the AJHSME) is the lack of a technical manual. The seven mathematical societies sponsoring these examinations may have assured the content validity of the items. Yet, little technical information (e.g., reliability and validity) is afforded the user. The test authors should consult the *Standards for Educational and Psychological Testing* (AERA, APA, & NCME, 1985) and provide test consumers with crucial psychometric information.

The AJHSME is one way of identifying and promoting exceptional mathematics achievement. Rewarding exceptional mathematics achievement on the basis of scores on the AJHSME appears appropriate in light of the commitment of the mathematics organizations sponsoring this testing program. Further technical information would support this speculation with data.

REVIEWER'S REFERENCE

American Educational Research Association, American Psychological Association, & National Council on Measurement in Education. (1985). *Standards for educational and psychological testing.* Washington, DC: American Psychological Association, Inc.

Review of the American Junior High School Mathematics Examination by DARRELL SABERS, Professor of Educational Psychology, University of Arizona, Tucson, AZ:

This is an unusual test to be reviewed in the *MMY* series. There is no manual for interpretation and no information on development, test or item bias studies, reliability, validity, scaling, norming, or equating. The materials reviewed for this review consist of the 1985 exam booklet and the solutions pamphlet. Each year a new exam booklet and a new solutions pamphlet are developed, permitting complete disclosure of all of the items used the previous year.

The exam booklet includes simple directions informing the student there is no penalty for guessing and that the answers can often be obtained by eliminating options and estimating. Calculators are not permitted. The 40-minute time limit for 25 five-option items permits hand calculation for some of the problems for a fast student, but many students may find that estimation and elimination need to be used to finish the test in the allotted time.

Anyone questioning whether computation must be included in an instrument to assess mathematical reasoning is encouraged to examine this test. All of the problems can be answered without routine computation, although some computation may be useful in finding the answer. Graph paper and rulers are permitted, although I did not find it necessary to use more than a small piece of scratch paper in order to answer all 25 items in less than 25 minutes. Taking the test was a very enjoyable experience, and it is likely the exam does indeed serve its purpose "to increase student interest in mathematics."

There are no "tricky" items in the exam. The items are fair and very well written. They appear to be good measures of mathematical reasoning, although there are no item statistics provided to support this belief. Content validity typically should be evaluated by considering relevance and representation. Every item in this exam appears to be relevant. Because there is no implication that high scorers have learned the mathematics intended for their grades, there is no need for the test to be representative of the complete seventh and eighth grade curriculum. Also, given the nature of the program in which this exam is used, there is no implication that the low scorers have failed to learn necessary prerequisites for further instruction. Thus, it is difficult to suggest cautions about misuses of the test. However, if there were any attempt to use the number (or percentage) correct scores for purposes of comparing performances across years, all the problems associated with volunteer samples and all the concerns about representative sampling of curriculum content, meaning of scores for low-scoring examinees, and others that plague the SAT and ACT would immediately become issues.

The solutions pamphlet contains the correct choice and at least one solution for each item. Several items have more than one solution included. There is no implication that any of these solutions is better than any other one the student could have used. One of the praiseworthy features of the solutions pamphlet is that for most problems so little computation is done in the solutions presented.

As an overall evaluation, it should be stated the exam really delivers what the program intends and suggests. The exam appears to be a fair and good measure of mathematical reasoning. As long as it is used for the purpose intended, there is no need for the additional supporting material that definitely would be required if selection or placement decisions were to be influenced by students' scores on the exam.

[16]

Ann Arbor Learning Inventory.
Purpose: To evaluate competencies in visual, memory, aural, and comprehension skills.
Population: Grades K–1, 2–4, 5–8.
Publication Dates: 1977–89.
Administration: Group.
Price Data, 1991: $10 per manual (specify Level A ['82, 62 pages], Level B ['87, 58 pages], or Level C ['89, 64 pages]); $12 per 10 student booklets (specify level); $8 per Level C stimulus cards.
Time: Administration time not reported.
Authors: Barbara Meister Vitale and Waneta B. Bullock.
Publisher: Academic Therapy Publications.
  a) SKILL LEVEL A.
  Population: Grades K–1.
  Scores, 7: Body Image, Visual Discrimination Skills, Visual Motor Coordination Skills, Visual Sequential Memory Skills, Aural Discrimination Skills, Aural Sequential Memory Skills, Aural Conceptual Skills.

b) SKILL LEVEL B.
Population: Grades 2–4.
Scores, 5: Visual Discrimination Skills, Visual Motor Coordination Skills, Sequential Memory Skills, Auditory Discrimination Skills, Comprehension Skills.
c) SKILL LEVEL C.
Population: Grades 5–8.
Scores, 6: Visual Discrimination Skills, Visual Motor Coordination Skills, Visual Sequential Memory Skills, Auditory Discrimination Skills, Auditory Sequential Memory Skills, Comprehension Skills.

Review of the Ann Arbor Learning Inventory by JUNE ELLEN SHEPHERD, Postdoctoral Pediatric Psychology Fellow in the Pediatric Comprehensive Neurorehabilitation Unit at the Kennedy Institute at Johns Hopkins University School of Medicine, Baltimore, MD:

The Ann Arbor Learning Inventory (AALI) test series was designed "to give a teacher a comprehensive picture of a student's basic disabilities . . . . By looking at the strong central processing areas as indicated on the Ann Arbor Inventory, the teacher can identify the student's modality strength and adopt the student's curriculum to the modality" (Level A manual, p. i). The tests are for the purpose of evaluating through group administration, the visual, memory, aural, and comprehension skills of children in grades K–8. Test scores are used to determine the proper selection of text materials or series of text materials, specifically the Ann Arbor Publishers materials, needed "to ease their difficulties" (Level C manual, p. ii).

Unsuccessful attempts were made to secure information concerning the AALI's development, standardization, reliability, and validity. Before the AALI can be taken seriously, the authors should provide a description of the test construction, a description and discussion of the test's psychometric properties, evidence that the AALI contributes to improved student grades, and simple, clear, step-by-step instructions for administration and scoring. Possibly this instrument might be of help to the classroom teacher if it were adequately researched; however, the authors have not met their professional responsibility of reporting data to support the reliability and validity of the instruments they have designed. Because it is unacceptable educational practice to promote tests of unknown quality, the AALI is not recommended for use at this time.

Review of the Ann Arbor Learning Inventory by RUTH E. TOMES, Assistant Professor of Family Relations and Child Development, Oklahoma State University, Stillwater, OK:

The Ann Arbor Learning Inventory is designed to serve two purposes: first, to identify specific competencies and deficiencies in central processing abilities, and second, to provide suggestions for remediations and/or placement in the publisher's text materials. The inventory is available at three levels: Level A (kindergarten and first grade), Level B (second through fourth grade), and Level C (fifth through eighth grade). The test authors advise that Level C may be used with older students and adults who are functioning at the grade 5–8 level. Separate manuals and student assessment booklets are available for each level. Level A consists of 21 subtests, each of which has five to 14 items purporting to measure a specific processing ability (e.g., visual discrimination). Level B has 14 subtests consisting of 6 to 40 items each, and Level C has 15 subtests of 9 to 50 items per subtest. All three levels assess Visual Discrimination, Visual Motor Coordination, Sequential Visual and Auditory Memory, and Auditory Discrimination Skills. In addition, Level A includes a test for Body Image, and Levels B and C include tests for Comprehension Skills.

Instructions for administration of individual subtests are generally clear and easy to follow by the classroom teacher, the intended user. The teacher gives oral instructions and the children mark in their test booklets. Several important omissions in the manuals, however, leave to guesswork certain aspects of administration. First, no report of administration time is included. Given the large number of subtests, it would seem, to this reviewer, necessary to space the tests over several days. Also, the manuals fail to state whether the test is group or individually administered. Careful reading of instructions for each subtest is necessary to learn that most may be group administered whereas a few require individual administration.

Scoring of the test is easily accomplished. Each subtest yields a score based on number of errors and percent correct. A student score summary page is provided for compiling the information from the subtests. No summary or composite score is obtained for the entire test, however. Rather, the subtest error scores are used as cutoffs for decisions on the need for remediation of a particular process. Suggestions for remediation that can be carried out by the classroom teacher are presented in the manuals for each process tested. These instructional suggestions are followed by information regarding remediation materials available from the test publisher.

This test suffers from many serious problems. No theoretical or empirical link between test items and the processing abilities purportedly measured is discussed in the manuals. No rationale is provided for cutoff points underlying decisions for remediation. No information is presented pertaining to item or subtest selection. No statistical information whatsoever is available regarding standardization, reliability, or validity. Finally, the use of paper-and-pencil format and group administration are viewed by early childhood educators as inappropriate testing procedures with young children. Overall, this test has little to recommend its use for any purpose.

[17]
Arizona Articulation Proficiency Scale, Second Edition.

Purpose: Intended as a "clinical measure of articulatory competence in children."
Population: Ages 1-6 to 13-11.
Publication Dates: 1963–86.
Acronym: AAPS.
Scores: Total score only.
Administration: Individual.
Price Data, 1991: $80 per complete kit; $49.50 per set of picture test cards; $10.50 per 25 protocol booklets; $19.50 per 100 survey forms; $22.50 per manual.
Time: (10–15) minutes.
Comments: Total score is provided in the form of severity rating, percentile, standard score, developmental age equivalent, and intelligibility description.
Authors: Janet Barker Fudala and William M. Reynolds.
Publisher: Western Psychological Services.
Cross References: For information regarding an earlier edition, see T3:200 (8 references); for reviews by Raphael M. Haller and Ronald K. Sommers, and an excerpted review by Barton B. Proger, see 8:954 (6 references); see also · T2:2065 (2 references), 7:948 (2 references), and 6:307a (2 references).

TEST REFERENCES

1. Bralley, R. C., & Stoudt, R. J., Jr. (1977). A five-year longitudinal study of development of articulation proficiency in elementary school children. *Language, Speech, and Hearing Services in Schools, 8,* 176-180.
2. Schissel, R. J., & James, L. B. (1979). An investigation of the assumptions underlying the scoring system of the Arizona Articulation Proficiency Scale: Revised. *Language, Speech, and Hearing Services in Schools, 10,* 241-245.
3. Kumin, L., Saltysiak, E., Bell, K., Forget, K., Goodman, M., Padden, J., Goytisolo, M., Schroeter, N., & Thomas, S. (1984). Functional method for assessing oral perceptual skills in children. *Perceptual and Motor Skills, 58,* 635-639.
4. Rastatter, M., & DeJarnette, G. (1984). EMG activity of orbicularis oris superior, orbicularis oris inferior, and masseter muscles of articulatory disordered children. *Perceptual and Motor Skills, 58,* 191-196.
5. Madison, L. S., George, C., & Moeschler, J. B. (1986). Cognitive functioning in the fragile-x syndrome: A study of intellectual, memory and communication skills. *Journal of Mental Deficiency Research, 30,* 129-148.
6. Ragsdale, J. D., & Dauterive, R. (1986). Relationships between age, sex, and hesitation phenomena in young children. *The Southern Speech Communication Journal, 52,* 22-34.
7. Powers, L. A., & Madison, C. L. (1987). Effects of presentation mode on discrimination skills of articulatory disordered children. *Perceptual and Motor Skills, 64,* 775-779.
8. Rastatter, M., McGuire, R., & Blair, B. (1987). EMG activity with the jaw fixed of orbicularis oris superior, orbicularis oris inferior and masseter muscles of mild and moderate articulatory disordered children. *Perceptual and Motor Skills, 64,* 1213-1214.
9. Abraham, S., Stoker, R., & Allen, W. (1988). Speech assessment of hearing-impaired children and youth: Patterns of test use. *Language, Speech, and Hearing Services in Schools, 19,* 17-27.
10. DeJarnette, G. (1988). Formant frequencies (F₁, F₂) of jaw-free versus jaw-fixed vowels in normal and articulatory disordered children. *Perceptual and Motor Skills, 67,* 963-971.
11. Klee, T., Schaffer, M., May, S., Membrino, I., & Mougey, K. (1989). A comparison of the age-MLV relation in normal and specifically language-impaired preschool children. *Journal of Speech and Hearing Disorders, 54,* 226-233.
12. Tallal, P., Ross, R., & Curtiss, S. (1989). Familial aggregation in specific language impairment. *Journal of Speech and Hearing Disorders, 54,* 167-173.

Review of the Arizona Articulation Proficiency Scale, Second Edition by PENELOPE K. HALL, Associate Professor of Speech Pathology and Audiology, The University of Iowa, Iowa City, IA:

The 1986 Second Edition of the Arizona Articulation Proficiency Scale (AAPS) provides information about an individual's speech-sound system for consonants and vowels using traditional sound-by-sound analysis. The consonant phonemes are assessed in initial and final word positions, while 20 vowels and diphthongs, including · rhotics, are assessed in appropriate word positions. The inclusion of vowel assessment in this instrument is important to note because these phonemes are often neglected by speech-sound assessment instruments. The AAPS assesses the phonemes in both picture and sentence formats, thus extending the test's usefulness to include older individuals with speech-sound disorders.

The format of the AAPS is user friendly. Thirty-four of the 48 picture stimuli and 58 of the 63 sentence stimuli assess only one phoneme within a response, while the remaining stimuli assess both a consonant and a vowel contained in the word. Of course, whole-word transcription could informally reveal information in addition to that on which the test is standardized. The administration instructions are easy to follow, with relevant information clearly presented.

The appearance of the Picture Test stimuli is unchanged from the 1970 test revision and consists of black and white line drawings. They may not be as inherently interesting to children as the pictures included in other assessment tools, but they are adequate for the test's purposes. The Sentence Test has also remained unchanged from the 1970 revision.

This edition of the AAPS has undergone a number of important changes that strengthen its psychometric characteristics.

ITEM ANALYSIS. The systematic analysis used in the development of the original picture stimuli is described in the test manual. The potential pictured stimuli were administered to 7,000 children whose responses resulted in the stimuli selections and picture style used in the original 1963 test. Some modifications were included in the 1970 revision, and they are described in the manual. The actual development of the stimuli used in the Sentence Test is not described, although the manual notes that a first grade reading level is used.

DEFINITION AND SIZE OF STANDARDIZATION SAMPLE. This edition of the AAPS was standardized on 5,122 children. Subject selection criteria are not specified. The number of subjects for each of the 13 age groups ranged from 112 to 742. The manual states that the sample of children was representative of the general population of children based on 1980 census information. Females made up 52.2% of the norm group, while males made up 47.8%. In addition, 83.7% of the group were White, 9.6% were Black, 3.4% were Hispanic, and 3.3% were Asian. The children were described as living in "four western states," with English as their primary language. No socio-economic information is provided.

MEASURES OF CENTRAL TENDENCY AND VARIABILITY. A considerable amount of effort was devoted to creating the measures of central tendency and variability included in this edition of the AAPS. Means, standard deviations, and ranges of scores are included for 18 age levels (at 6-month intervals between the ages of 1 year 6 months and 6 years 11 months, and at yearly intervals between the ages of 7 years 0 months and 13 years 11 months). Also included are percentile ranks by age levels, standard scores in the form of normalized *T*-scores, and standard errors of measurement.

Statistically based severity ratings are also provided. Examinees with scores within plus or minus one standard deviation of the mean are described as having "normal" articulation; those with scores within the range of -1.5 to -1.01 standard deviations are described as having a "mild" problem; those whose scores fall within the range of -2.00 to -1.51 standard deviations are described as having a "moderate" problem; and those whose scores fall below -2.01 standard deviations are described as having a "severe problem" with articulating sounds correctly.

Two criterion-based methods of test interpretation are also provided. Developmental age norms for each assessed consonant and vowel phoneme, collected as a part of the Second Edition standardization, are presented in two formats. The age by which 90% of the subjects correctly articulated each phoneme is included in the test manual. Tables present this same data across all tested ages.

The authors also suggest that the ratings of intelligibility index is a criterion-referenced measure. This interpretation of articulatory proficiency is suggested by the total scores achieved on the AAPS but no information about the development of the index is given. The authors correctly note that the suggested intelligibility interpretations do not take into account either a child's age and articulatory developmental level or the impact of the various types of articulatory errors upon overall intelligibility.

VALIDITY. Concurrent validity for the AAPS was demonstrated during the development of the 1963 edition when 10 judges rated one minute of spontaneous speech of 45 children (6 to 12 years of age, with test results ranging from normal to severely disordered articulation). The reported correlation between the listeners' ratings and examinees' test scores was .92. During the renorming process for the 1986 Second Edition, 2,485 children

in the standardizing population were also administered one of three other commercially available speech-sound inventories. The correlations between scores from these tests and the AAPS were very high. Other forms of validity are not discussed by the authors.

RELIABILITY. Several forms of reliability are reported: interrater, intrarater, test-retest, and internal consistency. Two raters who listened to the randomized responses to the AAPS of 21 children achieved an interrater reliability of .86. The authors also report two studies that produced intra-examiner reliabilities of .95 and .99. These studies used a small number of trained examiners as raters, and no indication of the severity of the problems being transcribed is given. Internal consistency reliability coefficients were also computed for each age level in the standardization sample. The range across all ages tested was .77 to .94, with a median of .89. Thus, the AAPS Second Edition appears to be a reliable assessment instrument.

USER QUALIFICATIONS/ADEQUACY OF TEST MANUAL. The manual clearly states that: "The AAPS should be administered only by qualified communication disorders specialists, persons with appropriate certification (Certificate of Clinical Competence) or students in training as speech-language pathologists or audiologists" (p. 2). The test administration, scoring, and interpretation procedures are also clearly described in the manual.

In summary, the 1986 AAPS Second Edition appears to have been developed with careful considerations being given to its psychometric characteristics. As a result, it is perhaps the strongest norm-referenced speech-sound assessment instrument commercially available at the present time.

Review of the Arizona Articulation Proficiency Scale, Second Edition by CHARLES WM. MARTIN, Assistant Dean, University College, Ball State University, Muncie, IN:

Fudala and Reynolds have made a commendable attempt to enhance the clinical utility of the Arizona Articulation Proficiency Scale (AAPS). The AAPS Second Edition provides the diagnostician with both quantitative and qualitative data for analysis of articulatory performance. Although there are some notable shortcomings, there are also some very positive attributes to data provided in the revised manual.

The AAPS is a well-researched, standardized, diagnostic instrument that was constructed to assess articulatory proficiency in children from 1.5 to 13 years of age. It assesses the articulation of single consonants in prevocalic and postvocalic positions and selected consonant clusters and vowels. The Second Edition uses the same stimulus items as previous editions. Client responses are elicited by using either 48 black and white line drawings or 25 first-grade-level sentences. Two additional stimulus cards showing a child performing an activity may be used to obtain spontaneous speech samples, but these items are not included in the basic scoring procedures.

The test manual provides clear and concise instructions for basic scoring, which is augmented by the scoring form structure. The AAPS total score (raw score) is the weighted percentage of the individual's correctly articulated sounds. Conversion tables are provided to determine global ratings of the child's level of proficiency (severity ratings and intelligibility level), percentile ranks, and standard scores. Another series of tables indicates the percentage of children at each age level who have mastered each particular sound. Discussions of clinical implications and limitations of the norm-referenced scores and descriptive statistical data (e.g., standard deviations) are provided and should facilitate interpretation of test results.

Test reliability is well documented for rater reliability, internal consistency, and test-retest performance. A test-retest reliability is reported as .96 among 19 examiners, but the exact procedure followed to determine this reliability is not reported. Concurrent and construct validity for the test are acceptable.

A major shortcoming of the AAPS Second Edition is the frequency-of-occurrence values used to determine the severity of a communication disorder. Although the authors provide extensive restandardized data based on 5,122 children, the most fundamental component of the test scoring procedure, the frequency-of-occurrence values, was not revised. These values were abstracted from Barker and England (1962) who used relative frequencies reported by French, Carter, and Koenig (1930). The authors note that the many subtle factors influencing children's acquisition of language and concept development necessitate that a test be renormed periodically. Unfortunately, one of the most critical components of this test was not reanalyzed. The relative frequency of occurrence of a given sound must vary as a function of the language structure. Current literature documents different relative frequency-of-occurrence values for different sounds. Frequency of occurrence is also a function of chronological age, a result of a child's language system. Using the adult frequency-of-occurrence value for a phoneme establishes as a criterion a standard that is not representative of the development of a child's phonological system. Weighted percentages should reflect the sound system under investigation in order to carry out differential diagnostics. These factors suggest that these important weights should have been considered as part of the renorming process.

The age of phoneme mastery on the AAPS was defined as the earliest age at which 90% of the particular age group achieved mastery of the phoneme. Clinicians should be aware that the ages presented on the test form do not reflect this criterion. The Tables of Percentages for Correct Articulation of Consonants indicate that this criterion was inconsistently applied to the test form. For example, prevocalic [v] is reported on the test form to be mastered at $5^1/_2$ years of age, but reaches 100% mastery according to the tables when the child is between 4 and $4^1/_2$ years of age. Although the percentage for correct articulation drops below 90% during the next two age ranges, the criterion had been met. In other instances, the early age for mastery was used even though the percentage dropped below 90% in subsequent age ranges. From a clinical standpoint, ages presented on the test form should reflect criteria established for age of mastery in a consistent manner in order to avoid misinterpretation of test results.

The "marginally significant" difference reported by the authors on gender would be expected when employing a t-test with a large sample. This statistical test is generally considered more appropriate for small sample sizes because it tends to be sensitive to small differences in subjects when applied to large samples. Given the large sample size (5,122), a more robust statistical test may not have suggested this difference.

In summary, the AAPS Second Edition provides the clinician with a traditional measurement of articulatory performance of single-word utterance comparable to the original edition. The data analysis procedures provided make it an appropriate part of a complete test battery, but the clinician should not rely on the results as a sole predictor of articulatory development or sole indicator of the therapeutic intervention strategy to be used.

REVIEWER'S REFERENCES

French, N. R., Carter, C. W., Jr., & Koenig, W., Jr. (1930). The words and sounds of telephone conversations. *Journal of Acoustical Society of America, 9,* 290-324.

Barker, J., & England, G. (1962). A numerical measure of articulation: Further developments. *Journal of Speech and Hearing Disorders, 27,* 23-27.

[18]
Assessing Linguistic Behaviors: Assessing Prelinguistic and Early Linguistic Behaviors in Developmentally Young Children.

Purpose: To assess "children's performance in five areas of cognitive-social and linguistic development: cognitive antecedents to word meaning, play, communicative intentions, language comprehension and language production."
Population: Children functioning below 2 years of age.
Publication Date: 1987.
Acronym: ALB.
Scores: 5 scales: Cognitive Antecedents to Word Meaning Scale, Play Scale, Communicative Intention

Scale, Language Comprehension Scale, Language Production Scale.

Administration: Individual.

Price Data, 1989: $40 per copy of Assessing Prelinguistic and Early Linguistic Behaviors in Developmentally Young Children in binder format (165 pages); $125 per copy of ½-inch VHS format of accompanying video; $250 per copy of ¾-inch U-Matic format of accompanying video.

Time: Administration time varies with scales administered.

Comments: Behavior checklist; other test materials (e.g., windup toy, doll) must be supplied by examiner.

Authors: Lesley B. Olswang, Carol Stoel-Gammon, Truman E. Coggins, and Robert L. Carpenter.

Publisher: University of Washington Press.

a) COGNITIVE ANTECEDENTS TO WORD MEANING SCALE.

Purpose: "To examine the cognitive skills for three particular early emerging semantic notions and their related pragmatic functions: Nomination, Agent, Location."

Acronym: CAWM.

Scores: 7 tasks: Nomination Task (Naming Box), Agent Tasks (Unobserved Agent, Observed Agent), Location Tasks (Doll and Cup, Containers, Block Structure and Doll, Nesting Cups).

Time: (20–30) minutes.

Authors: Lesley Olswang with contributions by Carla Brooks, Judith Cooper, and Mary Pat Daly.

b) PLAY SCALE.

Purpose: "A practical means for observing practice play and symbolic play behaviors in a clinical setting for the purpose of gleaning information about a child's understanding of objects and their functions."

Scores, 12: Single Play Episodes (Mouthing Objects, Banging Objects, Visual Regarding, Manipulating Objects, Approximating Objects, Semi-appropriate Toy Use, Nesting Objects, Grouping, Appropriate Toy Use), Multiple Play Episodes (Same-action Multiple Play Episode, Different-action Multiple Play Episode, Extended Multiple Play Episode).

Time: (35–45) minutes.

Authors: Robert L. Carpenter with contributions by Judith Cooper, Janet Ringle-Bartels, and Shelley Tinsley.

c) COMMUNICATIVE INTENTION SCALE.

Purpose: "For observing and coding several intentional behaviors in children functioning in the latter stages of sensorimotor development."

Scores: 5 categories: Commenting, Requesting, Requesting Information, Acknowledging, Answering.

Time: Administration time not reported.

Comments: "Criterion-referenced."

Authors: Truman E. Coggins with contributions by Lori Harris, Linda Pelligrini, and Susan Vethivelu.

) LANGUAGE COMPREHENSION SCALE.

Purpose: "To obtain an accurate developmental assessment of children's comprehension during the latter stages of sensorimotor development."

Parts: 3 subsections: Action Games, Single Words, Comprehension of Word Combinations.

Levels: 3 levels corresponding to 3 subsections respectively: functional level 9–15 months, 15–24 months, 18–24 months.

Time: Administration time not reported.

Authors: Truman E. Coggins with contributions by Susan E. Kellogg.

e) LANGUAGE PRODUCTION SCALE.

Purpose: "To examine the vocalizations and verbalizations of children 9 to 24 months of age."

Parts, 5: Prelinguistic Utterances, Meaningful Speech Production (Phonetic, Phonological, Syntactic, Semantic).

Time: Administration time not reported.

Authors: Carol Stoel-Gammon with contributions by Charlene Kelly, Shelly Tinsley, and Susan Kellogg.

Review of Assessing Linguistic Behaviors: Assessing Prelinguistic and Early Linguistic Behaviors in Developmentally Young Children by JEFFREY A. ATLAS, Deputy Chief Psychologist and Assistant Clinical Professor, Bronx Children's Hospital, Albert Einstein College of Medicine, Bronx, NY:

Assessing Linguistic Behaviors is an assessment procedure, explained via a large looseleaf-binder manual, packaged as a criterion-referenced scale. It falls short of a satisfactory criterion-referenced scale due to inadequate reliability, inadequate internal and external validity, and problems in construct validity. Assessing Linguistic Behaviors does sample the universe of prelinguistic and early linguistic behaviors in wide fashion, demonstrating good content validity.

The assessment procedure was developed from an early 1980 15-month longitudinal study of 40 children at 9, 12, 15, 18, 21, and 24 months. The original sample comprised 20 male and 20 female 9-month-olds, but due to attrition or illness sometimes as few as 34 subjects participated in data collection, leaving the sampling problem of "empty cells." In addition the sample is skewed by inclusion criteria specifying that the subject be the only child in the family at the onset of the study and that s/he be from an English-speaking home. Inspection of the Bayley mental scale scores provided in the manual shows developmental indices about a standard deviation above average. Finally, although degree of agreement between two raters on 24 subjects is provided, there are not sufficient data on some measures to evaluate whether interrater reliability was consistently above chance level. Problems in the internal validity of the assessment procedures and the constricted nature of the sample thus limit the usefulness of Assessing Linguistic Behaviors as a criterion-referenced scale.

A strength of the instrument is that it does sample a wide spectrum of prelinguistic and linguistic behaviors of infancy. The five assessment areas, which call for overlapping test materials (toys) but may be evaluated independently, are: Cognitive Antecedents to Word Meaning; Play; Communicative Intention; Language Comprehension; and Language Production. In choosing assessment items the authors have gleaned and integrated approaches deriving from Piagetian and neo-Piagetian theory and the linguistic competence and language pragmatics work of Elizabeth Bates and colleagues. There are some debatable aspects of the authors' attempted ordinal scaling of measurement items. The Play module is especially weak, probably because play precursors have not been as well studied as language precursors. Piagetians such as Inhelder (Inhelder, Lezine, Sinclair, & Stambak, 1972) have included conventional object use (e.g., child's running comb through own hair) as an early stage in play activity. This is controversial. But some action sequences identified in Assessing Linguistic Behaviors, such as "Mouthing Objects," surely seem gratuitous as play constructs. In fact the first 5 of 12 play behaviors assessed, namely Mouthing Objects, Banging Objects, Visual Regarding, Manipulating Objects, and Approximating (juxtaposing) Objects showed no ordinal pattern and were not well distinguished from one another in frequency of occurrence. This is not surprising inasmuch as autistic children, for example, might show a lot of these behaviors and yet never go on to demonstrate pretend play, or language.

The strongest part of this assessment is the Communicative Intention Scale deriving from an inventory previously published by two of the authors (Coggins & Carpenter, 1981). This measure assesses children's progressing abilities in dyadic commenting, requesting, acknowledging, answering, and requesting information.

In summary, Assessing Linguistic Behavior recommends itself as a guide in assessment of early communication disorders and in identification of areas needing remediation or enrichment. It is more likely to be of use to students or beginning language practitioners than to experienced speech pathologists, whose informal diagnostic-therapeutic knowledge likely surpasses the validity of this instrument.

REVIEWER'S REFERENCES

Inhelder, B., Lezine, I., Sinclair, H., & Stambak, M. (1972). Les debuts de la fonction symbolique. [The beginnings of the symbolic function]. *Archives de Psychologie, 41,* 187-243.

Coggins, T., & Carpenter, R. (1981). The communicative intention inventory: A system for observing and coding children's early intentional communication. *Applied Psycholinguistics, 2,* 235-251.

Review of Assessing Linguistic Behaviors: Assessing Prelinguistic and Early Linguistic Behaviors in Developmentally Young Children by LYNN S. BLISS, Professor of Communication Disorders and Sciences, Wayne State University, Detroit, MI:

Assessing Linguistic Behaviors (ALB) was developed as a clinical assessment tool for children functioning below a 2-year level. The author cites a need for a comprehensive assessment procedure geared to very young children who are often difficult to test.

CONTENT. The ALB is a comprehensive assessment measure that comprises five scales: Cognitive Antecedents to Word Meaning, Play, Communicative Intention, Language Comprehension, and Language Production. The tasks used in each section were based on reviews of the literature and identify basic prerequisites for further development.

ADMINISTRATION. The authors recommend that all the scales be administered; they can be grouped or given and interpreted separately. The time required for each scale is approximately 30 minutes. For each scale, an overview, administration guidelines, and interpretation section are presented in the manual. The examiner must purchase a wide range of stimuli, many of which are useful in more than one scale. The child's parent is used to elicit some behaviors. A videotape accompanies the manual and should be watched for administration and scoring purposes, especially for the Communicative scale.

SCORING AND INTERPRETATION. Scoring guidelines are presented for each of the scales. Descriptions for the scoring are clearly presented with many examples provided. The videotape enhances the scoring descriptions and presents a detailed format for the Communicative Intention scale. The Language Production scale requires considerable background in the areas of phonetics, prelinguistic and linguistic phonology, semantics, and syntax. The coding and scoring of the Language samples are very comprehensive and will require considerable time.

For each scale, some interpretive remarks are provided. These comments vary in detail and relate to clinical applications.

STANDARDIZATION. For every scale there is a section that describes the "normative data" on which the scale is based. The sample consisted of approximately 37 normal children divided almost equally between males and females. The children were selected randomly. No information is provided describing their socioeconomic status or racial background. The children were required to: exhibit, according to their parents, no unusual health or sensory problems; be from English-speaking homes; and have normal hearing and intellectual functioning. The children were evaluated longitudinally from 9 to 24 months of age in 3-month intervals. The data were analyzed by obtaining the percentage of subjects who exhibited specific target behaviors at six age levels (9, 12, 15, 18, 21, and 24 months). Mastery was defined when at least 85% of the children at each age level exhibited the behavior. The authors acknowledge the ALB is based on preliminary normative data. The data presented do not constitute a normative sample. Any results from the ALB must be interpreted cautiously.

RELIABILITY AND VALIDITY. Interexaminer reliability information is presented. Interexaminer reliability measures that were reported for the scales range from 63% to 100%. Generally 10% of the sample was used to obtain the reliability information. Validity is not addressed directly. The authors refer only to content validity in terms of the selection of behaviors to be examined as based on a review of the literature in each area.

CONCLUSIONS. The strength of the ALB is in the broad and comprehensive nature of each scale. The behaviors and the tasks appear appropriate for the target population. Further, there is a need for such an instrument with very young children. The manual is clearly written. The weaknesses fall into the area of test administration and construction. The scales are time consuming to administer and score if all are given. The use of the videotape is essential but also will require additional time. Nevertheless, the time spent should be worthwhile. However, the scales cannot be used for differentiating normal and impaired children because of the absence of a normative sample as well as reliability and validity information. The ALB is recommended as a descriptive measure. It will provide a broad and comprehensive evaluation of a child.

[19]
Assessment and Placement Services for Community Colleges.

Purpose: "Directed toward identifying the appropriate level of study for each entering student in each subject" and "to provide predictive information about performance in an entry-level course."
Population: Entering community college students.
Publication Dates: 1984–85.
Scores, 4: Reading, Writing, Mathematics (Computation, Elementary Algebra).
Administration: Group.
Forms, 2: A, B.
Price Data, 1988: $1.75 per reusable test booklet (specify Form A or Form B); $.15 per NCS or MRC answer sheet; $.95 per self-scoring answer sheet (specify Form A or Form B); $.50 per student placement inventory; $.25 per student essay sheet; $.25 per student essay booklet; $2.50 per manual for Using and Interpreting Scores ('85, 41 pages); no charge for Supervisor's Instructions for Test Administration ('84, 4 pages).
Time: 70(90) minutes plus 20 minutes for optional essay.
Comments: English and mathematics tests are derived from the Comparative Guidance and Placement Program (9:253); only one mathematics test is administered depending on previous algebra experience; Student Placement Inventory and optional essay test also available.
Author: Administered for the College Entrance Examination Board by Educational Testing Service.
Publisher: The College Board.

Review of the Assessment and Placement Services for Community Colleges by MARCIA J. BELCHER, Senior Research Associate, Miami-Dade Community College, Office of Institutional Research, Miami, FL:

Building on its predecessor, the Comparative Guidance and Placement Services (CGP), the College Board's Assessment and Placement Services for Community Colleges aims to provide a package that community colleges and other open-admissions institutions can use to place their diverse student population in entry-level English and mathematics courses. Known commonly as the MAPS (Multiple Assessment Programs and Services), this battery reports results on four subtests using scaled scores with a mean of 50 and a standard deviation of 10 for each test. In Reading, the abilities tested include understanding the main idea, the secondary idea, vocabulary in context, and the ability to make inferences. The multiple-choice Writing test includes testing of sentence recognition, sentence structure, pronoun problems, language and style, logic, verb problems, and recognition of error-free construction. Computation measures knowledge of basic arithmetic operations with whole numbers, fractions, decimals, and percents. The Elementary Algebra test includes operations with real numbers and algebraic expressions, solving linear equations and inequalities, and reading graphs.

NORMING GROUP. The program norms presented in the manual consist of a random sample of 30,912 students who were tested during 1976–77 and 1977–78. Based on current enrollment in community colleges, the norm group appears to underrepresent students from the western and southwestern portions of the United States, including Hispanic students and part-time enrollees. It is extremely helpful, however, that the College Board includes sufficient information that such conclusions can be drawn. Many manuals of other instruments remain conspicuously silent on this subject.

STATISTICAL CHARACTERISTICS. The manual is very readable and straightforward on the topics of reliability and standard error of measurement, providing definitions in lay language. Estimates of reliability and errors of measurement are based on approximately 1,500 students. Using KR-20 as an estimate of reliability, the highest reliability was found for Reading (.90) and the lowest for the two-part Writing test (.83). The Computation and Elementary Algebra tests had estimates ranging from .84 to .88 depending on the sample used. All of these estimates are in acceptable ranges for reliability.

Information on errors of measurement are provided using both the standard error of measurement (*SEM*) and the conditional *SEM*. All *SEM*s ranged from 2.2–4.7 scaled score points, with the lowest *SEM* for groups scoring well on the Elementary Algebra test and the highest for those scoring at or below the mean on the Writing test.

The Reading and Computation subtests are more highly speeded than the other two subtests. Writing was the only subtest that fits the definition of unspeeded (all students reaching 75% of the questions). This fact may pose problems for students whose native language is not English, a growing group in the community college. The difficulty level of most of the subtests appears to be such that the "average" student knows the answers to about half the questions.

VALIDITY. The assertion of content validity for the test is boosted by the fact that community college English and mathematics faculty were involved with test development. Apparently the items selected were based on skills identified by faculty as necessary for students to succeed in an open-door institution.

Predictive validity hinges on data provided between 1975 and 1978 by CGP-user institutions. The manual notes the number of studies (29) used in mathematics and the selectivity of the sample weakens the findings from the research. The median correlation reported ranged from .28 for Reading to .43 for Mathematics using the criterion of end-of-course grades in related courses. Users are urged to norm and validate their tests locally, and the end of the manual provides a quick overview on how to conduct such studies. Personal experience indicates that community colleges that do conduct validity studies usually find results similar to these.

In all, this is a well-designed test of basic skills aimed at the community college population. It has proved popular and is used at a variety of institutions. The package comes with a number of options, including an essay, student placement inventory, and several English-as-a-Second-Language modules. The College Board provides optional services including scoring, local norming and validity studies, and free training in holistic scoring of student essays.

Review of the Assessment and Placement Services for Community Colleges by JAMES B. ERDMANN, Associate Dean, Jefferson Medical College, Thomas Jefferson University, Philadelphia, PA:

The Assessment and Placement Services for Community Colleges (APSCC) program appears to have the potential to be a useful service to the faculty of community colleges. However, the elements of the placement service are not presented in a manner that maximizes their utility to potential users. In fact, in the view of this author, there are points of misdirection in the descriptions of the test materials and the interpretation of scores that suggest that purposes other than placement of students were contemplated by the developers of the materials.

A case in point is the detailed attention that is afforded the development and the interpretation of national norms. It is not really very clear why this choice has been made or why the sponsor believes this is one of the selling points of the test instruments. One can speculate that this emphasis is a holdover from the Comparative Guidance and Placement Program of which major portions of

Form A were previously a part and that there was reluctance to "throw away" the national data collected for that program. However, because the tests in the APSCC are intended for improving the accuracy of placement into classes in a specific community college and not, by the sponsor's own statements, for selection purposes or the evaluation of the comparative quality of the entering students at various colleges, all of the discussion surrounding national norms, their development, and interpretation, is not only of questionable relevance but confusing to the typical user.

This focus on what might be considered the usual topics germane to admissions tests is maintained throughout, both in terms of what is presented and what is not presented. For example, three to seven clusters of test questions are identified as representing different dimensions of each of the battery components (i.e., Reading, Writing, Computation, and Elementary Algebra). In the case of the Reading test, for example, these clusters include "Understanding the main idea," "Understanding the secondary idea," "Ability to make inferences," and "Understanding vocabulary in context." This identification of these subskills of the Reading test is precisely the kind of information which, in a placement situation, will be of significant interest to faculty. Admittedly, the user's guide does state that while the reliability of a score for a given cluster is not adequate to provide a measure for an individual student, it can provide a fairly reliable measure of the *average* [my emphasis] level of skill for a group of students. Unfortunately, this is where the guide stops. No further information is provided as to what the level of reliability is for this measure of group performance or how such cluster scores might be computed. It would appear pertinent to discuss whether any additional value might be gained from a closer examination of the cluster performance of individual students and, specifically, what the restrictions or limitations should be in drawing additional conclusions or inferences. This omission seems especially strange because considerable effort was expended to identify the questions belonging to a cluster in each test as well as the level of difficulty associated with each question; yet no guidance was provided as to how this information might be used.

The user's manual does support the notion of a college developing its own database of experience. Unfortunately, it does this by suggesting that "a college should develop its own norms" and by stating that placement "is most *systematic* [my emphasis] when it is based on the results of a [local] validity study." Again, unfortunately, the manual does not make clear what it means by norms, because on subsequent pages tables of percentile ranks are entitled "Norms." It is not clear how the process of converting student scores to percentile ranks would inform the placement decision. Further, the use of the term "systematic" is somewhat curious and vague. Ostensibly, one should be striving to be more accurate and not more systematic. Some of this confusion is dispelled by the last section, "Procedures for Norming and Validating the Tests." Here again, however, the most useful information is given the least attention and comes last. Reference is made to the creation of a graph describing the relationship between a predictor (test score) and a criterion, and the preparation of an associated two-way table of test scores and grades. This kind of analysis would appear to be of greatest value to the typical faculty member of a community college because it requires relatively less exposure to interpreting the practical meaning of bivariate and multivariate correlation coefficients. Greater space could profitably be devoted to the creation and interpretation of expectancy tables and their value in selecting cutoff points as well as the errors one makes when setting a high cutoff versus one that may be too low. Principles that should be followed in adopting a compromise cutoff score and situations where one type of error might be more acceptable than another should be presented. This would seem to be where the primary attention should be focused given that the purpose of the battery is placement into the course of a given faculty member at a specific community college.

Much of this desirable supporting information is apparently available but is presented as the role of the MAPS Placement Research Service. Thus, valuable analysis of local information is available to the college, but one must pay an additional fee to learn about the best use and interpretation of the data. The latter guidance would seem to be the expected responsibility of the test publisher/sponsor.

Before concluding consideration of this service, a few additional comments of a more technical nature are appropriate.

No data are provided on differences, if any, among various ethnic or racial subgroups. Particularly in the setting for which this program was ostensibly designed, minorities are present in significant proportions. Therefore, an assessment of subgroup differences and the possible presence of bias in such differences needs to be reviewed. This is an area where national studies have particular relevance because sizeable numbers reflecting criteria across a variety of institutions are required for a meaningful analysis.

It is acknowledged in the manual that the Elementary Algebra test of Form B contains questions of a type different from those of Form A and that, therefore, the properties of the two may be different. Unfortunately, that is the only reference to the differing formats of questions and one is otherwise led to believe that the two tests are equivalent forms. No data are presented to support that conclusion.

The reliability data cited appear to have been calculated on combined samples from various colleges. Rather it may have been more appropriate to calculate the reliability estimates for each sample separately. This would have allowed a determination of whether there were important differences among a variety of colleges, and if so, the reporting of a median reliability coefficient for colleges of a given type may have been more appropriate. Such information would appear to be more useful and relevant to a given application. A similar line of thought would indicate that it is desirable to cluster colleges by types similar to categories reported when describing the norming sample. This too should lead to a better indication of the kind of validity a particular college might expect when considering the value the service program might hold for it.

In conclusion, the tests would seem to hold promise for placement applications, but the supporting materials fall short not only of what might be its real potential but also of what should be expected of a professionally prepared examination program. For those colleges that have in-house testing expertise, the deficiencies in the supporting systems of the program may be offset by the availability of such personnel.

[20]
Assessment of Competencies for Instructor Development.

Purpose: To measure six competencies important to being an effective instructor in an industrial setting.
Population: Instructors in industrial settings.
Publication Date: 1986.
Scores, 7: Analyzing the Needs and "Entering Behavior" of the Learner, Specifying Outcomes and "Terminal Behaviors" for a Course, Designing Instructional Sequences and Learning Materials, Instructing in Both the Inductive and Deductive Modes, Maintaining Adult-to-Adult (not "Parent-Child") Relationships in Class, Staying Learner-Centered not Information-Centered, Overall Instructional Competency.
Administration: Individual or group.
Manual: No manual.
Price Data, 1988: $40 per 20 questionnaires; $40 per 20 interpretation brochures; $20 per 20 response sheets.
Time: Administration time not reported.
Comments: Self-administered, self-scored.
Author: Training House, Inc.
Publisher: Training House, Inc.

Review of the Assessment of Competencies for Instructor Development by STEPHEN F. DAVIS, Professor of Psychology, Emporia State University, Emporia, KS:

The examination materials provided for review of this instrument included a copy of the Proficiency Test, a Response Sheet, and an Interpretation Sheet booklet. Based upon the assumption that the good trainer/teacher possesses both content (knowledge) and process (the "ability to arrange learning experiences and deliver instruction effectively") skills, this instrument was developed to measure one's process skills. Although never clearly specified, it is apparent that this is a completely self-administered instrument. The test booklet consists of 30 situational items requiring a course of action decision(s). For each item four alternative actions are listed. The examinee must allocate a total of 3 points among these alternatives. All of the points may be given to one alternative, or they may be weighted and divided among the alternatives. The example provided is reasonably clear, but it is not specified whether one is allowed to use *only* whole numbers when allocating points. As the majority of the situations deal with business/industry-related workshops and short (2-to-3-day) courses, this instrument clearly is limited to evaluation of instructor effectiveness in that area. A 1-hour period should be sufficient for the administration, scoring, and interpretation.

One's distribution of points is recorded on a two-page NCR Response Sheet that reiterates the basic instructions contained in the test booklet. An examination of the second page of the answer sheet suggests that some alternatives are weighted more heavily or are more desirable than others. This page also indicates that the instrument measures one's proficiency in six major domains or competencies. These competencies include: (*a*) Analyzing the needs and "Entering Behavior" of the Learner, (*b*) Specifying Outcomes and "Terminal Behaviors" for a Course, (*c*) Designing Instructional Sequences and Learning Materials, (*d*) Instructing in Both the Inductive and Deductive Modes, (*e*) Maintaining Adult-to-Adult (not "Parent-Child") Relationships in Class, and (*f*) Staying Learner-Centered, not Information-Centered. Ideally, the examinee should not turn to the second page of the Response Sheet until the test has been completed and he or she is ready to actually score the responses that have been made. If this information is reviewed prior to completion of the test, then one's score could be influenced rather easily and dramatically.

Once the scoring has been completed the examinee is encouraged to read the six-page "Interpretation Sheet" for a fuller description of each of the six competencies. For each competency a brief, descriptive introduction is provided. Subsequently, the four alternative actions are analyzed on an item-by-item basis in order to show their relationship to the successful attainment of the competency in question. Although such information may be helpful in achieving an understanding of each competency and how to better achieve skill in that area, one must be concerned with the lack of precaution to insure that this material is not read before the test is taken. The

examinee is *never* told the appropriate sequence and/or cautions to be observed in interacting with these testing materials.

As a total of 15 points can be accumulated for each of the six competencies, a maximum score of 90 is possible. The Interpretation Sheet indicates that "A score of 75 or better reflects a good degree of proficiency in the competencies needed to be successful as an instructor. How did you do?" The answer to this question is to be obtained via plotting one's scores on a Proficiency Profile provided in the Interpretation Sheet booklet.

Although the six competencies this instrument purports to evaluate appear to have considerable face validity, no information has been provided to indicate their derivation for the present testing instrument. The same concern is expressed for each of the items that make up the six competencies. Similarly, the *complete* lack of normative data, content validity, predictive validity, and reliability indices must be viewed as rather strong indictments of this instrument. Such information, as well as a clear indication of the most effective uses/applications of this instrument, should be incorporated into a technical manual to accompany this test. Until this is done, potential users will find this a rather disappointing test.

[21]
Assessment of Individual Learning Style: The Perceptual Memory Task.

Purpose: "To provide measures of the individual's perception and memory for spatial relationships; visual and auditory sequential memory; intermediate term memory; and discrimination of detail."
Population: Ages 4 and over.
Publication Date: 1984.
Acronym: PMT.
Scores: 7 scores, 3 alternate scores: Spatial Relations, Visual Designs Recognition, Visual Designs-Sequencing, Auditory-Visual Colors Recognition, Auditory-Visual Colors Sequencing, Discrimination Recall, Total PMT, Visual-Visual (alternate), Auditory-Auditory (alternate), Visual-Auditory (alternate).
Administration: Individual.
Price Data, 1988: $280 per complete kit including carrying case containing various subtest components, 25 scoring forms, 25 alternate forms, and manual (129 pages); $12 per 25 scoring forms; $7.75 per 25 alternate forms; $29 per manual.
Time: (30–40) minutes.
Author: Lawrence McCarron.
Publisher: McCarron-Dial Systems.

TEST REFERENCES
1. Bihn, E. M., & McCarron, L. T. (1988). Vocational-neuropsychological evaluation of psychiatrically disabled patients. *Psychological Reports, 62,* 104–106.

Review of the Assessment of Individual Learning Style: The Perceptual Memory Task by STEVEN FERRARA, Chief, Measurement, Statistics, and Evalu-

ation Section, Maryland State Department of Education, Division of Instruction, Baltimore, MD:

The Perceptual Memory Task (PMT) is intended to assess "type and degree of memory dysfunction . . . [and] to assist in formulating appropriate educational and rehabilitation programs for diverse groups of handicapping conditions" (PMT manual, p. 7). It is intended for use by special educators, rehabilitation counselors, and other professionals to diagnose "strengths and weaknesses in essential memory processes" (PMT manual, p. 40).

Providing such diagnostic-prescriptive information is a laudable goal. However, it is rather a tall order for a 52-task, four-subtest instrument that is administered in 30–40 minutes. The PMT fails to provide a useful "operational definition of essential memory processes" (PMT manual, p. 40) because of failure to (*a*) define perceptual memory in theoretical or behavioral terms; (*b*) describe the relationship between definitions of perceptual memory as portrayed in subtest tasks, and perceptual memory as it functions in learning and working situations; and (*c*) demonstrate the efficacy of remedial instruction and accommodations designed from PMT score profiles. It is also noteworthy that the manual is not well organized and is sometimes difficult to use. However, some diagnosticians are likely to find the PMT useful as a rough screening device to identify examinees with significant deficits in visual and auditory memory that could (*a*) hinder learning and performance in vocational, training, and educational settings, and (*b*) indicate preferred learning style.

DEVELOPMENT AND CONSTRUCTION OF THE PMT. Description of the contents, purposes, rationales, and theoretical and empirical origins and underpinnings for the four subtests in the PMT is inadequate. In addition, a description of item development and selection procedures and criteria is missing from the manual. The appropriateness of the PMT's construction procedures cannot be evaluated without these descriptions. Three paragraphs under the heading "Test Development" provide no specific information on item and test development procedures. Likewise, the content validity section does not include test content specifications or other relevant information.

In the Spatial Relations subtest, examinees are required to replicate from memory 12 block designs displayed on cards. In Discrimination Recall, the fourth subtest administered, examinees are asked to separate the 13 Spatial Relations subtest block-design cards from 13 distractor cards. Together these two subtests are scored and interpreted as a "conceptual memory" factor. In the Visual Designs subtest, examinees are shown up to six abstract visual designs on 12 display cards, and then asked to replicate from memory the sequence of designs on each card by selecting from among 12 blocks that each display one visual design. In the Auditory-Visual Colors subtest, the examiner recites 14 sequences of up to seven colors; examinees are asked to replicate from memory the sequence of the colors by selecting from among 12 colored blocks. Both completeness and sequential accuracy of examinee responses are scored in the visual and auditory subtests. These two subtests are scored and interpreted separately as "visual memory" and "auditory memory" factors; likewise, the recognition and sequencing scores from these two subtests are interpreted as "recognition" and "sequencing" factors. Users might note the asymmetry in the visual and auditory memory tasks: The abstract visual designs may inhibit verbalization that could support visual recall, whereas the recited colors may allow visualization to support auditory recall. Factor analyses of memory functioning differences across handicapped subgroups should address a more fundamental issue: the validity of the six within-subtest and five across-subtest memory "factor" scores that form the basis of interpretations of performance on the PMT.

NORMS AND SCORES. Descriptions of norming samples suggest that important examinee groups are inadequately represented. The norming sample comprises 1,500 nonhandicapped people ranging in age from 4 to 35 years who participated in standardization and norming administrations over a 5-year period. Examinees were located in seven states (no states in the West Coast or Southeast population centers). Although percentages of the sample in various SES and race-ethnic subgroups are specified, numbers of examinees in each age group are not given, and the years and sites in which data were collected are not specified. Separate male and female norms to account for gender-related developmental differences are not provided.

The "Individual Profile of Perceptual Memory Skills" provides six within-subtest linear standard scores, a total PMT standard score, and five across-subtest "factor" standard scores, based on nonhandicapped norming samples. The six within-subtest standard scores can be hand plotted onto a graph that is conveniently marked off in standard score units to create a diagnostic profile of an examinee's relative strengths and weaknesses. The "general population" mean (100; $SD = 15$) and "special population" mean (55; $SD = 15$) are also indicated on the profile to aid interpretation of subtest scores. However, no indication is given as to whether the latter group's raw score mean is actually 3 standard deviations lower than the former's mean, or only constrained to be so through standard score calculations. PMT users should note that a one or two subtest raw score change often corresponds to a 5-point change in standard score. This correspondence is especially important because subtest standard score discrepancies greater than 15 are said to indicate a disability.

RELIABILITY EVIDENCE. Test-retest (1-month delay) and split-half reliability coefficients for 150 4- to 6-year-old normal children (.91 and .89, respectively) and 51 neuropsychologically disabled adults (.93 and .92) are good, as is a split-half reliability estimate for an unspecified group of normal adults (.91). These coefficients are calculated on total PMT scores (probably based on 77 items) and then inappropriately used to calculate standard errors for subtest scores (based on 12–14 items). In addition, it is not clear whether the standard errors are calculated on raw or standard scores. And although the manual suggests that standard errors can be used to create 68 percent score confidence intervals, it does not provide score bands in the norms tables. No other reliability information is given for subgroups or subtest scores.

VALIDITY EVIDENCE. Results from more than 20 studies described in the manual's reliability and validity chapter include (a) correlations of the PMT with external measures of neuropsychological functioning, perceptual memory, intelligence, vocational competence, educational achievement, and college-level musical literacy, and with teacher ratings of student memory functioning; and comparisons of (b) PMT scores, using factor analysis and within quasi-experimental designs, from cognitively and physically handicapped and nonhandicapped children and adults; and (c) real and apparently hypothetical PMT score profiles for various subgroups. Although the organization, relevance, and persuasiveness of much of this evidence is questionable, some of it—particularly the correlations with measures of vocational competence and perceptual memory—suggests the PMT actually does tap memory processes and distinguishes poor from good memory performances. However, questions remain: What memory processes are activated and can be inferred from PMT performance? And are these inferences meaningful for designing training and accommodations? This latter question may be best addressed within the context of use of PMT scores.

USE FOR DESIGNING INSTRUCTION, TRAINING, AND ACCOMMODATIONS. The PMT may be useful because PMT scores probably (a) indicate general level of memory performance compared to nonhandicapped norm groups, (b) suggest whether an examinee is likely to best process and remember visually or auditorally presented information, and because (c) the PMT provides a structured context for observing learning behaviors (e.g., focused attending and impulsivity) and sensory limitations (e.g., visual acuity and auditory reception threshold). Unfortunately, the chapter entitled "Interpretation of Individual Performance" includes no

evidence to support suggested interpretations and interventions based on PMT performance. The discussion in this chapter includes reasonable but nonvalidated guidelines for planning interventions based on PMT scores.

CONCLUSION. Special educators and other diagnosticians use similarly nebulous measures of cognitive functioning (see Shepard, 1983). Why might they use the PMT? Perhaps because few standardized and normed memory assessments exist, and perhaps because the PMT provides an alternative to memory instruments that require oral response. (The PMT requires only manual responses). But the available evidence does not support interpretation and use of PMT scores for designing vocational, training, and educational accommodations. Some diagnosticians may want to use PMT scores as general indicators of memory strengths and weaknesses. However, they should try to remember that the phrase "lack of clarity" might best characterize the PMT.

REVIEWER'S REFERENCE

Shepard, L. (1983). The role of measurement in educational policy: Lessons from the identification of learning disabilities. *Educational Measurement: Issues and Practice, 2* (3), 4-8.

Review of the Assessment of Individual Learning Style: The Perceptual Memory Task by ARLENE COOPERSMITH ROSENTHAL, Educational Psychologist and Consultant, Olney, MD:

The development of the Perceptual Memory Task (PMT) is based on the premise that the essential processes of learning largely depend on conceptual, visual, and auditory memory. Consequently, dysfunction in memory functioning has a direct impact on learning-skill acquisition. A major goal of the PMT is to aid in the development of individually tailored educational and/or rehabilitative programs based on the nature of an individual's memory-processing style. A large portion of the manual is devoted to translating diagnostic PMT information into training and educational strategies. The purpose and goals of the PMT are reflected by the test author's background in the field of vocational evaluation and rehabilitation.

The test manual is 122 pages long and is divided into four chapters. These chapters respectively describe the test's purpose and development; administration and scoring procedures and norms; reliability and validity; and interpretation of PMT performance. Development of the PMT was extended over a 7-year period. The manual reflects the extensive work done on this test prior to its publication.

The test is administered individually in 30–40 minutes. It comprises four subtasks (three alternate subtasks are available for individuals with visual or hearing impairments and/or as a supplement to the assessment process). Standard administration and scoring procedures are well detailed to assist the examiner. Subtask performance requires visual and auditory input modalities and visual-motor output modalities. This is to avoid the influence of poor expressive communication skills. It does not avoid the influence of motor dysfunction.

The Spatial Relations subtask requires the individual to reproduce from memory increasingly difficult spatial configurations using 1-inch cubes and results in one score. The Visual Designs subtask requires the individual to reproduce from memory a sequence of visual designs and results in a sequencing and recognition score. The Auditory Visual Colors subtask requires the individual to reproduce a spoken sequence of colors (auditory input modality) motorically (visual-motor output modality) using colored blocks. A sequencing and recognition score is obtained. The Discrimination Recall subtask tests the individual's recall of the stimuli used in the first two subtasks and results in two scores.

A total PMT score is derived by summing the six scores; tables are provided for conversion of raw to standard scores. The use of standard scores permits a direct comparison of relative strengths and weaknesses. The six subtasks have been grouped into three factors: conceptual, visual, and auditory memory. A recognition and sequencing factor can also be derived. The use of standard scores permits direct comparisons to be made between subtask performance and between performance on the three factors. A range of values for normal and dysfunctional performance is provided. Scoring is simple and the scoring protocol is clearly and well designed. The back page provides a visual display of standardized performance scores.

NORMS. The PMT was developed for use with normal children and adults with a variety of handicapping conditions. Developmental norms are not provided for the sample of handicapped adults but are based on 1,500 average individuals between 4 years of age and young adult. One set of conversion tables from raw to standard scores is used for all examinees.

The study upon which this set of developmental norms is based is buried in the section on construct validity. A specific section on norms development is not provided. Apparently, this section is based solely on conversion tables. No rationale is provided as to why the group of neuropsychologically disabled individuals is not included in the norming of the tests. The manual explicitly states this test is to be used with such individuals. The population upon which the test is based remains unclear.

RELIABILITY. Two types of reliability are described. Test-retest reliability over a 1-month interval was .91 for a group of 150 4–6-year-olds and .93 for a group of 51 neuropsychologically disabled adults. The mean and standard deviation of the

PMT is 100 and 15, respectively. The standard error of measurement of the total PMT based on split half reliability estimates is 6.94, 8.10, and 8.24 for a group of normal children, normal adults, and neuropsychologically disabled adults, respectively.

VALIDITY. This section is 50 pages long; published and unpublished studies are cited to support the test's content, criterion, construct, and predictive validity. The author supports the test's content validity by interpreting subtask performance within a neuropsychological framework. For example, the Spatial Relations subtask requires skills mediated by a variety of brain regions. Test development was based on the principles of neuropsychological functioning. The specific procedures used to generate and analyze the test items are not provided. This would seem to weaken the test's content validity.

Concurrent validity was assessed using teacher ratings of student's memory functioning and music literary performance. Statistically significant correlations were found between the PMT and each of the two criterion measures. Further studies are needed using a wider variety of criteria, for example, other measures of perceptual memory, neuropsychological functioning, and vocational competency. The merit of criterion-related validity studies depends on the appropriateness of the criterion measures. Further, the validity of the criterion measures used in these studies is not reported.

Construct validity was assessed in nine different ways including factor analysis. The findings are reported in 34 pages of the test manual. Construct validity is supported by the test's ability to, for example, identify subgroups of learning disabled children and reflect normal development of memory skills with age. This group of studies lends support to the construct validity of the PMT.

Four studies are used to support the test's predictive validity. They assess the ability of the PMT to predict: ability to benefit from training; vocational competency of psychiatrically disabled; and acquisition of horticultural skills and vocational competency of mentally retarded adults. These studies support the use of the PMT as an approach to vocational evaluation and rehabilitation.

The final chapter provides guidelines for translating assessment data into training/rehabilitation strategies. PMT data provide an overall level of memory function; a comparison of relative strengths in a variety of mnestic processes; behavioral observations (e.g., cognitive flexibility); clinical indicators; and educational, vocational, and neuropsychological implications. This section is well detailed with research and case studies. A section is included on special remedial strategies for accommodating specific memory deficits.

To summarize, the PMT is useful as one component in a comprehensive assessment for aiding in the development of educational and/or vocational strategies. The research that went into the test is impressive and lends support for its stated purposes.

The test name itself may be a misnomer and its greatest weakness. No single test is an assessment of "learning style." Evaluation on the PMT is not synonymous with assessment of learning style. Learning style does include, but is not limited to, memory functioning. The test author recognizes that PMT data must be analyzed and corroborated by multiple data sources before developing remedial procedures. Despite this recognition, perhaps too many conclusions are drawn solely from PMT performance. Even though a tremendous amount of research is cited, some critical information is still lacking in the manual. For example, subtest reliability coefficients are not provided, neither are the intercorrelations among the subtests. Other weaknesses have been mentioned. A number of validity studies used total versus subtask PMT scores so that the validity of individual factors may be tenuous. A clinical comparison of an individual's performance on conceptual, visual, and auditory factors should take into account that each factor comprises only two brief tasks. The test user must be cautioned against overinterpretation of subtest performance and PMT profiles of strengths and weaknesses. Despite some weaknesses, the studies cited have yielded promising empirical data for this instrument.

[22]
Assessment of School Needs for Low-Achieving Students: Staff Survey.

Purpose: Designed to measure "staff perceptions as to whether certain behaviors are occurring in their school."
Population: Teachers and administrators.
Publication Date: 1988–89.
Acronym: ASNLAS.
Scores, 9: School Programs and Policies, Classroom Management, Instruction, Teacher Expectations, Principal Leadership, Staff Development, Student Involvement in Learning, School Climate, Parent Involvement.
Administration: Group.
Price Data, 1991: $2 per survey booklet; $.25 per scoring form; $16.95 per manual ('89, 44 pages).
Time: (45–50) minutes.
Authors: Francine S. Beyer and Ronald L. Houston.
Publisher: Research for Better Schools.

Review of the Assessment of School Needs for Low-Achieving Students: Staff Survey by DEAN H. NAFZIGER, Executive Director, and ANN M. MUENCH, Research Associate, Far West Laboratory for Educational Research and Development, San Francisco, CA:

The Assessment of School Needs for Low-Achieving Students: Staff Survey (ASNLAS) is a 177-item survey designed "to help educators at the school and district level identify needs within the school programs, operations, staff, and environment for working successfully with low-achieving students." The survey consists of nine scales, each containing from 14 to 27 items. Each item is answered by selecting one of five Likert-type responses: 1— *Almost Never*, 2— *Seldom*, 3— *Sometimes*, 4— *Frequently*, and 5— *Almost Always*. Every person receives an average score for each scale. These average scores for each scale are then averaged across respondents to create group summary scale scores. When combined within a scale, low scores indicate need for improvement. Scoring may be done by the school staff (estimated time for scoring not provided) or by the test publishers.

According to the manual, the basis for choosing the nine scale areas involved a thorough review of the research on at-risk, low-achieving students and a determination that the school could have an influence in each area. Although the areas seem consistent with those identified in the literature on effective schools, the manual itself contains little specific research information in support of these choices and provides only summary descriptions and assurances that the original 228 items were carefully developed and reviewed.

Although the item content was "tailored for low-achieving students," many statements represent sound teaching practices for all students, and such tailoring may unnecessarily imply that a certain practice is recommended for low achievers but not for all students in general. For example, consider the item "Teachers respond to the inappropriate behavior of low-achieving students early." A high response (*Frequently* or *Almost Always*) may indicate that the teachers respond to misbehavior more quickly from a low achiever than from a high-achieving student, thus implying preferential treatment for students who are not low achievers. Some educators may take issue as to whether other items necessarily imply good instructional practices for low or high achievers. Without supporting research or explanations, the distinction becomes blurred as to when to treat students alike (as with discipline and teacher expectations) and when to treat at-risk students differently (as with special programs, focusing curriculum, and educational goals).

Along the same line, it is also possible that an average scale score could be high (indicating no perceived need for change) when in reality there could be a great need for improvement. For example, a high score in School Climate indicates only that teachers perceive the activities and attitudes of low-achieving students to be in agreement with those of students in general. Someone could mark the following statement *Almost Always*: "Low achieving students participate as much as other students in extracurricular activities." If students in general do not participate very much, then School Climate rates high in an area that needs improvement. Other items also contain problematic wording: "The school develops coping skills for low-achieving students." Does the school cope with the low achievers, or does the school help the students to cope?

When completing the survey, staff members are instructed to answer items by determining the extent to which the statement is true of the school. Although they are to give their opinions, no instructions are provided for the person who does not know or have any idea about the frequency of some event. Indeed, some items may be difficult enough for a teacher to answer about her or his own classes (particularly if the teacher does not interact with low-achieving students) without generalizing about the frequency in which something happens throughout the school. Likewise, many of the questions involving the parents of low-achieving students seem beyond the knowledge of most teachers. The assumption seems to be that a teacher who doesn't know or doesn't want to answer an item will simply skip the item. However, this option is not stated in the instructions, perhaps because many items would (appropriately) go unanswered.

This also brings into question the meaning of an average scale score. Although allowances are made for nonresponses (averages are calculated by dividing the sum of the response points by the number of items answered), interpretation of averaged results may be tricky when one person answers every item in a set and another answers only a few, or when half of the respondents mark *Almost Never* on almost all the items in a scale and the other half almost always mark *Almost Always*.

The original survey was pilot tested in four nonurban schools in the mid-Atlantic region (Beyer & Smey-Richman, 1988). Participation was mandatory in three of the schools, and 56% of the teachers in the fourth school returned their survey. The manual recommends that responses be confidential, and that respondents be given the opportunity to make additional comments on a separate sheet of paper. It also suggests that a staff meeting period be used for administration. Although not mentioned directly in the manual, it is important to note that the ASNLAS was pilot tested with response choices ranging from 1— *Strongly Disagree* to 5— *Strongly Agree* —rather than the *Almost Never* to *Almost Always* choices that appear in the present survey. In a disagree/agree situation, a respondent may be Undecided about an item, and not simply skip the item if he or she is unable to determine the frequency at which it occurs. This difference in choices alters the nature of the question for the respondent. Marking a 3 in the present survey to indicate that "Parents of low-achieving students participate often in some type of parent involvement activity" happens *Sometimes* not only seems nonsen-

sical, it is also quite a bit different than marking a 3 to the same item in the piloted version because you are Undecided.

RELIABILITY. The scales have high coefficient alphas—between .88 and .95—based on the piloted version. No data were provided, however, to indicate how the present survey, with its response choices revised to reflect perceived frequencies of statements, relates to the piloted survey, in which responses represent agreement. No information was provided about the reliability of the revised instrument.

VALIDITY. The validity of the ASNLAS, as described in the manual, comes from the review of the literature and identifying school features or areas that can be influenced at the school level. And the final evaluation of its validity depends on a school's purpose and objectives. No other validity data are provided.

NORMATIVE DATA. The ASNLAS is designed to be used at the district or school level, and no normative data are included in the manual. The results of each scale can be reported descriptively, with comparisons made among scales, among respondent groups, or over time. The school or district must decide for itself such things as how low a scale score should be to indicate a perceived need for improvement, whether one area actually is in more need than another based on scale averages, whether most staff members perceive the same needs or have conflicting perceptions. The manual does not indicate how sensitive the instrument is to each area of perceived needs. Although more advanced score reports and analyses can be obtained from the survey developers, it is not clear from the manual just how these statistics will be useful.

SUMMARY. The ASNLAS was designed to help schools identify needs in order to implement change to help low-achieving students. The survey is comprehensive in terms of categories or scales; and the items within each scale appear reasonably related and somewhat distinct from items in other scales. However, the user should take the time to review each scale to determine whether or not the survey will provide useful information. For some uses, the number of items (177) may be excessive and the length of time to complete the survey (45 minutes) may require more effort than some staff are willing to put forth. Perhaps one or more scales could be omitted if a school or district cannot impact the area or wishes to use an abbreviated form of the test.

Whether the ASNLAS is used as a diagnostic planning instrument or a comparative evaluative instrument, users should inspect individual items to be sure the survey provides useful information for school improvement for low-achieving students. Because options were changed from the piloted survey to the survey in its present form, the reported coefficient alphas may not represent the actual internal consistencies of the scales. ASNLAS developers may wish to reanalyze this instrument based on samples using their revised survey.

REVIEWER'S REFERENCE

Beyer, F., & Smey-Richman, B. (1988, April). *Addressing the "at-risk" challenge in the nonurban setting*. Paper presented at the annual meeting of the American Educational Research Association, New Orleans.

[23]
Australian Biology Test Item Blank.

Purpose: To assess a wide range of biological information and abilities.
Population: Australian years 11–12.
Publication Date: 1984.
Administration: Group.
Manual: No manual.
Price Data, 1989: A$10 per Volume I; $10 per Volume II.
Time: Administration time not reported.
Comments: Consists of nearly 1,500 multiple-choice items to assist teachers in preparing diagnostic and achievement tests.
Authors: Edited by David W. Brown and Jeffrey J. Sewell.
Publisher: Australian Council for Educational Research Ltd. [Australia].

a) VOLUME I: THE LIVING WORLD.
Population: Years 11–12.
Scores: Items in 8 areas: Investigating the Living World, The Variety of Life, Organisms and Environments, Reproduction, Nutrition/Development and Growth, Populations, Interaction and Change in the Natural World, The Living World.
Comments: 1 volume (220 pages).

b) VOLUME II: THE FUNCTIONING ORGANISM.
Population: Year 12.
Scores: Items in 9 areas: The Organism, Function and Structure in Plants, Function and Structure in Animals, Integration and Regulation in Multicellular Organisms, Cellular Processes, Heredity, Life—Its Continuity and Change, The Human Species, Science and the Scientific Process.
Comments: 1 volume (242 pages).

[24]
Automated Office Battery.

Purpose: Aptitude tests designed for the selection of staff to work in offices with a high degree of automation.
Population: Student and employed clerical staff.
Publication Dates: 1985–86.
Acronym: AOB.
Scores: 3 tests: Numerical Estimation, Computer Checking, Coded Instructions.
Administration: Group.
Price Data, 1986: £108 per administration set; £110 per 10 test booklets; £55 per 50 answer sheets; £27.50 per 50 profile charts; £5.50 per administration card; £15 per 50 practice leaflets; £55 per manual and user's guide ('86, 57 pages); £500 Automated Office Battery User's Fee.
Time: 40(60) minutes for entire battery.
Comments: "Tests may be used individually or as a complete battery as particular requirements dictate."
Authors: Bill Mabey and Hazel Stevenson.
Publisher: Saville & Holdsworth Ltd. [England].

a) NUMERICAL ESTIMATION.
Purpose: A test to measure the ability to estimate the answer to a calculation.
Acronym: NE-1.
Time: 10(15) minutes.

b) COMPUTER CHECKING.
Purpose: A test to measure the ability to check machine input information with the corresponding output.
Acronym: CC-2.
Time: 12(17) minutes.

c) CODED INSTRUCTIONS.
Purpose: A test to measure the ability to comprehend and follow written instructions when a form of coded language is used.
Time: 18(23) minutes.

Review of the Automated Office Battery by PHILIP ASH, Director, Ash, Blackstone and Cates, Blacksburg, VA:

The Automated Office Battery (AOB) is a handsome test product, including very helpful support items. The presentation binder includes: (*a*) helpful hints for takers of the AOB; (*b*) the manual; (*c*) materials for each test (booklet, answer sheet, "administration instructions"); (*d*) scoring stencil for hand scoring; (*e*) individual profile chart marked out in percentiles and *T*-scores; (*f*) score roster sheet; and (*g*) a test log.

The AOB was developed from job analyses of highly automated clerical work. The tests, intended for international use, should be comprehensible to examinees in English-speaking countries. The answer sheets are scannable by a British portable Evalmatic microcomputer, but cannot be read by U.S. scanners, such as the NCS series.

PRICE. The cost in American dollars (calculated at the November 1991 exchange rate) of administering the AOB to a sample of 50 applicants, tested 10 at a time with reusable test booklets, is around $1,000, plus a user's fee of $905, or a cost-per-applicant of almost $40. U.S. test batteries that are nonproprietary (the user purchases the manual, tests, and key, and scores and interprets the results) cost from under a quarter or less of the AOB price. The seven-part Short Tests of Clerical Ability (SRA/London House, 1989) costs $9.80 per applicant; the nine-part General Clerical Test (Psychological Corporation, 1989) costs $4.20 per applicant; the Short Employment Tests (Psychological Corporation, 1989) costs $4.80 per applicant. In comparison, the Bank Basic Skills Battery (London House, undated) is a proprietary test which includes four mental abilities and seven attitudinal and achievement measures. The publisher scores, interprets, and provides an extensive norm-based report. The complete package, including legal counsel and other support, costs from $6.50 to $15 per applicant, depending upon volume of use.

The manual, clearly and concisely written, includes 14 chapters; the main ones are described below. Saville & Holdsworth Ltd. (SHL) abides by the British Psychological Association standards for test distribution, which are similar to the APA A-level standards. The AOB is available to individuals who are qualified and to institutions other than educational institutions.

THE TESTS. NE-1, Numerical Estimation, includes 50 arithmetic (addition, subtraction, multiplication, division, percentages, and decimals) items. The examinee is strongly urged to *estimate* the right answer, not to *compute* it from the stem. With a 10-minute limit, it is highly speeded. Each item includes five alternatives, one of which is correct, one or two that might be close, and two or three that are incorrect by orders of magnitude (e.g., 25 correct, 2,500 distractor).

CC-2, Computer Checking Test, is representative of a real-life task. Eight sets, each of four to six input data items (prices for goods, train tickets, etc.), must be compared with the contents of a video display monitor screen or a computer printout, and discrepancies identified. This is the most difficult of the tests.

CI-3, Coded Instructions, calls for entry of items into a computerized filing system, using systems of two to six character codes. Eight sets of five entry tasks are presented, each set comprising items of various types of files (e.g., airline flight information, international money transfer).

NORMS. First, descriptions of various kinds of norms (e.g., percentiles, "five division grades," standard scores, and *T*-scores) are presented. They are all exhibited under the usual normal curve display. The reported norms were computed on the basis of four groups of clerical employees and one group of secondary school and college students. No demographic data (age, gender, ethnic group) are provided. The groups included building society clerical staff ($N = 166–193$, depending on test), bank clerical staff ($N = 78$), food retailer clerical staff ($N = 54$), mail order clerical staff ($N = 44–60$, depending on test), and student group ($N = 43$). A reviewer-computed analysis of variance over the five groups for each test found that in each case the *F*-ratio was significant beyond the .01 level, suggesting that the subsamples were not drawn from a common population. Percentile and *T*-score norms are provided for three subsample combinations: total clerical staff/student group; "financial group," which combines building society clerical staff and bank clerical staff; and "retail group," combining food retailer and mail order clerk clerical staffs.

However, the apparent heterogeneity of the subsamples, the lack of demographic data, and the absence of data on applicant samples would make these norms inapplicable to U.S. (and probably British) applicant samples. The manual does indicate that SHL plans to publish additional norm data, and suggests that users develop their own norms.

RELIABILITY. An explanation, covering test-retest, alternate form, and internal consistency reliability, the standard error of measurement, and related issues, precedes the reliability data. They include two Cronbach alpha coefficients for each test, one based on the building society clerical subgroup, the other based upon a "mixed" group (i.e., three of the four subsamples combined). The internal consistency estimates are uniformly high: NE-1, .90; CC-2, .88; CI-3, .85 and .86. However, internal consistency measures are inappropriate for speeded tests; these measures assume that the test is *untimed*, with the opportunity to respond to every item (cf. Guion, 1965, p. 44).

The intercorrelations of the tests are also high: NE-1 and CC-2, .52; NE-1 and CI-3, .57; CC-2 and CI-3, .61. It is obvious that they share a large amount of common variance, which this reviewer suspects is simply "G."

VALIDITY. A brief presentation is given of the major forms of validity strategies: face, content, concurrent, predictive, and construct, as well as of the problems of low criterion reliability and of the difficulty of predictive validity studies. One concurrent validity study is reported, based upon a sample of 187 employed clerical workers distributed among an undisclosed number of participating companies, and selected by the managers who rated them. The authors comment that "There appears to have been a tendency for somewhat better candidates to have been put forward for this exercise." No demographic or length-of-service data are given. The criterion was a rating scheme consisting of eight 9-point scales (e.g., "speed of work," "ability to handle complex tasks," "overall evaluation re: clerical staff"). Neither the intercorrelation matrix for the nine scales nor any estimates of the reliabilities of the ratings are provided.

The three most predictable ratings for all three tests were "ability to handle complex tasks," "ability to understand quickly when something is wrong," and "good at working with numbers." The correlations with "overall evaluation re: clerical staff" were almost as high. The correlations with the total score were marginally higher than the correlations for each test separately. For these 16 (four ratings by four scores) correlations, the range was from .19–.34; the median was .28.

The authors also present a two-way expectancy table, with both the "overall evaluation re: clerical staff" and the AOB total score dichotomized at the approximate midpoints of their respective scales. The "hit rate" is about 61% (59% for "good performers"; 64% for "poor performers"). A reviewer-computed phi-coefficient was .22 over this four-fold table.

TESTING AND EQUAL EMPLOYMENT OPPORTUNITY. The English Sex Discrimination Act (1975) and the Race Relations Act (1976) are described. Both are similar to the *U.S. Civil Rights Act of 1964, as amended* (1982), and the *Guidelines on Employee Selection Procedures* (1978). The bottom line in both countries is similar: If a test results in adverse impact (lower pass rates for women and protected minorities than for white males) the validity and business necessity of the selection device must be demonstrated. Several practical steps for reducing discrimination in testing are outlined, and the option of exploring for and acting on "differential validity" are mentioned. SHL indicates that it "will provide separately analysed norms (broken down by sex and/or ethnic minority group) for users' information." None of the data provided so far, however, include age, gender, or ethnic group information. In the U.S. it has been found that highly speeded tests result in adverse impact particularly against ethnic minorities. If such impact were found, the validity evidence given would, in this reviewer's opinion, constitute a very inadequate defense.

SUMMARY. The AOB is a very handsomely assembled clerical battery. However, it is considerably overpriced in comparison with U.S. clerical batteries, the internal consistency reliabilities are inappropriate, the self-selection of an undescribed validity sample, the fact that the sample was limited to employed workers, and the unknown reliability and intercorrelations of the rating scales all reduce confidence in the AOB as a useful selection instrument. Extensively researched and validated clerical selection batteries are available; better alternatives exist.

REVIEWER'S REFERENCES

Guion, R. L. (1965). *Personnel testing.* New York, NY: McGraw-Hill.
Uniform guidelines on employee selection procedures. (1978). 29 Code of Federal Regulations Part 1607. Washington, DC: Bureau of National Affairs.
Civil Rights Act of 1964, as amended. (1982). 29 United States Code 621. Washington, DC: U.S. Government Printing Office.
Psychological Corporation. (1989). *Catalog.* San Antonio, TX: The author.
SRA/London House. (1989). *Test catalog for business.* Park Ridge, IL: The author.
London House. (undated). *Systems catalog for business.* Park Ridge, IL: The author.

[25]
The Bangs Receptive Vocabulary Checklist.

Purpose: "To provide a developmentally sequenced list of words that emerge in children's lexicons between the third birthday and entry into the first grade."
Population: Mentally retarded, hearing impaired, language/learning disabled, or autistic children ages 3-0 to 7-0.
Publication Date: 1990.
Scores: Total score only.

Administration: Individual.
Price Data, 1991: $49 per complete kit, including manual (48 pages); $15 per 25 score sheets; $12.95 per 25 achievement profiles.
Time: [60] minutes or less.
Comments: Other test materials (e.g., coins) must be supplied by examiner.
Author: Tina E. Bangs.
Publisher: Communication Skill Builders.

Review of The Bangs Receptive Vocabulary Checklist by LEO M. HARVILL, Professor and Assistant Dean for Medical Education, James H. Quillen College of Medicine, East Tennessee State University, Johnson City, TN:

The Bangs Receptive Vocabulary Checklist is a test of 95 vocabulary words and phrases that children are expected to acquire prior to entry into first grade. These words and phrases are contained in 40 test items, 10 items for each of four age levels. Information from the checklist can be used to assist teachers and clinicians in preparing goals and objectives for individualized educational programs.

Items were selected from an initial list of 175 words and phrases. The initial list was administered to 542 children in preschools, kindergartens, and first and second grades in Texas. The group of children ranged in age from 2-0 years to entry into second grade, lived primarily in low-middle to high-middle income areas, had no known deficits in language or the ability to learn, and included equal numbers of males and females. Children ranging in age from 3-0 to 4-0 years were in Level I, those from 4-0 to 5-0 years were in Level II, children entering kindergarten (5-0 to 6-0) were in Level III, and those entering first grade (6-0 to 7-0) were in Level IV.

Items were selected for a particular level of the checklist if 80% or more of the children within and above the specified age level passed the item and less than 80% of the children below that level passed the item.

The checklist does appear to effectively measure a child's receptive vocabulary. If face validity of this instrument were of any import, it appears it could provide information that would assist teachers and clinicians in developing individualized educational programs. For the most part, the testing materials provided for the administration of the checklist are of high quality and would seem to hold the attention of a young child. The only exception to this is Picture Set 26 in the stimulus book which is used to determine the child's knowledge of whole and half. Each row in the picture set includes a whole, a half, and a quarter of an object but it seems that it might be difficult for a young child to distinguish between the pictures of a half and a quarter.

There is no mention of reliability or validity in the manual. It is important for a checklist of this type to be able to report, at least, adequate test-retest reliability if educational decisions are to be made from the test results. No norms are reported. A developmental age can be determined from the test based on the child's performance on test items in the four age levels. Users may have difficulty judging the appropriateness of this test for their particular purposes with no norm group information being available.

Three items in the checklist measure the concept of quantity at three different levels of difficulty (Items 9, 19, 30). It is unclear from reading the manual and the score sheet exactly how these items are to be administered and recorded on the score sheet. Clearer directions for administering and recording the responses for each of these items would be helpful.

A description of entry and termination levels is provided in the manual. It is obvious that the appropriate entry level is based on a number of factors and cannot be stated directly in the manual. However, a clear description of a termination level could be provided. The only statement concerning this states, "If so, a rule of thumb might be to start the assessment with the ten items below the child's developmental age and continue until five consecutive items are failed." It is unclear from this sentence whether the examiner should definitely conclude the testing after five consecutive items are failed or whether this should only be used as a guideline. In the example in Appendix B in the manual, three different test administrations on the same examinee show stopping points after fifteen, three, and two consecutive failed items, respectively. If the examiner wishes to determine the developmental age group of the examinee at the conclusion of the test, it is necessary to have a definitive rule for concluding the testing session. If the results of the test are to be used to simply determine the child's knowledge of the 40 test items, it would seem appropriate to administer as many of the test items as the child can tolerate and now worry about a specific "stopping" rule.

The manual indicates that a developmental age group can be determined and a place is provided for recording this on the score sheet and on the achievement profile. However, there is no description in the manual for determining this. Material presented in Appendices A and B in the manual imply how to do this by providing some examples but it is never explicitly stated in the manual.

In summary, the development of the test seems to have been appropriate, the test materials are generally of excellent quality, and the directions for the administration of the individual items are generally good. The test does seem to be useful for determining the nature of a child's receptive vocabulary and for assisting in the development of goals and specific objectives for individualized educational programs.

The manual could be improved by reporting upon the reliability of the test, mentioning the validity of the test, and clarifying the descriptions of when to terminate the test and how to determine the developmental age group of an examinee.

[26]
Bankson Language Test—2.

Purpose: Constructed "to establish the presence of a language disorder and identify areas in need of further, in-depth testing."
Population: Ages 3-0 to 6-11.
Publication Dates: 1977–90.
Acronym: BLT-2.
Scores, 4: Semantic Knowledge, Morphological and Syntactic Rules, Language Quotient, Pragmatic Knowledge (optional).
Administration: Individual.
Forms, 2: BLT-2; BLT-2 Screen.
Price Data, 1990: $84 per complete kit including 25 profile/examiner's record booklets, 25 screen record forms, picture book, and manual ('90, 32 pages); $29 per picture book; $24 per 25 profile/examiner's record booklets; $10 per 25 screen record forms; $25 per manual.
Time: (30) minutes.
Comments: Revision of Bankson Language Screening Test.
Author: Nicholas W. Bankson.
Publisher: PRO-ED, Inc.
Cross References: For a review of an earlier edition by Barry W. Jones, see 9:107 (1 reference).

TEST REFERENCES
1. Beitchman, J. H., Nair, R., Clegg, M., & Patel, P. G. (1986). Prevalence of speech and language disorders in 5-year-old kindergarten children in the Ottawa-Carleton region. *Journal of Speech and Hearing Disorders, 51*, 98-110.
2. Fujiki, M., & Brinton, B. (1987). Elicited imitation revisited: A comparison with spontaneous language production. *Language, Speech, and Hearing Services in Schools, 18*, 301-311.
3. Abraham, S., & Stoker, R. (1988). Language assessment of hearing-impaired children and youth: Patterns of test use. *Language, Speech, and Hearing Services in Schools, 19*, 160-174.
4. Densem, J. F., Nuthall, G. A., Bushnell, J., & Horn, J. (1989). Effectiveness of a sensory integrative therapy program for children with perceptual-motor deficits. *Journal of Learning Disabilities, 22*, 221-229.

Review of the Bankson Language Test—2 by RONALD B. GILLAM, Assistant Professor of Communicative Disorders, University of Missouri-Columbia, Columbia, MO:

The Bankson Language Test—2 (BLT-2), a revision of the Bankson Language Screening Test (BLST; 9:107), samples a wide variety of early developing semantic and syntactic properties of language. The BLT-2 differs significantly from the BLST. The Visual Perception, Visual Association/Sequencing, and Auditory Perception Subtests are not included on the BLT-2. In the Semantic Knowledge subtest, the color knowledge section was removed. This subtest now targets expressive knowledge of body parts, nouns, verbs, categories, functions, prepositions, and opposites. Like the BLST, receptive knowledge of the semantic items may be evaluated for clinical purposes. The Morphological-

Syntactic Rules subtest has been expanded to more completely assess the child's use of subject, object, and possessive pronouns; present progressive, present, irregular past, and regular past verb tenses; modal, auxiliary, and copula verbs; plurals; comparative/superlatives; negatives; and questions. A supplemental subtest that targets pragmatic abilities has been added. The examiner is required to note whether ritualizing, informing, controlling, and/or imagining behaviors were evidenced during prior testing. A 20-item screening test composed of selected items from the BLT-2 is also included. Percentiles and standard score equivalents are presented for Semantic Knowledge, Morphological-Syntactic Knowledge, and Screening raw test scores. The sum of the standard scores from the Semantic Knowledge and Morphological-Syntactic Knowledge subtests can be converted to a composite quotient.

Targets are elicited by showing children black-and-white line drawings while presenting verbal stimuli. The majority of the drawings are 2 x 3 inches in size and appear in groups of three, four, or six per page. The verbal stimuli for the semantic knowledge items are in question form. Cloze sentences are primarily used to elicit morphological and syntactic items. Item analysis was undertaken on 200 protocols from 50 children at each age level between 3-0 years and 6-11 years. Statistically significant item-total correlations support item validity for all four age ranges. Median percentages of difficulty were within acceptable limits for all but the 6-year-old children. Test items should elicit desired responses from older preschool and kindergarten children. Although ceiling effects may interfere with the evaluation of 6-year-olds, the cloze format and the small, crowded, and colorless pictures could be confusing for some 3-year-olds.

The BLT-2 was standardized on 1,108 children in 18 states. This sample is twice the size of that used for the BLST. Demographics for the standardization sample are representative of the national population. Internal reliability coefficients (Cronbach's alpha) averaged across the four age levels range between .91 and .97. Test-retest reliability studies are not reported. Thus, although internal consistency appears to be adequate, test stability is unknown.

Concurrent validity was assessed by correlating BLT-2 results from 22 children with their performance on the Screening Children for Related Early Educational Needs (Hresko, Reid, Hammill, Ginsburg, & Baroody, 1988). The resulting coefficients range from .43 to .74. Although these correlations are well within acceptable limits, the small subject sample and the use of an achievement screening test as a criterion measure for a test of language

production compromise the interpretability of these results.

Several types of evidence were presented to support the construct validity of the BLT-2. The test appears to measure developmental properties of language. Correlations between raw scores and chronological age were .54 for Semantic Knowledge, .40 for Morphological-Syntactic Knowledge, .10 for Pragmatic Knowledge, and .45 for the screening test. The BLT-2 may differentiate between language-delayed and normally developing children. Mean standard scores earned by a group of 26 language-delayed children were 1 standard deviation below the mean. Unfortunately, information about the percentage of language-delayed children whose performance was better than 1 standard deviation below the mean is not provided. Therefore, readers have no basis for judging the actual predictive power of this test. The Semantic Knowledge and Morphological-Syntactic Knowledge subtests correlated at .75 across the four age levels, suggesting that they measure interrelated language skills. Moderate correlations are also reported between performance on the BLT-2 and a test of general aptitude.

Construct validity was also evaluated in terms of the extent to which the test reflects its underlying theoretical foundation. The author contends that Bloom and Lahey's (1978) interactional perspective of language as a three-dimensional system of content, form, and use served as the rationale for test construction. The BLT-2 represents language content as vocabulary. Certainly, knowledge of the critical features that underlie word meaning is one aspect of language content. However, the BLT-2 does not purport to measure knowledge of the ways that meanings and events relate to each other, an equally important aspect of language content. Similarly, the BLT-2 represents language form as morphology and syntax, and omits phonology. Finally, the BLT-2 represents language use as four language functions. Other aspect of language use such as conversational devices, presuppositions, and linguistic/contextual contingencies are omitted.

One critical feature of Bloom and Lahey's (1978) theory of language concerns the interrelationships between content, form, and use. Having examiners base judgements about pragmatic items on language behaviors evidenced during earlier testing incorporates content-use and form-use relationships into the test's structure. The BLT-2 does not measure content-form or content-form-use interactions, but neither does any other norm-referenced test of child language. However, failure to account for these interrelationships threatens construct validity because it is inconsistent with the theoretical model that serves as the foundation for this test.

In summary, as a test of semantic, morphological, and syntactic language functioning, the BLT-2 is a substantial improvement over the BLST. Internal consistency meets minimum reliability requirements, but test stability cannot be evaluated because test-retest reliability studies are not reported. Concurrent and construct validity have been only tentatively established, and users should be cautious. The BLT-2 is not an adequate representation of Bloom and Lahey's (1978) language theory. Like all other norm-referenced tests of early language development, the BLT-2 treats language content and form as discrete entities. To date, careful observation of children using language in context remains the best way to obtain evidence about interactions between the development of content, form, and use.

REVIEWER'S REFERENCES

Bloom, L., & Lahey, M. (1978). *Language development and language disorders*. New York: Wiley.
Hresko, W. P., Reid, D. K., Hammill, D. D., Ginsburg, H. P., & Baroody, A. J. (1988). Screening Children for Related Early Educational Needs. Austin, TX: PRO-ED, Inc.

Review of the Bankson Language Test—2 by ROGER L. TOWNE, *Assistant Professor of Speech Pathology and Audiology, Illinois State University, Normal, IL:*

PURPOSE. The Bankson Language Test—2 (BLT-2) represents a major revision of the Bankson Language Screening Test (BLST; 9:107) first published in 1977. The BLT-2 is based upon the premise that language can be regarded as a composite of content, form, and use (Bloom & Lahey, 1978). Three major subtests, Semantic Knowledge, Morphological and Syntactic Rules, and Pragmatic Knowledge assess these areas through a variety of tasks. The author notes that there are three major uses for the BLT-2: to serve as a norm-referenced survey of language skills; to provide an informal diagnostic inventory of strengths and weaknesses; and to serve as a research tool when language assessment is desired.

ADMINISTRATION, SCORING, AND INTERPRETATION. Administration of the BLT-2 involves eliciting verbal and nonverbal responses to verbal cues that are presented with a series of line drawings. The Semantic Knowledge subtest is designed to measure expressive vocabulary as one aspect of language content. It consists of seven inclusive sections, with six items in each section, specifically dealing with body parts, nouns, verbs, categories, functions, prepositions, and opposites. The Morphological and Syntactic Rules subtest assesses language form. Seven sections, each with 5 to 24 items, specifically assess use of pronouns, verb tense, verb usage, plurals, comparatives and superlatives, negation, and questions. Language use is assessed by the supplemental Pragmatic Knowledge subtest. This subtest consists of a checklist of pragmatic language behaviors related to ritualizing, informing, controlling, and imagining.

Each test item is scored as either correct (1) or incorrect (0) and the cumulative raw scores for the Semantic Knowledge and Morphological and Syntactic Rules subtests are recorded. Tables are provided from which the raw scores can be converted to percentiles and standard scores based on the child's age (3-0 years through 6-11 years). Further, these two subtest standard scores can be added together and converted to a composite quotient. A child's overall performance level on the BLT-2 is determined by comparing the standard scores and quotient obtained to performance criteria provided in the manual. Overall performance can then be categorized as very poor, poor, below average, average, above average, superior, or very superior. In addition, 20 items have been selected to comprise a separate screening procedure for which separate standard scores and percentiles are provided.

EVALUATION OF TEST ADEQUACY. The norming procedures, reliability, and validity information of the BLT-2 represents a significant improvement over those of the Bankson Language Screening Test. The three subtests were selected to represent traditional areas that language clinicians frequently test and remediate in younger children. Individual test items were selected from a much larger pool of items and were analyzed for level of difficulty and discriminating power. These analyses suggest that difficulty and discriminating power are appropriate for 3- to 5-year-olds and acceptable for 6-year-olds. Test reliability was measured through both content sampling and standard error of measurement procedures. The results of these procedures suggest that the individual test items on the BLT-2 have a relatively high degree of homogeneity and that individual test scores are reasonably reliable measures. Concurrent validity was established with the Screening Children for Related Early Educational Needs (Hresko, Reid, Hammill, Ginsburg, & Baroody, 1988). Analyses of six hypotheses related to test performance also suggest that the BLT-2 has strong construct validity. Finally, normative data were gathered from a demographically representative sample of 1,108 children from 18 states. This sample closely represents the U.S. population as a whole on such important characteristics as sex, residence, race, geographic region, and family income.

The content of the BLT-2 has also been significantly improved over the original screening version of the test. Subtests for visual and auditory perception related to memory, discrimination, and sequencing, which have questionable value in assessing language skill and function, have been eliminated. The original Syntactic Rules subtest has been completely revised to also include morphological rules. The new Morphological-Syntactic Rules subtest now assesses important language use skills including use of pronouns, verb tense, verb usage, plurals, comparatives/superlatives, negation, and questions. The test items selected to assess these areas appear to sample a broad range of behaviors at a succession of developmental levels. Thus, the BLT-2 should be more able to reliably and accurately assess language problems throughout the entire targeted age range.

SUMMARY. The BLT-2 has been significantly improved over the original BLST. The content of the BLT-2 has been revised to more comprehensively assess relevant areas of language as reflected in language content, form, and use. The stimulus material has been simplified and improved so as to lessen its potential negative influence on test performance. Finally, the standardization of the BLT-2 was considerably more rigorous, resulting in a test that is much more valid and reliable.

Complete and comprehensive assessment of children's language abilities is probably beyond the scope of any one test to accomplish. All tests must focus on selected language skills and be targeted for a selected population. Therefore, clinically useful tests are often those that can reliably evaluate a broad range of language abilities and specify those areas which may require additional in-depth assessment. The BLT-2 appears to qualify as such a clinically useful evaluation tool. Persons should find the BLT-2 an efficient means of assessing general language abilities of younger children.

REVIEWER'S REFERENCES

Bloom, L., & Lahey, M. (1978). *Language development and language disorders*. New York: Wiley.
Hresko, W. P., Reid, D. K., Hammill, D. D., Ginsburg, H. P., & Baroody, A. J. (1988). Screening Children for Related Early Educational Needs. Austin, TX: PRO-ED, Inc.

[27]
Basic Economics Test.

Purpose: "An updated economics achievement test for curriculum development, for the assessment of student understanding, and for determining the effectiveness of educational materials and teaching strategies."
Population: Grades 4–6.
Publication Dates: 1980–81.
Acronym: BET.
Scores: Total score only.
Administration: Group.
Forms, 2: A, B.
Price Data, 1987: $8 per 25 test booklets (specify Form A or B); $5 per Examiner's Manual ('81, 38 pages) which includes scoring keys and model answer sheet which may be duplicated locally.
Time: 50(55) minutes.
Comments: Substantive revision of the Test of Elementary Economics.
Authors: John F. Chizmar and Ronald S. Halinski.
Publisher: Joint Council on Economic Education.
Cross References: For reviews by Mary Friend Adams and James O. Hodges of an earlier edition, see 8:901 (1 reference).

Review of the Basic Economics Test by IRVIN J. LEHMANN, Professor of Measurement, Michigan State University, East Lansing, MI:

The authors state that the Basic Economics Test (BET) "represents a substantive revision" of the 1971 Test of Elementary Economics. In fact, the only similarity between this form and the 1971 Revised Experimental Edition is the sponsor (the Joint Council on Economic Education), the number of forms (two), and the applicable population (it was designed for students in grades 4–6). Other than that, the authors are different, the number of items is reduced from 40 to 38, and the content of the test is different. In the 1971 edition, students' understanding of seven basic economic concepts—Household, Business, Government, Exchange, Technology Market, and the National Economy—were assessed. The present edition of the Basic Economics Test is based on the *Master Curriculum Guide (MCG) Framework*. The test is based on the view that "economic literacy hinges on effectively applying basic economic concepts to problems in order to reach decisions." The authors attempt to do this by developing a 38-item test that stresses producing a reasoned approach to five major facets—Basic Economic Concepts, Economic Systems, Microeconomics, Macroeconomics, and Economic Institutions—and 17 specific concepts such as supply and demand, banking, inflation, and the like. Whether or not the quality of the test has improved is the concern of the forthcoming discussion.

The authors discuss the five criteria that were established and followed (or at least an attempt was made to follow them) in the test's development. The criteria were as follows:

1. The test had to reflect current curricular thinking in economics education.

2. The test had to consist of items that reflected curricular validity (i.e., the items should differentiate between students who did and did not receive economic education).

3. The items had to be written at an appropriate reading level.

4. The test had to meet "acceptable levels of reliability."

5. The test had to be a *power* rather than a speeded test.

A working committee "which consisted of two economists, one educator, one reading specialist, and three elementary teachers who had attended workshops conducted by the Illinois Council on Economic Education" developed the test.

It appears that the conventional principles to be employed in the development of an achievement test such as preparation of a test blueprint, writing more items than needed, developing several forms, try out of the preliminary form, conducting item analyses, undertaking necessary revisions, and the like were followed. This resulted in the development of two tests, each with 38 four-choice multiple-choice items.

The authors state that the items were developed to measure three levels of cognition: knowledge, comprehension, and application. In contrast to the 1971 edition, more emphasis is placed on comprehension and application—55% versus 45% and 32% versus 22% respectively and significantly less on knowledge—13% versus 32%. Nearly two-thirds of the items deal with basic economic concepts (29%) and microeconomics: resource allocations (37%). Although some teachers may feel that these two areas are overemphasized, we must remember that the test was built on a conceptual framework contained in the *Master Curriculum Guide Framework* as well as on a test blueprint which was sent to a National Advisory Committee for review.

Two criticisms noted by Hodges (1978) of the first experimental edition, were (a) although the test is designed for students in grades 4–6, there were no fourth and fifth graders in the piloting and revision stages and (b) there is limited emphasis on the higher-order thinking skills of interpretation or analysis of charts, tables, and documents. These criticisms were attended to in the revision. The BET used fourth, fifth, and sixth graders in the piloting and norming stages. With reference to the lack of emphasis on higher order thinking skills, this criticism has also been addressed (albeit in a limited fashion) in the revision. Also, we should remember that the test is designed for students in the upper elementary grades. How much can we expect from these students? Even though the test matrix does not have categories of analysis, synthesis, and evaluation per se, the authors state that "our application items primarily require students to apply economic concepts, although occasionally they need to analyze and synthesize as well."

Hodges (1978) also commented on the representativeness of the norming sample—pupils primarily from middle-class homes—and the reading level required. This reviewer has the same concern as Hodges insofar as the representatives of the sample is concerned. Although the authors state that "approximately 90 percent of the students who took the norming test were Caucasian, and more than 80 percent were classified as belonging to upper or middle class families," we are not provided with sufficient information to infer the norming sample's representativeness. For example, of the approximately 10 percent who were *not* Caucasian, how many were Afro-Americans, native Americans, Hispanics, Orientals, and the like?

Raw scores can be converted to standard scores and to percentile ranks by grade level and amount of instruction in economics. The former permits the user to use pre- and post-test scores for evaluative purposes.

The norms were obtained from a national sample of 15,052 students (7,652 for Form A and 7,400 for Form B) in 56 school districts. Separate norms tables are provided for each form and for each of grades 4, 5, and 6. The percentile ranks tables are further reported in terms of the amount of economics education received: (a) without economics instruction, (b) with at least 1 week of instruction, and (c) with 13 + weeks of instruction. A conversion table is given equating Form A scores to Form B scores. The forms appear to be comparable.

Cronbach's alpha varies from .810 to .849 for Form A and from .760 to .821 for Form B. Standard error of measurement ranges from 2.60 to 2.72.

With respect to the readability of the items, a Dale-Chall readability analysis showed that the test's reading level was appropriate for the average fifth grader. It should be noted that the use of technical economic terms such as *profit*, *capital*, and *productivity* no doubt may attenuate the readability index. But, as the authors state, "all such words . . . are used in one or more of the economic teaching materials for grades 4–6." They further believe that if pupils exposed to economic instruction fare poorly on technical terms, this is suggestive of the teachers' attention.

Generally, the quality of the 38 items in each form is very good. There are, however, some instances, where (a) there may be two correct answers, or (b) a clue may be provided in the stem that aids the test-wise student. For example, Item 5 in Form B asks, "Pick which 'good' is not scarce: A. Time; B. Spinach; C. Water in a big city; D. Air to breathe in the country," and has "D" keyed as the correct answer. Might a student not argue that "A" is also a correct answer? Also, wherever possible, negatives should be avoided, but if they are used, they should be *italicized*, in **bold**, or underlined to draw the student's attention to the negative.

Another suggestion for writing multiple-choice items is to avoid having a word in the stem that might provide a clue of the correct answer to the test-wise student. Item 8, Form B, asks who decides how something is "produced in a market economy" and "producers," which is a correct answer, is one of the foils.

In the majority of instances, the distractors are reasonable, although an item asking for an example of an indirect cost has "a beautiful lake" as a foil.

The authors made the BET a more difficult test than its predecessor. Whereas, in the experimental edition, 39/40 correct answers placed a student at the 99th percentile, and students who answered one-half the items correctly were at the median, the number of items to be correctly answered in the revision to place pupils at these percentile point are about 34–35 and 20–21 respectively for Forms A and B depending on grade level and level of instruction.

The Examiner's Manual is well written. It includes an explanation of the test's development, instructions for administration and scoring, and the test's psychometric characteristics (e.g., validity, reliability, and discrimination coefficients). In addition, for each of the 38 items in both forms there is an explanation of the educational objective the item is designed to measure (e.g., the student is required to "show an understanding of the concept of scarcity by recognizing the dilemma of scarcity"). The evidence presented attests to the test's content and its instructional and construct validity as well as to its reliability. Of the 76 items in the two forms, there are only three items—one in Form A (Item 32) and two in Form B (items 10 and 34) where it appears the greater the exposure to instruction, the poorer the pupils' performance.

Some sections of the manual should be of more value to the classroom teacher than are other parts. For example, the statistics (means, standard deviations) for each form by gender, grade, type of community, and teacher's participation in an economic education workshop should help teachers interpret the performance of their students. Regretfully absent in this edition (it *was* in the experimental form) is a table showing the percentage of students responding to each foil. Such data would be valuable for necessary reteaching.

If any criticism could be levied against the technical data provided, it would be that the material pertaining to the validity evidence, specifically the Analysis of Variance reporting, is likely to be beyond the scope of the ordinary classroom teacher. As noted earlier, many of the concerns raised in regard to the first experimental edition appear to have been addressed.

In summary, the Basic Economics Test is a well-constructed instrument. The authors have attended to many of the concerns raised by reviewers of its predecessor (Adams, 1978; Hodges, 1978). Elementary school teachers who teach economics should give serious attention to using this test when they are interested in norm-referenced interpretation.

REVIEWER'S REFERENCES

Adams, M. F. (1978). [Review of the Test of Elementary Economics, Revised Experimental Edition.] In O. K. Buros (Ed.), *The eighth mental measurements yearbook* (pp. 1434-1435). Highland Park, NJ: The Gryphon Press.

Hodges, J. O. (1978). [Review of the Test of Elementary Economics, Revised Experimental Edition.] In O. K. Buros (Ed.), *The eighth mental measurements yearbook* (pp. 1435-1437). Highland Park, NJ: The Gryphon Press.

Review of the Basic Economics Test by A. HARRY PASSOW, Schiff Professor of Education, Teachers College, Columbia University, New York, NY:

The Joint Council on Economic Education's (JCEE) Basic Economics Test (BET) aims at assessing the achievement of children in grades 4 through 6 in the basic principles of economics. It presumably represents a substantive revision of the JCEE's Test of Elementary Economics, published in 1971.

The JCEE *Master Curriculum Guide in Economics for the Nation's Schools* provided the base for the test's content categories. The *Master Curriculum Guide (MCG) Framework* views economic literacy as hinging on being able to apply basic economic concepts to problems in order to reach decisions. Both practice in applying a decision-making model and mastery of the basic economic concepts are required and are presumably reflected in the five content categories of the BET: Basic Economic Concepts, Economic Systems, Microeconomics (resource allocation), Macroeconomics, and Economic Institutions (banking). The BET focuses on modified Bloom taxonomy cognitive categories of knowledge, understanding, and application. The Examiner's Manual provides a text matrix for the test with the five content categories and the three cognitive categories as the correlates, with the number of items per cell reflecting the weights the authors decided were appropriate for each content-cognitive category.

The procedures by which the test was developed are described in sufficient detail. Four forms of the test, each containing 35–38 items, were constructed for the initial trial and given to approximately 1,500 children in grades 4–6 (with and without instruction in economics), with the results analyzed for item difficulty, reliability, and responsiveness to instruction. Two forms (A and B), each with 40 items, were then developed for norming. Schools that were JCEE Centers for Economic Education or those enrolled in its Developmental Economic Educational Program were asked to volunteer for norming and provided information about whether or not they were providing instruction in economics, the nature of that instruction, the type of community, and their students' socioeconomic status. Of the total number of usable tests returned for processing, 5,080 were from students with instruction and 8,728 from those without instruction in economics. Based on the analysis of item difficulty, item reliability, and item responsiveness to instruction, two items were deleted from each form, and the forms were rescored and reanalyzed. The final forms reflect the authors' "judgment in balancing the demands of the various criteria [they] attempted to meet with the sometimes conflicting reactions . . . received from different sources."

The reliability data are, as the authors report, "well within the range necessary for use in the evaluation of group instruction." They suggest, however, that in making decisions about individual students, the BET score should be supplemented by other evidence of achievement. A Dale-Chall readability analysis indicated that the reading level was appropriate for an average fifth grader. The authors note the uncommon words that raise the reading level are basically technical terms from the discipline of economics itself.

In discussing the test validity, the authors note that consensus is required on two issues: the concepts to be tested for and the extent to which the items chosen actually test these concepts. With respect to the concepts to be tested, the authors assert that the *MCG Framework* represents a consensus within the discipline of economics so that the tests do have content validity. An analysis of variance was used to study the impact of instruction on student score and to establish the construct validity of the BET. The analysis of variance data indicate that the BET does respond to instruction and that the effect increases with a longer period of instruction. The Examiner's Manual provides teachers with the economic content and cognitive category of each of the items.

If the *MCG Framework* does indeed represent a consensus within the discipline of economics concepts important and appropriate for fourth, fifth, and sixth graders, then these concepts must be at a very basic level—otherwise, it is hard to conceive of consensus among economists about very many economic events. That is, students are tested primarily on whether they understand what demand, supply, markets, and similar basic—almost definitional—economic concepts mean, and, to a lesser extent, whether they can apply this understanding in simple situations. In sum, the Basic Economics Test appears to be a reliable and valid test for assessing the achievement of students who have had instruction in economics using the framework and the teaching strategies of the Joint Council on Economic Education's *Master Curriculum Guide in Economics for the Nation's Schools.* How useful it is for fourth through sixth graders who have had instruction in economics following another curriculum guide or who have had only incidental instruction in social studies classes, for example, is not clear.

[28]
Basic English Skills Test.

Purpose: Designed to test listening comprehension, speaking, reading, and writing skills at a basic level when information on the attainment of basic functional language skills is needed.
Population: Limited-English-speaking adults.
Publication Dates: 1982–88.
Acronym: B.E.S.T.
Scores, 9: Oral Interview Section (Listening Comprehension, Communication, Fluency, Pronunciation, Reading/Writing, Total) and Literacy Skill Section (Reading Comprehension, Writing, Total).

Subtests, 2: Oral Interview Section, Literacy Skills Section.
Administration: Individual in part.
Parts: 4 forms (Forms B and C only in current circulation).
Price Data, 1989: $100 per complete test kit; $9 per picture cue book ('88, 15 pages); $10 per 5 interviewer's booklets ('88, 13 pages); $20 per 100 interview scoring sheets ('88, 2 pages); $40 per literacy skills testing package including 20 literacy skills test booklets ('88, 20 pages) and 20 literacy skills scoring sheets ('88, 2 pages); $15 per manual ('88, 79 pages).
Time: [75] minutes.
Comments: Orally administered in part; subtests available as separates; other test materials (e.g., 3 $1 bills, 2 dimes, etc.) must be supplied by examiner.
Authors: Center for Applied Linguistics (test), Dorry Kenyon (revised manual), and Charles W. Stansfield (revised manual) with assistance from Dora Johnson, Allene Grognet, and Dan Dreyfus.
Publisher: Center for Applied Linguistics.

Review of the Basic English Skills Test by ALAN GARFINKEL, Associate Professor of Spanish and Foreign Language Education, Purdue University, West Lafayette, IN:

The Basic English Skills Test is advertised as a standardized, criterion-referenced, elementary-level test for determining placement, progress, diagnosis, screening decisions, and program evaluation. It is a well-constructed test that provides qualitative and quantitative evidence of its validity. Further, despite the fact that the test does not achieve all of its declared purposes equally well, it is a superb instrument, especially for assessment of progress and for overall evaluation in basic programs.

Face validity is clearly self-evident. The test was developed and published by The Center for Applied Linguistics (CAL) under a U.S. government contract. This center is widely known across the nation as the operator of two ERIC Clearinghouses and as perhaps the single most important source of information on second- and foreign-language teaching and learning. The instrument was field tested in several of the nation's best known centers for bilingual education.

Content validity is similarly well established. The test is intended to function in classes where survival skills have been emphasized and its content is clearly aimed at this kind of instruction. It is, however, partly a content issue that makes the test less valuable as a placement test. Its focus on survival skills has been provided at the expense of knowledge about English (linguistic competence). The Basic English Skills Test could still be used for placement when placement is not a matter of selecting one of several levels. In those cases, the Test of English Proficiency Level (433; TEPL; Rathmell, 1985) would be a better choice because its content includes some (but admittedly fewer) emphases on survival skills along with a focus on more knowledge about language, and because the TEPL uses a scale of results labeled in letters rather than numbers to avoid confusion with chronologically labeled levels.

The Basic English Skills Test manual provides extensive information on quantitative efforts to establish validity. It cites the *Standards for Educational and Psychological Testing* (AERA, APA, & NCME, 1985) and indicates both the oral interview and the literacy skills portions have reliability quotients (.911 and .966, respectively) that exceed the .90 standard. Means and standard deviations are provided for each of seven student-performance levels. Interscorer reliability is only slightly lower. Subsequent efforts to establish interscorer reliability should include a larger N than 29 and more than two scorers.

An exceptionally well-written manual with clear instructions for testing without contaminating results completes the Basic English Skills Test package. This reviewer recommends the test very highly for assessment of progress or program evaluation in elementary survival-skills-oriented English as a Second Language classes.

REVIEWER'S REFERENCES

American Educational Research Association, American Psychological Association, & National Council on Measurement in Education. (1985). *Standards for educational and psychological testing.* Washington, DC: American Psychological Association, Inc.
Rathmell, G. (1985). Test of English Proficiency Level. Hayward, CA: The Alemany Press.

Review of the Basic English Skills Test by PATSY ARNETT JAYNES, Second Language Program Evaluation Specialist, Jefferson County Public Schools, Golden, CO:

The purpose of the Basic English Skills Test (BEST) is to assess the English as a Second Language (ESL) skills of adults using a nonacademic format. The authors describe the BEST as a standardized, criterion-referenced test of basic functional skills in English at an elementary level.

The battery consists of two sections: the Oral Interview Section and the Literacy Skills Section. These two sections can be used in tandem or separately. The Oral Interview Section (15 minutes) is an individually administered interview that simulates basic, real-life language tasks. The three subtests of this section consist of Listening Comprehension, Communication, and Fluency. Other items included in the Oral Interview Section are a rater-judgement of the student's pronunciation and a screening device for the Literacy Skills Section.

The Literacy Skills Section (1 hour) can be individually or group administered. The student is expected to complete a variety of reading and writing tasks in a consumable student book. The reading items are increasingly more difficult as the student goes through the exercises and include multiple-choice cloze passages. The writing tasks are

in short paragraph format asking for three to four sentences on a given informal topic. Verbal and written answers are given a numerical score. These scores are added for a total score.

The training and testing procedures are presented in the Test Manual in a step-by-step, clearly understood manner. The authors emphasize very strongly that test examiners must have guided training prior to administering the BEST. Practice and interrater agreement are essential for compliance to the standardization component, especially in the Oral Interview Section. The instructions are brief, explicit, and complete. The scoring directions are clear, and extra samples for examiner training are included in Appendix C for additional practice prior to giving the exam. There is a Student Performance Level Document (Appendix B) in the Test Manual that describes survival English in 10 different levels of proficiency. The emphasis given to having a complete understanding of test administration is important, as the examiner must make scoring decisions quickly during the actual test procedure. There is no time to stop and reference the manual for guidance. Examiner preparation is also required to assemble the $3.84 before testing occurs. The exercises using these bills and coins reflects the authors' desire to have a language assessment that is pragmatic, with natural content that is suitable to the target population.

The BEST content has been structured to include items similar to real-life adult language situations. The topics of survival English situations for adults have been selected to include (*a*) basic grammar, and (*b*) language functions of seeking, giving, and clarification of information within a U.S. cultural context. This attention to survival skills suggests the BEST has high content validity. This measure may also address what Cohen (1980) points to as a problem of validity in language assessment: interference with communicative competence. His definition of a language proficiency test requires that the measure of a student's knowledge in a language be applied functionally. Thus, strong support can be given to the BEST's construct validity as well.

Perhaps the BEST's solid predictive validity is of most value. The normative group of 987 for the Oral Interview Section and 632 for the Literacy Skills Section was drawn from adult speakers of Vietnamese, Hmong, Lao, Cambodian/Khmer, Chinese, Spanish, and Polish. Items were selected for level of difficulty and discrimination with an r-biserial coefficient item analysis, and the performance of the normative group was used to establish seven Student Performance Levels (SPL) using a modified contour analysis on all subsections of the test. These seven student levels were correlated to the most frequent performance levels of the preexisting Mainstream English Language Training Project

(M.E.L.T.) funded by the Office of Refugee Resettlement that included geographically as well as linguistically diverse populations. Even though affective factors such as personality, cognitive style, and motivation cannot be taken into account, this instrument matched student ability to existing instructional program levels. The BEST does very well at predicting appropriate levels of instruction for adult English class placement and instruction. The test is able to identify different levels for lower level placement which other instruments are unable to do (Eakin & Ilyin, 1987).

The authors report their test has high internal reliability. By section, the Oral Interview has a reliability factor of .911 for Form B and the Literacy Skills Section has a reliability factor of .966. This provides stable classification of language performance to the language-learning continuum. For those instructors who followed the authors' directions, the interrater reliability for Form B ranged from .842 to .999.

The BEST can provide achievement information as well as predictive information. For program screening, student placement, student evaluation, and exit criteria data, this assessment will meet the needs of adult ESL programs. Student progress can be documented, diagnostic information on the student's ability to respond in linguistic form and appropriate situational context is available, and most importantly, accurate student placement in levels of instruction is assured. The BEST also provides pre/post data that are so necessary for program funding survival. It is an appropriate screening instrument for English-medium vocational training programs. The one drawback to using the BEST is having to juggle multiple books and scoring sheets. Having a consumable booklet for an adult learner seems unnecessary.

· In summary, the BEST responds to a real need in the field of adult ESL education. It is technically strong, normed to an appropriate group, and addresses the typology of situations students will encounter.

REVIEWER'S REFERENCES

Cohen, A. D. (1980). *Testing language ability in the classroom*. Rowley, Massachusetts: Newbury House Publishers.

Eakin, E., & Ilyin, D. (1987). Basic English Skills Test. In J. Alderson, K. J. Krahnke, & C. W. Stansfield (Eds.), *Reviews of English language proficiency tests* (pp. 9-10). Washington, DC: Teachers of English to Speakers of Other Languages.

[29]
Basic Tests Series.

Purpose: To assess basic skills and knowledge relevant to the world of work or postsecondary education.
Population: High school seniors and college entrants and job applicants.
Publication Dates: 1981–90.
Scores: Total scores only.
Administration: Group.

Restricted Distribution: Distribution restricted and tests administered at licensed testing centers.
Price Data, 1990: £4.25 entry fee per test (£5.25 Basic Tests [Special] and Basic English; £2.50 Proficiency Test in Arithmetic); 60p per Basic Tests booklet containing syllabus and specimen papers (specify test); price data for additional supplementary materials available from publisher.
Comments: Tests administered each May and December at centers established by the publisher (Basic Tests in [Special] subjects available only in May); tests available as separates.
Author: The Associated Examining Board.
Publisher: The Associated Examining Board [England].
  a) BASIC TEST (SPECIAL) IN ELECTRONICS.
Time: 90(95) minutes.
  b) BASIC TEST IN ARITHMETIC.
Time: 10(15) minutes for Paper 1 (mental arithmetic test); 75(80) minutes for Paper 2 (written test).
    1) *Proficiency Test in Arithmetic.*
    Time: 90(95) minutes.
    Comments: To enter this test, candidate must enter for Basic Test in Arithmetic at the same time.
  c) BASIC TEST IN ENGLISH.
Time: 30(40) minutes for Paper 1 (listening); 60(65) minutes for Paper 2 (reading and writing).
  d) BASIC TESTS IN LIFE SKILLS.
Time: 90(100) minutes.
  e) BASIC TEST IN COMPUTER AWARENESS.
Time: 90(95) minutes.
  f) BASIC TEST IN GRAPHICACY.
Time: 90(100) minutes.
  g) BASIC TEST IN HEALTH, HYGIENE AND SAFETY.
Time: 75(85) minutes.
  h) BASIC TEST IN GEOGRAPHY.
Time: 90(95) minutes.
  i) BASIC TEST IN SCIENCE.
Time: 90(95) minutes.
  j) BASIC TEST IN WORLD OF WORK.
Time: 90(100) minutes.
  k) BASIC TEST (SPECIAL) IN BOOKKEEPING.
Time: 90(100) minutes.
  l) BASIC TEST (SPECIAL) IN GEOGRAPHY FOR TOURISM AND LEISURE.
Time: 90(100) minutes.

Review of the Basic Tests Series by STEVEN FERRARA, Chief, Measurement, Statistics, and Evaluation Section, Maryland State Department of Education, Division of Instruction, Baltimore, MD:

The prefaces to the specimen booklets for the 12 Basic Tests reveal several purposes for the series. These purposes fall into three categories: (*a*) Demonstrate mastery of basic skills and knowledge considered necessary to succeed in a first job or to benefit from post-secondary job training, (*b*) reflect existing vocational courses or provide a framework for designing new ones, and (*c*) provide "incentive" and a "major challenge and stimulus" for students not planning to take other external examinations at the end of secondary school. Determining if the tests meet the first purpose is a question of predictive validity; if they meet the second, a question of content and curricular validity; if they meet the third, a matter of asking potential examinees and their teachers. The publisher also claims that employers use Basic Test results to guide hiring decisions and that they can be used to indicate the effectiveness of employee training.

This review is based on my examination of an introduction booklet that describes the 12 tests and their purposes, and of specimen test booklets dated 1985–88 and updated in 1988–89. Each specimen booklet includes an intact test and accompanying course syllabus. The publisher made no technical or other information available for this review. The Basic Tests are not currently available outside of the more than 2,500 publisher-approved testing centers in the United Kingdom.

Content, Format, and Development of the Basic Test Series.

CONTENT AND FORMAT. The Basic Tests Series includes tests of basic academic skills and knowledge (the Arithmetic, English, Geography, Graphicacy, and Science tests), basic life skills and knowledge (the Computer Awareness, Health, Hygiene and Safety, Life Skills, and World of Work tests), and basic skills and knowledge for specific occupations (the Bookkeeping, Electronics, and Geography for Tourism and Leisure tests). The skills and knowledge assessed in many of these tests should be familiar to educators who know about minimum-competency (MCT) and other basic skills tests in wide use in the U.S. What makes the Basic Tests unique is their almost exclusive use of short-answer items (i.e., a few words to one or two sentences) rather than machine-scorable multiple-choice items. This observation may seem mundane to educators in Europe but not to U.S. educators who only in the last few years have seen increasing use of open-ended test questions and the rise of the performance assessment movement. What may seem even more surprising to U.S. educators is that each test's content is detailed in a syllabus for a course designed to prepare examinees specifically for each test, similar to the U.S. College Board's Advanced Placement examinations and courses. There is no concern apparent in Basic Tests materials over measurement-driven instruction as there has been in discussions of assessment in the U.S. That these tests are openly intended to drive instruction in a specific course appears to be routine and accepted.

In general, the Basic Tests include items requiring short written answers plus one or more exercises requiring more extensive responses (e.g., essays; completing forms; constructing or completing diagrams, graphs, or maps) or clusters of sometimes interdependent short-answer items. In several of the tests, both short-answer and extended or multistep tasks may be more difficult and perhaps more "authentic" than items on typical U.S. MCTs, but

many probably are not (e.g., "Should a letter ready for mailing be placed in an in-box or out-box?" from World of Work). Many of the short-answer items could be presented in selected-response format to improve efficiency. However, even multiple-choice items (which appear in quantity only in the Bookkeeping test) are hand scored rather than machine scored.

COMMENTS ON SELECTED INDIVIDUAL TESTS. Most items on all Basic Tests require a considerable amount of reading and writing, which may hinder examinees' abilities to display their skills and knowledge. Some tests appear to require general skills and knowledge that are acquired as part of schooling in general (e.g., the Arithmetic and English tests), while others probably require specialized skills and knowledge that would be acquired only from a specialized course (e.g., the Electronics test), or perhaps only from a course designed around a Basic Test's syllabus (e.g., the Health, Hygiene, and Safety test). The Graphicacy test, which assesses primarily understanding of symbols (e.g., in electronics and computer programming) and signs, charts, and graphs, also includes tasks similar to those on visual-spatial aptitude tests (e.g., paper-folding tasks). Similarly, the test on Health, Hygiene, and Safety requires both general and job-specific health and hygiene knowledge (e.g., for food-handling industries) and even knowledge probably irrelevant to health and hygiene in the workplace (e.g., labeling internal human organs). Interestingly, examinees must show evidence they have had actual and/or simulated work experience before they can take the World of Work test and that they have had practical experience in using a computer.

The production quality and artwork in the test booklets is excellent in general, although there are punctuation and other errors in some tests, one error is hand-corrected (and appears in updated booklets), some of the artwork is amateurish looking (but improved in updated versions of some tests), and responses to some items are cued by other items (e.g., in the Health, Hygiene, and Safety and the World of Work tests).

DEVELOPMENT. The publisher states in the introduction booklet that the Basic Tests are validated by employers and elsewhere that each course syllabus was developed in consultation with employers and educators. However, information important for evaluating test development is missing, including information on item review and selection procedures, balance of coverage of each test's accompanying syllabus, standard setting procedures, equivalence of test difficulty and scores produced from various forms of the tests, and whether alternate forms exist.

Technical Characteristics of the Basic Tests.

SCORING, REPORTING, AND NORMS AND INTERPRETIVE INFORMATION. No information is available from the publisher regarding scoring criteria and procedures, or training, qualifications, accuracy, and consistency of scorers of open-ended exercises. Similarly, no information is available on how the 60% and 75% correct passing standards (leading, respectively, to "pass" and "pass with merit" certificates) were set and by whom, their relationship to performance in future training and employment, and why they are the same for all tests (because they are set on the raw score metric). Examinees receive a score report that includes their percent-correct score rounded to the nearest 5% and a "description of the skills and knowledge area that they have mastered" (introduction booklet, p. 3). This report is intended to serve as a profile of skills strengths and weaknesses. Examinees receive a certificate if they pass. Reports of examinee pass-rates and score distributions could allow normative comparisons and aid interpretation, if they were available.

SCORE RELIABILITY AND VALIDITY EVIDENCE. Likewise, scorer performance and score reliability information is not available. And, as discussed above, no information on content nor predictive validity is available. The usefulness of the basic tests cannot be evaluated without this information.

CONCLUSION. The Basic Tests may or may not be useful in the United Kingdom, depending on whether potential users consider their contents to cover relevant skills and knowledge. They are probably not useful in their current forms outside the United Kingdom, partly because of some content (e.g., inclusion only of areas popular with United Kingdom travelers in the Geography for Tourism and Leisure test), symbols (e.g., for British pounds and pence), and terminology (e.g., "zebra crossing" for "cross walk"). Predictive validity evidence is not available nor is evidence of the tests' purported motivational potential. Without such information concluding comments must be mostly speculative. One speculation is that the Basic Tests should be considered for use only after close scrutiny of their contents and only if the publishers provide technical and other information necessary to evaluate the tests' usefulness for specific interpretations and populations.

Review of the Basic Tests Series by ANNE R. FITZPATRICK, Manager of Applied Research, CTB Macmillan/McGraw-Hill, Monterey, CA:

The main series of the Basic Tests consists of tests in Arithmetic, English, Geography, Computer Awareness, Science, Graphicacy, Health/Hygiene and Safety, Life Skills, and World of Work. These tests cover skills described by the publisher as "essential for a wide range of jobs in industry and commerce." In addition, there is a special set of tests in Bookkeeping, Electronics, Geography for Tourism and Leisure that assess knowledge and skills specific to employment in particular industries.

Each test except Life Skills is a mastery test on which two cut scores have been set. One cut score is set at 60% of the total test score, and individuals scoring at or above this cut score achieve at least a Pass rating. The second cut score is set at 75% of the total test score, and individuals who score at or above this cut score achieve a Pass with Merit rating.

For this review the publisher provided for each test only a detailed description of the content covered by the test, a "specimen paper" (which is a sample test), and a table showing the number of candidates tested and their passing rates in the 1987–88 school year. No documentation was provided that explains how the tests were developed, how the tests are administered and scored, or how the cut scores were set. Also no data describing the items, nor the tests' reliability and validity, were made available for review.

Correspondence from the publisher indicated the position of the Basic Tests is currently under government review. In light of these circumstances and the paucity of information that was provided, only commentary on the content of each test and the reported pass rates seem reasonable to include in this review.

TEST CONTENT. A notable quality of each test is the absence of multiple-choice items; all but a few items in the series are short-answer, completion-type items. Between 1,000 and 20,000 candidates sat for at least one of the Basic Tests in May and June of 1988. It is surprising the considerable number of candidates did not compel the publisher to succumb to the scoring efficiencies of multiple-choice tests.

The Arithmetic Test consists of a Mental Arithmetic Test and a Written Test. In the Mental Arithmetic Test, a candidate must write an answer to each of 20 questions that is read aloud twice. Although this test undoubtedly assesses understanding of number concepts and basic arithmetic operations, it probably also measures listening skills, oral comprehension, and memory as well. Apropos the Written Test, about half of its 50 items also cover number concepts and arithmetic operations; these items should be easy for candidates with at least a high school education because they involve mostly operations on whole numbers, common fractions, or simple mixed decimals. The remaining 25 items pertain to straightforward problems involving percentages, money, concepts of length, area, volume, mass, and perimeter, as well as time and speed. Only 2 of the 50 items had graphics of any kind. For test-takers unfamiliar with British currency, British decimal notation, and imperial and metric units, the Written Test will be an inappropriate measure of their arithmetical knowledge and skills.

The English Test consists of a Listening section and a Reading and Writing section. In the first part of the Listening section, candidates are read three passages consisting of instructions, messages, or other communications likely to arise in the work place. After hearing a passage, they respond to questions that assess their literal comprehension and recall of the details given in the passage. In the second part of the Listening section, examinees must write and punctuate a short, dictated passage. The Reading and Writing Test has four components. A passage accompanied by questions resembles the typical reading comprehension task posed in standard achievement batteries, although answering the questions requires only literal comprehension or very low level inference. The second component requires the examinee to arrange a list of words in alphabetical order, thereby assessing what seems to be a trivial clerical skill. In the third component, the examinee must use information that is provided to complete a form, and in the fourth component the examinee must compose a letter in response to a situation that is described. The third and fourth components appear to be effective devices for assessing a candidate's ability to comprehend and use information and for assessing his or her skill in written communication, respectively.

The Basic Test in Geography focuses on locational knowledge, map skills, and route planning. Approximately one-third of this test involves questions that require a candidate to recall specific information about towns, cities, counties, and regions of the British Isles and their environs, limiting the usefulness of the test outside the United Kingdom.

The Basic Test in Computer Awareness is highly practical in nature, designed to assess the degree to which a candidate understands the nature and function of basic components of computer systems and understands the strengths and limitations and the economic and social implications of computer systems. Knowledge of programming languages and specific types of hardware and software is intentionally not covered by this test. It is a test of computer literacy, not technical expertise.

The Basic Test in Science measures candidates' general knowledge of the human body; heat; electricity; basic circuitry; energy storage, conversion, and transfer; levers, gears, and wheels; internal combustion; plant structure and function; ecology; properties of materials; and how telephones, radios, and TVs operate. Commendably, quite a few of the test questions require not the recall but the application of knowledge. The quality and number of graphics accompanying the items, however, could be improved considerably.

The Basic Test in Graphicacy is unusual. It is designed to assess a candidate's skill in using diagrammatic means of communication. The items assess the candidate's understanding of common signs and symbols, charts and graphs, flow charts, circuit diagrams, orthographic sketches, and isometric projection. Most of these methods of representation would be learned in everyday life or in school. In its explanation of the test, the publisher makes it clear this test is intended to promote the teaching of the skills assessed in British schools. However, it is not at all clear to this reviewer that the results of this test would be valuable to prospective employers.

The Tests in Life Skills was designed to reflect the core of a wide range of courses in social and life skills being taught in British schools. The items appear to vary substantially in difficulty. About half the test consists of short-answer knowledge questions about job-seeking, money management, government subsidy programs, health, and practical problems that arise in everyday life. The other half of the test consists of more challenging questions that require a candidate to complete forms, to make plans, and to analyze and explain decisions they are asked to make.

The Basic Test in Health, Hygiene, and Safety includes questions that concern the safe handling of toxic substances, equipment, electricity, and food, and questions that concern the causes and treatment of diseases and other physical disorders. The knowledge tested is basic and likely to be covered in courses on health, life skills, and general science.

The Basic Test in World of Work is novel in that candidates can sit for this test only after they have learned a specified set of practical skills in an actual or simulated work environment. The test itself appears to measure a candidate's understanding of the components of organizations and how they work. For example, in the specimen paper there are questions that assess the understanding of organization charts, the roles of managers and unions, and the role of marketing, quality control, productivity, and public relations in a business. Some questions that concern wages and job opportunities overlap with content covered in the Tests in Life Skills.

The Basic Test (Special) in Bookkeeping covers content likely to comprise the curriculum for a general, practical course in the subject. Candidates are tested for their understanding of balance sheets, profit and loss statements, transaction records, ledgers, bank statements, single- and double-entry bookkeeping, methods of calculating depreciation, and the meaning of concepts such as liquidity, working capital, and cash flow. Some terminology that is used will be foreign to candidates not trained in British schools.

The Basic Test (Special) in Electronics covers the content likely to comprise a course introducing students to the basic principles of electronics and the components of electrical and electronic systems.

Graphics accompany most items, which pertain to the functioning of capacitors, transistors, diodes, and integrated circuits; the components and operation of microcomputer, audio, and radio systems; types of measurements and measurement instruments; as well as procedures for fault finding and safety.

The Basic Test (Special) in Geography for Tourism and Leisure covers the content of particular courses intended for students or trainees interested in a career in an industry related to tourism and travel. About half of the test involves questions about major tourist attractions in the British Isles and Western Europe. The remainder of the test entails the use of maps, charts, and diagrams to plan routes and solve very realistic problems that a traveler might confront.

PASS RATES. The percentage of candidates tested in the 1987–88 school year who received a Pass or Pass with Merit rating ranged from 41.9% to 80.1% over the 12 Basic Tests. For the nine tests in the main series, the lowest pass rates occurred in Science (46.4%) and Computer Awareness (49.4%), and the highest passing rate occurred in Graphicacy (84.1%). About 75% of the candidates who took the English Test passed, and about 64% of the candidates who took the Arithmetic Test passed. Without information about the candidate populations who sat for these tests, interpretation of these pass rates is difficult.

[30]
Battelle Developmental Inventory Screening Test.

Purpose: For general screening, preliminary assessment, and/or initial identification of possible developmental strengths and weaknesses.
Population: Birth to age 8.
Publication Date: 1984.
Acronym: BDI Screening Test.
Scores, 10: Personal-Social, Adaptive, Motor (Gross Motor, Fine Motor, Total), Communication (Receptive, Expressive, Total), Cognitive, Total.
Administration: Individual.
Price Data, 1988: $70 per screening test including 30 test booklets, test item book (108 pages), and examiner's manual (52 pages); $15 per 30 screening test booklets.
Time: (10–30) minutes.
Comments: Short form of the Battelle Developmental Inventory (10:25); other test materials must be supplied by examiner.
Authors: Initial development by Jean Newborg, John R. Stock, and Linda Wnek; pilot norming study by John Guidubaldi; completion and standardization by John Svinicki.
Publisher: DLM Teaching Resources.

Review of the Battelle Developmental Inventory Screening Test by DAVID W. BARNETT, Professor of School Psychology and Counseling, University of Cincinnati, Cincinnati, OH:

The Battelle Developmental Inventory Screening Test (BDI Screening Test) is described as a short form of the Battelle Developmental Inventory (BDI; 10:25). The authors suggest that applications of the BDI Screening Test include general screening of preschool and kindergarten children, monitoring of individual student progress, assessing the "preliminary" status of at-risk children, and identifying strengths and weaknesses of children to determine the need for comprehensive assessments. The instrument is intended to be administered by program staff members and assessment specialists within a 10-to-30-minute time span.

The BDI Screening Test comprises 96 items selected from the more extensive BDI. There are two items for every age level in each domain, except for the Communication and Cognitive Domains for the 12-to-17- and 18-to-23-month age groups. The Screening Test is not recommended for children less than 6 months of age. Another feature is the availability of administrative adaptations for handicapped children. Many materials need to be supplied by the examiner. The domains and subdomains are as follows:

Personal-Social Domain (20 items): Adult interaction, expression of feelings/affect, self-concept, peer interaction, coping, and social role.

Adaptive Domain (20 items): Attention, eating, dressing, personal responsibility, and toileting.

Motor Domain (20 items representing fine and gross motor skills): Muscle control, body coordination, locomotion, fine muscle, and perceptual motor.

Communication Domain (18 items representing receptive and expressive skills): Receptive communication and expressive communication.

Cognitive Domain (18 items): Perceptual discrimination, memory, reasoning and academic skills, and conceptual development.

A significant feature of the BDI Screening Test is that three assessment methods may be used: administration of items to children, observations in natural settings, and interviews with caregivers. Examiner judgment is used to determine which procedures should be used to acquire test information. Even though the authors state, "Regardless of the procedure used, examiners can be confident that scoring and interpretation will be equally sound because the criteria are so clearly stated" (p. 7), a considerable amount of research indicates that agreement between observations and ratings may be modest, and that rater differences (i.e., parents, teachers) are often significant. Furthermore, the authors suggest that under ideal circumstances, observations should occur over "a few weeks' time" (p. 10)—a sound practice but also an important qualification for a "brief" screening instrument. In fact, many places in the manual describe procedures applicable to the BDI rather than the screening instrument.

The normative information for the BDI Screening Test is based on the development of the parent BDI. The authors used stratified random sampling to select children by geographic region, race, and sex. Children of poverty may be underrepresented. A total of 42 test administrators represented by a broad array of backgrounds and training levels (including elementary school teachers, paraprofessionals, specialists in early childhood education, psychologists, nursery school and day-care center staff) administered the BDI at sites in 24 states. Data collection was carried out in 1982–83. The sample is collapsed into 6-month age levels for infants and 1-year age levels for toddlers and older children. While the total norming sample contained 800 children, the actual decisions are based on subsamples that vary from 49 to 108 children. The overall sample included approximately 16% minority children. However, depending on the specific age level and sex, the subsample may be quite small (i.e., $n = 1$ for a minority male in the age range 12 to 17 months).

The validity information for the BDI Screening Test is limited to correlations between items on the Screening Test and the parent BDI ($n = 164$). As may be expected, the correlations are quite high.

In the manual, reliability information for the parent BDI is stressed rather than for the Screening Test. Test-retest and interrater reliabilities for the BDI (*not* the Screening Test) are generally quite high. The retest interval is not reported in the manual, nor is the method used to calculate interrater reliability.

Scoring criteria are based on three categories. Two points are credited based on the child meeting the specified criteria; 1 point for the child's *attempts* at the task; and 0 points for the circumstances when a child will not or cannot attempt the item, the performance is judged as "extremely poor," or for tasks that the child has no opportunity to perform. Basal and ceiling rules are used to guide decisions concerning the beginning (first item is at the child's estimated developmental age) and ending of testing (when 0 points are scored for both items at an age level). The five domain raw scores are summed to yield a total score.

In order to assist with screening decisions, cutoff scores are provided both in standard deviations and probabilities (from a z table based on properties of the normal curve). Levels are provided that vary presumably with state criteria (or selection ratios) from -1 standard deviation (probability of .16) to -2.33 standard deviations (probability of .01). However, "if the raw score is higher than all five cutoff scores," the " *largest* " cutoff score is entered (i.e., -1 standard deviation) and the column is marked as passed. This practice may lead to misinterpretations.

The authors recommend a cutoff score of -1 standard deviation, which is described as a borderline performance. For children falling at or below this level, a complete administration of the more extensive BDI is recommended. Although many major assessment sources argue against the use of age-equivalent scores and cautions are described in the manual, tables are provided for determining scores and are prominently featured on the child's summary. Another problem is that the manual refers to screening decisions as *placement decisions* (emphasis added, p. 13), and points out the use of the Screening Test for eligibility and placement purposes on page 18 of the manual.

The potential concerns for the wide-scale use of the BDI Screening Test are many. Beyond basic concerns with reliability and validity, there is an inadequate ceiling and floor for domain scores. Also, item gradients are inadequate. These factors seriously affect the reliable use of cutoff scores and profile interpretations.

The following examples illustrate some of the concerns. For many age levels and domains, one or two raw score points separate a performance of -1 standard deviation from -2.33 standard deviations. In fact, for 46% of the age levels, the range of raw scores used to "discriminate" a severely discrepant performance (-2.33 standard deviations) from a "borderline score" (-1 standard deviation) was either 0, 1, or 2 points. As another example, for the Receptive Score at age level 18 to 23 months, a raw score of 5 is described as being from -1 to -2.33 standard deviations below the mean. Children receiving nearly perfect scores at the upper age levels (e.g., 39/40 for the Motor Domain) have performances described as -1 standard deviation. To sum, in many cases the number of items separating extreme from marginal (or average) performances is small or even nonexistent. This factor is likely to lead to unreliable *decisions* (as distinct from test reliability) and unreliable profiles. A problem described by Boyd (1989) for the parent BDI is particularly potent for the Screening Test Total Score for children whose birthdays are at the borderlines of the age intervals. The difference of a day can alter significantly the way a child's performance is interpreted.

In summary, the BDI Screening Test cannot be recommended for use in consideration of stated purposes of the measure. The interpretation chapter is two paragraphs long. Reliability and validity information is based on the parent BDI. The differentiation of reliable and meaningful profiles is untenable, given its reported technical characteristics. Furthermore, the error rates associated with screening decisions may be considerable. Alternatively, those interested in early childhood screening will need to consider a wide range of factors including educational experiences provided to children, parent needs, parent-child and other interactions, and curricular-based methods of assessment.

REVIEWER'S REFERENCE

Boyd, R. D. (1989). What a difference a day makes: Age-related discontinuities and the Battelle Developmental Inventory. *Journal of Early Intervention, 13,* 114-119.

Review of the Battelle Developmental Inventory Screening Test by JOAN ERSHLER, Postdoctoral Student, School Psychology Program, and STEPHEN N. ELLIOTT, Professor of Educational Psychology University of Wisconsin-Madison, Madison, WI:

INTRODUCTION. The Battelle Developmental Inventory Screening Test (BDI) is a relatively new norm-referenced and criterion-referenced measure of early development. A shortened (96-item) version of the 341-item Battelle Developmental Inventory (10:25; Newborg, Stock, Wnek, Guidubaldi, & Svinicki, 1984), it is an individually-administered instrument using a combination of direct observation and interview assessment methods to evaluate developmental skills in children from birth to 8 years. Intended as a general screening measure for preschool and kindergarten children, the BDI Screening Test has as its purpose the identification and placement of infants and young children "at risk" for developmental delay, as well as the identification of specific areas for educational remediation. It may also be used to identify normally developing children's areas of strengths and weaknesses and to evaluate the effectiveness of intervention programs. The 96 items on the test represent five areas, or domains, of functioning with 18 to 20 items on each: Personal-Social, Adaptive, Motor, Communication, and Cognitive. Examiner-gathered materials are administered in a 10- to 30-minute period of time.

PRACTICAL FEATURES OF THE TEST. The examiner presents each item in one of three ways, depending on which is most appropriate for the particular testing situation: directly administering an item to the child, observing the child performing an item, or interviewing a parent or teacher. The decision of whom to interview is left to the best judgment of the tester. Some items are more suited for administration according to one of the three methods; in fact, most of the items measuring the Personal-Social domain are best obtained through interview. Nonetheless, instructions for giving the items in alternative ways are included. Although instructions for interviewing are given, the examiner is encouraged to adjust the questioning to obtain enough information. Thus, the actual administration of this test may vary for individual children, making comparability of scores questionable. In addition, the items are to be administered in order. This aspect of this test has been criticized because it prevents the flexibility considered necessary when working with very young children (Boyd, Welge, Sexton, & Miller, 1989; McLean, McCormick, Bruder, & Burdg, 1987). However, administering the items in the specified order is necessary for applying the basal and ceiling rules that permit normative comparisons to be made on this test.

Several other points regarding the features of the BDI Screening Test are noteworthy. For those items requiring specific materials, descriptions of the materials are given, and it is the examiner's responsibility to provide them, again raising the question of the standardized nature of the test. There is one form of the BDI Screening Test, and the authors recommend becoming thoroughly familiar with the items and administration formats through conducting at least one practice administration with a normally developing child before administering the test. It has been suggested, however, that for the complete BDI, one administration is insufficient preparation for accurate administration (McLean et al., 1987). Finally, the authors report testing time to be one-half hour or less, but there is no available research addressing the accuracy of this assessment time.

Children's responses to the items are scored according to a 3-point system that allows one to "capture" skills in the process of being acquired, an advantage when measuring progress over time. Computing raw scores for each domain and a total raw score is described straightforwardly. However, difficulties and inaccuracies in scoring have been reported by those investigating the characteristics of the complete BDI. In their study of administration of the BDI, Bailey, Vandiviere, Dellinger, and Munn (1987) found that only 14.5% of their sample of experienced test administrators had no scoring errors.

Raw scores are not converted to standard scores, but are instead compared to cutoff raw scores corresponding to different standard deviations and probabilities for false positives (based on a standardized distribution of z-scores). The derivation of each of the cutoff scores is not explained, and there is no information provided regarding the mean scores achieved by each age group in the normative sample, or standard score equivalents. In the absence of standard scores, one cannot assume the scores from each test are comparable (Anastasi, 1988), and with a test that purports to determine placement, the process of deriving cutoff scores needs to be made explicit. Age-equivalent scores are also provided in table form, but again, no explanation as to their derivation is given.

CHARACTERISTICS OF THE MANUAL. The BDI Screening Test Manual provides clear and complete descriptions of the subtests and the areas within each subtest that are tapped. An example of a protocol and scoring instructions are also provided, as is a listing of the items both on the complete BDI and on the Screening Test. This enables one to see the scope of the screening test in relation to the complete BDI.

Administration and scoring instructions are presented in the Manual, but not clearly enough to ensure standardization and objectivity. For example, a score of 1 point is earned for some items according to a criterion of "attempts but is often unsuccessful." This descriptive criterion does not represent objective, consistent scoring. Although many items do contain objective criteria for scoring in the test book itself, this standard is not consistently applied across all items. A good deal of clinical judgment in interviewing is necessary for acquiring information, which may provide a rich pool of information but does not lend itself to consistent, objective scoring criteria. To the authors' credit, the Manual does provide extensive examples of interviews in the Appendix.

The BDI Screening Test Manual also makes note of specific administration instructions for use with children having a variety of handicapping conditions that are further described in conjunction with specific items in the test book. Adaptations are provided for children with speech and hearing, vision, motor, and emotional difficulties. With regard to the complete BDI, however, only half of these adaptations have been found to be appropriate (Bailey et al., 1987).

Although there is little research reported in the Manual, psychometric properties of the BDI Screening Test are addressed in an organized manner. The standardization process, including date of standardization and characteristics of the normative sample, is adequately described. There is no information regarding the reliability of the Screening Test, however; readers are referred to a table for information regarding the complete BDI's test-retest and interrater reliability. Unfortunately, there is no information provided concerning the methods for obtaining reliability, characteristics of the sample (size, age), or interval of time elapsed, in the case of test-retest reliability. Thus, it is not possible to evaluate completely the reliability of the BDI Screening Test from the information presented in the Manual.

Validity information is limited, as well, with the criterion for selecting the Screening Test items described without the provision of supporting data, and only one study comparing the Screening Test with the complete BDI is reported in the manual. It is thus also difficult to evaluate the validity of the BDI Screening Test based on the information given. Finally, interpretive guidelines are described, but an explanation of their derivation is missing.

In summary, the Manual is strongest in its description of domains, interviewing techniques, and the standardization process. It is somewhat helpful in its provision of guidelines for administering the test to handicapped children. It is inadequate in providing scoring criteria, the rationale for interpreting raw scores, and a description of reliability and validity.

Psychometric characteristics of the test.

NORMS. The normative sample for the BDI Screening Test was part of the complete BDI's norming sample of 800 children. The number of children identified as the normative sample for the Screening Test is not mentioned, however, nor are the number of children and descriptive data regarding their BDI Screening Test scores included for each age group. Normative data for the complete BDI was collected over a 4-month period from 1982 to 1983 (Newborg et al., 1984). Using a stratified random sampling procedure, children were selected on the basis of sex, age, geographic location, and race. The proportions of children in each of these categories were equivalent to U.S. Bureau of the Census data.

Several problems exist with the sample chosen for the complete BDI. First, of the total 800 children in the standardization sample, 301 comprised the 0-to-35-month range. Of these, approximately 50 children were selected for each of the infant age groups (0 to 5 months, 6 to 11 months, 12 to 17 months, and 18 to 23 months), and 99 were selected for the 24-to-35-month range. The number of children comprising this age component of the sample has been considered inadequate (Boyd et al., 1989), especially when one compares these figures to the Bayley Scales of Infant Development (1,262 children from 0 to 30 months, with 90 children representing 1- or 2-month intervals within the 30-month range).

A second problem deriving from the relatively broad sampling across ages during infancy is the likelihood of obtaining very different scores for identical performance of children whose chronological age falls close to either side of the cutoff points between age groups (Boyd, 1989). These potential differences in scores could result in the under- or overestimation of developmental levels, important to note when considering the placement, educational remediation, and program evaluation decisions for which the authors are recommending the BDI be used.

There was also no effort made, across the entire sample, to obtain a representative number of children according to parental socioeconomic status, occupation, or income level. The authors do address this issue, stating they controlled for this potential bias through selection of test sites that included a wide range of socioeconomic levels. No data about socioeconomic status are provided, however, and one is left with the impression that little is known about the socioeconomic levels represented in the normative sample.

Another difficulty lies in the nature of the minority population represented. Although the total proportion of minority children is comparable to the overall proportion in the United States, the authors make no mention of including Asian or Native American children. Minorities included in the normative sample were Black and Hispanic. There is no mention of handicapped children being included in the normative sample, an important omission considering the authors promote this test as a means of assessing children with a variety of handicapping conditions. One final point worth reiterating is the fact that no information is provided about the exact nature—size and characteristics—of the normative sample for the Screening Test. Only normative information about the complete BDI is provided.

RELIABILITY. There is no published reliability information for the BDI Screening Test. The limited information available related to reliability refers to the complete BDI.

Test-retest reliability of the complete BDI, using an "item-by-item" procedure, has been reported in two studies. The first, reported in the BDI Screening Test Manual and further described by McLinden (1989), reported total test-retest reliability on a sample of 183 children, tested with a 4-week interval, to be .88, with coefficients ranging from .81 to .97. The "item-by-item" procedure is not described, however; nor are the means and standard deviations for the two testings provided. The second study, using the same procedure with a sample of five children and a 6-week interval, reported a coefficient of .80 (Boyd et al., 1989). Again, the method of determining reliability is not described, and there are no data presented concerning means and standard deviations. This lack of procedural and data specificity contributes to the tentativeness of concluding adequate test-retest reliability for the complete BDI.

Internal consistency of the complete BDI using Cronbach's Alpha procedure has been evaluated with a sample of 40 children from birth to 30 months with a variety of handicapping conditions (McLean et al., 1987). The coefficients for all five domains were found to be very high, ranging from .89 to .96.

The majority of the reliability research with the complete BDI has been concerned with interrater reliability. As reported in the BDI Screening Test Manual, for the complete BDI (no method described, no means and standard deviations presented, no sample size provided), this was very high, with a total interrater reliability of .97, ranging from .95 to .99 across domains. Mott (1989) further elaborated this finding, reporting that the sample comprised the same 148 children from the norming sample used to determine test-retest reliability, as well as a group of handicapped children. However, no additional information is presented regarding the number of children in differing age groups in the normative sample or the characteristics of the handicapped children. Additional evidence for test-retest reliability is reported by Boyd et al. (1989), who found in a sample of seven children (few sample characteristics provided) a reliability coefficient of .97. Similarly, McLean et al. (1987) reported an overall interrater reliability of .93 in their sample of 20 children (no sample characteristics provided). Again, the lack of method specification, descriptive statistics, and information about the samples used in these studies causes us to question the evidence for interrater reliability.

VALIDITY. Validation studies concerning the complete BDI have been conducted, investigating its content, construct, and criterion validity. In addition, the issue of the content validity of the BDI Screening Test has been addressed.

As with the complete BDI, each item on the BDI Screening Test was assigned to an age category, based on the age level in the normative sample at which approximately 75% of the children earned full credit. One can assume that the 96 items comprising the Screening Test qualified for inclusion, but there are no data concerning the proportion of children in each age level in the norming sample achieving full credit for the items placed in each age category. In addition, the 75% criterion has been considered a conservative criterion compared, for example, to the 50% criterion for the Bayley, and most likely contributes to the significantly lower total age-equivalent scores that have been found on the BDI when compared to those earned on the Bayley (Boyd et al., 1989). However, McLean et al. (1987) did not find the two tests to yield significantly different composite scores.

Other information is lacking regarding content validity of the BDI Screening Test. Items included in the complete BDI, however, were selected by experts from 4,000 items found in a variety of developmental tests. Although the sequence and placement of skills generally have been deemed appropriate, there has been some criticism concerning the equivalency of increasing item difficulty between age levels. For example, McLinden (1989) identified a math item requiring addition and subtraction and noted the absence of any items assessing prerequisite number skills. Bracken (1987) also noted the problem of gaps in the sequence of skills that are assessed on the BDI.

Although there will necessarily be a steep gradient of skills assessed on a screening measure designed to sample behavior across a wide age range, a slightly different problem is evident on the BDI Screening

Test. The items selected to tap each domain do not systematically represent their respective subdomains. That is, the subdomains that are measured vary from level to level, so that for different age groups, the subskills being assessed differ. Thus, the degree to which items are representative of their respective domains and the functional equivalence of items across age levels within each domain are questionable.

Although evidence of the construct validity of the BDI Screening Test is lacking, several investigators have evaluated the complete BDI. As mentioned above, McLean et al. (1987) found high internal consistency between the BDI total score and the five domains, ranging from a low of .89 for Cognition to a high of .96 for Motor. There is no information, however, regarding the internal consistency of items within domains. Newborg et al. (1984) presented similar evidence for internal consistency among the BDI domains in the BDI Manual. Although the specific domain scores are omitted and the correlation between the total score and the Cognitive domain score is missing, intercorrelations for the other domains are given, equal to .98 (for Personal-Social) and .99 (for Adaptive, Communication, and Motor). Again, no data are mentioned concerning the intercorrelation of items within domains. Finally, Boyd et al. (1989) found a wide range of intercorrelations among the BDI component scores, with coefficients ranging from a low of .52 (between the Motor and Communication domains) to a high of .97 (between the Adaptive domain and the Total Age Equivalent score). The majority of coefficients were in the .70s and .80s, suggesting good internal consistency between the domain and total scores. Again, the specific domain scores are not included, the sample size of 30 was relatively small, and there is no information regarding item consistency within each domain.

Factor analysis has revealed an age-related factor structure for the complete BDI, with only the performance of children between 2 and 5 years of age explained by five factors consistent with the five domains (Newman & Guidubaldi, cited in Newborg et al., 1984). This lends partial support to the construct validity of the complete BDI, but it should be noted that this research was based on pilot data, and its applicability to the final version of the BDI is unknown.

Two final aspects of construct validity evidence are again provided by Newborg et al. (1984). In developing the BDI, the authors found that with increasing age, scores reflected increasingly mature performance. McLinden (1989) has questioned the meaningfulness of this finding, however, given the wide age groupings on the BDI. In addition, Newborg et al. (1984) found no significant differ-

ences in scores between boys and girls and between White and minority groups in the normative sample.

Probably the most investigated aspect of validity regarding the BDI has been criterion-related validity. Again, most of the evidence has come from studies evaluating the complete BDI, rather than the BDI Screening Test.

Several investigations of the concurrent validity of the complete BDI have yielded mixed findings. In their investigation of the relationships among the BDI, the Bayley Scales of Infant Development, and the Vineland Adaptive Behavior Scale, McLean et al. (1987) found, in their sample of 40 children from birth to 30 months with a variety of handicapping conditions, high correlations between the BDI and the Bayley total scores ($r = .88$ and .90), as well as high correlations between their respective domains, ranging from .74 to .92. Correlations between the BDI and the Vineland were also high, with coefficients for the BDI total scores and Vineland subdomain scores ranging from .86 to .92, and coefficients for the BDI domain scores and Vineland subdomain scores ranging from .73 to .95. Information concerning the concurrent validity of the BDI and the Bayley also has come from the research of Boyd et al. (1989), comparing the scores of his sample of handicapped children ranging in age from birth to 36 months on these two measures. Unlike the findings of McLean et al. (1987), the mean total age-equivalent score of the BDI was significantly lower than the Bayley. Further analysis revealed the discrepancy to be due to the significantly different motor domain scores. In an attempt to remediate the problem of small sample size, Sexton, McLean, Boyd, Thompson, and McCormick (1988) pooled the McLean and Boyd samples and subjected them to canonical correlational analysis. Their findings revealed correlation coefficients for the BDI domain scores and Bayley total scores ranging from .65 to .95, and they included means and standard deviations for the scores presented.

Strong relationships were found by Newborg et al. (1984) when they compared the complete BDI to the Vineland Social Maturity Scale, Developmenal Activities Screening Inventory, Stanford-Binet Intelligence Scale, Wechsler Intelligence Scale for Children—Revised, and Peabody Picture Vocabulary Test. McLinden (1989) has pointed out, however, that the number of children used in these comparison groups was very small (from 13 to 37 subjects), and several of the criterion measures themselves have outdated norms.

One final investigation of the BDI's concurrent validity looked at the relationship between the Communication domain and several measures of expressive and receptive language. In this study of 20 speech- and language-disordered children, ages 35 to 60 months, Mott (1987) compared performance on the BDI Communication domain with performance on the Peabody Picture Vocabulary Test—Revised, Preschool Language Scale—Revised, and Arizona Articulation Proficiency Scale—Revised. Results showed that the BDI domain of Communication was most highly related, although moderately, to the Peabody Picture Vocabulary Test—Revised. The BDI total Communication domain score also was most strongly related to the Preschool Language Scale—Revised ($r = .81$), but its Expressive Communication subdomain and Cognitive domain were comparably correlated ($r = .75$, $r = .79$, respectively), indicating the overlap between the content measured by these two areas of the BDI. With regard to the Arizona Articulation Proficiency Scale—Revised, only the BDI Expressive Communication subdomain correlated moderately ($r = .68$). Thus, there is moderate evidence for the criterion validity of the Expressive Communication subdomain of the BDI, but the Receptive Communication domain does not appear to be measuring the same content as other measures of receptive language.

The only investigation concerning the criterion validity of the BDI Screening Test itself examined its predictive validity. A sample of 164 children was administered the BDI Screening Test prior to their inclusion in the normative sample for the complete BDI. High correlations between the components of the Screening Test and the components of the complete BDI were found, with coefficients ranging from .92 to .98. Correlations between the BDI Screening Test total score and the BDI components were similarly high, with coefficients ranging from .96 to .98, while the correlation between the total scores of the two measures was .99. Although it is unfortunate that characteristics of the sample (e.g., number of children per age group) and the scores on which the correlations are based were not given, it is not surprising that the BDI Screening Test appears to be measuring the same skills as the complete BDI.

Three final points regarding the evidence for validity of the BDI Screening Test warrant mention. First, only one study has reported validity findings using the Screening Test itself, and that has provided incomplete data. Second, the evidence for the concurrent validity of the complete BDI must be considered in light of the caveat argued by Boyd (1989), that group studies hide the inherent problem with the BDI's cutoff scores (explained above), contributing to either over- or underestimation of developmental scores and lending doubt as to their validity. Third, there is a noticeable absence in the literature of evaluation studies that have employed the BDI or the BDI Screening Test. Thus, while gross age-related differences in scores have been found, evidence for changes in scores over time as a result of intervention is still lacking.

SUMMARY OF OVERALL TEST QUALITY AND CONCLUSIONS. It is difficult to evaluate the Battelle Developmental Inventory Screening Test comprehensively at this time because of the lack of research concerning its psychometric properties, both in the Manual and in the literature. It appears that this test is reliable across examiners and successive testing times, but the omission of complete data regarding these types of reliabilities diminishes the strength with which this conclusion can be made. It also appears the BDI Screening Test is highly related to the complete BDI, and based on the BDI's content validity, seems to have a valid group of items. However, criticisms noting the inconsistent representation of subdomains across age levels, as well as an unequal succession of items in terms of their difficulty levels across age categories, also lessen the strength with which one may conclude the test has good content validity. The final bit of information relating directly to the Screening Test concerns its standardization process, and one would be well advised to use caution when applying the cutoff scores. There is much that is unknown (or at least unwritten) about the normative sample, including the age groups evaluated, their mean scores, the variability of their scores, and their socioeconomic status.

Additional information concerning the psychometric properties of the Battelle Screening Test must be inferred from the complete BDI, a less than satisfactory occurrence. Evidence from the standardization of the BDI has revealed a limited sample size, especially in the youngest age ranges, and wide age groupings that can result in over- or underestimation of developmental levels. Moreover, minority populations are underrepresented, and handicapped children are not included in the normative sample. All of these factors make one uneasy about using this test to make normative comparisons.

Although reports of test-retest and interrater reliability reveal high consistency, the data provided are inadequate and the sample sizes are small. Internal consistency between the domains and the total BDI scores does seem adequate, but the research is limited in scope and there is no research concerning the internal consistency within domains.

The complete BDI has been shown to be related to a variety of other measures of early development and expressive language. However, using group means may misrepresent the scores derived on the BDI, the validation studies that have been conducted have been based on small sample sizes, and several of the measures used as criteria have outdated norms. Thus, sound conclusions concerning the validity of the BDI cannot clearly be made at this time.

Given the paucity of research, the unclear findings, and original deficiencies of the normative process, what recommendations can be made regarding use of the BDI Screening Test? The test does include relevant items for assessing young children, and the use of multiple assessment methods lends itself to flexible assessment that could provide a wealth of information. The use of a developmental milestone approach also lends itself easily to remedial planning and intervention. For these reasons, the BDI Screening Test could be a useful *adjunct* in one's assessment repertoire. The Screening Test provides a relatively quick assessment of areas of weakness, and it indicates areas to assess more fully for possible educational programming. These advantages would increase one's clinical judgment about individual children. At this point, however, it would be imprudent to use the Screening Test cutoff scores alone for placement decisions, in spite of the enthusiasm noted in the literature (e.g., McLean et al., 1987).

The BDI Screening Test, like its parent measure, has the potential of being a valuable addition to the assessment options available to practitioners and researchers working with young children. However, additional research needs to be done concerning the psychometric properties of the Screening Test, for it should be judged on its own merits, not on the qualities of the BDI. Moreover, a useful addition to the literature would be longitudinal evaluation research using the Screening Test as a measure of change. The addition of this research to the existing literature would enable potential consumers of the BDI Screening Test to make informed decisions about its utility.

REVIEWER'S REFERENCES

Newborg, J., Stock, J., Wnek, L., Guidubaldi, J., & Svinicki, J. (1984). Battelle Developmental Inventory. Allen, TX: DLM Teaching Resources.

Bailey, D. B., Vandiviere, P., Dellinger, J., & Munn, D. (1987). The Battelle Developmental Inventory: Teacher perceptions and implementation data. *Journal of Psychoeducational Assessment, 3*, 217-226.

McLean, M., McCormick, K., Bruder, M. B., & Burdg, N. B. (1987). An investigation of the validity and reliability of the Battelle Developmental Inventory with a population of children younger than 30 months with identified handicapping conditions. *Journal of the Division for Early Childhood, 11*, 238-246.

Mott, S. E. (1987). Concurrent validity of the Battelle Developmental Inventory for speech and language disordered children. *Psychology in the Schools, 24*, 215-220.

Anastasi, A. (1988). *Psychological testing* (6th ed.). New York: Macmillan.

Sexton, D., McLean, M., Boyd, R. D., Thompson, B., & McCormick, K. (1988). Criterion-related validity of a new standardized developmental measure for use with infants who are handicapped. *Measurement and Evaluation in Counseling and Development, 21*, 16-24.

Boyd, R. D. (1989). What a difference a day makes: Age-related discontinuities and the Battelle Developmental Inventory. *Journal of Early Intervention, 13*, 114-119.

Boyd, R. D., Welge, P., Sexton, D., & Miller, J. H. (1989). Concurrent validity of the Battelle Developmental Inventory: Relationship with the Bayley Scales in young children with known or suspected disabilities. *Journal of Early Intervention, 13*, 14-23.

McLinden, S. E. (1989). An evaluation of the Battelle Developmental Inventory for determining special education eligibility. *Journal of Psychoeducational Assessment, 7*, 66-73.

Beck Depression Inventory [Revised Edition].

Purpose: To detect possible depression and to assess severity of depression.
Population: Ages 13–80.
Publication Date: 1961–87.
Acronym: BDI.
Comments: Self-administered; may be orally administered.
Scores: Total score; item score ranges.
Administration: Group.
Price Data, 1990: $39.50 per complete kit including 25 record forms and manual ('87, 30 pages); $21.50 per 25 record forms; $77.50 per 100 record forms; $19 per manual.
Time: (5–15) minutes.
Authors: Aaron T. Beck and Robert A. Steer.
Publisher: The Psychological Corporation.

TEST REFERENCES

1. Crowther, J. H., & Chernyk, B. (1986). Bulimia and binge eating in adolescent females: A comparison. *Addictive Behaviors, 11*, 415-424.
2. Deluty, B. M., Deluty, R. H., & Carver, C. S. (1986). Concordance between clinicians' and patients' ratings of anxiety and depression as mediated by private self-consciousness. *Journal of Personality Assessment, 50*, 93-106.
3. Edwards, F. E., & Nagelberg, D. B. (1986). Personality characteristics of restrained/binge eaters versus unrestrained/nonbinge eaters. *Addictive Behaviors, 11*, 207-211.
4. Godfrey, H. P. D., & Knight, R. G. (1986). Reading difficulty levels of eleven self-report depression rating scales. *Behavioral Assessment, 8*, 187-190.
5. Greenberg, B. R., & Harvey, P. D. (1986). The prediction of binge eating over time. *Addictive Behaviors, 11*, 383-388.
6. Hayden, R. M., Allen, G. J., & Camaione, D. N. (1986). Some psychological benefits resulting from involvement in an aerobic fitness from the perspectives of participants and knowledgeable informants. *The Journal of Sports Medicine and Physical Fitness, 26*, 67-76.
7. Schulman, R. G., Kinder, B. N., Powers, P. S., Prange, M., & Gleghorn, A. (1986). The development of a scale to measure cognitive distortions in bulimia. *Journal of Personality Assessment, 50*, 630-639.
8. Antonuccio, D. O., Davis, C., Lewinsohn, P. M., & Breckenridge, J. S. (1987). Therapist variables related to cohesiveness in a group treatment for depression. *Small Group Behavior, 18*, 557-564.
9. Ayers, M. R., Abrams, D. I., Newell, T. G., & Friederich, F. (1987). Performance of individuals with AIDS on the Luria-Nebraska Neuropsychological Battery. *The International Journal of Clinical Neuropsychology, 9*, 101-105.
10. Beutler, L. E., Scogin, F., Kirkish, P., Schretlen, D., Corbishley, A., Hamblin, D., Meredith, K., Potter, R., Bamford, C. R., & Levenson, A. I. (1987). Group cognitive therapy and alprazolam in the treatment of depression in older adults. *Journal of Consulting and Clinical Psychology, 55*, 550-556.
11. Bolton, W., & Oatley, K. (1987). A longitudinal study of social support and depression in unemployed men. *Psychological Medicine, 17*, 453-460.
12. Brannon, S. E., & Nelson, R. O. (1987). Contingency management treatment of outpatient unipolar depression: A comparison of reinforcement and extinction. *Journal of Consulting and Clinical Psychology, 55*, 117-119.
13. Caldwell, R. A., Pearson, J. L., & Chin, R. J. (1987). Stress-moderating effects: Social support in the context of gender and locus of control. *Personality and Social Psychology Bulletin, 13*, 5-17.
14. Christopoulos, C., Cohn, D. A., Shaw, D. S., Joyce, S., Sullivan-Hanson, J., Kraft, S. P., & Emery, R. E. (1987). Children of abused w Adjustment at time of shelter residence. *Journal of Marriage and the Family, 49*, 611-619.
15. Dobson, K. S. (1987). Marital and social adjustment in depressed and remarried married women. *Journal of Clinical Psychology, 43*, 261-265.
16. Doyne, E. J., Ossip-Klein, D. J., Bowman, E. D., Osborn, K. M., McDougall-Wilson, I. B., & Neimeyer, R. A. (1987). Running versus weight lifting in the treatment of depression. *Journal of Consulting and Clinical Psychology, 55*, 748-754.
17. Eckert, E. D., Halmi, K. A., Marchi, P., & Cohen, J. (1987). Comparison of bulimic and non-bulimic anorexia nervosa patients during treatment. *Psychological Medicine, 17*, 891-898.

18. Emery, R. E., & Wyer, M. M. (1987). Child custody mediation and litigation: An experimental evaluation of the experience of parents. *Journal of Consulting and Clinical Psychology, 55*, 179-186.

19. Fennell, M. J. V., Teasdale, J. D., Jones, S., & Damlé, A. (1987). Distraction in neurotic and endogenous depression: an investigation of negative thinking in major depressive disorder. *Psychological Medicine, 17*, 441-452.

20. Fincham, F. D., & Bradbury, T. N. (1987). Cognitive processes and conflict in close relationships: An attribution-efficacy model. *Journal of Personality and Social Psychology, 53*, 1106-1118.

21. Foelker, G. A., Jr., Shewchuk, R. M., & Niederehe, G. (1987). Confirmatory factor analysis of the short form Beck Depression Inventory in elderly community samples. *Journal of Clinical Psychology, 43*, 111-118.

22. Foley, F. W., Bedell, J. R., LaRocca, N. G., Scheinberg, L. C., & Reznikoff, M. (1987). Efficacy of stress-inoculation training in coping with multiple sclerosis. *Journal of Consulting and Clinical Psychology, 55*, 919-922.

23. Frank, R. G., Umlauf, R. L., Wonderlich, S. A., Askanazi, G. S., Buckelew, S. P., & Elliott, T. R. (1987). Differences in coping styles among persons with spinal cord injury: A cluster-analytic approach. *Journal of Consulting and Clinical Psychology, 55*, 727-731.

24. Freund, B., Steketee, G. S., & Foa, E. B. (1987). Compulsive Activity Checklist (CAC): Psychometric analysis with obsessive-compulsive disorder. *Behavioral Assessment, 9*, 67-77.

25. Goldberg, J. O., Shaw, B. F., & Segal, Z. V. (1987). Concurrent validity of the Millon Clinical Multiaxial Inventory depression scales. *Journal of Consulting and Clinical Psychology, 55*, 785-787.

26. Greenberg, B. R., & Harvey, P. D. (1987). Affective lability versus depression as determinants of binge eating. *Addictive Behaviors, 12*, 357-361.

27. Hawton, K., McKeown, S., Day, A., Martin, P., O'Connor, M., & Yule, J. (1987). Evaluation of out-patient counselling compared with general practitioner care following overdoses. *Psychological Medicine, 17*, 751-761.

28. Hong, S. (1987). Factor structure of the depression-proneness rating scale. *Psychological Reports, 61*, 863-866.

29. Hops, H., Biglan, A., Sherman, L., Arthur, J., Friedman, L., & Osteen, V. (1987). Home observations of family interactions of depressed women. *Journal of Consulting and Clinical Psychology, 55*, 341-346.

30. Johnston, J. R., Gonzalez, R., & Campbell, L. E. G. (1987). Ongoing postdivorce conflict and child disturbance. *Journal of Abnormal Child Psychology, 15*, 493-509.

31. Keane, T. M., Wolfe, J., & Taylor, K. L. (1987). Post-traumatic stress disorder: Evidence for diagnostic validity and methods of psychological assessment. *Journal of Clinical Psychology, 43*, 32-43.

32. Kuiper, N. A., Olinger, L. J., & Swallow, S. R. (1987). Dysfunctional attitudes, mild depression, views of self self-consciousness, and social perceptions. *Motivation and Emotion, 11*, 379-401.

33. Love, A. W. (1987). Depression in chronic low back pain patients: Diagnostic efficiency of three self-report questionnaires. *Journal of Clinical Psychology, 43*, 84-88.

34. McLaren, J., & Bryson, S. E. (1987). Hemispheric asymmetries in the perception of emotional and neutral faces. *Cortex, 23*, 645-654.

35. Monteiro, W. O., Noshirvani, H. F., Marks, I. M., & Lelliott, P. T. (1987). Anorgasmia from clomipramine in obsessive-compulsive disorder: A controlled trial. *British Journal of Psychiatry, 151*, 107-112.

36. Morin, C. M., & Azrin, N. H. (1987). Stimulus control and imagery training in treating sleep-maintenance insomnia. *Journal of Consulting and Clinical Psychology, 55*, 260-262.

37. Nelson, L. D. (1987). Measuring depression in a clinical population using the MMPI. *Journal of Consulting and Clinical Psychology, 55*, 788-790.

38. Nietzel, M. T., Russell, R. L., Hemmings, K. A., & Gretter, M. L. (1987). Clinical significance of psychotherapy for unipolar depression: A meta-analytic approach to social comparison. *Journal of Consulting and Clinical Psychology, 55*, 156-161.

39. Nulty, D. D., Wilkins, A. J., & Williams, M. G. (1987). Mood, pattern sensitivity and headache: A longitudinal study. *Psychological Medicine, 17*, 705-713.

40. Olinger, L. J., Shaw, B. F., & Kuiper, N. A. (1987). Nonassertiveness, dysfunctional attitudes, and mild levels of depression. *Canadian Journal of Behavioural Science, 19*, 40-49.

41. Platt, S. D., & Dyer, J. A. T. (1987). Psychological correlates of unemployment among male parasuicide in Edinburgh. *British Journal of Psychiatry, 151*, 27-32.

42. Ranieri, W. F., Steer, R. A., Laurence, T. I., Rissmiller, D. J., Piper, G. E., & Beck, A. T. (1987). Relationships of depression, hopelessness, and dysfunctional attitudes to suicide ideation in psychiatric patients. *Psychological Reports, 61*, 967-975.

43. Rape, R. N. (1987). Running and depression. *Perceptual and Motor Skills, 64*, 1303-1310.

44. Rehm, L. P., Kaslow, N. J., & Rabin, A. S. (1987). Cognitive and behavioral targets in a self-control therapy program for depression. *Journal of Consulting and Clinical Psychology, 55*, 60-67.

45. Robbins, P. R., & Tanck, R. H. (1987). A study of diurnal patterns of depressed mood. *Motivation and Emotion, 11*, 37-49.

46. Rubin, R. T., Poland, R. E., Lesser, I. M., Martin, D. J., Blodgett, A. L. N., & Winston, R. A. (1987). Neuroendocrine aspects of primary endogenous depression III. Cortisol secretion in relation to diagnosis and symptom patterns. *Psychological Medicine, 17*, 609-619.

47. Saigh, P. A. (1987). In vitiro [*sic*] flooding of an adolescent's posttraumatic stress disorder. *Journal of Clinical Child Psychology, 16*, 147-150.

48. Schwartz, R. M., & Michelson, L. (1987). States-of-mind model: Cognitive balance in the treatment of agoraphobia. *Journal of Consulting and Clinical Psychology, 55*, 557-565.

49. Shapurian, R., & Hojat, M. (1987). Descriptive statistics, reliability and validity of a short form of Rotter's locus of control scale given to Iranian college students. *Perceptual and Motor Skills, 65*, 229-230.

50. Shaw, D. S., & Emery, R. E. (1987). Parental conflict and other correlates of the adjustment of school-age children whose parents have separated. *Journal of Abnormal Child Psychology, 15*, 269-281.

51. Sigmon, S. T., Nelson, R. O., & Brannon, S. E. (1987). Situational-specificity of motivational differences between depressed and nondepressed subjects. *Perceptual and Motor Skills, 65*, 860-862.

52. Steer, R. A., Beck, A. T., Brown, G., & Berchick, R. J. (1987). Self-reported depressive symptoms that differentiate recurrent-episode major depression from dysthymic disorders. *Journal of Clinical Psychology, 43*, 246-250.

53. Swallow, S. R., & Kuiper, N. A. (1987). The effects of depression and cognitive vulnerability to depression on judgments of similarity between self and other. *Motivation and Emotion, 11*, 157-167.

54. Tanaka, J. S., & Huba, G. J. (1987). Assessing the stability of depression in college students. *Multivariate Behavioral Research, 22*, 5-19.

55. Thompson, L. W., Gallagher, D., & Breckenridge, J. S. (1987). Comparative effectiveness of psychotherapies for depressed elders. *Journal of Consulting and Clinical Psychology, 55*, 385-390.

56. Williams, J. M., Little, M. M., Scates, S., & Blockman, N. (1987). Memory complaints and abilities among depressed older adults. *Journal of Consulting and Clinical Psychology, 55*, 595-598.

57. Wilson, R. S., Como, P. G., Garron, D. C., Klawans, H. L., Barr, A., & Klawans, D. (1987). Memory failure in Huntington's disease. *Journal of Clinical and Experimental Neuropsychology, 9*, 147-154.

58. Young, J. P. R., Coleman, A., & Lader, M. H. (1987). A controlled comparison of fluoxetine and amitriptyline in depressed out-patients. *British Journal of Psychiatry, 151*, 337-340.

59. Zekoski, E. M., O'Hara, M. W., & Wills, K. E. (1987). The effects of maternal mood on mother-infant interaction. *Journal of Abnormal Child Psychology, 15*, 361-378.

60. Zeldow, P. B., Daugherty, S. R., & Clark, D. C. (1987). Masculinity, femininity, and psychosocial adjustment in medical students: A 2-year follow-up. *Journal of Personality Assessment, 51*, 3-14.

61. Zettle, R. D., & Hayes, S. C. (1987). Component and process analysis of cognitive therapy. *Psychological Reports, 61*, 939-953.

62. Acklin, M. W., & Bernat, E. (1987). Depression, alexithymia, and pain prone disorder: A Rorschach study. *Journal of Personality Assessment, 51*, 462-479.

63. Anderson, C. A., & Harvey, R. J. (19880. Discriminating between problems in living: An examination of measures of depression, loneliness, shyness, and social anxiety. *Journal of Social and Clinical Psychology, 6*, 482-491.

64. Anderson, C. A., Jennings, D. L., & Arnoult, L. H. (1988). Validity and utility of the attributional style construct at a moderate level of specificity. *Journal of Personality and Social Psychology, 55*, 979-990.

65. Angold, A. (1988). Childhood and adolescent depression: I. Epidemiological and aetiological aspects. *British Journal of Psychiatry, 152*, 601-617.

66. Ashton, H., Golding, J. F., Marsh, V. R., Thompson, J. W., Hassanyeh, F., & Tyrer, S. P. (1988). Cortical evoked potentials and clinical rating scales as measures of depressive illness. *Psychological Medicine, 18*, 305-317.

67. Bargh, J. A., & Tota, M. E. (1988). Context-dependent automatic processing in depression: Accessibility of negative constructs with regard to self but not others. *Journal of Personality and Social Psychology, 54*, 925-939.

68. Barkley, R. A., Fischer, M., Newby, R. F., & Breen, M. J. (1988). Development of a multimethod clinical protocol for assessing stimulant drug response in children with attention deficit disorder. *Journal of Clinical Child Psychology, 17*, 14-24.

69. Barnett, P. A., & Gotlib, I. H. (1988). Dysfunctional attitudes and psychosocial stress: The differential prediction of future psychological symptomatology. *Motivation and Emotion, 12*, 251-270.

70. Barrera, M., Jr., & Garrison-Jones, C. V. (1988). Properties of the Beck Depression Inventory as a screening instrument for adolescent depression. *Journal of Abnormal Child Psychology, 16*, 263-273.

71. Birtchnell, J. (1988). Depression and family relationships: A study of young, married women on a London housing estate. *British Journal of Psychiatry, 153*, 758-769.

72. Birtchnell, J., Masters, N., & Deahl, M. (1988). Depression and the physical environment: A study of young married women on a London housing estate. *British Journal of Psychiatry, 153*, 56-64.

73. Bond, M. J., & Feather, N. T. (1988). Some correlates of structure and purpose in the use of time. *Journal of Personality and Social Psychology, 55*, 321-329.

74. Brodie, D. A., & Slade, P. D. (1988). The relationship between body-image and body-fat in adult women. *Psychological Medicine, 18*, 623-631.

75. Brophy, C. J., Norvell, N. K., & Kiluk, D. J. (1988). An examination of the factor structure and convergent and discriminant validity of the SCL-90R in an outpatient clinic population. *Journal of Personality Assessment, 52*, 334-340.

76. Brown, R. G., MacCarthy, B., Gotham, A. M., Der, G. J., & Marsden, C. D. (1988). Depression and disability in Parkinson's disease: A follow-up of 132 cases. *Psychological Medicine, 18*, 49-55.

77. Burchill, S. A. L., & Stiles, W. B. (1988). Interactions of depressed college students with their roommates: Not necessarily negative. *Journal of Personality and Social Psychology, 55*, 410-419.

78. Campbell, N. B., Franco, K., & Jurs, S. (1988). Abortion in adolescence. *Adolescence, 23*, 813-823.

79. Carver, C. S., LaVoie, L., Kuhl, J., & Ganellen, R. J. (1988). Cognitive concomitants of depression: A further examination of the roles of generalization, high standards, and self-criticism. *Journal of Social and Clinical Psychology, 7*, 350-365.

80. Crocker, J., Alloy, L. B., & Kayne, N. T. (1988). Attributional style, depression, and perceptions of consensus for events. *Journal of Personality and Social Psychology, 54*, 840-846.

81. Cunningham, C. E., Bennes, B. B., & Siegel, L. S. (1988). Family functioning, time allocation, and parental depression in the families of normal and ADDH children. *Journal of Clinical Child Psychology, 17*, 169-177.

82. Deal, S. L., & Williams, J. E. (1988). Cognitive distortions as mediators between life stress and depression in adolescents. *Adolescence, 23*, 477-490.

83. Friedrich, W. N., Reams, R., & Jacobs, J. H. (1988). Sex differences in early adolescents. *Psychological Reports, 62*, 475-481.

84. Furnham, A., & Brewin, C. R. (1988). Social comparison and depression. *Journal of Genetic Psychology, 149*, 191-198.

85. Goldberg, J., & Sakinofsky, J. (1988). Intropunitiveness and parasuicide: Prediction of interview response. *British Journal of Psychiatry, 153*, 801-804.

86. Gotlib, I. H., Mount, J. H., Cordy, N. I., & Whiffen, V. E. (1988). Depression and perceptions of early parenting: A longitudinal study. *British Journal of Psychiatry, 152*, 24-27.

87. Ingram, R. E., Cruet, D., Johnson, B. R., & Wisnicki, K. S. (1988). Self-focused attention, gender, gender role, and vulnerability to negative affect. *Journal of Personality and Social Psychology, 55*, 967-978.

88. Jacobsen, R. H., Tomkin, A. S., & Hyer, L. A. (1988). Factor analytic study of irrational beliefs. *Psychological Reports, 63*, 803-809.

89. Jahanshahi, M., & Marsden, C. D. (1988). Depression in torticollis: A controlled study. *Psychological Medicine, 18*, 925-933.

90. Johnson, D. A. W. (1988). The significance of depression in the prediction of relapse in chronic schizophrenia. *British Journal of Psychiatry, 152*, 320-323.

91. Kaslow, N. J., Rehm, L. P., Pollack, S. L., & Siegel, A. W. (1988). Attributional style and self-control behavior in depressed and nondepressed children and their parents. *Journal of Abnormal Child Psychology, 16*, 163-175.

92. Kelley, M. L., & Carper, L. B. (1988). The Mothers' Activity Checklist: An instrument for assessing pleasant and unpleasant events. *Behavioral Assessment, 10*, 331-341.

93. Kraemer, D. L., & Hastrup, J. L. (1988). Crying in adults: Self-control and autonomic correlates. *Journal of Social and Clinical Psychology, 6*, 53-68.

94. Labbé, E. E., Welsh, M. C., & Delaney, D. (1988). Effects of consistent aerobic exercise on the psychological functioning of women. *Perceptual and Motor Skills, 67*, 919-925.

95. Lambert, M. J., Masters, K. S., & Astle, D. (1988). An effect size comparison of the Beck, Zung, and Hamilton rating scales for depression: A three-week and twelve-week analysis. *Psychological Reports, 63*, 467-470.

96. Larsen, R. J., & Cowan, G. S. (1988). Internal focus of attention and depression: A study of daily experience. *Motivation and Emotion, 12*, 237-249.

97. Lewin, L., Hops, H., Aubuschon, A., & Budinger, T. (1988). Predictors of maternal satisfaction regarding clinic-referred children: Methodological considerations. *Journal of Clinical Child Psychology, 17*, 159-163.

98. Logsdail, S. J., Callanan, M. M., & Ron, M. A. (1988). Psychiatric morbidity in patients with clinically isolated lesions of the type seen in multiple sclerosis: A clinical and MRI study. *Psychological Medicine, 18*, 355-364.

99. Mauro, R. (1988). Opponent processes in human emotions? An experimental investigation of hedonic contrast and affective interactions. *Motivation and Emotion, 12*, 333-351.

100. McAdams, D. P., Lensky, D. B., Daple, S. A., & Allen, J. (1988). Depression and the organization of autobiographical memory. *Journal of Social and Clinical Psychology, 7*, 332-349.

101. Meisner, S. (1988). Susceptibility of Rorschach distress correlates to malingering. *Journal of Personality Assessment, 52*, 564-571.

102. Meyers, L. S., & Wong, D. T. (1988). Validation of a new test of locus of control: The Internal Control Index. *Educational and Psychological Measurement, 48*, 753-761.

103. Mezey, G. C., & Taylor, P. J. (1988). Psychological reactions of women who have been raped: A descriptive and comparative study. *British Journal of Psychiatry, 152*, 330-339.

104. Michelson, L., Manchione, K., Manchione, N., Testa, S., & Mavissakalian, M. (1988). Cognitive correlates and outcome of cognitive, behavioral and physiological treatments of agoraphobia. *Psychological Reports, 63*, 999-1004.

105. Miller, S. M., Brody, D. S., & Summerton, J. (1988). Styles of coping with threat: Implications for health. *Journal of Personality and Social Psychology, 54*, 142-148.

106. Nezu, A. M., & Ronan, G. F. (1988). Social problem solving as a moderator of stress-related depressive symptoms: A prospective analysis. *Journal of Counseling Psychology, 35*, 134-138.

107. Nezu, A. M., Nezu, C. M., & Blissett, S. E. (1988). Sense of humor as a moderator of the relation between stressful events and psychological distress: A prospective analysis. *Journal of Personality and Social Psychology, 54*, 520-525.

108. Nielson, W. R., & MacDonald, M. R. (1988). Attributions of blame and coping following spinal cord injury: Is self-blame adaptive? *Journal of Social and Clinical Psychology, 7*, 163-175.

109. Norman, P. D., & Antaki, C. (1988). Real Events Attributional Style Questionnaire. *Journal of Social and Clinical Psychology, 7*, 97-100.

110. Parker, G., Blignault, I., & Manicavasagar, V. (1988). Neurotic depression: Delineation of symptom profiles and their relation to outcome. *British Journal of Psychiatry, 152*, 15-23.

111. Pinkley, R., LaPrelle, J., Pyszczynski, T., & Greenberg, J. (1988). Depression and the self-serving search for consensus after success and failure. *Journal of Social and Clinical Psychology, 6*, 235-244.

112. Pollard, A. C., & Cox, G. L. (1988). Social-evaluative anxiety in panic disorder and agoraphobia. *Psychological Reports, 62*, 323-326.

113. Radenhausen, R. A., & Anker, J. M. (1988). Effects of depressed mood induction on reasoning performance. *Perceptual and Motor Skills, 66*, 855-860.

114. Ramirez, L. F., McCormick, R. A., & Lowy, M. T. (1988). Plasma cortisol and depression in pathological gamblers. *British Journal of Psychiatry, 153*, 684-686.

115. Robins, C. J. (1988). Attributions and depression: Why is the literature so inconsistent? *Journal of Personality and Social Psychology, 54*, 880-889.

116. Robins, C. J., & Block, P. (1988). Personal vulnerability, life events, and depressive symptoms: A test of a specific interactional model. *Journal of Personality and Social Psychology, 54*, 847-852.

117. Rosenblatt, A., & Greenberg, J. (1988). Depression and interpersonal attraction: The role of perceived similarity. *Journal of Personality and Social Psychology, 55*, 112-119.

118. Roth, D. L., Harris, R. N., & Snyder, C. R. (1988). An individual differences measure of attributive and repudiative tactics of favorable self-presentation. *Journal of Social and Clinical Psychology, 7*, 159-170.

119. Russell, P. O., Epstein, L. H., Johnston, J. J., Block, D. R., & Blair, E. (1988). The effects of physical activity as maintenance for smoking cessation. *Addictive Behaviors, 13*, 215-218.

120. Sacco, W. P., Milana, S., & Dunn, V. K. (1988). The effect of duration of depressive episode on the response of others. *Journal of Social and Clinical Psychology, 7*, 297-311.

121. Scott, J., Barker, W. A., & Eccleston, D. (1988). The Newcastle chronic depression study: Patient characteristics and factors associated with chronicity. *British Journal of Psychiatry, 152*, 28-33.

122. Sidrow, N. E., & Lester, D. (1988). Locus of-control and suicidal ideation. *Perceptual and Motor Skills, 67*, 576.

123. Viglione, D. J., Jr., Brager, R. C., & Haller, N. (1988). Usefulness of structural Rorschach data in identifying inpatients with depressive symptoms: A preliminary study. *Journal of Personality Assessment, 52*, 524-529.

124. Watson, D., Clark, L. A., & Tellegen, A. (1988). Development and validation of brief measures of positive and negative affect: The PANAS Scales. *Journal of Personality and Social Psychology, 54*, 1063-1070.

125. Webster-Stratton, C., & Hammond, M. (1988). Maternal depression and its relationship to life stress, perceptions of child behavior problems, parenting behaviors, and child conduct problems. *Journal of Abnormal Child Psychology, 16*, 299-315.

126. Wenzlaff, R. M., Wegner, D. M., & Roper, D. W. (1988). Depression and mental control: The resurgence of unwanted negative thoughts. *Journal of Personality and Social Psychology, 55*, 882-892.

127. Wilhelm, K., & Parker, G. (1988). The development of a measure of intimate bonds. *Psychological Medicine*, 18, 225-234.

128. Wilson, J. T. L., Wiedmann, K. D., Phillips, W. A., & Brooks, D. N. (1988). Visual event perception in alcoholics. *Journal of Clinical and Experimental Neuropsychology*, 10, 222-234.

129. Acklin, M. W., Sauer, A., Alexander, G., & Dugoni, B. (1989). Predicting depression using earliest childhood memories. *Journal of Personality Assessment*, 53, 51-59.

130. Agras, W. S., Schneider, J. A., Arnow, B., Raeburn, S. O., & Telch, C.F. (1989). Cognitive-behavioral and response-prevention treatments for bulimia nervosa. *Journal of Consulting and Clinical Psychology*, 57, 215-221.

131. Alden, L. (1989). Short-term structured treatment for avoidant personality disorder. *Journal of Consulting and Clinical Psychology*, 57, 756-764.

132. Alexander, P. C., Neimeyer, R. A., Follette, V. M., Moore, M. K., & Harter, S. (1989). A comparison of group treatments of women sexually abused as children. *Journal of Consulting and Clinical Psychology*, 57, 479-483.

133. Barnes, T. R. E., Curson, D. A., Liddle, P. F., & Patel, M. (1989). The nature and prevalence of depression in chronic schizophrenic in-patients. *British Journal of Psychiatry*, 154, 486-491.

134. Berrios, G. E., & Chiu, H. (1989). Obsessive-compulsive disorders in Cambridgeshire: A follow-up study of up to 20 years. *British Journal of Psychiatry*, 154 (Suppl. 4), 17-20.

135. Bishay, N. R., Petersen, N., & Tarrier, N. (1989). An uncontrolled study of cognitive therapy for morbid jealousy. *British Journal of Psychiatry*, 154, 386-389.

136. Booth, C. L., Mitchell, S. K., Barnard, K. E., & Spieker, S. J. (1989). Development of maternal social skills in multiproblem families: Effects on the mother-child relationship. *Developmental Psychology*, 25, 403-412.

137. Breen, M. J. (1989). Cognitive and behavioral differences in AdHD boys and girls. *Journal of Child Psychology and Psychiatry and Allied Disciplines*, 30, 711-716.

138. Brewin, C. R., Furnham, A., & Howes, M. (1989). Demographic and psychological determinants of homesickness and confiding among students. *British Journal of Psychology*, 80, 467-477.

139. Brewin, C. R., McCarthy, B., & Furnham, A. (1989). Social support in the face of adversity: The role of cognitive appraisal. *Journal of Research in Personality*, 23, 354-372.

140. Burns, M. O., & Seligman, M. E. P. (1989). Explanatory style across the life span: Evidence for stability over 52 years. *Journal of Personality and Social Psychology*, 56, 471-477.

141. Charision, J., Jackson, H. J., Boyle, G. J., Burgess, P., Minas, I. H., & Joshua, S. D. (1989). Are employment-interview skills a correlate of subtypes of schizophrenia? *Psychological Reports*, 65, 951-960.

142. Christensen, L., Krietsch, K., & White, B. (1989). Development, cross-validation, and assessment of reliability of the Christensen Dietary Distress Inventory. *Canadian Journal of Behavioural Science*, 21, 1-15.

143. Clark, D. A., Beck, A. T., & Brown, G. (1989). Cognitive mediation in general psychiatric outpatients: A test of the content-specificity hypothesis. *Journal of Personality and Social Psychology*, 56, 958-964.

144. Cole, D. A., & Milstead, M. (1989). Behavioral correlates of depression: Antecedents or consequences? *Journal of Counseling Psychology*, 36, 408-416.

145. Conrad, M., & Hammen, C. (1989). Role of maternal depression in perceptions of child maladjustment. *Journal of Consulting and Clinical Psychology*, 57, 663-667.

146. Cox, B. J., Norton, G. R., Dorward, J., & Fergusson, P. A. (1989). The relationship between panic attacks and chemical dependencies. *Addictive Behaviors*, 14, 53-60.

147. Dobson, K. S. (1989). A meta-analysis of the efficacy of cognitive therapy for depression. *Journal of Consulting and Clinical Psychology*, 57, 414-419.

148. Draucker, C. B. (1989). Cognitive adaptation of female incest survivors. *Journal of Consulting and Clinical Psychology*, 57, 668-670.

149. Dumas, J. E., Gibson, J. A., & Albin, J. B. (1989). Behavioral correlates of maternal depressive symptomatology in conduct-disorder children. *Journal of Consulting and Clinical Psychology*, 57, 516-521.

150. Duricko, A. J., Norcross, J. C., & Buskirk, R. D. (1989). Correlates of the egocentricity index in child and adolescent outpatients. *Journal of Personality Assessment*, 53, 184-187.

151. Dykman, B. M., Abramson, L. Y., Alloy, L. B., & Hartlage, S. (1989). Processing of ambiguous and unambiguous feedback by depressed and nondepressed college students: Schematic biases and their implications for depressive realism. *Journal of Personality and Social Psychology*, 56, 431-445.

152. Ennis, J., Barnes, R. A., Kennedy, S., & Trachtenberg, D. D. (1989). Depression in self-harm patients. *British Journal of Psychiatry*, 154, 41-47.

153. Fincham, F. D., Beach, S. R. H., & Bradbury, T. N. (1989). Marital distress, depression, and attributions: Is the marital distress-attribution association an artifact of depression? *Journal of Consulting and Clinical Psychology*, 57, 768-771.

154. Fleming, J. E., Offord, D. R., & Boyle, M. H. (1989). Prevalence of childhood and adolescent depression in the community: Ontario Child Health Study. *British Journal of Psychiatry*, 155, 647-654.

155. Flett, G. L., Pliner, P., & Blankstein, K. R. (1989). Depression and components of attributional complexity. *Journal of Personality and Social Psychology*, 56, 757-764.

156. Friedman, T., & Gath, D. (1989). The psychiatric consequences of spontaneous abortion. *British Journal of Psychiatry*, 155, 810-813.

157. Fromuth, M. E., & Burkhart, B. R. (1989). Long-term psychological correlates of childhood sexual abuse in two samples of college men. *Child Abuse & Neglect*, 13, 533-542.

158. Goodwin, G. M., Shapiro, C. M., Bennie, J., Dick, H., Carroll, S., & Fink, G. (1989). The neuroendocrine responses and psychological effects of infusion of L-tryptophan in anorexia nervosa. *Psychological Medicine*, 19, 857-864.

159. Gotlib, I. H., & Lee, C. M. (1989). The social functioning of depressed patients: A longitudinal assessment. *Journal of Social and Clinical Psychology*, 8, 223-237.

160. Gotlib, I. H., & Whiffen, V. E. (1989). Stress, coping, and marital satisfaction in couples with a depressed wife. *Canadian Journal of Behavioural Science*, 21, 401-418.

161. Gotlib, I. H., Whiffen, V. E., Mount, J. H., Milne, K., & Cordy, N. I. (1989). Prevalence rates and demographic characteristics associated with depression in pregnancy and the postpartum. *Journal of Consulting and Clinical Psychology*, 57, 269-274.

162. Greene, P. G., Zeichner, A., Roberts, N. L., Callahan, E. J., & Granados, J. L. (1989). Preparation for cesarean delivery: A multicomponent analysis of treatment outcome. *Journal of Consulting and Clinical Psychology*, 57, 484-487.

163. Greene, S. M. (1989). The relationship between depression and hopelessness: Implications for current theories of depression. *British Journal of Psychiatry*, 154, 650-659.

164. Hakstian, A. R., & McLean, P. D. (1989). Brief screen for depression. *Psychological Assessment*, 1, 139-141.

165. Harris, B., Huckle, P., Thomas, R., Johns, S., & Fung, H. (1989). The use of rating scales to identify post-natal depression. *British Journal of Psychiatry*, 154, 813-817.

166. Hewitt, P. L., Mittelstaedt, W., & Wollert, R. (1989). Validation of a measure of perfectionism. *Journal of Personality Assessment*, 53, 133-144.

167. Hibbert, G. A., & Chan, M. (1989). Respiratory control: Its contribution to the treatment of panic attacks: A controlled study. *British Journal of Psychiatry*, 154, 232-236.

168. Hibbert, G., & Pilsbury, D. (1989). Hyperventilation: Is it a cause of panic attacks? *British Journal of Psychiatry*, 155, 805-809.

169. Huber, S. J., Freidenberg, D. L., Shuttleworth, E. C., Paulson, G. W., & Clapp, L. E. (1989). Neuropsychological similarities in lateralized Parkinsonism. *Cortex*, 25, 461-470.

170. Ingram, R. E. (1989). Unique and shared cognitive factors in social anxiety and depression: Automatic thinking and self-appraisal. *Journal of Social and Clinical Psychology*, 8, 198-208.

171. Jorgensen, R. S., & Richards, C. S. (1989). Negative affect and the reporting of physical symptoms among college students. *Journal of Counseling Psychology*, 36, 501-504.

172. Judd, F. K., Stone, J., Webber, J. E., Brown, D. J., & Burrows, G. D. (1989). Depression following spinal cord injury: A prospective in-patient study. *British Journal of Psychiatry*, 154, 668-671.

173. Kaplan, A. S., Garfinkel, P. E., & Brown, G. M. (1989). The DST and TRH test in bulimia nervosa. *British Journal of Psychiatry*, 154, 86-92.

174. Kazdin, A. E., Bass, D., Siegel, T., & Thomas, C. (1989). Cognitive-behavioral therapy and relationship therapy in the treatment of children referred for antisocial behavior. *Journal of Consulting and Clinical Psychology*, 57, 522-535.

175. Kelly, J. A., St. Lawrence, J. S., Hood, H. V., & Brasfield, T. L. (1989). Behavioral intervention to reduce AIDS risk activities. *Journal of Consulting and Clinical Psychology*, 57, 60-67.

176. Klein, D. N. (1989). The Depressive Experiences Questionnaire: A further evaluation. *Journal of Personality Assessment*, 53, 703-715.

177. Klein, D. N., Dickstein, S., Taylor, E. B., & Harding, K. (1989). Identifying chronic affective disorders in outpatients: Validation of the General Behavior Inventory. *Journal of Consulting and Clinical Psychology*, 57, 106-111.

178. Laessle, R. G., Tuschl, R. J., Waadt, S., & Pirke, K. M. (1989). The specific psychopathology of bulimia nervosa: A comparison with restrained and unrestrained (normal) eaters. *Journal of Consulting and Clinical Psychology*, 57, 772-775.

179. Lefkowitz, M. M., Tesiny, E. P., & Solodow, W. (1989). A rating scale for assessing dysphoria in youth. *Journal of Abnormal Child Psychology*, 17, 337-347.

180. Leigh, I. W., Robins, C. J., Welkowitz, J., & Bond, R. N. (1989). Toward greater understanding of depression in deaf individuals. *American Annals of the Deaf, 134,* 249-254.

181. Lester, D. (1989). Locus of control, depression and suicidal ideation. *Perceptual and Motor Skills, 69,* 1150.

182. Lewinsohn, P. M., Hoberman, H. M., & Clarke, G. N. (1989). The Coping with Depression Course: Review and future directions. *Canadian Journal of Behavioural Science, 21,* 470-493.

183. Lopez, F. G., Campbell, V. L., & Watkins, C. E., Jr. (1989). Constructions of current family functioning among depressed and nondepressed college students. *Journal of College Student Development, 30,* 221-228.

184. Maag, J. W., & Behrens, J. T. (1989). Depression and cognitive self-statements of learning disabled and seriously emotionally disturbed adolescents. *The Journal of Special Education, 23,* 17-27.

185. MacCarthy, B., & Brown, R. (1989). Psychosocial factors in Parkinson's disease. *British Journal of Clinical Psychology, 28,* 41-52.

186. Mallinckrodt, B. (1989). Social support and the effectiveness of group therapy. *Journal of Counseling Psychology, 36,* 170-175.

187. Martin, P. R., Nathan, P. R., Milech, D., & vanKeppel, M. (1989). Cognitive therapy vs. self-management training in the treatment of chronic headaches. *British Journal of Clinical Psychology, 28,* 347-361.

188. McCombs, A., & Forehand, R. (1989). Adolescent school performance following parental divorce: Are there family factors that can enhance success? *Adolescence, 24,* 871-880.

189. Mclean, P. D., & Carr, S. (1989). The psychological treatment of unipolar depression: Progress and limitations. *Canadian Journal of Behavioural Science, 21,* 452-469.

190. Miller, S. M., Leinbach, A., & Brody, D. S. (1989). Coping style in hypertensive patients: Nature and consequences. *Journal of Consulting and Clinical Psychology, 57,* 333-337.

191. Nezer, A. M., & Perri, M. G. (1989). Social problem-solving therapy for unipolar depression: An initial dismantling investigation. *Journal of Consulting and Clinical Psychology, 57,* 408-413.

192. Olioff, M., Bryson, S. E., & Wadden, N. P. (1989). Predictive relation of automatic thoughts and student efficacy to depressive symptoms in undergraduates. *Canadian Journal of Behavioural Science, 21,* 353-363.

193. Peselow, E. D., Stanley, M., Filippi, A. M., Barouche, F., Goodnick, P., & Fieve, R. R. (1989). The predictive value of the dexamethasone suppression test: A placebo-controlled study. *British Journal of Psychiatry, 155,* 667-672.

194. Pyszczynski, T., Hamilton, J. C., & Herring, F. H. (1989). Depression, self-focused attention, and the negative memory bias. *Journal of Personality and Social Psychology, 57,* 351-357.

195. Rhodewalt, F., & Zone, J. B. (1989). Appraisal of life change, depression, and illness in hardy and nonhardy women. *Journal of Personality and Social Psychology, 56,* 81-88.

196. Ron, M. A., & Logsdail, S. J. (1989). Psychiatric morbidity in multiple sclerosis: A clinical and MRI study. *Psychological Medicine, 19,* 887-895.

197. Rybicki, D. J., Lepkowsky, C. M., & Arndt, S. (1989). An empirical assessment of bulimic patients using multiple measures. *Addictive Behaviors, 14,* 249-260.

198. Schofield, M. A. (1989). The contribution of problem drinking to the level of psychiatric morbidity in the general hospital. *British Journal of Psychiatry, 155,* 229-232.

199. Segal, Z. V., Shaw, B. F., & Vella, D. D. (1989). Life stress and depression: A test of the congruency hypothesis for life event content and depressive subtype. *Canadian Journal of Behavioural Science, 21,* 389-400.

200. Shapiro, D. A., Firth-Cozens, J., & Stiles, W. B. (1989). The question of therapists' differential effectiveness: A Sheffield psychotherapy project addendum. *British Journal of Psychiatry, 154,* 383-385.

201. Shulman, R., Price, J. D. E., & Spinelli, J. (1989). Biopsychosocial aspects of long-term survival on end-stage renal failure therapy. *Psychological Medicine, 19,* 945-954.

202. Steer, R. A., Beck, A. T., & Brown, G. (1989). Sex differences on the revised Beck Depression Inventory for outpatients with affective disorders. *Journal of Personality Assessment, 53,* 693-702.

203. Stiffman, A. R. (1989). Physical and sexual abuse in runaway youths. *Child Abuse & Neglect, 13,* 417-426.

204. Stoltz, R. F., & Galassi, J. P. (1989). Internal attributions and types of depression in college students: The learned helplessness model revisited. *Journal of Counseling Psychology, 36,* 316-321.

205. Suis, J., & Wan, C. K. (1989). The relation between Type A behavior and chronic emotional distress: A meta-analysis. *Journal of Personality and Social Psychology, 57,* 503-512.

206. VanGorp, W. S., Miller, E. N., Satz, P., & Visscher, B. (1989). Neuropsychological performance in HIV-1 Immunocompromised patients: A preliminary report. *Journal of Clinical and Experimental Neuropsychology, 11,* 763-773.

207. Whisman, M. A., Strosahl, K., Fruzzetti, A. E., Schmaling, K. B., Jacobson, N. S., & Miller, D. M. (1989). A structured interview version of the Hamilton Rating Scale for Depression: Reliability and validity. *Psychological Assessment, 1,* 238-241.

208. Whitaker, A., Davies, M., Shaffer, D., Johnson, J., Abrams, S., Walsh, B. T., & Kalikow, K. (1989). The struggle to be trim: A survey of anorexic and bulimic symptoms in a non-referred adolescent population. *Psychological Medicine, 19,* 143-163.

209. Wierzbicki, M., & Carver, D. (1989). Children's engagement in antidepressive activities. *Journal of Genetic Psychology, 150,* 163-174.

210. Williams, D. E., & Page, M. M. (1989). A multi-dimensional measure of Maslow's hierarchy of needs. *Journal of Research in Personality, 23,* 192-213.

211. Witt, V. (1989). Premarital abuse: What is the effect on the victim? *Journal of College Student Development, 30,* 339-344.

212. Barkley, R. A., DuPaul, G. J., & McMurray, M. B. (1990). Comprehensive evaluation of attention deficit disorder with and without hyperactivity as defined research criteria. *Journal of Consulting and Clinical Psychology, 58,* 775-789.

213. Bentall, R. P., & Thompson, M. (1990). Emotional Stroop performance and the manic defence. *British Journal of Clinical Psychology, 29,* 235-237.

214. Blackburn, I. M., Roxborough, H. M., Muir, W. J., Glabus, M., & Blackwood, D. H. R. (1990). Perceptual and physiological dysfunction in depression. *Psychological Medicine, 20,* 95-103.

215. Chadwick, P. D. J., & Lowe, C. F. (1990). Measurement and modification of delusional beliefs. *Journal of Consulting and Clinical Psychology, 58,* 225-232.

216. Chartrand, J. M. (1990). A causal analysis to predict the personal and academic adjustment of nontraditional students. *Journal of Counseling Psychology, 37,* 65-73.

217. Connell, D. K., & Meyer, R. G. (1991). Adolescent suicidal behavior and popular self-report instruments of depression, social desirability, and anxiety. *Adolescence, 26,* 113-119.

218. Costello, E. J., & Caggiula, A. W. (1990). Influences of natural menopause of psychological characteristics and symptoms of middle-aged healthy women. *Journal of Consulting and Clinical Psychology, 58,* 345-351.

219. DeRubeis, R. J., Evans, M. D., Hollon, S. D., Garvey, M. J., Grove, E. M., & Tuason, V. B. (1990). How does cognitive therapy work? Cognitive change and symptom change in cognitive therapy and pharmacotherapy for depression. *Journal of Consulting and Clinical Psychology, 58,* 862-869.

220. Dumas, J. E., & Gibson, J. A. (1990). Behavioral correlates of maternal depressive symptomatology in conduct-disorder children: II. Systemic effects involving fathers and siblings. *Journal of Consulting and Clinical Psychology, 58,* 877-881.

221. Ehrenberg, M. F., Cox, D. N., & Koopman, R. F. (1990). The Millon Adolescent Personality Inventory profiles of depressed adolescents. *Adolescence, 25,* 415-424.

222. Ehrenberg, M. F., Cox, D. N., & Koopman, R. F. (1990). The prevalence of depression in high school students. *Adolescence, 25,* 905-912.

223. Field, T., Healy, B., Goldstein, S., & Guthertz, M. (1990). Behavior-state matching and synchrony in mother-infant interactions of nondepressed versus depressed dyads. *Developmental Psychology, 26,* 7-14.

224. Flett, G. L., & Hewitt, P. L. (1990). Clinical depression and attributional complexity. *British Journal of Clinical Psychology, 29,* 339-340.

225. Gallagher-Thompson, D., Hanley-Peterson, P., & Thompson, L. W. (1990). Maintenance of gains versus relapse following brief psychotherapy for depression. *Journal of Consulting and Clinical Psychology, 58,* 371-374.

226. Gilbert, P., & Reynolds, S. (1990). The relationship between the Eysenck Personality Questionnaire and Beck's concepts of sociotrophy and autonomy. *British Journal of Clinical Psychology, 29,* 319-325.

227. Greene, G. W., Achterberg, C., Crumbaugh, J., & Soper, J. (1990). Dietary intake and dieting practices of bulimic and non-bulimic female college students. *Journal of the American Dietetic Association, 90,* 576-578.

228. Hains, A. A., & Szyjakowski, M. (1990). A cognitive stress-reduction intervention program for adolescents. *Journal of Counseling Psychology, 37,* 79-84.

229. Hock, E., & DeMeis, D. K. (1990). Depression in mothers of infants: The role of maternal employment. *Developmental Psychology, 26,* 285-291.

230. House, A., Dennis, M., Warlow, C., Hawton, K., & Molyneux, A. (1990). The relationship between intellectual impairment and mood disorder in the first year after stroke. *Psychological Medicine, 20,* 805-814.

231. Imber, S. D., Pilkonis, P. A., Sotsky, S. M., Elkin, I., Watkins, J. T., Collins, J. F., Shea, M. T., Leber, W. R., & Glass, D. R. (1990). Mode-specific effects among three treatments for depression. *Journal of Consulting and Clinical Psychology, 58,* 352-359.

232. Johnston, C., & Pelham, W. E., Jr. (1990). Maternal characteristics, ratings of child behavior, and mother-child interactions in families of children with externalizing disorders. *Journal of Abnormal Child Psychology, 18,* 407-417.

233. Kazdin, A. E. (1990). Premature termination from treatment among children referred for antisocial behavior. *Journal of Child Psychology and Psychiatry, 31,* 415-425.

234. Klimes, I., Mayou, R. A., Pearce, M. J., Coles, L., & Fagg, J. R. (1990). Psychological treatment for atypical non-cardiac chest pain: A controlled evaluation. *Psychological Medicine, 20,* 605-611.

235. Kovacs, M., Iyengar, S., Goldston, D., Obrosky, D. S., Stewart, J., & Marsh, J. (1990). Psychological functioning among mothers of children with insulin-dependent diabetes mellitus: A longitudinal study. *Journal of Consulting and Clinical Psychology, 58,* 189-195.

236. Larson, L. M., Piersel, W. C., Iamo, R. A. K., & Allen, S. J. (1990). Significant predictors of problem-solving appraisal. *Journal of Counseling Psychology, 37,* 482-490.

237. Linaker, O. M., & Nitter, R. (1990). Psychopathology in institutionalised mentally retarded adults. *British Journal of Psychiatry, 156,* 522-525.

238. Mallinckrodt, B. (1990). Satisfaction with a new job after unemployment: Consequences of job loss for older professionals. *Journal of Counseling Psychology, 37,* 149-152.

239. Moffett, L. A., & Radenhausen, R. A. (1990). Assessing depression in substance abusers: Beck Depression Inventory and SCL-90R. *Addictive Behaviors, 15,* 179-181.

240. Mohr, D. C., Beutler, L. E., Engle, D., Shoham-Salomon, V., Bergan, J., Kaszniak, A. W., & Yost, E. B. (1990). Identification of patients at risk for nonresponse and negative outcome in psychotherapy. *Journal of Consulting and Clinical Psychology, 58,* 622-628.

241. Parsons, O. A., Schaeffer, K. W., & Glenn, S. W. (1990). Does neuropsychological test performance predict resumption of drinking in posttreatment alcoholics? *Addictive Behaviors, 15,* 297-307.

242. Peveler, R. C., & Fairburn, C. G. (1990). Measurement of neurotic symptoms by self-report questionnaire: Validity of the SCL-90-R. *Psychological Medicine, 20,* 873-879.

243. Piper, W. E., Azim, H. F. A., McCallum, M., & Joyce, A. S. (1990). Patient suitability and outcome in short-term individual psychotherapy. *Journal of Consulting and Clinical Psychology, 58,* 475-481.

244. Pitcairn, T. K., Clemie, S., Gray, J. M., & Pentland, B. (1990). Non-verbal cues in the self-presentation of Parkinsonian patients. *British Journal of Clinical Psychology, 29,* 177-184.

245. Ranseen, J. D., Bohaska, L. A., & Schmitt, F. A. (1990). An investigation of anosognosia following traumatic head injury. *The International Journal of Clinical Neuropsychology, 12,* 29-36.

246. Richards, A., & Whittaker, T. M. (1990). Effects of anxiety and mood manipulation in autobiographical memory. *British Journal of Clinical Psychology, 29,* 145-153.

247. Robins, C. J., Block, P., & Peselow, E. D. (1990). Endogenous and non-endogenous depressions: Relations to life events, dysfunctional attitudes and event perceptions. *British Journal of Clinical Psychology, 29,* 201-207.

248. Rotheram-Borus, M. J., Trautman, P. D., Dopkins, S. C., & Shrout, P.K. (1990). Cognitive style and pleasant activities among female adolescent suicide attempters. *Journal of Consulting and Clinical Psychology, 58,* 554-561.

249. Sakinofsky, I., Roberts, R. S., Brown, Y., Cumming, Y., Cumming, C., & James, P. (1990). Problem resolution and repetition of parasuicide: A prospective study. *British Journal of Psychiatry, 156,* 395-399.

250. Salkovskis, P. M., Atha, C., & Storer, D. (1990). Cognitive-behavioural problem solving in the treatment of patients who repeatedly attempt suicide: A controlled trial. *British Journal of Psychiatry, 157,* 871-876.

251. Schotte, D. E., Cools, J., & Payvar, S. (1990). Problem-solving deficits in suicidal patients: Trait vulnerability or state phenomenon? *Journal of Consulting and Clinical Psychology, 58,* 562-564.

252. Shapiro, D. A., & Firth-Cozens, J. (1990). Two-year follow-up of the Sheffield Psychotherapy Project. *British Journal of Psychiatry, 157,* 389-391.

253. Shek, D. T. L. (1990). Reliability and factorial structure of the Chinese version of the Beck Depression Inventory. *Journal of Clinical Psychology, 46,* 35-43.

254. Stanton, A. L., Garcia, M. E., & Green, S. B. (1990). Development and validation of the Situational Appetite Measures. *Addictive Behaviors, 15,* 461-472.

255. Sutker, P. B., Galina, Z. H., West, J. A., & Allain, A. N. (1990). Trauma-induced weight loss and cognitive deficits among former prisoners of war. *Journal of Consulting and Clinical Psychology, 58,* 323-328.

256. Swoboda, J. S., Dowd, E. T., & Wise, S. L. (1990). Reframing and restraining directives in the treatment of clinical depression. *Journal of Counseling Psychology, 37,* 254-260.

257. Telch, C. F., Agras, W. S., Rossiter, E. M., Wilfley, D., & Kenardy, J. (1990). Group cognitive-behavioral treatment for the nonpurging bulimic: An initial evaluation. *Journal of Consulting and Clinical Psychology, 58,* 629-635.

258. Whissell, C., Whissell, R., & Kneer, R. (1990). Speed and content of affective self-description as a function of the personality characteristics of the respondent. *Perceptual and Motor Skills, 70,* 803-815.

259. Wilson, G. L. (1990). Psychotherapy with depressed incarcerated felons: A comparative evaluation of treatments. *Psychological Reports, 67,* 1027-1041.

260. Beutler, L. E., Engle, D., Mohr, D., Daldrup, R. J., Bergan, J., Meredith, K., & Merry, W. (1991). Predictors of differential response to cognitive, experiential, and self-directed psychotherapeutic procedures. *Journal of Consulting and Clinical Psychology, 59,* 333-340.

261. Burns, D. D., & Hoeksema, S. (1991). Coping styles, homework compliance, and the effectiveness of cognitive-behavioral therapy. *Journal of Consulting and Clinical Psychology, 59,* 305-311.

262. Butter, G., Fennell, M., Robson, P., & Gelder, M. (1991). Comparison of behavior therapy and cognitive behavior therapy in the treatment of generalized anxiety disorder. *Journal of Consulting and Clinical Psychology, 59,* 167-175.

263. Chan, D. W. (1991). The Beck Depression Inventory: What difference does the Chinese version make? *Psychological Assessment, 3,* 616-622.

264. Christensen, A. J., Turner, C. W., Smith, T. W., Holman, J. M., & Gregory, M. C. (1991). Health locus of control and depression in end-stage renal disease. *Journal of Consulting and Clinical Psychology, 59,* 419-424.

265. Drennen, W. T. (1991). Negative schemas and depression in normal college student volunteers. *Psychological Reports, 68,* 521-522.

266. Emery, R. E., Matthews, S. G., & Wyer, M. M. (1991). Child custody of mediation and litigation: Further evidence on the differing views of mothers and fathers. *Journal of Consulting and Clinical Psychology, 59,* 410-418.

267. Foa, E. B., Olasor Rothbaum, B., Riggs, D. S., & Murdock, T. B. (1991). Treatment of posttraumatic stress disorder in rape victims: A comparison between cognitive-behavioral precedures and counseling. *Journal of Consulting and Clinical Psychology, 59,* 715-723.

268. Follette, V. M., Alexander, P. C., & Follette, W. C. (1991). individual predictors of outcome in group treatment for incest survivors. *Journal of Consulting and Clinical Psychology, 59,* 150-155.

269. Heppner, P. P., Cook, S. W., Strozier, A. L., & Heppner, M. J. (1991). An investigation of coping styles and gender differences with farmers in career transition. *Journal of Counseling Psychology, 38,* 167-174.

270. Hollon, S. D., Shelton, R. C., & Loosen, P. T. (1991). Cognitive therapy and pharmacotherapy for depression. *Journal of Consulting and Clinical Psychology, 59,* 88-99.

271. Holroyd, K. A., Nash, J. M., Pingel, J. D., Cordingley, G. E., & Jerome, A. (1991). A comparison of pharmacological (amitriptyline HCL) and nonpharmacological (cognitive-behavioral) therapies for chronic tension headaches. *Journal of Consulting and Clinical Psychology, 59,* 387-393.

272. Ivanoff, A., & Jang, S. J. (1991). The role of hopelessness and social desirability in predicting suicidal behavior: A study of prison inmates. *Journal of Consulting and Clinical Psychology, 59,* 394-399.

273. Jacobson, N. S., Dobson, K., Fruzzetti, A. E., Schmaling, K. B., Salusky, S. (1991). Marital therapy as a treatment for depression. *Journal of Consulting and Clinical Psychology, 59,* 547-557.

274. Joe, G. W., Knezek, L., Watson, D., & Simpson, D. D. (1991). Depression and decision-making among intravenous drug users. *Psychological Reports, 68,* 339-347.

275. Kelly, A. E., McKillop, K. J., & Neimeyer, G. J. (1991). Effects of counselor as audience on internalization of depressed and nondepressed self-presentations. *Journal of Counseling Psychology, 38,* 126-132.

276. Kelly, J. A., St. Lawrence, J. S., & Brasfield, T. L. (1991). Predictors of vulnerability to AIDS risk behavior relapse. *Journal of Consulting and Clinical Psychology, 59,* 163-166.

277. Nelson, L. D., & Cicchetti, D. (1991). Validity of the MMPI depression scale for outpatients. *Psychological Assessment, 3,* 55-59.

278. Ogles, B. M., Lambert, M. J., & Craig, D. E. (1991). Comparison of self-help books for coping with loss: Expectations and attributions. *Journal of Counseling Psychology, 38,* 387-393.

279. Pyant, C. T., & Yanico, B. J. (1991). Relationship of racial identity and gender-role attitudes to Black women's psychological well-being. *Journal of Counseling Psychology, 38,* 315-322.

280. Reynolds, S., & Gilbert, P. (1991). Psychological impact of unemployment: Interactive effects of vulnerability and protective factors on depression. *Journal of Counseling Psychology, 38,* 76-84.

281. Ruehlman, L. S., & Karoly, P. (1991). With a little flak from my friends: Development and preliminary validation of the test of negative social exchange (TENSE). *Psychological Assessment, 3,* 97-104.

282. Safran, J. D., & Wallner, L. K. (1991). The relative predictive validity of two therapeutic alliance measures in cognitive therapy. *Psychological Assessment, 3,* 188-195.

283. Sharpe, M. J., & Heppner, P. P. (1991). Gender role, gender-role conflict, and psychological well-being in men. *Journal of Counseling Psychology, 38,* 323-330.

284. Stroebe, M., & Stroebe, W. (1991). Does "grief work" work? *Journal of Consulting and Clinical Psychology, 59,* 479-482.

285. Sutker, P. B., Bugg, F., & Allain, A. N. (1991). Psychometric prediction of PTSD among POW survivors. *Psychological Assessment, 3,* 105-110.

286. Whisman, M. A., Miller, I. W., Norman, W. H., & Keitner, G. I. (1991). Cognitive therapy with depressed inpatients: Specific effects on dysfunctional cognitions. *Journal of Consulting and Clinical Psychology, 59,* 282-288.

Review of the Beck Depression Inventory [Revised Edition] by COLLIE W. CONOLEY, *Associate Professor of Educational Psychology, University of Nebraska-Lincoln, Lincoln, NE:*

The Beck Depression Inventory (BDI) was designed to measure the severity of depression in adolescents and adults already diagnosed as depressed. An important use of the BDI is examining the specific items as significant information about a person's experience of depression. The BDI has been shown to be predictive of suicidal behavior (Emery, Steer, & Beck, 1981; Lester & Beck, 1975; Silver, Bohnert, Beck, & Marcus, 1971). However, an important issue in the use of the BDI is its fakability (Beck & Beamesderfer, 1974; Davis, 1978) and relationship to social desirability (Beck, 1972; Langevin & Stancer, 1979; Strosahl, Linehan, & Chiles, 1984). Caution is imperative in using the BDI with persons who might wish to hide their suicidal intentions or, conversely, would like to overestimate their depression.

The BDI consists of 21 items with four options per item. The BDI is estimated to take the average person 5 to 10 minutes. The reading level is estimated at fifth grade level with the test designed for ages 13 years and older. The test may be administered orally in about 15 minutes.

The BDI has been used for over 25 years. The original version was developed in 1961 with a revision made in 1971. A brief search of the psychological literature revealed over 1,900 articles using the BDI. The BDI has been translated into many languages in addition to English. There are translations into Chinese, Spanish, French, German, Dutch, Arabic, and Persian. There are studies including many different U.S.A. cultural groups and people residing in other countries.

With the abundant information about the BDI it is disappointing that the manual is so meager. An invaluable addition to the information in the manual is the Beck, Steer, and Garbin (1988) review and meta-analysis of the reliability and validity literature for the BDI. The manual and review article in combination provide an abundance of information. Much of this review relies on information from the review article.

The manual suggests that cognitive, affective, vegetative, and somatic symptoms are identified by the BDI. However, these items are not identified as subscales or individually. Nor is there validity or reliability information differentially for these suggested functions. Two subscales are referred to in the manual: the cognitive-affective subscale and the somatic-performance subscale. The manual is not clear about the utility or origin of the subscales.

There are 13 factor analytic studies in the review article (Beck, Steer, & Garbin, 1988). Reported factor structures vary from one to seven. Beck, Steer, and Garbin attribute the variability of factors to the statistical analysis and population used by the different researchers.

The internal consistency rated by Cronbach's coefficient alpha (Beck et al., 1988) for 25 studies ranged from .73 to .95. The mean coefficient alphas for the nine psychiatric populations was .86. The mean coefficient alphas for the 15 nonpsychiatric populations was .81. The test-retest stability correlations for depression are troublesome because of the variability of a person's experience of depression. Pearson correlations for the nonpsychiatric samples ranged from .60 to .83. The psychiatric samples had correlations from .48 to .86. The time periods between testing ranged from hours to 4 months.

Content, construct, concurrent, and factorial validity studies are plentiful. The content validity is substantiated by comparing the BDI to the criteria of the American Psychiatric Association's Diagnostic and Statistical Manual on Mental Disorders. The BDI investigates six of the nine criteria. Steer and Beck (1985) defend the exclusions arguing that if all of the criteria were included in a self-report inventory the rate of false positives would increase to an unacceptable level.

The review article presented discriminate validity via 14 studies that tout fairly strong discriminate validity. It is important to consider that the BDI was not developed for discriminating between populations. As Beck (1967, Chapter 2) reminds us, depression is a phenomenon that occurs as part of many other mental and physical disorders.

The review article lists studies addressing construct validity. The BDI correlates as predicted with biological and somatological issues, suicidal behaviors, alcoholism, adjustment, and life crisis.

Concurrent validity studies are in abundance. Thirty-five such studies are listed in the review article. The BDI is compared to clinical ratings, the Hamilton Psychiatric Rating Scale for Depression (Hamilton, 1960), the Zung Self-Reported Depression Scale (Zung, 1965), the MMPI depression scale, and the Multiple Affect Adjective Checklist Depression Scale (Zuckerman & Lubin, 1965). The mean correlations for the concurrent validity studies ranged from .60 to .76.

Although not included in the manual, there are validity and reliability studies based upon an eight-item version of the BDI. It is referred to in the literature as the short form of the Beck Depression Inventory. Information about the short form is given in the review article. The short form is not commercially published.

There are some concerns about the use of the BDI. At times the BDI has been used for screening purposes for identification of depressed persons. The manual cautions about the use of the BDI for identification because of the false positive inflation. The manual provides cutoff scores for different levels of depression with warning about their use. It is unfortunate that the cutoff scores are given. Their only usefulness might be in research applications. Additionally, the cutoff scores are based upon the previous edition of the BDI.

The BDI has demographic correlates. Gender correlates with BDI scores. Women have been found to have slightly higher scores than men (e.g., Knight, 1984; Nielsen & Williams, 1980; Oliver & Simmons, 1985). Relative to age, adolescents score higher than adults (Albert & Beck, 1975; Levine, 1982; Teri, 1982). However, Schnurr, Hoaken, and Jarrett (1976) found that younger psychiatric patients scored lower than older psychiatric patients. Education attainment is negatively correlated to BDI scores (Beck, 1967; Dorus & Senay, 1980; Oliver & Simmons, 1985). Non-White persons were at times found to score higher than White persons (e.g., Oliver & Simmons, 1985). Beck, Steer, and Garbin (1988) suggest that although the demographic correlates are statistically significant, they are probably more important for researchers to attend to than for clinicians.

In summary, the BDI is a well-researched assessment tool with substantial support for its reliability and validity. When used clinically, care should be taken to use it as an indicator of extent of depression not as a diagnostic tool. Additionally, if used as a suicide screening tool its high fakability should be remembered.

REVIEWER'S REFERENCES

Hamilton, M. (1960). A rating scale for depression. *Journal of Neurology, Neurosurgery, and Psychiatry, 23*, 56-62.

Zuckerman, M., & Lubin, B. (1965). *Manual for the Multiple Affect Adjective Checklist*. San Diego, CA: Educational and Industrial Testing Service.

Zung, W. W. K. (1965). A self-rating depression scale. *Archives of General Psychiatry, 12*, 63-70.

Beck, A. T. (1967). *Depression: Causes and treatment*. Philadelphia: University of Pennsylvania Press.

Silver, M. A., Bohnert, M., Beck, A. T., & Marcus, D. (1971). Relation of depression of attempted suicide and seriousness of intent. *Archives of General Psychiatry, 25*, 573-576.

Beck, A. T. (1972). Measuring depression: The depression inventory. In T. A. Williams, M. M. Katz, & J. A. Shield, Jr. (Eds.), *Recent advances in the psychobiology of the depressive illnesses* (pp. 299-302). Washington, DC: U.S. Government Printing Office.

Beck, A. T., & Beamesderfer, A. (1974). Assessment of depression: The depression inventory. In P. Pichot (Ed.), *Modern problems of pharmacopsychiatry: Psychological measurements in psychopharmacology* (pp. 151-169). Basel, Switzerland: Karger.

Albert, N., & Beck, A. T. (1975). Incidence of depression in early adolescence: A preliminary study. *Journal of Youth and Adolescence, 4*, 301-307.

Lester, D., & Beck, A. T. (1975). Suicidal intent, medical lethality of the suicide attempt, and components of depression. *Journal of Clinical Psychology, 31*, 11-12.

Schnurr, R., Hoaken, P. C. S., & Jarrett, F. J. (1976). Comparison of depression inventories in a clinical population. *Canadian Psychiatric Association Journal, 21*, 473-476.

Davis, T. W. (1978). *"Faking good" and "faking bad" on the Beck Depression Inventory and variables which might contribute to "faking" by adult clients of a community mental health center*. Unpublished doctoral dissertation, Duke University, Durham, NC.

Langevin, R., & Stancer, H. (1979). Evidence that depression rating scales primarily measure a social undesirability response set. *Acta Psychiatrica Scandanavica, 59*, 70-79.

Dorus, W., & Senay, E. C. (1980). Depression, demographic dimensions, and drug abuse. *American Journal of Psychiatry, 137*, 699-704.

Nielsen, A. C., & Williams, T. A. (1980). Depression in ambulatory medical patients: Prevalence by self-report questionnaire and recognition by nonpsychiatric physicians. *Archives of General Psychiatry, 37*, 999-1004.

Emery, G. D., Steer, R. A., & Beck, A. T. (1981). Depression, hopelessness, and suicidal intent among heroin addicts. *International Journal of the Addictions, 16*, 425-429.

Levine, M. E. (1982). Depression in psychiatric admission to a military medical center. *Military Medicine, 147*, 752-755.

Teri, L. (1982). The use of the Beck Depression Inventory with adolescents. *Journal of Abnormal Child Psychology, 10*, 277-284.

Knight, R. G. (1984). Some general population norms for the short form Beck Depression Inventory. *Journal of Clinical Psychology, 40*, 751-753.

Strosahl, K. D., Linehan, M. M., & Chiles, J. A. (1984). Will the real social desirability please stand up? Hopelessness, depression, social desirability, and the prediction of suicidal behavior. *Journal of Consulting and Clinical Psychology, 52*, 449-457.

Oliver, J. M., & Simmons, M. E. (1985). Affective disorders and depression as measured by the Diagnostic Interview Schedule and the Beck Depression Inventory in an unselected adult population. *Journal of Clinical Psychology, 41*, 469-477.

Steer, R. A., & Beck, A. T. (1985). Modifying the Beck Depression Inventory: Reply to Vredenburg, Krames, and Flett. *Psychological Reports, 57*, 625-626.

Beck, A. T., Steer, R. A., & Garbin, M. G. (1988). Psychometric properties of the Beck Depression Inventory: Twenty-five years of evaluation. *Clinical Psychology Review, 8*, 77-100.

Review of the Beck Depression Inventory [Revised Edition] by NORMAN D. SUNDBERG, Professor Emeritus of Psychology, University of Oregon, Eugene, OR:

The Beck Depression Inventory (BDI) is probably the most widely used clinical self-report test of depression. Originally developed by Aaron Beck and his associates in 1961 as a structured interview, it came to be used as a short questionnaire and was revised at Beck's Center for Cognitive Therapy of the University of Pennsylvania in 1971. It was not until 1987 that a manual was published by Beck and Robert Steer. Beck is well known for his cognitive therapy approach, but the BDI is not tied to that theory. Over the years the usage has expanded from clinical settings to screening operations and research on many non-clinical samples.

The BDI consists of 21 items, or sets of statements, answered on a 0 to 3 scale of severity of depressive problems. Items and item weights were derived judgmentally, not empirically. The answer sheet is entitled BDI; depression is not mentioned, but most respondents would know the intent of the test. Instructions tell the respondent to consider feelings in the last week. Each of the 21 items has four sentences, ranging from no complaint to a severe complaint (e.g., "0—I do not feel sad" to "3—I am so sad or unhappy that I can't stand it"). On one side of the form the first 13 items cover the cognitive-affective subscale (on such topics as pessimism, guilt, self-accusations, crying, and indecisiveness), and on the reverse side 8 items form the somatic-performance subscale (on topics such as body image, work and sleep difficulties, and loss of interest in sex). The BDI is easily administered and scored by paraprofessionals. It can be answered in 5 to 10 minutes, and if the person answers more than one choice in an item, the highest answer is used in adding to obtain the total.

Typically, only the total score is used. In the manual, Beck and Steer suggest general guidelines with patients: 0 to 9 are within the normal range; 10 to 18, mild-moderate depression; 19 to 29, moderate-severe depression; and 30 and above, extremely severe depression. These suggestions are based on clinical ratings of patients. With normals, scores greater than 15 may suggest depression.

The 1987 manual by Beck and Steer is well done; it is readable, short but comprehensive (30 small pages including about 50 references), and useful for finding fundamental information about psychometrics. Data on six normative samples, including major depressive groups, dysthymics, alcoholics, heroin addicts, and a mixed diagnostic group are presented in tabular form. From various studies they report test-retest reliability with patients ranging from .48 to .86 and with nonpsychiatric samples from .60 to .90. The internal consistency is high—.86 with psychiatric patients (Beck, Steer, & Garbin, 1988), .88 with outpatients (Steer, Beck, & Brown, 1989), and .81 with nonpsychiatric subjects (Beck et al., 1988).

The manual and a review (Beck et al., 1988) report a studies of concurrent and construct validity. Meta-analyses have reported high mean correlations between the BDI and clinical ratings of depression both in psychiatric samples (.72) and normals (.60). BDI correlations with MMPI-D, Zung Self-rating Depression Scale, Hopelessness Scale, and Hamilton Scale are moderate to high. Studies of discriminant validity differentiate psychiatric patients from normals and dysthymics from major depressive disorders. The authors recognize that depression is common in many disorders but claim that the BDI can differentiate between major depression and anxiety disorders. Further study should be done, however, because anxiety and depression often overlap.

In regard to content validity, Beck and Steer defend the BDI items for not covering some parts of the *DSM-III* criteria for affective disorder; specifically they omit excesses of sleeping, appetite, and motor activity, saying that these are infrequent among depressives but common with normals. The manual reports a variety of results from factor analyses. One recent study with VA domiciliary patients shows a dominant first factor emphasizing cognitive aspects of depression (Louks, Hayne, & Smith, 1989); Steer (personal communication, December 17, 1990) raises questions about the adequacy of that sample and analysis, and elsewhere Beck et al. (1988) note that factors vary in different clinical samples.

In general, sex and age differences are small or nonsignificant. Reading requirements are low, and the BDI can be used with adolescents. It is used with the elderly, but Item 14 is age biased and may be wrongly scaled (Talbott, 1989). Empirical evidence for scaling all items is missing. There are indications of differences between socioeconomic groups. Differences related to membership in various cultural groups are not discussed in the manual but have received attention elsewhere. The BDI has been used extensively in both Great Britain and North America. A recent study shows no significant differences between Mexican-American and Caucasian elders (Gatewood-Colwell, Kaczmarek, & Ames, 1989). Translations of the BDI show variable applicability. Authors of a Chinese translation (Zheng, Wei, Lianggue, Guochen, & Chenggue, 1988) concluded the BDI could not be applied effectively in China. However, another report on usage in diverse languages is positive about cross-cultural application (Steer, Beck, & Garrison, 1986).

The manual mentions response sets briefly but does not attend adequately to intentional distortion. Dahlstrom, Brooks, and Peterson (1990) have demonstrated that changes in the order of the items affect BDI scores, and they point out the BDI items are obvious and susceptible to faking. At least one study (Cappeliez, 1989) has shown a negative correlation between social desirability and BDI scores among clinical elderly. The test user should be aware of a respondent's test-taking attitudes. Also the BDI is relatively state-oriented, because answers are based on the past week; results may not reflect earlier depressive episodes and may change over time. For certain purposes, it is useful to note differences between the cognitive and somatic subscales. For epidemiological studies, the CES-D (The Center for Epidemiological Studies—Depression, Radloff, 1977), specifically designed for that purpose, is probably better than the BDI.

In conclusion, the Beck Depression Inventory has made an important contribution to clinical and research work on depression. It is a simple, short, and specific measure for depression. For clinical purposes, of course, diagnosis must involve much more than this test alone.

REVIEWER'S REFERENCES

Radloff, L. S. (1977). The CES-D scale: A self-report depression scale for research in the general population. *Applied Psychological Measurement, 1*, 385-401.

Steer, R. A., Beck, A. T., & Garrison, B. (1986). Applications of the Beck Depression Inventory. In N. Sartorius & T. A. Ban (Eds.), *Assessment of depression* (pp. 121-142). Geneva, Switzerland: World Health Organization.

Beck, A. T., Steer, R. A., & Garbin, M. G. (1988). Psychometric properties of the Beck Depression Inventory: Twenty-five years of evaluation. *Clinical Psychology Review, 8*, 77-100.

Zheng, Y., Wei, L., Lianggue, G., Guochen, Z., & Chenggue, W. (1988). Applicability of the Chinese Beck Depression Inventory. *Comprehensive Psychiatry, 29*, 484-489.

Cappeliez, P. (1989). Social desirability response set and self-report depression inventories in the elderly. *Clinical Gerontologist, 9* (2), 45-52.

Gatewood-Colwell, G., Kaczmarek, M., & Ames, M. H. (1989). Reliability and validity of the Beck Depression Inventory for a White and Mexican-American gerontic population. *Psychological Reports*, 65, 1163-1166.

Louks, J., Hayne, C., & Smith, J. (1989). Replicated factor structure of the Beck Depression Inventory. *Journal of Nervous & Mental Disease*, 177, 473-479.

Steer, R. A., Beck, A. T., & Brown, G. (1989). Sex differences on the revised Beck Depression Inventory for outpatients with affective disorders. *Journal of Personality Assessment*, 53, 693-703.

Talbott, N. M. (1989). Age bias in the Beck Depression Inventory: A proposed modification for use with older women. *Clinical Gerontologist*, 9 (2), 23-35.

Dahlstrom, W. G., Brooks, J. D., & Peterson, C. D. (1990). The Beck Depression Inventory: Item order and the impact of response sets. *Journal of Personality Assessment*, 55, 224-233.

[32]
Beck Hopelessness Scale.

Purpose: Measures an individual's expectations about the long-range and short-range future.

Population: Ages 13–80.

Publication Date: 1978–88.

Acronym: BHS.

Comments: Self-administered; may be orally administered; used as a tool for detecting hopelessness and as an indirect indicator of suicidal risk; most appropriate for adults over age 17.

Scores: Total score only.

Administration: Group.

Price Data, 1990: $45 per complete kit including 25 record forms, scoring template, and manual ('88, 34 pages); $21.50 per 25 record forms (includes scoring template); $80 per 100 record forms; $4.50 per scoring template; $19 per manual.

Time: (5–10) minutes.

Authors: Aaron T. Beck and Robert A. Steer.

Publisher: The Psychological Corporation.

TEST REFERENCES

1. Platt, S. D., & Dyer, J. A. T. (1987). Psychological correlates of unemployment among male parasuicide in Edinburgh. *British Journal of Psychiatry*, 151, 27-32.

2. Wade, D. T., Legh-Smith, J., & Hewer, R. A. (1987). Depressed mood after stroke: A community study of its frequency. *British Journal of Psychiatry*, 151, 200-205.

3. Bond, M. J., & Feather, N. T. (1988). Some correlates of structure and purpose in the use of time. *Journal of Personality and Social Psychology*, 55, 321-329.

4. O'Brien, G., Hassanyeh, F., Leake, A., Schapira, K., White, M., & Ferrier, I. N. (1988). The dexamethasone suppression test in bulimia nervosa. *British Journal of Psychiatry*, 152, 654-656.

5. Cole, D. A., & Milstead, M. (1989). Behavioral correlates of depression: Antecedents or consequences? *Journal of Counseling Psychology*, 36, 408-416.

6. Greene, S. M. (1989). The relationship between depression and hopelessness: Implications for current theories of depression. *British Journal of Psychiatry*, 154, 650-659.

7. DeRubeis, R. J., Evans, M. D., Hollon, S. D., Garvey, M. J., Grove, W. M., & Tuason, V. B. (1990). How does cognitive therapy work? Cognitive change and symptom change in cognitive therapy and pharmacotherapy for depression. *Journal of Consulting and Clinical Psychology*, 58, 862-869.

8. Salkovskis, P. M., Atha, C., & Storer, D. (1990). Cognitive-behavioural problem solving in the treatment of patients who repeatedly attempt suicide: A controlled trial. *British Journal of Psychiatry*, 157, 871-876.

9. Schotte, D. E., Cools, J., & Payvar, S. (1990). Problem-solving deficits in suicidal patients: Trait vulnerability or state phenomenon? *Journal of Consulting and Clinical Psychology*, 58, 562-564.

10. Connell, D. K., & Meyer, R. G. (1991). Adolescent suicidal behavior and popular self-report instruments of depression, social desirability, and anxiety. *Adolescence*, 26, 113-119.

11. Dixon, W. A., Heppner, P. P., & Anderson, W. P. (1991). Problem-solving appraisal, stress, hopelessness, and suicide ideation in a college population. *Journal of Counseling Psychology*, 38, 51-56.

12. Ivanoff, A., & Jang, S. J. (1991). The role of hopelessness and social desirability in predicting suicidal behavior: A study of prison inmates. *Journal of Consulting and Clinical Psychology*, 59, 394-399.

13. Whisman, M. A., Miller, I. W., Norman, W. H., & Keitner, G. I. (1991). Cognitive therapy with depressed inpatients: Specific effects on dysfunctional cognitions. *Journal of Consulting and Clinical Psychology*, 59, 282-288.

Review of the Beck Hopelessness Scale by E. THOMAS DOWD, Professor and Director of Counseling Psychology, Kent State University, Kent, OH:

Aaron T. Beck and his colleagues have, over the years, developed a reputation for constructing and publishing several well-crafted and extensively validated and researched psychological instruments to measure a variety of cognitive phenomena. The present Beck Hopelessness Scale (BHS) follows in this tradition. Although it is relatively short (20 items), it possesses good psychometric characteristics and is backed by clinical data as well.

A major conceptual problem from the start is the definition of hopelessness. The construct, as measured by this scale, was defined by Stotland (1969) as negative expectancy about the future. As such, however, it overlaps with the third component of Beck's cognitive triad of depression, a negative view of the future. In addition, the manual refers to the concept of pessimism as if it were functionally equivalent to hopelessness. But the latter is future-oriented, whereas the former simply refers to a negative view of events. Exacerbating this problem is the ongoing debate in the literature, summarized in the manual and apparently not yet resolved, regarding the conceptual overlap of hopelessness and social desirability. Hopelessness, according to one view, can be seen as measuring the tendency to describe oneself in socially undesirable ways.

The manual provides a great deal of information linking hopelessness with suicide and indeed the assessment of suicide potential seems to be the primary purpose of the scale. Two clinical vignettes in the manual, however, describe how the scale can be used to resolve a clinical impasse and to facilitate movement in therapy. There are considerable data provided indicating that, although hopelessness is moderately correlated with depression, the former is a significantly better prediction of suicide intention and behavior than the latter.

The internal consistency reliability is excellent, with coefficients between .82 and .93 reported for seven different norm groups. The test-retest reliability is substantially lower, .69 after 1 week and .66 after 6 weeks. However, one might question just how stable the construct of hopelessness really is. Depression, a related construct, is known to be highly labile so perhaps it might be expected that hopelessness would be as well. If it is not stable, then of course the test-retest reliability coefficient would not be expected to be high. This issue is not addressed anywhere in the manual and represents one of the few deficits in the conceptualization and data collection on the scale. The amount of reliability data provided, especially test-retest, is quite skimpy and I would recommend that further data be incorporated in the next edition of the manual.

The validity information provided is more extensive, including content, concurrent, discriminant, construct, predictive, and factorial studies. Data are provided indicating that age and sex adjustments are not necessary. The predictive validity information indicates the scale has a very low false negative rate of prediction, between 6% and 9%. However, little information is given on the false positive rate of prediction; what there is seems to indicate a much higher rate, about 58%. Although false negatives are more important in suicide assessment than false positives, this is definitely an area for further study. The factorial validity is confusing. Different studies have found different factor structures. The remainder of the validity information is fairly straightforward.

Normative data are provided for seven groups: suicide ideators, suicide attempters, alcoholics, heroin addicts, single-episode major depressives, recurrent-episode major depressives, and dysthymics. Although the rationale for the selection of some of these groups is clear, it is not for others. I would recommend that data on additional norm groups be provided in the future.

A real strength of the manual is the section on the clinical uses of the BHS. Four clinical vignettes are provided, with a good description of how the BHS was used in each. I would suggest this section be expanded in future editions, with additional vignettes.

The manual provides detailed descriptions of the administration and scoring of the BHS, as well as appropriate uses and user qualifications. A scoring template is provided, although the instrument is so easy to score that one is not really necessary. However, it is obvious the manual's authors, Aaron Beck and Robert Steer, have done a thorough job in describing the characteristics of the scale and its uses.

In summary, the BHS is a well-constructed and validated instrument, with adequate reliability. Although it appears to overlap conceptually with other psychological constructs, its use in suicide assessment is well demonstrated. Additional normative data and other uses should be developed in the future, as well as further data on the stability of hopelessness in various populations.

REVIEWER'S REFERENCE

Stotland, E. (1969). *The psychology of hope*. San Francisco: Jossey-Bass.

Review of the Beck Hopelessness Scale by STEVEN V. OWEN, Professor of Educational Psychology, University of Connecticut, Storrs, CT:

The Beck Hopelessness Scale (BHS) has been used experimentally and clinically since 1974. It is a brief and straightforward measure: 20 self-report items inquire about negative beliefs concerning the respondent's future. The negative future orientation is built on a theoretical base, and fits with Beck's own model of depression.

The response format is True-False, so responding can be rapid. Some persons will vacillate, or be perturbed that they cannot squeeze between True and False. The possible complaint that a T–F response scale is too limited is an empirical question; the psychometric evidence for the BHS suggests the format is satisfactory. Interpretation of BHS scores is assisted by suggested ranges (e.g., a score of 15–20 indicates severe hopelessness), but the authors caution that cut scores are situational and therefore flexible. Cut points are readily modified to reduce false positives or, depending on the circumstances, to reduce false negatives. A second caution is that the BHS is not meant to give definitive diagnostic advice, but to serve as a rapid screening tool. The authors provide several realistic vignettes to illustrate such uses.

The most extensive normative data for the BHS have been gathered at the Center for Cognitive Therapy at the University of Pennsylvania Medical School. It is difficult to guess how generalizable these normative data are, although the validity studies reported by Beck and Steer in the (1988) BHS manual suggest that hopelessness manifestations are similar throughout English-speaking countries.

In the manual, Beck and Steer offer evidence of strong internal consistency for the BHS (mean coefficient = .87). Stability estimates are considerably smaller (mean = .68), suggesting that hopelessness is somewhat transient, which should be a positive sign for clinicians. A moderate stability coefficient implies the construct can be altered with a suitable intervention. A significant omission is information about standard errors of measurement, essential for scores that focus on individual assessment.

Validity evidence is partitioned into six categories, which seems contrary to the more modern trend to treat all such evidence as special cases of construct validity. The use of multiple categories of validity also increases the likelihood of definitions in disagreement with those of other analysts. For example, Beck and Steer's category "Discriminant Validity" has no bearing on Campbell and Fiske's (1959) classic use of the same phrase. Nevertheless, the forms of validity evidence are largely supportive of the BHS, particularly regarding its relationship to suicidal behaviors.

A conspicuous weakness in evidence occurs with "Factorial Validity." As though exploratory principal components could steer theory, Beck and Steer used the analysis "[t]o determine whether or not the BHS represents a homogeneous set of items reflecting hopelessness, as opposed to complex subsets of items representing distinct scales" (p. 18). The description and detail of the components analyses are very sketchy, and the different results (three versus five components) suggest factorial variability. The lack of congruence could also result from one of the analyses having far too few subjects to produce a stable structure. Or possibly the solutions were forced into orthogonal structures when oblique components fit the data better. No matter what the explanation, there is no excuse for ignoring much more powerful analyses to inspect the latent structure of the construct. In particular, confirmatory factor procedures are especially well suited for measures that are carefully embedded in theory, such as the BHS.

The last few pages of the manual detail a somewhat tedious debate about the confounding of social desirability and hopelessness responses. Because the authors' conclusion—false positives are better than false negatives—is persuasive, this space could be put to more effective use with additional validity evidence, particularly from confirmatory factor analysis.

In summary, the BHS is a simple tool with fairly robust psychometric properties. As such, it can be a useful screening tool in the clinician's workbox of diagnostic measures.

REVIEWER'S REFERENCE

Campbell, D. T., & Fiske, D. W. (1959). Convergent and discriminant validation by the multitrait-multimethod matrix. *Psychological Bulletin, 56,* 81-105.

[33]
Becker Work Adjustment Profile.

Purpose: Provides "information about the work habits, attitudes and skills of individuals in sheltered and competitive work."
Population: Mentally retarded, physically disabled, emotionally disturbed, learning disabled, and economically disadvantaged, ages 15 and over.
Publication Date: 1989.
Acronym: BWAP.
Scores, 5: Work Habits/Attitudes, Interpersonal Relations, Cognitive Skills, Work Performance Skills, Broad Work Adjustment.
Administration: Individual.
Price Data: Available from publisher.
Time: (10–15) minutes for Short Scale; (20–25) minutes for Full Scale.
Comments: Ratings by teachers, counselors, or other vocational professionals; 2 forms: Short Scale, Full Scale.
Authors: Ralph L. Becker.
Publisher: Elbern Publications.

Review of the Becker Work Adjustment Profile by BRIAN BOLTON, *Professor, Arkansas Research and Training Center in Vocational Rehabilitation, University of Arkansas, Fayetteville, AR:*

The Becker Work Adjustment Profile (BWAP) is an observer rating instrument designed for use with persons with physical, intellectual, and emotional disabilities who are clients in vocational rehabilitation programs. The primary purpose of the BWAP is to identify deficits in clients' work behavior that can be remediated in vocational training facilities. Use of the BWAP assumes the evaluator has had ample opportunity to observe the client in a simulated or real work setting.

The conceptual domain measured by the BWAP includes work skills, habits, attitudes, and personal traits that comprise "vocational competency," a construct of central importance in vocational rehabilitation. The BWAP consists of 63 items that are allocated to four subscales: Work Habits/Attitudes (10), Interpersonal Relations (12), Cognitive Skills (19), and Work Performance Skills (22). A total score, called Broad Work Adjustment, is also calculated.

Each of the 63 BWAP items is briefly defined with a description 6 to 12 words in length. The standard 5-point rating format is behaviorally anchored for each item. The instrument is published in an attractive consumable booklet that expedites the approximately 20-minute rating process. The Manual is well organized, with helpful sections describing the instrument and giving directions for administration, scoring, and interpretation of the resulting profile.

Scoring the four subscales is accomplished by summing the raw item ratings, which range from 0 to 4. The total score is the sum of the four subscale scores. Raw scale scores are translated into percentile equivalents, normalized *T*-scores, and stanines using standardization samples representing four populations of vocational rehabilitation clients: mental retardation, medical disabilities, emotional disturbance, and learning disabilities. All clients in the normative samples were participating in vocational adjustment programs conducted in workshop facilities.

Potential BWAP items were located by reviewing existing work behavior scales and the professional literature on work evaluation of persons with disabilities, supplemented by suggestions given by experienced work evaluators during interviews. The four subscales were constructed by factor analysis of preliminary item pools (principal factor condensation and varimax rotation of four factors retained by the scree criterion).

Because the BWAP subscales are scored by summing raw item ratings, the subscales are not uncorrelated. The intercorrelations range from .55 to .79, with Cognitive Skills having somewhat lower correlations with the other subscales. Considering the good reliability (see below), there is still substantial variance unique to the subscale profile; at the same time, a total vocational competency score is also warranted.

Three types of reliability evidence are given for the BWAP subscales: internal consistency, rerating by the same evaluator after 2 weeks, and interrater agreement by independent evaluators. The median coefficients for the three kinds of reliability are .87, .86, and .82 respectively. Although these three reliability estimates have somewhat different interpretations, it can be concluded that the BWAP is a reliable rating instrument.

Several kinds of evidence support the validity of the BWAP. The multiple item sources and developmental factor analysis that pertain to content sampling have already been mentioned. The pattern of relationships obtained with the concurrently administered Adaptive Behavior Scale includes high positive correlations with social and vocational competencies and negative correlations with maladaptive behavior indices. These data indicate the BWAP measures the presence of prosocial capabilities and the absence of maladaptive tendencies.

Average BWAP scores for four diagnostic categories of mentally retarded clients (profound, severe, moderate, mild) correspond to the degree of intellectual handicap present. Emotionally disturbed clients scored lower on Interpersonal Relations, a result consistent with the central feature of the disabling condition (i.e., difficulty with social and emotional adjustment). One important type of validity evidence missing is data relating BWAP scores to successful completion of different types of vocational placements (see below).

There are no sex differences on the BWAP, and older clients tend to score only slightly lower on Cognitive Skills. However, measured intelligence is very highly correlated with the Cognitive Skills subscale. The correlation of .81 approaches the theoretical maximum, reflecting the nature of the Cognitive Skills items (e.g., memory, reading level, problem solving, and job task learning). Hence, the Cognitive Skills subscale may be regarded as an index of intellectual functioning. Although the correlations of IQ with Work Performance Skills (.57), Habits/Attitudes (.39), and Interpersonal Relations (.30) are somewhat lower, it is apparent that the BWAP is, in part, measuring intelligence.

The considerable impact of intelligence on BWAP ratings has implications for the interpretation of normative scores. First, the mentally retarded (MR) norm group includes clients from four classifications with widely varying mean IQs (given in parentheses): mild (66), moderate (46), severe (28), and profound (13). Second, the other three normative samples contain many clients with below-average intelligence (mean IQs in parentheses): physically disabled (66), emotionally disturbed (82), and learning disabled (83). Two suggestions follow: (a) The single MR norm group is too heterogeneous and should be separated into subgroups, and (b) client intellectual level should be taken into account when interpreting BWAP scores using the other norm samples.

Providing separate norms for each of the four mentally retarded subgroups would substantially reduce the influence of IQ on BWAP normative scores for this client population. The use of an independent measure of client intellectual functioning in conjunction with the interpretation of scores derived from the physically disabled, emotionally disturbed, and learning disabled norm groups would accomplish a similar objective, especially for low-scoring clients from these populations.

A major problem concerns the recommended procedure for translating BWAP profiles into five competency levels located on a continuum of job placement potential (i.e., community-competitive, transitional sheltered, extended workshop, work activity, day care). As noted above, there are no empirical data to support this interpretation and, moreover, the suggested procedure entails the use of normative scores. Thus, the placement level identified is contingent on the norm group selected. Instead, program placement should be determined on the basis of absolute performance level. Criterion-related validity studies are essential to this type of predictive interpretation of the BWAP profile.

A BWAP Short Scale composed of the "best" 32 items (i.e., those with the highest subscale factor loadings and the highest item-total score correlations) is also available. The main problem with the Short Scale is the loss of diagnostic information. Fully half of the behaviors and traits comprising vocational competency are omitted. Because the rater time saved is minimal (10 minutes or less), the Short Scale should not be used for standard evaluation purposes.

In summary, the BWAP is a comprehensive and easily administered behavior rating instrument for use with vocational rehabilitation clients. The manual clearly presents directions for administering, scoring, and interpreting BWAP results. The behaviorally anchored items generate reliable information for diagnostic purposes and the validity evidence supports the interpretation of the BWAP as a measure of vocational competency. The recommended procedure for deciding program placement levels should be disregarded, however.

Review of the Becker Work Adjustment Profile by ELLIOT L. GORY, Psychologist, Getz School for the Developmentally Disabled, Tempe, AZ:

The Becker Work Adjustment Profile (BWAP) is a norm-referenced questionnaire scale designed to assess the work habits, attitudes, and skills of individuals in sheltered and competitive work. The BWAP is useful for individuals age 15 years through adulthood. Four separate norm reference groups used in test construction and for whom the

BWAP is appropriate include: mentally retarded, emotionally disturbed, learning disabled/economically disadvantaged, and physically disabled/cerebral palsy. Single reference group conversion tables were constructed for learning disabled and economically disadvantaged as well as physically disabled and cerebral palsy. A combined norm table for learning disabled/economically disadvantaged and combined norm table for physically disabled/cerebral palsy is justified adequately in terms of statistical analysis and rationale.

The BWAP is simple in design and used appropriately with minimal training or after review of the Evaluator's Manual. The scale is designed to be completed by those familiar with an individual's work behavior such as counselors, vocational trainers, teachers, and vocational evaluators. The BWAP consists of an Evaluator's Manual and questionnaire booklets available in a Short (32 items) or Long (63 items) Form. The Long Form takes about 20 minutes to administer, and the Short Form requires about half that time. The Short Form was constructed of the items with the highest factor loadings and item-score correlations. However, the brevity with which the Long Form can be completed minimizes the need for a Short Form. Completion of the Long Form permits consideration of data provided by 31 additional items, which may be helpful in constructing specific individualized vocational training programs.

Test content consists of items factor analyzed and distributed within four domains: (a) Work Habits/Attitudes—attendance, punctuality, personal hygiene, motivation, work posture; (b) Interpersonal Relations—social interaction, emotional stability, cooperation; (c) Cognitive Skills—knowledge, reasoning, recognizing, judging, functional academics; and (d) Work Performance Skills—motor, job responsibility, communication, work efficiency.

The domains are well described in the manual, and brief item definitions in the questionnaire booklets are helpful in accurately understanding a given item. Test items are scored by using a 5-point rating scale. Each point on the scale corresponds to a recognizable or generally definable behavior pattern. Each test item is developmental in nature, as descriptions of each item behavior progress in vocational competency from the lower through the upper end of the 5-point scale. The items are logical and easy to understand.

Once the scale is completed and raw scores listed, reference to the appropriate norm reference group in the manual permits the ready conversion of raw score data to *T*-scores, percentiles, and stanines that describe an individual's performance with respect to his/her respective norm reference group. These derived scores are based on a representative sample of subjects working in vocational training programs

and work centers throughout the United States and Canada. Further, percentiles can be used to generate a graphic Peer Profile of an individual's relative domain strengths and weaknesses. An Employability Status Profile can also be developed that rates an individual's vocational competency level from Low to High and yields decision and prognostic information for placement options that include: day care, work activity, extended workshop, transitional sheltered, and community-competitive. A summary Broad Work Adjustment score based on total test performance is available and is helpful in global summaries or general decisions about an individual's vocational status.

Reliability and validity information is clearly presented in the manual. Reliability coefficients are high and are based on content, test-retest, and interrater comparisons. Content, concurrent, and construct validity data are also described in the manual and provide strong support that the BWAP measures the vocational behaviors and characteristics for which the test is intended. The manual describes a norm sample that is geographically representative of the United States, is current, and includes sufficient numbers of individuals with specified characteristics for assignment to the various norm reference groups. Means and standard deviations are available in the manual related to different levels of mental retardation.

In conclusion, the Becker Work Adjustment Profile is an inexpensive, clear, useful rating scale designed to assess vocational proficiency in teenagers and adults who have learning disabilities, mental retardation, physical disability, emotional disabilities, cerebral palsy, or economic disadvantage. The use of different norm-reference groups represents an advantage of the BWAP over other scales such as the San Francisco Vocational Competency Scale and Camelot Behavioral Checklist which have single norm-reference groups of adults who have mental retardation. The BWAP is easy to understand, administer, and score following brief training or review of the manual. Results are summarized in a manner that permits comparison of an individual with a norm-reference group specific to the individual's area of disability or economic background. The BWAP yields information useful in constructing individual training activities, making individual program placement decisions, assessing progress, and making general program plans for groups of individuals based on BWAP scores of individuals within the group. The Becker Work Adjustment Profile is recommended as an efficient and useful instrument for assessment of work behavior, work related behavior, and attitudes. The instrument is suitable for use both on a selective case basis and for broad routine administration in vocational centers, workshops, and public school vocational and special education programs.

[34]
Bedside Evaluation and Screening Test of Aphasia.

Purpose: "To provide clinicians with a profile of a patient's language residuals in each modality on a continuum of severity ranging from no impairment to global impairment."
Population: Patients with language deficits.
Publication Date: 1987.
Acronym: BEST.
Scores, 8: Conversational Expression, Naming Objects, Describing Objects, Repeating Sentences, Pointing to Objects, Pointing to Parts of a Picture, Reading, Total.
Administration: Individual.
Levels, 4: A, B, C, D.
Price Data: Available from publisher.
Time: (15–25) minutes.
Authors: Joyce Fitch-West and Elaine S. Sands.
Publisher: Aspen Publishers, Inc.

Review of the Bedside Evaluation and Screening Test of Aphasia by MALCOLM R. McNEIL, Professor of Communicative Disorders, University of Wisconsin-Madison, Madison, WI:

The Bedside Evaluation and Screening Test of Aphasia (BEST) is designed for use with patients who have acquired language deficits. It is designed for the efficient assessment of acute aphasic patients for whom a comprehensive test battery is not indicated. Conditions of this contraindication are not discussed. It is recommended for administration in hospital settings, nursing homes, rehabilitation centers, and patient residences. Although designed by and for speech/language pathologists, it is recommended for use without formal training "by other health care professionals such as registered nurses, occupational therapists, and psychologists" (manual, p. 2). Presumably it would also be appropriate for use by other professionals concerned with the assessment of aphasia such as neurologists, psychiatrists, physiatrists, etc.

The stated goals of the test are to profile language residuals in several language modalities in order to determine the overall severity of impairment, type of aphasia, degree of aphasia, and presence of bilateral hemispheric brain damage so as to aid diagnosis, discharge, and follow-up. The criterion for administration of the BEST is that the patient is able to sit in bed and maintain eye contact with the examiner (presumably for the duration of the test administration).

The stated main advantages of the BEST over other aphasia tests include: (*a*) the ease of physical manipulation of the test objects which is achieved through a magnetic board and magnetized objects which can be placed easily on a patient's lap or bedside traytable; (*b*) the test's portability; (*c*) the ease of test administration with instructions contained on the test form itself, eliminating the need for a separate test manual; (*d*) the test items are "relatively 'culture free'"; and (*e*) a rapid administration time (maximum of 20 minutes), which is achieved through the design of the test's administration in which the examiner can alternate levels of stimulus item difficulty based on the patient's performance. The test is accompanied by (*a*) a scoring summary sheet with descriptive severity adjectives for subtest and overall scores, and (*b*) a prose summary (Summary of Test Results Form) in which the test scores are entered into a descriptive evaluation of the patient's strengths and weaknesses in speaking, auditory comprehension, reading, general cognitive and linguistic/communicative characteristics, and a statement of prognosis with a recommendation for or against a period of "trial . . . language therapy."

It is stated explicitly that a comprehensive aphasia battery be administered, in addition to the BEST, before any long-term course of action with a patient is planned or executed. However, the written summary (Part VII Prognosis) recommended for placement into the medical charts or patient's folders invites prognostic statements, decisions for treatment candidacy, treatment focus, discharge, etc., based on BEST results.

CONTENT VALIDITY. The magnetized items used to elicit the responses to be scored are: three replications of postage stamps, three nails, three candles, three buttons, three door-style keys, five large-print single words, five large-print subject-verb-object sentences, one pictured cartoon with caption, and one medium large-print factual paragraph. One nonmagnetized laminated page contains five sentences with the final word of the sentence eliminated and a three-choice closed set printed below the sentence for the answers to the reading subtest.

The authors state that these items are relatively culture free; however, no information is provided about such critical psycholinguistic variables as frequency of occurrence with which these words or sentence structures occur within the English language, the items' operativity, semantic prototypicality, or imageability. With the exception of two of the simulated stamps, and perhaps the clarity of the *New Yorker* magazine cartoon, the objects of the test are large enough and clearly printed to be identifiable. The items are easily manually manipulable and the written stimuli are easily legible.

The tasks performed by the patient on each of the seven subtests (each subtest having five items with Subtest VII having three separate subparts with five items in each) are similar to tasks on other aphasia tests and, therefore, may have some degree of concurrent validity. However, the validity of some of the subtests must be questioned. For example, it is not obvious that the Conversational Expression subtest (Subtest I) measures much information that is critical to the description of conversational spoken or unspoken intercourse. Without well-constructed logical arguments or correlational data from tests purported to measure similar functions, this subtest must be considered to be mislabeled, though perhaps a valid measure of personally relevant and automatic word selection and production (naming and serial counting). The BEST may not assess any verbal skills that are traditionally assessed in a syntactic (e.g., sentence types used or number of agrammatic sentences), pragmatic (e.g., ability to maintain or change topic), or discourse (e.g., coherence or cohesion indices) analyses of spoken language. The single imperative (Item 1), the three interrogative (Items 2, 3, and 4) sentences that are correctly answered by one or two word phrases, and the 1-to-20 counting task (Item 5) require only the correct lexical selection and production. By most standards, this does not provide a valid sample of speech with which to judge interpersonal conversational skills.

Instructions for test administration are generally, but not always, clear. For example, it is not clear to the examiner whether all 15 test objects are present on the magnetic board or whether only those five items to be named are presented for Subtest II, Naming Objects. The orientation of the objects on the board is not specified for any of the subtests, a factor that could conceivably be a source of performance variability for some subjects, especially those with concomitant visual perceptual deficits.

Subtest III, Describing Objects, requires the patient to give a short answer for Items 1, 3, and 4 and to select the correct lexical color name for Item 2 or the correct shape for Item 5. There is sufficient cognitive and linguistic heterogeneity among these commands to conclude that at least two of the items are better characterized as lexical retrieval than object description tasks per se (acknowledging that word retrieval is a rudimentary form of object description and identifying object attributes is a form of word retrieval).

Subtest IV, Repeating Sentences, requires the repetition of five different six-word prepositional phrases. Subtest V, Pointing To Objects, requires the differential identification of objects from a short description. Subtest VI, Pointing to Parts of a Picture, requires the identification of one or two men from a picture, given the context of a prepositional phrase. These sentences appear to be relatively homogeneous within subtests as do the cues. Subtest VII requires reading the paragraph within a 2-minute time limit and pointing to one of three closed set answers that completes a written sentence about the story for Level A, pointing to objects in the cartoon from declarative sentences in

Level B, or pointing to objects in the cartoon from single printed words in Level C.

The internal consistency of the subtests has not been addressed by the test authors. There is, however, considerable reason to question it. For example, on Subtest I, Item 1, the Level B cue following the command to "tell me your name" is a sentence completion task, "My name is _____," with the patient's first name given as a stimulus for the last name. The Level C cue is the same sentence completion task with the first name and the first phoneme of the patient's last name given. However, the Level B cue for the interrogative, "How old are you?" for Item 2 of this subtest is "I am _____ years old." The equivalency of these two items and their respective cues must be demonstrated in order to have confidence that these two test items represent two exemplars of the same task. In addition, the syntactic difference between the imperative and the interrogative forms provides sufficient concern for their equivalency. The same concerns for the heterogeneity of items within subtests are apparent in Subtest III. Although it appears from a cursory inspection of the within-subtest items for the other four subtests (excluding the Reading subtest which has three distinct subparts) that they are more homogeneous, no item analyses are reported for any of the subtests.

The BEST contains no elicitation or evaluation of writing, gesture, or pantomime. Writing tasks were said to have been eliminated following "extensive field testing . . . [because] they gave relatively little useful diagnostic information" (manual, p. 1). No data are presented to substantiate these conclusions. No explanation for omitting the evaluation of gesture or the assessment of pantomime was offered. The elimination of these modalities from the BEST is counter to the majority of aphasia tests and antithetical (particularly for the writing) to the test's sensitivity for detection or differential diagnostic and therapeutic information likely gained by their inclusion.

The "Patient Profile" is judged on the presence of what the authors refer to as: (a) Bilateral Signs, (b) Response Appropriateness, and (c) Fluency Rating. "Functional" bilateral cerebral hemisphere involvement is determined by a positive answer to a questionnaire for any one of the following signs: Incontinence; Emotional lability; Orientation to time, place, or person; Swallowing and drooling problems; Persisting dysarthria. Although the authors suggest obtaining these data from the medical records, no methods for eliciting any of these behaviors or criteria for detecting the presence of any of them are offered by the test's authors. In addition, no differential diagnosis is required for the etiology of the incontinence or the emotional lability, in spite of the possibility for their presence for several reasons other than bilateral cerebral hemisphere involvement. Likewise, if a person *is* oriented to where they are in time, where they are in space, and who they are, they are typically considered to be *normal* rather than show any sign of pathology. The simple presence of dysphagia or persisting dysarthria are not pathognomonic of bilateral cerebral involvement and are well documented to be caused from unilateral (typically, though not exclusively, lower motor neuron) involvement. Similar validity concerns are present for selecting candidates for treatment from the "Response Appropriateness" questionnaire and from the "Fluency Rating" characteristics used for classifying the patient into *fluent* or *nonfluent* aphasia categories.

CONSTRUCT AND PREDICTIVE VALIDITY. The authors provide no theoretical framework within which they define aphasia or from which the BEST was constructed. Likewise, there are no predictive validity data presented, in spite of the call for a prognostic statement of "recovery of functional language" and a recommendation for or against a "trial period of language therapy" based on the test results.

CONCURRENT VALIDITY. Twenty undefined and undescribed aphasic patients were reported to have been given the Porch Index of Communicative Ability (PICA; Porch, 1969), the Body-Part Identification, Word Discrimination, and the Severity Rating of the Boston Diagnostic Aphasia Examination (BDAE; Goodglass & Kaplan, 1983), the "Token Test" (TT), and the BEST. The BDAE Body-Part Identification and Word Discrimination subtests along with the Severity Rating was correlated with the BEST. The reliability with which the BDAE can measure these aphasic behaviors has not been reported (McNeil, 1989), thus making any correlation with the BEST uninterpretable. The authors report a coefficient of +.85 between the BEST Auditory subtests and the "Token Test." They do not, however, provide a reference for the "Token Test," and there is no published test by that name (although there are other published tests with "Token Test" as part of their title). In general, the most reliable and interpretable concurrent validity data for the BEST was derived from its correlation with the PICA. In general (though not invariably), those subtests on the BEST correlated more highly with subtests on the PICA that shared the same descriptions (e.g., Auditory = +.76, Verbal = +.88).

SCORING. No information is provided about the ordinality or intervality of the test's scoring system. In addition, no attempt has been made to establish that any one score on one subtest is equivalent to that score on any other subtest (in terms of the severity of the aphasia or the degree of impairment of communicative ability). Though the issues of ordinality, intervality, and score equivalency are difficult to explicate experimentally, they are necessary to address before the scores of the BEST can be summed, before the test is interpretable as a measure of aphasia severity, or before it can be used for any of the other purposes for which it was designed.

In some instances, the target "correct" response is not clear to the examiner. For example, on Subtest I, Item 1, the command is to give his/her name. However, it is not specified if a first and last name is needed for a score of 6. Given that only a last name is required for the Levels B and C cues, it might be reasonable to assume that only the final name is required.

The ability to supply a cue for the elicitation of a correct response following an incorrect one (e.g., the close technique or a phoneme cue) is rare among aphasia tests, though found in others such as the Porch Index of Communicative Ability (Porch, 1969) and the Boston Naming Test (Goodglass, Kaplan, & Weintraub, 1983). The use of a bracketing procedure for administering the stimuli within a subtest (the level of cues provided) is unique in aphasia testing; however, without experimental evidence that failure on one item leads reliably to failure on subsequent items, the procedure of administering subsequent items at a particular level of cuing must be questioned. Likewise, the procedure of discontinuing testing following two consecutive failures at the C level of cuing must be validated with experimental evidence that failure at that level leads reliably to failure on all subsequent items within that subtest. No such confirmatory data are provided in the test's manual.

RELIABILITY. The authors state that "Since the items are intentionally few in number and the intended patients are at their most acute and, accordingly, most variable phase, traditional reliability assessments are not possible" (manual, p. 7). There are, therefore, no scorer or test reliabilities reported for the BEST.

TEST DEVELOPMENT AND STANDARDIZATION. There are no data presented on the process of selecting test stimuli, tasks, or scoring procedures. No normal or pathological reference data are reported for the test.

SUMMARY. The BEST represents an attempt to fill a much needed void for an adequate screening tool for aphasia. No adequate screening test precedes the BEST. Although there is much to like about the physical attributes of the BEST and to potentially like about the hierarchical organization of the test administration (i.e., the test levels or levels of cuing), without clear evidence of high test-retest, interjudge, and intrajudge reliabilities there is insufficient evidence to have confidence in the test's ability to elicit the behaviors necessary for detecting, differentiating, describing, or quantifying aphasic behavior. Without better concurrent validity (logic or data) there is insufficient evidence to believe that the BEST adequately captures the relevant behavior necessary for achieving any of the test's stated purposes. There is no theoretical context in which to place the test's development or to interpret the test data that are obtained. There is a complete absence of reliability and reference (pathological or normal) data. The validity with which the BEST's main purpose of detecting the presence of aphasia is shown has not been addressed by the test's creators. These factors conspire to yield sufficient concern for all aspects of the test to prevent recommending its use for any of the purposes for which it was designed.

REVIEWER'S REFERENCES

Porch, B. E. (1967). *Porch Index of Communicative Ability. Vol. II. Administration, scoring and interpretation.* Palo Alto, CA: Consulting Psychologists Press, Inc.
Goodglass, H., & Kaplan, E. (1983). The Assessment of Aphasia and Related Disorders (2nd ed.). Philadelphia: Lea & Febiger.
Goodglass, H., Kaplan, E., & Weintraub, S. (1983). Boston Naming Test. Philadelphia: Lea & Febiger.
McNeil, M. R. (1989). [Review of The Assessment of Aphasia and Related Disorders.] In J. C. Conoley & J. J. Kramer (Eds.), *The tenth mental measurements yearbook* (pp. 37-43). Lincoln, NE: Buros Institute of Mental Measurements.

[35]
Behavior Analysis Language Instrument.

Purpose: "Identifies student/client deficits across a range of beginning language skill areas."
Population: Individuals with severe and profound handicaps.
Publication Date: 1988.
Acronym: BALI.
Scores: Item scores only; 4 language skill areas: Receptive Skills, Expressive Labeling Skills, Requesting Skills, Beginning Conversational Skills.
Administration: Individual.
Price Data: Available from publisher.
Time: Administration time not reported.
Comments: "Criterion-referenced"; other test materials (e.g., pictures of items) must be supplied by examiner.
Authors: Ennio Cipani, Dionyse Johnston, Susan Burger, Liz Torres, Twyla Rowe, and Holly Reynolds.
Publisher: Edmark Corporation.

Review of the Behavior Analysis Language Instrument by MARY ELLEN PEARSON, Professor of Special Education, Mankato State University, Mankato, MN:

PURPOSE. The Behavior Analysis Language Instrument (BALI) was designed for practitioners who work with severely and profoundly handicapped children, adolescents, or adults. The BALI is a criterion-referenced instrument intended to identify specific language deficits for the purpose of developing individualized behavioral objectives. The authors state that functional language skills should be high priority objectives for persons with severe/profound handicaps; thus, the BALI was developed to provide functional objectives at the beginning level of language.

CONTENTS. The BALI is a spiral-bound 184-page book that includes directions, four areas of language to assess, word lists for substituting appropriate vocabulary, and an appendix, which provides sample data, objectives, and an individual educational plan. Each of over 150 data sheets provides space for documenting 10 trials for 10 language items. The examiner must provide many everyday items or pictures of the everyday items to complete the test materials. The BALI may be used alone or with the Behavior Analysis Language Program (BALP), which is an explanation of the behavioral approach to language.

TECHNICAL WORK. The authors provided no technical work regarding validity or reliability.

ASSESSMENT ITEMS. The instrument assesses four areas of language in the following parts: (*a*) Receptive, (*b*) Expressive Labeling, (*c*) Requesting, and (*d*) Beginning Conversational Skill. The practitioner chooses the areas to be assessed and chooses from many possible items in each of the four areas. The Receptive items that assess receptive language consist of 20 commands such as "Look at me." The items in the area of expressive language require the examinee to provide the names of 32 objects, most of them through the question, "What is this?" The five Requesting items include a contrived situation in which the client requests a missing object by name, such as an article of clothing. The section assessing Beginning Conversational Skills includes 98 items, which are direct questions or commands such as "What do you eat for breakfast?" and "Name some cold drinks," for the client to answer. Most of the items can be expanded by choosing several examples from the word lists provided. For instance, the item requesting clothing could also include pants, socks, a coat, and a sweater. Consequently, the instrument provides a potential bank of hundreds of items.

STRENGTHS OF THE INSTRUMENT. The authors have provided a format developed from the behavioral model for gathering data at the beginning level of language. The BALI is flexible, easy to use, and provides data sheets and specific, well-written behavioral objectives. The instructions are satisfactory, and the authors have attempted to choose words that are functionally appropriate for persons with severe/profound handicaps. Examples include words for money, kitchen and laundry objects, leisure activities, clothing, emergency numbers, name and address, as well as school objects.

WEAKNESSES OF THE INSTRUMENT. Although the BALI has several strengths, it also has some weaknesses. The most obvious weakness is the lack of technical information. Because the purpose of the BALI is to develop objectives for program planning, the practitioner would not expect a great deal of technical information; however, the authors did not address this issue at all. The practitioner should expect a complete rationale concerning the development of the instrument, and a discussion of the face validity of the instrument, of the content validity as judged by specialists in the field, and of reliability issues. The absence of technical information should also be addressed.

Another weakness of the BALI is that it tends to focus on the client's deficits without emphasizing and reinforcing his or her acquired communication skills. In addition, most of the items are more appropriate for older clients, and the example of an IEP in the appendix is very poor. Furthermore, it is not clear whether the applicable data sheets may be photocopied or if an entirely new book is necessary for each client.

The most pervasive weakness of the BALI is that it does not emphasize skills that are truly communicative and functional. The most functional skill assessed by the BALI is the examinee's ability to request, but the vast majority of items are in the other test areas. The instrument does not address the power of one's communicative skills in the environment and may lead to objectives that are memorized, splinter skills that are not connected to the client's functioning in everyday activities. Some practitioners will be able to use the BALI and match it well to the needs of a client; however, the authors should have provided more emphasis on matching this instrument to the demands of the environment. For instance, conversation items should require more than answering questions; conversation initiations should be documented; turn-taking should be recorded; and one-word vocabulary should be evaluated more in terms of functional holophrases (e.g., want, hungry, help, sick, happy) to measure true communication. Practitioners want to measure the extent to which the client can meet the demands of his or her environment, and successfully name and acquire an object. This functional use of language often involves more than naming pictures.

In a 1989 review of the BALI, Kent-Udolf emphasized the "need for assessment and instruction that promote acquisition of functional relevant communication and language skills in natural contexts and that facilitate social interaction" (p. 80). She believed the BALI fell short of this need, and this reviewer concurs. The first author of the BALI responded to Kent-Udolf (Cipani, 1989) but did not address her major concern about the extent to which the skills measured on the BALI were truly functional (useful, powerful) in the client's environment.

CONCLUSION. Practitioners would best use the BALI to observe a client's level of communication skills in the natural context. It provides a wealth of situations and vocabulary to consider. However, it is not best used alone or exactly as the authors propose because it focuses on skills that may not become integrated and useful in one's everyday life.

REVIEWER'S REFERENCES

Cipani, E. (1989). In response: A reply to Kent-Udolf's review of Behavior Analysis Language Instrument and Behavior Analysis Language Program. *The Behavior Analyst, 12* (2), 249.
Kent-Udolf, L. (1989). Behavior Analysis Language Instrument and Behavior Analysis Language Program: A short review. *The Behavior Analyst, 12* (1), 79-80.

Review of the Behavior Analysis Language Instrument by GERALD TINDAL, Assistant Professor of Special Education, University of Oregon, Eugene, OR:

The Behavior Analysis Language Instrument (BALI) is a criterion-referenced measure of simple vocabulary for students with severe handicaps. It provides a cogent, though limited, theoretical perspective, utilizing Skinner's mands (directives) and tacts (declaratory information). The manual has explicit directions that are easy to follow, though quite repetitive. After the first few administrations, much of the text is probably not very useful. The variety of language behavior sampled is somewhat diverse, given the singular focus on functional vocabulary, including many important words from different environments (e.g., household oriented, occupations, foods, clothing, anatomy). These words are used with four basic formats: (*a*) directives, which the authors describe as receptive mand compliance; (*b*) identification using either language or pictures, called "expressive labeling"; (*c*) use, referred to as "requesting mands"; and (*d*) naming, described as "beginning conversational intraverbal skills." Administration directions and student summary sheets are presented together on the same sheet, which is separate from the actual lists of words within the different functional categories. Although this format allows greater flexibility, it also requires extra preparation for the administrator.

This instrument has some major limitations. A criterion of 90% accuracy over 10 trials is used for scoring the responses, which need to occur within specified time limits (always set to a range of 1 to 5 seconds). None of these conditional criteria are justified logically, empirically, or psychometrically. Also, correctness of the response itself is never defined, which allows slippage to occur within and across administrations.

Although the student is required to respond overtly to different verbal and pictorial stimuli, the contingencies for such responses are obviously out of context. Even the items demanding use (e.g., toothbrushing, dressing, bed-making) are not embedded within any larger response classes or considered within an environmental contingency. This aspect, therefore, leaves the instrument awkwardly based upon Skinner's work in an academic sense only. The use of mands and tacts requires a more contingent and environmental perspective. For example, an observational and functional analysis would provide more and better data on student understanding or use of these vocabulary words. A more appropriate framework for viewing such verbal behavior may well come from considering the pragmatic aspects of language, an area well developed in speech and language (see Prutting & Kirchner, 1987). Alternatively, the interactional context of language may also be considered (see Grunewald & Pollak, 1989).

No psychometric data are presented on this instrument. Reliability and validity information is completely lacking. Although this instrument is criterion-referenced, the authors still need to provide appropriate technical information about the stability of mastery, the relationship between performance on this instrument, examinee functioning in the environment, and the kinds of decisions that can properly be made from data collected using this instrument.

In summary, the BALI is a well-organized instrument for sampling a limited range of verbal behaviors, but it lacks sufficient theoretical information and technical data to warrant its use for quantifying and summarizing student performance.

REVIEWER'S REFERENCES
Prutting, C. A., & Kirchner, D. M. (1987). A clinical appraisal of the pragmatic aspects of language. *Journal of Speech and Hearing Disorders, 52,* 105-119.
Grunewald, L. J., & Pollak, S. A. (1990). *Language interaction in curriculum and instruction.* Austin, TX: PRO-ED, Inc.

[36]
Behavior Change Inventory.

Purpose: Developed to assess the effects of a head injury on the behavior of an individual.
Population: Patients with head injury.
Publication Date: 1989.
Scores: No scores.
Administration: Individual.
Price Data, 1990: $5 per 25 test forms; $9 per manual (37 pages).
Time: (5–10) minutes.
Author: Lawrence C. Hartlage.
Publisher: Clinical Psychology Publishing Co., Inc.

Review of the Behavior Change Inventory by MARK ALBANESE, Adjunct Associate Professor of Biostatistics and Educational Statistics and Director, Office of Consultation and Research in Medical Education, The University of Iowa College of Medicine, Iowa City, IA:

OVERVIEW. The Behavior Change Inventory is a relatively brief checklist of 68 behaviors research has shown to be commonly affected by head injury. These are documented at the current time and retrospectively prior to injury. The instrument can be completed by the injured individuals and/or someone familiar with their behavior before injury. The Inventory is not intended for use as a diagnostic instrument, but rather was developed to help the examiner have at hand a systematic approach to determining whether behaviors or feelings have changed after a given point of reference. The author states that the Behavior Change Inventory can "represent perhaps the single most important scale for documenting the presence of such disorders as Organic Personality Syndrome . . . or Organic Affective Syndrome." This claim is based upon research suggesting that change in behavior before and after an assault to the central nervous system is a better index of the degree of injury than simply the presence or absence of indicator symptoms. The author also states that documentation of this type of behavior change is especially crucial in situations involving litigation.

DESCRIPTION OF INSTRUMENT. The Behavior Change Inventory was developed by reviewing relevant literature and surveys of practicing clinicians regarding behaviors observed to be affected following assault to the central nervous system. Following the development of the instrument, data were collected from 29 children (ages 6 to 17) with documented mild head injury, 43 young adults with positive history for head injury with positive neurological examination findings, 48 adults who had sustained head trauma, 14 adults and 20 young adults who had been exposed to Ethylene Oxide, 40 young adult controls with no known neurologic change or exposure, and a normative group of 100 individuals with no known neurologic impairment.

The results of these studies showed that patients with documented assaults to their central nervous system showed substantially more changes in behaviors measured by the Behavior Change Inventory than did the control groups. The type of behavior changes experienced varied by the type of injury, but showed some relative ordering in prevalence.

CRITIQUE OF STRENGTHS. Among the strengths of the Behavior Change Inventory are that it is quick and easy to complete. The test manual gives a good description of how to administer the instrument and interpret the results. The Behavior Change Inventory has been used by the author in 11 studies to identify its properties. The instrument's focus on changes in patients' behavior since experiencing a central nervous system assault was well documented as effective in discriminating between injured and control patients.

CRITIQUE OF WEAKNESSES. One of the weaknesses of the Behavior Change Inventory is that because it is a straightforward self-report instrument, the potential exists for the results to be susceptible to faking. This would be particularly true when the stakes are high such as when the instrument was being used as evidence during litigation. The author addressed this issue in one study by arguing that faking would be difficult to sustain under the 8 hours of intensive assessment to which the patients were subjected. In addition the Minnesota Multiphasic Personality Inventory (MMPI) was administered with the validity scale serving as an indicator of faking. The precautions of time-consuming assessment and use of lie scales seem to reduce the attractiveness of the Behavior Change Inventory at least in terms of economy of administration time.

Because the Behavior Change Inventory seeks only the presence or absence of various behaviors, it will not be sensitive to behaviors that existed before the injury that became worse afterward and vice versa. Any clinician using the instrument may need to supplement the information on the inventory with follow-up on items marked as present before injury.

There is no overall score derived from the instrument. The author recommends an item-by-item interpretation and gives examples of how to report results in sample cases. However, there will be a strong tendency for users to report the total number of items showing change. The author indirectly supports this practice by reporting total percent change in his tables. Data on the validity and reliability of such a total score would be useful in either encouraging or discouraging the computation of a total score.

Although the author encourages users to obtain results from friends and relatives in addition to the patient, he notes in the test manual that these other individuals may not produce results identical to that of the patient. He offers only a discussion covering differences in perspective others may offer. More research on the bias associated with the specific data source would benefit interpretation.

There are no data reported on the reliability of item responses. Of particular value would be data on the stability of the before-injury responses. Because this is a recall item from a person who may be suffering memory loss, the likelihood is high that pre-injury responses are unstable. Data on test-retest reliability would be especially helpful.

A final observation is that the presence of the before-injury responses at the same time one is completing the after-injury portion raises administration issues for long-term follow-up assessments. Among the issues that arise are: Do responses vary if the pre-injury ratings are not available as the post-injury ratings are made and on long-term follow-up, should the entire history of earlier ratings be provided as the respondent makes his/her current status ratings.

SUMMARY. In summary, the Behavior Change Inventory offers a quick and easy method of obtaining a sense for whether patients have had any changes in behavior since experiencing an injury to their central nervous systems. The arguments used by the test developer for the importance of change as opposed to current functioning are compelling and well documented. The data used to support the validity of the instrument indicate that it effectively

discriminates between individuals with a known injury to the central nervous system and controls who have had no such known injury. As a tool to aid clinicians in assessing a patient's status following injury, the Behavior Change Inventory offers a standard mechanism for collecting such data. This may be useful for training purposes as well as chart documentation of a patient's progress. The degree of utility will depend on the clinical judgment of the user to determine if the information obtained offers a useful supplement to existing assessment procedures.

The use of the instrument in litigation, however, presents difficulties because of the simplicity with which patients could fake responses to assist their case in court. The author has not provided sufficient evidence to indicate the results from the instrument could not be manipulated in ways that would bias its use in legal actions.

ACKNOWLEDGEMENT. The reviewer wishes to acknowledge Steven W. Anderson, M.D., Postdoctoral Associate, Department of Neurology at the University of Iowa, for providing consultation regarding the clinical application of this instrument with patients suffering injury to the central nervous system.

Review of the Behavior Change Inventory by ROBERT A. REINEKE, *Evaluation Specialist, Lincoln Public Schools, Lincoln, NE:*
The Behavior Change Inventory (BCI) is described as an instrument to measure behavior change resulting from head injury. The BCI is not intended to be used as a diagnostic test. Its author suggests that most available measures of behavior and/or affect provide a current assessment only. A primary feature of the Behavior Change Inventory is information relative to the patient's current behavior as well as his or her pretrauma behavior. The instrument is designed to be completed by the patient and, if available, family members or close friends. It is described as requiring only 5 to 10 minutes to complete. A checklist approach is used to indicate behaviors such as "absentminded," "cheerful," "temperamental" which, in the raters mind, describe the patient "Now" and/or "Before" some (traumatic) event. The author suggests the inventory may also be administered as a series; in this case only the "Now" column need be completed.

The BCI provides a very economical approach to assessing behavior change in patients with head injury. Administering and scoring the inventory are straightforward. Relying on self-report, this indirect method of collecting clinical information is subject to patient-induced distortions. Recognizing this potential problem, particularly as part of a compensation-oriented strategy on the part of the patient, the author reported special efforts to insure candor, and eliminated cases from the clinical study where candor was in question or validity scales on the Minnesota Multiphasic Personality Inventory were questionable. This or some similar procedure is recommended to help insure valid responses when using the Behavior Change Inventory.

No concurrent behavior change data are described, such as might be provided by family or friends, nor is any corroborating evidence, such as direct observation, presented. Inclusion of such information, based on the norming sample, would be helpful.

The procedure followed for developing the inventory is described. Although reasonable care seems to have been exercised, some question remains in terms of criteria used to select behaviors. The list apparently includes behaviors that have been mentioned in the literature or which practicing clinicians have observed in patients "following insult to the central nervous system."

No direct evidence of reliability for the BCI is given. A control group showing substantially less change in reported behaviors over a 1-year period (obtained at a single administration) than patients under care for head injuries (less than 1 year) does not adequately address the question of reliability. Similarly, validity is addressed in terms of self-report rather than in terms of actual behavior, or even behavior as reported by friends or close family members.

The Behavior Change Inventory may provide a reasonable and economical approach to obtain information about behavior change resulting from head injury or other similar trauma. The information included in the manual provides some measure of face validity. However, in view of its limited use, lack of reliability information and concurrent validity, it is suggested that the BCI be used only as an adjunct measure for clinical applications.

[37]
Behavior Dimensions Rating Scale.

Purpose: Developed to screen for emotional/behavior disorders and for monitoring behavior change.
Population: Grades K–11.
Publication Date: 1989.
Acronym: BDRS.
Scores, 5: Aggressive/Acting Out, Irresponsible/Inattentive, Socially Withdrawn, Fearful/Anxious, Total.
Administration: Individual.
Price Data, 1991: $65 per complete kit including 25 rating/profile forms and manual (77 pages); $24 per 25 rating/profile forms; $50 per manual.
Time: [5–10] minutes.
Comments: Ratings by teachers, parents, and psychologists.
Authors: Lyndal M. Bullock and Michael J. Wilson.
Publisher: DLM Teaching Resources.

TEST REFERENCES
1. Bullock, L. M., Wilson, M. J., Sparnacki, R. L., & Campbell, R. E. (1990). Behavior Dimensions Rating Scale: A comparison of elementary and secondary school student ratings. *Measurement and Evaluation in Counseling and Development, 23,* 77-82.

Review of the Behavior Dimensions Rating Scale by MARTHA W. BLACKWELL, *Associate Professor of Psychology, Auburn University at Montgomery, Montgomery, AL:*

The Behavior Dimensions Rating Scale (BDRS) presents 43 bipolar descriptors of behaviors related to emotional/behavioral problems for use with K–11 grade students. Items representing four major areas—aggression, irresponsibility, social withdrawal, and fearfulness—are rated on a 7-point scale according to extent of fit for the target child.

The BDRS presents a well-designed format that fosters ease and efficiency in simultaneously recording the ratings on both the form and scoring page beneath. General directions and references to pertinent sections of the BDRS Examiner's Manual are clearly stated and accurately referenced. The BDRS Examiner's Manual is noteworthy in clarity, organization, and thoroughness. The working definitions for the bipolar descriptors in chapter 2 represent precise polar extremes with the exceptions of two items: Item 15, Responsible/Irresponsible (p. 9); and Item 21, Poor/Adequate Social Relationships (p. 10). Item 15 obfuscates by combining unobservable moral judgments and thinking with observable age-appropriate behaviors. Perhaps adding another item with bipolar extremes of reflective/impulsive could produce greater interscorer reliability. Item 21 defines Poor Social Relationships as "an ability to get along with peers." For congruence with the item title, *inability* is more appropriate.

Overall, the instructions and illustrations in the Examiner's Manual and the shaded areas of the Subject Profile in the BDRS Rating Form aid in the interpretation of ratings. Users' understanding could be accelerated in the Examiner's Manual (p. 12) by adding the page number of the Subject Profile in the BDRS Rating Form (Step 4) and the sex and age-grade range for the Figure 2-1 illustration (Step 7).

Development procedures and sequences are generally explicit and documented. Disconcerting discrepancies and incongruities appear, however, between development delineations and later claims that the BDRS was constructed to be "sensitive to (*a*) differences in environment, (*b*) personal perspective, and (*c*) actual behavior differences" (p. 40). Although analyses of students' ratings in a variety of educational/therapeutic settings (p. 30) were conducted, no differences attributable to environment/setting were reported in the manual. A similar concern applies to "personal perspective." The authors suggest the BDRS can be used by parents, teachers, and psychologists; however, an important assumption (p. 52) for an assortment of raters is the sharing of similar beliefs and theories regarding normal/disturbed behavior and behavior distributions. The interscorer agreement between teacher and teacher's assistant (p. 40) ranged from .64–.68, certainly less than adequate for interrater reliability. Whereas these results could reflect sensitivity to individual perceptions they could also suggest the necessity for adequate training of raters prior to administration and interpretation of ratings. More information is needed regarding differences attributable to environments and to personal perspectives and the impact of both on ratings and interpretation.

The technical properties of the BDRS were addressed thoroughly and clearly. Reliability documentation included internal consistency as determined by Cronbach's alpha in the good to excellent range (.87–.98), test-retest over 3- to 4-week intervals by Pearson product-moment (.82–.91), and standard errors of measurement based on T-score standard deviation of 10 at the 68% and 95% confidence levels. These results establish consistency across age-grade levels and over time. The interscorer reliability is, however, inadequate.

Content, criterion-related, and construct validities were investigated. Content validity was determined by agreement among seven experts. On their recommendation, 14 items were added to the original 30 items with one omitted due to ill fit. No mention was made of further content analysis after the additions were made.

Criterion-related validity was evaluated by discriminant function analysis on all nationally collected BDRS data. These results indicated that three out of four correct identifications of being emotionally disturbed or not being emotionally disturbed could be made, which means that one of four such identifications would be erroneous. The authors urge caution in the use of the BDRS for identification and placement purposes and recommend the use of additional measures and judgments for decision-making.

Construct validity was evaluated by factor analysis and multitrait-multimethod analysis. The results of several factor analyses, as well as research by others (Wilson, Moore, & Bullock, 1987), suggest the invariance of the factor structure of responses permits using the BDRS for people with and without emotional disturbances, for females and males, for all levels of school populations, and, possibly, for longitudinal studies. Less clear-cut results were yielded by multitrait-multimethod analyses. Data from a total of only 54 subjects were used for BDRS interscale reliabilities. Of the 54 elementary and secondary subjects, only 30 elementary students were used in BDRS/Walker Problem Behavior Identification Checklist (9:1345) comparisons and 24 secondary students in BDRS/Revised Behavior Problem Checklist (332) comparisons. Convergent validity for Subscale 1—Aggressive/Acting Out and for Subscale 2—Irresponsible/Inattentive was moderate to strong (.68–.81); for Subscale 3—Socially Withdrawn, weak (.48–.60); for Subscale 4—Fearful/Anxious, weak (.59). Support for discriminant validity was variable and confounded by overlap among the four BDRS subscales, by poor reliabilities of the Walker Problem Identification Checklist scales, and by comparisons of perhaps different behavioral traits.

In summary, the BDRS is easy to understand, administer, score, and interpret using the tables provided in the Examiner's Manual. The interscorer reliability should be further investigated for effects of varying personal perspectives resulting from observer-target roles and for effects of different educational/therapeutic settings. Training of raters should occur prior to using the BDRS Rating Form. The convergent validity is adequate but the discriminant validity is questionable. Data from diverse environments and personal perspectives should continue to be collected and analyzed and any differences in ratings attributable to these sources should be made known. Caution is reiterated in making diagnosis and placement decisions on the basis of only BDRS ratings.

REVIEWER'S REFERENCE

Wilson, M. J., Moore, A. D., & Bullock, L. M. (1987). Factorial invariance of the Behavior Dimensions Rating Scale. *Measurement and Evaluation in Counseling and Development, 20,* 11-17.

Review of the Behavior Dimensions Rating Scale by ROSEMERY O. NELSON-GRAY, *Professor of Psychology and Director of Clinical Training, University of North Carolina at Greensboro, Greensboro, NC:*

The Behavior Dimensions Rating Scale (BDRS) is a 43-item rating scale "designed to measure patterns of behavior related to emotional problems" (p. 2, all page numbers refer to Examiner's Manual). Each behavior has two specified anchor points; the teacher, parent, or psychologist is to describe the school-aged child or adolescent on each behavior by using a 7-point rating scale.

Positive features of the BDRS include the following. First, the rating scale is convenient and relatively easy to use. According to page 2: "A significant feature of the BDRS is its easy-to-use format. It can be completed and scored in less than 30 minutes." An illustration of the convenience is that the rating form is equipped so that the initial ratings of the 43 items are automatically copied onto the scoring sheet without requiring manual transmission of scores. Scoring is facilitated by the easy identification of specific items comprising each of the four subscales. Tables to translate raw scores to standard scores are highly usable. The scoring form contains an annotated subject profile sheet, which facilitates interpretation of the standard scores for the four subscales and for the total score.

A second positive feature is that the Examiner's Manual is, for the most part, clearly written. The instructions and explanations seem to be directed to classroom teachers. Suitable explanations are provided for technical psychometric findings.

Third, the rating scale was standardized on a national sample of normal and emotionally disturbed youths, with an additional sample of juvenile delinquents. Four subscales were identified via factor analyses; and the same four subscales are reported as being replicated across the three distinct subject groups. Reliability and validity studies are described in adequate detail with generally good results, with exceptions noted below. Both the internal consistency (interrelationship of items within a subscale) and test-retest reliability data (relationship of subscale scores given at 3–4 weeks' temporal separation) are good. Adequate procedures were followed to ensure content validity: Items were generated by a literature review and by classroom teachers, and were subsequently evaluated by expert judges. Criterion-related validity was demonstrated in that the scale scores discriminated between students in emotionally disturbed placements and in regular classrooms.

Fourth, the test manual provides appropriate cautions about the uses and interpretations of test results. A designated use of the test is "screening individuals who may have emotional/behavior disorders" (p. 4). It is recommended that test results be used only to generate hypotheses that form the bases of further assessment: "interpretations should be limited to hypotheses about the level of need for further observation and assessment rather than attempts to identify causes of the student's possible problems, to assign diagnostic labels to the student, or to recommend placement or other treatment or management solutions" (p. 5). Another caution that is appropriately issued is that ratings provided by different raters may be discrepant. Indeed, the average interrater agreement for the four subscale scores was moderate ($r = .68$). The test authors rightfully note that discrepancies may be a result of actual differences in student behaviors across different environments or of different rater perceptions. It is recommended that discrepant ratings be discussed among the differing raters. Finally, additional caution is recommended in interpreting the scores from the four separate subscales: "This caution is warranted not only because inferences based on the small number of items in a Subscale are generally less reliable than those based on all the BDRS items combined . . . but also because their use as predictors is not yet fully understood or completely accurate" (p. 18).

On the other hand, negative aspects of the BDRS include the following. First, it is not clear if there is a need for additional child behavior rating scales. There are at least three well-established and similar rating scales available: the Revised Problem Behav-

ior Checklist (332; RPBC) (Quay & Peterson, 1987), the Walker Problem Behavior Identification Checklist (9:1345; WPBIC) (Walker, 1983), and the Achenbach Child Behavior Checklist (64; CBCL) (Achenbach & Edelbrock, 1988). Indeed, correlations between BDRS subscale scores and RBPC and WPBIC subscale scores for very small samples of children ($n = 24$ and 30, respectively) are reported to help establish the construct validity of the BDRS. The CBCL is well established with good normative data and many subscale scores ($n = 9$), including internalizing versus externalizing subscale sets. It is not clear what the BDRS adds to existing child behavior rating scales.

A second weakness relates to the four subscales. The manual states that the same four subscales were repeatedly identified in samples of normal, emotionally disturbed, and juvenile delinquent youths. References and short summaries of research substantiating this statement are provided, but much of the cited research is not readily available. In this reviewer's opinion, insufficient research data are provided in the manual. The eigenvalues for the four factors across the different studies are not provided, nor are the intercorrelations among the four factors. One set of intercorrelations is reported on page 49 ($n = $ difficult to determine from text) with values varying from .27–.71. Item loadings on the four factors for three data sets are appropriately provided. Examination of these factor loadings indicates some overlap of items across subscales: Items 15 and 25 are assigned to Subscale 2, but they also load highly on Subscale 1; Items 2, 19, and 38 are assigned to both Subscales 3 and 4. Another concern about the BDRS subscales is their variable convergent and discriminant validity with the subscales of the RBPC and the WPBIC; validity for Subscales 1 and 2 is much better than for Subscales 3 and 4. The manual conveys that test users should interpet the subscale scores cautiously, as noted earlier, but the concern is that it may be tempting to some users to perform subscale interpretations.

A third weakness is the nature of some of the 43 test items. The manual states that: "The BDRS covers a wide range of observed behavior" (p. 2). To its credit, the manual provides operational definitions of both anchor points of all 43 items. Nonetheless, some of the items seem to require a high degree of rater inference (e.g., Item 2 "self-conscious . . . confident"; Item 8 "shy . . . sociable"; Item 16 "dislikes school . . . enjoys school"; Item 19 "fearful . . . self-confident"; Item 36 "receptive to new ideas . . . hostile to new ideas"; Item 39 "trusts others . . . distrusts"). Perhaps the moderate interrater agreement is partly attributable to the inferential nature of some test items, a reason not hypothesized in the test manual.

Fourth, two psychometric features of the BDRS are worth questioning. In the standardization sample, the number of Blacks with emotional disturbance (32.1%) exceeds the percent of Blacks in the 1980 U.S. Census (14.7%), whereas the number of Caucasians with emotional disturbance (63.3%) is less than the percent of Caucasians in the Census (82.3%). The sample may be representative of emotionally disturbed youth nationally, but no data are provided to allow this conclusion. Another concern is that a stated use of the test is "as a tool to assist in monitoring behavior change" and similarly "to develop a baseline for a subject's behavior against which progress in behavioral intervention may be measured" (both on p. 4). But no construct validity data are provided to show that the BDRS scores are sensitive to changes produced by treatment, intervention, or special education placement.

Finally, the manual is clearly written on the whole but with some important exceptions. It is stated that a subject should be observed for at least 2 weeks prior to rating (p. 8). But the amount of time during the 2 weeks is not suggested. Surely, the amount of time available to psychologists differs greatly from classroom teachers or parents. On page 18, a confusing example is provided regarding comparing the four subscale scores that may be due to a typographical error, substituting Subscale 4 for Subscale 2. Finally, it is stated that all 43 items must be rated (p. 8) with the inference that the test is invalid if any item is incomplete. No information is provided on prorating subscale or total scores, in case of one or more incomplete items.

In conclusion, the BDRS is noteworthy because of its easy-to-use format and promising psychometric data. Conversely, additional studies are needed to show why this test should replace other alternative and well-established child behavior checklists.

REVIEWER'S REFERENCES

Walker, H. M. (1983). Walker Problem Behavior Identification Checklist. Los Angeles: Western Psychological Services.
Quay, H. C., & Peterson, D. R. (1987). Revised Behavior Problem Checklist. Coral Gables, FL: The Authors.
Achenbach, T. M., & Edelbrock, C. (1988). Child Behavior Checklist. Burlington, VT: Thomas M. Achenbach.

[38]

Behavioral Characteristics Progression.

Purpose: Identifies specific skills exhibited during an individual's development.
Population: Physically and mentally handicapped children and adults.
Publication Date: 1973.
Acronym: BCP.
Comments: "Criterion-referenced"; manual title is BCP Observation Booklet; also available in binder format.
Scores: Item scores only.
Administration: Individual.
Price Data, 1990: $12.95 per manual ('73, 205 pages); $12.95 per binder; $125 per set of 5 method books (also available as separates).
Time: Administration time not reported.

Authors: The Office of the Santa Cruz Superintendent of Schools.
Publisher: VORT Corporation.

Review of the Behavioral Characteristics Progression by ROSEMERY O. NELSON-GRAY, Professor of Psychology and Director of Clinical Training, University of North Carolina at Greensboro, Greensboro, NC:

The Behavioral Characteristics Progression (BCP) is an assessment device designed to determine specific skills or behaviors that may or may not be in the repertoire of "mentally and behaviorally exceptional children." It consists of 59 behavioral areas or "strands," which are subdivided into up to 50 specific behaviors, for a total of 2,400 specific assessed behaviors.

The BCP is intended to be used in special education settings for: assessment of individuals, instruction in conjunction with an individualized educational plan, and communication regarding a pupil's progress. It is intended that the classroom teacher be the primary assessor, with assistance as needed from specialized professionals, such as speech therapists, physical therapists, nurses, or school psychologists.

Assessment within all 59 behavioral strands for each pupil would be a formidable undertaking. Hence, the manual provides some suggestions to limit the workload. For example, "identifying behaviors" are listed that may frequently occur in individuals with handicaps. It is suggested that the behavioral strand be assessed for an individual if the individual displays many of the identifying behaviors within that strand. For another example, it is suggested that assessment can begin anywhere within the strand, depending on the level of the particular assessed individual. No more specific guidelines regarding suggested starting points are provided.

One positive feature of the manual is its recommendation for handling unusual assessment situations. For example, if a student's performance is variable across different trials of the same task, it is suggested that demonstration of the skill on 75% of the trials be used as a guideline for presence of the skill. For another example, if there is interobserver disagreement on specific behaviors, then either re-observation or acceptance of the lower-level behavior is suggested. For a third example, scoring codes are provided if a physical handicap permanently prevents acquisition of a particular behavior, or if necessary equipment to assess a particular behavior is not available.

Another positive feature of the BCP is that curriculum materials are available to teach assessed missing skills. There are five "method books" to teach self-help, motor, communication, social, and learning/academic skills.

The critical negative feature of the BCP is that no reliability and validity data are reported. The assessment device is intended to be criterion-referenced, as opposed to norm-referenced; hence, no normative data are provided. An acknowledgement is made in the manual that the specific behaviors within each behavioral strand "may not reflect exact developmental sequencing or spacing." No reliability and validity data that may be appropriate to a criterion-referenced assessment tool are provided. To illustrate, there are no interobserver reliability data or test-retest reliability data. Content validity is difficult to judge because no information is provided regarding the source or refinement of the specific behaviors or behavioral strands. Criterion-related validity data (e.g., changes in observed behaviors as a result of curricular interventions focused on teaching specific behaviors) are also absent.

A second negative feature of the BCP is that it is potentially difficult to administer. Different materials are required to assess different skills; however, no list of necessary or suggested equipment is provided in the manual. Similar items within a behavioral strand that require the same materials are not necessarily grouped together, nor is an index of related items provided. Assessment data are recorded in a BCP observation booklet and then transferred to a BCP chart. Finally, these data are transferred to a BCP Learner Objectives Worksheet. Samples of the observation booklet and of the objectives worksheet are supplied in the manual; but no sample of the BCP chart is provided, making it difficult to follow and understand the manual directions related to the chart.

In summary, some centers, schools, or teachers may find the BCP to be a useful device to assess specific behaviors in individuals with handicaps due to both the very large number of behaviors listed and the curriculum materials available to teach specific absent behaviors. Conversely, lack of psychometric data and certain potential administration difficulties may prevent wide-scale adoption of the BCP.

Review of the Behavioral Characteristics Progression by HARVEY N. SWITZKY, Professor of Educational Psychology, Counseling, and Special Education, Northern Illinois University, DeKalb, IL:

The Behavioral Characteristics Progression (BCP) is an atlas of 2,400 observable, criterion-referenced behavioral characteristics organized into 59 behavioral strands (i.e., domain-specific functional developmental and practical sequences of adaptive behavior consisting of self-help, perceptual-motor, language, social, academic, recreational, and vocational skills). Behavioral strands are available in the skill domains of sign language use, orientation, mobility, wheelchair use, and ambulation for individuals who are deaf, blind, or orthopedically handicapped. The BCP is designed as an observational tool to provide assessment, instructional, and communication functions for educators of children and adults with handicaps. The assessment information provided by the BCP may provide the educator with an extensive and comprehensive chart of student behaviors and behavioral characteristics that are and are not a part of the student's behavioral repertoire. From the information collected, appropriate individualized learning objectives can be developed for each student. As a communication tool, the BCP may function as a historical recording device that can be used throughout the life span of the student to document progress and to help communicate this information to the educational/habilitation team.

Behavioral strands can have up to 50 behavioral characteristics roughly ordered in terms of increasing developmental level and complexity of behavior. Each behavioral strand has identifying behaviors describing behavioral deficits that students might display. These identifying behaviors assist the educator in identifying the basic needs for each student and in determining priorities of learner objectives. The BCP provides a very fine-grained set of behavioral objectives for all degrees of handicap, ranging from mildly handicapped to profoundly multiply handicapped and is basically an assessment/curricular tool for educators (Switzky, 1979; Switzky, Rotatori, & Fox, 1985).

Each behavioral characteristic is evaluated according to the following scoring criteria: (*a*) Behavior not displayed. No opportunity offered to pupil; (*b*) Behavior not displayed. Pupil offered opportunities to display it; (*c*) Behavior displayed a portion of the time but less than the 75% required incidence level; (*d*) Behavior displayed at the required 75% incidence level without any physical or verbal assistance; (*e*) Physical handicap prevents demonstration of this behavior; and (*f*) The equipment/materials required to observe the behavior are unavailable.

The scoring criteria are vague and difficult to use because the manual provides very few guidelines regarding how many trials per day or for how many days each assessment item should be presented to determine the student's level of behavioral functioning. The criterion responses for simpler behavioral characteristics are more clearly defined than for complex behavioral characteristics. However, guidelines do suggest the importance of cross-checking one's observations regarding students' behavioral characteristics in varied situations, with different observers, and at different times of the day or week, but no substantive details are provided.

The strength of the BCP is its breadth and depth of criterion-referenced behavioral characteristics covering functional developmental and practical skill sequences of adaptive behavior, which can be used for students with mild to profound multiple handicaps. The main weaknesses of the BCP are its ambiguity and vagueness as regards the details of the behavioral assessment process and its time-consuming nature.

Alternative omnibus atlases of assessment/curriculum models that may prove more useful because of their more specific details and guidelines for use include: (a) *The Adaptive Behavior Curriculum*, Volume 1 (Popovich & Laham, 1981) and *The Adaptive Behavior Curriculum*, Volume 2 (Popovich & Laham, 1982), which can be used with students having moderate, severe, and profound handicaps (see Switzky, 1979: and Switzky, Rotatori, & Fox, 1985 for a discussion of the assessment/curricular approach); and (b) The Behaviour Assessment Battery, Second Edition (10:29; Kiernan & Jones, 1982), which is an extremely sophisticated, fine-grained, criterion-referenced, and psychometrically advanced behavioral inventory useful for the assessment of the cognitive, communicative, and self-help skills of individuals with severe and profound mental handicaps. (See Switzky, 1985 for a detailed review of this assessment instrument.)

In summary, the BCP is what it claims to be, an observational tool, not a testing instrument, to enable educators to identify which behavioral characteristics are part of exceptional students' behavioral repertoires so that appropriate learner objectives can be designed for each student. The BCP may be useful for many practitioners; however, other assessment/curricular models are available that are as good or better.

REVIEWER'S REFERENCES

Switzky, H. N. (1979). Assessment of the severely and profoundly handicapped. In D. A. Sabatino & T. L. Miller (Eds.), *Describing learner characteristics of handicapped children and youth* (pp. 415-478). New York: Grune & Stratton.

Popovich, D., & Laham, S. L. (1981). *The Adaptive Behavior Curriculum* (Vol. 1). Baltimore, MD: Paul H. Brookes.

Kiernan, C., & Jones, M. C. (1982). Behaviour Assessment Battery, Second Edition. Windsor, England: NFER-Nelson Publishing Co., Ltd.

Popovich, D., & Laham, S. L. (1982). *The Adaptive Behavior Curriculum* (Vol. 2). Baltimore, MD: Paul H. Brookes.

Switzky, H. N. (1985). [Review of Kiernan & Jones' Behaviour Assessment Battery.] In D. J. Keyser & R. C. Sweetland (Eds.), *Test critiques* (Vol. 4). Kansas City, MO: Test Corporation of America.

Switzky, H. N., Rotatori, A. F., & Fox, R. (1985). Assessment of adaptive behavior. In A. F. Rotatori & R. Fox (Eds.), *Assessment for regular and special education teachers* (pp. 311-334). Austin, TX: PRO-ED, Inc.

[39]
Behaviour Problems: A System of Management.

Purpose: "A systematic means of recording and analysing information on children's problem behaviour."
Population: Problem behavior children in a classroom situation.
Publication Date: 1984.
Scores: 8 areas of behavior: Classroom Conformity, Task Orientation, Emotional Control, Acceptance of Authority, Self-Worth, Peer Relationships, Self Responsibility/Problem Solving, Other.
Administration: Individual.

Price Data, 1987: £13.75 per complete set including manual (15 pages), pad of 50 Daily Records, and pack of 10 Behaviour Checklist/Monthly Progress Charts; £4.50 per pad of 50 Daily Records; £3.50 per pack of 10 Behaviour Checklist/Monthly Progress Charts; £5.95 per manual.
Time: Administration time not reported.
Authors: Peter P. Galvin and Richard M. Singleton.
Publisher: NFER-Nelson Publishing Co., Ltd. [England].

Review of the Behaviour Problems: A System of Management by KATHRYN M. BENES, Assistant Professor of Psychology, Iowa State University, Ames, IA:

Behaviour Problems: A System of Management (BPSM) is published in Great Britain and designed to provide a structured means of objectively measuring children's behavior in the classroom. Galvin and Singleton, the authors of the BPSM, state that "the need for specificity when describing behaviour, and the importance of the role of the teacher in this process, are the guiding principles for this approach" (p. 3).

Indeed, the importance of structured methods of directly assessing behaviors has become a major focal point in the school psychology literature over the past decade (Alessi, 1988). A study by the National Academy of Sciences recommends that systematic behavioral assessment is necessary when considering children for eligibility in special education classrooms (Alessi, 1988; Heller, Holtzman, & Messick, 1982). Moreover, monitoring behavioral data, from assessment throughout intervention, is deemed to be vital in providing children with appropriate educational services (Reschly, Kicklighter, & McKee, 1988).

COMPONENTS AND UTILIZATION. The BPSM consists of three components: (a) the Behaviour Checklist; (b) the Daily Record; and (c) the Monthly Progress Chart. The Behaviour Checklist and the Monthly Progress Chart are displayed back to back on an $11^3/4$ -inch by $16^1/2$ -inch sheet of paper. The Daily Record is on a separate $8^1/4$ -inch by $11^3/4$ -inch sheet of paper.

BEHAVIOUR CHECKLIST. The Behaviour Checklist is made up of 111 items divided into seven categories (Classroom Conformity, Task Orientation, Emotional Control, Acceptance of Authority, Self-Worth, Peer Relationships, and Self-Responsibility/Problem Solving). An additional category, titled Other Descriptions, is available for teachers to add behaviors that are not found in the specified categories. The items are not meant to provide a behavioral profile or to measure relative degrees of behavior. Rather, the aim of the collection of items is meant to provide a guide to facilitate greater behavioral specificity. The manual indicates that the Behaviour Checklist can be placed on a clipboard and kept beside the teacher at all times. The teacher is to monitor one child's behavior at a time. In the initial or assessment phase of data collection, the teacher is to record the presence of any of the listed behavioral items when they occur, without regard to frequency. After a "sufficient time" (2 weeks is recommended), the teacher begins to monitor the frequency or duration of each of the previously observed behaviors. After 6 weeks, the authors maintain that the teacher should have a sufficient record of the target behaviors; however, the actual time period may be left to individual discretion. Following the assessment phase (which could last as long as 8 weeks), the teacher identifies behaviors that "demand his or her immediate attention." The authors recommend selecting no more than two priority behaviors because of the difficulty of attempting to change too many behaviors at one time.

DAILY RECORD. Once priority behaviors have been identified, the Daily Record provides a structured means for the teacher to collect specific behavioral data during a 1-week period. Space is provided for two priority behaviors, two spaces for "other significant items," and one space for positive behaviors. The behavioral descriptors are followed by columns for morning and afternoon sessions of each day. The teacher is to assign a numeric code to each specific behavioral incident in the appropriate column and to write a narrative report at the bottom of the form describing specific details of the event (i.e., duration, others involved, intensity, antecedents, consequences, etc.). The authors indicate that the teacher may choose to record whatever information is deemed necessary regarding specific incidents and children.

MONTHLY PROGRESS CHART. The Monthly Progress Chart serves as a 3-month summative profile of the child's behavior and intervention goals. The teacher is to write short-term goals related to the child's prioritized behaviors and to outline strategies that will be used to accomplish these goals. In addition, weekly results, comments, strengths and positive aspects of behavior, and long-term goals can be documented on the chart. The Monthly Progress Chart also contains a graph that provides a visual display of intervention results.

DISCUSSION OF THE STRENGTHS AND WEAKNESSES OF THE BPSM. The manual states the authors' aim for developing the BPSM was to provide a structured means for teachers to collect objective behavioral information in order to assess and provide treatment interventions. Structured forms that Galvin and Singleton have developed make the paperwork associated with collecting and monitoring a child's behavior over several months a relatively easy task. The BPSM framework, however, goes beyond facilitating data collection to represent a direct link between assessment, intervention, and continuous monitoring that is lacking in service delivery methods that rely on norm-referenced instruments. By providing space on the Monthly Progress Chart to document short- and long-term goals, individuals who work with the child are continually prompted as to their intervention objectives and the effectiveness of those interventions.

Although the development of the BPSM is noteworthy, three critical areas call for further attention. First, the BPSM was designed with an underlying behavioral philosophy; however, many of the items are written in vague or subjective terms. For example, "Lacks confidence task-wise" (Task Orientation, Item 9) is ambiguous and lends itself to a broad array of metric indices. Items are also written in a manner that infers internally based motives. Terms such as "manipulates," "provokes," "cannot," and "deliberately" all imply that the child's behavior is strategic and planful. In order to describe behavior objectively within an environment, such a priori assumptions cannot be made. Moreover, all items are worded to focus on inappropriate behavior. Galvin and Singleton draw an analogy to having car problems, "You do not take it to a garage to be told what is right." However, it is important to remember that a reduction in the frequency of inappropriate behavior does not necessarily lead to concurrent increases in the frequency of appropriate behavior (Evans & Nelson, 1977). Therefore, in order for the BPSM to be a useful observation tool (i.e., facilitate the development of effective interventions), data for inappropriate *and* appropriate behavior must be collected.

The second area of the BPSM in need of further attention is related to the unrealistic expectations of classroom teachers. Few teachers would be able to collect behavioral data accurately and continuously throughout each day for several weeks. In addition, the length of time suggested for baseline data collection is excessive. Many teachers would not be willing to stand by passively and collect data for 8 weeks before behaviors are prioritized and intitial interventions implemented. By requiring unreasonable demands of the teacher, the entire assessment-intervention process is placed in jeopardy.

The final and greatest drawback of the BPSM is the lack of attention given to measurement qualities. Galvin and Singleton state that items are grouped into specific categories based on their subjective attempt "to place each item in the most appropriate category." The authors concede that item specificity is "open to debate." The absence of empirical analysis to support behavioral categories in conjunction with the lack of information regarding the selection of behavioral items, setting events, behavioral norms, control comparisons, structured observation methods, or interrater reliabilities raises serious concerns regarding use of the BPSM. As Lentz (1985) points out, "even within . . . nontraditional assessment model[s], empirical data are necessary to guide user behavior."

SUMMARY. The BPSM provides a convenient, inexpensive "packaged product" that facilitates behavioral observation, intervention, and evaluation in the classroom setting. Lack of attention, however, to empirical issues in constructing the BPSM and user guidance in structured data collection, make the BPSM inferior to existing "unpackaged" strategies of behavioral observation (e.g., Alessi & Kaye, 1983).

REVIEWER'S REFERENCES

Evans, I. M., & Nelson, R. O. (1977). Assessment of child behavior problems. In A. R. Ciminero, K. S. Calhoun, & H. E. Adams (Eds.), Handbook of behavioral assessment. New York: Wiley.

Heller, K. A., Holtzman, W. H., & Messick, S. (Eds.). (1982). Placing children in special education: A strategy for equity. Washington, DC: National Academy Press.

Alessi, G. J., & Kaye, J. H. (1983). Behavior assessment for school psychologists. Kent, OH: National Association of School Psychologists.

Lentz, F. E., Jr. (1985). [Review of Behavior Analysis Forms for Clinical Intervention.] In J. V. Mitchell, Jr. (Ed.), The ninth mental measurements yearbook (pp. 158-159). Lincoln, NE: Buros Institute of Mental Measurements.

Alessi, G. J. (1988). Direct observation methods for emotional/behavior problems. In E. S. Shapiro & T. R. Kratochwill (Eds.), Behavioral assessment in schools (pp. 14-75). New York: Guilford.

Reschly, D., Kicklighter, R., & McKee, P. (1988). Recent placement litigation, Part III: Analysis of differences in Larry P., Marshall, and S-1 and implications for future practices. School Psychology Review, 17, 39-50.

Review of the Behaviour Problems: A System of Management by TERRY OVERTON, *Assistant Professor of Special Education, Longwood College, Farmville, VA:*

DESCRIPTION AND PURPOSE. The purpose of Behavior Problems: A System of Management is to provide teachers with a systematic method of evaluating, observing, and monitoring problematic classroom behaviors. The system consists primarily of a behavioral checklist, daily records, monthly progress reports, and the manual. The authors of the system recommend using frequency counting as a means for observing the 111 behaviors listed on the checklist. The system assists teachers in analyzing student behaviors and writing short-term target objectives that are monitored for a period of weeks or months.

The behaviors included on the checklist are divided into the seven categories of Classroom Conformity, Task Orientation, Acceptance of Authority, Peer Relationships, Self-Responsibility/Problem Solving, Emotional Control, and Self-Worth. An additional category named Other Descriptions is provided for teacher input of other behaviors. A majority of the items are stated negatively, using terms such as "cannot" or "does not" before the stated behavior. No positive behaviors are listed on the checklist.

SCORES. The checklist is first scored with a check to indicate the behaviors of concern. The student is observed for a period of about 2 weeks, as recommended by the authors, using a frequency counting method of recording. The individual time periods of observation during the 2 weeks are unspecified and left to the teacher's discretion. The observation periods may range from a few minutes to several hours or longer. The information obtained on the checklist is used as a basis for writing objectives, which are monitored on the daily record forms and the monthly progress chart. No standard quantitative scores are obtained and no derived scores are provided. This system may be used to establish criteria that may then provide a criterion-referenced type of scoring to meet the objectives.

RELIABILITY AND VALIDITY. The only mention of validity is found in statements by the authors in the Rationale section of the manual. No reliability or validity studies are presented nor do the authors include any reference to research on the instrument. No comments are made regarding the interrater reliability of this instrument.

EVALUATION. The authors purport to have created a system to help teachers become more specific and systematic in behavioral observation and monitoring techniques. The relative strength of the system appears to be the behavioral checklist that is laden with inadequacies. The behavioral items that make up the checklist are somewhat problematic. Several items contain subjective terminology and describe unobservable "feelings" of the student. Other items are so subjective in nature that by marking them the teacher would clearly be using conjecture, speculation, or inference about the student's feelings. Actual meaning of some of the behaviors is questionable even though a brief explanation of a few of the items is presented in the Appendix. Other items cannot be accurately measured quantitatively, because no criteria are given to guide the teacher in determining whether or not a behavior has occurred. Although the authors recommend using frequency counting during the evaluation period, many items cannot be counted or would more appropriately be recorded using duration recording. Other items would be more appropriately included in self-reporting, inventory, or interview formats. In addition, no rating of behaviors (always, sometimes, never) is provided.

No positive behaviors are included on the checklist, which may give the overall appearance of a very negative outlook for a specific student. While the authors use the analogy of the uselessness of finding out what is right with a car that needs repairing, the analogy seems inappropriate in an educational field where strengths are regarded as at least as important as weaknesses in children with behavioral problems. A student's overall behavioral functioning includes positive, as well as negative, behaviors, and provision for assessing all behaviors would paint a more objective diagnostic picture.

Overall, this behavioral system appears to lack what the authors were striving to attain: a system that helps teachers by providing specificity when describing and analyzing behaviors. At best, this instrument could cautiously be adapted and used as a criterion-referenced behavioral observation checklist. For measuring classroom behavior, employing the use of more researched instruments, such as the Behavior Rating Profile (10:27; Brown & Hammill, 1983) or the Revised Behavior Problem Checklist (332; Quay & Peterson, 1983), along with multiple objective systematic behavioral classroom observations, is recommended. To call for further research on the validity and reliability of the Behaviour Problems: A System of Management is an overwhelming understatement.

REVIEWER'S REFERENCES

Brown, L., & Hammill, D. (1983). Behavior Rating Profile. Austin, TX: PRO-ED, Inc.

Quay, H., & Peterson, D. (1983). Revised Behavior Problem Checklist. Coral Gables: Author.

[40]
[Bender-Gestalt Test.]

Purpose: Measures perceptual-motor abilities.
Scores: Scores vary depending on adaptation used.
Administration: Individual.
Comments: The original Bender Gestalt is listed as a below; the modifications listed as b–g consist primarily of alterations in administration procedure, new scoring systems, or expanded interpretive procedures, rather than changes in the test materials; c and d provide, in addition, for use of the materials as projective stimuli for associations.

a) BENDER VISUAL MOTOR GESTALT TEST DESIGN CARDS.
Population: Ages 4 and over.
Publication Dates: 1938–46.
Acronym: VMGT.
Price Data, 1990: $15 per set of cards ('46, 9 cards), directions ('46, 8 pages), and manual ('38, 187 pages).
Time: (10) minutes.
Comments: No reliability data.
Author: Lauretta Bender.
Publisher: Western Psychological Services.

b) THE BENDER GESTALT TEST.
Population: Ages 4 and over.
Publication Date: 1951.
Acronym: BGT.
Price Data, 1990: $13.50 per 100 scoring sheets (1 page); $61.80 per manual (287 pages).
Time: (10) minutes.
Comments: Utilizes same test cards as a.
Authors: Gerald R. Pascal and Barbara J. Suttell.
Publisher: Western Psychological Services.

c) THE HUTT ADAPTATION OF THE BENDER-GESTALT TEST.
Population: Ages 10 and over.
Publication Dates: 1944–85.
Acronym: HABGT.
Price Data, 1989: $24.50 per set of test figures (9 cards); $42.90 per template; $14.50 per set of 25 record forms; $43 per manual (4th edition, '85, 241 pages).

Time: Administration time not reported.
Comments: No reliability data on scored factors.
Author: Max L. Hutt.
Publisher: Grune & Stratton, Inc.

d) THE BENDER VISUAL MOTOR GESTALT TEST FOR CHILDREN.
Population: Ages 4–12.
Publication Date: 1962.
Price Data, 1990: $8.70 per 25 record forms; $18.90 per manual ('62, 92 pages).
Time: (10) minutes without associations.
Comments: Utilizes same test cards as a.
Author: Aileen Clawson.
Publisher: Western Psychological Services.

e) THE BENDER GESTALT TEST FOR YOUNG CHILDREN.
Population: Ages 5–10.
Publication Dates: 1963–75.
Price Data, 1990: $125 per complete set including 2 volumes (Volume I, 195 pages; Volume II, 205 pages); $61.50 per Volume I; $67.50 per Volume II.
Time: Administration time not reported.
Comments: Includes developmental scoring system; utilizes same test cards as a.
Author: Elizabeth M. Koppitz.
Publisher: Western Psychological Services.

f) THE WATKINS BENDER-GESTALT SCORING SYSTEM.
Population: Ages 5–14.
Publication Date: 1976.
Acronym: WBSS.
Price Data, 1990: $19.50 per 100 record forms; $18.75 per manual ('76, 137 pages); $41 per complete kit including cards described in a.
Time: Administration time not reported.
Author: Ernest O. Watkins.
Publisher: Western Psychological Services.

g) THE CANTER BACKGROUND INTERFERENCE PROCEDURE FOR THE BENDER GESTALT TEST.
Population: Ages 12 and over.
Publication Dates: 1966–76.
Acronym: BIP; also called BIP-Bender.
Price Data, 1990: $32 per complete kit including 25 test forms ('75, 4 pages) and manual ('76, 95 pages); $18.50 per 25 test forms; $14.50 per manual.
Time: Administration time not reported.
Author: Arthur Canter.
Publisher: Western Psychological Services.
Cross References: For reviews by Kenneth W. Howell and Jerome M. Sattler, see 9:139 (65 references); see also T3:280 (159 references), 8:506 (253 references), and T2:1447 (144 references); for a review by Philip M. Kitay, see 7:161 (192 references); see also P:415 (170 references); for a review by C. B. Blakemore and an excerpted review by Fred Y. Billingslea, see 6:203 (99 references); see also 5:172 (118 references); for reviews by Arthur L. Benton and Howard R. White, see 4:144 (34 references); see also 3:108 (8 references).

TEST REFERENCES

1. Elliott, S. N., Piersel, W. C., & Galvin, G. A. (1983). Psychological re-evaluations: A survey of practices and perceptions of school psychologists. *Journal of School Psychology, 21,* 99-105.

2. Ritvo, E., Shanok, S. S., & Lewis, D. O. (1983). Firesetting and nonfiresetting delinquents: A comparison of neuropsychiatric, psychoeducational, experiential, and behavioral characteristics. *Child Psychiatry and Human Development, 13,* 259-267.

3. Teglasi, H., & Freeman, R. W. (1983). Rapport pitfalls of beginning testers. *Journal of School Psychology, 21*, 229-240.

4. Champion, L., Doughtie, E. B., Johnson, P. J., & McCreary, J. H. (1984). Preliminary investigation into the Rorschach response patterns of children with documented learning disabilities. *Journal of Clinical Psychology, 40*, 329-333.

5. Gordon, M., Post, E. M., Crouthamel, C., & Richman, R. A. (1984). Do children with constitutional delay really have more learning problems? *Journal of Learning Disabilities, 17*, 291-293.

6. Guidubaldi, J., & Perry, J. D. (1984). Concurrent and predictive validity of the Battelle Development Inventory at the first grade level. *Educational and Psychological Measurement, 44*, 977-985.

7. Holmes, C. B., & Stephens, C. L. (1984). Consistency of edging on the Bender-Gestalt, Memory-For-Designs, and Draw-A-Person tests. *The Journal of Psychology, 117*, 269-271.

8. Holmes, C. B., Dungan, D. S., & Medlin, W. J. (1984). Reassessment of inferring personality traits from Bender-Gestalt Drawing Styles. *Journal of Clinical Psychology, 40*, 1241-1243.

9. Horn, W. F., & O'Donnell, J. P. (1984). Early identification of learning disabilities: A comparison of two methods. *Journal of Educational Psychology, 76*, 1106-1118.

10. Lesiak, J. (1984). The Bender Visual Motor Gestalt Test: Implications for the diagnosis and prediction of reading achievement. *Journal of School Psychology, 22*, 391-405.

11. Lewandowski, L. J. (1984). The symbol digit modalities test: A screening instrument for brain-damaged children. *Perceptual and Motor Skills, 59*, 615-618.

12. Lothstein, L. M., & Roback, H. (1984). Black female transsexuals and schizophrenia: A serendipitous finding? *Archives of Sexual Behavior, 13*, 371-386.

13. Margalit, M., & Zak, I. (1984). Anxiety and self-concept of learning disabled children. *Journal of Learning Disabilities, 17*, 537-539.

14. McCormick, T. T., & Brannigan, G. G. (1984). Bender-Gestalt signs as indicants of anxiety, withdrawal, and acting-out behaviors in adolescents. *The Journal of Psychology, 118*, 71-74.

15. Merritt, F. M., & McCallum, R. S. (1984). The relationship between simultaneous-successive processing and academic achievement. *The Alberta Journal of Educational Research, 30*, 126-132.

16. Oas, P. (1984). Validity of the Draw-A-Person and Bender Gestalt Tests as measures of impulsivity with adolescents. *Journal of Consulting and Clinical Psychology, 52*, 1011-1019.

17. Obrzut, A., Nelson, R. B., & Obrzut, J. E. (1984). Early school entrance for intellectually superior children: An analysis. *Psychology in the Schools, 21*, 71-77.

18. Siegel, R. K. (1984). Hostage hallucinations: Visual imagery induced by isolation and life-threatening stress. *The Journal of Nervous and Mental Disease, 172*, 264-272.

19. Taylor, R. L., & Partenio, I. (1984). Ethnic differences on the Bender-Gestalt: Relative effects of measured intelligence. *Journal of Counseling and Clinical Psychology, 52*, 784-788.

20. Taylor, R. L., Kauffman, D., & Partenio, I. (1984). The Koppitz developmental scoring system for the Bender-Gestalt: Is it developmental? *Psychology in the Schools, 21*, 425-428.

21. Thomas, A. D. (1984). Bender scores and the horse as a distinct item on object assembly of the WISC. *Perceptual and Motor Skills, 56*, 103-106.

22. Wendler, C. L. W., & Roid, G. H. (1984). A cost analysis approach to optimizing test selection. *Journal of Learning Disabilities, 17*, 400-405.

23. Zagar, R., Arbit, J., Stuckey, M., & Wengel, W. W. (1984). Developmental analysis of the Wechsler Memory Scale. *Journal of Clinical Psychology, 40*, 1466-1473.

24. Arnold, L. E., Clark, D. L., Sachs, L. A., Jakim, S., & Smithies, C. (1985). Vestibular and visual rotational stimulation as treatment for attention deficit and hyperactivity. *The American Journal of Occupational Therapy, 39*, 84-91.

25. Beutler, L. E., Storm, A., Kirkish, P., Scogin, F., & Gaines, J. A. (1985). Parameters in the prediction of police officer performance. *Professional Psychology: Research and Practice, 16*, 324-335.

26. Blackwell, S. C., Dial, J. G., Chan, F., & McCollum, P. S. (1985). Discriminating functional levels of independent living: A neuropsychological evaluation of mentally retarded adults. *Rehabilitation Counseling Bulletin, 29*, 42-52.

27. Breen, M. J., Carlson, M., & Lehman, J. (1985). The Revised Developmental Test of Visual Motor Integration: Its relation to the VMI, WISC-R, and Bender Gestalt for a group of elementary aged learning disabled students. *Journal of Learning Disabilities, 18*, 136-138.

28. Furlong, M. J., & LeDrew, L. (1985). IQ = 69 = mildly retarded?: Factors influencing multidisciplinary team recommendations on children with FSIQs between 63 and 75. *Psychology in the Schools, 22*, 5-9.

29. Hellkamp, D. T., & Hogan, M. E. (1985). Differentiation of organics from functional psychiatric patients across various IQ ranges using the Bender-Gestalt and Hutt Scoring System. *Journal of Clinical Psychology, 41*, 259-264.

30. Hilgert, L. D. (1985). A graphic analysis Bender-Gestalt Test. *Journal of Clinical Psychology, 41*, 505-511.

31. Hilgert, L. D., & Treloar, J. H. (1985). The relationship of the Hooper Visual Organization Test to sex, age, and intelligence of elementary school children. *Measurement and Evaluation in Counseling and Development, 17*, 203-206.

32. Johnston, C. W., & Lanak, B. (1985). Comparison of the Koppitz and Watkins scoring systems for the Bender Gestalt Test. *Journal of Learning Disabilities, 18*, 377-378.

33. Kermani, E. J., Borod, J. C., Brown, P. H., & Tunnell, G. (1985). New psychopathologic findings in AIDS: Case report. *Journal of Clinical Psychiatry, 46*, 240-241.

34. McKay, M. F., & Neale, M. D. (1985). Predicting early school achievement in reading and handwriting using major 'error' categories from the Bender-Gestalt Test for young children. *Perceptual and Motor Skills, 60*, 647-654.

35. McNamara, K. M., Wechsler, F. S., & Larson, P. (1985). Neuropsychological investigation in cerebral Whipple's disease: A case study. *Clinical Neuropsychology, 7*, 131-137.

36. Moon, C., Marlowe, M., Stellern, J., & Errera, J. (1985). Main and interaction effects of metallic pollutants on cognitive functioning. *Journal of Learning Disabilities, 18*, 217-221.

37. Neale, M. D., & McKay, M. F. (1985). Scoring the Bender-Gestalt Test using the Koppitz Developmental System: Interrater reliability, item difficulty, and scoring implications. *Perceptual and Motor Skills, 60*, 627-636.

38. Ninness, H. A. C., Graben, L., Miller, B., & Whaley, D. (1985). The effect of contingency management strategies on the Bender Gestalt diagnostic indicators of emotionally disturbed children. *Child Study Journal, 15*, 13-28.

39. Okasha, A., Kamel, M., Lotaif, F., Khalil, A. H., & Bishry, Z. (1985). Academic difficulty among male Egyptian university students: II. Associations with demographic and psychological factors. *British Journal of Psychiatry, 146*, 144-150.

40. Rao, A. V., & Potash, H. M. (1985). Size factors on the Bender-Gestalt Test and their relation to trait anxiety and situationally induced anxiety. *Journal of Clinical Psychology, 41*, 834-838.

41. Sherman, R. G., Berling, B. S., & Oppenheimer, S. (1985). Increasing community independence for adolescents with spina bifida. *Adolescence, 20*, 1-13.

42. Sohlberg, S. C. (1985). Personality and neuropsychological performance of high-risk children. *Schizophrenia Bulletin, 11*, 48-60.

43. Taylor, R. L., Ziegler, E. W., & Partenio, I. (1985). An empirical investigation of the Adaptive Behavior Inventory for Children. *Psychological Reports, 57*, 640-642.

44. Aylward, E. H., & Schmidt, S. (1986). An examination of three tests of visual-motor integration. *Journal of Learning Disabilities, 19*, 328-330.

45. Black, F. W. (1986). Digit repetition in brain-damaged adults: Clinical and theoretical implications. *Journal of Clinical Psychology, 42*, 770-782.

46. Black, F. W. (1986). Neuroanatomic and neuropsychologic correlates of digit span performance by brain-damaged adults. *Perceptual and Motor Skills, 63*, 815-822.

47. Bowers, T. G., Washburn, S. E., & Livesay, J. R. (1986). Predicting neuropsychological impairment by screening instruments and intellectual evaluation indices: Implications for the meaning of Kaufman's Factor III. *Psychological Reports, 59*, 487-493.

48. Huebner, E. S., & Cummings, J. A. (1986). Influence of race and test data ambiguity upon school psychologists' decisions. *School Psychology Review, 15*, 410-417.

49. Itskowitz, R., Bar-El, Y., & Gross, Y. (1986). Thought processes in culturally deprived and learning disabled children—A comparative study. *Journal of Learning Disabilities, 19*, 432-437.

50. Knoff, H. M., Cotter, V., & Coyle, W. (1986). Differential effectiveness of receptive language and visual-motor assessments in identifying academically gifted elementary school students. *Perceptual and Motor Skills, 63*, 719-725.

51. Lewis, D. O., Pincus, J. H., Feldman, M., Jackson, L., & Bard, B. (1986). Psychiatric, neurological, and psychoeducational characteristics of 15 death row inmates in the United States. *American Journal of Psychiatry, 143*, 838-845.

52. Livesay, J. R. (1986). Clinical utility of Wechsler's deterioration index in screening for behavioral impairment. *Perceptual and Motor Skills, 63*, 619-626.

53. Malatesha, R. N. (1986). Visual motor ability in normal and disabled readers. *Perceptual and Motor Skills, 62*, 627-630.

54. Rantakallio, P., & von Wendt, L. (1986). Mental retardation and subnormality in a birth cohort of 12,000 children in Northern Finland. *American Journal of Mental Deficiency, 90*, 380-387.

55. Stevenson, H. W., & Newman, R. S. (1986). Long-term prediction of achievement and attitudes in mathematics and reading. *Child Development, 57*, 646-659.

56. Stone, M. H. (1986). Exploratory psychotherapy in schizophrenia-spectrum patients: A reevaluation in the light of long-term follow-up of schizophrenic and borderline patients. *Bulletin of the Menninger Clinic, 50,* 287-306.

57. Tarbox, A. R., Connors, G. J., & McLaughlin, E. J. (1986). Effects of drinking pattern on neuropsychological performance among alcohol misusers. *Journal of Studies on Alcohol, 47,* 176-179.

58. Uzzell, B. P., & Oler, J. (1986). Chronic low-level mercury exposure and neuropsychological functioning. *Journal of Clinical and Experimental Neuropsychology, 8,* 581-593.

59. Vance, B., Fuller, G. B., & Lester, M. L. (1986). A comparison of the Minnesota Perceptual Diagnostic Test Revised and the Bender Gestalt. *Journal of Learning Disabilities, 19,* 211-214.

60. Werner, E. E. (1986). Resilient offspring of alcoholics: A longitudinal study from birth to age 18. *Journal of Studies on Alcohol, 47,* 34-40.

61. Bach, Z. (1987). Keep "Gestalt" in the name of the test: The curious name permutations of the Bender-Gestalt Test. *Journal of Personality Assessment, 51,* 109-111.

62. Canavan, P., Kraemer, D., Brannigan, G. G., & Hijikata, S. (1987). Torque as a predictor of reading achievement. *Journal of Genetic Psychology, 148,* 349-356.

63. Eliason, M. J., & Richman, L. C. (1987). The Continuous Performance Test in learning disabled and nondisabled children. *Journal of Learning Disabilities, 20,* 614-619.

64. Grunau, R. V. E., & Low, M. D. (1987). Cognitive and task-related EEG correlates of arithmetic performance in adolescents. *Journal of Clinical and Experimental Neuropsychology, 9,* 563-574.

65. Hart, R. P., Kwentus, J. A., Taylor, J. R., & Harkins, S. W. (1987). Rate of forgetting in dementia and depression. *Journal of Consulting and Clinical Psychology, 55,* 101-105.

66. Ivnik, R. J., Sharbrough, F. W., & Laws, E. R., Jr. (1987). Effects of anterior temporal lobectomy on cognitive function. *Journal of Clinical Psychology, 43,* 128-137.

67. O'Brien Towle, P., & Schwarz, J. C. (1987). The Child Behavior Checklist as applied to archival data: Factor structure and external correlates. *Journal of Clinical Child Psychology, 16,* 69-79.

68. Rossini, E. D., & Kaspar, J. C. (1987). The validity of the Bender-Gestalt emotional indicators. *Journal of Personality Assessment, 51,* 254-261.

69. Boudreault, M., Thivierge, J., Coté, R., Boutin, P., Julien, Y., & Bergeron, S. (1988). Cognitive development and reading achievement in pervasive-add, situational-add and control children. *Journal of Child Psychology and Psychiatry and Allied Disciplines, 29,* 611-619.

70. Bow, J N. (1988). A comparison of intellectually superior male reading achievers and underachievers from a neuropsychological perspective. *Journal of Learning Disabilities, 21,* 118-123.

71. Davis, D. D., & Templer, D. I. (1988). Neurobehavioral functioning in children exposed to narcotics in utero. *Addictive Behaviors, 13,* 275-283.

72. Finch, A. J., Jr., Blount, R., Saylor, C. F., Wolfe, V. V., Pallmeyer, T. P., McIntosh, J. A., Griffin, J. M., & Carek, D. J. (1988). Intelligence and emotional/behavioral factors as correlates of achievement in child psychiatric inpatients. *Psychological Reports, 63,* 163-170.

73. Mallinger, B. L., & Longley, K. F. (1988). BIP-Bender protocols of learning disabled and regular education students. *Perceptual and Motor Skills, 67,* 193-194.

74. Matilainen, R., Heinonen, K., & Siren-Tiusanen, H. (1988). Effect of intrauterine growth retardation (IUGR) on the psychological performance of preterm children at preschool age. *Journal of Child Psychology and Psychiatry and Allied Disciplines, 29,* 601-609.

75. Smith, T. C., & Smith, B. L. (1988). The Visual Aural Digit Span Test and Bender Gestalt Test as predictors of Wide Range Achievement Test—Revised scores. *Psychology in the Schools, 25,* 264-269.

76. Wagner, E. E., & Flamos, O. (1988). Optimized split-half reliability for the Bender Visual Motor Gestalt Test: Further evidence for the use of the maximization procedure. *Journal of Personality Assessment, 52,* 454-458.

77. Aptekar, L. (1989). Characteristics of the street children of Colombia. *Child Abuse & Neglect, 13,* 427-437.

78. Bieliauskas, L. A., & Glantz, R. H. (1989). Depression type in Parkinson disease. *Journal of Clinical and Experimental Neuropsychology, 11,* 597-604.

79. Calev, A., Ben-Tzvi, E., Shapira, B., Drexler, H., Carasso, R., & Lerer, B. (1989). Distinct memory impairments following electroconvulsive therapy and imipramine. *Psychological Medicine, 19,* 111-119.

80. Coursey, R. D., Lees, R. W., & Siever, L. J. (1989). The relationship between smooth pursuit eye movement impairment and psychological measures of psychopathology. *Psychological Medicine, 19,* 343-358.

81. Goddard, R., & Tuber, S. (1989). Boyhood separation anxiety disorder: Thought disorder and object relations psychopathology as manifested in Rorschach imagery. *Journal of Personality Assessment, 53,* 239-252.

82. Lownsdale, W. S., Rogers, B. J., & McCall, J. N. (1989). Concurrent validation of Hutt's Bender Gestalt screening method for schizophrenia, depression, and brain damage. *Journal of Personality Assessment, 53,* 832-836.

83. Snow, J. H., & Desch, L. W. (1989). Characteristics of empirically derived subgroups based on intelligence and visual-motor score patterns. *Journal of School Psychology, 27,* 265-275.

84. Snow, J. H., & Desch, L. W. (1989). Subgroups based on medical, developmental, and growth variables with a sample of children and adolescents referred for learning difficulties. *The International Journal of Clinical Neuropsychology, 11,* 71-79.

85. Suzuki, L. A., & Leton, D. A. (1989). Spontaneous talkers among students with learning disabilities: Implications of right cerebral dysfunction. *Journal of Learning Disabilities, 22,* 397-399.

86. Hirt, M., & Pithers, W. (1990). Arousal and maintenance of schizophrenic attention. *Journal of Clinical Psychology, 46,* 15-21.

87. Lorandos, D. A. (1990). Change in adolescent boys at Teen Ranch: A five-year study. *Adolescence, 25,* 509-516.

88. Svensson, P. W., & Hill, M. A. (1990). Interrater reliability of the Koppitz Developmental scoring method in the clinical evaluation of the single case. *Perceptual and Motor Skills, 70,* 615-623.

89. Zagar, R., Arbit, J., Sylvies, R., Busch, K. G., & Hughes, J. R. (1990). Homicidal adolescents: A replication. *Psychological Reports, 67,* 1235-1242.

90. Campbell, J. W., D'Amato, R. C., Raggio, D. J., & Stephens, K. D. (1991). Construct validity of the computerized Continuous Performance Test with measures of intelligence, achievement, and behavior. *Journal of School Psychology, 29,* 143-150.

91. Harrison, K. A., & Romanczyk, R. G. (1991). Response patterns of children with learning disabilities: Is impulsivity a stable response style? *Journal of Learning Disabilities, 24,* 252-255.

92. Schachter, S., Brannigan, G. G., & Tooke, W. (1991). Comparison of two scoring systems for the Modified Version of the Bender-Gestalt Test. *Journal of School Psychology, 29,* 265-269.

Review of the Hutt Adaptation of the Bender-Gestalt Test by JACK A. NAGLIERI, Professor of School Psychology, Ohio State University, Columbus, OH:

The Hutt Adaptation of the Bender-Gestalt Test is a system of analyzing performance on the Bender-Gestalt to "maximize projective features of the test performance and to provide both clinical and objective methods for its analysis" (Hutt, 1985, p. 25). The technique involves several approaches to obtaining information about the individual from a phase when the designs are copied in the typical fashion. Other phases include, for example, an elaboration phase where the subject is asked to modify the drawings, a recall phase where the subject is requested to draw all the figures from memory, and an interview analysis where questions are asked about the drawings. In general, the Hutt Adaptation of the Bender-Gestalt is a classic example of insightful clinical expertise that remains to be substantiated by experimental results. This was recognized by Hutt in the beginning of the text when he stated "there is still a lack of fully adequate, empirical evidence for some of the statements that follow" (p. 67). This remark understates the need and should lead those who advocate this approach to obtain validity evidence prior to its use as a screening test for psychopathology.

Any attempt to evaluate the Hutt Adaptation of the Bender-Gestalt according to current standards inevitably gives the reviewer the sense of being in a time warp. Although obviously written by an accomplished clinician, the text is devoid of the kinds of psychometric information required for any test published according to today's standards. These limitations will become obvious as the norms, reliability, validity, and test interpretation are evaluated.

The quality of the norms for the Hutt Adaptation of the Bender-Gestalt can be described only as inadequate. "Normative" data are provided for normals ($n = 140$), outpatient neurotics ($n = 150$), inpatient neurotics ($n = 55$), unipolar depressives ($n = 68$), outpatient schizophrenics ($n = 60$), chronic schizophrenics ($n = 155$), and organic brain-damaged ($n = 147$) adults. Hutt's description of these data is minimal and these data certainly cannot be considered to represent normal or clinical populations described. To his credit, Hutt recognized the limits of these "norms" when he stated the "organic group is a very heterogeneous group and is not claimed to be representative of typical organic cases" (p. 110). The importance of this limitation, however, was not adequately recognized. That is, a problem of this magnitude should be corrected prior to publication of any test. Therefore, because of the paucity of information on the normative samples and the ambiguity that results, the "norms" presented by Hutt cannot be seriously considered as useful for determining typical performance. The "normative" data for children aged 10 to 12 years is similarly unacceptable.

According to the studies cited by Hutt, the test-retest and interrater reliabilities of the Hutt Adaptation of the Bender-Gestalt appear to be acceptable; however, given the limitations of the "norms" this seems to be a moot issue. Similarly, the usefulness of the validity evidence presented in Hutt's text is questioned by the failure to provide adequate normative values for the system and the serious limitation this places on those who may wish to use the procedure.

Perhaps the only advantage of the Hutt Adaptation of the Bender-Gestalt is that it is an excellent example of the clinical approach to test interpretation. The thorough analysis of the manner in which the Bender-Gestalt figures are reproduced under different conditions and the manner in which additional information can be obtained from this process is impressive. If there were acceptable norms and experimental validation of the wealth of information presented in the Hutt Adaptation of the Bender-Gestalt, this approach could have value. In its present form, however, the approach is a complex, rich, and academically interesting technique that needs appropriate norms and experimental validation.

In summary, the Hutt Adaptation of the Bender-Gestalt is an excellent example of good clinical interpretation and hypothesis generation, and at the same time, an example of the kind of test that cannot meet today's standards. The "norms" provided in Hutt's text cannot be used to gauge the performance of individuals because of the extremely small sample sizes, ambiguity of the samples, and overall lack of information about the nature of the groups. This fundamental weakness precludes the use of the system in making defensible decisions about individuals. Although it may have utility for developing initial hypotheses, users of the Hutt Adaptation of the Bender-Gestalt must be cognizant of the fact that their interpretations may not withstand careful criticism or experimental analysis.

Review of the Hutt Adaptation of the Bender-Gestalt Test by JOHN E. OBRZUT, Professor of Educational Psychology, and CAROL A. BOLIEK, Assistant Research Scientist, Speech and Hearing Sciences, University of Arizona, Tucson, AZ:

The Hutt Adaptation of the Bender-Gestalt Test (HABGT) was designed initially to help delineate personality problems, assess impoverished mental capabilities, and to analyze possible consequences of neurological impairment or deficit. The fourth edition (Hutt, 1985) was undertaken to present current clinical and research findings relative to the use of this technique to the practicing clinician. In such an attempt, the entire work has been reorganized, and a final chapter has been added to present the test rationale and principles of application in clinical practice and therapeutic work. Additional research to confirm the validity of certain test indices in discriminating between well-adjusted and poorly adjusted children and adolescents is presented.

The nine designs contained in the fourth edition are modifications of Bender's original designs (smaller and more uniform in size) and are similar to those used in the second and third editions (Hutt, 1969; 1977). Although interpretation using projective theory remains the focus of the fourth edition, objective methods of scoring and interpretation are provided as well. Essentially, the projective approach tries to understand the individual's personality style; needs, conflict, and defenses; level of maturity; and coping methods and ego strength. The tacit assumption is that the HABGT, a perceptual-motoric test, taps aspects of behavior not available in verbal tests such as earlier levels of meaningful and conflictual experience and allows for less distortion of interpretation.

In order to maximize the projective features of the test, administration of the HABGT involves three phases: copy, elaboration, and association. In the copying phase the subject is asked to copy the drawings as accurately as possible. In the elaboration phase the subject is asked to modify or change the drawings to make them more acceptable to self. In the association phase the subject is asked what each copied design or modified design resembles or suggests. Other methods of administration including the tachistoscopic method (limited exposure time of stimulus card), the recall method, group methods, and other experimental methods are offered as well. However, interpretations derived from the projective approach are seriously questioned due to the subjective nature of this approach and lack of concrete research to validate such interpretation.

The objective approach, involving the use of a Psychopathology Scale, Adience-Abience Scale, and/or configural analysis approach, may be more useful to the clinician, although reliability and validity data are still lacking. The Psychopathology Scale is designed to determine the general pathology of individuals and consists of 17 factors (e.g., sequence, position of first drawing, use of space, curvature difficulty, change of angulation) based on scores derived from subjects' productions in the copy phase only. Hutt purports the factors were first derived from extensive clinical experience similar to the work done by Thweatt, Obrzut, and Taylor (1972) and then from research studies; therefore, the factors were not derived statistically. However, the fourth edition does relate additional research primarily by Lacks (1984), Marley (1982), and Monheit (1983) to confirm the stability and significance of several factors (specifically—sequence, collision, retrogression, fragmentation, overlapping difficulty, and preservation). It is important to note, however, that Lacks and Marley used Orthopsychiatric cards rather than the HABGT cards in their research. Several other current research studies are alluded to, but the breadth of investigation and explanation of additional research pertinent to the reliability and validity of Hutt's factorial structure, based on use of his cards and approach, remains in question. Although scale values for factors have not been statistically derived, scale values vary from 1 (no problems) to 10 (severe problems). Of note, scale values for Factor 2, "Position of the First Drawing," have been modified from those depicted in the third edition (Hutt, 1977).

No attempt has been made in the fourth edition to improve the extremely limited and poorly described norming samples used to form the Psychopathology Scale. The adult norming sample consists of 140 normal individuals (of whom 80 were screened for signs of psychiatric disturbance and 60 were unselected college students) and six groups with various forms of psychopathology. Subjects were not randomly assigned; rather they were Hutt's or other clinical psychologists' clients or were derived from state mental hospitals. The norming sample of younger subjects consisted of groups of 28 to 39 children each composed of ages 10, 11, or 12. To gain entry into the "normal" group only one restriction applied—they could not have been referred for special study by the school psychologist or clinic. Those classified as "disturbed" children

had only to be reported by teachers as showing problems in their personal or social adjustment. The mean and standard deviations are supplied for each norming group, but standard scores are not provided.

Interscorer reliability of the Psychopathology Scale is reported to be .96 and .90 (from two experienced scorers and one experienced/one inexperienced scorer, respectively). Test-retest reliability with a group of hospitalized patients yielded a correlation of .87 for males and .83 for females. The Psychopathology Scale distinguishes psychotic individuals from normal individuals, and research provided by Lacks (1984) suggests use of the scale distinguishes those with organic brain syndrome from normals and other psychotic groups. However, no evidence is presented to show the utility of the HABGT in distinguishing those with chronic schizophrenia from those with organic brain damage. This primary weakness was noted by Sattler (1985) in his review of the second edition and remains an issue.

The Adience-Abience Scale (perceptual openness vs. closeness) as well as a configural analysis approach is presented to help identify psychiatric conditions and may be used within the objective approach. The Adience-Abience Scale attempts to measure the individual's perceptual orientation toward the world and has not been modified since the second edition. The items of this scale correlate .69 with those on the Psychopathology Scale, indicating significant overlap between the scales. The scale consists of 12 factors assigned a weight from +2 (high adience) to -2 (high abience). The norming sample consists of 500 individuals composed of five of the seven groups comprising the Psychopathology Scale. Tentative norming data for children are provided, based on a sample of 331 "normal," "disturbed," and "boys/girls club" subjects ages 10–16. Additional description of the norming sample is lacking. Interrater reliability coefficients range from .90 to .94 and test-retest reliability over an interval of 2 weeks for each of two different groups was found to be .84. Some evidence of the scale's construct validity is offered even though Hutt admits the need for further research.

The configural approach assumes that groups of people may be distinguished from other groups based on configurations expressed in the HABGT. The sparse research presented supports the configural approach as a useful procedure to screen and differentiate individuals with organic brain syndrome from other psychiatric patients and normals. However, further research is warranted to substantiate such an approach and to validate whether the positive identification of other psychiatric conditions can be determined. The test factor and scores as well as the weights for the configural approach have been modified (e.g., Essential Psychoneurosis and Mental

Retardation) and the test factor, scores, and weights for a new sign—"Emotional Disturbance in Adolescents"—have been added to the five signs presented in the third edition (e.g., brain damage, schizophrenia, depression, psychoneurosis, and mental retardation). The weights were assigned empirically on the basis of the discriminatory capacity of the components.

Only a couple of case studies using the HABGT have been retained in this edition. Rather, Hutt discusses some of the special characteristics of the test figures, general problems in psychodiagnosis, and illustrates the Testing-the-Limits Method. Unfortunately, because he does not validate his statements with pertinent research, they are of little use to the clinician.

Overall, the HABGT may be useful when screening for organic brain damage or psychiatric disturbance. However, further research using the HABGT on clearly specified samples is warranted before any of the scales or the configural analysis approach can be used for differential diagnosis. Finally, continued insufficient reliability and validity data should caution the clinician from using the projective approach in personality assessment.

REVIEWER'S REFERENCES

Hutt, M. L. (1969). The Hutt adaptation of the Bender-Gestalt Test (2nd ed.). New York: Grune & Stratton.

Thweatt, R. C., Obrzut, J. E., & Taylor, H. D. (1972). The development and validation of a soft-sign scoring system for the Bender-Gestalt. *Psychology In The Schools, 9,* 170-174.

Hutt, M. L. (1977). The Hutt adaptation of the Bender-Gestalt Test (3rd ed.). New York: Grune & Stratton.

Marley, M. L. (1982). *Organic brain pathology and the Bender-Gestalt Test: A differential diagnostic scoring system.* New York: Grune & Stratton.

Monheit, S. (1983). The Bender-Gestalt Test as a discriminator of normal, severely disturbed, and delinquent male adolescents. Unpublished doctoral dissertation, University of San Francisco.

Lacks, P. (1984). *Bender Gestalt screening for brain dysfunction.* New York: John Wiley & Sons.

Hutt, M. L. (1985). The Hutt adaptation of the Bender-Gestalt Test (4th ed.). Orlando: Grune & Stratton.

Sattler, J. (1985). [Review of the Hutt Adaptation of the Bender-Gestalt Test.] In J. V. Mitchell, Jr. (Ed.), *The ninth mental measurements yearbook* (pp. 184-185). Lincoln, NE: Buros Institute of Mental Measurements.

[41]
Bennett Mechanical Comprehension Test.

Purpose: "Measure(s) the ability to perceive and understand the relationship of physical forces and mechanical elements in practical situations."

Population: Industrial employees and high school and adult applicants for mechanical positions or engineering schools.

Publication Dates: 1940–80.

Acronym: BMCT.

Scores: Total score only.

Administration: Group.

Forms, 2: S, T (equivalent forms).

Price Data, 1987: $30 per examination kit; $55 per 25 test booklets (Form S or T); $27 per 50 IBM answer sheets; $11 per hand-scoring key (Form S or T); $12 per manual ('69, 14 pages); $52 per cassette or reel-to-reel recording of test questions (Form S or T); scoring service offered by publisher.

Time: 30(35) minutes.

Comments: Tape recordings of test questions read aloud are available for use with examinees who have limited reading abilities.

Author: George K. Bennett.

Publisher: The Psychological Corporation.

Cross References: See T3:282 (7 references) and T2:2239 (9 references); for reviews by Harold P. Bechtoldt and A. Oscar H. Roberts, and an excerpted review by Ronald K. Hambleton, see 7:1049 (22 references); see also 6:1094 (15 references) and 5:889 (46 references); for a review by N. W. Morton of earlier forms, see 4:766 (28 references); for reviews by Charles M. Harsh, Lloyd G. Humphreys, and George A. Satter, see 3:683 (19 references).

TEST REFERENCES

1. Lowman, R. L., Williams, R. E., & Leeman, G. E. (1985). The structure and relationship of college women's primary abilities and vocational interests. *Journal of Vocational Behavior, 27,* 298-315.

2. Hamilton, J. W., & Dickinson, T. L. (1987). Comparison of several procedures for generating J-coefficients. *Journal of Applied Psychology, 72,* 49-54.

3. Bordieri, J. E. (1988). Reward contingency, perceived competence, and attribution of intrinsic motivation: An observer simulation. *Psychological Reports, 63,* 755-762.

Review of the Bennett Mechanical Comprehension Test by HILDA WING, Personnel Psychologist, Federal Aviation Administration, Washington, DC:

The Bennett Mechanical Comprehension Test (Bennett) is a venerable measure of mechanical ability, an ability important for success in a wide variety of technical skilled and professional occupations. I have a number of concerns about the Bennett, concerns that some test users might share and the publisher might be encouraged to correct. However, I believe the Bennett to be a reasonably well-developed and well-documented instrument whose use should be considered whenever the assessment of mechanical ability in youth and adults is required.

My most critical remarks concern the appearance of the test. It just looks old. The test copy I reviewed listed "copyright renewed" no later than 1969, and figures in test item diagrams reflect their pre-Civil Rights Act origins. Of the 68 test items in Form S, 5 had male figures while 3 had female figures. All of the figures were Caucasians. The males were all active: workmen, soldier, hiker. The female figures were decidedly more passive: One young woman was on a hammock (!), another was demonstrating a trapeze, and two girls were on swings. Tests should not have items that inadvertently offend examinees, as offensive items could bias test scores. The current work force is much more female and much more minority than when these test items were developed.

The Test Manual, also copyrighted in 1969, is mostly helpful. In describing the history of the forms of the Bennett, the Manual includes the item budget, a list of the number of items in each of 18 content categories covered by the test. It would be useful to have more detailed information, such as, for example, the average and spread of item difficulties within each category. Such information would be very helpful to the test user in developing a content validity justification for use of the Bennett.

The 1969 Manual presents much useful data. First, there are correlations with other tests, including the Differential Aptitude Test (DAT) of Mechanical Reasoning, Forms L and M, as a parallel version of the Bennett. The Psychological Corporation publishes both these tests. In addition, Mechanical Comprehension as measured by the Bennett is not very independent of verbal and numerical ability, although it is more strongly related to spatial ability and tool knowledge.

Additional statistics are included whose utility depends somewhat on the test user's tolerance for the psychometric attitudes shared over 20 years ago. The Bennett's normative data in this 1969 Manual are elderly and mostly limited to male samples. The discussion of sex differences struck me as patronizing. Because the Bennett was developed for occupations that are traditionally male and are only now opening up to women, it is perhaps unfair to fault a 1969 Manual with sexism. However, using the Bennett effectively with women now will require, at the least, better norms, a deficit partially met by the 1980 Manual Supplement, discussed below.

The critical employment statistics of the Bennett, albeit based on all male samples, are given in the 1969 Manual and are mostly acceptable. On the one hand, corrected reliabilities are in the high .80s; validities for a variety of criteria range from .10 to .64, with median validities in the mid-30s. It is not clear whether these validity coefficients were corrected for attenuation. On the other hand, the studies of form equivalence and short-term practice effects did not strike me as sufficiently rigorous.

The 1980 Manual Supplement would be required for anyone seriously considering the use of the Bennett for employment in today's environment. It includes additional normative and validity data collected in business organizations between 1969 and 1977. First, there are nine new norms groups and more recent data for three of the 1969 norms groups, with some separate norms for race and gender groups. Both applicant and employee groups are included. One norms group combines white females with minority males, the logic of which is not clear. Second, there are 14 additional validity studies, with two-digit *Dictionary of Occupational Titles* codes. (I cannot help but wonder why, with an instrument of the age and quality of the Bennett, there are not many more cited validation studies.) Third, the 1980 Supplement includes a discussion of critical issues in validity studies, such as the relevance of the test and the quality of the criteria. Fourth, there is also a table providing raw score equivalents of the DAT Mechanical Reasoning

(Form T) and the Bennett. For a sample of 175 employees, the correlation between these two tests is over .80.

In summary, if you need a test of mechanical aptitude for occupational guidance or selection, the Bennett is worth your consideration. Its positive attributes include an adequate description of its character and contents, acceptable normative data and validity, and a history of useful service. On the negative side is the datedness of the test contents and statistics for new members of applicant pools for traditionally male jobs: women and minorities. I would surmise that most of the older statistics would generalize adequately to new situations, but I would recommend that individual users decide for themselves how serious this datedness is for any prospective use. A more positive recommendation I will make is based on information in both the 1969 Manual and the 1980 Supplement that supports the parallel forms equivalence between the Bennett and the DAT Mechanical Reasoning. I would judge that improvements in appearance and norms for the more recently revised DAT might permit the expansion of the generalizability of the reliability and validity statistics for the older Bennett. Perhaps in subsequent editions, the Psychological Corporation will do this for prospective test users.

[42]

Bilingual Home Inventory.
Purpose: Assesses "students with severe disabilities" within a context that is culturally and linguistically appropriate.
Population: Nonnative speakers of English.
Publication Dates: 1985–86.
Acronym: BHI.
Scores: No scores reported.
Administration: Individual.
Price Data, 1989: $9 per manual (specify edition).
Time: Administration time not reported.
Comments: Family interview assessing student skills.
Authors: Susan M. Pellegrini and Herbert Grossman.
Publisher: San Jose State University.
  a) FILIPINO EDITION.
  Publication Date: 1986.
  Author: Ma. Luisa Villongco.
  b) PORTUGUESE EDITION.
  Publication Date: 1986.
  Authors: Heraldo G. Da Silva and Maria A. Da Silva.
  c) SPANISH EDITION.
  Publication Dates: 1985–86.
  Authors: Paula Hughes, Evelyn Ortiz-Stanley, and Michele Thomas.
  d) VIETNAMESE EDITION.
  Publication Date: 1985.
  Authors: Mai Dao and Kim-Lan Nguyen.

Review of the Bilingual Home Inventory by ANDRES BARONA, Associate Professor of Psychology in Education, Arizona State University, Tempe, AZ:

The Bilingual Home Inventory (BHI) is a semistructured instrument designed to obtain information useful in the development of ecologically functional Individual Education Programs (IEPs). The authors state that the BHI is culturally and linguistically appropriate and is to be used when interviewing parents and family members of culturally and linguistically different handicapped students. The BHI is available in Vietnamese, Filipino, Portuguese, and Spanish.

The present review focuses on the Spanish version of the BHI. This version was developed by a group of special educators who work with severely handicapped Hispanic students and specialize in the use of environmental assessment procedures. The authors reiterate the PL 94-142 mandate requiring that minority students be assessed using culturally and linguistically appropriate measures and contend that the use of assessment procedures standardized on English-speaking handicapped students is biased and inappropriate for ethnic minorities with limited proficiency in English. Based on the authors' experiences with environmental approaches, they consider the BHI a more appropriate and practical option.

The BHI provides cells for recording and organizing a child's activities and skills in a variety of home and community sub-environments (e.g., the kitchen or living room). Although the subenvironments are not specifically defined, they are represented by nine activities performed by the child. These include: eating, dressing, toilet/grooming, leisure, daily living, friends or relatives, stores, recreation, and a miscellaneous "other" cell. Six variables delineate the information to be solicited about the child: likes and dislikes, mode of communication, current skill level, learning style, projected goals, and language preference. Each activity is described according to one of six variables. The inventory ranks three types of information related to current level of skills, long-term goals, and short-term objectives. The long-term goals are evaluated and ranked using a Goal Priority Rating Form, which is included in the manual. Each goal is evaluated on a scale of 1 to 3 on the basis of pre-established criteria provided in the manual.

Administration of the BHI, which takes approximately 2 hours, may be conducted by any individual familiar with IEP development, provided there is an awareness of the cultural influences that interact with the child's functioning. Ideally, the interview should be conducted in the preferred home language, although this is not required. The manual provides instructions to facilitate the interview process if an interpreter is needed. The authors recognize that some Hispanic families may not wish to conduct meetings in Spanish and suggest that the interviewer inquire about the preferred language as a demonstration of acceptance and respect. The manual includes a review of Hispanic cultural characteristics to assist users in maximizing their client rapport, heightening their sensitivity to individual differences, and encouraging them to refrain from stereotyping.

Although the protocol does not provide specific questions to be asked during the interview, the manual contains sample questions to guide examiners in developing their own. Steps to be taken before, during, and after the interview are also provided. According to the authors, this process of information collection and organization is based on other, unspecified protocol methods used in the United States, Mexico, and South America. The authors also report that the BHI was evaluated by professionals participating in the field testing: The BHI's usefulness as well as its cultural and linguistic appropriateness was reported to be highly approved by a consensus of these professionals. However, neither validity nor reliability studies are reported; this omission substantially limits the use of the BHI.

In summary, the BHI (Spanish version) seems well suited for use with a culturally and linguistically different population (Hispanics). It is relatively easy to administer, the materials are well designed, and the items appear to be directly related to the type of information associated with IEP development. On face value, the BHI can be (and has been) judged to be appropriate for use with diverse Spanish-speaking populations, although the psychometric properties of this inventory are unknown. Given that validity and reliability studies have not been conducted, a comparison of the BHI to other environmental approaches cannot be undertaken. This is unfortunate because the approach suggested seems quite sensible; the intrinsic involvement of family members and home life styles suggests that such an approach should be used for culturally and linguistically different students, as well as for handicapped students regardless of ethnicity. Nonetheless, until more rigorous studies are undertaken and more data are provided, the BHI will likely remain a potentially good instrument with undetermined psychometric properties and usefulness.

Review of the Bilingual Home Inventory by DAN DOUGLAS, Associate Professor of English, Iowa State University, Ames, IA:

The Bilingual Home Inventory (BHI) was developed in 1985 in response to a California law requiring that culturally and linguistically different handicapped students be assessed with culturally and linguistically appropriate instruments. The authors of the BHI, special education professionals, based it on an "ecological assessment approach to educational decision making" (p. 2), which involves completing an environmental inventory of the student's home and family life. The information from the inventory is used to establish goals and objectives for the student's Individual Education

Program (IEP). The BHI has been published in four editions, Spanish-English, Vietnamese-English, Filipino-English, and Portuguese-English. The BHI manual, with the two languages printed on facing pages, was designed to facilitate the interviewer's ability to alternate between the two languages as necessary. BHI materials consist of a manual and a blank protocol form for recording responses during the interview. The manual contains a rationale for the BHI, a short summary of information about home and family life in the target culture, instructions for completing the inventory, which include sample questions, and instructions for using the inventory to complete the Individual Education Program. This final step involves rating the importance of each of the educational goals stated by the student's family during the interview on a 3-point scale. Approximately 900 copies of the BHI have been sold, with permission to duplicate as needed.

FORMAT. The BHI interview may be conducted by the interviewer alone or with the assistance of an interpreter. It may be tape recorded, with the permission of the family. The interview requires about 2 hours to complete and covers a number of age-appropriate, functional environments or activities: eating, dressing, toilet/grooming, leisure, daily living, family and friends, stores, recreation, and "other" environments (e.g., transportation, church, library, or doctor's office). Each environment is discussed in terms of six student-centered descriptors: likes and dislikes, preferred mode of communication, skill level, learning style, preferred language of instruction, and the family's projected goals for the student's education. Suggested questions are provided for eliciting information from the family about each of the environments and descriptors. Notes on the responses are recorded on the protocol form provided with the manual, and this information is then used to complete an Individual Education Program in terms of the student's present level of functioning, long-term goals and short-term objectives. Projected educational skill goals are rated on a 3-point scale by the interviewer in terms of their importance, frequency, and appropriateness. The ratings for each skill are then totalled to produce a final rating with a 22-point range.

RELIABILITY. No information on interrater or intrarater reliability is provided, so it is not known how stable the assessment may be from one occasion or interviewer to the next.

VALIDITY. As a field test, the BHI was sent to special education professionals in a number of states. They evaluated it on its overall usefulness and its linguistic and cultural appropriateness. The evaluations were uniformly positive. No other information concerning the validity of the BHI or the goal priority rating has been reported.

SUMMARY. The Bilingual Home Inventory appears to be a theoretically sound interview schedule that attempts to quantify a number of behavioral and psychological features related to educational goals for disabled students in linguistically and culturally appropriate format. Its reliability and validity as an evaluative instrument have yet to be demonstrated empirically.

[43]

Biofeedback Certification Examination.

Purpose: A certification examination covering "the knowledge needed by providers of biofeedback services at the time they begin practice."
Population: Entry-level biofeedback service providers.
Publication Dates: 1980–84.
Scores: 4 performance domains: Instrumentation, Clinical Intervention, Professional Conduct, Health and Education.
Administration: Group.
Manual: No manual.
Price Data: Available from BCIA.
Time: Administration time not reported.
Comments: Administration schedule available from BCIA.
Author: Biofeedback Certification Institute of America.
Publisher: Biofeedback Certification Institute of America.

[44]

Biographical and Personality Inventory, Series II.

Purpose: Serves as a measure of recovery potential and as an aid in determining a treatment plan.
Population: Delinquent youths.
Publication Dates: 1971–85.
Acronym: BPI.
Scores, 4: Amenability, Drug Proclivity, Estimate of Treatment Length, Behavioral Classification with Optimum Milieu and Treatment Environment.
Administration: Individual or group.
Price Data, 1987: $120 per 100 reusable test booklets ('85, 13 pages); $10 per 100 answer sheets; $10 per 100 profiles; $25 per scoring kit including key, secondary scale worksheets, and manual ('82, 9 pages).
Time: (60) minutes.
Authors: Ronald C. Force, Charles A. Burdsal, and James Klingsporn.
Publisher: Test Systems International.

Review of the Biographical and Personality Inventory, Series II by ROBERT J. DRUMMOND, Professor of Education and Program Director, Counselor Education, University of North Florida, Jacksonville, FL:

The Biographical and Personality Inventory (BPI) is a 200-item inventory designed for use to help counselors make decisions about the recovery potential of delinquent youth. The BPI identifies youthful offenders who are more or less ready to respond to an opportunity to change their behavior. The author purports the test will help well-read correctional workers to make or recommend selective placement and to augment the judgment of the judge, probation officer, or clinicians in working with the youth.

Currently there is a revised test booklet (Force, Burdsal, & Klingsporn, 1985), but the manual has not been revised. Previously there were two forms of the BPI (Force, 1971): Form A for males and Form B for females. The items are both in the true-false and multiple-choice formats.

The BPI provides a profile of the youth on eight scales: Responsive versus Hostile, Legal Involvement, Police Contacts, Inactive versus Active, Anxiety, Sensitive versus Callous (also called Self-Assurance), Depression, and Deviance. The BPI also provides a Predicted Coping Score, a General Drug Use/Addiction-Proneness Score, a Predicted Length of Treatment Score, and an Amenability Score.

The BPI reports predictive validity studies based upon youth who had been in the residential treatment program at the St. Francis Boys Home and were followed for 2 to 5 years after their release. The correlation between the coping criteria and amenability/coping score was .53. No construct validity studies are reported. There are no studies correlating the BPI with other personality measures having similar scales. There are no studies reported of the factor structure of the test. Items were derived from work at the St. Francis Boys Home and from other researchers and their instruments.

No reliability data are presented. The norming group is not described other than as part of a comprehensive 5-year post-treatment outcome study of up to 200 predelinquents or adjudged delinquents in each study. No age, grade, or gender information is presented on the norming group. No means and standard deviations are given for the scales on the BPI.

Instructions are provided the test administrator on how to score the items and compute the predicted coping score. The manual provides description of the Amenable Scores, the Coping, and the Length of Treatment Criterion.

The BPI is a specialized inventory designed for use with delinquent youth. There are a number of problems with the instrument that need to be addressed before it can be recommended for use. The authors must provide information on the construct validity and criterion-referenced validity of the BPI. There are no studies of the reliability of the instrument. The preliminary studies and norms were based upon youth who were involved in treatment at one time or another at the St. Francis Boys Home. A much larger sample of youth is needed, including youth from other treatment facilities, before the results can be generalized to delinquent youth. There is a need to cross-validate the results. The norms and weighing of scores in the predictive scales

might be completely different with another group of youth. The earlier edition had separate forms for males and females. We do not know whether there were any gender differences on the scales or whether the analysis is just based on males. We do not have any empirical evidence of the accuracy of the placement scores. Workers with delinquent youth might find the Jesness Behavior Check List (8:594; Jesness, 1984) a more useful instrument to use.

REVIEWER'S REFERENCE

Jesness, C. F. (1984). Jesness Behavior Check List. Palo Alto, CA: Consulting Psychologists Press, Inc.

[45]

Birth to Three Assessment and Intervention System.

Purpose: To identify and assess developmental delays in young children and to help develop individual programs to remediate those delays.

Population: Birth to 3 years.

Publication Dates: 1979–86.

Administration: Individual.

Price Data, 1989: $130 per complete kit including 25 screening test record forms, 25 checklist record forms, screening test manual ('86, 85 pages), checklist manual ('86, 107 pages), and intervention manual ('86, 77 pages).

Time: Administration time not reported.

Comments: 2 tests: Screening Test of Learning and Language Development, Checklist of Learning and Language Behavior; tests available as separates; other test materials (e.g., small toys, bell) must be supplied by examiner.

Authors: Tina E. Bangs and Susan Dodson (coauthor of screening test).

Publisher: DLM Teaching Resources.

a) SCREENING TEST OF LEARNING AND LANGUAGE DEVELOPMENT.

Purpose: "To serve as a screening instrument that will identify children who are at high risk for developmental delay."

Scores, 5: Language Comprehension, Language Expression, Avenues to Learning, Social/Personal Development, Motor Development.

Comments: Earlier edition called Birth to Three Developmental Scale.

b) CHECKLIST OF LEARNING AND LANGUAGE BEHAVIOR.

Purpose: "(a) To determine a child's developmental strengths and weaknesses in basic behavioral categories, (b) to provide the information necessary for writing behavioral goals and objectives for a child's Individual Developmental Plan (IDP), and (c) to provide the information needed to select activities and write lesson plans."

Scores: 5 Developmental Age scores: Language Comprehension, Language Expression, Avenues to Learning, Social/Personal Behaviors, Motor Behaviors.

Comments: "Criterion-referenced."

Cross References: For a review by Bonnie W. Camp of an earlier edition, see 9:152.

Review of the Birth To Three Assessment and Intervention System by DONNA SPIKER, Senior

Research Associate, Department of Psychiatry and Behavioral Sciences, Stanford University School of Medicine, and Stanford Center for the Study of Families, Children and Youth, Stanford, CA:

The Birth To Three Assessment and Intervention System is a set of materials for screening, program planning, and monitoring developmental progress of at-risk or delayed children below a 3-year level. It is an updated, expanded version of the Birth to Three Developmental Scale (Bangs & Dodson, 1979; 9:152). Included are three spiral-bound notebooks: an examiner's manual for a norm-referenced screening test, the Birth To Three Screening Test of Learning and Language Development; an examiner's manual for a criterion-referenced measure to monitor developmental progress and identify behavioral objectives for developing lesson plans, the Birth To Three Checklist of Learning and Language Behavior; and an intervention program planning guide, the Intervention Manual: A Parent-Teacher Interaction Program. A 4-page record form accompanies the Screening test; an 11-page form accompanies the Checklist. The Screening test contains 85 items divided into five areas: Language Comprehension; Language Expression; Avenues to Learning (cognitive and perceptual-motor items); Social/Personal Development; and Motor Development (fine and gross motor items). The Checklist instrument contains 240 items, 48 in each of these same areas, with 8 items for each area in each 6-month developmental age range from birth to 36 months.

The construction of items was based on existing infant/preschool developmental tests and assessment instruments (see Screening test manual, p. 67), and they will seem familiar to those trained in infant assessment. Both manuals contain detailed instructions for administering and scoring items. Standard materials for administering items are not provided, but the manuals contain lists of needed materials.

Instructions for items on both instruments include descriptions of needed materials, procedures for administering the item, required number of trials, and definitions for scoring performance as Pass, Emerging, and Fail. Many items require three trials, with Pass defined as successful performance on at least two trials, Emerging as successful performance on one trial or success with a portion of the task requirements, and Fail defined as no proficiency on the task. Generally, these definitions are stated as clear observable behaviors, with sufficient detail for unambiguous scoring.

The standardization sample for the Screening test consisted of 357 children from 4–36 months from California, Tennessee, and Utah, with 20 children from each state in each of the following age ranges: 4–6, 10–12, 16–18, 22-224, 28–30, 34-36 months,

to represent each 6-month age range from 0–36 months. The test is appropriate for children who are functioning between 4–36 months, and is not useful for very young infants. Each age group was balanced for gender and urban versus rural residence. The manual states that: "An attempt was made to include children of varying ethnic backgrounds and socioeconomic statuses" (p. 9), but no data are presented to describe these sample characteristics or to indicate test performance based on them. Items were selected for the Screening test if at least 80% of the children at the particular age level passed them.

Raw scores (items passed) for each subtest are converted to three derived scores: T-scores, percentile ranks, and stanines. No provision is made for a global score. For reasons that are not clearly stated, the norms are based on data from the earlier 1979 sample rather than the current standardization sample.

The instructions for using the norms tables (p. 61) are confusing and inadequate. Although the raw scores are in whole numbers, the norms are presented in tenths. The averaging method described usually does not result in one of the entries in the norms table, and for some raw scores for some ages there are multiple raw score entries. A call to the publishers failed to clarify the problem, but it is now being reviewed by them.

Issues of reliability and validity of the Screening test as a norm-referenced test are poorly addressed. Lack of standard test materials limits comparability of scores for different children. Interrater reliabilities for scoring protocols were reported to be between .88 and .99 for pairs of raters consisting of the senior author of the test, a nurse, and a speech pathologist. No test-retest reliability data are presented.

An additional problem concerns examiner qualifications. The manual states that the test can be used by "any person who can reliably observe child behaviors, follow the designated procedures in Part II of the examiner's manual, and assess a sampling of at least six children who are in the birth to 3 years chronological or developmental age range" (p. 17). Such requirements are inadequate because such a test is likely to be used with infants and toddlers who have developmental delays, sensory, social-emotional, and/or neurodevelopmental impairments. The standardization work was conducted by graduate students in speech pathology and practicing speech pathologists, examiners who are hardly naive about child development and psychometric assessment principles.

More serious is the lack of attention to test validity. No data are presented comparing test results to those for any other available standardized test. Nor are other data presented to support concurrent or predictive validity. Standard scores of less than 1.5 standard deviations below the mean are "indications of possible developmental delay" (p. 63), but this contention is not supported with validity studies. These omissions and the lack of detailed descriptive data about the standardization sample limit this instrument as a norm-referenced test.

The Checklist manual contains no information on how that instrument was constructed, nor about reliability or validity. Scoring of items is similar to scoring for the Screening test. Raw scores are converted to developmental age scores for each subscale. No provision is made for a global score. The cover page of the record form is used for recording subscale scores in both graphical and numerical form for three different evaluations. As with the Screening test, the lack of reliability and validity data seriously limits the user's ability to interpret scores. The Checklist manual contains no discussion of how to interpret scores.

The third component of the system, the Intervention Manual, is a 75-page handbook for use in program development by early intervention program staff for "handicapped children in the birth to 3 years developmental age range" (p. 1) and their parents. The manual contains 12 chapters divided into four major sections covering: (a) the rationale behind the assessment and intervention approach; (b) brief descriptions of the Screening test and the Checklist and their assessment uses; (c) a brief outline of some basic features of early intervention programs (e.g., program sites, curriculum content, lesson planning); and (d) descriptions of teaching strategies. The authors provide sample lesson plans that include explicit reference to parent involvement.

The Intervention Manual gives a good outline of some basic program features to consider in designing an early intervention program. The curriculum focus is on cognition and language skill development, with an emphasis on defining clear observable behavioral objectives that dictate the learning activities. Although there is mention of the communicative functions of language and the importance of social-emotional development, these developmental issues appear to be secondary in the espoused intervention model. These are issues that need more attention, given that the manual is to be used with at-risk or handicapped infants and young preschoolers. Similarly, the section on parent groups provides brief sketches of key issues to consider when establishing such groups, but the manual is limited in providing substantive content about such groups.

On the whole, the Intervention Manual is too brief and lacks sufficient depth to provide the basis for establishing or developing an early intervention program or as a curriculum package. Paraprofessionals with limited training in early childhood special education might be misled by this manual into thinking that assessing and intervening with handicapped infants and parents is a simple, straightforward enterprise. The early childhood special education field continues to struggle with many basic questions about effectiveness of different curriculum models, parent involvement models, approaches toward screening and assessment, and training requirements for staff. The Intervention Manual would be better titled: "Intervention Program Issues: An Introduction and Overview."

SUMMARY. The Birth To Three Assessment and Intervention System is a three-part set of materials for screening, program planning, and monitoring developmental progress of at-risk or delayed children below a 3-year level. It contains a screening test, a criterion-referenced checklist, and an intervention manual. The data presented on reliability, validity, and the standardization sample for the Screening test make it inadequate as a norm-referenced test, but additional studies could remedy that situation. The Checklist has face validity and could be useful in charting developmental progress in early intervention programs, providing extreme care is taken not to interpret performances in a strictly normative way until further validation studies are done. Data on reliability and concurrent or predictive validity are not available. The Intervention manual provides a good overview and introduction to early intervention program issues, but program specialists will need many additional resources for the in-depth coverage for implementing early childhood special education programs.

REVIEWER'S REFERENCE
Bangs, T. E., & Dodson, S. (1979). Birth to Three Developmental Scale. Allen, TX: DLM Teaching Resources.

[46]
Boehm Test of Basic Concepts—Preschool Version.

Purpose: To "measure a child's knowledge of twenty-six basic relational concepts considered necessary for achievement in the beginning years of school."
Population: Ages 3-0 to 5-0.
Publication Dates: 1984–86.
Scores: Total score only.
Administration: Individual.
Price Data, 1987: $45 per complete kit including picture book ('86, 112 pages), 35 individual record forms ('86, 5 pages), manual ('86, 35 pages), and class record ('86, 5 pages); $25 per picture book; $17.50 per 35 individual record forms; $2.50 per class record form; $10 per manual.
Time: (15) minutes.
Comments: Downward extension of the Boehm Test of Basic Concepts (10:32).
Author: Anne E. Boehm.
Publisher: The Psychological Corporation.

TEST REFERENCES

1. Zucker, S., & Riordan, J. (1988). Concurrent validity of new and revised conceptual language measures. *Psychology in the Schools, 25,* 252-256.

Review of the Boehm Test of Basic Concepts— Preschool Version by JUDY OEHLER-STINNETT, Assistant Professor of Psychology, Eastern Illinois University, Charleston, IL:

The Boehm Test of Basic Concepts—Preschool Version (BTBC-PV) is designed to assess knowledge of basic relational concepts such as up/down and tallest/shortest in 3- to 5-year-old children. The BTBC-PV represents a continuation of several decades of work for the author and is a downward extension of the Boehm Test of Basic Concepts (BTBC; 10:32). Considerable research on the BTBC has demonstrated that a child's knowledge of basic concepts is related to kindergarten readiness, school achievement, and performance on psychoeducational test instruments. Two studies have contributed to norms on the BTBC for preschool children (Levin, Henderson, Levin, & Hoffer, 1975; Smith, 1986), and the test has been used frequently with these children for research and assessment purposes. There is an established need for preschool norms or a preschool version of the BTBC. The author chose to publish two separate tests in 1986, the BTBC—Revised, appropriate for grades K–2, and the BTBC-PV. Users working with handicapped populations are encouraged in the BTBC-PV manual to use it with older handicapped children who find the BTBC-R too difficult as well as with preschoolers. An easel format is used. The child is required only to point to the correct answer. The test is individually administered. Thus, administration is easier than for the BTBC with distractible children or those with limited pencil-and-paper skills.

The test is designed for individual criterion-referenced assessment and can identify a child's specific concept weaknesses to be remediated by those working directly with the child. This use of the test is especially relevant for teachers. To facilitate teaching of basic concepts, the manual describes the stages of concept acquisition, specific recommendations for instructional planning, and refers the reader to the *Boehm Resource Guide for Basic Concept Teaching* (Boehm, 1976). Also included with the test are an Error Analysis Form and a Class Record Form. Although brief, the manual is written in a clear, straightforward manner that can be easily understood by those who are likely to use the test.

Item selection was based on a "careful review of relevant educational and psychological research literature, analyses of tape recordings made of classroom 'teacher talk,' and surveys of widely used curriculum materials." Existing psychological tests, the major source of item selection for another measure of basic concepts, the Bracken Basic Concept Scale (BBCS; 10:33), were not surveyed

for the BTBC-PV. However, all but one item on the BTBC-PV also appear on the BBCS. After a tryout of 110 items measuring 40 concepts with 214 children (Black, White, and Hispanic), and two smaller samples, solicited reviewers gave the author feedback regarding item bias and validity. The standardization version contains 26 concepts, each tested by two items, for a total of 52 items. Inclusion of two items per concept adds to the stability of the test. Users can compare a child's performance on pairs of items in order to better determine whether a child has mastered a particular concept.

Unfortunately, the manual does not describe the manner in which the test was reduced from 40 to 26 concepts. Discriminative ability of items at each age level, contributions to internal consistency, etc., were omitted. The manual simply states that from the solicited reviews and the tryout testing, the number of items and concepts was reduced. It is also interesting to note that while the original BTBC reported a list of 35 items rejected partly for being too easy for kindergartners, only three of these concepts appear on the BTBC-PV (two others appear as practice items), suggesting perhaps the need for an even further downward extension to 2-year-olds. Additionally, there are only three items that overlap with the BTBC-R, all of which occur on the BTBC-R's more difficult Booklet 2.

The BTBC-PV yields *T*-scores and percentiles. Age norms for older and/or handicapped children on the BTBC-PV are not provided and would be useful. An additional complication occurs for examiners trying to use both Boehm tests as upward or downward extensions of the other. Only grade norms are reported for the BTBC-R (K–2, presumably age 5 and above), and only age norms are reported for the BTBC-PV (3 years, 0 months to 5 years, 0 months). Therefore, examiners encountering floor effects on the BTBC-R or ceiling effects on the BTBC-PV cannot obtain standard scores for one child on both tests.

Standardization was conducted in 1985–86 with 433 children using a stratified sample respectively reflective of 1980 census data. While a minority sample was included in standardization (23% of total sample), there is no indication of percentage of Blacks, Hispanics, or Asians within the minority sample. Socioeconomic status (SES) was stratified using educational level of the child's parents. The BTBC-R contains separate norms for low and high SES based on different levels of performance of these children on concept mastery. However, the BTBC-PV does not provide separate norms or data indicating similar performance by high and low SES children. Separate means and standard deviations should be reported, along with criterion-referenced validity studies, by race and SES. Children from day-care, nursery school, and Head Start programs were used. No home-based children were sampled; therefore, users should be cautious when assessing children who have not had any school or group care experience.

There is no reporting of changes being made in the test based on standardization administration. For example, item order was based on estimated difficulty, and this was not changed following standardization. Percent of children passing each item at each age level is not reported.

Content and concurrent validity data are reported. Content validity is inferred from the fact that concepts tested were based on those actually used in classrooms and curriculum materials. The fact that similar concepts were derived from a different source and used in the BBCS adds support for the content validity of the BTBC-PV. Information regarding item retention would be useful to further judge this aspect of the test. In an assessment of the construct validity of the BTBC-PV, Zucker and Riordan (1988) found the BTBC-PV to be significantly correlated with the BBCS for a group of 99 White preschoolers. Zucker and Riordan state that for their sample the BTBC-PV had a significantly higher mean than the BBCS, perhaps due to a low ceiling on the BTBC-PV. Also, while there is 50% shared variance between the two tests, the BBCS measures other skills than relational concepts, such as readiness skills (colors, shapes).

Concurrent validity is reported in the manual and by Zucker and Riordan. The BTBC-PV is significantly related to the Peabody Picture Vocabulary Test—Revised, a measure of receptive language but not limited to relational concepts, for both normal and language-delayed children. Both studies employed very small samples and while the manual reports that "whites and nonwhites" were included, no demographic data are provided. A review of the literature revealed no other validity studies to date. Studies of the ability of the BTBC-PV to predict academic achievement and school readiness are needed to validate the test for use as a norm-referenced assessment instrument for preschool children for whom school decisions must be made. Analysis of the standardization data and other studies are needed to determine the predictive validity of the BTBC-PV specifically for minorities.

Internal consistency (alpha) coefficients range from .85 at age 4 to .91 at age 3, lending support for the internal stability and also the validity of the instrument. Split-half reliability coefficients range from .80 at age $4^{1}/_{2}$ to .87 at ages 3 and 4, slightly lower than the alpha coefficients. The manual does not indicate whether the two halves of the test, which measure each concept twice, were used for split-half reliability or whether an odd-even split was used. An estimate of the reliability of testing each concept only once versus twice would be useful.

There is no alternate form of the BTBC-PV as there is with the BTBC-R. Test-retest reliability (7–10 day intervals) reported for 78 children from the standardization sample is reported as .94 at age $3^{1}/_{2}$ and .87 at age $4^{1}/_{2}$, adequate for screening purposes and for diagnosis as part of a multimethod assessment. Again, additional research with larger samples and minority samples is needed to further establish the appropriate use of this instrument for diagnostic purposes.

Administration is easy and quick, facilitated by the easel presentation and pointing responses. Scoring is straightforward, requiring minimal manipulation of test data in order to obtain percentiles and T-scores. Users are cautioned that the table indicating percentiles for ages 3, $3^{1}/_{2}$, 4, $4^{1}/_{2}$, and 5 does not directly correspond to typical use of years in many psychological tests. For example, year 4 actually consists of standardization sample subjects ranging from 3 years, 9 months to 4 years, 2 months. Use of the correct table is essential.

In conclusion, the BTBC-PV does measure a child's knowledge of 26 specific basic relational concepts, useful for criterion-referenced assessment and remediation. Until further research is conducted regarding the ability of the test to predict future academic performance, users are cautioned (by the author as well as the reviewer) to include it in a multimethod assessment for diagnostic purposes only as an adjunct to more comprehensive language measures. Those wishing to employ an assessment device measuring similar concepts as well as school readiness items, with norms for a wider age range, should consider the BBCS. Additionally, those working directly with children are cautioned by Boehm (1983) herself to assess a child's understanding of basic concepts informally over time and across different contexts (e.g., assessing understanding of "before" in both time and space), as well as formally with one instrument such as the BTBC-PV. Expressive use of concepts is not measured by the BTBC-PV, so this would also be an area which could be informally assessed or for which an additional assessment instrument could be developed.

REVIEWER'S REFERENCES

Levin, G. R., Henderson, B., Levin, A. M., & Hoffer, G. L. (1975). Measuring knowledge of basic concepts by disadvantaged preschoolers. *Psychology in the Schools, 12,* 132-139.

Boehm, A. E. (1976). *Boehm resource guide for basic concept teaching.* New York: The Psychological Corporation.

Boehm, A. (1983). Assessment of basic concepts. In K. D. Paget & B. A. Bracken (Eds.), *The psychoeducational assessment of preschool children.* New York: Grune and Stratton.

Smith, E. F. (1986). The Boehm Test of Basic Concepts: An English standardization. *British Journal of Educational Psychology, 56,* 197-200.

Zucker, S., & Riordan, J. (1988). Concurrent validity of new and revised conceptual language measures. *Psychology in the Schools, 25,* 252-256.

Review of the Boehm Test of Basic Concepts—Preschool Version by STEPHANIE STEIN, Assistant

Professor of Psychology, Central Washington University, Ellensburg, WA:

The Boehm Test of Basic Concepts—Preschool Version (Boehm-Preschool) is designed to be a downward extension of the Boehm Test of Basic Concepts (BTBC; 10:32) for use with children between the ages of 3 and 5. The preschool version differs from the original BTBC in two important ways. First of all, the Boehm-Preschool specifies the child should be tested individually whereas the BTBC allows for either group or individual administration. Secondly, the child is asked to respond to the items by pointing instead of having to provide a written response. Both of these adaptations appear to be appropriate for assessment of the young child.

The rationale given in the manual for assessing basic relational concepts is logical and convincing. Some of the uses for the Boehm-Preschool specified in the manual include "an indicator of school readiness," "a guide for planning language instruction," to "help assess possible developmental delays in language acquisition," and to "help teachers identify those concepts that preschoolers have not yet mastered." There is no information in the manual on how to use the results to determine school readiness but there are some suggestions and guidance as to how the test results can be used to address the remaining three uses. The manual is careful to caution that the Boehm-Preschool "should *not* be used as the sole readiness or screening determinant, but is most useful when combined with other information about the child."

The manual is well organized, clear, and easy to read. It appears to be designed with the interests of the teacher in mind and avoids the use of overly technical jargon and theory. The types of information provided that are directly applicable to the teaching process include an optional error analysis, a class record form, a review of the typical developmental process of acquiring knowledge of concept pairs, concrete suggestions for remediation, and a table for determining difficulty of various concepts by indicating the percent of children who pass each concept at different ages.

Twenty-six concepts are assessed through the Boehm-Preschool, with two items per concept resulting in 52 test items. The test items are easy to administer and score and the materials appear to be attractive and interesting enough to hold the attention of most young children. The child can earn either a score of 2, 1, or 0 on each concept. A score of 2 indicates the child is familiar with the concept and its meaning and a score of either 1 or 0 indicates the need for further instruction on the concept. The child's total raw score can be converted to a percentile and a *T*-score for purposes of normative comparison. The author should be congratulated for avoiding the use of the problematic age-equivalent scores that are so popular with test developers of other preschool measures.

The only apparent problem with the test directions/scoring is in reference to the five warm-up items that are administered prior to the test items. The directions indicate that the examiner can "help" the child with the warm-up items, if necessary, but it does not specify what "help" entails (repeating the item, eliminating one of the distractors, teaching a strategy, giving the answer, etc.). Because the manual directs the examiner to discontinue the test if two of the last four warm-up items are missed even with additional help, the degree of help provided on these items would obviously affect the decision about whether or not to discontinue the test.

The technical characteristics of the Boehm-Preschool appear to be adequate for the purposes of screening. The two internal consistency measures of reliability resulted in a range from .85 to .91 for alpha coefficients (average of .88) and a range from .80 to .87 for split-half coefficients (average of .85). The test-retest reliability for the test is fairly good, with coefficients of .87 and .94.

There is less consistent support for the concurrent validity data of the test because of the small sample sizes. The validity coefficient for the Boehm-Preschool and the Peabody Picture Vocabulary Test—Revised (PPVT-R), Form L of .63 is based on a sample size of 29 preschool children. Likewise, the Boehm-Preschool and PPVT-R, Form M coefficient of .57 is based on a sample size of 19 children identified as language delayed. Larger sample sizes and additional comparison measures are needed to provide convincing support in the area of concurrent validity.

The strongest support of the technical characteristics of the test is in the area of content-validity. The manual provides detailed guidelines for the selection of test content based on a review of the professional literature, surveys of kindergarten and grade 1 curriculum materials, and, most importantly, analysis of tape-recorded teacher verbal behavior when teachers are giving directions to or conversing with preschool-age students. The manual states that "teachers used over 70% of the concept terms . . . from the Boehm-Preschool during their instructional talk with children. Clearly, knowledge of basic concepts is necessary for preschoolers to comply with teacher's verbal instructions in the classroom."

The standardization group for the Boehm-Preschool, though not impressively large (only 433 children), appears to be adequately representative with respect to sex, race, region, and socioeconomic status. The proportions for race, region, and education level of parents coincides closely with the proportions found in the United States population, based on 1980 census data.

In summary, the Boehm-Preschool is a well-constructed, technically adequate measure of the preschool child's familiarity with and understanding of relational concepts commonly encountered in the classroom and curriculum materials. The test provides only a small portion of the information necessary in screening for school readiness and possible language delays but the information it does provide is potentially very useful for teachers and evaluators.

[47]

The BrainMap™.
Purpose: "A tool for determining the world-building (or thinking/information-processing) style of individuals and of groups."
Population: Adults.
Publication Dates: 1981–86.
Scores: 4 scales: Posterior Brain Scale, Anterior Brain Scale, Left Brain Scale, Right Brain Scale.
Administration: Group.
Price Data: Available from publisher.
Time: [30–40] minutes.
Comments: Self-administered, self-scored.
Author: Dudley Lynch.
Publisher: Brain Technologies Corporation.

Review of The BrainMap™ by MANFRED J. MEIER, Professor of Neurosurgery, Psychiatry, and Psychology, and Diplomate in Clinical Neuropsychology, University of Minnesota, Twin Cities, Minneapolis, MN:

This test is described as a "self-assessment profile" that is designed to yield a set of "major BrainFrame profiles" that are then converted into a "BrainMap™" for subsequent interpretation. The procedure begins with a questionnaire that relates to personal characteristics, interests, problem-solving style, activities, and related attributes. These are grouped under headings such as Characteristics, Insights, Pastimes and Activities, Information Sources, and Comparisons. The individual completing the questionnaire is instructed to distribute points across a set of alternatives for each item. The points are to be assigned on the basis of a heuristic scheme that is not fully articulated in the questionnaire. There is reference to a BrainMap Workbook that can be purchased and may contain more information relating concepts about brain-behavior relationships to this questionnaire. In any case, the respondent is asked to apportion these points and then computes subtotals which are used to derive Posterior, Anterior, Left Brain, and Right Brain scores. These scores are then entered on a graph that divides the brain into quadrants and depicts the individual's "primary BrainFrame" as the largest area demarcated by the scores. An assortment of individual characteristics is then derived from a compendium of attributes under each frame as a

"special case profile" appearing on the "BrainMap™."

The procedure is claimed to have been derived from "research into brain functions and cognitive activities in the past decade" and is presented as "one of the first biologically based educational testing instruments." Two general areas of research are mentioned but there are no specific citations that would link those areas of research to the particular applications the user is encouraged to pursue with this procedure. This appears to be a superficial attempt to relate the procedure to the work of "a brilliant group of scientists" (unnamed) engaged in research in brain-behavior relationships. To the informed reader, these areas would appear to be the clinical and experimental studies done on individuals who had undergone a commissurotomy for the treatment of intractable seizures or a prefrontal lobotomy for the treatment of chronic psychiatric disorders. To the uninformed reader, the basis for the connection to this imagined supporting literature must be taken on faith. Without exploring this literature in any detail for the reader, the manual then appears to take an enormous leap into "the basic ideas about the brain used to develop the BrainMap." After deriving (a priori) four "essential insights—call them Great Discoveries for modern brain science," the authors summarize their view of the cognitive and personality functions of "the Posterior Brain," "the Left Brain," "the Anterior Brain," and "the Right Brain." These characteristics are then converted (following the derivation of the BrainMap from the self-administered and self-scored questionnaire) into an elaborate set of descriptors, traits, and personal characteristics that purportedly will guide the individual into increased role effectiveness in managerial and personal activities. Presented in this fashion, the procedure appears to be a vehicle for encouraging the application of concepts of brain-behavior relationships to individuals without training or familiarity with the literature in that area for the purpose of self-improvement and increased effectiveness in interpersonal and group situations.

This is not a psychological test in terms of the criteria in the *Standards for Educational and Psychological Testing* (1985) prepared by a joint committee of the American Educational Research Association, the American Psychological Association, and the National Council on Measurement in Education. The absence of normative data (even for the audiences being served), reliability or validity studies, program evaluation studies for applications with managerial personnel, or an identifiable empirical basis for these applications raises ethical implications relating to misrepresentation of this product if the authors are psychologists. Even when applied to the leadership, organizational, or team-effectiveness contexts by nonpsychologists, appropriate qualifications and disclaimers would appear to be dictated by conventional truth-in-advertising principles. The use of these procedures by other than mental health professionals to facilitate discussion (hopefully without misleading the audience or creating gross misunderstandings with respect to the implications of these exercises for the individual) might possibly engender potentially serious emotional reactions in predisposed individuals. Presented as an exercise (and with a more modest introduction with respect to the scientific basis of the procedure as derived from unidentified "Great Discoveries"), the procedure could conceivably achieve some of the purposes for which it was designed.

Whether or not such effectiveness can be demonstrated remains an empirical question. In the meantime, conceptually generalized and empirically unsubstantiated applications of this type should be tempered by ethical contraints based on truth-in-representation principles. This reviewer advises against publishing a review of this procedure in the Buros *Mental Measurements Yearbook* because the procedure does not constitute a psychological test in terms of accepted criteria and practices within the psychology profession.

REVIEWER'S REFERENCE

American Educational Research Association, American Psychological Association, & National Council on Measurement in Education. (1985). *Standards for educational and psychological testing.* Washington, DC: American Psychological Association, Inc.

[The Buros Institute does not endorse testing products by way of including or excluding them from our reference works. We attempt to provide potential consumers with information about the wide array of tests they may be considering for any professional use.—Ed.]

[48]
Bricklin Perceptual Scales.

Purpose: Yields information on a child's unconscious or nonverbal perception of his or her parents; for determining which of the parents would make the better primary caretaker for a particular child in child-custody decisions.
Population: Ages 6 and over.
Publication Dates: 1984–90.
Acronym: BPS.
Scores, 10: 5 scores each for mother and father: Perception of Competency, Perception of Supportiveness, Perception of Follow-Up Consistency, Perception of Admirable Character Traits, Total.
Administration: Individual.
Price Data, 1990: $89 per complete kit including 4 sets of 64 test cards, 4 scoring sheets, stylus-pen, foam insert and test box, manual ('90, 102 pages), instructions, and Bricklin Updates; $59 per 5 additional sets of test cards.
Time: (20) minutes.
Author: Barry Bricklin.
Publisher: Village Publishing.

Review of the Bricklin Perceptual Scales by ROSA A. HAGIN, Professor of Psychological and Educational Services, Graduate School of Education, Fordham University-Lincoln Center, New York, NY:

The Bricklin Perceptual Scales (BPS) are less a formal test than a structured technique developed by an experienced and sensitive clinician for use in child custody decisions when parents divorce. The Scales have been designed to tap children's perceptions of each parent's actions through verbal and nonverbal responses to a series of 32 questions dealing with specific parent-child situations. These situations are grouped under four headings: Competency (e.g., ability to cope with emergencies, to be reliable sources of information, to help a child deal with a bully); Supportiveness (e.g., degree of patience, ability to help a child deal with fears); Follow-up Consistency (e.g., enforcing bedtime limits, homework assignments); Admirable Character Traits (e.g., trustworthiness, positive mood, altruism). The author states that the BPS measures "a child's gut-level, unconscious perception of parental behavior where this perception is, in largest part, based on the behavior's utility for the child."

The child is asked to respond verbally and by indicating along a continuum on a series of grid-printed cards responses ranging from *very well* to *not so well* to describe how each parent is perceived as handling the specific situations. The nonverbal response scores are used to calculate three scores: (*a*) which parent is the "winner" or "loser" on the total number of items, (*b*) point scores based on the place on the grid the child assigns to each parent on each item in the continuum of ratings, and (*c*) difference scores between ratings for each parent on individual items.

A manual and four periodic supplements are provided to instruct users in interpretation of BPS results in clinical work and in courtroom testimony. These support materials are informal in style, so that it is necessary to search among the theoretical observations and clinical insights for data on the statistical characteristics of the scale. Data that are presented are limited by very small samples (ranging from 12 to 36). The usual descriptive statistics are not presented; samples are only described as adversarial and nonadversarial.

The matter of reliability is dismissed by the BPS manual with the statement that there is no reason to expect stability of measurement because responses might be expected to vary with changes in children's perceptions of their parents. However, it does report there were no "significant changes" in 12 retest cases with the measure. Validity data are reported in terms of percentages of agreement between the BPS and an unpublished test that utilizes children's drawings (83%); children's and parent's questionnaires (70%); judgments based on clinical and historical information, and courtroom decisions on custody (94%).

Although described as a research-based test, the BPS manual leaves many questions unanswered. What conceptual framework guided item selection? How do items relate to each other? How reliable are the four area scores? How meaningful are the difference scores? What do long-term followup data show about predictive validity?

It must be conceded that the area of child custody decisions presents many hazards for test design. It may be that conventional expectations of reliability and validity cannot, as the manual suggests, be applied appropriately. The BPS is an interesting approach that draws upon many years of distinguished clinical practice. However, insufficient data are presented to justify its use as an independent measure in what must be regarded as a major decision in a child's life, the selection of the parent who will be the primary caretaker.

Review of the Bricklin Perceptual Scales by MARCIA B. SHAFFER, School Psychologist, Lancaster, NY:

Practitioners in psychology who evaluate children tend to think of the word "perceptual" as related to comprehension of sensory stimuli. For them, a caveat: The Bricklin Perceptual Scales deal with *emotional* comprehension. They are intended to tap a child's intellectual processing of parental behaviors, the "'meaning' of parental behavior . . . in terms of its UTILITY to a particular child" (from brochure advertising the Bricklin Perceptual Scales).

Bricklin set out to develop a technique that would assist psychologists in custody cases involving the choice of a particular parent as the primary caregiver. He sees it as useful for children 6 years of age and up, sometimes even for youngsters as young as 4 years of age. How well he has succeeded in his purpose is at best a moot question.

The Scales consist of $8\frac{1}{2}$-inch by $3\frac{1}{2}$-inch cards containing questions about parents. The child can respond both verbally and nonverbally, the latter by punching, with a stylus, a heavy black continuum line on each card. The stylus is poked through the card into a styrofoam pad. The questions are paired. The pairs are separated, but the same questions are eventually asked regarding both mother and father. Areas covered, according to Bricklin, are parental competence, supportiveness, followup consistency, and possession of admirable character traits. Also, according to Bricklin, the data derived are to be trusted for legal use.

The manual accompanying the Scales, three manual supplements, and a letter from Bricklin, are impressive. Detailed descriptions of the problems of custody decisions are given, and the events which led up to the Scales' development are delineated, as are the psychological premises on which Bricklin believes them to be based. There is a chapter telling "expert" psychological witnesses what to say in court. This chapter is worthy of being written, on its own, as a journal article.

Despite all of Bricklin's effort, however, one cannot help urging caution in the use of his Scales, for the following reasons:

1. The Scales rest on too many assumptions, the most egregious of which is that children who stick a stylus into a long black line have unconsciously chosen the spot on the line which reveals their unconscious attitudes. (Unconscious is otherwise defined as "action tendencies.") Even this reviewer, who is a believer in Freud and in clinical intuition, has difficulty with that idea, especially in view of the meager theories and statistics presented in its defense.

2. The Scales really have no more than face validity. Numbers tested are small and the external criteria are shaky: judges' decisions; parents' opinions. Reliability is not considered significant, perhaps with good reason. Bricklin points out that reliability is not to be expected because, especially in these family configurations, conditions of life change and with them children's perceptions.

3. The instructions for administering and scoring the Scales are obfuscating, wordy, and somewhat prone to error. For example, reference is made to the "green arabic numbers" on the test cards; the cards have only black numbers. And the reviewer, after several perusals (and perhaps some oversight) of the manual, does not know what happens to the verbal responses. The manual supplements indicate, by inference, how difficult it is to find absolutes in this area of life.

4. It is expensive. A new set of cards is used for every administration. This brings the cost for materials to almost $10 each time the test is given.

5. Over and over, Bricklin cautions readers not to use the word "winner" in verbal or written reports. Over and over, Bricklin uses the words "winner" or "the parent who wins." Because the choice of words is an important consideration, it would seem that he himself should have sought a more desirable term. Preferred parent? More compatible parent? Or even a nonsense word like "upkin"?

One must conclude that, contrary to Bricklin's hopes, the Scales may be of clinical rather than statistical help. It would, in this reviewer's opinion, be more appropriate to refer to the results as trends rather than thinking of them as hard data. And here, a second caveat to users is in order: These Scales are not for the inexperienced or for those psychologists of a behavioristic bent.

It should be emphasized that Dr. Bricklin's personal expertise and integrity are not in question. One does not doubt, reading the material that accompanies his Perceptual Scales, that he is well acquainted with the situations and the people his work encompasses, nor that he understands them and treats them with sympathetic competence. Unfortunately, he has set himself a well-nigh impossible task: he has tried to quantify information which may not yield itself to quantification.

NOTE. A revised manual for the Scales arrived just after the above review had been submitted. It is larger in physical size than the original. Comparison of the two manuals, however, reveals no appreciable difference in the general content. One chapter has been added, and seven, instead of three, manual supplements have been included. This reviewer's opinion remains the same: The manual contains valuable information and advice for the psychologist in custody cases, but use of the Scales continues to raise the same questions.

[49]

BRIGANCE® Early Preschool Screen for Two-Year-Old and Two-and-a-Half-Year-Old Children.

Purpose: "Criterion-referenced" screen designed "to provide a sampling of a child's learning, development, and skills in a broad range of areas."
Population: Ages 2 to 2¹/₂ years.
Publication Date: 1990.
Administration: Individual.
Price Data, 1990: $46 per manual (69 pages with building blocks); no charge for Spanish directions.
Foreign Language Edition: Spanish component available.
Time: (15–20) minutes.
Comments: Most skills included in the assessments were excerpted from the BRIGANCE® Diagnostic Inventory of Early Development (9:164).
Author: Albert H. Brigance.
Publisher: Curriculum Associates, Inc.
  a) TWO-YEAR CHILD.
  Scores, 9: Builds Tower with Blocks, Visual-Motor Skills, Identifies Body Parts, Picture Vocabulary, Identifies People in Picture by Pointing, Identifies Objects According to Use, Gross-Motor Skills, Verbal Fluency, Total.
  Price Data: $15.95 per 30 data sheets.
  b) TWO-AND-A-HALF-YEAR CHILD.
  Scores, 10: Builds Tower with Blocks, Visual-Motor Skills, Identifies Body Parts, Picture Vocabulary, Identifies People in Picture by Naming, Knows Use of Objects, Quantitative Concepts, Gross-Motor Skills, Verbal Fluency, Total.
  Price Data: $16 per 30 data sheets.

Review of the BRIGANCE® Early Preschool Screen for Two-Year-Old and Two-and-a-Half-Year-Old Children by WILLIAM M. BART, Professor of Educational Psychology, University of Minnesota, Minneapolis, MN:

The Brigance Early Preschool Screen for Two-Year-Old and Two-and-a-Half-Year-Old Children is an assessment device that is composed of eight tasks used for the assessment of 2-year-old children and nine tasks used for the assessment of 2¹/₂-year-old

children. The tasks assess concepts and skills such as quantitative concepts and visual-motor skills.

For each task performance, the examinee is provided a certain number of points. A total point total which is the sum of the points provided for the individual task performances of the examinee is then calculated for the examinee. The child's score is generated by dividing the total point total for the child by 100. The child's score for each examinee is compared to the scores of other children in a sample. Each child's score is categorized as being either lower, or average, or higher, based on the position of the child's score in relation to the other children's scores for the children in the sample.

The Brigance Preschool Screen is attractive and well made by Curriculum Associates. It can be used to assess English-speaking children and Spanish-speaking children, because there are directions in English and in Spanish. The tasks are appealing. Also, the tasks seem to be very reasonable and appropriate if one considers tasks for young children in other tests of mental abilities for young children.

Despite these positive features, the test has many drawbacks, which could be readily resolved through psychometric research. First of all, the child's score is interpreted from a comparison with a small sample of other children's scores. Thus, a child's score of 70/100 could be categorized as a higher score in one sample of children and a lower score in another sample of children. Such elasticity in score interpretation leads to undesirable variation in the classification of students for educational programs and interventions. The test would benefit from having national norms and two cutoff scores so that an examiner could determine whether a child is fit for certain preschool programs and is performing at least at an average level among same age peers.

The test is objective in that different examiners would very likely produce equivalent child's scores from analyses of the same set of task performances for the same child. However, it is uncertain how reliable the screen is. For example, no information is given in the manual as to how stable children's scores and their component task scores are over time in terms of test-retest reliabilities. The manual should provide detailed information as to the reliability of the screen.

Also, no information is provided as to how valid the test is. I would contend that the test has a certain level of face validity from an examination of the tasks in the test and a comparison of those tasks with other tasks assessing mental abilities in well-established cognitive tests for young children. However, I have no idea how much concurrent validity or predictive validity or construct validity the screen has. As a result, let me suggest that the manual should also provide detailed information as to the validity of the screen.

In summary, the Brigance Preschool Screen is an efficient measure of some basic cognitive capabilities of young children. Its brevity in test administration time and its ease in scoring are definite advantages. However, the screen lacks clarity and meaning in the interpretation of its test scores. Also, the screen manual lacks information regarding the reliability and the validity of the screen. These drawbacks are serious but could be readily handled through a program of psychometric research. I hope that Brigance and Curriculum Associates initiate such a research program, because the screen, although appealing, could benefit from the completion of such a program of psychometric research.

Review of the BRIGANCE® Early Preschool Screen for Two-Year-Old and Two-and-a-Half-Year-Old Children by JOSEPH M. RYAN, Associate Professor of Education, University of South Carolina, Columbia, SC:

The Brigance Early Preschool Screen for Two-Year-Old and Two-and-a-Half-Year-Old Children (EPS) continues the process of supplementing the Brigance Diagnostic Inventory of Early Development (9:164) designed for use with children from birth to 7 years with shorter inventories focused in a narrower segment of the birth to 7 years period. In rationale, history, and procedures for development, this Early Preschool Screen has much in common with the Brigance K & 1 Screen (9:166) and the Brigance Preschool Screen (10:36; ages 3 and 4). There are eight assessment tasks for 2-year-olds, nine tasks for 2¹/₂ -year-olds, and a total score for each level. The tasks are traditional for the ages involved and receive varying weights in calculating the total. Slightly different Data Sheets are used for the 2-year-olds and the 2¹/₂ -year-olds and both forms are well organized and facilitate the recording and interpreting of results. Supplementary Screening Observations Forms and Parent's and Teacher's Rating Forms are provided for collecting additional information.

The major strength of the EPS is that it is easily administered, brief, and reflects a certain degree of common sense in its assessment tasks. With modest training and experience, almost any adult can administer the instrument as prescribed and most children can be screened in 15 minutes (or less). The assessment tasks are extracted from the Brigance Diagnostic Inventory of Early Development and thus are familiar to those using this other instrument. In addition, the tasks represent a sampling from activities that are developmentally appropriate for children at the target ages. They are the fairly traditional tasks one expects to see in an informal inventory designed for these age groups.

The EPS has two major weaknesses: a lack of appropriate technical information about instrument development and pilot testing, and an absence of guidelines or standards for interpretation. A brief description of the instrument's history, field testing, and revisions through professional critiques is provided in an appendix. The elements combined to produce the Field Test/Critique Edition include the author's own professional training and experience, an "extensive review of related publications," and consultations with interested parties. A list of field test participants is provided with no information about the nature or extent of their involvement. The field test review and critique appear to have been qualitative in nature because no empirical information is presented. The field test critique resulted in the retention of the assessments selected for both levels on the field test edition; elimination of the use of the concept "many" in the "Quantitative Concepts" assessment (2-and-a-half-year level); and a set of 10 "Other Significant Changes." These changes dealt with modifications in directions, word choices, scoring criteria, order of assessments, and items within assessments. Some examples of these changes are:

3. In "Visual Motor Skills" scribbling using a jumbo crayon was substituted for using a pencil.

6. When assessing the skill of "Walks backward six steps" (two-and-a-half-year level), the children tended to terminate performance prior to taking the fifth or sixth step. Most of the time this appeared to happen as a result of losing concentration rather than the result of a lack of gross motor skills or development. The criterion for this skill was changed from "six steps" to "four steps."

9. The skill "Uses three-word sentences" in the "Verbal Fluency" assessment at the two-and-a-half-year level was changed. The scorability of some three-word responses was questionable. (Was the response a phrase or sentence?) To avoid this questionable scoring, the skill was changed to "Uses three words that relate in combination" (manual, p. 40).

The changes described seem both reasonable and wise, in most cases. However, the lack of empirical information about the development or field testing makes it difficult to offer the conventional evaluation of the instrument's objectivity, reliability, and validity.

A second difficulty deals with guidelines for interpreting children's scores. The author writes that "The primary purpose of screening is to obtain a sampling of a child's skills and behavior in order to identify the child who should be referred for a more comprehensive evaluation or diagnostic assessment." One important guideline the author emphasizes by repeating is the suggestion that no important decisions about a child be made based exclusively on the score from the inventory. The author urges the inclusion of information from as many pertinent sources as possible.

The author offers two additional guidelines related to the use of the screen. In a section headed, "Establish a Program 'Cutoff' score, if Needed," a norm-referenced approach is recognized when the author observes that "a procedure or policy may be that a certain percent of a group be referred for additional assessment." An example is provided of a policy that "twenty percent of the group be referred for additional assessment." A criterion-referenced approach is described in the same section when the author recommends that a child "who scores 60 or below should be evaluated in more detail."

The norm-referenced approach is not particularly helpful because all groups, no matter how developmentally able or unable, have a bottom 20% and upper 80%: the bottom 20% of an able group may not need additional assessment whereas the upper 80% of a less able group may benefit from a detailed assessment.

Some rational or empirical evidence for a criterion score of 60 would be useful. Technical procedures for establishing cutscores or standards are well described in the psychometric literature and could be applied. In addition to substantiating the use of a particular cutscore, a description of the assessment tasks that most sharply differentiate students above and below the cutscore would be helpful.

The Brigance EPS is a straightforward, efficient, and easy-to-administer inventory that many will find efficient and practical. The value of the information obtained by its application, however, depends heavily on the expertise and experience of the user. Guidelines for interpretation are not particularly helpful and information about the instrument's objectivity, reliability, and validity is not provided.

[50]
Burks' Behavior Rating Scales.

Purpose: Identify "particular behavior problems and patterns of problems shown by children."
Population: Preschool–grade 9.
Publication Dates: 1968–77.
Acronym: BBRS.
Administration: Individual.
Price Data, 1990: $12.50 per 25 test booklets and profile sheets; $10.50 per 10 parents' guides; $13.50 per 10 teacher's guides; $21.75 per practitioner-oriented handbook.
Time: Administration time not reported.
Comments: Ratings of problem children by teachers or parents.
Author: Harold F. Burks.
Publisher: Western Psychological Services.
a) PRESCHOOL AND KINDERGARTEN.
Population: Ages 3–6.
Scores, 18: Excessive Self-Blame, Excessive Anxiety, Excessive Withdrawal, Excessive Dependency, Poor Ego Strength, Poor Physical Strength, Poor Coordination, Poor Intellectuality, Poor Attention, Poor Impulse Control, Poor Reality Contact, Poor Sense of Identity, Excessive Suffering, Poor Anger Control,

Excessive Sense of Persecution, Excessive Aggressiveness, Excessive Resistance, Poor Social Conformity.
Price Data, 1988: $25 per complete kit including 25 test booklets and profile sheets and manual ('77, 41 pages); $14.50 per manual.
b) GRADES 1–9.
Population: Grades 1–9.
Scores, 19: Same scores as *a* above plus Poor Academics.
Price Data, 1988: $52 per complete kit including 25 test booklets and profile sheets, manual ('77, 53 pages), 2 parents' guides, 2 teacher's guides, and practitioner-oriented handbook; $16.50 per manual.
Cross References: See T3:328 (1 reference), T2:1115 (1 reference), and 7:46 (2 references).

TEST REFERENCES

1. LeVine, E., Rittenhouse, J. A., Smith, G., & Thompson, T. (1981). A cojoint, operant model for assisting profoundly behaviorally disordered adolescents. *Adolescence, 16,* 299-307.
2. Lewis, S., Horton, F. T., & Armstrong, S. (1981-82). Distress in fatally and chronically ill children: Methodological note. *OMEGA, 12,* 293-306.
3. Fontenelle, S., & Alarcon, M. (1982). Hyperlexia: Precocious word recognition in developmentally delayed children. *Perceptual and Motor Skills, 55,* 247-252.
4. LeVine, E., & Greer, M. (1984). Long-term effectiveness of the Adolescent Learning Center: A challenge to the concept of least restrictive environment. *Adolescence, 19,* 521-526.
5. Sabornie, E. J., Kauffman, J. M., Ellis, E. S., Marshall, K. J., & Elkshin, L. K. (1987). Bi-directional and cross-categorical social status of learning disabled, behaviorally disordered, and nonhandicapped adolescents. *The Journal of Special Education, 21* (4), 39-56.
6. Thompson, R. A. (1987). Creating instructional and counseling partnerships to improve the academic performance of underachievers. *The School Counselor, 34,* 289-296.
7. Davis, D. D., & Templer, D. I. (1988). Neurobehavioral functioning in children exposed to narcotics in utero. *Addictive Behaviors, 13,* 275-283.

Review of the Burks' Behavior Rating Scales by LISA G. BISCHOFF, *Assistant Professor of Educational Psychology, University of Nebraska-Lincoln, Lincoln, NE:*

The Burks' Behavior Rating Scales (BBRS) is designed to "identify patterns of pathological behavior" in children grades one to nine. The BBRS, Preschool and Kindergarten Edition, is meant for use with children ages 3 through 6. The only difference between the BBRS and the Preschool and Kindergarten Edition is the presence of the Poor Academics category in the former. Although the BBRS is described as a "preliminary device," it is not recommended for use as a screening instrument. Rather, it is recommended for use with children already known to have behavioral difficulties. The BBRS is not intended to be a measure of "how the child's inner world is experienced." However, subscales are nearly all described in terms of internal states (e.g., Self-Blame, Dependency, Ego Strength), rather than in terms of behavior. Furthermore, information contained in the manual interprets the subtests in terms of defense mechanisms, desires, and needs.

The BBRS consists of 110 items (105 items for the Preschool and Kindergarten Edition) rated from 1 (*You have not noticed this behavior at all*) to 5 (*You have noticed the behavior to a very large degree*). Category scores ranging from 5 (not significant) to 40 (very significant) are obtained through plotting scores on a profile. Only one form of the BBRS is provided for each edition and may be completed by parents or teachers. Although some of the items provide a clear indication of the behavior to be rated (e.g., follows directions poorly, rotates or rocks his body), many items require the rater to interpret behavior (e.g., seems to welcome punishment, deliberately puts himself in position of being criticized). Furthermore, items contain sexist language as children are consistently referred to using masculine pronouns.

The standardization sample for the BBRS included 494 primary age children and 69 middle school children. Ratings were provided by teachers. An approximately equal number of boys and girls were included. Seventy percent of the sample were Mexican American and the remainder were Anglo American. The standardization sample for the BBRS Preschool and Kindergarten Edition included 127 preschool children (70 boys and 57 girls) from San Bernardino County, California rated by parents and 337 kindergarten students (184 boys, 153 girls) in Los Angeles and Orange counties rated by teachers. Seventy-five percent of the children were Anglo American and the remainder were Mexican American. The sampling strategy associated with norming the BBRS is a weakness. The usefulness of the test is questionable beyond those children in the norm group.

Stated psychometric properties of both editions of the BBRS are based on studies with small sample sizes, limited populations, and questionable assumptions. Test-retest reliability of items in the original edition was collected through the rating and rerating by teachers of 95 "disturbed children" grades one through six. Reliability for the Preschool and Kindergarten Edition was obtained using 84 kindergarten children, described as "normally behaved" by teachers. Test-retest correlation coefficients for original items ranged from .60 to .83. Correlation coefficients for preschool and kindergarten items ranged from .74 to .96. No other information regarding reliability is provided. Data concerning interrater reliability are needed for the BBRS.

The BBRS is said to possess face validity based on the "long established . . . relationship between particular personality difficulties and the outward expression of these conflicts" and on the "extensive use of the scales over the past eight years." Criterion validity is claimed based on studies conducted using the Burks' Behavior Rating Scale of Organic Brain Dysfunction and on the authors' hypothesis that "defense systems could be identified and related to particular problems faced by children." Content validity was established through review of the

original scale by 22 school psychologists in Los Angeles county who used the scale in their practice. Comments were also solicited from teachers of both regular and special education. Content validity of the Preschool and Kindergarten Edition was assessed through review by 26 kindergarten teachers.

Discriminant validity is claimed based upon a study in which the BBRS was found to identify as troubled a significantly greater percentage of children from a group of 153 referred children than from a group of 494 nonreferred children. The referred children had been referred by regular education teachers, had been determined by school guidance staff to need assistance, and had already been provided special services either in the regular classroom or in a special classroom. The soundness of this procedure to establish validity must be questioned. Teachers' referrals had already been validated by special placement of children and the children were rated by teachers who had referred them for assistance.

Finally, a case for factorial validity is made based upon factor analysis of category scores for various samples of children. Factors vary by age of children. Variables other than behavior related to higher category scores include gender (kindergarten boys received higher parent ratings than girls on the Aggressive-Disinhibited factor) and intellectual ability as defined by performance on an intelligence test (children with lower intellectual ability received higher scores than children with higher intellectual ability). No differences were noted for ethnicity. Additional studies investigating concurrent validity with other behavior checklists would prove useful for clinicians and educators.

Both editions of the BBRS provide descriptions of categories with "cookbook-type" listings of causes, manifestations, and possible interventions. Booklets for teachers and parents provide similar information directed toward their level of understanding and specific environments. Finally, an expanded, handbook version, containing information regarding diagnosis and remediation, is available for clinicians and educators using the BBRS.

In summary, the BBRS and BBRS Preschool and Kindergarten Edition are rating scales based on the assumption that behavior problems may be indicative of childhood pathology. Rating scales and profile sheets are nearly identical for both boys and girls in preschool through ninth grade and the same form is used for both parent and teacher ratings. The psychometric properties of the BBRS are poor and studies are based on unrepresentative, small samples. Finally, interpretations suggested in the manuals and other publications focus on internal pathology rather than observable behavior. Professionals desiring a behavior checklist with better psychometric properties, a broader standardization sample, and forms and profiles specifically designed for particular age and gender children, as well as specific forms for parents, teachers, and children, would be advised to consider the Child Behavior Checklist (64; Achenbach & Edelbrock, 1983).

REVIEWER'S REFERENCE

Achenbach, T. M., & Edelbrock, C. S. (1983). *Manual for the Child Behavior Checklist and Revised Child Behavior Profile*. Burlington, VT: Thomas M. Achenbach.

Review of the Burks' Behavior Rating Scales by LELAND C. ZLOMKE, *Clinical Coordinator of Intensive Treatment Services, and* BRENDA R. BUSH, *Psychologist, Beatrice State Developmental Center, Beatrice, NE:*

The Burks' Behavior Rating Scales, first published in 1977, is a revision of an earlier checklist developed by the author in 1966. The current scales were developed to assist in the identification of problem behavior patterns in children who are already perceived as having difficulty in controlling their behavior in school or community settings. The instrument consists of two versions of the rating scales with accompanying manuals. One version is the Burks' Behavior Rating Scales (110 items) designed for children in grades 1 through 9 (BBRS). The second version is the Burks' Behavior Rating Scales Preschool and Kindergarten (105 items). The instrument's items describe negative symptoms (behaviors) often displayed by children demonstrating significant behavioral difficulties. The BBRS provides a profile of the severity of a child's inappropriate behavior in 19 categories and in 18 categories (Poor Academics deleted) on the Preschool and Kindergarten Scale. The categories assessed include: Excessive Self-Blame, Excessive Anxiety, Excessive Withdrawal, Excessive Dependency, Poor Ego Strength, Poor Physical Strength, Poor Coordination, Poor Intellectuality, Poor Academics, Poor Attention, Poor Impulse Control, Poor Reality Contact, Poor Sense of Identity, Excessive Suffering, Poor Anger Control, Excessive Sense of Persecution, Excessive Aggressiveness, Excessive Resistance, and Poor Social Conformity. Category scores consist of raw scores summed from the 1–5 Likert-type individual item ratings. The category scores are plotted on a profile sheet that is divided into "not significant," "significant," and "very significant" ranges. An extensive amount of information is provided in the manuals to assist in the interpretation of high scores. Intervention approaches are also suggested.

DESCRIPTION. The complete Burks' Behavior Rating Scales consists of two manuals: Burks' Behavior Rating Scales (53 pages) and the Burks' Behavior Rating Scales Preschool and Kindergarten (41 pages). The protocols are four-page booklets each with a profile sheet. Added to the complete Burks' Behavior Rating Scales package after initial publication are individual Teacher's (11 pages) and Parent's (8 pages) Guide(s) to the Interpretation and Application of the Burks' Behavior Rating Scales (1980). A further addition in 1985 was the Diagnosis and Remediation of Learning and Behavior Problems in Children Using the Burks' Behavior Rating Scales: A Handbook (181 pages). This handbook provides information describing aspects of individual categories including theoretical background, diagnostic considerations, associated characteristics, adjunctive checklists, and intervention/data collection formats. Also provided are suggested interventions for use by both school professionals and parents.

ADMINISTRATION. Both versions of the Burks' Behavior Rating Scales are completed by a rater who has daily contact with the child and has observed the child for at least 2 weeks. The author recommends multiple rater perceptions particularly from teachers and parents. The rater must rate the child's behavior on each item. Ratings are marked directly on the rating scale booklet beside each item. The severity level displayed by the child is scored on a 5-point Likert-type scale. Descriptive statements on the severity scale for each item range from *You have not noticed this behavior at all* (1) to *You have noticed the behavior to a very large degree* (5). Category scores are obtained by summing item raw scores vertically by column on each page. These category scores are transferred to the profile sheet where they can be plotted allowing a visual analysis of the significance of each category score. In the manual raters are warned against personally summing the item raw scores or plotting the categories on the profile sheet to avoid a "halo effect." When the profile sheet is completed the clinician is directed to the manuals, interpretive guides, and the diagnosis and remediation handbook for information to assist in the interpretation of scores. This information includes general considerations, 19 separate category descriptions, theoretical considerations for individual categories, and a set of suggested remedial approaches that include suggestions from various theoretical backgrounds.

SCALE DEVELOPMENT. A varied population of children (N = approximately 100 per item) constituted the sample for item development. The sample included students classified as normal, educable mentally retarded, educationally handicapped, orthopedically handicapped, speech/hearing impaired, and "disturbed." Each of the 110 scale items met certain standards before being accepted into the scale. These standards included statistically significant differences between handicapped and nonhandicapped populations, high test-retest reliability, content validity to educational specialists, and a statistical propensity to be grouped with other items into a category. The items were then submitted to a factor analysis. Professional educators labeled and judged the appropriateness of each derived category factor or category name. Thus, the development of the behavioral categories appears to have been objectively derived and is statistically sound. The cut scores related to the category ratings of "not significant," "significant," and "very significant," however, lack the statistical support achieved by the item selection process. The manual indicates that these classifications "are merely arbitrary at this point." The scale does not separate student performance on the basis of age except for preschool–kindergarten versus grades 1–9. All ages are held to the same criteria (i.e., raw score) for significance.

RELIABILITY. Item reliability averaged .705 based on a sample of 95 disturbed children with the test/retest ratings occurring over 10 days. Other standardized behavior rating scales show complete scale test-retest reliability of .80 (9:1345; Walker Problem Behavior Identification Checklist, 1983) to .97 (9:128; Behavior Evaluation Scale, 1983). The reliability of the Burks' Behavior Rating Scales was not assessed using normal children due to the author's theory that the correlations would be unduly inflated due to the absence of aberrant behavior. The test-retest reliability procedure showed statistically significant differences in the scores from individual raters but the authors concluded that these disagreements were not of practical importance.

VALIDITY. Extensive validation studies have been conducted using the BBRS. The authors have shown significant differences between referred/nonreferred populations across the arbitrarily assigned classifications of significance. Analyses based on age differences were conducted with the conclusion that the categories differ across age groups. The authors state, for example, an "immature" factor is found at the primary age level that disappears at older age levels. However, they do not include in their instrument a method of eliminating a developmentally normal 6-year-old child from appearing "very significantly immature" based on BBRS scores. Construct validity is well documented. Study samples were from a variety of handicapping conditions.

CRITIQUE. The BBRS is a useful tool in rating the behavior of children. It provides easy-to-understand, simple, clear instructions. The scales can be administered and scored with relative ease. This instrument is helpful in quantifying the severity of referred children's perceived deviance as observed by authority figures in their environment. The manual provides a large number of useful interventions for areas of assessed deficits. Several of the suggested interventions are psychodynamic in nature but the overall content logically follows the behavioral indicators. The development of the tool, although based on psychodynamic theory of defense mechanisms and neurotic characteristics, utilizes behavioral criteria and sound statistical development of the individual items and categories.

The psychometric properties of the scales contain several areas of concern. Problems arise when one considers the arbitrary development of the "significant" classification levels and the knowledge that age is not taken into consideration when classifying behavioral performance as "significant." The use of the term "significant" easily leads to a misrepresentation of the actual information being conveyed as it is not currently based on empirical evidence. When all ages are rated on a comparative scale false levels of significance can occur because some behavior categories may be developmentally appropriate at one age but significantly inappropriate at older ages and vice versa. It is not developmentally appropriate to expect a first grade student to demonstrate the same level of attention span and coordination that is expected of a ninth grade student. Now that data are available, from studies conducted subsequent to the scales' publication, norm tables could be constructed and standard scores determined. These tables could provide classifications based on empirically based statistical differences within age groups rather than arbitrary cutoffs. Another area of concern is the negative direction of the items and categories of this instrument. This reliance on measuring only the child's inappropriate behavior accentuates the negative and ignores the positive aspects and strengths of the child's complete development.

Overall, the Burks' Behavior Rating Scales should be considered a criterion-referenced tool to assess the behavioral characteristics of children. However, one must be careful not to overinterpret the information as indicative of deep-seated emotional problems. Other information sources must also be considered as well as the age of the child before making diagnostic or placement decisions. There are several behavior checklists and rating scales (e.g., Achenbach & Edelbrock, 1986 [64], and McCarney, Leigh, & Cornbleet, 1983 [9:128]) that more adequately address the psychometric concerns and negative measurement bias so prominent in the Burks' Behavior Rating Scales.

REVIEWER'S REFERENCES

McCarney, S., Leigh, J. E., & Cornbleet, J. A. (1983). Behavior Evaluation Scale. Columbia, MO: Educational Services.
Walker, H. (1983). Walker Problem Behavior Identification Checklist. Los Angeles: Western Psychological Services.
Achenbach, T. M., & Edelbrock, C. (1986). Manual for the teacher's report form and teacher version of the Child Behavior Profile. Burlington, VT: Thomas M. Achenbach.
Wilson, M. J., & Bullock, L. M. (1989). Psychometric characteristics of behavior rating scales: Definitions, problems, and solutions. Behavioral Disorders, 14 (3), 186-200.

[51]

California Achievement Tests Writing Assessment System.

Purpose: "To aid educators in evaluating writing programs and students' writing skills."

Population: Grades 3–12.
Publication Dates: 1986–87.
Scores: 6 scores using a 4-point scale: 1 Holistic, 5 Analytic (Content, Organization, Sentence Construction, Vocabulary/Grammar, Spelling/Capitalization).
Administration: Group.
Levels, 8: 13–20; level tests available as separates.
Forms, 1: E.
Price Data, 1988: $20 per examination kit including 1 sample 4-page writing booklet for each type of writing prompt, sample administration and scoring manual, test coordinator's directions, and answer sheet; $18 per test including 35 writing booklets per prompt with 1 administration and scoring manual (specify level and writing type); $9.50 per 50 answer sheets (for CTB scoring service); $6 per each additional administration and scoring manual (specify level and writing type); $12 per each writing assessment guide ('87, 51 pages); scoring service offered by publisher.
Time: [20–40] minutes per level.
Comments: 4 types of writing prompts: Descriptive, Narrative, Expository, Persuasive.
Author: CTB/McGraw-Hill.
Publisher: CTB Macmillan/McGraw-Hill.
a) LEVEL 13.
Population: Grades 2.6–4.2.
Comments: 2 prompts: Descriptive, Narrative.
b) LEVEL 14.
Population: Grades 3.6–5.2.
Comments: 2 prompts: Descriptive, Narrative.
c) LEVEL L5.
Population: Grades 4.6–6.2.
Comments: 3 prompts: Descriptive, Narrative, Expository.
d) LEVEL 16.
Population: Grades 5.6–7.2.
Comments: 3 prompts: Descriptive, Narrative, Expository.
e) LEVEL 17.
Population: Grades 6.6–8.2.
Comments: 3 prompts: Narrative, Expository, Persuasive.
f) LEVEL 18.
Population: Grades 7.6–9.2.
Comments: 3 prompts: Narrative, Expository, Persuasive.
g) LEVEL 19.
Population: Grades 8.6–11.2.
Comments: 3 prompts: Narrative, Expository, Persuasive.
h) LEVEL 20.
Population: Grades 10.6–12.9.
Comments: 2 prompts: Expository, Persuasive.

Review of the California Achievement Tests Writing Assessment System by DONALD L. RUBIN, Professor of Language Education, The University of Georgia, Athens, GA:

Direct assessment of writing ability by rating actual writing performance (as opposed to indirect assessment on the basis of multiple-choice testing) has become standard practice even in large-scale testing situations. It is true that direct writing assessment poses formidable logistic and psychomet-ric difficulties. Nevertheless, the washback to class-room practice is so valuable that increasing numbers of state and local systems have adopted writing samples into their competency testing programs. The California Achievement Tests (CAT) Writing Assessment System offers a conveniently packaged set of procedures for direct writing assessment. Test users may elect to avoid training their own raters and to instead contract for rating with CTB Macmillan/McGraw-Hill's own Composition Evaluation Center. Other than these conveniences, however, there is little in the Writing Assessment System that could not be similarly developed at the local level.

In particular, potential users of this System should not believe that, because this product bears the imprimatur of CAT, it is necessarily of higher psychometric quality than anything they might develop in their own shops. The System uses standard methods for eliciting writing samples, sometimes less than acceptable procedures for rating, and fairly unimaginative techniques for reporting scores. Moreover, no strong effort is evident in validating or even in establishing acceptable reliabilities for this assessment.

The Writing Assessment System quite rightly recognizes that writing quality is highly task-specific. What makes for good narration is not the same as what makes for good exposition. Therefore, each of eight graded levels allows for collecting writing samples in either two or three rhetorical modes (Descriptive, Narrative, Expository, or Persuasive writing). No claim is made for equivalence between writing prompts, and therefore, the Writing Assessment Guide recommends that students be evaluated by means of more than just a single writing sample. Indeed, intercorrelations between tasks, as reported in the Writing Assessment Guide, show remarkably low levels of association even within age levels.

At the same time, the lack of equivalence between writing prompts also obviates comparisons between age levels. In general, systematic developmental sequencing in grade level expectations is hard to pinpoint. Presumably, pilot testing of writing topics resulted in appropriate sequencing of the elicitation prompts. This sequencing reflects the common presumption that narration and description are developmentally prior to exposition and persuasion. In light of young children's considerable persuasive skills in speech, however, it is likely that the alleged late onset of persuasive writing competence is more an artifact of school curricula than student abilities. Age appropriate evaluation standards are presumably also built into the quality of the anchor papers, which provide different models for each writing prompt against which raters calibrate their judgments. The criteria that describe the levels of quality expected at each rating point, however, do not change systematically from one testing level to the next. Thus, for example, all rating criteria and quality indicators for the Level 10 persuasive writing assessment are identical to the criteria and indicators for Level 12 persuasive writing.

The Writing Assessment System provides for two types of ratings: Holistic and Analytic. Holistic ratings are general impressions of composition quality expressed on a 4-point scale. Two raters assign Holistic scores to each paper. If those two scores differ by more than 1 point, a third rater resolves the difference. The Writing Assessment Guide presents the results of a pilot administration. (The pilot instrument was slightly different than the current published version.) At lease 200 students wrote in response to each of the prompts. Exact agreement between raters on the 4-point scale was achieved only 60% of the time (without correction for chance agreement). Correlations between raters for the various prompts ranged from .45 to .78, with the poorest interrater reliabilities occuring in judgments of high school writing. Although judgments of composition quality are admittedly susceptible to a variety of extraneous rater variables, research studies typically report interrater reliabilities above .85. The degree of reliability reported here would not withstand legal challenge.

No interrater reliabilities are available at all for analytic scores. This is because procedures specify that only one reader assigns analytic scores to papers. The analytic scores comprise separate ratings on (a) content, (b) organization, (c) sentence construction, (d) vocabulary and grammar, and (e) spelling and capitalization. These categories are not entirely distinct conceptually (e.g., uses of subordinating conjunctions like "whereas" to connect ideas could fall under at least three of the above scales); nor, however, are they intended to sum into any single composite rating.

Analytic rating procedures attempt to maintain the integrity of each of the five items and to guard against contamination across the items that could result when raters form general impressions of the papers they are reading. The resulting rating protocol apparently asks Analytic raters to read each paper five different times focusing on a separate Analytic scale on each pass. This method of Analytic rating differs from standard Analytic rating procedures reported elsewhere, and renders the Analytic ratings impractical. Together with the lack of any sort of reliability check on the Analytic ratings, the tedious reading procedures militate against adopting this method of assessment. In fact, the Administration and Scoring Manuals provide much less adequate instructions for Analytic rating than they do for Holistic (e.g., no sample papers are provided to calibrate raters' Analytic scores).

Consistent with the poorly developed reliabilities, little work is evident to establish the validity of Writing Assessment System scores. The pilot study reported in the accompanying Guide suggests divergent validity between several measures of writing ability. Low to moderate correlations are found among Holistic scores, Analytic scores, and scores derived from the CAT/E Language Tests. It is curious that the Guide regards this divergence as validation. When holistic composition rating was first developed as a psychometrically sound procedure, it was validated by demonstrating its convergence with indirect measures of writing ability (as well as by demonstrating convergence among multiple writing samples; Godshalk, Swineford, & Coffman, 1966).

Finally, potential users of the System ought to be aware of the nature of the writing sample upon which scores are based. For most prompts, students write for a total of 30 minutes. Test booklets provide a blank space for outlining and planning, and two lined pages, enough space for a maximum of about 250 words. These constraints hardly support the kind of rich writing process—including incubation of ideas, prewriting activities, drafting, revision, and editing—which the Writing Assessment Guide itself espouses. Thus, results are likely to seriously underestimate students' actual writing abilities.

The CAT Writing Assessment System is helpful because it does promote direct writing assessment. It also educates users about the importance of well-designed writing prompts, about conditions for eliciting and rating writing samples, and especially about methods of training raters. Most test users, however, could develop superior writing assessment programs by following the practices described in practical guides like *Measuring Growth in English* (Diederich, 1974).

REVIEWER'S REFERENCES

Godshalk, F. I., Swineford, F., & Coffman, W. E. (1966). *The measurement of writing ability.* New York: College Entrance Examination Board.
Diederich, P. (1974). *Measuring growth in English.* Urbana: National Council of Teachers of English.

Review of the California Achievement Tests Writing Assessment System by TERRY A. STINNETT, *Assistant Professor of Psychology, Eastern Illinois University, Charleston, IL:*

The California Achievement Tests (CAT) have been well established for more than half a century as measures of basic academic skills. There is now available a Writing Assessment System (WAS) as part of Forms E and F. The WAS has eight levels (13–20) that cover the grade ranges 2.6 through 12.9. Contiguous levels of the test overlap with one another by .6 year so that two levels of the test can be appropriate for students in the target grade range. This overlap allows different levels of the test to be administered during fall and spring of a school year.

The complete CAT-WAS package includes writing booklets, administration and scoring manuals for each level, CompuScan supplementary answer sheets, and the Writing Assessment Guide. The Administration and Scoring manuals and the Writing Assessment Guide are the primary administrative and interpretive materials and they are written in a concise and clear manner. Directions for administering the test are in the Administration and Scoring manuals and are unambiguous. These manuals also provide detailed information for training scorers and for scoring writing samples. The Writing Assessment Guide is designed to aid in interpretation. The majority of the Writing Assessment Guide is focused on writing activities that could be used in the classroom.

The WAS assessment model is also described in detail. The writing activities and description of the WAS model comprise 59% of the Writing Assessment Guide at the expense of other relevant sections. For example, the technical section of the Guide is sparse and generally lacks adequate detail. Important reliability and validity information is neglected and specific procedures used to analyze the WAS standardization data are imprecise.

TEST FORMAT. The WAS can yield direct and indirect measures of student writing skill (actual writing samples versus multiple-choice test performance data). The indirect measures are secondary to the direct measures and the WAS administration and scoring manuals suggest they can be CAT Forms E and F or any other CTB Macmillan/McGraw-Hill language and spelling multiple-choice tests. The primary writing assessment is direct and requires that an actual sample of student writing be obtained. Descriptive, Narrative, Expository, and Persuasive writing samples are elicited by prompts (writing assignments) that are in each writing book. The prompts are reported to be appropriate for their respective grade levels in terms of topic and form. The authors indicate the development of prompts involved several stages including reviews of the writing assessment research, teacher recommendations, and an item tryout of various prompts. However, an exact description of how the final selection and assignment of prompts to the various test levels was done is not presented.

Descriptive prompts are available for Levels 13–16 (grades 2.6 through 7.2) and are designed to elicit a description of a place or event that can be constructed based on previous experiences and imagination. Narrative prompts are available for Levels 13–19 (grades 2.6 through 11.2) and should elicit descriptions of eventful situations from an expressive and personal perspective. Plot and setting clues are included in an attempt to encourage sequencing of events and a narrative perspective. Expository prompts are available for Levels 15–20

(grades 4.6 through 12.9) and specifically ask the student to explain and inform the reader about topics based on knowledge and insights to which the average student who would take these levels of the test would have access. The final type of writing assessed is Persuasive writing (Levels 17–20, grades 6.6 through 12.9). The student is prompted to present and support a position with persuasive reasons. The Persuasive prompts provide focus on the topic, and imply a particular audience and the type of writing required. Users should note that the type of writing prompt that is available varies depending on the level of the test selected, so fall and spring testing of students in a particular grade using different levels may not provide two samples of the same type of writing for comparison (Levels 14–15, 16–17, and 19–20).

SCORING PROCEDURES. Two methods are used to score the student writing samples: Holistic and Analytic. Holistic scoring reflects the overall quality of the writing sample by having trained evaluators numerically rank papers that have been written from the same prompt. Evaluators learn to rank papers in training sessions and scoring is guided by representative anchor papers that have been chosen from compositions obtained during the CAT-WAS standardization, to exemplify the numeric criteria.

The anchor papers were selected to reflect the "middle point" in the range of papers that could earn the same score. The rankings are based on a 4-point system: 1 = *unacceptable*, 2 = *below average*, 3 = *acceptable*, and 4 = *good*. In special circumstances, papers may be scored as (N), *no response*; (I) *illegible*; or (0), *off prompt*. Each student paper is read by two or three evaluators and they are blind to any score(s) a paper has previously obtained. Typically, scores from two separate evaluators are averaged and a final score is obtained. However, if there is more than 1 point difference between the first two evaluators' ratings then a third reader evaluates the writing sample and the third reader's ranking becomes the final score. Anchor papers and scoring explanations are presented in the administration and scoring manuals for each type of prompt, every score point, and for each grade level. The scoring guidelines reportedly have been carefully designed to focus on specific qualities that are expected in writing at a given grade level.

Analytic scoring is used in conjunction with the Holistic method and evaluates the writing samples in terms of important isolated elements of compositions: content, organization, sentence construction, vocabulary and grammar, and spelling and capitalization. Evaluators score each analytic component on the 4-point scoring system: 1 = *unacceptable*, 2 = *below average*, 3 = *acceptable*, and 4 = *good*. The administration and scoring manual describes the analytic criteria in detail. However, evidence for the reliability of analytic scoring is absent and discussion of validity is minimal.

General scoring guidelines are modified for use depending on the type of writing to be analyzed (Descriptive, Narrative, Expository, or Persuasive) and the grade level of the examinee. It is suggested in the Writing Assessment Guide that strengths and weaknesses in the particular analytic writing skill areas can be identified and this information can be used to design remedial instruction. This reviewer thinks the authors have overstated the power and potential usefulness of the WAS. No evidence for reliability of Analytic scoring is available. Additionally, because validity data are not described in detail, it is unknown how much of the variance in overall writing proficiency each of the Analytic elements can account for and whether the elements are in fact good predictors of writing proficiency.

The Writing Assessment Guide also suggests that writing samples can be evaluated on the basis of a primary trait. A primary trait is defined as a selected skill that has been chosen to be the exclusive scoring criterion and any of the analytic elements could be designated as the primary trait. The authors offer no guidelines for selecting a particular analytic element to serve as the primary trait on which writing samples will be scored. This reviewer assumes that test users would select criteria that are directly linked to the curriculum in place at their schools, but no suggestions are offered by the WAS authors.

The writing samples can be scored locally by evaluators who have been trained to use the two scoring systems specified in the Writing Assessment Guide (Holistic and Analytic) or the CTB Macmillan/McGraw-Hill Composition Evaluation Center can be contracted to score the papers. If the tests are scored locally, an Answer Sheet Supplement for each student can be submitted to CTB Macmillan/McGraw-Hill and computer-generated reports can be obtained that detail the student's performance on the various writing samples. A Writing Assessment System Class Record Sheet (CRS) can also be obtained from the scoring service and is a computer-generated list of students and their respective scores. The authors suggest that the CRS will be useful to determine individual class members' strengths and weaknesses and the strengths and weaknesses of the class as a whole. This information is suggested to be used to develop or target specific instructional objectives in a curriculum.

The Individual Test Record (ITR) is the computer-generated report that can be obtained for each student. The ITR summarizes the child's performance on the writing samples and presents the numeric Holistic and Analytic ratings the child received. The Holistic score points are reported in .5 increments because the Holistic score is an average of two ratings and half points are thus possible (e.g.,

rating one = 2 and rating two = 3, Holistic score = 2.5). However, only the whole numbers have interpretive statements. Canned descriptive interpretive statements are listed on the ITR for the four whole number Holistic score points (e.g., 4 = *good*, 3 = *acceptable*, 2 = *below average*, and 1 = *unacceptable*) and for each of the four possible score points for the five Analytic elements. The Analytic interpretive statements are also standard but do vary to reflect the particular type of writing sample (Descriptive, Narrative, Expository, or Persuasive) that was obtained for the individual student. The interpretation is accomplished by having an arrow placed next to each of the student's earned score points and their associated interpretive statements.

An additional WAS computer-generated report is the class summary Frequency Distribution (FD) that is based on the local writing samples that have been obtained. The FD contains means, medians, and standard deviations for the Holistic and Analytic scores. Also the number and percentage of students in the sample group receiving a score and the cumulative percentage and frequency for the group are provided.

TEST CONSTRUCTION. The exact procedures adhered to for the WAS test construction and refinement are unclear. The descriptive demographic information for the standardization sample student examinees or for the teachers who helped develop the prompts for the initial tryout of the system is not available in the test materials. No details are provided about the CTB Macmillan/McGraw-Hill Composition Evaluation Center trained scorers who evaluated all of the standardization writing samples. The sampling procedures are not described. The Writing Assessment Guide simply states that districts from Arkansas, California, Delaware, Maine, Massachusetts, Mississippi, Missouri, Montana, North Carolina, Ohio, and South Carolina participated in the tryout. Apparently in the test tryout there were twice as many writing prompts as are now in the final form. The number of prompts was reduced, wording of some prompts was changed, and two expository prompts were moved to higher levels. No detailed rationale for these changes is offered in the technical information. To their credit, the authors of the guide do caution that the data presented in the guide apply only to the writing samples elicited by the initial "tryout" prompts. No data are available for the final prompts.

RELIABILITY. Of the traditional test reliability estimates, only scorer reliability estimates (Pearson product-moment correlations) are available for the WAS. Test-retest and alternate-form estimates would be appropriate for the WAS but are not reported in the technical manual. To further exacerbate this technical problem, interrater reliabilities for *only* the Holistic scores by type of prompt are presented. No reliability estimates are reported for the Analytic scores. Interrater reliabilities were calculated for scoring of the writing samples by having two CTB Macmillan/McGraw-Hill Composition Evaluation Center independent evaluators score each Holistic sample. Samples that were scored by more than two raters were excluded from the computations and the authors estimate this to be approximately 1.5% of the total samples. It is unclear how many evaluators participated or if different evaluators were used for each type of prompt. The reliabilities by level and type of prompt are lower than are desirable. Reliabilities for the Descriptive prompts ranged from .65 to .72 across four levels (median $r = .68$). Reliabilities were also consistently low for the Narrative prompts at all seven possible levels and ranged from .47 to .70 (median $r = .62$). Scorer reliabilities for the Expository prompts ranged from .45 to .78 (median $r = .66$) and for the Persuasive writing samples from .54 to .69 (median $r = .66$). Scoring the WAS consistently is likely to be a significant problem for WAS users. Low interrater reliabilities were obtained by CTB Macmillan/McGraw-Hill trained evaluators at the Composition Evaluation Center. This reviewer thinks it is likely the reliabilities will be even lower if the scorers are school staff who have not been trained by CTB Macmillan/McGraw-Hill personnel who are expert in the Holistic scoring system.

VALIDITY. The developers of the WAS have accentuated content validity. The test does yield direct samples of writing. The authors provide a bibliography in the Writing Assessment Guide and it seems they have done a good job of producing relevant test content. Research studies pertaining to writing assessment and scoring were reviewed and teachers were surveyed to develop and place the writing prompts at the appropriate test/grade levels. However, users of the WAS should be cognizant that no information is reported to describe the demographic characteristics of the teachers who participated in the test development. Typically, content validity is developed with the assistance of subject-matter experts; however, without specific teacher information it is impossible for WAS users to estimate the level of the teachers' expertise.

Correlations are presented in the CAT-WAS Writing Assessment Guide between various Holistic scoring prompts in an attempt to demonstrate construct validity. The correlations are for prompts within levels only, not across levels. They range from .50 to .71 (median $r = .65$). These correlations suggest a moderate to low degree of intercorrelation among some of the prompts, thus the separate prompts might be measuring a similar construct (i.e., overall writing ability, within levels). Additionally, the authors are implying that the various

prompts are divergent enough to warrant their inclusion in the test. Test users should interpret these results with caution. The authors did not adequately describe the procedures used to derive the correlations. It is unclear whether the correlations are derived based on ratings given to different prompts by the same scorer, or whether the correlations were derived by correlating ratings from different scorers. Also, the complete picture of the relationships among the prompts is not available. The authors did not report the relationship of each prompt with every other prompt within levels. Also, the authors fail to report the relationship of the prompts across levels so test users cannot determine if there is a developmental effect associated with overall writing ability.

The authors also correlated each of the Holistic scores for the writing prompts with CAT Form E Language Mechanics, Language Expression, and Total Language scores. The correlations were generally low and the authors indicate this provides evidence for CAT-WAS divergent validity. The correlations ranged from .35 to .65 (median $r = .52$), .32 to .69 (median $r = .58$), and .37 to .73 (median $r = .58$) for Language Mechanics, Language Expression, and Total Score respectively.

Multiple correlations among the WAS Analytic scores and CAT Form E Language Mechanics, Language Expression, and Total Language scores were also computed. The multiple correlation coefficients were reported as .55 to .76, .53 to .79, and .58 to .81 for Language Mechanics, Language Expression, and Total Score respectively. The authors do not report all obtained correlations and it is not clear which of the reported correlations are associated with which Analytic scores. The results could, however, provide further evidence for the divergent validity of the WAS if more detail was available.

Another multiple regression analysis was conducted to examine the relationship among the Analytic scores and the Holistic scores. Multiple Rs are reported to range from .65 to .86, which means analytic elements accounted for 42% to 74% of the variance in the Holistic scores. Unfortunately the authors do not report all of the obtained correlations from this analysis and they also neglect to indicate which of the particular Analytic elements are associated with the specific multiple Rs. Considering that is was earlier suggested that Analytic elements could be targeted as strengths or weaknesses for instruction, it would be helpful to know which element best predicts the Holistic score, because the Holistic score is reportedly a measure of overall writing proficiency.

SUMMARY. The CAT Writing Assessment System might eventually develop into a state-of-the-art system for evaluating actual student writing samples. The direct measurement of behavior will allow test users to link assessment with treatment more efficiently. The CAT-WAS appears to be a well-planned system that has good potential to address these direct assessment needs on a large scale level. However, until reliability and validity of the WAS scoring systems can be improved, indirect, multiple-choice tests likely will continue to be the dominant assessment technology. If CTB Macmillan/McGraw-Hill is able to bring the WAS to the level of technical quality of the objective battery, the WAS will certainly find a niche in the assessment field. The CAT-WAS cannot be recommended for any use other than research at the present time. Test users who need direct samples of writing to design remediation and treatment would do just as well to informally assess writing by matching their assessment with the content of the curriculum that is in use.

[52]
California Diagnostic Mathematics Tests.

Purpose: Developed to assess mathematics achievement for use in instructional planning and program evaluation.
Publication Date: 1989.
Acronym: CDMT.
Administration: Group.
Price Data, 1991: $10.50 per 35 practice tests (select Levels A, B–C, D–F); $17.15 per 35 locator tests (select Levels A–C, D–F); $16 per 50 locator test answer sheets (Levels D–F); $9.60 per set of hand scoring stencils (select Levels D, E, F); $26 per 100 student diagnostic profiles; $1 per class report form; $5.65 per locator test directions; $7.35 per examiner's manual and answer keys (select level); $10.35 per teacher's guide (select Levels A–B, C–D, or E–F); $7.35 per norms book (31 pages); $7.35 per technical report; $35.30 per specimen set; TestMate software available for local scanning and scoring; scoring service available from publisher.
Time: Administration time not reported.
Author: CTB/McGraw-Hill.
Publisher: CTB Macmillan/McGraw-Hill.

  a) LEVEL A.
  Population: Grades 1.1–2.9.
  Scores, 3: Number Concepts, Computation, Applications.
  Price Data: $44.10 per 35 hand-scorable test books; $72.10 per 35 machine-scorable (NCS) test books.
  b) LEVEL B.
  Population: Grades 2.6–3.9.
  Scores, 3: Same as *a* above.
  Price Data: Same as *a* above.
  c) LEVEL C.
  Population: Grades 3.6–4.9.
  Scores, 3: Same as *a* above.
  Price Data: Same as *a* above.
  d) LEVEL D.
  Population: Grades 4.6–6.9.
  Scores, 3: Same as *a* above.
  Price Data: $32.90 per 35 reusable tests; $15 per 25 SCOREZE answer sheets for hand scoring; $11.50 per 50 CompuScan machine-scorable answer sheets; $11.50

per 50 SCANTRON machine-scorable answer sheets for use with computer-linked scanners.
  e) LEVEL E.
  Population: Grades 6.6–8.9.
  Scores, 3: Same as *a* above.
  Price Data: Same as *d* above.
  f) LEVEL F.
  Population: Grades 8.6–12.
  Scores, 3: Same as *a* above plus Life Skills.
  Price Data: Same as *d* above.

Review of the California Diagnostic Mathematics Tests by MICHAEL B. BUNCH, Vice President, Measurement Incorporated, Durham, NC:

Title I of the Elementary and Secondary Education Act of 1965 (ESEA Title I) and subsequent evaluation regulations and models created a tremendous market for hybrid tests that could perform the program evaluation role of standardized norm-referenced tests and the diagnostic role of informal inventories. The basic idea of that legislation exists today in Chapter 1 of the Educational Consolidation and Improvement Act of 1981 (ECIA Chapter 1). The evaluation models have changed very little since 1976. Evaluation that provides national norms is still a standard feature of Chapter 1 programs. At the same time, because Chapter 1 is a compensatory program, planners and practitioners demand tests that are diagnostic. Most major test publishers have rushed to fill this demand with hybrid tests that have both norm-referenced and domain-referenced features. The California Diagnostic Mathematics Tests (CDMT) is a recent entry in this market. Its teacher's guides and technical report make it very clear that the CDMT was designed with Chapter 1 in mind. The publisher's candor in this matter is very refreshing.

CONTENT. The content of the CDMT is similar to that of the California Achievement Tests Forms E and F (CAT E/F; 10:41). Indeed, items for the CDMT and CAT E/F were selected from the same pool. Similarly, items in the locator tests and practice tests were drawn from this pool. The primary difference in the two tests is the fact that the CDMT items are easier than CAT E/F items for a given grade. In addition to the general item categories listed above, the CDMT measures whole number concepts, whole number place value and estimation, rational number concepts, algorithms, advanced number concepts, whole number addition and subtraction, whole number multiplication, whole number division, rational number computation, modeling word problems, solving word problems, measurement and geometry, graphing, and life skills problems. These strands are further divided into dozens of specific objectives that are shown in Table 2 of the teacher's guides. Individuals considering adopting the CDMT would do well to study these tables as well as individual items to determine the degree to which the content of the CDMT matches local curriculum.

BOOKLETS AND MANUALS. Test booklets and examiner's manuals are well conceived and executed. Particularly at the lower levels, student test booklets are uncluttered and inviting. Maximum use of graphics and pictures is made. Pictures and drawings are fairly generic; a dog, for example, is depicted with enough detail to show that it is a dog but not so much detail that the student is likely to be distracted from the task of counting the dogs. Examiner's manuals contain scripts as well as miniature student test booklet pages so that the examiner can read along without having to hold the manual in one hand and the student booklet in the other.

The teacher's guides are quite well done. They are concise, convey a great deal of information about the tests and their use, and are generally user friendly. Discussions of score reports and possible classroom activities are extremely helpful. Each guide contains several kinds of classroom activities ranging from whole-class to independent practice, from bulletin boards to higher order thinking skills. Not surprisingly, many of the activities bear a great resemblance to the test items with which they are associated.

SCORE REPORTS. The various score reports are uncluttered and highly informative. The individual test record, for example, has only 45 numbers and 27 symbols for Level C. Some publishers' tests provide student score reports at this grade level (4) with as many as 200 numbers and symbols to decipher and remember. The class record sheet is very easy to read and understand. Nearly one-third of it is set aside for teacher comments. Although some of the reports are less well designed (e.g., the Objectives Performance Report and the Parent Report), overall, the score reports reflect a great deal of concern for the user.

Although most scoring of the CDMT is done by machine, a norms booklet is available for those who prefer to score by hand. The best feature of the norms booklet is the provision of standard errors of measurement for every obtainable scale score. The worst feature of the booklet is its organization. First, there are no tables for total score. Second, the booklet provides only raw score to scale score conversion tables. To convert scale scores to percentiles or NCEs, the user must obtain a set of norms tables for the CAT E/F (there are three, one each for fall, winter, and spring). The norms booklet also provides cut scores for three levels of proficiency for each objective. Unfortunately, no support for these cut scores is ever given. Teachers might just as effectively set their own cut scores.

TECHNICAL. Technical information about the tests is summarized in an undated preliminary technical report. A final report is promised, but two years after the publication date of the tests, none is available. The preliminary report reveals some disturbing facts. First the tests were normed in the fall of 1987 (October) one grade below level. Although IRT (Item Response Theory) linking requires only one point in time and is indifferent to student ability level, a spring administration would have been consistent with more Chapter 1 evaluation cycles, and response patterns of average third graders are not likely to be identical to those of below-average fourth graders. At the very least, an average third grader's growth expectation would be greater than that of a below-average fourth grader. In contrast, the Stanford Diagnostic Mathematics Test (SDMT; 9:1177) was empirically normed in fall and spring on grade level.

Reliability is reported at the subtest level but not at the total test level. Yet, score reports clearly show total scores. Particularly for program evaluation, total scores are very important as is information about their reliability. Validity information is mentioned but will not be forthcoming until publication of the final technical report, along with bias data. These two omissions are serious shortcomings but seem to reflect a common practice; CTB Macmillan/McGraw-Hill is not alone in delaying publication of important technical data. Indeed, for the SDMT, the latest Psychological Corporation catalog does not even list a technical report.

Although the norm-referenced aspects of the CDMT are well documented, there is little information provided about the diagnostic or domain-referenced aspects of the tests. As noted above, no support is given for the many cut scores. Similarly, there is no discussion of instructional sensitivity. Ideally, tests would have been given before and after instruction and items selected on the basis of pre-post p value differences. For diagnostic purposes, items would have been selected on the basis of their agreement with teacher ratings of student strengths and weaknesses.

The use of IRT techniques raises important questions about the content of the CDMT. The technical report does not discuss relationships among the subtests and objectives. The fact that all the items in a given level had to fit a model that assumes unidimensionality suggests that divergent validity is low. This condition is highly desirable in a norm-referenced test of general mathematics achievement but not in a diagnostic test of specific mathematics skills.

On balance, the CDMT technical report provides difficulty indices (p values) at the objective level, provides a thorough and generally readable discussion of the linking process (with sufficient references for those who wish to gain a deeper understanding), and provides standard errors of measurement

(*SEM*) for the entire range of scores for each level. A more common practice is simply to report *SEM*s at the mean or median. Similarly, item selection and score construction are well defined.

SUMMARY. The CDMT was created to serve a well-defined market niche. It shares that niche with several other like instruments. Most (like the SDMT mentioned above) are hybrids. In terms of content, the CDMT covers a reasonable range of the objectives most teachers are likely to want to see. The publisher has developed an attractive and highly useful set of materials (especially the teacher's guides) to support effective instruction. Technically, the tests are well conceived and fairly well documented. In a norm-referenced world, the CDMT performs as well as any of the other contenders in its niche. In absolute terms, the potential user is advised to compare actual test content to local objectives and instruction, use the standard errors of measurement provided by the publisher, and avoid hand scoring, particularly if the CDMT is to be administered any time other than October.

Review of the California Diagnostic Mathematics Tests by JERRY JOHNSON, Professor of Mathematics, Western Washington University, Bellingham, WA:

The California Diagnostic Mathematics Tests (CDMT) are a series of diagnostic tests designed to measure "achievement in the skills that underlie success in mathematics." As objective-based, criterion-referenced diagnostic instruments, the tests' primary purpose is to provide reliable information about students who tend to get mathematics scores below the 50th percentile on standardized, norm-referenced achievement tests. Furthermore, the authors of the CDMT claim to offer the best of two worlds—the relative ranking of students against an appropriate normed population and useful information that pinpoints the specific instructional needs of students on an individual basis.

The six tests (A, B, C, D, E, F) in the CDMT series are classified according to the grade ranges 1–2, 2–3, 3–4, 4–6, 6–8, and 8–12. All of the tests assess student performance in three primary areas, each separated into several subtopics. First, Number Concepts includes the subtopics of whole number concepts, whole number place value, estimation, rational number concepts, algorithms, and advanced number concepts. Computation includes the subtopics of whole number addition, subtraction, multiplication, division, and rational number computation. Applications includes the subtopics of modeling word problems, solving word problems, measurement, geometry, and graphing. The sixth test (F) also includes the area of Life Skills which focuses on consumer-related problems. A minimum of four test items are used to assess each objective associated with a subtest.

The Teacher's Guide claims the CDMT measures of mathematical content comply with the well-publicized recommendations of both the *Position Statement on Basic Skills* (National Council of Supervisors of Mathematics, 1977) and the *Agenda For Action* (National Council of Teachers of Mathematics, 1980). Two key ingredients are the measure of higher-order thinking skills and the measure of computational skill within the context of real-world applications and concepts. As worthy as these claims may be, they are already outdated, given the current attention in the mathematical community on the more recent documents, *Essential Mathematics For The 21st Century* (National Council of Supervisors of Mathematics, 1989) and *Curriculum and Evaluation Standards for School Mathematics* (National Council of Teachers of Mathematics, 1989).

Although designed to be administered to groups of students, the CDMT are not timed. The CDMT examiner manual for each test suggests approximate time limits for each subtest (more than 3 hours for Level F), with the caution to "make sure that at least 90 percent of the students" finish a section. For the tests directed at the lower grade levels, many of the questions are oral, which places a greater burden on the test examiner in a group situation. If grade level is not a good indicator of test appropriateness, special locator tests can be used to determine which level of the CDMT to administer. Practice books for some CDMT levels (D–F) are available to give students experience with both test-taking mechanics and the format of test items.

Examiner's manuals guide both the proper administration of the CDMT and the scoring of the student responses to the multiple-choice items. If the tests are scored by hand, instructions are included to guide the completion of the two report forms, the Student Diagnostic Profile and the Class Record Sheet for Hand Scoring, and the use of the CDMT Norms Book. If the tests are scored by the CTB Macmillan/McGraw-Hill machine-scoring service, the types of information available include a norm-referenced Class Record Sheet, a criterion-referenced Individual Test Record, a group-based Objectives Performance Report, an instructional-based Class Grouping Report, and a Parent Report. When the CDMT is machine scored, an option is the use of pattern scoring, which uses Item Response Theory to build scale scores from the overall pattern of correct and incorrect responses in contrast to the number of correct items.

Additional information in the CDMT Teacher's Guide includes a helpful discussion of the test content, how it is measured, and how it can be taught. The specific content is organized using the format of instructional strand, content range, illustrative test items, common errors (distractors), learning activities, and instructional strategies.

To produce the CDMT, more than 3,000 items were written and tested using a tryout sample during October, 1987. Structured to be both homogeneous and representative of students "across the country," the sample included approximately 800 to 1,000 students per test level. Each student took both a subset of the tryout items and the California Achievement Tests, Form E (CAT E). Using nominal ranges—CAT E and F scale scores for fall (5th percentile) and the spring (50th percentile)—for each test level, items were selected for the six tests and the locator tests. The item selection was refined to ensure coverage of the prescribed content domains.

During the tryout of items, the CAT E was included so that the CDMT items could be calibrated to the CAT E Mathematics Computation or Mathematics Concepts and Applications scales. Although the CDMT is criterion referenced by intent, the calibrations of its items allow the use of the CDMT raw scores and a norms book to derive norm-referenced scores (based on the CAT E scales) such as percentile ranks, stanines, and grade equivalents. Underlying the entire process of calibration is a statistical analysis using the three-parameter logistic model known as Item Response Theory, with a dependance on the discrimination and location parameters.

Only a preliminary report is available regarding the technical aspects regarding the reliability and validity of the CDMT. To measure internal consistency, Kuder-Richardson formula 20 was used to calculate the average of all possible split-half coefficients, which is a lower bound to a classical reliability value. The range of KR-20 values over the six tests was .73 to .96. As another measure of reliability, the standard error of measurement (SEM) was calculated and varies considerably among the six tests. Because the CDMT items were selected using a nominal range based on a 5th–50th percentile comparison, the SEM will be the smallest (and the test more reliable) when a student scores in this range rather than near the possible floor or ceiling values.

Validity of the CDMT is given little attention in the preliminary edition of the technical report. An informal discussion and some cautions are provided regarding the validity of using criterion-performance indicators such as the Objective Performance Index in the CDMT. It is also reported that a cross-validation study was conducted in 1988 to "confirm" the correspondence of the CDMT raw scores to CAT E scale scores. No data or results were available from this study. Similarly, data regarding ethnic/gender bias in the tests have been collected with no analysis reported.

In summary, the CDMT are criterion-referenced tests designed to help diagnose the instructional needs of low-achieving students, that is, those who normally score below the 50th percentile on a standardized, norm-referenced achievement test. In addition to its diagnostic function, the CDMT can be used for district-wide evaluations or program evaluation (e.g., Chapter 1). One concern is the preliminary nature of the technical data supporting the tests and their proposed functions, as to validity and reliability. A second concern is the compatability of the CDMT with the current direction in assessment being proposed by the professional community of mathematics educators.

REVIEWER'S REFERENCES
National Council of Supervisors of Mathematics. (1977). Position paper on basic skills. *Arithmetic Teacher, 25* (1), 19-22.
National Council of Teachers of Mathematics. (1980). *An agenda for action.* Reston, VA: The Council.
National Council of Supervisors of Mathematics. (1989, September). Essential mathematics for the 21st century. *Mathematics Teacher,* pp. 470-474.
National Council of Teachers of Mathematics. (1989). *Curriculum and evaluation standards for school mathematics.* Reston, VA: The Council.

[53]

California Diagnostic Reading Tests.

Purpose: Developed to assess reading achievement for use in instructional planning and program evaluation.
Publication Date: 1989.
Acronym: CDRT.
Administration: Group.
Price Data, 1991: $10.50 per 35 practice books (select Levels A, B–C, D–F); $17.85 per 35 locator tests (select Levels A–C, D–F); $16 per 50 locator test answer sheets (Levels D–F only); $28.80 per set of scoring stencils (Levels D–F only); $26 per 100 student diagnostic profiles; $1 per class record sheet for hand scoring (select level); $5.65 per locator test directions; $7.35 per examiner's manual including answer keys (select level); $10.35 per teacher's guide (select Levels A–B, C–D, E–F); $7.35 per norms book (32 pages); $7.35 per technical report; $35.40 per specimen set; TestMate software available for local scanning and scoring; scoring service available from publisher.
Time: Tests are untimed.
Author: CTB/McGraw-Hill.
Publisher: CTB Macmillan/McGraw-Hill.

a) LEVEL A.
Population: Grades 1.1–2.9.
Scores, 3: Word Analysis, Vocabulary, Comprehension.
Price Data: $44.10 per 35 hand-scorable test books; $72.10 per 35 machine-scorable test books.

b) LEVEL B.
Population: Grades 2.6–3.9.
Scores, 3: Same as *a* above.
Price Data: Same as *a* above.

c) LEVEL C.
Population: Grades 3.6–4.9.
Scores, 3: Same as *a* above.
Price Data: Same as *a* above.

d) LEVEL D.
Population: Grades 4.6–6.9.
Scores, 4: Same as *a* above plus Applications.
Price Data: $32.90 per 35 reusable test books; $29.75 per 25 SCOREZE answer sheets; $20 per 50

machine-scorable answer sheets (select CompuScan or SCANTRON).

e). LEVEL E.
Population: Grades 6.6–8.9.
Scores, 4: Same as *d* above.
Price Data: Same as *d* above.

f) LEVEL F.
Population: Grades 8.6–12.
Scores, 3: Vocabulary, Comprehension, Applications.
Price Data: Same as *d* above.

Review of the California Diagnostic Reading Tests by T. STEUART WATSON, Assistant Professor of Educational Psychology, Mississippi State University, Starkville, MS:

The California Diagnostic Reading Tests (CDRT) is a lengthy battery of group-administered reading tests that claims to provide diagnostic information to assist the classroom teacher in planning instructional reading activities for children in kindergarten through 12th grades. Other stated purposes of the CDRT are to provide district-wide program evaluations and a reliable reading test for students scoring below the 50th percentile. Norms are provided in a preliminary edition norms book for each subtest at each level. Kindergarten norms are not printed in the norms book but are available upon request.

Like most group-administered achievement tests, the CDRT supplies an examiner's manual and test booklet for each level. The examiner's manual includes chapters on Description of the CDRT, Advance Preparation, Directions for Administration, and Processing Completed Tests. Description of the CDRT would be more appropriate in a technical manual rather than in a teacher examination manual. The remaining sections are concise and clearly written to permit ease of administration and handling.

A Teacher's Guide accompanies the test materials. The most relevant sections in the guide discuss interpreting the results (Part 3) and using a diagnostic/prescriptive approach in the classroom (Part 4). Part 3 contains a glossary of measurement terms and concepts that should assist the novice tester in understanding this and other tests. Part 4 attempts to illustrate how a student's performance on the test translates to classroom instructional activities. Noticeably lacking are data to support a significant diagnostic by treatment interaction. The activities suggested often appear to have little or no relationship to reading. Part 2 of the Teacher's Guide (The Theoretical Basis of the CDRT) would be more appropriate in a technical manual.

TEST CONTENT. The CDRT comprises four subtests that are made up of instructional strands. Within each instructional strand are objectives related to reading. For example, instructional strands of the Word Analysis subtest are visual and auditory discrimination, whole word recognition,

and structural analysis. Although the objectives vary according to level, whole word recognition objectives include sight words, encoding, and decoding. A convenient table is included in the teacher's guide and examiner's manual that shows complete test content by level.

The items within each objective are grade appropriate and have relevance beyond classroom reading, particularly in the upper levels. For example, items in Level F include reading resumes, job applications, food packaging labels, etc. At Level A, the first items of each objective may not extend far enough downward for kindergartners or first graders who are having difficulty with reading. Overall, item content and sampling are good to excellent.

SCORING. Both norm- and criterion-referenced scores may be derived from the CDRT. The norm-referenced score is a scale score that is the basic score for the California Achievement Tests (CAT), Forms E and F (10:41). Scale scores range from 0–999 and are units on a single, equal-interval scale that is applied across all levels regardless of grade or time of year of testing. The advantage of such scores is that they allow for comparisons among classes, schools, or entire districts.

Scale scores may be obtained by pattern scoring and number-correct scoring. Pattern scoring is based on Item Response Theory and can be obtained only through machine scoring. The more useful number-correct scoring can be obtained through hand scoring. This score is converted to a scale score in the conversion table. The scale scores can be converted to norm-referenced scores based on the normative sample of the CAT E and F. Thus, a CAT E and F Norms Book is required in order to obtain norm-referenced scores.

To obtain derived scores (i.e., percentile ranks, normal curve equivalents, stanines, and grade equivalents) from scale scores, one must also have the appropriate CAT E and F Norms Book. To further complicate scoring, there are three CAT E and F Norms Books, depending on the time of year testing was done.

The task of obtaining norm-referenced and derived scores would be much simpler if the test publisher reproduced the necessary tables from the CAT for the CDRT. This is an unnecessary burden for the test user who wishes to quickly produce usable scores without requiring tables from other tests.

The criterion-referenced scores are also called objectives performance scores. These scores reflect each student's level of proficiency on each CDRT objective. Three scores are possible: "+," "P," and "-." A "+" score reflects the highest level of proficiency and indicates that the student is ready to move to the next instructional level. A "P" means that the student has some proficiency or knowledge, but is not ready to move to the next instructional level. A "-" means that the student is performing at the guess or chance level and needs to be introduced to or retaught the content area.

Objective performance cut scores, which are specific to each objective and each level, were established by determining: the average item difficulty for each objective at each relevant grade level; the importance of each objective at the level in which it is tested; and the number of items measuring the objective. The cut scores for the objective performance scores at each level (+, P, -) are presented in tabular form in the norms book. To obtain a "+" for each objective across tests, the student must answer 80–90% of the items correctly. To receive a "P," 47–82% of the items must be answered correctly, and 0–46% of the items must be answered correctly for the student to obtain a "-." These cut scores correspond to mastery, instructional, and frustration levels of performance.

At Levels D, E, and F, an approximate reading rate score may be computed based on the reading rate items of each objective. Tables are also provided that give the average reading rate in words per minute by grade level.

REPORT FORMS. Computer-generated and hand-scoring report forms are available when using the CDRT. The computer-generated scoring provides norm-referenced reports (Class Record Sheet), criterion-referenced reports (Objectives Performance Report and Class Grouping Report), reports containing both types of information (Individual Test Record), and a Parent Report. All reports are clear, useful, and understandable except the Parent Report. On the Parent Report, under the section entitled "Interpretation of Student's Results," strengths and weaknesses are listed. Unless a parent is knowledgeable about reading vernacular, some of the results may be meaningless. For example, a weakness given in the sample parent report in the Teacher's Guide (p. 18) is multinyms. An alternative would be to define and give examples of words not familiar to those outside of the educational system.

Hand-scored test results can be summarized on the Class Record Sheet and Student Diagnostic Profile. The Class Record Sheet requires the CDRT and CAT E and F Norms Books. Norm- and criterion-referenced information can be entered on the Class Record Sheet and is used for grouping students according to instructional need. The Student Diagnostic Profile summarizes normative and criterion information. It is said to be useful in discussions with parents and students.

TECHNICAL CHARACTERISTICS. Although no technical characteristics are provided in the CDRT materials, one can consult the CAT manual to determine technical adequacy because the tests are very closely related and the norm-referenced scores are taken from the CAT. This is an inconvenience in that the test user has to consult another source to find basic reliability and validity data.

CONCLUSIONS. Given the educational system's emphasis on standardized testing, the CDRT is another instrument destined for wide use. It provides administrators, teachers, and parents the types of information they are accustomed to seeing and using to evaluate individual performance and program success. However, the validity of using the CDRT to diagnose skill deficits and design remediative activities based on those results is not supported.

With the advent of curriculum-based assessment (CBA), teachers can directly assess those reading skills they deem important and that are part of their curriculum. The appropriate use of CBA takes less time, has a direct relationship to teaching reading, and provides accurate feedback regarding individual skill development.

Noticeably lacking are a technical manual and CAT norms book to obtain norm-referenced information and derived scores. Having to consult other sources to obtain basic data makes the CDRT less user friendly. This does, however, increase the reinforcing value of using the computer-scoring service.

Ultimately, use of this test cannot be recommended. It is noted in the purpose and rationale section of the Teacher's Guide that traditional standardized achievement tests do not help teachers develop instructional programs based on test results. Neither does the CDRT. The instructional activities recommended based on test performance are not supported by research presented in the CDRT materials or elsewhere.

[54]
California Psychological Inventory, Revised Edition.

Purpose: To assess personality characteristics and to predict what people will say and do in specified contexts.
Population: Ages 13 and over.
Publication Dates: 1956–87.
Acronym: CPI.
Scores, 20: Dominance (Do), Capacity for Status (Cs), Sociability (Sy), Social Presence (Sp), Self-Acceptance (Sa), Independence (In), Empathy (Em), Responsibility (Re), Socialization (So), Self-Control (Sc), Good Impression (Gi), Communality (Cm), Well-Being (Wb), Tolerance (To), Achievement via Conformance (Ac), Achievement via Independence (Ai), Intellectual Efficiency (Ie), Psychological-Mindedness (Py), Flexibility (Fx), Femininity/Masculinity (Fm).
Administration: Group.
Price Data, 1987: $18.75 per 25 tests; $6 per 50 hand-scored answer sheets; price data for 100 profiles (specify male or female) available from publisher; $39 or less per 10 prepaid CPI answer sheets; price data for 10 prepaid answer sheets producing Gough Interpretive Report or McAllister Interpretive Report available from publisher; price data for computer-administered version and

computer scoring available from publisher; price data for scoring stencils available from publisher; $13.50 per Administrator's Guide ('87, 134 pages); $17 per specimen set.

Foreign Language Editions: French, German, Italian, and Spanish editions available in previous edition.

Time: (45–60) minutes.

Comments: Previous edition (9:182) still available; 1 form.

Author: Harrison G. Gough.

Publisher: Consulting Psychologists Press, Inc.

Cross References: For reviews by Donald H. Baucom and H. J. Eysenck, see 9:182 (61 references); see also T3:354 (195 references); for a review by Malcolm D. Gynther, see 8:514 (452 references); see also T2:1121 (166 references); for reviews by Lewis R. Goldberg and James A. Walsh and an excerpted review by John O. Crites, see 7:49 (370 references); see also P:27 (249 references); for a review by E. Lowell Kelly, see 6:71 (116 references); for reviews by Lee J. Cronbach and Robert L. Thorndike and an excerpted review by Laurance F. Shaffer, see 5:37 (33 references).

TEST REFERENCES

1. Friesen, W., & Andrews, D. (1982). Self-management during counseling sessions: The behavioral assessment of process. *Criminal Justice and Behavior, 9*, 204-216.
2. Suedfeld, P., Ramirez, C., Deaton, J., & Baker-Brown, G. (1982). Reactions and attributes of prisoners in solitary confinement. *Criminal Justice and Behavior, 9*, 303-340.
3. Dollinger, S. J., Reader, M. J., Marnett, J. P., & Tylenda, B. (1983). Psychological-mindedness, psychological-construing, and the judgment of deception. *Journal of General Psychology, 108*, 183-191.
4. Davidson, W. B. (1984). Personality correlates of the Matching Familiar Figures Test in adults. *Journal of Personality Assessment, 48*, 478-482.
5. Dworkin, R. H., & Saczynski, K. (1984). Individual differences in hedonic capacity. *Journal of Personality Assessment, 48*, 620-626.
6. Erdwins, C. J., & Mellinger, J. C. (1984). Mid-life women: Relation of age and role to personality. *Journal of Personality and Social Psychology, 47*, 390-395.
7. Gough, H. G. (1984). A managerial potential scale for the California Psychological Inventory. *Journal of Applied Psychology, 69*, 233-240.
8. Hedlund, B. L., & Lindquist, C. U. (1984). The development of an inventory for distinguishing among passive, aggressive, and assertive behavior. *Behavioral Assessment, 6*, 379-390.
9. Helson, R., Mitchell, V., & Moane, G. (1984). Personality and patterns of adherence and nonadherence to the social clock. *Journal of Personality and Social Psychology, 46*, 1079-1096.
10. Holliman, N. B., & Montross, J. (1984). The effects of depression upon responses to the California Psychological Inventory. *Journal of Clinical Psychology, 40*, 1373-1378.
11. Jannarone, R. J., & Roberts, J. S. (1984). Reflecting interactions among personality items: Meehl's paradox revisited. *Journal of Personality and Social Psychology, 47*, 621-628.
12. Kohlberg, L., Ricks, D., & Snarey, J. (1984). Childhood development as a predictor of adaptation in adulthood. *Genetic Psychology Monographs, 110*, 91-172.
13. McAuliffe, T. M., & Handal, P. J. (1984). PIC delinquency scale: Validity in relation to self-reported delinquent acts. *Criminal Justice and Behavior, 11*, 35-46.
14. Rapaport, K., & Burkhart, B. R. (1984). Personality and attitudinal characteristics of sexually coercive college males. *Journal of Abnormal Psychology, 93*, 216-221.
15. Stevenson, D. T., & Romney, D. M. (1984). Depression in learning disabled children. *Journal of Learning Disabilities, 17*, 579-582.
16. Vargo, M. E., & Black, F. W. (1984). Psychosocial correlates of death anxiety in a population of medical students. *Psychological Reports, 54*, 737-738.
17. Zeldow, P. B., & Pavlou, M. (1984). Physical disability, life stress, and psychosocial adjustment in multiple sclerosis. *The Journal of Nervous and Mental Disease, 172*, 80-84.
18. Barnes, M. L., & Buss, D. M. (1985). Sex differences in the interpersonal behavior of married couples. *Journal of Personality and Social Psychology, 48*, 654-661.
19. Burisch, M. (1985). I wish it were true: Confessions of a secret deductivist. *Journal of Research in Personality, 19*, 343-347.

20. Friedrich, W. N., Tyler, J. D., & Clark, J. A. (1985). Personality and psychophysiological variables in abusive, neglectful, and low-income control mothers. *The Journal of Nervous and Mental Disease, 173*, 449-460.
21. Goldberg, L. R., & Kilkowski, J. M. (1985). The prediction of semantic consistency in self-descriptions: Characteristics of persons and of terms that affect the consistency of responses to synonym and antonym pairs. *Journal of Personality and Social Development, 48*, 82-98.
22. Gough, H. G. (1985). A work orientation scale for the California Psychological Inventory. *Journal of Applied Psychology, 70*, 505-513.
23. Graziano, W. G., Feldesman, A. B., & Rahe, D. F. (1985). Extraversion, social cognition, and the salience of aversiveness in social encounters. *Journal of Personality and Social Psychology, 48*, 971-980.
24. Haan, N. (1985). Processes of moral development: Cognitive or social disequilibrium? *Developmental Psychology, 21*, 996-1006.
25. Hare, R. D. (1985). Comparison of procedures for the assessment of psychopathy. *Journal of Consulting and Clinical Psychology, 53*, 7-16.
26. Heilbrun, A. B., Jr., & Heilbrun, M. R. (1985). Psychopathy and dangerousness: Comparison, integration and extension of two psychopathic typologies. *British Journal of Clinical Psychology, 24*, 181-195.
27. Honts, C. R., Raskin, D. C., & Kircher, J. C. (1985). Effects of socialization on the physiological detection of deception. *Journal of Research in Personality, 19*, 373-385.
28. Larsen, J. J., & Juhasz, A. M. (1985). The effects of knowledge of child development and social-emotional maturity on adolescent attitudes toward parenting. *Adolescence, 20*, 823-839.
29. Lifton, P. D. (1985). Individual differences in moral development: The relation of sex, gender, and personality to morality. *Journal of Personality, 53*, 306-334.
30. Loehlin, J. C., Willerman, L., & Horn, J. M. (1985). Personality resemblances in adoptive families when the children are late-adolescent or adult. *Journal of Personality and Social Psychology, 48*, 376-392.
31. Maceyko, S. J., & Nagelberg, D. B. (1985). The assessment of bulimia in high school students. *Journal of School Health, 55*, 135-137.
32. Mattes, J. A. (1985). Methylphenidate in mild depression: A double-blind controlled trial. *Journal of Clinical Psychiatry, 46*, 525-527.
33. Mellinger, J. C., & Erdwins, C. J. (1985). Personality correlates of age and life roles in adult women. *Psychology of Women Quarterly, 9*, 503-514.
34. Moore, R. H. (1985). Construct validity of the MacAndrew Scale: Secondary psychopathic and dysthymic-neurotic character orientations among adolescent male misdemeanor offenders. *Journal of Studies on Alcohol, 46*, 128-131.
35. Mossholder, K. W., Bedeian, A. G., Touliatos, J., & Barkman, A. I. (1985). An examination of intraoccupational differences: Personality, perceived work climate, and outcome preferences. *Journal of Vocational Behavior, 26*, 164-176.
36. Newlin, D. B. (1985). Offspring of alcoholics have enhanced antagonistic placebo response. *Journal of Studies on Alcohol, 46*, 490-494.
37. Paunonen, S. V., & Jackson, D. N. (1985). On ad hoc personality scales: A reply to Burisch. *Journal of Research in Personality, 19*, 348-353.
38. Seeman, K., Yesavage, J., & Widrow, L. A. (1985). Correlations of self-directed violence in acute schizophrenics with clinical ratings and personality measures. *The Journal of Nervous and Mental Disease, 173*, 298-302.
39. Voelz, C. J. (1985). Effects of gender role disparity on couples' decision-making processes. *Journal of Personality and Social Psychology, 49*, 1532-1540.
40. White, M. S. (1985). Ego development in adult women. *Journal of Personality, 53*, 561-574.
41. Wyatt, C., O'Neill, B., Harder, R., & Noth, N. (1985). Affective changes in teacher corps interns during one year of the traineeship. *College Student Journal, 19*, 176-184.
42. Assor, A., Aronoff, J., & Messé, L. A. (1986). An experimental test of defensive processes in impression formation. *Journal of Personality and Social Psychology, 50*, 644-650.
43. Buss, D. M., & Barnes, M. (1986). Preferences in human mate selection. *Journal of Personality and Social Psychology, 50*, 559-570.
44. Clay, H., Lindgren, C., Moritsch, B., Thulin, E. K., & Mich, G. (1986). Validity studies of three measures of achievement motivation. *Psychological Reports, 59*, 123-136.
45. DeFrancesco, J. J., & Taylor, J. (1986). Confirmatory item factor analysis of Gough's Socialization scale. *Psychological Reports, 58*, 759-762.
46. Edwards, F. E., & Nagelberg, D. B. (1986). Personality characteristics of restrained/binge eaters versus unrestrained/nonbinge eaters. *Addictive Behaviors, 11*, 207-211.
47. Fleischer, R. A., & Chertkoff, J. M. (1986). Effects of dominance and sex on leader selection in dyadic work groups. *Journal of Personality and Social Psychology, 50*, 94-99.
48. Fuqua, D. R., Newman, J. L., Anderson, M. W., & Johnson, A. W. (1986). Preliminary study of internal dialogue in a training setting. *Psychological Reports, 58*, 163-172.
49. Gough, H. G., & Lanning, K. (1986). Predicting grades in college from the California Psychological Inventory. *Educational and Psychological Measurement, 46*, 205-213.

50. Harris, R. N., & Snyder, C. R. (1986). The role of uncertain self-esteem in self-handicapping. *Journal of Personality and Social Psychology*, *51*, 451-458.

51. Johnson, D. W., Johnson, R. T., & Krotee, M. L. (1986). The relation between social interdependence and psychological health on the 1980 U.S. Olympic ice hockey team. *The Journal of Psychology*, *120*, 279-291.

52. Martin, J. D., Grah, C. R., & Harris, J. W. (1986). Closed-mindedness: Effect on achievement. *Psychological Reports*, *59*, 611-614.

53. McClure, R. F., & Mears, F. G. (1986). Videogame playing and psychopathology. *Psychological Reports*, *59*, 59-62.

54. Schroer, A. C. P., & Dom, F. J. (1986). Enhancing the career and personal development of gifted college students. *Journal of Counseling and Development*, *64*, 567-571.

55. Schuerger, J. M., & Allen, L. C. (1986). Second-order factor structure common to five personality questionnaires. *Psychological Reports*, *58*, 119-126.

56. Shaw, D. S., & Gynther, M. D. (1986). An attempt to obtain configural correlates for the California Psychological Inventory. *Psychological Reports*, *59*, 675-678.

57. Werner, E. E. (1986). Resilient offspring of alcoholics: A longitudinal study from birth to age 18. *Journal of Studies on Alcohol*, *47*, 34-40.

58. Werner, P. D., & Pervin, L. A. (1986). The content of personality inventory items. *Journal of Personality and Social Psychology*, *51*, 622-628.

59. Brook, J. S., Gordon, A. S., & Brook, D. W. (1987). Fathers and daughters: Their relationship and personality characteristics associated with the daughter's smoking behavior. *Journal of Genetic Psychology*, *148*, 31-44.

60. Dyer, E. D. (1987). Can university success and first-year job performance be predicted from academic achievement, vocational interest, personality and biographical measures? *Psychological Reports*, *61*, 655-671.

61. Gold, B. D. (1987). Self-image of punk rock and nonpunk rock juvenile delinquents. *Adolescence*, *22*, 535-544.

62. Hakstian, A. R., Woolsey, L. K., & Schroeder, M. L. (1987). Validity of a large-scale assessment battery in an industrial setting. *Educational and Psychological Measurement*, *47* (1), 165-178.

63. Helson, R., & Moane, G. (1987). Personality change in women from college to midlife. *Journal of Personality and Social Psychology*, *53*, 176-186.

64. Helson, R., & Wink, P. (1987). Two conceptions of maturity examined in the findings of a longitudinal study. *Journal of Personality and Social Psychology*, *53*, 531-541.

65. Loehlin, J. C. (1987). Heredity, environment, and the structure of the California Psychological Inventory. *Multivariate Behavioral Research*, *22*, 137-148.

66. Martel, J., McKelvie, S. J., & Standing, L. (1987). Validity of an intuitive personality scale: Personal responsibility as a predictor of academic achievement. *Educational and Psychological Measurement*, *47* (4), 1153-1163.

67. Moore, R. H. (1987). Effectiveness of citizen volunteers functioning as counselors for high-risk young male offenders. *Psychological Reports*, *61*, 823-830.

68. Schuerger, J. M., Foerstner, S. B., Serkownek, K., & Ritz, G. (1987). History and validities of the Serkownek subscales for MMPI scales 5 and 0. *Psychological Reports*, *61*, 227-235.

69. Vaughn, B. E., Bradley, C. F., Joffe, L. S., Seifer, R., & Barglow, P. (1987). Maternal characteristics measured prenatally are predictive of ratings of temperamental "difficulty" on the Carey Infant Temperament Questionnaire. *Developmental Psychology*, *23*, 152-161.

70. Assor, A. (1988). Types of power motivation, sense of security, and style of power-seeking in groups. *Psychological Reports*, *63*, 91-105.

71. Bennett, J. B. (1988). Power and influence as distinct personality traits: Development and validation of a psychometric measure. *Journal of Research in Personality*, *22*, 361-394.

72. Bergin, A. E., Stinchfield, R. D., Gaskin, T. A., Masters, K. S., & Sullivan, C. E. (1988). Religious life-styles and mental health: An exploratory study. *Journal of Counseling Psychology*, *35*, 91-98.

73. Brook, J. E., & Brook, J. S. (1988). A developmental approach examining social and personal correlates in relation to alcohol use over time. *Journal of Genetic Psychology*, *149*, 93-110.

74. Curtis, J., Billingslea, R., & Wilson, J. P. (1988). Personality correlates of moral reasoning and attitudes toward authority. *Psychological Reports*, *63*, 947-954.

75. Johnson, J. A., Germer, C. K., Efran, J. S., & Overton, W. F. (1988). Personality as the basis for theoretical predilections. *Journal of Personality and Social Psychology*, *55*, 824-835.

76. Lanning, K. (1988). Individual differences in scalability: An alternative conception of consistency for personality theory and measurement. *Journal of Personality and Social Psychology*, *55*, 142-148.

77. Mayer, J. E. (1988). The personality characteristics of adolescents who use and misuse alcohol. *Adolescence*, *23*, 383-404.

78. Moran, P., & Barclay, A. (1988). Effect of father's absence on delinquent boys: Dependency and hypermasculinity. *Psychological Reports*, *62*, 115-121.

79. Pederson, D. M. (1988). Correlates of privacy regulation. *Perceptual and Motor Skills*, *66* (2), 595-601.

80. Petrie, K., Chamberlain, K., & Clarke, D. (1988). Psychological predictors of future suicidal behaviour in hospitalized suicide attempters. *British Journal of Clinical Psychology*, *27*, 247-257.

81. Plescia-Pikus, M., Long-Suter, E., & Wilson, J. P. (1988). Achievement, well-being, intelligence, and stress reaction in adult children of alcoholics. *Psychological Reports*, *62*, 603-609.

82. Raskin, R., & Terry, H. (1988). A principal-components analysis of the narcissistic personality inventory and further evidence of its construct validity. *Journal of Personality and Social Psychology*, *54*, 890-902.

83. Swan, G. E., Carmelli, D., & Rosenman, R. H. (1988). Psychological characteristics in twins discordant for smoking behavior: A matched-twin-pair analysis. *Addictive Behaviors*, *13*, 51-60.

84. Tesser, A., Millar, M., & Moore, J. (1988). Some affective consequences of social comparison and reflection processes: The pain and pleasure of being close. *Journal of Personality and Social Psychology*, *54*, 49-61.

85. Torki, M. A. (1988). The CPI Femininity scale in Kuwait and Egypt. *Journal of Personality Assessment*, *52*, 247-253.

86. Westman, A. S., & Canter, F. M. (1988). Diurnal changes on the California Personality Inventory [sic] on work and leisure days. *Psychological Reports*, *62*, 863-866.

87. Assor, A. (1989). The power motive as an influence on the evaluation of high and low status persons. *Journal of Research in Personality*, *23*, 55-69.

88. Babor, T. F., Kranzler, H. R., & Lauerman, R. J. (1989). Early detection of harmful alcohol consumption: Comparison of clinical, laboratory, and self-report screening procedures. *Addictive Behaviors*, *14*, 139-157.

89. Block, J. (1989). Critique of the act frequency approach to personality. *Journal of Personality and Social Psychology*, *56*, 234-245.

90. Botwin, M. D., & Buss, D. M. (1989). Structure of act-report data: Is the five-factor model of personality recaptured? *Journal of Personality and Social Psychology*, *56*, 988-1001.

91. Davis, B. M., & Gilbert, L. A. (1989). Effect of dispositional and situational influences on women's dominance expression in mixed-sex dyads. *Journal of Personality and Social Psychology*, *57*, 294-300.

92. Domino, G., & Hannah, M. T. (1989). Measuring effective functioning in the elderly: An application of Erikson's theory. *Journal of Personality Assessment*, *53*, 319-328.

93. Freeman, B., & Lanning, W. (1989). A multivariate analysis of the relationship between social power motivation and personality characteristics in college students. *Journal of College Student Development*, *30*, 522-527.

94. Hargrave, G. E., & Hiatt, D. (1989). Use of the California Psychological Inventory in law enforcement officer selection. *Journal of Personality Assessment*, *53*, 267-277.

95. Jenkins, S. J., Fisher, G., & Applegate, R. L. (1989). Analysis of the relations between personality characteristics and education majors' sex and grade-level focus. *Psychological Reports*, *64*, 583-589.

96. Kamakura, W. A., & Balasubramanian, S. K. (1989). Tailored interviewing: An application of item response theory for personality measurement. *Journal of Personality Assessment*, *53*, 502-519.

97. Mayer, J. E., & Ligman, J. D. (1989). Personality characteristics of adolescent marijuana users. *Adolescence*, *24*, 965-976.

98. Picano, J. J. (1989). Development and validation of a life history index of adult adjustment for women. *Journal of Personality Assessment*, *53*, 308-318.

99. Schuerger, J. M., Zarrella, K. L., & Hotz, A. S. (1989). Factors that influence the temporal stability of personality by questionnaire. *Journal of Personality and Social Psychology*, *56*, 777-783.

100. Williams, D. E., & Page, M. M. (1989). A multi-dimensional measure of Maslow's hierarchy of needs. *Journal of Research in Personality*, *23*, 192-213.

101. Albano, R. A., & Glenwick, D. S. (1990). Predicting the effectiveness of telephone crisis counselors: A comparison of two approaches. *Journal of College Student Development*, *31*, 81-82.

102. Higgins-Lee, C. (1990). Low scores on California Psychological Inventory as predictors of psychopathology in alcoholic patients. *Psychological Reports*, *67*, 227-232.

103. Houldin, A. D., & Forbes, E. J. (1990). Nursing students' personalities as measured by the California Psychological Inventory: Participant vs. nonparticipants in a program of research. *Psychological Reports*, *67*, 1119-1122.

104. Sloan, J., & Slane, S. (1990). Personality correlates of anxiety about public speaking. *Psychological Reports*, *67*, 515-522.

105. VanHutton, V. (1990). Test review: The California Psychological Inventory. *Journal of Counseling and Development*, *69*, 75-77.

106. Cooney, N. L., Kadden, R. M., Litt, M. D., & Getter, H. (1991). Matching alcoholics to coping skills or interactional therapies: Two-year follow-up results. *Journal of Consulting and Clinical Psychology*, *59*, 598-601.

107. Lynn, R., Yamauchi, H., & Tachibana, Y. (1991). Attitudes related to work of adolescents in the United Kingdom and Japan. *Psychological Reports*, *68*, 403-410.

108. Novelli, L., Jr., & Gryskiewicz, N. (1991). Reliability and factor structure of the Managerial Potential Scale. *Educational and Psychological Measurement*, *51*, 227-229.

Review of the California Psychological Inventory, Revised Edition by BRIAN BOLTON, Professor, Arkansas Research and Training Center in Vocational Rehabilitation, University of Arkansas, Fayetteville, AR:

The 1987 edition of the California Psychological Inventory (CPI) is a self-report questionnaire that measures 20 features of the normal personality. The 20 basic scales were conceptualized as dimensions of interpersonal behavior that exist in all human societies, hence, the label "folk concepts." The author's goal was to develop a clinical instrument that would enable psychologists to accurately describe individuals and to predict their behavior. Consistent with this practical objective, the CPI scales were constructed using observer judgments and measurable performance as criteria.

In addition to the 20 folk concept scales, the 1987 CPI is scored on three structural or vector scales (described below) that comprise a typology of modes of personal adjustment. Thirteen special purpose scales, such as Managerial Potential and Creative Temperament, may also be scored. Standard *T*-score profiles are calculated with reference to demographically representative norm groups for males and females. Descriptive statistics for a variety of specialized normative samples are also provided. Respondents typically complete the 462 true/false items in about 1 hour. A wealth of interpretive data and resources are available to CPI users.

The 1987 CPI is a revision of the 1956 edition of the instrument. Because only small changes were made in the items composing the inventory and the basic scales appear to be essentially the same, the extensive normative data and the exceptional validity evidence accumulated over a period of more than 40 years were not lost. Briefly, just six items (that referred to sexual thoughts or practices and excretory functions) were actually deleted from the 1956 edition and slight adjustments to eliminate sexist language and dated expressions were made in 29 items. Although it is probably safe to conclude that the item pool is unchanged, all modifications should be specified in the manual (called the Administrator's Guide).

Of somewhat greater concern are the changes that were effected in the composition of 18 folk concept scales. (Two basic scales, Independence and Empathy, are new to the 1987 CPI.) As many as 18 items were dropped and as many as 13 items were added to the 1956 scales to produce the revised 1987 folk concept scales. The net result is that the 20 scales in the 1987 CPI consist of between 28 and 46 items and the pairwise correlations between the old and new scales range from .88 to .99, with a median of .96. However, the manual provides no explanation of the procedures by which item deletions and additions were accomplished.

Because the normative samples for the 1987 CPI "were assembled from the CPI archives" and much of the interpretive information for the folk concept scales was carried forward from studies with the 1956 edition, the assumption of equivalence between the 1956 and 1987 versions of the CPI is critical. In fact, construct equivalence is fundamental to the legitimate use of the 1987 CPI. Although the assumption of equivalence does appear warranted to this reviewer, the manual should provide a thorough discussion of the issues and a full description of the methods by which the basic scales were revised.

Another issue that CPI users should be aware of is the inclusion of 194 items from the Minnesota Multiphasic Personality Inventory that refer to symptoms of pathology. Of these items, 70 are clearly indicators of depression, paranoia, hysteria, hypochondriasis, and similar problems. Although none of the items would be offensive to most respondents, some items might be annoying or upsetting to sensitive individuals. Of course, the larger question is whether it is necessary to employ items that suggest psychiatric disturbance to assess variations in normal personality functioning.

The three structural scales that frame the cuboid model of interpersonal functioning measure the higher-order dimensions of Involvement, Norm-Acceptance, and Realization. These three scales, which are based on just 128 CPI items, generate a 28-cell typology that is predictive of practical criteria, such as college attendance by high school students. It is ironic that Gough, who is highly critical of what he refers to as the "orthogonality model" of personality scale construction, should have developed the vector scales with the explicit requirement that they be mutually uncorrelated!

It is this reviewer's opinion that the CPI (and all other instruments that assess normal personality dispositions) should be scored on the "Big Five" dimensions of Extraversion, Adjustment, Sensitivity, Autonomy, and Discipline. The results of several dozen factor analyses indicate that the CPI encompasses the Big Five. It is especially appropriate that the CPI should be scored for the Big Five, because these dimensions were discovered and replicated in observer ratings of personality, which is the primary data source by which most of the CPI folk concept scales were developed and validated.

To explain interscale relationships, Gough formulated the principle of psychosocial topography, which maintains that the intercorrelations among the folk concept scales should reflect the way in which people actually use the concepts in describing each other. This entirely reasonable point of view, called the criterion of "folk usage," is consistent with the author's goal of mapping the domain of interpersonal appraisal. The intercorrelations among the 20 folk concept scales range from -.15 to .83, with a median of .44. However, it is not clear how much of the scale covariation is due to construct overlap and how much is attributable to common items. About one-half of the 462 CPI items are scored on two or more scales.

Three types of reliability data are presented in the manual: (*a*) internal consistency coefficients, which may not provide optimal estimates for empirically developed scales; (*b*) parallel form correlations based on English and French versions of the CPI; and (*c*) test-retest correlations with a 1-year interval between administrations. Considering the lengths of the 20 folk concept scales (a minimum of 28 items) and the high test/retest reliabilities given for the individual items in Appendix D of the manual, as well as the reported median reliability of .70 obtained under the inappropriately stringent conditions noted above, it is reasonable to guess that the actual reliabilities of the scales range from .70 to .90, with a median in the low .80s. In other words, users can have considerably more confidence in the accuracy of the CPI score profile than is suggested by the reliability data provided in the manual.

The validity of the CPI folk concept scales derives from (*a*) the method of scale construction utilized, (*b*) the numerous investigations that have been carried out over the years, and (*c*) the extensive interpretive information summarized in the manual. Most of the scales were developed using the empirical-keying strategy, which requires external criteria (nontest data) as the basis for identifying items that compose the scales. The CPI has been validated as a predictor of academic achievement (e.g., high school, college, medical school), creativity, (e.g., architects, engineers, mathematicians), occupational performance (e.g., police officers, accountants, nurses), personal and social problems (delinquency, alcoholism, illness susceptibility), and various other behaviors such as leadership and mate selection. Because one of the primary purposes of the CPI is to describe individuals in "interpersonally significant ways," it follows that especially relevant interpretive information would come from standardized descriptions by interviewers, peers, and spouses. These data have been assembled for each of the 20 folk concept scales in a handy format in the manual.

Three scales (Well-Being, Good Impression, Communality) are incorporated into a decision-tree strategy that assesses tendencies to fake good, fake bad, and answer carelessly. About 97% of all protocols are judged to be "valid," with only 3% assigned to one of the invalidating categories. In addition to the regular profile scoring service, the publisher offers a comprehensive computer-generated narrative report that includes a standardized description of what observers would say about the respondent. Validity studies using actual descriptions by observers who were familiar with respondents produced correlations ranging from the .40s to the .60s, indicating that this feature possesses substantial accuracy.

SUMMARY. Gough initiated work on the CPI when he was a graduate student at the University of Minnesota in the late 1940s, studying under Starke Hathaway and Paul Meehl. He adapted the criterion-keying approach to scale development that was used with the famous Minnesota Multiphasic Personality Inventory to the task of constructing a self-report measure of normal personality. Gough's goal for the CPI was from the beginning practical, that is, to develop an instrument that would describe the respondent's salient personality characteristics and predict his/her behavior in specific situations. After more than 40 years of developmental and validation studies, it can be concluded that the author's objective has been fully realized. The 1987 CPI is an excellent normal personality assessment device, more reliable than the manual advertises, with good normative data and outstanding interpretive information. The manual is well organized and the scoring and reporting services provide useful information. The only shortcoming is the failure to give essential technical information in the manual, and this deficit can be remediated easily.

Review of the California Psychological Inventory, Revised Edition by GEORGE ENGELHARD, JR., Associate Professor of Educational Studies, Emory University, Atlanta, GA:

After 30 years, Harrison Gough has prepared a revised version of the California Psychological Inventory (CPI). In addition to the 18 scales included in the original CPI, scales for Independence and Empathy (Hogan, 1969) have been added. Three new structural scales are proposed that yield scores for interpersonal orientation (externality vs. internality), normative perspective (norm-favoring vs. norm-questioning), and self-realization (little to superior realization of potential). These structural scales are used to define four personality types (Alpha, Beta, Gamma, and Delta) and seven levels that reflect self-actualization. There are 462 items in the revised CPI (some of the items are included in more than one scale); 18 items were deleted from the original (12 of which were repeated items) and 29 items have revised wording. Items have also been added to and deleted from many of the scales. There are 194 items in the revised CPI taken from the Minnesota Multiphasic Personality Inventory (MMPI); (Hathaway & McKinley, 1943). The correlations between the old and new scales tend to be high; for males, the median correlation across all of the scales is .96, and for females, the median correlation is .96. As might be expected, revised scales with more items added, subtracted, or revised tend to have lower correlations.

One of the distinctive characteristics of the original CPI as compared to other personality inventories was the large normative samples (6,200 males and 7,150 female); the revised CPI presents norms based on 1,000 males and 1,000 females derived from archival data. The details of this process are not reported in sufficient detail. For example, it is not clear how the 18 deleted and 29 revised items were handled; very minor changes in wording can have a major impact on the meaning of an item. Descriptions of the racial, ethnic, social class, and geographic representation of the normative sample are also noticeably absent. Further, the age of the archival CPI data is not clear; the percent answering "true" to certain items may have changed over time and this may affect the meaning of the scores. Although standards for reporting normative data are generally lower for personality assessment instruments than for instruments designed to measure ability and achievement, the basic normative sample in the revised version of the CPI is not adequate. Minimally, some new normative data should have been gathered to verify the current accuracy of the archival data.

A major earlier criticism of the CPI was that evidence regarding the internal consistency of the scales was not provided. For the revised CPI, Gough (1987) reports alpha coefficients as indices of internal consistency, as well as test-retest correlations as evidence of the stability of the scores. Unfortunately, alpha coefficients are not reported for the normative sample. Alpha coefficients for a sample of college students (200 males and 200 females) are provided, and are generally within the range that would be expected for subscales of self-report inventories; for males, the alpha coefficients range from .45 to .85 with a median of .72, whereas for females they range from .39 to .83 with a median of .73. The test-retest correlations are based on 102 male and 128 female high school students who took the CPI in 11th grade and again in 12th grade; for males, the test-retest correlations ranged from .43 to .76 with a median across scales of .65, whereas for females, they ranged from .58 to .79 with a median of .69. Standard errors of measurement (SEMs) are not reported for the CPI scales. Although SEMs are less frequently reported for personality inventories, they are still necessary for meaningful interpretations of the relative strengths and weaknesses within an examinee's profile. Related to the interpretation of the CPI Profiles, Gough may have compounded the problem of an inadequate normative sample by making adjustments in the standard deviations of four scales (Dominance, Capacity for Status, Social Presence, and Self-Acceptance) in order to make them more similar to earlier configurations based on

old forms; this is questionable practice, and additional description and justification should be provided.

A great deal of effort has gone into discovering and defining the meaning of the scores on the CPI scales. The voluminous research on the validity of the original CPI provides empirical support for the usefulness of the CPI for a variety of purposes, such as the prediction of high school dropout, high school and college achievement, and occupational performance. When the CPI is used for clinical purposes, the low reliabilities of a few scales must be carefully considered and SEMs should be provided. It cannot be stressed strongly enough that individual assessments must be interpreted by trained and competent clinicians; this applies even with the interpretive narratives provided by computer.

Evidence is provided relative to the construct validity of the CPI. Extensive research on the original CPI is reported in Megargee (1972), McAllister (1986), and Gough (1987), although changes in the revised CPI will require revisions in the prediction equations. Nevertheless, problems related to the development of the earlier version of the CPI remain. Because the CPI was developed based on criterion keying rather than personality theory, problems related to the definition of meaningful criterion groups still exist. As pointed out by Thorndike, "the weakness lies in the possibility that this criterion dimension may not have clear, distinctive, and unequivocal psychological meaning" (1959, p. 99).

Another major criticism of the original CPI was that Gough did not recognize that whatever the method of test construction, deductive, inductive, or empirical (criterion-keying), the test author should conduct post hoc statistical analyses to examine how well the items and scales are functioning. The user should have all the information possible, including statistical information (item intercorrelations and factor analyses) in order to determine the meaning of the scales. Gough has responded to this criticism and conducted a factor analysis of the CPI. He has also acknowledged, through the reporting of three structural scales, that the 20 CPI scales may reflect significantly fewer basic dimensions of personality than previously hypothesized. In the development of the structural scales, Gough used factor analysis and smallest space analysis for guidance, and then proceeded with a set of vaguely described procedures to develop "three vectors." Another approach, that Gough should consider in future revisions, is full-information item factor analysis (Bock, Gibbons, & Muraki, 1988; Muraki & Engelhard, 1985); this approach is based on recent advances in psychometrics, and eliminates some of the arbitrariness in Gough's approach by providing empirical criteria for scale development.

In an earlier review, Gynther (1978) pointed out the need for further research on the invariance of the CPI across groups; this may have implications for profiles of minorities that may not share, or even value, the same "folk concepts." As pointed out by Cronbach (1959), many of the items and scales in the CPI have ethical overtones, which tend to be evaluative and suggest that certain personality characteristics are "better" than others. Valued personality characteristics may vary by culture and also over time within the same society; relevant information on this issue is not provided. New procedures for examining differential item functioning (Holland & Thayer, 1988) would have contributed to our understanding of how the meaning of the items may vary for different cultural groups.

In summary, the revisions in the CPI appear to contribute to an improvement in the instrument. The CPI remains a classic example of a criterion-keyed instrument that should be studied by anyone interested in the assessment of personality. The usefulness of the three new structural scales and the proposed personality typology will require further research. Unfortunately, the normative sample is clearly not adequate for the revised CPI. It is also recommended that standard errors of measurement be provided and taken into account when the scales are used for individual assessment. The CPI is useful for instructional purposes in classes on psychological testing, for research and prediction purposes with groups, and when used by a trained and competent clinician can also provide useful information for individual assessment and counseling. The strong points of the CPI remain in the revised version and many of the earlier weaknesses still stand. Gough is to be commended for his continuing contributions to the field of personality assessment. In spite of its weaknesses, the CPI remains one of the best personality inventories of its type.

REVIEWER'S REFERENCES

Hathaway, S. R., & McKinley, J. C. (1943). The Minnesota Multiphasic Personality Inventory. Minneapolis: University of Minnesota Press.
Cronbach, L. J. (1959). [Review of the California Psychological Inventory.] In O. K. Buros (Ed.), The fifth mental measurements yearbook (pp. 97-99). Highland Park, NJ: The Gryphon Press.
Thorndike, R. L. (1959). [Review of the California Psychological Inventory.] In O. K. Buros (Ed.), The fifth mental measurements yearbook (p. 99). Highland Park, NJ: The Gryphon Press.
Hogan, R. (1969). Development of an empathy scale. Journal of Consulting and Clinical Psychology, 33, 307-316.
Megargee, E. I. (1972). The California Psychological Inventory handbook. San Francisco: Jossey-Bass.
Gynther, M. D. (1978). [Review of the California Psychological Inventory.] In O. K. Buros (Ed.), The eighth mental measurements yearbook (pp. 733-736). Highland Park, NJ: The Gryphon Press.
Muraki, E., & Engelhard, G. (1985). Full-information item factor analysis: Applications of EAP scores. Applied Psychological Measurement, 9, 417-430.
McAllister, L. W. (1986). A practical guide to CPI interpretation. Palo Alto, CA: Consulting Psychologists Press.
Gough, H. G. (1987). California Psychological Inventory: Administrator's guide. Palo Alto, CA: Consulting Psychologists Press.
Bock, R. D., Gibbons, R., & Muraki, E. (1988). Full-information item factor analysis. Applied Psychological Measurement, 12, 261-280.
Holland, P. W., & Thayer, D. T. (1988). Differential item performance and the Mantel-Haenszel procedure. In H. Wainer & H. I. Braun (Eds.), Test validity (pp. 129-145). Hillsdale, NJ: Lawrence Erlbaum Associates, Inc.

[55]
Canadian Tests of Basic Skills, Forms 7 and 8.

Purpose: Constructed to measure growth in the fundamental skills crucial to day-to-day learning.
Publication Dates: 1955-90.
Acronym: CTBS.
Administration: Group.
Price Data, 1992: $9 per multilevel test booklet (select Levels 9-14 or 15-18); $9 per 35 pupil profile charts (select Levels 5-14 or 15-18); $5 per 10 profile sheets for averages (select Levels 5-14 or 15-18); $5 per 10 class record sheets (select Levels 5-14 or 15-18); $9 per 35 reports to parents (Levels 5-8); $9 per 35 How are Your Basic Skills? (Levels 9-14); $16 per teacher's guide (select Levels 5-6 or 7-8); $15 per teacher's guide (select Levels 9-14 or 15-18); $40 per manual ('90, 138 pages); $15 per Level 5-8 examination kit; $25 per examination kit (select Levels 9-14 or 15-18); scoring service available from publisher.
Comments: 2 forms: 7, 8; forms 5 and 6 still available; Form 8 not available for Levels 5-8 and 15-18.
Authors: A. N. Hieronymus, H. D. Hoover, E. F. Lindquist, and others (original Level 5-14 tests); Dale P. Scannell and others (original Level 15-18 tests); Ethel King-Shaw and others (Canadian adaptation).
Publisher: Nelson Canada [Canada].
a) LEVEL 5.
Population: Grades K.1-1.5.
Scores, 6: Listening, Word Analysis, Vocabulary, Language, Mathematics, Total.
Price Data: $38 per 25 test booklets; $22 per set of scoring masks.
Time: (150) minutes over 5 days.
b) LEVEL 6.
Population: Grades K.8-1.9.
Scores, 7: Listening, Word Analysis, Vocabulary, Reading, Language, Mathematics, Total.
Price Data: Same as *a* above.
Time: (205) minutes over 5 days.
c) LEVEL 7.
Population: Grades 1.7-2.6.
Scores, 17: Listening, Word Analysis, Vocabulary, Reading, Language (Spelling, Capitalization, Punctuation, Usage and Expression, Total), Work-Study Skills (Visual Materials, Reference Materials, Total), Mathematics (Concepts, Problems, Computation, Total), Total.
Price Data: Same as *a* above.
Time: (227) minutes over 5 days.
d) LEVEL 8.
Population: Grades 2.7-3.5.
Scores, 17: Same as *c* above.
Price Data: Same as *a* above.
Time: Same as *c* above.
e) LEVEL 9.
Population: Grade 3.
Scores, 15: Vocabulary, Reading Comprehension, Language (Spelling, Capitalization, Punctuation, Usage and Expression, Total), Work-Study (Visual Materials,

Reference Materials, Total), Mathematics (Concepts, Problem Solving, Computation, Total), Total.
Price Data: $18 per 35 answer sheets; $12 per set of scoring masks.
Time: (256) minutes in 4–8 sessions.
f) LEVEL 10.
Population: Grade 4.
Scores, 15: Same as *e* above.
Price Data: Same as *e* above.
Time: Same as *e* above.
g) LEVEL 11.
Population: Grade 5.
Scores, 15: Same as *e* above.
Price Data: Same as *e* above.
Time: Same as *e* above.
h) LEVEL 12.
Population: Grade 6.
Scores, 15: Same as *e* above.
Price Data: Same as *e* above.
Time: Same as *e* above.
i) LEVEL 13.
Population: Grade 7.
Scores, 15: Same as *e* above.
Price Data: Same as *e* above.
Time: Same as *e* above.
j) LEVEL 14.
Population: Grades 8–9.
Scores, 15: Same as *e* above.
Price Data: Same as *e* above.
Time: Same as *e* above.
k) LEVEL 15.
Population: Grade 9.
Scores, 6: Reading Comprehension, Mathematics, Written Expression, Using Sources of Information, Total, Applied Proficiency Skills.
Price Data: Same as *e* above.
Time: 160(190) minutes in 2 sessions.
l) LEVEL 16.
Population: Grade 10.
Scores, 6: Same as *k* above.
Price Data: Same as *e* above.
Time: Same as *k* above.
m) LEVEL 17.
Population: Grade 11.
Scores, 6: Same as *k* above.
Price Data: Same as *e* above.
Time: Same as *k* above.
n) LEVEL 18.
Population: Grade 12.
Scores, 6: Same as *k* above.
Price Data: Same as *e* above.
Time: Same as *k* above.
Cross References: See T3:363 (15 references) and 8:11 (1 reference); for a review by L. B. Birch of an earlier edition, see 7:6.

TEST REFERENCES

1. Carey, S. T., & Cummins, J. (1983). Achievement, behavioral correlates and teachers' perceptions of francophone and anglophone immersion students. *The Alberta Journal of Education Research, 29,* 159-167.
2. Pravica, S. S., & McLean, S. D. (1983). The effects of principal participation in curriculum implementation: Support from an evaluation of a new mathematics curriculum. *The Alberta Journal of Educational Research, 29,* 46-53.
3. Evans, C. S. (1984). Writing to learn math. *Language Arts, 61,* 828-835.
4. Rampaul, W. E., Singh, M., & Didyk, J. (1984). The relationship between academic achievement, self-concept, creativity, and teacher expectations among native children in a northern Manitoba school. *The Alberta Journal of Educational Research, 30,* 213-225.
5. Violato, C., White, W. B., & Travis, L. D. (1984). Some concurrent, criterion-related data on validity for the Quick Test based on three Canadian samples. *Psychological Reports, 54,* 775-782.
6. Hanna, G., & Lei, H. (1985). A longitudinal analysis using the LISREL-model with structured means. *Journal of Educational Statistics, 10,* 161-169.
7. Hoge, R. D., & McKay, V. (1986). Criterion-related validity data for the Child Behavior Checklist—Teacher's Report Form. *Journal of School Psychology, 24,* 387-393.
8. Fletcher, J. D., Hawley, D. E., & Piele, P. K. (1990). Costs, effects, and utility of microcomputer assisted instruction in the classroom. *American Educational Research Journal, 27,* 783-806.
9. Meyer, M., Wilgosh, L., & Mueller, H. H. (1990). Effectiveness of teacher-administered tests and rating scales in predicting subsequent academic performance. *The Alberta Journal of Educational Research, 36,* 257-264.

Review of the Canadian Tests of Basic Skills, Forms 7 & 8 by JOHN O. ANDERSON, Faculty of Education, University of Victoria, Victoria, B.C., Canada:

The Canadian Tests of Basic Skills (CTBS) provides "comprehensive measurement of growth in the fundamental skills: listening, word analysis, vocabulary, reading, language, work study and mathematics," according to the *Manual for Administrators, Supervisors and Counsellors* (p. 5). The adaptation of the Iowa Tests of Basic Skills (184) to develop the CTBS consisted of a review and minor revision of test content by the Canadian editor and a panel of educators, and a norming of the revised tests with a Canadian sample of English-speaking students. The test results are reported as national percentiles, grade-equivalent scores, standard scores, and for the high school level of the tests "minimal competency scores." The tests are entirely composed of multiple-choice items and require substantial investments of time to complete ($2^1/_2$ to $4^1/_2$ hours distributed over 1 to 4 days depending on level). The teacher guides and administrator manual provide suitable guidance on the administration and interpretation of the tests. A broad range of scoring services are available through the publisher.

The Primary battery of the CTBS (Levels 5 to 8) consists of separate test booklets for each level and the student is expected to enter his/her response into the booklet; this seems to be a relatively straightforward task given adequate support by the teacher. However, for Levels 9 to 18, the mechanics of writing the test are relatively complicated. The test booklets each contain several levels of each subtest, so that from the student's perspective the test is not a consistent sequence of items but rather clusters of items located through the booklet. The student has to be aware of the level of the test he/she is writing and be able to locate the starting and finishing locations for each subtest written. Further, the student has to enter responses on a separate answer sheet. This assertion of complicated test mechanics is supported by completion rates as low as 47% for some subtests as reported in the *Manual for Adminis-*

trators, Supervisors and Counsellors (Table 6.17) and elsewhere (Nagy, 1986).

The norms for the tests were established in the 1987/88 school year. The sample was stratified by school size and province, and the grades were linked in that the grade 3 school was randomly selected and its "receiving schools" served as the sample for the remaining grades. The number of students participating in the standardization administration averaged 2,625 for grades 1 to 8, and 1,427 for grades 9 to 12. However, it is not clear how many students actually wrote each form of the test for the development of Fall, Winter, and Spring norms.

Forms 7 and 8 of the CTBS are intended to be parallel, yet no empirical support is offered to support this assertion. In fact, information to the contrary is tabulated in the CTBS manual. For example, in the Mathematics Problem Solving subtest, Form 7 is testing 64 "operations" of computational skills at Level 14, whereas Form 8 is testing 68 "operations." This does not lend credibility to the concept of parallel forms.

The validity of the CTBS is described primarily in terms of the skills it is intended to measure. A brief descriptor of each "skills objective" within each subtest is listed along with the related test items. This approach is in the right direction but further work should be done to describe fully the skills being tested and to articulate clearly the link of skill to item response demands. Some work has been conducted on the predictive validity of the test in regard to predicting readiness of students for grades 1 and 2. Correlations between Fall test scores and teacher rating of readiness (in the following Spring) ranged from .35 to .67 across various subtests. The level of agreement offers some support for the use of the test in predicting academic readiness but further study is required.

The reliability of the tests is described in terms of internal consistency indices (KR20) for each subtest. These reliabilities average .77 for Levels 5 and 6, .85 for Level 8 to 14, and .90 for Level 15 to 18. For tests consisting of 30 or more items, with average scores of approximately 50% (which CTBS subtests are), these reliabilities are not outstanding but adequate.

The test scores are reported as both national percentiles and grade-equivalent scores for subtests and composites. The manuals explain what the percentile scores are and how they can be used in a reasonable and comprehensive manner. However, the suggested use of grade-equivalent scores does raise concern. The manuals promote the use of the grade-equivalent scores by describing them as indicators of a student's position on a developmental or growth scale. If this use is to be made of test results, the scale should be fully described and a sound rationale offered for its use; this is not done. This interpretation of the test scores as indicators of student position on a developmental continuum cannot be supported.

The CTBS provides a standardized norm-referenced, multiple-choice format approach to estimating student academic skills. However, the authors recommend a broader base of interpretation and use can be made. The suggestion that the test can also serve an objectives-based function does strain credulity. Although we are assured that steps were taken to align the test with common elements in Canadian curriculum, to suggest that the test measures the essential components of kindergarten through grade 12 is an exaggerated claim. Further, the "minimal competency scores," which are simply labels for percentile score ranges on the high school levels, can serve no useful purpose.

The strength of the CTBS is that it is a widely used standardized test of general academic skills with Canadian norms that is supported by relatively comprehensive resource documents and scoring service. As such it provides a useful external referent for student performance but the claims of measuring development and the implied general curricular validity detract from its basic utility in schools.

REVIEWER'S REFERENCE

Nagy, G. P. (1986). Validity of CTBS from an analysis of speededness and item response patterns. *Canadian Journal of Education, 11* (4), 536-556.

Review of the Canadian Tests of Basic Skills, Forms 7 and 8 by JEAN-JACQUES BERNIER, Professor, and MARTINE HEBERT, Assistant Professor, Department of Measurement and Evaluation, University Laval, Quebec, Canada:

The Canadian Tests of Basic Skills (CTBS), Forms 7 and 8 is a group-administered achievement test designed to assess pupils' abilities in seven fundamental skills: Listening, Word Analysis, Vocabulary, Reading, Language, Work-Study, and Mathematics. According to the authors, information obtained from the CTBS might serve several purposes. For example, the determination of a subject's developmental level in fundamental skills may permit educators to adjust educational material to the pupil's needs and level of ability, to determine an individual's strengths and weaknesses, and to plan individualized study programs.

The CTBS provides 14 different levels (Level 5 through 18) that were conceived to correspond roughly to chronological age. The different levels are represented into three batteries. The Primary Battery (Levels 5 to 8) emphasizes readiness skills, "the developed abilities needed to profit from learning experiences in the basic skills." In addition to a total score, results are given for five to seven areas depending on the level administered: Listening, Word Analysis, Vocabulary, Reading (not available for Level 5), Language, Mathematics, and Work-Study (not available for Levels 5 and 6). The

Elementary Multilevel Battery (Levels 9 to 14) covers the range of achievement of grades 3 to 8. It has 11 subtests covering five major areas: Vocabulary, Reading, Language, Work-Study, and Mathematics. The High School Multilevel Battery (Levels 15 to 18) is designed for pupils in grades 9 to 12 and assesses skills in four major areas: Reading Comprehension, Mathematics, Written Expressions, and Using Sources of Information. Administration time varies for each battery from 3 to 5 hours. Authors suggest testing periods be distributed over 2 days (High School Multilevel Battery) to 5 days (Primary Battery).

The 1990 version of the CTBS presents some improvements over its previous version, but some of the criticisms voiced before remain pertinent. The test is a norm-referenced instrument providing two kinds of scores: developmental and status with different norms depending on the battery. Norms were developed in the fall of 1987 from a stratified random sample of some 241 schools in which English was the major language of instruction in all provinces of Canada. Norms are expressed as grade equivalents. Conversion tables for translating a pupil's grade equivalent into a percentile score are provided in the Teacher's guides. Norms are available for the fall, the midyear, and the spring period of the year. The authors should provide age-based norms. This addition would facilitate the applicability of the CTBS in Canadian contexts where one can find great variation in schools' organization systems.

The reported reliabilities of the various CTBS subtests and composite scores are in general quite acceptable. Internal consistency measures based on KR-20 range from the .70s to the low .90s for the subtest scores and from .90 to .98 for the composites. Two subtest scores provide lower reliability coefficients in the Primary Battery: the KR-20 coefficient for the Listening subtest is .67 for Levels 6 and 7 and for the Reading subtest at Level 6 the internal consistency coefficient is .69. Although these coefficients are not extremely weak, one must consider the lower consistency measures generally found in testing young children.

The CTBS was based originally on the Iowa Tests of Basic Skills (184). Although the latter was submitted to extensive research, and detailed information concerning its psychometric properties is available to users, the former has not yet demonstrated evidence regarding some of its psychometric characteristics. For example, no data are yet available on a nationally representative Canadian sample regarding the stability coefficients. Studies on the equivalence of forms as well as on the factorial composition of the CTBS based on a Canadian sample have yet to be completed.

Content validity was ascertained by procedures of item selection based on a rational strategy and on

studies of the Iowa Tests of Basic Skills. Items were reviewed by Canadian educators and in the fall of 1986, approximately 2,000 pupils from 17 schools participated in a tryout testing. Characteristics of the items in terms of difficulties and discrimination indices were used for the final item selection. However, these are not clearly and sufficiently detailed in the manual for the administrators.

Criterion-related validity was investigated by correlating CTBS subtest scores with results of the Canadian Cognitive Abilities Test (CCAT). The correlations were of the expected nature: Generally the correlations of the Verbal, Quantitative, and Non-verbal scores of the CCAT were higher with corresponding subtests of the CTBS than with other subtests measuring different domains. However, the authors note the difficulty in comparing abilities and achievement scores emphasizing the extensive overlapping of the two constructs or in this case of the predictor and the criterion. It is important that authors proceed to a complete investigation of the construct validity in order to validate the interpretation of the expected test results.

Although some information is still to come, the authors have nonetheless taken great care in providing users with a useful instrument designed to measure fundamental educational skills.

[56]
Canfield Instructional Styles Inventory.

Purpose: Constructed to identify instructional preferences.
Population: Instructors.
Publication Dates: 1976–88.
Acronym: ISI.
Scores, 21: Conditions for Instruction (Peer, Organization, Goal Setting, Competition, Instructor, Detail, Independence, Authority), Areas of Interest (Numeric, Qualitative, Inanimate, People), Modes of Instruction (Lecturing, Readings, Iconic, Direct Experience), Influence (A-influence, B-influence, C-influence, D-influence, Total Influence).
Administration: Group or individual.
Price Data, 1991: $45 per complete kit including 5 inventory booklets and manual ('88, 55 pages); $29.50 per 10 inventory booklets; $32.50 per manual.
Time: (30–40) minutes for individual administration; (35–40) minutes for group administration.
Comments: May be self-administered.
Authors: Albert A. Canfield and Judith S. Canfield.
Publisher: Western Psychological Services.
Cross References: For reviews of an earlier edition by Thomas B. Bradley and C. Dean Miller, see 9:514.

Review of the Canfield Instructional Styles Inventory by NANCY L. ALLEN, Research Scientist, Educational Testing Service, Princeton, NJ:

According to its authors, the Canfield Instructional Styles Inventory (ISI) can be used to compare preferences in teaching style to those of other instructors, to match teachers' teaching styles to students' learning styles, and to identify the teaching style with which a teacher is most comfortable. There is, however, limited evidence the inventory can be used to do these things well. The use of this inventory could help to clarify roles in the classroom and to generate an examination of what is really happening in a teaching/learning setting.

The inventory is self- or group-administered and easily scored. Administration time is about 30 minutes. Twenty-one scores are produced from 25 items. For each item, instructors rank four alternatives in order of their preference, making five sets of four scales dependent upon each other.

The four scales associated with Areas of Interest (Numeric, Qualitative, Inanimate, People) and with Modes of Instruction (Lecturing, Readings, Iconic, Direct Experience) are not unexpected given the early literature on learning and thinking styles. They are also mutually exclusive within each set of four scales, thus, ordering responses by preference makes sense. This is also true for four of the Influence scales (A, B, C, D).

However, the eight scales associated with Conditions for Instruction (presented in two sets of four related scales) are not so mutually exclusive. For instance, it is not obvious that scoring high on Detail ("emphasizes specific and detailed information about what is to be done, in what form, and at what time," manual, p. 2) should imply a low score for authority ("concerned with controlling the classroom and the direction in which study activity will occur," manual, p. 2). This is a construct validity issue and no evidence is given for the final form of the inventory. In fact, no information is available about the development of the inventory and, other than the areas of interest and modes of instruction, the scales appear to be based on no theory or research.

The purpose of the Influence scales is also unclear. If the instructor (or, perhaps, his/her supervisor) did not think a particular method affects learning in some way, why would the instructor be responding to the inventory? The weighted sum of the four Influence scales is presented as another scale, without explanation or interpretation.

A new addition to this edition of the ISI is an instructor typology. This typology is concise and easy to describe. It has nine cells based on two dimensions: a social/neutral/independent continuum and an applied/neutral/conceptual continuum. This way of looking at instructional or learning style is common in the literature, and the simplification of the 21 scales makes it easier to match teachers' instructional styles with students' learning styles, as measured by the Canfield Learning Styles Inventory (LSI; 57). The typology is based on only 10 of the 21 scales. The development of the instructor typology was highly dependent on the learning style

typology. Factor analytic evidence is provided to justify this, but no justification is given for ignoring high loadings for Lecturing on the applied/neutral/conceptual continuum, especially for the LSI.

Comparisons of an instructor's own preferences in teaching style to the styles of other instructors may be limited by the use of midwestern junior college instructors as the original norm group. Apparently (based on sample sizes), no new norming of the inventory was completed for this edition. The date of the previous edition is 1976. Responses for a sample of 200 instructors used in the factor analysis mentioned above were used to produce percentages of instructors in each typology cell. No other information is available about this sample.

Test-retest reliabilities range from .81 to .96, whereas average phi coefficients for the items within each subscale range from .59 to .85. Higher phi coefficients tend to be associated with the Areas of Interest and Modes of Instruction scales. Correlations between scale scores are difficult to interpret because of the dependency among sets of scales. The test-retest reliabilities are based on data collected 7 days apart from 62 students in a classroom. The other reliability and correlational information is based on a sample of 200 community college instructors (100 males and 100 females). No other information about the samples is available, including how the samples were selected.

The authors have included information about the validity of the Canfield Learning Styles Inventory (LSI). It is possible the two inventories are equivalent so that the validity results are generalizable. However, the ISI is meant for an adult audience, whereas the LSI is most often used with children and young adults. It would have been appropriate to have at least one study that addresses directly the validity of the ISI, or at least the validity of some of the scales. For instance, a comparison of the subject area taught by the instructors in the original norm sample with the ISI Areas of Interest would have been simple to complete and report. The manual describes several studies that examined the value of matching a student's learning style with a teacher's instructional style. These studies and others in the literature indicate this type of matching is not always useful. This is the opinion of some imminent psychologists as well. For instance, Sternberg (1990, pp. 369–370) says, "Students need to develop ways to capitalize on their stylistic strengths, but they also need to develop the ability to move from one style to another." More detailed evidence is needed about when a careful match between learning and instructional styles should be made. Evidence of this kind may not be expected in a manual for an inventory, however.

Despite the addition of the instructor typology and its usefulness in matching instructional and learning styles (as measured by the LSI), the ISI is still not based on a theory of student learning and does not borrow from the rich advances made recently in developmental psychology. Validity evidence for the ISI is nonexistent, although there is some validity evidence for the parallel LSI. Evidence of reliability is not overwhelming. There is danger, as expressed by Gordon (Rabianski-Carriuolo, 1989, p. 22) about learning style inventories, that instruments of this type "lead novices to think that they have made a more precise and definitive diagnosis than I think is possible right now. My advice would be to use a learning style test with the awareness that it is a probe: a sample of one's behavior." If used for research purposes or for encouraging an examination and/or discussion of current classroom practice, the ISI could be used appropriately. However, care should be used in comparisons with the norms, and one should not blindly accept that learning styles, as measured by the LSI, should be matched by instructor styles, as measured by the ISI.

REVIEWER'S REFERENCES

Rabianski-Carriuolo, N. (1989). Learning styles: An interview with Edmund W. Gordon. *Journal of Developmental Education, 13* (1), 18-22.
Sternberg, R. J. (1990, January). Thinking styles: keys to understanding student performance. *Phi Delta Kappan, 71,* 366-371.

Review of the Canfield Instructional Styles Inventory by JERRILYN V. ANDREWS, Coordinator Research/Statistics, Department of Educational Accountability, Montgomery County Public Schools, Rockville, MD:

The 1988 publication of the Canfield Instructional Styles Inventory (ISI) uses 25 items to assess 21 dimensions of instructional style grouped into four clusters. The ISI is intended to give instructors a picture of the instructional techniques with which they may be more or less comfortable. The manual says the ISI is most commonly and effectively used in conjunction with the Canfield Learning Styles Inventory (57); the objective is to examine matches and mismatches between teaching style and student learning style with the intent of improving the match.

The items, norms, and technical information in the 1988 version appear to be identical to the earlier, 1976 version. What appears new is having 21 scales rather than 17, but this is simply the result of counting the four components of the Total Influence scale as scales themselves. The Total Influence scale is a weighted sum of the four individual influence scales; the scales are given weights ranging from negative one to three but no rationale for the weights is provided.

What really is new is the addition of a 3 x 3 instructor typology based on 10 of the scales. The new version of the ISI extends the interpretation

and uses suggested in the earlier version. Almost a third of the manual is devoted to matching or comparing instructors and students by using the Learning Styles Inventory (LSI) and ISI. The technique used is intuitively appealing but no theoretical, logical, or empirical basis for the calculations is given. Further, no evidence is presented that student or teacher satisfaction with the instructional process is changed if the styles are compared and adjustments made to bring the two sets of preferences into better alignment.

Unfortunately, nothing appears to have been done to shore up the shaky psychometric underpinnings of the inventory. All the technical problems cited in the earlier reviews (9:514) of the ISI remain. Although the internal consistency appears satisfactory, the sample on which it was calculated is described only as 100 male and 100 female instructors; no demographic data are provided. Test-retest reliability also appears satisfactory. However, the retest interval, 7 days, is too short to establish stability of a measure of instructional style. Further, the sample on which this reliability was established consisted of a class of 62 students; again, no demographic data are provided.

The validity of the ISI itself is never addressed directly. The manual cites a few studies involving the companion LSI and contends that studies on the LSI provide indirect evidence for the validity of the ISI. Even if one accepts that proposition, the study by Braunard and Ommen, from which much of the empirical information in the section on validity is said to be taken, is not included in the references, which is certainly a major oversight.

The ISI manual states the inventory is designed to be used by adult instructors in educational and business settings, a rather broad group, and cautions that results may not be accurate if the respondents differ substantially from typical college instructors. All the normative data, however, come from instructors in midwestern junior colleges, a much narrower population. Other than sex, the manual contains no demographic information about the norm group. Further, no indication is given concerning when the inventory was normed, but the N s reported in the current manual match those of the norm group used in the earlier (1976) publication. If the norms are that old, one must question how well they represent even current instructors in midwestern junior colleges.

The lack of any data relating the preferences expressed as scores on the ISI to actual behavior in the classroom is a serious concern. These data would seem to be the key to establishing the validity of the measure. The idea of an instructional style is appealing and if a valid measure were available, it might be a useful self-assessment and training tool. However, with the current lack of information about the technical properties of the inventory coupled with old norms from a very limited population, it is difficult to recommend using it regardless of its intuitive appeal.

[57]
Canfield Learning Styles Inventory.

Purpose: Designed to assess learning preferences.
Population: Junior High School, High School, College, Adults in business settings.
Publication Dates: 1976–88.
Acronym: LSI.
Scores, 21: Conditions for Learning (Peer, Organization, Goal Setting, Competition, Instructor, Detail, Independence, Authority), Area of Interest (Numeric, Qualitative, Inanimate, People), Mode of Learning (Listening, Reading, Iconic, Direct Experience), Expectation for Course Grade (A-expectation, B-expectation, C-expectation, D-expectation, Total expectation).
Administration: Group.
Forms, 4: A (College), B (High School), C (Junior High School), E (College-Easy).
Price Data, 1991: $80 per complete kit including 2 each of Forms A, B, C, and E inventory booklets, 1 Form ABC computer-scorable booklet, 1 Form E computer-scorable booklet, and manual ('88, 76 pages); $35 per 10 inventory booklets (specify form); $7.35–$9.50 per computer-scorable booklet (price depends on quantity ordered and includes scoring service by publisher); $35 per manual; $185 per IBM microcomputer disk.
Time: (30–40) minutes.
Author: Albert A. Canfield.
Publisher: Western Psychological Services.
Cross References: For reviews of an earlier edition by John Biggs and C. Dean Miller, see 9:609 (1 reference).

TEST REFERENCES

1. Buell, C., Pettigrew, F., & Langendorfer, S. (1987). Effect of perceptual style strength on acquisition of a novel motor task. *Perceptual and Motor Skills, 65,* 743-747.
2. Pettigrew, F., & Buell, C. (1989). Preservice and experienced teachers' ability to diagnose learning styles. *The Journal of Educational Research, 82,* 187-189.

Review of the Canfield Learning Styles Inventory by STEPHEN L. BENTON, *Associate Professor of Educational Psychology, Kansas State University, Manhattan, KS:*

The Canfield Learning Styles Inventory (LSI) is a self-report questionnaire intended to identify the kinds of educational experiences students most prefer. Teachers can presumably use test results to help students select courses or environments compatible with their style or to adapt course structures to student preferences. Although the author consistently refers to learner "preferences" and makes no claims that students perform better under conditions compatible with their learning styles, there is little sound theoretical and empirical support for the instrument's validity and reliability.

For example, no theoretical rationale underlies the content validity of the test. The author fails to tie the LSI to current cognitive theory and ignores the plethora of research that emphasizes the important role of *domain specific knowledge* in academic achievement. Psychologists recognize that knowledge and interest affect one's approach to learning and presumably one's preferences for learning conditions, modes, and expectations. No attempt is made, however, to explain how learning style is influenced by or related to these variables.

One must also question the face validity of specific items. For example, on a question asking about preferred learning content, mathematics and physical science are grouped together, which assumes students who prefer mathematics must also prefer the physical sciences. In addition, the similarities in descriptive phrases across multiple items could create a response bias on the part of respondents who simply respond stereotypically.

An examination of specific test items also revealed two that might be culturally biased. One listed "carrying on a conversation with a stranger" as an option for a preferred activity that is tied to the People subscale. It is assumed that individuals who score high on this scale prefer working with people. It may also be possible that in some cultures talking with a stranger is a dangerous activity and has little to do with preference for working with others. Another alternative listed on an item was "ask the teacher questions when the course is confusing or when the purpose isn't clear." This alternative is tied to the Organization subscale and, if ranked high, presumably characterizes someone who desires well-organized, meaningful coursework. It is also possible that in some cultures asking the teacher questions is a challenge to omniscient authority and is considered inappropriate (e.g., Schommer, 1990). No attempts to examine whether any of the test items are culturally biased are reported by the author.

There is also very little support for construct validity. Although the claim is made that 21 scales and nine distinct categories of learning styles can be derived from a mere 30 items, a factor analysis identified only two underlying constructs: Conceptual/Applied and Social/Independent. The table of factor loadings reveals, however, that even these two scales are ambiguous. The author claims that the Independence subscale loads heavily (-.30) on the Social/Independent factor, when it actually loads more heavily (-.44) on the Conceptual/Applied factor. The nine mutually exclusive Learner Typologies that are based on these two supposedly orthogonal factors are therefore of questionable validity.

In an attempt to establish criterion-related validity, the author cited studies that have correlated scores on LSI scales with actual achievement. Of the three studies cited, however, none controlled for students' aptitude in the relevant content area. On the basis of one study, weights were assigned to six

LSI subscales such that raw scores could be converted and summed to obtain a low-achievement risk score. Although this was a worthy effort, it is unclear exactly how the achievement weights were derived for each of the six LSI scales involved, and so the validity of the low-achievement risk score must be questioned. In addition, the lack of research correlating the LSI with scores on other learning style inventories further threatens validity.

The reliability of the instrument is also suspect. The preponderance of negative correlations reported among the subscales results from the forced-choice format of the test questions. The author sees this format as a strength because he believes it is not possible to maximize one kind of educational experience without giving up other alternatives. No theoretical justification is given for this stance. It is important to note that the correlations are corrected for attenuation but that the correlations prior to attenuation are not reported.

A test of equivalence and stability was conducted with students who took both Forms A and E of the LSI on the same day. None of the subscale reliabilities were equal to or greater than .90 which seems somewhat surprising given the similarity between the two instruments and the brief interval between test administrations. It should be noted that with longer intervals (e.g., 30 days, 5 weeks, and 3 months) researchers (e.g., Atkinson, 1989) have failed to obtain high correlations among equivalent forms of other learning style inventories. In spite of this, the author gave no justification for administering the tests on the same day. Finally, it should be noted that no standard errors of measurement are reported for any subscale.

Although several sources of evidence are offered for the LSI's validity and reliability, most are flawed for the reasons already mentioned. Despite their apparent widespread use, it is still unclear exactly what learning style inventories measure and if they are related to improved learning (Atkinson, 1989; Sims, Veres, & Shake, 1989; Veres, Sims, & Shake, 1987). Prospective users should consider student knowledge and interest as more important than concerns about style.

REVIEWER'S REFERENCES

Veres, J. G., Sims, R. R., & Shake, L. G. (1987). The reliability and classification stability of the Learning Style Inventory in corporate settings. *Educational and Psychological Measurement, 47,* 1127-1133.

Atkinson, G. (1989). Kolb's Learning Style Inventory—1985: Test-retest deja vu. *Psychological Reports, 64,* 991-995.

Sims, R. R., Veres, J. G., & Shake, L. G. (1989). An exploratory examination of the convergence between the Learning Styles Questionnaire and the Learning Style Inventory II. *Educational and Psychological Measurement, 49,* 227-233.

Schommer, M. (1990). Effects of beliefs about the nature of knowledge on comprehension. *Journal of Educational Psychology, 82,* 498-504.

[58]

Capitalization and Punctuation Tests.

Purpose: Measures skills in capitalization and punctuation before and after direct instruction.

Population: Students of English.
Publication Date: 1985.
Scores: Item scores only.
Administration: Group.
Forms, 2: Diagnostic, Achievement.
Manual: No manual.
Price Data, 1989: $15.95 per complete kit including 25 Diagnostic tests, 25 Achievement tests, and answer keys; $8.95 per 25 tests (Diagnostic or Achievement) with answer key; $.36 per additional copy.
Time: Administration time not reported.
Comments: For use as pre- and post-tests.
Authors: Kenneth Stratton and George Christian.
Publisher: Stratton-Christian Press, Inc.

[59]

Career Assessment Inventory, Second Edition (Vocational Version).

Purpose: "A vocational interest assessment tool for individuals planning to enter occupations requiring a four-year college degree or less."
Population: Grade 10 through adult.
Publication Dates: 1973–84.
Scores, 125: 2 Administrative Indices (Total Responses, Response Patterning), 4 Nonoccupatonal (Fine Arts-Mechanical, Occupational Extroversion-Introversion, Educational Orientation, Variability of Interests), 6 General Themes (Realistic, Investigative, Artistic, Social, Enterprising, Conventional), 22 Basic Interest Area Scales (Mechanical/Fixing, Electronics, Carpentry, Manual/Skilled Trades, Agriculture, Nature/Outdoors, Animal Service, Science, Numbers, Writing, Performing/Entertaining, Arts/Crafts, Social Service, Teaching, Child Care, Medical Service, Religious Activities, Business, Sales, Office Practices, Clerical/Clerking, Food Service), 91 Occupational Scales (Aircraft Mechanic, Auto Mechanic, Bus Driver, Camera Repair Technician, Carpenter, Conservation Officer, Dental Laboratory Technician, Drafter, Electrician, Emergency Medical Technician, Farmer/Rancher, Firefighter, Forest Ranger, Hardware Store Manager, Janitor/Janitress, Machinist, Mail Carrier, Musical Instrument Repair, Navy Enlisted, Orthodontist/Prosthetist, Painter, Park Ranger, Pipefitter/Plumber, Police Officer, Printer, Radio/TV Repair, Security Guard, Sheet Metal Worker, Telephone Repair, Tool/Die Maker, Truck Driver, Veterinary Technician, Chiropractor, Computer Programmer, Dental Hygienist, Electronic Technician, Math-Science Teacher, Medical Laboratory Technician, Radiological Technician, Respiratory Therapeutic Technician, Surveyor, Advertising Artist/Writer, Advertising Executive, Author/Writer, Counselor-Chemical Dependency, Interior Designer, Legal Assistant, Librarian, Musician, Newspaper Reporter, Photographer, Piano Technician, Athletic Trainer, Child Care Assistant, Cosmetologist, Elementary School Teacher, Licensed Practical Nurse, Nurse Aide, Occupational Therapist Assistant, Operating Room Technician, Physical Therapist Assistant, Registered Nurse, Barber/Hairstylist, Buyer/Merchandiser, Card/Gift Shop Manager, Caterer, Florist, Food Service Manager, Hotel/Motel Manager, Insurance Agent, Manufacturing Representative, Personnel Manager Private Investigator, Purchasing Agent, Real Estate Agent, Reservation Agent, Restaurant Manager, Travel Agent, Accountant, Bank Teller, Bookkeeper, Cafeteria Worker, Court Reporter, Data Entry Operator, Dental Assistant,

Executive Housekeeper, Medical Assistant, Pharmacy Technician, Secretary, Teacher Aide, Waiter/Waitress).
Administration: Group.
Price Data, 1988: $4.15 or less per Profile Report; $8.25 or less per Narrative Report; $14 per manual ('84, 152 pages).
Foreign Language Editions: Spanish and French editions available.
Time: (30–45) minutes.
Author: Charles B. Johansson.
Publisher: National Computer Systems, Inc.
Cross References: For a review of The Enhanced Version by James B. Rounds, see 10:43 (2 references); see also T3:367 (1 reference); for additional information and reviews of an earlier edition by Jack L. Bodden and Paul R. Lohnes, see 8:993.

TEST REFERENCES

1. Naylor, F. D., & Kidd, G. J. (1991). The predictive validity of the investigative scale of the Career Assessment Inventory. *Educational and Psychological Measurement, 51,* 217-226.

Review of the Career Assessment Inventory, Second Edition (Vocational Version) by JERARD F. KEHOE, District Manager, Selection and Testing, American Telephone & Telegraph Co., Morristown, NJ:

The Career Assessment Inventory (CAI) is a comprehensive occupational interest assessment system designed specifically for persons seeking occupations not largely dependent on 4 years of college education. In many ways the CAI is closely related to the Strong-Campbell Interest Inventory (SCII; 9:1195), as described in the earlier reviews (10:43 and 8:993). And even though the 1982 version includes a few significant changes from the 1976 version, the link with the SCII remains. This 1982 version has eliminated the Infrequent Response administrative index and added four new nonoccupational style scales to the set of Administrative Indices: Fine Arts-Mechanical, Occupational Extroversion-Introversion, Educational Orientation, and Variability of Interests. Also, the 1982 version has increased the number of Occupational Scales to 91, and perhaps most significantly, has introduced 32 combined-gender Occupational Scales. The 1982 CAI continues to include Holland's six types of general themes and 22 basic interest areas.

The reliability and validity data presented are extensive and supportive of CAI applications. Of particular interest is the result that the concurrent validities of the 32 combined-gender Occupational Scales decreased only slightly due to the exclusion of items not valid for both males and females. This slight loss of "gender-related uniqueness" is an acceptable price to pay for the increase in generality and reduction in complication of these Occupational Scales.

The purpose of the Fine Arts-Mechanical Scale is to represent a meaningful overall orientation to work without explicit gender labels. The Fine Arts-Mechanical Scale capitalizes on the typical result that fine arts, creative, and culturally oriented interests are associated with a feminine orientation and mechanical and trades-type interests are associated with a masculine orientation. The remaining three new administrative indices derive from earlier research with the Strong inventories. The Extroversion-Introversion Scale is well understood and is likely to be useful based on its relationship to occupational groups. The Educational Orientation Scale and the Variability of Interests Scale together seem to form what might be described as a CAI relevancy scale. The CAI has been developed primarily as a tool for persons generally not oriented to education and generally not focused on a particular occupational category. As a result, I would expect these scales to have relatively low value in aiding the interpretation of CAI profiles. More likely, they would provide an indication that some other type of assessment might be more appropriate.

The manual continues to be an excellent example of a comprehensive, yet focused and easy-to-use, document. Although it is now up to 142 pages, it continues to report succinctly a large volume of supporting evidence. Previous reviews suggested more descriptive information about the normative samples for the general themes and basic interests and more information about the predictive validity of interests both for the CAI in particular and as represented in the literature. Unfortunately, there are no improvements in these areas, in spite of the fact that requests for additional descriptive information about normative samples should be easy to accommodate and that at least some literature review of predictive validity for interests would be well worth the modest effort required. Previous reviewers were divided about the merits of more Occupational Scales. In my view, the additional Occupational Scales make the CAI better, not worse. The disadvantage of somewhat more crowded (if not more complex) profiles is more than offset by the benefits of the wider range of occupations. The CAI is more likely to have value to a wider range of potential users. The profiles are presented clearly enough that the relatively uninformative information on the Occupational Scales does not interfere with the more distinctive information. In fact, for most profiles that have an orderliness about the grouping of interests and occupations, the additional occupations may actually increase the meaningfulness to users of the relationship between interests and specific occupational choices.

SUMMARY. The CAI continues to be an excellent inventory that deserves widespread application. The combined-gender Occupational Scales reflect and facilitate significant progress toward freer access by males and females to desired occupations.

Review of the Career Assessment Inventory, Second Edition (Vocational Version) by NICHOLAS A. VACC, Professor and Chairperson, Department of Counselor Education, University of North Carolina, Greensboro, NC:

The Career Assessment Inventory, Vocational Version (CAI-VV), is designed to be used by counselors and other educators who work with non-college-bound students or adults seeking immediate career entry, or with individuals interested in work requiring some postsecondary education. In essence, the CAI-VV is intended for use with individuals seeking careers that do not require a baccalaureate degree. Another version (i.e., the Career Assessment Inventory, Enhanced Version [10:43]) exists, for which the intended audience is individuals seeking professional careers. Readers should not confuse the two versions; although the titles are deceptively similar, the purpose and intended audiences of the two versions are dissimilar.

The rationale for the CAI-VV's development was a need for what has been described as a "blue collar version" of the Strong-Campbell Interest Inventory (SCII; 9:1195), because a large percentage or a majority (estimated at 80%, p. 3) of the work force is characteristically employed in technical, vocational, or other nonprofessional types of employment. (The SCII is now called the Strong Interest Inventory.) As reported by the author, the inventory has been designed to (*a*) be applicable for careers requiring no postsecondary training or those requiring training from, in general, a vocational-technical level through 4 years of postsecondary college; (*b*) be applicable for lower reading levels; (*c*) be reflective of the three levels of analysis, types (Theme Scales), and traits (Basic Interest Areas Scales), as well as specific career levels (Occupational Scales); and (*d*) provide a reporting format that is easy to understand, applicable for employment selection, and useful in career exploration.

The CAI-VV is a comprehensive instrument that comprises only one form for both males and females. More specifically, the 305 items included in the CAI-VV, as reported by the author, contain 151 items (i.e., 50%) that are "activity items," 43 items (i.e., 14%) that are related to school subjects, and 111 items (i.e., 36%) that are associated with job titles. The manual reports that wording of the items was designed to reduce biasing, be responsive to low reading levels (i.e., sixth-grade level, p. 10), and be relevant to individuals interested in vocational-technical jobs. Test takers respond to items using one of five alternatives as follows: *Like Very Much, Like Somewhat, Indifferent, Dislike Somewhat,* and *Dislike Very Much.* The inventory takes approximately 30 minutes to complete by an adult. It appears to require somewhat longer for adolescents or individuals with reading problems.

The organizational format of the CAI-VV is essentially the same as previous versions and is very similar to that of the Strong Interest Inventory. No apparent changes appear to have been made in the 1984 version compared to the 1982 version; the inventory has remained the same. The content of the manual and the test was appreciably changed between the 1976 and 1982 versions. Changes between the 1976 and 1978 versions existed basically in the Occupational Scales. The 1978 version contained 68 gender-common occupations, and 21 separate male and female occupations, whereas the 1982 and 1984 versions contained 91 gender-common occupations. The Occupational Scales were designed to help individuals understand how their preferences fit with those of employed persons in a variety of occupations that are relevant to individuals who are interested in nonprofessional occupations. The specific occupational groups included were derived from surveys of high school counselors in 1975 and community college counselors sometime after 1978 (p. 66).

The organizational format of the CAI-VV and the scoring profiles for both the test taker (Narrative Scoring Report) and counselor (Counselor's Summary) are attractive and appealing. The main subsection includes General Theme Scales (Holland's six types), Basic Interest Area Scales (developed using the organization of Holland's typologies), and the Occupational Scales. The manual provides technical information, interpretative guidelines, and two case studies. Also included are illustrative score reports and informative interpretative information. The manual would be enhanced if the interpretative information was separated from the inventory's development procedures and data. Otherwise, the manual is very functional for acquiring knowledge concerning the interpretation of scores.

The major focus of the technical presentation is scale construction; lacking is adequate information supporting the predictive validity of the instrument. Although the instrument has been in existence about a decade, the manual is void of reported studies that examined the CAI-VV. It would be helpful if greater focus was directed toward reporting evidence that the CAI-VV has been successful in helping clients find highly satisfying occupations (prediction). Many of the relevant data in the manual need updating; some of the empirical information presented reflects work done in the mid-seventies. It is also unfortunate the manual does not document the reading levels for both the inventory and the narrative-scoring report using a standardized readability index, because the sensitivity to level of reading was such an important component in the construction and merchandizing of the inventory. Lastly, the author reports the instrument can be used for employment selection, but no evidence is presented to support this claim. Because the technical information has not changed appreciatively, the reader is directed to earlier reviews for additional comments.

In summary, the CAI-VV has merit, particularly because it addresses a population for which comprehensive instruments are needed, and the items and manual are presented in gender-neutral terms. However, it is difficult to judge adequately some of the psychometric aspects of the inventory due to insufficient information. The noticeable small number of cases used in the development of some of the Occupational Scales is of concern. Also of questionable value is the construction of Theme Scales by choosing the items "rationally" or by inspection, rather than empirically demonstrating that the Themes adequately reflect the hexagonal model of Holland.

I would use the CAI-VV selectively with its intended population. Its cost and the time needed for appropriate interpretation preclude using it with large groups. It also should be noted that although the instrument is targeted for individuals with lower reading levels, the narrative scoring report will require an individual who has greater command of reading and a good ability to conceptualize.

[60]
Career Exploration Series, 1988 Revision.

Purpose: Designed for career guidance using "a series of job interest inventories that focus on specific occupational fields."
Population: Grades 7–12 and college and adults.
Publication Date: 1979–89.
Acronym: CES.
Scores: 6 areas: Agriculture-Forestry-Conservation, Business, Consumer Economics, Scientific-Mathematical-Health, Industrial, Design-Art-Communications.
Subtests, 6: [AG-O ('89, 17 pages), BIZ-O ('89, 17 pages), CER-O ('88, 17 pages), SCI-O ('89, 17 pages), IND-O ('89, 17 pages), DAC-O ('88, 17 pages)] available as separates.
Administration: Group.
Price Data, 1989: $50 per class set of 36 (6 of each title) including User's Guide ('89, 4 pages); $50 per 35 reusable booklets (specify title); $1.60 per reusable booklet (specify title); $.30 per answer form (specify title); $49.95 per computer edition (specify title); $249.95 per set of 6 computer editions; $8 per specimen set.
Time: (50–60) minutes per subtest.
Comments: Self-administered and self-scored interest inventories for 6 areas.
Authors: Arthur Cutler, Francis Ferry, Robert Kauk, and Robert Robinett.
Publisher: CFKR Career Materials, Inc.
Cross References: For reviews by Bruce R. Fretz and Robert B. Slaney of the original edition, see 9:196.

Review of the Career Exploration Series, 1988 Revision by MARK POPE, President, Career Decisions, San Francisco, CA:

The Career Exploration Series (CES) is a series of six self-administered, self-scored inventories which focus on broad occupational areas: agricultural occupations (AG-O), business occupations (BIZ-O), consumer economics-oriented occupations (CER-O), design-art-communications-related occupations (DAC-O), industrial occupations (IND-O), and scientific and health occupations (SCI-O). The materials for the CES include a general user's guide for use with all six of the inventories as well as separate question booklets and an answer insert folder, a combination answer sheet/report form, for each of the six inventories. No other materials are supplied with the CES.

The user's guide is a four-page booklet that contains general information on the background, format, administration, and development of the CES. The background section explains why specific occupations and occupational clusters were chosen for this series. In the description section, the CES instruments are described as having the same basic format. The question booklet and the answer insert folder are also described here. In the administration section, specific step-by-step procedures are presented to assist in the administration of these inventories. Administration time and other specific guidelines on how to present certain information from the inventories are also included. The development section contains some general information on the construction of the six inventories. Administration time for each inventory requires 45–50 minutes for "90% of those taking the instruments" (user's guide, p. 3). To obtain a comprehensive profile of a client using the CES measures would take 5 to 6 hours of testing time. A more efficient way of using these inventories would be to administer one or two of the inventories to help identify some additional, specific occupations after general career themes have been identified using a more comprehensive inventory.

Each of the six inventories uses a unique, 18-page, reusable question booklet designed to serve as a step-by-step guide for the client. Directions are presented in large type in an easily read format. This question booklet also serves as the inventory scoring key. Each of the six question booklets has the same format, beginning with a statement of the purpose and goals for the particular inventory and directions for the client. The next three sections respectively request clients to report the level of their educational aspirations (how much school they wish to attend), the types of work activities they prefer, and a rating of their work interests on a Likert-type scale (*usually or often, sometimes or occasionally, seldom or rarely*). The work interests and work activities change for each inventory and are based on the *Guide for Occupational Exploration* (U.S. Department of Labor, 1977) categories.

The answer insert folder for each inventory is a four-page, expendable booklet that serves as an answer sheet when used in conjunction with the question booklet and as a report form for the results of the completed career exploration process.

No specific reliability or validity data are presented in any of the available components of the CES. When this reviewer telephoned CFKR for additional information, they responded by sending the *JOB-O Professional Manual* (Cutler, Ferry, Kauk, & Robinett, 1985) stating that the same methodology was used in the development of both the JOB-O and the CES. It is important to note that this statement does not relieve the authors of responsibility for performing validation studies for each of the six CES inventories. Further, the authors do not address the issue of gender differences, which most research has reported as having importance in interest measurement. Overall, there is simply not enough data presented for the test user to use these inventories with confidence.

The authors go to great pains to tell the user that the CES inventories are not tests, but merely "'open inventories' with no norms" (user's guide, p. 4). Also, the user's guide (p. 2) contains the disclaimer: "The CES instruments are EXPLORATORY only. They are not designed as tests." Even if the instruments were not designed to be tests, the authors are still required to provide appropriate technical information to support their use. The only mention of research in the CES user's guide concerns field tests (although no data are provided about when, where, how many, or the results) and the *National Ag Occupations Study* conducted by the U.S. Department of Health, Education, and Welfare in 1978. Even the JOB-O inventory is based on limited research conducted in the mid- to late 1970s, according to the *JOB-O Professional Manual.*

The authors offer some validity evidence by citing a variety of Department of Labor general publications as sources of the educational aspirations, work interests, and work activity variables. This is primarily face validity which is not the strongest type of validity evidence for career measures. The authors hint at criterion-related validity in the user's guide (p. 4): "field testing indicates that the questions adequately measure these personal characteristics"; however, no research citation is provided.

The user's guide states that job "ACTIVITY GROUPS have sufficient variability and content to insure the accurate placement of the job titles in a specific group according to the DOMINANT CHARACTERISTICS of the job." This is an important statement if it is true; however, nowhere is specific research cited to verify it. This is not an adequate substitute for objective measures of content validity.

The above validity information as well as some form of reliability measurement should be available in a technical manual. Test-retest reliability, a relatively simple procedure, would assist in establishing some of the necessary data.

These inventories were last reviewed in *The Ninth Mental Measurements Yearbook* (Fretz, 1985; Slaney, 1985) where many of these same issues were originally reported. Because the copyright statements on the six inventory question booklets are quite recent (1988 or 1989), some changes may have been made. It appears that any such changes did not include the report of new validation research. Test users are given no information on which to determine how reliable and valid these inventories really are.

This model of self-reported aspirations/ activities/interests may be too broad to be useful. For example, the same configuration/code is assigned to teacher, psychologist, counselor, and social worker. These four do not belong to the same DOT group (teacher does not) and the Dictionary of Holland Occupational Codes gives each one a different three letter code (first two letters the same, the third letter is different for each). These are differences that the CES inventories are not able to measure.

Also, there is a carelessness about the quality of some of the materials, which should make the user suspicious about less obvious aspects of the CES. Typographical errors in the user's guide, inappropriate use of abbreviations in the narrative, and inconsistent and incorrect citation format may all be important clues to the kind of development that has gone into these inventories.

These instruments may indeed have some use in career interest measurement. They may be useful starting places for career exploration discussions. However, they cannot be a substitute for a good career interest inventory such as the Strong Interest Inventory (9:1195) or a more efficient self-assessment inventory such as the Self-Directed Search (10:330). There continues to be a substantial amount of basic research yet to be done on these instruments before they can be used for any reason in the career area, but especially as interest inventories. Further, the CES is in need of a technical manual, which would make data easily available to users.

REVIEWER'S REFERENCES

U.S. Department of Labor. (1979). *Guide for occupational exploration.* Washington, DC: U.S. Government Printing Office.

Cutler, A., Ferry, F., Kauk, R., & Robinett, R. (1985). *JOB-O professional manual.* Meadow Vista, CA: CFKR Career Materials, Inc.

Fretz, B. R. (1985). [Review of the Career Exploration Series.] In J. V. Mitchell, Jr. (Ed.), *The ninth mental measurements yearbook* (pp. 273-274). Lincoln, NE: The Buros Institute of Mental Measurements.

Slaney, R. B. (1985). [Review of the Career Exploration Series.] In J. V. Mitchell, Jr. (Ed.), *The ninth mental measurements yearbook* (pp. 274-275). Lincoln, NE: The Buros Institute of Mental Measurements.

Review of the Career Exploration Series, 1988 Revision by WILLIAM I. SAUSER, JR., Associate Vice President and Professor, Office of the Vice President for Extension, Auburn University, Auburn, AL:

It should be clearly understood from the outset that the Career Exploration Series (CES) is not a test. It was not designed to be a test or measurement tool; it does not possess the psychometric characteristics required of an acceptable test; the authors clearly state on every booklet that the CES is not a test; and it should certainly not be used by vocational guidance counselors—either professionally trained or voluntary—as a test. Rather, the CES can be viewed as a guided tour of the world of work and the many possible vocations available to someone who is searching for an appropriate career choice. When used as intended, the CES can be a valuable curriculum supplement in a vocational education course, a useful tool for volunteers who are attempting to assist others in a search for an initial or new career, and an appropriate self-administered introduction to career guidance techniques employed by professional counselors.

Too often individuals find themselves working in unsatisfying jobs that do not match their interests or abilities. Career or vocational guidance is a process conducted by both professionals and volunteers that is intended to help persons find jobs and careers for which they are well suited, with the intention of preventing job dissatisfaction and its attendant problems in general adjustment and life satisfaction. The process typically consists of helping individuals gather and use information to accomplish three purposes: (*a*) to make a valid assessment of personal abilities, aptitudes, interests, and behavioral tendencies; (*b*) to explore and gain an understanding of the myriad career and job options available, with particular attention to realistic views of career options of significant interest; and (*c*) to select one or more options well suited to the individual's identified personal characteristics. Following this career guidance process, the individual is in a far better position to search for appropriate jobs or to enter training or educational programs to prepare for appropriate jobs.

Reviewers of the original version of the CES (Fretz, 1985; Slaney, 1985) correctly point out that the CES is not an appropriate instrument for assisting in the first step of the career guidance process (i.e., producing a valid assessment of vocational interests). The absence of a manual describing how the CES was constructed and how the job reviews it contains were selected, the lack of standard reliability and validity data, and the fact that no norms are reported for the CES are serious concerns which preclude its use as a measurement tool. Potential users who are seeking such a device would do well to consider instead the Strong Interest Inventory (9:1195), the Kuder Occupational Interest Survey (10:167), Holland's Self-Directed Search (10:330), or one of the many comprehensive career planning programs on the market today, such as the Career Planning Program sponsored by the American College Testing Program (T3:77), the Career Development Program conducted by Science Research Associates, and the Career Skills Assessment Program conducted by the College Board (see Mehrens & Lehmann, 1991, pp. 421–423, for reviews of these and other programs). Several entries in Watkins and Campbell's (1990) edited volume are also useful references for professionals seeking innovative assessment devices to aid in vocational guidance.

Although the CES is not appropriate for use in the first stage of career guidance, it appears to have considerable merit for use in the second stage, helping the individual explore and gain realistic views of potential career options, the process for which the CES was designed.

The specific steps by which the CES was constructed are not described in the user's guide (an oversight which should be addressed by the authors in a future release), but it appears that 300 popular jobs, as described in the U.S. Department of Labor publications *Occupational Outlook Handbook* (1980) and *Dictionary of Occupational Titles* (1977), were analyzed by the authors and rated on a series of variables, such as required education and training; working with data, people, and things; required physical stamina; and such characteristics as autonomy and job content. These jobs were grouped into six convenient categories and laid out in attractive booklet forms with engaging content and titles, such as AG-O and BIZ-O. Each booklet is designed for 45–50 minute exploration by high school students or adults and provides a wealth of information in digestible form. Jobs range from semiskilled occupations through skilled crafts and paraprofessional positions to professions, making the CES usable for a population with a wide range of interests, aptitudes, and abilities.

Career exploration with the CES consists of four steps. First, the individual performs a brief, guided self-assessment regarding preferences for various job characteristics. This step can be enhanced considerably by using information derived from professionally prepared assessment devices, such as those previously mentioned. Second, using an insert folder, the individual compares the self-assessment scores with job ratings for 60 occupations within the broad grouping considered in the booklet, and counts the number of matches between the self-assessment and the job ratings. Third, the individual reviews brief descriptions (job title and duties, required training, pay range, outlook, and related jobs) of those jobs which most closely match the self-assessments, and completes a brief questionnaire about the three best liked jobs from among those identified. Fourth, the individual reads some general information about the job grouping and identifies sources for additional information. Further steps are suggested, such as writing to one of the many addresses provided in the booklet for additional information; reading the *Occupational Outlook Handbook, Dictionary of Occupational Titles,* or the authors' own JOB-O Dictionary; or seeking more information from job incumbents and counselors. All further steps taken are at the option of the individual.

The booklets are well laid out and illustrated, easy to work through, and intrinsically interesting, although tackling all six in one sitting is a daunting task! They also seem to provide useful information. This reviewer, an industrial/organizational psychologist with responsibilities in university administration, teaching, and editing, was intrigued after working through all six of the booklets to be guided by the CES to explore such career options as psychologist, personnel or labor relations worker, public administrator, teacher, and editor! Apparently it is to this kind of anecdotal experience that the authors are referring when they state in the user's guide that "Field-testing indicates a high degree of satisfaction with the information in the insert folder" (p. 4). They also invite users to share their experiences in the use of the CES. Testimonials from satisfied users, however, are not a strong enough basis for encouraging the widespread use of the CES. Its authors are strongly urged to conduct systematic evaluative research with the CES, and to report the results of such work, along with other information noted earlier in this review, in a CES manual. The four-page user's guide is simply not sufficient.

In summary, the CES is not suitable for use in identifying occupational interests, but appears to be a helpful tool for the second phase of the career guidance process: exploring a variety of jobs and searching for viable options. Vocational education teachers, volunteers, and professional guidance counselors may find these attractive, information-packed booklets to be an effective way to help youth and adults gain a realistic understanding of available jobs and career options.

REVIEWER'S REFERENCES

U.S. Department of Labor. (1977). *Dictionary of occupational titles.* Washington, DC: U.S. Government Printing Office.
U.S. Department of Labor. (1980). *Occupational outlook handbook.* Washington, DC: U.S. Government Printing Office.
Fretz, B. R. (1985). [Review of the Career Exploration Series.] In J. V. Mitchell, Jr. (Ed.), *The ninth mental measurements yearbook* (pp. 273-274). Lincoln, NE: The Buros Institute of Mental Measurements.
Slaney, R. B. (1985). [Review of the Career Exploration Series.] In J. V. Mitchell, Jr. (Ed.), *The ninth mental measurements yearbook* (pp. 274-275). Lincoln, NE: The Buros Institute of Mental Measurements.
Watkins, C. E., Jr., & Campbell, V. L. (Eds.). (1990). *Testing in counseling practice.* Hillsdale, NJ: Lawrence Erlbaum Associates.
Mehrens, W. A., & Lehmann, I. J. (1991). *Measurement and evaluation in education and psychology* (4th ed.). Fort Worth, TX: Holt, Rinehart and Winston.

[61]

Career Guidance Inventory.

Purpose: "Designed to provide measures of relative interest in postsecondary instructional programs."

Population: Students and prospective students at trade, vocational, or technical school, or at community college.

Publication Dates: 1972–89.

Acronym: CGI.

Scores, 47: Agribusiness and Agricultural Production, Renewable Natural Resources, Business (Accounting and Finance, Data Processing, Clerical/Typing/Word Processing, Office Supervision and Management, Secretarial), Marketing and Distribution (General Marketing, Financial Services, Hospitality/Recreation/Tourism, Real Estate), Communications and Communications Technologies, Computer and Information Sciences, Cosmetology and Barbering, Engineering and Related Technologies (Architectural, Civil, Electrical and Electronic, Environmental Control, Industrial Production, Mechanical Engineering, Mining and Petroleum), Allied Health (Dental Services, Diagnostic and Treatment Services, Miscellaneous Services, Medical Laboratory Technologies, Mental Health/Human Services, Nursing and Related Services, Rehabilitation Services), Vocational Home Economics (Child Care and Guidance, Clothing/Apparel/Textiles, Food Production/Management/Services, Institutional/Home Management/Supporting Services), Protective Services, Construction Trades (Brickmason/Stonemason/Tile Setting, Carpentry, Electrical and Power Transmission Installation, Plumbing/Pipefitting/Steamfitting), Mechanics and Repairers (Electrical and Electronic Equipment Repair, Heating/Air Conditioning/Refrigeration Mechanics, Industrial Equipment Maintenance and Repair, Vehicle and Mobile Equipment), Precision Production (Drafting, Graphic and Printing Communication, Precision Metal Work, Wookworking), Transportation and Material Moving, Visual Arts (Fine Arts).

Administration: Group.

Price Data, 1991: $3 per reusable test booklet; $35 per 25 answer sheet/interpretation guides; $6 per administrator's manual ('89, 43 pages); $10 per specimen set of all Career Guidance Inventory and Educational Interest Inventory (123) components.

Time: [45–60] minutes.

Comments: Self-administered, self-scored.

Author: James E. Oliver.

Publisher: Orchard House, Inc.

Cross References: For a review by James B. Rounds, Jr., of an earlier edition, see 9:197; for a review by Bert W. Westbrook, see 8:996.

Review of the Career Guidance inventory by E. JACK ASHER, Jr., Professor Emeritus of Psychology, Western Michigan University, Kalamazoo, MI:

The Career Guidance Inventory (CGI) by J. E. Oliver is designed to assess student interests in the instructional programs offered by Trade, Vocational, and Technical Schools, and by Community Colleges. The first edition of the inventory (1972) provided scores for 25 programs. The current edition, published in 1989, provides scores for 47 instructional programs. According to the manual, the inventory is intended for use in an educational and career guidance program. The results are supposed to be of use in helping a student select an academic major. The author also has a companion instrument: the Educational Interest Inventory (EII; 123). The latter is intended for students planning to attend a college or university. The two instruments are available in either paper-and-pencil or computer format.

The CGI consists of a set of 235 paired activity descriptions for which the student is asked to (a) choose which activity they prefer, and (b) choose whether that activity is of high (Hi) or low (Lo) interest. The student is then asked to find the number of this activity on the answer sheet and mark the sheet accordingly. The answer sheet lists the 47 programs. Many students completing this inventory will very likely find the directions for completing the inventory difficult and confusing. As a result, it should be expected that a number of marking errors will occur.

Directions for scoring the inventory are provided on the answer sheet but not in the manual. The scoring system uses a rather arbitrary 3 for a Hi response and a 1 for a Lo response. A student's score for a particular program is the sum of the Hi and Lo responses marked for that program. The highest and lowest possible interest scores for a program are 30 and zero, respectively. The authors provide high, middle, and low interest cutoff points. However, there are neither norms nor a description of how the cutoff points were established.

The manual for the CGI and the EII, both of which are covered in the same document, is almost totally lacking in basic technical test information. This was apparently true in the prior edition of the inventory. There are no norms, no reliability coefficients, and little discussion of validity. The method of selecting the 235 activities from the 47 instructional programs is described in brief terms. The 47 instructional programs were selected from the U.S. Department of Education's Classification of Instructional Programs (CIP) code system. This system is the Department of Education's method of classifying instructional programs in postsecondary education. The 235 activities are supposed to represent activities of persons who complete the 47 programs. However, no discussion of the scaling procedure used to select the activities is included other than to note that six professionals were involved in selecting the statements.

The validity of the inventory is entirely dependent upon the content of the items because no other supporting data are presented. Therefore, the research to support the development of the activities that make up the inventory should have been explained in much more detail. The major questions that remain unanswered are: How did the authors of the items move from CIP code program descriptions to work activities, and how does all of this relate to a student's interest in an academic program of study?

According to the manual, the reliability of the inventory cannot be calculated by the normal procedures. This is supposedly true because the responses are not normally distributed. The manual also states that the test-retest reliability would be inaccurately low because of changing conditions and multiple Hi–Lo responses. In previous editions, a split-half reliability coefficient was reported. Why was it omitted this time? The reliability of this instrument should be seriously questioned, if for no other reason than the likelihood of mistakes by students filling out the answer sheet.

The new edition of the CGI attempts to answer some of the earlier criticisms about the lack of a strong rationale for the 25 scales. This edition identifies 47 scales taken from the U.S. Department of Education's CIP. However, the relation between these programs and the 235 activities that make up the inventory is poorly established.

It is clear from the CGI manual that the basic research to support the theoretical basis of the inventory still has not been completely reported. The need for norms is also essential to establish the usefulness of the inventory. Norms by sex should also be provided. Finally, the reliability of the instrument is suspect due to both the absence of supportive research cited within the manual and the complex administrative directions. All of this work should be completed and reported in the manual prior to the use of the instrument in guidance and counseling situations.

Review of the Career Guidance Inventory by MICHAEL B. BUNCH, Vice President, Measurement Incorporated, Durham, NC:

The stated purpose of the Career Guidance Inventory (CGI) is to help students match their interests to established fields of study. The publisher has chosen for this purpose fields of study defined by the Classification of Instructional Programs (CIP; U.S. Department of Education, 1981, 1985). These CIP codes are used by schools throughout the United States.

The CGI consists of a reusable student booklet, the answer sheet/profile/interpretation guide, and the examiner's manual. A computerized version of the CGI has been withdrawn from the market and thus is not reviewed.

The test booklet is a 12-page reusable document consisting of 235 pairs of forced-choice statements. Each statement is followed by a category number. For example, the student is presented the following pair of statements: "Manage a prison" (33) and "Work as a typist and general clerk" (5). The numbers in parentheses refer to the CGI categories associated with the statements.

The student reads pairs of statements from the test booklet and marks responses in the answer sheet/profile/interpretation guide. If the student had preferred to manage a prison in the example above, he or she would have turned to row 33 of the answer sheet and circled "Hi" or "Lo," depending on the intensity of preference. The student repeats this process 234 times, then tallies Hi's, Lo's, and total score for each of the 47 rows. This process seems awkward.

The format and use of the answer sheet, although apparently awkward, are actually reasonable ways to allow students to enter 235 responses on a single sheet of paper and tally scores in 47 categories. Other means of recording responses would no doubt be easier to follow, but would not allow for quick tabulation of results for the 47 scales.

As noted in previous reviews (Westbrook, 1978; Rounds, 1985), problems with this inventory are legion. To their credit, the author and publisher have responded to the criticism of arbitrary selection of fields of study by using the CIP-defined fields. However, item-construction deficiencies remain, and the publisher makes no attempt to establish the reliability or validity of the instrument.

The examiner's manual claims content validity for the instrument by arguing that the CIP classification system has been the focus of many years of research. Whereas such a claim would be weak if the CGI followed the system precisely, it is even weaker when one considers that the publisher has modified the system rather extensively. Further, there appears to have been no participation in item writing or review by content experts. According to the examiner's manual, six individuals with expertise in psychometrics wrote, edited, and reviewed the 235 items.

As with previous editions of the CGI, the publisher offers no empirical evidence of reliability or validity, Indeed, the author claims that instruments like the CGI are exempt from such standards. He argues that because scores on the 47 scales of the CGI are derived in relation to other scales on the CGI, rather than relative to other individuals' scores on the same scales, traditional measures of reliability are inappropriate. This argument is valid only as it relates to internal consistency. However, the argument absolutely does not apply to measures of profile stability. Profile similarity or stability over time is the essence of interest batteries.

Similarly, validity of ipsative scales can be established by comparing students' scores with outcome measures such as successful completion of a program or persistence in a program. Students completing a course in nursing, for example, should generally have higher scores on the nursing and allied health scales than they have on agriculture or building trades scales. Given the technical limitations of ipsative scores, it is not necessary to use correlational methods. Simple classification measures would suffice and would certainly be better than nothing.

The author and publisher have responded only minimally to strong and justifiable criticism. The redefinition of skill areas has at least shown an attempt to link the CGI to a known entity. However, the instrument remains totally unproven. The publisher continues to fail to provide the most meager evidence of reliability and validity and argues that such information is not needed. This test may be suitable for research projects, but it should definitely not be considered for guiding students.

REVIEWER'S REFERENCES

Westbrook, B. W. (1978). [Review of the Career Guidance Inventory.] In O. K. Buros (Ed.), *The eighth mental measurements yearbook* (pp. 1557-1558). Highland Park, NJ: The Gryphon Press.

U.S. Department of Education. (1981, 1985). *A classification of instructional programs (CIP)*. Washington, DC: U.S. Government Printing Office.

Rounds, J. B., Jr. (1985). [Review of the Career Guidance Inventory.] In J. V. Mitchell, Jr. (Ed.), *The ninth mental measurements yearbook* (pp. 275-277). Lincoln, NE: Buros Institute of Mental Measurements.

[62]

Carolina Picture Vocabulary Test (for Deaf and Hearing Impaired).

Purpose: "To measure the receptive sign vocabulary in individuals where manual signing [is] the primary mode of communication."

Population: Deaf and hearing-impaired children ages 2.5–16.

Publication Date: 1985.

Acronym: CPVT.

Scores: Total score only.

Administration: Individual.

Price Data, 1988: $69 per complete program; $55 per test; $7.50 per 50 record forms; $7.50 per manual (38 pages).

Time: (10–30) minutes.

Authors: Thomas L. Layton and David W. Holmes.

Publisher: PRO-ED, Inc.

TEST REFERENCES

1. Kline, M., & Sapp, G. L. (1989). Carolina Picture Vocabulary Test: Validation with hearing-impaired students. *Perceptual and Motor Skills, 69,* 64-66.

[63]

Chicago Early Assessment and Remediation LaboratorY.

Purpose: To assess individual abilities and provide remedial instructional activities in weak areas of functioning.

Population: Ages 3–6.

Publication Dates: 1981–84.

Acronym: Chicago EARLY.

Scores, 5: Gross Motor, Fine Motor, Language, Visual Discrimination, Memory.

Administration: Individual.

Price Data, 1989: $129 per complete kit including Assessment Pictures, Puzzles, Drawing Worksheets, Score Sheets, Social/Emotional Checklist, Individual Progress Record Sheets, Class Summary Sheets, 3 jars of blocks, bean bag, bag with zipper, small cardboard box, box of crayons, Assessment Manual ('84, 58 pages), Instructional Activities Guide ('84, 264 pages); $3.95 per 25 Drawing Worksheets; $3.95 per 25 score sheets; $4.95 per 50 Social/Emotional Checklists; $3.95 per 25 Individual Progress Record Sheets; $2.95 per 15 Class Summary Sheets; $9.95 per Assessment Manual; $17.95 per Instructional Activities Guide.

Foreign Language Edition: Spanish edition available.

Time: (15–30) minutes.

Comments: Screening instrument.

Author: Board of Education of the City of Chicago.

Publisher: Educational Teaching Aids.

Review of the Chicago Early Assessment and Remediation LaboratorY by NORMAN A. CONSTANTINE, Director of Assessment Services, Far West Laboratory for Educational Research and Development, San Francisco, CA, and Lecturer in Pediatrics, Stanford University School of Medicine, Stanford, CA:

The Chicago Early Assessment and Remediation LaboratorY (EARLY) "is designed to help early childhood teachers determine which skills a child has and has not mastered and to help the teacher implement special supplemental instruction in the child's weak areas of functioning." It consists of an assessment component and an instruction component, each with a separate manual and set of materials. This evaluation focuses on the assessment component.

The assessment component comprises a series of 23 developmental items keyed to items on other developmental tests, such as the Bayley Scales of Infant Development and the Stanford-Binet Intelligence Scale. Each item is scored on a scale ranging from zero through an upper limit of 2 to 8, depending on the item. Item scores are summed into five separate subtest scores. Decile norms (percentiles grouped in intervals of 10) are provided for each subtest based on samples of Chicago school children. These samples cover 6-month age intervals for ages 3 through 6 years. The sample sizes range from 159 to 727.

The total sample across all age groups is 54% Black, 30% White, 11% Hispanic, and 5% other. This ethnic breakdown is approximately representative of the Chicago school system's enrollment during the development of the test.

Little information is provided in the manual regarding test reliability and validity. Two conference presentation papers were provided by the publisher as a source of further information. Unfortunately, these papers were poor reproductions and were very difficult to read. Additional copies provided by the publisher upon request were equally poor reproductions.

RELIABILITY AND VALIDITY. A coefficient alpha of .89 is reported in the manual for the full test. One-week test-retest reliabilities ranging from .72 to .91, and interrater reliabilities from .87 to .98, are reported for the five subscales. The source of these reliability estimates is not explained.

The manual reports, without further explanation, that "content validity was determined through a careful process of test construction and item selection." Concurrent validity is reported to have been determined by a discriminant analysis yielding a match of 90% accuracy between EARLY assessment results and 3 hours of diagnostic testing. Predictive validity is described as "currently the focus of a longitudinal study." No further psychometric information is provided in the manual.

SUPPLEMENTAL ARTICLES. I decided to brave the barely legible text of the two available papers to try to obtain more information on reliability and validity. The first thing I noticed was that the Naron (1978) article refers to the assessment as a "screening test," and that the work she reports is consistent with this orientation as opposed to an orientation appropriate to the more ambitious advertised purpose of the test. A validation study based on a sample of 140 children is described. A 3-hour diagnostic battery was administered along with the EARLY, and children were classified into groups of normal versus learning disabled based on the diagnostic testing. Using a series of discriminant analysis comparisons with the EARLY items as dependent variables, the author concludes that 18 learning disabled children were identified with over 90% accuracy by the EARLY. A factor analysis also is reported, yielding four factors which roughly overlap with the five subscales. A strained explanation is given to try to tie these results into the actual structure of the test items.

In the Perlman, et al. (1981) article I learned that the coefficient alpha estimate reported in the manual was based on a sample of 160 Chicago school children, and that individual subtest alphas range from an unimpressive .56 for Visual Discrimination to a more adequate .86 for Language. The paper also indicates that the test-retest and interrater reliability estimates were based on samples of 57 and 61 children respectively. The validity analyses examined predictability, by the EARLY, of achievement tests, teacher ratings, and special education referral at ages 5 through 8. This involved a series of regressions that unfortunately contain a number of serious design flaws. For example, subtest scores and two versions of the total score were all evaluated simultaneously as independent variables in the same equations. The authors concluded that "the EARLY Assessment definitely has some validity in predicting later school learning problems." Depending on how one defines "some validity," this interpretation of the reported results is at best unedifying and at worst unfounded.

SUMMARY. The EARLY manual inadequately addresses the topics of reliability and validity. The two supplemental articles present a variety of complex and poorly applied statistical analyses, which provide little evidence the test is valid for its stated purpose (profiling developmental skills predictive of later functioning). These analyses tend to be the wrong techniques, set up in the wrong ways, to answer the wrong questions. A straightforward examination of the appropriate validity issues is missing. At the same time the reliability analyses are disappointingly minimal, especially given the availability of the much larger samples used in determining norms.

Somewhere during its developmental course the advertised mission of this test grew from a gross screening device to a comprehensive assessment tied to a full remediation curriculum. The original intent may or may not be appropriate; the more ambitious one clearly is not. Early childhood teachers seeking developmental criteria with which to compare their students would be better served by the Battelle Developmental Inventory (10:25; Newborg, Stock, Wnek, Guidubaldi, & Svinicki, 1984), or the Brigance Diagnostic Inventory of Early Development (9:164; Brigance, 1978).

REVIEWER'S REFERENCES

Brigance, A. H. (1978). Brigance Diagnostic Inventory of Early Development. North Billerica, MA: Curriculum Associates, Inc.

Naron, N. K. (1978, November). A tested approach to the prediction and treatment of learning disabilities at a preschool level. In T. Rowland & T. Lovitt (Eds.), Proceedings of the Second National Invitational Conference on Communication Research in Mental Retardation and Learning Disabilities. Monmouth, OR: Oregon College of Education.

Perlman, C. L., Naron, N. K., Hiestand, N. I., & Sarther, C. M. (1981, April). Chicago EARLY program followup: A longitudinal analysis. Paper presented at the annual meeting of the American Educational Research Association, Los Angeles.

Newborg, J., Stock, J. R., Wnek, L., Guidubaldi, J., & Svinicki, J. (1984). Battelle Developmental Inventory. Allen, TX: DLM Teaching Resources.

Review of the Chicago Early Assessment and Remediation LaboratorY by MARGARET ROGERS WIESE, Assistant Professor of School Psychology, Appalachian State University, Boone, NC:

DESCRIPTION. The Chicago Early Assessment and Remediation LaboratorY (EARLY), developed by the Chicago Public Schools, is an individually administered screening device designed to identify potential learning disabilities in children between the ages of 3 and 6. An instructional package, designed for children between 3–5, is also included and covers 194 behavioral objectives. The test consists of 23 items which cluster into five skill areas: Language, Memory, Visual Discrimination, Fine Motor, and Gross Motor and yields subtest scores for each area. Raw scores for each subtest are translated into percentile ranks based on the child's age. These scores are used to guide instructional grouping decisions. The test is available in English and Spanish versions and takes between 15–20 minutes to administer.

TEST ADMINISTRATION. Directions for administering and scoring the test items are included in the assessment manual. For each item, standardized directions for the child are set apart from those that are specific to the examiner by capital letters and underlining. This format is somewhat unclear. Color coding directions intended for the child would be an improvement.

Test materials contained in a large red plastic carrying case include a set of eight crayons, three plastic jars, puzzles, one open-ended box, a variety of blocks, one soft beanbag, a drawing pad, and one zippered pouch. Also included are six sets of stimulus cards, each used as a different test item. The pictures depicted in the cards are rather bland, represented on a white background, and outlined in black. Colorized versions of these cards would greatly improve their presentation. Another point concerning these cards is the stimulus side of the card depicts not only the stimulus, but also copyright data and the subtest title and number. This information could have been listed on the back of the card and would have allowed for a cleaner stimulus presentation.

There appear to be relatively minor problems in the test administration guidelines. For example, examiners are encouraged to maintain a neutral stance by making nonevaluative comments regarding test performance. However, the examiner is also instructed to say "good," a positively evaluative comment, to the child after task completion. These conflicting directions are confusing. Test materials may be used as toys before the test proper in order to improve rapport. I would suggest examiners avoid contaminating test responses by using nontest toys (as needed) prior to the test administration.

Classroom summary sheets, individual scoring sheets, and individual progress sheets are provided separately for the examiner's use. A social/emotional checklist is also provided but no explanation for this index was located in the test manual. Scoring items requires simple computations and minor numerical manipulations. Subtest raw scores are based on only three to eight tasks, suggesting there may be too few items for each subtest to insure reliability. Also, a review of the conversion tables suggests minute differences in raw scores translate into large differences in percentile ranks. In interpreting student performance, a subtest score of 30% is the cutoff for decisions regarding referrals for remedial activities but no explanation is provided for how this cutoff was determined.

TECHNICAL DATA. Technical information is provided as a one-page summary in the manual. Under separate cover, the publisher supplied articles containing test development, reliability, and validity information. All technical psychometric information relevant to the test should be included in the manual. The test development process began in 1976 in Chicago with field testing of 1,900 urban preschoolers ranging in age from 3 to 5 years. The composition of that group was 54% Black, 30% White, 11% Hispanic, and 5% other. Further field testing was performed in 1982 on 500 5- to 6-year-old children but information regarding the racial/ethnic composition of this group was not reported. Males and females were equally represented during the 1976 field testing. A review of the norm tables suggests that the number of children at each age level was not evenly distributed. Item selection was based on a review of the literature. Parts of the data collected during field testing were factor analysed suggesting the existence of four underlying factors. Despite these results, the test items are arranged into five subtests.

Reliability data were compiled by studies employing about 160 3–4-year-olds. Based on these studies, coefficient alphas are reported for each of the five subtests (ranging from .56 to .86) as well as for the total scale (.89). Test-retest reliabilities for the five subtests over a 1-week period ranged from .72 to .91. Further reliability data concerning 5- and 6-year-olds are also needed. Evidence of predictive validity is provided. No data regarding the standard error of measurement are provided although this information is needed.

REMEDIAL ACTIVITIES. An important component of this program is the EARLY instructional activities that were designed to remediate specific skill weaknesses identified by the EARLY assessment and to supplement the regular preschool curriculum. The EARLY instructional package covers 194 skills representing three major skill areas: language, body image/gross motor, and perceptual motor/arithmetic. Each of these skills has been sequentially ordered and painstakingly operationalized with task objectives, recommended teaching procedures, teaching materials, and criterion for task success clearly specified.

SUMMARY. The purpose of the EARLY assessment and instructional program is to assess potential learning disabilities and provide remedial assistance to preschool children with skill deficits. This instrument has been regionally normed with an urban preschool and kindergarten population. Caution needs to be exercised in using this instrument for populations that depart from the norming group. The strengths of the program include the multicultural orientation with test instructions in Spanish and English versions, the structure and high degree of specificity of the instructional materials, and the preliminary predictive validity data. Weaknesses of the program relate to the lack of content validity information regarding test development and item selection, limited sample sizes used to gather reliability information, and small number of test items. Overall, before this instrument can be recommended for use, more information is needed regarding its reliability and validity.

[64]
Child Behavior Checklist.

Purpose: To assess the competencies and problems of children and adolescents through the use of ratings and reports by different informants.
Population: Ages 4–18.
Publication Dates: 1980–88.
Price Data, 1989: $25 per 100 Child Behavior Checklists (specify Ages 2–3 or Ages 4–16); $25 per 100 CBCL profiles (specify level); $5 per CBCL scoring template (specify level); $25 per 100 Teacher Report Forms; $25 per 100 TRF profiles; $5 per TRF template; $25 per 100 Youth Self-Report Forms; $25 per 100 YSR profiles; $25 per 100 Direct Observation Forms; $18 per CBCL manual ('83, 243 pages); $18 per TRF manual ('86, 205 pages); $18 per YSR manual ('87, 222 pages); computer programs available for computer scoring and profiling.
Comments: Behavior checklists; forms available as separates.
Authors: Thomas M. Achenbach and Craig Edelbrock.
Publisher: Thomas M. Achenbach, Ph.D.
  a) CHILD BEHAVIOR CHECKLIST.
  Purpose: "To record in a standardized format the behavioral problems and competencies of children . . . as reported by their parents or others who know the child well."
  Comments: Ratings by parents.
    1) *Ages 2–3.*
    Population: Ages 2–3.
    Publication Dates: 1986–88.
    Acronym: CBCL/2–3.
    Scores: 6 scales: Social Withdrawal, Depressed, Sleep Problems, Somatic Problems, Aggressive, Destructive.
    Time: (15) minutes.
    2) *Ages 4–16.*
    Population: Ages 4–16.
    Publication Dates: 1980–83.
    Acronym: CBCL/4–16.
    Parts: 6 profiles: Boys Aged 4–5, 6–11, 12–16; Girls Aged 4–5, 6–11, 12–16.
    Scores: 13 to 14 scores depending on profile used: Boys Aged 4–5 Profile: Behavior Problems (Internalizing, Externalizing, Social Withdrawal, Depressed, Immature, Somatic Complaints, Sex Problems, Schizoid, Aggressive, Delinquent), Social Competence (Activities, Social, School); Boys Aged 6–11 Profile: Behavior Problems (Internalizing, Externalizing, Schizoid or Anxious, Depressed, Uncommunicative, Obsessive-Compulsive, Somatic Complaints, Social Withdrawal, Hyperactive, Aggressive, Delinquent), Social Competence scores same as above; Boys Aged 12–16 Profile: Behavior Problems (Internalizing, Externalizing, Somatic Complaints, Schizoid, Uncommunicative, Immature, Obsessive-Compulsive, Hostile Withdrawal, Delinquent, Aggressive, Hyperactive), Social Competence scores same as above; Girls Aged 4–5 Profile: Behavior Problems (Internalizing, Externalizing, Somatic Complaints, Depressed,

Schizoid or Anxious, Social Withdrawal, Obese, Aggressive, Sex Problems, Hyperactive), Social Competence scores same as above; Girls Aged 6–11 Profile: Behavior Problems (Internalizing, Externalizing, Depressed, Social Withdrawal, Somatic Complaints, Schizoid-Obsessive, Hyperactive, Sex Problems, Delinquent, Aggressive, Cruel), Social Competence scores same as above; Girls Aged 12–16 Profile: Behavior Problems (Internalizing, Externalizing, Anxious Obsessive, Somatic Complaints, Schizoid, Depressed Withdrawal, Immature Hyperactive, Delinquent, Aggressive, Cruel), Social Competence scores same as above.

Time: (15) minutes.

b) TEACHER'S REPORT FORM.

Purpose: "To obtain teachers' reports of their pupils' problems and adaptive functioning in a standardized format."

Population: Ages 6–16.

Publication Dates: 1982–86.

Acronym: TRF.

Forms: 4 profiles: Boys Aged 6–11, 12–16; Girls Aged 6–11, 12–16.

Scores: 16 to 17 scores depending on profile used: Boys Aged 6–11 Profile: Behavior Problems (Internalizing, Externalizing, Anxious, Social Withdrawal, Unpopular, Self-Destructive, Obsessive-Compulsive, Inattentive, Nervous-Overactive, Aggressive), Adaptive Functioning (School Performance, Working Hard, Behaving Appropriately, Learning, Happy, Sum of Items); Boys Aged 12–16 Profile: Behavior Problems (Internalizing, Externalizing, Social Withdrawal, Anxious, Unpopular, Obsessive-Compulsive, Immature, Self-Destructive, Inattentive, Aggressive), Adaptive Functioning scores same as above; Girls Aged 6–11 Profile: Behavior Problems (Internalizing, Externalizing, Anxious, Social Withdrawal, Depressed, Unpopular, Self-Destructive, Inattentive, Nervous-Overactive, Aggressive), Adaptive Functioning scores same as above; Girls Aged 12–16 Profile: Behavior Problems (Internalizing, Externalizing, Anxious, Social Withdrawal, Depressed, Immature, Self-Destructive, Inattentive, Unpopular, Delinquent, Aggressive), Adaptive Functioning scores same as above.

Time: (15) minutes.

Comments: Ratings by teachers.

c) YOUTH SELF-REPORT.

Purpose: "To obtain 11- to 18-year-olds' reports of their own competencies and problems in a standardized format."

Population: Ages 11–18.

Publication Dates: 1983–87.

Acronym: YSR.

Forms: 2 profiles: Boys Aged 11–18, Girls Aged 11–18.

Scores: 10 to 11 scores depending on profile used: Boys Aged 11–18 Profile: Problem Scales (Internalizing, Externalizing, Depressed, Unpopular, Somatic Complaints, Self-Destructive/Identity Problems, Thought Disorder, Delinquent, Aggressive), Competence Scales (Activities, Social); Girls Aged 11–18 Profile: Problem Scales (Somatic Complaints, Depressed, Unpopular, Thought Disorder, Aggressive, Delinquent), Competence Scale scores same as above.

Time: (15) minutes.

Comments: Ratings by self.

d) DIRECT OBSERVATION FORM.

Purpose: "To obtain direct observational data in situations such as school classrooms, lunchrooms, recess, and group activities."

Population: Ages 4–16.

Publication Date: 1981.

Acronym: DOF.

Scores, 10: Behavior Problems, Internalizing, Externalizing, Withdrawn-Inattentive, Nervous-Obsessive, Depressed, Hyperactive, Attention-Demanding, Aggressive, On-Task Behavior.

Time: (10) minutes for each observation period.

Comments: Ratings by trained observer.

Cross References: For additional information and reviews by B. J. Freeman and Mary Lou Kelley, see 9:213 (5 references). [The following reviews pertain to the Teacher's Report Form and Youth Self-Report. The CBCL/4–16 and Direct Observation Form were reviewed in an earlier *MMY*. The CBCL/2–3 will be reviewed at a future time.—Ed.]

TEST REFERENCES

1. Larson, C. P., & Lapointe, Y. (1986). The health status of mild to moderate intellectually handicapped adolescents. *Journal of Mental Deficiency Research, 30,* 121-128.
2. Aram, D. M., Ekelman, B. L., & Nation, J. E. (1984). Preschoolers with language disorders: 10 years later. *Journal of Speech and Hearing Research, 27,* 232-244.
3. Bond, C. R., & McMahon, R. J. (1984). Relationships between marital distress and child behavior problems, maternal personal adjustment, maternal personality, and maternal parenting behavior. *Journal of Abnormal Psychology, 93,* 348-351.
4. Dishion, T. J., Loeber, R., Stouthamer-Loeber, M., & Patterson, G. R. (1984). Skill deficits and male adolescent delinquency. *Journal of Abnormal Child Psychology, 12,* 37-54.
5. Emery, R. E., & O'Leary, K. D. (1984). Marital discord and child behavior problems in a nonclinic sample. *Journal of Abnormal Child Psychology, 12,* 411-420.
6. Feinstein, C., Blouin, A. G., Egan, J., & Conners, C. K. (1984). Depressive symptomatology in a child psychiatric outpatient population: Correlations with diagnosis. *Comprehensive Psychiatry, 25,* 379-391.
7. Ferrari, M. (1984). Chronic illness: Psychosocial effects on siblings—I. Chronically ill boys. *The Journal of Child Psychology and Psychiatry and Allied Disciplines, 25,* 459-476.
8. Garbarino, J., Sebes, J., & Schellenbach, C. (1984). Families at risk for destructive parent-child relations in adolescence. *Child Development, 55,* 174-183.
9. Garrison, W., Earls, F., & Kindlon, D. (1984). Temperament characteristics in the third year of life and behavioral adjustment at school entry. *Journal of Clinical Child Psychology, 13,* 298-303.
10. Gordon, M., Post, E. M., Crouthamel, C., & Richman, R. A. (1984). Do children with constitutional delay really have more learning problems? *Journal of Learning Disabilities, 17,* 291-293.
11. Kazdin, A. E., & Heidish, I. E. (1984). Convergence of clinically derived diagnoses and parent checklists among inpatient children. *Journal of Abnormal Child Psychology, 12,* 421-436.
12. Kazdin, A. E., Matson, J. L., Esveldt-Dawson, K. (1984). The relationship of role-play assessment of children's social skills to multiple measures of social competence. *Behaviour Research and Therapy, 22,* 129-139.
13. Kendall, P. C., & Fischler, G. L. (1984). Behavioral and adjustment correlates of problem solving: Validational analyses of interpersonal cognitive problem-solving measures. *Child Development, 55,* 879-892.
14. Loeber, R., & Dishion, T. J. (1984). Boys who fight at home and school: Family conditions influencing cross-setting consistency. *Journal of Consulting and Clinical Psychology, 52,* 759-768.
15. Rosenberg, L. A., Harris, J. C., & Singer, H. S. (1984). Relationship of the Child Behavior Checklist to an independent measure of psychopathology. *Psychological Reports, 54,* 427-430.
16. Seagull, E. A. W., & Weinshank, A. B. (1984). Childhood depression in a selected group of low-achieving seventh-graders. *Journal of Clinical Child Psychology, 13,* 134-140.

17. Stiffman, A. R., Feldman, R. A., & Evans, D. A. (1984). Children's activities and their behavior: Are activities worth manipulating? *Child Psychiatry and Human Development, 14*, 187-199.

18. Telzrow, C. F. (1984). Practical applications of the K-ABC in the identification of handicapped preschoolers. *The Journal of Special Education, 18*, 311-324.

19. Walker, E., Bettes, B., & Ceci, S. (1984). Teachers' assumptions regarding the severity, causes, and outcomes of behavioral problems in preschoolers: Implications for referral. *Journal of Consulting and Clinical Psychology, 52*, 899-902.

20. Webster-Stratton, C. (1984). Predictors of treatment outcome in parent training for conduct disordered children. *Behavior Therapy, 16*, 223-243.

21. Webster-Stratton, C. (1984). Randomized trial of two parent-training programs for families with conduct disordered children. *Journal of Consulting and Clinical Psychology, 52*, 666-678.

22. Cantrell, V. L., & Prinz, R. J. (1985). Multiple perspectives of rejected, neglected, and accepted children: Relation between sociometric and behavioral characteristics. *Journal of Consulting and Clinical Psychology, 53*, 884-889.

23. Cohen, N. J., Gotlieb, H., Kershner, J., & Wehrspann, W. (1985). Concurrent validity of the internalizing and externalizing profile patterns of the Achenbach Child Behavior Checklist. *Journal of Consulting and Clinical Psychology, 53*, 724-728.

24. Cooley, E. J., & Ayres, R. (1985). Convergent and discriminant validity of the mental processing scales of the Kaufman Assessment Battery for Children. *Psychology in the Schools, 22*, 373-377.

25. Costello, E. J., Edelbrock, C. S., & Costello, A. J. (1985). Validity of the NIMH Diagnostic Interview Schedule for Children: A comparison between psychiatric and pediatric referrals. *Journal of Abnormal Child Psychology, 13*, 579-595.

26. Dulcan, M. K., & Piercy, P. A. (1985). A model for teaching and evaluating brief psychotherapy with children and their families. *Professional Psychology: Research and Practice, 16*, 689-700.

27. French, D. C., & Waas, G. A. (1985). Behavior problems of peer-neglected and peer-rejected elementary-age children: Parent and teacher perspectives. *Child Development, 56*, 246-252.

28. French, D. C., & Waas, G. A. (1985). Teachers' ability to identify peer-rejected children: A comparison of sociometrics and teacher ratings. *Journal of School Psychology, 23*, 347-353.

29. Hasselt, V. B. V., Hersen, M., & Kazdin, A. E. (1985). Assessment of social skills in visually-handicapped adolescents. *Behaviour Research and Therapy, 23*, 53-63.

30. Heath, G. A., Hardesty, V. A., Goldfine, P. E., & Walker, A. M. (1985). Diagnosis and childhood firesetting. *Journal of Clinical Psychology, 41*, 571-575.

31. Janos, P. M., Fung, H. C., & Robinson, N. M. (1985). Self-concept, self-esteem, and peer relations among gifted children who feel "different." *Gifted Child Quarterly, 29*, 78-82.

32. Kolko, D. J., Kazdin, A. E., & Meyer, E. C. (1985). Aggression and psychopathology in childhood firesetters: Parent and child reports. *Journal of Consulting and Clinical Psychology, 53*, 377-385.

33. Last, J. M., & Bruhn, A. R. (1985). Distinguishing child diagnostic types with early memories. *Journal of Personality Assessment, 49*, 187-192.

34. McConaughy, S. H. (1985). Using the Child Behavior Checklist and related instruments in school-based assessment of children. *School Psychology Review, 14*, 479-494.

35. McConaughy, S. H., & Ritter, D. R. (1985). Social competence and behavioral problems of learning disabled boys aged 6-11. *Journal of Learning Disabilities, 18*, 547-553.

36. Resnick, G. (1985). Enhancing parental competencies for high risk mothers: An evaluation of prevention effects. *Child Abuse & Neglect, 9*, 479-489.

37. Stolberg, A. L., & Garrison, K. M. (1985). Evaluating a primary prevention program for children of divorce. *American Journal of Community Psychology, 13*, 111-124.

38. Webster-Stratton, C. (1985). Comparison of abusive and nonabusive families with conduct-disordered children. *American Journal of Orthopsychiatry, 55*, 59-69.

39. Webster-Stratton, C. (1985). The effects of father involvement in parent training for conduct problem children. *The Journal of Child Psychology and Psychiatry and Allied Disciplines, 26*, 801-810.

40. Wolfe, D. A., Jaffe, P., Wilson, S. K., & Zak, L. (1985). Children of battered women: The relation of child behavior to family violence and maternal stress. *Journal of Consulting and Clinical Psychology, 53*, 657-665.

41. Wood, B. (1985). Proximity and hierarchy: Orthogonal dimensions of family interconnectedness. *Family Process, 24*, 487-507.

42. Campbell, S. B., Breaux, A. M., Ewing, L. J., & Szumowski, E. K. (1986). Correlates and predictors of hyperactivity and aggression: A longitudinal study of parent-referred problem preschoolers. *Journal of Abnormal Child Psychology, 14*, 217-234.

43. Campbell, S. B., Ewing, L. J., Breaux, A. M., & Szumowski, E. K. (1986). Parent-referred problem three-year-olds: Follow-up at school

entry. *Journal of Child Psychology and Psychiatry and Allied Disciplines, 27*, 473-488.

44. Davis, J. M., Elfenbein, J., Schum, R., & Bentler, R. A. (1986). Effects of mild and moderate hearing impairments on language, educational, and psychosocial behavior of children. *Journal of Speech and Hearing Disorders, 51*, 53-62.

45. Dodge, K. A. (1986). A social information processing model of social competence in children. *The Minnesota Symposia on Child Psychology, 18*, 77-125.

46. Dodge, K. A., Petit, G. S., McClaskey, C. L., & Brown, M. M. (1986). Social competence in children with commentary by John M. Gottman. *Monographs of the Society for Research in Child Development, 51* (2, Serial No. 213).

47. Elander, G., Nilsson, A., & Lindberg, T. (1986). Behavior in four-year-olds who have experienced hospitalization and day care. *American Journal of Orthopsychiatry, 56*, 612-616.

48. Friedlander, S., Weiss, D. S., & Traylor, J. (1986). Assessing the influence of maternal depression on the validity of the Child Behavior Checklist. *Journal of Abnormal Child Psychology, 14*, 123-133.

49. Fuhrman, M. J., & Kendall, P. C. (1986). Cognitive tempo and behavioral adjustment in children. *Cognitive Therapy and Research, 10*, 45-50.

50. Guidubaldi, J., Cleminshaw, H. K., Perry, J. D., Nastasi, B. K., & Lightel, J. (1986). The role of selected family environment factors in children's post-divorce adjustment. *Family Relations, 35*, 141-151.

51. Hoge, R. D., & McKay, V. (1986). Criterion-related validity data for the Child Behavior Checklist—Teacher's Report Form. *Journal of School Psychology, 24*, 387-393.

52. Jacob, T., & Leonard, K. (1986). Psychosocial functioning in children of alcoholic fathers, depressed fathers and control fathers. *Journal of Studies on Alcohol, 47*, 373-380.

53. Jaffe, P., Wolfe, D., Wilson, S. K., & Zak, L. (1986). Family violence and child adjustment: A comparative analysis of girls' and boys' behavioral symptoms. *American Journal of Psychiatry, 143*, 74-77.

54. Jaffe, P., Wolfe, D., Wilson, S., & Zak, L. (1986). Similarities in behavioral and social maladjustment among child victims and witnessess to family violence. *American Journal of Orthopsychiatry, 56*, 142-146.

55. Kazdin, A. E., & Kolko, D. J. (1986). Parent psychopathology and family functioning among childhood firesetters. *Journal of Abnormal Child Psychology, 14*, 315-329.

56. Kazdin, A. E., Colbus, D., & Rodgers, A. (1986). Assessment of depression and diagnosis of depressive disorder among psychiatrically disturbed children. *Journal of Abnormal Child Psychology, 14*, 499-515.

57. Kazdin, A. E., Rodgers, A., & Colbus, D. (1986). The Hopelessness Scale for Children: Psychometric characteristics and concurrent validity. *Journal of Consulting and Clinical Psychology, 54*, 241-245.

58. Kendall, P. C. (1986). Comments on Rubin and Krasnor: Solutions and problems in research on problem solving. *The Minnesota Symposia on Child Psychology, 18*, 69-76.

59. Li, A. K. F. (1986). Low peer interaction in kindergarten children: An ecological perspective. *Journal of Clinical Child Psychology, 15*, 26-29.

60. McConaughy, S. H. (1986). Social competence and behavioral problems of learning disabled boys aged 12-16. *Journal of Learning Disabilities, 119*, 101-106.

61. McConaughy, S. H., & Ritter, D. R. (1986). Social competence and behavioral problems of learning disabled boys aged 6-11. *Journal of Learning Disabilities, 19*, 39-45.

62. McIntyre, A., & Keesler, T. Y. (1986). Psychological disorders among foster children. *Journal of Clinical Child Psychology, 15*, 297-303.

63. Nussbaum, N. L., & Bigler, E. D. (1986). Neuropsychological and behavioral profiles of empirically derived subgroups of learning disabled children. *Clinical Neuropsychology, 8*, 82-89.

64. Nussbaum, N. L., Bigler, E. D., & Koch, W. (1986). Neuropsychologically derived subgroups of learning disabled children: Personality/behavioral dimensions. *Journal of Learning Disabilities, 19*, 57-67.

65. Patterson, G. R., & Bank, L. (1986). Bootstrapping your way in the nomological thicket. *Behavioral Assessment, 8*, 49-73.

66. Pianta, R. C., Egeland, B., & Hyatt, A. (1986). Maternal relationship history as an indicator of developmental risk. *American Journal of Orthopsychiatry, 56*, 385-398.

67. Rosenberg, L. A., & Joshi, P. (1986). Effect of marital discord on parental reports on the Child Behavior Checklist. *Psychological Reports, 59*, 1255-1259.

68. Shiller, V. M. (1986). Joint versus maternal custody for families with latency age boys: Parent characteristics and child adjustment. *American Journal of Orthopsychiatry, 56*, 486-489.

69. Shoemaker, O. S., Erickson, M. T., & Finch, A. J., Jr. (1986). Depression and anger in third- and fourth-grade boys: A multimethod assessment approach. *Journal of Clinical Child Psychology, 15*, 290-296.

70. Stiffman, A. R., Jung, K. G., & Feldman, R. A. (1986). A multivariate risk model for childhood behavior problems. *American Journal of Orthopsychiatry, 56*, 204-211.

71. Stouthamer-Loeber, M., & Loeber, R. (1986). Boys who lie. *Journal of Abnormal Child Psychology, 14*, 551-564.

72. Tharinger, D. J., Laurent, J., & Best, L. R. (1986). Classification of children referred for emotional and behavioral problems: A comparison of PL 94-142 SED criteria, DSM III, and the CBCL system. *Journal of School Psychology, 24*, 111-121.

73. Van Hasselt, V. B., Kazdin, A. E., & Hersen, M. (1986). Assessment of problem behavior in visually handicapped adolescents. *Journal of Clinical Child Psychology, 15*, 134-141.

74. Weisz, J. R. (1986). Contingency and control beliefs as predictors of psychotherapy outcomes among children and adolescents. *Journal of Consulting and Clinical Psychology, 54*, 789-795.

75. Wolfe, D. A., Zak, L., Wilson, S., & Jaffe, P. (1986). Child witnesses to violence between parents: Critical issues in behavioral and social adjustment. *Journal of Abnormal Child Psychology, 14*, 95-104.

76. Yu, P., Harris, G. E., Solovitz, B. L., & Franklin, J. L. (1986). A social problem-solving intervention for children at high risk for later psychopathology. *Journal of Clinical Child Psychology, 15*, 30-40.

77. Achenbach, T. M., Verhulst, F. C., Baron, G. D., & Althaus, M. (1987). A comparison of syndromes derived from the Child Behavior Checklist for American and Dutch boys aged 6-11 and 12-16. *Journal of Child Psychology and Psychiatry and Allied Disciplines, 28*, 437-453.

78. Bathurst, K., & Gottfried, A. W. (1987). Untestable subjects in child development research: Developmental implications. *Child Development, 58*, 1135-1144.

79. Bierman, K. L., & McCauley, E. (1987). Children's descriptions of their peer interactions: Useful information for clinical child assessment. *Journal of Clinical Child Psychology, 16*, 9-18.

80. Burke, A. E., Solotar, L. C., Silverman, W. K., & Israel, A. C. (1987). Assessing children's and adults' expectations for child self-control. *Journal of Clinical Child Psychology, 16*, 37-42.

81. Campbell, S. B. (1987). Parent-referred problem three-year-olds: Developmental changes in symptoms. *Journal of Child Psychology and Psychiatry and Allied Disciplines, 28*, 835-845.

82. Capaldi, D., & Patterson, G. R. (1987). An approach to the problem of recruitment and retention rates for longitudinal research. *Behavioral Assessment, 9*, 169-177.

83. Christopoulos, C., Cohn, D. A., Shaw, D. S., Joyce, S., Sullivan-Hanson, J., Kraft, S. P., & Emery, R. E. (1987). Children of abused women: I. Adjustment at time of shelter residence. *Journal of Marriage and the Family, 49*, 611-619.

84. Concept Scale (The Way I Feel About Myself): Tong, L., Oates, K., & McDowell, M. (1987). Personality development following sexual abuse. *Child Abuse & Neglect, 11*, 371-383.

85. Hanson, C. L., Henggeler, S. W., & Burghen, G. A. (1987). Social competence and parental support as mediators of the link between stress and metabolic control in adolescents with insulin-dependent diabetes mellitus. *Journal of Consulting and Clinical Psychology, 55*, 529-533.

86. Johnston, J. R., Gonzalez, R., & Campbell, L. E. G. (1987). Ongoing postdivorce conflict and child disturbance. *Journal of Abnormal Child Psychology, 15*, 493-509.

87. Kashani, J. H., Shekim, W. O., Burk, J. P., & Beck, N. C. (1987). Abuse as a predictor of psychopathology in children and adolescents. *Journal of Clinical Child Psychology, 16*, 43-50.

88. Kazdin, A. E. (1987). Children's Depression Scale: Validation with child psychiatric inpatients. *Journal of Child Psychology and Psychiatry and Allied Disciplines, 28*, 29-41.

89. Kazdin, A. E., Esveldt-Dawson, K., French, N. H., & Unis, A. S. (1987). Problem-solving skills training and relationship therapy in the treatment of antisocial child behavior. *Journal of Consulting and Clinical Psychology, 55*, 76-85.

90. Kazdin, A. E., Rodgers, A., Colbus, D., & Siegel, T. (1987). Children's Hostility Inventory: Measurement of aggression and hostility in psychiatric inpatient children. *Journal of Clinical Child Psychology, 16*, 320-328.

91. Kurdek, L. A., & Berg, B. (1987). Children's Beliefs About Parental Divorce Scale: Psychometric characteristics and concurrent validity. *Journal of Consulting and Clinical Psychology, 55*, 712-718.

92. Lobato, D., Barbour, L., Hall, L. J., & Miller, C. T. (1987). Psychosocial characteristics of preschool siblings of handicapped and nonhandicapped children. *Journal of Abnormal Child Psychology, 15*, 329-338.

93. McCauley, E., Kay, T., Ito, J., & Treder, R. (1987). The turner syndrome: Cognitive deficits, affective discrimination, and behavior problems. *Child Development, 58*, 464-473.

94. Mooney, K. C., Thompson, R., & Nelson, J. M. (1987). Risk factors and the Child Behavior Checklist in a child mental health center setting. *Journal of Abnormal Child Psychology, 15*, 67-73.

95. O'Brien Towle, P., & Schwarz, J. C. (1987). The Child Behavior Checklist as applied to archival data: Factor structure and external correlates. *Journal of Clinical Child Psychology, 16*, 69-79.

96. Reich, W., & Earls, F. (1987). Rules for making psychiatric diagnoses in children on the basis of multiple sources of information: Preliminary strategies. *Journal of Abnormal Child Psychology, 15*, 601-616.

97. Reid, J. B., Kavanagh, K., & Baldwin, D. V. (1987). Abusive parents' perceptions of child problem behaviors: An example of parental bias. *Journal of Abnormal Child Psychology, 15*, 457-466.

98. Rey, J. M., Plapp, J. M., Stewart, G., Richards, I., & Bashir, M. (1987). Reliability of the psychosocial axes of DSM-III in an adolescent population. *The British Journal of Psychiatry, 150*, 228-234.

99. Rovet, J., Ehrlich, R., & Hoppe, M. (1987). Behaviour problems in children with diabetes as a function of sex and age of onset of disease. *Journal of Child Psychology and Psychiatry and Allied Disciplines, 28*, 477-491.

100. Shaw, D. S., & Emery, R. E. (1987). Parental conflict and other correlates of the adjustment of school-age children whose parents have separated. *Journal of Abnormal Child Psychology, 15*, 269-281.

101. Sollee, N. D., & Kindlon, D. J. (1987). Lateralized brain injury and behavior problems in children. *Journal of Abnormal Child Psychology, 15*, 479-490.

102. Stark, K. D., Reynolds, W. M., & Kaslow, N. J. (1987). A comparison of the relative efficacy of self-control therapy and a behavioral problem-solving therapy for depression in children. *Journal of Abnormal Child Psychology, 15*, 91-113.

103. Susman, E. J., Inoff-Germain, G., Nottelmann, E. D., Loriaux, D. L., Cutler, G. B., Jr., & Chrousos, G. P. (1987). Hormones, emotional dispositions, and aggressive attributes in young adolescents. *Child Development, 58*, 1114-1134.

104. Weisz, J. R., Suwanlert, S., Chaiyasit, W., & Walter, B. R. (1987). Over- and undercontrolled referral problems among children and adolescents from Thailand and the United States: The *Wat* and *Wai* of cultural differences. *Journal of Consulting and Clinical Psychology, 55*, 719-726.

105. Weisz, J. R., Weiss, B., & Langmeyer, D. B. (1987). Giving up on child psychotherapy: Who drops out? *Journal of Consulting and Clinical Psychology, 55*, 916-918.

106. Wertlieb, D., Weigel, C., & Feldstein, M. (1987). Stress, social support, and behavior symptoms in middle childhood. *Journal of Clinical Child Psychology, 16*, 204-211.

107. Wolfe, V. V., Finch, A. J., Jr., Saylor, C. F., Blount, R. L., Pallmeyer, T. P., & Carek, D. J. (1987). Negative affectivity in children: A multitrait-multimethod investigation. *Journal of Consulting and Clinical Psychology, 55*, 245-250.

108. Angold, A. (1988). Childhood and adolescent depression: I. Epidemiological and aetiological aspects. *British Journal of Psychiatry, 152*, 601-617.

109. Asarnow, J. R. (1988). Peer status and social competence in child psychiatric inpatients: A comparison of children with depressive, externalizing, and concurrent depressive and externalizing disorders. *Journal of Abnormal Child Psychology, 16*, 151-162.

110. Barkley, R. A., Fischer, M., Newby, R. F., & Breen, M. J. (1988). Development of a multimethod clinical protocol for assessing stimulant drug response in children with attention deficit disorder. *Journal of Clinical Child Psychology, 17*, 14-24.

111. Bodiford, C. A., Eisenstadt, T. H., Johnson, J. H., & Bradlyn, A. S. (1988). Comparison of learned helpless cognitions and behavior in children with high and low scores on the Children's Depression Inventory. *Journal of Clinical Child Psychology, 17*, 152-158.

112. Cohen, J. A., & Mannarino, A. P. (1988). Psychological symptoms in sexually abused girls. *Child Abuse & Neglect, 12*, 571-577.

113. Edelbrock, C., & Costello, A. J. (1988). Convergence between statistically derived behavior problem syndromes and child psychiatric diagnoses. *Journal of Abnormal Child Psychology, 16*, 219-231.

114. Evenson, R. C., Frankel, M. T., Sirles, E. A., & Parsons, R. (1988). Factor structure for Child Behavior Checklist scores of young boys in St. Louis. *Psychological Reports, 63*, 279-282.

115. Finch, A. J., Jr., Blount, R., Saylor, C. F., Wolfe, V. V., Pallmeyer, T. P., McIntosh, J. A., Griffin, J. M., & Carek, D. J. (1988). Intelligence and emotional/behavioral factors as correlates of achievement in child psychiatric inpatients. *Psychological Reports, 63*, 163-170.

116. Gordon, M., Diniro, D., & Mettelman, B. B. (1988). Effect upon outcome of nuances in selection criteria for ADHD/hyperactivity. *Psychological Reports, 62*, 539-544.

117. Kashani, J. H., Barbero, G. J., Wilfley, D. E., Morris, D. A., & Shepperd, J. A. (1988). Psychological concomitants of cystic fibrosis in children and adolescents. *Adolescence, 23*, 873-880.

118. Lewin, L., Hops, H., Aubuschon, A., & Budinger, T. (1988). Predictors of maternal satisfaction regarding clinic-referred children: Methodological considerations. *Journal of Clinical Child Psychology, 17*, 159-163.

119. Massman, P. J., Nussbaum, N. L., & Bigler, E. D. (1988). The mediating effect of age on the relationship between Child Behavior Checklist hyperactivity scores and neuropsychological test performance. *Journal of Abnormal Child Psychology, 16*, 89-95.

120. McConaughy, S. H., Achenbach, T. M., & Gent, C. L. (1988). Multiaxial empirically based assessment: Parent, teacher, observational, cognitive, and personality correlates of child behavior profile types for 6- to 11-year-old boys. *Journal of Abnormal Child Psychology, 16*, 485-509.

121. McIntyre, L. L. (1988). Teacher gender: A predictor of special education referral? *Journal of Learning Disabilities, 21,* 382-383.

122. Romano, B. A., & Nelson, R. O. (1988). Discriminant and concurrent validity measures of children's depression. *Journal of Clinical Child Psychology, 17,* 255-259.

123. Rosenbluth, L. A., Harris, J. C., & Reifler, J. P. (1988). Similarities and differences between parents' and teachers' observations of the behavior of children with learning problems. *Journal of Learning Disabilities, 21,* 189-190.

124. Smets, A. C., & Hartup, W. W. (1988). Systems and symptoms: Family cohesion/adaptability and childhood behavior problems. *Journal of Abnormal Child Psychology, 16,* 233-246.

125. Verhulst, F. C., Achenbach, T. M., Althaus, M., & Akkerhuis, G. W. (1988). A comparison of syndromes derived from the Child Behavior Checklist for American and Dutch girls aged 6-11 and 12-16. *Journal of Child Psychology and Psychiatry and Allied Disciplines, 29,* 879-895.

126. Wallander, J. L., Hubert, N. C., & Varni, J. W. (1988). Child and maternal temperament characteristics, goodness of fit, and adjustment in physically handicapped children. *Journal of Clinical Child Psychology, 17,* 336-344.

127. Watkins, J. M., Asarnow, R. F., & Tanguay, P. E. (1988). Symptom development in childhood onset schizophrenia. *Journal of Child Psychology and Psychiatry and Allied Disciplines, 29,* 865-878.

128. Watson, B. V., & Goldgar, D. E. (1988). Evaluation of a typology of reading disability. *Journal of Clinical and Experimental Neuropsychology, 10,* 432-450.

129. Webster-Stratton, C., & Hammond, M. (1988). Maternal depression and its relationship to life stress, perceptions of child behavior problems, parenting behaviors, and child conduct problems. *Journal of Abnormal Child Psychology, 16,* 299-315.

130. Wierzbicki, M., & McCabe, M. (1988). Social skills and subsequent depressive symptomatology in children. *Journal of Clinical Child Psychology, 17,* 203-208.

131. Achenbach, T. M., Conners, C. K., Quay, H. C., Verhulst, F. C., & Howell, C. T. (1989). Replication of empirically derived syndromes as a basis for taxonomy of child/adolescent psychopathology. *Journal of Abnormal Child Psychology, 17,* 299-323.

132. Ammerman, R. T., VanHasselt, V. B., Hersen, M., & Moore, L. E. (1989). Assessment of social skills in visually imparied adolescents and their parents. *Behavioral Assessment, 11,* 327-351.

133. Baldwin, D. V., & Skinner, M. L. (1989). Structural model for antisocial behavior: Generalization to single-mother families. *Developmental Psychology, 25,* 45-50.

134. Christopher, J. D., Giuliani, R., Holte, C. S., Beaman, A. L., & Camp, G. C. (1989). Predictor variables related to the classification of learning disabilities. *Journal of Learning Disabilities, 22,* 588-589.

135. Compas, B. E., Howell, D. C., Phares, V., Williams, R. A., & Giunta, C. T. (1989). Risk factors for emotional/behavioral problems in young adolescents: A prospective analysis of adolescent and parental stress and symptoms. *Journal of Consulting and Clinical Psychology, 57,* 732-740.

136. Compas, B. E., Howell, D. C., Phares, V., Williams, R. A., & Ledoux, N. (1989). Parent and child stress and symptoms: An integrative analysis. *Developmental Psychology, 25,* 550-559.

137. Connolly, J. (1989). Social self-efficacy in adolescence: Relations with self-concept, social adjustment, and mental health. *Canadian Journal of Behavioural Science, 21,* 258-269.

138. Conrad, M., & Hammen, C. (1989). Role of maternal depression in perceptions of child maladjustment. *Journal of Consulting and Clinical Psychology, 57,* 663-667.

139. Custrini, R. J., & Feldman, R. S. (1989). Children's social competence and nonverbal encoding and decoding of emotions. *Journal of Clinical Child Psychology, 18,* 336-342.

140. Doering, R. W., Zucker, K. J., Bradley, S. J., & MacIntyre, R. B. (1989). Effects of neutral toys on sex-typed play in children with gender identity disorder. *Journal of Abnormal Child Psychology, 17,* 563-574.

141. Downey, G., & Waller, E. (1989). Social cognition and adjustment of children at risk for psychopathology. *Developmental Psychology, 25,* 835-845.

142. Dumas, J. E., Gibson, J. A., & Albin, J. B. (1989). Behavioral correlates of maternal depressive symptomatology in conduct-disorder children. *Journal of Consulting and Clinical Psychology, 57,* 516-521.

143. Einbender, A. J., & Friedrich, W. N. (1989). Psychological functioning and behavior of sexually abused girls. *Journal of Consulting and Clinical Psychology, 57,* 155-157.

144. Fleming, J. E., Offord, D. R., & Boyle, M. H. (1989). Prevalence of childhood and adolescent depression in the community: Ontario Child Health Study. *British Journal of Psychiatry, 155,* 647-654.

145. Fombonne, E. (1989). The Child Behavior Checklist and the Rutter Parental Questionnaire: A comparison between two screening instruments. *Psychological Medicine, 19,* 777-785.

146. Gallucci, N. T. (1989). Personality assessment with children of superior intelligence: Divergence versus psychopathology. *Journal of Personality Assessment, 53,* 749-760.

147. Hamdan-Allen, G., Stewart, M. A., & Beeghly, J. H. (1989). Subgrouping conduct disorder by psychiatric family history. *Journal of Child Psychology and Psychiatry and Allied Disciplines, 30,* 889-897.

148. Johnston, C., & Mash, E. J. (1989). A measure of parenting satisfaction and efficacy. *Journal of Clinical Child Psychology, 18,* 167-175.

149. Kazdin, A. E. (1989). Identifying depression in children: A comparison of alternative selection criteria. *Journal of Abnormal Child Psychology, 17,* 437-454.

150. Kazdin, A. E., Bass, D., Siegel, T., & Thomas, C. (1989). Cognitive-behavioral therapy and relationship therapy in the treatment of children referred for antisocial behavior. *Journal of Consulting and Clinical Psychology, 57,* 522-535.

151. Keogh, B. K., Juvonen, J., & Bernheimer, L. P. (1989). Assessing children's competence: Mothers' and teachers' ratings of competent behavior. *Psychological Assessment, 1,* 224-229.

152. Klaczynski, P. A., & Cummings, E. M. (1989). Responding to anger in aggressive and nonaggressive boys: A research note. *Journal of Child Psychology and Psychiatry and Allied Disciplines, 30,* 309-314.

153. Kline, M., Tschann, J. M., Johnston, J. R., & Wallerstein, J. S. (1989). Children's adjustment in joint and sole physical custody families. *Developmental Psychology, 25,* 430-438.

154. Konstantareas, M. M., & Homatidis, S. (1989). Parental perception of learning-disabled children's adjustment problems and related stress. *Journal of Abnormal Child Psychology, 17,* 177-186.

155. Lambert, M. C., Weisz, J. R., & Knight, F. (1989). Over- and undercontrolled clinic referral problems of Jamaican and American children and adolescents: The culture general and the culture specific. *Journal of Consulting and Clinical Psychology, 57,* 467-472.

156. Lambert, M. C., Weisz, J. R., & Thesiger, C. (1989). Principal components analyses of behavior problems in Jamaican clinic-referred children: Teacher reports for ages 6-17. *Journal of Abnormal Child Psychology, 17,* 553-562.

157. Leblanc, R., & Reynolds, C. R. (1989). Concordance of mothers' and fathers' ratings of children's behavior. *Psychology in the Schools, 26,* 225-229.

158. McArdle, J., & Mattison, R. E. (1989). Child behavior profile types in a general population sample of boys 6 to 11 years old. *Journal of Abnormal Child Psychology, 17,* 597-607.

159. Pettit, G. S., & Bates, J. E. (1989). Family interaction patterns and children's behavior problems from infancy to 4 years. *Developmental Psychology, 25,* 413-420.

160. Phares, V., Compas, B. E., & Howell, D. C. (1989). Perspectives on child behavior problems: Comparisons of children's self-reports with parent and teacher reports. *Psychological Assessment, 1,* 68-71.

161. Poal, P., & Wiesz, J. R. (1989). Therapists' own childhood problems as predictors of their effectiveness in child psychotherapy. *Journal of Clinical Child Psychology, 18,* 202-205.

162. Pryor, C. W., Wilkinson, S. C., Harris, J., & Trovato, J. (1989). Grade repetition and psychological referrals in relation to Child Behavior Checklist scores for students in elementary school. *Psychology in the Schools, 26,* 230-242.

163. Ramsey, E., Walker, H. M., Shinn, M., O'Neill, R. E., & Stieber, S. (1989). Parent management practices and school adjustment. *School Psychology Review, 18,* 513-525.

164. Raymond, K. L., & Matson, J. L. (1989). Social skills in the hearing impaired. *Journal of Clinical Child Psychology, 18,* 247-258.

165. Rey, J. M., Plapp, J. M., & Stewart, G. W. (1989). Reliability of psychiatric diagnosis in referred adolescents. *Journal of Child Psychiatry and Allied Disciplines, 30,* 879-888.

166. Ritter, D. R. (1989). Social competence and problem behavior of adolescent girls with learning disabilities. *Journal of Learning Disabilities, 22,* 460-461.

167. Sater, G. M., & French, D. C. (1989). A comparison of the social competencies of learning disabled and low achieving elementary-aged children. *The Journal of Special Education, 23,* 29-42.

168. Schneider, B. H., & Byrne, B. M. (1989). Parents rating children's social behavior: How focused the lens? *Journal of Clinical Child Psychology, 18,* 237-241.

169. Stiffman, A. R. (1989). Physical and sexual abuse in runaway youths. *Child Abuse & Neglect, 13,* 417-426.

170. Szapocznik, J., Rio, A., Murray, E., Cohen, R., Scopetta, M., Rivas-Vazquez, A., Hervis, O., & Posada, V. (1989). Structural family versus psychodynamic child therapy for problematic Hispanic boys. *Journal of Consulting and Clinical Psychology, 57,* 571-578.

171. Szatmari, P., Offord, D. R., & Boyle, M. H. (1989). Correlates, associated impairments and patterns of service utilization of children with attention deficit disorder: Findings from the Ontario Child Health Study. *Journal of Child Psychology and Psychiatry and Allied Disciplines, 30,* 205-217.

172. Trieber, F. A., Mabe, P. A., III, Riley, W., Carr, T., Levy, M., Thompson, W., & Strong, W. B. (1989). Assessment of children's Type A behavior: Relationship with negative behavioral characteristics and children and teacher demographic characteristics. *Journal of Personality Assessment, 53,* 770-782.

173. Verhulst, F. C., & Akkerhuis, G. W. (1989). Agreement between parents' and teachers' ratings of behavioral/emotional problems of children aged 4-12. *Journal of Child Psychology and Psychiatry and Allied Disciplines, 30*, 123-136.

174. Weigel, C., Wertlieb, D., & Feldstein, M. (1989). Perceptions of control, competence, and contingency as influences on the stress-behavior symptom relation in school- age children. *Journal of Personality and Social Psychology, 56*, 456-464.

175. Weisz, J. R., & Weiss, B. (1989). Assessing the effects of clinic-based psychotherapy with children and adolescents. *Journal of Consulting and Clinical Psychology, 57*, 741-746.

176. Weisz, J. R., Suwanlert, S., Chaiyasit, W., Weiss, B., Achenbach, T. M., & Trerathan, D. (1989). Epidemiology of behavioral and emotional problems among Thai and American children: Teacher reports for ages 6-11. *Journal of Child Psychology and Psychiatry and Allied Disciplines, 30*, 471-484.

177. Williams, C. L., & Butcher, J. N. (1989). An MMPI study of adolescents: I. Empirical validity of the standard scales. *Psychological Assessment, 1*, 251-259.

178. Williams, C. L., & Butcher, J. N. (1989). An MMPI study of adolescents: II. Verification and limitations of code type classifications. *Psychological Assessment, 1*, 260-265.

179. Wood, B., Watkins, J. B., Boyle, J. T., Nogueira, J., Zimand, E., & Carroll, L. (1989). The "psychosomatic family" model: An empirical and theoretical analysis. *Family Process, 28*, 399-417.

180. Woodward, C. A., Thomas, H. B., Boyle, M. H., Links, P. S., & Offord, D. R. (1989). Methodologic note for child epidemiological surveys: The effects of instructions on estimates of behavior prevalence. *Journal of Child Psychology and Psychiatry and Allied Disciplines, 30*, 919-924.

181. Achenbach, T. M., Hensley, V. R., Phares, V., & Grayson, D. (1990). Problems and competencies reported by parents of Australian and American children. *Journal of Child Psychology and Psychiatry, 31*, 265-286.

182. Banez, G. A., & Compas, B. E. (1990). Children's and parents' daily stressful events and psychological symptoms. *Journal of Abnormal Child Psychology, 18*, 591-605.

183. Barkley, R. A., DuPaul, G. J., & McMurray, M. B. (1990). Comprehensive evaluation of attention deficit disorder with and without hyperactivity as defined research criteria. *Journal of Consulting and Clinical Psychology, 58*, 775-789.

184. Beitchman, J. H., Hood, J., & Inglis, A. (1990). Psychiatric risk in children with speech and language disorders. *Journal of Abnormal Child Psychology, 18*, 283-296.

185. Fletcher, J. M., Ewing-Cobbs, L., Miner, M. E., Levin, H. S., & Eisenberg, H. M. (1990). Behavioral changes after closed head injury in children. *Journal of Consulting and Clinical Psychology, 58*, 93-98.

186. Hammen, C., Burge, D., & Stansbury, K. (1990). Relationship of mother and child variables to child outcomes in a high-risk sample: A causal modeling analysis. *Developmental Psychology, 26*, 24-30.

187. Howes, C. (1990). Can the age of entry into child care and the quality of child care predict adjustment in kindergarten? *Developmental Psychology, 26*, 292-303.

188. Johnston, C., & Pelham, W. E., Jr. (1990). Maternal characteristics, ratings of child behavior, and mother-child interactions in families of children with externalizing disorders. *Journal of Abnormal Child Psychology, 18*, 407-417.

189. Kazdin, A. E. (1990). Premature termination from treatment among children referred for antisocial behavior. *Journal of Child Psychology and Psychiatry, 31*, 415-524.

190. Livingston, R. L., Dykman, R. A., & Ackerman, P. T. (1990). The frequency and significance of additional self-reported psychiatric diagnoses in children with attention deficit disorder. *Journal of Abnormal Child Psychology, 18*, 465-478.

191. Lovejoy, M. C., & Rasmussen, N. H. (1990). The validity of vigilance tasks in differential diagnosis of children referred for attention and learning problems. *Journal of Abnormal Child Psychology, 18*, 671-681.

192. McIntyre, L. L. (1990). Teacher standards and gender: Factors in special education referral? *Journal of Educational Research, 83*, 166-172.

193. Norford, B. C., & Barakat, L. P. (1990). The relationship of human figure drawings to aggressive behavior in preschool children. *Psychology in the Schools, 27*, 318-324.

194. Phares, V., & Compas, B. E. (1990). Adolescents' subjective distress over their emotional/behavior problems. *Journal of Consulting and Clinical Psychology, 58*, 596-603.

195. Pianta, R. C., Erickson, M. F., Wagner, N., Kruetzer, T., & Egeland, B. (1990). Early predictors of referral for special services: Child-based measures versus mother-child interaction. *School Psychology Review, 19*, 240-250.

196. Ritter, D. R. (1990). Adolescent suicide: Social competence and problem behavior of youth at high risk and low risk for suicide. *School Psychology Review, 19*, 83-95.

197. Sawyer, M., Sarris, A., Quigley, R., Baghurst, P., & Kalucy, R. (1990). The attitude of parents to the use of computer-assisted interviewing in a child psychiatry service. *British Journal of Psychiatry, 157*, 675-678.

198. Wahler, R. G., & Sansbury, L. E. (1990). The monitoring skills of troubled mothers: Their problems in defining child deviance. *Journal of Abnormal Child Psychology, 18*, 577-589.

199. Watson, S. M., Henggeler, S. W., & Whelan, J. P. (1990). Family functioning and the social adaptation of hearing-impaired youths. *Journal of Abnormal Child Psychology, 18*, 143-163.

200. Webster-Stratton, C. (1990). Enhancing the effectiveness of self-administered videotape parent training for families with conduct-problem children. *Journal of Abnormal Child Psychology, 18*, 479-492.

201. Westerman, M. A. (1990). Coordination of maternal directives with preschoolers' behavior in compliance-problem and healthy dyads. *Developmental Psychopathology, 26*, 621-630.

202. Worchel, F. F., Hughes, J. N., Hall, B. M., Stanton, S. B., Stanton, H., & Little, V. Z. (1990). Evaluation of subclinical depression in children using self-, peer-, and teacher-report measures. *Journal of Abnormal Child Psychology, 18*, 271-282.

203. Capaldi, D. M., & Patterson, G. R. (1991). Relation of parental transitions to boys' adjustment problems: I. A linear hypothesis. II. Mothers at risk for transitions and unskilled parenting. *Developmental Psychology, 27*, 489-504.

204. Dishion, T. J., Patterson, G. R., Stoolmiller, M., & Skinner, M. L. (1991). Family, school, and behavioral antecedents to early adolescent involvement with antisocial peers. *Developmental Psychology, 27*, 172-180.

205. Dykman, R. A., & Ackerman, P. T. (1991). Attention deficit disorder and specific reading disability: Separate but often overlapping disorders. *Journal of Learning Disabilities, 24*, 96-103.

206. Fantuzzo, J. W., DePaola, L. M., Lambert, L., & Martino, T. (1991). Effects of interparental violence on the psychological adjustment and competencies of young children. *Journal of Consulting and Clinical Psychology, 59*, 258-265.

207. Gillmore, M. R., Hawkins, D., Catalano, R. F., Day, L. E., & Moore, M. (1991). Structure of problem behaviors in preadolescence. *Journal of Consulting and Clinical Psychology, 59*, 499-506.

208. Henggeler, S. W., Cohen, R., Edwards, J. J., Summerville, M. B., & Ray, G. E. (1991). Family stress as a link in the association between television viewing and achievement. *Child Study Journal, 21*, 1-10.

209. Hynd, G. W., Semrud-Clikeman, M., Lorys, A. R., Novey, E. S., Eliopulos, D., & Lyytinen, H. (1991). Corpus callosum morphology in attention deficit-hyperactivity disorder: Morphometric analysis of MRI. *Journal of Learning Disabilities, 24*, 141-146.

210. Mattison, R. E., Morales, J., & Bauer, M. A. (1991). Elementary and secondary socially and/or emotionally disturbed girls: Characteristics and identification. *Journal of School Psychology, 29*, 121-134.

211. McNally, R. J. (1991). Assessment of posttraumatic stress disorder in children. *Psychological Assessment, 3*, 531-537.

212. Patterson, G. R., & Stoolmiller, M. (1991). Replications of a dual failure model for boys' depressed mood. *Journal of Consulting and Clinical Psychology, 59*, 491-498.

213. Ralph, N., & Morgan, K. A. (1991). Assessing differences in chemically dependent adolescent males using the Child Behavior Checklist. *Adolescence, 26*, 183-194.

214. Tarnowski, K. J., King, D. R., Green, L., & Ginn-Pease, M. E. (1991). Congenital gastrointestinal anomalies: psychosocial functioning of children with imperforate anus, gastroschisis, and omphalocele. *Journal of Consulting and Clinical Psychology, 59*, 587-590.

215. Trickett, P. K., Aber, J. L., Carlson, V., & Cicchetti, D. (1991). Relationship of sociometric status to the etiology and developmental sequelae of physical child abuse. *Developmental Psychology, 27*, 148-158.

216. Weiss, B., Weisz, J. R., Politano, M., Corey, M., Nelson, W. M., & Finch, A. J. (1991). Developmental differences in the factor structure of the Children's Depression Inventory. *Psychological Assessment, 3*, 38-45.

Review of the Child Behavior Checklist by SANDRA L. CHRISTENSON, *Associate Professor of Educational Psychology, University of Minnesota, Minneapolis, MN:*

The purpose of the Child Behavior Checklist (CBCL) is to obtain parents' reports of their children's problems and competencies. Items were selected for inclusion on this checklist because of a significant relationship between the item and referral for social-emotional problems. The development of the Teacher's Report Form (TRF) and Youth Self-Report (YSR) of the Child Behavior Checklist creates a comprehensive assessment approach for describing the social-emotional development of children and youth. These two new self-report checklists are the focus of this review.

The TRF was designed to provide standardized descriptions of behavior rather than diagnostic inferences. Similarly, the YSR was designed to provide standardized self-report data on adolescents' competencies and problems rated by teachers on the TRF and parents on the CBCL. A comparison of parent, teacher, and student perceptions of items significantly related to referral for social-emotional problems in children and youth is facilitated by similarity in items across the three checklists.

Assessing social-emotional development for students or describing problems in social-emotional development in a standardized way is a difficult and complex task. The use of the TRF and YSR by well-trained professionals (e.g., master's level) is highly recommended for several reasons. Specific strengths include:

1. The manuals are well written, informative, and very "user friendly." Information presented in each manual follows a consistent format. Essential information about users' qualifications, checklist purposes, scoring and administration procedures, reliability and validity data, and interpretation of data are clearly provided. The authors are to be commended for the instructive value of the manual. Definitions of technical terms, such as *criterion-related validity*, are given, and many explicit illustrations are provided in varied ways, such as graphic portrayal of assessment results, case studies, and descriptions of interpretations of the TRF profile score or YSR profile scores for specific cases. The manuals, which are organized similarly, are so well written that either could serve as a prototype for development of other instruments.

2. The comprehensiveness of the CBCL, TRF, and YSR is a major strength. The use of these checklists allows professionals to gather standardized information in the area of social-emotional assessment from multiple sources. The congruence of items across parents, teachers, and students allows for an ecological perspective and greater understanding of student behavior. Although the purpose of these checklists is to provide standardized descriptions of behavior, the authors' assessment approach and interpretation of data are directed at achieving an assessment-to-intervention link for students. The authors provide information on how the empirically derived scales relate to commonly used clinical diagnoses, but are very explicit that the names of the scales were selected to summarize item content of each scale, not to be used as diagnostic categories or equivalents of particular diagnoses. Rather, the authors provide examples about how the differing perceptions of parent, teacher, and student must be considered, in relation to *all* other assessment information available on the student, to plan an intervention program. In addition, the gathering of qualitative information is encouraged on both the TRF and YSR. Thus, major strengths of these instruments (CBCL, TRF, and YSR) are that (*a*) examiners are provided with a means to gather multiple sources of data in the assessment of children and adolescents, and (*b*) examiners are instructed in the benefits of a multiaxial approach. No one type of informant is likely to provide the same information as other informants because the student's functioning may be different under different conditions. It is precisely this comprehensive and ecological interpretation of student behavior that makes the CBCL, TRF, and YSR so valuable to clinicians.

3. The TRF and YSR are reliable and valid checklists. The authors have provided strong, sound evidence for an explanation of three forms of reliability data (test-retest reliability, stability of ratings, and interrater agreement) and three forms of validity data (content, construct, and criterion related). Of particular importance is the evidence provided for criterion-related validity of the TRF and YSR. Using referral for professional help with behavioral and social/emotional problems as a criterion, the authors found significant differences in TRF and YSR ratings between demographically similar referred and nonreferred pupils. In addition, explicit information is provided about the empirical derivation of the behavior-problem scales and item scores for both the TRF and YSR.

The development of norms based on empirical evidence for both checklists is a major strength. Norms are available separately for age groups of 6–11 years and 12–18 years by sex. The authors examined effects of race and SES but found that differences were too small to warrant separate norms. In sum, the norming procedures are impeccable.

4. The authors should be commended for their strong commitment that assessment practices (and interpretation) should be firmly grounded in research. The instrument typologies are based on empirical evidence. For example, the authors eliminated a typology of teacher-profile patterns on the TRF, despite the fact there was an analogous empirically derived parent typology found on the CBCL. The authors are engaged in an ongoing research program using CBCL, TRF, and YSR data, and advise users of the checklists to be aware that interpretation of scores could be subject to change. Users of the CBCL, TRF, and YSR are responsible for staying informed and need to be certain they are using the most recent manuals.

In addition to these four strengths of the checklists, specific features make the use of the checklists strongly recommended. Examples of these features include:

1. Specific directions for use of the checklists in unusual situations, such as appropriate use of norms when comparing a student who crosses from one age range to the next between ratings.

2. Specific directions for hand scoring, the provision of templates to assist scoring, and availability of computer scoring.

3. Clear description of multiple applications of the TRF and YSR, such as research, reevaluation of students after intervention implementation, and comprehensive evaluation of students for special services.

4. The last chapter in each manual addresses commonly asked questions and reviews salient points for accurate administration, scoring, and interpretation of TRF and YSR ratings.

In summary, the TRF and YSR, as part of the multiaxial assessment approach of the CBCL, are well-designed and well-researched instruments to provide standardized descriptions of students' problems and competencies in the social-emotional area. Use of these instruments by mental health professionals is highly recommended because of the conceptual and empirical basis for the checklists.

Review of the Child Behavior Checklist by STEPHEN N. ELLIOTT, Professor of Educational Psychology, and R. T. BUSSE, Graduate Student, Department of Educational Psychology, University of Wisconsin-Madison, Madison, WI:

The following review is divided into two parts. The first section critiques the Teacher Report Form and the second, the Youth Self-Report of the Child Behavior Checklist (CBCL).

The Teacher's Report Form or TRF is a teacher version of the Child Behavior Checklist "designed to provide standardized *descriptions* of behavior, rather than diagnostic inferences" (p. iii). The TRF is an empirically derived rating scale that covers a wide range of potential problem behaviors and a small number of academic and prosocial competencies. It is used by many psychologists and educators to screen and to classify children in need of special services. Achenbach and Edelbrock's record of scholarly research and sensitivity to psychometric and practical issues with the CBCL has done much to establish the TRF as one of the most frequently used problem-behavior rating scales with children ages 6 to 16 years.

CONTENT AND USE. The TRF has a separate user's technical manual, one rating form, and four (girls 6–11, girls 12–16, boys 6–11, and boys 12–16 years) Child Behavior Profile sheets for scoring and interpretation. The TRF includes 118 items, 5 comprising the Adaptive Functioning Scale and 118 the Behavior Problems Scale.

The Adaptive Functioning Scale items (e.g., How hard is he/she working? How happy is he/she?), the first items confronted on the rating form, are rated on a 7-point scale whereby a teacher compares the target child to "typical pupils of the same age." This scale seems poorly named and, consequently, may be misleading to many consumers familiar with adaptive behavior scales for assessing potentially retarded children. More importantly, it is of limited practical use. Furthermore, the development of the Adaptive Behavior Profile sheet for reporting results from individual items on this brief scale is likely to lead to overinterpretation of the ratings in this area.

The Behavior Problems Scale is the centerpiece of the TRF and, unlike the Adaptive Functioning Scale, is quite comprehensive and is conceptually consistent with several other problem-oriented behavior rating scales. Items are assumed to characterize objectively an overt behavior or state of functioning and are rated on a 3-point scale (0 = *Not True*, 1 = *Somewhat or Sometimes True*, and 2 = *Very True or Often True*). For the most part, the items are objective and clearly interpretable; however, several cause puzzlement, such as Item 5 ("Behaves like opposite sex") or Item 51 ("Feels dizzy"). The first example is highly subjective and the latter item is more reliably handled through self-report. Several items are designed to allow the rater to personalize the content. For example, Item 84 reads "Strange behavior (describe): _____" and Item 73 reads "Behaves irresponsibly (describe): _____." Such personalized items can be a plus, but often are a minus; the plus is that a rater can do a more accurate job of communicating about the behavior of a given child. The minus involves the scoring and interpretation of these items within a normative subscale structure. This structure includes eight to nine scorable subscales (e.g., Anxious, Social Withdrawal, Unpopular, Self Destructive, Aggressive) and a large (19 to 30 items depending on the sex and age of the student) catch-all subscale appropriately titled "Other Problems." The Other Problems subscale items are scored but do not contribute to a specific subscale; they are for descriptive use. A Profile sheet with percentile and *T*-score scales is used when the TRF is hand scored and provides a graphic portrayal of a teacher's ratings. The use of the now familiar broad-band Internalizing and Externalizing characterizations of problem behavior is a featured interpretive schema for the ratings.

Completion of this rating scale is rather easy and can be done by most teachers in 20 to 25 minutes. Scoring, on the other hand, is more complicated; hand scoring is tedious work and can take up to 25 minutes if one double-checks his/her work of transferring ratings from the rating form to the Profile sheet and the subsequent addition and graphing of subscale rating totals. A computer-scoring option is available, but is not described in the manual. A final and somewhat minor point about scoring: An error was observed in the raw score ranges for girls 6–11 that are equivalent to a T-score of 71 (see page 151 of the Manual). The raw score range should be 67 to 71 rather than 70 to 71. [More recently printed manuals have corrected this error.—Ed. Note]

STANDARDIZATION SAMPLES AND NORMS. Two separately collected samples of students, a nonreferred and a referred group, were used to standardize and norm the TRF. Specifically, a sample of 1,100 students in grades 1 through 10 from schools in three large cities (Omaha, Nashville, and Pittsburgh) was used to norm both the Adaptive Functioning Scale and the Behavior Problems Scale. This sample had equal numbers of girls and boys and was characterized racially as 77% White and 23% Black. This sample's racial mix slightly overrepresents both Whites and Blacks, and obviously underrepresents Hispanics, Asians, and Native Americans. Sex and race information about the teachers ($N = 665$) who completed all the ratings was not provided.

Before the Behavior Problems Scale was normed, a sample of 1,700 students referred for school and mental health services were rated and their scores analyzed to determine the factor structure of the scale. An equal number of girls and boys characterized as 76% White, 24% Black, and 2% mixed and other comprised this referred sample. Thus, the interpretive structure for the core of the TRF is based on referred children, but the norms were derived from a smaller sample of nonreferred children, somewhat unrepresentative of the U.S. population. This approach to determining a factor structure is reasonable, although infrequently done without confirming the structure for the second known group.

RELIABILITY AND VALIDITY. The authors of the TRF have demonstrated a sound knowledge of psychometric issues and techniques in constructing this rating scale. With regard to the scale's reliability, they report test-retest reliabilities for a 2-week period (mean $r = .89$), test stability for periods of 2 months ($r = .74$) and 4 months ($r = .68$), and interrater (teacher with teacher aides) reliabilities or agreements (median $r = .57$). No coefficient alphas or internal consistency data are presented as evidence for reliability. These latter traditional forms of scale reliability are assumed to be high and technically are unnecessary, given the factor analytic data presented in the manual. The reliabilities reported for the TRF are very respectable and compare well to other teacher rating scales such as the Revised Behavior Problem Checklist (Quay & Peterson, 1983) or the Social Skills Rating System (Gresham & Elliott, 1990).

The validity of the TRF, the authors argue, is based on its substantive content and the congruence of its constructs with many of the problem behaviors cited in the child psychopathology literature. Thus, the primary validity data for the TRF focus on the Behavior Problems Scale and are the result of factor analytic work and a concurrent validity study with the Conners Revised Teacher Rating Scale. The validity coefficient resulting from Pearson correlations between total problems scores on the TRF and the Conners scale was high ($r = .85$). In addition, good convergent validity was documented for TRF subscales concerning Aggressive, Nervous-Overactive, and Inattentive behaviors and those subscales respectively labelled Conduct Disorder, Hyperactivity, and Inattentive-Passive on the Conners.

The authors of the TRF spent significant effort to examine its criterion-related validity. Using multiple regression methods, the authors found for all ages and both sexes that referral status consistently accounted for the largest percent of the variance in ratings on the TRF. This is a desirable result, considering the purpose of the TRF.

In addition to this multiple regression approach to criterion-related validity, the authors conducted discriminant analysis to test the classification accuracy of the TRF for known referred and nonreferred samples. Overall, using just TRF scores, they misclassified approximately 28% of the sample with false-positives and false-negatives being observed almost equally. This level of classification accuracy is considered adequate, given that only one measure was used and the stated purpose of the TRF is for description, not classification!

CONCLUSIONS. The TRF is a useful contribution to the assessment arsenal of psychologists interested in gaining a broad picture of the behavioral functioning of a school-aged child. It is consistent with the presently popular empirical/descriptive approach to childhood psychopathology and generally has good to very good reliability and validity data to support its use as a method for describing children's behavior. The instrument was standardized on a sample of adequate size; however, it was unrepresentative of the U.S. population with regard to racial status and regional representation. The TRF's Adaptive Functioning Scale is weak conceptually and psychometrically, and consequently detracts from an otherwise rather attractive instrument. The Behavior Problems Scale is comprehensive, although we believe that eliminating the Other Problems items would be desirable and would not significantly affect the end product. Hand scoring is time consuming and tedious; computer scoring seems desirable, but little information is provided about it in the otherwise readable, informative TRF manual. (Other manuals are available for computer scoring.)

On balance, the TRF offers one a reasonable instrument for documenting the problem behaviors of school-age children. It has been developed from the mold of the CBCL, which has become one of the most frequently used descriptive tools of child psychopathology researchers. It is not as user friendly as some of its competition (e.g., Walker Problem Behavior Identification Checklist [9:1345]), but its psychometric qualities and research base are superior to much of its competition (e.g., Behavior Rating Profile [10:27], Devereux Elementary School Behavior Rating Scale II [9:330]). The TRF Manual is well written, which suggests its authors are knowledgeable developers and users of rating scales. This scale should be considered for use by those looking for more teacher input into the assessment and decision-making process for children referred for severe behavior difficulties.

The Youth Self-Report (YSR) is a relatively brief (120 items) multidimensional scale designed to measure adolescents' ratings of their personal competencies and problems. The scale requires reading abilities at the fifth-grade level and provides a potentially useful measure for cross-informant comparisons when employed concurrently with parent and teacher reports, such as the Child Behavior Checklist and the Teacher's Report Form. The Competence Scales are designed to assess adolescents' involvement in activities, their social relationships, and their academic performance. The Problem Scales yield scores for total behavior problems, broad-band problems (Internalizing and Externalizing), and several narrow-band syndromes (e.g., Unpopular, Depressed, Aggressive). Scoring is done by hand or by a computer program available from the author. The separate YSR scoring profiles for boys and girls allow for ready comparison between a respondent's ratings and those of the normative group. The manual is thoughtfully laid out, with ample information regarding scale usage and psychometrics. A section answering commonly asked questions concerning the YSR is a particularly useful feature.

STANDARDIZATION. The YSR was standardized in 1985–86 with 344 boys and 342 girls aged 11–18 from eight communities in Worcester, Massachusetts. Adolescents included in the norms had not received mental health services within 12 months prior to their ratings. Random cluster sampling in 34 residential census tracts stratified by income yielded similar proportions and mean Hollingshead ratings of upper, middle, and lower socioeconomic status families. Racial distribution was 81% White, 17% Black, and 3% mixed/other. Unfortunately, age distribution and handicap/nonhandicap status are not presented.

SCALE CONSTRUCTION. The YSR is an extension of the Achenbach Child Behavior Checklist (CBCL). Most of the items from the CBCL were retained or altered slightly, appearing in a parallel first-person format. The response format for prob-lem behaviors is identical to the Likert-type rating used in the CBCL (0 = *Not True*, 1 = *Somewhat or Sometimes True*, 3 = *Very True or Often True*). Sixteen problem behaviors deemed inappropriate for adolescents were replaced by socially desirable items. The Competence Scales also parallel the CBCL, with the exception of a separate academic competence scale that is not used in the YSR.

Separate problem-behavior syndromes were empirically derived from statistical analyses of YSRs completed by adolescents referred for mental health services. Data were obtained between 1981–86 for 486 boys and 441 girls from 25 mental health services located predominantly in the eastern United States. Orthogonal varimax rotations were performed, with loadings $\geq .30$ as the criterion for retention on eight principal components and resulted in seven narrow-band syndromes for boys and six narrow-band syndromes for girls. Items that did not meet the criterion level are listed under Other Behaviors. In contrast to the Aggressive syndrome on the CBCL, the Depressed syndrome on the YSR accounted for the largest proportion of variance for both sexes. The remaining syndromes are similar across the measures, with the exception of the Self-Destructive/Identity Problems factor for boys.

Unfortunately, several problems exist with the referral group. As with the normative sample, no age distribution is reported. A further problem is that socioeconomic status (SES) is "unknown" for a rather large percentage of the sample (38%). Thus, the representativeness of SES is questionable. Finally, information concerning the selection and the presenting problems of the referred sample is lacking. Although the author states the purpose of employing referred adolescents was to "detect the syndromes that characterize individuals having severe enough problems to warrant referrals," the level of severity within the sample remains unknown and, as such, the validity of the derived syndromes is suspect.

A final note regarding scale construction concerns the inclusion of the 16 socially desirable items. These items do not effectively discriminate between referred and nonreferred youths and, as such, are not scored on the YSR profile. They do provide mitigation for the problem items and may help ensure against indiscriminate responding.

RELIABILITY AND VALIDITY. Given that the YSR is an empirically derived scale, internal consistency is not required to establish reliability. Therefore, reliability for the YSR is appropriately presented as test-retest stability. The authors used Pearson correlations and *t* tests to calculate rank order *and* mean differences in the determination of the reliability of the scale.

Overall scale test-retest reliability for a 1-week interval is satisfactory (median $r = .81$), with adequate broad-band and total behavior reliabilities (range $r = .83–.87$), and small mean differences. Reliabilities for age differences indicate lower stability for 11- to 14-year-olds (median $r = .77$) than 15- to 18-year-olds (median $r = .89$). The small sample size (22 boys, 28 girls), however, limits strong conclusions regarding stability. Further, the range of narrow-band and Competence Scale reliabilities (.39–.83) for the total sample is somewhat large for the small retest interval. Eight-month stability of YSR ratings with a "general population sample" of 48 boys and 54 girls yielded very small mean differences and satisfactory broad-band and total behavior reliabilities (range $r = .64–.67$), although overall scale stability was somewhat low (median $r = .51$). Unfortunately, the 8-month reliabilities were calculated on a restricted sample of 12- to 14-year-olds. Given the age differences reported above, reliability data for older adolescents should have been included to provide an indication of the stability of the scale for different age groups.

Although content validity is not a principal requirement for the validation of an empirical scale, content validity is offered and appears adequate. By employing referral status as the validity criterion, the authors have demonstrated satisfactory concurrent validity, as evidenced by lower competence and higher problem scores for referred adolescents. The YSR also appears to possess adequate discriminant validity for the Problem Scales, but not for the Competence Scales. The Competence Scales have limited, if any, clinical utility. To their credit, the authors acknowledge the shortcomings of the Competence Scales.

The overall validation of the YSR was managed appropriately and is well documented. However, a possible problem exists with the cross-validation study. Cross-validation with a sample other than the derivation group is a necessary component of the validation of any empirical scale. Although cross-validation was performed, it is unclear whether a new sample was employed. If, as it appears, the same sample or subsamples of the derivation group were used in cross-validation, there is a high probability that the results are inflated.

Validity for the use of the YSR as a means to obtain cross-informant data is clearly presented by correlations with the CBCL and its counterpart in the school setting, the TRF. Correlations between these measures also provide an index of construct validity. Mean correlations are acceptable between the YSR and CBCL ($r = .41$ for boys, .45 for girls). Similar correlations are reported for the YSR and TRF. Interestingly, nonreferred adolescents and referred girls reported significantly more problems than parents or teachers, whereas the YSR problem scores of referred boys exceed only teacher ratings. These differences underscore the need for measures such as the YSR to ascertain cross-information regarding the functioning of youths.

More direct evidence for the concurrent and construct validity of the YSR is not provided in the YSR Manual, due to the reported paucity of relevant child and adolescent self-report measures. Recent research, however, has provided some evidence that the YSR Problem Scales correlate negatively ($r = -.33$) with prosocial behaviors and that the Competence Scales correlate positively ($r = .23$) with the prosocial behaviors as measured by the Social Skills Rating System (Gresham & Elliott, 1990).

SUMMARY. The YSR is a useful self-report measure of the problems and competencies of adolescents. The instrument is *not* to be used for diagnosis or classification, but rather to provide an adjunct to decision making and for guiding clinical interviews. Clinicians and researchers will find the measure particularly useful for cross-informant comparisons. To date, the YSR has been employed in only a handful of published studies. Continued research is needed to further substantiate the reliability and validity of the scale.

REVIEWER'S REFERENCES

Quay, H. C., & Peterson, D. (1983). Revised Behavior Problem Checklist. Coral Gables, FL: University of Miami.
Gresham, F. M., & Elliott, S. N. (1990). Social Skills Rating System. Circle Pine, MN: American Guidance Service.

[65]
The Childhood Autism Rating Scale.

Purpose: "To identify children with autism, and to distinguish them from developmentally handicapped children without the autism syndrome."
Population: Ages 2 and over.
Publication Dates: 1986–88.
Acronym: CARS.
Scores: 16 rating scores: Relating to People, Imitation, Emotional Response, Body Use, Object Use, Adaptation to Change, Visual Response, Listening Response, Taste/Smell/Touch Response and Use, Fear or Nervousness, Verbal Communication, Nonverbal Communication, Activity Level, Level and Consistency of Intellectual Response, General Impressions, Total.
Administration: Individual.
Price Data, 1989: $25 per complete kit including 25 rating scales and manual ('88, 20 pages); $8.70 per 25 rating scales; $17.50 per manual.
Time: Administration time not reported.
Comments: Revision of the Childhood Psychosis Rating Scale; ratings by professionals trained to administer the CARS.
Authors: Eric Schopler, Robert J. Reichler, and Barbara Rochen Renner.
Publisher: Western Psychological Services.

TEST REFERENCES

1. Lord, C., & Schopler, E. (1989). Stability of assessment results of autistic and non-autistic language-impaired children from preschool years to early school age. *Journal of Child Psychology and Psychiatry and Allied Disciplines, 30,* 575-590.
2. Yirmiya, N., Kasari, C., Sigman, M., & Mundy, P. (1989). Facial expressions of affect in autistic, mentally retarded and normal children.

Journal of Child Psychology and Psychiatry and Allied Disciplines, 30, 725-735.

3. Dawson, G., Hill, D., Spencer, A., Galpert, L., & Watson, L. (1990). Affective exchanges between young autistic children and their mothers. *Journal of Abnormal Child Psychology, 18,* 335-345.

4. Ozonoff, S., Pennington, B. F., & Rogers, S. J. (1990). Are there emotion perception deficits in young autistic children? *Journal of Child Psychology and Psychiatry, 31,* 343-361.

Review of the Childhood Autism Rating Scale by BARRY M. PRIZANT, *Professor, Division of Communication Disorders, Emerson College, Boston, MA:*

According to the authors, The Childhood Autism Rating Scale (CARS) was developed in order to fill the need for an observational instrument that could reliably distinguish children with the autistic syndrome from children with other developmental disorders, as well as differentiate among levels of severity within the autistic syndrome. It can be used during observations of child behavior in a variety of settings, or may be used with information gleaned from chart or record reviews. The CARS is composed of 15 4-point scales on which a child's behavior is rated on a continuum from *within normal limits* (1) to *severely abnormal* (4) for chronological age. Half-point values can be given allowing for the use of a 7-point continuum in practice. Peculiarity, frequency, intensity, and duration of behavior are all to be considered in making ratings, and specific descriptive examples of point values for each scale are provided within the manual to assist raters. Total scores are then used to categorize a child on a continuum ranging from nonautistic, to mild to moderate autism, to severe autism. The CARS is purported to be an initial aid in the classification process. Depending on the results, it may be necessary to conduct in-depth follow-up assessments of behavioral, psychoeducational, communication and language, and biological functioning. To this end, a concerted effort was made to construct the CARS to be immediately useable with minimal training by professionals from a variety of disciplines.

The scales include behavioral characteristics noted in Kanner's (1943) original description of the syndrome, as well as characteristics published in other diagnostic schemes. The authors of the CARS claim that none of the most widely used diagnostic schemes for autism are tied to a rating scale or checklist, thus diagnosis has remained largely subjective. The CARS rating scales cover a broad range of behavior, and include symptomatology that overlaps, to some degree, with most diagnostic schemes for autism. For each scale there is a short descriptive paragraph indicating whether the behavioral domain assessed is a primary or secondary feature, or is not included for each of five other published diagnostic schemes. Thus, a child's presenting profile can be related to other prominent schemes for diagnosis.

The authors report a variety of reliability and validity studies, all with acceptable findings. Internal consistency (coefficient alpha) are found to be .94. Interrater reliability, using two raters and 280 cases, was found to be .71, with a range of .55 (Level and Consistency of Intellectual Response) to .93 (Relating to People). Test-retest reliability of CARS scores for 91 cases assessed 1 year apart resulted in a correlation of .88. Test-retest reliability of CARS diagnoses (i.e., nonautistic, mild/moderate autism, or severe autism) from the second to third annual evaluation resulted in a coefficient kappa of .64. The authors did not report the findings for reliability of diagnosis between the first and second evaluation, claiming that the symptom picture often changes dramatically due to improvement following the first year of intensive treatment. These data would have been useful, as would data on test-retest reliability over longer periods of time. Well-informed clinicians should be aware of the changing developmental picture of autism, and such data would provide important and useful information about how improvement is reflected on the CARS.

Comparison of subjective clinical ratings to total CARS scores made from observations of the same assessment session yielded a correlation of .84. The correlation between total CARS scores and independent clinical ratings made by a child psychiatrist or psychologist based on referral records, parent interviews, and unstructured clinical interviews with a child was .80. Validity of the CARS across different settings revealed no significant differences among these settings with coefficient kappas of .75 (parent interview vs. psychoeducational testing), .86 (classroom observation vs. psychoeducational testing), and .63 (case history review vs. psychoeducational testing). Thus, valid CARS ratings were found when the CARS was used in a variety of settings as compared to the setting for which it was originally designed to be used (i.e., during psychoeducational testing).

Finally, validity of CARS ratings across different disciplines was tested by having 18 raters from five disciplines use the CARS following a review of the manual, and for some raters, viewing of a teaching videotape. In comparing the ratings with those of "expert clinical directors," a coefficient alpha of .81 was found, indicating that valid CARS ratings can be made by professionals from different disciplines with little training in autism.

Compared with the few other instruments designed to identify children with autism, the CARS has a number of notable strengths. First, it is not constructed with any strong bias towards a particular diagnostic framework or orientation concerning the autistic syndrome. As noted, its content was derived from behavioral characteristics that have been noted in many diagnostic schemes over the past four decades, and clinicians can compare their ratings with how areas assessed fit with other frameworks.

Second, it is designed to be used easily by professionals of different backgrounds with limited experience with autistic children. Observations may be made in classrooms, clinics, or other contexts. It may also be used in interviews with parents and in reviewing records.

Third, total scores place a child on a continuum of severity from nonautistic, to mild/moderate autism, to severe autism, rather than a simple yes/no diagnostic decision. This approach is consistent with the widely used *Diagnostic and Statistical Manual of Mental Disorders* (DSM-III-R; American Psychiatric Association, 1987) classification of Pervasive Developmental Disorders (PDD), where Autistic Disorder represents the most extreme end of severity, and PDD Not Otherwise Specified is thought of as representing less severe points on the continuum, typically including children with some characteristics of the autistic syndrome. Finally, information gathered on the CARS may be used for treatment or educational planning, although the instrument was not designed primarily for this purpose.

Its weaknesses emanate from some of the same sources of its strengths. First, the CARS uses a wide range of symptoms in its scales with no weighting of each scale in calculating final total scores. However, recent theory and research on autism have moved the field close to a consensus that the primary and necessary criteria for a diagnosis of autism include qualitative impairments in reciprocal social relations, communication and imaginative activity, and a markedly restricted range of interests as manifest in stereotypic behavior and resistance to change. Some areas assessed on the CARS are no longer considered necessary, and certainly not sufficient, for a diagnosis of autism (e.g., taste, smell and touch response, activity level, fear or nervousness). An unintended effect of having scales for these behavioral domains is that it may imply to some CARS users that these are important criteria in diagnosing autism. Furthermore, given the wide array of behavioral domains explored, a determination of severity is so multidimensionally based that it may be of limited meaning. For example, severity on the CARS clearly would increase with degree of cognitive impairment. However, it may not necessarily reflect degree of social impairment to the same degree. Given that current approaches to understanding autism focus primarily on social and communicative limitations, a severity rating should give greater weight to social relatedness and social communication measures. Second, use of the CARS assumes knowledge of chronological age-appropriate functioning across the domains assessed. Given that the CARS is recommended for a wide range of professionals, this assumption may not hold. Thus, professionals with a limited developmental background should work closely with other professionals

with such a background when using the CARS. The problems in rating appropriateness of behavior would seem to be most pronounced when observing preschoolers and toddlers.

Third, the manual includes some minor inaccuracies and conceptual inconsistencies. For example, Imitation, one of the CARS scales, was noted not to be included in the *DSM-III-R* (American Psychiatric Association, 1987) diagnostic scheme, yet it is. The Visual Response scale includes and confounds issues of use of gaze to other persons in establishing and regulating social interaction, with gaze used nonsocially for object exploration. The developmental literature has viewed these phenomena as somewhat distinct. Finally, users of the CARS may have some reservations about complying with the following suggestion in the manual: "For direct observation of the child's response to pain, it may be necessary to pinch the child" (p. 10). Surely, this information can be obtained in other ways.

In summary, within the limitations noted above, the CARS appears to be the best instrument available for initial classification of children suspected of having the autistic syndrome. It is useful in organizing one's observations, and its ease and range of use makes it readily accessible to a variety of potential users. It is recommended particularly for professionals who have limited experience with autistic children, especially given the danger of misdiagnosis that has plagued clinical and educational efforts.

REVIEWER'S REFERENCES

Kanner, L. (1943). Autistic disturbance of affective contact. *Nervous Child*, 2, 217-250.

American Psychiatric Association. (1987). *Diagnostic and statistical manual of mental disorders—revised* (3rd ed.). Washington, DC: Author.

Review of The Childhood Autism Rating Scale by J. STEVEN WELSH, Assistant Professor, Nicholls State University, Thibodaux, LA:

The Childhood Autism Rating Scale (CARS) is a behavior rating scale developed to identify children with autism, to discriminate between children with autism and other developmental disorders, and to assess the severity of autistic disorder in children within a range of mild to severe. The 15-item rating scale has been in development since 1971 and in its original form was referred to as the Childhood Psychosis Rating Scale. The authors have gone to great length to include diagnostic criteria from multiple classification systems and various theoretical perspectives of autism in the development of this instrument. Cited in the manual are criteria and perspectives from Kanner (1943), Creak (1961), the National Society for Autistic Children (NSAC, 1978), Rutter (1978), and the *Diagnostic and Statistical Manual of Mental Disorders* (*DSM-III-R*; American Psychiatric Association, 1987).

DEVELOPMENT OF THE CARS. The scale was developed in North Carolina to evaluate autistic children participating in the statewide Treatment and Education of Autistic and Related Communication handicapped Children (TEACCH) program and represents a compilation of approximately 1,600 cases spanning a 15-year period of development. Approximately 75% of cases were male with approximately 57% entering the initial investigation below age 6, 32% between ages 6 to 10, and 11% above age 10. Sixty-seven percent of the sample were white, 30% black, and 3% represented other ethnic groups. Approximately 71% of the sample had measured IQs below 70, with 17% having IQs between 70 and 84, and 13% having IQs at or above 85. Approximately 60% of the sample fell within the bottom two categories of the Hollingshead-Redlich (1958) index.

The authors indicated the development of the CARS classification procedure was based on a behaviorally based (empirically derived) observational system. The 15 behavioral domains included: (a) Relating to People, (b) Imitation, (c) Emotional Response, (d) Body Use, (e) Object Use, (f) Adaptation to Change, (g) Visual Response, (h) Listening, (i) Taste/Smell/Touch Response and Use, (j) Fear or Nervousness, (k) Verbal Communication, (l) Nonverbal Communication, (m) Activity Level, (n) Level and Consistency of Intellectual Response, and (o) General Impressions. The manual includes a weighting of each of the first 14 domains with its importance within each of the five diagnostic systems mentioned previously. Items were rated as either "primary," "secondary," or "not included" with regard to item relationship with the five major diagnostic or theoretical systems. Examiners are required to rate each domain on a 7-point Likert scale ranging from within normal limits to severely abnormal for a child of that age. The manual offers detailed behavioral descriptors to be observed for each domain taking into account the perculiarity, frequency, intensity, and duration of each behavior. Data may be collected from a variety of sources including direct observation in home and classroom settings, psychological testing, parent reports, and "history" records. A CARS Rating Sheet with limited space for recording observations is provided. The examiner is instructed to complete the rating form, transfer obtained scores to the face of the protocol, and generate the "Total Score." Based on the total score, which may range from 15 to 60, the examiner rates a child as either nonautistic, mild to moderately autistic, or severely autistic. The manual does not provide an explanation of the metric of the Total Score.

RELIABILITY AND VALIDITY. The CARS manual provides extensive reliability and validity information; however, these 1980 data may be somewhat dated in the current edition of this instrument. Internal consistency is high with a coefficient alpha of .94. Test-retest data ($n = 91$) collected at a 1-year interval resulted in a correlation coefficient of .88 ($p < .01$) and mean scores for each rating period were not significantly different. Interrater reliability obtained from 280 cases was moderate with an interrater reliability score of .71. When compared to "independent clinical" ratings by child psychologists and psychiatrists, criterion-related validity was high, with a resulting correlation of .80 ($p < .001$). However, the manual did not indicate degree of agreement between CARS level scores and clinical judgments. Numerous additional validity studies are reported of CARS scores obtained under "alternate conditions" in the CARS manual.

SUMMARY. The CARS is a well-constructed rating scale for assessing autism in young children. The authors' carefully developed rating scale is based on a credible review of a wide variety of classification systems and theoretical perspectives. The manual is well written, straightforward, and well referenced. However, reliability and validity data were reported from a 1980 study and should be updated. Whereas the authors have successfully developed a behaviorally based data collection procedure, cutoff scores appeared rationally derived based on Wing and Gould's (1978) conception of a continuum of autistic disability. Psychometrically, the Total Score lacks definition as to its metric and specific means and the standard errors of measurement for various age groups are not reported. However, the authors do provide false positive and false negative percentage rates in the manual based on the TEACCH data base. The scale user is cautioned that all reported data used in the manual of this instrument were collected in North Carolina. A welcome addition to the technical data would be the inclusion of reliability and validity studies from other regions of the country, which have recently been reported in the literature (e.g., Garfin, McCallon, & Cox, 1988, and Teal & Wiebe, 1986). Aptly, the authors indicate that the CARS is not intended to be and should not be used as the sole instrument in making diagnostic decisions. Whereas they indicate the CARS is a useful decision-making tool, they recommend a multimodal, multidisciplinary decision-making process in the identification of autistic children. Overall, the CARS appears to be a useful, reliable, and valid instrument for the identification and classification of autistic children.

REVIEWER'S REFERENCES

Kanner, L. (1943). Autistic disturbance of affective contact. *Nervous Child, 2*, 217-250.

Hollingshead, A., & Redlich, F. (1958). *Social class and mental illness.* New York: Wiley.

Creak, M. (1961). Schizophrenia syndrome in childhood: Progress report of a working party. *Cerebral Palsy Bulletin, 3*, 501-504.

National Society for Autistic Children. (1978). National Society for Autistic Children definition of the syndrome of autism. *Journal of Autism and Developmental Disorders, 8*, 162-167.

Rutter, M. (1978). Diagnosis and definition of childhood autism. *Journal of Autism and Developmental Disorders, 8*, 139-161.

Wing, L., & Gould, V. (1978). Systematic recording of behaviors and skills of retarded and psychotic children. *Journal of Autism and Childhood Schizophrenia, 8* (1), 79-98.

Teal, M. B., & Weibe, M. J. (1986). A validity analysis of selected instruments used to assess autism. *Journal of Autism and Developmental Disorders, 16* (4), 485-494.

American Psychiatric Association. (1987). *Diagnostic and statistical manual of mental disorders—revised* (3rd ed.). Washington, DC: Author.

Garfin, D. G., McCallon, D., & Cox, R. (1988). Validity and reliability of the Childhood Autism Rating Scale with autistic adolescents. *Journal of Autism and Developmental Disorders, 18* (3), 367-378.

[66]
Children's Depression Inventory.

Purpose: A self-rating assessment of children's depression.

Population: Ages 8–17.

Publication Dates: 1977–82.

Acronym: CDI.

Scores: Total score only.

Administration: Individual and small groups.

Price Data: Available from publisher for test, instructions for administration, scoring template, reference list, and manuscripts.

Foreign Language Editions: Translations available in Arabic, Bulgarian, Italian, Hungarian, Hebrew, Spanish, German, French, and Portuguese.

Time: [10–15] minutes.

Comments: For research use only.

Author: Maria Kovacs.

Publisher: Western Psychiatric Institute and Clinic.

TEST REFERENCES

1. Borden, K. A., Brown, R. T., Jenkins, P., & Clingerman, S. R. (1987). Achievement attributions and depressive symptoms in attention deficit-disordered and normal children. *Journal of School Psychology, 25,* 399-404.

2. Carey, M. P., Faulstich, M. E., Gresham, F. M., Ruggiero, L., & Enyart, P. (1987). Children's Depression Inventory: Construct and discriminant validity across clinical and nonreferred (control) populations. *Journal of Consulting and Clinical Psychology, 55,* 755-761.

3. Feshbach, N. D., & Feshbach, S. (1987). Affective processes and academic achievement. *Child Development, 58,* 1335-1347.

4. Finch, A. J., Saylor, C. F., Edwards, G. L., & McIntosh, J. A. (1987). Children's Depression Inventory: Reliability over repeated administrations. *Journal of Clinical Child Psychology, 16,* 339-341.

5. Jouriles, E. N., Barling, J., & O'Leary, K. D. (1987). Predicting child behavior problems in maritally violent families. *Journal of Abnormal Child Psychology, 15,* 165-173.

6. Kazdin, A. E. (1987). Children's Depression Scale: Validation with child psychiatric inpatients. *Journal of Child Psychology and Psychiatry and Allied Disciplines, 28,* 29-41.

7. Matson, J. L., & Nieminen, G. S. (1987). Validity of measures of conduct disorder, depression, and anxiety. *Journal of Clinical Child Psychology, 16,* 151-157.

8. Schaughency, E., Frame, C. Y., & Strauss, C. C. (1987). Self-concept and aggression in elementary school students. *Journal of Clinical Child Psychology, 16,* 116-121.

9. Stark, K. D., Reynolds, W. M., & Kaslow, N. J. (1987). A comparison of the relative efficacy of self-control therapy and a behavioral problem-solving therapy for depression in children. *Journal of Abnormal Child Psychology, 15,* 91-113.

10. Trieber, F. A., & Mabe, P. A., III. (1987). Child and parent perceptions of children's psychopathology in psychiatric outpatient children. *Journal of Abnormal Child Psychology, 15,* 115-124.

11. Vincenzi, H. (1987). Depression and reading ability in sixth-grade children. *Journal of School Psychology, 25,* 155-160.

12. Weisz, J. R., Weiss, B., & Langmeyer, D. B. (1987). Giving up on child psychotherapy: Who drops out? *Journal of Consulting and Clinical Psychology, 55,* 916-918.

13. Wolfe, V. V., Finch, A. J., Jr., Saylor, C. F., Blount, R. L., Pallmeyer, T. P., & Carek, D. J. (1987). Negative affectivity in children: A multitrait-multimethod investigation. *Journal of Consulting and Clinical Psychology, 55,* 245-250.

14. Worchel, F., Nolan, B., & Willson, V. (1987). New perspectives on child and adolescent depression. *Journal of School Psychology, 25,* 411-414.

15. Altmann, E. O., & Gotlib, I. H. (1988). The social behavior of depressed children: An observational study. *Journal of Abnormal Child Psychology, 16,* 29-44.

16. Angold, A. (1988). Childhood and adolescent depression: I. Epidemiological and aetiological aspects. *British Journal of Psychiatry, 152,* 601-617.

17. Benfield, C. Y., Palmer, D. J., Pfefferbaum, B., & Stowe, M. L. (1988). A comparison of depressed and nondepressed disturbed children on measures of attributional style, hopelessness, life stress, and temperament. *Journal of Abnormal Child Psychology, 16,* 397-410.

18. Bodiford, C. A., Eisenstadt, T. H., Johnson, J. H., & Bradlyn, A. S. (1988). Comparison of learned helpless cognitions and behavior in children with high and low scores on the Children's Depression Inventory. *Journal of Clinical Child Psychology, 17,* 152-158.

19. Gates, L., Lineberger, M. R., Crockett, J., & Hubbard, J. (1988). Birth order and its relationship to depression, anxiety, and self-concept test scores in children. *Journal of Genetic Psychology, 149,* 29-34.

20. Kaslow, N. J., Rehm, L. P., Pollack, S. L., & Siegel, A. W. (1988). Attributional style and self-control behavior in depressed and nondepressed children and their parents. *Journal of Abnormal Child Psychology, 16,* 163-175.

21. Knight, D., Hensley, V. R., & Waters, B. (1988). Validation of the Children's Depression Scale and the Children's Depression Inventory in a prepubertal sample. *Journal of Child Psychology and Psychiatry and Allied Disciplines, 29,* 853-863.

22. Robins, C. J. (1988). Attributions and depression: Why is the literature so inconsistent? *Journal of Personality and Social Psychology, 54,* 880-889.

23. Romano, B. A., & Nelson, R. O. (1988). Discriminant and concurrent validity measures of children's depression. *Journal of Clinical Child Psychology, 17,* 255-259.

24. Rowlison, R. T., & Felner, R. D. (1988). Major life events, hassles, and adaptation in adolescence: Confounding in the conceptualization and measurement of life stress and adjustment revisited. *Journal of Personality and Social Psychology, 55,* 432-444.

25. Slotkin, J., Forehand, R., Fauber, R., McCombs, A., & Long, N. (1988). Parent-completed and adolescent-completed CDIS: Relationship to adolescent social and cognitive functioning. *Journal of Abnormal Child Psychology, 16,* 207-217.

26. Spirito, A., Williams, C. A., Stark, L. J., & Hart, K. J. (1988). The Hopelessness Scale for Children: Psychometic properties with normal and emotionally disturbed adolescents. *Journal of Abnormal Child Psychology, 16,* 445-458.

27. Strauss, C. C., Last, C. G., Hersen, M., & Kazdin, A. E. (1988). Association between anxiety and depression in children and adolescents with anxiety disorders. *Journal of Abnormal Child Psychology, 16,* 57-68.

28. Strauss, C. C., Lease, C. A., Last, C. G., & Francis, G. (1988). Overanxious disorder: An examination of developmental differences. *Journal of Abnormal Child Psychology, 16,* 433-443.

29. Wierzbicki, M., & McCabe, M. (1988). Social skills and subsequent depressive symptomatology in children. *Journal of Clinical Child Psychology, 17,* 203-208.

30. Allen, D. M., & Tarnowski, K. J. (1989). Depressive characteristics of physically abused children. *Journal of Abnormal Child Psychology, 17,* 1-11.

31. Belter, R. W., Lipovsky, J. A., & Finch, A. J., Jr. (1989). Rorschach Egocentricity Index and self-concept in children and adolescents. *Journal of Personality Assessment, 53,* 783-789.

32. Christopher, J. D., Giuliani, R., Holte, C. S., Beaman, A. L., & Camp, G. C. (1989). Predictor variables related to the classification of learning disabilities. *Journal of Learning Disabilities, 22,* 588-589.

33. Cole, D. A. (1989). Validation of the Reasons for Living Inventory in general and delinquent adolescent samples. *Journal of Abnormal Child Psychology, 17,* 13-27.

34. Conrad, M., & Hammen, C. (1989). Role of maternal depression in perceptions of child maladjustment. *Journal of Consulting and Clinical Psychology, 57,* 663-667.

35. Einbender, A. J., & Friedrich, W. N. (1989). Psychological functioning and behavior of sexually abused girls. *Journal of Consulting and Clinical Psychology, 57,* 155-157.

36. Hall, C. W., & Haws, D. (1989). Depressive symptomatology in learning-disabled and nonlearning-disabled students. *Psychology in the Schools, 26,* 359-364.

37. Hodges, J. B., & McCoy, J. F. (1989). Distinctions among rejected children on the basis of peer-nominated aggression. *Journal of Clinical Child Psychology, 18,* 121-128.

38. Kazdin, A. E. (1989). Identifying depression in children: A comparison of alternative selection criteria. *Journal of Abnormal Child Psychology, 17,* 437-454.

39. Kennedy, E., Spence, S. H., & Hensley, R. (1989). An examination of the relationship between childhood depression and social competence amongst primary school children. *Journal of Child Psychology and Psychiatry and Allied Disciplines, 30,* 561-573.

40. Lipovsky, J. A., Finch, A. J., Jr., & Belter, R. W. (1989). Assessment of depression in adolescents: Objective and projective measures. *Journal of Personality Assessment, 53,* 449-458.

41. Meyer, N. E., Dyck, D. G., & Petrinack, R. J. (1989). Cognitive appraisal and attributional correlates of depressive symptoms in children. *Journal of Abnormal Child Psychology, 17,* 325-336.

42. Nelms, B. C. (1989). Emotional behaviors in chronically ill children. *Journal of Abnormal Child Psychology, 17,* 647-668.

43. Nieminen, G. S., & Matson, J. L. (1989). Depressive problems in conduct-disordered adolescents. *Journal of School Psychology, 27,* 175-188.

44. Politano, P. M., Edinger, D. L., & Nelson, W. M. III. (1989). Comparisons of conduct and affective disordered youth: A psychometric investigation of responses to the Children's Depression Inventory. *Journal of Child Psychology and Psychiatry and Allied Disciplines, 30,* 431-438.

45. Rodriguez, C. M., & Routh, D. K. (1989). Depression, anxiety, and attributional style in learning disabled and non-learning disabled children. *Journal of Clinical Child Psychology, 18,* 299-304.

46. Wierzbicki, M., & Carver, D. (1989). Children's engagement in antidepressive activities. *Journal of Genetic Psychology, 150,* 163-174.

47. Armsden, G. C., McCauley, E., Greenberg, M. T., Burke, P. M., & Mitchell, J. R. (1990). Parent and peer attachment in early adolescent depression. *Journal of Abnormal Child Psychology, 18,* 683-697.

48. Banez, G. A., & Compas, B. E. (1990). Children's and parents' daily stressful events and psychological symptoms. *Journal of Abnormal Child Psychology, 18,* 591-605.

49. Curry, J. F., & Craighead, W. E. (1990). Attributional style in clinically depressed and conduct disordered adolescents. *Journal of Consulting and Clinical Psychology, 58,* 109-115.

50. Joffe, R. D., Dobson, K. S., Fine, S., Marriage, K., & Haley, G. (1990). Social problem-solving in depressed, conduct-disordered, and normal adolescents. *Journal of Abnormal Child Psychology, 18,* 565-575.

51. Kendall, P. C., Stark, K. D., & Adam, T. (1990). Cognitive deficit or cognitive distortion in childhood depression. *Journal of Abnormal Child Psychology, 18,* 255-270.

52. Kovacs, M., Iyengar, S., Goldston, D., Obrosky, D. S., Stewart, J., & Marsh, J. (1990). Psychological functioning among mothers of children with insulin-dependent diabetes mellitus: A longitudinal study. *Journal of Consulting and Clinical Psychology, 58,* 189-195.

53. Ollendick, T. H., & Yule, W. (1990). Depression in British and American children and its relation to anxiety and fear. *Journal of Consulting and Clinical Psychology, 58,* 126-129.

54. Spirito, A., Hart, K., Overholser, J., & Halverson, J. (1990). Social skills and depression in adolescent suicide attempters. *Adolescence, 25,* 543-552.

55. Stark, K. D., Humphrey, L. L., Crook, K., & Lewis, K. (1990). Perceived family environments of depressed and anxious children: Child's and maternal figure's perspectives. *Journal of Abnormal Child Psychology, 18,* 527-547.

56. Vernberg, E. M. (1990). Psychological adjustment and experiences with peers during early adolescence: Reciprocal, incidental, or unidirectional relationships? *Journal of Abnormal Child Psychology, 18,* 187-198.

57. Whitman, P. B., & Leitenberg, H. (1990). Negatively biased recall in children with self-reported symptoms of depression. *Journal of Abnormal Child Psychology, 18,* 15-27.

58. Worchel, F. F., Hughes, J. N., Hall, B. M., Stanton, S. B., Stanton, H., & Little, V. Z. (1990). Evaluation of subclinical depression in children using self-, peer-, and teacher-report measures. *Journal of Abnormal Child Psychology, 18,* 271-282.

59. Worchel, F., Little, V., & Alcala, J. (1990). Self- perceptions of depressed children on tasks of cognitive abilities. *Journal of School Psychology, 28,* 97-104.

60. Garber, J., Walker, L. S., & Zeman, J. (1991). Somatization symptoms in a community sample of children and adolescents: Further validation of the Children's Somatization Inventory. *Psychological Assessment, 3,* 588-595.

61. Hall, C. W., Beougher, K., & Wasinger, K. (1991). Divorce: Implications for services. *Psychology in the Schools, 28,* 267-275.

62. McNally, R. J. (1991). Assessment of posttraumatic stress disorder in children. *Psychological Assessment, 3,* 531-537.

63. Weiss, B., Weisz, J. R., Politano, M., Corey, M., Nelson, W. M., & Finch, A. J. (1991). Developmental differences in the factor structure of the Children's Depression Inventory. *Psychological Assessment, 3,* 38-45.

Review of the Children's Depression Inventory by MICHAEL G. KAVAN, *Director of Behavioral Sciences and Assistant Professor of Family Practice, Creighton University School of Medicine, Omaha, NE:*

The Children's Depression Inventory (CDI) is a 27-item self-report instrument aimed at measuring depression in children and adolescents between the ages of 8 and 17. According to the author, the CDI was modeled after the Beck Depression Inventory (an adult scale) due to support in the literature that overlap exists among the salient manifestations of depressive disorders in children, adolescents, and adults. This viewpoint has been echoed by the recently revised *Diagnostic and Statistical Manual of Mental Disorders—Third Edition* (DSM-III-R) (APA, 1987). The DSM-III-R indicates the essential features of depression in children and adolescents are similar to those in adults with some recognition of age-specific effects. With this in mind, CDI items cover fully or partially all nine of the DSM-III-R symptom categories for diagnosing major depressive syndrome in children.

ADMINISTRATION AND SCORING. The CDI was designed for individual administration in clinical research settings, but may also be administered in a group format to "normal" individuals. The respondent is handed a copy of the scale and asked to read along silently, marking the appropriate response as the administrator reads the items aloud. Older children and adolescents may continue on their own after a few items, because reading level for the CDI is estimated at the first-grade level (although Berndt, Schwartz, & Kaiser [1983] estimate reading level to be at the third-grade level). Each item contains a three-choice response format (i.e., 0, 1, or 2) reflecting increasing severity of disturbance. Respondents are requested to select the statement from each group that "describes you best for the past two weeks." Scoring simply involves the addition of numerical values assigned to each selected item response. Total scores may therefore range from 0 to 54. Although the CDI is not meant to be a diagnostic instrument, the author does provide cutoff scores for determining depression.

Unfortunately, a cutoff score of 11 has a sensitivity of 67% (i.e., about 33% of the clinically depressed cases will be missed) and a specificity of 60% (i.e., 40% of children taking the CDI will be identified mistakenly as having a depressive disorder). A cutoff score of 13 has a sensitivity of 51% and a specificity of 75%. Predictive values (i.e., the number of true positivies *divided* by the number of true positivies and false positivies multiplied by 100) for the cutoff scores of 11 and 13 are 62% and 67%, respectively.

RELIABILITY. The unpublished manuscript that accompanies the CDI provides information on several reliability studies. Internal consistency (coefficient alpha) has been found to be .86 with a diagnostically heterogeneous, psychiatrically referred sample of children ($n = 75$), .71 with a pediatric-medical outpatient group ($n = 61$), and .87 with a large sample of Toronto public school children ($n = 860$). Item-total score correlations for these three samples range from .08 to .62. One-month test-retest data on 29 recently diagnosed children with diabetes were .43 (when two outlying subjects were dropped in subsequent analysis, reliability improved to .82). Nine-week test-retest data on a subsample of 90 school children were .84. Because the CDI is supposed to measure a state as opposed to a trait, however, the author recommends a 2-week test-retest interval may be most appropriate. No data are provided in the accompanying manuscript to indicate level of stability of the CDI over this time period. Saylor, Finch, Spirito, and Bennett (1984) found 1-week test-retest reliability to be .87 in 28 emotionally disturbed children and .38 in 69 normal fifth and sixth grade children.

VALIDITY. Concurrent validity of the CDI was determined against two self-rating instruments that assess constructs related to depression. CDI scores were found to correlate positively with scores from the Revised Children's Manifest Anxiety Scale and to correlate negatively with scores from the Coopersmith Self-Esteem Inventory. Evidence of criterion-related validity and construct validity of the CDI was provided by Carlson and Cantwell (1979) and Cantwell and Carlson (1981), who examined the relationship between CDI scores and independent psychiatric diagnoses in 102 children aged 7 to 17 years who were undergoing inpatient or outpatient psychiatric treatment. Results indicated that patients with higher self-rated depression as measured by the CDI received higher global severity ratings of depression on the basis of a semistructured interview administered without knowledge of patients' CDI results. The high-scoring patients were also more likely to receive a formal diagnosis of major depressive disorder. Factor analysis completed on data collected from the Toronto public school system yielded one principal factor, whereas studies with clinic-referred children yielded as many as seven separate factors.

NORMS. Limited normative data are available on several groups. Information is presented in a disjointed manner in the accompanying manuscript. Means, modes, standard deviations, ranges, and standard errors are made available on recently diagnosed juvenile diabetics ($n = 61$), child psychiatric outpatients ($n = 75$), and Toronto public school children ($n = 860$). In addition, means, standard deviations, and standard errors are provided for various small psychiatric diagnostic samples (range of $n = 10$–40). Means are not provided for specific age groups nor for minority populations. In light of the age-specific features associated with depression (highlighted in DSM-III-R) and recent research suggesting age-related (Helsel & Matson, 1984) and race-related (Politano, Nelson, Evans, Sorenson, & Zeman, 1986) differences on the CDI, these would seem most important for proper interpretation. As a result, the clinician is

left with little information on how to appropriately interpret CDI score results.

SUMMARY. The CDI is a self-report instrument designed to assess depressive symptomatology in school-aged children and adolescents. Its easy and efficient administration and scoring are very beneficial to clinicians. Although further studies need to be completed on the test-retest reliability of the CDI, internal consistency and validity appear adequate for a research instrument. As a result, the CDI shows promise as an instrument to measure childhood depression. However, limited normative data are provided by the author, and thus, the CDI should be interpreted cautiously.

Until more research is collected on the CDI, its use, as its author suggests, should be limited to that of "clinical research settings." Unfortunately, due to the absence of a solid self-report instrument to assess childhood and adolescent depression, many clinicians may be pressed to use this scale for purposes beyond those recommended by the author.

REVIEWER'S REFERENCES

Carlson, G. A., & Cantwell, D. P. (1979). A survey of depressive symptoms in a child and adolescent psychiatric population. *Journal of the American Academy of Child Psychiatry, 18,* 587-599.

Cantwell, D. P., & Carlson, G. A. (1981, October). *Factor analysis of a self-rating depressive inventory for children: Factor structure and nosological utility.* Paper presented at the annual meeting of the American Academy of Child Psychiatry, Dallas, TX.

Berndt, D. J., Schwartz, S., & Kaiser, C. F. (1983). Readability of self-report depression inventories. *Journal of Consulting and Clinical Psychology, 51,* 627-628.

Helsel, W. J., & Matson, J. L. (1984). The assessment of depression in children: The internal structure of the Child Depression Inventory (CDI). *Behaviour Research and Therapy, 22,* 289-298.

Saylor, C. F., Finch, A. J., Spirito, A., & Bennett, B. (1984). The Children's Depression Inventory: A systematic evaluation of psychometric properties. *Journal of Consulting and Clinical Psychology, 52,* 955-967.

Politano, P. M., Nelson, W. M., Evans, H. E., Sorenson, S. B., & Zeman, D. J. (1986). Factor analytic evaluation of differences between black and Caucasian emotionally disturbed children on the Children's Depression Inventory. *Journal of Psychopathology and Behavioral Assessment, 8,* 1-7.

American Psychiatric Association. (1987). *Diagnostic and statistical manual of mental disorders* (3rd ed. rev.). Washington, DC: Author.

Review of the Children's Depression Inventory by HOWARD M. KNOFF, *Associate Professor of School Psychology and Director of the School Psychology Program, University of South Florida, Tampa, FL:*

In formulating this review, the following documents were read and considered: (*a*) the Children's Depression Inventory (CDI) protocol along with its two-page photocopied "Instructions for the Administration of the Children's Depression Inventory" dated March, 1978; (*b*) an unpublished manuscript (April, 1983) by Maria Kovacs, the CDI's author, entitled "The Children's Depression Inventory: A Self-Rated Depression Scale for School-Aged Youngsters"; (*c*) an article describing the CDI's construction and some psychometrically-related research (Kovacs, 1985); and (*d*) a three-page list of references of research with the CDI copyrighted 1982 but dated October 1987. The review of these documents is notable given the fact that the CDI is available only from the author and that a user might not have access to these materials so as to understand how to best use (if at all) this inventory.

As noted correctly by the author, the CDI should be used only as a research tool. However, given the scale construction and psychometric concerns discussed below, it is recommended that research with the CDI be used only for further scale refinement or to demonstrate its own reliability and validity across multiple samples, both clinically-involved and normal. Any other use of the CDI at this time, for example as a functional dependent or independent variable, would be premature and unsupportable.

Currently the CDI is a 27-item self-report scale that is purported to be suitable for school-aged children and adolescents aged 8 to 17. Based on the adult Beck Depression Inventory (Beck, 1967), the CDI has been developed in four phases from 1975 to 1979, the most significant of which used data from 39 consecutively admitted 8- to 13-year-old patients from a child guidance center, 20 age-matched "normal" controls, and 127 children from the Toronto public schools aged 10 to 13. While the use of such small and geographically confined samples for a scale's initial development might be acceptable, the CDI has never been nationally normed using appropriate stratification processes, its use with and generalizability to multiple (research) samples has been unsystematic, and its evaluation has consisted of various reliability and validity studies that have been equivocal in their results.

Yet, the CDI's author recommends this inventory for research, and in her unpublished April, 1983, manuscript states that "it is best used as a severity measure in appropriately selected samples . . . [because] . . . the investigator who does not have the resources to conduct clinical interviews does need a tool for subject selection" (p. 19). The author then continues by suggesting a CDI cutoff score, to identify children with depressive disorders in research studies, that, by her own admission, misses "about 49% of the clinically depressed cases . . . [yet] . . . will include the lowest number of false positives" (p. 21). Given the CDI's construction and lack of systematic and consistent psychometric data, the author's recommendations regarding the use of the CDI in research and her suggestion of a clinical cutoff score appear premature and ill-advised. In fact, many recommendations for the scale have gone beyond the evaluation data thus far collected. Indeed, even in such a basic area as test administration, a conclusion that CDI group administration procedures appear acceptable because a number of studies using this approach "reported no difficulties" is based more on anecdotal reports than actual research data.

Expanding on administration, the CDI's items are written at the first grade level, and children respond to each item by identifying which of three choices best describes their feelings and ideas over the past 2 weeks. Fifty percent of the items start with the choice reflecting a "more depressed" status or correlate, and the rest start with the "less depressed" choice. Although the directions and protocol are clear and easy to read, separate booklets for younger (elementary school) versus older (high school) respondents are suggested. The former booklet might provide fewer items per page and more space between item choices, while the latter might be printed to appear more "grown up." Relative to actual administration, examiner directions are clear, and appropriate recommendations for individualization for children with reading or attentional problems are made. Overall, the CDI's administration procedures appear clear-cut and efficient. Perhaps the instruction sheet provided for the test will soon be integrated into a comprehensive manual including both administration and technical data.

Relative to reliability, a number of studies using different normal and clinical samples have reported inconsistent results. For example, reported studies suggest that the CDI's internal consistency is acceptable for separate samples of clinically referred, psychiatrically distressed youngsters and normal children, but that less consistency was noted for a pediatric-medical outpatient group. Similar inconsistent results occurred with the same samples when item-total score correlations were evaluated. These inconsistencies were of such a magnitude the author concluded that the CDI "does not have the same 'reality' to different respondent groups" (Kovacs, 1983, p. 12). Although test-retest reliability ranged from .43 over a 4-week period for diagnosed juvenile diabetics to .84 over a 9-week period with 90 children from the Toronto "standardization" sample, overall a number of serious reliability questions exist that must be addressed by future research. Among the most important questions are (a) to what degree does the CDI test-response pattern truly vary across research and/or clinical samples, and if it does vary, how can it be used with any consistency relative to interpretation and generalization; and (b) to what degree is the CDI a state-related versus trait-related instrument (i.e., what results should be expected when test-retest reliability is measured)?

Relative to validity, the CDI again seems to yield inconsistent results. While concurrent validity with such scales as the Revised Children's Manifest Anxiety Scale and the Coopersmith Self-Esteem Inventory appear acceptable, construct, discriminant, and predictive validity data are problematic. For example, CDI factor analyses with the Toronto student sample yielded one principal factor, yet with a psychiatric-clinic referred sample, *seven* factors were found. Thus, again, the CDI appears to vary from sample to sample in its psychometric reactivity, making its research or clinical use difficult. CDI discriminant and predictive validity studies indicated the instrument (a) could not discriminate a normal from a heterogeneous child psychiatric sample; and (b) that it could discriminate certain outpatient children with major depressive disorders from children with adjustment disorders, with depression in remission, and with other pathologies but not depression even though *the actual score differences were not that substantive.* To summarize, the CDI has not been thoroughly validated, and more research in this area is critical. The author's caution not to use the CDI for patient selection, but as an adjunct to other diagnostic screening tools is important and should be heeded.

Although the author is very forthright in describing the limitations and equivocable results of the CDI, it may be too early to conclude, as she does, that it "has clear promise as an assessment tool in treatment-outcome studies" (Kovacs, 1985, p. 998) depending on how one operationalizes "promise." For now, the CDI needs a great deal more research on its own psychometric properties. This is recommended *before* utilizing it as a dependent or independent variable in research investigating, for example, different characteristics of depressed children or the ability of certain interventions to decrease children's depression. The CDI *cannot* be used diagnostically at this time, thus it is disconcerting to find a cutoff score to identify children with major depressive disorders even suggested—the fear being that someone not familiar with the CDI's current status might actually use the test and the cutoff in clinical practice. To summarize, there is clearly a need for a sound children's depression inventory in our field. While the CDI has the potential to be one of those scales, a great deal more research on its own psychometric properties is needed at this time.

REVIEWER'S REFERENCES

Beck, A. T. (1967). *Depression: Clinical, experimental, and theoretical aspects.* New York: Harper & Row.

Kovacs, M. (1983). *The Children's Depression Inventory: A self-rated depression scale for school-aged youngsters.* Unpublished manuscript, University of Pittsburgh School of Medicine, Pittsburgh.

Kovacs, M. (1985). The Children's Depression Inventory (CDI). *Psychopharmacology Bulletin, 21,* 995-998.

[67]
CID Phonetic Inventory.

Purpose: To evaluate the hearing-impaired "child's speech ability at the phonetic level."
Population: Hearing-impaired children.
Publication Date: 1988.
Scores, 7: Suprasegmental Aspects, Vowels and Diphthongs, Initial Consonants, Consonants with Alternating Vowels, Final Consonants, Alternating Consonants, Average.
Administration: Individual.

Price Data, 1989: $24 per complete kit including manual (24 pages), 25 rating forms, and 166 stimulus cards; $5 per 25 rating forms.
Time: (30–35) minutes.
Author: Jean S. Moog.
Publisher: Central Institute for the Deaf.

Review of the CID Phonetic Inventory by VINCENT J. SAMAR, Associate Professor of Communication Research, National Technical Institute for the Deaf, Rochester Institute of Technology, Rochester, NY:

The CID Phonetic Inventory is a clinical evaluation instrument for rating children's phonetic productions of various suprasegmental and segmental aspects of speech. It closely follows the first three sections of Ling's (1976) Phonetic Level Evaluation. It is intended for classroom teachers and speech pathologists to use diagnostically as a basis for selecting specific speech training objectives, and as an objective measure of children's progress in acquiring phonetic skills. The manual asserts that the Phonetic Inventory should be useful for quantitatively comparing children's rates of acquisition of phonetic skills, and for research on the impact of hearing aids, tactile aids, and cochlear implants on speech development.

The Phonetic Inventory includes a broad sample of 361 specific vocal behaviors and phonemic sequencing tasks to assess suprasegmental and segmental control at the syllabic level. Like Ling's instrument, the Phonetic Inventory provides teachers and speech pathologists with the opportunity to systematically elicit and judge the acceptability of a representative range of specific syllabic productions. And like Ling's instrument, teachers and speech pathologists may use the Phonetic Inventory to develop a subjective clinical profile, a professional mental understanding that integrates the child's successes and failures with the evaluator's knowledge and experience of speech acquisition patterns. But, in these respects the Phonetic Inventory offers nothing new for testing phonetic competence. Actually, Ling's instrument is more comprehensive because it also tests phonetic blends.

The Phonetic Inventory's novelty lies in the quantitative section scores it provides. This innovation putatively endows the Phonetic Inventory with the ability to objectively document progress in clinical and research settings. Unfortunately, the manual provides no validity data showing these scores achieve psychometrically valid diagnostic detail.

TEST DESCRIPTION. The Phonetic Inventory consists of six sections: Suprasegmental Aspects, Vowels and Diphthongs, Initial Consonants, Consonants with Alternating Vowels, Final Consonants, and Alternating Consonants. The Suprasegmental Aspects section rates children's elicited productions on: (a) vocal duration and repetition timing, (b) vocal intensity, (*c*) continuous and discrete pitch modulation, (*d*) breath control for single-breath syllable repetitions, and (*e*) voice quality of single, repetitive, and alternating syllable patterns. The remaining five sections rate productions of 16 vowels and diphthongs in consonant-vowel-consonant (CVC) syllables, and of 22 initial and 14 final consonants in CV and VC syllables involving different vowel heights. Single and repetitive syllable productions and vowel or consonant alternation sequences are separately rated. Graphic and syllabic cue cards aid test administration.

RELIABILITY AND VALIDITY DATA. Surprisingly, the manual presents only a single Pearson interrater reliability coefficient of .93 to justify the quantitative use of this test. This coefficient was based on two very experienced teachers' overall ratings of only 20 students. Importantly, the author acknowledges that achieving such a high reliability coefficient requires practice in rating. Unfortunately, we do not know whether this practice-enhanced reliability represents accurate phonetic competency measurement due to the suppression of idiosyncratic rater biases, or conversely reflects the institutional standardization of rater biases at the expense of accurate phonetic competency measurement.

No additional reliability or validity data are presented. Given that the Phonetic Inventory purports to be a quantitative diagnostic test, it is inexcusable that separate reliability coefficients were not computed for the six sections. Given the amount of time required to administer the six sections (30 + minutes), it is equally inexcusable that no attempt was made to validate their metric distinctiveness. Are the sections' intercorrelations low enough to believe their scores provide usefully different information?

CONSTRUCT VALIDITY. I accept without hesitation that teachers and speech pathologists may form diagnostically valid mental profiles of a child's phonetic competence using the Phonetic Inventory to elicit speech samples. However, it is questionable whether the construct validity of such a mental profile is preserved in the process of generating 361 independent categorical ratings. Evaluators might not assign equal importance to each test item in forming their mental profiles. Rather, an item's importance may depend complexly on an evaluator's perceptions and professional criteria. Yet, arithmetically, each item contributes an equal weight to its final section summary score. Consider, for example, that a hearing-impaired person's speech, even at the single syllable level, can be complexly disordered acoustically without being terribly distorted phonetically. Syllabic utterances may have unnatural pitch, conspicuous breathiness, or be perceptibly speeded or slowed without necessarily triggering phonemic misidentifications by normal listeners. Given an acoustically disordered but phonetically acceptable speech event an evaluator faces a fundamental perceptual conflict, and ratings of speech events appear to be inherently sensitive to that conflict (Samar & Metz, 1988; 1991). However, that conflict may not carry the same weight in the rater's eventual mental profile as the forced categorical rating associated with that conflict carries in the section's summary score. The construct validity of Phonetic Inventory summary scores is therefore suspect a priori and requires empirical support. For example, do clinicians' subjective holistic ratings of children's phonetic performance on the test's six sections correlate closely with the test's tally of acceptable individual ratings assigned by the same clinicians? The answers to this and many other empirical validity questions are required to justify the quantitative use of this test.

More generally, the diagnostic specificity of the six subscales of the Phonetic Inventory is not guaranteed just because they were designed to include distinct classes of target syllable productions. Speech-property ratings do not necessarily faithfully measure the speech behavior that they target when speech samples are complexly disordered. For example, several validly measured segmental and suprasegmental factors have been shown to determine a hearing-impaired person's speech intelligibility in factor analytic studies (e.g., see Metz, Schiavetti, Samar, & Sitler, 1990). However, we recently factor analyzed published correlational data from Subtelny's (1977) study of 249 hearing-impaired adults involving an articulatory measure and six different rating scales reputedly sensitive to different segmental and suprasegmental aspects of speech intelligibility (e.g., pitch control, speaking rate). A single segmental-control factor described 80% of the data variance. No stable suprasegmental factor emerged despite the strong focus of the rating scales on suprasegmental diagnostics. Apparently, raters could not adequately suppress competing segmental information while rating specific suprasegmental dimensions of complexly disordered speech. Do the six rating scales of the Phonetic Inventory possess an appropriately differentiated factor structure? Again, appropriate validation studies are necessary.

CONCLUSION. Teachers and speech pathologists may find the CID Phonetic Inventory useful for qualitative diagnostics in lieu of competing phonetic evaluation procedures such as Ling's Phonetic Level Evaluation. I cannot recommend it as a *quantitative* test of the suprasegmental and segmental integrity of a child's phonetic control at this stage of the test's development. Immediate use of the CID Phonetic Inventory to document a child's progress quantitatively, to compare rates of phonetic skill acquisition among different children, or to evaluate and document quantitatively the effectiveness of assistive devices would be scientifically (and possibly clinically) irresponsible. A foundation of reliability and validity statistics and normative data is absolutely essential before quantitative use can be recommended.

REVIEWER'S REFERENCES

Ling, D. (1976). *Speech and the hearing impaired child: Theory and practice.* Washington, DC: Alexander Graham Bell Association.
Subtelny, J. (1977). Assessment of speech with implications for training. In F. Bess (Ed.), *Childhood deafness* (pp. 183-194). New York: Grune and Stratton.
Samar, V. J., & Metz, D. E. (1988). Criterion validity of speech intelligibility rating-scale procedures for the hearing-impaired population. *Journal of Speech and Hearing Research, 31,* 307-316.
Metz, D. E., Schiavetti, N., Samar, V. J., & Sitler, R. W. (1990). Acoustic dimensions of hearing-impaired speakers' intelligibility: Segmental and suprasegmental characteristics. *Journal of Speech and Hearing Research, 33,* 476-487.
Samar, V. J., & Metz, D. E. (1991). Scaling and transcription measures of intelligibility for populations with disordered speech: Where's the beef? *Journal of Speech and Hearing Research, 34,* 699-702.

[68]
CID Picture SPINE.

Purpose: To "provide a measure of speech intelligibility for severely and profoundly hearing-impaired children and adolescents."
Population: Hearing-impaired children ages 6–13.
Publication Date: 1988.
Scores: Total score only.
Administration: Individual.
Price Data, 1989: $100 per complete kit including 300 picture cards, 25 response forms (4 pages), and test manual (31 pages); $5 per 25 response forms.
Time: (20–30) minutes.
Authors: Randall Monsen, Jean S. Moog, and Ann E. Geers.
Publisher: Central Institute for the Deaf.

Review of the CID Picture SPINE by VINCENT J. SAMAR, Associate Professor of Communication Research, National Technical Institute for the Deaf, Rochester Institute of Technology, Rochester, NY:

The CID Picture Speech Intelligibility Evaluation (Picture SPINE) is an easy-to-use speech intelligibility assessment test for use with severely to profoundly hearing-impaired children who do not yet read. Its design is logical and empirically well motivated; limited initial data suggest that it is reliable and shows predictive validity. A reasonably principled framework for meaningful intelligibility assessment has emerged from recent empirical and theoretical work on the hearing-impaired population; the Picture SPINE follows the prescriptions of that framework nicely.

TEST DESCRIPTION. The Picture SPINE consists of four sets of picture cards containing 75 cards each: a 25-card rehearsal deck and a 50-card test deck. Each rehearsal-deck card contains a distinct picture; two duplications of the rehearsal-deck cards compose the test deck. For each set, the examiner trains the child using the rehearsal deck and then blindly presents each test-deck card to the child for naming. For each card, the examiner records the word the child's utterance most closely resembles

from among the set's 25 possible consonant-vowel-consonant (CVC) picture names. The percentage of correct responses represents the child's overall intelligibility.

EMPIRICAL MOTIVATION. The choice of the picture names used is empirically well motivated. They include voicing contrasts in word-initial and word-final positions (e.g., pear/bear, bed/belt) and vowel-height contrasts (e.g., pin/pen). Previous studies have demonstrated a strong predictive relationship between the integrity of hearing-impaired speakers' acoustic cues for these phonemic contrasts and various intelligibility measures (Monsen, 1978, 1981; Metz, Schiavetti, Samar, & Sitler, 1990; Samar, Metz, Schhiavetti, Sitler, & Whitehead, 1989). Within each test set the picture names share a similar place of articulation for their initial phonemes. Consequently, the picture names within a given set are easily confusable, requiring the child to specifically control the voicing and vowel height contrasts in order to be understood by the evaluator. The four test sets broadly span several phonemes over several places of articulation, providing a global sampling of a child's articulatory repertoire.

PARADIGMATIC STATUS. Three general paradigms are typically used to assess intelligibility: (*a*) The *Rating Scale* paradigm: Listeners assign ratings to a speaker's read or spontaneous utterances; various speech properties can be rated separately (e.g., pitch register, prosody, speaking rate); (*b*) The *Transcription* paradigm: A speaker reads lists of sentences or words and listeners record the speaker's utterances verbatim without consulting a fixed utterance set; percent of key words correctly identified represents intelligibility; and (*c*) The *Forced-Choice* paradigm: The speaker utters a set of individual speech items, usually CVC words, and listeners identify the utterances from among a closed set of alternatives. The Picture SPINE is a forced-choice, isolated word, overall-performance intelligibility test.

Good intelligibility tests must overcome some important problems to be useful and valid (see Boothroyd, 1985). They should suppress the effects of professional listener experience on test scores. They should control the effects of material-specific syntactic/semantic context on word recognition probabilities. They should ensure that intelligibility is measured, not some other speech dimension. It is also useful if an intelligibility test is based on a paradigm with the potential to provide valid analytic detail about the articulatory/acoustic problem underlying reduced intelligibility. Even if the test is not itself diagnostic, it will fit more validly into a comprehensive testing program if it shares fundamental psychometric design features with specialized follow-up tests. Finally, a good intelligibility test should generalize to natural speech performance.

The Picture SPINE possesses all these properties. Using CVCs greatly reduces the effects of listener experience and eliminates the material-specific effects of semantic/syntactic context on word recognition probabilities (Boothroyd, 1985). The Picture SPINE largely measures intelligibility, not some perceptually conspicuous but linguistically irrelevant speech behavior. This is because it requires listeners to identify speech sounds based on the speaker's control of the obligatory feature distinctions of English (Monsen, 1981; Samar & Metz, 1991). Specialized forced choice tests can assess various specific segmental and suprasegmental speech properties. Thus, the Picture SPINE belongs to a psychometrically flexible paradigm with general diagnostic capability. Finally, the Picture SPINE appears to generalize to natural speech performance because (*a*) it is based on phonemic contrasts that strongly predict *contextual* intelligibility (Monsen, 1978; Metz, et al., 1990), and (*b*) speakers' Picture SPINE scores can be converted very accurately to contextual intelligibility scores with a power function formula developed by Boothroyd (Schiavetti, Sitler, Metz, & Houde, 1984). This conversion would place speakers' Picture SPINE scores onto a scale possessing the correct metric relationships for comparative contextual intelligibility assessments among speakers.

COMPARISON TO OTHER TESTS. No transcription test for easy use with preliterate children is available to compete with the Picture SPINE. Rating scales are visible competitors because they can be applied to preliterate children simply by eliciting spontaneous speech samples. However, the Picture SPINE is unquestionably superior for valid quantitative assessment.

Intelligibility rating scales violate their equal-interval assumption, display gross validity violations for individuals in the clinically critical midrange of intelligibility, and are approximately three times less accurate than transcription and forced-choice measures (Schiavetti, Metz, & Sitler, 1981; Samar & Metz, 1988). Rating scales seem inordinately sensitive to listener experience and to conspicuous vocal qualities unrelated to intelligibility. Some recent factor analytic results show that rating scales are psychometrically insensitive to the very diagnostic dimensions of speech that they purport to distinguish and quantify (Samar & Metz, 1988, 1991). Unlike the Picture SPINE, speech-property rating scales evidently do not satisfy the generally acknowledged paradigmatic requirements for valid and useful intelligibility measurement.

RELIABILITY AND VALIDITY. The psychometric information provided by the Picture SPINE manual, although encouraging, is deficient. The Picture SPINE is a particularly attractive new test precisely because it promises easy, reliable, and valid intelligibility assessment of preliterate hearing-impaired children. Yet, the reliability and criterion-validity data reported are mostly based on children old enough to read. These psychometric data do not necessarily generalize to preliterate children. Additionally, the authors' study sample was restricted to a mere 20 children with contextual intelligibility ratings above about 40%. The test's reliability and validity for children with less than 40% intelligibility remains unattested. One of the validity correlations in the manual is erroneously reported. The criterion-validity correlation coefficients between the Picture SPINE and a sentence transcription test for examiners A and B are reported as .96 and .91, respectively. The same correlations computed directly from data in Table 1 of the manual are .85 and .91, respectively. Finally, no normative data are presented that would permit evaluators to make norm-referenced interpretations of children's intelligibility test performance at different ages. Considerable additional psychometric work is necessary to develop the full assessment potential of the Picture SPINE.

ACHILLES HEEL. Valid intelligibility assessment using the Picture SPINE depends critically on the examiner remaining ignorant of the picture name presented on each test trial. However, I find it easy to see the test pictures right through the backs of the test cards under normal office lighting conditions. Examiners using the Picture SPINE must consistently conceal the identity of the test pictures from themselves. I suggest that the examiner hold the cards in one stack facing the child and peel off the front-most card on each test trial after recording the child's utterance. Thick cardboard can be used to mask the back of the deck from the examiner.

CONCLUSION. The Picture SPINE is among the best currently available tests for easy and valid quantitative assessment of the speech intelligibility of severely to profoundly hearing-impaired children. Combined with specialized mathematical tools like Boothroyd's contextual intelligibility transformation and with properly designed follow-up diagnostics, the Picture SPINE has the potential to significantly improve the evaluation of a child's progress in speech intelligibility, and the speech intelligibility research enterprise.

REVIEWER'S REFERENCES

Monsen, R. B. (1978). Toward measuring how well hearing-impaired children speak. *Journal of Speech and Hearing Research, 21,* 197-219.

Monsen, R. B. (1981). A usable test for the speech intelligibility of deaf talkers. *American Annals of the Deaf, 126,* 845-852.

Schiavetti, N., Metz, D. E., & Sitler, R. W. (1981). Construct validity of direct magnitude estimation and interval scaling of speech intelligibility: Evidence from a study of the hearing impaired. *Journal of Speech and Hearing Research, 24,* 441-445.

Schiavetti, N., Sitler, R. W., Metz, D. E., & Houde, R. A. (1984). Prediction of contextual speech intelligibility from isolated word intelligibility measures. *Journal of Speech and Hearing Research, 27,* 623-626.

Boothroyd, A. (1985). Evaluation of speech production of the hearing-impaired: Some benefits of forced-choice testing. *Journal of Speech and Hearing Research, 28,* 185-196.

Samar, V. J., & Metz, D. E. (1988). Criterion validity of speech intelligibility rating-scale procedures for the hearing-impaired population. *Journal of Speech and Hearing Research*, 31, 307-316.

Samar, V. J., Metz, D. E., Schiavetti, N., Sitler, R. W., & Whitehead, R. L. (1989). Articulatory dimensions of hearing-impaired speakers' intelligibility: Evidence from a time related aerodynamic, acoustic, and electroglottographic study. *Journal of Communication Disorders*, 22, 243-264.

Metz, D. E., Schiavetti, N., Samar, V. J., & Sitler, R. W. (1990). Acoustic dimensions of hearing-impaired speakers' intelligibility: Segmental and suprasegmental characteristics. *Journal of Speech and Hearing Research*, 33, 476-487.

Samar, V. J., & Metz, D. E. (1991). Scaling and transcription measures of intelligibility for populations with disordered speech: Where's the beef? *Journal of Speech and Hearing Research*, 34, 699-702.

[69]

Class Achievement Test in Mathematics.

Purpose: "To survey the extent to which individual students and class groups have mastered aspects of primary mathematics."
Population: Years 4–5, 6–7 in Australian schools.
Publication Dates: 1979–86.
Acronym: CATIM.
Scores, 6: Counting and Place Value, Whole Numbers and Money, Fractions, Measurement I, Measurement II, Total.
Administration: Group.
Levels, 2: Years 4/5, Years 6/7.
Price Data, 1989: A$1.45 per test and answer strip sheet; $.55 per additional answer strip sheets; $1.45 per class analysis sheet; $5.85 per teacher's manual ('86, 31 pages) (specify Year 4/5 or Year 6/7).
Time: 45(55) minutes.
Comments: Levels available as separates.
Authors: Greg Cornish, John Foyster, Peter Jeffery, David Sewell, Robin Wines, John Izard, and Graham Ward.
Publisher: Australian Council for Educational Research Ltd. [Australia].

Review of the Class Achievement Test in Mathematics by GARY J. STAINBACK, Senior Psychologist, Department of Pediatrics, East Carolina University School of Medicine, Greenville, NC:

The Class Achievement Test in Mathematics (CATIM) has two forms for Year 4/5 and Year 6/7, and has been developed for use in the Australian Schools to survey the basic mathematical skills of school children. Year 4/5 and 6/7 corresponds to grades 4/5 and 6/7 in the United States and Canada. Each test contains 45 items and students record their answers on long, thin answer strips for further analysis. The manual is neatly organized and is easy to follow. The reusable test booklets have good separation of items and clear readability. Some items are more appropriate for Australian children than for students of different nationalities. Measurement tasks are only of the metric system, and counting of money reflects the currency of Australia. Placement of decimal points may also be confusing to some children, because that placement is at a midnumeral height rather than on the lower horizontal level of the numeral. Intelligent children, comfortable with the required tasks, will probably make the transition without difficulty;

however, those experiencing some achievement difficulty in mathematics and of other than Australian education will surely find those items even more confusing.

Scoring of the test is simple. The items are of multiple choice, and the answer key is on the Class Analysis Chart. This Class Analysis Chart provides an item code for item difficulty (four levels of difficulty from easiest to most difficult). The Teacher's Manual reviews scoring procedures for either one student at a time, or scoring one item at a time (for the class of students). In addition the manual provides direction on how the teacher can perform an item analysis with the aid of the Class Analysis Chart. No suggested values are given, however, for determining if meaningful differences exist between mastery levels of different subject areas. This Class Analysis Chart is a large spread sheet ($23^5/_8$ x $16^1/_2$ inches), and allows the teacher to record information on the student's test performance, with the possibility to group student answer strips by student group or alphabetically.

Technical information in the manual explains the selection process of types of schools involved in the standardization study (November, 1983), and separates schools by Catholic, Government, or Independent. No information is available regarding sex, age, or racial composition of the total standardization reference group. These variables would prove very important if the tests and available norms are used outside of the Australian educational system. Reliability coefficients reported are satisfactory; however, the only validity reported is face validity as determined by the teacher. Due to differences existing in the instructional objectives between the Australian schools and schools in the United States, validity of the test could be suspect.

The November standardization of the norms would prove a disadvantage in the United States. Educators employing the CATIM near the beginning of the school year would prefer an early standardization time (November is near the end of the Australian school year). In this way, student strengths and weaknesses with respect to mathematical skills could be evaluated early in the academic year, and educational plans developed for teaching those objectives for which the student has not yet demonstrated mastery. Likewise, if the test is used for any postmeasure, another standardization date in the latter portion of the academic year should be established (e.g., February or March in U.S. and Canadian schools).

In summary the CATIM is not appropriate for use in the United States because of potential differences existing in some educational objectives as well as the use of some terms which would confuse the reader and complicate the task. Neither do the norms contain information relating to the age, sex, or racial composition of the reference group, so comparison to classrooms of children tested outside of Australia would be risky. An interesting feature of the CATIM, however, is the encouragement by the instrument to item analyze the student responses, so that more appropriate educational interventions can be planned. With some item rewriting and further standardization, the instrument would prove useful to a broad international audience.

Review of the Class Achievement Test in Mathematics by RICHARD M. WOLF, Professor of Psychology and Education, Teachers College, Columbia University, New York, NY:

The Class Achievement Test in Mathematics (CATIM) consists of two tests, one for students in Years 4/5 and one for students in Years 6/7 in Australian schools (public and non-public). Each test consists of 45 items measuring mathematics performance in five major content areas and covering four process areas (knowledge, computation, application, and understanding). The quality of the printing in the test booklets is among the best this reviewer has ever seen.

The Teacher's Manual furnishes a clear set of directions for administration for the teacher to follow. Students record their answers on a perforated answer strip sheet which can then be torn off and pasted onto a Class Analysis Chart by a teacher to facilitate an item analysis for the class. The answer strip appears to be cumbersome and could possibly present problems for younger students.

The test blueprint for each level is the same and there are a few items that are common to both levels. The content topics and skills accord well with those included in a numeration test developed to assess the status of Australian students (Keeves, & Bourke, 1976, pp. 33-34). Each test item number is shown in the blueprint so it is possible to assess the content validity of the items. The items match the test specifications quite well on the whole. There is one interesting exception. Several of the items appear to be more a measure of numerical reasoning and spatial relations than achievement in mathematics. In the United States, these items would likely be found in a test such as the Differential Aptitude Tests (9:352). They seem questionable to include in a mathematics achievement test.

The reliability of the total test scores at each level was estimated using KR20 and range from .85 to .88. These are satisfactory considering the somewhat diverse content of the tests. The manual recommends obtaining subscores in five areas: Counting and Place Value, Whole Numbers and Money, Fractions, Measurement I (spatial relations, graphs, length, area and volume, and capacity), and Measurement II (mass and weight and time). The number of items comprising these subscores ranges from 6 to 13. Applying the Spearman-Brown

formula to the total score reliabilities yields estimates of subscore reliability ranging from .43 to .62. These are unacceptably low. The use of subscores in interpreting individual test performance is, at best, questionable.

Norms for the CATIM were developed using a two-stage sampling design. At the first stage, schools were selected from each state and territory from among government, Catholic, and independent schools. The acceptance rate was over 80% at each year level. In the second stage, students were selected randomly within each school by the test publisher. Four different tests were distributed within each class at each testing session. The procedure aimed for a group of about six students per class group. This was done to reduce the design effect caused by testing intact classes within the schools. This seems to be a reasonable compromise between the goals of obtaining precise estimates of performance and a minimum of disruption in the schools.

The number of schools in the norm group at each year level ranged from 67 to 72 and the number of students ranged from 414 to 490. These numbers are somewhat low but probably minimally satisfactory given the high participation rate and the way in which the within school sampling was done. Unfortunately, no information was reported on the actual design effects.

Norms reported in the test manual are percentile ranks and stanines for total scores along with means and standard deviations, item difficulties, and average item difficulties for the subscores at each year level. The manual contains appropriate cautions regarding the interpretation of percentile ranks given the imprecision of the tests. Lower and upper limits for a 68% confidence interval are supplied with each percentile rank at each year level to reduce the tendency to overinterpret small score differences.

The norms for the CATIM furnish some useful information regarding the construct validity of the tests. Because one level of the test is intended for Years 4 and 5 and the other level is intended for Years 6 and 7, the means at adjacent levels indicate how much growth occurs from one year to the next. At the total test level, the higher year level is about one half of a standard deviation above the lower year level. There are also notable increases in item difficulties from one year to the next. In addition, there are several items that are included in both levels of the test. They also show generally sizable increases over the four year levels.

The Teacher's Manual provides a number of useful suggestions to the teacher on how the test scores can be used for individual students as well as for classes. The accompanying Class Analysis Chart is a useful device for displaying and summarizing the test data. The norms for the test, however, were obtained in November, one month before the end of the school year (the Australian school year ends in December). Beginning of the year norms would seem to be more appropriate for the kinds of instructional uses of the test that are presented in the manual.

SUMMARY. The Class Achievement Test in Mathematics are survey tests of mathematics designed for use in Years 4, 5, 6, and 7 in Australian schools. They are the product of a careful development process and a well-designed, albeit limited, standardization. The content validity of the tests closely agrees with other mathematics tests developed for use at this level in Australia although several items in the tests appear to be more a measure of aptitude (spatial relations and numerical reasoning) than of achievement in mathematics. The reliability of the total test scores is high. Subtest reliability is questionably low, however. The test should be able to furnish a teacher with a serviceable estimate of student achievement in mathematics. How much instructional use can be made of the scores is problematic. Only end-of-year norms are supplied. If the teacher gives the test at the end of the year, there is apt to be little time left to remedy deficiencies. If the test is given at the beginning of the year, the appropriateness of the norms is questionable.

REVIEWER'S REFERENCE

Keeves, J. P., & Bourke, S. F. (1976). *Australian studies in school performance: Vol. I. Literacy and numeracy in Australian schools: A first report.* Canberra, Australia: Government Publishing Service.

[70]

Classroom Communication Screening Procedure for Early Adolescents: A Handbook for Assessment and Intervention.

Purpose: "To identify early adolescents who have not acquired some basic thinking strategies and communication skills considered to be essential for success in secondary school."
Population: Grades 5–10.
Publication Dates: 1986–87.
Acronym: CCSPEA.
Scores: Total score only.
Forms, 2: Short, long.
Administration: Individual or group.
Price Data, 1988: $35 for handbook ('87, 173 pages) including tests, information, scoring key, and answer sheets.
Time: Short form, (50–70) minutes; long form, (80–110) minutes.
Comments: Only to be administered to students who scored below the 40th percentile on the last annual reading test and/or teacher referral; "criterion-referenced."
Author: Charlann S. Simon.
Publisher: Communication Skill Builders.

Review of the Classroom Communication Screening Procedure for Early Adolescents: A Handbook for Assessment and Intervention by ESTHER E. DIAMOND, Educational and Psychological Consultant, Evanston, IL:

The Classroom Communication Screening Procedure for Early Adolescents (CCSPEA) draws on research from cognitive psychology, speech-language pathology, and education, indicating that communication deficits are the single most critical factor for students diagnosed as learning disabled or emotionally handicapped. A criterion-referenced, paper-and-pencil screening procedure for high-risk junior high students likely to drop out of school prematurely, it is designed to measure competence in comprehending directions, scanning for information in text, analyzing language, making inferences, interpreting math story problems, recognizing vocabulary, and engaging in written composition.

Both the long and short forms, which are suitable for classroom administration, have an accompanying observational checklist for observing the test-taking and interactive behaviors of students in grades 6–9. The procedure can also be administered individually or in small groups. Approximately 75% accuracy in performance on CCSPEA tasks is claimed to be predictive of successful classroom performance in the middle and upper grades. The CCSPEA is administered only to students making the transition from elementary to secondary school who have scored below the 40th percentile on their last annual standardized reading test and/or have been referred by a teacher for underachievement in the classroom. The reading test requirement is based on research cited by the author indicating a strong relationship between reading performance and communication and thinking skills. The CCSPEA can be administered by teachers and a variety of specialists— speech-language pathologists, learning disability (LD) specialists, psychologists, and reading specialists. Ideally, it is administered at the "feeder" school.

RATIONALE. The author questions the clinic model of intervention and the practice of pinning diagnostic labels on marginal students such as those the CCSPEA is designed to identify. Ninety percent of language-learning special education students, according to the research literature cited, need to acquire school socialization skills and practical strategies to help them learn to learn. They are generally of normal intelligence, but they exhibit only marginal mastery of skills, strategies, and basic knowledge in subject areas. They generally do not qualify for special education. A teacher-student ratio between 1:12 and 1:18 is recommended in basic core subject classes—English, social studies, and science.

The CCSPEA can also be used with bilingual students who have been enrolled for 3 or more years in an elementary school transitional bilingual program or have been living in the United States for at least 3 years. Students from other than mainstream cultural backgrounds can also benefit from the CCSPEA. Because of their failure to use language and logic as well as middle-class children do, they are often perceived as lacking in ability rather than in training.

The rationale for the CCSPEA draws heavily from relevant research literature on communications skills, language proficiency, metalinguistic awareness, reading disabilities, and language and learning disabilities, which the author cites throughout the Handbook. CCSPEA tasks are designed to probe the underlying cognitive strategies and communication skills that research has shown to affect classroom performance in language proficiency, independent problem solving, language processing and analysis, and task persistence. No research studies on the CCSPEA itself are reported, although there is mention of preliminary reports from schools using the CCSPEA, including one instance in which the Screening Test of Adolescent Language (STAL), a one-to-one instrument, was administered to all students who failed the CCSPEA. An 85% overlap of the two measures was found.

CONTENT. The CCSPEA is divided into four sections:

1. This section taps content comprehension and metalinguistic skills. The administrator reads aloud a passage and the directions for each task, and the student must be able to understand numbers presented as words as well as in figures; write a clear phrase or sentence that includes all information requested; figure out a definition from the context; determine the noun or noun phrase to which a pronoun refers; and determine the total number of subpoints in a text that are related to the main topic.

2. This section contains 10 separate direction-following tasks involving listening to details within an oral direction, understanding multipart written directions, and other tasks requiring active listening and monitoring of task performance.

3. This section involves 10 different types of tasks, some with overlapping features—for example, unscrambling or rearranging words to make a sentence, solving riddles, adding a meaningful word to the end of an unfinished sentence, deciding if statements make sense, combining several short sentences into one, choosing an example that demonstrates a given fact, solving math story problems, finding the noun referent for a pronoun in a story, identifying terms in a story that have been substituted for a given term, and using all of a given set of words to make up a descriptive sentence about a picture.

4. This section requires students to match synonyms or brief definitions with vocabulary words.

The CCSPEA is not a timed test, but approximately 80–90 minutes are generally needed for the long form and 50–60 minutes for the short form. The short form has been found useful with incoming and current seventh graders, while the long form is recommended for students above grade 7. The item sequence is identical for the two forms.

A specific rationale is given for each task, and complete scoring instructions are provided. The CCSPEA administrator and a colleague from the feeder school make notations on the Observational Checklist during the session, rating as "good" or "inappropriate" such behaviors as on-task persistence, attention to directions, amount of time taken to settle down, daydreaming, and so on.

DETERMINING LOCAL PASSING SCORES. The CCSPEA is not a standardized test, and there are no norms. Two procedures are suggested for comparing achieving and nonachieving students and establishing local norms. The first, to be used where students are grouped by reading ability, is to administer the CCSPEA to approximately 30 students in average-ability classes at the grade level being screened, and to compute a mean percentage correct score for that grade level. The second procedure, to be used where grouping is heterogeneous, is to administer the CCSPEA to two classrooms at the grade level being screened, compute the percentage correct score, rank the students from highest to lowest, isolating the middle third of the students, and determine, in discussions with classroom teachers, grade-level classroom communication behavior. If all agree, compute a mean score for the middle-third group. It is suggested then that 15 points be subtracted from the mean percentage correct score for average students at the appropriate grade level for use with incoming students to that grade. No psychometric reason is cited, but the author claims the formula has been found to predict validly which students will have difficulty with curriculum content.

The authors do not suggest using the CCSPEA as a pre/post test, although at one school a preliminary version was used as part of a total assessment of an experimental curriculum in English, science, and social studies. A 6.5% increase in performance among seventh graders and a 9.4% increase among eighth graders between September and May was found.

FOLLOW-UP SCREENING. A procedure for follow-up screening is suggested for cases where students show borderline performance (just above or below the passing score) on the CCSPEA, and where students display exceptional difficulty, compared with classmates, in language processing and analysis, expressive language, and cognitive strategies, or where another teacher observes difficulties in a particular subject area. Some other follow-up screening suggestions are using supplementary measures—

for example, STAL scores (Prather, Breecher, Stafford, & Wallace, 1980), any one of several suggested observational checklists, an adaptation of the Token Test and the Reporter Test included in the Handbook, and the Learning Style Inventory (Carbo, 1984).

SUMMARY. In summary, this revised edition of the CCSPEA is a practical handbook that offers the promise of being a useful screening instrument for identification of grade 6–9 students who are marginal in their school skills and at risk for dropping out of school. However, users are well advised to use it only on an experimental basis—advice with which the author concurs—until there is clear-cut evidence of internal consistency, test-retest reliability, and construct and predictive validity to support the inferences drawn from performance on the instrument. Schools using the CCSPEA should be encouraged to engage in well-designed research studies toward that end, and also to examine more completely the relationship between the CCSPEA and related instruments, such as STAL and other measures that deal with speech and other communication disabilities.

In addition, although the Handbook offers a wealth of background historical, research, and philosophical information, the information is scattered too widely throughout the content, and much of it tends to be repetitious. It would be more helpful to the researcher to have all the background information that is not *directly* pertinent to CCSPEA rationale and development, such as "Notable Quotes: An Introduction to Philosophical Biases," placed in a separate section.

REVIEWER'S REFERENCES

Prather, E., Breecher, S., Stafford, M., & Wallace, E. (1980). Screening Test of Adolescent Language. Seattle, WA: University of Washington Press.

Carbo, M. (1984). Research in learning style and reading: Implications for instruction. *Theory Into Practice, 23,* 72-76.

Review of the Classroom Communication Screening Procedure for Early Adolescents: A Handbook for Assessment and Intervention by GARY J. STAIN-BACK, Senior Psychologist, Department of Pediatrics, East Carolina University, School of Medicine, Greenville, NC:

The Classroom Communication Screening Procedure for Early Adolescents: A Handbook for Assessment and Intervention (CCSPEA) is a criterion-referenced, paper-and-pencil screening procedure to help identify students in the sixth through ninth grades who possess communication difficulties. It was designed by a speech-language clinician who has strong interest and experience in learning-disabled adolescents, in addition to those with emotional handicapping and speech-language disorders. The CCSPEA is experimental, and can be either individually or group administered by a variety of educational personnel (teachers, speech-language patholo-

gists, learning disability specialists, psychologists, and reading specialists). There are both short and long forms. Only a difference of six tasks separate the two forms. A recommended 50 minutes is allocated for the short form and 80 minutes for the long form. Scoring is done by hand and is reportedly (and apparently) uncomplicated.

The manual for the CCSPEA is inadequately organized. It is extremely difficult to find essential parts for administration or scoring instructions. There is extensive review of research supporting the need for the CCSPEA, why certain kinds of tasks are included, and discussion of speech pathologists' role; however, it would be better for the test user if such information was contained in a separate handbook.

The personal and professional feelings and thoughts of the author regarding the need for supportive services for early adolescents who may not respond adequately to established regular educational or special educational practices are very apparent from a reading of the CCSPEA. Ms. Simon (the author) makes a strong argument for providing a group intervention approach to help improve communication skills.

The CCSPEA is a screening measure for competence in comprehending directions, scanning for information in a textbook, analyzing language, making inferences, interpreting language in math story problems, recognizing vocabulary, engaging in written composition, and demonstrating task persistence. It is intended to be given to students who score below the 40th percentile on a recent standardized reading test, or by teacher referral for classroom underachievement. Ideally it can be given to students entering into the middle school or junior high from a "feeder school," so students who may require intervention can be identified early and planning done prior to their first day in the new school. The short form is intended for incoming seventh grade students (second semester sixth graders) and current seventh graders, whereas the long form is intended for students above the seventh grade. A cutoff of 70% accuracy level (conversion table available in the manual) is used to make a determination of whether or not a student should participate in a cognitive/communication development program.

The manual contains both the long and short forms of the CCSPEA, along with scoring directions, test directions, sample letters that can be sent to the teachers and parents, adaptions to some other test items, and some classroom activities. Test forms are reproducible from the manual. Directions are the same for the short and long forms, with an asterisk denoting short-form items. Care has been taken to develop the items to be equal to or below a fifth-grade ability level, so that communication skills are actually being measured; however, statistical data supporting this are lacking. The examiner is instructed to reread portions in the manual during the test administration. It is, however, difficult to find these portions quickly. Bold facing the type for the examiner's script and repeating those portions of the directions intended to be repeated will help reduce examiner confusion and aid in administration. Scoring is provided in the manual; however, it is not clear how misspellings should be scored except in vocabulary where the reader cannot recognize the letter.

Follow-up screening is recommended when a student shows a borderline level of performance on the CCSPEA, or if a student exhibits exceptional difficulty with language processing, language analysis, expressive language, and cognitive strategies. The author recommends specific recourse in some instances, to the exclusion of others. The recommendations are not explained or justified. Throughout the manual it is impossible to distinguish facts from opinions because necessary citations are not provided.

In summary, the CCSPEA is introduced as an experimental screening instrument to help identify early adolescents who may possess language disorders, and who might benefit from some group cognitive-communication intervention. The manual is poorly organized, and contains an excessive amount of material related to the personal and professional beliefs of the author regarding underachieving adolescents, in addition to the role of the speech-language pathologist in the school system. There are two forms available, short and long, separated only by a small number of items and about 30 minutes of allotted administration time. No statistical data exist to support whether the test items measure their purported skills, nor to indicate whether the screening procedure actually identifies children who have a mild language disability separate from some other handicapping condition. However, there appears to be excellent thought and planning given to initial item development. The test shows promise as an instrument worthy of further development, but is not developed sufficiently for application in the school system as a screening instrument or diagnostic tool.

[71]
Clerical Abilities Battery.
Purpose: Assesses clerical abilities "for use in hiring and promoting clerical personnel."
Population: Clerical applicants and employees and business school students.
Publication Dates: 1985–87.
Acronym: CAB.
Scores: 7 tests: Filing, Comparing Information, Copying Information, Using Tables, Proofreading, Addition and Subtraction, Reasoning with Numbers.
Administration: Group.

Forms, 2: A, B.
Restricted Distribution: Distribution of Form A restricted to personnel departments in business and industry.
Price Data, 1987: $75 per complete kit including 5 test booklets of each test, 7 keys, and manual ('87, 22 pages); $23 per 25 test booklets (Filing ['87, 7 pages], Copying Information ['87, 6 pages], Comparing Information ['87, 5 pages], Using Tables ['87, 6 pages], Proofreading ['87, 6 pages], Addition and Subtraction ['87, 7 pages], Reasoning with Numbers ['87, 7 pages]); $35 per set of scoring stencils; $15 per manual.
Time: 70(105) minutes for the battery; 5(10) minutes each for first four tests, 15(20) minutes each for next two tests, 20(25) minutes for last test.
Comments: Tests available as separates.
Author: The Psychological Corporation.
Publisher: The Psychological Corporation.

Review of the Clerical Abilities Battery by JOSEPH C. CIECHALSKI, Assistant Professor of Counselor Education, East Carolina University, Greenville, NC:

The Clerical Abilities Battery (CAB) was designed to measure seven tasks performed by clerical personnel. In order to measure these tasks, the CAB includes the following tests: (*a*) Filing, (*b*) Comparing Information, (*c*) Copying Information, (*d*) Using Tables, (*e*) Proofreading, (*f*) Addition and Subtraction, and (*g*) Reasoning with Numbers. Each test is included in a separate booklet.

There are two forms of the CAB, A and B. Form A is restricted for use in personnel departments in business and industry. Form B may be used by employment agencies, vocational training programs, business and technical schools, and business and industry personnel departments.

TEST ADMINISTRATION AND SCORING. The general and specific directions for administering and scoring the CAB are explicit. Directions read to the examinees are blocked in gray for easy identification.

The tests may be given in any combination. However, if all of the tests are administered, the manual includes suggestions on appropriate sequencing.

Each booklet includes specific directions and sample problems. The answers to the sample problems are found at the bottom of the page. Examinees place their responses in the test booklet. Sufficient work space is provided in the test booklets.

The CAB is hand scored using templates. The manual provides a clear description on scoring the tests. To avoid errors, this reviewer suggests that two persons score the tests to insure accuracy.

STANDARDIZATION AND NORMS. The norming population consisted of 515 individuals including 145 part-time clerical workers and applicants and 370 business school students. The norms are described in a table according to sex, ethnic origin, age, educational level, and years of clerical experience. It is interesting to note that 85% of the clerical workers and 94% of the business school students were females. Males are not adequately represented in the norming sample.

RELIABILITY. Alternate form reliability coefficients for each of the seven tests are reported in the manual. The reliability coefficients range from a low of .77 to a high of .93 and the authors state this is "quite good." However, these coefficients are based on a sample of 64 for Form A and 26 for Form B. A larger sample size is needed. In addition, the standard error of measurement is reported using the above sample. The standard error of measurement for the tests ranges from a low of 1.34 for Reasoning with Numbers to a high of 5.13 for Filing.

Intercorrelations among the seven tests are reported using a sample size of 90 part-time clerical workers. The intercorrelations range from a low of .22 for Reasoning with Numbers and Copying Information to a high of .76 for Using Tables and Filing. The authors state "it is clear that the various tests really do measure different types of clerical skills."

VALIDITY. Evidence of predictive validity was demonstrated in Tables 8 and 9 of the manual. Correlations between the CAB and business school grade point averages ($n = 117$) for each of the seven tests range from a low of .23 with Copying Information to a high of .56 with the Proofreading Test. All of the coefficients reported were significant at the .01 level.

In Table 9, three CAB tests (Copying Information, Using Tables, and Reasoning with Numbers) were correlated with final exam scores for teller trainees ($n = 23$). Correlations of .37, .45, and .37 were reported. Although these correlations were significant at, at least, the .05 level, this reviewer would have liked to see a larger sample and the inclusion of the other four tests of the CAB.

To establish concurrent validity, the CAB tests were correlated with the General Clerical Test (GCT) using 90 part-time clerical workers. The correlation coefficients ranged from a low of .13 to a high of .74. The correlation between Addition and Subtraction (CAB) with Checking (GCT) was significant at the .05 level. Correlations between Reasoning with Numbers (CAB) with Checking (GCT) and Copying Information (CAB) with Grammar (GCT) were not significant. However, the remaining correlations were reported to be significant at the .01 level.

INTERPRETATION. Separate tables are provided for part-time clerical workers and applicants and business school students. Using these tables, one can easily convert raw scores into percentiles. The authors suggest that percentiles be reported as "zones of performance" rather than a single percentile.

Space is provided on each test booklet for reporting the raw score, clerical percentile, and business percentile.

SUMMARY. The Clerical Abilities Battery (CAB) is a quick and easily administered instrument. Although the manual is in its preliminary stage, it is very easy to read and understand. The validity, reliability, and conversion tables are clear. The authors are cautious and realize that additional normative data and validity studies are needed. It is this reviewer's opinion that many new tests also share this need. Given additional research and data, the CAB will serve its intended purpose.

Review of the Clerical Abilities Battery by BIKKAR S. RANDHAWA, Professor of Educational Psychology, University of Saskatchewan, Saskatoon, Canada:

The Clerical Abilities Battery (CAB) is intended for use in hiring and promoting clerical personnel. It comprises seven tests. Two forms, A and B, of each of the seven CAB tests are available. Form A is available only to personnel departments in business and industry. Form B is available to other users and to those purchasing Form A. Any rationale for this is not provided, nor is it evident in the manual.

The CAB grew out of a contract between the author (The Psychological Corporation) and General Motors Corporation (GMC) to develop a battery of tests measuring clerical abilities. The tests of the CAB were supposed to be representative of clerical jobs in a variety of contexts. The GMC, according to the author, employed individuals from all the major clerical occupational groupings listed in the *Dictionary of Occupational Titles* (U.S. Department of Labor, 1977). A job analysis was performed and 27 general clerical behaviors were identified. Almost 50% of these were not suitable for measurement with a paper-and-pencil test. The CAB tests are supposed to include 11 behaviors, which were rated as most frequent for clerical jobs and were amenable to paper-and-pencil measurement. However, only seven scores, one score for each test, are available. Also, it is not clear from the list of behaviors given in the manual (Table 1), what constitutes each of the 11 behaviors included in these tests. How one can infer the clerical behavior corresponding to each of the critical behaviors identified by the job analysis and measured with these tests is not obvious.

Tasks in the CAB tests represent important components of clerical work. However, the sampling and range of tasks represented in these tests are restricted and narrow. For example, only one type of test item is used on three of the tests: Copying Information Test, Comparing Information Test, and Using Tables Test. In the Copying Information Test an alphabetical listing of policy holders with their respective policy numbers is presented in six blocks of 20 names. In the corresponding response block the examinee is provided 10 of the names, which are not in alphabetical order, and the task requires the examinee to copy the policy number from the alphabetically listed block. The same and repetitive task not only has a tendency to be monotonous, it also does not test the copying accuracy for other types of information pertinent for clerical work. Also, content representativeness and generalizability of assessed ability will be problematic from such a limited content sampling.

Another related problem is the use of information in the item content of the CAB tests. For instance, the Filing Test requires the examinee to indicate where in the shown set of nine records of a file drawer a given new record should be filed. For a selected file drawer, four new records are provided. When the filing situations in alphabetical order are presented, each file draw record, as well as the new record, consists of a last name followed by an initial. Out of the 32 such tasks, in only one does the examinee have to pay attention to the initial following the last name. Thus, all the stimulus information is not necessary for the remaining 31 tasks involving alphabetical filing. Similarly, all 32 numerical filing tasks do not use all the information in the stimulus items consisting of seven integers. At most four of the seven integers of the stimulus set are necessary to determine the filing sequence in the given response set. However, the above criticism does not apply to the chronological filing tasks; most of these seem to utilize all the stimulus components to determine where a record should be filed.

The readability level for the directions of each test, as well as for the items in two tests with sufficient verbal content, is provided. This information is helpful to consumers. Between 92% and 99% of the words in the directions of these tests are at, or below, the sixth grade level, and almost 100% of the words are at or below the eighth grade level. This evidence ensures the users that problems in comprehension of the directions would not be a factor in the obtained test scores.

It is emphasized in the manual that the CAB tests should be useful for recruitment and promotion decisions regarding clerical workers. However, it is not clear how the recommended use of these tests is justified for testing purposes of business and technical schools and vocational training programs. Other than the fact that the CAB tests were administered to 370 business school students for producing norms and for reliability and validity evidence, no rationale for using these tests for other groups has been provided. The test manual should indicate clearly for what purposes the tests should be used when testing various groups of examinees.

The most troubling aspect of these tests is their standardization, and reliability and validity evidence. The manual encourages the users to develop their "local" norms and provides a sensible reason for doing this. However, the manual reports the norms of two standardization groups, applicants and part-time clerical workers ($N = 145$) and business school students ($N = 370$). The number of subjects in the clerical workers' group is so small that the representativeness of this group to a mix of clerical workers in the domain of interest could hardly be justified. The appropriateness of using the business school standardization group for personnel departments of business organizations or for business schools is not explained either in the development approach taken or in the section on the intended use of the CAB. The manual does not indicate how the standardization samples were selected, and what regions, businesses, and schools they represent. Therefore, it is highly recommended that potential users develop local norms and conduct their own validation studies before using the CAB either for recruitment and promotion of clerical workers or for whatever purpose can suitably be served when testing business school students. However, I do not see the appropriateness of the CAB for any purpose other than for hiring and promoting clerical workers unless the users are willing to develop their local norms and to establish satisfactory validity evidence.

The reliability evidence is weak and misleading. It is weak because: (a) It is based on a sample of only 90 part-time clerical workers, so the evidence is appropriate only for this type of examinees; (b) it is reporting only the alternate form reliability, so only if the alternate forms are intended to be used can the corresponding standard error of measurement be used for interpreting the variability in scores; (c) the reliability sample is not described at all; and (d) the design of the study appears to be ad hoc because the number of examinees tested first with each form were not equalized. This problem was resolved by computing the weighted average of the two correlations, a questionable procedure, obtained from 64 and 26 pairs of observations. Table 6 in the manual reports the mean and standard deviation of each test only for the first administration of each form. The corresponding statistics for the second administration should also be given.

The reliability evidence is misleading because: (a) It does not acknowledge the limitation of the evidence given; (b) other forms of reliability such as a stability coefficient, appropriate for some uses of tests have not been reported; (c) the evidence is generalized, such as the case with the use of the standard error of measurement in this context; and (d) the comparison of the range of reliabilities is interpreted without acknowledging the influence of test length and the number of subjects tested. Also, no justification is given for weighting the correlations in order to estimate the equivalent-form reliability.

Again, in the validity section, the manual recommends local investigation. However, it goes on to report three sets of evidence based on 117 business school students, 23 teller trainees, and presumably the same 90 part-time clerical workers used for the reliability evidence. I find the weakness not in what is reported, but in that which is not reported. These samples have not been described at all. Also, portions of the General Clerical Test (GCT), administered to 90 part-time clerical workers who were also given the CAB for establishing criterion-related validity, were not described. Details (beyond mere names) of what was selected from the GCT and its reference should be available to those who would like to replicate the study. Because the validation samples were small, the purpose of the studies was not clearly established, and the evidence seems to have been obtained from convenience samples, the utility of the validation evidence is questionable.

In summary, though the CAB tests have impressive developmental background and format, the range and scope of content of a number of these tests is narrow. The reliability and validity evidence is not satisfactory, and it is therefore necessary for the prospective users to establish this evidence for their specific situation and context. Unless a good rationale can be provided and satisfactory reliability and validity evidence is found, the CAB should be used with extreme caution with business school students. There is good reason to believe that with proper validation the CAB could be an excellent instrument for recruitment and promotion of clerical workers.

REVIEWER'S REFERENCE

U.S. Department of Labor. (1977). *Dictionary of occupational titles.* Washington: Author.

[72]

Clinical Evaluation of Language Fundamentals—Revised.

Purpose: "For the identification, diagnosis, and follow-up evaluation of language skill deficits in school-age children."
Population: Ages 5-0 to 16-11.
Publication Dates: 1980–87.
Acronym: CELF-R.
Scores, 14: Linguistic Concepts, Word Structure, Sentence Structure, Oral Directions, Formulated Sentences, Recalling Sentences, Word Classes, Sentence Assembly, Semantic Relationships, Word Associations, Listening to Paragraphs, Receptive Language Score, Expressive Language Score, Total Language Score.
Administration: Individual.
Levels: 2 overlapping levels: Ages 5–7, Ages 8 and over.
Price Data, 1989: $198 per total battery; $98 per 2 stimulus manuals; $35 per examiner's manual ('87, 219 pages); $35 per technical manual ('87, 95 pages); $19 per package of 12 record forms.
Time: (60–80) minutes for administration of all subtests.

Comments: Revised edition of Clinical Evaluation of Language Functions; 11 subtests.
Authors: Eleanor Semel, Elisabeth H. Wiig, and Wayne Secord.
Publisher: The Psychological Corporation.
Cross References: For additional information and a review by Dixie D. Sanger of the earlier edition, see 9:233 (2 references); see also T3:474.

Review of the Clinical Evaluation of Language Fundamentals—Revised by LINDA CROCKER, Professor in Foundations of Education, University of Florida, Gainesville, FL:

In this revision of the Clinical Evaluation of Language Fundamentals (CELF-R) the authors have changed the title from the Clinical Evaluation of Language Function to the Clinical Evaluation of Language Fundamentals. Other changes from the earlier version include shorter administration time, clarification of directions, improved pictorial stimuli, empirical evidence of criterion-related validity, age norms (rather than grade norms), deletion of four old subtests, addition of two new subtests, and major revisions of several other subtests. Thus, although previous users may find the format of the test familiar, the CELF-R is a substantially different test from the CELF. Any attempt to measure examinee growth over time using scores from the previous version and the present version would be especially inappropriate.

The CELF-R comprises 11 subtests. Some subtests, however, are considered to be more important than others at given age levels for discriminating between normal and subnormal language performance. In general, the tests are designed to assess memory, syntax, and semantics, which the authors deem to be critical components of language skills.

The examiner's manual is clearly written and well organized. Examiners should be experienced with individual test administration procedures. The estimated times for administration range from approximately 60 to 90 minutes if all subtests are given, with the longer testing times required for younger children. The technical manual is comprehensive, informative, and well written.

Scoring instructions and norms tables are easy to use. The subtest raw scores are converted to standard scores with a mean of 10 and standard deviation of 3 points. Three subtest scores are then combined to compute the Receptive Language score and three others are combined to compute the Expressive Language score; however, the configuration of subtests used for these composites varies for different age levels. The Total Language score is the composite of the six subtests used to compute Expressive and Receptive Language Scores at each age level. Percentile ranks, NCEs, and stanines are also available in the norm tables. Age equivalents are available for Total Language scores. Norms were established separately for samples at each age level from 5 to 16 years with sample sizes ranging from 151 to 267 across age levels. The total norm group appears to be reasonably balanced in terms of gender and geographical distribution.

Reliability evidence is presented in the form of internal consistency, test-retest, and interrater reliability coefficients. Internal consistency estimates ranged from .49 to .92 across different subtests and age levels. Receptive, Expressive, and Total Language internal consistency estimates were in the .80s and .90s. Median coefficients for the stability estimates were in the .70s for these three composites, but were generally lower for individual subtests. Standard errors of measurement and confidence bands for interpretation of the standard scores are provided.

Evidence of concurrent criterion-related validity is found in a study using data from 157 students ages 7, 9, 12, and 15. Approximately half of this sample had been previously classified as learning disabled and half as normal using independent criteria. Results of a discriminant function analysis indicated that both subtest scores and composite scores resulted in functions that led to correct classifications for approximately 90% of the cases. These results must be interpreted with some caution, however, because the sample used to develop the discriminant function weights was the same as used for the classification. There was no cross validation. Additional validity evidence is presented in the form of moderately low correlations with Wechsler Intelligence Scale for Children—Revised (WISC-R) and Peabody Picture Vocabulary Test—Revised (PPVT-R) scores, demonstrating some discriminant validity with verbal aptitude. Finally, differences in performance of gender and racial groups were found to be smaller than the difference in performance of normal and learning disabled students.

The authors have further attempted to establish construct validity by reporting factor analytic results. These results, however, raise questions about the creation of the composite for Expressive and Receptive Language scores. For example, for ages 5–7, Word Structure, Formulated Sentences, and Recalling Sentences are combined to form the Expressive Language score, but the factor analytic results suggests that Word Structure actually loads much more heavily on the factor that underlies the Receptive Language composite. Similar anomalies occur with other subtests at other age levels. This detracts from the confidence that can be placed in interpretation of the Expressive and Receptive score composites, and particularly from interpretation of the observed score difference between these two composites, even though such interpretation is recommended in the manual.

In summary, the CELF-R is a viable contender when seeking an individual test for assessment of language skills in school-age children. Reliability data and standardization samples are reasonable. The authors' recommended creation of composite scores and their interpretations, however, are not well justified by the empirical evidence.

Review of the Clinical Evaluation of Language Fundamentals—Revised by DAVID A. SHAPIRO, Associate Professor of Communication Disorders, School of Education and Psychology, Western Carolina University, Cullowhee, NC:

The components of the Clinical Evaluation of Language Fundamentals—Revised (CELF-R) include an examiner's manual, two stimulus manuals, a technical manual, and record forms. The title of the original instrument, Clinical Evaluation of Language Functions (CELF, 1980), was changed in order to clarify that it and its revision are not measures of language function or pragmatics. In addition to the purpose stated in the examiner's manual and identified in the descriptive information preceding this review, the authors contend that the CELF-R "was designed to identify children in grades K–12 who lack the basic foundations of form and content that characterize mature language use: word meanings (semantics), word and sentence structure (morphology and syntax), and recall and retrieval (memory)." However, the authors caution succinctly that the "CELF-R should never be used as the only measure to diagnose a language disorder or to determine eligibility for special services such as language intervention or placement in a special class." The following review, therefore, assumes that the CELF-R will be utilized as a complement to other formal and informal evaluation measures, such as analysis of conversational speech, measures of concept development and receptive vocabulary, behavioral observations from the classroom and other more natural contexts, evaluations of pragmatic and interpersonal communication skills, etc.

The CELF-R is an individually administered test containing 11 subtests. Although any subtest may be administered to a child aged 5 years or older, rarely are all of the subtests needed to differentiate between normal and subnormal language performance. For children aged 5 to 7 years, a Receptive Language score is computed from administration of the Linguistic Concepts, Sentence Structure, and Oral Directions subtests; an Expressive Language score is computed from Word Structure, Formulated Sentences, and Recalling Sentences subtests. For children aged 8 and above, a Receptive Language score results from administration of the Oral Directions, Word Classes, and Semantic Relationships subtests; and an Expressive Language score results from the Formulated Sentences, Recalling Sentences, and Sentence Ability subtests. For any student, Listening to Paragraphs and Word Associations may be used to replace one of the subtests in figuring the Receptive or Expressive Language scores, respectively, or may be used as supplementary measures.

Raw scores on each subtest are converted into standard scores for each 1-year age interval from 5.0 to 16.11. These standard scores have a mean of 10 and a standard deviation of 3. Receptive and Expressive Language standard scores are each computed by summing the standard scores of the three subtests that probe primarily that aspect of language. The CELF-R Total Language score is computed by summing the standard scores of the six subtests required to figure the Receptive and Expressive Language scores. The sums of these subtest standard scores are converted into Receptive, Expressive, and CELF-R Total Language standard scores, which have a mean of 100 and a standard deviation of 15. This is the same metric used by a number of other psychoeducational instruments. All standard scores can be converted into percentile ranks or normal curve equivalents. In addition, an age-equivalent score for each CELF-R Total score can be reported. This score provides "a gross estimate" of performance by reporting the approximate chronological age of the students in the standardization sample at which each CELF-R Total Language score was the average.

The instructions provided in the examiner's manual for administering and scoring all subtests are clearly stated. All visual stimuli are presented neatly and without distraction in the stimulus manuals. Unless otherwise noted in the discussion that follows, all subtests are untimed, allow for no repetition of the item instructions by the examiner, present demonstration and trial items preceding the test items, score 1 for correct response or 0 for incorrect or no response, begin with the first item and are discontinued when completed or when the student makes four consecutive responses earning a 0. All responses/scores are recorded on the Record Form, which contains a grid for error analysis and space for additional observations. Subtests include the following:

1. Linguistic Concepts: This 20-item subtest is intended to assess the ability to interpret oral directions containing linguistic concepts requiring logical operations such as *and, either/or, if/then*, etc. The examiner directs the student to point to colored bars that relate to the verbal instructions.

2. Word Structure: In order to assess acquisition of morphological rules, the student is directed to complete sentences presented orally that relate to pictured stimuli. The test items may be repeated one time if requested. All 36 items must be administered.

3. Sentence Structure: Assessing acquisition of a variety of structural rules at the sentence level, the student points to one of four pictures that depicts the sentence presented orally by the examiner (26 items).

4. Oral Directions: To evaluate the ability to interpret, recall, and execute oral commands of increasing length and complexity, the student points in the appropriate sequence to geometric figures (22 items).

5. Formulated Sentences: To assess the ability to construct compound and complex sentences, the student is directed to make a sentence with a particular word or words that relates to the picture presented. The 20 sentences are recorded verbatim and are scored 3, 2, 1, or 0 according to the clear instructions and models provided. The examiner is permitted to repeat the item or instructions one time if requested.

6. Recalling Sentences: Evaluating the ability to recall and reproduce sentence surface structure of increasing length and syntactic complexity, this 26-item subtest directs the student to imitate sentences that are orally presented. The elicited imitation is scored 3, 2, 1, or 0 based upon the number of errors.

7. Word Classes: Evaluating the ability to perceive the associative relationship between word concepts, the student is orally presented four words and directed to say the two "that go together best" (27 items).

8. Sentence Assembly: To assess the ability to assemble syntactic structures into sentences, the student is directed to construct two sentences from visually presented words or word clusters. Test items may be repeated one time (22 items).

9. Semantic Relationships: Assessing the ability to interpret different semantic relationships in sentences, the student is presented a verbal problem and directed to select two of four visually presented word choices. The discontinue rule (i.e., four consecutive errors) applies to each of the four sections (i.e., comparative, spatial, passive, and temporal relationships) (28 items).

10. Word Associations: Evaluating the ability to recall labels for members of a semantic class, the student is directed to name as many animals, modes of transportation, and kinds of work as possible. Rather than apply a discontinue rule, each of the three sections is timed for a duration of 60 seconds.

11. Listening to Paragraphs: To evaluate the ability to interpret factual information presented in spoken paragraphs, the student is read two paragraphs, each of which is followed by four questions. The paragraphs used are determined on the basis of the student's age. One repetition of the questions only is allowed if requested. No discontinue rule is imposed (8 items).

These 11 subtests provide a comprehensive and organized system for assessing selected aspects of language fundamentals. In the Semantic Relationships subtest, selection of two responses, rather than one, reduces the chance of successful guessing. The guidelines and examples for correct and incorrect responses provided in the examiner's manual are particularly helpful. The space provided in the Formulated Sentences, Recalling Sentences, Sentence Assembly, and Word Associations subtests for verbatim recording provides a useful opportunity for more in-depth language analysis. The organization and color coding of the record form are excellent for space utilization and ease of scoring.

Warranting attention from an ecological perspective are the procedures utilized in the Recalling Sentences subtest (i.e., sentence imitation). Although the authors justify the procedures used, inferences regarding a student's ability to use, rather than recall, different grammatical forms in spoken language must be considered as tentative based upon the method of elicitation. Also, the instructions in the Word Classes subtest might confound the intended task. Assessing recognition of semantic, opposite, spatial, and temporal relationships among words, the examiner directs the student to "tell me the two that go together best." These procedures do not facilitate the examiner's understanding of the student's creative "errors" specifically in terms of his or her knowledge of language and the world. For example, it would be more useful to know that a student associated seconds and yards on the knowledge basis of football, rather than only to interpret the response as an error in forming a semantic and temporal association (i.e., seconds and minutes). Likewise, truth and success might "go together best" based upon a knowledge of morals and advancement, rather than simply indicating failure to associate word opposites (i.e., success and failure).

Tables providing normative data and guidelines for computing and interpreting normed scores are included in the examiner's manual. Because the guidelines appear in different sections (e.g., "Recording Subtest Scores and Confidence Intervals" in Administration and Scoring; "Using a Range of Scores to Reflect Confidence in Obtained Scores" and "Age Equivalent Scores" in Test Interpretation; etc.), integrating and following these guidelines renders some confusion. Effects of this weakness are reduced by providing a list of guidelines for interpreting CELF-R scores, a completed scoring summary, and four case studies. Not included in the test materials but available from the publisher is critical information regarding establishing CELF-R confidence intervals and determining confidence levels (Secord, 1989). Also available is an examination of the process and rationale for interpreting CELF-R scores including composite and subtest scores, supplementary tests, qualitative analysis, and extension and additional testing. This material is summarized in an invaluable interpretation flowchart including 21 steps (Wiig, 1989). Test

users are advised to obtain and use this information when interpreting CELF-R scores.

Offsetting this reviewer's concern that scores (i.e., abstractions of language behavior) rather than language behavior receive primary focus, the authors include a most practical final section entitled "Extension Testing and Instructional Objectives." Providing objectives, procedures, and related resources for each subtest area, this section should prove helpful to public school clinicians who address on a daily basis students' language needs and the requirements of recent legislation.

The technical aspects of the test are presented clearly. These include discussions of development and standardization, validity, and reliability.

Addressing the test's development, the authors carefully review and justify the purpose and design of the CELF-R and identify the revisions that resulted from the original CELF. Field testing included a pilot test with 63 students representing grades K, 1, 3, 5, 7, 9, and 11. The revision tryout utilized 50 examiners and 233 students from six school systems. The latter sample clustered around ages 7, 9, 11, and 15, equally represented LLD (language-learning disabled) and nonLLD (assumed to be normally developing) students, and balanced for sex, race, and Spanish origin. The results from 157 of the 233 administrations entered into a stepwise discriminant analysis and revealed 90.4% classification agreement with that already completed by the school systems.

Standardization was completed from test administration to 2,426 students between the ages of 5 and 16 from 33 school districts located in 18 states. No identified handicapped students were included. This sample is representative, on the basis of age, region of the nation, race, and sex, of nonhandicapped (nonLLD) students enrolled in school.

The normative information addresses the types of norms reported and differential performance between genders and races. The types of norms presented are within-group standard scores by age and an across-group score expressed as an age equivalent. The within-group standard scores may be converted into percentile ranks. The authors explain the percentile rank associated with each raw score was converted into a normalized Z-score and then into a standard score. Standard scores for each subtest were assigned a mean of 10 and a standard deviation of 3. Standard scores for Receptive Language, Expressive Language, and Total Language were computed by adding the standard scores for each of the relevant subtests. Standard scores of the summed subtests standard scores were assigned a mean of 100 and a standard deviation of 15. The rationale and procedure for developing age equivalents are presented clearly. An analysis of 150 matched pairs indicated that there is minimal difference in performance between males and females on the CELF-R. Another matched sample (291 pairs matched on age, sex, and Spanish origin; 60 pairs when a variable related to socioeconomic status was added) indicated that Blacks score approximately one-third to one-half of a standard deviation lower than Whites on composite scores. The authors address these findings and implications.

Evidence for content validity, criterion-related validity, and construct validity is provided. The content validity is supported adequately by discussion of the rationale, purpose, and design of the test and item selection. However, this reviewer remains cautious regarding choice of procedures already noted.

The results of the discriminant analysis already mentioned are provided as evidence of criterion-related validity. Not reported, however, is the method by which the examinees were selected or the information (e.g., previous test results, identified exceptionality, etc.) that was available to the speech-language pathologists who administered all of the protocols. This information is critical to evaluate the procedures utilized to establish criterion-related (i.e., predictive) validity. Nevertheless, when all CELF-R subtest standard scores were used, 91% of the students classified by the school systems as LLD were so classified by the CELF-R; 90% classified as nonLLD by the school were so classified by the CELF-R. These figures reduce when only those CELF-R subtest standard scores used to compute Receptive and Expressive Language scores were used, or when Receptive and Expressive Language scores only or Total Language scores only were used. These results indicate a high level of agreement between the school-based and CELF-R results. The authors do not, however, identify the specific procedures or comment on the validity of these diagnostic methods used in the schools. Evidence of concurrent validity is provided by reviewing two studies, one in which 43 10-year-old students not identified as LLD and another in which 42 students identified as LLD were given both the CELF and CELF-R in counterbalanced order. Results indicate that the CELF-R is more sensitive to language difficulties evidenced by low-scoring students. However, the CELF-R is not more difficult for the average or above average student. Additional evidence of concurrent validity is provided by comparing the results of the CELF-R with those of the Test of Language Development—Intermediate, the TOLD-I (436; Hammill & Newcomer, 1982; $n = 24$), the Peabody Picture Vocabulary Test—Revised, PPVT-R (9:926; Dunn & Dunn, 1981; $n = 53$), and the Wechsler Intelligence Scale for Children—Revised, WISC-R (9:1351; Wechsler, 1974, $n = 48$). The authors emphasize that the correlations between the CELF-

R and the CELF and the TOLD-I present evidence of the relationship between the CELF-R and other measures of language. The correlations with the PPVT-R and the WISC-R reportedly indicate the CELF-R better identifies language deficient students than do these tests of general ability. Of all the pairwise correlations reported, 22 are significant at the .01 or .05 level and range from .29 to .73. It is interesting to note that 19 are less than .60 and only 3 are greater than .60. The relationships being reported between the CELF-R and other measures suggest a moderate association.

Construct validity is established by providing intercorrelations among the subtests. The correlations are generally low to moderate. Only one coefficient is above .50 in the combined-age samples and the range is .25 to .51, suggesting that the CELF-R subtests are not measuring the same concept. Factor analysis of subtest intercorrelations indicated that the CELF-R is a one-factor test; that is, the individual subtests do not measure separate components which, when used in combination, comprise "normal language." Nevertheless, individual subtests may provide clues to areas of language deficiency. The construct is supported further by a section addressing the CELF-R Purpose and Design, mention of the model presented by Bloom and Lahey (1978), and frequent reference to Wiig and Semel (1984). However, an integration of these would more clearly support the coherence of the construct.

Evidence for reliability in terms of internal consistency, test-retest, interscorer, and intrascorer is provided. Internal consistency reliability was investigated using coefficient alpha on the items represented by all subtests used in computing that subscale or total score, and using a composite-score formula. Relating to the subjects' internal consistency on individual subtests, 59 of the 114 coefficients reported fall short of .80, the minimum level for indicating educational usefulness. Although the authors explain this in terms of the effect of test length on estimates of reliability (i.e., length was reduced to shorten administration time for examiners), these findings raise concern over internal consistency on individual subtests. Pertaining to the composite scores, all coefficients exceed .80. Standard errors of measurement are reported for each age interval and are smaller for individual subtests than for composite scores.

The time sampling reliability is reported from a 4- to 8-week test-retest of 116 students aged 6, 10, or 14 years. The 39 test-retest coefficients reported for the subtests range from .17 to .90, 33 of which fall below the .80 criterion. The 12 test-retest coefficients associated with the composite scores range from .49 to .90, nine of which fall below .80. On the basis of these data, this reviewer remains cautious regarding the authors' interpretation that the coefficients "indicate adequate stability for the CELF-R subscale and total scores." These data do support, however, the interpretation "that the composite scores are the most reliable CELF-R measures of language ability and that subtests should be viewed as opportunities to probe more specific aspects of language for the purpose of setting priorities for more in-depth assessment prior to planning an intervention program."

Interscorer reliability was investigated by having "several practicing speech/language clinicians" score three sets of five Formulated Sentences protocols, the final set yielding a range of 83% to 91% agreement (86% average) between the scorers and trainer. Interscorer reliability among experienced scorers was investigated by having 40 Formulated Sentences protocols of students aged 6, 10, and 14 scored by three scorers. Percentage of agreement between scorers was 80% to 94%. Similar procedures were utilized for the Word Associations subtest. The third set of five protocols resulted in 70% agreement between the scorers and trainer. The 40 protocols resulted in percentages of agreement between scorers ranging from 68% to 82%. Additional data for the other subtests and composite scores would prove useful in determining interscorer reliability for the CELF-R.

Intrascorer reliability was investigated by having the scorers (i.e., who participated in the interscorer reliability of Formulated Sentences and Word Associations) rescore the protocols 1 week later. Percentage of agreement between first and second scoring was 86% to 96% for Formulated Sentences, and 78% to 89% for Word Associations. Because of the difference in range of percentage of agreement between the two subtests and because the different subtests both assess different language skills and require different administration procedures, additional data on other subtests and the Expressive, Receptive, and Total Language composites are necessary to determine intrascorer reliability.

In summary, the CELF-R is a carefully developed, organized, and comprehensive system for assessing selected aspects of language fundamentals. Taking seriously the authors' caution that results gained from the CELF-R should be supplemented by other formal and informal evaluation measures including conversational language analysis, this test should prove useful as one aspect of an assessment and intervention program.

REVIEWER'S REFERENCES

Wechsler, D. (1974). Wechsler Intelligence Scale for Children—Revised. San Antonio: The Psychological Corporation.
Bloom, L., & Lahey, M. (1978). *Language development and language disorders.* New York: John Wiley & Sons.
Dunn, L. M., & Dunn, L. M. (1981). Peabody Picture Vocabulary Test—Revised. Circle Pines, MN: American Guidance Services.
Hammill, D. D., & Newcomer, P. L. (1982). Test of Language Development—Intermediate. Austin, TX: PRO-ED, Inc.
Wiig, E. H., & Semel, E. (1984). *Language assessment and intervention for the learning disabled* (2nd ed.). Columbus, OH: Charles E. Merrill Publishing Company.
Secord, W. (1989). CELF-R confidence: Understanding confidence intervals. *CELF-R Update 2,* 2, 3-4, 6-7. [Available from The Psychological Corporation, Harcourt Brace Jovanovich, Inc.]
Wiig, E. H. (1989). The interpretation of CELF-R results: A process. *CELF-R Update 2,* 2, 8-12. [Available from The Psychological Corporation, Harcourt Brace Jovanovich, Inc.]

[73]

C.O.A.C.H.: Cayuga-Onondaga Assessment for Children with Handicaps, Version 6.0.

Purpose: A tool to assist in educational planning.
Population: Preschool and school-aged learners with moderate, severe, or profound handicap.
Publication Dates: 1985–90.
Acronym: COACH.
Scores: Item scores only.
Administration: Individual.
Price Data, 1990: $5.50 (plus $1 postage and handling) per manual/test booklet ('90, 81 pages).
Time: (60) minutes (part 1 of 3 parts).
Comments: "Criterion-referenced"; ratings by a team including a parent, student (where appropriate), educators, related service personnel, and family advocate.
Authors: Michael F. Giangreco, Chigee J. Cloninger, and Virginia S. Iverson.
Publisher: National Clearing House of Rehabilitation Training Materials.

Review of the C.O.A.C.H.: Cayuga-Onondaga Assessment for Children with Handicaps, Version 6.0 by JAY KUDER, Associate Professor and Chairperson, Department of Special Educational Services/Instruction, and DAVID E. KAPEL, Dean, School of Education and Related Professional Studies, Glassboro State College, Glassboro, NJ:

DESCRIPTION OF TEST. The Cayuga-Onondaga Assessment for Children with Handicaps, Version 6.0 (C.O.A.C.H.) is both an assessment tool and a planning procedure designed to be used in the development of educational goals for students with moderate to severe disabilities. Although designed to be used for students placed in regular education classrooms, its results can be applied to students in other settings as well.

The C.O.A.C.H. is divided into three levels of assessment and planning. Level 1 (General) is designed to help families and professionals identify learning priorities. In Level 2 (Refined) the priorities established by the Level 1 process are translated into educational goals suitable for an individualized education plan (I.E.P.). Level 3 (Ongoing) is designed to facilitate the implementation of goals in the regular education classroom and to provide a framework for evaluation of these goals.

The General level of assessment is divided into seven parts. In Part 1.1 the parents of the students being evaluated are asked to complete a "Quality of Life" survey. This survey, based on previous research by two of the authors, attempts to identify broad areas of family concern. In the next section

(Part 1.2) team members work with the parents to identify curriculum areas that will be included in developing goals, using a checklist provided for this purpose. In Parts 1.3 through 1.5 the parents are asked to rate their child (on a scale of 1 to 4) on skills in three areas. Part 1.3 (Cross-Environmental Activities) consists of the following domains: Socialization, Communication, Personal Management, Leisure/Recreation, and Applied Academics. Part 1.4 (Environment-Specific Activities) measures the child's skills at home, in school, in the community, and in the vocational setting. Part 1.5 focuses on sensory learning skills. In Parts 1.6 and 1.7 participants are directed to prioritize the previously identified activities that need work. Two methods are provided for this purpose.

In Level 2 of the C.O.A.C.H. (Refined) the previously established priorities are first restated as annual goals (Part 2.1). There is no prescribed format for this section, although some examples of goals are provided. In Part 2.2 the team identifies curriculum areas in both special and regular education that should be included in the student's educational plan using a worksheet provided for this purpose. In Part 2.3 the team identifies what will be required in terms of training, staff, and equipment to implement the student's educational plan. In Part 2.4 annual goals are translated into short-term objectives. Some suggestions are provided for this purpose. In Level 3 of the C.O.A.C.H. these objectives are translated into an instructional plan for the regular education setting. Some suggestions for this process are provided as well as a form, but the authors of the test note the inadequacy of the information and suggest that consumers refer to previous research.

The C.O.A.C.H. was designed to be administered to families of learners ages 3 through 21 who are identified as having moderate, severe, or profound handicapping conditions. The authors state that Level 1 (General Assessment/Planning) takes approximately one hour to administer. They further report that the time required to use Levels 2 and 3 is difficult to estimate because the time depends on several factors, including the number of annual goals, short term objectives, lesson plans, etc.

The C.O.A.C.H. can be administered by any professional member of an evaluation team. It is administered to the parents of the student being evaluated. It can be administered in any location at any time of the school year.

PURPOSE AND MODEL. The purpose of the C.O.A.C.H. is to better enable students with moderate to severe handicapping conditions to participate in regular education settings. The authors have attempted to accomplish this purpose by developing a procedure that will facilitate the identification of goals for persons with moderate to severe disabilities and translate these goals into educational practice.

The C.O.A.C.H. is based on several assumptions and models. One implicit assumption is that students with moderate to severe disabilities are best taught through the use of a "functional curriculum." Such an approach emphasizes the use of teaching activities that have direct, practical applications in daily life. This is a widely supported instructional approach for students with serious disabilities, but there is a danger of ignoring curriculum areas that some teachers may find useful—particularly when working with young children. Specifically, cognitive, motor, and language development are not identified as specific areas of focus in this instrument. Rather, the authors state that these domains are integrated into functional skills such as "makes requests," "uses telephone," and "selects clothing to wear."

The C.O.A.C.H. model separates functional activities and skills into three categories: Cross-Environmental Activities, Environment-Specific Activities, and Sensory-Learning Skills. The distinction between the first two categories is somewhat artificial. Many activities identified as environment-specific would seem to apply to several environments (e.g., cares for personal hygiene, participates in small groups, uses vending machines). Yet, the distinction may be a useful way of conceptualizing goals as long as participants do not take the categories literally. A more serious problem with the model is in how it treats sensory skills. Rather than including these with cognitive, language, and motor skills, as integrated into functional activities, the authors treat these skills as a separate curricular domain. This could be potentially confusing to test users who were looking for a functional curriculum approach.

Another component of the C.O.A.C.H. is the use of the "Osborn-Parnes Creative Problem-Solving Process." This procedure has been used to help participants in the C.O.A.C.H. process select the most appropriate goals for the student. Although the C.O.A.C.H. does not use the Osborn-Parnes model in its entirety, the inclusion of the approach does enhance the power of the C.O.A.C.H. as a decision-making tool.

CONCLUSIONS. The Cayuga-Onondaga Assessment for Children with Handicaps, Version 6.0 (C.O.A.C.H.) is a highly structured, comprehensive system for assessing the learning needs of students with moderate to severe disabilities and developing an educational plan for such students. As an assessment instrument it has significant limitations. No standardization information is provided. Minimally, some data on the validity of the rating scales should have been included. In addition, because parents are the respondents for the assessment portion of the procedure, the accuracy of responses depends on the parents' ability and willingness to participate. The authors report that they have had success in using this instrument in field studies, but provide no details.

As an instructional planning procedure, the C.O.A.C.H. could be useful. Its strengths lie in its involvement of the family in planning, in the clarity with which underlying assumptions are expressed, and in the use of a prioritization procedure. Unfortunately, despite some reported modifications, the manual is still difficult to follow. As a result, the planning model appears to be more complex than is actually the case.

The C.O.A.C.H. planning process would be best utilized in conjunction with a standardized assessment of functional and academic skills.

[74]
Cognitive Behavior Rating Scales.

Purpose: "To allow a family member, or other reliable observer, to rate the presence and severity of cognitive impairment, behavioral deficits, and observable neurological signs."
Population: Patients with possible neurological impairment.
Publication Date: 1987.
Acronym: CBRS.
Scores: 9 scales: Language Deficit, Apraxia, Disorientation, Agitation, Need for Routine, Depression, Higher Cognitive Deficits, Memory Disorder, Dementia.
Administration: Group.
Price Data, 1989: $32 per complete kit including manual, 25 reusable item booklets, and 50 rating booklets.
Time: (15–20) minutes.
Author: J. Michael Williams.
Publisher: Psychological Assessment Resources, Inc.

Review of the Cognitive Behavior Rating Scales by RON EDWARDS, Professor of Psychology, University of Southern Mississippi, Hattiesburg, MS:

The Cognitive Behavior Rating Scales (CBRS) are designed to provide information regarding the cognitive functioning of brain-damaged individuals who are unable or unwilling to complete more formal tests of cognitive abilities. The items are rated by a family member or other reliable observer familiar with the everyday functioning of the client. Materials include a reusable Item Booklet containing 104 descriptive statements and 12 ability items (e.g., spelling, reading, drawing ability) and a separate Rating Booklet. The first 104 items are rated on a 5-point scale from *not at all* (1) to *very much* (5) like the person being rated. Items 105–116 rate the person's ability from *very low* (1) to *very high* (5). Completion of the CBRS is reported to take 15–20 minutes with raters generally needing assistance in completing only the first two or three items.

Identifying populations that can be expected to complete the CBRS reliably and validly may be a problem. No information is provided as to the age, race, ethnic, educational, or social class characteristics of the raters used in the development of the CBRS. The ability of informants to complete the CBRS may be influenced by such characteristics.

CBRS item ratings are entered in corresponding blocks in the Rating Booklet. The blocks are arranged so that column and/or row totals represent raw score totals or subtotals for each of the nine CBRS scales. The total raw scores for the nine CBRS scales are transformed to T-scores ($M = 100$, $SD = 15$) and percentiles using a table contained on the last page of the Rating Booklet. Because score distributions for the Apraxia and Disorientation scales were significantly skewed, only percentiles are provided for these scales. Higher raw scores on the CBRS represent more pathological ratings and yield lower T-scores and percentiles.

DEVELOPMENT OF THE CBRS. An initial pool of 170 nonredundant items was created based on interviews with families with a demented member, review of the literature on dementia-related illnesses, and popular guides describing behavioral aspects of cognitive impairment. The initial item pool was arranged into the nine CBRS scales and reviewed by 10 practicing neuropsychologists. Items that at least eight raters agreed belonged to a particular scale were placed in that scale. Items failing to meet this criterion were dropped, resulting in the final set of 116 items.

RELIABILITY AND VALIDITY. Reliability and validity data were obtained by analyzing CBRS ratings provided by either a child or spouse for three groups of subjects. A demented group consisted of 30 patients with a diagnosis of Alzheimer's disease but no other brain disease, psychiatric disorder, or cerebral vascular accident. A second group consisted of 30 normals matched on age and years of education. The third group consisted of 400 normal subjects with no history of brain disease or psychiatric disorder. Test-retest reliabilities (1-week interval) based on 31 of the normal subjects ranged from .61 to .94. Internal consistency reliability using the 400 normals yielded alpha coefficients ranging from .78 to .92. Although the reliability data would seem adequate, especially for a research instrument, the fact they are based solely on normal subjects limits their value. Reliability data for subjects similar to those for which the instrument is intended to be used are clearly needed.

Normative data were obtained for 688 individuals recruited by public newspaper advertisements and by "announcements to the membership of an Alzheimer's Disease and Related Disorders Association and the American Association of Retired People." All volunteers were screened for neurological and psychiatric disorders. The resulting data were used to construct the T-score and percentile tables for the CBRS.

Validity was assessed by comparing the scores of the 30 demented patients with those of the 30 matched normals. Based on paired *t*-test comparisons, the demented group received significantly higher ratings on all scales except Depression. A nonstepwise discriminant analysis resulted in 100% correct classification of the demented and normal subjects. These data suggest that the CBRS can discriminate between moderately impaired Alzheimer's patients and normals. Whether the CBRS can also discriminate mildly impaired patients or patients with other forms of brain damage is unknown.

A couple of puzzling aspects of the CBRS scoring system were noted. First, the initial 104 items are statements of pathology, with higher ratings reflecting greater pathology. On the other hand, higher ratings on the "ability" items (105–116) reflect positive characteristics. Although one would assume the normative data would control for this idiosyncracy, examination of data reported in the manual raises additional questions. For example, the Language Deficit (LD) scale consists of four pathology items (Cannot maintain a simple conversation, Has difficulty communicating thoughts, Substitutes an incorrect word that sounds similar to the correct word, and Has difficulty following instructions) and six ability items (Spelling, Writing, Reading, Ability to use language, Following directions or instructions, and Speaking). The LD mean for the normative group is 12.32 which, assuming the lowest ratings on the pathology items, means that they were rated as low or very low on all the ability items. Ratings of average ability would yield an LD scale score of 22. Anomalies of this sort raise questions as to the accuracy of the instructions for rating items 105–116.

Another curious situation occurs with items 98 and 101. Item 98 states "When asked to recall something, he or she is quick to say 'I don't know' rather than make up something," whereas item 101 states "Guesses or makes up an answer rather than saying 'I don't know.'" Ratings on these items would appear to cancel each other.

SUMMARY. The CBRS manual identifies the scale as a research instrument intended to document a family member's observations of cognitive impairments in the everyday functioning of brain-damaged individuals. The information yielded by the CBRS is intended to supplement other data available to the clinician and to suggest areas for further exploration. Based on available data, the CBRS would appear to be a useful instrument for obtaining such information for patients with Alzheimer's disease. Whether it will be as useful for patients with other forms of brain damage remains to be demonstrated. Advantages of the CBRS include its standardized format and normative data. The apparent ability of the CBRS to discriminate dementia from depression in the elderly, if substantiated by further research, would be another significant advantage. As a research instrument, the CBRS would seem to be an excellent alternative to informal interviews with family members.

Review of the Cognitive Behavior Rating Scales by DAVID J. MEALOR, Chair of Educational Services Department, College of Education, University of Central Florida, Orlando, FL:

The Cognitive Behavior Rating Scales (CBRS) is a 116-item instrument designed to rate the presence and severity of cognitive impairment, behavioral deficits, and observable neurological signs. The CBRS was published as a research edition to "interest other experimenters in the further development of the scales." Persons with cognitive impairment may be unable or unwilling to complete formal test batteries. The CBRS is designed to allow a family member or other reliable observer to rate an individual in nine specific areas (scales) designed to "elicit information about deficits as they are revealed in everyday behaviors." The nine scales are: Language Deficit (LD)—10 items; Apraxia (AP)—5 items; Disorientation (DO)—5 items; Agitation (AG)—6 items; Need for Routine (NR)—7 items; Depression (DEP)—24 items; Higher Cognitive Deficits (HCD)—12 items; Memory Disorders (MD)—21 items; and Dementia (DEM)—26 items.

The items were selected "from interviews with families who have a demented member, the scientific literature that describes dementia-related illnesses and their diagnoses . . . and the popular guides for families which describe behavioral aspects of cognitive impairment in everyday terms." An initial item pool of 170 items was reduced to the present number using an expert judge methodology. Ten practicing neuropsychologists were asked to group items, and items remained if at least eight of these experts agreed that an item belonged in a particular scale.

The CBRS consists of a reusable item booklet, rating booklet, and manual. The Item Booklet is divided into three sections and the respondent rates the first 92 items on a scale of 1 (*not at all like this person*) to 5 (*very much like this person*). The second section has 12 items and assesses memory and intellectual stability. Completion of the second section is optional and the third section (12 items) employs a slightly different rating with 1 (*this person's ability is very low*) to 5 (*this person's ability is very high*). The method used to determine the rating descriptors is not mentioned. The actual ratings for the 116 items are recorded on the Rating Booklet. Respondents are instructed to read the instructions in the item booklet and record only one number in each box. Each item from the item booklet has a corresponding box in the Record Booklet. Scoring is entered in a horizontal direction and the total score for each scale is derived by summarizing in a vertical direction. It would be beneficial if the respective ratings were listed on the pages with the items. This would save the need to keep referring to the front page of the Item Booklet.

Total ratings for each of the scales are computed and transferred to the scoring grid on the back page of the Rating Booklet. It would be helpful if the boxes for total scale scores were provided. Transferring total scores to the scoring grid may result in errors. According to the author, most persons should be able to complete the CBRS in 15–20 minutes.

Although the intent of the CBRS appears to be very good, the technical aspects of the test present some major shortcomings. The CBRS manual is inadequate at best. The section dealing with reliability and validity simply does not provide enough information to determine if the CBRS is capable of doing what it purports to do. In addition, there is insufficient information provided about the subjects used in the reliability and validity study(ies). For example, comparisons were made utilizing three groups: "Demented" ($N = 30$), "Matched-Normal" ($N = 30$), and "Normal" ($N = 400$). The demented subjects came from a local chapter of the Alzheimer's Disease and Related Disorders Association. No other demographic information relating to any of the subjects is given. Any comparisons with others would be most difficult. The mean age of the "Normal" group is 2 standard deviations below that of the other two groups.

Test-retest reliability was conducted with the "Normal" subjects. Considering the intent of the CBRS, a test-retest study is needed with the "Demented" group. Concurrent validity studies centered on comparing the performance of the "Matched-Normals" with the ratings given the "Demented" group. It is inferred that "family members were able to judge reliably the disabilities of a demented family member," yet, no test-retest studies were conducted with this group.

The normative sample ($N = 688$) ranged in age from 30–89 years. Means and standard deviations for each of the nine scales by age group and total group for the normative sample are provided. However, a note appears at the bottom of the table informing the reader "ratings [were] not available for all subjects for all scales."

If the CBRS is to be used as a measure of cognitive decline, its use is not supported by the performance of the normative sample, where performance differed little between the 30–39-year age group and the 70–89-year age group. The data from all age groups were combined for purposes of normative comparisons. It is the use of the CBRS for comparative purposes that may present the most difficulty. The manual refers readers to the Appendix of percentile rankings and normalized T-scores for the CBRS scales. This same Appendix appears in the Rating Booklet. The basic tenets of measurement appear to be misunderstood. The means and standard deviations do not match the numbers presented in the Appendix, and measures of central tendency are ignored. The author notes that the appendix contains normalized T-score transformations ($x = 100$, $SD = 15$); however, most T-scores have a mean of 50 and a standard deviation of 10. Regardless, the appendix yields maximum scores to only 1 standard deviation above the mean. Higher scores are reported below a percentile ranking of 1 and are carried to 3 standard deviations below the mean. This Appendix forms the basis for the CBRS Rating Booklet.

In summary, any potential usefulness of the CBRS in its current form appears to be outweighed by the serious psychometric deficiencies with standardization, norming, and reliability. A great deal of technical work needs to be done before the test should be used for any clinical purpose. At best the CBRS item booklet may serve as an initial survey for clinicians to gain insight about a person's present level of functioning in certain areas.

[75]
Cognitive Control Battery.

Purpose: Helps "to predict, diagnose, and treat learning disabilities."
Population: Ages 4–12.
Publication Dates: 1987–88.
Acronym: CCB.
Scores: Scattered Scanning Test, 6 scores: Motor Tempo, Number Correct Shapes Marked, Ratio I, Total Distance, Ratio II, Mean Distance; Fruit Distraction Test, Time and Errors scores for each of the following: Card 2, Card 3/Card 2, Card 4/Card 2; Leveling-Sharpening House Test, 3 scores: First Stop, Number Correct Changes, Ratio.
Administration: Individual.
Parts, 3: Scattered Scanning Test, Fruit Distraction Test, Leveling-Sharpening House Test.
Price Data, 1989: $235 per complete set including picture book ('88, 132 pages), stimulus materials, 25 Form 1 Test Sheets, 25 Form 2 Test Sheets, Line Measure, 25 Motor Tempo Sheets, 25 Training Forms, 25 Record Booklets, and manual ('88, 213 pages); $135 per complete kit for Leveling-Sharpening House Test; $97.50 per complete kit for Fruit Distraction Test; $98 per complete kit for Scattered Scanning Test; $85 per picture book; $47.50 per stimulus materials; $13.50 per 100 Form 1 Test Sheets; $14.40 per 25 Form 2 Test Sheets; $27.50 per Line Measure; $13.50 per 100 Motor Tempo Sheets; $13.50 per 100 Training Forms; $8.70 per 25 Record Booklets; $45 per manual.
Time: (28–33) minutes.
Author: Sebastiano Santostefano.
Publisher: Western Psychological Services.

TEST REFERENCES

1. Cotugno, A. J. (1987). Cognitive control functioning in hyperactive and nonhyperactive learning disabled children. *Journal of Learning Disabilities, 20,* 563-567.

2. Cotugno, A. J., & Levine, D. S. (1990). Cognitive functioning in learning-disabled and nonlearning-disabled secondary level students. *Psychology in the Schools, 27,* 155-162.

Review of the Cognitive Control Battery by SCOTT W. BROWN, Associate Professor of Educational Psychology, University of Connecticut, Storrs, CT:

The Cognitive Control Battery (CCB) is intended to assess individual differences in performance "based on a theoretical model that conceptualizes cognitive functioning *within* personality functioning and development" for children between 3 and 16 years of age. The CCB assesses the interaction of emotion and cognition according to the cognitive control model. Each subtest is designed to assess "discrete, nonverbal, cognitive activity that takes place unconsciously." The resulting patterns of these subtests are intended to be used for identifying children with learning disabilities, diagnosing existing learning disabilities, diagnosing cognitive dysfunctions in school adjustment problems, and for assessing cognition in studies of personality and cognitive functioning.

The CCB focuses on three of the five components of the cognitive control model: Focal Attention, Field Articulation, and Leveling-Sharpening. These three components are assessed through the Scattered Scanning Test (SST), Fruit Distraction Test (FDT), and Leveling-Sharpening House Test (LSHT). Each test produces several measures that are converted to *T*-scores and percentiles for interpretation.

The SST provides a measure of the manner in which an individual scans a stimulus field. The child scans a sheet of paper containing an array of geometric shapes and marks only the circles and crosses among the shapes. The results of the SST generate scores for Motor Tempo, the Number of Correct Shapes Marked, the Total Number of Shapes Marked, Total Distance, Mean Distance, Ratio I, and Ratio II. These scores indicate: the time it takes the child to mark a shape; the total and average distance between shapes marked based on the order of the marks; the vigor of scanning (Ratio I); and the breadth of scanning (Ratio II).

The FDT measures the principle of field articulation. Field articulation concerns the manner in which a person selectively directs attention. The child identifies the colors of a series of different objects on a stimulus card. The FDT yields measures based on the time required to complete a card of figures and the number of errors on each stimulus card. These measurements are used to calculate scores related to changes from one card to another.

The LSHT measures the cognitive control principle of leveling-sharpening. Leveling-sharpening refers to the manner in which an individual constructs images and compares these images with present perceptions. The child compares an image that they have in memory from a stimulus presentation to changes that may or may not have occurred in the currently presented stimulus. Slight changes between the presented picture and the image in memory may or may not exist. The child is requested to identify those changes when they exist. The LSHT yields: a First Stop score, the number of the card on which the first correct change is perceived; a Number of Correct Changes, the total number of correct changes perceived; and a Leveling-Sharpening Ratio, accounting for "correct changes not perceived, correct changes perceived, and how soon those perceived were detected after the change was introduced."

The normative data reported in the manual for over 1,100 children were stratified on age, sex, ethnicity, geographic area, and socioeconomic status variables. Although the CCB is intended to assess children between the ages of 3 and 16, the normative data include only children between the ages of 4 and 12 and the SST normative data include only ages 4 through 9.

Test-retest reliability indices reported in the manual for the subtests vary greatly according to the study reported and the time span between testings. The manual reports numerous studies over the last 30 years examining the reliability of one or more subtests for time periods of 1 week up to 5 years. A 5-year study of the stability of the three subtests of the CCB cited in the manual reports reliability estimates across the three subtests ranging from -.27 to .74 through the 5 years of testing. Nearly 50% of the reported correlations reached statistical significance. Only test-retest reliability coefficients for the LSHT of 1 week (.67 to .70) and 4 weeks (.02 to .82) were reported but these were for experimental studies employing variables that may have affected the reliability of the test. Alternate forms reliability was indirectly assessed by comparing the scores on different forms as part of an apparent experiment. These reliabilities may also have been affected by the experimental manipulations and resulted in coefficients ranging from .30 and .55 for the SST, from .40 to .71 for the FDT, and from .08 to .75 for the LSHT.

The validity of the CCB is supported by an extensive discussion of several research studies examining the factor structure of the three tests, and the relationship between the CCB measures and various other instruments. The data reported in the manual detailing these studies appear to support the fit between the cognitive control model and the abilities assessed by the CCB. Criterion-related studies suggest that the CCB is measuring abilities similar to those measured by other tests of attention, intelligence, and achievement. Additional studies reported the predictive validity of the CCB in identifying children "suspected" of having learning disabilities.

In summary, the CCB provides a viable tool for assessing components of the cognitive control model for research purposes. It has the potential for presenting a new system for identifying children with specific learning dysfunctions and, through the linkage with the theoretical model, provides suggestions for interventions. However, until the reliability indices of this instrument achieve acceptable levels for each of the subtests, it should not be used in clinical settings for identification or intervention purposes. Adequate reliability is a must for clinical instruments and this is no exception. Further reliability analyses must be done to indicate various coefficients at each age range not on the conversion tables. The norm groups should be extended to include ages 3 through 16.

Review of the Cognitive Control Battery by HOPE J. HARTMAN, Associate Professor of Social & Psychological Foundations, School of Education, The City College, City University of New York, New York, NY:

The Cognitive Control Battery (CCB) was developed to assess nonverbal, unconscious cognition that affects learning. Santostefano extended Klein's work with adults on cognitive controls to children. The three tests comprising this battery measure fundamental processes of focal attention, field articulation, and comparison of past and immediately present information. Santostefano's biodevelopmental theory (1978) emphasizes shifts from global to differentiated cognitive functioning. Valuable components of Santostefano's work are recognition of the intimate link between cognition and affect, and placement of this work within the contexts of Piagetian theory, cognitive style, and other related constructs. However, Santostefano does not relate it to modern, information-processing views of cognition, including work on intelligence, metacognition, and learning strategies.

Extensive research was conducted in developing and refining CCB tests, each of which has undergone substantial revisions. Cross-sectional and longitudinal studies addressed hypothesized developmental changes in cognitive control functioning. Scoring is based on the obtained developmental age trends.

The CCB was developed for several users: clinicians, teachers, and parents who want a profile of the developmental status of aspects of a child's cognitive control functioning. It has broad applicability: well-adjusted as well as clinical populations, including mentally retarded, brain-damaged, learning disabled, and autistic children. Although the battery is intended for children and adolescents, ages 3–16 years, it has been used successfully with adults. Test results are used to diagnose cognitive and/or affective difficulties; to prescribe classroom teaching strategies, tutoring, and several types of therapy; and to evaluate the effectiveness of intervention strategies. Administration, training, and scoring procedures are carefully and thoughtfully presented. Test scores and statistics have a clear rationale. Score conversion tables are easy to use. Alternative interpretations of results, in conjunction with other clinical data sources, are demonstrated through numerous and varied cases, although most involve a narrow chronological age span.

The Scattered Scanning Test (SST), an elegant measure of focal attention or surveying a stimulus field, was developed as an improvement over the Focal Attention Circles Test for use with children. It can help diagnose cognitive impairments that prevent success in developing basic academic skills. The Motor Tempo Test controls for the effect of motor performance when responding on the SST. Alternate forms reliability was studied indirectly with the SST and three forms varying the emotional content of test items. Correlations ranged only from .30 to .55, suggesting that scanning varies to some degree with the type of distractions.

The Fruit Distraction Test (FDT) measures field articulation, or selective attention to relevant/irrelevant information. It was developed as an improvement over the Stroop Test for children with academic difficulties. There is empirical support for the relationship between field articulation and reading; field articulation differentiates young children with and without reading disabilities. Alternate forms reliability evidence is indirect. Some consistency data were obtained by comparing performance on cards from the same test with each other and with a baseline. Correlations were significant, ranging from .40–.71, and provide some support for the consistency of the FDT. In three studies, subjects were in grades K–4; ages were not reported for the clinical sample.

The Leveling-Sharpening House Test (LSHT) measures constructing and retaining images of past information and comparing them with immediately present information. The LSHT was designed to compare to the Schematizing Squares Tasks. The Matching Familiar Figures Test (9:662; Kagan, 1971) measures somewhat similar cognitive functions, reflective versus impulsive cognitive style. Santostefano views cognitive control as relatively stable, but capable of flexibly adapting to the situation. In contrast, he views cognitive style as more general and stable, and less flexible. Two studies provide some evidence of consistency based on alternate forms of the LSHT. A study of young adults showed the standard form of the LSHT correlated significantly with an alternate form featuring a parachutist scene ($r = .38$, $p < .01$). Another study ($N = 45$ boys, ages 7–11) showed significant correlations between the standard form of the LSHT and an alternate form featuring a doctor standing in a hospital room. Although 13 of 18 correlations were statistically significant, they ranged from only .08–.75, but provide some support for consistency of the construct being measured.

Test-retest reliability studies of the CCB were unusually ambitious, extending from 1 week to 5 years. The 5-year study followed children from kindergarten through fifth grade; the ratio of boys to girls was approximately 2:1. CCB performance in one grade was correlated with CCB performance in other grades. Two of the four SST variables, Motor Tempo and Number of Correct Shapes Marked, correlated significantly across grades. The two distance variables generally did not show significant stability. Although the three FDT time variables showed significant test-retest correlations, the recall variable generally did not. Three of the four LSHT variables, First Stop score, Number of Correct Changes, and Ratio Score, appear relatively stable over the 5-year period. The number of incorrect Type A changes showed some significant stability across grades; the number of incorrect Type B changes did not. A 4-year study following children from kindergarten through fourth grade showed inconsistent results. In one sample, 8/16 CCB variables showed significant test-retest correlations; in the other sample, only 3/16 variables had significant correlations. No data related to different ethnic groups were reported in the manual for any of the reliability or validity studies.

Both construct and criterion-related validity studies were conducted. Construct validation studies suggested cognitive controls exist in children. Analyses of IQ, sex, and 27 cognitive variables yielded factors that resembled the cognitive control dimensions found in the CCB. Unfortunately, the sample sizes used in these studies with public school, orphaned, and brain-damaged children were too small for drawing meaningful conclusions about validity. CCB performance was compared with personality measures and teachers' ratings. Factor loadings for personality variables were moderate and in the predicted directions; factor loadings with teacher ratings were low, but in the predicted directions. Performance on the CCB was compared with performance on other cognitive measures, including Piagetian tasks. The results indicated the solution of Piagetian tasks depends upon more basic cognitive processes, including those assessed by the CCB.

Criterion-related validity studies compared earlier versions of the CCB tests with similar instruments including: The Benton Visual Retention Test, the Incomplete Figures Test, and the Marble Board Test. Some positive and significant correlations were found; however, the sample size was very small and

it is questionable whether results can be generalized to the current versions of the tests or across various ethnic groups. Predictive validity studies demonstrated that CCB scores in kindergarten were moderately predictive of classroom behavior (e.g., attention deficits) observed in later grades and that CCB scores could discriminate between learning disabled and typical learners.

Research on the effect of moderator variables on CCB performance tentatively suggests that although age was consistently related to CCB performance, sex, intellectual ability, and, in general, academic achievement and SES were not. Ethnicity was not systematically examined. The FDT was the only CCB test that consistently related to skills tests. In various studies, some CCB variables had significant correlations with SES. Lower SES was associated with lower levels of cognitive control functioning. The FDT also differentiated between reading disabled boys (ages 8–13) and controls; the SST and LSHT did not. FDT and SST data from kindergarten discriminated between attentive and inattentive first graders.

Normative studies were better than most, taking into account age, ethnicity, sex, geographic area, and SES. The standardization sample consisted of well-adjusted, public school children. The results showed no significant effect for sex or race. Although a substantial number of Black and White students were included in the studies, Hispanics and Asians were not. Because age emerged as a significant factor, the norms for each test were stratified by age. The manual clearly cautions against using current norms for older groups than those in the standardization sample. It recommends restricting use with older adolescents and adults to research studies that include relevant comparison groups. Although no data are reported for them, the manual states the CCB has been used successfully with children from several countries, as well as with Hispanics, and middle and lower SES children from the United States.

No standard error of measurement data were reported and test security was not mentioned. Otherwise, the test manual is outstanding in its comprehensiveness, clarity, emphasis on testees' understanding of each test task, and use of tests with other clinical data sources. It provides step-by-step directions for training, administration, scoring, and interpretation. The CCB may be used by clinical, school, and counseling psychologists; psychiatrists; psychiatric nurses; rehabilitation counselors; and related professionals with formal training in administering and scoring educational and psychological tests. The manual says users *must* have experience administering intelligence scales and other perceptual-motor tests to well-adjusted children. Social skills for working with children are emphasized. The manual may be too detailed to be user friendly. More information could be in appendices.

The CCB is appealing and impressive. It appears to discriminate successfully between children in terms of levels of cognitive control functioning. Each test makes a valuable contribution to the assessment of basic cognitive processes. Both quantitative and qualitative indices are provided for each test. The CCB consistently shows respect for the complexity of mental functioning and its measurement. However, before it can be recommended without reservation, the following issues should be addressed. First, more psychometric information is needed. Stronger evidence is needed to bolster reliability claims. Validation studies should use larger samples and *current* CCB tests. Ethnicity should be addressed systematically in studies of reliability and validity. Standard error of measurement data should be provided. There is no empirical base for generalizing the current norms to Hispanic or Asian students. Research on the test and its psychometric properties should be expanded beyond the characteristically narrow age range of preadolescents. Second, the manual should be edited and reorganized, perhaps by presenting some illustrative cases and/or caveats regarding use in appendices.

REVIEWER'S REFERENCES

Kagan, J. (1971). Matching Familiar Figures Test. Cambridge, MA: The author.
Santostefano, S. (1978). *A biodevelopmental approach to clinical child psychology: Cognitive controls and cognitive control therapy.* New York: Wiley.

[76]

College Basic Academic Subjects Examination.

Purpose: Designed to assess skills and competencies typically achieved through the general education component of a college curriculum.
Population: College students having completed the general education component of a college curriculum (i.e., late sophomores or early juniors).
Publication Dates: 1989–90.
Acronym: College BASE.
Administration: Group.
Price Data, 1991: $27.45 per registration form per group or partial group of 50 students (48 for the Institutional Matrix Form).
Comments: "Criterion-referenced."
Author: Steven J. Osterlind.
Publisher: The Riverside Publishing Co.
a) LONG FORM.
Scores, 40: Competency (Interpretive Reasoning, Strategic Reasoning, Adaptive Reasoning), Skill (Social Science Procedures, Political/Economic Structures, Geography, Significance of U.S. Events, Significance of World Events, Physical Sciences, Life Sciences, Interpreting Results, Laboratory/Field Techniques, Observation/Experimental Design, Geometrical Calculations, 2- & 3-Dimensional Figures, Equations & Inequalities, Evaluating Expressions, Using Statistics, Properties and Notations, Practical Applications, Expository Writing Sample, Conventions of Written

English, Writing as a Process, Understanding Literature, Reading Analytically, Reading Critically), Cluster (Social Sciences, History, Fundamental Concepts, Laboratory & Field Work, Geometry, Algebra, General Mathematics, Writing, Reading & Literature), Subject (Social Studies, Science, Mathematics, English), Composite.
Price Data, 1991: $17.10 per student with writing exercise, $10.80 per student without writing exercise (includes all test materials, scoring, and delivery of score reports); materials package consists of 50 test books ('90, 44 pages), 50 answer books ('90, 8 pages), Manual for Examiners and Test Coordinators ('90, 27 pages), Guide to Test Content ('90, 27 pages), Coordinator's Data Sheet, and Examiner's Data Sheet.
Time: 210(240) minutes with writing exercise; 160(180) minutes without writing exercise.
Comments: Writing exercise is optional.
b) SHORT FORM.
Scores, 24: Same as Long Form without Social Studies and Science sections.
Price Data, 1991: $14.85 per student with writing exercise, $8.55 per student without writing exercise (includes all test materials, scoring, and delivery of score reports); materials package same as *a* above.
Time: 110(120) minutes with writing exercise; 60(80) minutes without writing exercise.
Comments: Writing exercise is optional.
c) INSTITUTIONAL MATRIX FORM.
Scores, 5: Composite Score, Subject Scores, Cluster Scores, Skill Scores, Competency Scores.
Price Data, 1991: $6.30 per student; materials package includes 4 matrix test books each for Forms 1–12, 48 matrix answer sheets, Coordinator's Data Sheet, Examiner's Data Sheet, Manual for Examiners and Test Coordinators ('90, 26 pages), and Guide to Test Content.

Review of the College Basic Academic Subjects Examination by WILLIAM E. COFFMAN, E. F. Lindquist Professor Emeritus, University of Iowa, Iowa City, IA:

The College Basic Academic Subjects Examination (College BASE) is being marketed as a criterion-referenced achievement battery designed particularly for students completing the general education component of their college experience. Testing would be typically near the end of the sophomore year, but users are encouraged to test at different times to assess changes resulting from college experience. Primary emphasis is given to the criterion-referenced aspect, that is, interpretation can be made directly in terms of the location of individuals and groups on a total of 40 ability scales. These scales were developed using item response theory. The College BASE can also be used to monitor changes on the 40 ability scales over time. Although these uses are described, given the nature of the population represented by the sample and on the scaling method itself, it is doubtful that such objectives can be achieved.

The College BASE includes a scoring service as well as test booklets and manuals describing various aspects of the program. One option is an Institutional Matrix Form that generates institutional averages while administering only one-sixth of the examination to an single student. The published materials contain copious description and rationale but are somewhat lacking in supporting data. This reviewer was provided with a copy of a technical manual that appears to be a preliminary draft of one that will eventually be offered by the publisher.

At first glance, the manual is impressive: over 150 pages of text, 69 tables, and 11 figures. It is rare that this amount of information is available for tests when they are first published. In the main, however, the manual is primarily an expansion of the rationales set forth in the published material. The data analyses result from the application of readily available computer statistical packages to the responses of an aggregate of college students. The students responded to test Forms LC and LD, forms with 154 items in common, plus self-report background questions. The content of the manual raises many questions and provides few answers regarding the technical quality of the examination.

The procedures followed in developing the examination lead one to expect that it will contain well-written items covering a wide range of educational achievement, and a detailed review of Form LD indicates that this expectation is met. The test plan calls for a content by skills framework that characterizes good achievement batteries. In addition, each of the 180 items is based on a different set of detailed specifications. There is an expectation that new items written to the same specifications will generate parallel test forms, but no supporting evidence is provided. Because plans call for introducing approximately 20% new items each year, it will be some time before two forms with no item overlap are available.

The specifications imply the examination is assessing multidimensional domains and the manual includes a discussion of this implication. The content specifications call for four general dimensions: English, Mathematics, Science, and Social Studies. Each of these is divided into clusters, the clusters into skills, and the skills into subskills. Scores are generated at each level except the last, thus implying a hierarchical structure of the four subject domains. The abilities specifications call for competencies that form a hierarchy with higher order competencies depending on lower ones.

Thus, each content domain would be expected to generate a factor structure somewhat like that described by Humphreys (1962) and the abilities domain a simplex as described by Guttman (1954). The authors recognize the appropriateness of factor analysis for validating the multidimensional model,

and they do provide some evidence. Unfortunately, the method employed (principal component analyses and orthogonal rotation of item intercorrelations separately at each level) does not do justice to the clarity and complexity of test planning.

Given the complexity of the test specifications and the evidence, however fragmentary, that the domains being assessed are multidimensional, the method of scaling is questionable. The authors argue correctly that whenever a single score is reported, it provides an estimate of a location on a single reference vector through a domain. Therefore, it is acceptable to generate scales for English, Mathematics, Science, and Social Studies using an item response model (IRT). The problem comes when the same IRT item statistics are also used to estimate scores for the several subscales. Because the item statistics locate the item on the general scale, each subscore should be an estimate of an individual's location on the overall scale; and intercorrelations among subscales, corrected for attenuation, should be 1.00. In other words, differences among subtest scores and total scores for the four areas are due to errors of measurement or to the fact that the students taking the test do not belong to the population represented by the scale.

The total sample, all or parts of which were used in item analyses, norming, scaling, and validity studies, consists of 4,375 college students, 2,013 of whom took Form LC and 2,362 Form LD. The two samples differ little in composition, and the total is distributed as follows: 19.3% seniors, 33.6% juniors, 30% sophomores, and 16.2% freshmen. Only 18% are males and 82% are females. The authors argue that the sample is representative of groups that will use the examination; they do not report scores either by class groups or by sex. Any institution wishing to test groups significantly different in composition must develop local norms.

One must be skeptical regarding the reported reliabilities of the several scales. First, they are internal consistency coefficients and provide no evidence regarding parallel form or test-retest stability. Also, to the extent that there is growth over the college years, coefficients based on samples including all four classes generate inflated coefficients. This practice is not in keeping with modern psychometric techniques. It seems the aura of IRT methods may be blinding users to some of the truths readily accepted with classical methods.

The arguments for validity of the College BASE are well stated, but the measures chosen for comparison are essentially irrelevant. Relationships between the four College BASE area scores and total scores on the ACT Assessment Program (ACT), the Scholastic Aptitude Test (SAT-V and SAT-M), and grade-point average (GPA), the so-called criterion measures, are what any experienced educator would have expected given a description of the College BASE. What one would like to know, however, is the relationship of subscores to particular curricular experiences.

In summary, Form LD of the College BASE appears to be a carefully written examination following a careful set of specifications. Whether or not the specifications meet the objectives of a particular institution must be decided by representatives of that institution. Whether or not the expectations of sample-free scales and parallel forms needed for longitudinal measurement can be met is still to be demonstrated.

REVIEWER'S REFERENCES

Guttman, L. (1954). A new approach to factor analysis: The radex. In P. F. Lazarsfeld (Ed.), *Mathematical thinking in the social sciences* (pp. 258-348). Glencoe, IL: Free Press.
Humphreys, L. G. (1962). The organization of human abilities. *American Psychologist, 17*, 475-483.

Review of the College Basic Academic Subjects Examination by DELWYN L. HARNISCH, Associate Professor of Educational Psychology, University of Illinois at Urbana-Champaign, Champaign, IL:

NATURE OF THE TEST. The College BASE (Basic Academic Subjects Examination) is a criterion-referenced achievement test designed to assess examinees' proficiency in English, Mathematics, Science, and Social Studies. It is also claimed that the test measures cognitive processing skills in three cross-disciplinary competencies: Interpretive Reasoning, Strategic Reasoning, and Adaptive Reasoning. The test is intended for students who have completed the general educational program which, at most institutions, will be near the end of the sophomore year.

The focus of the College BASE is to determine the degree of student mastery of particular skills and competencies rather than ranking and comparing students. Hence it is clear that the main purpose of the test is to diagnose the strengths and weaknesses of both individual students and curricula rather than to provide criteria for student selection into particular educational programs.

GENERAL DESCRIPTION OF THE TEST. The College BASE is available in three forms: Long Form, Short Form, and Institutional Matrix Form. The Long Form is the complete test battery recommended for assessing individual achievement levels in depth. The Short Form includes only English and Mathematics, appropriate when administration time is limited or when only the two disciplines are of interest. The Institutional Matrix Form yields only aggregate data about an institution and does not include individual student information. This form, which requires less individual testing time, is recommended for institutional program review and evaluation.

TEST CONTENT AND ITEM TYPE. The complete form contains 180 multiple-choice test items and a Writing test to assess achievements in four subject areas: English, Mathematics, Science, and Social Studies. The four areas are further divided into nine clusters which "represent natural groupings of topics within a subject" (technical manual, p. 14). Twenty-three skills within each of the nine clusters "represent particular abilities within a subject" (p. 14). Together, these subskills form one dimension of the test matrix, the knowledge base, which is intercepted by the other dimension of the matrix, three levels of cognitive processing skills: Interpretive, Strategic, and Adaptive Reasoning. According to the authors of the test, Interpretive Reasoning is an even more basic level of information processing that factual recall, including such abilities as paraphrasing, summarizing, and explaining. In contrast, Strategic Reasoning includes skills related to definition, comparison, and classification. Adaptive Reasoning includes the skills of synthesis and evaluation. It is claimed that "all of the items on the test represent the conjunction of a content element and a cognitive act; that is, every item represents a skill *and* a competency" (technical manual, p. 15).

The Short Form is identical to the Long Form in both the content and the format. The difference is that the Short Form contains only English and Mathematics. The Writing exercise is optional with the Short Form.

The Institutional Matrix Form is derived from dividing, following a matrix sampling scheme, 2 Long Form tests into 12 shorter forms, 10 of which contain 36 multiple-choice test items each and 2 of which contain the Writing exercise. Together, 12 matrix form tests constitute one complete matrix of College BASE. All 12 forms should be used to get an overall assessment of an institution's program.

TEST ADMINISTRATION AND SCORING. The College BASE is administered in a large group setting to the whole group of examinees. Administration guidelines should be strictly followed. The Long Form requires about 4 hours to complete, 40 minutes of which are for the Writing exercise. The Short Form requires about 1 hour and 20 minutes or about 2 hours if the Writing exercise is included. The Institutional Matrix Form requires about 50 minutes to complete.

All College BASE test forms are scored by the test publisher. Individual scores are reported on the Student Score Report and institutional averages are reported on the Institutional Summary Report. Interpretive guides are provided to each examinee and to every institution.

For both reports, the College BASE yields 40 scores in accordance with the test structure: one score each for the 4 subjects, 9 clusters, 23 skills, and 3 competencies. A composite score is also reported.

The numerical scale is adopted for subject and cluster scores, which range from 40 to 560 with a mean of 300 and a standard deviation of 65. The subject score is not an average of the cluster scores.

The skills and competencies are reported using three ranking levels: High, Medium, and Low. The distinction among High, Medium and Low is ± 1 standard deviation from the mean score of the standardization population. The available information indicates that the cutoff score was carefully and well selected via a standard setting process.

The composite score is a single scaled number representing the level of achievement across all subjects. For individual examinees, this score is the arithmetic mean of the four subject scores; and for institutional reports, it is the median score for the particular group of examinees who took the complete test.

TEST NORMS. The authors of the College BASE subjected all test items to rigorous item analysis. The authors, however, failed to provide an informative description of the population on which the College BASE was normed. The information and data available to the reviewer indicate that the test was normed in April 1988 on approximately 4,000 students in 36 colleges and universities stratified on the basis of size and type of the institutions, race, gender, and educational level (e.g., freshman, sophomore, etc.). The authors of the test believe the norm population represents postsecondary student populations anticipated to take the College BASE. However, as the test was designed as a national assessment of a specified level of achievement common to many colleges and universities, it would be desirable to include in the norming samples such variables as geographical locations, SES, and student intended majors. Due to insufficient information, it is difficult to judge the representativeness of the norming sample.

RELIABILITY. Three types of reliability indices are available for every subject, cluster, and skill: (a) internal consistency measures reported as KR-20, (b) standard error associated with each score point, and (c) consistency of mastery-nonmastery classifications.

For the four subjects, the KR-20 reliabilities range from .77 for English to .89 for Mathematics. For the nine clusters, reliability indices range from .59 for Writing to .82 for Algebra. For the 23 skills, reliabilities range from .30 for Understanding Literature to .73 for Equations and Inequalities. Median skill reliabilities are .51 for English, .64 for Mathematics, .48 for Science, and .54 for Social Studies. Reliabilities for competencies range from .72 for Adaptive Reasoning to .86 for Strategic Reasoning. Reliability indices decrease as the number of test items is reduced.

The reliability coefficients appear to be moderate for an achievement test with a limited number of items considered for the specific scores of interest. It should be taken into consideration that these coefficients are computed from eight to nine test items per skill, and from about 27 items per cluster. Therefore, review of performance should be evaluated across several indicators versus a single indicator of subject matter performance in a specific domain. Reliabilities for competencies are quite strong considering the difficulty in obtaining accurate measurements of cognitive skills and abilities.

VALIDITY. Classical test theory makes distinctions among three types of validity: content validity, criterion-related validity, and construct validity. The authors of the College BASE, however, argue that the study of validity is a dynamic process, and that validity is a unitary concept that involves the interpretability of test scores, their utility, and the value implications of the scores as a basis for actions. Hence the authors' hypothesis argues that performance on the College BASE is more closely related to the constructs intended to be measured than it is to competing constructs.

Two factor-analytic studies of over 2,000 examinees using Forms LC and LD indicate that factor compositions are consistent with the intended structures. The external component was examined using canonical correlational analyses, multiple regression analysis, and the discriminant function analysis. The results reported support the hypothesis that the College BASE is similar to other measures but yet different enough to contribute independent assessment of the underlying achievement attribute. The findings also indicate that College BASE scores correlate positively and strongly with the examinees' ACT Assessment Program (ACT) composite scores. The correlation between College BASE scores and the examinees' scores on the Scholastic Aptitude Test (SAT) verbal skills tests, the SAT quantitative skills tests, and examinees' grade point average are moderate in magnitude and positive in direction.

OVERVIEW. The College BASE is a well-developed test designed to assess proficiency in four major subject areas: English, Mathematics, Science, and Social Studies. It also measures students' general knowledge. The test was organized into a structure which consists of subjects, clusters, skills, and competencies originally derived from the Educational Equality Project. The objectives assessed by the College BASE stem from the summary report of the Educational Equality Project, "Academic Preparation for College: What Examinees Need to Know and Be Able to Do" (cited in the technical manual, p. 31). The original test items were developed by consulting 50 institutions of higher learning from 20 states. The information and data available to the reviewer indicate that each test item was subjected to rigorous item analysis and that effort was made to control for test bias.

The College BASE correlates positively and strongly with the ACT and positively and moderately with the SAT-V, SAT-Q, and grade-point average. Scores for both individuals and institutions are available. The scores are particularly useful for diagnostic purposes. Both individuals and institutions are provided score interpretation guides. A technical manual offers detailed analyses and relevant information and data.

The number of specific subscores provided by the College BASE and the evidence of the construct validity of those subscores are impressive. However, each institution considering this assessment tool should examine the extent of overlap of the test content with its general education goals. Pike (1991) reports that only 36% of the general education goals at the University of Tennessee at Knoxville were covered on the College BASE. As is true of all assessment measures, judgment is needed to determine the appropriateness of the College BASE for specific contexts and purposes. Additional measures, such as performance assessments, should be used to supplement the College BASE in order to provide additional information that can guide decisions concerning the adoption of modification of an educational program.

REVIEWER'S REFERENCE

Pike, G. (1991). Assessment measures. *Assessment Update: Progress, Trends & Practices in Higher Education, 3,* 6-7.

[77]
Communication Knowledge Inventory.

Purpose: To measure knowledge about person to person communication practices.
Population: High school through adult.
Publication Dates: 1970–78.
Acronym: RCK.
Scores: Total score only.
Administration: Group.
Manual: No manual; fact sheet available.
Price Data: Available from publisher.
Time: (10–20) minutes.
Comments: Self-administered.
Authors: W. J. Reddin and Ken Rowell.
Publisher: Organizational Tests Ltd. [Canada].

Review of the Communication Knowledge Inventory by GREGORY J. BOYLE, Senior Lecturer in Psychology, University of Queensland, St. Lucia, Queensland, Australia:

The Communication Knowledge Inventory (RCK) is an 80-item true/false self-report instrument designed to index an individual's knowledge about effective interpersonal communication skills. In the accompanying Fact Sheet, the RCK is described as "a test of general communication knowledge for managers" (but it is also recommended for use with a diversity of vocational categories—see below). The RCK is composed of 40 true statements (e.g., "People don't like to listen to or read about things they disagree with") and 40 false

statements (e.g., "People who say less have less to offer"). Twenty true statements and 20 false statements pertain to verbal communication, and 20 true and 20 false statements concern nonverbal methods of expressing feelings and thoughts. Although the RCK is recommended for use with the general adult population, nevertheless, it was intended primarily to be used with management, supervisory, leadership, and human relations training, and for assisting in screening, appraisal, and selection decisions.

The instrument is self-scored (there is an underlying carbon sheet). The maximum possible score is 80 points (with higher scores being associated with superior communication knowledge). Raw total scores may be converted into one of five separate categories (Very Low, Low, Average, High, Very High) depending on the particular score obtained. However, the RCK is an informal instrument, and obtained responses are used more for discussion purposes rather than for formal testing as such. Users should be alerted to this limit of valid use of the RCK. The RCK is only one of a battery of six instruments, which together comprise the Behavioral Inventory Battery.

Administration of the RCK is straightforward (self-administered) and usually takes a maximum of 10 to 20 minutes. Norms for the RCK were derived from a sample of 648 managers (although it is intended for use with any individual who wishes to improve the effectiveness of his/her communication skills). Approximately 20% of individuals are said to fall within each of the five competency categories. However, the norms are extremely simple, being merely a crude translation of raw scores into one of the five separate proficiency categories. Strictly speaking, they should not be regarded as norms at all. Moreover, there are no conversion tables with respect to the significant variables of Years in Position, Age, Years of Education, and Job Function.

Test-retest reliability (stability) over a retest interval or 2 months was found to be .87 for a sample of 107 first and second level manager—as indicated in the RCK manual (although the fact sheet refers to 108 managers). Other than this single coefficient, no other reliability evidence is provided in the test manual. No information is presented on the immediate test-retest (dependability) of the inventory. Additional test-retest reliability data obtained from widely differing samples across a whole spectrum of retest intervals is clearly desirable. Moreover, no evidence is presented as to the item homogeneity of the RCK, so it is not known whether the instrument enables either broad or narrow measurement of the communication knowledge construct, or of its subcategories.

The RCK manual provides some validity data for the RCK. The initial normative sample of 648 managers was subdivided into various subgroups, which had significantly different mean scores. Results obtained indicate that RCK scores are lower for individuals who: stay in the same job longer; are older than the managers; and have less formal schooling, all suggesting less interpersonal effectiveness within the workplace. It was also reported that production, finance, accounting, and purchasing managers scored lower than did personnel and training managers. The RCK manual advises that those interested in ascertaining the validity of the instrument should undertake their own validity studies, by comparing various between-group differences in scores. It would be useful if the RCK manual also provided empirical evidence as to other forms of validity, such as concurrent validity, predictive validity, and construct validity.

Item responses can be interpreted in terms of three separate categories (pertaining to communication fallacies; verbal communication; nonverbal communication, respectively). However, no factor analytic evidence (either exploratory or confirmatory) is presented in the RCK manual to substantiate the validity of the purported three-factor structure of the instrument. Until such evidence (based on methodologically sound procedures) is provided, the structural dimensionality of the RCK remains somewhat uncertain. The most appropriate methodology would be to undertake a confirmatory factor analysis of the item intercorrelations using statistical packages such as LISREL (Joreskog & Sorbom, 1989). Only then can the goodness of fit of the subscale structure claimed for the RCK be assessed, in an hypothesis testing sense (cf. Cuttance & Ecob, 1987).

The RCK instrument itself, together with the built-in answer keys is a professionally presented inventory, which should serve as a useful stimulus for individual analysis and group discussion. When the RCK is administered to large groups ($N \geq 200$) computer scoring facilities are available (although it is not clear from the manual precisely how to organize such scoring). Also, an interpretation guide is useful for both training and coaching applications.

REVIEWER'S REFERENCES
Cuttance, P., & Ecob, R. (1987). *Structural modeling by example: Applications in educational, sociological, and behavioral research*. New York: Cambridge University Press.
Joreskog, K. G., & Sorbom, D. (1989). *LISREL 7: User's reference guide*. Mooresville, IN: Scientific Software Inc.

[78]
Communication Response Style: Assessment.

Purpose: To assess an individual's communication response style.
Population: Adults.
Publication Dates: 1981–87.

Scores, 4: Empathic Response Score, Critical Response Score, Searching Response Score, Advising Response Score.
Administration: Group.
Manual: No manual.
Price Data, 1988: $60 per set of 20 including test booklets, answer sheets, and interpretation sheets ('81, 4 pages).
Time: Administration time not reported.
Comments: Self-administered, self-scored.
Author: Madelyn Burley-Allen.
Publisher: Training House, Inc.

Review of the Communication Response Style: Assessment by JANET NORRIS, Associate Professor of Communication Disorders, Louisiana State University, Baton Rouge, LA:

The Communication Response Style (CRS) consists of an assessment exercise, a corresponding answer sheet, and a four-page interpretation and summary guide. According to the publishers (personal communication, January 15, 1990) this instrument was developed for use as an exercise for courses and workshops in business management offered by their corporation. It is not promoted as a standardized test or instrument that is readily understood outside of the context for which it was designed. Consequently, there is no manual describing the theoretical constructs underlying the CRS, procedures used in test construction, or in-depth administration and scoring instructions.

The publishers indicated that the CRS is based upon the work of McGregor (1960, 1966) and his notions of Theory X versus Theory Y as management frameworks adopted by supervisors within organizations such as corporations. These two perspectives differ in the manner in which they view the role of authority, assumptions made regarding the inherent attitudes people maintain toward work, and the needs of individuals that motivate behavior. Management style, corporate decisions, and interpersonal relationships within an organization are strongly influenced by the theory to which an individual ascribes. McGregor's work focuses upon the validity of Theory Y as a fundamental framework for generating and interpreting management policies and practices.

Theory Y regards management as a dynamic process that is founded in establishing strong interrelationships and interdependence between the needs of the organization and individuals. Authority and control are regarded as selective and adaptive, rather than absolute and rule or law governed. Poor motivation and performance are viewed as symptoms of a system that provides limited opportunities for individuals to achieve personal goals and to develop a commitment to the organization, and are directly attributable to the methods or organization and control established by management. Employees are regarded as valuable and capable resources, and emphasis is placed upon developing individual potentiality. It is contrasted with the more traditional management principles proposed by Theory X, in which management is viewed as the upper level of authority where decisions are made that must be adhered to unquestioned by those on lower levels of the hierarchy. Emphasis is placed upon the needs of the organization, even when they are inconsistent with the needs of the individual.

The items on the CRS are designed to assist course/workshop participants in evaluating their personal style of response to situations that are commonly encountered in the workplace. Twenty situations are presented related to topics such as job satisfaction, difficulties with superiors or subordinates, evaluation of job performance, and establishing one's role within the organization. Each situation is presented as a quote or statement made by a hypothetical co-worker. The responder is asked to select from four response statements the one or ones that are in closest agreement with his/her preferred response to the situation. Three points are to be assigned to each situation, so that all 3 points may be awarded to one response choice if the participant fully agrees with that behavior, or the points may be distributed, with the first preference given 2 points and the second preference assigned 1 point, or each of three responses assigned 1 point.

Responses are categorized according to response style. The order of presentation for the four possible response style alternatives is randomized for each of the 20 situations. One of the four choices is rated as an Empathic response, that is, a nonjudgmental reply that is conducive to open communication and encourages the other person to elaborate upon his/her own needs or feelings. One statement is categorized as a Searching response, or one that asks for additional information. These two styles of responding are deemed to be consistent with Theory Y management, and therefore are desirable response types. The CRS Interpretation guide describes them as responses that encourage two-way interaction and joint problem solving, and are sensitive to the personal needs of the individual. They place the person initiating the concern in the role of an adult who is capable of making decisions, and focus on personal needs as well as seeking solutions that are beneficial to the organization.

A third response choice is categorized as a Critical response, or one that expresses judgment or evaluation. The fourth choice consists of an Advising response, in which a recommendation is made. Both Critical and Advising responses are considered to be consistent with the authoritarian and controlling style of interaction characteristic of Theory X. According to the CRS Interpretation guide, they reflect the biases of the responder and therefore tend to reject or present a closed attitude toward the beliefs of the other individual. They remove the decision-making power from the person initiating the concern, create dependency, and establish a differential in power or status between the interlocutors.

No information is available regarding item selection, the assignment of response choices to response style categories, the reliability of the instrument in eliciting a most preferred response style, or any other issue related to test construction. The assessment exercise is completed individually by reading each situation and response choices, and then writing point values on the answer sheet. Three points must be distributed among one or more of the alternate responses for each of the 20 situations. All of the instructions are provided on the front page of the assessment booklet, including an example situation and possible scoring profiles. The format of the assessment exercise booklet and answer sheet are straightforward and easy to follow.

The answer sheet consists of a double-page form, the top page presenting a column of four boxes for each response situation. The responder is asked to write numbers corresponding to the point values assigned based upon agreement with the responses, ranging from 0 to 3. The bottom page is yellow noncarbon reproducing paper that duplicates the answers onto a score sheet that is coded for response style type. Instructions for scoring are contained on the yellow copy, and generally consist of totalling the number of points assigned to each response style category. On this yellow form, response choices are coded according to style, so that Empathic response statements appear in triangles, Critical statements appear in squares, and Searching and Advising statements appear in circles and diamonds, respectively. Scoring is thus clear and easy to complete.

The CRS Interpretation guide consists of a short description of each of the response style types, followed by a discussion of the relative value of response style types and their relationship to the views proposed by transactional analysis (Harris, 1973). Each participant is asked to profile his/her personal response style based upon the most to least frequently occurring response choice, and to draw conclusions about his/her communication response style, the implications for change, and expected outcomes in communicating with others as a result of this change. The CRS is designed to be used in the context of a course or workshop, where these concepts are explored in more detail (personal communication with publishers, January 15, 1990).

In summary, the Communication Response Style was developed as an exercise to be used in creating a personal awareness of an individual's interpersonal interaction style and how other persons might respond to that style. It was not developed as a standardized instrument or an assessment device to be used by clinical professionals to analyze the communication style of others, or to make judgments on personality or adaptive abilities. The validity of the instrument is dependent upon the extent to which the situations and response choices measure a person's actual response style, and the extent to which the response alternatives accurately represent the four categories of response style. Because no information on test construction is available, the validity is unknown. The CRS thus represents an interesting exercise that may be useful to individuals interested in understanding more about their own interpersonal interaction style. It is inappropriate for any clinical or assessment purposes.

REVIEWER'S REFERENCES

McGregor, D. (1960). *The human side of enterprise.* New York: McGraw Hill.

McGregor, D. (1966). *Leadership and motivation: Essays of Douglas McGregor.* Cambridge, MA: The M.I.T. Press.

Harris, T. (1973). *I'm OK, you're OK.* New York: Avon.

Review of the Communication Response Style: Assessment by GARGI ROYSIRCAR SODOWSKY, Assistant Professor of Educational Psychology, University of Nebraska-Lincoln, Lincoln, NE:

This is a self-report measure that purports to assess four kinds of response styles in the verbal communications of adults: the Empathic Response, the Critical Response, the Searching Response, and the Advising Response. In the self-interpretation section of the test, the author states, "your response style serves as a model for those you communicate with, and it is likely to influence their response style when it's their turn to listen." Thus, effective communication includes being aware of how one affects another person's response. For instance, one becomes aware that an Empathic Response influences the other person to elaborate on his or her ideas and feelings. The Critical Response makes the other person feel threatened, and he or she may choose not to respond. A Searching Response that is well-timed and does not arouse the feeling of being given the "third degree" elicits additional information from a person and enables the communicator to understand the person better. The Advising Response prevents the listener from talking through a problem and tends to build a dependency relationship between the communicator and the listener.

Although the author does not state the test is for a specific adult population, the contents of the response items and imaginary statements are suggestive of the experiences and interactions of people in the corporate world and in business. The test-taker is provided a test booklet with items and instructions for responding, an answer-cum-score sheet with instructions for self-scoring, and an interpretation handout for self-analysis.

The test items consist of a series of 20 imaginary spoken statements. Beside each are four responses representing the four response styles. For each item,

the test-taker, imagining that he or she is responding face-to-face to a speaker presenting an imaginary statement, has 3 points to assign. Each of the four responses is rated in terms of how much the test-taker "agrees" with or "likes" the response, giving the 3 points to one or more of the alternate responses. Thus the assigning of the points can have three possible patterns: 3 points can be assigned to one response; 2 points can be assigned one response, and 1 point to another; or 1 point can be assigned to each of three responses.

The 20 statements and the four responses to each statement are printed in the test booklet. The answer sheet printed on NCR (non-carbon reproducing) paper generates beneath it a yellow score sheet. On the answer sheet, beside each numbered item, there are four boxes corresponding to the four responses in the test booklet for each item. The test-taker uses a pencil or ball-point pen with enough pressure, so that the scoring shows up on the yellow score sheet. This score sheet provides instructions to the test taker for self-scoring. The scoring is reported in raw scores.

The interpretation section defines and elaborates the four response styles and evaluates descriptively their respective effects. A self-analysis sheet follows. On this sheet, the test-taker rank orders his or her response styles based on the total raw scores obtained for each response style, and then, the test-taker answers three free response items (incomplete sentences) describing his or her response style, the implications of such a style, and his or her communication effectiveness based upon the listener's initial response. The self-analysis is subjective and clinical in nature.

The instructions to the test-taker for the self-administration, self-scoring, and self-analysis are simple, clear, and reader-friendly and are accompanied with examples. However, the self-scoring system could encourage cheating. When turning to the score sheet to check whether the assigned scores show up (which the test-taker does, according to the test administration instructions), the distinct symbols given to each response style—triangle, square, circle, and diamond—are accompanied by their respective response style names. The instructions on the score sheet for scoring the symbols also repeat what each symbol represents. Even though the test-taker is requested not to read the scoring instructions while taking the test, some might be tempted to read what is so obviously presented.

The four responses across the whole measure are not in any particular order and, therefore, may prevent a response set. On the other hand, the Empathic Responses on the average are longer than the other responses, and some test-takers may correctly conclude that the longer response is the "best" response. Then, when turning the answer sheet to check the score sheet, one can see that the longer answers are coded as triangles which total up to an Empathic Response Score. Because adult test-takers are generally familiar with the word "empathy," their responses may indicate content-dependent response biases such as social desirability, faking good, or defensiveness.

Despite its objective responding and scoring techniques, giving it the face validity of a test, this measure is more similar to an exercise in a workbook on communications or one following a chapter in a textbook (for review purposes) than to an objective assessment instrument. The assessment approximates a form of self-evaluation to increase personal awareness rather than a systematic procedure for measuring a sample of behavior, personality characteristics, or certain attitudes toward a referent. In the instructions for taking the test, the test-taker is told to select the response(s) "you most agree with," "like" the most, and "would be most likely to make." The instructions use interchangeably the constructs of cognition, affect, and behavior which are, however, distinct psychological processes; for instance, what one agrees with (cognitive reasoning) may not be what one likes (affective attitude) and what one does. The instructions should make clear whether the device is measuring evaluation (agreement), preference (liking), or behavior (actual response). Otherwise, the test-taker may get confused or may respond superficially or with vague understanding.

A test manual is not provided. Therefore, there is no information about the development, reliabilities, validity, and homogeneity of the test. Although in the section "Analyzing Your Scores," the author states, "The instrument has been completed by thousands of people," there is no information on a norm group and normative data that can be used as the basis for interpretation of individual test scores. Therefore, this is not a standardized test. The author should demonstrate the content validity of the 20 items for each response style, showing that each set of items does, in fact, representatively sample the underlying response style domain. The construct validity of the measure must be examined, both theoretically and psychometrically, showing the degree to which it measures the response styles it is designed to measure.

There is a significant problem related to a lack of acknowledgement of psychological theories and counseling practice, where the types of responses measured by the test were originally proposed. The empathic response is associated with the work of Carl Rogers (1957); the confrontational (critical) response with those of Perls (1969), Ellis (1973), and Glasser (1965); the listening, searching, and advising responses with those of Carkhuff (1969), Egan (1975), Koile (1977), and Yalom (1970); and the

ego state responses with that of Berne (1964). A manual is needed where the author can provide the necessary review of psychological literature to discuss the sources of and theoretical rationale for the constructs measured by the instrument. Also in the interpretation section of the test, the author should reference the primary information sources.

The strength of the measure is that it has provided clear, readable examples of responses illustrating a certain hypothesized response style, thus operationalizing a construct. Researchers of the dyadic process of communication would perhaps be interested in such a measure. At the same time, the following are needed to make the measure acceptable: research into the development, psychometric properties, and uses of the measure; a test manual; standardization and normative data; standard or transformed scores; protected scoring keys; the control of response sets; and reference to original sources.

REVIEWER'S REFERENCES

Rogers, C. R. (1957). The necessary and sufficient conditions of therapeutic personality change. *Journal of Consulting Psychology, 21,* 95-103.
Berne, E. (1964). *Games people play.* New York: Grove Press.
Glasser, W. (1965). *Reality therapy: A new approach to psychiatry.* New York: Harper & Row.
Carkhuff, R. R. (1969). *Helping and human relations.* New York: Holt, Rinehart, & Winston.
Perls, F. S. (1969). *Gestalt therapy verbatim.* Moab, Utah: Real People Press.
Yalom, I. D. (1970). *The theory and practice of group psychotherapy.* New York: Basic Books.
Ellis, A. (1973). *Humanistic psychotherapy: The rational-emotive approach.* New York: Julian Press.
Egan, G. (1975). *The skilled helper.* Monterey, CA: Brooks/Cole.
Koile, E. (1977). *Listening as a way of becoming.* Waco, TX: Word Books.

[79]

Community Opinion Inventory.

Purpose: "To identify areas the public sees as being done well, and areas seen as not done well" in the local school.
Population: Adults who do not have children enrolled in school.
Publication Date: 1990.
Scores: 5 subscales: General Support Climate, Program Awareness, Responsiveness to the Community, Equality of Opportunity, Resource Stewardship.
Administration: Group.
Parts, 2: A (Likert-scale items), B (open-ended items).
Price Data, 1991: $4 per 25 inventories (Part A); $3 per 25 inventories (Part B); $3 per 25 machine-scored answer sheets; $3 per Administrator's Manual (12 pages).
Time: Untimed.
Author: National Study of School Evaluation.
Publisher: National Study of School Evaluation.

[80]

Comprehensive Assessment of School Environments.

Purpose: Developed to assess perceptions of the school climate and student, teacher, and parent satisfaction with each individual's personal environment in order "to foster data-based decision making for school improvement."
Population: Junior and senior high schools.
Publication Dates: 1986–89.

Acronym: CASE.

Administration: Group.

Price Data, 1991: $5 per 35 surveys (specify form) and manual ('87, 36 pages); $4 per 35 machine-scorable answer sheets; $3 per examiner's manual; $95 per microcomputer scoring package (Apple IIe, IBM-PC); $5 per specimen set; scoring service available from publisher: $50 (minimum fee) plus $5 per 100 answer sheets.

Time: Administration time not reported.

Comments: Test booklet titles are School Climate Survey, Parent Satisfaction Survey, Teacher Satisfaction Survey, and Student Satisfaction Survey.

Authors: Cynthia Halderson (manuals and climate survey), Edgar A. Kelley (manuals and climate survey), James W. Keefe (manuals and climate survey), Paul S. Berge (technical manual), John A. Glover (climate survey), Carrie Sorenson (climate survey), Carol Speth (climate survey), Neal Schmitt (satisfaction surveys), and Brian Loher (satisfaction surveys).

Publisher: National Association of Secondary School Principals.

a) SCHOOL CLIMATE SURVEY.

Scores: Student, Teacher, and Parent scores for the following 10 subscales: Teacher-Student Relationships, Security and Maintenance, Administration, Student Academic Orientation, Student Behavioral Values, Guidance, Student-Peer Relationships, Parent & Community-School Relationships, Instructional Management, Student Activities.

b) PARENT SATISFACTION SURVEY.

Scores, 9: Parent Involvement, Curriculum, Student Activities, Teachers, Support Services, School Building/Supplies/Maintenance, Student Discipline, School Administrators, School Information Services.

c) TEACHER SATISFACTION SURVEY.

Scores, 9: Administration, Compensation, Opportunities for Advancement, Student Responsibility & Discipline, Curriculum and Job Tasks, Co-workers, Parents and Community, School Building/Supplies/Maintenance, Communication.

d) STUDENT SATISFACTION SURVEY.

Scores 8: Teachers, Fellow Students, Schoolwork, Student Activities, Student Discipline, Decision-Making Opportunities, School Building/Supplies/Upkeep, Communication.

Review of the Comprehensive Assessment of School Environments by NANCY L. ALLEN, Research Scientist, Educational Testing Service, Princeton, NJ:

The intention of the Task Force on Effective School Climate of the National Association of Secondary School Principals (NASSP) was to make suggestions about how to assess and improve school climate after examining the research literature and current measures of school climate. From the task force's careful review and consensus process came a useful model of the school environment and the Comprehensive Assessment of School Environments (CASE). The CASE model includes student productivity as the major outcome variable, with school climate and student satisfaction as mediating variables, and teacher and parent satisfaction as two of the many input variables in the model. School climate, and student, teacher, and parent satisfaction are measured by four different CASE surveys. The School Climate Survey is appropriately administered to students, teachers, and parents. The model recognizes effective and efficient achievement of student goals as the major purpose of junior and senior high schools. This is an important improvement over school environment models which emphasize improvement in teacher, student, or community satisfaction as a primary goal. The use of standardized instruments in this setting is laudatory, as it will provide a comparison among schools of different types as well as a comparison of a particular school's characteristics over time.

The survey instruments have been carefully constructed using group consensus and factor analytic techniques. The subscales for each instrument are appropriate to the target populations for which they were intended, and a special effort was made to keep the reading level necessary to respond to each survey as reasonable as possible. The individual survey questions have been carefully screened and selected. Information about the reliability of subscores across time is readily available, albeit for relatively small sample sizes (from 38 to 95 people), and correlations range from .62 to .92. Estimates of internal consistency of subscales range from .67 to .93. On the basis of the information presented in the technical manual, the items within each subscale are consistent with one another. A statement is made that the School Climate Survey should not be given to the same group just before or after the appropriate satisfaction survey, because perception of climate and satisfaction may be confused. No correlations between responses to the School Climate Survey and the satisfaction surveys are provided.

The results of the surveys are meant to be interpreted on a school-wide basis; however, little information is available in the examiner's manual or the technical manual about characteristics of the instruments on the school level. Means and standard deviations of school means are available in the manuals, but the number of schools contributing to these is very small (35). The large preponderance of evidence for reliability and validity is based on individual-based subscale means. This contributes to the information about the across-school, and between- and within-people characteristics of the instruments. No information is available on the within-school and between-school characteristics. It would require an infeasible number of schools to conduct a complete hierarchical analysis of the CASE model. However, if school level standard scores are produced or school level scale scores are compared to a national mean, then more must be known about the distribution of school level subscores.

In addition, no evidence is presented that the instruments are valid in reflecting changes or differences in school environments. The examiner's manual proposes a very sensible five-step plan for the use of the instruments that includes an initial administration of the instruments, the use of the results to identify strengths and weaknesses, specification of goals, a plan of action, and evaluation of the results of the action taken. In order for this five-step plan to work, results from the initial instruments must be shown to identify strengths and weaknesses that can be acted upon. Only content and construct (at the individual, not school level) validity is available. There is no evidence that very different schools have school level results on the instruments that are very different. If the plan of action includes interventions to impact school climate or satisfaction with the school (particularly for the student) then it should be shown that the CASE instruments can reflect this change.

This thorough collection of surveys of perception of and satisfaction with the school environment is well founded. After a careful review of the literature, and careful attention to consensus of educators within the field of school improvement, the National Association of Secondary School Principals has produced a package that can contribute to study of the effects of specific changes on perceptions of and attitudes toward the school environment. The extensive framework for the school environment begs for confirmation on statistical grounds, and initial work in this area has begun, although studies using the CASE instruments are only unpublished technical reports. However, there is a real need for within-school and between-school information about the characteristics of the instruments. In addition, there is no evidence that changes acted upon by administrators, teachers, parents, or students would contribute to changes in responses to the surveys. It is unknown whether the instruments would actually be sensitive enough to pick up differences in school environment, across schools or for a single school across time.

Review of the Comprehensive Assessment of School Environments by FREDERICK T. L. LEONG, Assistant Professor of Psychology, The Ohio State University, Columbus, OH:

The Comprehensive Assessment of School Environments (CASE) is an assessment package that consists of four separate surveys. The first three are satisfaction surveys for three constituent groups, namely students, teachers, and parents. The fourth survey is a measure of school climate. The CASE is an ambitious project that has been based on a systematic process of instrument development and extensive collection of normative data (i.e., 1,768 teachers, 8,022 students, and 3,797 parents). The advantage of the CASE is that it makes an important theoretical distinction between satisfaction and climate. This distinction is often lacking in other instruments assessing school climates. Another advantage of the CASE is that it is based on the theoretical model of school climate and its correlates and predictors. In addition, the constructs within the school climate scale are also multidimensional (e.g., teacher-student relationships, student academic orientation, and guidance).

There are, however, some major problems with the CASE in its present form. First, the CASE measure of school climate, although it claims to be comprehensive in its title, omits a very important dimension within our schools. Namely, it does not measure cultural diversity as an important element in school climates. The importance of this dimension to school climate cannot be overemphasized given the changing demographics of American society (Johnston & Packer, 1987).

Secondly, the theoretical model and the manual describing the model do not make a distinction between organizational climate and organizational culture. In fact the terms "climate" and "culture" are used interchangeably in a loose fashion in the test materials. As Rentsch (1990) has pointed out, the climate approach has usually been the quantitative avenue to understanding an organization, whereas the culture approach has been more qualitative or anthropological. The disadvantage of the climate approach (viz., the culture approach) is that in being quantitative, it does not get at the *meaning* of various perceptions, behaviors, and activities within organizations.

Another significant problem with the CASE is that the items for the instrument were developed based on a rational process, but none of the constituent groups were consulted in the generation of the dimensions. For example, students may have been able to identify additional dimensions that are important to them, either in the school climate or in their satisfaction with their schools.

In addition, respondent sets have not been investigated. For example, a set to answer items in socially desirable ways is always a threat to the validity of satisfaction measures. Yet no attempt has been made either to evaluate or discuss the possible impact of social desirability on clients responding to such a survey.

Another conceptual problem with the CASE is that it does not address an important point raised by Schneider and Reichers (1983) concerning the measurement of organizational climate. As Schneider and Reichers (1983) have pointed out, there is really no single organizational climate as such, but rather there are multiple climates within any organization. Accurate attempts to characterize an organization's climate needs to be domain specific, in other words, to assess specific organizational climates. For example, within organizations there might be a service climate, a research climate, a climate for safety, and so forth. Some climates are more crucial than others to certain organizations or particular outcomes within the organizations. Although the CASE recognizes that an organizational climate is multidimensional, there is no attempt to delineate the different climates that are important to students' and teachers' performance and behavior within the school environment.

The attempt to develop organization-specific surveys (i.e., schools) of satisfaction is commendable and suggests the need for this measure to be compared to similar existing measures (i.e., the Teacher Satisfaction Survey could be compared to the Job Descriptive Index [9:550]).

Validity evidence must be gathered concerning teacher, parent, and student parts of the CASE. For example, although there is sufficient evidence of the internal consistency (r ranges .67–.93), test-retest reliability (r ranges .63–.92) and factorial validity of the instruments, evidence regarding the criterion validity for the instruments, particularly the School Climate Survey, is rather weak at this point. Specifically, there has been no evidence to demonstrate that the climate scale can differentiate between different environments that are successful or not successful. In other words, strong validity for the CASE, particularly the School Climate Survey, can come about only from a criterion-related validity approach to instrument development. A climate measure is useful only to the extent that it can identify climates that are predictive of a specific criterion, for example, student performance, student satisfaction, or overall morale. According to the theoretical model guiding the CASE, school climate is posited as a causal factor in student outcomes such as satisfaction and productivity. Yet, even though the data appear to be available, none were presented to support the criterion-related validity of the CASE (i.e., school climate predicted levels of student satisfaction).

In summary, the Comprehensive Assessment of School Environments is an ambitious project to develop scales for measuring the key variables influencing the organizational effectiveness, productivity, and constituents' satisfaction within schools. The scales have promising levels of reliability. Extensive normative data have been collected. However, the evidence for the validity of the scale is still very limited and there are some conceptual problems with the underlying model (e.g., omission of cultural diversity element in school climate). Research is also lacking comparing the CASE to similar instruments such as Moos' Work Environment Scale (WES; 9:1398) and Classroom Environment Scale (CES; 10:60). The CASE is ready for research use but until more validity data are collected, its role in program planning, policy changes, and organizational interventions seems premature.

REVIEWER'S REFERENCES

Schneider, B., & Reichers, A. E. (1983). On the etiology of climates. *Personnel Psychology, 36,* 19-39.
Johnston, W. B., & Packer, A. H. (1987). *Workforce 2000: Work and workers for the 21st century.* Indianapolis: Hudson Institute.
Rentsch, J. R. (1990). Climate and culture: Interaction and qualitative differences in organizational meanings. *Journal of Applied Psychology, 75,* 668-681.

[81]

Comprehensive Tests of Basic Skills, Fourth Edition.

Purpose: "Designed to measure achievement in . . . reading, language, spelling, mathematics, study skills, science, and social studies."
Publication Dates: 1968–90.
Acronym: CTBS/4.
Administration: Group.
Price Data, 1991: $26 per 100 basic/complete battery profile sheets (specify level); $1 per class record sheet; $7.35 per examiner's manual (specify level and edition); $7.40 per multi-level norms book ('89, 125 pages); $17.20 per class management guide ('90, 192 pages); $10.40 per test coordinator's handbook ('90, 146 pages); $5.20 per technical bulletin; $1.80 per preview materials book; scoring service available from publisher.
Comments: Forms U and V still available.
Author: CTB/McGraw-Hill.
Publisher: CTB Macmillan/McGraw-Hill.

a) LEVEL K.
Population: Grades K.0–K.9.
Scores, 7: Reading (Visual Recognition, Sound Recognition, Vocabulary, Comprehension, Total), Mathematics Concepts and Applications, Total.
Editions, 3: Complete, Survey, Benchmark.
Price Data: $62.30 per 35 complete battery or benchmark machine-scorable test books; $42 per 35 complete battery or benchmark hand-scorable test books; $52.85 per 35 survey machine-scorable test books; $35.35 per 35 survey hand-scorable test books; $7.35 per 35 practice tests.
Time: (117) minutes.
b) LEVEL 10.
Population: Grades K.6–1.6.
Scores, 6: Reading (Word Analysis, Vocabulary, Comprehension, Total), Mathematics Concepts and Applications, Total.
Editions, 3: Same as *a* above.
Price Data: Same as *a* above.
Time: (113) minutes.
c) LEVEL 11.
Population: Grades 1.0–2.2.
Scores, 13: Reading (Word Analysis, Vocabulary, Comprehension, Total), Language (Mechanics, Expression, Total), Mathematics (Computation, Concepts and Applications, Total), Science, Social Studies, Total.
Editions, 6: Same as *a* above plus Basic, Reading, and Mathematics.
Price Data: $79.80 per 35 basic machine-scorable test books; $53.90 per 35 basic hand-scorable test books; $58.45 per 35 reading or mathematics machine-scorable test books; $38.50 per 35 reading or mathematics hand-

scorable test books; $92.40 per 35 complete battery or benchmark machine-scorable test books; $59.85 per 35 complete battery or benchmark hand-scorable test books; $79.45 per 35 survey machine-scorable test books; $52.50 per 35 survey hand-scorable test books; $19.95 per 35 locator tests; $7.70 per 35 practice tests; $15.50 per 50 locator test answer sheets; $5.60 per locator test directions.

Time: (242) minutes.

d) LEVEL 12.
Population: Grades 1.6–3.2.
Scores, 14: Scores same as *c* above plus Spelling.
Editions, 6: Same as *c* above.
Price Data: Same as *c* above.
Time: (287) minutes.

e) LEVEL 13.
Population: Grades 2.6–4.2.
Scores, 14: Same as *d* above.
Editions, 6: Same as *c* above.
Price Data: Same as *c* above.
Time: (325) minutes.

f) LEVEL 14.
Population: Grades 3.6–5.2.
Scores, 15: Same as *d* above plus Study Skills.
Editions, 6: Same as *c* above.
Price Data: $75.60 per 35 basic reusable test books; $37.45 per 35 reading or mathematics reusable test books; $79.10 per 35 complete battery or benchmark reusable test books; $67.20 per 35 survey reusable test books; $9.80 per 35 practice tests; $19.95 per 35 locator tests; $20 per 50 basic, complete, or benchmark CompuScan answer sheets; $11.50 per 50 reading or mathematics CompuScan answer sheets; $15 per 25 basic or complete battery SCOREZE answer sheets (specify subject area); $15 per 25 survey SCOREZE answer sheets (specify subject area); $15.50 per 50 locator answer sheets; $28.20 per basic, complete, battery, or benchmark hand-scoring stencils; $18.80 per survey hand-scoring stencils; $5.60 per locator test directions.

Time: (341) minutes.

g) LEVEL 15.
Population: Grades 4.6–6.2.
Scores, 15: Same as *f* above.
Editions, 6: Same as *c* above.
Price Data: Same as *f* above.
Time: Same as *f* above.

h) LEVEL 16.
Population: Grades 5.6–7.2.
Scores, 15: Same as *f* above.
Editions, 6: Same as *c* above.
Price Data: Same as *f* above.
Time: Same as *f* above.

i) LEVEL 17/18.
Population: Grades 6.6–9.2.
Scores, 15: Same as *f* above.
Editions, 6: Same as *c* above.
Price Data: Same as *f* above.
Time: Same as *f* above.

j) LEVEL 19/20.
Population: Grades 8.6–11.2.
Scores, 15: Same as *f* above.
Editions, 6: Same as *c* above.
Price Data: Same as *f* above.
Time: Same as *f* above.

k) LEVEL 21/22.
Population: Grades 10.6–12.9.
Scores, 15: Same as *f* above.
Editions, 6: Same as *c* above.
Price Data: Same as *f* above.
Time: Same as *f* above.

Cross References: For reviews by Robert L. Linn and Lorrie A. Shepard of an earlier form, see 9:258 (29 references); see also T3:551 (59 references); for reviews by Warren G. Findley and Anthony J. Nitko of an earlier edition, see 8:12 (13 references); see also T2:11 (1 reference); for reviews by J. Stanley Ahmann and Frederick G. Brown and excerpted reviews by Brooke B. Collison and Peter A. Taylor (rejoinder by Verna White) of Forms Q and R, see 7:9. For reviews of subtests of earlier editions, see 8:721 (1 review), 8:825 (1 review), 7:685 (1 review), 7:514 (2 reviews), and 7:778 (1 review).

TEST REFERENCES

1. Conrad, K. J., & Eash, M. J. (1983). Measuring implementation and multiple outcomes in a Child Parent Center Compensatory Education Program. *American Educational Research Journal, 20*, 221-236.
2. Ehri, L. C., & Wilce, L. S. (1983). Development of word identification speed in skilled and less skilled beginning readers. *Journal of Educational Psychology, 75*, 3-18.
3. Llabre, M. M., & Cuevas, G. (1983). The effects of test language and mathematical skills assessed on the scores of bilingual Hispanic students. *Journal for Research in Mathematics Education, 14*, 318-324.
4. O'Tuel, F. S., Ward, M., & Rawl, R. K. (1983). The SOI as an identification tool for the gifted: Windfall or washout? *Gifted Child Quarterly, 27*, 126-134.
5. Powers, S., Slaughter, H., & Helmick, C. (1983). A test of the equipercentile hypothesis of the TIERS norm-referenced model. *Journal of Educational Measurement, 20*, 299-302.
6. Webb, N. M., & Cullian, L. K. (1983). Group interaction and achievement in small groups: Stability over time. *American Educational Research Journal, 20*, 411-423.
7. Wheeler, L. J., & McNutt, G. (1983). The effect of syntax on low-achieving students' abilities to solve mathematical word problems. *The Journal of Special Education, 17*, 309-315.
8. Asher, S. R., Hymel, S., & Renshaw, P. D. (1984). Loneliness in children. *Child Development, 55*, 1456-1464.
9. Bos, C. S., & Filip, D. (1984). Comprehensive monitoring in learning disabled and average students. *Journal of Learning Disabilities, 17*, 229-233.
10. Carlin, J., Kodman, F., & Moore, C. W. (1984). Researching a spelling method with third and fourth graders. *Psychological Reports, 55*, 180-182.
11. Charles, R. I., & Lester, F. K., Jr. (1984). An evaluation of a process-oriented instructional program in mathematical problem solving in grades 5 and 7. *Journal for Research in Mathematics Education, 15*, 15-34.
12. Coladarci, T., & Gage, N. L. (1984). Effects of minimal intervention on teacher behavior and student achievement. *American Educational Research Journal, 21*, 539-555.
13. Griswold, P. A. (1984). Elementary students' attitudes during 2 years of computer-assisted instruction. *American Educational Research Journal, 21*, 737-754.
14. McDermott, P. A. (1984). Comparative functions of preschool learning style and IQ in predicting future academic performance. *Contemporary Educational Psychology, 9*, 38-47.
15. Miller, L. B., & Bizzell, R. P. (1984). Long-term effects of four preschool programs: Ninth- and tenth-grade results. *Child Development, 55*, 1570-1587.
16. Paradise, L. V., & Block, C. (1984). The relationship of teacher-student cognitive style to academic achievement. *Journal of Research and Development in Education, 17* (4), 57-61.
17. Parkerson, J. A., Lomax, R. G., Schiller, D. P., & Walberg, H. J. (1984). Exploring causal models of educational achievement. *Journal of Educational Psychology, 76*, 638-646.
18. Reynolds, C. R., & Willson, V. L. (1984). Standardized grade equivalents: Really! No. Well, Sort of, but they are more confusing than helpful. *Journal of Learning Disabilities, 17*, 326-327.
19. Saracho, O. N. (1984). Young children's academic achievement as a function of their cognitive styles. *Journal of Research and Development in Education, 18* (1), 44-50.
20. Saville-Trolke, M. (1984). What *really* matters in second language learning for academic achievement? *TESOL Quarterly, 18*, 199-219.
21. Slavin, R. E., Madden, N. A., & Leavey, M. (1984). Effects of team assisted individualization on the mathematics achievement of

academically handicapped and nonhandicapped students. *Journal of Educational Psychology*, 76, 813-819.

22. Slavin, R. E., Madden, N. A., & Leavey, M. (1984). Effects of cooperative learning and individualized instruction on mainstreamed students. *Exceptional Children*, 50, 434-443.

23. Valencia, R. R. (1984). The McCarthy Scales and Kaufman's McCarthy Short Form correlations with the Comprehensive Test of Basic Skills. *Psychology in the Schools*, 21, 141-147.

24. Waxman, H. C., & Sulton, L. D. (1984). Evaluating effects of nonclass experiences on students' educational aspirations and academic achievement. *Psychological Reports*, 54, 619-622.

25. Atkins, M. S., Pelham, W. E., & Licht, M. H. (1985). A comparison of objective classroom measures and teacher ratings of attention deficit disorder. *Journal of Abnormal Child Psychology*, 13, 155-167.

26. Beck, F. W., Black, F. L., & Doles, J. (1985). The concurrent validity of the Peabody Picture Vocabulary Test—Revised relative to the Comprehensive Tests of Basic Skills. *Educational and Psychological Measurement*, 45, 705-710.

27. Frick, S. B. (1985). Diagnosing boredom, confusion, and adaptation in school children. *Journal of School Health*, 55, 255-257.

28. Haller, E. J. (1985). Pupil race and elementary school ability grouping: Are teachers biased against black children? *American Educational Research Journal*, 22, 465-483.

29. Hopkins, K. D., George, C. A., & Williams, D. D. (1985). The concurrent validity of standardized achievement tests by content area using teacher ratings as criteria. *Journal of Educational Measurement*, 22, 177-182.

30. Kickbusch, K. (1985). Minority students in mathematics: The reading skills connection. *Sociological Inquiry*, 55, 402-416.

31. Kistner, J., White, K., Haskett, M., & Robbins, F. (1985). Development of learning-disabled and normally achieving children's causal attributions. *Journal of Abnormal Child Psychology*, 13, 639-647.

32. Leal, L., Crays, N., & Moely, B. E. (1985). Training children to use a self-monitoring study strategy in preparation for recall: Maintenance and generalization effects. *Child Development*, 56, 643-653.

33. Schwartz, H., & Papier, S. (1985). A head start in mathematics for girls in elementary school: A pilot study. *Urban Education*, 19, 357-364.

34. Slavin, R. E., & Karweit, N. L. (1985). Effects of whole class, ability grouped, and individualized instruction on mathematics achievement. *American Educational Research Journal*, 22, 351-367.

35. Slife, B. D., Weiss, J., & Bell, T. (1985). Separability of metacognition and cognition: Problem solving in learning disabled and regular students. *Journal of Educational Psychology*, 77, 437-445.

36. Tolfa, D., Scruggs, T. E., & Bennion, K. (1985). Format changes in reading achievement tests: Implications for learning disabled students. *Psychology in the Schools*, 22, 387-391.

37. Valenzuela de la Garza, J., & Medina, M., Jr. (1985). Academic achievement as influenced by bilingual instruction for Spanish-dominant Mexican American children. *Hispanic Journal of Behavioral Sciences*, 7, 247-259.

38. Yen, W. M. (1985). Increasing item complexity: A possible cause of scale shrinkage for undimensional item response theory. *Psychometrika*, 50, 399-410.

39. Baglin, R. F. (1986). A problem in calculating group scores on norm-referenced tests. *Journal of Educational Measurement*, 23, 57-68.

40. Bender, W. N. (1986). Instructional grouping and individualization for mainstreamed learning disabled children and adolescents. *Child Study Journal*, 16, 207-215.

41. Dirgi, D. R. (1986). Does the Rasch model really work for multiple choice items? Not if you look closely. *Journal of Educational Measurement*, 23, 283-298.

42. Gersten, R., Carnine, D., Zoref, L., & Cronin, D. (1986). A multifaceted study of change in seven inner-city schools. *Elementary School Journal*, 86, 257-276.

43. Jesness, C. F. (1986). Validity of Jesness Inventory classification with nondelinquents. *Educational and Psychological Measurement*, 46, 947-961.

44. Naglieri, J. A., & Hill, D. S. (1986). Comparison of WISC-R and K-ABC regression lines for academic prediction with black and white children. *Journal of Clinical Child Psychology*, 15, 352-355.

45. Pedersen, K., Elmore, P., & Bleyer, D. (1986). Parent attitudes and student career interests in junior high school. *Journal for Research in Mathematics Education*, 17, 49-59.

46. Rembert, W. I., Calvert, S. L., & Watson, J. A. (1986). Effects of an academic summer camp experience on black students' high school scholastic performance and subsequent college attendance decisions. *The College Student Journal*, 20, 374-384.

47. Risko, V. J., & Alvarez, M. C. (1986). An investigation of poor readers' use of thematic strategy to comprehend text. *Reading Research Quarterly*, 21, 298-316.

48. Seymour, H. L. (1986). Peer academic rankings and the Piers-Harris Children's Self-Concept Scale. *Perceptual and Motor Skills*, 62, 517-518.

49. Veit, D. T., & Scruggs, T. E. (1986). Can learning disabled students effectively use separate answer sheets? *Perceptual and Motor Skills*, 63, 155-160.

50. Dalton, D. W., & Hannafin, M. J. (1987). The effects of word processing on written composition. *The Journal of Educational Research*, 80, 388-342.

51. Davis, Z. T. (1987). Effects of time-of-day of instruction on beginning reading achievement. *The Journal of Educational Research*, 80, 138-140.

52. Ditton, P., Green, R. J., & Singer, M. T. (1987). Communication deviances: A comparison between parents of learning-disabled and normally achieving students. *Family Process*, 26, 75-87.

53. Griswold, P. C., Gelzheiser, L. M., & Shepherd, M. J. (1987). Does a production deficiency hypothesis account for vocabulary learning among adolescents with learning disabilities? *Journal of Learning Disabilities*, 20, 620-626.

54. Hirsch, B. J., & Rapkin, B. D. (1987). The transition to junior high school: A longitudinal study of self-esteem, psychological symptomatology, school life, and social support. *Child Development*, 58, 1235-1243.

55. Holcomb, W. R., Hardesty, R. A., Adams, N. A., & Ponder, H. M. (1987). WISC-R types of learning disabilities: A profile analysis with cross-validation. *Journal of Learning Disabilities*, 20, 369-373.

56. Mandeville, G. K., & Anderson, L. W. (1987). The stability of school effectiveness indices across grade levels and subject areas. *Journal of Educational Measurement*, 24, 203-216.

57. Miramontes, O. (1987). Oral reading miscues of Hispanic students: Implications for assessment of learning disabilities. *Journal of Learning Disabilities*, 20, 627-632.

58. Sidles, C., & MacAvoy, J. (1987). Navajo adolescents scores on a primary language questionnaire, the Raven's Progressive Matrices (RSPM) and the Comprehensive Test of Basic Skills (CTBS): A correlational study. *Educational and Psychological Measurement*, 47 (3), 703-709.

59. Tollison, P., Palmer, D. J., & Stowe, M. L. (1987). Mothers' expectations, interactions, and achievement attributions for their learning disabled or normally achieving sons. *The Journal of Special Education*, 21 (3), 83-93.

60. Carrier, C. A., & Williams, M. D. (1988). A test of one learner-control strategy with students of differing levels of task persistence. *American Educational Research Journal*, 25, 285-306.

61. Kagan, D. M. (1988). Measurements of divergent and complex thinking. *Educational and Psychological Measurement*, 48, 873-884.

62. Pomplun, M. (1988). Retention: The earlier, the better? *The Journal of Educational Research*, 81, 281-287.

63. Valencia, R. R., & Rankin, R. J. (1988). Evidence of bias in predictive validity on the Kaufman Assessment Battery for Children in samples of Anglo and Mexican American children. *Psychology in the Schools*, 25, 257-263.

64. Wilkinson, I., Wardrop, J. L., & Anderson, R. C. (1988). Silent reading reconsidered: Reinterpreting reading instruction and its effects. *American Educational Research Journal*, 25, 127-144.

65. Atkins, M. S., Pelham, W. E., & Licht, M. H. (1989). The differential validity of teacher ratings of inattention/overactivity and aggression. *Journal of Abnormal Child Psychology*, 17, 423-435.

66. Meisel, C. J. (1989). Interpersonal problem solving and children's social competence: Are current measures valid? *Psychology in the Schools*, 26, 37-47.

67. Waller, M. I. (1989). Modeling guessing behavior: A comparison of two IRT models. *Applied Psychological Measurement*, 13, 233-243.

68. Allred, R. A. (1990). Gender differences in spelling achievement in grades 1 through 6. *Journal of Educational Research*, 83, 187-193.

69. Marks, D. (1990). Cautions in interpreting district-wide standardized mathematics achievement test results. *Journal of Educational Research*, 83, 349-354.

70. Bear, G. G., Clever, A., & Proctor, W. A. (1991). Self-perceptions of nonhandicapped children and children with learning disabilities in integrated classes. *The Journal of Special Education*, 24, 409-426.

Review of the Comprehensive Tests of Basic Skills, Fourth Edition by KENNETH D. HOPKINS, Professor of Education, University of Colorado, Boulder, CO:

The Comprehensive Tests of Basic Skills (CTBS/4) is a revision of one of the established general achievement test batteries. The changes are minor, but not inconsequential. Most appear to be improvements. There are now 11 (instead of 10) test (difficulty) levels that collectively span the 13 (K–12) grade levels. The grade-level range encompassed by the tests designed for grades 1–5 (Levels

11–14) has been increased by 3 months, apparently by developing a higher ceiling to these tests. In the previous version, Level G was purported to be appropriate for grades 4.6–6.9; now two separate test levels cover approximately the same range. This modification should increase the quality of the information provided to users in the upper elementary grades. Similarly, in the previous edition, the next most difficult level was designed to be appropriate for grades 8.6–12.9; the corresponding range in CTBS/4 has been reduced to 8.6–11.2—a definite improvement. The principal consequence of these changes should be a slight gain in reliability and validity resulting from fewer students taking tests of inappropriate difficulty.

Another important step forward is the availability of a brief "locator test"—a pretest that can be used to determine the appropriate test level for each student. Because Levels 14–22 (grades 4–12) are designed so that several different test levels can be administered concurrently within a class, the *potential* of the locator test for improving the quality and usefulness of results from the standardized testing at these grade levels is substantial. A locator test is also available for the earlier grade levels, but the logistic costs associated with its application are great because the time limits for the various test levels differ below Level 14. Indeed, the test publishers appear to realize that potential users are unlikely to opt for more testing (the locator test must be scored before it can be used in assigning students to test level, hence another period of time devoted to the standardized testing program is required). Nevertheless, the procedure has much to recommend it (dating back at least to Hopkins, 1964). A much stronger case for its use must be made before users will be willing to give the extra time required. Unfortunately, CTB Macmillan/McGraw-Hill did not collect data during the standardization process that could have demonstrated the increased validity accruing from the use of the locator test (such as higher correlations with the concurrent, independent proficiency ratings of students' classroom teachers).

CTBS/4 has moved somewhat away from atomistic objectives toward slightly broader objectives (e.g., stated objectives have been reduced from 11 to 4 for Language Mechanics, and from 16 to 10 in Mathematics Computation). The broader designations result in more items per objective (at least four) and a step away from the appealing, but impossible, task of making survey tests diagnostic for very narrow objectives.

All items are classified not only with respect to content strata/objectives, but also using a six-category cognitive taxonomy similar to Bloom's: Gather Information, Organize Information, Analyze Information, Generate Ideas, Synthesize Elements, and Evaluate Outcomes. Although this information is useful for descriptive and content validity purposes (and to researchers who may wish to evaluate outcomes in the various taxonomy categories), CTB does not capitalize on the potential advantages of the taxonomy for CTBS/4 users. For example, a district profile across the six taxonomy categories in the context of a normative backdrop could have important curricular implications. Certain curricula are criticized for being too fact/drill/algorithmic oriented, assuming higher level conceptual skills would suffer as a consequence. Two curricula could result in the same mean, but one yield better performance on rote knowledge items, yet poorer performance on problem-solving items—a taxonomy profile could illuminate what otherwise might appear to be a standoff in outcomes.

CTB correctly states that "it is essential that students be given adequate time to attempt all items in a test section," yet fails to document that the tests are power tests (e.g., the percent of students completing the tests in the allowed time limits is not reported). There is no mention of why a correction for chance was not considered to aid slow-working examinees; it is unrealistic to assume all tests are pure power tests. The procedures used to estimate reliability (KR-20) assume power tests, and are inflated to the extent that speed is a component of any of the tests.

CTB can be forgiven for using the "buzz" words ("whole language," "information processing," "holistic design," "critical thinking," "inferential reasoning")—this is a market economy, and we should expect best-foot-forward promotional literature from commercial enterprises. Nevertheless, such descriptions must be taken with the usual grain of salt by the potential user.

The weakest aspect of the CTBS/4 (and its competitors) is in the area of norming and standardization. CTB is to be commended for using the Practice Test during the standardization for grades K through 6 (the Practice Test apparently was not given above grade 6). The CTBS/4 literature, however, presents the use of the Practice Test as an option for all test levels. If the Practice Test is inconsequential to performance, why use it at all? On the other hand, if it does serve as an advanced organizer for the tests (and it probably does), it should not be left as an option to the user. This option tarnishes the term standardized, and introduces unnecessary noise into the meaning of the norms.

The three-parameter item response theory (IRT) model was used in the standardization of all CTBS/4 tests. There is no mention of the controversial IRT homogeneity assumption in curricular achievement assessment. Information provided is insufficient to determine whether the IRT model attenuated curricular validity by eliminating items ("lack of model fit") that assess relevant, but idiosyncratic content/skills. Interestingly, the user is allowed the option of either traditional number-correct scoring, or scoring resulting from IRT procedures. CTB should have provided the correlation between the two scoring modes, as well as their relative concurrent validities. The IRT scoring is associated with smaller standard errors of measurement, which suggests greater precision, but the reviewer was not provided with corresponding reliability data.

The user is given the options of three "test formats"—Complete Battery, Survey, and Benchmark. The Survey and Benchmark versions provide only norm-referenced information (reporting is at a more general level—Reading Vocabulary, Language Expression, etc.), whereas the Complete Battery is said to provide both norm-referenced and curriculum-referenced data. Paradoxically, the Benchmark version typically has a few more items than the Complete Battery, whereas the Survey has 30–50% fewer items. How the standardization procedures accommodated all three versions is not made clear; they obviously could not be given within the same classes because their time limits vary. Such "flexibility" introduces even more noise into the meaning of the already fuzzy norms.

The description of the procedures used to select the standardization sample is incomplete. In addition, the resulting norm group is not compared with national parameters on relevant variables such as the percentage of large-city urban districts and percentages of various ethnic minorities (specific districts are not listed). In addition, in the high schools, the choice of classes to be tested was left to the districts! CTB also fails to report the critical statistic—what percent of the selected districts refused to participate!

SUMMARY. The CTBS/4 continues to be among the very best general achievement test batteries. Some new ground is broken that could eventually improve the validity of standardized achievement tests. The principal weakness in the area of norms is that there are major unanswered questions about the representativeness of the norming sample. In an effort to be flexible, the meaning of "standardized test" has been compromised. Unfortunately, the same can be said for the competitors of the CTBS/4.

REVIEWER'S REFERENCE

Hopkins, K. D. (1964). Extrinsic reliability: Estimating and attenuating variance from response styles, chance, and other irrelevant sources. *Educational and Psychological Measurement, 24,* 271-281.

Review of the Comprehensive Tests of Basic Skills, Fourth Edition by M. DAVID MILLER, Associate Professor of Foundations of Education, University of Florida, Gainesville, FL:

The Comprehensive Tests of Basic Skills, Fourth Edition (CTBS/4) is the latest edition of a widely used achievement test battery with 11 overlapping levels. Many of the positive features of the third edition (Forms U and V) have been retained including the use of functional level testing and item response theory (IRT) for test construction, scaling, and equating; item analysis and item bias detection; and the estimation of conditional standard errors of measurement.

Several positive changes have occurred since the third edition, including the reporting of estimates of internal consistenly (KR-20) and the use of three different versions of the test battery: Benchmark, Survey (Forms A and B), and Complete Battery (Forms A and B). The selection of each version for administration is dependent upon the intended uses of the battery. However, the most substantial change in the Fourth Edition reflects recent changes in the curriculum resulting in a shift in the conceptual approach to testing as well as a shift in the content and skills to be tested.

The test areas covered in CTBS/4 are similar to CTBS Forms U and V, but the new test battery is a more integrative, holistic approach to assessment with increased emphasis on process and thinking skills. For example, the Reading Comprehension test requires students to construct meaning from literature-based passages, the Mathematics Concepts and Applications test uses a problem-solving approach, and the Science test includes process skills. Although some of the content and objectives in CTBS/4 were present in CTBS Forms U and V, the addition of new and more complex objectives, the use of new item formats, and the use of items to measure multiple objectives has increased the complexity of the testing process to more closely resemble the current emphases in instruction and curriculum.

FEATURES. The 11 overlapping levels of CTBS/4 have been designed to be used on grade level, or students can be matched to their functional level via two short locator tests covering grades 1 to 6 and grades 6 to 12. In her review of CTBS Forms U and V, Shepard (1985) noted that functional level testing is a positive feature that provides better information on students' strengths and weaknesses. However, no evidence was presented to show that the locator tests reliably or validly assign students to the correct test level. On the other hand, some inaccuracy in the assignment can be tolerated because all test levels, except Level K, overlap by more than half a year, and a clear emphasis is also given to the importance of using teacher judgments in assigning students to their correct functional level.

The tests and the examiner's manuals are clearly written and well edited. The instructions for test administration and the directions for the students taking the tests are clear and simple to follow. The items appear to be well constructed and reflect the test objectives.

CTBS/4 is available in three different versions: the Benchmark, the Survey, and the Complete Battery. The Benchmark provides the most accurate norm-referenced information on test and total battery scores; and can be used to evaluate the overall effectiveness of a program, to place students in programs, or for other administrative functions. However, curriculum-referenced interpretations are not given for planning instruction for individuals or classes. That is, scores are not reported at the objective level, because items that provide the best norms may cover multiple objectives and some of the curriculum-based objectives are not measured.

The Survey is an abbreviated version of the Benchmark that also is used only for norm-referenced information. The shorter test can be completed in about half the time of the Benchmark and is recommended for group level assessment only. For individuals, the norms are not as accurate and the reliability is lower (see Reliability Section below). However, no recommendations nor evidence are provided for determining the minimum size of a group that is needed for reliable and valid interpretation.

The Complete Battery (Forms A and B) may become the most popular version of CTBS/4 as it provides both norm- and curriculum-referenced interpretations. The Complete Battery is comparable in length to the Benchmark, but sacrifices accuracy in norm-referenced interpretation by the addition of curriculum-referenced items. Individual reports of objective level performance can be used to diagnose students' strengths and weaknesses and to plan instruction. A minimum of four items are given for each tested objective.

Other features of CTBS/4 include a short practice test for grades K to 6 that provides students with examples of item formats and practice in responding to multiple-choice items, numerous scoring options (local or at CTB Macmillan/McGraw-Hill), an expanded reporting system for group and individual level results, and linkage to other CTB Macmillan/McGraw-Hill tests. In addition, the Norms Books, which are used to convert locally scored tests to the desired scales, have been expanded to cover three time periods: beginning, middle, and end of the school year. As in the previous edition, the Test Coordinator's Handbook provides directions for effective administration of a testing program, and the Class Management Guide facilitates use of the test results from the Complete Battery by explaining in detail the content, skills, and objectives tested; how to interpret various scales; and how to interpret the various score reports available to the classroom teacher.

TEST CONSTRUCTION. The process of test development, as described in Technical Bulletin #1, is state of the art, and was planned and executed well. The test design was created from a review of state and district curriculum guides, textbook series, instructional programs, and other assessment instruments to measure basic academic and critical thinking skills that are commonly found throughout the nation. Item development was done by a professional staff who had previously taught in the schools. The item pool (about twice the number of items needed) was reviewed by editors and researchers. The vocabulary level and sensitivity of the items to subpopulations (ethnic, gender, and age) were examined using published guidelines.

In Spring 1987, an item tryout was completed with the Benchmark items. Using item statistics from the three-parameter IRT model (item parameters, a model fit index for each item, and bias indices) in conjunction with the test content specifications, parallel forms of the Survey and anchor items for the Complete Battery were selected from the Benchmark tryout. The advantages of IRT in test development were noted in Linn's (1985) and Shepard's (1985) reviews of Forms U and V. In 1988, standardization and equating data were collected using the Benchmark. In addition, scale scores were created, and the full item tryout for the Complete Battery was completed.

Overall, the content and bias reviews as well as the technical procedures used in the construction of CTBS/4 reflected current "best practice" and led to a well-developed test. However, two potential problems with the tests, noted in the Test Coordinator's Handbook and Technical Bulletin #2, were the readability of the Reading Comprehension tests at selected levels and the statistical indices of bias for three tests.

The median readability indices for the Reading Comprehension passages were reported for the Complete Battery. For most test levels, the median readability indices were below the upper grade level measured on the test. However, Level 15, which is intended for grades 4.6 to 6.2, has a median readability on the Fry index of 6.95 and 6.53 for Forms A and B, respectively. In addition, Level 16 (grades 5.6–7.2) has a median Fry readability index of 7.36 for Form B. Even for the other test levels, selected passages may have readability indices above the grade levels tested, but only the median readability for a test was reported. No doubt readability is difficult to control with literature-based passages and this problem may be more common with the emphasis on using intact literature passages. In addition, the Dale-Chall and the Spache readability formulas led to lower and acceptable indices of readability for all test levels.

Item bias was measured for ethnicity (Black, Hispanic, and White) and sex, using an index proposed by Linn and Harnisch (1981) that approximates IRT indices of bias but does not require as large of a sample size. The number of biased items required to fill the content specifications was relatively small and spread evenly across tests, with three exceptions. The Language Mechanics test for Level 11 had large numbers of items biased against Blacks (15 of 30), Hispanics (16 of 30), and males (10 of 30). The science test had large numbers of items biased against Hispanics on Level 17/18 (12 of 40) and Level 19/20 (16 of 40). In addition, the Level 19/20 Science test was biased against Blacks (16 of 40) and females (21 of 40). On the other hand, the differential item functioning that was detected by the item bias indices may be explained by other factors such as differences in instruction (Miller & Linn, 1988) or multidimensionality (Oshima & Miller, 1990). Consequently, maintaining the content specifications may be more crucial and was done with the least bias possible on all tests.

RELIABILITY. The only classical index of reliability reported is the KR-20 for the subtests (e.g., Vocabulary), total tests (e.g., Reading), and total battery. For both forms and all levels of the Complete Battery, total battery (KR-20 > .94), total test (KR-20 > .80), and subtest (KR-20 > .80 for Levels 13 and above ranging to .70 in the lower levels) internal consistency was reasonably high with one exception. For Level 11, the Language Mechanics subtest had fall KR-20 coefficients of .55 and .59 for Forms A and B, respectively. This suggests that the subtest may be multidimensional, which could explain the biased items mentioned above. Uniformly higher internal consistency coefficients were found for the Benchmark, whereas uniformly lower coefficients were found for both forms of the Survey. The lower reliability of the shorter test confirms the recommendation that the Survey should not be used for individual decisions.

Despite the STANDARDS FOR EDUCATIONAL AND PSYCHOLOGICAL TESTING (AERA, APA, & NCME, 1985) requirements that relevant reliability coefficients be reported for any score that is to be used (Standard 2.1), no reliability estimates were given for the objective-based scores that are reported with the Complete Battery. Given that an objective can be measured by as few as four items, some of the objective reliabilities could presumably be too low for valid use, especially for identifying students' strengths and weaknesses. However, the practice of reporting objective-based scores without reliability coefficients is commonly seen in the other major achievement batteries also.

Alternate form reliabilities were not reported, but were unnecessary. Conditional standard errors of measurement (CSEM) reported in the Norms Books and the IRT standard error curves in Technical Bulletin #1 provide more information than traditional measures of reliability and show consistency across forms on all tests. In addition, CSEM provide information needed for better interpretation of individual scores. The use of CSEM continues to be an important positive feature of CTBS/4.

As noted in previous editions, no evidence of stability across time is reported.

VALIDITY. Little information has been provided to assist users in interpreting and using test scores beyond the rich description of the content and skills measured by the test battery. Consistent with the Standards for Educational and Psychological Testing (AERA, APA, & NCME, 1985) and its emphasis on content validation (Standard 1.6), CTBS/4 has provided substantial documentation on the universe represented by the test battery and the procedures followed to generate the test from the universe. However, little evidence has been reported for specific uses of the scores. For example, no evidence has been provided for how scores should be used in instructional planning (suggested use of the Complete Battery), evaluation, or placement (suggested uses of the Benchmark). On the other hand, Standards for Educational and Psychological Testing (AERA, APA, & NCME, 1985) clearly pointed to the responsibility of the user in providing evidence of validity when not available (Standard 6.3). In addition, other major achievement batteries have reported the same type of validity evidence as found in the CTBS/4 test materials.

Content validity will continue to be a major portion of the school district's responsibility in selecting a test battery. CTBS/4 has provided enough information to facilitate the district's validation studies including general descriptions of the content and skills tested, descriptions of the objectives, and the item-objective and item-subskill match for the Complete Battery and Benchmark. As discussed above, the content and skills seem to reflect the current curricular emphases across the nation, but local users will need to examine the match with their own curriculum.

SCALES. CTBS/4 has provided the standard norm-referenced scores: percentile rank, normal curve equivalent, grade equivalent, and stanine, as well as the grade mean equivalent for the class. However, the crucial score is the scale score derived from IRT pattern scoring, and ranges from 0 to 999. The scale score spans the 11 test levels and provides an estimate of achievement that is comparable from fall to spring and across grade levels. It is assumed to be equal interval. As in Forms U and V, the standard deviations do not remain constant across grade levels as expected from an equal interval scale. Instead, the standard deviations decrease as the grade levels increase, particularly in the lower grade levels. For example, the standard deviations on Total Reading for grades 1, 4, 7, and 10 are 70, 50, 44, and 43, respectively. The largest changes are in grades 1 to 3. As noted by Linn (1985), this has important implications for score interpretation because a student with a percentile rank of 10 would need to gain more points on the scale to maintain the same percentile than a student with a percentile rank of 90.

In addition to the norm-referenced scores, an objective performance index (OPI) is reported for each curriculum-referenced objective. The OPI is a Bayesian estimate of the probability that a student will respond correctly to a randomly selected item for the objective. The objective reporting shows if a student has mastered (.75–1.00), partially mastered (.50–.74), or not mastered (.00–.49) the objective. The OPI may be a useful index, but the standards applied to decide mastery seem to be arbitrary and the reliability of the OPI is unknown.

Finally, the Test of Cognitive Skills (TCS; 9:1248) can be used to obtain anticipated achievement scores for Levels 12 through 21/22. Using age, grade, and the four TCS subtests, predicted achievement scores can be obtained in the form of percentiles, grade equivalents, normal curve equivalents, or scale scores.

NORMS. Norm Books are available for three time periods of the school year—September to November, December to February, and March to June. The books provide the user with conversion tables to convert the raw scores to scale scores and each of the norm-referenced scores. For each scale score, a *CSEM* is given that is larger for the raw score conversion than for IRT pattern scoring. Consequently, greater accuracy in estimating achievement is obtained through IRT pattern scoring than is possible with local scoring. However, the Norms Books provide a simple and efficient method for districts to obtain results quickly.

The norms are based on a stratified random sample of 166,848 students in the fall and 156,042 students in the spring. A rich description of the standardization schools and students was reported in Technical Bulletin #2. Comparing the fall and spring samples, few important or sizable differences can be found except that the fall sample was more rural (59% vs. 53%) whereas the spring sample was more urban/inner city (25% vs. 20%). Compared with national estimates of the population, the standardization samples had about 4% more Blacks and appeared to be lower in SES on several variables (parents' earning, parents' education levels, and percent single parents). However, given the large number of variables reported for the samples, they seem to be fairly representative of the nation on most measures. One statistic not reported for the standardization samples, which could affect the

norms, is the percent participation of those initially contacted.

SUMMARY. CTBS/4 is one of the better achievement test batteries available to school districts. It has several positive features including functional level testing, different versions of norm-referenced and curriculum-referenced testing, and three sets of norms a year. In addition, it is a technically sound test battery that includes strong features such as conditional standard errors of measurement. Many of the criticisms of CTBS/4 in this review are common to other major achievement batteries (e.g., no objective level reliabilities reported). However, there is some reservation about the use of the Language Mechanics test for Level 11 in terms of reliability and bias. In the end, districts must conduct their own content validity studies to select an achievement test battery and the CTBS/4 should be considered in the selection process.

REVIEWER'S REFERENCES

Linn, R. L., & Harnisch, D. L. (1981). Interactions between item content and group membership on achievement test items. *Journal of Educational Measurement, 18*, 109-118.
American Educational Research Association, American Psychological Association, & National Council on Measurement in Education. (1985). *Standards for educational and psychological testing.* Washington, DC: American Psychological Association, Inc.
Linn, R. L. (1985). [Review of the Comprehensive Tests of Basic Skills, Forms U & V.] In J. V. Mitchell, Jr. (Ed.), *The ninth mental measurements yearbook* (pp. 382-386). Lincoln, NE: Buros Institute of Mental Measurements.
Shepard, L. A. (1985). [Review of the Comprehensive Tests of Basic Skills, Forms U & V.] In J. V. Mitchell, Jr. (Ed.), *The ninth mental measurements yearbook* (pp. 386-389). Lincoln, NE: Buros Institute of Mental Measurements.
Miller, M. D., & Linn, R. L. (1988). Invariance of item characteristic functions with variations in instructional coverage. *Journal of Educational Measurement, 25*, 205-219.
Oshima, T. C., & Miller, M. D. (1990). Multidimensionality and IRT-based item invariance indices: The effect of between-group variation in trait correlations. *Journal of Educational Measurement, 27*, 273-283.

[82]
Computer Literacy and Computer Science Tests.

Purpose: "The tests of Computer Literacy measure concepts related to understanding the capabilities, applications, and implications of computer technology." The Computer Science test assesses "skills related to software development, the design and operation of hardware, and specific problem solving applications."
Publication Date: 1984.
Administration: Group.
Price Data, 1987: $39.95 per 35 student test booklets (specify Computer Literacy Test [Grade 4, Grade 7, or Grade 11] or Computer Science Test [Grades 9–12]) and examiner's manual (37 pages); $14.95 per specimen set including copy of each test and examiner's manual.
Time: 45(60) minutes per test.
Comments: Examiner's manual title is Computer Literacy and Science Tests.
Author: Roy M. Gabriel.
Publisher: Northwest Regional Educational Laboratory.
a) COMPUTER LITERACY TEST.
Population: Grades 4, 7, and 11.

Scores, 5: Interacting with Computers, Functions and Uses of Computers, Problem Solving, Computers' Impact on Society, Total.
Levels, 3: Grade 4, Grade 7, Grade 11.
b) COMPUTER SCIENCE TEST.
Population: Grades 9–12.
Scores, 4: Writing Programs, Hardware Operations, Problem Solving with Computers, Total.

TEST REFERENCES

1. Fletcher, J. D., Hawley, D. E., & Piele, P. K. (1990). Costs, effects, and utility of microcomputer assisted instruction in the classroom. *American Educational Research Journal, 27,* 783-806.

Review of the Computer Literacy and Computer Science Tests by GARY L. MARCO, Executive Director, Statistical Analysis, College Board Programs Division, Educational Testing Service, Princeton, NJ:

This test battery attempts to measure computer literacy and computer science skills. Computer literacy is defined as "understanding the capabilities, applications, and implications of computer technology" (Examiner's Manual, p. 2). Computer literacy is subdivided into several subdomains representing four "program" objectives and four or five instructional objectives within each. Computer science covers "skills related to software development, the design and operation of hardware, and specific problem solving applications" (Examiner's Manual, p. 2). Computer science is represented by three program objectives and three or four instructional objectives within each for grade levels 9–12.

The section in the Examiner's Manual devoted to technical characteristics provides information on item and test statistics, which were derived from samples of students who participated in the Spring 1983 field test in the Department of Defense Dependents Schools System. The statistics for the Computer Literacy Test were based on approximately 900 fourth graders, 650 seventh graders, and 430 eleventh graders; those for the Computer Science test were based on 745 eleventh and twelfth graders who had had formal course work in computer programming. No normative score distributions are provided because the field test sample was not a nationally representative sample. Perhaps the most meaningful "normative" information the publisher could have provided about the test would have been summary statistics on these convenience samples of students by amount and kind of computer experience.

It is disturbing to note that significant percentages of the students who took the Computer Literacy Test spent no time learning about computers in class—51% to 62%, depending on grade level. These percentages suggest that the field test samples were not appropriate for item and test analysis because too small a proportion of students had been exposed to instruction about computers. It is not surprising, given the lack of exposure of the students to computers, that the average percentage correct

was about 50 for a given grade level and that the percentages correct for a number of test items fell into the chance score range. Almost all of the analysis sample for the Computer Science Test reported that they had spent 1 hour a week or more in class learning about computers and had worked at a computer terminal keyboard more than 10 times. Even though this sample seemed to be a more appropriate analysis sample than the samples for the Computer Literacy Test, the average percentage of items correctly answered was still about 50 and the percentages correct for a number of items were in the chance score range. Thus, the test was difficult for the group; middle difficulty for a test composed of four-choice items is 62.5% correct.

The test manual is clear about the type of reliability used (split-half) and the meaning of reliability, whether for the Computer Literacy or Computer Science Test. It also reports standard errors of measurement. The point-biserial item-test correlation was used as the index of item discrimination, although it is not clear whether the item used on the calculation was included in or excluded from the total score. The high item-test correlations suggest that the item was included in the criterion, thus causing the correlations to be spuriously high.

The manual provides no statistical information about test validity for either test. The manual states simply there was a high relationship between Computer Literacy Test scores and experience with computers, as would be expected for an instrument measuring computer literacy. Some assessment of instructional validity might have been possible had the test authors noted the progression from grade to grade in percentages correct on common questions. One would generally expect to see a gradual progression in percentages correct from fourth grade to eleventh grade for students with exposure to computers.

More information about the validity of these tests is needed. The manual does deal with content validity in that information is provided about what topics are measured. However, it is not clear whether the tests adequately measure the construct they are intended to measure.

A review of the test questions uncovered a few problems to which the test authors would want to attend when the tests are revised. For example, in the Grade 4 Computer Literacy Test, the answers to a few items depend on the answer to a previous question, and a small number of questions seem to have more than one correct answer. In addition, a few questions are somewhat dated in that they assume that the student is using a keyboard rather than a mouse and 5.25-inch rather than the newer 3.5-inch diskettes. This reviewer noted no such problems with the Computer Literacy Test questions at the other grade levels. However, some of the questions at the higher grade levels could seemingly be answered correctly by students with good common sense and thus might not be good measures of computer literacy.

The wording of some questions on both the Computer Literacy Test and the Computer Science Test is problematic in that it calls for test takers to choose the answer they *feel* is most correct or to choose what *they* would do—rather than to choose the correct answer. Strictly speaking, to score such questions would require knowledge of how the test taker felt or what he or she would do—but this is not what the test is intended to measure. Directions like these should be avoided.

All three versions of the Computer Literacy Test cover a wide range of material. The specific questions asked may or may not be appropriate to a given classroom situation. The material covered by the Computer Science Test is more narrowly focused but introductory in nature. The material covered by the Computer Science Test is more technical, but the name "computer science" is perhaps misleading. The material covered is introductory in nature rather than what might be implied by the descriptor, "computer science." Again, depending on the testing situation, the test questions may or may not be appropriate.

Prospective users of the Computer Literacy Test and the Computer Science Test are advised to look beyond the interpretive data available on these tests, particularly the Computer Literacy Test, and to judge the tests' merit by reviewing actual test questions and evaluating their appropriateness to the measurement situation at hand. Prospective users should not depend upon the publisher's interpretive data to evaluate the quality of the Computer Literacy Test because a relatively large proportion of the analysis samples lacked computer experience. Presumably there are applications, such as program evaluation, for which one or more of the tests may appropriately be used despite the lack of adequate technical data.

[83]
Computer Managed Articulation Diagnosis.

Purpose: "Evaluates articulation in connected speech for 23 single phonemes and 24 blends and tests stimulability for sounds in error."
Population: Students with articulation disorders.
Publication Date: 1985.
Scores: 4 error scores (Distortion, Substitution, Omission, Total) in each of 17 areas: Total Responses, Prevocalic, Postvocalic, Unvoiced, Voiced, Plosives, Fricatives, Affricates, Nasals, Glides, Bilabials, Labiondentals, Linguadentals, Lingua-Alveolars, Linguapalatals, Linguavelars, Glottals.
Administration: Individual.
Parts: 2 tests: Single Phonemes, Blends.

Price Data, 1989: $65 per complete kit including diskette, backup diskette, and manual (36 pages).
Time: Administration time not reported.
Comments: Use restricted to trained speech pathologists only; Apple II microcomputer necessary for administration.
Author: James L. Fitch.
Publisher: Communication Skill Builders.

Review of the Computer Managed Articulation Diagnosis by STEVEN H. LONG, Assistant Professor of Speech Pathology and Audiology, Ithaca College, Ithaca, NY:

Computer Managed Articulation Diagnosis (CMAD) is a computer program that cross tabulates articulation data entered by the user and prints an analysis report. Though it is described as a "test" in the manual, the CMAD presents no reliability, validity, or normative data. Nevertheless, it is clearly intended to be an assessment tool and anyone considering the CMAD should compare it both to standardized articulation tests and to other computer programs that produce a phonological analysis.

As a test, the CMAD consists of 47 sentences containing target words that evaluate production of 23 initial and final consonant "sounds" (i.e., singletons) and 24 initial blends. The sections for sounds and blends are independent of one another so they can be administered separately or in combination. It is also possible to enter stimulability ratings for each consonant singleton or blend produced incorrectly. The recommended elicitation procedure is for the student to read or repeat each test sentence. In the absence of norms, however, students can instead be asked to repeat only the target words. As with all articulation tests, the user must be mindful of the potential effects of imitative rather than spontaneous productions and of the differences between single-word and connected speech responses.

The CMAD evaluates phonetic responses in a traditional way that seems to lag behind current research and clinical practice in the area of child phonology. Each student response must be classified as a normal production, substitution, omission, or distortion. Distortions, in turn, are rated as mild, moderate, or severe. The effect of using a global category of "distortion" is to discard valuable information which would be captured in a narrow phonetic transcription. Hence, the CMAD discourages good clinical technique by using an insufficiently discriminating error category and produces an error analysis that merely lists responses as distorted. This leaves the clinician without important diagnostic and remedial planning information.

The analysis yielded by the program is a set of three tables that present different views of the entered data. The first table simply lists the sounds tested, the student's production of each, and the stimulability rating, if one was entered. The second table, described as a "distinctive features analysis," shows the productions in a position by place by voicing by manner matrix. The third table lists the number of distortion, substitution, and omission errors and the number of opportunities for error in each of the position, voicing, place, and manner categories. This analysis has three significant flaws: (a) Each sound and blend is produced only once in the test. Hence the report gives no information regarding variability of production that might indicate developmental changes already underway or suggest the influence of lexical or phonetic factors on production. (b) The test assesses only prevocalic and postvocalic consonants, almost exclusively in monosyllabic words. This approach is vaguely justified by citation of two older studies in motor speech production. It seems rather archaic, however, when compared to more recent work in child phonology which explicitly recognizes the importance of "ambisyllabic" consonants (Ingram, 1981) and the common tendency of children to simplify multisyllabic words. (c) Given the test's weakness in providing important qualitative information about error patterns, it is especially surprising not to find normative data that would allow a quantitative interpretation of the test results.

As a piece of software, the CMAD is functional but hardly up-to-date. It uses the older Apple II DOS 3.3 operating system, which means that disks formatted to store CMAD files cannot also be used to store files from modern programs that use the ProDOS operating system. The program is written in BASIC and is interpreted, not compiled. This results in performance which, by today's standards, is very slow.

The operation of the program is straightforward and well explained by the manual. Data files are stored on separate diskettes so that an unlimited number may be created. Files may be edited to correct any typographical errors committed during data entry. A major weakness of the program is that there is no procedure for handling missing data (i.e., cases where the student is either unable or unwilling to produce a response on the test). This makes the instrument difficult to use with any student who is not fully cooperative. The only output option for the program's reports is to a printer and it is assumed—but not stated in the manual—that the printer is loaded with continuous-feed paper. Finally, the program operates entirely with capital letters. This feature, along with the program's use of "alphabetic conversions" for certain phonetic symbols, results in reports which are difficult to read, especially by other professionals who might receive the reports but are not familiar with the CMAD's conventions.

In summary, the CMAD is a combination of an articulation test and a phonological analysis computer program, which fails to satisfy as either. As a test,

it does not meet even minimal requirements of standardization and careful reliability and validity assessment. Speech-language pathologists who must make normative comparisons in their diagnostic reports cannot consider the CMAD. Those clinicians who desire a time-efficient way of obtaining qualitative information from a set of articulation test data should consider computer software such as *Interactive System for Phonological Analysis* (ISPA) (Masterson & Pagan, 1989) or *Programs to Examine Phonetic and Phonologic Evaluation Records* (PEPPER) (Shriberg, 1986). Both of these programs, though slightly more difficult to learn, will generate comprehensive phonological analyses with data taken from any articulation test or from spontaneous speech.

REVIEWER'S REFERENCES

Ingram, D. (1981). *Procedures for the phonological analysis of children's language.* Austin, TX: PRO-ED, Inc.

Shriberg, L. (1986). *Programs to examine phonetic and phonologic evaluation records (PEPPER) Version 4.0* [Computer program]. Madison, WI: Software Development and Distribution Center, University of Wisconsin.

Masterson, J., & Pagan, F. (1989). *Interactive system for phonological analysis (ISPA)* [Computer program]. University, MS: The author.

Review of the Computer Managed Articulation Diagnosis by ELIZABETH M. PRATHER, Professor of Speech and Hearing Science, Arizona State University, Tempe, AZ:

The Computer Managed Articulation Diagnosis samples articulation in connected speech for 23 single phonemes and 24 blends. Each sound is presented in a prevocalic and a postvocalic position embedded within a short sentence for oral reading or sentence imitation. The author cites Stetson (1951) and McDonald (1964) to support the premise that sampling in connected speech in arresting and releasing positions gives a better indication of true phonological performance than single word tests, and is more efficient than spontaneous sampling. No consonants abut the phoneme or blend being tested.

The computer program (Apple II+, IIe, or IIc) is designed for use during a diagnostic or treatment session. As the student reads or repeats each sentence, the clinician inputs the data on accuracy of each response and judges type and severity of misarticulations. Input on stimulability is also possible.

Three different reports for each student can be computer generated. The first resembles a standard test form showing actual errors by sound in the prevocalic and postvocalic position, and level of stimulability. A similar table is printed for the Sound in Blends subtest. The second report (called "Distinctive Features Analysis") shows misarticulations by place, manner, and voicing, and is tabled separately for the prevocalic and postvocalic positions. The third report counts errors by type (distortion, substitution, and omission) for each manner, voicing, and position distinction.

In summary, this program provides computerized test forms which separate and count errors along several dimensions for the clinician. The sentence stimuli seem an effective way to obtain a representative speech sample, and the phonetic contexts are carefully controlled for vowel-only abutment. Interpretation of these summary reports, however, rests totally with the clinician. No data are provided for comparison with age, grade, sex, or racial peers. Thus, this program provides no justification for enrolling a student into a treatment program. Because it lacks normative data, it is limited clinically in its usefulness. To label it a test is inappropriate because no scores are obtained and no direct comparisons across students are possible. It provides instead a protocol for sampling speech and a computerized program for obtaining completed test forms.

REVIEWERS REFERENCES

Stetson, R. (1951). *Motor phonetics*. Amsterdam: North-Holland Publishing Company.

McDonald, E. (1964). *Articulation testing and treatment*. Pittsburgh: Stanwix House, Inc.

[84]
Computer Managed Screening Test.

Purpose: "Screens children for communicative disorders in articulation, receptive language, expressive language, voice and fluency."
Population: Ages 3–8.
Publication Date: 1985.
Scores, 3: Receptive Language, Articulation, Expressive Language; 2 ratings: Voice Test (pass/fail), Fluency Test (pass/fail).
Administration: Individual.
Price Data, 1989: $79.95 per complete kit including diskette, backup diskette, and manual (29 pages).
Time: (4) minutes.
Comments: Apple II microcomputer necessary for administration.
Author: James L. Fitch.
Publisher: Communication Skill Builders.

Review of the Computer Managed Screening Test by RONALD K. SOMMERS, Professor of Speech Pathology and Audiology, Kent State University, Kent, OH:

Screening tests seem particularly vulnerable to criticism. These tests invariably can be found wanting in one area or another, one common deficiency being that they skim the surface of factors evaluated and thus lose their sensitivity. The Computer Managed Screening Test has this deficiency, but it also has some potential for use for rapid screening and reporting if the user has an Apple computer available for use wherever screening is conducted. Apparently, this small program will not run on other microcomputers at this time.

Field testing was limited to 50 Head Start children 4–6 years of age. The examiners were laypersons who received 2.5 hours of training prior to testing these children. The Receptive Language

portion subtest scores agreed with unspecified criterion measures of receptive language at 88%, the Expressive Language subtest 88%, and the Articulation subtest 68%. Thus, criterion-related validity is grossly understudied, and what was accomplished is meagerly described.

Basic test-construction information and a stated rationale for the selection of the subtests and items incorporated in the test are not provided. These deficiencies are reflected in the absence of information concerning any aspect of test validity, except that limited to the small tryout of the test that included the use of unidentified criterion measures of language and speech, as previously mentioned.

The construct validity, although not tested, may be promising. For example, the Receptive Language assessment uses colored blocks and verbal instructions on how they are to be manipulated, a strategy for testing comprehension similar to that of The Token Test for Children (9:1295), a test with a reasonably good reputation as a measure of children's language comprehension. The Expressive Language subtest is one of sentence imitation. At young age levels, imitative tests of this type seem to have more power to detect children's language impairments. However, after ages 4–5, there is some evidence that sentence imitation tests may not be adequate measures to reflect the overall quality of children's spoken language. The Articulation subtest is simple word imitation. Children with significant delays in articulation development will largely be identified on such a test, but some marginal cases will likely escape detection. Because rapid screening, data analysis, and reporting are major objectives of this computerized test, the word-imitation model may fit into this scheme. However, although a rapid assessment procedure, the practice of having a child count to 10 to judge whether a voice or fluency problem exists is a "bare-bones" determination. The author needs to provide some data to show how effective counting to 10 is in the detection of these two disorders. Some children may count to 10 without noticeable voice defects but have difficulty in connected speech, because simple counting fails to assess important aspects of vocal behavior.

Another vital consideration, test reliability, was not reported. Data showing interjudge reliability for examiners on the total test and its subtests were not reported. Determinations of test-retest reliability were also not included in the test manual.

This evaluator tried this screening test with a young child and found it very easy to use. The time required is essentially that stated by the author. The computer program is very simple to operate and user friendly. Student files are easily established and can be reentered easily. Three reports can be generated. The Individual Test Report shows the child's scores on each item of the five subtests. The Student List is a printed list of all students filed on a data disc, along with the date and whether or not a student has been tested. The Age Analysis Report is a breakdown of the Student List by 6-month age levels, listing each student's overall scores for the subtests. This appears helpful in comparisons of performances of children at different age levels. However, a user may accumulate data on children's performances (which may prove helpful as "local norms"), but test norms were needed to compare children's performances by age and other variables. This screening test was not standardized in any fashion.

The target population is children 3–8 years of age. However, the author feels, but does not justify with information, that the screening test is most useful with the middle range of this distribution. This vagary is typical of the greatest deficiency in the use of this instrument: good scientific reporting of the accuracy of the screening test in the identification of children impaired in communication skills. Factors such as age, sex, ethnic background/race, and handicapping/nonhandicapping status were also needed to clarify the nature of the test scores and their interpretations.

Based upon a flurry of investigations reported in recent years of the validity of children's language tests, it seems likely that others will use and investigate this screening instrument. One would hope its author is a prominent member of this group.

[85]
Computer Programmer Aptitude Battery.

Purpose: To "measure abilities related to success in computer programmer and systems analysis fields."
Population: Applicants for training or employment as computer programmers or systems analysts.
Publication Dates: 1964–85.
Acronym: CPAB.
Scores, 6: Verbal Meaning, Reasoning, Letter Series, Number Ability, Diagramming, Total.
Administration: Group.
Price Data, 1987: $85 per 5 reusable test booklets; $52 per 25 hand-scorable answer sheets; $10 per examiner's manual ('85, 32 pages).
Time: 79(89) minutes.
Authors: Jean Maier Palormo and Bruce M. Fisher (manual revision).
Publisher: Science Research Associates, Inc.
Foreign Adaptations: British edition; 1964–71; standardization supplement by Peter Saville; NFER-Nelson Publishing Co., Ltd. [England].
Cross References: See also T3:557 (1 reference); for additional information and a review by Nick L. Smith, see 8:1079 (3 references); see also T2:2334 (2 references); for reviews by Richard T. Johnson and Donald J. Veldman, see 7:1089 (2 references).

Review of the Computer Programmer Aptitude Battery by RODERICK K. MAHURIN, Clinical Assistant Professor, Department of Psychiatry, University of Texas Health Science Center, San Antonio, TX:

PURPOSE. The Computer Programmer Aptitude Battery (CPAB) was developed to aid managers of data-processing centers and personnel directors in selecting persons with the aptitudes for computer programming and systems analysis. This is the third (1985) edition of the examiner's manual, which was first published in 1967.

CONTENT. The CPAB comprises five separate subtests: (*a*) Verbal Meaning: A vocabulary test of words commonly used in mathematical, business, and systems-engineering literature; (*b*) Reasoning: A test requiring translation of mathematical word problems into their corresponding numeric notation; (*c*) Letter Series: A test of sequential pattern analysis; (*d*) Number Ability: A test of mental computational problem solving; and (*e*) Diagramming: A test of the ability to interpret flow charts. Each subtest is timed, ranging from 6 minutes for Number Ability to 35 minutes for Diagramming.

All questions are in a 4- or 5-item multiple-choice format. Answers are marked on a separate carbon-backed scoring sheet, which when separated from the top sheet allows viewing of an easily tallied scoring key. The test booklet and instructions are clearly written. Test items of the CPAB apparently have undergone little or no change since they were first published in 1964, and some are in need of updating. For example, an item on the Reasoning subtest refers to the cost of "IBM cards" and the pay rate for a key-punch machine operator, both of which will rarely be encountered by today's programmers.

RELIABILITY. Reliability coefficients for the CPAB were drawn from experimental versions of the test. Part-whole reliability for the total battery was .95. Reliabilities of individual subtests ranged from .67 for Letter Series to .94 for Diagramming. Subtest intercorrelations were calculated on final forms, revealing Verbal Meaning and Diagramming to have the greatest independence from other subtests; Number Ability and Reasoning shared the most common variance across subtests.

No data are provided on test-retest reliability, practice effects, or reliability across different testing sites. A parallel form of the battery was used in determining some of the psychometric properties of the CPAB. However, the manual does not suggest that the parallel form be used for applied testing (e.g., as a retest measure), and no data are supplied on correlations between the forms.

VALIDITY. A total of 19 validity studies are briefly described in the manual. Outcome criteria included training program and job performance measures from a variety of settings such as banking, insurance, military, and manufacturing organizations. Validity coefficients for training programs ranged from .30 to .71 for the total score, and from .09 to .69 for individual subtests. Predictions based on job performance criteria were more modest, ranging from .02 to .61 for the total score, and from .03 to .57 for subtests. The most extensive ($n = 865$) and recently cited validation study from 1983 involved newly hired applicants from 53 financial service companies. Validity coefficients between CPAB total score and job performance ratings at 3 and 6 months were .21 and .15 respectively, although these scores were somewhat attenuated because of restricted range. Validity generalization analysis (combining studies utilizing both training and performance criteria) yielded a "true validity" of .59 for the CPAB total score. The best predictor of programming performance was the Diagramming score, with a coefficient of .63. Coefficients for the remaining subtests were .62 for Reasoning, .39 for Letter Series, .38 for Number Ability, and .29 for Verbal Meaning.

Analysis of the relationship between demographic variables and test scores revealed no significant effect for age or gender. Higher education was related to better performance on all subtest and total mean scores. Racial status also had a significant effect. Implications of the latter finding for use of the CPAB with minority applicants are discussed in a separate section of the manual.

Normative data are provided for a total of 1,739 applicants or trainees drawn from a variety of governmental, manufacturing, financial, and educational settings. The demographic characteristics of the normative sample are well described. Normative percentiles are given for each subtest and the CPAB total score, and are separately listed for Trainees, Nonwhite Trainees, Experienced Applicants, Entry-Level Positions, and College Data Processing Majors.

DISCUSSION. Supporting data suggest that the CPAB is a reliable test battery with acceptably high validity for predicting performance in the field of computer programming. A potential user of the test may want to consider several issues related to information provided in the manual.

First, incremental validity of the CPAB over other tests of reasoning is not well established. For example, the content of Word Meaning, Letter Series, and Numerical Reasoning subtests is similar to that found in sections of the Wechsler Adult Intelligence Scale—Revised (9:1348) or the Shipley Institute of Living Scale (360). The manual reports high correlations (.50 to .87) between CPAB subtests and the Thurstone Test of Mental Alertness and the Programmer Aptitude Test, but states that the CPAB "appears to measure some variance not measured by the other tests." Direct comparison of the CPAB with other commonly used employment tests would aid in demonstrating an advantage in predictive validity.

Second, validity studies reported in the manual need updating, an admittedly difficult task given the rapid changes in the computer field. Of the 19 validation studies reported in the manual, 16 were conducted prior to 1980. The recent validation study cited was conducted in 1983. Many aspects of programming style have changed over the past decade. For example, flow charting is less emphasized on the job than in classroom training, and complex calculational skills are of limited importance to many programming tasks. Further, the rationale for including a subtest of Word Meaning (the weakest predictor of job performance)—"the ability of the computer programmer to communicate with and understand the problems of specialists in a variety of fields will become increasingly important"—is unconvincing. More likely, this subtest fares even modestly well not because of its specific content, but because vocabulary scores in general are a strong predictor of overall verbal IQ (Wechsler, 1981). Because validity studies commendably have continued since the introduction of the CPAB, updated research presumably will be conducted and reported in future editions of the manual.

Third, the manual appropriately cautions that the CPAB should not be used alone in making employment decisions, but that other relevant evidence (e.g., education, experience, motivation, and interest) should also be weighed. The test has better predictive value for training programs than for actual job performance, presumably because job success depends on a richer set of variables. For example, creative abilities are not addressed by the CPAB (although an Ingenuity subtest was tried out and dropped from the initial battery because of low predictive value). It is possible that a slower, perhaps more thoughtful, programmer would not fare well on the test, but would do quite well in the job setting.

As a final note, current developments in computer technology now allow a test like the CPAB to be administered as an interactive, computer-based assessment. To adapt the test would require restandardization and reestablishment of psychometric properties, but indications are that computer-based testing will become increasingly common in the near future. A test of programming aptitude would be a logical candidate for such adaptation.

CONCLUSIONS. In summary, the CPAB provides acceptably high predictive validity for use in computer programmer training courses, and can be recommended in that regard. It has more modest utility as a predictor of job performance, and should be considered in conjunction with other relevant factors when used for personnel selection. The test has differential validity for minority groups, which must be considered if it is used for employment screening. The minority norms that are included in the manual will aid in this process. The content of the CPAB apparently has not changed since the original 1964 version, and the test seems due for an updated version. Further, although a large validation study was performed in the early 1980s, the bulk of reported studies were done in the 1960s and 1970s. The battery may require additional validation studies for the changing job demands faced by a new generation of programmers.

REVIEWER'S REFERENCE

Wechsler, D. (1981). *Wechsler Adult Intelligence Scale—Revised: Manual.* San Antonio: The Psychological Corporation.

Review of the Computer Programmer Aptitude Battery by WILLIAM D. SCHAFER, *Associate Professor of Educational Measurement, Statistics, and Evaluation, University of Maryland, College Park, MD:*

This battery consists of five subtests: Verbal Meaning (38 items; 8 minutes), Reasoning (24 items; 20 minutes), Letter Series (26 items; 10 minutes), Number Ability (28 items; 6 minutes), and Diagramming (35 items grouped into 7 sets of 5, each set referring to an incomplete flowchart for a described problem; 35 minutes). The Letter Series and Number Ability subtests are designed to be speeded. Psychometric and normative data are given for each subtest and for a total score.

The development of the battery was motivated by a desire to improve on the validity of more general aptitude and mental ability tests for success in computer programming in two reasonable ways: by focusing on those traits that are most related to the job of a computer programmer, and by including only items that are of a difficulty level appropriate for applicants for employment in the computer programming field. A review of the literature and a job analysis yielded seven traits deemed most pertinent (the above five along with Number Series and Ingenuity). The manual does not describe how either of these investigations were accomplished, nor are there operational descriptions of the roles of a computer programmer and how they relate to the subtests (there is a statement that programming was expected to change toward increased need for communication with software users). It is probable that the validities of the subtests and likely the entire battery differ depending on the particular activity of the computer programmer, such as defining software requirements, making structural programming decisions, writing code, testing code, correcting code, site-testing, documentation, and maintenance.

Based on four validity studies using experimental forms, the original seven subtests were reduced to five. The sample sizes ranged from 18 to 69. The Number Series subtest was eliminated because it contributed little unique variance (although the Number Ability subtest, which was retained, contributed less in the partial data that are reported in the manual) and the Ingenuity subtest was eliminated because it showed small validity coefficients in all samples. This approach to the selection of subtests (correlations with criteria, such as supervisor ratings) is appropriate, but the small sample sizes are inadequate for making decisions as important as what traits to include on a battery.

All coefficient alpha and split-half (for the two speeded subtests) data reported in the manual are from the experimental forms, which are not well described; no reliability data are reported for the final forms. Median difficulty and mean point-biserial correlations are given for the experimental forms, but the latter are difficult to interpret because the numbers of items on each of the subtests are not given nor do we know the relation between these items and those that are on the final forms.

Data from an impressive array of 19 validity studies are succinctly reported and summarized using a validity generalization technique and several references to the validity generalization literature are given in the manual. Although generally supportive of the battery's validity, the results of the validity generalization study should be interpreted cautiously because there is no discussion of the assumptions that were made in applying the various corrections the technique demands. Readers of the manual should be aware that validity generalization outcomes, although expressed as correlations, must be interpreted differently from the correlations observed in the studies themselves, because they result from a series of corrections for bias that tend in general to increase the numerical value of the combined estimate. That these corrections also affect the generalizability portion of the analysis is a consideration that should moderate the claims for generalizability found in the manual. However, the authors of the manual are to be congratulated on their use of a quantitative strategy for combining the results of the various validity studies. As the manual points out, the validity generalization study provides greater support for the total score and the Diagramming and Reasoning subtests than for the other subtests.

Comparisons on subtest and total test scores are given within subgroups of examinees (trainees and experienced applicants) among several examinee groups using data supplied by various companies. The groups include status (hired or not hired), sex, age (three ranges), education (three ranges), and race (white or nonwhite). Although the sex differences are relatively small, the race differences are more marked and the manual appropriately includes a discussion on the use of the test with minorities. Unfortunately, the sample sizes for many of these groups are very small (e.g., only 13 nonwhite experienced applicants are represented).

The manual repeats norms from its earlier editions and gives new norms based on data collected in the early 1980s from over 5,000 (for each subtest) entry-level programmer applicants from 53 companies and from over 700 (for each subtest) data processing majors collected from two community colleges. These norms represent a distinct improvement in sample size and the characteristics of the norming sample are described in terms of the above five groups. However, the nature of the sample of companies is not described and there are some striking differences between the newer norm samples and earlier ones regarding the breakdowns of the various groups. Both community colleges are from the Midwest, but there is no further discussion of the demographics of those students. Because of these shortcomings, the inclusion of a helpful section in the manual on developing and using local norms is valuable.

The validity studies that have been added to the manual since the last revision provide information that generally supports the usefulness of the Computer Programmer Aptitude Battery. When used in conjunction with locally developed validity and normative data, information that is particularly important given the differential validities of the subtests, this battery should prove to be a valuable tool for predicting success in computer programming.

[86]

[Computer Programmer Test Package].

Purpose: "To assist in the screening and selection of applicants most likely to succeed in the programming area" and to assist a supervisor in quantifying an "objective evaluation of a programmer's work performance."
Administration: Group.
Parts, 2: Aptitude Profile Test, Performance Rating Scale.
Price Data, 1987: $30 per complete set including all materials below plus research summary ('84, 9 pages).
Author: Industrial Psychology International, Inc.
Publisher: Industrial Psychology International, Inc.
  a) APTITUDE PROFILE TEST.
Population: Applicants for computer programming jobs.
Publication Dates: 1981–84.
Scores: 5 subtests: Office Terms, Numbers, Judgment, Parts, Perception.
Price Data: $16 per instruction kit including manual ('84, 4 pages) and all aptitude profile material; $10 per set of subtests and profile sheet.
Time: 30(40) minutes.
  b) PERFORMANCE RATING SCALE.
Population: Computer programmers.
Publication Date: 1984.
Scores: Item scores only.
Price Data: $16 per instruction kit including 3 performance rating scales, manual ('84, 4 pages), and norms sheet; $21 per 20 performance rating scales.
Time: Administration time not reported.

Comments: Ratings by supervisor.

Review of the [Computer Programmer Test Package] by DAVID O. HERMAN, President, Measurement Research Services, Inc., Jackson Heights, NY:

This special-purpose "package" should be of interest to businesses that employ groups of entry-level programmers. The five brief aptitude tests are simple to administer and score, and the manual offers clear guidelines for using test scores for the identification of qualified applicants. The Performance Rating Scale is tailor-made for use in appraising the job performance of employed programmers. Convenience is an obvious asset of these materials; yet, for the reasons given below, potential users should approach them with a questioning attitude.

The five aptitude subtests appear to have existed in some form for many years (their copyright dates go back to the late 1940s). Their developmental work as a package for use with computer programmers is much more recent and has focused on a single group of 118 programmers employed by a large insurance company. The subtests, each printed as a consumable booklet, cover familiar territory. All of the items are in a multiple-choice format. Office Terms is a vocabulary test that emphasizes knowledge of business terms. Numbers requires examinees to perform arithmetic operations on two to four numbers arranged horizontally on the page; parentheses are used in some of the items to clarify the desired order of operations. Judgment, a measure of reasoning, consists of three item types: completion of letter series, completion of number series, and identification of which group of four letters does not belong with the other groups. Parts provides a measure of two-dimensional space perception, and Perception taps speed and accuracy of perceiving clerical detail. All of the subtests have 6-minute time limits and are more or less speeded.

Generally speaking, the items appear suitable for their purpose, with the exception of some of those on Office Terms. Some of the keyed definitions of the target words or phrases on this subtest are rather loose, and one is simply wrong (a mortgage, regardless of its type, is not a chattel). This quality, coupled with the fact that some of the words tested are specialized business terms, suggests that the subtest may discriminate against applicants whose primary language is not English. Finally, six antonym items are scattered about the second half of the test; it would be preferable to avoid such items entirely or at least to group them together in their own section.

Percentile norms for four of the five subtests appear to be based on the sample of 118 employed programmers mentioned above. For Numbers, however, the normative sample has 159 cases; the manual does not identify this larger group.

Test-retest reliability coefficients range from .72 (Perception) to .84 (Office Terms) for unidentified samples of about 90 cases. Kuder-Richardson reliability estimates are also provided, but are spuriously inflated and therefore meaningless, because the tests are speeded.

The five subtests were validated against a set of work-performance ratings. The job elements rated were similar to, but not the same as, those of the Performance Rating Scale that is the other half of the package. The validity efforts were properly conducted separately for three different types of programming personnel—58 applications programmers, 22 technical services staff members, and 38 advanced applications programmers and systems analysts. (The Ns vary somewhat from rating to rating.) Consistent with findings in other prediction situations, the tests were most highly correlated with the criterion measures for entry-level personnel, in this case the applications programmers.

On the basis of the validity coefficients, the manual presents suggested cutoff points on each subtest for selecting qualified applicants. According to these standards, examinees should score at or above the 50th percentile on Office Terms, Numbers, and Judgment, and at or above the 25th percentile on Parts and Perception. A few comments are in order. The manual provides an explanation regarding the use of higher cutoff points for three of the five subtests. Unfortunately, it presents no evidence to support the particular cutoffs selected. Because the available norms were developed for employed programmers, the use of these multiple cutoffs may eliminate a large proportion of applicants who typically score lower on the average than do employees. The manual does not discuss the selectivity of the recommended procedure, nor does it indicate what proportion of the employees studied would have been classified as underqualified by use of the cutoff guidelines.

Also not addressed in the validity section of the manual is the effect of using a reduced set of predictor tests. For example, if only the three most valid subtests were used instead of the entire battery, how, if at all, would the quality of prediction be compromised? In this connection, the intercorrelations of the subtests are not given—an important omission.

The 17 separate scales of the Performance Rating Scale provide good coverage of significant job functions for entry-level programmers. Each rating statement is responded to on a 7-point scale. The statements are clearly written and show little overlap of content.

The manual accompanying the Scale is brief, but includes many useful, commonsense pointers on such topics as who should do the rating, how often it should be undertaken, the training of raters, inter-

preting the ratings, and presenting feedback to both employees and management.

Percentile norms are presented for each rating and for the summary rating of overall job performance. The group whose performance is reflected by these norms is not identified, but the number of individuals represented in the data varies from 63 to 118; the maximum N of 118 indicates that it is the same insurance company programmers who were involved in developing the aptitude test battery. Because rater training, leniency effects, and levels of programming experience and skill will vary in different settings, the manual properly cautions that the norms should be considered only as guidelines, and that local norms should be more meaningful.

SUMMARY. One would be more enthusiastic about the Computer Programmer Test Package if the Office Terms subtest were better constructed and if the test manual were more generous with the kind of descriptive and psychometric detail that is expected today. On the other hand, limited evidence from a single employer supports the use of the tests as an aid in selecting entry-level computer programmers. Users are cautioned that applying the recommended multiple cutoff scores may result in eliminating more applicants than they would wish. The rating scale portion of the package is well designed for its purpose, and its manual contains helpful supplementary material.

Review of the [Computer Programmer Test Package] by KEVIN L. MORELAND, Associate Professor of Psychology, Fordham University, Bronx, NY:

The Computer Aptitude Profile Test (CAPT) consists of five brief (6 minutes each) 54-item aptitude tests listed in the test description preceding this review. That battery, along with the complementary Computer Performance Appraisal Scale (CPAS), will be reviewed here.

DEVELOPMENT. Office Terms is a vocabulary test that involves choosing synonyms and antonyms for terms commonly used in business, for example, "Salary means the same as: (1) commission (2) bonus (3) wages (4) dividend." Numbers assesses applicants' abilities to add, subtract, multiply, and divide. Judgment is a test of abstract reasoning that includes items like "Which group does NOT BELONG?: (1) EXHM (2) LMNO (3) ABCD (4) RSTU." Parts is a test of spatial perception that requires applicants to indicate which in a series of four designs can be constructed from component parts displayed at the beginning of each item. Perception is a test of clerical aptitude including matching items like "Wilbur E. Stone: (1) Wilbur F. Stone (2) William E. Stone (3) Wilbur E. Stone (4) Wilbur E. Stine." Obviously, this is a general aptitude battery not linked to computer programming per se on the basis of item content.

The Computer Programmer Test Examiner's Manual describes the selection of the five tests as follows: "Based upon the statistical data resulting from [a study of 118 incumbents at a major insurance company], the following IPI tests have been shown to be related to job performance for entry level computer programming positions, and therefore, are recommended for inclusion in the test battery: Office Terms . . ." This statement raises two points that are worth noting. First, it suggests that other tests may have been tried in the developmental study; IPI publishes a number of other brief aptitude tests. An undated summary of the developmental study explicitly indicates that IPI's Contact Personality Factor Inventory was tried, but no data are presented on its performance. Second, it suggests that the developers relied on data from incumbent applications programmers ($N = 58$) in deciding which tests to retain in the battery. (The other two job categories included in the study were Advanced Applications Programmers and Systems Analysts [$N = 38$], and Technical Services Staff [$N = 22$].) This inference is supported by the fact that data on the complete CAPT are presented only for the applications programmer sample. No cross-validation data are presented, suggesting that the CAPT battery may have been composed by the selective use of a limited data base. In fairness, it should be pointed out that the CAPT may have been put together on a rational basis by examining the items on the performance measure described next. If so, it stands a much better chance of holding up on cross-validation.

IPI developed an 18-item Computer Performance Appraisal Scale that was used, along with five items that were subsequently dropped, in the developmental study described briefly above. Persons familiar with an individual's job performance are asked to judge the employee's performance against that of others in the same job. In order to merit a rating of "excellent" on "Quickly estimates reasonable answers to arithmetic computations" the "employee [had to] consistently [perform] in an outstanding manner; in the top 5% of employees with similar responsibilities for this factor." No information is provided about which job analysis method was used to develop the CPAS. Nor is there information about why five items were dropped in the final version of the scale. It contains only four items unique to computer programming (e.g., "Writes accurate, complete and clearly understood program documentation.").

NORMS AND INTERPRETATION. Normative data for all the CAPT tests except Numbers are percentile ranks based on the 118 insurance company data processing employees. The norms for the currently employed version of Numbers are based on an undescribed sample of 159. Norms for the CPAS are also based on the insurance company sample. These choices are puzzling in light of the fact that the CAPT and CPAS are both touted for use with entry level programmers.

The manual provides the following guidelines for interpretation of the CAPT: "Since Office Terms, Numbers, and Judgment are highly related to successful job performance, applicants should be scoring at or above the 50th percentile for these tests. A cut-off score at or above the 25th percentile is satisfactory for the Parts and Perception tests." These guidelines are evidently judgmental; no expectancy data are presented. The authors do say that "The norms given [here] are useful as reference points but local norms should be developed by the test user whenever possible."

The manual for the CPAS suggests that "Ratings below 3 and above 5 [on each item] should be examined since they reflect the extreme end of the job performance scale." It goes on to caution that "the distribution of performance ratings . . . are slightly distorted in the positive direction . . . [b]ecause the sample of employees used to compile this [sic] data had . . . on-the-job experience . . . Therefore, it is important to remember that these norms are only guidelines, but local norms developed with your own employees will provide more meaningful and relevant data."

RELIABILITY. The five CAPT tests have test-retest reliabilities ranging from .72–.84 in an undescribed sample of about 90 over an undescribed interval. "Kuder-Richardson" internal consistencies for this sample ranged from .75–.90. No reliability data are available for the CPAS.

VALIDITY. The only validity data available for the CAPT are correlations between four of the tests and a superceded version of Numbers, and each of 23 items on the precursor of the final CPAS. In the applications programmer sample, 86 correlations (out of 115) were significant beyond the .05 level. The significant correlations ranged from .26 to .66, averaging .38. Few validity data are presented for the other two groups studied: correlations of three tests with six outcome measures for the Technical Services Staff, and two tests and nine criteria for the more experienced programmers. Prospective studies of applicants are badly needed. No validity data are available for the CPAS.

ADVERSE IMPACT. No data are presented regarding adverse impact. Indeed, no data are presented on the gender and ethnic mix of the insurance company employees who were used to develop virtually all of the data currently available on the CAPT and the CPAS. This is a critical omission, especially in light of all the evidence suggesting that ability tests often have adverse impact on ethnic minorities and that spatial tests like Parts may adversely impact women.

SUMMARY AND EVALUATION. The CAPT and CPAS are clearly the result of a single consulting engagement. Even those data are not reported as completely as one trying to comply with Equal Employment Opportunity guidelines would wish. As the authors imply in several instances, neither the CAPT nor the CPAS should be used at this point without local evidence of their utility.

[87]
Conners' Rating Scales.

Purpose: Designed to "evaluate the reported problem behavior of the child."

Population: Ages 3–17.

Publication Date: 1989.

Administration: Individual.

Price Data, 1991: $90 per complete kit including 25 CPRS-48, CPRS-93, CTRS-28, and CTRS-39 QuikScore forms and manual; $18 per 25 QuikScore forms (select form); $25 per manual; $145 per IBM microcomputer software.

Author: C. Keith Conners.

Publisher: Multi-Health Systems, Inc.

a) CONNERS' PARENT RATING SCALES.

Comment: Ratings by parents.

1) *Conners' Parent Rating Scales-93.*

Acronym: CPRS-93.

Scores, 8: Conduct Disorder, Fearful-Anxious, Restless-Disorganized, Learning Problem, Psychosomatic, Obsessive Compulsive, Antisocial, Hyperactive-Immature.

Time: (30) minutes.

2) *Conners' Parent Rating Scales-48.*

Acronym: CPRS-48.

Scores, 6: Conduct Problem, Learning Problem, Psychosomatic, Impulsive-Hyperactive, Anxiety, Hyperactivity Index.

Time: (20) minutes.

b) CONNERS' TEACHER RATING SCALES.

Time: (15) minutes.

Comments: Ratings by teachers.

1) *Conners' Teacher Rating Scales-39.*

Acronym: CTRS-39.

Scores, 7: Hyperactivity, Conduct Problem, Emotional Overindulgent, Anxious-Passive, Asocial, Daydream-Attention Problem, Hyperactivity Index.

2) *Conners' Teacher Rating Scales-28.*

Acronym: CTRS-28.

Scores, 4: Conduct Problem, Hyperactivity, Inattentive-Passive, Hyperactivity Index.

TEST REFERENCES

1. Epstein, M. H., & Nieminen, G. S. (1983). Reliability of the Conners Abbreviated Teacher Rating Scale across raters and across time: Use with learning disabled students. *School Psychology Review, 12,* 337-339.
2. Wynne, M. E., & Brown, R. T. (1984). Assessment of high incidence learning disorders: Isolating measures with high discriminant ability. *School Psychology Review, 13,* 231-237.
3. Kehle, T. J., Clark, E., Jenson, W. R., & Wampold, B. E. (1986). Effectiveness of self-observation with behavior disordered elementary school children. *School Psychology Review, 15,* 289-295.
4. Murphy-Berman, V., Rosell, J., & Wright, G. (1986). Measuring children's attention span: A microcomputer assessment technique. *The Journal of Educational Research, 80,* 23-28.
5. Schell, R. M., Pelham, W. E., Bender, M. E., Andree, J. A., Law, T., & Robbins, F. R. (1986). The concurrent assessment of behavioral and psychostimulant interventions: A controlled case study. *Behavioral Assessment, 8,* 373-384.
6. Abramowitz, A. J., O'Leary, S. G., & Rosén, L. A. (1987). Reducing off-task behavior in the classroom: A comparison of encouragement and reprimands. *Journal of Abnormal Child Psychology, 15,* 153-163.
7. Aman, M. G., Mitchell, E. A., & Turbott, S. H. (1987). The effects of essential fatty acid supplementation by Efamol in hyperactive children. *Journal of Abnormal Child Psychology, 15,* 75-90.
8. Borden, K. A., Brown, R. T., Wynne, M. E., & Schleser, R. (1987). Piagetian conservation and response to cognitive therapy in attention deficit disordered children. *Journal of Child Psychology and Psychiatry and Allied Disciplines, 28,* 755-764.
9. Brito, G. N. O. (1987). The Conners Abbreviated Teacher Rating Scale: Development of norms in Brazil. *Journal of Abnormal Child Psychology, 15,* 511-518.
10. Carlson, C. L., Lahey, B. B., Frame, C. L., Walker, J., & Hynd, G. W. (1987). Sociometric status of clinic-referred children with attention deficit disorders with and without hyperactivity. *Journal of Abnormal Child Psychology, 15,* 537-547.
11. Cullinan, D., Gadow, K. D., & Epstein, M. H. (1987). Psychotropic drug treatment among learning-disabled, educable mentally retarded, and seriously emotionally disturbed students. *Journal of Abnormal Child Psychology, 15,* 469-477.
12. Cunningham, C. E., & Siegel, L. S. (1987). Peer interactions of normal and attention-deficit-disordered boys during free-play, cooperative task, and simulated classroom situations. *Journal of Abnormal Child Psychology, 15,* 247-268.
13. Grenell, M. M., Glass, C. R., & Katz, K. S. (1987). Hyperactive children and peer interaction: Knowledge and performance of social skills. *Journal of Abnormal Child Psychology, 15,* 1-13.
14. Kuehne, C., Kehle, T. J., & McMahon, W. (1987). Differences between children with attention deficit disorder, children with specific learning disabilities, and normal children. *Journal of School Psychology, 25,* 161-166.
15. Sprafkin, J., & Gadow, K. (1987). An observational study of emotionally disturbed and learning-disabled children in school settings. *Journal of Abnormal Child Psychology, 15,* 393-408.
16. Sprafkin, J., Gadow, K. D., & Grayson, P. (1987). Effects of viewing aggressive cartoons on the behavior of learning disabled children. *Journal of Child Psychology and Psychiatry and Allied Disciplines, 28,* 387-398.
17. Taylor, E., Schachar, R., Thorley, G., Wieselberg, H. M., Everitt, B., & Rutter, M. (1987). Which boys respond to stimulant medication? A controlled trial of methylphenidate in boys with disruptive behaviour. *Psychological Medicine, 17,* 121-143.
18. Waldron, K. A., Saphire, D. G., & Rosenblum, S. A. (1987). Learning disabilities and giftedness: Identification based on self-concept, behavior, and academic patterns. *Journal of Learning Disabilities, 20,* 422-427.
19. Walker, J. L., Lahey, B. B., Hynd, G. W., & Frame, C. L. (1987). Comparison of specific patterns of antisocial behavior in children with conduct disorder with or without coexisting hyperactivity. *Journal of Consulting and Clinical Psychology, 55,* 910-913.
20. Zentall, S. S., & Meyer, M. J. (1987). Self-regulation of stimulation for ADD-H children during reading and vigilance task performance. *Journal of Abnormal Child Psychology, 15,* 519-536.
21. Abikoff, H., Ganeles, D., Reiter, G., Blum, C., Foley, C., & Klein, R. G. (1988). Cognitive training in academically deficient ADDH boys receiving stimulant medication. *Journal of Abnormal Child Psychology, 16,* 411-432.
22. Benezra, E., & Douglas, V. I. (1988). Short-term serial recall in ADDH, normal, and reading-disabled boys. *Journal of Abnormal Child Psychology, 16,* 511-525.
23. Borcherding, B., Thompson, K., Kruesi, M., Bartko, J., Rapoport, J. L., & Weingartner, H. (1988). Automatic and effortful processing in attention deficit/hyperactivity disorder. *Journal of Abnormal Child Psychology, 16,* 333-345.
24. Boudreault, M., Thivierge, J., Coté, R., Boutin, P., Julien, Y., & Bergeron, S. (1988). Cognitive development and reading achievement in pervasive-add, situational-add and control children. *Journal of Child Psychology and Psychiatry and Allied Disciplines, 29,* 611-619.
25. Clark, M. L., Cheyne, J. A., Cunningham, C. E., & Siegel, L. S. (1988). Dyadic peer interaction and task orientation in attention-deficit-disordered children. *Journal of Abnormal Child Psychology, 16,* 1-15.
26. Cohen, M. (1988). The Revised Conners Parent Rating Scale: Factor structure replication with a diversified clinical sample. *Journal of Abnormal Child Psychology, 16,* 187-196.
27. Cohen, M., DuRant, R. H., & Cook, C. (1988). The Conners Teacher Rating Scale: Effects of age, sex, and race with special education children. *Psychology in the Schools, 25,* 195-202.
28. Cunningham, C. E., Bennes, B. B., & Siegel, L. S. (1988). Family functioning, time allocation, and parental depression in the families of normal and ADDH children. *Journal of Clinical Child Psychology, 17,* 169-177.
29. Douglas, V. I., Barr, R. G., Amin, K., O'Neill, M. E., & Britton, B. G. (1988). Dosage effects and individual responsivity to methylphenidate

in attention deficit disorder. *Journal of Child Psychology and Psychiatry and Allied Disciplines*, 29, 453-475.

30. Gualtieri, C. T., & Evans, R. W. (1988). Motor performance in hyperactive children treated with imipramine. *Perceptual and Motor Skills*, 66, 763-769.

31. Landau, S., & Milich, R. (1988). Social communication patterns of attention-deficit-disordered boys. *Journal of Abnormal Child Psychology*, 16, 69-81.

32. Luk, S. L., Lee, P. L. M., Leung, W. L. P., & Lieh-Mak, F. (1988). Teachers' referral of children with mental health problems: A study of primary schools in Hong Kong. *Psychology in the Schools*, 25, 121-129.

33. Malone, M. A., Kershner, J. R., & Siegel, L. (1988). The effects of methylphenidate on levels of processing and laterality in children with attention deficit disorder. *Journal of Abnormal Child Psychology*, 16, 379-395.

34. Milich, R., & Landau, S. (1988). Teacher ratings of inattention/overactivity and aggression: Cross-validation with classroom observations. *Journal of Clinical Child Psychology*, 17, 92-97.

35. Schachar, R., Logan, G., Wachsmuth, R., & Chajczyk, D. (1988). Attaining and maintaining preparation: A comparison of attention in hyperactive, normal, and disturbed control children. *Journal of Abnormal Child Psychology*, 16, 361-378.

36. Sprafkin, J., & Gadow, K. D. (1988). The immediate impact of aggressive cartoons on emotionally disturbed and learning disabled children. *Journal of Genetic Psychology*, 149, 35-44.

37. Sprafkin, J., Gadow, K. D., & Grayson, P. (1988). Effects of cartoons on emotionally disturbed children's social behavior in school settings. *Journal of Child Psychology and Psychiatry and Allied Disciplines*, 29, 91-99.

38. Zentall, S. S. (1988). Production deficiencies in elicited language but not in the spontaneous verbalizations of hyperactive children. *Journal of Abnormal Child Psychology*, 16, 657-673.

39. Atkins, M. S., Pelham, W. E., & Licht, M. H. (1989). The differential validity of teacher ratings of inattention/overactivity and aggression. *Journal of Abnormal Child Psychology*, 17, 423-435.

40. Barkley, R. A. (1989). Hyperactive girls and boys: Stimulant drug effects on mother-child interactions. *Journal of Child Psychology and Psychiatry and Allied Disciplines*, 30, 379-390.

41. Breen, M. J. (1989). Cognitive and behavioral differences in AdHD boys and girls. *Journal of Child Psychology and Psychiatry and Allied Disciplines*, 30, 711-716.

42. Brown, R. T., & Pacini, J. N. (1989). Perceived family functioning, marital status, and depression in parents of boys with attention deficit disorder. *Journal of Learning Disabilities*, 22, 581-587.

43. Bylsma, F. W., & Pivik, R. T. (1989). The effects of background illumination and stimulant medication on smooth pursuit eye movements of hyperactive children. *Journal of Abnormal Child Psychology*, 17, 73-90.

44. Chee, P., Logan, G., Schachar, R., Lindsay, P., & Wachsmuth, R. (1989). Effects of event rate and display time on sustained attention in hyperactive, normal, and control children. *Journal of Abnormal Child Psychology*, 17, 371-391.

45. Conrad, M., & Hammen, C. (1989). Role of maternal depression in perceptions of child maladjustment. *Journal of Consulting and Clinical Psychology*, 57, 663-667.

46. Day, A. M. L., & Peters, R. D. (1989). Assessment of attentional difficulties in underachieving children. *The Journal of Educational Research*, 82, 356-361.

47. Felton, R. H., & Wood, F. B. (1989). Cognitive deficits in reading disability and attention deficit disorder. *Journal of Learning Disabilities*, 22, 3-13.

48. Gluson, D., & Parker, D. (1989). Hyperactivity in a group of children referred to a Scottish child guidance service: A significant problem. *British Journal of Educational Psychology*, 59, 262-265.

49. Hinshaw, S. P., Buhrmester, D., & Heller, T. (1989). Anger control in response to verbal provocation: Effects of stimulant medication for boys with ADHD. *Journal of Abnormal Child Psychology*, 17, 393-407.

50. Horn, W. F., Wagner, A. E., & Ialongo, N. (1989). Sex differences in school-aged children with pervasive attention deficit hyperactivity disorder. *Journal of Abnormal Child Psychology*, 17, 109-125.

51. Hynd, G. W., Nieves, N., Connor, R. T., Stone, P., Town, P., Beclar, M. G., Lahey, B. B., & Lorys, A. R. (1989). Attention deficit disorder with and without hyperactivity: Reaction time and speed of cognitive processing. *Journal of Learning Disabilities*, 22, 573-580.

52. Jones, M. B., & Offord, D. R. (1989). Reduction of antisocial behavior in poor children by nonschool skill-development. *Journal of Child Psychology and Psychiatry and Allied Disciplines*, 30, 737-750.

53. Kaplan, B. J., McNicol, J., Conte, R. A., & Moghadam, H. K. (1989). Overall nutrient intake of preschool hyperactive and normal boys. *Journal of Abnormal Child Psychology*, 17, 127-132.

54. Lahey, B. B., Hynd, G. W., Stone, P. A., Piacentini, J. C., & Frick, P. J. (1989). Neuropsychological test performance and the attention deficit disorders: Clinical utility of the Luria-Nebraska Neuropsychological Battery—Children's Revision. *Journal of Consulting and Clinical Psychology*, 57, 112-116.

55. Lahey, B. B., Russo, M. F., Walker, J. L., & Piacentini, J. C. (1989). Personality characteristics of the mothers of children with disruptive behavior disorders. *Journal of Consulting and Clinical Psychology*, 57, 512-515.

56. Lam, C. M., & Beale, I. L. (1989). Relationship between the Delay Task and rating scale measures of inattention and hyperactivity. *Journal of Abnormal Child Psychology*, 17, 625-631.

57. Levy, F., & Hobbes, G. (1989). Reading, spelling, and vigilance in attention deficit and conduct disorder. *Journal of Abnormal Child Psychology*, 17, 291-298.

58. Luk, S. L., & Leung, P. W. L. (1989). Conners' teacher's rating scale—A validity study in Hong Kong. *Journal of Child Psychology and Psychiatry and Allied Disciplines*, 30, 785-793.

59. McHale, S. M., & Gamble, W. C. (1989). Sibling relationships of children with disabled and nondisabled brothers and sisters. *Developmental Psychology*, 25, 421-429.

60. Moehle, K. A., & Fitzhugh-Bell, K. B. (1989). Factor analysis of the Conners Teacher Rating Scale with brain-damaged and learning-disabled children. *Psychology in the Schools*, 26, 113-125.

61. Pisterman, S., McGrath, P., Firestone, P., Goodman, J. T., Webster, I., & Mallory, R. (1989). Outcome of parent-mediated treatment of preschoolers with attention deficit disorder with hyperactivity. *Journal of Consulting and Clinical Psychology*, 57, 628-635.

62. Rapport, M. D., Quinn, S. O., DuPaul, G. J., Quinn, E. P., & Kelly, K. L. (1989). Attention deficit disorder with hyperactivity and methylphenidate: The effects of dose and mastery level on children's learning performance. *Journal of Abnormal Child Psychology*, 17, 669-689.

63. Sanders, M. R., Rebgetz, M., Morrison, M., Bor, W., Gordon, A., Dadds, M., & Shepard, R. (1989). Cognitive-behavioral treatment of recurrent nonspecific abdominal pain in children: An analysis of generalization, maintenance, and side effects. *Journal of Consulting and Clinical Psychology*, 57, 294-300.

64. Sobol, M. P., Ashbourne, D. T., Earn, B. M., & Cunningham, C. E. (1989). Parents' attributions for achieving compliance from attention-deficit-disordered children. *Journal of Abnormal Child Psychology*, 17, 359-369.

65. Tannock, R., Schachar, R. J., Carr, R. P., Chajczyk, D., & Logan, G. D. (1989). Effects of methylphenidate on inhibitory control in hyperactive children. *Journal of Abnormal Child Psychology*, 17, 473-491.

66. Vyse, S. A., & Rapport, M. D. (1989). The effects of methylphenidate on learning in children with ADDH: The stimulus equivalence paradigm. *Journal of Consulting and Clinical Psychology*, 57, 425-435.

67. Zentall, S. S., & Dwyer, A. M. (1989). Color effects on the impulsivity and activity of hyperactive children. *Journal of School Psychology*, 27, 165-173.

68. Beitchman, J. H., Hood, J., & Inglis, A. (1990). Psychiatric risk in children with speech and language disorders. *Journal of Abnormal Child Psychology*, 18, 283-296.

69. Cohen, M., Becker, M. G., & Campbell, R. (1990). Relationships among four methods of assessment of children with Attention Deficit-Hyperactivity Disorder. *Journal of School Psychology*, 28, 189-202.

70. Crouter, A. C., MacDermid, S. M., McHale, S. M., & Perry-Jenkins, M. (1990). Parental monitoring and perceptions of children's school performance and conduct in dual- and single-earner families. *Developmental Psychopathology*, 26, 649-657.

71. Douglas, V. I., & Benezra, E. (1990). Supraspan verbal memory in attention deficit disorder with hyperactivity normal and reading-disabled boys. *Journal of Abnormal Child Psychology*, 18, 617-638.

72. Halperin, J. M., Newcorn, J. H., Sharma, V., Healey, J. M., Wolf, L. E., Pascualvaca, D. M., & Schwartz, S. (1990). Inattentive and noninattentive ADHD children: Do they constitute a unitary group? *Journal of Abnormal Child Psychology*, 18, 437-449.

73. Kupietz, S. S. (1990). Sustained attention in normal and in reading-disabled youngsters with and without ADDH. *Journal of Abnormal Child Psychology*, 18, 357-372.

74. Livingston, R. L., Dykman, R. A., & Ackerman, P. T. (1990). The frequency and significance of additional self-reported psychiatric diagnoses in children with attention deficit disorder. *Journal of Abnormal Child Psychology*, 18, 465-478.

75. Lovejoy, M. C., & Rasmussen, N. H. (1990). The validity of vigilance tasks in differential diagnosis of children referred for attention and learning problems. *Journal of Abnormal Child Psychology*, 18, 671-681.

76. Merrell, K. W. (1990). Teacher ratings of hyperactivity and self-control in learning-disabled boys: A comparison with low-achieving and average peers. *Psychology in the Schools*, 27, 289-296.

77. Roberts, M. A. (1990). A behavioral observation method for differentiating hyperactive and aggressive boys. *Journal of Abnormal Child Psychology*, 18, 131-142.

78. Schachar, R., & Logan, G. (1990). Are hyperactive children deficient in attentional capacity? *Journal of Abnormal Child Psychology*, 18, 493-513.

79. Schachar, R., & Wachsmuth, R. (1990). Hyperactivity and parental psychopathology. *Journal of Child Psychology and Psychiatry*, *31*, 381-392.

80. Stern, L. M., Walker, M. K., Sawyer, M. G., Oades, R. D., Badcock, N. R., & Spence, J. G. (1990). A controlled crossover trial of fenfluramine in autism. *Journal of Child Psychology and Psychiatry*, *31*, 569-585.

81. Campbell, J. W., D'Amato, R. C., Raggio, D. J., & Stephens, K. D. (1991). Construct validity of the computerized Continuous Performance Test with measures of intelligence, achievement, and behavior. *Journal of School Psychology*, *29*, 143-150.

82. Halperin, J. M., Sharma, V., Greenblatt, E., & Schwartz, S. T. (1991). Assessment of the continuous performance test: Reliability and validity in a nonreferred sample. *Psychological Assessment*, *3*, 603-608.

83. Mattison, R. E., Morales, J., & Bauer, M. A. (1991). Elementary and secondary socially and/or emotionally disturbed girls: Characteristics and identification. *Journal of School Psychology*, *29*, 121-134.

Review of the Conners' Rating Scales by BRIAN K. MARTENS, Associate Professor of Psychology and Education, Syracuse University, Syracuse, NY:

Four instruments comprise the Conners' Rating Scales: two teacher-rating scales and two parent-rating scales. Each pair of measures consists of a long and short form, and all scales contain a 10-item Hyperactivity Index in addition to the Hyperactivity subscale. Items are rated using a common 4-point scale (*Not at All, Just a Little, Pretty Much, Very Much*), and all items are negatively worded. Scoring is extremely easy using answer sheets that automatically transfer ratings on the first page to a second page where the examiner is required to copy the scores into adjacent columns. The ratings in each column are summed to yield the subscale scores which are then circled on a separate sheet called the Profile Form. Profile Forms are provided for each scale, and except for the Conner's Parent Rating Scales-93 (CPRS-93), are separated by the sex and age range of the child. These forms replace typical conversion tables by indicating the *T* score that corresponds to each raw score while simultaneously generating a profile of the ratings.

The author states the Conners' Ratings Scales have been used extensively in research, particularly in studies of childhood hyperactivity and its sensitivity to drug treatment. In support of this claim, a litany of studies published between 1969 and 1988 involving at least one version of the scales is included as a bibliography. Relevant studies from this bibliography are described briefly or acknowledged in Chapter 5 of the manual, which addresses the scales' psychometric properties. Overall, the manual is well written and well organized, and Chapter 1 provides an excellent discussion of the uses and limitations of informant reports. Chapter 2 contains numerous examples of scoring, whereas Chapter 3 discusses relevant issues such as threats to the validity of results, factors contributing to differences in teacher and parent ratings, and developmental trends in scores by sex of the child. Also presented in Chapter 3 is a stylized sequence of steps that users are likely to find helpful when interpreting the assessment data. Microcomputer programs that can be used for administration, scoring, or interpretation are available for the two longer forms of the scales. These programs contain several interesting features including a use counter that limits the number of administrations per disk and a toll-free number for computer support in the United States and Canada.

SCALE DEVELOPMENT AND STANDARDIZATION. Despite the voluminous research base supporting the Conners' Rating Scales, virtually no information is presented in the manual concerning scale development and standardization. Based on descriptions of the scales presented in Chapter 1 and discussions of the factor structures in Chapter 5, it appears that norms for the Conners' Teacher Rating Scales-28 (CTRS-28) and the Conners' Parent Rating Scales-48 (CPRS-48) were taken from a study conducted by Goyette, Conners, and Ulrich (1978). The normative sample is described, however, only by the number of children included in the study and their age range.

Examination of the primary source revealed that norms for the CPRS-48 were based on a sample of 529 almost exclusively White children residing in the greater Pittsburgh area. Subjects in the sample were between the ages of 3 and 17, and approximately half were male. Norms for the CTRS-28 were based on a subset of 383 children drawn from the same sample. Although separate norms are reported by sex and age range of the child, the number of subjects included at each level ranged from as few as 11 for 3–5-year-old females on the CTRS-28 to as many as 76 for 6–8-year-old males on the CPRS-48.

Norms for the Conners' Teacher Rating Scales-39 (CTRS-39) were apparently taken from a restandardization study conducted by Trites, Blouin, and Laprade (1982). The study involved 9,583 children ranging in age from 4 to 12 years who were attending school in Ottawa, Canada. Despite the age range of the subjects, columns on the Profile Form for the CTRS-39 are inclusive of children aged 3 years to 14 years. Demographic information for the children is reported elsewhere, further obscuring the sample's characteristics. Again, separate norms are reported by sex and age range of the child for the CTRS-39, although in this case several hundred to more than a thousand subjects are included at each level.

Norms for the CPRS-93 are based on a reanalysis by Conners and Blouin (1988) of data from the original 1970 standardization sample. Only the size ($n = 683$) and age range of this sample (6 to 14 years) are presented in the manual. Clearly, it is the responsibility of the author to make descriptive information about the standardization samples readily accessible to the user. This information is not presented for the Conners' scales nor is scale development described beyond providing the references of initial research studies. Examination of the primary sources suggests that detailed demographic information is available as well as the means and standard deviations of the subscale scores by sex and age. Three of the scales (CTRS-28, CPRS-48, and CTRS-39) employ norms of questionable representativeness because data were apparently collected in only a single metropolitan area. For two scales (CTRS-28 and CPRS-48), it appears that the number of children included at each level of sex and age is too small to support separate norms. This situation may be difficult to remedy because the idiosyncratic nature of research with the Conners' Scales precludes the aggregation of norms across studies.

PSYCHOMETRIC PROPERTIES. As a result of more than 20 years of research, extensive reliability and validity evidence exists in support of the Conners' Rating Scales. This evidence is summarized in Chapter 5, although two characteristics of the presentation deserve mention. First, as stated by the author on page 37, "much of the research literature fails to differentiate between the long and short forms [of the instruments], or individual investigators have chosen to develop their own study-specific scales." Thus, although a wealth of information is presented, only a portion of these data apply to the specific subscales advocated in the manual. Second, different versions of the rating scales are not equally represented across studies. As would be expected, most of the data concerning reliability and validity were collected using the original CTRS-39.

Despite inconsistencies in the research literature, the results obtained across studies have been similar. Generally speaking, test-retest reliability for the scales is high to moderate (range = .91 to .33) with intervals ranging from 2 weeks to 1 year. Interrater reliability has been evaluated between teachers, parents, and teachers and parents. Moderate to high correlations (range = .23 to .94) are reported, with lower values being obtained for parent-teacher comparisons. The internal consistency of the scales is adequate, with alpha coefficients ranging from .61 to .95.

Validity evidence for the Conners' Rating Scales is substantial, and can be classified into the following categories: (a) sensitivity to changes in behavior resulting from drug therapy; (b) correlations with other rating scales, independent observations, and peer ratings; (c) ability to discriminate among various diagnostic groups; and (d) correlations with other measures of childhood pathology including depression and coronary-prone Type A behavior. Finally, numerous studies are reported in the manual demonstrating the stability of factor scores across different samples.

SUMMARY. According to the author, the Conners' Ratings Scales are "among the most widely used assessment instruments for childhood problem behaviors in the world" (p. 1). A substantial research base supports this claim, although comparing the results across studies is hindered by inconsistencies in deriving the subscales. The manual represents a much needed attempt to standardize the manner in which these various scales are used and interpreted. As noted by the author, appropriate uses of the scales include screening and, in conjunction with other assessment methods, clinical diagnosis. Extensive psychometric data are presented for the scales collectively, although the information reported differs across measures. The manual is well organized and offers information that is likely to be helpful in interpreting results. In contrast, the standardization samples are inadequately described, and the representativeness of these samples seems questionable.

REVIEWER'S REFERENCES

Goyette, C. H., Conners, C. K., & Ulrich, R. F. (1978). Normative data on revised Conners parent and teacher rating scales. *Journal of Abnormal Child Psychology, 6,* 221-236.

Trites, R. L., Blouin, A. G. A., & Laprade, K. (1982). Factor analysis of the Conners Teacher Rating Scale based on a large normative sample. *Journal of Consulting and Clinical Psychology, 50,* 615-623.

Conners, C. K., & Blouin, A. G. (1988, August). *Hyperkinetic syndrome and psychopathology in children.* Paper presented at the meeting of the American Psychological Association, Montreal.

Review of the Conners' Rating Scales by JUDY OEHLER-STINNETT, Assistant Professor of Psychology, Eastern Illinois University, Charleston, IL:

This review encompasses all of the scales bearing the Conners name which, although having been in use for decades, have been recently published (1989) by Multi-Health Systems, Inc. One manual, written by Conners, has also been published containing information on all the scales. This publication does not represent new work, such as updated norms, but is a compilation of previous work conducted by a variety of researchers. Although it is the intent of this reviewer to critically evaluate the scales for what they are, simple behavior rating scales, it is impossible to ignore the fact that these scales have been used extensively to identify "hyperactive" children for research and clinical purposes.

If the Conners' scales are to be used for critical decision making, they must stand up under the highest scrutiny of their reliability and validity for this purpose. Continuing use of the scales simply for comparison to previous studies is not acceptable from a psychometric perspective. There is a state of confusion (including incomplete and inaccurate citations) in the research literature, previous reviews, and also the new manual, regarding which version of which scale was actually used from one research study to the next. It is also inappropriate to continue to combine results of investigations employing several different versions of the scale to support the "Conners' Scales" as if they were one test. The manual's minimal reporting of separate psychometric data for each version of each scale is a major drawback.

39-ITEM CONNERS' TEACHER RATING SCALES (CTRS-39). Conners (1969) published the 39-item Teacher Rating Scales in an effort to obtain ratings in response to medication, with a *mixed* clinical group of behavior disordered, hyperactive, and inattentive students. The original goal, to obtain relatively objective ratings from a source in the child's actual environment, was an admirable one. However, Conners does not describe, in his original study or in the 1989 manual, his conceptualization of behavior disorders in general, or of the specific constructs of conduct disorder, hyperactivity, inattention, anxiety, or social skills. In particular, nowhere is item selection or retention adequately described. Although the intent of the scale was to determine response to medication given for inattention/hyperactivity, the majority of the items measure behavior more related to conduct disorder and load on such a factor accounting for over one third of the variance. A remarkably few items (fewer than 10) were written which specifically address the inattention-overactivity dimensions of behavior. Several items appear to measure traits rather than specific behavior (e.g., "shy," "impudent") or can apply to a wide variety of behaviors (e.g., "inattentive, easily distracted"). When comparing the description of test construction and item selection of the CTRS-39 to that of such scales as the Child Behavior Checklist (64), it is found wanting. In fact, the problem with factor stability of the scale, which has frequently been discussed as instability of the constructs themselves, could be an artifact of an inadequate initial item pool and retention of compounded items and those which load on more than one factor.

In 1973, Conners reported a slightly revised version of the CTRS-39 in order to have 10 items in common with the parent scale, a fact that is frequently overlooked in the literature and is not clarified in the manual. Seven items (18%) were significantly reworded or completely changed. Many investigators have presumably employed this revised version using the factor structure of the original version. Subsequent factor analyses of the revised version have not replicated the 1969 factor structure, indicating it is inappropriate to continue using the 1969 factor structure with the 1973 revised version. Relatively few studies have been conducted using the factors of the 1989 published version which are based on a 1982 factor analysis of the 1973 version.

The factor structure of the CTRS-39 is a troubling aspect of the scale. A complete discussion is beyond the space limitations of a review. Potential users of the test should consult a number of studies before deciding to interpret factor scores (e.g., Arnold, Barnebey, & Smeltzer, 1981; Cohen & Hynd, 1986; Glow, 1981; Moehle & Fitzhugh-Bell, 1989; Taylor & Sandberg, 1984; Trites, Blouin, & Laprade, 1982; Ullmann, Sleator, & Sprague, 1985; Werry & Hawthorne, 1976; Werry, Sprague, & Cohen, 1975). Conners (1989) chose to retain the factor analysis of Trites, Blouin, and Laprade (1982) for the factor structure of the published CTRS-39. This investigation is particularly noteworthy as it employed a very large stratified random sample ($n = 9,583$) from Canada. The manual does not adequately describe the characteristics of this sample.

There are several problems with this factor solution that make it particularly difficult to interpret. First, the Conduct Disorder factor has been described as a combination Conduct Disorder/Hyperactivity factor, which compounds the two constructs the test purportedly discriminates between. Second, approximately one-half or more of the items in each factor load on more than one factor, making the factors uninterpretable. Finally, although the Anxious-Passive and Asocial factors contain few items and account for small amounts of variance, retention of the final factor, Daydreams/Attention Problem, is particularly troublesome. It contains only three items, two of which load on other factors. Item 39 ("Attendance problem") does not seem to fit appropriately into any of the stronger factors.

An additional problem with the choice to use the Trites et al. (1982) factor structure for test subscales and norms is generalizability. Although these results are quite useful for the Canadian population from which they were derived, their applicability to an American population, particularly minorities, is questionable. Second, there are considerable data to suggest that the CTRS-39 factor structure differs within subtypes of clinical populations. Application of the Trites et al. (1982) factor structure and norms may be inappropriate for children from these populations (Cohen & Hynd, 1986; Moehle & Fitzhugh-Bell, 1989). Unfortunately, Conners (1989) does not report these alternative factor solutions or norms for clinical populations. Those who insist on continuing to use the CTRS-39 should utilize the appropriate factor structure for the children they are assessing. Those wishing to assess minority children in the United States should use a scale which has appropriately addressed its validity for this population.

Total scores are not available on the CTRS-39 and item-total score internal consistency values are not reported. Given the number of items loading on more than one factor in the Trites et al. (1982) analysis used for scoring, and a presumed correlation among factors (the manual reports correlations for the 1969 version), this information would be useful.

Adequate short- and long-term test-retest reliability have been established for the 1969 and 1973 versions of the CTRS-39 (Conners, 1969, 1973; Glow, Glow & Rump, 1982; Roberts, Milich, Loney, & Caputo, 1981; Taylor & Sandberg, 1984; Trites, Dugas, Lynch, & Ferguson, 1979). However, Glow et al. (1982) demonstrate that the stability of the CTRS is poor with younger children, and other studies (see Barkley, 1988) suggest that scores consistently regress to the mean on second administration. Although administering two pretests may obviate this problem, in practice it is not typically done. For measurement of treatment effects, this is imperative. No studies employing the Trites et al. (1982) factor structure have been reported.

Interrater reliability data with teachers as raters indicate adequate correlations among ratings (Trites et al., 1979; Taylor & Sandberg, 1984) for the 1969 factor version of the CTRS-39, and the Adelaide version employed by Glow (1981). Homatidis and Konstantareas (1981) obtained a .94 interrater coefficient for the 1969 version using clinic raters who had access to data from a multidisciplinary team assessment.

There are no interrater reliability studies with the Trites et al. (1982) factors. This deficiency, along with that of test-retest reliability, should have been addressed prior to publication of the 1989 manual. As with any behavior rating scale, if the CTRS-39 is used for diagnostic decisions, more than one teacher should rate the child and ratings should be compared (not averaged as the manual suggests) for congruence.

The current form of the protocol/profile sheet is user friendly. Users are cautioned to use the right gender/age when calculating T-scores. Users should also note that the Trites et al. (1982) norms include only children ages 4–12, and the age groups described in the manual reflect this. However, the protocol has scoring for children ages 3–5 and 12–14, which is incorrect.

Although scoring may not be problematic, there are discrepancies in the manual regarding interpretation. One part of the manual suggests first interpreting factor scores and then considering individual items (the most appropriate analysis), and another section suggests conducting an item analysis first. As there are limited data regarding critical items or item reliability, this is not recommended. A more confusing recommendation concerns use of cutoff scores. The table and text in the manual recommend the traditional 2 standard deviation cutoff as indicative of behavior problems; however, the author suggests a *higher* cutoff for screening. Also, treatment is recommended for children scoring above the cutoff. The author recommends use of a profile analysis for which there is no empirical support. The manual does not report standard error of measurement for the CTRS-39 or any of the other scales, which

greatly hampers interpretation and questions the reliability of scores.

The author refers to the CTRS-39 and the CTRS-28 (Conner Teacher Rating Scales-28) as "alternate measures." They are not alternate forms in the true sense of the term and cannot be compared as equivalent. Therefore, alternate-form reliability is not available for the CTRS.

Discriminant and convergent evidence for construct validity can be examined through correlations of CTRS-39 factors, as well as the stability of the factor structure which has already been discussed. For the most part, the 1969 factors of Conduct Disorder, Hyperactivity, and Inattention have been found to be correlated in clinical samples, indicating a lack of discriminant validity (Lahey, Green & Forehand, 1980; Roberts et al., 1981; Werry, Sprague, & Cohen, 1975).

Regarding convergent validity, Trites et al. (1982) provide the only information regarding the factor structure of the scale in its current form. When coefficients of congruence calculated for their solutions were compared to those of Conners (1969) and Werry et al. (1975), the strongest support emerged for the Conduct Disorder and Asocial factors, with inconsistent support (modest to good) for the other factors. Correlations among purportedly unrelated factors are not reported, so discriminant validity cannot be assessed with these data.

In traditional studies of construct validity, several investigations have compared the earlier versions of the CTRS-39 to other behavior rating scales. Moderate correlations have been found with the Quay-Peterson Behavior Problems Checklist (Arnold et al., 1981; Campbell & Steinert, 1978), the Primary-Secondary Checklist and Teacher Off-Task Scale (Roberts, Milich, Loney, & Caputo, 1981), the Behavior Problem Checklist (Campbell & Steinert, 1978) and the Child Behavior Profile (Edelbrock, Greenbaum, & Conover, 1985). Adequate convergent but not discriminant validity has been established. The CTRS-39 factors are routinely correlated as much with other tests' factors purporting to measure dissimilar constructs as with those measuring the same constructs. Remarkably, no studies were found which specifically correlated the various other versions of the Conners' scales with the CTRS-39.

The 1989 published version of the CTRS-39 has not been studied. Thus, although it appears from previous versions that adequate convergent validity has been established, this cannot be assumed for the current version of the scale. Discriminant validity of the factors has not been strongly supported through research conducted so far. Given the considerable overlap of the Trites et al. (1982) factors, it is likely that discriminant validity will not be forthcoming.

The final issue in the review of the CTRS-39 is in regard to treatment validity. As stated above, the scale gained popularity as a measure of treatment effects, specifically to medication. The CTRS-39 appears to have circumvented the diagnostic problem by demonstrating that it is sensitive to medication treatment effects for children evidencing behavior problems (e.g., Arnold, Wender, McCloskey, & Snyder, 1972; Hoffman et al., 1974). The CTRS-39 has also been shown to be sensitive to behavioral and cognitive treatment effects, and these in combination with medication, although results are mixed (Cohen, Sullivan, Minde, Novak, & Helwig, 1981; Horn, Chatoor, & Conners, 1983). Hoffman, Engelhardt, Margolis, Polizos, Waizer, and Rosenfeld (1974) did control for pretest effects by obtaining multiple pretest ratings. Effects are typically demonstrated on both the Conduct Disorder and Hyperactivity factors. There is no evidence to suggest the scale is capable of determining changes in discrete domains of behavior. Use of the current factor structure for measurement of treatment effects has not been examined, and the manual does not address this issue. Continued use of the CTRS-39 as the primary measure in hyperactivity research is not recommended.

28-ITEM TEACHER RATING SCALE (CTRS-28). In 1978, Goyette, Conners, and Ulrich published a revised version of the CTRS containing 28 items. The 1989 published version of the CTRS-28 is based on this 1978 work. Item retention was based on results of factor analyses of the original version. Rather than adding items to strengthen the Tension-Anxiety and Asocial factors of the CTRS-39, the authors chose to exclude items from these weak factors from the revised version. Additionally, some items from the Conduct Problems factor were eliminated and other scale items were reworded or combined. It is unclear why items concerning lying, stealing, and destructive behavior were eliminated. The result is a scale that measures more limited dimensions of behavior but is more easily interpreted.

This version of the scale was normed on 383 children ages 3–17 from the Pittsburgh area. The group contained both normal children and those referred or tested for behavior or learning problems. It is unfortunate that the norms are already relatively outdated and based on a local sample. Also, only 2% of the sample was minority children, an inadequate representation. Despite psychometric improvements over the original scale, the CTRS-28 cannot be heartily recommended until updated national norms are available.

Goyette et al. (1978) factor analyzed the revised items and derived a three-factor scale which measures Conduct Problems, Hyperactivity, and Inattention-Passivity. Convergence with analyses of the original version is adequate (.82–.92). Although the Conduct Problems and Hyperactivity factors are conceptually purer than those of the CTRS-39, the Inattentive-Passive factor contains items not clearly associated with this construct. This makes interpretation difficult. Additionally, five items related to sociability were retained, which did not load significantly on any factor and are not used in scoring the CTRS-28. Alpha coefficients for the factors and/or items were not reported, data that would be helpful for evaluating item contributions.

Wilson and Kiessling (1988) have more recently replicated the CTRS-28 factor analysis employing a sample of children who were referred to a clinic for possible neurological problems. As with the Cohen and Hynd (1986) analysis of the CTRS-39, these results may have more utility with a clinic sample than does the factor interpretation in the published version of the CTRS-28. Age and grade norms based on this analysis, as well as replication, would be useful.

A strength of the CTRS-28 is that it was normed on essentially the same group as the revised parent scale, so comparisons can be made (limited by different item content on the scales). Correlations between the revised parent and teacher scales indicate modest but significant correlations between corresponding factors (.33–.45). However, intercorrelations among the teacher factors show that all factors are correlated (.49–.68), with the Hyperactivity factor having correlations of (≥ .60 with both the Conduct Problem and Inattentive-Passive factors.

Edelbrock, Greenbaum, and Conover (1985) correlated the CTRS-28 with the Teacher Version of the Child Behavior Profile (CBP) and found adequate convergent validity for the three factors (.62–.90), particularly for the Conduct Disorder factor. However, they also found the Hyperactivity factor to be highly correlated with the CBP Aggressive factor (.83) and all CTRS-28 factors were significantly correlated with the three corresponding CBP factors. There was support for the CTRS-28 as a broad-band measure of externalizing behaviors, as the three factors were significantly correlated with the externalizing scores but not, for the most part, the internalizing scores on the CBP. They also found the CTRS-28 to be significantly negatively correlated with the CBP measures of school performance and adaptive functioning.

This study, combined with the original study by Goyette et al. (1978), suggests that the CTRS-28 evidences adequate convergent but not disciminant validity for the factors of Conduct Problem, Hyperactivity, and Inattentive-Passive. The lack of discriminant validity between the Conduct Problem and Hyperactivity factors is particularly troublesome, as with the CTRS-39, given the clinical use of the scale in discriminating these two groups.

Regarding reliability, one study has been conducted (contrary to what is reported in the manual). Edelbrock, Greenbaum, and Conover (1985) found 1-week test-retest reliability coefficients ranging from .88–.96. Even accepting that coefficients from a longer retest interval would likely be lower, these results are excellent. However, users are cautioned that scores are likely to regress to the mean on second administration. Interrater reliability has not been reported, information which is essential for establishing adequate psychometric properties of the scale. Additional reliability studies are needed.

Scoring is straightforward and the age ranges on the protocol are correct for this scale. Scoring and profile examples in the manual are helpful for all forms of the scale. Until norms are updated and treatment validity is examined, this scale cannot be recommended.

93-ITEM PARENT RATING SCALE (CPRS-93). The 1989 manual and previous literature do not adequately describe test conceptualization or item selection/analysis for the CPRS-93. Number of items has ranged from 73 to 85 to 93 in early studies (Conners, 1970; 1973). The current version of the CPRS-93 overlaps with the teacher versions on some items but includes items concerning psychosomatic complaints, anxious/shy behavior, and other items not found on the other scales. Some items relate to home and are logically contained only on the parent scale. The rationale for inclusion of other items on the parent and not the teacher scale is, however, unclear. The parent and teacher scales are not equivalent, which makes comparisons more difficult.

The 1989 version is based on an unpublished 1988 item factor analysis of the 93-item scale using the original (1970) local sample ($n = 683$), combining normal and clinic-referred children. Users should be aware that the norms are, therefore, already over 20 years old. Critical data, such as factor loadings, alpha coefficients, percent of variance accounted for, and means and standard deviations by age and gender are not reported in the manual.

The protocol and scoring directions indicate that 24 items which parents are asked to complete apparently did not load significantly on any factor and are not used in scoring. Of the 69 items used to compute factor scores, 20 load and are scored on more than one factor.

Internal consistency of the current factor structure cannot be determined due to lack of reported alpha coefficients. Conners (1973) reported a total score interrater reliability coefficient of .85 between mothers and fathers on the original scale. O'Connor, Foch, Sherry, and Plomin (1980) reported test-retest reliability coefficients ranging from -.08 to .91

on their 12 factors of the scale; Glow et al. (1982) reported modest but significant test-retest reliability coefficients (.38–.76) for their 13-factor version. No reliability data are available for the original factor structure or for the 1989 published version of the test. Until these basic psychometric data have been reported, the test cannot be recommended for use and all validity data must be considered questionable. This should be kept in mind when evaluating the following data.

In an investigation of concurrent validity, Campbell and Steinert (1978) found modest correlations (in a clinic sample) between the 1970 CPRS-93 factors and those of the Behavior Problems Checklist (.14–.82), with the highest correlations being between the Hyperactivity (.82) and Conduct Problem (.75) factors and the BPC Conduct Problem factor. Results did not support discriminant validity of the factors. Achenbach and Edelbrock (1983) correlated the 1970 version of the CPRS-93 with the Revised Child Behavior Profile. Moderate support was found for convergent validity, with the highest correlations (> .80) for conduct problems. The two factors purporting to measure hyperactivity were correlated .46 for boys and .85 for girls. Discriminant validity coefficients were not reported. There is not strong overall support for discriminant validity of the specific factors, either from factor analytic or correlational studies. None of the studies employed the current factor structure of the CPRS-93; therefore, validity has not been adequately established. The scale's relationship to measures of behavior other than rating scales or to criteria such as home or school performance has not been reported.

The CPRS-93 has been adopted in clinical settings and used for over two decades; however, basic psychometric data are lacking which would support such use of the scale. For the 1989 published version, no reliability or validity data are available. Data on the original scale suggest that the CPRS-93 can be useful as a general screening measure of behavior problems; however, norms for a total score are not reported. Use of the current factors for differential diagnosis cannot be recommended until adequate research has been conducted and updated norms are available. As stated at the outset of this review, we cannot assume reliability and validity of one scale based on studies conducted with a different scale.

8-ITEM CONNERS PARENT RATING SCALE (CPRS-48). In 1978, Goyette, Conners, and Ulrich reported an abridged version of the CPRS containing 48 items. From these, a five-factor scale was formed (Conduct Problem, Learning Problem, Psychosomatic, Impulsive-Hyperactive, and Anxiety). The factors include 22 items loading significantly for both mother and father analyses. The 1989 published version includes factor scoring for these items plus two more which loaded significantly on Factor 5 for mothers and not for fathers (the factor structure reported in the manual does not list these items or a rationale for their inclusion). Thus, nearly one-half of the 48 items parents are asked to complete are not used in scoring factors. Norms for a total score are not reported. Although the factor structure is cleaner than with the CPRS-93 (no item is scored on more than one factor), four of the five factors contain only four items, including the Impulsive-Hyperactive factor. The two items which measure inattention load on the Learning Problems factor. Internal consistency of the factors cannot be determined as alpha coefficients were not reported. Factor intercorrelations range from .01 to .55, with the Psychosomatic and Anxiety factors evidencing discriminant validity. The Conduct Problem, Learning Problem, and Impulsive-Hyperactive factors all intercorrelated >.40. However, the Conduct Problem and Impulsive-Hyperactive appear to contain more pure items of these constructs than any of the other Conners scales.

Only one study (Pollard, Ward, & Barkley, 1983) has studied the utility of the CPRS-48 in measuring treatment effects, and no published study has determined its utility in response to medication. Therefore, even though the scale has been available for over a dozen years and the author and reviewers recommend its use in clinical settings, basic validity data have never been reported. Additionally, reliability data are minimal, making validity studies such as the one cited above questionable. For example, no test-retest reliability data are reported, making use of the scale as a measure of treatment outcome questionable. Researchers and clinicians have, in effect, put the cart before the horse.

HYPERACTIVITY INDEX. If potential users of the 1989 Conners' Rating Scales are hoping for comprehensive coverage of the abbreviated scale(s), along with standardization of items across versions of the CRS, they will be disappointed in the 10-item scales contained in each of the longer versions. The author fails to adequately describe how or why users should use the 10-item scales separately from the factors of the longer scales or from each other. It is particularly disturbing that he chose to use the label "Hyperactivity Index" for the 10-item scales and suggested their continuing use for the identification of "hyperkinesis" when he concedes that the scales are "more a general index of child psychopathology than a syndrome specific to the diagnostic category of hyperactivity or Attention Deficit Disorder" (Conners, 1989).

Conners (1973) first reported a 10-item scale as part of the revised 39-item CTRS created by modifying the 39-item scale to have 10 items in common with the parent scale. These 10 items are contained on the 1989 published versions of the CTRS-39 and the CPRS-93. The items have been described as those most sensitive to drug change and most frequently checked by parents and teachers (Werry et al., 1975). However, the item selection process and data supporting the superiority of these 10 items over others have never been adequately described. Despite this, numerous studies have demonstrated that the 10-item scale can contribute to a multimethod assessment of drug treatment effects (Conners, 1972; Henker, Whalen, & Collins, 1979; Rapport, DuPaul, Stoner, & Jones, 1986; Rapport, Stoner, DuPaul, Birmingham, & Tucker, 1985). Although most studies show behavioral improvement with drug treatment, some do indicate that behavioral improvement deteriorates rapidly if medication is removed (Brown, Borden, Wynne, Schlesser, & Clingerman, 1986) and that at long-term follow-up children receiving medication continue to experience learning and adjustment problems (Charles & Schain, 1981).

Despite the support for the scale cited above, there are concerns regarding reliability which would affect its use. The most critical factor is a practice effect, evidenced by a decrease in scores, which has been documented from the first to second administration (Conners, 1972; Werry & Sprague, 1974; Zentall & Barack, 1979). It is critical that users conduct at least two pretests, and preferably multiple ratings, when using the scale as a treatment outcome measure. Test-retest coefficients are acceptable (.89) between second and third administrations (Zentall & Barack, 1979).

Another major consideration in use of the 10-item scale is construct validity. Although items were *not* selected to discriminate among conduct disordered, hyperactive, inattentive, or anxious children, the 1973 10-item scale has been widely adopted for use in identifying hyperactive children. Werry et al. (1975) reported a cutoff score based on a local sample of 291 children. Despite the fact that age and gender differences were observed, other researchers have routinely used the one reported cutoff score for identification of children as hyperactive. Since the 1975 study, many investigators have demonstrated that this cutoff score yields a disproportionate number of false positives in the general population, only identifies children who are hyperactive *and* aggressive, and underidentifies children with attention problems (Holborow, Berry, & Elkins, 1984; Prinz, Connor, & Wilson, 1981; Satin, Winsberg, Monetti, Sverd, & Foss, 1985; Ullmann, Sleator, & Sprague, 1985).

What is needed are multitrait-multimethod studies to establish both the convergent and discriminant validity of the scale. An excellently designed study by Reynolds and Stark (1986) suggests the scale is related to teacher and student measures of self-control but not to direct measures such as matching familiar figures. They also obtained reliability information. Unfortunately, they, like many researchers, do not adequately describe the version of the 10-item scale they used and they incorrectly referenced their sources. Because of this, it is unclear which version this study supports.

Of particular concern for the 1989 published version of the 1973 10-item scale are the norms. There are no parent norms for the CPRS-93, despite its being in existence for almost 20 years. Therefore, this reviewer cannot recommend parent use of the scale for diagnostic purposes. Use of teacher-derived cutoff scores for parent informants is inappropriate due to low interrater reliability.

Construct validity of the 1978 version as a global measure of hyperactivity has also been questioned (Wilson & Kiessling, 1988). Kuehne, Kehle, and McMahon (1987) found the teacher and parent versions to be capable of discriminating between learning disabled, attention deficit, and normal children. The scale's ability to discriminate between conduct disordered and hyperactive children has not been established. Edelbrock et al. (1985) did find the teacher version to be significantly (.87) correlated with the Externalizing and not the Internalizing (.25) of the Child Behavior Profile. However, it was significantly correlated with all subscales except Anxious and Social Withdrawal, indicating a lack of discriminant validity for Conduct Disorder and Hyperactivity. In fact, the highest correlation was with the Aggressive subscale (.82).

The addition of norms, although almost a dozen years old, is a strength of the 1978 version of the 10-item scale; however, it is not recommended as the sole criterion for diagnostic or treatment measurement. A version of the 10-item scale which merits some consideration, but is not part of the 1989 published tests, is the IOWA Conners developed by Loney and Milich (1982). This scale contains two subtests, Inattention/Overactivity and Aggression, which were derived by examining the factor loadings of the original 39-item scale. This research represents a move toward differentiating the components measured by the most widely used 10-item scale but is limited by the few items measuring each component and a compounding of attention and overactivity.

Except for the quick and easy administration and scoring of a 10-item scale, its advantages are not apparent. Making critical diagnostic and treatment decisions based on such an instrument is simply not justified. The limitations of rating scales in general have been widely documented; these should be taken doubly into consideration when using a short screening instrument such as the Hyperactivity Index. Also, the fact that several versions remain available for use only adds to the confusion already in the literature regarding the Conners' scales and

questions the contention that there is a set of 10 best items.

CONCLUSIONS. It is this reviewer's conclusion that much additional work is needed on all versions of the Conners' scales, despite their age, and that the 1989 manual does not represent an effort to complete this work. It was particularly disappointing to see the lack of comprehensive coverage of the scales in the manual, the retention of all versions of the scales, use of outdated norms, inappropriate interpretive advice, and a general lack of caution to readers regarding shortcomings of the scales.

Readers are advised to keep up with the literature rather than the status quo. For overall behavioral measures, scales such as the Child Behavior Profile exhibit more adequate psychometric properties. For the measurement of hyperactivity, inattention, and impulsivity, scales such as the ADD-H Comprehensive Teacher's Rating Scale (7), the Yale Children's Inventory, and the Attention Checklist may prove to be useful instruments. Users should select the scale that measures the specific behavior of interest. The Conners' scales have simply been relied upon too heavily in research and clinical practice. Rating scales should be the beginning component of an assessment, comparable to interview data, not the last word.

REVIEWER'S REFERENCES

Conners, C. K. (1969). A teacher rating scale for use in drug studies with children. *American Journal of Psychiatry, 126,* 884-888.

Conners, C. K. (1970). Symptom patterns in hyperkinetic, neurotic, and normal children. *Child Development, 41,* 667-682.

Arnold, L. E., Wender, P. H., McCloskey, K., & Snyder, S. H. (1972). Levoamphetamine and dextroamphetamine: Comparative efficacy in the hyperkinetic syndrome. *Archives of General Psychiatry, 27,* 816-822.

Conners, C. K. (1972). Psychological effects of stimulant drugs in children with minimal brain dysfunction. *Pediatrics, 49,* 702-708.

Conners, C. K. (1973). Rating scales for use in drug studies with children [Special Issue]. *Psychopharmacology Bulletin,* pp. 24-84.

Hoffman, S. P., Engelhardt, D. M., Margolis, R. A., Polizos, P., Waizer, J., & Rosenfeld, R. (1974). Response to methylphenidate in low socioeconomic hyperactive children. *Archives of General Psychiatry, 30,* 354-359.

Wherry, J. S., & Sprague, R. L. (1974). Methylphenidate in children—effect of dosage. *Australian and New Zealand Journal of Psychiatry, 8,* 9-19.

Werry, J. S., Sprague, R. L., & Cohen, M. N. (1975). Conners' Teacher Rating Scale for use in drug studies with children—an empirical study. *Journal of Abnormal Child Psychology, 3,* 217-229.

Werry, J. S., & Hawthorne, D. (1976). Conners Teacher Questionnaire—norms and validity. *Australian and New Zealand Journal of Psychiatry, 10,* 257-262.

Campbell, S. B., & Steinert, Y. (1978). Comparisons of rating scales of child psychopathology in clinic and nonclinic samples. *Journal of Consulting and Clinical Psychology, 46,* 358-359.

Goyette, C. H., Conners, C. K., & Ulrich, R. F. (1978). Normative data on revised Conners Parent and Teacher Rating Scales. *Journal of Abnormal Child Psychology, 6,* 221-236.

Henker, B., Whalen, C. K., & Collins, B. E. (1979). Double-blind and triple-blind assessments of medication and placebo responses in hyperactive children. *Journal of Abnormal Child Psychology, 7,* 1-13.

Trites, R. L., Dugas, E., Lynch, G., & Ferguson, H. B. (1979). Prevalence of hyperactivity. *Journal of Pediatric Psychology, 4,* 179-188.

Zentall, S. S., & Barack, R. S. (1979). Rating scales for hyperactivity: Concurrent validity, reliability, and decisions to label for the Conners and Davids abbreviated scales. *Journal of Abnormal Child Psychology, 7,* 179-190.

Lahey, B. B., Green, K. D., & Forehand, R. (1980). On the independence of ratings of hyperactivity, conduct problems, and attention deficits in children: A multiple regression analysis. *Journal of Consulting and Clinical Psychology, 48,* 566-574.

O'Connor, M., Foch, T., Sherry, T., & Plomin, R. (1980). A twin study of specific behavioral problems of socialization as viewed by parents. *Journal of Abnormal Child Psychology, 8,* 189-199.

Arnold, L. E., Barnebey, N. S., & Smeltzer, D. J. (1981). First grade norms, factor analysis and cross correlation for Conners, Davids, and Quay-Peterson behavior rating scales. *Journal of Learning Disabilities, 14,* 269-275.

Charles, L., & Schain, R. (1981). A four-year follow-up study of the effects of methylphenidate on the behavior and academic achievement of hyperactive children. *Journal of Abnormal Child Psychology, 9,* 495-505.

Glow, R. A. (1981). Cross-validity and normative data on the Conners' Parent and Teacher Rating Scales. In K. D. Gadow & J. Loney (Eds.), *Psychosocial Aspects of Drug Treatment for Hyperactivity* (pp. 107-115). Boulder, Colorado: AAAS Westview Press.

Homatidis, S., & Konstantareas, M. M. (1981). Assessment of hyperactivity: Isolating measures of high discriminant ability. *Journal of Consulting and Clinical Psychology, 49,* 533-541.

Prinz, R. J., Connor, P. A., & Wilson, C. C. (1981). Hyperactive and aggressive behaviors in childhood: Intertwined dimensions. *Journal of Abnormal Child Psychology, 9,* 191-202.

Roberts, M. A., Milich, R., Loney, J., & Caputo, J. (1981). A multitrait-multimethod analysis of variance of teachers' ratings of aggression, hyperactivity, and inattention. *Journal of Abnormal Child Psychology, 9,* 371-380.

Glow, R. A., Glow, P. H., & Rump, E. E. (1982). The stability of child behavior disorders: A one year test-retest study of Adelaide versions of the Conners Teacher and Parent Rating Scales. *Journal of Abnormal Child Psychology, 10,* 33-60.

Loney, J., & Milich, R. S. (1982). Hyperactivity, inattention, and aggression in clinical practice. In M. Wolraich & D. Routh (Eds.), *Advances in developmental and behavioral pediatrics* (pp. 113-147). Greenwich, CT: JAI Press.

Trites, R. L., Blouin, A. G. A., & Laprade, K. (1982). Factor analysis of the Conners Teacher Rating Scale based on a large normative sample. *Journal of Consulting and Clinical Psychology, 50,* 615-623.

Achenbach, T. M., & Edelbrock, C. (1983). *Manual for the Child Behavior Checklist and Revised Child Behavior Profile.* Burlington, VT: University of Vermont Department of Psychiatry.

Pollard, S., Ward, E. M., & Barkley, R. A. (1983). The effects of parent training and Ritalin on the parent-child interactions of hyperactive boys. *Child and Family Therapy, 5,* 51-69.

Holborow, P. L., Berry, P., & Elkins, J. (1984). Prevalence of hyperkinesis: A comparison of three rating scales. *Journal of Learning Disabilities, 17,* 411-417.

Taylor, E., & Sandberg, S. (1984). Hyperactive behavior in English schoolchildren: A questionnaire survey. *Journal of Abnormal Child Psychology, 12,* 143-155.

Edelbrock, C., Greenbaum, R., & Conover, N. C. (1985). Reliability and concurrent relations between the teacher version of the Child Behavior Profile and the Conners Revised Teacher Rating Scale. *Journal of Abnormal Child Psychology, 13,* 295-303.

Rapport, M. D., Stoner, G., DuPaul, G. J., Birmingham, B. K., & Tucker, S. (1985). Methylphenidate in hyperactive children: Differential effects of dose on academic, learning, and social behavior. *Journal of Abnormal Child Psychology, 13,* 227-243.

Satin, M. S., Winsberg, B. G., Monetti, C. H., Sverd, J., & Foss, D. A. (1985). A general population screen for Attention Deficit Disorder with Hyperactivity. *Journal of the American Academy of Child Psychiatry, 24,* 756-764.

Ullmann, R. K., Sleator, E. K., & Sprague, R. L. (1985). A change of mind: The Conners Abbreviated Rating Scales reconsidered. *Journal of Abnormal Child Psychology, 13,* 553-565.

Brown, R. T., Borden, K. A., Wynne, M. E., Schleser, R., & Clingerman, S. R. (1986). Methylphenidate and cognitive therapy with ADD children: A methodological reconsideration. *Journal of Abnormal Child Psychology, 14,* 481-497.

Cohen, M., & Hynd, G. (1986). The Conners Teacher Rating Scale: A different factor structure with special education children. *Psychology in the Schools, 23,* 13-23.

Rapport, M. D., DuPaul, G. J., Stoner, G., & Jones, J. T. (1986). Comparing classroom and clinic measures of Attention Deficit Disorder: Differential, idiosyncratic, and dose-response effects of methylphenidate. *Journal of Consulting and Clinical Psychology, 54,* 334-341.

Reynolds, W. M., & Stark, K. D. (1986). Self-control in children: A multimethod examination of treatment outcome measures. *Journal of Abnormal Child Psychology, 14,* 13-23.

Shaywitz, S. E., Schnell, C., Shaywitz, B. A., & Towle, V. R. (1986). Yale Children's Inventory (YCI): An instrument to assess children with attentional deficits and learning disabilities: I. Scale development and psychometric properties. *Journal of Abnormal Child Psychology, 14,* 347-364.

Kuehne, C., Kehle, T. J., & McMahon, W. (1987). Differences between children with Attention Deficit Disorder, children with Specific Learning Disabilities, and normal children. *Journal of School Psychology, 25,* 161-166.

Barkley, R. A. (1988). Child behavior rating scales and checklists. In M. Rutter, A. H. Tuman, & I. S. Lann (Eds.), *Assessment and Diagnosis in Child Psychopathology* (pp. 113-155). New York: The Guilford Press.

Wilson, J. M., & Kiessling, L. S. (1988). What is measured by the Conners' Teacher Behavior Rating Scale? Replication of factor analysis. *Developmental and Behavioral Pediatrics, 9,* 271-278.

Conners, C. K. (1989). *Manual for Conners' Rating Scales.* Toronto, Canada: Multi-Health Systems, Inc.

Das, J. P., & Melnyk, L. (1989). Attention checklist: A rating scale for mildly mentally handicapped adolescents. *Psychological Reports, 64,* 1267-1274.

Moehle, K. A., & Fitzhugh-Bell, K. B. (1989). Factor analysis of the Conners Teacher Rating Scale with brain-damaged and learning-disabled children. *Psychology in the Schools, 26,* 113-125.

[88]

Cornell Critical Thinking Tests.

Purpose: Assesses general critical thinking ability including "induction, deduction, evaluation, observation, credibility (of statements made by others), assumption identification, and meaning."

Publication Dates: 1961–85.

Acronym: CCTT.

Scores: Total score only for each level.

Administration: Group.

Levels, 2: X, Z.

Price Data, 1988: $16.95 per 10 test booklets (specify level); $4.95 per 10 machine-gradable answer sheets; $6.95 per manual ('85, 32 pages); $10 per specimen set including both tests, answer sheet, and manual.

Time: (50) minutes.

Comments: Identical to 1971 edition except for minor format and wording changes; 1 form.

Authors: Robert H. Ennis, Jason Millman, and Thomas N. Tomko (manual).

Publisher: Midwest Publications/Critical Thinking Press.

a) LEVEL X.

Population: Grades 4–14.

b) LEVEL Z.

Population: Advanced and gifted high school students and college students and adults.

Cross References: See 9:269 (1 reference), T3:606 (7 references), T2:1755 (2 references), and 7:779 (10 references).

TEST REFERENCES

1. Norris, S. P. (1985). Synthesis of research on critical thinking. *Educational Leadership, 42,* 40-45.
2. Frisby, C. L. (1990). A meta-analytic investigation of the relationship between grade level and mean scores on the Cornell Critical Thinking Test (Level X). *Measurement and Evaluation in Counseling and Development, 23,* 162-170.
3. Mines, R. A., King, P. M., Hood, A. B., & Wood, P. K. (1990). Stages of intellectual development and associated critical thinking skills in college students. *Journal of College Student Development, 31,* 538-547.

Review of the Cornell Critical Thinking Tests by JAN N. HUGHES, *Associate Professor of Educational Psychology, Texas A&M University, College Station, TX:*

The 1985 edition of the Cornell Critical Thinking Tests (CCTT) is identical to the 1971 version with the exception of minor format and wording changes and an expanded manual with an updated review of published literature on the CCTT. The content of the test was selected based on Ennis's conceptualization of critical thinking skills. Level X is intended for use with elementary and junior high school students, and Level Z is intended for advanced and gifted high school students and adults and for college students. Both tests consist of multiple-choice items, and the 50 minutes allocated for test administration appears adequate for the 71 items on Level X and the 52 items on Level Z.

Both levels employ a story format that is likely to maintain the test taker's interest. All questions in Level X pertain to a science fiction story about a rescue mission to a planet, whereas different scenarios are employed in each section of Level Z.

The CCTT has many positive aspects. The developers caution the reader against using subscale scores to make individual comparisons. This caveat is important given the small number of items on some scales and the lack of evidence from factor analytic studies that the subscales measure distinct skills. The developers avoid describing the CCTT as a measure of intelligence or innate reasoning abilities and, indeed, emphasize the view that critical thinking skills are learned by students. Given the common misinterpretation of cognitive measures as measures of innate ability, their emphasis on learned skills is laudable. The manual is clearly written at a level of sophistication appropriate for the most likely potential test users—educators. For example, the manual includes the caution that if the recommended time limits are extended the normative data provided should not be used. The developers exercise appropriate caution in their claims for the test's reliability and validity. They warn that if the test is used as a criterion for selecting students into graduate school, it should not be the sole criterion.

Despite these positive aspects, there are several weaknesses that limit the test's usefulness. It is disappointing these shortcomings have not been addressed with more rigor in the 14 years since the 1971 edition of the test.

The norms are described as user norms to emphasize that they are not representative of some well-described group. Thus, for Level X, the manual lists means, standard deviations, and selected percentile rank equivalents for 15 elementary and junior high school groups and 14 high school and college groups. These samples are only sketchily described (e.g., high school students from a rural area in Washington State), and sample sizes range from 19 to 1,673. Similar data are provided for Level Z for 15 groups ranging in size from 22 to 224. Most of the studies report means and standard deviations for multigrade samples, and separate norms by grade level are not provided. The norms do not permit the user to compare a student's or group's performance with a normative group. However, norms are not as important to the use of the CCTT as a teaching evaluation tool, the use the authors recommend most highly.

Several studies on the internal consistency reliability are reported, with results suggesting adequate but somewhat low reliability for an ability measure. The split-half reliability estimates range from .76 to .87 (Mean of .83) for Level X and from .55 to .76 (Mean of .69) for Level Z. The Kuder-Richardson reliabilities are somewhat lower, as expected for a heterogeneous test. No test-retest data are available, probably due to the lack of an alternate form of the test. Nevertheless, variance due to time sampling is an important source of error variance in ability tests and remains an unknown source of variance for the CCTT.

The developers rely primarily on content validity data for demonstrating the test's validity. Test content was selected to measure each skill in Ennis's conceptualization of critical thinking. If one accepts Ennis's conceptualization, one would probably agree that the items adequately sample these skills. However, the developers should have convened a panel of independent experts in critical thinking to select item content from a pool or, at the least, to have classified test items according to the specific skills the item is intended to test. Neither of these procedures were followed, although members of the Illinois Critical Thinking Project agreed the items test for the indicated aspects of critical thinking. Similarly, a panel of experts should have independently rated the answers to determine if experts agree on the keying of answers to items. The manual includes the statement that members of the Illinois Critical Thinking Project reached unanimous agreement on the correctness of the keyed answers, but these judges are not described and may not represent independent ratings by persons not associated in the test's development. Another manner relevant to the content validity of the test is the extent to which test scores measure reading comprehension proficiency. No information on reading level of the test is provided, and the test might measure reading comprehension as much as critical thinking skills, especially among elementary students. In support of this possibility is evidence provided in the manual that the CCTT correlates as highly with reading comprehension scores as with measures of scholastic aptitude or intelligence.

The manual includes the statement that criterion validity is not an appropriate test of validity for the CCTT because "there is no established criterion for critical thinking ability" (p. 14). If a test does not correlate with some external criterion, the importance of the trait purportedly measured by the test is called into doubt. Despite the developers' statement, they do provide data on the test's correlations with external criteria as evidence of construct validity. Correlations with other tests of critical thinking are similar to correlations with measures of scholastic aptitude, averaging in the .50s. Correlations with measures of intelligence are somewhat higher. The two studies reporting correlations with grades show very low correlations (.15 and .17). Results of factor analytic studies have been inconclusive. In summary, the pattern of correlations suggests the CCTT measures some ability relevant to scholastic ability, intelligence, and reading comprehension. However, it is not clear what construct best explains these correlations.

Because the developers suggest the best use of the test is in the evaluation of teaching and curriculum development, studies demonstrating the test's sensitivity to instruction would provide important validity data. It is disappointing that after 14 years, only a few studies have investigated the test's sensitivity to instruction. These studies are not well conceptualized and the results do not lead to any definitive conclusions as to the test's construct validity. In summary, evidence that the CCTT measures some ability different from existing measures of intelligence and reading comprehension is far from conclusive. Multiple regression studies using the CCTT along with measures of intelligence and achievement to predict success in endeavors presumably calling for critical thinking skills would help to assess the construct validity of the CCTT.

The potential user of the CCTT should refrain from making decisions affecting individuals on the basis of this test. It may be an appropriate choice for evaluating instruction designed to improve critical thinking skills or for selecting specific critical thinking skills to teach in a course. Even for these purposes, however, the test has not demonstrated adequate validity. Of particular concern is the failure to find convincing evidence of the test's construct validity. A better, although far from perfect choice for a test of critical thinking skills is the Watson-Glaser Critical Thinking Appraisal (9:1347), which has the advantage of alternative forms and well-constructed norms.

Review of the Cornell Critical Thinking Tests by **KORESSA KUTSICK MALCOLM,** *School Psychologist, Augusta County School System, Fishersville, VA:*

The Cornell Critical Thinking Tests (CCTT) are an outgrowth of 30 years of research conducted by the authors. The tests were designed originally to assess critical thinking competencies as a way to evaluate the effectiveness of various curricular and teaching interventions. Throughout the manual, the authors indicate the CCTT is still a research tool which is undergoing refinement, yet state the current third edition has immediate utility as a screening device and teaching aid.

Critical thinking is a difficult concept to define. There are differences of opinion as to what components comprise critical thinking. The test authors (Ennis, Millman, & Tomko) define critical thinking as the process of deciding what to believe and do.

Using works of B. Othanial Smith, and Ennis' early writings on critical thinking, the authors have attempted to construct assessment tasks that measure seven aspects. These aspects are ones they believe to be most indicative of the critical thought process: Induction, Deduction, Value Judgment, Observation, Credibility, Assumptions, and Meaning. The authors provide information regarding which items correspond to these aspects. Future revisions of the CCTT might include more detailed descriptive information as to what each of these concepts involves and how the various test items fit these concepts.

There are two levels of the CCTT. Level X was designed for students in grades 4 through college sophomore year. Level Z was designed for advanced or gifted high school students, college students, and "other adults." There is an obvious overlap between these levels. Descriptions of which level users should select for high school and college students are somewhat vague. The vocabulary and readability of Level Z is more difficult than Level X. There are also some differences between the two levels in the weighting of items that were designed to measure the seven components of critical thinking. The authors suggest Level Z may be too difficult for younger and "less sophisticated" subjects. The term "less sophisticated" is not well defined in the test manual. To resolve the issue of which test to use, the authors recommend an examiner take the test herself to determine which level would be more suitable for her client. This level selection process sounds a bit awkward and would warrant additional attention. The authors suggest future test development will help clarify level identification issues.

The materials used to assess critical thinking on both levels are interesting and challenging. Adult and high school subjects who volunteered to take the CCTT and provide subjective comment about the test for this review stated the items were thought provoking, engrossing, and fun. The test authors' suggestion that the test be administered in a relaxed atmosphere should be followed. It seems likely that test anxiety would interfere with a subject's test performance. Analysis of the information provided by the various tasks would require sustained concentration and a calm mental set.

The administration and scoring procedures for both levels are very clear and relatively simple. Brief rationales are provided for item answers. These rationales might spark discussions on reasoning when the Cornell Critical Thinking Tests were used as part of a lesson on critical thinking.

As for the technical merits of the CCTT, the authors provide information regarding a number of validity, reliability, item, and factor analytic studies which they and other researchers have conducted. The validity of the CCTT has been somewhat difficult to establish. The authors maintain they have achieved content validity because of the procedures they followed in writing items for the test (i.e., expert review and scrutiny of the items). They claim construct validity through review of various convergent and divergent validity studies using the CCTT. Correlations of .27 to .74 were cited for studies comparing scores on the CCTT to scores on other tests purporting to measure critical thinking, or involving some aspect of this process, such as scholastic aptitude. Variables such as age, SES, and gender carried correlations of CCTT scores that ranged from -.07 to .39. Despite this, factor analytic studies have not yielded clear factor structures of the CCTT. The authors admit there is no definitive information regarding the construct validity of their test and concede additional work is needed to examine this issue.

Reliability information on the CCTT is provided through a brief review of studies conducted to examine this aspect of the test. Split-half and interitem correlations were reported to range from .67 to .90 for Level X and from .50 to .77 for Level Z. Rationales for the range differences between these two forms are not discussed. Normative information is provided on selected groups of individuals who have taken the CCTT. For example, one might compare a subject's test performance to those of freshmen in a small upstate New York university. Sample sizes for these groups range from 19 to 1,673. The authors have been cautious about noting the specificity of the norms established for their test.

The information provided about the CCTT suggests the test may hold good potential as a tool to be used in the examination and teaching of critical thinking. As the authors concede, however, additional exploration into the reliability and validity of the test is warranted. A consolidation of the normative data would also help improve the utility of this test. The use of this instrument as a screening device for any purpose, especially when used alone, is not recommended.

[89]
Cosmetology Student Admissions Evaluation.

Purpose: To "determine the aptitude and dexterity of an applicant to the cosmetology field."
Population: Cosmetology school applicants.
Publication Dates: 1977–85.
Scores, 5: Interest Inventory, Word Analogies, Comprehension and Reasoning, Manual Dexterity, Total.
Administration: Individual in part.
Price Data, 1989: $18.37 List, $13 School price per examination kit including 12 examination booklets ('85, 23 pages) and 12 evaluation sheets; $9.93 List, $6.95 School price per manual ('85, 40 pages); $7.07 List, $4.95 School price per 50 remedial work guide cards;

$17.14 List, $12 School price per examination plus audio cassette tape.
Foreign Language Edition: Spanish edition available.
Time: (34) minutes.
Comments: Examiner must be trained to score Manual Dexterity; other test materials (e.g., mannequin, professional comb, etc.) must be supplied by examiner.
Authors: Anthony B. Colletti and Robert M. Denmark (manual).
Publisher: Keystone Publications.

Review of the Cosmetology Student Admissions Evaluation by CRAIG N. MILLS, Executive Director, GRE Testing and Services, Educational Testing Service, Princeton, NJ:

The Cosmetology Student Admissions Evaluation is designed "to measure certain components of aptitude for the appreciation of the principles and practice of cosmetology." The evaluation consists of four separate components: an Interest Inventory, Word Analogies, Comprehension and Reasoning, and Manual Dexterity. Four part scores and a total score are generated. A quick review of the test content leads one to the conclusion that the test probably has content validity. For example, the Interest Inventory covers topics such as working with people and running a small business. The Word Analogies are limited to words that are clearly related to cosmetology. Similarly, Reasoning and Comprehension items require examinees to distinguish between tools and concepts one would expect to be used in cosmetology. The Manual Dexterity section uses a mannequin to determine the examinee's skillfulness in shaping hair and using combs, clips, etc. Evidence is not provided, however, to support the notion that these four areas are important predictors of success in either a cosmetology course or in practice. In addition, the scoring procedures and technical information on the reliability and validity of the test do not provide substantial evidence that the test is useful for selecting students for a cosmetology course.

TEST USE. The manual that accompanies the test states "This test was designed to be used for predicting the successful training of an applicant in the field of cosmetology, and not to be used as a device for rejecting applicants." Statements such as this, which describe appropriate and inappropriate test use, are an indication the test sponsor has devoted substantial attention to the use of the test and is interested in promoting proper use. Unfortunately, the remainder of the manual does not maintain this orientation. Only four pages later, the manual states that a score lower than 68 on the total battery "indicates that the applicant may not benefit from the training provided by the school and *should not be accepted*" [emphasis added].

SCORING. In the first three sections of the test, each question has a correct, an acceptable, and two incorrect options. Two points are awarded for a correct response, one for an acceptable response, and none for an incorrect response. A list of appropriate techniques is provided for each task in the Manual Dexterity section. Points are awarded based on the number of acceptable techniques used. Acceptable techniques include, for example, picking up instruments in the proper order, holding them appropriately, and combing hair completely prior to initiating the task. It is not clear why an applicant for cosmetology training should know these techniques before being admitted to a course. As a result, it appears this section may be testing the extent to which applicants already know basic concepts rather than whether they have sufficient dexterity to learn the techniques. No judgments are required that are strictly related to dexterity.

SCORE INTERPRETATION. The battery is especially weak in providing justification for score interpretation. In each of the first three sections, remediation is suggested for individuals with poor or failing scores. Low, weak, or failing scores are never defined. Further, prescriptions for remediation are made on the basis of a single item in some cases. In the Interest Inventory, for example, a recommendation is made that remedial work in "attitude" be provided if any one of a series of statements is responded to incorrectly. As mentioned previously, the manual recommends not accepting persons for training who score lower than 68 on the entire battery. No justification is given for this cutoff score. The manual simply states that such a score is "respectively below average." The further interpretation that the individual may not benefit from instruction and should not, therefore, be admitted lacks support. Further, because each section except the Interest Inventory contains 10 items, an examinee could conceivably receive no points in one of those sections and still be accepted. Such compensatory practice may be appropriate, but should be justified.

TECHNICAL INFORMATION. The technical information provided is scant and, in some cases, inaccurate. Further, the samples used to generate the data are not optimal. For example, reliability statistics were computed on a sample of 486 subjects, including licensed cosmetologists, advanced cosmetology students, beginning students, and noncosmetologists (including bus drivers, homemakers, clerks, etc.). This latter group made up over half of the sample. Not surprisingly, mean scores were highest for licensed cosmetologists and declined as cosmetology experience declined.

The overall reliability of the test was computed to be .78 using a Kuder-Richardson 21. This low reliability raises serious concern over the usefulness of the test for decision-making purposes. For the beginning cosmetology students, the reliability was .03. The manual itself states that this low reliability suggests that the results for beginning students may be a reflection of "random or chance experiences." Regardless of the reason for the results, they indicate that the test is not a useful measure for assessing incoming cosmetology students.

The manual also incorrectly interprets the reliability coefficient. It states that a reliability of .70 indicates that 70% of the variance in the test is systematic variance. This is simply inaccurate.

The manual uses data from a sample of 4,000 individuals as evidence of the validity of the test. Included in the sample are individuals who both scored above 68 on the test and passed a cosmetology course. The group was divided into four subgroups: (1) High Test Score, High Course Grade; (2) High Test Score, Low Course Grade; (3) Low Test Score, High Course Grade; and (4) Low Test Score, Low Course Grade. Seventy-six percent of the sample were in the "High, High" and "Low, Low" groups. This is cited as evidence that the test predicts likelihood of profiting from instruction. An alternate hypothesis is that individuals who already know cosmetology techniques will do well in a cosmetology course. Restricting a validity sample just to individuals who are successful on both the predictor and criterion variables does not provide particularly useful validity evidence.

Standard scores and percentile ranks are provided for each of the four groups used to compute the reliability estimates. It is unclear why these data are provided, however, because neither the standard score nor the percentile rank is ever used in score interpretation. However, it is interesting to note that the cutoff score is at the first percentile for beginning students, the ninth for advanced students, and the fifth for licensed cosmetologists. The result may be due primarily to sample sizes, but it could also indicate problems with the test content. The fact that the standard deviation of scores in the licensed cosmetologist group is about three times as large as for the beginning student group raises additional questions about the test.

SUMMARY. The Cosmetology Student Admissions Evaluation is of dubious value. Inspection of the content suggests it may be more of a measure of how much an individual already knows about cosmetology than of the likelihood that the individual will be successful in a cosmetology course. Score interpretations are not supported by the information provided and there is no evidence the recommended cutoff score was derived by a typically accepted method. Technical information suggests that the test is not useful for decision-making purposes, particularly for beginning cosmetology students.

Review of the Cosmetology Student Admissions Evaluation by STEVEN J. OSTERLIND, Associate Professor and Director, Center for Educational Assess-

ment, University of Missouri-Columbia, Columbia, MO:

The Cosmetology Student Admissions Evaluation (CSAE) is a battery of four subtests apparently designed to screen examinees for admission into a cosmetology training program. The four subtests are Interest Inventory, Word Analogies, Comprehension and Reasoning, and Manual Dexterity. Looking at this test from one point of view, it is appealing. Specifically, the test booklet is attractively presented with clearly labeled parts and well-done illustrations. The Examiner's Manual is likewise approachable. In fact, when administering the test, the directions may be read from scripted pages in the manual or a tape may be played to ensure standardization of administration. These features make the CSAE an attractive instrument insofar as its surface features.

Looking at the CSAE from a technical point of view, however, is a more troublesome task. In examining the only technical information available (a section of the Evaluator's Manual entitled "Reliability, Validity, and Standard Score Information"), one is left cold. There is much important information unexplained or not reported. Further, there are several instances of misleading and even inaccurate information. All of this leaves one to wonder what is the confidence of score interpretations. For example, as a measure of aptitude, the CSAE is undocumented. The psychological constructs to be assessed are not stated. Their factor structure among the items is likewise unreported. The specifications for these items are not given. One simply cannot determine what is being measured. By examination of the items themselves, one notices that they are diverse: Some are analogies, some are content specific, and some seem to aim at having examinees figure something out. What they measure, however, is anybody's guess.

The section of the test on Manual Dexterity is a bit more straightforward. Still, measures of internal consistency are inappropriately reported. A more useful bit of information would have been to describe a rationale for including the particular dexterity tasks that examinees are asked to do. In sum, one can only conclude the statement prominently printed on the cover of the test and manual, "A Valid and Reliable Measure of Aptitude and Dexterity," is unsubstantiated.

[90]
Counselor and Client Verbal Response Category Systems.
Purpose: To "provide a standardized method for analyzing counselor and client verbal behavior."
Population: Counselors in training.
Publication Date: 1981.
Scores: 23 categories: Counselor (Minimal Encourager, Silence, Approval/Reassurance, Information, Direct

Guidance, Closed Question, Open Question, Restatement, Reflection, Interpretation, Confrontation, Verbal Referent, Self Disclosure, Other), Client (Simple Responses, Requests, Description, Experiencing, Exploration of Counselor-Client Relationship, Insight, Discussion of Plans, Silence, Other).
Administration: Group.
Price Data, 1989: $10 per manual (62 pages).
Time: Administration time not reported.
Comments: 2 systems: Counselor, Client; interaction must be taped and transcribed.
Authors: Clara E. Hill, Carole Greenwald, Kathryn G. Reed, Darlene Charles, Mary K. O'Farrell, and Jean A. Carter.
Publisher: Marathon Consulting and Press.

[91]
The Couples BrainMap™.
Purpose: "To help partners gain new perspective of, and value for, their relationship."
Population: Couples.
Publication Dates: 1981–86.
Scores, 4: I-Organize, I-Explore, I-Pursue, I-Preserve.
Administration: Group.
Price Data: Available from publisher.
Time: 40(50) minutes.
Comments: Self-administered, self-scored.
Authors: Sherry Lynch, Dudley Lynch, Phyllis Miller, and Sherod Miller.
Publisher: Brain Technologies Corporation.

Review of The Couples BrainMap™ by ALICIA SKINNER COOK, Professor of Human Development and Family Studies, and RICHARD E. GUEST, Assistant Professor of Human Development and Family Studies, Colorado State University, Fort Collins, CO:

The Couples BrainMap™ is presented by its authors as an instrument for use by couples to more clearly understand and integrate differences in cognitive, affective, and behavioral styles. By better understanding these differences couples presumably are able to be more tolerant, achieve greater complementarity, and maximize their ability to relate in mutually supportive, creative fashion. The instrument is attractively designed with clear and easily followed instructions. It is self-scored and includes a readily understood worksheet format.

The instrument is described as a learning tool, rather than a standardized psychological test. As such, the authors do not report any data on reliability or validity. The only reference to basic elements of test construction is a vague statement regarding face validity. The authors do, however, make strong claims about the scientific basis of the instrument. Although no specific research is cited, the authors report that they have been able to construct a questionnaire that precisely measures how humans think and interact based on an extensive review of the literature on brain theory and research. This approach (*a*) does not provide sufficient information to allow the user to evaluate the merits of the instrument, (*b*) assumes erroneously that the instrument is valid and reliable if it is based on a literature review, and (*c*) overgeneralizes and oversimplifies the available information on neuropsychological functioning and its relationship to behavior. At best, this approach is pseudo-scientific and lacks the sophistication required for instruments used in the field of marriage and family therapy. Based on these points, the instrument has little value in research on couple interaction or compatibility.

The questionnaire also has limited use in applied settings. Although the authors state the primary function of the instrument is educational—to stimulate interpersonal awareness and discussion in couples, will the ensuing discussion be meaningful if it is based on test results with questionable validity and reliability? The authors report the instrument will help couples understand themselves better including their similarities, differences, strengths, and current limitations. It also refers to "systems gaps" that couples need to address. Many of these concepts, supposedly derived from the test results, are not substantiated by any evidence.

The major criticisms of this instrument concern the lack of reliability and validity data and its simplistic representation of brain function. The authors claim face validity related to general references to neuropsychological findings on brain lateralization and differences between posterior and anterior brain functions, coupled with "insights of philosophy, psychology, artificial intelligence, cultural anthropology, the neurosciences, linguistics and cognitive science." No supporting information is offered to assess claims that the instrument does indeed measure its purported constructs.

The instrument's model of neuropsychological function is based on the assumption that human behavior reflects the interactive influence of four grossly defined quadrants of the brain (the left anterior, right anterior, left posterior, and right posterior quadrants). The instrument purports to identify personal strengths and preferred styles for any given subject, based on relative dominance of specific brain quadrants. This approach is a marked oversimplification of neuropsychological research and, at best, provides a vague, reductionistic model by which couples may become more tolerant and supportive of each other's differences. At worst, it may contribute to the creation of simplistic stereotypes by which subjects could label themselves and others and to dissemination of questionable understandings of brain-mind phenomena. Other instruments already available (e.g., the Myers-Briggs Type Indicator [10:206], The Taylor-Johnson Temperament Analysis [10:357]) appear to address the issue of understanding and acceptance of differences without making claim to questionable interpretation of neuropsychological findings.

In conclusion, the Couples BrainMap can possibly be a useful format for stimulating discussion in couple relationships, but it claims to offer more than it can actually deliver. The major criticisms are that the items on the questionnaire have not been shown to actually measure the construct of interest, the dimensions of variance are only loosely based on scientific knowledge, and the instrument relies largely on a questionable oversimplification of neuropsychological findings.

[92]

Couple's Pre-Counseling Inventory, Revised Edition, 1987.

Purpose: "Provides a comprehensive portrait of couples' strengths and concerns—the basis for planning specific treatment strategies."
Population: Married or cohabiting couples beginning counseling.
Publication Dates: 1972–87.
Acronym: CPCI.
Scores: 13 areas: Demographic Data, General and Specific Happiness with the Relationship, Caring Behaviors, Conflict Management, Communication Assessment, Sexual Interaction, Moods and Management of Personal Life, Decision Making, Division of Home/Child Care/Work Responsibilities, Child Management, Goals of Counseling, Previous Marriages and/or Relationships, Additional Information.
Administration: Group.
Price Data, 1989: $19.95 per set including 25 forms and counselor's guide ('87, 38 pages); $25 per couple computer scoring service available from COMPUSCORE, Inc.
Time: Administration time not reported.
Comments: Revision of the Marital Pre-Counseling Inventory; may be scored by hand or by computer.
Authors: Richard B. Stuart and Barbara Jacobson.
Publisher: Research Press.
Cross References: For reviews by Lee N. June and Marlene W. Winell of an earlier edition, see 9:277; see also T3:1373 (1 reference).

Review of the Couple's Pre-Counseling Inventory, Revised Edition, 1987 by DAVID N. DIXON, Professor and Department Chair, Department of Counseling Psychology and Guidance Services, Ball State University, Muncie, IN:

The current Couple's Pre-Counseling Inventory (CPCI) evolved from the Marital Pre-Counseling Inventory (T3:1373) and an earlier edition of the CPCI (9:277). Its evolution has resulted in a longer instrument for couples to complete, a computer-scoring system to compute scores on 32 topics with up to seven summary scores for many topics, and a more eclectic conceptual/theoretical base. Whereas the earliest version of the Inventory relied primarily on content-valid items to gather information directly tied to a particular social-learning-based model of relationship-enhancement therapy, the current Inventory includes a broadened content (e.g., indices of individual psychopathology, Section F; information related to boundary problems, Section I:3). The expanded content seems to have resulted primarily from input/requests from practitioners experienced in the use of earlier versions. Users may not find all of the scored information directly relevant to their therapeutic approach. On the other hand, a wider array of therapists may find useful material to warrant using the Inventory with couples in treatment.

The major strength of the Inventory remains the relationship between assessment and treatment for both couples and therapists. For couples the Inventory serves to (a) socialize couples into therapy by creating a positive set that focuses on strengths in the relationship and (b) introduce a pattern of thinking about the relationship in self-responsible, reciprocal terms. For therapists the Inventory is a tool for (a) planning couples therapy and (b) evaluating the outcome of treatment.

The major weakness of the Inventory continues to be the lack of psychometric development. The validation of the current version is based on a sample of 55 couples. This is a limited sample, and no replications or cross validations are reported. Many of the summary scores report internal consistency scores that are good (e.g., Section A: General and Specific Happiness with the Relationship, Cronbach alpha = .91). Validity indices for summary and some individual scores are primarily based on correlations with the Dyadic Adjustment Scale (Spanier, 1976). This standard measure of marital satisfaction correlated highly with more global measures from the CPCI and adequately with more focused scales.

No attempt is made to organize the various scales/dimensions using factor analytic or related procedures. This is especially problematic when items are grouped into summary scales. How does the score for Decision Making from the specific section on Decision Making differ from the composite Decision Making score (see also Sexual Interaction, Child Management)? When the focus of the Inventory is gathering specific information about a narrow band of behavior, questions of underlying structure may be less important. When the focus of the Inventory is providing composite, summary scores for broad areas of marital interaction, questions of underlying structure are important for test development.

Normative data are limited to the sample of 55 couples (43 who requested marital therapy and 12 who participated in a marriage enrichment program). Satisfying and successful relationships are not based, however, on norms, but on the experience of participants. The authors provide some limited, normative information but direct the users to the relational meanings for a particular couple. The authors state that the Inventory is "principally designed for ideographic [sic] assessment, i.e., for planning an individualized approach to helping each couple change" (p. 1).

The manual is more extensive than in the past. This is partly due to the increased number of scales reported through the computer analysis. The manual includes a great deal of information about the meaning of scores based on the research literature and about how to integrate results with treatment. Suggestions are given for potential follow-up questions and for specific ways to proceed with treatment. The manual provides information for both hand scoring and computer scoring, with hand scoring estimated to take between 60 and 75 minutes. No estimate is given for time of administration, although it is clearly an instrument that requires a considerable time commitment from couples. Completion of the Inventory may be a better measure of commitment and motivation for counseling than is a person's reported willingness to change (Section J).

The available Computer Analysis Results seemed quite cumbersome (24 pages). The labels for some scores differed from those used in the manual and thus were unclear. The average user would require specific training or extensive experience before feeling comfortable with the computer results. There are a great number of scores provided, but learning what they all mean and how they can be used would take some time and effort.

The CPCI is at a critical threshold. The authors, in their attempt to provide complete assessment information, may have expanded the Inventory to the point where it is practical only with highly motivated, verbally fluent clients. The reviewer's recommendation is that future revision should focus on simplification. Analyses of underlying structure may demonstrate that several of the current items and scales are redundant.

The CPCI is of great benefit for the treatment of a couple who completes the instrument. Not only does the therapist have a wealth of information about the strengths and weaknesses of the relationship and suggested directions for treatment, but also the couple is well into the process of new understanding and changed behaviors.

The CPCI remains, perhaps, the most useful instrument available for the professional doing therapy with couples. It provides information for the therapist directly related to effective treatment design. The psychometric properties of selected scales make them useful for the researcher. Future revisions need to consider a shortened, simplified version that is practical with a broader clientele.

REVIEWER'S REFERENCE

Spanier, G. B. (1976). Measuring dyadic adjustment: New scales for assessing the quality of marriage and similar dyads. *Journal of Marriage and the Family, 38*, 15-38.

Review of the Couple's Pre-Counseling Inventory, Revised Edition, 1987 by GERALD L. STONE, Professor of Counseling Psychology and Director, University Counseling Service, The University of Iowa, Iowa City, IA:

The Couple's Pre-Counseling Inventory (CPCI) was first published in 1973 and revised in 1983. The current revision of 1987 was reported to be based on new data, a broadened array of cognitive-behavior therapy methods applicable to marriage counseling, and feedback from therapists and researchers. Because of previous reviews (June, 1985; Winell, 1985) this review will be selective.

The purpose of the CPCI is "to collect data for planning and evaluating relationship enhancement therapy based on principles of social learning theory." The purpose is accomplished through an idiographic assessment of each couple in 13 areas. The assessment is descriptive, multidimensional, strength oriented, and focused on the present situation. The information gained can be used to help therapists plan and evaluate couples counseling, socialize couples in therapy, and help the couple participate in therapy through their contemplation of changes in the way they think about issues that arise in therapy.

The CPCI yields 347 bits of information provided by each partner. The 16-page Inventory includes requests for open-ended responses or endorsement of scale values. Hand or computer scoring is available. Hand scoring takes 60–75 minutes. Computer services offer a printout of 18 to 24 pages for use by the therapist and a two-page printout for the couple. A Counselor's Guide is also available that includes a description of the history and the development of the CPCI, instructions about administration, scoring, and interpretation, presentation of psychometric data, explanations about each section, and scale definitions.

Many of the strengths and weaknesses mentioned in earlier reviews remain. Some of the strengths (and weaknesses) relate to the Guide including the sections on problems and issues on assessment, test administration instructions, and cautions about computer scoring. Given the revisions made on the CPCI, the Guide should identify changes and how the data provided relate to various revisions. It was very difficult to note specific changes in the CPCI for the current revision. The issue of a limited evidential warrant remains. In the current revision, a standardization sample of 55 couples is used, although a pool of data assembled from responses of 1,200 couples whose forms were computer scored is to be published soon. It seems to be time for the authors to devote resources to comprehensively evaluate their instrument (e.g., behavior validation of self-report responses, effectiveness of instrument with various theoretical approaches) before another

revision is completed with more promises of evaluation. As part of the evaluation, standardized samples of nonmarried heterosexual as well as gay and lesbian couples should be included if the Inventory is to be a couples inventory rather than a heterosexual, marital inventory with simple label changes. The Guide seems oriented to marriage counseling. Moreover, the scoring alternatives, hand and computer scoring, need to be evaluated in terms of client, therapist, and economical considerations.

In summary, the Inventory continues to yield potentially useful information for couples counseling. There are no clear competitors, but it is time for the promise and potential of the CPCI to be realized. The lack of a solid evidential warrant mentioned in reviews in the past for an instrument that has been around in various forms for over 15 years needs to be comprehensively and substantially addressed. It is time for the authors to follow the purpose they set for CPCI and to apply it to their research task, that is, "collect data" and "evaluate."

REVIEWER'S REFERENCES

June, L. N. (1985). [Review of the Couple's Pre-Counseling Inventory.] In J. V. Mitchell, Jr. (Ed.), *The ninth mental measurements yearbook* (pp. 403-404). Lincoln, NE: Buros Institute of Mental Measurements.
Winell, M. W. (1985). [Review of the Couple's Pre-Counseling Inventory.] In J. V. Mitchell, Jr. (Ed.), *The ninth mental measurements yearbook* (pp. 404-405). Lincoln, NE: Buros Institute of Mental Measurements.

[93]
Creative Behavior Inventory.

Purpose: Designed to measure "behavioral characteristics associated with creativity."
Population: Grades 1–6, 7–12.
Publication Date: 1989.
Acronyms: CBI1, CBI2.
Scores, 5: Contact, Consciousness, Interest, Fantasy, Total.
Administration: Individual.
Levels, 2: I (elementary), II (secondary).
Price Data: Price data for materials including manual (70 pages) available from publisher.
Time: Administration time not reported.
Comments: Ratings by teachers; manual title is Understanding the Creative Activity of Students.
Author: Robert J. Kirschenbaum.
Publisher: Creative Learning Press, Inc.

Review of the Creative Behavior Inventory by RICHARD M. CLARK, Chair, Department of Educational Psychology and Statistics, State University of New York at Albany, Albany, NY:

Many schools in the United States have developed programs for students designated as gifted or talented. Often students are selected for such programs based on their performance on standardized achievement or intelligence tests. The Creative Behavior Inventory (CBI) was developed with the notion that individuals possess creative abilities that may be independent of intelligence or academic achievement.

It is not surprising that the CBI is included in a larger publication titled *Understanding the Creative Activity of Students.* Much emphasis is given to reviewing literature about creativity, principally from the 1960s and 1970s. The CBI is almost an afterthought.

According to the author, the CBI was designed to measure four of nine postulated dimensions of creativity. These four: Contact, Consciousness, Interest, and Fantasy, are presumed to be important to the preparation phase of creativity. Teachers are asked to rate children in their classes, using a scale of 1 to 10, to evaluate how often each child exhibits a particular behavior compared to his or her peers (e.g., "Notices and remembers details"). The instrument consists of a total of 10 items. One dimension is assessed with only one item, and the other three dimensions are assessed with three items each.

During the development stage of the instrument, an earlier and longer version of it (25 items) was a given to 10 teachers from one school and each teacher provided ratings of three boys and three girls. Cronbach's alpha was then calculated for each subscale based on the 60 children who had been rated. Although the reported alphas were typically .93 or higher, one can hardly be confident of the reliability of the instrument. Keep in mind that an assessment of a child is made based on the judgement of a teacher. Certainly one can assume that teachers will vary greatly in how they perform the task. No data are provided concerning how the 10 teachers used the scale provided. We are not told whether some teachers consistently rated children higher or lower, how much of the scale range was used, or what variance was found for any item. The author makes no apology for the fact that the instrument discussed in the reliability section of the manual is different from the instrument presented for use.

The validity claims for the instrument are based on a study published by the author in 1984, also with an earlier version of the instrument. Fifty-six talented children from one of the two participating school districts, for whom the author also had IQ and achievement test scores, were divided into two groups depending on whether they completed a "Type III" product in the course of their enrichment program. Then, a discriminant function analysis was performed. Using CBI scale subscores, 49 children were correctly classified and 11 children were misclassified.

As in the section on reliability, the predictive validity section provides no data on basic psychometric aspects of the studies. For example, means and standard deviations are not provided either for the total sample or for the groups that did and did not produce a Type III product. A definition of a Type III product is also not provided. The author does not state whether the teachers who provided ratings in the validation phase had special interest and instruction related to creativity. Considering the context in which the validation studies were set, a description of the teachers is essential.

At this stage of its development, the Creative Behavior Inventory is not ready to be used in a situation in which serious decisions are being made about appropriate educational programs for children. Kirschenbaum's review of the creativity literature may be useful for discussing this complex topic with teachers and parents, but much more work is needed on the Creative Behavior Inventory.

[94]
The Creative Reasoning Test.

Purpose: Measures the ability to generate and evaluate problem solutions in a variety of categories.
Population: Presecondary to college.
Publication Date: 1989–90.
Acronym: CRT.
Scores: Total score only.
Administration: Group and individual.
Levels, 2: A, B.
Price Data, 1990: $5.95 per specimen set including test booklet and manual ('90, 6 pages; Level A or Level B); $3.95 per manual (Level A or Level B); $6.95 per 8 test booklets.
Time: 30(35) minutes.
Comments: Each level has 2 equivalent forms: 1, 2.
Author: John H. Doolittle.
Publisher: Midwest Publications/Critical Thinking Press.

Review of The Creative Reasoning Test by ROBERT J. DRUMMOND, Professor of Education and Program Director, Counselor Education, University of North Florida, Jacksonville, FL:

The Creative Reasoning Test (CRT) is a 20-item test that purports to measure creative reasoning of individuals. The problems are set in riddle format. The author states that "these tests provide problems whose solution requires word association, and/or open-ended generation of categories" (manual, p. 3). The author claims the test can be used as a criterion measure in studies dealing with creative reasoning, as a criterion measure in nonexperimental classroom settings to measure the changes that might occur over the course of a semester or year in creative reasoning, and as a means of assessing the achievement level of individuals or groups.

There are two levels of the CRT: Level A for presecondary students, and Level B for secondary and college students. Each level has two forms, Form 1 and Form 2. The test booklets contain four pages. The first page contains a place for recording student information and the scores and the set of instructions for the test. The author provides two examples of the type of items that are on the test. The next three pages contain the 20 items in double columns. Each riddle is included in a box and the test taker is asked "What am I?" A blank is left for the test taker to record the answer.

Reliability coefficients for Level A are presented for both forms for third grade to sixth grade. The manual lists the coefficients as alpha, but split-half procedures are described. The coefficients range from a low of .63 for a group of 14 third graders to a high of .99 for a group of 139 fourth graders. The coefficients for Form A2 are higher than for Form A1. The median coefficient for A1 is .76 and for Form A2, .90. For Form B the split-half reliability corrected by Spearman-Brown is .90 for 53 students. The level or type of students is not described. There is no information on the age, gender, or type of school indicated. The author does not present any alternate form reliability information. Are the two forms really equivalent? One would question the equivalence of the two forms because the reliability of the second form tends usually to be higher than on the first form. The means differ on the two forms also.

The author claims that the test has content validity because the items were written to fulfill the purpose of the test. One study of the construct validity of the CRT is presented. The CRT correlated .70 for a group of 50 college students with the Remote Associations Test. There is no correlation matrix of the items or factor analytical evidence presented. Norm tables for both forms are presented. There are separate norms available for grade 3 to grade 6. For Level B there is just one norm table for secondary level and college level students based upon slightly over 50 college students. Raw scores can be converted into percentile ranks. The standard error of measurement by grade level is not provided users. The norming groups are not described.

The CRT is an interesting type of test because it uses riddles as a mechanism to test problem solving. There are, however, a number of problems with the test as far as the reliability, validity, and interpretability are concerned. Two forms are available at each level, but no alternate form reliability studies are reported. Are the forms really equivalent? The author reports exclusively split-half coefficients for each form at each level. No evidence is available on the stability of the CRT over time.

Only one study is given to support the construct validity of the CRT. No studies are available on the criterion-referenced validity of the instrument. How does the test relate to measures of scholastic aptitude, critical thinking, and achievement?

There is no demographic description of the norming groups. Level B norms are based entirely on just 53 and 54 college students. No data are reported on secondary school students. No distribution of scores are presented by grade or by gender.

The CRT might be appropriate for use in instructional units on creative reasoning and could be used as a tool to focus student attention on problem-solving strategies. The CRT, however, has limited value as a psychological test of the construct or as a research tool until more development is done on the reliability, validity, and interpretability of the instrument.

Review of The Creative Reasoning Test by KA-THRYN D. HESS, Consultant, Montgomery, AL:

The Creative Reasoning Test (CRT), putatively measuring the construct of that name, consists of parallel forms: Level A, Forms 1 and 2 for presecondary students and Level B, Forms 1 and 2 for secondary and college students. The two 20-item forms for each level can serve as pre- and post-tests. Each item consists of a four line riddle such as: "I drop from the clouds, A king's term of rule; The northernmost deer, Think Santa, not mule" (manual, p. 4), with the last line asking "What am I?"

The six-page manual begins with a statement regarding the importance of teaching problem-solving skills to children as well as an acknowledgement that there is considerable disagreement about which problem-solving processes should be taught. The author, Doolittle, proposes that one approach is to focus on the kinds of problems to be solved, the information (clues) one uses to solve the problems, and the possible solutions to the problem. He then discusses four problem types: deductive reasoning, deductive search, creative reasoning, and creative search. Doolittle defines creative reasoning problems as those in which the clues are all given, the solutions are not all given, and the task is to generate solutions and evaluate them against the given clues.

Doolittle writes that the CRT "uses the skills required in other creative reasoning tests, but it differs in the following way: problems are set in riddle format, allowing students to evaluate and validate their answers by disconfirming their initial unsatisfactory ideas through various words within the riddles" (manual, p. 3). The CRT manual suggests its use as a criterion in both experimental and classroom settings.

The instructions for administration are clear as are the scoring instructions. The manual suggests converting raw scores into t scores or percentile ranks using the tables provided. The Level A manual includes norms on grades 3, 4, 5, and 6. The Level B manual, although written for secondary and college levels, includes norms only for college ($N = 53$ for Form B-1, and $N = 54$ for Form B-2). Because the gathering of normative data is in the early stages, the percentile ranks may be based on as many as 168 or as few as 14 cases, with no description of the geographical, racial, cultural, or gender characteristics of the "norm" group. Use of the CRT in appraisal of an individual may well render a pseudo-precise score wholly unrepresentative of that individual's actual standing in her or his own norm group.

Sections on reliability and validity are included in the manuals. Reliabilities are presented via odd-even correlations corrected for test length. The manual claims content validity by definition "because test items were written to fulfill the stated purposes of the test" (manual, p. 6), as circular a line of (creative) reasoning as this reviewer has ever heard. Doolittle acknowledges that if translated into different languages or different cultures its content validity would be "greatly diminished"; however, he does not describe the parameters for the groups for whom he feels the CRT is valid. This confounds an already perplexed reviewer because creative reasoning is often theoretically described as *less* culture bound than other types of reasoning. This is one more example of a set of items searching for a construct, a theoretical link, a set of normative data, and a reason for being.

In sum, although the CRT is a novel, interesting collection of items it is in its earliest stages of development. Publication and use of the CRT is premature.

[95]
The Creatrix Inventory.

Purpose: "To help people identify their levels of creativity as well as their orientations toward risk taking."
Population: Members of organizations.
Publication Dates: 1971–86.
Acronym: C&RT.
Scores, 2: Creativity, Risk Taking; plotted on matrix to determine 1 of 8 styles: Reproducer, Modifier, Challenger, Practicalizer, Innovator, Synthesizer, Dreamer, Planner.
Administration: Group.
Price Data, 1987: $5.95 per manual ('86, 26 pages) including inventory and scoring instructions plus administrator's guide (2 pages).
Time: Administration time not reported.
Comments: Catalog uses the test title Creativity and Risk-Taking.
Author: Richard E. Byrd.
Publisher: Pfeiffer & Company International Publishers.

Review of The Creatrix Inventory by HARRISON G. GOUGH, Professor of Psychology, Emeritus, University of California, Berkeley, CA:

The Creatrix Inventory for "risk-taking" and "creativity" consists of two 28-item self-report scales. Each item is answered on a 9-step scale, going from 1 (*complete disagreement*) to 9 (*complete agreement*). Three illustrative items for Risk Taking are "I feel free to be myself whatever the consequences," "Sometimes I cheat a little," and "I can accept my mistakes." For Creativity, defined as the ability to generate unconventional ideas, three representative items are "Daydreaming is a useful activity," "I often see the humorous side when others do not," and "Complete ambiguity is more desirable than complete clarity."

The items within each scale appear to be reasonably homogeneous, but no intrascale reliability data are presented. The only statement in the manual concerning reliability reports a test-retest correlation of .72 for 25 persons readministered the test after a 1-week interval. Whether this coefficient refers to one scale, both scales, or some sort of index based on the 56 items is unspecified.

Also, nothing is said in the manual about the correlation between the two scales, even though the major interpretive model for the Inventory depicts them in a conjoint display. Eight regions on the bivariate surface are marked off and designated as discrete "orientations." Persons scoring very high on both scales are classified as Innovators, those scoring very low on both as Reproducers. Challengers are very high on Risk Taking but low on Creativity, and Dreamers are very high on Creativity but low on Risk Taking. In the center of the grid are found Practicalizers (average on Creativity, above average on Risk Taking), Synthesizers (average on Risk Taking, above average on Creativity), Planners (average on Creativity, below average on Risk Taking), and Modifiers (average on Risk Taking, below average on Creativity). No evidence is provided concerning the expected number of respondents to be found in each category.

The implications of each of the eight categories are elaborated in one-page digests suggesting how individuals in each class will think and approach problems, the positive contributions they might make to an organization, and the difficulties that can be anticipated. The sketches are plausible, but no data are furnished to substantiate the claims made for each way of functioning, or for the predicted assets and liabilities.

The manual closes with a one-page discussion of "norms," "effects of faking or extraordinary stress," and "validity." Under "norms," no means or standard deviations for any sample are given, although it is stated that women score higher than men on Risk Taking, whereas on Creativity no differences were detected.

Under "faking" it is asserted that attempts to fake good should seriously depress Risk Taking scores, but only moderately depress those for Creativity. Unfortunately, no data are given for samples tested under normal and fake-good instructions. Considering that the goal of the Inventory is to assess creative potential, the "fake creativity" set as explored in depth by Harrington (1975) is more relevant than that for "fake good."

The short paragraph on validity offers no data whatsoever, and in fact carries the anomalous sentence, "Although the statistics necessary to support concurrent validity are not available, face validity is generally attested to by respondents." This assertion is an unacceptable substitute for the validity data that should have been provided.

Another serious deficiency in the manual is the absence of any attempt to relate Risk Taking and Creativity scores to widely used and well-known measures of these two phenomena. For instance, in the creativity domain, good examples are Welsh's (1975) scales for origence and intellectence, Barron's (1953, 1965) scales for independence of judgment and originality, and Cattell's (Cattell, Eber, & Tatsuoka, 1970) creativity equation for the 16PF. In the risk-taking domain, a good example is the scale of that name in the Jackson Personality Inventory (Jackson, 1976). Scores on the Creatrix Inventory should also be related to performance measures of creativity, such as those of Guilford (Wilson, Guilford, & Christensen, 1953), Harris (1960), and Torrance (1966), and linkage should also be established with the Innovator-Adaptor categories as defined by Kirton's (1976) measures.

To conclude, there may well be good potential in the scales of this Inventory, but at the present time there is little, if any, evidence of their value. Until such time as adequate evidence becomes available, the Inventory should be viewed only as a research device of undetermined worth.

REVIEWER'S REFERENCES

Barron, F. (1953). Some personality correlates of independence of judgment. *Journal of Personality, 21*, 287-297.
Wilson, R. C., Guilford, J. P., & Christensen, P. R. (1953). The measurement of individual differences in originality. *Psychological Bulletin, 50*, 362-370.
Harris, D. (1960). The development and validation of a test of creativity in engineering. *Journal of Applied Psychology, 44*, 254-257.
Barron, F. (1965). The psychology of creativity. *New directions in psychology* (Vol. 2, pp. 3-134). New York: Holt, Rinehart & Winston.
Torrance, E. P. (1966). Torrance Tests of Creative Thinking. Princeton, NJ: Personnel Press.
Cattell, R. B., Eber, H. W., & Tatsuoka, M. M. (1970). *Handbook for the Sixteen Personality Factor Questionnaire (16PF)*. Champaign, IL: Institute of Personality and Ability Testing.
Harrington, D. M. (1975). Effects of explicit instructions to "be creative" on the psychological meaning of divergent thinking test scores. *Journal of Personality, 43*, 434-454.
Welsh, G. S. (1975). *Creativity and intelligence: A personality approach.* Chapel Hill, NC: University of North Carolina Institute for Research in Social Science.
Jackson, D. N. (1976). *Jackson Personality Inventory manual*. Goshen, NY: Research Psychologists Press.
Kirton, M. J. (1976). Adaptors and innovators: A description and measure. *Journal of Applied Psychology, 61*, 622-629.

Review of The Creatrix Inventory by JOHN F. WAKEFIELD, Associate Professor of Education, University of North Alabama, Florence, AL:

The Creatrix Inventory (C&RT) is a 56-item instrument designed to measure creativity and risk-taking orientations on a grid-like matrix. Each variable is measured by degree of agreement or disagreement with 28 statements. Degrees range from 1 (*complete disagreement*) to 9 (*complete agreement*), and the instrument is self-scored. Total scores for Creativity and Risk Taking are then plotted by the respondent on the two axes of the matrix. The matrix itself is divided into eight areas to indicate different types of individuals. The four central personality types (Modifier, Practicalizer, Synthesizer, and Planner) are purportedly more socialized than the other four, which lie at corners of the grid. Individuals are encouraged to interpret their combined orientation in light of descriptions of all eight types supplied in the C&RT booklet.

The strength of the C&RT lies in the logic of the rationale. If one accepts the author's definition of creativity as "the ability to produce unconventional ideas," it follows that people who live "in a phantasmagoric world of wildly imaginative ideas" are highly creative. This definition also permits the Inventory author to distinguish risk-taking from creativity and describe four extreme types based on this distinction. The Dreamer (creative but not a risk-taker) is described as an underachiever, while the Challenger (a risk-taker but not creative) is described as critical of others' ideas. The other two extreme types (Reproducer and Innovator) are self-explanatory and represent extremely low or high scores on both scales.

The weakness of the Inventory lies in the absence of statistical data to support the instrument. Means for the Creativity and Risk Taking scales can be estimated from the matrix, but standard deviations are not reported in the manual or the administrator's guide. Reliability is only reported through a test-retest coefficient (.72) for 25 subjects over 1 week. Statistical evidence of validity is not available, although the claim is made that respondents attest to face validity.

In the absence of more evidence of reliability and validity, the user should compare the C&RT with The Kirton Adaption-Innovation Inventory (KAI; Kirton, 1976). The KAI is also intended for use with organizational members, but it measures a personality dimension with an "Adaptive" type at one end and an "Innovative" type at the other. This continuum seems generally comparable to combined dimensions of the C&RT with Reproducer and Innovator at the extremes. The KAI measures a simpler construct than the C&RT, but the clear documentation of some of its psychometric characteristics would lead many potential users to prefer it over the C&RT.

Use of the KAI is made somewhat problematic, however, by the fact that at the time of this writing, it was no longer available from a publisher or distributor in the United States or Canada. This situation creates a possible dilemma for potential test users. Either they can request the KAI from its author at the Occupational Research Centre in Hatfield, England, or risk using the C&RT. The deciding factor in favor of the KAI is not that it is necessarily a better measure, but that it is a more thoroughly documented one.

At a minimum, efforts to document psychometric soundness should include descriptive statistics for both scales, scale reliabilities, and evidence of the validity of the matrix construct. Validation might begin with a factor analysis of scale items to demonstrate the distinction between creativity and risk taking, but to be convincing, it should also include correlations of the C&RT scales with other measures.

Overall, the C&RT presents a logical rationale for an inventory with inadequate research support. Currently, the Kirton Adaption-Innovation Inventory is a more thoroughly documented measure of a similar concept. The C&RT is more theoretically sophisticated and more easily accessible than the KAI, but the C&RT is not presented with adequate supportive information.

REVIEWER'S REFERENCE

Kirton, M. J. (1976). Adaptors and innovators: A description and measure. *Journal of Applied Psychology, 61,* 622-629.

[96]
Criterion Validated Written Tests for Clerical Worker.

Purpose: For selection of clerical employees.
Population: Candidates for clerical positions.
Publication Dates: 1984–90.
Scores: 9 scores for 2 equivalent forms: Memorization, Information Ordering, Number Facility, Time-Sharing, Problem Sensitivity, Dealing with People, Deductive Reasoning, Verbal Comprehension, Total.
Administration: Group.
Manual: No manual.
Restricted Distribution: Restricted to Civil Service Commissions, Personnel Directors, City Managers, and other "responsible officials."
Price Data, 1991: Rental and scoring service, $175 for the first 5 candidates; $7.50–$12.50 for each additional candidate ($175 minimum).
Time: 210(230) minutes.
Author: McCann Associates, Inc.
Publisher: McCann Associates, Inc.

[97]
CRS Placement/Diagnostic Test.

Purpose: Designed to diagnose and locate the student's CRS (Crane Reading System) level.
Population: Grades Preprimer–2.
Publication Dates: 1977–78.
Scores: Total score only.
Administration: Group.
Price Data: Price information for test materials including general directions ('77, 7 pages) available from publisher.
Foreign Language Edition: Spanish version available.
Time: Administration time not reported.
Author: Barbara J. Crane.
Publisher: Bilingual Educational Services.

a) ENGLISH VERSION.
1) *Level A.*
Population: Grade Preprimer.
Subtests, 4: Rhyming, Words That Begin Alike, Long Vowel Recognition, Consonant Sounds.
2) *Levels B, C, and D (Beginning Consonant Sounds).*
Population: Preprimer–primer.
Comments: Levels determined by number of errors.
3) *Level E (Blends).*
Population: Grade 1.
4) *Level F (Vowel Recognition).*
Population: Grade 1.
5) *Level G (Digraphs).*
Population: Grade 1.
6) *Levels H, I, and J (Special Vowel Patterns).*
Population: Grades 1–2.
Comments: Levels determined by number of errors.
b) SPANISH VERSION.
1) *Level A.*
Subtests, 2: Rhyming, Words That Begin Alike.
2) *Level B (Beginning Consonant Sounds—S, M, F, R, N, L, Z).*
3) *Level C (Beginning Consonant Sounds—B, P, T, D, V, CH).*
4) *Level D (Beginning Consonant Sounds—C, G, LL, Q, J, Y).*
5) *Level E (Special Patterns).*

[98]
The Custody Quotient.

Purpose: Provides relevant information about the knowledge, attributes, and skills of adults involved in custody disputes.
Population: Parents or other adults seeking access or custody.
Publication Dates: 1987–88.
Acronym: CQ.
Scores, 13: Emotional Needs, Physical Needs, No Dangers, Good Parenting, Parent Assistance, Planning, Home Stability, Prior Caring, Acts/Omissions, Values, Custody Quotient, Joint Custody Quotient, Frankness.
Administration: Individual.
Price Data, 1989: $35 per complete kit including manual ('88, 180 pages) and 5 protocols; $150 per person for training workshop.
Time: Administration time not reported.
Comments: Research edition; ratings by trained examiner based on an interview and observations; orally administered.
Authors: Robert Gordon and Leon A. Peek.
Publisher: The Wilmington Institute.

Review of The Custody Quotient by LISA G. BISCHOFF, Assistant Professor of Educational Psychology, University of Nebraska-Lincoln, Lincoln, NE:

The Custody Quotient (CQ) is a research instrument that is not considered by the authors to be a fully developed psychological technique. Its primary purpose is to provide information relevant to the resolution of child custody disputes. The Custody Quotient provides information regarding parental knowledge and attitudes about parenting, ability to apply concepts and to practice parenting skills, parenting history, personality dynamics that impact upon parenting, and the parent-child relationship. Items included in the CQ are based on research literature in the areas of child psychology and psychiatry, sociology, and child development. Legal statutes and case law were also reviewed in order to assess the propriety of CQ items in child custody cases and attitude and opinion surveys were conducted in order to obtain additional information from parents, children, district judges, and family law specialists. It is important to note that legal statutes and case law in the state of Texas were used in the construction of the CQ. It would be vital for examiners using the CQ to be aware of child custody laws and legal standards in the state in which they practice.

The CQ is a structured interview designed to be administered by a qualified psychological examiner. Respondents may include parents (biological or adoptive) or nonparents (adults related to the child or unrelated adults with substantial past contact with the child). Interview items are rated on a 3-point scale ranging from *highly competent/very competent* to *weak/defective*. Ratings are made based on information obtained by the examiner through a variety of sources. Structured interview with parents, historical information, diagnostic interviews, child interviews, interviews with other relevant individuals (e.g., teachers, babysitters), observations of parent-child relationships, review of documents (e.g., legal records, medical and psychological reports), as well as additional psychological assessment procedures may be used to obtain information pertinent to CQ items. Ratings based only upon information obtained through structured interview with parents should be interpreted with extreme care.

The construct validity of the CQ appears to be sound. The CQ is stated to be a measure of parenting knowledge, attributes, attitudes, skills, and behavior determined by the law to be relevant to custody decisions. "Good parenting" is defined by review of research literature, assessment of parental attitudes, and survey of legal opinions. As the items of the CQ are based directly on research literature and legal standards relevant to the question of parenting and child custody, the CQ is determined to be valid in terms of item and scale content. No information is provided regarding the predictive validity of the CQ at this time. However, the authors are currently involved in conducting validity studies and in developing validity scales for the standard interview.

Reliability information pertaining to the internal consistency and interrater reliability of the CQ is not available at this time. A preliminary study of interrater reliability, based on observations of video-taped interviews, suggests interrater reliability to range from 50% (Good Parenting scale) to 100% (No Dangers scale) for five of the factors. However, the sample for this study was small ($n = 10$) and the authors were included as participants.

Directions for administering and scoring the CQ are contained within the manual. Instructions are presented in a step-by-step format and information concerning assessment of families from minority culture groups is included. Furthermore, gender differences in parenting roles and styles are addressed. Standards for the scoring of individual items, additional information concerning administration of items, and methods of corroborating parental responses are also provided.

The CQ provides a "Custody Quotient" which is expressed as a standard score with a mean of 100 and a standard deviation of 15. Ten subscale scores, a Frankness Scale (FS), and a Joint Custody Quotient (JQ) provide stanine scores. Standard scores are obtained by summing raw score ratings within each of the 12 factors and converting the total raw scores to "stanine type" scores. Stanines are then averaged to yield the CQ summary score. It is important to note that the standard scores and stanines provided by the CQ are based on information obtained through pilot studies and the assumption that parenting attributes are normally distributed within the population. Tables included in the manual are based on pilot studies and should not be considered to be statistical norm tables.

The CQ provides information that can be used to provide recommendations for remediation with parents. The attributes assessed within the CQ are not considered to be static properties of a parent, but rather skills, knowledge, and behavior which may be amenable to change. Recommendations for types of remediation needed range from dynamic psychotherapy to parent training to directed reading. The basis for remediation recommendations is not detailed in the manual.

In summary, the CQ is a research instrument designed to assist in the determination of child custody disputes. This instrument should be administered and interpreted only by qualified examiners and should not be considered to be a fully developed psychological instrument. The CQ appears to be valid in terms of the construct of "good parenting" and in terms of item and scale content. No predictive validity and scant reliability data are available at the present time. The CQ provides a format for gathering and interpreting information provided by a variety of sources. It would be a useful tool for professionals involved in the determination of child custody disputes. However, professionals using the CQ in practice should continue to consider all sources of information carefully and not to rely upon scores in determining custody issues.

[99]
Customer Reaction Survey.

Purpose: Assesses customers' perceptions of salespeople's interpersonal skills.
Population: Salespeople.
Publication Date: 1972–79.
Acronym: CRS.
Scores, 4: Observed Exposure, Observed Feedback, Preferred Exposure, Preferred Feedback.
Administration: Group.
Price Data, 1990: $5.95 per test, including score interpretation guide ('79, 4 pages).
Time: Administration time not reported.
Comments: Ratings by customers; also called Customer Reaction Index; based on the Johari Window Model of interpersonal relations.
Authors: Jay Hall and C. Leo Griffith.
Publisher: Teleometrics International.

[100]
DABERON-2: Screening for School Readiness.

Purpose: Developed to "identify . . . students who may not be ready to enter formal academic instruction."
Population: Ages 3-0 to 7-11.
Publication Dates: 1972–91.
Scores: Total score only.
Administration: Individual.
Price Data, 1990: $79 per complete kit including 24 presentation cards, 25 screen forms, 25 readiness reports, 5 classroom summary forms, object kit of manipulatives, and manual ('91, 38 pages); $5 per set of presentation cards; $14 per 25 screen forms; $14 per 25 readiness reports; $5 per 5 classroom summary forms; $23 per object kit of manipulatives; $24 per manual.
Time: (20–40) minutes.
Authors: Virginia A. Danzer, Mary Frances Gerber, Theresa M. Lyons, and Judith K. Voress.
Publisher: PRO-ED, Inc.

TEST REFERENCES

1. Stoner, S., & Purcell, K. (1985). The concurrent validity of teachers' judgments of the abilities of preschoolers in a daycare setting. *Educational and Psychological Measurement, 45,* 421-423.

Review of the DABERON-2: Screening for School Readiness by STEPHEN N. AXFORD, Faculty Member, University of Phoenix, Colorado Campus, Aurora, CO, and School Psychologist, Academy District Twenty, Colorado Springs, CO:

According to its authors, the DABERON-2 is a screening instrument designed to assess school readiness and student strengths and weaknesses, and to monitor student progress. Cautioning the user about the limitations of screening instruments, the authors provide helpful guidelines for interpreting and using the DABERON-2. The authors acknowledge that "inaccurate responses" or relatively deficient performances may indicate the need for "further diagnostic and prognostic study" (p. 2., Examiner's Manual). Nevertheless, in stating the DABERON-2 is to be used in identifying children "who may not be ready to enter formal academic instruction" (p. 2, Examiner's Manual)—meaning

children entering preschool, prekindergarten, and kindergarten—it is clear that the instrument is to be used primarily as a "selection" tool for entrance into educational programs, not as a screening test as the name of the instrument suggests. Given the gravity of this issue, the standard to which the DABERON-2 should be compared is high relative to "screening" instruments used primarily for providing direction for further assessment.

Although referred to as a "screening tool," the apparent primary purpose of the DABERON-2 is similar to that of other school readiness tests (e.g., Developmental Indicators for the Assessment of Learning—Revised [DIAL-R; 10:89]) and aptitude tests (e.g., Cognitive Abilities Test [CogAT; 10:66], ACT Assessment Program [9:43], College Board Scholastic Aptitude Test [SAT; 9:244], Graduate Record Examinations [GRE; 9:448]) used at higher educational levels for selection into academic programs. Specifically, this relates to issues of promotion and program qualification. The authors are correct in specifying the interpretive limitations of the DABERON-2, for which they should be commended. Nevertheless, use of the term "screening" and qualifying statements do not preclude the potential implications, good or bad, DABERON-2 test results might have on children's academic futures.

Regarding the authors' second stated purpose for the DABERON-2, identifying student strengths and weaknesses, the claim is made that the instrument may be used to identify "apparent delays in development" and "learning problems" (p. 2, Examiner's Manual). As identified by the authors, general areas assessed include: Body Parts, Color Concepts, Number Concepts, Prepositions, Following Directions, Plurals, General Knowledge, Visual Perception, Gross Motor Development, and Categories.

From a cognitive developmental perspective, task analysis of the DABERON-2 items by this reviewer indicated assessment of the following skills: position concepts and directionality, receptive and expressive vocabulary, functional relations (i.e., comprehension of cause-and-effect relationships), one-to-one correspondence, the identity principle (i.e., notion of sameness), a rudimentary sense of number and quantity, ordering, a rudimentary sense of classification, and motor integration involving verbal direction. The level of development characteristic of these skills is what cognitive developmentalists refer to as "preoperations" (Elkind, 1981; Furth, 1970; Ginsburg & Opper, 1979; Kegan, 1982; Piaget, 1967).

The major characteristics of preoperations (approximately ages 2 to 5 years) include: representational thought (i.e., language, symbolic play, deferred imitation); centration (tendency to focus attention on one feature of a situation to the exclusion of others); understanding of the "identity principle" (notion of sameness); categorization skill (assignment of objects to single classes); a lack of a stable classification system (is not able to simultaneously consider the particular or subclasses and the general or supersets); syncretism (tendency to connect a series of separate but not necessarily meaningfully related ideas); and juxtaposition or the failure to fully comprehend relations between events, even with ordered relations (e.g., counting as this relates to quantity).

The DABERON-2 appears designed to measure early- to late-preoperational skills, which is appropriate for a kindergarten screening instrument. The instrument does not measure more advanced classification and quantitative reasoning skills characteristic of higher developed kindergarten-aged students. Thus, the range of development measured by the DABERON-2 is somewhat limited given its stated purposes. Although this range is indeed probably sufficient for screening, it is questionable as to whether it is sufficient for monitoring student progress at the kindergarten level, except for slower developing students. For higher functioning kindergarten students (if statistical discrimination is needed), additional items should be added measuring comprehension of the inverse operation (notion that something changed can be returned to its original state by reversing the action), transitive seriation (e.g., if $a > b$, & $b > c$, then $a > c$), multiple classification, and conservation of quantitative relations (i.e., number, length, volume, area, mass).

Regarding item construction, it is apparent that the DABERON-2 developers exercised care. Nevertheless, the essentially dichotomous (right/wrong) scoring system is somewhat inconsistent with the authors' claim that the instrument is designed to measure development, as a more qualitative scoring system sensitive to gradations/transitions in development is psychometrically preferable, as such an approach considers the critical issue of answer rationales.

The authors indicate that items were carefully constructed to avoid ambiguity. The authors note "few qualitative judgements are required in scoring; responses, in most cases, are obviously right or wrong" (p. 5, Examiner's Manual). Certainly, such an approach offers advantages in terms of training and ease of scoring. However, such an approach also provides less diagnostic utility in terms of inferring thought processes, a critical aspect in any cognitive developmental assessment.

Another concern, with regard to the developmental assessment issue, is that the authors provide no detailed discussion of theoretical rationale underlying item development. This seems to be a common problem with early childhood developmental measures. Despite the absence of theoretical rationale, examination of test content indicates the authors

nevertheless were reasonably careful about item construction and content. Overall, the instrument content is consistent with current theoretical understanding of early childhood development.

Regarding its technical aspects, the DABERON-2 is commendable. Percentiles, age equivalent scores, and standard scores (mean $= 100$, $SD = 15$) are provided, with clear descriptions and interpretive guidelines for each. The standardization sample ($n = 1,647$) is adequate with reasonable demographic representation. Reliability of the DABERON-2 (homogeneity or internal consistency) is good. The authors report that Cronbach's coefficients alpha were computed by age (3, 4, 5, 6, and 7 years), with all values exceeding .80 and four of the five coefficients exceeding .90. In addition, the standard errors of measurements by age are quite adequate, being comparable to those representing individual intellectual batteries such as the Wechsler series. This provides further evidence of the instrument's reliability.

Concurrent validity for the DABERON-2 was established by correlating the instrument with the Metropolitan Readiness Tests. A total battery Pearson product moment correlation of .83 ($p < .05$) is reported, which is quite adequate.

Predictive validity for the DABERON-2 was established by correlating 1979–1980 kindergarten-aged standardization subjects' DABERON-2 scores with follow-up behavior checklist ratings involving 15 "experts." A correlation of .84 ($p < .001$) is reported.

Regarding construct validity, the authors researched: (a) the relationship between DABERON-2 subtest scores and chronological age, assuming the instrument measures development; (b) the relationship between DABERON-2 scores and aptitude, assuming early achievement as measured by the DABERON-2 is related to the child's intellectual skills; (c) cluster intercorrelations, assuming the DABERON-2 subtests measure readiness skills; and (d) item validity, assuming the DABERON-2 items measure similar traits.

Regarding the "developmental" construct, examination of group means for ages 3, 4, 5, 6, and 7 years indicates a consistent increase, thus supporting the hypothesis. Also of note, however, is a consistent decrease in standard deviations across younger to older groups (standard deviations of 20.5, 15.2, 11.2, 7.6, and 3.3, respectively). This result should be expected, as with increased maturation more students would be expected to answer correctly the test items, as they have limited range of difficulty (i.e., early to late preoperational). This relates to the earlier noted problem of the likelihood that many kindergarten-aged subjects would be at late preoperational to transitional-into-early-concrete operational levels of development. In short, older and more mature students may quickly "ceiling out" when assessed by the DABERON-2. This should not be a problem when the test is used for selection purposes. However, as discussed earlier, it may pose a problem when using the instrument to monitor progress of more mature students. Again, addition of developmentally more advanced items may alleviate this problem.

In researching the "relationship to aptitude" hypothesis, DABERON-2 scores for 27 children were correlated with the children's subtest performances on the Detroit Tests of Learning Aptitude—Primary. Correlations ranged from .49 to .69. All correlations were significant beyond the .05 level of confidence.

Regarding cluster intercorrelations, coefficients range from .16 to .68, according to Table 46 of the Examiner's Manual (p. 25). An apparent error in the text (p. 24, Examiner's Manual) states that all the cluster intercorrelations "exceed .30 and are statistically significant beyond the .01 level." Correspondence by this reviewer with a PRO-ED, Inc. (publisher of the DABERON-2) representative verified the accuracy of the reported intercorrelations in the table and the statistical significance of the coefficients at the .01 level. The observed statistical significance is not surprising (and perhaps should be expected) given the relatively large sample size. More importantly, the higher intercorrelations reported are what would be expected theoretically, thus supporting the validity of the DABERON-2.

Regarding item validity, median item discriminating powers for ages 3, 4, 5, 6, and 7 years are: .41, .34, .33, .29, and .25, respectively. The magnitudes of these discriminating powers provide support for the construct validity of the DABERON-2. However, the apparent trend of diminishing values also suggests that discrimination power decreases as the subjects mature, supporting earlier concerns regarding a ceiling effect and the need for adding developmentally higher level items.

Overall, the DABERON-2 appears to be among the better screening instruments for school readiness. It compares favorably to other such instruments such as, for example, the Developmental Indicators for the Assessment of Learning—Revised (DIAL-R; Mardell-Czudnowski & Goldenberg, 1983; 10:89). Psychometrically, the DABERON-2 is quite adequate. In addition, the Examiner's Manual, Screen Form (protocol sheet), and Report on Readiness (test results summary for parents) are very well constructed. However, further explanation by the authors of theoretical foundation is needed. Also, any subsequent revision should include developmentally higher level items if the instrument is to continue to be used for monitoring academic progress. Nevertheless, the DABERON-2 represents an improvement over many instruments currently in use for early childhood educational screening.

REVIEWER'S REFERENCES
Piaget, J. (1967). *Six psychological studies* (A. Tenzer, Trans.). New York: Random House.
Furth, H. G. (1970). *Piaget for teachers*. Englewood Cliffs, NJ: Prentice-Hall.
Ginsburg, H., & Opper, S. (1979). *Piaget's theory of intellectual development* (2nd ed.). Englewood Cliffs, NJ: Prentice-Hall.
Elkind, D. (1981). *The hurried child: Growing up too fast too soon.* Reading, MA: Addison-Wesley Publishing Company.
Kegan, R. (1982). *The evolving self: Problem and process in human development.* Cambridge: Harvard University Press.
Mardell-Czudnowski, C. D., & Goldenberg, D. S. (1983). *Developmental Indicators for the Assessment of Learning—Revised (DIAL-R) Manual.* Edison, NJ: Childcraft Education Corp.

Review of the DABERON-2: Screening for School Readiness by SELMA HUGHES, Professor of Psychology and Special Education, East Texas State University, Commerce, TX:

The DABERON-2 is a 1991 revision of the original test published in 1972. It provides a standardized assessment for the screening of preschool children ages 4 through 6. It takes 20–40 minutes to administer and is intended for use with presumably normal children to determine if they are ready to begin formal instruction.

The kit is comprehensive, contains everything needed to give the test, and is easy to handle. The 122 items have not changed from the original test but the normative data have been revised.

The Examiner's Manual outlines examiner qualifications. These seem appropriate because the test requires minimal knowledge of psychological appraisal or child development. As with the original test the items are scored "right" (R), "wrong" (W), "no response" (N), or "inappropriate" (I). The category I is intended to provide valuable clinical information on the types of errors the child makes. Use of the I category may also be an indication of the ambiguity of the scoring on some of the items where a specific answer is required more so than a thoughtful answer which may not meet the criteria for correctness.

There is a good technical discussion of item development and analysis. Much effort has been made to justify the statistical soundness of the items included. Although the items may satisfy the statistical criteria cited, they represent a very limited range of skills. There is considerable emphasis on knowledge of letters, numbers, colors, and shapes, and little emphasis on language and cognition skills.

The first edition of the test was criticized by Kelble (1986) for its overemphasis on motor and social development to the detriment of cognitive development. Her criticism still applies. The DABERON-2 is not as well designed as the Screening Children for Related Early Educational Needs (SCREEN; Hresko, Reid, Hammill, Ginsburg, & Baroody, 1988; 346). The SCREEN is an individually administered screening test, relatively simple to administer, score, and interpret. The construction of the tasks and the wording of the items are carefully done. The SCREEN is more interesting than the DABERON-2 and may, therefore, be more motivating for students.

TECHNICAL ASPECTS. The DABERON-2 was standardized on a stratified sample of 1,647 children in 16 states. Data are provided indicating the sample is representative of the U.S. population relative to age, sex, place of residence, geographic region, family income, and ethnicity.

The raw score obtained from the 122 items is converted to an age equivalent score (which the manual suggests should be used with caution), to percentile ranks, and a standard score or quotient (e.g., <70 very poor; 70–79 poor, etc.). Kelble (1986) and this reviewer feel this categorization influences attitudes towards the child whatever cautions we take to ensure that such negative attitudes do not form.

Good measures of internal reliability or consistency are reported for the test. Coefficients alpha were computed by age for the sample and four of the five coefficients exceeded .90. This indicates that the test is a homogeneous instrument.

Validity (i.e., the extent to which a test measures what it says it measures) must be derived from studies done on the DABERON because the items have not been changed on the current version of the test. The first edition of the test was found to correlate positively and adequately (.83, $p < .05$) with the Metropolitan Readiness Tests (Nurss & McGauvran, 1976). These tests have been revised so current coefficients are difficult to extrapolate. The predictive validity was confirmed by correlating the DABERON with an independent behavioral checklist completed on some of the standardization sample children during their kindergarten year. The result was again positive and adequate (.84, $p < .001$) in relation to the first edition.

What is still somewhat nebulous is the validity of the constructs underlying the screening instrument. The fourth author makes a good attempt at satisfying the criteria suggested by Hammill, Brown, and Bryant (1989). She identifies four testable questions related to the DABERON-2; whether the test measures skills that progress over time, which it does; whether the clusters of items correlate with one another, which they do; and correlate with the total score, which they do. The fourth question is whether the DABERON-2 correlates with a measure of general aptitude and is a measure of cognitive ability. Here the author demonstrates the weakness of the test which was pointed out earlier. The DABERON-2 is not a good measure of cognitive functioning and shows low correlation (around .60) on the average with the Detroit Tests of Learning Aptitude—Primary (DTLA-P).

SUMMARY. The DABERON-2 is a standardized, easily administered and scored measure of at least some generally acknowledged aspects of preschool development. The usefulness of the test needs to be balanced against the limited nature of the abilities tested and the questionable validity of the test. Nevertheless, the test may be helpful for those who need baseline information to assist in the individualization of the curriculum for a young child.

REVIEWER'S REFERENCES
Kelble, E. S. (1986). DABERON Screening for School Readiness. In D. J. Keyser & R. C. Sweetland (Eds.), *Test critiques: Vol. V* (pp. 86-89). Kansas City, MO: Test Corporation of America.
Nurss, J. R., & McGauvran, M. E. (1986). Metropolitan Readiness Tests. San Antonio, TX: The Psychological Corporation.
Hresko, W. P., Reid, D. K., Hammill, D. D., Ginsberg, H., & Baroody, A. J. (1988). Screening Children for Related Early Educational Needs. Austin, TX: PRO-ED, Inc.
Hammill, D. D., Brown, L., & Bryant, B. R. (1989). *A consumer's guide to tests in print.* Austin, TX. PRO-ED, Inc.

[101]
Daily Stress Inventory.

Purpose: Constructed to measure "the number and relative impact of common minor stressors frequently experienced in everyday life."
Population: Ages 18 and over.
Publication Dates: 1988–89.
Acronym: DSI.
Scores, 3: Event, Impact, I/E Ratio.
Administration: Group or individual.
Price Data: Available from publisher.
Time: Administration time not reported.
Authors: Phillip J. Brantley and Glenn N. Jones (manual).
Publisher: Psychological Assessment Resources, Inc.

Review of the Daily Stress Inventory by STEVEN C. HAYES, Professor of Psychology and Director of Clinical Training, University of Nevada, Reno, NV:

The Daily Stress Inventory is a 58-item occurrence and rating inventory that asks clients to indicate each day the number of minor, annoying events that occurred, and to rate their impact on a 7-point scale from "occurred but was not stressful" (rating of 1) to "caused some stress" (rating of 4) to "caused me to panic" (rating of 7). As is the case within similar inventories developed within this wing of behavioral assessment, the items have high face validity. Professionals' perception of the value of the instrument would probably depend heavily on their perception of the sensibility of the items themselves. The items are explicitly minor, daily items, a strength for those wishing clients to rate items of this kind. The inventory yields scores for frequency of occurrence, overall impact (the sum of stress ratings, this score is sensitive to occurrence and rated stress per se), and the amount of rated stress per occurrence. Items are logically organized into "clusters" but the developers caution that these clusters should not be used diagnostically, presumably because they are not factors or clusters in a statistical sense.

Seventy-one items were originally developed from diaries kept by graduate students, clinic patients, and community volunteers (the mix is not specified). These 71 items were rated for a period of time (not specified) by 418 people, 61% undergraduate students. Five items occurred in less than 15% of the sample, but three were retained anyway because they seemed to be nonstudent items. Eleven items were eliminated because they did not correlate well with rated stress for the overall items. The original pool of items seems unfortunately small, especially given possible unrepresentativeness of the population.

The original normalization was on 473 southern nonstudent adults, although how they were recruited is not described. Other normalization samples have been used, including college students and medical patients. Some of the patterns seen there seem strange. For example, the average impact score is 51 for college students, but only 20 for medical patients. Some of these patients had very severe diseases. A similar pattern is shown for the frequency of occurrence of items. This pattern could be due to the student-oriented item selection procedure— perhaps these items occur more often to students.

It is always difficult to interpret certain kinds of reliability with these kinds of inventories. Why, for example, would a person who "spoke or performed in public" be more likely also to have "had car trouble"? Nevertheless, the internal consistency even of the frequency of occurrence of items is above .80 (alpha coefficient). This may in part be due to subjective reactions included in the items themselves (see below). Test-retest reliability showed a more complex picture, with day-to-day stability that was high for mere occurrence and low for rated impact, and week-to-week stability that was low for occurrence and high for impact.

The inventory has shown moderate validity in its correlation with various anxiety and stress scales and biochemical indicants of stress. In general, impact scores (the sum of rated stress) correlate more highly than mere occurrence. The number of validity studies is still fairly limited, as might be expected with a relatively new inventory.

The scale does not correlate with the Marlow-Crowne (few do), but no correlation is reported with the Edwards Social Desirability (ESD) scale, with which many scales correlate highly. Given its pattern of correlation with other scales, a correlation with the ESD seems likely.

The method of item collection seems basically sound, although with limitations caused by the population used. The items themselves are the major strength of the inventory, especially if a college-oriented sample does not present a problem. The editing of the wording of the items and the rating scale selected seems more questionable for the following reasons:

1. The DSI asks clients not only to indicate the amount of perceived "stress," but also asks the client to infer causality. Some clients may have noticed that the felt stress was associated with a given event, but may have interpreted its cause differently (e.g., "I felt stress when the bus was late but I know it was really due to that argument I had with my wife"). It would have been better to ask for less interpretation on the part of the client (e.g., how much felt stress was *associated*, or *followed* a given event).

2. The 7-point rating scale itself uses the term "stress" without definition or clarification. Stress is already a highly interpreted and metaphorical concept, and the professional literature has a difficult time agreeing what it means. Perhaps for this reason, the authors included the word "stress" itself in the rating scale (it makes it hard to disagree that this inventory measures "stress" whatever you might take "stress" to mean). The end result, however, is that responsibility for the meaning of the concept actually measured by the instrument is, in a sense, moved from the authors to the respondents. Someone may reasonably view "stress" to mean muscle tension, whereas someone else may interpret it to mean annoyance, and so on.

3. The seventh item on the rating scale is "caused me to panic." Panic and stress seem to be different concepts, and the authors are not presenting the instrument merely as an anxiety inventory. The presence of this item as an end point, however, probably causes clients to define stress to mean anxiety. This interpretation is strengthened by a moderately large correlation between impact scores and the State-Trait Anxiety Inventory (STAI).

4. The authors define stress as the subjectively perceived impact of minor daily annoying events. This definition, however, puts subjective reactions both into the events ("annoying events") and into further reactions to the reacted to events ("stress"). Perhaps as a consequence, several of the items to be rated include anxiety-laden terms in their description such as "upsetting," "discomfort," "problems," "concern," "fear," or "worry." For example, one item asks if subjects were "Worried about another's problems" and another asks if clients were "exposed to upsetting TV shows." It is hard to image "upsetting" events that are not aversive and at least in that sense the mere occurrence of the item seems by definition stressful.

Overall, the DSI seems to be a reasonable collection of minor, annoying items useful for daily stress ratings. However, normalization populations are limited, and the inventory may be fairly student oriented due to its means of development. The rating scale descriptions used seem unfortunate and somewhat ambiguous.

Review of the Daily Stress Inventory by BERT W. WESTBROOK, Professor of Psychology, and

THOMAS E. POWELL, Doctoral Candidate, Department of Psychology, North Carolina State University, Raleigh, NC:

The Daily Stress Inventory (DSI) was designed to measure "the number and relative impact of common minor stressors frequently experienced in everyday life" (Manual, p. 1). Its recommended uses include: (*a*) A measure for assessing the frequency and impact of daily stressors, facilitating assessment and treatment planning for clinicians who treat individuals with stress-related disorders and complaints; (*b*) A method of monitoring and evaluating the outcome of treatment interventions aimed at ameliorating the adverse impact of stressors; and (*c*) A sensitive measure of stress that can be administered frequently to assist in explicating the relation between stress and its biological, psychological, and social correlates.

The DSI is described as "unique" because "it provides a current measure of stress over a 24-hour period and can be administered serially over several days or weeks" (p. 1).

The DSI purports to measure the following dimensions: Interpersonal Problems (e.g., Was interrupted while talking), Personal Competency (e.g., Performed poorly at task), Cognitive Stressors (e.g., Heard some bad news), Environmental Hassles (e.g., Your property was damaged), and Varied Stressors (e.g., Someone spoiled your completed task).

The DSI can be administered over three different time periods: (*a*) once in a single day, (*b*) daily for 1 week, or (*c*) daily for multiple weeks. "One-week or multiweek administration is recommended to provide an adequate sample of clinical data. One-day administration procedures are primarily for use in research or clinical situations that do not permit longer periods of data collection" (p. 5). Administration suggestions include that the administrator should "discuss the nature and importance of the task" (p. 5) with the respondent immediately before administration to establish rapport and enlist full cooperation. It is not clear why the test administrator is directed to complete the information requested on the front of the Rating Booklet, such as the respondent's name, sex, age, occupation, education, rating period, and rating time. This information can be provided by the respondent. The procedures for administration, including directions for completing the ratings, recording the dates of the days to be rated, the rating scale values and anchors, and the format for rating each item on each day of the rating period are clear. Selecting a consistent time in the evening—preferably just before retiring—for completing the ratings is considered to be an important aspect of correct administration.

The 1-day administration procedures are simple and straightforward because only one set of ratings is obtained from the respondent. The 1-week administration procedures are more involved because the respondent takes the Rating Booklet with him/her and must take responsibility for rating himself/herself *at the same time each day* and recording each day's ratings in the appropriate column. A minimum of 6 days of ratings is required to permit calculation of weekly summary data. Basically, the DSI is self-administering if the respondent has been given the general instructions and if subsequent administrations are monitored.

The multiweek administration procedures are similar to the 1-week administration procedures except that a new Rating Booklet will be issued for each successive week to be rated. The completed Rating Booklet should be returned before a new Rating Booklet is issued.

The DSI is hand scored. The directions for scoring are clear and complete. The raw score calculations are simple: Count the number of items that are rated to get an Event score; sum the item ratings to get an Impact score; and divide the Impact score by the Event score to get an I/E Ratio score. Using the table of normative data for adults, college students, or medical patients (pp. 22–27), the three raw scores (for Event, Impact, and I/E Ratio) can be converted to T scores and percentiles; and they can be recorded on a Scoring Grid provided on the fourth page of the Rating Booklet.

The DSI items were generated by the author(s). First, graduate students ($N = 85$), community volunteers, and clients at a university psychology clinic were recruited and asked to keep a diary of stressful events. "After 2 weeks, the diaries were collected and examined for recurring similar events. An item was then written for every event that had appeared in at least one of the diaries." A total of 71 items were generated and constituted the initial item pool of the DSI (Brantley, 1980/1981). The 71-item form was then administered to a pilot sample of 254 undergraduates and 164 noncollegiate adults from the local community (Brantley, Waggoner, Jones, & Rappaport, 1987). Item analysis statistics were used to determine which items would be retained, but the data are not presented in the manual. Apparently, an item was retained if it was endorsed as having occurred by 15% of the sample and correlated .30 or greater with Impact scores. A total of 58 items were retained and constitute the final version of the DSI. This final version was then administered to 433 adults "recruited from within the local community," but there is no evidence of an item analysis for the final version with the 433 adults sample.

The items are statements of stressful events such as "Was embarrassed," "Experienced money problems," "Had car trouble," etc. The respondent is instructed to read the statements and if an event occurred in the past 24 hours, rate how stressful it was. If the event did not occur during the past 24 hours, the respondent does not make a rating. For each event that occurred, respondents assign a rating of 1 to 7 as follows: 1 = occurred but was not stressful; 2 = caused very little stress; 3 = caused a little stress; 4 = caused some stress; 5 = caused much stress; 6 = caused very much stress; 7 = caused me to panic.

Normative data were collected from 473 adults whose occupation was "other than full-time students in a community surrounding a large state university in the southeastern United States." A table showing the demographic breakdown by sex, race, marital status, education, and occupational status for the normative sample is in the manual. Compared to the general population, the sample appears to have more females (67%), fewer nonwhites (17%), and more college educated individuals (47%). Ages ranged from 18 to 72 years with a mean of 33.4 and a S.D. of 12.2. To provide descriptive statistics for the normative sample of 473 adults, DSI data were collected for 7 consecutive days and comprise the data base from which T scores and percentile scores were derived. Means, standard deviations, ranges of scores, normalized T scores, and percentiles for daily and weekly DSI scores are available. Gender differences were found only in Impact/Event Ratio weekly scores. No significant race differences were found for any of the DSI scores. Correlations between age and DSI scores were found to be very low (-.03 to -.13). Because the above analyses found little or no difference in DSI scores associated with gender, race, and age, all data were combined and the normative tables are based on the entire sample of adults.

A college normative sample was composed of 252 students enrolled in undergraduate psychology classes at a large southeastern university. A table showing the means, standard deviations, ranges of scores, normalized T scores, and percentiles is presented for the college sample.

The third norm group was a sample of medical patients ($N = 223$). These were adults living in two metropolitan areas in the southeastern portion of the United States. All subjects were volunteers for research studies. The medical disorders were asthma, Crohn's disease, chronic renal failure, angina, and headaches.

T scores and percentiles for daily and weekly Event, Impact, and I/E Ratio raw scores are provided. The possible range of Impact raw scores is from 0 to 406. An Impact raw score of 90 would be a percentile of 95 for adults, a percentile of 88 for college students, and a percentile of 98 for medical patients. An Impact raw score of 5 would be a percentile of 10 for adults, a percentile score of 2 for college students, and a percentile of 25 for medical

patients. The DSI comprises 58 items, so the maximum Event score is 58. If an adult rated only 11 of the 58 statements (meaning he or she had had 11 experiences in the last 24 hours), the score would be at the 50th percentile. For a college student, an Event score of 16 is the 49th percentile. On the average the typical college student in the normative sample experienced five more events than the typical adult in the normative sample.

Under the heading, Concurrent Validity, the authors cite the Brantley et al. (1987) study with the 418 pilot sample subjects (254 undergraduate plus 164 noncollegiate adults) mentioned earlier. They correlated scores on the DSI with global ratings of daily stress (GR scale), "a 10-point Likert-type rating scale that requests subjects to rate the daily experience of stress on a scale of 0 (No stress) to 10 (The most stressful day I have had)." Correlations of GR scale ratings with Event, Impact, and I/E Ratio scores were .13, .35, and .49, respectively. All correlations were statistically significant.

Using a sample of 35 adults who participated in a 28-day study on headaches, Brantley et al. (1987) found significant correlations of .07, .40, and .25 between GR ratings and DSI Event, Impact, and I/E Ratio scores.

In another study reported in the manual, Brantley, Dietz, McKnight, Jones, and Tulby (1988) found that significantly higher levels of biochemical stress indices were associated with the presences of high scores on the DSI. Time-series analyses of the data suggested a "positive association between psychological stress and biochemical stress indices."

Under the heading, Convergent and Discriminant Validity, the manual cites the Brantley et al. (1987) study as a "multitrait-monomethod approach for gathering evidence for the validity of the DSI" (p. 15). The study does not meet the criteria of a multitrait-multimethod design because the authors did not include clearly different traits. Although the study involved inventories with different names, the authors did not provide the rationale for their theoretical expectation. These hypotheses were that stress should have (a) most in common with the construct measured by the Hassles Scale; (b) less in common with state anxiety, and (c) least in common with state hostility and whatever constructs are measured by the Uplifts Scale. It is not clear why DSI scores would be expected to correlate substantially with state anxiety scores and Hassles scores, but not with state hostility and Uplifts scores.

A series of studies are reported in the manual to establish Construct Validity. For example, Brantley, Cocke, Jones, and Goreczny (1988) found differences between weekdays and weekends Event, Impact, and I/E Ratio scores. Although it is not clear if these differences are statistically significant, the authors suggest they are "consistent with prior expectations of reduced stress during the weekends for the average person" (p. 16). Goreczny, Brantley, Buss, and Waters (1988) reported that scores on the DSI were related to daily functions in the physical symptoms associated with asthma and chronic obstructive pulmonary disease. A similar study by Nathan, Brantley, Goreczny, and Jones (1988) found that daily asthma symptoms were significantly related to scores on the DSI. Garrett, Brantley, Jones, and McKnight (1988) found a relationship between DSI scores and the presence of Crohn's disease symptoms. Rubman, Brantley, and Jones' (1988) subjects reported poorer quality of sleep on high-stress days. The last study (Everett, 1989) summarized in the manual "revealed that subjects endorsed significantly more depressive and physical symptoms on high-stress than on low-stress days" (p. 17).

The manual summarizes a *test-taking response style* study (Brantley, Waggoner, McAnulty, Rappaport, & Jones, 1987) that the authors interpret as suggesting that "DSI scores may be influenced by the response styles reflected in the MMPI *F* and *K* scales," "individuals who appear open and more self-disclosing tend to obtain higher DSI scores" (p. 17), and finally that DSI Event and Impact scores were not significantly correlated with a measure of social desirability.

Little evidence is offered to support the validity of the content clusters. Judges were asked to sort the 58 items into "meaningful groups" and to provide category names after completing the sorting task. Categories were examined for similar themes and were given the six names that are presented earlier in this review. Why the authors did not carry out a factor analysis is unclear. Hence, there is no statistical support for the content clusters.

Internal consistency reliability (alpha) coefficients were obtained for 433 subjects in the adult sample. The coefficients were .83 for Event and .87 for Impact. Coefficients of stability were obtained "from 35 adults in the local community who were participants in a 28-day research study on headache pain." The average test-retest reliability coefficient over the four 1-week periods was .28 for Event and .89 for Impact. These results suggest that *frequency* of minor stressful events (Event scores) is moderately stable within short periods but variable from week to week. In contrast, the *perceived impact* of minor life events (Impact scores) is variable from day to day but quite stable when examining scores derived from 7 consecutive days of ratings. The authors suggest that daily Impact ratings represent state measures of stress whereas weekly Impact scores are more similar to trait measures.

For the most part, the technical manual is complete, accurate, and clear, and it provides important information regarding the appropriateness

and technical adequacy of the test. The intent of the *Standards for Educational and Psychological Testing* (AERA, APA, & NCME, 1985) seems to have been clearly satisfied by the test authors and the test publisher. The DSI has potential for useful applications in research and clinical practice.

Despite its promise, there are concerns: Statistical data are not presented to support the assignment of items to content clusters and to support the independence of the content clusters. Item-total statistics are not reported in the manual. The adult normative sample may not be representative of the adult population. Most of the validity data presented in the manual are summaries of studies carried out by the authors themselves and reported earlier in various journals. The kind of statistical data called for earlier should be included or summarized in the technical manual. Additional and more representative adult normative data must be collected. More research is needed to determine the DSI's value as an assessment instrument, as a method of monitoring and evaluating the outcome of treatment interventions, and as a measure that can explicate the relation between stress and life's circumstances.

REVIEWER'S REFERENCE

American Educational Research Association, American Psychological Association, & National Council on Measurement in Education. (1985). *Standards for educational and psychological testing.* Washington, DC: American Psychological Association, Inc.

[102]
Dallas Pre-School Screening Test.

Purpose: "Designed to screen the primary learning areas for children from three to six years of age."
Population: Ages 3–6.
Publication Date: 1972.
Scores, 6: Psychological, Auditory, Visual, Language, Motor, Articulation Development (optional).
Administration: Individual.
Price Data, 1987: $27.50 per 25 pupil record forms, stimuli book, and manual (42 pages).
Time: (15–20) minutes.
Authors: Robert R. Percival and Suzanne C. Poxon (stimuli book).
Publisher: Dallas Educational Services.

Review of the Dallas Pre-School Screening Test by JAMES E. YSSELDYKE, *Professor of Educational Psychology, University of Minnesota, Minneapolis, MN:*

The Dallas Pre-School Screening Test (DPST) was developed by a school psychologist and a speech therapist to eliminate excessive and unnecessary testing of small children, and to screen weaknesses and strengths in learning areas. The test falls very short of meeting even minimal criteria specified in *Standards for Educational and Psychological Testing* (AERA, APA, & NCME, 1985).

There are six subtests in the DPST: Psychological, Auditory, Visual, Motor, Language, and Articulation Development. These are not described adequately enough for the reader to decide what they are intended to assess. The author claims these are the major areas of learning for preschool children, but offers no evidence to support his conclusions. There is a list of references in the manual, but these are not cited in the text of the manual. Children who take this test are graded successful or unsuccessful in each of the areas relative to "expected normal development." Expected normal development is not defined.

The manual for the DPST is in need of a good editor. There are many spelling, grammatical, and typographical errors. Some of the sections are just incomprehensible. The test stimuli are clear, though crudely drawn.

The DPST was standardized on a random sample of approximately 3,000 children in a single community (Richardson, Texas). The authors describe the community as "above average in education, social and financial status." The authors do not specify the demographics of the standardization population, though they do say that at least half the population tested was enrolled in private schools. They report that "approximately one hundred black children were evaluated."

Evidence for the technical adequacy of this scale is very poorly presented in the manual, and the evidence presented looks inadequate and inappropriate. The concepts of standardization and standardized scores are confused. Procedures for establishing reliability were incorrect and inadequate. Evidence for validity is based on correlations of performance of an unspecified sample on this test (or parts of it) and the Columbia Mental Maturity Scale (more than likely an old edition, because the scales were both published in 1972), the motor subtest of the Detroit Tests of Learning Aptitude (old edition), and the Draw-A-Man Test. There is little here to suggest the scale is reliable and valid.

The DPST is a very dated scale that falls far short of criteria necessary for a good test.

REVIEWER'S REFERENCE

American Educational Research Association, American Psychological Association, & National Council on Measurement in Education. (1985). *Standards for educational and psychological testing.* Washington, DC: American Psychological Association, Inc.

[103]

DANTES Subject Standardized Tests.

Purpose: Gives "colleges and universities the opportunity . . . to offer civilian students credit for education acquired in nontraditional environments."

Population: College students wishing to earn credit by examination.

Publication Dates: 1983–90.

Acronym: DANTES.

Administration: Group.

Parts: 49 tests in 7 areas.

Price Data, 1987: $25 for each test administered by the institution which may set its own fee to students; scoring by publisher included in price.

Time: Untimed, requiring approximately (90) minutes per test.

Comments: Originally available only to military personnel through Defense Activity for Non-Traditional Education Support (an agency of the U.S. Department of Defense), but since 1983 available to institutions of higher education for all their students; "testing-on-demand" program administered by individual institutions under agreement with publisher.

Author: Defense Activity for Non-Traditional Education Support.

Publisher: Educational Testing Service.

a) MATHEMATICS.

Scores: Total score for each of 3 tests:
1) *Introductory College Algebra.*
2) *Calculus I.*
3) *Principles of Statistics.*

b) SOCIAL SCIENCE.

Scores: Total score for each of 9 tests:
1) *History of Western Civilization to 1500 (Revised).*
2) *Geography.*
3) *War and Peace in the Nuclear Age.*
4) *Lifespan Developmental Psychology.*
5) *General Anthropology.*
6) *Introduction to Law Enforcement.*
7) *Criminal Justice.*
8) *Fundamentals of Counseling.*
9) *Art of the Western World.*

c) PHYSICAL SCIENCE.

Scores: Total score for each of 7 tests:
1) *Astronomy.*
2) *Physics for Non-Majors.*
3) *Physics with Calculus: Mechanics.*
4) *Physics with Calculus: Electricity & Magnetism.*
5) *ACS General Chemistry.*
6) *Principles of Physical Science I.*
7) *Physical Geology.*

d) BUSINESS.

Scores: Total score for each of 12 tests:
1) *Principles of Finance.*
2) *Principles of Financial Accounting.*
3) *Personnel/Human Resource Management.*
4) *Organizational Behavior.*
5) *Introduction to Computers with BASIC Programming.*
6) *Introduction to Business.*
7) *Risk and Insurance.*
8) *Principles of Real Estate.*
9) *Money and Banking (Revised).*
10) *Basic Marketing (Revised).*
11) *Business Mathematics.*
12) *Business Law II.*

e) FOREIGN LANGUAGE.

Scores: Total score for each of 5 tests:
1) *Beginning German I.*
2) *Beginning German II.*
3) *Beginning Spanish I.*
4) *Beginning Spanish II.*
5) *Beginning Italian I.*

Comments: Cassettes available for all tests except Beginning German II.

f) APPLIED TECHNOLOGY.

Scores: Total score for each of 11 tests:
1) *Basic Automotive Service.*
2) *Automotive Electrical/Electronics.*

3) *Introduction to Carpentry.*
4) *Basic Technical Drafting.*
5) *Fundamentals of Electronics (Revised).*
6) *Electric Circuits.*
7) *Electronic Devices.*
8) *Technical Writing (Revised).*
9) *Principles of Electronic Communication Systems.*
10) *Television Theory and Circuitry.*
11) *Principles of Refrigeration Technology.*
g) HUMANITIES.
Scores: Total score for each of 2 tests:
1) *Ethics in America.*
2) *Principles of Public Speaking.*

Review of the DANTES Subject Standardized Tests by LAURA L. B. BARNES, Assistant Professor Applied Behavioral Studies, Oklahoma State University, Stillwater, OK:

The DANTES subject tests are intended for individuals seeking college credit by examination. Forty-nine tests cover subjects in the social sciences, humanities, natural and physical sciences, foreign languages, business, mathematics, and technological areas. The tests are primarily multiple choice. The test content generally corresponds to that learned in a single-semester college-level course. The DANTES program differs from the ETS-developed College Level Examination Program (CLEP; 9:245), according to the publisher, in that the DANTES tests may be given on demand, whereas the CLEP tests have specified administration dates; the DANTES tests are semester-oriented, whereas the CLEP tests cover an entire academic year's worth of content; the DANTES tests have no time limits (most tests are reported to take about 90 minutes to complete), whereas a number of the CLEP tests are timed; and the DANTES tests offer a variety of subject tests in technological areas which the CLEP tests do not have. The publisher suggests that the two programs be considered complementary.

For each subject area test there is a reproducible fact sheet containing technical information (norming statistics, reliability, recommended passing score, standard error of measurement, etc.), the percent of items related to each topic area, and sample questions with answers and a recommended reading list to help the student prepare for the exam. The fact sheet also contains American Council on Education recommendations regarding courses to be credited and the number of semester hours credit for each test. Separate technical summaries providing a more detailed description of the norming samples and procedures, relevant statistical procedures, and other test and item characteristics are also available upon request for approximately 36 of the subject tests. The tests are to be administered under unspeeded standardized conditions and an accompanying manual details administrative procedures.

Normative data for the tests were obtained between 1985 and 1989 depending on the subject test. For each test, the norming sample consisted of institutions selected from a list of approximately 1,000 schools representing a national cross section of public and private universities, colleges, and junior colleges that offered a course in the specific subject content. Norm groups ranged in size from approximately 300 to 600 students and were selected to be representative of various geographic regions and institution types. To achieve representation, schools with classes larger than 100 were not included, although in response to this reviewer's inquiry, the publisher reported that schools with large lecture classes may be included if they tested in groups smaller than 100.

All faculty participants in the norming process were requested to administer the respective DANTES subject area test to their students at the end of the semester and to compute the final course grade without the DANTES score. In response to reviewer's request for clarification, the publisher stated that to ensure comparability of assigned grades across institutions, all faculty were requested to compute the final course grade without a final exam score because some faculty used the DANTES test in lieu of the final exam, whereas other administered the DANTES test in addition to their own final exam. The passing score for a subject test was determined to be the mean subject test score obtained by students who were assigned a grade of C for the course by their instructor. To some extent, the validity of the passing score depends on how similarly students would have been graded had all their work up through a final exam (excluding the DANTES) been utilized in computing the final course grade.

Internal consistency reliabilities are reported for 45 of the 49 tests and are generally quite satisfactory. KR-20 coefficients range from .81 to .95 with a median reliability of .89. Some of the tests contain both essay and multiple-choice sections. KR-20 reliabilities for the essay portions range from .80 to .95 and composite score reliabilities range from .90 to .96. The standard error of measurement is reported for both raw scores and scaled scores (mean of 50 and standard deviation of 10) and for scaled scores at the passing score.

Content validity was established through the test development process. DANTES tests were developed by the publisher in consultation with faculty who taught courses for which tests were being developed. Test content was determined by surveying commonly used texts in the field supplemented with input from the faculty committees. For two of the tests, War and Peace in the Nuclear Age, and Ethics in America, test content was based on the Annenberg/CPB Project video courses. Faculty committees were involved with test developers in creating, reviewing, and revising test specifications and questions. Sensitivity analyses were conducted to eliminate offensive or stereotypical material, and when sufficient data were available statistical analyses were conducted to detect differential item functioning (DIF) by gender classifications. According to the publisher, the tests are reviewed periodically to update items and/or include new topics, and new tests are developed yearly.

Test results are used to determine a pass/fail status, so the ability of the tests to classify students in the same way instructors do is of critical importance. Thirty-four technical summaries report the proportion agreement between the pass/fail classification on the test and the pass/fail classification for the course. Because all students receiving a grade of C for the course are considered to have passed the course but only those receiving above the mean DANTES score for C students are classified as passing the test, the upper limit for perfect agreement is less than 1.00. The ratio of the observed proportion agreement to the maximum possible proportion agreement may be a useful index for evaluating the decision accuracy of the subject tests. This ratio was computed to range from .82 to 1.00 with a median value of .91. As a correction for chance agreement (i.e., that agreement which could be expected to occur even if no relationship exists between the two classification methods), the kappa coefficient was also reported. The upper bound of kappa is also constrained by the method of establishing the passing score, so the ratio of observed kappa to the maximum possible kappa is presented. The value of this index ranged from .35 to .95 with a median value of .56. In addition, the correlation between subject scores and course grades (weighted by sample size for each institution) ranged from .38 to .74 with a median value of .58. For the norming sample, the tests appear to correlate well with course grades and pass/fail decisions.

The recommended passing score based on the norming sample is reported for each test. However, the publisher suggests that some schools may wish to set their own standards for credit and may require a higher score. Users may wish to obtain technical summaries for the tests they are considering and review the distribution of course grades for the norming sample as an aid in making this decision. For several of the tests, course grades tended to be heavily concentrated in the A and B range, thus establishing a relatively low passing score. Assistance in conducting local norming is said to be available from the publisher.

In summary, the DANTES program presents a very well-developed and well-documented set of instruments for use by colleges or universities that wish to grant college credit by examination.

Review of the DANTES Subject Standardized Tests by WILLIAM A. MEHRENS, Professor of Educational Measurement, Michigan State University, East Lansing, MI:

The original DANTES (Defense Activity for Nontraditional Education Support) mission was "to help service members obtain credit for knowledge and skills acquired through nontraditional educational experiences" (p. 2, ETS booklet on DANTES). Since 1983 this same opportunity has been made available to all American colleges and universities. For each of the 47 tests there exists a Fact Sheet/Study Guide. There were, at the time of this review (February, 1990), technical summaries for 30 of these tests. [Ed. Note: Several more have been made available since that time.] This review is based on the above mentioned material, a booklet describing the program, a booklet containing administration instructions, and copies of the tests themselves (which are secure).

All DANTES tests are developed by ETS which follows the same basic procedures used for other ETS achievement test development programs. Faculty test committees, with the assistance of ETS test development staff, generate a set of test specifications based on a study of the most commonly used textbooks and/or a survey of faculty currently teaching the course. These draft specifications, some sample questions, and a list of reference texts are all reviewed by the faculty committee and test questions are written following the test specifications. A series of reviews of these questions are conducted which include reviews for quality, clarity, etc., by an independent expert and for sensitivity by a panel trained for this task.

Following the test development and reviews, the test is administered to a national sample of students who are completing or had recently completed a course for credit in the specified area. Descriptive statistics are obtained from this sample. Faculty members submit the grades they would have given the students *if the test scores were not included* and the correlation between these grades and the test scores is computed. The minimum passing score for credit is the average score of students in the norming sample who received a grade of C for the course.

This general procedure seems acceptable. However, the process could be made stronger by insisting on a formal survey of current teachers of the relevant courses regarding the test content. Sample sizes could be larger to allow for ethnicity Differential Item Functioning (DIF) statistics on the items (at least 500 total and 100 in the subgroup).

Although the general process is acceptable, the information provided the users could be more thorough and explicit. For example, none of the material I received makes it clear whether the faculty who supply the "grades" have access to the students' test scores. Although I assume they do not, the descriptive material should make it clear whether there was any possibility for criterion contamination.

Technical summaries currently (February, 1990) exist for only 30 of the 47 tests. Although these are generally well done, more information about the representativeness of the norming samples should be presented. Typically the technical summaries provide information about how the mailing list of colleges was obtained. For example, for the Geography test (Form SJ470) institutions "were selected from mailing lists of approximately 1000 schools compiled by the Association of American Geographers and the CMG Mailing List . . . . These schools were sent a mailing that invited faculty to participate in the norming process." It is not clear whether "these" in the sentence above is the total of the 1,000 on the mailing list, or a subset "selected from" the mailing list. At any rate, we are told that 22 schools agreed to participate but only 19 actually supplied data. These institutions are listed in the appendix but we are not given any information regarding how these 19 compare to the original list of approximately 1,000 with respect to various relevant characteristics.

Information on the Fact Sheet/Study Guides is occasionally incomplete. For example, 5 of the 47 tests do not provide percentage breakdowns on their content specifications, 2 do not provide sample sizes, 3 do not provide internal consistency reliability estimates, 10 do not provide a correlation between grades and test scores, 2 do not provide a T-score cut score, 4 do not provide a percentage correct cut score, and 9 do not give the year the norm data were gathered. (Some of this information is found in some of the technical summaries but, as mentioned, only around 30 of the 47 tests have such summaries available.)

Although the data are not as complete or extensive as one would ideally hope, in general the most necessary data are provided—and in a very user friendly format. The Fact Sheet/Study Guides are typically three to four pages long and present the information in a very straightforward manner.

The technical summaries provide an expansion of the information on the Fact Sheets as well as some additional information. The organization of these summaries provides for quick and easy understanding. The format of the more recent technical summaries which place a "summary of principal findings" at the beginning is particularly appealing. All the technical summaries provide information on the appropriateness of the difficulty of the items, information on speededness, criterion-referenced decision consistency (based on the score and whether the students obtained a grade of C or greater), the standard error at the cut score, and item statistics

distributions (but not identified with each item). Starting somewhere around 1988, Differential Item Functioning (DIF) statistics were computed for tests where the total number of examinees exceeds 500 and the number in the smaller of the comparable subgroups is greater than 100 (this results only in gender DIF statistics, not ethnicity DIF statistics).

The Fact Sheet/Study Guides generally contain a description of the test content, sample questions, appropriate study references, some technical information, some norming statistics, and the recommended cut score for the test. The technical information and norming statistics typically include the number of colleges participating in the norming study, the date of the norming study, the total number of students in the study, and some descriptive statistics on the test including the number of items, mean, median, standard deviation, KR-20 reliability, standard error of measurement, and average grade/test score correlation. However, some of this information is missing on some of the Fact Sheets.

The data that are presented for the tests are generally adequate. For example, all reliabilities are at or above .85 with the exception of five between .81 and .85 and three unspecified; the correlations with course grades are typically between .50 and .69 (the lowest given was .38 and 10 were unspecified). As mentioned earlier, some sample sizes could be larger (the sample sizes are 500 or greater for all but eight tests, six are below 500, and two are unspecified).

In summary, the DANTES tests are well developed. The information provided on them suggests they may be used with some confidence, and for subject matter areas where CLEP (College Level Examination Program; 9:245) tests do not exist DANTES tests should be made available. For those subject matter areas where there is overlap with CLEP tests, the decision should be based on whether the college wishes to give credit for a total year (use CLEP) or only a term (use DANTES).

For future development of new tests and/or revisions, I suggest consideration of the following: (*a*) Insist on a survey of faculty teaching the course regarding the test specifications, (*b*) consider giving a two-way breakdown on the specifications—rather than just a content breakdown, (*c*) provide more information on the representativeness of the norming samples, and try to obtain sufficient minority students for DIF analyses, and (*d*) provide information on the subsequent success rate of individuals who have "passed" the test and have taken the next more-advanced course. Information on this latter point is absolutely necessary to make more informed decisions about the benefits of the DANTES program to both the individuals and the institutions.

[104]
Defining Issues Test.

Purpose: "Gives information about the process by which people judge what ought to be done in moral dilemmas."
Population: Grades 9–12 and college and adults.
Publication Dates: 1979–87.
Acronym: DIT.
Scores, 12: Consistency Check, M (meaningless items) score, P (principled moral thinking) score, U (utilizer) score, D (composite) score, A (antiestablishment) score, and stage scores (2, 3, 4, 5A, 5B, and 6).
Administration: Group.
Forms, 2: Short form, long form.
Price Data, 1987: $25 per manual including both forms and scoring information ('86, 96 pages); scoring service available from publisher; $1.90 or less per prepaid scoring sheet including all reports, handling costs, etc.
Time: (30–40) minutes for short form; (40–50) minutes for long form.
Comments: 2 optional companion booklets available: *Development in Judging Moral Issues* from the Center for the Study of Ethical Development, and *Moral Development: Advances in Theory and Research* from Praeger Press.
Authors: James R. Rest, with model computer scoring programs by Steve Thoma, Mark Davison, Stephen Robbins, and David Swanson.
Publisher: Center for the Study of Ethical Development.
Cross References: For reviews by Robert R. McCrae and Kevin L. Moreland, see 9:304 (22 references); see also T3:666 (8 references).

TEST REFERENCES

1. Simmons, D. D. (1983). Identity achievement and axiological maturity. *Social Behavior and Personality, 11* (2), 101-104.
2. Welfel, E. R., & Lipsitz, N. E. (1983). Ethical orientation of counselors: Its relationship to moral reasoning and level of training. *Counselor Education and Supervision, 23,* 35-45.
3. DeWolfe, T. E., & Jackson, L. A. (1984). Birds of a brighter feather: Level of moral reasoning and similarity of attitude as determinants of interpersonal attraction. *Psychological Reports, 54,* 303-308.
4. Gibbs, J. C., Arnold, K. D., Morgan, R. L., Schwartz, E. S., Gavaghan, M. P., & Tappan, M. B. (1984). Construction and validation of a multiple-choice measure of moral reasoning. *Child Development, 55,* 527-536.
5. Hanson, R. A., & Mullis, R. L. (1984). Moral reasoning in offender and nonoffender youth. *The Journal of Genetic Psychology, 144,* 295-296.
6. Lutwak, N. (1984). The interrelationship of ego, moral, and conceptual development in a college group. *Adolescence, 19,* 675-688.
7. McNergney, R., & Satterstrom, L. (1984). Teacher characteristics and teacher performance. *Contemporary Educational Psychology, 9,* 19-24.
8. Mullis, R. L., & Hanson, R. A. (1984). Adult judgments of delinquent and non-delinquent reasoning. *Child Psychiatry and Human Development, 14,* 261-267.
9. Park, J. Y., & Johnson, R. C. (1984). Moral development in rural and urban Korea. *Journal of Cross-Cultural Psychology, 15,* 35-46.
10. Renwick, S., & Emler, N. (1984). Moral reasoning and delinquent behavior among students. *British Journal of Social Psychology, 23,* 281-283.
11. Sternberg, R. J., & Grajeck, S. (1984). The nature of love. *Journal of Personality and Social Psychology, 47,* 312-329.
12. Walker, L. J. (1984). Sex differences in the development of moral reasoning: A critical review. *Child Development, 55,* 677-691.
13. Zeidler, D. L., & Schafer, L. E. (1984). Identifying mediating factors of moral reasoning in science education. *Journal of Research in Science Teaching, 21,* 1-15.
14. Givner, N. (1985). Cognitive and noncognitive characteristics of medical school applicants. *Journal of Medical Education, 60,* 798-799.
15. Guthrie, K. H. (1985). Locus of control and field independence-dependence as factors in the development of moral judgment. *The Journal of Genetic Psychology, 146,* 13-18.
16. Kelly, R. B., & Chovan, W. (1985). Yet another empirical test of the relationship between self-actualization and moral judgment. *Psychological Reports, 56,* 201-202.
17. Ma, H. K. (1985). Consistency of stage structure in objective moral judgment across different samples. *Psychological Reports, 57,* 987-990.
18. Malinowski, C. I., & Smith, C. P. (1985). Moral reasoning and moral conduct: An investigation prompted by Kohlberg's theory. *Journal of Personality and Social Psychology, 49,* 1016-1027.
19. Muehleman, T., Robinson, F., & Emerson, D. (1985). Shifts in preference for moral reasoning. *The Journal of Social Psychology, 125,* 287-293.
20. Presley, S. L. (1985). Moral judgment and attitudes toward authority of political resisters. *Journal of Research in Personality, 19,* 135-151.
21. Preston, D. D., & Napier, J. D. (1985). Effects of a cognitive-moral approach on moral reasoning ability in a health and physical education curriculum. *The High School Journal, 68,* 75-82.
22. Rest, J. R., & Thoma, S. J. (1985). Relation of moral judgment development to formal education. *Developmental Psychology, 21,* 709-714.
23. Shaver, D. G. (1985). A longitudinal study of moral development at a conservative, religious, liberal arts college. *Journal of College Student Personnel, 26,* 400-404.
24. Taylor, J. B., Waters, B., Surbeck, E., & Kelley, M. (1985). Cognitive, psychosocial, and moral development as predictors of pre-service teachers' ability to analyze child behavior. *College Student Journal, 19,* 65-72.
25. Zeidler, D. L. (1985). Hierarchial relationships among formal cognitive structures and their relationship to principled moral reasoning. *Journal of Research in Science Teaching, 22,* 461-471.
26. Kessler, G. R., Ibrahim, F. A., & Kahn, H. (1986). Character development in adolescents. *Adolescence, 21,* 1-9.
27. Propper, S., & Brown, R. A. (1986). Moral reasoning, parental sex attitudes, and sex guilt in female college students. *Archives of Sexual Behavior, 15,* 331-340.
28. Locke, D. C., & Zimmerman, N. A. (1987). Effects of peer-counseling training on psychological maturity of Black students. *Journal of College Student Personnel, 28,* 525-532.
29. McGraw, K. M., & Bloomfield, J. (1987). Social influence on group moral decisions: The interactive effects of moral reasoning and sex role orientation. *Journal of Personality and Social Psychology, 53,* 1080-1087.
30. Shaver, D. G. (1987). Moral development of students attending a Christian, liberal arts college and a Bible college. *Journal of College Student Personnel, 28,* 211-218.
31. Curtis, J., Billingslea, R., & Wilson, J. P. (1988). Personality correlates of moral reasoning and attitudes toward authority. *Psychological Reports, 63,* 947-954.
32. Sprinthall, N. A., & Scott, J. R. (1989). Promoting psychological development, math achievement, and success attribution of female students through deliberate psychological education. *Journal of Counseling Psychology, 36,* 440-446.
33. Sanders, C. E. (1990). Moral reasoning of male freshmen. *Journal of College Student Development, 31,* 5-8.
34. Hendel, D. D. (1991). Evidence of convergent and discriminant validity in three measures of college outcomes. *Educational and Psychological Measurement, 51,* 351-358.

Review of the Defining Issues Test by ROSEMARY E. SUTTON, Associate Professor of Education, Cleveland State University, Cleveland, OH:

The Defining Issues Test (DIT) is an objective test of moral judgement derived from Kohlberg's theory of moral development. Traditionally, assessment of stages derived from cognitive development theories, like Kohlberg's, involves a clinical interview in which the subject is presented with a situation or dilemma and asked to make a decision and give a rationale for that decision. The scoring depends predominantly on the nature of the explanation. This kind of assessment is difficult to perform because it requires trained interviewers, is time consuming, expensive, and has been especially difficult with respect to Kohlberg's theory because the criteria for scoring were not clear and changed over time. There is evidence that it also tends to underestimate an individual's developmental level because it requires the subject to provide a clear rationale of her or his thinking.

The DIT is an easy-to-use and practical application of this technique. Six dilemmas that are the same or similar to those used in Kohlberg's interview schedule, are printed on the page, along with 12 questions. Subjects are asked to rate how important each question is in making a decision, what their decision is, and to rank the four most important questions. From the test the researcher gains a P score (percentage of principled thinking) and a D score (a composite needing computer scoring to calculate), as well as checks for consistency and the number of meaningless items the subject checks. These items are written as lofty and pretentious sounding but are meaningless. Too high a score indicates that the subject does not understand test directions. The test requires a reading age of approximately 12–13 years.

The manual contains extensive information on the reliability, validity, and norms for the test. These data appear to have been collected carefully, and are appropriate for the stated purpose.

RELIABILITY. The reliability of the DIT is good. Test-retest correlations range from .71 to .82 for the P index, and .67 to .92 for the D index. For a shorter three-story test version test-retest correlations range from .58 to .77 for the P index, and .63 to .83 for the D index. The values for Cronbach's alpha are .77 for the P score and .79 for the D score. Alpha values for the shorter version are .76 for the P score and .71 for the D score.

VALIDITY. To establish criterion-group validity, mean scores for graduate students in moral philosophy and political science, college students, senior high school students, and ninth grade students were compared. Significant differences were found among the groups. Any developmental measure should show longitudinal change in the direction of higher stages. Significant upward trends over 6 years and four testings ($F = 17.6$, $p < .0001$) for the P score are reported. Research has indicated that individuals are unable to fake good on the DIT. Additional information in the manual may be found on validation studies related to experimental enhancement, and multidimensional scaling and latent trait analysis.

NORMATIVE DATA. Normative data provided in the manual are very extensive. They are broken down by educational level: junior high, high school, college, professional school and graduates, and nonstudent adults. Scores on the DIT are positively correlated with education, IQ, and age (for student groups). No consistent relationship has been found with DIT scores and gender, socioeconomic status, and college major. The majority of the normative samples were drawn from the midwest and no information is provided about ethnic differences. In a recent book Rest (1986) discusses non-U.S. cross-cultural comparisons from 15 cultures.

The problems with this test are associated with its age. Two of the dilemmas in the test involve real issues surrounding the Vietnam war. To high school and college students these are obviously not completely hypothetical dilemmas, but they are not part of their personal memory (or, perhaps, interest). One dilemma is the classic case of whether Heinz should steal to get money for drugs to save his wife's life. This dilemma has been summarized and reprinted so widely that it may be difficult to find a group of naive college graduates, or even undergraduates. The lack of norms and discussion of moral reasoning for U.S. ethnic minority groups, always a serious omission, appears more glaring in the 1990s because of the increased number of minorities in the country. Finally, cognitive developmental theory, which assumes that a stage reflects a level of reasoning that can be generalized across situations and content, is seriously challenged with recent work. In particular, researchers are more likely to assume that reasoning or problem solving is domain specific. Although the test developer, Rest, takes a "soft" stage position, his test gives a summary score of principled thinking, not separate scores within domains. In contrast, separate moral developmental histories have been proposed in rights versus conventional rules (Turiel, 1983) or friendship, justice, fairness, obedience and authority, and social rules and conventions (Damon, 1977). However, easy-to-use tests are not, to my knowledge, available for these newer approaches.

In summary, in many aspects this test is a model of instrument development in social sciences. It has good psychometric properties, has a full and informative manual, is easy to administer, is inexpensive, and was based on an established theory. There are a wealth of data on the use of the DIT including two detailed books by Rest (Rest, 1979, 1986). However, the test is dated and so should be used with caution, especially with ethnically diverse groups.

REVIEWER'S REFERENCES
Damon, W. (1977). *The social world of the child*. San Francisco: Jossey-Bass.
Rest, J. R. (1979). *Development in judging moral issues*. Minneapolis: University of Minnesota Press.
Turiel, E. (1983). *The development of social knowledge: Morality and convention*. New York: Cambridge University Press.
Rest, J. R. (1986). *Moral development: Advances in theory and research*. New York: Praeger Press.

Review of the Defining Issues Test by BERT W. WESTBROOK, Professor of Psychology, and K. DENISE BANE, Graduate Student, North Carolina State University, Raleigh, NC:

The Defining Issues Test (DIT) was designed to measure an individual's level of moral reasoning or moral judgment. Moral judgment is purportedly one component of the construct of morality.

The DIT yields several different scores for each respondent. The most important scores are the stage scores and "P" scores. Stage scores indicate different levels of moral reasoning. The stages are enumerated 2, 3, 4 5a, 5b, and 6. Stage 2 represents the least mature response. Stage 6 represents the most mature response. The Principled morality score, or "P" score, is the sum of Stages 5a, 5b, and 6. It indicates the relative importance an individual gives to "principled moral considerations in making a decision about moral dilemmas" (manual, p. 5.2).

The DIT comprises six problem stories. Each problem story describes a "social problem." For each social problem story, the respondent is asked to indicate his or her recommendation for what a person should do. Next, the respondent is given a list of 12 statements of issues about the story and is asked to indicate the extent to which the issue is important in making a decision. The respondent is asked to rank what he or she considers to be the four most important issues in order of importance. These four most important items are the only items that enter into the scoring.

The manual does not discuss the source of the items or the design of the DIT, nor does it explain how the items were classified into the different stages of moral reasoning. Also, the manual does not provide justification for the weighting of the items in terms of degree of maturity of moral reasoning. Instead, it provides a brief discussion of how the DIT stages differ from Kohlberg's moral reasoning stages. It also refers the reader to a more detailed discussion in a book (Rest, 1979) published by the author.

There are four possible means of scoring the test: (a) It may be hand scored, (b) it may be computer scored by the user, (c) it may be computer scored by mailing one's data to the Center for the Study of Ethical Development, or (d) one may soon be able to use computer-scoring sheets currently under development.

The hand-scoring procedure can be described as involved. The manual provides detailed instructions for scoring but the opportunity for clerical error is considerable. The manual does not present data from studies indicating the accuracy of scoring.

The manual does not present item analysis data for any of the items. Some questions about the items can be raised. To what extent do moral philosophers endorse the individual items? What is the relation between importance ratings of the items and P scores? What is the relation between age of respondent and item rating of importance?

Apparently, the author has relied heavily upon the data that have been collected by others. Unfortunately, such a procedure may compromise the integrity of the data, inasmuch as it is impossible to verify the accuracy of the data and the test administration.

The manual provides norm tables presenting the P scores for junior high, high school, college, graduate school students, and adults. On the average, graduate school students score higher than college students, who score higher than high school students, who score higher than junior high students. However, one of the problems with presenting norms in this manner is that it assumes that there are no meaningful differences between the scores of 9th and 12th grade students, between college freshmen and college seniors, and between first year graduate students and third year graduate students, etc. Pooling data from different levels tends to spuriously inflate the variability of the scores as well. The effect of all this is that we really do not have norms and statistics for 9th graders, 10 graders, etc., and we do not have means and standard deviation estimates for each grade separately.

The validity evidence presented in the manual does not provide sufficient details of the many studies that are cited in the manual. Relying heavily upon his book (Rest, 1979), the author chose merely to "outline the logic of our building a case for validity and the major findings" (manual, p. 6.1). However, these major findings are not clearly presented. Although a wide variety of different kinds of evidence are presented, they are not well described. The validation strategy is not explained in the manual, and practically none of the typical descriptive statistical and correlational tables are included.

Under the subheading, "Face validity," the Guide for the Defining Issues Test, a companion to the manual, states that the DIT "does not only ask what line of action the subject favors (i.e., to steal or not to steal a drug), but is concerned with a subject's reasons behind the choice" (Center for the Study of Ethical Development, 1987, p. 19). Although the manual claims the DIT task "obviously" involves making judgments about moral problems, no empirical evidence is provided to support this statement.

To provide support for "Criterion-group validity," the author describes the different groups being contrasted (Ph.D. philosophy students, college, high school, and ninth grade students) but does not provide the necessary details of the studies (i.e., sample sizes and relevant mean scores for the different groups). The manual states that the differences were "highly significant" (manual, p. 6.5), but without providing the necessary statistics, this is not meaningful.

The manual states that the 1979 book reports significant changes in the direction of "higher stages" for subjects who are retested over 4 years at three testings; this is referred to as "Longitudinal change validity," but the relevant statistical data are not presented; nor does it state the length of the intervals between tests or the sample sizes.

Under the subheading, "Convergent-divergent correlational validity," the Guide states the DIT correlates about .50 (on the average) with "variables which are theoretically more similar to moral judgment" (Center for the Study of Ethical Development, 1987, p. 23); and it correlates .36 (on the average) with variables that are "theoretically dissimilar" (Center for the Study of Ethical Development, 1987, p. 23), such as measures of cognitive development and intelligence. Raw data and details of these studies, such as which tests were used, are not presented in the Guide or manual.

To provide support for what Anastasi (1988) calls "experimental interventions," the manual refers the reader to a study which found that a logic class moved subjects up on a logic test but not on the DIT, whereas an ethics class moved subjects up on the DIT but not on the logic test. Data for this study are not presented in the manual.

Under the heading "Validation through experimental manipulation of test taking sets," the author describes a study testing the DIT's susceptibility to faking. No difference was found between scores of subjects responding normally and those of subjects asked to fake good. The author claims this is a positive result because it suggests that "under usual conditions, subjects are giving their best notions of the highest principles of justice" (manual, p. 6.6). However, is it possible that respondents' "best notions" are what is socially desirable?

The Guide presents a table showing the test-retest correlation for the six-story DIT. The highest test-retest reliability coefficient for the P score is reported to be .82 for Sample A, based upon "123 subjects pooled together from various moral education projects" (Guide, p. 19). However, the .82 value is practically meaningless because the interval between testing is so variable (1 week to 5 months), the range in age is so great (16 to 56), and the educational background is so diverse (junior high to graduate school). These kinds of data do not provide a basis for making statements about the validity of the DIT with specific populations such as ninth graders tested over a 2-week period.

The *Standards for Educational and Psychological Testing* stipulate that test publishers "should provide enough information for a qualified user or a reviewer of a test to evaluate the appropriateness and technical adequacy of the test" (American Educational Research Association, American Psychological Association, & National Council on Measurement in Education, 1985, p. 35). The manual for the DIT points out that "the DIT is the most widely used instrument of moral judgment and the best documented in terms of reliability and validity" (manual, p. ii). However, we cannot judge the technical adequacy of the DIT on the basis of information in the manual and the *Guide for the Defining Issues Test*. In the opinion of the reviewers, the intent of the *Standards* has not been satisfied by the developer of

the DIT. Future revision of the DIT should include a revised technical manual that includes detailed technical data to support the reliability and validity of the DIT.

REVIEWER'S REFERENCES

Rest, J. R. (1979). *Development in judging moral issues*. Minneapolis: University of Minnesota Press.
American Educational Research Association, American Psychological Association, & National Council on Measurement in Education. (1985). *Standards for educational and psychological testing*. Washington, DC: American Psychological Association, Inc.
Center for the Study of Ethical Development. (1987). *Guide for the Defining Issues Test*. Minneapolis: Center for the Study of Ethical Development.
Anastasi, A. (1988). *Psychological testing* (6th ed.). New York: MacMillan Publishing Co.

[105]
DeLong Interest Inventory.

Purpose: Designed to identify areas of interest for use in developing a remedial program.
Population: Special education students.
Publication Date: 1988.
Scores: No scores.
Administration: Individual.
Price Data, 1991: $8 per 25 recording forms; $10 per manual (48 pages).
Time: [10] minutes.
Author: Ruth Simpson DeLong.
Publisher: Academic Therapy Publications.

Review of the DeLong Interest Inventory by ROBERT F. McMORRIS, Professor of Educational Psychology and Statistics, State University of New York at Albany, Albany, NY:

The DeLong Interest Inventory is a relatively brief, informal set of 14 topics that an examiner can use to interview a student/client. The examiner completes a brief demographic section about the student/client, then asks questions about use of free time, pets and favorite animals, best friend(s), hobbies, music, activities, scariest experiences, movies and TV, career, school, etc. The fourth and final page of the Inventory provides an opportunity for the examiner to integrate and comment on the responses. The age range is given as age 7 to adult.

Let us consider first what the Inventory is *not*, then what it is and what it might be used for, what questions a user/interpreter might wish answered, and then summarize.

This measure is not a fancy test replete with psychometrically sophisticated bells and whistles. It has no forced-choice, Likert, or rating-scale items. It has no standard errors of measurement and no profiles.

It is a set of topics to be used as a basis for an interview. The examiner can refer to the manual for two to five alternate questions or probes per topic, for several vignettes and four case studies illustrating previous applications, and for words of encouragement and caution presented in a conversational style. The measure is approachable, and it apparently has assisted the developer in designing interventions and remedial programs tailored to the interests of the student.

Certainly our laws (e.g., P.L. 94-142) and our humanity support designing instructional treatments appropriate to the student/client, and not depending solely on intelligence-test results, especially for any student designated as "special." (And what student/client is not special?) The suggested approach does provide an examiner an opportunity to listen (probably more like a 20-minute than the 10-minute opportunity suggested by the publishers). In my opinion, the instrument would be better administered and interpreted by an examiner who conceptualizes himself/herself as a counselor, an educator, a psychologist, an observer, and an advocate than by one conceptualizing himself/herself as a critic or judge.

Ideally, the examiner should have the competencies and attitudes of all the professionals referred to in the first part of the previous sentence, but the manual is silent on requisite competencies for examiners. What level and type of training is recommended for administering and interpreting the Inventory? Many interpretations illustrated in the manual could be handled safely even by untrained examiners, but judgements of emotional development, for example, especially when such generalizations could become part of a written record supported by a "test," could be unprofessional. Some potential interpretations could be both unreliable and harmful. A related question is one of confidentiality: To what extent, under what conditions, and with whom should the examiner share sensitive revelations? Should the examiner seek the student/client's permission before any discussion of this information with parents or with other professionals?

The manual contains no information on reliability. It would help the interpreter to know the extent to which themes are likely to be stable over even short periods of time and also whether two observers hearing the same responses are likely to report the same themes.

The manual contains anecdotal information on validity. That is, the developer has applied the Inventory and has noted information and insights that assisted in devising interventions and remedial programs tailored to individual interests, and students/clients have improved. Although it seems reasonable for other professionals to expect to find positive results with at least some students/clients, empirical support for such application is at best thin. Questions the developer and other users might address to help the interpreter include:

What is the rationale for including these particular 14 topics? What important topics are not included?

Do users find the Inventory assists in making Individual Instructional Plans (IEPs) more constructive and effective?

Would a greater number of potential probes help examiners elicit additional insights? Would additional probes be too difficult for the examiner to deal with?

Does the type of report relate to the training, orientation, or role of the examiner? For example, would examiners tending to use *Diagnostic and Statistical Manual—IIIR* (American Psychiatric Association, 1987) categories report and interpret differently from those tending to use behavioral objectives? Would a psychodynamic therapist and a cognitive-behaviorist both find the Inventory helpful but write down very different descriptions and interpretations? Would a teacher's report differ predictably from a school psychologist's report?

What educational or personal gains are made by student/client participants beyond gains made by other experimental or control groups not so treated?

Do examiners who have used the instrument reuse it with later students/clients? With what kinds of students/clients, and for what purposes?

Further, we might ask whether the Inventory would be an unnecessary crutch for the sophisticated interviewer and a dangerous cloak of professionalism for the untrained or incompetent interviewer.

To summarize, the DeLong Interest Inventory provides a means for a student or client to express thoughts and feelings on 14 topics. These interests could help professionals develop an instructional or remedial plan tailored for the individual and presumably a more effective and encouraging approach than a generic plan where one size fits all. The conversational and anecdotal manual could encourage constructive and creative use of the instrument, but there is also great potential for misuse. For a variety of reasons, this Inventory could help the student/client take stock, and with the help of professionals, help plan an effective and humane course of action. The potential user is cautioned, however, that a myriad of questions regarding interpretation have not even been acknowledged in the manual, let alone given a response. A few such questions have been included in this review.

REVIEWER'S REFERENCE

American Psychiatric Association. (1987). *Diagnostic and statistical manual of mental disorders* (3rd ed. rev.). Washington, DC: Author.

Review of the DeLong Interest Inventory by ANNIE W. WARD, President of Ward Educational Consulting, Inc. and of The Techne Group, Inc., Daytona Beach, FL:

PURPOSE. The DeLong Interest Inventory is designed to identify areas of interest for use in developing a remedial program.

The Inventory is simply a form to facilitate recording student's responses to questions in 14 areas. Only the general areas are provided on the form;

the specific questions are left up to the interviewer, although some suggestions are provided in the manual.

Although the manual is delightfully written and provides four case histories that provide interesting reading, there is little assistance for a novice interviewer who might try to use this inventory. In order for the Inventory to be useful, the interviewer would need to be trained in clinical interviewing and would need to have experience in both interviewing techniques and in making the inferences necessary to interpreting the responses.

No validity or reliability evidence is provided, there are no norms, and scoring is intuitive. In short, there is little to commend this instrument. Most trained and experienced interviewers would do as well constructing their own interview form. They might profit from reading the manual. It provides a rationale for the areas addressed and contains suggestions for followup activities.

[106]
Deluxe Detention Promotion Tests.
Purpose: Specifically prepared and tailor-made test for promotion of detention workers.
Population: Detention workers under consideration for promotion.
Publication Date: 1990.
Scores, 7: Detention-Related Technical Knowledges, Knowledge of the Behavioral Sciences and Human Relations, Supervisory Knowledge and Ability, Administrative Knowledges and Abilities, Knowledge of Inmate Legal Rights, Detention-Related Abilities, Total.
Administration: Group.
Price Data, 1991: Rental and scoring services, $645 per first 5 candidates; $15–$37 for each additional candidate ($645 minimum).
Time: [210] minutes.
Author: McCann Associates, Inc.
Publisher: McCann Associates, Inc.

[107]
Dementia Rating Scale.
Purpose: Measures the cognitive status of individuals with known cortical impairment.
Population: Individuals suffering from brain dysfunction.
Publication Dates: 1973–88.
Acronym: DRS.
Scores, 6: Attention, Initiation/Perseveration, Construction, Conceptualization, Memory, Total.
Administration: Individual.
Price Data, 1990: $45 per complete kit including 25 scoring/recording forms, stimulus cards, and manual ('88, 28 pages); $24 per 25 scoring/recording forms; $15 per set of stimulus cards; $9 per manual.
Time: (15–45) minutes.
Author: Steven Mattis.
Publisher: Psychological Assessment Resources, Inc.

TEST REFERENCES
1. Salmon, D. P., Shimamura, A. P., Butters, N., & Smith, S. (1988). Lexical and semantic priming deficits in patients with Alzheimer's Disease. *Journal of Clinical and Experimental Neuropsychology, 10,* 477-494.
2. Squire, L. R., & Zouzounis, J. A. (1988). Self-ratings of memory dysfunction: Different findings in depression and amnesia. *Journal of Clinical and Experimental Neuropsychology, 10,* 727-738.

Review of the Dementia Rating Scale by R. A. BORNSTEIN, Associate Professor of Psychiatry, Neurosurgery and Neurology, The Ohio State University, Columbus, OH:

The Dementia Rating Scale (DRS) consists of 36 tasks distributed among five subscales. The test was designed to "provide a brief measure of cognitive status in individuals with known cortical impairment." The DRS was developed in the context of the examination of patients with progressive dementia. It was recognized that although most neuropsychological measures can discriminate normal from brain-impaired individuals, there are few measures that can discriminate reliably between different levels of dementia. Most available neuropsychological measures reach "floor effects" and are insensitive to progressive levels of dementia. The DRS was designed specifically to assess that lower level of cognitive function. Therefore, the DRS fills a needed and important niche in the assessment of higher cognitive function.

The DRS was designed to sample a broad range of functions based on clinical observations of the types of deficits observed in patients with dementing illnesses. There are five subscales measuring areas of specific ability including Attention, Initiation/Perseveration, Construction, Conceptualization, and Memory. The items are unevenly distributed among the five scales. The test also yields a summary score that enables users to examine a global level of performance in addition to specific abilities. In contrast to other scales, the broad range of measurement inherent in the DRS (total of 144 points) permits much better assessment and discrimination of different levels of impairment. The instructions for administration and scoring are clear and explicit. In addition, the DRS is structured with "skip patterns" so that satisfactory performance of certain tasks assumes normal performance of subordinate tasks. Therefore, considerable time saving can be achieved in some patients.

As would be expected, and by design, the DRS does not discriminate well at higher levels of performance. However, at the lower end of ability, the DRS is vastly superior to other measurement approaches in the discrimination of different levels of performance. This is based on the intentional structuring of the task to have a low floor effect which permits evaluation of even severely demented patients. This is an important feature in the longitudinal study of patients with progressive dementing disorders.

There have been relatively few studies of the reliability and validity of the DRS. However, those data that are available are very supportive. Split-half reliability and test/retest reliability greater than .9 have been reported. Further, internal reliability (Cronbach's alpha) of .75 to .95 have been reported in control subjects and groups of mild and moderate dementia. Other validity data have demonstrated the correlation between DRS total scores and cerebral glucose metabolism in patients with Alzheimer's dementia. The demonstration of a relationship between degree of impairment and reduction in cortical glucose metabolism is strong evidence of the validity of the DRS. The one important potential use of the DRS relates to the differential diagnosis of dementia and depression. In this context, one study directly examining depressed and demented patients found that none of the depressed patients but 62% of the demented patients obtained scores below an identified cutoff score. This provides further construct validity support for the DRS.

The normative data base for the DRS is relatively weak. The largest control sample reported in the manual consists of 85 community living subjects between the ages of 65 and 81. Table 2 in the manual (p. 20) contains the actual frequency distributions of performance for the total DRS score as well as each of the subscales. Cutoff scores are proposed based on criteria of two standard deviations below the mean of the control subjects. The manual also presents means and standard deviations as well as normalized T-scores for a group of 30 dementia patients. Therefore, the manual provides the basis for comparison of an individual patient's performance with both a normal control group and a dementia group. Users of the DRS should be aware the percentiles and T-scores presented in Table 4 are in reference to a dementia population. Users who are interested in comparing the performance of an individual patient with a normal group can compute mean standard deviations and T-scores based on the frequency distribution presented in Table 2.

In summary, the DRS was developed to discriminate among individuals at the low end of the performance range. As such, the DRS is intended to represent an anchor point in the continuum of neuropsychological examination techniques. The DRS examines a broad range of functions and generates a wide range of scores. These clear strengths allow the DRS to accomplish its intended mission of discriminating between different levels of dementia. The DRS is the best measure of its kind and is strongly recommended for clinical and research evaluations designed to examine or differentiate among patients with various dementing disorders.

Review of the Dementia Rating Scale by JULIAN FABRY, Clinical supervisor, Department of Rehabilitation Psychology, Immanuel Medical Center, Omaha, NE:

The Dementia Rating Scale (DRS) is a brief measure of cognitive status for individuals with known cortical impairment, particularly Senile Dementia, Alzheimer's Type. It was designed to measure the progression of behaviorial, neuropathological, and cognitive decline. The author has reported the DRS is sensitive to the differences at the lower end of functioning but it will not detect impaired cognitive ability in individuals who function within the average range of intellectual potential.

The assessment consists of 36 tasks subdivided into 5 subscales: (*a*) Attention (8 items), (*b*) Initiation/Perseveration (11 items), (*c*) Construction (6 items), (*d*) Conceptualization (6 items), and (*e*) Memory (5 items).

The tasks were derived from clinical procedures and what the author described as traditional assessment methods. They are presented in a fixed order with the most difficult item (within each subscale) presented first. If the person being examined passes the first item or two, credit is given for the remaining tasks (i.e., items). The examiner can then move to the next subscale, thereby shortening the total testing time. It would appear the DRS is easily administered and scored. It is portable and can be given in an office, in an examining room, or at bedside.

The Dementia Rating Scale consists of a technical manual, booklet of stimulus cards, and individual scoring form. The booklet containing the stimulus cards is used to complete several of the construction and memory tasks contained within the assessment. The manual contains four chapters: (*a*) Introduction, (*b*) Administration and Scoring, (*c*) Interpretation, and (*d*) Development and Validation of the procedure. The information contained in the manual is easily accessed and it is clearly written.

The DRS individual scoring form should assist the examiner in administering, scoring, and interpreting the assessment. Most of the instructions contained within the scoring form make the administration easy to accomplish even without the use of the manual. Subscale raw scores are calculated by summing the task scores under each section. These scores can then be transferred to the front page of the form to a scoring grid. The grid provides for the raw score, cutoff scores, percentile, and T scores using the Senile Dementia, Alzheimer's Type normative sample.

Norms are presented in chapter 3 of the manual. Cutoff scores for each of the subscales as well as the total score were derived from 85 normal elderly subjects ranging in age from 65 to 81. The test performance of 30 Senile Dementia, Alzheimer's Type patients is also available.

As was previously indicated, specific test administrative instructions are contained in the manual and on the individual scoring form. The criteria for correct responses are available only in the manual. The author suggests practicing both the administration and scoring procedures prior to administration. The instructions to the patients can be repeated except for the attention tasks. Points are awarded for the correct response on the various tasks. the author maintains a liberal attitude toward scoring in general.

Test-retest correlations for a sample of Alzheimer patients range from .94 for the Conceptualization subscale to .61 for the Attention subscale. A coefficient of .97 was calculated for the total score.

On the basis of the total score, 62 percent of demented patients were correctly classified, whereas no depressed patients were found to have a score below the cutoff for cognitive impairment. The author reports a study that suggests the Initiation/Perseveration subscale, which is the longest subscale, differentiates controls from those with mild dementia. Apparently all scales differentiated mild from moderately demented subjects under study. Albert, Naeser, Duffy, and McNulty (1986) reported significant negative correlations between fluid volume in the lateral ventricle of the brain and the Initiation subtest score, as well as the total score on the Dementia Rating Scale for senile Alzheimer's patients.

Some criticism can be made regarding the composition of each of the scales. For example, the Initiation/Perseveration subscale contains questions that deal with language, movement, and drawing. The scale seems heavily weighted with naming objects and articulating consonants, compared to drawing designs and figures and making alternative hand movements. Actual perseverations within the context of these tasks is not accounted for in the scoring. Individuals suffering from dysnomia, apraxia, lack of visual synthesis, and/or memory deficits could have problems responding to the items within this particular scale, thereby giving the impression of having difficulty initiating or perseverating. For example, a person with apraxia will not initiate, thereby earning a poor score. In addition, someone with frontal lobe deficits and possible memory deficits may perseverate.

Other criticisms center on having only limited information regarding internal consistency coefficients for the scale and the small number of subjects used in many of the studies. The Dementia Rating Scale does warrant further research use with Alzheimer's patients, especially longitudinal research in order to continue in its development, and to establish both its validity as a diagnostic device and the reliabilities associated with its structure and its administration.

REVIEWER'S REFERENCE

Albert, M., Naeser, M., Duffy, F., & McNulty, G. (1986). CT and EEG validators for Alzheimer's disease. In L. Poon (Ed.), *Clinical memory assessment of older adults*. Washington, DC: American Psychological Association.

[108]
Descriptive Tests of Language Skills.

Purpose: "To help college teachers assign entering students to appropriate English courses, identify students who may need special assistance in particular aspects of reading and language use before undertaking college-level work, tailor instruction in reading and composition to individual student needs, and plan instruction for classes or groups of students."

Population: Beginning students in two- and four-year institutions.

Publication Dates: 1978–88.

Acronym: DTLS.

Administration: Group.

Price Data, 1989: $.25 per student guide ('88, 16 pages); $.25 per score interpretation; $2.50 per user's guide (first copy free; '88, 34 pages); $7.50 per specimen set.

Comments: Revised edition; tests may be used independently or in combination with other tests in the series.

Author: The College Board.

Publisher: The College Board.

a) READING COMPREHENSION.

Scores, 4: Identifying Word and/or Phrase Meaning Through Context, Understanding Literal and Interpretive Meaning, Understanding Writers' Assumptions/Opinions and Tone, Total.

Price Data: $3 per reusable test booklet (minimum order of 25); $.25 per optional essay booklet (minimum order of 25); $.95 per self-scoring answer sheet (minimum order of 25); $1 per instructor's guide (first copy free; '88, 43 pages); $.50 per scoring guide for writing sample ('88, 20 pages).

Time: 45(50) minutes; 50(55) minutes for optional essay section.

b) CRITICAL REASONING.

Scores, 4: Interpreting Information, Using Information Appropriately, Evaluating Information, Total.

Price Data: $.25 per essay booklet (minimum order of 25); $1 per instructor's guide ('88, 27 pages); $.50 per scoring guide for writing sample ('88, 16 pages); other price data same as *a* above.

Time: Same as *a* above.

c) CONVENTIONS OF WRITTEN ENGLISH.

Scores, 4: Maintaining Consistency, Using Standard Forms, Connecting Ideas Appropriately, Total.

Price Data: $3 per reusable test booklet (minimum order of 25); $.25 per essay booklet (minimum order of 25); $1 per instructor's guide ('88, 41 pages); $.50 per scoring guide for writing sample ('88, 11 pages); other price data same as *a* above.

Time: 60(70) minutes for entire test, 35(40) minutes for multiple-choice section, and 25(30) minutes for essay section.

d) SENTENCE STRUCTURE.

Scores, 4: Using Complete Sentences, Relating Ideas in Sentences Logically, Making Meaning Clear, Total.

Price Data: $3 per reusable test booklet; $.95 per self-scoring answer sheet; $1 per instructor's guide ('88, 39 pages).

Time: 30(35) minutes.

Cross References: See T3:685 (1 reference).

TEST REFERENCES

1. Francis, K. C., McDaniel, M., & Doyle, R. E. (1987). Training in role communication skills: Effect on interpersonal and academic skills of high-risk freshmen. *Journal of College Student Personnel, 28*, 151-156.

2. Evans, R., Venetozzi, R., Bundrick, M., & McWilliams, E. (1988). The effects of sentence-combining instructions on writing and on standardized test scores. *The Journal of Educational Research, 82*, 53-57.

3. Boyle, G. J., Start, B., & Hall, E. J. (1989). Prediction of academic achievement using the School Motivation Analysis Test. *British Journal of Educational Psychology, 59*, 92-99.

4. Gerardi, S. (1990). Academic self-concept as a predictor of academic success among minority and low-socioeconomic status students. *Journal of College Student Development, 31*, 402-407.

Review of the Descriptive Tests of Language Skills by FRANCIS X. ARCHAMBAULT, JR., *Professor of Educational Psychology and Department Head, The University of Connecticut, Storrs, CT:*

The Descriptive Tests of Language Skills (DTLS) were developed in 1978 to help college teachers and administrators assess the needs of entering college students. The tests were updated in 1988 to reflect The College Board's Basic Academic Competencies, a set of skills that several hundred experts determined students needed to succeed in college. The six fundamental skills that comprise the Basic Academic Competencies are reading, writing, reasoning, speaking and listening, mathematics, and studying. The DTLS assesses the first three of these skill areas with four multiple-choice tests: (*a*) Reading Comprehension, (*b*) Critical Reasoning, (*c*) Sentence Structure, and (*d*) Conventions of Written English. Optional writing samples are also available, two for the Reading Comprehension test, two for the Critical Reasoning test, and two for either the Conventions of Written English test or the Sentence Structure test.

The multiple-choice tests are easy to administer and generally interesting to take. The essays also deal with interesting subject matter, but the Reading Comprehension and Critical Reasoning essays present activities that may be unfamiliar to some students. For the former, respondents must complete a prewriting exercise; for the latter, students must evaluate two statements or positions and compare them using certain specified criteria. Nonetheless, the competencies measured by the essays are important to success in college. Moreover, the well-written Student Guide gives examples of the questions, thereby eliminating, or at least reducing, a possible novelty effect.

A guide for interpreting test scores is also available for students. Because they can score their own exams, this is a useful aid. Also useful are the Instructors' Guides for each skill area and the Scoring Guides for each of the three types of essays. The Instructors' Guides provide good overviews of the Basic Academic Competencies measured by the test, as well as a good description of the tests themselves and the meaning of test scores. More importantly, they provide very good advice and strategies for remediating deficiencies uncovered by the tests. For example, the Reading Comprehension Guide provides an interview technique for determining a student's level of metacognitive awareness, a reading/study strategy and suggestions for helping students internalize it, and a set of sample lessons in areas such as identifying word meaning through context and understanding literal and interpretive

meaning. The manuals are quick to point out that they are just guides for teachers to construct their own lessons and strategies, but they are very good. Likewise, although the Scoring Guides are not meant to be prescriptive, they provide sound advice and solid strategies for rating the essays. They also provide details on how one might have the essays scored through the Educational Testing Service, should that option be preferred.

It is clear that a great deal of work has gone into the development of the DTLS and that the tests are likely to be useful to a number of institutions. It is also clear from the User's Guide, which provides what little technical information is available on the tests, that much more work needs to be done. At this writing, only one of the two forms of the multiple-choice tests is available, but it is expected the alternate forms will be available soon. Some normative data, such as means, standard deviations, and scaled scores, are available, but these are based on relatively small samples. Moreover, there is no discussion of how the colleges participating in the standardization sample were selected, and no information on the ability levels of the students taking the tests. Perhaps because sound normative data are lacking, the authors suggest institutions develop their own norms, including cutoff scores for assigning students to different categories of instruction. Although some institutions may prefer this approach, it is hoped the authors will also provide normative data in the future, preferably separately for 2-year and 4-year institutions.

At present, only internal consistency measures of reliability are available for the multiple-choice tests. The coefficients of .88 for both Reading Comprehension and Conventions of Written English, .86 for Sentence Structure, and .78 for Critical Reasoning are within acceptable ranges, as are the standard errors of measurement. The same does not appear to be true, however, for the subscores, or cluster scores as they are called by the authors. As a result, caution must be exercised in interpreting these scores.

In addition to internal consistency estimates, the authors also plan to provide stability coefficients for the separate forms, as well as stability and equivalence measures across forms. These data will be useful in assessing the quality of the tests. It will also be informative to have data on the degree of overlap among the tests. It appears from the items that some redundancy may exist. Also desirable will be correlations between DTLS scores and measures such as the Scholastic Aptitude Test or the Academic Tests of the ACT Assessment because some of the information available from the DTLS may be available from these other measures. Some predictive validity data also should be provided.

In summary, the Descriptive Tests of Language Skills may be a valuable resource for institutions wishing to assess the needs of incoming students for planning, placement, and remediation purposes. Before these tests can be fully recommended, however, more technical information must be provided. Even without this information, some institutions may be interested in using these instruments with an eye toward determining how they perform at their location.

[109]
Descriptive Tests of Mathematics Skills.

Purpose: Designed to help colleges place students in appropriate entry-level courses in mathematics, assess students' skills in particular areas of mathematics, and measure student performance upon completion of a program of instruction in mathematics.
Population: Beginning students in 2- and 4-year institutions.
Publication Dates: 1978–88.
Acronym: DTMS.
Administration: Group.
Price Data, 1989: $.25 per student guide (16 pages); $.25 per student score interpretation (4 pages); $2.50 per user's guide (first copy free, 31 pages); $7.50 per specimen set.
Time: (30) minutes per test.
Comments: Revised edition; 4 tests; tests may be used independently or in combination with other tests in the series.
Author: The College Board.
Publisher: The College Board.

a) ARITHMETIC SKILLS.
Scores, 6: Operations with Whole Numbers, Operations with Fractions, Operations with Decimals, Ratio/Proportion and Percent, Applications, Total.
Price Data: $3 per reusable test booklet (minimum order of 25, '88, 8 pages); $.95 per self-scoring answer sheet (minimum order of 25, 2 pages); $1 per instructor's guide (first copy free, 23 pages).

b) ELEMENTARY ALGEBRA SKILLS.
Scores, 5: Operations with Real Numbers, Operations with Algebraic Expressions, Solutions of Equations and Inequalities, Applications, Total.
Price Data: $1 per instructor's guide (21 pages); other price data same as *a*.

c) INTERMEDIATE ALGEBRA SKILLS.
Scores, 5: Algebraic Operations, Solutions of Equations and Inequalities, Geometry, Applications, Total.
Price Data: $3 per reusable test booklet (minimum order of 25, '88, 12 pages); $.95 per self-scoring answer sheet (minimum order of 25, 2 pages); $1 per instructor's guide (first copy free, 19 pages).

d) FUNCTIONS AND GRAPHS (CALCULUS READINESS).
Scores, 4: Algebraic Functions, Exponential and Logarithmic Functions, Trigonometric Functions, Total.
Price Data: $1 per instructor's guide (13 pages); other price data same as *a*.

Review of the Descriptive Tests of Mathematics Skills by STEPHEN B. DUNBAR, Associate Professor of Measurement and Statistics, The University of Iowa, Iowa City, IA:

The Descriptive Tests of Mathematics Skills (DTMS) were designed as a general achievement battery in mathematics for use by post-secondary educators in diagnosis and placement. The four subtests of this battery are patterned after the typical content of a 3- or 4-year mathematics curriculum at the high school level. The interpretive materials that accompany the DTMS clearly emphasize interpretation of scores with respect to the content specifications for each component of the test battery to ensure well-informed decisions regarding placement and counseling into appropriate entry- or advanced-level mathematics courses at the college level.

The test booklets themselves show a great deal of care and editorial guidance during item writing and test construction. Items are worded precisely and laid out clearly on each page of the booklet. The selection and sampling of content domains in Arithmetic, Elementary Algebra, Intermediate Algebra, and Functions and Graphs strikes a nice balance between coverage and depth, such that reliable diagnostic information about specific strengths and weaknesses can be secured in a reasonable amount of testing time. Cluster scores are provided in four areas of the Arithmetic Skills test, and in three areas of each of the other tests. The interpretive manual also introduces appropriate cautions in the interpretation of such scores.

Technical information for these tests is described in a concise section of the Guide to the Use of the DTMS. Average item difficulties do not imply any serious floor or ceiling effects in the raw score distributions of these tests. Completion rates indicate that time limits and test length were carefully determined during test construction. KR-20 reliability estimates range from .84 for the Functions and Graphs test to .91 for the Elementary Algebra Skills test. Validity evidence in the form of exhaustive documentation of test content and an extensive supplementary report issued by the College Board (Bridgeman, 1980) together support the use of the DTMS in placement and academic counseling. The Bridgeman report reviews evidence regarding the use of the DTMS to measure gain as a result of instruction, as well as concurrent, predictive, and construct-related evidence of validity. Given the present emphasis in higher education on the measurement of outcomes and the likely use of these tests for evaluation purposes, it would be nice to see the kind of evidence presented by Bridgeman updated to the current generation of college students. Presently, users need to provide local justification for interpreting scores on the DTMS in the context of outcome evaluations.

Raw scores on each of the DTMS subtests are converted to scaled scores by a simple method in which chance-level scores and below are assigned a value of 1 and the maximum possible raw score is assigned a value of 25. A linear conversion function is then established by these two points. As new forms of the test are introduced, raw-score equatings provide links to the same scaled scores. In reporting scaled scores, different constants are added to scaled scores in each test area so that users are discouraged from comparing scores across subtests. In order to have a clear basis for comparisons across subtests, users would have to develop local norms for the DTMS, as no national norms have been developed by the College Board.

The lack of general norms for the DTMS deserves special comment. All of the interpretive materials for these tests, including guides prepared for students and course instructors, emphasize that scores are most meaningful when understood in the context of local curricula and local expectations for student achievement. It is certainly convenient to encourage such practice when national norms do not exist. However, given the ascribed purposes of the DTMS, the advice is probably appropriate and well taken.

Although somewhat dated, results are reported in the Guide to the Use of the DTMS from a 1978 study of 7,789 students from 27 two- and four-year colleges and universities. Four samples were drawn from these data on the basis of students' level of preparedness in mathematics. Scaled score to percentile rank conversions in these samples establish a limited frame of reference for normative interpretations and analysis of relative strengths and weaknesses across content areas. In fact, the datedness of these data is not likely to undermine their use for the latter purpose. The manual is careful not to overinterpret the results of this study and encourages the development of local norms when there is a strong need to compare scores across subtests.

The DTMS is a carefully constructed set of instruments, with good technical documentation and supporting interpretive materials. The publisher has painstakingly outlined the proper niche for this battery, and the test manual articulates its role in clear and concise language. The emphasis on local frames of reference for score interpretation is a strength in view of the primary purposes of the DTMS.

REVIEWER'S REFERENCE

Bridgeman, B. (1980). *Validation of the Descriptive Tests of Mathematics Skills* (Research Report RR-80-6). Princeton, NJ: Educational Testing Service.

Review of the Descriptive Tests of Mathematics Skills by JOHN R. HESTER, Associate Professor of Psychology, Francis Marion College, Florence, SC:

The Descriptive Tests of Mathematics Skills (DTMS) was originally published in 1978 and revised in 1988. The tests purport to assist college administrators in placing students in appropriate entry-level and upper-level math courses, while also identifying math deficiencies for individual students. The DTMS is composed of the following four tests that can be administered individually or in any combination: Arithmetic Skills, Elementary Algebra Skills, Intermediate Algebra Skills, and Functions and Graphs (Calculus Readiness). Each of the four tests is subdivided into 3–5 clusters. For instance, the Arithmetic Skills Test yields cluster scores for: Operations with Whole Numbers; Operations with Fractions; Operations with Decimals; Ratio, Proportion, and Percent; and Applications.

Each of the four tests consists of 30–35 four-choice, multiple-choice items. Students are allowed 30 minutes to complete each of the tests. A two-ply, self-scoring answer sheet is available to allow students to score their own tests. Answer sheets allow students to calculate both total and cluster raw scores, with a table for converting total raw scores to scale scores and percentiles. The answer sheet lists math competencies compiled by the College Board's Educational Equality Project, and directs the student to those competencies measured by that particular test. A microcomputer scoring system is also available.

Items for the tests were chosen by a special advisory committee, field tested, and then reviewed by the advisory committee. No information is provided as to the advisory committee's training or experience with instruments such as the DTMS. The revision of the DTMS is actually not a total revision. The Functions and Graphs Test is actually Form A from the 1978 version of the test; content of the three revised tests and scaling of scores have changed such that scores cannot be used interchangeably with those from the earlier edition. Currently, only one (M-3KDT) of the planned two forms of the tests is available. The User's Guide accompanying the tests, in providing technical data and suggestions for interpretation of scores, is written as if the second form was available. Parenthetical comments as to the second form not being available are provided, but such a presentation does yield some initial confusion. It appears the second form being developed will include a revision of the Functions and Graphs Test and scale scores on the two forms will be equated.

Demographic data including ethnic group, type of math course enrolled in, and English as the primary language, are provided for the normative groups of each of the revised tests (Arithmetic, Elementary Algebra, and Intermediate Algebra), but similar data for the Functions and Graphs Test are not available. The number of students in each normative group varied widely from a low of 297 for Intermediate Algebra Skills to 803 for Arithmetic Skills. It is unclear whether some students were in more than one normative group. The normative groups do appear to be representative of 2- and 4-year institutions from various geographic regions and representative of students in both remedial and regular math courses.

Reliability coefficients (internal consistency) fall in the low .80s for the four tests and appear to be adequate. Unfortunately, current data do not include test-retest reliability information. To assist in interpreting individual scores, not only is a general *SEM* provided, but also, an estimated *SEM* is provided for four selected points along the range of scores for each of the four tests. This is a useful feature given the stated purpose of the tests to assist in placing students in mathematics courses. Such a use of the tests may necessitate multiple cutoff points. When tests are subdivided into clusters the number of items in each cluster typically varies between 7–9 questions resulting in reliability coefficients generally in the range of .51 to .72. Given the limited number of items in each cluster, *SEM* of 1.0–1.3 items per cluster, and no factor analysis, users should be cautious in using cluster scores to make decisions about remedial activities for individual students.

Although the DTMS purports to assist in placing students in the appropriate math class, no data are presented in the test material to validate using the tests for placement purposes. The User's Guide offers useful suggestions as to how institutions might conduct their own validity studies, and the publisher offers technical assistance for institutions in analyzing data. Certainly in establishing the validity of an instrument such as the DTMS, where the criterion measure is something as subjective as success in a course at an individual college, it would be expected that each college would need to pilot the instrument. However, the lack of validity data comparing the DTMS to currently used and accessible placement measures such as the SAT and high school grades is a weakness. The prospect of establishing the validity of the DTMS is encouraging given data (Bridgeman, 1982; Suddick & Collins, 1984) from the 1978 edition of the tests.

In summary, users of the 1988 revision of the DTMS may find it more valuable than more general predictors (SAT) of success in college-level math courses. The tests are well normed, reliable (internal consistency) and easy to administer and score. Yet, the DTMS can best be characterized as an instrument in process. An alternate form with accompanying reliability data is being developed and validity of the test must be established in the field. The test is recommended to users with the stipulation that considerable time be allotted to piloting the instrument to verify its superiority to current systems of placement and to establish acceptable DTMS cutoff scores.

REVIEWER'S REFERENCES

Bridgeman, B. (1982). Comparative validity of the College Board Scholastic Aptitude Test—Mathematics and the Descriptive Tests of Mathematics Skills for predicting performance in college mathematics courses. *Educational and Psychological Measurement, 42,* 361-366.

Suddick, D., & Collins, B. (1984). Descriptive Tests of Mathematics Skills: A follow-up of performance of older master's level students. *Perceptual and Motor Skills, 58,* 465-566.

[110]
Developing Cognitive Abilities Test [Second Edition].

Purpose: "Measures learning characteristics and abilities that contribute to academic performance."

Population: Grades 1–2, 3, 4, 5, 6, 7–8, 9–10, 11–12.

Publication Dates: 1980–91.

Acronym: DCAT.

Scores, 7: Verbal, Quantitative, Spatial, Basic Abilities, Application Abilities, Critical Thinking Abilities, Total.

Administration: Group.

Levels, 8: C/D, E, F, G, H, I/J, K, L.

Price Data, 1991: $41.20 per 25 machine-scorable test booklets (specify Level C/D or Level E only) with 1 Directions for Administration; $31.90 per 25 reusable test booklets (specify Level E–L) with 1 Directions for Administration; $13.75 per 35 answer sheets; $33.20 per 100 answer sheets; $4.30 per Directions for Administration (specify Level C/D ['89, 43 pages], Level E [machine-scorable] ['89, 19 pages], or Levels E-L ['89, 19 pages]); $22 per Norms Book ('91, 44 pages); $17 per Technical Manual; scoring service available from publisher.

Comments: Gifted population norms and regular population national norms are available.

Authors: John W. Wick, Donald L. Beggs, and John T. Mouw.

Publisher: American Testronics.

a) LEVEL C/D.
Population: Grades 1–2.
Time: (83–90) minutes.
Comments: Examiner-paced.

b) LEVEL E.
Population: Grade 3.
Time: 60(70) minutes.

c) LEVEL F.
Population: Grade 4.
Time: 60(70) minutes.

d) LEVEL G.
Population: Grade 5.
Time: 60(70) minutes.

e) LEVEL H.
Population: Grade 6.
Time: 60(70) minutes.

f) LEVEL I/J.
Population: Grades 7–8.
Time: 60(70) minutes.

g) LEVEL K.
Population: Grades 9–10.
Time: 60(70) minutes.

h) LEVEL L.
Population: Grades 11–12.
Time: 60(70) minutes.

Cross References: For a review by Lynn H. Fox of the original edition, see 9:321.

TEST REFERENCES

1. Karnes, F. A., & Lee, L. A. (1984). Correlations of scores on the Developing Cognitive Abilities Test and the Wechsler Intelligence Scale for Children—Revised for intellectually gifted students. *Psychological Reports, 54,* 373-374.

2. Johnson, S. T., Starnes, W. T., Gregory, D., & Blaylock, A. (1985). Program of assessment, diagnosis, and instruction (PADI): Identifying and

nurturing potentially gifted and talented minority students. *Journal of Negro Education, 54*, 416-430.

3. Karnes, F. A., Whorton, J. E., Currie, B. B., & Cantrall, S. W. (1986). Correlations of scores on the WISC-R, Stanford-Binet, the Slosson Intelligence Test, and the Developing Cognitive Abilities Test for intellectually gifted youth. *Psychological Reports, 58*, 887-889.

4. Henry, P., & Bardo, H. R. (1987). The predictive validity of the Developing Cognitive Abilities Test. *Educational and Psychological Measurement, 47* (1), 207-214.

5. Henrey, P., & Bardo, H. R. (1990). Relationship between scores on Developing Cognitive Abilities Test and scores on Medical College Admissions Test for nontraditional premedical students. *Psychological Reports, 67*, 55-63.

Review of the Developing Cognitive Abilities Test [Second Edition] by GLEN P. AYLWARD, Associate Professor of Pediatrics and Psychiatry, Southern Illinois University School of Medicine, Springfield, IL:

The Developing Cognitive Abilities Test (DCAT) [Second Edition] is a revision of the 1980 DCAT. This multiple-choice, group test is applicable to grades 1–12; in conjunction with the National Achievement Test (254) and the School Attitude Measure (344), the DCAT is a component of the Comprehensive Assessment Program. This program reportedly is geared to evaluating curriculum objectives gleaned from a survey of "most" major programs. The DCAT may be used independently, however.

The DCAT is described as assessing cognitive characteristics that contribute to academic performance and that can be altered or modified in the school environment. The emphasis therefore is not on stable traits, but rather on those skills developed through instructional interventions. To this end, the test is unique in its utilization of Bloom's *Taxonomy of Educational Objectives* (Bloom, Englehart, Furst, Hill, & Krathwohl, 1956). This taxonomy provides a conceptual framework for the test items. These test items are grouped into eight levels (C/D–L): grades 1–2, 3, 4, 5, 6, 7–8, 9–10, and 11–12. Each level has the same design and contains 81 total items, grouped into three timed, 27-item content areas: Verbal, Quantitative, and Spatial. Within each content area the first nine items measure Basic Cognitive Abilities, the second grouping of nine measures Application Abilities, and the remaining nine involve Critical Thinking. The technical manual contains helpful tables that classify individual items in terms of their "cognitive class," namely, knowledge, comprehension, application, analysis, and synthesis. Testing takes approximately 60 minutes although Form C/D (grades 1 and 2) requires somewhat more time. Scoring services are similar to other comparable tests; scores for the Verbal, Quantitative, and Spatial content areas and the five cognitive levels are provided.

Whereas conceptually this test is quite attractive, there are some minor practical problems. The Spatial items often involve more science-related items than purely spatial conceptualization: pulleys, volumes, and occasionally difficult-to-discriminate pictures. However, the authors indicate the Spatial items are less aligned with traditional curricula than are the other two content areas.

The standardization sample was stratified by school district size, geographic region, public versus private classification, and socioeconomic status (although using poverty level for socioeconomic measurement is questionable). No mention is made of racial/ethnic distributions. The authors report that 150,000 students participated in the fall standardization, and more than 150,000 in the spring standardization. DCAT raw scores were transformed into Equal Interval Scores via the Rasch method; two or three levels of the DCAT (e.g., below, at, and above grade level) were administered to 7,000 students for scaling purposes.

Reliability (KR-20) for the total DCAT ranges between .88 and .96, depending upon grade; figures for the individual content or thinking skills areas are lower, but still acceptable. The lowest reliability figures are found in Level C/D (grade 1). This finding is likely due to more examiner participation in test administration, as compared to later grades. No test-retest reliability figures are reported.

The technical manual (prepublication edition) is a bit weak in regard to presentation of validity data. Much emphasis is placed on the aforementioned content area and cognitive taxonomies, and how these two dimensions bridge school curricula and Bloom's classifications. The points made are both reasonable and convincing; however, the only criterion-related validity figures are those involving correlations with the reading, language, mathematics, social studies, and science areas of the National Achievement Test. Multiple Rs from grade 2 onwards were acceptable (generally in the .70 to .85 range); those for grade 1 were somewhat lower. Relationships between the DCAT Verbal subtests and achievement were higher than were those between achievement and the Quantitative and Spatial subtest scores. In general, the Spatial subtest correlations were less than .25, suggesting that this area may measure something that is not related to traditional academic achievement. Because this finding could have significant implications, the need for further investigation is apparent. Presently, no studies are reported correlating the DCAT with other measures. Therefore, although content and construct validity appear sound, criterion-related validity requires further documentation.

Test statistics suggest that the grade 1 (fall) data are the weakest, particularly in the Quantitative area; there appear to be too few easy items. Sample administrations revealed that some items may be difficult for younger students to comprehend. As in the case of many similar tests, reading or processing problems effectively preclude adequate evaluation of even the Quantitative or Spatial content areas. Perhaps standardization of alternative administration strategies for such cases should be considered by the test authors.

In summary, the DCAT is well designed. Perhaps the most attractive feature of this test, and one which augments its potential as a prime diagnostic and prescriptive device, is its conceptual base and broad range of assessment. Recall and recognition of learned content material, application of acquired knowledge in practical reasoning tasks, and transformation and integration of information are all involved. Comparison of scores on these cognitive dimensions in the Verbal, Quantitative, and Spatial content areas, respectively, would be an excellent means of identifying a student's strengths and weaknesses and of designing proper interventions. Therefore, the DCAT should be highly competitive with other aptitude tests, and may, in fact, surpass most if some of the aforementioned issues are clarified.

REVIEWER'S REFERENCE

Bloom, B., Englehart, M., Furst, E., Hill, W., & Krathwohl, D. (Eds.). (1956). *Taxonomy of educational objectives, Handbook I: Cognitive domain.* New York: David McKay.

[111]
Differential Ability Scales.

Purpose: Designed to measure cognitive abilities and achievement.
Population: Ages 2-6 to 17-11.
Publication Date: 1990.
Acronym: DAS.
Administration: Individual.
Price Data, 1991: $495 per complete kit with briefcase; $24 per 20 preschool record forms; $24 per 20 school-age record forms; $8 per 20 basic number skills and spelling worksheets; $8 per 10 speed of information processing booklets (select A, B, C); $12 per 10 sequential and quantitative reasoning booklets; $50 per administration manual ('90, 445 pages); $20 per technical handbook ('90, 379 pages).
Author: Colin D. Elliott.
Comments: Based on The British Ability Scales (9:172).
Publisher: The Psychological Corporation.
  a) COGNITIVE BATTERY.
    1) *Preschool.*
    Population: Ages 2-6 to 7-11.
    Time: (25–65) minutes.
      (*a*) Ages 2-6 to 3-5.
      Scores, 7: Block Building, Verbal Comprehension, Picture Similarities, Naming Vocabulary, Total General Conceptual Ability, Recall of Digits, Recognition of Pictures.
      (*b*) Ages 3-6 to 5-11.
      Scores, 14: Verbal Ability (Verbal Comprehension, Naming Vocabulary, Total), Nonverbal Ability (Picture Similarities, Pattern Construction, Copying, Total), Early Number Concepts, Total General Conceptual Ability, Block Building, Matching Letter-Like Forms, Recall of Digits, Recall of Objects, Recognition of Pictures.
    2) *School-Age.*

Population: Ages 5-0 to 17-11.
Scores, 13: Verbal Ability (Word Definitions, Similarities, Total), Nonverbal Reasoning Ability (Matrices, Sequential and Quantitative Reasoning, Total), Spatial Ability (Recall of Designs, Pattern Construction, Total), Total General Conceptual Ability, Recall of Digits, Recall of Objects, Speed of Information Processing.
Time: (40–65) minutes.
  b) SCHOOL ACHIEVEMENT.
Population: Ages 6-0 to 17-11.
Scores, 3: Basic Number Skills, Spelling, Word Reading.
Time: (15–25) minutes.

TEST REFERENCES

1. Platt, L. O., Kamphaus, R. W., Keltgen, J., & Gilliland, F. (1991). An overview and review of the Differential Ability Scales: Initial and current research findings. *Journal of School Psychology, 29,* 271-277.

Review of the Differential Ability Scales by GLEN P. AYLWARD, Associate Professor of Pediatrics and Psychiatry, Southern Illinois University School of Medicine, Springfield, IL:

The Differential Ability Scales (DAS) is an individually administered battery of subtests that measures cognitive abilities in children ages $2^1/_2$ – 17. Derived from the British Ability Scales (9:172), the DAS is designed to provide a composite measure of conceptual and reasoning abilities useful for diagnostic and placement purposes. The test is unique in that it incorporates a developmental and an educational perspective.

The DAS contains 17 cognitive and 3 achievement subtests, grouped in two overlapping levels: Preschool and School-Age. Twelve core subtests contribute to the General Conceptual Ability Score (GCA), and five additional diagnostic subtests measure short term memory, perceptual skills, and speed of information processing. The School-Age achievement tests assess spelling, word decoding, and arithmetic skills. The number of subtests that are administered varies, depending on age: four core subtests for the lower Preschool level (ages 2-3 to 3-5 years), six core subtests for the upper Preschool level (ages 3-6 to 5-11), and six for School-Age children (ages 6-0 to 17). The number of diagnostic subtests ranges from two to five, once again depending on age. In addition to the GCA, Verbal Ability and Nonverbal Ability Cluster Scores are obtained for upper Preschool children, whereas Verbal Ability, Nonverbal Reasoning Ability, and Spatial Ability Cluster Scores are produced for the School-Age level. Raw scores are converted first to ability scores (Rasch model). These scores are not normative, but provide a scale of performance within a subtest. The ability scores, in turn, are translated into T scores and percentiles. T scores are then summed to produce the GCA (considered to best reflect g) and Cluster Scores ($M = 100, SD = 15$). Cluster Standard Scores range from approximately 50–150; the GCA from 45–165. Therefore, three levels of interpretation are available; the GCA, Cluster Scores, and subtest scores. Testing requires 25–65 minutes for the Preschool level and 40–65 minutes for the School-Age level. Achievement testing necessitates 15–25 minutes. A Special Nonverbal Composite (consisting of pointing, drawing, and object manipulation) is recommended for nonverbal or hearing-impaired children.

The DAS was standardized on 3,475 U.S. children, 175–200 per age group. The sample was stratified for age, gender, race/ethnicity, parental education, geographic region, and preschool enrollment, based on 1988 Census figures. Special education categories represented in the normative sample include learning disabled, speech impaired, emotionally disturbed, physically impaired, mentally retarded, and gifted children (percentages being relative to those found in the general population).

Mean internal consistency reliabilities (based on item response theory [IRT]) ranged from .70–.92 for individual subtests, .88–.92 for composite scores, and .90–.95 for the GCA. The mean reliability for the Special Nonverbal Composite was .81–.94, depending on age. Test-retest reliabilities (2–6 weeks) for the Preschool subtests and composites generally ranged from .56–.94 (the exception being delayed recall of objects, $r = .38$); for the School-Age level, .53–.97. Interrater reliabilities for four subtests with open-ended responses, and for out-of-level testing are also provided.

Confirmatory and exploratory factor analyses were employed to evaluate internal validity. A single factor provided the best fit for the core subtests at the youngest level, two factors for upper Preschool, and three factors for the School-Age level. Subtests not loading sufficiently ($> .50$) on the general factors were retained as diagnostic subtests and were not included in the GCA. Concurrent validity was assessed by comparing the DAS composites and GCA with the Wechsler Preschool and Primary Scale of Intelligence—Revised (WPPSI-R) (r s = .72–.89); Stanford-Binet Intelligence Scale, Fourth Revision (SB-IV) (.69–.77); McCarthy Scales of Children's Abilities (MSCA) (.55 = .84); Kaufman Assessment Battery for Children (K-ABC) (.63–.68); as well as the Peabody Picture Vocabulary Test—Revised (PPVT-R); Basic Achievement Skills Individual Screener (BASIS); Kaufman Test of Educational Achievement (K-TEA); and Woodcock Reading Mastery Tests—Revised (WRMT-R). These correlations were found for younger children; those for older ages were somewhat higher. In addition, a Bias Review Panel evaluated test materials to eliminate item or subtest bias based on gender, racial, ethnic, or cultural factors. Additional samples of Black and Hispanic children were collected for item bias analysis.

Out-of-level testing and extended norms can be used with exceptional children, namely, bright younger children or older, less able ones. These enhance diagnostic accuracy, and normative tables are provided to allow determination of T scores, percentiles, and age equivalents in these cases. Examiners accustomed to other, similar test batteries are advised to review the Handbook and the Administration and Scoring Manual in detail, because some procedures differ from the routine. For example, age is not rounded upwards, raw scores do not include items the child would have passed had all items been given, no basal or ceiling levels are required, a decision point concept (regarding starting and stopping) is utilized, and some subtests are administered differently than they are on similar batteries (e.g., Recall of Digits is presented at the rate of two digits per second). Nonetheless, the Preschool and the School-Age record forms are well designed and help to simplify these differences.

In summary, the DAS is a well-constructed and standardized test instrument. It appears psychometrically sound, allows for "tailored" testing, and the items are appealing and conducive to maintaining a high interest level in children. The recommended sequence of administration is good, and the procedures are not difficult. Documentation in the Handbook and Administration manual is excellent. The DAS contains many subtle "perks" such as performance analysis in Word Reading, the Informal Behavior Scale, and scoring templates for drawing tests. Comparisons can be made between Cluster scores, the GCA, subtest scores, and achievement, thereby allowing for more precision in the identification of strengths and weaknesses.

The DAS is competitive with tests such as the WPPSI-R, MSCA, K-ABC, and SB-IV; examiners, therefore, may be reluctant to invest the time, effort, and expense in developing proficiency with yet "another test." However, the DAS should not be considered a "johnny-come-lately" in the burgeoning field of cognitive testing. The combination of developmental and educational perspectives makes the DAS unique and particularly useful in the evaluation of young ($3^1/2$–6 year) children suspected of having developmental delays, children with hearing or language difficulties, or school-age students with LDs or mild mental retardation. The first point is particularly important, given the reported problem on the WPPSI-R and SB-IV of low sensitivity for mild or even moderate developmental delays in young children. However, reciprocally, the DAS may not be as useful for young, gifted children or lower preschool children with significant delays.

Review of the Differential Ability Scales by ROBERT C. REINEHR, Associate Professor of Psychology, Southwestern University, Georgetown, TX:

The Differential Ability Scales (DAS) is an outgrowth of the earlier British Ability Scales (9:172). It is an individually administered battery of cognitive and achievement tests for children and adolescents. The Cognitive Battery includes 17 subtests and yields a composite score called the General Conceptual Ability (GCA) score, some lower level composite scores, and some specific-ability measures. In addition, three School Achievement Tests yield measures of arithmetic, spelling, and word reading.

The DAS is very comprehensive and almost everything about it is correspondingly complex, including administration procedures, scoring, and interpretation. Even the record form, although beautifully designed and reproduced, is very dense and complex, containing a great deal of administration and scoring information, including 12 tables for the conversion of raw scores to ability scores. It is 22 pages long and the pages are not numbered. The summary page requires a complex 12-step process to complete.

The manual suggests that a trained examiner should be able to administer the entire battery to children older than 5 years in less than $1^{1}/_{2}$ hours. It seems likely that this would be possible only for a very experienced examiner. There are many complex stimulus materials to be handled, and starting and stopping points are determined by finding levels at which the child passes and then fails a given number of consecutive items. Although stimulus exposure is often timed, for most subtests the examiner must exercise clinical judgement concerning the length of time to allow before scoring an item incorrect. In general, administration of the DAS resembles the administration of the Stanford-Binet Intelligence Scale (10:342).

Raw scores are converted to scaled scores called "Ability Scores" by use of tables in the record form. For the cognitive subtests, these ability scores are then converted to T scores with a mean of 50 and a standard deviation of 10. The T scores are in turn converted into five Cognitive Composite Scores and the GCA score, each with a mean of 100 and a standard deviation of 15. For the achievement tests, the ability scores are converted directly into standard scores with a mean of 100 and a standard deviation of 15.

The manual contains over 130 pages of tables for the conversions of scores and for comparisons of scores to various reference groups. Standardization data and reliability and validity information are presented in a separate Introductory and Technical Handbook.

The Handbook is a model of how information concerning test development should be presented. It covers the rationale behind the test, the history of development, description and interpretation of the subtests and clusters, norms, reliability, and validity information. Many different estimates of reliability, and dozens of comparisons of the DAS with other cognitive and achievement measures are presented. It is very technical, but very comprehensive: Very few instruments provide such detailed information regarding development, reliability, and validity.

From a psychometric perspective, the DAS is more than satisfactory. Internal and test-retest reliabilities are high for both subtest and composite scores at all ages, and standard errors of measurement are low. Correlations between the DAS and other cognitive measures are high, particularly so for children of school age. WISC-R (Wechsler Intelligence Scale for Children—Revised) FSIQs and Stanford-Binet IV IQs tend to be slightly higher than the GCA, but correlations between the GCA and other measures of global intellectual function are high across all age groups.

Moderate correlations are reported between the three DAS Achievement Test Scores and the Cognitive Composite Scores. The relationship between the DAS achievement tests and scores on other individually administered achievement batteries is very high. Correlations with group-administered achievement tests are lower but still substantial: There is little question that the same domain is being assessed.

In general, the DAS is an excellent instrument for intellectual evaluation and is at least as good as other well-known instruments for achievement evaluation. It is difficult to administer and to score, however, and yields results so like the WISC-R and Stanford-Binet IV that, for most assessment situations, some consideration needs to be given to whether it is worth the considerable effort required to train examiners in its use. The detailed presentation of the psychometric characteristics of the DAS makes it an outstanding choice for research applications.

[112]

Dimensions of Excellence Scales.

Purpose: To assess the quality and effectiveness of a school or district.
Population: Schools or districts.
Publication Date: 1988.
Acronym: DOES.
Administration: Group.
Price Data: Available from publisher.
Comments: Ratings by students, parents, and school staff.
Authors: Russell A. Dusewicz and Francine S. Beyer.
Publisher: Research for Better Schools.
a) STUDENT SCALE.
Scores: 4 dimensions: School Climate, Teacher Behavior, Monitoring and Assessment, Student Discipline and Behavior.
Time: (30) minutes.
b) PARENT SCALE.

Scores, 8: same as *a* above plus Leadership, Curriculum, Staff Development, Parent Involvement.
Time: (20–30) minutes.
c) SCHOOL STAFF SCALE.
Scores, 8: Same as *b* above.
Time: (45) minutes.

Review of the Dimensions of Excellence Scales by JANET F. CARLSON, Assistant Professor of Education, Graduate School of Education, Fairfield University, Fairfield, CT:

The Dimensions of Excellence Scales (DOES) consists of three survey instruments completed by school staff, parents, and students of a school or district. Although the scales are apparently intended "for school improvement," as attested to on the cover of the manual, they actually are only appropriate for gathering information related to various dimensions of school performance. Their utility for even this limited purpose, however, is dubious.

The *Standards for Educational and Psychological Testing* (AERA, APA, & NCME, 1985) note that test manuals should provide enough technical information for the potential user to evaluate the test's appropriateness for the user's intended purpose. The DOES manual falls far short of this objective. The basis of research from which the dimensions themselves were derived is not specified, either in summary fashion or via citations of relevant literature. Indeed, no references are cited in the manual and no list of resources, such as a bibliography, is provided. The test authors do note that they chose to include only dimensions that were considered modifiable.

The scales demonstrate the potential for the occurrence of many of the problems commonly associated with rating scales. These issues are compounded further by the dearth of supportive psychometric evidence. "One of the conditions that affects the validity of ratings is the extent of the rater's *relevant contact* with [what is] to be rated . . . In many rating situations, it is desirable to include a space to be checked in lieu of a rating if the rater has had no opportunity to observe the particular trait in a given [situation]" (Anastasi, 1988, p. 646). The lack of an option stating that there has been insufficient opportunity to observe seems particularly problematic when one considers the student survey is administered in grades as low as fourth, and that it asks students to rate such things as whether "teachers are fair in grading all students." Similarly, when parents are asked to render a judgment regarding the extent to which "most parents provide a place for their children to study at home," the omission of a "cannot say" option is troublesome.

Rating errors, such as errors of central tendency and leniency errors, pose a problem for rating scales such as the DOES because they act to "reduce the effective width of the scale and make ratings less discriminative" (Anastasi, 1988, p. 646). Although such errors may be eliminated by employing rankings or other *order-of-merit procedures*, these systems are not employed by the DOES and, consequently, one may suspect that these common rating errors may influence the validity of the results.

Despite these potential problems, the test authors state boldly that the scales' reliability and validity are supported by the results of field testing. They note elsewhere, however, that only one scale—the School Staff Scale—has been subjected to this form of scrutiny. Regarding reliability and validity, the data presented are extremely sparse. It seems unlikely that more persuasive data exist that are not presented in the test manual.

The test authors represent the DOES as both criterion- and norm-referenced. Although insufficient support is presented for either claim, a particularly grave concern arises from a statement contained in the DOES manual that "normative comparisons also may be made" (p. 4). The statement implies that a normative sample exists, from which estimates of population parameters have been derived. Because such a standardization sample apparently does not exist, it seems the test authors' intention is simply to point out that potential users may develop their own local norms by administering the scales on a district-wide basis and then make comparisons between one school's performance and that of the entire district. The implication that the scales thus constitute norm-referenced instruments is irresponsible, because virtually any criterion-referenced measure may be used in this manner.

In summary, the authors of the DOES intended to provide an instrument to accurately and reliably evaluate school performance, with the hope of improving school practices and policies that impact performance. They fail to achieve these goals primarily due to the failure of establishing the soundness of the instrument and the procedures governing its administration. Of deepest concern are the lack of specificity regarding the research basis on which the instrument was developed, the paucity of studies to establish reliability and validity, and the disregard for several important standards of test construction promulgated by the American Educational Research Association, the American Psychological Asociation, and the National Council on Measurement in Education in the form of the *Standards for Educational and Psychological Testing* (1985).

REVIEWER'S REFERENCES

American Educational Research Association, American Psychological Association, & National Council on Measurement in Education. (1985). *Standards for educational and psychological testing.* Washington, DC: American Psychological Association, Inc.

Anastasi, A. (1988). *Psychological testing* (6th ed.): New York: Macmillan.

Review of the Dimensions of Excellence Scales by
WILLIAM P. ERCHUL, *Associate Professor of Psychology and Director of the School Psychology Program, North Carolina State University, Raleigh, NC:*

OVERVIEW. The Dimensions of Excellence Scales (DOES) consists of three survey scales (i.e., School Staff, Parent, and Student) that assess respondents' perceptions of eight dimensions shown to be related to school effectiveness. The eight dimensions, identified through a careful review of the research literature, are: School Climate, Leadership, Teacher Behavior, Curriculum, Monitoring and Assessment, Student Discipline and Behavior, Staff Development, and Parent Involvement. Evaluating these dimensions at the school district and/or school building level would seem to be valuable in documenting the perceived impact of current educational programs and in targeting areas for future improvement.

Respondents to the DOES are instructed to rate each item on a 5-point Likert scale having the anchors, *Almost Always* and *Almost Never*. Examples of items include: "The school motivates students to learn" (School Staff scale/School Climate dimension) and "Usually I am not bored in class" (Student scale/Teacher Behavior dimension). The School Staff scale, containing 200 items grouped by the eight dimensions, is completed by teachers, support staff, administrators, and school board members. The Parent scale addresses the same dimensions, but in a briefer, 71-item form. There are two Student scales, each containing 44 items and addressing only the four dimensions appropriate to students. One form is for students in grades 7 and higher, and the other form, which uses a 3-point Likert scale, is for those in grades 4 through 6.

NORMS AND SCORE INTERPRETATION. Given that the authors of the DOES consider the individual school the smallest relevant unit of analysis, one might expect to find norms reported in the Manual based on a national sample of respondent groups associated with elementary, junior high, and secondary schools. However, it appears that the DOES was "normed" on only 26 schools located in Maryland, and the Manual provides no descriptive statistics. Therefore, a traditional, norm-referenced interpretation of DOES scores is not possible. Dusewicz and Beyer instead suggest a norm-referenced interpretation based on comparing: (*a*) different schools across the same dimensions, (*b*) different respondent groups across the same dimensions, and (*c*) different dimensions within the same school. With no normative data, no data supporting the equivalency of dimension scores across respondent groups, and no data supporting the equivalency of scores across dimensions, any conclusions drawn from the authors' suggested "norm-referenced"

comparisons should be viewed skeptically. Fortunately, a criterion-referenced interpretation (e.g., a relative comparison between a high dimension score established as an a priori goal and an obtained dimension score) is meaningful and defensible.

RELIABILITY. Coefficient alphas for the eight dimensions on the School Staff scale range from .89 to .98 ($M = .93$). These high alphas attest to the internal consistency of the DOES. Although the authors report no reliability data pertaining to the Parent and Student Scales, it may be assumed that the reliability of these two scales will be lower because they contain many fewer items than does the School Staff scale. Because the DOES could be used for pre- and post-testing purposes, it is imperative that test-retest reliability data be compiled.

VALIDITY. The authors note that content validity is the most important kind of validity for a measure such as the DOES, and offer sufficient evidence in that regard. Although the emphasis on content validity seems warranted, concurrent, construct, and criterion-related validity studies also must be conducted. The case for concurrent and construct validity studies is clear, given the existence of several reliable and valid instruments in use that measure organizational climate and related factors in schools. Examples include the Stern-Steinhoff Organizational Climate Index (OCI), first described by Steinhoff (1965), and the Profile of a School (POS) (Likert & Likert, 1976). Both instruments are theoretically based and have been well researched.

The case for conducting (or at least reporting) criterion-related validity studies is equally clear, given the authors' claim on page 2 of the Manual: "Each dimension has evidence linking it to student achievement. If the school takes action to affect a given dimension, achievement will be improved. When the relationship between a dimension and student achievement is strong, or when the action that a school takes is strong, the level of achievement rises significantly." This statement is not only a bold claim, but also a reflection of the authors' mistaken belief that correlation regularly implies causation. Although one would expect to find correlational evidence in the Manual linking dimension scores with student achievement, there is none.

The potential user of the DOES must realize that Dusewicz and Beyer provide no validity data for the Parent and Student scales. As the "data are currently being analyzed" (Manual, p. 15), one may expect a revised Manual to contain additional information that will address many of the issues raised in this review.

CONCLUSION. The DOES impresses one as a well-planned, potentially useful instrument that currently lacks fundamental empirical validation. The scales are viewed most fairly as incomplete rather than psychometrically inadequate. This review has noted several concerns related to norming, score interpretation, and test-retest reliability as well as concurrent, construct, and criterion-related validity. Although the OCI and POS do not measure exactly what the DOES purports to measure, these two instruments offer better documentation of their psychometric properties and thus, should be considered for use instead of the DOES at this time.

REVIEWER'S REFERENCES

Steinhoff, C. R. (1965). *Organizational climate in a public school system.* (U.S.O.E. Cooperative Research Program, Contract No. OE-4-255, Project No. S-083). Washington, DC: U.S.O.E.
Likert, R., & Likert, J. G. (1976). *New ways of managing conflict.* New York: McGraw Hill.

[113]
Dimensions of Self-Concept.

Purpose: Designed to "measure non-cognitive factors associated with self-esteem or self-concept in a school setting."
Publication Dates: 1976–89.
Acronym: DOSC.
Scores, 5: Level of Aspiration, Anxiety, Academic Interest and Satisfaction, Leadership and Initiative, Identification vs. Alienation.
Administration: Group.
Price Data, 1991: $8.15 per 25 tests (specify form); $3 per technical manual ('89, 23 pages); $5.80 per specimen set.
Comments: Self-report instrument.
Authors: William B. Michael, Robert A. Smith, and Joan J. Michael.
Publisher: EdITS/Educational and Industrial Testing Service.
a) FORM E.
Population: Grades 4–6.
Time: (20–40) minutes.
b) FORM S.
Population: Grades 7–12.
Time: (15–35) minutes.
c) FORM H.
Population: College.
Time: (15–35) minutes.
Cross References: For reviews by Herbert G. W. Bischoff and Alfred B. Heilbrun, Jr., see 9:353 (4 references); see also T3:734 (5 references).

TEST REFERENCES

1. Darakjian, G. P., Michael, W. B., & Knapp-Lee, L. (1984). The predictive validity of subscales of an academic self-concept measure administered nine semesters prior to acquisition of criterion data reflecting school achievement. *Educational and Psychological Measurement, 44,* 715-720.
2. Halote, B., & Michael, W. B. (1984). The construct validity of two college-level academic self-concept scales for a sample of primarily Hispanic community college students. *Educational and Psychological Measurement, 44,* 993-1007.
3. Michael, W. B., Denny, B., Knapp-Lee, L., & Michael, J. J. (1984). The development and validation of a preliminary research form of an academic self-concept measure for college students. *Educational and Psychological Measurement, 44,* 373-381.
4. Michael, W. B., Kim, I. K., & Michael, J. J. (1984). The factorial validity of the Dimensions of Self-Concept (DOSC) measure for a sample of eighth-grade children and for one of community college adults. *Educational and Psychological Measurement, 44,* 413-421.
5. Darakjian, G. P., Michael, W. B., & Knapp-Lee, L. (1985). The long-term predictive validity of an academic self-concept measure relative to criteria of secondary school grades earned over eleven semesters. *Educational and Psychological Measurement, 45,* 397-400.
6. Gold, Y., & Michael, W. B. (1985). Academic self-concept correlates of potential burnout in a sample of first-semester elementary-school practice teachers: A concurrent validity study. *Educational and Psychological Measurement, 45,* 909-914.
7. Caracosta, R., & Michael, W. B. (1986). The construct and concurrent validity of a measure of academic self-concept and one of locus of control for a sample of university students. *Educational and Psychological Measurement, 46,* 735-744.
8. Crowder, B., & Michael, W. B. (1989). The construct validity of a revised form of a self-concept measure for employees in a work setting. *Educational and Psychological Measurement, 49,* 421-428.
9. Crowder, B., & Michael, W. B. (1989). The measurement of self-concept in an employment setting. *Educational and Psychological Measurement, 49,* 19-31.
10. Freeman, J. G., & Hutchinson, N. L. (1989). The concurrent validity of the Dimensions of Self-Concept (DOSC), Level E. *Educational and Psychological Measurement, 49,* 429-431.

Review of the Dimensions of Self-Concept by SHARON JOHNSON-LEWIS, Director of Research, Evaluation, and Testing, Detroit Public Schools, Detroit, MI:

GENERAL DESCRIPTION. The Dimensions of Self-Concept (DOSC) is a self-reported measure of noncognitive factors associated with self-concept in a school setting. Each of the three forms—elementary, secondary, and college—contains between 70 and 80 statements that are designed to assess five dimensions of school-related self-concept: (*a*) Level of Aspiration, (*b*) Anxiety, (*c*) Academic Interest and Satisfaction, (*d*) Leadership and Initiative, and (*e*) Identification versus Alienation. The five self-concept dimensions are each measured by 14 to 16 statements. Elementary school students respond to three answer choices— *always or almost always*, *sometimes*, and *never or almost never*. However, students in grades 7–12 and college students are given five choices— *never, seldom, about half the time, very often,* and *always*.

The three different forms of the DOSC were designed to contain parallel items for each of the five self-concept dimensions. The underlying construct for each form is the same; however, the reading and language level varies to correspond to the approximate age group of the students. The readability level for the tests is not provided. The manual indicates that the test items for the elementary and secondary forms were first developed in 1975–76 and the college form in 1980–84.

A review of the items indicates that there is some need to revise the statements so that they better reflect the language of today's youth. For example, the term "recess" in the elementary form is probably outdated. The test statements were reviewed by the professional staff of Los Angeles Unified School District and if, in their judgement, items were threatening to teachers, parents, citizen groups, or significant others, they were removed or altered. This review procedure provides limited control. It would have been more efficient if parents, teachers, and representatives of citizen groups had also participated in the review process.

TEST ADMINISTRATION. The test forms are short and appear to be easy to administer. Although the tests are untimed, the authors suggest that the approximate working time should not exceed 55 minutes. This reviewer did not receive a separate test administration manual. Directions were included as part of the technical manual and on the cover of the test books. This may prove to create a problem in that there are no common directions for preparing students for testing.

The statements contained in the manual for test administrators are not extremely specific in nature. For instance, for the elementary form, the manual states that "it *may* be advisable . . . to read the directions aloud." In order to preserve the standardization of the test administration, it would be better to advise examiners either to read aloud or not to read aloud, but not both.

Although the directions fail to provide illustrative items, they do suggest that the teacher "go through" a sample item that is not a part of the test in order to show students how to use their answer sheets. Again, this omission limits test standardization however minimal for this type of test. It also requires teachers to develop their own samples. Sample items may be of particular importance in the elementary grades where students may be less familiar with Likert-type formats.

TEST INTERPRETATION. The authors provide percentile ranks corresponding to the raw scores on each of the five dimensions of self-concept. Unfortunately, the percentiles were developed with data from only one school district and with fairly small samples. In addition, the method used to select the sample lacked statistical rigor. The manual states that "In the professional judgement of high-level personnel within the Los Angeles Unified School District, classes were selected in a variety of schools to constitute what would be representative samples of students."

Although the manual provides other normative information, it too is limited. Additional data are provided for a group of eighth grade students in a suburban middle school, grades 13 and 14 in a suburban community college, and undergraduates in a private university located in a suburban area. Although it is not mentioned, this reviewer assumes that these samples were also from the Los Angeles area. Only means and standard deviations of the five DOSC scales are given for these samples. Percentile ranks are not provided.

In general, concurrent and predictive validity data indicate that the Level of Aspiration dimension has positive correlation with the achievement measures used, whereas the Level of Anxiety dimension tends to have a negative one. The authors do note that the patterns of correlations differ somewhat from study to study which is likely to be due in part to the differences of the populations involved. These data were derived by examining grade point averages and achievement test scores of samples of students from the Los Angeles Unified School District, a private university, and a Texas Mexican-American community.

The technical manual also provides a fairly comprehensive selection of activities to assist test users in score interpretation. The activities are specifically designed to increase student self-concept and may be quite helpful to teachers.

SUMMARY. In summary, the DOSC is a short, easy-to-administer instrument designed to assess self-concept in a school setting. The elementary and secondary forms were developed in 1975–76, and there is evidence to suggest that the language of these forms should be revised. In addition to language revision, the authors need to extend the normative sample beyond the Los Angeles area. The manual lacks specific directions to be read by test administrators and would be enhanced greatly by the inclusion of sample items.

Before selecting a student self-concept instrument, this reviewer would recommend examining the School Attitude Measure (SAM; 344) published by American Testronics. The SAM has been recently normed on an adequate sample, has clear and concise directions, and does not have many of the limitations of the DOSC.

[114]

Draw A Person: A Quantitative Scoring System.
Purpose: "To meet the need for a modernized, recently normed, and objective scoring system to be applied to human figure drawings produced by children and adolescents."
Population: Ages 5–17.
Publication Date: 1988.
Acronym: DAP.
Scores, 4: Man, Woman, Self, Total.
Administration: Group or individual.
Price Data, 1989: $59 per complete kit including 25 student record/response forms, scoring chart, and manual ('88, 100 pages); $40 per scoring chart and manual; $19 per 25 student record/response forms.
Time: 15(25) minutes.
Author: Jack A. Naglieri.
Publisher: The Psychological Corporation.

TEST REFERENCES
1. Prewett, P. N., Bardos, A. N., & Naglieri, J. A. (1989). Assessment of mentally retarded children with the Matrix Analogies Test—Short Form, Draw A Person: A Quantitative Scoring System, and the Kaufman Test of Educational Achievement. *Psychology in the Schools, 26*, 254-260.

Review of the Draw A Person: A Quantitative Scoring System by MERITH COSDEN, Associate Professor of Education, University of California, Santa Barbara, CA:

The Draw A Person (DAP) is a revision of the popular Goodenough-Harris Drawing Test (Harris, 1963; 9:441), which was itself a revision of Goodenough's Draw-A-Man Test published in 1926. Harris adapted the original test by adding a drawing of a woman and a self-drawing to the drawing of a man, developing a more objective coding system, obtaining a nationally representative normative sample, expanding the age range of the normative group, and replacing the ratio IQ used to evaluate performance with a deviation IQ. One prescient reviewer (Dunn, 1972) predicted the Harris revision would add 20 years to the life of the Goodenough procedure. Indeed, over 25 years have elapsed between the Harris revision and the current one.

The manual states the DAP was developed in response to criticisms of the Goodenough-Harris test. The following changes from the Goodenough-Harris system are reported: use of smaller (half-year and quarter-year) norm intervals, development of a more recent standardization sample, reduction in the ambiguity of the Goodenough-Harris scoring criteria, and development of norms for the self-drawing to permit calculation of a composite (man, woman, self) standard score. Although the value of updating the standardization sample and using smaller norm intervals is evident, the effects of the other changes on the utility of the test are less clear.

The changes to the scoring system are perhaps the most difficult to evaluate. The criteria used to score the DAP differ from those of the Goodenough-Harris, as do the total number of items for which one can gain credit. Although the manual describes the conceptualization of the DAP scoring system in some detail, its relationship to the Harris system is not addressed. This is surprising, as the DAP is promoted as a revision of the earlier test. It appears, however, the DAP scoring system was developed independently and without consideration of the Harris system. Nevertheless, the manual reports correlations between the two systems that range from .84 to .87. Further, the relationship between the two scoring systems and other measures of cognitive functioning appear similar. The advantage of one set of scoring criteria over another has not been demonstrated empirically.

Some internal problems with the DAP scoring system are apparent. Although the standardization sample was expanded to include children from ages 5 to 18, the system does not differentiate scores equally well for children at each age. Scores at quarter-year intervals could be developed only for children from ages 5 to 8-11, whereas half-year intervals could be obtained for 9- and 10-year-olds. For ages 11–18, mean scores on the DAP were too similar to provide separate age norms, so their scores are grouped together. The Goodenough-Harris system, on the other hand, yields progressively increasing raw scores for children at yearly intervals from age 5 to 15. Given the low age ceiling in the DAP scoring system, its utility as a measure of cognitive functioning for children over age 11 should be questioned.

The major weakness of this test, however, is the limited scope of its revision. The DAP follows the basic structure of the Goodenough-Harris test without substantively questioning its content or purpose. For example, the DAP adopts the Goodenough-Harris' use of three figures: drawings of the man, woman, and self. The DAP, in fact, reifies what was the experimental, auxiliary use of the self-drawing in the Goodenough-Harris test; in the DAP, all three figures are scored by the same criteria and summed to provide a composite score. What is missing in the manual is the rationale for the use of these particular three drawings. Why not rely on only one or two drawings? Is it essential that the drawings be of a man, woman, and self? We may assume the author of the test was interested in obtaining several samples of behavior in order to increase the reliability of the test results. However, one still needs to question the selection of these particular samples of behavior, and whether other samples (e.g., two drawings of a man; one of a man and one of a woman) would provide more accurate or reliable information. The lack of theoretical or empirical support for the structure of the test is troublesome.

The use of the three-figure composite score is supported only partly by the psychometric data presented in the manual. Internal consistency coefficients (coefficient alphas) for the individual drawings are lower (ranging from .56 to .78) than those for the composite score (.83 to .89). Interrater reliabilities are high for individual as well as composite scores (.86 to .95) and are comparable to those obtained for the Goodenough-Harris system.

Test-retest reliabilities are less impressive, however. The major study presented in the manual was conducted on a sample of 112 students over a 4-week period. Mean reliability coefficients were .74 for the composite score, .70 for the man, .65 for the woman, and .58 for the self-drawing. Examination of the reliability coefficients as a function of grade level, however, found some of the self-drawing coefficients strikingly low (.30 for sixth graders and .21 for seventh graders). Thus, one can question the inclusion of the self-drawing in the composite score on both psychometric and conceptual grounds. Given the self-drawing's intended experimental use on the Goodenough-Harris test, and the lack of a validated study to support its relationship to other measures of cognitive functioning, the nature of its contribution to a composite score warrants further study.

The validity of the DAP as a "nonverbal measure of ability" is a fundamental concern. The validity data presented in the manual are similar to those associated with the Harris scoring system: DAP scores increase as the child gets older, reflecting the effects of development on performance, and statistically significant correlations are obtained between the DAP and other measures of intellectual functioning. The manual reports that correlations between the DAP and the Matrix Analogies Test— Short Form (MAT-SF) and the Multilevel Academic Survey Test (MAST) range from .17 to .31. Although statistically significant, these correlations indicate the DAP accounts for only a small portion of the variance in the other cognitive tests. Similar correlations are obtained between the Goodenough-Harris system and the MAST and MAT-SF; this is not surprising, given the relatively high correlations between scores obtained from the DAP and Goodenough-Harris tests. These data suggest the two scoring systems are sampling similar cognitive skills, but that these skills vary in substantive ways from those sampled by other tests of cognitive functioning.

There is, in fact, a vast literature on the use of figure drawings for both emotional and intellectual assessment. The results of the studies on ability assessment have been inconclusive. Some have demonstrated statistically significant, if functionally low, relationships between figure drawings and other measures of ability, although others have found no relationship between children's drawings and other measures of cognitive performance. What is striking in the literature is the lack of attention given to defining the conditions under which one would select drawings to assess intellectual functioning over other available assessment devices. The DAP manual suggests the test may be particularly useful for some special populations. Included in this list are children with language impairments, individuals from minority cultures (particularly American Indians), and individuals with motor problems (including cerebral palsy) as the child is credited for the inclusion of body parts but not penalized for the precision of the drawings. The manual does not provide any data, however, to support these contentions. Normative data for individuals from the aforementioned special groups are not readily available. The manual provides normative data on two ethnic-minority groups, Blacks and Hispanics; the mean scores of these groups do not significantly differ from those of the rest of the sample. These data are suggestive, but the hypothesized role of the DAP as an ability assessment device for special populations remains unsubstantiated.

It is my feeling that despite the lack of "hard" data to support their use, figure drawings will continue to be a popular part of many assessment batteries. In addition to the ease with which they can be administered, drawings provide the clinician with a nonthreatening way to obtain information that is intuitively very rich. In fact, the implicit rationale for the use of the three figures in the DAP is that these drawings can serve double duty in a test battery; that is, they can be used for projective purposes as well as for ascertaining the child's cognitive abilities. The utility of the test for assessing ability, however, remains a question. The conditions under which figure drawings should be preferred over other tests of ability have neither been well defined nor empirically validated.

In sum, the major advantage of the DAP over the Goodenough-Harris system is that it uses a more recent normative sample. The advantage of one set of scoring criteria over the other has not yet been determined, and the high correlations between the two systems add to the ambiguity in choosing between them. Although the DAP appears to be as good an assessment tool as the Goodenough-Harris, it is unfortunate the revision stays so close to its predecessor. Dunn (1972) criticized the Goodenough-Harris manual for its limited discussion of the theoretical relevance of the Draw-A-Man test and its implications for future conceptualizations of intelligence. One finds similar flaws in the presentation of the DAP. Further theoretical and empirical analysis of the role of figure drawing in the assessment of ability is needed to make this test a more useful tool.

REVIEWER'S REFERENCES

Harris, D. (1963). *Children's drawings as measures of intellectual maturity.* New York: Harcourt, Brace and World.

Dunn, J. (1972). [Review of the Goodenough-Harris Drawing Test.] In O. K. Buros (Ed.), *The seventh mental measurements yearbook* (pp. 671-672). Highland Park, NJ: The Gryphon Press.

Review of the Draw A Person: A Quantitative Scoring System by W. GRANT WILLIS, Associate Professor of Psychology, University of Rhode Island, Kingston, RI:

The Draw A Person: A Quantitative Scoring System (DAP) is a carefully constructed and well-normed procedure that should prove useful in accomplishing its goal of providing a screening measure of nonverbal ability. The examinee is required to produce time-limited (i.e., 5 minutes) pencil drawings of three pictures (man, woman, and self) on separate pages of a response form. Instructions are provided for both individual and group administration. The DAP is intended for ages 5 through 17 years, but it does not provide enough discriminative power at the upper-age ranges to be of much utility for adolescents. The maximum age-equivalent score reported for the DAP is 11 years, which "results from a ceiling effect at the upper age levels of the normative sample" (p. 63); standard-score equivalents ($M = 100$, $SD = 15$) of raw scores are collapsed across the 11- through 17-year-old age range.

The quantitative scoring system is unambiguous and the record form is clearly organized along 14 criteria. High levels of interrater reliability ($rs =$

.86 to .95), intrarater reliability (rs = .89 to .97), interrater agreement (91% to 94%), and intrarater agreement (94% to 96%) are reported in the test manual. The manual includes an excellent chapter on the scoring system, which provides explicit procedures, practice exercises, competency criteria, and (if needed) even remedial exercises.

The test manual is comprehensive and clearly organized. In addition to material on the scoring system, introductory (e.g., history, goals, appropriateness, user qualifications), test development and standardization, statistical properties, administration and scoring, and interpretation sections are included. The manual provides sufficient information for qualified users to evaluate the appropriateness and technical adequacy of the DAP.

The standardization sample is sufficiently large (N = 2,622) to ensure stability of the norms. Between 99 and 267 participants were included at each of 13 one-year age levels from 5 through 17 years stratified according to age, gender, racial, ethnic, and geographical proportions documented by 1980 U.S. Census data. Socioeconomic indicators of annual income and occupational type, documented on a district-wide basis, also closely matched 1980 U.S. Census data. Finally, community size was documented in the standardization sample as well. No gender differences were found for raw scores, and therefore norms were collapsed across gender. Age-related changes in raw scores showed the most rapid increase between 5 and 9 years, and then increased less rapidly. Thus, norms were established for quarter-year intervals for 5- through 8-year-olds, half-year intervals for 9- and 10-year-olds, and, as noted, one combined interval for the remaining 11-through 17-year-olds (for a total of 21 age intervals). Naglieri (p. 11) noted that "Because the raw score distributions are approximately symmetrical at all ages, they were not normalized," and argued that obtained standard scores closely matched those that would have resulted from a normalizing procedure. It is unfortunate no data were presented to support this claim, because the symmetry of a distribution of scores is unrelated to its kurtosis. This is an isolated weakness, however, in an otherwise exemplary test manual. Proper interpretation of standard scores, of course, rests on the assumption that those scores are based on a normal distribution; users of the DAP must trust this indeed is the case.

The internal consistency of DAP scores is good (median r = .86 for Total scores across the 13 one-year age groups in the standardization sample), and standard errors of measurement range from 5 to slightly over 6 standard score units. The stability of DAP scores was assessed for 112 individuals in one geographic region of the standardization sample. The mean test-retest coefficient for Total scores, computed over a 4-week interval for seven separate age levels (i.e., grades 1 through 7) was .74. The lowest coefficient was reported at grade 7 (r = .60) and the highest at grade 4 (r = .89). Clearly, additional stability data should be collected, but DAP Total scores show promise of adequate stability for screening purposes, at least during childhood.

The construct and concurrent validity studies reported in the manual also show promise of the validity of the DAP Total score as a screening measure during childhood. Here, age-related increases in total raw scores were found in the standardization sample from ages 5 through 11, but not thereafter. DAP Total standard scores showed a fairly high correlation (r = .87) with the sum of the Man, Woman, and Self standard scores from the Goodenough-Harris for 100 9-year-olds, and, in other samples, low to moderate correlations with matrix analogies (rs = .27 and .31), reading (r = .24), and math (r = .21) tests. In addition to the analysis of gender differences, DAP total standard scores were compared to investigate potential Black/White and Hispanic/non-Hispanic differences. Results suggested that scores are unlikely to be influenced by these factors.

In summary, the recently published DAP is a carefully developed and well-described nonverbal screening test of general ability. Evidence for the reliability and validity of the standard scores is accruing, and although inadequate for individual diagnosis, it is promising as a screening tool. The normative sample is stable and representative of 1980 U.S. Census data. The scoring system and test manual are clear. Results do not seem to be influenced by cultural (Hispanic/non-Hispanic) or racial (Black/White) factors. I would recommend its use through about age 11 for the purposes intended over other scoring systems, such as the Goodenough-Harris. As would be expected, use of the Total score is associated with substantially improved reliability relative to the Self, Man, or Woman drawings when scored separately. Thus, especially considering the minimal increase in administration time for the three drawings rather than only one, examiners should administer the DAP in its entirety. Finally, I would caution potential users that the DAP was neither intended nor validated as a personality measure, and it clearly should not be used for this purpose.

[115]
Draw-a-Story: Screening for Depression and Emotional Needs.

Purpose: "To facilitate the early identification of depressed individuals."
Population: Ages 5 and over.
Publication Dates: 1987–88.
Acronym: DAS.
Scores: Total score only.
Administration: Group.

Price Data, 1989: $19.95 per manual ('88, 80 pages) including test forms which may be photocopied.
Time: Administration time not reported.
Author: Rawley A. Silver.
Publisher: Ablin Press Distributors.

Review of the Draw-a-Story: Screening for Depression and Emotional Needs by WALTER KATKOVSKY, Professor of Psychology, Northern Illinois University, DeKalb, IL:

The aim of the Draw-a-Story (DAS) task is "the early identification of depressed individuals," especially of "masked" depression that is not readily identifiable using self-report measures. The instructions involve an interesting combination of projective methods: first, selecting two pictures from 14 about which the subject imagines a story; second, drawing a picture that tells a story based on his/her selections; and third, writing the story presented by the drawing. The theme of the story is scored on a 7-point scale from "strongly negative" to "strongly positive," and scoring examples of drawings and stories for each scoring category are presented in the manual. Negative themes, consisting of references to "sad, dead/dying, helpless, or isolated" story characters and "hopeless" futures, are considered signs of depression. Administration of the DAS is uncomplicated and brief, can be done individually or in groups, and is likely to elicit the cooperation of most subjects.

Although the reported research on the DAS is very limited, information on scoring reliability and the stability of scores over time is promising. Significant interscorer reliability is reported on 20 drawings with correlations ranging from .749 to .816 for three registered art therapists. These coefficients demonstrate acceptable scoring agreement among persons trained in the scoring method. Concerning the stability of scores, the manual briefly describes one reliability study, noting little change after 1 month in the scores of 12 children with negative scores, and after 2 years in children with positive scores. In a private communication, the author provided additional test-retest data on a small sample. A significant test-retest correlation of .87 was found after a 1-week interval on eight public school children, ages 9–11, who displayed signs of being emotionally disturbed.

Unfortunately, limited validity data provide sparse evidence that the DAS fulfills its aim as a measure of the early identification of depression. The one validity study reported in the manual compared the scores of 350 subjects heterogeneous for age and geographical location, divided into seven groups consisting of five groups of children/adolescents (35 depressed, 74 emotionally disturbed and nondepressed, 18 deaf, 64 learning-disabled, and 117 normal) and two groups of adults (15 depressed and 27 elderly). Subjects were classified into groups based on questionnaire responses about their histories and behavior by therapists and teachers, but detailed information about the questionnaire and criteria for group classification are not presented. The results of the validity study indicate that responses of depressed children and adolescents, but not those of depressed adults, were more likely to be scored "strongly negative" than the responses of the other groups. However, it is important to note that more negative than positive themes were given by all groups, and that themes scored as "moderately" or "mildly negative" did not discriminate between groups. Thus, the limited evidence of validity pertains only to children and adolescents and involves a dichotomous distinction between strongly negative themes and all others. No information is presented concerning relationships between DAS scores and scores on other widely used measures of depression. The author concludes with appropriate caution that the instrument "might be useful . . . in identifying some, but not all, depressed children and adolescents."

Norms on the DAS are presented in the manual for the 350 subjects used in the validity study. However, these are of limited value for the interpretation of scores because of the small numbers in some of the groups and the absence of standard demographic subject identification. Norms are needed for age, gender, race, and ethnic background. Also, a more extensive sample of adults, both normal and depressed, is necessary if the measure is to be meaningfully applied to adults.

In addition to the above limitations, several problems inherent in the DAS seem likely to lessen its validity. First, as presented, the measure provides limited and uneven amounts of data on subjects. Because the instructions call for only one drawing and story, subject data result in a single score, which eliminates the possibility of investigating internal consistency and sequential aspects of responses. Moreover, the examples of stories presented in the manual range from a title of a few words to several sentences, suggesting the possibility that scores are influenced by the length of the narrative response. To enhance the discriminatory power of the measure, the instructions for the narrative story could be expanded to include a past, present, and future to the story similar to instructions used in other thematic apperception tasks, and more than one story per subject could be obtained. Second, the 14 pictures from which the subject selects two were chosen for the DAS because earlier studies suggested they "prompted negative fantasies." Their limited and negative stimulus content probably accounts for the preponderance of negative themes in responses and restricts the measure's potential discrimination between depressed and nondepressed subjects as well as between degrees of depression. Third, the instructions in the rating scale deal only with the story content and do not make clear the extent to which the content of the drawing, including such features as its size, shading, and placement, should be used in evaluating the theme of the story. Also, two of the scoring rules invite questions without data to support them. Aggressive humor is scored 6 (moderately positive) even though responses of sarcasm and cynicism may be associated with depression, especially with "masked" depression. Another question involves the scoring of unemotional and ambivalent themes which are scored 4 (neutral) even though such responses may reflect detachment, lack of will, or hopelessness which are often signs of depression. The finding that 60% of the depressed adults who were tested were given a score of 4 points indicates this scoring category clearly needs refinement.

In a private communication, the author noted that a number of art therapists have reported using the DAS clinically for assessing a variety of factors, such as self-image, concerns, creativity, and reactions to traumatic experiences such as sexual abuse. Based on the limited research reported, the DAS is likely to be most useful with children and adolescents as a semistructured interview rather than as a specific measure of depression. Available data do not support its use for the early identification or screening of depression, for which self-report measures appear more appropriate despite their limitations and likelihood of missing individuals who are reluctant to report feelings of depression. Still, the DAS's aim of assessing depression without relying on self-report and its use of picture selection as a way of structuring projective drawings and story telling warrant further development and research.

Review of the Draw-a-Story: Screening for Depression and Emotional Needs by DAVID LACHAR, Associate Professor of Psychiatry and Behavioral Sciences, University of Texas Medical School at Houston, Houston, TX:

This diagnostic technique is based upon the following assumptions: (*a*) Signs of significant depression are often masked in childhood and adolescence, (*b*) stories accompanying original drawings often reflect unconscious conflict, and (*c*) expression through drawing tends to be less guarded than expression through language. These assumptions have received little or no empirical support, and are by and large, no longer in theoretical favor (see, for example, the assessment of childhood depression as defined in *DSM-III-R*).

In Draw-a-Story (DAS) the examinee is asked to select 2 line drawings from the 14 that are presented and to develop a story from the subjects represented (these drawings include five people, five animals, one object, one building, and two landscapes). The examinee is then asked to draw a picture from this

story and then to write the story, or at least provide a title for the drawing. Silver has presented similar task formats in other assessment procedures (The Stimulus Drawing Technique: Sandberg, Silver, & Vilstrup, 1984; Drawing from Imagination: Silver, 1990).

The DAS scoring system reflects the following assumptions: (*a*) Children perceive the same drawings differently, (*b*) perceptions are influenced by personal experiences, and (*c*) drawings can reflect elements of personality that can be quantified. The DAS stimuli were selected from 65 drawings. Story content, rather than formal drawing characteristics, is classified using a 7-point scale, "1" reflecting strongly negative themes (such as suicide) and "7" reflecting strongly positive themes. Scores of 2 and 3 reflect moderately and mildly negative themes, while 5 and 6 reflect mildly and moderately positive themes. A score of 4 suggests either ambivalent, unemotional, or unclear content.

Evidence of interrater reliability is presented for 20 varied protocols that were rated by three registered art therapists. Correlations between rater pairs were .749, .806, and .816. As for evidence of test-retest reliability, the manual (and Silver, 1988) presents a description of the results of 24 third graders tested twice. Following publication of the manual, a 1-week reliability of .87 was obtained for drawings from eight 9-to-11-year-old public school children (Silver, 1990, personal communication). These results are promising, although larger samples and the inclusion of the assessment of diagnostic agreement (1 versus 2–7; see below) will be necessary to provide stable and representative estimates.

Although this first DAS manual dedicates 58 pages to the 7-point scoring system, chapter 7 (and Silver, 1988) demonstrates that only the score of "1" significantly separates the depressed from the nondepressed—and then only for children and adolescents (percent scoring 1: depressed children and adolescents, 63%; normal children and adolescents, 10%; nondepressed emotionally disturbed children and adolescents, 19%). It is interesting to note that 39% of a sample of normal children and adolescents obtained a score of 2 (moderately negative response) compared to only 9% of a sample of same-age depressed. Considering that these 14 pictures were selected because of their tendency to generate negative content, it is not surprising that the majority of stories for normal children were classified as negative (60%) (the remainder obtain neutral = 15%, or positive = 25% content). The diagnostic utility of a score of 1 is further compromised by the observation that learning disabled adolescents (presumably not depressed) obtained this score 30% of the time. These data question the appropriateness of calling DAS a "screening" instrument that identifies the presence of depression.

This reviewer is impressed with the potential therapeutic and communicative value of a drawing-and-interpretation task. It is certainly a fairly popular diagnostic practice to use a drawing task with uncommunicative clients and to employ the idiographic interpretation of pictorial material as a projective technique. It does seem rather perplexing that a complex, multidimensional task has been reduced to a single dimension with only two meaningful categories. Silver's previous parametric analyses that demonstrated age and sex differences for the Stimulus Drawing Technique (Silver, 1987) suggest that similar analyses are necessary for the DAS.

It is possible the selection of drawings that pull for negative content over more ambiguous or neutral drawings that would generate a broader range of content has attenuated the validity of the 7-point rating procedure. It is important to document that the selected drawings are those that discriminate the best among meaningful groups. It is also necessary to determine if this time-consuming complex procedure is any more accurate than simple single-dimension self-report measures of child depression, such as the Children's Depression Inventory (67; Kovacs, 1982) and the Reynolds Child Depression Scale (334; Reynolds, 1989). The differential validity of the DAS must be established through comparison of the test performance of relatively homogeneous subgroups of behaviorally and emotionally disturbed children and adolescents, as well as through correlational study of the DAS score and multidimensional measures of child and adolescent adjustment.

REVIEWER'S REFERENCES

Kovacs, M. (1982). The Children's Depression Inventory. Pittsburgh, PA: Western Psychiatric Institute and Clinic.
Sandburg, L., Silver, R., & Vilstrup, K. K. (1984). The Stimulus Drawing Technique with adult psychiatric patients, stroke patients, and in adolescent art therapy. Art Therapy, 1, 132-140.
Silver, R. (1987). Sex differences in the emotional content of drawings. Art Therapy, 4, 67-77.
Silver, R. (1988). Screening children and adolescents for depression through Draw-a-Story. The American Journal of Art Therapy, 26, 119-124.
Reynolds, W. M. (1989). Reynolds Child Drepression Scale. Odessa, FL: Psychological Assessment Resources, Inc.
Silver, R. A. (1990). Silver Drawing Test of Cognitive Skills and Adjustment. Mamaroneck, NY: Ablin Press.

[116]
Drumcondra Verbal Reasoning Test 1.

Purpose: A measure of the ability to use and reason with verbal symbols.
Population: Ages 10-0 to 12-11.
Publication Date: No date.
Acronym: DVRT.
Scores: Total score only.
Administration: Group.
Restricted Distribution: Restricted to qualified psychologists.

Price Data, 1990: 30p per test booklet; £2 per scoring stencil; £2 per administrator's manual (no date, 18 pages); £5 per specimen set.
Time: 40(60) minutes.
Comments: Practice test available.
Author: Educational Research Centre.
Publisher: Educational Research Centre [Ireland].
Cross References: For reviews by Allen K. Hess and Neil H. Schwartz and William K. Wilkinson, see 10:97.

Review of the Drumcondra Verbal Reasoning Test 1 by ARTHUR B. SILVERSTEIN, Professor of Psychiatry, University of California, Los Angeles, CA:

The Drumcondra Verbal Reasoning Test 1 (DVRT) was designed as a group measure of the ability of children aged 10 through 12 years to use and reason with verbal symbols. It is made up of six types of items—following directions, classification, number series, opposites, analogies, and classes and relations—but yields just one score. The manual contains a brief description of the construction and standardization of the test, data on its reliability and validity, instructions, scoring, and norms. For further information on all these topics, one is referred to an unpublished doctoral dissertation from University College, Dublin.

At the time the DVRT was constructed, no objective ability or achievement tests had been standardized for use with an Irish population. Over 250 items were tried out on a group of students judged to be fairly representative of Irish 10-, 11-, and 12-year-olds, and 110 items survived the tryout. These items had the following properties: Roughly 75% had difficulty levels between .25 and .75, all had item-total correlations and regressions on age that were significant at the .01 level, and every distractor in the multiple-choice items attracted at least 10% of the incorrect responses at each of the three age levels.

The test was standardized in 1967 on a sample of almost 6,000 children, virtually all the pupils in the relevant age range in a stratified sample of all the Catholic primary schools in Ireland, to which a small number of Protestant primary schools, private schools, and secondary schools had been added. Norms, in the form of standard scores with a mean of 100 and a standard deviation of 15, are provided for every month of age from 10 years 0 months to 12 years 11 months.

The manual reports two types of reliability estimates. Internal consistency (Kuder-Richardson) coefficients ranged from .96 to .98 for the three age groups, and stability coefficients over both a 2-week and a 9-week interval were .94. These values are excellent. The manual also presents assorted evidence of criterion-related validity. A summary: Correlations ranged from .77 to .90 with standardized measures of general ability, from .72 to .81 with teachers' estimates of pupils' scholastic aptitude, and from .50 to .76 with standardized measures of achievement. All these values are very respectable.

The DVRT was designed primarily for use in research, and to judge from the data given in the manual it appears to have fared quite well in the small number of studies in which it has been employed. Nevertheless, its potential usefulness for psychoeducational assessment in the United States appears rather limited, not only because it was standardized on Irish school children, but also because the norms are now more than 20 years old.

Review of the Drumcondra Verbal Reasoning Test 1 by LINDA F. WIGHTMAN, Vice President—Test Development and Research, Law School Admission Services, Newtown, PA:

The Drumcondra Verbal Reasoning Test 1 (DVRT) is a 40-minute, 110-item, paper-and-pencil verbal aptitude test developed for use with primary school children in Ireland. At the time it was initially developed (1967), there were no standardized objective tests of ability or achievement for use with an Irish population. The test was designed primarily for use in research, but it is now commercially available. The published materials do not provide adequate data and instruction for score users. Specifically, the information available in the Administrator's Manual is unacceptably sparse. It does not include sufficient data to evaluate the technical adequacy of the instrument for the use for which it is intended and it is equally inadequate to guide potential users to appropriate interpretation of scores earned by students. Apparently, more detailed information about the development of the instrument is included in the author's unpublished doctoral dissertation, but the Educational Research Centre does not include the dissertation or relevant sections from it with its specimen set nor does it offer it for sale or provide an option to obtain a complimentary copy of it.

NORMS AND STANDARDIZATION. The norming sample was drawn from all Catholic primary schools in the country. After the Catholic primary schools were stratified by location, sex, type of administration, and size, a sample within each stratum was selected randomly. A small number of Protestant primary schools, private schools, and secondary schools were also included. The manual provides no information about the proportion of the selected schools that participated nor about what procedures were used to replace those schools that were unwilling or unable to participate. Consequently, there is no information from which to judge whether the norms are representative.

The manual is most lacking in the information for interpretation of scores. The manual claims that norms are available for every month of age from age 10 years 0 months to 12 years 11 months, but in fact, only a standardized score conversion table is provided. The test was standardized to a mean of 100 and a standard deviation of 15 based on the 1967 test data. A conversion table, allowing the test administrator to convert a raw score to the standardized score, is included in the manual. Although the table is not so labelled, it apparently is based on the 1967 standardization sample. Score users are instructed to find the column corresponding to the child's exact age and to find the row corresponding to the child's raw score, noting that the cell where the row and column intersect contains the child's standardized score. There are no further data or information to help the score user know what the score in the intersecting cell means for the student. There are no descriptive statistics, no percentile ranks, grade equivalents, age equivalents, or any other interpretive data. The publisher proffers that the test might be of use in the guidance of students at the point of transfer from primary to secondary education, but fails to provide even minimum data to aid the score user in making such use of the scores.

One might assume that the same standardized score represents the same amount of verbal reasoning ability across different age groups and that 100 represented the average for each age group in 1967, but there is no additional performance information. More importantly, this test was standardized on a group of students who apparently had no experience with standardized objective tests. This characteristic of the test-taking population is likely to have changed over time. Even leaving test-taking experience aside, the data in the tables are nearly 25 years old. Interpreting scores earned by students in 1991 or later relative to 1967 data seems of dubious value.

RELIABILITY. Internal consistency measures for this test are reported to range between .98 and .96, apparently based on the 1967 norming data. Reliability estimates should be recalculated using current data. The manual addresses the issue of unreliability in test scores and provides an explanation of standard error of measurement. The example provided confuses true score and observed score labels and is inaccurate as presented. This should be corrected in the next edition of the manual.

ADMINISTRATION. The instructions for administration do not adhere to the same rigors of standardized administration that are required by more commonly used primary school ability measures. Most notably, administrators are encouraged to identify individual children who are not working as quickly as the other children in the class and encourage them to select an answer. Presumably this instruction is intended to help pace the child through the test, but this subjective judgement about when a child is working too slowly would have differential impact on students who were noticed and encouraged at different times during the test.

There is no penalty for incorrect responses, so the advice to select an answer and move on would not harm the child who received it, but would differentially advantage children who received it earlier rather than later. Further, the instructions on the cover of the test book tell the child to skip a question if (s)he does not know the answer, so that the child who received individual encouragement might engage in a guessing strategy that was specifically discouraged for the other children.

Although there is a single time limit, administrators are instructed to ensure that the test book is folded over so that the students can look at only one page at a time. The glued binding on the test books makes it somewhat awkward to fold the pages to comply with this request. There is no information in the manual about whether the test is speeded for some students, but the concern about exact time limits suggests that all students might not have time to finish. There seems little to gain by insisting that the test book be folded rather than allowed to lay flat on the student's desk, especially because the directions at the bottom of each page instruct the student to go on to the next page.

VALIDITY. Results from a variety of validity studies are reported in the manual. Correlations between scores on the DVRT and other established measures of general ability such as the Wechsler Intelligence Scale for Children verbal scale and the California Short-Form Test of Mental Maturity and the Standard Progressive Matrices are reported to range from .77 to .84. Reported correlations with measures of performance that the DVRT purports to predict, such as academic achievement tests (.50 to .76) and teacher's estimates of pupils' aptitude (.72 to .81) are somewhat higher than expected; the studies referenced in the manual should be reviewed carefully by score users. The six item types on the test are combined to produce a single score, implicitly assuming a single construct referred to as verbal reasoning ability. No factor analysis or other data are provided to support this assumption.

CONCLUSION. The DVRT was developed specifically for use with Irish students age 10 years 0 months to 12 years 11 months. Validity data suggest the test is acceptable for its intended purpose. The major problem with the DVRT is the lack of normative information. The material provided with the test is inadequate to provide meaningful score interpretation, resulting in a measurement instrument of little utility to the practitioner. The administration manual and technical materials are not sufficiently developed. Prospective users should anticipate establishing their own local norms. There is nothing to recommend the use of this instrument in preference to other available instruments such as the Cognitive Abilities Test (10:66).

[117]

Dyadic Adjustment Scale.

Purpose: Designed to measure the quality of adjustment in marriage and similar dyadic relationships.
Population: People who have any committed couple relationship including unmarried cohabitation.
Publication Date: 1989.
Acronym: DAS.
Scores, 5: Dyadic Consensus, Dyadic Satisfaction, Affectional Expression, Dyadic Cohesion, Total.
Administration: Group or individual.
Price Data, 1989: $32 per complete kit including test manual (55 pages) and 20 QuikScore forms; $16 per 20 QuikScore forms; $18 per QuikScore manual; $100 per disk for computer administration (specify IBM $5^1/_4$ inch, IBM $3^1/_2$ inch or Apple).
Time: (5–10) minutes.
Comments: Computer program allows for 50 administrations.
Author: Graham B. Spanier.
Publisher: Multi-Health Systems, Inc.

TEST REFERENCES

1. Bowen, G. L. (1987). Wives employment status and marital adjustment in military families. *Psychological Reports*, *61*, 467-474.
2. Brand, E., & Clingempeel, W. G. (1987). Interdependencies of marital and stepparent-stepchild relationships and children's psychological adjustment: Research findings and clinical implications. *Family Relations*, *36*, 140-145.
3. Brannon, S. E., & Nelson, R. O. (1987). Contingency management treatment of outpatient unipolar depression: A comparison of reinforcement and extinction. *Journal of Consulting and Clinical Psychology*, *55*, 117-119.
4. Dobson, K. S. (1987). Marital and social adjustment in depressed and remarried married women. *Journal of Clinical Psychology*, *43*, 261-265.
5. Grossman, F. K., Pollack, W. S., Golding, E. R., & Fedde, N. M. (1987). Affiliation and autonomy in the transition to parenthood. *Family Relations*, *36*, 263-269.
6. Hops, H., Biglan, A., Sherman, L., Arthur, J., Friedman, L., & Osteen, V. (1987). Home observations of family interactions of depressed women. *Journal of Consulting and Clinical Psychology*, *55*, 341-346.
7. Kessler, R. C., Turner, J. B., & House, J. S. (1987). Intervening processes in the relationship between unemployment and health. *Psychological Medicine*, *17*, 949-961.
8. Rachlin, V. C. (1987). Fair vs. equal role relations in dual-career and dual-earner families: Implications for family interventions. *Family Relations*, *36*, 187-192.
9. Watson, R. E. L., & DeMeo, P. W. (1987). Premarital cohabitation vs. traditional courtship and subsequent marital adjustment: A replication and follow-up. *Family Relations*, *36*, 193-197.
10. Lewin, L., Hops, H., Aubuschon, A., & Budinger, T. (1988). Predictors of maternal satisfaction regarding clinic-referred children: Methodological considerations. *Journal of Clinical Child Psychology*, *17*, 159-163.
11. Holtzworth-Munroe, A., Jacobson, N. S., Deklyen, M., & Whisman, M. A. (1989). Relationship between behavioral marital therapy outcome and process variables. *Journal of Consulting and Clinical Psychology*, *57*, 658-662.
12. Assh, S. D., & Byers, E. S. (1990). Effects of behavioural exchanges and cognitions on the relationship satisfaction of dating and married persons. *Canadian Journal of Behavioural Science*, *22*, 223-235.
13. Baucom, D. H., Sayers, S. L., & Sher, T. G. (1990). Supplementing behavioral marital therapy with cognitive restructuring and emotional expressiveness training: An outcome investigation. *Journal of Consulting and Clinical Psychology*, *58*, 636-645.
14. Houser, R., Kanstam, V., & Ham, M. (1990). Coping and marital satisfaction in dual-career couples: Early stage dual-career couples—wives as college students. *Journal of College Student Development*, *31*, 325-329.
15. Jacobson, N. S., Dobson, K., Fruzzetti, A. E., Schmaling, K. B., & Salusky, S. (1991). Marital therapy as a treatment for depression. *Journal of Consulting and Clinical Psychology*, *59*, 547-557.
16. Kurdek, L. A. (1991). Predictors of increases in marital distress in newlywed couples: A 3-year prospective longitudinal study. *Developmental Psychology*, *27*, 627-636.
17. Levy-Shiff, R., Goldshmidt, I., & Har-Even, D. (1991). Transition to parenthood in adoptive families. *Developmental Psychology*, *27*, 131-140.

Review of the Dyadic Adjustment Scale by KAREN S. BUDD, Associate Professor of Psychology, and NANCY HEILMAN, Graduate Student in Psychology, Illinois Institute of Technology, Chicago, IL:

The Dyadic Adjustment Scale (DAS) is a 32-item rating instrument designed to measure the quality of adjustment between marital couples or other partners in a dyadic relationship. Respondents indicate the extent to which they agree or disagree with their partner on some items, and they rate how often they engage in various activities with their mate on other items. The DAS yields a total adjustment score and four subscales (Dyadic Consensus, Dyadic Satisfaction, Dyadic Cohesion, and Affectional Expression).

STRENGTHS. The DAS is likely the most frequently used and well-researched paper-and-pencil instrument for assessing relationship satisfaction. The manual states the DAS has been used in "more than 1,000 scientific investigations." Reliability studies by various experimenters indicate good internal consistency among items and stable scores over time for the total measure and two of four subscales. Somewhat lower reliability indices have been reported for two other subscales (Affectional Expression and Dyadic Cohesion), which probably is related to the few items (4–5) comprising these subscales. Validity studies indicate that the DAS correlates significantly with other criteria of marital or dyadic satisfaction. Spanier (1976) demonstrated differences between married and divorced persons on the DAS, and other research supports its concurrent and predictive validity. Because Spanier originally derived DAS items from other marital adjustment scales, one would expect the DAS to correlate with related paper-and-pencil marital satisfaction measures, which it does. However, in addition, the DAS has been shown to correlate positively with measures such as marital communication and self-esteem, and to correlate negatively with measures such as social anxiety and depression.

A major virtue of the DAS is its pragmatic nature. Item wording and response anchors are brief, clear, and universal in their applicability to diverse couples (including marriage partners and cohabiting couples of the opposite or same sex). The measure takes 5 to 10 minutes to complete and an equally brief time to score. The DAS can be administered in written form or in computerized format. Scores of one respondent can be analyzed individually, or the independent ratings of both partners can be compared to ascertain how their ratings converge and differ. These features make the DAS appealing for both clinical and research purposes.

Commercial publication of the DAS manual, administration, and scoring forms facilitates use of the DAS as a clinical instrument. The manual provides clear instructions for administration, scoring, and some aspects of clinical interpretation of the DAS. The manual is written in a "user-friendly" style for clinicians or students in training who are unfamiliar with the technical aspects of assessment. Scores on the DAS can be used clinically to assess the need to initiate therapy, identify specific areas of agreement and disagreement between partners, monitor therapy progress, or assess marital/dyadic adjustment in clients who are referred for other concerns. The manual provides appropriate cautions that the DAS is subject to response biases and is not intended to be the only instrument of clinical diagnosis or treatment planning.

LIMITATIONS. One limitation of the DAS concerns the normative data used to develop response profiles. Norms were derived from a study published by Spanier in 1976. Participants in this study were quite homogeneous and are not representative of many populations who would complete the DAS in a clinical setting. The normative sample consisted of 218 white, married persons residing in one county of Pennsylvania. In addition, 94 individuals comprising the divorced sample were mailed their questionnaires and therefore received a different administration procedure than the typical client or research participant would receive. Several studies have reported normative DAS scores with various populations. It is surprising that data from these studies were not used to establish norms for the DAS scoring profile.

Another related limitation concerns the interpretation of *T*-scores derived from the DAS total and subscale scores. The manual presents differing information regarding the significance of particular *T*-scores. In one place the manual indicates that there is no cutoff score for determining a problematic relationship, whereas in another place it states that *T*-scores below 30 (or elsewhere below 20 or 25) are clinically significant. The latter discussion is based on common interpretation of other psychological tests, but it does not appear that any research with the DAS substantiates the use of particular *T*-scores as clinical indicators. Future research directed at determining appropriate clinical cutoffs based on heterogeneous normative samples would enhance the interpretability of DAS scores.

A minor point of note is the publisher's use of the DAS manual as a means to promote the commercial use of the QuikScore™ Forms and the computer administration and scoring program. Indeed, the manual states that the "QuikScore™ Forms are the only legal and ethical way to administer a hand-scored version of the DAS to a respondent" (p. 5). This statement belies the fact that the DAS has been published in a variety of journals and reference books that are part of the public domain. Other written forms of the DAS have been widely used both clinically and in research evaluations of the measure.

SUMMARY. The Dyadic Adjustment Scale is a convenient and widely used means of measuring individual and couples' perceptions of a dyadic relationship. The research literature generally supports the reliability and validity of the DAS. The manual provides explicit, easy-to-follow guidance regarding administration, scoring, and interpretation, thus enhancing the clinical usefulness of the instrument. Users are advised to take care in applying the norms and assigning clinical significance based on T-scores, given limitations in the research relating to these aspects of the instrument.

REVIEWER'S REFERENCE

Spanier, G. B. (1976). Measuring dyadic adjustment: New scales for assessing the quality of marriage and similar dyads. *Journal of Marriage and the Family, 38*, 15-28.

Review of the Dyadic Adjustment Scale by RICHARD B. STUART, Clinical Professor of Psychiatry, University of Washington School of Medicine, Seattle, WA:

The Dyadic Adjustment Scale (DAS) was developed by Graham B. Spanier to serve as a rapid measure of the adjustment of partners "in any committed couple relationship." The instrument has been widely used in research applications. In addition, the author strongly promotes use of the DAS as a "formal clinical assessment tool . . . . providing a comprehensive description of the marital relationship." Accordingly, it is necessary to evaluate the DAS for both research and therapeutic applications.

Although the latest edition of the DAS has been converted to a quick-scoring format, the instrument's content has not been altered since its original publication in 1976 (Spanier, 1976). It was developed by compiling a pool of 300 items that had appeared in approximately 17 previously used inventories dating back to 1933. After eliminating duplicate items, three judges "other than the author" deleted those items they deemed to be lacking in content validity. The remaining pool of some 200 items were submitted to two test groups whose responses were used to construct the instrument, which consists of 32 items that can be converted to T scores for standard comparisons.

These test groups yield the norms offered as a standard against which couples' responses are evaluated. The appropriateness of the norm group is compromised by the fact that these groups are not representative of the broad populations with which the DAS is being used. The married sample consists of 109 white, lower-middle-class couples residing in rural Pennsylvania. This is hardly a comprehensive sample. With similar characteristics, the divorced group used to test criterion validity has a further limitation. These 90 individuals (or 94—the data vary) are 22.5% of the sample contacted by mail up to one year after their marriages ended. Asked to

evaluate retrospectively their failed marriages using the DAS, their responses were more negative than those of the married sample, and accordingly their scores are offered as norms for divorced partners. Unfortunately, there is no way to correct for the biasing effect of the almost inevitable post-decision dissonance reduction in such a sample.

Users of the DAS frequently assume that couples with scores of 100 or more are well adjusted, a standard the author acknowledges as somewhat arbitrary. Unfortunately, no norms exist for some of the groups with which the author recommends the DAS be used (e.g., homosexual couples or families with a psychiatrically disturbed or alcoholic member).

Alpha reliabilities of .90 and above have been found consistently by the author and many other researchers. Data collected by other investigators show that partners achieve a moderate level of agreement (from .44 to .58 for various subscales) in ratings of their relationship, and it has been shown that the DAS has a high test-retest reliability of .96 after 11 weeks.

The author's factor analysis of responses to the instrument's 32 items yielded four components: Dyadic Consensus (13 items), Affectional Expression (4 items), Dyadic Satisfaction (10 items), and Dyadic Cohesion (5 items). However, subsequent researchers (Kazak, Jarmas, & Snitzer, 1988; Sabatelli, 1988; Sharpley & Cross, 1982) have suggested these factors are not as independent as originally reported. Inspection of the instrument supports this view. For example, the Affectional Expression subscale consists of only four items, three of which refer directly to physical affection, and one of which (agreement about "not showing love") does so obliquely. Yet the frequency of kissing loads on the Dyadic Satisfaction subscale. Thus it may be most accurate to regard the DAS as a somewhat lengthy global measure of relationship satisfaction (Fowers, 1990).

Data from many studies are presented by the author to establish the concurrent and predictive validity of the DAS. For example, low scorers have a higher probability of domestic violence, greater depression, more family dysfunction, and poorer communication. Not surprisingly, high convergent validity is reported between the DAS and the Locke-Wallace Marital Adjustment Scale (Locke & Wallace, 1959) to which it is closely related. Finally, use of the DAS to measure group differences tentatively supports finding no differences between married versus cohabiting couples, heterosexual versus gay versus lesbian couples, and men versus women. This latter finding raises a question, however, about validity of the DAS in light of the growing number of studies that do report gender differences in the perception of, and satisfaction with, domestic relationships (e.g., Margolin, Talovic, & Weinstein, 1983). In addition, the absence of data on the influence of social desirability in responses is unfortunate because this factor has been found to influence respondents' self-assessments of their marriages (Hansen, 1981).

The DAS is currently the most widely used measure in research on many aspects of couples' interaction. Yet there is still confusion about what it measures. The author refers interchangeably to marital "adjustment" and marital "quality" despite the fact that the former may refer more to behaviors while the latter may refer to emotional responses (Trost, 1985). The content validity of the DAS has also been challenged by critics who contend that its items do not address issues that may influence many partners' salient evaluations of their relationships (Norton, 1983). For example, 17 of the items measure agreement, 13 the frequency of certain kinds of interaction, and 2 address present and anticipated satisfaction. With no item weights available, agreement on "religious matters," "friends," and "ways of dealing with parents or in-laws" is no less important than the frequency with which partners confide in each other or regret that they married, or their rating of their marriage on a Likert scale from "extremely unhappy" to "perfect." On an a priori basis, it seems improbable that such diverse items would contribute equally to partners' assessments of their relationships.

In part because of the foregoing limitations, the DAS does not yet live up to the author's claim that it is a "fully developed and formal clinical assessment tool." Among its clinical limitations is the fact that many important relationship issues are addressed by a single item, some addressing agreement, others frequency, but none both. In addition, it is well recognized that instruments used to formulate treatment plans are most useful when they are closely tied to the theoretical logic of the therapeutic approach to be used. Because the DAS was derived inductively from items drawn from many different approaches to relationship assessment, its content is not closely tied to any particular theory of relationships. Therefore, it may lack dimensions of assessment that are at the core of any given clinical effort. In addition, many of the issues that arise in counseling contemporary couples (e.g., coparenting and managing alcohol and drug use) are not addressed by the DAS.

In summary, despite its limitations, the DAS is one of the best of the currently available instruments for use in studies of many aspects of marital and family functioning. Used in this way, it provides a valuable standard of comparison of the way couples in diverse subject populations evaluate their relationships. The author recognizes that the DAS is "not perfectly valid" and therefore may or may not make a positive contribution to any given clinical assessment. If the DAS is used in clinical settings, it would be best to make it one of several measures of relationship strength and concerns, and to verify the findings of all such paper-and-pencil instruments during clinical assessment interviews.

REVIEWER'S REFERENCES

Locke, H. J., & Wallace, K. M. (1959). Short marital adjustment and prediction tests: Their reliability and validity. *Marriage and Family Living*, *21*, 251-255.

Spanier, G. B. (1976). Measuring dyadic adjustment: New scales for assessing the quality of marriage and similar dyads. *Journal of Marriage and the Family*, *38*, 15-30.

Hansen, G. L. (1981). Marital adjustment and conventionalization: A reexamination. *Journal of Marriage and the Family*, *43*, 855-863.

Sharpley, C. F., & Cross, D. G. (1982). A psychometric evaluation of the Spanier Dyadic Adjustment Scale. *Journal of Marriage and the Family*, *44*, 739-741.

Margolin, G., Talovic, S., & Weinstein, C. (1983). Areas of Change Questionnaire: A practical approach to marital assessment. *Journal of Consulting and Clinical Psychology*, *51*, 920-931.

Norton, R. (1983). Measuring marital quality: A critical look at the dependent variable. *Journal of Marriage and the Family*, *45*, 141-151.

Trost, J. E. (1985). Abandon adjustment! *Journal of Marriage and the Family*, *47*, 1072-1073.

Kazak, A. E., Jarmas, A., & Snitzer, L. (1988). The assessment of marital satisfaction: An evaluation of the Dyadic Adjustment Scale. *Journal of Family Psychology*, *2*, 82-91.

Sabatelli, R. M. (1988). Measurement issues in marital research: A review and critique of contemporary survey instruments. *Journal of Marriage and the Family*, *50*, 891-915.

Fowers, B. J. (1990). An interactional approach to standardized marital assessment: A literature review. *Family Relations*, *39*, 368-377.

[118]

Dysarthria Profile.

Purpose: To describe the dysarthric client's problems, and to supply the speech therapist with indications of where to begin in treatment.

Population: Dysarthric adults.

Publication Dates: 1982–87.

Scores: 8 sections: Respiration, Phonation, Examination of Facial Musculature, Diadochokinesis, Reflexes, Articulation, Intelligibility, Prosody and Rate.

Administration: Individual.

Price Data, 1988: $16.95 per Dysarthria Profile including 25 scoring forms, 25 profile summary sheets, 5 stimulus cards, and manual ('87, 21 pages); $13.95 per 25 scoring forms and 25 summary sheets.

Time: Administration time not reported.

Comments: Based on Mayo Clinic study of Darley, Aronson, and Brown (1975); checklist; other test materials (stopwatch, digital counter, penlight, tape recorder, tongue depressor) must be supplied by examiner.

Author: S. J. Robertson.

Publisher: Communication Skill Builders.

Review of the Dysarthria Profile by KATHARINE G. BUTLER, Professor and Chair, Communication Sciences and Disorders, Syracuse University, Syracuse, NY:

PURPOSE. The author, S. Robertson, based much of the Dysarthria Profile's substance on earlier research by Darley (1975), Darley, Aronson, and Brown (1975) and Lundeen (1950). Acknowledging the importance of the work of Darley and colleagues, the author notes that the 38 dimensions of assessment specified by those authors was too great in number for use in settings beyond hospital-based research settings. Therefore, Robertson selected from among them and added a section on Reflexes and Diadochokinesis, noting the clinical usefulness of assessing chewing, swallowing, and coughing reflexes and speed of movement of the articulators. *No* attempt was made by Robertson to construct a profile that might be used to classify different types of dysarthria, but rather, "to describe the dysarthric client's problems, whatever the underlying neurological etiology" (manual, p. 2).

From the materials provided, it appears that no attempt has been made to standardize this instrument (referred to as a profile, but identified as having "test equipment and instruction for test administration and scoring"). This instrument owes its existence to the careful work of others, particularly the text *Motor Speech Disorders*, by Darley, Aronson, and Brown (1975), and very early work from the 1950s including that of Lundeen (1950), Blomquist (1950), and Irwin and Becklund (1953).

TEST CONSTRUCTION. Limited information is provided on test construction. Statistical and technical information is drawn from the work of researchers completed in 1950–1975. The small, stapled manual (19 pages) carries no information on the criteria used to select the 5 items used to evaluate Respiration, the 12 items used to measure Phonation, the 20 items utilized to measure Facial Musculature ability, the 11 items for Diadochokinesis, nor the remainder of the items to measure Articulation, Intelligibility, and Prosody and Rate. Articulation is measured via five tasks, using 48 single words, and four sentences. Intelligibility is measured by having the client read aloud and engage in spontaneous speech. The author then notes: "This section should be recorded and played back to a relative or friend and a stranger, if none of these are present during the assessment." A 5-point grid, entitled *Normal, Good, Fair, Poor, None* is provided as the evaluation form for all items on the test. Such items require the subjective interpretation of the examiner, with the exception of some broad norms provided in the section on Diadochokinesis (although there is no attribution of the source of those norms). Articulation is scored according to "overall impression of accuracy of vowel sounds" (p. 14).

MATERIALS. This product includes a white manila folder, containing 25 four-page scoring forms and a 19-page manual, stapled and of doubtful durability. Five stimulus cards, produced on heavy, coated white stock, include a reading passage, "My Grandfather," which is difficult reading for poor readers of any age. No total score is computed (nor would one be useful, if it were). Presumably the totality of the clinician's impressions gathered from the check sheet matrix and the underlined descriptive information is to provide the substance for the item which appears at the beginning of the Dysarthria Profile entitled Summary of Type and Severity of Dysarthria, for which less than two lines are provided. The remainder of the heading involves the recording of name, hospital number, date of birth, Medical Diagnosis, Physical Condition, Date of onset of Dysarthria, Date of Testing, Name of Tester, and Dates of Retest. There is no suggestion in the manual itself that retesting is optional or obligatory. Specifically, the manual (p. 2) states "The profile has been compiled with treatment planning as a priority. It is hoped that the profile will supply the speech therapist with indications of *where* [emphasis added] to begin in treatment."

ADMINISTRATION TIME. No estimate of administration time is provided by the author. This reviewer found that with a cooperative client, administration of the first three areas specified (Respiration, Phonation, and Facial Musculature), some of which required the use of equipment not included in the profile materials (e.g., stopwatch, counter, penlight, tongue depressor, tape recorder) required about 15–18 minutes to evaluate and record. Measurement of Diadochokinesis ranged from 3–5 minutes, and Reflexes (i.e., assessing the client's chewing, swallowing, and coughing reflexes) using a glass of water and cracker, as indicated by the test's author, took approximately 5 minutes. The Articulation section provides limited measurement of 49 items, ranging from one syllable to six syllables, plus four sentences, ranging from three to seven syllables, and requiring approximately 5 minutes. Because measuring intelligibility (Section VII) requires the examiner plus two other individuals to perform an evaluation, time is difficult to determine, and will probably vary considerably. Prosody and Rate can also be scored from the client's performance in Section VI, or further attempts at spontaneous speech may be sought. Total administration time is estimated to be no less than 30 to 40 minutes, and quite possibly an hour or more.

STRENGTHS AND WEAKNESSES. This profile/assessment instrument is of relatively limited value, because it is based upon the work of others, has no reliability, validity, or normative data of its own, and is time consuming to administer. A more finely focused and better standardized instrument is The Assessment of Intelligibility of Dysarthric Speech (10:19) by Yorkston, Beukelman, and Traynor. It is available in both a computerized and noncomputerized version.

SUMMARY. The Dysarthria Profile is an inexpensive, nonstandardized instrument which has little to offer other than a structure for reporting data selected from other instruments. Its format would permit only the broadest of measurements if increase in functional skills of a dysarthric patient is required as evidence of therapeutic progress.

REVIEWER'S REFERENCES

Blomquist, B. L. (1950). Diadochokinetic movements of nine-, ten-, and eleven-year-old children. *Journal of Speech and Hearing Disorders, 15,* 159-164.

Lundeen, D. J. (1950). The relationship of diadochokinesis to various speech sounds. *Journal of Speech and Hearing Disorders, 15,* 54-59.

Irwin, J. V., & Backlund, O. (1953). Norms for maximum repetitive rates for certain sounds, established with the Sylrater. *Journal of Speech and Hearing Disorders, 18,* 149-160.

Darley, F. L. (1975). Diagnosis of motor speech disorders. *Australian Journal of Human Communication Disorders, 3* (1), 19-27.

Darley, F. L., Aronson, A. E., & Brown, J. R. (1975). *Motor speech disorders.* Philadelphia: W. B. Saunders.

Review of the Dysarthria Profile by DAVID A. SHAPIRO, Associate Professor of Communication Disorders, School of Education and Psychology, Western Carolina University, Cullowhee, NC:

First published in England in 1982, the Dysarthria Profile reportedly is based upon a now classic study of motor speech disorders (Darley, Aronson, & Brown, 1969a, 1969b) conducted at the Mayo Clinic in Rochester, Minnesota. The author indicated that the Mayo Clinic procedures would not be appropriate for the day-to-day clinical situation. Therefore, in addition to the purpose stated in the manual and in the descriptive information preceding this review, the author conveyed that "a brief, objective assessment procedure is required—one that will cover as many areas as possible of the Mayo Clinic study." This instrument was designed to provide the clinician with: "(1) a profile of the client's abilities and disabilities; (2) descriptive information to help in classification of the dysarthric problem; [and] (3) a sound basis on which to build a therapy and management program" (manual, p. 1).

The resulting system is an individually administered, nonstandardized, high inference checklist by which the examiner estimates the degree to which a behavior or quality exists along a continuum from present to absent. Eight different areas are assessed with suggested instructions provided for each task within the areas. The clinician demonstrates each task and then scores the client's attempt. "If the client is unable to perform the task or has misunderstood the instruction," the client is asked to try again in which case the second attempt is scored. All attempts are scored one of the following: normal, good, fair, poor, none. Where descriptive information is required, the clinician underlines the appropriate description provided. When the protocol is completed, scores are transferred from the scoring form to the summary form.

The Dysarthria Profile contains eight sections: (*a*) Respiration: Assessing the pattern, capacity, and control of respiration at rest and during speech, the client is directed to breathe with and without phonation (5 tasks, 6 additional descriptive observations); (*b*) Phonation: This section assesses voice quality in addition to the ability to initiate and sustain voice and to control volume, pitch, and intonation (12 tasks, 5 observations); (*c*) Examina-

tion of Facial Musculature: This oral peripheral examination assesses movement of the lips, jaw, tongue, and soft palate, symmetry and muscle tone of the face, and appearance of the tongue (20 tasks, 7 observations); (*d*) Diadochokinesis: This section assesses articulatory rate and movement with and without phonation and articulation (11 tasks, 11 observations); (*e*) Reflexes: This section assesses the client's chewing, swallowing, and coughing reflexes (7 tasks, 0 additional observations); (*f*) Articulation: Assessing the ability to produce consonant/vowel combinations, the client is directed to imitate words and sentences of increasing length and complexity when presented a verbal model and cards containing printed stimuli (5 tasks, description requested for each of 52 responses); (*g*) Intelligibility: This section assesses the client's speech intelligibility during reading and spontaneous conversation by the clinician, a relative or friend, and a stranger (6 tasks, 0 observations); (*h*) Prosody and Rate: Based on the reading and conversation collected during the previous section, this component assesses the prosodic features of speech (e.g., rhythm, stress, intonation, rate) (5 tasks, 2 observations).

These eight sections provide a system for guiding clinical observations when assessing dysarthric speech. The sections focus on areas that are critical to communication and are supported by current literature on assessing dysarthric speakers. The scoring and summary forms in addition to the five stimulus cards are well organized. The manual is readable and easy to follow. A particular strength of the manual is the inclusion of descriptions of the purpose for each section. This reviewer particularly appreciates that the author is a clinician who, in designing the Dysarthria Profile, responded to the needs expressed to her by students and fellow speech-language pathologists.

In its current form, however, the Dysarthria Profile contains several major limitations:

1. The instrument lacks standardization for providing instructions and demonstration and for analyzing, scoring, and interpreting responses. Although the author presents suggested instructions and methods for elicitation, the variety in clinician procedures can confound the intended tasks. Exacerbating the well-documented difficulty in making perceptual judgments (Darley, Aronson, & Brown, 1975; Rosenbek & LaPointe, 1985; Yorkston, Beukelman, & Bell, 1988), the author presents scoring guidelines for less than a third of the 71 tasks. The 5-point rating scale is, at best, imprecise and fails to achieve the objectivity intended. The Mayo Clinic study to which the author refers but does not reference (Darley et al., 1969a, 1969b) utilized 38 speech dimensions on a 7-point equal-appearing interval scale. Other instruments have adapted such scales for more objective perceptual,

component, and overall assessment of dysarthric speech, for interpreting intelligibility, comparing with normal performance, monitoring change, and planning treatment (Yorkston & Beukelman, 1981).

2. This instrument fails to provide any guidelines for planning treatment or monitoring change, an application that was stated as a major objective.

3. Of relatively minor concern, no guidelines are provided regarding the rationale or procedures for transferring data from the scoring to summary forms. The one mention ("When the test has been completed, transfer the scores to the Profile Summary Form by drawing a bold line at the appropriate level and shading in the area to the right of the score") has no clear referent when examining the summary form.

4. The author has provided no technical information regarding test construction, standardization, validity, reliability, or uses/applications of the test. This represents a shortcoming of considerable magnitude. This reviewer believes that it is incumbent upon test authors and publishers to present such detailed information, the absence of which should register a major concern among clinicians who are potential test consumers.

In summary, the Dysarthria Profile is a nonstandardized checklist that focuses on eight areas that are critical for assessment of dysarthric speech. Potential test users will find this profile useful for guiding observation and generating description. Because of the lack of standardization for administration and scoring and absence of technical information regarding test design and construction, the objectivity and utility of the results will be a reflection of the examiner's diagnostic experience and competence.

REVIEWER'S REFERENCES

Darley, F. L., Aronson, A. E., & Brown, J. R. (1969a). Differential diagnostic patterns of dysarthria. *Journal of Speech and Hearing Research, 12,* 246-269.

Darley, F. L., Aronson, A. E., & Brown, J. R. (1969b). Clusters of deviant speech dimensions in the dysarthrias. *Journal of Speech and Hearing Research, 12,* 462-496.

Darley, F. L., Aronson, A. E., & Brown, J. R. (1975). *Motor speech disorders.* Philadelphia: W. B. Saunders.

Yorkston, K. M., & Beukelman, D. R. (1981). Assessment of Intelligibility of Dysarthric Speech. Austin, TX: PRO-ED, Inc.

Rosenbek, J. C., & LaPointe, L. L. (1985). The dysarthrias: Description, diagnosis, and treatment. In D. F. Johns (Ed.), *Clinical management of neurogenic communicative disorders* (2nd ed.; pp. 97-152). Boston: Little, Brown and Company.

Yorkston, K. M., Beukelman, D. R., & Bell, K. R. (1988). *Clinical management of dysarthric speakers.* Boston: Little, Brown and Company.

[119]

Early Child Development Inventory.

Purpose: "A brief screening inventory . . . designed to help identify children with developmental and other problems that may interfere with the child's ability to learn."

Population: Ages 1-3 to 3-0.

Publication Date: 1988.

Acronym: ECDI.

Scores: General Development Score, Possible Problems List (24); 4 ratings: Child Description, Major Problem, Parent's Questions Regarding Child, Parent's Functioning.

Administration: Individual or group.

Price Data, 1990: $7 per 25 Question-Answer sheets; $5 per manual (15 pages).

Time: Administration time not reported.

Comments: Parent-completed questionnaire.

Authors: Harold Ireton.

Publisher: Behavior Science Systems, Inc.

Review of the Early Child Development Inventory by ROBERT W. HILTONSMITH, Associate Professor of Psychology, Radford University, Radford, VA:

OVERVIEW. The Early Childhood Development Inventory (ECDI) is described by the author as a "brief screening inventory for use with children ages 15 months to three years . . . designed to help identify children with developmental and other problems that may interfere with the child's ability to learn." The ECDI consists of a questionnaire for the parent and a brief 12-page manual for the professional. The author suggests that the ECDI is best used in conjunction with a developmental screening test, but adds that it can also be used as a pre-evaluation questionnaire. The ECDI is divided into six sections: General Development, Possible Problems, Child Description, Special Problems or Disabilities, Questions or Concerns, and Parent's Functioning. The ECDI is part of a family of measures that has evolved from the author's "twenty-year research experience with the use of mothers' reports to measure the development of young children." Other related measures include the Minnesota Child Development Inventory (MCDI; 9:712) and the Preschool Development Inventory (10:291).

TEST MATERIALS AND PROCEDURES. The ECDI questionnaire fills two sides of one page. Sixty "yes" or "no" questions (taken from the Minnesota Child Development Inventory) are concerned with overall development and cover seven developmental areas: language comprehension, expressive language, gross motor skills, fine motor skills, self-help skills, situational comprehension, and personal-social skills. A 24-item list of general symptoms and problems, also answered "yes" or "no," follows. Four small boxes complete the measure. These ask the parent to write a brief description of their child, note the child's special problems or disabilities, list any questions or concerns the parent has about the child, and then respond to the question "How are you doing, as a parent or otherwise, at this time?" Three of the four boxes provide a small area of only 1 inch x 4 inches to write in what would appear to often be a considerable amount of information. No information is given regarding approximate times needed to complete the questionnaire and score it.

Scoring on the 60-item General Development Scale is simply the number of "yes" answers noted for these items. The child's score is then compared to that of other children. The "cutoff" score for suspected developmental problems is the average score for children who are 20% younger than the child in question. The 24-item scale for "possible problems" is scored by counting the number of "yes" answers and assigning this number to one of three categories: "possible major problem," "possible problem," and an unnamed category when all items on this scale are answered "no." Next, parents' written responses to the four open-ended questions are examined and individually assigned to one of 3 categories under each of the four questions. Finally, guidelines are provided for examining the entire scored measure and then judging the need for any follow-up evaluation.

NORMS AND STANDARDIZATION. Users refer to a table in the manual listing means and cutoff scores for the 60-item General Development Scale. These scores are based on 138 males and 137 females. No demographic information on these children is presented. The manual alludes to normative research with the MCDI, but none is presented. MCDI norms are known to be based on White, middle-class, nonhandicapped children from intact families of successfully employed fathers and mothers who do not work outside the home. If ECDI norms are taken from the MCDI group, then there are obvious, serious limitations in addition to the small norm sample size. Finally, there is no rationale presented for the use of the 20%-below-age-level cutoff.

RELIABILITY. No reliability data are reported. Test-retest data would be particularly helpful, because a range of only 2 "yes" responses separates "normal" children from children with "possible major problems."

VALIDITY. No validity data are presented. The author contends that "a low score on the General Development Scale is a strong indicator of a significant, possibly major, developmental problem," but no information is presented to support that claim. Particularly disturbing is the lack of criterion-related validity, both predictive and concurrent. Without these data, it is virtually impossible to determine what scores on this measure might mean, either for current or for future functioning.

SUMMARY. The ECDI is a brief parent-report screening inventory for developmental problems in young children ages 15 months to 3 years. The measure does provide parents with the opportunity to provide their own perceptions of their child's problems, which should always be an important part of the data collected in any child evaluation. As such, it can provide a springboard for parents to talk in earnest with the professional about their child.

Unfortunately, the ECDI has a variety of serious problems which drastically limit its usefulness. The measure is basically problem-based rather than needs-based, and therefore not in the spirit of P.L. 99-457. Norms are based on a very small group of children with unknown demographic characteristics. Reliability data are lacking, and there is no information on the measure's validity. Particularly troubling is the lack of either concurrent or predictive validity data—essential information for judging any screening measure of this type. The ECDI might be considered as an adjunct or supplement to a parent interview done within the context of a comprehensive evaluation, but under no circumstances should it stand alone as an indicator of the child's developmental status or of developmental problems.

[120]
Early Coping Inventory.
Purpose: Measures adaptive behavior.
Population: Ages 4–36 months.
Publication Date: 1988.
Scores, 4: Sensorimotor Organization, Reactive Behavior, Self-Initiated Behavior, Total.
Administration: Individual.
Price Data, 1989: $30 per complete kit including manual (62 pages) and 20 inventories (9 pages); $18 per 20 inventories; $15 per manual; $15 per specimen set.
Time: Administration time varies.
Comments: Downward extension of the Coping Inventory (9:268); ratings of adaptive behavior by an adult.
Authors: Shirley Zeitlin and G. Gordon Williamson with Margery Szczepanski.
Publisher: Scholastic Testing Service, Inc.

Review of the Early Coping Inventory by HARLAN J. STIENTJES, School Psychologist, Heartland Educational Agency 11, Johnston, IA:

The Early Coping Inventory (ECI) is a downward extension of the Coping Inventory (10:74) by the same principal author. Although the ECI is called a coping inventory and it is claimed to be a measure of adaptive behavior, the definitions for these constructs are inconsistent with current literature regarding coping (Lazarus & Folkman, 1984) as well as with the most prominent thinking on adaptive behavior (Reschly, 1990). The authors attempt to clarify the distinctions but seem to confuse rather than illuminate. It may be the Early Coping Inventory measures something important and unique; however, the theoretical framework seems befuddled.

The instrument consists of 48 items that are distributed equally into three descriptive categories (Sensorimotor Organization, Reactive Behavior, and Self-Initiated Behavior). The items, gleaned from research, are descriptors of coping-related behaviors. Coping-related behaviors, the authors maintain, are the repertoire of behavior the child uses to manage the motives, opportunities, challenges, and frustration encountered in daily living. The descriptors are intended to be distinct from developmental milestones or any single contributing variable such as intelligence, language, temperament, or social competence. The authors claim the formal characteristics of coping-related behaviors are the same for all individuals regardless of age, sex, culture, or intelligence, but specific actions by which a coping related behavior is demonstrated vary. For example, "initiates action to communicate a need" is representative of coping at all ages but would be exhibited differently by various age individuals.

Nevertheless, some descriptors of the ECI lack the specificity that would make them meaningful (e.g., "maintains visual attention to people and objects" or "engages in reciprocal social interactions"). Each of the 48 items is to be rated for the individual on a 5-point scale from *not effective* (1) through *situationally effective* (3) to *consistently effective across situations* (5). Computation of scores for scales is straightforward and easy. The score on each scale is nothing more than an average of the ratings given the items in the scale. Interpretation is based on the key words of the rating system. Scoring is totally distinct from and is never compared to a norm group performance.

The technical data section is descriptive of the processes used in development of the ECI; however, reliability and validity study is extremely incomplete. In fact, it appears the data collection was done after the instrument was devised and no revisions were made in the instrument despite some readily apparent major problems. For example, principal component factor analysis was conducted using three samples of children (disabled children, nondisabled with family income above $10,000, nondisabled with family income below $10,000). The pattern of factors for the three groups has little consistency and would not seem to support the descriptive categories used in the structure of the instrument. Major technical difficulties also exist with the reliability reported for the instrument. Reliability testing was done using 25-minute videotaped sessions of children with written narration describing the child to be assessed. It would seem that such a procedure would yield spuriously high test-retest and interrater agreement reliability ratings in a manner very atypical from actual usage of the instrument. No meaningful evidence of concurrent validity is reported to support the construct of coping as presented in this instrument.

In summary, the ECI is far from a completed instrument. Some initial field study has been conducted; however, the data have not been allowed to influence the instrument. Additionally, the construct of coping is inadequately defined and far more empirical study remains to be done. Although the authors maintain coping is not influenced by

intelligence, language, temperament, or social competence, evidence to support such a claim is not available at this time. Additional research is needed to clarify the construct of coping and its relationship to other adaptive behavior, as well as the stability and function of the Early Coping Inventory.

REVIEWER'S REFERENCES
Lazarus, R. S., & Folkman, S. (1984). *Stress, appraisal, and coping*. New York: Springer.
Reschly, D. J. (1990). Adaptive behavior. In A. Thomas & J. Grimes (Eds.), *Best practices in school psychology II* (pp. 22-41). Washington, DC: National Association of School Psychologists.

Review of the Early Coping Inventory by LOGAN WRIGHT, Professor of Psychology, and WADE L. HAMIL, Research Assistant, University of Oklahoma, Norman, OK:

The Early Coping Inventory (ECI) is billed as the only instrument available specifically to assess coping-related behaviors in infants and toddlers. The authors define coping as the "repertoire of behaviors the child uses to manage the routines, opportunities, challenges, and frustrations encountered in daily living." The ECI is designed primarily for developmentally delayed or disabled children, in order to determine which behavior patterns these children use to manage their environment (coping style), and to assess whether their coping style is effective. The ECI contains 48 items organized into three categories of 16 items each: Sensorimotor Organization, Reactive Behavior, and Self-Initiated Behavior. Behaviors are scored in each category using a 5-point scale. The inventory is intended for use with children possessing a developmental age of 4 to 36 months, irrespective of their chronological age.

Implicit in the materials associated with the ECI scale is the notion that the construct "early coping" somehow differs from the more global construct of early developmental status. However, the authors make no statements supporting such a rationale. And, upon inspection, the ECI items appear extremely similar to those of early developmental scales such as the Brazelton Neonatal Assessment Scale (9:157), Bayley Scales of Infant Development (10:26), Denver Developmental Screening Test (9:311), Home Observation for Measurement of the Environment (9:481), etc. Because the above mentioned developmental scales are far more refined psychometrically than the ECI, some question remains as to whether a legitimate need for the ECI exists. No statements demonstrating its unique properties are articulated by the authors.

A variety of *internal* problems plague the ECI. One is that its 5-point rating scale combines two separate dimensions into a single rating. This prevents the ratings from yielding even ordinal (not to mention interval) data. The recording of simple behavioral observations is made extremely convoluted by a complex scale. The Inventory would benefit from the elimination of Point 3 (*situationally effective*), as well as the "situational" component that pervades some of the other points on the 5-point rating scale. This would leave a much more functional 1–4 point Likert-type scale with categories as follows: (1) *not effective*, (2) *minimally effective*, (3) *mostly effective*, (4) *consistently effective*.

No normative data for the ECI are provided.

The authors use unacceptable methods in attempting to demonstrate the objectivity and reliability of the ECI. In order to assess interrater reliability, they asked 24 raters to view four videotapes of disabled and normal children in various environments. Differences between raters' estimates for first and second viewings were then analyzed by an ANOVA method. The resulting F scores were then used to provide coefficients of correlation using the Guilford (1965) translation formula. Although those coefficients fell within what is generally an acceptable range (.80 to .94), they describe what might best be labeled a form of *intrarater* reliability.

The reported test-retest reliability of the ECI is, in reality, a measure of the observers' ratings of the same videotapes after a 6-week interval. These data, therefore, tell us nothing about the reliability of young children's scores on the ECI or of the reliability of the behaviors being measured. The issue of the internal consistency of the ECI is not addressed. Split-half correlations and/or coefficient alpha data should have been provided.

In regard to validity, nothing is provided beyond item content validity. Although the ECI manual claims to report on the Inventory's construct validity, the authors appear to have confused construct validity with item content validity. No criterion-based data relating to actual construct (or other forms of postconstruction) validity are reported.

In summary, the ECI: (*a*) lacks clarity from a construct standpoint, (*b*) relies on scaling techniques which are flawed, (*c*) provides no normative data, (*d*) fails to offer defensible data for objectivity and reliability, and (*e*) provides no information concerning validation of the scale beyond the initial item content validity data used in its construction. At best, the ECI might be regarded as a potential research instrument, but its value as a predictive or diagnostic tool remains unsupported. Offering it at this stage for commercial publication and marketing seems premature.

REVIEWER'S REFERENCE

Guilford, J. P. (1965). *Fundamental statistics in psychology and education* (4th ed.). New York: McGraw-Hill.

[121]

Early Mathematics Diagnostic Kit.

Purpose: "To provide the teacher with an effective means of diagnosing early difficulties in the learning of mathematics."

Population: Ages 4–8.
Publication Dates: 1977–87.
Acronym: EMDK.
Scores: 10 areas: Number, Shape, Representation, Length, Weight, Capacity, Memory, Money, Time, Foundation.
Administration: Individual.
Price Data, 1989: £63.25 per complete kit including 25 record booklets, book of test items, set of coloured cubes, set of 3 small boxes, manual ('87, 32 pages); £6.35 per 10 record forms; £8.05 per manual.
Time: 30(35) minutes.
Comments: Item checklist.
Authors: David Lumb and Margaret Lumb.
Publisher: NFER-Nelson Publishing Co., Ltd. [England].

Review of the Early Mathematics Diagnostic Kit by JOHN M. ENGER, Professor of Education, Arkansas State University, State University, AR:

As evident from the price given in pounds, the Early Mathematics Diagnostic Kit (EMDK) is a British product. It was developed and field tested in England over a number of years. The administration of the EMDK to a young child, aged 4 to 8 years, is similar to the administration of an individualized IQ test. The intent, however, is to identify any deficiencies in mathematics in 10 different areas.

THE MANUAL. A 28-page instruction manual accompanies the EMDK. Background information about the test and administration procedures are included in the manual. It is imperative the user of the EMDK be well versed on the procedures covered in the manual prior to administering the instrument to a young child. These procedures are quite explicit and are explained very well. However, the American reader will sense a different culture base inherent throughout the manual in both the examples used (e.g., pence for coins) and the spellings of some words (e.g., colour, metre, programme).

In the manual, each of the 110 items of the EMDK is classified into 1 of 10 content areas. A table of specifications is not provided, so weights by content areas are not obvious to the reader. In constructing a table of specifications for the EMDK, the user will find a heavy representation on numbers (47 of 110 items, or 43 percent), yet there are fewer than 10 items in each of six content areas.

Information on reliability, validity, and normative data are scant in contrast to the recommendations of information for the publisher to provide given in the 1985 *Standards for Educational and Psychological Testing* (AERA, APA, & NCME). Validity is addressed in reporting the development of the instrument by groups of teachers in northeast England over a period of 7 years. Specific procedures and numbers of teachers involved in the development are not given.

A single reliability exercise was reported in which the EMDK was administered to 40 boys and 40 girls aged 7–8 who were judged by their teachers to have mastered the objectives covered by the EMDK. The items were administered by 20 individuals, and each child took a single administration of the instrument. The intent of this investigation was to examine the clarity of the items. This exercise resulted in the elimination of two of the original 112 items used in the instrument. Ten or more of the children failed these items. It is suggested in the manual that any normative data would be inappropriate because the instrument is intended only for those perceived to have deficiencies in mathematics.

THE INSTRUMENT. All of the 110 items or a subset of the items in the EMDK are presented by the examiner to a young child, aged 4 to 8. A convenient presentation is made through a loosely bound book, which lies flat, showing one item per page. A handy eight-page score sheet is kept by the examiner to record if the child's response to an item is correct or incorrect. If the child makes no response, the box is left blank.

Because the instrument is intended to be administered to young children and the children will be touching the pages of the test booklet, the pages should probably be plastic coated. In its present form, the pages are sturdy, but will soil with use. The cardboard boxes that accompany the instrument are loosely constructed and tend to come apart with use.

In administering the EMDK, the user will note little difference from administering an individual IQ test. Many of the items parallel the items and procedures found in commonly used intelligence tests, such as the WISC-R, the WPPSI, the WAIS-R, the Stanford-Binet, and the K-ABC. However, no reference is made to these or other tests.

Little information is given in the manual to guide the user in interpreting the child's performance. Learning difficulties are said to be identified by responses to the individual items. It is noted that a child's teacher would be in the best position to contrast achievement with expectations, based upon what had been covered in class.

USE OF EMDK RESULTS. In addition to the examination, the EMDK includes information on follow-up activities for the mathematics learning difficulties identified by the examination. More than half of the manual presents follow-up activities that correspond to the topics covered by various item groupings. Suggested follow-up activities are listed by referencing pages in 13 primarily British commercial textbooks.

In the suggested activities section, the items are grouped as 24 subtests containing from one to 26 items. Sixteen of the 24 subtests contain three or fewer items. A checklist of commonly taught mathematical topics is appended. Here, key concepts (called items) are grouped into eight content areas. Teachers are advised to record (*a*) when the student is introduced to the item, (*b*) when further involvement occurs with the item, and (*c*) when the item is consolidated (mastered).

OVERALL EVALUATION. By all appearances, the content and administration procedures of the EMDK model many of the commonly used individual IQ tests. In interpreting a child's performance on the EMDK, the user is advised to examine responses to individual items to determine deficiencies in mathematics achievement. The user could use subtests from IQ tests in much the same manner.

In the EMDK the test items are classified by topic and referenced to pages in various British commercial textbooks. To be applicable in American education, some items and the references should be changed.

For a young child suspected of having learning difficulties in mathematics, the EMDK would provide a systematic evaluation of performance on specific items. In writing an individualized education plan (IEP), commonly used in special education, the EMDK might be quite useful.

REVIEWER'S REFERENCE

American Educational Research Association, American Psychological Association, & National Council on Measurement in Education. (1985). *Standards for educational and psychological testing.* Washington, DC: American Psychological Association, Inc.

Review of the Early Mathematics Diagnostic Kit by G. MICHAEL POTEAT, *Associate Professor of Psychology, East Carolina University, Greenville, NC:*

The Early Mathematics Diagnostic Kit (EMDK) was designed as part of a curriculum package. It was developed in England and is designed for use with children from 4 to 8 years of age who are experiencing learning difficulties in mathematics. The kit consists of a spiral-bound booklet of test items, a handbook (28 pages), test record booklets, a box of small cubes, and three small boxes of identical size and shape but of different weights. A pencil and sheet of paper for the child to make written responses are also required.

The EMDK has 110 items; all are contained in the test booklet. The spiral-bound booklet is placed between the child and the examiner and all of the items are presented by simply turning the page. The examiner's inquiry is printed on the page opposite the test item and the test materials and inquiries are oriented toward the child and examiner respectively. The instrument is designed to be administered not only by psychologists but by teachers and other school staff without training in assessment. Administration is relatively straightforward but is hampered by directions that are occasionally too abbreviated. The record booklet does not provide spaces for recording responses to all of the questions contained in the test booklet, nor is a system provided for grouping or summarizing performance in the variety of areas assessed. No guidelines are provided for where to start and stop administering items, and the handbook states only that the test may be administered in its entirety or as a collection of shorter subtests. The test-item hierarchy is ineffective in structuring the items in order of difficulty (e.g., Item 55 asks which of two fishes is smaller, whereas Item 50 requires the construction of sets of 2, 5, and 9 blocks).

The 110 items are inequitably divided into 10 areas of mathematics: Number (47 items), Shape (8 items), Representation (1 item), Length (11 items), Weight (2 items), Capacity (5 items), Memory (3 items), Money (11 items), Time (9 items), and Foundation (15 items). The content coverage of the instrument is consequently disparate. The Number area (the content areas are poorly defined by the authors) consists of items measuring everything from determining if there are equal numbers of knives and forks in a picture to naming two-digit numerals. All the mathematical operations (e.g., multiplication and addition) are also classified as in the Number area. The Foundation area includes several items reminiscent of the picture vocabulary on the Stanford-Binet. For the Memory area, a measure of "short-term" memory (Item 49) is obtained by asking the child what the two children shown in the Item 5 picture were doing. However, on Item 110 the same question is construed as a measure of "delayed recall." The 11 Money items are inappropriate for use in U.S. schools because they all involve British coins. The EMDK does contain some unusual items of potential value (e.g., weight discrimination). Still, no rationale for the selection and structure of the test content is given, although an appendix does contain a list of mathematical topics assigned to 8 of the 10 categories.

Almost no technical information is provided for the EMDK. The technical information consists of the report that the majority of a group of 80 seven- and eight-year-old boys and girls identified as not having problems in mathematics passed most of the items included on the instrument. No attempt to measure reliability and validity is mentioned. There is no evidence the information provided by the instrument is of any additional value other than that derived from the informal observations of teachers. No attempt is made to empirically link failure on any item or group of items to particular problems in mathematics, and only the most cursory attempt is made at the conjectural linking of test and classroom performance.

The EMDK cannot be considered to meet even the most minimal criteria for an educational test. No formal content analysis, or even a rationale, is provided. No data on reliability, validity, or norma- tive performance are presented. The authors also state that attempts to norm reference the instrument are considered inappropriate. To be fair, the authors generally avoid the use of the word "test," referring to the materials as a "kit." Nonetheless, it is apparent the instrument is designed as a diagnostic, criterion-referenced measure. An essential requirement for any criterion-referenced measure is a well-defined domain of knowledge or skills to be assessed. Even this most basic requirement has not been achieved. The classroom teacher might find some of the information provided by the EMDK useful, but this information could be collected less expensively using informal materials. Also, several other, better, instruments are available. These include the KeyMath Revised: A Diagnostic Inventory of Essential Mathematics (191) and the Sequential Assessment of Mathematics Inventories (359). The EMDK can be recommended only as a supplemental instrument of limited value. It would probably be of most interest to researchers involved in the assessment and teaching of mathematics to young children.

[122]

Early Screening Inventory.

Purpose: "A brief developmental screening instrument . . . designed to identify children who may need special educational services in order to perform adequately in school."

Population: Ages 3–6.

Publication Dates: 1976–87.

Acronym: ESI.

Administration: Individual.

Levels, 2: Three Year Olds, Four to Six Year Olds.

Price Data, 1987: $39.95 per complete kit including test and manual ('83, 64 pages), score sheets, screening materials, and parent questionnaires; $10.95 per test and manual; $9.95 per 30 score sheets; $11.95 per screening materials; $9.95 per 30 parent questionnaires.

Foreign Language Edition: Spanish version ('87) available.

Time: (15–20) minutes.

Comments: Originally introduced as the Eliot-Pearson Screening Inventory; test also includes a parent questionnaire; manual for Revision for Three Year Olds and Spanish version available directly from S. J. Meisels.

Authors: Samuel J. Meisels and Martha Stone Wiske.

Publisher: Teachers College Press.

a) THREE YEAR OLDS.

Scores: 4 areas: Draw-a-Person, Visual-Motor/ Adaptive, Language and Cognition, Gross Motor/ Body Awareness.

b) FOUR TO SIX YEAR OLDS.

Scores: Same as *a*.

c) PARENT QUESTIONNAIRE.

TEST REFERENCES

1. Meisels, S. J., Wiske, M. S., & Tivnan, T. (1984). Predicting school performance with the Early Screening Inventory. *Psychology in the Schools, 21*, 25-33.

Review of the Early Screening Inventory by DEN-ISE M. DEZOLT, Instructor in School Psychology, Illinois State University, Normal, IL:

The Early Screening Inventory (ESI) is a brief, developmentally based survey designed to identify 4–6-year-old children "who may need special educational services in order to perform adequately in school." A 3-year-old version and two Spanish versions (3-year and 4–6-year) are also available. Performance in speech, language, cognition, perception, and motor domains is screened by individual administration. Several sources of data about the child are used including the child's performance on the tasks, observations by the examiner, and information from a parent questionnaire also included in the test kit. The parent questionnaire administered prior to the child's screening elicits information about the child's family history, school history, medical history, health, development, and related concerns. The authors further recommend a medical examination and vision and hearing screening as additional and necessary sources of information to make an appropriate status determination.

The ESI consists of three primary sections: Visual-Motor/Adaptive, Language and Cognition, and Gross Motor/Body Awareness. It comprises 13 sections, including a Draw-a-Person task and an unscored letter-writing item, that have been developed by the authors or derived from several diagnostic and screening instruments. Included in the screening kit are the examiner's manual, 3-inch x 5-inch cards for copy forms and visual sequential memory, ten 1-inch cubes, objects for verbal expression tasks, ESI protocols, and parent questionnaires. The examiner must provide manila paper, two 2-inch x 2-inch squares each of red, blue, green, and yellow paper, large pencil, plain white paper, and an optional 8.5-inch x 11-inch cardboard.

This instrument can be readily administered by examiners with knowledge of early childhood development and standardized test procedures. The authors, however, recommend a three-step training process including observation of a trained examiner, review of the manual, and supervised practice. The extent to which one requires supervised practice is influenced by one's experience with children in this age range. English and Spanish training videotapes are also available. Test administration procedures are generally straightforward and concise, although one of the motor items seems to be difficult to administer and score as it requires the examiner to demonstrate the item concurrent with attending to and scoring the child's performance. Each item presented in the manual includes a list of materials needed, standard administration procedures, and scoring criteria. Specific examples of pass/fail responses are included within each item description to facilitate scoring. On several items, alternative forms

are provided when the child fails to master the initial, more difficult task. Standardized administration procedures are also provided on the protocol itself to facilitate administration. The 3-year-old version is similar, with minor age-appropriate modifications. The authors recommend following the order of administration presented in the manual, but recognize the need to be flexible and responsive to the child's needs.

The ESI Score Sheet is designed for quick scoring by checking one of three boxes following each item in a Pass, Fail, or Refuse column with space for examiner comments. The Total Points Possible on each item is provided. The examiner need only calculate Total Points Received for each item and sum these to determine the Total Screening Score. The child's total ESI score is compared to the mean score for the appropriate age group derived from the standardization sample to ascertain one of three possible categories. The cutoff scores for the 5-6 to 5-11 age range are extrapolated from standardization scores for the other subjects. Thus, results for this age group must be viewed with caution. The "OK" category reflects a total score less than one standard deviation below the mean and assumes normal development. A total score falling between 1 and 2 standard deviations below the mean is in the "rescreen" category, indicating another screening within 8–10 weeks. A total score lower than 2 standard deviations below the mean, the "refer" category, indicates the need to refer. The manual provides sample score sheets and brief case summaries of three children, one from each of the categories. A description of the normative sample is not provided and needs to be included in the revision that is currently underway. The revision will incorporate the 3-year and 4- to 6-year versions into one manual.

The value of any instrument lies in its ability to discriminate between children who have problems and those who do not. Item analysis indicates that although certain components of two items do not discriminate referred from nonreferred children, examination of all the items as a whole lends to clear performance differentiation. Other psychometric qualities of the ESI are also provided in the manual. Interscorer reliability and test-retest reliabilities are acceptable at .91 and .82 (for the total ESI) respectively. With regard to the validity of the ESI, the manual presents concurrent, short-term predictive, and longitudinal predictive studies. To demonstrate the relationship between ESI and criterion results, data are presented as correlation coefficients and contingency tables. Results generally indicate acceptable levels of validity. Specificity and sensitivity rates are also found to be moderate to high in kindergarten, subsequently becoming less stable through grade 4.

Standardization of the 3-year-old version and the two Spanish versions is currently underway. Mean scores and standard deviations are available for the 3-year-old English version as of July 1989. These versions should be used with care until such data are available.

In summary, the ESI appears to be a useful screening instrument with 4- to 6-year-olds when used as part of a multidimensional approach. As with any screening instrument, results of the ESI should be viewed with caution as such measures sample small parts of a child's range of behaviors and focus on the product of development. Ecological variables that influence child development should also be included when making determinations and recommendations. A formal attempt to measure the child's personal/social-emotional functioning especially needs to be incorporated.

Review of the Early Screening Inventory by KEVIN MENEFEE, Certified School Psychologist, Barkley Center, University of Nebraska-Lincoln, Lincoln, NE:

The Early Screening Inventory (ESI) is a brief (15–20 minutes), individually administered screen of verbal, visual-motor, and gross motor development in children ages 4 to 6 years. The ESI has undergone four revisions since its introduction in 1975 as the Eliot-Pearson Screening Inventory, and, according to the developers, is currently in the process of being normed nationally on 3- to 6-year-old children (with a Spanish version in production as well).

Administration of the test is generally quick, easy, and enjoyable on the part of both examiner and child. Scoring, for the most part, is very easy and concrete, although this reviewer feels that more elaboration and clarification of scoring criteria on some of the verbal subtests would be helpful.

The ESI consists of three sections (Visual-Motor/Adaptive, Language and Cognition, and Gross Motor/Body Awareness) yielding a single total score. Also provided is a Parent Questionnaire. This questionnaire is not scored but includes questions on a variety of developmental, medical, and family topics. The authors recommend using the ESI total score to classify children into one of three referral groups: "OK" (between the mean and 1 standard deviation below the mean), "rescreen" (between 1 and 2 standard deviations below the mean), and "refer" (lower than 2 standard deviations below the mean).

The manual includes tables giving cutoff scores corresponding to the limits of the three referral decision groups by age (in 6-month intervals, from age 4-0 to 5-11). These initial norms were based upon a sample of 465 Caucasian, English-speaking children, "randomly selected from public preschool and elementary school programs in a predominantly working- and lower-middle-class urban community."

As previously mentioned, the ESI is currently in the process of being nationally normed; the developers have indicated (personal communication) that preliminary results suggest that the final cutoff scores will be very similar to those given in the manual.

Test-retest reliability for the total score on the ESI is presented by the manual as a "percent agreement" correlation of .82 between two administrations given approximately a week apart to 57 children. Interrater reliability, again based on "percent agreement" between examiners and observers scoring a very limited number (18) of administrations, is similarly reported as a correlation of .91 between scorers for the total score. The manual does not clearly state the exact statistic these correlations represent, nor the procedure for calculating the "percent agreement" upon which they are based (e.g., point-by-point, total score, etc.). Without this information, it is difficult to evaluate these indices of the test's reliability.

Three studies are described in an attempt to establish the concurrent validity, short-term predictive validity, and long-term predictive validity of the ESI. The concurrent validity study compares the scores of 102 children on both the ESI and the McCarthy Scales of Children's Abilities, yielding a favorable overall correlation of .73. The authors then claim a strong association between the referral classifications yielded by the two instruments on what seems to be a rather questionable basis; the three classification groups (refer, rescreen, OK), as produced by scores on both instruments, are selectively collapsed into two groups (refer, OK) in a way that seems to boost the apparent agreement in classification between them.

Short-term predictive validity data are presented in the manual by way of a study of 472 children who were administered the ESI at the beginning of their kindergarten year and the Metropolitan Readiness Test (MRT) at the end of the year, yielding a modest correlation of .45 overall between the ESI and the MRT Prereading Skills composite score. The authors claim a high (83%) rate of agreement between the ESI and the MRT in terms of the children who would be classified as "low" (at or below the 15th percentile) versus "high" (above the 15th percentile) by each instrument without acknowledging the substantial effects of the base rate for the "high" classification. That is an instrument that classified *all* the subjects as belonging to the "high" group, in this case, would be in agreement with the results of the MRT 85% of the time. In addition, the data presented in the manual indicate that 67% of the children rated "low" on the MRT were rated "high" on the ESI, and that 63% of the children rated "low" on the ESI were rated "high" on the MRT, raising further doubt about these claims.

The manual also describes a longitudinal study that examines the accuracy of ESI scores in predicting later school success. Scores from three outcome variables (cumulative grade score, referral for special educational service, and promotion vs. retention) for 115 children, grades kindergarten through fourth, were "correlated" with the scores they received from administration of the ESI near the beginning of kindergarten. Although many of the coefficients presented are both significant and of moderate magnitude, more information about how they were calculated (two of the outcome variables are binary in nature, but the "correlation" statistic used is not stated) and about how the cumulative grade score outcome variable was computed is needed before the data can be wholeheartedly accepted as evidence of the ESI's predictive power. Making use of the same data, the authors again tried to establish a strong association between the ESI and the three outcome variables in identifying the lowest 15% of the population on each variable, and again ignored the powerful effect of the base rate in elevating agreement between predictor and outcome.

In summary, the Early Screening Inventory is a quick, easy, and attractive instrument whose contents lend it an undeniable face validity, and whose manner of administration makes it well suited to typical school or clinic settings. Some of the claims made in the instrument's manual for its validity appear to have a rather dubious basis. In all fairness, however, the purpose for a screening instrument should not be the making of perfectly accurate diagnoses, but rather, the identification of subjects for whom further evaluation is warranted. In this, the data presented suggest the ESI is on the right track. This reviewer, however, feels that further work is needed in validating the instrument (particularly in comparison to other screening instruments) before it can be unreservedly endorsed.

[123]

Educational Interest Inventory.

Purpose: Designed to identify personal preference for different college educational programs.
Population: Prospective college students.
Publication Date: 1989.
Acronym: EII.
Scores: 47 scales: Agriculture (Agribusiness/Agricultural Production, Agricultural Sciences, Renewable Natural Resources), Architecture and Environmental Design, Area/Ethnic Studies, Business/Management (Accounting and Finance, Administration and Management, Human Resources Management, Marketing/Distribution), Communications, Computer and Information Sciences, Education (Pre-Elementary and Elementary, Secondary and Post-Secondary, Special Education, Physical Education, Industrial Arts), Engineering (Chemical, Civil, Electrical/Electronic, Mechanical), Foreign Languages,

Health Sciences (General Medicine, Dentistry, Nursing, Pharmacy, Medical Laboratory), Home Economics, Law, Letters, Library and Archival Sciences, Life Sciences/General Biology, Mathematics, Philosophy and Religion, Theology, Physical Sciences (Chemistry, Geological Sciences, Physics), Psychology, Protective Services, Public Affairs/Social Work, Social Sciences (Economics, History, Political Sciences/Government, Sociology), Visual and Performing Arts (Fine Arts, Drama, Music).
Administration: Group.
Price Data, 1991: $3 per reusable test booklet; $35 per 25 answer sheets and profile guides; $6 per manual (43 pages); $10 per specimen set of all Educational Interest Inventory and Career Guidance Inventory components.
Time: [45–60] minutes.
Comments: Self-administered; self-scored; manual is for the EII and the Career Guidance Inventory (62).
Author: James E. Oliver.
Publisher: Orchard House, Inc.

Review of the Educational Interest Inventory by LOIS T. STRAUSS, Associate Professor of Psychology, and DAVID E. KAPEL, Dean, School of Education and Related Professional Studies, Glassboro State College, Glassboro, NJ:

The Educational Interest Inventory (EII) is intended to "measure relative interest in formal, postsecondary educational programs as they are presented in both public and private schools." The paper-pencil version presents a 235-item, forced-choice format that corresponds to 47 instructional programs, based on the U.S. Department of Education's (1985) Classification of Instructional Programs (CIP). The computer format (CEP), when it is released, will be available to those who are able to narrow their interests. The CEP allows students to preselect 11 of the 47 programs, thus, reducing the inventory to 110 forced-choice items.

According to its author, the EII was "Primarily" revised to increase the number of scales that correspond to the growing number of options available in postsecondary educational programs. Indeed, the credibility of the process is enhanced by utilizing this classification system. However, the procedures for item development, scoring, and interpretation, as well as the reliability and validity of the instrument itself, remain in question.

The following caveats should be considered before selecting the EII for use. No data that demonstrate the inventory's predictive validity accompany the present revision. Each section describing the construction of the inventory provides dubious generalizations unsupported by data and unsubstantiated by inspecting the instrument, its administration, scoring, and interpretation.

Methodology for item development and selection (10 items correspond to each scale) is unreported. The user is asked to accept "the collective effort and judgement [sic] of three men and three women with extensive experience in the area of psychometrics." A review of items representing their "collective judgment" yielded several systematic flaws: items that ask two questions rather than one, items that appear to be unrelated to the scale or the corresponding program's description, items that are either too broad or too narrow, and items within a scale that are redundant.

For example, the item "Direct all housekeeping activities and meal plans for a wealthy family" asks two questions, perhaps ruling out a student who would enjoy the activity in a different setting. The item "Teach courses in early childhood development" is said to correlate with the program K–8th grade teacher; however, in practice this expertise is outside the province of the elementary school teacher. The item "Study why seasonal changes cause variation in the coat color of foxes" does not appear to have face validity for a secondary student completing the inventory by virtue of its narrowness and esoteric quality within the broad area of Life Sciences. The Law scale is exceedingly redundant and narrow, with 7 of 10 items asking if one would prefer to defend, counsel, or advise clients. Both the language and the process referred to are redundant, leaving three items to tap the plethora of skills and abilities necessary for the study and practice of law.

Directions for the self-scoring, pencil-paper version of the EII are opaque, requiring guidance by the examiner. Although the author defends the length of the inventory, 235 items appear to be indefensible for the attention span of the target population. The format of the answer sheet creates several pitfalls for the student, while at the same time providing ease of profiling the student's preferences by the examiner. The format of the answer sheet, which allows 10 responses to each of 47 scales, is transparent to the student who wishes to manipulate responses to maximize, minimize, or normalize interests. Further, neither the inventory booklet nor the answer sheet is arranged by consecutive numbers. Thus, despite a warning by the authors, students can easily lose their place and have to begin again.

An incomplete or "partial pair" design has been used for the 235 forced-choice comparisons. The author argues that a two-step process (i.e., choosing between activities and then assigning high or low interest weights to that choice) significantly reduces the systematic error that is inherent in ipsative measures with incomplete pairs. The author cites supportive research from 1953, but fails to provide enough information on samples or design to evaluate outcomes.

Reliability and validity are dismissed in the following manner: Reliability coefficients are considered unnecessary in the pencil-paper version, which is based on ipsative rather than normative measures. Construct validity is based on the "longi-tudinal 'public' agreement" for the CIP. Finally, content validity is said to rest on the representative nature of each activity statement, which has been shown above to have little credibility.

Guidelines for interpretation fall short; for example, it would have been useful to provide a threshold above which a high interest or a secondary interest should be explored in depth. An interpretive guide of skills and abilities correlated with each of the 47 scales could have been provided to assist students in self-exploration, which is universally accepted as the first step in sound decision making. Unfortunately, the examiner's manual does not provide the professional counselor with any additional interpretive guidelines for best utilizing the inventory.

The CEP, for which no costs were provided, appears to have greater reliability because of its complete, rather than incomplete, forced-choice pairings. It has a capability for utilizing a data base that could provide information on colleges that correlate with student preferences. It also has a letter-writing program that can generate various formats for communicating with college personnel. Ease of administration, scoring, and item selection remain a concern.

Because of limitations regarding item development and selection, a difficult and unwieldy scoring procedure, disregard for providing reliability and validity data, and lack of in-depth guidelines and accompanying interpretive material for users, this inventory is not recommended. There are numerous inventories that can be suggested by counselors, such as the Kuder inventories (T3:1269 and 10:167) and the Strong Interest Inventory (9:1195), which are known for their research base and the accompanying interpretive materials that are available to better inform and guide prospective postsecondary students.

Review of the Educational Interest Inventory by JIM C. FORTUNE, Professor of Educational Research and Evaluation, and JAVAID KAISER, Associate Professor of Educational Research and Evaluation, College of Education, Virginia Tech, Blacksburg, VA:

The Educational Interest Inventory (EII) and its companion Career Guidance Inventory (CGI) are designed to identify personal preferences for the content of different postsecondary instructional programs. The EII, through preference indications, permits the identification of one or more major interest areas from 47 different instructional college programs. The CGI uses the same response format to identify one or more major interest areas from 47 different postsecondary or vocational programs. The response format of the scales uniquely uses both an open-response format (the student makes a judgment concerning interest in a given activity) and a closed-response format (the student has to choose between competing activities). This response format involves the selection of the most preferred of two activities and then the subsequent weighting of the selected activity by either a "high" or "low" interest designation. The authors in the examiner's manual state that this process of weighting the forced selection tends to "diminish the impact of non-random distribution of error." Further discussion and explanation of this point seems in order.

The inventory involves 235 pairs of activities from which preferences are to be made and then rated in terms of high or low interest. The inventory can be self-administered and self-scored. Overall, the process takes between 45 and 90 minutes. The scoring format and the interpretation scale are included and are clearly written. Interest levels are generated for all 47 programs, with focus to be placed on those with the highest scores.

In the examiner's manual, terse, superficial statements are made concerning reliability and validity. The author argues that due to the ipsative nature of the scores the computation of reliability would produce "spuriously low" results, because the methods would involve linearity assumptions. This argument appears reasonable on the surface, but is weak with regard to the basic intent of reliability. Generalizability theory would permit an analysis of response differences across time. Also, using the notion of classification as an outcome, the phi correlation provides a method for estimating reliability. The issue of reliability appears to be too easily dismissed.

Again, in the examiner's manual, a terse treatment of validity is made. First, there is the question of the validity of the 47 areas chosen by the author. Should there be a lesser or greater number of programs listed? There is no doubt that the 47 programs are instructional programs, but how were these selected from the long listings of curricular offerings? The author states that "content validity is inherent in the behaviors described by the paired items." Is this really true? Do the paired items produce equally competing activities across program areas? Were principal activities omitted? In taking the inventory, we do not remember any references to "flying," "race-car driving," "military science," "forestry," and so forth. Again, rationales for activity inclusion would be useful.

In a study of an earlier version of the scale, Morrill, Miller, and Thomas (1970) reported a split-half reliability ranging from .63 to .89 and test-retest reliabilities of .71 to .93. These researchers also reported significant and positive correlations of the instrument with the Strong Vocational Interest Blank (Thomas, Morrill, & Miller, 1970).

The examiner's manual is made more complex by the inclusion of discussion concerning a computerized version of the scales that is scored differently from the two pencil-paper versions. This computerized version is not yet available for distribution and discussion of it detracts from the well-written directions. This inclusion could well be replaced by two or three case histories and interpretations that would provide additional insight for those self-administering the instrument.

The instrument may provide needed self-reflection to those wishing to continue their education, but who are undecided about the area or curriculum to pursue. We suspect that profiles for some will contain several "very high" interest areas, whereas profiles for others may contain only an occasional "high" interest area. To still others, the scale will point out the obvious. With additional information, the scale should be useful in counseling high school seniors.

REVIEWER'S REFERENCES

Morrill, W. H., Miller, C. D., & Thomas, L. E. (1970). Educational and vocational interest of college women. *Vocational Guidance Quarterly, 19* (2), 85-90.
Thomas, L. E., Morrill, W. H., & Miller, C. D. (1970). Educational interests and achievement. *Vocational Guidance Quarterly, 18* (3), 199-202.

[124]

Educational Leadership Practices Inventory.

Purpose: Reflects Ideal versus Actual attitudes for individual and group teaching style patterns.
Population: Teachers and administrators.
Publication Dates: 1955–79.
Acronym: ELPI.
Scores, 2: Ideal, Actual.
Administration: Group.
Price Data, 1988: $12.75 per specimen set including reusable test booklet, 25 self-scoring answer sheets, and manual ('67, 14 pages).
Time: (30–45) minutes.
Comments: Computer form available.
Authors: Charles W. Nelson and Jasper J. Valenti (inventory).
Publisher: Management Research Associates.

Review of the Educational Leadership Practices Inventory by ERNEST J. KOZMA, *Professor of Education, Clemson University, Clemson, SC:*

The Educational Leadership Practices Inventory is a self-scored survey consisting of 50 problem situations. Each problem has two practices offered as choices. The respondent must choose the ideal practice and the actual practice. The 50 problem situations are categorized into four styles of leadership. After categorizing the responses, teams of participants are formed to discuss the various categories and leadership styles. Group profiles can be determined and the scores in each area can be compared to a table of ideal scores for various known groups such as police department heads, auto manufacturing organizations, and route sales organizations.

The manual for administration, analysis, and interpretation contains the directions, explanations, and tables for interpretation. No statistical data concerning reliability or validity are included. The tables included in the manual do not have references or statistical explanations. One reference used to show that progress was made by the management of a company using the material was referenced to the years 1954, 1955, and 1956. The manual indicated a copyright date of 1967. The actual survey instrument indicates a revised form made in 1979. Accompanying material and references were all somewhat dated. Most of the sources cited, in the manual and the supportive material provided, were dated prior to 1974. Users of the survey should be cautious concerning the use of the tables and the ideal and actual scores. The material might be used by an effective discussion leader to introduce management development activities, particularly if some of the more recent materials and practices concerning leadership were added.

Review of the Educational Leadership Practices Inventory by DARRELL SABERS, Professor of Educational Psychology, University of Arizona, Tucson, AZ:

The Educational Leadership Practices Inventory (ELPI) is intended for in-service workshops and is not intended to be an instrument for providing assessments of individuals' leadership practices. Any evaluation of the survey based on criteria for tests and inventories will result in an extremely negative summation, especially when there is no evidence available to suggest the scores obtained from the survey are reliable or valid.

Most of the information presented to suggest the system of classifying styles is useful is dated (so dated that a footnote refers to a 1974 article as "recently published"). Some quantitative data supporting the obtained scores are from 1954 training results. These are most certainly not relevant to the 1979 revision. Other data are presented in two tables that might be used with in-service participants, but one cannot determine from reviewed materials where these data were obtained (or whether they are actual scores or examples of score differences). The information regarding reliability and validity is very limited, pertains to judgments made during development of the theory that guided the construction of this survey, and is based on data from a 1949 Ph.D. thesis.

While reading the material for the ELPI, I kept thinking the editors of the *Mental Measurements Yearbook* series must be using me for some experimental purpose. It is difficult to believe anyone would seriously propose the use (much less the purchase) of materials without better documentation. Based on these materials, one cannot judge the appropriateness of the in-service training provided by the authors (or others) who might use these materials. However, unless substantially better materials to support its use are made available to potential consumers, the ELPI cannot be recommended for any assessment purpose.

[125]
Educational Process Questionnaire.

Purpose: "To aid teachers in their own self-development by providing objective information about the processes used in the teacher's own actual classroom."
Population: Grades 4–12.
Publication Dates: 1973–87.
Acronym: EPQ.
Scores: 5 scale scores: Reinforcement of Self-Concept, Academic Learning Time, Feedback, Expectations, Development of Multiple Talents.
Administration: Group.
Price Data, 1988: $20 per 35 reusable booklets; $3 per 35 answer sheets; $5 per specimen set including booklet, answer sheet, and administration manual ('87, 22 pages); $30 per 35-pupil classroom scoring services (scoring performed during first week of November, February, and May); $.75 per student (above 35 in classroom) scoring services.
Time: 35(45) minutes.
Comments: Ratings by students.
Author: Institute for Behavioral Research in Creativity.
Publisher: Institute for Behavioral Research in Creativity.

Review of the Educational Process Questionnaire by WILLIAM L. CURLETTE, Professor of Educational Foundations, Georgia State University, Atlanta, GA:

The Educational Process Questionnaire Administration Manual and Technical Documentation (1987), states that the purpose of the Educational Process Questionnaire (EPQ) is to "provide direction to a teacher's self-improvement efforts, by identifying five key educational processes." To accomplish this objective students answer 54 items, each having five possible responses. This results in scores on five subscales with the following number of items in each subscale: Reinforcement of Self-Concept (11 items), Academic Learning Time (7 items), Feedback (5 items), Expectation (12 items), and Development of Multiple Talents (18 items). According to the manual, it is recognized that these subscales "do not exhaust the set of all processes important within classrooms, but are five of the more important processes defined by the literature" (p. 15).

Many items on these subscales are high inference. For example, Item 11 asks "Do your teachers expect everyone to do his/her best in class?" In other words, a student is asked to infer about what a group of teachers have as their set of expectations for all their students. In contrast, one of the items that requires the least inference is "How often do you prepare information for a debate with someone else?"

The test manual supplied by The Institute for Behavioral Research in Creativity is produced with only a moderately attractive format. The manual contains a clear set of numbered instructions for administering the EPQ. A flyer with ordering information indicates that scoring is available during the first week of November, February, and May. Scoring at other times of the year is available if the EPQ has been administered in 20 or more classrooms.

A unique score-reporting feature of the EPQ is the availability of reports at three different levels: individual classrooms, entire grades, and particular schools. To obtain these reports, the special code section on an optical scan answer sheet must be marked on each of the student answer sheets. It is suggested in the manual that students taking the EPQ code in the number for their classroom.

A graphical presentation of a teacher's percentile rank is furnished on each of the five subscales using bell-shaped curves. (Do the scores on each scale actually follow a bell-shaped curve?) Underneath each bell-shaped curve are two different ranges of scores labeled as "low" and "high." No rationale is presented in the manual for these labels. Accuracy in scoring is attended to by the detection of random responses, extreme responses, or missing data. However, more details are needed in the manual regarding how missing data are handled.

Two practical concerns for using any test are the amount of time required to administer the test and its reading level. On both accounts the EPQ appears very good. The test manual reports that it requires approximately 45 minutes to take the 54 items in the test which should fit well with most class periods in schools. The manual states the EPQ is appropriate for grades 3 to 12 and has a reading level of third grade. A quick check of the reading level using the SMOG formula indicates that third or fourth grade appears to be a reasonable estimate of reading level.

Norming was done in Utah with a sample of approximately 1,700 students in grades 3 to 6. Although user norms are acceptable by APA Standards, the difficulty in this instance is knowing where a teacher being rated might stand compared to a typical teacher from other states or a national sample. Furthermore, it would be helpful if narratives and descriptive statistics of the schools used in the norm sample were provided. A free service of The Institute for Behavioral Research in Creativity that tends to compensate for limitations in the norms is their willingness to prepare local norms for users.

Of the five subscales in the test, two have low intrascore reliability. Academic Learning Time has a reliability of .57 and Feedback has a reliability of .44. As indicated in the manual, this may be due to the heterogeneity of content within a scale and the low number of items on these scales. Typically, the effect of the low reliability for a subscale with few items is to make the standard error of measurement

so large that it encompasses a relatively large portion of the possible scores. However, despite the low reliabilities, several correlations between educational outcomes and each of these two scales are statistically significant.

Often the motivation for developing a test becomes important for understanding the test. Some insight into the EPQ is obtained by realizing that "the EPQ was originally constructed to monitor the implementation of talent developing activities" (manual, p. 3) of classroom teachers for their students. It seems then, based on the manual, that a rationale approach was employed in test development rather than the empirical approach that often involves using group differences or a factor analytic approach. For instance, no factor analysis is discussed in the manual as a justification for arriving at the five subscales in the EPQ.

The validity section of the manual emphasizes the grounding of the EPQ in literature on classroom educational process as evidence for content validity. Empirical data supporting construct validity are provided in tables of correlations as well as cited studies. Of the 10 correlations from a classroom level analysis of the five subscales on the EPQ with the CTBS Reading and the CTBS Mathematics scores, the lowest correlation was -.02 ($p > .05$) and the highest correlation was .30 ($p < .05$). This indicates that the EPQ subscales, which are related to teacher practices, vary with student academic achievement from essentially no degree to perhaps a moderate degree. In the same study, correlations of the five EPQ subscales with affective educational outcomes varied from .02 ($p < .05$) to .56 ($p < .05$).

A computer search of several data bases (Psych-ALERT, PsychINFO, ERIC, and Dissertations Abstracts International) turned up one citation (Embley, 1987), which was not listed in the test manual. Embley (1987) administered the EPQ along with multiple talent tests to students in grades 4 through 6. In the program group classes, a new inservice program of learn/teaching multiple talents was implemented. Student pretest data on the EPQ and multiple talents tests were given to their teachers. In comparison to the control group, the students in the program group reported change in their teachers' methodology. This provides some evidence for the instructional validity of the EPQ.

There is lack of information in the test manual on topics considered necessary (primary standards) in the *Standards for Educational and Psychological Testing* (AERA, APA, & NCME, 1985). Missing from the manual are standard errors of measurement and information on cultural fairness.

In a broad sense, one way to view the EPQ is to ask what other methods of obtaining data on teaching are possible to meet the objective of improving teaching. As previously indicated, the EPQ is based on student perceptions of teaching. Other ways involve observations of teaching by professionals such as in the System for Teaching and Learning Assessment and Review (Ellett, Loup, & Chauvin, 1990) or the Georgia Teacher Evaluation Program (Rogers, 1989). More recently, the National Center for Research on Teacher Education is looking at evaluating teaching based in part on portfolios representing teachers' work or assessment centers.

In conclusion, the concerns regarding high inference items, some low reliabilities on scales with few items, and the lack of standard errors of measurement, place some limits on the usefulness of the EPQ. Nevertheless, the EPQ does moderately satisfy its objective of providing a teacher with student perceptions to help improve teaching.

REVIEWER'S REFERENCES

American Educational Research Association, American Psychological Association, & National Council on Measurement in Education. (1985). *Standards for Educational and Psychological Testing.* Washington, DC: American Psychological Association, Inc.

Embley, P. T. (1987). Learn/Teach inservice and formative student feedback: Educational change with multiple talents. (Doctoral dissertation, Brigham Young University, 1987). *Dissertation Abstracts International, 48* (11), 2797A.

Rogers, W. (1989). *Georgia Teacher Evaluation Program Evaluation manual.* Atlanta, GA: Georgia Department of Education.

Ellett, C., Loup, K., & Chauvin, S. (1990). *System for teaching and learning assessment and review annotated guide to teaching and learning.* Baton Rouge, LA: College of Education, Louisiana State University.

[126]
Einstein Assessment of School-Related Skills.

Purpose: "To identify children who are at risk for, or are experiencing, learning difficulties; and who therefore should be referred for a comprehensive evaluation."
Population: Grades K–5.
Publication Dates: 1988–90.
Administration: Individual.
Levels, 6: Kindergarten, First Grade, Second Grade, Third Grade, Fourth Grade, Fifth Grade.
Price Data: Available from publisher.
Time: (10) minutes.
Authors: Ruth L. Gottesman and Frances M. Cerullo.
Publisher: Modern Curriculum Press.

a) KINDERGARTEN LEVEL.
Scores, 5: Language/Cognition, Letter Recognition, Auditory Memory, Arithmetic, Visual-Motor Integration.
b) FIRST GRADE LEVEL.
Scores, 7: Language/Cognition, Word Recognition, Oral Reading, Reading Comprehension, Auditory Memory, Arithmetic, Visual-Motor Integration.
c) SECOND GRADE LEVEL.
Scores: Same as *b* above.
d) THIRD GRADE LEVEL.
Scores: Same as *b* above.
e) FOURTH GRADE LEVEL.
Scores: Same as *b* above.
f) FIFTH GRADE LEVEL.
Scores: Same as *b* above.

TEST REFERENCES

1. Gottesman, R. L., Cerullo, F. M., Bennett, R. E., & Rock, D. A. (1991). Predictive validity of a screening test for mild school learning difficulties. *Journal of School Psychology, 29,* 191-205.

Review of the Einstein Assessment of School-Related Skills by GLORIA A. GALVIN, School Psychologist, Dodgeville School District, Dodgeville, WI:

The Einstein test, according to the authors, was designed "to identify children who are at risk for, or are experiencing learning difficulties, and who therefore should be referred for a comprehensive evaluation." It is made up, at each level from kindergarten through fifth grade, of approximately 20–25 items typically found in general cognitive or achievement tests for children including: (*a*) words to define orally; (*b*) letters, words, or sentences to identify or read; (*c*) arithmetic problems to solve; (*d*) designs to copy; (*e*) strings of numbers or sentences to remember and recite; and (*f*) a drawing of a human figure to create. Administration of the test requires, at each grade level, an eight-page Examiner's Form and a four-page Test Booklet. The Examiner's Form contains the total available information on administration and scoring of the test. The companion Test Booklet contains the stimulus materials for the student taking the test and normative scores for comparison purposes from which a decision whether to refer the student for a comprehensive evaluation is made.

There are major problems with this test. First, although the authors assert that the Einstein measures "the major skill areas underlying school achievement," no logical or theoretical rationale for the specific choice of items and how they relate to achievement is presented. No information is presented on any aspect of the test's development. Second, there is no technical information of any kind presented by the authors so that the Einstein can be judged fairly in comparison to other screening tests. The authors do not present a manual, do not cite a norm group (although the test contains "Norms" cited on the Test Booklets), and do not present any reliability or validity information.

In summary, the value of this test is highly questionable. Despite fairly attractive materials and well-written and easy-to-follow administration and scoring directions, this test is not ready for use. The decision that the authors would have examiners make following administration of the test (i.e., whether to refer a student for a comprehensive evaluation) is a decision of significant consequence. Given the emotional and economic costs of overreferral, and the emotional and educational consequences of underreferral, it is important that any screening test be rigorously and carefully developed and that basic information on its reliability and validity be presented to prospective users before it is commercially available. At this time, alternatives to this test should be sought by those needing a screening test at these grade levels.

ADDENDUM. A two-part technical manual for the Einstein became available following the preparation of the preceding review. Part 1 describes in clear detail administration and scoring of the test and Part 2 describes the test's development, validity, and reliability.

The Einstein's norm group was of very adequate size with an average of 297 children per grade level, and was well balanced by sex. The norm group, however, was restricted to children from a few urban and suburban New York state schools. Therefore, users should consider development of local norms if their population or school curricula are likely to differ.

Validity data presented by the authors indicate that the Einstein leans toward overidentification of students at risk for learning difficulty with a median false positive rate of 22.5% (false negative rate 1–2%) among six grade levels. Users should consider following the Einstein's selected children with another screening measure (e.g., teacher judgment to reduce unnecessary referrals for full evaluation).

Reliability data are presented for both decision consistency and interrater decision consistency; however, the latter was based on only 10 students who were not from the norm group. Additional, more comprehensive data are needed to establish the Einstein's reliability.

In summary, the Einstein shows promise in the area of screening for learning difficulties in grades K–5 and the provision of a technical manual has enhanced its usefulness.

[127]

Electrical and Electronics Test.

Purpose: "Examines knowledge of fundamental laws, symbols and definitions and requires the application of them to familiar equipment."
Population: Students in electrical or electronics programs ages 15 and over.
Publication Date: No date on test materials.
Scores: Total score only.
Administration: Group.
Price Data, 1987: £1.25 per test booklet; £2.50 per answer key; £9 per manual; £11 per specimen set.
Time: (15–30) minutes.
Author: The Test Agency Ltd.
Publisher: The Test Agency Ltd. [England].

[128]

Electronics Test.

Purpose: "To measure the knowledge and skills required for electronics jobs."
Population: Electronics employees and applicants for electronics positions.
Publication Dates: 1987–88.
Scores: Total score only.
Administration: Group.
Forms: 2 equivalent forms (Form F and Form G).

Price Data, 1989: $498 per 10 reusable booklets (Form F or G), 1 test manual ('88, 12 pages), 1 scoring key, and 100 blank answer sheets.
Time: (120) minutes.
Author: Roland T. Ramsay.
Publisher: Ramsay Corporation.

[129]

Elicited Articulatory System Evaluation.

Purpose: Evaluates traditional phoneme and phonological process usage.
Population: Ages 3 and over.
Publication Date: 1988.
Acronym: EASE.
Scores, 15: Consonant/Vowel Production (Patterns of Substitution Errors, Patterns of Omission Errors, Patterns of Distortion Errors, Patterns of Addition Errors), Phonological Process (Deletion of Final Consonant, Consonant Cluster Reduction, Deletion of Unstressed Syllable, Fronting of Velar, Fronting of Fricatives, Stopping of Fricatives, Stopping of Affricates, Affrication, Gliding, Prevocalic Voicing of Consonant, Vocalization).
Administration: Individual.
Price Data, 1988: $89 per complete kit; $12 per 25 score sheets; $23 per examiner's manual (37 pages); $29 per analysis booklets; $29 per picture book.
Time: (15–20) minutes.
Authors: Susie Finn Steed and William O. Haynes.
Publisher: PRO-ED, Inc.

Review of the Elicited Articulatory System Evaluation by KATHARINE G. BUTLER, Professor and Chair, Communication Sciences & Disorders, Division of Special Education & Rehabilitation, Syracuse University, Syracuse, NY:

The Elicited Articulatory System Evaluation (EASE) claims to be the only single assessment instrument that provides a measurement of articulation and phonological processes. Although the test was designed for children 3 years and older, the authors indicate that it can also be administered to adults with some modification. The second strength, as viewed by the authors, is that articulation and phonology are measured in a number of imitative contexts (337 consonants and 187 vowel productions), as well as 10 phonological processes, occurring in the tests at least 13 times.

TEST CONSTRUCTION. The test involves sentence imitation, sometimes to pictured stimuli. The sentences are constructed to call forth certain phonemic contexts, and as such are somewhat artificial. For example, although a "story" format is used with pictured stimuli, the sentences of the story tend to be awkwardly constructed (e.g., Plate 20: "Now let's learn another story: The lady is nice. His name is Jim. The valentine was a letter. He will give her a necklace").

The test's standardization group appears to consist of nine articulation-disordered children, with a mean age of 5.0 (range 4–7 years). All were Caucasian and all were enrolled in a treatment program for articulation disorders. Testing revealed that the children had varying degrees of articulation difficulty (one "mild," four "mild-moderate," three "moderate-severe," and one "severe"). It appears that no other speech-disordered children or normal control subjects were used. Apparently a preliminary version was developed and copies given to four experienced speech-language pathologists who gave the test three times and made suggestions prior to the publication of this test in its present form. This appears to be the extent of the standardization of the instrument and attempts to establish content validity.

Interjudge reliability was found to be 85% and test-retest reliability was 88%, in point-by-point computations. These statistics were drawn from inexperienced student clinicians, who "had never administered the test prior to the three times they had seen the subjects" (manual, p. 11).

Content validity is said by the authors to have been demonstrated because the items "have been included in many other widely accepted tests of articulation" (manual, p. 14). The specific test items selected from other instruments are not identified. The authors concluded by noting that "the EASE is intended to be a tool for use as an adjunct to other procedures in articulatory assessment" (p. 14), which is somewhat at variance with earlier comments regarding the purpose and use of the test.

MATERIALS. The materials (manual, spiral-bound picture book, score sheet, and analysis booklet) are minimally acceptable. In particular, the picture book containing the visual stimuli for the sentence imitative tasks is flimsily made and would fail to stand up to repeated use. The black and white drawings show groups of children and some adults, and reflect cultural and ethnic diversity. The stories used are, as indicated above, not true narratives. They hold moderate interest for young children. The scoring sheet is difficult to use, and consists of hundreds of tiny squares, utilizing a wide spectrum of colors, which tend to obscure the phonetic symbols printed thereon. The space left for recording the child's production of the phonemes is minuscule. The score sheet data must then be transferred to a 24-page "Analysis Booklet," that presents deep grey spaces for re-recording the material from the score sheets. Presumably, the insertion of the deep grey background is to discourage the unauthorized copying of the booklet. There is no other apparent reason for making the recording and reading process so visually difficult.

TEST ADMINISTRATION. The authors indicate that the mean administration time is 18 minutes and scoring of both portions of the test with summary is 77 minutes, but may take as long as 98 minutes. This time is reduced if not all portions of the test are administered (i.e., the vowel portion is not administered if no vowel distortions or omissions are noted in the child's running speech). Administration and scoring require considerable time and effort, but yield considerable information. This is a fine-grained instrument which rewards its user with an extensive analysis.

SUMMARY. The EASE is a complex instrument designed to satisfy examiners' needs for an instrument that will evaluate both particular performance and the existence of nonsuppressed phonological processes. As such, it may be particularly important for use with severely impaired speech-disordered children ages 3 to 5 or 6. It permits the examiner to measure articulation and phonology in a number of linguistic contexts in imitative contexts. The weaknesses of the EASE have to do with poor standardization, very complex scoring procedures, and transfer of data to a 24-page analysis book which also requires resummarizing of data. The test is costly and of limited durability. Evaluation of articulatory skills in running speech requires an expert ear, well beyond that which is required in single word production tasks. It is this reviewer's suggestion that the use of the test be reserved for fine-grained analysis of severely speech-handicapped young children.

Review of the Elicited Articulatory System Evaluation by STEVEN H. LONG, Assistant Professor of Speech Pathology and Audiology, Ithaca College, Ithaca, NY:

The Elicited Articulatory System Evaluation (EASE) is intended to help speech-language pathologists obtain a broad sample of articulation data and analyze it using both "traditional" and "phonological" methods. The test is not normed though it does contain a worksheet that allows comparisons to be made between a child's productions and the age-of-acquisition data gathered by Sander (1972). The primary goal of the authors, it appears, was to create a time-efficient instrument (hence the acronym) yielding a comprehensive phonological sample that could be analyzed at various levels of detail according to the needs of the clinician.

The efficiency of the EASE results from its imitative elicitation procedure and cleverly designed scoring and analysis worksheets. Articulatory productions are elicited by presenting a set of "stories" depicted in 30 stimulus plates. In order to learn the stories, a child must repeat a total of 65 sentences, each of which contains two target words scored by the examiner. The authors suggest that administration takes around 15 minutes and this seems a reasonable estimate. Because responses are obtained imitatively, the test can be criticized as unrepresentative of natural speech, an issue which the authors duly address in the manual. Perhaps more significantly, the imitative format imposes a lower age boundary for use of the test. It is suggested that "in normal language development, this would be from age 3 years and older." On the presumption that the test would likely be used with children who are *not* developing language normally, this age estimate should probably be adjusted upward.

Phonetic responses are recorded on a multicolored score sheet using different notations for substitution, omission, distortion, addition, and syllable deletion errors. The data are then transferred to a 24-page analysis booklet to organize the information into consonant, vowel, and phonological process sections as well as a series of "summary" pages. The three sections of the booklet are independent of one another and the authors discuss how time may be saved by scanning the responses and omitting unnecessary portions of the analysis. Transferring the data from score sheet to analysis booklet is a laborious process but is facilitated by a scheme of numbered columns, which indicate the word position of various sounds, and different colors, which identify place and manner distinctions. The authors' pilot study with the test indicated that it took clinicians an average of 77 minutes to complete the entire analysis booklet. Their data suggest the amount of time varied considerably among clinicians ($SD = 21.75$). This reviewer's intuition is that users will react differently to the number and color scheme: Some will find it easy and time saving to use, others will think it exasperating. Consequently, this is one instrument where a "test drive" is strongly recommended.

Reliability and validity studies of the EASE are clearly reported in the manual. The data are described as "preliminary" and this is indeed so, judging from the very small sample size ($N = 9$). A more adequate sample is desirable but, as the test cannot be used for normative comparisons anyway, this is not a fatal flaw. Test-retest and interjudge reliability were computed using both total score and point-by-point methods. Test-retest correlations were quite high using both methods (.90 and .88); interjudge reliability was somewhat lower (.80 and .85). Reliability measures for articulation tests are always difficult to interpret because of the performance variability, which is inherent in certain types of phonological disorders, and because of the complexity of phonetic transcription. The statistics reported for the EASE seem consistent with those of other articulation instruments.

The content validity of the EASE is one of its strengths. Although the method of elicitation is imitative, it produces responses in the more representative context of connected speech. The length and complexity of the stimulus sentences is well controlled so as not to produce interactions between grammatical and phonological disabilities. Best of all, the EASE yields a corpus of 130 words, which is substantially larger than other tests designed to generate traditional and phonological articulation

analyses. For example, the Goldman Fristoe Test of Articulation (Goldman & Fristoe, 1986; 10:126) and the accompanying Khan-Lewis Phonological Analysis (Khan & Lewis, 1986; 10:164) are based on a set of 44 words; the Compton-Hutton Phonological Assessment (Compton & Hutton, 1978) is based on 50 responses. The value of a larger sample, as the authors of the EASE correctly point out, is that it provides a more accurate estimate of the strength of individual phonological processes as well as indicating the role of variability in a child's disability.

Speech-language pathologists will want to evaluate the EASE in terms of what it does and how efficiently it does it. As a qualitative instrument for phonological assessment, the EASE would be a good choice, provided that it is intended for use with children capable of sentence imitation. If normative comparisons are necessary, clinicians should turn to something like the Goldman Fristoe Test of Articulation and Khan-Lewis Phonological Analysis, which are well standardized and yield similar kinds of analyses. Judged for its efficiency alone, the EASE also rates highly when compared to other paper-and-pencil analysis systems. Nowadays, however, the analysis component of all articulation tests must be compared with microcomputer-assisted methods. Several computer programs, such as the *Interactive System for Phonological Analysis* (ISPA; Masterson & Pagan, 1989) or *Programs to Examine Phonetic and Phonologic Evaluation Records* (PEPPER; Shriberg, 1986), will generate phonological analyses comparable to those of the EASE. These programs can analyze any set of data, including the responses which would be obtained from the EASE. If efficiency is a paramount concern, clinicians might wish to consider using the EASE to elicit articulatory responses and some type of computer software to analyze them.

REVIEWER'S REFERENCES

Sander, E. (1972). When are speech sounds learned? *Journal of Speech and Hearing Disorders, 37*, 55-63.
Compton, A., & Hutton, S. (1978). Compton-Hutton Phonological Assessment. San Francisco: Carousel House.
Goldman, R., & Fristoe, M. (1986). Goldman Fristoe Test of Articulation. Circle Pines, MN: American Guidance Service.
Khan, L. M. L., & Lewis, N. (1986). Khan-Lewis Phonological Analysis. Circle Pines, MN: American Guidance Service.
Shriberg, L. (1986). *Programs to examine phonetic and phonologic evaluation records (PEPPER) Version 4.0* [Computer program]. Madison, WI: Software Development and Distribution Center, University of Wisconsin.
Masterson, J., & Pagan, F. (1989). *Interactive system for phonological analysis (ISPA)* [Computer program]. University, MS: Department of Communication Disorders, University of Mississippi.

[130]
Emotional Behavioral Checklist.

Purpose: To assess an individual's overt emotional behavior.
Population: Children and adults.
Publication Date: 1986.
Acronym: EBC.

Scores, 8: Impulsivity-Frustration, Anxiety, Depression-Withdrawal, Socialization, Self-Concept, Aggression, Reality Disorientation, Total EBC.
Administration: Individual.
Manual: No manual.
Price Data, 1988: $10.50 per 25 checklists.
Time: Administration time not reported.
Authors: Jack G. Dial, Carolyn Mezger, Theresa Massey, and Lawrence T. McCarron.
Publisher: McCarron-Dial Systems.

Review of the Emotional Behavioral Checklist by WILLIAM A. STOCK, Professor of Exercise Science, Arizona State University, Tempe, AZ:

The Emotional Behavioral Checklist (EBC) is a 35-item, behavior checklist that purports to measure seven factors, each with five items (Frustration-Impulsivity, Anxiety, Depression-Withdrawal, Self-Concept, Socialization, Aggression, and Reality Disorientation). Each of the 35 items can require three ratings. First, each behavior is rated as *definitely not observed* (0), *observed, but inconclusive* (1), or *definitely observed* (2). If an initial rating of 1 or 2 is given for an item, a second rating calls for a judgment as to whether treatment or intervention is or is not needed. Promotional materials claim the EBC may be used in school, rehabilitation, and/or clinical settings. However, technical and psychometric information accompanying the instrument fail to meet minimal standards, and, in this reviewer's opinion, potential users should be extremely cautious about adopting the instrument.

Absent from the documentation provided by the test publisher are (*a*) a rationale for the measure (including recommended uses and specific cautions against potential misuses); (*b*) a statement of qualifications required to administer and interpret the instrument; (*c*) a theoretical framework and definitions for the seven constructs; (*d*) specifications of observational domains for each construct; (*e*) descriptions of how behavior observations were selected; and (*f*) directions guiding judgments of the test user (who rates the client). Further, the evidence for reliability and validity claims seems to be primarily derived from data collected in settings where intervention programs of the test vendor were in operation.

Although recommended for school, clinical, and vocational settings, characteristics of the 567 adults (60% Caucasian, 26% Black, 11% Hispanic, 3% other) who comprise the normative sample do not support this recommendation. The sample is one of convenience and not from a well-specified population. About 40% of the sample were characterized as "diagnosed with neuropsychological disabilities (congenital or adventitious brain damage or dysfunction, mental retardation, CP, etc.) and were placed in various rehabilitation work settings." Forty-two further suffered either some or complete visual impairment. Of the 322 remaining individuals in the sample, 195 were visually impaired or blind, and 92 were *nondisabled*. An absence of systematic sampling from educational and clinical populations, and the opportunistic character of the sample with regard to vocational and rehabilitation populations, pose serious threats to inferences drawn from scores obtained from the scale.

Because primary evidence for reliability and validity of the EBC is also derived from this sample, an extremely cautious view on its adoption must be taken. Further, evidence provided for both the reliability and validity of the instrument suffers from several shortcomings. A single reliability estimate, reported for the total score of the EBC, of .83 is derived from a subsample ($N = 100$) of the 245 subjects with neuropsychological and visual impairments. The estimate is obtained by correlating scores obtained from two different raters at an interval of 7–14 days. As there are identifiable subgroups within this subsample, a portion of the variance attributed to reliability of the instrument may, in fact, be attributed to subgroup mean differences on behaviors rated. The estimate of .83 should be regarded as generous. Further, with respect to reliability, there is an absence of attention to a number of test standards of primary importance. There are no standard errors of measurement reported. There are no separate reliability estimates for the seven purported observational domains comprising the instrument. There are no estimates for the subgroups comprising the sample, nor for populations where the instrument is claimed to be applicable (educational and clinical settings). Information regarding the qualifications, training, and selection of judges is absent. Internal consistency estimates are absent. In short, evidence for reliability is extremely restricted.

Evidence for the validity of the scale is not adequate. There is an absence of evidence for the validity of decisions made on the basis of the EBC in clinical or educational settings. Two of the primary pieces of validity evidence are correlations with two other instruments offered by this test vendor. As the EBC is a shorter version of one of these additional measures, characterizing the reported correlation of .91 as validity evidence stretches the concept of validity too far. Of the other validity evidence reported, a concurrent correlation of .70 between the EBC and placement level in a vocational program suggests the instrument may have applicability in that setting.

In sum, potential users are advised that this instrument falls short of professional standards for educational and psychological testing. Its adoption for clinical and educational settings is not recommended, and its adoption in vocational settings is questionable at present.

Review of the Emotional Behavioral Checklist by HOI K. SUEN, Associate Professor of Educational Psychology, Pennsylvania State University, University Park, PA:

The Emotional Behavioral Checklist is a 35-item rating scale. For most items, ratings are to be assigned directly based on overt behaviors of the subject (e.g., "repetitive physical movements"; "repeated expressions of worry"). For other items, however, ratings are assigned based on the rater's inference of a subject's covert attributes (e.g., "does not understand impact his/her behavior has on others"; "limited self-awareness"). Based on these ratings, a norm-referenced score is derived. Subjects can then be classified as average, below average, or "deficit."

Whereas technical reliability and validity information is available for review, clearly stated explanations of purpose, theoretical background, or scoring scheme are not provided. Consequently, the intended appropriate use of the checklist is not clear. From various documents, the purpose of the checklist has been described as "to assess an individual's overt emotional behavior"; "prediction of actual vocational functioning level"; a measure of "emotional/behavioral functioning and adaptive behavior"; and a substitute for the existing McCarron-Dial System measures of emotional functioning and adaptive behavior. It would be most helpful if the authors could provide clear statements specifying the purpose of the checklist, the intended use, and the situations under which the use of the checklist is appropriate.

SCORING SYSTEM. After ratings are assigned, the total raw score is converted into a standard score or a *T*-score based on a conversion table. Several problems are noted with the scoring procedure. First, the mean and standard deviation, which are needed to interpret standard scores meaningfully, are not provided. Second, the " *T*-score" does not appear to be based on the conventional *T*-score transformation. Specifically, conventional *T*-scores have a mean of 50 and a standard deviation of 10. This suggests that a score of 50 is average and scores less than 50 are below average. Based on the scoring instruction of the checklist, however, "*T*-scores" of above 70 are considered "average" and those at or below 70 (or standard scores below 85) are all considered "below average." If this is indeed a conventional *T*-score, this implies that 95% of the subjects will be considered "below average." Some clarification of this scoring system is needed. Finally, it is suggested in the scoring instruction that standard scores between 70 and 85 (i.e., "*T*-scores" between 60 and 70) indicate "below average" and standard scores below 70 (i.e., "*T*-scores" below 60) indicate "deficit" or "significant problem ratings." There is no explanation as to how these cutoff scores were

chosen for this classification process. It might be helpful to a consumer if the authors would present percentile scores in addition to the standard and *T*-scores.

NORMATIVE SAMPLES. The subjects for the normative samples consisted of 567 adults. Of these 567 subjects, 475 (or 84%) had been diagnosed as neuropsychologically disabled and/or visually impaired, with a mean IQ of 85. All subjects had functioned successfully in community employment situations. From this normative sample, it appears that the Emotional Behavioral Checklist might be intended to be used for subjects with various disabilities. If this is true, it would have been helpful to a consumer had the authors stated clearly as such. The ethnic and gender composition of the normative sample appears to be quite representative. It should be pointed out that 70% of the subjects were from southwestern United States. Should this instrument be used in other regions of the United States, local norms need to be established. This accentuates the need to clarify the scoring and transformation process so that consumers may establish their own norms when needed.

RELIABILITY. A high estimate of test-retest reliability (.83) with a 7- to 14-day period between the first and the second administration is reported. A crossover method was used to estimate this test-retest reliability. Specifically, a subject was rated by one rater in the first administration and by a different rater in the retest. As a result, the estimate of interrater reliability is embedded in the test-retest reliability estimate. Given this design, the reliability estimate of .83 can be considered excellent. A drawback is the lack of information on the qualifications and training needed for a rater. Perhaps the authors should provide a description of the characteristics of the raters as well as any rater training procedures used in the reliability studies. This would assist the consumer in the choice of raters in order to sustain the high level of score reliability.

VALIDITY. Validity is not an absolute entity. Rather, it is relative to the intended use of an instrument. The scores on a given instrument may be valid for certain uses but not for others. Given the intended use of this checklist is not clear, it is difficult to judge if sufficient evidence has been derived to indicate the validity of such usage.

As evidence of validity, the authors reported relatively high and statistically significant correlations between scores on the Emotional Behavioral Checklist and various measures of emotional functioning and adaptive behavior in the McCarron-Dial System. This provides good evidence of concurrent validity and indicates that scores on the checklist are a valid substitute for scores attained through the McCarron-Dial System. It also provides very limited evidence of construct validity in interpreting the scores on the checklist as measuring "emotional functioning and adaptive behavior."

It should be noted that the checklist is divided into seven sections with labels of Impulsivity-Frustration, Anxiety, Depression-Withdrawal, and so on. There is no statistical or other systematic evidence that scores from these sections form distinct subscores. For example, there is no evidence that a subject who scores high in the section labelled Impulsivity is different from one who scores high in the section labelled Anxiety. As such, the section scores should be considered convenient groupings of items, but not distinct subscales.

SUMMARY. The major limitation of the Emotional Behavioral Checklist is the lack of information on its intended use and the situations under which its use is appropriate. Without this information, many aspects of the quality of the instrument cannot be judged adequately. Based on the available information, scores on the instrument have an excellent level of reliability. However, the scoring procedure and interpretation need clarifications and justifications. Without a clear intended use, it is difficult to judge the validity of scores from the instrument. Local norms need to be established for uses of this instrument in areas outside of the Southwestern region of the United States. In its present form, the Emotional Behavioral Checklist can best be considered experimental. Until the exact intended use of the checklist is clarified, the scoring scheme and rater training requirements clarified, and the classification criteria justified, the checklist is susceptible to misuse and abuse.

[131]
The Emotional Empathic Tendency Scale.

Purpose: To measure an individual's vicarious emotional response to perceived emotional experiences of others.
Population: Adults.
Publication Date: 1972.
Acronym: EETS.
Scores: Total score only.
Administration: Group or individual.
Manual: No manual.
Price Data: Price data for test kit available from publisher.
Time: [15] minutes.
Author: Albert Mehrabian and Norm Epstein.
Publisher: Albert Mehrabian.

[132]
Employability Maturity Interview.

Purpose: "Developed to assess readiness for the vocational rehabilitation planning process."
Population: Rehabilitation clients.
Publication Date: 1987.
Acronym: EMI.
Scores: Total score only.
Administration: Individual.
Price Data, 1990: $7 per complete kit; $5 per 50 test forms; $4 per manual (29 pages).

Time: (15–20) minutes.
Comments: Based upon the Adult Vocational Maturity Assessment Interview.
Authors: Richard Roessler and Brian Bolton.
Publisher: Arkansas Research & Training Center in Vocational Rehabilitation.

Review of the Employability Maturity Interview by WILLIAM R. KOCH, *Associate Professor of Educational Psychology, The University of Texas, Austin, TX:*

DESCRIPTION. The Employability Maturity Interview (EMI) is an individually administered structured interview consisting of 10 open-ended questions and requiring 15–20 minutes for administration. The EMI questions are presented orally by the examiner in a prescribed sequence. After each question, the examiner writes the examinee's responses in the test booklet. Upon completion of the EMI, the examiner scores the responses according to the scoring guidelines provided on the back of the booklet. Each response is scored on a 3-point, low-to-high scale to indicate the examinee's level of maturity. Curiously, question number 5 actually counts as two questions because it is scored twice—once for "specificity" and once for intrinsic and extrinsic "work orientation"—but no justification for this scoring procedure is provided. The authors of the EMI should reconsider the wisdom of requiring a single question to perform dual functions. The 11 item scores are summed to obtain a total score ranging from 0 to 22. Percentile ranks are also provided.

The basic purpose of the EMI is to assess the readiness of vocational rehabilitation clients to begin the vocational choice planning process. The 10 questions that constitute the EMI were selected with permission from the four scales of Manuele's more comprehensive Adult Vocational Maturity Assessment Interview (1980). The EMI manual states that the rationale for choosing these 10 questions is that they measure self-knowledge and occupational information, both of which are important for deciding if a rehabilitation client is ready for vocational planning. However, no specific justification or criteria are provided for selecting these particular 10 questions. (Were they the best discriminating questions? Were they good predictors? Were they the most reliably scored?)

NORMS. Norms for the EMI are based entirely on a single sample ($N = 106$) of disabled, vocational rehabilitation clients who received assistance from the Arkansas Rehabilitation Services at the Hot Springs Rehabilitation Center during a 5-month period in 1984. The norming sample was two-thirds male and relatively young (73% under 30 years of age). However, the types of disabilities represented in the sample included a fairly balanced cross-section of sensory, orthopedic, emotional, learning, and retardation problems. Slightly more than half the sample had received 12 years of education, but as a group the sample was below average on standardized aptitude and achievement measures. The existing norms for the EMI are inadequate. The size of the normative sample needs to be expanded substantially. Normative data are needed from multiple sites across several regions of the U.S. before they could be considered to be somewhat representative. A larger sample, broadly based, would also make possible subgroup norms, which would be highly desirable.

TECHNICAL ELEMENTS. Interscorer reliability, based on a single study with an unspecified coefficient, was estimated for each item and for the total score on the EMI based on intercorrelations among independently scored protocols obtained from the norming sample. The protocols were scored by three Master's degree students who had been trained to use the EMI scoring guidelines. These interscorer reliability estimates were fairly high at the item level (median = .80) and very high at the total score level (range from .90 to .93). Additionally, corrected split-half reliability estimates ranged from .74 to .82. Test-retest reliability estimates are not provided.

Efforts to provide evidence to support the validity of the EMI centered on the convergent aspect of construct validity. Scores on the EMI protocols obtained from the norming sample were found to be correlated significantly with a variety of other measures, including standardized aptitude and achievement test scores, vocational interest measures, and employment potential indices. However, EMI scores were found not to be correlated significantly with personality characteristics or with outcome measures of the rehabilitation training program. Little or no evidence was provided in support of the content or criterion-related validity of the EMI.

SUMMARY. Based on the reliability and validity data gathered from a very limited norming sample, the EMI appears to have promise for use as a brief, individually administered, structured interview procedure. The preliminary evidence reported in the manual indicates that the EMI fulfills its intended purpose of providing a reliable assessment of the readiness of rehabilitation clients to begin the vocational planning process. However, considerable further research needs to be conducted with the EMI. The norming sample needs to be larger and broadened substantially, and additional reliability studies need to be conducted with new samples. Finally, more attention needs to be paid to the content validity of the EMI. Efforts to provide evidence of criterion-related validity should be undertaken.

REVIEWER'S REFERENCE

Manuele, C. A. (1980). The Adult Vocational Maturity Assessment Interview. New York: Fordham University at Lincoln Center.

Employee Involvement Survey.

Purpose: Assesses employees' actual and desired opportunities for personal involvement and influence in the workplace.
Population: Business and industry employees.
Publication Date: 1988.
Acronym: EIS.
Scores, 5: Basic Creature Comfort, Safety and Order, Belonging and Affiliation, Ego-Status, Actualization and Self-Expression.
Administration: Group.
Price Data, 1990: $6.95 per test booklet (14 pages).
Time: Administration time not reported.
Comments: Self-administered, self-scored.
Authors: Jay Hall.
Publisher: Teleometrics International.

Employment Screening Test and Standardization Manual.

Purpose: Provides procedures for performing a person-job analysis comparing the performance requirements of a job with the behavioral capabilities of the client.
Population: Developmentally disabled persons.
Publication Date: 1985.
Acronym: EST.
Scores: Behavioral capability and performance requirements for 26 physical demands (Standing, Walking, Sitting, Reclining, Lifting, Carrying, Pushing, Pulling, Climbing, Bending, Crouching, Crawling, Reaching, Handling, Fingering, Touching, Talking, Hearing, Tasting/Smelling, Visual Acuity, Depth Perception, Field of Vision, Numbering, Reading, Writing, Driving) and 11 temperament requirements (Directing/Controlling and/or Planning Activities of Others, Performing Repetitive and/or Short Cycle Work, Influencing People, Performing a Variety of Duties, Creative Expression, Working Alone, Performing Effectively Under Stress, Attaining Precise Measurement, Working Under Specific Instructions, Dealing With People, Making Judgments and Decisions).
Administration: Group.
Price Data, 1987: $25 per manual including analysis sheets ('85, 49 pages).
Time: Administration time not reported.
Comments: Analysis completed by professional to determine Goodness-of-Fit Index and Discrepancy Analysis for client-job match.
Authors: Robert L. Schalock, Deborah L. Johnsen, and Thomas L. Schik.
Publisher: Mid-Nebraska Mental Retardation Services, Inc.

Review of the Employment Screening Test and Standardization Manual by BRIAN BOLTON, Professor, Arkansas Research and Training Center in Vocational Rehabilitation, University of Arkansas, Fayetteville, AR:

The Employment Screening Test (EST) is a procedure for assessing the congruence between persons with developmental disabilities and their work environments. The EST is premised on an ecobehavioral approach to rehabilitation that emphasizes training functional skills in the natural environment. The purpose of the EST is to enhance the successful job placement of clients with disabilities through the process of Person-Job Analysis.

Research indicates that clients' behavioral capabilities assessed in relation to specific job performance requirements are the best predictors of successful work adjustment for persons with severe disabilities. The EST generates two profiles, one reflecting the client's behavioral capabilities and the other summarizing the performance requirements of a target job, and assesses the congruence between the two profiles by computing a Goodness-of-Fit Index. It is recommended that profile disparities identified by a Discrepancy Analysis be reduced through skill training, prosthetics, or environmental modification.

The EST involves judgments about 26 physical demands and 11 temperamental requirements of the job, all adapted from materials developed by the U.S. Department of Labor's programmatic research on job analysis. For each job, the 26 physical demands (see test entry above for complete list) are evaluated on a 3-point frequency scale (required constantly; required frequently; required seldom or never). The 11 temperamental or adaptability requirements (see test entry) are also rated on a 3-point scale (independence required; required, but assistance provided; not required). The person analysis procedures parallel the job analysis with judgments made on each of the 37 behavioral competencies using a 3-point scale of independent functioning (can do independently; does with assistance; does not do).

The EST consists of a Person-Job Analysis scoring sheet that provides spaces for the ratings of the client's behavioral capabilities and the job's performance requirements, with accompanying scoring forms for the Goodness-of-Fit Index and the Discrepancy Analysis. The Goodness-of-Fit Index gives an *overall* assessment of person-job congruence, while the Discrepancy Analysis identifies the *specific* matches and mismatches between the client's capabilities and the job's requirements. The Manual presents concise guidelines and suggestions for conducting the Person-Job Analysis.

Interrater reliabilities were generated for each of the 37 EST items for a sample of clients employed in semiskilled and unskilled jobs. The average coefficients for ratings of 26 physical demands for jobs (.71) and employees (.85) were somewhat higher than the reliabilities for the 11 temperamental requirements for jobs (.64) and employees (.57). Considering the nature of the procedure, these reliabilities are minimally acceptable. However, professionals who use the EST should not place too much emphasis on any single person-job match or mismatch.

Evidence for the validity of the EST Goodness-of-Fit Index was obtained for two groups of employees classified as "good" and "poor" in their actual work performance, measured by skill acquisition, incident reports, and behavioral interventions needed. A significant ($p < .01$) difference between the two criterion groups was observed. Further analyses found significant ($p < .01$) correlations between the Index and monthly wages ($r = .55$) and a quality of life asessment ($r = .46$). Although these data support the validity of the global EST assessment, it is important to recognize that the typical counseling application of the EST depends primarily on the subsequent Discrepancy Analysis that establishes a basis for intervention strategies designed to enhance the person-job correspondence.

The EST is a carefully developed procedure for assessing the job potential of persons with developmental disabilities. Although the Person-Job Analysis is limited to just two categories of employment functioning, these comprise the most important job features for workers with severe handicaps. Completing the EST is clearly a time-consuming process, requiring a thorough evaluation of both jobs and clients on 37 work competencies using information obtained from descriptions, observations, and/or interviews. The most appropriate use of the EST would be to assemble a computer bank of job profiles so that clients with disabilities could be optimally matched to jobs in the local labor market. The manual is straightforward and well written, but should be updated with minor errors and typos corrected.

Review of the Employment Screening Test and Standardization Manual by LELAND C. ZLOMKE, Clinical Coordinator of Intensive Treatment Services, and BRENDA R. BUSH, Psychologist, Beatrice State Developmental Center, Beatrice, NE:

The Employment Screening Test (EST) is a revision of the Vocational Training Screening Test developed by Schalock and Gadwood in 1981. The current instrument attempts to provide a standardized person-job assessment procedure and to identify skills and abilities that individual clients need to maximize their success in a specific job placement. The EST also attempts to provide a Goodness-of-Fit Index (GOFI) to produce a statistic that would be comparable across jobs and environments and to provide an index representing better or worse person-job congruence. With the relatively recent change from sheltered workshop training situations to actual job stations for training and employment of persons with developmental disabilities, the measurement of these skills, abilities, and job requirements is certainly important.

DESCRIPTION. The EST comprises a test/standardization manual (49 pages). The manual provides an excellent basic summary of job analysis procedures that can provide a basic standardization of the skills and procedures used by examiners who are already skilled in developmental disabilities vocational service delivery and skill assessment. Several tables are provided listing 26 physical and 11 temperament job demands with accompanying definitions. Scoring sheets and formats for copying are provided to complete the summarization of raw data, for completion of the GOFI, and to perform the Person Behavioral Capability versus Job Performance Requirements Discrepancy Analysis.

ADMINISTRATION. The EST is performed by an examiner well acquainted with the client and proposed job station. The manual provides a general overview of procedures through which examiners should systematically proceed to analyze the client's capabilities and the job's requirements. The examiner assesses both physical and temperament job requirements and the abilities of the client. Person-Job analysis scoring is recorded on 3-point Likert-type scales. These scales rate the required frequency of performance, degrees of independence needed for a specific job, and the degree to which the client possesses these skills and abilities. These raw scores are tabulated on the person-job analysis scoring sheet and receive an arbitrary weighting factor according to "required skills" contributing 200 points versus "not required skills" contributing 100 points. This procedure provides a GOFI metric between "0" signifying no fit between client skills and job requirements and "300" indicating a maximum fit. A Discrepancy Analysis Matrix also uses raw scores to identify the frequency of important person-job matches and mismatches.

TECHNICAL ADEQUACY. There are several significant problems with the psychometric properties of the EST as it is reported in the manual: (a) As the field testing was confined to Nebraska, the results may not easily generalize to other settings, (b) there was an indication that the items of the EST were similar to those established by the Department of Labor but there is no precise indication of the exact changes made or why the Guide from the Department of Labor was not used, and (c) the sample of 44 clients was very homogeneous in nature in that the average age was 40 ± 1.3 and the Full Scale I.Q. was 54 ± 1.8.

A Pearson product-moment correlation coefficient was computed between two independent raters' evaluations on each item of the EST making a total of 176 coefficients of which 161 were statistically significant ($p < .05$). With so many comparisons there is a danger of overestimating the true number of significant relationships.

In further reliability investigations, using the chi square to test the statistical independence of the GOFI, the median (172) was used as the measure of

central tendency while the mean GOFI (164.5) was used to compute independent t-tests. The sample sizes also varied with these separate tests. The chi square test had an N of 20 while the t-test had an N of 30. The chi square test was *not* significant in discriminating "good" versus "bad" performers. The t-test was significant. The authors concluded the GOFI "accurately reflects 'success' in that particular environment." It is unclear as to why the t-test results were felt to be more reliable than the chi square results.

The validity of the EST raises several areas of concern. The groups ($n = 50$) used to validate the GOFI were of equal size and similar ages (35 and 36 years) but size and age were, seemingly, the only common variables. From these data, the authors claim scale validity because the groups were significantly different in their GOFI scores. The marked differences between the groups in other reported areas undermines confidence in the discriminatory value of the Index. For example, the "good" group was in the training program 1.9 years longer than the "poor" group. The "poor" group also had an average of 4.1 more incident reports as well as 4.2 more behavior intervention hours per month. The "good" group earned an average of $107.16 more per month and had a higher rating on the quality of life index. So, one could say if a client was in a program longer, had fewer incident reports, required less behavior intervention and earned over $50 per month they would probably score higher on the GOFI. Few professionals need a specialized index to make such predictions.

From a test construction perspective the EST fails to meet the standards for reliability and validity necessary for the GOFI to be useful. The primary role of the EST may be to provide descriptions of client skills and capabilities while matching these to specific job requirements. The identification of matches and mismatches in a criterion-referenced format is a major contribution to a treatment team's planning information base.

SUMMARY. The EST has value as a standardized guide to performing a job-person analysis and identifying mismatches between individual client capabilities and specific job requirements. When the EST is used in such a comparison analysis format its weaknesses in establishing reliability and validity become less important. The psychometric weaknesses of the EST make the use of the GOFI, however, of questionable utility. This is especially true when much of the GOFI is based on an arbitrary weighting factor using "clinical or experiential knowledge" of examiners. Such clinical judgement is what most decisions in vocational training are already based upon. The GOFI could be useful if standard scores were available that would indicate a cutoff for successful job performance or other peer group comparison information. In its present form the GOFI does not add to the pool of useful information in vocational training planning. In most cases, training programs for clients with developmental disabilities do not need another index to rank "good workers" from other clients. Ecobehavioral assessments and actual work record data are more accurate and useful in planning. The EST can be viewed as a criterion-based-comparison screening test for making comparisons between client capabilities and specific job requirements.

[135]
End-of-Course Tests.
Purpose: "To measure the subject matter taught in a selected number of junior and senior high school courses."
Population: Secondary school students.
Publication Date: 1986.
Scores, 9: Algebra, Geometry, Physics, Chemistry, Biology, World History, American History, Consumer Economics, Computer Literacy.
Subtests: Available as separates.
Administration: Group.
Price Data, 1987: $21 per complete kit including 35 test booklets (Algebra [10 pages], Geometry [10 pages], Physics [11 pages], Chemistry [9 pages], Biology [13 pages], World History [9 pages], American History [10 pages], Consumer Economics [9 pages], or Computer Literacy [14 pages]) and examiner's manual (27 pages); $7.65 per 50 answer sheets; $6.20 per scoring stencil per subtest; $10 per specimen set including examiner's manual with answer key, answer sheet, and 1 each of the test booklets; machine scoring available through publisher.
Time: 405(410) minutes for the battery; 45(50) minutes for any one test.
Author: CTB/McGraw-Hill.
Publisher: CTB Macmillan/McGraw-Hill.

Review of the End-of-Course Tests by ERNEST W. KIMMEL, Executive Director, Test Development, Educational Testing Service, Princeton, NJ:

There are nine End-of-Course tests in subjects commonly taught as one-year courses in secondary school. They are intended to be administered at the end of the appropriate course, "regardless of the grade in which the course is offered," as a "supplement or substitute for basic skills achievement testing" at that level. The results will provide a school with a basis for comparing the achievement of its students in a particular course with a broad sample of students who were taking similarly titled courses in 1985. The tests can be hand scored or machine scored by the CTB Macmillan/McGraw-Hill scoring service. If a school chooses to hand score the tests, a Class Record Sheet is provided in the manual to help a teacher summarize the test results for the group of students.

The publisher appears to have been quite successful in getting schools to participate in the standardization study which took place in the spring of 1985.

A total of 134 schools, representing 109 districts in 29 states, took part in the study. A preponderance of the schools participated in the administration of several different subjects. The number of cases ranged from a low of 1,500 in Consumer Economics to over 8,000 in Biology. Frequency distributions of raw scores are provided for each test. Tables for converting the number of items correct to percentile ranks, stanines, and normal curve equivalents are also provided as part of the Examiner's Manual.

Based on data from the standardization administration, none of the tests appears to be speeded. The KR-20 reliability estimates range from .798 for Physics to .889 for Consumer Economics. The "Technical Information" supplement for test users provides a well-worded caution about the limitations of internal consistency measures of reliability, identifying sources of error that are not reflected in such estimates. The reported reliability estimates are at a level where it would be appropriate to use the scores in evaluating the performance of a group or as one source of information for making a decision about an individual (e.g., to be used as one factor but not the sole basis for determining a student's end-of-year grade).

The tests, with the exception of Biology and Consumer Economics, proved very difficult for the standardization samples. For each of the other seven tests, the mean raw score was from one-half to one standard deviation below middle difficulty for the test. The most difficult was World History where the mean number right was 21.87 out of 50 items.

The Examiner's Manual provides a brief description of the content of each test and a chart relating each item to a particular category within the specifications for the test. Although the Manual asserts that "The tests represent the most commonly taught curricula in a one-year course in each of these content areas," no evidence is provided to demonstrate the test content represents what is taught in similarly titled courses. None of the documentation describes how the specifications were developed, what subject matter experts were involved, or what information was used as a basis for deciding on the categories and relative weighting of topics within each test.

Consequently, schools or teachers contemplating the use of an End-of-Course test would be well advised to analyze the content of the test against the learning objectives of their particular curriculum in order to determine if there is sufficient congruence for the test to be considered a reasonable sample of the curriculum.

Most of the questions in the several tests are of a factual recall nature with a sprinkling of items requiring simple inferences. There is little attempt to measure problem solving or critical reasoning skills within the context of a particular subject. For example, only 10% of the Algebra questions are posed as "real world" problems, the balance measure one's ability to manipulate an algorithm. The two history tests measure knowledge of traditional political/military events and do not reflect the multicultural, social, and intellectual emphases of many secondary history curricula. For example, the American History test ignores the pre-European cultures of the Americas and does not mention any contribution by a woman or a member of an ethnic or racial minority.

In summary, the End-of-Course tests have acceptable psychometric properties and reflect considerable technical care in providing interpretable normative information. However, no basis is provided for evaluating the appropriateness of the content of each test; the user is left with the burden of establishing the comparability of test content to the learning outcomes to be assessed.

Review of the End-of-Course Tests by BIKKAR S. RANDHAWA, Professor of Educational Psychology, University of Saskatchewan, Saskatoon, Canada:

These tests are supposedly designed to measure the most commonly taught subject matter content in a one-year course in Algebra, Geometry, Physics, Chemistry, Biology, World History, American History, Computer Literacy, and Consumer Economics, regardless of the grade (although specified to be between 7 and 12). Also, it is the stated purpose of these tests that they can be used to "supplement or substitute for basic skills achievement testing at these levels" (Examiner's Manual, p. 1).

The multigrade or multiage coverage of achievement tests for testing common curricular emphasis is usually defended by using grade-specific or age-specific levels. Also underlying the development of such tests is the commonly held knowledge that within certain limits, cognitive processing skills and strategies of individuals improve with development. Tests developed with these considerations in mind, therefore, provide grade-specific or age-specific norms and validity evidence. These common approaches to constructing multigrade tests have not been followed in the End-of-Course Tests (ECT).

An argument in support of the development approach to the ECT, however, would be that these tests measure only what is covered in a one-year course in these areas, therefore, the grade level at which a course is offered does not matter. But this argument would not hold against appropriate principles of human and curriculum development and pedagogical considerations. One would be hard pressed to justify that a one-year course in algebra or geometry for grade 7 would be appropriate for grade 12. The fact that the same test is intended for use in each case with students in grades 7 to 12 is one of the fundamental weaknesses of these tests.

Extending the argument that any curricular content can be taught to anybody, a Brunerian hypothesis, coverage of the nine areas of the ECT does not seem to follow from a content-specific analysis of a large number of courses typically taught in the U.S.A. and Canada. It is not what can be taught that is of concern here but rather the appropriateness of these tests for grades 7 to 12. My judgment is that all nine ECTs, in terms of the reading level, cognitive sophistication, and breadth and depth of content, would be too difficult for junior high school students (grades 7 to 9). There is no evidence accompanying these tests for general consumption (Examiner's Manual) or for sophisticated consumers (Technical Manual) that convinces me otherwise. In fact, the technical information confirms my belief that these tests might be more appropriate for measuring the knowledge and understanding of high school students in these areas. The standardization of the ECT was done involving nine different groups of only secondary school students in the spring of 1985. The fact that there was no representation from the junior high school student population in the standardization sample makes the claim of suitability of these tests for grades 7 to 9 impossible to support. The remainder of my comments will address the issues associated with the use of these tests with the secondary school students and with technical issues.

The Examiner's Manual for the ECT provides classification by content for each test item. Tables showing correspondence of these classifications contain two columns entitled Objective and Item Number, respectively. I would have been pleased to see these tables provide content information through objectives because then one would be in a position to discern the cognitive complexity of the items in each test. Alas, that is not the case! These tables list only brief headings of the content, as one would find in chapter headings of a text. These descriptions are too global to be of much analytic use. To make an informed judgment on the content and cognitive demand of each item the prospective test user must examine each item. In spite of this limitation, it appears that content coverage of these tests reflects reasonably the domain of interest in a first one-year course in each case.

One answer sheet (costing about 15 cents each) is required for each test. Both time for administration and cost of purchasing answer sheets could have been reduced if the same answer sheet had been so designed that each could be used for administering at least five tests. There is enough room for doing this and I do not see any need for the space provided for administering optional tests on these answer sheets.

Each test is in a separate booklet. This is a desirable feature of this set of tests because the users can choose to buy only those which are appropriate for their intended purposes and courses. The booklets are reusable and stapled together with four distinctive and colorful bond paper covers. The color codes represent mathematics, history, science, and consumer studies areas. The cost of test booklets is reasonable. Machine-scoring service is available at cost; however, hand-scoring masks are available as an option. These are attractive considerations for the consumer.

Item difficulties indicate the ECT are not assembled systematically in order of difficulty, from easiest to most difficult items. The reason, if any, for not following the well-established principle in assembling standardized achievement tests is not given. For these tests the typical excuse, the influence on achievement of item context and placement in test, of not doing this after the standardization testing was done could not apply because from each test a number of items were dropped after standardization samples were tested.

The Consumer Economics and Biology tests were the easiest for the standardization samples, with average difficulty indices of .65 and .63 respectively. The most difficult test was World History, difficulty index of .44. The other tests were of moderate difficulty, from .47 to .54. As these difficulties were reported for the combined secondary school standardization samples, it is not possible to determine how these tests should be expected to function at each secondary grade level.

With the above limitation in mind, the ECT produced reasonable discriminating power, in each case the average discrimination index was .31 or higher. The highest value was for the Consumer Economics test, .51.

Reliability estimates of the ECT were obtained by the Kuder-Richardson formula 20. These ranged from .798 for the Physics test to .889 for the Consumer Economics test. These internal consistency estimates are moderate for tests of length 42 to 50 items. Unfortunately, no other reliability evidence is available.

These tests do not provide any statistical validity evidence. This is another major weakness and users should be cautious of this limitation. The publication of this test prior to gathering validity data is inappropriate.

The above weakness is further augmented when one attempts to understand the representativeness of the standardization samples. No demographic breakdown is provided. Therefore, it is not possible to assess whether these tests are biased for any subgroups. Furthermore, it is not clear how the standardization samples were selected.

For the weaknesses indicated above, the two sets of norms available for these tests, percentile ranks and the normalized ranks, are limited. Norms are meaningful only to the extent that the user is able to relate the performance of the tested student to the performance of a well-defined normative population. Also, the final forms of these tests emerged from trimmed down versions of tests administered to the standardization samples. One can only guess as to what influence the items eliminated from the existing tests had on the performance of the standardization samples. For the extent to which this influence is a factor the norms are not realistic, and they, therefore, do not characterize properly the interpretive vehicle for the user.

Although the tests seem to have a reasonable domain coverage for one-year courses in secondary schools, there is no evidence on the appropriateness of these tests for junior high grades. Only internal consistency reliability is reported. No statistical validity evidence is provided. Norms are global and do not provide grade-specific interpretation. Standardization samples of secondary school students have not been described in detail and it is not possible to assess their representativeness. Users must be willing to establish local norms and validation evidence for an effective use of any of the ECT.

[136]
English as a Second Language Oral Assessment, Revised.

Purpose: Measures "students' ability to speak and understand English."
Population: Adult nonnative speakers of English.
Publication Dates: 1978–80.
Acronym: ESLOA.
Scores, 4: Auditory Comprehension, Basic Survival Vocabulary, Information Questions, Past/Future/Conditional Tenses.
Administration: Individual.
Price Data, 1989: $7.25 per manual ('80, 75 pages) including test; $2 per 50 answer sheets.
Time: Administration time not reported.
Authors: Joye Jenkins Coy, David R. Gonzalez, and Kathy Santopietro.
Publisher: Literacy Volunteers of America, Inc.

Review of English as a Second Language Oral Assessment, Revised by JAMES D. BROWN, Director, English Language Institute, Honolulu, HI:

The English as a Second Language Oral Assessment, Revised (ESLOA) is, initially, an attractive test for several reasons. It comes in an appealing flip folder format that is relatively easy to use. It uses attractive line drawings as part of the stimulus for some items, and the General Instructions and Directions for each level subtest are clear and easy to follow. However, the moment a user attempts to discover how the test was designed or what its testing characteristics are, there is absolutely no information available. A number of other problems also surface upon closer inspection of the testing materials.

Consider, for instance, the line drawings. They appear to be adequate in quality; however, there is little discussion of the rationale for choosing these particular drawings (other than some presupposition that the pictures represent common situations that will elicit survival language). In addition, no mention is made of the problems that students from some societies (e.g., Hmong immigrants) may have with these pictures because their cultures do not traditionally use such line drawings to represent reality.

Perhaps more important is the difficulty that any reader will have with determining the purpose of the test. The authors state on page 3 that the information gained from the test is "meant to serve as a guide to help the tutor meet the needs of the individual learner as quickly and efficiently as possible, and not the basis for grouping or classifying students." It is therefore difficult to decide just what the purpose of this test is. Clearly, the test is not meant as a general ESL proficiency test, nor are the authors claiming that it should be used for placement. They seem to be suggesting that, in a limited way, the ESLOA might serve as a diagnostic tool in the specific areas which it tests, as well as a way to monitor subsequent "student progress levels." Naturally, this would be true only if the students' proficiency levels and the curriculum of a particular program happened to correspond to the very low level and limited types of vocabulary and syntax included in the test.

The areas tested coincide with the four "levels" (subtests) as follows: (a) Auditory Comprehension and vocabulary identification; (b) Basic Survival Vocabulary and elementary structures; (c) ability to answer Information Questions and use more complex structures (present and present progressive as well as transforming statements to questions and positives to negatives); and (d) use of past and future tenses and responses to questions using the conditional tense.

The ESLOA is clearly a product of the structural tradition of language teaching as indicated by the types of items and by the "Suggested Lessons" for each level. The test is also influenced throughout by what appears to be the audiolingual approach to language teaching as exemplified in the last appendix which provides the following categories of "Useful Teaching Techniques": repetition drills, substitution drills, transformation drills, expansion drills, and minimal pairs. Even though these techniques are replete with examples, they are far from innovative. Although the structural orientation and audiolingual approach are clearly represented on the test, there is no indication that any of the developments in language teaching since those paradigms were dominant (25 years ago) have had any effect on the test. Thus, unless a program is isolated from current practices in language teaching, this test will probably not match the institutional goals or classroom objectives.

The majority of the items in all four sections of the test rely on a combination of pictures and interviewer questions as the stimuli. "Responses in complete sentences are encouraged" (p. 4). These responses must then be judged by the interviewer as "correct," "incorrect," or "no response given." These terms are never defined. Must a correct response match exactly the "correct responses" given on the answer sheet? Or could they be counted as correct if the message is essentially correct, but with a small grammatical error? What about a correct response that is not a complete sentence, but is what a native speaker would say? Too many questions are left unanswered about how the ratings should be assigned for this test to be of much help to practicing ESL teachers.

There are also four "free expression" questions provided in the appendix, which can be rated in five linguistic categories for three levels of performance. However, again, the categories—Fluency, Vocabulary, Pronunciation, Structure, and Intonation—are not defined or characterized in any way, nor are there even minimal descriptions of what performance described as Good, Satisfactory, or Needs Instruction might mean.

Finally, the test manual provides no technical information about how the test was developed and revised, nor is there any evidence of norms or arguments supporting the reliability and validity of the test. In short, no effort was made to comply with the *Standards for Educational and Psychological Testing* (AERA, APA, & NCME, 1985). In addition, there are no suggestions made for training raters or standardizing scoring at a particular institution.

In sum, at first glance this test is attractive. However, on closer inspection, it turns out to be a relatively naive product, the use of which would be inappropriate from a serious language tester's point of view. It is recommended only for use in programs that restrict their teaching to very low levels and focus primarily on teaching structures through transformation and substitution drills. Even then, the test results should be carefully analyzed to determine the degree to which the ESLOA is appropriate for the program in terms of descriptive statistics, reliability, and validity.

REVIEWER'S REFERENCE

American Educational Research Association, American Psychological Association, & National Council on Measurement in Education. (1985). *Standards for educational and psychological testing.* Washington, DC: American Psychological Association, Inc.

Review of the English as a Second Language Oral Assessment, Revised by CHARLENE RIVERA, *Director, The Evaluation Assistance Center East, The George Washington University, Arlington, VA:*

The English as a Second Language Oral Assessment (ESLOA) is a measure of English listening and speaking proficiency for limited English proficient (LEP) adults functioning at a survival level of English. The test was developed in the mid 1970s as part of a Right to Read project in Colorado. The field-tested version was adopted by Literacy Volunteers of America (LVA) for use by its network of volunteer tutors of LEP adults. LVA published the ESLOA in 1978 and reprinted the revised ESLOA in 1980.

Detailed information about the ESLOA is not available. Many of the particulars provided here are drawn from several telephone conversations with Joye Jenkins Coy, one of the test authors, and with representatives of LVA. In addition, data is drawn from an undated, unpublished manuscript (Coy, ca. 1976) describing the origins of the ESLOA.

In 1975, a review of literature was conducted to identify an instrument for use with an adult population with very limited English skills. Because no appropriate instrument was identified, the authors developed a test and named it the English as a Second Language Assessment (ESLA). It was piloted in 1975 on Spanish-speaking migrant and rural workers in Colorado. Subsequently, the test was revised and field-tested on 88 subjects in the fall of 1976. It was published in 1978 under its present title.

The revised ESLOA is an individually administered discrete-point instrument intended to differentiate between four basic levels of oral English language proficiency: ability to comprehend oral speech, ability to use basic survival vocabulary, ability to provide informational answers, and ability to use verb tenses (LVA, 1980). The test is designed to serve three functions: (*a*) as a placement measure, (*b*) as a pre-/post-measure of progress, and (*c*) as a diagnostic measure of specific receptive and expressive skills (e.g., ability to follow directions, ability to follow English patterns, and ability to use specific vocabulary).

The ESLOA item formats are based on those employed in several oral language assessment instruments used in the 1970s and early 1980s, for example, the Oral Placement Test for Adults (Timiraos & Perrel, 1971), the James Language Dominance Test (James, 1974), and the Ilyin Oral Interview (Ilyin, 1974). With the possible exception of the Ilyin Oral Interview (9:498), these tests are not currently in use.

The ESLOA test kit includes a 75-page, spiral-bound, 5-inch by 8-inch combined manual and student cue book and a double-sided answer sheet. The manual provides a brief introduction to the test where the purpose, rationale, and the four levels of English language proficiency the ESLOA is designed to assess are outlined. The test manual provides no information about the rationale for the test other than a list of works and authors consulted prior to the development of the test. The manual also contains general instructions for administering the test and picture cues for students. At the end of each level of assessment, the content for suggested follow-up lessons is outlined. Finally, the appendices include an optional assessment called Free Expression (Appendix A) and Useful Suggested Teaching Techniques (Appendix B). The teaching techniques recommended include: repetition, substitution, transformation, expansion, and minimal pair drills.

The ESLOA is individually administered and has no defined time limitations; however, it should take no more than 20 minutes to administer, depending upon an examinee's level of proficiency. Each section has a set number of items that must be answered correctly in order for an examinee to progress to a higher level. The manual does not recommend any special training for the test administrator except to read the manual and to become familiar with how to complete the answer sheet.

The four levels of the ESLOA correspond to four stages of English language instruction. Level I is designed to measure auditory comprehension and recognition of specific vocabulary items. After each stimulus, the examinee selects the corresponding image from a set of pictures in the test manual. No verbal response is required. At Level II the intent is to elicit basic vocabulary and rudimentary English structures. The examinee is presented with 10 simple questions that require a verbal response. Some items require identification of several related elements such as parts of the body, buildings, etc. The first five items, which are not linked to specific pictures, include questions about such things as time, money, work, etc. The items demonstrate a high reliance on limited samples of vocabulary. The levels of questions also range from simple (e.g., What is this?) to complex (e.g., What do you do when you need work?). The 12 Level III items focus on the ability to use specific verb forms (present and present progressive tenses) and sentence transformations (changing positive statements to questions and to negative statements). At this level, the examinee is encouraged to answer in complete sentences, a concept that is not defined for the test administrator. The ability to use additional verb tenses (past, future, and conditional) is assessed at Level IV. Examinees are expected to respond to prompts in full sentences and to expand their answers. If the examinee is successful at Level IV, the authors recommend that a more advanced assessment be administered. As Jackson (1990) in a review of the ESLOA noted, even if an individual successfully completes Level IV, he/she may not be able to understand and participate in a conversation in English.

For $20, LVA has developed a training kit for the ESLOA—English as a Second Language (ESL) Tutor Training Workshop (1980). It includes a script, audio tape, answer sheet, and test manual. The script includes an overview of the ESLOA and an audiotape demonstration of an examinee taking the ESLOA. Little discussion of the quality of the examinee's responses is presented and issues related to scoring are not discussed. The narrator acknowledges that there may be discrepancies in how to score an item because "testing is partly a matter of judgement" (LVA, 1980).

A double-sided answer sheet is used to record responses for all levels. Directions for scoring each level are provided on the answer sheet. The scoring procedures and format at each level vary slightly and are not always apparent. For example, some Level II items are numbered and others are lettered, yet each correct response receives 1 point. On Level III items, the raw score is multiplied by 3, 2, or 1 based on the quality of the response.

The passing score for each level is a range: Level I—at least 6 out of a possible 9 points; Level II—at least 21 out of a possible 29 points; Level III—26 out of a possible 36 points; and Level IV—8 out of a possible 10 points. Items are to be scored or responses noted while the test is being administered. No instructions are given to the test administrator about what the student should be told about the levels or that, most probably, some pause will need to be taken between levels to allow for scoring.

The ESLA was tested in 1975 by 15 tutors who received a total of 4 hours of training. The test was revised and field-tested in 1976 on a sample of 88 students. Coy (ca. 1976) reports that the Kuder Richardson Formula 20 was used to establish reliability for the sets of items pertaining to Levels I, III, and IV. Reliability for the items pertaining to Level II was established using Cronbach's alpha, another measure of internal consistency reliability. The reliability of each set (level) of items is high, indicating that these items measure the same ability.

The reliability of the ESLOA is difficult to assess because the data presented by Coy exhibit certain anomalies (e.g., the number of items at each level do not correspond to the number of items on the revised ESLOA). No data on reliability are included in the combined manual and student cue book, nor are any data presented on correlational or criterion-related validity.

The ESLOA is used extensively by LVA volunteer tutors (approximately 50,000). It is also used by a limited number of other educators who work with limited English proficient adults.

In conclusion, the ESLOA is a low-level test of English language proficiency intended for adults learning English as a second language. It is easy to administer and keyed to instruction. This makes the ESLOA useful within the LVA context. However, given this use, it would also be helpful if more careful explanations were given in the instructions that are provided on the answer sheet (e.g., "Encourage students to use complete sentences," "More credit is given for a more complete answer").

The ESLOA suffers from a lack of technical information on reliability and validity. Also, the item formats employed on the ESLOA are outdated and represent a discrete-point, decontextualized approach to language use. The vocabulary used in the test is extremely limited and does not include reference to basic survival competencies normally required of adults learning English as a second language. Moreover, if an adult had not learned certain related vocabulary (e.g., body parts) he or she could be held back from taking other sections of the test that he or she might, in fact, comprehend and successfully pass. That is, the rationale or basis for the hierarchical nature of the test is not articulated.

LVA is currently in the process of creating a new instrument to replace the ESLOA. It is anticipated that this new measure will incorporate relevant context into the testing of English language proficiency.

An alternative measure currently available and designed for low level adult learners of English as a second language is the Basic English Skills Test (B.E.S.T.) (Center for Applied Linguistics, 1984; 28). The B.E.S.T. is both reliable and valid and offers a more context-based approach to language proficiency assessment.

REVIEWER'S REFERENCES

Timiraos, C., & Perrel, A. (1971). Oral Placement Test for Adults. New Mexico: SWCEL.

Ilyin, D. (1974). Ilyin Oral Interview. Rowley, MA: Newbury House Publishers.

James, P. (1974). James Language Dominance Test. Austin, TX: Learning Concepts.

Coy, J. J. (ca. 1976). *A measure of oral proficiency in English for adults: The English as a Second Language Assessment (ESLA)*. Unpublished manuscript.

Literacy Volunteers of America, Inc. (1980). English as a second language (ESL) tutor training workshop. New York: Author.

Center for Applied Linguistics. (1984). *Basic English Skills Test manual*. Washington, DC: Author.

Jackson, G. (1990). [Review of English as a Second Language Oral Assessment.] In T. Sticht (Ed.), *Testing and assessment in adult basic education and English as a second language programs* (p. 17). San Diego, CA: Applied Behavioral and Cognitive Sciences, Inc.

[137]

English Language Skills Assessment in a Reading Context.

Purpose: Assesses English language skills "measuring the understanding of meaning in a context, as well as grammatical ability."

Population: Beginning, intermediate, and advanced students of English as a Second Language from upper elementary to college and adult students.

Publication Dates: 1980–84.

Acronym: ELSA.

Administration: Group.

Levels, 3: Beginning, Intermediate, Advanced.
Price Data, 1987: $9.95 per 25 tests, 50 answer sheets, and answer key (specify test/level BC, BN, IC, IN, AN, or AL); $7.95 per 50 answer sheets and keys for use with all forms; $4.50 per technical manual ('81, 37 pages).
Time: (30) minutes per test.
Comments: "Criterion-referenced."
Authors: Cecelia Doherty and Donna Ilyin (technical manual) and others listed below.
Publisher: Newbury House Publishers, Inc.

a) BEGINNING LEVEL.
Scores: 2 tests: Conversation, Narrative.
Comments: Separate answer sheet/practice test for each test.
Authors: Donna Ilyin, Lynn Levy (Conversation test), and Lauri E. Fried Lee (Narrative test).

b) INTERMEDIATE LEVEL.
Comments: Details same as *a* above.

c) ADVANCED LEVEL.
Scores: 2 tests: Narrative, Letter.
Comments: Separate answer sheet/practice test for each test.
Authors: Cecelia Doherty, Donna Ilyin (Narrative test), and Philip Carleton (Letter test).

TEST REFERENCES

1. Spurling, S., & Ilyin, D. (1985). The impact of learner variables on language test performance. *TESOL Quarterly, 19*, 283-301.
2. Mori, C., & Yamada, J. (1988). Copying span as an index of written language ability. *Perceptual and Motor Skills, 66* (2), 375-382.

Review of the English Language Skills Assessment in a Reading Context by LYLE F. BACHMAN, Professor of Applied Linguistics, University of California at Los Angeles, Los Angeles, CA:

The English Language Skills Assessment in a Reading Context (ELSA) was developed for the purpose of placing adult students of English as a Second Language (ESL) into different language ability levels in ESL courses. Tests at three levels (beginning, intermediate, and advanced) are available and all utilize a four-choice, multiple-choice cloze test format. Passages are written to represent typical English conversational and narrative styles. The authors claim that the test is criterion-referenced and that it measures "understanding of meaning in a context" and "grammatical ability."

FEATURES. The ELSA has several desirable features. The test materials have been carefully edited, with reusable test booklets and separate hand-scorable answer sheets that provide clear instructions to test takers. There is a practice test to familiarize students with the multiple-choice cloze format. There are clear directions for the administration and scoring of the test, including scoring stencils. Each test can be administered to a group in about 30 minutes and scored in a few seconds per subject. The Technical Manual provides information on norms and tables for converting raw scores to placement levels based on the levels in the San Francisco Community College District. Discussions of the reliability and validity of the test are also included.

TEST CONSTRUCTION. The content of the ELSA is based on "the ESL structural syllabus curriculum taught in open enrollment adult centers" of the San Francisco Community College District. Two passages—one conversational and one narrative—were written specifically for the ELSA for each of the three levels. These passages were written in such a way that every seventh word was deleted, for a total of 33 deletions per passage. Each deletion is intended to elicit the specific grammatical and semantic features to be measured. These original passages were pretested as open-ended cloze tests with native speakers and students of the same levels of ability as those for which the test is intended. Errors made by students in this pretest were used as distractors for constructing 33-item four-choice multiple-choice cloze tests, which were then administered to a representative sample of ESL students. On the basis of classical item statistics, 25 items for each form were retained and the passages were revised a final time. These revised tests were then used for norming studies to establish cutoff points for placement levels.

VALIDITY. Although the Technical Manual discusses validity, the section headings do not provide accurate indications of the aspects of validity that are discussed, and evidence supporting the recommended interpretations and uses of the ELSA is scant. Under "face validity" (a concept that has long since been abandoned by the measurement profession), the authors make passing reference to what is essentially content validity, by stating that instructors reported that the ELSA "contained material that was taught at corresponding levels of instruction" (Technical Manual, p. 26). In the section entitled "content validity," the authors present evidence that pertains most directly to the predictive utility of the ELSA in placing students, and say virtually nothing about content validity. Evidence that pertains to the predictive utility (validity) of ELSA scores for placement is also presented in a separate section that describes the norming procedures. It would be most helpful if a summary of the curriculum on which the ELSA is based, along with the content specifications for the deletions that were made in the different forms, could be provided here. In this reviewer's opinion, content relevance is a strength of the ELSA, and it is disappointing to see that this is the aspect to which the authors have paid the least attention. The next section, entitled "empirical validity" should more accurately be called "concurrent validity," because it reports the results of studies designed to investigate the correlations among the ELSA and other measures of English language proficiency.

VALIDITY OF SCORE INTERPRETATIONS. Despite the authors' claim that the ELSA measures "understanding of meaning in a context" and "grammatical ability," they cite as a rationale for using the cloze, research that they interpret as supporting the interpretation of cloze test scores as indicators of "global proficiency," rather than of "specific skills or components in isolation" (p. 11). This research indicates that the cloze correlates highly with overall placement batteries, traditional tests of reading comprehension, speaking and listening, dictation, structure, and writing. In the section on "empirical validity," the authors cite studies of their own in which the ELSA correlates highly with a wide variety of language tests, including not only measures of grammatical structure and reading, but of listening. The fact that the cloze in general, and the ELSA in particular, is highly correlated with a wide variety of different types of language tests suggests indeterminacy in the definition of the construct measured by the ELSA, rather than support for the interpretation of scores as indicators of the specific language abilities it is claimed to assess. Furthermore, the authors ignore the considerable research in reading assessment, in which the nature of the constructs measured by the cloze has been controversial. More recent research in foreign language testing challenging the notion of "general language proficiency," which has led many language testers to abandon this as a viable construct in testing, is not discussed. Because of these problems, the construct validity of the proposed interpretations of ELSA scores has not been adequately demonstrated.

VALIDITY OF TEST USES. The research that the authors cite in support of the use of the ELSA in placement is problematic in that this research was not designed to address adequately the use of multiple forms across multiple ability levels. The authors would like to demonstrate that the ELSA has been equated vertically, or more accurately, scaled so that scores on the three level tests achieve comparability on a single developmental scale. However, the design of the studies they cite is inadequate for equating the three forms across even the levels for which they are intended. The vertical equating design that the authors used is essentially an equivalent-groups design, in which test takers from adjacent proficiency levels should be aggregated into a single group and then randomly assigned to two groups, each of which takes one of the two tests intended for the two levels. However, their implementation of this design was flawed in that they did not randomly assign the test takers to the forms to be taken, and they did not replicate the design for all pairs of proficiency levels. Thus, their results cannot be interpreted clearly as evidence that the three test levels form a multilevel ability scale. Although this does not necessarily vitiate the usefulness of the ELSA as a placement instrument, it certainly places in doubt the recommendation that

it be used for achievement testing, especially for measuring gains in achievement.

RELIABILITY. Although the authors provide an extensive discussion of reliability, much of it is inappropriate in that it is based on classical internal consistency estimates, and does not report information relevant to the uses for which the test is intended. It is well-known that the internal consistency coefficients reported—Kuder-Richardson 20 and 21—overestimate reliability to the extent that test items are dependent upon each other. This is particularly problematic for a cloze test, in which the items are part of a whole text, and thus inescapably interrelated to each other. Thus, even though the reliability coefficients reported are lower-bounds estimates, they are nevertheless likely to exaggerate the actual reliability. A more critical problem is the fact that even though the authors claim that the ELSA is criterion-referenced (CR), no CR dependability or agreement indices are provided. Test users are given no information about the consistency of ELSA scores as domain score estimates, nor about the consistency of placement decisions at the specific cutoff scores recommended for placement levels. Because the consistency of placement decisions will vary as a function of both the reliability of test scores and the cutoff score, a single reliability estimate and standard error of measurement for a given form provides inadequate information about how consistent placement decisions are across different levels. The authors do provide internal consistency reliability estimates for the different forms at different placement levels, but it would be most useful if they could take this a step further and provide the agreement indices and corresponding standard errors at each of the different cutoff scores they recommend for placement.

NORMS. Norms for placement were established with students in ESL classes in adult centers in the San Francisco Community College District and in intensive ESL programs at two universities in the San Francisco area. The samples used were all relatively small, ranging in size from over 100 per form per level for the beginning level forms to under 25 per form per level for the intermediate and advanced level forms. It is thus appropriate that the authors caution test users that the raw score to placement level conversion tables in the Technical Manual are a general guide only, and that programs should establish their own placement norms (p. 6). Although multilevel tests offer many advantages for test users, such tests also place upon test users the responsibility for assuring that each test taker is administered the appropriate level test. Neither the ELSA Technical Manual nor the instructions to test administrators offers adequate information about how to determine which level of ELSA is correct for a given student or group of students. The descriptions of ESL proficiency levels provided (p. 7) are too general to be of much use in this regard. Furthermore, if the test user knows the proficiency level of students in advance, there would appear to be little need to use the ELSA for placement. It would therefore be very useful if the authors could provide detailed procedures, including a locator test, for determining which level of the ELSA should be administered to a given group.

SUMMARY. The ELSA is a well-constructed ESL test, utilizing a procedure that offers efficient testing and at the same time requiring test takers to process complete texts, as opposed to single items, of language. It is referenced to a specific content domain, and in this regard differs from many other ESL tests that are currently available for use. However, the evidence provided does not adequately support the intended interpretations of test scores as indicators of grammatical ability and the understanding of meaning in context. And although there is evidence that within the context of adult ESL classes in community colleges and university intensive programs the ELSA may provide useful information for placement purposes, the evidence does not support the use of the ELSA for the measurement of achievement or gains in achievement.

Review of the English Language Skills Assessment in a Reading Context by ALEX VOOGEL, Assistant Professor, TESOL/MATFL Program, Monterey Institute of International Studies, Monterey, CA:

The English Language Skills Assessment (ELSA) is a carefully designed test of reading and grammar in a multiple-choice, cloze format. It was developed in conjunction with a program for adult resident immigrants. For this reason, the ELSA appears most appropriate for use with adult education or beginning level university intensive language institutes. The test manual also indicates possible use with high school and upper elementary students. However, the beginning and intermediate test passages are written from an adult perspective, so the younger the population the more questionable the ELSA's appropriateness.

The ELSA's test passages reflect the ESL curriculum of the San Francisco Community College District. In the sense that the ELSA contains structures and semantic content that relate to this curriculum as well as cutoff scores that refer to the performance of students proceeding through this curriculum, the ELSA is criterion referenced. However, the test manual does not give specific information about skills, structures, or vocabulary domains covered by the test. Without this information the score ranges in the manual cannot serve as criteria for mastery.

Interpretation of scores for placement is based on a table that converts raw scores into one of the levels

of the San Francisco curriculum. No normative data are provided. Unless users follow a curriculum similar to San Francisco's, these score ranges cannot serve for placement. Local criteria or norms will have to be developed in these cases. The San Francisco ESL Master Plan, as well as information about establishing local levels, may be obtained by writing the ESL Resource Instructor at the San Francisco Community College District.

Some theory and research have suggested that the cloze format could provide a global picture of language proficiency (Oller, 1979). In addition to assessment of structure and vocabulary built into the ELSA, the authors hoped this test could serve as a more global measure of language proficiency. To explore this possibility they ran correlations between ELSA and several other tests. One finding is that the ELSA correlates well (.70s and .80s) with tests that emphasize structure and vocabulary (Michigan Test of English Language Proficiency, Structure Tests-English Language, Comprehensive English Language Test-Structure), but not so well (.56–.61) with listening comprehension tests (Comprehensive English Language Test-Listening, and the Listening Comprehension Picture Test, respectively). This finding is consistent with more recent research (Cohen, 1984) that disputes the global quality of cloze tests. Rather, student answers are seen as responses to contexts, structure, and vocabulary at a sentence or even more local level. In any case, the ELSA is at least appropriate for identifying degree of proficiency in sentence level reading skills.

In addition to the ELSA's use to sort students into different levels, the authors suggest that the ELSA may be used as a pretest and posttest to generate accountability data for federal funding. In this case stability over time is important, but no test-retest reliability data are reported. However, other aspects of reliability for which data are available look very favorable.

Internal consistency for each form of the ELSA is in the low .80s (KR-20). These are very respectable values, especially considering that a test form only contains 25 items. Equivalent form reliabilities for the beginning and intermediate levels are also in the .80s. Thus, alternate forms of the beginning and intermediate levels of the tests can be used with relative confidence. No statistics are given for the alternate advanced form (which is a more recent publication).

In addition to good reliability, the ELSA has several practical advantages. Administration of the ELSA does not require skilled personnel. Simple step-by-step instructions for the administrator are on the front of every test booklet. The front page of the test booklet also reports summary statistics for the test form, and the answer key has a conversion table for placing individual scores into levels in the San

Francisco curriculum. The ELSA is time efficient. It takes 30 minutes and can be done in groups. Also, because of the multiple-choice format, scores can be generated quickly and reliably, either by hand or machine. Student answer sheets easily fit into a student's file. The test booklets are reusable and the cost of additional copies is nominal. These features make the ELSA very desirable from a practical standpoint. Finally, the technical manual is comprehensive and quite readable for the interested practitioner.

In summary, the ELSA appears to be a carefully designed test that has good reliability and practicality, especially where large numbers of adult students are tested. It can be used to identify placement and proficiency levels in sentence level reading skills, provided local norms are established or the program is similar to the one on which the ELSA is based.

REVIEWER'S REFERENCES

Oller, J. W. (1979). *Language tests at school.* London: Longman.
Cohen, A. D. (1984). On taking language tests: What the students report. *Language Testing, 1,* 70–81.

[138]
ESL/Adult Literacy Scale.

Purpose: Developed to identify "the appropriate starting level for ESL and literacy instruction."
Population: Adults.
Publication Date: 1989.
Scores, 6: Listening, Grammar, Life Skills, Reading, Composition, Total.
Administration: Individual.
Manual: No manual.
Price Data, 1991: $14 per 25 test booklets; $3 per scoring overlay; $3 per instruction sheet.
Time: [15–20] minutes.
Author: Michael Roddy.
Publisher: Academic Therapy Publications.

Review of the ESL/Adult Literacy Scale by ANNE L. HARVEY, Measurement Statistician, Educational Testing Service, Princeton, NJ:

There is certainly a use in an ethnically diverse society for a test of English as a second language (ESL) that can be given in 15 to 20 minutes. The benefits of such a test over the 2 hours plus required for a test such as the Test of English as a Foreign Language (9:1257) are obvious. I would encourage the author of the ESL/Adult Literacy Scale (EALS) to pursue the task begun in developing this screening tool. However, the usefulness of the EALS test has yet to be proven.

When purchasing the EALS, the test user is given fairly clear instructions on how to administer the test, but no instruction in how to interpret the results. Test takers are classified as advanced, intermediate, or beginner, but by what standard? No normative information, standardization sample, or examples of capabilities are given. Neither is any information given about the reliability or validity of the test. To be brief, no information is given beyond how to administer and score the test. This is a disservice to both the test user, who must use the results, and to the test taker, who will have no idea how to interpret the fact they have been labeled as "beginning," "intermediate," or "advanced" in the English language.

When I contacted the company, I was told that the test was developed over a 5-year period using actual field practice, although no published references could be given. This suggests careful consideration of the content and usefulness of the test. I would strongly encourage Academic Therapy Publications to see this information is given to users of their test so that informed decisions can be made about the quality and usefulness of this test for particular populations.

Information is also needed about the intended uses of this test. I gather that it is intended for adult education classes, rather than college level remediation, etc. This assumption is by inference, however, rather than information. Informed decisions about the quality of this test over a cheaper, locally developed, screening tool (or for that matter, over spending 20 minutes conversing with the test taker) are impossible to make.

Beyond my reservations about the test as a whole, I am very concerned with the implicit assumption, based on the way in which the scores are recorded, that this test is made up of subskills. Three "listening" items should not suggest a "Listening" score. One six-sentence paragraph should not suggest a "Composition" score. Should the test user decide to use this test rather than developing a local screening tool, I strongly recommend against any attempt at using the subscores.

On a more specific level, the test user should be aware the instructions for Part III of the test are incorrect (this is noted on the scoring template), and that there may be some confusion on Item 3 of this section as to which of the housing ads depicted is meant by the answers of "1," "2," etc.

In summary, without more information than I was able to obtain, this test should not be considered more useful than a locally developed, untested screening tool. Care should be taken, if it is decided to use this test, that no inferences are made regarding ability in the five subskills listed in the scoring instructions. I would recommend that Academic Therapy Publications return to the author of this test for additional information on the development and quality of the EALS, and that test quality and score interpretation information be made available.

Review of the ESL/Adult Literacy Scale by DIANNA L. NEWMAN, Associate Professor of Educational Theory and Practice, University at Albany/SUNY, Albany, NY, and KATHLEEN T. TOMS, Assistant Professor of Education, College of St. Rose, Albany, NY:

DESCRIPTION OF THE TEST: The ESL/Adult Literacy Scale, published by Academic Therapy Publications and written by Michael Roddy, was developed with the stated purpose of identifying the appropriate starting level for English second language and literacy instruction with adult learners. Published in 1989, the test scores five areas of language use. These are defined by the author of the test. They are: Grammar, Life Skills, Reading, Composition, and Listening. This is contrary to widely used pedagogic delineations of four areas of language use pertinent to the measure of language proficiency, for example, the receptive areas of listening and reading and the productive areas of speaking and writing (Wilkins, 1972). The ESL/Adult Literacy Scale does not measure the productive level of spoken language. No justification is given for the decision to exclude this measure.

Instructions for the administration and scoring of the test are given on a separate sheet; there is no manual provided with this test. No information pertaining to validity or reliability of the instrument is provided, therefore, a short content analysis of each of the sections follows.

Additional instructions for each section are provided in the booklet to be read by the test taker. The level of complexity of the instructions in terms of syntactic and semantic competence necessary for their comprehension is greater than that being measured by the test itself.

LISTENING SECTION. Number of items: three; Format: multiple choice with three options presented, all verbally (there is no written copy of the questions or the options available to testee). Two of the items are single clause questions, the third is a five-sentence description of a movie theater's charges followed by a single clause question. Instructions to testee: (To be read by the tester) "Listen to the question or statement and the three answers. Mark the correct answer in column A on the far right side." (Printed on the testee answer sheet) "Your instructor will read a question or a statement and three answers. Mark an 'x' over the correct answer." There are no statements followed by alternatives, only questions. Item content: The content reflected in the Listening section is very narrow. The responses for the first question are based on an understanding of the question-word "where." The responses for the second item are based on the understanding of the verb compliment noun phrase "the hours of your job." The final item response is based on the understanding of a single fact from a stream of facts about one phenomenon.

GRAMMAR SECTION. Number of items: ten; Format: multiple choice with four options presented. Instructions to testee: (Printed on the answer sheet, to be read by the examinee) "Mark an 'x' over the letter that matches the correct sentence or question." Item content: There is heavy emphasis on the syntax of verb phrase manipulations (8 out of 10 items). This focus on verb phrase manipulation is not counterbalanced. Four of the items test knowledge of the construction of questions. One item tests the syntax of negatives when formed as part of the verb phrase. Three of the items question the use of tense and aspect within the verb phrase; there is one item on continuous aspect (past tense), one on perfect aspect (past tense), and one on future aspect.

LIFE SKILLS SECTION. Number of items: three; Format: Three contextual presentations followed by one question on each. Instructions to testee: (Printed on the question paper) "Refer to the calendars and circle the letter that corresponds to the correct answer." This section is extremely confusing for a number of reasons. Primarily, the print format leads the reader to believe the instructions meant for the first item refer to all items. Indeed, there are no instructions for the second item, and, although there are instructions for the third item, it is unanswerable (see below). Item content: The first item is a question based on the reading of information from a calendar. Response is multiple choice from among three possible answers. The second item is a question with three multiple-choice responses based on a set of instructions from the label of a cough medicine bottle. The third item gives some information about a person and his housing needs and asks for the respondent to choose the most suitable from among five housing ads. The ads are not, however, marked in any way to indicate which ad should be considered response (a), which (b), and so forth. It is, therefore, impossible to answer this question at all. In addition, the print is so small as to be almost illegible.

READING SECTION. Number of items: three; Format: A single passage of approximately 120 words followed by three standard question-word (who, what, where, etc.) initiated questions (one containing the nonsubstantive do construction). The passage is written in the simple past with some complex clause constructions. Instructions to testee: (Printed on the answer form) "Read the following paragraph and give the correct answer to the questions following it." Item content: The subject matter of the reading passage is culture specific. For example, the character described dials 911 for emergency assistance, although there are many areas in the United States where there is no 911 service. It also asks for inferences that may be possible only for those who are familiar with driving and traffic situations. Choice of a context, say on shopping, might prove more neutral and, therefore, more informative for the purposes of this test.

WRITING SECTION. Number of items: one paragraph written on a prescribed topic; Format: Open-ended writing of a paragraph on "My Favorite

City." Instructions to testee: (Printed on the test answer form) "Write at least 6 sentences in a paragraph form about 'My Favorite City'. Explain why." Item content: The instruction "Explain why" is itself a fragment and misleading. The lack of focus for students who are being assessed for basic English proficiency is problematic. Levels of writing are better assessed through the completion of writing tasks of increasing difficulty presented in a sequence that follows established research on the developmental stages of written language.

SCORING THE TEST. Each section of the test carries a different scale value for the computation of an overall score. They are: Listening: 18; Grammar: 30; Life Skills: 18; Reading: 16; Composition: 16. These values appeared to reflect a weighted scale of points awarded for the items within each subscale, according to a notion of the degree of differentiation between levels of difficulty. However, this is not explained; no justification for the points is given and the validity of the weighting is debatable. These subscales are to be summed to a total score which converts to the following levels: 85–100 = Advanced, 61–84 = Intermediate, and 0–60 = Beginning. Again, no explanation, either theoretically or psychometrically, of these levels is given. Based on the item content analysis detailed above, the scales are questionable. The use of the terms "Advanced, Intermediate, and Beginning" are also subject to question, because they are relative terms and not defined or delineated by the test author.

SUMMARY. This test is poorly constructed, inadequately documented, and appears to have limited use. These reviewers would not recommend it for use under any circumstances.

The items included appear to be narrow in their focus. They reflect only three of the four commonly accepted areas of language use. The instructions are, at times, too difficult and at times totally lacking. The scoring is not documented and is confusing. In addition, the lack of a manual leaves the user with no theoretical reasons for the selection of the test concepts or its subsequent interpretation.

REVIEWER'S REFERENCE

Wilkins, D. A. (1972). *Linguistics in language teaching*. Bungay, United Kingdom: Edward Arnold Pub.

[139]

ETSA Tests.

Purpose: To measure "aspects of intelligence, specific abilities or aptitudes, and certain personality characteristics . . . to supplement the other factors upon which hiring, placing, training and promotion decisions are based."
Population: Employees and job applicants.
Publication Dates: 1959–85.
Scores: 8 tests: General Mental Ability Test, Office Arithmetic Test, General Clerical Ability Test, Stenographic Skills Test, Mechanical Familiarity Test,

Mechanical Knowledge Test, Sales Aptitude Test, Personal Adjustment Index.
Administration: Individual.
Price Data: Available from publisher.
Comments: Publisher recommends use of General Mental Ability Test (1A) and one or more others depending on nature of job.
Authors: Manual by Charles K. Stouffer and Susan Anne Stouffer; technical handbook by S. Trevor Hadley and George A. W. Stouffer.
Publisher: Educators'/Employers' Tests & Services Associates.

a) GENERAL MENTAL ABILITY TEST (1A).
Time: 45(50) minutes.
b) OFFICE ARITHMETIC TEST (2A).
Time: 60(65) minutes.
c) GENERAL CLERICAL ABILITY TEST (3A).
Time: 30(35) minutes.
d) STENOGRAPHIC SKILLS TEST (4A).
Subtests, 2: Typing Test, Shorthand Test.
Time: 45(50) minutes.
e) MECHANICAL FAMILIARITY TEST (5A).
Time: 60(65) minutes.
f) MECHANICAL KNOWLEDGE TEST (6A).
Time: 90(95) minutes.
g) SALES APTITUDE TEST (7A).
Time: 60(65) minutes.
h) PERSONAL ADJUSTMENT INDEX (8A).
Time: 45(50) minutes.
Cross References: For additional information, see 9:399 and T3:846; for reviews by Marvin D. Dunnette and Raymond A. Katzell of an earlier edition, see 6:1025.

Review of the ETSA Tests by ROLAND H. GOOD, III, Assistant Professor of Counseling and Educational Psychology, College of Education, University of Oregon, Eugene, OR:

PURPOSE. The stated purpose of the ETSA Tests is to "help provide . . . more satisfactory hiring, better employee placement, better selection of employees for special training, more effective measurement of training progress and more effective promoting with an objective data base." However, serious concerns regarding the reliability and validity of the tests as well as their normative samples, derived scores, and item selection severely limit the tests' ability to accomplish their stated purposes.

DESCRIPTION. Test 1A consists of 75 selection-type vocabulary, arithmetic reasoning, and visual analogies items. Test 2A has 50 items including computations, word problems, and graph and chart interpretations. Test 3A consists of 131 items measuring skills in alphabetizing, verifying, spelling, office vocabulary, and knowledge of postal rates and regulations. Test 4A consists of 120 items covering proofreading for spelling and grammar, alphabetical filing, and office procedures. Supplemental shorthand and typing tests also are available.

Test 5A requires selection of the corresponding picture for 50 tool or part names. Test 6A consists of 121 agree/disagree and matching items covering electrical, mechanical, drafting, and carpentry tools and terms. Test 7A includes 80 agree/disagree items representing sales lore/attitudes and 20 items matching a product to a slogan or sales pitch. Test 8A consists of 105 statements rated agree/disagree representing attitudes toward the community and employment.

The authors recommend administering Test 1A to all examinees and Test 8A when characteristic mode of life adjustment is a job consideration. Tests 2A through 7A assess job-specific skills and are to be used selectively.

ITEM SELECTION. Two concerns pertain to item selection. First, items for the specific tests were selected primarily from standard textbooks, handbooks, parts books, and other literature. It would be desirable instead to base item selection on an analysis of the knowledge, skills, and abilities necessary for successful job performance. Second, some items contain outdated material. For example, postcard postage of 13 cents is scored as correct.

SCORES. The primary score reported for the ETSA Tests is a performance classification that characterizes performance as either Poor, Questionable, Average, Good, or Excellent. The authors claim that "any further refinement of the derived scores obtained from ETSA Tests would not be helpful and might possibly be misleading" (p. 4). Two problems limit the utility of these performance categories. First, no information is provided on the criteria used to establish the performance categories; there is no explanation of just what made a questionable performance questionable. Second, there is a great deal of variability across tests in the proportion of examinees placed in each category. For example, based on the normative information provided, 12% of Test 8A examinees and 32% of Test 3A examinees obtained scores of Poor or Questionable.

RELIABILITY. The authors do not provide adequate information to judge whether the ETSA Tests have sufficient reliability to accomplish their purpose. The primary derived score for the ETSA Tests is the performance category—no reliability estimates are provided for performance categories. Performance categories will be less reliable than the raw scores because considerable variability is discarded in the conversion. In addition, subtest scores are reported for Tests 7A and 8A with *no* estimate of their reliability. No estimate of the standard error of measurement was provided for any scores.

Although reported raw score reliability estimates ranged from .77 to .94, insufficient information limits their value in evaluating the tests. On four tests, the sample used to estimate the reliability was not described at all; on none of the tests was the sample described adequately. Detailed descriptions are necessary to determine if the tests have sufficient reliability for the user's context and intended

decisions. Furthermore, an unreliable test can appear highly reliable when using a sample of extreme scorers. Without a description of the samples used to estimate reliability, consumers must rely on hope that sample characteristics match their application.

NORMATIVE SAMPLE. Two problems severely limit the utility of the normative samples. First, an adequate description of the normative sample was not provided for any of the tests. Without the year(s) in which normative data were collected and a description of the sampling design and participation rates, the norms cannot be evaluated for appropriateness. Test 8A provides more information on the normative sample than the other tests, with serious limitations apparent. Although the occupational level of the normative sample was representative of the U.S., according to the 1958 Census, more recent comparative information was not reported. Furthermore, the sample was geographically restricted to the eastern United States and the distribution of the normative sample by age, educational level, racial/ethnic group, or community size was not reported.

Second, the normative samples often do not represent groups with whom users of the ETSA Tests would wish to compare examinees. Test 7A has the most appropriate normative sample: "2300 employed salesmen representing four aspects of the sales field" (p. 18). However, other norms were based, in part, on respondents from a college psychological clinic (4 tests), college applicants or students (4 tests), and high school students (2 tests).

VALIDITY. When tests are used to make performance predictions and employment decisions, the *Standards for Educational and Psychological Testing* (AERA, APA, & NCME, 1985) stress that "the principal obligation of employment testing is to produce reasonable evidence for the validity of such predictions and decisions" (p. 59). The most troubling limitation of the ETSA Tests is the lack of empirical support for the performance categories. For example, on Test 8A an applicant scoring 65 or below is reported to be a poor risk for employment on a personal adjustment basis. However, no information is provided on the proportion of poor-risk applicants who are indeed unsatisfactory employees. Conversely, there is no indication that excellent-risk applicants have fewer personal adjustment problems. Predictive validity was not reported for any of the tests.

Although concurrent validity was reported for seven of the eight tests (raw scores only), a job performance criterion with job applicants or employees was employed for only two tests. Test raw scores were correlated with supervisor ratings of job performance for Tests 6A (.87) and 7A (.71 to .82). Instructor rating of student peformance in college was the criterion for three tests, and college student test performance was the criterion for three tests.

Content validity was claimed for Tests 2A, 3A, and 4A. However, that assertion was based solely on the item selection procedure: Items were obtained from standard textbooks. The extent to which test content corresponds to job requirements based on a job analysis was not reported.

Support for the construct validity of Tests 4A and 5A was reported. Group means were significantly different for those with and without mechanical experience. However, the extent to which the tests are effective in differentiating individuals was not examined.

CONSUMER RESPONSIBILITY. Throughout the test manuals, the authors stress the desirability of the consumer developing local norms, conducting local reliability and validity studies, and developing local cutoff scores. In addition, the consumer is responsible for establishing the content validity of the ETSA Tests. If these tests are to be used for hiring, training, and promotion decisions, *all* supporting data must be provided by the consumer.

SUMMARY. The manuals provide little data to support the use of these tests to assist with hiring, training, and promotion decisions. Thus, the consumer is responsible for all empirical support in defense of such uses. The concluding comment from the review of an earlier edition (6:1026) remains appropriate: Caveat emptor! Let the buyer beware!

REVIEWER'S REFERENCE

American Educational Research Association, American Psychological Association, & National Council on Measurement in Education. (1985). *Standards for educational and psychological testing.* Washington, DC: American Psychological Association, Inc.

Review of the ETSA Tests by HILDA WING, Personnel Psychologist, Federal Aviation Administration, Washington, DC:

The Educators'/Employers' Tests & Services Associates (ETSA) have published, in the Test and Personal Adjustment Index, a battery of eight measures: General Mental Ability, Office Arithmetic, General Clerical Ability, Stenographic Skills Test, Mechanical Familiarity Test, Mechanical Knowledge Test, Sales Aptitude Test, and Personal Adjustment Index. The copyright dates on these components of the test battery are 1984 and 1985. In addition to having copies of the tests, I also had access to the Administrator's Manual, copyrighted 1985, and the Technical Handbook of Norms and Testing Guidance, revised edition, copyrighted 1972.

The contents of these tests make the battery interesting and potentially useful, but evaluation is very difficult because the information available to me contained very few statistics providing critical details about the tests, such as item and test construction, reliability, validity, norms, and statistics. Any test user would be required to have or to develop such statistics to justify implementation of these measures. Although my general predilection is to require local norms whenever a test is used, I also believe test publishers should be required to provide an adequate psychometric and content foundation for this test selection process. The ETSA publishers have not met these requirements for this battery. Although I will describe the materials that were available to me, without the necessary psychometric and conceptual information I cannot recommend these tests.

The first six tests are power tests of cognitive abilities or skills. The remaining two are biodata instruments. All have fairly generous time limits; they are each scored Rights Only. There is no information about item characteristics and selection, or about test construction. Minimal information about reliability is provided, but the available statistics appear to be in acceptable ranges. The characteristics of the group(s) supplying the test data are mostly unknown. Validity statistics are few, as well as being inadequately described. There was an almost complete absence of information about normative groups.

The General Mental Ability Test includes different item types assembled in a spiral omnibus fashion, reminiscent of tests constructed decades ago, such as the Wonderlic (475). These types appear to include vocabulary, arithmetic reasoning, and figural/spatial analogies. More modern tests might cluster all items of a given type together, to minimize possible examinee confusion. The selection of item types was not documented here. For this, as for the other ETSA tests, several score categories are recommended (Poor, Questionable, Average, Good, Excellent) with little if any information concerning the origin of such scoring categories or their utility. Without appropriate justification, such scoring categories should not be used.

Each of the remaining seven measures are assembled to include several sections. The next three (Office Arithmetic, General Clerical Ability, Stenographic Skills) appear to tap clerical abilities and to include such traditional clerical item types as arithmetic, percentages, arithmetic reasoning, tables, graphs, alphabetizing, number and name matching, spelling, vocabulary, filing, and grammar. The sections on mailing, in the General Clerical Ability Test, and on general information, in the Stenographic Skills Test, should be checked for currency. The latter also provides for a test of shorthand and typing, with scoring rules to be provided by the test user.

Each of these clerical tests has generous time limits, although most clerical ability tests are quite speeded. No explanation is provided for this difference in speededness, and there are minimal validity data. It could be that power tests are appropriate for clerical abilities, perhaps more so than traditional speeded tests. However, without a good explanation, including supporting data, I am dubious.

Mechanical Familiarity and Mechanical Knowledge both appear to be getting at some version of mechanical ability, with insufficient discussion of the benefits and drawbacks of either approach. The former test presents sets of pictures of tools and the examinee has to select the picture to go with a tool name. This approach might be useful for applicants with low levels of written English, but the representativeness of the selected tools is not documented. The latter test includes primarily statements with which the examinee agrees or disagrees, along with questions about diagrams exhibiting mechanical principles. Again, the content representativeness of the items requires more documentation. Verbal descriptions are provided concerning the procedures used to select and develop items used to assemble these tests of mechanical ability. Because part of the validity for each test appears to rest on a content strategy, item and test statistics combined with item budgets would have been useful. It would be interesting to know the correlations of these tests to each other and to similar tests such as the Bennett Mechanical Comprehension Test (41). It is also important to have normative data and differential validity studies separately by gender and race.

The Sales Aptitude Test includes several categories: sales judgment, interest in selling, personality factors, matching occupations, level of aspiration, insight into human nature, and awareness of sales approach. Because sales occupations are purportedly poorly predicted by cognitive ability tests, the prospect of this biodata measure developed for prediction of successful salespeople is an exciting one. The information provided for this ETSA measure does not dampen such enthusiasm, but it does not enhance it greatly, either. Although the content categories used may be right for sales jobs, insufficient data are presented in their support. Why these seven categories? Is each category unique or at least conceptually independent? Is there any theory behind this? A small table of validity data is provided for this test; the value of the median coefficient is .40. The table is a good start in providing adequate data for an instrument of potentially great utility, but highlights the insufficiency of the information.

The final ETSA measure, a biodata index of Personal Adjustability, is based on a theory of vocational adjustment that is not linked to the research literature by any citation. The format selection was not justified in an adequate manner. No criterion-related validity data are provided. Without more explicit reference to current research in personality theory and vocational adjustment, and with the minimal documentation provided here, it

would not be wise to use this measure in employment selection.

To summarize: This is a potentially interesting test battery that requires extensive research and data collection before being used operationally. I would recommend the Sales Aptitude Test and the mechanical ability tests as the most worthy of the effort, although the impact of (the lack of) speededness on the assessment and validity of clerical abilities is an interesting question as well. The test user who selects one or more of these tests for operational purposes with only the available data does so at his/her own peril. The publisher has provided insufficient information.

[140]
FACES III.

Purpose: To determine the structure of the family, in terms of the Circumplex Model.
Population: Families.
Publication Date: 1985.
Acronym: FACES III.
Scores: 2 dimensions: Family Cohesion, Family Adaptability.
Administration: Group.
Price Data, 1987: $30 per set of inventory materials including FACES III scale, which may be copied for use after obtaining permission, and manual (49 pages).
Special Edition: Couple version available for couples without children.
Time: [15] minutes.
Comments: Also known as Family Adaptability & Cohesion Evaluation Scales; self-report instrument.
Authors: David H. Olson, Joyce Portner, and Yoav Lavee.
Publisher: Family Social Science.

TEST REFERENCES

1. Kunce, J. T., & Priesmeyer, M. L. (1985). Measuring family dynamics. *Journal of Counseling Psychology, 32,* 40-46.
2. Lavee, Y., McCubbin, H. I., & Patterson, J. M. (1985). The Double ABCX model of family stress and adaptation: An empirical test by analysis of structural equations with latent variables. *Journal of Marriage and the Family, 47,* 811-825.
3. Goldklank, S. (1986). My family made me do it: The influence of family therapists' families of origin on their occupational choice. *Family Process, 25,* 309-319.
4. Olson, D. H. (1986). Circumplex model VII: Validation studies and FACES III. *Family Process, 25,* 337-351.
5. Vega, W. A., Patterson, T., Sallis, T., Nader, P., Atkins, C., & Abramson, I. (1986). Cohesion and adaptability in Mexican-American and Anglo families. *Journal of Marriage and the Family, 48,* 857-867.
6. Christopoulos, C., Cohn, D. A., Shaw, D. S., Joyce, S., Sullivan-Hanson, J., Kraft, S. P., & Emery, R. E. (1987). Children of abused women: I. Adjustment at time of shelter residence. *Journal of Marriage and the Family, 49,* 611-619.
7. Day, R. D., & Hooks, D. (1987). Miscarriage: A special type of family crisis. *Family Relations, 36,* 305-310.
8. Friedman, A. G., Utada, A., & Morrissey, M. R. (1987). Families of adolescent drug abusers are "rigid": Are these families either "disengaged" or "enmeshed," or both? *Family Process, 26,* 131-148.
9. Maynard, P. E., & Olson, D. H. (1987). Circumplex model of family systems: A treatment tool in family counseling. *Journal of Counseling and Development, 65,* 502-504.
10. Mertensmeyer, C., & Coleman, M. (1987). Correlates of inter-role conflict in young rural and urban parents. *Family Relations, 36,* 425-429.
11. Geber, G., & Resnick, M. D. (1988). Family functioning of adolescents who parent and place for adoption. *Adolescence, 23,* 417-428.
12. Kuehl, B. P., Schumm, W. R., Russell, C. S., & Jurich, A. P. (1988). How do subjects interpret items in Olson's Family Adaptability

and Cohesion Evaluation Scales (FACES)? *Educational and Psychological Measurement, 48,* 247-253.

13. Morrison, G. M., & Zetlin, A. (1988). Perceptions of communication, cohesion, and adaptability in families of adolescents with and without learning handicaps. *Journal of Abnormal Child Psychology, 16,* 675-685.

14. Peek, C. W., Bell, N. J., Waldren, T., & Sorell, G. T. (1988). Patterns of functioning in families of remarried and first-married couples. *Journal of Marriage and the Family, 50,* 699-708.

15. Smets, A. C., & Hartup, W. W. (1988). Systems and symptoms: Family cohesion/adaptability and childhood behavior problems. *Journal of Abnormal Child Psychology, 16,* 233-246.

16. Tolan, P. (1988). Socioeconomic, family, and social stress correlates of adolescent antisocial and delinquent behavior. *Journal of Abnormal Child Psychology, 16,* 317-331.

17. Needle, R., Su, S., & Lavee, Y. (1989). A comparison of the empirical utility of three composite measures of adolescent overall drug involvement. *Addictive Behaviors, 14,* 429-441.

18. Wampler, K. S., Halverson, C. R., Jr., Moore, J. J., & Walters, L. H. (1989). The Georgia Family Q-Sort: An observational measure of family functioning. *Family Process, 28,* 223-238.

19. Allen, S. F., Stoltenberg, C. D., & Rosko, C. K. (1990). Perceived psychological separation of older adolescents and young adults from their parents: A comparison of divorced versus intact families. *Journal of Counseling and Development, 69,* 57-61.

20. Anderson, S. A., & Gavazzi, S. M. (1990). A test of the Olson Circumplex Model: Examining its curvilinear assumption and the presence of extreme types. *Family Process, 29,* 309-324.

21. Baldwin, S. E., & Baranoski, M. V. (1990). Family interactions and sex education in the home. *Adolescence, 25,* 573-582.

22. Edman, S. O., Cole, D. A., & Howard, G. S. (1990). Convergent and discriminant validity of FACES III: Family adaptability and cohesion. *Family Process, 29,* 95-103.

23. Masselam, V. S., Marcus, R. F., & Stunkard, C. L. (1990). Parent-adolescent communication, family functioning, and school performance. *Adolescence, 25,* 725-737.

24. Papini, D. R., Farmer, F. F., Clark, S. M., Micka, J. C., & Barnett, J. K. (1990). Early adolescent age and gender differences in patterns of emotional self-disclosure to parents and friends. *Adolescence, 25,* 959-976.

25. Perosa, L. M., & Perosa, S. L. (1990). Convergent and discriminant validity for family self-report measures. *Educational and Psychological Measurement, 50,* 855-868.

26. Watson, S. M., Henggeler, S. W., & Whelan, J. P. (1990). Family functioning and the social adaptation of hearing-impaired youths. *Journal of Abnormal Child Psychology, 18,* 143-163.

[141]

Family Day Care Rating Scale.

Purpose: Assesses the quality of family day care.

Population: Consumers of day care services, day care providers, agency supervisors, and researchers.

Publication Date: 1989.

Acronym: FDCRS.

Scores, 6: Space and Furnishings for Care and Learning, Basic Care, Language and Reasoning, Learning Activities, Social Development, Adult Needs.

Administration: Group.

Price Data, 1989: $8.95 per manual (48 pages); $6.95 per 30 scoring sheets.

Time: (2) hours.

Authors: Thelma Harms and Richard M. Clifford.

Publisher: Teachers College Press.

Review of the Family Day Care Rating Scale by ANNETTE M. IVERSON, Assistant Professor of School Psychology, University of Missouri, Columbia, MO:

The need for a reliable and valid assessment instrument of family day care environments is great. Half of the infants in the United States today have employed mothers (Clarke-Stewart, 1989). By 1990 it was estimated that 23 million children under the age of six would be cared for in day care settings (Salkind & Ambron, 1987). Family day care is the most widely utilized; twice as many children are in

family day care as in center day care. However, most assessment tools and most child development research have been constructed/conducted for center day care populations.

The Family Day Care Rating Scale (FDCRS) is a rating scale for day care homes and is an adaptation of the Early Childhood Environment Rating Scale (ECERS, 9:365), a rating scale for center-based settings. The FDCRS is designed to provide users with an environmental assessment of health and safety provisions, cognitive and social development opportunities, and day care worker and parent development. Potential uses include self-evaluation by care providers, supervision and monitoring by agency staff, and research and program evaluation.

The instrument has been field tested on approximately 150 Los Angeles family day care homes. No norms are available. Individual item scores, subscale scores, and total score are best interpreted in a criterion-referenced manner (i.e., what competencies the day care environment does or does not exhibit).

The manual explicitly describes the development and rationale of the FDCRS. Ratings are based on observation and interview; instructions for using the test are accordingly thorough. Items are operationally defined, thus aiding scoring procedures. The scale includes additional items to assess the environment of children with disabilities.

Individual item median interrater reliabilities were all greater than or equal to .90 for two raters observing in 55 family day care homes and for two different observers in 101 family day care homes, all in Los Angeles. Given proper observer training, the FDCRS can be a reliable measure of family day care home environments. Internal consistencies were also high (Cronbach's alpha > .83) on every subscale except the Adult Needs subscale (.70). No test-retest reliability is reported in the manual.

Content validity of the FDCRS is linked by the authors to the validity of the ECERS. ECERS validity was established by a panel of experts who rated each item on importance to child care and relevance to the scale. A relationship between environment (as defined by ECERS) and language and social development outcomes in child care center children has been demonstrated. Further evidence of content validity of the FDCRS is observed in the authors' preparation of items which match the six Child Development Association goals made nationally available for family day care providers in 1985.

The expectation for validity of the FDCRS is thus far supported by the study of family day care homes in Los Angeles in which FDCRS results correlated positively with both observed behaviors and regulatable aspects of family day care environment (Howes & Stewart, 1987). Jones and Meisels (1987) found that training could improve family day care home environments as measured by the FDCRS.

Weaknesses of the instrument include the lack of guidance in interpretation of scores and recommendations for improving environments based on FDCRS results.

The FDCRS appears to be a promising assessment tool for evaluating family day care environments. Although the items have been developed on the basis of professionals' judgments of face value, it is not a carelessly conceived checklist. Additional research to establish test-retest reliability and construct validity is needed before this instrument can be recommended for widespread evaluation of family day care environments or as a psychometrically sound addition to an ecological assessment plan for a preschooler. The authors conscientiously note final determination of validity depends on a wide range of studies documenting the ability of the scale to discriminate among quality of environments and the relation of quality to child development outcomes.

REVIEWER'S REFERENCES

Howes, C., & Stewart, P. (1987). Child's play with adults, toys, and peers: An examination of family and child care influences. *Developmental Psychology, 23*, 423-430.
Jones, S. N., & Meisels, S. J. (1987). Training family day care providers to work with special needs children. *Topics in Early Childhood Special Education, 7* (1), 1-12.
Salkind, N. J., & Ambron, S. R. (1987). *Child Development.* New York: Holt, Rinehart, and Winston.
Clarke-Stewart, K. A. (1989). Infant day care: Maligned or malignant? *American Psychologist, 44*, 266-273.

[142]
Family Relations Test: Children's Version.

Purpose: "To assess the relative importance that different family members have for children" and to explore the child's emotional relations with his or her family.

Population: Ages 3–7, 7–15.

Publication Dates: 1957–85.

Administration: Individual.

Levels, 2: Form for Young Children, Form for Older Children.

Price Data, 1988: £70.15 for complete set including manual ('85, 59 pages), test figures and item cards, scoring and record sheets for older children, and record/score sheets for young children.

Time: 25(40) minutes.

Authors: Eva Bene (test and revised manual) and James Anthony (test).

Publisher: NFER-Nelson Publishing Co., Ltd. [England].

a) FORM FOR YOUNG CHILDREN.

Population: Ages 3–7.

Scores, 8: Outgoing Feelings (Positive Total, Negative Total), Incoming Feelings (Positive Total, Negative Total), Dependency Feelings, Sum of Positive, Sum of Negative, Total Involvement.

b) FORM FOR OLDER CHILDREN.

Population: Ages 7–15.

Scores, 12: Sum of Outgoing Positive, Sum of Outgoing Negative, Sum of Incoming Positive, Sum of Incoming Negative, Total Involvement, Sum of Positive Mild, Sum of Positive Strong, Sum of Negative Mild, Sum of Negative Strong, Maternal Overprotection, Paternal Overindulgence, Maternal Overindulgence.

Cross References: For information on the complete test, see 9:409 (3 references), T3:874 (33 references), 8:558 (18 references), and T2:1182 (4 references); for an excerpted review by B. Semeonoff of the Children's Version and the Adult Version, see 7:79 (7 references); see also P:81 (2 references); for reviews by John E. Bell, Dale B. Harris, and Arthur R. Jensen of the Children's Version, see 5:132 (1 reference).

Review of the Family Relations Test: Children's Version by CINDY I. CARLSON, Associate Professor of Educational Psychology, University of Texas at Austin, Austin, TX:

The Family Relations Test (FRT) for children is a clinical tool for examining the direction and intensity of a child's feelings toward family members, as well as his/her estimates of their reciprocal feelings. The measure is based upon psychoanalytic theory. Consideration of Piagetian cognitive development theory is employed in the construction of items for the younger and older child version, with items for older children reflecting greater complexity of emotions. The FRT is physically designed as a manipulation of objects (test figures) that are sufficiently stereotyped to permit the child to select figures that represent the members of his/her family. The test consists of the placement of items, each printed on a separate card, onto the figure(s) which the child associates with the item. Children have the option of selecting multiple family figures for items as well as selecting no family member for a particular item. The physical properties of the FRT are designed to maximize the collection of family relationship information from children less able or willing to express their thoughts and feelings about family members, such as younger, less verbal, or defensive children.

A comprehensive manual is available for the FRT. Directions for the administration and scoring of the test are clearly written. The primary shortcoming of the administration directions of the FRT is the limited guidance provided regarding the use of the younger or older form of the test. For children between the ages of 6 and 8, FRT users are directed to use their clinical judgment in determining the applicability of forms when it would appear that more specific guidelines could be identified (e.g., based on Piagetian cognitive measures, standard intelligence tests, or a series of prescreening questions designed to identify the complexity of emotions understood by the child).

A considerable portion of the FRT manual is devoted to the clinical interpretation of test results. Numerous clinical examples are provided and discussion is organized around clinical syndromes (e.g., egocentric auto-aggressive, idealizing, paranoid). It would appear that use of the FRT is limited to the creation of hypotheses and clinical judgments, as neither the information regarding interpretation of scores nor the evaluation studies of the FRT are adequate to permit differential diagnosis based upon the test. A further shortcoming of the manual and interpretative information is that it does not conform to the widely used *Diagnostic and Statistical Manual—III*. Information contained in the FRT manual, therefore, may be limited in relevance to those clinicians who have been trained in and who practice within the psychodynamic framework.

Regarding the reliability of the FRT, the internal consistency of the measure was determined using a modification of the split-half procedure yielding corrected correlation coefficients ranging from .68 to .90. Although the FRT authors assert that the test-retest method of reliability is unsuitable for the test due to retest memory effects with short-term retest reliability or changes in home environment with longer retest intervals, this reviewer does not agree. Because the authors argue that children will be unable to remember their placement of items *within* the test administration, it seems unlikely they could remember placement *across* administrations. Short-term (1 week to 1 month) retest reliability evaluation appears both warranted and feasible with the FRT. Moreover, the occurrence of mediating home environmental changes could be measured and statistically controlled in retest analyses. It would appear that a critical concern regarding the FRT is the degree to which stable versus momentary subjective family relationship conditions are being measured.

The validity of the FRT, as a projective measure of "psychic reality," cannot be determined in the conventional manner, according to the authors (citing Cronbach & Meehl, 1955). The authors, however, have made an effort to examine the construct validity of the FRT from several points of view, including a comparison of the reciprocity of parent-child responses, the correspondence and reciprocity of sibling attitudes, the differentiation of theoretically relevant "pre-genital" and "genital" syndrome groups, and a comparison of child report with parent questionnaire responses. Although the FRT authors cite these data as supportive of construct validity of the measure, their primary reliance upon descriptive data without accompanying qualitative statistical analyses to confirm conclusions leaves this reviewer skeptical. In addition, current developmental research increasingly acknowledges the "nonshared reality" of members within a family suggesting that efforts to establish construct validity by comparing within family member responses may be inappropriate. Rather,

examining the relationship of FRT responses with other tests of the same construct would be more fruitful (see Grotevant & Carlson, 1989, for a review of relevant parent-child measures).

Adequate normative data are not available for the FRT. In the manual descriptive data are provided that differentiate the ascribed parent items of nonclinical children and adolescents. This provides the clinician with an estimate of the differences between these developmental stages in children's parental perceptions. Similar data are provided regarding children's differing perceptions for brothers versus sisters and younger versus older siblings. Data are not provided that differentiate clinical from nonclinical child and adolescent perceptions of relevant family members. This would appear crucial for clinical use of the measure. Ideally cutoff scores that have been empirically validated would be available for users of the FRT. Finally, available descriptive data rely upon a single nonclinical sample (55 school-age children and 40 adolescents) and provide limited information regarding the characteristics of the sample. Without normative data, use of the FRT as a method of clinical diagnosis is inappropriate.

In summary, the strength of the FRT is its unique physical construction, which optimizes the collection of subjective family relationship information from children who are either developmentally or clinically less capable of completing objective self-report measures or reticent to share such information in a clinical interview. Given the few family relationship measures designed for children (see Grotevant & Carlson, 1989), the FRT provides an invaluable adjunct interview technique. Unfortunately, use of the FRT for clinical diagnostic or research purposes must await a more stringent test of the measure's psychometric properties. This reviewer does not agree with the FRT authors that such psychometric validation cannot be accomplished due to the "psychic reality" basis of the FRT. Rather, social scientists have increasingly recognized the importance of the subjective cognitive realities of individuals as determinants of their behavior, and have measured these in family and other close relationships (see Huston & Robbins, 1982). Rigorous psychometric standards are considered essential for family assessment measures, whether used in research or clinical practice (Carlson, 1989). Thus, the lack of adequate reliability, validity, and normative data on the FRT seriously limits its current utility in either clinical or research contexts except as an interview method.

REVIEWER'S REFERENCES

Huston, T. L., & Robins, E. (1982). Conceptual and methodological issues in studying close relationships. In L. H. Brown & J. S. Kidwell (Eds.), Methodology: The other side of caring (Special issue). *Journal of Marriage and the Family, 44* (4), 901-925.

Carlson, C. I. (1989). Criteria for family assessment in research and intervention contexts. *Journal of Family Psychology, 3* (2), 158-176.

Grotevant, H. D., & Carlson, C. I. (1989). *Family assessment: A guide to methods and measures.* New York: Guilford Press.

Review of the Family Relations Test: Children's Version by STEVEN I. PFEIFFER, Director, Institute of Clinical Training and Research, The Devereux Foundation, Devon, PA:

The Family Relations Test: Children's Version (FRT:C) is a semistandardized procedure that allows children to express their feelings and attitudes toward their families, as well as the children's perceptions of the families' reciprocal feelings toward them. The test consists of 21 cardboard schematic human figures representing a variety of family members of various ages and sizes, a set of red cardboard boxes with openings in the top, and a group of cards with printed statements reflecting a range of feelings and attitudes.

The FRT:C is presented in a play-like format and is individually administered. The child is asked to select a set of test figures to represent important family members, including the child, and a figure representing "Nobody." The child next reviews each of the statements—from 48 printed cards for younger children and 100 cards for older children—and sorts each card into the box behind the family figure for which each statement is most representative. Statements reflect feelings of like and dislike, love and hate, and attitudes such as overprotection and overindulgence. Administration time is 20–30 minutes, and scoring time is an additional 15 minutes. Scoring is straightforward—tallying statements for each particular family role. The manual provides some rather meager normative data and detailed clinical profiles for a few case vignettes to assist in interpreting a child's performance.

The test was originally published in 1957, with minor revisions in 1978 and 1985 that incorporated changes to five items and slight modifications in the administration procedure. The task is intrinsically appealing; it is easy to elicit the cooperation and interest of the child; and, as a relatively objective personality measure, the test has considerable heuristic value. In addition, the procedure is an ingenious device to assess the child's perceptions of emotional relationships within the family.

Although the test has strong face validity and inherent clinical appeal, the manual provides very little evidence to support the validity of the specific inferences made from the test profiles. The only validity studies compare test results with case history material for several small groups of clinical subjects, and equate profiles with predictions made from psychiatric diagnoses. Interpretation requires considerable clinical wisdom and extensive experience with the instrument, and is based on highly speculative and inferential psychological constructs founded in psychoanalytic thinking.

Reliability studies are somewhat more encouraging. However, the manual does not provide the user with enough information to judge whether the scores are sufficiently accurate for individual clinical decision making. As mentioned above, normative data are sketchy—apparently local norms, with only a very small number of "normal families" included.

The test does not follow a standard administration procedure. For example, only the first and last two items are presented in a uniform sequence; all other items are simply presented in a "mixed order." In addition, it is left to the discretion of the examiner to determine whether items for the older children need to be read to the child. Perhaps the most telling procedural weakness is that the child is permitted to select from the 21 cardboard figures which family members to include or exclude. The family members the child selects may not necessarily coincide with his true family system—a not unlikely occurrence for younger children or for children whose parents are separated, divorced, or remarried, or with absent or deceased family members.

This test is innovative in design and of considerable heuristic value. However, until administration is restandardized, more extensive and carefully selected norms are obtained, and more rigorous examination of the technical adequacy of the scale is procured, the FRT:C should be used only as a clinical research instrument.

[143]

Firefighter Selection Test.

Purpose: "To rank-order applicants according to their probability of success in training and success on the job" as a firefighter.

Population: Applicants for firefighter trainee positions.

Publication Date: 1983.

Acronym: FST.

Scores: Total score only.

Administration: Group.

Price Data, 1990: Leasing fee, $155 for package of 10 tests including administrator's guide, technical manual, and scoring key.

Time: 150(170) minutes.

Comments: Measures mechanical comprehension, reading comprehension, and report interpretation.

Author: Psychological Services, Inc.

Publisher: Psychological Services, Inc.

Review of the Firefighter Selection Test by DAVID O. ANDERSON, Senior Measurement Statistician, Educational Testing Service, Princeton, NJ:

The Firefighter Selection Test (FST) was developed as a written selection instrument for entry-level firefighters. Each of the two alternate forms of the FST consists of 100 multiple-choice questions, divided into three sections: comprehension of mechanical principles (39–40 items), report/table interpretation (10 items), and reading comprehension (50–51 items). Rights-only scoring is employed to calculate a Total Score. The 2½ -hour test is intended to be used for ranking candidates, and for providing a cutoff score. No guidance is provided for setting legally defensible cutoff scores.

The Technical Report, dated April 1983, contains detailed information about test development, reliability, validity, and fairness analyses. All quotes are from this Technical Report.

TEST DEVELOPMENT. "The Firefighter Selection Test items were developed to have job-relevant content and be free of bias against minorities and women." Although mention is made of a job analysis having been carried out, the Technical Report contains no details.

The Technical Report states that "the pictorial items depict males and females and minorities and non-minorities"; in actuality, no Black or Hispanic figures are used on Form A. Three items use female figures, in one instance jumping from a diving board and in another on a carnival ride. Five items show male figures in neutral or work situations. Uni-sex figures are used in two other items. This reviewer did not see Form B.

Because "a firefighter needs mechanical ability to perform many job duties (e.g., operating pumps, making hose connections, raising and securing ladders, maintaining tools and equipment)," the test includes items requiring comprehension of mechanical principles. These three-option items consist of drawings (planes and slopes, hydraulics, levers, shape and volume, gears, etc.) and require the candidate to determine the consequences of certain actions. Although the claim is made that "the items were written to test job-related knowledge rather than textbook knowledge or information learned in a physics course," the items appear to be quite general in nature and not related specifically to firefighting tasks.

"The Reading Comprehension passages . . . are based on the actual training materials that entry-level firefighters in a metropolitan fire department are required to read as part of their training. . . . Firefighters must be able to read and understand written materials including instructions, directions, procedures, warnings, manuals, bulletins, and training materials." No job analysis evidence is presented to document these statements. To their credit, however, the test authors have virtually eliminated all third-person pronoun references (he/she, his/her) in these four-choice items.

The five-choice Report Interpretation items test the ability to read charts and interpret correctly the numbers contained therein. The charts contain numerical data related to firefighting.

The initial field test was conducted using data from 3,010 firefighter applicants; only the best items were retained—"best" defined as those items having maximum item-total point-biserial correlations, maximum effectiveness of the distractors, and

moderate level of difficulty. In addition, items found to be possibly biased (ethnic, racial, and gender) using the delta approach (Angoff & Ford, 1973) were eliminated. No mention was made of the total number of items originally used in the field test, the item-attrition rate by content category, the range of point-biserial correlations, nor the number of candidates by gender and ethnicity/race.

RELIABILITY. The remaining items were then used to develop two alternate 100-item forms of the Firefighter Selection Test. The relevant statistics for each form are reported to be: Form A (Mean = 70.7, SD = 13.56, KR-20 = .91, SEM = 4.07) and Form B (Mean = 70.7, SD = 14.97, KR-20 = .87, SEM = 5.40). The uncorrected and corrected interform correlations are adequate at .83 and .93, respectively. However, the Technical Report indicates that only half of the Reading Comprehension and Mechanical Comprehension items on Form B were administered in the field test. Consequently, the means reported must be Percent Correct, rather than Total Score, and the KR-20 reliabilities must be based on different numbers of items.

VALIDITY. The Technical Report states that three criterion-related validity studies were conducted in 1975 and 1977, using a total of 335 candidates. The criteria included three from fire college (work samples, training tests, and job knowledge tests) and seven post-graduation (officer and peer ratings of overall knowledge, overall performance and their composite, and termination as firefighter probationer). The correlations between FST and criterion scores ranged from .55 (for fire college training test) to .19 (officer composite rating). Because of the restricted range of the criterion scores, these validity values are underestimated. No evidence was presented as to the validity and reliability of these criterion measures. More recent studies with larger numbers of candidates and more detailed descriptions of the criteria would be welcome.

FAIRNESS. To determine whether or not the test was fair to all subgroups, analyses of covariance (Gulliksen & Wilks, 1950) were carried out. "This procedure tests for significant differences in validities for different racial and ethnic groups and also tests for systematic underestimation of criterion scores for a racial or ethnic subgroup." The five criteria used were: work samples, fire college training tests, a job knowledge test, officers' ratings after graduation, and peer ratings after graduation. Standard errors, regression line slopes, and regression line intercepts were checked for significant differences. No fairness studies were reported for gender differences.

In one study, no significant differences between racial/ethnic groups (Hispanic, Black, and non-minority) were found for the fire college work samples and the three officer ratings. The fire college training tests and job knowledge tests showed significantly different regression line slopes and intercepts, respectively. In a second study, the regression line slopes were significantly different for the training tests and the work samples. Although they concluded that the FST over predicted minority criterion scores and under predicted non-minority scores, no plots or other detailed post hoc results were offered to bolster this claim.

Not discussed in the Technical Report is the fact that Hispanic and Black candidates score, on average, 6 and 7 points, respectively, below non-minority candidates. This will have serious consequences to minority candidates in the ranking process and the use of cut scores.

SCORING OPTIONS. Answer sheets can be returned to Psychological Services, Inc. (PSI) for scanning and scoring or they can be manually scored on site. The PSI scoring service provides a listing of examinees in score order, as well as alphabetically. Only the total score is reported, not part scores. No normative information is provided.

SUMMARY. The Firefighter Selection Test could be an adequate device for testing a candidate's ability to handle material taught in fire college and to succeed as an entry-level firefighter. However, without an adequate and current job analysis of the skills and knowledge required for successful completion of fire college and firefighter probation, it is difficult to recommend this test as a stand-alone assessment. Perhaps it would best be used with several other measures, such as the assessment of physical ability related to firefighting tasks, map-reading skills, spatial visualization, interpersonal skills, and others determined by the job analysis.

REVIEWER'S REFERENCES

Gulliksen, H., & Wilks, S. S. (1950). Regression tests for several samples. *Psychometrika, 15,* 91-114.

Angoff, W. H., & Ford, S. F. (1973). Item-race interaction on a test of scholastic aptitude. *Journal of Educational Measurement, 10,* 95-106.

Review of the Firefighter Selection Test by CYN-THIA ANN DRUVA-ROUSH, Assistant Director, Evaluation and Examination Service, The University of Iowa, Iowa City, IA:

The Firefighter Selection Test is a 100-item multiple-choice test used as a selection instrument for entry-level firefighters. The test is composed of three sections. Thirty-nine items involve mechanical comprehension, 10 items report interpretation, and 51 items test reading comprehension. Only a total score is reported. The manual indicates the test was developed to measure abilities important for the successful job performance of firefighters. Although all items seem to tap job-relevant content, no job analysis in pursuit of critical skills needed for successful job performance as a firefighter is mentioned. The mechanical comprehension items consist of drawings illustrating various mechanical princi-

ples (e.g., resolution of forces, hydraulics, center of gravity). The reading comprehension passages are based on training materials that entry-level firefighters in a metropolitan fire department used. The report interpretation items require the examinee to refer to a report about fires and other fire department information and then make interpretations. All items were piloted on a sample of 3,010 firefighter applicants. Items chosen for the test were of moderate difficulty and maximum discrimination. No average difficulty or discrimination for items included on the exam are provided. Items biased toward protected groups (i.e., women and minorities), as determined by the delta transformation method (Angoff & Ford, 1973), were eliminated.

Two forms of the test are available. Both forms report a high internal consistency reliability (KR20) of .87 and .91. The manual describes in detail how similar these two forms are, both in content and psychometric properties. No attempt was made, however, to equate the two forms through scaling.

Evidence for the criterion-related validity of the test as a tool used for selection of firefighters was collected in three studies. The sample for the first study consisted of 144 firefighter applicants who took the firefighter selection test, completed fire college, and became firefighter probationers. The criterion measures included work samples, training tests, a job knowledge test, officers' ratings, and firefighters' ratings. No assessment as to the reliability of these criterion measures is made. Although the validity coefficients were not high (.19 to .55, .55 being the correlation with the training test), all were significantly different from zero. The low correlations might be explained by a restriction in range due to selection. The second study, replicating the first study with a larger sample size of 335, still reported only moderate validity coefficients. In study three, a criterion measure of termination was examined on the study two sample. Those individuals scoring below 70% on the test had a higher rate of termination. However, only 9% of the sample scored at this level.

A fairness analysis (ns = 119–321) was conducted to determine whether or not the test is equally accurate in predicting various criterion outcomes (work samples, training tests, job knowledge tests, officers' rating of overall knowledge, officers' ratings of overall job performance, officers' composite, academy training tests, and training work samples) for Blacks, Hispanics, and non-minorities. Descriptive statistics for each criterion by subgroup are provided. Although standard errors of estimate were not significantly different between the subgroups, a significant difference in the regression slope coefficients was found. The interpretation offered in the manual suggests this results from more precise estimation of Blacks than for other subgroups. Although this is, in fact, true, no mention is made that this difference may lead to a selection bias, depending upon where a cut score is set. Blacks had a higher slope coefficient. If cut scores were set using all the subjects, Blacks would be underestimated on their performance on both the academy training tests and training work samples at a .01 level.

Overall, the test seems to be well developed. The administrator's guide is clear and gives instructions that explain how to achieve a standardized test environment. An attempt has been made to link test scores to criteria actually used in the work place. However, a concern should be raised that test items were not developed as the result of a thorough job analysis. The *Standards for Educational and Psychological Testing* state clearly that a tool used for employment selection must have established the construct validity of the instrument from a job analysis. Criterion validity is not enough. Further, no interpretation of scores is provided as no norm studies were reported.

REVIEWER'S REFERENCES

Angoff, W. H., & Ford, S. F. (1973). Item-race interaction on a test of scholastic aptitude. *Journal of Educational Measurement, 10* (2), 95-106.
American Educational Research Association, American Psychological Association, & National Council on Measurement in Education. (1985). *Standards for educational and psychological testing.* Washington, DC: American Psychological Association, Inc.

[144]
Forms for Behavior Analysis with Children.

Purpose: A collection of assessment measures "designed to provide a comprehensive portrait of childhood problems with an eye to how the information can be used to design behavioral treatments."
Population: Children.
Publication Date: 1983.
Scores: 21 measures: Behavior Analysis History Questionnaire, Behavior Status Checklist, Reinforcement Survey Schedules, Assertive Behavior Survey Schedule, Bodily Cues for Tension and Anxiety, Fear Inventory, Medical History Inventory, Parental Reaction Survey Schedule, Physical Complaint Survey Schedule, School Behavior Status Checklist, Self-Evaluation Scale, Parents' and Children's Reinforcement Survey Schedule, Reinforcement Menu, Response Cost Survey Schedule, School Reinforcement Survey Schedule, Behavior Record Form, Home Visit Observation Form, Behavior Rating Card, Motivation Assessment of Parents and Children, Progress Chart, Session Report.
Administration: Group.
Forms, 5: C (child), A (adolescent), P (parent), S (school personnel), T (therapist).
Price Data, 1991: $39.95 per manual (206 pages) including reproducible forms.
Time: Administration time not reported.
Comments: Forms (C, A, P, S, T) refer to the person who is to complete the form; "Different assessment formats are encompassed, ranging from direct observations and interviews to informant ratings and self-report."

Authors: Joseph R. Cautela, Julie Cautela, and Sharon Esonis.
Publisher: Research Press.

Review of the Forms for Behavior Analysis with Children by SARAH J. ALLEN, Assistant Professor of Psychology, The University of Rhode Island, Kingston, RI:

The Forms for Behavior Analysis with Children were developed for use in behavioral assessment within the context of clinical work with children and adolescents. These forms include a variety of questionnaires, self-report inventories, behavior monitoring forms, and informational handouts on topics related to childhood behavior problems. Many of the forms may be administered using either an interview or self-report format. Premised on a behavioral assessment model, the forms are intended to provide a systematic approach to data collection that allows for operational definition of target behaviors, identification of the antecedents and consequences that influence them, and development of an efficacious treatment program.

With regard to presentation and packaging, the forms are organized according to the phase of treatment in which they are mostly commonly used, including intake, intervention development, and intervention recording and guidelines. A codification system is provided to facilitate selection of materials relevant to specific therapeutic tasks. In addition, the authors outline the rationale and purpose underlying each form. In general, each description specifies the type of client that might complete the form, the type of information expected to be derived, and briefly, the potential utility of such information. It is expected that these descriptions will be helpful to consumers in determining the inclusion of forms on one type of problem over another.

Also accompanying the forms are directions that clearly outline the procedures and guidelines for administration of each instrument. Specifically, clear instructions are provided for the individual administering the forms (e.g., identification of the person who should complete each form, the settings that might be assessed, the type of responses that can be expected). The instructions provided to respondents are brief, but appear sufficiently explanatory to facilitate completion of the forms.

In contrast, some questions arise regarding the potential utility of the information derived from these forms. Specifically, little guidance is provided regarding the use of information generated from the forms within a behavioral therapy format. Further, some of the information derived from these forms is in a format that will be difficult to quantify and thus, may limit the potential utility of these instruments for developing therapeutic interventions and/or for application in research.

With regard to content validity, some forms (e.g., Behavior Analysis History Questionnaire) provide very thorough coverage of a topic. Unfortunately, other forms appear to cover rather trivial content and/or omit potentially useful content. Overall, these forms provide useful suggestions regarding information that might be obtained from clients with specific problems. However, it is expected that consumers may wish to adapt the content and/or construction of the forms to fit their own clinical practice needs.

Finally, also accompanying each form is a listing of the constructs that the items comprising it are intended to measure. Unfortunately, identification of these constructs appears to be based solely on the authors' clinical judgement; no empirical validation of the item content is provided.

In fact, it is the almost complete lack of any data within the manual relating to the psychometric qualities of the various forms that represents the most serious problem with the Forms for Behavior Analysis with Children. Specifically, no information is provided regarding development of these measures. Moreover, no evidence is provided relative to even basic measurement questions such as the validity and reliability of the forms. As a result, little is known about whether the forms measure what they intend to measure, how these forms relate to other instruments, whether responses are stable over time, or whether they are biased relative to particular samples. Further, it would be useful to know how the individual forms that comprise this manual compare to each other, in terms of basic measurement qualities.

A number of positive features identified in the Forms for Behavior Analysis with Children also deserve mention. For example, the forms encourage solicitation of information from respondents with different perspectives relative to child assessment, including parents, teachers, child, and therapist. Secondly, the means used to solicit child assessment information encompass a number of different formats, including direct observation, interview, informant ratings, and self-report. Further, consideration is given to client strengths as well as weaknesses, and client preferences for situations and procedures. Finally, the forms encourage consideration of target behaviors relative to environmental conditions and in a variety of settings, such as home and school.

In summary, the Forms for Behavior Analysis with Children provide a variety of instruments related to the assessment and treatment of behavior problems with children and adolescents. These forms can aid clinical practice by prompting useful questions and providing a systematic method of collecting intake data. Further, they could function as adjunctive tools useful in maintaining records of therapeutic intervention. Unfortunately, however, no empirical evidence is provided in the manual to support the validity or reliability of the forms. Given the dearth of information available regarding even the basic measurement qualities of these forms, it is recommended they be used with great caution.

Review of the Forms for Behavior Analysis with Children by KAREN T. CAREY, Assistant Professor of Psychology, California State University, Fresno, Fresno, CA:

The Forms for Behavior Analysis with Children is a compilation of observation, interview, rating, and self-report measures to assist professionals with the identification of children's and adolescents' behavioral difficulties. The Forms are contained in a spiral-bound book and are divided by three stages of treatment: Intake, Intervention Development, and Intervention Recording and Guidelines.

Four interview forms are included in the Intake Packet. These are the Behavior Analysis History Questionnaire, the Behavior Status Checklist, the Behavior Status Checklist for Children and Adolescents, and the Reinforcement Schedules. The Intervention Development Packet is composed of self-report, rating, interview, and observation measures for Pinpointing Target Behaviors, Discovering Reinforcers, and Recording Baseline Data. The Intervention Recording and Guidelines section consists of a Behavioral Rating Card for the school staff, a Progress Chart for the child or adolescent to complete, 12 Guidelines for Parental Discipline, and Guidelines for Time-Out. A form to determine the motivation of the parents and child for treatment and a Session Report form are available to the therapist.

Preceding each form, the authors have included a rationale/purpose for the form, information relative to administration, guidelines for administration, item breakdowns, and a "use of information" section. Each form is also compared to other forms within the collection and a listing of recommended readings is provided.

The majority of the forms are self-report or rating measures that are completed by the referred child's parents, the child or adolescent, or members of the school staff. Three-point Likert scales are used for the child forms (e.g., *dislike* to *like very much*), and 5-point Likert scales are used for forms completed by parents and school staff (e.g., *not at all* to *very much*). Some of the forms for adolescents utilize a 3-point scale whereas others use a 5-point scale. The amount of time needed for the completion of each form is not provided.

For many of the self-report forms it is recommended that a therapist oversee the completion of these forms. However, the authors state in the preface of the manual that "many other professionals" may find the forms useful. Concerns related to interpretation must be raised as it appears that clinical judgment, based on the professional's previous experience, is needed in order to identify target behaviors and develop interventions based on such information.

Although item breakdowns are included for each form, no information is presented as to the methods by which these breakdowns were determined. It appears that item breakdowns were based on clinical judgment rather than statistical analyses.

The "Use of Information" section for some of the forms might be useful for those unfamiliar with behavior therapy. Unfortunately, this information is very basic for those who use behavioral treatments. For example, the Use of Information section for the Bodily Cues for Tension and Anxiety form suggests that relaxation treatment be used to assist the child in coping with tension and anxiety. Other suggestions for treatment include modeling, role-playing, and imagery, although specifics for intervention development are not provided. One useful portion of this section, for some forms, are questions provided for the professional to ask him/herself relative to the rating of items. By prioritizing item response the professional can propose potential targets for intervention. The recommended reading included for each form would also be useful for the development of interventions.

Each form is compared to the other available forms within the collection. However, no statistical analyses were completed to determine whether or not the forms are correlated. From statements made by the authors it appears that such comparisons are based on their own use of the instruments.

Two observation forms are included in the collection: the Behavioral Record Form and the Home Visit Observation Form. Limited information is provided for the inexperienced behavior therapist in the utilization of such forms. Furthermore, these two forms utilize primarily an anecdotal format, which is of limited use for identifying target behaviors and developing interventions.

The most serious limitation of these forms is that no technical information is available. Although several of the measures include forms for both parents and children to complete, the interview and self-report formats may allow respondents to present the family situation or the child's behavior in adaptive or maladaptive directions.

In conclusion, the forms may be useful for developing hypotheses related to diagnosis and intervention design, and for research purposes. Furthermore, the use of such forms can be useful when collaborating with parents, teachers, and children to gain insight into their perceptions of the presenting problem. However, it is strongly recommended that the forms be used in conjunction with formal, structured behavioral observations and instruments that are psychometrically sound when making diagnostic and treatment decisions for children and adolescents.

[145]
Frenchay Aphasia Screening Test.

Purpose: "To screen for aphasia as an aid to appropriate diagnosis, referral, and treatment."
Population: Normals and aphasics.
Publication Date: 1987.
Acronym: FAST.
Scores, 5: Comprehension, Expression, Reading, Writing, Total.
Administration: Individual.
Price Data, 1988: £25 per complete set including 25 record forms, picture card, and manual (12 pages); £5 per 24 record forms.
Time: (3–10) minutes.
Authors: Pamela Enderby, Victorine Wood, and Derick Wade.
Publisher: NFER-Nelson Publishing Co., Ltd. [England].

Review of the Frenchay Aphasia Screening Test by ROGER L. TOWNE, Assistant Professor of Speech Pathology and Audiology, Illinois State University, Normal, IL:

PURPOSE. The Frenchay Aphasia Screening Test (FAST) is purported by the authors to be "a valid, reliable, sensitive and simple method of identifying patients with aphasia." It is not specifically intended for use by speech pathologists or psychologists, but by other health workers who must also make decisions regarding the presence of aphasia in patients. The patients' language competency is judged on their cumulative performance of four subtests: Auditory Comprehension, Verbal Expression, Reading Comprehension, and Writing.

ADMINISTRATION, SCORING, AND INTERPRETATION. A card with a picture scene and shapes and five cards with written commands are the basic elements of the test. Auditory comprehension is tested by having the patient respond to verbal instructions of increasing length and linguistic difficulty by pointing to shapes and objects in the picture scene. One point is assigned for each correct response for a maximum of 10. Verbal Expression is evaluated in two ways. First, the patient is asked to describe the picture scene. A score of 1 to 5 is assigned based on the number of objects named and the linguistic normalcy of the responses. Second, Word Fluency is assessed by having patients name as many animals as they can in 60 seconds with a score of 1 to 5 assigned depending on the number of animals named. Reading Comprehension is tested by having the patient read and respond to five picture-related instructions of increasing difficulty. Correct responses receive 1 point. A maximum of 5 points is possible. Finally, the patient is asked to write aobut the scene with a score of 1 to 5 assigned based on the number of appropriate words and the linguistic content of the response. The total number of points is calculated (maximum 30 points) and compared to cutoff scores for patients up to 60 years of age (27 points) and for those over 60 years (25 points). Scores below the cutoff score are indicative of abnormal performance.

EVALUATION OF TEST ADEQUACY. Normative data and cutoff scores on the FAST were obtained on 123 normal people ranging in age from 20 to 81+ years. The established cutoff scores were validated on 50 stroke patients, 20 of whom had a known aphasia. According to the authors, the FAST successfully identified all 20 aphasic patients and 16 nonaphasic patients. There were, however, 14 false positives based on ancillary problems such as visual neglect and confusion. When the authors used the highest score obtained by an aphasic patient as the cutoff score the number of false positives was reduced to 7.

Interobserver reliability (three observers; 17 patients) and test-retest reliability (39 patients) were reported as adequate.

Two areas of concern relate to the items used for testing specific skills and to the procedure by which the cutoff scores were established. First, with the FAST Auditory Comprehension is based solely on the ability of the patient to point correctly to objects—a potentially serious limitation for apraxic individuals. The incorporation of "yes/no" questions along with the pointing tasks would provide alternate means of demonstrating comprehension. Second, the use of shape identification as a test of Auditory Comprehension appears to have limited value. Shape naming is not linguistically potent, has little pragmatic value, and is susceptible to error due to visual closure and visual spatial limitations. Finally, the picture scene contains a person paddling what is obviously a kayak; however, the patient is asked to point to a "canoe," increasing the likelihood of error.

Another concern is the procedure by which the cutoff scores for the test were established. First, the authors provide no explanation or rationale as to how the cutoff scores were derived. From inspection of their data, it appears the cutoff scores represent simply the point at which the normal subjects in the two age groups stopped making errors. The nature of the errors made by the subjects is not described nor are interitem or intersubtest correlations provided. Curiously, the authors report that use of a lower cutoff score (23) representing maximum aphasic performance resulted in a significant decrease in false positives with no increase in false negatives. Despite this apparent improvement in test validity, no explanation is provided as to why this cutoff score was not adopted. Finally, to measure the relationship between test performance and severity of aphasia the authors provide a scattergram of test scores of acute aphasics (3–32 days post onset) and chronic aphasics (1–3.5 years post onset). Although there is a visual grouping of the acute aphasics at the low performance end, this tells us little regarding performance and severity of aphasia as we cannot equate severity solely with post-onset time. Therefore, the test's sensitivity to the mild aphasic patient is not known.

SUMMARY. The potential value of this test, perhaps, rests on whether one believes a screening test for aphasia is necessary or desirable. If a test is truly a screening tool its function should be limited to detecting the presence of a potential problem and to indicating the need for further testing. It might be argued, therefore, that a screening test for aphasia would not be very useful as the typical aphasic patient will adequately demonstrate the need for further testing based on structured conversation. Further, the necessarily limited scope of a screening test makes it easier for mildly involved patients potentially to avoid detection. However, if one does desire a standardized screening format, the FAST might have some usefulness within the limitations discussed. It also must be kept in mind that the test does not actually screen for aphasia as there are other nonaphasic deficits that could also result in a patient not attaining the cutoff score. Clearly, a patient's performance on the FAST should not be the only criterion used for decisions regarding the patient's management.

[146]
Gates-MacGinitie Reading Tests, Third Edition.
Purpose: Measures reading achievement.
Population: Grades K.6–12.
Publication Dates: 1926–89.
Administration: Group.
Levels: 9; 2 forms: K, L.
Price Data, 1990: $1.95 per scoring booklet for any one level; $9 per 35 class summary sheets; $9 per technical report ('89, 92 pages); $1.95 per administrator's summary; $66 per score conversion package.
Authors: Walter H. MacGinitie and Ruth K. MacGinitie.
Publisher: The Riverside Publishing Co.
a) LEVEL PRE.
Population: Grades K.6–1.2.
Scores, 5: Literacy Concepts, Reading Instruction Relational Concepts, Oral Language Concepts, Letters and Letter-Sound Correspondences, Total.
Price Data, 1990: $51 per 35 MRC machine-scorable test booklets (includes administration directions and machine-scoring materials); $60 per 35 NCS machine-scorable test booklets (includes administration directions); $39 per 35 hand-scored test booklets (includes administration directions, scoring key, class summary sheet); $4.95 per administration directions ('89, 75 pages); $6 per manual for scoring and interpretation ('89, 41 pages).
Time: (85–105) minutes.
b) LEVEL R.
Population: Grades 1.0–1.9.

Scores, 5: Initial Consonants, Final Consonants, Vowels, Use of Context, Total.

Price Data, 1990: $48 per 35 MRC machine-scorable test booklets (includes same materials as Level PRE above): $56.25 per 35 NCS machine-scorable test booklets (includes same materials as Level PRE above); $34.50 per 35 hand-scored test booklets (includes same materials as Level PRE above); $3.99 per directions for administration ('89, 58 pages); $6 per manual for scoring and interpretation ('89, 45 pages).

Time: (55–70) minutes.

c) LEVEL 1.

Population: Grades 1.3–1.9.

Scores, 3: Vocabulary, Comprehension, Total.

Price Data, 1990: $48 per 35 MRC machine-scorable test booklets (includes same materials as Level PRE above); $56.25 per 35 NCS machine-scorable test booklets (includes same materials as Level PRE above); $34.50 per 35 hand-scored test booklets (includes same materials as Level PRE above, plus a decoding skills analysis); $3.99 per directions for administration, Levels 1 and 2; $6 per manual for scoring and interpretation, Levels 1 and 2.

Time: 55(60) minutes.

d) LEVEL 2.

Population: Grade 2.

Scores, 3: Same as Level 1 above.

Price Data, 1990: Same as Level 1 above.

Time: Same as Level 1 above.

e) LEVEL 3.

Population: Grade 3.

Scores, 3: Same as Level 1 above.

Price Data, 1990: Same as Level R above.

Time: Same as Level 1 above.

f) LEVEL 4.

Population: Grade 4.

Scores, 3: Same as Level 1 above.

Price Data, 1990: $34.95 per 35 reusable test booklets; $33 per 100 MRC answer sheets; $21 per 35 self-scorable answer sheets; $117 per 250 self-scorable answer sheets; $99 per 250 NCS 7010 answer sheets; $9 per MRC scoring templates; $3.99 per directions for administration; $6 per manual for scoring and interpretation.

Time: Same as Level 1 above.

g) LEVEL 5/6.

Population: Grades 5–6.

Scores, 3: Same as Level 1 above.

Price Data, 1990: Same as Level 4 above.

Time: Same as Level 1 above.

h) LEVEL 7/9.

Population: Grades 7–9.

Scores, 3: Same as Level 1 above.

Price Data, 1990: Same as Level 4 above.

Time: Same as Level 1 above.

i) LEVEL 10/12.

Population: Grades 10–12.

Scores, 3: Same as Level 1 above.

Price Data, 1990: Same as Level 4 above.

Time: Same as Level 1 above.

Cross References: For reviews by Robert Calfee and William H. Rupley of an earlier edition, see 9:430 (15 references); see also T3:932 (77 references) and 8:726A (34 references); for reviews by Carolyn L. Burke and

Byron H. Van Roekel and an excerpted review by William R. Powell of an earlier edition, see 7:689.

TEST REFERENCES

1. Ysseldyke, J. E., & Marston, D. (1982). A critical analysis of standardized reading tests. *School Psychology Review, 11,* 257-266.
2. Arlin, M., & Webster, J. (1983). Time costs of mastery learning. *Journal of Educational Psychology, 75,* 187-195.
3. Weed, K., & Ryan, E. B. (1983). Alphabetical seriation as a reading readiness indicator. *Journal of General Psychology, 109,* 201-210.
4. White, M., & Miller, S. R. (1983). Dyslexia: A term in search of a definition. *The Journal of Special Education, 17,* 5-10.
5. Bohannon, J. N., III, Warren-Leubecker, A., & Hepler, N. (1984). Word order awareness and early reading. *Child Development, 55,* 1541-1548.
6. Cecil, N. L. (1984). Impact of interest on the literal comprehension of beginning readers—A West Indian study. *The Reading Teacher, 37,* 750-753.
7. Duffelmeyer, F. A. (1984). The effect of context on ascertaining word meaning. *Reading World, 24* (1), 103-107.
8. Halpern, H. G. (1984). An investigation of reading and conceptual tempo measures. *Reading World, 24* (1), 90-96.
9. Haynes, J. E., & Fillmer, H. T. (1984). Paraphrasing and reading comprehension. *Reading World, 24* (1), 76-79.
10. Heydorn, B. L. (1984). Symbol reversals, reading achievement, and handedness of first grade students. *Perceptual and Motor Skills, 58,* 589-590.
11. Hoge, R. D., & Butcher, R. (1984). Analysis of teacher judgments of pupil achievement levels. *Journal of Educational Psychology, 76,* 777-781.
12. Johns, J. L. (1984). Equivalence of forms 1 and 3, Level 3, Gates-MacGinitie Reading Tests. *Journal of Reading, 28,* 48-51.
13. Learner, K. M., & Richman, C. L. (1984). The effect of modifying the cognitive tempo of reading disabled children on reading comprehension. *Contemporary Educational Psychology, 9,* 122-134.
14. Manning, B. H. (1984). Problem-solving instruction as an oral comprehension aid for reading disabled third graders. *Journal of Learning Disabilities, 17,* 457-461.
15. Oakhill, J. (1984). Inferential and memory skills in children's comprehension of stories. *British Journal of Educational Psychology, 54,* 31-39.
16. Paris, S. G., & Jacobs, J. E. (1984). The benefits of informed instruction for children's reading awareness and comprehension skills. *Child Development, 55,* 2083-2093.
17. Paris, S. G., Cross, D. R., & Lipson, M. Y. (1984). Informed strategies for learning: A program to improve children's reading awareness and comprehension. *Journal of Educational Psychology, 76,* 1239-1252.
18. Reutzel, D. R. (1984). Story mapping: An alternative approach to comprehension. *Reading World, 24* (2), 16-25.
19. Roehler, L. R., Duffy, G. G., & Meloth, M. S. (1984). The effects and some distinguishing characteristics of explicit teacher explanation during reading instruction. *National Reading Conference Yearbook, 33,* 223-229.
20. Shanahan, T. (1984). Nature of the reading-writing relation: An exploratory multivariate analysis. *Journal of Educational Psychology, 76,* 466-477.
21. Stanovich, K. E., Cunningham, A. E., & Feeman, D. J. (1984). Relation between early reading acquisition and word decoding with and without context: A longitudinal study of first-grade children. *Journal of Educational Psychology, 76,* 668-677.
22. Wong, B. Y. L., & Wilson, M. (1984). Investigating awareness of and teaching passage organization in learning disabled children. *Journal of Learning Disabilities, 17,* 477-482.
23. Zenke, L., & Alexander, L. (1984). Teaching thinking in Tulsa. *Educational Leadership, 42,* 81-84.
24. Connelly, J. B. (1985). Published tests—which ones do special education teachers perceive as useful? *Journal of Special Education, 19,* 149-155.
25. Dunn, R., Krimsky, J. S., Murray, J. B., & Quinn, P. J. (1985). Light up their lives: A review of research on the effects of lighting on children's achievement and behavior. *The Reading Teacher, 38,* 863-869.
26. Erickson, L. G., Stahl, S. A., & Rinehart, S. D. (1985). Metacognitive abilities of above and below average readers: Effects of conceptual tempo, passage level, and error type on error detection. *Journal of Reading Behavior, 17,* 235-252.
27. Gagñe, E. D., Bell, M. S., Yarbrough, D. B., & Weidemann, C. (1985). Does familiarity have an effect on recall independent of its effect on original learning? *The Journal of Educational Research, 79,* 41-45.
28. Geva, E., & Ryan, E. B. (1985). Use of conjunctions in expository texts by skilled and less skilled readers. *Journal of Reading Behavior, 17,* 331-346.
29. Gibson-Harman, K., & Austin, G. F. (1985). A revised form of the Tennessee Self-Concept Scale for use with deaf and hard of hearing persons. *American Annals of the Deaf, 130,* 218-225.

30. Heydorn, B. L. (1985). Effect of practice of correct symbol reversals on reading achievement by first-grade children. *Perceptual and Motor Skills, 60,* 509-510.

31. Horowitz, R., & Samuels, S. J. (1985). Reading and listening to expository text. *Journal of Reading Behavior, 17,* 185-198.

32. Leung, J. J., & Foster, S. F. (1985). Helping the elderly: A study on altruism in children. *Child Study Journal, 15,* 293-309.

33. Smith, E. R. (1985). Community college reading tests: A statewide survey. *Journal of Reading, 28,* 52-55.

34. Walters, K., & Gunderson, L. (1985). Effects of parent volunteers reading first language (L1) books to ESL students. *The Reading Teacher, 39,* 66-69.

35. Berninger, V. W. (1986). Normal variation in reading acquisition. *Perceptual and Motor Skills, 62,* 691-716.

36. Crocker, R. K., & Brooker, G. M. (1986). Classroom control and student outcomes in grades 2 and 5. *American Educational Research Journal, 23,* 1-11.

37. Davenport, L., Yingling, C. D., Fein, G., Galin, D., & Johnstone, J. (1986). Narrative speech deficits in dyslexics. *Journal of Clinical and Experimental Neuropsychology, 8,* 347-361.

38. Dirgi, D. R. (1986). Does the Rasch model really work for multiple choice items? Not if you look closely. *Journal of Educational Measurement, 23,* 283-298.

39. Duffy, G. G., Roehler, L. R., Meloth, M. S., Vavrus, L. G., Book, C., Putnam, J., & Wesselman, R. (1986). The relationship between explicit verbal explanations during reading skill instruction and student awareness and achievement: A study of reading teacher effects. *Reading Research Quarterly, 21,* 237-252.

40. Firestone, P., Crowe, D., Goodman, J. T., & McGrath, P. (1986). Vicissitudes of follow-up studies: Differential effects of parent training and stimulant medication with hyperactives. *American Journal of Orthopsychiatry, 56,* 184-194.

41. Hinshaw, S. P., Carte, E. T., & Morrison, D. C. (1986). Concurrent prediction of academic achievement in reading disabled children: The role of neuropsychological and intellectual measures at different ages. *Clinical Neuropsychology, 8,* 3-8.

42. Kuhns, C. O., Moore, D. W., & Moore, S. A. (1986). The stability of modified miscue analysis profiles. *Reading Research and Instruction, 25,* 149-159.

43. Malatesha, R. N. (1986). Visual motor ability in normal and disabled readers. *Perceptual and Motor Skills, 62,* 627-630.

44. Melson, G. F., Fogel, A., & Toda, S. (1986). Children's ideas about infants and their care. *Child Development, 57,* 1519-1527.

45. O'Brien, D. G. (1986). A test of three positions posed to explain the relation between word knowledge and comprehension. *National Reading Conference Yearbook, 35,* 81-86.

46. Rinehart, S. D., Stahl, S. A., & Erickson, L. G. (1986). Some effects of summarization training on reading and studying. *Reading Research Quarterly, 21,* 422-438.

47. Shanahan, T., & Lomax, R. G. (1986). An analysis and comparison of theoretical models of the reading-writing relationship. *Journal of Educational Psychology, 78,* 116-123.

48. Stahl, S. A., Rinehart, S. D., & Erickson, L. G. (1986). Detection of inconsistencies by above and below average reflective and impulsive sixth graders. *The Journal of Educational Research, 79,* 185-189.

49. Svec, H. (1986). Overestimation of academic competence by high school dropouts. *Psychological Reports, 59,* 669-670.

50. Taylor, K. K. (1986). Summary writing by young children. *Reading Research Quarterly, 21,* 193-208.

51. Wells, L. E., & Sweeney, P. D. (1986). A test of three models of bias in self-assessment. *Social Psychology Quarterly, 49,* 1-10.

52. Wolf, M., Bally, H., & Morris, R. (1986). Automaticity, retrieval processes, and reading: A longitudinal study in average and impaired readers. *Child Development, 57,* 988-1000.

53. Zutell, J., & Rasinski, T. (1986). Spelling ability and reading fluency. *National Reading Conference Yearbook, 35,* 109-112.

54. Berninger, V. W. (1987). Global component, and serial processing of printed words in beginning reading. *Journal of Experimental Child Psychology, 43,* 387-418.

55. Davey, B. (1987). Relations between word knowledge and comprehension: Generalization across tasks and readers. *The Journal of Educational Research, 80,* 179-183.

56. Feldt, R. C., & Witte, K. L. (1987). Metamemorial knowledge of good and poor readers: A developmental perspective. *Journal of Genetic Psychology, 148,* 415-426.

57. Kitty, T., Charney, N., & Leviton, A. (1987). Headaches, performance in high school, and handedness. *Perceptual and Motor Skills, 65,* 159-163.

58. Solan, H. A. (1987). A comparison of the influences of verbal-successive and spatial-simultaneous factors on achieving readers in fourth and fifth grade: A multivariate correlational study. *Journal of Learning Disabilities, 20,* 237-242.

59. Warren-Leubecker, A. (1987). Competence and performance factors in word order awareness and early reading. *Journal of Experimental Child Psychology, 43,* 62-80.

60. Berninger, V. W., Proctor, A., Bruyn, I. D., & Smith, R. (1988). Relationship between levels of oral and written language in beginning readers. *Journal of School Psychology, 26,* 341-357.

61. Cahn, L. D. (1988). Sex and grade differences and learning rate in an intensive summer reading clinic. *Psychology in the Schools, 25,* 84-91.

62. Eldredge, J. L., & Quinn, D. W. (1988). Increasing reading performance of low-achieving second graders with dyad reading groups. *The Journal of Educational Research, 82,* 40-46.

63. Feldt, R. C., & Witte, K. L. (1988). Mnemonic benefits of digit-list organization: Test of the developmental lag hypothesis of reading retardation. *Journal of Genetic Psychology, 149,* 459-469.

64. Gallivan, J. (1988). Concept knowledge as a predictor of first- and fourth-grade reading achievement. *Perceptual and Motor Skills, 66* (2), 407-410.

65. Levinson, H. N. (1988). The cerebellar-vestibular basis of learning disabilities in children, adolescents and adults: Hypothesis and study. *Perceptual and Motor Skills, 67,* 983-1006.

66. Morrison, D. C., & Hinshaw, S. P. (1988). The relationship between neuropsychological/perceptual performance and socioeconomic status in children with learning disabilities. *Journal of Learning Disabilities, 21,* 124-128.

67. Mungas, D. (1988). Psychometric correlates of episodic violent behavior: A multidimensional neuropsychological approach. *British Journal of Psychiatry, 152,* 180-187.

68. Musselman, C. R., Lindsay, P. H., & Wilson, A. K. (1988). An evaluation of recent trends in preschool programming for hearing-impaired children. *Journal of Speech and Hearing Disorders, 53,* 71-88.

69. Rinehart, S. D. (1988). Conceptual tempo, studying, and reading. *The Journal of Educational Research, 81,* 138-142.

70. Foorman, B. R., & Liberman, D. (1989). Visual and phonological processing of words: A comparison of good and poor readers. *Journal of Learning Disabilities, 22,* 349-355.

71. Gibbs, K. W. (1989). Individual differences in cognitive skills related to reading ability in the deaf. *American Annals of the Deaf, 134,* 214-218.

72. Eldredge, J. L., Quinn, B., & Butterfield, D. D. (1990). Causal relationships between phonics, reading comprehension, and vocabulary achievement in the second grade. *Journal of Educational Research, 83,* 201-214.

73. Kupietz, S. S. (1990). Sustained attention in normal and in reading-disabled youngsters with and without ADDH. *Journal of Abnormal Child Psychology, 18,* 357-372.

74. Reutzel, D. R., & Cooter, R. B. (1990). Whole language: Comparative effects on first-grade reading achievement. *Journal of Educational Research, 83,* 252-257.

75. Taylor, B. M., Frye, B. J., & Maruyama, G. M. (1990). Time spent reading and reading growth. *American Educational Research Journal, 27,* 351-362.

76. Zagar, R., Arbit, J., Sylvies, R., Busch, K. G., & Hughes, J. R. (1990). Homicidal adolescents: A replication. *Psychological Reports, 67,* 1235-1242.

77. Forman, B. R., Francis, D. J., Novy, D. M., & Liberman, D. (1991). How letter-sound instruction mediates progress in first-grade reading and spelling. *Journal of Educational Psychology, 83,* 456-469.

78. Jenkins, J. R., Jewell, M., Leicester, N., Jenkins, L., & Troutner, N. M. (1991). Development of a school building model for educating students with handicaps and at-risk students in general education classrooms. *Journal of Learning Disabilities, 24,* 311-320.

Review of the Gates-MacGinitie Reading Tests, Third Edition by MARK E. SWERDLIK, Professor of Psychology, Illinois State University, Normal, IL:

The Third Edition of the Gates-MacGinitie Reading Tests (GMRT) represents the most recent in a series that began in 1926 with the publication of the Gates Silent Reading Test and Gates Primary Reading Tests. The second revision occurred in 1976–77. An effort was made to minimize the overlap between the Second and Third Editions with no more than one-third of the items in any field test or final form of the Third Edition also included in the Second Edition. The Third Edition also adds a Level PRE (Pre-Reading evaluation). For all but three of the nine levels, two parallel forms of the Third Edition are available.

USES OF THE TEST. The authors suggest the levels designed for the early grades (PRE and R) have somewhat different uses than the higher Levels 1–10/12. PRE was designed to assess the child's knowledge of important background concepts upon which beginning reading skills are built. PRE can assist in identifying concepts with which children beginning reading instruction may need additional help. Level R can be useful in measuring reading skills of children who make less than average progress in reading by the end of grade 1. The other levels of the GMRT were developed to provide a general assessment of reading achievement.

The manuals for scoring and interpreting of PRE and R further specify the scores can assist in making individual and program evaluation decisions. For example, the test results can yield data that can help determine how strong a background the individual student has in concepts important for success in reading instruction and in identifying children who are likely to have difficulty in learning to read unless they receive a modified instructional program. For a classroom, the test results can assist in determining how strong a reading background the children possess, what types of beginning reading materials will be needed, and what instructional emphasis would be useful. In addition, the GMRT can be helpful in determining if a new set of materials or curriculum used in kindergarten has made any difference in the background the children bring to first grade reading instruction.

For those levels appropriate for older students, the authors suggest the results can help answer questions such as which, if any, children should receive further evaluation or be encouraged to do more additional work in reading; whether each child is continuing to progress in reading at the rate one would expect; and to identify children who need special help with comprehension and in developing a larger vocabulary. As a group, the scores can help answer questions relating to how the children read; are the children progressing in reading and at a rate one would expect; are the children falling behind or catching up; what reading materials will be needed; and are new sets of materials having an effect on the children's ability to read?

TEST CONSTRUCTION. The test construction process is described in clear and sufficient detail in the separate Technical Report. The GMRT was carefully constructed and created from a detailed test blueprint. The authors also delineate clearly when and how the final form deviated from the predetermined test blueprint prior to field testing. A clear rationale is given for items included in the Third Edition. Words chosen for the various levels of the test were selected from either Harris and Jacobson

(1982) or the list of *The Living Word Vocabulary* (Dale & O'Rourke, 1976). The blueprint included such factors as selecting words for vocabulary representing various parts of speech. In addition, passages were chosen for the comprehension sections that represented different subject areas and both narrative and expository writing styles. A panel of experts including the test authors, editors, and consultants also reviewed the various vocabulary words included in the GMRT.

Efforts were also made to minimize bias and offensiveness of the test content by having a panel of Asian, Black, Hispanic, and Native American consultants review all items. If judged to be biased or offensive by the panel, items were either revised or eliminated. In addition to employing a content analysis approach to item bias, item difficulty levels were also reviewed for Black and Hispanic students and for males and females as a group. If items were differentially more difficult for any of these groups they were carefully examined. For gender differences, items were balanced so an equal number favoring males and females were included in the final forms of the tests. Items written by both male and female authors were also included in the comprehension section of the various levels.

ADMINISTRATION AND SCORING. The separate Directions for Administration booklets for each level of the GMRT are clearly written and complete. The directions are presented with enough detail so that personnel with minimal training can administer the test in a way consistent with how the norms were collected. For example, the directions to be read by the person administering the test are shaded. The directions also include test-taking strategies including guessing and cautions against skipping items. These directions will promote more consistent use of test-taking strategies that will enhance reliability and validity of the results. Helpful suggestions for the examiner on how to deal with common problems that occur during testing are also offered such as when testing is interrupted or a child misses the first testing session.

A several page summary of the technical data, called Technical Notes, is also provided in each of the Directions for Administration booklets with the test user encouraged to consult the more detailed Technical Manual for additional information. This manual does not, however, include specific cautions against misuses of the test.

The GMRT is a power test with all students expected to complete all of the items in the time allotted. Data are presented in the Technical Manual to support this claim.

Responses can be recorded on separate answer sheets or in the test booklet. The authors present data to support the ability of younger students to mark the answer sheets accurately as well as providing a rationale as to why circles were chosen at Levels PRE–3 as the shape of the answer space.

Several options are available for scoring and interpreting the GMRT. Standard machine scoring is available as well as a hand-scorable test booklet. Self-scorable answer sheets are available for Levels 4 through 10/12. More extensive scoring and interpretation is available from the publisher including narrative reports, pre- and post-testing analyses, and frequency distributions.

The separate Manual for Scoring and Interpretation provides instructions on hand scoring in sufficient detail and clarity to maximize accuracy. A discussion of the various types of test scores yielded by the GMRT, including the limitations of each, is provided in the Scoring and Interpretation manual at each level. The appropriate way of using various derived scores is presented in an easy-to-read question-and-answer format. This manual also includes a section on interpolating between fall and spring norms.

In addition, interpretation aids are provided in the form of a score report form and a listing of instructional activities and materials to use in teaching those with low scores on various sections of the GMRT. However, no support is provided relative to the effectiveness of these suggestions.

NORMATIVE DATA. The Technical Report includes an adequate description of the timing and process by which the normative data for the Third Edition were collected. The extensive field testing is discussed in appropriate detail and allows the test user to determine the appropriateness of the standardization sample for the population with whom the user is working.

The Third Edition was standardized on 77,413 students enrolled in 222 schools which were affiliated with 67 public and private school systems located in 30 states. Students were tested in both fall (October) and spring (April) and a longitudinal sample was constructed. The standardization sample was stratified on geographic region, district enrollment, socioeconomic status of the community determined by the median years of education of the population 25 years and older, and median family income. All information for the standardization was based on the 1980 U.S. Census data.

The standardization sample is described in sufficient detail in the manual to determine that it is very well constructed and representative. Schools were randomly selected within cells by region by size by SES. Schools were then contacted by the representatives of the publishing company to participate. If they refused, another system was randomly selected within that area. Each school system that agreed to participate was asked to select two classrooms or about 50 students in each of grades K–12 who were representative of each system.

Weighted norms were used to improve the representativeness of the norms. This is described in adequate detail. The unweighted sample closely approximated the weighted sample for the fall but not the spring. Each scoring and interpretation manual also includes a discussion of out-of-level norms and when they can be useful.

A number of derived scores are yielded from GMRT raw scores including Normal Curve Equivalents (NCEs), percentile ranks, grade equivalents, and Extended Scale Scores (ESSs). Each manual for scoring and interpretation provides a full explanation of how the scaled scores were derived and the strengths and limitations of each. This is particularly useful in that a complete discussion of the limitations of grade equivalents is included.

Three equating studies on 25,210 students during the fall standardization period were conducted. Although the authors report the samples came from a geographically dispersed, heterogenous sample of schools across the United States and that some of the schools in the norming sample were also included in the equating studies, support for this assertion is lacking because a detailed analysis is not provided other than a listing of the participating schools. Efforts were made to equate the Second and Third editions, adjacent test levels, and alternate forms.

The correlations between the two editions were quite high and suggest that the Third Edition measures essentially the same reading abilities as the Second Edition. ESS scores were modified so that a given ESS for the Third Edition represents the same level of reading achievement as the same ESS for the Second Edition. The results of correlational analyses also indicate that each level of the test measures essentially the same reading skills as the adjacent levels except for PRE and R. The magnitude of the correlations for the total scores (except for PRE and R) were all .84 and higher.

RELIABILITY. The authors provide internal consistency (KR-20) along with means and standard deviations for total scores and subscales for each level of the GMRT for both spring and fall administrations. These are quite satisfactory and fall in the upper .80s and .90s for Levels 1–10/12. KR 20s for PRE and R are somewhat lower, falling in the .70s and .80s for the individual subtests with the total score in the mid-.90s. These lower levels of reliability can be attributed to these levels corresponding to the lower age levels and fewer items being included on these forms. Although standard errors of measurement expressed in ESSs for Levels 1–10/12 and NCEs for all levels of the test are provided in the Technical Report for Levels R-10/12, confidence intervals are not.

Reliability estimates of stability are also provided in the manual. Students in the standardization sample took Form K of the level for their grade in both the fall and spring administrations. Correlations between their scores during the two testing sessions were computed and served as a measure of stability. Correlations between fall and spring scores for grade 1 were smaller than at the other grades and the authors provide a reasonable rationale relating to the differential amount of reading instruction received in kindergarten by various children prior to being tested in the fall. By the spring administration, all children had received considerable reading instruction and the amount received in kindergarten had less of an impact on their score. All students in the standardization sample could not be included in the stability study due to differences in the way the subjects coded their names on the fall and spring administrations of the test, and loss of subjects due to mobility and absences. Reliability of differences between vocabulary and comprehension subtests was also provided.

A high level of alternate form reliability for each subtest and total scores were also reported with coefficients in the .80s and low .90s. Each form was administered 3 weeks apart. Each of the forms were given in one order in some schools and in the reverse order in others. Although it is reported that approximately half of the students took one test first and half took the other test first, exact data were not provided. In addition, the rationale for including 3 weeks as the interval was not provided.

VALIDITY. The authors rely on expert judgement to develop content validity. Although the sources of the test content are delineated, it is unclear how close of a relationship exists between the test content and the reading curriculum used or skills taught in most American school systems. The authors also do not provide a rationale for why they chose the Harris and Jacobson and the Dale and O'Rourke lists.

Other validity data reported include: the inter-correlations among subtests; the high percentage (over 80% in the fall and 90% in the spring administrations) of students completing the tests providing evidence that the GMRT is a power test; and data supporting that the test has an excellent ability to assess reading achievement at the lower and upper levels.

The bulk of the validity evidence relates to providing data that support substantial relationships between the GMRT and other instruments that are assumed to measure the same constructs of reading vocabulary and comprehension. These tests include general achievement screening batteries such as the Iowa Test of Basic Skills (ITBS), Tests of Achievement and Proficiency (TAP), the Comprehensive Tests of Basic Skills (CTBS), California Achievement Test (CAT), Metropolitan Achievement Test (MAT), the Survey of Basic Skills (SBS), the Verbal and Mathematics sections of the Preliminary Scholastic Aptitude Test (PSAT) and the Scholastic Aptitude Test (SAT), and the English, Math, Social Science, Natural Science, and Composite sections of the American College Testing Program (ACT).

In addition, teacher assigned grades awarded in reading, language, English, and total GPA are also used as criteria for supporting the validity of the GMRT. Correlations with reading, English, and language grades and total GPA tend to be quite high through grade 6 providing support for the authors' contention that the GMRT measures those aspects of reading that teachers regard as representative of reading achievement. The correlations of GMRT and grades decrease as the students get older which the authors attribute to a restriction of range because many students who receive reading at the higher grade levels are exhibiting reading problems.

For all of these validity studies, the composition of the validation samples such as community characteristics, gender, and ethnic composition are not provided in detail nor are measures of central tendency or variability. It is difficult for the test user to determine if these validity data can be generalized to their test population. The amount of time between administrations of the GMRT and the criterion test is also not reported. In addition, although a number of instructional strategies are provided for use by the test user in remediating reading deficits based on low GMRT scores, no validity data are provided on their use or effectiveness.

Further, validity data are not provided for the major uses for which the test is recommended such as selecting students who may benefit from additional instruction or different types of reading instruction. No validity data unique to the purposes of level PRE are provided.

The GMRT underwent a comprehensive test development process. The test authors were sensitive to the issue of potential cultural and gender bias of items. Test materials are attractively packaged. The GMRT is simple and time efficient to administer and score. Special scoring and interpretation services are also available. The GMRT is a well-standardized instrument with a large and representative norm sample. Adequate reliability and validity data are presented to use the test as a useful measure of reading achievement or as a first level screening to be followed-up by more of a diagnostic reading test. The GMRT could also be used as a tool in an evaluation of a school's reading program if the test content related to the reading curriculum of the individual school system being evaluated. The test lacks validity evidence for use as more than a general screening achievement test in reading. For example, no validity evidence was presented for the use of the instructional strategies recommended based on low scores or for selecting students who would benefit from more instruction in comprehension. It is also somewhat limited at the upper levels because it does not include reading/study skills important to assess at the upper grades such as ability to use reference tools, reading graphic illustrations, notetaking, and outlining. In addition, the reporting of the GMRT comprehension score does not include different types of comprehension such as literal and inferential. Based on the information presented above, the GMRT is recommended for use as a screening test.

REVIEWER'S REFERENCES

Dale, E., & O'Rourke, J. (1976). *The living word vocabulary*. Chicago: Field Enterprises Educational Corporation.

Harris, A. J., & Jacobson, M. D. (1982). *Basic reading vocabularies*. New York: Macmillan.

[147]
Global Assessment Scale.

Purpose: "For evaluating the overall functioning of a subject during a specified time period on a continuum from psychological or psychiatric sickness to health."

Population: Psychiatric patients and possible psychiatric patients.

Publication Dates: 1976–85.

Acronym: GAS.

Scores: Mental Health-Illness rating of individual on a continuum of 1 to 100.

Administration: Individual.

Price Data, 1988: $.25 per scale; $1.50 per case vignettes and keys ('85, 16 pages); $.50 per instructions ('78, 2 pages).

Authors: Robert L. Spitzer, Miriam Gibbon, and Jean Endicott.

Publisher: Department of Research Assessment and Training, New York State Psychiatric Institute.

TEST REFERENCES

1. Abraham, I. L. (1986). Cognitive set and clinical inference: Referral information may not (always) affect psychosocial assessment. *Social Behavior and Personality, 14*, 51-58.

2. Allen, J. G., Coyne, L., & David, E. (1986). Relation of intelligence to ego functioning in an adult psychiatric population. *Journal of Personality Assessment, 50*, 212-221.

3. Mallon, J. C., Klein, D. N., Bornstein, R. F., & Slater, J. F. (1986). Discriminant validity of the General Behavior Inventory: An outpatient study. *Journal of Personality Assessment, 50*, 568-577.

4. Affleck, G., Tennen, H., Pfeiffer, C., & Fifield, J. (1987). Appraisals of control and predictability in adapting to a chronic disease. *Journal of Personality and Social Psychology, 53*, 273-279.

5. Bowden, C. L., Koslow, S., Maas, J. W., Davis, J., Garver, D. L., & Hanin, I. (1987). Changes in urinary catecholamines and their metabolites in depressed patients treated with amitriptyline or imipramine. *Journal of Psychiatric Research, 21*, 111-128.

6. David, A. S. (1987). Tachistoscopic tests of colour naming and matching in schizophrenia: Evidence for posterior callosum dysfunction? *Psychological Medicine, 17*, 621-630.

7. Kochanska, G., Kuczynski, L., Radke-Yarrow, M., & Welsh, J. D. (1987). Resolutions of control episodes between well and affectively ill mothers and their young children. *Journal of Abnormal Child Psychology, 15*, 441-456.

8. Thompson, L. W., Gallagher, D., & Breckenridge, J. S. (1987). Comparative effectiveness of psychotherapies for depressed elders. *Journal of Consulting and Clinical Psychology, 55*, 385-390.

9. Tienari, P., Lahti, I., Sorri, A., Naarala, M., Moring, J., Wahlberg, K., & Wynne, L. C. (1987). The Finnish adoptive family study of schizophrenia. *Journal of Psychiatric Research, 21*, 437-445.

10. Archer, R. P., Gordon, R. A., Giannetti, R. A., & Singles, J. M. (1988). MMPI scale clinical correlates for adolescent inpatients. *Journal of Personality Assessment, 52*, 707-721.

11. Holcomb, W. R., & Otto, R. L. (1988). Construct validity of the Global Assessment Scale. *Psychological Reports, 62*, 279-282.

12. Nimgaonkar, V. L., Wessely, S., Tune, L. E., & Murray, R. M. (1988). Response to drugs in schizophrenia: The influence of family

history, obstetric complications and ventricular enlargement. *Psychological Medicine, 18*, 583-592.

13. Zheng, Y., Zhao, J., Phillips, M., Liu, J., Cai, M., Sun, S., & Huang, M. (1988). Validity and reliability of the Chinese Hamilton Depression Rating Scale. *British Journal of Psychiatry, 152*, 660-664.

14. Archer, R. P., Gordon, R. A., Anderson, G. L., & Giannetti, R. A. (1989). MMPI special scale clinical correlates for adolescent inpatients. *Journal of Personality Assessment, 53*, 654-664.

15. Dodwell, D., & Goldberg, D. (1989). A study of factors associated with response to electroconvulsive therapy in patients with schizophrenic symptoms. *British Journal of Psychiatry, 154*, 635-639.

16. Harding, C. M., McCormick, R. V., Strauss, J. S., Ashikaga, T., & Brooks, G. W. (1989). Computerised life chart methods to map domains of function and illustrate patterns of interactions in the long-term course trajectories of patients who once met the criteria for DSM-III schizophrenia. *British Journal of Psychiatry, 155* (Suppl. 5), 100-106.

17. Klein, D. N. (1989). The Depressive Experiences Questionnaire: A further evaluation. *Journal of Personality Assessment, 53*, 703-715.

18. Moller, H. J., Hohe-Schramm, M., Cording-Tommel, C., Schmid-Bode, W., Wittchen, H. U., Zaudig, M., & von Zerssen, D. (1989). The classification of functional psychoses and its implications for prognosis. *British Journal of Psychiatry, 154*, 467-472.

19. Sohlberg, S. (1989). There's more in a number than you think: New validity data for the global assessment scale. *Psychological Reports, 64*, 455-461.

20. Van Mechelen, I., & De Boeck, P. (1989). Implicit taxonomy in psychiatric diagnosis: A case study. *Journal of Social and Clinical Psychology, 8*, 276-287.

21. Goodman, S. H., & Brumley, H. E. (1990). Schizophrenic and depressed mothers: Relational deficits in parenting. *Developmental Psychology, 26*, 31-39.

22. Talley, P. F., Strupp, H. H., & Morey, L. C. (1990). Matchmaking in psychotherapy: Patient-therapist dimensions and their impact on outcome. *Journal of Consulting and Clinical Psychology, 58*, 182-188.

Review of the Global Assessment Scale by MICHAEL J. SUBKOVIAK, Professor of Educational Psychology, University of Wisconsin-Madison, Madison, WI:

The Global Assessment Scale (GAS) elicits a single, subjective rating of an individual's overall mental health as perceived by a psychiatrist, psychologist, or other mental health professional. Assigned ratings range from 1 to 100, representing the hypothetically sickest individual (1) to the healthiest (100). The scale is subdivided into 10 equal intervals: 1–10, 11–20, . . ., 91–100, which are defined by a subject's symptoms, behaviors, and characteristics. The rater selects the interval which best describes the subject's current functioning and then considers the defining characteristics of the two adjacent intervals to determine whether the final rating should fall closer to one or the other.

The manual for the instrument consists of: (a) six pages of instructions that attempt to clarify (only somewhat successfully) distinctions between the 10 scale intervals and (b) a set of 23 case summaries to provide practice in using the scale. The psychometric properties of the instrument are discussed by its authors in an article (Endicott, Spitzer, Fleiss, & Cohen, 1976) in which they conclude that "the relative simplicity, reliability, and validity of the GAS suggests that it would be useful in a wide variety of clinical and research settings." However, it would appear that further development is needed in a number of these areas before the instrument could be recommended for general use.

RELIABILITY. Interrater correlations of GAS scores are reported for five separate reliability studies involving small, convenience groups of subjects. In all of these studies, each rater observed and scored the same sample of a subject's behavior. Day-to-day variations in a subject's behavior were not considered in the way the data were collected. Thus, the reported correlations, which have a median value of only .76 and a range of .61–.91, may be somewhat inflated estimates of the instrument's actual reliability. More accurate estimates would require studies involving larger and more representative groups of subjects rated on more than one occasion.

Developers of standardized instruments often strive for reliabilities exceeding about .90. In light of the discussion above, it seems unlikely that the GAS, as currently used, could consistently achieve this level of consistency. However, reliability could be enhanced if a subject's final GAS score was computed as the *average* of two or more independent ratings. This approach is sometimes used, for example, to increase the reliability of grades assigned to writing samples on standardized cognitive tests.

VALIDITY. Evidence regarding the potential usefulness of GAS scores for certain purposes is suggestive rather than conclusive. The previously cited journal article provides information regarding: (*a*) the correlation of GAS scores with other standardized measures, (*b*) the sensitivity of GAS scores to changes in a patient's condition while undergoing treatment, and (*c*) the potential usefulness of GAS scores for predicting subsequent rehospitalization. However, results are again based on relatively small, convenience data sets which limit the accuracy and generalizability of the findings.

Data were collected on patients assessed at admission and 6 months later using a number of mental health measures: (*a*) GAS, (*b*) Mental Status Examination Record (MSER), (*c*) Psychiatric Status Schedule (PSS), and (*d*) Family Evaluation Form (FEF). GAS ratings correlated moderately with a 7-point scale of overall severity from the MSER (-.44 at admission and -.62 at 6 months), which suggests the GAS is a global measure of mental health. Correlations with total score on the FEF, another composite index of psychopathology, were small (-.25 and -.19) at admission and moderate (-.52 and -.45) at 6 months. GAS ratings were generally uncorrelated with items measuring specific symptoms of psychological disturbance on other instruments which further suggests the global nature of GAS scores.

In the previous study, the sensitivity of GAS ratings to change in a patient's mental health from admission to 6 months later was compared to other mental health measures noted above. GAS ratings did appear to be somewhat more sensitive than the PSS, FEF, and MSER. However, it is impossible to judge the statistical significance or nonsignificance

of these differences because no further analysis of the apparent trends is reported.

The usefulness of GAS scores for predicting rehospitalization was also studied. Three months after admission for hospitalization, patients then living in the community were rated on the GAS by their therapist ($N = 117$) and independently by a researcher ($N = 133$). From that point, readmission status was determined for the succeeding 3-, 6-, and 9-month periods. One would expect higher GAS ratings to be associated with lower readmission rates. For researchers' data, weak trends were statistically confirmed at the 3- and 6-month intervals, but none at the 9-month. There were no statistically significant trends in the therapists' data. The existing trends in the data were weak, corresponding to a correlation less than .20 (reviewer's estimate) between GAS ratings and readmission status. Thus, the GAS does not appear to be a useful predictor of rehospitalization.

NORMS. One of the most serious limitations of the GAS is the absence of tables providing norm-referenced interpretations for various possible GAS scores. For example, where does a GAS score of 75 fall within the distribution of scores for an appropriate comparison group? Tables of percentiles or standard score equivalents for raw scores on the GAS are essential for complete understanding of results. The GAS interval 71–80 is associated with "minimal symptoms and everyday worries," so a rough criterion-referenced interpretation can be given to a score of 75. However, it would also be essential to know how far above or below the population mean the score of 75 lies and what percentage of the population score lower.

In summary, there are reasons to question the reliability of GAS ratings and to question their usefulness for measuring change in a patient's condition or for predicting the likelihood of rehospitalization. Also there are no tables for deriving norm-referenced interpretations of results. Given these limitations, the GAS should not be recommended for general use at this time. However, because there is some evidence for the validity of GAS scores as global measures of mental health, further development of the instrument may be warranted.

REVIEWER'S REFERENCE

Endicott, J., Spitzer, R. L., Fleiss, J. L., & Cohen, J. (1976). The Global Assessment Scale. *Archives of General Psychiatry, 33,* 766-771.

[148]

Grammatical Analysis of Elicited Language—Simple Sentence Level, Second Edition.

Purpose: "To assess the deaf child's facility in producing the structures of English" using expressive skills at the simple sentence level.

Population: Hearing-impaired ages 5–9.

Publication Dates: 1978–85.
Acronym: GAEL-S.
Scores: 2 overall scores (Prompted Productions, Imitated Productions) plus Mastery Points in 11 categories (Articles, Noun Modifiers, Pronouns, Subject Nouns, Object Nouns, WH-Questions, Verbs, Verb Inflections, Copulas, Prepositions, Conjunctions/Negatives).
Administration: Individual.
Price Data, 1988: $320 per complete kit including scoring forms, profile sheets, toys, manual ('85, 157 pages), and videotape; $17 per 25 transcription sheets and record forms; $6 per 50 summary and profile sheets; $25 per 1/2-inch videotape demonstrating administration of the test to a hearing-impaired child (if not purchased with the kit); $22 per manual.
Time: (60) minutes.
Comments: Pre-Sentence Level (GAEL-P) and Complex Sentence Level (GAEL-C) also available; Mastery Points are "criterion-referenced" and overall scores are norm-referenced.
Authors: Jean S. Moog and Ann E. Geers.
Publisher: Central Institute for the Deaf.

TEST REFERENCES

1. Abraham, S., & Stoker, R. (1988). Language assessment of hearing-impaired children and youth: Patterns of test use. *Language, Speech, and Hearing Services in Schools, 19,* 160-174.
2. Geers, A. E., & Schick, B. (1988). Acquisition of spoken and signed English by hearing-impaired or hearing patients. *Journal of Speech and Hearing Disorders, 53,* 136-143.

Review of the Grammatical Analysis of Elicited Language—Simple Sentence Level by JUNE ELLEN SHEPHERD, Postdoctoral Pediatric Psychology, Fellow in the Pediatric Comprehensive Neurorehabilitation Unit at the Kennedy Institute of Johns Hopkins School of Medicine, Baltimore, MD:

The Grammatical Analysis of Elicited Language (GAEL) instruments are standardized, norm-referenced language evaluation instruments developed for persons interested in evaluating and improving the English language curricula and methods of instructional intervention for children, ages 3 to 12, who are either hearing impaired or language impaired. The GAEL test series consists of three separate tests designed to elicit a representative sample of a child's syntactic mastery of language production. The tests purport to provide in-depth analyses of children's language from the first use of vocalizations up through the use of complex sentences. Language samples obtained during the assessment procedure are evoked through the technique known as "elicited imitation" in which the examiner uses a model sentence to describe a given situation, has the child imitate it, and then prompts the child to produce a sentence of exactly the same structure but with different vocabulary, words, or morphemes.

The rationale given by the authors of the GAEL for choosing the elicited imitation method as the means for obtaining language samples for analyses is that they consider the method to be objective, efficient, and comprehensive. The method is considered objective because the examiner simply notes errors on a score sheet on which target sentences have been preprinted. It is considered efficient because it takes approximately one hour to administer and is easy to score because the child either does or does not produce the target structure. It is considered comprehensive because by providing specific target language in advance, contextual support is given which results in a comprehensive sampling of the child's language proficiency, a sampling that might not have been obtained if only a sample of the child's spontaneous language had been analyzed.

The elicited imitation method used in the GAEL test series is one of the two most commonly used techniques for obtaining language samples for assessment of expressive language. The other commonly used technique is the spontaneous language sampling method in which a spontaneous language sample of approximately 50 utterances is collected in a variety of discourse settings. The method is time consuming and requires the examiner to make word-for-word judgments and, at times, guesses as to precisely what a child said, which is often difficult or impossible if the child's intelligibility is poor or the child has poor signing skills. In addition, when only spontaneous samples are collected for analyses, it is difficult to determine why particular linguistic structures do not appear in the child's spontaneous language sample. When a spontaneous sample fails to yield specific structures, was it because the situation failed to call for the structures, or because the child simply chose not to produce the structures, or in fact, was it because the child was unable to produce the structures (Hughes & Till, 1982)?

On the other hand, when the method of elicited imitation is used to evoke language samples, are the resultant samples an accurate representation of the child's level of grammatical performance and rate of progress in language acquisition, or does the method measure a child's rote memory abilities because imitation relies heavily on rote memory? In the case of oral stimulus sentences, the method may result in an assessment score that represents the measure of a child's speechreading and/or audition receptive skills (de Villiers, 1988). Also, elicited imitation tasks have been criticized because of their lack of communicative intent, an important characteristic of conversational speech (Connell & Myles-Zitzer, 1982).

The answers to such questions are of importance to the clinician or language evaluator involved in the development of intervention procedures for hearing-impaired children or for evaluating the success of language teaching programs for the hearing impaired. Because of the obvious strengths and weaknesses of the two commonly employed language sampling methods, current research efforts are being directed toward the extension of those methods and the development of various other types of elicitation procedures (de Villiers, 1988) that may be more sensitive to a hearing-impaired child's best grammatical performances.

The Grammatical Analysis of Elicited Language—Simple Sentence Level (GAEL-S), one of the three GAEL tests and the subject of the present review, is a standardized procedure to be used in a clinical setting to evaluate the level of language development of hearing-impaired or language-impaired children ranging in age from 5 years to 9 years, 11 months. When one of the goals of assessment is to compare a hearing-impaired child's level of structural English development to normal-hearing children the same age and/or to other hearing-impaired children the same age with the same degree of hearing loss, the GAEL-S is one of the few structural measures available that has norms on a large number of signing and speaking hearing-impaired children with various degrees of hearing impairments.

DESCRIPTION AND ADMINISTRATION. The GAEL-S takes approximately $2^1/_2$ hours to administer and score. The testing session is videotaped so that deviations from target sentences can be transcribed and scored after the administration of the test. Twenty-one games and activities are used to evoke a total of 94 target sentences. The 11 grammatical structures sampled on the test include Articles, Noun Modifiers, Pronouns, Subject Nouns, Object Nouns, WH-Questions, Verbs, Verb Inflections, Copulas, Prepositions, and Conjunctions/Negatives.

To facilitate the administration of the test, the examiner should have the Examiner's Testing Sheet available during the test and should be familiar enough with the procedures described in the test manual to need the testing sheet only as a cue for executing the games and activities constructed to evoke target sentences. All test items should be removed from the kit and arranged on the floor or on a table near the examiner but out of reach of the child. A clear guide to the administration of each of the activities is provided in the test manual. A companion video is also available that demonstrates the administration of the test. The hearing-impaired child selected for the test administration on the video is a model child who is exceptionally well behaved, cooperative, and has an above average attention span. Perhaps a valuable addition to the video would have been to include the demonstration of ways to handle children who have a very short attention span, are oppositional, and/or want to play instead of be tested.

SCORING. After the testing session, the entire session of both the child's Prompted Productions and Imitated Productions are transcribed separately from the video recording on the GAEL-S Transcription Sheet. Guidelines for transcribing spoken productions, signed productions, and total communication productions as well as what deviations not to transcribe are provided in the manual. Most deviations from the target sentence are scored as incorrect; however, the following deviations are scorable: omissions, substitutions, transpositions, and additions.

Errors are then noted on the Score Sheet where every word in each target sentence has been analyzed into one of 11 grammatical categories. The number of correctly produced imitated structures and prompted structures are easily determined by subtracting the number of errors made in each grammatical category from the total number of target structures in each category. The total number of correctly imitated and prompted productions within each grammatical category is then assigned a point that is used for graphing purposes on the front page of the Score Sheet. The resultant Grammatical mastery Profile illustrates the grammatical categories that a child has acquired (MASTERED), is just developing (EMERGING), and those that are BARELY DEVELOPED. A Total Mastery Score is then computed which can be compared to four different reference groups: normal hearing, severely hearing-impaired (orally educated), profoundly deaf (orally educated or total communication), and total communication. Most often hearing-impaired children are compared to children of the same age and hearing ability who either have been orally educated or have participated in a total communication program. Their level of language acquisition can also be compared to normal-hearing children of the same age. This comparison can serve as one index for determining how well the hearing-impaired child might fare in mainstream classes.

STANDARDIZATION. The 1985 edition of the GAEL-S included several improvements over the original 1978 edition, specifically an expansion of the normative sample and a revision of the scoring system; however, no data are provided to establish the representativeness of the final norm sample. The GAEL-S was individually administered to each of the 700 children in the standardization sample: 200 normal-hearing children and 500 hearing-impaired children. The normal-hearing children were obtained from 16 different preschool and day care centers in the St. Louis, Missouri area. Hearing-impaired children were selected from 28 different programs across the country that have received national recognition as a result of their high quality oral or total communication instructional approaches. These programs had been in existence for more than 5 years and had at least eight children who met the criteria for the hearing-impaired subjects.

All of the hearing-impaired children in the sample shared the following characteristics: Their hearing impairment was congenital or acquired during infancy; they had received a consistent communication approach, either oral only or total communication since the age of 3; and they had no other educationally significant handicaps as determined by the administrators of their programs. The hearing-impaired normative sample was divided into three subgroups: severely hearing-impaired children educated in oral programs ($n = 163$), profoundly deaf children educated in oral programs ($n = 160$), and profoundly deaf children educated in total communication programs ($n = 177$).

Four certified teachers of the deaf from the Central Institute for the Deaf in St. Louis, extensively trained in GAEL-S administration procedures, tested both the hearing and hearing-impaired children. The examiner of all the children in the Total Communication programs was a hearing person with deaf parents and was adept at a wide continuum of sign languages ranging from American Sign Language to Signed English.

RELIABILITY AND VALIDITY. Concise summaries are offered to substantiate test-retest reliability (range $r = .88–.96$) and transcriber/scorer reliability for the prompted responses of the orally educated (range $r = .87–.99$), the imitated responses of the orally educated (range $r = .69–1.0$), prompted responses of the total communication samples (range $r = .77–.99$), and the imitated responses of the total communication samples (range $r = .84–.97$). No data or discussion of the test's internal consistency reliability are offered. Because the test items are scored dichotomously, the Kuder-Richardson Formula 20 could have been used to determine the coefficient of internal consistency. In addition, no standard error of measurement was calculated so as to construct the *range* in which the examinee's *true criterion score* (Mastery Points) is likely to fall given their obtained score. This deficit prohibits the examiner from being able to describe the degree of accuracy with which a child's score can be predicted.

A high degree of concurrent validity was established with three measures of expressive language: Scales of Early Communication Skills for Hearing-Impaired Children (Moog & Geers, 1975) (range $r = .81–.83$), Northwestern Syntax Screening Test—Expressive (Lee, 1971) (range $r = .81–.83$), and Grammatical Analysis of Elicited Language—Complex Sentence Level (Moog & Geers, 1979) (range $r = .84–.87$). Predictive validity was reported for identifying preschoolers with significant language delays at or below the 15th percentile for their age groups. Because neither an evaluation of the instrument by other experts nor coefficients of internal consistency were reported, the question of content validity is left unanswered.

SUMMARY. The GAEL-S was standardized on a large number ($n = 500$) of hearing-impaired children and appears to be a useful tool. Elicitation tasks are clever and are enjoyable to children. The test was designed to be used to evaluate hearing and hearing-impaired children with language disabilities who use either spoken or signed English. "This test is appropriate for hearing-impaired children enrolled in oral-aural programs, mainstreamed programs, or total communication programs if the manual communication system used is signed English" (manual, p. 135). Although many clinicians prefer to use the spontaneous language sampling method for language assessment purposes (Muma, 1978), because of presumed ecological validity (i.e., this method can evaluate the communicative intent of a child's conversational speech), the elicited imitation method employed by the GAEL-S can provide an objective comparison of a child's level of English language development to normal hearing children of different ages and to hearing-impaired children with similar backgrounds and hearing losses (de Villiers, 1988). Because the GAEL-S provides an objective means for evaluating a child's progress over time, it can also be used as an objective program evaluation tool. Whenever a hearing-impaired child is being considered for mainstreaming with normal hearing children, the GAEL-S can provide objective data to support or not support the decision to mainstream and can be used to identify children who are language impaired and in need of special education services. Because the overall purpose of most language evaluations is to provide information sufficient to develop effective Individualized Education Plans (IEPs), a norm-referenced tool such as the GAEL-S in combination with a spontaneous language sample would provide a rich, representative sample of a child's current level of language development.

REVIEWER'S REFERENCES

Lee, L. L. (1971). Northwestern Syntax Screening Test. Evanston, IL: Northwestern University Press.

Moog, J. S., & Geers, A. E. (1975). Scales of Early Communication Skills for Hearing-Impaired Children. St. Louis, MO: Central Institute for the Deaf.

Muma, J. R. (1978). *Language handbook: Concepts, assessment, intervention.* Englewood Cliffs, NJ: Prentice-Hall, Inc.

Moog, J. S., & Geers, A. E. (1979). Grammatical Analysis of Elicited Language—Simple Sentence Level. St. Louis, MO: Central Institute for the Deaf.

Connell, P. J., & Myles-Zitzer, C. (1982). An analysis of elicited imitation as a language evaluation procedure. *Journal of Speech and Hearing Disorders, 47,* 390-396.

Hughes, D., & Till, J. A. (1982). A comparison of two procedures to elicit verbal auxiliary and copula in normal kindergarten children. *Journal of Speech and Hearing Disorders, 47,* 310-320.

de Villiers, P. A. (1988). Assessing English syntax in hearing-impaired children: Eliciting production in pragmatically-motivated situations. In R. R. Kretschmer & L. W. Kretschmer (Eds.), *Communication assessment of hearing-impaired children: From conversation to classroom. The Journal of the Academy of Rehabilitative Audiology, 21,* 41-71.

[149]

Gray Oral Reading Tests—Diagnostic.

Purpose: Developed to assess oral reading proficiency in students having difficulties in reading continuous print.

Population: Ages 5-6 to 12-11.
Publication Date: 1991.
Acronym: GORT-D.
Scores, 4: Total Reading, Meaning Cues, Graphic/Phonemic Cues, Function Cues.
Administration: Individual.
Forms, 2: A, B.
Price Data, 1991: $99 per complete kit including student book, 25 each Form A and B record forms, and examiner's manual (78 pages); $19 per student book; $29 per 25 record forms; $26 per manual; $79 per computer scoring system (Apple or IBM).
Time: (50–90) minutes.
Comments: Expanded edition of the Gray Oral Reading Tests—Third Edition.
Authors: Brian R. Bryant and J. Lee Wiederholt.
Publisher: PRO-ED, Inc.

TEST REFERENCES

1. Wolff, P. H., Michel, G. F., Ovrut, M., & Drake, C. (1990). Rate and timing precision of motor coordination in developmental dyslexia. *Developmental Psychology, 26*, 349-359.

Review of the Gray Oral Reading Tests—Diagnostic by WILLIAM R. MERZ, SR., Professor and Coordinator, School Psychology Training Program, California State University, Sacramento, Sacramento, CA:

The Gray Oral Reading Tests—Diagnostic is intended for children 5–12 years old. Seven subtests including Paragraph Reading, Decoding, Word Attack, Word Identification, Morphemic Analysis, Contextual Analysis, and Word Ordering are aggregated to form four composite scores. These scores are Total Reading, Meaning Cues, Graphic/Phonemic Cues, and Function Cues. Subtest raw scores are converted to percentile ranks, standard scores with means of 10 and standard deviations of 3, and grade equivalents. Composite scores are converted to a quotient with a mean of 100 and a standard deviation of 15. The test takes 50–90 minutes to administer. Clear purposes are listed in the manual: identifying readers with problems, determining strengths and weaknesses, documenting progress, and conducting research.

The Gray allows users to conduct miscue analysis along with assessing other skills typically examined by reading tests for children at this age level. Two well-accepted word lists are used along with sequence charts to develop tasks and items for this test. Two experimental versions were tried with small numbers of children at a Texas school prior to 1988. Tasks and items were selected to conform to difficulty and discrimination criteria set by the authors and publisher. The test was normed on 831 examinees from 13 states. Numbers in each age group varied from 70 twelve-year-olds to 130 eight-year-olds. Demographic characteristics of the norm group approximated percentages reported in the *Statistical Abstracts of the United States* (1985).

Evidence that scores can be interpreted reliably is presented through internal consistency reliabilities (Cronbach's alpha) and test-retest reliabilities with alternate forms. Internal consistency reliabilities varied from .73–.99. Alternate form reliabilities ranged from .72–.89. Stability coefficients calculated from alternate form reliability utilizing Anastasi's (1988) procedure ranged from .72–.96.

Three types of evidence are presented for validity of generalizations from scores to the domain being assessed. Content evidence of validity is presented through the description of the development of the subtests. Criterion-referenced evidence is presented from two studies on children in Austin, Texas. Here, the Gray was correlated with either the Screening Children for Related Early Education Needs (Hresko, Reid, Hammill, Ginsburg, & Baroody, 1988) or the Diagnostic Achievement Battery—Second Edition (Newcomer, 1990). Students in both studies were also given the Gray Oral Reading Test—Revised (Wiederholt & Bryant, 1986). Students in grades K–2 were administered the Test of Early Mathematics Ability—Second Edition (Ginsburg & Baroody, 1990). Coefficients for the Screening Children ranged from .30–.83. The lowest correlations were with the math subtests. For the Test of Early Mathematics Ability correlations ranged from .35–.59. For the Gray Oral Reading Tests—Revised, from .20–.68. Correlations for subtests were lower than were correlations for composites. Correlations between the Gray Oral Reading Tests—Diagnostic and the Diagnostic Achievement Battery ranged from .22–.88. In addition, another study related scores on the Gray Diagnostic and the Scholastic Aptitude Scale (Bryant & Newcomer, 1991). Intercorrelations among subtests and composite scores were of acceptable magnitude.

Overall, conclusions drawn from these data support the notion that scores on the Gray Oral Reading Tests—Diagnostic may be used to generalize to ability to read. Difficulties in generalizing from samples of oral reading to silent reading are problematic. However, for children who are acquiring basic reading skills, oral reading samples may be a necessary way to assess what has been learned. This version of the test escapes many of the difficulties associated with coding miscues. The number of deviations from print are counted as the error score rather than counting each kind of miscue separately. The examiner is encouraged to record the miscues.

An erratum sheet was included with the manual to correct several errors related to comprehension responses. Two users queried by this author also challenged the accuracy of yet other comprehension questions.

The Gray Oral Reading Tests—Diagnostic is a valuable instrument in assessing the acquisition of reading skills by 5–12-year-olds. It provides a supplementary look at the process of reading by having the child perform orally and by providing a way of systematically recording correct responses and miscues. It is restricted to paragraph-length passages, so it does not tap comprehension with longer passages; however, neither do the paper-and-pencil reading tests available today. By having the child read orally, it may confound reading ability with performance anxiety or shyness. Possibly, this happens only with a small number of children and can be detected by an observant examiner. The test must be administered individually, so it cannot be used for large scale assessment programs.

REVIEWER'S REFERENCES

Statistical Abstracts of the United States. (1985). Washington, DC: U.S. Bureau of the Census.

Wiederholt, J. L., & Bryant, B. R. (1986). Gray Oral Reading Test—Revised. Austin, TX: PRO-ED, Inc.

Anastasi, A. (1988). *Psychological testing* (6th ed.). New York: Macmillan.

Hresko, W. P., Reid, D. K., Hammill, D. D., Ginsburg, H. P., & Baroody, A. J. (1988). Screening Children for Related Early Education Needs. Austin, TX: PRO-ED, Inc.

Ginsburg, H. P., & Baroody, A. J. (1990). Test of Early Mathematics Ability—Second Edition. Austin, TX: PRO-ED, Inc.

Newcomer, P. L. (1990). Diagnostic Achievement Battery—Second Edition. Austin, TX: PRO-ED, Inc.

Bryant, B. R., & Newcomer, P. (1991). Scholastic Aptitude Scale. Austin, TX: PRO-ED, Inc.

Review of the Gray Oral Reading Tests—Diagnostic by STEVEN A. STAHL, Associate Professor of Reading Education, The University of Georgia, Athens, GA:

The Gray Standardized Oral Reading Paragraphs were the first standardized measure of oral reading fluency. Since 1915, the Gray has undergone four reincarnations. The first two were supervised by William S. Gray; the last two by Brian R. Bryant and J. Lee Wiederholt. The latest version, the Gray Oral Reading Tests—Diagnostic (GORT-D), has to be considered both on its own terms and in the terms of its history.

In 1915, precise and expressive oral reading was the hallmark of a well-educated person; silent reading tended to be deemphasized, even in the upper grades. Since then, oral reading has become less a performance art than an indication of the processes a person uses while reading, as a "window onto the mind" (Goodman & Goodman, 1977), and the emphasis in oral reading tests has shifted from rating enunciation to providing process information. In an attempt to provide better diagnostic information, the GORT-D has been expanded from an oral reading test to a full diagnostic battery consisting of seven subtests—Paragraph Reading, Decoding, Word Attack, Word Identification, Morphemic Analysis, Contextual Analysis, and Word Ordering.

The Paragraph Reading subtest consists of nine passages to be read orally. The first passage was taken from the second edition of the Gray (GORT-R); the remainder from the Formal Reading Inventory (Wiederholt, 1986). Passages were not taken from the GORT-R so that the GORT-D could be used to reassess students who have already taken the GORT-R, and vice versa. (However, I would *not* recommend this, because the concurrent validity correlations between the paragraph subtest on the GORT-D and the GORT-R range between .50 and .59, suggesting that the two measures are correlated only moderately.) Scores on this subtest are based on the child's (*a*) reading rate, (*b*) accuracy, and (*c*) a set of comprehension questions asked following reading.

Traditionally, oral reading miscues are marked so that the test protocol is a transcription of the child's reading. Substitutions, omissions, insertions, and repetitions are all marked, so that the examiner can perform a miscue analysis. Unlike the second edition of the Gray, the GORT-D inexplicably has the examiner mark errors only with slashes, limiting the ability to make interpretive analyses. (Of course, one can use a richer marking system if desired.) Examination of a child's use of contextual and orthographic cues is done through separate subtests. It would be better to get data from *both* the passage reading and the separate subtests, to reinforce diagnostic conclusions.

The manner in which comprehension is assessed is also unusual, at least for an individually administered test. For each passage, there are five multiple-choice questions, which are read aloud as the student follows along. Open-ended questions, the norm in tests like this, would be preferred.

The second subtest, Decoding, consists of 15 sets of consonants or blends and phonograms which, when blended, form nonsense words (e.g., *tr*, *ope*, *trope*). The third subtest, Word Attack, contains eight polysyllabic words in which the child is to find as many little words as possible. For *complacent*, for example, points are given for *cent*, *place*, *lace*, *ace*, and *comp*. These two subtests begin at a relatively advanced stage, knowledge and use of spelling patterns (see Frith, 1985) and may not be suitable for early readers. Although examples are given, the tasks are very different from those children are expected to do in school or elsewhere. Decoding and word attack are best measured by having children read words aloud, as they would be expected to do when reading (Adams, 1990), not through such artificial tasks.

The Word Identification subtest also uses a somewhat unconventional format. Instead of word lists, this test presents words in groups of four. The child is to both read the four words out loud and say which two of the four are related. An item is scored correct only if both conditions are met. The rationale here is that a word should not be considered known if the child does not know its meaning. Children could do poorly on this either because they could not recognize the words or because they did not grasp the relationships between the words. It would be better to avoid the confound and provide separate scores for identification and meaning.

The Morphemic Analysis subtest assesses knowledge of inflectional endings, contractions, and compound words. Inflectional endings are assessed by having the student choose which of four choices fits a cloze blank. This seems to be especially susceptible to dialect interference and should be interpreted cautiously with speakers of nonstandard English. The contraction section has the child give the full form for a series of contractions and the compound word section again uses a cloze format, but provides part of the compound and has the student provide the remainder.

The Contextual Analysis subtest consists of 30 cloze sentences, with an initial consonant or blend provided as a cue for the unknown word. The Word Ordering subtest presents a set of sentence anagrams, which the student is supposed to order into a coherent sentence. Both the Contextual Analysis and Word Ordering subtests are also confounded with word knowledge. On both subtests, the sentences and the words used in the sentences are progressively more difficult.

All seven scores could be combined for a Total reading score, Paragraph Reading and Word Identification for a Meaning Cues score, Decoding and Word Attack for a Graphic/Phonemic Cues score, and Morphemic Analysis, Contextual Analysis, and Word Ordering for a Function Cues score. No justification is given for these groupings. For example, Contextual Analysis would seem to fit better in the Meaning Cues area than would Word Identification, and Morphemic Analysis would seem closer to Word Attack than to Word Ordering.

Reliability of the GORT-D is measured by correlating alternate forms and by examining internal consistency. Alphas range from .96 (Decoding) to .72 (Morphemic Analysis), with three of the coefficients below .80. Overall, reliability is weak for an individually administered test. Alternate form reliabilities tend to be somewhat lower, with five coefficients below .80 and two subtests (Morphemic Analysis and Contextual Analysis) below .70. Only the Paragraph Reading (.87 alternate form and .94 alpha), the Decoding subtest (.90 and .96), and the composites that contain these subtests have adequate reliability. I would advise caution in interpreting scores from the other subtests and certainly would look at alternative data sources before making a recommendation based on these scores.

Concurrent validity for this test is also lower than desired. The median correlation with a number of different measures is .53. The test manual calls this correlation "moderate," but such a moderate correla-

tion does not provide evidence that the GORT-D is measuring reading in the same way as the comparison tests. Looking at a few randomly chosen, oral reading measures, these concurrent validity coefficients are markedly below those of the Durrell Analysis of Reading Difficulty (Durrell & Catterson, 1980) which range from .56 to .96 for similar subtests and the Qualitative Reading Inventory (Leslie & Caldwell, 1990) which range from .73 to .27, with the median of .71.

One reason for low concurrent validity may be the artificiality of some of the passages. This was especially true of the older Gray, written in the era of *Fun with Dick and Jane* by its author. This is inexcusable now, with the emphasis on more "natural" texts. It has been found that children will deviate from poorly written "primerese" in order to make sense of what they read (Simons & Ammon, 1988). Thus, poorly or awkwardly written texts could add to the number of errors children make. Because the coding system recommended does not lend itself to analysis, an examiner might not distinguish between miscues that make the text sound better and real oral reading errors.

Many of the flaws of the GORT-D—the less-than-adequate reliabilities and concurrent validity coefficients for some of the subtests, and the awkward or artificial subtests and passages—can be found on some competing diagnostic batteries. But it is the heritage of the Gray that makes one expect more.

REVIEWER'S REFERENCES

Goodman, K. S., & Goodman, Y. M. (1977). Learning about psycholinguistic processes by analyzing oral reading. *Harvard Educational Review, 47*, 317-333.

Durrell, D. D., & Catterson, J. H. (1980). Durrell Analysis of Reading Difficulty. San Antonio, TX: The Psychological Corporation.

Frith, U. (1985). Beneath the surface of developmental dyslexia. In K. E. Patterson, J. C. Marshall, & M. Coltheart (Eds.), *Surface dyslexia: Neuropsychological and cognitive studies of phonological reading* (pp. 301-330). Hillsdale, NJ: Erlbaum.

Wiederholt, J. L. (1986). Formal Reading Inventory. Austin, TX: PRO-ED, Inc.

Simons, H. D., & Ammon, P. (1988). Primerese miscues. In J. E. Readence & R. S. Baldwin (Eds.), *Dialogues in literacy research: Thirty-seventh yearbook of the National Reading Conference* (pp. 115-124). Chicago: National Reading Conference.

Adams, M. J. (1990). *Beginning to read: Thinking and learning about print.* Cambridge, MA: M.I.T. Press.

Leslie, L., & Caldwell, J. (1990). Qualitative Reading Inventory. New York: Harper Collins.

[150]

Group Achievement Identification Measure.

Purpose: "To determine the degree to which children exhibit the characteristics of underachievers so that preventative or curative efforts may be administered."
Population: Grades 5–12.
Publication Date: 1986.
Acronym: GAIM.
Scores, 6: Competition, Responsibility, Achievement Communication, Independence/Dependence, Respect/Dominance, Total.
Administration: Group.

Price Data, 1988: $10 per individual inventory including prepaid computer scoring by publisher; $80 per class set of 30 inventories including prepaid computer scoring by publisher; manual for administration and interpretation (12 pages) included with test orders.
Time: (30) minutes.
Comments: Self-report inventory.
Author: Sylvia B. Rimm.
Publisher: Educational Assessment Service, Inc.

Review of the Group Achievement Identification Measure by ROBERT K. GABLE, Professor of Educational Psychology, and Associate Director, Bureau of Educational Research and Service, University of Connecticut, Storrs, CT:

The Group Achievement Identification Measure (GAIM) is a 90-item self-report measure that employs a 5-point Likert response format (*No, To a Small Extent, Average, More Than Average, Definitely*). No empirical evidence is presented to support the "equal interval" nature of this atypical Likert scale.

The 10-page Manual for Administration and Interpretation is extremely superficial and presents little comprehensive information regarding theoretical or empirical support for the measure. For example, the author states the "GAIM was created based on the psychological practice" of the author (p. 1) and refers readers to her nontheoretical book containing case studies of children's problems and strategies for assistance. No literature or appropriate judgmental data are presented to properly support the content validity of the measure.

Although the manual indicates the GAIM is appropriate for grade 5–12 students, this reviewer doubts if lower grade students can reliably respond to a 90-item measure. Brief mention is made of percentiles, normal curve equivalents, and stanine scores; these scores are inadequately defined in a footnote (p. 3).

The most serious problems with the GAIM rest in the vague description of the process followed in its development and the empirical support offered for reliability and validity, which fall inexcusably short of the criteria set forth in the *Standards for Educational and Psychological Testing* (AERA, APA, & NCME, 1985). For example, reference is made to an item analysis that indicated "some items discriminated well for one sex and not the other" (p. 4), but no data are presented. Respectable Hoyt reliability coefficients were calculated for male (.92) and female (.90) scores on the 90 items, but no reliability data are presented for the five subscore areas assessed. Users are presented no empirical evidence that the subscore items are adequate samples of student characteristics from the intended domains of content, and thus cannot be confident that the subscores yield accurate assessments. Further, no stability reliabilities are reported.

A section on construct validity (p. 4) states the "construct validity of GAIM was based on items which Rimm used in developmental history interviews with parents of underachieving children." This evidence appears to address content validity and is not sufficient to support construct validity. The comment that "further theoretical background is provided" in the available book (p. 4) is insufficient, given the flyer for the book states that "the book is not theoretical." Construct validity evidence in the form of factor analysis of the items to support empirically the judgmentally designated item clusters is essential, but missing. No evidence is presented to indicate the factor structure of the student responses is constant across grades 5–12.

A section is presented on criterion-related validity that states GAIM scores were compared with teacher ratings of student achievement (p. 4). A criterion-related validity correlation of .43 is reported for a sample of 215 students. No description of the sample (i.e., grade level) is presented and no data are presented for the subscales. The overall correlation of .43, while not interpreted in the context of theoretical expectations, appears more likely to address construct validity than criterion-related validity.

A section on norms states that the GAIM was normed on "over 950 school aged children" from various community types and geographic areas (p. 5). A more specific description of the norms is appropriate. The norms are apparently provided during the computer-scoring service, but no norm tables appear in the Manual for Administration and Interpretation. A final section in the manual offers well-written interpretive descriptions of the five subscales included in the 90 items. Unfortunately, the manual provides little judgmental (i.e., content validity) and no empirical (i.e., construct validity and alpha reliability) support for the item groupings employed to define the subscales.

Overall, in its current form the GAIM manual provides inadequate judgmental and empirical support for the validity and reliability of the proposed assessment of the "characteristics which distinguish achieving students from underachievers" (p. 1). Until these data are available in a manner consistent with the *Standards*, users cannot be confident that scores on the GAIM are meaningful or accurate.

REVIEWER'S REFERENCE

American Educational Research Association, American Psychological Association, & National Council on Measurement in Education. (1985). *Standards for educational and psychological testing.* Washington, DC: American Psychological Association, Inc.

Review of the Group Achievement Identification Measure by JEFFREY JENKINS, Attorney, KeLeher & McLeod, P.A., Albuquerque, NM:

On its face, the Group Achievement Identification Measure (GAIM) seems to offer the user a thoughtful measure of student "underachievement."

Closer examination, however, reveals shortcomings that leave the instrument with questionable usefulness.

GAIM was based on a theory of underachievement derived from the clinical psychology practice of its author, Sylvia B. Rimm. This theory is summarized in general terms in the GAIM Manual for Administration and Interpretation as "the inability to deal with competition was key to causing children to underachieve." The user is referred to Dr. Rimm's book, *Underachievement Syndrome: Causes and Cures* for further theoretical background and suggestions on reversing underachievement. Because the theoretical debate over the concept of underachievement continues, such lack of more specific theoretical justification for GAIM presents a significant stumbling block to confident recommendation of the instrument.

The measure is presented in a format clearly readable for students in grades 5–12, and simply consists of a series of 90 statements with which students are to agree *definitely, more than average, average, to a small extent,* or *no*. The items, such as "The most important part of school for me is my social life" and "I believe I am smarter than my grades show me to be," comprise five dimensions and are scored by the publisher. The manual offers no guidance on how scoring is accomplished, nor is any indication given of which items fall into the various dimensions. Brief descriptions of the five dimensions are given. Total scores are reported as percentiles and NCEs (normal curve equivalents) with dimension scores reported as stanines.

Instructions for administration are straightforward, and teachers are free to explain words to students. No time limit is imposed, but the suggested usual time required is 30 minutes. Students mark in pencil on the instrument itself.

The manual offers very brief sections on reliability, validity, and norms, which are altogether inadequate for weighing the sufficiency of these characteristics. Hoyt reliability coefficients are reported as .92 for males and .90 for females, but no specific information is given on how these coefficients were computed, raising questions about the GAIM's actual reliability. A more common measure of reliability should have been reported with a simple explanation of its basis. In addition, although dimension scores are reported, no evidence of their reliability is offered.

Criterion-related validity was explored by correlating the GAIM scores of 215 students with teacher ratings of student achievement, resulting in a validity coefficient of .43. A value of this magnitude is generally adequate for this type of measure, and may support the instrument's purpose of differentiating between underachievers and achieving students.

In support of construct validity, the manual offers the following: "Construct validity of GAIM was based on items which Rimm used in developmental history interviews with parents of underachieving children." A one-sentence explanation of Dr. Rimm's theory is then offered. Given the theory-laden nature of this instrument, construct validity is of central importance. However, essentially no information is offered in support of the instrument's construct validity. Moreover, the five specific dimensions on which scores are obtained purport to reflect student strengths and weaknesses, yet no support for their presentation as separable constructs is offered. An article by Rimm (1985) suggests the dimensions are derived from a factor analytic study, but no specific information from such a study was given. These are flaws that should be remedied before any user gives serious consideration to the instrument.

Normative information is derived from "950 school aged children" including "rural, urban and suburban children as well as those representing different geographical areas of the country." Although more specific information about the norm group would be helpful, such as numbers of male and female students in each grade, the norm group is probably sufficient for the instrument's purpose.

The GAIM is an instrument presenting itself as a measure of underachievement, yet the publisher offers little specific information to support this claim. The instrument may have some usefulness for tentative assessments of students' underachievement, but insufficient evidence is available to warrant recommendation of even this. At this time, use of the GAIM should be limited to research settings.

REVIEWER'S REFERENCE

Rimm, S. (1985, November-December). Identifying underachievement: The characteristics approach. *G/C/T*, pp. 2-5.

[151]
Group Process Questionnaire.

Purpose: "Designed to help groups assess how effective they are."
Population: Adults.
Publication Date: 1988.
Scores, 29 to 145: My Rating, Group Rating, and How I Did scores for Behavior Scale (Task Behavior, Maintenance Behavior), for Total Scale, and for 12 optional categories (Initiating, Seeking Information or Opinions, Giving Information or Opinions, Clarifying and Elaborating, Summarizing, Consensus-Testing, Listening, Harmonizing, Gatekeeping, Encouraging, Compromising, Standard Setting/Testing), and My Rating and Group Rating scores for 5 additional optional categories (Leadership, Time Utilization, Results, Acceptance, Inclusion).
Administration: Group.
Price Data: Available from publisher.
Time: (60) minutes.

Comments: Scale for ratings by group members and for self-ratings.
Authors: Richard Hill, D. Joseph Fisher, Tom Webber, and Kathleen A. Fisher.
Publisher: Orion International, Ltd. (also distributed by Organization Design and Development, Inc.)

[152]

Guidance Centre Classroom Achievement Tests.

Purpose: "To assist teachers in making informed decisions about the success of their instructional practices and the progress of their students."
Publication Dates: 1979–85.
Acronym: GC CATS.
Administration: Group.
Levels, 2: Elementary, Secondary.
Price Data, 1987: $1.75 per test; $55 per 35 of any 1 test; $1.75 per teacher's manual for any test.
Time: (45–60) minutes per test.
Comments: Curriculum-based achievement tests.
Author: Merlin Wahlstrom (Background, Scope, and Interpretation manual).
Publisher: Guidance Centre [Canada].
a) ELEMENTARY LEVEL.
Population: Grades 3–8.
Scores: 24 tests in 6 domains: Summative Mathematics, Scientific Processes, Scientific Literacy/Knowledge: Mathematics, Summative Reading, Reading, Language Arts: Writing.
Comments: Subtests available as separates.
b) SECONDARY LEVEL.
Population: Grades 9–12.
Scores: 22 tests in 9 domains: Reading, English/Writing, Chemistry, Consumer Education, Consumer Mathematics, Algebra, Number and Number Operations, Geometry and Measurement, Summative Mathematics.
Comments: Subtests available as separates.
[The publisher advised in June 1990 that this test is now out of print—Ed.]

Review of the Guidance Centre Classroom Achievement Tests by PAUL C. BURNETT, Lecturer in Psychology, Queensland University of Technology—Kelvin Grove Campus, Brisbane, Australia:

The Guidance Centre Classroom Achievement Tests (GC CATS) consist of 46 curriculum-based achievement tests designed and developed as classroom achievement tests based upon the instructional objectives for each curriculum domain. The tests are based on the instructional objectives from the Canadian Province of British Columbia's curriculum guide. The use of these tests in other provinces and countries is extremely limited, given the differences in curriculum content and the variation in the sequence of instruction that exist from classroom to classroom, province to province, and country to country. The eight-page manual, which addresses the background, scope, and interpretation of the tests, partly addresses this issue by stating all items should be reviewed by teachers outside the Province of British Columbia (B.C.) to determine if instruction in their classrooms has covered the knowledge and skills required to answer each item. Consequently, the use of this test outside B.C. is questionable because of (*a*) the differences that exist in curriculum and instruction across educational environments, and (*b*) the laborious task of evaluating the suitability of each item for a particular classroom.

This review will now focus on the use of the GC CATS in British Columbia. The tests were developed using a curriculum-based criterion-referenced approach. There are 24 tests in three curriculum areas (Mathematics, Reading, and Language Arts: Writing) for elementary children (grades 3–8) and 22 tests in six curriculum areas (Consumer Education, Mathematics, Reading, Chemistry, Algebra, and English: Writing) for secondary level students (grades 9–12). The elementary tests are interpreted using either broad classifications such as (*a*) at or above grade expectations, (*b*) below grade expectations, and (*c*) inconclusive; a 5-point scale, A = Excellent, B = Very Good, C = Average, P = Pass, and F = Fail; means, standard deviations, percentile ranks, and stanines; or a combination of the above. The secondary level tests are interpreted using percentile ranks, stanines, means, and standard deviations, or grades of A, B, C, P, and F as above. Each of the 46 tests has its own manual, which addresses test development, administration, scoring, and interpretation. The content of these manuals varies greatly and the criteria for interpreting the results are not always consistent. For example, an "A" on one test means an excellent performance in terms of some set criteria, but "A" on another test indicates the student is reading at an independent level. Some manuals report norm-referenced data and statistical characteristics such as means, standard deviation, reliability, and standard error of measurement, but most do not. The few reliability coefficients reported are computed using different methods such as Hoyt's analysis of variance procedure for examining internal consistency and the Kuder-Richardson 20 formula. Each manual presents a different combination of information for interpreting the results of the test and for evaluating the psychometric properties of the instrument. No information pertaining to validity is presented. The inconsistent presentation of information is a major weakness of these tests.

One problem inherent in an externally developed evaluation of curriculum objectives is that many teachers view the tests as an assessment of their teaching effectiveness and consequently teach to the tests' content. Additionally, it is hoped each curriculum is tailored to the needs of the students in the class. Tailoring a curriculum to student needs requires flexibility, and teachers are not likely to be flexible if an externally developed curriculum evaluation is used to assess student achievement. An alternative exists with teachers assessing student performance in terms of curriculum objectives but with the understanding of the uniqueness of their class. The curriculum implemented in individual classrooms to cater adequately to student needs may vary from the general curriculum outlined by an educational authority.

In summary, the GC CATS is a curriculum-based criterion-referenced test developed using the Province of British Columbia's curriculum. It is not recommended for use outside British Columbia because of curriculum differences and questionable suitability of items. The test manuals are inconsistent in the presentation of necessary information. The 46 manuals present little reliability data and there is no information about validity. A variety of methods for interpreting results are presented. Teachers in British Columbia may find the tests useful because they are based on familiar curriculum goals and instructional objectives.

Review of the Guidance Centre Classroom Achievement Tests by ROLAND H. GOOD, III, Assistant Professor of Counseling and Educational Psychology, College of Education, University of Oregon, Eugene, OR:

The Guidance Centre Classroom Achievement Tests (GC CATS) consist of 46 tests covering Mathematics (24 tests), Reading (10 tests), Science (6 tests), English (4 tests), and Consumer Education (2 tests). Only 41 tests were available for review. The tests are intended for use in grades 3 through 12, with 11 of the tests intended for the 7/8 grade level. Between 1 and 6 tests are available for other grade levels. Although the mathematics area and the 7/8 grade level are well represented, there is little consistency in the availability of tests for other academic areas across grade levels.

The purpose, description, instructions, norms, and interpretive guidelines are available in a separate Teacher's Manual for each test. All of the teacher's manuals contain information that is partially redundant with other manuals, and yet there also are substantial differences among the tests. Separate manuals allow test users to read and evaluate only that material directly relevant to the tests they are using. However, no overall teacher's manual or technical manual is available, which makes evaluation of the package of tests more difficult as, for example, when a school district would consider adopting the entire set of tests. This review focuses on those characteristics that typify the entire set of tests, although individual exceptions can usually be found. In the materials reviewed, the manual labeled Grade 4/5 Reading: Content Areas contained instead the manual for another test by mistake. Consequently, the Grade 4/5 Reading: Content Areas test is not included in this review.

Two types of tests are included in the GC CATS. The eight tests intended to provide only summative information regarding the mastery of curriculum objectives are to be used at only one grade level. The remaining tests are intended to provide summative information at one grade level and formative information at the next grade level. For example, a 3/4-level test covers the curriculum objectives for grade 3. When administered at the end of grade 3, the test provides summative information regarding student mastery of the curriculum. When administered at the beginning of grade 4, the test is intended to provide formative information regarding pupil strengths and weaknesses to guide instruction.

Most of the tests are timed tests consisting of 40 multiple-choice items to be completed in 45 minutes. The six Reading tests, two Consumer Education tests, and two Summative Mathematics tests are not timed, however. The grade 11 and 12 summative tests are timed and require 100 to 120 minutes to administer. Production-type responses are required for three English tests where the students are required to write two letters, a newspaper article, and several short paragraphs, and to edit several short passages. Production-type responses also are required for the grade 11 and 12 Algebra tests where the students are required to solve problems and graph functions. Scoring of production-type responses is subjective, although detailed scoring rules and criteria are provided. In addition, optional, open-ended questions with scoring criteria are provided for the six Reading tests.

SCORES. Letter grades (A, B, C, P[Pass], and F) indicating the level of student performance are available for all but two of the tests. For the most part, letter grades are based on experienced teacher judgment. The difficulty inherent in this approach is illustrated for the two Language Arts, grade 7/8 tests which were the only tests to report the frequency of each letter grade. For one of the tests, 6% of the normative sample received an A or a B. In contrast, 47% received an A or a B for the other test. Relying on teacher judgment to establish letter-grade criteria may have resulted in similar disparities for other tests as well. A variety of other scores also are available, including percentiles (21 tests), quartiles (6 tests), stanines (14 tests), and percent correct (14 tests). For 11 of the tests, the only norm-referenced information provided is whether the score is above or below the mean. Although the interpretation of subtest performance is recommended for 27 tests, subtest percentile ranks are provided only for 3 tests. For the remaining 24 tests, whether the subtest raw score is above or below the mean is the only nomative information provided.

NORMS. Norm-referenced information is provided for all but two of the tests, based on sample sizes ranging from 556 students to 30,000 students. All normative samples consist of students in British Columbia, Canada. The normative sample is described as either random or representative of British Columbia students for 14 of the tests. However, none of the tests describe the sample distribution by gender, race, socioeconomic status, geographic location within the province, or language spoken in the home. Test consumers would be wise to exercise caution in their interpretation of normative information when the tests are used with students in British Columbia. The norms are not appropriate for use in other locations.

RELIABILITY. No evidence of test reliability is reported for 16 of the tests. For those subtests without reliability information, the test consumer is completely responsible for demonstrating test reliability sufficient for intended uses. Reliability estimates sufficient for important individual educational decisions (.90 or above) are reported for 7 tests and reliability estimates sufficient for screening decisions (.80 to .89) are reported for 12 tests. Reliability estimates sufficient for group data and administrative decisions only (.71 to .79) are reported for 5 tests. Internal consistency estimates are the only type of reliability information provided, although the type of reliability was not indicated for 10 of the tests.

Estimates of interrater agreement are not provided for those tests requiring production-type responses. Less than satisfactory interrater agreement is reported for selected items and scales of the English 12: Writing test, but the standards by which satisfactory/unsatisfactory agreement were judged are not reported. The test consumer is left with some doubt regarding the extent to which the scoring criteria are clear enough for acceptable interrater consistency.

VALIDITY EVIDENCE. In general, excellent support is provided for the content validity of the tests with respect to the curriculum employed in the province of British Columbia as represented by the 1978 (24 tests), 1981 (4 tests), and 1982 (2 tests) curriculum guides. The close correspondence of the tests to the British Columbia Curriculum is a significant strength of the GC CATS, although it also limits the range of settings where the GC CATS would be appropriate. A table of specifications is provided for all of the tests, and 29 of the tables directly reference the objectives of the British Columbia Curriculum. In addition, teachers in British Columbia contributed substantially to the design and development of most, if not all, of the tests. The limited number of production-type responses limits both the types of objectives and the level of mastery that can be evaluated. For most items, the students must only select the correct answer from four alternatives.

No evidence is provided regarding the tests' criterion-related or construct validity. In particular, evidence that students performing well on the GC CATS were also judged by their classroom teachers to be mastering the curriculum objectives would provide valuable support for the GC CATS.

SUMMARY. Teachers in British Columbia using the British Columbia Curriculum of 1978 who are seeking a classroom achievement test for one of the grade-academic area combinations supplied by the GC CATS will want to consider these tests carefully. Teachers in other settings using other curricula would be well advised to keep looking.

[153]
The Hall-Tonna Inventory of Values.

Purpose: To be used for "identifying present value priorities and the skills needed for future growth in this area."

Population: Ages 16 and over.

Publication Dates: 1985–90.

Scores: 125 values comprising 50 descriptors: Self-Preservation, Wonder/Awe, Safety/Survival, Security, Sensory Pleasure, Property/Economics, Family/Belonging, Self Worth, Belonging (Liked), Care/Nurture, Control/Duty, Tradition, Social Prestige, Work/Confidence, Worship/Creed, Play, Achievement/Success, Administration/Management, Institution, Patriotism/Loyalty, Education, Workmanship/Technology, Law/Duty, Equality, Actualization/Wholeness, Service, Autonomy, Empathy/Generosity, Law/Guide, Personal Authority, Adaptability/Flexibility, Health/Well-Being, Search, New Order, Dignity/Justice, Art/Beauty, Insight, Contemplation, Accountability, Community/Support, Detachment, Corporate Mission, Research/Knowledge, Intimacy, Wisdom, Word/Prophet, Community/Simplicity, Transcendence/Ecority, Convivial Technology, Rights/World Order.

Administration: Individual or group.

Editions, 2: Lifestyle (secular), Discern (religious).

Price Data, 1990: $25 per individual prepaid report including workbook (indicate Lifestyle, Discern, Lifestyle II [group member], or Discern II [group member]; $5 per specialized supplementary options (indicate Leadership, Faith and Ethics, or Skills/Time and Vocation); price data for manual ('86, 148 pages) and other test materials available from publisher.

Time: (30–40) minutes.

Comments: Self-administered; must be computer scored by publisher who returns a 15–35-page personalized report and workbook appropriate to the setting.

Authors: Brian P. Hall, Benjamin Tonna (Inventory), Oren Harari (manual), Barbara D. Ledig (manual and workbooks), and Murray Tondow (manual).

Publisher: Behaviordyne, Inc.

Review of The Hall-Tonna Inventory of Values by ELEANOR E. SANFORD, Research Consultant, Division of Accountability Services/Research, North Carolina Department of Public Instruction, Raleigh, NC:

The Hall-Tonna Inventory of Values (H-T) is based on over 20 years of research on the nature of values by Brian P. Hall (1986) and reported in *The Genesis Effect: Personal and Organizational Transformations*. The H-T is based on the rationale that values are developmental; that is, the development of an individual's value system is divided into discernable phases (technical manual, p. 2). The test can be administered individually or in a group setting to individuals age 16 and older and takes approximately 30–40 minutes to complete.

The results of the H-T can be reported for an individual and/or for a group as a whole and for secular or religious environments. The test can be scored only by a computer algorithm by Behaviordyne, Inc., and produces a 15- to 35-page report. It is suggested the results be interpreted with a counselor as part of the counseling process using the workbooks supplied with the type of report received. Three additional reports may also be received for the individual or the group: Leadership; Faith and Ethics; and Skills, Time, and Vocation.

The H-T consists of 77 forced-choice items measuring 125 values, 50 value descriptors, 8 developmental stages, and 7 developmental cycles. Each item consists of four responses assessing four different values and a "not applicable at this time" response. The technical manual does not explain which items measure which values, how the value descriptor scores are derived, or how a developmental cycle is specified.

The H-T has adequate reliability—stability and consistency. The test-retest reliabilities range from .66 for specific values to .75 for developmental level (unclear in manual whether this is the developmental stage or cycle). Using the two versions of coefficient alpha (one correcting for the possibility of unequal variances in the two halves of the test and one more general), the internal consistency reliability coefficients ranged from .66 for specific values to .92 for developmental level.

The H-T was subjected to two content validity investigations. The first study was to standardize the language of the items so that they accurately reflected the value definitions and stage of development. From this process 120 value definitions were confirmed and 5 new ones were added. The second investigation asked a group of respondents to match H-T items with value definitions with a criterion of 80% agreement between the respondents. It is unclear from Hall's book, *The Genesis Effect* (where much of the technical information for the test is found), how many items failed to meet the 80% criterion (one source says 25% and another says 25 items—16.4%). These items were classified as ambiguous, but have not been removed from the test, and therefore could reduce the validity of any further results obtained from the test. The specific

values are not identified and it is possible they could all be from one particular developmental stage.

The intercorrelations of the 125 values on the H-T appear to be relatively independent (intercorrelations range from -.50 to .53, but cluster around 0). Values are assigned to a developmental stage based on theory only—nothing has been done to investigate the underlying factor structure of the values to see if they accurately measure the eight developmental stages they are hypothesized to measure.

The construct validity of the H-T has been investigated by administering it in conjunction with the Allport-Vernon-Lindzey Study of Values (AVL). The authors of the H-T state that is has a broader domain of values than the AVL and that the AVL categories relate primarily to the Phase I and II categories of the H-T (i.e., the AVL Economic category corresponds with seven of the H-T values). Only 31 of the 125 values on the H-T matched with the AVL categories (from Phase I and II only). Moderate consistency was found between the top three value categories on the H-T and the AVL (generally two of the three matched, but in a different order). Nothing has been done to examine the construct validity of the remaining 94 H-T values.

The contrasted groups method was suggested to examine the construct validity of the H-T by making "predictions about how different groups with 'known' characteristics should score on the H-T and then test these hypotheses" (technical manual, p. 25). The value selections from gender groups, age groups, cultural groups, and occupational groups were described and do appear to differentiate the various groups, but none of the hypotheses concerning differences were presented and/or empirically tested. Further construct validity studies were suggested and should be undertaken such as peer studies, individual assessments, and studies modeled after the multitrait-multimethod design of Campbell and Fiske (1959). Longitudinal support should be obtained to discover if the H-T is instrumental in the process of values clarification for individuals over time given the premise that values are learned and developed over time and are modified and shaped by circumstances.

Additional empirical support must be obtained for the Hall-Tonna Inventory of Values before it can be used to make predictions and judgements about the value development and change of individuals. The Technical Manual should be revised to include the information presented in Hall's book *The Genesis Effect*. The H-T is a descriptive tool for the exploration of values for the individual and for groups (such as the values of an organization or department as a whole). The workbooks aid the individual and/or group in a thought-provoking and insightful process of values examination where the individual is a participant in the process rather than a spectator.

REVIEWER'S REFERENCES

Campbell, D. T., & Fiske, D. W. (1959). Convergent and discriminant validation by the multitrait-multimethod matrix. *Psychological Bulletin, 56,* 81-105.

Hall, B. P. (1986). *The Genesis effect: Personal and organizational transformations.* New York: Paulist Press.

[154]
Happiness Measures.

Purpose: Assesses a respondent's perception of amount of happiness or unhappiness and estimate of time experienced as happy or unhappy.
Population: Ages 16 and over.
Publication Dates: 1980–87.
Acronym: HM.
Scores, 5: Scale, Happy Percentage Estimate, Unhappy Percentage Estimate, Neutral Percentage Estimate, Combination.
Administration: Group.
Manual: No manual.
Price Data: Available from publisher.
Time: (1–5) minutes.
Comments: Test booklet title is *Emotions Questionnaire.*
Author: Michael W. Fordyce.
Publisher: Cypress Lake Media.

Review of the Happiness Measures by WILLIAM A. STOCK, Professor of Exercise Science, Arizona State University, Tempe, AZ:

The Happiness Measures (HM) is most appropriately considered a social indicator instrument, historically linked to research in the domain of subjective well-being—a domain whose origins are primarily in general social survey research and social gerontology. Well-established constructs in this domain include mood, happiness, life satisfaction, and morale. The HM is a two-item instrument requiring a global assessment of degree of happiness, and of amount of time spent in happy, neutral, and unhappy states. The principal item, tapping degree or intensity of happiness, may be modified to assess any reasonable span of time. Although appropriate for a variety of research settings in which a global index of happiness is required, users are advised not to adopt it for clinical or diagnostic purposes.

In reviewing research on happiness, the test author (Fordyce, in press) competently places the HM in a network of theoretical constructs and empirical evidence. Further, he provides a variety of reliability and validity information on the instrument. Based on this reviewer's knowledge, Fordyce's claim that the HM displays equivalent or better reliability and validity than comparable subjective well-being measures is reasonable.

Generally, Fordyce obtained psychometric information using samples of community college students, a population younger than the general population. Use of representative samples from the general population would not, in my opinion, significantly alter the magnitude of estimates of reliability. However, these estimates would likely lead to lower mean scores than those reported by Fordyce, because samples from older populations historically have self-reported lower levels of happiness. Therefore, empirical support for the HM would be strengthened by expanding the normative base to include persons more representative of the general population. Also needed are estimates of standard errors of measurement (currently absent from the documentation). As significant gender, age, and ethnic differences have been consistently reported for subjective well-being measures, the empirical base of the HM should include reliability and validity information obtained within levels of these classifications.

Reported, short-term, test-retest reliabilities range from .98 to .62 as the retest period goes from 2 days to 4 months, and are consistent with results reported in psychometric summaries of the field (Okun & Stock, 1987a). Further, numerous concurrent validity estimates are reported both with other scales of subjective well-being (e.g., happiness, life satisfaction, positive mood), and with a variety of divergent constructs (e.g., anxiety, depression, negative affect). These estimates are consistent in magnitude and direction with those found in the field. Finally, experimental evidence from studies conducted by Fordyce indicates that HM scores change in a theoretically relevant manner after interventions designed to evaluate happiness.

This instrument is acceptable for use in research where happiness is the construct of interest and where the user is interested in assessment of a present-oriented time perspective (e.g., the last two weeks, the past few months, the past year). In addition, the user should be aware that subjective indices of well-being have stronger relationships with each other than with objective indicators of quality of life (Okun & Stock, 1987b). Therefore, a subjective index should not be used as a substitute in situations where objective quality of life is the construct of primary interest. Some appropriate uses of the HM would be as an outcome measure in program evaluations, in general and local social surveys, and in research assessing *mild* interventions designed to increase feelings of well-being. The measure should not be used as a diagnostic tool, nor should it be used to evaluate the impact of clinical interventions. Clinical interventions deal with stable negative traits (e.g., depression and neuroticism) that are manifestations of an independent construct, negative affectivity (Watson & Clark, 1984), and a different measurement tool is required. In clinical settings, the objective is to demonstrate effective long-term decreases in behaviors associated with negative affectivity, and here the user should select from among the well-established clinical scales.

REVIEWER'S REFERENCES

Watson, D., & Clark, L. A. (1984). Negative affectivity: The disposition to experience aversive emotional states. *Psychological Bulletin, 96*, 465-490.

Okun, M. A., & Stock, W. A. (1987a). The construct validity of subjective well-being measures: An assessment via quantitative research syntheses. *Journal of Community Psychology, 15*, 481-492.

Okun, M. A., & Stock, W. A. (1987b). Correlates and components of subjective well-being among the elderly. *Journal of Applied Gerontology, 6*, 95-112.

Fordyce, M. W. (in press). A review of research on the Happiness Measures: A sixty-second index of happiness of mental health. *Social Indicators Research.*

[155]

Hassles and Uplifts Scales, Research Edition.

Purpose: To identify sources of stress and positive aspects of daily living that help counteract the damaging effects of stress.
Population: Adults.
Publication Date: 1989.
Administration: Group.
Price Data, 1990: $13.50 per 25 test booklets (specify Hassles or Uplifts Scale); $16 per 25 Combined Scales test booklets; $19.50 per manual (43 pages); $20 per specimen set (includes manual and 1 of each test booklet).
Time: (10–15) minutes per test.
Comments: Self-administered; tests available as separates.
Authors: Richard S. Lazarus and Susan Folkman.
Publisher: Consulting Psychologists Press, Inc.
a) THE DAILY HASSLES SCALE.
Scores, 2: Frequency, Severity.
b) THE UPLIFTS SCALE.
Scores, 2: Frequency, Intensity.
c) THE COMBINED HASSLES AND UPLIFTS SCALES.
Scores, 2: Hassles, Uplifts.

TEST REFERENCES

1. Zarski, J. J., Bubenzer, D. L., & West, J. D. (1986). Social interest, stress, and the prediction of health status. *Journal of Counseling and Development, 64*, 386-389.
2. Barone, D. F., Caddy, G. R., Katell, A. D., Roselione, F. B., & Hamilton, R. A. (1988). The Work Stress Inventory: Organizational stress and job risk. *Educational and Psychological Measurement, 48*, 141-154.
3. DeLongis, A., Folkman, S., & Lazarus, R. S. (1988). The impact of daily stress on health and mood: Psychological and social resources as mediators. *Journal of Personality and Social Psychology, 54*, 486-495.
4. Swan, G. E., Denk, C. E., Parker, S. D., Carmelli, D., Furze, C. T., & Rosenman, R. H. (1988). Risk factors for late relapse in male and female ex-smokers. *Addictive Behaviors, 13*, 253-266.
5. Banez, G. A., & Compas, B. E. (1990). Children's and parents' daily stressful events and psychological symptoms. *Journal of Abnormal Child Psychology, 18*, 591-605.
6. Cinelli, L., & Ziegler, D. J. (1990). Cognitive appraisal of daily hassles in college students showing Type A or B behavior patterns. *Psychological Reports, 67*, 83-88.

Review of the Hassles and Uplifts Scales, Research Edition by KAREN S. BUDD, Associate Professor of Psychology, and NANCY HEILMAN, Graduate Student in Psychology, Illinois Institute of Technology, Chicago, IL:

The Hassles and Uplifts Scales consist of three self-report inventories measuring how individuals appraise their encounters of everyday life experiences. The Daily Hassles Scale assesses the frequency and severity of 117 irritants or minor annoyances (e.g., concerns about job security, legal problems, wasting time). The Uplifts Scale assesses the frequency and severity of 135 presumably positive experiences (e.g., nature, making a friend, laughing). The Combined Hassles and Uplifts Scales assesses 53 events that may have *both* negative and positive qualities, and respondents indicate the frequency and severity of items separately as hassles and as uplifts. The scales are designed primarily for research use in studying psychological stress and coping. The authors articulate the research focus of the tests and also suggest potential clinical uses.

STRENGTHS. The conceptual basis for the scales is clearly described in the manual, and issues regarding the role of psychological stress as both a dependent variable and an independent variable are addressed. The test manual provides a persuasive and well-researched rationale for studying the effects of psychological stress by assessing hassles and uplifts rather than life events. Studies reviewed in the manual indicate that, although hassles and life events are overlapping constructs, hassles scores account for more variance in psychological symptoms and somatic health status than do life events.

The scales are designed to be adaptable to various research uses. For example, respondents are instructed to indicate a time frame (e.g., past month, today) to keep in mind as they complete items. The time frame can be specified by the experimenter, which allows the scales to be administered repeatedly at intervals appropriate to the research question. Hassles and uplifts may be assessed in the combined form or separately. Estimated administration time of 10–15 minutes is short enough for frequent use. Scoring is simple and straightforward.

Reliability and validity data included in the manual provide preliminary support for the methodological soundness of the scales. More research has been conducted on the Daily Hassles Scale than the other two scales, with correspondingly stronger evidence supporting this measure. The authors cite other research that has replicated some or all of the findings of their own research group, but unfortunately they do not describe the results of these studies. To the authors' credit, alternative conceptual frameworks and critiques of the scales also are cited and discussed.

LIMITATIONS. Normative data provided on the scales are insufficient to allow for interpretation of scores with reference to other samples. In part, the limitations stem from the fact that normative data from different studies are summarized in varying ways across several tables rather than as consistent information from each study. The sampled populations (e.g., elderly persons, married couples) are diverse, and their representativeness is questionable. No scores on clinical samples are provided, and no suggested clinical ranges are identified. Less normative research has been conducted on the uplifts and combined scales than on the Daily Hassles Scale.

Given the limitations in normative data, intra-individual comparisons and correlational analyses with other variables would be more appropriate than diagnostic applications.

The validity and clinical feasibility of the Combined Hassles and Uplifts Scales are open to question based on the information available in the manual. The authors note that lack of specificity in some of the generically worded items may limit their interpretability. In addition, it seems cumbersome for respondents to consider each of 53 items alternately as hassles and uplifts in order to rate the items on both negative and positive dimensions. This task probably requires more than 10–15 minutes time, and it may be difficult to get respondents to complete it systematically on repeated administrations.

The term "daily" in the title Daily Hassles Scale appears to be confusing and unnecessary, because the instructions to respondents indicate they are to specify a time frame to think about while completing items.

The manual includes a discussion of state versus trait characteristics as they relate to interpretation of hassles and uplifts test scores. This discussion would be enhanced by clear specification of the concepts of state and trait personality variables.

SUMMARY. The three scales assess respondents' subjective appraisals of their experiences in everyday living on negative and positive dimensions. The scales are distinguished from other available instruments assessing psychological stress and coping factors by (a) focusing on the subject's perception of events rather than discrete occurrences, (b) including a wide range of minor events that may add up to significant stressors or buffers of stress over time, and (c) allowing researchers to select time frames and negative, positive, or combined valences of items according to experimental questions.

The scales are simple to administer and score; however, interpretation is limited by absence of sufficient normative data. Reliability and validity investigations on the Daily Hassles Scale provide preliminary evidence that overall test scores are stable and measure what they are designed to measure, but more research is needed to determine the methodological soundness of the other two scales. The authors' statements regarding the preliminary status of their findings, and their stated interest in hearing from other researchers who use the scales, suggest an openness to empirical evidence and plans to continue refining the scales.

Review of the Hassles and Uplifts Scales, Research Edition by BARBARA A. REILLY, Assistant Professor of Psychology, Clemson University, Clemson, SC:

Three scales will be discussed in this review, The Daily Hassles Scale (Hassles), The Uplifts Scale (Uplifts), and The Combined Hassles and Uplifts Scales (Combined). It is important to note that the Combined scale is not the sum of the two aforementioned scales but serves as a unique and quite different measure. Before examining each scale individually, some overriding issues will be discussed.

PSYCHOLOGICAL APPRAISAL. The scales are based on the idea that an event is not stressful or uplifting unless a person views the event as such. The scales take into account individual differences regarding the appraisal of various events and thus do not assume that what is stressful or uplifting for one is stressful or uplifting for all. This is an important component that has been missing from other stress measures.

MAJOR LIFE EVENTS VERSUS DAILY HASSLES. The three scales all focus on ongoing daily hassles and uplifts rather than major life events (Holmes & Rahe, 1967). Researchers have begun to take note of the importance of daily occurrences as stressors and these scales will do much to stimulate research in this area.

TIME FRAME. Each of the scales requires the researcher/test user to give explicit instructions as to the time frame to be considered while completing the inventories. This presents two problems, one practical and one theoretical. The practical problem is brought on by the wording on the surveys which states, "Please indicate the time period you will be thinking about: Past month, Past week, Yesterday, Today, or Other." The wording implies that the subject is to choose his/her own time period whereas the test manual and scientific rigor suggest that all subjects should be considering the same time period. Clear instructions by the researcher can rectify any confusion. A second, theoretical, problem occurs by having the researcher/test user choose a time frame. At the present time there is no clear evidence supporting the endorsement of one specific time frame. Too long a time frame might lead to distortion and too short a time frame might not allow for adequate sampling of events. The most commonly used time frames are 1 month and 1 week, but no evidence is provided in support of these choices.

GENERAL VERSUS SPECIFIC. The two individual scales, The Daily Hassles Scale and The Uplifts Scale, include very specific items (e.g., "Concerns about weight," "Rising prices of common goods," "Relating well with your spouse and lover," "Getting enough sleep"). The Combined scale includes similar dimensions but in broader terms (e.g., "Your physical appearance," "Your spouse"). When a test user has a need for specificity, the Combined scale should not be used or should be used with caution.

THE THREE SCALES: HASSLES, UPLIFTS, AND COMBINED. The authors state in the test manual, "We regard all three versions of the Hassles and

Uplifts Scales as research tools in their formative stages." The three scales, however, are clearly not in the *same* formative stages. The Uplifts Scale and the Combined Hassles and Uplifts Scales are in early formative stages and thus not much is known regarding their reliability, validity, or normative structure. The Daily Hassles Scale is in a much more advanced stage and, as expected, much more information is known regarding its reliability, validity, and normative structure.

THE DAILY HASSLES SCALE. The scale provides two scores, one for Frequency and one for Severity. The normative information provided in the test manual ($N = 980$ distributed over three samples) is well presented and easy to interpret. One sample of the normative data was collected over nine repeated administrations ($N = 100$) and the other two samples ($N = 432$ and $N = 448$) were gathered from a single observation. Item statistics are reported for Frequency and average Severity. Reliability, as measured by stability (the correlation of scores in successive time periods), was higher for the Frequency measure (.79) than for the Severity measure (.48). Validity evidence is strong. Daily hassles were related to somatic health problems (.30–.40) and psychological symptom scores (.50–.60). In addition, when daily hassles and life events were used as predictors of psychological and somatic health, the daily hassles explained more variance than did life events. The factor structure of the Hassles scales reveals eight factors: future security, time pressures, work, household responsibilities, health, inner concerns, financial responsibilities, and neighborhood and environmental concerns. The stability of these factors over time and with multiple samples is yet to be determined. If the factors do prove to be stable they could provide a very useful dimension to the measure of daily hassles via the factor subscales.

THE UPLIFTS SCALE. Normative information for this scale is based on nine repeated observations of 100 adults. No item statistics are reported. Additional normative data are needed. No reliability, stability, or validity information is known at this time.

THE HASSLES AND UPLIFTS SCALE. Normative information is based on three samples (Combined $N = 748$). One sample of the normative data was collected over 16 repeated administrations ($N = 115$) and the other two samples ($N = 150$ and $N = 448$) were gathered from a single observation. Item statistics are reported.

No reliability or stability information is presented. In general, there is evidence that an increase in daily hassles as measured by the Combined scale precedes an increase in dysphoric affect and symptoms of illness. There are large individual differences, however, with some individuals reporting increases in stress that were accompanied by increased health

and mood. More validity evidence is needed regarding the combined scale.

In conclusion, there is a clear and pressing need for a scale like The Daily Hassles Scale and the evidence suggests that it is a sound measure of daily stress. More information is needed on The Uplifts Scale and The Combined Hassles and Uplifts Scales before a fair evaluation can be provided.

REVIEWER'S REFERENCE

Holmes, R. H., & Rahe, R. H. (1967). The Social Readjustment Rating Scale. *Journal of Psychomatic Research, 11,* 213-218.

[156]
Health Attribution Test.

Purpose: Constructed to measure "beliefs about the causes and cures of illness."
Population: High school and college and adult patients.
Publication Date: 1990.
Acronym: HAT.
Scores, 3: Internal Scale, Powerful Others Scale, Chance Scale.
Administration: Group.
Price Data, 1989: $20 per complete kit including 10 test booklets and manual (24 pages); $21.75 per 25 test booklets; $12 per manual.
Time: (10) minutes.
Authors: Jeanne Achterberg and G. Frank Lawlis.
Publisher: Institute for Personality and Ability Testing, Inc.

Review of the Health Attribution Test by DIANNA L. NEWMAN, Associate Professor of Educational Theory and Practice, University at Albany/SUNY, Albany, NY:

The Health Attribution Test (HAT) is a self-report questionnaire designed to measure respondents' attitudes toward health control. The authors indicate the findings could be used to aid in health management, health maintenance, or health treatment. Although the instrument and the user's guide are professionally prepared and appear to be appropriate for clinical use, the authors are labeling the current version a research instrument.

The HAT consists of 22 statements describing causes of ill health, treatment and prevention measures, and individuals' roles in those activities. These statements reflect Rotter and Levenson's theories of Locus of Control and provide individual (but not independent) measures of forces affecting or causing ill health and its treatment. Twenty-one of the items reflect content related to health, the last is a direct reflection of overall control by powerful others. Although the items are all appropriate in content, it should be noted the reading level of the instrument may be too high for some respondents. In addition, several items are composed of multiple clauses or modifying phrases that may provide ambiguity in respondents' understanding of the item content.

Response to the scale is easy and accommodating to most individuals. Using a 6-point Likert-type format (ranging from *Strongly Disagree* to *Strongly Agree*) the instrument produces three subscores. The first subscale, Internal, assesses the "degree to which people believe they control their physical health"; the second subscale, Powerful Others, measures the "degree to which individuals believe doctors, nurses, and other medical professionals are responsible for their health"; the third subscale reflects perceptions of Chance: the belief that "chance, fate, or other external, uncontrollable factors affect health." The instrument also provides a HAT profile code, which is a verbal descriptive code summarizing the interrelationship of the three attributes (e.g., "Average Joe," "High I," "Super High I," "C"). According to the authors, these codes allow the user to interpret the three scores as a whole and are followed by suggestions for clinical interpretations. The User's Guide provides very little, if any, documentation for these summary codes; hence, users should be very careful in their application. Although possibly the most useful of all the scores when all determinations of validity have been provided, their current validity is weak.

The physical presentations of the instrument and the user's guide are extremely well done and make the scale easy for clinicians and researchers to use. The questionnaire is attached to its own scoring pad and worksheet allowing immediate scoring of responses by either the respondent or the test giver. This provides the clinician or other supporting health professionals the opportunity to discuss scores with individual respondents and to provide information on health responsibility. The inclusion of graphics makes the presentation of results more compatible with lay populations' understanding of scores. Again, a caveat must be expressed; there is only limited data available for the validity of the sten scores (i.e., standard scores) and the profile graphs.

The User's Guide provides an excellent set of directions for administering and scoring the instrument. A description of the validation sample is also provided. Information pertaining to the theoretical background for the locus of control concept and the need for the instrument is adequate and well presented; unfortunately, when presenting the information that would document predictive or construct validity for the instrument, only generalized statements with no factual support are provided. For example, readers are informed there is a significant correlation between scores and successful treatment but no numerical values are provided that would allow readers to make their own judgements. Data for scale reliabilities and interscale correlations are provided in a single table with only limited footnotes indicating the numbers and types of subjects. To the authors' credit, they do indicate that subject numbers are small and that more validation

is needed; however, this caveat appears at the end of the guide and may not be found by many users.

In summary, the Health Attribution Test is a promising instrument that is now ready for intensive research to determine its true usefulness. If its promise holds, and the instrument can be shown to reflect accurately individuals' perceptions of their own and others' role in health care, it will be of benefit to clinicians and practitioners in prescribing treatment and predicting success. Until this research is completed, clinicians should be conservative in its use. The current physical status of the instrument makes it easily adaptable to multiple research settings and should greatly enhance and increase the information available about the scale.

Review of the Health Attribution Test by STEPHEN OLEJNIK, Professor of Educational Psychology, University of Georgia, Athens, GA:

The Health Attribution Test (HAT) is based on the premise that an individual's belief about the causes of good health is an important factor related to the treatment of an illness and the recovery process. Based on attribution theory and the concept of locus of control, the authors have identified 22 statements that reflect what the individual thinks about the role that personal involvement, powerful others, and chance play in health maintenance. Many of the items are similar to items found on other locus of control instruments but the statements here focus on health issues. Individuals indicate on a 6-point scale the degree to which they disagree or agree with each statement. Because there are no correct responses to the HAT, some respondents may find the instrument's title a bit misleading.

The two-page test booklet is attractive. Health statements are well-spaced, one- or two-line sentences and respondents can indicate their beliefs easily without confusion. The use of NCR paper for the first page allows the responses to be recorded on the second page and the scoring of the instrument by hand is quick and simple. An Internal Scale, a Powerful Others Scale, and a Chance Scale are provided by summing responses to eight items identified by the authors to reflect the three sources believed to have an influence on one's health. Two items on the inventory have dual weights for the scales. One item on the Internal Scale and one item on the Powerful Others Scale are inversely weighted and added to the six-item Chance Scale. The raw scores are converted to a 10-point standard score called a sten score. Finally, the sten scores are used to classify the respondent as High, Average, or Low in each of the three areas to provide a profile. The 27 possible profile codes are then classified into eight categories. The authors use these categories to describe the patient and predict the likely response to treatment. The basis of the predictions rests primarily on the authors' experiences and limited research with burn patients. The authors do not provide a clear justification for the grouping of the profile codes.

Although over a thousand individuals have responded to this instrument and descriptive statistics are reported for the three scales, the sten scores on which the profile codes are based were created using only 100 subjects. The authors do not discuss the procedure they used to identify and select these individuals nor do they provide any descriptive statistics on this "norm" group. The sten scores are described as a standard score with a mean of 5.5 and a standard deviation of 2. The authors treat these scores as if the distribution is normal (i.e., "about 67% of all the people taking the test will score between 4 and 7"). But there is no indication that the distribution of scores is, in fact, normal nor do the authors mention the use of any normalizing transformation. Because the sten scores were based on only 100 respondents, it is unlikely that these scores can be thought to be representative of the general population. The authors do caution users, however, that the norms are tentative and they are continuing to collect additional data.

Reliability estimates are provided for each scale in the form of test-retest (7 to 14 days), split-half correlations, and coefficient alpha. All reliability estimates are in an acceptable range (.75 to .92). However, because the authors stress the interpretation of profile patterns, the reliability coefficients associated with profile patterns would have been more useful. In particular, it would have been useful to provide some index of stability for the patient's categorization based on the profile pattern. Because the categorization of a patient can be changed dramatically by a change in the coding of one scale, it would be important to provide some evidence the patterns of profile codes are not likely to change over short periods of time. It might be suspected that the stability of the codes may vary as a function of patient illness. More information in this area is needed.

Data supporting the instrument's validity are very limited. The authors use the results of a factor analysis study based on the responses from 121 undergraduate students to support the scale formation. It is very doubtful that this sample can be thought of as being representative of a general population of people likely to take this test. Furthermore, there is no indication that a cross-validation study has been conducted. Additional support for the scale formation is needed.

The authors mention briefly three studies that might provide some support for the instrument's validity. One study conducted by the first author found a correlation between scale scores and recovery time for burn patients. These results are difficult to interpret because the manual contains only a discussion of the profile code interpretations. A second study conducted by an independent investigator found that scores predicted success or failure in a drug and alcohol treatment. Again, the use of the profile codes or classifications are not mentioned. The third study did mention the profile codes and found different patterns for successful spinal pain patients than for presumably unsuccessful patients. Because this third study is not described in any detail, alternative explanations such as the severity of the illness cannot be discarded. Contrary to the author's suggestion, these studies do not provide strong support for the usefulness of the instrument. No other data are provided to support the instrument's validity, thus reducing the usefulness of the scores.

The instrument was designed to assess health attributions and is based on a very popular and powerful psychological construct that has extensive support in many behavioral areas. Although there may be little question regarding the importance of the construct, the present instrument provides only sparse data to support its use in a clinical setting. The authors have designated the current edition of the instrument as a "research instrument" and do caution users on the tentative nature of the scaled scores. Additional development and research with the instrument are clearly needed and the authors have expressed an interest in collaborating with others who may be interested in the construct. Perhaps with additional research and development a useful inventory can evolve.

[157]

HELP Checklist (Hawaii Early Learning Profile).

Purpose: Assesses developmental skills/behaviors.
Population: Ages birth–3.
Publication Dates: 1984–88.
Acronym: HELP Checklist.
Scores: Item scores only; 6 developmental areas: Cognitive, Language, Gross Motor, Fine Motor, Social, Self-Help.
Administration: Individual.
Price Data, 1990: $2.95 per checklist.
Time: Administration time not reported.
Comments: Ratings by professionals.
Authors: Setsu Furuno, Katherine A. O'Reilly, Carol M. Hosaka, Takayo T. Inatsuka, Barbara Zeisloft-Falbey, and Toney Allman.
Publisher: VORT Corporation.

Review of the HELP Checklist (Hawaii Early Learning Profile) by WILLIAM STEVE LANG, Assistant Professor of Educational Leadership, Technology and Research, Georgia Southern University, Statesboro, GA:

The HELP Checklist (Hawaii Early Learning Profile) is not a formal psychometric instrument, but a list of developmental skills and behaviors that would be typical of infants from birth to 3 years of age. The Checklist contains skills that, according to the authors, come from the developmental areas of "Cognitive, Language, Gross Motor, Fine Motor, Social-Emotional, and Self Help skills." The Checklist is reportedly intended to facilitate a comprehensive assessment of an infant with a team that includes psychologists, educators, speech pathologists, and physical therapists. The Checklist skills are crosslisted by the authors with a set of handouts for parents, an activity guide, and charts to mark a child's progress.

The Checklist structure includes 16 pages of items with approximately 45 items per page. These items are arranged by skill area (such as Cognitive) and ordered by age in months. According to the authors, "The skills are not necessarily listed in a hierarchical or exact sequential order." The items typically are clauses describing infant behavior such as: "Plays with paper" or "Grasps crayon adaptively." The directions request that the user of the instrument record whether the skill was observed, reported by the parent, assessed but not observed, or is "emerging, but not complete." The authors then suggest that a professional plan be devised to teach the appropriate skills (if teachable) that have not been observed. The test developers do not suggest that any particular skills are prerequisite or necessary for other listed skills.

Developmental checklists are not new and checklists that measure similar constructs such as motor skills, social development, and cognitive development are relatively common. The only possible advantage of the HELP Checklist over any other instrument might reside in the larger than usual number of items. Longer instruments often overcome the weakness of longer administration times and more difficult scoring by giving a more reliable score for the attribute measured. Unfortunately, the HELP Checklist has no norms or criterion-based scoring that would allow the user to assess strengths and weaknesses of a child in any of the developmental areas suggested. The HELP Checklist suggests that it might take several sessions up to an hour each to complete the entire instrument. This seems to be an excessive use of time when the resulting information is rather limited.

If a "multi-disciplinary team" is available, then each expert should be able to assess the functional level of the child within his or her domain using specific tests already available for each professional's concern. On the other hand, a parent or layman likely would not understand the meaning of many of the items or that item's importance. An example would be "Imitates several invisible gestures" or "Releases object voluntarily."

No reliability assessment of this instrument was provided by the authors. Even though observational checklists are assumed to be reliable compared to traditional testing, this assumption should be determined empirically. Many of the items of the HELP Checklist are abstract and call for inference from the observer. Examples are "Grasps toy actively" and "Enjoys looking at pictures in books." In reviewing this instrument, two school psychologists disagreed on the performance of their own child with regard to several items. The items on the HELP Checklist are not objective enough to suggest reliability, and it is a serious weakness that reliability data are not available.

The HELP Checklist provides no validity arguments for its construction. Some of the items on the HELP Checklist might have construct validity with regard to theories of human development, but none of those arguments are mentioned by the authors. Defense of the items, skill areas, and age ranges are lacking. More importantly, there is no concurrent validity reported even though numerous tests that measure infant development are available. Predictive validity studies are not reported even though these are of crucial importance to developmental assessment. This instrument is suspect until its utility is demonstrated.

No norms, descriptive data, or item analysis are provided for the HELP Checklist. Again, this limits its usefulness. If a child "appears" weak or strong in an area of the instrument, no comparison score such as percentile rank or an expected developmental criterion is provided; thus, no conclusion can be reached regarding the child's progress. No variance with regard to any items or subtests is provided. One could only say which items were observed and which were not observed, but not how typical that observation was for that age.

The most serious weakness of the HELP Checklist is the observational methodology employed. If the observer had to wait for many of the items suggested to occur spontaneously, a single assessment might require many sessions and the behavior in question would never be observed. Meanwhile, the items require so much trained judgment and inference, it is unlikely parents would observe the behavior accurately and objectively.

If diagnosis of a child's progress and specific weakness is a goal, instruments with better standardization are available such as the Bayley Scales of Infant Development (10:26). If the prediction of later functioning is important, the Denver Developmental Screening Test (9:311) is a better choice. In fact, there is little reason to recommend the HELP Checklist because many better known assessment instruments have established validity and reliability parameters. The authors' intent to "facilitate comprehensive individualized assessment, program planning, and recording of child progress" has not been achieved in a way preferable to existing and more thoroughly designed instruments. The lengthy and passive administration format, the lack of standardization, and the absence of validity and reliability data suggest skepticism with the use of this checklist and extreme caution in the assessment of infants with the HELP Checklist.

Review of the HELP Checklist (Hawaii Early Learning Profile) by KORESSA KUTSICK MALCOLM, School Psychologist, Augusta County Public Schools, Fishersville, VA:

VORT Corporation publishes a series of educational and evaluative materials for children ages 0–3 years under the acronym of HELP (Hawaii Early Learning Profile). Included in these materials are the HELP Activity Guide, HELP . . . At Home (curriculum ideas for teachers and parents), and the HELP Charts (a profile for recording a child's developmental progress). The HELP Checklist, which is the focus of this review, was constructed in order to provide a comprehensive, yet easy-to-use, developmental assessment tool which complements the other HELP materials.

The HELP Checklist comprises 685 developmental items that cover age equivalencies of 0 to 36 months. With this number of items a broad sampling of behavior can occur. Six separate functioning domains are tapped by the Checklist. These include: Cognitive, Language, Gross Motor, Fine Motor, Social/Emotional, and Self-Help skills. Items within each domain are roughly arranged in a developmental progression; however, an item is not necessarily prerequisite to a subsequent item.

The HELP Checklist is a criterion-referenced instrument. No standard scores can be computed from a child's test performance. Specific reliability and validity information is not provided. The lack of this information in a test manual greatly detracts from this instrument.

Items comprising the HELP Checklist are relatively similar to those of other developmental assessment tools for young children. The unique feature of the HELP Checklist lies in its relationship to the other HELP materials. Items on the Checklist are numbered to correspond to related items on the HELP Charts and in the HELP Activity Guide. Page numbers corresponding to activities found in the HELP . . . At Home manual are provided for each item. This cross referencing of assessment tasks and instructional activities would be extremely valuable to those engaged in educational programming for young children. A quick reference to the HELP . . . At Home or HELP Activity Guide would provide direct suggestions for teachers or parents to use in the remediation of a child's developmental weaknesses and the building of his or her strengths.

The HELP Checklist can be completed by one or more professionals. It is possible for different professionals to administer separate domains in order to obtain a multidisciplinary assessment of a child from one assessment tool. The HELP Checklist protocols can also be used for multiple evaluations of a child. This allows examiners to note a child's developmental gains over time.

Authors of the HELP Checklist maintain their assessment tool is useful for evaluations of children who possess a wide variety of handicapping conditions. The authors encourage examiners to adapt items to accommodate any handicap which might interfere with a child's response; however, specifics as to how to adapt items are not provided. Other missing guidelines involve suggested basals and ceilings. The authors recommend examiners use their own judgment for these. The major problems examiners face when specific starting and stopping points are not developed include overtiring children when too many unnecessary items are administered, or missing splinter skills if too few items are given.

In summary, the HELP Checklist may be a useful tool to those who need to monitor a young child's developmental status on a regular basis. The Checklist would best be used in conjunction with other HELP materials. Examiners searching for a criterion-referenced assessment tool for the 0–3-year age group might consider the Brigance Diagnostic Inventory of Early Development (9:164). The HELP materials could be useful, however, to those who not only need to monitor and record a child's developmental progress but who also must provide specific recommendations to themselves, other professionals, and parents regarding the educational programming of a child. With its lack of technical data, caution should be used when considering this test for selection or placement purposes.

[158]
Help for Special Preschoolers ASSESSMENT CHECKLIST: Ages 3–6.
Purpose: Comprehensive screening and assessment of developmentally delayed children.
Population: Ages 2-6 to 6-0.
Publication Date: 1987.
Scores: Ratings in 5 developmental areas: Self Help, Motor Development, Communication, Social Skills, Learning/Cognitive; 28 goals areas: Self-Help (Eating and Drinking, Toileting, Grooming, Dressing, Undressing, Oral and Nasal Hygiene, Self-Identification), Motor Development (Sensory Perception, Fine Motor, Gross Motor, Wheelchair, Swimming), Communication (Auditory Perception, Language Comprehension, Language, Sign Language, Speechreading), Social Skills (Adaptive Behaviors, Responsible Behaviors, Interpersonal Relationships, Personal Welfare, Social Manners), Learning/Cognitive (Attention Span, Basic Reading, Math, Writing Skills, Reasoning Skills, Music/Rhythm).
Administration: Individual.
Price Data, 1990: $2.95 per test booklet (20 pages).
Time: Administration time not reported.

Comments: Adaptation of Behavioral Characteristics Progression (BCP); upward extension of Hawaii Early Learning Profile (157); "criterion-referenced."
Author: The Santa Cruz County Office of Education.
Publisher: VORT Corporation.

Review of the Help for Special Preschoolers ASSESSMENT CHECKLIST: Ages 3–6 by HARLAN J. STIENTJES, School Psychologist, Heartland Educational Agency 11, Johnston, IA:

The Help for Special Preschoolers ASSESSMENT CHECKLIST: Ages 3–6 (HSPAC) is a developmental checklist for children aged 3 to 6. It is designed to continue beyond the age range of birth to age 3 covered by the widely used Hawaii Early Learning Profile (157). The HSPAC is adapted from a broad-based criterion-referenced assessment originally developed by the Santa Cruz County Office of Education. The items selected were compared to existing instruments and literature and edited by field reviewers. The skills covered are thought to be developmentally sequenced, but not necessarily prerequisite nor related to each other. Each skill has age ranges which represent "normal" developmental milestones. The HSPAC covers 625 skills in 28 separate goal areas. Some skill areas cover topics not often found in developmental checklists (e.g., Wheelchair, Swimming, Speech-reading Skills).

The instructions for assessment are general procedures; neither directions nor criteria are specific for the individual skills. Observation, unobtrusive play interaction, as well as parent interviews, are suggested formats, but no other guidance is provided. As with most other developmental checklists, it is suggested that the HSPAC can be used as a guide to instruction with the addition of criteria for instructional measurement. More specific criteria are also necessary to make this instrument effective as an assessment and programming guide.

Additionally, there is no manual to accompany the checklist and no technical data are available. Item characteristic data, as well as the procedures utilized to provide the developmental age ranges, would be helpful, and indeed are essential to understanding the instrument. Furthermore, the ranges may be meaningless and subject to grave misuse by parents or well-intentioned but uninformed child-care professionals.

The checklist itself is printed on plain white paper in 8¹/₂ x 11 inch booklet format. No color coding or other useful divisions are provided to help the user. Arrangement of the items and the recording section, although understandable, offer little advantage over previously published checklists.

Without technical information on items and skill areas, the HSPAC should be used with caution. The large number of items and coverage of some innovative areas makes the instrument somewhat attractive. Nevertheless, the use of the HSPAC cannot be recommended until further technical data are available.

Review of the Help for Special Preschoolers ASSESSMENT CHECKLIST: Ages 3–6 by GERALD TINDAL, Assistant Professor of Special Education, University of Oregon, Eugene, OR:

This instrument is designed to identify young children's needs, set instructional objectives, and monitor their progress. The manual provides a very limited description of the instrument, consisting primarily of lists that identify important behaviors. A screening instrument gives five general areas: (a) Self Help, (b) Motor Development, (c) Communication, (d) Social Skills, and (e) Learning/Cognitive. Further breakdowns of specific behaviors within these areas are then provided for assessment. Administration directions are very brief, indicating that information for completing the checklist can be gathered from any of three sources: (a) observation of the student, (b) interview with the parent, or (c) play interactions with the student. The administrator is directed to check those areas in which the student has either current mastery or need. The essential data compiled by using this instrument are dates in which the student was given an opportunity and (a) failed to display the behavior, (b) exhibited emerging but incomplete behavior, (c) could not display the behavior because of inherent physical limitations, or (d) engaged in the behavior at a mastery level. A comment column is also provided for each behavior on the checklist. Other directions for administration are simply vague statements that provide suggestions only. For example, several sessions may be needed, criteria for mastery may vary by skill area (although 75% is suggested), and adaptations for student physical limitations might be needed but are left open-ended.

The instrument is riddled with problems in its development, format, and technical adequacy. For example, the authors describe only that the instrument was developed from an analysis of a broader criterion-referenced checklist, selecting items according to age appropriateness. No other information on the selection criteria is provided. No theoretical perspective is provided regarding behavior sampling and no selection criteria are presented. The checklist is purportedly developmentally sequenced and "the age ranges represent 'normal' developmental milestones, making this Checklist appropriate for use with disabled and non-disabled children in a variety of preschool settings" (p. 1). Ages are shown as year-month numbers. Although disclaimers are provided about the problems with developmental ages, the bottom line is that the instrument depends upon them.

No administration directions are included, so that, with any of the three assessment techniques, wide variation may occur. Indeed, all three formats are left undefined, so the administrator is given no help on how to observe, interview parents, or play interactively as a means for collecting data.

No technical adequacy data are presented. Both reliability and validity data are essential even for a criterion-referenced instrument. For example, reliability estimates are needed both for the dates of attainment and the judgments of behavior adequacy ("emerging" or "mastered"). Validity data are also needed to confirm the instrument is actually a developmental measure that is useful in making decisions about children. Although the checklist is designed for setting objectives and tracking progress, the consumer is provided no guidance to complete either.

In summary, the Help for Special Preschoolers ASSESSMENT CHECKLIST is an instrument that fails to meet even minimal professional standards and should probably not be used until the authors address the many problems described above.

[159]
Herrmann Brain Dominance Instrument.

Purpose: Designed to measure "human mental preferences" and thinking styles.
Population: Adults.
Publication Dates: 1981–1990.
Acronym: HBDI.
Scores, 12: Left Mode Dominance, Right Mode Dominance, Quadrant (Upper Left, Lower Left, Lower Right, Upper Right), Adjective Pairs (subset of 4 Quadrant Scores), Cerebral Mode Dominance, Limbic Mode Dominance.
Administration: Individual or group.
Manual: No manual.
Price Data: Prices and validation studies available from publisher.
Time: (15–20) minutes.
Comments: Survey booklet title is Participant Survey Form of the Herrmann Brain Dominance Instrument; self-administered; must be scored by publisher or certified practitioner.
Author: Ned Herrmann.
Publisher: Applied Creative Services, Ltd. dba The Ned Herrmann Group.

Review of the Herrmann Brain Dominance Instrument by RIK CARL D'AMATO, Associate Professor of School Psychology and Director of the School Psychology Programs in the Division of Professional Psychology, University of Northern Colorado, Greeley, CO:

Interest in brain functions has been apparent for centuries. Unfortunately, early proponents of brain-behavior relationships offered erroneous correlates as illustrated by the study of phrenology, where bumps on the skull were related to personality functioning (Aiken, 1989; Dean, 1986a). It is important to note such a misconception because it provides a cautionary example of techniques utilized in the field which were not empirically evaluated before being applied

to practice. More recently, the study of neuropsychology has again been offered as a means to relate the inner processes of the brain to outward behavior (Whitten, D'Amato, & Chittooran, 1992). Neuropsychological assessment has become popular since the opportunities for its use have become more available. Thus, instruments that claim a neuropsychological foundation must be rigorously scrutinized if measures are to be used ethically (Anastasi, 1988; D'Amato, 1990).

The Herrmann Brain Dominance Instrument (Herrmann) consists of a six-page Herrmann Participant Survey Form and an Appendix A (from Herrmann, 1988) entitled The Validity of the Herrmann Brain Dominance Instrument. The copy of the Appendix pages provided to this reviewer are not numbered; therefore, references to the Appendix in this review are not page numbered. The Herrmann test purports to evaluate "different types of thinking, feeling, and doing" and these behaviors are seen as representing "an outward manifestation" of underlying "clusters of mental activity" (Appendix). The measure is offered as appropriate for personal growth evaluation, group processes, counseling, enhanced productivity through teamwork, better management, diagnosis, enhanced teaching and learning, modeling, and design. From this view, it is not clear if the instrument evaluates personality, intelligence, or some type of neuropsychological functioning. In fact, it would seem that the use of the words *brain dominance* may be misleading and an unfortunate choice for naming this measure; it may be more a measure of personality.

The instrument is a forced-choice, self-report inventory consisting of 120 items representing various formats. These questions are grouped into 11 major areas including (*a*) biographical information, (*b*) handedness, (*c*) best/worst subjects, (*d*) work elements, (*e*) key descriptors, (*f*) hobbies, (*g*) energy level, (*h*) motion sickness, (*i*) adjective pairs, (*j*) introversion, extroversion, and (*k*) twenty questions. Subjects are directed to answer "each question by writing in the appropriate words or numbers or checking the boxes provided" (Participant Survey, p. 2). Response requirements vary drastically in these sections with individuals first filling in basic descriptive information such as name, gender, and job title. Next, questions in the handedness section require individuals to select one of four pictures that correspond to how individuals hold pencils. No choice is provided for alternative ways of grasping pencils. Questions also ask the strength and direction of each individual's handedness, this time through the selection of one of five handedness options. In the best/worst subject area individuals must choose from three subject choices; again no direction is provided for individuals who would like to select academic subjects outside of math, foreign language, or native language courses.

The work elements, key descriptors, and hobbies sections provide adjective lists which subjects rate but they are asked to do the ratings in *different ways* for each section. In the key descriptors section individuals select eight adjectives which best describe themselves by placing a 2 next to words selected from a list of 25 adjectives. Then they are directed to erase one adjective and put a 3 next to the adjective which best describes them. For example, in the key descriptors section, some sample adjectives include musical, rational, and symbolic. In the hobbies section, individuals are asked to identify up to six major, primary, and secondary hobbies such as golf, sewing, and fishing. Many of the test areas as well as individual items appear unusual. For instance, motion sickness questions evaluate how often you have become nauseous and if you can read in the "car without stomach awareness, nausea, or vomiting" (Participant Survey, p. 4). In a sample administration by this reviewer, subjects reported confusion with some of the instrument's directions and indicated that they often did not *fit* into what were seen as artificial categories. The test cannot be individually scored and must be returned to the publisher (Ned Herrmann) for scoring and interpretation.

The Appendix indicates that scoring of the instrument by the publisher produces nine main scores: left and right dominance, four quadrant scores relating to a four-fold model of brain dominance (upper left, lower left, lower right, upper right), cerebral and limbic preferences, and an introversion/extroversion score. Normative data are sketchy and appear inadequate at best. It seems that the instrument was administered to about 8,000 participants taking part in workshops conducted by Ned Herrmann and his colleagues during 1984, 1985, and 1986 and analyzed as part of a doctoral dissertation (Appendix A). It is distressing that little additional information about the normative sample is presented (Anastasi, 1988).

Validity and reliability information concerning the Herrmann is also relatively absent. One exception is a study of 143 college students and Ned Herrmann workshop participants who completed 15 instruments. A factor analysis with what seemed to be 31 variables claimed to provide support for some of the Herrmann constructs. A troubling aspect of this study is the fact that a large number of variables were analyzed with very few subjects, which, because of the poor variable-subject ratio, results in a statistically flawed study. Additional validity and reliability studies are reported, again using small numbers of subjects. For example, in a study of coincidental test-retest reliability performed with 78 subjects as part of a doctoral dissertation, back-

ground information on the subjects was not provided and no indication of the test-retest time interval was offered; this renders the study basically irrelevant. Given these many technical limitations, the Herrmann seems inappropriate for use with Ned Herrmann workshop participants as well as with others. It should be apparent that studies of validity and reliability, utilizing sound scientific procedures, are needed if sound psychometric conclusions are to be reached (Anastasi, 1988). Another disturbing feature is the instrument's focus on cerebral localization, a practice that has been abandoned as of late (D'Amato, 1990; Dean, 1986a, 1986b; Whitten, D'Amato, & Chittooran, 1992).

In summary, the Herrmann cannot presently be recommended for use in any of the areas suggested. Obviously, the test cannot measure all constructs for all purposes as it currently purports to do. Validity of the instrument remains in question, and the test's reliability has not been adequately demonstrated. Moreover, the test's Appendix is misleading and serves more as a vehicle for cheerleading than providing an accurate understanding of the instrument. If practitioners are interested in finding a test to use in global, applied areas such as career counseling, group process evaluation, teaching, learning, and personal growth evaluation, the Myers-Briggs Type Indicator (10:206) or the Sixteen Personality Factor Questionnaire (16PF; 9:1136) may be more appropriate tests to consider (see Aiken, 1989; Anastasi, 1988). If individuals are interested in neuropsychologically evaluating brain laterality the Lateral Preference Schedule (196) would seem apropos (see Dean, 1986a, 1986b). It should be noted, however, that the Herrmann appears of interest for research, which is sorely needed if the instrument can be recommended in the future.

REVIEWER'S REFERENCES

Dean, R. S. (1986a). Lateralization of cerebral functions. In D. Wedding, A. M. Horton, & J. Webster (Eds.), *The neuropsychology handbook: Behavioral and clinical perspectives* (pp. 80-104). New York: Springer.

Dean, R. S. (1986b). Perspectives on the future of neuropsychological assessment. In B. S. Plake & J. C. Witt (Eds.), *Buros-Nebraska symposium on measurement and testing: The future of testing* (pp. 203-244). Hillsdale, NJ: Erlbaum.

Anastasi, A. (1988). *Psychological testing* (6th ed.). New York: Macmillan.

Herrmann, N. (1988). *The creative brain*. Lake Lure, NC: Brain Books.

Aiken, L. R. (1989). *Assessment of personality*. Boston: Allyn & Bacon.

D'Amato, R. C. (1990). A neuropsychological approach to school psychology. *School Psychology Quarterly, 5* (2), 141-161.

Whitten, C. J., D'Amato, R. C., & Chittooran, M. M. (1992). The neuropsychological approach to intervention. In R. C. D'Amato & B. A. Rothlisberg (Eds.), *Psychological perspectives on interventions: A case study approach to prescriptions for change* (pp. 112-136). New York: Longman.

[160]

High-School Subject Tests.

Purpose: Developed to assess student achievement in English, mathematics, social studies, and science.

Population: Grades 9–12.

Publication Dates: 1980–90.

Administration: Group.

Price Data, 1991: $33.85 per 35 test booklets with administration directions (select test); $13.25 per 35 machine-scorable answer sheets; $4.30 per directions for administration; $19.45 per Teacher's Manual ('90, 110 pages); $12.60 per specimen set (specify English, mathematics, social studies, or science); $26.55 per all-subjects specimen set; scoring service available from publisher.

Time: (40) minutes per test.

Comments: Tests have been equated to the original Form A for purposes of pre- and posttesting.

Authors: Louis A. Gatta, John W. Wick, Robert B. Adams, Larry M. Faulkner, Karen J. Kuehner, Vincent F. Malek, and John W. McConnell.

Publisher: American Testronics.

a) LITERATURE AND VOCABULARY.
Scores, 5: Literal Comprehension, Inferential Comprehension, Vocabulary, Literary Terms, Total.

b) LANGUAGE.
Scores, 4: Spelling, Punctuation/Capitalization, Correctness of Expression, Total.

c) WRITING AND MECHANICS.
Scores, 4: Paragraph Development, Grammar/Word Choice/Usage, Paragraph Structure, Total.

d) GENERAL MATHEMATICS.
Scores, 6: Computation (Recall, Comprehension), Geometry and Measurement, Tables/Graphs/Charts, Calculators and Decision-Making, Total.

e) PRE-ALGEBRA.
Scores, 6: Numbers and Operations, Equations and Inequalities, Geometry, Expressions, Applications, Total.

Forms, 2: B-1, B-2.

f) ALGEBRA.
Scores, 8: Polynomials, Exponents and Rational Expressions, Definitions and Theory, Linear Equations and Inequalities, Systems and Coordinates, Radicals and Quadratics, Word Problems, Total.

g) ADVANCED ALGEBRA.
Scores, 7: Linear Sentences and Applications, Algebraic Expressions, Exponents and Logarithms, Polynomial and Radical Equations, Analysis of Graphs, Systems, Total.

Forms, 2: B-1, B-2.

h) GEOMETRY.
Scores, 6: Angles, Segments/Lines/Rays, Similarity and Congruence, Perimeter and Area, Circles, Total.

i) COMPUTER LITERACY.
Scores, 6: Information Processing-Input/Output, Computer Hardware-Processors and Storage Devices, Computer Software and Applications, Networking and Telecommunications, Computer Issues and Problems, Total.

j) PHYSICAL SCIENCE.
Scores, 9: Measurement/Mass/Volume/Density, Particle Nature of Matter, Heat Energy, Structure of the Atom and Chemical Formulas, Solutions and Behavior of Matter, Energy and Motion, Electricity, Light and Sound, Total.

k) BIOLOGY.
Scores, 10: Cell Structure and Function, Cellular Chemistry, Viruses/Monerans/Protists/Fungi, Plants, Animals, Human Body Systems and Physiology, Genetics, Ecology, Biological Analysis and Experimentation, Total.

l) CHEMISTRY.
Scores, 8: Chemical Symbols/Equations/Moles, Solutions, The Gaseous Phase, Atomic/Molecular Structure and Bonding, Energy/Reaction Rates/Equilibrium, Acids and Bases, Oxidation/Reduction, Total.

Forms, 2: B-1, B-2.

m) PHYSICS.
Scores, 10: Linear Motion, Analyzing Graphs and Using Vectors, Dynamics and Momentum, Motion in Two Dimensions, Energy and Work, Gravitation, Kinetic Theory/Heat/Nuclear Reactions, Light and Optics, Electricity and Magnetism, Total.

n) WORLD HISTORY.
Scores, 8: Anthropology and Archeaology, Economic History, Biography, Philosophy and Religion, Interpretation of Information, Governmental History, General Knowledge, Total.

o) AMERICAN HISTORY.
Scores, 9: Chronology, Government, Ideology, Foreign Policy, Geography, Politics, Economic History, Social History, Total.

p) AMERICAN GOVERNMENT.
Scores, 10: Principles of Government, Guarantees of Liberty, American Symbols and Political Traditions, Governmental Powers, Law Making and the Amendment Process, Duties and Qualifications of Federal Officials, Branches of Government-Duties and Checks, Presidential Succession and Appointment, Elections and Voting Procedure, Total.

q) CONSUMER ECONOMICS.
Scores, 9: Insurance, Credit, Banking and Investment, Economics, Consumer in the Marketplace, Money Management, Housing, Taxes, Total.

Cross References: For reviews by Robert K. Gable and Francis X. Archambault and by Gary W. Phillips, see 9:476.

Review of the High School Subject Tests by JIM C. FORTUNE, Professor, Educational Research and Evaluation, and JOHN M. WILLIAMS, Graduate Assistant, Coordinator of Educational Research Computing Laboratory, College of Education, Virginia Tech, Blacksburg, VA:

The High School Subject Tests are described by the authors as useful tools in the assessment of individual student performance, in the diagnosis of individual student achievement problems, in the evaluation of instructional programs, and in assisting career counseling. The tests are reported to provide both criterion-referenced and norm-referenced information in four subject areas, Mathematics, Social Studies, English, and Science across four grade levels, 9th, 10th, 11th, and 12th. Form B of the tests was the specimen set reviewed for this entry. Form A was reviewed by Gable and Archambault in 1985 (Gable & Archambault, 1985).

The norm referencing refers to norms created on a sample of 25,741 students selected randomly from a sample of public and private high schools across the country. The technical manual does not report the number of high schools, the mix of public/private auspices, nor the number of students taking each test in a content area. Instead, the technical manual includes a caution of comparing a student's performance across subjects due to different norm groups for individual content areas and grades. The overall sample size of 25,741 is not as impressive as it appears on the surface because this number includes composite groups of 9th, 10th, 11th, and 12th graders taking each subject area. No information that is descriptive of the norming sample is reported, but in the technical manual the user is assured that the sample was weighted to ensure that "geographical region and socioeconomic status were represented in the proper proportions." No mention is made as to representativeness of age and gender. Raw scores, percentile ranks, and standard scores are reported in Appendix B of the technical manual for each test. In the technical manual the biserial correlation and the mean raw score are reported as measures of item discrimination and difficulty respectively in Appendix C.

The criterion referencing refers to the referencing of the specific tests to an array of content objectives. The objectives are written clearly and are reported by test in the *High School Subject Tests Teacher's Manual and Technical Information* booklet. No cut scores are reported and the cross index reported in the technical manual links items to broad categories of objectives, rather than to specific objectives. For instance, in the test for Literature and Vocabulary four objectives are listed under this category of Inferential Comprehension and 15 items are linked to the category. No item linkage is made to any of the four objectives. This linkage does not permit one to reference performance on an item to a specific objective, except where the content linkage is simple. It appears that for some objectives there is inadequate domain sampling (sparse or no redundancy in content measurement due to too few items for the objective) to make objective-referenced interpretations.

The Kuder-Richardson Formula 20 was used to estimate reliability. Reliabilities for the 29 tests in the four content areas across the four grades range from .85 to .93 with a median of .88. The standard errors of measurement are reported with raw score means and standard deviations in the technical manual; however, the sample sizes on which the reported statistics were computed are not reported.

Content coverage is very difficult to judge without cross indexing items to objectives. The objectives that are reported in Appendix D of the technical manual are major objectives in the specific content areas and appear to cover a reasonable range of appropriate content for each course that is being measured. In Appendix A are reported the number of items by categories of objectives and the means of

subgroups of items at each quartile division. For example, there are four categories of objectives in the tests for Literature and Vocabulary. They include: Literal Comprehension, Inferential Comprehension, Vocabulary, and Literary Terms. In Literal Comprehension, there is one objective and 4 items. In Inferential Comprehension, there are four objectives and 15 items. In Vocabulary, there are two objectives and 18 items, and in Literary Terms, there is one objective and 13 items.

Each test requires 40 minutes for completion with approximately 10 minutes required for distribution and collection. The tests are easy to administer and complete instructions are provided in the administration manual. The major responding strategy appears to be recognition in the language-arts related tests and to some extent in all of the tests. Costs are competitive and scoring services can be purchased from the distributor. The tests range from 40 to 70 items in length.

The availability of Forms A and B permit using the test as pretest-posttest measures given the availability of comparative statistics on the two forms. True criterion-referenced interpretations appear unlikely and the utility of the tests for diagnosis is questioned without the item-to-objective cross indexing. Norm-referenced uses of the tests are also limited due to the inadequate reporting of the norming study. The tests can be recommended for use as a global measure of the content area, perhaps as a measure of effectiveness in an evaluation of instruction or curriculum.

Subtests have been used to test the preservice knowledge level of prospective elementary teachers in three studies (Gilmore, 1988; Ford, 1988; and McKinney, 1988). The subtests used were (a) American Government, (b) American History, and (c) World Geography. In all three subtests, student performance was below levels established by the researchers for "satisfactory" teacher-level knowledge. McKinney (1988) reported a computed reliability using the Kuder-Richardson Formula 20 of .88. This coefficient was on the 50 items for the World Geography test.

The researchers involved in each study felt the High School Subjects Tests were fair representations of content for these subject areas in high school curricula. Considering these researchers primarily studied students recently graduated from high school, their observations support the content validity of the subtests.

REVIEWERS' REFERENCES

Gable, R. K., & Archambault, F. X. (1985). [Review of the High School Subject Tests.] In J. V. Mitchell, Jr. (Ed.), *The ninth mental measurements yearbook* (pp. 656-657). Lincoln, NE: Buros Institute of Mental Measurements.

Ford, M. J. (1988). *Preservice elementary education majors' knowledge of American history.* Alexandria, VA. (ERIC Document Reproduction Service No. ED 305 314)

Gilmore, A. C. (1988). *Preservice elementary education majors' knowledge of American government.* Alexandria, VA. (ERIC Document Reproduction Service No. ED 305 315)

McKinney, C. W. (1988). *Preservice elementary education majors' knowledge of world geography.* Alexandria, VA. (ERIC Document Reproduction Service No. ED 305 313)

Review of the High School Subject Tests by ROBERT A. REINEKE, Evaluation Specialist, Lincoln Public Schools, Lincoln, NE:

The High School Subject Tests (Form B) are described as being both norm-referenced and criterion-referenced tests covering 17 subject areas. Subject area coverage is similar to that described in the original form of the High School Subject Tests (1980) with a few exceptions. The Health and World Geography tests have been deleted. Additions include Pre-Algebra (Forms B1 and B2), Advanced Algebra (Forms B-1 and B-2), Computer Literacy, and Physics. Consumer Economics has replaced Consumer Education. These subject area changes would seem to better reflect current curriculum emphasis than the earlier version of the High School Subject Tests (Form A).

Reasonable care seems to have been exercised in development of the tests. Teacher comments were used to guide early review and revision of items. A group of 25,741 students was used to establish national norms. The norming data were collected in 1988. Although reportedly based on a random sample of schools across the country, the representativeness of the actual participating schools cannot be determined because it is not known what percentage of schools actually responded to the invitation to participate in the norming study. The authors report the data were weighted to insure that geographic region and socioeconomic status were appropriately represented. Because norming populations differed among subtests, users are advised to be cautious when comparing a student's performance in various subject areas.

Reliabilities (Kuder-Richardson Formula 20) for the various subject tests are quite high. Reported reliability values ranged from .85 to .93. Users are cautioned to be aware that local reliability values may be lower than those [reported] based on national norms. Additional supporting data regarding characteristics such as subject test standard errors, item difficulty levels, and item discrimination coefficients are provided in extensive tables. This information should help users with local score interpretation.

The validity of the tests is described in terms of their accuracy in reflecting subject areas as taught throughout the United States. Appropriately, the user is cautioned to examine the "validity" of the test in terms of local coverage. Classification tables and objective lists are provided to assist local users in establishing the match between the stated test objectives and local objectives.

It appears that the item development and selection was done primarily to enhance norm-referenced interpretation of test scores, particularly given the item difficulties reported. Item difficulty coefficients appeared to center at or just above the .50 level, at least for most of the subtests.

Use of the tests for criterion-referenced or mastery decisions should be avoided. In addition to the item difficulties being inappropriate, the number of items per test is too small to make decisions about individual student mastery of unique skill areas. For this norm group and set of items, only about one in four students would achieve a "mastery" score much above 50% correct, at least for some subtests.

The High School Subject Tests (Form B) may provide a reasonable approach to compare local performance, particularly for a class, school, or school district, with a national norm group. Also these tests may be useful as a rough objectives-based measure if the match between stated test objectives and local objectives is high and if the items are judged to be at a difficulty level that is locally appropriate. Again, the classification tables and objectives lists should prove useful in ascertaining the match between the tests objectives and local objectives.

[161]
Hilson Adolescent Profile.

Purpose: "Designed as a screening tool to assess the presence and extent of adolescent behavior patterns and problems."
Population: Ages 10 to 19.
Publication Dates: 1984–87.
Acronym: HAP.
Scores, 16: Guarded Responses, Alcohol Use, Drug Use, Educational Adjustment Difficulties, Law Violations, Frustration Tolerance, Antisocial/Risk-Taking, Rigidity/Obsessiveness, Interpersonal/Assertiveness Difficulties, Homelife Conflicts, Social/Sexual Adjustment, Health Concerns, Anxiety/Phobic Avoidance, Depression/Suicide Potential, Suspicious Temperament, Unusual Responses. Temperament, Unusual Responses.
Administration: Group.
Price Data, 1990: $50 per starter kit including manual ('87, 82 pages); scoring service offered by publisher.
Special Edition: Audiotape edition available.
Time: (45–55) minutes.
Comments: Self-administered; computer-scored.
Authors: Robin E. Inwald, Karen E. Brobst (manual only), and Richard F. Morrissey (manual only).
Publisher: Hilson Research, Inc.

Review of the Hilson Adolescent Profile by ALLEN K. HESS, Professor and Department Head, Auburn University at Montgomery, Montgomery, AL:

The Hilson Adolescent Profile (HAP) is a 310-item true-false inventory intended to screen adolescents "at risk" for personality, behavior, and adjustment problems. The items are grouped into four domains; the first domain is a validity scale,

Guarded Responses (21 items); the second is an Acting Out Behavior with subdomains consisting of "External Behavior," which has scales regarding Alcohol Use (13 items), Drug Use (15 items), Educational Adjustment Difficulties (19 items), and Law/Society Violations (21 items), and Attitudes and Temperament with subdomains consisting of scales concerning Frustration Tolerance (23 items), Antisocial/Risk Taking (19 items), and Rigidity/Obsessiveness (21 items). The third domain is titled Interpersonal Adjustment and consists of scales labelled Interpersonal/Assertiveness Difficulties (26 items), Homelife Conflicts (33 items), and Social/Sexual Adjustment (22 items). The fourth domain is called "Internalized Conflict" and is composed of scales focussed on Health Concerns (14 items), Anxiety/Phobic Avoidance (25 items), Depression/Suicide Potential (25 items), Suspicious Temperament (17 items), and Unusual Responses (10 items).

Fourteen items appear on more than one scale, avoiding the heavy item-scale contamination problem that plagues some other inventories. By contrast, the Millon Clinical Multiaxial Inventory has over 90% item overlap, precluding differential validity, differential diagnosis, and any research based on correlation due to the collinearity problem. The HAP avoids this problem.

Section One of the test manual describes the rationale for the HAP, citing the tumultuous nature of adolescence and the large number of youth enmeshed in emotional turmoil, substance abuse, and legal trouble.

Section Two describes the scales' content, and Section Three provides clear directions for test administration. Scoring can be done by subscribing to The Hilson Mail-In Service, or purchasing software for scoring by one's own computer. Hand-scoring keys are unavailable. A tape-recorded version of the HAP is available for those unable to read this test, scaled for the fifth grade reading level.

Section Four describes psychometric properties of the HAP. The norming sample of 465 males and 251 females ranged from 10 to 19 years of age with a mean of 15 years, 9 months. Norms for the sample, plus subsamples of delinquents, psychiatric inpatients and outpatients, and college students are presented.

Internal consistency (KR 20) coefficients range from .67 to .90 for the 16 HAP scales. Two- to four-week test-retest reliabilities for the scales range from .74 to .95 for 33 students in one study, and .60 to .86 for a sample of 72 high school dropouts in a second 2- to 4-month test-retest study.

Factor analytic research for the 716-adolescent normative study reveals a three-factor solution with an "Internalized Difficulty" factor, an "Acting Out" factor, and a minor factor best characterized as gross disturbance.

Finally, criterion validity is addressed via a set of discriminant function analyses in which six groups were defined with problems of suicide, drug, alcohol, substance or sexual abuse, or conduct disturbance. Each group was contrasted with the remainder of the norm group. "Hits" or correct classifications ranged in the .70s, a modest level of prediction. These results require cross-validation and the coefficients will likely shrink in such studies. Moreover, false positives and negatives in classification applications have drastically different consequences, an issue not addressed in the manual.

Section Five presents several cases to show the HAP in action. The authors duly note that no inventory should be used in isolation.

So what does one make of all this description? The HAP addresses an important group, adolescents, with a set of obvious content items grouped in meaningful scales of decent reliability. Yet, the HAP, developed over the decade of the 1980s, is incipient in such areas as the correlation of items to scales, development of a national norm base, and criterion validity of the concurrent and predictive types. Although the HAP is supposed to be behavioral, the only criterion studies presented concern factor structure and classification. There are no studies, for example, on whether those scoring high on Frustration Tolerance (FT) differ on tasks tapping that quality when contrasted with low FT scorers. Specific, behavioral validity studies are needed.

Similarly, before the HAP can be useful in clinical settings where dissimulation may be a problem, studies concerning response distortion are needed. We simply do not know how the Guarded Response scale works, though we do know that youth, particularly troubled ones, are prone to exaggerations.

In sum, the HAP is akin to a hypothesis that is yet to be tested. There seems to be a set of obviously stated, readable items that cluster in three areas, and have some reasonable reliabilities and modestly representative norms groups. The intrepid test user may wish to use the HAP in concert with other information sources and inventories, and develop local norms. The HAP, however, is an inventory in search of validity.

[162]
Hilson Personnel Profile/Success Quotient.

Purpose: To identify individual "strengths," behavior patterns, and personality characteristics "leading to success in a variety of work settings."
Population: High school through adult.
Publication Date: 1988.
Acronym: HPP/SQ.

Scores, 13: Candor, Achievement History, Social Ability (Extroversion, Popularity/"Charisma," Sensitivity to Approval), "Winner's" Image (Competitive Spirit, Self-Worth, Family Achievement Expectations), Initiative (Drive, Preparation Style, Goal Orientation, Anxiety About Organization), Success Quotient.
Administration: Group.
Price Data, 1991: $60 per complete starter kit including 3 scorings; $1.50 per test booklet; $2.50 per 10 answer sheets; $12.50 per manual (83 pages); $9–$12 per test (according to volume) for computer scoring.
Time: (20–30) minutes.
Authors: Robin E. Inwald.
Publisher: Hilson Research, Inc.

Review of the Hilson Personnel Profile/Success Quotient by JOSEPH G. LAW, JR., Associate Professor of Behavioral Studies, University of South Alabama, Mobile, AL:

The Hilson Personnel Profile/Success Quotient (HPP/SQ) follows in the tradition of the Inwald Personality Inventory (IPI; 183) by using behavioral descriptors and historical data rather than symptom-oriented questions. The HPP/SQ is based on Inwald's Success Quotient theory. It attempts to operationalize the hypothesis that an employee's successful adaptation to the workplace is based on such factors as social ability, initiative, and competitive spirit as well as academic ability. Rather than infer job-related characteristics from personality tests, Inwald has designed the HPP/SQ to measure directly how well examinees have developed crucial social skills, good work habits, and the self-confidence to do well on a job. Although the IPI enables the user to screen *out* prospective employees based upon negative factors, the HPP/SQ was developed originally to screen *in* those most likely to be successful. However, recent research suggests the HPP/SQ is equally successful in identifying negative traits, for example, correlations between low scores on some scales and poor performance in management and sales positions have been obtained. According to the publisher, new computer programs are under development which will enable the narrative reports to pinpoint strengths and weakness with greater precision (R. Inwald, personal communication, January 22, 1991).

The inventory measures these "success" factors with five basic scales: Candor (16 items), Achievement History (33 items), Social Ability (40 items), "Winner's" Image (28 items), and Initiative (33 items). The Candor scale is used to determine how frank the examinee was in responding. When combined with other scales, Candor may also indicate how an individual responds to criticism and the expectations of others. Profile interpretation focuses on the five basic scales and the overall summary score or Success Quotient (SQ). Component items from the basic scales have been grouped into areas with labels such as Competitive Spirit and

Drive to facilitate further analysis. The 10 content areas range from a low of 5 items (Anxiety about Organization) to a high of 19 items (Extroversion), with an average of about 10 items per content area. The manual's authors stress the need to realize the limitations of the shorter area scores when interpreting the profiles of individual examinees.

A normative sample of 985 applicants for entry-level jobs in a city agency were administered the HPP/SQ, as well as 5 company samples and 12 job category samples (e.g., sales professionals, psychiatrists). Although socioeconomic status is not mentioned in the manual, it appears by the job titles of the 12 job category samples that white-collar workers in skilled occupations are overrepresented in contrast to blue-collar and semiskilled/unskilled workers. The entry-level sample contains more blue-collar representation. In the sample of city job applicants there are data on 272 Black females, but only 9 White females and 25 Hispanic females. Similarly, there are data on 395 Black males, but only 130 White males and 140 Hispanic males. Although the size of the sample should be large enough to make this a useful screening instrument, the authors note that care should be exercised in the interpretation of White females' scores.

Studies of internal consistency and test-retest reliability are reported in the 83-page manual. Cronbach's alpha coefficient is reported for the five basic scales on a sample of 931 entry-level applicants. Coefficients range from .76 to .80, with a mean of .78. A sample of 300 current employees produced a mean alpha of .81 for the first five scales. To assess test-retest reliability, a sample of 100 entry-level job applicants was administered the HPP/SQ at 4–6 week intervals. The mean correlation coefficient for the first five scales was .78. Factor analyses reported in the manual support the construct validity of the test scales.

The HPP/SQ and its manual have quite a few strengths. The inventory is based upon a strong theory and research base, with adequate information on reliability and validity in the manual. Ongoing studies of validity are evident by numerous studies completed since the publication of the manual.

The manual contains 13 pages of data and narrative addressing the issue of validity. Thorough, in-depth studies of small occupational groups such as computer programmers, psychologists, administrative assistants, and top level managers are reviewed to illustrate how high scores on the HPP/SQ contribute to success in these jobs. Concurrent validity studies using the Minnesota Multiphasic Personality Inventory (MMPI), the IPI, and the California Psychological Inventory (CPI) are reported in the manual. The Social Ability scale correlated .44 with the CPI Sociability scale, .36 with the CPI Dominance scale, and .37 with the CPI Self-Acceptance scale. The "Winner's" Image scale on the HPP/SQ correlated .41 with CPI Dominance and .38 with CPI Self-Acceptance. Negative correlations with the CPI were in expected directions (e.g., "Winner's" Image inversely related to Psychological Mindedness and Femininity). The MMPI Lie Scale correlated -.40 with the HPP/SQ Candor scale and -.53 with the IPI Guardedness scale, lending support to a conceptualization of the Candor scale as a validity index for the HPP/SQ.

The manual contains 41 pages of tables on normative samples and 21 individual sample profiles to assist in learning profile interpretation. A section on interpretation reinforces the importance of developing local norms and looking for relative strengths in each examinee's individual profile. Test scores are stored in a data bank by the test publisher so that individual agency norms can be maintained and cutoff points for future selection decisions can be adjusted as needed to ensure fairness. Occupational norms are provided in the manual for 12 job categories.

An analysis of 931 entry-level applicants found Black and Hispanic males scoring significantly higher than White males on a number of scales, with no differences between Black and Hispanic females. Mean scores for males were higher than those of females on a number of scales, including Competitive Spirit and "Winner's" Image. There were no significant racial differences in a separate sample of 391 employed individuals (Inwald & Kaufman, 1985). Normative data are reported by race and sex in the manual.

The short examination time required, sixth grade reading level, nonthreatening nature of item content, and flexibility of administration (individual and group) contribute to the utility of the HPP/SQ. Correction of some minor errors, further discussion of item development and content validity, and the addition of a table of contents and index would greatly improve the manual, which largely follows guidelines set forth in the *Standards for Educational and Psychological Testing* (AERA, APA, & NCME, 1985).

Overall, the HPP/SQ is a very promising instrument for employee selection and should prove useful to industrial/organizational psychologists, personnel administrators, and researchers. The availability of item responses with the computer-generated scores may also assist therapists and counselors in formulating treatment plans for clients, especially those in vocational rehabilitation settings.

REVIEWER'S REFERENCES

American Educational Research Association, American Psychological Association, & National Council on Measurement in Education. (1985). *Standards for educational and psychological testing.* Washington, DC: American Psychological Association, Inc.

Inwald, R. E., & Kaufman, J. C. (1990). *Race and sex differences on the Hilson Personnel Profile/Success Quotient.* Kew Gardens, NY: Hilson Research Inc.

[163]
Hogan Personnel Selection Series.

Purpose: "Four inventories to identify personality characteristics important to specific job requirements."
Population: High school seniors and adults.
Publication Date: 1986.
Acronym: HPSS.
Scores: 4 inventories, 19 scales: Prospective Employee Potential Inventory (Service Orientation, Stress Tolerance, Reliability, Validity), Clerical Potential Inventory (Clerical Potential, Service Orientation, Stress Tolerance, Reliability, Validity), Sales Potential Inventory (Sales Potential, Service Orientation, Stress Tolerance, Reliability, Validity), Managerial Potential Inventory (Managerial Potential, Service Orientation, Stress Tolerance, Reliability, Validity).
Administration: Group.
Price Data, 1989: $5.95 or less per prepaid answer sheets including test items and cost of scoring and reports (indicate Prospective Employee, Clerical Potential, Sales Potential, or Managerial Potential Inventory) via mail-in scoring service; $8.50 per manual (43 pages); $11 per specimen set (indicate inventory) including combined test booklet and answer sheet, Guide to Interpreting a Report for the Hogan Personnel Selection Series ('85, 1 page), and manual; $9.25 or less per 25 answer sheets for use with ARION II Teleprocessing or Microtest Assessment Software scoring; $5.95 or less per scoring via ARION II Teleprocessing; $48 per 10-use disk ($240 per 50-use, $450 per 100-use) for Microtest Assessment Software for on-site scoring and reports for all four inventories (for use with IBM PC or PC/XT).
Time: (20–30) minutes per inventory.
Comments: Derived from the Hogan Personality Inventory (10:140); inventories available as separates.
Authors: Joyce Hogan and Robert Hogan.
Publisher: National Computer Systems.

Review of the Hogan Personnel Selection Series by S. ALVIN LEUNG, Assistant Professor of Educational Psychology, University of Houston, Houston, TX:

(Scales from the Hogan Personnel Selection Series being reviewed included: Service Orientation, Reliability, Stress Tolerance, Clerical Potential, Sales Potential, Management Potential, and Validity.)

According to the User Manual, the Hogan Personnel Selection Series (HPSS) is designed as a personnel selection device for organizations. The HPSS purports to help organizations in two areas of employee selection. The first is to identify the kinds of people who will perform well within various organizational roles, and the second is to identify individuals who will perform well in a particular organizational role.

Information relevant to the first area is to be found in the first section of the HPSS, called the Prospective Employee Potential Inventory (PEPI). The PEPI consists of three scales: Service Orientation, Reliability, and Stress Tolerance. The authors of the HPSS suggest that people who are service-oriented, reliable, and tolerant of stress will perform well within various organizational roles.

The second concern is addressed in the second section of the HPSS. Three scales are offered to measure potential in specified organizational roles: Clerical Potential, Sales Potential, and Managerial Potential. A Validity Scale is included to detect whether the HPSS items are answered properly by a respondent.

All the items in the HPSS are in true-false format. The PEPI has a total of 198 items, including 87 items for Service Orientation, 69 items for Reliability, and 55 items for Stress Tolerance. However, the total number of items obtained by adding up the totals for the three scales (resulting in 211 items) does not match the 198 items total printed in the test booklet. Although the discrepancy may be due to some items being used twice, it is not addressed in the manual, creating confusion for the reviewer and perhaps, for some users. The total number of items for the Clerical, Sales, Managerial, and Validity scales are 25, 24, 57, and 16 respectively. It takes about 20–25 minutes to complete the HPSS.

Items for the various scales of the HPSS were abstracted from a personality inventory called the Hogan Personality Inventory (Hogan, 1986). Core items from the Hogan Personality Inventory were recombined to form the scales of the HPSS. Correlational techniques were used to form the HPSS scales. Scores from the various scales of the Hogan Personality Inventory were used to correlate with certain criterion variables, and low to moderate correlations (usually between .10 and .30) were used as rationale for forming the new scales of the HPSS. The resulting HPSS scales were not confirmed by factor analytic techniques. In addition, the samples used to generate data for scale formation were of questionable appropriateness. For example, to demonstrate the Reliability scale discriminated between reliable and unreliable workers, the responses of two groups of known felons were compared with those of blue-collar men and undergraduate students. In another place, the Stress Tolerance scale was developed based on data collected from a group of 56 truck drivers (assumed here to be mostly males). The Clerical scale was formed based on data collected from 107 women holding clerical positions (no males included). To show that the HPSS is valid for men and women in various organizational settings, more representative samples have to be used.

Reliability information was rather incomplete. The reliability estimates reported in the manual were those from the Hogan Personality Inventory. The authors suggested that because the HPSS items were abstracted from this Inventory, they shared the same psychometric properties. This assumption may bear some reexamination. Four-week test-retest reliabilities for the HPSS scales for a sample of 36 male and female working adults (the male and female distribution was not reported) ranged from .70 to .90. The internal consistency of the scales, based on data from 43 male and 47 female undergraduate students, was rather low, ranging from .19 (the Clerical scale) to .63 (the Reliability scale), with an average of .46. There is a need to generate more reliability information based on larger and more representative samples.

Although the authors were able to demonstrate low to moderate correlations between the HPSS scales and specific criterion variables as evidence of construct and concurrent validity, the studies reported have several limitations. First, it is not clear how some of the criterion variables were operationally measured. For example, job performance was often used as a criterion variable to correlate with the Service Orientation scale, but how job performance was measured, and information concerning raters and interrater reliability, were not reported. This information is important as it indicates the validity of the criteria variables.

Second, in the studies reported in the manual concerning scale information and validity, the sample distribution concerning males and females was seldom given. It is crucial to document that the HPSS is both valid and fair for both males and females.

Third, other information concerning samples, such as age and educational background, was omitted. For example, no such information was provided concerning the samples used to compute the norm table. It is not clear whether the individuals were students, working adults, or others. Because the percentile scores and interpretation in the individual reports are generated from the norm table, it is distressing to have such information omitted.

Fourth, the authors included normative data for both Whites and Blacks, but there was no discussion concerning possible cross-cultural applications and limitations.

Aside from the absence of some essential information mentioned above, the manual is quite well organized and concise, and has some information that a user will find helpful. An example of a score report given in the User Manual (p. 28) appears to be well written, presenting clearly the implications and limitations of the scores.

The HPSS is essentially a "reframing" of the Hogan Personality Inventory into a personnel selection device. After reviewing the information concerning scale formation, reliability, and validity, it appears the HPSS must be improved in a number of areas to make it a valid instrument for the intended purposes. More planned research with appropriate samples is needed to generate information concerning reliability and construct validity. Because of the limitations discussed above, practitioners should use it with caution.

REVIEWER'S REFERENCE

Hogan, R. (1986). *Hogan Personality Inventory Manual*. Minneapolis, MN: National Computer Systems, Inc.

Review of the Hogan Personnel Selection Series by NORMAN D. SUNDBERG, *Professor Emeritus of Psychology, University of Oregon, Eugene, OR:*

Despite earlier studies showing limited utility of personality tests in predicting job success, Joyce and Robert Hogan have accepted the challenge to create a valid measure. The Hogan Personnel Selection Series (HPSS) literally comes out of the Hogan Personality Inventory (HPI, reviewed in the 1989 *Tenth Mental Measurements Yearbook* [10:140] by Hennessy and Peterson, and elsewhere by Lifton and Nannis, 1987). The Hogans state their assumptions about personality and personnel selection in the HPSS Manual and other publications (Hogan & Hogan, 1989; Hogan, Hogan, & Busch, 1984; Hogan, Hogan, & Gregory, in press; Hogan, Hogan, & Murtha, in press). For instance, they assert that personality is closely related to the interpersonal aspects of work effectiveness, that their test measures the "big five" variables (i.e., neuroticism, extraversion, agreeableness, conscientiousness, and openness) found by many personality researchers, and that the so-called "self-report" inventories are really self-presentations of the public self (as opposed to the private self) reflecting one's interpersonal style in everyday life. An innovative aspect of these measures is the use of small groups of highly correlated items, Homogeneous Item Composites (HICs) as units to form scales on the HPI and HPSS, rather than individual items.

The HPSS consists of seven scales arranged in four inventories. The items, all selected from the 310 items of the HPI, are easily read, phrased in the first person, and answered true or false. Examples are "It is easy for me to talk to strangers," and "I have been in trouble for drinking too much." Most people finish the test in 20 to 30 minutes. The three core personality scales are Service Orientation, Reliability, and Stress Tolerance. These three and the Validity scale are combined in the 198-item Prospective Employee Potential Inventory (PEPI), which may be administered alone for general assessment. The three scales oriented to specific occupational areas, the Clerical Potential (CLE), Sales Potential (SAL), and Managerial Potential (MAN) are integrated with PEPI items to produce three inventories. As an example, the Managerial Potential Inventory has 223 true-false items on a form for scoring by the National Computer Systems.

Development of scales involved empirical selection using ratings and records in various applied settings. The purpose of the Service Orientation Scale is to identify people who work well with the public and other staff members; it was developed mainly by choosing HICs which correlated with supervisor nominations of nursing aides in a large Baltimore hospital. The purpose of the Reliability Scale is to identify potential employees who are honest and rule-abiding (the opposite of "organizational delinquency," Hogan & Hogan, 1989); it was developed using responses of felons as compared with those of nondelinquents. The purpose of the Stress Tolerance Scale is to identify people whose work is seldom interfered with by accidents or illness, and it was developed by using reports in a trucking company.

The foregoing three scales, used on the PEPI, have only a small amount of item overlap, but they correlate around .50 with each other. The three occupational scales use some PEPI items and some additional items. The Clerical Potential scale (CLE) was developed by using ratings of women in various clerical positions in a large insurance company. The development of the Sales Potential scale (SAL) made use of sales representatives in a large trucking firm. The development of the Managerial Potential scale (MAN) involved managers in the same trucking firm. The three occupational scales exhibit great variability in correlations with each other and with the personality scales, ranging from .01 (Reliability & SAL) to .73 (Service Orientation & MAN). All of these six scales have been developed on limited samples, and generalization to other populations is a question which the Hogans take up in some of their research. The seventh scale, a part of the PEPI, is the Validity scale. It consists of 16 items answered 92% of the time in the scored direction. A low score suggests the person was careless or did not understand. The authors briefly discuss faking or self-misrepresentation but present no studies with the HPSS.

The HPSS manual is a well-written document of 38 pages, including 14 pages of appendices and over 50 references. It has a helpful discussion of expectancy tables and utility. The manual provides brief descriptions of the development of each of the seven scales. Norms are given for men and women and for Blacks and Whites, though in general there are few gender or ethnic differences. Internal consistency of the scales tends to be only moderate because of the heterogeneity of the HICs, but test-retest reliability is higher. For each of the scales, the authors present validity information using measures from job performance and tests. These are too numerous to cover in a short review but, in general, performance criteria correlate in the expected directions, but at low to moderate levels; very few reached .30. Correlations with the California Psychological Inventory (CPI) scales were also low and mostly in expected directions; surprisingly the SAL showed little correlation with CPI scales. Correlations with the Self-Directed Search are reported but are complex to interpret; in this case the CLE showed few correlations of magnitude. The Hogans continue to investigate the HPSS. For example, their 1989 article is a useful review of research on employee reliability, including an extensive study showing positive results using the HPSS with caretakers in an Idaho facility for the retarded.

What can be said about the strengths and weaknesses of the HPSS? On the positive side, it is an interesting new approach in relating personality to job selection and performance. The authors have carried out a knowledgeable and extensive set of investigations. The test is relatively short, clear, self-administrable, and usable with people of high school education or somewhat less. It covers important core personality characteristics and three common occupational domains. NCS provides computer scoring and interpretation for individuals and groups. On the negative side, the test is quite new and untried in many settings. There are very few reports by researchers other than the authors. Much work needs to be done to demonstrate validity with other populations, especially predictive validity. As with all computerized interpretations, these from NCS need separate validity research. Apparently no hand-scoring forms are provided. There are still many questions about test-taking attitudes, not covered by the so-called Validity scale.

In conclusion, the HPSS is a promising test, grounded in an interesting theoretical viewpoint and worthy of further research and consideration for applications. As with most tests, it needs studies of incremental utility for employee selection beyond such common procedures as biodata information and against other tests, such as the CPI. Because there is a limited amount of research on the HPSS, potential users in applied settings should study the excellent manual carefully, and perhaps consult with the authors and consider development of local norms and cutoff scores for decisions.

REVIEWER'S REFERENCES

Hogan, J., Hogan, R., & Busch, C. M. (1984). How to measure service orientation. *Journal of Applied Psychology, 69,* 167-173.

Lifton, P. D., & Nannis, E. D. (1987). Hogan Personality Inventory and Hogan Personnel Selection Series. In D. J. Keyser & R. C. Sweetland (Eds.), *Test critiques,* Vol. VI (pp. 216-225). Kansas City, MO: Test Corporation.

Hennessy, J. J. (1989). [Review of the Hogan Personality Inventory.] In J. C. Conoley & J. J. Kramer (Eds.), *The tenth mental measurements yearbook* (pp. 352-354). Lincoln, NE: Buros Institute of Mental Measurements.

Hogan, J., & Hogan, R. (1989). How to measure employee reliability. *Journal of Applied Psychology, 74,* 273-279.

Peterson, R. A. (1989). [Review of the Hogan Personality Inventory.] In J. C. Conoley & J. J. Kramer (Eds.), *The tenth mental measurements yearbook* (pp. 354-355). Lincoln, NE: Buros Institute of Mental Measurements.

Hogan, J., Hogan, R., & Gregory, S. (in press). Validation of a sales representative selection inventory. In F. Landy (Ed.), *Handbook of test validity.* Pacific Grove, CA: Brooks/Cole.

Hogan, J., Hogan, R., & Murtha, T. (in press). Validation of a personality measure of managerial performance. In F. Landy (Ed.), *Handbook of test validity.* Pacific Grove, CA: Brooks/Cole.

The Houston Test for Language Development, Revised Edition.

Purpose: Developed to assess "linguistic and non-verbal communication ability in children."
Publication Dates: 1958–78.
Scores: 4 categories: Self Talk, Auditory, Non-Verbal, Oral Communication.
Administration: Individual.
Price Data, 1991: $90 per complete kit; $17 per set of vocabulary cards; $16 per 25 record forms; $28.50 per manual ('78, 56 pages).
Author: Margaret Crabtree.
Publisher: Stoelting Co.

a) INFANT SCALE.
Population: Birth to 18 months.
Time: (20–30) minutes.
b) 2–6 YEAR TEST.
Population: Ages 2–6.
Time: (30–40) minutes.
Cross References: For reviews by Margaret C. Byrne and Lawrence J. Turton and an excerpted review by C. H. Ammons, see 7:954; see also 6:310 (1 reference).

Review of the Houston Test for Language Development, Revised Edition by JEFFREY A. ATLAS, Deputy Chief Psychologist and Assistant Clinical Professor, Bronx Children's Hospital, Albert Einstein College of Medicine, Bronx, NY:

A *test* of *language* development optimally comprises valid indices of language, standardized administration procedures, reliability data, and population norms. Because The Houston Test fulfills these conditions only partially, it might be better conceptualized as a *scale* of *early communicative competence.*

The Houston Test is made up of an infant scale for children 0 to 18 months (administration time of 20 to 30 minutes) and a 2- to 6-year-old component (30 to 40 minutes) having 18 measures, including assessments of vocabulary, gesture, and drawing. Some of the items of the infant scale, such as "babbles," are clear language (word) precursors, whereas others such as "smiles," "laughs," "holds out arms," "waves," and "points," are precursors to gestural development or more generally indices of communicative competence. For example, the absence of a social smile within the first 6 months may not necessarily be prodromal to impairment in the formal (semantic) properties of language, but may augur derailment in social-emotional development and attendant impairment in the pragmatics of communication, as seen in echolalia, perseveration, and telegraphic speech. As The Houston Test assesses some of these dimensions of communication it recommends itself as a useful adjunctive instrument in screening for severe emotional disorder, specifically early childhood psychoses.

The attractively packaged manual for The Houston Test details a set of administration procedures that strike a harmonious balance between standardized approach and individualized parameters, enhancing the likelihood of demonstrated performance and diminishing false negative results. For example, the "smile" item necessitates a smile in response to another person (not a reflexive smile), but procedures permit the mother or some other familiar person to elicit the smile. The manual has too many typographical errors for a test that has been in circulation since 1978. The test materials, although simple enough and engaging, also show some oddities: The vocabulary cards are not numbered and the bendable toy family's package bears the inscription "not recommended for child under four." As with other toys small enough to be ingested or sharp enough to be stuck into orifices, one would want to ensure against unmonitored handling of the test materials.

The manual gives a test-retest correlation coefficient, based on a 1-week retest of 25 children aged 6 months to 6 years, of .98. There are no figures for interrater reliability. It is stated in the manual that the "norms" were based on a study of 370 children but no normative data are provided that would allow for evaluation of significant deviations. The validity of placement of items in the scale was determined by percentages passing at specified age levels as compared to the year below or above (chi square yielding differences at .01 level of confidence). The author, Mary Crabtree, gives sensible suggestions for deviations warranting clinical attention.

The sample population is said to be from Standard American English speaking backgrounds, located in both rural and metropolitan areas of Texas and Oregon. In interpreting test results the author recommends using broader cutoffs for a child with Black Dialect or Spanish background in identifying deviation but this seems unsatisfactory. Given the test's exclusive derivation from children of standard English speaking backgrounds the present reviewer would restrict its use to this population. The scale, although useful, is impressionistic enough without extrapolating to groups outside the study sample.

The Houston Test yields categorizations of strength or concern ("above age," "below age") in Self Talk, Auditory Function, Non-Verbal Communication, and Oral Communication. Given the heterogeneity of subtest groupings (Non-Verbal Communication includes assessment of preposition understanding along with reproduction of geometric designs and production of a house, tree, and person) one should use the "Category Analysis" with caution. The "Clinical Observations" illustrated in the manual are sometimes suspect—of most concern is the author's loose usage of the term "hyperactivity" (e.g., "The two year old is normally hyperactive if he is given all of the toys at once").

The most useful summary score for this scale is, paradoxically, the most general, the derived "Communication Age." Although one may challenge the factor groupings and loadings of the "Category Analysis," the Communication Age is a summated score that takes into account all of the wide variety of communicative behaviors sampled by The Houston Test, ranging from expressive and receptive language, imitation of prosodic patterns, to drawing. The Communication Age is also the one score grounded in statistical data, yielding an ordinal scale.

The Houston Test may be recommended as a potentially useful adjunctive instrument in pediatric-psychiatric and early-educational settings. It may assist in screening for emotional problems reflected through formal and qualitative aspects of communication, may identify areas of strength and leverages for intervention in language-disordered children, and may identify candidates for early educational enrichment/remediation.

Review of The Houston Test for Language Development, Revised Edition by DOLORES KLUPPEL VETTER, Professor and Associate Dean, University of Wisconsin-Madison, Madison, WI:

The author states that the revision of The Houston Test for Language Development was undertaken as a response to questions raised by users of the test concerning scoring and interpretation. It contains two scales, for birth to 18 months and ages 2 to 6 years, which were previously assessed by the two parts of the test. A single administration and interpretation manual was produced and duplicate items on the scales were deleted or rewritten. The manual provides details of scoring and interpretation and contains illustrative examples and case histories.

Unfortunately, the author does not appear to have responded to the criticisms of the psychometric adequacy of the original scales (Hatten, 1979). The manual for the revised test provides the rationale for the revision and all psychometric information in a single page of text. There is a paucity of information on either the validity or the reliability of the instrument and little information on the 370 normative subjects. They were from rural and urban backgrounds in Texas and Oregon in which Standard American English was spoken, but there is no information concerning the number, gender, or ethnic heritage of children at each age level. In addition, the author apparently expects the use of the earlier publications of the test for the rationale for the weighting values of items for the total score and the interpretation of Communication Age because neither of these are contained in the manual for the revised edition.

The Houston Test for Language Development requires a minimal amount of testing sophistication for its use. Directions for scoring the scales are detailed and examples are given. The examiner should, however, be a skilled observer, know how to interact with children, and have a knowledge of the abilities and behaviors of children in the age range specified.

There are four categories of observations scored in the Infant Scale: Self Talk, Auditory, Non-Verbal, and Oral Communication. Either the examiner or another more familiar adult may set the conditions for many of the behaviors to be observed. Items are scored as plus or minus depending upon whether or not the specific behavior (e.g., laughs out loud) occurs during the testing period. If it does not occur, it is impossible to know whether it is because the child is not capable of producing the response or because the adult was not capable of setting the conditions for the response to occur. Because there is no information on how items were chosen for inclusion on the scale, item validity is not addressed. There are no data on the variation in the normative infants' productions of these behaviors; therefore, a valid interpretation of the scores on the Infant Scale is not possible.

There are 18 subtests on the 2–6-Year Test. Some have general face validity for language assessment (e.g., vocabulary), others are problematic (e.g., copying geometric designs). No evidence nor rationale are provided for the inclusion of any of the subtests. Performance on a subtest is determined at yearly intervals. A total score (Communication Age) is obtained by summing the number of items at each age level, weighting the score by the item value, and then summing across age levels. This score reflects an assumption that each item passed is equivalent to months of communication. There are no data presented to support such an assumption and none are available in the research literature.

To obtain gross indicators of strengths and weaknesses in a child, performance above or below age on each of the subtests is assigned to one of the same four categories as on the Infant Scale. Although this is presented as a norm-referenced instrument the author suggests the knowledge of these strengths and weaknesses may be used in planning language intervention.

The revised Houston Test of Language Development falls substantially short of the minimal standards required for a standardized test. At best, it presents a systematic way to record observations of some linguistic and nonlinguistic behaviors of children. The interpretation of Communication Age, subtest scores, and strengths and weaknesses by category are not an improvement on clinical observation.

REVIEWER'S REFERENCE

Hatten, J. T. (1979). The Houston Test for Language Development. In F. L. Darley (Ed.), *Evaluation of appraisal techniques in speech and language pathology* (pp. 29-30). Reading, MA: Addison-Wesley.

[165]
How Well Do You Know Your Interests.

Purpose: Designed to identify "an individual's attitudes of liking, disliking, or apathy toward . . . work activities."
Population: Grades 9–12, college, adults.
Publication Dates: 1957–75.
Scores, 54: Numerical, Clerical, Retail Selling, Outside Selling, Selling Real Estate, One-Order Selling, Sales Complaints, Selling Intangibles, Buyer, Labor Management, Production Supervision, Business Management, Machine Operation, Repair & Construction, Machine Design, Farm or Ranch, Gardening, Hunting, Adventure, Social Service, Teaching Service, Medical Service, Nursing Service, Applied Chemistry, Basic Chemical Problems, Basic Biological Problems, Basic Physical Problems, Basic Psychological Problems, Philosophical, Visual Art (Appreciative, Productive, Decorative), Amusement (Appreciative, Productive, Managerial), Literary (Appreciative, Productive), Musical (Appreciative, Performing, Composing), Sports (Appreciative, Participative), Domestic Service, Unskilled Labor, Disciplinary, Power Seeking, Propaganda, Self-Aggrandizing, Supervisory Initiative, Bargaining, Arbitrative, Persuasive, Disputatious, Masculinity (for males only) or Femininity (for females only).
Administration: Group.
Levels, 3: Secondary School, College, Personnel.
Price Data, 1991: $11 per complete kit including 3 test booklets of each edition, scoring keys, and manual ('74, 24 pages); $20 per 25 test booklets (select level); $6.75 per set of scoring keys; $6.75 per manual; $6.75 per handbook on interpretation ('75, 19 pages).
Time: (15–20) minutes.
Authors: Thomas N. Jenkins (test booklets, manual), John H. Coleman (manual, handbook), and Harold T. Fagin (manual).
Publisher: Psychologists and Educators, Inc.
Cross References: See 7:1022 (2 references); for a review by John R. Hills and an excerpted review by Gordon V. Anderson, see 6:1059 (1 reference); for reviews by Jerome E. Doppelt and Henry S. Dyer, see 5:859.

[166]
How Well Do You Know Yourself?

Purpose: Developed to assess personality characteristics.
Population: Grades 9–12, college, office and factory workers.
Publication Dates: 1959–76.
Scores, 19: Irritability, Practicality, Punctuality, Novelty-Loving, Vocational Assurance, Cooperativeness, Ambitiousness, Hypercriticalness, Dejection, General Morale, Persistence, Nervousness, Seriousness, Submissiveness, Impulsiveness, Dynamism, Emotional Control, Consistency, Test Objectivity.
Administration: Group.
Levels, 3: Secondary School, College, Personnel.
Price Data, 1991: $11 per complete kit including test booklets (3 of each level) and manual ('74, 30 pages); $20 per 25 test booklets (select level); $6.75 per set of scoring keys; $6.75 per manual.
Time: Administration time not reported.
Authors: Thomas N. Jenkins, John H. Coleman (manual), and Harold T. Fagin (manual).
Publisher: Psychologists and Educators, Inc.

Cross References: See T2:1220 (2 references); see also P:113; for reviews by Lee J. Cronbach and Harrison G. Gough and excerpted reviews by Edward S. Bordin and Laurence Siegel, see 6:118 (2 references).

TEST REFERENCES

1. Westbrook, B. W., Sanford, E. E., & Donnelly, M. H. (1989). The reliability and validity of the Self-Appraisal Scale of the Career Maturity Inventory. *Educational and Psychological Measurement, 49,* 929-935.

[167]
Hudson Education Skills Inventory.

Purpose: Assesses "the academic performance level of students with dysfunctional learning patterns."
Population: Grades K–12.
Publication Date: 1989.
Acronym: HESI.
Scores: Item scores only.
Subtests, 3: Mathematics, Reading, Writing; available as separates.
Administration: Individual.
Price Data, 1989: $169 per complete battery including 1 each of complete Mathematics, Reading, and Writing kits; $59 per complete Mathematics, Reading, or Writing kit; $19 per student book; $22 per instructional planning form; $21 per examiner's manual (Mathematics, 119 pages; Reading, 86 pages; Writing, 177 pages); $69 per software report system (Apple and IBM versions available).
Time: Administration time not reported.
Comments: "Criterion-referenced."
Publisher: PRO-ED, Inc.

a) MATHEMATICS.
Acronym: HESI-M.
Scores: 14 skill areas: Numeration, Addition of Whole Numbers, Subtraction of Whole Numbers, Multiplication of Whole Numbers, Division of Whole Numbers, Fractions, Decimals, Percentages, Time, Money, Measurement, Statistics/Graphs/Tables, Geometry, Word Problems.
Authors: Floyd G. Hudson and Steven E. Colson.

b) READING.
Acronym: HESI-R.
Scores: 5 skill areas: Readiness, Vocabulary, Phonic Analysis, Structural Analysis, Comprehension.
Authors: Floyd G. Hudson, Steven E. Colson, and Doris L. Hudson Welch.

c) WRITING.
Acronym: HESI-W.
Scores: 3 parts, 14 skill areas: Composition (Capitalization, Punctuation, Grammar, Vocabulary, Sentences, Paragraphs), Spelling (Readiness, Consonants, Vowels, Structural Changes, Selected Word Groups), Handwriting (Readiness, Manuscript, Cursive).
Authors: Floyd G. Hudson, Steven E. Colson, Alison K. Banikowski, and Teresa A. Mehring.

Review of the Hudson Education Skills Inventory by RONALD K. HAMBLETON, *Professor of Education and Psychology, University of Massachusetts at Amherst, Amherst, MA:*

This 1989 mathematics, reading, and writing testing system is fairly typical of objectives-based testing systems that have been commercially available since the early 1970s with the advent of criterion-referenced testing practices in the schools. The tests are intended to be used in diagnosing student learning problems and in providing a basis for planning effective instruction. The complete package of materials including background, philosophy, tests, instructional planning forms, etc., is nicely organized and presented. The materials appear to have been carefully put together. However, some of the terminology used in the material is confusing.

The terms, *skills* and *objectives*, which are often used interchangeably in the criterion-referenced testing literature, mean very different things in the Hudson Education Skills Inventory (HESI) series. Skills or skills areas are so broad in the HESI series that 14 areas (in Mathematics, for example) comprehensively cover the curriculum. In other testing packages, perhaps the term "strand" would be used. Skills are further divided into subskills and objectives are matched to subskills. But then there are slips, too, in the writing and the term *skill* was used when the term *objective* should have been. This made for confusing reading! This reviewer had to read the three manuals (one for each content area) several times to sort things out. Only then did this reviewer learn that the use of these and other terms was somewhat inconsistent both across and within the three manuals.

Another confusing term is "test item," which has a very uncommon meaning in the HESI series. This reviewer was alerted to the problem in Chapter 2 of the Mathematics manual where it was stated "if the student achieves 100 percent mastery on a test item" (p. 14). What is the meaning of 100% mastery on an *item?* Why not talk about students answering items correctly or incorrectly? But in Chapter 3, a unique (i.e., unusual) definition of a test item can be inferred: "Each test item, which is keyed to a single objective . . . consists of at least two problems" (Mathematics manual, p. 16). Being labelled a master of an objective in the HESI series means answering "all problems correctly within the test item." This is strange measurement language indeed. The readability of the manuals would be enhanced with the inclusion of a glossary. Also, more conventional testing language would be desirable. Perhaps the authors should talk about sets of test items being carefully matched to objectives, and performances on these sets of test items being used to make instructional decisions.

One of the strengths of the testing system from this reviewer's perspective was the use of multiple-item formats: free response, manual response, oral response, etc. Such use of multiple formats, while creating some problems for examiners/scorers, should be very much appreciated by teachers, many of whom are currently asking for more "authentic measurements."

From a psychometric viewpoint, the biggest shortcoming of the HESI series is the lack of supporting technical documentation. What is the evidence that a group of curriculum specialists, teachers, and graduate students in Missouri and Kansas are capable of judging the appropriateness of objectives (especially) and items for a national testing program? Were other persons used? How many? What were their qualifications? How exactly were the ratings made? What about the details of test development and of reliability and validity information? Apparently some of my questions were addressed for the Mathematics area in a doctoral thesis by one of the authors, but according to the 1985 AERA/APA/NCME *Standards for Educational and Psychological Testing*, answers to these and other psychometric questions should be reported in the manual. Only a few technical points were addressed in the manuals. For example, there was a reference to some evidence of "curriculum validity" of the Mathematics objectives and items. In the Reading area, there is a general statement addressing validity: "Numerous validity checks have been made by the authors, outside reviewers, teachers, and curriculum specialists" (p. 6). I do not doubt the accuracy of the statements, but technical readers need more details to form their own judgments about the quantity as well as the quality of psychometric evidence to support the HESI series.

Some evidence for (*a*) the reliability of various scores and instructional decisions, (*b*) the choice of 100% as a cutoff score, and (*c*) the validity of the scores for diagnosing learning problems, is needed. Basically, the objectives, items, and packaging look good but some hard empirical evidence would certainly be desirable for those persons who want to conduct a comprehensive evaluation of the system prior to making a purchase decision.

One of the authors' claims for an improved approach to assessing children in the HESI series over other testing systems is the "Test-Down/Teach-Up" model. In this model "The teacher/examiner begins testing at the highest level that appears appropriate for the individual student . . . If the student is unable to achieve mastery of the entry level chosen, the teacher then *tests down* with the next band of assessment items and continues to test down until the student meets the criterion for success." The advantage claimed by the authors is that "this procedure tends to leave the student with a successful experience." That may be so but what are the psychological effects on students of *not* being able to successfully answer many of the early questions in their tests? Will this discourage students and cause them to feel frustrated? Where is the evidence on either side of the hypothesis? I would agree that the authors have an interesting hypothesis, but claims for the advantage of this testing model

over others are only that, claims. Empirical evidence bearing on the psychometric and psychological impact of the authors' "Test-Down/Teach-Up" model is needed before this model can be claimed as an advantage. After all, there is empirical evidence to support a "Test-Up" testing strategy. In any case, the burden of proof falls to the authors because they are making claims for an alternate testing model.

Another psychometric problem with the available documentation was that there was almost *no* mention of the problem of measurement error in criterion-referenced testing and with the scores and related decisions from this series, in particular. (There were a few references in one of the appendices.) The fact is that teachers using a testing package must be made aware of the possibilities of *both* false-positive and false-negative errors in instructional decision making. And, teachers need to know that these errors are especially prevalent for students performing near the cutoff scores. Sometimes these measurement errors are due to luck, to loss of attention, to carelessness, and sometimes to examiner errors and less than perfectly clear test items. Users, such as teachers, must be warned about measurement errors. This reviewer does not have a problem with instructional decisions being made on the basis of two or three test items particularly when the objectives to which the items are attached are narrow. Teachers and other users must be reminded, however, about (*a*) measurement errors and instructional decision errors, (*b*) overinterpreting test results, and when necessary, (*c*) the use of professional judgment to resolve inconsistent test results.

Another important measurement problem, which goes unaddressed by the authors, is the validity of the sequence of objectives within each subskill area. Whatever the merits of a "Test-Down/Teach-Up" model, the validity of such a model for testing depends on the correctness of the sequences of objectives. No satisfactory evidence is offered in the manuals for the validity of the sequences, although there are vague references to how experts, teachers, school districts, and basals would sequence the objectives.

In summary, the HESI series seems to have many fine features from a curriculum and teaching standpoint—but judging the package on strict psychometric grounds, the HESI series is rather disappointing because of the various claims that are made without supporting evidence, and the nearly total absence of technical information for use in a criterion-referenced test evaluation. Evidence seems especially important to document features like the "Test-Down/Teach-Up" model when the model departs 180 degrees from standard testing practice. I am sure those technical points can be rectified in an improved and expanded manual, and they must be, if the HESI series is to meet current standards of psychometric acceptability.

REVIEWER'S REFERENCE

American Educational Research Association, American Psychological Association, & National Council on Measurement in Education. (1985). *Standards for educational and psychological testing.* Washington, DC: American Psychological Association, Inc.

Review of the Hudson Education Skills Inventory by ERNEST W. KIMMEL, *Executive Director, Test Development, Educational Testing Service, Princeton, NJ:*

The Hudson Education Skills Inventory (HESI) is an assessment tool designed to assist teachers and other educators to judge the academic performance level of students in grades K–12 who have dysfunctional learning patterns and to make decisions about the appropriate instruction for these students. The inventory is directed toward the basic skills in mathematics, reading, and writing that are commonly taught in the K–6 curriculum. The materials are designed for individualized assessment and assume that, in most cases, the teacher will conduct the assessment and use the student's performance on the selected exercises to plan subsequent instruction.

The HESI materials provide a well-articulated rationale for the series and an extensive description of why a "curriculum-based assessment" using criterion-referenced techniques is appropriate to the intended application. Central to the HESI package is an "Instructional Planning Form." If used as suggested, this form should reinforce the principle that assessment data should be used in the context of all other available information about the student. The Instructional Planning Form appears to be a useful device for collating a wide range of information about a student to help a teacher plan what to teach or to develop an Individualized Educational Plan (IEP) that complies with P.L. 94-142. This form asks the teacher or examiner to record and analyze formal test data, the student's instructional history, student work samples, and grade placement scores. The teacher is then asked to estimate the appropriate grade-level placement in the skill of interest, to state diagnostic hypotheses based on the analysis of previous data, and to determine the subskills and instructional objectives that are most in need of assessment. The Instructional Planning Form then guides the teacher or examiner to particular assessment activities and provides the mechanism for recording the student's mastery or nonmastery of each objective. The form also provides space to record subsequent assessments of the nonmastered objectives.

The authors claim the HESI "is representative of basic curriculum skills from current basal series and school districts across the country." Various basal texts are referenced in the Resources section of the materials, along with curriculum guides and scope and sequence charts from a modest number of school districts. Many of the texts and guides cited were issued in the early to mid-1970s, hardly "current" for an assessment published in 1989. The school districts providing curriculum guides or scope and sequence information are hardly representative of the nation's schools: One Kansas district is included for Reading; the Writing references include curricula from two California districts, two Kansas districts, one Arizona district, a Georgia collaborative, and the Missouri Department of Education; the Mathematics references are similar to those for Reading with the addition of two more Kansas districts and the substitution of a checklist from Ohio for the one from Georgia. No information is provided about how these several sources were collated or evaluated to determine the learning objectives included in the HESI. Brief references are made to unpublished curricular validation studies for Writing and Mathematics; the HESI materials do not provide enough information to judge the credibility of these efforts. There is no reference to any curricular validation study for Reading. Thus, although the authors premise their inventory on the need for a close link between assessment and learning goals, they do not provide evidence of the congruence between the skills assessed in the HESI and current curricular practices throughout the United States. Prospective users would need to examine *with care* the curriculum skills included in the HESI to determine their appropriateness to the user's situation.

Although the careful development of specifications and decision rules for classifying mastery/nonmastery performance is a critical step for criterion-referenced assessment, there is also a need to ask a number of fundamental measurement questions about the resulting assessment instrument. Among the questions that need to be asked are: Would the student be classified the same way (i.e., master or nonmaster) if given this exercise on another occasion? or if given a parallel exercise? Is this an adequate sample of the behavior to make a reliable classification of the student? How difficult is this exercise for a group of students who are classified as "masters" by some other means? How does one know that this exercise is classified at the appropriate grade level? Most of these questions are not addressed in the HESI materials; we are told that the authors followed "strict guidelines in determining adequacy of sample" but no indication of the nature of those guidelines is provided. No empirical evidence is provided to answer any of these questions. Consequently, it is impossible to evaluate the measurement characteristics of the Inventory.

The HESI claims to be designed for "assessing the basic skill level of dysfunctional students in elementary, junior high, and senior high school settings." Virtually all available data suggest that a disproportionate number of such students are members of racial or ethnic minorities. Yet the language and illustrations in the HESI materials are almost exclusively that of white middle-class America. Only one illustration in the entire series is of a nonwhite person and that is a picture of a female Native American in traditional dress used to test the sound of "squ." The names of the people in the stories are of the Jan, Dan, Bill, Bob, Jill, and Mary variety except for one mathematics problem that includes a player called "Perez." The makers of the HESI seem to be oblivious of the backgrounds of the students to be assessed and fail to reflect the multicultural/multi-ethnic composition of the student population of the United States.

In summary, Hudson and his colleagues set out to develop a series of criterion-referenced exercises for use by teachers and schools in planning instruction for dysfunctional students. The philosophy and approach to assessment are clearly articulated. Importantly, the HESI stresses the use of the assessment results in the context of other information about the student. However, the basis for the content specifications (and curricular validity) of the instruments appears to be both limited and dated. No empirical evidence is provided about the instruments and the decisions based on their results. Finally, the surface features of the tests seem to ignore the diverse backgrounds and cultural sensitivities of the students currently in American schools.

[168]
Human Activity Profile.
Purpose: Measures physical activity level.
Population: Ages 20–79.
Publication Dates: 1980–88.
Acronym: HAP.
Comments: Earlier version called Additive Activities Profile Test; may be orally administered.
Scores: 8 scores/classifications: Primary Scores (Maximum Activity Score, Adjusted Activity Score, Activity Age), Fitness Classification, Activity Classification, Energy Analysis (Expected Energy Potential, Lifestyle Energy Consumption), Dyspnea Scale Score.
Administration: Group or individual.
Price Data, 1990: $36.95 per complete kit including 50 test booklets and manual ('88, 30 pages); $29.95 per 50 test booklets; $9 per manual.
Time: (10) minutes or less.
Authors: A. James Fix and David M. Daughton.
Publisher: Psychological Assessment Resources, Inc.

[169]
Human Resource Development Report.
Purpose: Assesses an individual's management style, "provides insights into the individual's personality, describes personal strengths, and identifies areas for potential growth and development."
Population: Managerial candidates.

Publication Dates: 1982–87.
Acronym: HRDR.
Scores: 5 dimensions: Leadership, Interaction with Others, Decision-Making Abilities, Initiative, Personal Adjustment.
Administration: Group.
Price Data, 1987: $27.95 per introductory kit including 16PF test booklet, answer sheet, prepaid processing form to receive Human Resource Development Report, and user's guide ('87, 47 pages); $17.50 per 25 16PF reusable test booklets; $6.25 per 25 16PF machine-scorable answer sheets; $12 per user's guide; $30 or less per Human Resource Development Report available from publisher scoring service.
Time: 45(60) minutes.
Comments: Based on the Sixteen Personality Factor Questionnaire (9:1136); must be scored by publisher.
Author: IPAT staff.
Publisher: Institute for Personality and Ability Testing, Inc.

Review of the Human Resource Development Report by S. ALVIN LEUNG, Assistant Professor of Educational Psychology, University of Houston, Houston, TX:

The Human Resource Development Report (HRDR) is based on the Sixteen Personality Factor Questionnaire (16PF; 9:1136), a personality inventory. The scores from a number of 16PF (Form A) scales are used to generate an interpretive report concerning the potential effectiveness of an individual in a managerial position. The interpretive report is a narrative summary outlining the individual's personality, strengths, and areas for growth and development. The HRDR is designed to assist organizations in making personnel-related decisions.

The HRDR has five composite scales and each has several subscales. The five composite scales are: Leadership, Interacting with Others, Making Decisions, Initiative, and Personal Adjustment. These five dimensions of management are regarded as common characteristics of successful managers. Short-term (2 days to 2 weeks) test-retest reliabilities for the subscales are within a desirable range, between .58 and .94, with a mean of about .81. Long-term reliabilities (from 2.5 months to about 8 years) range between .08 and .89, with a mean of about .52. These reliability data were collected from a number of groups, including college students and working adults. However, information concerning internal consistency reliability is not available in the User's Guide.

The User's Guide provides only limited information concerning validity. It is suggested that because the 16PF was well documented as a valid instrument, users who are interested in validity information of the HRDR should refer to other sources. Although this may be true, the HRDR is actually extending the application of the 16PF to personnel selection and development. Past research data concerning the 16PF may not be relevant to the objectives and claims of the HRDR. The HRDR targets management personnel who are not trained in psychological testing and are unlikely to have knowledge about the 16PF. Consequently, it is reasonable to expect the User's Guide to give a more informed summary concerning the validity of the 16PF, as related to the composite scales and subscales being used in the HRDR.

A key to the utility of the HRDR is whether the interpretive statements are accurate and valid. The interpretive statements are derived from a statement library, and the selection of specific statements is determined by the elevation and configuration of the scales. The authors are rather vague on how statements were constructed. Although empirical findings served as a general background, specific statements were linked to the scores based on expert opinions, not on findings of specific research studies. The User's Guide indicates the statement library was written by a team consisting of "a number of specialists" (p. 28) who had at least 4 years of experience in interpreting the 16PF profile. Information concerning the experts, such as training, educational background, and sex, were omitted. It is also not clear as to how many experts actually participated in writing the statements, and no information regarding reliability checks (e.g., inter-expert reliability) was provided. One gets the impression from this procedure that the statements were written based more on the experts' experience in interpreting the 16PF than on specific research findings. This is a very risky process. The interpretive statements should be based on specific research findings and if expert opinions are used, there has to be some form of reliability check. A review of the example statements in the User's Guide (pp. 11–12) suggests some statements are quite definitive (e.g., "He is not very trusting of the behaviors and motives of others") and extreme (e.g., "He may frequently seem inconsistent and prone to suddenly change his mind about things"). These statements can easily be abused by a user in making personnel-related decisions. If the statements are of questionable validity and accuracy, users who are not trained or experienced in psychological testing can be misled.

A so-called "stop-light model" is recommended for using the HRDR. The user initially generates a description of the ideal employee in a specified position. The user will then read the HRDR of a candidate, marking in red those interpretive statements that do not indicate a good match, marking in yellow those that are questionable, and green those that are indicative of a good match. The user is then encouraged to integrate and compare the marked statements with data from other sources, such as those from an interview. The stop-light model appears to be a useful method, particularly in its emphasis on integrating data from multiple sources.

The user is also encouraged to discuss and share the results of the HRDR with the respondent. Several useful guidelines and answers for commonly asked questions are provided in the User's Guide. Although interpretation of test scores is necessary, it is doubtful whether the user has the necessary skills, training, and information to perform such an interpretation, particularly when the HRDR includes so many extreme and definitive statements about an individual. The typical user is not likely to be equipped with basic knowledge about psychological measurement and the 16PF. Inaccurate interpretations could create confusion and problems for both the user and the test taker. This is perhaps an expected undesirable effect of having a nontrained person to interpret psychological test reports.

The 16PF may be a well-documented personality measurement, but the authors of the HRDR have to show how past and current research findings support the validity of the interpretive statements printed in the HRDR. The information reported in the User's Guide is not adequate. It is troubling to read the interpretive statements as they are rather extreme and definitive, and to think about the possibility they may be abused by users. Consequently, users of the HRDR have to be aware of its limited validity, and not use it as the only source of information when making personnel and hiring decisions.

Review of the Human Resource Development Report by MARY A. LEWIS, Director, Organizational and Employment Technology, PPG Industries, Inc., Pittsburgh, PA:

The Human Resource Development Report (HRDR) is a five- to six-page computer-based analysis of Cattell's Sixteen Personality Factor Questionnaire (16PF; 9:1136) designed to measure those personality dimensions that relate to management potential. The narrative portion of the report is organized around five areas: Leadership, Interaction with Others, Decision-Making Abilities, Initiative, and Personal Adjustment. The report is supported by a score summary sheet that reports and displays graphically the sten (standard ten) scores for the scales that correspond to each of the five areas.

The User's Guide for the HRDR refers the user to the 16PF Handbook (Cattell, Eber, & Tatsuoka, 1970) for information on construction, reliability, and validity of the 16PF Scale, and contains a technical supplement describing both the development of the scales and the process by which the computer-generated report was developed.

SCALES IN THE HRDR. Four of the five topical scales in the HRDR (Interaction with Others, Decision-Making Abilities, Initiative, and Personal Adjustment) are second or third order factors of the primary 16PF scales that were developed and documented in other literature. The Leadership scale was developed specifically for this instrument and is a third order factor developed for the HRDR. This scale is based on Sweney's (1970) model of organizational power, and was developed through multiple correlations of 16PF scores with the Response to Power Measure (RPM; Sweney, 1977). The correlations of the scales with the RPM scores ranged from .42 to .51, although the specific correlations are not reported.

The documentation includes a description of the literature review that led to the selection of the scales used for the HRDR, and information about the validity and scale reliability. The average short-term reliability of the scales used in the HRDR is .81 for the basic scales and .87 for the composite scales. The long-term reliability average is .52 for the basic scales and .67 for the composite scales.

The validity of the scales is based on a content analysis of the management literature that identified 88 studies using 54 assessment instruments. No validity coefficients for the scales are reported; however, specific references are provided to studies that support the use of each of the subscales.

COMPUTER-GENERATED REPORT. The computer-generated report for the HRDR is built from a statement library that was built from summary reports prepared for managers who were candidates for hiring or promotion. A team of experts, each with at least 4 years of experience in interpreting the 16PF profiles, was involved in developing the statement library. The themes identified from the 88 studies mentioned above were linked to the statement library and to the logic that triggered the statements.

USE OF THE HRDR IN HUMAN RESOURCE DECISIONS. The HRDR User's Guide includes a detailed section on how to use the HRDR for personnel decision making, as a supplement to a selection interview, and as a developmental tool. It also includes instructions of feeding results back to the candidate. These sections are easy to follow and include detailed instructions on how to tie the report statements to the job, or to integrate the report into a selection interview.

STRENGTHS AND WEAKNESSES OF THE HRDR. Use of computer-generated interpretive statements to write reports such as the HRDR helps alleviate reliability problems associated with raters. The fact that the same answers will generate the same report on two different occasions assures consistency. The use of a team of experts to generate the statements and logic to generate the report should also help to improve the content validity of the report.

However, the long-term scale reliabilities of .52 raise questions about the use of instruments such as the 16PF for selection purposes. Although the User's Guide provides some detail on how to conduct a job analysis and tie the statements from the report to desirable job behaviors, the use of the

report as a stand-alone decision maker would be difficult to justify, particularly if the dimensions being measured can change over time. Using it as a developmental tool, or as a tool to guide the development of a structured selection interview, seems more appropriate.

An additional concern with the use of instruments such as the 16PF in organizational settings is that nonprofessionals may have access to scale scores and may use them inappropriately. The User's Guide instructs the individual receiving the report to separate the attached scale scores from the report to prevent this, but the potential remains.

REVIEWER'S REFERENCES
Cattell, R. B., Eber, H. W., & Tatsuoka, M. M. (1970). *Handbook for the Sixteen Personality Factor Questionnaire (16PF)*. Champaign, IL: Institute for Personality and Ability Testing.
Sweney, A. B. (1970). Organizational power roles. *Professional Management Bulletin, 10,* 5–12.
Sweney, A. B. (1977). *Response to power measure handbook.* Wichita, KS: Test Systems, Inc.

[170]
Humanics National Child Assessment Form.

Purpose: To serve as developmental checklists of skills that occur during the first 6 years of life.
Population: Ages 0–3, 3–6.
Publication Dates: 1981–83.
Administration: Group.
Levels, 2: Birth to age 3, ages 3 to 6.
Price Data, 1987: $1 per checklist (specify level).
Time: Administration time varies.
Comments: Behavior checklists to be completed by parents or teachers.
Publisher: Humanics Limited.

a) BIRTH TO THREE.
Scores: Item scores in 5 areas: Social-Emotional, Language, Cognitive, Gross Motor, Fine Motor.
Price Data: $14.95 per user's guide entitled *Humanics National Infant-Toddler Assessment Handbook* ('81, 167 pages).
Authors: Marsha Kaufman (checklist), T. Thomas McMurrain (checklist), Jane A. Caballero (handbook), and Derek Whordley (handbook).
b) AGES THREE TO SIX.
Scores: Item scores in 5 areas: Social-Emotional, Language, Cognitive, Motor Skills, Hygiene/Self-Help.
Price Data: $.25 per individualized educational program form; $16.95 per user's guide entitled *Humanics National Preschool Assessment Handbook* ('83, 235 pages).
Authors: Derek Whordley (handbook) and Rebecca J. Doster (handbook).

Review of the Humanics National Child Assessment Form by ARTHUR S. ELLEN, Assistant Professor of Psychology, Pace University, New York, NY:

The purpose of the Humanics National Child Assessment Form (HNCAF) is to help parents and preschool teachers to observe and better understand children. To do this, a parent or preschool teacher completes an informal checklist of early childhood activities. The activities are grouped into broad areas of development such as Social-Emotional, Fine Motor, and Cognition. Each area includes 18 activities, presumably placed in a developmental sequence. The HNCAF consists of a user's guide and its companion assessment form—the check-list—one for birth to 3 and another for ages 3 to 6.

The easy-to-read user's guides include chapters on nutrition, child development, and the mechanics of assessment. In addition, each broad area of development has its own chapter. Within these chapters, each one of the 18 activities is presented in the same format: An activity label and description, its devel-opmental significance, a task description, a sample objective, and suggested activities. The activity label and its number link the user's guide to the assessment form. The activity description provides a short concrete statement that identifies the activity. A parent or teacher reads this description to decide if a child exhibits the activity. Next follows the statement of developmental significance, which briefly relates the activity to a developmental concept such as object permanence, visual discrimi-nation, or locomotion. Following this is a task description, a more inclusive and general statement describing the activity. This task description is very useful because it will often add to and clarify the activity description. Next to last, the sample objec-tive provides a clearly written criterion-referenced goal for instruction. Finally, the list of suggested activities provides interesting remedial exercises.

Like the user's guides, the two assessment forms employ a clear and consistent format. When the assessment form is opened like a book, each area's 18 activities are clearly listed on a single page. For each activity, the assessment form includes the activity number, label, and description; this links the assessment form to its user's guide. Next to each activity, the test format provides space for rating a child over several different ages. There are three possible ratings. If the activity is absent, the space is left blank. If the child exhibits the activity, one must decide whether to make a check in the *occurs occasionally* or *occurs consistently* column. Only activi-ties that occur consistently are tallied at the back of the assessment form. These tallies are grouped by their respective areas with space for ratings at several different ages. This final page of the test form provides a profile of the child's activities, either at a single time or over several ratings.

To evaluate this product, one must look at both what the publisher does not and does intend as the HNCAF's purpose. Because the publisher does not intend the HNCAF be a normative or diagnostic test (as indicated in the fine-print disclaimer on the front page of the assessment form), one does not find norms, reliability indices, and validity informa-tion. Because the publisher does want parents and teachers to share what they know about a child's developmental activities, one must, however, mini-mally consider (*a*) how well a parent and teacher might agree that a child displays an activity (i.e., interjudge reliability), and (*b*) how accurately the activities cover and follow a growth sequence (i.e., developmental validity).

If there is low interjudge reliability, parents and teachers may not mutually understand a child, but instead they will disagree about what activities a child can accomplish. If the activities do not extend adequately over the actual ages, parents may feel the activities do not permit them to provide an accurate description of their child's skills. And if the activities do not approximate childhood maturation, parents may find the child unready for, or bored with, the remedial activities. Therefore, until evidence is presented for at least interjudge reliability and developmental validity, one must look upon the HNCAF not as an informal assessment procedure but as a list of interesting early childhood activities that *perhaps* are given added appeal by their test-like presentation.

Review of the Humanics National Child Assessment Form by DAVID MacPHEE, Associate Professor of Human Development and Family Studies, Colorado State University, Fort Collins, CO:

This behavior checklist is structured much like the Minnesota Child Development Inventory (Ire-ton & Thwing, 1974) but with a crucial difference: The Humanics National Child Assessment Form is not designed for diagnostic or predictive purposes and so has no psychometric data. Instead, it provides a structured format for observing young children, alerts caregivers to potential handicapping condi-tions, and can be used to guide Individualized Educational Programs (IEPs). The two manuals are largely devoted to the latter purpose. Each item is described in terms of its developmental significance and how the behavior is to be observed, and then a number of activities are recommended to promote the given behavior. Therefore, it would be more accurate to describe the manuals as curriculum guides for developmentally appropriate learning activities.

From a curricular rather than assessment perspec-tive, there is much to recommend. The manuals provide complete, concrete guidelines for how to observe children, how to use the assessments, and when referral for professional evaluation is merited. The learning activities do not require expensive materials and are easy enough for most parents to implement, although one wonders about the use-fulness of some general suggestions such as setting aside time to walk with the child and listening to the birds, an airplane, or a siren. For the caregiver who wishes to improve his or her teaching skills, the authors recommend specific observational exercises and supplemental resource materials.

There are some concerns related to the use of these checklists. First, although the item descriptions and activities in the manual appear to be at a sixth to ninth grade reading level, the Assessment Form's instructions are written for college-educated adults. Second, even with assistance from the manual, the most skilled observer would have difficulty coping with some general items on the 3–6 year form (e.g., "shows creativity," "exhibits appropriate values," and "demonstrates judgment"). Third, expected ages are not given for the items. Although this omission is consistent with the purpose of the checklist ("it is not to be used to compare one child with another"), a *range* of ages would provide more specific anchors for teachers in making referral decisions. As well, for parents who are not astute observers of their children's behavior, age ranges might help them to match activities to their children's actual developmental level.

A semantic issue with implications for test misuse is that the manuals refer to these checklists as developmental assessments or screening devices for early handicapping conditions. Yet making such a claim is indefensible given the absence of data of any kind, especially expected ages. Clearly, the authors intend to provide a format for documenting everyday observations of child behavior so that appropriate referrals can be made, but their word choices could mislead a naive user into drawing inappropriate conclusions about developmental delays.

A final concern is that many of the activities in the 0–3-year manual are decontextualized and seem to be directly tied to helping children pass items on the Bayley Scales. That is, the purpose seems to be to *train* children in specialized skills, rather than to provide integrated experiences that would promote development in several domains. Theory (Feuerstein, 1980) and research (MacPhee, Ramey, & Yeates, 1984) indicate that cognitive growth is most likely when learning is embedded in everyday experiences with caregivers. On a related note, the authors do not discuss content validity, or why these particular activities were chosen instead of others, nor do they present evidence that their activities actually promote development. Such data would be valuable to educators who are considering this curriculum for adoption.

In sum, the Humanics National Child Assessments are recommended as curriculum guides for early childhood education. The manuals nicely balance concrete writing and suggestions with adequate detail on normal and atypical child development. However, more information on content validity, expected ages, and program evaluation would be extremely helpful. These checklists should not be used for screening or any other diagnostic purpose, given the absence of normative or psychometric data. Instead, one might consider the Minnesota Child Development Inventory (9:712; Ireton & Thwing, 1974) because it has been validated for screening and predictive purposes.

REVIEWER'S REFERENCES

Ireton, H., & Thwing, E. (1974). *Manual for the Minnesota Child Development Inventory.* Minneapolis: Behavior Science Systems.
Feuerstein, R. (1980). *Instrumental enrichment.* Baltimore: University Park.
MacPhee, D., Ramey, C. T., & Yeates, K. O. (1984). The home environment and early cognitive development: Implications for intervention. In A. W. Gottfried (Ed.), *Home environment and early cognitive development: Longitudinal research.* New York: Academic Press.

[171]

Hunter-Grundin Literacy Profiles.

Purpose: Designed to monitor the written and spoken language skills of children.
Population: Ages 6.5–8, 7.10–9.3, 9–10, 9.10–11.5, 10.10–12.7.
Publication Dates: 1979–89.
Scores: 6 tests: Attitude to Reading (Levels 1 and 2 only), Reading for Meaning, Spelling, Free Writing, Spoken Language, Profile of Personal Interests (Levels 4 and 5 only).
Administration: Individual and group.
Levels: 5 overlapping levels.
Manual: Separate manual for each level.
Price Data: Available from publisher.
Time: (3–10) minutes per test at any one level.
Comments: Ratings by teacher in part.
Authors: Elizabeth Hunter-Grundin and Hans U. Grundin.
Publisher: The Test Agency Ltd. [England].
  a) LEVEL 1.
  Population: Ages 6.5–8.
  b) LEVEL 2.
  Population: Ages 7.10–9.3.
  c) LEVEL 3.
  Population: Ages 9–10.
  d) LEVEL 4.
  Population: Ages 9.10–11.5.
  e) LEVEL 5.
  Population: Ages 10.10–12.7.
Cross References: For reviews of a previous edition by Martha C. Beech and Patricia H. Kennedy, see 9:491.

[172]

IDEAS: Interest Determination, Exploration and Assessment System.

Purpose: "To help individuals explore their personal vocational preferences."
Population: Grades 7–12 and adults.
Publication Dates: 1977–90.
Acronym: IDEAS.
Scores, 16: Mechanical/Fixing, Protective Services, Nature/Outdoors, Mathematics, Science, Medical, Creative Arts, Writing, Community Service, Educating, Child Care, Public Speaking, Business, Sales, Office Practices, Food Service.
Administration: Group or individual.
Price Data, 1991: $57 per 50 booklets; $8.50 per manual ('90, 88 pages); $11.90 per preview package.

Time: (40–45) minutes.
Comments: Self-administered, self-scored.
Author: Charles B. Johansson.
Publisher: National Computer Systems.
Cross References: For a review by M. O'Neal Weeks of an earlier edition, see 9:516.

Review of IDEAS: Interest Determination, Exploration and Assessment System by ROBERT J. MILLER, Assistant Professor of Special Education, Mankato State University, Mankato, MN:

IDEAS: Interest Determination, Exploration and Assessment System is a vocational interest inventory. It is a shortened version of the Career Assessment Inventory (CAI; 59) by the same author. In contrast to the CAI, IDEAS was designed only to differentiate among broad categories of interest. As stated in the test manual, "IDEAS is intended to be used in a career introduction unit and as a career exploration vehicle." As such, it is of limited utility for predicting vocational choice or as an instrument on which to base career decisions.

The instrument consists of 128 items in 16 career areas. Subjects answer the 128 items regarding their likes and dislikes including the titles of occupations, school subjects, and various work- or school-related activities. The five-choice response options for the individual include: *like very much* (L); *like somewhat* (l); *indifferent* (I); *dislike somewhat* (d); *dislike very much* (D). Subjects are to circle the response that most represents their perceptions of the activity, subject, or occupation. Each of the 128 items consists of a single phrase of no more than eight words. Each phrase is gender neutral. The reading level is appropriate for the average junior high aged student. This is important because the purpose of the instrument lends itself well to administration during the junior high years. The directions for test administration are clearly stated and the test booklet is well designed. The inventory is easily administered to an individual or group. It can be self-administered and self-scored in approximately 40 minutes, thus providing immediate feedback to the individual completing the inventory.

A profile of high and low interest is created as the subject converts raw scores into standard scores with the instructions included in the test booklet. Three norm tables are included. These norm tables are for grades 7–9, grades 10–12, and adult. Norms for males and females are not included based on a concern for sex stereotyping. As a result, the test booklet norms are based on a composite average of an equal representation of females and males. The test manual does, however, include information relating the individual's score to the average ranges for males and females for each of the corresponding norm tables.

This edition of IDEAS is an updated version of an original instrument. It contains several changes.

First, the number of items in the inventory has been increased from 112 to 128. Second, the number of career-related scales has been increased from 14 to 16. Adult norms have been added. The instrument no longer includes norms for grade 6. Norm tables for school aged population have been changed to include one table for grades 7–9 and one table for grades 10–12. Finally, the manual provides procedures for calculating the relationship of the individual's scores to the Holland R-I-A-S-E-C theoretical vocational model (Holland, 1975).

Sex equity and concern for minority representation were issues well addressed in the test manual. The sample for standardization was very adequate and included: (*a*) grades 7–9 ($N = 1,770$; 950 female, 820 males); (*b*) grades 10–12 ($N = 2,891$; 1,683 females, 1,208 males); (*c*) adult ($N = 900$; 450 females, 450 males). Separate female and male data were statistically weighted to provide equal representation. Minority representation in the sample was addressed. At least 7.8% of the adult sample, at least 15% of the grade 10–12 sample, and at least 45% of the sample for grades 7–9 were minorities.

Test-retest correlations were included for 1 week, 2 weeks, and 30 days to document the reliability of the interest inventory over time. The correlation data were excellent ($r = .75$ and above). However, limitations of these data should be considered. First, no information was included regarding the reliability of the instrument for junior high school aged students (grades 7–9). The reliability study contained mostly high school and college students, with the remainder being employed adults. Second, the number of persons included in the reliability study were very small (1 week, $N = 54$; 2 weeks, $N = 31$; 30 days, $N = 42$). Perhaps these limitations will be addressed in future revisions of the inventory.

Validity of the test instrument was assessed by three methods: content validity, construct validity, and concurrent validity. Content validity was very well addressed in the manual. Information regarding item-scale correlations was presented for each of the 16 scales and was separated by gender, race, and grade level. Internal scale consistency values were computed as an overall measure of homogeneity of the items on each scale and were all in the .80s and low .90s. Data across the demographic samples consistently reflected similar and adequate internal consistencies for each scale regardless of gender, race, or age. To determine concurrent validity of the IDEAS scales, data from over 100 samples of students in career programs and adults in occupations were used. Although the test manual reports overall good concurrent validity for the scales of the IDEAS inventory, statistical information regarding the sample was incomplete. To support the construct validity of the inventory, correlations were computed between IDEAS and the Strong Interest Inventory. The values for this comparison were quite high, .80s and above. The test manual also presents correlations between IDEAS and the CAI. Although the correlations were very high, this information would seem to be of limited value because the IDEAS scales are based on items directly from the CAI. Finally, to support construct validity of the instrument, intercorrelations were presented between Holland's six interest domains and the IDEAS scales. Overall, the intercorrelations among scales in the same interest domain in Holland's model were moderately high ($R = .40s$ to $.60s$) and the correlations with other scales outside the interest domain were lower ($r = .00s$ to $.40s$). These data generally support the construct validity of the instrument.

In conclusion, IDEAS is a well-designed and well-researched interest inventory. It is easy to administer, easy to score, and easy to interpret. Great care has been given to address sex equity and inclusion of minority populations in the norming of this edition of the instrument. Information concerning the validity of the inventory is adequate. Additional information concerning reliability of the inventory for junior high aged groups is needed. IDEAS is an adequate instrument and a valuable tool for career exploration.

REVIEWER'S REFERENCE

Holland, J. L. (1975). *Making vocational choices: A theory of careers.* Englewood Cliffs, NJ: Prentice-Hall.

[173]

Independent Mastery Testing System for Writing Skills.

Purpose: "To monitor the student's mastery of basic grammar and writing skills, to diagnose specific student weaknesses, to recommend a program of further study, and to provide the teacher with a comprehensive record of student progress."
Population: Adult students.
Publication Date: 1984.
Acronym: IMTS.
Scores: 15 tests: Recognizing Sentences, Verb Tenses, Subject-Verb Agreement—Part A, Subject-Verb Agreement—Part B, Pronouns—Part A, Pronouns—Part B, Plurals and Possessives, Adjectives and Adverbs—Part A, Adjectives and Adverbs—Part B, Sentence Structure, Prepositions and Conjunctions, Logic and Organization, Capitalization, Punctuation, Spelling.
Administration: Individual.
Forms: 3 parallel forms (1, 2, 3) of each test.
Price Data, 1987: $96 per software package including 3 program disks with a backup for each; $35 per individual disk (specify Mastery Disk, Question Disk, or Teacher's Disk); $20 per replacement disk; $7.50 per Writing Implementation Manual (49 pages).
Time: Administration time not reported.
Comments: Computer-administered instructional management system; Apple II, Apple II+, Apple IIe, or Apple IIc computer necessary for administration.

Author: Cambridge, The Adult Education Company, in association with Moravian College, Bethlehem, PA.
Publisher: Simon & Schuster Higher Education Group.

Review of the Independent Mastery Testing System for Writing Skills by PAMELA A. MOSS, Assistant Professor, University of Michigan, Ann Arbor, MI:

According to the manual, the Independent Mastery Testing System for Writing Skills (IMTS) is a computer-administered testing program for adult learners intended to "monitor the student's mastery of basic grammar and writing skills, to diagnose specific student weaknesses, to recommend a program of further study, and to provide the teacher with a comprehensive record of student progress" (p. 1). This statement promises a somewhat more powerful testing program than the IMTS delivers, because much of the diagnostic and instructional information is not generated by the computer but must be laboriously developed by hand. Moreover, the format and substance of the tests reflect an approach to literacy pedagogy that is currently under attack by a number of literacy educators.

The IMTS consists of 15 computer-administered (APPLE II) multiple-choice tests. Each test covers a different surface level "writing skill" (such as Sentence Structure, Verb Tenses, Capitalization, and so on) broken down into two or more subskills (such as regular verbs, irregular verbs, simple verb tenses, perfect verb tenses, and forms and uses of the verb *to be* for the Verb Tenses test). The Logic and Organization test is the only test that deals with rhetorical structures beyond the sentence level. There are three fixed "parallel" forms per test, typically comprising about 20 items each. One test requires the teacher to duplicate reading passages contained in the implementation manual.

For students, the system reports a score and an evaluative message indicating level of "mastery" (e.g., "very good," "This unit needs more work"). Students may request "corrective feedback," which consists of a table of item numbers, the student's answers, the correct answers (which is largely useless information, because the student does not have access to the original items), and a subskill code for each item. Students wishing to take advantage of the subskill information must look up the meaning of the code in a table provided in the manual. There they will find the name of the subskill and the page numbers in texts (available from the same publisher) that present relevant instructional information.

For teachers, the system stores and reports item level information on each student, organized by test form rather than subskill, as well as a list of students' names with the scores they have received on each test form taken. In a separate subprogram, the system also provides item difficulties (percentages of students correctly answering each item), also organized by test form as opposed to subskill.

Unfortunately, because the system can store only 200 test form results, its monitoring function is quite limited. For instance, a teacher with a class of 25 students could store information on only eight test forms per student.

The teacher wishing a class profile must complete, by hand, a "Group Profile Worksheet" for each test form. Completing the worksheet involves using two subprograms, one program to obtain the subskill code for each item which must then be decoded by referring to the table in the manual, and another program to obtain the percentage of students correctly answering the item. Because worksheets are organized by item and form rather than by subskill, the diagnostic information relevant to a particular subskill must still be searched out and aggregated across items and forms.

Teachers have the option to revise the items, assuming they have access to an Apple II-compatible word processing program. This is a somewhat complex and risky process for the computer novice, as the revisions must be written in a format that only computers can appreciate and errors in entry will cause problems with subsequent test administration. Clearly, such revisions may change the nature of the tests, including the parallelism of the forms.

The manual provides no normative information, no information on reliability and validity, and no indication of where such information might be obtained. It does not even provide information on how the tests were developed or on how parallelism in test forms was evaluated. Moreover, the manual contains occasional undocumented empirical assertions and just plain bad advice. For example, the manual reader, having been told that a student will not see the same form twice until the fourth administration of a test, is reassured that, "by that time, however, the student is unlikely to remember correct responses from previous exposure." For another example, the manual informs the reader that the "best measure of an item's effectiveness is its difficulty level" and that "a difficulty quotient of 40 to 60 is considered within the acceptable range. Quotients significantly above 60 reflect items that are too easy" (pp. 17–18). With mastery tests, one would expect (in fact, hope) to see item difficulties (proportions of students answering an item correctly) considerably above .60 for items representing material already covered.

Beyond my concern with the technical limitations of the IMTS is my concern with the reductionist form and substance of the tests. Although multiple-choice tests of surface level language skills may serve as adequate predictors of writing skill in some contexts, in a mastery learning context they provide seriously limited targets for instruction. As many educators of both children and adults have recently argued, language skills are best learned as holistic, meaning-centered processes (e.g., Rose, 1989; Kazemek, 1988) rather than as decontextualized, atomistic processes divorced from the making of meaning.

In summary, I cannot recommend the IMTS for the purposes its developers intended. It may be unfair to evaluate a computerized test published in 1984 against 1990 expectations. Prospective users, however, have the right to expect far more from their 1990 expenditures than IMTS offers. As the above description illustrates, the test developers have not taken adequate advantage of a computer's capabilities to store, aggregate, organize, and report information. Much of the summary and diagnostic reports promised to teachers and students must be completed by hand. Further, the technical quality of the test is neither documented nor referenced in the manual. Most importantly, because the tests are intended as mastery learning tools, users should evaluate carefully the targets for instruction that they present. The pedagogical choices implied in these tests, that is, isolated and decontextualized language skills, will be unacceptable for users who value more holistic approaches to language instruction.

REVIEWER'S REFERENCES

Kazemek, F. E. (1988). Necessary changes: Professional involvement in adult literacy programs. *Harvard Educational Review, 58,* 464-487.

Rose, M. (1989). *Lives on the boundary.* New York: The Free Press.

[174]
Independent Schools Entrance Examination.

Purpose: Developed to assess verbal ability, quantitative ability, reading comprehension, and mathematics achievement for use in admissions into independent schools and to provide independent schools with a candidate's writing sample given under standard conditions.

Population: Grades 5–7, 8–11, or candidates for grades 6–8 and 9–12.

Publication Date: 1989.

Acronym: isee.

Scores, 4: Verbal Ability, Quantitative Ability, Reading Comprehension, Mathematics Achievement.

Administration: Group.

Levels, 2: Middle, Upper.

Forms, 2: A, B.

Price Data: Price data including technical manual ('89, 104 pages) available from publisher.

Time: 130 minutes; 30 minutes for essay component.

Comments: Test book name is isee; essay component is not scored but is sent to schools.

Author: Educational Records Bureau, Inc.

Publisher: Educational Records Bureau, Inc.

Review of the Independent Schools Entrance Examination by MARY ANNE BUNDA, Director, University Assessment, Western Michigan University, Kalamazoo, MI:

The Independent Schools Entrance Examination (isee) is a relatively new instrument with little public information available. Potential users will have to rely on information from the publisher for a discussion of the instrument. The technical report provided by the publisher contains a detailed description of the development of standard scores, the norms, and the internal statistical characteristics of the test in 130 pages of tables supported by 10 pages of narrative. There is, unfortunately, a great deal of missing information in the technical manual. There is no discussion of the possible uses and misuses of the instrument. There is no discussion of the rationale for the integers selected to represent the scale. The scale selected for the middle level form was from 801 to 850 and from 850 to 900 for the upper level form. There is no discussion of the definition of the skills or traits measured by the instrument. There is no discussion of the kind of reports provided to either the student or the school. There is no discussion of the cost constraints or the time constraints that are implied by this test (i.e., the turnaround time in scoring). What the technical manual gives the potential user is a fine description of the internal consistency reliability of the instrument, the percentile norm equivalents for each grade for the standard scores which are equated both horizontally and vertically with cutting edge psychometric precision, subscore intercorrelations, and item difficulty information.

Reliability of the tests is presented solely in terms of internal consistency. Some information on test-retest reliability is required in a situation such as this. The KR-20 coefficients for each of the four subtests have within grade level coefficients in the mid .80s. Coefficients developed by form on the more heterogeneous samples are predictably higher in the upper .80s and low .90s. At the point of discussing the internal consistency of the test, part scores for Reading, Verbal Ability, and Quantitative Ability are introduced with reported KR-20s. One wonders about the relevance of the information, because scores associated with the parts are presumably not reported back to the schools nor are standard scores developed for them.

The part scores, however, do allow some inferences to be made about the meaning of the three tests which have parts, even though the descriptors for the parts are less than satisfying. The Verbal Ability parts are called: Synonyms and Sentence Completion. Across the seven grade levels, the correlation between the two parts is .76. The Quantitative Ability parts are described as Regular Multiple Choice and Quantitative Comparisons. Across the seven grade levels, the correlation between the two parts is .72. The Reading parts are characterized as Social Science passages and Science passages. Across the seven grade levels, the average correlation between the scores derived from the two types of passages is .78. Similarity between parts of the test generally support an inference of common underlying trait even though one of the traits is defined in terms of the item format. But additional inferences can be drawn from the relationship among the four scores provided to schools. The within grade level correlations between the Verbal Ability and the Reading scores are in the high .50s and the low .60s and the cross grade level coefficients are .76 and .71. The relationship between the Quantitative Ability score and the Mathematics Achievement scores within grade level is in the .70s and the .80s and the cross grade level coefficients are .84 and .85. One has to wonder whether four meaningful scores are reported. The suspicions become stronger when you look at the relationships reported between Verbal Ability or Reading with Quantitative Ability or Mathematics. These are in the low .60s, slightly higher than the degree of variation one finds in the Scholastic Aptitude Test (SAT) or the Graduate Record Examinations (GRE).

Validity of the test is very difficult to defend with the information presented. The model for the development of this device may have been the SAT or the Preliminary Scholastic Aptitude Test (PSAT), but no information is given with respect to the rationale for development nor to possible validity studies with outside criteria. No discussion is given as to the use of the test as a possible aid to course selection for accepted students. It is difficult to see how this test is an improvement over any other achievement test developed for these grade levels. If the problem with other achievement or aptitude tests is a ceiling effect with the population of independent school students, the solution might be out of grade level testing. In any case, there is some evidence of a ceiling effect with the middle level form where most normative samples are negatively skewed. The skewness increases from the lowest to the highest recommended grade level.

The only benefit of this test is that the norm group has been specifically designed for independent schools. But the group is composed of current students, not students who might apply. Although the manual regrets the student population in the norms and indicates this is a problem, it does not go on to discuss the problem with setting admission cut scores when the norm group is composed of only currently enrolled students.

The number of schools that participated in the pilot and the development stage of the instrument, and the fact the test was developed under contract may mean that it fills a market niche. However, independent schools should be careful concerning the validity of this instrument. Use as a selection device without validation (local or national) is unwise no matter how reliable the instrument is.

Review of the Independent Schools Entrance Examination by JOYCE R. McLARTY, Director, Work Keys Development, Center for Education and Work, American College Testing, Iowa City, IA:

The Independent Schools Entrance Examinations (isee) consists of two levels (middle and upper) with two forms each (A and B) of a multiple-choice test used with students attending or wishing to enter grades 5–11 in independent schools. Although the test description indicates that a writing sample is also offered, no information on it was supplied so it will not be discussed.

The subtest structure of each of the four tests (two levels, two forms each) is identical. The Verbal Ability subtests (20 minutes) contain 24 synonym and 16 sentence completion items. These are essentially vocabulary tests in varying formats. The Quantitative Ability subtests (35 minutes) contain 20 regular multiple-choice and 20 quantitative comparisons items. The regular multiple-choice items cover a variety of mathematical reasoning tasks; the quantitative comparison items require the student to compare two quantities to determine whether they are equal, which is greater, or whether insufficient information is provided to determine the relationship. The Reading Comprehension subtests (35 minutes) contain 20 science and 20 social science items. The items are based on 10 reading passages of varying lengths and focus on material stated or implied in the passages. The Mathematics Achievement subtests (40 minutes) contain 50 items. The middle level Mathematics Achievement subtest consists of a variety of computational problems ranging from basic operations on integers to prealgebra. The upper level begins with prealgebra and includes coordinate and plane geometry and algebra.

All items have four choices. Some of the same items repeat from Form A to Form B and from the middle to the upper level within a subtest content area. Because of the passage content, the reuse of passage sets on the Reading Comprehension test is quite obvious.

The Technical Report provided with the isee is extremely thorough and detailed but not very "user friendly." The 10 pages of explanation are terse and focus on test score analysis (scaling, equating, and norming). They are supported by 73 tables, in various formats, and 5 appendices. Fortunately, the tables are fairly complete and well labeled. Unfortunately, they provide little help to the technically naive reader. At least, it seems unlikely that the reader who does not know the term "skewness" will be enlightened by the footnote "Standardized third moment of the distribution of scaled scores."

All items were pretested. Within-subject pretests were administered in spiralled order to samples of independent school students, the middle level test to seventh grade and the upper level test to eighth and ninth grades. Final forms were administered for scaling, equating, and norming purposes to a stratified sample of independent school students in grades 5–11. Stratification was based on the school's geographic region and its type (boarding or day).

Common items equating was used for both horizontal (Form B to Form A) and vertical (middle to upper level) equating. Scale scores for the equated tests were placed on a scale from 860–900. The scores on the Mathematics Achievement tests were not vertically equated because the item types were different across levels. Scale scores for the middle level Mathematics Achievement test were set from 801 to 850; those on the upper level from 851 to 900. It is important to recognize that it is inappropriate to compare isee scale scores across subject areas, even though they appear to be on the same numeric scale.

Raw scores (number right) for the subtests range from an average of about 50% correct for the youngest students (fifth grade for the middle level and eighth grade for the upper level) to about 75% correct for the oldest (seventh grade for the middle level and eleventh grade for the upper level). Some aspects of the mathematics tests were quite difficult for fifth graders (Quantitative Comparison had an average of 38% correct on one form) whereas some aspects of Verbal Ability were quite easy for the eleventh graders (Sentence Completion on one form had an average of 87% correct). On the whole, the difficulty levels appear appropriate. Although the isee is intended to be used primarily with local norms, percentile rank tables are offered. It is important to note, however, that these were compiled on current independent school students; students desiring admission may or may not score at these levels.

Internal consistency reliabilities also appear generally appropriate, in the range of .8 to .9 for individual test scores and somewhat lower, as expected, for the shorter subtests. Lower reliabilities were generally reported for the fifth grade students, for whom speededness was also somewhat of a problem, especially in Reading Comprehension where about 25% of the students were unable to complete the test. About 90% or more of the students at other grade levels and of fifth graders in other subject areas were able to complete the test.

Validity evidence is absent from the materials provided. There is no discussion of the basis for selecting the test content. There is no statistical evidence the isee identifies students likely to succeed, or that it is correlated with other measures that relate to student success in independent schools (e.g., achievement test scores, course grades). Schools considering the use of these materials will, therefore, need to conduct their own validity investigations beginning with a careful consideration of whether the content of each test is appropriate for their intended student population (either current students or applicants). If the test is to be used for selection, care should be taken to ensure that the isee both identifies students who are successful and does not screen out students who would also be successful. If the isee is to be used with current students, the specific use intended for the scores should be considered. If students or teachers are to be judged on the basis of test results, for example, it will be important to assess the degree to which the test measures the institution's curriculum. Although no data are presented separately by race or gender, tests of this type sometimes manifest subgroup differences that may or may not be relevant, so this should also be considered.

In summary, the isee is a reliable test that should be at an appropriate level of difficulty for independent school students in grades 5 through 11. Schools will find it essential to judge for themselves whether this test is likely to be valid for their specific purposes, whether as a selection device or as an indicator of current student status and progress, and to monitor its effectiveness.

[175]
Index of Personality Characteristics.

Purpose: "To screen the personal and social adjustment of school-aged children and adolescents."
Population: Ages 8-0 to 17-11.
Publication Date: 1988.
Acronym: IPC.
Scores, 9: Personality Quotient, Academic Scale, Nonacademic Scale, Perception of Self Scale, Perception of Others Scale, Acting In Scale, Acting Out Scale, Internal Locus of Control Scale, External Locus of Control Scale.
Administration: Group.
Price Data, 1989: $59 per complete kit; $23 per 50 student response booklets; $17 per 50 profile and record forms; $22 per manual (69 pages).
Time: (30–45) minutes.
Comments: Self-ratings scale; may be orally administered.
Authors: Linda Brown and Margaret C. Coleman.
Publisher: PRO-ED, Inc.

Review of the Index of Personality Characteristics by PATRICIA A. BACHELOR, *Associate Professor of Psychology, California State University, Long Beach, CA:*

The Index of Personality Characteristics (IPC) was developed as a screening device of affective adjustment of school-aged children and adolescents. The IPC is a self-report inventory of perceptions of behavior and feelings intended to be incorporated with additional observational data into a socioemotional appraisal. The IPC may be administered as a group or individual test in approximately 30 to 45 minutes. Subjects respond to 75 items using a 4-point scale (*Almost always like me, Usually like me, Usually not like me,* or *Almost never like me*). Using the Profile and Record Form, the IPC yields a Personality Quotient plus eight scale scores, which can be converted to percentile ranks, deviation quotients, and/or standard scores by using the tables presented in the manual.

Four dimensions, each measured by a pair of dichotomous scales, comprise the eight scales of the IPC. By design, each item is assigned to two, three, or four scales. I would have preferred a more simple structure. The Ecological dimension's scales are Academic (28 items) and Nonacademic (47 items), which attempt to assess if problems are pervasive or situational. The Social Perception dimension inquires if problems deal with self-esteem (Perception of Self scale—40 items) or interpersonal relationships (Perception of Other—35 items). The Behavioral dimension's scales are Acting In (22 items) and Acting Out (22 items). These assess if one turns problems inward to oneself or outward to others or the environment, respectively. The Locus of Control dimension indicates if the student assumes responsibility for his or her own behavior (Internal—22 items) or deflects responsibility to chance or others (External—33 items).

The manual adequately presents the rationale for test development, procedures and techniques utilized in test construction, administration and scoring instructions, and guidelines for interpretation of test results. Data from reliability and validity studies are reported clearly. Standard score transformations are presented in tables. Hand scoring at the scale level is quite tedious and prone to clerical error. It is hoped that future editions of this test will be machine scorable because the present procedure is too time-consuming for most educational professionals.

The normative sample consisted of 2,704 students from ages 8-0 to 17-11. Randomly selected students or classes from 30 states were included. Demographic variables such as age, sex, race, ethnicity, geographic location, place of residence (urban or rural), parents' education and occupation, and principal language spoken at home were captured on each subject. The size and demographic characteristics of the normative sample when contrasted to recent U.S. Census data suggested the sample was adequate.

RELIABILITY ESTIMATES. Based upon the Salvia and Ysseldyke (1985) guidelines of acceptable evidence of reliability for a screening device, a critical value of .80 or greater was adopted by the authors. Internal consistency coefficients were computed on the standardization sample consisting of 500 students (50 at each one-year age level). Coefficient alphas were reported for each of the eight IPC scales plus the Total test across the 10 age levels. Alphas (with only six exceptions) met or surpassed the .80 criteria. The exceptions, which were confined to the Acting Out and Internal Locus of Control scales, ranged between .76 and .79. Hence, the reported estimates of internal consistency are adequate to excellent.

Estimates of internal consistency were also computed on special populations sampled from nine states. Fifty-nine institutionalized emotionally disturbed, 39 Public School emotionally disturbed, 34 learning disabled, and 49 nonhandicapped behaviorally disordered subjects comprised this sample. Alphas were presented for the eight IPC scales as well as the Total Test. With one exception (.78), the computed Alphas met the aforementioned criteria of .80.

Test-retest reliability coefficients for a sample (234) of subjects over a 10- to 14-day interval were adequate. Pearson correlations were computed on each of the eight IPC scales as well as the Total Test across five age intervals. Ten of the reported reliability coefficients were in the .70s with the remaining coefficients ranging from .80 to .91.

VALIDITY ESTIMATES. The authors base the IPC's content validity on the development, selection, and review of the items. Three hundred twenty-five items were reviewed initially by a panel of university professors in psychology and special education, psychologists in private practice, and school personnel who identify or serve serious emotionally disturbed students. This panel reduced the item pool to 227 items. These items were then classified into the eight scales. Items that did not contribute to at least two scales were omitted and thus, 150 items formed the experimental version. Through item analyses, 75 items emerged as the final form of the IPC. The analysis of the item validity conforms adequately to Guilford's (1956) criteria.

Concurrent validity was claimed by four correlational studies. IPC scores were correlated with (a) teachers' evaluation of socioemotional maturity; (b) the Piers-Harris Children's Self-Concept Scale, Revised; (c) the Coopersmith Self-Esteem Inventory, School Form; and (d) the Behavior Rating Profile Scales. Although the correlations were of reasonable magnitude, the choice of comparative variables and small and unrepresentative samples limit confidence in the concurrent validity of the IPC. More empirical evidence is warranted.

Using the responses of the standardization sample, a factor analysis was performed at the item level to establish construct validity. Four factors were revealed that most closely resembled the hypothesized Acting Out scale, Acting In scale, External Locus of Control scale, and Perception of Self scale. The eight hypothesized dimensions were not supported by the evidence.

Discrimination among groups of personality disordered and normal students was preliminary and not compelling to this reviewer. Further investigation is needed in order to verify this claim.

SUMMARY. The manual of the IPC was clearly written and data supporting each claim were presented in a straightforward manner. The IPC appears to have only moderately strong psychometric qualities. Estimates of reliability and content validity suggest the IPC is a promising instrument for screening personal and social adjustment disorders. However, a lack of sufficient evidence of construct and concurrent validity demands further study. Scoring should be mechanized in future versions.

REVIEWER'S REFERENCES

Guilford, J. P. (1956). *Fundamental statistics in psychology and education* (3rd ed.). New York: McGraw-Hill.

Salvia, J., & Ysseldyke, J. E. (1985). *Assessment in special and remedial education* (3rd ed.). Boston: Houghton-Mifflin.

Review of the Index of Personality Characteristics by JAYNE E. STAKE, *Professor of Psychology, University of Missouri-St. Louis, St. Louis, MO:*

The Index of Personality Characteristics (IPC) is designed to provide information about the social and personal adjustment of children. The IPC Manual contains descriptions of the test development procedures, characteristics of the normative sample, indices of reliability and validity, administrative and scoring procedures, and interpretation of test profiles. The manual includes appropriate cautions regarding the administration and interpretation of the IPC and is written in clear language that those unfamiliar with personality assessment can understand readily.

The IPC comprises a total of 75 items, each of which is designated for at least two of the eight scales of the IPC. The eight subscales represent four dimensions: (a) The Ecological Dimension refers to the setting of feelings and behaviors—school settings (the Academic Scale) and nonschool settings (the Nonacademic Scale); (b) the Social Perception Dimension refers to the targets of perceptions—self (the Perception of Self Scale) and others (Perception of Others Scale); (c) the Behavioral Dimension refers to the behavioral manifestations of disordered personality development—feelings turned inward (the Acting In Scale) and feelings expressed in outward action (the Acting Out Scale); and (d) the Locus of Control Dimension refers to perceptions of control and responsibility for events and one's own behavior (the Internal Locus of Control Scale) and perceptions of lack of control (the External Locus of Control Scale).

The authors do not provide a rationale for including these four dimensions or the eight scales, but do describe in detail their procedure for selecting items for the scales. Final item selection was made on the basis of: (a) correlations between items and scale and total scores and (*b*) the percentage of normal children endorsing unfavorable responses. Unfortunately, the authors did not confirm during test development that the items selected represent the eight constructs they were intended to measure. A factor analysis performed after the IPC was completed yielded only four factors: Acting Out, Acting In, External Locus of Control, and Perception of Self. Hence, the presence of eight factors has not been substantiated. These findings suggest the eight scales do not yield distinct indices of adjustment and that differential interpretation of all eight scale scores is not justified.

Three types of normative scores are provided. These scores are based on a sample of 2,704 students, ages 8 to 17, from 30 U.S. states. Demographic information for the normative sample is provided and contrasted to 1985 U.S. Census data. The normative sample closely resembles the national sample in social class and ethnicity. The normative scores are provided in the Appendices of the manual. Standard scores (mean = 10, standard deviation = 3) and percentile ranks are given for each scale. "Personality quotients" (mean = 100, standard deviations = 15) are given for total scores only.

Test users should be aware that the summing of scale scores may produce misleading total scores. As the authors themselves state, deviance may be expressed by either higher or lower scale scores. By summing scale scores, deviantly high and deviantly low scores occurring within the same profile are obscured. Hence, standard total scores may significantly misrepresent a testee's level of adjustment.

Two indices of reliability were obtained for each scale and for total scores: internal consistency and test-retest stability. Coefficient alpha was .96 for total scores and means for the individual scales ranged from .82–.95. Stability tested after a 10–14 day interval was .85 for total scores and .80–.87 for individual scores. This means that not all of the scales meet accepted standards of reliability for making decisions about individual cases, but that all meet minimum standards for research purposes.

Validity was tested through two procedures. First, scores of subjects from special populations were compared with the normative sample. The special samples included a total of 44 girls and 137 boys from three groups: emotionally disturbed, learning disabled, and behavior disordered. Given that the purpose of the scale is to detect problems in social and emotional adjustment, the size of these groups should be larger, particularly the female sample. Girls and boys tend to differ in the ways they express their adjustment problems, but separate findings by gender are not provided. The authors state that scores from these samples were significantly different from the normative group, but most of

the average scale scores of the learning disabled and emotionally disabled samples were within the normal range, including the Acting Out scores of the behavior disordered sample. Hence, children with significant adjustment problems may not be detected by the IPC scales.

A further study of validity was accomplished by correlating IPC scale and total scores with teacher, parent, and peer ratings, the Piers-Harris Children's Self-Concept Scale, and the Coopersmith Self-Esteem Inventories, School Form. The IPC scale and total scores were highly correlated with these other measures, providing evidence that IPC scores do reflect social and emotional adjustment. However, there is little evidence for the discriminate validity of the individual scales. That is, the scales were not shown to be uniquely successful in predicting behaviors and feelings within the domains they are purported to measure. In the few cases in which differential validity was tested, generally the results did not follow expectations. For example, the Academic Scale correlated higher with the Piers-Harris Anxiety Scale than with the Piers-Harris Intellectual and School Status Scale, and the Coopersmith School-Academics Subscale correlated higher with the Perception of Self Scale than with the Academic Scale. These findings cast further doubt on the value of the IPC scales for representing the constructs they are intended to measure.

In summary, the IPC has some strengths, including normative data based on a representative sample of U.S. students and relatively high levels of internal consistency and stability. However, the presence of the eight constructs has not been confirmed by factor analysis, there is considerable overlap between scores of behavior disordered and normal children, and validity data for the individual scales are weak. Test users should be aware that the eight scale scores must be interpreted with caution and may not represent distinct measures of adjustment. As the authors suggest, decisions should never be made on the basis of the IPC alone, but on a broader range of information. It is not recommended that total scores be used, even for screening purposes, because the profiles of normal and maladjusted children can yield similar total scores.

[176]
Individualised Classroom Environment Questionnaire.
Purpose: "An instrument for measuring perceptions of the classroom environment among secondary school students or their teachers."
Population: Junior and senior high school students and teachers.
Publication Date: 1990.
Acronym: ICEQ.
Scores, 5: Personalisation, Participation, Independence, Investigation, Differentiation.
Administration: Group.

Forms, 4: Actual Classroom-Long Form, Actual Classroom-Short Form, Preferred Classroom-Long Form, Preferred Classroom-Short Form.

Price Data, 1991: A$49.95 per complete materials including manual (39 pages).

Time: (10–15) minutes for short form; (15–30) minutes for long form.

Comments: Test forms contained in manual may be photocopied by purchaser.

Author: Barry J. Fraser.

Publisher: Australian Council for Educational Research Ltd. [Australia].

Review of the Individualised Classroom Environment Questionnaire by LAWRENCE M. ALEAMONI, Associate Head and Professor of Educational Psychology, University of Arizona, Tucson, AZ:

The description and purpose of the Individualised Classroom Environment Questionnaire (ICEQ) is laudable in that it is designed to assess the actual and preferred dimensions of Personalisation, Participation, Independence, Investigation, and Differentiation, which distinguish individualized secondary classrooms from conventional ones. The respondents can be either students or teachers. The uses of the ICEQ are identified as: providing teachers with feedback about their classrooms, evaluating innovations, investigating which types of classroom environment best promote student learning, and determining whether students and teachers differ in the ways they perceive the environment of the same classroom.

The primary support for the above uses of the ICEQ is found in Appendix A: Research with the ICEQ, of the Handbook. The only other section of the Handbook that deals with uses of the ICEQ is the two-page section: Using Information from the ICEQ, which provides a somewhat limited description of how the ICEQ data could be used to improve classroom learning. For most users of this questionnaire this would be the most important section and, therefore, should contain extensive detail as well as examples. Although the Handbook emphasizes, in the section Using Information from the ICEQ, the desirability of comparing the actual classroom environments in different school subjects as well as large and small classes, there are no tables or strategies provided to show how such normative comparisons could be accomplished.

The Handbook is very well done and easy to follow with excellent, eye-catching headings for each section. The long and short forms for both the actual and preferred classrooms are very well described including actual copies of the forms. The Handbook, however, does not recommend the use of the short form when the perceptions of individual students or teachers are being assessed because "it is less reliable than the long form." This is a curious statement in light of the fact that the reliabilities reported for the long form with individuals as the unit of analysis are lower than those reported for the short form. In order to support this statement Table I should also contain reliabilities based on individuals as the unit of analysis. Also no mention is made of the fact that the long form reliabilities will necessarily be higher than the short form due to the larger number of items.

The Statistical Information: Long Form section of the Handbook raises certain concerns about the data presented and analyzed. Two nonrandom samples of students and teachers were selected from two states (New South Wales and Tasmania) in Australia. It appears that the characteristics of the students, teachers, and types of classes were also different in the two samples. In spite of this difference, the data from these two samples were combined to generate statistical information for the ICEQ as if they represented some common "population." At the very least, means and standard deviations on the two separate samples, stratified by gender, grade, and science and social science classes should have been provided and also tested for significant differences. This would have provided the necessary evidence to determine if these samples and/or subsets of them should be combined for statistical purposes.

The Handbook provides mean correlations of each scale with the other four scales as evidence of scale independence. However, there is no indication about the range and frequency of these correlations which would shed more light on the reality of the purported independence.

Finally, the fact that three of the five scales have reliabilities of .80 and below (with class as the unit of analysis) does not bode well for a 50-item questionnaire. One reason for the lower reliabilities could be that the response scale of *almost never, seldom, sometimes, often,* and *very often* is probably not a quasi-interval scale because *seldom* and *sometimes* are probably not distinguishable by the respondents. A more appropriate scale would probably have been *always, often, neither often nor never, almost never,* and *never.* Also, the use of a numeric scale on the answer sheet instead of abbreviations or acronyms for the response scale will contribute to the instrument's unreliability as well as its validity.

In summary, although the ICEQ appears to be a well-constructed and researched instrument, the Handbook reveals there is a dearth of information on how it should be and has been used to improve classroom learning. In fact, the four uses identified are actually suggestions for future research rather than documented applications. Also, the statistical information presented raises some questions about the appropriateness of the samples and the reliabilities reported.

[177]
Infant Mullen Scales of Early Learning.
Purpose: Assesses a child's cognitive abilities and gross motor base for learning.
Population: Birth to 36 months.
Publication Dates: 1984–89.
Acronym: Infant MSEL.
Scores: 5 scales: Gross Motor Base, Visual Receptive Organization, Visual Expressive Organization, Language Receptive Organization, Language Expressive Organization.
Administration: Individual.
Price Data: Available from publisher.
Time: (10–45) minutes.
Authors: Eileen M. Mullen.
Publisher: T.O.T.A.L. Child, Inc.

Review of the Infant Mullen Scales of Early Learning by VERNA HART, Professor of Special Education, University of Pittsburgh, Pittsburgh, PA:

Passage of P.L. 99-457, the preschool amendment to P.L. 94-142, has increased interest in assessing young children, particularly those from birth to 3 years of age. The publication of the Infant Mullen Scales of Early Learning (IMSEL) should interest some of those who are looking for such an instrument.

The author, Dr. Eileen M. Mullen, is a developmental psychologist with many years of experience diagnosing children with multihandicaps, severe physical handicaps, and learning disabilities. She explains at length her test model, an interactive one with intrasensory as well as intersensory components. Central motor control and mobility are seen to have an impact on visual spatial organization, fine motor ability, auditory and auditory/visual reception, and verbal communication. With normal motor development, a state of motor equilibration exists that allows responsivity and learning to occur. With abnormal motor development, patterns essential to movement do not develop and the child is unable to take full advantage of sensory input. Receptive sensory levels emphasize comprehension whereas expressive levels target output. Visual and auditory comprehension and expression are viewed as intrasensory entities as well as intersensory, where vision and hearing, visual-motor, or vocal-motor interact.

The test is based on norms of typical early development. Its purpose is to identify specific areas of delay rather than to give a developmental or intelligence quotient. Each scale has its own score, available as a developmental age score or as a *T*-score. The author recommends that standard scores be used for program eligibility and test age scores for those with little background in measurement. Early intervention is recommended if a child falls 1.5 or more standard deviations below the mean in two or more subscales or if a single *T*-score falls 2 or more standard deviations below the mean. Intervention and educational decisions are to be designed relative to the domain where weaknesses are noted.

The test kit contains many simple testing materials of interest to young children. Most of the items are quite durable. An exception is the various colors and sizes of shapes, which are made of a thin poster type of paper and which bend and can tear. It would also be desirable to have the Picture Vocabulary and Picture Cards booklets covered with the same easy-to-wipe surfaces as those found in the Show and Tell Me booklet.

The scales are easy to administer and flexibility is allowed in presentation. Some items can be scored by caregiver's report. The manual is written in nontechnical terms and is easy to follow. Scoring is quite simple. The time to administer the scales is relatively short. All five of the scales may be given, or separate subscales administered individually; each subscale can stand on its own administratively and for scoring. A strength of the scales is availability of separate scores for receptive and expressive responses.

Ease of administration should make this unrestricted test attractive to many early intervention programs. Although the author offers workshops in its administration, those with experience testing young children should have no difficulty with this particular instrument. A variety of professionals from many disciplines were used in the standardization of the scales. Seventy-one clinicians representing psychology, speech pathology, special education, occupational therapy, pediatric nursing, physical therapy, and social work were used to gather normative data. Interscorer reliability ranged from .88 to .99 from 6 to 36 months and .78 to 1.00 from 1–4 months.

Standardization data are available on a sample of 1,231 children from birth to 38 months of age. These data and revised *T*-scores, available from the author, replace those found in the kit. Standardization testing was completed over an 8-year period and began in the northeast. Later, children were included from the west, south, north, and south central areas of the country. Stratified variables of age, sex, race, parental occupation, and urban/rural residence were considered, as was minority representation. The sample's description suggests that it is fairly representative of the U.S. population. Some ages within the groups, however, are under- or overrepresented. Age groups tested were 2, 4, 6, 8, 10, 12, 14, 18, 24, 30, and 36 months. In addition, users should remember the sample includes only children whose parents consented to the testing.

The psychometric properties of the instrument present some concern. Data presented show a Cronbach alpha coefficient of .97 for internal consistency of the intrasensory subscales. Concurrent validity was reported using three instruments with different age ranges. The IMSEL gross motor subscale showed a correlation of .95 with the Bayley

Motor Scale. However, these data were compiled using only a group of 7–14-month-old infants. Correlation of the IMSEL composite score with the Bayley Mental Scale was .97 for the 7–14-month-old children. The language subscales of the IMSEL were correlated with the Preschool Language Assessment with coefficients of .78 to .98. These coefficients are based on small sample size and data only from 18- and 24-month-old children. Correlations with the Birth to Three Scale were .94 and .95. These reflect an N of only 25 and an age range of 26 to 35 months. No data were available from birth to 6 months. Test-retest reliability ($N = 68$) ranged from .70 to .99 across the ages of 10 to 36 months, but did not include the gross motor area after 16 months.

The test is new and additional information on reliability and validity is needed. An item analysis is lacking and should be obtained. Only one item is presented for each age group. That item must be highly discriminating. Minor things also need attention: vestiges of older versions found in the manual, an incomplete list of materials needed for testing, and inclusion in the test kits of all of the materials listed (mine had several items missing).

However, the test, if used with other test results obtained by the multidisciplinary team members as recommended by the author, should offer insight into a child's particular problems for programming purposes. Separate scoring for the receptive and expressive areas as well as cross-modal associations are its strengths.

[178]
Informal Reading Comprehension Placement Test.

Purpose: Assesses the instructional and independent comprehension levels of students from prereadiness (Grade 1) through level eight plus (Grade 8).
Population: Grades 1–6 for typical learners and Grades 7–12 remedially.
Publication Date: 1983.
Scores, 3: Word Comprehension, Passage Comprehension, Total Comprehension.
Administration: Individual.
Price Data, 1989: $49.95 per complete kit including 1 diskette, 1 back-up diskette, management, and documentation (15 pages).
Time: (35–50) minutes for the battery, (15–20) minutes for Part 1 and (20–30) minutes for Part 2.
Comments: Test administered in 2 parts; Apple II or TRS-80 microcomputer necessary for administration.
Authors: Ann Edson and Eunice Insel.
Publisher: Educational Activities, Inc.

Review of the Informal Reading Comprehension Placement Test by GLORIA A. GALVIN, School Psychologist, Dodgeville School District, Dodgeville, WI:

This test consists of two types of tasks: word analogies and a series of eight graded paragraphs.

The paragraphs were developed using readability formulas to control for vocabulary and sentence length. Each paragraph is followed by four multiple-choice questions (each with three one-word answer choices) designed to test comprehension of each of the following: detail, main idea, inference, and vocabulary from the context. The major purpose of the test is to enable a student to be placed in curricular materials at the appropriate reading comprehension level. The authors' rationale for the test is "to use the findings to prescribe a developmental, corrective, or remedial reading program for the individual student."

The main advantage of this test over other commercial tests or typical teacher-made tests of this type is the computer format that lets the child take the test largely independent of a test administrator. However, this advantage is limited because there are points within the program where the student may be given the instruction, "Please call your teacher," so that an examiner must be available to advance or terminate the program appropriately. Further, there is a fundamental problem in having beginning or poor readers do a reading test independently when the instructions are printed on the screen and must be read and comprehended to be executed correctly. Children whose reading comprehension is at the lower reading levels may not be validly tested because they do not understand the printed program commands, and not because they cannot comprehend the lower level paragraphs. This limits the usefulness of the test with many young children and also with older children with reading problems.

A major problem with this test is the complete lack of reliability, validity, and normative information. Although the test is claimed to have been used with 3,000 children, no data are presented. Furthermore, how well this test places children into various curricular materials at various grade levels is not known. For the purpose of placing children accurately into reading materials, teachers would be better served by their own teacher-made materials that fit their specific curricula.

A second problem with this test is the authors' failure to fully utilize the computer technology. Although the variety of comprehension questions accompanying each paragraph is laudable, greater numbers of questions could have been incorporated to make the measurement more reliable. For example, questions could have been arranged so that a student answering 100% of the four basic questions would be given some higher level inferential questions, whereas the student falling below the criterion would be given additional easier questions. The process should lead to a fuller understanding of the student's level of comprehension. In addition, qualitative information on the student's test performance should be made available using computer technology, rather than limiting the output to a few summary scores. Given the rationale for the test by the authors as a way of helping plan for prescriptive and remedial help for the individual student, information on the (a) number and types of errors made, (b) amount of rereading the student did (each paragraph can be recalled once per question), and (c) rate at which the student completed the test should also be made available. Such information would be available in many, typical paper-and-pencil, examiner-administered tests.

In summary, this test offers some positive features such as the variety of comprehension questions uniformly applied to each paragraph, minimum examiner time per student, and a test that ends smoothly without showing the student how many items were not presented. However, this test lacks the basic foundation for adequate measurement by ignoring the concepts of reliability and validity. Further, the test fails to utilize the computer format to provide analysis of student errors and actually is more limited in the information it provides and the flexibility with which it can be used than a well-constructed teacher-made test for a specific curriculum. Therefore, although time is saved in administration of this test, the information gleaned is much less than it could have been. This test may be useful for a quick screening of reading placement level, but does not have much to offer the educator who has the goal of remediation for the individual student.

Review of the Informal Reading Comprehension Placement Test by CLAUDIA R. WRIGHT, Assistant Professor of Educational Psychology, California State University, Long Beach, CA:

The Informal Reading Comprehension Placement Test was developed by two educators with backgrounds as reading specialists in elementary and secondary school settings who also have worked as curriculum development consultants for public school districts located in New York. This test was designed to serve as a computer-facilitated screening and placement test providing a measure of reading comprehension levels for students in grades 1 through 6 who may range in reading ability from prereadiness through eighth-grade levels and beyond. In addition, the test has been employed for remediation purposes with secondary and special education students.

The Informal Reading Placement Test is divided into two parts. The first section, identified as the Word Comprehension Test (Part 1) is made up of eight sets of eight word-meaning analogies for a total of 64 test items in a multiple-choice response format. Approximately 15 to 20 minutes is required for testing. Vocabulary levels for this part of the test have been validated, in part, by the employment of the EDL and Dolch Word lists as referents in the selection of words for each level. The second section,

the Passage Comprehension Test (Part 2), is composed of eight reading passages which range in reading difficulty from prereadiness to eighth-grade plus levels. Vocabulary and sentence length have been controlled for each level using Spache, Frye, and Dale Chall readability formulas. Each of the eight passages is followed by four multiple-choice test items that purportedly measure comprehension of detail, main idea, inference, and vocabulary. Completion time for Part 2 is 20 to 30 minutes. In addition to the two reading comprehension components, estimates of a respondent's total instructional level, independent reading level, and frustration level are also provided.

The entire test is administered and scored on the microcomputer. The test manual provides the teacher with clear instructions for the operation of the program through a sample testing session. The process is facilitated further by illustrations of the sequence for several test segments. The computer displays are personalized with the student's name, the content is easy to read and hierarchically organized, and the program is well suited for independent or teacher-assisted testing. In addition, explicit directions are provided for the interpretation of student performances. Teachers have access to five types of information for each student: (a) a word comprehension score that identifies the number of incorrect responses at each of the eight reading levels; (b) a passage comprehension score for each of the eight reading levels; (c) the total instructional level, which is a composite indicator made up of a comparison of the word comprehension and passage comprehension levels to determine by how many levels the two scores differ; (d) a total independent level that identifies the level at which the student can read independently (operationally defined as that level at which the student correctly identifies words with 99% accuracy and passes the comprehension items at the 95% level); and (e) the total frustration level, which signifies the lowest level of comprehension (less than 90% word accuracy and 50% or below in correct responses to the comprehension items) and is thought to indicate the extent to which the reading material is too difficult for the student. This reviewer assumes that conventional mastery-learning rationales have been employed for the selection of these particular percentages as cutoff scores, even though no rationales have been cited.

No reliability or validity information has been provided with the test materials. The authors acknowledge that the psychometric properties of the instrument are "undoubtably not the same as a typical standardized reading test," however, they fail to report what information may have led them to this conclusion. Further, a relatively thorough search of the literature revealed that very little, if any, research has employed the Informal Reading Placement Test to support the validity of the instrument.

As noted in the test manual, the Informal Reading Placement Test has been used with over 3,000 students enrolled in grades 1 through 6 as a tool for the classroom teacher to assess reading comprehension for placement and to provide information for remedial instruction. It would appear that with such a broadly based usage of the instrument, some data from standardized achievement tests could be made available for estimating construct and criterion-related validities.

The authors are encouraged to incorporate within the test manual any additional information that may be obtained from empirical studies to establish the reliability of the instrument as well as the construct and criterion-related validities of the Informal Reading Placement Test. These data could serve to support the placement and remedial functions for which the test was developed. Even though a test has been designed to afford a "quick" assessment of behavior, the brevity of the assessment does not reduce the demand for an instrument with sound psychometric properties.

Overall, the Informal Reading Placement Test as a computer-assisted assessment device would appear to provide a promising approach for classroom applications. Caution, however, should be exercised in the use of this instrument if it is employed as the only criterion for placement or remediation purposes particularly in light of the absence of reliability and validity data.

[179]
Informal Writing Inventory.
Purpose: To measure an individual's skills in written expression.
Population: Grades 3–12.
Publication Date: 1986.
Acronym: IWI.
Scores, 4: Formation Errors, Grammar Errors, Communication Errors, Total Errors.
Administration: Individual or group.
Price Data, 1988: $32.95 per complete set including 50 response forms, 20 student record folders, 14 picture prompts, and administrator's manual (36 pages).
Time: Administration time not reported.
Author: Gerard Giordano.
Publisher: Scholastic Testing Service, Inc.

Review of the Informal Writing Inventory by GABRIEL DELLA-PIANA, Professor of Educational Psychology, University of Utah, Salt Lake City, UT:
The Informal Writing Inventory (IWI) is designed as a "diagnostic procedure . . . for evaluating writing samples . . . . analyzing [them] into categories that simplify a judgment about the presence, degree, and [to some extent] cause of writing disability . . . . [It also] specifies remedial exercises . . . . for writers who commit errors that

interfere with . . . formation [handwriting], grammar, and communication [comprehensibility]" (p. 1, manual, bracketed words added). The instrument makes use of pictorial prompts to "motivate students to write." This review focuses on the procedures specified in the administrator's manual. Although the reviewer found much innovative about the IWI, it was found limited in its current stage of development.

The procedures for administration do not appear adequate for the uses intended. The test administrator is to "choose one from a set of 14 pictures" (p. 7, manual) for the student to write about. However, no data are presented describing the differential effects of the writing prompts for the wide range of ages for which the test is designed. Furthermore, the instructions to the writer leave so much to the discretion of the test administrator that it is not clear what writing prompt will be presented. A portion of one key sentence is "ask the students to think about the picture you display and to create a record of their responses" (p. 7, manual). One teacher following these instructions said to the students, "Look at the picture and write what the girl is thinking about." These instructions certainly focused attention differently than others would with the same general guide to administration. Additionally, the instructions indicate that there are "No limits . . . for . . . length of passage." However, they also suggest that "Typically, a minimum of twenty errors is required for an analysis" (p. 7). With such instructions, the "diagnosis" can certainly be quite different when conducted by different test administrators.

Scoring procedures could be improved with respect to the help given to the test user doing the scoring. The writing sample elicited is scored for three kinds of errors, which are transformed into an "error index" and a "communication index." The error index is the percent of words analyzed that indicate any kind of error including: Formation (handwriting), Grammar, or Communication (formation and grammar errors that interfere with comprehension and another category of communication error to be noted below). The communication index is the percent of total errors that are Communication errors. The scoring difficulty arises from the lack of detailed descriptions of the categories and the lack of sample analyses representing "disabled writers." On the latter point, there are three complete illustrative analyses none of which represent "disabled writers" (a writer who has *not* developed "functional writing skills"). For writers *with* functional writing skills, "at least 77% of [their] writing errors do not impede communication." Yet, of the three illustrative analyses, two of them have *no* Communication errors (well above 77% that do not impede communication) and one has only three Communication errors out of a total of 31 errors (or about 90% of the errors being those that do not impede communication). As to the detail on description of scoring categories, Grammar errors are listed and well illustrated. However, Formation errors (handwriting) are not clearly described or illustrated. The only Communication error other than Formation errors that is illustrated or described is "joining of semantically irreconcilable concepts, e.g., 'He took a bite from the sleeping stone.' " Because the definition of disabled and nondisabled rests primarily on the extent of communication errors these examples in the manual raise questions about the construct or domain definition of "disability."

Suggestions for correcting writing problems are outlined under 24 activities keyed to weaknesses in handwriting, spelling, grammar, and communication. These activities are of varying quality. What is most significant, however, is the lack of a clear guide to selection of an activity based on the diagnostic data. For example, once one eliminates instructional activities that are relevant to communication errors due to spelling, handwriting, or grammar, there are 14 of the 24 activities that are targeted to improve communication and many of them indeed do appear to be helpful for this purpose. However, the diagnostic test does not identify kinds of communication errors in a way that would help in selecting among the activities. Also, there are six activities relevant to "spelling," three of which are independent of spelling error due to handwriting difficulties. But again there is no diagnosis of *kinds* of spelling difficulties (e.g., phonetically regular spellings, mispronunciations, regular spelling inappropriately generalized) and remediation relevant to the kind of spelling difficulty.

Perhaps what is most problematic about the IWI is that even though it is intended as an "informal" assessment instrument, its development does not appear to be guided by systematic procedures for performance assessment. There are no intercoder reliability data for the scoring system. The achievement domain is not defined clearly enough so that one can interpret a "communication index" or decide if the scoring operations appear to tap the domain or construct intended. The idea of using pictorial prompts is excellent because it can sidestep the difficulties in reading instructions that tell what to write about. But the IWI has too many problems in its current stage of development. What this reviewer would recommend to potential consumers of an informal writing inventory is that they read up on what is involved in writing skills assessment (e.g., Faigley et al., 1985; Ruth & Murphy, 1988; Quellmalz, 1986) and then survey available instruments.

REVIEWER'S REFERENCES

Faigley, L., Cherry, R. D., Jolliffe, D. A., & Skinner, A. M. (1985). *Assessing writers' knowledge and processes of composing.* Norwood, NJ: Ablex.

Quellmalz, E. (1986). Writing skills assessment. In R. A. Berk (Ed.), *Performance assessment: Methods and applications* (pp. 492-508). Baltimore: Johns Hopkins University Press.

Ruth, L., & Murphy, S. (1988). *Designing writing tasks for the assessment of writing.* Norwood, NJ: Ablex.

Review of the Informal Writing Inventory by DONALD L. RUBIN, *Professor of Language Education, The University of Georgia, Athens, GA:*

In recent years, educational reformers have decried the once common medical pathology-oriented metaphor of teaching and learning. Rather than diagnosing and curing skill deficits, the new generation of metaphors instead urges educators to acknowledge the considerable prowess of even novice learners. The new models enjoin educators to nurture students as they move through predictable stages of development. The skill domain of written communication is at the forefront of this new order. Under slogans like "writing to learn" and "composing processes not written products," and in tandem with growing interest in teaching critical thinking, the teaching of writing is enjoying a strong revitalization as something a great deal more than just error-free scribing.

A writing assessment procedure that focuses exclusively on errors, therefore, is an anachronism, a throw-back to deficit remediation models. Such is the case of the Informal Writing Inventory. The purpose of this instrument is to identify the writing problems of potentially disabled writers. The category of disabled writer to which the Inventory is aimed seems quite broad; the administrator's manual refers to students who experience difficulty forming letters, suffer from writer's block, and manifest inability to distinguish relevant from extraneous details. At least some of these disabling conditions are quite normal occurrences for most writers at least some of the time. They hardly serve to define some special population.

Moreover, the entire issue of error in writing is a good deal more complex than this Inventory acknowledges. The instrument analyzes elicited writing samples for relative frequencies of three kinds of errors: Formation errors (spelling and penmanship), Grammatical errors, and Communication errors. One issue not adequately addressed is the identification of error. For example, the society—if not the grammar handbooks—is rapidly moving toward acceptance of "they" as a generic third person *singular* pronoun (e.g., "If a person wants to write well they need to know what to say"). And although many people would regard starting a sentence with a conjunction as gravely egregious, the administrator's manual shows one such example (on page 8) but fails to mark it as a violation. As it happens, it is difficult to define the concept of error in writing. The phrase "gravely egregious" contains an element of redundancy. Is it therefore an error?

Beyond the issue of defining reliably the concept of error, categorizing types of errors can be problematic. Consider the sentence, "The manuscript went to the printed." It contains a formation error if one assumes that the final "d" should be "r." It contains a grammatical error if one assumes that a verb form cannot serve as object of a sentence (but compare, "The toils went to the vanquished"). It constitutes a communication error, the administrator's manual rightly points out, only if one cannot make sense of it in context. Communicative errors are particularly important to interpreting results of the Informal Writing Inventory; the greater the proportion of communicative errors to total errors, the more disabled is the writer. Most teachers of basic writing are painfully aware, however, that in context—for example in the context of a conversation with the writer—virtually all student sentences do make sense. The critical issue in judging writing quality is not so much one of sense as negotiating effort: How much effort ought the reader, relative to the writer, expend in order to reveal the sense of a text?

These concerns about the Inventory's emphasis on error, the fuzziness of the very concept of writing error, and lack of clear definition between categories of error all speak to the procedure's poor construct validity. They also bear on matters of reliability. The test publisher's materials provide no information about interrater reliability in identifying or categorizing error.

Test users will also be operating in the dark with regard to the reliability of elicitation procedures. The Inventory includes 14 stimulus pictures to be used in eliciting writing samples. The pictures depict incongruent events, intended to arouse mild anxiety in writers. According to the administrator's manual, this is an optimal way to elicit "meaningful writing samples." Optimal or not, the various pictures are likely not equivalent forms of the same test. (Elicitation instructions even permit the option of test-takers drawing their own stimulus pictures.) Students may produce different quantities of writing, or different modes of writing, in response to the different stimuli. Test users would also be interested in learning about test-retest reliabilities. To what extent does a student's error production represent a stable trait? Because motivation and attentiveness are important factors in error detection and correction, reliability across time is likely small. The administrator's manual does recommend that writing samples ought to include at least 20 errors. Too small a sample, according to the manual, "decreases . . . one's confidence in the validity of the analysis of these errors." Using the number of errors as an index of sample length results in an odd enigma, however. An adequate language sample for a poor writer might be five sentences but a good writer might need to produce five pages. Still the two writers' error proportions might end up looking quite similar.

The basic strength of the Informal Writing Inventory is that it attempts to measure writing ability directly. It samples holistic writing performance rather than isolated word writing and rather than indirect measures of error identification in supplied sentences. In using the Inventory with learning disabled populations, test administrators will be acknowledging that all students are capable of authentic composing. In addition, the Inventory quite properly recognizes that not all errors are created equal; those that disrupt communication engender greater concern than those that are mere violations of surface-level mechanics. Finally, as a diagnostic instrument the Inventory links various error profiles to one of 24 remedial writing exercises. These exercises range from simple procedures in which students label illustrations with descriptive words to more complex and diffuse activities such as writing to request information from foreign consulates. The activities are sound instructional practices, though there is little reason to believe that any single exercise will remediate a pattern of error. In short, the Informal Writing Inventory is inadequate psychometrically, and it does reflect a paradigm of instruction generally regarded as outmoded, if not bankrupt. But at least it gets students writing, and that's not bad.

[180]
Intermediate Measures of Music Audiation.
Purpose: "To identify children with exceptionally high music aptitude . . . who can profit from the opportunity to participate in additional group study and special private instruction . . . to evaluate the comparative tonal and rhythm aptitudes of each child with exceptionally high music aptitude."
Population: Grades 1–4.
Publication Dates: 1978–82.
Acronym: IMMA.
Scores, 3: Tonal, Rhythm, Composite.
Administration: Group.
Price Data, 1986: $62 per complete kit containing 1 tonal tape and 1 rhythm tape, 100 tonal answer sheets, 100 rhythm answer sheets, 2 sets of scoring masks, 100 profile cards, 4 class record sheets, and test manual ('82, 44 pages); $13 per tonal tape; $13 per rhythm tape; $8 per 100 tonal answer sheets; $8 per 100 rhythm answer sheets; $1 per set of tonal or rhythm scoring masks; $13 per 100 profile cards; $1.75 per 10 class record sheets; $12.95 per manual.
Time: (20) minutes per Tonal test; (20) minutes per Rhythm test.
Comments: Advanced version of the Primary Measures of Music Audiation (9:988); tests administered by $7^1/_2$ ips tape recordings.
Author: Edwin E. Gordon.
Publisher: G.I.A. Publications, Inc.

[181]
Interpersonal Relations Questionnaire.
Purpose: "To identify specific problems in connection with interpersonal relations and identity formation."

Population: "White pupils" in Standards 5–7 in South African schools.
Publication Dates: 1981–88.
Acronym: IRQ.
Scores, 13: Self-Confidence, Self-Esteem, Self-Control, Nervousness, Health, Family Influences, Personal Freedom, Sociability A, Sociability T, Sociability D, Moral Sense, Formal Relations, Lie Scale.
Administration: Group.
Price Data: Available from publisher.
Time: (105–120) minutes.
Comments: Supplementary manual in English and Afrikaans.
Authors: Marianne Joubert and Dawn Schlebusch (supplementary manual).
Publisher: Human Sciences Research Council [South Africa].

[182]
Inventory for Counseling & Development.

Purpose: An attempt to identify "strengths, assets and coping skills of college students seeking assistance with vocational, educational and personal problems."
Population: College students.
Publication Dates: 1981–87.
Scores, 23: Agreement, Favorable Impression, Infrequent, Insecurity, Alienation, Exam Tension, Ambition, Persistence, Practicality, Sociability, Teacher-Student Interaction, Intellectuality, Originality, Adaptability, Orderliness, Liberal-Conservative, Socio-Political Interest, Sexual Beliefs, Sex Role Differences, Academic Performance, Academic Excellence, Academic Capacity, Academic Motivation.
Administration: Group or individual.
Price Data, 1990: $12.45 per 10 reusable test booklets; $31.50 per handscoring key; $8.35 per 25 handscoring answer sheets; $3.55–$4.55 per mail-in scoring answer sheet (includes cost of scoring and profile report); $14.75 per 25 Microtest answer sheets; $3.55–$4.55 per Microtest profile report (for on-site scoring); $8.35 per 25 handscoring profile sheets; $11.25 per manual ('88, 106 pages).
Time: (60–120) minutes.
Authors: Norman S. Giddan, F. Reid Creech, and Victor R. Lovell.
Publisher: National Computer Systems.

Review of the Inventory for Counseling & Development by NAMBURY S. RAJU, Professor of Psychology, Illinois Institute of Technology, Chicago, IL:

The Inventory for Counseling & Development (ICD) is an objective and multiscale personality questionnaire specifically designed for assessing the academic, personal, and social functioning of college students. It consists of 449 items and yields scores on 23 different scales grouped into three categories: 3 validity scales, 15 substantive scales, and 5 criterion scales. The true-false (dichotomous) format is used for all items in the ICD, and it is designed for both machine and hand scoring.

The ICD has gone through many phases of development over the last 15 years, with each succeeding phase (form) resulting in an improved version over the preceding one. The latest version of the ICD, Form F, reflects a high degree of psychometric soundness and a strong research base. The scales in the validity category measure test-taking attitudes and response styles. The clinical and counseling value of the 15 substantive scales is well documented in the manual (Chapter 5). The reported validity of the academic scales (contained in the criterion category) in predicting college academic achievement (GPA) is empirically based and appears to be superior to validities obtained with SAT scores and high school GPAs (manual, p. 85).

NORMS. The standardization of Form F was based on 660 female and 520 male college undergraduates, most of whom came from seven universities. The raw score scales associated with the 23 ICD scales were converted to T scores with a mean of 50 and a standard deviation of 10. In addition, national percentiles were developed for each scale. The development of both T scores and national percentiles was done separately for women and men. However, the description of the standardization procedures leaves this reviewer with some unanswered questions. How were the students from the seven participating universities chosen for the standardization? Was there a statistical sampling design for the ICD standardization? Without a well-designed and implemented sampling plan, it is sometimes difficult to interpret the derived percentile scores.

RELIABILITY. Internal consistency estimates of reliability (KR-20) and test-retest correlations are reported for the ICD. The KR-20 estimates for all 23 scales were based on Form D. The KR-20 estimates for the scales in the substantive category are also available from Forms B, C, and E. The KR-20 estimates are in the .70s and .80s for scales in the substantive category. These reliabilities appear to be reasonable for the types of scales included in the ICD, with the exception of the Agreement and Infrequent Scales in the validity category (manual, p. 54). None of the reported KR-20 estimates was based on Form F. The authors of the ICD could have easily generated the KR-20 estimates from the Form F standardization data. The fact they did not is a surprise to this reviewer.

The two sets of Form F test-retest reliability estimates are mostly in the .70s and .80s. The time interval between the two testings was 3 weeks for the first set and 7 weeks for the second set.

No standard errors of measurement (*SEM*s) are reported for the ICD scales. As previously noted with respect to the generation of KR-20 estimates of reliability, the authors of the ICD could have also generated the necessary *SEM* statistics from the Form F standardization data. The *SEM* data would be particularly useful for counselors. Also, the printing of *SEM* bands (± *SEM*, for example) with the computer-generated score reports would have been very helpful in facilitating the interpretation of score profiles, especially in minimizing the overinterpretation of small to moderate differences between any two scale scores.

VALIDITY. The authors present various types of data for assessing the content, construct, and criterion-related validity of the ICD (manual, pp. 58–88). The reported information is impressive and speaks to the high psychometric quality of the ICD. As the authors correctly point out, the validity of a psychometric instrument depends upon the appropriateness of the inferences made from the use of scores. Because the type of inferences made could vary from one set of situations to another, there is a need for continuous monitoring of the validity of an instrument such as the ICD. The authors should be commended for articulating this view point and for proposing a plan for ongoing validation of the ICD (manual, p. 88).

With respect to construct validation, the manual presents correlations between the ICD scores and other relevant inventories such as the Strong-Campbell Interest Inventory, Self-Description Inventory, and Personality Description Inventory. Correlations between certain ICD scales and the corresponding scales from the other inventories are carefully summarized and discussed to underscore the construct validity of the ICD. These are very useful data and their utility could have been substantially enhanced by noting which reported correlations are statistically significant. Information about statistical significance would be very helpful in delineating the evidence for divergent and convergent validation.

Information about criterion-related validity of the ICD is presented for various criteria. As previously noted, correlations between the ICD Academic Scales and (Stanford) Freshman GPA are statistically significant and vary from .37 to .53 for males and females. Significant correlations with GPAs are also reported for other colleges.

Alienation, creativity, student activism, and student-teacher interactions were also used as criteria for assessing the validity of the ICD scales. The experimental group sample sizes in the Creativity and Student Activism studies were extremely small compared to the control group sample sizes. The definition of control groups in these two studies appears to be somewhat arbitrary and may explain some of the noted inconsistencies in the reported results.

Overall, the ICD is a solid psychometric instrument for assessing the academic, personal, and social functioning of college students. The research base for the ICD is impressive, with detailed documentation about its development, reliability, validity, and standardization. Empirical as well as theory-based claims of validity for the ICD scales are carefully summarized to minimize the potential misinterpretation of scale scores.

Review of the Inventory for Counseling & Development by ELEANOR E. SANFORD, Research Consultant, Division of Accountability Services / Research, North Carolina Department of Public Instruction, Raleigh, NC:

The Inventory for Counseling & Development (ICD) is an objective, multiscale measure of personality that is linked to academic success in college. It is a very timely measure considering all the controversy surrounding the use of the Scholastic Aptitude Test (SAT; 9:244) for college admissions. It was initially designed to be used in conjunction with the SAT, high school GPA, and nonintellective measures of personality and motivation to predict success in college. The ICD (Form F being reviewed here) considers personal, social, and academic functioning and has developed into a "comprehensive device for use in counseling, evaluating, and educating college students" as well as a predictor of academic success (technical manual, p. 1).

The ICD is based on three psychological paradigms: psychodynamic-clinical, cognitive-social learning, and developmental (Erikson). The test consists of 449 true/false items that comprise 23 scales (3 validity scales, 15 substantive scales, and 5 criterion scales).

The ICD may be administered individually or in a group setting and takes approximately 50–60 minutes. The test is designed for an individual of any age entering college. The test can be individually scored using templates for each scale or computer scored (locally or by National Computer Systems) for large administrations of the test. A profile of the 23 scale raw scores is obtained with raw scores graphically converted to *t*-scores for interpretation across the scales. The authors state acceptable ranges for the scale scores and the technical manual has numerous interpretative case studies to aid the counselor in the interpretation of ICD profiles with the individual.

The ICD has undergone extensive development through six versions with large samples of college students at each stage (920 to 1985). The development process of the substantive scales was guided by the criteria that an item should correlate more highly with its own scale than with other scales and that the scales should be independent. During each phase of development an iterative procedure was employed where items were removed, scales were reorganized, and new items and scales were developed in order to meet this criteria of maximum discrimination and convergence. This iterative procedure of test development was repeated five times (nine iterations were required for Form B and less for Forms C-F). The validity and the criterion scales were developed through an empirical procedure with the criteria that the item must correlate highly with expected GPA or its residual (regression equation based on SAT-V, SAT-M, and high school GPA) and lower with other predictors. Separate male and female scales were developed for the criterion scales based on research with the first form of the ICD.

The ICD (Form E) has adequate stability and internal consistency reliability. The KR-20 estimates of the internal consistency range from .75 to .83 for the substantive scales and from .49 to .66 for the criterion scales. Estimates of the internal consistency of the validity scales are not stated. The test-retest reliability coefficients range from .46 to .88 over a 3-week period and from .55 to .89 over a 7-week period.

Numerous research investigations concerning the validity of the ICD are reported in the technical manual. The content validity of the ICD was built into the development process. Items were written to measure clinical and personality constructs of an ideal student. Profiles of accepted students were examined by admissions staff concerning their responses to the ICD and another inventory and the results were consistent. Also the scales of the ICD correlate moderately with each other where applicable (e.g., Insecurity scale with Exam Tension is .63). The results from the third administration of the ICD were factor analyzed and five interpretable factors were derived.

The construct validity of the ICD has been examined by correlating the theoretically meaningful ICD scales with scales from other tests (Career Assessment Inventory, Self-Description Inventory, Personality Description Inventory, and Strong-Campbell Interest Inventory). The correlations range from the .30s to the .50s generally, and higher where the match between ICD scale and another scale is very close (e.g., ICD Orderliness with Self-Description Inventory Unorganized-Orderly is .73). The investigation of the construct validity of the ICD is extensive while being very judicious in the comparisons that were investigated.

The Inventory for Counseling & Development is an excellent test that has undergone extensive psychometric and theoretical development and comes at a time when many universities are under fire concerning their admissions procedures. The ICD offers an objective measure of nonintellective factors empirically related to academic performance and has been developed to enhance the prediction of academic success within a university and to aid in the planning and counseling of students. Once specific studies are undertaken to examine the effect of the inclusion of the ICD results in selection decisions, admissions officers may be able to improve the selection process.

[183]
Inwald Personality Inventory.

Purpose: To aid public safety and security agencies in selecting new officers who require psychological screening.
Population: Public safety and security applicants (police, correction, fire, security).
Publication Dates: 1980–82.
Acronym: IPI.
Scores, 26: Guardedness, Externalized Behavior Measures (Actions [Alcohol, Drugs, Driving Violations, Job Difficulties, Trouble with the Law and Society, Absence Abuse], Attitudes [Substance Abuse, Antisocial Attitudes, Hyperactivity, Rigid Type, Type A]), Internalized Conflict Measures (Illness Concerns, Treatment Programs, Anxiety, Phobic Personality, Obsessive Personality, Depression, Loner, Unusual Experiences/Thoughts), Interpersonal Conflict Measures (Lack of Assertiveness, Interpersonal Difficulties, Undue Suspiciousness, Family Conflicts, Sexual Concerns, Spouse/Mate Conflicts).
Administration: Group.
Price Data, 1990: $50 per complete starter kit including test booklet, 3 computer-scorable answer sheets, manual ('82, 54 pages); $1.50 per test booklet; $2.50 per 10 scantron/standard answer sheets; $3 per 10 Sentry answer sheets; $12.50 per manual; scoring service offered by publisher at $9–$12.50 per test; (all prices may be adjusted for volume discounts).
Time: (30–45) minutes.
Author: Robin Inwald.
Publisher: Hilson Research, Inc.
Cross References: For reviews by Brian Bolton and Jon D. Swartz, see 9:530.

TEST REFERENCES

1. Shusman, E. J., Inwald, R. E., & Landa, B. (1984). Correction officer job performance as predicted by the IPI and MMPI: A validation and cross-validation study. *Criminal Justice and Behavior, 11*, 309-329.
2. Shusman, E. (1987). A redundancy analysis for the Inwald Personality Inventory and the MMPI. *Journal of Personality Assessment, 51*, 433-440.

Review of the Inwald Personality Inventory by SAMUEL JUNI, *Professor of Applied Psychology, New York University, New York, NY:*

This review is based on a critical analysis of the test booklet, manual, sample reports, and a collection of over two dozen articles, unpublished papers, presentation summaries, and assorted literature submitted by the author to document the merits of the Inwald Personality Inventory (IPI). Some of these works attempt to address inadequacies pointed out in the most recent reviews of the IPI (9:530), whereas others raise new issues which have not been noted earlier.

The IPI was designed to facilitate screening of law enforcement candidates. The 310 true-false questions are introduced to the respondent as "designed to reflect your feelings about yourself and life in general." This introduction is a misstatement; just on the first page of 29 items, less that 1/3 can be seen as being consistent with the introduction. (Consider, for example, "I have collected unemployment," "I am at least ten pounds overweight," and "I have been suspended from school.") Although the booklet states, "There are no right and wrong answers" and "Do not dwell on any one item," this orientation is apparently contradicted in the actual administration procedures; this is particularly clear in the instructions used in one validation study where candidates were warned that lying would be grounds for job dismissal.

Other than Guardedness (GD), which is intended for use as a lie scale, the other 25 scores are grouped into three sets that are labeled as "Acting Out Behavior" (which includes two subsets: *specific "external" behaviors* and *attitudes and temperament*), "Internalized Conflict," and "Interpersonal Conflict." It seems that although the author may well be familiar with the field, and that the IPI was prefaced by "over 2,500 pre-employment interviews with law enforcement candidates," the actual item selection algorithms and the overall rationale of scale and subset definition are intuitive and undefined. In fact, the factor analysis reported in the manual shows one predominant and two minor factors, with no support for the IPI scaling. Clearly, no theoretical base was used in the procedure, leaving the instrument open to possible errors of subjectivity and exclusion in its design.

The lack of reported item-selection and item-writing procedures, moreover, serves to skew the items, and minimizes the potential validity of the instrument. Because the manual does not specify which items comprise each scale, it is impossible to evaluate the content validity of the instrument. The following item flaws are intended as examples, and not as an exhaustive listing:

10. I have had periods of spending more money than I had available to me. The definition of "periods" is unclear and its intention not evident.

36. I have had no fist fights since I was twenty years old. How is an 18-year-old to answer this item, and how would that response be interpreted?

39. I was never in trouble in the service. How are responses of nonservicemen interpreted?

79. I have been arrested in my life. The qualification of "in my life" is perplexing as it reads.

95. I have held the same job for longer than two years. How is the response of a candidate who just finished school interpreted? Is it deemed equivalent to that of the habitual unemployed?

106. I have been divorced. The response of the never divorced is equivalent to that of the never married.

163. My mother has made life harder for me today. The latter word is a floating misplaced modifier, rendering the sentence ambiguous.

191. I am not stretching the truth on this questionnaire. Cf. #118: I am being completely honest on this questionnaire. Do these items contribute twice to the same scale?

232. It is all right to take certain unauthorized actions in your life, provided you are not apprehended. Unauthorized by whom? Father? Police? Teacher?

250. My mate/spouse thinks I am a good provider. If single, is the correct response "no"?

The computerized test result package features *t*-scores on each of the 26 scales, normed specifically for correction or police officer (separately for each gender). These scores should form the crux of the test results. Also included are critical items that represent single responses which reveal emotional or adjustment problems, with the notion that the evaluator's attention should be directed to those areas. Finally there is a narrative report.

Because most interviewers are not psychometricians, it can be assumed that the narrative report is the most salient, vis-a-vis the intended use of the IPI. Here, too, there is a lack of systematic procedure or algorithm evident in the origin of these narratives, other than the assurance that they were developed following several thousand interviews and questionnaire/test administrations. Also noted are inconsistencies in the narrative interpretation of low scores on scales. (For example, a low score on Scale 6 is interpreted as "Denial of a pattern of antisocial behaviors," whereas a low score on Scale 8 is interpreted as "No apparent tendency towards risk taking." The deficit in scientific test development rigor is further exacerbated by the inclusion into the narrative statements not only of references to item content but also "clinical impressions and interpretations based on experience with the test results and interview behavior of . . . candidates."

What will inevitably occur in the utilization of such a narrative report is the transmission of an implicit (and undefined) personality theory which is divined by the evaluator based on the intuitive clustering and scaling in the presentation. Thus, a narrative statement referring to a presumed antisocial construct will state that the pattern "may" include arrests, dismissal from military duty, etc. It is clear that the examples are intended to point to an overall construct which suggests that the specifics are likely to occur, whether they in fact happened or not. In reality, all that exists is a grouping of items which falls into a logical category. In keeping with the avowed purpose of offering a "behavioral orientation" instrument, would it not make more sense to have the narrative spell out whether the particular respondent has indeed had trouble with arrests or the military, rather than suggesting a personality trait which subsumes the details unwittingly? It appears evident that despite the avowed intention of the test author to limit the IPI to behavioral rather than personality constructs, the narrative and the very scale names are often quite trait oriented.

Furthermore, the intention of the IPI to "differentiate between individuals who express pathological or socially deviant attitudes and those who *act* on them" is obscure. For an instrument focusing on behaviors, why bother with the nonbehavioral attitudes? Just how do those scales affect the synthesized interpretation? It might also be added, in view of the absence of item-scale information, that the integrity of such a demarcation is not at all clearly presented. The distinction becomes even more obscure when we find such areas as drug use (or antisocial) under *attitudes and temperament* as well as under the *behavioral* heading; the temperament of drug use is an obscure construct indeed. Similarly, when we find the IPI focusing on the "behavioral tendencies" of acting out, one wonders about the distinction between that construct and acting out proper.

Several studies demonstrated the usefulness of the IPI in predicting which candidates will show attendance, lateness, and disciplinary problems. It is noted that these studies also include past experience in counseling as an index of maladjustment, a position which is also reflected in Item 41 on the IPI. This stance is inconsistent with that of counseling intervention, a field that is devoted to assist people's mastery of life's events in a productive fashion. Indeed, from the latter perspective, unwillingness to be counseled in times of crisis can well be seen as connoting significant underlying problems.

Other than the potential misuse of the IPI by consumers who will inevitably choose to ignore the author's warning not to base selection solely on the instrument, the utility of the test is quite impressive based on the growing validation literature. Although not cited consistently, it is assumed that the studies were carried out with professional integrity, so that the IPI was not allowed to influence the very employment decisions (or ratings) which were subsequently used to validate the instrument. There are, nonetheless, some exceptions to this assumption. Consider, for example, the validation study of the IPI drug scale, where items were discussed with candidates who were forced to give excuses for responding in a specific manner, and the merits of these excuses were then evaluated for their legitimacy. Such a verification procedure is clearly contaminating, rendering alleged validity findings meaningless.

The validity and reliability concerns cited in the previous reviews have been addressed to a large extent by the accumulating research on the IPI. There are, however, some issues raised by the use of officers already hired as subjects for validation studies, because their response sets in taking the IPI cannot be equated with those of candidates who are not volunteers, but instead take the test as an employment prerequisite. Another shortcoming is to be found in many of the *t*-test statistics, where significant findings are proffered which are not meaningful at the practical level, because the mean differences fall shy of half of the standard deviations.

The IPI manual presents separate norms for male versus female, police versus correction, and officers versus candidates, although those for females are often relatively few in number. Critical scores are defined as falling 2 standard deviations above the mean. Test-retest reliability (for 6 to 8 weeks) figures are reported, and these seem to range from poor to good. The latter aspect is quite significant, because the test is intended to be used as a long term predictor. The stability of scores may drop further yet if retests were done with longer intervals. Alpha coefficients range from the very poor to good, reinforcing our notion that some of the scales are unitary only on the experience and judgement of the author and lack empirical documentation. Concurrent validity is established by moderate correlations between IPI and Minnesota Multiphasic Personality Inventory (MMPI) scales. It is noted, however, that one consistent correlation (between the IPI scales and the MMPI K scale) bodes poorly for the IPI as it demonstrates significant susceptibility to social desirability.

A series of validation studies focus on developing discriminant function equations predicting retained versus terminated officers (for Whites, Blacks, and Hispanics separately), positive commendations, disciplinary events, negative reports, absences, latenesses, and times on restrictive duty. In many of these studies, the predictive validity of the IPI is juxtaposed to that of the MMPI.

Construct validity studies presented in the manual include the administration of the IPI to diagnosed phobics, correlating IPI scales with interview performance of officers, and correlating the IPI with personal history data connoting adjustment problems. The scope of these studies is rather constricted and the resulting correlations vary considerably in magnitude. In addition, reliability of these criterion measures is not established. Other studies focus on variations of these validations with different populations, adjusting time periods from the IPI administration to the criterion measures, and modifications of the latter indices.

In summary, the IPI, which is presented as a test of behaviors (in contrast to personality) to test consumers, and as a survey of feelings to candidates, is, in fact, neither. Instead, it combines facets of each and is objectively indistinguishable from the major inventories, such as the MMPI. What differentiates it from the other inventories is that the items were conceived specifically to tap areas deemed relevant to law enforcement. This advantage is mitigated, however, by a lack of appropriate psychometrics in item selection, item writing, and scale construction; content validity seems totally neglected. These attributes contribute to a test that is intrinsic to law enforcement only vis-a-vis the intentions of the author, and whose scales are composed according to the author's judgement. In addition to problems with items per se, there is no a priori evidence the scales relate to their assigned names, and no objective reason to use the scale scores as specified by the IPI.

There is no arguing with the predictive validity of the IPI, and the host of studies showing its efficacy certainly present an impressive argument for the utility of the inventory. It is feasible, however, that the predictive validity of the IPI is not all due to the content-related attribution by its authors based on the suggested scale foci, but that it is also an artifact of such non-law-enforcement constructs as response sets and social desirability.

At this stage of the development of the test, it is clear that the form of the items is already fixed and not easily modifiable. It may be suggested to go back to the original test protocol records which were used in the various studies and reexamine the item intercorrelations. Factor analysis can be established as the primary determinant of scale construction, using factor weightings as criteria for scaling. These scales can then be named, as is usually the case, by appealing to expertise in the field. The validation studies can then be reanalyzed using the new scale scores. Such a procedure could increase the psychometric value of the scales, but may necessitate the deletion of constructs which are not sufficiently supported empirically, albeit intuitively salient. The specific characteristics of various items would then be expected to have less significant effects on test validity.

Review of the Inwald Personality Inventory by NIELS G. WALLER, Assistant Professor of Psychology, University of California, Davis, Davis, CA:

When the Inwald Personality Inventory (IPI) was first published in the early 1980s, it was one of the first tests designed specifically for the assessment of law enforcement personnel (defined broadly to include police officers, correction officers, transit officers, court officers, and security officers). Since its debut, routine screening of officer recruits has become an established practice in many metropolitan areas, and the IPI has become one of the leading instruments for officer selection. The IPI was first reviewed in *The Ninth Mental Measurements Yearbook* (9:530). Because neither the test nor its manual has been revised since the publication of these reviews, many of the previously noted strengths and weaknesses of the instrument are still valid. Therefore, instead of repeating the accolades and criticisms of my predecessors, I will restrict my comments to aspects of the test not previously discussed. Interested readers are encouraged to consult the *9th MMY* for further information.

The IPI includes 26 scales grouped into four rationally based content categories: (*a*) Validity (a measure of Guardedness); (*b*) Acting Out Behaviors (e.g., Alcohol Use, Drug Use, Driving Violations, and Type A Behavior); (*c*) Internalized Conflicts (e.g., Illness Concerns, Anxiety, Obsessive Personality, Depression, and Unusual Experiences); and (*d*) Interpersonal Conflicts (e.g., Lack of Assertiveness, Family Conflicts, Sexual Concerns, and Spouse/Mate Conflicts). Items were developed using rational criteria; the manual notes that the items were drawn from over 2,500 pre-employment interviews of law enforcement candidates. Scales were formed by rationally grouping items of similar content, and it appears that no empirically based scale refinement procedures (e.g., factor analysis) were used during scale construction. Thus, at every level of the inventory, the IPI was rationally constructed.

The manual reports a variety of statistics, including means, standard deviations, internal consistencies, and test-retest reliabilities for each of the IPI scales. These statistics were generated from several impressively large relevant samples (e.g., 2,544 officer recruits). Many of these samples, furthermore, were appropriately broken down by gender and ethnicity. Unfortunately, several important statistics are not reported in the manual. For example, neither coefficients of skewness or kurtosis, nor tables of percentiles are reported for the scales. One cannot determine, therefore, whether a T-score of 70 (the recommended cutoff value) on one scale is equivalent, in terms of representing the same percentile value, as a T-score of 70 on a different scale (this problem was recently addressed in the revision of the Minnesota Multiphasic Personality Inventory [MMPI], where *uniform* T-scores are now routinely reported). Tables describing the item keying and item composition of the scales are also conspicuously absent from the manual. This latter point is particularly troublesome, and thus deserves further comment.

In contrast to other widely used inventories for officer selection (e.g., the MMPI, the California Psychological Inventory [CPI], and the Sixteen Personality Factor Questionnaire [16PF]), scoring keys for the IPI scales are not commercially available. Users of the instrument, therefore, are forced to rely on either an electronic scanner or a mail-in scoring system in order to obtain test results. In effect, this precludes researchers, other than the test developers, from empirically investigating the structural properties of the scales. For example, it is not possible to factor analyze the items of a scale to determine whether the items empirically, rather than merely rationally, hang together.

Validity data for the scales are reported under three headings in the manual: Concurrent Validity, Predictive Validity, and Construct Validity. Correlations among the IPI scales and other personality measures used in law enforcement selection (e.g., the MMPI, CPI, and 16PF) are reported as evidence for the concurrent validity of the instrument. A more appropriate title for this section would have been: MORE IS BETTER. The manual notes, for example, that: "For male correction officers, 199 total correlations were obtained between the IPI and MMPI, with 118 (or 59%) showing values above .30 . . . . [and] From a total of 203 correlations between IPI and CPI scales, 186 (or 92%) were above .30" (IPI manual, p. 19). If a plethora of significant correlations between randomly selected scales supported the concurrent validity of an instrument, the IPI would be in good shape. However, rather than support the concurrent validity of the IPI, these data argue cogently for the *lack* of convergent and discriminant validity of the IPI scales. A scale that measures everything measures nothing!

Evidence in support of the predictive validity of the instrument is, unfortunately, not much better. Table 15 of the manual, for example:

shows results of a study of 545 retained ("successes") and 51 terminated correction officers ("failures") where the prediction equation was obtained using Wilks' stepwise method . . . . Using IPI scales developed to measure "acting out" behaviors, suspiciousness and rigidity, this equation correctly predicted a total of 72% of the officers as to whether they were retained by or terminated from the department. The canonical correlation coefficient was .26 . . . MMPI scales correctly predicted 62% of the male correction officers, and the canonical correlation was .18. (IPI manual, p. 20)

After reading this passage one might conclude that the IPI is a good test for predicting "successful" versus "unsuccessful" correction officers; one might also conclude that it is a better test for this purpose than the MMPI. However, if our objective is merely to make "correct" predictions about who will be retained and who will be terminated, then the best test to use, in this example, is no test at all!

To follow this logic assume that no test is given, and that all candidates are predicted to be successes. From data provided in the IPI manual we determine that 91% of the officers who our (non)test predicted would be successes later turned out to be successes. To obtain this result, we divide the base rate of successes ($n = 545$) by the sample size ($n = 596$). Of course, there is more to prediction than merely picking the successes out of the applicant pool.

Clearly, it makes a difference to police departments in particular, and society more generally, whether a test predicts more false positives (officers

predicted to be successes who later must be terminated due to inappropriate behavior), or more false negatives (candidates denied positions who would have become successes). A comprehensive validation study will consider base rates and selection ratios when evaluating the effectiveness of a test (c.f., Cronbach & Gleser, 1965; Wiggins, 1973). Recent work on the IPI (Inwald, 1988) has begun to address these issues, so perhaps the results of this work will be included in future versions of the IPI manual.

The IPI appears to be a promising tool for the assessment of law enforcement personnel. The aforementioned limitations of the inventory, however, as well as limitations noted by previous reviewers (9:530), preclude me from recommending use of this test for anything other than research purposes. If the concerns pointed out in these reviews are adequately addressed, the IPI may become an important adjunct to existing measures for officer selection.

REVIEWER'S REFERENCES

Cronbach, L. J., & Gleser, G. C. (1965). *Psychological tests and personnel decisions* (2nd ed.). Urbana: University of Illinois Press.
Wiggins, J. S. (1973). *Personality and prediction: Principles of personality assessment.* Reading, MA: Addison-Wesley Publishing Company.
Inwald, R. E. (1988). Five year follow-up study of departmental terminations as predicted by 16 preemployment psychological indicators. *Journal of Applied Psychology,* 73 (4), 703-710.

[184]

Iowa Tests of Basic Skills, Form J.

Purpose: Constructed to "provide for comprehensive measurement of growth in the fundamental skills: Listening, word analysis, vocabulary, reading, the mechanics of writing, methods of study, and mathematics."
Publication Dates: 1955–90.
Acronym: ITBS.
Administration: Group.
Price Data, 1991: $3 per scoring key booklet; $9 per 35 pupil profile charts; $9 per 35 profile charts for averages; $9 per 35 class record folders (select Levels 5–8 or 9–14); $7.95 per 35 reports to parents (select English or Spanish); $8.40 per teacher's guide (select Level 5–6, 7–8, or 9–14); $2.10 per teacher's guide for practice tests (select Level 5–6, 7–8, 9–14); $21 per school administrator's manual; $6 per school administrator's supplement ('90, 53 pages); $1.98 per administrator's summary ('90, 30 pages); $8.10 per skills objectives booklet ('90, 129 pages); $8.10 per norms booklet (select large city, Catholic, high socioeconomic, or low socioeconomic); $21 per examination kit.
Comments: Forms G and H, parallel forms, available from publisher; Form G Listening Supplement and Writing Supplement may be used with Form J; earlier Forms 7 and 8 still available from publisher.
Authors: A. N. Hieronymus, H. D. Hoover, K. R. Oberley (everything except school administrator's supplement), N. K. Cantor (everything except school administrator's supplement), D. A. Frisbie (everything except teacher's guides for practice tests), S. B. Dunbar (everything except teacher's guides for practice tests), J. C. Lewis (everything except teacher's guides for practice

tests and school administrator's supplement), and E. F. Lindquist (teacher's guide for practice tests, Levels 9–14).
Publisher: The Riverside Publishing Co.

a) EARLY PRIMARY BATTERY.
Price Data: $7.35 per 35 practice tests including teacher's guide; $4.20 per administrator's directions (select level).

1) *Level 5.*
Population: Grades K.1–1.5.
Scores, 6: Listening, Word Analysis, Vocabulary, Language, Mathematics, Basic Composite.
Price Data: $63 per 35 MRC machine-scorable test booklets including teacher's guide and materials needed for machine scoring; $72.15 per 35 NCS test booklets including administration directions; $27 per set of scoring stencils.
Time: (125–150) minutes, including 10-minute practice test.

2) *Level 6.*
Population: Grades K.8–1.9.
Scores, 8: Listening, Word Analysis, Vocabulary, Language, Mathematics, Basic Composite, Reading, Complete Composite.
Price Data: $86.25 per 35 MRC machine-scorable test booklets including teacher's guide and materials needed for machine scoring; $100.35 per 35 NCS test booklets including administration directions; $36.75 per set of scoring stencils.
Time: (125–205) minutes, including 10-minute practice test.

b) PRIMARY BATTERY.
Scores: Basic Battery, 12 scores: Word Analysis, Vocabulary, Reading Comprehension (Pictures, Sentences, Stories, Total), Spelling, Mathematics (Concepts, Problem Solving, Computation, Total), Basic Composite; Complete Battery, 22 scores: Listening, Word Analysis, Vocabulary, Reading Comprehension (Pictures, Sentences, Stories, Total), Language (Spelling, Capitalization, Punctuation, Usage and Expression, Total), Work-Study (Visual Materials, Reference Materials, Total), Mathematics (Concepts, Problem Solving, Computation, Total), Complete Composite, Social Studies (optional), Science (optional).
Forms, 3: Basic, Complete, Complete Plus Social Studies and Science.
Price Data: $72 per 35 MRC machine-scorable basic battery tests including teacher's guide and materials needed for machine scoring (select level); $86.25 per 35 MRC machine-scorable complete battery tests including teacher's guide and materials needed for machine scoring (select level); $90.75 per 35 MRC machine-scorable complete battery plus Social Studies and Science tests including teacher's guide and materials needed for machine scoring (select level); $83.10 per 35 NCS basic battery tests including administration directions (select level); $100.35 per 35 NCS complete battery tests including administration directions (select level); $12.30 per 35 practice tests; $51.45 per set of scoring stencils (select level); $4.20 per administrator's directions (select level).
Time: (134–180) minutes for Basic Battery; (227–285) minutes for Complete Battery; (267–335) minutes for Complete Battery Plus Social Studies and Science.

1) *Level 7.*
Population: Grades 1.7–2.6.
2) *Level 8.*
Population: Grades 2.5–3.5.

c) MULTILEVEL BATTERY.
Scores: Basic Battery, 8 scores: Vocabulary, Reading Comprehension, Spelling, Mathematics (Concepts, Problem Solving, Computation, Total), Basic Composite; Complete Battery, 17 scores: Vocabulary, Reading Comprehension, Language (Spelling, Capitalization, Punctuation, Usage and Expression, Total), Work-Study (Visual Materials, Reference Materials, Total), Mathematics (Concepts, Problem Solving, Computation, Total), Complete Composite, Social Studies (optional), Science (optional).
Forms, 3: Basic, Complete, Complete Plus Social Studies and Science.
Price Data: $90.75 per 35 Level 9 machine-scorable booklets (Complete Plus Social Studies and Science) including administration directions and materials needed for machine scoring; $4.95 per complete battery multilevel test booklet containing Levels 9–14; $3.90 per basic battery multilevel test booklet containing Levels 9–14; $68.75 per 35 complete battery plus Social Studies and Science test booklets including administration directions (select level); $36 per 35 multilevel Social Studies/Science test booklets including administration directions; $51 per 100 practice tests including 3 teacher's guides; $21.30 per 35 MRC answer sheets including teacher's guide, 35 pupil report folders, and class record folder (select level); $129 per 250 NCS answer folders (select level); $18 per 100 practice test answer sheets; $16.35 per set of scoring stencils (select level); $4.05 per administrator's directions; $3.15 per Social Studies/Science directions for administration.
Time: (135–167) minutes for Basic Battery; (256–305) minutes for Complete Battery; (326–385) minutes for Complete Battery Plus Social Studies and Science.

1) *Level 9.*
Population: Grade 3.
2) *Level 10.*
Population: Grade 4.
3) *Level 11.*
Population: Grade 5.
4) *Level 12.*
Population: Grade 6.
5) *Level 13.*
Population: Grade 7.
6) *Level 14.*
Population: Grades 8–9.

Cross References: For reviews by Robert L. Linn and Victor L. Willson of Forms G and H, see 10:155 (45 references); for reviews by Peter W. Airasian and Anthony J. Nitko of Forms 7 and 8, see 9:533 (29 references); see also T3:1192 (97 references); for reviews by Larry A. Harris and Fred Pyrczak of Forms 5–6, see 8:19 (58 references); see T2:19 (87 references) and 6:13 (17 references); for reviews by Virgil E. Herrick, G. A. V. Morgan, and H. H. Remmers, and an excerpted review by Laurence Siegel of Forms 1–2, see 5:16. For reviews of the modern mathematics supplement, see 7:481 (2 reviews).

TEST REFERENCES

1. Ysseldyke, J. E., & Marston, D. (1982). A critical analysis of standardized reading tests. *School Psychology Review, 11*, 257-266.

2. Bachman, E. E., Sines, J. O., Watson, J. A., Lauer, R. M., & Clarke, W. R. (1986). The relations between Type A behavior, clinically relevant behavior, academic achievement, and IQ in children. *Journal of Personality Assessment, 50*, 186-192.

3. Pedersen, K., Elmore, P., & Bleyer, D. (1986). Parent attitudes and student career interests in junior high school. *Journal for Research in Mathematics Education, 17*, 49-59.

4. Cialdini, R. B., Eisenberg, N., Shell, R., & McCreath, H. (1987). Commitments to help by children: Effects on subsequent prosocial self-attributions. *British Journal of Social Psychology, 26*, 237-245.

5. Donovan, J. F., Sousa, D. A., & Walberg, H. J. (1987). The impact of staff development on implementation and student achievement. *The Journal of Educational Research, 80*, 348-351.

6. Estrada, P., Arsenio, W. F., Hess, R. D., & Holloway, S. D. (1987). Affective quality of the mother-child relationship: Longitudinal consequences for children's school-relevant cognitive functioning. *Developmental Psychology, 23*, 210-215.

7. LaVoie, J. C., & Hodapp, A. F. (1987). Children's subjective ratings of their performance on a standardized achievement test. *Journal of School Psychology, 25*, 73-80.

8. Nelson-LeGall, S. A. (1987). Necessary and unnecessary help-seeking in children. *Journal of Genetic Psychology, 148*, 53-62.

9. Wehr, S. H., & Kaufman, M. E. (1987). The effects of assertive training on performance in highly anxious adolescents. *Adolescence, 22*, 195-205.

10. Bleakley, M. E., Westerberg, V., & Hopkins, K. D. (1988). The effect of character sex on story interest and comprehension in children. *American Educational Research Journal, 25*, 145-155.

11. Blume, G. W., & Schoen, H. L. (1988). Mathematical problem-solving performance of eighth-grade programmers and nonprogrammers. *Journal for Research in Mathematics Education, 19*, 142-156.

12. Juel, C., & Leavell, J. A. (1988). Retention and nonretention of at-risk readers in first grade and their subsequent reading achievement. *Journal of Learning Disabilities, 21*, 571-580.

13. Soto, L. D., Grellen, M. I., & Morris, J. D. (1988). School perceptions of Puerto Rican mothers and achievement of their children. *Psychological Reports, 62*, 187-192.

14. Wilson, M., Suriyawongse, S., & Moore, A. (1988). The effects of ceiling rules on the internal consistency reliability of a mathematics achievement test. *Educational and Psychological Measurement, 48*, 213-217.

15. Allen, J. P., Weissberg, R. P., & Hawkins, J. A. (1989). The relation between values and social competence in early adolescence. *Developmental Psychology, 25*, 458-464.

16. Harris, D. J., & Kolen, M. J. (1989). Examining the stability of Angoff's data item bias statistic using the bootstrap. *Educational and Psychological Measurement, 49*, 81-87.

17. Knudson, R. E. (1989). Effects of instructional strategies on children's informational writing. *Journal of Educational Research, 83*, 91-96.

18. Melamed, L. E., & Rugle, L. (1989). Neuropsychological correlates of school achievement in young children: Longitudinal findings with a construct valid perceptual processing instrument. *Journal of Clinical and Experimental Neuropsychology, 11*, 745-762.

19. Phelps, L. (1989). Comparison of scores for intellectually gifted students on the WISC-R and the fourth edition of the Stanford-Binet. *Psychology in the Schools, 26*, 125-129.

20. Reynolds, A. J., & Bezruczko, N. (1989). Assessing the construct validity of a life skills competency test. *Educational and Psychological Measurement, 49*, 183-193.

21. Cameron, M. B., & Wilson, B. J. (1990). The effects of chronological age, gender, and delay of entry on academic achievement and retention: Implications for academic redshirting. *Psychology in the Schools, 27*, 260-263.

22. Clements, D. H., & Battista, M. T. (1990). The effects of Logo on children's conceptualizations of angle and polygons. *Journal for Research in Mathematics Education, 21*, 356-371.

23. Marks, D. (1990). Cautions in interpreting district-wide standardized mathematics achievement test results. *Journal of Educational Research, 83*, 349-354.

24. Gottesman, R. L., Cerullo, F. M., Bennett, R. E., & Rock, D. A. (1991). Predictive validity of a screening test for mild school learning difficulties. *Journal of School Psychology, 29*, 191-205.

Review of the Iowa Tests of Basic Skills, Form J by SUZANNE LANE, *Associate Professor of Education, University of Pittsburgh, Pittsburgh, PA:*

The Iowa Tests of Basic Skills (ITBS) measures the development of general cognitive skills in the areas of Listening, Word Analysis, Vocabulary, Reading Comprehension, Language, Mathematics, Work-Study, Social Studies, and Science. The ITBS are well-known, widely used standardized achievement test batteries appropriate for kindergarten through grade 9. The name of the batteries implies that the tests measure the development of "basic" skills; however, the ITBS appears to measure the development of general cognitive skills. An important criterion for selecting a standardized achievement test is the extent to which it measures valuable learning outcomes. If the acquisition of general cognitive skills is a valuable learning outcome and the ITBS is aligned with a school's curriculum, adoption of the ITBS is recommended.

Form J is one of three alternate forms (the other two being Forms G and H) and comprises three batteries: Early Primary (Levels 5 and 6), Primary (Levels 7 and 8), and Multilevel (Levels 9 through 14). The levels are numbered to correspond roughly with ages. Form J should be used in conjunction with the Manual for School Administrators (Forms G and H), the supplement to the manual (Form J), and the Teacher's Guides. The supplement to the manual provides technical information on Form J as well as documentation of the procedures used to obtain 1988 norms for Forms G, H, and J. Users of Forms G, H, and J have the option to use norms that were established in 1984-1985 or to use more recent norms that were established in 1988. The attempt to provide a comprehensive body of evidence for the reliability and validity of the ITBS and the clarity in which the evidence is reported are impressive.

Form J was developed in 1988 using the same content and difficulty specifications that were used in 1983 and 1984 in the development of Forms G and H. In the Manual for School Administrators, the authors provide a strong rationale for the inclusion of each of the tests. The skill objectives and ways to test these skills were identified based on a thorough review of the literature, analysis of state and local curriculum guides, analysis of instructional materials and methods, and consultation with teachers and school curriculum specialists. A booklet containing all of the skills with item norms for the fall, midyear, and spring is available. To ensure fairness and avoid bias, commonly used approaches were adopted including the review of the test items by a national team of professionals selected on the basis of geographic region and ethnic composition. The Listening Supplement and Writing Supplement in Form G may be used with Form J.

A difference between Form J and Forms G and H is that in the Early Primary and Primary Battery, fewer items appear on each page. This allows for picture responses to be larger than in the previous forms. A good practical addition in the Early Primary Battery is the inclusion of page locators (i.e., artwork used to identify test pages) that are at the top of the booklet pages to facilitate administration of the tests. This was added based on a study conducted at the University of Iowa indicating that a time-consuming task associated with the administration of tests to kindergarten and beginning grade 1 students involves the location of the correct page in the test booklet. Similar to Forms G and H, the Reading Comprehension test involves longer reading passages and questions that attempt to measure more complex thinking skills than those used in the earlier forms. For example, some of the reading passages consist of a number of paragraphs and are on an entire page, and the associated items require students to make inferences and generalizations. These additions to the Reading Comprehension test enhance its logical validity.

The Administrator's Summary written by the Riverside Publishing Company indicates the ITBS includes a large number of items that measure higher-order thinking skills. The Summary defines higher-order thinking skills as "those that require students to associate at least two pieces of nonconsecutive information and process that information to find the correct response" (p. 9). Although it is true the tests include a large number of items requiring multiple steps for solution as well as items requiring analysis and inference, this definition of higher-order thinking skills is a bit narrow. As an example, the Mathematics Problem Solving Tests include multistep word problems; however, mathematics reformers may argue the tests do not adequately reflect the current goals of the mathematics curriculum as outlined in the *Curriculum and Evaluation Standards for School Mathematics* (NCTM, 1989). For example, the tests are limited in terms of the degree to which the items require students to find structure in the problem situation, to formulate conjectures, to find a path for a solution that is not immediately visible, to evaluate the reasonableness of answers, and to justify answers. This is not a criticism aimed solely at the ITBS but pertains to most standardized achievement batteries.

Form J was equated to Form G in the fall of 1988 using a nationwide sample of 32 schools. The equating process was based on a national probability sample stratified in terms of public and private schools, geographic region, socioeconomic status, and school district size. Across grade levels the number of students responding to a subtest ranged from 557 to 2,959. The supplement to the Manual for School Administrators provides a clear description of the equating process. As the authors state, the differences between the 1984–1985 and 1987–1988 national norms reflect the trend toward increased achievement test scores in this nation.

Reliability coefficients and standard errors of measurement for Form J are reported in the supplement to the manual. Most of the equivalent-forms reliability coefficients for the tests range from .70–.90. Exceptions are the coefficients for the Listening test (Levels 5–8), which range from .494 to .695. Most of the internal-consistency reliability (K-R20) coefficients are above .85. A notable exception is the coefficient for the Listening test (Level 8), which is .577.

A number of reports describing individual student as well as class and school performance are available. The most useful reports for teachers and parents are those that identify an individual student's strengths and weaknesses so that instruction can be tailored to the student's needs and abilities. Three reports that would be most helpful in shaping instruction to meet individual student needs are the Student Criterion-Referenced Skills Analysis Report, the Individual Performance Profile, and the Class Diagnostic Report. They allow the teacher (and parents) to examine a student's strengths and weaknesses in a large number of skill areas as well as to make a relative comparison of the student's performance to the class and to the nation. An attractive feature of the Individual Performance Profile is that in reporting a student's performance in the skill areas the error of measurement is accounted for by the plotting of percentile bands.

The Teacher's Guides are excellent. They provide a description of the nature and purposes of the tests, preparations for testing, directions for administering and scoring, interpreting test results, use of test results in improving instruction, and the 1988 norms and conversion tables. In particular, the sections on interpreting test results and how to use test results to improve instruction provide valuable information to the teachers to ensure valid interpretation of the test scores. It should be noted that the ITBS was not designed to facilitate day-to-day instructional decision making, but was designed to facilitate more long-term, broader instructional decision making. When describing how to interpret the various scores provided, the authors should be commended for also identifying improper interpretations of some scores (e.g., grade equivalents). However, I believe teachers would profit from a more in-depth discussion on how to use the standard error of measurement when interpreting test scores and differences in test scores. Sound pedagogical advice is provided for each of the major skill areas, and for additional information on instructional methods teachers may consult the well-selected references that are provided. An example of a suggestion for developing mathematical skills follows: "Children may find the concept of measurement more meaningful if they begin by measuring objects in units that are familiar to them. For instance, ask pupils to find out how many new pencils 'long' the table is" (Teacher's Guide [Levels 5–6], p. 60).

Educators as well as the general public would benefit greatly from reading the section on the use of test results in evaluating the effectiveness of instruction on page 59 in the manual. The authors describe clearly how the use of standardized test results *in conjunction* with other information should be used in evaluating the effectiveness of instructional programs. In their description, they emphasize that interpretation of test scores must be considered in light of other available information. They further state that "the wisest use of tests involves a full recognition of their limitations" (p. 59).

SUMMARY. The ITBS are widely used standardized achievement tests that measure general cognitive skills. Form J was developed based on sound measurement practices and meets high standards of technical quality. The associated manuals for school administrators and teachers are informative and well written. The ITBS Batteries and accompanying score reports provide information useful for shaping instruction to meet students' needs.

REVIEWER'S REFERENCE

National Council of Teachers of Mathematics, Commission on Standards for School Mathematics. (1989). *Curriculum and evaluation standards for school mathematics*. Reston, VA: The Council.

Review of the Iowa Tests of Basic Skills, Form J by NAMBURY S. RAJU, *Professor of Psychology, Illinois Institute of Technology, Chicago, IL:*

Form J of the Iowa Tests of Basic Skills (ITBS) was designed to parallel Forms G and H (which were published in 1985) in psychometric characteristics and content coverage. Therefore, this review will be confined mostly to some of the specific features of Form J. Interested readers are strongly advised to read the two excellent reviews of Forms G and H by Robert L. Linn (1989) and Victor L. Willson (1989) for a more complete evaluation and discussion of the ITBS.

The ITBS, intended for basic skills assessment in kindergarten through grade 9, is one of the premier assessment batteries currently available to teachers, school administrators, and evaluation specialists in the United States. The research base underlying this well-known and well-regarded battery is voluminous and impressive. The latest version of the ITBS (Forms G, H, and J) reflects much of the current thinking in measurement and psychometrics.

Form J was published in 1990, four years after the publication of its counterparts, Forms G and H. The test and item development specifications for Form J were, however, very similar to those used with the development of Forms G and H, thus ensuring a high degree of parallelism among the three forms. Form J consists of three batteries, each with several levels of individual tests: The Early

Primary Battery (Levels 5–6) for grades K.1 to 1.9, the Primary Battery (Levels 7–8) for grades 1.7 to 3.5, and the Multilevel Battery (Levels 9–14) for grades 3.0 to 9.9. Compared to Forms G and H, the Early Primary and Primary Batteries of Form J reflect a better layout of test items (with more white space between items and fewer items per page), thus potentially contributing to more test-taking comfort for the student. The Listening and Writing supplements, originally developed for use with Forms G and H, are also available for supplemental assessment in conjunction with Form J.

CONTENT VALIDITY. Content validity is an essential and important requirement for an achievement test. One way to assess the content validity of Form J is to study the material contained in the following documents: *Detailed Skills Objectives With Item Norms* (Levels 5–14) and Teacher's Guides (Levels 5–6, Levels 7–8, and Levels 9–14). These documents offer a thorough description of skill objectives and number of items by skill level included in Form J. They are written clearly and are detailed enough to make it fairly straightforward for teachers and curriculum experts to assess the degree of congruence between item content coverage available in Form J and the instructional content emphasized in a given school, district, or state level instructional program. The information articulated in the three Teacher's Guides, as well as the availability of a wide variety of score-report services, should be of enormous help to teachers and curriculum experts in identifying the strengths and weaknesses of individual students and in delineating appropriate prescriptions for remedial action and instructional change. Based on the content of the above-mentioned documents, this reviewer concludes that the content validity of Form J is excellent.

No direct evidence of other types of validity (criterion-related and construct) is presented in the ITBS Manual for School Administrators: Supplement for Form J but, in light of the reported high correlations between Form J and Form G subtests (manual, p. 14) and previously documented evidence of such types of validity for Form G, it can be inferred that Form J subtests are also valid for such purposes.

RELIABILITY. Internal consistency estimates of reliability (Kuder-Richardson Formula 20) for Form J are presented in the manual (pp. 11–13) by level and subtest. Also presented in this manual are the means, standard deviations, and standard errors of measurement, separately for raw score, grade equivalent, and standard score metrics. The reported KR-20 estimates of reliability are quite good, with most in the .80s and .90s.

Equivalent-form estimates of reliability are also provided in the manual (p. 14). Both Forms G and

J were administered, using a counter-balanced design, to the same groups of students to gather the alternate-form or parallel-form estimates of reliability. The correlations between comparable Form J and Form G subtests were adjusted for differences in variability between the 1988 samples and the fall and spring 1985 national standardization samples. A great majority of the reported equivalent-form estimates of reliability are quite good; however, in general, they appear to be somewhat lower than the KR-20 estimates as well as the 1985 (Forms G and H) equivalent-form estimates. The equivalent-form estimates for the Listening tests in the Primary Batteries are generally low.

STANDARDIZATION. There was an important difference between the 1985 standardization of (or norms development for) Forms G and H and the 1988 standardization of Form J (and also of the restandardization of Forms G and H). In 1985, Forms G and H were administered to students from a nationally representative sample of schools and districts. Appropriate sampling weights were used in generating percentile data to ensure that the standardization sample was adequately representative with respect to geographic region, public/nonpublic schools, and the socioeconomic status. In 1988, the process of standardization was different in that it consisted of only ITBS customers; it did not require any new testing. The 1985–86 and 1986–87 ITBS growth patterns were carefully assessed and scale-score increments were attached to the 1985 norms distributions to generate 1988 norms for Forms G and H as well as for Form J. The differences in achievement levels from 1985 to 1988 were 1 to 3 Grade Equivalent (GE) months, with the 1988 sample doing better than the 1985 sample. According to the manual (pp. 4–6), appropriate weighting procedures were incorporated into the growth analysis to make sure that the final estimates of growth were adequately reflective of the achievement growth patterns in the target population.

This new (Iowa) procedure for developing national percentiles appears (to this reviewer, at least) to reflect two relatively recent developments in the measurement community: the high cost of national standardizations and the call for annual or biannual norms for achievement test batteries based, in part, on Cannell's (1988) controversial commentary on how all 50 states are testing above the national average. The Iowa procedure seems to offer a viable alternative to a full-blown annual or biannual standardization, which is financially prohibitive for all commercial test publishers if reasonable prices are to be maintained. Even though the new procedure appears to be promising, this reviewer feels that this and other financially feasible alternatives must be carefully scrutinized for their statistical validity prior to their acceptance as sound, viable alternatives to

national standardizations. The sampling bias associated with using customer-based data and the attendant standard errors must be critically examined in future investigations of the proposed alternatives to representative national standardizations.

TEST FAIRNESS AND DIFFERENTIAL ITEM FUNCTIONING. The Form J content was examined carefully for its appropriateness to "members of demographic groups defined by sex, race, ethnicity, or socioeconomic status" (manual, p. 30). An external panel of judges, known for their expertise in fair test development, also reviewed the Form J test items. There was no mention in the manual, however, of any DIF (differential item functioning) analysis for Form J items, as there was for Forms G and H.

SCORE REPORTS. The score report services for the ITBS are many and varied, ranging from typical Class Reports to specialized Individual Item Analysis and Profile Narratives. They are designed to serve the diverse needs of students, parents, teachers, and school administrators. Taken as a whole, these reports are well designed, easy to read, and offer valuable, instructionally relevant norm-referenced and criterion-referenced interpretations of achievement data.

Overall, Form J is an excellent addition to the ITBS family, reflecting up-to-date school curricula and national student achievement levels. The well-known ITBS multi-level format, well-designed score reports, and well-documented skill objective specifications should make Form J very attractive to teachers and school curriculum specialists and administrators.

REVIEWER'S REFERENCES

Cannell, J. J. (1988). Nationally normed elementary achievement testing in America's public schools: How all 50 states are above the national average. *Educational Measurement: Issues and Practice*, 7 (2), 5-9.

Linn, R. L. (1989). [Review of the Iowa Tests of Basic Skills, Forms G and H.] In J. C. Conoley & J. J. Kramer (Eds.), *The tenth mental measurements yearbook* (pp. 393-395). Lincoln, NE: Buros Institute of Mental Measurements.

Willson, V. L. (1989). [Review of the Iowa Tests of Basic Skills, Forms G and H.] In J. C. Conoley & J. J. Kramer (Eds.), *The tenth mental measurements yearbook* (pp. 395-398). Lincoln, NE: Buros Institute of Mental Measurements.

[185]

IPI Job-Tests Program.

Purpose: "Screening, selection, and promotion of job applicants and employees."
Population: Job applicants and employees in industry.
Publication Dates: 1948–87.
Administration: Group.
Price Data, 1990: $155 per Test Examination Kit and $399 per Job-Field Examination Kit which include all test forms, hiring summary worksheets, aptitude profile sheets, and scoring keys for all job fields; $16 per instruction kit including 1 copy of each recommended test in the job field battery, instructions for administration, scoring, and interpreting tests, and scoring keys; $10 per test package for each job field.

Foreign Language Edition: French, Spanish, Dutch, German, Japanese, and Brazilian Portuguese editions available.

Comments: Program is composed of 18 tests "used in different combinations to form specific batteries for each of the job-test fields."

Author: Industrial Psychology International, Ltd.

Publisher: Industrial Psychology International, Ltd.

a) OFFICE TERMS.

Price Data: $21 per 20 test booklets; $6 per manual ('81, 5 pages); $9 per specimen set including 3 test booklets, administration directions, scoring key, and interpretation and technical manual.

Time: 6(11) minutes.

b) NUMBERS.

Price Data: $21 per 20 test booklets; $6 per manual ('81, 7 pages); $9 per specimen set (including manual).

Time: 6(11) minutes.

c) PERCEPTION.

Price Data: Same as *a* above.

Time: Same as *a* above.

d) JUDGMENT.

Price Data: Same as *a* above.

Time: Same as *a* above.

e) FLUENCY.

Price Data: $21 per 20 test booklets; $6 per manual ('81, 5 pages); $9 per specimen set.

Time: Same as *a* above.

f) PARTS.

Price Data: $21 per 20 test booklets; $6 per manual ('81, 6 pages); $9 per specimen set.

Time: Same as *a* above.

g) MEMORY.

Price Data: $35 per 20 test booklets; $6 per manual ('81, 5 pages); $14 per specimen set.

Time: Same as *a* above.

h) BLOCKS.

Price Data: $21 per 20 test booklets; $6 per manual (for use with Blocks, Dexterity, Dimension, Precision, Tools, and Motor, '87, 7 pages); $9 per specimen set.

Time: Same as *a* above.

i) DEXTERITY.

Price Data: Same as *h* above.

Time: Same as *a* above.

j) DIMENSION.

Price Data: Same as *h* above.

Time: Same as *a* above.

k) PRECISION.

Price Data: Same as *h* above.

Time: Same as *a* above.

l) TOOLS.

Price Data: Same as *h* above.

Time: Same as *a* above.

m) MOTOR.

Price Data: Same as *h* above.

Time: Same as *a* above.

n) SALES TERMS.

Price Data: $21 per 20 test booklets; $6 per manual; $9 per specimen set.

Time: Administration time not reported.

o) FACTORY TERMS.

Price Data: Same as *n* above.

Time: Same as *n* above.

p) CONTACT PERSONALITY FACTOR.

Acronym: CPF.

Price Data: $21 per 20 test booklets; $9 per specimen set.

Time: Same as *n* above.

Authors: R. B. Cattell, J. E. King, and A. K. Schuettler.

q) NEUROTIC PERSONALITY FACTOR.

Acronym: NPF.

Price Data: Same as *p* above.

Time: Same as *n* above.

Authors: Same as *p* above.

r) 16 PERSONALITY FACTOR TEST: INDUSTRIAL EDITION A.

Acronym: 16PF.

Price Data: $35 per 20 test booklets; $14 per specimen set.

Time: Same as *n* above.

Author: R. B. Cattell.

Review of the IPI Job-Tests Program by LAURA L. B. BARNES, Assistant Professor Applied Behavioral Studies, Oklahoma State University, Stillwater, OK:

The IPI Job-Tests Program comprises a comprehensive set of tools for personnel selection, placement, and promotion decisions. Included are aptitude batteries for clerical fields, entry level computer programmers, and factory and mechanical workers. Tests may also be used with sales and technical fields, and professional fields such as dental office assistant, dental technician, and optometric assistant. The Employee Attitude Series includes three personality measures: Contact Personality Factor, Neurotic Personality Factor, and the 16 Personality Factor.

The Job-Tests Program has undergone a series of revisions in content, procedures, and packaging since it was first developed in 1949. The tests themselves were revised in 1956 and again in 1978. Procedures related to developing and interpreting test profiles have changed and, according to a spokesperson for the current publisher (M. Stivers, personal communication, June 5, 1991), procedures were being revised again at the time this review was prepared. Recommended batteries for some jobs have also been changed from earlier versions. A discussion of issues relevant to the use of tests in personnel decisions and guidelines for conducting local validation studies and job analysis are no longer included in the current package, although reportedly these materials are being revised and should be available at a later date. Given that modifications are still being made, readers are advised that this review is based on the most current information and materials available.

Tests and supplementary materials are professional in appearance and conveniently packaged. All tests come with an easy-to-use answer key and, in most cases, the raw test score is determined by counting the number of correct responses.

The original versions of the Job-Tests Program utilized Hiring Summary Worksheets that indicated recommended test batteries and interpreted scores on a stanine system. Under the old system an applicant's stanine rank was converted to a "Qualification Level" ranging from underqualified to overqualified. Ranks were assigned to the qualification levels and then averaged across the tests to get an overall qualification level. However, at the time this review was begun, this system was being phased out and replaced with Aptitude Profile Sheets that use percentile norms. The Aptitude Profile system is less cumbersome and does not involve qualification levels or average ranks. Applicants' raw scores are easily converted to percentile ranks by referring to norms tables attached to each profile sheet. It is said that the "preferred applicant" will score highest on the "most important" tests (indicated and listed in order of importance on the profile sheets) and should score between the 25th and 75th percentiles or higher on all recommended tests. This system provides the interviewer with an immediate visual profile of the applicant's test performance and a means of making comparisons among applicants. Aptitude Profile Sheets are currently (at the time of the review) available for only 14 of the 30 job test fields. In the meantime, Hiring Summary Worksheets are available for the other 16 fields, as well as for several fields for which the Aptitude Profile Sheets were also developed. However, according to the most recent information from the publisher, a new method is being developed to supplement or replace both previous systems.

Normative data are presented in the Examiner's Manual for the tests. Norming samples ranged in size from 219 to 1,003 and were obtained from "various employee groups from a number of corporations utilizing both white-collar and blue-collar job classifications." Norming for the clerical tests was completed in 1981 and for the factory/mechanical tests, the norming date is given as 1986. Both percentile and stanine norms are reported. For the clerical tests, percentile norms are reported separately for different clerical and factory/technical positions and there are separate norms for minority and nonminority employees. The factory/mechanical tests report norms only for a general category of factory/mechanical employees and separate data are not available by minority status. The authors encourage test users to develop local norms whenever possible; however, when this is not possible, they advise test users to choose the norm groups most resembling their particular employee group and organization.

Most tests in the clerical battery report both internal consistency and 4-month test-retest reliabilities. Stability coefficients for the seven-test clerical battery range from .70 to .84 with a median of .74 indicating adequate temporal stability for the tests. However, the Numbers test was revised and length-ened by 20% between the two administrations and reliability data for the Memory test were reported only for an earlier version of the test. The coefficients for internal consistency range from .75 to .90 with a median of .84. The authors correctly note that due to the considerable speededness of the tests (6-minute time limits in most cases), the internal consistency coefficients are inflated estimates of reliability. Stability coefficients are available for only Dexterity ($r = .79$) and Motor ($r = .75$) in the factory/mechanical battery with intervals of a few hours and 3 weeks, respectively. The other four tests report internal consistency coefficients ranging from .76 to .85 with a median of .84 (again these tests are speeded, resulting in overestimates of reliability). Two of the tests appear to be carryovers from an earlier version of the package. Although Sales Terms and Factory Terms are recommended for several job fields when utilizing Hiring Summary Worksheets, there are no reliability or validity data available, nor, except for their intercorrelations with other tests, are current psychometric data of any kind presented for these two tests.

In compliance with the Uniform Guidelines and perhaps in an attempt to address earlier reviewers' criticisms regarding absence of adequate validity data, the authors present criterion-related evidence for validity through simple correlations between the individual test scores and concurrently obtained supervisors' ratings of various performance criteria. The criteria were developed by research staff "based on clients' job descriptions or by job analyses." Validity coefficients are reported separately for a variety of geographic regions, occupations, and organizations (e.g., clerical employees at a west coast trucking organization). These data are reported in the Test Examiner's Manuals and in a series of validation studies available upon request from the publisher. Most reported validity coefficients show correlation in the expected direction with their respective criteria and most are greater than .20, the average reported by Ghiselli (1966) for employment tests, and many are greater than .50. However, it appears that only significant ($p < .10$) correlations were reported, because for some groups only one correlation is given and it seems reasonable that a group would have more than one job criterion. Intercorrelations between the tests are also presented and indicate at least a moderate (.30 to .50) degree of overlap, although some are higher (e.g., .71 for Sales Terms with Office Terms). The authors advise against using redundant tests for the same individuals; however, the recommended Aptitude Profile Sheet battery for several of the positions includes Memory and Judgment which correlate .63.

The validity information presented seems consistent with generally accepted practice for personnel testing; that is, the significant zero order correlations provide evidence that the tests correlate with some "relevant" aspects of job performance. However, several important kinds of information are lacking. For one, there is insufficient detail regarding how the job performance criteria were developed as evidence of their relevance. How frequently was job analysis used in developing these criteria, and how extensive were the job analyses? Second, the manual fails to provide any theoretical or empirical justification for the recommended combinations of tests for various jobs, nor does it explain why certain tests in a recommended battery are to be considered more important than others in interpreting applicant profiles. Third, although the tests have no established cut scores per se, the 25th percentile is the recommended cutoff for tests when using Aptitude Profile Sheets. Again, no rationale is given for this recommendation.

The failure to consider validity as a characteristic, not of the test itself, but rather as a function of the use of the test—the interpretation of scores and, more importantly, the decisions based upon those scores, is reflected in statements such as: "Validity is assessed by obtaining correlation coefficients between test scores and specified criteria of job performance" (Fluency Test Examiner's Manual) and "a valid test will correlate statistically with actual job performance . . . . Where the coefficients are significant, one can conclude that the tests are valid and predictive of job performance" (Industrial Psychology Incorporated, undated). Although technically correct, these statements suggest a simplistic view of validity. If tests with arbitrarily defined cutoffs correlate individually with some arbitrarily selected criteria, and are then arbitrarily combined to form a "recommended battery," there is no basis for judging the validity of any decisions based on those test batteries. This is not to say the cutoffs, criteria, or recommended batteries necessarily are arbitrary, but rather that the authors have failed to provide sufficient evidence that they are not.

A step in the right direction would be to describe clearly the steps involved in selecting the criteria reported in the validation studies. In all fairness to the authors, the previous hiring manual contained an excellent section on conducting a job analysis. If they indeed followed their own advice, the criteria probably were justified. Second, to evaluate the concurrent validity of the batteries and the relative importance of individual tests in relation to job success, it would be useful to conduct cross-validation studies using multiple regression analysis. An expectancy table approach could be used to establish guidelines for interpreting profiles and establishing cutoffs. I would also suggest the inclusion of a discussion on the role of base rates, selection ratios, and validity in helping clients decide the extent to which the tests are likely to be useful in improving hiring decisions.

The IPI Job-Tests Program has undergone several revisions and apparently is still being revised. The most well-developed aspects of the program are the Aptitude Series for Clerical fields and Computer Programmers. The availability of separate norms for minority employees and the separate norms and validity coefficients for various positions addresses concerns expressed by previous reviewers. Although tests in the factory/mechanical aptitude series have also undergone revision and renorming, the information provided for these tests is less complete. The section of the old Hiring Manual pertaining to testing issues and personnel practices was extremely well written and it is hoped it will again be included when revisions are complete.

This version of the IPI appears to be an improvement over the versions reviewed previously; however, there are still notable shortcomings. Validity evidence for recommended batteries is weak to nonexistent and there is a total lack of technical information for two of the tests. Reliability data on one clerical test are available only for an earlier version. During the phasing in of the Aptitude Profile Sheets, the concurrent use of the old Hiring Summary Worksheets with different scoring systems and the reported development of yet another scoring system may be confusing. It is this reviewer's opinion that although the IPI Job-Tests Program has its strong points, prospective users should approach this series with caution until revisions are more complete.

REVIEWER'S REFERENCES

Ghiselli, E. (1966). *The validity of occupational aptitude tests.* New York: Wiley.

Industrial Psychology Incorporated. (undated). *A statistical summary of recent validation studies for dental technicians.* New York: Author.

Review of the IPI Job-Tests Program by MARY A. LEWIS, Director, Organizational and Employment Technology, PPG Industries, Inc., Pittsburgh, PA:

The IPI Job-Tests Program (IPI) is packaged in a hiring manual that is intended to contain everything necessary, from soup to nuts, for selecting people for jobs in clerical, mechanical, sales, technical, supervision, and professional positions. The manual is divided into six sections.

Section 1 describes the six major job areas and 24 job fields and includes an index of job titles for each field. Although some new job titles have been added, and some job titles have been changed, the fifties origin of this book is clear when you see job titles such as "Girl Friday" listed with a job test area of secretary.

Section 2 contains general information about tests and personnel practices and is designed as an introductory text on testing, including sections on test utility, government guidelines, conducting your own validation study, interpreting test norms, how to do a job analysis, how to recruit, and how to conduct interviews. This section also lists in the table of contents a summary of validation studies on IPI tests; however, this information is not included in the section, although a form is provided to send off for seven reports. A major disappointment in this section is that no comprehensive research on the IPI tests is included. In fact, the annotated bibliography in this section does not include a single reference to any research on the IPI tests.

Section 3 describes the IPI clerical test battery, and Section 4 describes the batteries for the other five areas. These two sections include copies of the tests and administrator's manuals and also make unsupported recommendations about which tests to use for each of the 24 job fields. Scattered through these two sections is limited information on the design, reliability, and validity of the tests for their prescribed purposes.

The tests from the IPI Job-Tests program have been around for 42 years. They were reviewed as the Factored Aptitude Series in 1953 by D. Welty Lefever (see 4:712) who concluded that the manual provided then did not adequately document the validity, that the authors appeared to present only a few exceptionally favorable examples of aptitude test validation, that the norms sample was arbitrary, and that claims of validity should be documented by thorough research.

In 1959, the tests were again reviewed, under the name Aptitude-Intelligence Tests, by Harold P. Bechtoldt (see 5:602), who also said that the data to support the validity claims were "entirely inadequate" and that the manual did not provide information about test intercorrelations to evaluate the validity coefficents that were reported. Bechtoldt concluded the tests may be appropriate for research but not for selection.

In 1965 the tests, now called the Job-Tests Program, were reviewed by two people, William H. Helme and Stanley I. Rubin (see 6:774). Both reviewers concluded that the evidence for validity was inadequate or inappropriate and that they could not recommend the use of the tests for selection purposes. Helme said:

With all the participating companies [using the tests], and with use of other research resources, it is hard to see why a really comprehensive validation program has not already been carried out in the more than 15 years since these tests were released. (p. 1036)

It has now been 42 years since the tests became available, and the above criticism is as true in 1989 as it was in 1953, 1959, and 1965. Rather than repeat the same criticisms that were published in the earlier reviews (I would not change a word of the Helme review), I will add to and build on their criticism.

The technical documentation for the reliability and validity of the cognitive ability tests is inadequate. Samples are only vaguely described; the sample sizes for test intercorrelation matrices vary from column to column with no indication about the source of the sample size variation. They appear to be a collection of smaller studies, but that is not specified.

The validity information reported is even more problematic. For example, for the Office Terms test, validities are reported for seven different samples that ranged in size from 24 to 77 people. It appears that each sample was given the test and a performance measure of unspecified length. What is reported for the sample are those univariate correlations of the test with any item from the criteria that was significant at the .1 level or higher.

An analysis of data presented in the manual suggests the IPI is reporting only the significant univariate correlations and that an unknown number of these correlations were calculated. We do not know if there were 6 or 60 job performance measures for any of the samples reported, and cannot determine the full extent of the "multiple T fallacy." This selective reporting clearly prohibits drawing conclusions from the validity evidence provided. In summary, the technical information provided is insufficient to draw conclusions about the validity of the tests or about the appropriateness of the recommended test batteries.

Section 5 of the manual contains three personality tests with a warning that personality tests have been challenged as not being job related and as potentially discriminatory. In the next paragraph, the manual goes on to say that thousands have been administered by IPI clients who "maintain" that they are useful. Given that this manual is intended for unsophisticated users, the inclusion of these tests and their unsupported interpretation guides raises serious concerns that go beyond the question of validity to include the possibility that the tests will be inappropriately applied and interpreted.

Section 6 is a merit rating program with copyright dates of 1956, although the instructions have a copyright date of 1983. Much has changed in the world of work since 1956, such as the introduction of the computer, and legal precedents about questions relating to marriage, assumptions about the gender of applicants, etc. These forms are a product of their time and include questions that are so clearly out of date that they would be embarrassing to ask, and of little use. For example, the clerical biographical questionnaire includes a multiple-choice question about desired salary range that starts with a salary of $3,000 per year and goes to a high of $6,000.

In summary, these tests have been around for over 42 years, and in all four previous reviews of them, as well as in this review, their documentation has been judged inadequate, and the validation techniques have been suspect. I do not recommend using these tests or this hiring manual.

If you are interested in using tests such as this for selection, I recommend you consider tests with sound technical documentation and clear evidence of validity and reliability. Tests such as the Employee Aptitude Survey (T3:799) and Flanagan Industrial Tests (T3:900) have been in use for a long time and are well documented. Newer tests such as the Basic Skills Tests for Industry by Psychological Services, Inc., the Clerical Assessment Battery by The Psychological Corporation, the Supervisory Profile Record (402) by Richardson, Bellows and Henry, and the Automated Office Battery (24) by Saville & Holdsworth, Ltd. are well designed and documented.

REVIEWER'S REFERENCES

Lefever, D. W. (1953). [Review of the Factored Aptitude Series.] In O. K. Buros (Ed.), *The fourth mental measurements yearbook* (pp. 681-683). Highland Park, NJ: The Gryphon Press.

Bechtoldt, H. P. (1959). [Review of the Aptitude-Intelligence Tests.] In O. K. Buros (Ed.), *The fifth mental measurements yearbook* (pp. 667-669). Highland Park, NJ: The Gryphon Press.

Helme, W. H. (1965). [Review of the Job-Tests Program.] In O. K. Buros (Ed.), *The sixth mental measurements yearbook* (p. 1036). Highland Park, NJ: The Gryphon Press.

Rubin, S. I. (1965). [Review of the Job-Tests Program.] In O. K. Buros (Ed.), *The sixth mental measurements yearbook* (pp. 1036-1039). Highland Park, NJ: The Gryphon Press.

[186]

Job Attitude Scale.

Purpose: Designed to assess intrinsic and extrinsic job orientations.
Population: Adults.
Publication Dates: 1971–88.
Acronym: JAS.
Scores, 17: Praise and Recognition, Growth in Skill, Creative Work, Responsibility, Advancement, Achievement, Salary, Security, Personnel Policies, Competent Supervision, Relations-Peers, Relations-Subordinates, Relations-Supervisor, Working Conditions, Status, Family Needs-Salary, Total Intrinsic.
Administration: Group.
Forms, 2: Full, Abbreviated.
Price Data: Available from publisher.
Time: Administration time not reported.
Author: Shoukry D. Saleh.
Publisher: Shoukry D. Saleh [Canada].
Cross References: See 8:1049 (9 references).

Review of the Job Attitude Scale by GREGORY J. BOYLE, Senior Lecturer in Psychology, University of Queensland, St. Lucia, Queensland, Australia:

The Job Attitude Scale (JAS), originally developed in 1962 and first published in 1971, is a 120-item forced-choice questionnaire (a total 16 statements paired with each other two at a time) wherein the adult respondent is required to indicate "which of the two factors will be more satisfying to him/her as s/he performs his/her job." Six statements pertain to *intrinsic* motivational factors, and 10 statements

are purported to index *extrinsic* factors. In addition, there is an abbreviated form of the JAS comprising only the 60 items from pairing the intrinsic and extrinsic statements. Both the full and short forms provide a general intrinsic score. The full form also provides a separate score for each of the 16 factors/statements. Although there are no specific instructions provided in the JAS manual, in practice, administration and scoring of responses is straightforward, and a separate answer sheet is provided in addition to the stimulus materials.

The assumption underlying construction of the instrument is that "intrinsic/extrinsic job orientation, as measured by the JAS, is a meaningful and stable motivational work related variable" and that "we should expect differences between the intrinsically oriented individuals (IO) and the extrinsically oriented individual (EO) in task perception." However, this assumption may be somewhat unjustified. It is conceivable that individuals may experience different IO/EO levels in regard to different jobs. That is, the IO/EO variable may be more a function of a particular job or milieu rather than of the individual alone.

Reliability data were summarized in the JAS manual in a single brief paragraph. In terms of item homogeneity, a split-half coefficient of .94 was reported for the general intrinsic scale based solely on a now rather dated 1964 study. However, as more recent discussion has indicated (e.g., Boyle, 1991), high levels of item homogeneity may suggest significant item redundancy and associated narrow measurement of the relevant construct. A high level of item homogeneity is not necessarily indicative of scale reliability. In terms of actual reliability evidence, a test-retest (stability) coefficient of .88 obtained across a 2-week interval was reported for a small sample of 25 employees from a large international manufacturing company. Unfortunately, no information was provided as to the test-retest reliability (both dependability and stability for immediate and longer term retest respectively) of the JAS for different occupational groups. It is difficult to assess the general reliability of the JAS on the basis of this single coefficient, obtained from such a small and specific sample.

In regard to validity evidence, the JAS manual reported correlations between the general intrinsic score and a number of personality variables as measured by the California Psychological Inventory, the Eysenck Personality Inventory, and with the Ghiselli Self-Description Inventory. In general, these correlations were mostly rather small and trivial. Of the total 32 correlations reported, only 13 were statistically significant at the 5% level or better (two-tailed test). The author concluded that "In sum, the portrait of the IO person revealed by the associations with other self-report instruments is that of a) one who is more independent, confident, self-assuared [*sic*] and takes risks; b) one who shows more initiative, persistant [*sic*] and achievement oriented; c) one who is more flexible, permissive, mature and accepting of others' differences; d) one who possesses higher intellectual and supervisory abilities and value work and effort for its own sake; e) one who is generally approach oriented." Nevertheless, given the unreliability usually associated with correlation coefficients (cf. Detterman, 1979), this composite picture of the IO individual may be less robust than the test author would like us to believe.

In an attempt to provide psychometric evidence regarding the structure of the JAS, an exploratory factor analysis of the responses of 413 male students was reported in the test manual. Unfortunately, the factor analytic methodology employed was rather unsophisticated. Use of principal components rather than an iterative principal factoring or maximum likelihood procedure precluded the possibility of obtaining accurate communality estimates, and ignored the fact that only part of the variance was attributable to common factors. No details were provided as to the criteria used for determining the appropriate number of factors, nor was any information regarding the rotational strategy supplied. Perusal of the factor pattern solution reported in the JAS manual (p. 12) indicates its inadequacy because the approximation to simple structure was poor (only 32.5% of the factor loadings were $\leq \pm .10$). Because the factor analysis of the JAS was defective (cf. Cattell, 1978; Gorsuch, 1983), the question of the actual factor structure of the JAS remains largely unresolved.

One irritating feature of the JAS manual relates to the numerous typographical spelling errors scattered throughout the document. Also, although there are several tables of means and standard deviations for the 16 job attitude statements and total intrinsic scores across different subgroups, there are no corresponding statistical tests to indicate which differences in mean scores are significant. Other descriptive information such as the size of groups (p. 5) is also missing. Together with the large number of obviously dated references (mostly 1960s publications) it would seem time for a major revision and upgrading of the JAS manual.

In summary, the JAS is a measure of intrinsic versus extrinsic job orientation which is easily administered and scored. However, evidence as to its reliability and validity remains uncertain, given the lack of adequate test-retest (both immediate/dependability and longer-term/stability retest) information, and in view of the inadequacy of the reported factor analysis. On the positive side, the several tables of normative data for five different age groups, and for eight different occupational categories, as well as for males and females separately, are based on respectably large sample sizes. However, even assuming that the IO/EO distinction is an appropriate conceptualization, and that the JAS is a reliable and valid measure of this variable, such information may be of little interest to employers in their selection of suitable personnel. It is likely that many employers will be more concerned with demonstrated achievements rather than whether the employee is intrinsically or extrinsically motivated to perform on the job. Even so, the JAS does enable measurement of some interesting aspects of job orientation not assessed by other instruments.

REVIEWER'S REFERENCES

Cattell, R. B. (1978). *The scientific use of factor analysis in behavioral and life sciences.* New York: Plenum Press.
Detterman, D. K. (1979). Detterman's laws of individual differences research. In R. J. Sternberg & D. K. Detterman (Eds.), *Human intelligence: Perspectives on its theory and measurement.* Norwood, NJ: Ablex Publishing Corp.
Gorsuch, R. L. (1983). *Factor analysis* (2nd ed.). Hillsdale, NJ: Lawrence Erlbaum Associates.
Boyle, G. J. (1991). Does item homogeneity indicate internal consistency or item redundancy in psychometric scales? *Personality and Individual Differences, 12,* 291-294.

[187]

A Job Choice Decision-Making Exercise.

Purpose: Serves as a behavioral decision theory measurement approach to need for affiliation, need for power, and need for achievement.
Population: High school and college and adults.
Publication Dates: 1981–86.
Acronym: JCE.
Scores, 3: Affiliation, Power, Achievement.
Administration: Group.
Price Data, 1988: $4 per exercise booklet; $150 per scoring software program including scoring manual ('85, 28 pages); $35 per *Managerial and Technical Motivation* book ('86, 178 pages, available from Praeger Publishers, in lieu of manual).
Time: [15–20] minutes.
Comments: IBM or compatible computer required for scoring program.
Authors: Michael J. Stahl and Anil Gulati (scoring software and scoring manual).
Publisher: Assessment Enterprises.

Review of A Job Choice Decision-Making Exercise by NICHOLAS A. VACC, Professor and Chairperson, and J. SCOTT HINKLE, Assistant Professor, Department of Counselor Education, University of North Carolina, Greensboro, NC:

The Job Choice Decision-Making Exercise (JCE) measures need for achievement (n Ach), power (n Pow), and affiliation (n Aff) by requiring the subject to make 30 decisions about hypothetical jobs described in n Ach, n Pow, and n Aff criteria. Need for power and need for achievement have been found to be positively related to leadership/managerial performance and individual performance, respectively. Need for affiliation, which is associated with the establishment of deeper friendships, may also lead to poor job performance if it is replacing work-related needs such as n Ach and n Pow.

The JCE is an objectively scored paper-and-pencil test based on McClelland's theory that needs for achievement, power, and affiliation are dominant factors in human motivation and are acquired at an early age (McClelland, 1961, 1962, 1975; McClelland & Winter, 1969; McClelland & Burnham, 1976). Scores are based on the decision-making behavior of subjects rather than the subjects' self-reports of their motivation. The objective scoring procedures result in separate scorers procuring the same profiles from the same data. Because it is self-administered, the JCE has no confounding problems with inconsistent administrations.

The JCE is scored quickly—in approximately 15 to 20 minutes. An alternate administration using the JCE-B can be implemented with individuals with lower reading levels (i.e., between 6th and 7th grades). The instrument also has a computer-assisted scoring disk for IBM or compatible microcomputers. Although this may enhance the scoring process once the program is running, the computer-scoring procedure is difficult to learn and operate. For instance, client identification codes are confusing, and mistakes in entry are difficult to replace. A calculator that performs regression analyses is required for the hand-scoring procedure.

Acceptable test-retest reliability on four different samples has been reported for n Ach (.81), n Pow (.82), and n Aff (.84). Overall reliability averages have been found in the .70 range, which is acceptable. Supporting data indicate adequate validity information. All samples appeared to reflect high-ranking individuals such as junior and senior management majors, presidents of fraternities and sororities, student senators, and 26 "nonleader" college juniors. The samples are reported to be representative of a "random" population, but they appear to be predominantly male. The JCE does not appear to have any significant age or minority biases.

The JCE is somewhat confusing to take, and may only be appropriate for people who can think abstractly. For example, subjects must make a decision on the attractiveness of a job on one dimension, and then make a second decision on the same job on another dimension. Each job is presented more than once, making it seem rather circular and boring.

There is a lack of reported research for applying the JCE in actual situations, and the author makes inferences that are not supported by data. For example, although the author suggests that n Ach is lower among executives, possibly because this need has already been met, there is no evidence that this is true. The author also suggests that high n Ach would be a motivational basis for the selection of engineers and scientists, but this does not take into account other selection criteria such as intelligence, cultural background, and personal values. Further, according to the author, n Ach scores can be used to select athletes. However, the research supporting this statement was not on athletes but on football players, 16% of whom could not complete the JCE due to low reading ability. Also, ministers and nurses are categorized into "helping professionals," and the author suggests that moderate to high n Pow and n Aff would be helpful in making selection decisions among this group. In making such a statement, other helping professionals (i.e., social workers, counselors, psychologists), for which no empirical evidence was reported, could be inappropriately selected or not selected. The research does not include them in the sample.

For its intended purposes of assessing and selecting managers and executives, the JCE appears to be somewhat useful, but limited.

REVIEWER'S REFERENCES

McClelland, D. C. (1961). *The achieving society.* New York: Van Nostrand.

McClelland, D. C. (1962). Business drives and national achievement. *Harvard Business Review, 40* (4), 99-112.

McClelland, D. C., & Winter, D. (1969). *Motivating economic achievement.* New York: The Free Press.

McClelland, D. C. (1975). *Power: The inner experience.* New York: Irvington Publishers.

McClelland, D. C., & Burnham, D. H. (1976). Power is the great motivator. *Harvard Business Review, 54* (2), 100-110.

[188]
Jr.-Sr. High School Personality Questionnaire.

Purpose: Measures primary personality characteristics in adolescents.

Population: Ages 12–18.

Publication Dates: 1953–84.

Acronym: HSPQ.

Scores, 18: 14 primary factor scores (Warmth, Intelligence, Emotional Stability, Excitability, Dominance, Enthusiasm, Conformity, Boldness, Sensitivity, Withdrawal, Apprehension, Self-Sufficiency, Self-Discipline, Tension), 4 second-order factor scores (Extraversion, Anxiety, Tough Poise, Independence).

Administration: Group.

Forms, 4: A, B, C, D (authors recommend administration of 2 or more forms).

Price Data, 1987: $14.25 per 25 reusable test booklets (specify Form A, B, C, or D); $9.50 per scoring keys for all forms; $7.50 per 25 machine-scorable answer sheets; $7.50 per 50 hand-scoring answer sheets; $9.50 per 50 hand-scoring answer-profile sheets; $7.50 per 50 profile sheets; $7.50 per 50 second-order worksheets; $9.95 per manual ('84, 101 pages); $21.10 per introductory kit; computer scoring and interpretive services available from publisher at $16 or less per individual report depending upon quantity requested.

Time: (45–60) minutes per form.

Authors: Raymond B. Cattell, Mary D. Cattell, and Edgar Johns (manual and norms).

Publisher: Institute for Personality and Ability Testing, Inc.

Foreign Adaptation: British adaptation; ages 13–15; 1973; supplement by Peter Saville and Laura Finlayson; NFER-Nelson Publishing Co., Ltd. [England].

Cross References: See 9:559 (8 references), T3:1233 (22 references), 8:597 (68 references), and T2:1253 (37 references); for reviews by Robert Hogan and Douglas N. Jackson, see 7:97 (53 references); see also P:136 (29 references); for reviews by C. J. Adcock and Philip E. Vernon of an earlier edition, see 6:131 (17 references); see also 5:72 (4 references).

TEST REFERENCES

1. Bamber, J. H., Bill, J. M., Boyd, F. E., & Corbett, W. D. (1983). In two minds—Arts and science differences at sixth-form level. *British Journal of Educational Psychology, 53,* 222-233.
2. Castelli-Sawicki, D., Wallbrown, F. H., & Blixt, S. L. (1983). Developing a Motivational Distortion Scale for the High School Personality Questionnaire. *Measurement and Evaluation in Guidance, 16,* 43-51.
3. Gilbert, J. (1983). Deliberate metallic paint inhalation and cultural marginality: Paint sniffing among acculturating central California youth. *Addictive Behaviors, 8,* 79-82.
4. McGiboney, G. W., Carter, C., & Jones, W. (1984). Hand Test and the High School Personality Questionnaire: Structural analysis. *Perceptual and Motor Skills, 58,* 287-290.
5. Munson, R. F., & Blincoe, M. M. (1984). Evaluation of a residential treatment center for emotionally disturbed adolescents. *Adolescence, 19,* 253-261.
6. Munson, R. F., & LaPaille, K. (1984). Personality tests as a predictor of success in a residential treatment center. *Adolescence, 19,* 697-701.
7. Cattell, R. B., Rao, D. C., & Schuerger, J. M. (1985). Heritability in the personality control system: Ego strength (C), super ego strength (G) and the self sentiment (Q3); by the Mava Model, Q-data, and maximum likelihood analyses. *Social Behavior and Personality, 13,* 33-41.
8. Cattell, R. B., & Krug, S. E. (1986). The number of factors in the 16PF: A review of the evidence with special emphasis on methodological problems. *Educational and Psychological Measurement, 46,* 509-522.
9. Drummond, R. J. (1986). A review of the High School Personality Questionnaire. *Journal of Counseling and Development, 65,* 218-219.
10. Handford, H. A., Mayes, S. D., Bagnato, S. J., & Bixler, E. O. (1986). Relationships between variations in parents' attitudes and personality traits of hemophilic boys. *American Journal of Orthopsychiatry, 56,* 424-434.
11. Howard, R. C., Haynes, J. P., & Atkinson, D. (1986). Factors associated with juvenile detention truancy. *Adolescence, 21,* 357-364.
12. Richman, C. L., Brown, K. P., & Clark, M. (1987). Personality changes as a function of minimum competency test success or failure. *Contemporary Educational Psychology, 12,* 7-16.
13. Winkel, M., Novak, D. M., & Hopson, H. (1987). Personality factors, subject gender, and the effects of aggressive video games on aggression in adolescents. *Journal of Research in Personality, 21,* 211-223.
14. Speck, N. B., Cinther, D. W., & Helton, J. R. (1988). Runaways: Who will run away again? *Adolescence, 23,* 881-888.
15. Karnes, F. A., & D'Ilio, V. R. (1989). Personality characteristics of student leaders. *Psychological Reports, 64,* 1125-1126.
16. Karnes, F. A., & D'ilio, V. R. (1990). Correlations between personality and leadership concepts and skills as measured by the High School Personality Questionnaire and the Leadership Skills Inventory. *Psychological Reports, 66,* 851-856.
17. Campbell, J. F. (1991). The primary personality factors of Hawaiian, middle adolescents. *Psychological Reports, 68,* 3-26.

Review of the Jr.-Sr. High School Personality Questionnaire by RICHARD I. LANYON, Professor of Psychology, Arizona State University, Tempe, AZ:

The Jr.-Sr. High School Personality Questionnaire (HSPQ) is described as a self-report personality inventory for adolescents (ages 12–18) that measures 14 primary personality characteristics. It is one of the 16PF series of tests that share a common core of personality concepts. There are four forms (A, B, C, and D), and norms exist to use them in combination (A + B; C + D; A + B + C + D). Each form uses a common answer sheet and scoring key. Computerized scoring and interpretation services are available. The HSPQ was first published

nearly 40 years ago (1953) as the *Junior Personality Quiz.* The current manual states that although minor revisions have been made in the test, the last being in 1968, the test has remained essentially the same.

The test booklet provided to this reviewer was entitled Jr.-Sr. HSPQ, Form A, 1968–1969 Edition. This appears to be exactly the same test that was reviewed in detail by Robert Hogan and by Douglas Jackson in the *Seventh Mental Measurements Yearbook* (1972), and the reader is referred to those reviews. To summarize them, Hogan found the HSPQ to be convenient and easy to use. However, "the reliability of the scales is modest, and their validity is indeterminate." Jackson's conclusions were even more negative, citing "deceptive misuse of the concept of validity" in reporting test data, low equivalent-form correlations, low homogeneity of single scales, and the failure to report the specific procedures by which scales were constructed and items were selected. He found the HSPQ to be "perhaps characteristic of personality tests as they existed three decades ago."

The HSPQ manual, updated in 1984, provides considerable additional validity and other data beyond what was available in 1972. However, it is noted that the *format* of the test was changed in the 1968/69 edition (to trichotomous from dichotomous items) and that some items were reworded. Thus, one cannot assume the pre-1968/69 HSPQ is the same as the current (1968/69) HSPQ. A cursory examination of the relevant references indicates that roughly half of them were published prior to the early 1970s, and thus may not be relevant to the current form of the test. This problem is not mentioned in the manual. Another problem with the validity data is that the form of the HSPQ used is not indicated in any of the studies cited. Because the interform correlations are so low, it cannot be assumed that the forms are interchangeable. The median scale correlations of the combined Forms A and B with the combined Forms C and D is less than .60, based on the largest sample cited in the manual.

Examination of the validity data leads to the conclusion that the promotional literature continues to oversell the test. For example, the *IPAT Catalog* states the computer interpretation "provides a complete report for . . . all personality characteristics of significance, as well as the individual's promise in areas of academic achievement, leadership, creativity, and vocational success." The accompanying brochure adds to this list tendencies for delinquency, chemical dependency proneness, longitudinal research, and rapid mental health screening.

The manual cites only one longitudinal research study, in England and Wales. Regarding chemical dependency, the only published work cited is on glue sniffers, also in England. An examination of this and several unpublished studies shows some group differences, but no evidence of utility for individual assessment. The claim of utility for mental health screening relies mainly on group differences on Anxiety, which is a second-order factor to be computed as a weighted composite of seven regular scales. The brochure states that "since the HSPQ has been translated into German, French, Italian, Hebrew, Japanese, Spanish, and other languages, it is especially useful for cross-cultural studies." However, not a word about any of these translations is given in the manual, let alone any recognition that the process of translating a personality inventory is a complex and tricky business that may not result in a test that is equivalent to the original-language version. Overall, the presentation of validity data falls far short of the 1985 *Standards for Educational and Psychological Testing* developed jointly by the American Psychological Association and other organizations.

There are many other problems and annoyances with the HSPQ. For example: (*a*) Although the norms are based on a large, geographically diverse sample, no information is given as to how the children were selected, so it is uncertain whether they are representative of teenagers in general. (*b*) One section of the manual continues to refer to the scales by Cattell's neologisms (Sizia/Affectia, Harria/Presmia, etc.), a practice that is guaranteed to befuddle potential users. (*c*) The sample items on the front of the booklet are written as statements (they are the same sample items as on the 16PF booklet), but the items themselves are in question format. (*d*) The HSPQ uses the obsolete "sten" (standard ten) scale-score system, rather than a percentile or deviation score system. (*e*) Age corrections for the norms can be made only by applying an algebraic formula individually to each score, and this correction is not available for all forms of the test. (*f*) Despite the promotional literature, no substantive information is given to support computer interpretation of the HSPQ.

There is little else to say except that Jackson's conclusions still hold, nearly 20 years later. The HSPQ is not a viable test for contemporary use. Readers are steered toward the Personality Inventory for Children (10:281) for children up to the age of 16, and also to the Minnesota Multiphasic Personality Inventory (MMPI; 9:715) adolescent data. (The MMPI-2 for adolescents has been promised but is not yet available at the time of writing this review.) Regarding the assessment of normal-range personality characteristics in adolescents, no alternative instrument comes readily to mind. However, in view of the recent activity in developing inventories based on the five-factor

system, it is hoped that an adolescent form of such an inventory will soon be forthcoming.

REVIEWER'S REFERENCES

Hogan, R. (1972). [Review of the Jr.-Sr. High School Personality Questionnaire.] In O. K. Buros (Ed.), *The seventh mental measurements yearbook* (pp. 207-208). Highland Park, NJ: The Gryphon Press.

Jackson, D. N. (1972). [Review of the Jr.-Sr. High School Personality Questionnaire.] In O. K. Buros (Ed.), *The seventh mental measurements yearbook* (pp. 208-211). Highland Park, NJ: The Gryphon Press.

American Educational Research Association, American Psychological Association, & National Council on Measurement in Education. (1985). *Standards for educational and psychological testing*. Washington, DC: American Psychological Association, Inc.

Review of the Jr.-Sr. High School Personality Questionnaire by STEVEN V. OWEN, Professor of Educational Psychology, University of Connecticut, Storrs, CT:

The Jr.-Sr. High School Personality Questionnaire (HSPQ) is a multifactor battery whose aim is to measure a variety of personality characteristics of high-school-aged youngsters. Superficially, the HSPQ seems to assess 14 traits, but a careful reading will produce ambiguity about exactly what is being measured. Fourteen primary scores are produced. Although the authors claim each scale "measures a unique personality dimension" (Cattell, Cattell, & Johns, 1984, p. 1), one of the scores is termed *Intelligence*, a construct not usually considered to be a portion of personality. Further, the scale intercorrelations are so strong the claim of unique dimensions is misleading.

Modeled on Cattell's Sixteen Personality Factor Questionnaire (16PF; 9:1136), the HSPQ has evolved through four versions—the original, published in 1953 under a different title, and revisions in 1958, 1963, and 1968. The current test version is thus more than two decades old; item wording occasionally reflects an earlier vocabulary (e.g., "Are there times when you think, 'People are so unreasonable, they can't even be trusted to look after their own good'?"). The most recent manual (1984) is a consolidation of earlier references and later research, but the norms appear to be from students in 1968.

There are four versions (A, B, C, and D) of the HSPQ that appear to be equivalent forms, each requiring 45 to 60 minutes to complete. Equivalence estimates for each scale across the four versions are given in the manual, but the authors argue that one should not consider these versions equivalent forms. Rather, "they are better thought of as *extension* forms" (Cattell et al., 1984, p. 26) and the authors propose that every effort be made to administer two or more forms. No matter what the forms are called, the equivalence coefficients are low. In the worst cases, Factors E (Dominance) and J (Withdrawal) show average coefficients of .19 and .18, respectively. For Factor J, double forms (A + B versus C + D) give a coefficient of only .06. A quick scan of the table of equivalence coefficients suggests the "extension" scales share only about 50% of their variance.

Stability estimates are also given. Coefficients for brief intervals (misleadingly called "dependability coefficients" as though derived from generalizability analysis) average .79 for a single form. For longer intervals, the mean is .56. Internal consistency estimates are conspicuously absent. Reliability estimates would not be expected to be especially high, because the scales are so brief.

The standard error of measurement is mentioned briefly, and a very hopeful example is offered. An analyst interested in confidence intervals around obtained scores will have to calculate his or her own standard errors; the results may reduce optimism about the HSPQ. Here is an example using the scale with the best psychometric properties—Intelligence—measured on Form A, for a male with a raw score of 7. Using the long-interval reliability estimate, a 95% confidence interval gives a range of percentile ranks from 23 to 89, or an IQ range of 88 to 120.

Even test users with adequate measurement skills might be confused by the wide variation in reliability data, coupled with a notably upbeat narrative in the manual. In classical test theory, of course, there is no rule that various reliability estimates must be consistent; sources of error variance are different for each type of coefficient. For two decades, advances in generalizability theory and covariance modeling have offered ways to improve and consolidate reliability information. Some consolidation would have been useful here.

The intended users of the HSPQ—teachers, guidance counselors, and clinical psychologists—likely will be befuddled as they try to wade through the validity evidence presented for the test. Perhaps the authors assume users will believe promises that the test is psychometrically sound because the procedures sound impressive. The statement introducing factorial data is typical: "Factor analysis, another technique for establishing construct validity, is becoming the standard procedure for confirming the existance of a construct" (Cattell et al., p. 27). Even before the widespread use of covariance structural modeling, this statement would have exaggerated the confirmatory use of principal factor analysis.

When the scale scores from the four test versions are factor analyzed, inspection of the pattern matrices shows a sizable departure from simple structure, especially for males. Here, six of the scales show very weak evidence of factorial validity. Oblique rotations might be expected to produce correlated scale scores (15% of the scale intercorrelations for females are greater than .50), but they cannot explain such vague structure. Second-order factoring of the 14 scales gives pattern matrices that

are even more opaque. As if to justify the covariation among factors, the authors give a table showing unique variance for each factor. Even these figures are unimpressive. The average unique variance for the factors is less than 40%.

Abundant validity evidence is presented. A frequent form is a known groups comparison, where, for example, the profiles of high- and low-achieving students are contrasted. The profile comparisons are somewhat inconsistent. The most authentic contrast would use a multivariate approach to take into account the scale covariances; none is seen. A few comparisons are based on visual inspection of the largest apparent scale differences, and others are based on significance tests for each scale. The repeated statistical tests offer a good object lesson in psychometric sleight of hand. Each test assumes the variance analyzed is error-free. When significances pop up, they are treated as genuine, with no mention of statistical power or experimentwise alpha. Under a different assumption—that the measures are fallible—the comparisons can be done using standard errors of measurement to construct confidence intervals. Using this method, the apparent display of significant differences (and thus validity evidence) evaporates.

Other validity arguments, too tedious to detail, can be summarized as a small question with no answer: What do we have here? Despite the authors' persuasive remarks, putting the HSPQ scale scores to practical use is doubly difficult for the practitioner. First, the psychometric evidence is not at all convincing. Second, it is not clear how a counselor or teacher might use scores to diagnose or to guide students. Neither does it seem clear to the authors, who resort to a long table of standard scores from a different measure (the 16PF/) to suggest how the HSPQ can provide occupational advice.

Although earlier reviewers have given straightforward advice about improving the psychometric properties of the HSPQ, the comments have gone largely unheeded. The HSPQ now seems so distant from current psychometric practice that it might be regarded as a relic in the history of measurement.

REVIEWER'S REFERENCE

Cattell, R. B., Cattell, M. D., & Johns, E. (1984). *Manual and norms for the High School Personality Questionnaire*. Champaign, IL: Institute for Personality and Ability Testing.

[189]
Kendrick Cognitive Tests for the Elderly.
Purpose: To detect early dementia and depressive psychosis by assessment of short-term memory and speed of responding.
Population: Ages 55 and over.
Publication Dates: 1979–85.
Subtests, 2: Object Learning Test, Digit Copying Test.
Administration: Individual.
Price Data, 1989: £39.70 per complete set (contains 1 of each item); £16.10 per Object Learning Test; £4.05

per Digit Copying Test; £8.05 per 25 record forms; £11.50 per manual ('85, 32 pages).
Time: (15–20) minutes.
Comments: Formerly known as Kendrick Battery for the Detection of Dementia in the Elderly; battery should be repeated 6 weeks after initial testing.
Author: Don C. Kendrick.
Publisher: NFER-Nelson Publishing Co., Ltd. [England].
a) OBJECT LEARNING TEST.
Acronym: KOLT.
Scores: Total score only.
Forms, 2: A, B (4 cards).
Comments: Test of recall of everyday objects.
b) DIGIT COPYING TEST.
Acronym: KDCT.
Scores: Total score only.
Forms: 1 form (2 pages).
Comments: Test of speed performance.
Cross References: For reviews by Joseph D. Matarazzo and K. Warner Schaie of the earlier form, see 9:566 (2 references).

TEST REFERENCES

1. Orrell, M. W., Sahakian, B. J., & Bergman, K. (1989). Self-neglect and frontal lobe dysfunction. *British Journal of Psychiatry, 155*, 101-105.
2. Abas, M. A., Sahakian, B. J., & Levy, R. (1990). Neuropsychological deficits and CT scan changes in elderly depressives. *Psychological Medicine, 20*, 507-520.

[190]

Keyboard Skills Test.

Purpose: Designed to measure typing skills both in terms of speed and accuracy.
Population: High school and college and adults.
Publication Date: 1988.
Acronym: KST.
Scores, 3: Gross Words Per Minute and Number of Errors, Net Words Per Minute, Error Rate.
Administration: Group.
Forms: 4 equivalent forms: A, B, C, D.
Price Data, 1989: $9 per 10 test form booklets; $6.60 per 35 typing worksheets; $5.50 per 10 practice exercise booklets; $12 per Administration and Scoring Manual (41 pages); $16.45 per Technical Manual (51 pages).
Time: 13(45) minutes.
Authors: J. A. Gordon Booth and Carol DeCoff.
Publisher: Nelson Canada [Canada].

Review of the Keyboard Skills Test by ROBERT FITZPATRICK, Consulting Industrial Psychologist, Pittsburgh, PA:

The Keyboard Skills Test (KST) is a straight-copy typing test intended to be used primarily in the selection of people for jobs in which typing skill is important. It may also be used to evaluate progress of student typists. It was developed in 1978 by a Canadian governmental agency which screens and refers applicants for employment to both public and private employers. Its distribution was taken over by Nelson Canada in 1987.

The technical manual provides a readable and meticulous description of the development and characteristics of the test. Included is a review of literature and a rationale for the choice of test characteristics. The manual gives a fair hearing to the point of view that a typing test should resemble a typical office typing task in (*a*) presenting a job-relevant text at least some of which is handwritten, usually in the form of corrections or interpolations to a printed passage, and (*b*) requiring the typist to plan format and to find and correct errors. But the authors argue that such tests are time consuming, difficult to score reliably, and otherwise flawed. Further, they point out that the basic stroking skills are obviously fundamental to the development of advanced typing skill. Hence, they chose to develop a straight-copy test, that is, one that requires the examinee merely to copy a printed text, with margins and spacing specified in the instructions. The examinee is told not to correct errors.

The test was designed to have a level of difficulty typical of office typing tasks. All passages to be typed have a syllabic intensity (average number of syllables per dictionary word) of 1.54; the stroke intensity (average number of typewriter strokes per dictionary word) varies in the narrow range of 5.91 to 6.01. An effort was also made to keep the level of difficulty fairly constant throughout each passage. The passages are narrative, without the complication of numbers or special symbols.

A 3-minute practice exercise is provided. Each alternate form of the test consists of two equivalent passages to be typed in separately timed 5-minute periods. The examinee is to choose one of the resulting texts for scoring.

The test directions are clear and should be followed readily by people with any training in typing. The rules for scoring are also clear and are supported by stroke counts of the passages.

Alternate forms reliability was studied using student typists as subjects. Score distributions and correlation coefficients indicate a level of reliability similar to other straight-copy typing tests. Also shown, partly by the same data, is an impressive degree of equivalence among the forms of the test. (The materials reviewed include the four English-language forms; four French-language forms are also available with a separate set of manuals.)

Norms are not provided in the usual way. The mean and standard deviation for speed and errors of the student sample for each passage are reported. In addition, there are graphic representations of speed and error distributions. The Administration and Scoring Manual suggests that standards used by the Canadian Federal Public Service be adopted. These standards, or cutoff scores, are couched in terms of words per minute and error rate.

No evidence of validity is provided. Because the KST is similar to other straight-copy typing tests, it seems safe to assume that it is valid to the extent it can be shown to relate to job content.

A problem for typing tests, especially in these days of proliferating word-processing equipment, is the extent to which scores may be affected by the particular type of equipment used or by the examinee's familiarity with the equipment. The Administration and Scoring Manual indicates that a study in 1987/88 compared the performance of subjects on electric typewriter keyboards and word-processor keyboards, and implies that the study supports the use of the KST with either type of equipment. However, there is no report of this study in the technical manual (dated 1988 but otherwise apparently unchanged since its original publication in 1978); the publisher has indicated that such a study was under way but not yet completed at the end of 1989.

Employers who use the Keyboard Skills Test will find a minor annoyance in that the test instructions and even the content of the practice exercise are worded to be appropriate for an employment agency rather than a direct employer. Reference is made in the practice exercise, for example, to the fact that "many employers" place importance on both speed and accuracy of typing.

On the whole, however, the Keyboard Skills Test is blessedly free of annoyances and imperfections. It was developed with considerable care and appears eminently suitable for use by a wide variety of employers.

[191]

KeyMath Revised: A Diagnostic Inventory of Essential Mathematics.

Purpose: Designed to assess understanding and applications of mathematics concepts and skills.
Population: Grades K–9.
Publication Dates: 1971–88.
Acronym: KeyMath-R.
Scores, 17: Basic Concepts (Numeration, Rational Numbers, Geometry, Total), Operations (Addition, Subtraction, Multiplication, Division, Mental Computation, Total), Applications (Measurement, Time and Money, Estimation, Interpreting Data, Problem Solving, Total), Total.
Administration: Individual.
Forms, 2: A, B.
Price Data, 1991: $269 per complete kit including Form A and B test easels, 25 each Form A and B test records, sample report to parents and manual ('88, 349 pages); $147.50 per single form (A or B) kit including test easels, 25 test records, sample report to parents, and manual; $30 per 25 test records (select A or B); $15.50 per 25 report to parents; $30 per manual.
Time: (35–50) minutes.
Comments: Revision of KeyMath Diagnostic Arithmetic Test.
Author: Austin J. Connolly.
Publisher: American Guidance Service.
Cross References: See T3:1250 (12 references); for an excerpted review by Alex Bannatyne, see 8:305 (10 references).

TEST REFERENCES

1. Obrzut, J. E., Hynd, G. W., Obrzut, A., & Pirozzolo, F. J. (1981). Effect of directed attention on cerebral asymmetries in normal and learning-disabled children. *Developmental Psychology, 17,* 118-125.
2. Sandoval, J. (1982). Light's Retention Scale does not predict success in first-grade retainees. *Psychology in the Schools, 19,* 310-314.
3. Harris-Stefanakis, E. (1983). Developing a learning disabilities program in an overseas community school: American Community School in Athens, Greece. *Journal of Learning Disabilities, 16,* 198-201.
4. Leon, J. A., & Pepe, H. J. (1983). Self-instructional training: Cognitive behavior modification for remediating arithmetic deficits. *Exceptional Children, 50,* 54-60.
5. Ritvo, E., Shanok, S. S., & Lewis, D. O. (1983). Firesetting and nonfiresetting delinquents: A comparison of neuropsychiatric, psychoeducational, experiential, and behavioral characteristics. *Child Psychiatry and Human Development, 13,* 259-267.
6. Breen, M. J., Lehman, J., & Carlson, M. (1984). Achievement correlates of the Woodcock-Johnson Reading and Mathematics subtests, Key Math, and Woodcock Reading in an elementary aged learning disabled population. *Journal of Learning Disabilities, 17,* 258-261.
7. Eaves, R. C., & Simpson, R. G. (1984). The concurrent validity of the Peabody Individual Achievement Test relative to the KeyMath Diagnostic Arithmetic Test among adolescents. *Psychology in the Schools, 21,* 165-167.
8. Haywood, H. C., Burns, S., Arbitman-Smith, R., & Delclos, V. R. (1984). Forward to fundamentals: Learning and the 4th R. *Peabody Journal of Education, 61* (3), 16-35.
9. Price, P. A. (1984). A comparative study of the California Achievement Test (Forms C and D) and the Key Math Diagnostic Arithmetic Test with secondary LH students. *Journal of Learning Disabilities, 17,* 392-396.
10. Sandoval, J. (1984). Repeating the first grade: How the decision is made. *Psychology in the Schools, 21,* 457-462.
11. Sapp, G. L., Chissom, B. S., & Horton, W. O. (1984). An investigation of the ability of selected instruments to discriminate areas of exceptional class designation. *Psychology in the Schools, 21,* 258-263.
12. Connelly, J. B. (1985). Published tests—which ones do special education teachers perceive as useful? *Journal of Special Education, 19,* 149-155.
13. Estes, R. E., Hallock, J. E., & Bray, N. M. (1985). Comparison of arithmetic measures with learning disabled students. *Perceptual and Motor Skills, 61,* 711-716.
14. Reynolds, C. R., Willson, V. L., & Chatman, S. P. (1985). Regression analyses of bias on the Kaufman Assessment Battery for Children. *Journal of School Psychology, 23,* 195-204.
15. Sherman, R. G., Berling, B. S., & Oppenheimer, S. (1985). Increasing community independence for adolescents with spina bifida. *Adolescence, 20,* 1-13.
16. Swanson, H. L. (1986). Do semantic memory deficiencies underlie learning disabled readers' encoding processes? *Journal of Experimental Child Psychology, 41,* 461-488.
17. Voeller, K. K. S. (1986). Right-hemisphere deficit syndrome in children. *American Journal of Psychiatry, 143,* 1004-1009.
18. Wharry, R. E., & Kirkpatrick, S. W. (1986). Vision and academic performance of learning disabled children. *Perceptual and Motor Skills, 62,* 323-336.
19. Beden, I., Rohr, L., & Ellsworth, R. (1987). A public school validation study of the achievement sections of the Woodcock-Johnson Psycho-educational Battery with learning disabled students. *Educational and Psychological Measurement, 47* (3), 711-717.
20. Tollison, P., Palmer, D. J., & Stowe, M. L. (1987). Mothers' expectations, interactions, and achievement attributions for their learning disabled or normally achieving sons. *The Journal of Special Education, 21* (3), 83-93.
21. Rivers, D., & Smith, T. E. C. (1988). Traditional eligibility criteria for identifying students as specific learning disabled. *Journal of Learning Disabilities, 21,* 642-644.
22. Eaves, R. C., Darch, C., Mann, L., & Vance, H. R. (1989). Cognition and academic achievement: The relationship of the Cognitive Levels Test to the KeyMath and Woodcock Reading Mastery Tests. *Educational and Psychological Measurement, 49,* 973-983.
23. Simner, M. L. (1989). Predictive validity of an abbreviated version of the Printing Performance School Readiness Test. *Journal of School Psychology, 27,* 189-195.
24. Eaves, R. C., Darch, C., Mann, L., & Vance, R. H. (1990). The Cognitive Levels Test: Its relationship with reading and mathematics achievement. *Psychology in the Schools, 27,* 22-28.
25. Eaves, R. C., Vance, R. H., Mann, L., & Parker-Bohannon, A. (1990). Cognition and academic achievement: The relationship of the Cognitive Levels Test, the KeyMath Revised, and the Woodcock Reading Mastery Tests—Revised. *Psychology in the Schools, 27,* 311-318.

26. Forness, S. R., Cantwell, D. P., Swanson, J. M., Hanna, G. L., & Youpa, D. (1991). Differential effects of stimulant medication on reading performance of boys with hyperactivity with and without conduct disorder. *Journal of Learning Disabilities, 24,* 304-310.

Review of the KeyMath Revised: A Diagnostic Inventory of Essential Mathematics by MICHAEL D. BECK, President, BETA, Inc., Pleasantville, NY:

KeyMath Revised (KeyMath-R) is an individually administered content-referenced test of student achievement in 13 strands of elementary mathematics. Designed primarily for use in grades K–9, the test provides both norm- and criterion-referenced assessment of a student's quantitative strengths and weaknesses. In the galaxy of educational tests, KeyMath-R can only be described as a brightly shining star. From all aspects—content development, technical and normative underpinnings, and presentation of materials—the test is an outstanding example of the test-maker's craft.

CONTENT. KeyMath-R content is organized in the usual three areas of Basic Concepts, Operations, and Applications. Each area is broken down into three or five strands as indicated in the score summary above. Strands are further subdivided into three or four domains. (The choice of the term "domain" is a curious one; this term is more typically applied to more global content constellations.) Each domain is assessed by six individually administered items; thus, each content strand is a subtest of 18 to 24 items.

Item content objectives and domain groupings, presented in the manual, are comprehensive and unambiguous. Item development procedures were soundly planned and carried out. The care with which content was developed and pilot tested is perhaps most clearly demonstrated in an appendix of the manual, which portrays the relative difficulty of all items by strand. Sound content coverage in a test results only from a combination of careful blueprinting, professional item development and editing, and comprehensive pretesting of sufficient numbers of items. The final product demonstrates that the KeyMath development team accomplished all of these steps in a high-quality manner.

FORMAT AND ADMINISTRATION. KeyMath-R is packaged in a useful and very attractive manner. Test items are presented to children on individual item sheets from two cleverly assembled comb-bound easel books. The flip side of each item sheet contains the examiner-read directions, the correct item response and, as needed, elaboration of the keyed response. Tabs separate the items for each strand.

Materials presented to students are very attractive, using a full range of colors and high-quality artwork. These materials highlight the superb graphics and production energies and expenditures of the publisher. The examiner directions are clear and complete; with very few exceptions, test items are well written, crisply presented, and unambiguously scored. Artwork reinforces the examiner-dictated items, easing the test-taking burden for many young children.

Overall administration and scoring directions are presented in the manual. General and specific directions are clear and informative; scoring procedures are presented (almost too) completely, with helpful illustrations of the Test Record Form, extracts of various normative tables, and examples of score conversions.

Student item responses (including some written computations) are recorded on an Individual Test Record (ITR). The ITR is well designed, cleverly using color and shading to distinguish the content areas and strands. Although the ITR is attractive, functional, and probably optimally usable, the plethora of content combinations, score types, and interpretive metrics is somewhat overwhelming. Most users typically would not use all of the possible score types or attempt to interpret all of the content configurations and thus probably adapt quickly to use of the ITR. However, the ITR is somewhat cumbersome in the effort to provide all of the score and content flexibility built into the instrument.

The test manual clearly and completely presents the test features, content and organization, directions for administering and scoring, interpretation of both norm- and content-referenced scores, and normative and technical data. The comprehensiveness of the manual is perhaps best illustrated in its length—339 pages. This includes well over 230 pages of normative conversions and other interpretive tables! The bulkiness of the manual, although certainly preferable to the sketchy corresponding pieces for far too many commercial test products, is somewhat troubling. Surely some way of reducing, for example, 200 pages of raw score-to-scaled/standard score tables to a more manageable length would be possible.

Test administration begins with the Numeration strand. A student's score on this strand determines the starting point for administration of each of the other strands. There is a sound pedagogical as well as technical justification for this administration procedure and it appears to function efficiently and accurately.

The full range of norm-referenced scores available for KeyMath-R includes both grade-based and age-based percentile ranks, stanines, and NCEs. Grade equivalents and, unfortunately, age equivalents are also provided. Another positive feature of the interpretive system is the integral inclusion of a confidence-band approach to score presentation. User-selected 68% or 90% confidence intervals are tabled for each score conversion. Sound explanations of both the derivation and use of all metrics are provided in the manual.

The intermediate conversion metric to obtain all of the normative scores is a scaled score (mean of 10, *s.d.* of 3) for strands, and standard score (mean of 100, *s.d.* of 15) for the area and total-test scores. Although cautions concerning appropriate interpretation of the scaled scores are provided, it is unfortunate that the publisher chose to present the area and total scores in terms of a DIQ-type metric. For example, direct comparison of a KeyMath Operations standard score of 89 with a WISC-R Performance DIQ of 97 is simply ill-advised. Such comparisons seem far more likely to lead to bad rather than good interpretation and decision making.

The manual chapter on test interpretation is excellent, with helpful examples and illustrations. Interpretive suggestions and cautions are practical, with the instructional tips especially well developed. I expect that most KeyMath-R users would have preferred several more pages of this type of material and fewer norms tables. For example, over 20 pages of tables are devoted to average domain scores. These norm-referenced cutoffs, development of which involved several assumptions and a great deal of combining and smoothing of data, seem of little technical or interpretive value. A criterion-referenced interpretive scheme for those scores would be as sound—and clearly simpler.

The supplementary Report to Parents illustrated and discussed briefly in the manual is a good idea; its content is less good than that of the other components, however. For example, the report layout is crowded and confused, key information is not highlighted, and some of the explanations are redundant or unclear.

The above quibbles notwithstanding, the Key-Math-R manual could well be used as a model for a graduate course in test construction. It is comprehensive, yet well written and organized. I am aware of no comparable publication that is as sound and complete.

TECHNICAL AND NORMATIVE DATA. Again the manual could well serve as a model for all test publishers. Explanations are clear and forthcoming, even about (generally minor) flaws or shortcomings. Data are presented in a comprehensive and disaggregated fashion, easing review and analysis of the procedures and outcomes. The technical section, in both its description of procedures used and results obtained, is extraordinarily complete. Relevant research articles on the first edition of KeyMath are referenced. A brief summary of these studies would have been helpful.

SUMMARY. I wholeheartedly recommend this test to anyone seeking an individually administered mathematics achievement test. In content development, material attractiveness and quality, and technical characteristics, KeyMath-R is unsurpassed. The author and publisher have built upon the soundness of the original KeyMath test and created a truly outstanding and useful assessment tool. It should be in the testing armamentarium of every psychometrist or counselor who conducts individualized testing of elementary students.

Review of the KeyMath Revised: A Diagnostic Inventory of Essential Mathematics by CARMEN J. FINLEY, Research Psychologist, retired, Santa Rosa, CA:

KeyMath, an individual-administered test originally developed in 1971, has been revised and updated to reflect the many changes that have occurred in mathematics instruction since its original development. Based on recommendations of the National Council of Teachers of Mathematics, new emphasis has been placed on such skills as estimation, prediction, reasoning, interpretation of data, and solving situational problems.

According to the publisher, the test has five major uses: (*a*) assessment for general instruction, (*b*) assessment for remedial instruction, (*c*) contribution to global assessment (part of a larger test battery), (*d*) pre- and post-testing (to measure educational growth), and (*e*) curriculum assessment.

The present reviewer must agree with Bannatyne, who reviewed the 1971 edition (1978; MMY 8:305), that KeyMath-R is well thought out and nicely constructed, with excellent stimulus material and manual. Illustrations on cards contained in two ring-backed free-standing easels provide attractive stimulus material for all items except the Operations subtests (Addition, Subtraction, Multiplication, and Division). These items are printed in the individual test record. Instructions are clearly presented. The individual test record is well designed and provides both for scoring by the test administrator and for work space for the pupil, thus preserving the information for future use.

Seventeen scores are provided, one for each of the 13 subtests (or strands); subtests are grouped into three areas, Basic Concepts, Operations, and Applications and are scored accordingly; and a total test score is provided. In addition, each subtest consists of three or four domains, each domain being based on six test items. (For example, the domains under Interpreting Data consist of "charts and tables," "graphs," and "probability and statistics.") Domain scores can also be summarized and by comparison with a table of average scores, are classified as weak, average, or strong.

The latter, domain-referenced interpretation, is a major change in format over the original KeyMath. According to the publisher, this change was made because of "the demand for more specific information about skill acquisition, stemming in part from mastery learning and diagnostic-prescriptive teaching . . . another factor stemmed from using the content domains as the vehicle for linking assessment with remediation."

This reviewer gets a little nervous when conclusions are drawn based on six items. However, it is probably best to withhold further judgment until research can be directed toward the utility of using this approach. Another scoring option includes a microcomputer package that provides automatic score conversion. This package, in addition to the basic scores, also provides a tailor-made performance report in narrative style. A typical student report from this package includes a score summary much like that found on the front page of the test record, a score profile (like the back page of the test record), a summary of domain performance (like the inside back cover of the test record) and five pages of narrative interpreting the preceding score records.

KeyMath-R is Binet-like in that the administrator must establish a basal and ceiling score for each of the 13 subtests. This is a practical component for a test that spans grade levels from K through 9. After the basal score has been established for the first subtest, Numeration, it is used to direct the starting point for each subsequent subtest. However, if the basal is not established using this starting point, it is necessary to work backwards until the child has three consecutive correct responses immediately preceding the easiest item missed. The mere manipulation of testing materials could become cumbersome if this were to happen on many of the subtests. The publisher claims that preliminary research by the test author and analysis using Rasch item calibration was used to arrive at their decision to use Numeration as the best predictor and to locate starting points on the other subtest areas.

Using the KeyMath-R does require some training on the part of the test administrator, not unlike other individually administered tests. A previous reviewer recommended at least five trial administrations should be done before an administrator could feel confident in using the results. Although the exact number of trials may vary depending on the previous experience of the administrator, the point is well taken that some degree of training and practice is needed.

The most typically anticipated uses of KeyMath-R and how it compares with other possible measures are probably best indicated by previous research studies on KeyMath. One of the more interesting is a study by Connelly (1985). He surveyed 398 special education teachers from 92 school districts in 42 states. The teachers specified the type of students with whom they worked (learning disabled, emotionally, behaviorally, socially maladjusted, mentally retarded, or multicategory) and were asked to list published tests they perceived as useful in making diagnostic and placement decisions. KeyMath was the most frequently mentioned test across groups

(63%) with the Peabody Individual Achievement Test (55%), Woodcock Reading Mastery Tests (42%), Peabody Picture Vocabulary Test (38%), and Wide Range Achievement Test (30%) following. Tinney (1975) compared KeyMath with the California Arithmetic Test. He concluded there was a significant positive relationship between the two tests for a learning disabled population and that KeyMath had the added advantage of providing individual diagnostic information as well as achievement data. He also concluded KeyMath was more in line with then current math curricula, had the advantage of requiring no reading or writing, "offers a simplified visual presentation, and allows the skilled diagnostician to observe behavior closely during the individual administration" (p. 315). Evidence of use with Chapter I populations is given by the test publisher. The number of requests they received for Normal Curve Equivalent (NCE) scores for KeyMath led them to add these conversion tables to the current version of KeyMath-R.

In summary, KeyMath-R has been revised and updated to reflect current mathematics curricula. It is well designed, attractively packaged, and apparently popular with educators who must make diagnostic and placement decisions.

REVIEWER'S REFERENCES

Tinney, F. A. (1975). A comparison of the KeyMath diagnostic arithmetic test and the California arithmetic test used with learning disabled students. *Journal of Learning Disability, 8* (5), 313–315.

Bannatyne, A. (1978). [Excerpted review of the KeyMath Diagnostic Arithmetic Test.] In O. K. Buros (Ed.), *The eighth mental measurements yearbook* (p. 452). Highland Park, NJ: The Gryphon Press.

Connelly, J. B. (1985). Published tests—which ones do special education teachers perceive as useful? *Journal of Special Education, 19* (2), 149–155.

[192]

Kilmann-Saxton Culture-Gap Survey.

Purpose: "Provides a systematic tool for surfacing and diagnosing cultural norms" in the workplace.

Population: Organizational work group members.

Publication Date: 1983.

Scores, 4: Task Support, Task Innovation, Social Relationships, Personal Freedom.

Administration: Group.

Price Data, 1987: $6.25 per manual ('83, 24 pages) including survey and scoring sheet.

Time: [15] minutes.

Authors: Ralph H. Kilmann and Mary J. Saxton.

Publisher: XICOM, Inc.

Review of the Kilmann-Saxton Culture-Gap Survey by ANDRÉS BARONA, Associate Professor, Division of Psychology in Education, Arizona State University, Tempe, AZ:

The Kilmann-Saxton Culture-Gap Survey is a 28-item instrument designed to identify organizational norms that influence the performance and morale of a work group. The authors refer to norms as the unwritten rules or policies that work group members are pressured to follow. The difference between what actually occurs and what is desired is defined as the culture-gap. The authors assert that large culture-gaps indicate a likelihood that the existing "norms" hinder morale or performance.

The survey yields four culture-gap scores which are differentiated by their emphasis on the technical versus human norms of the work situation, and on short-term versus long-term concerns: (*a*) *Task Support* refers to norms that are primarily technical and involve a short time frame, such as those that entail day to day concerns; (*b*) *Task Innovation* overlaps with technical norms but involves a longer time frame and may affect the organization's future; (*c*) *Social Relationships* refer to more personally oriented, short term norms; (*d*) the norms involved in *Personal Freedom* are also more individually oriented but may have long term effects.

Respondents first assess each of the 28 items according to the perceived pressures exerted by the work group (actual norms). They then evaluate the same 28 items according to how each should influence the work group to promote high performance and morale (desired norms). The difference between the actual and desired norms in each cluster represents the culture-gaps.

The four culture-gap scores can be plotted in bar graph form for interpretive purposes. Diagnostic guidelines, derived from more than 1,000 responses from over 25 profit and nonprofit organizations, indicate that a score of +3 or greater in any cluster represents a very significant culture-gap and "signifies a desire for more Task Support, more Task Innovation, more Social Relationships, or more Personal Freedom" (p. 16). A score of +1 suggests an insignificant culture-gap whereas a score of +2 is considered to be borderline. A negative score represents a potentially significant culture-gap and may signify a desire for less of one of the previously mentioned aspects.

The authors state that all members of an organization should complete the Kilmann-Saxton Culture-Gap Survey in order to accurately diagnose separate divisions within an organization. The authors indicate that computer software is available to calculate culture-gap profiles for large units but provide no specific information on its availability.

The items on the Kilmann-Saxton Culture-Gap Survey reportedly were selected from more than 400 items generated through interviews and group discussions with employees from a wide range of organizations. Specific item selection information was not provided; the authors state only that statistical analyses were used to arrive at the final 28 items. No data regarding these analyses are included in the manual. Similarly, information pertaining to reliability and validity is not included.

Although the Kilmann-Saxton Culture-Gap Survey appears to be useful for diagnosing the need for organizational change, several limitations exist.

First, the authors consistently err on the side of brevity. Although instructions generally are clear, little rationale for the use of the specific culture-gap clusters is provided. Only one example of a culture-gap profile is provided and this illustration describes a situation where significant culture-gaps exist in a number of areas. The lack of examples illustrating less extreme or marginal culture-gap profiles may limit interpretation for those using the instrument.

Second, those who opt for manual scoring may find transferring items to a separate scoring sheet for computing the four culture-gap scores both cumbersome and prone to error. Although computer scoring appears to be a possibility, the lack of details regarding this option may deter those considering its use for large groups. Third, information regarding the procedures used in the instrument's development and the characteristics of the organizations that participated in item selection were not specified. Such omissions create difficulty in determining the type(s) of organizations for which the survey's use is most appropriate. Finally, although personal communication with the author revealed that more detailed information is available in Saxton's dissertation, omitting such critical data from the manual may result in decisions against its use.

In sum, the Kilmann-Saxton Culture-Gap Survey *appears* to hold considerable promise for diagnosing the need for change within an organization. However, based on the absence of technical, statistical, and development information in the manual this reviewer regretfully concludes that until such information is readily available the survey as presented does not meet the requirements described in the *Standards for Educational and Psychological Testing* (AERA, APA, & NCME, 1985).

REVIEWER'S REFERENCE

American Educational Research Association, American Psychological Association, & National Council on Measurement in Education. (1985). *Standards for educational and psychological testing.* Washington, DC: American Psychological Association, Inc.

Review of the Kilmann-Saxton Culture-Gap Survey by GARGI ROYSIRCAR SODOWSKY, *Assistant Professor of Educational Psychology, University of Nebraska-Lincoln, Lincoln, NE:*

According to the authors, corporate "culture is the unwritten, often unconscious, message that fills in the gaps between what is formally decreed and what actually takes place" (p. 12). The implicit culture of an organization "thus determines how formal statements get interpreted and translated, and provides what the written documents leave out" (p. 12). Every work group develops norms or silent "rules of the game" (p. 1) and pressures each of its members to follow them. Such a description of culture is a limited, albeit utilitarian, application of the broader and more inclusive constructs of culture and worldviews which have been defined comprehensively in anthropology and cross-cultural psychology.

The authors' term "culture-gap" could be understood from the acculturation concepts of "culture shock," which is suffered by minority individuals, and "value conflicts," which occur between the dominant and minority cultures. However, the authors do not provide a theoretical rationale for their terms. Culture-gap is described as the "differences between the actual norms operating" in one's work group "versus the desired norms," and "materialize[s] as an unwillingness to adopt new work methods and innovations, as a lack of support for programs to improve quality and productivity, as lip-service when changes in strategic directions, goals, and objectives are announced and, at the extreme, as efforts to maintain the status quo at all costs" (p. 12).

The survey is not for individual assessment and interpretation. The survey must be administered to all members of the work group (a unit, department, and/or whole organization), and scores are averaged across all or most members. The authors warn against making recommendations for organizational changes that are based on the responses of only one or a few members.

To diagnose the culture-gap of one's place of work, an individual responds in Part 1 to 28 pairs of norms in a forced-choice format (choosing Statement A or Statement B), as according to the pressures one's work group puts on its members. In Part 2, the individual responds to the same 28 pairs of statements according to how the individual believes the norms should be. Four culture-gaps, Task Support, Task Innovation, Social Relationships, and Personal Freedom, are calculated by subtracting the sum of scores obtained in Part 1 for each of the above dimensions from the sum of scores obtained in Part 2 for the same dimensions.

On a profile, the four culture-gap scores can be plotted in a bar graph. A raw score of +3 represents "potentially, a very significant Culture-Gap," signifying a desire for more support, innovation, social relationships, or personal freedom. A raw score of -3 also represents "potentially, a very significant Culture Gap," signifying a desire for less support, less innovation, etc. A raw score of +2 means a borderline culture-gap, and a score of +1 means an insignificant culture-gap. Except for stating that minus scores are infrequent, the authors do not provide diagnostic guidelines for -2 and -1. If as many as three or four culture-gap scores in the profile are significant, the authors diagnose a broad-based culture problem in an organization.

Computer software is available to calculate the average culture-gaps of each unit in an organization. A computerized organizational culture-gap profile can provide a summary picture of culture-gaps for each unit in an organizational flowchart. Thus, an organizational profile permits diagnoses across a whole organization.

The authors do not indicate whether the diagnostic criteria were empirically derived with the use of criterion groups. The only information available is that the sample consisted of 1,000 subjects from approximately 25 profit and nonprofit organizations. No information is provided about norm groups. Raw scores which are reported on the profile need to be replaced by standard scores, so that standard deviations from the mean (and also possibly percentile ranks) could make interpretations more meaningful and facilitate comparisons with scores on other measures.

The authors do not provide information about the psychometric properties of the survey, specifically its reliability, homogeneity, and validity. Therefore, because of the lack of predictive validity data, one could question the authors' claim that organizational decision making and action taking and, in turn, job performance and morale are hindered by culture-gaps. It appears that an examination of the survey is currently under way in an ongoing research program of the authors who have also requested respondents to volunteer their score sheets to help them establish a data bank.

The pairs of statements in the survey are easy to read and the instructions for answering, scoring, and doing the bar-graph profile are reader-friendly. However, Part 1 may elicit particular response sets. For example, the use of pronouns "you" (e.g., "dress as you like") and "your" (e.g., "live for your job or career") may obtain responses that reflect the individual's personal reactions to the work group, level of professional development, current mood, or frustrations rather than the group's actual norms.

In Part 2, where respondents circle the desired norms, the authors' assumption is that in a given pair of norms, one norm is more beneficial than the other. However, both norms could have drawbacks. For instance, "help others complete their tasks" could lead to the neglect of one's own tasks or to the experience of a role overload. The alternate choice of "concentrate on one's own tasks" could lead to unhealthy competitiveness or social isolation. Both choices could also have their respective benefits. Thus, respondents may be confused over which statement to circle and may either respond inaccurately, randomly, or leave some items unanswered. Likert and semantic differential answer formats, offering more response choices, could prevent such difficulties.

Individuals may desire both norms such as "believe in your own values" as well as "believe in the organization's values" because the values may not necessarily be contradictory. If they are contradictory, some could privately follow their personal values and adhere to organizational values at work.

Additionally, there are some pairs of statements that are not opposites such as "try new ways of doing things" and "don't rock the boat." Social desirability could also operate when responding to Part 2. Owing to the obviousness of the statements, the individual could give socially acceptable responses for the "ideal organizational environment" rather than indicate personal preferences.

The application of the constructs of culture and values to explain the work place is commendable. However, the major concerns about the survey are as follows: Inadequate theoretical rationale for definitions; a lack of information about the development and psychometric properties of the survey; problems with the pairing of some statements and with some item wordings; and the influence of social desirability.

[193]
Kirton Adaption-Innovation Inventory.

Purpose: A measure . . . of a person's preference for, or style of, creativity, problem solving and decision making.
Population: British and U.S. adults.
Publication Dates: 1976–87.
Acronym: KAI.
Scores, 4: Sufficiency v. Proliferation of Originality, Efficiency, Rule/Group Conformity, Total.
Administration: Group.
Price Data: Available from publisher.
Time: (5–10) minutes.
Comments: Translations available for Italian adults and Slovak adults.
Author: Michael Kirton.
Publisher: Occupational Research Centre [England]; U.S. Distributor: Mercatus, Inc.

TEST REFERENCES

1. Masten, W. G., & Caldwell-Colbert, A. T. (1987). Relationship of originality to Kirton's scale for innovators and adaptators. *Psychological Reports, 61,* 411-416.
2. Robertson, E. D., Fournet, G. P., Zelhart, P. F., & Estes, R. E. (1987). Relationship of field dependence/independence to adaption-innovation in alcoholics. *Perceptual and Motor Skills, 65,* 771-776.
3. Isaksen, S. G., & Puccio, G. J. (1988). Adaption-innovation and the Torrance Tests of Creative Thinking: The level-style issue revisited. *Psychological Reports, 63,* 659-670.
4. Joniak, A. J., & Isaksen, S. G. (1988). The Gregorc Style Delineator: Internal consistency and its relationship to Kirton's adaptive-innovative distinction. *Educational and Psychological Measurement, 48,* 1043-1049.
5. Masten, W. G., & Colbert-Caldwell, A. T. (1988). Self-estimates of adaptors and innovators on the Kirton Adaption-Innovation Inventory. *Psychological Reports, 63,* 587-590.
6. Goldsmith, R. E., McNeilly, K. M., & Russ, F. A. (1989). Similarity of sales representatives' and supervisors' problem-solving styles and the satisfaction-performance relationship. *Psychological Reports, 64,* 827-832.
7. Robertson, E., Fournet, G., Zelhart, P., & Estes, R. (1989). Response to Kirton. *Perceptual and Motor Skills, 69,* 1037-1038.
8. Cutright, P. S. (1990). Predicting adaption-innovation styles: Selected demographic characteristics and the Kirton inventory. *Perceptual and Motor Skills, 70,* 173-174.

Review of the Kirton Adaption-Innovation Inventory by GREGORY J. BOYLE, Senior Lecturer in Psychology, University of Queensland, St. Lucia, Queensland, Australia:

The Kirton Adaption-Innovation Inventory (KAI) is a self-report scale designed to measure the degree to which adults are characteristically either "adaptive" or "innovative" in their cognitive style in regard to decision making, problem solving, and creativity. The instrument is based on adaptive-innovation theory, which was originally postulated to account for the occurrence of qualitatively different solutions to ostensibly the same problem. Adaption-Innovation theory predicts that responses on the KAI are normally distributed with most individuals exhibiting scores in the midrange (80 to 112, on a scale from 32 to 160, as indicated on the KAI Report Back Form).

The reliability of the KAI has been examined in terms of its item homogeneity. For example, several Alpha and Kr^{20} coefficients ranging from .76 to .91 were reported for various large samples taken from the general population, managers, and students. However, evidence has been presented (cf. Boyle, 1991) which shows that the reliability of a scale can be either high or low, irrespective of the level of item homogeneity. Indeed, the high levels of item homogeneity reported for the KAI suggest that the instrument provides rather narrow measurement of the adaption-innovation dimension (cf. Cattell, 1978; Kline, 1986). Yet, in terms of the test-retest reliability data provided in the KAI manual, the stability coefficients across substantial intervals of several months are all quite good (ranging from .82 to .86). Therefore, while the KAI is a respectably reliable instrument, it appears to be a limited measure of the adaption-innovation construct itself.

The KAI has high face validity and a high level of item transparency. It is therefore prone to motivational distortion ranging all the way from inadequate self-insight to blatant dissimulation (faking good/faking bad), as well as being unduly influenced by various well-documented response sets. Use of reverse-scored items (in order to minimize the possible influence of such response sets) has been shown elsewhere to be potentially problematic (Boyle, 1979), wherein the reversed items have been found (using factor analysis) to measure an entirely different construct. From the data reported in the KAI manual it is not clear whether this caveat applies also to the KAI reverse-scored items.

In support of its construct validity, the KAI manual reports a factor analysis of the item inter-correlations. A table is presented showing the item-scale loadings in terms of the first unrotated principal component. Because principal components are not iterated and communality estimates are treated as unities, those loadings below .40 would generally be considered as being of no "practical significance" (as opposed to statistical significance) (cf. Gorsuch, 1983). Perusal of this table indicates that 12 of the 32 scored KAI items failed to exhibit conceptually meaningful loadings. In other words, more than a third of the present KAI items appear to have only a trivial overlap with the adaptive-innovative dimension, and therefore probably should be removed from future versions of the scale. In any event, this method of analysis is a somewhat crude one. It would have been more satisfactory had the item analysis been undertaken using a one-factor congeneric model in LISREL (cf. Joreskog & Sorbom, 1989).

As for the exploratory factor analysis, the KAI manual reported that varimax rotation indicated that the KAI scale comprised three subscales measuring different aspects of the adaption-innovation dimension. However, although the sample was respectably large ($N = 532$), the specific factor analytic methodology employed was inappropriate on several counts. Failure to iterate the initial solution ensured that the communality estimates and concomitant factor loadings were spuriously inflated. The decision to extract three factors was based on subjective application of the scree test. However, it is extremely unlikely that the scree test would have suggested only three factors. Given the 32 input variables, the scree test would more typically suggest that 9 or 10 factors should be extracted (e.g., Hakstian, Rogers, & Cattell, 1982)! Use of orthogonal varimax rotation, which provides only a special resolution of the whole gamut of possible factor solutions, was unjustified. An oblique rotational strategy should have been employed in view of the reported intercorrelations of the three "factors" (see KAI manual, p. 18). Moreover, there was no assessment of the degree to which simple structure had been achieved in terms of, for instance, the ($\pm.10$) hyperplane count (cf. Cattell, 1978; Boyle & Stanley, 1986; Gorsuch, 1983). The above difficulties with the factor analytic methodology necessarily render interpretation of the structural dimensionality of the KAI uncertain. Other factor analytic studies cited in the KAI manual were also defective, and by and large also employed the "Little Jiffy" approach which has been shown to be seriously defective (cf. Gorsuch, 1983).

Nevertheless, the KAI is easily administered, taking only 5–10 minutes testing time. Normative data for a large sample as well as for a replication sample are provided in the KAI manual. It is potentially a very useful instrument which enables quantitative insights into the cognitive style of individuals. Such information could be invaluable in certain employment contexts. Thus, the KAI is an interesting and novel instrument which may have a useful role in a number of research and applied settings.

REVIEWER'S REFERENCES

Cattell, R. B. (1978). *The scientific use of factor analysis in behavioral and life sciences.* New York: Plenum Press.

Boyle, G. J. (1979). Delimitation of state-trait curiosity in relation to state anxiety and learning task performance. *Australian Journal of Education, 23,* 70-82.

Hakstian, A. R., Rogers, W. T., & Cattell, R. B. (1982). The behavior of number-of-factors rules with simulated data. *Multivariate Behavioral Research, 17,* 193-219.

Gorsuch, R. L. (1983). *Factor analysis* (2nd ed.). Hillsdale, NJ: Lawrence Erlbaum Associates.

Boyle, G. J., & Stanley, G. V. (1986). Application of factor analysis in psychological research: Improvement of simple structure by computer-assisted graphic oblique transformation: A brief note. *Multivariate Experimental Clinical Research, 8,* 175-182.

Kline, P. (1986). *A handbook of test construction: Introduction to psychometric design.* London & New York: Methuen.

Joreskog, K. G., & Sorbom, D. (1989). *LISREL 7: A guide to the program and applications.* Chicago: SPSS, Inc.

Boyle, G. J. (1991). Does item homogeneity indicate internal consistency or item redundancy in psychometric scales? *Personality and Individual Differences, 12,* 291-294.

Review of the Kirton Adaption-Innovation Inventory by GERALD E. DeMAURO, Senior Examiner, Educational Testing Service, Princeton, NJ:

The Kirton Adaption-Innovation Inventory (KAI) is designed to locate respondents on an adaptive-innovative continuum of cognitive style. Adaptors are characterized as extending the application of available procedures and approaches to problems, and innovators are characterized as restructuring problems and designing less conventional approaches and solutions (Kirton, 1984). An impressive body of research is devoted to the definition of the construct measured by the KAI.

Respondents are asked to rate the difficulty of presenting themselves for long times in manners consistent with each of 33 statements. Difficulty can be rated as *Very Hard, Hard, Easy,* and *Very Easy,* with enough space left between the *Hard* and *Easy* categories to permit the ascription of a middle, unlabeled rating. The first statement is unscored. Although it is untimed, the KAI is said to take individuals and small groups from 5–10 minutes and larger groups a few more minutes to complete.

The 32 scored statements describe attributes such as problem attack, disposition toward team work, consistency, and thoroughness. Each is scored from 1 to 5, yielding a theoretical range of 32–160. As a consequence of item-selection procedures, the theoretical mean is 3 for each statement and 96 for the total. In fact, the observed mean for 532 subjects from the London area was 95.33 and the range was 46–145. Scores above 96 characterize innovators and those below characterize adaptors.

INVENTORY DEVELOPMENT. The KAI was developed using expert judgment. A preliminary list of statements was reviewed during interview by 20 senior business managers who were also invited to add any other statements which discriminated adaptors from innovators. Twenty other managers divided the resulting statements into favorable and unfavorable groups. The managers sorted these groups further into a minimum number of groups, each of which would present an internally consistent description of an individual. The managers then joined groups of statements to give a portrait of a balanced individual. The interviewed managers and the managers used in the sorting task agreed on which statements described adaptors and which described innovators. This statement list was then increased by literature review and further interview.

In an inventory format, the statements were presented to a pilot sample of 121 people. Statements in which 80% or more of the sample reported the task of describing themselves as being *Very Hard* or *Hard* or as being *Very Easy* or *Easy* were dropped. Statements with ratings that correlated less than .20 with the sum of the rest of the statement ratings were also dropped. The resulting form of the KAI was tested on a sample of 355 split into two subsamples matched for sex, age, education, and socioeconomic status. Statements that met the two empirical criteria described above and contributed to internal reliability in both subsamples were retained in the inventory.

NORMS. Normative data are presented for three samples: a main sample of 532 composed of subsamples that took different constellations of various other measures; a replication sample of 276; and a combined sample of 562 combining members of the main sample and the replication sample who took many of the same tests. Intact, English groups having demographic characteristics of interest were included in the samples. Raw score means and standard deviations are also presented in the manual from Italian (translated version) and American studies. Women are slightly, but significantly, more adaptive.

Principal factor analyses with varimax rotations revealed three subscales that conformed to descriptions of Sufficiency of Originality (SO) by Rogers (1959), Efficiency (E) by Weber (1970), and Rule/Group Conformity (R) by Merton (1957). Factor trait means, standard deviations, and constants to compute expected factor trait scores from observed total scores are presented for the combined main subsample and replication sample. These constants equal the ratios of the sample trait mean to the sample total inventory mean.

RELIABILITY. Kuder-Richardson 20 (KR-20) coefficients of .88 are reported both for the main sample ($n = 532$) and for the replication sample tested 1 year later ($n = 276$). A Cronbach alpha coefficient of .88 is reported for the combined main subsample and replication sample ($n = 562$). It is not clear how the KR-20 was obtained from statements that have values of 1 to 5. Reported KR-20 coefficients for the factor traits are between .76 and .84 although these traits were based on the sums of scores for only 13, 7, and 12 statements. Standard errors of measurement for the total score, and the SO, E, and R factor-trait scores are given as 6.20, 3.77, 2.74, and 3.63, respectively. Test-retest coefficients vary from .82 for a 7-month interval (KAI manual) to .86 for a 5-month interval (as noted in

KAI manual from an unpublished study by Prato Previde).

VALIDITY. Some of the ample validity evidence which addresses the capacity of the KAI to measure the adaptor-innovator construct is summarized below, first focusing on evaluations of the convergent properties of the KAI and then on evaluations of the discriminant properties of the KAI.

A study of organizational departments, first classified by Kirton as innovative or adaptive in function, showed the innovative departments averaged 105.18 (innovator) on the KAI and adaptive departments averaged 91.63 on the KAI (Kirton, 1980). Means characteristic of innovators were observed both for research and development personnel and for those selecting innovative training courses as compared to those assigned to courses (Kirton & Pender, 1982).

Reported KAI score correlations only range from -.14 to .12 with intelligence measures in several cited studies. In a principal factors analytic study of measures of creativity, two factors emerged, one attributed to creative style and one to level of creativity. The KAI loaded .66 on the first factor, but less than .30 on the second.

During interviews, innovators attributed to adaptors several traits (called the "Adorno" characteristic by Kirton) that people identified by the KAI as adaptors denied. Analyses of extensive measures of these traits showed them to be better related to each other than to KAI scores. Such analyses help define the characteristics of adaptors and innovators.

CONCERNS. The major concern focuses on item response distributions. Data suggest a normal distribution of inventory scores, related to the careful statement development and screening procedures. However, the deletion of statements that attract extreme responses could limit the capacity of the KAI to distinguish reliably among extreme examples of adaptors or innovators. On the other hand, much of the research concerns "innovators" and "adaptors" as groups (see Kirton, 1980, for example), which requires reliable discrimination at the theoretical dividing point rather than at the extremes. Reporting conditional standard errors of measurement would help evaluate the reliability of the KAI in making these discriminations.

A second concern about the item response distributions is the absence of a descriptor on the inventory for a middle level response (neither hard nor easy). It appears (from the KAI manual) that this unlabeled option attracts only between 1% and 7% of respondents, which raises some concern about the treatment of data for statistical procedures involving item responses and the interpretation of item averages.

SUMMARY. The KAI appears to be a valuable research tool for identifying a style of defining and attacking problems. A large body of research documents what it is and what it is not. Considerable potential may be realized with improved documentation and some additional attention to item level procedures.

REVIEWER'S REFERENCES

Merton, R. K. (Ed.). (1957). *Bureaucratic structure and personality in social theory and social structure.* New York: Free Press of Glencoe.

Rogers, C. R. (1959). Towards a theory of creativity. In H. H. Anderson (Ed.), *Creativity and its cultivation.* New York: Harper.

Weber, M. (1970). In H. H. Gerth & C. W. Mills (Eds. and Trans.). From *Max Weber: Essays in sociology* (pp. 196-244). London: Routledge & Kegan Paul. (Original work published 1948).

Kirton, M. J. (1980). Adaptors and innovators in organizations. *Human Relations, 33* (4), 213-224.

Kirton, M. J., & Pender, S. (1982). The adaption-innovation continuum, occupational type and course selection. *Psychological Reports, 51,* 883-886.

Kirton, M. J. (1984). Adaptors and innovators—why new initiatives get blocked. *Long Range Planning, 17* (2), 137-143.

[194]
Kundu Neurotic Personality Inventory.

Purpose: Designed to measure neurotic tendencies.
Population: Adults.
Publication Dates: 1965–87.
Acronym: KNPI.
Scores: Item scores only.
Administration: Group.
Price Data: Available from publisher.
Foreign Language Edition: Bengali edition available.
Time: (20–40) minutes.
Author: Ramanath Kundu.
Publisher: Ramanath Kundu [India].
Cross References: See T2:1257 (2 references) and P:140 (5 references).

[195]
Language-Structured Auditory Retention Span Test.

Purpose: Designed to assess the ability to maintain short-term memory for linguistically significant information.
Population: Ages 3.7–adult.
Publication Dates: 1973–89.
Acronym: LARS.
Scores, 2: Mental Age (MA), "Quotient" (MA/CA).
Administration: Individual.
Forms, 2: A, B.
Price Data, 1991: $40 per complete kit including manual ('89, 64 pages), 50 recording Form A, and 50 remedial checklists; $12 per manual; $18 per 50 recording Form A; $18 per recording Form B; $7 per pad of 50 remedial checklists; $12 per specimen set (manual and sample forms).
Time: (12–15) minutes.
Comments: Immediate recall of words and sentences presented orally; new edition includes remedial activities; "norm-referenced."
Author: Luis Carlson.
Publisher: Academic Therapy Publications.
Cross References: For a review of old edition by James B. Lingwall, and an excerpted review by Alan Krichev, see 8:941 (1 reference).

Review of the Language-Structured Auditory Retention Span Test by RODNEY W. ROTH, Professor of Educational Research and Dean, College of Education, The University of Alabama, Tuscaloosa, AL:

The purpose of the Language-Structured Auditory Retention Span (LARS) Test is to define disabilities in language functioning for children of mental age 3 years, 7 months through adult. The test has 58 sentences varying in length from 1 word to 12 words. The total number of sentences passed is the raw score. A conversion table is provided to convert the raw scores to "mental ages." A quotient, derived by dividing "mental age" by chronological age, is suggested by the test author for test interpretation. The quotient is not, however, an intelligence quotient.

The manual for the LARS does not provide adequate information to meet the technical standards for test construction and evaluation as presented in the *Standards for Educational and Psychological Testing* (AERA, APA, & NCME, 1985). The manual does not present validity or reliability data, equivalent forms data between Forms A and B, or adequate data to evaluate the conversion of the raw score to "mental age" conversion table.

The LARS was first published in 1973 and the current "revised" edition is dated 1989. The new edition is really the 1973 test with two additions. The 1989 LARS has added a remedial checklist to provide teachers with remedial activities to help students improve their auditory retention span. Most of the activities suggest presenting to students sentences with some nonsense words. No data, however, are provided that support the effectiveness of the activities in improving retention. The other new addition to the 1989 LARS is a Mental Retroflection Learning Disability (MRLD) Test. This assessment was added because there are times when persons perform adequately on the LARS, but whose test performance suggests an auditory recall dysfunction. The MRLD is administered by having the testee respond to a series of numerals, letters, and colors by repeating them as they were presented. The testee also responds to a series of numerals, letters, and colors by repeating them backward. The scoring procedures produce a quotient. This quotient is then converted into one of the five probability levels, ranging from zero to almost certain, for having mental retroflection learning disability. The documentation to evaluate the MRLD is even less than provided for the LARS. This reviewer cannot recommend the MRLD.

In conclusion, my assessment of the current LARS is very similar to the assessment of the original LARS by Lingwall (1979). He also found a complete absence of information on the construction, standardization, reliability, and validity of the test. He stated, and I would agree, that the use of this test cannot be recommended.

REVIEWER'S REFERENCES

American Educational Research Association, American Psychological Association, & National Council on Measurement in Education. (1985). *Standards for educational and psychological testing.* Washington, DC: American Psychological Association, Inc.

Lingwall, James B. (1979). [Review of the Language-Structured Auditory Retention Span Test.] In O. K. Buros (Ed.), *The eighth mental measurements yearbook* (pp. 1463-1464). Highland Park, NJ: The Gryphon Press.

[196]
Lateral Preference Schedule.

Purpose: "To meet the research and clinical needs for a standardized measure of lateral preference."
Population: Ages 7 and over without physical disabilities.
Publication Dates: 1978–88.
Acronym: LPS.
Scores, 9: General Laterality, Visually Guided Activities, Visual Activities, Auditory Activities, Strength, Foot Use, Total, Maternal, Paternal.
Administration: Group.
Price Data, 1989: $32 per complete kit (includes manual ['88, 21 pages], 50 test booklets, and 50 profile forms); $16 per 50 test booklets; $9.50 per 50 profile forms; $8 per manual.
Time: (15–30) minutes.
Comments: Formerly called Laterality Preference Schedule.
Author: Raymond S. Dean.
Publisher: Psychological Assessment Resources, Inc.
Cross References: For reviews by Patti L. Harrison and John E. Obrzut of the original edition, see 9:591 (2 references); see also T3:1289 (6 references).

TEST REFERENCES

1. Rothlisberg, B. A., & Dean, R. S. (1985). Reading comprehension and lateral preference in normal readers. *Psychology in the Schools, 22,* 337-342.
2. Dean, R. S., & Rattan, G. (1986). Cerebral laterality and paired associate learning in young children: A dual processing model. *Clinical Neuropsychology, 8,* 118-123.
3. Dean, R. S., Schwartz, N. H., & Hua, M. (1986). Lateral preference patterns in schizophrenia and affective disorders. *Clinical Neuropsychology, 8,* 145-148.

Review of the Lateral Preference Schedule by ALIDA S. WESTMAN, Professor of Psychology, Eastern Michigan University, Ypsilanti, MI:

The Lateral Preference Schedule (LPS) is a 59-item, untimed self-report. It assesses relative left-right preference on a 5-point Likert scale with alternatives from *Left Always* (5 points) to *Right Always* (1 point) with *Left and Right Equally* as midpoint. The LPS's strengths include taking laterality as a continuous rather than a dichotomous variable and as a multidimensional rather than a simple variable. Six factors and three additional variables are calculated. The six factors are General Laterality (13 items), Visually Guided Activities (17 items), Visual (eye preference; 5 items), Auditory (ear preference; 5 items), Strength (of the hands; 5 items), and Foot Use (4 items). The three additional variables are total score, mother's lateral preference (5 items), and father's lateral preference (5 items). Parents are included because laterality is influenced by both biological and environmental

factors. The nine indices can be analyzed as a profile. The manual includes two useful sample profiles. The interpreter is warned appropriately to look not only at profiled sums but also at answers to individual items.

Despite these positive aspects, the LPS needs some editorial and research effort before use can be recommended without qualification.

TEST BOOKLET AND PROFILE. Some fairly simple changes in format would make the materials easier to use. First, the alternatives of the Likert scale should be defined on the booklet, so respondents can refer to them easily. Second, in the booklet below each factor a row should be added to record the number of times each alternative is checked. These numbers must be multiplied by their respective Likert-scale weights. Currently, there is space only for the results of the multiplication. This format makes checking for simple computational errors difficult. Third, for ease of reference the scales on the profile should be indicated by abbreviated names instead of numbers. (The first example in the LPS Manual is on page 5 and concerns factor 3 and not 1. Without name labels on the profile, or number of the factor in the manual, the example is initially confusing.)

Representing both content and format problems are the next four criticisms. First, some of the items are dated. Given changing family structure and work patterns, many moms today do not iron or throw balls, and many dads are not observed kicking balls. These changes may cause respondents to answer from a general response set. Second, although the strategy for initial item selection was good, the current presentation of items about self invites a response set. For example, all items for a factor are together and the alternatives are always indicated in the same order. Third, some questions are not appropriate for younger children. For example, 7-year-old children may not know how they would thread a needle or look through a microscope. The last point is just a personal opinion but I would prefer the author use an item about stepping on a lever or a pedal rather than a bug.

MANUAL: NORMATIVE DATA. Normative data are given for elementary school children. The data presented for adults are based on a sample of people who have an average age of about 20. This fairly young norm group may present a problem for those who use the test with older adults.

RELIABILITY. For later elementary school children and the young adults, reliability on the six factors was obtained by checking internal consistency and by test-retest with a 1-week delay. The reliability was moderate to very good. Alpha coefficients measuring internal consistency ranged from .62 to .98 and test-retest reliability varied from .58 to .93. Only internal consistency was provided for the parental scales, but the values were similar. No reliability data were provided for early elementary school children. An appropriate warning was included to check that the young children know left from right and to provide concrete signs during testing if needed.

Interpretation of obtained differences among factors would be enhanced if the author incorporated reliability data and standard error of measurement information into the guidelines. Such information will enable test users to know which differences have statistical and/or clinical significance.

SUMMARY. Several authors have pointed out the need for a good profile of laterality (Federico, 1984; Thompson, Heaton, Matthews, & Grant, 1987) for basic research and clinical applications. The LPS is an acceptable index, but it could be improved. It is a good tool for gathering data on lateral preferences. Application of the information gained from the test requires substantial expertise. Test users will require some sophistication in neuropsychology to make proper use of the scores.

REVIEWER'S REFERENCES

Federico, P. A. (1984). *Cerebral lateralities and individualized instruction.* San Diego, CA: Final Report, Navy Personnel Research and Development Center.

Thompson, L. L., Heaton, R. K., Matthews, C. G., & Grant, I. (1987). Comparison of preferred and nonpreferred hand performance on four neuropsychological motor tasks. *Clinical Neuropsychologist, 1,* 324-334.

Review of the Lateral Preference Schedule by THOMAS A. WROBEL, *Assistant Professor of Psychology, University of Michigan-Flint, Flint, MI:*

The Lateral Preference Schedule (LPS) is a self-administered inventory of an individual's hand of preference for various activities. The author, Raymond S. Dean of Ball State University and the Indiana University School of Medicine, states that lateral preference should be thought of as a continuous, bipolar dimension with right and left preference at the extremes. He further reports that the indication of cortical laterality, a result of the interaction of complex genetic and environmental factors, is not readily obtained from single measures such as hand preference for writing. The LPS not only attempts to assess the degree of hand preference for the activities of the individual taking the schedule, but assesses the degree of parental laterality demonstrated as well.

The four-page test booklet consists of 59 questions that ask the subject to report which hand they prefer to use, and the strength of that preference for various arm, leg, eye, and ear tasks and five questions regarding each parent. The item responses are summed over the eight dimensions measured and may be compared to normative results using tables found in the manual or by plotting the results on a profile sheet. Norms and profile sheets are provided for both adults and children from age 7 to 13.

The LPS originated with a pool of 153 items that were administered to 97 undergraduates. These students were observed performing the activities and then retested. Forty-nine items demonstrating stability and criterion correlations of above .80 were retained. The 49 items were factor analyzed using the responses of 1,000 adults with the six resulting factors used to classify the items into the LPS's dimensions. Reliability estimates using coefficient alpha range from .62 to .98 for the six dimensions. Test-retest coefficients range from .58 to .93 with correlations being higher, as expected, for adults than for children and for the longer scales. Validation studies reported have investigated the relationship between LPS scores and poor reading (Dean, 1978); learning disability (Dean, 1979; Dean, Schwartz, & Smith, 1981; and Schwartz & Dean, 1978); WISC-R scores (Dean, 1979); psychiatric disorders (Dean, 1986); reading comprehension (Rothlisberg & Dean, 1985); and giftedness (Lewandowski & Kohlbrenner, 1985).

The test has clear instructions and scoring directions that contribute to its high degree of reliability. The abilities also are clearly linked to the underlying concept of laterality of function.

The test form could be improved regarding the experimental parental items by adding a place to report if the parent is or is not the biological parent. The author acknowledges the potential influence of both genetic and environmental factors. An opportunity for those from blended or adoptive families to clarify their responses might provide some potentially interesting data.

Another area of concern is the manner in which the normative data have been pooled across all 1,000 adult and 308 child subjects, regardless of their hand preference. Interpretation of factor scores is done based on the bimodal population as a whole. As a result, the scores have not been normalized and the resulting *T*-scores are not comparable to other *T*-scores, nor are they clearly interpretable. The author has provided helpful prototype profiles for individuals of right, left, and mixed preference. The user is cautioned when interpreting the aggregate dimension scores to look at the constituent items as the same total dimension score may be obtained from widely discrepant individual items responses. With these cautions in mind, the LPS appears well suited for research and clinical applications where a clear self-report of hand preference is needed.

REVIEWER'S REFERENCES

Dean, R. S. (1978). Cerebral laterality and reading comprehension. *Neuropsychologia, 16,* 633-636.

Schwartz, N. H., & Dean, R. S. (1978). Laterality preference patterns of learning disabled children. *Perceptual and Motor Skills, 47,* 869-870.

Dean, R. S. (1979). Cerebral laterality and verbal-performance discrepancies in intelligence. *Journal of School Psychology, 17,* 145-150.

Dean, R. S., Schwartz, N. H., & Smith, L. S. (1981). Lateral preference patterns as a discriminator of learning difficulties. *Journal of Consulting and Clinical Psychology, 49,* 227-235.

Lewandowski, L., & Kohlbrenner, R. (1985). Lateralization in gifted children. *Developmental Neuropsychology, 1* (3), 277-282.

Rothlisberg, B. A., & Dean, R. S. (1985). Reading comprehension and lateral preference in normal readers. *Psychology in the Schools, 22,* 337-342.

Dean, R. S. (1986). Neuropsychological aspects of psychiatric disorders. In J. E. Obrzut & G. Hynd (Eds.), *Child neuropsychology* (pp. 83-112). New York: Academic Press.

[197]

Learned Behaviors Profile—Self/Other.

Purpose: "Designed to help people explore their patterns of behavior."
Population: Adults.
Publication Date: 1990.
Acronym: LBP.
Scores, 6: Caretaker, People-Pleaser, Workaholic, Martyr, Perfectionist, Tap Dancer.
Administration: Group.
Editions, 2: Self, Other.
Price Data, 1990: $7.95 per LBP: Self inventory (31 pages); $2.95 per LBP: Other inventory (6 pages); each includes administrator's guide (no date, 2 pages).
Time: Administration time not reported.
Comments: Self-administered, self-scored.
Authors: J. William Pfeiffer and Judith A. Pfeiffer.
Publisher: Pfeiffer & Company International Publishers.

Review of the Learned Behaviors Profile— Self/Other by DIANE BILLINGS FINDLEY, Doctoral Candidate, Louisiana State University, Baton Rouge, LA:

The Learned Behaviors Profile (LBP) is a self-administered inventory designed to help individuals identify their patterns of learned behaviors and change those that are undesirable. Included in the package are a Self inventory, to be completed by the individual, and an Other inventory, to be completed by persons who are well acquainted with the individual. It is not necessary for others to complete the inventory to obtain a profile, however. Except for the appropriate grammatical change in person, the items for both inventories are identical.

The Self inventory is presented in a five-part booklet. Part 1 presents the questionnaire, and Parts 2 through 5 present scoring and interpretation procedures. The questionnaire consists of 60 items that are rated on a Likert-type scale (1 = *strongly disagree* through 6 = *strongly agree*). Each item is a statement that describes a particular behavior. All are easy to read and understand. In Part 2, the scores for each of the six scales are totaled and then transferred to a graph highlighted to indicate high scores. Part 3 provides interpretative information for the LBP. Part 4 provides instructions for scoring and recording results from both the Self and Other inventories. Part 5 offers questions to guide the individual's thinking when comparing his or her Self and Other scores.

The interpretive section includes a brief description of codependency and references for additional reading. This is followed by a description of each of the six scales. Under each scale description is a

behavior profile that describes the characteristics of the typical person scoring high on that scale. Guidance about ways to change their behavior are offered for high-scoring individuals. Following this, space is provided for the respondent to write how his or her behaviors can be changed and the steps that can be taken to accomplish this.

The LBP requires no special training for administration or scoring and seems to have been designed as a self-help tool to allow individuals to assess their own patterns of behavior and guide them in changing their own behavior. Although an instrument that would serve this purpose might be beneficial, the LBP appears to have several problems. First, the authors provide no information about test construction. For example, no information is given for how the items were selected or how the scales were derived. Second, the authors provide no rationale for the particular cutoff scores used to determine the highlighted, high-score range on a particular scale. There is no indication of how the cutoff scores were chosen. Finally, the authors provide no reliability or validity data. For these reasons, this reviewer cannot recommend this instrument for clinical use at this time. Without adequately demonstrated psychometric properties and empirical support for the scales and cutoff scores, the LBP may lead individuals to place more confidence in the results than can be justified.

In conclusion, the LBP is an easily administered and scored instrument designed to help individuals assess their patterns of learned behaviors and guide them in changing undesirable ones. As a self-help tool in the field of codependency, the LBP has potential for being a useful instrument if it could be demonstrated to have adequate psychometric properties and a sound empirical base for its development. Until these concerns are adequately addressed, the LBP cannot be recommended by this reviewer for clinical or self-help purposes.

Review of the Learned Behaviors Profile— Self/Other by JOHN R. GRAHAM, Professor of Psychology, Kent State University, Kent, OH:

Although the authors do not state so explicitly in the manual, the purpose of the Learned Behaviors Profile (LBP) appears to be to help individuals understand learned behavioral styles that may at times be dysfunctional. The materials made available for this review were a manual for the LBP— Self and a test booklet for the LBP—Other.

One form of the instrument is to be completed by the test subject, and the other form is to be completed by five to eight other persons who know the test subject well and have observed the test subject in a variety of settings. Each form of the instrument contains 60 items that are rated on a 6-point scale (1 = *strongly disagree* to 6 = *strongly agree*).

The manual includes instructions for subjects to obtain scores on each of six scales by summing the ratings for the 10 items in each scale. Scores can be plotted on a profile sheet. Subjects are told that scores falling in shaded areas on the profile sheet may indicate learned behaviors that are dysfunctional. The manual includes brief behavioral descriptions for each scale and recommendations for persons who score high on each scale. Subjects are encouraged to read and consider the descriptions for their highest ranked scales. The manual also includes a table for summarizing scores on the scales based on others' ratings. Questions are provided to encourage test subjects to compare their self-perceptions with the perceptions of others.

The six scales of the LBP (Caretakers, People-Pleasers, Workaholics, Martyrs, Perfectionists, Tap Dancers) are based on the ideas of Larsen (1985). The scales correspond to behavioral styles that persons have learned as ways of trying to assure that their needs are met.

The manual for the LBP provides no information about scale construction, internal consistency, temporal stability, or validity. There are no data available concerning the extent to which the scales are independent of each other. The authors do not indicate how the shaded areas on the profile sheet, which are supposedly suggestive of dysfunctional behaviors, were determined. Although they imply some comparison of test subjects with a normative sample, no information is given about normative subjects. No consideration is given to possible gender differences and their meaning. A letter to the publisher from this reviewer requesting more information about the instrument was not answered.

In summary, the notion underlying the LBP is interesting. Helping persons to understand learned behavioral styles could be beneficial, particularly in counseling situations. The names of the scales are catchy, and the descriptions seem reasonable. However, complete absence of psychometric information about the instrument makes it impossible to recommend the LBP for routine use.

REVIEWER'S REFERENCE

Larsen, E. (1985). *Stage II recovery: Life beyond addiction*. Minneapolis, MN: Winston Press, Inc.

[198]
Learning and Study Strategies Inventory.
Purpose: "To measure students' use of learning and study strategies and methods."
Population: College students.
Publication Date: 1987.
Acronym: LASSI.
Scores, 10: Attitude, Motivation, Time Management, Anxiety, Concentration, Information Processing, Selecting Main Ideas, Study Aids, Self Testing, Test Strategies.
Administration: Group or individual.
Price Data, 1990: $3 per packet including test booklet, manual (15 pages), and score interpretation information;

$2 per computer administration; information on volume discounts available from publisher.
Time: (30) minutes.
Comments: Manual title is LASSI User's Manual; Apple II and IBM PC microcomputer versions available.
Authors: Claire E. Weinstein.
Publisher: H and H Publishing Co.

TEST REFERENCES

1. Haynes, N. M., Comer, J. P., & Hamilton-Lee, M. (1988). Gender and achievement status differences on learning factors among Black high school students. *The Journal of Educational Research, 81*, 233-237.
2. Haynes, N. M. (1990). A comparison of learning and motivation among high school students. *Psychology in the Schools, 27*, 163-171.
3. McGuire, J. M., Hall, D., & Litt, A. V. (1991). A field-based study of the direct service needs of college students with learning disabilities. *Journal of College Student Development, 32*, 101-108.

Review of the Learning and Study Strategies Inventory by MARTHA W. BLACKWELL, Associate Professor of Psychology, Auburn University at Montgomery, Montgomery, AL:

This single-form inventory is designed to be self-administering, self-scoring, and self-interpreting for beginning college students to identify standard areas of attitudes, motivations, and study practices that might be improved with educational intervention. The 77 items yield 10 separate scale scores. There is no total test score.

The inventory booklet contains item-answer sheets, scoring sheet, and profile chart. Directions on the booklet's front page are presented in two columns and are confusing as to reading sequence and to detachment and separation of sheets for testing and scoring. For example, the Likert-type key, presented prior to detachment instructions, necessitates rereading before proceeding to respond. Caution should be urged to mark response choices heavily and to "X" any response changes to improve scoring ease and accuracy.

Although generally well written, the items overlap within and between scales. For example, intrascale overlap occurs in the Time Management scale, Item 36, "When it comes to studying, procrastination is a problem for me," and Item 66, "I put off studying more than I should." Interscale overlap is exemplified in the Time Management scale, Item 3, "I find it hard to stick to a study schedule," and the Motivation scale, Item 33, "I talk myself into believing some excuse for not doing a study assignment." Although such redundancy is not uncommon, it appears too much in this inventory.

The test manual describes the 9-year inventory development with numerous item tryouts and reductions, field testing, questioning examinees, and content inspection by experts. Items correlating .50 or better with a measure of social desirability were eliminated. Supporting data are not presented, however.

For test administrators, directions and scoring procedures presented in the inventory booklet are summarized. Score interpretation for each scale score is its comparison to "national norms" and also to what is cited as a common cutoff of 75% used on many campuses to derive scale percentile ranks. The only description of the composition of the "national norms" was a sample of 880 entering freshmen from a large southern university with no mention of age, sex, geographical origin, or other. Presumably, the correlations of coefficient alpha (.68 for Study Aids to .86 for Time Management) were derived from the 880 entering freshmen. Test-retest correlations (.72 for Information Processing to .85 for both Time Management and Concentration) were derived from 209 students in an introductory communications course at the same large southern university.

Undocumented claims for external validity consist of vague, broad, and brief references to comparisons of scale scores "where possible" to other tests/subscales measuring similar factors and to "performance measures" with "several of the scales." Unanswered reliability issues include intercorrelations of all items with scale scores and with a total test score which should be easy to compute although no summed total score was presented in the manual. Unanswered validity issues include the relationships of inventory scores to high school or first-semester grade-point averages, to scholastic ability, and to improvement in grades after mastery of study skills. In essence, informative statistical data are sorely lacking.

Examination of the Learning and Study Strategies Inventory (LASSI) manual and inventory and the Brown-Holtzman Survey of Study Habits and Attitudes, Forms C and H, manual and test (Brown & Holtzman, 1967) accentuates the deficiencies in technical data with regard to thorough analyses of internal consistency, of relationships of differences in test scores between different groups and other variables, and of correlations of test scores with other tests and variables with which a relationship would be expected. The Brown-Holtzman is somewhat old and has a high vocabulary load, but may still be the superior test.

In conclusion, the LASSI is an innocuous means to orient beginning college students to some of the attitudes and study practices that may be needed to succeed academically. The lack of statistical evidence regarding discrete scales, criterion-related validity, and construct validity will preclude the use of the LASSI by those who require important validity and reliability data on measures they choose.

REVIEWER'S REFERENCE

Brown, W. F., & Holtzman, W. H. (1967). *Survey of Study Habits and Attitudes, Forms C and H: Manual.* New York: Psychological Corporation.

Review of the Learning and Study Strategies Inventory by STEVEN C. HAYES, Professor of Psychology and Director of Clinical Training, University of Nevada, Reno, NV:

The Learning and Study Strategies Inventory (LASSI) is a 77-item Likert-type rating inventory that purports to measure students' use of learning and study strategies. It is organized into 10 scales: Attitude toward college, Motivation to work hard, Time Management, Anxiety, Concentration, use of Study Aids, Self Testing, Test-taking Strategies, Selection of Main Ideas, and the use of Information Processing strategies. Nine of the scales have eight items, one has five. Items are scored on a 5-point rating scale from *Not at all typical of me* to *Very much typical of me*. The sum of the rating score (sometimes inverted depending upon the direction of keying of the item) of the items in the scale yields the scale score. Raw scores are converted to percentiles for each scale. The LASSI is self-scoring and is designed for group administration.

The items all have high face validity: "I find it hard to stick to a study schedule" or "When they are available, I attend group review sessions." Information on how they were grouped is vague, but they seem to have been grouped primarily on the basis of apparent content.

The user's manual presents extremely limited information about the psychometric properties of the instrument. Alpha coefficients and test-retest reliability for each scale are presented. The test-retest data are apparently from a sample of 209 students in an introductory communications course who took the LASSI twice over 3 weeks. Normative data are from 880 incoming freshmen at a large southern university. Scale intercorrelations and specific validity data of any kind are missing. The author claims the inventory has been correlated with "other tests . . . measuring similar factors" and has been "validated against performance measures" but the tests used or results obtained are not described. The author emphasizes the items all tap areas that can be changed through educational intervention, and that the device will yield an "accurate diagnosis of entry-level skills" that can lead to "individualized prescriptions for improvement" but no data on the intervention utility of the instrument are provided.

The appeal of the LASSI seems to be in its common-sense format, face-valid items, and ease of mass administration and student scoring. The specific areas examined are well suited to entry-level "study skills" programs. The lack of documented validity or utility, however, means that as an empirical matter the instrument is currently of unknown value.

[199]
Learning Behaviors Scale, Research Edition.
Purpose: Identifies dysfunctional learning behaviors for an early assessment of how a child will perform academically.
Population: Kindergarten.

Publication Dates: 1981–88.
Acronym: LBS.
Comments: Manual title is Learning Behaviors Scale and Study of Children's Learning Behaviors; ratings by teachers; manual also used with the Study of Children's Learning Behaviors (SCLB; 388).
Scores, 4: Impulsive-Distractible, Apprehensive-Avoidant, Moody-Uncooperative, Total.
Administration: Individual.
Price Data, 1990: $36 per complete kit including 5 LBS and 5 SCLB Ready-Score™ questionnaires and manual ('88, 113 pages); $29 per 25 Ready-Score™ questionnaires; $24 per manual.
Time: (1–2) minutes per child.
Authors: Denis H. Stott, Paul A. McDermott, Leonard F. Green, and Jean M. Francis.
Publisher: The Psychological Corporation.

TEST REFERENCES

1. Glutting, J. J., Kelly, M. S., Boehm, A. E., & Burnett, T. R. (1989). Stability and predictive validity of the Boehm Test of Basic Concepts—Revised among black kindergarteners. *Journal of School Psychology, 27,* 365-371.

Review of the Learning Behaviors Scale, Research Edition by LIZANNE DESTEFANO, Assistant Professor of Educational Psychology, University of Illinois at Urbana-Champaign, Champaign, IL:

The Learning Behaviors Scale (LBS) is a 22-item scale developed to assess kindergarten pupils' "physical acts and expressions of motivation" (manual, p. 1) that influence success in school. Items on the scale were derived from two instruments, the Preliminary Guide to the Child's Learning Skills (Stott, Green, & Francis, 1983) and the appendix to the Flying Start Learning-to-Learn Kit entitled Guide to the Child's Learning Skills (Stott, 1971), both of which grew out of the observations of teachers working with children with learning problems in a laboratory school in Ontario in the 1960s. To complete the scale, teachers who are familiar with a child for at least 50 days are asked to read each item and mark whether the item "most often applies," "sometimes applies," or "doesn't apply" to the child's day-to-day school experience. The LBS yields a Total Score and three dimension or Dysfunctional Learning Behavior scores, obtained by summing the scores from all or a subset of items. It is recommended that the Total Score be used as an estimate of the child's general approach to learning. The score could serve as the basis for identifying students who are "at risk" for school failure. The Dysfunctional Learning Behavior scores can then be used to evaluate specific areas of weakness and the individual items can be used to develop intervention strategies or individualized education plan (IEP) goals.

The authors claim the test is based on a behavioral model that views a child's learning behavior as the outcome of the interaction among cultural, educational, environmental, and individual influences and they review the literature to that effect.

However, it is not clear how the proposed model relates to the construction and use of the test. First, the meaning of the construct, learning behavior, is not well differentiated from similar constructs such as temperament and cognitive style. Second, it is not demonstrated empirically how measures of learning behavior should relate to other variables in the model such as social status, race, attitudes, and ability. To add to the confusion, the construct is referred to alternately as learning behavior and learning-related behavior throughout the manual. Inspection of the content of the items suggests that the scale measures teacher perceptions of a child's attention, approach to tasks, persistence, and level of motor activity.

Although the version of the test reviewed was labelled "research edition," purposes and uses of the test as stated by the authors emphasized heavily the use of the scale in schools to identify at an early age students who are likely to fail academically due to deficits in learning behavior and to design interventions to remediate those deficits. Because the prescribed use of the test is to identify children very early in their school career, one might presume that during standardization and norms development, careful consideration would be given to the developmental nature of the behaviors being assessed. Beyond the fact that teachers are asked to take the child's age into consideration when making the ratings, however, age is given little consideration. In fact, the issue of age is treated so loosely, the authors suggest that if normative data are not needed, the scale may be used with students of any age. No data are provided to support this use.

Internal consistency reliability, computed using coefficient alpha, ranges from .81 for the Apprehensive-Avoidant and Moody-Uncooperative dimensions to .90 for the overall test. Standard errors of measurement are reported for each dimension and for the overall test. They appear reasonable (1.03 to 2.26). Although it is suggested that data from individual items serve as the basis for individualized planning, the reliability of individual items is not reported. Although the authors do not claim they are measuring a construct that is stable over time, they are advocating the use of the test for long term educational planning and for diagnosis. Evidence of stability over time would seem to be essential for this purpose. No data on test-retest reliability are reported. Because the test relies on teacher ratings, interobserver reliability would seem to be necessary to provide evidence of the objectivity of the measure. None is reported. The authors address objectivity by recommending that even when a single child is the target of the evaluation, the teacher should be asked to rate several children of similar age and ethnicity. In this way the response set or possible biases of the teacher can be detected.

The authors make no recommendations for scoring or interpretation if a response set is found.

Much of the interpretation of the test is based on the use of *T*-scores, derived from the entire standardization sample. The distribution of *T*-scores was not normalized, it remains positively skewed, with scores ranging from 40 to 100. The authors recommend a criterion score of 60 and above to identify students who are at risk (approximately 10% of all students based on the standardization sample). A criterion score of 70 and above identifies students who are seriously at risk (5%). The basis for setting these scores is not discussed and does not seem to fit with the performance of the standardization sample.

This sample itself is quite problematic, comprising 1,227 children, ranging in age from 60 to 97 months (although they are treated as a single age group of kindergartners in the norms tables), from various geographical locations including a Newfoundland fishing village, a large Australian industrial city, rural Georgia, and suburban Arizona. It is not clear why these sites were chosen, what procedures were used to select subjects and in what year data were collected. The sample is not well described in terms of socioeconomic status, ethnicity, or ability. Furthermore, the patterns of performance of the various subgroups appear quite different. For example, in the Newfoundland subgroup, only 3.5% of the sample met the criterion of "at risk," that is having Total Scores greater than 60. The subgroups belonging to the United States sample had much higher rates of identification, ranging from a low of 16% in the Arizona suburbs to 33.1% in rural Georgia. Given the diversity of the various subgroups, subsequent analyses based on the entire sample (such as the *T*-score tables and the factor analyses) are difficult to interpret and are questionable. Differentiated norms or summary information about differences in gender, ethnicity, or age groups would aid in understanding patterns of performance on the scale. In general, norms that are presented should represent clearly described groups with whom the users of the tests will ordinarily wish to compare the people who are tested. It is difficult to imagine a group of children to which these data would generalize. If the test is to be used in a local school district, test publishers should encourage the development of local norms.

The factor structure solution for the LBS was based on the entire standardization sample (*N* = 1,227). A three-factor solution was found, with all factors meeting criteria for minimum eigenvalues and scree, explaining a large enough percentage of the overall variance, containing enough items with appreciable loadings, and possessing sufficient reliability. Items 11 and 20 loaded on two factors. Items 5, 9, and 16 did not load on any of the three factors, but were retained on the scale. Intercorrelations among the three factors: Impulsive/Distractible, Moody/Uncooperative, and Apprehensive/Avoidant ranged from .46 to .71, indicating some uniqueness in what was measured by each factor. Although technically sound, the limitations of the standardization sample call into question whether this factor structure will hold for other groups of kindergarten children. This concern is heightened by the practice of using different factor analytic solutions for scoring purposes in several of the validity studies. Although the authors state that the solutions were similar to those of the standardization sample, the solutions themselves are not reported in the manual.

Evidence of predictive, concurrent, and discriminant validity is presented in the manual. The composition of the validation samples is not well described, but they appear to vary considerably from the standardization sample. The results of the validity studies show consistent negative correlations among LBS scores and ability and academic achievement as measured by standardized test scores and teacher ratings. However, differential prediction equations are not derived for different demographic groups and the validity of the scale for the purposes outlined in the introduction is not clearly demonstrated. For example, one of the major uses of the scale is the use of individual items to develop IEP goals. In fact, a computer program has been developed to select IEP goals based on scores on the LBS. Unfortunately, the validity of items for prescribing or evaluating the effects of interventions is not shown. In addition, the relationship between scale ratings and the factors contributing to faulty learning behaviors is not demonstrated.

In summary, problems with the representativeness of the standardization sample, failure to establish interrater and test-retest reliability, and lack of validity studies to support the use of the test for long term planning and evaluation of interventions limit the use of the LBS in school settings. Its content and format make it a potentially desirable instrument, however. Further research is warranted.

REVIEWER'S REFERENCES
Stott, D. H. (1971). *Manual to the Flying Start Learning-to-Learn Kit.* Guelph, Ontario: Brook International.
Stott, D. H., Green, L. F., & Francis, J. M. (1983). *Guide to the child's learning skills.* Stafford, England: National Association of Remedial Education.

Review of the Learning Behaviors Scale, Research Edition by BRIAN K. MARTENS, Associate Professor of Psychology and Education, Syracuse University, Syracuse, NY:

The Learning Behaviors Scale (LBS) is a brief teacher-rating scale intended for use with kindergartners. Unlike global rating scales that measure a broad range of adjustment problems, the LBS focuses exclusively on the manner in which children approach schoolwork. The LBS contains 22 items that describe task-related behavior (e.g., "Is very hesitant about giving an answer"), and each item is rated using a 3-point scale (*Most often applies, Sometimes applies, Doesn't apply*). Both negatively and positively worded items are included on the scale, and the wording of items is clear and unambiguous. Scoring the LBS is easily accomplished using answer sheets that automatically transfer non-numerical ratings on the front of the answer sheet to numerical ratings on the back. The numerical ratings are then copied by the examiner into adjacent columns which are summed to yield the respective subscale and total scores. The final step in scoring involves converting the summed raw scores to *T* scores using a one-page conversion table presented in the appendix.

The manual is well organized and contains a generous number of figures and tables that complement the text. Helpful recommendations for using the scale provided in the first two chapters include the suggestion that a student be taught for at least 50 days prior to completing the scale and that classroom norms be collected to aid interpretation. Chapter 3 contains supplementary material describing dimensions measured by the subscales, items of particular diagnostic significance, and factors that contribute to specific deficits as well as principles for their remediation. Many of the references in this section are dated, and the discussion is likely to be of only general use in programming. The authors state that a microcomputer software program is available for developing IEP objectives on the basis of the item responses.

SCALE DEVELOPMENT. Items appearing on the LBS were adapted from two previous scales, the Guide to the Child's Learning Skills (GCLS) and the Preliminary Guide to the Child's Learning Skills (PGCLS). The GCLS was developed on the basis of case conferences involving tutors of approximately 200 kindergarten children in a laboratory school at the University of Guelph, Ontario. According to the authors, problems expressed during the case conferences were "progressively classified into a schedule of 14 regularly observed faults of learning behavior" (p. 37) over a 4-year period. The PGCLS consisted of seven statements describing appropriate learning behavior that were abstracted from the original GCLS. The interview data from which items were developed appears substantial, and this information was collected on a population appropriate for the intended uses of the scale (i.e., kindergarten children exhibiting learning problems).

The resulting 22-item LBS was standardized on a sample of 1,227 primarily white kindergarten (and kindergarten equivalent) students in the United States, Canada, and Australia during January of the school year. Approximately half of the subjects were male ($n = 607$), and the children ranged in age from 60 to 97 months. Subjects in the United States sample were drawn from geographically diverse regions that included Arizona, New Jersey, and Georgia. The size and diversity of the standardization sample are good for a screening instrument, and subjects are described by sex, age, race classification, and school classification (urban, suburban, rural). Despite the large sample size, however, separate norms are not reported by age or sex.

Subscales appearing on the LBS were based on the results of a principal components factor analysis using ratings from the entire standardization sample. Factor loadings for each item as well as the percentage of variance explained by each factor are presented in the manual. The three-factor solution accounted for 49% of the variance in teachers' ratings, with intercorrelations among the factors ranging from .46 to .71. Procedures involved in obtaining the factor solution and labeling the subscales are well articulated, although the stability of factors across different subject samples is not discussed.

PSYCHOMETRIC PROPERTIES. The only reliability data reported for the LBS are the internal consistency (using Cronbach's alpha) and standard error of measurement of the subscale and total scores. This is somewhat puzzling given that three measures of reliability (internal consistency, test-retest, and interrater) are presented in the same manual for the related scale, the Study of Children's Learning Behaviors (SCLB; 388). The latter two indices (i.e., test-retest and interrater reliability) are particularly relevant to behavior rating scales and should be reported for the LBS (Edelbrock, 1988, p. 371). As would be expected, the reliability coefficient associated with the total score (.90) is higher than those associated with the subscale scores (range = .81 to .87), although all values indicate adequate internal consistency.

The authors describe two studies examining the predictive and concurrent validity of the LBS, both of which appeared to employ appropriate criterion measures. Results of the first study indicated moderate correlations between ratings on the LBS and teacher ratings of achievement 6 months later (range = -.40 to -.62). Similar results were obtained in the second study which correlated ratings on the LBS with three standardized measures of preschool readiness obtained concurrently (range = -.38 to -.72). Discriminant validity evidence is also presented from two studies in which ratings on the LBS were used to identify children who had been classified previously on the basis of (*a*) emotional indicators from the Bender Gestalt and (*b*) teacher recommendations for instructional groupings. In each study, the LBS accurately classified a significant proportion of the subjects.

SUMMARY. The authors claim the LBS is appropriate for use in research and educational decision making as a screening instrument, an aid in diagnosis, and an outcome measure of instructional programming. The LBS seems well suited to screening with its relatively small number of items that can be completed quickly. In addition, adequate normative data are reported for kindergarten populations, and evidence is provided concerning the scale's predictive, concurrent, and discriminant validity. The scale may also be helpful in identifying learning problems because it measures behavior that is more task-specific than classroom deportment but more general than academic achievement. Although the scale exhibits adequate internal consistency, test-retest and interrater reliability are not addressed. Finally, the LBS may be suitable as an outcome measure, although this remains unknown in the absence of data demonstrating the scale's sensitivity to short-term instructional modifications.

REVIEWER'S REFERENCE

Edelbrock, C. (1988). Informant reports. In E. S. Shapiro & T. R. Kratochwill (Eds.), *Behavioral assessment in schools: Conceptual foundations and practical applications* (pp. 351-383). New York: Guilford.

[200]

The Learning Channel Preference Checklist.

Purpose: Intended as an "indicator of learning style preference."
Population: Grades 5–13.
Publication Date: 1990.
Acronym: LCPC.
Scores, 3: Visual, Auditory, Haptic.
Administration: Group.
Price Data, 1991: $10.95 per complete kit including manual (8 pages) and 25 checklists.
Time: [15–20] minutes.
Author: Lynn O'Brien.
Publisher: Research for Better Schools.

Review of The Learning Channel Preference Checklist by WILLIAM L. DEATON, Professor and Associate Dean, College of Education, Auburn University, Auburn University, AL:

The Learning Channel Preference Checklist (LCPC) is described as "the quickest, most up-to-date, reliable indicator of learning style preference for students in grades 5–13." The seven-page manual contains three pages of general information about learning styles, a brief discussion of three profiles of scores on the LCPC, three pages of suggestions for visual, auditory, and haptic learners, and a copy of the instrument itself (printed with very light blue ink, presumably to prevent duplication). The 36 sentences to which students respond are written in a clear and understandable manner. Readability analyses of the items conducted by the reviewer produced estimates of reading grade level from 5.0 to 6.0. These estimates do not, of course,

mean that students in grade 5 will be able to read or understand the sentences.

The LCPC manual does not provide evidence to support the claims of the author. Information *not* provided includes the research or theoretical base upon which the LCPC is drawn; the instrument development process; selection of items; item characteristics; item analyses; reliability estimates; evidence of validity; normative data; administration time; appropriateness for different ages, ethnic groups, languages, socioeconomic levels, and gender; and cautions in score interpretation. The manual states that approximately 40% of students demonstrate a visual learning style, less than 15% of the student population shows auditory as their strongest learning channel, and the haptic style is represented by 45% of students on the LCPC. However, because supporting data are not presented, these percentages are not helpful.

The use of three learning styles by the LCPC implies that these are the only learning styles used by individuals. The Learning-Style Inventory (reviewed in the *Tenth Mental Measurements Yearbook*, 10:173), uses four dimensions of learning style: Concrete Experience (feeling), Reflective Observation (watching), Abstract Conceptualization (thinking), and Active Experimentation (doing). The LCPC manual does not address the possibility that learning style may include modes of learning other than visual, auditory, and haptic.

Conflicting terms are used to describe the process of responding to the 36-item instrument. On page 1 of the manual, it is a "self rating inventory" that asks students "to rank their learning preferences." The page containing the LCPC instructs students to "write the number that best describes your reaction to each sentence." The response scale is 5 = *Almost Always*; 4 = *Often*; 3 = *Sometimes*; 2 = *Rarely*; and 1 = *Almost Never*. Thus, it appears that the LCPC is not a checklist nor are ranks used; it is a self-rating inventory.

Three scores are obtained by summing responses to the 12 items presented for each of the three categories to create a Visual, an Auditory, and a Haptic score. The Total score is a sum of the three category scores. The category scores, also referred to as clusters in the manual and channels in the title of the instrument, are converted to percentages by dividing each category score by the total score (the result is a proportion, not a percentage as stated in the manual). The presence of a common denominator for the three category scores produces ipsative scores. Because minimum and maximum scores within the three categories are 12 and 60, respectively, the minimum and maximum percentage scores for each category are 9.1% and 71.4%, respectively, assuming responses to all items. No provisions are made for missing responses to items.

Sample items are not given. Sample responses to items are not provided. No information is provided to explain the basis or rationale for creating the three category scores nor is an explanation given for the unit weighting of responses within each category.

The items in each category are not always conceptually similar. For example, one item in the visual category is "I am able to visualize pictures in my head." Another is "It's hard for me to understand what a person is saying when there is background noise." The second item would appear to belong more to the Auditory category than Visual. "I like to complete one task before starting another" appears in the Auditory category but, because no description of how items were selected is provided, one is left to question the appropriateness of this item as an indicator of auditory learning preference. The manual states, "Students are intensely curious about what the scores mean." The reviewer, too, is intensely curious of the meaning of the scores.

Suggestions for learners in the visual, auditory, and haptic styles are provided for teachers to distribute to students after individual learning styles are assessed. Many of the recommendations restate items on the LCPC. The possibility that learning style may be context specific is not mentioned.

The many shortcomings of the LCPC and manual preclude consideration of its use. No research is referenced to support the claims of the author and, as mentioned previously, no evidence of the psychometric properties of the scores is provided. Users may consider using the LCPC to initiate discussions with students on different study habits, but it cannot be recommended for the assessment of students' learning styles or learning style preferences.

[201]
Learning Preference Inventory.

Purpose: "To assist teachers in the task of identifying individual student learning preferences or styles."
Population: Elementary through adult students.
Publication Dates: 1978–80.
Acronym: LPI.
Scores: 6 preference scores: Sensing-Feeling, Sensing-Thinking, Intuitive-Thinking, Intuitive-Feeling, Introversion, Extraversion.
Administration: Group.
Price Data, 1988: $175 per complete kit including 35 inventories, 35 Student Diagnostic Behavior Checklist folders, 35 individual computer printouts, 1 class profile printout, 1 copy each of Learning Style Inventory and Teaching Style Inventory (for teacher self-assessment), Learning Styles and Strategies Manual, and user's manual ('80, 60 pages); $142 per complete kit without computer scoring; $3 per inventory with prepaid computer scoring; $2 per inventory without computer scoring.
Time: [30] minutes.
Comments: Identifies learning styles based on Jungian typology.
Authors: Harvey F. Silver and J. Robert Hanson.

Publisher: Hanson Silver Strong & Associates, Inc.

TEST REFERENCES
1. Cahill, R., & Madigan, M. J. (1984). The influence of curriculum format on learning preference and learning style. *The American Journal of Occupational Therapy, 38*, 683-686.
2. Ricca, J. (1984). Learning styles and preferred instructional strategies of gifted students. *Gifted Child Quarterly, 28*, 121-126.

Review of the Learning Preference Inventory by BRUCE H. BISKIN, *Senior Psychometrician, American Institute of Certified Public Accountants, New York, NY:*

As described in its User's Manual, the Learning Preference Inventory (LPI) "is designed to assist teachers in the task of identifying individual student learning preferences or styles." The LPI is based on Jung's theory of psychological types and attempts to classify students in terms of their information-processing attitude (introversion [I] vs. extraversion [E]), perceptual function (sensing [S] vs. intuition [N]), and judgment function (thinking [T] vs. feeling [F]). Six scores are calculated—one for each attitude (I and E) and one for each possible combination of functions (ST, SF, NT, NF). Descriptions of "ideal" types representing the four function combinations, as well as the two attitudes, are included in the User's Manual.

Many readers may be familiar with the Myers-Briggs Type Indicator (MBTI; 10:206), which is also a Jungian-based measure of psychological types. The LPI differs from the MBTI in several important ways. First, the LPI is targeted at school-aged children, whereas the MBTI was developed for adults. Second, whereas the MBTI items were written to measure single dimensions (e.g., S-N), the LPI items yield scores for dimensional combinations (e.g., SF). Third, the MBTI items require that a choice be made among two or three statements, whereas the LPI requires that preferences be rank ordered.

The LPI comprises 36 item stems, each intended to assess different preferences for learning. Each item is followed by four choices that students rank order in terms of their preference for each.

Hand scoring the LPI is more complex than on many inventories, and some teachers may have trouble manually scoring the LPI accurately in the 2–3 minutes estimated in the User's Manual. Although the User's Manual suggests "older students can score their own inventories," answer sheets should be computer-scanned and scored whenever possible to ensure accuracy. The weighting scheme used in the scoring is not intuitive and, unfortunately, its rationale is not explained.

The LPI booklet I examined was printed in black and white on glossy paper. Because glossy paper is sometimes difficult to read, the publisher should consider printing the LPI on nonreflective paper.

The LPI comes with considerable documentation. My review materials included the *LPI User's*

Manual, a *Teaching Styles & Strategies* manual, and two research monographs. These materials are geared to help the teacher understand Jung's typology, interpret results from the LPI, and provide examples of teaching exercises to use with students having different learning preferences. Teachers may find the pedagogical material useful in developing lesson plans.

Although the documentation may help teachers think about different ways to teach different types of students, it lacks the technical information needed to evaluate the LPI fairly. I was unable to find a statement about the minimum grade or age level for which the LPI is appropriate. The User's Manual does contain instructions for administering the LPI to "younger children" orally, but it provides no evidence to suggest that oral administration results in scores similar to the standard paper-pencil administration. The User's Manual reports no norms or reliability estimates.

The section in the User's Manual describing LPI profiles is confusing because it illustrates various profile configurations, but then does not suggest how the interpretations of these profiles differ.

Documentation to support the LPI's validity was limited to one research monograph describing a factor analysis of the LPI. The monograph was ambiguous about which of the two groups of students reported had its LPI responses factor analyzed. It was also unclear about which factoring method (principal factors or principal components) was used. The LPI's partially ipsative scoring, a result of the ranking procedure, places constraints on the factor structure that probably enhances the appearance of the results. Thus, this study's findings have limited value until they can be supported by further research.

As I noted earlier, I found much of the pedagogical material provided for review interesting. For those teachers who are comfortable with Jung's model, this material may be a useful source of ideas. However, the documentation includes no evidence of validity for differential effectiveness of teaching methods across student LPI types.

SUMMARY. The fundamental problem with the Learning Preference Inventory is the lack of technical information documented in materials available to users. Basic information is missing about its reliability, its validity in classifying student learning preferences, and its usefulness for increasing teaching effectiveness. The manuals and other information provided are aimed at the classroom teacher rather than the measurement specialist. It is laudable to provide "nuts and bolts" information in an administrator's manual and other documents. However, such information is not sufficient for users who wish to evaluate whether a measure suits their purposes. Because the authors include no informa-

tion on norms, reliability, and validity in the documentation, the LPI's adequacy and usefulness as a measure of learning preference is questionable.

I would expect to see information regarding a measure's psychometric characteristics in its manual. A published measure without such information falls far short of the ideals set forth in the *Standards for Educational and Psychological Testing* (AERA, APA, & NCME, 1985). In the absence of information that would allow a user to evaluate its psychometric qualities, the Learning Preference Inventory should be considered a research measure at best. Any teacher using the LPI for diagnostic purposes should interpret student scores with extreme caution.

REVIEWER'S REFERENCE

American Educational Research Association, American Psychological Association, & National Council on Measurement in Education. (1985). *Standards for educational and psychological testing.* Washington, DC: American Psychological Association, Inc.

Review of the Learning Preference Inventory by JEFFREY JENKINS, *Attorney, KeLeher & McLeod, P.A., Albuquerque, NM:*

The Learning Preference Inventory (LPI) is based on Carl Jung's Theory of Psychological Type; such a basis forms a well-known and studied theoretical foundation for assessing student preferences and learning styles. As a component of a larger kit that includes measures for assessing teachers' teaching and learning styles as well as student behaviors, the LPI is an integral part of a program developed to "create a classroom environment that will work for different teaching and learning styles."

The User's Manual outlines five phases for exploring learning styles: Phase 1, Teacher Self Assessment; Phase 2, Collecting Student Data; Phase 3, Scoring, Analyzing and Plotting Student Learning Styles; Phase 4, Using Student Data; and Phase 5, Sharing Student Data. In each phase are step-by-step instructions for analyzing and using learning styles in the classroom. Phases 4 and 5 comprise half of the manual and outline instructional techniques and classroom exercises for teachers. Thus, the User's Manual, unlike a typical test manual, actually serves as an instructional manual that outlines a method of assessing learning styles as well as procedures for applying learning styles in the classroom. This review is limited to consideration of the LPI apart from its companion measures.

The authors of the LPI adapt the Jungian theory of psychological type to theoretically define styles of learning. This adaptation is one of many that have appeared for the measurement of aspects of personality, with perhaps the most well-known of these being the Myers-Briggs Type Indicator (10:206). Whereas the Myers-Briggs provides a broad measure of personality constructs by assessing personal preferences suggested by the Jungian theory, the LPI simplifies these constructs and focuses on those preferences that are found to be most relevant to learning styles.

Briefly, the authors of the LPI characterize learning style in terms of two sets of "functions," Perception and Judgment. The Perception functions are methods of "finding out" about the world either through Sensing ("The sensor assumes that what he sees is what exists") or Intuition ("The intuiter . . . looks at what the potential significance or interpretations of what the situation might be"). Judgment involves the analysis of the perceived information either by Thinking ("based on external and verifiable information") or Feeling (based on "likes and dislikes"). The authors also identify the dimension of Introversion/Extraversion as typifying two "attitudes" that mediate "how the mind processes those data perceived and judged."

The LPI is a 144-item self-report measure that yields a student profile in terms of four learning styles: Sensing-Feeling, Sensing-Thinking, Intuitive-Thinking, and Intuitive-Feeling. Preference scores are computed in each of these areas and ordered according to a student's "dominant" learning style, "auxiliary" style, "supportive" style, or "least used" style. In addition, students' attitudes are designated as either Introversion or Extraversion. Although the 144 items are scored separately, they are presented as 36 statements with four choices each; students rank the choices according to preference. For example, statement number 1 is: "I'm good at: 1._____helping others, 2._____getting things done, 3._____organizing things, 4._____discovering things." The directions for responding are clear and the items are presented on three pages in an easy-to-read format.

Student responses can be hand scored, and detailed but uncomplicated instructions are given. Scoring results in numerical values of 0–125 for each of the four learning styles and a value of 0–80 for attitude. Values indicate the strength of a student's preference for each style and profiles can be summarized graphically.

Although the authors of the User's Manual state the LPI was developed "over a period of five years on a population of 3,000 students in inner city, urban, and suburban environments," no summary of technical characteristics of the Inventory is offered. Thus, although the instrument appears to measure clearly defined and theoretically supportable constructs, there is no evidence the instrument provides any valid or reliable information about learning styles. This is a fatal flaw that should cause any user alarm.

Although teachers may be tempted to try the LPI and its kit as an interesting exploration in learning styles, they are forewarned that use of the LPI as a measure of learning style may be a futile and unwarranted exercise. Although the program of which the LPI is a part may be useful for sensitizing teachers to the potential differences in learning styles that may exist, there is currently little reason to believe the instrument should be used as a diagnostic tool for teaching, learning, and curriculum planning, as claimed by the authors.

[202]
Learning Process Questionnaire.

Purpose: "To assess the extent to which a secondary school student endorses different approaches to learning and the more important motives and strategies comprising those approaches."

Population: Secondary students.

Publication Dates: 1985–87.

Acronym: LPQ.

Scores, 9: Surface Motive, Surface Strategy, Deep Motive, Deep Strategy, Achieving Motive, Achieving Strategy, Surface Approach, Deep Approach, Achieving Approach.

Administration: Individual or group.

Price Data, 1989: A$4.65 per 10 questionnaires; $2.50 per 10 answer sheets; $3 per score key; $29.95 per monograph entitled *Student Approaches to Learning and Studying* ('87, 151 pages); $12.70 per manual ('87, 36 pages).

Time: 20(40) minutes.

Comments: Tertiary counterpart of the Study Process Questionnaire (389).

Author: John Biggs.

Publisher: Australian Council for Educational Research Ltd. [Australia].

Cross References: For a review by Cathy W. Hall of the Study Process Questionnaire, see 389.

TEST REFERENCES
1. Ramsden, P., Martin, E., & Bowden, J. (1989). School environment and sixth form pupils' approaches to learning. *British Journal of Educational Psychology, 59,* 129-142.

Review of the Learning Process Questionnaire and the Study Process Questionnaire by ROBERT D. BROWN, Carl A. Happold Distinguished Professor of Educational Psychology, University of Nebraska-Lincoln, Lincoln, NE:

The Learning Process Questionnaire (LPQ) and the Study Process Questionnaire (SPQ) are highly related instruments designed to assess the motives, strategies, and approaches that students use to learn and to study. The LPQ is intended for high school students and the SPQ for college students. The instruments were designed by Australian John Biggs and much of the research performed on the instruments is based on Australian subjects.

The self-report questionnaires ask students questions that attempt to measure whether they approach learning and studying primarily from a Surface Motive (to meet minimal standards), a Deep Motive (an intrinsic interest in learning), or from an Achieving Motive (interest in competition and doing well). Corollary strategies are assessed to again determine whether strategies used are Surface (bare essentials learned through rote learning), Deep (attempts to grasp meaning and interrelationships), or Achieving (being well organized). Subscale scores are obtained for Motive and Strategy within each of the three basic approaches: Surface, Deep, and Achieving. The summation of the Motive and Strategy scores yield scale scores for each, referred to as the Approach scores. The sum of the Approach Scores for the Deep and Achieving scales is used as a Composite Approach Score. Thus, there are six subscale scores: Surface Motive and Surface Strategy, Deep Motive and Deep Strategy, and Achieving Motive and Achieving Strategy; three scale scores: Surface Approach, Deep Approach, and Achieving Approach; and one composite score.

The LPQ has 36 items (6 items per subscale) and the SPQ has 42 items (7 items per subscale). Each item asks the respondent to indicate whether the item is 1 = "never or only rarely true of me" or on up the 5-point scale to "is always or almost always true of me." Norms are available for secondary and tertiary students.

The instruments are derived from research on the learning and study process that has centered in Australia. The basic theory is cognitive and assumes that students vary in motives and strategies, study and learn differently, and should be taught differently. Students using surface strategies will learn unintegrated details, those using deep strategies will learn the meaning and interrelationships, and those using achieving strategies will study whatever is necessary to achieve high grades. Students may have a typically used strategy for all subjects, but may also vary their strategies from subject matter to subject matter depending on their interests.

The Research Monograph accompanying the test materials is replete with scale analysis data and reliability and validity information obtained in numerous studies involving the two instruments with correlations available between the scales and a variety of other student variables ranging from fathers' education to locus of control scores. The test author characterizes the test-retest reliability coefficients ranging from .49 to .72 for the subscales across two studies as "highly satisfactory" given that the responses could be affected by interventions, time of year of administration (e.g., just before final exams), and other variables that could affect responses. As might be expected, the scale scores have reported higher test-retest reliability (.60 to .78) and measures of internal consistency are typically in the .70s. These reliability estimates might be more accurately characterized as "good" or "satisfactory" and minimally sufficient for use in working with individual students.

Validity studies lend support to the construct validity of the instruments. Factor analysis supports the scale structure and though labelled differently, other researchers have also reported the distinctions between motivations and strategies, and between deep and surface approaches. Generally, the results support the instruments at the same time they provide disquieting information about what happens to students. Students with high LPQ scores on Deep Approach and Achieving Approach, for example, were more likely to have plans for future education and parents who had more education. Gender differences interacted with the various scale scores with boys, for example, scoring lower on Deep Approaches on the LPQ with increasing years in school. Studies of college students on the SPQ yielded similar results, but interactions were found between the kind of institution and score patterns.

More work needs to be done before these instruments can be highly recommended for use in counseling individual students, but these instruments and others like them can prove to be valuable tools for research on how college and high school students learn and study. The author provides general thoughts about counseling students with different profiles on the scales. As rough guidelines, these can be useful, but counselors must be alert to how the specific context of the test administration may have affected the student's responses. The implications of patterns of group scores for teaching may be more useful as instructors gain insights as to what will and will not work for students who use primarily deep strategies as opposed to those who use primarily surface strategies. The instruments could be invaluable for researchers investigating the impact of intervention programs, particularly the value of teaching metacognition skills and trying to strengthen the metalearning capabilities, on student learning.

Before deciding whether or not to use this particular set of instruments for counseling individual students, intervening with different instructional strategies, or conducting research on the cognitive process, the decision maker should at least examine other available tools such as the Approaches to Studying Inventory (Entwistle & Ramsden, 1983) and the Inventory of Learning Processes (Schmeck & Ribich, 1978). These instruments were designed by researchers pursuing similar lines of inquiry and their instruments and their respective subscales are similar to those of the LPQ and SPQ. Research results thus far are not sufficient to make conclusive comments about how much these instruments are measuring similar or identical constructs (Speth & Brown, 1988). Test users for any purpose will want to read carefully the specific items in these instruments to determine whether or not the phrasing is appropriate for American students.

These instruments, and others like them, could have a significant impact on future education even if they do no more than sensitize school and college instructors to individual differences among their students and alert them that how they teach and test affects what and how students learn.

REVIEWER'S REFERENCES

Schmeck, R. R., & Ribich, F. D. (1978). Construct validation of the Inventory of Learning Processes. *Applied Psychological Measurement, 2*, 551-562.

Entwistle, N. J., & Ramsden, P. (1983). *Understanding student learning.* London: Croom Helm.

Speth, C., & Brown, R. D. (1988). Study approaches, processes and strategies: Are three perspectives better than one? *British Journal of Educational Psychology, 58*, 247-257.

Review of the Learning Process Questionnaire by CATHY W. HALL, Assistant Professor of Psychology, East Carolina University, Greenville, NC:

The Learning Process Questionnaire (LPQ) is a 36-item, self-report questionnaire that measures the process factors of learning strategies and learning motives used by secondary students. The Study Process Questionnaire is an extended version of the LPQ for use with tertiary students. A student's approach to a given learning situation is seen as a function of both a motive and a strategy. A surface approach would entail meeting the basic requirements of a learning situation by the rote learning of information for the sole purpose of passing a test. The student demonstrating intrinsic motivation with a strong desire to gain additional information and knowledge would be employing a deep approach. The achieving approach is concerned with being regarded as competent in the subject area and the strategy employed would be organized and systematic study in order to obtain this goal. These three approaches are not necessarily exclusive, however. It is possible for a student to demonstrate a deep-achieving or surface-achieving approach.

Three primary learning approaches are measured (Surface, Deep, and Achieving) with each factor having two subscales consisting of motives and strategies for a total of nine scores. The range of scores is 6 to 30 for each of the motive and strategy subscales. Scoring of the LPQ may be done by hand, machine, computer, or by sending the protocols to the Australian Council for Educational Research.

The purpose of the LPQ is to better assess students' approaches to learning and make appropriate instructional decisions as well as possible referrals. Profiles are obtained for the students and possible implications for learning are discussed. For example, a student demonstrating a surface-achieving profile is cognizant of the need to do well but he/she may be approaching the learning situation by using rote memory and reproduction. This may lead to a lower achievement level than he/she wants and counseling could be warranted to help modify his/her strategies.

The LPQ was standardized on an Australian student population of 14-year-olds ($N = 1,366$) and Year 11 students ($N = 985$). A random sampling was achieved through the assistance of the Australian Council for Educational Research. Tables of norms are provided in the manual for males ($N = 1,117$) and females ($N = 1,234$) to be used in converting raw scores to decile scaled scores for Motives and Strategies (Surface, Deep, and Achieving) and Approaches (Surface, Deep, and Achieving). Significant effects for gender and year level supported the utilization of separate norms for the two age groups and genders (Biggs, 1987). Decile standard scores provide information on where a student falls (low, average, high) on the scales in comparison to the standardization group.

Reliability and validity data are presented in the manual. Test-retest reliability data yielded correlations ranging from .49 to .72 and demonstrated reasonable stability over a 4-month period. Internal consistency data also demonstrated satisfactory results with a range of .45 to .78. Construct validity was assessed by utilizing students' estimates of their performance, how satisfied they were with their performance, future educational goals, and correlations with a performance exam administered 15 months after the LPQ administration.

The manual does not provide information on minority representation, demographic variables, or socioeconomic status. However, a detailed account of these variables can be found in *Student Approaches to Learning and Studying* (Biggs, 1987). In addition to the above variables, Biggs' text offers detailed information concerning theoretical development, relevant research, and implications for the use of the LPQ.

Utilization of the LPQ outside Australia needs to be done with the understanding that the norms are limited. Future research with the LPQ in other countries needs to determine if the three factors (Surface, Deep, and Achieving) are identified in other populations. For example, in one study by Ramsden and Entwistle (1981) four factors emerged, three very similar to Biggs' and one additional factor they termed "disorganized and dilatory."

The LPQ provides a promising research tool for the assessment of learning approaches and for studying the development of metacognition. The author in no way suggests that the surface, deep, and achieving approaches are the only factors. Biggs (1987) suggests that certain strategies may indeed be taught. He also stresses the importance of future research in this area. The distinction between availability and production is made in regard to the teaching of strategies as well as personality factors such as internal versus external locus of control. It is strongly suggested that anyone choosing to utilize the LPQ also acquire the text, *Student Approaches to Learning and Studying* (Biggs, 1987).

REVIEWER'S REFERENCES

Ramsden, P., & Entwistle, N. (1981). Effects of academic departments on students' approaches to studying. *British Journal of Educational Psychology, 51*, 368-383.

Biggs, J. (1987). *Student approaches to learning and studying.* Melbourne: Australian Council for Educational Research Ltd.

[203]
Learning Style Inventory [Price Systems, Inc.].

Purpose: "Identifies those elements that are critical to an individual's learning style . . . [and] aids in prescribing the type of environment, instructional activities, social grouping(s), and motivating factors that maximize personal achievement."

Population: Grades 3–12.

Publication Dates: 1976–87.

Acronym: LSI.

Scores: 22 areas: Noise Level, Light, Temperature, Design, Motivation, Persistent, Responsible, Structure, Learning Alone/Peer Oriented, Authority Figures Present, Learn in Several Ways, Auditory, Visual, Tactile, Kinesthetic, Requires Intake, Evening/Morning, Late Morning, Afternoon, Needs Mobility, Parent Figure Motivated, Teacher Motivated, plus a Consistency score.

Administration: Group.

Price Data, 1987: $2.50 per 10 answer sheets for grades 3 and 4 or for grades 5 and above; $.40 per individual interpretative booklet; $9.50 per manual ('87, 109 pages); $3.25 per research report; $295 per computerized self-administered inventory program with 100 administrations ($60 per 100 additional administrations) (specify IBM or Apple); $395 per Scan and Score program; $.60 per answer forms to use with Scan and Score; $4 or less per individual profile available from publisher's scoring service; $7.50 or less per group and subscale summaries summaries available from publisher only in addition to individual profiles.

Time: (20–30) minutes.

Comments: Apple, IBM, or IBM-compatible computer required for (optional) computerized administration; 3000 or 3051 NCS scanner required for (optional) Scan and Score system.

Authors: Rita Dunn, Kenneth Dunn, and Gary E. Price.

Publisher: Price Systems, Inc.

TEST REFERENCES

1. Carbo, M. (1984). Research in learning style and reading: Implications for instruction. *Theory Into Practice, 23* (1), 72-76.
2. Dunn, R. (1984). Learning style: State of the science. *Theory Into Practice, 23* (1), 10-19.
3. Dunn, R., Krimsky, J. S., Murray, J. B., & Quinn, P. J. (1985). Light up their lives: A review of research on the effects of lighting on children's achievement and behavior. *The Reading Teacher, 38,* 863-869.
4. Biberman, G., & Buchanan, J. (1986). Learning style and study skills differences across business and other academic majors. *Journal of Education for Business, 61,* 303-307.
5. Della Valle, J., Dunn, K., Dunn, R., Geisert, G., Sinatra, R., & Zenhausern, R. (1986). The effects of matching and mismatching students' mobility preference on recognition and memory tasks. *The Journal of Educational Research, 79,* 267-272.
6. Atkinson, G. (1990). Kolb's Learning Style Inventory: a practitioner's perspective. *Measurement and Evaluation in Counseling and Development, 23,* 149-161.

Review of the Learning Style Inventory [Price Systems, Inc.] by JAN N. HUGHES, Associate Professor of Educational Psychology, Texas A&M University, College Station, TX:

Research and test development in the field of individual learning styles has been plagued by poor attention to issues of construct validity and theoretical development. The authors of the Learning Style Inventory (LSI) have not improved upon this state of affairs. Rather, their instrument exemplifies all of the problems characteristic of instruments designed to measure learning styles.

The authors' failure to provide a clear, theoretically based definition of learning styles contributes to their difficulty in establishing the content and construct validity of the LSI. The authors state the purpose of the LSI is to aid "in prescribing the type of environment, instructional activities, social grouping(s), and motivating factors that maximize personal achievement" (p. 5, manual). In the authors' published articles concerning the LSI (e.g., Griggs & Dunn, 1984), they clearly state the instrument is a diagnostic one, permitting educators to match instructional environments and activities to individual characteristics. This claim is not supported by the limited published data on the LSI.

The LSI has undergone several revisions since 1974, and it is impossible to know to which version information in the manual on reliability, item development, and construct validity pertains. In its current form, the inventory consists of 104 items that are grouped into 22 scales. Scores for each scale are reported as standard scores with a mean of 50 and a standard deviation of 10. The relationship between the subscales and the four types of preferences the instrument purportedly measures is not addressed, and the number of items on each scale is not provided. Given the small number of items on which at least some of the scale scores are based, it is likely the scales do not possess adequate reliability to make the type of diagnostic decisions for which the authors recommend the test's use. The authors do report reliability coefficients on the internal consistency for the scales, which range from .40 to .84. Most of these reliability coefficients are too low to justify making instructional decisions. Furthermore, the groups on which these coefficients were obtained are not adequately defined.

The types of student preferences the scale purports to measure include temperature (defined simply as "Many students 'can't think' when they feel hot, and others can't when they feel cold"); structure (student needs or does not need structure); and modality (e.g., auditory, kinesthetic, tactile, visual). The authors ignore an impressive amount of literature that lends no support to the educational usefulness of such factors on learning.

The authors do not provide evidence of the instrument's test-retest reliability, with the exception of one unpublished study that found one scale to be consistent across administrations. Given the instrument's widespread use in schools and the importance of demonstrating test-retest in any measure used to predict optimal learning environments, the lack of test-retest data is appalling.

The authors provide no information on the normative group on which the standard scores are derived, other than to state that the norms are based on "more than 500,000 students" (p. 11). In light of this paucity of information, the provided norms are meaningless.

The authors state the LSI was developed through "a content and factor analysis" (p. 6). Evidently, content validity refers to the authors' intuition as to which types of student preferences affect achievement. Results of factor analysis are reported for an earlier version of the LSI, for which the number of items is not given in the manual but is something less than 223 items. The principal components factor analysis resulted in 32 factors, each with an eigenvalue greater than 1.0, which collectively explained 62% of the variance. Because factor analysis is a device for simplifying correlations between related variables, the 32-factor solution does not accomplish what factor analysis is intended to do. Of greater significance is that the relationship between the factor structure and the authors' conceptualization of learning style is not addressed. Thus, the factor analysis represents a confused use of a sophisticated statistical tool, and the reported results obfuscate rather than clarify the constructs underlying the LSI. The authors do not apply acceptable rules for retaining factors, do not provide data on the number of items that load on each factor, and do not provide factor loadings of items.

A well-conducted factor analysis of the 104-item version of the LSI was reported by Ferrell (1983). Ferrell extracted four factors from the LSI, accounting for 23.5% of the variance. Sixty of the items loaded on one factor only. Twelve items had salient loadings on more than one factor, and 32 had no salient loadings. An inspection of the factor loadings provided no support for the authors' conceptualization of learning styles. Only the first factor was interpretable.

The manual is written to sell rather than to inform. The heavy use of statistical jargon and the exaggerated claims of the test's construct and predictive validity will impress the psychometrically naive reader. The unsophisticated reader will assume the 147 references provided attest to the instrument's scientific respectability. A closer inspection of these references reveals that a majority are unpublished dissertations, most of which were conducted under the supervision of one of the authors, Gary Price. The remaining references are nonempirical studies with titles such as "Breakthrough: How to Improve Early Reading Instruction" (Dunn, Carbo, & Burton, 1981). A search of PsychLIT (1974–1988) revealed two empirical studies on the LSI,

both of which provided negative results (Pettigrew & Buell, 1986; Ferrell, 1983). Neither of these studies were referenced in the LSI manual.

The critical test of the validity of a prescriptive instrument is evidence the test predicts the conditions under which learning is optimized. The manual includes numerous recommendations for individualizing instruction based on students' scores on the 22 scales. Although it would be easy to design an experiment to test for such aptitude-treatment interactions, these investigations have not been undertaken.

In summary, the LSI has no redeeming values. Many of its limitations also apply to other measures of individual learning styles. Research to date has not supported the individual learning-styles paradigm. Whether this failure is attributable to inadequate measurement or to a faulty paradigm cannot yet be determined. If one is determined to use a measure of learning styles, he or she should consider Kolb's Learning-Style Inventory (Kolb, 1976; 10:173), for which some evidence of construct validity is available. Currently, no instrument provides a good substitute for a teacher's careful observations of student behavior and systematic collection of data to provide confirming or disconfirming evidence of hypotheses based on such observations.

REVIEWER'S REFERENCES

Kolb, D. A. (1976). *Learning-Style Inventory: Technical manual*. Boston, MA: McBer and Company.
Dunn, R., Carbo, M., & Burton, E. (1981). Breakthrough: How to improve early reading instruction. *Kappan, 62* (9), 675.
Ferrell, B. G. (1983). A factor analytic comparison of four learning styles instruments. *Journal of Educational Psychology, 75*, 33-39.
Griggs, S. A., & Dunn, R. (1984). Selected case studies of the learning style preferences of gifted students. *Gifted Child Quarterly, 28* (3), 115-119.
Pettigrew, F. E., & Buell, C. M. (1986). Relation of two perceptual styles to learning a novel motor skill. *Perceptual and Motor Skills, 63*, 1097-1098.

Review of the Learning Style Inventory [Price Systems, Inc.] by ALIDA S. WESTMAN, Professor of Psychology, Eastern Michigan University, Ypsilanti, MI:

The Learning Style Inventory (LSI) consists of 104 questions which take about 20 to 30 minutes to answer. The items are meant to explore some important aspects of the way in which a pupil prefers to learn (see the test entry above). The LSI explores some environmental, personality, social, and biological factors. The factors are well described and interpretation is easy. Application of the findings assumes that a pupil is adjusted enough to learn and that the pupil and teacher can implement the findings (for example, the time of day when learning is easiest).

ANSWER SHEET AND QUESTIONS. Some aspects of the LSI decrease ease of use and reliability. I will describe five of these. First, the instructions are in small print against the side of the identification box on the answer sheet and are easily overlooked. The vocabulary (e.g., "reliable") is too advanced for children. Second, some questions are repeated as a consistency check. However, the instructions not only point out that there are repetitions, they also tell the child to answer the questions the same way the second time as the first time. This means the child is urged to remember his or her answers. The child also may feel compelled to look back. Therefore, the consistency check is confounded by the instructions. Third, only three response alternatives are used with grades 3 and 4, whereas a five-alternative Likert scale is used with older children. This incompatibility is not explained and in my experience is unnecessary. Fourth, some of the questions are simplistic and thereby may contribute to unreliability. For example, one question asks whether quiet is needed to study, but the material to be studied is not indicated and the answer may depend on what comes to the child's mind. The problem is noted in the Manual (pp. 34–35) but not resolved. Fifth, some questions are confusing. For example, Item 31 states, "I like to feel what I learn inside." Inside a classroom or the body? And is the subject matter bacteria, poisonous snakes, or shapes?

RESEARCH DESIGN AND STATISTICS. There are some attempts to establish a research base for the LSI, but many statistical problems are apparent. On occasion, the number of pupils studied was far too low to permit statistical analysis. For example, in one study the number of pupils in each condition was 3, 2, 4, 3, and 7, respectively (Manual, p. 41). In an analysis by grade, 11 boys and 11 girls represented the first grade (Research Report, p. 4). Much research is cited, which could be a strength, but usually only probability levels are indicated, whereas means, SDs, or F-values are not, and therefore interpretation of the research is difficult or impossible. For example, sometimes significant interactions are cited, but the results are described as main effects. Sex is said to interact with learning style in one case, such that both sexes do better in one condition than in another (Manual, p. 62, number 2). This is not interpretable without means. Sometimes the probability level indicates nonsignificant results, but subsequent interpretations are made as though the probability levels were significant (see Manual, pp. 51–52 and 79 for examples). With respect to the type of statistics used, 48 separate one-way analyses of variance were done for sex (Research Report, p. 12), even though much better statistical procedures are available. The corresponding table is mislabelled; it reads ANOVA *within* grades and should read *across* grades. It also is not clear which 500,000 people's scores were used to develop the standard scores (Manual, p. 11).

EXPENSIVE AND DIFFICULT TO USE. For many schools the test may cost $1 for each student if answer sheets need to be sent to the publisher for scoring. Group summaries cost extra. One group of principals found the LSI too expensive and demanding to use (NASSP, 1979, pp. 83–84). Sale of a template overlay for hand scoring would be very welcome.

VALIDITY. Content validity is based, in part, on a factor analysis. The factors seem logical.

RELIABILITY. The reliability coefficients cited are low to moderate. It would be worthwhile to investigate further why they are so low. A few reasons are mentioned above. Hoyt reliability for the English test showed a range of .35 to .85 for grades 3 and 4 combined and a range of .40 to .84 for grades 5 through 12 combined. The French edition showed a range of .18 to .85 for grades 6 through 12 combined. Test-retest reliability on an unspecified population with delay of unknown duration showed reliability coefficients between .43 and .69, except for one of .74 and one of .00 (Manual, p. 102, Table 4, which seems not to be mentioned in the text anywhere).

SUMMARY. The LSI provides some good indices on aspects of learning style. Application assumes that pupils are sufficiently adjusted to learn and that both they and their teachers can use the information gathered (e.g., whether to permit food intake during study). Many other learning-style indicators exist that also are helpful and many of these will be cheaper and less cumbersome to obtain than the LSI. To put the indices and learning styles into perspective, I recommend the books listed below.

REVIEWER'S REFERENCES

National Association of Secondary School Principals (NASSP). (1979). *Student learning styles.* Reston, VA: The Association.
National Association of Secondary School Principals (NASSP). (1982). *Student learning styles and brain behavior.* Reston, VA: The Association.
Wittrock, M. C. (Ed.). (1986). *Handbook of research on teaching* (3rd ed.). New York: Macmillan.

[204]

Learning Styles and Strategies.

Purpose: "Assists teachers and administrators in better understanding their own learning and teaching styles."
Population: Teachers.
Publication Date: 1980.
Scores, 4: Sensing/Feeling, Sensing/Thinking, Intuitive/Thinking, Intuitive/Feeling.
Administration: Group.
Price Data, 1988: $25 per manual (130 pages) including Learning Style Inventory and Teaching Style Inventory.
Time: Administration times not reported.
Comments: Self-administered, self-scored; tests available as separates.
Authors: Harvey F. Silver and J. Robert Hanson.
Publisher: Hanson Silver Strong & Associates, Inc.

a) LEARNING STYLE INVENTORY.
Purpose: "A self-diagnostic tool for adults to assess learning styles preferences."
Price Data: $2 per inventory including scoring key and information.

b) TEACHING STYLE INVENTORY.

Purpose: "A self-diagnostic tool to identify one's preferred teaching style."

Price Data: $2 per inventory including scoring key and information.

Review of Learning Styles and Strategies by BERT A. GOLDMAN, Professor of Education, University of North Carolina, Greensboro, NC:

The Teacher Self-Assessment (Learning Styles and Strategies) Manual includes information concerning two instruments: the Learning Style Inventory and the Teaching Style Inventory.

Authors Hanson and Silver based their instruments on Carl Gustav Jung's Theory of Psychological Types about which they provide the reader a description and explanation. Their description and explanation of Jung's theory is detailed and informative.

Following the presentation of Jungian theory, the reader is led through a series of "warm-up" activities to introduce the process of self-analysis of one's learning style. These activities are followed by the Learning Style Inventory which, contrary to the authors' statement of being a "simple self-descriptive instrument," appears to this reviewer to be rather complex. It includes the four processes of (*a*) choosing self-descriptors through a weighting system, (*b*) preparing the self-analysis profile by rank ordering the styles, (*c*) computing the learning preference score for each of the learning styles, and (*d*) analyzing the learning preferences by plotting a learning profile. All of this is succeeded by a description of four possible profiles, any one of which might emerge. Next the reader is asked to read descriptions of each of the four basic learning styles and to rank order them according to how characteristic each one is of the reader. Following this task the reader is asked to compare the ranking with the results obtained from the Learning Style Inventory by being led through a series of 17 self-diagnostic questions. This exercise is succeeded by a checklist of abilities for each of the learning styles. Those the reader would like to expand are to be checked and the strongest abilities identified by placing a plus sign next to them.

Any reader not exhausted at this point should not despair for there is more to come. Now the authors provide the reader with a series of "warm-up" activities to prepare for the self-analysis of one's teaching style. These activities include three sets of myriad tasks and questions. Then the Teaching Style Inventory is proclaimed by the authors to be a simple self-descriptive instrument. First there are 10 sets of four behaviors, each set to be ranked in order of preference. Next, the reader is asked to rank the four teaching styles according to how characteristic each is of the reader. This is followed by a request to complete the Teaching Style Profile. Now the reader

is ready to compare the reader's personal analysis of teaching style preference with the style obtained from the Teaching Style Inventory. Next, the reader is led through a procedure for scoring teaching preferences and a few ways of interpreting the inventory are presented. Then several pages of detailed descriptions of the four teaching styles are presented so that the reader can rank them to further analyze the reader's teaching style. For the eager reader who has survived the preceding exercises there are yet several pages of questions and checklists and checklists and questions to enable the teacher to indulge in further self-assessment of teaching.

Having read through the entire manual, which includes both the Learning Style Inventory and the Teaching Style Inventory, it appears to this reviewer that one cannot just respond to each of the instruments in order to evaluate one's learning and teaching styles. Instead it appears to this reviewer that one should engage in all of the exercises compiled in the manual in addition to addressing all items of both instruments in order to gain a comprehensive understanding of one's learning and teaching styles. A very cumbersome task, indeed!

The introduction to the manual indicates that its purpose "is to assist classroom teachers in diagnosing learning styles" and the Teaching Style Inventory indicates that its purpose is "to help you identify your own teaching profile based on your preferences for particular behaviors." Thus, the entire manual and the two instruments that it contains appear to be designed for teachers. However, publisher's promotional materials tout the manual as a publication "for teachers and administrators." Nowhere does the manual indicate its use by administrators. However, it is conceivable that administrators may be interested in identifying their learning style but for administrators, there appears to be no application for teaching style.

C. G. Jung's treatment of psychological type is nicely described in the manual as is its use as a basis for the development of the Teaching Style and Learning Style Inventories. This reviewer finds the initial chapter of the manual entitled "Dealing with Diversity" to be trite, trivial, and warranting deletion. Further, the illustrations included in the chapter as well as those throughout the publication are childishly insulting for any educator attempting to take the material seriously.

Not a single shred of evidence concerning the reliability and validity of either the Learning Style or the Teaching Style Inventories appears in the manual. Nor is there presented any evidence of validity supporting the Jungian personality theory upon which the two inventories are based.

Authors Hanson and Silver have identified two important educational processes that, if accurately assessed, could no doubt provide teachers with valuable information useful to their teaching decisions. Until the authors provide evidence their instruments are indeed reliable and valid, however, one should proceed with caution in their use.

Review of Learning Styles and Strategies by DAN WRIGHT, School Psychologist, Ralston Public Schools, Ralston, NE:

The Learning Styles and Strategies manual is one of a series of manuals developed by the authors to promote more effective teaching through processes of self-assessment and self-guided study. The entire series is based on the Jungian theory of personality types and its application to the teaching/learning process. Central to the part of the process embodied in this manual is the self-assessment by teachers of their own learning and teaching styles. Two brief inventories are employed in this task: the Learning Style Inventory and the Teaching Style Inventory. Each of these purports to analyze one's mode of functioning according to the feeling/thinking and sensing/intuiting dimensions of personality proposed by Jung. Results of the inventories are intended to give a measure of one's relative predisposition toward each of the four categories or styles yielded by the conjunction of these dimensions. The manual also provides some interpretive information dealing with the assets and liabilities that typify each style.

The inventories themselves are brief and simple, requiring test-takers to rate descriptions of behavioral or classroom characteristics according to preference. The Learning Style Inventory presents 20 sets of behavioral descriptors to be rated and should take less than half an hour to complete, including scoring. The Teaching Style Inventory presents 10 sets of classroom descriptions to be rated, and should take a bit longer to complete. Results are self-scored and self-interpreted according to guidelines presented in the manual.

Very little can be said about the adequacy of these two inventories for their intended purposes. The authors provide absolutely no information regarding test development. Although results from the inventories are ipsative, indicating only the strength of an individual's preferences relative to each other, items should have been developed through trials with various pools of subjects. However, there is no reference to any sort of subject group, nor any information supporting the reliability of results. According to a research monograph provided by the publisher at the reviewer's request (Research Monograph #4, undated), initial item development for an apparently similar inventory (the Learning Preference Inventory) was accomplished with a sample of 600 third through sixth grade students in New Jersey. If the methodology employed for the development of the teachers' inventories was similar,

there is some cause for concern. Factory analytic treatment of item responses appears to have been somewhat unorthodox. Responses were compared *across* items after having been ranked *within* items; this would compromise the correlation matrix by restricting the variance for the group of responses presented with each item stem. The implications of this practice are unclear, but troubling.

Despite the basis of the inventories in recognized theory, there is no information presented regarding validity. According to the research monograph, the inventories were patterned, at least in part, on the Myers-Briggs Type Indicator (Briggs, K. C., Myers, I. B., & McCaulley, M. H., 1985; 10:206). Validity studies with the Myers-Briggs inventory would appear to be a necessary and early step in development, but no references to such appear in either the manual or the monograph. These inventories rest on face validity, period. Because of this, as well as the lack of information on reliability and item development, the inventories cannot literally be considered assessment instruments at all; at the present time, they must be considered as more similar to the self-assessment quizzes that frequently appear in popular magazines.

The unfortunate implication is that the process of guided study that follows the inventories is without foundation. Theory, educational practice, and test validity are all tightly linked in these inventories. As Wiggins (1989) observed of the Myers-Briggs Type Indicator, a construct-oriented test cannot be validated outside the bounds of the theory on which it is based. Thus, the soundness of the authors' observations and recommendations cannot be separated from the applicability of Jung's theories to education or from the validity of these inventories in particular. The authors may have much to say that is relevant to the improvement of teaching, but there is no reason to be confident their insights can be directed to individuals based on their learning or teaching styles. For example, teachers who complete the inventories are referred to descriptions of their type of learner or teacher, based on their dominant and auxiliary styles of functioning. The descriptions read rather like a horoscope, with many general statements that are either flattering or challenging. Most readers will likely identify with some of the characteristics in each of the descriptions, which is to be expected of an ipsative profile and which is acknowledged by the authors. Although one is directed by the inventories to a description of a dominant style, we must ask: If the descriptions were scrambled so they no longer matched inventory results, would anyone suspect? Without further information, we cannot suppose they would.

In summary, the inventories contained in the Learning Styles and Strategies manual must be considered of tentative utility at best. No great harm is likely to come of their use, but there is no reason to consider them adequate for their intended purpose. It is incumbent upon the authors to provide support for the technical adequacy of the inventories, because they provide the foundation for users' further self-study. This is a minimal and necessary (but not sufficient) step in demonstrating the overall value of their materials.

REVIEWER'S REFERENCES

Briggs, K. C., Myers, I. B., & McCaulley, M. H. (1985). Myers-Briggs Type Indicator. Palo Alto, CA: Consulting Psychologists Press, Inc.

Wiggins, J. S. (1989). [Review of the Myers-Briggs Type Indicator.] In J. C. Conoley & J. J. Kramer (Eds.), *The tenth mental measurements yearbook* (pp. 537-538). Lincoln, NE: Buros Institute of Mental Measurements.

Research Monograph #4. (undated). Moorestown, NJ: Hanson Silver Strong & Associates, Inc.

[205]
Leatherman Leadership Questionnaire.

Purpose: "To aid in selecting supervisors, providing specific feedback to participants on their leadership knowledge for career counseling, conducting accurate needs analysis, and screening for assessment centers or giving pre/post assessment feedback."

Population: Managers, supervisors, and prospective supervisors.

Publication Date: 1987.

Acronym: LLQ.

Scores, 28: Assigning Work, Career Counseling, Coaching Employees, One-on-One Oral Communication, Managing Change, Handling Employee Complaints, Dealing with Employee Conflicts, Counseling Employees, Helping an Employee Make Decisions, Delegating, Taking Disciplinary Action, Handling Emotional Situations, Setting Goals/Planning with Employees, Handling Employee Grievances, Conducting Employee Meetings, Giving Positive Feedback, Negotiating, Conducting Performance Appraisals, Establishing Performance Standards, Persuading/Influencing Employees, Making Presentations to Employees, Problem Solving with Employees, Conducting Selection Interviews, Team Building, Conducting Termination Interviews, Helping an Employee Manage Time, One-on-One Training, Total.

Subtests: May be administered in separate sessions.

Administration: Individual or group.

Price Data, 1989: $600 per complete set including 12 overhead transparencies, manual (336 pages), 10 sets of reusable test booklets (may be reproduced for local use), NCS computer-scored answer sheets, and scoring service for 10 participants; $30 for each additional set of test booklets; $30 for each additional set of answer sheets including scoring service; $75 per additional manual; $1 each for "confidential service" (participant's scoring sheet sealed in an envelope).

Time: (300–325) minutes for battery; (150–165) minutes per part.

Comments: Complete test administered in 2 parts; machine scored by publisher only (present norm of 5,000 participants); use of overhead projector for group instructions recommended; materials and scoring for legitimate research provided without charge.

Author: Richard W. Leatherman.

Publisher: International Training Consultants, Inc.

Review of the Leatherman Leadership Questionnaire by WALTER KATKOVSKY, Professor of Psychology, Northern Illinois University, DeKalb, IL:

Carefully packaged in a carrying case, the Leatherman Leadership Questionnaire (LLQ) consists of 339 multiple-choice questions, divided into 27 supervisory tasks, that require 5 to 6 hours of testing time. A detailed administrative guide and overhead transparencies are included for group administration. Designed to be a "knowledge-based" measure of supervisory leadership, the criteria of "correct" responses and of the differential weights given items for scoring purposes were determined by the judgments of eight experts in management, supervision, and human resource development. Correct answers, item weights, and scoring procedures are not presented in the manual, and scoring and analysis require sending the completed answer sheet to a scoring service.

Two reports are returned. The first is directed to the organization and compares the scores on the 27 supervisory tasks of all subjects in that group with one another and with an "international population's average" (based on "everyone who has taken the LLQ") so that the group's strengths and weaknesses (needs) can be identified. The second report is on the individual, presenting and comparing his or her scores with other subjects in the organization and with the international averages, and designating the individual's strengths and needs.

A lengthy research report is included in the Administrator's Manual that contains commentary on competing measures and describes research conducted on the LLQ. The first phase of the research reports on the development of the instrument and its content validity. Beginning with the identification of distinctive supervisory tasks and effective ways of dealing with them culled from the literature, the instrument's content validity was established by agreement of six out of eight of the expert panel members on the importance of the tasks and the "correct" answers to items. Apparently, however, judgments concerning correct answers involved a suggestive bias in that the "correct" answers were presented to the judges with instructions to "agree" or "disagree" with them, rather than have the judges answer the actual test items independently.

An apparent problem in the construct validity of the LLQ concerns the differential weights assigned to items. The report notes that in addition to the experts, 229 subjects from seven organizations also "ranked" (actually rated) the tasks for their importance in a supervisory job, and that these ratings, together with the experts' ratings of the importance of tasks and behaviors, were "used in calculating the final score." Not only are the procedures for using the judgments of the different groups not explained clearly, but the report misinterprets the findings.

A statistically significant analysis of variance F of 2.4 is reported between groups' judgments, indicating differences in the importance they attached to the tasks for supervisory leadership. These findings, however, are erroneously cited in the report as a "correlation" that indicates the groups rated the tasks "similarly" (p. 77). The differences in judgments found concerning the importance of the tasks for supervision calls into question an underlying assumption of the LLQ, that distinctive areas of supervisory skill and knowledge can be identified that represent "an essential portion of the leadership part of a supervisor's job" (p. 45).

The second phase of research pertained to the internal reliability of the LLQ. Preliminary findings on the extent to which items correlated with task scores and with the total score resulted in the elimination of items and revision of the questionnaire. The internal consistency reported for the final version of the LLQ based on the Kuder-Richardson formula 20 is .9706 (KR-20 correlations of .91 and above also are reported for each of nine separate organizations). However, not presented are correlations between the 27 tasks and between the items within each task that are needed to establish the distinctiveness of the tasks or skill areas. The reporting format used by the author is difficult to decipher. Users would feel more confident in the internal reliability coefficients if all the necessary data were offered in the research report.

Given its reported high internal consistency, the LLQ appears to measure a homogeneous factor, rather than knowledge about 27 different supervisory tasks as intended. A factor analysis would help in determining the extent to which different factors are measured by the questionnaire. Also, data on the test-retest reliability of the LLQ are needed because no information on the stability of scores is given in the manual.

Concurrent criterion validity is the topic of the third phase of the research using assessment center findings as criteria. Three studies involving three separate assessment centers were conducted, in which Spearman *rho* correlations were obtained between rankings of subjects based on their assessment center evaluations of supervisory potential and rankings of their LLQ total scores. The findings indicated no relationship for the first study and significant relationships for the next two, with *rhos* of .01, .71, and .89 on samples of 23, 6, and 10 respectively. These inconsistent findings on small samples leave open to question the predictive validity of the LLQ for identifying and selecting leadership potential in accord with assessment centers. Without detailed information about the procedures of the different assessment centers, the

meaning of the inconsistent findings remains obscure. Perhaps analyses of LLQ scores with ratings on separate assessment center dimensions would help determine the nature of possible relationships between these two measures. Also, as noted by the author of the test, additional validity studies are needed using a variety of criteria, such as job performance evaluations as a supervisor, promotions, and scores on other tests of supervisory abilities. In addition, if future analyses do, in fact, demonstrate that separate supervisory tasks or factors are measured by the LLQ, separate criterion validity research for each factor would be desirable.

Another weakness of the LLQ at present is the absence of norms in the manual and the failure to identify the subjects and groups included in the "international population's average" used in scoring analyses. The manual states "over 250 organizations have purchased the LLQ" (Introduction, p. 7). However, the research reported refers to only ten organizations that participated in the reliability studies and three in the validity studies. To interpret scores meaningfully, norms are needed for different organizations and for subjects based on gender, education, race, and job level.

A question that must be addressed is, what does the LLQ measure? Inspection of items raises two issues. First, the assumption that a single "correct" answer exists for each item ignores the importance of situational variations and individual differences in subordinates. Second, many of the items appear to tap general intelligence rather than supervisory knowledge. If true, as may be determined readily by correlating LLQ scores with IQ, the value of the measure for the selection of supervisors may be no better than that of a general abilities measure that could be administered in one fifth the time required for the LLQ.

In conclusion, many questions exist concerning the LLQ and its potential value in evaluating supervisory leadership. And its claim of being a "lower cost alternative to assessment centers" for identifying effective supervisors is neither demonstrated nor justified. Additional research and clear presentations of findings are needed to further refine the measure and to determine its utility. The research report presently included in the Administrator's Manual would benefit considerably from careful editing to remove redundancies, shifts back and forth between topics, occasional errors, inconsistent use of the terms "ratings" and "rankings," and text references to materials not included in the appendices.

Review of the Leatherman Leadership Questionnaire by WILLIAM D. PORTERFIELD, Academic Coordinator and Adjunct Assistant Professor of Educational Administration, Commission on Interprofessional Educa-

tion and Practice, The Ohio State University, Columbus, OH:

The Leatherman Leadership Questionnaire (LLQ) is part of a packet of training materials that includes the instrument, full reports of normative data, training and presentation materials, and suggestions for the use of the instrument. The packet is presented as a comprehensive assessment center for managers, supervisors, and individuals interested in testing their leadership knowledge. One complete set of the materials is priced at $600 (1989), with additional materials available at prices ranging from $30 for scoring services and additional questionnaires to $75 for additional administration guides. While such prices may be reasonable market values for larger organizations and businesses, the costs will significantly reduce the possibilities of the LLQ being used for graduate research and furthering the validity of the instrument through the academy.

The theoretical base for the instrument is problematic in terms of a distinctive theoretical orientation. The author used a panel of eight human resource development specialists to validate the appropriateness of the questions and the subscales on the instrument. Thus, although providing some support for content validity, the theoretical base is diffuse and unclear. If application of the instrument in organizational settings is the primary use, such an instrument-development process may be acceptable. However, if the LLQ is intended as a research tool, a more clearly defined theoretical approach to leadership, human behavior, and perception should be developed and incorporated into the instrument.

The author makes a strong claim the instrument measures leadership knowledge versus perceptions of leadership knowledge. The questionnaire consists of 339 multiple-choice items, directed toward 27 subscales of leadership tasks. Within each of the questions are preferred responses that indicate the respondent's leadership knowledge. The instrument is designed to yield scores for each of the subscales that can be compared to normative data collected in eight different organizations ($N = 301$). Reliability and validity studies were conducted for the instrument and are extensively described in the packet of research materials. Data from test-retest reliability studies are missing and should be conducted with the instrument to increase the reliability data base. Additionally, continued item verification could strengthen the reliability of the instrument and its internal consistency. Validity studies were conducted using assessment center ratings for identified leaders, and comparing these ratings with scores on the LLQ. Validity studies might also be conducted by reviewing literature for each item and for each subscale.

Any new instruments in the leadership area must be designed in such a way that perspectives from various minority groups and both sexes are incorporated in the instrument. The author does not indicate if the panel of experts included minority individuals or a balance of men and women, or if any attention was given to these concerns in the actual design of the instrument. Additionally, the author notes there are little data on whether there are significant differences in test scores across racial and ethnic groups.

This lack of information is a serious weakness for the LLQ. Certainly, any instrument that is to be utilized in staff selection, needs assessment, career counseling, assessment centers, and evaluation should be thoroughly reviewed for sensitivity to various cultural and racial perspectives that may affect the theoretical basis and/or actual scores. This is a rich area for further research if the LLQ receives credibility for organizational development and planning.

The LLQ is a very lengthy instrument. It can be administered in 4 to 5 hours or in two separate sessions. This is a costly time commitment for respondents and for organizations choosing to employ the results of the LLQ for further planning and training purposes. The author makes the claim the LLQ yields comprehensive data on leadership knowledge. Such a claim suggests to businesses and trainers that time invested in administration may save time later. However, the practical barriers to an individual testing for a period of 4 hours may inhibit individual use of the LLQ and certainly would inhibit use of the LLQ by researchers. If possible, a consolidated version of the LLQ should be developed with a maximum administration time of $1\frac{1}{2}$ hours.

Scoring for the LLQ is completed electronically by the author for a price of $30. It seems much more practical, given current computer technology, to offer users a scoring package for test-site scoring. Additionally, it would be helpful for a hand-scoring key to be made available to users. On-site, reasonably priced scoring options might serve to broaden the use of the LLQ in nonbusiness settings.

Aside from the instrument, the packet of materials also contains an administrator's guide, research documentation, overhead transparencies, and a carrying case for materials, all quite nicely developed. The research documentation is more detailed than many instruments and provides potential users with the data necessary to make further judgments about the use of the LLQ in various settings.

In summary, the LLQ may be useful as a practical tool for assessing leadership knowledge in organizations. Attention should be given to explicating the theoretical base of the "knowledge" that is being tested. Further research needs to be conducted on the theoretical and practical validity of the instrument cross-culturally and with respect to gender differences. Due to the length of administration and the cost of the package, the instrument may not be the choice of researchers in the leadership arena at the academy. This is unfortunate, in that the LLQ needs more research and normative data in order for test results to be meaningful and generalizable. As a comprehensive assessment center, the LLQ may have some merits for organizations willing to commit themselves to the validity of the leadership knowledge incorporated in the instrument. However, businesses and trainers would be well advised to compare the LLQ to other instruments available in the areas of selection, needs assessment, career counseling, and evaluation.

[206]
Let's Talk Inventory for Children.

Purpose: "To identify children who have inadequate or delayed social-verbal communication skills; provides a uniform and standardized method of eliciting and probing selected speech acts, representing the ritualizing, informing, controlling, and feeling functions of verbal communication."
Population: Ages 4–8.
Publication Date: 1987.
Acronym: LTI-C.
Scores, 2: Formulation, Association.
Administration: Individual.
Price Data, 1989: $69 per complete kit including 25 record forms, stimulus manual, and examiner's manual (82 pages); $15 per 25 record forms; $30 per stimulus manual; $25 per examiner's manual.
Time: 30(40) minutes.
Comments: Downward extension of Let's Talk Inventory for Adolescents (9:613).
Authors: Candice M. Bray and Elisabeth H. Wiig.
Publisher: The Psychological Corporation.

Review of the Let's Talk Inventory for Children by MERITH COSDEN, Associate Professor of Education, University of California, Santa Barbara, CA:

The Let's Talk Inventory for Children (LTIC) provides a standardized method for assessing the verbal social-communication skills of children who have a background in standard American spoken English. It is not intended to identify the bases of verbal-communication problems nor to be used as the sole criterion to determine placement in special programs. The LTIC is designed primarily for descriptive use. As such, it is structured to provide specific information on the ability of children to formulate or identify speech acts that perform different communicative functions.

The LTIC is based on a "parametric" taxonomy of social-verbal communication. Within this taxonomy, all interpersonal communications are defined by four controlling variables: participants, setting, topic, and task. Speech acts are categorized into five communicative functions: ritualizing, informing, controlling, feeling, and imagining. The first four of

these are sampled in the Inventory. Omission of the fifth area is only weakly justified in the manual. Although at least four items using different situational communicative contexts were constructed to assess each speech act, no systematic method for analyzing the impact of the four control variables is provided.

There are three parts to the LTIC. The first, Speech Act Formulation-Peers, contains 24 items. Each item consists of a picture of a peer interaction and a short narrative describing the intent of the depicted communication. The examiner reads the narrative aloud and then instructs the child to verbalize the next communication that should occur between the characters. For example, in a trial story Mike and Debbie are shown playing together. Mike has a new toy; Debbie doesn't know the name of the toy and wants to ask him about it. The child taking the test is asked to formulate a verbal response to the question "What did Debbie say to Mike?"

The second part of the Inventory, Speech Act Formulation-Adults, follows the same format. These 10 items are taken directly from the Peer Formulation section and rewritten to feature child/adult interactions in the same social contexts. Only two of the five speech functions, feeling and controlling, are sampled. The lack of complete crossover between audience (adult or child) and speech function is not well explained. The manual states that the Adult Formulation items are designed to indicate emerging formality features in the child's verbal repertoire; that is, to assess the child's skill in making distinctions between peer and adult communications.

The third part of the LTIC, Speech Act Associations, is optional and designed to assess receptive understanding of communicative intent in children who have difficulty formulating verbal responses. Items were selected from the informing, controlling, and feeling functions and were redesigned to reflect new task demands. The child is shown a stimulus page on which three interpersonal communicative contexts are pictured. Two of the pictures represent targeted speech acts and the third is a foil. The child is asked to point to the picture that best represents the intent of a speech act read by the examiner; then a second speech act is read and the child asked to make another selection from the same page. The authors' use of two targeted responses per stimulus page is a concern, however, as children who are sure of one answer can eliminate it when considering a response to the second item.

The LTIC is individually administered and does not require specialized training beyond familiarity with the test and general assessment procedures. The test easel is placed between the child and examiner so that the child can see the stimulus pictures while the examiner reads the accompanying narratives. There is no time limit for testing, but administration is estimated at 30 minutes. Demonstration items are provided at the beginning of the test and trial items are available for each section. Rules for determining when to discontinue testing are vague. Each narrative may be repeated once; repetition is not reflected in the child's score, although it may be noted in qualitative interpretation of the results.

All responses are transcribed on the Record Form. The manual suggests audiotaping Formulation responses for later transcription rather than noting them during the session. Preference for taping is based on a desire to increase accuracy in transcription without disrupting the flow of the test. It is this reviewer's experience, however, that one should not rely solely on taping, as machines may malfunction or children's voices may prove too soft to hear. The additional time required to transcribe taped data may also be too costly. Thus, examiner recording of verbal responses, with tape recording as a backup, is preferable to tape recording alone.

The manual presents both qualitative and quantitative systems for interpretation of test results. More emphasis is placed on the qualitative system. This system as described in the manual is highly subjective and relies on the clinical skills of the examiner. The manual provides several examples of this type of interpretation (e.g., if a child fails to understand the perspective of others across stories, a need to develop awareness of others' perspectives may be indicated). The manual suggests testing hypotheses generated in this manner through observation of the child in natural settings. Given the lack of knowledge on the empirical validity of the scale (discussed below), testing for the occurrence of problem behavior in natural settings should be mandatory.

Quantitative measures are obtained for each part of the LTIC. All Formulation items are scored for whether the intent of the speech act is "realized and expressed" in the response. An additional score is given to Formulation-Adult items to reflect the presence of formality structures, that is, the ability of the child to differentiate social communications between adults and peers. Association items are scored for correct identification of speech intent. Scoring is straightforward with adequate guidelines and examples provided. The utility of some of the scores, however, is unclear. No norms are provided for the scores of formal verbal structures obtained on Adult Formulation items nor for scores on the Association items. Qualitative interpretation of scores reflecting formality is suggested, but not enough age-relevant information is provided to allow one to do this in an informed manner. Similarly, Association scores are discussed in regard to differentiating children who formulate poor responses but understand social communications

from children who have problems in both areas. Unless the child provides a clear pattern of positive or negative scores on these subtests, however, interpretation of results based on the information provided in the manual will be difficult.

Normative data are provided only for the total intent score obtained by summing across all 34 (24 Child and 10 Adult) Formulation items. The normative data represent a small sample of children ($N = 214$), ages 4–8, and are presented for 1-year intervals. Although the manual states that the total score is the most reliable, the data supporting this statement are limited. Internal consistency coefficients (coefficient alphas) for the combined Child and Adult Formulation score range from .69 to .85 across age groups. Only one small study of interscorer reliability is reported, with high levels (94–96%) of agreement across categories. No studies substantiating reliability of responses or scores across test administrations are cited.

Using the total score as a representation of speech act formulation skill is questionable because speech acts are not equally sampled by the Inventory. The total score is more heavily weighted by controlling and feeling functions (13 items apiece) than by ritualizing or informing functions (4 items apiece). To the extent that students are differentially hampered by these communicative functions, the total test score will present a biased picture of skill level.

Although the instrument has a strong theoretical base, its validity as a measure of pragmatics is not apparent from the manual. The authors are very careful to frame the purpose of the test with caveats, noting that the Inventory is not designed to provide a diagnosis of language disorder, but rather to complement existing standardized tests and procedures. Nevertheless, the LTIC should contain items that tap into the needs of students known to have language and learning disorders. Recent literature reviews on pragmatic deficits in children are presented in the manual; however, test items were not selected to address these issues. Items were generated on the basis of their content validity for normal children; in fact, the small normative sample used to develop the scoring system consists solely of students with normal language skills. The only manner in which validity is addressed in the manual is by noting that test scores change as a function of age; that is, older children score higher on the test than do younger children, as would be predicted by developmental theories on social language development. Two types of studies are needed to determine the efficacy of this instrument even as an informal description of language skills. First, one needs to examine the validity of the test items for differentiating children known to have language deficits from those who do not. Second, given the novelty of this instrument's subject matter, there is a need to evaluate the effectiveness of this type of inventory for obtaining accurate information regarding children's skills in natural settings.

In sum, the LTIC presents an interesting model for systematically studying developing skills in the area of pragmatics. The importance of this area is well developed in the manual. The authors describe the LTIC as an informal assessment instrument to be used in association with other standardized tests. The advantages of using the Inventory over other types of informal observations, however, are unclear. It should be noted that the items in this Inventory correspond to an intervention program, *Let's Talk for Children*, also developed by the co-authors (Wiig & Bray, 1983). This Inventory opens a promising area for understanding more subtle social-communication problems in young children, but the utility of the test itself has not been established.

REVIEWER'S REFERENCE

Wiig, E., & Bray, C. (1983). *Let's talk for children.* Columbus, OH: Charles E. Merrill Publishing Co.

Review of the Let's Talk Inventory for Children by JANET NORRIS, Associate Professor of Communication Disorders, Louisiana State University, Baton Rouge, LA:

The purpose of the Let's Talk Inventory for Children (LTIC) is to assess the ability to express and interpret speech acts representing the communication functions of ritualizing, informing, controlling, and feeling. Specifically, the ability to formulate or recognize speech acts that express the appropriate intent and degree of formality or politeness in both peer and adult/authority contexts is evaluated. The Speech Act Formulation Items require the child to generate a speech act appropriate to a pictured situation presented with a lead-in narrative describing the situation. The Speech Act Association items probe the ability to associate spoken speech acts with pictured situational contexts, and is designed to be used in addition to or in place of the Formulation Items when a child performs poorly on the latter.

The LTIC assesses a very limited aspect of language, measuring only one component of pragmatics and only four communication functions within this domain. However, the manual states that the test is not designed to be used as a single diagnostic tool, to determine educational placement, or to identify the bases for a delay. Rather, the primary purpose is to assist in the identification of children with inadequate or delayed social-verbal communication skills. To achieve this goal the four communication functions assessed were selected because they are acquired early in development, are readily pictured and elicited by the task, reflect common experiences for young children (ages 4 to 8 are targeted), have been shown to be delayed in populations of children with language disorders or

special needs, reflect increasing competence with increasing age, and correlate with items on the Let's Talk Inventory for Adolescents (Wiig, 1982; 9:613).

The test stimuli elicit natural communication to the degree that any contrived task is able to do so. The pictures and narratives used depict situations that are similar to the experiences of young middle-class children. They provide a meaningful situation and present characters with clear goals. The child is allowed to formulate a speech act using his/her own language rather than being limited to single word responses or imitations. The procedure has the advantage over spontaneous language assessment of assuring that a variety of speech acts are sampled. It is difficult to determine from naturally occurring interactions whether various language functions do not occur because of a lack of communicative competence or because the context failed to elicit the response.

However, the current task may present difficulties to young and/or language-disordered children. To formulate an appropriate speech act in response to the test stimuli, the child must be capable of understanding the situation from the perspective(s) of the characters depicted and be able to function in the role of another person. A language-disordered child may fail to formulate an appropriate response because of an inability to shift perspectives, while successfully performing similar communicative functions in real situations.

Minimal reliability data are reported. The manual does not report any stability of performance data, such as test-retest results. This is particularly problematic in that results from the adolescent version of the Inventory reported only moderate correlations for test-retest scores. Thus, the cautions that the Inventory not be used to provide a diagnosis of a language disorder or to determine educational placement must be taken seriously. Internal consistency coefficients for groupings of items by intent were relatively low. The author suggests that the Inventory is designed to assess a variety of speech acts that are not necessarily similar in function.

Only one preliminary study is reported concerning the interrater reliability for scoring the LTIC. This involved only five protocols and the scoring was conducted by trained professionals with backgrounds in test administration and linguistics. Although the percentage of interscorer agreements was high (94%–97%), this level of reliability cannot be assumed for practitioners who have not received training. The extensive rules and examples of possible responses provided in the manual would seem to enhance interscorer agreement and are a strength.

No measures of validity are reported. However, the manual provides an extensive literature review that describes various taxonomies used to categorize speech acts and establishes the rationale for the categories selected for inclusion in the Inventory. Literature is cited establishing the relative sequence and ages of acquisition of the functions assessed, ways in which the communicative functions are realized linguistically, and patterns of difficulty in using communicative functions exhibited by language-learning-disabled children. The author states that items were carefully designed to probe the functions targeted and to be developmentally appropriate, but no data are provided to support this claim. Thus, although the literature may indicate that children exhibit certain communicative functions at various stages of development, there is no evidence that these children are able to exhibit behaviors in response to the tasks required by the LTIC at these same ages.

Some support for validity is reported in a pilot study that showed increasing performance in speech act formulation on the test with increasing age, and moderate but significant correlations between groups of items that assessed similar functions expressed to peers versus adults.

The LTIC does not represent the universe of speech acts used by young children, but only four functions. More information is needed in order to determine if these four categories are sufficient to sample speech acts used by this population, or whether content validity is weakened by this restricted range. No studies establishing concurrent or construct validity are reported.

The Inventory does not purport to be a norm-referenced test. Results are evaluated based upon both quantitative and qualitative interpretations. Means and standard deviations are provided by age intervals of 1 year. These are based upon a small, nonrepresentative sample of 214 children who participated in field testing. In general, the sample consisted of normally developing, urban, middle-class, standard-English-speaking children from five eastern states. Language-disordered or special-needs children were not included by design. The author states that the score obtained on the LTIC can be compared to the means and standard deviations from the field-test group, with a substantial difference from the mean serving as a possible indication that the child's overall communication competence needs to be more completely examined. The examiner is further encouraged to make comparisons in relation to the standard error of measurement rather than the raw score.

Qualitative interpretations are recommended as well. The author suggests evaluating the speech acts obtained for patterns of inadequate responding, such as multiple examples of poor perspective taking across items, or a general inability to modify speech acts to reflect more polite forms in the adult context.

These patterns can then be substantiated by interviews with individuals such as parents and teachers, as well as observations of the child in various settings. Confirmation of difficulties would suggest the need for specific intervention. An intervention program designed by the authors, *Let's Talk for Children* (Wiig & Bray, 1983), provides a set of objectives and therapy materials for developing the functions assessed by the Inventory and thus provides continuity between assessment and intervention.

Use of the Inventory is time-consuming. Administration (30 minutes), transcription of the child's responses from audiotape, and scoring can take 2–3 hours. This represents a considerable amount of time that may not be clinically worthwhile in that only one limited aspect of pragmatic abilities is examined, there is no evidence that the results are reliable or valid, and no diagnostic claims beyond probable strengths and weaknesses can be made based upon results. There is considerable danger in attributing too much importance or emphasis on the types of behaviors assessed, particularly given the existence of the parallel intervention program. The speech acts included represent a restricted sample and not a comprehensive representation of the types of social-verbal communications produced by young children.

SUMMARY. Let's Talk Inventory for Children is an assessment instrument that has some appealing features. It provides an efficient method for eliciting four categories of early-developing, high-frequency speech acts. The Inventory is easy to administer and score (although time-consuming) and provides implications for intervention. However, the instrument is not well constructed, lacks evidence of both reliability and validity, and does not provide useful norms. The use of the LTIC for purposes of diagnostics is thus severely limited. Even more problematic is the test-teach paradigm that is encouraged by the authors of the Inventory. The focus upon discrete pragmatic language skills results in the perpetuation of the "splinter skill" approach to language assessment and remediation that has been largely ineffective in dealing with the language disorders of children in the past. If the Inventory is used, the examiner must be careful to interpret the results cautiously and to go beyond the narrow scope of the instrument when planning intervention.

REVIEWER'S REFERENCES

Wiig, E. (1982). *Let's talk inventory for adolescents.* Columbus, OH: Charles E. Merrill Publishing Co.
Wiig, E., & Bray, C. (1983). *Let's talk for children.* Columbus, OH: Charles E. Merrill Publishing Co.

[207]

Life Orientation Inventory.

Purpose: To "assess the presence of suicide risk in an individual."

Population: Ages 13 and over.

Publication Date: 1988.

Acronym: LOI.

Scores, 7: Private Opinions About Me, Love/Work/What is Important to Me, Getting What I Want, Reacting to Situations, Being with Other People, Reasons for Living or Dying, Total.

Administration: Group.

Editions, 2: Screen Response Form, Profile and Response Form.

Price Data, 1991: $66 per complete kit including 25 profile/response forms, 50 screen response forms, manual (67 pages); $24 per 25 profile/response forms; $18 per 50 screen response forms; $27 per manual.

Time: (10–60) minutes.

Authors: Brian Kowalchuk and John D. King.

Publisher: John D. King (the author).

Review of the Life Orientation Inventory by JAN-ICE G. WILLIAMS, Assistant Professor of Psychology, Clemson University, Clemson, SC:

The Life Orientation Inventory (LOI) is a self-report measure of suicide risk. There are two versions of the scale: a 30-item screening inventory, and the 113-item full LOI. Response format is a 4-point rating scale which ranges from *I am sure I disagree* to *I am sure I agree*. The full LOI consists of six subscales: Self-Esteem Vulnerability, Overinvestment, Overdetermined Misery, Affective Domination, Alienation, and Suicide Tenability. These areas are believed by the authors to reflect the belief systems that differentiate suicidal individuals from nonsuicidal individuals. The short Screen contains a subset of items from the full scale. Administration and scoring instructions are clear and precise. The Overinvestment scale is considered supplementary and is not included in calculating the total LOI score. Some information about interpretation of subscale differences is provided and standard errors are given for subscale scores as well as full scale scores.

TEST DEVELOPMENT. The LOI was developed through a review of the literature on suicide and formulation of a model for predicting suicidal orientation. Items were generated by looking through other measures of suicide risk, including the Beck Hopelessness Scale (Beck, Weissman, Lester, & Trexler, 1974) and constructing items related to the six belief systems. A pool of 150 items was reviewed by a panel of judges (including four individuals with a history of suicidal ideations) who retained 120 items for analysis. These 120 items were administered to a group of college students and a group of hospitalized psychiatric patients. Items not reaching the criterion of a .30 correlation with total subscale scores were eliminated or rewritten, resulting in the 113-item total. Item-total score correlations are presented in the test manual for a sample drawn from the standardization sample.

NORMS. The LOI was standardized on a sample of 1,347 individuals in 23 states. Data are given to allow comparison of the standardization sample with the national population. Norms are presented in standard score form and in percentile ranks. The manual gives clear instructions for the appropriate use of these norm tables.

RELIABILITY. The six subscales were constructed for internal consistency and reported coefficient alphas indicate reasonable internal consistency. Low alphas were obtained for the Overinvestment scale for subjects under 19 years of age, probably because the items about work, relationships, and life goals are not as closely related for young respondents as for the older ones. Both the Screen and total LOI scale scores were internally consistent for all age groups. Data are also provided for test-retest reliability, which is modest but appropriate for the nature of the concept being measured.

VALIDITY. Information is presented about content, concurrent, and construct validity. Initial item generation and selection procedures were aimed at ensuring content validity. Because the measure assesses beliefs associated with suicidal ideation, few of the items appear face valid. Concurrent validity was assessed using the Hopelessness Scale, resulting in nonsignificant to moderate correlations (nonsignificant for Affective Domination to .60 for Overdetermined Misery). These relationships might have been expected, as the Hopelessness Scale addresses only some of the beliefs represented on the LOI. Moderate correlations were also obtained between LOI scores and Beck Depression Inventory (Beck & Beck, 1972) scores and a rating of patients' suicidal ideations. Comparison of known groups indicated that the LOI does distinguish between suicidal patients and nonsuicidal patients. The manual reports a .94 correlation between Screen scores and full LOI scores.

STRENGTHS. The LOI is a carefully planned measure with a basis in theory. Test development procedures included attention to internal consistency and content validity. The scale's focus on beliefs, rather than suicidal behaviors or intentions, may enable assessment of suicide potential in individuals who are reluctant to discuss suicide directly, although the manual cautions appropriately against reaching any decisions on the basis of a test score. When used with other indicators of suicide risk, such as sociodemographic characteristics (Lewinsohn & Lee, 1981) or suicidal intentions and behaviors (Rehm, 1981), this measure may allow sensitive assessment in a difficult area. The manual provides much useful information, including references to relevant literature and a discussion of issues of self-report measurement (such as social desirability and concealment). Data presented in the manual indicate reasonable reliability and validity for a new measure. This scale offers many possibilities for research on suicidal individuals. Additionally, the

Screen may be administered and scored quickly and easily, with little loss of total score information.

WEAKNESSES. Assessing suicide risk is an inherently difficult task. Suicide itself is a low-frequency event and, thus, difficult to predict successfully. Establishing the appropriate criterion for examining the validity of the scale is a problem, because individuals considered at risk for suicide will be targets for intervention aimed at reducing the risk of actually engaging in suicidal behavior. Further research on the validity of the measure would considerably enhance confidence in LOI scores.

SUMMARY. The LOI is a new measure of beliefs associated with suicidal ideation. The Screen gives a unidimensional measure of suicide risk, whereas the full LOI gives six subscale scores in addition to a total score. The manual provides a clear description of the theory underlying the scale; complete instructions for administration, scoring, and interpretation; and information on the psychometric properties of the scale. The authors have given careful consideration to appropriate uses of the instrument. Further research is necessary to clarify the validity of the LOI, but with appropriate caution, the LOI will be a useful tool for both clinicians and researchers.

REVIEWER'S REFERENCES

Beck, A. T., & Beck, R. W. (1972). Screening depressed patients in family practice: A rapid technique. *Postgraduate Medicine, 52,* 81-85.
Beck, A. T., Weissman, A., Lester, D., & Trexler, L. (1974). The measurement of pessimism: The Hopelessness Scale. *Journal of Consulting and Clinical Psychology, 42,* 861-865.
Lewinsohn, P. M., & Lee, W. M. L. (1981). Assessment of affective disorders. In D. H. Barlow (Ed.), *Behavioral assessment of adult disorders* (pp. 129-179). New York: Guilford Press.
Rehm, L. (1981). Assessment of depression. In M. Hersen & A. S. Bellak (Eds.), *Behavioral assessment: A practical handbook* (pp. 246-295). New York: Pergamon.

[208]
Light's Retention Scale [Revised Edition 1991].

Purpose: Aids the school professional in determining whether the student would benefit from grade retention.
Population: Grades K–12.
Publication Dates: 1981–91.
Acronym: LRS.
Scores, 20: Sex of Student, Student's Age, Knowledge of English Language, Physical Size, Present Grade Placement, Previous Grade Retentions, Siblings, Parents' School Participation, Experiential Background, Transiency, School Attendance, Estimate of Intelligence, History of Learning Disabilities, Present Level of Academic Achievement, Student's Attitude About Possible Retention, Motivation to Complete School Tasks, Immature Behavior, Emotional Problems, History of Delinquency, Total.
Administration: Individual.
Price Data, 1991: $60 per complete test kit including manual ('91, 78 pages), 50 recording forms, and 50 parent guides; $17 per manual; $22 per 50 recording forms; $18 per 50 parent guides; $14 per 25 parent consent forms; $17 per specimen set.
Time: (10–15) minutes.

Comments: Ratings by teachers and parents; a nonpsychometric instrument used as a counseling tool with a specific retention candidate.
Author: H. Wayne Light.
Publisher: Academic Therapy Publications.
Cross References: For reviews by Michael J. Hannafin and Patti L. Harrison of an earlier edition, see 9:622; see also T3:1328 (1 reference).

TEST REFERENCES

1. Vasa, S. F., Wendel, F. C., & Steckelberg, A. L. (1984). Light's Retention Scale: Does it have content validity? *Psychology in the Schools, 21,* 447-449.
2. Willis, W. G. (1987). Retention/promotion decisions: Selective use of data? *Perceptual and Motor Skills, 64* (1), 287-290.

Review of the Light's Retention Scale [Revised Edition 1991] by BRUCE K. ALCORN, Director of Certification, Teachers College, Ball State University, Muncie, IN:

In the manual of the 1991 Edition of Light's Retention Scale (LRS), the author states:

This Revised Light's Retention Scale (LRS) provides a format that aids the school professional in determining if the elementary or secondary student would benefit from grade retention. The scale consists of 19 categories derived from an exhaustive review of the literature and addresses such factors as attendance, intelligence, physique, age, sex, history, participation of parents, motivation of the student, absenteeism, emotional problems, behavior patterns, and other information. Each of these factors is evaluated on a scale of one to five, and the total score is broken down into several "retention candidacy" categories. The evaluation takes approximately ten to fifteen minutes to complete.

The 1991 edition is also intended to be used as a counseling tool by the school professional. . . . the LRS has been used in . . . parent teacher conferences. . . . as a general guide for the entire school staff, including the school psychologist. The LRS is intended to provide guidance in determining if a student should be retained and should not be used as the sole criterion when making a decision whether to retain or promote a child. Findings by . . . other professionals should always be considered. (p. 9)

The LRS manual provides a useful review, including an extensive bibliography, of the sometimes very controversial issue of school retention: whether or not students should be made to repeat school grades, why or why not, and the factors or reasons involved. It should be on the required reading list of every practicing teacher and teacher-to-be, regardless of the reader's position relative to the issue. It would also be a helpful resource to schools during the development of retention policies, even in those schools that decide against all or almost all retention. The author is also commended for placing references containing criticisms of the LRS in the bibliography.

The 1991 edition of the LRS is essentially the same as the 1986 edition. Although the manual for the latest edition has been strengthened in a few ways, it has at the same time been weakened. Several additional research studies have been referenced in the text, the citations in the bibliography have been increased from 203 to 249, and the recording form has been revised to make the tabulation of the results easier. However, I believe that the additional credibility has been lost by the inclusion of the incredible claim that the LRS "is now used in most elementary schools throughout North America" (p. 11).

The problems with the LRS are not as a source of information, but as an instrument. These problems fall into two categories: conceptual and technical.

CONCEPTUAL PROBLEMS. School retention is analogous to medicine in that it is administered as a remedy for a problem, but, whereas the medicine may have positive effects, it may also have negative side effects. The question that must be answered in each case is, do the positive effects outweigh the negative side effects? Although the LRS was designed to provide some answers to that question, it does not even attempt to deal with the important question of etiology.

Although the LRS presupposes that a lack of academic achievement is the sole reason for retention it does not, in any way, take into consideration the cause of this failure. Before the factors in the LRS are even considered, the overriding question should be answered: Will retention for this student provide the missing elements that caused the lack of achievement or will it just be another year of failure? If the answer is the former, then the 19 factors in the LRS might be helpful in determining the extent of the possible negative side effects. Although the manual claims that the "LRS . . . aids the school professional in determining if the . . . student would benefit from grade retention" (p. 9), it does not start with the correct question, nor does it even suggest that to the reader. It starts with the assumption that there will be retention and then proceeds to evaluate whether there are enough other reasons to reject that assumption.

TECHNICAL PROBLEMS. Although the 19 factors per se can impact retention, some of their descriptions and/or scale values need improvement. Some of them overlap. The Knowledge of English Language factor does not take into account interest in acquiring such knowledge, whereas other factors do; the Physical Size factor should be related to the group into which retention will be made rather than to the student's age; the Previous Retention factor assumes that the normal starting grade for all schools is kindergarten rather than first grade; the School Attendance factor measures only absence and leaves no room to account for the reason for absence and neither do any other factors. The Transiency factor does not take into account the reasons for a student to be in two schools. The selection of 80% in

Motivation to Complete School Tasks may mislead the decision maker for the student who works hard and persists but does so less than 80% of the time due to other factors. The Immature Behavior factor contains weak or incomplete descriptors of immaturity, and the Emotional Problems factor allows a student to be rejected for retention even though his or her behavior is because of being retained rather than because of basic emotional problems. The scale values for a number of the factors jump from 0 to 3 or higher or, as determined by the interpretation guidelines in Table 2, from *Excellent retention candidate* to *Poor retention candidate*, skipping three levels.

Once the LRS has been administered, the values from all of the factors are summed and meaning is given to the total by entering it into Table 2. The interpretation guidelines contain six scale levels by which each candidate for retention can be measured, from *excellent* to *should not be retained*. A student who receives any score of 5 is automatically considered a poor candidate for retention by this table, but it is not hard to see retention benefits for individuals receiving a 5 for the Parents School Participation factor. In addition, using the 19 factors, it is easy to attribute enough points to a student to classify him or her as a marginal or poor candidate for retention, while simultaneously coming to the conclusion that the positive benefits of retaining this individual would outweigh the negative aspects.

The single most important technical problem of the LRS relates to the complete absence of documentation supporting its use as a measurement instrument, even though the documentation is present to support it as a source of information. No data or other information is presented for validity, reliability, derivation of the scale values, determination of the descriptors or levels for each factor, or rationale for the interpretation guidelines.

The LRS manual is a very useful document for teachers as a source of information on the topic of school retention and as a reference for identifying some of the issues. It may also be useful for schools in the development of retention policies. It has little or no value as a measurement instrument in its present form.

Review of Light's Retention Scale [Revised Edition 1991] by FREDERIC J. MEDWAY, Professor of Psychology, University of South Carolina, Columbia, SC:

Light's Retention Scale (LRS) is a rating scale designed as a counseling tool for use by school professionals, in conjunction with parents, to determine if an elementary or secondary school student would benefit from repeating a school grade. The idea behind the scale is controversial because the bulk of research evidence on retention argues against this practice. However, in view of rising retention rates caused by strict promotion policies enacted during the last two decades, a scale that could differentiate children who should not be retained would be of great value in slowing the nonpromotion tide. The 1991 revision updates two earlier editions (1981 and 1986). The complete LRS kit includes a 77-page manual describing scale administration and interpretation, a sample school retention policy, parental retention consent forms, and analysis of a good and a poor retention candidate; scale recording forms; and parent guides to retention.

The LRS consists of 19 broad areas under which ratings are made chosen as a result of an "exhaustive review of the literature." Examples of areas are students' attendance history, intelligence, physical size, school motivation, gender, mobility history, and presence of possible handicapping conditions (e.g., learning disabilities, emotional problems). Five factors are assigned points ranging from 0 to 4, and the remaining factors are assigned points ranging from 0 to 5, although some factors do not have every value represented. Area scores are summed and totals are compared with a chart indicating how good the child is for retaining. Lower scores (those in the 0–31 range out of a possible total of 89) indicate good retention candidates. Retention is not recommended for children receiving any scores of 5. For example, if even after counseling, a child remains upset over possible retention, a rating of 5 is given and the child is viewed as having a minimal chance of benefitting from retention regardless of the total score. The manual states clearly that the scale should not be the sole criterion in making retention/promotion decisions; however, because the scale can be used without the manual, users might overlook this caution.

The manual represents the LRS as a nonpsychometric device, the scores of which should not be considered comparable to those of a standardized test and should not have to meet conventional standards of test construction. Reviewers of the 1981 edition and independent researchers found this to be a weak argument inasmuch as use is made of numerical weights and values, and retention guidelines based on total score cutoffs are presented. No reliability, validity, or normative data are provided for the LRS despite the fact that several studies have found that the scale is not reliable and has no concurrent or predictive validity (Sandoval, 1980, 1982; Vasa, Wendel, & Steckelberg, 1984).

Perhaps even more problematic than the failure to include research on the LRS in the manual is the attempt to use some of this research to justify the scale. For example, one study (Vasa et al., 1984) found that school personnel did not use most scale factors to make retention decisions and questioned the scale's content validity. The manual concludes that this study merely shows that educators have failed to recognize significant factors, which the scale includes.

The argument that the scale is content valid despite educators' views might have merit had the selection of the scale's factors been based on a careful research review; however, this does not appear to be the case. According to the 1986 version of the manual, the 19 factors were selected based on review of 175 studies "that lend some clear guidance and are . . . of good design" (p. 27). However, no guidelines are listed for inclusion and exclusion of studies, thus resulting in a selective and potentially biased review. For example, local school district technical reports and unpublished studies are given the same status as empirical articles in refereed journals and syntheses of multiple research studies. In the 1991 version of the test, an additional 25 studies are reviewed in the manual. However, the actual scale does not differ from earlier versions. The only change made in the 1991 edition is in the format of the scoring sheet. Interestingly, Light does not cite any studies published in the last 7 years that support the practice of grade retention but does summarize several recent papers that argue against it.

The inclusion of some of the 19 retention factors makes some intuitive sense (e.g., that absence due to illness may justify grade retention); however, the criticism remains that many of the broad factors and corresponding items have no empirical basis and/or weak conceptual basis. For example, the scale assumes that retaining a child in the same grade as a sibling and retaining a child who associates with older students is harmful. No literature is cited directly to support these claims other than the author's clinical judgement. The scale claims that smaller children are less likely to be penalized by retention than larger ones. The manual even goes so far as to include a height and weight chart to allow users to gauge the relative height of children prior to the retention decision. This physical size argument is one of the myths of retention contradicted by research (e.g., Vance, 1991), that, unfortunately, use of the LRS perpetuates. There may be others as well.

When the psychological literature is cited to support inclusion of factors, the reasoning often is circular and confuses association with cause and effect. For example, it is stated that because average intelligence children are retained the least, such children are the best retention candidates. Some statements in the manual contradict the whole notion of the scale. The manual states that "it is unusual to find a child above the fourth grade level that would do better if retained" (p. 20). Yet, the scale itself is intended for use through grade 12, and the sample retention policy in the manual endorses retention beyond the elementary level.

Over and above the concerns about content and validity, the wording of scale items is problematic. The item content does not cover all possible combinations, and teachers who have used the scale have left items unanswered due to vague wording.

SUMMARY. The LRS has been and is likely to be widely used by school personnel looking for a guide to assess the appropriateness of grade retention. In fact, Light claims that the scale "is now used in most elementary schools throughout North America" (p. 11). The scale's only positive feature is that it encourages consideration of a broad range of factors rather than basing retention decisions solely on immaturity, low achievement, or some other reason. However, many of the factors in isolation do not relate to a successful retention experience and total scores have no predictive validity. Based on technical adequacy, content, and basic psychometric considerations, there is little to recommend the LRS even as a crude guide during counseling. Given the importance of retention decisions, recommendations based on LRS interpretation guidelines could have legal ramifications for the user, even if used in conjunction with other data. It is recommended that there be a moratorium on the use of the LRS until independent research shows that it can differentiate prospective good retention candidates and can do so better than other methods (e.g., teacher and parent judgement). It will be necessary to show not only that the LRS can identify children who will do well during the retained year but that it can also distinguish children who are not likely to be retained again and those who will continue to show good progress in subsequent years. The LRS has a long way to go to prove its merit and justify its existence.

REVIEWER'S REFERENCES

Sandoval, J. (1980). Reliability and concurrent validity of Light's Retention Scale. *Psychology in the Schools, 17*, 442-445.
Sandoval, J. (1982). Light's Retention Scale does not predict success in first-grade retainees. *Psychology in the Schools, 19*, 310-314.
Vasa, S. F., Wendel, F. C., & Steckelberg, A. L. (1984). Light's Retention Scale: Does it have content validity? *Psychology in the Schools, 21*, 447-449.
Vance, M. D. (March, 1991). *Short stature and psychological risk: Don't retain based on standing height.* Paper presented at the meeting of the National Association of School Psychologists, Dallas, TX.

[209]

Living Language.

Purpose: "Remedial teaching programme, concentrating on spoken language, for use with all children who are failing to develop adequate language skills"; includes assessment of prelanguage/language skills for placement in this program.
Population: Language-impaired children.
Publication Date: 1985.
Scores: No scores.
Administration: Individual.
Levels, 3: Pre-Language, Starter, Main Programme.
Manual: No manual.
Price Data, 1989: £55.20 per complete kit including general manual (57 pages), subtest manuals (Before Words [31 pages], First Words [16 pages], Putting Words

Together [67 pages], set of 10 record booklets (Pre-Language [8 pages], Starter Programme [8 pages], Main Programme [12 pages]), and assessment pictures (50 pages); £4.45 per 10 Pre-Language or Starter Programme record booklets; £5.45 per 10 Main Programme record booklets; £10.10 per general handbook; £5.75 per Before Words manual; £12.10 per First Words or Putting Words Together manual; £48.30 per Introductory Video.
Time: Administration time variable.
Comments: General manual title is Teaching Spoken Language; subtest manual titles are Before Words, First Words, and Putting Words Together; test booklet titles are Pre-Language Record Booklet, Starter Programme Record Booklet, and Main Programme (Level I) Record Booklet; subtests available as separates.
Author: Ann Locke.
Publisher: NFER-Nelson Publishing Co., Ltd. [England].

[210]

The Lollipop Test: A Diagnostic Screening Test of School Readiness—Revised.

Purpose: "A screening test to identify the child's deficits (and strengths) in readiness skills."
Population: First grade entrants.
Publication Dates: 1981–89.
Scores, 5: Identification of Colors and Shapes and Copying Shapes, Picture Description and Position and Spatial Recognition, Identification of Numbers and Counting, Identification of Letters and Writing, Total.
Administration: Individual.
Price Data, 1990: $29.95 per complete kit including 5 test booklets, stimulus cards, and manual ('89, 35 pages); $24.95 per 25 test booklets; $10.95 per set of stimulus cards; $14.95 per manual.
Foreign Language Edition: Available in Spanish.
Time: (15–20) minutes.
Author: Alex L. Chew.
Publisher: Humanics Publishing Group.
Cross References: For reviews by Isabel L. Beck and Janet A. Norris of an earlier edition, see 9:629.

TEST REFERENCES

1. Chew, A. L., & Morris, J. D. (1984). Validation of the Lollipop Test: A diagnostic screening test of school readiness. *Educational and Psychological Measurement, 44*, 987-991.
2. Chew, A. L., Kesler, E. B., & Sudduth, D. H. (1984). A practical example of how to establish local norms. *The Reading Teacher, 38*, 160-163.
3. Chew, A. L., & Morris, J. D. (1987). Investigation of the Lollipop Test as a pre-kindergarten screening instrument. *Educational and Psychological Measurement, 47* (2), 467-475.
4. Chew, A. L., & Morris, J. D. (1989). Predicting later academic achievement from kindergarten scores on the Metropolitan Readiness Tests and the Lollipop Test. *Educational and Psychological Measurement, 49*, 461-465.
5. Chew, A. L., & Lang, W. S. (1990). Predicting academic achievement in kindergarten and first grade from prekindergarten scores on the Lollipop Test and DIAL. *Educational and Psychological Measurement, 50*, 431-437.

Review of The Lollipop Test: A Diagnostic Screening Test of School Readiness—Revised by SYLVIA T. JOHNSON, Professor, Research Methodology and Statistics and Acting Editor-In-Chief, Journal of Negro Education, Howard University, Washington, DC:

OVERVIEW. The Lollipop Test was originally designed to meet the need for a "quick, yet valid, individually administered instrument for evaluating school readiness." The 1989 revisions include additional validity studies with larger samples (*ns* from 129 to 293) than the initial study of 69 children. The test booklet provides space for scoring and reporting two sets of scores for each child. Test materials are simply and adequately drawn stimulus cards in a spiral booklet, presented to subjects with spoken directions from the examiner. Individual testing time is about 15 minutes.

RATIONALE AND TEST CONSTRUCTION. The author provides background on the concept of readiness and the criterion-referenced approach to assessment, but does not indicate the criteria to which the subtests of the Lollipop should be referenced. As noted in the *Ninth Mental Measurements Yearbook* review by Beck (1985), tasks involving identification of colors, identification of shapes, and copying of shapes are contained in the same subtest, and thus, strengths or deficiencies in one of these areas could not be identified from the subtest score.

NORMS AND INTERPRETATIVE MATERIALS. Although tables are not provided for converting raw scores to scores based on normative groups, complete descriptive statistics are reported for all four subtests and the total score, based on spring testing of 293 kindergartners with a mean age of 74.4 months, and 129 prekindergarten children with a mean age of 62.1 months. The mean ages are not reported in the body of the table, but rather, in a side note. No information on variability of ages is reported. The table of data for the end of the kindergarten year is not so labelled, and may thus be misunderstood. The author suggests the development of local norms, and detailed instructions for setting up frequency distributions, computing percentile ranks, and interpreting the meaning of the local percentile rank are provided.

All data reported are from a county in rural Georgia. From a quarter to a third of the children are African American and the rest are White, about evenly divided by gender. Suggested score ranges for above average to below average readiness are provided, based on this sample. The author suggests the use of criterion-referenced interpretations of scores, but provides no specific information to do so. It is suggested that teachers make a list of items passed and not passed, and if a deficit is demonstrated, plan remedial strategies. It is not clear how a deficit is to be identified, that is, which items or how many items must be failed before a deficit is discovered.

The administration and scoring booklet contains space for the recording of individual pre- and post-test scores, but no information is provided to assist in interpreting these data. Given the general problems associated with the measurement of change, this seems an important omission.

VALIDITY AND RELIABILITY. The manual reports an extended and ongoing program of research on the Lollipop Test. Later studies make reference to earlier studies, and a clear attempt has been made to gradually build a network of useful test information largely based on the local population on which the test was developed.

The relationship between test scores and socioeconomic status was investigated. No significant relationships were found between any of the subtests or total score with parental occupational level or income. However, no information is provided on the distributions of income or educational level. The finding could have resulted from lack of variability on these constructs among this sample.

Factor analysis was used to build construct validity for the instrument. Item scores for 69 kindergarten and Head Start children were factored. However, this sample is extremely small for meaningful factor analysis, especially at the test item level, and no factoring is reported for the larger samples that are used for score interpretation. Scores obtained for single test items have much more variability and are less reliable than scores obtained for a subtest, or for an entire test. Thus, if factoring is done at the item level, it is important to have a sample large enough to obtain stable estimates of item parameters. From this limited factoring, four factors were identified and labelled as reflecting Visual-Perceptual Abilities, Numerical Ability, Color Recognition and/or Visual Discrimination, and Position and Spatial Recognition. There is no information indicating which items loaded onto each of the four factors.

The examination of the extent to which the Lollipop Test predicts school grades is essential for an instrument designed to measure school readiness, and is thus a further construct validation for the instrument. The four subtests were used to predict grade 1 and grade 3 Stanford Achievement Test scores and teacher assigned grades, among 246 of the 293 children in the score interpretation sample. The six subtests of the Metropolitan Readiness Test (MRT) were similarly analyzed.

For predicting first grade scores and grades, multiple correlation coefficients ranged from .47 to .75 for the Lollipop Test, and from .49 to .73 for the MRT. For grade 3, the Lollipop multiple correlation coefficients ranged from .36 to .58, and those for the MRT ranged from .44 to .68. In addition to the longer time period, the lower third grade results may be due to using the earlier test data to modify instruction, and thus to appropriately reduce the predictive power of the tests.

To support its use as a shorter test of readiness, two studies compared the Lollipop Test and the MRT. The first study, on 69 children, reported a correlation coefficient of .86 for the total test scores, and the later study reported $r = .76$. The author attributes this difference to the use of an earlier edition of the MRT and to the administration of the MRT to students in groups of threes in the first study. However, the age range for the first study was broad, including both Head Start and kindergarten children. Failure to control for age is a probable cause of the higher coefficient. Lollipop and MRT scores for younger children are both likely to be lower, and those for older children are likely to be somewhat higher.

The manual reports another concurrent validation study comparing the Lollipop with an individually administered readiness test, the Developmental Indicator for the Assessment of Learning (DIAL). Subtest correlations between scales designed to measure similar constructs ranged from .53 to .70. For the Lollipop, the internal consistency reliability coefficient of the total score was .93. However, this was obtained for the sample of 69 kindergarten and Head Start children. A reliability coefficient computed over this wide developmental range would be larger than one obtained within a more restricted age range. This finding is due to the fact that when the reliability coefficient is computed, the variability in performance on the test that is a function of age would be treated as "true" variance, and would increase the reliability coefficient. For children in this age range, the variability would be rather large. No test-retest reliability coefficients are reported for the total score, and no subtests reliabilities are reported.

In conclusion, the Lollipop is a school readiness test with a growing body of data based on a local community to support its use in estimating readiness for school. The samples are balanced by race and sex, and an attempt has been made to avoid socioeconomic effects. However, there are flaws in many of the supporting studies, and the way in which important tables are labelled and presented may be misleading. The test can serve a useful purpose if it is cautiously used and considered as a research instrument from which one can build a local data base for interpretation. Reliability is quite high for a short instrument, and materials are clearly drawn. Instructions for administration are adequate, but scoring and interpretation problems limit its usefulness severely.

REVIEWER'S REFERENCE

Beck, I. L. (1985). [Review of The Lollipop Test: A Diagnostic Screening Test of School Readiness.] In J. V. Mitchell, Jr. (Ed.), *The ninth mental measurements yearbook* (pp. 866-867). Lincoln, NE: The Buros Institute of Mental Measurements.

Review of The Lollipop Test: A Diagnostic Screening Test of School Readiness—Revised by ALBERT C. OOSTERHOF, Professor of Education, Florida State University, Tallahassee, FL:

The Lollipop Test is an individually administered instrument designed to diagnose and screen pre-school and kindergarten children for school readiness. The test presents visual stimuli on seven cards. Three of the cards contain color drawings of lollipops, these pictures suggesting the name for the test. In the first of the four subtests, a child is asked to identify lollipops by color, and then using a separate card, to identify common geometric shapes such as a rectangle and square. The child is also asked to draw freehand a circle, cross, and square. In the second subtest, the child looks at a drawing of an adult cat with several kittens and is asked to point to the kitten being referenced by words such as "on top" and "on the left side." The child then looks at a series of large to small lollipops and is asked to identify the one matching words such as "biggest" and "in the middle." In the third subtest, the child is shown a random series of the numbers 1 through 10 and asked to point to and also name the numbers. Then the child is shown sets of lollipops and asked to perform arithmetic operations with each set. In the fourth subtest, the child is shown a random series of letters from the alphabet and then asked to identify, name, and then copy several of the letters. The child is also asked to print his or her name.

The Lollipop Test was copyrighted in 1981 and has remained unchanged since that time, although the manual was expanded (copyright 1989) to include information concerning additional statistical studies. The graphics on the stimulus cards are of appropriate quality. The administration directions are quite clear and the manual accompanying the test is easy to read and nicely formatted. For reasons that follow, the Lollipop Test unfortunately appears to be of limited value with respect to its proposed purpose, that of diagnosing and screening children for school readiness.

The manual indicates the Lollipop Test can be used to provide a quick (15-minute) screening of a child's school readiness. The primary evidence supporting this potential is correlations between the various scores on the Lollipop Test with scores on the Metropolitan Readiness Tests (MRT). As would be expected, there is a high correlation ($r = .86$) between total test scores on the two instruments. Although this correlation is fairly high, two important constraints must be observed. First, the usefulness of the MRT in part is established through the correlation of that test with a criterion external to the MRT. The correlation of the Lollipop Test with that external criterion would be substantially less than .86. Second, virtually no normative information is provided for the Lollipop Test (elaboration of this point provided later). Consequently, from information provided in the manual, one cannot determine whether a child scored high or low on the Lollipop Test, and likewise cannot estimate how the child might score on the MRT.

The above referenced correlations were based on an original sample of 69 kindergarten and Head Start students. The current manual reports more recent studies. In 1984, correlation of the Lollipop Test with the MRT was revisited, with the correlation between total test scores then estimated to be .76 based on 293 kindergarten students. Using prekindergarten children, a similar study observed a correlation of .71 between the Lollipop Test and the Developmental Indicator for the Assessment of Learning (DIAL). The two constraints addressed previously concerning the interpretation of the correlations also apply to these more recent studies.

Correlations ranging from .37 to .61 are reported between scores on the Lollipop Test and teacher ratings. These correlations are fairly low, and very limited information is provided as to what it is the teachers were rating. Multivariate correlations are reported between scores on the Lollipop Test and scores on the Stanford Achievement Test at the end of grade 1, and also at the end of grade 3. Similar correlations are presented between scores on the Lollipop Test and teacher assigned grades. These correlations were also computed substituting scores on the MRT for those of the Lollipop Test. It is assumed that the multivariate analysis allowed for differential weighting of the respective subtest scores, although these weights are not discussed. How one can make use of these correlations is also not addressed.

Means and standard deviations of scores are reported for pre and end of kindergarten administrations of the Lollipop Test. Suggested descriptors or categories of these scores are provided ranging from "below average readiness" to "above average readiness." The below and above ranges appear to begin at points one-half standard deviation from the mean. Justification for these interpretations is not provided. Very limited information is provided about the reference group. This instrument does not (and does not propose to) allow norm-referenced interpretations.

The Lollipop Test manual does propose criterion-referenced interpretations of performance. The only interpretative assistance the manual provides the user is "make a list of those items passed, and not passed, for each subtest." Other than indicating that other readiness tests measure similar skills, the domain being measured by the instrument is not defined. Likewise, the relevance of these skills to school readiness is not addressed. No information is provided as to how children with varying scores are to be differentially treated. The only benefit the Lollipop Test does appear to provide is the opportunity to observe children's performance on a selected series of academic tasks. But this activity can be accomplished conveniently with any of a number of instructional materials readily available to teachers in most kindergarten and early elementary classrooms.

[211]

Luria-Nebraska Neuropsychological Battery: Children's Revision.

Purpose: "To diagnose general and specific cognitive deficits, including lateralization and localization of focal brain impairments, and to aid in the planning and evaluation of rehabilitation programs."

Population: Ages 8–12.

Publication Date: 1987.

Acronym: LNNB-C.

Scores, 16: Clinical scales (Motor Functions, Rhythm, Tactile Functions, Visual Functions, Receptive Speech, Expressive Speech, Writing, Reading, Arithmetic, Memory, Intellectual Processes), Optional scales (Spelling, Motor Writing), Summary scales (Pathognomonic, Left Sensorimotor, Right Sensorimotor).

Administration: Individual.

Price Data, 1988: $270 per complete kit including manual (266 pages) and all required materials in a carrying case; $11.50 per 10 patient response booklets; $37.50 per 10 administration and scoring booklets; $165 per Adult Form I cards plus 3 additional cards and audiotape; $39.50 per supplementary test materials including the 4 additional cards and audiotape; $47.50 per manual; $7.90 per prepaid WPS Test Report answer sheet; $119.50 per 25 use microcomputer diskette (specify Apple [IIc, IIe, II+] or IBM [PC, XT, AT] scoring program).

Time: (90–120) minutes.

Comments: Uses the same stimulus materials, with the addition of 3 extra cards and an audiotape, as Form I of the adult version of the Luria-Nebraska Neuropsychological Battery; other test materials (e.g., tape recorder, stopwatch, eraser, door key) must be supplied by examiner.

Author: Charles J. Golden.

Publisher: Western Psychological Services.

TEST REFERENCES

1. Karras, D., Newlin, D. B., Franzen, M. D., Golden, C. J., Wilhening, G. N., Rothermel, R. D., & Tramontana, M. J. (1987). Development of factor scales for the Luria-Nebraska Neuropsychological Battery—Children's Revision. *Journal of Clinical Child Psychology*, 16, 19-28.
2. Pfeiffer, S. I., Naglieri, J. A., & Tingstrom, D. H. (1987). Comparison of the Luria-Nebraska Neuropsychological Battery—Children' Revision and the WISC-R with learning disabled children. *Perceptual and Motor Skills*, 65, 911-916.
3. Lahey, B. B., Hynd, G. W., Stone, P. A., Piacentini, J. C., & Frick, P. J. (1989). Neuropsychological test performance and the attention deficit disorders: Clinical utility of the Luria-Nebraska Neuropsychological Battery—Children's Revision. *Journal of Consulting and Clinical Psychology*, 57, 112-116.

Review of the Luria-Nebraska Neuropsychological Battery: Children's Revision by STEPHEN R. HOOPER, Assistant Professor of Psychiatry, Psychology Section Head, The Clinical Center for the Study of Development and Learning, University of North Carolina School of Medicine, Chapel Hill, NC:

The Luria-Nebraska Neuropsychological Battery: Children's Revision (LNNB-C) was designed to be a multidimensional battery that could assess a broad range of neuropsychological functions in children 8 through 12 years of age in a relatively efficient manner (i.e., approximately 2 hours). Its use with children slightly older (i.e., ages 13 and 14) is mentioned, but not described further. The LNNB-C purportedly is based on principles of brain development and, as noted above, its main purposes are to diagnose general and specific cognitive deficits and to contribute to intervention programs.

The LNNB-C is an individually administered instrument that is nicely packaged and easily transported. For examiners familiar with the adult version of the LNNB, Form I (212), only a few additional materials are required as noted above. The LNNB-C provides the examiner with standardized *T*-scores for 11 clinical scales, 2 additional scales derived from the clinical scales, 3 summary scales, and 11 factor scales. Two additional supplementary scales also have been developed, the Acute Injury and Early Injury Scales, but these remain to be investigated further. The LNNB-C can be hand or computer scored, with the latter offering a considerable time savings to the clinician. Items are scored based on a 0 (normal), 1 (weak evidence of brain disorder), and 2 (strong evidence of brain disorder) format.

The manual of the LNNB-C is somewhat disorganized in its presentation of information (e.g., instrument development, standardization, and psychometric properties are presented last) and riddled with inconsistencies, but it does provide most of the relevant information necessary to evaluate the instrument effectively. The manual also provides cautions with respect to user qualifications, ethical and legal issues, and instrument limitations, areas particularly important for potential examiners. Each scale is described in detail, and the administration and scoring of each item is described adequately. A qualitative scoring system also is presented in detail but, although intriguing and potentially useful, no data are provided with respect to its use. The manual does note that normative data are being collected on the qualitative scoring system, but this is not described further. The case studies described in Chapter 7 of the manual also are interesting and provide the user with a nice range of clinical applications and referral questions; however, in all of the cases described additional instruments were used without any stated rationale. Although one could clinically deduce why these instruments may have been utilized, one also is left questioning whether these additional tools were used to compensate for selected deficiencies in the LNNB-C.

Theoretically, the LNNB-C purportedly was constructed on the basis of principles of developmental neuropsychology. The test construction procedures described, however, suggest otherwise. Specifically, the 269-item adult version of the LNNB (Form I) was administered to a group of children having above average intelligence and, based on the scores obtained, a group of items were delineated for further study. Although this is not an unusual practice in terms of generating an initial item pool, there is no stated rationale as to why children with above average abilities were used. Further, the use of the adult version of the scale suggests that the LNNB-C is little more than a scaled-down version of the adult battery. This has contributed to perhaps the chief weakness of the LNNB-C as it does not appear firmly grounded in developmental neuropsychology.

For example, Hynd, Snow, and Becker (1986) have criticized the battery for its exclusion of items assessing frontal lobe functions based on Golden's (1981) assumption that the frontal lobes do not begin to reach functional maturation until adolescence. This is contrary to available evidence that suggests that frontal lobe functions develop in a stepwise fashion, with some functions being developed by about 6 to 7 years of age and others continuing to mature into adolescence. It also is contrary to Luria (1973), whose theory guided the construction of the LNNB-C, as well as the discussion of developmental neuropsychology presented in the LNNB-C manual. Moreover, developmental considerations hardly could have been taken into account in the omission of test items specifically assessing attention and learning.

Despite these conceptual and psychometric difficulties, one attractive feature of the LNNB-C is the relative simplicity and range of coverage of its test items. A skilled examiner can utilize these items to obtain a detailed specification of functional strengths and weaknesses in a componential fashion. Users should note, however, that the LNNB-C tends to have many items that address language functions and far too few items that assess visual-perceptual abilities.

In addition to concerns regarding the conceptual basis of the LNNB-C and the development of its initial item pool, the strength of the normative data is highly suspect. The final version of the LNNB-C was normed on 125 children (i.e., 60 males and 65 females), 25 at each age level from 8 through 12. All of the children were Caucasian and issues with respect to race and socioeconomic status were not addressed. In comparison to other child neuropsychological batteries (e.g., Halstead-Reitan Neuropsychological Battery for Older Children), these normative data are superior; however, when evaluated against current psychometric standards, these normative data are woefully inadequate.

To date, a fair amount of research has been generated in a relatively short amount of time with respect to the LNNB-C's reliability and validity (see Tramontana & Hooper, 1988). Reliability estimates for the clinical and summary scales fall within acceptable limits (i.e., alpha coefficients ranging from .13 to .92 across all samples), with higher estimates being obtained from the clinical samples as would be expected given their greater variability in performance. Internal consistency estimates ranged from .70 to .94 for the 11 factor scales. The use of multiple comparison samples (i.e., nonimpaired, brain damaged, suspected brain damage, psychiatric, and learning disabled) represents a relative strength in the exploration of the internal consistency of the LNNB-C given the potential wide range of populations in which a child neuropsychological battery may be applicable. It is curious, however, that the clinical scales are described in the manual to be "intentionally heterogeneous," with the "scale names intended only as convenient mnemonic devices"; but, when calculating the reliability, estimates are provided that would suggest otherwise to the reader. Also, the discussion of the determination of ipsative strengths and weaknesses leaves one to question the interpretation of these scales (i.e., should they be considered homogeneous or heterogeneous in their make-up). It would appear that the scales should be treated as heterogeneous summary indices and that users should use caution when attempting to decipher ipsative strengths and weaknesses based on these indices.

The validity of the LNNB-C also has been addressed with some vigor. Generally, the LNNB-C appears to discriminate brain dysfunction in children about as well as the Halstead-Reitan Neuropyschological Test Battery (9:463) and, at least for general classification purposes, the two batteries yield highly comparable results. This could be deemed a relative strength of the LNNB-C in that it requires about half the time for administration when compared to the Halstead-Reitan. There is some indication that it adds to the discriminant validity achieved by the Wechsler Intelligence Scale for Children—Revised (WISC-R; 9:1351) alone in children manifesting milder forms of brain dysfunction. In the case of children with learning disabilities, however, the discrimination probably is no better than what would be achieved when standard measures of intelligence and academic achievement are combined. The factorial validity of the LNNB-C is well done and provides additional interpretive information for users. Users should be careful, however, to recognize that many of the factor scales have very few items and, consequently, if an individual child makes an inadvertent error on one of these items, an abnormal score could be obtained.

The LNNB-C was designed to be a comprehensive measure of neuropsychological functioning for children. Although the battery is described as a developmental neuropsychology measure, it more than likely represents a downward extension of a test battery designed primarily for adults. Significant questions plague the battery with respect to its conceptualization and psychometric properties, particularly with respect to its item generation, the representativeness of the constructs purportedly tapped, and its normative base. The ease of administration and the computer scoring format are relative strengths of this instrument, but they also represent a seductive feature with respect to the complexities of child neuropsychology. In general, given these concerns, clinicians and researchers should use caution in employing this battery. Until these conceptual and psychometric deficiencies are addressed, users may be better off to employ an eclectic approach in their neuropsychological assessments so as to ensure a more reliable and representative coverage of neuropsychological functions than that provided by the LNNB-C.

REVIEWER'S REFERENCES

Luria, A. R. (1973). *The working brain.* New York: Basic Books.
Golden, C. J. (1981). The Luria-Nebraska Children's Battery: Theory and formulation. In G. W. Hynd & J. E. Obrzut (Eds.), *Neuropsychological assessment and the school-age child: Issues and procedures* (pp. 277-302). New York: Grune & Stratton.
Hynd, G. W., Snow, J., & Becker, M. G. (1986). Neuropsychological assessment in clinical child psychology. In B. Lahey & A. Kazdin (Eds.), *Advances in clinical child psychology* (Vol. 9, pp. 35-86). New York: Plenum Press.
Tramontana, M. G., & Hooper, S. R. (1988). Child neuropsychological assessment: Overview of current status. In M. G. Tramontana & S. R. Hooper (Eds.), *Assessment issues in child neuropsychology* (pp. 3-38). New York: Plenum Press.

[212]

Luria-Nebraska Neuropsychological Battery: Forms I and II.

Purpose: Designed "to diagnose general and specific cognitive deficits, including lateralization and localization of focal brain impairments, and to aid in the planning and evaluation of rehabilitation programs."

Population: Ages 15 and over.

Publication Dates: 1980-85.

Acronym: LNNB.

Scores, 27: Clinical and Summary scales (Motor Functions, Rhythm, Tactile Functions, Visual Functions, Receptive Speech, Expressive Speech, Writing, Reading, Arithmetic, Memory, Intellectual Processes, Intermediate Memory [Form II only], Pathognomonic, Left Hemisphere, Right Hemisphere, Profile Elevation, Impairment), Localization scales (Left Frontal, Left Sensorimotor, Left Parietal-Occipital, Left Temporal, Right Frontal, Right Sensorimotor, Right Parietal-Occipital, Right Temporal), Optional scales (Spelling, Motor Writing), plus 28 Factor scales.

Administration: Individual.

Forms, 2: I, II.

Price Data, 1991: $365 per Form I set including manual ('85, 423 pages), test materials, 10 administration and scoring booklets, 10 patient response booklets, and 2 computer-scored answer sheets; $345 per Form II set; $190 per Form I test materials; $175 per Form II test materials; $42.50 per 10 administration and scoring booklets (Form I); $37.50 per 10 administration and scoring booklets (Form II); $9.80 per 10 patient response booklets (Forms I and II); $95 per manual; $9.80–$14.50 per computer-scored answer sheet; $350 per IBM microdisk for LNNB, Forms I, II, and Children's Revision; $225 per Apple disk (provides scoring only, no interpretation).

Time: (90–150) minutes.

Comments: Uses cards adapted from Luria's Neuropsychological Investigation by Anne-Lise Christensen (Form II includes improved, spiral-bound stimulus cards); tape provided for rhythm subtest; Form I can be scored by hand or computer; Form II is computer scored only.

Authors: Charles J. Golden, Arnold D. Purisch, and Thomas A. Hammeke.

Publisher: Western Psychological Services.

Cross References: For a review by Russell L. Adams, see 9:637 (41 references); see also T3:1346 (8 references).

TEST REFERENCES

1. Golden, C. J., & Berg, R. A. (1983). Interpretation of Luria-Nebraska Neuropsychological Battery by item intercorrelation: The memory scale. *Clinical Neuropsychology, 5,* 55-59.

2. Golden, C. J., & Berg, R. A. (1983). Interpretation of the Luria-Nebraska Neuropsychological Battery by item intercorrelation: Intellectual processes. *Clinical Neuropsychology, 5,* 23-28.

3. Golden, C. J., & Berg, R. A. (1983). Interpretation of the Luria-Nebraska Neuropsychological Battery by item intercorrelation: The Arithmetic scale. *Clinical Neuropsychology, 5,* 122-127.

4. Horton, A. M., Jr., Scott, M. L., & Golden, C. J. (1983). Discrimination of brain damaged schizophrenics from non-brain-damaged schizophrenics: Value of the Wiggins MMPI content scales. *Clinical Neuropsychology, 5,* 21-22.

5. Knight, R. G., & Godfrey, H. P. D. (1983). The interpretation of retest scores on the Luria-Nebraska Neuropsychological Battery. *Clinical Neuropsychology, 5,* 171-173.

6. McKay, S., & Ramsey, R. (1983). Correlation of the Weschler Memory Scale and the Luria-Nebraska Memory Scale. *Clinical Neuropsychology, 5,* 168-170.

7. Moses, J. A., Jr. (1983). An orthogonal factor solution of the Luria-Nebraska Neuropsychological Battery items: I. Motor, rhythm, tactile and visual scales. *Clinical Neuropsychology, 5,* 181-185.

8. Shelly, C., & Goldstein, G. (1983). Discrimination of chronic schizophrenia and brain damage with the Luria-Nebraska Battery: A partially successful replication. *Clinical Neuropsychology, 5,* 82-85.

9. Tramontana, M. G., Sherrets, S. D., & Wolf, B. A. (1983). Comparability of the Luria-Nebraska and Halstead-Reitan Neuropsychological Batteries for older children. *Clinical Neuropsychology, 5,* 186-190.

10. Webster, J. S., & Scott, R. R. (1983). The effects of self-instructional training on attentional deficits following head injury. *Clinical Neuropsychology, 5,* 69-74.

11. Berg, R. A., Bolter, J. F., Ch'ien, L. T., Williams, S. J., Lancaster, W., & Cummins, J. (1984). Comparative diagnostic accuracy of the Halstead-Reitan and Luria-Nebraska Neuropsychological Adult and Children's Batteries. *Clinical Neuropsychology, 6,* 200-204.

12. Carr, E. G., & Wedding, D. (1984). Neuropsychological assessment of cerebral ventricular size in chronic schizophrenics. *Clinical Neuropsychology, 6,* 106-111.

13. Dorman, C., Hurley, A. D., & Laatsch, L. (1984). Prediction of spelling and reading performance in cerebral palsied adolescents using neuropsychological tests. *Clinical Neuropsychology, 6,* 142-144.

14. Dorman, C., Laatsch, L. K., & Hurley, A. D. (1984). A study of reading disability among neurologically impaired students using the Luria-Nebraska Neuropsychological Battery. *Clinical Neuropsychology, 6,* 197-199.

15. Franzen, M. D., & Golden, C. J. (1984). Multivariate statistical techniques in neuropsychology: II. Comparison of number of factor rules with the motor scale of the Luria-Nebraska Neuropsychological Battery. *Clinical Neuropsychology, 6,* 165-171.

16. Freeland, J., & Puente, A. E. (1984). Relative efficacy of the Luria-Nebraska Neuropsychological Battery and the Wechsler Adult Intelligence Scale in discriminating schizophrenics with and without brain damage. *Clinical Neuropsychology, 6,* 261-263.

17. Geary, D. C., & Gilger, J. W. (1984). The Luria-Nebraska Neuropsychological Battery—Children's Revision: Comparison of learning disabled and normal children matched on full scale IQ. *Perceptual and Motor Skills, 58,* 115-118.

18. Hutchinson, G. L. (1984). The Luria-Nebraska Neuropsychological Battery controversy: A reply to Spiers. *Journal of Consulting and Clinical Psychology, 52,* 539-545.

19. Johnson, G. L., & Moses, J. A., Jr. (1984). An empirical evaluation of the decision tree procedure for the Luria-Nebraska Neuropsychological Battery. *Clinical Neuropsychology, 6,* 98-102.

20. Johnson, G. L., Moses, J. A., Jr., & Bryant, E. (1984). Development of an impairment index for the Luria-Nebraska Neuropsychological Battery. *Clinical Neuropsychology, 6,* 242-247.

21. McCue, M., Shelly, C., Goldstein, G., & Katz-Garris, L. (1984). Neuropsychological aspects of learning disability in young adults. *Clinical Neuropsychology, 6,* 229-233.

22. McKay, S., & Ramsey, R. (1984). Neuropsychological correlates of sociometric status in alcoholics. *Clinical Neuropsychology, 6,* 191-195.

23. Miran, M., & Miran, E. (1984). Cerebral asymmetries: Neuropsychological measurement and theoretical issues. *Biological Psychology, 19,* 295-304.

24. Moses, J. A., Jr. (1984). An orthogonal factor solution of the Luria-Nebraska Neuropsychological Battery items: II. Receptive speech, expressive speech, writing and reading scales. *Clinical Neuropsychology, 6,* 24-28.

25. Moses, J. A., Jr. (1984). An orthogonal factor solution of the Luria-Nebraska Neuropsychological Battery items: III. Arithmetic, memory and intelligence scales. *Clinical Neuropsychology, 6,* 103-106.

26. Moses, J. A., Jr. (1984). An orthogonal factor solution of the Luria-Nebraska Neuropsychological Battery items: IV. Pathognomonic, right hemisphere and left hemisphere scales. *Clinical Neuropsychology, 6,* 161-165.

27. Moses, J. A., Jr. (1984). Luria-Nebraska Neuropsychological Battery performance as a function of sensorimotor impairment in a brain damaged sample. *Clinical Neuropsychology, 6,* 123-126.

28. Moses, J. A., Jr. (1984). Performance of schizophrenic and schizoaffective disorder patients on the Luria-Nebraska Neuropsychological Battery. *Clinical Neuropsychology, 6,* 195-197.

29. Moses, J. A., Jr. (1984). The effect of presence or absence of neuroleptic medication treatment on Luria-Nebraska Neuropsychological Battery performance in a schizophrenic population. *Clinical Neuropsychology, 6,* 249-251.

30. Moses, J. A., Jr. (1984). The relative effects of cognitive and sensorimotor deficits on Luria-Nebraska Neuropsychological Battery performance in a brain-damaged population. *Clinical Neuropsychology, 6,* 8-12.

31. Moses, J. A., Jr., & Johnson, G. L. (1984). The relative contributions of WAIS and Luria-Nebraska Neuropsychological Battery variables to cognitive performance level: A response to Chelune. *Clinical Neuropsychology, 6,* 233-239.

32. Reynolds, C. R. (1984). On melding psychometric science and clinical acumen in neuropsychological assessment: Reply to Snow and Hynd. *Journal of Consulting and Clinical Psychology, 52,* 697-699.

33. Sawicki, R. F., & Golden, C. J. (1984). Multivariate statistical techniques in neuropsychology: I. Comparison of orthogonal rotation methods with the receptive scale of the Luria-Nebraska Neuropsychology Battery. *Clinical Neuropsychology, 6,* 126-134.

34. Sawicki, R. F., Leark, R., Golden, C. J., & Karras, D. (1984). The development of the Pathognomonic, Left Sensorimotor, and Right Sensorimotor scales for the Luria-Nebraska Neuropsychological Battery—Children's Revision. *Journal of Clinical and Child Psychology, 13,* 165-169.

35. Snow, J., & Hynd, G. W. (1984). Determining neuropsychological 'strengths' and 'weaknesses' on the Luria-Nebraska: Good practice or wishful thinking? *Journal of Consulting and Clinical Psychology, 52,* 695-696.

36. Spiers, P. A. (1984). What more can I say? In reply to Hutchinson, one last comment from Spiers. *Journal of Consulting and Clinical Psychology, 52,* 546-552.

37. Steinmeyer, C. H. (1984). Are the rhythm tests of the Halstead-Reitan and Luria-Nebraska batteries differentially sensitive to right temporal lobe lesions? *Journal of Clinical Psychology, 40,* 1464-1466.

38. Taylor, M. A., & Abrams, R. (1984). Cognitive impairment in schizophrenia. *American Journal of Psychiatry, 141,* 196-201.

39. Tramontana, M. G., Klee, S. H., & Boyd, T. A. (1984). WISC-R interrelationships with the Halstead-Reitan and Children's Luria Neuropsychological Batteries. *Clinical Neuropsychology, 6,* 1-8.

40. Webster, J. S., Dostrow, V., & Scott, R. R. (1984). A decision-tree approach to the Luria-Nebraska Neuropsychological Battery. *Clinical Neuropsychology, 6,* 17-21.

41. Webster, J. S., Jones, S., Blanton, P., Gross, R., Beissel, G. F., & Wofford, J. D. (1984). Visual scanning training with stroke patients. *Behavior Therapy, 15,* 129-143.

42. Dorman, C., Laatsch, L. K., & Hurley, A. D. (1985). The applicability of neuropsychological test batteries for assessment of the congenitally brain disordered. *Clinical Neuropsychology, 7,* 111-117.

43. Gilger, J. W., & Geary, D. C. (1985). Performance on the Luria-Nebraska Neuropsychological Test Battery—Children's Revision: A comparison of children with and without significant WISC-R VIQ-PIQ discrepancies. *Journal of Clinical Psychology, 41,* 806-811.

44. Hermann, B. P., & Melyn, M. (1985). Identification of neuropsychological deficits in epilepsy using the Luria-Nebraska Neuropsychology Battery: A replication attempt. *Journal of Clinical and Experimental Neuropsychology, 7,* 305-313.

45. Kemali, D., Maj, M., Galderisi, S., Ariano, M. G., Cesarelli, M., Milici, N., Salvati, A., Valente, A., & Volpe, M. (1985). Clinical and neuropsychological correlates of cerebral ventricular enlargement in schizophrenia. *Journal of Psychiatric Research*, 19, 587-596.

46. Kivlahan, D. R., Harris, M. D., Moore, J. E., Powel, J., & Donovan, D. M. (1985). Validation of the Luria-Nebraska Intellectual Processes Scale as a measure of intelligence in male alcoholics. *Journal of Clinical Psychology*, 41, 287-290.

47. Larrabee, G. J., Kane, R. L., Schuck, J. R., & Francis, D. J. (1985). Construct validity of various memory testing procedures. *Journal of Clinical and Experimental Neuropsychology*, 7, 239-250.

48. Malloy, P. F., Webster, J. S., & Russell, W. (1985). Tests of Luria's frontal lobe syndromes. *Clinical Neuropsychology*, 7, 88-95.

49. McCue, M., Shelly, C., & Goldstein, G. (1985). A proposed short form of the Luria-Nebraska Neuropsychological Battery oriented toward assessment of the elderly. *Clinical Neuropsychology*, 7, 96-101.

50. McNamara, K. M., Wechsler, F. S., & Larson, P. (1985). Neuropsychological investigation in cerebral Whipple's disease: A case study. *Clinical Neuropsychology*, 7, 131-137.

51. Mittenberg, W., Kasprisin, A., & Farage, C. (1985). Localization and diagnosis in aphasia with the Luria-Nebraska Neuropsychological Battery. *Journal of Consulting and Clinical Psychology*, 53, 386-392.

52. Moses, J. A., Jr. (1985). Relationship of the profile elevation and impairment scales of the Luria-Nebraska Neuropsychological Battery to neurological examination outcome. *Clinical Neuropsychology*, 7, 183-190.

53. Moses, J. A., Jr. (1985). Replication of internal consistency reliability values for the Luria-Nebraska Neuropsychological Battery summary, localization, factor and compensation scales. *Clinical Neuropsychology*, 7, 200-203.

54. Moses, J. A., Jr. (1985). The relative contributions of Luria-Nebraska Neuropsychological Battery and WAIS subtest variables to cognitive performance level. *Clinical Neuropsychology*, 7, 125-130.

55. Moses, J. A., Jr., & Schefft, B. K. (1985). Interrater reliability analyses of the Luria-Nebraska Neuropsychological Battery. *Clinical Neuropsychology*, 7, 31-38.

56. Silverstein, M. L., & Arzt, A. T. (1985). Neuropsychological dysfunction in schizophrenia. Relation to associative thought disorder. *The Journal of Nervous and Mental Disease*, 173, 341-346.

57. Sweet, J. J., Osmon, D. C., Rozensky, R. H., & Tovian, S. M. (1985). Comparison of the decision-tree and standard methods of the Luria-Nebraska Neuropsychological Battery. *Journal of Consulting and Clinical Psychology*, 53, 185-188.

58. Taylor, M. A., & Abrams, R. (1985). Short-term cognitive effects of unilateral and bilateral ECT. *British Journal of Psychiatry*, 146, 308-311.

59. Vannieuwkirk, R. R., & Galbraith, G. G. (1985). The relationship of age to performance on the Luria-Nebraska Neuropsychological Battery. *Journal of Clinical Psychology*, 41, 527-532.

60. Carr, M. A., Sweet, J. J., & Rossini, E. (1986). Diagnostic validity of the Luria-Nebraska Neuropsychological Battery—Children's Revision. *Journal of Consulting & Clinical Psychology*, 54, 354-358.

61. Fowler, P. C., Macciocchi, S. N., & Ranseen, J. (1986). WAIS-R factors and performance on the Luria-Nebraska's Intelligence, Memory, and Motor Scales: A canonical model of relationships. *Journal of Clinical Psychology*, 42, 626-635.

62. Hucker, S., Langevin, R., Wortzman, G., Bain, J., Handy, L., Chambers, J., & Wright, S. (1986). Neuropsychological impairment in pedophiles. *Canadian Journal of Behavioural Science*, 18, 440-448.

63. Koffler, S., & Zehler, D. (1986). Correlation of the Luria-Nebraska Neuropsychological Battery with the WAIS-R. *Clinical Neuropsychology*, 8, 68-71.

64. Magner, J. R., Kirzinger, S. S., & Spector, J. (1986). Viral encephalitis: Neuropsychological assessment in differential diagnosis and evaluation of sequelae. *Clinical Neuropsychology*, 8, 127-132.

65. Mensch, A. J., & Woods, D. J. (1986). Patterns of feigning brain damage on the LNNB. *Clinical Neuropsychology*, 8, 59-63.

66. Moses, J. A., Jr. (1986). Factor analysis of the Luria-Nebraska Neuropsychological Battery by sensorimotor, speech, and conceptual item bands. *Clinical Neuropsychology*, 8, 26-35.

67. Moses, J. A., Jr. (1986). Orthogonal factor structure of the Luria-Nebraska Neuropsychological Battery localization scale items for the left and right hemispheres. *Clinical Neuropsychology*, 8, 148-155.

68. Moses, J. A., Jr. (1986). The relative efficiency of WAIS IQ and subtest variables as predictors of Luria-Nebraska Neuropsychological Battery performance level. *Clinical Neuropsychology*, 8, 90-94.

69. Newman, P. J., & Sweet, J. J. (1986). The effects of clinical depression on the Luria-Nebraska Neuropsychological Battery. *Clinical Neuropsychology*, 8, 109-114.

70. Silverstein, M. L., & Hallman, K. (1986). Derived IQ estimates from the Luria-Nebraska Neuropsychological Battery in neuropsychiatric disorders. *Journal of Consulting and Clinical Psychology*, 54, 398-399.

71. Stahl, S. M., Thiemann, S., Faull, K. F., Barchas, J. D., & Berger, P. A. (1986). Neurochemistry of dopamine in Huntington's dementia and normal aging. *Archives of General Psychiatry*, 43, 161-164.

72. Strauss, B. S., & Silverstein, M. L. (1986). Luria-Nebraska measures in neuropsychologically nonimpaired schizophrenics: A comparison with normal subjects. *Clinical Neuropsychology*, 8, 35-38.

73. Taylor, A. E., Saint-Cyr, J. A., & Lang, A. E. (1986). Frontal lobe dysfunction in Parkinson's disease: The cortical focus of neostriatal outflow. *Brain*, 109, 845-883.

74. Tramontana, M. G., & Boyd, T. A. (1986). Psychometric screening of neuropsychological abnormality in older children. *Clinical Neuropsychology*, 8, 53-59.

75. Abrams, R., & Taylor, M. A. (1987). Cognitive dysfunction in melancholia. *Psychological Medicine*, 17, 359-362.

76. Ayers, M. R., Abrams, D. I., Newell, T. G., & Friederich, F. (1987). Performance of individuals with AIDS on the Luria-Nebraska Neuropsychological Battery. *The International Journal of Clinical Neuropsychology*, 9, 101-105.

77. Dorman, C. (1987). Verbal, perceptual, and intellectual factors associated with reading achievement in adolescents with cerebral palsy. *Perceptual and Motor Skills*, 64, 671-678.

78. Greene, R. S., & Dawson, J. E. (1987). Hand Test, WAIS-R and Luria-Nebraska intercorrelations. *Perceptual and Motor Skills*, 64, 906.

79. Gur, R. E., Resnick, S. M., Alavi, A., Gur, R. G., Caroff, S., Dann, R., Silver, F. L., Saykin, A. J., Chawluk, J. B., Kushner, M., & Reivich, M. (1987). Regional brain function in schizophrenia: A position emission tomography study. *Archives of General Psychiatry*, 44, 119-125.

80. Kane, R. L., Parsons, O. A., Goldstein, G., & Moses, J. A., Jr. (1987). Diagnostic accuracy of the Halstead-Reitan and Luria-Nebraska Neuropsychological Batteries: Performance of clinical raters. *Journal of Consulting and Clinical Psychology*, 55, 783-784.

81. Langell, M. E., Purisch, A. D., & Golden, C. J. (1987). Neuropsychological differences between paranoid and nonparanoid schizophrenics on the Luria-Nebraska Battery. *The International Journal of Clinical Neuropsychology*, 9, 88-95.

82. Moses, J. A. (1987). Item analyses of the Luria-Nebraska Neuropsychological Battery clinical and summary scores. *The International Journal of Clinical Neuropsychology*, 9, 83-88.

83. Moses, J. A., & Maruish, M. E. (1987). A critical review of the Luria-Nebraska Neuropsychological Battery literature: I. Reliability. *The International Journal of Clinical Neuropsychology*, 9, 149-157.

84. Moses, J. A., Vinogrador, S., & Berger, P. A. (1987). Serial neuropsychological evaluation of a case of bilateral frontal lobe brain tumor. *The International Journal of Clinical Neuropsychology*, 9, 106-110.

85. Tramontana, M. G., & Hooper, S. R. (1987). Discriminating the presence and pattern of neuropsychological impairment in child psychiatric disorders. *The International Journal of Clinical Neuropsychology*, 9, 111-119.

86. Wagner, E. E., Greene, R. S., Adair, H. E., & Dawson, J. (1987). Maximized reliability coefficients for LLNB factor scales. *The International Journal of Clinical Neuropsychology*, 9, 132-135.

87. Yun, X., Yao-Xian, G., & Matthews, J. R. (1987). The Luria-Nebraska Neuropsychological Battery Revised in China. *The International Journal of Clinical Neuropsychology*, 9, 97-101.

88. Dorman, C. (1988). Relationships between reading disability subtypes in neurologically impaired children. *The International Journal of Clinical Neuropsychology*, 10, 165-177.

89. Moses, J. A., & Maruish, M. E. (1988). A critical review of the Luria-Nebraska Neuropsychological Battery literature: II. Construct validity. *The International Journal of Clinical Neuropsychology*, 10, 5-11.

90. Moses, J. A., & Maruish, M. E. (1988). A critical review of the Luria-Nebraska Neuropsychological Battery literature: III. Concurrent validity. *The International Journal of Clinical Neuropsychology*, 10, 12-19.

91. Moses, J. A., & Maruish, M. E. (1988). A critical review of the Luria-Nebraska Neuropsychological Battery literature: IV. Cognitive deficit in schizophrenia and related disorders. *The International Journal of Clinical Neuropsychology*, 10, 51-62.

92. Moses, J. A., & Maruish, M. E. (1988). A critical review of the Luria-Nebraska Neuropsychological Battery literature: V. Cognitive deficit in miscellaneous psychiatric disorders. *The International Journal of Clinical Neuropsychology*, 10, 63-73.

93. Moses, J. A., & Maruish, M. E. (1988). A critical review of the Luria-Nebraska Neuropsychological Battery literature: VI. Neurologic cognitive deficit parameters. *The International Journal of Clinical Neuropsychology*, 10, 130-140.

94. Moses, J. A., & Maruish, M. E. (1988). A critical review of the Luria-Nebraska Neuropsychological Battery literature: VII. Specific neurologic syndromes. *The International Journal of Clinical Neuropsychology*, 10, 178-188.

95. Moses, J. A., Csernansky, J. G., & Leiderman, D. B. (1988). Neuropsychological criteria for identification of cognitive deficit in limbic epilepsy. *The International Journal of Clinical Neuropsychology*, 10, 106-112.

96. Silverstein, M. L., & McDonald, C. M. (1988). Personality trait characteristics in relation to neuropsychological dysfunction in schizophrenia and depression. *Journal of Personality Assessment*, 52, 288-296.

97. Golden, C. J. (1989). Abbreviating administration of the LNNB in significantly impaired patients. *The International Journal of Clinical Neuropsychology*, 11, 177-181.

98. Heinrichs, R. W. (1989). Neuropsychological test performance and employment status in patients referred for assessment. *Perceptual and Motor Skills, 69,* 899-902.

99. McCue, M., Goldstein, G., & Shelly, C. (1989). The application of a short form of the Luria-Nebraska Neuropsychological Battery to discrimination between dementia and depression in the elderly. *The International Journal of Clinical Neuropsychology, 11,* 21-29.

100. Meyers, J. E., & McMordie, W. R. (1989). The LNNB memory scale and WMS as memory screening instruments. *The International Journal of Clinical Neuropsychology, 11,* 137-142.

101. Moses, J. A., Jr. (1989). Construct validation of the Luria-Nebraska Neuropsychological Battery clinical and summary scales with the WAIS-R subtests. *The International Journal of Clinical Neuropsychology, 11,* 80-89.

102. Altman, E., Hedeker, D., Davis, J. M., Comaty, J. E., Jobe, T. H., & Levy, D. L. (1990). Neuropsychological test deficits are associated with smooth pursuit eye movement impairment in affective disorders but not in schizophrenia. *The International Journal of Clinical Neuropsychology, 12,* 49-59.

103. Moses, J. A., Jr. (1990). Comparative factor structure of the Luria-Nebraska Neuropsychological Battery C1 and C2 scales for neurologic and psychiatric samples. *The International Journal of Clinical Neuropsychology, 12,* 60-73.

104. Silverstein, M. L., Strauss, B. S., & Fogg, L. (1990). A cluster analysis approach for deriving neuropsychologically-based subtypes of psychiatric disorders. *The International Journal of Clinical Neuropsychology, 12,* 7-13.

105. Stephens, C. W., Clark, R. D., & Kaplan, R. D. (1990). Neuropsychological performance of emotionally disturbed students on the LNNB and LNNB-C. *Journal of School Psychology, 28,* 301-308.

Review of the Luria-Nebraska Neuropsychological Battery: Forms I and II by JEFFREY H. SNOW, Neuropsychologist, Capital Rehabilitation Hospital, Tallahassee, FL:

The Luria-Nebraska Neuropsychological Battery (LNNB) is a multidimensional battery designed to measure various neuropsychological processes. The authors state the instrument can be used as a screening device as well as a more comprehensive diagnostic measure. The manual further states the battery represents a standardized version of the diagnostic procedures first employed by the Russian neuropsychologist, A. R. Luria, with advantages being standardized administration and scoring as compared to the more subjective, classic clinical/qualitative technique which Luria employed.

There are two published forms of the LNNB (Form I and Form II). The two forms are meant to be parallel versions, although there are some differences. Form I employs the stimulus cards first developed by Anne-Lise Christensen. Form II uses cards developed in the United States, with larger, more clearly delineated pictures for individuals who may have impaired visual systems. Form I has a total of 269 items. Form II has 279 items. Forms I and II have 84 common items. The scales are similar for both forms, except Form II has an additional memory scale. The tests are designed for individuals 15 years of age and older, although the manual reports they have been used successfully with adolescents in the 13- to 14-year-old age range.

A number of scores can be derived for each form of the LNNB. Each item is given a score of either 0 (normal performance), 1 (mildly dysfunctional performance suggesting possible brain disorder), or 2 (severely dysfunctional performance indicating brain dysfunction). Raw scores for item clusters can

then be converted to scale scores in four general areas (Clinical scales, Summary scales, Localization scales, and Factors scales). Form I contains 11 Clinical scales. Form II has 12 Clinical scales. Both forms contain two optional Clinical scales. The Clinical scales are designed to provide overall summaries of function and range from such scales as Motor Functions to Receptive Speech to Intellectual Processes. The Summary and Localization scales are designed to provide more detailed diagnostic information. The Summary scales consist of lateralization as well as impairment indices. The Localization scales are specific measures designed to provide information as to localization of brain dysfunction. The Factor scales consist of clusters of items which reportedly measure discrete neuropsychological functions.

Raw scores for each scale are converted to a *T*-score with a mean of 50 and a standard deviation of 10. Form I can be hand scored, or there is an optional computer-scoring program. The manual states that Form II is only computer scored. The computer-scoring program is available through either mail-in service to the publisher or a disk can be purchased that will score the measure on a microcomputer. The resulting output gives a detailed analysis of all of the various scales and provides clinical interpretation. Also provided within the computerized report form are estimated WAIS (Wechsler Adult Intelligence Scale) Verbal, Performance, and Full Scale IQ scores, a profile of strengths and weaknesses, background information, and individual item responses. A sample report is provided with the test kit.

The manual provides detailed instructions and criteria for administration and scoring of each individual item. Additionally, the authors have added a section on qualitative scoring. They report this system is designed to provide a method for recording behaviors observed during the testing session which are not included in more generalized standardized scales. The manual provides individual descriptions of a number of different behaviors that may be evidenced during the testing session. There is a scoring summary at the back of the booklet and the qualitative scoring of the behaviors is categorized and summed. A cutoff score is then derived for each category and can be compared with normative values.

The authors indicate there are several levels in terms of interpretation for the test battery. These levels range from identification of specific brain dysfunction, behavioral descriptions, underlying etiology for dysfunction, and integration/conclusions based on the entire test. The manual provides what is called a Critical Level. This is an adjustment for age and educational background. Additionally, if premorbid IQ is known, then a Critical Level can be based on this information. The Critical Level is then used for comparative purposes in order to determine potential pathology.

Limited information is provided concerning test development and standardization. The authors indicate items for the measure were derived from Luria's clinical/neuropsychological work, although they do not state how the various items were selected for inclusion in the battery. The standardization samples were also extremely small for both forms. Form I was standardized on a sample of 50 subjects who were in a hospital setting with a variety of medical disorders. Form II was standardized with a sample of 73 subjects, 51 of whom were normal individuals, 14 psychiatric inpatients, and 8 neurological patients. The manual lists basic demographic information for these subjects (i.e., age, education, and sex) but no other information is provided. The equivalence of the two forms has been examined using correlation analyses. The resulting coefficients for the various scales range from a low of .42 to a high of .91.

The manual provides information concerning reliability of the measure. Interrater comparisons indicated agreement of 95% in regard to scoring by different pairs of examiners. Split-half coefficients for the various scales range from a low of .89 to a high of .95. The manual also reports internal consistency coefficients for various diagnostic groups. These groups included normals, brain injured, schizophrenic, and mixed psychiatric. Internal consistency estimates were highest for the clinical groups, with resulting coefficients well within the .80 range. Finally, test-retest coefficients are also reported in the manual. Utilizing a sample of 27 neurological and psychiatric patients, these coefficients ranged from a low of .77 to a high of .96. The interval between test-retest averaged 167 days with a range from 10 to 469 days. Another study is reported which investigated test-retest reliability. Coefficients for the 14 original scales range from .83 to .96 with a mean of .89. The Localization scales evidenced coefficients ranging from .78 to .95 with a mean of .89. The most variability was evidenced with the Factor scale coefficients with an overall mean of .81 and a range from .01 to .96. The manual also provides a table listing standard errors of measurement for each of the scales.

Several studies were reported that provide validity evidence for the test battery. The majority of these studies focused on the ability of various test scores and criteria established for the measure to discriminate between brain-injured and non-brain-injured populations. Studies are also noted that examine the validity of various Localization scales, and the pattern of the LNNB scores within different clinical groups. There is some evidence which indicates the relationship between the LNNB and other measures. In general, the results of these studies suggest the battery to be fairly effective at discriminating brain-damaged patients from other clinical groups. Comparisons with other measures have yielded respectable coefficients in the predicted direction.

The manual also provides a number of other sections that may be of interest to examiners. There is a chapter which presents a number of case studies. There are also various tables listed in the back of the manual that provide such information as factor loadings for various items, item means and standard deviations, and item difficulty indices.

To summarize, there are several strengths to the LNNB. The battery includes a comprehensive array of items and appears to tap a wide variety of behaviors. Along these lines, however, users should be aware that when initially released, the battery was criticized for relying too heavily on language-based items. The heavy reliance on language is a legacy from Luria, who spent the majority of his clinical and research efforts investigating individuals with language-dominant hemisphere lesions. In any event, another strength of the battery is the establishment of specific reliability coefficients with the various scales. Those reported in the manual are certainly well within the acceptable range for a screening instrument and many meet criteria for use as a diagnostic tool. This is considered to be a strength because many neuropsychological instruments used in the field today do not have well-established reliability coefficients. Yet another strength is the specific instructions provided for administration of each individual item which should minimize interadministrator variability.

There are a number of specific weaknesses with the LNNB about which potential users should also be aware. Inadequate information is provided concerning item selection and the standardization samples are extremely limited. The fact that Form II is only computer scored is another significant weakness. This compels users to purchase the microcomputer scoring program, because it is not practical to have the long turnaround time associated with sending scoring sheets and receiving reports generated by the test publisher. The computer reports also seem to be excessively long and probably of little value to more experienced clinical neuropsychologists. One of the major weaknesses of these computer-generated reports is the assumption of an intact central nervous system prior to the onset of the injury and/or disease process. In this regard, it is assumed that demonstrated weaknesses are attributable to brain dysfunction rather than to developmental factors. In general, it is felt the computer-generated reports will add little in terms of diagnostic value for more experienced clinical neuropsychologists and can, in fact, be misleading and/or confusing to individuals in training in neuropsychology or less experienced neuropsychologists. The qualitative scoring system provides an interesting attempt to incorporate clinical observation into the procedure, yet the authors again try to quantify this information. As with the computer-generated scoring system, it is felt that the qualitative categories listed in the manual will be of little value to the experienced neuropsychologist and will be confusing to beginning level professionals. Finally, although the manual does provide some indication regarding the validity of the battery, further research is needed in this area. The majority of validity studies reported merely indicate the test to be effective at discriminating brain-damaged from non-brain-damaged individuals. This seems to add little to the area of clinical neuropsychology. There are a number of tests which are effective at providing this information. It would appear as if the authors as well as others should focus more effort on describing the sensitivity of the battery to variability within various clinical populations and establishing more clear-cut criterion-related validity. When such data are available, meaningful decisions can be made about the clinical and research utility of the LNNB.

Review of the Luria-Nebraska Neuropsychological Battery: Forms I and II by WILFRED G. VAN GORP, Assistant Professor in Residence, Department of Psychiatry and Biobehavioral Sciences, UCLA School of Medicine, and Chief, Neuropsychology Assessment Laboratory, Department of Veterans Affairs Medical Center West Los Angeles, Los Angeles, CA:

The Luria-Nebraska Neuropsychological Battery (LNNB) represents an American quantitative/empirical orientation to the behavioral assessment of neurologic disorders. It is an outgrowth of the original work of the Soviet behavioral neurologist/neuropsychologist, A. Luria, who studied many patients with brain injuries and attempted to diagnose and localize their injury using a bedside mental status examination tailored for each patient. Though essentially antithetical to Luria's individualized, hypothesis-driven examination, Golden and colleagues developed the LNNB to "diagnose general and specific cognitive deficits, including lateralization and localization of focal brain impairments, and to aid in the planning and evaluation of rehabilitation programs" (Golden, Purisch, & Hammeke, 1985, p. 1). This goal is attempted through administration of a standard battery of 269 items for Form I or 279 items for Form II, assessing motor and cognitive skills using both a quantitative and qualitative scoring system. Clinical, Summary, Localization, and Factor scores are produced from the patient's responses. Several reviews (e.g., Adams, 1980, 1984; Delis & Kaplan, 1982; Spiers, 1981, 1982) have discussed methodologic limitations of the LNNB, whereas others (e.g., Golden, 1980;

Moses & Maruish, 1989a, 1990) have defended the battery. Certainly, whatever one's final conclusions regarding the battery, it must be acknowledged that few assessment instruments have generated as much attention and literature as the LNNB so soon after its development, a testament to its potential contribution to the field.

Careful review of the test manual and subsequent literature on the LNNB (cited below) yields a number of strengths but also key weaknesses of the battery. They will be summarized below.

1. Validation studies: Subject Selection and Description: The test manual devotes some 24 pages to issues of reliability and validity for the LNNB. However, many of the initial validation studies are suspect, leaving the reader with questions as to appropriateness of the "normal" or patient groups. For instance, in an early study by Golden, Hammeke, and Purisch (1978), the goldstandard for assignment of a subject to a "brain-damaged" group was clinical diagnosis by the attending physician, *"usually* a neurologist or neurosurgeon" (Golden, Purisch, & Hammeke, 1985, p. 269, emphasis added). No research criteria were used for diagnosis and physician determination of brain impairment alone may be less a sensitive criterion than is desired for the development of a new, and it is hoped, more sensitive neuropsychological measure. CT scans were used to aid in diagnosis in only 60% of the cases. Second, in many studies (e.g., Golden, Hammeke, & Purisch, 1978), the "normal" groups in the early studies actually consisted of *hospitalized patients*, "most . . . [of whom] were referred from *neurological* and orthopedic wards [while] none had medical histories, symptoms, or laboratory data suggestive of cerebral dysfunction in the opinion of the attending physician" [emphasis added] (Golden, Purisch, & Hammeke, 1985, p. 270). The fact that many were referred from neurologic wards is concerning and raises the possibility that subtle but discernable CNS effects were present.

Also of concern is the lack of data on degree of overall cognitive impairment of the patient samples across the various studies. This is almost never reported in the studies cited in the manual (i.e., are subjects mildly, moderately, or severely brain injured?). This is a key question because a test that discriminates mildly impaired subjects from controls will obviously be more useful than a test that is able to discriminate only moderately to severely impaired patients from normals.

2. Number of Subjects to Number of Analyses: The test manual is replete with studies reporting many (even thousands in some cases) of univariate analyses, oftentimes on a sample of 100 or fewer patients. For instance, in the initial validation article of 100 subjects (50 patients and 50 controls) described above, *t*-tests between the two groups were

performed on each individual item (scored 0, 1, or 2), violating assumptions, assuming continuous data which is distributed normally for parametric analyses, and often resulting in an increased alpha level. As another example, a study is cited in the manual in which 60 subjects were assigned to one of eight "localization groups." A discriminant function analysis was then performed using the 14 scales to distinguish localization group. "Although it was recognized that an insufficient number of patients were available to legitimately conduct a discriminant analysis, it was felt that such an analysis would yield some information bearing on the effectiveness of the battery in discriminating among the various criterion groups" (Golden, Purisch, & Hammeke, 1985). The tendency to conduct an unacceptably large number of analyses relative to subject number seems more the rule than the exception in the studies reported and reviewed in the test manual, only capitalizing on the possibility for a Type I error and greatly increasing the actual alpha level. In fairness, the authors sometimes incorporate the Bonferonni correction for multiple comparisons though the sheer number of analyses performed no doubt accounts for many of the significant findings reported in the manual.

3. Inadequate Sampling of Critical Cognitive Domains: Several critical cognitive domains are sampled inadequately by the LNNB. Most notable of these is memory. Although Form I includes no formal assessment of delayed (secondary) memory, Form II includes an Intermediate Memory scale. It will be important to determine the accuracy of this scale to detect and measure the severity of secondary verbal and nonverbal memory dysfunction in patients in the future.

4. Discrimination Between "Brain Damage" versus "Other": Considerable data are presented in the manual to substantiate the claim the LNNB discriminates well between those subjects who are "brain damaged" versus those who are normal. At least one subsequent study found the LNNB to discriminate as well as the Halstead Reitan battery and the WAIS (Wechsler Adult Intelligence Scale) between a sample of brain damaged subjects and normals (Kane, Parsons, & Goldstein, 1985). However, as Mapou (1988) has noted, this is only one of the questions frequently posed to the neuropsychologist. In fact, one might speculate that as neurodiagnostic imaging and other biochemical techniques increase in sophistication, providing biological markers and diagnostic armamenteria for clinicians, questions of "functional versus organic" will become less important and other questions (type of aphasia, dementia, level of overall impairment, functional implications, etc.) will become more important. Goldstein, Shelly, McCue, and Kane (1987) found that although stable clusters were found for the LNNB items, "they were relatively unrelated to actual diagnoses" (p. 215). The test manual reports several studies, unfortunately most of which contain significant methodologic weaknesses, suggesting that the LNNB is able to correctly identify quadrant of damage with hit rates of approximately 74% (Golden, Purisch, & Hammeke, 1985, p. 276). Despite evidence that the test may identify hemisphere, and somewhat less successfully, quadrant, at least two studies document the failure of the LNNB to accurately localize or discriminate accurately among aphasias (Delis & Kaplan, 1982; Ryan, Farage, Mittenberg, & Kasprisin, 1988). Ryan and colleagues administered the language scales of the LNNB to seven patients with left frontal (Broca's aphasia) or left posterior (Wernicke's aphasia) damage. They compared between groups on the standard scales and on 13 factor-analytically derived subscales reported in the test manual. Ryan and colleagues (1988) found the standard T-score profile did not successfully discriminate between the two aphasias, and only two of the factor scales discriminated between the groups. It must be noted that the Ryan et al. (1988) study is limited because of an n of only seven subjects per group, resulting in perhaps insufficient power to detect differences between the two groups.

5. Form II: It must be noted that the studies reviewed above essentially were performed on the LNNB—Form I. Although Form II may hold slightly more promise than Form I (the test stimuli are a bit larger and better organized and an Intermediate Memory scale is included), it is premature to draw any firm conclusions on the utility of Form II relative to Form I. As Moses and Maruish (1989b, p. 97) have pointed out, "cross-form equivalence has been an assumption rather than an established fact, and there is growing experimental evidence that the two forms of the test probably are not interchangeable." Hence, review of Form II must await a future edition of this *Yearbook*.

In summary, the LNNB has attracted much attention in the past decade, an enviable testament to its considerable impact on the field in a relatively short period of time. However, with its success has come difficulties as well. Many of the early studies contained significant methodologic weaknesses which provided critics with sufficient ammunition to assail the battery. It appears the LNNB discriminates between "functional versus organic" disorders as well as other standard neuropsychological batteries. The need, however, to answer this question will likely continue to wane. Although it may adequately localize hemisphere of damage, it appears to fail to adequately discriminate between language syndromes. The degree to which it adequately discriminates among other syndromes (e.g., among the dementias) has not been sufficiently studied. Considerable caution must be exercised when using the LNNB for tasks other than identification of the presence and hemisphere of central nervous system impairment.

REVIEWER'S REFERENCES

Golden, C. J., Hammeke, T. A., & Purisch, A. D. (1978). Diagnostic validity of a standardized neuropsychological battery derived from Luria's neuropsychological tests. *Journal of Consulting and Clinical Psychology, 46* (6), 1258-1265.

Adams, K. M. (1980). In search of Luria's battery: A false start. *Journal of Consulting and Clinical Psychology, 48,* 511-516.

Golden, C. J. (1980). In reply to Adams' "In search of Luria's battery: A false start." *Journal of Consulting and Clinical Psychology, 48,* 517-521.

Spiers, P. A. (1981). Have they come to praise Luria or to bury him?: The Luria-Nebraska Battery controversy. *Journal of Consulting and Clinical Psychology, 49,* 331-341.

Delis, D. C., & Kaplan, E. (1982). The assessment of aphasia with the Luria-Nebraska Neuropsychological Battery: A case critique. *Journal of Consulting and Clinical Psychology, 50,* 32-39.

Spiers, P. A. (1982). The Luria-Nebraska Neuropsychological Battery revisited: A theory in practice or just practicing? *Journal of Consulting and Clinical Psychology, 50,* 301-306.

Adams, K. M. (1984). Luria left in the lurch: Unfulfilled promises are not valid tests. *Journal of Clinical Neuropsychology, 6,* 455-458.

Golden, C. J., Purisch, A. D., & Hammeke, T. A. (1985). Luria-Nebraska Neuropsychological Battery: Forms I and II manual. Los Angeles: Western Psychological Services.

Kane, R. L., Parsons, O. A., & Goldstein, G. (1985). Statistical relationships and discriminative accuracy of the Halstead-Reitan, Luria-Nebraska, and Wechsler IQ scores in the identification of brain damage. *Journal of Clinical and Experimental Neuropsychology, 7,* 211-223.

Goldstein, G., Shelly, C., McCue, M., & Kane, R. L. (1987). Classification with the Luria-Nebraska Neuropsychological Battery: An application of cluster and ipsative profile analysis. *Archives of Clinical Neuropsychology, 2,* 215-235.

Mapou, R. L. (1988). Testing to detect brain damage: An alternative to what may no longer be useful. *Journal of Clinical and Experimental Neuropsychology, 10,* 271-278.

Ryan, J. J., Farage, C. M., Mittenberg, W., & Kasprisin, A. (1988). Validity of the Luria-Nebraska language scales in aphasia. *International Journal of Neuroscience, 43,* 75-80.

Moses, J. A., Jr., & Maruish, M. E. (1989a). A critical review of the Luria-Nebraska Neuropsychological Battery literature: X. Critiques and rebuttals. Part One. *International Journal of Clinical Neuropsychology, 11,* 145-162.

Moses, J. A., Jr., & Maruish, M. E. (1989b). A critical review of the Luria-Nebraska Neuropsychological Battery literature: IX. Alternate forms. *International Journal of Clinical Neuropsychology, 11,* 97-110.

Moses, J. A., Jr., & Maruish, M. E. (1990). A critical review of the Luria-Nebraska Neuropsychological Battery literature: X. Critiques and rebuttals. Part Two. *International Journal of Clinical Neuropsychology, 12,* 37-45.

[213]
Management and Graduate Item Bank.

Purpose: "For use in the selection, development or guidance of personnel at graduate level or in management positions."

Population: Graduate level and senior management applicants for the following areas: finance, computing, engineering, corporate planning, purchasing, personnel, and marketing.

Publication Dates: 1985–87.

Acronym: MGIB.

Scores, 2: Verbal Critical Reasoning, Numerical Critical Reasoning.

Administration: Group.

Price Data, 1986: £55 per administration set including manual ('87, 39 pages), supplementary norms manual ('87, 39 pages), test log, test booklets, answer sheets, administration instructions, and scoring stencils; £45 per 10 Verbal test booklets ('85, 16 pages); £65 per 10 Numerical test booklets ('85, 15 pages); £35 per 50 Verbal or Numerical answer sheets; £7 per Verbal or Numerical scoring stencil; £7 per Verbal (3 pages) or Numerical (3 pages) administration instructions; £22 per manual.

Time: 60(65) minutes.

Comments: Abbreviated adaptation of the Advanced Test Battery (9:57); subtests available as separates.

Authors: Saville & Holdsworth Ltd. and Linda Espey (supplementary norms manual).

Publisher: Saville & Holdsworth Ltd. [England].

Review of the Management and Graduate Item Bank by JAMES T. AUSTIN, Assistant Professor, University of Illinois, Urbana, IL, and H. JOHN BERNARDIN, University Professor of Research, Florida Atlantic University, Boca Raton, FL:

The tests of Verbal and Numerical Critical Reasoning from the Management and Graduate Item Bank are the first in a planned series of short tests with multiple parallel forms (hence the title Item Bank) for managerial selection and development in industry. Test takers are to be at the upper ranges of the respective ability distributions. The tests consist of short passages (Verbal) or statistical tables and figures (Numerical) with associated questions that call for critical evaluation by the examinee. Both entry-level college graduates and experienced managers are suggested as populations to which the tests apply. The authors acknowledge the tentative nature of inferences based on the scores at this stage in test and norm development.

The tests are short (1 hour total for both) to minimize practice effects and allow use throughout employees' careers. They were developed from the same firm's Advanced Test Battery (ATB; 9:57). The manual is available to anyone without restriction, but other materials are released only to those who meet the company's standards (based on British Psychological Society guidelines). Although internal and external selection is emphasized as a purpose for the tests in the Manual and User's Guide, no studies are cited or discussed that support this or other functions claimed for the tests. Moreover, the tests are based on the idea that critical reasoning is an important component in managerial and professional positions. One would therefore expect that construct validation or (at least) criterion-related validity evidence be presented (cf. Cook, 1988; Cronbach, 1988). Thus, the most critical flaw of the present tests and their supporting documentation is that no validity evidence is presented. This lack is especially distressing because the same firm has published other tests with no evidence of validity. Given the time lapse since the publication of the ATB, lack of time cannot serve as an excuse for this problem.

Reliability estimates (Cronbach's alpha) are presented in the Manual and User's Guide. Normative data from relatively large overall samples, in the form of T-scores and percentiles, appear in a publication entitled *Normline Supplement No. 1.*

These data, however, have problems of their own that we discuss below.

SPECIFIC EVALUATIONS. The tests have several strengths. One positive aspect is that the administration instructions are complete enough so that persons with relatively little training can give the test. Another is a discussion of equal employment opportunity in the context of British law (e.g., the Sex Discrimination Act and the Race Relations Act, 1975 and 1976, respectively). There is, however, no mention of the UK Commission on Racial Equality's Code (1984) and/or the Equal Employment Commission's Code (1985). There is a discussion of differential validity concepts with a question and answer section in the *Normline*. Third, the concept of a periodically updated norm supplement to which users can contribute data is a good one, provided that quality control is maintained. Finally, the authors seem to have a good grasp of basic psychometrics, as evidenced by their competent discussion of such concepts as standard scores, reliability and validity estimates, and user qualifications. A caveat to this final point is there is no discussion of range restriction, which is implied in the prescreening that many of the normative samples underwent. Taken as a whole, however, these strengths do not balance the test's critical flaws.

The reliability estimates (.74 and .82 for Verbal and Numerical respectively) are unimpressive, particularly given that the tests are recommended for important individual decisions. In addition, the samples for the final forms are too small (n s of 44), especially relative to the larger sample sizes for pilot forms. Oddly, the reliability estimates for both pilot forms (.77 for Verbal and .91 for Numerical) were higher than those of the final forms. Also, given that the test is supposed to discriminate at the high ends of the distribution, estimations of the standard error of measurement at different points along the test score distribution are advisable. There is no mention of any possible deficiencies in the reliability section of the manual other than a discussion of the advisability of considering the mean and variability of the sample when interpreting the standard error of measurement.

The lack of validity data is extremely troubling, although such information is promised in future editions of the *Normline*. Beyond a discussion of types of validity, no validity evidence for this test is presented, unless one considers a cursory discussion of a positive relationship between the two tests to be adequate (with no mention of the size of the relevant correlation; Manual, p. 23). Furthermore, evidence of construct validity is necessary, given that critical reasoning, a theoretical construct, is claimed as an important component of the managerial job.

The Watson-Glaser Critical Thinking Appraisal (9:1347), with forms for adults, appears to be the best alternative for assessing this construct at the present time. Although there are problems with the Watson-Glaser test, the authors of the tests under review here would do well to at least consider the conceptual work that went into the Watson-Glaser (i.e., the five-dimension structure) and to study the validation strategy used. An alternative assessment strategy might be to employ the techniques proposed and demonstrated by Borman, Rosse, and Abrahams (1980).

The norms presented consist of two sections: (*a*) Graduates (presumably recent undergraduates) and (*b*) Management. Sample sizes appear adequate at the overall level. There are some problems when the data are broken down into subsamples covering a wide range of occupations and firms. Overall sample sizes for the recent graduate group are 1,443 for Verbal and 1,439 for Numerical; the subsamples range in size from 72 (Mail Order Book Club) to 252 (Finance and Technical). The total sample for managers is 368 for both tests, with 277 managers who are graduates and 91 who are not. There is no discussion regarding the mean differences between the graduate and management samples. Even when managers who are graduates are compared to the graduate sample, there are mean differences in favor of the graduates (34.17 vs. 31.12 for Verbal; 23.63 vs. 20.56 for Numerical). These differences suggest the tests may assess aspects of schooling rather than job performance. This is a common complaint about general ability tests (cf. Frederiksen, 1986, although that critique was directed at "intelligence" tests). Some consideration and discussion should be given to the convenience sampling plan that apparently governed the development of the norms. *Large numbers do not compensate for improper sampling.* Perhaps the ideal procedure would be to use a multistage procedure, in which firms would be randomly sampled from the U.K. population, followed by random sampling of managerial personnel within the firms. When state-of-the-art test development strategies are not used, mention of these shortcomings should be made in supporting manuals.

In summary, we cannot recommend the use of these tests for selection or development until more evidence is produced. The reported reliability estimates are low for individual decision-making purposes. More importantly, there is virtually no evidence for validity. Finally, the process of norm development has problems as well. The Manual has several strong sections, but references to many of the concepts and findings are lacking. A more complete manual would allow less experienced test users to fairly evaluate the tests.

REVIEWERS' REFERENCES

Mintzberg, H. (1973). *The nature of managerial work.* New York: Harper & Row.

Borman, W. C., Rosse, R. L., & Abrahams, N. M. (1980). An empirical construct validity approach to studying predictor-job performance links. *Journal of Applied Psychology, 65,* 662-671.

Stewart, R. (1982). A model for understanding managerial work. *Academy of Management Review, 7,* 7-13.

Frederiksen, N. (1986). Toward a broader conception of human intelligence. *American Psychologist, 41,* 445-452.

Cook, M. (1988). *Personnel selection and productivity.* Chichester: Wiley.

Cronbach, L. J. (1988). Five perspectives on the validity argument. In H. Wainer & H. Braun (Eds.), *Test validity* (pp. 3-17). Hillsdale, NJ: Erlbaum.

Review of the Management and Graduate Item Bank by R. W. FAUNCE, Consulting Psychologist, Minneapolis, MN:

The Management and Graduate Item Bank (MGIB) is described as the first stage in a series of new higher level cognitive tests being developed to rescue the Advanced Test Battery (9:57) from the ravages of practice effects and "potential" overexposure. The first two tests in this proposed series are the Verbal Critical Reasoning test (VMG1) and the Numerical Critical Reasoning test (NMG1). These new tests are reported to be similar in appearance to the Verbal and Numerical Critical Reasoning tests of the Advanced Test Battery (VA3 and NA4).

The test of verbal reasoning, VMG1, consists of 52 questions to be answered within 25 minutes. Answers are made by filling in boxes on a separate answer sheet. Scoring may be done manually or by machine. Thirteen paragraphs are presented and four statements are made about each paragraph. Respondents indicate whether each statement is true (follows logically), untrue (the opposite follows logically), or if neither the statement nor its opposite is true (or if more information is needed to make a determination).

The numerical reasoning test, NMG1, consists of 40 multiple-choice questions to be answered within 35 minutes. Half the items have 5 response options and half have 10 options. Questions are based on a number of statistical tables containing data on such things as production rates, inflation rates, and life expectancy.

Both tests are attractively packaged, printed on sturdy, high-gloss paper, have clear instructions, and are easy to handle. Answer sheets are also of high quality construction. The hand-scoring plastic overlay keys make scoring simple and errors should be minimal. Scoring key instructions have one minor error. Scorers are directed to enter raw scores in a box at the top of the answer sheet; the box is actually at the bottom of the answer sheet.

The 41-page manual is also attractive and easy to read. More than a third of the manual (17 pages) is devoted to descriptions of the testing program, administration, and scoring. Another third (15 pages) presents boilerplate information on basic psychometric desiderata, which could apply to any test. Only nine pages refer to psychometric information specific to the MGIB. Eight pages present normative information and one page is devoted to reliability. No validity data are presented.

Users in the U.S. might be put off by language differences, such as instructions referring to the use of crayons, rubbers, and invigilators. Although language differences in instructions might have nuisance value, differences in item content could affect validity. It is hard to tell what impact questions involving petrol, pounds (instead of dollars), programmes, and tonnes would have on populations that do not speak "English."

The Management and Graduate Item Bank appears to be a direct competitor of another British developed test, Graduate and Managerial Assessment (10:129). Publishers of both tests appear to have pursued the same marketing approach of publishing the basic test materials and then supplying supportive information as it becomes available. This approach has the advantage of getting the tests before the public with plenty of time to review them. It has the disadvantage of not supplying the potential user with sufficient psychometric data on which an informed decision to use or not to use must be based. It would be difficult to choose between the two tests, considering the available information. It appears unlikely that either test will have a substantial impact on the domestic U.S. market.

STANDARDIZATION AND NORMS. Little information is provided about standardization procedures. No information is given on item statistics. Norms, initially presented in 1986, were based on 252 "graduate applicants to a public utility." Presumably, these college graduates were applying for entry-level jobs because their average age was 21. Means, standard deviations, percentile ranks, and *T* scores are given. Similar information is also given for subgroups of the graduate applicant sample, based on the type of occupation to which they applied: Finance and Technical, Administration, or Commercial. Sample sizes in these subgroups were small, with Administration having only 46 applicants.

According to information found in the manual, applicants who did well on the verbal test also tended to do well on the numerical test. No supporting data are given. Males were described as doing better than females on the numerical test, but no sex difference was found on the verbal test. Again, supporting data are lacking. All norms are based on combined male-female scores and no evidence of predictive validity is provided. The publisher "plans to provide data on likely differences in test scores for different groups and, when appropriate, to issue differential norms."

A subsequent publication, in 1987 (*Normline Supplement No. 1*), provides additional norms, using the same format as the original norms. The new norms provide scores for 1,443 people in a Total

Graduate Group and 368 members in a Total Management Group. Norms are also given for nine subgroups of the Graduate Group, with sample sizes ranging from 72 graduates applying for trainee positions at a mail-order book club to 252 graduate applicants for financial and technical positions in a public utility. Apparently, although not explicitly stated, this latter sample is the same sample included in the original norm group described in the manual. The sample sizes in the subgroups do not add up to the Total Graduate Group sample size for some unexplained reason.

The Total Management Group is divided into two subgroups: a Graduate Management Group and a Non-Graduate Group. Subgroup sample sizes do add up to the Total Management Group sample size. Mean scores for the Graduate Group were substantially higher than mean scores for the Non-Graduate Group, but large age differences between the two groups also existed. No studies of the influence of age have been reported thus far.

RELIABILITY AND VALIDITY. Information on reliability is sparse. Cronbach's alpha coefficients for 44 "young graduates in banking" were .74 for the verbal test and .82 for the numerical test. The reliability of the tests is critical to the success of the Management and Graduate Item Bank because a major purpose of the item bank is to permit the easy development of numerous alternate forms. Additional reliability information on larger and better described samples would be welcome and, of course, alternate form reliability needs to be established as the new tests are released.

Standard errors of measurement are provided for raw scores and T scores. Again, these measures are based on the 44 young graduates in banking and, presumably, on Cronbach's alpha coefficients. Standard errors typically were about 5 for the verbal test and about 4 for the numerical test.

The face validity of the two tests seems good, at least for Great Britain. No other validity information is presented, although it is promised.

SUMMARY. The Management and Graduate Item Bank is an attractively designed instrument that appears easy to administer and score. Its face validity is good for the British market. Its developers appear to be well aware of the criteria used to evaluate the adequacy of tests, and their descriptions of test desiderata are clearly presented in the manual. Up to this point, little evidence of reliability or validity has been offered. It remains to be seen if the developers can live up to their promising beginning. Until more information is forthcoming, the tests should be considered experimental.

[214]
Management Change Inventory.
Purpose: Measures knowledge of sound methods of introducing change.

Population: Managers and prospective managers.
Publication Dates: 1970–81.
Scores: Total score only.
Administration: Group.
Price Data, 1990: $40 per complete kit of 10 test booklets, fact sheet, and user's guide.
Time: (15–20) minutes.
Comments: Self-administered.
Authors: W. J. Reddin and E. Keith Stewart.
Publisher: Organizational Tests Ltd. [Canada].

Review of the Management Change Inventory by FREDERICK BESSAI, Professor of Education, University of Regina, Regina, Saskatchewan, Canada:

The Management Change Inventory (MCH) is an 80-item true-false test designed to measure knowledge of change relations. It yields a single score and is intended for use in management training sessions and seminars. The MCH has an attractive booklet and is self-scoring. The items are easily legible, and clear instructions for scoring are given on the carbon-backed score sheet. A four-page administration guide serves as a manual. The guide states that the test should not be used as a pretest and posttest to measure change in individuals' knowledge due to training. The authors state that the test can be used as a learning vehicle (by discussing items in group training sessions) or to identify training needs in a group.

The test appears to have good face validity for the purposes mentioned, but the accompanying information provides no statement or data about other validity evidence or score reliability. The authors only describe these characteristics and briefly suggest how they could be established. The only rationale given for the selection and wording of the items is that they were reviewed by more than 100 judges. A 10-point percentile scale in intervals of 10 from 5 to 95 is provided for users to convert raw scores to percentiles. The authors provide basic information for interpreting the percentiles. No norming information is provided and no statement about the group used to obtain these percentiles is given.

This reviewer cannot recommend this test (in its present form) for general use and, as the authors themselves state, the MCH should not be used as pretest and posttest measures in experimental research. At best, it might be used casually or as instructional material in situations where the substance of the items will be discussed in learning groups. A reasonable amount of information on validity and reliability and an adequate set of norms would make MCH scores much more meaningful either in professional practice or in research.

Review of the Management Change Inventory by RALPH F. DARR, JR., Professor of Education, Department of Educational Foundations, The University of Akron, Akron, OH:

The Management Change Inventory (MCH) Kit contains a Fact Sheet, the Instrument Administration Guide, and 10 copies of the MCH. The Fact Sheet provides a brief description of the MCH, states the purpose of the instrument, suggests ways the instrument data might be used, notes six "topics" that the instrument measures, offers 17 propositions about how effective change occurs, and concludes with a table for converting raw scores to percentile ranks. Norms are based on 1,895 subjects.

The goal of the instrument, according to the Fact Sheet, is to test "knowledge of sound methods of introducing change at a worker and supervisory level." Six topics are assessed: participation, speed, degree of information, training, resistance, and planning. The Instrument Administration Guide provides instruction on the mechanics of administering the inventory, suggests ways for dealing with confidential results, urges administrators to provide a relaxed atmosphere during the test, suggests several models for using the inventory in instructional settings, and offers a brief discussion of the concepts of reliability and validity. The guide concludes with suggestions for answering test takers' queries about reliability and validity. Test-retest is not recommended because respondents could simply memorize answers obtained during discussion and/or the theory lecture. Part of the value of the instrument is the self-scoring feature, which could also influence test-retest results. The guide suggests that frequent users might wish to validate the MCH within their own company by administering it to their most effective and least effective change managers and comparing the score ranges of the two groups. This paper-and-pencil instrument measures knowledge of practices that facilitate change, not whether the respondent employs these practices effectively.

The guide states that the instrument has good face validity because all items deal with the notion of affecting organizational change. Further, it notes that the face validity of the test renders it adequate for use as a training tool. As an additional defense of the instrument's validity, the guide states that the MCH was "constructed by skilled trainers" and "inspected" by "judges" (p. 4). Both trainers and judges are unidentified, as are their techniques for developing the instrument and judging its worth.

The MCH is an 80-item true-false instrument. Each booklet provides both test items and an answer sheet. The respondent marks the answers in the booklet, separates the pages, counts the marked boxes, and then converts the raw score into a percentile rank using the table provided in the Instrument Administration Guide.

All items are short, concise statements about effective practices for introducing change in the business sector. Statements vary in length from 6 to 19 words. The word *change* is used in 90% of the items. Although the manager's role in the change process is emphasized in the inventory's title, employees' roles in and reaction to change are not ignored in the inventory. The term *manager* or *management* is used in about 26% of the items, whereas the term *employees* is used in about 24% of them.

The MCH is a straightforward, efficient instrument for determining if managers know the right answers about how to affect desirable change in their organizations. The instrument can be completed in 15 to 20 minutes, and the answers can be scored and analyzed by the respondent in a few minutes more. This speed and ease of self-scoring makes the MCH a useful instructional tool in management change seminars. It stimulates the respondent to think about the roles of the employee and the manager in affecting institutional change.

This instrument has limited assessment and research value because some of the items do not conform to good item-writing practices. Several contain ambiguous, undefined concepts, and extensive use is made of specific determiners and ambiguous qualifiers. The usefulness of the MCH is seriously restricted by the absence of any evidence of reliability and the limited amount of validity evidence. The Instrument Administration Guide limits its discussion of reliability to warning consumers not to attempt to assess test-retest reliability. Because there is only one form, parallel-form reliability is not an issue. However, without parallel forms, studies that use gain scores would produce questionable results. Evidence of internal consistency is lacking as well.

The developers of the inventory appear to have given limited consideration to the issue of validity. Only face validity as it relates to the instrument's use as a teaching tool is addressed. No rationale for content validity is provided. Although 90% of the items contain the word *change*, there is no way for the consumer to determine how many aspects of change the MCH actually assesses or how much each of those aspects influences an individual's overall score. Although the Fact Sheet indicates that the test measures six topics, no information about how much each topic influences the total score is given.

Empirical and construct validity are also ignored. Although the authors note that knowledge of change strategies does not guarantee use of those strategies, they do not appear to have tested that hypothesis. Nor did they provide evidence of how scores on the MCH relate to other measures of the characteristics of successful managers. Knowledge is the primary construct measured by the MCH.

SUMMARY. This inventory appears to be more usable as a teaching tool than as an assessment or research instrument. The lack of parallel forms restricts the research potential of the MCH. Limited information about reliability and validity severely limit the instrument's interpretability and usability.

[215]
Management Coaching Relations.

Purpose: Measures "knowledge of sound methods of coaching subordinates who may be supervisors or managers."
Population: Managers and potential managers.
Publication Dates: 1970–81.
Acronym: MCR.
Scores: Total score only.
Administration: Group.
Manual: No manual; fact sheet available.
Price Data, 1990: $40 per complete kit including 10 test booklets, fact sheet, and user's guide.
Time: (15–20) minutes.
Comments: Self-administered; may be self-scored.
Authors: W. J. Reddin and E. Keith Stewart.
Publisher: Organizational Tests Ltd. [Canada].

[216]
Management Interest Inventory.

Purpose: "To assist both organizations and individuals in making decisions relating to selection, placement, and career development at management level."
Population: Managers.
Publication Dates: 1983–86.
Scores, 54: Management Functions Preference Scores and Experience Scores (Production Operations, Technical Services, Research and Development, Distribution, Purchasing, Sales, Marketing Support, Personnel and Training, Data Processing, Finance, Legal and Secretarial, Administration, Total, Spread Across Functions); Management Skills Preference Scores and Experience Scores (Information Collecting, Information Processing, Problem-Solving, Decision-Making, Modelling, Communicating Orally, Communicating in Writing, Organising Things, Organising People, Persuading, Developing, Representing, Total).
Administration: Group.
Price Data, 1987: £45 per administration set; £20 per 10 nonreusable booklets; £26.50 per scoring keys; £20 per manual and user's guide ('86, 51 pages).
Time: (20–40) minutes.
Authors: Roger Holdsworth (test), Ruth Holdsworth (test), Lisa Cramp (test), and Miranda Blum (manual).
Publisher: Saville & Holdsworth Ltd. [England].

Review of the Management Interest Inventory by DAVID M. SAUNDERS, Assistant Professor, Faculty of Management, McGill University, Montreal, CANADA:

The recently developed Management Interest Inventory measures employee interest in various management functions and skills. The inventory includes items that assess 12 Management Functions and 12 Management Skills. There are 144 items on the inventory, one item for each of the Management Functions/Management Skills pairings assessed. The items on the inventory are clearly

written, the questionnaire itself is quite accessible to people completing the inventory, and the manual is well written with appropriate cautions about the use of the inventory. Inventories may be scored by hand with a color-coded template, or sent to the publisher for computer scoring. There is a computerized version of the measure available from the publisher.

The manual presents no information about the reliability of the scales. Test-retest reliability studies are currently being conducted and the results are promised for future versions of the manual. Internal consistency measures (Cronbach's alpha) could have been calculated with the data collected for the initial validity studies but they are not reported.

The manual reports that no independent validity study has been conducted to date and invites test users to participate in such a study. Initial validation studies conducted by the inventory developers suggest the Management Interest Inventory has good convergent and discriminant validity. Evidence of convergent validity comes from a series of interesting and sensible correlations between the Management Interest Inventory and various personality characteristics (as measured with the Occupational Personality Questionnaire) [OPQ]). Evidence of discriminant validity comes from the fact that the Management Interest Inventory generally is not correlated with aptitude (as measured by the VA3 and NA4).

One disturbing aspect of the Management Interest Inventory is the degree to which the skills interests are highly intercorrelated (from .31 to .85). These strong intercorrelations suggest the different skills interests are not independent, and that treating them as such may not be appropriate. Although the Management Interest Inventory was developed rationally, and items are based on managers' descriptions of their jobs and existing models of managerial jobs, the intercorrelations of the skills interests suggest to this reader that there might be underlying dimensions of managerial skills that could be identified with factor analytic techniques. Many of the functions interests are also strongly intercorrelated, but not as strongly as the skills interests. However, factor analysis could also be used to investigate patterns of functions interests that appear to exist and that are discussed in the manual.

The manual recommends two methods of interpreting scores from the Management Interest Inventory and discusses many of the advantages and disadvantages of each. The intrapersonal method discussed allows the individual to explore his or her own differences in interest levels across the 12 Management Functions and 12 Management Skills. This method may be most appropriately used in counselling and managerial development activities. Even in these uses, however, it must be remembered that the scales are not as independent as they are described to be and that previous experience with a function or a skill is strongly correlated (above .65 based on my calculations of the group means from the manual) with interest. People may have latent interests in functions or skills of which they are unaware because they have yet to have experience with those activities.

The second method of interpreting the Management Interest Inventory discussed in the manual involves comparing individual scores with group norms. The manual suggests that the Management Interest Inventory may be used to improve selection decisions by selecting job applicants who have interests that are similar to those of job incumbents. This practice should be strongly discouraged for two reasons: (*a*) No evidence of the validity of this scale as a selection device was presented; and, (*b*) because experience with functions and skills is strongly correlated with interest in functions and skills, this inventory may fail to identify people with latent interests in various functions or skills but who have yet to gain experience with them.

An additional caution regarding the use of the norms provided in the manual is also necessary. The norms are based on a sample of British managers that reflect the "average British manager"; as such, production managers are represented heavily in the sample while Legal and Secretarial managers are infrequently represented. Because experience with functions and skills is strongly correlated with interest in functions and skills, the norms presented in the manual are substantially influenced by the frequency of the functions of the managers who completed the inventory for the norm sample. That is, because there are many production managers in the sample, the norms for the production scale are higher (because more experienced production workers who are also interested in production work are in the sample). Comparison of these managers' interests and experience with the other functions may not be appropriate. Rather, because of the experience-interest correlation, it would seem essential to report norms separately for the different functions.

In summary, the Management Interest Inventory should be adopted with caution. Its most appropriate use at this time may be as an aid in counselling and managerial development. The inventory should not be used as a selection device until its validity for this task is established. Finally, any comparisons of individual scores with the inventory norms should be done with caution until norms are presented separately for managers with different levels of experience in various functions.

[217]
Management Inventory on Performance Appraisal and Coaching.

Purpose: "To determine the need for training in 'performance appraisal and coaching'" and to stimulate discussion in a supervisory/management training program.
Population: Managers.
Publication Date: 1990.
Acronym: MIPAC.
Scores: Total score only.
Administration: Group.
Price Data, 1991: $30 per 20 tests and answer booklets; $5 per optional audiocassette; $2 per manual (7 pages); $5 per specimen set.
Time: (20–25) minutes.
Comments: Self-administered, self-scored.
Author: Donald L. Kirkpatrick.
Publisher: Donald L. Kirkpatrick.

[218]
Management Practices Update.
Purpose: To provide individuals with information about managerial behavior in areas of interpersonal relationships, the management of motivation, and personal "style" of management.
Population: Individuals involved in the management of others.
Publication Date: 1987.
Acronym: MPU.
Scores, 12: Section I (Exposure, Feedback), Section II (Basic, Safety, Belonging, Ego Status, Actualization), Section III (Team Management, Middle-of-the-Road Management, Task Management, Country Club Management, Impoverished Management).
Administration: Group.
Levels: 3 parts: I (Interpersonal Relationships), II (Management of Motivation), III (Analysis of Management Style).
Price Data, 1990: $10 per manual (25 pages).
Time: Administration time not reported.
Comments: Represents a shortened version of Personnel Relations Survey (289), Management of Motives Index (9:1189), and Styles of Management Inventory (9:1185).
Author: Jay Hall.
Publisher: Teleometrics International.

[219]
Management Relations Survey.
Purpose: To assess employees' perceptions of their practices toward their managers.
Population: Subordinates to managers.
Publication Date: 1970–87.
Acronym: MRS.
Scores, 2: Exposure, Feedback.
Administration: Group.
Price Data, 1990: $6.95 per manual ('87, 14 pages).
Time: Administration time not reported.
Comments: Companion instrument to Personnel Relations Survey (289); based on the Johari Window Model of interpersonal relations.
Author: Jay Hall.
Publisher: Teleometrics International.
Cross Reference: For a review by Walter C. Borman, see 8:1178 (1 reference).

[220]
Management Style Inventory [Training House, Inc.].

Purpose: "This exercise is designed to give you some insights into your management style and how it affects others."
Population: Industry.
Publication Dates: 1986–87.
Scores, 5: Team Builder, Soft, Hard, Middle of Road, Ineffective.
Administration: Group.
Price Data, 1988: $60 per 20 complete sets including test, answer sheet, and interpretation sheet.
Time: Administration time not reported.
Comments: Self-administered, self-scored.
Author: Training House, Inc.
Publisher: Training House, Inc.

Review of the Management Style Inventory [Training House, Inc.] by ERNEST J. KOZMA, Professor of Education, Clemson University, Clemson, SC:

The Management Style Inventory is self-scoring inventory designed to help an individual make a self-assessment of his/her management style. The inventory contains 10 sets of statements. Each set includes five statements concerning a topic covered by the set. The individual using the inventory assigns a number to each of the statements. The highest number indicates the statement most representative of his/her view. The 10 topics covered are role perception, view of authority, setting goals and standards, view of work and workers, planning and scheduling work, giving feedback, team building, implementation, evaluation, and management philosophy.

An answer sheet is provided and the numerical ratings given each statement are recorded. A scoring sheet is attached and the answer is recorded and assigned a category. The totals for each category are compiled. The five categories are supposed to reflect five different management styles. After compiling the score in each of the five categories, the individual is referred to a four-page self-assessment folder that provides more detail concerning each of the categories or management styles.

The self-assessment folder begins with a very short review of various management styles that have been advocated since the first quarter of this century. The review contains no references or mention of some of the major management criticisms of the 1980s. A chart of factors affecting a person's management style with brief descriptive statements about each is included.

The styles are Hard style, Soft style, Middle of Road style, Ineffective style, and Team Builder. The entire folder includes only a few paragraphs of information about each of these.

No data or information are supplied as to the validity or reliability of the material. The claim is made that the material will provide some insights into personal management style and how it affects others. It is difficult to guarantee this result. As with most inventory-type instruments, individual differences in examinees greatly affect the value of the test-taking experience. The material overly simplifies the complex problems of management.

Review of the Management Style Inventory [Training House, Inc.] by CHARLES K. PARSONS, Professor of Management, Georgia Institute of Technology, Atlanta, GA:

The stated purpose of this inventory is to give the respondent some insights into his/her management style and its possible effects on other people. The inventory consists of 10 sets of five self-descriptive statements, on which the respondent is to rank order the five statements within each set on the degree to which each one is representative of him/her. The inventory is then self-scored and the respondent ends up with five scale scores representing his/her tendency to be a Team Builder, a Soft manager, a Hard manager, a Middle of the Road manager, or an Ineffective manager. Some explanation of these styles and when they might be effective is provided in an accompanying four-page folder.

This instrument is reported to be based on the "Managerial Grid" of Blake and Mouton (1964) and Blanchard and Hersey (1977). The resulting styles are virtually identical to those described by Blake and Mouton. The styles are the result of varying degrees of concern for people and production.

On the surface, this instrument appears to have some desirable features. First, each scale score ends up being the function of the responses to 10 items, thus improving chances of reliability. Second, the five statements within each set appear to be somewhat equal in terms of social desirability. Each statement appears to represent a plausible statement by a manager. This characteristic could make the forced choice nature of the response format effective in eliminating social desirability effects.

The scoring routine is relatively easy, although I can imagine some respondents needing clarification. Because of the nature of the scoring, it is possible for a person to end up with five scores that are quite similar to each other (one for each of five styles) or five that are quite different (strongly suggesting one style is dominant). Neither the scoring instructions nor the four-page explanatory folder provides guidance on interpreting the differences in the scores. I recommend some guidance on what level of difference between scores suggests a dominant style. Also, I suggest providing guidance on interpreting a score profile for a person who scores about the same on all five scales.

One particular style and its description are problematic—that resulting from low concern for tasks and low concern for people and labeled "ineffective." For a respondent having this predominant style, the label could be devastating. Somewhat surprisingly, the explanation of the style goes on to describe situations in which this style might be effective. I recommend that a different label and description be associated with the low, low style.

Another shortcoming of this instrument is it provides only a report of how the manager sees him/herself, which might be quite different from how subordinates view this person. Although the sole use of a self-report instrument, like the Management Style Inventory, is an expedient way to get some information about one's management style, a more complete view can be obtained by getting parallel information from subordinates and coworkers. Several commercially available instruments provide this capability.

The theory upon which this instrument is based suggests that this sort of inventory is best used as a self-assessment tool prior to some form of management development intervention. It would be extremely useful if the author(s) included information regarding the intended use of the instrument. There is none provided presently.

A major disadvantage of this inventory is that it is not accompanied by a reference manual that includes standard psychometric characteristics of the instrument. There are no reports of reliability, validity, norms, and so on. The user is left only with the "face" validity of the items and the scales as the basis for use. I would strongly recommend the publisher of this inventory correct this glaring deficiency in the package.

REVIEWER'S REFERENCES

Blake, R. R., & Mouton, J. S. (1964). *The managerial grid*. Houston: Gulf Publishing Co.

Hersey, P., & Blanchard, K. H. (1977). *Management of organizational behavior: Utilizing human resources* (3rd ed.). Englewood Cliffs, NJ: Prentice-Hall.

[221]
Manager Profile Record.

Purpose: "To identify candidates with a high potential for success in managerial and professional classifications."
Population: Prospective managers.
Publication Date: 1985.
Acronym: MPR.
Scores, 11: Background Record (Achievements: Academic Years, Present Self Concept, Present Social Orientation, Present Work Orientation, Total), Judgment Record (Staff Communication/Participation, Employee Selection-Development, Employee Motivation-Labor Relations, Management Style/Decision-Making, Total), Total Record.
Administration: Group.
Price Data, 1989: $8 per reusable test booklet; $35 per answer sheet (includes scoring by publisher); $5 per administrator's guide (24 pages).
Time: (180) minutes.
Author: Richardson, Bellows, Henry & Co., Inc.
Publisher: National Computer Systems.

Review of the Manager Profile Record by WILLIAM I. SAUSER, JR., Associate Vice President and Professor, Office of the Vice President for Extension, Auburn University, Auburn, AL:

The early identification of management potential through the use of self-reported biographical, attitudinal, and judgmental data has been the focus of several major research projects over the past few decades (Bentz, 1990; Howard & Bray, 1990; Owens, 1976). The Manager Profile Record (MPR) is based upon one such project, a collaborative effort begun in the 1950s between Richardson, Bellows, Henry and Company (the authors of the MPR) and Standard Oil of New Jersey (Sparks, 1990).

This reviewer concurs with its authors that the MPR appears suitable for several purposes, including (*a*) to serve as an inexpensive prescreen for assessment center systems and as an objective check against center results; (*b*) to audit present staff to inventory potential managers; (*c*) to identify potential candidates for managerial training, particularly for affirmative action purposes; and (*d*) to be used as *one component* of a management recruitment and selection program. Throughout their descriptive materials the authors properly warn potential users that the MPR does *not* measure intellectual capacity or past achievement, thus it should certainly *not* be used as the sole selection device for promotion into managerial ranks.

The MPR test booklet is very professional in appearance. Part I contains 196 multiple-choice items, the last 57 of which are intended only for examinees with at least 5 years of full-time work experience. Items deal with such topics as high school, work, and college experiences; preferred work environment and managerial style; and personal habits and tendencies. The items are clearly worded, face valid, and not overly intrusive; no racial, gender, or cultural bias is evident in any of the items. Many of the items call for self-assessments, and may be subject to faking, social desirability, or other such response sets. Part II consists of 46 situational item stems followed by multiple-choice options, of which the examinee selects a first and second choice; it is clearly intended to measure managerial judgment. These items are more complex than those in Part I, are quite challenging, and are intrinsically interesting to potential and practicing managers; they appear much less susceptible to response set bias.

Instructions to the examinee are clear and easy to follow, the machine-scorable answer sheet presents no problems, and the authors provide useful suggestions to test administrators regarding such issues as standardization of testing conditions, test security, confidentiality, and interpretation. The test is not timed. Although the authors suggest providing a generous 3 hours or more to complete the MPR, this reviewer's experience indicates that most examinees likely will finish within 90 to 120 minutes.

Scoring procedures for the MPR are proprietary; they are evidently based on an empirically keyed profile matching technique. (Potential users should note that this approach tends to identify individuals with response patterns similar to successful *current* managers, and may serve to perpetuate current managerial styles while hindering the development of new approaches to management.) Results are reported for the 11 categories noted above, but the authors suggest using only the *overall* score for decision-making purposes; the others are for research use only (a caveat which this reviewer suspects is often ignored in practice).

The authors correctly note that longitudinal, predictive validation research would be ideal for the MPR, but admit that most of the validation and normative work has been concurrent in nature, employing various measures of managerial progression as the criterion. Sixteen such studies are outlined in the manual, typically employing several hundred managers and potential managers as subjects and yielding validity coefficients in the .27 to .70 range. Results of a cumulative study, based on the scores of over 5,000 examinees, show a correlation of .51 using progression to the top half of the hierarchy of management as the criterion. Results of this study are reported in the form of an expectancy chart for each of seven segments of the range of overall scores, making interpretation of MPR scores very easy for potential users. Users also are urged by the authors to carry out their own local validation studies, with the authors' assistance at little or no cost.

From a technical standpoint the MPR manual has several important shortcomings. For example, no reliability coefficients, standard error of measurement data, or standard error of estimate data are reported. There is no information given regarding the stability of scores or predictions over time. Norm tables are not provided. Although the authors claim that the MPR is equally as predictive for minorities and women as for white males, no evidence for this claim is displayed in the manual. (The authors do, however, offer to provide "Washington representation if MPR problems arise with federal equal employment agencies.") Another shortcoming is that the potential problems of faking and other response set difficulties are never addressed in the manual, nor are any procedures described to detect examinees who desire to portray themselves in a false but more favorable light. The authors are urged to address these issues in future editions of the test manual.

In summary, the MPR is a well-designed self-report measure which appears useful as an aid to the identification of prospective managers. Despite the technical shortcomings mentioned above, the test appears well grounded in research and theory and has an impressive track record for identifying individuals with a profile of biographical, attitudinal, and judgmental scores which relate to success in the managerial ranks. The MPR, when used in conjunction with measures of job-related aptitude and achievement, could be a valuable tool for management recruitment and selection.

REVIEWER'S REFERENCES

Owens, W. A. (1976). Background data. In M. D. Dunnette (Ed.), *Handbook of industrial and organizational psychology* (pp. 609-644). Chicago: Rand McNally.

Bentz, V. J. (1990). Contextual issues in predicting high-level leadership performance: Contextual richness as a criterion consideration in personality research with executives. In K. E. Clark & M. B. Clark (Eds.), *Measures of leadership* (pp. 131-143). West Orange, NJ: Leadership Library of America.

Howard, A., & Bray, D. W. (1990). Predictions of managerial success over long periods of time: Lessons from the management progress study. In. K. E. Clark and M. B. Clark (Eds.), *Measures of leadership* (pp. 113-130). West Orange, NJ: Leadership Library of America.

Sparks, C. P. (1990). Testing for management potential. In K. E. Clark & M. B. Clark (Eds.), *Measures of leadership* (pp. 103-111). West Orange, NJ: Leadership Library of America.

[222]

Managerial and Professional Job Functions Inventory.

Purpose: "For defining the basic dimensions of jobs and assessing their relative importance for the job" and "assessing one's ability to perform them."

Population: Middle and upper level managers and non-management professionals.

Publication Dates: 1978–86.

Acronym: MP-JFI.

Scores, 16: Setting Organizational Objectives, Financial Planning and Review, Improving Work Procedures and Practices, Interdepartmental Coordination, Developing and Implementing Technical Ideas, Judgment and Decision Making, Developing Group Cooperation and Teamwork, Coping with Difficulties and Emergencies, Promoting Safety Attitudes and Practices, Communications, Developing Employee Potential, Supervisory Practices, Self-Development and Improvement, Personnel Practices, Promoting Community-Organization Relations, Handling Outside Contacts.

Administration: Group.

Forms, 2: Ability Rating, Importance Rating.

Price Data, 1988: $13.75 per 25 Ability or Importance test booklets; $2.50 per 25 scoring sheets; $5 per interpretation and research manual ('86, 28 pages); $10 per specimen set; scoring service available from publisher.

Time: (30–60) minutes.

Comments: Hand or machine scored.

Authors: Melany E. Baehr, Wallace G. Lonergan, and Bruce A. Hunt.

Publisher: London House, Inc.

Review of the Managerial and Professional Job Functions Inventory by L. ALAN WITT, Personnel Research Psychologist, Civil Aeromedical Institute, Federal Aviation Administration, Oklahoma City, OK:

Job analyses of management positions are sufficiently expensive to justify not doing them. Many organizations could use an instrument that assesses, in a fairly standardized method, the job functions of management personnel. The 140-item Managerial and Professional Job Functions Inventory (MP-JFI) was designed to meet this need. Its manual lists five basic uses of the MP-JFI: (*a*) job description and design, (*b*) job clarification, (*c*) diagnosis of individual developmental needs, (*d*) diagnosis of group training needs, and (*e*) wage and salary administration. To accomplish these uses, the MP-JFI has two forms. One assesses the importance of the functions (categorized into dimensions) for a job. The other assesses the rater's self-perception of his/her ability to perform those functions.

MP-JFI authors contend there is considerable overlap in functions performed by higher level incumbents across occupational groups. This assumption led them to develop items listing functions (e.g., "ensuring that performance appraisal procedures are free from racial or other bias") that represent 16 dimensions presumed to be typical of managerial jobs: (*a*) Setting Organizational Objectives, (*b*) Financial Planning and Review, (*c*) Improving Work Procedures and Practices, (*d*) Interdepartmental Coordination, (*e*) Developing and Implementing Technical Ideas, (*f*) Judgment and Decision Making, (*g*) Developing Group Cooperation and Teamwork, (*h*) Coping with Difficulties and Emergencies, (*i*) Promoting Safety Attitudes and Practices, (*j*) Communications, (*k*) Developing Employee Potential, (*l*) Supervisory Practices, (*m*) Self-Development and Improvement, (*n*) Personnel Practices, (*o*) Promoting Community-Organization Relations, and (*p*) Handling Outside Contacts. Although it is unlikely that any instrument can tap all management functions, these dimensions may represent those present in most jobs and organizations. Moreover, the functions are relatively contemporary.

Another advantage of the MP-JFI is the instructions. These require rating the importance of each item (function) in two steps. First, raters are to indicate whether the item is of "below average" or "above average" importance for the job, with the items split about evenly between the two. Second, raters are to rate half of the "below average" items into "little or none" and the other half "less than average"; then they are to rate half of the "above average" items into "more than average" and the other half "outstanding." Determining the importance of one's job functions is typically a daunting task, and this procedure makes the rater's decision process easier and increases the likelihood of more evenly distributed ratings.

Administration and scoring appear relatively easy and straightforward. Administration of the Invento-ry is estimated to last 30 to 60 minutes and it may be given to individuals, to a group, or by mail. Both machine and hand scoring are available, although hand conversion of raw scores into normalized standard scores, conversion of normalized standard scores into centiles, and filling in the profile grid may be a bit tedious. For those experiencing problems, a test consultant phone number is provided.

Evidence is presented supporting the ability of the MP-JFI to differentiate within and across occupational hierarchies. Although the breakdown of the results by level (executive, manager, supervisor) and occupation (line, professional, sales, financial) was helpful, the sample sizes (e.g., executives in the sales group = 29) may be a bit low to be truly representative. Indeed, selection of the samples and their representativeness are somewhat curious. The initial trial form consisting of 122 items was administered to about 600 male industrial employees in nine occupational classifications. Why all males? What nine occupational classifications? An updated version was administered to a "vocationally heterogeneous sample of 893 employees," including public and private sector personnel. Explanation or definition of the phrase "vocationally heterogeneous" was not provided.

Reliability coefficients computed from data collected from 882 employees are acceptable for all but six of the 16 dimensions: (*a*) Financial Planning and Review (alpha = .62), (*b*) Improving Work Procedures and Practices (alpha = .63), (*c*) Interdepartmental Coordination (alpha = .64), (*d*) Judgment and Decision Making (alpha = .48), (*e*) Coping with Difficulties and Emergencies (alpha = .67), and (*f*) Communication (alpha = .63). These low alphas are cause for concern.

Normalized standard scores for the MP-JFI derived from a total sample of 893 (private sector personnel = 484, state transit department officials = 360, utility company managers = 49) provide helpful bases for comparison. However, it was not clear why these norms and the reliability coefficients were computed from different samples. A larger sample across a greater variety of industries would be preferable.

Aside from sampling inadequacies and reliability problems, the MP-JFI is a good attempt at a standardized job analysis-type instrument for management personnel. Using the ability form, however, may offer limited utility. Because it assesses self-perceptions of ability, which may reflect a number of biases, the MP-JFI has limitations as a diagnostic tool for individuals and groups. In addition, the lack of items assessing technical functions unique to the specific job may limit the utility of the MP-JFI as an instrument to be used for compensation functions.

Review of the Managerial and Professional Job Functions Inventory by SHELDON ZEDECK, Professor of Psychology and Director, University of California, Berkeley, CA:

The Managerial and Professional Job Functions Inventory (MP-JFI) is composed of two instruments intended to be used to provide information concerning the basic functions of managerial and professional jobs. One inventory requires ratings of the importance of each of 140 task statements for the respondent's position. The second inventory focuses on a general ability rating whereby the respondent indicates his or her perceived general ability to perform the tasks. The Manual for the inventory suggests there are a number of applications for the inventories such as (a) job description and design, (b) job clarification, (c) diagnosis of individual developmental needs, (d) diagnosis of group training needs, and (e) wage and salary administration. An important area for which job analytic methods such as the MP-JFI have been used, but ignored in the Manual, is that pertaining to the development of selection tests; the ability and task ratings should facilitate the development and validation of selection devices for managerial and professional jobs.

A factor analysis of responses from 893 employees, representing a putative vocationally heterogeneous sample, yielded a 16-factor solution for the MP-JFI. The 16 factors are slightly more comprehensive than the 13 factors provided by a competitive inventory, the Management Position Description Questionnaire (MPDQ; Tornow & Pinto, 1976). Whereas on the face of it, the MP-JFI contains items that appear to represent obvious tasks for managerial jobs, the sample of 893 is somewhat questionable on which to base the factor analysis. More specifically, the sample includes 484 private sector sales representatives, managers, and executives, 360 state transit department professionals, and 49 utilities managers. Whether this is a truly "vocationally heterogeneous sample" is questionable. Furthermore, the Manual does not indicate how many organizations are represented in this sample.

Another issue of concern related to the limited representativeness of the developmental sample is the use of norms to interpret scores derived from the MP-JFI. Are these norms appropriate for managerial jobs in the financial industry, high-technology industry, etc? More research and data are needed before the MP-JFI is to be considered generalizable to a broad range of positions and organizations.

A more important conceptual issue, related to interpretation of scores, deals with a proposed hierarchical model for occupational group profiles. The model suggests that scores can be viewed as representing three occupational levels (I, II, and III), with each of these levels existing within each of four managerial hierarchies (line, professional, sales, and financial). The Manual provides results from analyses of variance (ANOVA) statistics to support a conclusion that the profiles serve as meaningful reference standards, and that the MP-JFI can differentiate among the functions performed by the three levels of occupational groups within each managerial hierarchy. Unfortunately, the ANOVAs are global, main effect results and do not indicate whether a dimension can differentiate one level from each of the others; at best, all that can be stated is that there are differences among the three levels. In addition, there is no information on the effect size for the differences. This is important, because differences are a function of sample size, and as already pointed out, there is concern about the sample and its representativeness. For example, for sales representatives, the analyses were conducted on 29, 39, and 134 Level I, II, and III managers, respectively. Finally, there is no discussion as to whether there is linearity in the relationship between scores and level.

Though the *importance* ratings generated by one of the inventories can be useful for assessing and understanding jobs, the value of the *ability* ratings generated by the second inventory is equivocal. Of what value is it to know the profile of a "general ability"? What is "general ability"? Also, the context for the respondent is whether the respondent's general ability to perform the task is "below" or "above" average compared with his or her ability to do other functions that he or she *can* perform. Is this asking the respondent whether he or she *has* abilities to perform tasks as opposed to whether or not an ability *is needed* for the task or the position? For example, the respondent may have "above average" ability to make decisions on the basis of the organization's economic situation, but in actuality this ability and/or task is not part of the respondent's responsibility. In essence, there could be ambiguity with respect to what abilities are possessed by the respondent as opposed to the abilities needed to perform the tasks.

With regard to the instruments per se, the positive features are the rather straightforward, generic type statements, the internal consistency reliabilities, the apparent conceptual differentiation among the 16 factors, and the ease with which the instruments can be administered (untimed). One potential problem for a respondent, however, is the means by which ratings are provided. The process is such that the respondent "works" the inventory page by page, whereby he or she examines the 28 statements on the first page and initially dichotomizes the tasks into "below average" or "above average" importance. Once these ratings are provided, the respondent reviews the approximately 14 "above average" responses and rerates them with respect to "more than average" and "outstanding"; the approximately 14 "below average" importance ratings are, likewise, rerated into 7 "little or none" and "less than average" ratings. This process is then repeated for the second and subsequent pages of the inventory. This double rating of the statements appears to be cumbersome. Research is needed to determine whether this process yields any different result than when ratings are made directly on a 4-point scale, which would range from "little or none" to "outstanding."

In summary, the current form of the MP-JFI represents a preliminary device to gather information on jobs. Currently, it does not represent an improvement over a device such as the MPDQ. As more research is conducted and more data accumulated, a better understanding of the MP-JFI will be obtained. At that time, more information needs to be presented with respect to how the device can be used for the purposes stated at the outset of this review.

REVIEWER'S REFERENCE

Tornow, W. W., & Pinto, P. R. (1976). The development of a managerial taxonomy: A system for describing, classifying, and evaluating executive positions. *Journal of Applied Psychology, 61*, 410-418.

[223]
Managerial Assessment of Proficiency MAP™.

Purpose: "Shows a participant's strengths and weaknesses in twelve areas of managerial competency and two dimensions of management style."
Population: Managers.
Publication Dates: 1985–88.
Acronym: MAP.
Scores, 17: Administrative Competencies (Time Management and Prioritizing, Setting Goals and Standards, Planning and Scheduling Work, Administrative Composite), Communication Competencies (Listening and Organizing, Giving Clear Information, Getting Unbiased Information, Communication Composite), Supervisory Competencies (Training/Coaching/Delegating, Appraising People and Performance, Disciplining and Counseling, Supervisory Composite), Cognitive Competencies (Identifying and Solving Problems, Making Decisions/Weighing Risk, Thinking Clearly and Analytically, Cognitive Composite), Proficiency Composite.
Administration: Group.
Price Data, 1991: $15,000 initial investment for purchase with licensing agreement (for high-volume users) including set of 4 videocassettes, 50 sets of participant materials including workbook ('88, 60 pages) and booklet entitled Interpreting Your Scores ('88, 24 pages), personal computer floppy disk for in-house scoring, scoring by publisher of first 25 participants, 1½-day training and pilot cycle by senior instructor from publisher; $40 per person for additional participant materials; $30 per person for additional (optional) scoring by publisher; $300 per person (minimum 12 persons) for contracting for in-house program including materials, scoring, and instructor/consultant time; $200–$250 per person for

registration at public workshop held in Princeton, NJ by publishers.
Time: (360–420) minutes.
Comments: May be purchased with licensing agreement, contracted for in-house administration, or used by attending a public workshop provided by publisher; administered in part by videocassette.
Author: Scott B. Parry.
Publisher: Training House, Inc.

Review of the Managerial Assessment of Proficiency MAP™ by JERARD F. KEHOE, District Manager, Selection and Testing, American Telephone & Telegraph Co., Morristown, NJ:

The Managerial Assessment of Proficiency (MAP) is a video-based assessment exercise lasting 6½ hours designed to measure managers' competencies in 12 categories of performance and managers' style on two types of interaction, four types of communication, and four types of communication response. The developer suggests several applications: to diagnose individual and organizational training/development needs; to evaluate competency and style gains from training/development programs; and to make personnel selection decisions. Overall, a significant lack of evidence concerning reliability and validity makes the MAP a poor choice as a selection procedure. The lack of explanation about the origin of the 12 competencies and the development of the corresponding scoring rules limits the MAP's value as a diagnostic or evaluative tool to those training/development programs that adopt the MAP's companion training modules organized around the same competency categories and style dimensions.

ADMINISTRATION. The MAP can be administered in groups with a live "instructor" or individually with a PC-based guide. The MAP process has two basic components. One is a set of 12 videotaped exercises and the other is a set of 187 four-option items. In the videotaped exercises actors portray various combinations of managers playing out different, but sometimes related, scenarios. The scenarios consist of a staff meeting, an individual planning session, the preparation of a subordinate for a performance review, discussion of a problem situation, two examples of delegation, a job interview, a discussion of a problem employee, preparation of a memo, a performance review, counseling an employee with a performance problem, and reassignment meetings. The scenarios are uniformly well done with credible realism, plausible exchanges, and generally good acting. The 187 items are organized into 13 sets that are answered in turn after each scenario. One or more of the options in each item may be chosen, resulting in 748 scorable subitems. The items assess recall of facts, evaluations of depicted performance, beliefs and judgments about the specific situations depicted in the scenarios, and general beliefs and judgments about management principles related to the scenarios. Support materials include a participant's workbook, self-assessment procedures for the competencies and styles, development options and planning guides, a score interpretation workbook, and a personal interpretation worksheet with sample profiles and help materials describing the style dimensions. These participant-support materials are uniformly well organized and written at an informal level that is easy to use and avoids procedural confusion. However, they shed no light on the origin and development of the competency categories and style dimensions. With the exception of six style dimensions that are clearly derived from previous literature, the materials are virtually a closed system with no linkage to other research or theoretical domains in managerial assessment.

The following sections on scoring, reliability, and validity are based on two technical reports prepared by the developer in July 1985 and November 1986 describing results of field trials in 11 organizations.

SCORING. No information is presented to describe the theoretical or practical origins of the 187 items. Nor is any information presented describing what the scoring rules are or how they were developed. Some item revision took place during the field trials, based on participant input, resulting in changes in approximately 53 of the 187 items. Also, some unknown number of items were deleted because more than 90% of the participants answered in the same way. Because the same trials resulted in validity estimates as well as item revisions, this lack of information about item development and scoring rules creates uncertainty about the meaning of the validity results. The 12 competency scores, 10 style scores, and 5 composite scores are reported as percentile ranks based on normative data collected by the developer. In the 1986 report, normative data are reported for 1,400 participants from 52 organizations in 11 industry groups and one executive group. The value of this normative data is limited because sample sizes are not provided, nor are any subgroup norms provided except by industry group. Also, the appropriateness of normative scoring is questionable due to the high sensitivity of MAP scores to training and other experience differences.

RELIABILITY. The developer claims two types of reliability evidence "verify the reliability of MAP." In fact, no reliability evidence is presented. Instead, the developer severely misconstrues the meanings of test-retest and split-half reliability, and presents evidence showing substantial score-level changes within one group of 13 participants from pre- to post-training and presents other evidence showing substantial score-level differences between two matched groups of 22 and 27 participants, one with and the other without related training. The irony of

these data is that they indirectly imply the distinct possibility that the MAP has rather low reliability. In one case, intervening training changed the average percentile score on related competencies from 53 to 94. The average percentile score on competencies not directly addressed in training changed from 65 to 82. In the two-group study, the average percentile scores on the six training-relevant competencies for the trained and untrained groups were 49 and 30, respectively. For the six training-irrelevant competencies the difference was negligible, 45 and 47. These results have little utility because they are based on only 13 participants in the first case and 49 in the second. Nevertheless, they raise the distinct possibility that the MAP scores are highly sensitive to a variety of directly and indirectly relevant experiences, including the experience of taking the MAP itself. These types of influences are likely to negatively impact many types of reliability estimates. A further irony is the developer explicitly discounted the value of the appropriate split-half reliability estimation procedure that, in fact, would have provided the most appropriate estimate of reliability, given the available evidence.

VALIDITY. Most critical of all is the developer's claim that MAP scores predict managerial job performance. To evaluate its validity, the MAP was trialed in 11 organizations involving over 200 participants. Eight organizations complied by providing one or two managers' independent evaluations of the job performance of the participants. Within each organization, a validity estimate was computed as the correlation between ranked MAP scores and ranked performance evaluations. The number of participants within organizations varied from 18 to 32 with a total of 184 in the 1986 report. A number of inconsistencies plague the reports of these validity results, although the validities reported are remarkably high. In the 1985 report, seven validity coefficients for the overall composite competency score are reported ranging from .71 to .92. The 1986 report, which provides more detail about the same seven data sets plus one more, reports eight validities ranging from .71 to .90. For some reason, however, only three of the 1985 validity values are found in the 1986 report. No mention is made of any reason for the changes. Validities for the individual competency category scores are reported, although they were based entirely on one manager's rating of 12 participants on the 12 MAP competencies as his strategy for deriving an overall performance evaluation. Of course, using the predictor—the MAP—as the basis for producing the criterion artificially biases the validities. Nevertheless, the correlations between MAP competency scores and the corresponding manager-rated competency scores were reported and ranged from .39 to .83. No report was made of the correlations between different competency scores. Overall, the validity evidence is weak in spite of the high values reported. Sample sizes are small, differences in the two reports are not accounted for, the effects of item revision and scoring rule development in the same trials are not reported, individual competency validities are positively biased by the rating procedure, and MAP competency scores are likely to be sensitive to a variety of experiences.

SUMMARY. The ease, orderliness, and attractiveness of the MAP materials belie the significant lack of supporting evidence for the reliability and validity of MAP scores. Certainly, the available reliability and validity evidence fails to meet even the most minimal professional standards for assessment procedures and fails to meet the regulatory requirements for selection procedures. However, for managers and organizations who accept the MAP representation of manager competence and style, the entire MAP package of assessment and training modules may be an attractive tool for developmental activities. Even developmental applications will be flawed, however, by the lack of appropriately reliable and valid outcome measures.

[224]
Managerial Competence Index.

Purpose: "To assess the probable competence of one's approach to management."
Population: Individuals who manage or are being assessed for their potential to manage others.
Publication Date: 1980–89.
Acronym: MCI.
Scores, 5: Team Management, Middle-of-the-Road Management, Task Management, Country Club Management, Impoverished Management.
Administration: Group.
Price Data, 1990: $6.95 per manual ('89, 21 pages).
Time: Administration time not reported.
Authors: Jay Hall.
Publisher: Teleometrics International.

Review of the Managerial Competence Index by KURT F. GEISINGER, Professor of Psychology, Fordham University, Bronx, NY:

The Managerial Competence Index (MCI) is intended to measure not only managerial style, but also managerial competence. ("The *Managerial Competence Index (MCI)* is designed to assess the probable competence of one's approach to management," manual, p. 12.) The instrument is based on the managerial grid model of Blake and Mouton (1964). (This model proposes two primary factors that have been found to differentiate managers and their performance: concern for people and concern for production.) Hall, the test author, argues that the present instrument is a refinement of other measures that he had developed previously to measure managerial styles in that he has performed research to insure that, "the MCI goes beyond a

mere depiction of one's dominant style of management and addresses the relative *competence* of one's approach to management. That is, the MCI measures both a manager's preference for various 'grid' styles and, of more practical importance, the combined effects of these unique and highly personal preferences on one's success in managing others" (manual, p. 12). The research to which the test author refers is almost entirely published by his company and is not available in the test manual.

The test manual and the inventory are one document of roughly 20 pages. This document begins with the instrument and is followed by a guide to self-scoring and self-interpretation according to the Blake and Mouton grid model.

The inventory itself is composed of 12 unfinished sentences, each with five possible endings (similar to options on multiple-choice examinations). The author of the test refers to the sentence fragment/stems as situations and the five potential responses as solutions. In taking the inventory, a test taker reads each of the sentence fragments, then selects the options that are most and least typical of the respondent's behavior in that situation. The test taker then places these two options upon a 10-point rating scale which may be found under the sentence fragment. This 10-point rating scale has two extremes labeled *Completely Characteristic* (a value of 10) and *Completely Uncharacteristic* (a value of 1) with no other anchors. Once the two selected options are rated, the test taker is asked to rate the remaining three unselected solutions along the same 10-point scale. Thus, when a test taker has completed the inventory, 60 ratings have been made, five ratings for each of 12 stems.

Once test takers have completed their 60 ratings, they self-score their responses by summing the ratings given to specific options. Five sums are initially calculated, representing five "ideal-types" according to the managerial grid model of Blake and Mouton (1964). (These styles are denoted by 1/1, 1/9, 5/5, 9/1, and 9/9. A 9/1 manager, for example, is one who has maximal concern for production and minimal concern for people and a 1/9 manager is the opposite. A 5/5 manager depicts a manager with moderate amounts of each.) The sums for each of the five styles are next converted to normalized T scores (mean of 50, standard deviation of 10) using tables provided in the instrument. On the basis of the five converted scores, test takers then rank order their apparent preferences for the five styles using the differences (e.g., difference scores) among the five converted scales. At this point, test takers are encouraged to look to certain pages in the manual to learn what their probabilities are for being competent as managers. Finally, core scores are provided for four interpretative "components": Management Beliefs, Involvement Practices, Management of Motives, and Interpersonal Competence. Understanding these dimensions is supposed to give test takers insights into their management style and help them to become more effective as industrial managers.

TEST DEVELOPMENT AND STANDARDIZATION. The test author provides no information on the construction of this instrument, other than to say that it is built on the Blake and Mouton model. A previous reviewer of a related instrument remarked, "There is no rationale or empirical support provided to justify the 12 management situations included in the survey" (Bernardin, 1989). No information on the relative usefulness of individual questions is provided. Some of the language in specific questions is sexist and is not in conformance with APA standards in this regard (American Psychological Association, 1983).

The normalized *T* scores, which are converted from raw score sums, are based on a standardization sample of 440 managers. Apparently, these numbers change from time to time as research provides additional data. No description of this sample is provided. How the cutoff scores representing the five "pure" styles of management were determined is not presented.

RELIABILITY AND VALIDITY. Virtually no information is provided for either reliability or validity. The only information reported is that this instrument correlates "about .75 with Teleometrics' *Styles of Management Inventory/Management Appraisal Survey*" (Hall, 1986), previously reviewed in the *Mental Measurements Yearbook* series (Bernardin, 1989; Korman, 1978; Thornton, 1989).

OVERVIEW. In reviewing another inventory of this format, by this author and publisher, Korman (1978) wrote, "I do not know how many years it will take to get these types of measures off the market, but the process should begin" (p. 1763). Thornton (1989) concluded his review of a similar management inventory published by this test author and publisher with "No student in my undergraduate class on tests and measurements, and certainly no graduate student in my class on psychometric theory and test construction, would pass the course if he or she turned in such a deficient report of test construction efforts and data to support the instrument" (p. 459).

The MCI in its present form can be evaluated no more positively than those similar instruments cited in the above paragraph and is perhaps substantially more dangerous in that it goes beyond assessing styles and mistakenly alludes to the notion of estimating managerial competence.

The present manual is confusing and is appropriate primarily for self-scoring purposes of a naive test taker. It does not provide basic and requisite information such as is called for in the joint standards (American Educational Research Association, American Psychological Association, & National Council on Measurement in Education, 1985). Calls to the publisher provided neither more useful information nor additional evaluative data. This same test manual provided no information regarding test construction or refinement and precious little on the empirical evaluation of this instrument. The sample used for the normal conversion is far too small and completely undefined. It would be helpful to know if different norms are appropriate for the two sexes, various ethnic groups, different industries, etc. Similarly, the lack of empirical proof concerning the rules used to designate the different managerial styles is troubling. Yet more troubling is the lack of any attempt to work at construct validation. Cutoffs are not critical when it is not even clear what an instrument measures. Difference scores are used without any clue that such scores are typically unreliable (e.g., Cronbach & Furby, 1970).

This instrument should not be used for any purpose other than basic research. In its place, one could better use the Leader Behavior Description Questionnaire, Form XII (Stogdill, 1963; 9:596) or the Managerial Practices Survey (Yukl, Wall, & Lepsinger, 1990).

REVIEWER'S REFERENCES

Stogdill, R. M. (1963). *Manual for the Leader Behavior Description Questionnaire—Form XII*. Columbus, OH: Bureau of Business Research, Ohio State University.

Blake, R. R., & Mouton, J. S. (1964). *The managerial grid*. Houston: Gulf Publishing Co.

Cronbach, L. J., & Furby, L. (1970). How we should measure "change"—or should we? *Psychological Bulletin, 74*, 68-80.

Korman, A. K. (1978). [Review of Styles of Leadership and Management.] In O. K. Buros (Ed.), *The eighth mental measurements yearbook* (p. 1763). Highland Park, NJ: The Gryphon Press.

American Psychological Association. (1983). *Publication manual of the American Psychological Association* (3rd ed.). Washington, DC: American Psychological Association.

American Educational Research Association, American Psychological Association, & National Council on Measurement in Education. (1985). *Standard for educational and psychological testing*. Washington, DC: American Psychological Association, Inc.

Hall, J. S. (1986). Styles of Management Inventory. The Woodlands, TX: Teleometrics International.

Bernardin, H. J. (1989). [Review of the Management Appraisal Survey.] In J. C. Conoley & J. J. Kramer (Eds.), *The tenth mental measurements yearbook* (pp. 458-459). Lincoln, NE: The Buros Institute of Mental Measurements.

Thornton, G. C., III. (1989). [Review of the Management Appraisal Survey.] In J. C. Conoley & J. J. Kramer (Eds.), *The tenth mental measurements yearbook* (pp. 459-460). Lincoln, NE: The Buros Institute of Mental Measurements.

Yukl, G., Wall, S., & Lepsinger, R. (1990). Preliminary report on the validation of the Managerial Practices Survey. In K. E. Clark & M. B. Clark (Eds.), *Measures of leadership* (pp. 223-238). West Orange, NJ: Leadership Library of America, Inc.

[225]

Managerial Competence Review.

Purpose: To identify a manager's preferred managerial style and assess the relative competence of his/her approach to management.
Population: Subordinates to managers.
Publication Date: 1980–89.
Acronym: MCR.

Scores, 5: Relative measures of concern for people and concern for production ("9/9", "1/9", "5/5", "9/1", "1/1").
Administration: Group.
Price Data, 1990: $6.95 per manual ('89, 17 pages).
Time: Administration time not reported.
Comments: Companion instrument for Managerial Competence Index (224).
Authors: Jay Hall.
Publisher: Teleometrics International.

[226]

The Manson Evaluation, Revised Edition.

Purpose: Identifies alcoholics and potential alcoholics.
Population: Adults.
Publication Dates: 1948–87.
Scores, 8: Anxiety, Depressive Fluctuations, Emotional Sensitivity, Resentfulness, Incompleteness, Aloneness, Interpersonal Relations, Total.
Administration: Individual or group.
Editions, 2: Paper-and-pencil, microcomputer.
Price Data, 1989: $35 per complete kit; $22.50 per 25 test booklets/profiles ('87); $12.70 per manual ('87, 28 pages); $185 per IBM computer package including diskette (tests up to 25) and user's guide.
Time: (10–20) minutes.
Comments: Self-administered.
Authors: Morse P. Manson and George J. Huba.
Publisher: Western Psychological Services.
Cross References: See T2:1271 (2 references) and P:152 (1 reference); for a review by Dugal Campbell, see 6:137 (5 references); for reviews by Charles H. Honzik and Albert L. Hunsicker, see 4:68 (4 references).

Review of The Manson Evaluation, Revised Edition by TONY TONEATTO, Psychologist, Addiction Research Foundation, Toronto, Ontario, Canada:

The stated purposes of the Manson Evaluation (ME) are to identify individuals with personality structures common to alcoholics and those who may be prone to abusing alcohol. A third stated purpose of the test, to understand "the psychodynamic processes" in such individuals, is not addressed in the manual. The ME is deficient in several areas, particularly the conceptual basis of the test, characteristics of the samples used in its construction and validation, and in its psychometric properties.

The basic assumptions underlying the ME, that there is a personality structure common to alcoholics and alcohol-abuse prone individuals, can be seriously challenged. No work is cited to support this hypothesis. Current research suggests that the concept of an alcoholic personality is not a viable one. If such a concept is to be assessed, strong evidence for its existence needs to be well documented. Consequently, the construct validity of the ME is seriously undermined.

The authors make use of "risk group," which refers to the a priori probability of being an alcoholic (e.g., 5, 10, 20, 50%). In combination with the ME score, it yields the probability that the individual has an alcohol abuse prone personality. The authors do not discuss how one determines such a "risk" for a given individual but state that only skilled examiners can make such evaluations. If an examiner could assess such risk, what exactly would the purpose of the ME be? Furthermore, how are the probabilities that result from combining risk and ME scores to be interpreted, for example, what does a 67% chance of being alcohol prone really mean? And how is being alcohol prone different, conceptually, from being at "risk" for alcoholism? What are the social implications of designating someone who is not currently abusing alcohol as abuse prone? What is the predictive validity of such formulae?

The subject sample used in the original construction of the test is inadequately described. Mean age, sex composition, drinking history and patterns, marital status, and many other variables, are completely lacking. The sample is limited to Caucasians from one geographical area. Only alcoholics who are AA members or inpatients were studied. Are they representative of alcoholics as a whole? Of the nonalcoholics used in the construction of the test, two-thirds were individuals from families with a member in AA. Is this appropriate considering the possible risk for alcohol abuse inherent in individuals with this family background? In any case, no description of the nonalcoholics' actual drinking is presented making it impossible to evaluate their drinking. The authors also group abstainers with moderate drinkers. Might these two groups represent distinct populations?

In the original validation study, basic demographic and descriptive data are lacking (e.g., mean age, marital status, drinking history). As well, although one-third of the alcoholics were female (which does not reflect the proportion of alcohol abusers who are women), more female than male nonalcoholics were used. The authors also explicitly state that for the validation study nonalcoholics from AA circles were not included indicating that the validation of the ME used a nonalcoholic sample very different from that used in test construction (where 67% were from AA circles).

The quality of the sampling in the 1985 validation study is poor. Sampling was limited to those applying for jobs at one company. An alcoholic sample was not included, severely limiting the scope and relevance of this validation study, and necessitating the use of norms, reliability and validity information determined in 1965 in the case of alcoholics. Except for gender distribution, mean age, and education no other descriptive data are provided.

The authors do not describe how the seven subscales were derived. A perusal of the item content of the seven subscales, however, shows a poor fit with the subscale label. For example,

Incompleteness (a "trait"?) consists of items that do not easily satisfy the definition of this subscale.

About 18% of the items were keyed on more than one subscale and, in one case, on three subscales. This is indicative of the lack of conceptual clarity characteristic of the ME.

In the original analyses of the test's psychometric properties, reliability was limited to a KR-20 evaluation ($r = .94$) for the entire scale. The reliability data generated from the 1985 sample (which did not include an alcoholic group of subjects) are more extensive than in the original validation study but not more supportive. The KR-20 internal consistency coefficients for the subscales and full scale appear adequate although low.

The validity data presented by the authors are difficult to interpret. Although predictive validity appears to be the intention, the procedures described suggest that concurrent validity was actually assessed. Nor is it clear how significant sex differences in the full ME scores is evidence of predictive validity. The data presented for the validity of this test are not persuasive. For example, the item factor analysis yielded a general dimension of personality functioning despite the claim that the ME assesses two personality dimensions. A factor analysis of the seven trait scores yielded a two-factor solution that did reflect the two personality dimensions but only if males and females were analyzed separately. The data presented as factor loadings in Table 5 of the manual for the two-factor solution appear to be incorrect as several loadings exceed $\pm$ 1.0. It is possible that factor scores, not factor loadings, were reported. Norms based on the 1985 sample are limited to means and standard deviations for the males, females, and total sample, for the full scale and the subscales.

In summary, the conceptual, sampling, and psychometric limitations discussed in this review strongly suggest that the ME is an inadequate instrument that cannot be recommended for use either in clinical or in research contexts.

Review of The Manson Evaluation, Revised Edition by JALIE A. TUCKER, Professor of Psychology and Co-Director of Clinical Training, Auburn University, Auburn, AL:

Originally published in 1948, the 72-item Manson Evaluation was designed as a screening instrument to discriminate adult alcoholics from nonalcoholics in clinical and employment evaluations. Guided by then popular notions that alcoholism is subserved by a distinct constellation of psychopathological personality traits, the test purports to assess three personality dimensions viewed as reflecting psychoneurotic tendencies (Anxiety, Depressive Fluctuations, and Emotional Sensitivity) and four dimensions viewed as reflecting psychopathic tendencies (Resentfulness, Incompleteness, Aloneness,

and Interpersonal Relations). An indirect method of test construction guided the scale's original development. Final test items were selected from a pool of 470 general personality items that discriminated between alcoholics, who were recruited from Alcoholics Anonymous (A.A.) and institutional programs, and nonalcoholics, many of whom were family members of the alcoholic subjects. In Manson's original validation study that included 268 alcoholic and 303 nonalcoholic men and women, diagnostic accuracy was about 81% using an optimal cut point approach. Murphy (1956) subsequently replicated these findings using active alcoholics in treatment and nonalcoholics, but did not find the test effective in discriminating A.A. members who had been abstinent for 6 months or more.

The Manson Evaluation has been criticized previously on numerous grounds (see Campbell, 1965; Gibbins, Smart, & Seeley, 1959; Miller, 1976), including (*a*) the inequivalence and select nature of the alcoholic and nonalcoholic subjects included in the original validation research; (*b*) the lack of evidence supporting the seven scale dimensions, which were based on subjective/rational groupings of items; and (*c*) the use of a validation sample with a base rate of alcohol problems (50%) that greatly exceeds that found in the general population (10%).

The revised edition of the test does little to redress these concerns. The revision retains all original scale items grouped in the same seven dimensions, and the only apparent substantive change is the addition of new normative data collected from 326 job applicants who were seeking clerical, manual labor, or professional positions in a single company in Los Angeles, California. The use of subjects who were unselected along any index of psychological disturbance, including alcohol problems, would seem to have been prompted by the base rate concern noted above, but, remarkably, no data were collected on their drinking patterns or problems apart from the Manson Evaluation. Consequently, no basis exists for determining the test's ability to identify alcoholics within a nonclinical sample recruited in an employment setting, and, without such data, the claims made for the utility of the test as an employee screening device are unconscionable.

Another feature of the revised edition that also pertains to the base rate issue is the use of different norms and interpretative guidelines depending on the examiner's estimation that the test subject is a member of a population sample with a particular probability of alcoholism (5%, 10%, 25%, or 50% probability). The test manual gives rough guidelines for making this estimation, with a 5% probability viewed as applicable in personnel screening situations and a 50% probability viewed as applicable for individuals with a history of serious alcohol-related negative consequences, such a drunk driving arrests. Although these endpoints may seem self-evident, the basis for determining intermediate probabilities of risk is unclear, and the use of different probability levels has widely discrepant interpretative consequences for subjects who score in the intermediate range of the test. For example, based on assignment to the 5%, 10%, 25%, and 50% risk groups, respectively, a female's raw score of 35 (of 72 total) would yield an alcohol abuse proneness score of 27%, 44%, 70%, and 87%, respectively. Such latitude in scoring and interpretation further compounds the potential for abuse in using the test for personnel screening and for other purposes that entail substantive decisions about individuals' livelihood and well-being.

The manual for the revised edition contains new information about the test's internal consistency and factor structure derived using the employment sample, but these data do little to obviate earlier concerns about the test's subjectively determined personality dimensions. Alpha coefficients for the seven scales ranged from .44 to .75, and the factor analysis of scale scores yielded a single factor solution that was interpreted as reflecting general psychopathology. Although a two-factor solution also was presented and was interpreted as supporting the test's partition of traits into neurotic and psychopathic categories, the two factors were significantly correlated ($r = .68$), and the pattern of rotated factor loadings is unconvincing evidence for the hypothesized partition.

In reviewing the original Manson Evaluation, Miller (1976) noted the test's lack of empirical evaluation since the 1950s and observed that the scale had "fallen into disuse" (p. 651). The revised edition offers little to recommend its resurrection. The test's fundamental premise regarding a distinct alcoholic personality has been thoroughly discredited empirically in the decades since the test's initial publication, and it is disheartening that the revised edition is essentially unchanged from the original and thus is impervious to 40 years of relevant research. Great strides also have been made in the classification and measurement of alcohol-related disorders (e.g., Donovan & Marlatt, 1988; Lettieri, Nelson, & Sayers, 1985), and the revision is insensitive to this body of work as well. At best, the Manson Evaluation is of historical interest in reflecting views of alcoholism that were popular during its inception, but its contemporary use cannot be recommended. Readers interested in empirically supported, alternative procedures for the detection and evaluation of alcohol problems are referred to the comprehensive volumes on assessment edited by Donovan and Marlatt (1988) and by Lettieri et al. (1985).

REVIEWER'S REFERENCES
Murphy, D. G. (1956). The revalidation of diagnostic tests for alcohol addiction. *Journal of Consulting Psychology, 20*, 301-304.
Gibbins, R. J., Smart, R. G., & Seeley, J. R. (1959). A critique of the Manson Evaluation Test. *Quarterly Journal of Studies on Alcohol, 20*, 357-361.
Campbell, D. (1965). [Review of the Manson Evaluation.] In O. K. Buros (Ed.), *The sixth mental measurements yearbook* (pp. 285-286). Highland Park, NJ: Gryphon Press.
Miller, W. R. (1976). Alcoholism scales and objective assessment methods: A review. *Psychological Bulletin, 83*, 649-674.
Lettieri, D. J., Nelson, J. E., & Sayers, M. A. (Eds.) (1985). *Alcohol treatment assessment research instruments* (National Institute on Alcohol Abuse and Alcoholism Treatment Handbook Series #2, DHHS Publication No. ADM85-1380). Washington, DC: U.S. Government Printing Office.
Donovan, D. M., & Marlatt, G. A. (Eds.) (1988). *Assessment of addictive behaviors.* New York: Guilford Press.

[227]

The Marriage and Family Attitude Survey.

Purpose: "A diagnostic and educational instrument for understanding relationship attitudes" in marriage and family life.
Population: Adolescents and adults.
Publication Date: No date.
Scores: 10 areas: Cohabitation and Premarital Sexual Relations, Marriage and Divorce, Childhood and Child Rearing, Division of Household Labor and Professional Employment, Marital and Extramarital Sexual Relations, Privacy Rights and Social Needs, Religious Needs, Communication Expectations, Parental Relationships, Professional Counseling Services.
Administration: Group.
Price Data, 1988: $15 per 25 test forms; $4.50 per examiner's manual (no date, 8 pages); $5 per specimen set.
Time: (4–10) minutes.
Authors: Donald V. Martin and Maggie Martin.
Publisher: Psychologists and Educators, Inc.

Review of The Marriage and Family Attitude Survey by MARK W. ROBERTS, Professor of Clinical Psychology, Idaho State University, Pocatello, ID:

The Marriage and Family Attitude Survey (MFAS) was designed to measure adolescent and adult expectations of various components of married life. Testing time is reported at 4 to 10 minutes. Respondents complete 5-point Likert scales for each of 58 items. For example, Item 1, "I believe it is wrong to engage in sexual intercourse before marriage," must be rated from "strongly agree" to "strongly disagree." Both item responses and total scale scores are suggested for use in counseling formats with individuals or couples or in educational formats with adolescents. By detecting deviations or conformity with either the available normative data or one's partner, the counseling or educational process is thought to be enhanced. The authors suggest that test items could also be used as a therapeutic exercise in seeking agreements for typical marital conflicts. Unfortunately, like the Marriage Role Expectation Inventory (9:655), the MFAS is severely limited by psychometric difficulties.

The standardization sample (*n* "exceeded" 5,000, 14 to 35 years of age, attending six different high schools, colleges, and universities) seems too heterogeneous to accomplish the stated objectives of the MFAS. As demonstrated by the authors in the manual, such variables as age, gender, ethnic background, parental marital status, and dating experience are significantly associated with some or all of the 58 MFAS items. Consequently, the assertion of normative data begs the question of normative for which subpopulation? Subsequent to printing the MFAS manual, the authors (Martin & Martin, 1984) did publish norms for a more homogeneous sample (*n* = 5,237, 16 to 36 years, single, undergraduates). It is unclear if these are new subjects or a subset of the original sample.

Test items were generated following a review of the marriage and family literature and subsequently reviewed by a panel of clinical psychologists specializing in marital problems. The manual does not state the criteria used by the experts for item inclusion. A pilot study (*n* = 30 university students) was undertaken to determine readability and test duration and to perform item analyses for "offensive" or "unnaturally skewed" items. Each item was then compared to the five demographic and marital/dating variables cited above. Items yielding significant chi-square statistics with any two of these "criterion" variables were retained. All 58 items were retained. It is unclear if the pilot study sample data or the standardization sample data were used for the chi-square analyses.

Norms are provided in terms of the typical rating (strongly agree to strongly disagree) for each item by gender. Whether "typical" is a mean, median, or mode is not specified, nor are any data available on item variances. Recommended scoring consists of summing one point for each agreement with the categorical normative response across the 58 items. Total scores (0 to 58) are then categorized as "High Agreement" (48–58), "Normal" (39–47), "Low Agreement" (28–38), or "Conflicting" (27 or lower), using arbitrary 10-point cutoffs. Percent endorsement data for each category from strongly disagree to strongly agree are reported for 43 of the original 58 items by Martin and Martin (1984). These norms correspond closely to those in the manual, suggesting that the "typical" item rating in the manual is the modal endorsement and that the 1984 subjects were a subset of the original sample.

Additional psychometric problems with the MFAS are readily apparent. The manual does not report any reliability data. Martin and Martin (1984, p. 295), citing an earlier study (Martin, 1982), report "an internal reliability coefficient of .81 and a test rates and reliability coefficient of .79." This sentence does not include sufficient information for interpretation. Unfortunately, Martin

(1982) was referenced incorrectly and is actually Martin, Gawinski, and Medler (1982), an article describing premarital counseling that does not include any information about MFAS reliability. Scale reliability is, therefore, uncertain. The standard error of the total scores is unknown. There are no internal consistency data or factor analyses to demonstrate the level of homogeneity within each of the 10 scales or to justify the summing of data across 10 scales to form total scores. Validity data consist of the chi-square analyses described above, rather than measurements of behavior responsive to the stated purpose of the MFAS. For example, total scores or couple agreement scores could be validated against independent measures of marital satisfaction. Couple agreement levels before and after counseling could be obtained. MFAS use versus non-use in high school formats could be contrasted on tests of student awareness of marital issues. In the absence of such studies, one must conclude that the MFAS total score is without criterion validation.

As currently researched, the MFAS represents an unproven instrument of questionable utility. It is not recommended. In a similar lament, Markman (9:655) recommended an unpublished instrument by Epstein and Eidelson called the Relationship Belief Instrument (RBI). The RBI, however, focuses on pathological expectations (e.g., Scale A, "Disagreement is Destructive"), rather than the comprehensive set of marital expectations attempted by the MFAS. Therefore, there does not yet appear to be a psychometrically adequate test of marital expectations.

REVIEWER'S REFERENCES

Martin, D., Gawinski, B., & Medler, B. (1982). Premarital counseling using group process. *Journal for Specialists in Group Work*, 7, 102-108.
Martin, D., & Martin, M. (1984). Selected attitudes toward marriage and family life among college students. *Family Relations*, 33, 293-300.

Review of The Marriage and Family Attitude Survey by DONALD U. ROBERTSON, Professor of Psychology, and VIRGINIA L. BROWN, Director, Institute for Research and Community Service, Indiana University of Pennsylvania, Indiana, PA:

The Marriage and Family Attitude Survey is a 58-item inventory that consists of statements grouped into 10 areas such as Religious Needs and Communication Expectations. Test takers indicate on a 5-point Likert scale how strongly they agree or disagree with each attitudinal statement. The initial item pool was generated by the test authors based on a review of the literature in the field of marriage and family therapy. This pool was then submitted to a panel of 10 licensed psychologists who also had supervisor status in the American Association for Marriage and Family Therapy. Items approved by seven of the panel members were included in the final test. The test manual does not indicate what the panel members were instructed to evaluate to determine whether an item was acceptable.

The ways the test can be used include facilitating discussion in classrooms from junior high through college and clarifying attitudes in the context of individual and couple counseling. An answer key is used to obtain scores on the test. The total test score is then assigned to high, normal, low, or conflicting ranges. Brief interpretive statements are provided for each of these ranges. There are no guidelines for interpretation of scores in the 10 areas.

The normative population consisted of over 5,000 people between the ages of 14 and 35, with slightly more females than males. No further information is provided in the manual. A far more serious problem is that the authors seem to have confused norms and answer keys. The answer key, labelled "Normative Distribution" in the only table contained in the manual, consists of a listing of the 58 items and the "typical" response for males, females, and combined males and females. The table is confusing and contradictory. For example, both males and females receive a point toward the total score if they disagree with the statement that it is wrong to engage in sexual intercourse before marriage. However, if one uses the combined key/norm, one obtains a point for either disagreeing or strongly agreeing! There is no information about how this table was constructed.

Even if we can accept the rather unusual scoring scheme, the only information that could possibly serve as norms are the ranges for total scores. There is no information about how the cutting scores were established or the basis of the interpretive statements.

The manual contains no information about reliability. In fact, the word "reliability" does not appear in the manual. The only evidence of validity is a brief statement that face validity was evaluated by administering the test to 30 undergraduates who were asked about the readability of the items. The only analysis of test data contained in the manual is a brief description of the results of cross-classifying six demographic variables with responses to the 58 items. The reader is told that 254 of the 348 tables produced values of chi-square that were significant at the .05 level or greater [sic].

The Marriage and Family Attitude Survey is a nice sample of 58 attitudes about marriage and families. The items could serve as a useful list of discussion topics. In its current form, however, it is not a test. There are no norms, no evidence of reliability, and no evidence of validity. The authors do not provide necessary technical information and its publication as a test is clearly inappropriate.

[228]
Mathematical Olympiads.

Purpose: Constructed "to discover and challenge secondary school students with outstanding mathematical talent."
Population: Secondary school.

Publication Dates: 1972–89.
Scores: Total score only.
Administration: Group.
Manual: No manual.
Price Data: Available from publisher.
Author: Committee on the American Mathematic Competitions.
Publisher: Mathematical Association of America; American Mathematical Society.

a) MATHEMATICAL OLYMPIAD.
Acronym: USAMO.
Time: 210(220) minutes.
Comments: Test administered annually in April; "selection to participate . . . is based on both the AHSME and AIME scores."

b) INTERNATIONAL MATHEMATICAL OLYMPIAD.
Acronym: IMO.
Time: 540(550) minutes over 2 sessions.
Comments: Test administered annually in July; selection to participate is based on USAMO scores and other scores obtained during the training session.

Review of the Mathematical Olympiads by PHILLIP L. ACKERMAN, Associate Professor of Psychology, University of Minnesota, Minneapolis, MN:

The Mathematical Olympiads (MO) is the third hurdle test in a trilogy of tests used for selection of candidates for further training (and final selection) to the International Mathematical Olympiads competition. The only persons allowed to take this test are those who survive cuts made first on scores from the American High School Mathematics Examination (AHSME) (which is open to all secondary school students; typical sample is about $N = 400,000$), and second on scores from the American Invitational Mathematics Examination (AIME) (which is open to only about 1% of the top scorers on the AHSME; typical $N = 4,000$). The MO exam is then administered to the top 150 scorers on a composite of AHSME and AIME exams. The exam is constructed each year by a committee of mathematicians, and as such is administered only once before it is retired from use. No manual exists for the test—reliability, validity, and norming data are entirely unknown. Given that the MO exam is constructed by subject matter experts, it seems likely that the exam would have relatively high content validity, but this is a matter of conjecture, rather than objective inference.

The exam has been structured so as to yield substantial floor effects, that is, even for the .04% of the total sample completing the AHSME that are allowed to take the MO, approximately 30% of this highly selected group obtain scores that are less than 10 points (out of a total of 100 possible points). Given the small proportion of students at large who could be expected to obtain scores above zero, and the fact that current versions of the test are strictly unavailable to the testing community, this test has limited use outside of its rather specific purpose.

However, there is an implicit suggestion on the part of the testing committee that selection to take the MO exam, in and of itself, is recognition of mathematical giftedness. As such, it is not unusual for students to include reference to their selection to take the MO exam on college and university applications. While the severe selection ratio suggests that the inference of giftedness is reasonable, the lack of validity data makes the inference impossible to justify on objective grounds. What is clearly needed is an attempt by the test authors to establish both reliability and validity indexes for the test. Most critical would be correlational data between the first two hurdle tests (the AHSME and AIME exams) and extant measures of mathematical ability (e.g., Scholastic Aptitude Test, ACT Assessment, Graduate Record Examinations, and so on). Given the severe selection ratio for the MO exam, it may be more effective to establish convergent validity by stratified random sampling from the other two hurdle examinations, or merely to compare MO examinees with control groups of high school, college, and/or graduate student populations. Mean differences in Scholastic Aptitude Test or Graduate Record Examinations scores between these groups (especially with a contrast of verbal abilities, in an attempt to establish discriminant validity), may be especially useful in at least providing critical validity information. Given the lack of basic psychometric information at this point, no recommendation for interpreting the fact of an invitation to take the examination, or for interpreting actual test scores on the MO can be supported.

Review of the Mathematical Olympiads by WILLIAM R. KOCH, Associate Professor of Educational Psychology, The University of Texas, Austin, TX:

The Mathematical Olympiads is a small booklet that includes copies of two separate, annually administered examinations: the United States of America Mathematical Olympiad (USAMO) and the International Mathematical Olympiad (IMO). This booklet is published upon conclusion of the IMO each year to provide the actual problems and a sample of correct solutions to that year's exams and to assist students in preparing for the next year's USAMO and IMO. The USAMO is the third step that must be taken by secondary school students who are exceptionally talented in mathematics to qualify for possible participation in the IMO.

In the spring of each year, thousands of students in grades 7–12 participate in the American High School Mathematics Examination (AHSME) published by the Mathematical Association of America. The AHSME is a group-administered, timed exam (90 minutes) consisting of 30 multiple-choice items. A cutoff score is announced in the fall to select the highest scorers for participation (by invitation only) in the American Invitational Mathematics Exam

(AIME), which is also group administered and timed (3 hours) but consists of 15 free-response problems appropriate for very able mathematics students in grades 9–12. Both the AHSME and AIME are prepared and scored by a committee of the Mathematical Association of America; also, both exams measure math skills at the precalculus level with an emphasis on intermediate algebra and plane geometry. Thus the AHSME and AIME are used as a sequence of selection exams to identify exceptional students to be invited to compete in the U.S.A. and, possibly, the International Mathematical Olympiads.

The 1989 version of the USAMO consisted of five very difficult, free-response problems to be solved in 210 minutes. The 1989 IMO was designed to be taken over a 2-day period with three (even more difficult) problems to be solved each day in 270 minutes. Unfortunately, the very best that can be said about these two exams is that they have obvious face validity for their intended purpose. That is, to a knowledgeable observer, the exams appear to consist of quite difficult problems in mathematics that only exceptional secondary students could solve.

However, no data whatsoever are available to evaluate the technical or psychometric characteristics of these exams. No manual for administration is available, nor is there a technical handbook. There are no norms, no evidence of test validity, no reliability estimates, and no information about item difficulty or discrimination values. Apparently, items are not tried out with students before they are included on the exams, probably for reasons of test security, nor are the exams equated across forms. The inevitable result is that tests of varying difficulty are constructed from one year to the next. Presumably each free-response question is scored by more than a single judge, but no estimates of interrater reliability are available. Furthermore, there are usually several different methods that might be used by students to obtain the correct solution to a given problem. Also, with math problems of this sort there is always the danger than an unconventional solution could be judged to be incorrect or that a problem could have more than one correct answer.

SUMMARY. Given the very special and limited purposes of the USAMO and IMO, perhaps it is excusable that no information is available about the psychometric properties of these exams. Only about 300 exceptionally able students in mathematics worldwide participate in the IMO each year, and the exams function simply to determine the best performing national teams and the recipients of Olympiad medals. Still, it would be very desirable for the constructors of these exams to make available estimates of scorer reliability. Also, evidence for the content validity of the exams should be provided; that is, do the problems on these exams adequately sample and represent the content domain of secondary school mathematics curricula at the most advanced, precalculus level? Finally, it must be stated that the USAMO and the IMO do not meet generally accepted guidelines and criteria for proper educational test construction.

[229]

Mathematics Anxiety Rating Scale.

Purpose: To assess the "degree of mathematics anxiety."
Publication Dates: 1972–88.
Scores: Total score only.
Administration: Group.
Author: Richard M. Suinn.
Publisher: Rocky Mountain Behavioral Science Institute, Inc.
a) MATHEMATICS ANXIETY RATING SCALE-E.
Population: Grades 4–6.
Acronym: MARS-E.
Price Data, 1991: $30 per 100 tests.
Time: [15–20] minutes.
b) MATHEMATICS ANXIETY RATING SCALE-A.
Population: Grades 7–12.
Acronym: MARS-A.
Price Data, 1991: $60 per 100 tests.
Time: (20–30) minutes.
c) MATHEMATICS ANXIETY RATING SCALE.
Population: College and adults.
Acronym: MARS.
Price Data, 1991: $60 per 100 tests.
Time: (40–50) minutes.
Cross References: For reviews by Michael J. Hannafin and Thomas R. Knapp, see 9:663 (6 references); see also T3:1405 (9 references); for reviews by William E. Kline and James A. Walsh of *c*, see 8:610 (3 references).

TEST REFERENCES

1. Dew, K. M. H., Galassi, J. P., & Galassi, M. D. (1983). Mathematics anxiety: Some basic issues. *Journal of Counseling Psychology, 30*, 443-446.
2. Clute, P. S. (1984). Mathematics anxiety, instructional method, and achievement in a survey course in college mathematics. *Journal for Research in Mathematics Education, 15*, 50 58.
3. Dew, K. M. H., Galassi, J. P., & Galassi, M. D. (1984). Math anxiety: Relation with situational test anxiety, performance, physiological arousal, and math avoidance behavior. *Journal of Counseling Psychology, 31*, 580-583.
4. Fulkerson, K. F., Galassi, M. D., & Galassi, J. P. (1984). Relation between cognitions and performance in math anxious students: A failure of cognitive theory? *Journal of Counseling Psychology, 31*, 376-382.
5. Blackwell, R. T., Galassi, J. P., Gallassi, M. D., & Watson, T. E. (1985). Are cognitive assessment methods equal? A comparison of Think Aloud and Thought Listening. *Cognitive Therapy and Research, 9*, 399-413.
6. Kelly, W. P., & Tomhave, W. K. (1985). A study of math anxiety/math avoidance in preservice elementary teachers. *Arithmetic Teacher, 32* (5), 51-53.
7. Siegel, R. G., Galassi, J. P., & Ware, W. B. (1985). A comparison of two models for predicting mathematics performance: Social learning versus math aptitude-anxiety. *Journal of Counseling Psychology, 32*, 531-538.
8. Adams, N. A., & Holcomb, W. R. (1986). Analysis of the relationship between anxiety about mathematics and performance. *Psychological Reports, 59*, 943-948.
9. Battista, M. T. (1986). The relationship of mathematics anxiety and mathematical knowledge to the learning of mathematical pedagogy by preservice elementary teachers. *School Science and Mathematics, 86*, 10-19.
10. Ferguson, R. D. (1986). Abstraction anxiety: A factor of mathematics anxiety. *Journal for Research in Mathematics Education, 17*, 145-150.
11. Kostka, M. P., & Wilson, C. K. (1986). Reducing mathematics anxiety in nontraditional-age female students. *Journal of College Student Personnel, 27*, 530-534.
12. Lindbeck, J. S., & Dambrot, F. (1986). Measurement and reduction of math and computer anxiety. *School Science and Mathematics, 86*, 567-577.
13. Hadfield, O. D., & Maddux, C. D. (1988). Cognitive style and mathematics anxiety among high school students. *Psychology in the Schools, 25*, 75-83.
14. Alexander, L., & Martray, C. (1989). The development of an abbreviated version of the Mathematics Anxiety Rating Scale. *Measurement and Evaluation in Counseling and Development, 22*, 143-150.
15. Chiu, L. H., & Henry, L. L. (1990). Development and validation of the Mathematics Anxiety Scale for Children. *Measurement and Evaluation in Counseling and Development, 23*, 121-127.

Review of the Mathematics Anxiety Rating Scale by ROBERT F. McMORRIS, *Professor of Educational Psychology and Statistics, State University of New York at Albany, Albany, NY:*

This review of the Mathematics Anxiety Rating Scale emphasizes the Elementary (MARS-E) and Adolescent (MARS-A) forms, separately and together; most comments generalize to the parent (MARS) form for college students and adults.

ELEMENTARY FORM. The MARS-E contains 26 statements which students rate on a 5-point scale from *Not at all nervous* to *very, very nervous.* Nonschool situations, especially involving consumer situations such as making change, are portrayed in approximately one-quarter of the items. Situations also include testing, writing on the board, participating or being in math class more generally, and reading for class. Only two situations refer to difficulty understanding or performing. No items portray math in nonmath classes, measurement, statistics, or geometry. Most items referring to specific content target computation.

To study further the test's content, Komang Tantra and I performed a target partition analysis (Ambrosino, McMorris, & Noval, 1979; Pfeiffer & Pruzek, 1972). With this data-summarizing procedure, individuals sort items into their own categories, even providing category labels, and thereby allowing study of how individuals—uncontaminated by knowing the test's title, description, or specifications—perceive and organize the items. For the MARS-E, doctoral students in educational psychology and this reviewer each sorted the items in four to seven categories with an index of agreement (Pst) of .87. Sorters provided category titles such as word problems, basic computation, consumer/everyday math applications, public performance, threat of poor performance, and text anxiety.

INTENDED USES. The developer did not adequately specify or support uses for the instrument. To illustrate, in the three-page *Information for Users* booklet, the first paragraph of the procedure refers to "youngster," later paragraphs to "subject" and "client." The developer refers to forming a desensitization therapy anxiety hierarchy for a client based on five items, choosing one item at each level on the 5-point scale. Unfortunately, the developer did not cluster items to allow a more reliable or understandable estimate.

NORMS/RELIABILITY. Percentile norms are based on 1,000+ Fort Collins, Colorado public school fourth- through sixth-graders. Other percentile norms are based on 105 Hispanic students from Colorado differentiated only by gender. Means for Hispanic females were 50, for Hispanic males and for undifferentiated males and females were from 54 to 56. Ceiling exists: the 95th percentiles were in the 70s and 80s out of a possible 130. Cronbach's alpha of .88, the only reliability information provided, presumably is based on the total norm sample, and appears sufficiently high given only 26 items.

VALIDITY. Construct validity was addressed by negative rs, generally .20s and .30s, with Stanford Achievement mathematics subtest scores, and by factor analysis indicating two primary factors, mathematics test anxiety and mathematics performance adequacy anxiety, which account for less than 30% of the variance.

ADOLESCENT FORM. The MARS-A consists of 98 statements which "refer to things and experiences that may cause tension or apprehension" to be rated on a 5-point "How anxious" scale ranging from *Not at all* to *Very much*. Many situations are computationally oriented, and at least one-quarter of the items portray situations that could be outside of school, especially consumer type, with a few rather interesting and potentially thought provoking. About 5% of the situations specify failure or difficulty; another 5% indicate or suggest algebra. Other subjects are less well represented: two items in geometry, two or three in statistics, two graphs or charts, one each in science and computer (printouts), and none in trigonometry or calculus. A few items deal with memorizing numbers, fear of numbers per se, or mathematical voyeurism (i.e., watching someone else do something mathematical). Some items involve minimal participation, such as getting a mathematics book or reading the word "statistics."

PROPOSED USES. Judging from the three-page *Information for Users* booklet (1979) or a two-page *Informational Brief* (1979), the scale can be used to screen for placement in special mathematics courses, provide counseling, provide for intervention through programs such as desensitization for mathematics anxiety (including development of a hierarchy of desensitization based on five items), evaluate programs, and research mathematics anxiety.

At least four concerns or cautions are in order: (*a*) Is the author promoting a desensitization program? (*b*) A suggested cutoff for eligibility for such a program was the 75th percentile; why the 75th? (*c*) How easy would it be to show decreasing mathematics anxiety over time when evaluating a junior high/middle school program given the norm group's decreasing scores over grades? (*d*) How difficult would it be to determine causally "the role of curriculum content, parental characteristics, extracurricular activities, etc., in influencing mathematics anxiety" given the minimal control researchers have over most such variables? (Informational Brief, p. 1).

NORMS. Percentile norms for grades 7, 8, and 9 are based on 1,000+ students from two small cities in Colorado and Arizona (Suinn & Edwards, 1982) and for grades 10, 11, and 12 on 300+ students from the same cities. Norms are given for each grade and for each gender within grades 7–9 combined and 10–12 combined. No information is given about characteristics of the schools or the samples within schools. Although supposedly "some data is available on minority students," this reviewer has not been able to locate any.

RELIABILITY. Internal consistency coefficients based on the entire sample range from .89 to .96 depending on the specific formula used. Stability information and standard error of measurement are not provided.

VALIDITY. Mathematics anxiety was found to be negatively related to GPAs in mathematics courses, number of mathematics/science courses enrolled in, and expressed career choice in mathematics/science occupations. Factor analysis results (Suinn & Edwards, 1982) seem to support two factors termed "Numerical Anxiety" and "Mathematics Test Anxiety." Incredibly, reporting of validity took only half a page in the *Informational Brief* and was not even mentioned in the *Information for Users*.

COMMENTS/CONCLUSION. Mathematics anxiety would seem a concept that has a significant impact on many individuals of all ages and on the future of the nation. Instruments related to this construct are vital to consider and improve. Judging from an unpublished review of mathematics anxiety measures (Harrington, 1990), the parent MARS for college students and adults has more support for validity than has been reported above for the forms intended for younger students. Even a shorter version has been devised and supported (Plake & Parker, 1982).

Other information would help the interpreter: stability of the scores over time; relationships with anxiety more generally, with test anxiety, and with other measures of math anxiety; displays of the (potentially curvilinear) relationships between math anxiety and performance; discussion of the "ideal" level of anxiety; results of stress-reduction treatments; placement of the test in a multitrait-multimethod format; fakability; and national norms.

Additional questions this reviewer would hope to have addressed in the literature and in an appropriate manual include: How do the authors conceptualize mathematics anxiety? How does this conceptualization square with factor analyses typically producing two to three factors? Can clinical anxiety be distinguished from lack of confidence or from dislike of mathematics or the mathematics teacher or from competence in mathematics? To what extent do the scores reflect social anxiety or performance anxiety? Do the items in this test referring to word problems reflect mathematics anxiety generally, reading comprehension problems generally, or mathematics reading comprehension more specifically? Can adequate subscales be devised and supported?

Is a pedestrian view of mathematics promulgated by this set of measures, as suggested in the first paragraph of this review? Do students have reinforced by this measure a view that mathematics is essentially a "hurry up and compute" activity with little regard for process or special ways of thinking? Emphases on computation and basic consumer tasks may inadvertently mask conceptual development, problem solving more generally, visualization, generalization, and other ways to consider mathematics.

I hope the MARS family will be joined by "real" manuals with information to assist the interpreter. Serious users may consider at least supplementing MARS information with scores from the Fennema and Sherman (1976) measure, for example. Given the importance of the construct, additional or revised measures may be developed, perhaps even reflecting NCTM's Agenda for Action or the Standards (National Council of Teachers of Mathematics, 1980, 1989). The Commission developing the Standards emphasized mathematics as problem solving, communication, reasoning, and connections, and contrasted these approaches to the "long-standing preoccupation with computation and other traditional skills [which] has dominated both *what* mathematics is taught and the *way* mathematics is taught . . . . As a result, the present . . . curriculum is narrow in scope; fails to foster mathematical insight, reasoning, and problem solving; and emphasizes rote activities. Even more significant is that children begin to lose their belief that learning mathematics is a sense-making experience. They become passive receivers of rules and procedures rather than active participants in creating knowledge" (1989, p. 15). A secondary consequence of using a form of the MARS may be to limit the conceptualization of mathematics by the students and by the teacher.

The impact of such limited conceptualizing may be eased by supplementing with additional assessment methods; one source for developing such methods is the NCTM's Evaluation Standard 10 on Mathematical Disposition (1989, pp. 233ff). Further, supplements to the global warning of high mathematics anxiety given by a MARS should be made available to help diagnose the type or source of mathematics anxiety and help in developing a treatment plan. Currently, then, researchers and practitioners are urged to interpret any of the MARS forms cautiously and supplement appropriately.

REVIEWER'S REFERENCES

Pfeiffer, R. A., & Pruzek, R. M. (1972, October). *An illustration of an approach to analyzing partitioned data in the context of educational measurement.* Paper presented at the meeting of the Northeastern Educational Research Association, Boston.

Fennema, E., & Sherman, J. A. (1976). Fennema-Sherman mathematics attitudes scale: Instruments designed to measure attitudes toward the learning of mathematics by females and males. *JSAS Catalog of Selected Documents in Psychology, 6,* 31. (Ms. No. 1225)

Ambrosino, R. J., McMorris, R. F., & Noval, L. K. (1979). Partitioning methods for detecting misconceptions of content and test items. *Journal of Educational Measurement, 16,* 187-195.

National Council of Teachers of Mathematics. (1980). *An agenda for action: Recommendations for school mathematics of the 1980s.* Reston, VA: Author.

Plake, B. S., & Parker, C. S. (1982). The development and validation of a revised version of the Mathematics Anxiety Rating Scale. *Educational and Psychological Measurement, 42,* 551-557.

Suinn, R. M., & Edwards, R. (1982). The measurement of mathematics anxiety: The Mathematics Anxiety Rating Scale for Adolescents—MARS-A. *Journal of Clinical Psychology, 38,* 576-580.

National Council of Teachers of Mathematics. (1989). *Curriculum and evaluation standards for school mathematics.* Reston, VA: Author.

Review of the Mathematics Anxiety Rating Scale by SHARON L. WEINBERG, *Professor of Quantitative Studies, New York University, New York, NY:*

The Mathematics Anxiety Rating Scale (MARS) was developed in 1972 to measure mathematics anxiety in adults. Since then two other versions of this scale have been developed, one in 1979 for adolescents (MARS-A) and the other in 1988 for elementary students (MARS-E). Reviews of both the MARS and MARS-A have appeared in earlier *Mental Measurements Yearbook* editions. Because no new information has been published to date which might add to the psychometric profiles of either the MARS or MARS-A, the earlier reviews of the MARS and MARS-A remain current. Accordingly, this review will focus on the latest form of this test, the MARS-E.

Like its predecessors (MARS and MARS-A), described by Walsh (1978) and Knapp (1985) in their earlier *MMY* reviews as "deficient," the latest version of this test appears to be equally deficient. To begin, there is no manual, only a scant three-page document that attempts to supply both administration and technical information for users.

As described in this three-page document, the MARS-E is a 26-item self-rating scale that may be individually or group administered. Although each of the items is said to describe "a situation which may arouse anxiety for a youngster," information is not provided as to how the items were generated. Accordingly, we do not know whether the relevant content domain has been sampled appropriately; that is, whether the test is content valid.

Following information on scoring, the document suggests that the MARS-E may be used "as the basis for forming a desensitization therapy anxiety hierarchy"; however, the document fails to provide justification for the use of this test for such purposes.

With respect to technical detail, the document is equally fuzzy and incomplete. Although some omitted details are supplied by two references provided (Suinn, Taylor, & Edwards, 1988, 1989), problems remain. Normative data are based on what appears to be a convenience sample of 1,119 fourth, fifth, and sixth grade students from six public schools in the Poudre R-1 district, Fort Collins, Colorado. Close to 90% of the sample is Caucasian, and although "a broad range of socio-economic status" is purported to be represented, details of representation are not provided, making generalizations based on these normative data questionable. Separate norms are provided for the 105 Hispanics of this sample. Again, with so small a sample of Hispanics, and no information on socio-economic status, etc., one must question the generalizability of these data for Hispanics.

Internal consistency reliability is given at .88. Construct validity in the form of correlations of the test with various subscales of the Stanford Achievement Test (SAT) and a factor analysis are provided. Although correlations with the subscales of the SAT are statistically significant, they are only modest in size, being no greater than -.31. Important details are missing from the report of the factor analysis (e.g., eigenvalues, correlation between oblique factors, number of items per factor). Moreover, the two factors purported to underlie the structure of the test account for only 28% of the variance, suggesting that many more than two dimensions are needed to describe the construct mathematics anxiety, at least as measured by the 26 items of this test. To suggest, as do the authors, that the test comprises "two primary factors," without qualification, is therefore misleading.

In conclusion, this reviewer agrees with the authors of this test that mathematics anxiety is an important construct requiring attention. Accordingly, the authors are encouraged to compile information that would add to the psychometric integrity of the MARS-E and its predecessors. Until such information is forthcoming, however, it is recommended that researchers of mathematics anxiety use this test with caution.

REVIEWER'S REFERENCES

Walsh, J. A. (1978). [Review of the Mathematics Anxiety Rating Scale.] In O. K. Buros (Ed.), *The eighth mental measurements yearbook* (pp. 900-901). Highland Park, NJ: The Gryphon Press.

Knapp, T. R. (1985). [Review of the Mathematics Anxiety Rating Scale.] In J. V. Mitchell, Jr. (Ed.), *The ninth mental measurements yearbook* (p. 911). Lincoln, NE: Buros Institute of Mental Measurements.

Suinn, R. M., Taylor, S., & Edwards, R. W. (1988). Suinn Mathematics Anxiety Rating Scale for Elementary School Students (MARS-E): Psychometric and normative data. *Educational and Psychological Measurement, 48*, 979-986.

Suinn, R. M., Taylor, S., & Edwards, R. W. (1989). The Suinn Mathematics Anxiety Rating Scale (MARS-E) for Hispanic Elementary School Students. *Hispanic Journal of Behavioral Sciences, 11*, 83-90.

Mathematics 7.

Purpose: "Assess the mathematics attainment of children near the end of the school year in which they reach their seventh birthday."

Population: Ages 6-10 to 7-9.

Publication Date: 1987.

Scores: 1 individual total score, 4 item analysis categories: Understanding, Computational Skill, Application, Factual Recall.

Administration: Group.

Price Data, 1989: £6.25 per specimen set including Teacher's Guide (24 pages), test booklet, and group record sheet; £5.75 per Teacher's Guide; £10.30 per test booklets.

Time: (30–50) minutes.

Comments: Downward extension of Mathematics 8–12 Series; no norms for categories; orally administered.

Authors: Test Development Unit of the Foundation for Educational Research in England and Wales.

Publisher: NFER-Nelson Publishing Co., Ltd. [England].

Review of Mathematics 7 by CAMILLA PERSSON BENBOW, Professor of Psychology, Department of Psychology, Iowa State University, Ames, IA:

Mathematics 7 was designed to assess the mathematics attainment of children near the end of the school year in which they reach their seventh birthday. This represents the final year of infant school for students in England. The items selected for the test were written to reflect guidelines issued by a number of local education authorities and to match the content of mathematics texts used by schools in England. Because the test was designed to be easy, it is argued that the test is suitable for identifying those children not making progress rather than for identifying advanced students. With this in mind, the fact that questions are read to students can be viewed as an advantage. Limitations in reading ability should not affect performance.

The test can be administered to small groups in either one or two sittings. Because the examiner does not proceed until every student has attempted the problem, it may take between 30 to 50 minutes to complete the 28 items. Some students may become frustrated by this procedure, however.

It is strongly recommended by the authors that the test be administered in the month of June. It is argued that data obtained during that month would be most useful to the junior schools receiving the pupils the following year. The disadvantage, as I see it, is that little time is left for the teacher in the infant school to provide remediation.

The items selected for the test represent four content areas: number, measures, shape, and pictorial representation. Four objectives are also tapped: understanding of basic concepts, computational skills, application of concepts and skills, and recall of basic facts. These two dimensions are crossed to produce a 4 x 4 grid. In this grid of 16 possible cells, items were designed to measure 10 cells or domains. Many of the items, however, are clustered in just one cell, the understanding of the basic concept of number. As a result, performance within certain domains is measured by only one question. To provide a specific diagnosis (except in the case of number), the number of items is clearly insufficient. I, therefore, question the utility of this test for that purpose. Moreover, an alternate form of the test is lacking.

An appealing aspect of the test appeared to be its attempt at providing a diagnosis of wrong answers. Five types of errors were discussed. Although the potential user is instructed in how to approach such a diagnosis, there is little explicit information provided.

The accompanying manual or rather teacher's guide contains much information useful to an individual with little or no knowledge of psychometrics. Statistical terms, such as measurement scales, standardized scores, the normal curve, percentile ranks, errors of measurement, and confidence intervals are explained in depth. Much information is also provided as to how percentile ranks and confidence intervals can be computed and interpreted. The discussion assumes no knowledge on the part of the potential user and is clearly written. Finally, a strong emphasis was placed on controlling for the effects of age on performance. Scores were adjusted, with precision, according to age in months.

After such care was exhibited for providing clear explanations and instructions and for partialling out the effects of age, one became rather disappointed in the technical data available. The test was standardized on a sample of 3,965 students in various parts of Great Britain, who were administered the test in June 1986. The only reliability index reported, however, was the Kuder-Richardson 20, which was good (i.e., .90). Retest reliability estimates are most notably missing. In terms of test validity, the situation is perhaps even worse. The only evidence of test validity we are given are correlations between teacher's rankings of students and scores on Mathematics 7. The correlations ranged from .53 to .91 (median = .80) for the 16 classes studied. Even if one did not question the usefulness of these data, they are clearly insufficient to establish validity. Moreover, because the authors argue the test is especially suited for identifying students with deficient performance, one would have expected some sort of validation of this claim. But none was provided.

Finally, the test was explicitly made to be easy (mean difficulty index was 69%) so that low achievers could be identified. It is rather puzzling then that the authors did not choose to develop a criterion-referenced test. This would seem to coincide more closely with the stated purpose of the test.

In sum, this test was designed to assess children's performance in mathematics at the end of infant school in England. The authors claim that the test is especially useful for identifying students performing poorly. We are not provided, however, with sufficient evidence to know if the test is actually fulfilling this promise. On the other hand, the test may be useful in comparing performance of groups on mathematics items designed to measure content covered by most widely used textbooks and items included in guidelines issued by local education authorities in Great Britain.

Review of Mathematics 7 by KEVIN MENEFEE, Certified School Psychologist, Barkley Center, University of Nebraska-Lincoln, Lincoln, NE:

Mathematics 7 is a 28-item screening test, in booklet form, of mathematics skills in 7-year-old children. It is designed for oral administration to small groups or entire classes of children, with an estimated administration time of 30 to 50 minutes. The test covers a broad range of problems in number, money, measurement, and related concepts, and yields an overall standard score or percentile rank. Both the standardization sample and the content and language of items in this instrument restrict its usage to children in Great Britain.

The authors state the test's items were "written to reflect guidelines issued by a number of local education authorities and mathematics course books currently in use in schools" without specifying more precisely the exact authorities or course books consulted, or how this particular set of items was determined to be a balanced representation of the curricula in question. We are left, therefore, to presume that they do, in fact, fairly cover the typical mathematics content of "the final year of infant school." The authors' description of the development process, however (items were piloted to a stratified national sample in two consecutive trials, allowing ample opportunity for selection and modification of items based both on statistical findings and on input from participating schools), suggest a high probability of good content validity.

Standardization of the instrument, as reported in the manual, appears to have been very good, based on scores of nearly 4,000 students from 139 schools, proportionately stratified nationwide by region, type of school, class size, and rural versus urban counties throughout Great Britain. The authors base the test's claim to validity largely on its content (no predictive studies or comparisons to other instruments are reported), and on a concurrent validity study based on a sample of 11 schools involved in its standardization. In this study, teachers' rankings of their students' mathematics achievement were correlated with the students' ranked test scores, yielding a median Spearman's rank-order correlation of .80 between teachers' rankings and students' standard scores. The authors also report good internal consistency for the test, with a Kuder-Richardson 20 reliability of .90. No data regarding test-retest were reported.

As previously mentioned, Mathematics 7 yields a standard score for each age level (at monthly increments) from 6-6 to 7-11. The test was actually normed only on children ages 6-10 to 7-9; however, extrapolated scores are provided at each end of the age span. Children's scores change fairly dramatically with age in the norms tables, such that a raw score of 24 (for example) equates to a standard score of 100 for the oldest age level (7-11), but a standard score of 118 for the youngest (6-6). These substantial shifts in performance over a relatively narrow age span suggest the importance of adhering closely to the developers' recommendations for administering the test as near to the end of the school year (as was done with the standardization sample) as possible.

The test developers have also grouped the test items (with no supportive basis cited) into four item analysis categories (Understanding, Computational Skill, Application, and Factual Recall) based upon the hypothetical primary "processing" requirement of each item. The manual, however, provides no means of deriving or interpreting category scores, and the authors themselves appear to have completely ignored this feature of the test after having mentioned it, almost in passing, early in the manual. Users of the instrument are advised to likewise ignore these categorizations, as neither theoretical nor empirical support is provided for their validity, and, in fact, one of the categories is represented by only a single item on the test. It might have been more useful to provide a means of deriving category scores based upon a task analysis of item content (e.g., money vs. measurement vs. computation, etc.), but given the brevity of the test, it is unlikely that reliable subscales for this instrument could be derived from any kind of breakdown of the total test.

A final significant issue limiting the utility of Mathematics 7 concerns its ability to discriminate achievement among the varying levels of math skill in the target population. As the authors point out, most of the subjects in the standardization sample enjoyed a relatively high rate of success on the test, producing a significant ceiling effect and lack of discriminative power at the upper levels of achievement (in fact, there were only two items on the entire test that were failed by more than 50% of the standardization sample). The test, therefore, is not a good instrument for comparing student performance across the full range of achievement, but is best used

for detection of significantly underachieving students from amongst large groups. In other words, its true value is as a screening device for students in need of extra assistance in mathematics.

In summary, Mathematics 7 is limited to screening groups of children for underachievement in mathematics near the end of the school year in which they reach their seventh birthday. It is not a comprehensive test of an individual child's mathematics skills, and should not be used as the sole basis for making administrative decisions about a child's educational programming. It cannot be used for the identification of exceptionally high-achieving students. Only the total score should be utilized; item categories described by the manual should be disregarded. The test is applicable only to children who have been educated in the areas of Great Britain upon which it was standardized (which are listed in the manual). These limitations of Mathematics 7 are (to the authors' credit) discussed with clarity and candor in the test manual. Users who respect the authors' directions regarding use of the instrument are likely to find it to be valuable for its intended purposes.

[231]

McCarron-Dial System.

Purpose: A battery of neurometric and behavioral measures to be used for vocational, educational, and neuropsychological assessment particularly in meeting the programming needs of handicapped persons.
Population: Normal and handicapped individuals ages 3 to adult.
Publication Dates: 1973–86.
Acronym: MDS.
Scores: 5 factors: Verbal-Spatial-Cognitive, Sensory, Motor, Emotional, Integration-Coping.
Administration: Individual.
Parts: 3 components (Auxiliary Component, Haptic Visual Discrimination Test [HVDT], McCarron Assessment of Neuromuscular Development [MAND]).
Price Data, 1989: $1,710 per complete System including Auxiliary, HVDT, and MAND Components; price data for software for computer-assisted programs supporting the MDS available from publisher; price information for workshops and training available from publisher.
Comments: "A commitment to receive training is required for all purchasers of the McCarron-Dial System"; components available as separates.
Authors: Lawrence McCarron and Jack G. Dial.
Publisher: McCarron-Dial Systems.
a) AUXILIARY COMPONENT.
Publication Dates: 1973–86.
Price Data: $280 per set of materials in carrying case; $13 per 50 forms for Peabody (specify Form A or B); $11.50 per 25 forms for Peabody Form L; $11.50 per 50 IEP forms; $19 per 25 IPP forms; $59.95 per manual ('86, 259 pages).
Comments: Manual title is Revised McCarron-Dial Evaluation System Manual; kit includes Peabody Picture Vocabulary Test—Revised (9:926), Bender

Visual Motor Gestalt Test (9:139), and Koppitz Scoring Manual for The Bender Gestalt Test for Young Children, the McCarron-Dial System Individual Evaluation Profile (IEP), the McCarron-Dial Individual Program Plan (IPP), the Observational Emotional Inventory, and the Dial Behavior Rating Scale.

1) *Dial Behavior Rating Scale.*

Purpose: To provide an abbreviated assessment of essential personal, social, and work adjustment behaviors that relate to vocational placement, adjustment to work, and personal-social adjustment.

Publication Dates: 1973–86.

Acronym: BRS.

Price Data: $11.50 per 25 forms.

Author: Jack G. Dial.

2) *Observational Emotional Inventory.*

Publication Date: 1986.

Acronym: OEI.

Price Data: $11.50 per 25 forms.

Time: 120 minutes on each of 5 days.

Comments: Behavior checklist.

b) HAPTIC VISUAL DISCRIMINATION TEST.

Purpose: To measure an individual's haptic-visual integration skills.

Publication Dates: 1976–79.

Acronym: HVDT.

Scores, 4: Shape, Size, Texture, Configuration.

Price Data: $645 per complete kit including score forms, photographic plates, folding screen, sets of shapes, sizes, textures, and configurations, manual ('79, 261 forms) in a carrying case; $13.25 per 50 score forms; $40 per manual.

Time: (10–15) minutes per hand.

Comments: Manual title is Sensory Integration: The Haptic Visual Processes.

1) *Haptic Memory Matching Test.*

Population: Blind normal young adults and blind mentally disabled adults.

Publication Dates: 1976–79.

Acronym: HMMT.

Scores, 4: Shape, Size, Texture, Configuration.

Price Data: $675 per complete kit (not including the HVDT) including 50 scoring forms, screen, stimulus items in special carrying case; $13.25 per 50 score forms.

Time: Administration time not reported.

Comments: A modification and extension of the Haptic Visual Discrimination Test to be used with the visually impaired in conjunction with the HVDT (manual and some accessories).

c) MCCARRON ASSESSMENT OF NEUROMUSCULAR DEVELOPMENT.

Purpose: "A standardized and quantitative procedure for assessing fine and gross motor abilities."

Population: Ages 3.5 to young adult.

Publication Dates: 1976–86.

Acronym: MAND.

Scores, 3: Fine Motor, Gross Motor, Total.

Price Data: $785 per complete kit including score forms, a dynamometer, stopwatch-timer, components for fine and gross motor testing, and manual ('82, 221 pages) in carrying case; $17.50 per 25 score forms; $35 per 50 Score Forms for the Visually Impaired; $40 per manual.

Time: (15) minutes.

Comments: Manual title is Revised McCarron Assessment of Neuromuscular Development Manual.

Author: Lawrence T. McCarron.

TEST REFERENCES

1. Bihn, E. M., & McCarron, L. T. (1988). Vocational-neuropsychological evaluation of psychiatrically disabled patients. *Psychological Reports, 62,* 104-106.

Review of the McCarron-Dial System by CALVIN P. GARBIN, Associate Professor of Psychology, University of Nebraska-Lincoln, Lincoln, NE:

Having recognized proper functioning of the touch system and accurate integration of visual and touch information as developmentally and neuropsychologically important, the authors of the McCarron-Dial System have created these tests to facilitate both research and diagnostic efforts in these areas.

The manual begins with a good overview of the touch system and integrates this with a useful review of previous efforts to identify touch-based and integrative tasks that correlate with intelligence and neuropsychological damage. Based on these, the authors propose the utility of a well-standardized and normed integrative test—the Haptic Visual Discrimination Test (HVDT) and the importance of a parallel assessment device for use with the blind—the Haptic Memory Matching Test (HMMT). However, there have been several theoretical and procedural advances in these areas since the publication date (1979), particularly those that address whether vision and touch engage the same "salient attributes" (e.g., Klatzky, Lederman, & Reed, 1989; Biederman & Ju, 1988) and the impact the resulting limits of visual-touch perceptual equivalence have upon cross-modal discrimination (Garbin, 1988). Attention to these issues and a related reanalysis of the test items might make the stimulus selection and scoring procedures clearer and more compelling.

For both tests, the stimuli, scoring sheets, and associated materials are generally well made and packaged for administrative efficiency. However, the cloth-covered stimuli tend to fray, tear away from the shapes, and become matted with use, problems that are likely to detract from the validity of the scores.

The administrative procedures are clearly described and easily followed for both tests, and supplementary procedures for obtaining additional data are described (e.g., determining haptic skill in both hands). The scoring procedures are simple and tables are provided for converting both total and component (shape, size, texture, and configuration) results to scaled scores for ages 3 through adult for the HVDT (with somewhat finer age categories for the total score, particularly for adult age ranges) and for normal and blind young adults for the HMMT.

The reported reliability coefficients for the HVDT (test-retest and split-half) are in the .80–.93

range. Item analysis information is based upon patterns of item difficulties, discrimination (differentiating upper and lower 27% of samples), and item total correlations (presented for normal children, $N = 51$; and adult neuropsychologically disabled, $N = 51$). The data presented are generally impressive, and it is not surprising that some of the items contribute more in one validation sample than the other (though all are retained for scoring). Based on these data, the authors seem to have assembled a useful collection of items. However, the relatively small sample sizes (51 subjects to evaluate 48 items) and the use of only the two populations impose severe limitations on the confidence one should have in these tests. For the HMMT, reliability information is limited to estimates of the split-half reliability based upon the Spearman-Brown formula (.93–.95). Item analyses based on 66 legally blind and 41 totally blind subjects show good internal properties for the HMMT.

Construct validity was addressed via a factor analysis of the four subtests (Shape, Size, Texture, and Configuration) for each of the samples. There seem to be separable comparative analysis and spatial integration factors of the HVDT for the normal children, and a single general factor for the adult neuropsychologically impaired sample. In order to contribute to the validity argument, this factor structure difference must be explained within the theoretical context and intentions of the test. For the HMMT, there is a single factor among blind adults. Concurrent validity of the HVDT was assessed using a sample of 70 neuropsychologically disabled adults and a variety of criterion scales from the San Francisco Vocational Competency Scale and Behavioral Characteristics Progression, with most correlations in the .50–.60 range. As with the reliability data, the small sample sizes and incomplete population representation damage the argument that these are valid instruments. For the HMMT, predictive validity coefficients in the .50–.70 range are reported for blind subjects using the San Francisco Vocational Competency Scales and the Electrical Component Assembly.

The remainder of the manual presents a wealth of case studies and interpretive suggestions. These usually involve data from commonly used tests, and so the reader can develop and picture the possible utility of the McCarron-Dial tests in different types of evaluations. Although an explicit argument is not made, the authors seem to suggest their tests have considerable incremental validity, that they can contribute importantly to virtually any educational, clinical psychological, or neuropsychological evaluation battery. If the evidence from the case studies was expanded into more complete studies of the tests' concurrent and incremental validity, this might be the case. At present, the use of these tests

for these purposes should be considered exploratory, and perhaps a weight of positive evidence will accrue. Unfortunately, these tests do not seem to have acquired a large audience. Literature reviews revealed neither many uses of the tests for basic research in the areas of touch or visual-touch integration nor their regular inclusion in clinical diagnostic batteries.

In summary, these are a well-packaged set of tests that are readily administered and scored, with reasonable preliminary evidence for their reliability and internal validity with normal children, neuropsychologically impaired adults, and blind adults. There is some individual case-based evidence for their contribution to multitest battery approaches to educational, psychological, and neuropsychological assessment and diagnosis.

REVIEWER'S REFERENCES

Biederman, I., & Ju, G. (1988). Surface versus edge-based determinants of visual recognition. *Cognitive Psychology, 20*, 38-64.

Garbin, C. P. (1988). Visual-haptic perceptual nonequivalence for shape information and its impact upon cross-modal performance. *Journal of Experimental Psychology: Human Perception and Performance, 14*, 547-553.

Klatzky, R. L., Lederman, S., & Reed, C. (1989). Haptic integration of object properties: Texture, hardness, and planar contour. *Journal of Experimental Psychology: Human Perception and Performance, 15*, 45-47.

Review of the McCarron-Dial System by DAVID C. SOLLY, Associate Professor and Chairperson, Department of Psychology & Counseling, Pittsburg State University, Pittsburg, KS:

Unlike most of the instruments reviewed in this volume, the McCarron-Dial System (MDS) is actually a collection of several tests, or more appropriately, a system for analyzing and interpreting data from several tests. The System is a very sophisticated one, and as such, requires specialized training from the publisher for appropriate scoring and interpretation.

The MDS consists of a multifactor battery that employs a neuropsychological processing model as the basis for assessment of educational and vocational functioning. The authors' approach to the assessment process (Data Gathering–Hypothesis Formation–Hypothesis Testing–Feedback) follows scientific methodology and is laudable, particularly in the neuropsychological diagnostic-prescriptive model of assessment. The System's true strength at this time appears to be in the area of neuropsychological assessment. Although the MDS is often considered categorically with commercial work sampling systems, it is neither a work sample nor a vocational aptitude test. Vocationally, the System's aim is to provide a prediction of an individual's potential for overall occupational competency, but *not* an *area* of projected competence. It is probably more appropriately described as a prevocational or work adjustment assessment device.

The MDS provides factor scores in five areas. However, factor analytic research by the authors and others has revealed only three relatively pure factors

(Verbal-Spatial-Cognitive, Sensorimotor, and Emotional-Coping) emerging from the collection of test data.

MANUAL. The MDS manual is generally well organized and provides detailed instructions for developing individual evaluation profiles. The background and purpose are well presented and a good case for construct validity of the system is established, but technical data on the *overall system* are lacking. Individual manuals for the Haptic Visual Discrimination Test and the McCarron Assessment of Neuromuscular Development (two component tests of the system) are provided and include normative, reliability, and validity data on each of these individual instruments. No manuals or technical data are available for the Dial Behavior Rating Scale or the Observational Emotional Inventory. (Additional and/or optional tests included in the overall MDS interpretation include the Wechsler Adult Intelligence Scale—Revised [WAIS-R], the Wechsler Intelligence Scale for Children—Revised [WISC-R], or the Stanford-Binet Intelligence Scale, the Peabody Picture Vocabulary Test—Revised [PPVT-R], the Bender Visual-Motor Gestalt Test, and one of several achievement tests, each of which has its own manual.)

Technical Data.

STANDARDIZATION SAMPLE. The Haptic Visual Discrimination Test and the McCarron Assessment of Neuromuscular Development both were standardized on a sample in excess of 2,000 which appears to be representative in terms of age, geographic region, and S.E.S. No normative/standardization sample data are presented on the Dial Behavior Rating Scale, the Observational Emotional Inventory, or on the System as a whole.

RELIABILITY. Reliability of the MDS as a whole can arguably be derived from the reliabilities of each of the individual instruments included within the system. Reliabilities (including both test-retest and split-half) are generally high, with most coefficients falling in the .90s. Individual task reliability coefficients on the McCarron Assessment of Neuromuscular Development range from a low of .67 to a high of .97, but the total score reliability is a robust .99. High reliability coefficients are essential in a collective system of tests such as the McCarron-Dial to minimize the error of measurement. However, the user should be aware that in such a collection of instruments, the error factor is additive; the standard error of measurement of each of the tests included should be considered in reporting and interpreting data. Unfortunately, no reliability data are reported on either the Dial Behavior Rating Scale or the Observational Emotional Inventory.

VALIDITY. Validity is the major failing of the MDS as a whole. Although the manual presents an excellent description of the system's theoretical base, which provides a foundation for construct validity, little more than face validity is apparent in the manual for the system as a whole, as no concurrent or predictive validity data are provided. (The MDS manual includes references to studies relating to the validity of the MDS or its components, copies of which were provided to this reviewer by the publisher.) The validity of the MDS in discriminating level of independent living (Blackwell, Dial, Chan, & McCollum, 1985) and in making neuropsychological diagnoses (Chan & Dial, 1987; Dial, Chan, Norton, & Henke, 1984) has been demonstrated. However, these constitute only a part of the system's stated purposes. Predictive validity studies employing follow-up measurement of work performance across and within the various worker trait groups would considerably strengthen the System's value to practitioners.

Validity data are reported in the respective manuals for the Haptic Visual Discrimination Test (HVDT) and the McCarron Assessment of Neuromuscular Development (MAND). Each of these instruments demonstrates generally acceptable levels of concurrent and content validation, and reasonably well-defended construct validity. Predictive validity (which this reviewer sees as most crucial in vocational assessment) is not addressed in the MAND and is discussed only as a part of the McCarron-Dial Work Evaluation System for the HVDT.

COMPUTER-ASSISTED SUPPORT SYSTEMS. The MDS is seen as most useful to practitioners when the available computer software systems are also included. Particularly when used as a vocational assessment tool, the Occupational Exploration System is an indispensable component. This software uses worker trait group and *Dictionary of Occupational Titles* information to list potential vocational areas for exploration. It falls short of predicting competence in worker functions or occupational categories (which is regrettable), but adds considerable information to aid in the career decision-making/vocational training program placement process. Without the computer software systems, one is limited to a prediction of general vocational competency, which research has shown can be accomplished through extended interpretation of a Wechsler Scale (Heinlein, 1987; Miller, 1977).

SUMMARY. Overall, the McCarron-Dial System is a well-conceived, multifactor approach to assessment that has proven diagnostic value in the neuropsychological assessment arena. In this area, it is probably very close to instruments such as the Luria-Nebraska Neuropsychological Battery (212) and the Halstead-Reitan Neuropsychological Test Battery (9:463). The neuropsychological approach to vocational assessment is a very logical one, and in this area, the MDS shows great promise. In current form, however, it is limited to being a prevocational assessment device. Without predictive validity data on specific occupational categories or data on occupational interests, it lacks the practical utility of instruments such as the APTICOM, TRANSIT, or SAGE. Although the MDS is technically sound as a prevocational assessment device or broad vocational screening device, it is neither cost nor time efficient for use as such. The authors/publishers are urged to collect and publish predictive validity data on specific areas of occupational/vocational competency and to include a measure of vocational interests as a part of the system. (Established instruments such as the Self-Directed Search [10:330] or the Wide Range Interest-Opinion Test [WRIOT, 9:1366] could be included with no additional test development required.) With these additions, the MDS could prove to be unmatched as a vocational assessment system.

REVIEWER'S REFERENCES

Miller, J. T. (1977). A study of WISC subtest scores as predictors of GATB occupational aptitude patterns for EMH students in a high school occupational orientation course. (Doctoral Dissertation, Auburn University, 1977). *Dissertation Abstracts International, 38*, 7272A.

Dial, J., Chan, F., Norton, C., & Henke, R. (1984). Concurrent validation of the extended McCarron-Dial individual evaluation profile. *Vocational Evaluation and Work Adjustment Bulletin, 17* (3), 95-99.

Blackwell, S., Dial, J., Chan, F., & McCollum, P. (1985). Discriminating functional levels of independent living: A neuropsychological evaluation of mentally retarded adults. *Rehabilitation Counseling Bulletin, 29* (1), 42-52.

Chan, F., & Dial, J. G. (1987). Diagnostic validity of the McCarron-Dial System in neuropsychological rehabilitation assessment. *International Journal of Rehabilitation Research, 10* (2), 151-158.

Heinlein, W. E. (1987). Clinical utility of the Wechsler scales in psychological evaluation to estimate vocational aptitude among learning disabled young adults. (Doctoral Dissertation, Virginia Polytechnic Institute & State University, 1987). University Microfilms International No. 8719012.

[232]

The *m*Circle™ Instrument.

Purpose: "Tests for and explores appropriate uses for five strategies routinely used by individuals to solve problems and reach resolution in human interaction."
Population: Business and industry.
Publication Date: 1986.
Scores, 5: Get Out, Give In, Take Over, Trade Off, Breakthrough.
Administration: Group.
Price Data: Available from publisher.
Time: (30–40) minutes.
Comments: Self-administered, self-scored.
Authors: Paul Kordis and Dudley Lynch.
Publisher: Brain Technologies Corporation.

Review of The mCircle Instrument by STEPHEN JURS, Professor of Educational Psychology, Research, and Social Foundations, College of Education and Allied Professions, University of Toledo, Toledo, OH:

The mCircle Instrument is designed to be used in workshops to identify how an individual responds to difficult situations. The information can then be used to analyze the strengths and weaknesses of various strategies. It is based on the notion that the typical coping strategies of some persons or groups are inappropriate (i.e., that people work harder at doing more of the same thing rather than restructuring their approach to a problem).

The instrument is used to place persons on a "metanoics circle" so that they might better understand their typical coping strategies. Metanoics stands for a fundamental shift of mind or character, a term presumably invented by the authors.

The instrument assesses five strategies that are asserted to be used routinely by individuals to solve problems and reach resolution in human interaction:

Get Out —running away, doing nothing, rationalizing and resorting to internal self-talk without action.

Give In —letting others have their way regardless of the personal consequences or sacrifice involved.

Take Over —allowing others to sacrifice and suffer negative consequences to support one's own personal gain and dominion.

Trade Off —arriving at a balanced strategy that produces long-term sharing of gain and loss for all parties.

Breakthrough —going beyond the positive expectations of all parties toward a win/win-plus solution, typically by reframing the meaning of events. (Instructional Guide, p. 3)

The instrument consists of 10 stories, each calling for the examinee's response to a difficult situation. For each situation the examinee must allocate 10 points to five possible choices. One could give all 10 points to one choice or spread the points across the choices. The straightforward scoring procedures place the examinees somewhere on what the authors call a metanoics circle.

The metanoics circle is divided into five areas that display visually the typical coping strategies of group members. One diameter has Take Over and Give In as end points. A second, perpendicular diameter has Get Out and Breakthrough as end points. The fifth area, in the center of the circle, represents balanced or inconsistent coping strategies.

Examples of certain hypothetical groups' responses are given with accompanying interpretations of the patterns of scores. It would have been helpful to supplement the hypothetical examples with some real data. More important, there are no normative data provided so that potential users of the instrument have no idea how a typical group of machinists, accountants, school counselors, or anyone else might respond on this instrument. The authors imply this instrument would be useful with a wide array of audiences but there are no baseline data given for any potential user group.

There are no data presented pertaining to test reliability. The instrument is supposed to measure typical coping strategies so one would hope that the instrument would provide stable information. The absence of reliability evidence is a major concern.

Similarly, there are no data presented that would support the validity of the instrument. The only basis for the validity of the instrument is the rationale that is provided in the Instructional Guide. Unfortunately, the mCircle Instrument Instructional Guide was written to "equip seminar and workshop leaders with sufficient understanding of the theory behind the instrument, the process for administering it and the potential for applying the results for its successful use" rather than to provide information about the technical adequacy of the instrument.

The mCircle Instrument appears to be a nice technique for workshops. The data are obtained easily, can be displayed graphically, and would serve as the basis for assessing group characteristics so that present or potential problems in resolving conflict can be identified and addressed.

The lack of adequate technical data demand that the instrument be used cautiously and that conclusions be limited to the specific group being tested. Without normative data, reliability coefficients, or other construct validity evidence, it is premature to conclude that the mCircle Instrument is an improvement over existing conflict resolution/problem-solving measures.

Review of The mCircle Instrument by RICK LINDSKOG, Associate Professor of Psychology and Counseling, Pittsburg State University, Pittsburg, KS:

The mCircle Instrument was designed to identify how persons respond when placed in conflictual situations frequently encountered in business and organizational environments.

Administration is done on a group basis by a facilitator. The 10 test items consist of conflict scenarios followed by a series of five alternative responses, each representing a scoring category (Get Out, Give In, Take Over, Trade Off, Breakthrough). The participants must choose one of these five. The facilitator guides the group through self-scoring. The score reveals to each participant her or his personal style in responding to conflictual relationship issues. Individual scores are interpreted in terms of primary and secondary strategies based upon the five above mentioned categories. The manual contains examples to help the facilitator in interpreting each group's profile according to its unique constellation of individual strategies. There is careful attention paid to explaining strengths and weaknesses of each strategy, but clearly the mCircle Instrument favors the category entitled "Breakthrough," which is defined as "going beyond the positive expectations of all parties toward a win/win-plus situation, typically by reframing the meaning of events."

There are no reliability data available and the only validity is face validity, established by the five coping categories (Get Out, Give In, Take Over, Trade Off, Breakthrough).

In summary, the mCircle Instrument is intended to be used for organizational development activities. The purpose is to identify an individual's or group's typical response strategy when faced with conflictual situations. This information positions a facilitator to initiate discussion that will allow the participants to stimulate more creative alternatives in similar situations.

The instrument lacks reliability and validity data, but may be of some use in training for response creativity and flexibility, especially in personnel development.

[233]

Measures of Psychosocial Development.
Purpose: "Provides a measure of the positive and negative attitudes, or attributes of personality, associated with each developmental stage, the status of conflict resolution at each stage, and overall psychosocial health."
Population: Ages 13 and over.
Publication Date: 1980–88.
Acronym: MPD.
Scores, 27: 8 Positive scores (Trust [P1], Autonomy [P2], Initiative [P3], Industry [P4], Identity [P5], Intimacy [P6], Generativity [P7], Ego Integrity [P8]), 8 Negative scores (Mistrust [N1], Shame and Doubt [N2], Guilt [N3], Inferiority [N4], Identity Confusion [N5], Isolation [N6], Stagnation [N7], Despair [N8]), 8 Resolution scores (R1, R2, R3, R4, R5, R6, R7, R8), 3 Total scores (Total Positive [TP], Total Negative [TN], Total Resolution [TR]).
Administration: Individual or group.
Price Data, 1989: $49.95 per complete kit including 25 reusable item booklets, 50 answer sheets, 25 male profile forms, 25 female profile forms, and manual ('88, 34 pages); $12 per 25 item booklets; $14 per 50 answer sheets; $9 per 25 male or female profile forms; $9 per manual.
Time: (15–20) minutes.
Comments: Based upon Erikson's theory of human development.
Author: Gwen A. Hawley.
Publisher: Psychological Assessment Resources, Inc.

Review of the Measures of Psychosocial Development by JAMES C. CARMER, Clinical Psychologist, Immanuel Medical Center, Omaha, NE:

The Measures of Psychosocial Development (MPD) was designed to reflect and investigate Erik Erikson's theory of human development. The eight developmental stages proposed by Erikson's theory and the conflicts that characterize each of these eight stages are all represented on this 112-item inventory. The MPD is self-administered, taking 15–20 minutes to complete. Respondents use a 5-point scale to rate how accurately the brief statements and phrases represent themselves. Normative data have been provided for adolescents and adults ages 13 and over.

Each developmental stage assessed yields a Positive scale, a Negative scale, and a Resolution scale. The Positive scale for each of the developmental stages is an attempt to measure the developmentally desirable outcome of that developmental stage's conflict. The Negative scale represents the problematic side of the conflict, with the Resolution scale being the difference between the Positive and the Negative scales. Thus, for Erikson's first developmental stage, the MPD yields three scales: Trust, Mistrust, and Resolution (the difference between the attained scores on the Trust and Mistrust Scales). What emerges for each administration of the MPD is an indication of the relative importance and intensity of the conflicts involved in all eight of Erikson's developmental stages for that individual.

Norms for each scale, as well as total scores, have been developed for four age groups for both sexes. Normalized t scores for each norm group have been applied to a profile form lending itself to profile analyses. Three additional scales consist of the total attained on all Positive scales, the total attained on all Negative scales, and the total attained on the Resolution scales. These too are normed by age group and sex.

The MPD functions as an indicator of the developmental issues and conflicts that are salient for an individual. The assessment of all eight developmental stages relative to each individual regardless of the individual's age is consistent with Erikson's assertion that the conflicts characterizing each of the developmental stages are present at all times. Erikson's theory of human development states that the developmental conflict intensifies when psychological, social, and biological factors all lead to a focus on the central issues associated with a particular developmental stage. For example, although Erikson hypothesized the conflict between Ego Integrity versus Despair is the central developmental theme of late adulthood, the issues surrounding this conflict are present throughout life, not just late adulthood.

The manual is well written. There are clear rationales for the development of the MPD and a cautionary statement that familiarity with Erikson's theory of human development is required in order to competently administer and interpret the MPD. Interpretive guidelines are included in the manual along with three case studies including data from the MPD. A carbonless two-page answer sheet allows for easy hand scoring without the use of a template. The second sheet of the answer sheet allows for the simple addition of the values of items endorsed across rows to attain the scale scores. Transposing the raw scores onto the profile form adds additional interpretive dimensions to the individual's test performance.

The author reports test-retest reliability coefficients for the individual scales approaching or exceeding .80 with the lowest scale coefficient being .67. Internal consistency coefficients also are adequate, ranging from .65 to .84.

The manual presents data on a detailed effort to assess the construct validity of the MPD. The author utilized a multitrait-multimethod matrix design and the expected patterns of relative correlations for each block were found. The Inventory of Psychosocial Development (IPD), and the Self-Description Questionnaire (SDQ) were used as additional Eriksonian self-report measures of personality development. The manual emphasizes that a weakness of the MPD is the lack of representation of minority individuals in the normative sample.

The author cautions that the MPD is not intended to assess psychopathology. Within the scope of its design and development, the MPD is useful as part of a battery of tests to assess personality dynamics and functioning. The MPD also lends itself to research on human development as well as research specifically pertaining to Erikson's theory of human development. The MPD invites the development of additional norms for minority groups and different cultures.

In summary, the MPD provides a unique view of the individual's functioning within the framework of Erikson's theory of human development. It has usefulness as a clinical assessment tool and holds much promise as a research instrument.

Review of the Measures of Psychosocial Development by ROBERT K. GABLE, Professor of Educational Psychology, and Associate Director, Bureau of Educational Research and Service, University of Connecticut, Storrs, CT:

The Measures of Psychosocial Development (MPD) contains 112 self-descriptive statements responded to on a 5-point Likert scale (*Not at all like me* to *Very much like me*). Items are hand scored to obtain separate profiles for males and females reported in *T*-scores and percentiles. Norms are based upon 2,480 individuals aged 13 to 86 primarily representing single, white, Southern residents with greater than 12 years of education.

Extensive judgmental support from the literature and expert judgment is present for content validity. Realizing the difficulties in assessing the attitudes and dynamics associated with Erikson's developmental theory based upon stage conflicts, the author properly defends several instrument development decisions that lend further support to content validity.

Comprehensive and impressive empirical evidence of construct validity is offered through multitrait-multimethod correlational studies employing discriminant and convergent arguments consistent with clearly described theoretical expectations;

Constantinople's (1980) Inventory of Psychosocial Development and Boyd's (1966) Self-Description Questionnaire are employed in these studies based upon samples ranging from 136 to 372 for selected scales. Profiles depicting the relationship of MPD mean scores with age are presented and discussed in light of the developmental nature of Erikson's theory. Although some of the correlations presented need further clarification regarding their support or lack of support for construct validity, the author concludes "the majority of the positive scales showed positive linear relationships with age" (manual, p. 22). These findings relate to the construct validity of the MPD and the developmental nature of Erikson's dimensions assessed. The reviewer would have preferred a more lengthy discussion regarding the correlations reported by Roid and Ledbetter (1987) in the context of theoretical expectations.

Alpha internal consistency reliability coefficients ranging from .65 to .84 are reported for samples of 372 adolescents and adults; test-retest (from 2- to 13-week intervals) reliabilities mostly near .80 are presented for 108 adolescents and adults. The alpha coefficients reflect the adequacy of item sampling from the targeted domain of content; the test-retest correlations support the stability of the scores over appropriate time periods.

Overall, the MPD very adequately meets the challenge of assessing affective variables associated with a developmental theory. The technical manual is comprehensive, well written, and a model of desired professional test development standards. Support for accurate and meaningful score interpretations is clearly present.

REVIEWER'S REFERENCES

Boyd, R. D. (1966). Self-Description Questionnaire. Madison, WI: The University of Wisconsin.
Constantinople, A. (1980). *Inventory for psychosocial development (scales for stages 7 and 8)*. Unpublished paper.
Roid, G. H., & Ledbetter, M. F. (1987, August). *Age trends in personality development: Evidence for Erikson's psychosocial theory*. Paper presented at meeting of the American Psychological Association, New York City.

[234]

Mental Status Checklist for Adolescents.

Purpose: To assist professionals in the assessment of adolescents' mental status.
Population: Ages 13–17.
Publication Date: 1988.
Scores: Item scores only.
Administration: Individual.
Price Data, 1989: $26.95 per 25 checklists.
Time: Administration time not reported.
Comments: Reliability and validity data not reported; problems checklist.
Authors: Edward H. Dougherty and John A. Schinka.
Publisher: Psychological Assessment Resources, Inc.

Review of the Mental Status Checklist for Adolescents by JULIAN FABRY, Clinical Supervisor, Department

of Rehabilitation Psychology, Immanuel Medical Center, Omaha, NE:

The Mental Status Checklist for Adolescents is a 174-item nominal checklist containing the following categories: (*a*) presenting problem, (*b*) personal information, (*c*) physical and behavioral observations, (*d*) health and habits, (*e*) legal issues and aggressive behavior, (*f*) recreation and reinforcers, (*g*) family and peer relationships, (*h*) developmental status, (*i*) academic performance and attitudes, (*j*) impressions and recommendations, and (*k*) comments. It would appear the checklist has been offered by the authors as a means of organizing information under the various categories.

The checklist is in an easy-to-use booklet form. The items are a mixture of self-report (e.g., "desire to achieve in school"), observations made by the interviewer (e.g., "observed signs of anxiety in interview"), and inferences drawn by the interviewer (e.g., "hostile demeanor . . . appears capable of immediate, sudden violence"). Information obtained from interviews, review of records, and direct observation can be used to complete the checklist for most adolescents.

It seems that all of the information contained within the checklist could help the user in completing an evaluation of the adolescent under study although the checklist is more descriptive than inferential. Once the information in the booklet is completed, a classification of the adolescent can be made utilizing either the *DSM-III-R* or *ICM-9-CM*.

Other than the directions on the face sheet of the booklet, there are no instructions on how to complete the questionnaire. There is no manual containing technical information such as reliability and validity. At least interrater reliability should be calculated to estimate the extent to which observer bias might detract from the validity of the approach.

The items within some of the various categories seem to be inappropriately placed. For example, age, gender, race, and source of referral are contained in the presenting problem section rather than the personal information area. Coordinating the items with various *DSM-III-R* classifications and computerizing the analysis would be extremely beneficial. At this time, the Mental Status Checklist for Adolescents should be considered only a data organization system, not an assessment device.

[235]

Mental Status Checklist for Children.

Purpose: Assess childhood problems and plan for treatment approaches.
Population: Ages 5–12.
Publication Date: 1989.
Scores: Item scores only.
Administration: Individual.
Manual: No manual.

Price Data, 1990: $26.95 per 25 checklists; $295 per IBM Computer Report (specify $3^1/_2$ -inch or $5^1/_4$ -inch disk).
Time: (10–20) minutes.
Comments: Downward extension of the Mental Status Checklist—Adult; scale for ratings by parents, caregivers, or self-ratings; Computer Report package using item responses requires 256K and two disk drives.
Authors: Edward H. Dougherty and John A. Schinka.
Publisher: Psychological Assessment Resources, Inc.

Review of the Mental Status Checklist for Children by DAVID LACHAR, Associate Professor of Psychiatry and Behavioral Sciences, University of Texas Medical School at Houston, Houston, TX:

The Mental Status Checklist for Children (MSCC) is a 12-page booklet from this publisher's Clinical Checklist Series. A personal computer program from the associated Clinical Checklist Computer Reports generates a descriptive multipage narrative from responses to booklet items. The MSCC consists of 153 items grouped under 10 headings: Presenting Problem, Personal Information, Physical and Behavioral Observations, Health and Habits, Legal Issues and Aggressive Behavior, Recreation and Reinforcers, Family Relationships, Social and Developmental Status, Academic Performance and Attitudes, and Impressions and Recommendations. The format for the majority of checklist items allows the selection of one from multiple options, although 61 items allow the selection of multiple descriptors. The term "mental status" does not appear to be an adequate description of this checklist, as MSCC content includes a variety of content that is not usually associated with a traditional mental status evaluation.

The publisher describes these checklists as serving "to identify relevant problems, establish rapport, and provide written documentation . . . . They serve as ideal instruments for initiating the consultation process and introducing the client to formal diagnostic testing. The checklist items to be completed by the client are presented in common terms that are easily understood at the intended age or educational level. The checklists can be completed in 10–20 minutes and provide a convenient tool for a comprehensive review of clients' concerns or problems." These quotes are presented here as they may suggest how the MSCC booklet is to be completed, as neither the checklist booklet nor the software manual address this issue. "Checklist items to be completed by the client" and "common terms . . . easily understood at the intended age or educational level" might indicate the client either responds directly to the items, or the items are presented to the client by the clinician. These options are quite improbable, at least for this booklet and intended age range. For example, Item 96, "Self-perception of role in family" is a phrase that most 5–12-year-olds will not understand. It is unlikely that check- lists can be completed in an average of 10, or even 20 minutes (4–8 seconds per item), as many items call for subjective assessments of complex content.

The MSCC may be most helpful as a debriefing form at the conclusion of an interview or evaluation, or concurrently with the evaluation process. Similar forms assist in organizing information and in improving the consistency of the information collected. This sort of checklist is also useful in the development of a mental health data base, if response storage and retrieval are incorporated into the system (options not currently available with the MSCC computer program).

The majority of checklist items are clearly written, although ambiguities in interpretation can be found. Comprehensive evaluations of children usually integrate information obtained from the child, guardians, the school, and other referral sources. Much of the information requested by the MSCC is unlikely to be obtained directly from a young child (e.g., "100. Importance of religion in family; 102. Perceived support from parents"). Although some checklist items clearly request the *child's* opinion, the use of "perceived" in many other items may imply that this checklist requests the perception of guardian or clinician.

The MSCC Computer Report generates a readable five-page narrative from the MSCC items that incorporate the 10 item headings listed above. This program is user friendly and the program manual easily trains all but the totally computer naive in data entry and program options. Narratives are easily modified to reflect missing data and can be customized to incorporate client-specific information or unique recommendations.

In summary, the MSCC is not a test. There are no scales and no norms. Similar checklists may assist in clinical evaluation and clinical research. Although the MSCC should not be evaluated by the statistical standards established for psychometric instruments, use of the MSCC in clinical research requires the documentation of adequate interrater reliability. Improvement in the interpretive clarity of checklist items may be necessary to meet this goal.

Review of the Mental Status Checklist for Children by MARCIA B. SHAFFER, School Psychologist, Lancaster, NY:

The Mental Status Checklist for Children is extraordinarily detailed. There are 153 items, including sections with such titles as "presenting problem," "physical and behavioral observations," and "legal issues and aggressive behavior." It is almost impossible to think of an aspect of a child's life or a bit of behavior that is not covered.

There is no question of the usefulness of the information provided by the Mental Status Checklist to clinical or school psychologists, or to those doing research on children with problematic behavioral manifestations. It is a well-organized and easy way to collect data. Some words of warning are in order, however. First, although the Checklist form itself does not say so, the information given above indicates that it is to be filled out by parents, caregivers, or the subject him/herself. It is, therefore, subject to all of the biases to be found in any such instrument. Second, it is simply a list; it is not a test. There is no manual; there are no statistics, no norms, and no interpretations. Even if the ratings are completely accurate, there is no indication of what they mean. Only those who are familiar with the configurations and combinations that point to particular diagnostic categories should attempt to use this checklist. It is not a tool for the novice. For the experienced psychologist or psychiatrist, it could prove invaluable.

[236]
Milani-Comparetti Motor Development Screening Test.

Purpose: "The test provides the clinician with a synopsis of the child's motor development by systematically examining the integration of primitive reflexes and the emergence of volitional movement against gravity."
Population: Ages 1–16 months.
Publication Dates: 1977–87.
Scores, 27: Body Lying Supine, Hand Grasp, Foot Grasp, Supine Equilibrium, Body Pulled Up From Supine, Sitting Posture, Sitting Equilibrium, Sideways Parachute, Backward Parachute, Body Held Vertical, Head Righting, Downward Parachute, Standing, Standing Equilibrium, Locomotion, Landau Response, Forward Parachute, Body Lying Prone, Prone Equilibrium, All Fours, All Fours Equilibrium, Symmetric Tonic Neck Reflex, Body Derotative, Standing Up From Supine, Body Rotative, Asymmetrical Tonic Neck Reflex, Moro Reflex.
Administration: Individual.
Price Data: Price data for test including manual ('87, 48 pages) available from publisher.
Time: (10–15) minutes.
Comments: Behavior checklist.
Authors: Wayne Stuberg (Project Director), Pam Dehne, Jim Miedaner, and Penni White (Content Consultants).
Publisher: Meyer Children's Rehabilitation Institute.

Review of the Milani-Comparetti Motor Development Screening Test by LINDA K. BUNKER, Professor of Education and Associate Dean for Academic and Student Affairs, Curry School of Education, University of Virginia, Charlottesville, VA:

The Milani-Comparetti Motor Development Screening Test—Revised (M-C) was designed to provide an observational tool for the evaluation of primitive reflexes and their integration into volitional movement for children birth to age 2. The majority of the assessment judgments relate to children between 3–12 months of age.

Twenty-seven motor behaviors are evaluated in two categories: evoked responses and spontaneous behaviors. Evoked responses include equilibrium reactions (tilting), protective extension reactions (parachute), righting reactions, and primitive reflexes. Spontaneous behaviors include postural control and active movements such as sitting, crawling, and walking.

One of the major strengths of this instrument is that it incorporates both quantitative and qualitative judgments about motor performance. As has been pointed out by many researchers, it is essential to judge the process of motor performance, and not merely the outcome of a pattern.

The M-C was first published in 1967 as an instrument to identify infants with abnormal movement patterns (Milani-Comparetti & Gidoni, 1967). The test was created as a result of examining the ability of Italian infants to control their bodies against the effects of gravity. The test was later modified by the Meyer Children's Rehabilitation Institute at the University of Nebraska. Meyer staff also developed the first training manual. The revisions made centered primarily on reordering the items to minimize positional changes. Behavioral criteria were established for scoring each item.

The normative sample (155 male and 157 female children) used to establish criteria for the successful demonstration of reflex patterns was provided by Meyer Children's Rehabilitation Institute and was included in the 1987 manual. The Institute's efforts have focused on providing reliability data and clarifying the scoring procedures.

The manual states that the "primary value of the Milani-Comparetti is to provide an organized, clinical impression of a child's motor development" (p. 7). The danger is that the precision implied by the instrument may encourage practitioners to use it as a screening test to identify children with abnormal motor development.

TEST PROPERTIES. Test-retest reliability was reported in an acceptable range between 83–100% for 43 children. Due to the developmental nature of these behaviors, this reliability was determined with an interval of 5–7 days. Such a short period of time may have influenced the recall of initial judgments by the raters and resulted in an inflated value for test-retest reliability.

The validity of the M-C has not been effectively established. The manual reports that "content validity of the Milani-Comparetti test items to the domain of motor behavior has been recognized through their acceptance by physicians and therapists." Such a statement seems to be somewhat superficial. Certainly it is possible to determine content validity through a more acceptable process than appeal to those who use the test.

Secondary reports of validity estimates are provided in the manual. In particular the reported results from VanderLinden indicated validity scores ranging from 44–89%. In addition, the statement that the values were "inflated due to a small sample size" (p. 13) should raise serious caution.

If a motor skill was demonstrated by 85% of the children tested, it was judged to occur at that age. This criterion has helped to increase the test sensitivity from its original norms in 1967. In fact, the documentation is largely the work of the Meyer Children's Rehabilitation Institute which developed the manual in 1977 and continues to update the normative data. The manual rightfully alerts the user that currently the data provide documentation for item variability within the normal population, but that no attempt to determine item validity is made. Readers are cautioned that the "question of the test's validity remains unanswered and may adversely affect conclusions drawn from a project utilizing the test as the only method to quantify motor development" (p. 8). Later the manual states "caution should be exercised in interpreting the results for diagnostic input or programming recommendations" (p. 17).

It is troublesome that there has been no attempt to determine the validity of this test. For example, all subjects used to standardize the original norms were prescreened on the Denver Developmental Screening Test. It would seem that these test data and correlations (if any) to the M-C should have been reported.

The manual suggests that in order to acquire accurate data, children should be screened within a range of 5 days before or after a month anniversary. Given the known importance of "gestational days" versus days post-birth, this seems like an overemphasis on the date of birth. In addition, the fact that the sample included 92% white children, 49% of whose parents had 4 or more years of college makes the data somewhat difficult to generalize to the total population of this country. (It is also inaccurately reported that Table 2 (p. 11) will provide data for "distribution of sample by age and race," but provides only age data.)

The use of normative standards has the obvious advantage of ease and simplicity, but the shortcomings of a "stage approach." By using the data provided with this manual it is possible for professionals to detect early deviations from normal development. It is therefore primarily useful in detecting potential neurodevelopmental delays.

TEST ADMINISTRATION. Examiners are trained to administer this test through two mechanisms: a training manual (44 pages plus appendices) and a videotape. The manual itself suggests that "use of the training videotape, review of the administration and scoring sections of this manual, and practice in test fundamentals should provide the necessary background for routine clinical use." This seems to

be a minimal level of training for an instrument that is designed to detect developmental delays.

The test takes approximately 25 minutes to administer although the manual suggests only 15. The only equipment required is a firm cushion (used to test equilibrium reactions) and the scoring manual. There are specific directions provided for calculating the age of the child, so that rounding can occur to the half month. Unfortunately, there is no adjustment allowed for the degree of prematurity of a child. It is merely stated that this should be noted and considered in the interpretation of test results. This is a major weakness of the test, particularly at the youngest ages.

It is suggested that children who are judged to be at risk should be tested several times. Key ages appropriate for testing are purported to be $2^{1}/_{2}$–4, 6–8, 10–12, and 14–16 months of age.

Each of the 27 items is accompanied by a brief description of the procedure and criteria for evaluating. There are also descriptions and pictures of complete and incomplete responses. Overall the diagrams are helpful, but not totally inclusive of the behaviors one can expect to observe. The example in the manual suggests that a hand grasp should be observed in months 1–4.5. It states that a 6-month old who demonstrates the grasp should be at Level 4. However, it is also possible that the child is really at Level 2 or 3.

The manual suggests that there are both qualitative and quantitative judgments to be made. However, the manual seems to focus on the quantitative (developmental level in months) aspects of the skill and fails to provide guidance covering a qualitative analysis framework.

The appendix includes both the original score form and the revised form. It appears that the revised form is much more self-explanatory. However, the transition from the criteria to the use of the scoring form is woefully inadequate for both. Much more material should be provided here.

INTERPRETATION OF RESULTS. Each child's test results are recorded on a time line of "normal development." If an 8-month-old child demonstrates a grasp to be judged 6 month, the score would be recorded by placing an 8 (months of age) over the demonstrated skill (6 months). The behavior is judged to be delayed or advanced if it differs by at least 1 month from the norm for that chronological age. Asymmetries are also noted if the response is shown in only forward, backward, left, or right directions or sides.

The revised M-C score form is much easier to use than the original one. The organization moves from Body Lying through Sitting to a simple Moro Reflex. There is minimal room for comments or notations about the test administration.

In addition to the revised score form, it is suggested that a narrative profile be prepared for each child. This profile should record any recommendations for further diagnostic testing or follow-ups.

SUMMARY. The absence of suitable validity data reduces the usefulness of the M-C. The manual contains clear descriptions of 27 skills but the test should be used cautiously, and not as a diagnostic tool.

REVIEWER'S REFERENCE

Milani-Comparetti, A., & Gidoni, E. A. (1967). Pattern analysis of motor development and its disorders. *Developmental Medicine & Child Neurology*, 9, 625-630.

Review of the Milani-Comparetti Motor Development Screening Test by RUTH E. TOMES, Assistant Professor of Family Relations and Child Development, Oklahoma State University, Stillwater, OK:

The Milani-Comparetti Motor Development Screening Test (MC) is a neurodevelopmental examination designed to aid in early identification of developmental delay in movement patterns in the first 2 years of life. The examination provides information to the tester about basic components of an infant's movement through evoked tilting reactions, parachute reactions, righting reactions, and primitive reflexes; and through observation of the infant's spontaneous postural control and active movement. The MC is not intended to be a diagnostic test; therefore, infants who perform poorly on it are candidates for neurological evaluation.

The current (1987) version of the MC is the most recent in a series of revisions of the original test published in 1967 by Drs. A. Milani-Comparetti and A. E. Gidoni. According to the 1987 MC manual, the original scoring and interpretation system and a revised system described by Trembath in a 1978 publication provided the basis for the current revision. The 27 items of the original MC are retained in the revised edition. The ordering of the items, however, has been changed to minimize handling and changing position of the child. As in the original, most items pertain to motor behaviors that emerge in the first 16 months of life, with most detailed information over the 3–12 month range. The major new contribution of the 1987 manual to neurodevelopmental screening with the MC is the presentation of normative data. A standardization sample (discussed later) provided information on the range of item variability among normal children. The revised scoring form reflects the age at which 85% of the children in this sample demonstrated the assessed developmental milestones.

Administration of the MC takes only 10–15 minutes and requires no materials except a firm cushion supplied by the examiner. The test may be administered by a variety of professionals such as physicians, occupational and physical therapists, nurses, and developmental specialists. Thorough reading of the manual, use of a training videotape available for rent or purchase from the publisher, and practice are recommended preparations for examiners. Formal training is available upon request to the publisher.

Procedures for administration and scoring are very clearly described in the manual. Each item assesses a specific movement skill and is scored by comparing the infant's response to criteria both described and illustrated. The line-drawn illustrations are especially helpful in assessing the quality of an infant's response. All items are represented on a single scoring sheet marked off by age in months. The child's chronological age, computed to the nearest half-month, is written on the corresponding age line if the response is normal. A delayed or advanced response, defined as 1 month ahead or behind the chronological age, is marked on the age line that corresponds to the behavior and is highlighted with an asterisk. Asymmetrical responses are also highlighted and notations made as to side of delay.

No summary score is obtained for interpreting the MC. Rather, a child's level of performance on each item may be interpreted by reference to a table in the manual's appendix which presents data concerning the age at which 15, 50, and 85% of the children in the norming sample demonstrated a behavior. Examiners are advised that a child who shows significant delay should be given a neurological evaluation. However, no criteria are provided for determining what constitutes significant delay.

Normative data were obtained from a sample of 312 Omaha children ages 1 month to 16 months. Twins, adoptees, children who were more than 2 weeks premature, and those who had identified medical problems were excluded from the sample. No formal sampling procedures are described. According to data presented in the manual, the sample approximated the 1980 Omaha census in terms of racial composition. Sample composition in terms of occupation and education of head of household appear to be skewed toward overrepresentation of those in professions and those with 4 or more years of college. The monthly age samples are about equally divided between boys and girls. Sample sizes for the 16 age levels are quite small ranging from 14 children tested at 13 months to 22 at 6 months. It should be noted that although the test is intended for use with infants from birth to 24 months of age, no children over 16 months were included in the norming sample.

Interrater reliability estimates were obtained by calculating percent of agreement among three therapists who viewed 60 videotaped administrations. Mean percentages of agreement were respectable ranging from 90 to 93%. The manual presents only summary information on interrater reliability by age, and no data for individual items. The authors report test-retest reliability (5- to 7-day interval) for the performance of a sample of 43 children who were tested by the same examiner. Mean percent of agreement between the two sessions was 93%. No data are reported pertaining to test-retest reliability of individual test items.

Content validity of the MC is claimed on the basis of its long-term acceptance by physicians and therapists. The authors make no claims for the construct or criterion-related validity of the revised instrument. A stated goal of the authors is to conduct studies that will provide information on the instrument's predictive validity, specificity, and sensitivity.

SUMMARY. The Milani-Comparetti Motor Development Screening Test is recommended as a tool for initial screening of neuromotor delay over the 1- to 24-month age range. It may be quickly administered without special equipment. A major strength of the 1987 manual is the provision of normative data that may be used in item interpretation. Interrater and test reliability estimates are good. Weaknesses are those of sample limitations and the lack of validity data.

[237]
Military Environment Inventory.

Purpose: "Assesses the social environment of varied types of military contexts."
Population: Military personnel.
Publication Date: 1986.
Acronym: MEI.
Scores, 7: Involvement, Peer Cohesion, Officer Support, Personal Status, Order and Organization, Clarity, Officer Control.
Administration: Group.
Forms, 4: Real Form (Form R), Short Form (Form S), Ideal Form (Form I), Expectations Form (Form E).
Price Data, 1987: $10 or less per 25 tests; $9 or less per 50 answer sheets; $3.50 or less per 50 profiles; $9 per manual (30 pages); $16 per specimen set.
Time: Administration time not reported.
Comments: One of 10 Social Climate Scales.
Author: Rudolf H. Moos.
Publisher: Consulting Psychologists Press, Inc.

TEST REFERENCES

1. Solomon, Z., Mikulincer, M., & Hobfoll, S. E. (1987). Objective versus subjective measurement of stress and social support: Combat-related reactions. *Journal of Consulting and Clinical Psychology, 55*, 577-583.

Review of the Military Environment Inventory by DAVID O. HERMAN, President, Measurement Research Services, Inc., Jackson Heights, NY:

Like the author's other Social Climate Scales, the Military Environment Inventory (MEI) is a questionnaire for assessing various social characteristics in an organizational setting. To the extent that these characteristics influence the mood and behavior of people within the organization, scales of this type can be useful for comparing contrasted organizations, evaluating the effects of organizational change over time, forming a basis for suggesting changes in training or supervision to improve morale or productivity, and possibly helping to select or place new members whose personal styles are compatible with an existing organization.

This particular Social Climate Scale is, as its title makes clear, for use specifically with military organizations such as training companies in the armed forces. Form R, the standard form, consists of 84 statements that examinees mark as true or false according to their perceptions of the social and work environment of their unit. Responses are scored on each of seven 12-item scales. Form S, a short form with only four items per scale, may be used by marking and scoring only the first 28 items. For special applications, researchers may use Forms I and E of the inventory to describe examinees' preferred and expected military environments, respectively.

The MEI is designed for group administration. The directions are simple and clear. Nearly all of the item-statements strike me as clear as well. The principal exception is an item concerned with the "sharing of things among the enlisted members"; are the "things" work equipment, personal gear, or personal confidences?

Answer sheets are scored by hand using a transparent overlay key. The raw scores of individuals or the average raw scores of groups may be transformed to standard scores, which may in turn be plotted on a profile form. (The standard-score norms for the Involvement scale contain a typographical error that should be corrected in the next printing of the manual.)

The MEI appears to have been rigorously developed. Information obtained from interviews with military personnel was used to reword items from existing Social Climate Scales and to generate new items that were specifically relevant to military settings. The 84 items surviving from the original 146 experimental items were selected according to multiple criteria: factorial clarity, variation in endorsement rates among military units, an overall endorsement rate between 25% and 75% across military units, and low correlation with a social desirability scale. The seven scales of the MEI were chosen on the basis of a factor analysis of the original 146 items. As for face validity, the final scales and the items they comprise sound potentially relevant to the effectiveness of a military unit, where effectiveness may refer to morale as well as to work productivity.

Over 4,000 respondents from 32 military training companies are represented in the standard-score norms. The manual does not define the type of standard score, but it appears to have a mean of 50 and a standard deviation of 10. Separate tables present means and standard deviations of raw scores on the seven scales for Forms R and S. Unfortunately, the manual does not make it entirely clear whether the norms were computed from the individual scores of the more than 4,000 cases mentioned above, or from the average scores associated with the 32 companies. However, because the raw score standard deviations given in the manual are so small (they range from 0.55 to 1.05 points for the seven scales of Form R), it is likely they reflect the variability of group averages rather than of individual scores. Assuming this deduction is correct, the manual does not include the information needed to interpret an individual's scores. This is because the variability of individual scores is much greater than the variability of group means. Discussion of proper and improper interpretations made with the published norms should be added to the manual.

Reliability coefficients (internal consistency) for the seven scales ranged from .65 to .81, and their intercorrelations ranged from -.15 to .52. There is no suggestion in these data that any of the scales should be merged.

An impressive variety of validity studies is briefly summarized in the manual. The results must be called suggestive rather than definitive, but they do establish relationships between MEI scores and such external variables as scores for depression, hostility, and anxiety on the Multiple Affect Adjective Check List; decisions to reenlist among National Guard members; results of military performance tests; and rates of reporting for sick call. References to the complete studies are provided.

In summary, this specialized questionnaire, developed only for use with military units, appears to be carefully constructed, and scale content has logical appeal. The seven scales have relatively low intercorrelations and adequate reliability for comparing group averages. A significant criticism is that the manual's description of how the norms were computed (that is, whether individuals or groups were the units of sampling) is inadequate and potentially misleading. Nevertheless, the validity studies mentioned in the manual show that MEI results correlate with interesting and meaningful external measures. This instrument has no known competition, and can be recommended for use in evaluation studies and in social-psychological or sociological research conducted with military groups.

Review of the Military Environment Inventory by ALFRED L. SMITH, JR., Personnel Psychologist, Federal Aviation Administration, U.S. Department of Transportation, Washington, DC:

The Military Environment Inventory (MEI) is one of a set of 10 Social Climate Scales developed by R. H. Moos. The MEI contains seven empirically derived subscales within three cognitively determined dimensions. Involvement, Peer Cohesion, and Officer Support make up the Relationship Dimension. The Personal Growth Dimension contains a single Personal Status subscale. The remaining subscales, Order and Organization, Clarity, and Officer Control comprise the System Maintenance Dimension. The original Social Climate scales were modified expressly for the military and additional military-specific items were added. The manual indicates that the MEI's primary uses are to describe and contrast military units, compare perceptions of enlisted members, NCOs, and officers, monitor changes across time, and perform "other evaluations."

The MEI Manual (Second Edition) suggests adherence to rigorous procedures in its development. Item and factor analyses were used to create an 84-item instrument (12 items per subscale) from an initial 146 items. Four forms were produced: the Real Form (Form R), Short Form (Form S), Ideal Form (Form I), and Expectations Form (Form E). The latter two are rewordings of Form R so that respondents can describe an "ideal" or "expected" climate. The Short Form is contained within the first 28 items of Form R, providing ease of administration and scoring. The manual reports a high correlation between profiles obtained from Forms R and S. This strongly suggests that unless one is concerned with individual responses, it is probably preferable to use Form S.

Although the manual gives a commendable description of how the scale was developed and evaluated, a critical review highlights several concerns. These issues are related to the development/norming sample, item scoring, item selection, reliability, item content, norms, and overall scoring.

The initial form of 146 items was administered over 2 years to samples from military training companies identified as three different types: Basic Combat (BCT), Advanced Infantry (AIT), and Combat Support Training (CST). These courses are identified incorrectly. AIT stands for Advanced Individual Training, courses provided for specific Military Occupational Specialty (MOS). Similarly, CST stands for Common Skills Training. Given the varied nature of enlistees' status within these courses, it is distressing that the author failed to consider differences in responses across these companies and instead lumped them together for norming purposes. In fact, in a later section of the manual, the profiles of a BCT unit and a CST unit are shown to be substantially different. (There is nothing to indicate that these results are contrived, leading one to assume that they are actual results.) Clearly, the military is organized such that enlistees in Basic Training find themselves in an environment quite foreign to the civilian one from which they came. In describing the summary picture given by the established norms, the manual states, "Personal status and individuality are played down, whereas organization and strict control by officers are emphasized strongly" (p. 10). Indeed, this describes what is happening in basic training to acclimate enlistees to military regimentation. Later training experiences are colored by growing familiarity with military procedures and some relaxation of rules and mores. Furthermore, the training situation is a unique one within the military. It seems to be a questionable basis upon which to establish norms against which other (nontraining) companies should be compared.

The next area of concern relates to item scoring and item selection. After reviewing the manual, it was not until I looked at the answer sheets that I realized this is a true-false instrument. Nowhere in the manual does it state how determination of the "correct" answer was made, and it is not intuitively clear for all of the items. With regard to item selection for the final instrument, first, why did the author use only part of the sample to select items? One plausible answer would be to use the other part for cross-validation or replication purposes, but, unfortunately, this is not the case. Second, was item selection based only on individual responses or aggregate company responses or both? Four criteria were applied to items for selection. The first was that the item discriminate significantly among companies. The manual does not describe the method for determining this. The second criterion was straightforward: higher correlation with the item's own factor scale than with any other. The third criterion seems weak as it is stated: No more than 75% of the respondents answered the item in the same direction. Considering this to be "difficulty" level, one might want to know that there was an adequate range of "difficulty." Finally, on a more positive note, the author is to be lauded for inclusion of the criterion that items could not correlate highly with an established measure of social desirability.

Another concern relates to reliability. The manual indicates that some of the initial companies were assessed several times during their training. This provided the opportunity for examining the stability of the responses (test-retest reliability). The absence of any information about the results from repeated assessment leaves us to wonder why it was omitted. Given the nature of military training and the course of adaptation over time, it is likely that individual and group assessments of the social climate were highly dependent upon time of administration. Clarification on stability is warranted. Attention to other measures of reliability is satisfactory. Measures of internal consistency for the seven subscales are moderate to high. Average item-subscale correlations generally are adequate except for "Officer Control."

With regard to item content, one thing is salient. Many of the items refer to the joint reference group: NCOs and officers. This reference may confound responses because, typically, NCOs and officers act differently from one another, have disparate responsibilities, and are viewed dissimilarly by enlistees. Also, other items contain words that may be ambiguous (e.g., "not harsh," "more effective," "pretty interesting," "very"). These are words that tend to elicit different, unstable responses. For example, on an unstressful day, things may seem "very well-organized," whereas even mildly stress-provoking events may lead one to feel that "very" is too positive an adjective.

Although the manual stresses ease of scoring, this may not be the case. The MEI makes use of nonstandard answer sheets. These unique answer sheets could prove confusing to respondents who over the years have become familiar with standard mark-sensitive answer sheets in which they fill in a small circle or rectangle from choices laid out horizontally. On the MEI answer sheets, the choices are vertical and somewhat indistinct, and one must make a large X. People could easily mark the wrong space or spend extra time blackening. In addition, these answer sheets can only be scored by hand, which is impractical when administering to large groups. Also, the scoring template instructs the scorer to count up the number of Xs showing, not just the number of Xs showing within the circles indicating "correct" answers, another potential source of error. Finally, it is not fully clear to the user that one must sum all individual scores for a company and then take an average. Additional information on converting to standard scores would be helpful for the unsophisticated user as well.

The manual contains an extensive and valuable discussion on the predictive validity of the instrument and its research applications. It gives evidence of relationships between perceptions and expectations about company climate and a variety of factors from illness and moods to performance of duties and reenlistment. This discussion suggests, therefore, that continued use of the MEI would be beneficial to the military. Such use, however, may be limited in comparison to possibilities in civilian occupations where individual entities have more autonomy. Within the military, it is unlikely that subunits (e.g., companies, battalions) will look at themselves independently and initiate unit-specific change. That is, changes are more likely to be across-the-board (e.g., the entire Infantry School). However, overall, the MEI seems to have considerable merit. Additional research may be warranted, particularly relative to group data (where Ns are typically small), to replicate earlier findings and to demonstrate linkage of perception of social climate to other important criterion behaviors. A beneficial outcome would be to identify changes that will lead to results such as enhanced job performance or retention of better soldiers.

[238]
Miller-Yoder Language Comprehension Test (Clinical Edition).

Purpose: "A measure of mainstream American-English language comprehension."
Population: Ages 3-8.
Publication Date: 1984.
Acronym: MY.
Scores, 2: Error Analysis, Total.
Administration: Individual.
Price Data, 1991: $89 per complete kit including picture book, 25 scoring forms, and manual (54 pages); $14 per 25 scoring forms.
Time: (10-30) minutes.
Authors: Jon F. Miller and David E. Yoder (test); Gary Gill, Margaret Rosin, Nathanial O. Owings, and Karen A. Carlson (manual).
Publisher: PRO-ED, Inc.

TEST REFERENCES
1. Fox, L., Long, S. H., & Langlois, A. (1988). Patterns of language of comprehension deficit in abused and neglected children. *Journal of Speech and Hearing Disorders, 53,* 239-244.

Review of the Miller-Yoder Language Comprehension Test (Clinical Edition) by NATALIE L. HEDBERG, Professor of Communication Disorders and Speech Science, University of Colorado, Boulder, CO:

The Miller-Yoder Language Comprehension Test (Clinical Edition) (MY) consists of 42 different test plates, four line drawings on each, that are mostly black and white. The plates include five main characters illustrating various states or actions to represent 10 basic grammatical forms. Forms were selected that children in first to third grade would be expected to know. The inclusion of two items for each plate, both of which must be passed to gain credit for the item, minimizes the potential for passing an item on the basis of chance alone. Not only are the drawings clear and attractive, but characters' names are taught to the children prior to administering the sample items, adding to their appeal. Another strength of this measure is that administration time may range from 10 to 30 minutes depending on which presentation format is selected: random presentation of all 42 plates or presentation in a developmental progression based on either a 60% or 90% pass criterion where only age appropriate items need be administered. Guidelines for selecting the presentation format are included although they are confusing in places. Instructions for administering and scoring are clear, albeit somewhat complex given the various presentation formats. The score form is not only easy to use but also provides three levels of analysis: a total score, a developmental profile, and an error analysis.

The developmental profile and error analysis allow the examiner to assess the reliability of the test results as part of the interpretive process. This is a very helpful feature.

Although the MY is a useful and fairly sophisticated measure, it has several significant limitations. First, this measure assesses only one aspect of comprehension, grammatical form. It does not address other language components that are important to comprehension such as vocabulary and morphology. Secondly, the normative sample is quite small (24 to 30 subjects for each age 3 through 8) and includes only middle class subjects. No mention is made of the inclusion of varying cultural backgrounds or genders, a distinct disadvantage given the distribution of language-impaired children. Third, as with other similar measures of sentence comprehension, it does not differentiate between the contribution of syntactic versus semantic knowledge to the comprehension process or take into account the contribution of the context of the natural language environment. In its favor, the manual includes evidence to support excellent reliability and three types of validity. In addition, the authors acknowledge the limitations of their test as a basis for designing a comprehension intervention program and provide many useful suggestions as to the additional steps that must be involved in the assessment and program planning process.

In summary, although the MY has many strengths, it is a less useful test than the Test for Auditory Comprehension of Language (10:363) (which also has limitations) because of its narrow range of test items and its limited normative sample.

[239]
Millon Clinical Multiaxial Inventory—II.

Purpose: "Provides a profile of the scale scores and a detailed analysis of personality and symptom dynamics as well as suggestions for therapeutic management."
Population: Adults receiving "mental health services stemming from genuine emotional, social, or interpersonal difficulties."
Publication Dates: 1976–87.
Acronym: MCMI-II.
Scores, 25: Modifier Indices (Disclosure, Desirability, Debasement), Clinical Personality Pattern (Schizoid, Avoidant, Dependent, Histrionic, Narcissistic, Antisocial, Aggressive/Sadistic, Compulsive, Passive-Aggressive, Self-Defeating), Severe Personality Pathology (Schizotypal, Borderline, Paranoid), Clinical Syndrome (Anxiety Disorder, Somatoform Disorder, Bipolar-Manic Disorder, Dysthymic Disorder, Alcohol Dependence, Drug Dependence), Severe Syndrome (Thought Disorder, Major Depression, Delusional Disorder).
Administration: Individual or Group.
Price Data, 1990: $22.45–$29.75 per test booklet/answer sheet depending on quantity (includes scoring and interpretive report); $5.85–$8.25 per test booklet/answer sheet depending on quantity (includes

scoring and profile report); $23 per manual ('87, 258 pages).

Time: [25–30] minutes.

Comments: Designed to coordinate with DSM III-R categories of personality disorders and clinical syndromes; revision of the Millon Clinical Multiaxial Inventory (9:709).

Author: Theodore Millon.

Publisher: National Computer Systems.

Cross References: For reviews by Allen K. Hess and Thomas A. Widiger of an earlier edition, see 9:709 (1 reference); see also T3:1488 (3 references).

TEST REFERENCES

1. Auerbach, J. S. (1984). Validation of two scales for narcissistic personality disorder. *Journal of Personality Assessment, 48*, 649-653.
2. Berenson, C. K., & Grosser, B. I. (1984). Total artificial heart implantation. *Archives of General Psychiatry, 41*, 910-916.
3. Flynn, P. M., & McMahon, R. C. (1984). An examination of the factor structure of the Millon Clinical Multiaxial Inventory. *Journal of Personality Assessment, 48*, 308-311.
4. Greer, S. E. (1984). A review of the Millon Clinical Multiaxial Inventory. *Journal of Counseling and Development, 63*, 262-263.
5. Lanyon, R. I. (1984). Personality assessment. *Annual Review of Psychology, 35*, 667-701.
6. Prifitera, A., & Ryan, J. J. (1984). Validity of the Narcissistic Personality Inventory (NPI) in a psychiatric sample. *Journal of Clinical Psychology, 40*, 140-148.
7. Tango, R. A., & Dziuban, C. D. (1984). The use of personality components in the interpretation of career indecision. *Journal of College Student Personnel, 25*, 509-512.
8. Antoni, M., Tischer, P., Levine, J., Green, C., & Millon, T. (1985). Refining personality assessments by combining MCMI high point profiles and MMPI codes, Part I: MMPI code 28/82. *Journal of Personality Assessment, 49*, 392-398.
9. Antoni, M., Tischer, P., Levine, J., Green, C., & Millon, T. (1985). Refining personality assessments by combining MCMI high point profiles and MCMI codes. Part III: MMPI code 24/42. *Journal of Personality Assessment, 49*, 508-515.
10. Bartsch, T. W., & Hoffman, J. J. (1985). A cluster analysis of Millon Clinical Multiaxial Inventory (MCMI) profiles: More about a taxonomy of alcoholic subtypes. *Journal of Clinical Psychology, 41*, 707-713.
11. Craig, R. J., Verinis, J. S., & Wexler, S. (1985). Personality characteristics of drug addicts and alcoholics on the Millon Clinical Multiaxial Inventory. *Journal of Personality Assessment, 49*, 156-160.
12. Fowler, R. D. (1985). Landmarks in computer-assisted psychological assessment. *Journal of Consulting and Clinical Psychology, 53*, 748-759.
13. Levine, J., Tischer, P., Antoni, M., Green, C., & Millon, T. (1985). Refining personality assessments by combining MCMI high point profiles and MMPI codes. Part II: MMPI code 27/72. *Journal of Personality Assessment, 49*, 501-507.
14. McMahon, R. C., & Davidson, R. S. (1985). An examination of the relationship between personality patterns and symptom/mood patterns. *Journal of Personality Assessment, 49*, 552-556.
15. McMahon, R. C., Flynn, P. M., & Davidson, R. S. (1985). Stability of the personality and symptom scales of the Millon Clinical Multiaxial Inventory. *Journal of Personality Assessment, 49*, 231-234.
16. McMahon, R. D., Flynn, P. M., & Davidson, R. S. (1985). The personality and symptoms scales of the Millon Clinical Multiaxial Inventory: Sensitivity to posttreatment outcomes. *Journal of Clinical Psychology, 41*, 862-866.
17. Millon, T. (1985). The MCMI provides a good assessment of DSM-III disorders: The MCMI-II will prove even better. *Journal of Personality Assessment, 49*, 379-391.
18. Reich, J. (1985). Measurement of DSM-III, Axis II. *Comprehensive Psychiatry, 26*, 352-363.
19. Repto, G. R., & Cooper, R. (1985). The diagnosis of personality disorder: A comparison of MMPI profile, Millon Inventory, and clinical judgment in a workers' compensation population. *Journal of Clinical Psychology, 41*, 867-881.
20. Robert, J. A., Ryan, J. J., McEntyre, W. L., McFarland, R. S., Lips, O. J., & Rosenberg, S. J. (1985). MCMI characteristics of DSM-III Posttraumatic Stress Disorder in Vietnam veterans. *Journal of Personality Assessment, 49*, 226-230.
21. Shafii, M., Carrigan, S., Whittinghill, J. R., & Derrick, A. (1985). Psychological autopsy of completed suicide in children and adolescents. *American Journal of Psychiatry, 142*, 1061-1064.
22. Widiger, T. A., Williams, J. B. W., Spitzer, R. L., & Frances, A. (1985). The MCMI as a measure of DSM-III. *Journal of Personality Assessment, 49*, 366-378.

23. Antoni, M., Levine, J., Tischer, P., Green, C., & Millon, T. (1986). Refining personality assessments by combining MCMI high-point profiles and MMPI Codes, Part IV: MMPI 89/98. *Journal of Personality Assessment, 50*, 65-72.
24. Choca, J. P., Peterson, C. A., & Shanley, L. A. (1986). Factor analysis of the Millon Clinical Multiaxial Inventory. *Journal of Consulting and Clinical Psychology, 54*, 253-255.
25. Gibertini, M., Brandenburg, N. A., & Retzlaff, P. D. (1986). The operating characteristics of the Millon Clinical Multiaxial Inventory. *Journal of Personality Assessment, 50*, 554-567.
26. McMahon, R. C., & Davidson, R. S. (1986). An examination of depressed vs. nondepressed alcoholics in inpatient treatment. *Journal of Clinical Psychology, 42*, 177-184.
27. McMahon, R. C., & Davidson, R. S. (1986). Concurrent validity of the clinical symptom syndrome scales of the Millon Clinical Multiaxial Inventory. *Journal of Clinical Psychology, 42*, 908-912.
28. Piersma, H. L. (1986). The factor structure of the Millon Clinical Multiaxial Inventory (MCMI) for psychiatric inpatients. *Journal of Personality Assessment, 50*, 578-584.
29. Piersma, H. L. (1986). The Millon Clinical Multiaxial Inventory (MCMI) as a treatment outcome measure for psychiatric inpatients. *Journal of Clinical Psychology, 42*, 493-499.
30. Piersma, H. L. (1986). The stability of the Millon Clinical Multiaxial Inventory for psychiatric inpatients. *Journal of Personality Assessment, 50*, 193-197.
31. Tamkin, A. S., Hyer, L. A., & Carson, M. F. (1986). Comparison among four measures of depression in younger and older alcoholics. *Psychological Reports, 59*, 287-293.
32. Van Gorp, W. G., & Meyer, R. G. (1986). The detection of faking on the Millon Clinical Multiaxial Inventory (MCMI). *Journal of Clinical Psychology, 42*, 742-747.
33. Widiger, T. A., Williams, J. B. W., Spitzer, R. L., & Frances, A. (1986). The MCMI and DSM-III: A brief rejoinder to Millon (1985). *Journal of Personality Assessment, 50*, 198-204.
34. Antoni, M., Levine, J., Tischer, P., Green, C., & Millon, T. (1987). Refining personality assessments by combining MCMI high-point profiles and MMPI Codes, Part V: MMPI Code 78/87. *Journal of Personality Assessment, 51*, 375-387.
35. Emmons, R. A. (1987). Narcissism: Theory and measurement. *Journal of Personality and Social Psychology, 52*, 11-17.
36. Gabrys, J. B., Schumph, D., & Utendale, K. A. (1987). Short-term memory for two meaningful stories and self-report on the adult Eysenck Personality Questionnaire. *Psychological Reports, 61*, 51-59.
37. Goldberg, J. O., Shaw, B. F., & Segal, Z. V. (1987). Concurrent validity of the Millon Clinical Multiaxial Inventory depression scales. *Journal of Consulting and Clinical Psychology, 55*, 785-787.
38. Jaffe, L. T., & Archer, R. P. (1987). The prediction of drug use among college students from MMPI, MCMI, and Sensation Seeking Scales. *Journal of Personality Assessment, 51*, 243-253.
39. Montag, I., & Comrey, A. L. (1987). Millon MCMI scales factor analyzed and correlated with MMPI and CPS scales. *Multivariate Behavioral Research, 22*, 401-413.
40. Moreland, K. L., & Onstad, J. A. (1987). Validity of Millon's computerized interpretation system for the MCMI: A controlled study. *Journal of Consulting and Clinical Psychology, 55*, 113-114.
41. Reich, J. (1987). Brief communication: Prevalence of DSM-III-R self-defeating (masochistic) personality disorder in normal outpatient populations. *The Journal of Nervous and Mental Disease, 175*, 52-54.
42. Reich, J. (1987). Sex distribution of DSM-III personality disorders in psychiatric outpatients. *American Journal of Psychiatry, 144*, 485-488.
43. Reich, J., Noyes, R., Jr., & Troughton, E. (1987). Dependent personality disorder associated with phobic avoidance in patients with panic disorder. *American Journal of Psychiatry, 144*, 323-326.
44. Retzlaff, P. D., & Gibertini, M. (1987). Air Force pilot personality: Hard data on the "right stuff." *Multivariate Behavioral Research, 22*, 383-399.
45. Retzlaff, P. D., & Gibertini, M. (1987). Factor structure of the MCMI basic personality scale and common-item artifact. *Journal of Personality Assessment, 51*, 588-594.
46. Sexton, D. L., McIlwraith, R., Barnes, G., & Dunn, R. (1987). Comparison of the MCMI and MMPI-168 as psychiatric inpatient screening inventories. *Journal of Personality Assessment, 51*, 388-398.
47. Trull, T. J., Widiger, T. A., & Frances, A. (1987). Covariation of criteria sets for avoidant, schizoid, and dependent personality disorders. *The American Journal of Psychiatry, 144*, 767-771.
48. Widiger, T. A., & Sanderson, C. (1987). The convergent and discriminant validity of the MCMI as a measure of the DSM-III personality disorders. *Journal of Personality Assessment, 51*, 228-242.
49. Broday, S. F. (1988). Perfectionism and Millon basic personality patterns. *Psychological Reports, 63*, 791-794.
50. Campbell, N. B., Franco, K., & Jurs, S. (1988). Abortion in adolescence. *Adolescence, 23*, 813-823.

51. Choca, J., Bresolin, L., Okonek, A., & Ostrow, D. (1988). Validity of the Millon Clinical Multiaxial Inventory in the assessment of affective disorders. *Journal of Personality Assessment, 52,* 96-105.

52. Hyer, L., Woods, M. G., Boudewyns, P. A., Bruno, R., & O'Leary, W. C. (1988). Concurrent validation of the Millon Clinical Multiaxial Inventory among Vietnam veterans with posttraumatic stress disorder. *Psychological Reports, 63,* 271-278.

53. Kent, J. B., Utendale, K. A., Schumph, D., Phillips, N., Peters, K., Robertson, G., Sherwood, G., O'Haire, T., Allard, I., Clark, M., & Laye, R. C. (1988). Two inventories for the measurement of psychopathology: Dimensions and common factorial space on Millon's clinical and Eysenck's general personality scales. *Psychological Reports, 62,* 591-601.

54. Lumsden, E. A. (1988). The impact of shared items on the internal-structural validity of the MCMI. *Educational and Psychological Measurement, 48,* 669-678.

55. Silverstein, M. L., & McDonald, C. M. (1988). Personality trait characteristics in relation to neuropsychological dysfunction in schizophrenia and depression. *Journal of Personality Assessment, 52,* 288-296.

56. Alden, L. (1989). Short-term structured treatment for avoidant personality disorder. *Journal of Consulting and Clinical Psychology, 57,* 756-764.

57. Cash, T. F., Mikulka, P. J., & Brown, T. A. (1989). Validity of Millon's computerized interpretation system for the MCMI: Comment on Moreland and Onstad. *Journal of Consulting and Clinical Psychology, 57,* 311-312.

58. Lundholm, J. K. (1989). Alcohol use among university females: Relationship to eating disordered behavior. *Addictive Behaviors, 14,* 181-185.

59. Lundholm, J. K., Pellegreno, D. D., Wolins, L., & Graham, S. L. (1989). Predicting eating disorders in women: A preliminary measurement study. *Measurement and Evaluation in Counseling and Development, 22,* 23-30.

60. McCormack, J. K., Barnett, R. W., & Wallbrown, F. H. (1989). Factor structure of the Millon Clinical Multiaxial Inventory (MCMI) with an offender sample. *Journal of Personality Assessment, 53,* 442-448.

61. Moreland, K. L., & Godfrey, J. O. (1989). Yes, our study could have been better: Reply to Cash, Mikulka, and Brown. *Journal of Consulting and Clinical Psychology, 57,* 313-314.

62. Overholser, J. C., Kabakoff, R., & Norman, W. H. (1989). The assessment of personality characteristics in depressed and dependent psychiatric inpatients. *Journal of Personality Assessment, 53,* 40-50.

63. Robbins, S. B. (1989). Validity of the Superiority and Goal Instability scales as measures of defects in the self. *Journal of Personality Assessment, 53,* 122-132.

64. Streiner, D. L., & Miller, H. R. (1989). The MCMI-II: How much better than the MCMI? *Journal of Personality Assessment, 53,* 81-84.

65. Wetzler, S., Kahn, R., Strauman, T. J., & Dubro, A. (1989). Diagnosis of major depression by self-report. *Journal of Personality Assessment, 53,* 22-30.

66. Ahrens, J. A., Evans, R. G., & Barnett, R. W. (1990). Factors related to dropping out of school in an incarcerated population. *Educational and Psychological Measurement, 50,* 611-617.

67. Gallucci, N. T. (1990). On the synthesis of information from psychological tests. *Psychological Reports, 67,* 1243-1260.

68. Streiner, D. L., & Miller, H. R. (1990). Maximum likelihood estimates of the accuracy of four diagnostic techniques. *Educational and Psychological Measurement, 50,* 653-662.

69. Wetzler, S., & Marlowe, D. (1990). "Faking bad" on the MMPI, MMPI-2, and Millon-II. *Psychological Reports, 67,* 1117-1118.

70. Bagby, R. M., Gillis, J. R., & Rogers, R. (1991). Effectiveness of the Millon Clinical Multiaxial Inventory validity index in the detection of random responding. *Psychological Assessment, 3,* 285-287.

71. Bagby, R. M., Gillis, J. R., Toner, B. B., & Goldberg, J. (1991). Detecting fake-good and fake-bad responding on the Millon Clinical Multiaxial Inventory—II. *Psychological Assessment, 3,* 496-498.

72. Funari, D. J., Piekarski, A. M., & Sherwood, R. J. (1991). Treatment outcomes of Vietnam veterans with posttraumatic stress disorder. *Psychological Reports, 68,* 571-578.

73. McCann, J. T. (1991). Convergent and discriminant validity of the MCMI-II and MMPI personality disorder scales. *Psychological Assessment, 3,* 9-18.

74. Safran, J. D., & Wallner, L. K. (1991). The relative predictive validity of two therapeutic alliance measures in cognitive therapy. *Psychological Assessment, 3,* 188-195.

Review of the Millon Clinical Multiaxial Inventory—II by THOMAS M. HALADYNA, Professor of Educational Psychology, Arizona State University West, Phoenix, AZ:

INTRODUCTION AND OVERVIEW. The second edition of the Millon Clinical Multiaxial Inventory—II (MCMI-II) intends to assist clinicians in diagnosing psychopathology in patients. The original version (MCMI-I) had 175 items and 20 clinical scales and 2 validity scales. The new version (MCMI-II) also has 175 items and yields 22 clinical scales and 3 validity scales, including ones reflecting "response style." The MCMI-II greatly improves on its predecessor in many ways. The new manual documents these improvements. This review will begin with a summary of the past and the present, and then look toward its future.

ITS PAST. The 1977 MCMI-I version was viewed as a promising instrument but not a worthy rival of the vaunted Minnesota Multiphasic Personality Inventory (MMPI; Hess, 1985; Widiger, 1985). These reviewers have collectively stated that (*a*) the MCMI-I manual tends to oversell the virtues of the test, (*b*) the test is experimental, (*c*) the test results are very complex, and (*d*) that more validation research is needed on the test. Despite these limitations, both reviewers were positive about the existence of a theoretical basis for the test, the relationship to the American Psychiatric Association's DSM-III-R diagnostic categories and labels, and the formidable effort in test development and validation that had begun in the late 1960s. Clearly, the MCMI-I had a future.

ITS PRESENT. The MCMI-II is the product of an evolutionary pattern spanning the 1970s and 1980s. The new manual, published in 1987, is impressive both in size and scope when compared to the previous manual. For instance, the earlier manual has grown from 73 pages to the present 249-page version. The virtues of the test are numerous: (*a*) The author has developed a theory to guide the development of the test, and both the theory and the test have been modified as a result of continued research; (*b*) the test results continue to be keyed to the DSM-III-R diagnostic categories and labels; (*c*) extensive validation research has been completed, much of it in recent years; and (*d*) the MCMI-I has provided a strong foundation for the current, revised version.

However, it would be remiss not to discuss some limitations. First, the basis for test validation is dated. A more modern view can be drawn from the work of Messick (1988, 1989) and incorporates the broader conception of validity under the rubric "construct validation." There are many facets of construct validation that would be easily satisfied by the work of Millon and other researchers, but the technical detail in the manual is centered more around traditional correlational and reliability studies.

Some technical difficulties persist. Foremost is the overlap of items to scales, which affects interscale correlations. Much discussion is given to this issue and problem, but lamentably more work is needed.

The factor analytic work is not well described or documented, but recent advances in multivariate statistics should lead researchers to use confirmatory factor analysis as a technique of choice instead of traditional exploratory methods used in this validation effort.

The manual is written in highly technical language that will challenge most readers. The large amount of technical data is supported by many references in the literature. That this research appears in journals is laudable. The author gives sensible advice about how to use the test, based on the *Standards for Educational and Psychological Testing* (American Educational Research Association, American Psychological Association, & National Council on Measurement in Education, 1985). The mass of data presented could have been synthesized to be more readable. Periodic summaries communicate much more effectively than the lengthy prose passages punctuated with graphs or tables of data. Much of this could appear in appendices with chapters providing shorter, more insightful summaries of the impressive array of findings.

ITS FUTURE. During and since the time of these earlier reviews, the test has matured. Computerized reporting has improved, and validation research has mushroomed. For example, 46 validation studies were published in 1985 or later. The fact that the author, his colleagues, and others seem to be actively pursuing additional validation research and also that a brief research agenda is offered in the manual give an indication that the MCMI-II will continue to improve.

SUMMARY. The MCMI-II has grown impressively from its promising beginning. The theory base and extensive and growing validation research contribute to a growing respect for the instrument and its applications for the author's stated purposes. Although its chief competitor, the MMPI, will probably continue to be widely used instead of the MCMI-II, the manual offers impressive evidence for why clinicians should consider trying the MCMI-II.

REVIEWER'S REFERENCES

American Educational Research Association, American Psychological Association, & National Council on Measurement in Education. (1985). *Standards for educational and psychological testing.* Washington, DC: American Psychological Association, Inc.

Hess, A. K. (1985). [Review of the Millon Clinical Multiaxial Inventory.] In J. V. Mitchell, Jr. (Ed.), *The ninth mental measurements yearbook* (pp. 984-986). Lincoln, NE: Buros Institute of Mental Measurements.

Widiger, T. A. (1985). [Review of the Millon Clinical Multiaxial Inventory.] In J. V. Mitchell, Jr. (Ed.), *The ninth mental measurements yearbook* (pp. 986-988). Lincoln, NE: Buros Institute of Mental Measurements.

Messick, S. (1988). Validity. In R. L. Linn (Ed.), *Educational measurement* (3rd ed., pp. 13-104). New York: American Council on Education and MacMillan Publishing.

Messick, S. (1989). Meaning and values in test validation: The science and ethics of assessment. *Educational Researcher, 18* (2), 5-11.

Review of the Millon Clinical Multiaxial Inventory—II by CECIL R. REYNOLDS, Professor of Educational Psychology, Texas A&M University, College Station, TX:

The Millon Clinical Multiaxial Inventory—II (MCMI-II) is a revision of the original 175-item MCMI that includes an updating of item content (45 items were replaced), the addition of two new personality disorder scales, additional modification indexes to correct distortions in responding, an item-weighting system for scoring, and substantial changes in the interpretive text in its accompanying computerized scoring and interpretive system. The MCMI-II can be completed by individuals with at least an eighth grade reading level in 20–30 minutes.

The MCMI-II is divided into a complicated array of 22 clinical scales with frequent item overlap and variable item weighting across scales. This obfuscates scoring and interpretation to the point that the only practical choice for most clinicians is to use the computerized interpretive system. At this writing, hand scoring is not available for the MCMI-II although templates are in preparation by the publisher. The array of 22 clinical scales reflects Millon's decades of work in the development of personality theory and its links to psychopathology (e.g., Millon, 1969, 1981, 1986). This is at once a major strength of the MCMI-II and a serious practical limitation. Intelligent and compassionate use of the MCMI-II requires a working knowledge of Millon's approach to personality but also mastery of an extensive, impressive manual. Unfortunately, the manual, like the MCMI-II, is far more abstruse than necessary.

As one example of the latter, the differential item weighting and scale overlap (items typically appear on three scales with differential weighting on the three scales) complicates scoring tremendously and also makes certain of the internal validity studies more difficult—and to what end? The use of differential item weights has long been controversial in the measurement literature, principally because they fail to improve reliability or validity over unit weights. Despite arguments to the contrary in the MCMI-II manual (pp. 86-93), evidence for enhancement of key psychometric characteristics is not convincing. The case for overlapping items is a better one even if limited to the utility of this approach in generating a narrative report for MCMI-II results. Eliminating these complexities probably would require a 30–50% increase in the length of the MCMI-II, which should be tolerated easily, given its present brevity, and much simplify its use.

The norming of the MCMI-II also varies from prototypical practice. Rather than use population proportionate sampling techniques, Millon chose to attempt to sample the population of referred individuals who are typically administered the MCMI-II.

A sample of 1,292 individuals was obtained and demographic data are made available for the variables of: gender, age, marital status, religion, ethnicity (Black, White, Hispanic, Other), setting, patient's stated major problem (from the front of the MCMI-II protocol list), and duration of most recent episode of patient's problem. This is a controversial approach to norming with many potential problems. Further, its superiority to population proportionate sampling of the entire United States population has not been demonstrated and must be considered suspect until shown otherwise. On certain key demographic variables, the MCMI-II norms are problematic. Only 6.1% of the sample is age 56 or higher, thus its use with older Americans, the most rapidly growing segment of the population, may raise concerns, especially because scores are not age based. Ethnicity is another problem as is the stability of parameter estimates for scaling the raw scores of Blacks and Hispanics (with separate norms and all $Ns < 100$). The MCMI-II sample is 87.7% White with only 6.9% Black and 4.3% Hispanic representation. Level of education and other measures of socioeconomic status are not provided and the method of sampling seems to assure that the higher socioeconomic groups are the most strongly represented. As an analog to understanding the sampling problems inherent to this approach, consider the reaction to standardization of the Wechsler Adult Intelligence Scale—Revised (9:1348) if conducted only as a sampling of individuals typically administered the WAIS-R in clinical practice. Other assumptions and problems related to such sampling approaches have been discussed also by Reynolds, Gutkin, Elliott, and Witt (1984).

Scaling the MCMI-II 22 clinical scales presents some complex problems and, as accomplished by Millon, relies heavily on the estimation of base rates of various DSM-III-R Axis I and Axis II diagnoses. To the extent these estimates are in error, scaling of the MCMI-II will have distortion, especially at the upper end of the distribution, the most important range of scores in relation to the diagnosis of psychopathology. Considerably more information on the precise techniques of scaling would be of more than a passing or mere academic interest but would assist many clinicians in evaluating performance on the MCMI-II.

Reliability data are reported for the total sample by subscale using the well-known Kuder-Richardson formula 21 estimates, which with dichotomous scoring such as on the MCMI-II, is equivalent to coefficient alpha. However, this straightforward approach is not appropriate when differential item weighting is employed. The calculation of internal consistency reliability is more complex because the total score is an unequally weighted composite of the item scores and reliability must be determined based on the differential item weights. This is not difficult to do but is computationally quite laborious. The MCMI-II manual is unclear about whether the proper procedures were followed.

Considerable thought and decades of research and writing have gone into the conceptualization of the MCMI-II. Its greatest strengths lie in the relative validity of Millon's theories of personality and psychopathology. Millon's theory is a strong one and the evidence for construct validation of the MCMI-II is equally strong. Traditionally, as validity has been arbitrarily presented in its tripartite conceptualization, construct validity is considered of greatest importance for measures of personality and this is where the MCMI-II is at its best. True to Millon's approach, the MCMI-II provides a strong survey of a lengthy array of personality problems and emphasizes personality deficiencies, an approach, the efficacy of which deserves debate elsewhere, the MCMI-II accomplishes better than any other existing scale.

The computerized interpretive report also strongly emphasizes the problematic aspects of the patient's personality and fails to identify strengths that may be useful in the context of therapy. The printout contains appropriate cautions that are real and meaningful, and clinicians must take these cautions seriously or they will almost certainly overinterpret the MCMI-II profile.

The MCMI-II is a conceptual gem and psychometrically somewhere between a nightmare and an enigma. If carefully considered, the MCMI-II has a potentially key role to play in assessing personality and psychopathology and in clinical practice. Data on how nonreferral populations respond to the MCMI-II and its role in viewing normal variations in personality, especially in the very low range of scoring ($T < 30$), will be important in its future. Clinicians must be extremely careful in using the MCMI-II with nonclinical populations such as in child custody evaluations, foster-parent studies, employment testing in all settings but especially in police agencies, security, and nuclear energy settings where one might be strongly tempted to use the MCMI-II, and in criminal forensic work where one is presumed innocent and mentally healthy—the latter not being the assumption of the MCMI-II. This interesting scale deserves far more research attention by clinicians other than Millon who, with his students and colleagues, has been the primary source of key research to date. The MCMI-II has a unique role in providing the most thorough, most well-conceptualized evaluation of Axis II disorders available but much remains to be understood about its psychometrics and how its complex profile might be interpreted best.

REVIEWER'S REFERENCES

Millon, T. (1969). *Modern psychopathology*. Philadelphia: Saunders.

Millon, T. (1981). *Disorders of personality: DSM-III, Axis II.* New York: Wiley.

Reynolds, C. R., Gutkin, T. B., Elliott, S. N., & Witt, J. C. (1984). *School psychology: Essentials of theory and practice.* New York: John Wiley & Sons.

Millon, T. (1986). A theoretical derivation of pathological personalities. In T. Millon & G. Klerman (Eds.), *Contemporary directions in psychopathology: Toward the DSM-IV* (pp. 639-670). New York: Guilford.

[240]
MindMaker6™.

Purpose: To determine personality or personal style using hemispheric dominance theories for use in training, consulting, and counseling clients.
Population: Adults.
Publication Dates: 1985–87.
Scores, 6: Kins-Person, Loner, Loyalist, Achiever, Involver, Choice-Seeker.
Administration: Group.
Price Data: Price data for manual ('87, 22 pages), including test and scoring information, available from publisher.
Time: (30–40) minutes.
Authors: Kenneth L. Adams and Dudley Lynch.
Publisher: Brain Technologies Corporation.

Review of the MindMaker6™ by THOMAS A. WROBEL, Assistant Professor of Psychology, University of Michigan-Flint, Flint, MI:

The MindMaker6™ attempts to measure the values and belief systems of an individual, as presented in the authors' unique theory. They claim their theory is based on the developmental theories of Clare W. Graves, Abraham Maslow, Lawrence Kohlberg, Jean Piaget, Jane Loevinger, and Alvin Toffler, and reflects the notion that the building of values and beliefs occurs in stages. A detailed explanation of the theory may be found in Lynch (1984).

The test consists of a series of 20 items grouped under the headings of Self, Substance, Social, Work, Intimates, and Cosmic. Each item consists of a set of six statements, adjectives, or groups of statements. The test taker is asked to divide 9 points among one, two, or three of the statements for each item. The points are written on a color-coded answer sheet, and are added across the six possible systems (Kins-Person, Loner, Loyalist, Achiever, Involver, or Choice-Seeker). As there exists a possible total of 180 points, the sum of the system scores serves as a check on the addition of scores. The system scores are then combined to give a relative weighting for the individual on the continuua of Group versus Self, and Past versus Future. In addition, the individual's score is presented in terms of the three historical eras defined by the MindMaker model, including the nomadic and survival-oriented era; the era of development of agriculture, industrialization, and commerce; and the post-modern era.

Interpretation of the MindMaker6™ Systems presented in the test includes the concept of reality, concept of human nature, personal inner reality, and assessment of situations for each system as well as the preferred organization type, preferred environments, possible strengths, and possible limitations of each. In addition, suggestions are made for motivating, communicating with, and changing each of the system types.

The test booklet is attractive and easy to follow. Administration and scoring should take approximately half an hour.

Unfortunately, according to the publisher, no manual exists for the MindMaker6™ other than the test booklet itself. Therefore, no information on the construction, norms, reliability, or validity of the test apparently exists. Further, there appears to be no information as to when, where, why, or to whom the test is to be given. Given that an individual obtains scores on each of the six systems, it seems necessary to present the difference between scores considered to be significant.

Overall, the MindMaker6™ appears to be a rather entertaining test with unknown psychometric properties. It should only be used with caution.

REVIEWER'S REFERENCE

Lynch, D. (1984). *Your high-performance business brain: An operator's manual.* New York: Simon & Schuster.

[241]
Miner Sentence Completion Scale.

Purpose: Intended for use in "selection, vocational and career guidance, identifying talent supplies, and evaluating training primarily."
Population: Workers and prospective workers in management, professional, and entrepreneurial or task-oriented occupations.
Publication Dates: 1961–86.
Acronym: MSCS.
Administration: Group.
Forms, 3: Form H (Management domain), Form P (Professional domain), Form T (Task domain).
Price Data, 1989: $17.50 per 50 tests; $8.50 per scoring guide (Form H, '64, 64 pages, with '77 supplement, 15 pages, and '89 supplement, 4 pages; Form P, '81, 49 pages; Form T, '86, 56 pages).
Time: (20–30) minutes.
Comments: Form H available as free-response or multiple-choice version; directions included for scoring rare response patterns.
Author: John B. Miner.
Publisher: Organizational Measurement Systems Press.
a) FORM H.
Scores, 9: Authority Figures, Competitive Games, Competitive Situations, Assertive Role, Imposing Wishes, Standing Out from Group, Routine Administrative Functions, Supervisory Job, Total.
b) FORM P.
Scores, 6: Acquiring Knowledge, Independent Action, Accepting Status, Providing Help, Professional Commitment, Total.
c) FORM T.
Scores, 6: Self Achievement, Avoiding Risks, Feedback of Results, Personal Innovation, Planning for the Future, Total.

Cross References: See T2:1484 (4 references); for a review by C. J. Adcock, see 7:172 (2 references); see also P:450 (3 references) and 6:230a (2 references).

TEST REFERENCES

1. Eberhardt, B. J., Yap, C. K., & Basuray, M. T. (1988). A psychometric evaluation of the multiple choice version of the Miner Sentence Completion Scale. *Educational and Psychological Measurement, 48,* 119-126.
2. Stevens, G. E., & Brenner, O. C. (1990). An empirical investigation of the motivation to manage among blacks and women in business school. *Educational and Psychological Measurement, 50,* 879-886.

Review of the Miner Sentence Completion Scale by FREDERICK T. L. LEONG, *Assistant Professor of Psychology, The Ohio State University, Columbus, OH:*

The Miner Sentence Completion Scale (MSCS) consists of three forms. The original MSCS, which is Form H, was developed in the 1950s and published in 1964. It is a theoretically based projective measure of "motivation to manage" in the form of a sentence completion scale consisting of 40 items with 5 items as fillers. Responses are scored using a scoring guide (Miner, 1964) along three dimensions: *like-indifferent-dislike.* Examples of responses for each dimension on each item are provided in the scoring guide. An individual's motivation to manage is derived from two overall scores: the item score as well as a score of rare or unusual responses. The 35 items that are scored also provide a measure of seven dimensions considered to be important in the construct of motivation to manage. These dimensions include Authority Figures, Competitive Games, Competitive Situations, Imposing Wishes, Assertive Role (formerly labelled Masculine Role), Standing Out from Group, and Routine Administrative Functions.

There is also a multiple-choice version of Form H (Miner, 1977a). Owing to the extra time and training needed in order to obtain scores on the sentence completion version of Form H, a research group at Rennsselaer Polytechnic Institute constructed and tested a multiple-choice version of Form H (Miner, 1985). Miner eventually developed his own multiple-choice version of Form H consisting of a stem followed by six alternative responses, with two responses representing each of the *like-indifferent-dislike* dimensions similar to the original Form H. Total score correlations between the multiple-choice version and the original version have ranged from .38 to .68. The multiple-choice version also suffers from a score inflation when moving from the sentence completion to the multiple-choice version.

Whereas the original version of the MSCS was designed to measure managerial motivation in hierarchical (Form H for Hierarchical) and bureaucratic organizations, Miner eventually recognized that there were other forms of organizations and began to develop two alternative (not parallel) versions of the MSCS. Form P (for Professional) was developed in 1981 for professional organizations (Miner, 1981) using responses from faculty samples (Miner, 1985). The five dimensions or roles measured by Form P consist of Acquiring Knowledge, Independent Action, Accepting Status, Providing Help, and Professional Commitment. Form T (for Task) was developed in 1986 to measure managerial motivation in the task domain and has been tested primarily with entrepreneurs (Miner, 1986). The dimensions measured by Form T consist of Self-Achievement, Avoiding Risks, Feedback of Results, Personal Innovation, and Planning for the Future.

Much of the research and reliability and validity studies have focused on the original sentence completion version of Form H and this review will do the same. According to Miner, in his review (1985) of the MSCS research, interscorer reliability for experienced scorers ranged from .86 to .97 with less experienced scorers' median reliability around .80. How Miner distinguished between experienced and less experienced scorers is not specified in his review. Test-retest reliability across different samples with 10-week intervals have ranged from .68 to .84 with a median of .83 for the total score while subscale coefficients have ranged from .44 to .63 with a median of .48. Test-retest reliability for the multiple-choice version with 3-week intervals obtained a median coefficient of .78 for total score and a median of .63 for subscale scores. Miner (1985) points out that internal consistency reliability for the original version of Form H is quite low but provides no specific data. He argues that "at least for projective techniques, there are good reasons to believe that internal consistency reliability is not an essential condition for construct validity" (p. 168).

In terms of validity, there seem to be considerable data supporting the validity of Form H of the MSCS. Miner (1985), in his review, identified 26 validity studies with a median validity coefficient of .35 (p. 159). Twenty of the validity studies were concurrent with six using a predictive validity design. According to Miner (1985) the results of the predictive studies were quite similar to the concurrent studies. Validity coefficients are somewhat lower for the subscales than for the total scores with the stronger coefficients obtained for Competitive Situations and Imposing Wishes followed by Authority Figures and Routine Administrative Functions. Miner (1985) also noted that good validity (no specific coefficients are provided) was obtained with the multiple-choice version of Form H (p. 162). In another review, Miner (1978a) provided validity correlations between the MSCS and theoretically relevant subscales of Kuder Preference Record ($r = .45$ and $.38$), Strong Vocational Interest Blank ($r = .35$ to $.51$), Gough Adjective Checklist ($r = .32$ to $.38$), and Ghiselli Self-Description Inventory ($r = .24, .26, .35$) (p. 755). The validity of the

MSCS has also been supported by validity generalization techniques (Nathan and Alexander cited by Miner, 1985, p. 163). Miner (1978a, 1985) points out that studies conducted outside the theoretical domain of the MSCS Form H (i.e., studies not using hierarchical-bureaucratic organizations) should be expected to exhibit no significant results.

The picture is by no means totally positive and uncontroversial. Some studies have questioned the reliability and validity of the MSCS. For example, Brief, Aldag, and Chacko (1977), examined the convergent and discriminant validity of the MSCS using England's Personal Values Questionnaire and Ghiselli's Self-Description Inventory and concluded that the MSCS lacked both types of validity. They also raised questions about the level of interscorer reliability. Miner (1978b) provided a very comprehensive and credible response to the questions raised by Brief et al. (1977). However, one sparrow does not a summer make. More recently, Eberhardt, Yap, and Basuray (1988) assessed the multiple-choice version of Form H and found all the subscale scores had unacceptably low internal consistency scores (i.e., Authority Figures, $r = .34$; Competitive Games, $r = .40$; Competitive Situations, $r = .24$; Imposing Wishes, $r = .26$; Assertive Role, $r = .34$; Standing Out from Group, $r = .29$; and Routine Administrative Functions, $r = .15$) with only the total score ($r = .58$) passing Nunnally's suggested criterion of $r = .50$. Eberhardt et al.'s (1988) factor analysis also did not support Miner's seven-factor theoretical model of managerial motivation, yielding instead three factors (i.e., Being in Front of Groups, Sports, and Image).

Given that science is a cumulative process, the weight of the current evidence seems to support Miner's contention that the MSCS is a reliable and valid measure of the motivation to manage. With the Brief et al. (1977) and Eberhardt et al. (1988) studies duly noted, much more negative evidence will have to be accumulated before one can challenge Miner's contention. However, it should be noted the scoring guides for Form H of MSCS measures are totally inadequate if evaluated as manuals according to the *Standard for Educational and Psychological Testing* (American Educational Research Association, American Psychological Association, & National Council on Measurement in Education, 1985). These guides (Miner, 1964; 1977a) do not provide any information on the rationale, intended uses, and psychometric properties of the MSCS. The scoring guides for Form P and T (Miner, 1981; 1986) are somewhat better in including some reliability and normative data and information on intended uses. Although it may be argued the scoring guides are not intended to be technical manuals, no other materials are provided to the test user other than the scoring guides. Given

the lack of technical manuals and the inadequacies of the scoring guides, potential users may consult the following sources for information on the theory, development, and supporting research for the MSCS: Miner (1965, 1977b, 1978a, 1985).

Finally, it should be noted that the original MSCS, as a sentence completion scale, is vulnerable to all the problems usually associated with projective measures. These problems include excessive subjectivity in scoring due to the lack of standardization, heavy reliance on clinical expertise in obtaining reliable scoring, and difficulty in obtaining normative data.

REVIEWER'S REFERENCES

Miner, J. B. (1964). *Scoring guide for the Miner Sentence Completion Scale.* New York: Springer.
Miner, J. B. (1965). *Studies in management education.* New York: Springer.
Brief, A. P., Aldag, R. J., & Chacko, T. I. (1977). The Miner Sentence Completion Scale: An appraisal. *Academy of Management Journal, 20,* 635-643.
Miner, J. B. (1977a). *Scoring guide for the Miner Sentence Completion Scale: 1977 Supplement* (Multiple choice version). Atlanta: Organizational Measurement Systems Press.
Miner, J. B. (1977b). *Motivation to manage: A ten year update on the "Studies in Management Education" research.* Atlanta: Organizational Measurement Systems Press.
Miner, J. B. (1978a). Twenty years of research on the role-motivation theory of managerial effectiveness. *Personnel Psychology, 31,* 739-760.
Miner, J. B. (1978b). The Miner Sentence Completion Scale: A reappraisal. *Academy of Management Journal, 21,* 283-294.
Miner, J. B. (1981). *Scoring guide for the Miner Sentence Completion Scale: Form P.* Atlanta: Organizational Measurement Systems Press.
American Educational Research Association, American Psychological Association, & National Council on Measurement in Education. (1985). *Standards for educational and psychological testing.* Washington, DC: American Psychological Association, Inc.
Miner, J. B. (1985). Sentence Completion measures in personnel research: The development and validation of the Miner Sentence Completion Scales. In H. J. Bernardin & D. A. Bownas (Eds.), *Personality assessment in organizations.* New York: Praeger.
Miner, J. B. (1986). *Scoring guide for the Miner Sentence Completion Scale: Form T.* Atlanta: Organizational Measurement Systems Press.
Eberhardt, B. J., Yap, C. K., & Basuray, M. T. (1988). A psychometric evaluation of the multiple choice version of the Miner Sentence Completion Scale. *Educational and Psychological Measurement, 48,* 119-126.

Review of the Miner Sentence Completion Scale by LINDA F. WIGHTMAN, *Vice President—Test Development and Research, Law School Admission Services, Newtown, PA:*

The Miner Sentence Completion Scale (MSCS) has been expanded to include three free-response forms as well as a multiple-choice version of the original scale, now designated Form H. Each of the three forms of the instrument is intended for the same type of use—selection, vocational guidance, identifying talent, and evaluating training—but each is geared toward different management environments. Form H focuses on managers and aspiring managers in bureaucratic systems, Form P on professionals and aspiring professionals in professional systems, and Form T on entrepreneurs or other independent managers whose success derives from task performance.

Form H is essentially unchanged since it was reviewed by C. J. Adcock in the *Seventh Mental Measurements Yearbook* (1972). The concerns raised in that review regarding cultural dependency are of even greater concern today. The previous reviewer noted that some of the starters, such as "Getting my shoes shined" and "Country club dances" would be foreign to the New Zealand experience. These starters would be equally foreign to many of today's new and aspiring middle managers. One of this reviewer's greatest concerns with the MSCS is its insensitivity to and inappropriateness for the ethnic and gender diversity among today's managers and aspiring managers. This instrument is particularly insensitive to the expanded role of women in management positions as evidenced, for example, by reference to "Wearing a necktie," "shooting a rifle," or "When one of my men asks for advice." Neither the options offered in the multiple-choice version of Form H nor the credited response examples offered in the Scoring Guide provide plausible credited alternatives for female managers.

The Rare Score Scale, a score not for originality, but rather for rare patterns of response, is still an integral part of the original measure, Form H. The questions about interpretability and usefulness of this score that were raised by Adcock have not been addressed in Form H, but neither Form P nor Form T includes a Rare Score Scale. The author of the instrument acknowledges that "the time and effort involved in obtaining these scores are not justified by the results obtained, unless norming is based on a directly relevant sample of substantial size."

Potential users of the MSCS are provided with a scoring guide for the chosen test form. Each guide provides 10 or more examples of responses that should be designated +, ?, and -, for each item. Responses scored + are assigned 1 point each, responses scored ? receive no credit, and responses scored - are assigned -1 point each. Total score and subscale scores are obtained by summing the plus and minus score assignments. The Scoring Guides provide normative information for total score and for each of the subscores. The 1989 Supplement to the Form H Scoring Guide expands the normative data provided in the original 1964 Guide. In each Guide, the data cut across multiple organizations as well as across multiple levels within individual organizations. The sparse descriptions of the included organizations severely limit the usefulness of the data. But even more limiting are the clear value judgments that are inherent in the scoring instructions. Individual organizations are best advised to analyze carefully the underlying philosophy inherent in the scoring of individual items. This reviewer believes that even among organizations for whom the management philosophy underlying the MSCS is consistent with their own, they would find the instrument most useful if they were in a position to develop norms at least for their individual organiza-

tion and more likely for different levels of management responsibility within the organization.

The Guides for Forms P and T also provide limited information about the reliability of scoring. In both manuals, only the results of an independent rescoring of the same 20 records by the same individual after a period of 2 or 3 years are reported in the reliability of scoring section. The author candidly expresses his belief that it is perhaps unrealistic to expect to obtain comparable scorer reliabilities from two separate individuals. This reviewer finds inability to obtain interrater reliability an unacceptable deficiency.

The scoring guide itself does not provide any information about test validity of any type. The Bibliographic Note at the end of each manual directs the user to some related research.

Potential users cannot make an informed decision about the appropriateness of these instruments for their own organizational purposes without gathering and reading the suggested references. These references provide the underlying management philosophy on which the instruments were developed as well as the limited psychometric data available to support their validity. It would be most helpful if the underlying philosophy and the substantive findings from these various sources were added as an appendix to the scoring manual or if a comprehensive technical manual were developed.

A final observation is that, as is the case with many projective evaluation instruments, the testwise prospective manager can easily manipulate the instrument to produce a high score. This becomes increasingly true for the ambitious manager who spends a short time reviewing Miner's underlying management theory. During this time in which the ranks of entry level managers are swollen and there is increased competition for the shrinking number of upper management positions, the value of the instruments is potentially at its highest, but the motivation and reward for manipulating the results on the part of test takers are also at an apex. In summary, concern about the susceptibility of scores to manipulation, combined with insensitivity to managers who are women or minorities, the limited statistical data to support the use of the instruments, and the difficulty in obtaining supporting documentation necessary to understand the underlying philosophy inherent in the assigned scores limit the usefulness of this instrument for meeting today's management needs.

REVIEWER'S REFERENCE

Adcock, C. J. (1972). [Review of the Miner Sentence Completion Scale.] In O. K. Buros (Ed.), *The seventh mental measurements yearbook* (pp. 418-420). Highland Park, NJ: The Gryphon Press.

[242]
Mini Inventory of Right Brain Injury.
Purpose: To screen "for right hemisphere brain injury."
Population: Ages 18 and over.

Publication Date: 1989.
Acronym: MIRBI.
Scores, 16: Visual Scanning, Integrity of Gnosis, Integrity of Body Image, Visuoverbal Processing, Visuosymbolic Processing, Integrity of Praxis, Visual Processing Total, Affective Language, Higher Level Language Skills, Language Processing Total, Affect, Emotion and Affect Processing Total, General Behavior, General Behavior and Psychic Integrity Total, Total MIRBI Score, Right-Left Differentiation Subscale Score.
Administration: Individual.
Price Data, 1989: $59 per complete kit including examiner's manual (38 pages), 25 test booklets, and 25 report forms; $24 per 25 test booklets; $17 per 25 report forms; $21 per examiner's manual.
Time: (15–30) minutes.
Authors: Patricia A. Pimental and Nancy A. Kingsbury.
Publisher: PRO-ED, Inc.

Review of the Mini Inventory of Right Brain Injury by R. A. BORNSTEIN, Associate Professor of Psychiatry, Neurosurgery and Neurology, The Ohio State University, Columbus, OH:

The Mini Inventory of Right Brain Injury (MIRBI) consists of 27 items that purport to measure right-brain function. The rationale for the development of this test appears to be an alleged lack of appropriately standardized objective instruments for assessment of right-brain function, and the need to develop time-efficient assessment procedures. The latter rationale may well be true, but the former assertion is almost completely without merit. Numerous measures of a variety of right-hemisphere functions have been developed and are widely in use. The fact that some of these measures are time-consuming is not sufficient justification for development of a new test in the absence of demonstration that the proposed measure is as effective as those already available.

In addition to the questionable rationale, the theoretical basis and underlying assumptions for this test appear to be grossly flawed. The test manual on page 7 provides the classification scheme of syndromes that are assumed to reflect right-hemisphere function. It is noted on page 6 that available literature does not "provide an acceptable, comprehensive theoretical model of right brain injury." In spite of assertions presented in the manual, the classification of symptoms in Table 2 does not represent such a theoretical model. The items from the MIRBI are divided into 10 subsections, some of which have only one item and yield only 1 point. For example, Section 9 contains a single item in which the examiner rates the presence or absence of flat affect. Specific criteria for evaluation of this rather difficult concept are not provided. The items yield a total of 43 points that are used in a total point score to determine the severity of impairment. The content and structure of the MIRBI is apparently based on the principal author's understanding of disorders associated with right-hemi-sphere dysfunction. These disorders are listed in Table 1 on page 5 of the manual. It is clear from this table that the MIRBI is based on a flawed, incomplete, and unsophisticated understanding of brain-behavior relationships. Many of the deficits in Table 1 are equally associated with the left-hemisphere dysfunction, or typically require dysfunction in both hemispheres.

The flaws in test content become immediately apparent on review of the actual test items. In the second section on "Integrity of Gnosis," patients are asked to name a particular finger, as well as to name an object that is placed in their hand. These items are performed on the left hand, and one presumes the manual makes the assumption this is therefore a right-hemisphere task. However, because these tasks require a verbal response, there is some doubt about those assumptions. In contrast, comparable measures from the Halstead-Reitan Neuropsychological Test Battery (9:463) do not require a verbal response, and therefore make the presumption of right-hemisphere mediation somewhat more likely. The section on "Visuoverbal Processing" comprises approximately 25% of the MIRBI and is composed of unequivocally language-laden tasks. These tasks include reading and comprehension of a paragraph, writing to dictation and spontaneously, and writing alternating strings of letters. The section on "Higher Level Language Skills" consists of 16 points, or 37%, of the entire test. Again, the items in this section are expressly verbal and require such classic language-based tasks as proverb interpretation, a general comprehension of language, and verbal similarities. To assert that such tasks reflect right-hemisphere function ignores nearly 150 years of scientific investigation of the relationship between the left hemisphere and language function.

The item content, therefore, of the MIRBI is grossly flawed from a conceptual and theoretical point of view. The statistical development of the test is similarly flawed. In the selection of subjects, it is stated that patients in the unilateral lesion groups have confirmed cerebral lesions based on CT scans. It is not, however, stated whether there is any evidence of involvement of the other hemisphere. An initial pool of items was administered to 50 patients with right-brain injury to identify the most discriminating items. From this pool of 63 items, the final 27 items were selected and administered to 30 patients with right-brain injury, 13 patients with left-brain injury, and 30 controls. The manual alleges to evaluate the effects of age, education, sex, and duration of illness by computing Pearson correlations between these variables and the MIRBI total score within each group. Examining these relationships in the groups separately does not evaluate potential differences between the groups. This is particularly important in view of the goal of demonstrating that the MIRBI can discriminate between groups. In this context, it is a major problem that the duration of illness in the right-hemisphere group was approximately 158 days, whereas the duration of illness in the left-hemisphere group was 689 days. It is well known in neuropsychological evaluation that acute and chronic lesions have vastly different effects. Therefore, these data may simply be comparing the effects of acute versus chronic hemispheric lesions.

Comparison of the left- and right-lesions groups in Tables 6 and 7 (p. 21) also reveals the groups are not equivalent in terms of distribution of lesion location. Among those groups, 37 percent of the right- and 62 percent of the left-lesion groups have posterior lesions. As might be expected, the mean scores of the right- and left-lesion groups both differ from the controls, but do not differ from each other. Results of an analysis of covariance are presented that indicate a main effect for group, but no sex effect. No data on group by sex interaction are presented. Nevertheless, the manual reports a marginally significant difference between right- and left-lesion females. The manual then suggests the failure to detect differences between the left- and right-lesion groups may have been due to unequal sample size. The results of an unequal variances T-test are then presented without any evidence whatsoever that the groups, in fact, differ in regard to variance.

The manual presents a variety of reliability and validity data. Internal reliability using Cronbach's Alpha was acceptable at .92. Interrater reliability was based on four protocols and yielded coefficients from .65 to .87, which is unacceptable. This lack of interrater agreement is likely a function of an insufficient number of protocols examined and the inadequate criteria for evaluation of responses. Information purporting to demonstrate the content, criterion, and construct validity of the MIRBI is included in the manual. The evidence presented represents little more than wishful thinking.

In summary, this is a poorly conceptualized and poorly validated measure that does not reflect current understandings of brain-behavior relationships. The test is based on a questionable rationale and a myriad of faulty assumptions. In brief, this is a bad test that has little chance of providing any meaningful data in the evaluation of patients with brain injuries. It is not recommended for use in any circumstance.

Review of the Mini Inventory of Right Brain Injury by JOHN E. OBRZUT, Professor of Educational Psychology, and CAROL A. BOLIEK, Assistant Research Scientist, Speech and Hearing Sciences, University of Arizona, Tucson, AZ:

The Mini Inventory of Right Brain Injury (MIRBI) was developed as a standardized screening instrument for right-hemisphere injury, presumably because there is a dearth of assessment instruments and materials that specifically address suspected right-hemisphere dysfunction. Clinicians currently use subtests or portions of larger batteries in screening for right-hemisphere difficulties that were initially intended for cerebral assessment not specific to right-hemisphere functioning (Adamovich & Brooks, 1981). Furthermore, other examinations designed for right-hemisphere functioning lack test standardization and norming, and also experience inherent problems that occur when trying to combine subtests from a variety of other instruments (Adamovich & Brooks, 1981).

Pimental and Kingsbury (the MIRBI authors) state six general uses of the MIRBI: (a) identification of "deficits in visual, language, emotion, affect, general behavior, memory, orientation, and nonverbal processing"; (b) determination of the level of severity of right-brain injury ranging from "normal" to "profound"; (c) determination of specific areas of right-hemisphere dysfunction by linking various right-hemisphere syndromes with their specific underlying disorders of processing, based on Pimental's classification system of right-hemisphere syndromes (Pimental, 1987a, 1987b, 1987c); (d) determination of strengths and weaknesses for the purposes of differential diagnosis and development of individualized remedial strategies; (e) monitoring rehabilitative progress; and (f) research-related issues.

The MIRBI can be administered to English-speaking adults between the ages of 20 to 80 years. The inventory yields 10 subsections that cover four general domains, as follows: (a) Visual Processing, (b) Language Processing, (c) Emotion and Affective Processing, and (d) General Behavior and Psychic Integrity. The Visual Processing domain comprises six subsections including Visual Scanning, Integrity of Gnosis, Integrity of Body Image, Visuoverbal Processing, Visuosymbolic Processing, and Integrity of Praxis Associated with Visuomotor Skills. The Language Processing domain is characterized by two subsections including Affective Language and Higher Level Receptive and Expressive Language Skills. The Emotion and Affective Processing domain has Affect as its only subsection and the General Behavior and Psychic Integrity domain has General Behavior as its only subsection. The MIRBI also has a Right-Left Differentiation Subscale (RLDS), which contains 10 items that were statistically derived on the basis of their ability to differentiate right- from left-hemisphere injuries.

The MIRBI can be administered in approximately 15 to 30 minutes and requires the Examiner's Manual, the Test Booklet, and minimal additional materials (i.e., pencil, quarter, paper, etc.). There are no basal or ceiling levels because the administration rules require that all items be presented regardless of performance. Items are scored as correct (i.e., 3/3), partially correct (i.e., 2/3), or incorrect (0). The total MIRBI score is the sum of all correct responses: The higher the score, the better the performance.

A total of 63 items were initially developed based on Pimental's classification system and the deficit analysis paradigm (i.e., deficits can be identified by examining skill areas that are known to be diminished as a function of right-hemisphere involvement). All but two items were original. These initial 63 items were given to 50 right-hemisphere-injured patients (from 18 pilot sites), as documented by a neurological evaluation and a computer tomography (CT) scan. In addition, these patients were screened for medical problems, substance abuse, adequate vision and hearing acuity, mental retardation, and premorbid illiteracy, to name a few. The sample included 50% males and 50% females (mean age = 66.7 years). Using Cronbach's (1951) coefficient alpha technique, a .91 coefficient was obtained, indicating good internal consistency among items. Of the 63 original items, 27 items were retained in the final inventory, those that were failed by 54% to 98% of the right-brain-injured sample based on criteria recommended by Anastasi (1976).

The actual standardization sample consisted of 30 patients with a diagnosis of right-brain injury, 13 with left-brain injury, and 30 controls matched on the basis of age, education, and sex. Each brain-injured group was further divided into subgroups by site of lesion (right or left anterior, posterior, subcortical). The mean age for the standardization sample was between 59.06 to 63.9 years for the various groups. Using multiple Pearson product moment correlations, significant age effects were found for the normal and right-brain-injured groups. Using a two-way ANCOVA (age as a covariant) with total MIRBI points, the authors report that overall performances on the MIRBI were significantly different between the right-brain-injured and normal groups and left-brain-injured and normal groups. Only a borderline significant difference (p = .0493) was found between right- and left-brain-injured groups, even after an unequal variances t-test procedure was conducted.

The 27 MIRBI items were submitted to another ANCOVA comparing the least square mean values for each item. This analysis yielded 10 items that most strongly differentiated the right- from the left-hemisphere-injured groups. Optimal cutoff scores were determined for the purposes of differentiating among right-brain-injured, left-brain-injured, and normal groups resulting in a score of 10 (93.10% true positives and 78.57% true negatives). Severity levels were determined using univariate summary statistics, a frequency table, and a normal probability plot.

An alpha reliability coefficient of .9230 was reported as an index of internal consistency. Interrater reliability ranged from .65 to .87, but was performed on protocols of only four of the 73 participants for unacknowledged reasons. Standard error of measurement (SEm) was calculated for age groups by 10-year intervals and ranged from 0 to 5.5.

Content validity was established by selecting items that were representative of skill deficits often seen in right-hemisphere-impaired individuals. For example, making a string of cursive ms or ws, drawing a picture of a clock with a specific time, understanding a humorous sentence, and expressing emotional tone of voice during speaking activities. The authors state the items used in this screening device were selected for their representativeness of right-brain injury, according to their theoretical model and our current understanding of cerebral organization and function. Criterion-related validity was established using concurrent measures, and performance on the MIRBI was compared to CT scans of the right- and left-brain-impaired groups. In addition, the MIRBI RLDS was apparently successful at differentiating between right- and left-brain-injured groups.

Construct validity was demonstrated by correctly classifying patients as right- or left-hemisphere-injured, as confirmed by CT scan. High item intercorrelations also indicated the MIRBI items are related to each other, presumably because they are measuring the same construct domain. In addition, the MIRBI total point score and the RLDS cutoff scores correctly differentiated right- from left-brain-injured patients, which would indicate that right-brain injury phenomena are being measured (at least at a screening level). Initial diagnostic utility of the MIRBI also has been reported by the test authors.

Overall, Pimental and Kingsbury have accomplished the goal of developing a standardized instrument that screens for right-hemisphere injury and related dysfunction. The major strengths of the MIRBI are that it was normed on a group of right-hemisphere-injured patients and that it appears successfully to identify adults with such injury who are in need of further, more intensive evaluation. Additionally, the MIRBI demonstrates adequate internal consistency as well as initial criterion and construct validity.

Several limitations of the MIRBI are noted. There were no specific age ranges reported for any of the standardization groups. In addition, the MIRBI was not standardized on brain-injured or normal adults between the ages of 20–39 years and the 80–89 age group. The standardization sample was selected from hospital settings where patients were seen primarily for acute care. In order to use the MIRBI as a screening instrument in rehabilitative or long-term care settings, specific norms for these settings need to be developed. Most test sites were in the Midwest, and Blacks and Hispanics were underrepresented. Further, there are always difficulties in obtaining "pure" right-hemisphere-injured patients because often when there is an infarct in the right hemisphere there is also a concurrent lacunar infarct in the left hemisphere (the converse is true for left-hemisphere injuries). Thus, interpretations of "pure" cases should be made very cautiously when using the MIRBI. There was also no mention of determining handedness preferences, familial histories, or premorbid learning difficulties (with the exception of mental retardation) of patients in the standardization sample. A larger left-hemisphere-injured comparative population is also needed to further enhance the MIRBI's discriminative ability between right- and left-hemisphere-injured patients.

Most of the test items are straightforward with regard to administration and scoring; however, some subjective judgments must be made on general reading, writing comprehension, and expressive abilities. The authors have placed the scoring criteria for these items in the Test Booklet for easy reference. It would be helpful to have some examples from the standardization group on matters like poor spacing between words and letters (writing sample) and examples of scoring the spoken paragraph including typical mistakes. Also, the clinician should keep in mind that many of the items are given orally and require a verbal (primarily left-hemisphere) response from the patient.

It appeared the *SEm* was slightly larger for the right-hemisphere-injured group than for the left-hemisphere-injured group, with the lowest *SEm* reported for the normal group. This *SEm* difference would imply the targeted right-hemisphere-injured group was more variable in its performance on the MIRBI. This should be taken into consideration when assessing those patients who receive "border-line" scores and deciding upon a further evaluation. Whereas the MIRBI RLDS differentiated right- and left-brain-impaired groups and concurrent CT scans confirmed the classification, it is not evident whether the examiners were blind to the results of the CT scans prior to testing each patient. Diagnostic usefulness and clinical utility of the MIRBI will be obtained with the benefit of additional concurrent data from other more established neuropsychological instruments and achievement batteries. With these precautions, the practitioner will find this instrument a useful asset in clinical practice to determine further areas of needed assessment of right-brain injury.

REVIEWER'S REFERENCES

Cronbach, L. J. (1951). Coefficient alpha and the internal structure of tests. *Psychometrika, 16*, 297-334.
Anastasi, A. (1976). *Psychological testing.* New York: Macmillan.

Adamovich, B. L., & Brooks, R. L. (1981). A diagnostic protocol to assess the communication deficits in patients with right hemisphere damage. In R. H. Brookshire (Ed.), *Clinical Aphasiology Conference Proceedings* (pp. 244-253). Minneapolis, MN: BRK.
Pimental, P. A. (1987a, October). *The MIRBI revisited: The first standardized right brain injury screening.* Paper presented at a meeting of the National Academy of Neuropsychology, Chicago.
Pimental, P. A. (1987b, October). *Deficit patterns and lesion site in right brain injured subjects.* Paper presented at a meeting of the National Academy of Neuropsychology, Chicago.
Pimental, P. A. (1987c). *The Mini Inventory of Right Brain Injury (MIRBI): Development and standardization of a new screening instrument for assessment of right hemisphere brain injury.* Unpublished dissertation, The Chicago School of Professional Psychology.

[243]

Minnesota Importance Questionnaire.

Purpose: "To measure twenty psychological needs and six underlying values that have been found to be relevant to work adjustment, specifically to satisfaction with work."
Population: Ages 16 and over.
Publication Dates: 1967–81.
Acronym: MIQ.
Scores, 21: Ability Utilization, Achievement, Activity, Independence, Variety, Compensation, Security, Working Conditions, Advancement, Recognition, Authority, Social Status, Co-workers, Social Services, Moral Values, Company Policies, Supervision-Human Relations, Supervision-Technical, Creativity, Responsibility, Autonomy (ranked form only).
Administration: Group.
Forms, 2: Ranked form ('75, 9 pages), paired form ('75, 18 pages).
Price Data, 1988: $39.50 per complete kit including 50 answer sheets, 10 reusable booklets, manual ('81, 73 pages), and Occupational Reinforcer Patterns ('86); $.70 or less per reusable booklet ($7 minimum); $.12 or less per answer sheet ($6 minimum); $8.50 per manual; scoring service offered by publisher.
Foreign Language Edition: Spanish and French editions available.
Time: (30–40) minutes for ranked form; (15–25) minutes for paired form.
Authors: James B. Rounds, Jr., George A. Henly, René V. Dawis, Lloyd H. Lofquist, and David J. Weiss.
Publisher: Vocational Psychology Research.
Cross References: For additional information and reviews by Lewis E. Albright and Sheldon Zedeck, see 8:1050 (40 references); see also T3:1495 (14 references), T2:2283 (8 references), and 7:1063 (29 references).

TEST REFERENCES

1. Scarpello, V., & Campbell, J. P. (1983). Job satisfaction and the fit between individual needs and organizational rewards. *Journal of Occupational Psychology, 56*, 315-328.
2. Tziner, A. (1983). Correspondence between occupational rewards and occupational needs and work satisfaction: A canonical redundancy analysis. *Journal of Occupational Psychology, 56*, 49-56.
3. Pedro, J. D. (1984). Induction into the workplace: The impact of internships. *Journal of Vocational Behavior, 25*, 80-95.
4. Hancock, J. E. (1988). Needs and reinforcers in student affairs: Implications for attrition. *Journal of College Student Development, 29*, 25-30.

Review of the Minnesota Importance Questionnaire by BARBARA LACHAR, Vice-President, Psychological Assessment Services, Inc., Sugar Land, TX:

The Minnesota Importance Questionnaire (MIQ) is a measure of 20 vocational needs and six underlying values, for use in vocational counseling, career planning, and job placement. This measure is one product of more than 30 years of study by the Work Adjustment Project at the University of Minnesota whose theory proposes that work adjustment is related to both the worker's own job satisfaction and satisfactoriness to the employer. Satisfaction depends on the correspondence between the worker's needs and the rewards or reinforcers available from the job. Satisfactoriness is related to the match between worker's abilities and the job requirements. The Work Adjustment Project has produced the MIQ to measure worker needs, The Minnesota Job Description Questionnaire (T3:1497) to measure the presence of reinforcers in an occupation (ORPs), and the Minnesota Satisfaction Questionnaire (9:721) to assess worker satisfaction.

The MIQ is available in two self-administered, untimed, forms that use one statement to represent each of the 20 needs or scales. In the paired form, a statement is paired once with every other statement, creating 190 paired comparisons. Respondents decide which statement in the pair is more important in their ideal job. In the ranked form, statements are grouped in 21 sets of five, and respondents rank the five statements in terms of importance in an ideal job. Both forms ask the respondent to respond to statements (e.g., "I could be busy all the time") in terms of whether or not it is important for their own "ideal job" in order to obtain absolute judgments of importance.

Needs are determined by the number of times an individual selects a statement as important relative to others. Values are defined by a cluster of related needs.

There are two manuals, a user manual for vocational psychologists, counselors, and other professionals by Rounds, Henly, Dawis, Lofquist, and Weiss, 1981, and a second technical manual by Gay, Weiss, Hendel, Dawis, and Lofquist, 1971. A revised technical manual is scheduled for release in 1990, but was unavailable at the time of this review. The 19-year-old technical manual describes the progressive development and psychometric properties of the instrument through three revisions, ending in 1967. The currently available 1975 edition of the MIQ was produced in order to remove references to the respondent's sex from the items, but this is not clearly explained in either of the manuals.

Reliability and validity information in the technical manual refer to the 1967 revision and earlier forms. Reliability has been measured by (*a*) scale internal consistency, (*b*) stability of MIQ scales over time, and (*c*) stability of MIQ profiles over time. Scale internal consistency calculated by Hoyt reliability coefficients for nine groups of subjects ranged between .30 and .95, with median coefficients between .77 and .81. Test-retest coefficients were

used to assess scale stability for the same nine groups plus one additional. Scale stability coefficients ranged from .19 (9-month retest interval) to .93 (immediate retest). Median stability coefficients for the 10 groups ranged from .89 with immediate retesting to .48 after a 6-month interval. Median profile stability coefficients range from .95 with immediate retesting to .70 after a 4-month interval. Even though the reliability of the MIQ is well documented, it would be useful if the new manual contained information on the internal consistency and test-retest stability of individual scales. Currently, users are unable to ascertain differences in scale reliability. This could restrict utility. Additionally, research investigating the equivalence of the paired and ranked forms would be useful.

MIQ scales are relatively independent. Data from 5,358 individuals were used to compute scale intercorrelations which ranged from .05 to .77 with a median intercorrelation of .33. Paired scale intercorrelations are not presented. A factor analysis of these data yielded these six factors: Management, Autonomy, Conditions of Work, Altruism, Achievement, and Recognition. These factors accounted for approximately 50% of the total scale score variance.

Validity evidence for the MIQ is weaker than that supporting its reliability. More statistics and information should be included in the technical manual to allow the reader to evaluate the studies cited. No evidence of validity for the individual need scales is provided. The studies cited consist of 3 different kinds of information: structural evidence of content and discriminant validity, indirect evidence from studies of the pre-1967 forms, and direct evidence of validity produced with the 1967 form.

Evidence of discriminant validity comes from studies indicating low correlations with different abilities as measured by the General Aptitude Test Battery (GATB), while convergent validity is indicated by canonical correlations of .74 and .78 with scales on the Strong Vocational Interest Blank (SVIB). Results showing that MIQ scales correlate lower with the GATB than with the SVIB, support the MIQ's claim that it is less a measure of ability than one of vocational interest. However, the GATB also contains performance tests in addition to paper-and-pencil tests, so variations in method of measurement may contribute to the disparity in shared variance. Stronger evidence of validity could be obtained from studies comparing needs measured by the MIQ to needs scores obtained by Murray's Thematic Apperception Test (TAT) or to a priori predicted relationships with individual scales of other vocational counseling inventories.

Studies conducted with the first version of the MIQ, one using a Likert format containing five items for each of the 20 scales, have shown differences between disabled and nondisabled workers, and management and nonmanagement employees. The manual also reports that college students produced more variable scores and lower mean scores on all but three scales in comparison to managers and skilled white collar workers. Differences are also reported for men and women on the same jobs and between groups differing in tenure. While the results are described in terms of differences in scale elevations, variability, and rankings, there are no statistics provided.

The 1971 technical manual includes only concurrent validity studies using the 1967 revision. These data were generated for nine different groups, but only three occupations (vocational rehabilitation counselors, retail trade workers, and high school counselors) were represented in addition to students and vocational rehabilitation clients. Significant differences were found for all 20 scales, the largest between "those who had experienced work and those who had not." Further analysis of demographic data indicated that sex, age, education, tenure, and marital status were related to scores on MIQ scales. The authors suggest that the MIQ is measuring differences in vocational needs where it is reasonable to assume differences exist. However, a theoretical explanation for the differences should be presented along with the findings.

The manual cites studies that use the MIQ as a measure of vocational needs in investigating relationships between needs and occupational reinforcers predicted by the Work Adjustment Theory. Data are provided that indicate a similar rank ordering of needs and available reinforcers (ORPs) in occupations for two groups of retail trade workers, vocational rehabilitation counselors, and high school counselors. An additional study presents significant correlations between job satisfaction and MIQ-ORP correspondence for cashiers and sales clerks, but not for checker-markers, in a retail trade organization. These data indicate that needs of job incumbents on the MIQ relate to their perception of rewards available and that measured correspondence of MIQ needs and ORPs is related to individual job satisfaction in two of three positions studied.

The 1981 user manual provides instructions on the interpretation of the MIQ. This manual includes a description of the MIQ, recommendations for use, and detailed instructions for interpretation including different strategies for presenting information to clients, normative information, illustrative case summaries, and questions and answers for clarification. Although norms are provided for different sex and age classifications, an idiographic approach to interpretation highlighting needs and values of relative importance to the respondent would be preferred by this reviewer.

Computer scoring of the MIQ by Vocational Psychology Research at the University of Minnesota is suggested, as hand scoring is time consuming. Results consist of a two-part report containing first, a profile of need and value scores, and second, predictions of the likelihood of occupational satisfaction for 90 representative benchmark occupations, arranged in six clusters according to similarity of Occupational Reinforcer Patterns (ORPs).

Each MIQ report provides a Logically Consistent Triad (LCT) score as a measure of the validity or the response consistency of the individual's importance responses. "A logically consistent triad is defined as a pattern of response in which A is chosen over B, B over C, and A over C." LCT scores above 33% (paired form) or 50% (ranked form) allow the counselor to conclude that random responding is unlikely.

The MIQ is an instrument that has been well researched in the context of the Theory of Work Adjustment. Reviewers agree there is evidence to support its reliability, validity, and utility in vocational counseling. It should be noted that its use and interpretation appear to require training and indepth study. It is also recommended to human resource professionals, although additional data to support its utility for specific placement decisions in organizations is desirable.

Additional validity studies to support the use of the MIQ for job placement should investigate its ability to differentiate between various occupational groups, predict job satisfaction outside of the theory of work adjustment, and differentiate between satisfied and dissatisfied employees in the same vocation. In addition, sex, age, education, and tenure differences require appropriate citations and further research before they can be accepted as supporting evidence of validity. Further, these findings should be replicated as more than 20 years have elapsed since the initial research. The revised manual, for which release is anticipated, may already incorporate many of these suggestions.

Review of the Minnesota Importance Questionnaire by WILBUR L. LAYTON, Professor of Psychology, Iowa State University, Ames, IA:

The Minnesota Importance Questionnaire (MIQ) was developed from the Theory of Work Adjustment (Dawis, England, & Lofquist, 1964). The Theory of Work Adjustment stresses the interaction of an individual's abilities and vocational needs with the ability requirements and reinforcer systems of a job to determine the satisfactoriness and the satisfaction of the worker.

The Minnesota Importance Questionnaire purports to measure vocational needs. Vocational needs are preferences for certain kinds of reinforcers, satisfiers, or rewards in working.

According to the Theory of Work Adjustment, work adjustment is indicated by an individual's satisfactoriness and satisfaction. Satisfactoriness is best predicted by the correspondence of the individual's abilities and the ability requirements of the work environment. Satisfaction is best predicted by the correspondence of an individual's needs and the reinforcers in the work environment.

The MIQ was designed to measure 20 (21 for the ranked form) psychological needs and six underlying values found to be relevant to work adjustment, specifically to satisfaction with work. Needs reflect values. Six values are represented by the MIQ. They are: Achievement, Autonomy, Altruism, Comfort, Safety, and Status.

In completing the instrument, an individual expresses the relative importance of the 20 needs by responding to 210 items, 190 of which are in a paired comparison format in which each need dimension, represented by one item, is compared with all other need dimensions. The remaining 20 items require absolute judgments of the importance of each need dimension. All items are responded to in terms of "your ideal job, the kind of job you would most like to have."

The ranked form of the MIQ consists of 21 groups of five items each. The subject ranks the items within each group of five. The last 21 items require absolute judgments as in the paired form. The reading difficulty level for the two forms is equivalent to the fifth grade.

The MIQ answer sheets are computer scored by Vocational Psychology Research, Department of Psychology, University of Minnesota. A computer-generated printout provides a profile of need and value scores and a listing of occupations for which satisfaction is predicted or not predicted. A Logically Consistent Triad (LCT) score representing the degree of logical consistency (transitivity) of response of the individual is also reported. In the event that an individual's LCT score is below 33% for the paired form or 50% for the ranked form, the MIQ profile is considered suspect because of an extraordinarily high level of inconsistent responses. In such cases the MIQ report is accompanied by an additional report containing an analysis, by scale, of the response inconsistency.

Twenty need scores and six value scores are reported. The need scores are usually accompanied by an indication of the range within which this score might have varied had the individual been more consistent in responding. The MIQ report also lists 90 representative occupations grouped into six clusters. These clusters designate groups of occupations with similar Occupational Reinforcer Patterns. An Occupational Reinforcer Pattern (ORP) describes the reinforcers present in an occupation for the 20 MIQ needs.

A C-Index, a correlation coefficient, gives a correspondence index, the extent to which the individual's MIQ profile corresponds to the ORP

for each occupation. A prediction of satisfaction is also listed for each occupation. A prediction of satisfaction is also listed for each occupation. An extended report, which may be requested, provides correspondence information for all occupations for which ORPs are available (185 in 1986). The report form is difficult to read and should be redesigned to make the large amount of information more readily accessible.

Two manuals are available. The first provides information about the development and technical characteristics of the MIQ. The second describes the nature, purpose, administration, scoring, reporting of results, and counseling use and interpretation of the MIQ. The 1981 manual states the MIQ manual was written to aid vocational psychologists, counselors, and other professional persons in assessing the work-relevant needs of individuals through the use of the MIQ. Part I of the Manual is a Description of the MIQ and Part II is Interpretation of the MIQ. A Bibliography for the Minnesota Importance Questionnaire 1967–89 is available from the publishers. It would be desirable for the test authors to integrate the available information in a single manual.

The MIQ is reasonably reliable. Median internal consistency reliability coefficients for the 20 MIQ scales for nine different groups ranged from .77 to .81. Median scale test-retest correlations for the 20 MIQ scales ranged from .89 for immediate retesting to .53 for retesting after 10 months. Median profile test-retest correlations ranged from .95 for immediate retesting to .87 for retesting after 10 months. The latter two reliability results were based on college students. Results for high school students are somewhat lower. Lower reliability coefficients were also reported at various time intervals between testings.

The discriminant and convergent validity of the MIQ were demonstrated by the authors and presented in the 1971 manual. Additional research has demonstrated the concurrent and predictive validity of the instrument. This research has consequently testified to the construct validity of the MIQ. There are over 200 publications that have reference to the MIQ. Many of these references incorporate research results. As indicated earlier, there is a need for a collection of the published research reports into an integrated manual.

According to the test authors, the MIQ, as a measure of vocational needs, may be used in vocational counseling, career planning, and job placement. In vocational counseling, the counselor can use the MIQ to help individuals to understand their vocational needs and how these needs will relate to their expectations of particular work settings. In career planning, the MIQ profile of needs can be compared with profiles of the reinforcer systems (ORPs) for specific occupations. Job placement of workers is facilitated by employer knowledge of both the needs of workers and the reinforcer systems of jobs in the work organization.

The MIQ can be a valuable instrument for use in vocational counseling, career planning, and job placement. The theory of work adjustment provides a meaningful framework to guide users. The forthcoming book on a theory of counseling by Lofquist and Dawis (in press) will provide counselors with additional information.

REVIEWER'S REFERENCES

Dawis, R. V., England, G. W., & Lofquist, L. H. (1964). A theory of work adjustment. *Minnesota Studies in Vocational Rehabilitation*, 15.

Lofquist, L. H., & Dawis, R. V. (in press). *A person-environment-correspondence (P-E-C) theory of counseling*. Minneapolis: University of Minnesota Press.

[244]
Minnesota Multiphasic Personality Inventory-2.

Purpose: "Designed to assess a number of the major patterns of personality and emotional disorders."
Population: Ages 18 and over.
Publication Dates: 1942–90.
Acronym: MMPI-2.
Scores, 75: 7 Validity Indicators: Cannot Say (?), Lie (L), Infrequency (F), Correction (K), Back F (FB), Variable Response Inconsistency (VRIN), True Response Inconsistency (TRIN) (last 3 are supplementary validity scales); 10 Clinical Scales: Hypochondriasis (Hs), Depression (D), Conversion Hysteria (Hy), Psychopathic Deviate (Pd), Masculinity-Femininity (Mf), Paranoia (Pa), Psychasthenia (Pt), Schizophrenia (Sc), Hypomania (Ma), Social Introversion (Si); 15 Supplementary Scales: Anxiety (A), Repression (R), Ego Strength (Es), MacAndrew Alcoholism Scale-Revised (MAC-R), Overcontrolled Hostility (O-H), Dominance (Do), Social Responsibility (Re), College Maladjustment (Mt), Gender Role-Masculine (GM), Gender Role-Feminine (GF), 2 Post-Traumatic Stress Disorder Scales (PK & PS); 15 Content Scales: Anxiety (ANX), Fears (FRS), Obsessiveness (OBS), Depression (DEP), Health Concerns (HEA), Bizarre Mentation (BIZ), Anger (ANG), Cynicism (CYN), Antisocial Practices (ASP), Type A (TPA), Low Self-Esteem (LSE), Social Discomfort (SOD), Family Problems (FAM), Work Interference (WRK), Negative Treatment Indicators (TRT); 3 Si subscales: Shyness/Self-Consciousness (Si₁), Social Avoidance (Si₂), Alienation-Self and Others (Si₃); 28 Harris-Lingoes Subscales: Subjective Depression (D₁), Psychomotor Retardation (D₂), Physical Malfunctioning (D₃), Mental Dullness (D₄), Brooding (D₅), Denial of Social Anxiety (Hy₁), Need for Affection (Hy₂), Lassitude-Malaise (Hy₃), Somatic Complaints (Hy₄), Inhibition of Aggression (Hy₅), Familial Discord (Pd₁), Authority Problems (Pd₂), Social Imperturbability (Pd₃), Social Alienation (Pd₄), Self-Alienation (Pd₅), Persecutory Ideas (Pa₁), Poignancy (Pa₂), Naivete (Pa₃), Social Alienation (Sc₁), Emotional Alienation (Sc₂), Lack of Ego Mastery, Cognitive (Sc₃), Conative (Sc₄), Defective Inhibition (Sc₅), Bizarre Sensory Experiences (Sc₆), Amorality (Ma₁), Psychomotor Acceleration (Ma₂), Imperturbability (Ma₃), Ego Inflation (Ma₄).

Administration: Group.
Price Data, 1989: $17.70 per 10 reusable softcover test booklets; $24.60 per reusable hardcover test booklet; $39.30 per 100 hand-scorable answer sheets (select hardcover or softcover); Basic Service Profile Report: $15.05 per 25 Arion II or MICROTEST answer sheets; $36.30 per set of Basic Scales softcover scoring stencils; $32.30 per set of Basic Scales hardcover scoring stencils; $35.30 per set of Supplementary Scales scoring stencils (select hardcover or softcover); $44 per set of Content Scales scoring stencils (select hardcover or softcover); $45 per set of Harris-Lingoes Subscales scoring stencils (select hardcover or softcover); $35.40 per set of Wiener-Harmon Subtle-Obvious Subscales scoring stencils (select hardcover or softcover); $39.30 per 100 profiles (select scales); $57.20 per audiocassette; $23 per manual for administration and scoring ('89, 166 pages); $10 per Adult Clinical System User's Guide ('89, 71 pages); $10 per Personnel Selection System User's Guide ('89, 76 pages); price data available from publisher for IBM compatible microcomputer edition based on type of score or interpretive report desired; price data available from publisher for scoring service by publisher based on type of score or interpretive report desired.
Time: (90) minutes.
Comments: Revision of the Minnesota Multiphasic Personality Inventory; publisher recommends use of original MMPI for adolescents until norms become available for this group; may be administered by audiocassette or microcomputer.
Authors: S. R. Hathaway, J. C. McKinley, and James N. Butcher (user's guides).
Publisher: Published by University of Minnesota Press; distributed by National Computer Systems.
Cross References: See 9:715 (339 references); see also T3:1498 (749 references); for reviews of the original version by Henry A. Alker and Glen D. King, see 8:616 (1,188 references); see also T2:1281 (549 references); for reviews by Malcolm D. Gynther and David A. Rodgers, see 7:104 (831 references); see also P:166 (1,066 references); for a review by Arthur L. Benton, see 4:71 (211 references); for reviews by Arthur L. Benton, H. J. Eysenck, L. S. Penrose, and Julian B. Rotter, and an excerpted review, see 3:60 (76 references).

TEST REFERENCES

1. Alford, G. S. (1980). Alcoholics Anonymous: An empirical outcome study. *Addictive Behaviors*, 5, 359-370.
2. Gilbert, D. G. (1980). Introversion and self-reported reason for and times of urge for smoking. *Addictive Behaviors*, 5, 97-99.
3. Alterman, A. I., Petrarulo, E., & Tarter, R. (1982). Hyperactivity and alcoholism: Familial and behavioral correlates. *Addictive Behaviors*, 7, 413-421.
4. Edinger, J. D., Reuterfors, D., Logue, P. E. (1982). Cross-validation of the Megargee MMPI typology: A study of specialized inmate populations. *Criminal Justice and Behavior*, 9, 184-203.
5. Epperson, D. L., Hannum, T. E., & Datwyler, M. L. (1982). Women incarcerated in 1960, 1970, and 1980: Implications of demographic, educational, and personality characteristics for earlier research. *Criminal Justice and Behavior*, 9, 352-363.
6. Hatsukami, D., Owen, P., Pyle, R., & Mitchell, J. (1982). Similarities and differences on the MMPI between women with bulimia and women with alcohol or drug abuse problems. *Addictive Behaviors*, 7, 435-439.
7. MacAndrew, C. (1982). An examination of the relevance of the individual differences (A-Trait) formulation of the Tension-Reduction Theory to the etiology of alcohol abuse in young males. *Addictive Behaviors*, 7, 39-45.
8. O'Neil, P. M., Roitzsch, J. C., Giacinto, J. P., & Miller, W. C. (1982). Brief report: Disulfiram acceptors and refusers: Do they differ? *Addictive Behaviors*, 7, 207-209.

9. Rohsenow, D. J. (1982). Social anxiety, daily moods, and alcohol use over time among heavy social drinking men. *Addictive Behaviors, 7*, 311-315.

10. Rohsenow, D. J. (1982). The Alcohol Use Inventory as predictor of drinking by male heavy social drinkers. *Addictive Behaviors, 7*, 387-395.

11. Svanum, S., & Hoffman, R. G. (1982). Brief report: The factor structure of the MacAndrew Alcoholism Scale. *Addictive Behaviors, 7*, 195-198.

12. Williams, S. G., Hudson, A., & Redd, C. (1982). Cigarette smoking, manifest anxiety and somatic symptoms. *Addictive Behaviors, 7*, 427-428.

13. Biasco, F., Fritch, C. O., & Redfering, D. (1983). Personality differences between successfully and unsuccessfully treated drug abusers. *Social Behavior and Personality, 11* (1), 105-111.

14. Bolter, J. F., Stanczak, D. E., & Long, C. J. (1983). Neuropsychological consequences of acute, high-level gasoline inhalation. *Clinical Neuropsychology, 5*, 4-7.

15. Carbonell, J. L. (1983). Inmate classification systems: A cross-tabulation of two methods. *Criminal Justice and Behavior, 10*, 285-292.

16. Dahlstrom, W. G., & Moreland, K. L. (1983). Teaching the MMPI: APA-approved clinical internships. *Professional Psychology: Research and Practice, 14* (5), 563-569.

17. Dikmen, S., Hermann, B. P., Wilensky, A. J., & Rainwater, G. (1983). Validity of the Minnesota Multiphasic Personality Inventory (MMPI) to psychopatathology in patients with epilepsy. *The Journal of Nervous and Mental Disease, 171*,114-122.

18. Greenberg, R. P., & Dattore, P. J. (1983). Do alexithymic traits predict illness? *The Journal of Nervous and Mental Disease, 171*, 276-279.

19. Hanson, R. W., Moss, C. S., Hosford, R. E., & Johnson, M. E. (1983). Predicting inmate penitentiary adjustment: An assessment of four classificatory methods. *Criminal Justice and Behavior, 10*, 293-309.

20. Hill, C. E., Carter, J. A., & O'Farrell, M. K. (1983). A case study of the process and outcome of time-limited counseling. *Journal of Counseling Psychology, 30*, 3-18.

21. Horton, A. M., Jr., Scott, M. L., & Golden, C. J. (1983). Discrimination of brain damaged schizophrenics from non-brain-damaged schizophrenics: Value of the Wiggins MMPI content scales. *Clinical Neuropsychology, 5*, 21-22.

22. Johnson, D. L., Simmons, J. G., & Gordon, B. C. (1983). Temporal consistency of the Meyer-Megargee inmate typology. *Criminal Justice and Behavior, 10*, 263-268.

23. Johnson, W. G., Lake, L., & Mahan, J. M. (1983). Restrained eating: Measuring an elusive construct. *Addictive Behaviors, 8*, 413-418.

24. Koch, H. C. H. (1983). Changes in personal construing in three psychotherapy groups and a control. *British Journal of Medical Psychology, 56*, 245-254.

25. Lloyd, C., Overall, J. E., Kimsey, L. R., & Click, M., Jr. (1983). A comparison of the MMPI-168 profiles of borderline and nonborderline outpatients. *The Journal of Nervous and Mental Disease, 171*, 207-215.

26. Louscher, P. K., Hosford, R. E., & Moss, C. S. (1983). Predicting dangerous behavior in penitentiary using the Megargee typology. *Criminal Justice and Behavior, 10*, 269-284.

27. Moreland, K. L., & Dahlstrom, W. G. (1983). Professional training with and use of the MMPI. *Professional Psychology: Research and Practice, 14* (2), 218-223.

28. Mrad, D. F., Kabacoff, R. I., & Duckro, P. (1983). Validation of the Megargee typology in a halfway house setting. *Criminal Justice and Behavior, 10*, 252-262.

29. Ryan, J. J., & Robert, J. A. (1983). Caudality scale correlates of WAIS IQs: A failure to replicate. *Clinical Neuropsychology, 5*, 161-162.

30. Sbordone, R. J., & Jennison, J. H. (1983). A comparison of the OBD-168 and MMPI to assess the emotional adjustment of traumatic brain injured inpatients to their cognitive deficits. *Clinical Neuropsychology, 5*, 87-92.

31. Zager, L. D. (1983). Response to Simmons and associates: Conclusions about the MMPI-based classification system's stability are premature. *Criminal Justice and Behavior, 10*, 310-315.

32. Akiskal, H. S., Lemmi, H., Dickson, H., King, D., Yerevanian, B., & VanValkenburg, C. (1984). Chronic depressions: Part 2. Sleep EEG differentiation of primary dysthymic disorders from anxious depressions. *Journal of Affective Disorders, 6*, 287-295.

33. Alfano, A. M., Thurstin, A. N., Bancroft, W., Jr., Haygood, J. M., & Sherer, T. M. (1984). Development and validation of an automatic treatment referral system. *Journal of Clinical Psychology, 40*, 842-850.

34. Anderson, W. P., & Kunce, J. T. (1984). Diagnostic implications of markedly elevated MMPI Sc scale scores for nonhospitalized clients. *Journal of Clinical Psychology, 40*, 925-930.

35. Banks, S., Mooney, W. T., Mucowski, R. J., & Williams, R. (1984). Progress in the evaluation and prediction of successful candidates for religious careers. *Counseling and Values, 28*, 82-91.

36. Bartram, D., & Bayliss, R. (1984). Automated testing: Past, present and future. *Journal of Occupational Psychology, 57*, 221-237.

37. Bates, J. E., & Bayles, K. (1984). Objective and subjective components in mothers' perceptions of their children from age 6 months to 3 years. *Merrill-Palmer Quarterly, 30*, 111-130.

38. Baxter, L. R., Fairbanks, L., & Gerner, R. H. (1984). Clinical utilization of the dexamethasone suppression test in an inpatient setting. *Journal of Clinical Psychiatry, 45*, 393-396.

39. Berenson, C. K., & Grosser, B. I. (1984). Total artificial heart implantation. *Archives of General Psychiatry, 41*, 910-916.

40. Berman, J. J., Meyer, J., & Coats, G. (1984). Effects of program characteristics on treatment outcome: An interrupted time-series analysis. *Journal of Studies on Alcohol, 45*, 405-410.

41. Bernard, J. L., & Bernard, M. L. (1984). The abusive male seeking treatment: Jekyll and Hyde. *Family Relations, 33*, 543-547.

42. Biaggio, M. K., Godwin, W. H., & Baldwin, H. K. (1984). Response to interpersonal request styles by dependent and overcontrolled hostility personalities. *Journal of Clinical Psychology, 40*, 833-836.

43. Blackwell, B., Galbraith, J. R., & Dahl, D. S. (1984). Chronic pain management. *Hospital and Community Psychiatry, 35*, 999-1008.

44. Bliss, E. L. (1984). A symptom profile of patients with multiple personalities, including MMPI results. *The Journal of Nervous and Mental Disease, 172*, 197-202.

45. Carey, M. P., Faulstich, M. E., & Delatte, J. G., Jr. (1984). Age-group classification of male alcoholics as a function of MMPI experimental scales. *Psychological Reports, 55*, 697-698.

46. Carter, J. E., & Wilkinson, L. (1984). A latent trait analysis of the MMPI. *Multivariate Behavioral Research, 19*, 385-407.

47. Ceniti, J., & Malamuth, N. M. (1984). Effects of repeated exposure to sexually violent or nonviolent stimuli on sexual arousal to rape and nonrape depictions. *Behaviour Research and Therapy, 22*, 535-548.

48. Cernovsky, Z. (1984). Es scale level and correlates of MMPI elevation: Alcohol abuse vs. MMPI scores in treated alcoholics. *Journal of Clinical Psychology, 40*, 1502-1509.

49. Chodzko-Zajko, W. J., & Ismail, A. H. (1984). MMPI interscale relationships in middle-aged male Ss before and after an 8-month fitness program. *Journal of Clinical Psychology, 40*, 163-169.

50. Cole, K. D., & Zarit, S. H. (1984). Psychological deficits in depressed medical patients. *The Journal of Nervous and Mental Disease, 172*, 150-155.

51. Colligan, R. C., Osborne, D., & Offord, K. P. (1984). Normalized transformations and the interpretation of MMPI T scores: A reply to Hsu. *Journal of Consulting and Clinical Psychology, 52*, 824-826.

52. Colligan, R. C., Osborne, D., Swenson, W. M., & Offord, K. P. (1984). The MMPI: Development of contemporary norms. *Journal of Clinical Psychology, 40*, 100-107.

53. Coolidge, F. L., & Bracken, D. D. (1984). The loss of teeth in dreams: An empirical investigation. *Psychological Reports, 54*, 931-935.

54. Correll, R. E. (1984). Relationship of anxiety and depression to age and sex in an acute psychiatric population. *Psychological Reports, 55*, 979-986.

55. Costa, A., Bonaccorsi, M., & Scrimali, T. (1984). Biofeedback and control of anxiety preceding athletic competition. *International Journal of Sport Psychology, 15*, 98-109.

56. Craig, R. J. (1984). A comparison of MMPI profiles of heroin addicts based on multiple methods of classification. *Journal of Personality Assessment, 48*, 115-120.

57. Craig, R. J. (1984). MMPI substance abuse scales on drug addicts with and without concurrent alcoholism. *Journal of Personality Assessment, 48*, 495-499.

58. Craig, R. J. (1984). Personality dimensions related to premature termination from an inpatient drug abuse treatment program. *Journal of Clinical Psychology, 40*, 351-355.

59. Danton, W. G., May, J. R., & Lynn, E. J. (1984). Psychological and physiological effects of relaxation and nitrous oxide training. *Psychological Reports, 55*, 311-322.

60. deMendonca, M., Elliott, L., Goldstein, M., McNeill, J., Rodriguez, R., & Zelkind, I. (1984). An MMPI-based behavior descriptor/personality trait list. *Journal of Personality Assessment, 48*, 483-485.

61. Dhanens, T. P., & Jarrett, S. R. (1984). MMPI Pain Assessment Index: Concurrent and predictive validity. *Clinical Neuropsychology, 6*, 46-48.

62. Dietrich, D. R. (1984). Psychological health of young adults who experienced early parent death: MMPI trends. *Journal of Clinical Psychology, 40*, 901-908.

63. Dodrill, C. B., & Clemmons, D. (1984). Use of neuropsychological tests to identify high school students with epilepsy who later demonstrate inadequate performances in life. *Journal of Consulting and Clinical Psychology, 52*, 520-527.

64. Dworkin, R. H., & Saczynski, K. (1984). Individual differences in hedonic capacity. *Journal of Personality Assessment, 48*, 620-626.

65. Edell, W. S. (1984). The Borderline Syndrome Index: Clinical validity and utility. *The Journal of Nervous and Mental Disease, 172*, 254-263.

66. Elkins, G. R., Barrett, E. T., & Texas A & M University College of Medicine. (1984). The MMPI in evaluation of functional versus organic low back pain. *Journal of Personality Assessment, 48,* 259-264.

67. Evans, R. G. (1984). MMPI dependency scale norms for alcoholics and psychiatric inpatients. *Journal of Clinical Psychology, 40,* 345-346.

68. Evans, R. M., & Picano, J. J. (1984). Relationships between irrational beliefs and self-report indices of psychopathology. *Psychological Reports, 55,* 545-546.

69. Forgac, G. E., & Cassel, C. A. (1984). Chronicity of criminal behavior and psychopathology in male exhibitionists. *Journal of Clinical Psychology, 40,* 827-832.

70. Fuller, C. G., & Malony, H. N., Jr. (1984). A comparison of English and Spanish (Núnez) translations of the MMPI. *Journal of Personality Assessment, 48,* 130-131.

71. Gadzella, B. M., & Williamson, J. D. (1984). Differences between men and women on selected Tennessee Self Concept scales. *Psychological Reports, 55,* 939-942.

72. Gallucci, N. T. (1984). Prediction of dissumulation on the MMPI in a clinical field setting. *Journal of Consulting and Clinical Psychology, 52,* 917-918.

73. Gayton, W. F., Golden, J., Clark, R., & Bailey, C. (1984). Comparative validity of the MMPI-168 and the MMPI-168E in discrimination of neurotic and psychotic MMPI profiles. *Psychological Reports, 55,* 874.

74. Gellen, M. I., Hoffman, R. A., Jones, M., & Stone, M. (1984). Abused and nonabused women: MMPI profile differences. *The Personnel and Guidance Journal, 62,* 601-604.

75. Gilbertson, A. D. (1984). Perceptual differentiation among drug addicts: Correlations with intelligence and MMPI scores. *Journal of Clinical Psychology, 40,* 334-339.

76. Gotlib, I. H. (1984). Depression and general psychopathology in university students. *Journal of Abnormal Psychology, 93,* 19-30.

77. Greenblatt, R. L., Mozdzierz, G. J., & Murphy, T. J. (1984). Content and response-style in the construct validation of self-report inventories: A canonical analysis. *Journal of Clinical Psychology, 40,* 1414-1420.

78. Groff, M. G., & Hubble, L. M. (1984). A comparison of father-daughter and stepfather-stepdaughter incest. *Criminal Justice and Behavior, 11,* 461-475.

79. Hart, R. R. (1984). Chronic pain: Replicated multivariate clustering of personality profiles. *Journal of Clinical Psychology, 40,* 129-133.

80. Havel, Z., & Deimling, G. (1984). Social resources and mental health: An empirical refinement. *Journal of Gerontology, 39,* 747-752.

81. Heilbrun, A. B., Jr. (1984). Cognitive defenses and life stress: An information-processing analysis. *Psychological Reports, 54,* 3-17.

82. Heilbrun, A. B., Jr. (1984). The Adaptive-Style Theory of schizophrenic development: Current research with schizophrenics. *Genetic Psychology Monographs, 110,* 229-255.

83. Hembling, D. W. (1984). Rapid conversion of adolescent MMPI raw scores to T scores using the HP-67 programmable calculator. *Journal of Clinical Psychology, 40,* 149-156.

84. Hendler, N. (1984). Depression caused by chronic pain. *Journal of Clinical Psychiatry, 45* (3,2), 30-36.

85. Hermann, B. P., & Melyn, M. (1984). Effects of carbamazepine on interictal psychopathology in TLE with ictal fear. *Journal of Clinical Psychiatry, 45,* 169-171.

86. Hermann, B. P., Whitman, S., & Dikmen, S. (1984). Validity of the Goldberg rules of classifying psychopathology in epilepsy. *Psychological Reports, 54,* 747-751.

87. Hirschfeld, R. M. A., Klerman, G. L., Clayton, P. J., Keller, M. B., & Andreasen, N. C. (1984). Personality and gender-related differences in depression. *Journal of Affective Disorders, 7,* 211-221.

88. Holcomb, W. R., & Adams, N. A. (1984). Are separate black and white MMPI norms needed?: An IQ-controlled comparison of accused murderers. *Journal of Clinical Psychology, 40,* 189-192.

89. Holliman, N. B., & Montross, J. (1984). The effects of depression upon responses to the California Psychological Inventory. *Journal of Clinical Psychology, 40,* 1373-1378.

90. Holmes, C. B., Dungan, D. S., & Medlin, W. J. (1984). Reassessment of inferring personality traits from Bender-Gestalt Drawing Styles. *Journal of Clinical Psychology, 40,* 1241-1243.

91. Holmes, C. B., Wurtz, P. J., Waln, R. F., Dungan, D. S., & Joseph, C. A. (1984). Relationship between the Luscher Color Test and the MMPI. *Journal of Clinical Psychology, 40,* 126-128.

92. Holmes, G. R., Sabalis, R. F., Chestnut, E., & Khoury, L. (1984). Parent MMPI critical item and clinical scale changes in the 1970's. *Journal of Clinical Psychology, 40,* 1194-1198.

93. Howard, R. C. (1984). The clinical EEG and personality in mentally abnormal offenders. *Psychological Medicine, 14,* 569-580.

94. Howard, R. C., Fenton, G. W., & Fenwick, P. B. C. (1984). The contingent negative variation, personality and antisocial behaviour. *British Journal of Psychiatry, 144,* 463-474.

95. Hsu, L. M. (1984). MMPI *T* scores: Linear versus normalized. *Journal of Consulting and Clinical Psychology, 52,* 821-823.

96. Huesmann, L. R., Eron, L. D., Lefkowitz, M. M., & Walder, L. O. (1984). Stability of aggression over time and generations. *Developmental Psychology, 20,* 1120-1134.

97. Huesmann, L. R., Lagerspetz, K., & Eron, L. D. (1984). Intervening variables in the TV violence-aggression relation: Evidence from two countries. *Developmental Psychology, 20,* 746-775.

98. Hurt, S. W., Hyler, S. E., Frances, A., Clarkin, J. F., & Brent, R. (1984). Assessing borderline personality disorder with self-report, clinical interview, or semistructured interview. *American Journal of Psychiatry, 141,* 1228-1231.

99. Johnson, J. H., Null, C., Butcher, J. N., & Johnson, K. N. (1984). Replicated item level factor analysis of the full MMPI. *Journal of Personality and Social Psychology, 47,* 105-114.

100. Keane, T. M., Malloy, P. F., & Fairbank, J. A. (1984). Empirical development of an MMPI subscale for the assessment of combat-related Posttraumatic Stress Disorder. *Journal of Consulting and Clinical Psychology, 52,* 888-891.

101. King, M. G., Stanley, G. V., & Campbell, I. M. (1984). A statistical audit of the clinical utility of the 168 version of MMPI. *Journal of Clinical Psychology, 40,* 740-743.

102. Klein, H. E., Bender, W., Mayr, H., Niederschweiberer, A., & Schmauss, M. (1984). The DST and its relationship to psychiatric diagnosis, symptoms, and treatment outcome. *British Journal of Psychiatry, 145,* 591-599.

103. Klein, S., & Cross, H. J. (1984). Correlates of the MMPI L_B Scale in a college population. *Journal of Clinical Psychology, 40,* 185-189.

104. Kodman, F. (1984). Identifying the CBK personality. *Social Behavior and Personality, 12,* 139-142.

105. Kodman, F. (1984). Some personality traits of superior university students. *Social Behavior and Personality, 12,* 135-138.

106. Kohlberg, L., Ricks, D., & Snarey, J. (1984). Childhood development as a predictor of adaptation in adulthood. *Genetic Psychology Monographs, 110,* 91-172.

107. Lanyon, R. I. (1984). Personality assessment. *Annual Review of Psychology, 35,* 667-701.

108. Lanyon, R. I., & Lutz, R. W. (1984). MMPI discrimination of defensive and nondefensive felony sex offenders. *Journal of Consulting and Clinical Psychology, 52,* 841-843.

109. Lefebvre, R. C. (1984). A psychological consultation program for learning-disabled adults. *Journal of College Student Personnel, 25,* 361-362.

110. Levin, D., Bertelson, A. D., & Lacks, P. (1984). MMPI differences among mild and severe insomniacs and good sleepers. *Journal of Personality Assessment, 48,* 126-129.

111. Lichtman, H. (1984). Parental communication of holocaust experiences and personality characteristics among second-generation survivors. *Journal of Clinical Psychology, 40,* 914-924.

112. Lothstein, L. M., & Roback, H. (1984). Black female transsexuals and schizophrenia: A serendipitous finding? *Archives of Sexual Behavior, 13,* 371-386.

113. Lueger, R. J., & Hoover, L. (1984). Use of the MMPI to identify subtypes of delinquent adolescents. *Journal of Clinical Psychology, 40,* 1493-1495.

114. McCreary, C., & Colman, A. (1984). Medication usage, emotional disturbance, and pain behavior in chronic low back pain patients. *Journal of Clinical Psychology, 40,* 15-19.

115. McCreary, C., & Turner, J. (1984). Locus of control, repression-sensitization, and psychological disorder in chronic pain patients. *Journal of Clinical Psychology, 40,* 897-901.

116. McKnight, D. L., Nelson, R. O., Hayes, S. C., & Jarrett, R. B. (1984). Importance of treating individually assessed response classes in the amelioration of depression. *Behavior Therapy, 15,* 315-335.

117. Megargee, E. I. (1984). A new classification system for criminal offenders, VI: Difference among the type on The Adjective Checklist. *Criminal Justice and Behavior, 11,* 349-376.

118. Meier, S. T. (1984). The construct validity of burnout. *Journal of Occupational Psychology, 57,* 211-219.

119. Merluzzi, T. V., Burgio, K. L., & Glass, C. R. (1984). Cognition and psychopathology: An analysis of social introversion and self-statements. *Journal of Consulting and Clinical Psychology, 52,* 1102-1103.

120. Merritt, R. D., & Balogh, D. W. (1984). The use of backward masking paradigm to assess information-processing deficits among schizotypics. *The Journal of Nervous and Mental Disease, 172,* 216-224.

121. Moreland, K. L. (1984). A cost-effective means of improving the statistical validity of an MMPI short form. *Journal of Clinical Psychology, 40,* 134-136.

122. Moreland, K. L. (1984). Comparative validity of the MMPI and two short forms: Psychiatric ratings. *Journal of Personality Assessment, 48,* 265-270.

123. Moreland, K. L. (1984). Conversion equations for two modified MMPI short forms. *Journal of Clinical Psychology, 40,* 738-739.

124. Murphy, G. E., Simons, A. D., Wetzel, R. D., & Lustman, P. J. (1984). Cognitive therapy and pharmacotherapy. *Archives of General Psychiatry, 41,* 33-41.

125. Murphy, W. D., Krisak, J., Stalgaitis, S., & Anderson, K. (1984). The use of penile tumescence measures with incarcerated rapists: Further validity issues. *Archives of Sexual Behavior, 13*, 545-554.

126. Novack, T. A., Daniel, M. S., & Long, C. J. (1984). Factors related to emotional adjustment following head injury. *Clinical Neuropsychology, 6*, 139-142.

127. Ollendick, D. G. (1984). Scores on three MMPI alcohol scales of parents who receive child custody. *Psychological Reports, 55*, 337-338.

128. Ollendick, D. G., & Otto, B. J. (1984). MMPI characteristics of parents referred for child-custody studies. *The Journal of Psychology, 117*, 227-232.

129. Patrick, J. (1984). Characteristics of DSM-III borderline MMPI profiles. *Journal of Clinical Psychology, 40*, 655-658.

130. Paulhus, D. L. (1984). Two-component models of socially desirable responding. *Journal of Personality and Social Psychology, 46*, 598-609.

131. Pfost, K. S., Kunce, J. T., & Stevens, M. J. (1984). The relationship of MacAndrew Alcoholism Scale scores to MMPI profile type and degree of evaluation. *Journal of Clinical Psychology, 40*, 852-855.

132. Pollack, D. R., & Grainey, T. F. (1984). A comparison of MMPI profiles for state and private disability insurance applicants. *Journal of Personality Assessment, 48*, 121-125.

133. Posey, C. D., & Hess, A. K. (1984). The fakability of subtle and obvious measures of aggression by male prisoners. *Journal of Personality Assessment, 48*, 137-144.

134. Query, W. T., & Megran, J. (1984). Influence of depression and alcoholism on learning, recall, and recognition. *Journal of Clinical Psychology, 40*, 1097-1100.

135. Robyak, J. E., Donham, G. W., Roy, R., & Ludenia, K. (1984). Differential patterns of alcohol abuse among normal, neurotic, psychotic, and characterological types. *Journal of Personality Assessment, 48*, 132-136.

136. Ross, M. W., Goss, A. N., & Kalucy, R. S. (1984). The relationship of panic-fear to anxiety and tension in jaw wiring for obesity. *British Journal of Medical Psychology, 57*, 67-69.

137. Roy, R. E. (1984). The Goldberg Neurotic-Psychotic rule and MMPI 2-7-8 patients. *Journal of Personality Assessment, 48*, 398-402.

138. Saccuzzo, D. P., Braff, D. L., Sprock, J., & Sudik, N. (1984). The schizophrenia spectrum: A study of the relationship among the Rorschach, MMPI, and visual backward masking. *Journal of Clinical Psychology, 40*, 1288-1294.

139. Selby, M. J. (1984). Assessment of violence potential using measures of anger, hostility, and social desirability. *Journal of Personality Assessment, 48*, 531-544.

140. Shusman, E. J., Inwald, R. E., & Landa, B. (1984). Correction officer job performance as predicted by the IPI and MMPI: A validation and cross-validation study. *Criminal Justice and Behavior, 11*, 309-329.

141. Siegel, C., Waldo, M., Mizer, G., Adler, L. E., & Freedman, R. (1984). Deficits in sensory gating in schizophrenic patients and their relatives. *Archives of General Psychiatry, 41*, 607-612.

142. Siegel, R. K. (1984). Hostage hallucinations: Visual imagery induced by isolation and life-threatening stress. *The Journal of Nervous and Mental Disease, 172*, 264-272.

143. Sines, J. O. (1984). Relations between the Family Environment Scale (FES) and the MMPI. *Journal of Personality Assessment, 48*, 6-10.

144. Skoog, D. K., Andersen, A. E., & Laufer, W. S. (1984). Personality and treatment effectiveness in anorexia nervosa. *Journal of Clinical Psychology, 40*, 955-961.

145. Smith, P. E., Burleigh, R. L., Sewell, W. R., & Krisak, J. (1984). Correlation between the Minnesota Multiphasic Personality Inventory profiles of emotionally disturbed adolescents and their mothers. *Adolescence, 19*, 31-38.

146. Snowden, L. R., & Campbell, D. R. (1984). Reasons for drinking among problem drinker-drivers: Client and counselor reports during treatment. *Addictive Behaviors, 9*, 391-394.

147. Snowden, L. R., Campbell, D. R., & Nelson, L. S. (1984). The MMPI and problem drinking: Statistical controls and multifactor criteria. *Journal of Personality Assessment, 48*, 271-278.

148. Snyter, C. M., & Graham, J. R. (1984). The utility of subtle and obvious MMPI subscales based on scale-specific ratings. *Journal of Clinical Psychology, 40*, 981-985.

149. Solomon, G. S., & Ray, J. B. (1984). Irrational beliefs of shoplifters. *Journal of Clinical Psychology, 40*, 1075-1077.

150. Sothmann, M. S., Ismail, A. H., & Chodepko-Zajiko, W. (1984). Influence of catecholamine activity on the hierarchical relationships among physical fitness condition and selected personality characteristics. *Journal of Clinical Psychology, 40*, 1308-1317.

151. Swain-Holcomb, B., & Thorne, B. M. (1984). A comparison of male and female alcoholics with an MMPI classification system. *Journal of Personality Assessment, 48*, 392-397.

152. Takefman, J., & Brender, W. (1984). An analysis of the effectiveness of two components in the treatment of erectile dysfunction. *Archives of Sexual Behavior, 13*, 321-340.

153. Tan, T., Kales, J. D., Kales, A., Soldatos, C. R., & Bixler, E. O. (1984). Biopsychobehavioral correlates of insomnia, IV: Diagnosis based on DSM-III. *American Journal of Psychiatry, 141*, 357-362.

154. Templer, D. I., King, F. L., Brooner, R. F., & Corgiat, M. (1984). Assessment of body elimination attitude. *Journal of Clinical Psychology, 40*, 754-759.

155. Turner, J. A., & Romano, J. M. (1984). Self-report screening measures for depression in chronic pain patients. *Journal of Clinical Psychology, 40*, 909-913.

156. Valliant, P. M., Asu, M. E., Cooper, D., & Mammola, D. (1984). Profile of dangerous and non-dangerous offenders referred for pre-trial psychiatric assessment. *Psychological Reports, 54*, 411-418.

157. Walters, G. D. (1984). Empirically derived characteristics of psychiatric inpatients with DSM-III diagnoses of schizophreniform disorder. *Journal of Abnormal Psychology, 93*, 71-79.

158. Walters, G. D. (1984). Identifying schizophrenia by means of Scale 8 Sc of the MMPI. *Journal of Personality Assessment, 48*, 390-391.

159. Walters, G. D., Greene, R. L., & Jeffrey, T. B. (1984). Discriminating between alcoholic and nonalcoholic blacks and whites on the MMPI. *Journal of Personality Assessment, 48*, 486-488.

160. Ward, L. C., & Meyers, R. (1984). The utility of an improved readability short form of the MMPI with elderly male patients. *Journal of Clinical Psychology, 40*, 997-1000.

161. Watson, C. G., Klett, W. G., Walters, C., & Vassar, P. (1984). Suicide and the MMPI: A cross-validation of predictors. *Journal of Clinical Psychology, 40*, 115-119.

162. Wong, M. R. (1984). MMPI Scale Five: Its meaning, or lack thereof. *Journal of Personality Assessment, 48*, 279-284.

163. Woodward, J. A., Bisbee, C. T., & Bennett, J. E. (1984). MMPI correlates of relatively localized brain damage. *Journal of Clinical Psychology, 40*, 961-969.

164. Wooten, A. J. (1984). Efficiency of local MMPI norms in the detection of psychopathology. *Journal of Personality Assessment, 48*, 285-290.

165. Wormith, J. S., & Goldstone, C. S. (1984). The clinical and statistical prediction of recidivism. *Criminal Justice and Behavior, 11*, 3-34.

166. Ahmed, S. M. S., Valliant, P. M., & Swindle, D. (1985). Psychometric properties of Coopersmith Self-Esteem Inventory. *Perceptual and Motor Skills, 61*, 1235-1241.

167. Anderson, W., & Bauer, B. (1985). Clients with MMPI high D-PD: Therapy implications. *Journal of Clinical Psychology, 41*, 181-188.

168. Antoni, M., Tischer, P., Levine, J., Green, C., & Millon, T. (1985). Refining personality assessments by combining MCMI high point profiles and MMPI codes, Part I: MMPI code 28/82. *Journal of Personality Assessment, 49*, 392-398.

169. Antoni, M., Tischer, P., Levine, J., Green, C., & Millon, T. (1985). Refining personality assessments by combining MCMI high point profiles and MCMI codes. Part III: MMPI code 24/42. *Journal of Personality Assessment, 49*, 508-515.

170. Archer, R. P., Ball, J. D., & Hunter, J. A. (1985). MMPI characteristics of borderline psychopathology in adolescent inpatients. *Journal of Personality Assessment, 49*, 47-55.

171. Archer, R. P., Gordon, R. A., Zillmer, E. A., & McClure, S. (1985). Characteristics and correlates of MMPI change within an adult psychiatric inpatient setting. *Journal of Clinical Psychology, 41*, 739-746.

172. Baker, E. L., White, R. F., & Murawski, B. J. (1985). Clinical evaluation of neurobehavioral effects of occupational exposure to organic solvents and lead. *International Journal of Mental Health, 14* (3), 135-158.

173. Bartsch, T. W., & Hoffman, J. J. (1985). A cluster analysis of Millon Clinical Multiaxial Inventory (MCMI) profiles: More about a taxonomy of alcoholic subtypes. *Journal of Clinical Psychology, 41*, 707-713.

174. Bayer, B. M., Bonta, J. L., & Motiuk, L. L. (1985). The PD subscales: An empirical evaluation. *Journal of Clinical Psychology, 41*, 780-788.

175. Beatrice, J. (1985). A psychological comparison of heterosexuals, transvestites, preoperative transsexuals, and postoperative transsexuals. *The Journal of Nervous and Mental Disease, 173*, 358-365.

176. Berg, A. J., Ingersoll, G. M., & Terry, R. L. (1985). Canonical analysis of the MMPI and WAIS in a psychiatric sample. *Psychological Reports, 56*, 115-122.

177. Bernstein, I. H., & Garbin, C. P. (1985). A comparison of alternative proposed subscale structures for MMPI Scale 2. *Multivariate Behavioral Research, 20*, 223-235.

178. Bernstein, I. H., & Garbin, C. P. (1985). A simple set of salient weights for the major dimensions of MMPI scale variation. *Educational and Psychological Measurement, 45*, 771-787.

179. Beutler, L. E., Storm, A., Kirkish, P., Scogin, F., & Gaines, J. A. (1985). Parameters in the prediction of police officer performance. *Professional Psychology: Research and Practice, 16*, 324-335.

180. Birtchnell, J. (1985). The relationship between scores on Ryle's Marital Patterns Test and independent ratings of marital quality. *British Journal of Psychiatry, 146*, 638-644.

181. Bonta, J., & Motiuk, L. L. (1985). Utilization of an interview-based classification instrument: A study of correctional halfway houses. *Criminal Justice and Behavior, 12*, 333-352.

182. Brown, H. J. D., & Gutsch, K. U. (1985). Cognitions associated with a delay of gratification task: A study with psychopaths and normal prisoners. *Criminal Justice and Behavior, 12,* 453-462.

183. Burke, H. R., & Mayer, S. (1985). The MMPI and the Post-traumatic Stress Syndrome in Vietnam era veterans. *Journal of Clinical Psychology, 41,* 152-156.

184. Bushman, B. J. (1985). Standard errors of measurement for the various MMPI subscales. *Psychological Reports, 56,* 444-446.

185. Catchlove, R. F. H., Cohen, K. R., Braha, R. E. D., & Demers-Desrosiers, L. A. (1985). Incidence and implications of alexithymia in chronic pain patients. *The Journal of Nervous and Mental Disease, 173,* 246-248.

186. Cernovsky, Z. Z. (1985). MacAndrew Alcoholism Scale and repression: Detection of false negatives. *Psychological Reports, 57,* 191-194.

187. Cernovsky, Z. Z. (1985). Relationship of the masculinity-femininity scale of the MMPI to intellectual functioning. *Psychological Reports, 57,* 435-438.

188. Chambless, D. L., Caputo, G. C., Jasin, S. E., Gracely, E. J., & Williams, C. (1985). The Mobility Inventory for Agoraphobia. *Behaviour Research and Therapy, 23,* 35-44.

189. Christensen, L., Krietsch, K., White, B., & Stagner, B. (1985). Impact of a dietary change on emotional distress. *Journal of Abnormal Psychology, 94,* 565-579.

190. Colligan, R. C., Osborne, D., Swenson, W. M., & Offord, K. P. (1985). Using the 1983 norms for the MMPI: Code type frequencies in four clinical samples. *Journal of Clinical Psychology, 41,* 629-633.

191. Correll, R. E. (1985). Relationship of anxiety and depression scores to WAIS performance of psychiatric patients. *Psychological Reports, 57,* 295-301.

192. Costa, P. T., Jr., Zonderman, A. B., McCrae, R. R., & Williams, R. B., Jr. (1985). Content and comprehensiveness in the MMPI: An item factor analysis in a normal adult sample. *Journal of Personality and Social Psychology, 48,* 925-933.

193. Culkin, J., & Perrotto, R. S. (1985). Assertiveness factors and depression in a sample of college women. *Psychological Reports, 57,* 1015-1020.

194. Daniel, M., Haban, G. F., Hutcherson, W. L., Bolter, J., & Long, C. (1985). Neuropsychological and emotional consequences of accidental, high-voltage electrical shock. *Clinical Neuropsychology, 7,* 102-106.

195. Dobson, K. S. (1985). An analysis of anxiety and depression scales. *Journal of Personality Assessment, 49,* 522-527.

196. Dodrill, C. B. (1985). Incidence and doubtful significance of nonstandard orientations in reproduction of the key from the Aphasia Screening Test. *Perceptual and Motor Skills, 60,* 411-415.

197. Dralle, P. W., & Baybrook, R. M. (1985). Screening of police applicants: A replication of a 5-item MMPI research index validity study. *Psychological Reports, 57,* 1031-1034.

198. Dubinsky, S., Gamble, D. J., & Rogers, M. L. (1985). A literature review of subtle-obvious items on the MMPI. *Journal of Personality Assessment, 49,* 62-68.

199. Duckro, P. N., Margolis, R. B., & Tait, R. C. (1985). Psychological assessment in chronic pain. *Journal of Clinical Psychology, 41,* 499-504.

200. Ehrenworth, N. V., & Archer, R. P. (1985). A comparison of clinical accuracy ratings of interpretive approaches for adolescent MMPI responses. *Journal of Personality Assessment, 49,* 413-421.

201. Fairbank, J. A., McCaffrey, R. J., & Keane, T. M. (1985). Psychometric detection of fabricated symptoms of postraumatic stress disorder. *American Journal of Psychiatry, 142,* 501-503.

202. Falk, J. R., Halmi, K. A., & Tryon, W. W. (1985). Activity measures in anorexia nervosa. *Archives of General Psychiatry, 42,* 811-814.

203. Faulstich, M. E., Carey, M. P., Delatte, J. G., Jr., & Delatte, G. M. (1985). Age differences on alcoholic MMPI scales: A discriminant analysis approach. *Journal of Clinical Psychology, 41,* 433-439.

204. Fjordbak, T. (1985). Clinical correlates of high Lie Scale elevations among forensic patients. *Journal of Personality Assessment, 49,* 252-255.

205. Fowler, R. D. (1985). Landmarks in computer-assisted psychological assessment. *Journal of Consulting and Clinical Psychology, 53,* 748-759.

206. Gallucci, N. T. (1985). Influence of dissimulation on indexes of response consistency for the MMPI. *Psychological Reports, 57,* 1013-1014.

207. Gass, C. S., Russell, E. W. (1985). MMPI correlates of verbal-intellectual deficits in patients with left hemisphere lesions. *Journal of Clinical Psychology, 41,* 664-670.

208. Gentry, T. A., Wakefield, J. A., Jr., & Friedman, A. F. (1985). MMPI Scales for measuring Eysenck's personality factors. *Journal of Personality Assessment, 49,* 146-149.

209. Goldstein, G., Shelly, C., Mascia, G. V., & Tarter, R. E. (1985). Relationships between neuropsychological and psychopathological dimensions in male alcoholics. *Addictive Behaviors, 10,* 365-372.

210. Graham, J. R., & McCord, G. (1985). Interpretation of moderately elevated MMPI scores for normal subjects. *Journal of Personality Assessment, 49,* 477-484.

211. Guy, E., Platt, J. J., Zwerling, I., & Bullock, S. (1985). Mental health status of prisoners in an urban jail. *Criminal Justice and Behavior, 12,* 29-53.

212. Hagan, L. D., & Schauer, A. H. (1985). Assessment of depression in alcoholics: Comment on Hesselbrock et al. *Journal of Consulting and Clinical Psychology, 53,* 64-66.

213. Hare, R. D. (1985). Comparison of procedures for the assessment of psychopathy. *Journal of Consulting and Clinical Psychology, 53,* 7-16.

214. Heilbrun, A. B., Jr., & Heilbrun, M. R. (1985). Psychopathy and dangerousness: Comparison, integration and extension of two psychopathic typologies. *British Journal of Clinical Psychology, 24,* 181-195.

215. Heilbrun, A. B., Jr., & Pepe, V. (1985). Awareness of cognitive defences and stress management. *British Journal of Medical Psychology, 58,* 9-17.

216. Heppner, P. P., & Anderson, W. P. (1985). The relationship between problem-solving self-appraisal and psychological adjustment. *Cognitive Therapy and Research, 9,* 415-427.

217. Hesselbrock, M. N., Tennen, H., Hesselbrock, V., Workman-Daniels, K., & Meyer, R. E. (1985). Assessment of depression in alcoholics: Further considerations—reply to Hagan and Schauer. *Journal of Consulting and Clinical Psychology, 53,* 67-69.

218. Hoffmann, T., Dana, R. H., & Bolton, B. (1985). Measured acculturation and MMPI-168 performance of Native American adults. *Journal of Cross-Cultural Psychology, 16,* 243-256.

219. Holcomb, W. R., & Adams, N. A. (1985). Personality mechanisms of alcohol-related violence. *Journal of Clinical Psychology, 41,* 714-722.

220. Holcomb, W. R., Adams, N. A., & Ponder, H. M. (1985). The development and cross-validation of an MMPI typology of murderers. *Journal of Personality Assessment, 49,* 240-244.

221. Hovanitz, C. A., Gynther, M. D., & Green, S. B. (1985). Discriminant validity of subtle and obvious items: The MMPI Pa and Ma scales. *Journal of Clinical Psychology, 41,* 42-44.

222. Hsu, L. M. (1985). Efficiency of local versus standard MMPI norms: A comment. *Journal of Personality Assessment, 49,* 178-180.

223. Hurt, S. W., Clarkin, J. F., Frances, A., Abrams, R., & Hunt, H. (1985). Discriminant validity of the MMPI for borderline personality disorder. *Journal of Personality Assessment, 49,* 56-61.

224. Ingram, J. C., Marchioni, P., Hill, G., Caraveo-Ramos, E., & McNeil, B. (1985). Recidivism, perceived problem-solving abilities, MMPI characteristics, and violence: A study of black and white incarcerated male adult offenders. *Journal of Clinical Psychology, 41,* 425-432.

225. Jain, S. (1985). Autokinesis and personality. *Perceptual and Motor Skills, 60,* 963-970.

226. Josiassen, R. C., Shagass, C., Roemer, R. A., & Straumanis, J. J. (1985). Attention-related effects on somatosensory evoked potentials in college students at high risk for psychopathology. *Journal of Abnormal Psychology, 94,* 507-518.

227. Karol, R. L. (1985). MMPI omitted items: A method for quickly determining individual scale impact. *Journal of Counseling and Clinical Psychology, 53,* 134-135.

228. Keane, T. M., Scott, W. O., Chavoya, G. A., Lamparski, D. M., & Fairbank, J. A. (1985). Social support in Vietnam veterans with posttraumatic stress disorder: A comparative analysis. *Journal of Consulting and Clinical Psychology, 53,* 95-102.

229. Kline, R. B., & Snyder, D. K. (1985). Replicated MMPI subtypes for alcoholic men and women: Relationship to self-reported drinking behaviors. *Journal of Consulting and Clinical Psychology, 53,* 70-79.

230. Krueger, G. P., Armstrong, R. N., & Cisco, R. R. (1985). Aviator performance in week-long extended flight operations in a helicopter simulator. *Behavior Research Methods, Instruments, & Computers, 17,* 68-74.

231. Layne, C. C., Heitkemper, T., Roehrig, R. A., & Speer, T. K. (1985). Motivational deficit in depressed cancer patients. *Journal of Clinical Psychology, 41,* 139-144.

232. Leon, G. R., Lucas, A. R., Colligan, R. C., Ferdinande, R. J., & Kamp, J. (1985). Sexual, body-image, and personality attitudes in anorexia nervosa. *Journal of Abnormal Child Psychology, 13,* 245-257.

233. Levine, J., Tischer, P., Antoni, M., Green, C., & Millon, T. (1985). Refining personality assessments by combining MCMI high point profiles and MMPI codes. Part II: MMPI code 27/72. *Journal of Personality Assessment, 49,* 501-507.

234. Lifton, P. D. (1985). Individual differences in moral development: The relation of sex, gender, and personality to morality. *Journal of Personality, 53,* 306-334.

235. Lorr, M., Nerviano, V. J., & Myhill, J. (1985). Structural analysis of the MMPI and the 16 PF. *Psychological Reports, 57,* 587-590.

236. Makarec, K., & Persinger, M. A. (1985). Temporal lobe signs: Electroencephalographic validity and enhanced scores in special populations. *Perceptual and Motor Skills, 60,* 831-842.

237. McAnulty, D. P., Rappaport, N. B., & McAnulty, R. D. (1985). A a posteriori investigation of standard MMPI validity scales. *Psychological Reports, 57,* 95-98.

238. McCreary, C. (1985). Empirically derived MMPI profile clusters and characteristics of low back pain patients. *Journal of Consulting and Clinical Psychology, 53,* 558-560.

239. McGiboney, G., & Carter, C. (1985). Readability of MMPI short forms. *Psychological Reports, 57,* 1237-1238.

240. McSweeny, A. J., Grant, I., Heaton, R. K., Prigatano, G. P., & Adams, K. M. (1985). Relationship of neuropsychological status to everyday functioning in healthy and chronically ill persons. *Journal of Clinical and Experimental Neuropsychology, 7,* 281-291.

241. Megargee, E. I., & Carbonell, J. L. (1985). Predicting prison adjustment with MMPI correctional scales. *Journal of Consulting and Clinical Psychology, 53,* 874-883.

242. Meyer, B. E., & Hokanson, J. E. (1985). Situational influences on social behaviors of depression-prone individuals. *Journal of Clinical Psychology, 41,* 29-35.

243. Miller, H. R., & Streiner, D. L. (1985). The Harris-Lingoes subscales: Fact or fiction? *Journal of Clinical Psychology, 41,* 45-51.

244. Montgomery, G. T., & Orozco, S. (1985). Mexican Americans' performance on the MMPI as a function of level of acculturation. *Journal of Clinical Psychology, 41,* 203-212.

245. Moore, J. E., & Chaney, E. F. (1985). Outpatient group treatment of chronic pain: Effects of spouse involvement. *Journal of Consulting and Clinical Psychology, 53,* 326-334.

246. Moreland, K. L. (1985). Validation of computer-based test interpretations: Problems and prospects. *Journal of Consulting and Clinical Psychology, 53,* 816-825.

247. Morey, L. C., Waugh, M. H., & Blashfield, R. K. (1985). MMPI scales for DSM-III personality disorders: Their deviation and correlates. *Journal of Personality Assessment, 49,* 245- 251.

248. Morokoff, P. J. (1985). Effects of sex guilt, repression, sexual 'arousability,' and sexual experience on female sexual arousal during erotica and fantasy. *Journal of Personality and Social Psychology, 49,* 177-187.

249. Munjack, D. J., Rebal, R., Shaner, R., Staples, F., Braun, R., & Leonard, M. (1985). Imipramine versus propranolol for the treatment of panic attacks: A pilot study. *Comprehensive Psychiatry, 26,* 80-89.

250. Nakano, K., Saccuzzo, D. P. (1985). Schizotaxia, information processing and the MMPI 2-7-8 code type. *British Journal of Clinical Psychology, 24,* 217-218.

251. Nelson, L. D., & Marks, P. A. (1985). Empirical correlates of infrequently occurring MMPI code types. *Journal of Clinical Psychology, 41,* 477-482.

252. Newman, J. P., Widom, C. S., & Nathan, S. (1985). Passive avoidance in syndromes of disinhibition: Psychopathy and extraversion. *Journal of Personality and Social Psychology, 48,* 1316-1327.

253. Nichols, D. S., & Jones, R. E., Jr. (1985). Identifying schizoid-taxon membership with the Golden-Meehl MMPI items. *Journal of Abnormal Psychology, 94,* 191-194.

254. Norman, W. H., Keitner, G. I., & Miller, I. W. (1985). MMPI, personality dysfunction and the Dexamethasone Suppression Test in major depression. *Journal of Affective Disorders, 9,* 97-101.

255. Nuechterlein, K. H., & Dawson, M. E. (1985). Increased critical stimulus duration: Vulnerability or episode indicator? *Schizophrenia Bulletin, 11,* 344-346.

256. Piran, N., Kennedy, S., Garfinkel, P. E., & Owens, M. (1985). Affective disturbance in eating disorders. *The Journal of Nervous and Mental Disease, 173,* 395-400.

257. Pitts, W. M., Gustin, Q. L., Mitchell, C., & Snyder, S. (1985). MMPI critical item characteristics of the DSM-III Borderline Personality Disorder. *The Journal of Nervous and Mental Disease, 173,* 628-631.

258. Pogue-Geile, M. F., & Rose, R. J. (1985). Developmental genetic studies of adult personality. *Developmental Psychology, 21,* 547-557.

259. Posey, C. D., & Hess, A. K. (1985). Aggressive response sets and subtle-obvious MMPI scale distinctions in male offenders. *Journal of Personality Assessment, 49,* 235-239.

260. Post, R. D., Alford, C. E., Baker, N. J., Franks, R. D., House, R. M., Jackson, A. M., & Petersen, J. L. (1985). Comparison of self-reports and clinicians' ratings of unipolar major depression. *Psychological Reports, 57,* 479-483.

261. Post, R. D., Petersen, J. L., Jackson, A. M., House, R. M., Franks, R. D., Baker, N. J., & Alford, C. (1985). The Mezzich MMPI regression formula revisited. *Journal of Personality Assessment, 49,* 258-259.

262. Rehm, L. P., & O'Hara, M. W. (1985). Item characteristics of the Hamilton Rating Scale for Depression. *Journal of Psychiatric Research, 19,* 31-41.

263. Reich, J., Steward, M. S., Tupin, J. P., & Rosenblatt, R. M. (1985). Prediction of response to treatment in chronic pain patients. *Journal of Clinical Psychiatry, 46,* 425-427.

264. Repto, G. R., & Cooper, R. (1985). The diagnosis of personality disorder: A comparison of MMPI profile, Millon Inventory, and clinical judgment in a workers' compensation population. *Journal of Clinical Psychology, 41,* 867-881.

265. Rohsenow, D. J., Smith, R. E., & Johnson, S. (1985). Stress management training as a prevention program for heavy social drinkers: Cognitions, affect, drinking, and individual differences. *Addictive Behaviors, 10,* 45-54.

266. Roland, B. C., Zelhart, P. F., Cochran, S. W., & Funderburk, V. W. (1985). MMPI correlates of clinical women who report early sexual abuse. *Journal of Clinical Psychology, 41,* 763-766.

267. Schaefer, A., Brown, J., Watson, C. G., Plemel, D., DeMotts, J., Howard, M. T., Petrik, N., Balleweg, B. J., & Anderson, D. (1985). Comparison of the validities of the Beck, Zung, and MMPI Depression scale. *Journal of Consulting and Clinical Psychology, 53,* 415-418.

268. Schlank, M. B. (1985). A brief inquiry into deviant answers to selected Grayson items of the Minnesota Multiphasic Personality Inventory. *Journal of Personality Assessment, 49,* 256-257.

269. Senatore, V., Matson, J. L., & Kazdin, A. E. (1985). An inventory to assess psychopathology of mentally retarded adults. *American Journal of Mental Deficiency, 89,* 459-466.

270. Shorkey, C. T., & Armendariz, J. (1985). Personal worth, self-esteem, anomia, hostility and irrational thinking of abusing mothers: A multivariate approach. *Journal of Clinical Psychology, 41,* 414-421.

271. Silberman, E. K., Post, R. M., Nurnberger, J., Theodore, W., & Boulenger, J. (1985). Transient sensory, cognitive and affective phenomena in affective illness: A comparison with complex partial epilepsy. *British Journal of Psychiatry, 146,* 81-89.

272. Sinnett, E. R. (1985). What art thou MacAndrew scale? Confusion and errata in high places. *Psychological Reports, 56,* 384-386.

273. Skenazy, J. A., & Bigler, E. D. (1985). Psychological adjustment and neuropsychological performance in diabetic patients. *Journal of Clinical Psychology, 41,* 391-396.

274. Sklar, A. D., & Harris, R. F. (1985). Effects of parent loss: Interaction with family size and sibling order. *American Journal of Psychiatry, 42,* 708-714.

275. Smith, T. W., Follick, M. J., & Ahern, D. K. (1985). Life-events and psychological disturbance in chronic low back pain. *British Journal of Clinical Psychology, 24,* 207-208.

276. Snyder, D. K., Kline, R. B., & Podany, E. C. (1985). Comparison of external correlates of MMPI substance abuse scales across sex and race. *Journal of Consulting and Clinical Psychology, 53,* 520-525.

277. Solomon, R. (1985). Creativity and normal narcissism. *The Journal of Creative Behavior, 19,* 47-55.

278. Thieret, N. L., & Anderson, D. H. (1985). Cluster analytic methods applied to the Minnesota Multiphasic Personality Inventory in a psychiatric population. *Journal of Clinical Psychology, 41,* 197-202.

279. Torki, M. A. (1985). Achievement motivation in college women in an Arab culture. *Psychological Reports, 56,* 267-271.

280. Townes, B. D., Martin, D. C., Nelson, D., Prosser, R., Pepping, M., Maxwell, J., Peel, J., & Preston, M. (1985). Neurobehavioral approach to classification of psychiatric patients using a competency model. *Journal of Consulting and Clinical Psychology, 53,* 33-42.

281. Traub, G. S., & Bohn, M. J., Jr. (1985). Note on the reliability of the MMPI with Spanish-speaking inmates in the federal prison system. *Psychological Reports, 56,* 373-374.

282. Walters, G. D. (1985). Scale 4 (Pd) of the MMPI and the diagnosis antisocial personality. *Journal of Personality Assessment, 49,* 474-476.

283. Williamson, D. A., Kelley, M. L., Davis, C. J., Ruggiero, L., & Blouin, D. C. (1985). Psychopathology of eating disorders: A controlled comparison of bulimic, obese, and normal subjects. *Journal of Consulting and Clinical Psychology, 53,* 161-166.

284. Winters, K. C., Newmark, C. S., Lumry, A. E., Leach, K., & Weintraub, S. (1985). MMPI codetypes characteristic of DSM-III schizophrenics, depressives, and bipolars. *Journal of Clinical Psychology. 41,* 382-386.

285. Wishiewski, N. M., Glenwick, D. S., & Graham, J. R. (1985). MacAndrew Scale and sociodemographic correlates of adolescent alcohol and drug use. *Addictive Behaviors, 10,* 55-67.

286. Zetény, T., & Lukács, D. (1985). Masculinity-femininity and perceptual style on the Circles Test. *Perceptual and Motor Skills, 60,* 361-362.

287. Adam, K., Tomeny, M., & Oswald, I. (1986). Physiological and psychological differences between good and poor sleepers. *Journal of Psychiatric Research, 20,* 301-316.

288. Adams, K. M., Heilbronn, M., & Blumer, D. P. (1986). A multimethod evaluation of the MMPI in a chronic pain patient sample. *Journal of Clinical Psychology, 42,* 878-886.

289. Antoni, M., Levine, J., Tischer, P., Green, C., & Millon, T. (1986). Refining personality assessments by combining MCMI high-point profiles and MMPI Codes, Part IV: MMPI 89/98. *Journal of Personality Assessment, 50,* 65-72.

290. Archer, R. P., Stolberg, A. L., Gordon, R. A., & Goldman, W. R. (1986). Parent and child MMPI responses: Characteristics among families with adolescents in inpatient and outpatient settings. *Journal of Abnormal Child Psychology, 14,* 181-190.

291. Arsuaga, E. N., Higgins, J. C., & Sifre, P. A. (1986). Separation of brain-damaged from psychiatric patients with the combined use of an

ability and a personality test: A validation study with a Puerto Rican population. *Journal of Clinical Psychology, 42*, 328-331.

292. Atkinson, J. H., Ingram, R. E., Kremer, E. F., & Saccuzzo, D. P. (1986). MMPI subgroups and affective disorder in chronic pain patients. *The Journal of Nervous and Mental Disease, 174*, 408-413.

293. Barley, W. D., Sabo, T. W., & Greene, R. L. (1986). Minnesota Multiphasic Personality Inventory normal Kt and other unelevated profiles. *Journal of Consulting and Clinical Psychology, 54*, 502-506.

294. Barton, K., & Dreger, R. M. (1986). Prediction of marital roles from normal and pathological dimensions of personality: 16 PF and MMPI. *Psychological Reports, 59*, 459-468.

295. Batzel, L. W., & Dodrill, C. B. (1986). Emotional and intellectual correlates of unsuccessful suicide attempts in people with epilepsy. *Journal of Clinical Psychology, 42*, 699-702.

296. Birenbaum, M. (1986). Effect of dissimulation motivation and anxiety on response pattern appropriateness measures. *Applied Psychological Measurement, 10*, 167-174.

297. Bohn, M. J., Jr., & Traub, G. S. (1986). Alienation of monolingual Hispanics in a federal correctional institution. *Psychological Reports, 59*, 560-562.

298. Bond, J. A. (1986). Inconsistent responding to repeated MMPI items: Is its major cause really carelessness? *Journal of Personality Assessment, 50*, 50-64.

299. Burke, D. M., & Hall, M. (1986). Personality characteristics of volunteers in a companion for children program. *Psychological Reports, 59*, 819-825.

300. Carbotte, R. M., Denburg, S. D., & Denburg, J. A. (1986). Prevalence of cognitive impairment in Systemic Lupus Erythematosus. *The Journal of Nervous and Mental Disease, 174*, 357-364.

301. Carey, R. J., Jr., Baer, L., Jenike, M. A., Minichiello, W. E., Schwartz, C., & Regan, N. J. (1986). MMPI correlates of obsessive-compulsive disorder. *The Journal of Clinical Psychiatry, 47*, 371-372.

302. Cernovsky, Z. (1986). Attitudes of male alcoholics towards equal freedom for women: Personality correlates. *Social Behavior and Personality, 14*, 85-87.

303. Cernovsky, Z. (1986). Color preference and MMPI scores of alcohol and drug addicts. *Journal of Clinical Psychology, 42*, 663-668.

304. Cernovsky, Z. (1986). Masculinity-femininity scale of the MMPI and intellectual functioning of female addicts. *Journal of Clinical Psychology, 42*, 310-314.

305. Cernovsky, Z. Z. (1986). MMPI and nightmare reports in women addicted to alcohol and other drugs. *Perceptual and Motor Skills, 62*, 717-718.

306. Cernovsky, Z. Z. (1986). Psychopathology and women's attitudes towards equal rights: An MMPI study. *Social Behavior and Personality, 14*, 167-169.

307. Conte, H. R. (1986). Multivariate assessment of sexual dysfunction. *Journal of Consulting and Clinical Psychology, 54*, 149-157.

308. Coons, P. M. (1986). Treatment progress in 20 patients with multiple personality disorder. *The Journal of Nervous and Mental Disease, 174*, 715-721.

309. Coons, P. M., & Milstein, V. (1986). Psychosexual disturbances in multiple personality: Characteristics, etiology, and treatment. *Journal of Clinical Psychiatry, 47*, 106-110.

310. Coons, P. M., & Sterne, A. L. (1986). Initial and follow-up psychological testing on a group of patients with multiple personality disorder. *Psychological Reports, 58*, 43-49.

311. Costa, P. T., Busch, C. M., Zonderman, A. B., & McCrae, R. R. (1986). Correlations of MMPI factor scales with measures of the five factor model of personality. *Journal of Personality Assessment, 50*, 640-650.

312. Culver, L. C., Kunen, S., & Zinkgraf, S. A. (1986). Patterns of recall in schizophrenics and normal subjects. *The Journal of Nervous and Mental Disease, 174*, 620-623.

313. Dana, R. H. (1986). Personality assessment and Native Americans. *Journal of Personality Assessment, 50*, 480-500.

314. Dolce, J. J., Crocker, M. F., & Doleys, D. M. (1986). Prediction of outcome among chronic pain patients. *Behaviour Research and Therapy, 24*, 313-319.

315. Dykens, E. M., & Gerrard, M. (1986). Psychological profiles of purging bulimics, repeat dieters, and controls. *Journal of Consulting and Clinical Psychology, 54*, 283-288.

316. Elmore, P. B., & Vasu, E. S. (1986). A model of statistics achievement using spatial ability, feminist attitudes and mathematics-related variables as predictors. *Educationa and Psychological Measurement, 46*, 215-222.

317. Evans, R. W., Ruff, R. M., Braff, D. L., & Cox, D. R. (1986). On the consistency of the MMPI in borderline personality disorder. *Perceptual and Motor Skills, 62*, 579-585.

318. Faravelli, C., Ambonetti, A., Pallanti, S., & Pazzagli, A. (1986). Depressive relapses and incomplete recovery from index episode. *American Journal of Psychiatry, 143*, 888-891.

319. Fitting, M., Rabins, P., Lucas, M. J., & Eastham, J. (1986). Caregivers for dementia patients: A comparison of husbands and wives. *The Gerontologist, 26*, 248-252.

320. Fitzgerald, M., & Schoenfeld, L. S. (1986). MMPI: Scoring changes. *Psychological Reports, 58*, 957-958.

321. Gallucci, N. T. (1986). General and specific objections to the MMPI. *Educational and Psychological Measurement, 46*, 985-988.

322. Gass, C. S., & Russell, E. W. (1986). Differential impact of brain damage and depression on memory test performance. *Journal of Consulting and Clinical Psychology, 54*, 261-263.

323. Gass, C. S., & Russell, E. W. (1986). Minnesota Multiphasic Personality Inventory correlates of lateralized cerebral lesions and aphasic deficits. *Journal of Consulting and Clinical Psychology, 54*, 359-363.

324. Geron, E., Furst, D., & Rotstein, P. (1986). Personality of athletes participating in various sports. *International Journal of Sport Psychology, 17*, 120-135.

325. Gerson, M. J. (1986). The prospect of parenthood for women and men. *Psychology of Women Quarterly, 10*, 49-62.

326. Godfrey, H. P. D., & Knight, R. G. (1986). Reading difficulty levels of eleven self-report depression rating scales. *Behavioral Assessment, 8*, 187-190.

327. Graham, J. R., Smith, R. L., & Schwartz, G. F. (1986). Stability of MMPI configurations for psychiatric inpatients. *Journal of Consulting and Clinical Psychology, 54*, 375-380.

328. Grossman, H. Y., Mostofsky, D. I., & Harrison, R. H. (1986). Psychological aspects of Gilles de la Tourette Syndrome. *Journal of Clinical Psychology, 42*, 228-235.

329. Hall, G. C. N., Maiuro, R. D., Vitaliano, P. P., & Proctor, W. C. (1986). The utility of the MMPI with men who have sexually assaulted children. *Journal of Consulting and Clinical Psychology, 54*, 493-496.

330. Hart, R. R., McNeill, J. N., Lutz, D. J., & Adkins, T. G. (1986). Clinical comparability of the standard MMPI and the MMPI-168. *Professional Psychology: Research and Practice, 17*, 269-272.

331. Heiby, E. M. (1986). Social versus self-control skills deficits in four cases of depression. *Behavior Therapy, 17*, 158-169.

332. Heinicke, C. M., Diskin, S. D., Ramsey-Klee, D. M., & Oates, D. S. (1986). Pre- and postbirth antecedents of 2-year-old attention, capacity for relationships, and verbal expressiveness. *Developmental Psychology, 22*, 777-787.

333. Heisel, J. S., Locke, S. E., Kraus, L. J., & Williams, R. M. (1986). Natural killer cell activity and MMPI scores of a cohort of college students. *American Journal of Psychiatry, 143*, 1382-1386.

334. Hirschfeld, R. M. A., Klerman, G. L., Andreasen, N. C., Clayton, P. J., & Keller, M. B. (1986). Psycho-social predictors of chronicity in depressed patients. *British Journal of Psychiatry, 148*, 648-654.

335. Hogg, J. A., & Deffenbacher, J. L. (1986). Irrational beliefs, depression, and anger among college students. *Journal of College Student Personnel, 27*, 349-353.

336. Holcomb, W. R. (1986). Stress inoculation therapy with anxiety and stress disorders of acute psychiatric inpatients. *Journal of Clinical Psychology, 42*, 864-872.

337. Holmes, G. R., Sabalis, R. F., Chestnut, E., Sheppard, B., & Smith, M. E. (1986). Comparison of MMPI clinical scale and critical item changes of adult outpatients and parents of child psychiatry outpatients during the 1970s. *Journal of Clinical Psychology, 42*, 913-916.

338. Hovanitz, C. A. (1986). Life event stress and coping style as contributors to psychopathology. *Journal of Clinical Psychology, 42*, 34-41.

339. Hovanitz, C. A., & Jordan-Brown, L. (1986). The validity of MMPI subtle and obvious items in psychiatric patients. *Journal of Clinical Psychology, 42*, 100-108.

340. Hsu, L. M. (1986). Implications of differences in elevations of K-corrected and non-K-corrected MMPI T scores. *Journal of Consulting and Clinical Psychology, 54*, 552-557.

341. Hsu, L. M., & Betman, J. A. (1986). Minnesota Multiphasic Personality Inventory T score conversion tables, 1957-1983. *Journal of Consulting and Clinical Psychology, 54*, 497-501.

342. Hyer, L., Harkey, B., & Harrison, W. R. (1986). MMPI scales and subscales: Patterns of older, middle-aged, and younger inpatients. *Journal of Clinical Psychology, 42*, 596-601.

343. Hyer, L., O'Leary, W. C., Saucer, R. T., Blount, J., Harrison, W. R., & Boudewyns, P. A. (1986). Inpatient diagnosis of Posttraumatic Stress Disorder. *Journal of Consulting and Clinical Psychology, 54*, 698-702.

344. Keltner, N. L., McIntyre, C. W., & Gee, R. (1986). Birth order effects in second-generation alcoholics. *Journal of Studies on Alcohol, 47*, 495-497.

345. King, M. G., & Campbell, I. M. (1986). A manifest anxiety scale from the MMPI-168. *Journal of Clinical Psychology, 42*, 748-751.

346. Klonoff, P. S., Costa, L. D., & Snow, W. G. (1986). Predictors and indicators of quality of life in patients with closed-head injury. *Journal of Clinical and Experimental Neuropsychology, 8*, 469-485.

347. Kunzendorf, R. G., & Butler, W. (1986). Personality and immunity: Depressive tendencies versus manic and schizophrenic tendencies. *Psychological Reports, 59*, 622.

348. Levenson, H., Olkin, R., Herzoff, N., & Delancy, M. (1986). MMPI evaluation of erectile dysfunction: Failure of organic vs. psychogenic decision rules. *Journal of Clinical Psychology, 42*, 752-754.

349. Levor, R. M., Cohen, M. J., Naliboff, B. D., McArthur, D., & Heuser, G. (1986). Psychosocial precursors and correlates of migraine headache. *Journal of Consulting and Clinical Psychology*, 54, 347-353.

350. Lindgren, S. D., Harper, D. C., Richman, L. C., & Stehbens, J. A. (1986). 'Mental imbalance' and the prediction of recurrent delinquent behavior. *Journal of Clinical Psychology*, 42, 821-825.

351. Livesay, J. R. (1986). Clinical utility of Wechsler's deterioration index in screening for behavioral impairment. *Perceptual and Motor Skills*, 63, 619-626.

352. McClure, R. F., & Mears, F. G. (1986). Videogame playing and psychopathology. *Psychological Reports*, 59, 59-62.

353. McCrae, R. R. (1986). Well-being scales do not measure social desirability. *Journal of Gerontology*, 41, 390-392.

354. McCranie, E. W., & Kahan, J. (1986). Personality and multiple divorce. A prospective study. *The Journal of Nervous and Mental Disease*, 174, 161-164.

355. McGovern, F. J., & Nevid, J. S. (1986). Evaluation apprehension on psychological inventories in a prison-based setting. *Journal of Consulting and Clinical Psychology*, 54, 576-578.

356. McGrath, R. E., & O'Malley, W. B. (1986). The assessment of denial and physical complaints: The validity of the Hy scale and associated MMPI signs. *Journal of Clinical Psychology*, 42, 754-760.

357. McGrath, R. E., O'Malley, W. B., & Dura, J. R. (1986). Alternative scoring system of repeated items on the MMPI: Caveat emptor. *Journal of Personality Assessment*, 50, 182-185.

358. Mlott, S. R., Rust, P. F., Assey, J. L., & Doscher, M. S. (1986). Performance of male nursing students on the MMPI, fantasy, and self-esteem inventories. *Psychological Reports*, 58, 371-374.

359. Schill, T., Wang, S., & Thomsen, D. (1986). MMPI F, 4, and 9 as measure of aggression in a college sample. *Psychological Reports*, 59, 949-950.

360. Murstein, B. I., & Azar, J. A. (1986). The relationship of exchange-orientation to friendship intensity, roommate compatibility, anxiety, and friendship. *Small Group Behavior*, 17, 3-17.

361. Needham, W. E., Ehmer, M. N., Marchesseault, L., & DeL'Aune, W. R. (1986). Effectiveness of the Mini-Mult in detecting MMPI pathology in the blind. *Journal of Clinical Psychology*, 42, 887-890.

362. Nelson, W. M., III, & Gumlak, J. (1986). MMPI personality differences in various populations of the unwed mother. *Journal of Clinical Psychology*, 42, 114-119.

363. Nezu, A. M. (1986). Efficacy of a social problem-solving therapy approach for unipolar depression. *Journal of Consulting and Clinical Psychology*, 54, 196-202.

364. Nobo, J., & Evans, R. G. (1986). The WAIS-R Picture Arrangement and Comprehension Subtests as measures of social behavior characteristics. *Journal of Personality Assessment*, 50, 90-92.

365. Nocita, A., & Stiles, W. B. (1986). Client introversion and counseling session impact. *Journal of Counseling Psychology*, 33, 235-241.

366. Osborne, D., Colligan, C., & Offord, K. P. (1986). Normative tables for the F-K index of the MMPI based on a contemporary normal sample. *Journal of Clinical Psychology*, 42, 593-595.

367. Peniston, E. G., Hughes, R. B., & Kulkosky, P. J. (1986). EMG biofeedback-assisted relaxation training in the treatment of reactive depression in chronic pain patients. *The Psychological Record*, 36, 471-482.

368. Polyson, J., Peterson, R., & Marshall, C. (1986). MMPI and Rorschach: Three decades of research. *Professional Psychology: Research and Practice*, 17 (5), 476-478.

369. Post, R. D., Clopton, J. R., Keefer, G., Rosenberg, D., Blyth, L. S., & Stein, M. (1986). MMPI predictors of mania among psychiatric inpatients. *Journal of Personality Assessment*, 50, 248-256.

370. Post, R. D., Franks, R. D., Alford, C., Petersen, J. L., House, R. M., Jackson, A. M., & Baker, N. J. (1986). MMPI results associated with abnormal responses to the DST and TRH tests. *Psychological Reports*, 59, 35-38.

371. Preng, K. W., & Clopton, J. R. (1986). Application of the MacAndrew Alcoholism Scale to alcoholics with psychiatric diagnoses. *Journal of Personality Assessment*, 50, 113-122.

372. Prokop, C. K. (1986). Hysteria scale elevations in low back pain patients: A risk factor for misdiagnosis? *Journal of Consulting and Clinical Psychology*, 54, 558-562.

373. Query, W. T., Megran, J., & McDonald, G. (1986). Applying posttraumatic stress disorder MMPI subscale to World War II POW veterans. *Journal of Clinical Psychology*, 42, 315-317.

374. Rehm, L. P. (1986). A self-management therapy program for depression. *International Journal of Mental Health*, 13 (3/4), 34-53.

375. Robyak, J. E., Goodyear, R. K., Prange, M. E., & Donham, G. (1986). Effects of gender, supervision, and presenting problems on practicum students' preference for interpersonal power bases. *Journal of Counseling Psychology*, 33, 159-163.

376. Ross, S. M., Gottfredson, D. K., Christensen, P., & Weaver, R. (1986). Cognitive self-statements in depression: Findings across clinical populations. *Cognitive Therapy and Research*, 10, 159-166.

377. Rude, S. S. (1986). Relative benefits of assertion or cognitive self-control treatment for depression as a function of proficiency in each domain. *Journal of Consulting and Clinical Psychology*, 54, 390-394.

378. Russell, G. K. G., Peace, K. A., & Mellsop, G. W. (1986). The reliability of a micro-computer administration of the MMPI. *Journal of Clinical Psychology*, 42, 120-122.

379. Schulman, R. G., Kinder, B. N., Powers, P. S., Prange, M., & Gleghorn, A. (1986). The development of a scale to measure cognitive distortions in bulimia. *Journal of Personality Assessment*, 50, 630-639.

380. Scott, R. L., & Baroffio, J. R. (1986). An MMPI analysis of similarities and differences in three classifications of eating disorders: Anorexia nervosa, bulimia, and morbid obesity. *Journal of Clinical Psychology*, 42, 708-713.

381. Scott, R. L., & Stone, D. A. (1986). MMPI measures of psychological disturbance in adolescent and adult victims of father-daughter incest. *Journal of Clinical Psychology*, 42, 251-259.

382. Scott, R. L., & Stone, D. A. (1986). MMPI profile constellations in incest families. *Journal of Consulting and Clinical Psychology*, 54, 364-368.

383. Scott, R., & Thoner, G. (1986). Ego deficits in anorexia nervosa patients and incest victims: An MMPI comparative analysis. *Psychological Reports*, 58, 839-846.

384. Shadish, W. R., Jr. (1986). The validity of a measure of intimate behavior. *Small Group Behavior*, 17, 113-120.

385. Smith, T. W., Aberger, E. W., Follick, M. J., & Ahern, D. K. (1986). Cognitive distortion and psychological distress in chronic low back pain. *Journal of Consulting and Clinical Psychology*, 54, 573-575.

386. Smith, T. W., Follick, M. J., Ahern, D. K., & Adams, A. (1986). Cognitive distortion and disability in chronic low back pain. *Cognitive Therapy and Research*, 10, 201-210.

387. Snowden, L. R., & Campbell, D. (1986). Validity of an MMPI classification of problem drinker-drivers. *Journal of Studies on Alcohol*, 47, 344-347.

388. Snowden, L. R., Nelson, L. S., & Campbell, D. (1986). An empirical typology of problem drinkers from the Michigan Alcoholism Screening Test. *Addictive Behaviors*, 11, 37-48.

389. Streiner, D. L., & Miller, H. R. (1986). Can a good short form of the MMPI ever be developed? *Journal of Clinical Psychology*, 42, 109-113.

390. Tamkin, A. S., Hyer, L. A., & Carson, M. F. (1986). Comparison among four measures of depression in younger and older alcoholics. *Psychological Reports*, 59, 287-293.

391. Thurstin, A. H., Alfano, A. M., & Sherer, M. (1986). Pretreatment MMPI profiles of A.A. members and nonmembers. *Journal of Studies on Alcohol*, 47, 468-471.

392. Tosi, D. J., Eshbaugh, D. M., Raines, M. G., & Murphy, M. A. (1986). Typological analysis of MMPI personality patterns of drug dependent men. *The Journal of General Psychology*, 113, 329-339.

393. Trice, A. D. (1986). Informed consent: VI. Informing subjects of legal liabilities may decrease volunteering rates and item responses. *Perceptual and Motor Skills*, 63, 766.

394. Trulson, M. E. (1986). Martial arts training: A novel "cure" for juvenile delinquency. *Human Relations*, 39, 1131-1140.

395. Turner, J. A., Herron, L., & Weiner, P. (1986). Utility of the MMPI Pain Assessment Index in predicting outcome after lumbar surgery. *Journal of Clinical Psychology*, 42, 764-769.

396. Ursano, R. J., Wheatley, R., Sledge, W., Rahe, A., & Carlson, E. (1986). Coping and recovery styles in the Vietnam era prisoner of war. *The Journal of Nervous and Mental Disease*, 174, 707-714.

397. Valliant, P. M., & Leith, B. (1986). Impact of relaxation training and cognitive therapy on coronary patients post surgery. *Psychological Reports*, 59, 1271-1278.

398. Walters, G. D. (1986). Screening for psychopathology in groups of black and white prison inmates by means of the MMPI. *Journal of Personality Assessment*, 50, 257-264.

399. Ward, L. C. (1986). Estimation of MMPI scale scores from an improved comprehensibility short form. *Journal of Clinical Psychology*, 42, 602-604.

400. Ward, L. C. (1986). MMPI item subtlety research: Current issues and directions. *Journal of Personality Assessment*, 50, 73-79.

401. Werner, P. D., & Pervin, L. A. (1986). The content of personality inventory items. *Journal of Personality and Social Psychology*, 51, 622-628.

402. Westendorp, F., Brink, K. L., Roberson, M. K., & Ortiz, I. E. (1986). Variables which differentiate placement of adolescents into juvenile justice or mental health systems. *Adolescence*, 21, 23-37.

403. Widiger, T. A., Sanderson, C., & Warner, L. (1986). The MMPI, prototypal typology, and borderline personality disorder. *Journal of Personality Assessment*, 50, 540-553.

404. Wierzbicki, M. (1986). Similarity of monozygotic and dizygotic twins in level and lability of subclinically depressed mood. *Journal of Clinical Psychology*, 42, 577-585.

405. Worthington, D. L., & Schlottmann, R. S. (1986). The predictive validity of subtle and obvious empirically derived psychological test items under faking conditions. *Journal of Personality Assessment*, 50, 171-181.

406. Wright, K. N. (1986). An exploratory study of transactional classification. *Journal of Research and Delinquency*, 23, 326-348.

407. Ackerman, P. T., McGrew, M. J., & Dykman, R. A. (1987). A profile of male and female applicants for a special college program for learning-disabled students. *Journal of Clinical Psychology*, 43, 67-78.

408. Acklin, M. W., & Bernat, E. (1987). Depression, alexithymia, and pain prone disorder: A Rorschach study. *Journal of Personality Assessment, 51*, 462-479.

409. Ahembaugh, R. V. (1987). Contrast of the Gender-Identity Scale with Bem's Sex-Role measures and the MF Scale of the MMPI. *Perceptual and Motor Skills, 64* (1), 136-138.

410. Antoni, M., Levine, J., Tischer, P., Green, C., & Millon, T. (1987). Refining personality assessments by combining MCMI high-point profiles and MMPI Codes, Part V: MMPI Code 78/87. *Journal of Personality Assessment, 51*, 375-387.

411. Archer, R. P., Gordon, R. A., & Kirchner, F. H. (1987). MMPI response-set characteristics among adolescents. *Journal of Personality Assessment, 51*, 506-516.

412. Ayers, M. R., Abrams, D. I., Newell, T. G., & Friederich, F. (1987). Performance of individuals with AIDS on the Luria-Nebraska Neuropsychological Battery. *The International Journal of Clinical Neuropsychology, 9*, 101-105.

413. Baird, A. D., Brown, G. G., Adams, K. M., Shatz, M. W., McSweeny, A. J., Ausman, J. I., & Diaz, F. G. (1987). Neuropsychological deficits and real-world dysfunction in cerebral revascularization candidates. *Journal of Clinical and Experimental Neuropsychology, 9*, 407-422.

414. Bernstein, I. H., Teng, G., Grannemann, B. D., & Garbin, C. P. (1987). Invariance in the MMPI's component structure. *Journal of Personality Assessment, 51*, 522-531.

415. Biaggio, M. K., & Godwin, W. H. (1987). Relation of depression to anger and hostility constructs. *Psychological Reports, 61*, 87-90.

416. Bieliauskas, L. A., & Glantz, R. H. (1987). Use of the Mini-Mult D scale in patients with Parkinson's disease. *Journal of Consulting and Clinical Psychology, 55*, 437-438.

417. Brannon, S. E., & Nelson, R. O. (1987). Contingency management treatment of outpatient unipolar depression: A comparison of reinforcement and extinction. *Journal of Consulting and Clinical Psychology, 55*, 117-119.

418. Cannon, D. S., Bell, W. E., Andrews, R. H., & Finkelstein, A. S. (1987). Correspondence between MMPI PTSD measures and clinical diagnosis. *Journal of Personality Assessment, 51*, 517-521.

419. Cernovsky, Z. Z. (1987). A failure to detect MAC's false negatives in female alcohol and drug addicts. *Addictive Behaviors, 12*, 367-369.

420. Cohen, L., & Merchelbach, H. (1987). Dichotic listening in relation to dysphoria, sensation seeking, and other personality characteristics. *Perceptual and Motor Skills, 64*, 471-477.

421. Colligan, R. C., & Offord, K. P. (1987). The MacAndrew Alcoholism Scale applied to a contemporary normative sample. *Journal of Clinical Psychology, 43*, 291-293.

422. Daehnert, C., & Carter, J. D. (1987). The prediction of success in a clinical psychology graduate program. *Educational and Psychological Measurement, 47* (4), 1113-1125.

423. Davies, A., Lochar, D., & Gdowski, C. (1987). Assessment of PIC and MMPI scales in adolescent psychosis: A caution. *Adolescence, 22*, 571-578.

424. deMan, A. F., Balkou, S., & Iglesias, R. I. (1987). A French-Canadian adaptation of the Scale for Suicide Ideation. *Canadian Journal of Behavioural Science, 19*, 50-55.

425. Denburg, S. D., Carbotte, R. M., & Denburg, J. A. (1987). Cognitive impairment in systemic lupus erythematosus: A neuropsychological study of individual and group deficits. *Journal of Clinical and Experimental Neuropsychology, 9*, 323-339.

426. Eckert, E. D., Halmi, K. A., Marchi, P., & Cohen, J. (1987). Comparison of bulimic and non-bulimic anorexia nervosa patients during treatment. *Psychological Medicine, 17*, 891-898.

427. Edell, W. S. (1987). Relationship of borderline syndrome disorders to early schizophrenia on the MMPI. *Journal of Clinical Psychology, 43*, 163-176.

428. Edwards, L. K., & Clark, C. L. (1987). A comparison of the first factor of the MMPI and the first factor of the EMMPI: The PSD factor. *Educational and Psychological Measurement, 47* (4), 1165-1173.

429. Erickson, W. D., Luxenberg, M. G., Walbek, N. H., & Seely, R. K. (1987). Frequency of MMPI two-point code types among sex offenders. *Journal of Consulting and Clinical Psychology, 55*, 566-570.

430. Farrell, A. D., Camplair, P. S., & McCullough, L. (1987). Identification of target complaints by computer interview: Evaluation of the computerized assessment system for psychotherapy evaluation and research. *Journal of Consulting and Clinical Psychology, 55*, 691-700.

431. Fekken, G. C., & Holden, R. R. (1987). Assessing the person reliability of an individual MMPI protocol. *Journal of Personality Assessment, 51*, 123-132.

432. Friedrich, W. N., Smith, C. K., Harrison, S. D., Colwell, K. A., Davis, A. K., & Fefer, A. (1987). MMPI study of identical twins: Cancer patients and bone marrow donors. *Psychological Reports, 61*, 127-130.

433. Gallucci, N. T. (1987). The influence of elevated F scales on the validity of adolescent MMPI profiles. *Journal of Personality Assessment, 51*, 133-139.

434. Gerbing, D. W., Ahadi, S. A., & Pattar, J. H. (1987). Toward a conceptualization of impulsivity: Components across the behavioral and self-report domains. *Multivariate Behavioral Research, 22*, 357-379.

435. Greene, R. L. (1987). Ethnicity and MMPI performance: A review. *Journal of Consulting and Clinical Psychology, 55*, 497-512.

436. Hartmann, E., Russ, D., Oldfield, M., Sivan, I., & Cooper, S. (1987). Who has nightmares?: The personality of the lifelong nightmare sufferer. *Archives of General Psychiatry, 44*, 49-56.

437. Helson, R., & Wink, P. (1987). Two conceptions of maturity examined in the findings of a longitudinal study. *Journal of Personality and Social Psychology, 53*, 531-541.

438. Huesmann, L. R., Eron, L. D., & Yarmel, P. W. (1987). Intellectual functioning and aggression. *Journal of Personality and Social Psychology, 52*, 232-240.

439. Hyper, L., Fallon, J. H., Jr., Harrison, W. R., & Boudewyns, P. A. (1987). MMPI overreporting by Vietnam combat veterans. *Journal of Clinical Psychology, 43*, 79-83.

440. Jaffe, L. T., & Archer, R. P. (1987). The prediction of drug use among college students from MMPI, MCMI, and Sensation Seeking Scales. *Journal of Personality Assessment, 51*, 243-253.

441. Jonsdottir-Baldursson, T., & Horvath, P. (1987). Borderline personality-disordered alcoholics in Iceland: Descriptions on demographic, clinical, and MMPI variables. *Journal of Consulting and Clinical Psychology, 55*, 738-741.

442. Keane, T. M., Wolfe, J., & Taylor, K. L. (1987). Post-traumatic stress disorder: Evidence for diagnostic validity and methods of psychological assessment. *Journal of Clinical Psychology, 43*, 32-43.

443. Klonoff, H., Fleetham, J., Taylor, D. R., & Clark, C. (1987). Treatment outcome of obstructive sleep apnea: Physiological and neuropsychological concomitants. *The Journal of Nervous and Mental Disease, 175*, 208-212.

444. Kolotkin, R. L., Revis, E. S., Kirkley, B. G., & Janick, L. (1987). Binge eating in obesity: Associated MMPI characteristics. *Journal of Consulting and Clinical Psychology, 55*, 872-876.

445. Koppleman, M. C. S., Parry, B. L., Hamilton, J. A., Alagna, S. W., & Loriaux, D. L. (1987). Effect of bromocriptine on affect and libido in hyperprolactinemia. *The American Journal of Psychiatry, 144*, 1037-1041.

446. Lachar, D., Kline, R. B, Gdowski, C. L. (1987). Respondent psychopathology and interpretive accuracy of the Personality Inventory for Children: The evaluation of a "most reasonable" assumption. *Journal of Personality Assessment, 51*, 165-177.

447. Lang, R. A., Langevin, R., Checkley, K. L., & Pugh, G. (1987). General exhibitionism: Courtship disorder or narcissism? *Canadian Journal of Behavioural Science, 19*, 216-232.

448. Loehlin, J. C., Willerman, L., & Horn, J. M. (1987). Personality resemblance in adoptive families: A 10-year follow-up. *Journal of Personality and Social Psychology, 53*, 961-969.

449. Love, A. W. (1987). Depression in chronic low back pain patients: Diagnostic efficiency of three self-report questionnaires. *Journal of Clinical Psychology, 43*, 84-88.

450. Mac Millan, J. S., Valliant, P. M. (1987). Occupational stress and behavioral change. *Perceptual and Motor Skills, 64*, 1061-1062.

451. Montag, I., & Comrey, A. L. (1987). Millon MCMI scales factor analyzed and correlated with MMPI and CPS scales. *Multivariate Behavioral Research, 22*, 401-413.

452. Nelson, L. D. (1987). Measuring depression in a clinical population using the MMPI. *Journal of Consulting and Clinical Psychology, 55*, 788-790.

453. Nockleby, D. M., & Deaton, A. V. (1987). Denial versus distress: Coping patterns in post head trauma patients. *The International Journal of Clinical Neuropsychology, 9*, 145-148.

454. Paunonen, S. V. (1987). Test construction and targeted factor solutions derived by multiple group and procrustes methods. *Multivariate Behavioral Research, 22*, 437-455.

455. Pennebaker, J. W., Hughes, C. F., & O'Heeron, R. C. (1987). The psychophysiology of confession: Linking inhibitory and psychosomatic processes. *Journal of Personality and Social Psychology, 52*, 781-793.

456. Persinger, M. A. (1987). MMPI profiles of normal people who display frequent temporal-lobe signs. *Perceptual and Motor Skills, 64*, 1112-1114.

457. Rehm, L. P., Kaslow, N. J., & Rabin, A. S. (1987). Cognitive and behavioral targets in a self-control therapy program for depression. *Journal of Consulting and Clinical Psychology, 55*, 60-67.

458. Rhue, J. W., & Lynn, S. J. (1987). Fantasy proneness and psychopathology. *Journal of Personality and Social Psychology, 53*, 327-336.

459. Rounsaville, B. J., Dolinsky, Z. S., Babor, T. F., & Meyer, R. E. (1987). Psychopathology as a predictor of treatment outcome in alcoholics. *Archives of General Psychiatry, 44*, 505-513.

460. Scapinello, K. F., & Blanchard, R. (1987). Historical items in the MMPI: Note on evaluating treatment outcomes for a criminal population. *Psychological Reports, 61*, 775-778.

461. Schuerger, J. M., Foerstner, S. B., Serkownek, K., & Ritz, G. (1987). History and validities of the Serkownek subscales for MMPI scales 5 and 0. *Psychological Reports, 61*, 227-235.

462. Sexton, D. L., McIlwraith, R., Barnes, G., & Dunn, R. (1987). Comparison of the MCMI and MMPI-168 as psychiatric inpatient screening inventories. *Journal of Personality Assessment*, 51, 388-398.

463. Shusman, E. (1987). A redundancy analysis for the Inwald Personality Inventory and the MMPI. *Journal of Personality Assessment*, 51, 433-440.

464. Sigmon, S. T., Nelson, R. O., & Brannon, S. E. (1987). Situational-specificity of motivational differences between depressed and nondepressed subjects. *Perceptual and Motor Skills*, 65, 860-862.

465. Solovay, M. R., Shenton, M. E., & Holzman, P. S. (1987). Comparative studies of thought disorders: Mania and schizophrenia. *Archives of General Psychiatry*, 44, 13-20.

466. Tienari, P., Lahti, I., Sorri, A., Naarala, M., Moring, J., Wahlberg, K., & Wynne, L. C. (1987). The Finnish adoptive family study of schizophrenia. *Journal of Psychiatric Research*, 21, 437-445.

467. Tucker, D. M., Novelly, R. A., & Walker, P. J. (1987). Brief communication: Hyperreligiosity in temporal lobe epilepsy: Redefining the relationship. *The Journal of Nervous and Mental Disease*, 175, 181-184.

468. Tyson, G. M., & Range, L. M. (1987). Gestalt dialogues as a treatment for mild depression: Time works just as well. *Journal of Clinical Psychology*, 43, 227-231.

469. Vanderploeg, R. D., Sison, G. F. P., Jr., & Hickling, E. J. (1987). A reevaluation of the use of the MMPI in the assessment of combat-related posttraumatic stress disorder. *Journal of Personality Assessment*, 51, 140-150.

470. Walker, M., & Hailey, B. J. (1987). Physical fitness levels and psychological states versus traits. *Perceptual and Motor Skills*, 64 (1), 15-25.

471. Zettle, R. D., & Hayes, S. C. (1987). Component and process analysis of cognitive therapy. *Psychological Reports*, 61, 939-953.

472. Zika, S., & Chamberlain, K. (1987). Relation of hassles and personality to subjective well-being. *Journal of Personality and Social Psychology*, 53, 155-162.

473. Archer, R. P., & Gordon, R. A. (1988). MMPI and Rorschach indices of schizophrenic and depressive diagnoses among adolescent inpatients. *Journal of Personality Assessment*, 52, 276-287.

474. Archer, R. P., Gordon, R. A., Giannetti, R. A., & Singles, J. M. (1988). MMPI scale clinical correlates for adolescent inpatients. *Journal of Personality Assessment*, 52, 707-721.

475. Bergin, A. E., Stinchfield, R. D., Gaskin, T. A., Masters, K. S., & Sullivan, C. E. (1988). Religious life-styles and mental health: An exploratory study. *Journal of Counseling Psychology*, 35, 91-98.

476. Blanchard, E. B., Schwarz, S. P., Neff, D. F., & Gerardi, M. A. (1988). Prediction of outcome from the self-regulatory treatment of irritable bowel syndrome. *Behaviour Research and Therapy*, 26, 187-190.

477. Borzecki, M., Wormith, J. S., & Black, W. H. (1988). An examination of differences between native and non-native psychiatric offenders on the MMPI. *Canadian Journal of Behavioural Science*, 20, 287-301.

478. Brophy, C. J., Norvell, N. K., & Kiluk, D. J. (1988). An examination of the factor structure and convergent and discriminant validity of the SCL-90R in an outpatient clinic population. *Journal of Personality Assessment*, 52, 334-340.

479. Calvert, S. H., Beutler, L. E., & Crago, M. (1988). Psychotherapy outcome as a function of therapist-patient matching on selected variables. *Journal of Social and Clinical Psychology*, 6, 104-117.

480. Derins, G. M., & Edwards, P. J. (1988). Self-efficacy and smoking reduction in chronic obstructive pulmonary disease. *Behaviour Research and Therapy*, 26, 127-135.

481. Diamond, R., Barth, J. T., & Zillmer, E. A. (1988). Emotional correlates of mild closed head trauma: The role of the MMPI. *The International Journal of Clinical Neuropsychology*, 10, 35-40.

482. Edwards, L. K., Edwards, A. L., & Clark, C. (1988). Social desirability and the frequency of social-reinforcement scale. *Journal of Personality and Social Psychology*, 54, 526-529.

483. Ekman, P., Friesen, W. V., & O'Sullivan, M. (1988). Smiles when lying. *Journal of Personality and Social Psychology*, 54, 414-420.

484. Gorwier, W. D., Brown, L. M., & Cone, C. (1988). Concurrent validity of the OBD-168. *The International Journal of Clinical Neuropsychology*, 10, 156-157.

485. Green, S. B., & Kelley, C. K. (1988). Racial bias in prediction with the MMPI for a juvenile delinquent population. *Journal of Personality Assessment*, 52, 263-275.

486. Greenberg, R. P., & O'Neill, R. M. (1988). The construct validity of the MMPI alexithymia scale with psychiatric inpatients. *Journal of Personality Assessment*, 52, 459-464.

487. Grossman, L. S., & Wasyliw, O. E. (1988). A psychometric study of stereotypes: Assessment of malingering in a criminal forensic group. *Journal of Personality Assessment*, 52, 549-563.

488. Hiatt, D., & Hargrave, G. E. (1988). MMPI profiles of problem peace officers. *Journal of Personality Assessment*, 52, 722-731.

489. Hill, C. E., Helms, J. E., Spiegel, S. B., & Tichenor, V. (1988). Development of a system for categorizing client reactions to therapist interventions. *Journal of Counseling Psychology*, 35, 27-36.

490. Hyer, L., Boudewyns, P., Harrison, W. R., O'Leary, W. C., Bruno, R. D., Saucer, R. T., & Blount, J. B. (1988). Vietnam veterans: Overreporting versus acceptable reporting of symptoms. *Journal of Personality Assessment*, 52, 475-486.

491. Hyer, L., Woods, M. G., Boudewyns, P. A., Bruno, R., & O'Leary, W. C. (1988). Concurrent validation of the Millon Clinical Multiaxial Inventory among Vietnam veterans with posttraumatic stress disorder. *Psychological Reports*, 63, 271-278.

492. Jacobsen, R. H., Tomkin, A. S., & Hyer, L. A. (1988). Factor analytic study of irrational beliefs. *Psychological Reports*, 63, 803-809.

493. Lee, S. W., Piersel, W. C., Friedlander, R., & Collamer, W. (1988). Concurrent validity of the Revised Children's Manifest Anxiety Scale (RCMAS) for adolescents. *Educational and Psychological Measurement*, 48, 429-433.

494. Meisner, S. (1988). Susceptibility of Rorschach distress correlates to malingering. *Journal of Personality Assessment*, 52, 564-571.

495. Moses, J. A., & Maruish, M. E. (1988). A critical review of the Luria-Nebraska Neuropsychological Battery literature: III. Concurrent validity. *The International Journal of Clinical Neuropsychology*, 10, 12-19.

496. Mueller, S. R., & Girace, M. (1988). Use and misuse of the MMPI, a reconsideration. *Psychological Reports*, 63, 483-491.

497. Mullins, L. S., & Kopelman, R. E. (1988). Toward an assessment of the construct validity of four measures of narcissism. *Journal of Personality Assessment*, 52, 610-625.

498. Mungas, D. (1988). Psychometric correlates of episodic violent behavior: A multidimensional neuropsychological approach. *British Journal of Psychiatry*, 152, 180-187.

499. O'Leary, W. C., Hyer, L., Blount, J. B., & Harrison, W. R. (1988). Interest patterns among Vietnam-era veterans. *Psychological Reports*, 63, 79-85.

500. Pancoast, D. L., & Archer, R. P. (1988). MMPI adolescent norms: Patterns and trends across 4 decades. *Journal of Personality Assessment*, 52, 691-706.

501. Pancoast, D. L., Archer, R. P., & Gordon, R. A. (1988). The MMPI and clinical diagnosis: A comparison of classification system outcomes with discharge diagnoses. *Journal of Personality Assessment*, 52, 81-90.

502. Puente, A. E. (1988). Personality characteristics of individuals with chronic rheumatoid arthritis. *Perceptual and Motor Skills*, 66 (2), 639-642.

503. Ramirez, L. F., McCormick, R. A., & Lowy, M. T. (1988). Plasma cortisol and depression in pathological gamblers. *British Journal of Psychiatry*, 153, 684-686.

504. Robyak, J. E., Prange, M., & Sands, M. (1988). Drinking practices among Black and White alcoholics and alcoholics of different personality types. *Journal of Personality Assessment*, 52, 487-498.

505. Rogers, R., Gillis, J. R., McMain, S., & Dickens, S. E. (1988). Fitness evaluations: A retrospective study of clinical, criminal, and sociodemographic characteristics. *Canadian Journal of Behavioural Science*, 20, 192-200.

506. Roland, B. C., Zelhart, P. F., & Dubes, R. (1988). Selected MMPI items that identified college women who reported early sexual abuse. *Psychological Reports*, 63, 447-450.

507. Rose, R. J. (1988). Genetic and environmental variance in content dimensions of the MMPI. *Journal of Personality and Social Psychology*, 55, 302-311.

508. Ross, M. W., Burnard, D., & Campbell, I. M. (1988). Utility of the Gd scale for the measurement of gender-dysphoria in males. *Psychological Reports*, 63, 87-90.

509. Scott, R. L., & Flowers, J. V. (1988). Betrayal by the mother as a factor contributing to psychological disturbance in victims of father-daughter incest: An MMPI analysis. *Journal of Social and Clinical Psychology*, 6, 147-154.

510. Smith, L. B., Silber, D. E., & Karp, S. A. (1988). Validity of the Megargee-Bohn MMPI typology with women incarcerated in a state prison. *Psychological Reports*, 62, 107-113.

511. Spirito, A., Faust, D., Myers, B., & Bechtel, D. (1988). Clinical utility of the MMPI in the evaluation of adolescent suicide attempters. *Journal of Personality Assessment*, 52, 204-211.

512. Strassberg, D. S., Adelstein, T. B., & Chemers, M. M. (1988). Adjustment and disclosure reciprocity. *Journal of Social and Clinical Psychology*, 7, 234-245.

513. Tooke, W. S., & Ickes, W. (1988). A measure of adherence to conventional morality. *Journal of Social and Clinical Psychology*, 6, 310-334.

514. Venn, J. (1988). Low scores on MMPI scales 2 and 0 as indicators of character pathology in men. *Psychological Reports*, 62, 651-657.

515. Venn, J. (1988). MMPI profiles of Native-, Mexican-, and Caucasian-American male alcoholics. *Psychological Reports*, 62, 427-432.

516. Walters, G. D. (1988). Assessing dissimulation and denial on the MMPI in a sample of maximum security, male inmates. *Journal of Personality Assessment*, 52, 465-474.

517. Walters, G. D., & Greene, R. L. (1988). Differentiating between schizophrenic and manic inpatients by means of the MMPI. *Journal of Personality Assessment*, 52, 91-95.

518. Wasyliw, O. E., Grossman, L. S., Haywood, T. W., & Cavanaugh, J. L., Jr. (1988). The detection of malingering in criminal forensic groups: MMPI validity scales. *Journal of Personality Assessment, 52,* 321-333.

519. Andrucci, G. L., Archer, R. P., Pancoast, D. L., & Gordon, R. A. (1989). The relationship of MMPI and Sensation Seeking Scales to adolescent drug use. *Journal of Personality Assessment, 53,* 253-266.

520. Archer, R. P., Gordon, R. A., Anderson, G. L., & Giannetti, R. A. (1989). MMPI special scale clinical correlates for adolescent inpatients. *Journal of Personality Assessment, 53,* 654-664.

521. Archer, R. P., Pancoast, D. L., & Klinefelter, D. (1989). A comparison of MMPI code types produced by traditional and recent adolescent norms. *Psychological Assessment, 1,* 23-29.

522. Ben-Porath, Y. S., & Butcher, J. N. (1989). Psychometric stability of rewritten MMPI items. *Journal of Personality Assessment, 53,* 645-653.

523. Ben-Porath, Y. S., & Butcher, J. N. (1989). The comparability of MMPI and MMPI-2 scales and profiles. *Psychological Assessment, 1,* 345-347.

524. Ben-Porath, Y. S., Hostetler, K., Butcher, J. N., & Graham, J. R. (1989). New subscales for the MMPI-2 Social Introversion (Si) scale. *Psychological Assessment, 1,* 169-174.

525. Ben-Porath, Y. S., Slutske, W. S., & Butcher, J. N. (1989). A real-data simulation of computerized adaptive administration of the MMPI. *Psychological Assessment, 1,* 18-22.

526. Bieliauskas, L. A., & Glantz, R. H. (1989). Depression type in Parkinson disease. *Journal of Clinical and Experimental Neuropsychology, 11,* 597-604.

527. Boswell, D. L., Tarver, P., & Simoneaux, J. (1989). A study of the convergent and divergent validity of the Psychological Screening Inventory for adolescent inpatients. *Educational and Psychological Measurement, 49,* 165-170.

528. Brown, A., & Zeichner, A. (1989). Concurrent incidence of depression and physical symptoms among hostile young women. *Psychological Reports, 65,* 739-744.

529. Brown, D. R., Morgan, W. P., & Kihlstrom, J. F. (1989). Comparison of test construction strategies in an attempt to develop an athletic potential scale. *International Journal of Sport Psychology, 20,* 93-113.

530. Brown, R., Munjack, D., & McDowell, D. (1989). Agoraphobia with and without current panic attacks. *Psychological Reports, 64,* 503-506.

531. Christensen, L., Krietsch, K., & White, B. (1989). Development, cross-validation, and assessment of reliability of the Christensen Dietary Distress Inventory. *Canadian Journal of Behavioural Science, 21,* 1-15.

532. Colby, F. (1989). Usefulness of the K correction in MMPI profiles of patients and nonpatients. *Psychological Assessment, 1,* 142-145.

533. Coursey, R. D., Lees, R. W., & Siever, L. J. (1989). The relationship between smooth pursuit eye movement impairment and psychological measures of psychopathology. *Psychological Medicine, 19,* 343-358.

534. DiFrancesca, K. R., & Meloy, J. R. (1989). A comparative clinical investigation of the "How" and "Charlie" MMPI subtypes. *Journal of Personality Assessment, 53,* 396-403.

535. Dillon, E. A., & Ward, L. C. (1989). Validation of an MMPI short form with literate and illiterate patients. *Psychological Reports, 64,* 327-336.

536. Duricko, A. J., Norcross, J. C., & Buskirk, R. D. (1989). Correlates of the egocentricity index in child and adolescent outpatients. *Journal of Personality Assessment, 53,* 184-187.

537. Frick, P. J., Lahey, B. B., Hartdagen, S., & Hynd, G. W. (1989). Conduct problems in boys: Relations to maternal personality, marital satisfaction, and socioeconomic status. *Journal of Clinical Child Psychology, 18,* 114-120.

538. Friedlander, M. L., Siegel, S. M., & Brenock, K. (1989). Parallel process in counseling and supervision: A case study. *Journal of Counseling Psychology, 36,* 149-157.

539. Gartner, J., Hurt, S. W., & Gartner, A. (1989). Psychological test signs of borderline personality disorder: A review of the empirical literature. *Journal of Personality Assessment, 53,* 423-441.

540. Hakstian, A. R., & McLean, P. D. (1989). Brief screen for depression. *Psychological Assessment, 1,* 139-141.

541. Hall, G. C. N. (1989). WAIS-R and MMPI profiles of men who have sexually assaulted children: Evidence of limited utility. *Journal of Personality Assessment, 53,* 404- 412.

542. Harding, T., & Zimmerman, E. (1989). Psychiatric symptoms, cognitive stress and vulnerability factors: A study in a remand prison. *British Journal of Psychiatry, 155,* 36-43.

543. Hogan, J. (1989). Personality correlates of physical fitness. *Journal of Personality and Social Psychology, 56,* 284-288.

544. Holden, R. R., & Fekken, G. C. (1989). Three common social desirability scales: Friends, acquaintances, or strangers? *Journal of Research in Personality, 23,* 180-191.

545. Holmes, C. B., Kixmiller, J. S., & Larsen, R. K. (1989). Statistical versus clinical significance in research with the MMPI. *Psychological Reports, 64,* 159-162.

546. Hsu, L. M., Santelli, J., & Hsu, J. R. (1989). Faking detection validity and incremental validity of response latencies to MMPI subtle and obvious items. *Journal of Personality Assessment, 53,* 278-295.

547. Irving, J. B., Coursey, R. D., Buschsbaum, M. S., & Murphy, D. L. (1989). Platelet monoamine oxidase activity and life stress as predictors of psychopathology and coping in a community sample. *Psychological Medicine, 19,* 79-90.

548. Kelly, D. B., & Green, R. L. (1989). Detection of faking good on the MMPI in a psychiatric inpatient population. *Psychological Reports, 65,* 747-750.

549. Knowles, E. E., & Schroeder, D. A. (1989). Familial and personality correlates of alcohol-related problems. *Addictive Behaviors, 14,* 537-543.

550. Leon, G. R., McNally, C., & Ben-Porath, V. S. (1989). Personality characteristics, mood, and coping patterns in a successful North Pole expedition team. *Journal of Research in Personality, 23,* 162-179.

551. Lipovsky, J. A., Finch, A. J., Jr., & Belter, R. W. (1989). Assessment of depression in adolescents: Objective and projective measures. *Journal of Personality Assessment, 53,* 449-458.

552. Lownsdale, W. S., Rogers, B. J., & McCall, J. N. (1989). Concurrent validation of Hutt's Bender Gestalt screening method for schizophrenia, depression, and brain damage. *Journal of Personality Assessment, 53,* 832-836.

553. Meyers, J. E., & McMordie, W. R. (1989). The LNNB memory scale and WMS as memory screening instruments. *The International Journal of Clinical Neuropsychology, 11,* 137-142.

554. Minskoff, E. H., Hawks, R., Steidle, E. F., & Hoffmann, F. J. (1989). A homogeneous group of persons with learning disabilities: Adults with severe learning disabilities in vocational rehabilitation. *Journal of Learning Disabilities, 22,* 521-528.

555. Nagayama Hall, G. C. (1989). Self-reported hostility as a function of offense characteristics and response style in a sexual offender population. *Journal of Consulting and Clinical Psychology, 57,* 306-308.

556. Norton, N. C. (1989). Three scales of alexithymia: Do they measure the same thing? *Journal of Personality Assessment, 53,* 621-637.

557. Overholser, J. C., Kabakoff, R., & Norman, W. H. (1989). The assessment of personality characteristics in depressed and dependent psychiatric inpatients. *Journal of Personality Assessment, 53,* 40-50.

558. Pancoast, D. L., & Archer, R. P. (1989). Original adult MMPI norms in normal samples: A review with implications for future developments. *Journal of Personality Assessment, 53,* 376-395.

559. Raskin, R., & Novacek, J. (1989). An MMPI description of the narcissistic personality. *Journal of Personality Assessment, 53,* 66-80.

560. Roland, B., Zelhart, P., & Dubes, R. (1989). MMPI correlates of college women who reported experiencing child/adult sexual contact with father, stepfather, or with other persons. *Psychological Reports, 64,* 1159-1162.

561. Roth, C. R., Aronson, A. E., & Davis, L. J., Jr. (1989). Clinical studies in psychogenic stuttering of adult onset. *Journal of Speech and Hearing Disorders, 54,* 634-646.

562. Rybicki, D. J., Lepkowsky, C. M., & Arndt, S. (1989). An empirical assessment of bulimic patients using multiple measures. *Addictive Behaviors, 14,* 249-260.

563. Schuerger, J. M., Zarrella, K. L., & Hotz, A. S. (1989). Factors that influence the temporal stability of personality by questionnaire. *Journal of Personality and Social Psychology, 56,* 777-783.

564. Shields, S. A., Mallory, M. E., & Simon, A. (1989). The Body Awareness Questionnaire: Reliability and validity. *Journal of Personality Assessment, 53,* 802-815.

565. Snyder, D. K., & Wills, R. M. (1989). Behavioral versus insight-oriented marital therapy: Effects on individual and interspousal functioning. *Journal of Consulting and Clinical Psychology, 57,* 39-46.

566. Spring, B., Lemon, N., Weinstein, L., & Haskell, A. (1989). Distractibility in schizophrenia: State and trait aspects. *British Journal of Psychiatry, 155* (Suppl. 5), 63-68.

567. Suis, J., & Wan, C. K. (1989). The relation between Type A behavior and chronic emotional distress: A meta-analysis. *Journal of Personality and Social Psychology, 57,* 503-512.

568. Svanum, S., & McAdoo, Wm. G. (1989). Predicting rapid relapse following treatment for chemical dependence: A matched-subjects design. *Journal of Consulting and Clinical Psychology, 57,* 222-226.

569. Taylor, J. R., Strassberg, D. S., & Turner, C. W. (1989). Utility of the MMPI in a geriatric population. *Journal of Personality Assessment, 53,* 665-676.

570. Tienari, P., Lahti, I., Sorri, A., Naarala, M., Moring, J., & Wahlberg, K-E. (1989). The Finnish adoptive family study of schizophrenia: Possible joint effects of genetic vulnerability and family environment. *British Journal of Psychiatry, 155* (Suppl. 5), 29-32.

571. Velasquez, R. J., Callahan, W. J., & Carrillo, R. (1989). MMPI profiles of Hispanic-American inpatient and outpatient sex offenders. *Psychological Reports, 65,* 1055-1058.

572. Watkins, C. E., Jr., Campbell, V. L., McGregor, P., & Godin, K. (1989). The MMPI: Does it have a place in counseling psychology training? *Journal of Personality Assessment, 53,* 413-417.

573. Weiss, D. S., Zilberg, N. J., & Genevro, J. L. (1989). Psychometric properties of Loevinger's Sentence Completion Test in an adult psychiatric outpatient sample. *Journal of Personality Assessment, 53,* 478-486.

574. Wetzler, S., Kahn, R., Strauman, T. J., & Dubro, A. (1989). Diagnosis of major depression by self-report. *Journal of Personality Assessment, 53,* 22-30.

575. Whisman, M. A., Strosahl, K., Fruzzetti, A. E., Schmaling, K. B., Jacobson, N. S., & Miller, D. M. (1989). A structured interview version of the Hamilton Rating Scale for Depression: Reliability and validity. *Psychological Assessment, 1,* 238-241.

576. Williams, C. L., & Butcher, J. N. (1989). An MMPI study of adolescents: I. Empirical validity of the standard scales. *Psychological Assessment, 1,* 251-259.

577. Williams, C. L., & Butcher, J. N. (1989). An MMPI study of adolescents: II. Verification and limitations of code type classifications. *Psychological Assessment, 1,* 260-265.

578. Zgourides, G., Frey, P., Camplair, C., Tilson, M., & Ihli, K. (1989). Anxiety and perceived helplessness as measures by MMPI and Exner-scored Rorschach protocols in a sample of adolescent outpatients. *Perceptual and Motor Skills, 69,* 458.

579. Barsky, A. J., & Wyshak, G. (1990). Hypochondriasis and somatosensory amplification. *British Journal of Psychiatry, 157,* 404-409.

580. Celmer, V., & Winer, J. L. (1990). Female aspirants to the Roman Catholic priesthood. *Journal of Counseling and Development, 69,* 178-183.

581. Coons, P. M., & Fine, C. G. (1990). Accuracy of the MMPI in identifying multiple personality disorder. *Psychological Reports, 66,* 831-834.

582. Corrigan, S. A., Johnson, W. G., Alford, G. S., Bergerson, K. C., & Lemmon, C. R. (1990). Prevalence of bulimia among patients in a chemical dependency treatment program. *Addictive Behaviors, 15,* 581-585.

583. Faurie, W. C. (1990). Prediction of length of hospitalization of adolescent psychiatric inpatients utilizing the Pd scale of the MMPI and demographic data. *Adolescence, 25,* 305-310.

584. Gallucci, N. T. (1990). On the synthesis of information from psychological tests. *Psychological Reports, 67,* 1243-1260.

585. Gass, C. S., & Daniel, S. K. (1990). Emotional impact on trail making test performance. *Psychological Reports, 67,* 435-438.

586. Gillis, J. R., Rogers, R., & Dickens, S. E. (1990). The detection of faking bad response styles on the MMPI. *Canadian Journal of Behavioural Science, 22,* 408-416.

587. Greenwald, D. F. (1990). The Last and Weiss Rorschach Sum E in a normal sample. *Perceptual and Motor Skills, 70,* 889-890.

588. Harmon, T. M., Hynan, M. T., & Tyre, T. E. (1990). Improved obstetric outcomes using hypnotic analgesia and skill mastery combined with childbirth education. *Journal of Consulting and Clinical Psychology, 58,* 525-530.

589. Hier, S. J., Korboot, P. J., & Schweitzer, R. D. (1990). Social adjustment and symptomatology in two types of homeless adolescents: Runaways and throwaways. *Adolescence, 25,* 761-771.

590. Higgins-Lee, C. (1990). Low scores on California Psychological Inventory as predictors of psychopathology in alcoholic patients. *Psychological Reports, 69,* 227-232.

591. Johnson, M. E., & Brems, C. (1990). Psychiatric inpatient MMPI profiles: An exploration for potential racial bias. *Journal of Counseling Psychology, 37,* 213-215.

592. Lees-Haley, P. R., & Fox, D. D. (1990). Neuropsychological false positives in litigation: Trail Making Test findings. *Perceptual and Motor Skills, 70,* 1379-1382.

593. Lorandos, D. A. (1990). Change in adolescent boys at Teen Ranch: A five-year study. *Adolescence, 25,* 509-516.

594. Roberts, G., Schmitz, K., Pinto, J., & Cain, S. (1990). The MMPI and Jesness Inventory as measures of effectiveness on an inpatient conduct disorders treatment unit. *Adolescence, 25,* 989-996.

595. Rowe, D. C. (1990). As the twig is bent? The myth of child-rearing influences on personality development. *Journal of Counseling and Development, 68,* 606-611.

596. Schill, T., & Wang, S. (1990). Correlates of the MMPI-2 anger content scale. *Psychological Reports, 67,* 800-802.

597. Sutker, P. B., Galina, Z. H., West, J. A., & Allain, A. N. (1990). Trauma-induced weight loss and cognitive deficits among former prisoners of war. *Journal of Consulting and Clinical Psychology, 58,* 323-328.

598. Swoboda, J. S., Dowd, E. T., & Wise, S. L. (1990). Reframing and restraining directives in the treatment of clinical depression. *Journal of Counseling Psychology, 37,* 254-260.

599. Velasquez, R. J., & Callahan, W. J. (1990). MMPI comparisons of Hispanic- and White-American veterans seeking treatment for alcoholism. *Psychological Reports, 67,* 95-98.

600. Velasquez, R. J., & Callahan, W. J. (1990). MMPIs of Hispanic, black, and white DSM-III schizophrenics. *Psychological Reports, 66,* 819-822.

601. Wagner, E. E., Adair, H. E., & Foerstner, S. (1990). Maximized reliability estimates for some research scales of the MMPI. *Educational and Psychological Measurement, 50,* 775-783.

602. Walfish, S., Massey, R., & Krone, A. (1990). MMPI profiles of adolescent substance abusers in treatment. *Adolescence, 25,* 567-572.

603. Wetzler, S., & Marlowe, D. (1990). "Faking bad" on the MMPI, MMPI-2, and Millon-II. *Psychological Reports, 67,* 1117-1118.

604. Wilson, G. L. (1990). Psychotherapy with depressed incarcerated felons: A comparative evaluation of treatments. *Psychological Reports, 67,* 1027-1041.

605. Ben-Porath, Y. S., Butcher, J. N., & Graham, J. R. (1991). Contribution of the MMPI-2 content scales to the differential diagnosis of schizophrenia and major depression. *Psychological Assessment, 3,* 634-640.

606. Berry, D. T. R., Wetter, M. W., Baer, R. A., Widiger, T. A., Sumpter, J. C., Reynolds, S. K., & Hallam, R. A. (1991). Detection of random responding on the MMPI-R: Utility of F, Back F, and *VRIN* scales. *Psychological Assessment, 3,* 418-423.

607. Boulet, J., & Boss, M. W. (1991). Reliability and validity of the Brief Symptom Inventory. *Psychological Assessment, 3,* 433-437.

608. Caldwell, A. B. (1991). Commentary on "The Minnesota Multiphasic Personality Inventory-2: A review." *Journal of Counseling and Development, 69,* 568-569.

609. Cheung, F. M., Song, W., & Butcher, J. N. (1991). An infrequency scale for the Chinese MMPI. *Psychological Assessment, 3,* 648-653.

610. Dowd, E. T., Milne, C. R., & Wise, S. L. (1991). The Therapeutic Reactance Scale: A measure of psychological reactance. *Journal of Counseling and Development, 69,* 541-545.

611. Duckworth, J. C. (1991). Response to Caldwell and Graham. *Journal of Counseling and Development, 69,* 572-573.

612. Duckworth, J. C. (1991). The Minnesota Multiphasic Personality Inventory-2: A review. *Journal of Counseling and Development, 69,* 564-567.

613. Earl, W. L. (1991). Perceived trauma: Its etiology and treatment. *Adolescence, 26,* 97-104.

614. Funari, D. J., Piekarski, A. M., & Sherwood, R. J. (1991). Treatment outcomes of Vietnam veterans with posttraumatic stress disorder. *Psychological Reports, 68,* 571-578.

615. Gass, C. S. (1991). MMPI-2 interpretation and closed head injury: A correlation factor. *Psychological Assessment, 3,* 27-31.

616. Gass, C. S., & Lawhorn, L. (1991). Psychological adjustment following stroke: An MMPI study. *Psychological Assessment, 3,* 628-633.

617. Gaston, L. (1991). Reliability and criterion-related validity of the California Psychotherapy Alliance Scales—Patient Version. *Psychological Assessment, 3,* 68-74.

618. Graham, J. R. (1991). Comments on Duckworth's review of the Minnesota Mutliphasic Personality Inventory-2. *Journal of Counseling and Development, 69,* 570-571.

619. Hedayat, M. M., & Kelly, D. B. (1991). Relationship of MMPI dependency and dominance scale scores to staff's ratings, diagnoses, and demographic data for day-treatment clients. *Psychological Reports, 68,* 259-266.

620. Herkov, M. J., Archer, R. P., & Gordon, R. A. (1991). MMPI response sets among adolescents: An evaluation of the limitations of the subtle-obvious subscales. *Psychological Assessment, 3,* 424-426.

621. Kinder, B. N., Curtiss, G., & Kalichman, S. (1991). Cluster analyses of headache-patient MMPI scores: A cross-validation. *Psychological Assessment, 3,* 226-231.

622. Kivlighan, D. M., & Angelone, E. O. (1991). Helpee introversion, novice counselor intention use, and helpee-rated session impact. *Journal of Counseling Psychology, 38,* 25-29.

623. Kulka, R. A., Schlenger, W. E., Fairbank, J. A., Jordan, B. K., Hough, R. L., Marmar, C. R., & Weiss, D. S. (1991). Assessment of posttraumatic stress disorder in the community: Prospects and pitfalls from recent studies on Vietnam veterans. *Psychological Assessment, 3,* 547-560.

624. Lanyon, R. I., Dannenbaum, S. E., Wolf, L. L., & Brown, A. (1989). Dimensions of deceptive responding in criminal offenders. *Psychological Assessment, 1,* 300-304.

625. Lees-Haley, P. R., & Glenn, W. J. (1991). A fake and scale on the MMPI-2 for personal injury claimants. *Psychological Reports, 68,* 203-210.

626. Levy-Shiff, R., Goldshmidt, I., & Har-Even, D. (1991). Transition to parenthood in adoptive families. *Developmental Psychology, 27,* 131-140.

627. McCann, J. T. (1991). Convergent and discriminant validity of the MCMI-II and MMPI personality disorder scales. *Psychological Assessment, 3,* 9-18.

628. Meier, S. T. (1991). Tests of the construct validity of occupational stress measures with college students: Failure to support discriminant validity. *Journal of Counseling Psychology, 38,* 91-97.

629. Nelson, L. D., & Cicchetti, D. (1991). Validity of the MMPI depression scale for outpatients. *Psychological Assessment, 3,* 55-59.

630. Rogers, R., Gillis, J. R., Bagby, R. M., & Monteiro, E. (1991). Detection of malingering on the Structured Interview of Reported Symptoms (SIRS): A study of coached and uncoached simulators. *Psychological Assessment, 3,* 673-677.

631. Rogers, R., Gillis, J. R., Dickens, S. E., & Bagby, R. M. (1991). Standardized assessment of malingering: Validation of the structured interview of reported symptoms. *Psychological Assessment, 3,* 89-86.

632. Sutker, P. B., & Allain, A. N., Jr. (1991). MMPI profiles of veterans of WWII and Korea: Comparisons of former POWS and combat survivors. *Psychological Reports, 68*, 279-284.

633. Sutker, P. B., Bugg, F., & Allain, A. N. (1991). Psychometric prediction of PTSD among POW survivors. *Psychological Assessment, 3,* 105-110.

634. Trull, T. J. (1991). Discriminant validity of the MMPI-Borderline Personality Disorder scale. *Psychological Assessment, 3,* 232-238.

635. Valliant, P. M., & Antonowicz, D. H. (1991). Cognitive behaviour therapy and social skills training improves personality and cognition in incarcerated offenders. *Psychological Reports, 68*, 27-33.

636. Velasquez, R. J., Callahan, W. J., & Carrillo, R. (1991). MMPI differences among Mexican-American male and female psychiatric inpatients. *Psychological Reports, 68*, 123-127.

637. Wiggins, J. S., & Pincus, A. L. (1989). Conceptions of personality disorders and dimensions of personality. *Psychological Assessment, 1,* 305-316.

Review of the Minnesota Multiphasic Personality Inventory-2 by ROBERT P. ARCHER, Professor of Psychiatry and Behavioral Sciences, Eastern Virginia Medical School, Norfolk, VA:

Stark Hathaway reported that he encountered substantial difficulty, including several rejections, before successfully finding a publisher for the Minnesota Multiphasic Personality Inventory (MMPI) in the early 1940s (Dahlstrom & Welsh, 1960). From this humble beginning, the MMPI's climb in popularity was nothing less than phenomenal. Surveys of test usage conducted in 1946 listed the MMPI among the 20 most widely used psychological tests (Louttit & Browne, 1947). A survey conducted in 1959 showed the MMPI to be among the 10 leading tests, and the only objective personality assessment instrument included in this group (Sundberg, 1961). By 1982, a national survey of patterns of psychological test usage found the MMPI to rank second overall (behind the Wechsler Adult Intelligence Scale) among clinicians' reports of tests they had used, and first overall when ratings were adjusted for frequency of usage (Lubin, Larsen, & Matarazzo, 1984). Despite its primary focus in the assessment of adults, the MMPI is also the most popular objective personality measure used with adolescents (Archer, Maruish, Imhoff, & Piotrowski, 1991). Beyond issues of clinical popularity, the MMPI has been the focus of extensive research interest. Butcher and Owen (1978), for example, have estimated that 84% of all research conducted in the personality inventory domain has been centered on the MMPI. Butcher (1987) has estimated that over 10,000 articles and books have documented the use of the MMPI. Much of this research involves the use of MMPI results as a means of increasing the understanding of clinical phenomena (e.g., alcohol and substance abuse) or special groups of interest to researchers (e.g., parents of psychiatrically disturbed offspring). A very important component of this research, however, has centered on the test instrument in studies of the external correlates and validity of the MMPI.

The MMPI-2 represents the first revision of the test since its original publication in 1943. Given the phenomenal success of the MMPI, it was likely that any effort to revise this instrument would have generated some controversy. Conservative revision efforts which minimized changes to the original instrument might be criticized by those who viewed the MMPI as an anachronistic measure with many undesirable psychometric properties. On the other hand, efforts to undertake a substantial revision of this highly successful instrument would run the risk of alienating many strong supporters of the original test. As Butcher and Owen (1978) have observed, "If modifications [in the MMPI] are too drastic, the instrument may be unacceptable to present users . . . They may continue to use the present MMPI because it is a known entity" (p. 507). In short, the original MMPI was destined to be a "tough act to follow" for those attempting to set revision goals and directions.

The MMPI Restandardization Project began in the summer of 1982 and resulted in the publication of the MMPI-2 in August 1989. The University of Minnesota Press, represented by Beverly Kaemmer, appointed a Restandardization Committee to advise on the development of the MMPI-2. This Committee consisted of Drs. James Butcher and Auke Tellegen of the University of Minnesota, W. Grant Dahlstrom of the University of North Carolina, and John Graham of Kent State University. The major goals of the MMPI restandardization project have been summarized by Butcher, Graham, Williams, and Ben-Porath (1990) as follows: (*a*) Obtaining a contemporary normative sample; (*b*) Undertaking a revision of the original instrument which preserved sufficient continuity to allow for the generalizability of the massive MMPI research literature to the revised instrument; and (*c*) Creation of new items to address areas of behavior not adequately covered by the original MMPI, and the deletion or revision of offensive, outdated, or antiquated item content. When the MMPI-2 was published in August 1989, extensive test materials were also released including the MMPI-2 Test Manual (Butcher, Dahlstrom, Graham, Tellegen, & Kaemmer, 1989), hand-scoring templates, and a variety of computer-scoring options. Several computer-based test interpretation (CBTI) products have been marketed for the MMPI-2.

The MMPI-2 differs from the original test instrument in a variety of ways. Although the total lengths of the MMPI (566 items) and MMPI-2 (567 items) are almost identical, substantial changes have occurred on the item level. Levitt (1990) has stated that 394 unaltered items were carried over from the MMPI to the MMPI-2, as well as 66 items that were modified/rewritten. Thus, 84% of the MMPI items appear in the MMPI-2 in an original or modified form. The major reasons for item rewordings included replacing obsolete or idiomatic language with more contemporary wording, elimination of sexist language, and modifications designed to simplify or improve sentence structure. Ben-Porath and Butcher (1989) administered the MMPI and MMPI-2 to college students, in a counterbalanced design, in order to compare responses to the original and rewritten version of items. They concluded that the rewritten items did not significantly alter test response patterns and were psychometrically equivalent to the original items.

In addition to modified items, 90 items were deleted from the original MMPI, of which 13 came from a standard validity or clinical scale. The standard scales losing the most items were F and Mf, each scale losing four items. The deleted items often involved potentially offensive content concerning sexual adjustment, bodily functions, or religious views or attitudes. These types of items were particularly intrusive/inappropriate when the MMPI was used in personnel screening applications. In addition to these 90 item deletions, the 16 duplicate items that appear in the original MMPI, and which have been utilized in the Test-Retest (TR) Index, have also been deleted in the MMPI-2. In place of these original items, the MMPI-2 contains 107 new items, most of which are found on the new MMPI-2 scales in the latter half of the test booklet.

The standard validity and clinical scales of the MMPI have been carried over, or protected, into the MMPI-2. No efforts were made to reevaluate the external validity of these measures, or to reexamine the K-correction weights traditionally assigned to five of the standard clinical scales. Additionally, MMPI-2 profile sheets and scoring programs provide for the derivation of 18 supplementary scales, 15 content scales, the Harris-Lingoes Subscales, and the Subtle-Obvious Subscales. An important effect of the creation of the MMPI-2 may be in the area of standardizing the use of a specific body of special scales that will be widely used with this instrument. This may be contrasted with the use of the original MMPI, in which test users often combined standard scale data with individualistic (and often idiosyncratic) special scale selections from the body of several hundred such measures which had been developed over the past five decades.

Of the 18 MMPI-2 supplementary scales, 8 are carried over from the original MMPI, typically with some item modifications. For example, the popular MacAndrew Alcoholism Scale (1965) has been incorporated into the MMPI-2 with four item replacements as *MAC-R*. Other popular special scales that were retained in the MMPI-2 include Anxiety (*A*), Repression (*R*), Ego Strength (*Es*), and Overcontrolled Hostility (*O-H*). Several less widely used special scales were also carried over,

including College Maladjustment (*Mt*), Social Responsibility (*Re*), and Dominance (*Do*). The MMPI-2 supplementary scales also include two separate but overlapping measures of posttraumatic stress disorder based on contrasting development methodologies. These measures are the *Pk* Scale, developed by Keane, Malloy, and Fairbank (1984), and the *Ps* Scale by Schlenger and Kulka (1987).

Several New validity scales have been developed for the MMPI-2 including the F_b (Back F) Scale, the Variable Response Inconsistency Scale (VRIN), and the True Response Inconsistency Scale (TRIN). The F_b Scale consists of infrequently endorsed items which occur in the latter stages of the MMPI-2 test booklet, therefore allowing for the possibility of identifying individuals who adopt random response patterns during the latter portion of the test. The VRIN and TRIN are inconsistency scales, similar to the Carelessness Scale developed by Greene (1978) for the original MMPI, which allow for an evaluation of the degree to which a subject responded to items in an inconsistent or contradictory manner. Also included in new supplementary scales are Masculine Gender Role (*GM*) and Feminine Gender Role (*GF*) Scales, and three new subscales for the *Si* standard scale which are Shyness/Self Consciousness (Si_1), Social Avoidance (Si_2), and Alienation-Self and Others (Si_3).

In addition to the supplementary scales, a series of 15 content scales were developed by Butcher, Graham, Williams, and Ben-Porath (1990) based on content dimensions identifiable within the MMPI-2 item pool. In contrast to the criterion group method employed by Hathaway and McKinley in the development of the original MMPI scales, the MMPI-2 content scales employ what is described as a deductive scale construction method. This later approach combines the use of empirical, theoretical, and rational criteria in the construction of these MMPI-2 measures (Butcher, Graham, Williams, & Ben-Porath, 1990). The end result of this process was the development of a series of face-valid, narrow-band scales with high levels of internal consistency. Much work on the validity of the scales remains for future reseachers. The focus of the MMPI-2 content scales varies widely, from traditional measurement constructs including Anxiety (ANX) and Depression (DEP), to innovative scales including Work Interference (WRK) and Negative Treatment Indicators (TRT). Many of the MMPI-2 content scales appear similar to, and share items with, content scales developed by Wiggins (1966) for the original MMPI.

The development of the content scales may have also contributed to a resurrection of the debate concerning the utility of subtle items. Because the MMPI-2 content scales consist of obvious items (i.e., items bearing an easily discerned relationship to the constructs being measured), opponents and proponents of the use of subtle items are likely to have different views of the usefulness of the MMPI-2 content scales. Ambivalence concerning the use of subtle items may be reflected in the MMPI-2 manual statement concerning the use of the Weiner and Harmon (1946) Subtle-Obvious Subscales: "These scales are included in the manual because we recognize that some authorities recommend their use and because we wish to facilitate further research. Their inclusion does not represent the committee's endorsement of the scales. We urge that they be interpreted with caution" (Butcher et al., 1989, p. 47).

In addition to changes that have occurred on the item and scale levels, the MMPI-2 is based on a new normative sample. The MMPI-2 norms are based on responses of 1,138 males and 1,462 females between the ages of 18 and 84. In comparison with the ethnic, geographic, and sample size restrictions present in the norms developed for the original instrument, the MMPI-2 norms offer very substantial improvements. Normative data were collected for the MMPI-2 primarily in seven sites involving the west coast (California and Washington), the midwest (Minnesota and Ohio), and the eastern region of the United States (North Carolina, Pennsylvania, and Virginia). The ethnic origins of the MMPI-2 restandardization sample compare reasonably well to the data from the 1980 U.S. Bureau of the Census. Similarly, the age sampling of restandardization subjects, although somewhat underrepresenting the extreme ends of the age distribution, is reasonably well done. It is in the area of the educational and occupational levels of MMPI-2 normative subjects that substantial controversy has been focused. Roughly 50% of males and 42% of females included in the MMPI-2 restandardization sample reported an educational level of a bachelor's degree or higher. This may be compared with 20% of males and 13% of females in the 1980 U.S. Census data, which reported comparable educational levels. Similarly, approximately 42% of males and 40% of females reported occupations in professional groups, in contrast to a 16% Census figure for this category. Debate is still occurring concerning what effects, if any, this educational skewing might have on MMPI-2 interpretation. In the April 1990 issue of the *APA Monitor*, several MMPI experts raised concerns regarding the suitability of the MMPI-2 norms in interpreting test respondents from lower socioeconomic status levels. In contrast, Butcher (1990a) has argued that educational level has a minimum impact on MMPI-2 scores, and that MMPI-2 norms "appear to work quite well for all levels of education even when K-correction is involved" (p. 3).

Independent of this debate, it is clear that the response patterns of subjects in the MMPI-2 normative sample differ substantially from those produced by the subjects for the original MMPI (i.e., the "Minnesota normals"). This is most apparent in *T*-score elevations differences found between the two instruments. The MMPI-2 clinical scale profiles are typically lower in elevation than profiles produced for the original instrument. This shift is reflected in a reduction of the demarcation point for clinical range elevations from $T \geq 70$ on the original instrument to $T \geq 65$ on the MMPI-2 profile sheet. This aspect of the MMPI-2 is likely to surprise many individuals in the initial stages of making the conversion from the original instrument to the revised test. First-time users may find the MMPI-2 profiles for clinical patients appear "too normal." As experience is gained with the MMPI-2 profile, however, most test users rapidly acclimate to the differences in "calibration." Many have erroneously attributed these elevation differences to the use of uniform *T*-scores in the MMPI-2. Uniform *T*-scores represent composite or averaged linear *T*-scores which serve to standardize the percentile equivalents represented by a given *T*-score across MMPI-2 clinical and content scales (Tellegen, 1988). Uniform *T*-scores do not, however, have major effects on the underlying distribution of raw scores and were not a substantial factor in the reduction of *T*-score elevation in the MMPI-2. Research by Pancoast and Archer (1989) suggests that part of these MMPI versus MMPI-2 elevations differences may reflect long-standing problems in the original MMPI norms. These authors observed that samples of normal adults have consistently shown substantial *T*-score elevations on the original instrument since its publication.

The major area of controversy and debate concerning the MMPI-2 has centered on the degree to which the profiles produced by this instrument are comparable to, or congruent with, test findings from the original MMPI. More broadly stated, this issue relates to the degree to which the MMPI and the MMPI-2 are equivalent measures. This concern has received substantial focus because it determines the degree to which the vast research literature available on the traditional MMPI can be generalized to the MMPI-2.

Empirical research is slowly accumulating on this crucial issue. The MMPI-2 manual provides congruence data for 2-point high-point codes using MMPI-2 norms and the original test norms in a sample of 232 male and 191 female psychiatric patients. These data indicate a congruence rate of 70% for males and 65% for females when high points are defined as the most elevated scale regardless of the magnitude of that elevation. Graham, Timbrook, Ben-Porath, and Butcher (in press) have reexamined these data and report that when 2-point codetype elevations were "well defined," as reflected in at least a 5 T-score point difference between the second and third most elevated scale in the clinical codetype, the congruence rate increased to 81.6% for males and 94.3% for females. Honaker (1990) investigated the congruence issue in an independent sample of 101 adults receiving either inpatient or outpatient psychological treatment who received both the MMPI and MMPI-2 in counterbalanced administrations. Results indicated that single-point and 2-point codetype similarity was lowest between the MMPI and MMPI-2, in comparison with MMPI-2/MMPI-2 comparisons and MMPI/MMPI comparisons. Honaker concluded that it would be erroneous to assume that the MMPI clinical research literature may be generalized to MMPI-2 test findings for all patients.

At the present time, many individuals who are beginning to use the MMPI-2 have elected to create profiles based on MMPI-2 norms as well as T-score values generated from Appendix K of the manual using the original (Minnesota normals) norms. These test users feel more comfortable when being able to examine the ways in which the MMPI and MMPI-2 produce comparable, or divergent, findings for a specific patient, and believe that this approach facilitates learning about the new test instrument. Clinicians working from an MMPI-2 manual generated in the first printing, however, should consult the Appendix K erratum sheet which has been distributed by the University of Minnesota Press. Others have elected to profile and interpret the MMPI-2 based exclusively on MMPI-2 norms, preferring a "clean break" with the original instrument. Both approaches appeared reasonable and defensible, given the current state of our knowledge concerning the MMPI-2.

An extensive literature will develop for the MMPI-2 over the next few years. The MMPI-2 manual (Butcher et al., 1989) provides a solid overview of the instrument, including administration and interpretive guides and 11 appendices providing a wide variety of data concerning the instrument. A specialized text has been published on the use of MMPI-2 content scales (Butcher, Graham, Williams, & Ben-Porath, 1990) and general guides to the MMPI-2 have been provided by Butcher (1990b), Graham (1990), and Greene (1991). The MMPI text by Friedman, Webb, and Lewak (1989) contains a chapter providing information on the MMPI-2. A growing research literature is also rapidly evolving including studies of the use of the MMPI-2 in populations of college students (Butcher, Graham, Dahlstrom, & Bowman, 1990), substance abusers (Greene, Arredondo, & Davis, 1991), and active duty military personnel (Butcher,

Jeffrey, Cayton, Colligan, DeVore, & Minnegawa, 1990).

In conclusion, the MMPI-2 is a new instrument closely related to the original MMPI. The MMPI-2 and MMPI are not, however, equivalent measures. Until a substantial correlate literature is published for the MMPI-2 , the issue of the generalizability of findings from the original test will be very important. It is likely that the generalizability of findings will vary depending on variables including gender, codetype definition or "crispness," and other factors to be determined by future researchers. As the MMPI-2 ultimately amasses its own independent research base, this issue will assume decreasing emphasis. The MMPI-2 is a reasonable compromise of the old and the new; an appropriate balance between that which required change (norms) and that which required preservation (standard scales). It should prove to be a worthy successor to the MMPI.

REVIEWER'S REFERENCES

Weiner, D. N., & Harmon, L. R. (1946). Subtle and obvious keys for the MMPI: Their development. (Advisement Bulletin No. 16). Minneapolis: Regional Veterans Administration Office.

Louttit, C. M., & Browne, C. G. (1947). The use of psychometric instruments in psychological clinics. *Journal of Consulting Psychology, 11*, 49-54.

Dahlstrom, W. G., & Welsh, G. S. (1960). *An MMPI handbook: A guide to use in clinical practice and research*. Minneapolis: University of Minnesota Press.

Sundberg, N. D. (1961). The practice of psychological testing in clinical services in the United States. *American Psychologist, 16*, 79-83.

MacAndrew, C. (1965). The differentiation of male alcoholic outpatients from nonalcoholic psychiatric outpatients by means of the MMPI. *Quarterly Journal of Studies of Alcohol, 26*, 238-246.

Wiggins, J. S. (1966). Substantive dimensions of self-report in the MMPI item pool. *Psychological Monographs, 80* (22, Whole No. 630).

Butcher, J. N., & Owen, P. L. (1978). Objective personality inventories: Recent research and some contemporary issues. In B. Wolman (Ed.), *Clinical diagnoses of mental disorders* (pp. 475-546). New York: Plenum.

Greene, R. L. (1978). An empirically devised MMPI carelessness scale. *Journal of Clinical Psychology, 34*, 407-410.

Keane, T. M., Malloy, P. F., & Fairbank, J. A. (1984). Empirical development of an MMPI subscale for the assessment of combat-related posttraumatic stress disorder. *Journal of Consulting and Clinical Psychology, 52*, 888-891.

Lubin, B., Larsen, R. M., & Matarazzo, J. D. (1984). Patterns of psychological test usage in the United States: 1935-1982. *American Psychologist, 39*, 451-454.

Butcher, J. N. (1987). Computerized clinical and personality assessment using the MMPI. In J. N. Butcher (Ed.), *Computerized psychological assessment: A practitioner's guide* (pp. 161-197). New York: Basic Books.

Schlenger, W. E., & Kulka, R. A. (1987, August). *Performance of the Keane-Fairbank MMPI scale and other self-report measures in identifying posttraumatic stress disorder*. Paper presented at the 95th Annual Convention of the American Psychological Association, New York, NY.

Tellegen, A. M. (1988, August). *Derivation of uniform T-scores for the restandardized MMPI. Symposium presentation at the 96th Annual Convention of the American Psychological Association, Atlanta, GA*.

Ben-Porath, Y. S., & Butcher, J. N. (1989). Psychometric stability of rewritten MMPI items. *Journal of Personality Assessment, 53*, 645-653.

Butcher, J. N., Dahlstrom, W. G., Graham, J. R., Tellegen, A., & Kaemmer, B. (1989). *Minnesota Multiphasic Personality Inventory-2: Manual for administration and scoring*. Minneapolis: University of Minnesota Press.

Friedman, A. R., Webb, J. T., & Lewak, R. (1989). *Psychological assessment with the MMPI*. Hillsdale, NJ: Lawrence Erlbaum Associates.

Pancoast, D. L., & Archer, R. P. (1989). Original adult MMPI norms in normal samples: A review with implications for future developments. *Journal of Personality Assessment, 53*, 376-395.

Butcher, J. N. (1990a). *Educational level and MMPI-2 measured psychopathology: A case of negligible influence*. In J. N. Butcher (Ed.), MMPI-2 News and Profiles: A Newsletter of the MMPI-2 Workshops &

Symposia (Vol. 1, No. 2, p. 3). Minneapolis: University of Minnesota Department of Psychology.

Butcher, J. N. (1990b). *MMPI-2 in psychological treatment*. New York: Oxford University Press.

Butcher, J. N., Graham, J. R., Dahlstrom, W. G., & Bowman, E. (1990). The MMPI-2 with college students. *Journal of Personality Assessment, 54*, 1-15.

Butcher, J. N., Graham, J. R., Williams, C. L., & Ben-Porath, Y. S. (1990). *Development and use of the MMPI-2 content scales*. Minneapolis: University of Minnesota Press.

Butcher, J. N., Jeffrey, T., Cayton, T. G., Colligan, S., DeVore, J., & Minnegawa, R. (1990). A study of active duty military personnel with the MMPI-2. *Military Psychology, 2*, 47-61.

Graham, J. R. (1990). MMPI-2: Assessing personality in psychopathology. New York: Oxford University Press.

Honaker, L. M. (1990, August). MMPI and MMPI-2: Alternate forms or different tests? In M. Maruish (Chair), *The MMPI and MMPI-2 comparability examined from different perspectives*. Symposium conducted at the annual conference of the American Psychological Association, Boston, MA.

Levitt, E. E. (1990). A structural analysis of the impact of MMPI-21 on MMPI-1. *Journal of Personality Assessment, 55*, 562-577.

Archer, R. P., Maruish, M., Imhof, E. A., & Piotrowski, C. (1991). Psychological test usage with adolescent clients: 1990 survey findings. *Professional Psychology: Research and Practice, 22*, 247-252.

Greene, R. L. (1991). *The MMPI-2/MMPI: An interpretive manual*. Boston: Allyn & Bacon.

Greene, R. L., Arredondo, R., & Davis, H. G. (1991). *MMPI and MMPI-2 MacAndrew Alcoholism Scales: Comparability of classification rates*. Manuscript submitted for publication.

Graham, J. R., Timbrook, R. E., Ben-Porath, Y. S., & Butcher, J. N. (in press). Code-type congruence between MMPI and MMPI-2: Separating fact from artifact. *Psychological Assessment: A Journal of Consulting and Clinical Psychology*.

Review of the Minnesota Multiphasic Personality Inventory-2 by DAVID S. NICHOLS, Supervising Clinical Psychologist, Department of Psychology, Dammasch State Hospital, Wilsonville, OR:

The original Minnesota normal sample consisted of 724 relatives and other visitors at the University of Minnesota Hospitals. The data from this sample provided the needed contrast for the original criterion groups from which the clinical scales of the Minnesota Multiphasic Personality Inventory (MMPI) were developed. But this use made the normal sample unsuitable for the establishment of test norms. Unfortunately, funds that would have been required to gather a normative sample of adequate size and representation were unavailable. By making the Minnesota Normals serve as both a source of contrast for pathological samples and the reference for normative standards, the latter function was compromised. Forcing the Normals to perform this double duty in effect purged them of their normal levels of abnormality. The consequence of this bias became evident as data from subsequent normal groups became available. Plotted on the standard profile form, these groups appear overpathologized, their scores tending to hover at about 5 T-scores of elevation above the mean (Colligan, Osborne, Swenson, & Offord, 1983; Pancoast & Archer, 1989). Thus, the need for the restandardization of the MMPI has been present from the beginning.

But the pressures to revise came less from problems with the original norms than from developments that followed the test's release. Foremost among these was the overwhelming success of the MMPI in assisting clinical work, a success vastly underanticipated by the test's founders. The lack of a nationally representative normative sample began to stand out as the applications of the MMPI expanded outside the psychiatric ward to include general medicine, personnel screening and selection, forensic and child custody evaluations, outpatient psychotherapy, assessment of disability, and a host of others. The phrase "Minnesota farmers" became the standard term of opprobrium for this largely rural, eighth-grade educated, skilled or semiskilled, northern midwestern group of Scandinavian origins. The geographic, cultural, educational, and occupational atypicality of the normative sample grew increasingly conspicuous with the passage of half a century and the availability of competing instruments with broader based normative samples such as the Basic Psychological Inventory (Jackson, 1989), the Clinical Analysis Questionnaire (9:232), the Millon Clinical Multiaxial Inventory (239), and the NEO Personality Inventory (258).

There were internal problems as well. The lack of percentile equivalence among the linear T-distributions for the basic clinical scales, although not compromising interpretation from actuarially derived profile types, confounded inferences based on scale-by-scale comparisons because greater elevations did not necessarily correspond to greater statistical deviance. Many items suffered from ambiguous, awkward, agrammatical, or overly complex phrasing. Others employed sexist wording or language that has fallen into disuse: streetcars, sleeping powders, acid stomach, cutting up, cross, the funnies, trifling, hooky. In other cases obscurity surrounded the item as a whole: "I used to like drop-the-handkerchief." For some items, endorsement frequencies had drifted over time, or they had been found objectionable and represented potential violations of Equal Employment Opportunity Commission guidelines if included in testing for personnel decisions. Items covering bowel and bladder functioning, sexual adjustment, and religious beliefs might fall into this category.

THE RESTANDARDIZATION. Funded by the test's copyright holder, the University of Minnesota Press, the restandardization is based on a sample of 2,600 paid volunteer adults, recruited from newspaper advertisements and random mailing solicitations, and tested under supervision at prearranged sites in seven states. Collateral data included biographical information and recent stressful life events. Behavior ratings were collected from 928 couples with each spouse rating the other. The sample exceeds 1980 census values for education and occupational status but approximates them in terms of age and income ranges, ethnic diversity, and marital status. The consequences of census disparities appear minor. The effect of the educational bias, for example, is limited to scores on scales *F* and *MF* for men and *K* for both sexes.

Deviations from the norm for the basic clinical scales (excluding *Mf* & *Si* and the Minnesota Multiphasic Personality Inventory-2 (MMPI-2) content scales, to be discussed below, are represented in uniform *T*-scores such that the positive skew of the original scale distributions is preserved but a given *T*-score corresponds to nearly identical percentile values across the scales. For each sex and scale set, scores were represented in a composite distribution. Scales were then individually transformed to conform to the composite. The procedure reduced the skewness of Scales *1*, *7*, and *8*, and augmented it for Scales *3*, *4*, *6*, and *9* (the skew of Scale *2* was reduced for men, augmented for women). Compared with the normative shifts observed from the original to the restandardization sample, the effects of making uniform the new scale distributions are small. It is the normative differences that will require some getting used to. Scales *4* and *8*, for example, will be less prominent in MMPI-2 profiles than in the original MMPI; Scale *6*, more so. *T*-scores on Scale *MF* for men are 11 points lower throughout the raw score range. The *F* Scale that a consensus of expert opinion has viewed as elevating too fast now goes up even faster, partly as a consequence of eliminating high *F* protocols from the restandardization sample. This effect is especially dramatic for women: *T*-scores of 70, 80, and 90 on the MMPI become 79, 92, and 109 on the MMPI-2, respectively. The *L* Scale, however, long considered sluggish by MMPI experts, now elevates much more briskly on the MMPI-2.

From the beginning, normal and pathological groups have been most reliably discriminated on the MMPI by a point 1.5 standard deviations above the mean. On the original MMPI, a *T*-score of 70 reflected this amount of deviation *plus* an additional increment that can be traced to three major causes: (*a*) the hypernormalizing effect on the original normative sample of their service as the controls for clinical scale development (Pancoast & Archer, 1989), (*b*) the failure to discourage the use of the Cannot Say (*?*) category in the earlier work, and (*c*) the decision to exclude from the normal sample anyone "under a physician's care" (Hathaway & McKinley, 1980, p. 10). None of these three factors were operative in the restandardization, hence the movement of the line of demarcation between normals and patients from *T*-70 to *T*-65 on the MMPI-2 represents less a change than a point of continuity.

Considerable controversy has surfaced over the concordance between MMPI and MMPI-2 codetypes. Rates reported thus far cluster around 67%, about twice the value reported for 1–2-week codetype stabilities. The effect of the lack of complete concordance between the original MMPI and the MMPI-2 on clinical prediction/description will be unclear for some time, but sweeping claims for the superiority of the codetypes of either version, when the two disagree, should be viewed skeptically.

REVISED ASPECTS AND NEW FEATURES. One hundred fifty-four new items were written for the restandardization of which 107 appear in the MMPI-2. Others were rewritten for reasons given above. Although the new items expand clinically important areas of content like substance use, marital relations, and suicide, their phrasings do not always reflect the smooth, worn quality of common speech. The three new suicide statements, for example, employ the fixed operative expression, "kill(ing) myself," in preference to more varied and less violent locutions like "want to die," "end it all," "commit suicide," "get it over with." Most of the hundreds of scales developed from the original item pool are relatively intact unless they included significant religious content or were drawn mainly from the last 200 items of the original MMPI. In order to be scored, however, the older keys must be translated into MMPI-2 item numbers, a process aided by an appendix in the manual (Butcher, Dahlstrom, Graham, Tellegen, & Kaemmer, 1989).

Item order has been rearranged to permit the basic validity and clinical scales to be scored from the first 370 items. Permitting the inventory to be discontinued at this point is a practice to be deplored, however, because it sacrifices the assessment of consistency (VRIN) and the content scales that amount to conceptually (though not statistically) independent self-ratings of symptoms and attitudes.

The availability of the Harris-Lingoes subscales continues, but those for Scale *4* were altered by dropping the off scale items. The Serkownek subscales for Scales *5* (*Mf*) and *0* (*Si*) have been abandoned, though those for Scale *0* have been replaced by three new, internally consistent subscales (Ben-Porath, Hostetler, Butcher, & Graham, 1989). The first two of these nicely distinguish the subjective (visibility discomfort, ease of embarrassment, self-consciousness; the feeling component of shyness) from the objective (social withdrawal, avoidance of groups and crowds; the public component) aspects of introversion. The third subscale is a residual dominated by neuroticism. An attempt to develop new Scale *5* subscales reportedly failed (Hostetler, Ben-Porath, Butcher, & Graham, 1989), but this failure owed more to unrealistic internal consistency hurdles than to the lack of independent subdimensions.

Of many supplementary scales listed in the manual, Peterson's *GM* (Masculine Gender Role) and *GF* (Feminine Gender Role) scales are among those new on the MMPI-2. These scales tap independent dimensions related to gender identity and, by implication, to sex role differentiation or rigidity on the one hand, and "androgyny" or a lack of sex role differentiation on the other. Three scales, *Mt* (College maladjustment), *PK* (Post Traumatic Stress Disorder-Keane), and *PS* (PTSD-Schlenger) are experimental and of doubtful utility in the clinical arena, but may have value in epidemiological research. All are saturated with nonspecific variation, and none has demonstrated adequate discriminative validity. The use of any of these in clinical settings will result in an explosion of false positives. The manual section describing *PK* and *PS* contains the only howler I was able to find: "These two scales appear to be largely independent of each other" (p. 41). With 26 items in common, the scales neither appear independent, nor are they (*rs* about .90).

Two new features are especially noteworthy. The MMPI-2 permits a much more comprehensive and reliable ascertainment of protocol validity. A new inconsistency scale (VRIN) has been added, as has a content-free acquiescence scale (TRIN). Both consist of paired items and hand scoring for both is complicated and taxing. A new infrequency scale *F*-Back (F_B) takes over as items scored on *F* become exhausted midway through the test. Like *F*, the new scale is sensitive to flagging cooperation, negative dissimulation, reading difficulties, cognitive disorganization, and carelessness.

Expanding the item pool to include new areas such as suicide and substance use created an occasion for reassessing dimensions of content. Three of the 13 content scales developed by Wiggins (1966) lost 20% or more of their items in the revision. The development of the 15 MMPI-2 content scales is described in Butcher, Graham, Williams and Ben-Porath (1990). Half of these scales are essentially MMPI-2 versions of their Wiggins predecessors but show somewhat higher internal consistencies. New scales address anxiety, antisocial attitudes and behavior, anger, low self-esteem, work interference, obsessiveness, health concerns, Type A personality, and negative treatment indicators. Most of these scales are destined to become useful in their own right and as aids to interpreting the standard profile. An internally consistent anxiety scale to stand beside an internally consistent depression scale has been needed for years. The MMPI-2 has them. The low self-esteem scale is one of similar value. The Type A and negative treatment indicators scales, however, have a significant potential for misinterpretation and misuse, and should probably be ignored pending adequate evidence for their construct and discriminative validity. Subscales for most of the new content scales are under development and these should enhance the interpretation of the content and clinical scales.

DOCUMENTATION. The MMPI-2 manual is five times the size of its predecessor, and is divided between text and appendices in a ratio of 1:2. It is clearly written and strikes an appropriate balance between clinical and psychometric values. The restandardization is well described and tables are provided that compare the normative sample against 1980 census data. For the clinician, there are scoring keys and interpretative information for each scale mentioned in this review, a section on protocol validity, and a pair of interpreted protocols. Tables are provided that give interpretative implications of four or five levels of elevation for the standard scales. This feature serves a very useful orienting purpose, but these tables may be quite misleading when moderate to extreme response sets are present. Tables for converting raw scores to linear or uniform *T*-scores are provided for the standard scales, with and without *K*-corrections. For the psychometrician, there are test-retest and internal consistency values, itemmetric and codetype concordance data, and external correlates for most scales. Conversion tables for translating MMPI item numbers into MMPI-2, and vice versa, are provided. Three scoring key and a few other errors have been discovered so far and will be noted in forthcoming errata. A final appendix, *K*-1 and *K*-2, is given for converting *K*-corrected and non-*K*-corrected *T*-scores on MMPI-2 profiles into MMPI values. By an unfortunate oversight, the *T*-score values reported in these tables did not reflect the adjustments to the original normative data made by Hathaway and Briggs (1957). Corrected tables will appear in the next manual revision.

A second basic document, *Development and Use of the MMPI-2 Content Scales* (Butcher, Graham, Williams, & Ben-Porath, 1990), contains a more leisurely and comprehensive description of the MMPI-2 restandardization than that given in the manual, and describes the construction, psychometric characteristics, preliminary validation, and interpretive guidelines for this new set of scales. More extensive reviews of this monograph are available (Caldwell, 1991; Nichols, in press).

THE LIMITS OF REVISION. Some critics of the MMPI-2 will complain that the revision did not go far enough. The nosology of *fin de siecle* psychiatry persists in the clinical scales. Why not develop new scales based on new pathological criterion groups defined by *DSM-III-R* criteria? The 50 years of research devoted to the MMPI have contributed to the very definition of the test. To have abandoned the original clinical scales would have been to decouple the revision from a body of validating evidence that could require another half-century to replace. But there were three other reasons for stopping short of a thoroughgoing revision: Criterion samples for many of the original scale constructs are simply no longer available. The pervasive use of psychotropic medications in contemporary psychiatry, and judicial rulings covering the right to treatment have virtually eliminated access to unmedicated criterion cases needed for reconstituting the clinical scales. Second, even if unmedicated criterion cases were available, a new set of basic clinical scales developed from them would not necessarily be justified. The recent acceleration in the rate at which the defining criteria for mental disorders are revised would render such scales ephemeral, thereby defeating any hope of repeating the incremental but cumulatively massive elaboration of scale constructs that has occurred with the original scales. A final reason for preserving the original constructs was the discovery in the late 1940s that high-point pairs and triads (codetypes) were often associated with distinct and sometimes unanticipated homogeneities in the patients that produced them. Thus, to abandon these constructs would have been to hamper the means by which the covariation among the personal and symptomatic characteristics common to specific code patterns could be identified and studied in the future.

SUMMARY. So far as the standard validity and clinical scales are concerned, the statistical properties of the MMPI-2 with respect to reliability, validity, and standard error are those of its predecessor, for better or worse. The provision of uniform T-scores is a significant advance, the immediate benefit of which is to simplify the comparison of scale elevations against a fixed percentile standard. In the longer term, this change may enhance the understanding of common configural patterns. As in the past, the interpretive implications of the clinical scales and codetypes are significantly augmented by reference to subscales, content scales, and supplementary scales.

In general, the new features incorporated in the MMPI-2 are genuine improvements. The new validity scales will greatly aid the ascertainment of validity, something the original validity scales were never very good at. The restandardization was appropriately executed and provides a normative sample of suitable size and ethnic diversity. Some of the shortcomings in representativeness (few Hispanics, Asian-Americans, older women, unrepresentative Native Americans) appear unlikely to compromise the test in most settings. Other divergences from the census such as the limited number of subjects at the lowest educational and occupational levels, and the generally higher socioeconomic status of the restandardization sample are of uncertain consequence at present. In psychiatric contexts, the higher educational and occupational attainment of the normative group may well increase the discrimination of psychopathology over the original version (W. G. Dahlstrom, personal communication, 1991).

The University of Minnesota Press and the Restandardization Committee wisely chose to rehabilitate the MMPI at a time when it had never been more vigorous, well before it began to cackle and wheeze. The revision breathes new life into a test the utility and excellence of which have made it the most widely used device for personality measurement in the world. The accustomed user will find that most of what was broke was fixed, most of what was not broke was left alone, and that the iatrogenic disfigurements are few and mostly minor. The psychodiagnostician selecting a structured inventory for the first time will find that no competing assessment device for abnormal psychology has stronger credentials for clinical description and prediction. As an inventory of normal range personality attributes, the MMPI-2 retains all the weaknesses of its predecessor and will, for most purposes, prove less satisfactory than instruments like the NEO Personality Inventory.

REVIEWER'S REFERENCES

Hathaway, S. R., & Briggs, P. F. (1957). Some normative data on new MMPI scales. *Journal of Clinical Psychology, 13*, 364-368.
Wiggins, J. S. (1966). Substantive dimensions of self-report in the MMPI item pool. *Psychological Monographs, 80* (22, Whole No. 630).
Hathaway, S. R., & McKinley, J. C. (1980). Construction of the schedule. In W. G. Dahlstrom & L. E. Dahlstrom (Eds.). *Basic readings on the MMPI: A new selection on personality measurement* (pp. 7-11). Minneapolis: University of Minnesota Press.
Colligan, R. C., Osborne, D., Swenson, W. M., & Offord, K. P. (1983). *The MMPI: A contemporary normative study.* New York: Praeger.
Ben-Porath, Y. S., Hostetler, K., Butcher, J. N., & Graham, J. R. (1989). New subscales for the MMPI-2 Social Introversion (Si) scale. *Psychological Assessment, 1,* 169-174.
Butcher, J. N., Dahlstrom, W. G., Graham, J. R., Tellegen, A., & Kaemmer, B. (1989). *Minnesota Multiphasic Personality Inventory-2 (MMPI-2): Manual for administration and scoring.* Minneapolis: University of Minnesota Press.
Hostetler, K., Ben-Porath, Y. S., Butcher, J. N., & Graham, J. R. (1989, April). *New MMPI-2 subscales.* Paper presented at the annual meeting of the Society for Personality Assessment, New York, NY.
Jackson, D. N. (1989). Basic Personality Inventory. Port Huron, MI: Sigma Assessment Systems, Inc.
Pancoast, D. L., & Archer, R. P. (1989). Original adult MMPI norms in normal samples: A review with implications for future developments. *Journal of Personality Assessment, 53,* 376-395.
Butcher, J. N., Graham, J. R., Williams, C. L., & Ben-Porath, Y. S. (1990). *Development and use of the MMPI-2 content scales.* Minneapolis: University of Minnesota Press.
Caldwell, A. B. (1991). MMPI-2 content scales: What you say is what you get? *Contemporary Psychology, 6,* 560-561.
Nichols, D. S. (in press). *New MMPI-2 content scales. Journal of Personality Assessment.*

[245]

[Re Minnesota Multiphasic Personality Inventory/California Psychological Inventory.] Behaviordyne OnLine MMPI/CPI Reports.

Purpose: To provide scoring and interpretive reports.
Publication Dates: 1971–89.
Acronym: BOS.
Restricted Distribution: Clinical reports are available only to state-licensed psychologists or psychotherapists.
Price Data: Available from publisher.
Foreign Language Edition: Narrative reports available in Spanish.
Comments: Mail order or on-line IBM-PC computer service provides seven reports: Clinical (Comprehensive

Clinical Report, Diagnostic Report, Physicians Report), Non-Clinical (Correctional Report, Counseling Report, Personnel Report, Profile and Data Page).

Author: Behaviordyne, Inc.

[Note: This system evaluation is based on materials available as of February 1990—Ed.]

Publisher: Behaviordyne, Inc.

Review of the Behaviordyne OnLine MMPI/CPI Reports by L. MICHAEL HONAKER, Adjunct Professor, Florida Institute of Technology, Melbourne, FL:

The Behaviordyne OnLine System (BOS) is an IBM-PC-compatible, microcomputer-based system that provides scoring and narrative reports for the Minnesota Multiphasic Personality Inventory (MMPI) and/or the California Psychological Inventory (CPI). The BOS software does not administer the test items (as the name "OnLine" would imply) but instead allows the user to enter examinees' MMPI/CPI item responses on the PC and then transfer the data via modem to the Behaviordyne mainframe computer. Scoring and report generation are done by the mainframe system and then either retrieved directly over the modem hookup or mailed to the customer. If the report is obtained via modem the user can print the report directly and/or can use the BOS software to prepare the report for the user's word processor for modification. The system produces eight basic MMPI/CPI reports, ranging from a simple inventory profile and data summary to a Comprehensive Clinical Report. The latter includes a detailed analytic based analysis of personality functioning, including suggested DSM-III diagnoses and treatment recommendations, and a complete summary of over 150 scales. Options are available that allow for expansion or contraction of the basic reports and the production of a self-report for the examinee to read. The clinician can also obtain either a differential report which compares two MMPI-CPI administrations or full reports for both tests when an MMPI and CPI-268 short form are administered to the same subject.

SYSTEM REQUIREMENTS. The software runs on an IBM-PC or compatible with 256K RAM, PC-DOS/MS-DOS version 2.0 or higher, and two 5 1/4 - inch drives or a 5 1/4 -inch drive and hard disk. For data transfer and report retrieval a 1200 or 300 baud asynchronous modem is needed. If reports are to be printed by the user, a printer capable of doing hardware form feeds is required. The system requirements parallel those found for most commercial MMPI programs except for the additional need of the modem.

RUN TIME AND COSTS. Total *online* run time for a report is approximately 15 to 30 minutes; however, *total time* from data input to report retrieval is about 1.5 hours. Data input requires 5 to 15 minutes, depending on the user's familiarity with the system. Transfer of the responses to the

mainframe and retrieval of the report requires as much as an additional 10 to 15 minutes for each report processed. The main factor that extends the total time is that the user must first send the data to the Behaviordyne main frame and then retrieve the report at a later time. The manual indicates that "reports will usually be ready to receive within one hour" (p. 3). This delay in the availability of the report and the additional time required to transfer data and retrieve reports via a modem results in a total run time that is considerably longer than that found for most microcomputer-based interpretive systems.

The user is charged for each report generated, with prices ranging from $8 for the Profile Only to $40 for the Comprehensive Clinical Report, plus the cost of phone time for data transfer and report retrieval. Some of the available options result in additional charges of $.50 (critical items) to $6.75 (self-report). Overall, the cost is somewhat higher than most comparable systems on the market.

USER-COMPUTER INTERFACE. The system is generally easy to use; however, there are some areas that can be problematic. First, each separate function for the system requires that the user run a different program; the user must remember six different program names to use the system. Although the program names are straightforward (e.g., SEND for transmitting data over the modem), it would be helpful to provide a main menu which accesses the different programs via software control.

User feedback when errors occur is a second concern. The system in some cases displays inadequate and/or inaccurate feedback when the user provides improper input or when the system is not functioning properly. If the user inputs unacceptable data the system "beeps" and/or reprompts the user for input. However, the system does not inform the user what error was made or provide a help function with a listing or sample of appropriate input. Although the necessary information is available in the manual, provision of error feedback and help screens would be a useful addition to the system.

Inaccurate feedback occurs when the modem/phone line is not functioning properly. For example, if the phone line or modem become disconnected the system will continue to indicate that the call is being completed, that the Behaviordyne computer has answered the call and then state that the system is not available at this time. This inadequate error trapping and feedback is particularly problematic if a nonstandard modem is employed and the user is attempting to determine the appropriate modem configuration switches for use with the system.

The input program is a final concern regarding the user-computer interface. The user presses the T

(True), F (False), B (Blank), or D (Double) keys for data input. Also, for faster input, the system allows use of "," and "." in place of the T and F keys, respectively, and is flexible with respect to how many items (up to 60) can be typed in before pressing the <RETURN> key. However, this latter feature can be problematic in that the <RETURN> key must be pressed before the screen will indicate the current item number. If a fixed number of items is not input on each line it is difficult to scan the previously entered items for possible errors. Also, if you choose to press <RETURN> after each item, which provides continuous prompts of the current item number, then correcting mistakes becomes more difficult; the <BACKSPACE>, which is used to correct the previous response, is no longer functional and the <UP ARROW> backs the user up 10 items and then requires that all 10 items be entered a second time.

To circumvent these possible problems in data input, it would prove helpful for the publishers to combine the KEYIN and EDIT programs. The EDIT program, which is separate from the KEYIN program, allows the user to review and change data that have been input previously. Demographic and response data are presented on a single screen and the arrow keys can be used to move to the different data points which then can be changed as needed. Response data are presented on 12 lines and each line contains five separated blocks of 10 responses (except for the last line). As you move the cursor across items, the current item number is presented on the screen. This mode of item presentation allows for easy identification of errors and the correction procedures are straightforward and user-friendly. If a similar presentation and correction procedure could be adopted for inputting data it would improve the system.

VALIDITY ISSUES. (This section is based primarily on evaluation of the Comprehensive Clinical Report.) The BOS is a commercial outgrowth of the interpretive system developed at the University of Kentucky by Joseph C. Finney and Charles Dwight Auvenshine. The system reportedly includes over 23,000 statements, which are based primarily on configural combinations, rather than scale by scale evaluation, of subsets taken from more than 150 scales. More than half of the scales were developed specifically by Finney and are not used by other MMPI/CPI interpretation systems. At least 26 of Finney's scales are based on unpublished data.

A relative strength of the computer-based test interpretation (CBTI) produced by the BOS is that in contrast to many available CBTI products the BOS does provide documentation for the report. Included in the manual are references for the scales used in the report and descriptions of the formulae used for derivation of corrected scores and other indices. Also, the publisher provides additional materials, as requested, which give information regarding specific scales/indices and research findings. According to the documentation provided, statements included in the BOS reflect empirically developed formulae or expert opinion which Finney refers to as "rational combinations of empirically validated measures" (Finney, LeMaistre, Smith, Sward, Auvenshine, Tondow, & Skeeters, 1972, p. 4). Descriptions of the system indicate that "many important judgments" are based on simulation of "a flesh-and-blood psychologist" (Finney et al., 1972, p. 4), which suggests that a large proportion of the narrative statements are clinician rather than actuarial based.

At least some of the clinician-simulated statements are the result of a quasi-empirical validation procedure that is designed to validate the decision rule against the classification/decision of the simulated expert. This method entails selection of a sample of subjects known by the expert and rational selection of scale combinations by the expert to produce 100% classification agreement between the rule and expert. New subjects are then added to the sample and the classification rule is evaluated and revised if needed to maintain 100% concordance. Although this method does represent a unique strategy for the development of an expert simulation, it is unclear how many or which of the statements in the system were developed in this manner; this information is not presented clearly in the manual or in the report. More importantly, there is no information regarding cross validation of the decision rules with other samples in different settings. Also, the description of these simulation procedures does not indicate that any additional data were available for the subjects classified by the expert. Additional subject measures are necessary to evaluate the validity of and to strengthen the basis for the experts' judgements. This lack of external criteria represents a problem for most systems which are primarily expert based but is particularly problematic for the BOS because many of the interpretive algorithms involve scales specific to the Finney system.

The BOS uses normalized T-scores that are based on a sample of 2,048 normal men and women. (The characteristics of the sample are not reported in the manual.) In addition, for each MMPI scale three different corrected T-scores are computed which are designed to remove anxiety and response bias effects from the scores. The use of normalized T-scores, and the corresponding corrected values, produces scale scores which differ, sometimes considerably, from those which occur when traditional Minnesota MMPI norms are employed. For example, on a sample protocol run by this author there were differences of 30 or more *T*-score points on three scales and a difference of at least 25 points on two other scales. The BOS profile had different relative high points and was considerably lower than the Minnesota norm-based profile. The manual does not address the possible implications or ramifications of these discrepancies. Because most research on the MMPI has employed traditional norms (including many of the studies cited as references for the BOS) the generalizability of research findings to the Finney scores is questionable, particularly as it relates to the use and interpretation of high-point and two-point codes.

The report does present traditional Minnesota standard scores although the scores are apparently not used to generate the narrative. However, these scores are described as *similar* to those obtained with hand scoring and there is no information regarding how the scores were derived or how they differ from traditional scores. The latter information is important for clinicians who wish to evaluate the accuracy of the BOS report in light of their own interpretation of the profile.

REPORT CLARITY. The Comprehensive Clinical Report is considerably longer than that found in most CBTI systems. Reviewed sample reports ranged from 12 to 18 pages in length. There is a tendency for the narrative section to be repetitive and statements are included which are worded awkwardly and/or are ambiguous in content. For example, in the sample report provided in the manual, the following statements appear: "His strongest point, the one that can help him the most to succeed in his work, is his readiness to try new ideas. He is not at all strong in that quality, but it is stronger than some of his other points." Also, the reports can include contradictory statements but do not provide an explanation of how or why the discrepancies occur. Again from the sample report, the examinee is depicted first as: "He admits many small flaws or imperfections in himself," but then later in the same paragraph: "He seems somewhat defensive. He denies any faults." Information needs to be presented in the manual regarding what factors may lead to these contradictions so that the clinician can make an informed decision regarding which statement may be more accurate.

MAINTENANCE OF SOFTWARE AND HARDWARE. The report includes a listing of the raw responses which allow the clinician to verify whether information was accurately transmitted to and received from the Behaviordyne mainframe. Also, the publisher provides an 800 number to answer questions and address software problems. Because the main CBTI software is maintained on the mainframe system, the user has constant access to the current version of the system.

MANUAL. The manual sections for use of the BOS are written in an easy-to-read, straightforward manner. Many examples are provided and minimal computer experience is required to understand the material. The initial chapters sequentially parallel the steps that are followed when the program is used and progresses from installation and setup of the system to preparation of the received report for word processing. As mentioned earlier, documentation of the system is provided in the appendix as well as descriptions of the types of reports produced by the BOS and a sample MMPI and CPI comprehensive report. Additional sample reports are available from the publisher.

SECURITY ISSUES. The publisher restricts the availability of the clinical reports (i.e., Physician's Report, Diagnostic Report, and Comprehensive Clinical Report) to licensed clinicians. However, other "non-clinical" reports (i.e., Personnel Report, Counseling Report, and Correctional Report) are available to personnel workers and counselors. The clinical reports include comprehensive emotional evaluation and diagnostic and treatment implications, whereas the nonclinical reports do not. Although the nonclinical reports are written in a manner that deemphasizes the pathology components of the results and are written in less technical language, the practice of making any type of MMPI/CPI report available to individuals who are not specifically trained in test interpretation may be questionable. Based on the professional standards for providers of psychological services, the *Guidelines for Computer-Based Tests and Interpretations* recommends that "Professionals will limit their use of computerized testing to techniques with which they are familiar and competent to use" (APA, 1986, p. 9). Making the reports available to individuals without training in assessment seems to contradict our own standards. The validity/accuracy of the report cannot be evaluated effectively if the user does not have an understanding of the test and its limitations.

Confidentiality of examinee material is well protected by the BOS. On the computer system, examinees are identified by number only and no name is included in the user's or Behaviordyne's files. Also, reports for a particular individual are released only to the professional ordering the report, although the report will be rerun for another qualified professional if a written release is obtained from the examinee.

SUMMARY. The BOS provides a comprehensive array of reports for the CPI/MMPI which are not available in "one package" from other sources. The main strengths of the system include: The manual is clear and user friendly, the system is generally easy to use, documentation for the system is provided by the manual/publisher, the user has constant access to updated versions of the system, good customer support is provided, and the confidentiality of the examinee is well protected. The major drawbacks of the BOS include: The total time for report completion is longer and report cost is higher than that for other systems, some of the wording of the reports is awkward and at times contradictory, scores used by the system are not based on traditional MMPI/CPI norms thus making generalizability of previous validity research to the BOS scores questionable, and much of the report is based on scores/indices that are unique to the BOS and have not been adequately cross validated. Finally, preliminary research that examined the BOS MMPI report in comparison to six other available CBTI systems (Eyde, Kowal, & Fishburne, 1986, 1987) found the BOS contained the lowest rate of clinically relevant statements and had the lowest overall descriptive accuracy. (Each report was evaluated by 12 experienced clinicians who had access to case history data on the patients.) Although these results are definitely not conclusive they suggest the need for further research to examine the validity of the BOS interpretive system.

REVIEWER'S REFERENCES

Finney, J. C., LeMaistre, G., Smith, D. F., Sward, R., Auvenshine, C. D., Tondow, M., & Skeeters, D. E. (1972). Computer simulation of psychologists' decision-making. *Proceedings of the ACM Annual Conference.*
American Psychological Association. (1986). *Guidelines for computer-based tests and interpretations.* Washington, DC: Author.
Eyde, L. D., Kowal, D. M., & Fishburne, F. J., Jr. (1986, August). The validity of computer-based test interpretations of the MMPI. In A. D. Mangelsdorff (chair), *Computer-based clinical assessment for children, adults, and neuropsychological cases.* Symposium conducted at the annual meeting of the American Psychological Association, Washington, DC.
Eyde, L. D., Kowal, D. M., & Fishburne, F. J., Jr. (1987, September). Clinical implications of validity research on computer-based test interpretations of the MMPI. In A. D. Mangelsdorff (chair), *Practical test user problems facing psychologists in private practice.* Symposium conducted at the annual meeting of the American Psychological Association, New York.

Review of the Behaviordyne OnLine MMPI/CPI Reports by MATTHEW E. LAMBERT, Assistant Professor of Psychology, Texas Tech University, Lubbock, TX:

Behaviordyne, Inc. was established in 1971 as the sole franchisee of the Minnesota Multiphasic Personality Inventory (MMPI) and California Psychological Inventory (CPI) computerized narrative reporting system developed by Joseph C. Finney and Charles D. Auvenshine at the University of Kentucky between 1965 and 1970.

The Behaviordyne MMPI/CPI narrative program provides psychological reports based upon the MMPI Group Form or Form-R and the CPI Revised Form. From these any of seven report types can be produced: (*a*) the Profile and Data page—an inventory profile, scale scores, and an item response listing; (*b*) the Personnel Report—a narrative report designed for vocational assessment and counseling; (*c*) the Counseling Report—designed for personal counseling settings, it focuses on client strengths and coping abilities relative to the counseling process; (*d*) the Correctional Report—for case management and planning in correctional or legal settings; (*e*) the

Physician's Report—focused on personality and psychopathology characteristics related to physical functioning; (*f*) the Diagnostic Report—designed as a psychodiagnostic aid for use in hospital and clinic admission screenings; and (*g*) the Comprehensive Clinical Report—dedicated to a thorough analysis of a client's personality and psychopathology characteristics. Also available are companion reports, for each report type, that are designed for direct consumption by the client. The various report types may also be supplemented by several additional report options that can provide supplementary scores, DSM-II and DSM-III diagnoses, critical items, and extensive research data.

The Behaviordyne reports can be accessed via mail order submission of completed inventory protocols or by use of the ONLINE microcomputer software system. The ONLINE system allows for transmission of completed protocols directly to Behaviordyne's main computer facility and the subsequent downloading of completed reports a short time later. Furthermore, the ONLINE system provides for in-house optical scanning of answer sheets to facilitate scoring and the conversion of downloaded reports to documents that may then be edited in word processing programs. Reports produced by the ONLINE system are slightly less expensive than the mail order reports, yet long distance charges may easily offset any savings inherent to the current ONLINE system version (Ver. 2.5). For example, the estimated time to download six Comprehensive Clinical Reports with additional options that were submitted by this reviewer was 110 minutes. Version 3.0 of the ONLINE system planned for release in 1990, however, should dramatically reduce downloading times. The ONLINE software is provided free to Behaviordyne's clients.

Supporting documentation for the Behaviordyne reporting system primarily contains instructions and information regarding use of the system. Specific reliability and validity data for the system are not summarized in the user manuals or promotional materials. The company does, however, maintain a bibliography of over 100 articles related to the MMPI and CPI, the various clinical indices used to generate reports, and the overall reporting system that can be provided to users upon request. Much of the information contained in this review was drawn from those sources.

Although protocols may be submitted by mail or electronically, access to the various report types is not readily available to everyone. Report types 5 through 7 are restricted to licensed professionals (e.g., psychologists or psychiatrists) only. Such professionals must provide evidence of their qualifications through a statement indicating their license number and the state board holding jurisdiction over them. These statements may then be checked against membership listings from various professional organizations. Additionally, some report options are restricted to reports designed only for those qualified professionals (e.g., diagnoses restricted to reports 5 through 7). Although those restrictions control the specific content type in some reports they do not control against the inclusion of potentially inappropriate content in all reports. For example, the Penal/Correctional option could be included in the Personnel Report.

The content for each Behaviordyne report is drawn from a statement library numbering over 23,000 statements. From this library statement selections are made based upon complex rational decision rules that involve various combinations of 161 scale scores for the MMPI and 141 scale scores for the CPI, 12 factor scores, and 45 indices developed by the narrative program's original authors. These variables were derived from data collected on a sample of over 2,000 men and women who completed the MMPI and CPI, along with other tests, as part of an MMPI/CPI restandardization study conducted at the University of Kentucky during the late 1960s. This sample population differed considerably from the Minnesota sample originally used to standardize the MMPI in that it was stratified to match the United States census demographics available at the time.

The data collected from this population were factor analyzed and subjected to various rational combinations and statistical manipulations that resulted in the scores used with the narrative reporting system. The rational combinations and statistical manipulations of the data, however, were often not based upon traditional psychometric methods, but rather on the authors' personal psychodynamic theoretical approach to understanding psychopathology and their knowledge of patients with whom they would attempt to validate the indices. Specifically, the authors would statistically derive theoretically relevant indices and then empirically test those indices against groups of patients who would be expected to load in a particular direction on those variables. If the patient did not load on the variable as expected it was reevaluated, theoretically modified, and retested until it was deemed by the authors to be a satisfactory index. Dr. Finney likened this approach to the process of inventing a machine in that items are added and removed until the machine operates the way it is intended. Thus, these indices were constructed with the goal of increasing clinical utility versus insuring psychometric soundness. Ironically, subsequent research has demonstrated that many of these conceptually derived indices possess acceptable levels of reliability and validity for discerning personality or psychopathology characteristics.

This somewhat unconventional conceptual-rational approach to deriving the scale scores was also employed to develop diagnostic decision rules and select specific interpretive statements for the narratives. According to documentation available from Behaviordyne, decision rule development evolved as a trial-by-trial process by Dr. Finney. In developing decision rules, Dr. Finney began by taking groups of about 30 patients that he knew well and who had specific psychopathological complaints. He then combined their various MMPI or CPI scores in ways such that he could correctly diagnose or classify 100% of those patients. The scale combinations were guided by Dr. Finney's knowledge of his patients' psychological functioning, hypotheses about which scales the patients differentially load on, and his psychodynamic orientation (which is often seen in the narrative reports). Once he could correctly diagnose all patients in his test sample he would then add new patients and reevaluate the decision rules by adding to or modifying them to correctly diagnose the new patients while retaining the discriminative power found for the original sample. The majority of decision rules used in the Behaviordyne system were developed through this iterative process.

What is interesting about this unconventional developmental approach, however, is that subsequent research has demonstrated that the diagnostic decision rules seem to have considerable utility for producing reliable and valid DSM-II and DSM-III diagnoses as compared to structured interview techniques. (DSM-III-R diagnoses are not entirely supported in the current system, but plans are being formulated to fully integrate that diagnostic scheme.) Thus, the decision rules appear to offer considerable stability and utility for discriminating various pathonomonic signs and diagnostic classifications, although not having been tested by traditional reliability and validity standards. Behaviordyne also indicates the general decision base continues to be modified as additional research becomes available.

This same general developmental format was also applied to creating the interpretive statements used in the narratives. Descriptive statements were written to reflect Dr. Finney's knowledge of his patients, their individual and combined scores on the various MMPI or CPI scales, and for the CPI results of adjective checklist descriptions of patient types by other professionals. These descriptive statements were then revised in light of suggestions and feedback provided by the narrative reporting system's users. This feedback took the form of users indicating agreement or disagreement with the interpretive statements used to describe their clients as compared to their individual clinical impressions. The statement revisions were designed to make, whenever possible, the statements more accurately descriptive of the users' clients. As with the various scales and decision rules, therefore, the authors developed interpretive statements that emphasized clinical utility and were less concerned with their statistical properties. And as such, the resulting statement library contains statements that are primarily descriptive or comparative and that point out various personality or psychopathological traits relevant to the report's purpose or type.

Because the interpretive statements are primarily descriptive, however, the resulting narrative reports may not appear integrated or stylistically cohesive as is found with some other computerized reporting systems. Yet, this lack of stylistic integration should be viewed as a strength in that the intents of the interpretive statements are not compromised through any procedures designed to make the reports more readable. The narrative paragraphs present descriptions of a client and tend not to go beyond that. There is a down side, nevertheless, to the way the narratives are constructed—trying to make sense of the quantity of interpretive statements that can be generated. For example, a Comprehensive Clinical Report without any additional options can easily consist of 10 text pages and 3 or 4 statistical information pages. The professional using the report must, therefore, put forth considerable effort to discern which aspects of the reports are applicable to the purpose for which the MMPI or CPI was administered.

Although the professional must exercise diligence and care when reviewing a report, this task is made somewhat easier by the manner in which the reports are organized. Specifically, the reports are organized into sections dealing with various personality or pathonomic issues (e.g., diagnoses, aggressive tendencies, vocational behavior) that are clearly identified with distinct headings, appropriate cautionary statements, and adequate supporting information. A professional user could easily scan through the various sections and focus specifically on report sections having direct relevance to the professional's needs.

Given that the narratives are largely an accumulation of interpretive statements rather than integrated paragraphs, however, the reliability and validity of the overall reports are difficult to judge. At this point there do not appear to have been any systematic overall reliability and validity evaluations made of the various Behaviordyne reports. Although such evaluations are desirable, they are quite difficult to undertake and complete. In lieu of such data Behaviordyne indicates that its users have reported that about 80% of the information contained in the reports is accurately descriptive of their clients and that Behaviordyne reports have been accepted as legal evidence in several court cases. Nevertheless, the lack of psychometric data supporting the reports

is problematic, but the Behaviordyne system does not differ substantially from other computerized MMPI and CPI interpretation systems in this respect.

Finally, to test the Behaviordyne system and its reporting capabilities this reviewer submitted 12 MMPI score sheets to Behaviordyne's main computer for processing. The 12 score sheets were variations on four clients seen by a licensed clinical psychologist. The clients' ages and sex were systematically varied to test the reporting system's sensitivity when generating various report types. A unique identification number was required for each score sheet to insure client confidentiality because Behaviordyne will not process score reports with client names attached. All clients' score sheets were originally transferred to the ONLINE microcomputer software system (Ver. 2.5) for direct transmission to Behaviordyne's computer. Problems with review copy of the software, however, prevented score file transmission. Behaviordyne's valiant efforts to resolve the problems were unsuccessful and the score files were ultimately transmitted using alternative telecommunications software. It should be noted that Behaviordyne was quite responsive to the problems encountered and provided a beta test copy of the new ONLINE software which enabled six of the score sheets to be transmitted to the company's main computer in about 3 minutes. The resulting reports were available for retrieval about 45 minutes later and the downloading took approximately 5 minutes.

Across the 12 reports there was considerable consistency when age was manipulated and substantive changes when sex was varied. These results were as expected given previous research with the MMPI and CPI. Moreover, the reports' content was predominantly consistent with the types of clients who had completed the MMPIs. Appropriate caveats were also integrated into the reports, which cautioned against making decisions based upon the reports alone and without regard for other client data. Specifically lacking, however, were cautions about interpreting the reports without regard for cultural or extreme age differences. Such cautions are especially necessary because the demographic characteristics making up the population today are significantly different than when Drs. Finney and Auvenshine originally collected their data and because of the lack of specific adolescent or geriatric age norms for the Behaviordyne system.

In summary, the Behaviordyne system offers a variety of MMPI and CPI interpretive reports based upon the work of Drs. Finney and Auvenshine that are for use by professionals and nonprofessionals. The extensive number of scales and interpretive statements used in generating the reports provide focused descriptions and diagnoses for clients across a wide spectrum of personality and diagnostic characterizations. Furthermore, many of those characterizations appear to be quite reliable and valid, despite a less than desirable psychometric base. Users should feel comfortable in using a Behaviordyne report as only one of many components in an overall assessment process. Given that stipulation this reviewer would recommend use of the Behaviordyne system.

[246]
Missouri Kindergarten Inventory of Developmental Skills, Alternate Form.

Purpose: A screening battery providing a comprehensive assessment measure to use at or before kindergarten entrance.
Population: Ages 48–72 months.
Publication Dates: 1978–82.
Acronym: KIDS.
Scores: 6 areas: Number Concepts, Auditory Skills, Language Concepts, Paper and Pencil Skills, Visual Skills, Gross Motor Skills.
Administration: Individual.
Price Data, 1988: $.25 per answer sheet; $15 per specimen set including sample test materials, answer sheet, administration and scoring manual ('80, 78 pages), and instructional guide book ('81, 45 pages).
Time: (35) minutes.
Comments: Can be given anytime within the year preceding kindergarten as well as at kindergarten entrance.
Author: Missouri Department of Elementary and Secondary Education.
Publisher: Center for Educational Assessment, University of Missouri-Columbia.

Review of the Missouri Kindergarten Inventory of Developmental Skills, Alternate Form by MARY HENNING-STOUT, Assistant Professor of Counseling Psychology, Lewis and Clark College, Portland, OR:

The Missouri Kindergarten Inventory of Developmental Skills, Alternate Form (KIDS) is a broad-based screen of the developmental status of preschool children. The skills measured by this instrument were selected based on the learning objectives articulated in the Missouri Department of Elementary and Secondary Education report, *Focus on Early Childhood Education.*

The authors describe the inventory's coverage as including consideration of physical, cognitive, and behavioral development of children from 48 to 72 months of age. These areas are tapped via six subtests: Number Concepts, Auditory Skills, Paper/Pencil Skills, Language Concepts, Visual Skills, and Gross Motor Skills. The last subtest is the primary measure of physical development and behavior is gauged informally with observation during the assessment period (a period of approximately 35 minutes).

Cognitive development seems most directly screened with this instrument. The Guidebook

accompanying the inventory provides suggestions for interventions by parents and teachers that are linked to the results of this screen.

ADMINISTRATION. The KIDS-Alternate Form is designed to be administered by the child's current or potential teacher. In the introductory pages of the administration manual, there are cautions about the importance of giving only standardized instructions to the child. In addition, special directions for recording scores and determining whether to give all items are presented. These instructions are not overly complex and with substantial practice could be mastered by classroom teachers. The test seems, however, to have characteristics of an instrument more appropriately administered by trained assessment specialists. The time required to become proficient in this test's standardized presentation and scoring may likely be prohibitive for most teachers unless special provisions are made.

The authors emphasize that behavioral observations should be collected throughout the administration. The back page of the response protocol provides prompts for recording the presence or absence of specific behaviors and environmental conditions. An additional questionnaire is included with the scale for completion by the parents. This questionnaire provides the parents' perspective on the child's developmental progress and personality.

It is suggested the scales be completed in the order they appear in the administration manual. The Gross Motor scale may be given to the child at any time for a change of pace. Generally, the items are immediately scorable as pass or fail. The authors suggest that, at the end of each subtest, the raw score for that subtest be recorded. These raw scores can later be transformed into percentiles, stanines, or Normal Curve Equivalents (NCE). NCE transformations provide normalized standard scores by breaking the line beneath the normal curve into equal segments. The authors describe NCEs as indicating "how many tasks a child can perform in relation to the number of similar tasks that other children can perform" (Guidebook, p. 13). Although they indicate application of percentiles and stanines in determining the need a child has for supplementary learning opportunity, the authors give no indication of the utility of the NCE transformations.

When scoring is completed and a profile is developed, the results are surveyed to determine if any score falls below the 20th percentile or third stanine. According to the authors, if any of the six scores (there is no full-scale score) falls in this area, intervention should be implemented and reassessment should occur in 2–6 weeks to determine if additional assessment and long-term intervention might be necessary.

PSYCHOMETRIC PROPERTIES. This version of the KIDS includes a downward extension of the norms of earlier versions (1975, 1978) which were based on a sample of children aged 54–72 months. The sample for the KIDS-Alternate Form consisted of 4,709 children 48–72 months of age. These children were from school districts, preschools, and child care facilities throughout Missouri. Efforts to obtain a representative sample of Missouri children seems to have been largely successful.

The item development/selection information presented in the Guidebook is sparse. At least some items were selected by a panel of state experts. Additional item selection or development methods are not described.

Reliability and validity are also reported in the Guidebook. Internal consistency reliability was established. There are no other reports of reliability, however. Test-retest, split-half, or alternate forms data would strengthen the test user's understanding of the KIDS' psychometric characteristics. Content validity was described as emerging from the expert status of the individuals selecting the items for the inventory. The authors also demonstrate the instrument's construct validity; as children get older, their scores improve.

Four factors emerged with factor analysis of the inventory: visual-spatial relations, language development, recall of verbal material, and inferential-constructional skill. Of 29 subtasks, 24 loaded on at least one of these four factors. Most heavily represented was the visual-spatial relations factor where 11 tasks clustered. Items from the Gross Motor scale were not included in the factor analysis because of earlier evidence this was a noncognitive scale.

The results of the factor analysis are well substantiated by linking them with the test's discrete content and with the broader knowledge base of psychoeducational assessment. However, the relationship between the identified factors and the six scales into which the test is divided is left unarticulated. Careful comparison of the tasks making up the Number Concepts scale, for example, shows two tasks loading on the visual-spatial relations factor, one loading on the recall of verbal material factor, and two unaccounted for within the four-factor solution. The relationship between the Number Concepts scale and the findings of the factor analysis is unclear.

Because the KIDS is divided into six scales, and because there is no full-scale metric, the construct validity of these scales should be clearly established. More explicit linkage between factor analytic findings and scale construction seems necessary to clarify the statistical basis for the test's construct validity.

PRACTICAL UTILITY. This reviewer found it difficult to remember that the instrument under review was a screening measure. There are several ways in which the materials accompanying this test seem to overstretch its applicability. The authors suggest a direct link between the results of the inventory and intervention. They make good suggestions to parents about activities for preschoolers at home. The link between the data derived from the test and the interventions suggested is, however, unclear. If the activities are designed to teach the test, the link is evident. If, on the other hand, the activities are presented as ways to improve skills that are measured by the test and found lacking, the inferential leap from the inventory content to the specific intervention is great. The brief time and relatively few items devoted to assessment with this instrument provide an insufficient base for any intervention planning.

A step is missing. After the screen, there should be additional behavior-based assessment of what the child can and cannot do relative to her/his weak scale performance. With this additional data, remediation can be clearly focused, rather than inferentially derived with the potential for irrelevance or ineffectiveness.

SUMMARY. The Missouri KIDS provides a carefully conceived and constructed screening tool. However, the literature accompanying this instrument could encourage users to apply its results beyond what is psychometrically supported. This test is a screen for possible indications of cognitive and motor difficulties thought to be related to children's performance in early academic settings. The suggestions provided in the Guidebook are creative and would likely be helpful for any family readying their young child for school. However, by including these suggestions with the materials of this test, the authors imply a link between the test's results and the interventions they suggest.

The suggestions are good. The numbers derived from the test indicate children's standings relative to their peers and help parents and teachers know when to ask more questions about a child's particular academic needs. To prevent the overapplication of the numbers, perhaps it would be best to package the two sets of material separately. Both are helpful. This reviewer's concern is that the findings of this screen might be overapplied, sending children needlessly down the narrow path toward classification before sufficient exploration of their demonstrated abilities and resourcefulness in a classroom setting has occurred.

Review of the Missouri Kindergarten Inventory of Developmental Skills, Alternate Form by JAMES E. YSSELDYKE, Professor of Educational Psychology, University of Minnesota, Minneapolis, MN:

The Alternate Form of the Missouri Kindergarten Inventory of Developmental Skills (KIDS) is a 1982 revision of the scale originally developed in

1975–76. The Alternate Form is intended for use with children aged 48–72 months, a downward extension of the earlier scale. The KIDS is individually administered and takes about 35 minutes. The test includes a parent questionnaire designed to obtain relevant information about the child's development. Subtests are included for each of the six areas listed above; within each area are several subsections that sample a variety of activities ranging from easy to difficult.

The test manual and forms are clearly printed. The manual (Guidebook) for this scale includes learning objectives and activities for each subtest area, a section on communicating with parents, and an extensive section on additional related learning activities. There are many excellent suggestions for remediation. The manual could be described as long on intervention and short on assessment information.

The KIDS was standardized originally on a sample of 4,000 children representative of the kindergarten population of Missouri. The test was revised and restandardized in 1980. The current norms are for a sample of 4,709 children aged 48–72 months. The normative data were gathered from preschool measures administered to children in 1980 and were stratified on the basis of school district enrollment.

Data on reliability of this scale consist of internal consistency coefficients for five of the six subtests based on the performance of an unspecified sample of children. All coefficients exceed .78. The reliability of this scale is satisfactory for screening purposes. There are no data on test-retest reliability.

Three kinds of evidence for validity are presented in the manual. It is argued the scale has good content validity because the subtests and items were designed and selected by a task force of experts in early childhood education. The test is said to have good developmental or construct validity because the mean score increases as a function of age. A factor analysis was completed and was used to show the factors assessed in this scale are like those underlying other widely used measures of children's cognitive skills. There are no data on how performance on the KIDS compares to performance on other tests.

Use of the Missouri KIDS is limited by the fact that the scale was developed and normed in a single state. Those who use the scale outside of Missouri will be constrained to simple descriptions of their preschool and kindergarten children. Comparisons in the form of percentile ranks, stanines, and normal curve equivalents are relative to a population of children in Missouri. Data on technical adequacy of this scale are limited. The manual includes interesting and useful information on intervention, and limited information on the use of the scale.

[247]
The Modified Version of the Bender-Gestalt Test for Preschool and Primary School Children.

Purpose: Designed to "measure the development of visual-motor integration skill in preschool and early elementary school children."
Population: Ages 4-6 to 8-5.
Publication Date: 1989.
Scores: Total score only.
Administration: Individual or group.
Price Data, 1990: $15.95 per manual (53 pages); $5 per 25 scoring forms.
Time: [5–10] minutes.
Comments: "Utilizes six geometric designs (A, 1, 2, 3, 4, 6, 8)"; a six-point Qualitative Scoring System that ranges from 0 for "random drawing, scribbling, having no concept of the design" to 5 for "perfect representation" of the design.
Authors: Gary G. Brannigan and Nancy A. Brunner.
Publisher: Clinical Psychology Publishing Co., Inc.
Cross References: For reviews by Kenneth W. Howell and Jerome M. Sattler, see 9:139 (65 references); see also T3:280 (159 references), 8:506 (253 references), and T2:1447 (144 references); for a review by Philip M. Kitay, see 7:161 (192 references); see also P:415 (170 references); for a review by C. B. Blakemore and an excerpted review by Fred Y. Billingslea, see 6:203 (99 references); see also 5:172 (118 references); for reviews by Arthur L. Benton and Howard R. White, see 4:144 (34 references); see also 3:108 (8 references).

Review of The Modified Version of the Bender-Gestalt Test for Preschool and Primary School Children by BARBARA A. ROTHLISBERG, Associate Professor of Educational Psychology and School Psychology I Program Director, Ball State University, Muncie, IN and RIK CARL D'AMATO, Associate Professor of School Psychology and Director of the School Psychology Programs in the Division of Professional Psychology, University of Northern Colorado, Greeley, CO:

The Bender Visual Motor Gestalt Test is probably the best known paper-pencil visual-motor test employed today. Since its development in the 1930s (Bender, 1938), its nine figures and simple administrative procedures have spawned the creation of multiple scoring systems and interpretive schemes designed to diagnose everything from personality functioning to brain damage (for a review of scoring systems, see Cantor, 1985). Although the Bender-Gestalt can be administered to a broad age range, it may have found its greatest popularity in the assessment of the perceptual-motor status of children (Goh, Teslow, & Fuller, 1981). With this younger population, the Koppitz Developmental Bender Test Scoring System has emerged as the preferred scoring method. The Koppitz System counts the number of errors made through distortion of shape, rotation, poor integration, and perseveration during reproduction of the designs; the higher the score, the more errors the child has made in drawing. Deemed suitable for children aged 5 through 11, the Koppitz System may assist in the development of hypotheses about the perceptual motor skills of children when used in conjunction with other measures. However, critics state that, because the Koppitz System's reliability and validity have not been well established, any interpretation of perceptual-motor performance using the Bender-Gestalt must be cautiously undertaken (Salvia & Ysseldyke, 1988; Sattler, 1988).

The Modified Version of the Bender-Gestalt Test for Preschool and Primary School Children, authored by Brannigan and Brunner, is a competing scoring system for use with Jansky and deHirsch's (1972) shortened version of the original Bender-Gestalt Test. This shortened Bender-Gestalt employs six of the nine figures (A, 1, 2, 4, 6, and 8) with the original numbering system retained. It was purportedly tailored to fit requirements for inclusion in an educational screening battery suitable for use with young children at-risk for academic failure. Although the familiar administrative techniques that could be applied to either an individual or group format were retained, Jansky and deHirsch scored performance on their abbreviated Bender-Gestalt using a global inspection method (i.e., the totality of each design is judged pass/fail) rather than the more common error approach utilized by the Koppitz System. Justification for scoring the totality of each figure drawing rather than specific errors was provided through reference to Bender's (1970) conviction that discrete scoring systems ran counter to the principles of Gestalt theory and thus the intent of the Bender-Gestalt itself.

While acknowledging Bender's position regarding the global nature of the figures, Brannigan and Brunner's Qualitative Scoring System for the Modified Bender-Gestalt purportedly offers a refinement of the pass/fail method initially used by Jansky and deHirsch. After the Modified Version of the Bender-Gestalt Test is administered in the usual fashion, the scoring system suggested by Brannigan and Brunner allows for a 6-point rating (0–5) of each design, ranking each in terms of the "overall representation of each design" (Manual, p. 7). This expanded scoring system is intended to better provide a "global measure of maturity for visual-motor integration skill" (Manual, p. 36). Consequently, the examiner must judge the quality of the examinee's reproductions of the figure drawings and consider the level of distortion present. A rating of "0" indicates that the drawing shows no concept of the design element while a "5" evidences a perfect representation of the stimulus figure. For added assistance, the Qualitative Scoring Manual offers four sample drawings at each quality level for each design. Examiners are told to award points "at the level where a drawing is equal to or better than the sample" (Manual, p. 7). Scores depend upon a somewhat subjective view of a drawing's distortion based on the match between the subject's actual drawing and the rating samples provided. Unfortunately, neither the samples nor the scoring instructions offer guidance in addressing potential subject errors of orientation, perseveration, or integration other than to refer to the issue of level of distortion. Instead, sample figures all appeared to be well oriented spatially with little evidence of perseveration.

Once quality ratings have been awarded for each figure, the ratings are summed to yield a total score. The score can then be compared to the appropriate reference group within the normative sample of 994 children, aged 4 years, 6 months to 8 years, 5 months. Tables converting raw scores into percentile and T scores for various age (i.e., 4 years, 6 months, 0 days to 8 years, 5 months, 30 days) and grade (i.e., kindergarten through second grade, with fall and spring testing) levels are provided. Children within the standardization sample were grouped to furnish score information for 6-month age intervals. It is regrettable that sample sizes were so limited and varied so widely among age levels. For example, only 70 children were evaluated at one level (age 4-6-0 to 4-11-30), while 168 children were assessed at another (age 6-6-0 to 6-11-30). All members of the standardization sample resided in northeastern New York state and were predominantly white and middle class. While data are provided as to age, gender, ethnicity, residence, and certain parent variables (i.e., income and education), the manual did not indicate the type of administration (individual or group) used to gather the normative data.

Although the means and standard deviations of the raw scores are available for different age groups, the authors of the Qualitative Scoring System supplied no further information on the characteristics of the distributions of scores obtained. Indeed, Brannigan and Brunner forward no justification for the advisability of converting qualitative, ordinal data into a standard score format that presupposes an interval scale of measurement. In fact, for only one of the eight age subgroups in the standardization sample could children receive a score at the 50th percentile. Moreover, if one notes the means and standard deviations supplied for the normative age groups (Manual, p. 31) and assumes that the raw scores were normally distributed, the subsequent tabular information furnished to convert raw scores to percentiles and standard scores suggests that high scores for younger and low scores for older members of the sample may have had to be extrapolated because they would have been beyond the range of those actually obtained. In addition, use of the scores to differentiate among children of limited visual-motor ability would seem extremely restricted given the small number of children in each of the age groups and the high degree of overlap between the distributions of scores at successive age levels. For instance, the difference between the mean raw scores obtained by the most disparate age groups (i.e., 4-year-olds and 8-year-olds) was less than 9 raw score points.

Brannigan and Brunner provided only sparse reliability information on the Modified Bender-Gestalt. Reported interscorer reliability seemed reasonable although it was based on the level of agreement between two graduate students on 61 kindergarten through second grade records. Test-retest reliability data also were based on a small kindergarten through second grade sample ($N = 53$) using a 1-week testing interval; the correlation between scores was marginal (.80) even for screening purposes (Salvia & Ysseldyke, 1988). Given that one might intuitively expect the visual-motor productions of children to become more stable with age, the fact that this "older" sample (i.e., kindergarten through second grade) showed such inconsistencies in their ratings on the figures should raise concerns about the reliability one could expect with younger age groups. Because the Modified Bender-Gestalt was proposed to be part of an effective battery for screening at-risk preschool children, the lack of any reliability information for this age group should warn clinicians that interpretation of the performance of preschoolers could include a high degree of uncertainty and error.

The validity information available on the Modified Bender-Gestalt was equally limited and troubling. Criterion-related validity was addressed only through the use of kindergarten to second grade children ($N = 258$) in one study. The study compared the predictive capacity of the Qualitative Scoring System to Koppitz's Developmental Scoring System for either the Metropolitan Achievement or Readiness Test. Correlation coefficients between the two scoring systems and achievement subtests were provided in the manual. Interestingly, no information was available to explain the way in which the Koppitz system scores were computed. The manual stated that the Modified Bender-Gestalt was employed for this study, yet Koppitz's Developmental Scoring System requires the administration of all Bender-Gestalt figures. In addition, correlations reported between the Koppitz system and achievement subtests were positive. Because the Koppitz method counts errors, higher scores should denote greater difficulty. Regrettably, the lack of descriptive or background information dilutes the credibility of the argument favoring Brannigan and Brunner's approach. Results suggested that, although the qualitative system was significantly more related to academic achievement than the Developmental Scoring System for kindergarten children, the difference in predicted achievement disappeared for first and second grade youngsters. It seemed that no direct comparison between the scoring methods was undertaken.

In essence, the Modified Bender-Gestalt Test was promoted by the authors as an improvement over the global, pass/fail system currently in use in most screening situations. Unfortunately, the evidence presented by Brannigan and Brunner did little to demonstrate that their qualitative scoring should be preferred over preexisting scoring systems. First, it was unclear how the normative data were collected and how the qualitative system could address examinee reproductions that captured the essence of the figure but demonstrated orientation or perseveration difficulties. Second, the system's qualitative nature would not seem to translate appropriately into a standard score format dependent on a quantifiable, interval level of measurement. Third, if a case for such transformation of qualitative scores can be made, no support was provided for the reliability and validity of the scoring system with children prior to the kindergarten level. It should also be noted that the preschool age range included in the sample was restricted only to the later preschool period; there is no indication that the instrument should even be attempted before the age of 4 years, 6 months. Thus, it is questionable if this should be labeled a preschool test. Finally, given that the Qualitative Scoring System based its utility on its improved contribution to a screening battery's ability to distinguish at-risk children, it was puzzling why this function was not investigated in any way. Consequently, given the paucity of information available regarding this technique's merits, an examiner would be better served by employing other existing scoring systems until more support can be obtained for this qualitative approach.

REVIEWER'S REFERENCES

Bender, L. (1938). A Visual Motor Gestalt Test and its clinical use. *American Orthopsychiatric Association Research Monograph*, No. 3.
Bender, L. (1970). Use of the Visual Motor Gestalt Test in the diagnosis of learning disabilities. *Journal of Special Education, 4*, 29-39.
Jansky, J. J., & deHirsch, K. (1972). *Preventing reading failure: Prediction, diagnosis, intervention.* New York: Harper and Row.
Goh, D. S., Teslow, C. J., & Fuller, G. B. (1981). The practice of psychological assessment among school psychologists. *Professional Psychology, 12*, 696-706.
Cantor, A. (1985). The Bender-Gestalt Test. In C. S. Newmark (Ed.), *Major psychological assessment instruments* (pp. 217-248). Boston: Allyn and Bacon.
Salvia, J., & Ysseldyke, J. E. (1988). *Assessment in special and remedial education* (4th ed.). Boston: Houghton Mifflin.
Sattler, J. M. (1988). *Assessment of children*, (3rd ed.). San Diego: The Author.

Review of The Modified Version of the Bender-Gestalt Test for Preschool and Primary School Children by JEFFREY H. SNOW, Neuropsychologist, Capital Rehabilitation Hospital, Tallahassee, FL:

The assessment of visual-motor integration skills is an integral part of evaluations with school-aged children. This measure represents a modified version of the Bender-Gestalt Test, utilizing a Qualitative Scoring System. The authors report the overall purpose of this test is to assess visual-motor integration skills with preschool and early elementary children and provide a tool useful in identifying children with learning difficulties.

The Bender-Gestalt is an established measure, with a number of different scoring systems developed for this test. The Koppitz system is the most widely used with the Bender-Gestalt. The authors note that Bender was critical of this system, stating that she objected to any scoring that focused on discrete errors as opposed to global performance. The authors indicate this version is a modification of an earlier revision developed in collaboration with Bender. The authors suggest that research indicates the modified Bender-Gestalt, when used in conjunction with other measures, was useful at identifying children at risk for academic difficulties.

The modified version of the Bender-Gestalt uses six designs from the original measure (A, 1, 2, 4, 6, and 8). The administration is the same as with other versions, whereby the child is given a blank piece of paper and a number 2 lead pencil. The directions merely instruct the child to copy the design as best he/she can, with guidelines for encouragement of the child if needed. Erasing of designs is neither encouraged nor discouraged on the part of the examiner. As with other versions of the Bender-Gestalt there is no time limit although the child's total time to complete the task is noted. Instructions for both individual and group administration are provided.

Each design is scored based on a 6-point rating system. The authors state the Qualitative Scoring System is based on research findings, and focuses on overall analysis of each drawing. The authors do note that evaluation of each drawing does demand a certain degree of examiner judgement. The general guidelines for scoring each design are as follows: 0 = random drawing, no attempt at design; 1 = drawing represents an attempt to resemble the design although omissions and distortions may be present; 2 = major elements are present yet major distortions may also be indicated; 3 = all major elements are present and recognizable with only minor distortions; 4 = design is recognizable and performed with only slight inconsistencies; 5 = perfect representation. Examples for each score are provided within the manual.

The standardization sample consisted of 994 children between the ages of 4 years, 6 months and 8 years, 5 months. The sample was selected from schools in northeastern New York state and consisted of 51% females and 49% males. The ethnic composition of the group was 95% Caucasian, 3% Black, and 2% other. Various income levels were represented, although lower middle- and middle-class children were the majority of the sample.

In regard to psychometric properties, the test manual reports both reliability and validity data. In relation to reliability, interrater consistency was evaluated utilizing two clinical psychology graduate students, each scoring the same 61 protocols. The reported coefficient of agreement was .95. Test-retest reliability is also reported for a group of 53 kindergarten through second grade children. Using a 1-week interval, a product moment correlation was reported to be .80. Split-half reliability corrected by the Spearman-Brown formula was .79.

In regard to validity, the manual reports a study comparing the Qualitative Scoring System with the Koppitz Developmental scoring system. The sample consisted of 258 kindergarten through second grade children. Each was administered the Bender-Gestalt along with achievement assessments. Correlation coefficients are reported for a sample of 58 kindergarten children, examining the relations of the two scoring systems with the Metropolitan Readiness Test. Coefficients for the Qualitative Scoring System ranged from a low of .05 to a high of .52. Correlations for the Koppitz Developmental system ranged from a low of .15 to a high of .35. Additionally, correlations between the two Bender-Gestalt scoring systems and the Metropolitan Achievement Test are reported for first and second grade children. Significance is noted for both measures in regard to correlations with this achievement test, with coefficients ranging from the low to moderate range.

With respect to norms, means and standard deviations at 6-month intervals are provided for children 4 years, 6 months to 8 years, 6 months. The authors report no significant sex differences were found comparing 92 subjects, and therefore, scores for boys and girls were combined in these tables. Percentile scores and T scores for each age group are also provided. Percentiles and T scores by grade level are also listed.

The manual concludes with a chapter on test interpretation and illustrative cases. The authors note the importance of observation during test administration, and outline behaviors that may be exhibited during the testing procedures. The illustrative cases provide reproduced designs and scores for each. A brief interpretation is given for each case study.

This version of the Bender-Gestalt has apparent strengths and limitations. When compared to the Koppitz system, an advantage is that only six designs are administered as opposed to nine. The scoring system, however, does seem suspect. With the Koppitz method, clear criteria for scoring are provided for each design. The Qualitative Scoring System appears prone to subjective decision making.

For example, it is unclear what constitutes a "major distortion" as opposed to a "minor distortion." The illustrative designs are helpful yet not exhaustive. The standardization sample for the test is somewhat restricted, making generalizability problematic. In regard to psychometric properties, the test does have adequate reliability, at least in terms for use as a screening measure. The validity data are sketchy yet promising. In conclusion, this measure represents a modification of a well-established test. The scoring system is based on both empirical and theoretical foundations, which is a strength. Until more comprehensive research is completed with the instrument, however, it would seem wise to restrict use of the test to empirical studies and as a screening assessment.

[248]

Monroe Diagnostic Reading Test.

Purpose: Designed to measure achievements in reading and diagnose reading difficulties.
Population: Grades 1–4 and over.
Publication Date: 1979.
Scores: 9 analytic test scores: Alphabet Repeating and Reading, IOTA Word Test, b/d/p/q/u/n Test, Recognition of Orientation, Mirror Reading Test, Mirror Writing Test, Number Reversal Test, Word Discrimination Test, Sounding Test.
Administration: Individual.
Price Data, 1991: $50 per test kit including test cards, 50 record blanks, and manual (11 pages); $25 per 13 test cards; $15 per 50 record blanks; $15 per manual.
Time: (30) minutes.
Comments: Preliminary tests are recommended to obtain the child's educational profile.
Author: Marion Monroe.
Publisher: Stoelting Co.

[249]

Motor Skills Inventory.

Purpose: Brief screening instrument to assess skill development in the gross and fine motor area.
Population: 6–84 months and older handicapped children.
Publication Date: 1984.
Acronym: MSI.
Scores, 2: Fine Motor, Gross Motor.
Administration: Individual.
Price Data, 1985: $9 per manual (16 pages) and 15 administration booklets; $5 per 15 administration booklets; $5 per manual.
Time: (5–15) minutes.
Comments: Equipment (e.g., plastic cup, child's scissors, windup toy) must be supplied by examiner.
Author: John Aulenta.
Publisher: Stoelting Co.

TEST REFERENCES

1. Steffens, K. M., Semmes, R., Werder, J. K., & Bruininks, R. H. (1987). Relationship between quantitative and qualitative measures of motor development. *Perceptual and Motor Skills, 64,* 985-986.

Review of the Motor Skills Inventory by PHILIP ASH, Director, Ash, Blackstone and Cates, Blacksburg, VA:

The Motor Skills Inventory (MSI) is not, in any meaningful sense of the term, a standardized screening inventory or a test. It "was conceived . . . out of an *obvious* [italics added] need for a brief measure of motor functioning when evaluating younger children . . . a compilation of motor tasks from . . . some of the best (or only) tests . . . around" (personal communication from author, October 27, 1989). The MSI comprises 45 "gross motor" items divided among seven age levels (0–1 year to 6–7 years), and 41 "fine motor" items divided among the same seven levels. An age level is attached to each item (e.g., "66–72 mos_____ Ties shoelaces," "20 mos_____Holds cup well while drinking"). In the Manual ($2^1/_4$ double-column pages governing nature, purpose, administration, scoring and development and about 2 pages for ten case vignettes, plus two appendices and a reference list) we are told that the items were drawn from seven scales (Gesell Developmental Schedules, Bayley Scales of Infant Development, Brigance Inventory of Early Development, Stanford-Binet Intelligence Scale, etc.). On the Record Form (one page, two sides) the user is told to "utilize parental report and items scoreable from other tests whenever possible" (although the source of each item is not given). Neither the Manual, nor any other publication, includes any norm data, reliability estimates, validity studies, or other statistical materials that might support this particular combination of items. It is presumed the attached age levels derive from the source scales, but because these scales used differing criteria for age-level determinations, ranging from inclusion if the item was passed by 50% of the norm sample, to inclusion if the item was passed by 60%, 70%, or 80% of the norm sample, the age levels used in the MSI are probably not comparable. The case vignettes all refer to other (unnamed) "assessments" prior to use of the MSI. In each case, the MSI is purported to have provided significant additional descriptive information. On the basis of the materials available, however, the MSI could also be adding error variance.

The Manual indicates that the MSI should be used as a supplement to other (presumably psychometrically adequate) assessment devices. In this reviewer's opinion, the MSI is not needed as a supplement for such well-standardized, well-researched instruments as the Battelle Developmental Inventory (age range birth to 8 years, BDI; 10:25), the Bayley Scales of Infant Development (age range 2–3 months, BSID; 10:26, 9:126, 8:206, 7:402), the Denver Developmental Screening Test (age range 2 weeks–6 years, DDST; 9:311, 7:45) or even several older scales, some from which some of the MSI items were taken. The Battelle and the Bayley are clearly instruments of choice in the 1990s. Test authors commonly borrow items from extant instruments, but renorming, reliability estimation, and revalidation are essential for every new combination of old items.

Review of the Motor Skills Inventory by LINDA K. BUNKER, Professor of Education and Associate Dean for Academic and Student Affairs, Curry School of Education, University of Virginia, Charlottesville, VA:

The Motor Skills Inventory (MSI) was developed by John Aulenta as a brief screening for fine and gross motor skills of young children (6 months to 6 years). All items are scored on a pass/fail basis with age level guidelines.

The MSI was designed to be used by trained diagnostic personnel although it is also purported that teachers or other interested adults can administer it. The manual makes several good suggestions about establishing rapport with parents before beginning the inventory, but gives little advice about standard testing procedures.

Score sheets and general administrative guidelines are provided with the test and manual. However, none of the required equipment is provided (peg board, beads, tricycle, etc.) although reference is made to the fact that such equipment exists with many of the other batteries (e.g., Binet, Bayley, Cattell, etc.). The criteria for establishing MSI basal and ceiling levels is five consecutive successes and five consecutive failures on test items.

Test administration is estimated to take between 5 and 15 minutes. However, given the criteria of at least five items passed and five items failed, it appears that this time line is underestimated.

PSYCHOMETRIC PROPERTIES OF THE MSI. No information was provided about the reliability or validity of the MSI. The manual states the MSI is "based on existing knowledge and research in assessment and child development and items were chosen for their previously established usefulness, reliability, and validity." All items do appear in other scales: Bayley Scales of Infant Development, Cattell Infant Intelligence Test, Monterey Pupil Development Scale, and UCLA Neuropsychiatric Institute's Evaluation and Prescription for Exceptional Children Scales.

Testers are reminded that this is a "gross measure" and age estimates, if reported, should be in at least 6-month increments (e.g., $2^1/_2$- to 3-year level). Testers are not given much information about the specific criteria for determining whether an item has been passed or not. For example, the 16-month task of "completes pegboard when urged" merely tells the tester to "place the pegboard with the pegs in place in front of the child; remove the pegs, and place them in front of the child . . . score plus if the child puts all the pegs back in place." No mention is made of how many pegs are expected, any time constraints, or judgements necessary about the quality of the placing skills.

The test seems somewhat inconsistent in its objectives and the examples given in the manual. The test is titled a test of motor skills, yet several of the example cases related to language problems (e.g., "a diagnosis was made of developmental language disorder"). The author's stated ambitions were noble: "to clarify developmental discrepancies among cognitive, linguistic, social, and motor areas and contribute to differential diagnosis among the developmental delays and disabilities. The MSI can contribute significantly in the diagnosis of retardation, developmental language delays, learning disability, specific motor deficit, and general or specific developmental immaturities" (p. 1, manual). It is unclear from the manual whether the MSI is purported to help assess all of these areas, or only designed as a motor skills inventory.

In summary, the MSI is an extremely informal inventory, which presents little evidence of its validity or reliability. There are other more rigorous and well-documented instruments (e.g., Bruininks-Oseretsky Test of Motor Proficiency [9:174]; Bayley Scales of Infant Development [10:26]) that provide more adequate documentation, and should be used as alternatives to the MSI.

[250]
The Multidimensional Self-Esteem Inventory.

Purpose: "Provides measures of the components of self-esteem."
Population: College students.
Publication Dates: 1983–88.
Acronym: MSEI.
Scores, 11: Competence, Lovability, Likability, Self-control, Personal Power, Moral Self-approval, Body Appearance, Body Functioning, Identity Integration, Defensive Self-enhancement, Global Self-esteem.
Administration: Individual or group.
Price Data, 1989: $38 per complete kit including manual ('88, 22 pages), 25 reusable test booklets, 25 rating forms, and 25 profile forms; $12 per 25 reusable test booklets; $12 per 25 rating forms; $7 per 25 profile forms; $9 per manual.
Time: (15–20) minutes.
Comments: Originally called Self-Report Inventory.
Authors: Edward J. O'Brien and Seymour Epstein.
Publisher: Psychological Assessment Resources, Inc.

TEST REFERENCES
1. O'Brien, E. J. (1991). Sex differences in components of self-esteem. *Psychological Reports, 68,* 241-242.

Review of The Multidimensional Self-Esteem Inventory by BARBARA J. KAPLAN, Associate Professor of Psychology, State University of New York College at Fredonia, Fredonia, NY:

The Multidimensional Self-Esteem Inventory (MSEI) is grounded in extensive writing, thinking, and research on a theory of the self-concept. Proponents of the model suggest the components of self-evaluation comprising self-esteem and self-concept are organized hierarchically in several levels from the general to the specific. Global self-esteem is the highest, most general self-evaluation in the model. Intermediate levels, as identified by eight component scales of the MSEI, are aspects of self-evaluations that generalize across situations in predicting behavior. Lower levels, which are not explicit parts of the MSEI, are specific to particular situations.

Two of the 11 MSEI scores are global measures of self-evaluation and self-concept, eight are intermediate level scales, and the final scale is a validity check on the extent to which the test-taker is "defensively inflating his or her self-presentation." The MSEI requires a 10th grade reading level, and its authors suggest it is most appropriate for use with college students. The high reading level required may make it an inappropriate measure for populations with cognitive, educational, or psychological impairments.

There are 116 questions, each evaluated on a 5-point scale. The majority of scales contain 10 items. The validity scale contains 16 items. Items were selected only after they met fairly rigid standards. Among these were relative independence of the scales, internal consistency within the scales, range of response, balancing positive and negative presentation of items, and ensuring that items were free of gender bias.

Reliability studies of the MSEI show excellent internal consistency and test-retest reliability, with reliability coefficients ranging from a low of .78 to a high of .90. It is worth noting, however, that the original population on which the test was normed consisted primarily of college student volunteers.

The normative sample consisted of 785 college students, 487 women and 298 men, who were undergraduate volunteers. There are separate norms for males and females. The MSEI profile uses T scores with a mean of 50 and a standard deviation of 10. The test manual provides interpretive descriptions of high and low scorers on each scale.

As a research instrument the MSEI has a good deal to offer, not least of which is a coherent theory underlying its construction. It functions as well as other available self-esteem measures, and may be of interest to investigators who have reason to go beyond a global measure of self-esteem. As a clinical tool, MSEI scales may enhance treatment planning and goal setting.

Scores on the MSEI correlate with students' responses to success or failure on a major test, help-seeking behavior, and outcomes of depressed and/or alcohol-abusing inpatients. The range of populations studied using the MSEI suggests researchers are

finding it a useful measure of self-esteem, but the available norms do not reflect these broader applications. The usual cautions about interpreting obtained scores must be heeded. Clinical applications of the test must await the development of a more diverse set of population norms.

Review of The Multidimensional Self-Esteem Inventory by JOSEPH G. PONTEROTTO, Associate Professor of Education, Division of Psychological and Educational Services, Graduate School of Education, Fordham University—Lincoln Center, New York, NY:

The Multidimensional Self-Esteem Inventory (MSEI) (formerly the Self-Report Inventory, O'Brien, 1980) is a 116-item, self-report instrument designed to measure components of self-esteem among college students in the United States. The underlying conceptual base of the MSEI posits that self-evaluation is an important component of personality. This self-evaluation consists of self-perceptions (self-concept) and evaluations associated with these perceptions (self-esteem). The MSEI is based on Epstein's (1980) self-esteem/self-concept model which posits that self-esteem is organized in a three-stage hierarchical fashion. At the highest level of self-evaluation is global self-esteem, which represents the basic evaluation of self-worth. Influencing the global self-esteem are specific components of self-esteem linked to domains of life experience. These specific self-esteem domains represent the second level of self-esteem. The third and lowest level of self-esteem has minimal impact on global self-esteem, is situation-specific, and addresses self-evaluation in specific activities or tasks. The MSEI is designed to assess the two higher levels of self-esteem.

STRUCTURAL BASE OF THE MSEI. The MSEI operationalizes its multidimensional self-esteem/self-concept theory through the use of 11 scales divided into four categories: (*a*) Global Self-esteem; (*b*) eight components of self-esteem defined as Competence, Lovability, Likability, Personal Power, Self-control, Moral Self-approval, Body Appearance, and Body Functioning; (*c*) Identity Integration; and (*d*) Defensive Self-enhancement.

The rationale for the scales stems from the earlier conceptual and empirical work of the instrument developers (see Epstein, 1980; O'Brien, 1980; O'Brien & Epstein, 1985). Global Self-esteem is defined as a generalized summary of feelings of worthiness. The eight distinct components of self-esteem focus on broad domains representative of the types of experiences that effect self-esteem day-to-day. Identity Integration refers to the organization, processing, and the efficiency of integration of self-experiences into the overall self-concept. Finally, Defensive Self-enhancement examines one's tendency to be defensive and to overinflate his or her self-esteem to appear socially desirable. The MSEI assesses social desirability through the respondent's denial of common weaknesses and claiming of rare virtues.

ADMINISTRATION AND SCORING. The total MSEI package includes a 22-page Professional Manual, a four-page item booklet containing 116 items, a rating sheet, and a profile form. Section 1 of the item booklet presents 61 items written as self-descriptions. The respondents use a 5-point Likert scale (1 = *Completely false* to 5 = *Completely true*) to assess the veracity of the descriptions as they apply to them. In Section 2, respondents use a 5-point Likert scale (1 = *Almost never* to 5 = *Very often*) to report how often they experience thoughts and feelings reflected in 55 items.

The hand-scored rating sheet provides space for basic demographic information (i.e., name, date, age, and sex) and places items strategically so that the scorer simply adds numbered responses across rows to arrive at scale raw scores. Finally, the Profile Form provides a table of percentiles and T scores for both male and female norms onto which the raw scores can be easily plotted to develop a graphic profile.

The MSEI is appropriate for both individual and group administration with college students. A 10th-grade reading level is required to complete the instrument, and the average time of completion is 15–30 minutes. The MSEI reviewed here used rating form HS (hand scored). It took this reviewer 10–15 minutes to score and profile his own MSEI results. Although a computer-administered version of the MSEI was developed and validated (Fairchok & O'Brien, 1987), the availability of such, or of a computerized scoring version, was not mentioned in the manual.

Although paraprofessionals may administer and score the MSEI, the instrument should be interpreted only by professionals trained in personality assessment. To the extent that self-esteem can be perceived as an important component of personality, the instrument may be used as a personality measure; however, the MSEI *is not* a diagnostic instrument and *should not* be used to form any type of clinical diagnosis.

MSEI DEVELOPMENT AND ITEM ANALYSIS. The MSEI was developed, normed, and validated in a series of seven separate studies spanning a 7-year time period. Subjects in all studies were undergraduate college students from four different colleges and universities who volunteered to participate for course credit. Both qualitative and quantitative research methods were used in item selection. First, items were written to reflect the definitions of the 11 scales inherent in the theory. These items (approximately 30 per scale) were then evaluated by independent judges for congruence with the specific scale definitions. Second, the items remaining from this qualitative analysis were subjected to empirical item analysis. Criteria for the final selection of items included convergent and discriminant criteria, content representation, scale balancing in terms of positively and negatively worded items, a wide response range in an attempt to avoid ceiling and flooring effects, and sex balancing.

CONVERGENT CRITERIA. Using two subject samples from a large state university ($N = 645$ males and females), the authors (through item analysis) selected the 10 best items for each of the 11 scales. A point biserial correlation minimum of .50 served as the cutoff point. Ten of the 11 scales reached this minimum criteria, with correlations ranging from .52 for Likability to .69 for Body Functioning. The point biserial correlation for Defensive Self-enhancement was a low .35, necessitating that the developers add 6 items to bring the correlation up to the .50 cutoff point. Thus 10 scales include 10 items each, and the Defensive Self-enhancement scale consists of 16 items, bringing the grand total to 116.

DISCRIMINANT CRITERIA. There were two discriminant criteria for item selection: that items showed a higher correlation with their own scale than with any other MSEI scale, and that items demonstrated higher correlations with their own scale than with the Defensive Self-enhancement scale. This latter criteria served to minimize social desirability contamination.

In summary, the item analysis procedure was successful in selecting items that were homogeneous within scales and discriminant between scales. The practical considerations with regard to positively and negatively worded items, the avoidance of ceiling and flooring effects, and selecting items with nearly equal convergent and discriminant criteria results across sex were satisfactorily met.

Reliability and Validity.

RELIABILITY. The MSEI's internal consistency was examined using a sample of approximately 298 male and 487 female students from a large state university and a private university. An analysis of sex differences revealed no significant differences and thus alpha coefficients are reported for the full sample. The resultant consistency measures were quite satisfactory, ranging from .78 for Defensive Self-enhancement to .90 for both Body Functioning and Global Self-esteem. Test-retest stability correlations over a 1-month span for approximately 58 male and 151 female students (again, no sex differences found) from two private colleges ranged from a low of .78 for Identity Integration to .89 for Body Functioning. The MSEI clearly demonstrates satisfactory internal consistency and short-term test-retest stability.

CONVERGENT AND DISCRIMINANT VALIDITY. MSEI scale scores were examined in relation to a host of other instruments designed to measure constructs that could be hypothesized to have either a positive or negative relationship to self-esteem. A number of validation studies generally supported a high level of convergent and discriminant validity of the MSEI construct relative to other measures of self-esteem (i.e., the Eagly [1967] and Rosenberg [1965] self-esteem scales), expectancy for success, depression, ego strength, perceived peer and parental acceptance, body perceptions, defensiveness, temperament, academic achievement, leadership, influence in intimate relationships, athletic involvement, and self-control behaviors. Collectively, the comparative correlations between relevant scale comparisons are in the expected direction (e.g., positive with other self-esteem measures; negative with depression measures) and support the validity of the MSEI for American college students.

FACTOR ANALYSIS. Using 1,086 students from a large state university and a private university, a confirmatory factor analysis constrained to extract 11 factors was conducted with the correlations among the 116 items used as input. With a factor loading restriction set at .40, strong factorial support was found for 7 of the 11 scales. Moderate factorial support was found for the Likability and Body Appearance scales. The Global Self-esteem and Identity Integration scales did not separate out as distinct factors. This is not surprising, however, because both of these scales are conceptualized as generalized measures of self-adequacy, and therefore, their high intercorrelations with each other and with other MSEI scales would be expected. Thus the factorial validity of the MSEI contruct is supported.

NORMS AND SEX DIFFERENCES. MSEI normative data are based on a sample of 298 men and 487 women from a large state university and a small private university (geographical region not specified). Students from the private university were predominantly from middle- and upper-class backgrounds, whereas the state university students were more varied in terms of social class and ethnic background. Analyses of variance indicated no MSEI differences due to university setting or to university setting X sex interaction. However, there were a number of significant differences for the main effect of sex. Men scored higher on Global Self-esteem, Competence, Personal Power, Body Appearance, and Body Functioning. Women scored higher on Lovability, Likability, Moral Self-approval, and Defensive Self-enhancement. In most cases the significant sex differences are small in magnitude; however, given the significant findings, the test developers appropriately report separate norms (reflected in the Profile Form and Professional Manual) by sex.

THE PROFESSIONAL MANUAL. The 22-page manual is well prepared and, generally speaking, easy to follow. Clear directions for administering, scoring, and interpreting the instrument are provided. Descriptive profiles of high and low scores on each of the 11 scales are meaningfully presented and assist the MSEI interpreter. The qualitative and quantitative development of the MSEI items is well presented, as are the studies on its psychometric evaluation. Clear tables in the manual help the interested reader. A strength of the manual, and the MSEI generally, is that the limitations of the instrument are adequately and candidly presented. The generalizability limits of the norming and validation samples are highlighted. The manual closes with a section on Supporting Research that summarizes 13 studies (from 1981 to the present) in which the MSEI was used. Generally, these studies provide additional support for the utility of the MSEI self-esteem construct as a mediating variable in the study of other personality traits. Noteworthy among these supporting studies is the initial utility of the scale with adult, nonstudent populations, and with some psychiatrically hospitalized patients.

SUMMARY. The MSEI is a content-valid measure of diverse components of self-esteem and self-concept. The construct and factorial validities of the MSEI have also been established, and are based on a series of well-designed studies spanning 7 years. The internal consistency reliability and short-to-moderate-term stability of the MSEI are high. The instrument is fairly easy to administer and score, and the manual is well organized, comprehensive, and generally easy to follow. This is an excellent self-esteem measure for use with the traditional college student population. At this time, the scale has not been validated or normed on nontraditional student populations (e.g., racial/ethnic minority groups, the returning adult student) nor on any nonstudent populations.

REVIEWER'S REFERENCES

Rosenberg, M. (1965). *Society and the adolescent self-image.* Princeton, NJ: Princeton University Press.

Eagley, A. H. (1967). Involvement as a determinant of response to favorable and unfavorable information. *Journal of Personality and Social Psychology, 7,* 1-15.

Epstein, S. (1980). The self-concept: A review and the proposal of an integrated theory of personality. In E. Staub (Ed.), *Personality: Basic aspects and current research* (pp. 81-132). Englewood Cliffs, NJ: Prentice-Hall.

O'Brien, E. J. (1980). *The Self-Report Inventory: Development and validation of a multidimensional measure of the self-concept and sources of self-esteem.* Unpublished doctoral dissertation, University of Massachusetts, Amherst.

O'Brien, E. J., & Epstein, S. (1985). Unpublished research. Marywood College, Scranton, PA.

Fairchok, G. E., & O'Brien, E. J. (1987, October). *Computerization of paper-and-pencil psychological tests: Do custom and omnibus computerization procedures affect test validity?* Paper presented at the Third Eastern Small College Computing Conference, Marist College, Poughkeepsie, NY.

[251]

Multiscore Depression Inventory.

Purpose: "To provide an objective measure of the severity of self-reported depression."

Population: Ages 13 through adult.

Publication Date: 1986.

Acronym: MDI.

Scores, 11: Low Energy Level, Cognitive Difficulty, Guilt, Low Self-Esteem, Social Introversion, Pessimism, Irritability, Sad Mood, Instrumental Helplessness, Learned Helplessness, Total.

Administration: Group.

Forms, 2: Short Form version available by administering first 47 items of questionnaire.

Price Data, 1987: $65 per kit including scoring keys, 100 hand-scored answer sheets, 2 prepaid WPS Test Report answer sheets, 100 profile forms, and manual (111 pages); $12.50 per set of scoring keys; $13.50 per 100 hand-scored answer sheets; $9.25 or less per prepaid WPS Test Report answer sheet; $13.50 per 100 profile forms; $18.50 per manual; $185 per microcomputer diskette for administration, scoring, and interpretation (25 uses per diskette).

Time: (20–25) minutes; (10) minutes for Short Form.

Comments: Self-report format; IBM PC, XT, or AT or compatible computer required for optional computer administration or scoring.

Author: David J. Berndt.

Publisher: Western Psychological Services.

Review of the Multiscore Depression Inventory by DAVID N. DIXON, Professor and Department Chair, Department of Counseling Psychology and Guidance Services, Ball State University, Muncie, IN:

The Multiscore Depression Inventory (MDI) provides an overall measure of depression and 10 subscale scores. Not only is it a measure of severity of depression, but also it provides information related to sources of the depression.

The MDI is a well-constructed, objective measure of self-reported depression. The Inventory consists of 118 true-false items that typically can be completed in 20 to 25 minutes. For increased brevity a short form is available, requiring approximately half the administration time. The Inventory can be either hand or computer scored. A computer-generated interpretation is also available.

Development of the MDI followed the accepted methods of scale construction using a combination of rational and empirical approaches. The 10 subscales were identified initially from the literature on depressive symptoms and subsequently developed through empirical procedures such as item-total correlations, internal consistency and test-retest reliabilities, convergent-divergent validation, and cluster analysis. The Total Scale and subscales performed well in all of these tests, with the exception of the Learned Helplessness subscale. For example, average corrected item-total correlations with this subscale are no better than corrected item-total correlations with the Total Scale. This subscale is not included in the short form of the MDI. Validity data for the Learned Helplessness subscale are also not as impressive as are data for the other subscales.

Male and female norms for the MDI are available for adults, college students, and adoles-

cents. Normative data for special populations are also reported for anorexic, bulimic, and weight-preoccupied patients; several high school students from differing SES levels; gifted adolescents; and family practice outpatients.

In addition to scores on the Total Scale and subscales, the individual profile is compared to criterion-group scores. Criterion groups include depressed, conduct disordered, mixed (depressed and conduct disordered), psychotic, suicidal, endogenomorphic, anorexic women, bulimic women, chronic pain sufferers, and theoretical groups of nondepressed and unselected prototypes. The individual profile is compared to these criterion groups for probability of belonging to each criterion group. Thus, a person's depressive symptomology is reported as resembling that of each criterion group at a particular level of probability. Users are cautioned not to make a diagnosis based on MDI scores alone but to use MDI scores as input into the diagnostic process.

The manual for the MDI is quite complete. It provides a nice blend of conceptual and technical material. The case examples included in the manual illustrate how MDI results can be integrated into the diagnostic process. The emphasis throughout the manual is on the diagnostic process. As the Inventory gains wider acceptance and use, increased information integrating the MDI with treatment would be a welcome addition to the manual. The section of the manual on future research is particularly useful. The use of the MDI as a treatment outcome measure has promise for demonstrating differential effects for varied treatments.

It is difficult to compare the merits of the MDI to more established measures of depression. For example, the Beck Depression Inventory (BDI; 31) has demonstrated its use both for diagnostic and research purposes. The MDI, because of its strong conceptual and psychometric development, has perhaps equivalent potential for significant contributions to practice and research. Like Aaron Beck and the BDI, the author of the MDI is not solely a test developer but has a research program focused on the diagnoses and treatment of depression. This, coupled with the existing level of development of the MDI, holds great promise for the future.

The MDI is built on a sound theoretical and empirical base. It has demonstrated acceptable levels of reliability and a solid, and developing, validity base. The subscale scores (with the previously noted exception of the Learned Helplessness subscale) seem to provide a method for understanding the overall depression score and for suggesting potential areas for intervention. Additional research is needed to support fully the utility of subscales in diagnosis and treatment, but initial data are supportive.

The MDI is recommended for clinical and research uses. Its development is exemplary and its potential is great.

Review of the Multiscore Depression Inventory by STEPHEN G. FLANAGAN, Clinical Associate Professor of Psychology, The University of North Carolina at Chapel Hill, Chapel Hill, NC:

The Multiscore Depression Inventory (MDI) was developed as a measure of severity of depressive affect. It differs from other measures of depression in its standardization and use with nonclinical subjects, less intrusiveness of item content compared to other depression scales, and the availability of multiple subscales for interpretation, in addition to a full-scale depression score. The paper-and-pencil MDI includes forms that are intelligently designed for ease of scoring, profiling, and error checking. The computer report includes scoring and profile construction. The MDI is intended for use and interpretation by professionals with advanced training in psychological assessment. It can be administered to persons aged 13 and above with a sixth-grade reading level, and includes norms for adolescents, college students, and adults. This review is based on information provided in the MDI Manual.

The inventory consists of 118 true-false self-descriptive statements, nine scales of 12 items each, and a 10-item Guilt scale. Scale development started with rational derivation of 10 dimensions of depression, based upon clinical and research literature. An item pool was devised and a "character sketch" written for each concept. An initial pool of over 900 items was cut to 362, based on rated ambiguity and match to the character description from which each item was derived.

The remaining 362 items were administered to 200 college students who also completed a social desirability scale, and sequential criteria were used to select the final items: (*a*) rarely endorsed items were omitted; (*b*) corrected item-total correlations were computed and items removed if less than $r = .30$; (*c*) items were omitted if the corrected item-total correlation was lower than the item's correlation with another scale or the social desirability measure; (*d*) the final 118 items were selected on rational grounds considering the item's ranking in contribution to the scale independent of social desirability, and additional criteria of balancing true and false scored items, redundancy, and face validity.

Internal consistency (coefficient alpha) with five different samples ranged from .70 to .91 for subscales, and .96 to .97 for the full scale score. The MDI compared favorably on internal consistency to other measures of depression such as the Zung Scale and the Beck Depression Inventory. Test-retest reliabilities were likewise consistently significant and high for full scale and subscale scores immediately

and over a 3-week interval (except Instrumental Helplessness, .38 in one study).

The Full Scale MDI has had high correlations with concurrent measures, including the Beck Depression Inventory ($r = .69$) and Depression Adjective Check List ($r = .77$) in a sample of 200 college students. The MDI correlated ($r = .66$) with the Hamilton Depression Rating Scale for an inpatient sample. The manual reports the corrected item-total correlations with each subscale and with the full scale for each item, noting that all are highly significant ($p < .001$). A criterion measure was selected for each MDI subscale, and significant correlations are reported between each scale and its criterion. Correlations between subscale criterion measures and each of the other nine subscales are not reported. This makes the table of correlations less cluttered, but makes it difficult to evaluate the specificity of the correlation between criterion and subscale. A number of research studies are cited showing MDI validity for differentiating severity of depression in clinical samples. Results of factor and cluster analyses are supportive of construct validity.

Data are also presented in support of the Short Form, which consists of the first 47 items of the MDI (SMDI). There are nine subscale scores (Learned Helplessness was omitted) and a full scale score. Reliabilities are adequate, though generally lower than for the full MDI as expected with fewer items. Corrected item-total correlations are significant, as are correlations with criterion measures for each subscale. Significant correlations are reported between Full Scale SMDI and the Beck Depression Inventory ($r = .68$) and the Depression Adjective Check List ($r = .76$) among 133 college students. Depressed medical patients scored significantly higher on the SMDI than nondepressed patients.

The optional computer report includes analyses for unusual patterns of item responses or statistical validity scales, including unusual patterns of true-false responses (Runs Test) and endorsement of rare items (Frequency Test). Also in the computer report is a histogram of normalized *T*-scores for the 10 subscales (9 for the SMDI) and Full Scale score, and an interpretive report with statements derived from subscale evaluations. The subject's profile is compared with prototypic profiles for several groups (e.g., depressed, suicidal, chronic pain sufferers) and the probability of group membership is calculated. The manual does not report on separate validation of inferences generated by the computer interpretation program.

The interpretive section of the manual provides guidelines for estimating validity, and discussion of how to detect response biases and faking. The hand-scored version of the inventory cannot include the computer "runs test," which requires extensive rapid calculations. It is unclear whether the frequency test could be adapted for use with hand scoring. The manual includes the caution that the MDI is not intended to be used to establish a diagnosis of depression, which would require careful assessment of symptomatic status and differential diagnosis in addition to any test battery employed. Guidelines are provided for estimating severity of depression, and a table provides corresponding ranges of MDI *T*-scores and Beck Depression Inventory scores corresponding to Nondepressed, Mild, Moderate, and Severe ranges of depression as defined by Beck. After providing interpretive sketches for each of the subscales, there is discussion of profile interpretation. The author appropriately cautions the user that greater elaboration of profile analysis awaits further research explicating empirical correlates of profile configurations.

In sum, the MDI is a reliable and easily administered objective measure of severity of depression that can be used in a wide range of settings with diverse populations. Scale development and validation meet high quality standards. The straightforward nature of the item content permits distortion of MDI responding, and professionals using the scale need to evaluate these risks to validity carefully. The computer report provides statistical indices of test-taking biases and validity not available with the hand-scored version. The MDI's characteristics make it highly suitable for research and clinical applications with a wide range of people, from college students and normal adults to severely depressed clients. Because the MDI is a relatively new instrument, additional research will be necessary to establish more firmly its usefulness with clinical populations. The manual outlines recommendations for further research, including applications in family practice and medical settings, assessment of affective symptomatology in eating disorders such as anorexia and bulimia, and multiscore evaluation of response to treatment and changes in symptomatic status in depression.

[252]
Murphy-Durrell Reading Readiness Screen.
Purpose: "Provides information about a child's phonics abilities before entering a formal reading program."
Population: Grades K–1.
Publication Date: 1988.
Scores, 6: Lowercase Letter Names, Letter-Name Sounds in Spoken Words, Writing Letters from Dictation, Syntax Matching, Identifying Phonemes in Spoken Words, Total.
Administration: Individual or group.
Price Data, 1989: $29.95 per complete kit including 10 of each of 5 tests and manual (16 pages).
Time: (15–25) minutes per inventory.
Comments: "Developed from the Murphy-Durrell Prereading Phonics Inventory"; recommended that each of the 5 inventories be administered in separate sitting, over a period of 3 days.

Authors: Helen A. Murphy and Donald D. Durrell.
Publisher: Curriculum Associates, Inc.

Review of the Murphy-Durrell Reading Readiness Screen by DOUGLAS J. McRAE, Vice-President for Publishing, CTB Macmillan/McGraw-Hill, Monterey, CA:

PURPOSE. The Murphy-Durrell Reading Readiness Screen is designed to identify grades K–1 students who will be successful in a formal reading program. The instrument is also designed to identify "at risk" students and note their reading readiness deficiencies. The instrument is based entirely on a child's phonics abilities.

DESCRIPTION. The Murphy-Durrell Reading Readiness Screen consists of five separately administered inventories: Lowercase Letter Names (26 items), Letter-Name Sounds in Spoken Words (22 items), Writing Letters from Dictation (26 items), Syntax Matching (10 items), and Identifying Phonemes in Spoken Words (25 items). Simple raw scores are computed for each inventory, and a level letter (A, B, C, or D) is assigned to each inventory using a table in the Teacher's Manual. A total score may also be computed and a level letter assigned, but the directions in the Teacher's Manual are unclear as to whether the total score level letter should be assigned based on the single numerical score or based on the pattern of level letters assigned to the five separate inventories. In any case, the manual is clear in indicating that students achieving level letters of A or B in all five inventories are ready for formal reading instruction.

Each inventory takes 15–25 minutes to administer, for a total administration time of 75–125 minutes. Either group or individual administration is acceptable.

RATIONALE. A brief statement of rationale, including broad references to research findings, is presented in the Teacher's Manual for each of the five inventories. The Teacher's Manual also provides possible reasons for low scores for each of the five inventories, along with suggestions for remediation. References to materials for remediation are given in the Teacher's Manual.

TECHNICAL INFORMATION. The Teacher's Manual provides no technical information to describe the development of the instrument, or to support the validity or reliability of the instrument. The Scoring Table in the Teacher's Manual indicates the assignment of level letters for each inventory is based on a frequency distribution of scores from 633 students, but gives no description for this reference group. The table is not entirely consistent with the instrument itself—for instance, it indicates a maximum score of 7 for Syntax Matching while the instrument itself has 10 items. No evidence for reliability is provided. Despite the express purpose of screening and placement, no evidence of predictive validity is provided.

EVALUATION. The Murphy-Durrell Reading Readiness Screen is a potentially useful instrument for reading teachers who believe that phonics abilities are necessary prerequisites for formal reading instruction. The instrument is based on research that supports this perspective. No evidence is presented that would suggest the instrument is psychometrically sound; the justification for the scoring rules appears to be particularly weak. The instrument's primary value may well be its lead into prereading instructional materials based on phonics. These materials are produced by the same publisher as the instrument itself.

Review of the Murphy-Durrell Reading Readiness Screen by STEPHANIE STEIN, Assistant Professor of Psychology, Central Washington University, Ellensburg, WA:

At first glance, the Murphy-Durrell Reading Readiness Screen's modest claim of providing "information about a child's phonics abilities before entering a formal reading program" is difficult to challenge or debate. After all, a series of inventories on letter names and sounds must provide *some* information about phonics skills. However, a closer look at the five inventories suggests that phonics skills are actually a fairly insubstantial part of the test and that more peripheral skills are being tested that may or may not be prerequisites to reading.

The inventories, which take 15 to 25 minutes each, all involve a combination of oral and printed stimulus items and require nonverbal responses from the child (either circling a letter/word or writing a letter). The first inventory is a fairly straightforward test of letter name identification which, although not a direct measure of phonics, is clearly related to reading readiness. The matching of the initial sound in a spoken word with a printed letter is assessed in the second inventory. In this inventory, the first sound does not always correspond to the first letter in the word. For example, the correct answer for "arm" is "r" and the correct answer for "Esther" is "s." The lack of correspondence between initial letter and initial sound could understandably be confusing for many beginning readers.

The possibility for confusion increases, however, when the third inventory jumps back from a focus on letter sounds to letter names and asks the child to write the dictated letter in the space provided. No rationale is given as to why letter reversals are scored as correct responses in the initial administration but are scored as errors in follow-up assessments. The fourth inventory consists of short printed sentences that are read orally by the examiner. One word in the sentence is then repeated and the child is asked to circle that word on the worksheet. It is questionable what skill this inventory is actually testing, but

phonics does not appear to be a substantial part of it. Children could respond to their knowledge of the actual printed word, memory of where they heard the word in the sentence, or the potentially misleading information provided in the picture that precedes the item.

Finally, the fifth inventory involves the visual presentation of a series of printed letters and the oral presentation of a brief sentence that contains two words that begin with the same letter. The two key words are repeated and the child is asked to circle the letter that is at the beginning of each word.

In all the inventories, the individual test item is preceded by a picture. The presence of the picture on each item is supposed to ensure the children do not lose their places because they are directed to put a finger on the particular picture before the item is presented. However, the picture also serves another purpose adding confusion and potential error to the test.

On three of the inventories, children are directed to circle the picture if they do not know the correct answer. The stated purpose of this practice is that "since the child is circling either a letter or the picture, the child doesn't experience failure." Although the intent is admirable, it is not clear the test-naive young child would not just choose to circle the picture because it is the most stimulating symbol in the row and because it appears to be an acceptable response to the examiner. Furthermore, it is unclear why suddenly in the fourth inventory, if children are unsure of the correct answer, they are simply directed to circle the answer they think is right rather than the picture. Why isn't this simple direction given throughout the test, for the sake of consistency if nothing else?

Another problem with the pictures in every item is that they do not always relate to the item in a consistent fashion. Sometimes the name of the picture represents the letter the child is supposed to select and other times it is very indirectly related to the item. The degree of relationship between the picture and the test item not only varies between inventories but also varies within an inventory. This inconsistent use of pictures represents a major distraction and downfall of the test materials.

If the manual stopped here, the Murphy-Durrell Reading Readiness Screen would simply be a mediocre classroom inventory of questionable usefulness and validity. However, the authors go one fatal step further and attempt to roughly quantify the child's test results into one of four categories. The categories of A, B, C, and D supposedly correspond to the norm group's scores in the top third, middle third, lowest third, and lowest fifth percentile, respectively. No explanation is given on why there is no overlap between the "lowest third" performance and the "lowest 5th percentile." The child's raw score on each inventory is assigned a letter depending on where it corresponds to the scores in the standardization categories, which are presented as a median score and a range of scores. The total letter score is obtained by adding up the raw scores from the five inventories, essentially ignoring the obtained raw total score, and then somehow averaging the letter scores from the five inventories (examples provided in the manual include AAABD = B and AABBC = B).

Although already clearly beyond the level of questionable measurement practice, the authors go even further and definitively state that a child with a score of A or B is ready for "formal reading instruction," implying that a child with a score of C or D is not ready. No definition is given of "formal reading instruction," and no information is provided about how this cutoff was determined. The manual does not provide any information about reliability, validity, or norms (other than $N = 633$).

Additional minor problems and weaknesses are present throughout the test and manual but are essentially inconsequential in comparison to the major, indefensible problems already discussed. The Murphy-Durrell Reading Readiness Screen is fraught with problems of distracting test items, lack of correspondence between stated purpose and actual inventories, imprecise scoring procedures, unsupported interpretation of test results, and complete lack of technical data in the areas of reliability, validity, and norms. Teachers would be better off to avoid this test and use either the readiness tests of major group achievement batteries or to design their own brief measure of phonics skills.

[253]
NASA Moon Survival Task.
Purpose: To explore the performance characteristics of a decision-making group and the significance of member contributions to the quality of group production.
Population: Individuals who work, or anticipate working, in a group setting.
Publication Date: 1963–89.
Scores, 4: Commitment, Conflict, Creativity, Consensus.
Administration: Individual in part.
Price Data, 1990: $7.95 per manual ('89, 21 pages).
Time: Administration time not reported.
Authors: Jay Hall.
Publisher: Teleometrics International.

[254]
National Achievement Test [Second Edition].
Purpose: "Designed to measure student achievement in the skill areas commonly found in school curricula."
Population: Grades K, 1, 2, 3, 4, 5, 6, 7, 8, 9/10, 11/12.
Publication Dates: 1980–90.
Acronym: NAT.
Administration: Group.
Levels, 12: A, B, C, D, E, F, G, H, I, J, K, L.

Price Data, 1991: $47 per 25 machine-scorable test booklets (Level A or B); $64.25 per 25 machine-scorable test booklets (Complete Battery Level C, D, or E); $50 per 25 machine-scorable test booklets (Basic Battery Level C, D, or E); $52.65 per 25 reusable test booklets (specify Level E–L); $5.90 per 25 practice test booklets (specify Level A through F–J); 1 Directions for Administration provided free with each package of 25 tests; $6.30 per Directions for Administration (specify level); $1.10 per practice test Directions for Administration (specify level); $24.95 per Norms Book; $24.95 per Technical Manual ('90, 72 pages); scoring service available from publisher.
Comments: Formerly called CAP Achievement Series.
Author: John W. Wick, Jana Mason, Janice Stewart, Jeffrey Smith, Norman Wallen, Louis Gatta, and Jack Fraenkel.
Publisher: American Testronics.
a) LEVEL A.
Population: Grade K.
Scores, 11: Reading (Word Recognition, Book Concepts, Total), Language (Listening Vocabulary, Listening Comprehension, Total), Mathematics, Word Attack (Letter Identification, Word Sounds, Total), Basic Battery Total.
Time: (134–150) minutes.
Comments: Examiner-paced.
b) LEVEL B.
Population: Grade 1 (fall).
Scores, 9: Reading (Word Recognition, Book Concepts, Total), Language (Listening Vocabulary, Listening Comprehension, Total), Mathematics, Word Attack (or Word Analysis), Basic Battery Total.
Time: (144–180) minutes.
Comments: Examiner-paced.
c) LEVEL C.
Population: Grades 1 (spring) and 2 (fall).
Scores, 13: Reading (Word Recognition, Story Reading, Total), Language (Listening Vocabulary, Listening Comprehension, Total), Mathematics (Mathematics Computation, Mathematics Concepts and Problem Solving, Total), Social Studies, Science, Word Attack (or Word Analysis), Basic Battery Total.
Time: (195–225) minutes.
Comments: Examiner-paced.
d) LEVEL D.
Population: Grade 2.
Scores, 15: Reading (Vocabulary, Reading Comprehension, Total), Language (Spelling, Language Mechanics, Language Expression, Total), Mathematics (Mathematics Computation, Mathematics Concepts and Problem Solving, Total), Reference Skills, Social Studies, Science, Word Attack, Basic Battery Total.
Time: (291–321) minutes.
Comments: Test is partially examiner-paced.
e) LEVEL E.
Population: Grade 3.
Scores, 15: Same as *d* above.
Time: (321–351) minutes.
Comments: Word Attack subtest is partially teacher-dictated.
f) LEVEL F.
Population: Grade 4.
Scores, 14: Same as *d* above but without Word Attack score.
Time: 319(349) minutes.

g) LEVEL G.
Population: Grade 5.
Scores, 14: Same as *f* above.
Time: Same as *f* above.
h) LEVEL H.
Population: Grade 6.
Scores, 14: Same as *f* above.
Time: Same as *f* above.
i) LEVEL I.
Population: Grade 7.
Scores, 14: Same as *f* above.
Time: Same as *f* above.
j) LEVEL J.
Population: Grade 8.
Scores, 14: Same as *f* above.
Time: Same as *f* above.
k) LEVEL K.
Population: Grades 9 and 10.
Scores, 9: Reading (Vocabulary, Reading Comprehension, Total), Language, Mathematics, Reference Skills, Social Studies, Science, Basic Battery Total.
Time: 255(285) minutes.
l) LEVEL L.
Population: Grades 11 and 12.
Scores, 9: Same as *k* above.
Time: 255(285) minutes.
Cross References: For reviews by Gary W. Peterson and John H. Rosenbach of the original edition, see 9:191 (1 reference).

Review of the National Achievement Test [Second Edition] by MICHAEL B. BUNCH, Vice President, Measurement Incorporated, Durham, NC:

The National Achievement Test (NAT) is part of a larger Comprehensive Assessment Program (CAP), which also includes the Developing Cognitive Abilities Test (DCAT; 110) and the School Attitude Measure (SAM; 344). This review focuses on the NAT only. References to other components of the program are included as appropriate.

CONTENT. The content of the NAT was defined after an exhaustive review of textbooks and instructional guides in grades K–12. The publisher (American Testronics) polled state and local education agencies for instructional guides and textbook lists and sought the advice of several national curriculum groups such as the National Council of Teachers of Mathematics. The end result is a compendium of objectives within the domains listed above. The seven domains are divided into 12 subdomains or strands and hundreds of specific objectives. These are all defined in Objectives and Item Classifications.

Development of the NAT reflects the measurement philosophy of John W. Wick (Northwestern University) and a core group of content and measurement specialists. Their views are elaborated in a series of 13 position papers describing the development of the CAP as well as the proper place of measurement in science, social studies, reading, and the other domains measured. The position papers are extremely well written and provide a very clear rationale for test development.

Although they do not make such a claim, the authors seem to have set out to make the NAT different from its competitors. Groups of test items within a form are thematic, artwork departs from the clean (often sterile) renditions found in most standardized tests, and reading passages sometimes contain violent or disturbing content. Reading passages range from traditional literature (Walt Whitman, Langston Hughes, for example) to *Sports Illustrated*.

BOOKLETS AND MANUALS. The NAT consists of 12 levels (A–L) for grades K–12. Grades K–3 account for five of the levels, and grades 9–12 account for only two. Indeed, the authors have purposely overloaded the lower end of the battery because they hold that the rapid change in student abilities and achievements at the lower grades requires multiple forms.

As noted above, the authors seem to have deliberately tried to make their tests different from the norm. They have succeeded, but sometimes at the expense of the student. Artwork, in particular, is inconsistent and sometimes sloppy and unprofessional in appearance. In general, artwork for the upper grades is superior to that at the lower grades. Reading passages, which sometimes soar to great poetic heights, occasionally plummet to the equivalent of "See Spot run." The use of response options A–D (or E) for odd-numbered items and F, G, H, J (and sometimes K) for even-numbered items seems awkward and unnecessary.

Administration manuals are very well done. They seem to be longer and clearer than most other currently available manuals. The manual for Form A (kindergarten), for example, is over 100 pages long and contains miniatures of the items found in the student booklet. Each manual contains a brief section describing the content of the test, a verbatim script, and instructions for checking and returning materials. Copyrighted passages in the corresponding test booklet are cited in the administration manual.

SCORE REPORTS. Several levels of score reports are available: the Student Class List, Home Report, Individual Student Profile, Student Label, Frequency Distribution, Group Item Analysis, Class Objective/Item Analysis, Class Diagnostic Report, Building/District Profile, Evaluator's Summary, Pre/Post Class List, and Classroom Organizer. An interpretive manual will be available in the fall of 1991. The publisher provided a customized User's Guide for the Archdiocese of Detroit for review. The Guide explains the score reports very well and reveals several important points about the reports. First, virtually no attention is paid to standard error of measurement (*SEM*). Only one report, the optional Individual Student Profile, takes *SEM* into account, but its meaning is not explained in the Guide. Second, the reports are generally well designed and the explanations are clear. Third, the publishers have followed the lead of most other publishers in providing lots of information, some of which has little or no value. Fourth, users can customize their reports to a great extent through selection of optional reports and optional scores.

The Student Class List is well designed and easy to read. Under- and overachievement are indicated by + and - (if the SAM is administered). The use of * to indicate achievement as predicted is probably unnecessary because + and - are present otherwise (i.e., a blank would work just as well). The Home Report is very easy to read and contains a genuine narrative. Total Basic Battery score could be easier to find and space could be provided for teacher comments. The Individual Student Profile contains a great deal of information. Level H, for example, has 170 entries. Multiply this number by 30 students to obtain 5,100 bits of information for the teacher to process and it is easy to see why this report is optional. The class and building reports show how each student and groups of students performed on each item. Most other publishers provide similar reports but such reports seem irrelevant if items represent random samples from a larger universe of possible test items. The Class Diagnostic Report is awkwardly presented and does not, for example, tell how big a difference in student scores is worth noting. The Building and District Profiles and various summaries are well designed and very easy to read. The absence of *SEM* information in these reports could hamper proper use.

Those who prefer to score the tests themselves may use a Norms Booklet. This document is used to convert raw scores to scale scores (equal interval scores) and scale scores to percentiles and stanines. The final page contains a percentile to normal curve equivalent table. With a total of 43 tables, the booklet is fairly complete and easy to follow. Its one minor shortcoming is its lack of discussion of out-of-level testing.

TECHNICAL. A technical manual (Prepublication Edition, 1990) describes the technical characteristics of the tests as well as the development process. Procedures, which included significant teacher involvement, are thoroughly described. Rules for item development and selection are also given. Reading levels were assessed with Spache and Fry methods for Levels D and E, whereas Dale-Chall and Fry methods were used for Levels F–L. Reading levels appear to be appropriate for all levels of the tests. The sample of students included in the standardization was approximately 150,000 in the fall of 1988 and 150,000 in the spring of 1989. The number of students who participated in both administrations is not given. Because the NAT is part of the CAP

battery, relationships among tests are reported. Multiple correlations and standard errors of measurement are given for predicting NAT scores from DCAT scores.

Difficulty indices (p values) by subtest are given in 26 tables (K–12, fall and spring). For most grades, substantial increases in p values from fall to spring are shown. For Reading, however, grades 7–12 show little or no movement from fall to spring. In Mathematics, grades 9–12 show little or no fall-spring improvement. Although these results are generally consistent with the cessation of formal reading instruction at the beginning of junior high and the branching of mathematics instruction at grade 9, they may also show the tests' decreasing sensitivity to instruction. This trend at grades 9–12 also applies to the Science and Social Studies subtests. High School Subject Tests (160), available from the publisher, may be more appropriate at these grade levels.

Biserial correlations between item and test scores are generally high. Test reliability coefficients are reasonably high, ranging from the high .80s to mid .90s at the lower grades and high .80s to high .90s for the upper grades. Intercorrelations among tests are also high. In fact, in all cases except Level D, grade 2 (which yielded two factors), tests are essentially unidimensional. In all but one instance, one reliable factor emerged, accounting for 70–75% of total variance and generally 45–85% of variance in individual subtests.

Validity studies have been conducted but are not reported in the preliminary technical manual. Multiple correlations with DCAT subtests have been noted above. Additional factor analyses of matrices of correlations among NAT, DCAT, and SAM subtests revealed two stable factors for most grades (with a third factor consisting of a single SAM subtest for one grade). In every instance, all NAT subtests and all DCAT subtests defined one factor, whereas the attitude measures (SAM) defined the other(s). Thus, although there is a strong relationship between the NAT (achievement) and the DCAT (ability), there is little differentiation. For example, the Reading subtests of the NAT correlate highly with the Verbal subtests of the DCAT, but they also correlate highly with the Quantitative subtests of the DCAT.

SUMMARY. Test users who are looking for something different should consider the NAT. It has much to recommend it. Its underlying instructional and psychometric framework are well articulated. The tests are challenging and generally interesting, if sometimes marred by poor artwork. Score reports look very much like the reports provided by any other publisher, with most of the same strengths and weaknesses. Absence of information about the standard error of measurement limits interpretation of most reports. Support materials are useful and fairly complete.

This is a new entry in the standardized test market. If the publisher can improve the artwork, separate the subtests more clearly, complete the criterion validity studies, make minor modifications to the score reports, and make the User's Guide available to all users, it will be a tough competitor.

Review of the National Achievement Test [Second Edition] by JAMES TERWILLIGER, Professor of Educational Psychology, University of Minnesota, Minneapolis, MN:

The Second Edition of the National Achievement Test (NAT) is a revision of the Comprehensive Assessment Program (CAP) Achievement Series (9:191) first published in 1980. As was the case with the CAP Achievement Series, the NAT is one component of a tripartite assessment system which also includes measures of ability, the Developing Cognitive Abilities Test (DCAT; 110), and attitudes, the School Attitude Measure (SAM; 344).

The lead author of the CAP instruments makes the following claims. "Only the *Comprehensive Assessment Program* provides educators this opportunity to concurrently assess achievement, ability, and attitude. Each of the test series is a powerful instrument in and of itself, but, when used in conjunction with each other, the results of the three series provide educators with a student profile unsurpassed in its thoroughness and ultimately geared toward improving student achievement. This is the purpose of the CAP" (Wick, 1989). Although this review is restricted to the NAT, it is important to keep in mind the context within which it was developed.

GENERAL OVERVIEW. The NAT is an extremely ambitious undertaking. It attempts to measure common educational outcomes from grades K–12 by means of a battery using 12 different levels (A–L). Depending upon the level employed, the battery yields between 7 and 15 scores for each student. The total testing time for administering the battery ranges from 150 minutes (kindergarten) to 350 minutes (grades 4 through 8). The total testing time for grades 9–12 is 285 minutes. The time limits at each level are quite a bit longer than these suggested schedules.

All 12 levels provide total scores on Reading, Language, and Mathematics. For all grades except kindergarten the battery yields scores on Science and Social Studies. In addition, for grades 2 through 12 a Reference Skills test is included. The number of subtests included in these categories varies according to the grade level being tested.

NAT CONTENT. The test publishers provide a 91-page document that describes the objectives and item classifications employed in the NAT. The introduction states, "The NAT was designed to sample from instructional objectives within the major content and skill areas commonly found in school curricula, and each level reflects instructional objectives and item characteristics that are appropriate for its corresponding grade level." To assure the NAT content is indeed representative of school curricula the authors performed an exhaustive review of textbooks, curriculum guides, supplementary instructional materials, etc. The outcomes sampled in the NAT are classified according to general content categories identified as "objective strands" within which more specific behaviorally stated outcomes are listed. Every item in each level of the NAT is linked to a behaviorally stated learner outcome. The detail presented in the documentation that accompanies the NAT makes it extremely easy for a prospective test user to judge the match between the test content and a given school curriculum.

NAT NORMS. The standardization sample for the NAT was tested in the fall of 1988 and spring of 1989. The sample was selected in a multistage process in which public school districts were stratified by size (four strata) and geographical region (five strata) to assure proportional representation and adequate sample sizes for norms within subpopulations defined by strata. A total of 110 public school districts and 30 parochial districts participated in the norming study with data being collected on students from five attendance centers within each district. Approximately 150,000 students participated in the fall data collection and over 150,000 participated in the spring. A detailed probability weighting was performed to ensure that sample data accurately reflect the national student population both by geographical region and by school size. The care taken in the selection and weighting of the sample is quite impressive.

An extensive booklet of norms accompanies the NAT. The prospective user can choose from raw scores, percentile ranks, grade equivalents, equal interval scores (EIS), stanines, and normal curve equivalents (NCEs). Over 80 pages of tables are provided for converting from one score system to another in each subject area for all levels of the test. I seriously question how much of this is necessary or helpful to teachers and counselors. Although grade equivalents may appear intuitively meaningful at the elementary and middle school level, it seems questionable to employ this system through grade 12.

The EIS system is even more bothersome. First, the Rasch analysis upon which the EIS is based is likely to be understood by few, if any, school personnel. Second, the EIS name is misleading in that it implies that score differences of equal magnitudes signify equal changes in achievement regardless of the absolute scale values. Yet Table 20 of the technical manual for the NAT shows that annual EIS growth intervals decrease sharply from the early grades to the latter grades in all content areas. The NAT authors claim this is evidence for the construct validity of the test. They state, "This diminished rate should not be interpreted as less learning or less adequate instruction but rather as a broadening of the intellectual base." I suspect teachers will find this difficult to accept. The recommendation that users of the NAT "pay little, if any, attention to the EIS," which appeared in the *Ninth Mental Measurements Yearbook* (Rosenbach, 1985) still appears to be good advice.

Questions about the efficacy of the EIS system are particularly important due to the central role this scoring system plays in the interpretation of the NAT. The score conversion tables allow a user to transform raw scores into EIS values. Separate tables allow conversion from the EIS into percentile ranks and stanines. Consequently, users who score by hand are forced to employ the EIS system if they wish to obtain percentile ranks or stanines.

RELIABILITY AND VALIDITY. The technical manual provides a rich supply of psychometric data on the NAT. Tables present KR-20 values, standard deviations, and standard errors of measurement (in both raw score and EIS units) for each content area and subtest within each of the 12 levels. The reliabilities are typically in the high .80s and low .90s for all subject areas and test levels. These are certainly respectable levels given that typical subtest lengths range between 25 and 45 items.

Although there is a brief discussion of the standard error of measurement, there is no concrete illustration of how this index can be employed in the interpretation of individual scores. A simple example of an estimated confidence interval for a student's hypothetical "true score" using data from a specific subtest and level would likely give the user more appreciation of the significance of this information.

Correlation matrices are presented in the technical manual showing the relations among all subtests and total scores within each level of the NAT. As expected, the correlations are uniformly positive. Values range from .45 to .75 for the lower levels (kindergarten–grade 1), from .55 to .95 for the middle levels (grades 5–7), and from .60 to .79 for upper levels (grades 9–12). At all levels the strongest correlations tend to involve the Reading and Language tests suggesting a prominent verbal factor among the subtests. However, no factor analytic results are presented.

The primary claim to validity of the NAT rests on the content validity that results from the extreme care taken in sampling commonly valued educational outcomes. As previously noted, the evidence presented in this regard is impressive. References are made in the technical manual to studies designed to support the criterion-related validity of the test (e.g., studies of students from the standardization sample in gifted programs). However, no data are presented to bolster claims for criterion-related validity. With respect to construct validity, the authors argue that changes in EIS scores over grade levels fit the pattern that developmental theory generally predicts (i.e., "growth occurs from grade to grade, and the intervals of growth at the beginning are higher than at later stages"). Of course, this argument is premised upon the assumption that the underlying dimension upon which change is defined is comparable across all levels. Frankly, I find it difficult to believe that measures of Reading, Language, and Math at grade 1 have much in common with measures of Reading, Language, and Math at grade 12. Consequently, I do not find the "growth" rationale for construct validity very persuasive.

There is one other issue discussed in the technical manual that deserves comment. The notion of a discrepancy between actual and "anticipated" achievement is proposed in which the "anticipated" achievement is estimated by regressing NAT scores on the companion measure of ability, the DCAT. The manual states, "If the difference is positive, the student has performed higher than did a group of students at that grade and with that ability pattern; a negative difference shows the converse. Many characterize this as 'over-' or 'under-achievement,' respectively" (p. 23). The concepts of "over-" and "under-achievement" have been thoroughly discredited in serious psychometric circles (cf. Thorndike, 1963). Therefore, this proposed use of the NAT is entirely inappropriate.

SUMMARY. The NAT is a well-designed battery that reflects great care in both instrument design and standardization. Materials describing the objectives sampled and the classification of items by objective make it easy for a prospective user to judge the fit between the test content and a school curriculum. Reliabilities for various subtests are very respectable. The argument that EIS scores provide a psychometrically sound basis for assessing growth on a continuous scale should be viewed with skepticism. Also, the claim that the NAT offers a plausible indicator of "over-" and "under-achievement" should be ignored. Despite these caveats, the NAT should be given serious consideration by users who wish to assess a broad spectrum of educational outcomes at grade levels ranging from K–12.

REVIEWER'S REFERENCES

Thorndike, R. L. (1963). *The concepts of over- and underachievement.* New York: Bureau of Publications, Teachers College, Columbia University.

Rosenbach, J. H. (1985). [Review of the CAP Achievement Series.] In J. V. Mitchell, Jr. (Ed.), *The ninth mental measurements yearbook* (pp. 264-266). Lincoln, NE: The Buros Institute of Mental Measurements.

Wick, J. W. (1989). *Assessing achievement, ability, and attitude. Comprehensive Assessment Program, Second Edition* (No. 29602). Chicago, IL: American Testronics.

[255]
National Educational Development Tests.

Purpose: To provide students with information in their development of skills that are necessary to do well on college admissions tests and in college work itself.
Population: Grades 9–10.
Publication Dates: 1983–84.
Acronym: NEDT.
Scores, 6: English Usage, Mathematics Usage, National Sciences Reading, Social Studies Reading, Composite Score, Educational Ability.
Administration: Group.
Price Data: Available from publisher for combined test materials and standard scoring services, student materials consisting of test booklets and answer sheets, Student Handbook, Certificates of Educational Development, and Student Information Bulletin; administrative materials consisting of identification sheets, Supervisor's and Examiner's Manuals ('84, 14 pages), and Interpretive Manuals.
Time: 150(180) minutes.
Comments: Tests administered 2 times annually (October and February).
Authors: Science Research Associates, Inc.
Publisher: CTB Macmillan/McGraw-Hill, Del Monte Research Park, 2500 Garden Road, Monterey, CA 93940-5380.

Review of the National Educational Development Tests by PATTI L. HARRISON, Associate Professor of Behavioral Studies, College of Education, The University of Alabama, Tuscaloosa, AL:

The National Educational Development Tests (NEDT) assess ninth and tenth grade students' ability to apply what they have learned and to understand material that might be encountered in later education. Objectives for the tests include helping students, counselors, and administrators to understand students' strengths, weaknesses, and instructional and guidance needs. However, interpretive guidelines emphasize the use of test scores in making plans for college.

The four educational development tests, described in the Student Handbook as measures of intellectual skills, are English Usage, Mathematics Usage, Natural Science Reading, and Social Studies Reading. The term "intellectual" is misleading, as the tests are measures of academic skills, rather than general intelligence. The four tests are averaged to yield a composite. A fifth test, Educational Ability, contains five verbal and nonverbal subtests and is vaguely distinguished from the educational development tests as a measure of "developed abilities" associated with academic performance.

NEDT scores are comprehensively described in the manual, although several needed details are omitted from the interpretation section and are reported in the technical section only. For example, the interpretation section does not indicate that percentile bands and predicted test score ranges are based on a low 50% confidence level. The interpretation section also does not mention that predicted score ranges are based on data from tenth grade students only, and are inaccurate for ninth grade students.

Standard scores are non-normative and do not have the same meaning across tests, but guidelines for interpretation state incorrectly that standard scores may be used to compare performance on different tests. National, college-bound, and local percentile ranks are recommended as the best scores for interpreting performance. National percentile bands reflect measurement error and are used to compare performance on different tests. Expected percentile bands indicate predictions of performance on the educational development tests, given Educational Ability scores. Predicted ranges on the PSAT, SAT, and ACT are based on students' educational development scores.

Skill area data include percentages of items students answered correctly in specific categories. Strengths and weaknesses are identified by comparing percentages to average percentages of a norm group. Many skill areas are assessed with only a few items and data should be interpreted with caution.

Recommendations for using NEDT scores are directed toward making college plans, although materials appropriately state that other factors should also be considered. According to the manual, composite scores above the 85th percentile indicate students could succeed in most colleges; scores below the 75th percentile indicate possible college success; and scores below the 25th percentile indicate questionable college success. Interpretive guidelines also suggest that scores on individual tests and skill areas may be used to identify and correct weaknesses. It should be noted, however, the manual reports no validity data for using scores to predict college success or remediate academic weaknesses.

A confusing array of studies were conducted for equating and norms development. Unfortunately, norms development was not based on a national standardization study for the NEDT; equating, interpolation, and convenient samples were used extensively. Several samples had small numbers of students, are not adequately described, or contained large numbers of church-related schools. The resulting normative data are questionable.

Studies with about 4,000 students equated the four test forms to each other and to an old test form and equated NEDT standard scores to Growth Scale Values. National percentile ranks for Growth Scale Values were obtained from the fall standardization of the Survey of Basic Skills. Spring percentile ranks were developed through interpolation.

Skill area data were obtained from a sample of an unspecified number of students, selected from the equating study to match standardization composite scores. Data from four samples of 100 students, also selected from the equating study, supplied internal consistency coefficients and correlations for developing national and expected percentile bands. Data for predicted PSAT, SAT, and ACT scores were obtained from a sample of 1,200 tenth grade students in five schools participating in the NEDT program. College-bound percentile ranks were based on all students participating in the 1983–84 NEDT program who indicated they definitely planned to go to college (Ns = 21,178 to 34,945).

Kuder-Richardson 20 and Spearman-Brown reliability estimates were obtained from fall and spring samples of ninth graders and fall and spring samples of tenth graders; 100 students in each of the four samples were selected from the equating study to match national standardization score distributions. KR-20 coefficients range from .75 to .91 for the educational development tests, .90 to .92 for the composite, and .79 to .85 for Educational Ability. Several questions can be raised about the reliability coefficients: Did time limits used for educational development tests result in overestimates? Did the different Natural Science and Social Studies passages and different item types of Educational Ability subtests result in underestimates? Were coefficients based on one form or were data pooled across all forms?

An alternate forms reliability study was conducted with about 2,700 students in 16 NEDT schools. Students were administered one complete form and a minitest of one of the other three forms. Correlations range from .37 to .75 for the five tests and .67 to .85 for the composite. Over 50% of the coefficients for the five tests fall below .60. Although the manual suggests that equating error in the minitests or fatigue may have resulted in low coefficients, many coefficients are alarmingly low and cast doubt on using forms interchangeably.

Limited validity data were obtained by correlating test scores with course grades from 11 schools. Correlations range from .02 to .81. Many of the correlations are based on very small samples and should be interpreted with caution. Correlations between the NEDT and PSAT, SAT, and ACT were determined for a sample of 1,200 tenth grade students and range from .60 to .80.

In conclusion, use of the NEDT is not recommended for several reasons. Normative and reliability data are questionable. The use of scores to predict college success or remediate academic weaknesses is not supported. A well-developed achievement/ability battery, such as the Stanford Achievement Test/Otis-Lennon School Ability Test (SAT/OLSAT; 377/274), can better accomplish the NEDT objectives of determining students' academic skills and instructional and guidance needs.

Review of the National Educational Development Tests by HOWARD M. KNOFF, *Associate Professor of School Psychology and Director of the School Psychology Program, University of South Florida, Tampa, FL:*

The National Educational Development Tests (NEDT) consist of five tests designed "to test students' ability to understand the kinds of material they might encounter later in their education rather than to elicit recall of specific information." The first four tests assess students' educational development and correlate most highly with student grades in the specific curricular areas covered. These tests are: English Usage (50 items), Math Usage (40 items), Natural Sciences Reading (32 items), and Social Studies Reading (32 items). The fifth test assesses students' educational ability, those verbal, numerical, reasoning, and spatial abilities that students have developed over time and that correlate most highly with overall academic performance. This test is considered to be a power test in that it has been developed to provide all students with sufficient time to complete all items, and questions (55 items in all) in this test are grouped into verbal and nonverbal subtests.

Created for use with students in their early high school years (typically ninth and tenth grades), the NEDT was developed from a national standardization conducted in 1983–84 and a series of equating studies using representative samples of schools and students stratified by enrollment size, geographic region, and socioeconomic level. In all, the Fall 1983 standardization sample consisted of 96,185 ninth and tenth grade students from 208 schools in 55 districts. Significantly, this standardization process was preceded by an item development and test construction process in 1982 that involved (*a*) a curricular analysis of each test to ensure that individual items had appropriate content and difficulty; (*b*) an item selection analysis to eliminate items that were too easy or too difficult or that did not statistically conform to "best fit" lines; and (*c*) an item bias analysis to identify and eliminate any items that inherently differed across the black, white, and Hispanic groups that participated in the test revision, pretest process. Procedures and results of these three analyses and the standardization and equating process were well described in the NEDT Interpretive Manual. It appears that the NEDT's test construction was well organized, operationalized, and implemented, and that test bias was controlled to a large degree. While church-related schools seemed to be over-represented in the test revision sample (to an unknown degree as no data comparing public, private, and church schools was provided), the NEDT revision and standardization process appears to have yielded a test that accurately reflects its purported purpose.

As a result of the test revision process, four equivalent forms of the NEDT were developed. In the Natural Sciences and Social Studies Reading tests, these forms were balanced across a number of content dimensions (e.g., male versus female referents, urban versus suburban versus rural passage settings), as well as across passage readability and passage length. With average readability levels ranging from grade 8.5 (Form 33, Natural Sciences Reading) to 10.1 (Forms 32 and 34, Social Studies Reading) across the four forms, it is important to note that students whose reading skills fall below these tests' levels will be at a distinct disadvantage. While this may be desired given the NEDT's stated assessment goals (see above), the test's predictive validity will be questionable with students who can conceptually understand the material (e.g., if read orally to them), yet have reading decoding problems. Regardless, the four NEDT appear well equated from both statistical and content perspectives, and the Interpretive Manual again provides good documentation of this equating process.

From any of the four forms, the NEDT reports the following data: standard scores, national percentiles, college-bound percentiles, local (school-based) percentiles, national percentile bands, expected percentile bands, and predicted test scores. In addition, the NEDT Program Student Profile provides the number of correct items for specific skills in each test area (e.g., capitalization/punctuation, verb usage, pronoun usage), and if the student scored above, below, or equivalent to the national standardization group in those skill areas. The NEDT's standard scores range from 1 to 35 with a mean of 15 and a standard deviation of approximately 5 for students in the ninth and tenth grades combined. Although standard scores facilitate test interpretation and test-retest comparisons, the use of a more educationally familiar standard score format (e.g., a mean of 50 and standard deviation of 10; a mean of 100 and standard deviation of 15) would make interpretation even easier and allow functional comparisons across *other* tests of educational development.

The NEDT percentiles indicate an individual student's rank within a specific reference group. The national percentile ranks, for example, are based on data from the 1983 national standardization and are best interpreted alongside the national percentile bands that utilize each test's error of measurement and indicate the range of scores wherein a student's true score rests. The local percentiles reflect a student's performance as compared to his or her same-school or same-community peers, while the college-bound percentiles were generated from students taking the NEDT in the Fall of 1983 and Spring of 1984 who indicated that they would definitely attend college. Finally, the expected

percentile bands are generated from a student's performance on the NEDT's Educational Ability test, and they can be compared to a student's actual performance on the four Educational Development tests; while predicted test scores use NEDT standard scores to predict future student performance on the PSAT, SAT, and ACT college board tests. Overall, the derivation, interpretation, and implications of each type of percentile is clearly discussed in the NEDT Manual. The predicted test scores were based on data collected for the high school graduating class of 1983 (thus, their NEDT and PSAT data from 1980–1982 and their SAT and ACT data from 1982–1983). Correlations among the tests ranged from .631 to .764 for the NEDT and PSAT, from .477 to .610 for the NEDT and the SAT, and from .614 to .791 for the NEDT and the ACT.

Relative to reliability, the NEDT Manual reports both internal consistency data and alternative form data. The former form of reliability was obtained with the 1983–1984 standardization samples using the Kuder-Richardson Formula-20 (KR-20) and the Spearman-Brown Prophecy Formula (S-B). The KR-20 correlations ranged from .75 for Mathematics Usage (Grade 9 sample, First Semester) to .92 for the Composite Score (Grade 10 sample, First and Second Semesters), and the S-B correlations ranged from .85 for Mathematics Usage (Grade 9 sample, First Semester) to .93 for the English Usage test (Grade 10 sample, First and Second Semesters). Overall, these correlations indicate very acceptable internal reliability.

Alternative form reliability was assessed by administering a NEDT "minitest" consisting of 20% of the items of a complete test drawn from Forms 31, 33, and 34. Reliabilities here were acceptable, except that the Educational Ability test had the lowest correlations (.367 to .663). These correlations were considered lower than expected, but two hypotheses were forwarded to explain the results: the use of a minitest (as opposed to the full test) and fatigue due to the fact that the minitest was administered after the students had already completed a full NEDT. Regardless, additional research is needed to document the NEDT's alternative form reliability. Further, periodic updating of all of these reliability results is necessary as the test gets older and continues to depend on the 1983–1984 standardization.

Relative to validity, a series of concurrent validity studies were performed as part of the 1983 equating process by correlating students' NEDT scores and their year-end course grades. Approximately 2,000 students from 11 schools were utilized, and the data from each school were considered separately. While often statistically significant, the lower range of these correlations was quite low. For example, concurrent validity correlations were .253 and .34

for ninth and tenth graders, respectively, on English Usage; .14 and .244 in Mathematics Usage; .076 and .018 for Natural Sciences Reading; and .341 and .356 for Social Studies Reading. No other validity studies were noted in the NEDT Manual. Clearly, more validity research is needed, especially (a) concurrent validity studies involving other educational development/achievement tests, (b) predictive validity studies that confirm the utility of the predicted test scores, and (c) discriminant validity studies that demonstrate the NEDT's ability to discern successful from unsuccessful college-bound and college-matriculated students.

To summarize, the NEDT is designed to determine how well ninth and tenth grade students can apply what they have learned. The Interpretive Manual does an excellent job of describing all of the technical aspects of the test, from test construction to standardization to reliability/validity determination. The Manual is very well written, and it includes numerous examples that help to clarify critical interpretive elements and pragmatic uses of the test. Similarly, the other manuals reviewed (i.e., the Supervisor's and Examiner's Manual, the Student Information Bulletin, and the Student Handbook) were clear and easy to read. While additional research is needed in the areas of alternative form reliability and concurrent, predictive, and discriminant validity, the NEDT appears to be a well-developed test that successfully attains its primary goals and objectives: to help students—especially those with collegiate aspirations—to better understand their academic status and current educational potential.

[256]
National Proficiency Survey Series.

Purpose: Provides an evaluation of student proficiency in high school language arts, mathematics, social studies, and science courses.
Population: High school students completing specific courses.
Publication Date: 1989.
Acronym: NPSS.
Scores: Total score and objective data for each of 13 tests.
Administration: Group.
Price Data, 1990: $34.98 per 35 test booklets for any one test including directions for administration; $19.98 per 35 easy-score answer sheets for any one test; $108 per 250 NCS 7010 answer sheets; $3.60 per directions for administration (30 pages); $9 per technical manual (26 pages); $1.98 per administrator's summary.
Time: 40(45) minutes per test.
Comments: 13 separate high school end-of-course tests; available as separates.
Author: The Riverside Publishing Co.
Publisher: The Riverside Publishing Co.
  a) WRITING FUNDAMENTALS.
  b) LITERATURE.
  c) ENGLISH IV.
  d) GENERAL MATH.
  e) ALGEBRA 1.
  f) ALGEBRA 2.
  g) GEOMETRY.
  h) WORLD HISTORY.
  i) U.S. HISTORY.
  j) AMERICAN GOVERNMENT.
  k) BIOLOGY.
  l) CHEMISTRY.
  m) PHYSICS.

Review of the National Proficiency Survey Series by IRVIN J. LEHMANN, Professor of Measurement, Michigan State University, East Lansing, MI:

Criticism has been, and continues to be, levied against tests and testing programs. Standardized tests are particular targets. Nevertheless, such tests continue to be predictable components of school testing programs in nearly all our schools. In the race between such valid survey achievement batteries as the Stanford Achievement Test (377), the Metropolitan Achievement Tests (10:200), and the Sequential Tests of Educational Progress (9:1115), where does the National Proficiency Survey Series (NPSS) belong? Is it keeping stride or is it just one of the "also rans"?

When we examine the numerous survey batteries designed for high school (such as those just mentioned), we find more similarities than differences among them. These batteries typically contain subtests in language, science, social studies, and mathematics. The NPSS is no exception. It is "designed to offer a comprehensive evaluation of student proficiency in high school . . . . language arts, mathematics, social studies, and science" using 13 tests—three in each of language arts, social studies, and science and four in mathematics—each of which assesses 13–22 objectives that reflect the major content areas. For each objective, there are three items. Administration and testing time is about 50 minutes per test which is the usual high school class period.

ITEMS. The NPSS uses a four-option, multiple-choice format for all the tests. The description of the test's development—from formulating the test objectives to the item writing, editing, and item selection—regrettably is sparse. Other than telling us that the national field test in May 1987 involved 7,800 students from 13 school systems in seven states, that consideration was given to ethnic and gender groups, that the final items were selected from a large (how large is large?) item bank, and that the items were written by classroom teachers and curriculum experts, no further information is provided. The authors state that the items had to satisfy "stringent requirements . . . . and the highest statistical criteria" to be included in the test. But what are the stringent requirements? What are high statistical criteria? This reviewer does *not* question that this was done. However, he would like to see some data to support this claim. As of now, we only know that item selection was made using various criteria. Were the criteria appropriate? We do not know and we should be told!

Language Arts is measured by three tests—Writing Fundamentals, Literature, and English IV. The NPSS Writing Fundamentals test—as do nearly all survey batteries—measures spelling, vocabulary, grammar, usage, and mechanics in the traditional manner, that is, with 66 multiple-choice items. Personally, this reviewer would like to see these skills measured with a writing sample. However, this should *not* be construed as a criticism of the NPSS because other popular survey batteries are no different. The test authors are to be commended because they "have subtests of objectives and items that measure meaning of words in context" of the subject. For example, for mathematics, the students select the definition of the word given: *median score* A. minimum; B. total; C. middle; D. improbable. But there are also subsets of objectives and items that assess the students' vocabulary development— actually spelling—in specific subjects. For example, for mathematics, the student identifies the incorrectly spelled word: A. minus; B. paralell; C. remainder; D. approximately.

Measuring spelling, like measuring writing ability from multiple-choice formats, is difficult. Being able to recognize an error is *not* synonymous with being able to *produce* a correctly spelled word. All test authors, including those of the NPSS, should consider using a separate spelling test rather than have spelling as part of a larger test.

The literature test uses 66 items and is designed to assess "literal and inferential comprehension." With the exception of the first three items which measure basic concepts/knowledge of facts, the remaining items are based upon a series of reading passages—seven prose and two poems—with 3–5 items related to each passage.

This reviewer hopes the NPSS publisher, as well as those of other highly acclaimed survey batteries, will capitalize on the works of some state assessment programs that are now using lengthy passages of sometimes two to three pages to assess reading achievement.

The English IV test "evaluates a student's ability to use language effectively to organize and support ideas" with 42 items that test such skills as whether the student can combine two sentences into one, or whether the student can edit.

Social Studies is measured with three tests— World History, U.S. History, and American Government. World History "measures knowledge of world geography and historical information from early civilization to the current age" using 45 items. It is interesting to note that World Geography is assessed with only 3 items. This reviewer feels the

test developers stretched the point somewhat by inferring that the test measures both World Geography and Historical information. At the same time, it should be noted that some of the history items go beyond factual recall and assess understanding.

The student's knowledge of U.S. History is assessed with 42 items that range from the early exploration and colonization of America to the present. Although the majority of the items are what might be termed "verbal" with respect to the stimulus, there are 4 items for which the stimulus is pictorial—in this case, the items require students to recognize/interpret maps.

The American Government test has 45 items that measure students' knowledge "about state and federal governments, elections, and the Constitution." As might be expected, the majority of the questions assess students' factual knowledge.

Mathematics is measured by four tests—General Mathematics, Algebra 1, Algebra 2, and Geometry. The General Mathematics test measures the students' "computation skills with integers and the knowledge of basic geometric concepts" with 42 items. On careful inspection of the items, it appears that at times the test developers do not have a "match" between the test objective and the test item. For example, when can an item dealing with coordinates in a trigonometric sense be considered a basic geometry item? Can an item dealing with the solution of an equation be categorized as measuring exponents and variables? I think not! Why are some items that have a problem in the stem considered word problems whereas others are not?

There are some items where the distracters do not seem to be based on errors that students would be likely to commit. For example, in the item $4^1/_2 \div ^1/_4$, two distracters ($1^1/_8$ and $4^1/_8$) are plausible. But how would one get 36? Or for the item that deals with the perimeter of 3 x 5 square, how might one arrive at 18?

The Algebra 1 test "measures understanding of real numbers and variables and their operations in equations and inequalities" using 45 items. Once again, it would appear that there may not be a "match" between an objective and an item(s) designed to measure that objective. For example, Objective J is "graph and solve linear equations." Does this mean that the student will graph an equation and then solve it? If so, none of the three items given require this. Or does it mean that graphs have to be used to solve the equation? Again, if this is the task, one of the three items does not require graphing.

The Algebra 2 test "measures an understanding of real numbers and polynomials; the solving of linear, quadratic, and trigonometric equations, and the graphing of functions" by means of 39 items. Nearly one-fourth of the test (9 of 39 items) deals with the solution of linear, quadratic, and trigonometric equations. Isn't this a rather heavy weighting of these objectives? It also appears that minimum attention is paid to using word problems—something that would be expected at this grade level.

The Geometry test "measures an understanding of the nature and relationship of points, lines, angles, planes, circles, polygons, and solids," the content one would expect to find in high school geometry. This is accomplished with 39 items. Of the 13 objectives, one might question whether ratio and proportion belong in a geometry course or in an algebra course. If students are exposed to this objective in *both* algebra and geometry, this may explain why the standardization sample performed so well on this objective.

Science is measured by three tests—Biology, Chemistry, and Physics. The Biology test has 45 items and is designed to measure "knowledge about the living world ranging from single-celled organisms to the human body." On the whole, the items are good although there are a few exceptions. For example, Item 5, which deals with four drawings of a brain, might be a better item if the last drawing, which looks like an elongated sausage, were deleted. This, at least to this reviewer, is a "give-away" to the correct answer. Item 26, which deals with the purpose of a mirror on a microscope, and Item 28, which deals with sweating, do not have distracters that are all plausible.

The Chemistry test measures "understanding of atomic theory, the nature of matter, and its states." There are 42 items. Of the 14 objectives, only two had difficulty levels of more than .50 and one of them was about .52. Again, there were a few poor items: Item 30, for example, where all the distracters were not plausible, and Item 8 where there may be two correct answers. On the whole, however, the items are of good quality.

The Physics test has 45 items and is designed to examine "the nature of energy and the relationship between energy and matter from mechanics through nuclear reactions." Of the three science tests, this one is the most difficult with 5 of the 15 objectives (or one-third of the test objectives) not passed by at least one-half of the students. The Physics test had a heavier concentration of application-type items than either the Chemistry or the Biology tests. Whether this fact or whether the quality of instruction is responsible for so many students doing poorly is a matter of conjecture.

Some interesting findings reported on the national average level of achievement by objective for each of the 13 tests are as follows:

1. The easiest test appears to be Writing Fundamentals and the most difficult is Physics. In fact, the Language Arts tests are, as a group, easier than the History, Mathematics, or Science tests.

2. Of the Science tests, Biology appears to be the easiest.

3. Of the History tests, U.S. History appears to be the easiest; American Government appears the most difficult.

4. Of the Mathematics tests, all are of approximately equal difficulty.

5. Of the Language Arts tests, Literature is the most difficult.

In summary, the items seem to "match" the instructional objectives specified. For the most part, their development, try-out, selection, and relationship to national objectives may be appropriate and well done but we lack information to conclude this is the case.

FORMAT. The tests, the Administrator's Manual, and the Technical Manual are presented in 8½ by 11 inch booklets. All printing is in blue ink on white paper with the letters identifying the distracters printed in red ink. The quality of paper, reproduction, and illustrations are excellent. The illustrations in the General Mathematics, Geometry, Biology, and Physics tests are also printed in red ink.

STANDARDIZATION AND NORMS. The tests were normed in April and May 1988 on 22,616 public and Roman Catholic school students in grades 9–12 from 45 high schools in 20 states.

The sampling design stratified the public schools on (*a*) geographic regions (the nation was divided into two regions); (*b*) district enrollment (small, medium, and large); and (*c*) district socioeconomic status (low, average, and high). The national values for enrollment and socioeconomic status were determined from 1980 census data. Regrettably, information pertaining to the categorical values for enrollment and socioeconomic status was conspicuous by its absence. It is nice to be told that districts were classified but it is *not* acceptable to be uninformed as to the operational definition of terms such as "small, large, medium, high, low, and average." This reviewer has no criticism of the sampling design, per se, but the NPSS—and it should be emphasized that this criticism is levied against most, if not all standardized tests—provides no information on the number of primary sampling units that refused to participate and had to be replaced. Such information could help users immeasurably by providing them with data concerning the sample's representativeness. The sampling design and the weighting procedures *may* have been appropriate and well done but one *cannot* conclude they were. It behooves the publisher to provide enough data for users to draw conclusions that the overall standardization *was* correct.

The publishers are to be commended for providing percentile ranks (PRs) by grade level for the Writing Fundamentals and Literature tests. In fact, where appropriate, PRs reported for each grade level would be desirable (9 through 12) for all tests.

It should be noted that although weighting procedures were used to equate the sample with the population on the three stratification variables, some inequalities still were present. This was especially evident for the sample's overrepresentativeness of the percentage of students from "medium" high schools (39.1 vs. 33.3% for the sample and population respectively), and from "low" and "average" SES districts; and the underrepresentativeness from each of the other district and SES categories.

This reviewer considers himself a psychometrician rather than a sampling statistician. Possibly for this reason, he would have appreciated a description of the logic (or at least a reference) for the way in which the SES index was derived.

SCORES AND SCORING. Both machine-scorable (NCS) and self-scorable answer sheets are available. For users wishing to machine score their answer sheets, the publisher has a test scoring and reporting program available on diskette.

The publisher is to be particularly complimented for having a self-scorable answer sheet. Not only does this provide for quick and easy scoring but immediate feedback should help in providing for somewhat more rapid remediation/reteaching if necessary. In addition, with the exception of the Writing Fundamentals test, there are at least 35 spaces available on the NCS answer sheet for users to add their own supplemental questions. In a sense, the NPSS can be "tailored" to meet users' specific needs. Other test publishers would be well advised to emulate this practice.

Two types of scores are used: percentile rank and NCEs. Norms are available for only PRs. Whereas the PRs permit users to compare individual pupils' scores with some reference group, NCEs permit users to make comparisons involving *groups* of individuals such as classes, schools, etc. The instructions provided for computing group average NCEs are simple and concisely presented. If the NCS scoring diskette is used, group average scores will be computed automatically.

RELIABILITY. The Technical Manual reports the mean, median, standard deviation, KR20, and standard errors of measurement in terms of raw scores. With the exception of the Language Arts tests where the KR20s and standard errors of measurement are reported by grade level, the reliability data for the Mathematics, History, and Science tests are reported only in terms of composite grades. The KR20s range from .82 to .91 with a median of .86. The standard errors of measurement are all less than 3 raw score points. Although the reliabilities are acceptable, this reviewer contends that if *individual* decisions are made on the basis of

these results, the reliabilities should be higher. Stability estimates would also be desirable.

VALIDITY. The sine qua non of an achievement test is *content* validity. The publishers are to be congratulated for alerting potential users to the fact that "the test *user* [italics added] must determine the purpose of the test, then evaluate its validity based on a variety of information available about the test . . . but information should always be interpreted in relation to the user's own purpose for testing." The publisher indicated that after an extensive review of high school instructional materials and a national curriculum survey, objectives were written. We are informed regarding (a) who wrote, edited, and reviewed the test items; (b) the field trials and the statistical data they provided; (c) the bias reviews conducted; (d) the national *p*-values for each objective; (e) the item *p*-value distributions, means, and medians by test; and (f) the self-reported grade-point average for the standardization sample. All in all, the publisher provided some valuable information, albeit sparse. One additional piece of information would prove useful—test blueprints by test and taxonomical classification (knowledge, understanding, and higher order thinking skills). This would help users determine whether the NPSS (or just some of the tests) are valid for them.

TYPES OF REPORTS. From the test manuals, it would appear that persons using the NCS scoring are provided with no formal score reports, per se. If this is the case, it is indeed unfortunate. The Stanford Achievement Test, for example, provides at least 10 reports that can be used for instructional purposes. The Metropolitan Achievement Test, Sixth Edition (MAT6) and the Iowa Tests of Basic Skills (ITBS; 184) (which, incidentally, is also published by Riverside Publishing Company) provide a variety of output data.

It should be noted that those using the self-scorable answer sheet can obtain (a) scores by objective, and (b) objective/item match data which facilitates grouping items into objective clusters. This is a good beginning but is woefully inadequate.

HOW DOES THE NPSS RATE? You will recall that at the beginning of this review, I asked whether the NPSS is in the race with other standardized survey batteries or whether it is lagging behind and may even be an "also ran."

The first draft of this review was a rather critical evaluation. But after having a good night's sleep, I concluded the NPSS is still in the running and could be made a strong contender. It is running well when the traditional criteria used to evaluate an achievement battery are applied. Information, albeit limited, is provided on the test development and item selection phases. As noted earlier, a test blueprint and more information on the selection criteria for items would be very valuable in aiding the potential user. The reliabilities are respectable although not spectacular for a test whose results might be used for *individual* decisions. The content validity evidence presented is supportive. The quality of the items and reproduction are excellent. With such good things to say about the NPSS what are its major faults?

The heart of any achievement test in general, and survey batteries in particular, is to assist in the teaching-learning process. Regrettably, there is little information provided to help classroom teachers become better teachers using the test results. What kind of grouping might they undertake? How valid are interpretations made regarding mastery/no mastery of objectives measured with only three items? Can the test results be used by administrators and counselors? The publisher should provide more illustrations of how the test results could be used. Where feasible, *p*-values should be reported by grade because one would expect the items to become easier, especially in language arts, as students progress through school. The publisher must seriously consider the validity of the claim that the NPSS is designed "to provide nationally-normed criterion-referenced surveys." Is this not an oxymoron? How can a true criterion-referenced test have norms? It is possible for a domain-referenced test to have norms but the author(s) do not claim that the NPSS is domain referenced.

The authors state the tests may be administered as pre (beginning of course) and post (end of course) tests "to determine how much individual students and the class have learned." This reviewer contends this is possible but questions the validity of such a statement. How much faith can one have in objectives that are assessed with only three items? Would you wish to certify that a pupil has mastered, for instance, "solutions, mixtures, and ionizations" even if he or she answered all three items correctly? This reviewer would be loath to do this.

The authors also state that in order to instill a positive attitude in the test takers, there are in all but three of the subtests—English IV, Writing Fundamentals, and U.S. History—three items (they refer to them as Basic Concepts) that "are designed to be answerable by virtually all students." This effort is intriguing. Whether it works has not been demonstrated, however.

In conclusion, the NPSS earns a B. The final choice of a test rests, however, with the users after they have made their own critical evaluation.

[257]
Neale Analysis of Reading Ability, Revised British Edition.

Purpose: "To assess the reading attainment of individuals and to provide diagnostic information about reading difficulties."
Population: Ages 6–13.

Publication Dates: 1957–89.
Scores, 3: Rate, Accuracy, Comprehension; plus 4 supplementary diagnostic scores (Discrimination of Initial and Final Sounds, Names and Sounds of the Alphabet, Graded Spelling, Auditory Discrimination and Blending).
Administration: Individual.
Forms, 2: 1, 2.
Levels, 6: 1–6.
Price Data: Available from publisher.
Time: (10–15) minutes.
Comments: Demonstration cassette available for familiarization with administration procedure.
Authors: Marie D. Neale, British adaptation and standardization by Una Christophers and Chris Whetton.
Publisher: NFER-Nelson Publishing Co., Ltd. [England].
Cross References: See T3:1567 (13 references) and T2:1683 (7 references); for reviews by M. Alan Brimer and Magdalen D. Vernon, and an excerpted review, see 6:843.

TEST REFERENCES

1. Aman, M. G. (1979). Cognitive, social, and other correlates of specific reading retardation. *Journal of Abnormal Child Psychology, 7,* 153-168.
2. Bishop, D. V. M., & Butterworth, G. E. (1980). Verbal-performance discrepancies: Relationship to birth risk and specific reading retardation. *Cortex, 76,* 375-389.
3. Rutter, M., Chadwick, O., Shaffer, D., & Brown, G. (1980). A prospective study of children with head injuries: I. Design and methods. *Psychological Medicine, 10R,* 633-645.
4. Bradley, L., & Bryant, P. (1981). Visual memory and phonological skills in reading and spelling backwardness. *Psychological Research, 43,* 193-199.
5. Chadwick, O., Rutter, M., Brown, G., Shaffer, D., & Traub, M. (1981). A prospective study of children with head injuries: II. Cognitive sequelae. *Psychological Medicine, 11,* 49-61.
6. Lovegrove, W., Martin, F., Bowling, A., Blackwood, M., Badcock, D., & Paxton, S. (1982). Contrast sensitivity functions and specific reading disability. *Neuropsychologia, 20,* 309-315.
7. Oakhill, J. (1982). Constructive processes in skilled and less skilled comprehenders' memory for sentences. *The British Journal of Psychology, 73,* 13-20.
8. Yule, W., Lansdown, R., & Urbanowicz, M. (1982). Predicting educational attainment from WISC-R in a primary school sample. *British Journal of Clinical Psychology, 21,* 43-46.
9. Prior, M. R., Frolley, M., & Sanson, A. (1983). Language lateralization in specific reading retarded children and backward readers. *Cortex, 19,* 149-163.
10. Hulse, J. A. (1984). Outcome for congenital hypothyroidism. *Archives of Disease in Childhood, 59,* 23-30.
11. Jorm, A. F., Share, D. L., Maclean, R., & Matthews, R. (1984). Phonological confusability in short-term memory for sentences as a predictor of reading ability. *British Journal of Psychology, 74,* 393-400.
12. Oakhill, J. (1984). Inferential and memory skills in children's comprehension of stories. *British Journal of Educational Psychology, 54,* 31-39.
13. Share, D. L., Jorm, A. F., Maclean, R., & Matthews, R. (1984). Sources of individual differences in reading acquisition. *Journal of Educational Psychology, 76,* 1309-1324.
14. Harding, L. M., Beech, J. R., & Sneddon, W. (1985). The changing pattern of reading errors and reading style from 5 to 11 years of age. *British Journal of Ecucational Psychology, 55,* 45-52.
15. Limbrick, E., McNaughton, S., & Glynn, T. (1985). Reading gains for underachieving tutors and tutees in a cross-age tutoring programme. *The Journal of Child Psychology and Psychiatry and Allied Disciplines, 26,* 939-953.
16. Lindsay, G., Evans, A., & Jones, B. (1985). Paired reading versus relaxed reading: A comparison. *British Journal of Educational Psychology, 55,* 304-309.
17. Maughan, B., Gray, G., & Rutter, M. (1985). Reading retardation and antisocial behaviour: A follow-up into employment. *The Journal of Child Psychology and Psychiatry and Allied Disciplines, 26,* 741-758.
18. McKay, M. F., & Neale, M. D. (1985). Predicting early school achievement in reading and handwriting using major 'error' categories from the Bender-Gestalt Test for young children. *Perceptual and Motor Skills, 60,* 647-654.

19. McKay, M. F., Neale, M. D., & Thompson, G. B. (1985). The predictive validity of Bannatyne's WISC categories for later reading achievement. *British Journal of Educational Psychology, 55*, 280-287.

20. Pickering, D. M., & Bowey, J. A. (1985). Psycholinguistic performance of children varying in socioeconomic status and home-language background. *Perceptual and Motor Skills, 61*, 1143-1146.

21. Wilsher, C., Atkins, G., & Manfield, P. (1985). Effect of Piracetam on dyslexic's reading ability. *Journal of Learning Disabilities, 18*, 19-25.

22. Jorm, A. F., Share, D. L., Maclean, R., & Matthews, R. (1986). Cognitive factors at school entry predictive of specific reading retardation and general reading backwardness: A research note. *Journal of Child Psychology and Psychiatry and Allied Disciplines, 27*, 45-54.

23. Jorm, A. F., Share, D. L., Matthews, R., & Maclean, R. (1986). Behaviour problems in specific reading retarded and general reading backward children: A longitudinal study. *Journal of Child Psychology and Psychiatry and Allied Disciplines, 27*, 33-43.

24. Neale, M. D., McKay, M. F., & Childs, G. H. (1986). The Neale Analysis of Reading Ability—Revised. *British Journal of Educational Psychology, 56*, 346-356.

25. Riding, R. J., & Cowley, J. (1986). Extraversion and sex differences in reading performance in eight-year-old children. *British Journal of Educational Psychology, 56*, 88-94.

26. Ellis, N., & Large, B. (1987). The development of reading: As you seek so shall you find. *British Journal of Psychology, 78*, 1-28.

27. Gurney, P. W. (1987). The use of operant techniques to raise self-esteem in maladjusted children. *British Journal of Educational Psychology, 57*, 87-94.

28. Kirby, J. R., & Robinson, G. L. W. (1987). Simultaneous and successive processing in reading disabled children. *Journal of Learning Disabilities, 20*, 243-252.

29. Stevenson, J., Graham, P., Fredman, G., & McLoughlin, V. (1987). A twin study of genetic influences on reading and spelling ability and disability. *Journal of Child Psychology and Psychiatry and Allied Disciplines, 28*, 229-247.

30. Udwin, O., Yule, W., & Martin, N. (1987). Cognitive abilities and behavioural characteristics of children with idiopathic infantile hypercalcaemia. *Journal of Child Psychology and Psychiatry and Allied Disciplines, 28*, 297-309.

31. Carr, J. (1988). Six weeks to twenty-one years old: A longitudinal study of children with Down's syndrome and their families. *Journal of Child Psychology and Psychiatry and Allied Disciplines, 29*, 407-431.

32. Casey, W., Jones, D., Kugler, B., & Watkins, B. (1988). Integration of Down's Syndrome children in the primary school: A longitudinal study of cognitive development and academic attainments. *British Journal of Educational Psychology, 58*, 279-286.

33. McKay, M. F., & Neale, M. D. (1988). Patterns of performance on the British Ability Scales for a group of children with severe reading difficulties. *British Journal of Educational Psychology, 58*, 217-222.

34. Wilks, R. T. J., & Clarke, V. A. (1988). Training versus nontraining of mothers as home reading tutors. *Perceptual and Motor Skills, 67*, 135-142.

35. Goodman, R., & Stevenson, J. (1989). A twin study of hyperactivity-I. An examiniation of hyperactivity scores and categories derived from Rutter teacher and parent questionnaires. *Journal of Child Psychology and Psychiatry and Allied Disciplines, 30*, 671-689.

36. Outhred, L. (1989). Word processing: Its impact on children's writing. *Journal of Learning Disabilities, 22*, 262-264.

37. Said, J. A., Waters, B. G. H., Cousens, P., & Stevens, M. M. (1989). Neuropsychological sequelae of central nervous system prophylaxis in survivors of childhood acute lymphoblastic leukemia. *Journal of Consulting and Clinical Psychology, 57*, 251-256.

38. Yuill, N., Oakhill, J., & Parkin, A. (1989). Working memory, comprehension ability and the resolution of text anomaly. *British Journal of Psychology, 80*, 351-361.

39. Chadwick, O., Yule, W., & Anderson, R. (1990). The examination attainments of secondary school pupils who abuse solvents. *The British Journal of Educational Psychology, 60*, 180-191.

40. Leach, D. J., & Siddall, S. W. (1990). Parental involvement in the teaching of reading: A comparison of hearing reading, paired reading, pause, prompt, praise, and direct instruction methods. *The British Journal of Educational Psychology, 60*, 349-355.

41. Stevenson, J., & Fredman, G. (1990). The social environmental correlates of reading ability. *Journal of Child Psychology and Psychiatry, 31*, 681-698.

Review of the Neale Analysis of Reading Ability, Revised British Edition by CLEBORNE D. MADDUX, Professor and Chairman, Department of Curriculum and Instruction, University of Nevada-Reno, Reno, NV:

The Neale Analysis of Reading Ability is an individually administered, norm-referenced reading test that also includes some of the diagnostic provisions of informal reading inventories. The original edition of the test was published in 1958. In 1984, it was revised and restandardized for Australian use. The present British Edition provides standardization data for England and Wales and incorporates revisions designed to modernize certain reading passages and to provide more detailed suggestions for interpreting results, and also includes practice passages to familiarize subjects with the test format.

Test materials include a clearly written manual; color coded, consumable individual record forms; an attractive student reader; and an excellent cassette tape containing sample testing sessions and aids and cautions in administering the test. The test consists of two equivalent forms, each with six graded reading passages for assessing rate, accuracy, and comprehension in oral reading. Subjects read the passages orally and in ascending order until a ceiling is established. The examiner keeps a record of time and errors including mispronunciations, substitutions, refusals, additions, omissions, and reversals. The examiner then asks a series of eight comprehension questions (four in Level 1) designed to tap immediate recall of the main idea, sequence and other details, and some limited inference. Tables are provided to convert rate, accuracy, and comprehension raw scores to percentile ranks, stanines, reading ages, and reading age confidence intervals called equivalent age ranges.

Four non-norm-referenced, informal Supplementary Diagnostic Tests are also included to help assess Discrimination of Initial and Final Sounds, Names and Sounds of the Alphabet, Graded Spelling, and Auditory Discrimination and Blending. Some educators will object to the format of three of these tests because they emphasize producing and recognizing letter sounds in isolation.

In addition, the test includes a Diagnostic Tutor, which is a third set of graded passages provided without normative data. These passages are to be used for various informal activities at the examiner's discretion.

NORMATIVE DATA. The test was standardized on a sample of 1,760 children attending school in England and Wales. The original sample contained 400 students (200 males and 200 females) from each of the six age groups, 6–12 years. These students attended 317 schools, 62 secondary and 255 primary. Although it is impossible to determine whether or not the sample was systematically stratified, the manual states the sample was representative of schools in England and Wales in terms of type of school, age range, number of pupils, and type of county. Reference is made to schools that declined to participate, although no other details are given. Thus, the possibility of sampling bias exists, especially because school administrators, rather than the test authors, chose which children would participate. Although school administrators were instructed to use a table of random numbers, this procedure may not have been followed. Another possible biasing factor is that the standardization subjects were administered the test by their own teachers, rather than by disinterested examiners. Further, it does not appear that these examiners received special training in test administration, but were simply mailed the test kits and encouraged to administer five practice exams prior to conducting the standardization sessions. These teachers were asked to record the time taken to read each passage, the number and type of errors, and the answers given by subjects to the comprehension questions. The tests were then scored by the publishers. These procedures obviously represent a serious threat to accuracy of the standardization data. No information is provided on SES or on numbers or types of handicapped or minority children included in the standardization sample.

RELIABILITY. The manual comments on equivalent forms reliability and internal consistency. With reference to equivalent forms reliability, a small subsample of the standardization sample took both forms of the test. The numbers of students who took part were unacceptably small (all reported correlations are based on numbers of subjects that vary from 19 to 46), and there is no information on how these subjects were selected. In addition, no demographics of any kind are presented. Correlations were calculated separately for Form 1 followed by Form 2, and for Form 2 followed by Form 1, and separately for rate, accuracy, and comprehension. The six levels were combined to form only three levels for calculation of coefficients (thereby increasing the variability and introducing the possibility of spuriously high results). The coefficients ranged from .67 to .98. All but three of the 18 coefficients were .85 or higher. Two of the three unacceptably low coefficients were for rate. The low sample sizes and lack of description of the subjects or rationale for their selection makes these data difficult to interpret.

Internal consistency was investigated by calculating coefficients alpha for accuracy and comprehension scores. These coefficients were calculated separately for the two forms of the test. Sample sizes vary from 179 to 345 and fall in the low to mid .80s for accuracy, and in the low .90s for comprehension. Although data on selection and characteristics of the sample are again missing, internal consistency appears to be acceptable.

VALIDITY. The manual suggests the content validity of the test rests on acceptance of the importance of oral reading, and on procedures taken to ensure that the reading passages are suited to the age groups being considered. However, few data were presented to support this latter point. In addition, there is no discussion of the importance of the types of errors noted.

The manual addresses concurrent validity by presenting correlations of scores on the *original* 1958 edition of the test, Form A for 9- and 11-year-olds, with seven other standardized reading tests. These correlations, calculated for an unpublished doctoral dissertation in 1956, vary from .61 to .95. The manual does not present the number of subjects on which the correlations are based, and does not include demographics or further details of any kind. The manual also presents correlations of the Australian version of the test with the Schonell Graded Word Reading Test and the Vocabulary and Similarities subtests of the Wechsler Intelligence Scale for Children—Revised (WISC-R). For the Schonell, these correlations range from .76 for rate, to .96 for accuracy. Again, these correlations are presented without revealing numbers of scores and without demographics.

The manual presents data on predictive validity by referring to 1967 and 1973 studies of the original 1958 edition. Other studies of the Australian edition are also mentioned.

SUMMARY. The test is attractively and professionally bound and the manual and cassette are clear and helpful. The test is easy to administer and score. Standardization data are incomplete and suspect due to procedures used to obtain test scores from the normative sample. Even if these procedures were corrected, usefulness would be restricted to England and Wales. Reliability data are incompletely presented and validity is unknown, because nearly all substantiating data apply to other editions of the test. Until these problems are corrected through more scientific standardization; through complete presentation of reliability data performed with larger, respresentative samples; and through validity studies carried out with this version of the test rather than with earlier editions, the test should be regarded as promising, but experimental in nature.

Review of the Neale Analysis of Reading Ability, Revised British Edition by G. MICHAEL POTEAT, Associate Professor of Psychology, East Carolina University, Greenville, NC:

The Neale Analysis of Reading Ability was first developed in Great Britain and published in 1958 with a second edition issued in 1966. The revised edition was published in Australia in 1988 and in Great Britain in 1989. The Australian and British versions are identical except for minor changes in content and separate norms. The test kit contains a test booklet (reader), individual record sheets, a demonstration cassette tape, and a test manual of more than 100 pages. Instructions for administration and information on the establishment of norms, reliability, and validity are provided by the manual. The reader contains two parallel forms of six graded reading passages, for ages 6 through 12 years, and four supplementary diagnostic tests. A third parallel form (diagnostic tutor) is provided without norms and is intended for use as a criterion-referenced test. Except for a stopwatch and pencil, no additional materials are required for administration.

The Neale Analysis of Reading Ability is described by the author as a set of graded reading passages for assessing the accuracy, rate, and comprehension of oral reading. The test is intended to provide both diagnostic information and standardized scores. It is administered individually by asking the student to read the story aloud and to remember the story. Practice passages with comprehension questions are provided to ensure that the pupil understands the requirements of the task. The examiner codes errors as mispronunciations, substitutions, refusals, additions, omissions, or reversals on the individual record sheet which reproduces the reading passages. The test is designed to be administered by teachers and the directions are straightforward except when testing comprehension while establishing a basal reading level. For Form 1, the passages vary in length from 26 to 141 words. Each of the passages has a maximum accuracy score of 16 except for the most advanced, which has a maximum score of 20. One point is subtracted for each error (mispronunciation, etc.) made and the maximum raw accuracy score is 100 points. Errors in accuracy are corrected by the examiner. Testing is discontinued if more than 16 errors are made at a single level (20 at Level 6). Accuracy scores are converted to a Reading Age (a standard score) which may extend from 5 to 13 years. Percentile ranks and stanines for ages 6:0 to 11:11 are provided by 1-year intervals.

Reading comprehension is assessed through 8 oral questions about the passage (only 4 questions are given for the first passage). Most of the questions ask for factual information, but a few require the examinee to make an inference. One point is earned for each correctly answered question (the maximum score is 44) and then converted to a reading age score and percentile rank. A reading rate is obtained by dividing the total number of words read by the total reading time. The reading rate is also converted to a reading age and percentile rank.

The reading age scores and percentile ranks are based on a sample of 1,760 British children enrolled in 203 participating secondary and primary schools in England and Wales. The 203 schools were part of a sample of 317 schools drawn from a Department of Education and Science Register of Schools. The selection was designed to include a representative sample of schools stratified by type, age range of

pupils served, number of pupils, and type of county (i.e., metropolitan or rural). Schools were given a table of random numbers to select students for testing and the normative data were obtained by regular or special education teachers in the schools. The author concludes that the sample was adequate for standardization but a count of subjects by sex and age is the only information provided about the sample. The description of the normative process is incomplete and more information (e.g., socioeconomic data) is needed concerning the sample.

Reliability was assessed through the use of parallel forms and measures of internal consistency. Forms 1 and 2 had parallel form reliability coefficients ranging from .67 to .98 using a sample of 208 subjects divided into three age groups. Accuracy and comprehension scores were generally more reliable than reading rate. Internal consistency coefficients (Cronbach's alpha) for accuracy and comprehension were calculated using 1,633 subjects divided into three age groups. Alphas ranged from .81 to .93 and were consistent across age groups and equivalent for Forms 1 and 2. Some evidence for the validity of the test is provided. Moderate correlations (.41 to .68) were found between the Australian Edition and Wechsler Intelligence Scale for Children—Revised (WISC-R) Vocabulary and Similarities subtest scores for a sample of over 1,400 students. For the same sample, correlations ranging from .76 to .96 were found with the Schonell Graded Word Reading Test. Research supporting the predictive validity of the Australian Edition is referenced. Additional research using earlier versions of the Neale Analysis is reviewed and the correlation between Form A of the 1958 test and Form 1 of the revised edition suggests the two versions are more or less equivalent measures.

The four supplementary diagnostic tests consist of: (a) Discrimination of Initial and Final Sounds, (b) Names and Sounds of the Alphabet, (c) Spelling, and (d) Auditory Discrimination and Blending. No norms are provided for the diagnostic tests. The author recommends the examiner use the diagnostic tests to augment observations made by the student's teacher, but the information provided by these abbreviated exercises would probably have little diagnostic value.

Despite some attractive attributes, the routine use of the Neale Analysis of Reading Ability cannot be recommended in the United States. Positive characteristics include adequate reliability, evidence of validity, and a direct format which reflects elementary classroom reading demands. In addition, the norms are based on a large and possibly representative sample of the British school population. However, the application of these norms in the United States cannot be justified without further investigation. It is apparent that the author did not intend for the test to be used for populations other than the one on which the standardization was based. Also problematic for the American user is the British spelling (e.g., programme, metres) found, albeit infrequently, throughout. The potential U.S. purchaser should consider the Woodcock Reading Mastery Tests—Revised (10:391) or, for a diagnostic criterion-referenced measure, the Diagnostic Reading Scales (9:338). With the new standardization, the Neale Analysis of Reading Ability offers the British user the advantage of parallel forms for situations requiring repeated assessments. In the U.S., it is recommended only as a supplemental measurement in unusual circumstances.

[258]
The NEO Personality Inventory.

Purpose: To "measure . . . five major dimensions or domains of normal adult personality."
Population: Adults.
Publication Dates: 1978–89.
Administration: Group.
Price Data, 1990: $6 per 25 feedback sheets; $15 per manual ('85, 48 pages) and supplement ('89, 34 pages); $8 per supplement.
Authors: Paul T. Costa, Jr. and Robert R. McCrae.
Publisher: Psychological Assessment Resources, Inc.
a) NEO PERSONALITY INVENTORY.
Acronym: NEO-PI.
Forms, 2: Form S (self-reports), Form R (observer ratings).
Scores, 23: Neuroticism (Anxiety, Hostility, Depression, Self-Consciousness, Impulsiveness, Vulnerability, Total), Extraversion (Warmth, Gregariousness, Assertiveness, Activity, Excitement-Seeking, Positive Emotions, Total), Openness (Fantasy, Aesthetics, Feelings, Actions, Ideas, Values, Total), Agreeableness, Conscientiousness.
Price Data: $55 per complete kit including 10 reusable Form S test booklets, 25 answer sheets, scoring keys, 25 Form S profile forms, 25 feedback sheets, manual, and manual supplement; $12 per 10 reusable test booklets; $9 per 25 answer sheets; $16 per set of scoring keys; $9 per 25 profile forms; $40 per introductory kit including manual, supplement, scoring keys, 1 Form S test booklet, 1 Form S profile, 1 answer sheet, 1 feedback sheet; $195 per computer version.
Time: (30) minutes.
Comments: IBM or Apple computer-administered version requires 64K 80-column card, 2 floppy disk drives-Apple; 256K and 2 disk drives-IBM.
b) NEO FIVE-FACTOR INVENTORY.
Acronym: NEO-FFI.
Scores, 5: Neuroticism, Extraversion, Openness, Agreeableness, Conscientiousness.
Price Data: $55 per complete kit including manual, supplement, 25 test booklets (answer sheets and profiles included), and 25 feedback sheets; $35 per 25 test booklets.
Time: Administration time not reported.
Comments: Shortened version of Form S.
Cross References: For a review by Robert Hogan of *a*, see 10:214 (6 references).

TEST REFERENCES

1. Costa, P. T., Busch, C. M., Zonderman, A. B., & McCrae, R. R. (1986). Correlations of MMPI factor scales with measures of the five factor model of personality. *Journal of Personality Assessment, 50*, 640-650.
2. Costa, P. T., Jr., & McCrae, R. R. (1988). From catalog to classification: Murray's needs and the five-factor model. *Journal of Personality and Social Psychology, 55*, 258-265.
3. Costa, P. T., Jr., & McCrae, R. R. (1988). Personality in adulthood: A six-year longitudinal study of self-reports and spouse ratings on the NEO Personality Inventory. *Journal of Personality and Social Psychology, 54*, 853-863.
4. Bernieri, F., Koestner, R., & Rosenthal, R. (1989). To predict some of the people some of the time: In search of moderators. *Journal of Personality and Social Psychology, 57*, 279-293.
5. McCrae, R. R., & Costa, P. T., Jr. (1989). The structure of interpersonal traits: Wiggins's circumplex and the five- factor model. *Journal of Personality and Social Psychology, 56*, 586-595.

Review of the NEO Personality Inventory by ALLEN K. HESS, Professor and Department Head, Auburn University at Montgomery, Montgomery, AL:

The good news is that Costa and McCrae developed a fine measure of the five major dimensions of personality. And the bad news is that Costa and McCrae developed a fine measure of the five major dimensions of personality.

THE INVENTORY. The NEO Personality Inventory (NEO-PI) is a 181-item measure that initially assessed Neuroticism (N), with its facets, Anxiety, Hostility, Depression, Self-Consciousness, Impulsiveness, and Vulnerability; Extraversion (E), with its facets Warmth, Gregariousness, Assertiveness, Activity, Excitement-Seeking, and Positive Emotions; and Openness to Experience (O), with its facets Fantasy, Aesthetics, Feelings, Actions, Ideas, and Values. Later, Agreeableness (A) and Conscientiousness (C) were added. The 18 facets have eight items each in a 5-point format (*Strongly Agree* to *Strongly Disagree*). The facet scores are summed so the N, E, and O domains have a 48-item composition. The A and C scales have 18 items each. The last, and 181st item, is the validity item which asks whether the questions were honestly and accurately answered. One further important feature of the Inventory is that it is designed to be used both as a person's self-rating scale and as a rating scale of a person by others.

The manual begins with a chapter on professional qualifications for the NEO-PI's use, followed by one on administration and scoring. Chapter 3 presents interpretation of the facets and their domains, and includes four profiles and the authors' interpretations of the cases. These are rich in description but seem to lack empirical support, in part because the validity studies are not presented for two more chapters. Chapter 4 describes applications of the NEO-PI. These extend to health, vocational, clinical, and educational clientele. Finally, in Chapter 5 the development and validation of the NEO-PI are described.

ITS ORIGINS. Costa and McCrae developed the NEO-PI and its shortened version, the NEO-FFI, in the course of studying the aging process in two samples of normal adults. The Normative Aging

Study (NAS) sampled over 2,000 men, mostly White veterans, living in the Boston area. This sample was bolstered by the Augmented Baltimore Longitudinal Study of Aging (ABLSA) consisting of about 400 men and 300 women drawn from professional, managerial, and scientific occupations who were recruited by word of mouth.

The authors give no accounting about how the items were developed and refined. However, Costa and McCrae articulated their Inventory toward fitting what has been termed the Big Five (Goldberg, 1981). The Big Five refers to the consistent set of content categories or factors that are replicated across various personality inventories, first recognized by Tupes and Christal (1961). The NEO-PI items were rationally derived to define the facets that in turn were supposed to define the content domains of each scale with minimum overlap.

RELIABILITY. Alpha coefficients for the facets for men range from .61 to .79, for women from .60 to .82, and for ratings by others of the person from .64 to .86. The alphas for men are .91 for N, .89 for E, and .86 for O, and for women are .93 for N, .85 for E, and .88 for O. The 6-month test-retest reliability coefficients for 31 men and women are .87 for N, .91 for E, and .86 for O, all highly respectable. Estimates for coefficient alpha for A and C are .56 and .84 for self-ratings, and .89 and .91 for peer ratings. No retest data were presented for A and C, nor for Form R (other ratings).

VALIDITIES. Consensual validation, or the correspondence between self and spouse, and self and peer ratings lend support to the factors. Convergent correlations for men and women are .47 and .56 for N, .72 and .46 for E, and .60 and .45 for O.

Studies correlating the NEO-PI with other measures show positive affect related to E and negative affect correlated with N; E is related to Social and Enterprising interests in Holland's vocational taxonomy, whereas Artistic and Investigative interests are related to O. Costa and McCrae claim somatic complaints correlate with N as does immature and neurotic coping mechanisms. Their Manual Supplement provides norms for college students, and reports studies of the NEO-PI and such inventories as the MMPI (Minnesota Multiphasic Personality Inventory), the PRF (Personality Research Form), the IAS-R (Interpersonal Adjective Scales), and the MBTI (Myers-Briggs Type Indicator). Generally, the manual suggests that scales that one would expect to correlate, do correlate, and that some degree of discriminant validity is obtained as well.

RESPONSE STYLES AND SETS. The NEO-PI assumes an honest respondent. Thus, no subtle items nor validity scales were included. The singular validity item was not validated. To counter the acquiescence response set, an equal number of items are keyed in the positive and negative directions.

Rather than construe social desirability as a contaminant, Costa and McCrae opt to see the correlations between the Marlowe-Crowne Social Desirability Scale and the Edwards Personality Inventory Lie scale with their N scale as evidence that the Lie and Social Desirability scales bespeak elements of neuroticism in individuals so motivated as to distort their responding. This would pose a problem for the clinical use of the scale in distinguishing "true" neurotic styles from transient, extrinsically motivated distortion.

THE GOOD NEWS AND THE BAD NEWS. The NEO-PI seems to be a reliable and valid measure, derived from samples of adults ranging in age from their 20s into their eighth decade, that taps the Big Five personality content domain. It contains no item overlap (unlike the Millon Clinical Multiaxial Inventory [239] which has some 90% item overlap precluding any discriminant validity and differential diagnoses or predictions), has 6-year stability coefficients reported in the Manual Supplement, has nicely developed parallel forms for self and other ratings, has been translated into German for cross-cultural use, can be machine or hand scored, and is anchored in a network of theory and research.

So, what is the bad news? First, a researcher can use various adjective checklists (e.g., Goldberg, 1982; John, 1990) that tap the Big Five economically and that can be adapted to one's needs in terms of length and response format. Second, the personality assessment field is capricious as to which measures catch on and which fade into obscurity. Who would have guessed that biographical inventories would fade after the Woodworth, eclipsed by the "dust bowl" empiricist inventories, with diminished emphasis on content? Who would guess that a measure of how a person responded to ataraxic medication would grow into the heralded MMPI (244), whereas a well-developed PRF (10:282) goes underutilized? And how could a test based on splotches of ink with diverse scoring systems and even more diverse interpreters persist when an extremely sophisticated Holtzman Inkblot Technique (9:480) with reliable and valid scales, with parallel forms, and with group (slide) formats and well-anchored norms fades unnoticed into the psychometric Valley of the Bones? Given the vaguely charted shoals of personality and psychopathology domains, and the gusty winds of fad and fashion that buffet the assessment field, valid and reliable measures do not always prevail. It seems that scales developed out of a particular need, such as the MMPI, or a singular personality construct, such as locus of control, develop far beyond the authors' fancy. Researchers apply some measures to various and sundry problems and populations, with some measures becoming footnotes in the history of psychology while others become monuments in psychological measurement.

Whether the NEO-PI, a measure of the normal adult personality, meets a need in the marketplace, or whether this straightforward measure of the Big Five is useful when used in applied settings with clientele of diverse and complex motives, only time will tell.

REVIEWER'S REFERENCES

Tupes, E. C., & Christal, R. C. (1961). *Recurrent personality factors based on trait ratings.* Technical Report, USAF, Lackland Air Force Base, TX.

Goldberg, L. R. (1981). Language and individual differences: The search for universals in personality lexicons. In L. Wheeler (Ed.), *Review of personality and social psychology,* (Vol. 2, pp. 141-165). Beverly Hills, CA: Sage.

Goldberg, L. R. (1982). From ace to zombie: Some explorations in the language of personality. In C. D. Spielberger & J. N. Butcher (Eds.), *Advances in personality assessment* (Vol. 1, pp. 203-234). Hillsdale, NJ: Erlbaum.

John, O. P. (1990). The search for basic dimensions of personality: A review and critique. In P. McReynolds, J. C. Rosen, and G. J. Chelune (Eds.), *Advances in psychological assessment* (Vol. 7, pp. 1-37). New York: Plenum.

Review of the NEO Personality Inventory by THOMAS A. WIDIGER, Professor of Psychology, University of Kentucky, Lexington, KY:

Digman (1990) suggests there has been a convergence of views regarding the fundamental dimensions of personality, with a consensus support for the five-factor model. The NEO Personality Inventory (NEO-PI) is the best measure of these five dimensions of Neuroticism (N), Extraversion (E), Openness to Experience (O), Agreeableness (A), and Conscientiousness (C). The NEO-PI also differentiates underlying facets of each dimension that may have particular relevance in various applications. The facets of N, E, and O are presented above. Provisional facets of Agreeableness are trust, candor, altruism, meekness, modesty, and tender-mindedness; provisional facets of Conscientiousness are competence, order, dutifulness, achievement, self-discipline, and deliberation (Costa and McCrae, in press).

There are three versions of the NEO-PI: Form S for self-reports; Form R for observer ratings; and an abbreviated version of Form S, the NEO-FFI. Both hand-scoring templates and computerized interpretations are available. There is even a report form that can be given directly to a subject that provides one- or two-sentence descriptions for three levels on each of the five dimensions. The test administrator simply checks which options apply. This form could be useful when debriefing research subjects. The authors caution against its indiscriminate use, particularly within clinical settings.

Construction of the NEO-PI was itself conscientious. Initial item construction was governed by rational-theoretical considerations, and item selection by internal consistency and factor analytic data. Norms are based on 502 adult males, 481 adult females, 250 college males, 276 college females, 430 peer raters of adult males, and 313 peer raters

of adult females. One of the distinct advantages of the NEO-PI is the norms were not derived simply from college students but included instead a full range of adults. The normative sample was better educated and more intelligent than the average adult but there may not be a substantial relationship between these variables and most of the dimensions. Openness is correlated with vocabulary level and education, but this is consistent with theoretical expectations. N, E, and O are somewhat higher for younger subjects. The authors attribute this to either sampling biases or cohort effects, rather than to changes in personality with age. The magnitude of the differences is in any case minimal and the stability of the scores is frankly more impressive than the variability.

College students, however, do provide quite a different profile than adults, obtaining (for example) scores almost two standard deviations higher on the E facet of Excitement-Seeking. Separate norms are therefore provided. Providing separate norms is consistent with current practice (as one would provide different norms for males and females). However, if it is the case that college students tend to be excitement-seeking, then an average college student should not be described as being average in Excitement-Seeking but rather above average. Providing separate norms for conscientiousness for prisoners or neuroticism for psychiatric patients would similarly underestimate the magnitude of these traits in persons from these populations. This issue is not confined to the NEO-PI and concerns the appropriateness of the individual differences model for personality assessment (Lamiell, 1981). It is not a problem for the NEO-PI as long as one interprets the scores as being relative to a respective population.

NEO-PI validation research has been impressive, not only with respect to the findings but also the process. Validity data are typically submitted to peer-reviewed journals for critical review rather than being published solely in the test manuals. There is considerable empirical support for the internal structure and external validity of the dimensions and their facets that replicates across self-report, spouse ratings, and peer ratings (e.g., McCrae & Costa, 1987). Six-month test-retest reliability ranges from .86 to .91 for the dimensions and .66 to .92 for the facets. Six-year test-retest reliability is above .80 for N, E, and O for Form S and above .75 for Form R; six-year reliability values for the facet scales range from .68 to .79 (Costa & McCrae, 1988). Three-year test-retest reliability was .63 for Agreeableness and .79 for Conscientiousness. The NEO-PI is often used in research concerned with the validation of the five-factor model (e.g., McCrae & Costa, 1987), and the continued support for the five factors is as much a testament to the strength of the

NEO-PI as it is of this particular model of personality.

The NEO-PI lacks substantial validity or dissimulation scales. The only "scale" is the last item that asks whether the subject has tried to answer all questions honestly or accurately. This item could identify negligent subjects willing to acknowledge their indifference, as well as approximately 40% of the random responders who did not read it, but it is unlikely that a subject who is motivated to be inaccurate will acknowledge the falsehood. The authors do suggest how visual inspection can identify systematic "random" responders by the occurrence of a string of identical responses (e.g., more than six consecutive *strongly disagree* responses). The administration of the NEO-PI largely assumes the presence of a cooperative, honest subject. This is often a safe assumption, but it may be somewhat less safe in some applications (e.g., forensic, personnel, and psychiatric settings). Items are balanced for acquiescence and McCrae and Costa (1983) make a compelling argument for not being concerned with social desirability.

The test manuals suggest how the NEO-PI could be used in medical, psychiatric, business, and other applied settings. A test that purportedly provides a comprehensive assessment of the fundamental domains of personality will likely have a broad practical application. The most relevant psychiatric application is perhaps the assessment of maladaptive personality (Wiggins & Pincus, 1989). A limitation in the clinical application of current self-report measures of personality is the effect of current mood (state) on the subject's description of long-standing personality (trait). It is not yet clear whether the NEO-PI will be immune to this issue.

The construct validity of the NEO-PI is tied to the validity of the five-factor model and its representation by the constructs of Neuroticism, Extraversion, Openness to Experience, Agreeableness, and Conscientiousness.

The support is substantial but it is not without some controversy (Digman, 1990). It is still debated, for example, whether openness to experience is a fundamental dimension of personality and whether this factor might be better represented by other constructs, such as intellect. McCrae and Costa (in press), however, do provide compelling arguments and empirical support for the construct of openness. In any case, any study that purports to be addressing fundamental dimensions of personality should include the NEO-PI as a measure.

REVIEWER'S REFERENCES

Lamiell, J. (1981). Toward an idiothetic psychology of personality. *American Psychologist, 36*, 276-289.
McCrae, R., & Costa, P. (1983). Social desirability scales: More substance than style. *Journal of Consulting and Clinical Psychology, 51*, 882-888.

McCrae, R., & Costa, P. (1987). Validation of the five factor model of personality across instruments and observers. *Journal of Personality and Social Psychology, 52*, 81-90.
Costa, P., & McCrae, R. (1988). Personality in adulthood: A six-year longitudinal study of self-reports and spouse ratings on the NEO Personality Inventory. *Journal of Personality and Social Psychology, 54*, 853-863.
Wiggins, J., & Pincus, A. (1989). Conceptions of personality disorders and dimensions of personality. *Psychological Assessment: A Journal of Consulting and Clinical Psychology, 1*, 305-316.
Digman, J. (1990). Personality structure: Emergence of the five-factor model. *Annual Review of Psychology, 41*, 417-440.
Costa, P., & McCrae, R. (in press). The NEO Personality Inventory (NEO-PI). In S. Briggs & J. Cheek (Eds.), *Personality measures* (Vol. 1). Greenwich, CT: JAI Press.
McCrae, R., & Costa, P. (in press). Conceptions and correlates of openness to experience. In S. Briggs, W. Jones, & R. Hogan (Eds.), *Handbook of personality psychology*. NY: Academic Press.

[259]
New Jersey Test of Reasoning Skills—Form B.

Purpose: Assesses elementary reasoning and inquiry skills.

Population: Reading level grade 5 and over.

Publication Dates: 1983–85.

Scores: 22 skill areas: Converting Statements, Translating into Logical Form, Inclusion/Exclusion, Recognizing Improper Questions, Avoiding Jumping to Conclusions, Analogical Reasoning, Detecting Underlying Assumptions, Eliminating Alternatives, Inductive Reasoning, Reasoning with Relationships, Detecting Ambiguities, Discerning Causal Relationships, Identifying Good Reasons, Recognizing Symmetrical Relationships, Syllogistic Reasoning (Categorical), Distinguishing Differences of Kind and Degree, Recognizing Transitive Relationships, Recognizing Dubious Authority, Reasoning with 4-Possibilities Matrix, Contradicting Statements, Whole-Part and Part-Whole Reasoning, Syllogistic Reasoning (Conditional).

Administration: Group.

Manual: No manual.

Price Data, 1987: $2.40 per 12-month test booklet rental including scoring and analysis service for up to 4 answer sheets.

Time: (30–45) minutes.

Author: Virginia Shipman.

Publisher: Institute for the Advancement of Philosophy for Children.

TEST REFERENCES

1. Anderson, R. N., Greene, M. L., & Loewen, P. S. (1988). Relationship among teacher's and student's thinking skills, sense of efficacy, and student achievement. *The Alberta Journal of Educational Research, 34*, 148-165.

Review of the New Jersey Test of Reasoning Skills— Form B by ARTHUR S. ELLEN, Assistant Professor of Psychology, Pace University, New York, NY:

The New Jersey Test of Reasoning Skills—Form B (NJTRS) was designed to evaluate the Philosophy for Children program, an innovative curriculum that asks students to reflect on their thinking through carefully planned class discussion. The NJTRS is based upon a 22-category taxonomy of children's elementary reasoning. Elementary reasoning is here defined as logic learned by children while they acquire language. It differs from higher level thinking, which occurs when students apply elementary skills to more advanced disciplines or solve problems using more than one elementary skill. True to this definition, the questions on the test tap basic logical operations by using an elementary-school reading level (Flesch reading grade level of 4.5 and a Fogg Index of 5.0).

The test consists of 50 multiple-choice questions, each in the form of a short dialogue with three possible answers. Directions are clearly given in the test booklet along with one practice item. The test, according to the publisher, should take about 45 minutes and a 1-hour time limit is suggested. An optical scan form goes back to the publisher, who will return for each class: (a) the Kuder-Richardson reliability index, (b) the mean and standard deviation, (c) the percent correct for each item, (d) a report for each of the pupils telling them the number correct in each of the 22 skill areas of the test, and (e) a chart of available test averages by grade from the publisher's data base.

The NJTRS appears to be used mainly with middle-school students, although it has been given experimentally to students from first grade to college (M. Lipman, personal communication, December 14, 1989). For students under fourth grade, the publisher suggests reading the test aloud. However, this may not work because many younger students will not remember or comprehend the questions and answers. As the test has been used to evaluate a year-long curriculum project, pre- and post-testing are possible with the same form if testing is completed during one school year.

Technical information is not provided in a manual, but instead the publisher furnishes four sources of information: (a) a portion of a 1982–83 curriculum evaluation report that used an earlier 55-item version of the test; (b) a 1983 three-page brochure from Montclair State College that briefly describes the test; (c) a sheet that reports correlations of the NJTRS with college-level measures of achievement; and (d) a sheet that contains grades 4 through 8 test means as of February 1986.

Although the current test has 50 items, the bulk of the technical information apparently comes from a 55-item version used in the curriculum evaluation project. In 10 communities, that project sampled 2,346 fifth- through seventh-grade students in 74 experimental and 42 control classes. From these data the publishers derived item statistics, test reliability, and some of the rationale for the test's validity.

Item statistics included item difficulties and point-biserial correlations for item to total test score. Although not reported for each item, a good range of item difficulties with a preponderance of "moderately difficult items" was found. Seven items with low point-biserial correlations (.20 or less) were found, and perhaps these results helped to drop

items from the 55-item version to make the final 50-item test.

Test reliability in the form of coefficient alpha, an index of internal consistency, was obtained from a random and representative sample of classrooms in the curriculum project. From grades 5 to 7, the coefficient alphas consistently increased from .84 to .94. These reasonably high indices agree with the reliability index of .83 found for a previous version of the test. Unfortunately, test stability was not examined by generating test-retest correlations.

One claim to validity is based upon the test's sensitivity to experimental intervention found in the year-long curriculum evaluation project. From the fall to spring of that school year, the matched-control classes, on the average, increased their test scores approximately 3 points. In contrast, experimental classes, on the average, increased their total test scores a little more than 6 points. These significant differences led the publishers to conclude that the NJTRS responds to changes caused by the Philosophy for Children program.

The publishers argue for at least four additional kinds of validity: content, construct, developmental, and concurrent. Content validity exists because the NJTRS is supposed to sample adequately the elementary reasoning skills taxonomy. Construct validity is based upon the unreported test development research performed at the Educational Testing Service between 1976 and 1978.

Developmental validity usually means test scores exponentially increase with either age or grade. But from grades 4 through 8, the NJTRS's means do not exponentially increase; instead, they remain relatively flat, a test plateau. To explain this, the publishers hypothesize that students develop elementary reasoning skills at about grade 4. However, the interaction between a child's age and item format (O'Brien & Shapiro, 1968; Roberge, 1970) might partially explain the test's ostensible plateau.

Concurrent validity comes from two studies that correlated the NJTRS with measures of college achievement. The first study, with over 600 college freshmen, found moderate correlations with the New Jersey College Basic Skills Placement Test, an exam consisting of five academic achievement subtests in the areas of reading, math, and writing. The second study, with 150 college students, reported moderate correlations between the NJTRS and the Scholastic Aptitude Test math and verbal subtests, and small but significant correlations to college grade-point average. Both studies support the interrelationship between the NJTRS and achievement with college-level students, but not with middle-school students, the intended test takers.

A major shortcoming of the NJTRS is the absence of a comprehensive test manual. A manual minimally must include such missing technical information as: (a) definitions and examples for the taxonomy of logical reasoning; (b) which items correspond to particular skills in the taxonomy, a test plan; (c) what research served as the basis for construct validity; (d) which test statistics were derived with the 55-item evaluation instrument and which came from the 50-item test; and (e) item difficulties and point-biserial correlations for each item.

Another limit of the NJTRS is its lack of subtests. Although the test is intended to evaluate a complex curriculum project, there is only one global test score. This score, a composite of the 22 elementary reasoning skills, will not inform a teacher or program evaluator which skills a pupil has learned. It should be noted, however, that constructing a test with reliable subtests for this many skills would require a much longer test and evidence that the subtest constructs exist.

In sum, the NJTRS provides an internally consistent composite measure of a unique taxonomy of elementary reasoning skills using a clever item format. However, the publishers could make a better case for test use by providing a thorough and comprehensive report of test information.

REVIEWER'S REFERENCES

O'Brien, T. C., & Shapiro, B. J. (1968). The development of logical thinking in children. *American Educational Research Journal, 5*, 531-542.
Roberge, J. J. (1970). A study of children's abilities to reason with basic principles of deductive reasoning. *American Educational Research Journal, 7*, 583-596.

Review of the New Jersey Test of Reasoning Skills— Form B by ROSEMARY E. SUTTON, Associate Professor of Education, Cleveland State University, Cleveland, OH:

The New Jersey Test of Reasoning Skills was developed in the early 1980s to evaluate the Philosophy for Children Program (PCP). The purpose of the PCP program, developed by Dr. Matthew Lipman at Montclair State College, is to improve students' reasoning skills through classroom discussion that emphasizes generating ideas, discovering resemblances and differences, and finding reasons. Although the Philosophy for Children Program is intended for kindergarten through high school students, the New Jersey Test of Reasoning Skills was developed for use with students in the fifth through seventh grades.

The 50-item multiple-choice test represents 22 skill areas of inductive and deductive reasoning. The language is very simple and the test can be used for as low as fourth grade level. Because so many skill areas are covered, and no information is given about which questions cover which skill areas, this test can be used only to provide information about general critical thinking ability. Thus, this test may be used to evaluate a program such as the PCP, but cannot be used to diagnose specific strengths and weaknesses.

RELIABILITY. The technical information supplied was not in the form of a technical manual, but as part of a final report on the experimental Philosophy for Children Program intervention. Details about reliability indices are given only for an earlier 55-item version of this test. Cronbach's alpha for fifth grade classes ranged from .84 to .87, for sixth grade classes the range was .86 to .89, and for seventh grade classes the range was .91 to .94. The published version of the test has only 50 items. I assume five items with low point-biserial correlations (item to total test score) discussed in the technical information were eliminated, but there is no way to determine which items were eliminated or the new reliability coefficients. These reliability coefficients are high and are unlikely to be altered significantly with the elimination of five items, but the correct figures should have been supplied.

VALIDITY. Content validity was established by producing a taxonomy of the skills needed to perform the operations in the discipline of logic used in childhood and by developing questions from this taxonomy. No information is provided about why some logical skills were selected for inclusion in the test and others were not. Correlations between this test and measures of academic performance are also provided to support validity. These correlations were high and statistically significant for the majority of the measures (e.g., SAT Math, .59; SAT Verbal, .57; Reading Comprehension subtest of the New Jersey College Basic Skills Placement Test, .82). However, all of these data were gathered from samples of college students, even though this test was developed and pilot tested on middle-school children.

NORMS. Norms for 1986 were provided for fourth through eighth grade students. These norms are based on large samples, but no demographic information was provided. Earlier norms were based on 10 diverse subsamples including suburban, rural, and inner-city children. The recent norms show little change in the average number of right answers from fourth grade to eighth grade (31.1 for fourth grade and 34.1 for eighth grade, with standard deviation for both groups approximately 10).

Evaluating critical thinking and reasoning is a very difficult task and there are very few tests appropriate for this age group. While this test appears to be of some value for its original purpose of evaluating the Philosophy for Children Program, I do not recommend it for other purposes. The technical information provided is too limited. If the publishers develop an appropriate technical manual with accurate reliability indices, details about normative samples, and more information about validity, this test may be worth consideration.

New Technology Tests: Computer Commands.

Purpose: To "provide a measure of aptitude for those entering employment or training in occupations where computers are used as basic operational tools . . . it focuses on skills relating to the rapid identification of differences between two pieces of information, and the use of commands to bring about change."
Population: Applicants for computer-related jobs.
Publication Date: 1987.
Scores: Total score only.
Administration: Group.
Price Data, 1989: £34.50 per 10 test booklets (20 pages); £30.50 per set of answer sheets including 25 answer sheets, 25 command lists, 1 test record form, and 1 data collection form; £48.30 per specimen set including user's guide (34 pages), test booklet, command list, answer key, test record form, data collection form, and administration cards.
Time: 20[25] minutes.
Comments: New Technology Tests: Computer Rules (261) also available.
Author: NFER-Nelson Publishing Co., Ltd.
Publisher: NFER-Nelson Publishing Co., Ltd. [England].

Review of the New Technology Tests: Computer Commands by BRUCE W. HALL, Chair, Department of Educational Measurement and Research, University of South Florida, Tampa, FL:

The authors offer their New Technology Tests: Computer Commands as "a measure of aptitude for those entering employment or training in occupations where computers are used as basic operational tools." It is intended as an aid in the recruitment/selection of employees whose job involves the routine use of computers or word-processing equipment or in the identification of employees capable of retraining for such purposes. The authors argue that the test can be considered a "proactive speed and accuracy test," appropriate for computer-related clerical tasks.

The test is composed of 34 items, each of which presents the respondent with two six-by-two grids (12 cells) containing information in the form of letters. The respondent is required to identify the ways in which the information in the two grids differs, and then to select from a set of eight commands, the commands required to transform the first grid into the second. The commands consist of directives to copy, delete, shift, move, or replace information. Each item directs the respondent as to the number of commands (one to three) required to complete the item. The recommended time limit for the test is 20 minutes.

Scoring is such that the examinee must get all responses to an item correct to receive credit for the item. The second response to many of the two-command items, however, may be predictable to an alert examinee, because the first nine of these two-command items require the same basic command (e.g., delete) as the answer for both responses.

This reviewer found the User's Guide to be readable and well laid out and the instructions for test administration and test scoring to be explicit and easy to follow. The test answer sheets are designed for self-scoring; marks made on a top sheet are transferred by carbon to a second sheet that indicates the positions of the correct answers. The directions to the examinees are equally clear, thanks to two sample items that are provided. However, this reviewer questions the completeness of the directions. Nine of the 34 items on the test require recognition of the order in which commands are to be used. Yet no indication of the importance of order is stated or even implied in the directions to the examinees, nor is order implicated in the two sample items. This apparent oversight raises questions about the authors' depiction of the test as a measure of speed and accuracy. Another complication in the directions concerns the commands themselves. Examinees must learn the five commands and their functions as part of the test directions. Examinees are assured that they do not have to memorize the list of commands and that they can refer to the command list as often as needed. Yet, this learning requirement raises further questions as to the nature of the aptitude being measured.

The authors present a reasonable rationale for the selection of the item format and the focus on basic commands. But necessary information on the selection and refinement of items is lacking. Standardization data were collected in two phases, only the first of which was complete at the time of publication. In this first phase the standardization sample consisted of 580 college students, primarily female, in commerce-related courses from 16 colleges in Great Britain. The authors describe the sample as "a reasonably good cross-section" of college students likely to be applying for a first job in a field that involves the use of computers. Beyond this, little descriptive information is provided about the sample, and no information is given about the conditions under which the data were collected. Norms tables based on this sample are presented in percentiles, T-scores, and z-scores. Although females constitute three-quarters of this standardization sample and the authors report statistically significant differences in scores favoring males, they provide no gender-specific norms. Indeed, they insist that no importance whatsoever should be attached to these gender differences, but their rationale for this position is unclear. Because the authors provide no clear decision rules for determining who was to be included in the standardization sample, and because of the limited description of the sample, this reviewer places little confidence in the norms data presented to date.

The reliability of the test was estimated by means of KR-20 on the standardization sample and by a test-retest study of 39 subjects over a 1-month interval. The KR-20 estimate of .89 (with a standard error of measurement of 2.13) appears adequate. Attempts to determine the effects of speeding on the estimate suggest that it was not seriously inflated by speed. The test-retest estimate of .79 is more problematic due to the small number of subjects employed and due to the lack of a description of these subjects.

As is often the case with a new instrument, relatively little information is provided on the validity of the test scores. The authors recognize the need for criterion-related validation studies on the test, but at the time of publication only one study, a predictive validity investigation, had been completed. The study was designed to select, from among current employees of a warehousing company, those employees to be trained to handle new computerized functions being adopted within the company. Although the authors report that the findings of the study are encouraging, the number of subjects involved ($N = 26$) was too small to yield more than suggestive results. The authors report that larger studies on the predictive validity of the test are underway. To the authors' credit, guidelines are offered to users for conducting their own validation studies.

The authors report the results of two studies on variables that may impact performance on the test. Chronological age was found to correlate modestly ($r = -.17$) with test performance in the standardization sample, but as the authors point out, this age effect is likely to be confounded with course membership. Test performance is also shown to be affected by previous exposure to the test; on a 1-month retest, examinees showed a mean gain of 5.2 score points, a rather notable increase of almost one standard deviation. This reviewer agrees with the authors that the gain in scores may reflect learning that occurs with exposure to the test. But whether such a result is a strength or weakness is unclear. Certainly, it limits the freedom of the user to reuse the test with target subjects.

The New Technology Tests: Computer Commands appears to be a useful addition to instrumentation needed for selection and training decisions in the burgeoning field of computer applications in commerce and industry. However, data on the reliability and validity of the test are still quite limited, and the standardization and norming of the test leaves much to be desired. The test employs a format that seems pertinent for assessing computer-related capabilities, but this reviewer has difficulty with the notion that the key aptitude being mea-sured is one of speed and accuracy. The format appears to emphasize visual-perceptual factors to a high degree, and a learning element is clearly implicated in performance on the test. Until further, more complete validation studies can clarify the factor or factors being tapped by the instrument, this reviewer wishes to echo the suggestion of the authors that the test be considered for use in conjunction with other tests of a more specific nature (e.g., tests of spatial ability, mechanical reasoning, and verbal and abstract reasoning).

[261]
New Technology Tests: Computer Rules.

Purpose: To "provide a measure of aptitude for those entering employment or training in occupations where computers are used as a basic operational tool . . . the emphasis in this test is primarily on following rules."
Population: Applicants for computer-related jobs.
Publication Date: 1987.
Scores: Total score only.
Administration: Group.
Price Data, 1989: £34.50 per 10 test booklets (30 pages); £30.50 per set of answer sheets including 25 answer sheets, 25 command lists, 1 test record form, and 1 data collection form; £48.30 per specimen set including user's guide (30 pages), test booklet, answer sheet, test record form, data collection form, and administration cards.
Time: 30[35] minutes.
Comments: New Technology Tests: Computer Commands (260) also available.
Author: NFER-Nelson Publishing Co., Ltd.
Publisher: NFER-Nelson Publishing Co., Ltd. [England].

Review of the New Technology Tests: Computer Rules by BRUCE W. HALL, Chair, Department of Educational Measurement and Research, University of South Florida, Tampa, FL:

The New Technology Tests: Computer Rules, like its companion, Computer Commands (260), is presented as "a measure of aptitude for those entering employment or training in occupations where computers are used as basic operational tools." It is intended as an aid in the recruitment/selection of people whose work will involve the routine use of computers or word-processing equipment or in the identification of employees capable of retraining for such purposes. Because of the test's emphasis on following and inferring rules, the authors suggest that high scorers should prove particularly efficient at implementing fundamental housekeeping operations within a computer environment.

The test, comprising 75 three-option multiple-choice items, requires the examinee to learn certain rules about file management and usage (presented on information sheets) and then to apply these rules to solve given problems. The typical item presents a computer command or command sequence and asks the examinee to identify the effect or result of using that command or command sequence. Items toward the end of the test require the examinee to infer certain rules, based on common sense, before proceeding. The time limit for the test is 30 minutes.

The answer sheet for the test uses a scratch-off procedure. The examinee responds to an item by scraping away the silver coating on his or her answer choice. If correct, the scratch-off process will reveal a check mark. If incorrect, an "X" will appear, in which case the examinee is directed to continue responding until a check mark appears. A check mark earns 2 score points, and a point is then subtracted for every "X" uncovered. This partial credit system thus awards from 0 to 2 points per item, for a maximum total score of 150. The marking and scoring processes seem quite straight-forward. However, this reviewer is unclear whether the examinee is being well served by the directive to continue the scratch-off activity even after two "Xs" have been uncovered, in view of the limited test time available.

This reviewer found the User's Guide to be well organized and readable, with easy-to-follow instructions for test administration and scoring. The directions to the examinee are clear and complete, thanks to the five sample items provided and the warning examinees are given that, although some rules may be familiar to those who have used microcomputers, the test is based on no particular system.

The rationale for basing the test on a "spoof operating system" similar but not identical to such systems as MS-DOS and Unix seems sound, given the authors' intent to measure examinees' capability to learn and apply computer rules. However, little information is provided on the process whereby items were selected and refined for inclusion in the test. Standardization data were collected on a target population of students in business and computing courses who "on taking up employment will most probably be required to interact with micro-computers." The sample, consisting of 474 students with an average age of 17, was drawn from 11 further education establishments and contained more males than females. Beyond this information and a listing of the courses sampled, little is provided on the standardization sample, and no information is given about the conditions under which the data were collected. Norms tables based on the sample are presented in percentiles, T-scores, and z-scores. Although the authors report statistically significant differences in scores favoring males, they provide no gender-specific norms and insist, without clear rationale, that no importance be attached to these gender differences. Because of the limited information on the standardization sample and its selection,

this reviewer has little confidence in the norms data presented.

An internal consistency estimate of reliability (KR-20) of .95 is reported on the standardization sample, with a standard error of measurement of 5.80. The authors properly warn that test-retest estimates of reliability are inappropriate because of the expectation of ability-related differential gains on the test. Indeed, based on a small sample retested after 3 weeks, they report evidence of an increase in mean scores of almost three-quarters of a standard deviation. Despite this, they present the reader with a speculative estimate of test-retest reliability, which causes this reviewer some confusion in light of their previously stated warning.

At the time of publication, very little in the way of validity evidence was offered on the Computer Rules test. The authors recognize the necessity of criterion-related validity studies in the workplace, but report that such in-company studies have begun only recently. They do, however, offer the results of several small feasibility studies conducted on university students. One series of studies, presumably using a concurrent validity design, was conducted on a total of 60 computer science students and produced an overall correlation of .42 between a preliminary version of the test and end-of-year examinations in computer programing and theory. Another study, using 49 first-year students, produced a predictive validity coefficient of .63 between the final version of the test, given at the start of a programing course, and end-of-term examination marks. The authors suggest that these results indicate the usefulness of their test in predicting programing ability. This reviewer would urge that judgments on this point await the results of further, more careful studies. To the authors' credit, users are encouraged to conduct their own validity studies in the workplace.

The New Technology Tests: Computer Rules is an interesting and potentially useful addition to instrumentation needed for selection and training decisions in the area of computer applications in commerce and industry. The test appears to be sensibly designed, with a format that seems appropriate for the assessment of computer-adaptive capabilities within the context of printed verbal instruction. However, the authors' contention that the test is predictive of computer programing ability has yet to be empirically supported. The most critical needs are for improved standardization and norming, and for large-scale, well-documented validity studies within the workplace. Until these needs are met, the potential of the test will remain unfulfilled.

[262]
NOCTI Teacher Occupational Competency Test: Audio-Visual Communications Technology.

Purpose: To measure the individual's occupational competency in audiovisual communications technology.

Population: Teachers and prospective teachers.

Publication Dates: 1986–87.

Scores: 9 scores for Written part (Total and 8 subscores); 3 scores for Performance part (Process, Product, Total).

Administration: Group.

Parts, 2: Written, Performance.

Price Data, 1989: Available from publisher for test materials including Written test booklet ('87, 21 pages); Performance test booklet ('87, 11 pages); examiner's copy of Performance test ('87, 22 pages); manual for administering NOCTI TOCT Performance tests ('86, 17 pages); manual for administering NOCTI TOCT Written tests ('86, 20 pages).

Time: 180(190) minutes for Written part; 390(400) minutes for Performance part.

Comments: Test administered at least twice a year at centers approved by the publisher.

Author: National Occupational Competency Testing Institute.

Publisher: National Occupational Competency Testing Institute.

Cross References: For a review of the NOCTI program, see 8:1153 (6 references).

Review of the NOCTI Teacher Occupational Competency Test: Audio-Visual Communications Technology by JoELLEN V. CARLSON, Director of Testing Standards, New York Stock Exchange, New York, NY:

The NOCTI Teacher Occupational Competency Test: Audio-Visual Communications Technology is one of a number of tests designed to measure technical knowledge and manipulative skills in an occupational area. Successful completion of one of these tests is required for certification as a vocational teacher in a number of states and sometimes is used for the award of academic credit in degree programs. Each of the NOCTI tests comprises two parts: a written test and a performance evaluation.

For the Audio-Visual Communications Technology test, the written test consists of 180 four-option, multiple-choice items, distributed across content areas as follows: general AV, 31 items; broadcasting, 11 items; lighting, 10 items; multi-image, 10 items; graphics/visuals, 14 items; photography, 29 items; audio/radio, 31 items; and TV and film, 44 items. The test is typewritten, but its format is generally clear. The items reflect, in the main, principles of good item construction, although some could be improved with a bit of editing. The item stems seem to be straightforward and each seems to define the task clearly. Some of the items include some implausible options, and there is some use of "none of the above" and "all of the above" as response options. The major problem with the items is that they seem to be based simply on recall and do not require reasoning.

The performance test consists of 10 tasks, which the examinee must complete in the order given. The performance test is administered to small groups, and is expected to be under close supervision and observation by a performance examiner. The examiner rates the examinee on both process- and product-related aspects of the tasks. Even though part of the scoring involves simply checking whether or not a product exists, the examiner indicates whether the examinee's "performance is typical of a/an extremely skilled worker, above average worker, average worker, below average worker, [or] inept worker." This type rating would seem to require more explicit definition of the category and/or training of the rater. However, there is no mention of any examiner training nor of the criteria for selecting examiners.

The examinee's booklet for the performance test is careful formatted and produced, and is fairly well organized. Colored pages are included for the performance evaluation worksheet, making them easy to identify. The written directions are, for the most part, presented in a clear, straightforward, step-by-step fashion. It is unclear, however, why the examinee is directed to record the starting time and the "normal" completion time, and unclear what is meant by the "normal completion time." Presumably, this is to help the examinee keep a reasonable pace.

Aside from the absence of examiner training materials, the manuals for administering both the written test and the performance evaluation are quite thorough and well organized. They provide precise directions for all aspects of test center preparation, test administration, and follow-up, and stress the importance of following the directions exactly as given in the manual. The directions to be read to the candidates are precise and clear, and seem to cover all aspects of the performance test. However, there does not seem to be a guide to the testing program or a content outline of the tests for distribution to prospective candidates; both of these should be included in the program.

Several additional pieces of information are needed to permit an evaluation of these instruments. There is no technical manual, and this reviewer was unable to obtain any data on the psychometric characteristics of either instrument, even though there is reference to a pilot testing program. In fact, materials given to the examinee include the statement, "Candidates who participated in the pilot testing program said that the examinations were fair and covered items that a competent tradesperson should know and the problems one should be able to solve." This reviewer considers such a statement totally inappropriate. Not only is it biasing and potentially intimidating, it is also basing a judgment of content validity on the opinions of questionable judges.

Given the apparently quite careful preparation of these materials, data on reliability and validity, particularly content and predictive validity, correlations between written and performance test scores, and other data on psychometric characteristics and examinee performance must be made available immediately.

Review of the NOCTI Teacher Occupational Competency Test: Audio-Visual Communications Technology by ANNE L. HARVEY, Measurement Statistician, Educational Testing Service, Princeton, NJ:

Little information is available on the NOCTI Teacher Occupational Competency Test: Audio-Visual Communications Technology (AVCT) that would allow for a reasoned judgement as to its usefulness. Information on the general development process for the NOCTI Tests in general is available by calling NOCTI, but information is sparse regarding the specifics for this test.

The test materials include some instruction on how to set up and administer both the written and performance parts of the test. It is clear that some attempt has been made to standardize the administration procedures. The effort, however, has not gone far enough to expect generalization of test results beyond a given administration. Although the type of equipment is specified, a 35mm camera for example, there is, in my experience, wide variation in the ease of using different 35mm cameras. Greater standardization of the type of equipment and supplies provided would greatly improve this test. If practical considerations make this impossible, some information on the generalization of results when different equipment is used would be in order.

Some improvement could also be made in the performance evaluation scoring. Without further information, categories such as "Extremely Skilled Worker" versus "Above Average Worker" have little meaning. Are the scorers trained to make such distinctions? Are there specific standards associated with these categories? I would expect so, but could find no evidence to that effect.

A technical manual is also conspicuously missing. As this test is apparently used for job-related testing and teacher certification, it should be considered as a high-impact test, and thus be expected to meet high standards regarding development, reliability, and validity. Because these data are missing, no job-related judgements should be made based on this test.

It would also be expected that a test of this type would provide test takers with extensive information on the interpretation of their scores. I am told that national, state, and administration averages are provided to the test takers. However, assuming this to be a criterion-referenced test (the intended purposes of the test are never directly stated), I do not believe this information would be of much help

in interpreting scores. If the test is meant to be norm referenced, who makes up these samples? Are the test takers instructed in the interpretation of this information?

Lacking reports on the development, standards for scoring, reliability, validity, and score interpretation of this test, the AVCT should be used only as a formative evaluation tool for use in instruction. Although the AVCT makes an attempt at standardization of testing in this field, I believe there is need for improvement. I do not think this test is ready to be used in making decisions regarding jobs or certification of teachers.

[263]
NOCTI Teacher Occupational Competency Test: Scientific Data Processing.

Purpose: Designed to measure the individual's occupational competency in scientific data processing.
Population: Teachers and prospective teachers.
Publication Dates: 1988–90.
Scores, 18: 11 scores for Written part (Total and 10 subscores), 7 scores for Performance part (Process, Product, Total, and 4 subscores).
Parts, 2: Written, Performance.
Administration: Group.
Price Data: Price information available from publisher for test materials including manual for administering NOCTI TOCT Written tests ('89, 17 pages) and manual for administering NOCTI TOCT Performance tests ('90, 16 pages).
Time: (180) minutes for Written part; (360) minutes for Performance part.
Comments: Test administered at least twice a year at centers approved by publisher.
Author: National Occupational Competency Testing Institute.
Publisher: National Occupational Competency Testing Institute.
Cross References: For a review of the NOCTI program, see 8:1153 (6 references).

Review of the NOCTI Teacher Occupational Competency Test: Scientific Data Processing by WILLIAM M. BART, Professor of Educational Psychology, University of Minnesota, Minneapolis, MN:

The NOCTI Teacher Occupational Competency Test: Scientific Data Processing is a test intended to assess an individual's occupational competency in scientific data processing. The test is meant for prospective teachers and established teachers.

The test has two component subtests: a written test and a performance test. The written test involves answering 167 of 187 possible multiple-choice test items covering topics such as computer fundamentals, using software packages, applying numerical analysis, and using specific computer languages such as BASIC and C. The performance test involves solving several questions associated with one of four challenging problems.

The entire test provides 18 scores with 11 scores emanating from the written test and 7 scores emanating from the performance test. The 11 scores from the written test consist of a total score and 10 subscores with each subscore indicating performance on items assessing some specific topic. The 7 scores for the performance test consist of a process score (which indicates how the testee performed), a product score (which reflects the quality of the product of the testee), a total score, and four subscores assessing performance in steps such as the input of data and the use of software.

The entire test is lengthy. One is allotted 180 minutes to complete the written test and 360 minutes to complete the performance test. The test also appears to be demanding and comprehensive.

The manuals for examiners for both the written test and the performance test are quite clear in detailing how the test should be administered; however, there is no specific information provided regarding the psychometric properties of the test such as its reliability and its validity.

The written test is most likely objective, because multiple-choice test items are used for which there is likely a correct answer key. The performance test is probably less objective, because the scoring instructions permit variation in scores. For example, the examiner must evaluate various features of the performance as to whether the performance is at the level of an extremely skilled worker or at any of four other levels. The testee is awarded 5 points if the performance feature is at the highest level and fewer points if the performance feature is at one of the four lower levels. Examiners may have some difficulty making distinctions among five levels of performance for each performance feature and, as a result, the same examiners may provide different points for the same performance feature for the same testee performance.

Although the written test and the performance test appear to be stylistically adequate and workable, there is one stylistic feature that could be improved. There are three items in the written test that pertain to a diagram presented on a previous page such that the testee will likely have to flip pages in order to answer the items. The written test should be changed so that any items involving diagrams are opposite the diagrams so that testees do not have to flip pages to respond. In so doing, the test maker reduces the working memory requirements of those test items.

The test manual lacks any information regarding the reliability of the test or any of its constituent subtests. Empirical psychometric research would remedy this omission. Also, the test manual lacks information as to how the scores are to be interpreted.

Regarding the validity of the test, from an examination of the test items the test clearly has face validity. However, no information is provided regarding the concurrent validity, the predictive validity, and the construct validity of the test. Empirical psychometric research could be instituted to address that weakness.

In general, the test is professional and workable but lacks essential psychometric information that would improve its utility.

[264]
NOCTI Teacher Occupational Competency Test: Welding.

Purpose: To measure the individual's occupational competency in welding.
Population: Teachers and prospective teachers.
Publication Dates: 1986–87.
Scores: 11 scores for Written part (Total and 10 subscores); 3 scores for Performance part (Process, Product, Total).
Administration: Group.
Parts, 2: Written, Performance.
Price Data, 1989: Available from publisher for test materials including Written test booklet ('87, 21 pages); Performance test booklet ('87, 25 pages); examiner's copy of Performance test ('87, 25 pages); manual for administering NOCTI TOCT Performance tests ('86, 17 pages); manual for administering NOCTI TOCT Written tests ('86, 20 pages).
Time: 180(195) minutes for Written part; 300(320) minutes for Performance part.
Comments: Test administered at least twice a year at centers approved by the publisher.
Author: National Occupational Competency Testing Institute.
Publisher: National Occupational Competency Testing Institute.
Cross References: See 9:809 (1 reference); for a review by Richard C. Erickson, see 8:1152; for a review of the NOCTI program, see 8:1153.

[265]
North American Depression Inventories for Children and Adults.

Purpose: "Measure symptoms of depression in children and adults."
Population: Grades 2–9, Ages 15 and over.
Publication Date: 1988.
Acronym: NADI.
Scores: Total score only.
Administration: Group.
Editions, 2: Children, Adult.
Price Data, 1988: $57.50 per complete battery including examiner's manual (56 pages) and 50 of each of the two test forms (Form A, Form C); $15 per 50 test forms (specify form); $5 per scoring stencil; $7.50 per audio cassette tape; $15 per examiner's manual; $17.50 per specimen set including examiner's manual and one copy each of the two test forms.
Time: (10–20) minutes.
Comments: Self-administered; may be orally administered by audio cassette tape; originally entitled Battle's Depression Inventories for Children and Adults

and is a derivative of the Culture-Free Self-Esteem Inventories.

Author: James Battle.

Publisher: Special Child Publications.

TEST REFERENCES

1. Battle, J. (1987). Test-retest reliability of Battle's Depression Inventory for Children. *Psychological Reports, 61*, 71-74.

Review of the North American Depression Inventories for Children and Adults by PATRICIA A. BACHELOR, Associate Professor of Psychology, California State University, Long Beach, CA:

The North American Depression Inventories (NADI) for Children (Form C) and Adults (Form A) are self-report scales that purport to measure symptoms or characteristics of depression. The NADI may be administered as an individual or group test in 10 to 20 minutes. An audiocassette enables oral administration to nonreaders. Form C consists of 25 items to which children (grades 2 through 9) respond either "yes" or "no." Form A requires that adults (ages 15 to 60 years) respond to 40 items using a 5-point scale (*always, usually, sometimes, seldom,* or *never*). Scores are sums of responses indicating depression, hence, higher scores indicate more intense symptoms of depression. Depression scores are classified on a 5-point continuum ranging from "very high" to "very low." Battle suggested that the information gathered from client's responses may guide the discussion and effectively focus therapeutic sessions as well as provide quantitative evaluation of intervention strategy efforts.

The manual includes numerous tables of descriptive statistics, results of validity and reliability studies, and standard score conversions (percentile ranks and *T* scores). Administration and scoring, as facilitated by an acetate template, are simple and quick. Four case studies briefly detailing the use of the NADI in assessing the progress of therapy are also presented. However, the rationale for the development of the test was limited with respect to a theoretical or conceptual framework. Guidelines for interpretation were sparse. Most troublesome to this reviewer was the shocking lack of descriptive detail of the standardization sample. The only demographic information provided are grade level in general terms (i.e., elementary, junior high, or adult) and number of males and females who were from a "large midwestern city." Meaningful comparisons based on these data are not possible nor is an assessment of the representativeness of the norm group.

RELIABILITY ESTIMATES. Test-retest reliability coefficients for 764 elementary, 325 junior high, and 277 adult subjects over a 2-week period were presented. Pearson correlation coefficients were .79, .79, and .93, respectively, hence the stability of the

scores is acceptable. It is unfortunate, however, that no estimates of internal consistency were reported.

VALIDITY ESTIMATES. The evidence presented to support the claim of construct validity of the NADI "was built-in by our identifying and incorporating items that measure depression." This is not a method of construct validation that is accepted or endorsed by the *Standards for Educational and Psychological Testing* (AERA, APA, & NCME, 1985). Hence, the claim of construct validity is currently unwarranted.

Concurrent validity was claimed by several correlational studies. Scores on both forms of the NADI were correlated with the age-level-appropriate Beck's Depression Inventory. Correlations were .56, .73, and .66 for elementary, junior high, and adults, respectively. NADI scores correlated with the Culture-Free Self-Esteem Inventory (CFSEI) -.73 at the elementary level; -.72 at the junior high level; and -.74 at the adult level. The test user is reminded that the NADI is a derivative of the CFSEI, hence the reported correlations should be interpreted judiciously. The correlations presented in support of concurrent validity were minimally adequate; however, there was no information about the validation sample's socioeconomic status, ethnicity, psychological characteristics, or other demographic makeup. This omission is problematic to external validity interpretation as well as to the establishment of concurrent validity. Perhaps, other research studies using direct observation and/or interview data to measure the intensity of symptoms of depression, rather than another self-report inventory of depression or an extension of a self-esteem instrument would prove fruitful in demonstrating concurrent validity. Discriminant validity studies would also be welcomed.

SUMMARY. The NADI for Children and Adults may serve as a promising instrument to influence and focus therapeutic intervention; however, its psychometric qualities have not, to date, been sufficiently verified. Construct and concurrent validity have not been substantiated nor has internal consistency. Stability reliability was acceptable but the normative samples were not adequately described, hence, meaningful interpretations of scores are not possible. The weakness of the norming calls into question the applicability and sample comparability of the NADI. An enthusiastic endorsement for the widespread use of the NADI in schools and clinical settings awaits further research that establishes its psychometric properties.

REVIEWER'S REFERENCE

American Educational Research Association, American Psychological Association, & National Council on Measurement in Education. (1985). *Standards for educational and psychological testing.* Washington, DC: American Psychological Association, Inc.

Review of the North American Depression Inventories for Children and Adults by MICHAEL G.

KAVAN, Director of Behavioral Sciences and Assistant Professor of Family Practice, Creighton University School of Medicine, Omaha, NE:

The North American Depression Inventories (NADI) for Children (Form C) and Adults (Form A) are self-report instruments designed to measure symptoms of depression in the general population and in clinical settings. Form C comprises 25 items, whereas Form A contains 40 items. All items were selected on their ability to measure characteristics of depression. They also represent symptoms typical of those reported by individuals experiencing depression. The author claims that such information is not only useful for classification purposes, but items may also be used to facilitate discussion concerning the direction of therapeutic sessions.

ADMINISTRATION AND SCORING. The NADI Form C and Form A may be administered to individuals or groups. Group administration of Form C is not recommended for children below grade 2. Instead, these children should respond individually to the stimulus items while the clinician records the responses in the appropriate answer box. Older children (grade 3 and above) should be able to read and follow independently the directions provided on the answer sheet. An optional audiocassette tape is available for oral administration of both Forms C and A.

Directions for Form C request the respondent to make a check mark in a "yes" or "no" box to questions that describe "how you usually feel." A total score is obtained by adding the number of items selected that represent depression. Thus, total scores may range from 0 to 25. Administration and scoring time is estimated to be 10 to 15 minutes. For Form A, the respondent is asked to describe "how you feel" by selecting one of five options: *always, usually, sometimes, seldom,* and *never.* Responses are converted to scores ranging from 1 to 5 and are then totaled. Total scores may range from 40 to 200. Administration and scoring time is estimated to be 15 to 20 minutes. Acetate templates are available to facilitate the scoring of both forms.

RELIABILITY. Limited reliability data are provided in the test manual. The author provides 2-week test-retest information on two samples for Form C and one sample for Form A. For Form C, correlations were .79 for 764 boys and girls in grades 2 through 6 in a large metropolitan school district, and .79 for 325 adolescents in grades 7 through 9. For Form A, the correlation for 277 adults (ages 15 through 60) in a large midwestern city was .93.

VALIDITY. The author claims that construct validity for both Forms is "built-in" by the identification and incorporation of items that measure depression. Although the manual does not specifically address content validity, it may be demonstrated by NADI item coverage of major depressive syndrome as defined by the recently revised *Diagnostic and Statistical Manual of Mental Disorders—Third Edition* (DSM-III-R) (American Psychiatric Association, 1987). Recent viewpoints suggest the essential features of depression in children and adolescents are similar to those in adults (with some recognition of age-specific effects). In terms of the NADI, Form C items cover only five of the nine symptom categories, whereas Form A more adequately covers eight of the nine symptom groups. Both forms place heavy emphasis on the depressed mood and worthlessness/guilt symptoms of depression. No evidence exists that factor analytic studies were performed on this instrument.

Concurrent validity was determined by correlating Form C and Form A with other instruments designed to measure both depression and constructs associated with depression. Comparisons of scores obtained by elementary school children (grades 2 through 6) on Form C with scores obtained on a "modified version of Beck's Depression Inventory adapted for children" yielded correlations of .56. Form C scores were also found to be significantly correlated with scores obtained on the Culture-Free Self-Esteem Inventory for Children, Form A (-.73). Similar correlations were obtained when 248 junior high school students (grades 7 through 9) took Form C and the "adapted" Beck Depression Inventory (.73), and when a sample of 302 children in seventh through ninth grade took the Culture-Free Self-Esteem Inventory for Children, Form A (-.72).

Scores from 277 adults taking Form A correlated .66 with the Beck Depression Inventory and -.74 with the Culture-Free Self-Esteem Inventory for Adults, Form AD. NADI Form A scores have also been compared with those earned on the depression subscale of the "mini-mult version of the Minnesota Multiphasic Personality." Correlations between these two scales were .51, .24, and .64 for both sexes, males, and females, respectively. The manual fails to provide data concerning the relationship between NADI scores and independent ratings of psychiatric diagnosis. In addition, despite claims by the author that the NADI are "sensitive to change" and "have been used effectively to identify patients or clients experiencing depression, and to determine the amount of progress that has occurred as a result of psychotherapeutic treatment," no evidence (other than case reports) is provided in the manual for such contentions.

NORMS. Normative data provided in the manual are quite adequate for general samples, but are nonexistent for other important groups. Means, standard deviations, percentile ranks, and *T*-scores are provided for elementary school age, junior high school age, and adult samples. Unfortunately, no data are provided for psychiatric diagnostic samples nor are they available on minority populations. Because race-related differences have been noted on depression instruments (Politano, Nelson, Evans, Sorenson, & Zeman, 1986) it would behoove the author to provide such information in the test manual. With normative data being limited to only general groups of children, adolescents, and adults, it is quite difficult to use the information in the manual to differentiate "normals" from psychiatrically depressed groups or from individuals with other types of disorders not in the depressive domain. As a result, interpretation of NADI scores is difficult.

SUMMARY. The NADI Form C and Form A are easily administered self-report instruments designed to assess symptoms of depression in children and adults. Although more extensive reliability studies must be performed on these instruments, their validity appears to be adequate. Normative data are limited, and thus, are a weakness of this instrument. More extensive normative data would allow for the NADI to be used more confidently to identify individuals with depression in clinical settings. At the present time, use of the NADI should be limited to research settings. In this context, the NADI provides a useful and comprehensive assessment of the depressed mood and self-esteem components of depression. Those interested in an instrument that quantifies a wider range of depressive symptoms may want to examine better-researched scales such as the Beck Depression Inventory (31; Beck, Ward, Mendelson, Mock, & Erbaugh, 1961) and the Zung Self-Rating Depression Scale (Zung, 1965) for adults, or the Children's Depression Inventory (66; Kovacs, 1983) for younger groups.

REVIEWER'S REFERENCES

Beck, A. T., Ward, C. H., Mendelson, M., Mock, J., & Erbaugh, J. (1961). An inventory for measuring depression. *Archives of General Psychiatry, 4,* 561-571.

Zung, W. W. K. (1965). A self-rating depression scale. *Archives of General Psychiatry, 12,* 63-70.

Kovacs, M. (1983). *The Children's Depression Inventory: A self-report depression scale for school-aged youngsters.* Unpublished manuscript, University of Pittsburgh School of Medicine, Pittsburgh.

Politano, P. M., Nelson, W. M., Evans, H. E., Sorenson, S. B., & Zeman, D. J. (1986). Factor analytic evaluation of differences between Black and Caucasian emotionally disturbed children on the Children's Depression Inventory. *Journal of Psychopathology and Behavioral Assessment, 8,* 1-7.

American Psychiatric Association. (1987). *Diagnostic and statistical manual of mental disorders* (3rd ed. rev.). Washington, DC: Author.

[266]
Observational Emotional Inventory—Revised.

Purpose: "Provides a structure for observing and rating overt emotional behaviors which interfere with educational or vocational potential."
Population: Students.
Publication Date: 1986.
Acronym: OEI-R.
Scores, 8: Impulsivity-Frustration, Anxiety, Depression-Withdrawal, Socialization, Self-Concept, Aggression, Reality Disorientation, Total Score.

Administration: Group.
Price Data, 1988: $13.75 per package of 25 inventories.
Time: 120 minutes each day for 5 days.
Comments: Problems checklist.
Authors: Lawrence T. McCarron and Jack G. Dial.
Publisher: McCarron-Dial Systems.

Review of the Observational Emotional Inventory— Revised by JOSEPH G. PONTEROTTO, Associate Professor of Education, Division of Psychological and Educational Services, Graduate School of Education, Fordham University—Lincoln Center, New York, NY:

The Observational Emotional Inventory—Revised (OEI-R) is a 70-item instrument designed to assess overt emotional behaviors that interfere with educational and vocational functioning. The OEI-R is designed for use in classroom, prevocational, or work training settings.

Conceptually, the OEI-R is one of a number of instruments used in the McCarron-Dial System (MDS; 231), which is a battery of neurometric and behavioral measures designed to assess the educational and vocational potential of the neurologically disabled. The MDS focuses on five neuropsychological areas: Verbal-Spatial-Cognitive, Sensory, Motor, Emotional, and Integration-Coping. The OEI-R is the major assessment used in the Emotional category.

Normative data on the OEI-R are based on an adult sample (mean age = 30) possessing a mean IQ of 85 (using the Wechsler Adult Intelligence Scale—Revised [WAIS-R]). The sample included persons with various neuropsychological disabilities, the visually impaired or blind, and a subsample of nondisabled persons. (The normative sample will be described in detail in a subsequent section.)

OEI-R STRUCTURE, ADMINISTRATION, AND SCORING. The OEI-R is a revised and expanded version of the original OEI. Two factors have been added to the OEI-R: Aggression and Reality Disorientation. The five original factors and the observational and scoring procedures have been retained in the OEI-R.

The seven factors of the OEI-R are as follows: Impulsivity-Frustration, Anxiety, Depression-Withdrawal, Socialization, Self-Concept, Aggression, and Reality Disorientation. Each factor consists of 10 items organized along three subheadings: "Verbalization," that is, something spoken (3 items); "Physical," that is, a movement or physical response of some kind (4 items); and "Interactive," that is, an interaction with other people (3 items).

In scoring the OEI-R an evaluator observes a target student/client for 5 consecutive days, each for a 2-hour period in which the student/client is engaged in routine activities in his or her classroom, prevocational, or work training setting. For each day that any of the specific behaviors is noted, 1 point is scored. Thus, for each of the 70 items, a student/client can receive from 0 (the behavior was not observed in the 5 days) to 5 (the behavior occurred on each of the 5 days). The scoring range for each of the 10-item factors is 0 to 50; and the total OEI-R score can range for 0 to 350. The instrument authors appropriately suggest that to increase reliability, more than one evaluator can observe and rate the target student/client.

To interpret and profile a person's OEI-R scores, each factor and the total scale score is converted to either T scores or Standard Scores using a conversion table on the rating sheet. These eight scores are then plotted on a profile sheet (located on the face page of the rating sheet) to form a graphic profile.

The present reviewer completed the OEI-R by observing a hypothetical rehabilitation client for 2 hours a day over 5 days. Completing the ratings and summing up the scale and total scores proceeded smoothly. However, interpreting and plotting the scores was extremely difficult. Minimal directions are included on this process. There is no manual, no sample profiles, and no interpretive instructions. The T score and Standard Score ranges used in the profile sheet are not explained, and no information is presented on standard deviations and measurement error.

RELIABILITY AND VALIDITY. All norming, reliability, and validity data were garnered from a sample of 567 adults, ranging in age from 15 to 62 with a mean of 30 years. Fifty-one percent of the sample was male, and the ethnic breakdown was as follows: 60% Caucasian, 26% Black, 11% Hispanic, and 3% Other. Approximately 40% of the sample had diagnosed neuropsychological disabilities (e.g., congenital or adventitious brain dysfunction, mental retardation); 42 of these individuals were visually impaired or blind; and all were placed in rehabilitation settings. A larger subsample (57%) functioned within the normal range of intelligence; of these subjects, 195 were visually impaired, legally or totally blind. Ninety-two subjects in this group were nondisabled. The nondisabled and visually impaired members of this subsample were functioning successfully in community employment situations. Of the neuropsychologically disabled members, 70% were from the southwest, and 30% collectively from the western, northeast, and midwest regions of the United States.

Test-retest stability measures for the OEI-R are available over a 7–14 day period, using a sample of 100 neuropsychologically and visually disabled individuals selected from the normative sample. The resulting correlations range from .87 for the Anxiety factor to .96 for both the Socialization and Reality Disorientation factors. The OEI-R total score had a test-retest stability coefficient of .95. These are very acceptable measures of short-term stability.

An abbreviated checklist vesion of the OEI-R, known as the Emotional Behavioral Checklist (EBC; 130) is also available from the test publishers. The EBC does not require multiday observation periods, yet it is less stable over time with a 7–14 day test-retest correlation of .83.

There are minimal validity data on the OEI-R. Only concurrent validity figures are available, and the comparison measures are other McCarron-Dial System instruments. Using the original normative sample of 567 adults, the OEI-R correlated .89 with the original OEI, and .91 with the Emotional Behavioral Checklist (EBC). The OEI-R had a concurrent validity measure of .62 with the Survey of Functional Adaptive Behaviors (SFAB) [a measure of adaptive behavior], .49 with the Street Survival Skills Questionnaire (SSSQ) [an adaptive behavior measure], and .63 with the Dial Behavior Rating Scale (BRS) [a measure of integration-coping and adaptive behavior]. Finally, using a separate sample of 52 mentally retarded adults, the OEI-R correlated .66 with the SFAB.

SUMMARY. The 70 items on the OEI-R appear adequate; however, no description of the development and selection of items is presented. Again, there is no manual to accompany the inventory as a stand-alone measure. Use of the inventory presupposes familiarity and experience with the McCarron-Dial System. Although test-retest findings are encouraging, there is need for internal consistency reliability assessments. There is only moderate concurrent validity support for the OEI-R using other McCarron-Dial System instruments. There is no factorial validity research on the inventory.

The OEI-R was evaluated here as a "stand-alone" measure; however, this reviewer believes that given the minimal information available on using and interpreting the inventory, the OEI-R should not be used in this fashion. Conceptually, the OEI-R was developed within the framework of the McCarron-Dial System (MDS), and without a firm grounding in this system, meaningful interpretation and use of the OEI-R poses great difficulty. Only after contacting the McCarron-Dial System Testing Coordinator, and after requesting and receiving additional information on the full MDS, was this reviewer able to more fully understand the development and purpose of the OEI-R.

At this point in time, and until more psychometric data becomes available and a thorough interpretation/administration manual is developed, extreme caution must be exercised when using the OEI-R as a stand-alone measure.

[267]

Occupational Personality Questionnaire.

Purpose: "A self-report measure of personality and motivational characteristics, which are particularly relevant to the world of work."

Population: Business and industry.
Publication Dates: 1984–90.
Acronym: OPQ.
Scores, 31 in 4 areas: Relationships with People (Persuasive, Controlling, Independent, Outgoing, Affiliative, Socially Confident, Modest, Democratic, Caring), Thinking Style (Practical, Data Rational, Artistic, Behavioral, Traditional, Change Oriented, Conceptual, Innovative, Forward Planning, Detail Conscious, Conscientious), Feelings and Emotions (Relaxed, Worrying, Tough-Minded, Emotional Control, Optimistic, Critical, Active, Competitive, Achieving, Decisive), Social Desirability.
Administration: Group or individual.
Price Data, 1991: $26.50 per test booklet; $7 per publisher-scored, $6 per optic-scanned, and $5.50 per hand-scored answer sheet; $20 per hand-scoring key; $1.60 per hand-scored profile; $10 per sample manual ('90, 28 pages); $65 per manual/user's guide ('90, 229 pages); $35 per specimen set.
Foreign Language Editions: Available in British, French, German, Italian, Dutch, Norwegian, Spanish, Portuguese, Chinese (Mandarin), and Japanese with local norms.
Time: (35) minutes.
Comments: Machine, hand, Casio pocket computer, and IBM computer scoring available; OPQ Expert System produces narrative reports based on the scores of the OPQ for PC and compatibles.
Author: Saville & Holdsworth Ltd.
Publisher: Saville & Holdsworth Ltd.

Review of the Occupational Personality Questionnaire by THOMAS M. HALADYNA, Professor of Educational Psychology, Arizona State University West, Phoenix, AZ:

The Occupational Personality Questionnaire (OPQ) was originally created in the United Kingdom and adapted for a number of other countries, including the United States. Its purposes are (*a*) to predict how a person might behave in the work setting; (*b*) to help managers know themselves better and how they affect others, as part of developing work teams; (*c*) to understand relationships between personality and occupational groups; (*d*) to assist in career counseling; and (*e*) for personnel selection. This ambitious list of purposes is augmented by an attractively packaged specimen set including a manual and user's guide.

This review will focus on chapters in this guide and discuss strengths and weaknesses of the test along the way.

Chapter 1 briefly introduces the instrument and its purposes. It defines personality in a single sentence, which speaks for the surface level of treatment of topics throughout this guide. No reference is offered to the extensive past or present theoretical work and research on personality, which is remarkable for any instrument with such lofty purposes.

Chapter 2 addresses the development of the OPQ. The builders of this instrument appear to have followed standard procedures in instrument development, giving in outline form the steps they followed. Brief mention is made of notable personality inventories as a background for the development of the OPQ, but no rationale is offered why these are not worthwhile or why the OPQ is needed or better. The Repertory Grid Technique (by G. Kelly) is offered as the model for the development of this instrument. Again, no reference is made to Kelly's work and the significance of it for this stated purpose. In the standardization trial, 75% of the sample chosen returned "partially completed" answer sheets, so the actual response rate was 55%. No description was made of the population represented by this sample or the potential bias of nonresponse. Partial data may be included in data analysis, but this point was overlooked by the developers of the OPQ.

Chapter 3 presents the 31 scales of the OPQ, arranged in four conceptual areas. Each scale is effectively described and is supported by quotes from famous persons capturing the essence of what each scale represents.

Chapter 4 describes the administration, scoring, and profiling. Because five methods of scoring exist, the chapter is necessary. Profiling is nicely illustrated.

Chapter 5 presents U.S. norms, which are described as being very similar to those in the United Kingdom. Although more technical than other sections, the initial pages present beginner level statistical concepts. This section seems almost out of place in a test manual and guide. Nevertheless, the descriptions and illustrations are lucid.

Chapter 6 uniquely discusses the concept of providing feedback to examinees. Although extremely brief, the chapter provides useful ideas about how to report results to an examinee.

Chapter 7 discusses the concept of reliability, again at a beginner level, although the authors mistakenly describe the split-half technique as the "conventional method." The chapter provides a weak, apologetic argument that reliability coefficients should be moderate, because the concepts being measured are not highly unidimensional. Test-retest reliability estimates and stability coefficients are satisfactory for most scales, and range from the .70s to the low .90s. Internal consistency (alpha) reliability estimates range from the .50s to the high .80s. In some cases, these are too low.

Chapter 8 is the weakest of the chapters and points to the vulnerability of the OPQ. The chapter presents a very superficial discussion of validity. The developers would benefit by relying on a more recent conceptualization, such as the unified approach to validity embodied in Messick's chapter in *Educational Measurement* (Messick, 1988). Mention is made of criterion and construct validation studies, and these appear in Appendix B. Sweeping statements are made in this chapter, such as "the OPQ goes a long way explaining much of what is provided by the other scales while adding unique information which other scales fail to provide" (p. 8-5). Interestingly, these studies are seemingly unpublished and the summaries too brief to allow thoughtful evaluation.

Chapter 9 addresses the problem of social desirability not only in terms of its measurement but also with the goal of preventing examinees from faking their performance on the test.

Chapter 10 contains a description of the OPQ Expert System, a computerized report based on test results. Users of the system will want to read this chapter. An expert system report is included in the specimen set.

Chapter 11 discusses how to use test results but is a general discussion of the issue rather than a specific discussion of the OPQ's results.

Chapter 12 generally discusses issues related to the EEOC Uniform Guidelines for Employee Selection and fair use of the test. Specifically, the developers should have referred to the *Standards for Educational and Psychological Testing* (AERA, APA, & NCME, 1985).

Overall, although the test appears to be well developed and possesses a high degree of face validity, one has to question the scientific rigor and attention to standards for test development and validation necessary to support a high quality test. The frequent mention of well-known names and dates but no list of references, the unpublished validation studies, and the breezy, superficial discussions throughout these chapters seems intended for novices or beginner test users. The developers of this instrument should concentrate more on meeting the standards of professional testing and placing a higher value on scientific rigor but at the same time retaining the highly effective format for presenting information.

REVIEWER'S REFERENCES

American Educational Research Association, American Psychological Association, & National Council on Measurement in Education. (1985). *Standards for educational and psychological testing.* Washington, DC: American Psychological Association, Inc.

Messick, S. (1988). Validity. In R. L. Linn (Ed.), *Educational Measurement* (3rd ed., pp. 13-104). New York: American Council on Education and Macmillan Publishing.

[268]
Occupational Stress Indicator.

Purpose: To clarify the nature of stress in organisations by identifying sources of stress, intervening factors, and the effects of stress on employees.
Population: Employees.
Publication Date: 1988.
Acronym: OSI.
Scores, 28: Sources (Intrinsic to Job, Managerial Role, Relationships with Other People, Career and Achievement, Organisational Structure and Climate,

Home-Work Interface), Individual Characteristics (Attitude to Living, Style of Behavior, Ambition, Broad View Type A, Organisational Forces, Management Processes, Individual Influences, Broad View of Control), Coping (Social Support, Task Strategies, Logic, Home and Work Relationship, Time, Involvement), Effects (Achievement Value and Growth, Job Itself, Organisational Design and Structure, Organisational Processes, Personal Relationships, Broad View of Job Satisfaction, Mental Ill Health, Physical Ill Health).
Administration: Group.
Price Data, 1989: £125.35 per complete Management Set kit including 15 questionnaires (Indicators), 15 biographical questionnaires, score sheet, scoring stencils, administration card, and Management Guide (71 pages); £67.85 per Group Profiling Pack including 15 questionnaires (Indicators); £287.50 per Disk Pack-IBM PC compatible, 50 administrations (to be used in conjunction with the complete kit).
Time: 45(55) minutes.
Authors: Cary L. Cooper, Stephen J. Sloan, and Stephen Williams.
Publisher: NFER-Nelson Publishing Co., Ltd. [England].

Review of the Occupational Stress Indicator by MARK POPE, President, Career Decisions, San Francisco, CA:

The Occupational Stress Indicator (OSI) is a self-report inventory designed to describe and articulate the climate of an organization, to focus attention on problems, and to act as a prompt to address stress and related organizational problems. Two questionnaires are used to record responses of individuals in four general areas: sources of stress, stress coping strategies, the individual and organizational effects of stress, and the individual's characteristics. Both ipsative (for comparison with other individuals or groups within an organization) and normative (for comparison with general organizational scores published in the manual) interpretations are described in the management guide. It is designed not as an intensive professionally administered, scored, and interpreted instrument, but as a general instrument to be used by management in determining the stress factors in an environment. It was developed in Great Britain by a team of American and British industrial/organizational psychologists.

The components of the OSI include: a management guide, an administrator's card, a question booklet, a biographical questionnaire, scoring keys, a data collection form, and a group profile sheet. All of the components are available in a management set that comes in a vinyl trifold binder with a professionally produced brochure describing the OSI and with an order form.

The management guide is both a technical manual and an administrator's guide. It serves the purpose as an educational tool for those unfamiliar with the research concerning stress; a step-by-step guide to the administration, scoring, and interpretation of the OSI; and a manual regarding the development of the OSI. The management guide is divided into three separate sections: an introduction; a uses and applications section with chapters on background, use, and interpretation; and technical development information with chapters on research and development, scale construction, psychometric properties, normative tables, and an extensive bibliography. The guide is clearly organized and presented with extensive basic theoretical information concerning research into the causes of stress. Administration should require approximately 45 minutes but is untimed. The process to administer the OSI is outlined in the guide; however, a more specific, detailed administration process is included as the administrator's card, which is one sheet, front and back, laminated to extend use.

There are two question booklets, one for biographical information, the other to collect the individual's responses to the six parts of that questionnaire. The biographical questionnaire is a four-page booklet with 37 items, printed on white paper, and is used to collect important demographic data on each individual. It is divided into seven basic areas: individual and family, education, work history, commitments, habits, interests, and recent life history. Some of the items are language specific to Great Britain.

The other questionnaire, labeled "The Indicator," consists of 167 items divided into six areas: attitudes toward job, current state of mental and physical health, general behavior, individual interpretation of events, sources of job pressure, and stress coping strategies. Items are rated by the individual on a 6-point Likert-type scale, anchored appropriately. The Indicator booklet is an expendable booklet, printed on white pages with a dark blue cover in an $8^{1}/_{4}$ -inch by $11^{11}/_{16}$ -inch format (standard British paper size). The items are clear and understandable with a few Great Britain idiomatic sentences ("threat of impending redundancy or early retirement"). American translations should have been used in collecting data for the American normative study currently in progress.

The scoring keys are clear acetate, riveted at the upper right corner. The directions for scoring are included in the management guide, but are somewhat confusing and the process is a rather complicated one for either the professional or nonprofessional. There are two types of scoring windows on the acetate. Clear windows are scored as printed in the question booklet; however, so-called "tinted" windows are reverse scored. The tinting consists of a series of small dots in the window that are easily missed. The subtle nature of the tinting may cause scoring errors to occur creating an unfortunate source of irrelevant variability.

Further, the subscale raw score boxes on the bottom of each page of the question booklet are not labeled except generically ("1") with no special mnemonic code to enable the easy transfer of raw scores to the data collection form. A data collection form and the group profile sheets are also components of the OSI. A data collection form is used to collect the work group data in order to make comparisons between individuals as well as groups for an entire organization.

Substantial reliability and validity data are reported. Information is provided for content, construct, and "empirical" validity. Reliability data are reported only for split-half reliability coefficients, ranging from .12 to .78 based on a sample size of 156. According to the management guide (1988), test-retest reliability studies are currently under way. Scales were constructed using a factor-analytic method and data are presented for subscale intercorrelations ranging from -.38 to .81. Subscale intercorrelations in the +.50 range or higher are especially important because they indicate scales are potentially not independent and may suggest some problems with the manner in which the factor analysis was conducted. The presence of redundant scales on the instrument should be explained to users and be accounted for in interpretive statements.

The purpose, scope, and structure of this instrument are similar to the Moos' Social Climate Scale (T3:2227), but this instrument is more comprehensive. There are 28 stress subscales. These are subsets of each of the four major profile areas. Both ipsative and normative interpretations are possible and examples are provided. Normative data are given for British managers in a range of organizations as well as for American female bank clerks ($N = 67$). The narrative provided with the norms is rich with cultural variances but is tentative and only part of a larger study in American banking organizations.

In summary, the OSI has substantial reasons to recommend its use as a tool for industrial/organizational psychology. More data are needed, but the authors are aware of the limitations of the instrument and have advised appropriate caution in the use of the OSI. The usefulness for American organizations is somewhat limited if norms are required; however, if the instrument is used for comparisons of groups or individuals within an organization, the OSI could prove a helpful device.

Review of the Occupational Stress Indicator by L. ALAN WITT, Personnel Research Psychologist, Civil Aeromedical Institute, Federal Aviation Administration, Oklahoma City, OK:

The measurement of stress among organizational personnel is becoming increasingly critical. The Occupational Stress Indicator (OSI) provides a multidimensional approach to assessing employee stress. Based on a conceptually strong model of stress, the OSI consists of seven survey components:

(a) rater biographical information (37 items), (b) rater feelings about the job and organization (i.e., job satisfaction; 22 items), (c) rater assessment of personal mental and physical health (30 items), (d) rater report of dispositional behavior (i.e., Type-A orientation; 14 items), (e) rater report of dispositional orientation to want to control events (12 items), (f) rater report of sources of pressure on the job (61 items), and (g) rater report of six aspects of how he/she copes with stress (28 items). This multifacet approach may permit assessment of varying antecedents and outcomes of stress for individuals and their groups.

Employees rarely enjoy completing surveys, but they may not resist taking the OSI, as it looks as though it will provide salient information about themselves and their work environment. It appears to have face validity and to assess several of the relevant variables that probably influence stress. Moreover, instructions are straightforward (circle a number on a 1 to 6 scale; different anchors are provided for each scale), and raters are expected to take only about 45 minutes to complete it.

A recommended, standardized procedure for administration is provided, as is a laminated list of instructions for the administator(s). Scoring is less straightforward, particularly for the biodata, for which there are no interpretation guidelines. American administrators may choose not to use the biographical questionnaire, as some items may confuse American employees not familiar with the British educational system (e.g., "A level or equivalent" as a level of formal education). The manual does provide a fairly easy method to score the other sections, to develop individual profiles, and to examine the data at the group or higher level of analysis. Unfortunately, the appropriateness of the norms is questionable, because the size of the sample on which the British norms were based is not mentioned, and the American sample of female bank clerks ($N = 67$) is both small and unrepresentative.

Overall, the OSI appears to be a cleverly developed instrument tapping many elements key to the experience of stress in organizations. However, serious problems in the validation of the instrument threaten its utility. For example, a factor analysis on the 22 job satisfaction items was run on a sample of 90 individuals. A second factor analysis of these items was run on 156 individuals. The authors (p. 50) stated that "criteria for selection of significant factors were relaxed so that there was no loss of practical information." With little supporting evidence, they claimed (p. 51), "these results, and subsequent sets of analyses, revealed a similar factorial structure," and "whilst the overall integrity of the first solution was confirmed by the second analyses, this latter solution did not provide a structure that was quite so useful." Therefore, they elected to use the initial solution ($N = 90$) as a basis for construction. Not only is the sample size inadequate for factor analysis on 22 items, but also the selection of the first solution for the sake of convenience is incongruent with even liberal interpretations of empirical rigor. Additional factor analyses were also questionable, with "relaxed" criteria for the selection of factors and the use of the "larger" sample ($N = 156$). Given the relaxed interpretation of results, it is unlikely that confirmatory factor analysis would have yielded results supportive of a construct validity argument.

In addition, the reliability coefficients were unacceptably low. The authors presented an unconvincing argument for the use of split-half reliability coefficients, and then presented very low coefficients.

More validation work with larger and more varied samples is needed before the OSI should be recommended for use in organizations. Additional analyses are needed to refine the instrument, which may improve its psychometric properties. Given the plethora of attempts to measure stress, evidence of criterion-related validity would be helpful. At the very least, confirmatory factor analysis should be used to assess the OSI stress model and the instrument itself. Until these analyses are performed and reported, potential users should be wary.

[269]
Occupational Stress Inventory.

Purpose: To measure three dimensions of occupational adjustment: occupational stress, psychological strain, and coping resources.

Population: Adults employed in schools, service organizations, and large manufacturing settings.

Publication Dates: 1981–87.

Acronym: OSI.

Scores, 14: Occupational Roles Questionnaire [ORQ] (Role Overload [RO], Role Insufficiency [RI], Role Ambiguity [RA], Role Boundary [RB], Responsibility [R], Physical Environment [PE]), Personal Strain Questionnaire [PSQ] (Vocational Strain [VS], Psychological Strain [PSY], Interpersonal Strain [IS], Physical Strain [PHS]), Personal Resources Questionnaire [PRQ] (Recreation [RE], Self-Care [SC], Social Support [SS], Rational/Cognitive Coping [RC]).

Administration: Group.

Parts: 3 tests.

Price Data, 1989: $49 per complete kit including Research Version manual ('87, 25 pages), 25 reusable item booklets, 50 rating sheets, and 50 profile forms; $26 per 25 reusable item booklets; $14 per 50 rating sheets; $8.50 per 50 profile forms; $8 per manual.

Time: (20–40) minutes.

Authors: Samuel H. Osipow and Arnold R. Spokane.

Publisher: Psychological Assessment Resources, Inc.

TEST REFERENCES

1. Powell, T. E. (1991). A review of the Occupational Stress Inventory. *Measurement and Evaluation in Counseling and Development, 24*, 127-130.

Review of the Occupational Stress Inventory by MARY ANNE BUNDA, Director, University Assessment, Western Michigan University, Kalamazoo, MI:

The Occupational Stress Inventory is an unique battery in the arsenal for research on stress and coping behaviors. However, one needs to carefully separate the research use of the instrument from any clinical application. The evidence provided on the technical quality of the instrument supports use in the research realm, but not clinical use.

The three instruments printed in a single booklet consist of a modest 140 items which could easily be administered in one sitting. However, the normative information shows that very often the instruments have been used separately. Although the manual indicates that the normative base has 909 members, some subscores have as few as 68 individuals and no score is associated with more than 257 individuals. The size of the norm group is very important, because profiles are created using T scores and separate normative information is provided for male and female participants. This disaggregation reduces the sizes of the normative pool. The need for separate norm tables for each gender is not specifically discussed in the manual, although one study is reported with significant differences between gender groups. The authors suggest that local norms are necessary for any clinical use. This reviewer would go further to indicate that any individual interpretation, even in a research setting, should rely on local norms as well as the norms printed on the profile forms.

The internal consistency reliability of each of the three questionnaires is reported at .89 for the Occupational Roles Questionnaire (ORQ), .94 for the Personal Strain Questionnaire (PSQ), and .88 for the Personal Resources Questionnaire (PRQ). But given that the total score on the questionnaires has no explicit meaning, the more appropriate indices would be the 14 subscores that have alpha coefficients from .71 to .90 (6 in the .70s, 7 in the .80s, and one at .90). These coefficients were based on samples of 549 (ORQ), 419 (PSQ), and 453 (PRQ) for the questionnaires and were replicated fairly well in a subsequent study involving 155 participants. The standard errors are from 2.55 to 3.97 when the internal consistency index is used, but are not reported for test-retest indices. Test-retest reliabilities were reported for a much smaller sample ($n = 31$) with a range of .56 to .94 at the scale level. Before the inventory can be used with any clinical confidence, more information on the test-retest reliabilities must be forthcoming.

The validity evidence for the instruments comes from three separate sources. Two confirmatory factor analyses were performed yielding fairly good results for the ORQ (four scales corresponded closely to the factor structure) and the PRQ (three scales corres-

ponded closely to the factor structure). However, the scale structure of the PSQ was not well supported. Subscores on the PSQ and PRQ were moderately to highly intercorrelated (.22 to .71), but the relationship among the ORQ scales is not clear. Approximately 14 studies are reported with correlational evidence about some subsection of the inventory. The relationship between the scales on the inventory and measures of job satisfaction are in the predicted direction (negative for the ORQ and PSQ; positive for the PRQ) and generally quite respectable. Only the PSQ was related to measures of burnout, but the correlations are quite respectable. However, potential users should be aware that the scales are not equally rich in meaning. Finally, the authors provide a description of two small treatment-based studies that support the validity of the total scores on the PSQ and PRQ.

This instrument has been designed to yield information about both stressors and coping behaviors. The evidence for the validity of most of the scales is sufficient to recommend this instrument for use in a wide range of research studies. It is clearly a meaningful instrument. However, the quality of the normative information makes the interpretation of individual scores a much more difficult problem. The warning concerning the development of local norms prior to clinical use is not sufficient. Cases presented in the manual imply that the national norm base may be used. However, this use would clearly be unwise given the sparse norm population and the lack of test-retest reliability.

Review of the Occupational Stress Inventory by LARRY COCHRAN, Professor of Counselling Psychology, The University of British Columbia, Vancouver, BC, Canada:

The Occupational Stress Inventory (OSI) is an operationalization of the authors' model of stress in work. Based upon an extensive review of stress literature, three areas of importance for occupational adjustment were identified: perceived stresses of the work role, experienced strain in relation to stresses, and coping resources that can modify the strain experienced from occupational stress. The model was filled in by identifying facets of each area in stress research. From a comprehensive description of each facet, the authors constructed a pool of items, eventually selecting those items with the most face validity and the least overlap. Empirical studies of employed adults led to a revision of some items and a deletion of others, resulting in the current form (E-2) which contains 14 scales, each with 10 items. Responses are marked on a 5-point scale ranging from *rarely* or *never* true to true *most of the time*. The test requires about a seventh grade reading level and takes from 20 to 40 minutes to complete.

The OSI is composed of three questionnaires or sections, one for each major area. The scales of the questionnaires represent the facets of the model. The Occupational Roles Questionnaire consists of six scales: Role Overload, Role Insufficiency (i.e., whether one's work role allows satisfactory use of knowledge and skills), Role Ambiguity, Role Boundary (i.e., conflicting demands and loyalties), Responsibility, and Physical Environment (i.e., physical stressors such as noise). The Personal Strain Questionnaire consists of four scales concerned with Vocational, Psychological, Interpersonal, and Physical Strain. The Personal Resources Questionnaire consists of four scales: Recreation (i.e., enjoyable relaxation from work), Self-Care (e.g., sleep, exercise), Social Support, and Rational/Cognitive Coping (i.e., use of cognitive strategies to manage stresses).

Factor analytic studies of the individual questionnaires indicate an encouraging degree of agreement between the allocation of items to scales and patterns of factor loadings for items, supporting the internal structure of the test and the facets of the model. Using a sample of 549 working adults, alpha coefficients of reliability ranged from .89 to .99 for total questionnaire scores. Scale reliabilities ranged from .71 to .94. No test-retest reliabilities were reported for the current form (E-2), although 2-week reliabilities for Form E-1 were generally good.

In general, research involving the OSI has both strengthened confidence in the test and been empirically fruitful. Several studies provide reasonable evidence for concurrent validity, showing expected relations between various scales and variables such as job satisfaction, burnout, and locus of control. Other studies have related OSI scales to measures of job performance such as absenteeism and nonproductive behaviors. In a few empirical tests of the OSI model, the magnitude of effect for the coping resources has been estimated in relation to particular facets of stress and strain. Further, a few studies have shown that the OSI is a sensitive instrument for measuring the effects of stress management programs.

One limitation of the research base for the OSI is the lack of norm groups. The reported group of mostly technicians, managers, and professionals from which T scores were calculated for profile assessment reflects middle-aged men and women (average age is about 44 years) in upper level jobs. The span of fields, levels of work, and experience of different racial or ethnic groups are not represented in this sample. The authors appropriately advise users to develop local norms.

The difficulty with local norms, however, is that the average raw score for a particular group could reflect high or low stress and strain. For example, in the male norm group, a raw score of only 14 on Physical Environment (scale score ranges from 10 to 50) converts to a T score of 49! Thus, the average

T score reflects very little physical stress. In contrast, the average T score for a group of firefighters might reflect a high stress level. Statistical averages are potentially misleading and cannot be used as the sole basis for judging degree of stress. For this reason, it would be highly desirable to have a more balanced, general norm group and to conduct empirical studies to determine the work realities that raw score totals reflect. Quite apart from an average for a local group, what does a score of 20 or 40 indicate, given various scales? And does the meaning of scores vary with work contexts? For example, noise might be very stressful in mental work and much less so in physical work.

In summary, the OSI seems very promising. The manual is clearly and competently written. The model used to guide test construction seems useful. The OSI has stimulated or been involved in the inception of a vigorous and fruitful program of research that is apt to expand. Overall, it is a well-conceived, well-constructed, and worthwhile instrument for research and practice. However, the problem of norms has not been sufficiently addressed for practical applications, and advice to develop local norms does not solve the difficulty of using this test in practice.

[270]
Occupational Test Series: General Ability Tests.

Purpose: "Assessing persons without previous work experience; selection for supervisory and similar management posts."
Population: Employees and candidates for employment.
Publication Date: 1988.
Scores: 4 tests: Verbal, Non-Verbal, Numerical, Spatial.
Administration: Group.
Price Data, 1989: £51.75 per Reference Set; £28.75 per test booklet (specify Verbal, Non-Verbal, Numerical, or Spatial); £20.15 per Administration Pack (specify Non-Verbal, Numerical, or Spatial); £17.25 per Test Taker's Guide.
Time: 25(30) minutes for Verbal; 30(35) minutes for each (Non-Verbal, Numerical, Spatial).
Comments: Tests may be administered separately.
Authors: Pauline Smith and Chris Whetton.
Publisher: NFER-Nelson Publishing Co., Ltd. [England].

Review of the Occupational Test Series: General Ability Tests by PHILIP G. BENSON, Associate Professor of Management, New Mexico State University, Las Cruces, NM:

The General Ability Tests are four distinct tests published as part of the Occupational Test Series through the Test Development Unit of the National Foundation for Educational Research in England and Wales (NFER). The tests are designed for use in hiring employees in a variety of occupational groups. Other tests in the same series include the

Graduate and Managerial Assessment, which has previously been reviewed in *The Mental Measurements Yearbook* (10:129).

The authors of the test specify four general requirements that the tests are intended to meet. First, the test content is general to avoid any terms or characteristics that would limit them to a specific occupational group. Second, the difficulty level of the tests was targeted to make them appropriate for the general population. Third, the tests are reasonably short and easily administered in a group context. Finally, the tests were developed to avoid as far as possible any bias against particular subgroups of potential test takers. Overall, these requirements create the impression of a series of tests that measure general abilities, with an orientation to the work setting. Such is an appropriate description of the General Ability Tests.

The items and formats of the subtests are clearly general in nature and rely very little on specific factual knowledge. Rather, the emphasis is on processes involved in reasoning and problem solving. Four specific tests are included: the Verbal Test, the Non-Verbal Test, the Numerical Test, and the Spatial Test.

The Verbal Test is an analogies test, given under a 15-minute time limit. In addition, the test requires about 10 minutes for instructions to test takers. Items appear to vary in difficulty. In addition, almost all words used avoid British spellings; the items could be used in the United States as easily as in England in most cases.

The Non-Verbal Test was designed to require the same sorts of cognitive processes as the Verbal Test, but to do so using abstract shapes and figures rather than words. In fact, the Non-Verbal Test includes two types of items. There are analogies, based on shapes and patterns, but there are also a number of items that deal with the classification of shapes. A total of 36 items are included in the Non-Verbal Test, and the time limit is set at 20 minutes (plus about 10 minutes for instructions).

The Numerical Test was intended to measure numerical reasoning without undue limitations set by specific knowledge of mathematics. The items focus on basic arithmetic operations (i.e., addition, subtraction, division, and multiplication) and use an analogy format. Items include a variety of geometric shapes with cells. Most of the cells contain numbers, and the examinee's task is to determine the numbers that belong in the remaining cells to complete the pattern represented in the analogy. As a test of abstract reasoning, as opposed to one of specific mathematical training, the Numerical Test appears to be an interesting approach to measurement. As with the Non-Verbal Test, the Numerical Test requires about 10 minutes for instructions and 20 minutes for testing time.

The fourth test in the series is the Spatial Test. This test is more traditional in format, requiring the test taker to mentally envision a three-dimensional shape that could be made from a cut and folded two-dimensional drawing. Perspective drawings of various objects are presented, and the test taker must indicate which are possible representations of the two-dimensional form as manipulated. The user's guide states that this form of test is similar to the General Aptitude Test Battery (GATB) 3-D Space and other spatial tests that have proven useful in predicting occupational success in engineering, construction, and other jobs requiring spatial imagination. Unlike other spatial tests, however, the Spatial Test includes varied shapes. In contrast, many such tests focus on cubes and rectangles. Because more different types of shapes and irregular shapes are included, the difficulty level of the Spatial Test is probably higher than that of other such tests. The Spatial Test requires 20 minutes for administration, after approximately 10 minutes of instructions.

The instructions for administration and scoring the General Ability Tests are adequate but not exceptional. Although the information given will ensure reasonably consistent test administration, it would be helpful if the manual anticipated more questions and problems and gave guidelines on how to deal with specific difficulties. However, it is likely that any administrator who has a reasonable background in educational and psychological testing would be able to use these tests in a reasonably standardized fashion.

Three separate standardization samples were used to develop norms for the four tests. These are somewhat confusing for the North American user, because the description is based on the English school system. The samples include a 5th form secondary school sample, an "A" Level sample, and a sample of FE BTEC National Diploma students. However, a careful examination of the demographics involved is helpful. The first sample consists of 15-year-olds and 16-year-olds; the second sample consists primarily of 16-year-olds and 17-year-olds (with a range up to 21 years old); and the third sample consists primarily of 17- to 19-year-olds (with a range of 16 to 38 years of age). Taken together, these samples reflect the ages of high school and university students in the United States and represent ages at which many individuals enter the work force. However, all three samples are smaller than would be preferred. No normative data are given for groups larger than 700 examinees, and it would be helpful to have larger samples. Users would be well advised to maintain local norms and to check for any apparent discrepancies from the normative data given.

Reliabilities are reported for the four tests within each of the three standardization samples. Of the 12 values reported, all range from .80 to .93. The reliabilities are given as KR-20 estimates. The highest reliabilities are given for the Spatial Test, and the lowest are for the Non-Verbal Test. Other than the Spatial Test, all reported reliabilities are below .90, which is a bit low for a test of general ability.

Because the Non-Verbal and Numerical Tests showed evidence of speededness, the authors analyzed the reliability of these two tests using only those test takers who had completed all items. The resulting reliabilities were not appreciably different from those obtained with the whole sample. In addition, test-retest reliabilities were calculated for these two tests, with values of .81 and .87 reported for the Non-Verbal and Numerical Tests, respectively. Thus, it appears that the speeded nature of the tests did not artificially inflate the KR-20 reliabilities.

The General Ability Tests were developed with the intention of avoiding items that show excessive bias on the basis of gender or race. However, it is clear from data presented that the test does show differences in mean scores for male and female test takers. This is most apparent for the Numerical Test and least apparent for the Non-Verbal Test. In addition, the greatest differences are found in the sample for the 5th form pupils, but the manual states that this difference may be artificial. For this subsample, a greater number of schools were for boys only, and the single-sex schools in general had greater selectivity in admissions. Thus, a mean difference with males scoring higher may be spurious. The test authors also considered gender differences at the item level, but the results were not especially conclusive. Relatively few items seemed to favor either gender.

The analyses for race were somewhat less impressive. Specifically, because so few individuals in the normative sample were nonwhite, little can be firmly concluded. All tests showed mean differences between whites and blacks, but because samples were small, proper statistical tests could not be performed. In general, users should be cautioned about use of these tests in racially heterogeneous groups without careful consideration of potential biases.

The user's guide provides technical information in a final section and lacks sufficient data to draw firm conclusions regarding tests validity. Item total correlations are presented as well as some normative data for industrial trials of the tests, but little correlational data are presented to allow firm conclusions regarding criterion-related validity of the tests. Intercorrelations with the Personnel Tests for Industry and the Differential Aptitude Test are included, but these data are insufficient to draw solid conclusions. Overall, the validity of the tests remains an unanswered question.

The user's guide does given an outline of the procedures to be used to generate local norms and to conduct local validity studies. Most test users should be able to undertake such studies without the guidelines given; indeed, users unfamiliar with the level of detail presented should not be using tests without considerable outside assistance.

Overall, the developmental work on these tests is really quite impressive, and the tests would seem to have substantial promise in employee selection. This is especially true when general reasoning can be justified as necessary for job performance. The user's guide is in general very good, the lack of validity data being its greatest shortcoming. With proper additional research, these tests could prove very good indeed, and their potential should not be overlooked. However, until such data are presented, it would be best to view these tests as primarily experimental.

Review of the Occupational Test Series: General Ability Tests by MICHAEL S. TREVISAN, *Research Associate, RMC Corporation, Portland, OR:*

The General Ability Tests (GAT) are a collection of four group-administered tests designed to aid in the selection of job applicants. These four tests are part of the new Occupational Test Series developed by the NFER-Nelson Publishing Co., Ltd., Assessment and Selection for Employment Division. The four tests that comprise the GAT measure Numerical, Verbal, Non-Verbal, and Spatial Reasoning, respectively. The Basic Skills and Critical Reasoning components of the series will be published sometime in the future.

The GAT is a timely approach for identifying people who can effectively respond to the rapidly changing demands of the organizational work environment. These may be people with no prior work experience or those already working who may have potential for a supervisory or management position. The starting point for this endeavor was to ask "numerous employers" what they believed to be the essential intellectual qualities their employees should have. From these interviews an assessment blueprint was developed. In addition, competing tests were investigated (e.g., the Differential Aptitude Test [DAT] and the USES General Aptitude Test Battery [GATB]) to consider alternative approaches to test construction.

In contrast to the DAT and the GATB, the theoretical underpinnings for the GAT assessment of reasoning are based on the pioneering work of Sternberg (1977, 1985). In addition, two design decisions were made when developing the GAT that are quite different from the designs of its competitors. The first of these is the use of "text-free" questions for the Verbal and Numerical tests. After consulting with employers, it was decided that face validity should be sacrificed in an attempt to obtain a clearer measure of verbal and numerical reasoning by reducing the reading component in both of these tests. It was argued that the potential of bias due to culture and educational background would decrease if the reading component were reduced. The second decision was to use "separately-timed measures of reasoning in verbal, numerical and figural media" (guide, p. 23) in the GAT. This decision was made to make a clear distinction between the way the material is presented and the content of the aforementioned tests. This distinction is not clear in the DAT or GATB. The authors cite research (e.g., Cooper & Regan, 1982) that suggests that individuals who are stronger in a particular media develop strategies that will take advantage of their abilities when solving tasks. It is therefore entirely possible that an individual would obtain different reasoning scores from tests that use different media. Employers interviewed believed this to be useful information. Consequently, the distinction was made between the tests, making it possible to determine the media preference as well as the reasoning ability of an individual.

The four abilities measured by the GAT are: Verbal—36 analogy items that test the ability to understand verbal concepts; Nonverbal—36 analogy and classification items that test the ability to process information to compare and contrast; Numerical—36 items using the question grid, which involves seriation, analogies, and various cell combinations to test the ability to reason inductively and numerically; and Spatial—80 items that test the ability to recognize three-dimensional objects by determining what a flattened object would look like when folded.

The test review kit is housed in a ring-binder and is wonderfully compact and convenient to store. The information provided is quite readable and adequate for anyone charged with the responsibility of deciding whether to adopt the tests. The test development and technical sections are clear and concise. The informational discussions about norms, item bias, standard error of measurement, reliability, and validity are so complete that this reviewer would recommend the test review kit as a supplement to any introductory measurement course.

One can choose to administer only one of the tests or all four. These tests stand alone because there is no battery or total score. Percentile ranks and T scores are provided for each test. In addition, a 68% true score confidence interval is provided for each raw score. Norms tables were constructed for each of three different reference groups. The three norms are provided for each of the four tests. These reference groups roughly correspond to people with no prior work experience, people with work experi-

ence who may have potential for a managerial position, and those who may benefit from further training or coursework. Depending on one's purpose, a particular norm group would be chosen for comparison over another. Further descriptions of the norm groups and guidelines for choosing a particular group are provided in the review kit. However, missing from the technical section is an explanation of how the data were scaled.

The norm samples were chosen from the British population. Multistratified sampling plans were used, with the stratification variables being chosen specifically for each norm group. This reviewer is uncertain whether or not Americans can be realistically compared to British norms. However, there is some evidence that British psychologists routinely and successfully use American norms when administering the Stanford-Binet (Wright & Stone, 1985). Perhaps having local norms would be most useful to employers. A nice feature of the review kit is an easy-to-understand, step-by-step procedure for developing local norms, should a company have the time and inclination to do so.

Internal consistency reliability estimates (KR-20s) are acceptably high for the GAT. These estimates range from .80 to .93 depending on the test and norm group. However, no test-retest data are provided.

A thorough item bias study was conducted for all items within each test and norm group. Items found to be biased were either discarded or, to strike a balance, items biased in the opposite direction were included.

There is a dearth of validity evidence. In fact, despite the progressive approach to occupational testing, the lack of validity evidence is of major concern. It is this reviewer's opinion that before a test reaches the market it is incumbent upon the publisher to provide adequate validity evidence. No evidence of construct validity is given. Some criterion-related validity data are given. Correlations between the Spatial Test of the GAT and the DAT and the Personnel Tests for Industry are provided. Other than this, the publisher's offer to be a clearinghouse for the studies that users of the GAT might conduct themselves is an inadequate substitution for the lack of validity evidence.

In summary, the GAT is an innovative approach to occupational testing and has the beginnings of being a fine addition to the field. However, the lack of reliability and validity data warrant the use of the GAT for research purposes only. The use of the DAT, which has stood the test of time, or the GATB and its plethora of validity evidence are recommended when making personnel decisions. Until the publishers can provide more technical data, this reviewer will not recommend the GAT for commercial use.

REVIEWER'S REFERENCES

Sternberg, R. J. (1977). *Intelligence, information processing, and analogical reasoning: The componential analysis of human abilities.* Hillsdale, NJ: Lawrence Erlbaum Associates.
Cooper, L. A., & Regan, D. T. (1982). Attention, perception and intelligence. In R. J. Sternberg (Ed.), *Handbook of human intelligence* (pp. 123-169). New York: Cambridge University Press.
Sternberg, R. J. (1985). *Beyond IQ: A triarchic theory of human intelligence.* New York: Cambridge University Press.
Wright, B. D., & Stone, M. H. (1985). [Review of the British Ability Scales.] In J. V. Mitchell, Jr. (Ed.), *The ninth mental measurements yearbook* (Vol I, pp. 232-235). Lincoln, NE: Buros Institute of Mental Measurements.

[271]
Oliver Organization Description Questionnaire.

Purpose: Describes occupational organizations along four dimensions.
Population: Adults.
Publication Date: 1981.
Acronym: OODQ.
Scores, 4: H (Hierarchy), P (Professional), T (Task), G (Group).
Administration: Group.
Price Data, 1989: $17.50 per 50 tests; $3.50 per scoring guide (13 pages).
Time: (15–20) minutes.
Author: John E. Oliver, Jr.
Publisher: Organizational Measurement Systems Press.

Review of the Oliver Organization Description Questionnaire by PETER VILLANOVA, Assistant Professor of Psychology, Northern Illinois University, DeKalb, IL, and H. JOHN BERNARDIN, University Professor of Research, Florida Atlantic University, Boca Raton, FL:

The Oliver Organization Description Questionnaire (OODQ) is an application of Miner's (1980) four limited domain theories of organizations. Each of Miner's four theories describes a role that must be performed by individuals within an organization or subunit in order to direct and sustain effort toward organizational goal attainment. The questionnaire provides four scores, each corresponding to a specific inducement system within Miner's taxonomy. The four inducement systems are: Hierarchic, Professional, Task, and Group. The OODQ purports to measure the extent to which organizations, organizational subunits, or positions possess characteristics representative of each inducement system.

Potential uses of the scale scores derived from the test include: (*a*) identification of boundary variables that affect the applicability of various management styles and conflict resolution strategies; (*b*) assessment of the amount of change resulting from interventions such as training, organizational development, job enrichment, management by objectives, and socio-technical designs; and (*c*) a more complete report of the organizational domain in which research on organizational behavior is conducted.

Each of Miner's theories refers to a specific form of organizational inducement system operating within a prescribed domain. For example, Miner's

Hierarchic (H) inducement system operates in large bureaucratic organizations where members' energy is direct by individuals who occupy traditional management positions. Management obtains its energy from a variety of "intrinsic motivational constellations," such as, for example, a desire to compete and a desire to exercise power over others (Miner, 1980, pp. 274–275).

In contrast, the Professional (P) inducement system is said to operate among individuals or organizations whose role requirements and norms are largely a function of professional standards. Intrinsic motivational constellations for the roles germane to Professional inducement systems include, for example, a desire to learn and acquire knowledge, and an identification with the values of the profession to which one belongs. Individuals may be members of professional organizations, self-employed, or serve in some professional capacity. College professors, lawyers, and chaplains are occupations that fall within this form of inducement system.

According to the scoring guide of the OODQ, the Task (T) inducement system is characteristic of organizations or positions "that receive their energy from rewards and punishments that are built into the job or task." In this form of inducement system, individuals establish specific duties and goals, their own decisions based on the situation at hand, and alone bear the responsibility for failure or success. There is little cooperation with others and success is largely determined by the individual's ability and motivation. Entrepreneurs and commissioned sales personnel are examples of positions that feature some of these characteristics.

Group inducement systems possess democratic decision-making features. The group regulates individual behavior by the application of positive or negative sanctions. Group loyalty is considered important for group maintenance and growth, and independence is discouraged. Group inducement systems are present in work situations that require close coordination among work group members who share relatively equal status. Organizations that subscribe to the socio-technical philosophy of work design tend to have more of these features.

The questionnaire consists of 43 forced-choice items with a tetradic response format and is administered without a time limit. Oliver (1982) reports that respondents required approximately one-half hour to complete the test, though some individuals completed it within 15 minutes and others required nearly 50 minutes. Each item of the three-page questionnaire begins with the words "In my work" and is followed by statements that pertain to specific job characteristics, such as "Work rules and regulations are established by" and "My training is generally." Respondents are instructed to complete each statement by selecting the one answer that best describes their work situation. For example, the former statement is followed by the following choices: (*a*) me–in order to insure goal accomplishment, (*b*) management, (*c*) the work group, and (*d*) my profession or occupation.

Psychometric data on the instrument are sparse at this time. Those data that were reported indicate adequate psychometric properties for its use as a research device. Psychometric characteristics of the test are based on a study conducted by Oliver (1980) with a sample of 438 respondents drawn from a variety of occupations representative of each of the four domains. Occupations were classified a priori as corresponding to the various inducement strategies. For example, U.S. Army officers, NCOs, and enlisted men were hypothesized to score higher on the Hierarchic inducement scale relative to the P, T, and G scales. Likewise, lawyers and dentists were hypothesized to score higher on the P scale than the H, T, and G scales.

Results of this study indicated that 72% of the initial validation sample were classified correctly. Cross-validation with a holdout sample indicated that 71% of these respondents were classified correctly. Also, 90% of the organizational units were correctly classified. Coefficient alphas for each of the four scales ranged from .82 to .88. Test-retest coefficients based on 32 members of the original sample ranged from .77 to .87. Cutting scores for classification purposes were empirically derived and are characterized by relatively small standard errors of measurement. Thus, the scales of this questionnaire possess adequate evidence for criterion-related validity, internal consistency, temporal stability, and acceptable precision for classification purposes. However, these results were generated with relatively small derivation and cross-validation samples of approximately 50–60 respondents for each scale. Caution is required by users when interpreting the findings. Moreover, extra caution may be required if a user plans to study a sample of occupations or organizations not represented in the initial sample.

Overall, the OODQ reflects a careful approach to scale development and attention to detail. The instrument possesses characteristics that make it a promising instrument for organizational diagnosis and classification in the context of Miner's taxonomy. Considerable research is still needed on the psychometric characteristics of the instrument. In its present form, however, the OODQ could be useful to consultants and organizational scholars who share a concern about the boundary conditions of various work place interventions and who accept Miner's taxonomy.

REVIEWER'S REFERENCES

Miner, J. B. (1980). Limited domain theories of organizational energy. In C. C. Pinder & L. F. Moore (Eds.), *Middle range theory and the study of organizations*. The Hague, Netherlands: Martinus Nijhoff.

Oliver, J. E. (1980). *The development of an instrument for describing organizational energy domains*. Unpublished doctoral dissertation, Georgia State University, Atlanta, GA.

Oliver, J. E. (1982). An instrument for classifying organizations. *Academy of Management Journal, 25*, 855-866.

[272]
Oral Speech Mechanism Screening Examination—Revised.

Purpose: "To provide the speech/language pathologist with a method for assessing the adequacy of the oral mechanism for speech."
Population: Age 5 through adults.
Publication Dates: 1981–87.
Acronym: OSMSE-R.
Scores: 9 areas: Lips, Tongue, Jaw, Teeth, Hard Palate, Soft Palate, Pharynx, Breathing, Diadochokinesis.
Administration: Individual.
Price Data, 1987: $34 per complete kit including 50 scoring forms and examiner's manual ('87, 67 pages); $15 per 50 scoring forms; $21 per examiner's manual.
Time: (5–10) minutes.
Authors: Kenneth O. St. Louis and Dennis M. Ruscello.
Publisher: PRO-ED, Inc.

Review of the Oral Speech Mechanism Screening Examination—Revised by CHARLES WM. MARTIN, Assistant Dean, University College, Ball State University, Muncie, IN:

The Oral Speech Mechanism Screening Examination—Revised (OSMSE-R) provides systematic observation of the pharyngo-oral tract for trained specialists (speech/language pathologists, physical therapists, etc.). The OSMSE-R is a quick screening method that attempts to provide quantitative data for delineating an oral speech mechanism problem. Although the manual provides traditional guidelines for screening procedures, there are some major shortcomings.

The OSMSE-R is constructed to evaluate 31 structural features and 24 oral motor functions. The scoring system incorporates evaluation of the lips, tongue, jaw, teeth, hard and soft palate, pharynx, breathing, and diadochokinesis. Thirty responses are recorded as a plus sign (no deviations), minus sign (deviation in structure or function), NT (item not tested), NR (lack of functional movement), or X (incorrect execution of movement). Other test items are marked with a *check mark* to indicate which structural or functional characteristic best characterizes the client's response to a given test condition. Raw scores comprised the total number of items that demonstrated no deviations or abnormalities. The OSMSE-R derives raw scores for structure, function, total (combined raw scores of structure and function), and diadochokinesis rate. These data are compared to normative information to delineate which raw scores fall below proposed average values.

The test manual provides clear and concise instructions for its basic scoring, which is augmented by an extended discussion of overall guidelines. The authors provide an illustrated review of normal structure and function of the oral mechanism as well as a discussion of typical deviations that may be found when conducting an oral peripheral examination. This should facilitate interpretation of test results, but the test does require an experienced examiner.

The OSMSE-R is not a standardized test but a systematic procedure for observing oral speech mechanism which has been supported by a series of research studies. Intrajudge and interjudge reliability were reported to be 96.3% and 91% respectively. The authors provide no formal estimates of validity. Normative comparisons of raw scores with those presented by the authors are of limited value given the small sample sizes and use of multiple studies to derive these data.

When screening the oral speech mechanism, an experienced practitioner would typically observe four broad parameters: (a) overt characteristics (size, shape, coloration, etc.); (b) symmetry; (c) mobility and strength; and (d) precision and timing. The OSMSE-R provides a restricted set of behaviors and structures from these parameters. The clinician should be aware that OSMSE-R procedures do not include all parameters necessary for screening the oral speech mechanism.

In summary, the OSMSE-R does not differ significantly from traditional screening procedures. Data obtained through the scoring procedure merely indicate the necessity for further testing. This could be determined by an experienced diagnostician by employing an informal and qualitative screening method.

Review of the Oral Speech Mechanism Screening Examination—Revised by MALCOLM R. McNEIL, Professor of Communicative Disorders, University of Wisconsin-Madison, Madison, WI:

The Oral Speech Mechanism Screening Examination—Revised (OSMSE-R) is designed for the purpose of providing "the speech/language pathologist with a method for assessing the adequacy of the oral mechanism for speech" (p. 10) for children and adults. In addition to the examination score sheet, scoring template, and the manual (which is to have been studied and practiced thoroughly prior to administration to a patient/client), the examiner requires tongue depressors, a flashlight, tissues, and a stopwatch. The manual states clearly that academic training in anatomy and physiology of the speech mechanism along with "a substantial background in the various speech and language disorders with which they come in contact and in the experimental literature that relates anatomic or physiologic deviations to speech and language ability" (p. 1) are prerequisites for test administration. An optional videotape is available for purchase from the authors illustrating a speech/language pathologist administering the OSMSE-R to a normal child; however,

the authors state explicitly that the training tape is supplementary and that "this manual is self-contained and provides all the information necessary to learn to administer, score, and interpret the OSMSE-R" (p. 1). Reported test administration time ranges from 5 to 10 minutes.

ADMINISTRATION AND SCORING. The test scoring form outlines the speech structure to be observed and the movement/observation required for the function. The scoring system (+ = no deviation, - = deviation, NT = not tested, NR = no response, and x = wrong response) provides a rapid means of recording information that should enhance valid test administration and scorer reliability. The examiner totals the number of judgements in which no deviations or abnormalities are observed. The diadochokinetic rates are timed and counted. These judgments and counts are supplemented by descriptive notes.

Although the authors discuss, in better detail than many other examinations designed for the same purposes, "typical deviations" for each of the structures and functions, the greatest threat to the valid and reliable use of the OSMSE-R is the lack of explicit criteria for scoring a + (no deviation noted) or a - (deviation noted). In the absence of either specific physical measurements or an explicit training program for administration and scoring the perceptual judgments required of the examination, the OSMSE-R relies on the skills and biases of the examiner. In support of this criticism is the absence of demonstrated reliability data for persons who have been trained by reading the manual only.

The OSMSE-R has reference data for 10 age ranges of normal individuals (mean age [years and months] = 5.3, N = 13; 7.8, N = 15; 10.9, N = 31; 13.8, N = 13; 20.8, N = 36; 35.5, N = 16; 45.5, N = 16; 55.8, N = 16; 65.5, N = 16; 77.7, N = 16) and five groups of speech and language disordered subjects (Articulation Disordered: 5.7, N = 12; Articulation Disordered: 7.11, N = 12; Stutterers: 8.2, N = 10; Stutterers: 13.3, N = 10; and Head Injured: 29.2, N = 20). The percentage of subjects displaying the feature (deviation, descriptive feature of the structure, or measured function) are presented for each group for each of the 63 observations/judgments and measurement. Average and 2 standard deviations from the mean data are also presented for the mean of each of the normal subject groups for the total structure score, total function score, overall score, and diadochokinetic rates (in seconds) for the individual syllable repetition and two- and three-syllable sequential repetition.

It is apparent the number of subjects in any of the normal or pathological groups is likely insufficient to represent the population as a whole. As such, these data are inadequate to serve as normative data against which normalcy or pathology can be reliably assigned. In addition, no attempt has been made to establish criteria for identifying subjects for further evaluation or for any of the other purposes of the examination (outlined below).

RELIABILITY: INTRAJUDGE. The authors refer to intrajudge reliability as that derived from a single examiner retesting the same subject. As recognized by the authors, this procedure confounds the reliability of the administrator with the test-retest reliability of the test plus the subject. The separation of these factors was, however, attempted only for the diadochokinetic rates. Recorded test performance from 91 normal and pathological subjects was rescored by four different examiners and one examiner that originally scored the performance of 10 normal college-aged subjects. Thus, live-to-recorded inter-judge reliability data are reported from 81 subjects by four examiners and live-to-recorded intrajudge reliability data are reported from 10 subjects by one examiner. Overall, the difference between scorings (in repetitions per second) was small (range = .45) for the between judge reliability and small (-.09) for the single intrajudge measure.

Intrajudge (more correctly considered test-retest) reliability was also assessed by having eight examiners retest the same subject (total subject $N = 45$) on a second occasion. The point-to-point agreement for the structure/function judgments differed by as much as 9.4% and as little as 0% for normal subjects. It should be remembered, however, that all percentages for these subjects were above 90% correct. Percentage of agreement for the error scores was not discussed, a factor known to artificially inflate reliability scores. Agreement for three closed-head-injured patients from one judge differed from test to retest by 17%. Without knowledge of the test's sensitivity and specificity, it is difficult to evaluate the adequacy of these reliability data.

VALIDITY. Although the authors state that "Since the OSMSE-R is a screening instrument, formal estimates of validity were not derived," all tests, perhaps most importantly screening tests, must meet minimal requirements for established validity and reliability.

Construct. The stated goal of the examination is to reach one of four decisions (a–d) about the structure or function of lips, tongue, jaw, teeth, hard palate, soft palate, pharynx, breathing apparatus, and diadochokinesis: (a) The structure and function of these speech apparatuses are normal and no further evaluation is necessary, (b) deviations in structure or function exceed the appropriate reference (normative) sample and referral to another professional is warranted for management or further evaluation, (c) deviations in structure or function warrant further in-depth testing by the clinician, or (d) deviations in structure or function are found to be subtle enough

that further evaluation is not needed. The implied criterion for making the first decision is a score that falls within 2 standard deviations of the appropriate normative sample. The implied criterion for making the second decision is a score that falls outside of 2 standard deviations of the appropriate normative sample. Criteria for making either of the other two decisions are not addressed. That is, the test has not been evaluated for its sensitivity or specificity (hits, misses, false positives, and false negatives).

The OSMSE-R is based on the assumption that disorders of nonspeech oral gestures are predictive of disturbances of function for those articulators when used for speech purposes. It is also based on the assumption that maximum performance tasks of the speech structures are related to the physiological requirements of those same structures for speech purposes. Neither of these assumptions is well established and both have received serious challenge in the speech pathology/speech science literature.

The manual discusses two forms of data that are used to support the construct validity of the test. First, the functions evaluated by the OSMSE-R would be expected to be developmental and such trends were observed. Second, subjects with confirmed neurological disorders of speech would be expected to perform lower than their neurologically normal age matches, and structure, function, and total scores were "substantially lower than normal" (p. 36).

Content. The test manual does discuss the rationale for the selection of structures to be evaluated; however, little discussion is presented relative to the specific features to be observed and judged for the structural examination or the specific tasks for the examination of the function for specific structures. In general, some concurrent validity for the structures and functions assessed by the OSMSE-R can be assumed as they are similar to those found in most other protocols and discussions of structural/functional speech mechanism examinations. However, it is of critical concern that the larynx, the sound generator and an important articulator, is not evaluated either structurally or functionally in the OSMSE-R.

All functions are assessed through verbal instruction plus imitation ("watch me and do what I do") which is likely designed to optimize the probability that the task will be attempted. However, those populations that show a differential performance between tasks performed better with imitation or poorer upon command (e.g., oral nonspeech apraxia or conduction aphasia, respectively), might result in fallacious decisions for these pathologies, as opposed to those who would be expected to show no differences between presentation modes.

Predictive/Concurrent. The ability of OSMSE-R results to predict speech errors (the explicit primary purpose of the examination), the need for treatment, referral, or dismissal has not been addressed. No concurrent validity data are presented for the OSMSE-R.

SUMMARY. The OSMSE-R provides an organized system of observing and recording critical structural and functional aspects of the majority of the structures used for speaking. In this systematicity it exceeds many such protocols published as appendices to diagnostic texts. However, as with other speech structural/functional examinations, the manual of the OSMSE-R does not provide either enough objective measures of structure or function (save diadochokinesis) or the necessary training to make more holistic perceptual judgments of structures and functions to perform the assessment validly or reliably. The accuracy with which the scores derived from the examination can be used for any of its stated purposes has not been investigated. The normative samples are too small to be representative of normal or any particular pathological sample and offer inadequate guidance in clinical decision making.

Although the OSMSE-R offers a reasonable outline for the evaluation of structure and function of the speech mechanism, its lack of adequate validity, reliability, and standardization data preclude recommending it for any of the purposes for which it was designed. The OSMSE-R does, however, offer a systematic record of observations for the clinician that may be better than no such record-keeping procedures.

[273]
Organizational Competence Index.
Purpose: "To assess, describe, and pinpoint organizational conditions which may, or may not, support organizational productivity."
Population: Individuals who, as part of a group or organization, share in the responsibilities of attaining a goal or objective.
Publication Date: 1977–87.
Acronym: OCI.
Scores: 10: Collaboration (Management Values, Support Structure, Managerial Credibility, Climate), Commitment (Impact, Relevance, Community), and Creativity (Task Environment, Social Context, Problem Solving).
Administration: Group.
Price Data, 1990: $10 per Test Manual ('87, 15 pages) and Interpretation Manual ('87, 25 pages); $15 per Leader's Manual ('87, 39 pages).
Time: Administration time not reported.
Authors: Jay Hall.
Publisher: Teleometrics International.

[274]
Otis-Lennon School Ability Test, Sixth Edition.
Purpose: "To measure abstract thinking and reasoning ability."
Population: Grades K–12.

Publication Dates: 1977–90.
Acronym: OLSAT.
Scores, 3: Verbal, Nonverbal, Total.
Administration: Group.
Levels, 7: A, B, C, D, E, F, G.
Price Data, 1990: $16.50 per norms booklet (Level A or B); $20 per norms booklets (Levels C–G); $40 per multilevel norms booklet; $33 per preliminary technical manual ('89, 53 pages); $39.50 per technical manual ('90, 101 pages); $6.50 per directions for administering; $3 per class record; scoring service provided by publisher: $1.42 per test booklet, $1.05 per answer sheet.
Comments: Previous (1979) edition still available; originally called Otis-Lennon Mental Ability Test.
Authors: Arthur S. Otis and Roger T. Lennon.
Publisher: The Psychological Corporation.

a) LEVEL A.
Population: Grade K.
Price Data: $43 per 25 type 1 machine-scorable test booklets; $49.50 per 25 type 2 machine-scorable test booklets; $32 per 25 hand-scorable test booklets; $6.50 per 25 practice tests; $22 per set of scoring stencils; $3 per 25 bookmarkers.
Time: (75) minutes over 2 sessions.
Comments: Orally administered.

b) LEVEL B.
Population: Grade 1.
Price Data: Same as Level A above.
Time: Same as Level A above.
Comments: Orally administered.

c) LEVEL C.
Population: Grade 2.
Price Data: Same as Level A above.
Time: Same as Level A above.
Comments: Partially self-administered.

d) LEVEL D.
Population: Grade 3.
Price Data: Same as Level A above.
Time: (60) minutes.
Comments: Self-administered.

e) LEVEL E.
Population: Grades 4–5.
Price Data: $32 per 25 reusable test booklets; $13 per 25 type 1 machine-scorable answer sheets; $15.50 per 25 type 2 machine-scorable answer sheets; $13 per 25 hand-scorable answer sheets; $6.50 per 25 practice tests; $11 per set of scoring stencils.
Time: Same as Level D above.
Comments: Self-administered.

f) LEVEL F.
Population: Grades 6–8.
Price Data: Same as Level E above.
Time: Same as Level D above.
Comments: Self-administered.

g) LEVEL G.
Population: Grades 9–12.
Price Data: Same as Level E above.
Time: Same as Level D above.
Comments: Self-administered.
Cross References: For reviews by Calvin O. Dyer and Thomas Oakland, see 9:913 (7 references); see also T3:1754 (64 references), 8:198 (35 references), and T2:424 (10 references); for a review by John E. Milholland and excerpted reviews by Arden

Grotelueschen and Arthur E. Smith, see 7:370 (6 references).

TEST REFERENCES

1. Epperson, D. L., Hannum, T. E., & Datwyler, M. L. (1982). Women incarcerated in 1960, 1970, and 1980: Implications of demographic, educational, and personality characteristics for earlier research. *Criminal Justice and Behavior, 9*, 352-363.

2. Bouchard, T. J., Jr. (1983). Do environmental similarities explain the similarity in intelligence of identical twins reared apart? *Intelligence, 7*, 175-184.

3. Chodzinski, R. T. (1983). Validity concerns for counsellors using the 1978 edition of the Career Maturity Inventory. *Canadian Counsellor, 18*, 5-12.

4. O'Tuel, F. S., Ward, M., & Rawl, R. K. (1983). The SOI as an identification tool for the gifted: Windfall or washout? *Gifted Child Quarterly, 27*, 126-134.

5. Wall, S. M. (1983). Children's self-determination of standards in reinforcement contingencies: A re-examination. *Journal of School Psychology, 21*, 123-131.

6. Elbert, J. C. (1984). Short-term memory encoding and memory search in the word recognition of learning-disabled children. *Journal of Learning Disabilities, 17*, 342-345.

7. Ford, C. E., Pelham, W. E., & Ross, A. O. (1984). Selective attention and rehearsal in the auditory short-term memory task performance of poor and normal readers. *Journal of Abnormal Child Psychology, 12*, 127-142.

8. Gold, D., Crombie, G., Brender, W., & Mate, P. (1984). Sex differences in children's performance in problem-solving situations involving an adult model. *Child Development, 55*, 543-549.

9. Maheady, L., Maitland, G., & Sainato, D. (1984). The interpretation of social interactions by mildly handicapped and nondisabled children. *The Journal of Special Education, 18*, 151-159.

10. Moore, J. W., Hauck, W. E., & Denne, T. C. (1984). Racial prejudice, interracial contact, and personality variables. *The Journal of Experimental Education, 52*, 168-173.

11. Sapp, G. L., & Marshall, J., Jr. (1984). The Otis-Lennon School Ability Test: A study of validity. *Psychological Reports, 55*, 539-544.

12. Sherris, J. D., & Kahle, J. B. (1984). The effects of instructional organization and locus of control orientation on meaningful learning in high school biology students. *Journal of Research in Science Teaching, 21*, 83-94.

13. Swanson, H. L. (1984). Effect of cognitive effort on learning disabled and nondisabled readers' recall. *Journal of Learning Disabilities, 17*, 67-74.

14. Swanson, H. L. (1984). Effects of cognitive effort and word distinctiveness on learning disabled and nondisabled readers' recall. *Journal of Educational Psychology, 76*, 894-908.

15. Ahmann, J. S. (1985). [Review of the Otis-Lennon School Ability Test.] *Measurement and Evaluation in Counseling and Development, 17*, 226-229.

16. Garnett, P. D. (1985). Intelligence measurement by computerized information processing using inspection time. *Journal of General Psychology, 112*, 325-335.

17. Grant, S. M. (1985). The kinesthetic approach to teaching: Building a foundation for learning. *Journal of Learning Disabilities, 18*, 455-462.

18. Ismail, M., & Kong, N. W. (1985). Relationship of locus of control, cognitive style, anxiety, and academic achievement of a group of Malaysian primary school children. *Psychological Reports, 57*, 1127-1134.

19. Lynch, A. D., & Clark, P. (1985). Relationship of self-esteem, IQ, and task performance for a sample of USA undergraduates. *Psychological Reports, 56*, 955-962.

20. Miller, J., & Eller, B. F. (1985). An examination of the effect of tangible and social reinforcers on intelligence test performance of middle school students. *Social Behavior and Personality, 13*, 147-157.

21. Ormrod, J. E. (1985). Proofreading *The Cat in the Hat*: Evidence for different reading styles of good and poor spellers. *Psychological Reports, 57*, 863-867.

22. Ormrod, J. E. (1985). Visual memory in a spelling matching task: Comparison of good and poor spellers. *Perceptual and Motor Skills, 61*, 183-188.

23. Renner, J. W., Abraham, M. R., & Birnie, H. W. (1985). The importance of the form of student acquisition of data in physics learning cycles. *Journal of Research in Science Teaching, 22*, 303-325.

24. Rothlisberg, B. A., & Dean, R. S. (1985). Reading comprehension and lateral preference in normal readers. *Psychology in the Schools, 22*, 337-342.

25. Schmidt, S., & Perino, J. (1985). Kindergarten screening results as predictors of academic achievement, potential, and placement in second grade. *Psychology in the Schools, 22*, 146-151.

26. Shaw, G. A. (1985). The use of imagery by intelligent and by creative schoolchildren. *Journal of General Psychology, 112*, 153-171.

27. Abraham, M. R., & Renner, J. W. (1986). The sequence of learning cycle activities in high school chemistry. *Journal of Research in Science Teaching, 23*, 121-143.

28. Anderson, O. R., & Callaway, J. (1986). Studies of information processing rates in science learning and related cognitive variables. II: A first approximation to estimating a relationship between science reasoning skills and information acquisition. *Journal of Research in Science Teaching, 23*, 67-72.

29. Bjorklund, D. F., & Bernholtz, J. E. (1986). The role of knowledge base in the memory performance of good and poor readers. *Journal of Experimental Child Psychology, 41*, 367-393.

30. Carrier, C. A., Davidson, G. V., Williams, M. D., & Kalweit, C. M. (1986). Instructional options and encouragement effects in a microcomputer-delivered concept lesson. *The Journal of Educational Research, 79*, 222-229.

31. Crow, L. W., & Piper, M. K. (1986). A study of field independent biased mental ability tests in community college science classes. *Journal of Research in Science Teaching, 23*, 817-822.

32. Howard, R. C., Haynes, J. P., & Atkinson, D. (1986). Factors associated with juvenile detention truancy. *Adolescence, 21*, 357-364.

33. May, D. (1986). Relationships between the Gesell School Readiness Test and standardized achievement and intelligence measures. *Educational and Psychological Measurement, 46*, 1051-1059.

34. Pullis, M., & Cadwell, J. (1986). Temperament as a factor in the assessment of children educationally at risk. *Journal of Special Education, 19*, 91-102.

35. Roth, F. P., & Spekman, N. J. (1986). Narrative discourse: Spontaneously generated stories of learning-disabled and normally achieving students. *Journal of Speech and Hearing Disorders, 51*, 8-23.

36. Swanson, H. L. (1987). Verbal-coding deficits in the recall of pictorial information by learning disabled readers: The influence of a lexical system. *American Educational Research Journal, 24*, 143-170.

37. Whorton, J. E., & Karnes, F. A. (1987). Correlation of Stanford-Binet Intelligence Scale with various other measures used to screen and identify intellectually gifted students. *Perceptual and Motor Skills, 64*, 461-462.

38. Braden, J. P., & Weiss, L. (1988). Effects of simple difference versus regression discrepancy methods: An empirical study. *Journal of School Psychology, 26*, 133-142.

39. Cahn, L. D. (1988). Sex and grade differences and learning rate in an intensive summer reading clinic. *Psychology in the Schools, 25*, 195-202.

40. Cohen, M., DuRant, R. H., & Cook, C. (1988). The Conners Teacher Rating Scale: Effects of age, sex, and race with special education children. *Psychology in the Schools, 25*, 195-202.

41. Gadow, K. D., Sprafkin, J., Kelly, E., & Ficarrotto, T. (1988). Reality perceptions of television: A comparison of school-labeled learning-disabled and nonhandicapped children. *Journal of Clinical Child Psychology, 17*, 25-33.

42. Pasnak, R., Denham, S., & Groff, R. (1988). Accelerated cognitive development of kindergarteners: One year later. *Child Study Journal, 18*, 249-263.

43. Buckhalt, J. A., & Jensen, A. R. (1989). The British Ability Scales Speed of Information Processing subtest: What does it measure? *British Journal of Educational Psychology, 59*, 100-107.

44. Gadzella, B. M., Hartsoe, K., & Harper, J. (1989). Critical thinking and mental ability groups. *Psychological Reports, 65*, 1019-1026.

45. Hughes, J. N., Boodoo, G., Alcala, J., Maggio, M., Moore, L., & Villapando, R. (1989). Validation of a role-play measure of children's social skills. *Journal of Abnormal Child Psychology, 17*, 633-646.

46. Randhawa, B. S., & Hunt, D. (1989). Social-psychological environments and cognitive achievement. *Perceptual and Motor Skills, 69*, 1075-1082.

47. Yarborough, B. H., & Johnson, R. A. (1989). Sex differences in written language among elementary pupils: A seven-year longitudinal study. *Psychological Reports, 64*, 407-414.

48. Diamond, K. E. (1990). Effectiveness of the Revised Denver Developmental Screening Test in identifying children at risk for learning problems. *Journal of Educational Research, 83*, 152-157.

Review of the Otis-Lennon School Ability Test, Sixth Edition by ANNE ANASTASI, Professor Emeritus of Psychology, Fordham University, Bronx, NY:

THE SIXTH EDITION AND ITS BACKGROUND. The Otis-Lennon School Ability Test (OLSAT) has evolved through a series of tests that virtually spans the history of group testing, from the pioneering innovations of Otis in 1918, through the Otis Self-Administering Test of Mental Ability, to the Otis-Lennon Mental Ability Test and the Otis-Lennon

School Ability Test. While incorporating significant ongoing developments in test construction and use, the current edition still shows the influence of several Otis contributions, as in the nature and diversity of item content and form and in the spiral-omnibus arrangement of items. This ordering of items permits the testing of multiple functions with a single set of initial instructions and a single time limit, an arrangement that not only simplifies test administration but also reduces the chances of procedural errors in presenting instructions and in timing.

Innovations introduced in the preceding edition and retained in the present edition of the OLSAT include the change in test name, from "Mental Ability" to "School Ability," and the change in total score from "Deviation IQ" to "School Ability Index" (SAI). Both represent efforts to prevent common misinterpretations of test scores, such as overgeneralization of the intellectual domain covered by any given test and the various misconceptions associated with popular uses of "IQ."

Among the improvements made in the Sixth Edition is the provision of multiple scores, including the Total SAI, the separate Verbal and Nonverbal SAIs, and the further provision for more narrowly focused performance evaluation on item clusters within the two part scores. Again spanning grades Kindergarten to 12, the current OLSAT comprises seven levels, two more than the preceding edition, thereby providing separate levels (A, B, C, D) for kindergarten and grades 1, 2, and 3, in place of the Primary I and Primary II levels of the earlier edition.

All levels of the Sixth Edition are preceded by a Practice Test in a separate booklet. The four lower levels begin with full oral administration, with separate oral instructions for each item and item-by-item pacing by the teacher at Levels A and B. At these levels, there is also some grouping of similar item types to facilitate the giving and understanding of instructions. Self-administration is introduced gradually at Levels C and D. The upper three levels (E, F, G), spanning grades 4 to 12, are essentially similar in format and administration, consisting of a single, spiral-omnibus test. They are completely self-administered, with written instructions and separate answer sheets. The vocabulary level required to read instructions was found to be well below that corresponding to the appropriate grades.

Although all items in the Sixth Edition are new, many item types (with regard to form and content) that proved successful in earlier editions are represented. For purposes of test construction and for some performance evaluation, 21 item types were identified and grouped into five clusters. These clusters are listed below, with illustrative item types. *Verbal scores* are derived from two clusters: Verbal Comprehension (e.g., Antonyms, Sentence Completion) and Verbal Reasoning (e.g., Verbal Analogies, Verbal Classification, Arithmetic Reasoning with verbal problems and simple computation). *Nonverbal scores* are derived from two of three clusters, depending upon test level: Pictorial Reasoning—only on Levels A, B, C (e.g., Picture Classification, Picture Series), Figural Reasoning—on all levels (e.g., Figural Analogies, Pattern Matrix), and Quantitative Reasoning—only on Levels D, E, F, G (e.g., Number Series, Number Matrix). It should be noted that the nonverbal items in the OLSAT involve essentially comprehension and reasoning with nonverbal content, rather than requiring perceptual and spatial aptitudes as in many tests usually designated as nonverbal.

PERFORMANCE EVALUATION AND DERIVED SCORES. Total raw scores on the entire test and on verbal and nonverbal parts are converted to School Ability Indexes (SAIs). These are normalized standard scores ($M = 100$, $SD = 16$) within each 3-month age group, from 4-6 to 18-2. The SAIs may be further converted to percentile ranks and stanines within the same age groups. Raw scores may also be expressed as percentiles and stanines within grades, with fall and spring norms.

Individual performance can be further examined for more specific strengths and weaknesses through the item clusters. Raw scores on the four clusters within each level, obtained by students in each grade in the spring and fall standardization, were first expressed as stanines. Then the raw score ranges corresponding to stanines 1–3, 4–6, and 7–9 were reported as below average, average, and above average, respectively, in the normative tables for each level.

Finally, scaled scores were developed by administering two adjacent levels to each student sample from different grades. This permitted the expression of item difficulties on a single uniform scale. The resulting sample-free scaled scores are comparable across all levels, regardless of age or grade of the test taker.

TEST DEVELOPMENT AND STANDARDIZATION. A national item tryout of several parallel forms at each level was conducted with 35,000 students from 65 schools. Qualitative editorial and substantive evaluations of all items were obtained from representative judges for both tryout and final forms of all levels. Special attention was given to the avoidance of stereotypes and differential item functioning (DIF) with regard to gender and ethnic populations. Empirical checks of DIF used both Rasch-model and Angoff-delta analyses. Statistical criteria for final item selection included difficulty level, discriminative value (biserial *rs*), and adequate functioning of response options.

Standardization testing was conducted in the spring and fall of 1988, from which were prepared separate spring and fall norms by school grades. The spring testing included approximately 200,000 students from 1,000 school districts; approximately 156,000 other students were tested in the fall program. School systems were selected according to a stratified random sampling with regard to socioeconomic status (5 levels), urbanicity (urban, suburban, rural), region (Northeast, Midwest, South, West), and ethnicity (African-American, Hispanic, White, other). The percentages of students in the standardization program in each category agreed closely with the corresponding percentages in the total U.S. school enrollment from the 1980 census. Also represented in the standardization sample were students from Catholic and other nonpublic schools and some with various physical or psychological handicaps.

Like the preceding edition, the latest OLSAT was concurrently normed with an achievement test. Form 1 was normed with the Stanford Achievement Test (Eighth Edition) and Form 2 (to be published before the mid-1990s) will be normed with the Metropolitan Achievement Tests (Seventh Edition).

RELIABILITY. Kuder-Richardson reliabilities are reported for each level (A–G), computed separately for each year of age from 5 to 18 and for each grade from kindergarten to 12. In both cases the reliability coefficients are in the high .80s and .90s for Total scores and mostly in the .80s for Verbal and Nonverbal Scores. The standard error of measurement (*SEM*) is given for the same age and grade groups as is the reliability coefficient. For Total scores, this *SEM* is approximately 5 SAI units for most ages. No data on retest reliability are given in the Preliminary Technical Manual (PTM) or in the subsequently published Technical Manual (TM). Nevertheless, the *SEM* derived from the Kuder-Richardson reliabilities is discussed as though it referred to retest reliability (PTM, p. 4l; TM, p. 47). The Kuder-Richardson reliability coefficient, which is largely a measure of item homogeneity, provides no information on short-term fluctuations over time resulting from changing conditions in the individual or in the testing context.

VALIDITY. The treatment of validity (in both PTM and TM) reflects the somewhat outdated tripartite approach to test validation. Although there is an introductory sentence that states, "Establishing the validity of a test is an ongoing process and involves the accumulation of various types of evidence, many of which demonstrate more than one kind of validity" (TM, p. 48), the validity section comprises three distinct parts labelled "Content Validity," "Criterion-Related Validity," and "Construct Validity." There is no systematic integration of the findings of the three parts, nor of these findings with the commendable procedures followed in the planning and development stages of the present OLSAT, as described in earlier sections of the manual.

If test validation is truly regarded as a continuous process, extending from initial planning, through successive test development stages, to analysis of performance on the final form in operational use, there is much that could be said about the validity of the current OLSAT. The test development plan took into account available theoretical and empirical findings about the nature of intelligence, as well as prior information from earlier forms of the Otis-Lennon test series. Both the choice of content areas sampled and the types of available scores followed a hierarchical model of intelligence, wherein constructs of progressively narrower breadth serve to enrich the understanding of individual performance and to provide information appropriate for different testing purposes. The thorough item analysis procedures employed in the national item tryouts, as well as analyses of correlations between test levels, between Verbal and Nonverbal components, with the earlier edition of the OLSAT, with the current Stanford Achievement Test series, and with other measures obtained during the national standardization program should all contribute toward defining and refining the constructs assessed by the present test.

OVERVIEW. Designed to assess broad intellectual functions prerequisite for and developed by successive levels of schooling, the Sixth Edition of this well-established test series was constructed with totally new and thoroughly investigated items. Standardized on large, representative samples of the U.S. school population, it provides a variety of derived scores for separate age and grade groups, as well as sample-free scores comparable across levels. Test construction and evaluation procedures meet the same high technical standards as in the earlier forms, although an integrated, comprehensive discussion of validation procedures and findings would have been welcome.

Review of the Otis-Lennon School Ability Test, Sixth Edition by MARK E. SWERDLIK, Professor of Psychology, Illinois State University, Normal, IL:

The Sixth Edition of the Otis-Lennon School Ability Test (OLSAT) represents the most recent in a series that began over a half century ago with the publication of the Otis Group Intelligence Scale. The Otis Group Intelligence Scale had its roots in the original Binet Scale. The earlier versions of the OLSAT, growing out of the original Otis Group Intelligence Scale, have included the Self-Administering Tests of Mental Ability, Quick Scoring Mental Ability Tests, Otis Mental Ability Test, and in 1979, the fifth revision of the test was renamed the School Ability Test. The use of the term School

Ability to replace Mental Ability was intended to "discharge overinterpretation of the nature of the ability assessed."

A number of changes from the Fifth edition have been implemented. These include all new items; levels designated from A through G; two additional levels that include separate tests for Kindergarten through grade 3; Level D (grade 3) administered as a separate level; and both Verbal and Nonverbal part scores.

The OLSAT series is a multilevel test designed for use in kindergarten through grade 12. The test includes seven levels and one form. Test materials are labeled Form 1. Form 2 is to be developed but is not yet available.

USES OF THE TEST. The major purpose of the OLSAT is to "assess examinees' ability to cope with school learning tasks, to suggest their possible placement for school learning functions, and to evaluate their achievement in relation to the talents they bring to school learning situations." The basis of the OLSAT is that "to learn new things, students must be able to perceive accurately, to recognize and recall what has been perceived, to think logically, to understand relationships, to abstract from a set of particulars, and to apply generalizations to new and different contexts." Specific cautions against any possible misuses of the test such as educational placement based solely on the scores yielded from this group test are not specified.

TEST CONSTRUCTION. Twenty-one different item types are organized into five clusters. The major types of items were used in earlier editions of the series and reflect the objective of a broad sampling of reasoning tasks. For Levels A–C (grades K–2) the cluster of Verbal Comprehension includes the item type Following Directions. Verbal Reasoning includes Aural Reasoning and Arithmetic Reasoning. The cluster of Pictorial Reasoning is composed of Picture Classification, Picture Analogies, and Picture Series (K only). Figural Reasoning includes the item types of Figural Classification, Figural Analogies, Pattern Matrix, and Figural Series. Quantitative Reasoning is not included at grades K–2. Level D does not include all of the item formats of the upper levels but rather item types from both the upper and lower levels. For Levels D–G (grades 3–12), the additional Verbal Comprehension item types include Antonyms, Sentence Completion, and Sentence Arrangement. Verbal Reasoning includes Logical Selection, Word/Letter Matrix, Verbal Analogies, Verbal Classification, and Inference (Levels E–G only). Quantitative Reasoning is briefly sampled (seven items) at grade 3, and more extensively tapped at Levels E–G including item types of Number Series, Numeric Inference, and Number Matrix. Pictorial Reasoning item types are not included at Levels D–G.

Equal numbers of verbal and nonverbal items are included at each level. The classification of an item as verbal or nonverbal "hinges upon whether understanding of the English language is requisite to answering the items."

The OLSAT went through an extensive test development process. This process included 50 free-lance item writers initially submitting a total of 4,000 items. A thorough editorial review process was accomplished.

The test specifications for the OLSAT included an equal number of verbal and nonverbal items within each of the levels and appropriate coverage of the item types specified above. Four parallel forms were constructed at each of the three lower levels, and five parallel forms at each of the four upper levels. Items were eliminated that did not meet specifications.

Word and reading levels at each of the grade levels (Levels D and above) were checked. A final count of number of words at each vocabulary level according to EDL Core Vocabularies is presented. The count indicated that most of the word levels are below the recommended grades for the test level. Although the authors suggest these word levels insure the items are measuring reasoning skills and not reading ability, at each level there are words above the recommended level of the test. In addition, no data are presented relative to the difficulty level of the vocabulary of the items presented orally on the lower levels of the test.

Special attention was also paid to racial, ethnic, and gender balance of the content of the items. This included use of proper names, pronouns, pictures, activities, and implied status. However, no specific information as to criteria used to select items was provided. In addition to new items, each form of the new test included a core of items from corresponding levels of Form R of the Fifth Edition. The purpose of this set of items was to equate the tryout forms to one another and to place the new items and items from the previous edition on a common scale of difficulty.

National item tryout occurred in February 1987, with approximately 35,000 students from 65 schools across the United States. School systems were included in the national item tryout based on a stratified random sampling of socioeconomic status based on a composite measure of the median family income in thousands of dollars plus the percentage of adults in the community over 25 years of age with a high school diploma, average school district enrollment per grade, and geographic region. Specific information relative to the exact composition of the sample used for national tryouts was not provided in the Technical Manual.

Specific attention to eliminating item bias related to gender, socioeconomic status, ethnic, cultural, or regional groups was also a part of the test development process. The initial focus was on a content analysis approach using an extensive editorial review process focusing on whether the items depicted differences in activities, emotions, occupations, or personality attributes. This was accomplished throughout the test development process with the items reviewed and revised by editors and psychologists. In addition, items were reviewed by a separate panel of "prominent educator[s]; several having been outspoken critics of tests as being biased against minorities" representing various minority groups including a representative who was a strong advocate of women's rights and one representing rural areas. Teachers participating in the national item tryout were also asked to note the inappropriateness of any item.

In addition to a focus on the content of the items, statistical analyses for differential performance of various groups were conducted. Separate analyses were conducted for males, females, Blacks, Whites, and Hispanics. Items that showed significant differences for the five groups were targeted to be dropped from the final form. No specific information is provided regarding the number of items that were dropped or revised on the basis of these analyses.

A brief discussion of only one paragraph on the theoretical framework for the OLSAT is presented. The framework presented is that of the Hierarchical Theory of Human Abilities of Vernon and Burt. Spearman's general cognitive ability (g) factor is divided into two broad factors corresponding to "verbal-educational" and "practical-mechanical" abilities with the OLSAT designed to assess only the verbal-educational. These two broad factors are divided into a number of minor groups including verbal or numerical which are further divided into the specific factors or tasks involved in reasoning. The authors point out that the OLSAT does not assess all of the abilities considered to be "verbal-educational" but only a subpart of them. In addition, responding to much of the criticism surrounding IQ tests, the authors indicate that all of the tests are "considered to be measures of learned or developed abilities in the broadest sense. Performance on the samples of tasks included in the tests reflect a complex interaction of genetic and environmental factors influencing the ability to deal with the abstract manipulation of the verbal, numerical, and figural symbol systems of our culture." Although the test user is referred to Vernon's text, *The Structure of Human Abilities*, the brief discussion presented in the Technical Manual does not facilitate or provide a greater understanding on how to interpret the results of the OLSAT. It is unclear how this theory guided test development.

ADMINISTRATION AND SCORING. Levels A–B were created for younger children. The tests at these levels are dictated. Items are organized into three sections in a format that allows examinees to become familiar with the item types and not get discouraged. Items do not increase in difficulty but are spiraled by difficulty levels with harder items cushioned by easier ones. Level C, appropriate for grade 2 students, is identical in format to Levels A and B. However, the first two parts of Level C are self-administered with the remaining parts dictated. Levels D–G are entirely self-administered. Level D includes self-administered classification sections with figural and verbal items that are spiraled by difficulty levels similar to Levels A–C. Other items are arranged in a spiral omnibus format similar to Levels E–G. For Levels E through G, the spiral omnibus format is rotated throughout the test according to item type and difficulty. Items are not grouped.

Both hand- and machine-scoring formats are available. Levels E through G have separate answer sheets, whereas examinees at the lower levels (grades K–3), mark their responses directly in the test booklet for use on reflective scanners. At the lower levels, the spaces in which the examinees place their responses are quite small.

Each level of the OLSAT includes separate Directions for Administering that provides an overview of the OLSAT, general instructions regarding the process of test administration, and specific directions for administering the test. Each level of the hand-scorable test booklets also has an accompanying Class Record that provides a mechanism to summarize class performance on the OLSAT. It facilitates the analysis of the performance of individual students and the class as a whole. The Score Record is located on the back of each of the hand-scorable test booklets and is a form for summarizing each student's performance. It can also be used to provide test results to parents.

For Levels A–C, special markers are available that assist children's focus on the test question the teacher dictates. Test takers move the marker down from row to row in the test booklet. The use of the markers reduces the child's chance of getting lost or distracted.

The OLSAT administration instructions are clear, concise, and easy to follow. No specific training in test administration is required. Directions encourage students not to guess blindly. Although the authors suggest that ample time is given to complete the entire test, no data are presented to support the claim that the test is a power test.

The degree to which coaching and practice results in improvements in test scores is an issue frequently discussed regarding the use of individual and group intelligence tests. No information or data are presented relating to this issue. Practice tests are available for each level of the OLSAT. Each level includes one sample item for each new item type. Test takers are free to ask questions regarding the rationale for the correct responses for the sample items.

The Practice Test assists test takers in becoming familiar with the types of questions that are included on the actual test and the way they are to mark their responses. According to the authors, the practice test will allow students to "learn to recognize row finders, to use a marker, to follow a row across the page from left to right, to mark their answers properly, and to change their answers when necessary." Practice tests must be ordered separately and it is recommended they be administered one week prior to the regular test administration. The practice tests provide more opportunity than the sample items, which are part of the actual OLSAT, to practice test format and become familiar with the testing process thereby reducing or eliminating the effect of test-taking skills on test performance.

Hand-scorable record booklets and scoring keys are available. Directions are presented in sufficient detail and clarity to maximize the accuracy of scoring. Directions are clear and easy to follow.

The OLSAT manuals provide little information on interpretation. This is limiting to the test user and increases the likelihood of inappropriate uses of the test. No specific cautions regarding test use are included in the manual.

TYPES OF SCORES. The OLSAT yields a number of derived scores including School Ability Indexes (SAI), which are normalized standard scores with a mean of 100 and a standard deviation of 16. SAIs for Total scores and verbal and nonverbal part scores are provided. The SAIs seem very much like IQ scores and are somewhat ambiguous as to their meaning. In addition to SAIs, percentile ranks, stanines, and Normal Curve Equivalents useful for interpolating and averaging are provided. The scaled score system of the OLSAT provides a continuous scale that allows comparison of performance of students taking different levels of the test. The scaled scores are appropriate for comparing scores from different levels of the test, for studying changes in performance over time, and for testing out of level.

The manual includes a discussion of the advantages and limitations of each of the scores. According to the authors, the total score represents the best overall indicator of school-learning ability. Although the authors indicated that a higher verbal or nonverbal part score could suggest a student's greater proficiency with one type of content than another, instructional implications of this discrepancy are not addressed in any of the manuals.

NORMATIVE DATA. A separate Norms Booklet is available for each level of the OLSAT. The booklet contains information about the various derived scores yielded by the test, the meanings of these scores, norm tables, and basic statistical data relating to the tests. The instructions for hand scoring are also located in these Norms Booklets. In addition to separate booklets for each level of the test, a Multilevel Norms Booklet is also available. This booklet includes norms for all ages and grades for all levels of the OLSAT. It also provides information about the types and meanings of the various derived scores yielded. This booklet might be especially useful for out-of-level testing.

A Technical Manual provides statistical data and information about the test development and norming process. Needed information about the norm group including the year in which it was collected and sampling design are included. Norms are provided for both age and grade and were developed on the basis of data collected in both the fall and spring standardization programs.

The standardization sample was selected to approximate the school district composition of the United States. The population characteristics of school districts on which the sample was stratified included scoioeconomic status, urbanicity, geographic region, ethnicity, plus Catholic and other nonpublic schools. A stratified random sampling technique was utilized within each state. The spring standardization consisted of "approximately" 175,000 students from 1,000 school districts in 48 states and the District of Columbia with another 11,200 in the equating programs. The fall standardization consisted of "approximately" 135,000 students. The spring sample closely approximated the 1980 census.

Approximately 20% of the spring and 30% of the fall standardization invitations were accepted. No data are provided regarding the frequency and magnitude of sampling bias if a selected school elected not to participate in the standardization and a second, third, or fourth school was selected as a replacement.

The authors state that a Verbal/Nonverbal score difference "may . . . be indicative of some student's greater proficiency with one type of content than with the other." They go on to say that because students' ability to learn in the educational setting is dependent upon proficiency in both verbal and nonverbal reasoning abilities, it is recommended that the Total Score is the best overall indicator of a student's learning ability. The manual does not include an adequate explanation of the meaning of the verbal and nonverbal part scores.

RELIABILITY. Internal consistency estimates (Kuder-Richardson Formula 20 and 21) of reliability are presented for both age and grade. The estimates were calculated on the large number of cases included in the standardization sample. Raw score Standard Errors of Estimate and means and standard deviations are provided for the Total, Verbal, and Nonverbal scores, and for the clusters across all levels of the OLSAT. The authors also explain the meaning of the standard error of measurement. For all scores, internal consistency estimates of reliability for the Total, Verbal, and Nonverbal scores range from the low .70s to low .90s across all grade levels suggesting the OLSAT is an internally consistent and homogeneous measure of general ability. The authors point out that, as expected, due to the fewer number of test items in the clusters as compared to the other scores, the reliability estimates for these clusters are lower with one as low as .24 and some in the .60s. No estimates of the stability of scores are provided.

VALIDITY. Separate sections of the Technical Manual are devoted to the content, criterion-related, and construct validity evidence for the OLSAT.

Overall, the amount of validity data presented in the Technical Manual is quite adequate. However, validity evidence for the different uses of the OLSAT and for the interpretation of verbal/nonverbal differences are not specifically presented. These deficiencies deserve attention.

SUMMARY OF CONCERNS. Despite many positive features, the OLSAT developers should attend to continuing improvement of the instrument.

1. Although plans call for the availability of alternate forms for the Sixth Edition, none are available at the time of publication.

2. The levels administered orally (Levels A and B and part of C) can be considered qualitatively different from the other levels because of the content of the items and the nature of the tasks are different. The orally administered items take more time to administer and must be given in more than one sitting. Test performance on these levels can also be influenced by the variations in the timing and fluency of the speech by the examiner. These issues were not addressed by the authors.

3. Satisfactory internal consistency reliability data are presented but no data relating to the stability of OLSAT scores are reported.

4. Standard Errors of Measurement are provided to aid in interpretation of scores. However, differences in SEMs based on ability level are not provided.

5. Limited information is presented on what the OLSAT actually measures, and the instructional relevance of the verbal and nonverbal part scores are not discussed. Although validity data are presented that suggest the OLSAT measures similar abilities to other group-administered achievement tests, it is unclear what unique aspects are captured by the OLSAT.

6. Cautions about possible misuse of test scores or overinterpretation of the test results are also not provided.

If the test user accepts the limitations associated with group-administered school ability tests and accepts its use as only a screening instrument, the OLSAT represents a technically adequate test with a variety of strengths.

[275]
PACS Pictures: Language Elicitation Materials.

Purpose: "To elicit data for the phonological assessment of child speech."
Population: Ages 3–6.
Publication Date: 1987.
Scores: 3 evaluations: Phoneme Realizations, Cluster Realizations, Phonotactic Possibilities: Contrastive Analysis.
Administration: Individual.
Levels: 2 word lists: Word List I (including EAT words), Word List II.
Price Data, 1989: £43.15 per complete kit including 10 record booklets, picture book, and manual (25 pages); £11.80 per 10 record booklets; £7.50 per manual.
Time: (30–45) minutes.
Comments: Includes the 41 words of the Edinburgh Articulation Test (EAT); 200 words.
Authors: Pamela Grunwell with Grimsby Health Authority, Department of Speech Therapy.
Publisher: NFER-Nelson Publishing Co., Ltd. [England].

Review of the PACS Pictures: Language Elicitation Materials by REBECCA J. McCAULEY, Assistant Professor of Communication Science and Disorders, University of Vermont, Burlington, VT:

The PACS Pictures: Language Elicitation Materials is designed to elicit a "spontaneous and representative speech sample" from children ages 3:0 to 6:0 primarily for use in phonological assessment and, secondarily, for use in other types of language analyses. The instrument is recommended for use with the Phonological Assessment of Child Speech (PACS; 10:284) (Grunwell, 1985). The authors emphasize that these materials are not to be considered an articulation test and thus they state that users need not elicit all of the 200 words explicitly targeted by the pictures nor be constrained to elicit *just* those 200 words.

The instrument includes a manual, a 20-plate Picture Book based on 200 words, and preprinted data sheets. The 200 words have been grouped into two word lists: Word List I, a basic list that includes words taken from the Edinburgh Articulation Test (Anthony, Bogle, Ingram, & McIsaac, 1971), and Word List II, a parallel list that completes the recommended 200-word sample. Words were selected so that multiple tokens of commonly used sound classes, syllable structures, and sound sequences are elicited.

ADMINISTRATION AND INTERPRETATION. Use of the instrument is expected to involve two 30- to 45-minute individual sessions. The authors indicate that there are "no prescribed administrative procedures," but strongly recommend elicitation of spontaneous, rather than imitated, productions in order to obtain a sample representative of a child's habitual production patterns. The instrument is intended equally for use in the elicitation of picture-naming, picture description, and narrative samples. Specific elicitation strategies are described for some target words.

Responses are to be repeated by the examiner to facilitate later transcription, audio-recorded, and transcribed on-site using a narrow phonetic transcription, which is to be checked against the recording as soon as possible after the elicitation session. Although the data sheets facilitate examination of phoneme and cluster production at each syllable and word position, several tables must be consulted in order to examine the use of specific phonological processes in targeted words. In general, directions for scoring and interpretation will probably be most easily followed by users familiar with the PACS.

INSTRUMENT DEVELOPMENT. The elicitation materials were designed initially for use with children with developmental language learning problems. However, the single "validation" study reported for the elicitation materials used a nonclinical population in what might more appropriately have been termed an "item tryout." A sample of 20 children (10 boys and 10 girls) for each 6-month age interval from age 3 years to 5 years, 11 months was studied. The children were drawn from a variety of schools and nurseries in Grimsby, England. Responses were examined to determine the extent to which the children were familiar with targeted words, produced those words in response to PACS illustrations, and produced speech samples of sufficient size to be clinically useful. Word lists and illustrations were revised based on the results of this study. For example, illustrations were modified for several words that were elicited from fewer than 50% of the children.

Adult phonemic representations and syllable structures provided on response sheets are those of a speaker of a "non-rhotic, Southern British accent." Nonetheless, it appears that most of the target words and materials—with a few exceptions (for example, "pram" and "caravan")—can readily be used for speakers of other English dialects if response sheets are appropriately adapted.

RELIABILITY, VALIDITY, AND NORMS. The data suggesting this instrument's validity for the elicitation of "spontaneous and representative speech sample" consist almost solely of descriptions of the instrument's development and content. Neither normative data nor empirical data concerning reliability and validity are provided in the manual. Although the instrument appears to be an "unstructured behavior sample" to which the *Standards for Educational and Psychological Testing* (American Educational Research Association, American Psychological Association, & National Council on Measurement in Education, 1985) are often less rigorously applied, increased attention to those standards would contribute greatly to the quality of measurement in the area of developmental articulation-phonologic disorders. In its current form, this instrument might best be used experimentally.

REVIEWER'S REFERENCES

Anthony, A., Bogle, D., Ingram, T. T. S., & McIsaac, M. W. (1971). Edinburgh Articulation Test. Edinburgh: Churchill Livingstone.

American Educational Research Association, American Psychological Association, & National Council on Measurement in Education. (1985). *Standards for educational and psychological testing.* Washington, DC: American Psychological Association, Inc.

Grunwell, P. (1985). Phonological Assessment of Child Speech (PACS). Windsor: NFER-Nelson Publishing Co.

[276]
P.A.R. Admissions Test.

Purpose: To identify strengths and weaknesses of individual students in basic academic skills and other content areas and to provide a self esteem measure.

Population: Students ages 17 and over.

Publication Date: 1987–91.

Administration: Individual or group.

Tests, 3: Aptitude, Self-Esteem, Counseling Questionnaire.

Price Data: Available from publisher.

Foreign Language Edition: Spanish translation available.

Comments: Test booklet title for Self-Esteem Test is Personal Inventory; Counseling Questionnaire includes questions for use in interviewing failing or potential drop-out students.

Authors: Carol A. Long.

Publisher: P.A.R. Educational Publishers, Inc.

a) APTITUDE TEST, ALTERNATE FORM.

Scores: 6 basic skill scores (Identification of Facts and Terms, Reading, Writing, Computation, Problem Solving, Total).

Time: (45-50) minutes.

Comments: Equivalent Form B also available.

b) SELF-ESTEEM TEST.

Scores: Total Self-Esteem score only.

Time: (10-15) minutes.

Comments: Test booklet title is Personal Inventory.

c) COUNSELING QUESTIONNAIRE.

Scores: Item scores only.

Administration: Individual.

Time: Administration time not reported.

Comments: Questions for use in interviewing failing or potential drop-out students.

[The following review is based on materials received by the reviewer through January 1990.—Ed.]

Review of the P.A.R. Admissions Test by FREDERICK G. BROWN, Professor of Psychology, Iowa State University, Ames, IA:

The P.A.R. Admissions Test (formerly the Ability-to-Benefit Admissions Test) is a "screening instrument to identify the basic skill strengths and weaknesses" (manual, p. 3) of students attending proprietary schools. The test was designed to measure "functional skills that are relevant to everyday living" (p. 3). Accompanying the ability test are a self-esteem test (the Personal Inventory) and a counseling questionnaire.

P.A.R. ADMISSIONS TEST. The test items focus on five skills: Identification of Facts and Terms, Reading, Writing, Computation, and Problem Solving. The items use content and skills involved in daily living—for example, filling out a job application, reading a train schedule, and computing the number of calories in a meal. The process of developing and selecting the items, however, is described only briefly and incompletely in the manual. Adequate item statistics are not presented. The only item data included are the percentages of students in one ad hoc sample who selected each alternative to each question. These data indicate that many items are quite easy; 7 of the 40 items were answered correctly by over 90% of the sample. A total of 15 items were answered correctly by over 80% of the sample. No item discrimination indices or data on differential item functioning are presented, but the manual states that the items were reviewed for bias by an expert in this area.

KR21 reliability coefficients of .86 for total scores are reported for each of two samples (but the reliability for one sample is listed as .86 in one place and .87 in another). The manual states these reliabilities probably are underestimates due to the homogeneous nature of the samples. The data, however, suggest that the samples were relatively heterogeneous (the standard deviations were 7.4 and 5.5 points). No reliabilities are reported for the skill area scores. One also wonders why KR21 was used when item difficulties varied widely (from .29 to .97) across the items.

The manual states that content validity is one of the most important types of validity evidence for a test, yet no data or other supporting evidence are presented. The manual credits the American College Testing Program (ACT) with developing a prior version of the current test and states that studies by ACT showed that "all items . . . were meaningfully related to the other [sic]" (p. 24). The one criterion-related study reported showed $r =$ .24 with a criterion of grades in vocational curricula. (Other information, not in the manual, indicates that at least one other criterion-related study has been completed.)

Although the manual states the test was standardized on a national cross section of the proprietary school population, the normative data are based on a sample of 813 students from 16 proprietary schools, with no evidence that these schools were representative of proprietary schools across the United States. More disturbing, scores on each skill area (e.g., Reading, Writing) are converted to performance levels (definite need for more study and extra help, need for study and review, may need very little review) with no empirical or other support for these classifications. Categories (e.g., recommended for regular curriculum, recommended for probably tutoring and/or remedial classes, recommended for admission denial) also are suggested for total scores, again with no empirical support.

There are other problems. For example, the test is described as having a 50-minute time limit, but the test takers are not told about the time limit; "percentile" is used in several tables to refer to percentages; and there are discrepancies when the same statistic is reported more than once. Most seriously, a number of the statements made in the manual (e.g., the test was standardized on a national cross-section of proprietary school students, and there is "strong evidence for excellent reliability and validity as verified by empirical research" [p. 30]) are not supported by the data reported in the manual.

PERSONAL INVENTORY. The test publisher stresses that high self-esteem is needed for academic success. Thus, a 20-item self-report self-esteem inventory is included with the admissions test. However, no evidence is presented to support the contention that the inventory measures self-esteem. Only three sorts of data are given: the average score of several groups of the inventory, a table showing the number of students at each of five schools who endorsed each statement, and the reliability of the inventory. (The table, however, is for an inventory with 25 items and the Personal Inventory has only 20 items. No explanation is given of this discrepancy.) In short, there is no evidence to support the claim the Personal Inventory is a valid measure of self-esteem.

COUNSELING QUESTIONNAIRE. The purpose for this six-question form appears to be as documentation of an attempt to help students who are having academic trouble. The questions are not neutral. It is difficult to ascertain how the student's best interests are served by this questionnaire. Consider several of the questions: "Based on your strengths as we know them from your entrance tests, would you be willing to delay your decision to drop out for another month?" and "Given the fact that it is clear from your entrance tests that you do have the ability and motivation to complete our program, is there anything you can suggest that we haven't done that we might do to enable you to graduate?"

SUMMARY. The ideas underlying this testing program—that students who attend proprietary schools, many of whom have not had highly successful prior educational experiences, need "real life" skills, and that these students often lack academic motivation and self-esteem—are reasonable. However, in spite of the statements in the test manual, there is far from sufficient evidence that these tests measure the skills and personality attributes claimed or that they can validly and appropriately be used in the manner suggested.

[The following review is based on materials received by the reviewer through August 1990.—Ed.]

Review of the P.A.R. Admissions Test by GEOFFREY F. SCHULTZ, Associate Professor of Educational Psychology and Special Education, Indiana University-Northwest, Gary, IN:

The P.A.R. Admissions Test (PAR) has been used for various purposes by different developers and publishers during the last 20 years. In that time, the test has evolved from being an aptitude measure of functional literacy to its current proposed use as a screening test of basic skill achievement for postsecondary institutions that offer technical and vocational training programs. Surprisingly, despite being declared an invalid measure of literacy and basic skill competency by its original developers 15 years ago, this test had continued to be marketed and sold under various titles.

The PAR was developed initially as an aptitude test called the Adult Performance Level Test (APL) which was commissioned by the U.S. Office of Education in 1971. After being field tested and extensively researched, the APL was ultimately determined to be an invalid measure of adult functional literacy by the Adult Performance Level Project at the University of Texas in Austin. Shortly thereafter, in 1976, the APL project entered into an agreement with the American College Testing (ACT) program for further study and possible use of the test as part of their college admission testing program. The ACT program later determined the APL showed no significant correlation with college success and allowed the test to pass into the public domain due to serious concerns over its validity. Fearing unauthorized and unscrupulous use of the APL, the Adult Performance Level Project at the University of Texas attempted to reclaim the copyright of the instrument, but this attempt proved to be unsuccessful.

The APL reappeared in 1987 as the Ability-To-Benefit Test (ATB) published by P.A.R. Inc. in Providence, Rhode Island. Under the new name, the old APL remained essentially intact but now included a self-esteem measure and a background questionnaire. The test was marketed as a "screening and diagnostic" test for "ability-to-benefit" students identified to be without a high school diploma. The additional components and the renaming of the test suggest an attempt to capitalize on what was then newly passed federal legislation mandating a comprehensive assessment format be used in the identification of basic skill competency in students admitted to postsecondary institutions offering specific job training programs (Federal Guidelines 668.6; Student Assistance General Provision, effective June 3, 1987).

Needless to say, it appeared to some that a test that had been found to be an invalid measure of functional literacy was now being marketed as an appropriate assessment of basic skill competency (Cates & White, 1987; Schrank, 1990). No doubt, in response to the serious validity concerns being raised about the ATB, the publishers at P.A.R. Inc. reissued the ATB in 1989 under another name—the P.A.R. Admissions Test. An updated user manual accompanied this version and defined the instrument to be *only* a screening test of basic skill competency. Included in the new manual was a criterion-related validity study which attempted to establish the PAR for use by technical training schools. A year later, the user manual was again reissued with the 1990 version including still another criterion-related study involving cosmetology schools. This review will focus on the 1990 version of the P.A.R. Admissions Test.

ADMINISTRATION AND SCORING. The publisher claims the test is simple to give and that no skills in the area of testing are necessary in the administration and scoring of this instrument. The PAR may be given individually or in groups except for a counseling questionnaire (individual only). The basic skill section of the test is timed, taking 50 minutes to administer, whereas the self-esteem portion is untimed. There are 40 multiple-choice items on the basic skill section and each question is identified as one of five basic skill areas: (*a*) Identification of Facts and Terms, (*b*) Reading, (*c*) Writing, (*d*) Math Computation, and (*e*) Problem Solving. No penalty for guessing is indicated for the basic skill component. The self-esteem section consists of 20 items with the manual proposing that a respondent with a high score can overcome academic shortcomings. An 8-question background information questionnaire is also included.

Using a hand-scoring master, the basic skill and self-esteem sections yield raw score data which the publisher breaks down into three performance levels: (1) low, (2) average, and (3) high. The prescribed cutoffs are derived from two validation studies conducted by the publisher. However, the publisher points out that the recommended cutoffs are offered only as guidelines and suggests the users establish independent norms for their own particular student populations and schools.

NORMS. The manual provides information on two standardization samples. The first group included about 500 students from a "national cross-section" of postsecondary technical training schools. Raw score means on the basic skill and self-esteem measures are reported for various age groups, ethnic backgrounds, socioeconomic levels, etc. The publisher does not present information about this group in a manner that allows for easy interpretation. No standard score formats are used, as performance is reported only in raw score format and percentages. In addition, given that the number of schools contributing to the sample is only six, and that one school contributed nearly half the students present in the total sample, it is doubtful the norms are representative, as the publishers claim, of the rural, suburban, and urban backgrounds of the different geographical areas of the country.

The second norm sample included approximately 400 students from 14 cosmetology schools. This population does appear to be more representative. However, the presentation of norm information for this group also has similar problems as those mentioned above. Raw scores are inappropriately presented in rank order without using an appropriate standard score format that allows for easy interpretation. Moreover, each raw score is accompanied by cumulative percentages.

This reviewer would also like to point out the publisher should present norm-referenced data clearly and in a prominent place in the user manual. What normative information is given is presented in very difficult to read tables that are found in the various discussions of test validity. Additionally, description and explanation of these sampling data are very poorly organized and written. Moreover, the publisher's particular presentation and use of raw score means as evidence of criterion-related validity is both confused and incorrect—especially because no meaningful criterion to judge these scores is ever firmly established. See further discussion of test validity below.

RELIABILITY. Information on the reliability of the test is minimal as well as questionable. Two KR 21 internal consistency coefficients are reported for the basic aptitude skills ($r = .86$) and self-esteem ($r = .95$) measures. Though reasonably high, the basic skill measure of reliability is probably misleading given that internal consistency coefficients tend to be inflated for speeded tests. In order for this reliability measure to be considered accurate, the publisher must include evidence indicating that speed of work is a negligible factor in successful performance on this essential portion of the test. On the other hand, if speed is integral or believed important to successful performance on this component, test-retest measures of reliability should also be presented.

CONTENT VALIDITY. This reviewer strongly questions the content validity of the test to measure basic skills competency in terms of the five domains identified in the user manual. A careful examination of content indicates that every item requires that the student be able to read at a reasonably high comprehension level. Because the test requires the student work independently, this reading requirement confounds the instrument's ability to measure validly identification of math facts, computation, and problem solving skills. At the same time, the reviewer questions how the test could possibly be a valid measure of basic writing skill given the content and nature of items used. For example, two items indicated in the manual to be measures of writing skill ask the student, given four choices, to identify the appropriate way information should be presented on an application. None of the items identified to be measuring writing skill ever require that the respondent demonstrate this basic skill.

The self-esteem section of the test is also a concern. Careful examination of these items raises questions as to whether they actually measure self-esteem. Most items appear to be measuring the general disposition of the respondent as can be seen in the yes-no questions, "I'm easy to be with" and "I'm very often in a good mood." Moreover, the claim made by the publisher that high self-esteem can easily overcome academic shortcomings is, at best, misinformed.

CRITERION-RELATED VALIDITY. Despite considerable efforts made by the PAR publisher, the criterion-related validity of the test is not clearly established. The publisher has conducted two studies that have attempted to establish both concurrent and predictive validity of the basic skill component of the instrument.

The first study attempted to correlate basic skill scores on the P.A.R. with actual classroom performance of students as measured by grade point average. A total of 12 technical training schools provided both basic skill scores and corresponding grade information. The publisher notes, however, that insufficient return on classroom performance data prevented the reporting of any validity coefficients between PAR scores and grades. Additionally, the study attempted to establish predictive validity for the test by comparing PAR mean basic skill scores between dropouts and graduates of the schools involved in the study. The results of this investigation are also reported by the publisher to be uninterpretable because many students identified as dropouts left school for reasons not related to their academic success.

The second validity study is also very difficult to interpret. Using approximately 400 students from 14 cosmetology schools, basic skill mean scores of "enrolled" and "graduated" students were compared. Though the PAR basic skill scores for graduates appear to be higher than those of enrolled students, the conclusions to be drawn from this result are not clear—especially because the differences are not reported to be significant. More importantly, it does not necessarily follow that students who are "enrolled" are less skilled than students who have graduated; it would have made more sense to make comparisons between "dropped" students and "graduates." Moreover, the publisher's attempt to explain these differences adds to the confusion—especially when the claim is made that the differences between the two groups represent "evidence of the efficacy of the test for predicting success of cosmetology students."

A concurrent validity coefficient ($r = .317$) establishing relationship between grades and PAR basic skill scores of students in the cosmetology school is also mentioned. However, no discussion of the statistical significance (if any) of this validity coefficient is given.

CONSTRUCT VALIDITY. The PAR is constructed to measure two factors thought to be significant in determining success in postsecondary technical training programs: (a) basic skill competency, and (b) self-esteem. Although these two factors appear to provide a reasonable operational construct to begin defining and differentiating successful students in these kinds of educational settings, the necessary content and criterion-related validation of the overall instrument is lacking. Additionally, no cited documentation of empirical validation via factor analysis or cluster analysis is reported for either the basic skills or self-esteem sections of the test. This lack of empirical validation is particularly troublesome when one attempts to determine the rationale for assigning particular items to the five skill areas identified in the basic skill portion of the test.

SUMMARY. The P.A.R. Admissions Test cannot be recommended for its proposed use as a screening instrument for postsecondary technical and vocational training schools. The basic skill portion of the test has yet to be determined as reliable for the purposes intended; therefore, the validity of the overall test is immediately in question. Additionally, given the problems noted in the content of both sections of the test, it appears the test as constructed cannot be considered a valid measure of either basic skill competency or self-esteem. At the same time, the attempts to validate the basic skill portion of the test as a criterion measure for determining success in technical training or cosmetology schools are inconclusive and, therefore, further discourage the use of this test as an effective screening tool for these kinds of institutions.

REVIEWER'S REFERENCES

Cates, J., & White, S. (1987). *The people speak: A call for action and accountability.* Austin, TX: Adult Functional Literacy Project, University of Texas, College of Education.
Schrank, F. A. (1990). Ability-To-Benefit Admissions Test. In D. J. Keyser & R. C. Sweetland (Eds.), *Test Critiques* (Vol. 8, pp. 1-6). Austin, TX: PRO-ED, Inc.

[277]
Parent Behavior Form.

Purpose: "Designed to assess . . . dimensions of perceived parent behavior."
Population: Parents; ratings by ages 8–12, 12–18 and adults.
Publication Date: No date.
Acronym: PBF.
Scores, 15: Acceptance, Active Involvement, Egalitarianism, Cognitive Independence, Cognitive-Understanding, Cognitive Competence, Lax Control, Conformity, Achievement, Strict Control, Punitive Control, Hostile Control, Rejection, Inconsistent Responding, Social Desirability.
Administration: Group or individual.
Forms, 5: PBF, PBF-S, PBF Elementary, Form A, Form C-B.
Price Data: Available from publisher.
Time: Administration time not reported.
Comments: Ratings of parent behavior by their children; form for self-rating available.
Authors: Leonard Worell and Judith Worell.
Publisher: Judith Worell, Ph.D..

TEST REFERENCES

1. Schwarz, J. C., & Mearns, J. (1989). Assessing parental childrearing behaviors: A comparison of parent, child, and aggregate ratings from two instruments. *Journal of Research in Personality, 23,* 450-468.

Review of the Parent Behavior Form by JoELLEN V. CARLSON, Director of Testing Standards, New York Stock Exchange, New York, NY:

The Parent Behavior Form (PBF) may provide the basis for some potentially useful instruments, but fundamental information is missing. No manual, technical summary, or directions for administration are provided. The materials require cross-referencing without direction and are inconsistently labeled, incompletely labeled, or not labeled at all.

The PBF includes 13 main scales and 2 response-set scales, each containing nine items. Each item describes a parent behavior, for which the respondent indicates whether it is "like," "somewhat like," or "unlike" the parent. The materials are so poorly organized that a good bit of sorting is required to determine what constitutes which form. Two forms are labeled, "Parent Behavior Form, PBF," but one includes 135 items and the other 117 items for each parent. Apparently the form with 117 items excludes the response-set scales and is the short form, PBF-S. The authors say these forms are suitable for ages 12–18 and "adults recalling . . . behavior of their parents . . . when they were 'about age 16,'" but the only "norms" are for university sophomores.

There are two forms intended for children 8–12 years of age: the PBF-E, which contains "the same statements in simplified language," and the PBF-C-B, which contains 10 of the children's scales. The PBF-A, intended for parents reporting on their own behaviors, includes the same statements revised for first person. No data are labeled for the children's or adult forms, although the authors say that the 13 main scales of the PBF-E have been "cross-validated on this age group for readability." A page with no explanation other than the heading, "Appendix 0: Means and Standard Deviations for Mothers and Fathers," could include statistics for one of the children's or adult forms, as sample sizes indicated differ from those previously reported. These figures are uninterpretable; one table refers to its entries as both "mean scale scores" and "raw scale scores."

Some unreported number of items were administered to 490 male and female students, apparently from a single university, and data on items with correlations of at least +.35 with at least two scales of the Jackson Personality Research Form (PRF) were analyzed using a cluster analysis. The nine items that loaded highest on each cluster were considered a scale, and the scales were the 13 clusters that had the highest correlations with the "warmth" cluster. The warmth factor is described later. The authors indicate that they "resubmit(ted) scales for normative data, reliability, validity" (i.e., reanalyzed the same data) and provide raw score–standard score and raw score–percentile rank correspondence tables based on administration to sophomores at a single university.

No other information is given about demographic characteristics of samples, sample selection procedures, or circumstances of administration. Besides the apparent site restriction, the selection of university sophomores, who are unlikely to be in the primary target age range for the PBF, is questionable. It appears that the same data used in selecting the items were reanalyzed in computing "norms" and reliability coefficients. Given the inappropriateness of the sample and the analyses, all statistics reported are questionable.

Values for Cronbach's alpha are reported for each scale, described as "composite reliabilities . . . averaged across male and female respondents and mothers and fathers," although the authors state that "scale reliabilities vary according to the gender of both respondent and parent being described." Even if these composites were meaningful, high values for measures of internal consistency would be expected from item selection procedures and reanalysis of the same data set. Stability indices based on the responses of appropriately selected samples are definitely needed.

The authors claim support for the existence of three factors, called Warmth, Control, and Cognitive Mediation, and cite values for " r," but do not indicate what these "rs" represent. Because related tables indicate they are based on a "principal components factor analysis following varimax rotation" [sic], it is impossible to determine what the values represent. As evidence of convergent validity, the authors indicate the scales expected to show correlations with "W" (which may be either a

"factor" or a scale, as one scale is labeled "Acceptance" in some places and "Warmth" in others) have positive correlations with W ranging from .46 to .81 and cite the correlations of items with the PRF scales—used as the basis for item *selection*. As evidence of discriminant validity, the authors report that scales expected to show a negative correlation with W do so, citing "moderate to high" negative "loadings" on the Warmth factor ($-.85 \leq r \leq -.35$), and that scales not expected to correlate with W show only "minimal" relationships to W (reporting no values). As evidence of criterion validity, the authors report that these three major factors, not necessarily PBF measures, have been shown to predict cheating behavior, college grades, self-esteem, and other behaviors, but provide no specifics.

Inclusion of the "Inconsistent Responding" and "Social Desirability" scales is a worthwhile effort, but incomplete. There are neither directions for using the Inconsistent Responding scale nor indication of the items included in it. For the Social Desirability scale, item numbers are given and some interpretations (e.g., "A score of 13–26 indicates [the] parent is unusually self-critical") are offered without empirical support. There is no discussion of the relationship between the main scales and the response-set scales or guide to controlling for a response set.

In addition to grammatical and usage errors, the materials contain several objectionable expressions. For example, the directions for responding refer to "your real mother or father," even though the term "real" has long been rejected in reference to a birth parent. "Caretaker," also rejected for its dehumanizing implications, is used in lieu of "caregiver," and "boy child" appears prominently in the materials.

While there is not sufficient evidence of sound developmental procedures or psychometric properties of the PBF to warrant use in a counseling context, the instruments appear to be worthy of further developmental efforts. If results are held anonymous and there are no individual interpretations or consequences, it should be acceptable to use the instruments in research. Work is needed to improve areas of weakness, identify potential applications, and provide data on the soundness and appropriateness of the instruments.

Review of the Parent Behavior Form by STEPHEN OLEJNIK, Professor of Educational Psychology, University of Georgia, Athens, GA:

The Parent Behavior Form (PBF) is a quick and simple assessment tool designed to measure adolescent perceptions. The instrument was not developed with any single theoretical model of parental behavior in mind. Rather, the PBF is a collation of items written to reflect what are believed to be important parental behaviors, based on clinical literature and previous instrumentation. The instrument is easy to use but it has several important limitations.

Although the PBF is intended to be used with adolescents, ages 12 through 18, all test development activities including scale formation, validity, reliability, and normative data are based on samples of college students. There is no reported evidence to support the use of the instrument with middle school or high school populations. Four additional forms of the inventory are available for younger children and adults but even less information is provided for them regarding their psychometric properties.

Evidence for test validity is very limited. The 13 scales that make up the inventory were identified through a cluster analysis procedure with college students as the respondents. There is no indication of a cross-validation study nor a determination of the appropriateness of the scale formation for younger respondents. A factor analysis of the 13 scales revealed three latent factors: Warmth, Control, and Cognitive Mediation. Scales which make up these factors vary slightly depending on the gender of the parent and the gender of the respondent but in general the factor structures appear to be similar.

Construct validity rests on the finding of positive correlations between scales that were predicted to be positively related with the Warmth factor and discriminant validity is based on finding the predicted negative correlations between selected scales and the Warmth factor. Criterion validity is based on the predictive accuracy of the three factors for such measures as sex-role orientation, cheating behavior, grades, and ACT scores. It is not clear why such relations should exist. No attempt seems to have been made to correlate scores on the PBF with other measures of parental behavior. More importantly, comparisons of responses by adolescents from functional and dysfunctional families are not reported. Finally, because the PBF lacks a theoretical framework, no attempt seems to have been given to assess the content validity of the scales. It appears that little external professional judgement was involved in the formation and evaluation of the scales.

The only evidence of reliability reported in the test manual are measures of internal consistency based on coefficient alpha. Although it is stated that reliability estimates vary as a function of respondent gender and parent gender, only the average reliability coefficient is reported for each scale. Because the normative tables and factor structures are reported separately for male and female respondents and by parental gender, the separate reliability coefficients, not the average, should have been reported for each group.

The reliability coefficients that are reported are based on a sample of college students and may not be appropriate for a younger group of respondents.

It is somewhat surprising that estimates of scale stability (test-retest) are not reported. The instrument intends to measure the perceptions of adolescents. As such it would seem important to determine how consistent the responses are over time. With young respondents it might be suspected that answers would vary greatly depending on respondents' most recent experiences with their parents.

The test manual does not provide any guidance regarding how the instrument should be used or what the scores really mean. Although means, standard deviations, standard scores, and percentiles are provided, these data are based on samples of college students. It seems unlikely this information will be useful or appropriate for a younger group of adolescents, especially for those who are not college bound.

The test manual refers to the three factors that comprise the instrument and the authors report these are important parental behavioral constructs as indicated in the clinical literature. It appears, however, that the emphasis is on the separate scales and not the underlying factors because the manual does not provide any guidance as to how the scales should be weighted to form the factor scores.

Test items are short behavioral statements that reflect what a parent actually does. The readability level of these items appears appropriate for an adolescent population. This is a very positive feature of the instrument. Items are presented in two columns and ordered by column. Responses are recorded on a separate sheet consisting of a grid of nine rows and 13 columns. An X is placed in a box corresponding to a *Like, Somewhat Like,* and *Unlike* response. This answer sheet format makes scoring the instrument very easy but there is potential for confusion and possible recording errors because responses are recorded from left to right by row but items are read from top to bottom of each column. If a respondent is not careful, unintended responses could be recorded. Furthermore, spacing is a problem with this answer sheet. The items are placed so close together as to provide a cluttered appearance, which further increases the potential of a recording error.

The most positive features of this instrument are that: It is easy to read, it requires only about 30 minutes to complete, it is machine or hand scorable, and the internal consistency estimates are in an acceptable range. However, the current version of the PBF cannot be recommended for use in counseling contexts. Even in a research setting investigators may have difficulty interpreting the meaning of the scores. The lack of a theoretical framework and extremely limited normative data reduce the usefulness of the instrument significantly. Further developmental work is needed. Specifically, cross-validation of the scale formation and the factor structure is needed. This work must include a sample of younger respondents. Additional evidence of construct validity is essential. And finally, stability estimates, especially for younger respondents, should be obtained.

[278]

Parent Opinion Inventory, Revised Edition.

Purpose: Designed "to provide the school personnel or administrator(s) with the opinions of parents in regard to how they believe the school is meeting the needs of students."
Population: Parents of schoolchildren.
Publication Dates: 1976–88.
Scores: 7 subscales: Parent/School Relations, Instructional Outcomes, School Problems, Program Factors, Student Activities, Support Services, Psychosocial Climate.
Administration: Group.
Parts, 2: A (Likert-scale items), B (open-ended items regarding recommendations).
Price Data, 1991: $4 per 25 inventories (Part A); $3 per 25 inventories (Part B); $3 per 25 machine-scored answer sheets; $3 per manual ('88, 11 pages).
Time: Untimed.
Author: National Study of School Evaluation.
Publisher: National Study of School Evaluation.

[279]

Participative Management Survey.

Purpose: To assess the extent to which a leader provides opportunities and support for employee involvement.
Population: Individuals involved in a leadership capacity with others.
Publication Date: 1988.
Acronym: PMS.
Scores, 5: Basic Creature Comfort, Safety, Belonging, Ego-Status, Actualization.
Administration: Group or individual.
Price Data, 1990: $6.95 per manual (17 pages).
Time: Administration time not reported.
Authors: Jay Hall.
Publisher: Teleometrics International.

[280]

Peabody Individual Achievement Test—Revised.

Purpose: Measure academic achievement.
Population: Grades K–12.
Publication Dates: 1970–89.
Acronym: PIAT-R.
Scores, 9: General Information, Reading Recognition, Reading Comprehension, Total Reading, Mathematics, Spelling, Total Test, Written Expression, Written Language.
Administration: Individual.
Levels: 2 for Written Expression subtest (Level I: Grades K–1; Level II: Grades 2–12).
Price Data, 1990: $185 per complete kit; $52 (1–4) or $48 (5 or more) per 50 record books; $24.50 (1–4) or $23.50 (5 or more) per 50 Written Expression subtest response booklets; $10.75 for Pronunciation Guide cassette; $25 for AGS carrying case; $26.50 per manual ('89, 228 pages).
Time: (50–70) minutes.
Comments: This test (PIAT-R) is a revision of the PIAT (1970), with updated norms, more items, more contemporary item content, and the addition of the Written Expression subtest.
Author: Frederick C. Markwardt, Jr.
Publisher: American Guidance Service.
Cross References: See 9:923 (39 references); see also T3:1769 (67 references); for excerpted reviews by Alex Bannatyne and Barton B. Proger of the original edition, see 8:24 (36 references); see also T2:26 (2 references); for a review by Howard B. Lyman of the original edition, see 7:17.

TEST REFERENCES

1. Ysseldyke, J. E., & Marston, D. (1982). A critical analysis of standardized reading tests. *School Psychology Review*, 11, 257-266.
2. Algozzine, B., & Ysseldyke, J. (1983). Learning disabilities as a subset of school failure: The over-sophistication of a concept. *Exceptional Children*, 50, 242-246.
3. Epstein, M. H., & Cullinan, D. (1983). Academic performance of behaviorally disordered and learning-disabled pupils. *The Journal of Special Education*, 17, 303-307.
4. Walden, T. A., & Ramey, C. T. (1983). Locus of control and academic achievement: Results from a preschool intervention program. *Journal of Educational Psychology*, 75, 347-358.
5. White, M., & Miller, S. R. (1983). Dyslexia: A term in search of a definition. *The Journal of Special Education*, 17, 5-10.
6. Ysseldyke, J., Algozzine, B., & Epps, S. (1983). A logical and empirical analysis of current practice in classifying students as handicapped. *Exceptional Children*, 50, 160-166.
7. Barth, J. T., Macciocchi, S. N., Ranseen, J., Boyd, T., & Mills, G. (1984). The effects of prefontal leucotomy: Neuropsychological findings in long term chronic psychiatric patients. *Clinical Neuropsychology*, 6, 120-123.
8. Bookman, M. O. (1984). Spelling as a cognitive-developmental linguistic process. *Academic Therapy*, 20, 21-32.
9. Cermak, S. A., & Ayres, A. J. (1984). Crossing the body midline in learning-disabled and normal children. *The American Journal of Occupational Therapy*, 38, 35-39.
10. Champion, L., Doughtie, E. B., Johnson, P. J., & McCreary, J. H. (1984). Preliminary investigation into the Rorschach response patterns of children with documented learning disabilities. *Journal of Clinical Psychology*, 40, 329-333.
11. Colligan, R. C., & Bajuniemi, L. E. (1984). Multiple definitions of reading disability: Implications for preschool screening. *Perceptual and Motor Skills*, 59, 467-475.
12. Decker, S. N., & Corley, R. P. (1984). Bannatyne's "genetic dyslexic" subtype: A validation study. *Psychology in the Schools*, 21, 300-304.
13. Eaves, R. C., & Simpson, R. G. (1984). The concurrent validity of the Peabody Individual Achievement Test relative to the KeyMath Diagnostic Arithmetic Test among adolescents. *Psychology in the Schools*, 21, 165-167.
14. Eno, L., & Woehlke, P. (1984). Relationship between grammatical errors on Rotter's Scale and performance on educational tests for students suspected of having learning problems. *Perceptual and Motor Skills*, 58, 75-78.
15. Feagans, L., & Short, E. J. (1984). Developmental differences in the comprehension and production of narratives by reading-disabled and normally achieving children. *Child Development*, 55, 1727-1736.
16. Fox, B., & Routh, D. K. (1984). Phonemic analysis and synthesis as word attack skills: Revisited. *Journal of Educational Psychology*, 76, 1059-1064.
17. Frane, R. E., Clarizio, H. F., & Porter, A. (1984). Diagnostic and prescriptive bias in school psychologists' reports of a learning disabled child. *Journal of Learning Disabilities*, 17, 12-15.
18. Gordon, M., Post, E. M., Crouthamel, C., & Richman, R. A. (1984). Do children with constitutional delay really have more learning problems? *Journal of Learning Disabilities*, 17, 291-293.
19. Hall, R. J., Reeve, R. E., & Zakreski, J. R. (1984). Validity of the Woodcock-Johnson Tests of Achievement for Learning- Disabled Students. *Journal of School Psychology*, 22, 193-200.
20. Haywood, H. C., Burns, S., Arbitman-Smith, R., & Delclos, V. R. (1984). Forward to fundamentals: Learning and the 4th R. *Peabody Journal of Education*, 61 (3), 16-35.

21. Kaufman, A. S. (1984). K-ABC and controversy. *The Journal of Special Education, 18,* 409-444.

22. Lindsey, J. D., & Armstrong, S. W. (1984). Performance of EMR and learning-disabled students on the Brigance, Peabody, and Wide Range Achievement Tests. *American Journal of Mental Deficiency, 89,* 197-201.

23. McKinney, J. D. (1984). The search for subtypes of specific learning disability. *Journal of Learning Disabilities, 17,* 43-50.

24. Naglieri, J. A. (1984). Concurrent and predictive validity of the Kaufman Assessment Battery for Children with a Navajo sample. *Journal of School Psychology, 22,* 373-380.

25. Olson, J., & Midgett, J. (1984). Alternative placements: Does a difference exist in the LD populations? *Journal of Learning Disabilities, 17,* 101-103.

26. Schiller, J. J. (1984). Neuropsychological foundations of spelling and reading difficulty. *Clinical Neuropsychology, 6,* 255-261.

27. Schulte, A., Borich, G. D. (1984). Considerations in the use of difference scores to identify learning-disabled children. *Journal of School Psychology, 22,* 381-390.

28. Tobey, E. A., & Cullen, J. K., Jr. (1984). Temporal integration of tone glides by children with auditory-memory and reading problems. *Journal of Speech and Hearing Research, 27,* 527-533.

29. Wilson, L. R., & Cone, T. (1984). The regression equation method of determining academic discrepancy. *Journal of School Psychology, 22,* 95-110.

30. Connelly, J. B. (1985). Published tests—which ones do special education teachers perceive as useful? *Journal of Special Education, 19,* 149-155.

31. Cooley, E. J., & Ayres, R. (1985). Convergent and discriminant validity of the mental processing scales of the Kaufman Assessment Battery for Children. *Psychology in the Schools, 22,* 373-377.

32. Derr, A. M. (1985). Conservation and mathematics achievement in the learning disabled child. *Journal of Learning Disabilities, 18,* 333-336.

33. Estes, R. E., Hallock, J. E., & Bray, N. M. (1985). Comparison of arithmetic measures with learning disabled students. *Perceptual and Motor Skills, 61,* 711-716.

34. Johnson, S. T., Starnes, W. T., Gregory, D. & Blaylock, A. (1985). Program of assessment, diagnosis, and instruction (PADI): Identifying and nurturing potentially gifted and talented minority students. *Journal of Negro Education, 54,* 416-430.

35. Kerns, K., & Decker, S. N. (1985). Multifactorial assessment of reading disability: Identifying the best predictors. *Perceptual and Motor Skills, 60,* 747-753.

36. LaBuda, M. C., Vogler, G. P., DeFries, J. C., & Fulker, D. W. (1985). Multivariate familial analysis of cognitive measures in the Colorado Family Reading Study. *Multivariate Behavioral Research, 20,* 357-368.

37. Levin, E. K., Zigmond, N., & Birch, J. W. (1985). A follow-up study of 52 learning disabled adolescents. *Journal of Learning Disabilities, 18,* 2-7.

38. Masten, A. S., Morison, P., & Pellegrini, D. S. (1985). A Revised Class Play method of peer assessment. *Developmental Psychology, 21,* 523-533.

39. Naglieri, J. A. (1985). Assessment of mentally retarded children with the Kaufman Assessment Battery for Children. *American Journal of Mental Deficiency, 89,* 367-371.

40. Pellegrini, D. S. (1985). Social cognition and competence in middle childhood. *Child Development, 56,* 256-264.

41. Pennington, B. F., Heaton, R. K., Karzmark, P., Pendleton, M. G., Lehman, R., & Shucard, D. W. (1985). The neuropsychological phenotype in Turner syndrome. *Cortex, 21,* 391-404.

42. Pennington, B. F., vanDoorninck, W. J., McCabe, L. L., McCabe, E. R. B. (1985). Neuropsychological deficits in early treated phenylketonuric children. *American Journal of Mental Deficiency, 89,* 467-474.

43. Sandoval, J., & Lambert, N. M. (1985). Hyperactive and learning disabled children: Who gets help? *The Journal of Special Education, 18,* 495-503.

44. Seitz, V., Rosenbaum, L. K., & Apfel, N. H. (1985). Effects of family support intervention: A ten-year follow-up. *Child Development, 56,* 376-391.

45. Sherman, R. G., Berling, B. S., & Oppenheimer, S. (1985). Increasing community independence for adolescents with spina bifida. *Adolescence, 20,* 1-13.

46. Sinclair, E., Forness, S. R., & Alexson, J. (1985). Psychiatric diagnosis: A study of its relationship to school needs. *Journal of Special Education, 19,* 333-344.

47. Strawser, S., & Weller, C. (1985). Use of adaptive behavior and discrepancy criteria to determine learning disabilities severity subtypes. *Journal of Learning Disabilities, 18,* 205-211.

48. Thackwray, D., Meyers, A., Schleser, R., & Cohen, R. (1985). Achieving generalization with general versus specific self-instructions: Effects on academically deficient children. *Cognitive Therapy and Research, 9,* 297-308.

49. Wagner, S. R. (1985). Handedness and higher mental functions. *Claremont Reading Conference Yearbook, 49,* 258-266.

50. Webster, R. E. (1985). The criterion-related validity of psychoeducational tests for actual reading ability of learning disabled students. *Psychology in the Schools, 22,* 152-159.

51. Caskey, W. E., Jr. (1986). The use of the Peabody Individual Achievement Test and the Woodcock Reading Memory Tests in the diagnosis of a learning disability in reading: A caveat. *Journal of Learning Disabilities, 19,* 336-337.

52. Davis, J. M., Elfenbein, J., Schum, R., & Bentler, R. A. (1986). Effects of mild and moderate hearing impairments on language, educational, and psychosocial behavior of children. *Journal of Speech and Hearing Disorders, 51,* 53-62.

53. Feagans, L., & Appelbaum, M. I. (1986). Validation of language subtypes in learning disabled children. *Journal of Educational Psychology, 78,* 358-364.

54. Huebner, E. S., & Cummings, J. A. (1986). Influence of race and test data ambiguity upon school psychologists' decisions. *School Psychology Review, 15,* 410-417.

55. Marcus, A. M. (1986). Academic achievement in elementary school children of alcoholic mothers. *Journal of Clinical Psychology, 42,* 372-376.

56. Masten, A. S. (1986). Humor and competence in school-aged children. *Child Development, 57,* 461-473.

57. McCue, P. M., Shelly, C., & Goldstein, G. (1986). Intellectual, academic and neuropsychological performance levels in learning disabled adults. *Journal of Learning Disabilities, 19,* 233-236.

58. McRae, S. G. (1986). Sequential-simultaneous processing and reading skills in primary grade children. *Journal of Learning Disabilities, 19,* 509-511.

59. Palisin, H. (1986). Preschool temperament and performance on achievement tests. *Developmental Psychology, 22,* 766-770.

60. Rapport, M. D., Tucker, S. B., DuPaul, G. J., Merlo, M., & Stoner, G. (1986). Hyperactivity and frustration: The influence of control over and size of rewards in delaying gratification. *Journal of Abnormal Child Psychology, 14,* 191-204.

61. Shaughnessy, M. F., & Evans, R. (1986). Word/world knowledge: Prediction of college GPA. *Psychological Reports, 59,* 1147-1150.

62. Sinclair, E., & Alexson, J. (1986). Factor analysis and discriminant analysis of psychoeducational report contents. *Journal of School Psychology, 24,* 363-371.

63. Speece, D. L., McKinney, J. D., & Appelbaum, M. I. (1986). Longitudinal development of conservation skills in learning disabled children. *Journal of Learning Disabilities, 19,* 302-307.

64. Swanson, H. L. (1986). Do semantic memory deficiencies underlie learning disabled readers' encoding processes? *Journal of Experimental Child Psychology, 41,* 461-488.

65. Westendorp, F., Brink, K. L., Roberson, M. K., & Ortiz, I. E. (1986). Variables which differentiate placement of adolescents into juvenile justice or mental health systems. *Adolescence, 21,* 23-37.

66. Willows, D. M., & Ryan, E. B. (1986). The development of grammatical sensitivity and its relationship to early reading achievement. *Reading Research Quarterly, 21,* 253-266.

67. Ackerman, P. T., McGrew, M. J., & Dykman, R. A. (1987). A profile of male and female applicants for a special college program for learning-disabled students. *Journal of Clinical Psychology, 43,* 67-78.

68. Beden, I., Rohr, L., & Ellsworth, R. (1987). A public school validation study of the achievement sections of the Woodcock-Johnson Psycho-educational Battery with learning disabled students. *Educational and Psychological Measurement, 47* (3), 711-717.

69. Blount, R. L., Finch, A. J., Jr., Saylor, C. F., Wolfe, V. V., Pallmeyer, T. P., McIntosh, J., Griffin, J. M., & Carek, D. J. (1987). Locus of control and achievement in child psychiatric inpatients. *Journal of Abnormal Child Psychology, 15,* 175-179.

70. Cooper, J. A., & Flowers, C. R. (1987). Children with a history of acquired aphasia: Residual language and academic impairments. *Journal of Speech and Hearing Disorders, 52,* 251-262.

71. Curry, J. F., Anderson, D. R., Zitlin, M., & Guise, G. (1987). Validity of academic achievement measures with emotionally handicapped children. *Journal of Clinical Child Psychology, 16,* 51-56.

72. Dorman, C. (1987). Verbal, perceptual, and intellectual factors associated with reading achievement in adolescents with cerebral palsy. *Perceptual and Motor Skills, 64,* 671-678.

73. Friedman, D. E., & Medway, F. J. (1987). Effects of varying performance sets and outcome on the expectations, attributions, and persistence of boys with learning disabilities. *Journal of Learning Disabilities, 20,* 312-316.

74. Holcomb, W. R., Hardesty, R. A., Adams, N. A., & Ponder, H. M. (1987). WISC-R types of learning disabilities: A profile analysis with cross-validation. *Journal of Learning Disabilities, 20,* 369-373.

75. Jones, K. M., Torgesen, J. K., & Sexton, M. A. (1987). Using computer guided practice to increase decoding fluency in learning disabled children: A study using the Hint and Hunt I Program. *Journal of Learning Disabilities, 20,* 122-128.

76. LaBuda, M. C., DeFries, J. C., & Fulker, D. W. (1987). Genetic and environmental covariance structures among WISC-R subtests: A twin study. *Intelligence, 11,* 233-244.

77. Lovett, M. W. (1987). A developmental approach to reading disability: Accuracy and speed criteria of normal and deficient reading skill. *Child Development, 58,* 234-260.

78. Lytton, H., Maunula, S. R., & Watts, D. (1987). Moral judgements and reported moral acts: A tenuous relationship. *The Alberta Journal of Educational Research, 33,* 150-162.

79. Lytton, H., Watts, D., & Dunn, B. E. (1987). Twin-singleton differences in verbal ability: Where do they stem from? *Intelligence, 11,* 359-369.

80. Monastra, V. J., Kovaleski, M., & Kurkjian, J. (1987). Neuropsychological deficit and learning disability in children with psychiatric disorders: A preliminary report. *Psychological Reports, 61,* 110.

81. Pellegrini, D. S., Masten, A. S., Garmezy, N., & Ferrarese, M. J. (1987). Correlates of social and academic competence in middle childhood. *Journal of Child Psychology and Psychiatry and Allied Disciplines, 28,* 699-714.

82. Simpson, R. G., & Halpin, G. (1987). The effects of altering the ceiling criterion on the passage comprehension test of the Woodcock Reading Mastery Test. *Educational and Psychological Measurement, 47* (1), 215-221.

83. Bennett, D. E., & Clarizio, H. F. (1988). A comparison of methods for calculating a severe discrepancy. *Journal of School Psychology, 26,* 359-369.

84. Good, R. H., III, & Salvia, J. (1988). Curriculum bias in published, norm-referenced reading tests: Demonstrable effects. *School Psychology Review, 17,* 51-60.

85. Ho, H., Gilger, J. W., & Decker, S. N. (1988). A twin study of Bannatyne's "genetic dyslexic" subtype. *Journal of Child Psychology and Psychiatry and Allied Disciplines, 29,* 63-72.

86. Huebner, E. S. (1988). Bias in teachers' special education decisions as a function of test score reporting format. *The Journal of Educational Research, 81,* 217-220.

87. La Buda, M. C., & DeFries, J. C. (1988). Cognitive abilities in children with reading disabilities and controls: A follow-up study. *Journal of Learning Disabilities, 21,* 562-566.

88. Levinson, H. N. (1988). The cerebellar-vestibular basis of learning disabilities in children, adolescents and adults: Hypothesis and study. *Perceptual and Motor Skills, 67,* 983-1006.

89. Martin, R. P., Drew, K. D., Gaddis, L. R., & Moseley, M. (1988). Prediction of elementary school achievement from preschool temperament: Three studies. *School Psychology Review, 17,* 125-137.

90. McConaughy, S. H., Achenbach, T. M., & Gent, C. L. (1988). Multiaxial empirically based assessment: Parent, teacher, observational, cognitive, and personality correlates of child behavior profile types for 6- to 11-year-old boys. *Journal of Abnormal Child Psychology, 16,* 485-509.

91. McCurdy, B. L., & Shapiro, E. S. (1988). Self-observation and the reduction of inappropriate classroom behavior. *Journal of School Psychology, 26,* 371-378.

92. Moses, J. A., & Maruish, M. E. (1988). A critical review of the Luria-Nebraska Neuropsychological Battery literature: III. Concurrent validity. *The International Journal of Clinical Neuropsychology, 10,* 12-19.

93. Phelps, L., Bell, M. C., & Scott, M. J. (1988). Correlations between the Stanford-Binet: Fourth Edition and the WISC-R with a learning disabled population. *Psychology in the Schools, 25,* 380-382.

94. Pillen, B. L., Jason, L. A., & Olson, T. (1988). The effects of gender on the transition of transfer students into a new school. *Psychology in the Schools, 25,* 187-194.

95. Rivers, D., & Smith, T. E. C. (1988). Traditional eligibility criteria for identifying students as specific learning disabled. *Journal of Learning Disabilities, 21,* 642-644.

96. Simpson, R. G., & Buckhalt, J. A. (1988). Estimating general intellectual functioning in adolescents with the PPVT-R and PIAT using a multiple regression approach. *Educational and Psychological Measurement, 48,* 1097-1103.

97. Stroebel, S. S., & Evans, J. R. (1988). Neuropsychological and environmental characteristics of early readers. *Journal of School Psychology, 26,* 243-252.

98. Webster, R. E. (1988). Variability in reading achievement test scores as related to reading curriculum. *Educational and Psychological Measurement, 48,* 815-825.

99. Weinberg, W. A., McLean, A., & Brumback, R. A. (1988). Comparison of reading and listening-reading techniques for administrations of PIAT reading comprehension subtest: Justification for the bypass approach. *Perceptual and Motor Skills, 66* (2), 672-674.

100. Culbert, J. P., Hamer, R., & Klinge, V. (1989). Factor structure of the Wechsler Intelligence Scale for Children—Revised, Peabody Picture Vocabulary Test, and Peabody Individual Achievement Test in a psychiatric sample. *Psychology in the Schools, 26,* 331-336.

101. Eaves, R. C., Darch, C., & Haynes, M. (1989). The concurrent validity of the Peabody Individual Achievement Test and Woodcock Reading Mastery Tests among students with mild learning problems. *Psychology in the Schools, 26,* 261-266.

102. Finkelman, D., Ferrarese, M. J., & Garmezy, N. (1989). A factorial, reliability, and validity study of the Devereux Elementary School Behavior Rating Scale. *Psychological Reports, 64,* 535-547.

103. Mason, E. M., & Wenck, L. S. (1989). Differences in factor structures of cognitive functioning of learning disabled (LD) and emotionally handicapped (EH) children. *Educational and Psychological Measurement, 49,* 767-782.

104. Olson, R., Wise, B., Conners, F., Rack, J., & Fuller, D. (1989). Specific deficits in component reading and language skills: Genetic and environmental influences. *Journal of Learning Disabilities, 22,* 339-348.

105. Riley, N. J. (1989). Piagetian cognitive functioning in students with learning disabilities. *Journal of Learning Disabilities, 22,* 444-451.

106. Salend, S. J., & Sonnenschein, P. (1989). Validating the effectiveness of a cooperative learning strategy through direct observation. *Journal of School Psychology, 27,* 47-58.

107. Schonfeld, I. S., Shaffer, D., & Barmack, J. E. (1989). Neurological soft signs and school achievement: The mediating effects of sustained attention. *Journal of Abnormal Child Psychology, 17,* 575-596.

108. Tarnowski, K. J., & Nay, S. M. (1989). Locus of control in children with learning disabilities and hyperactivity: A subgroup analysis. *Journal of Learning Disabilities, 22,* 381-383, 399.

109. Weinberg, W. A., McLean, A., Snider, R. L., Rintelmann, J. W., & Brumback, R. A. (1989). Comparison of paragraph comprehension test scores with reading versus listening-reading and multiple-choice versus nominal recall administration techniques: Justification for the bypass approach. *Perceptual and Motor Skills, 69,* 1131-1135.

110. Zentall, S. S. (1989). Attentional cuing in spelling tasks for hyperactive and comparison regular classroom children. *The Journal of Special Education, 23,* 83-93.

111. Zentall, S. S., & Dwyer, A. M. (1989). Color effects on the impulsivity and activity of hyperactive children. *Journal of School Psychology, 27,* 165-173.

112. Davis, J. M., & Spring, C. (1990). The Digit Naming Speed Test: Its power and incremental validity in identifying children with specific reading disabilities. *Psychology in the Schools, 27,* 15-22.

113. LaBuda, M. C., DeFries, J. C., & Pennington, B. F. (1990). Reading disability: A model for the genetic analysis of complex behavioral disorders. *Journal of Counseling and Development, 68,* 645-651.

114. Pianta, R. C., Erickson, M. F., Wagner, N., Kruetzer, T., & Egeland, B. (1990). Early predictors of referral for special services: Child-based measures versus mother-child interaction. *School Psychology Review, 19,* 240-250.

115. Bowden, H. N., & Byrne, J. M. (1991). Use of the Hobby WISC-R Short Form with patients referred for neuropsychological assessment. *Psychological Assessment, 3,* 660-666.

116. Campbell, J. W., D'Amato, R. C., Raggio, D. J., & Stephens, K. D. (1991). Construct validity of the computerized Continuous Performance Test with measures of intelligence, achievement, and behavior. *Journal of School Psychology, 29,* 143-150.

117. Costenbader, V. K., & Adams, J. W. (1991). A review of the psychometric and administrative features of the PIAT-R: Implications for the practitioner. *Journal of School Psychology, 29,* 219-228.

118. Cunningham, A. E., & Stanovich, K. E. (1991). Tracking the unique effects of print exposure in children: Associations with vocabulary, general knowledge, and spelling. *Journal of Educational Psychology, 83,* 264-274.

119. Edwards, L. K. (1991). Fitting a serial correlation pattern to repeated observations. *Journal of Educational Statistics, 16,* 53-76.

120. Feagans, L. V., Merriwether, A. M., & Haldane, D. (1991). Goodness of fit in the home: Its relationship to school behavior and achievement in children with learning disabilities. *Journal of Learning Disabilities, 24,* 413-420.

121. Forness, S. R., Cantwell, D. P., Swanson, J. M., Hanna, G. L., & Youpa, D. (1991). Differential effects of stimulant medication on reading performance of boys with hyperactivity with and without conduct disorder. *Journal of Learning Disabilities, 24,* 304-310.

122. Halperin, J. M., Sharma, V., Greenblatt, E., & Schwartz, S. T. (1991). Assessment of the continuous performance test: Reliability and validity in a nonreferred sample. *Psychological Assessment, 3,* 603-608.

123. McLeskey, J., & Waldron, N. L. (1991). Identifying students with learning disabilities: The effect of implementing statewide guidelines. *Journal of Learning Disabilities, 24,* 501-506.

124. Vandell, D. L., & Ramanan, J. (1991). Children of the National Longitudinal Survey of Youth: Choices in after-school care and child development. *Developmental Psychology, 27,* 637-643.

125. Webster, R. E., & Braswell, L. A. (1991). Curriculum bias and reading achievement test performance. *Psychology in the Schools, 28,* 193-198.

Review of the Peabody Individual Achievement Test—Revised by KATHRYN M. BENES, Assistant

Professor of Psychology, Iowa State University, Ames, IA:

The Peabody Individual Achievement Test—Revised (PIAT-R) is a revision of the Peabody Individual Achievement Test (PIAT; 9:923). The PIAT-R retained many of the features of the original PIAT. It is an individually administered, norm-referenced, wide-ranged screening instrument that measures academic achievement. Administration of the PIAT-R requires approximately one hour and is designed to be used with students that range in age from 5-0 to 18-11. The PIAT-R subtests are contained in four volumes—three easel kits and a book. Similar to the original PIAT easel volumes, stimulus materials are presented to students at eye level on one side of the book plate, while the examiner's instructions and correct responses are presented on the reverse side.

The updated PIAT reflects an effort to address three primary areas: (*a*) contemporary educational priorities; (*b*) a balanced representation of gender, racial, cultural, and socioeconomic backgrounds; and (*c*) improved psychometric properties.

CONTEMPORARY EDUCATIONAL PRIORITIES. The manual indicates that a "primary reason for the revision was to make the test more representative of current curricular content." Although all of the five original subtests were retained, only about 35% of the original items within the subtests remain. In order to increased the breadth of the PIAT-R, Written Expression was added as a subtest to assess written language.

The six subtests of the PIAT-R include:

General Information. The General Information subtest is made up of 100 open-ended questions that are presented orally by the examiner and answered orally by the student. Items measure the student's factual knowledge related to science, social studies, humanities, fine arts, and recreation. The items within the General Information subtest were written to minimize knowledge specific to the United States. Rather, an attempt was made for the subtest to be appropriate for use in other countries.

Reading Recognition. The Reading Recognition subtest contains 100 items. Items 1–16 are multiple choice and measure prereading skills. Items 17–100 measure decoding skills and require the student to read orally individually presented words.

Reading Comprehension. The Reading Comprehension subtest consists of 82 items and measures the student's ability to draw meaning from printed sentences. Each item requires the presentation of two test plates. The student must silently read a sentence printed on the first test plate, then select one of four pictures that best depicts the meaning of the sentence on the second test plate.

Mathematics. The Mathematics subtest consists of 100 multiple-choice items ranging in difficulty from discrimination tasks to advanced mathematic concepts such as trigonometry. Mathematics items assess practical application (50%), understanding of concepts (30%), and computational skills (20%).

Spelling. The Spelling subtest is made up of 100 items. Items 1–15 are multiple-choice tasks that assess readiness skills. Items 16–100 require the student to select, from four possible choices, the correct spelling of a word read orally by the examiner.

Written Expression. The Written Expression subtest is divided into two levels. Level I assesses readiness skills that require the subject to: (*a*) print his/her first and last names; (*b*) copy letters and words; and (*c*) write letters, words, and sentences orally presented by the examiner. Level I consists of 19 copying and dictation items that are arranged in order of ascending difficulty.

Level II of the Written Expression subtest measures the student's writing skills. The student is presented with one of two picture plates (Prompts A and B) and given 20 minutes to write a story about the picture.

Three composites can be used to summarize achievement: Total Reading consists of Reading Recognition and Reading Comprehension subtests. Total Test provides an overall measure of the student's level of achievement and is made up of General Information, Reading Recognition, Reading Comprehension, Mathematics, and Spelling subtests. A Written Language composite is optional and consists of Written Expression and Spelling subtests.

Six types of derived scores can be obtained for the first five PIAT-R subtests: age equivalents, grade equivalents, percentile ranks, stanines, standard scores (mean = 100, standard deviation = 15), and normal curve equivalents (NCEs). Grade-based stanines (Levels I and II) and developmental scaled scores (Level II) are obtained for the Written Expression subtest.

BALANCED REPRESENTATION. The design and artwork of the PIAT-R attempts to update visual stimuli. In addition, an effort has been made to provide representation from a broad range of individual characteristics such as race, age, gender, socioeconomic, and cultural backgrounds. This wide-range representation is apparent in both verbal and visual stimuli.

PSYCHOMETRIC PROPERTIES:

Norms. The standardization sample for the PIAT-R consisted of 1,563 kindergarten through 12th grade students from 33 communities in the continental United States (Alaska and Hawaii were not included). In addition, 175 kindergarten students from 13 sites were tested later to provide beginning kindergarten information. Students from public school systems made up 91.4% of the standardization sample; the remainder of the sample consisted of students from private schools. Although a greater number of students from lower grades were tested because of the more frequent use of the PIAT-R in elementary school, statistical requirements were met for all grades. The standardization sample was balanced between sexes (50.1 females, 49.9 males). Geographic, socioeconomic, and ethnic group dimensions were consistent with proportional distributions of the general population in the continental United States.

Reliability. Four statistical methods were used to estimate reliability for the first five subtests, and Total Reading and Total Test composites of the PIAT-R: (a) split-half; (b) Kuder-Richardson; (c) test-retest; and (d) item response theory (using the Rasch model). Reliability coefficients for each of the four methods were very high, with the majority of coefficient medians being at or above .94 for both age and grade.

Reliability estimates for the Written Expression subtest were obtained by using interrater, internal consistency, and test-retest procedures for Level I. Interrater, internal consistency, and alternate-form procedures were used to determine reliability estimates for Level II.

Interrater reliabilities for Level I were obtained by correlating scores of two independent scorers. Estimates of interrater reliabilities were .90 for kindergarten and .95 for Grade 1. Interrater reliability estimates were also computed using Ebel's (1951) method. Ebel's estimates of reliability were .91 for kindergarten and .88 for Grade 1. Somewhat more moderate reliability coefficients resulted when estimates of internal consistency were conducted. Coefficient alpha reliabilites were .61 for the fall kindergarten sample, .60 for the spring kindergarten sample, and .69 for the first grade sample. Test-retest reliabilities were drawn from a subset of 45 kindergarten and first grade students who were retested 2 to 4 weeks following the initial test administration. Results indicated moderate (.56) reliability.

Level II interrater reliabilities were computed for both prompts (A and B) and for each grade. Interrater correlations ranged from .30 to .81 (median of .58) for Prompt A and from .53 to .77 (median of .67) for Prompt B. Ebel's (1951) method was also used for both prompts of Level II. Estimates of reliability ranged from .29 to .79 (median of .57) for Prompt A and from .53 to .77 (median of .67) for Prompt B. Measures of internal consistency were conducted for both prompts and each grade. Reliability coefficients ranged from .69 to .91, with total sample coefficients of .86 for Prompt A and .88 for Prompt B. Approximately 35 students, randomly selected from 3rd, 5th, 7th, 9th, and 11th grades were retested within 2- to 4-week

intervals. These students were administered the picture prompt that had not been given in the first testing. Estimates of reliability ranged from .44 to .61, with a coefficient of .63 for the total sample.

Validity. Content and construct validity methods were employed to determine whether the PIAT-R measures academic achievement. The purpose of content validity is to measure whether the test items adequately assess a particular performance domain. Content validity, as reported in the manual, is based on expert judgment used in the "extensive developmental process" to create each subtest. The development of the PIAT-R is documented in the manual. Reliability estimates from the Kuder-Richardson and split-half procedures are also cited as evidence that subtests measure specific content areas.

The construct validity of the PIAT-R was measured according to criteria recommended by Anastasi (1988): "developmental changes, correlations with other tests, and factor analysis." Evidence for developmental changes was drawn from an increase in subtest and composite raw score means for successive grade and age groups. One exception was cited in the manual for the 18-year-old sample. The author accounts for the exception by stating that a "smaller sample of subjects still in high school may be lower achieving than would be a truly representative sample of 18-year-olds."

Construct validity, as evidenced by correlations with other tests, was conducted by correlating the PIAT-R with the PIAT and the Peabody Picture Vocabulary Test—Revised (PPVT-R). Correlations between like subtest scores for the PIAT and PIAT-R ranged from .46 (General Information for the 12-year-old sample) to .97 (Total Test for the 14-year-old sample), with the majority of correlations in the moderate to high range. When the PPVT-R was correlated with the PIAT-R, median correlation coefficients ranged from .50 to .72, showing stronger correlations on those PIAT-R subtests that were more dependent upon verbal ability.

The underlying constructs of the PIAT-R were measured by conducting a factor analysis. The factor analysis was based on standard scores from grades 2–12 for the initial five subtests and stanines for those same grade levels for the Written Expression subtest. Six factors were identified; however, three of the factors accounted for "64.3% of the total variance." Therefore, a three-factor solution was used. Factor I appeared to represent general verbal ability, Factor II represented a more specific verbal factor requiring the student to recognize and combine letters and sounds in a meaningful manner, and Factor III appeared to measure a more advanced kind of verbal ability related to "complex grammatical and syntactic structures."

SUMMARY. In summary, the Peabody Individual Achievement Test—Revised represents a screening instrument designed to assess six academic skill areas. It is apparent that great effort was made to build upon the existing strength of the original PIAT and make it better. Additions and revisions made to the item pool, as well as the updated visual prompts, reflect attention to changes in educational priorities and sensitivity to differences in gender, racial, cultural, and socioeconomic backgrounds. Moreover, the psychometric properties of the PIAT-R are much stronger than the original PIAT, with high reliability coefficients for five of the six subtests. Validity measures would suggest that the strength of the PIAT-R lies in its ability to measure verbal performance. All of the factors mentioned make the PIAT-R an excellent screening instrument for use in the educational setting.

REVIEWER'S REFERENCES

Ebel, R. L. (1951). Estimation of the reliability of ratings. *Psychometrika, 16,* 407-424.
Anastasi, A. (1988). *Psychological testing* (6th ed.). New York: Macmillan.

Review of the Peabody Individual Achievement Test—Revised by BRUCE G. ROGERS, Professor of Educational Psychology and Foundations, University of Northern Iowa, Cedar Falls, IA:

The Peabody Individual Achievement Test—Revised (PIAT-R) is an individually administered achievement battery that provides norm-referenced measures, from kindergarten to grade 12, in the areas of reading, spelling, mathematics, and general information. The first edition was developed in 1970 by Lloyd M. Dunn and Frederick C. Markwardt, while Dunn was at the George Peabody College for Teachers; Markwardt alone was responsible for the revision. Previously, Dunn had prepared an individually administered intelligence test, the Peabody Picture Vocabulary Test (PPVT), which has also been revised. The two tests, having similar formats and administration procedures, are designed to be used together to measure both mental ability and achievement. Many of the essential features of the original PIAT are retained in the revised edition, including easel administration, 1-hour administration time, the measurement of widely accepted educational outcomes, training exercises, items in ascending difficulty, and minimal qualifications for administrators. However, several features of the test were revised, including a reordering of the subtests, the revision of about two-thirds of the items to conform to current curricular trends, an increase in the number of items in each subtest, and the introduction of a writing sample.

DESCRIPTION OF THE SUBTESTS. Six subtests comprise the PIAT-R. Items in each of the first five subtests are arranged in ascending difficulty. General Information, consisting of 100 open-ended questions given orally, covers the areas of science, social science, recreation, humanities, and fine arts. Many of the items begin with the words "why" and

"how," with the intent of measuring reasoning ability. By contrast, a few require the recall of a specific name (e.g., Bo Peep) in order to measure factual material. There may be instances, however, in which a person could recognize the factual name in a multiple-choice format, but have a so-called "mental block" and not be able to recall it in an open-ended format. In such cases, the person would receive no credit for the degree of knowledge that he or she possessed. Fortunately, there are few items of this type, so the resulting error in the total score is likely to be small. To show the relative weight for each content area, a scope chart is provided, which denotes a stronger emphasis for science and social studies than for the humanities and fine arts.

Because some open-ended items may elicit a variety of responses, the test booklet gives examples of both correct and incorrect responses, which are designed to help the examiner make the proper decision. Because this requires judgments on the part of the examiner, previous reviewers have been critical of the claim in the Manual that appears to downplay the need for professional training to administer the test. Users must be very careful in determining what level of training paraprofessionals will need to score this subtest properly.

Reading Recognition consists of 16 prereading items (e.g., naming letters) and 84 words to be pronounced by the pupil. For the pronunciation of some of the words, word attack skills will suffice, but for others above the fourth grade level, sight vocabulary is necessary. To the credit of the publisher, the Manual makes the reader aware that the interpretation of the scores may differ by level. The pronunciation guide is from *Webster's Ninth Collegiate Dictionary* (to emphasize usage typical in education), and an audiotape is available to help prepare the administrator. Once again, users must be careful in seeing that paraprofessionals receive the proper training for scoring these items. It would be beneficial to have evidence of interrater reliability for this subtest.

In Reading Comprehension, which consists of 82 sentences, the subject reads a sentence once, looks at four pictures, and selects, by recalling the sentence, the picture that best represents the meaning of that sentence. The words used in the sentences were selected according to difficulty level from graded vocabulary lists. The author explains that readability formulas were not used on the sentences because of their unreliability, but it might be advantageous if such formulas were applied to test that hypothesis. Subjective judgments were used to evaluate the complexity of the sentences and item analyses were performed to check the difficulty and discrimination of the items. A few of the items appear more complicated than may be necessary; for example, the two words "acrimonious invectives" seem to be redundant. In this reviewer's opinion, that type of repetition is not a common characteristic of high quality writing, and therefore, sentences with such words should be replaced with others that would be considered to be exemplary by writing experts. Item analysis data can assist in confirming or disconfirming that subjective judgment.

The Total Reading score is computed from the raw score sum of the Reading Recognition and the Reading Comprehension subtests. In future studies, it might be useful to investigate the optimal weighing of these components in the composite as evidence pertaining to the validity of score interpretations.

The Mathematics subtest consists of 100 multiple-choice items ranging from concepts of longer and shorter to elementary concepts in differential calculus. According to the Manual, this subtest reflects the view that the ultimate goal of mathematics is to deal with everyday tasks. Although most of the test items are consistent with that goal, there appear to be some exceptions; for example, most people do not factor trinomials or take derivatives in their everyday tasks. However, most people do perform mentally the four basic arithmetic operations and this subtest provides good examples that require an understanding of those processes. A scope and sequence chart was developed with instructional objectives for each cell, but only a scope chart is shown in the Manual, thus making it more difficult for the user to assess the content validity.

The Spelling subtest consists of 15 readiness items and 85 words presented orally. Some of the readiness items appear very appropriate, such as selecting a letter when given its sound, whereas the rationale for others is less readily seen, such as selecting what is different when given the printed letter "m" and three pictures of a fish. For each of the orally presented words, the student is asked to identify the correct spelling from a list of four words. There is controversy over whether the words on a spelling test should be dictated, requiring the pupil to write the words, or whether they should be presented in a multiple-choice format, requiring the student to recognize the correct spelling. This issue is addressed in a very professional manner and the research studies that were used are cited. The words were selected from research-based spelling scales, and item analysis data were used in the evaluation of the foils.

The Written Expression subtest was developed in response to the widespread use of such instruments in both elementary and secondary schools. It consists of two levels, the first measuring readiness skills (copying and writing from dictation), and the second measuring composition skills (composing a story, in 20 minutes, from a picture prompt). The detailed instructions for scoring are well written.

The conditions under which paraprofessionals can be trained to score this subtest as reliably as can professionals would be an appropriate direction for further research.

The Total Test score is defined as the sum of the first five subtest scores. Because of its lower reliability, the Written Expression subtest is excluded. When a similar problem was faced in the revisions of the General Tests of Educational Development (GED tests), composite weights were assigned to reflect the lower reliability of the written component (Patience & Swartz, 1987). In future studies of the PIAT-R, it might be rewarding to consider that approach.

SCORES AND NORMS. The PIAT-R was standardized in a field test involving approximately 100 students per grade. When both conventional item analysis and Rasch-Wright latent-trait analysis were applied to the data, the results were found to be similar. This normative sample of approximately 1,500 students was stratified by four geographic regions, grade level, sex, and parental education. With only a few exceptions, the proportions in each of the strata compared favorably with the United States Census figures. The use of current psychometric procedures is reflected in the details of the standardization procedure. The data were used to create norms for standard scores, grade and age equivalents, and percentile ranks. The resulting norms tables are easy to read. Whereas the normative sample for this revision was only about half the size of the normative sample for the first edition, there do not appear to be any obvious faults in the standardization procedure that would cause serious concern about the interpretation of the norms.

VALIDITY. Evidence is presented to support content, concurrent, and construct validity. For content validity, the evidence includes the selection of vocabulary words from validated vocabulary lists, the use of a number of school curriculum guides to determine appropriate content, and the use of content area specialists to review the items. Because the PIAT and PIAT-R share many features, evidence for concurrent validity consists of research studies using the PIAT. Correlation coefficients from studies that investigated relationships with about 10 other achievement tests are presented, and appear to support the concurrent validity of the test. To establish evidence for construct validity, some of these subtest intercorrelations were factor analyzed, and the resulting factors were reasonably supportive of the validity of the test. Another source of evidence for construct validity is given by the mean raw score differences between grade levels. Prior to grade five, these differences are reasonably large (approximately one standard deviation), but in grades 5 through 12, they tend to decrease. Above the seventh grade, the differences seem quite small (only about one-fourth of a standard deviation). This would suggest that the grade- and age-equivalent scores are more valid in the lower grades than in the upper grades.

RELIABILITY. Test-retest reliability coefficients were computed on samples of 50 students from even-numbered grades who were retested following a 2- to 4-week span. Whereas, the majority of the subtest correlations were above .90, a few were below .80. Further evidence pertaining to the reliability of the subtest scores is shown by the reliability coefficients computed from the one-parameter model of item response theory and the Kuder-Richardson formula 20. A majority of these coefficients, for each subtest by grade and by age, are above .94. The user needs to be aware that such high coefficients are due, in part, to the procedure of counting all items below the basal score as correct and all items above the ceiling as incorrect. It is to the credit of the publisher that this fact is pointed out in the Manual, but it might also be helpful if reliability studies were done which made appropriate psychometric adjustments to minimize these inflated values. Using the reliability data to establish confidence bands around the scores is a desirable procedure to reduce the emphasis on small differences between the subtest scores of an individual.

SUMMARY. In summary, the PIAT-R is a current, properly standardized, norm-referenced achievement test designed to provide screening information on six areas of cognitive development. When compared to the original edition, the revision is broader in scope and contains more items. The stratified standardization procedure appears comparable or superior to that of other individually administered achievement tests. For initial screening, the reliabilities of the subtests are sufficient. The inclusion of confidence bands improves the interpretation of the scores. At the lower grades, the mean score differences provide evidence of construct validity. The use of curriculum guides and subject matter experts in the development of the test provides evidence pertaining to content validity. Data from the first edition of the test are presented to support concurrent validity, but more evidence is needed for the revised edition. Overall, the PIAT-R appears to be a useful instrument both to practitioners in the schools and to researchers.

REVIEWER'S REFERENCE

Patience, W., & Swartz, R. (1987, April). *Essay score reliability: Issues in and methods of reporting GED Writing Test scores.* Paper presented at the annual meeting of the National Council on Measurement in Education, Washington, DC.

[281]

Pediatric Extended Examination at Three.

Purpose: "To aid in the early detection and clarification of problems with learning, attention, and behavior in three- to four-year-old children."
Population: Ages 3–4.

Publication Date: 1986.
Acronym: PEET.
Scores, 20: Developmental Attainment (Gross Motor, Language, Visual-Fine Motor, Memory, Intersensory Integration), Assessment of Behavior Rating Scale (Initial Adaptation, Reactions during Assessment), Global Language Rating Scale, Physical Findings (General Physical Examination, Neurological Examination, Auditory and Vision Testing), Task Analysis (Reception, Discrimination, Sequencing, Memory, Fine Motor Output, Gross Motor Output, Expressive Language, Instructional Output, Experiential Application).
Administration: Individual.
Price Data, 1987: $54.50 per complete kit including 24 record booklets, PEET kit (ball, target, key, wooden blocks, plastic sticks, car, crayon, doll, buttoning strip, checkers, and objects for stereognosis task), stimulus booklet (35 pages), and examiner's manual (63 pages).
Time: Administration time not reported.
Authors: James A. Blackman, Melvin D. Levine, and Martha Markowitz.
Publisher: Educators Publishing Service, Inc.

Review of the Pediatric Extended Examination at Three by WILLIAM B. MICHAEL, Professor of Education and Psychology, University of Southern California, Los Angeles, CA:

The Pediatric Extended Examination at Three (PEET) was prepared by two pediatricians and a psychologist with a strong medical orientation. This instrument was designed to assess a wide range of characteristics in neurological development, in cognitive and affective behaviors, and in physical and mental health of the 3-year-old child, with applicability to the child of 4 or 5 years of age. The authors have emphasized in the manual the lack of adequate standardized diagnostic evaluation and screening procedures for the 3-year-old. The PEET is actually one of three separate parent and school questionnaires within what is known as the Aggregate Neurobehavioral Student Health and Educational Review (ANSER) System that has been prepared to evaluate developmental factors of three age groups (ages 3 to 5 for preschool and kindergarten children, ages 6 to 11 corresponding to elementary school children, and ages 12 or more relative to secondary students).

Central to the PEET are 29 developmental tasks covering five broad functional areas: Gross Motor, Language, Visual-Fine Motor, Memory, and Intersensory Integration skills, for which there are 7, 8, 6, 5, and 3 tasks, respectively. Relative to each task, detailed and quite explicit instructions are given in the manual both for administration and for scoring and interpreting the responses.

The scoring instructions described in the manual are integrated within an 8-page fold-out record form, which itself needs to be studied to afford a comprehensive grasp of the organizational structure of the PEET. In this record form, space is provided for a tabulation of detailed results of a medical examination as well as for evaluative responses in rating scales covering (*a*) eight language skills and (*b*) 25 categories of behaviors. Although the multidimensional nature of the instrument prevents use of an interpretable total score, the record form does include one summary page to highlight information of developmental attainment, behaviors manifested during assessment, general language competency, medical status, and performance in nine global task areas.

Credit must be given to the authors for the caution they have exercised in numerous places within the manual concerning accurate interpretation of scores generated—especially the caveat not to overgeneralize the results or to draw extravagant inferences. They have encouraged the use of other indicators to supplement the outcomes of the assessment furnished by the PEET.

This refreshing postion may be, in part, a function of the fact that the amount of data regarding the reliability and validity of the PEET is quite limited. In fact, the only available psychometric information is presented in a 1983 article from *Developmental Behavioral Pediatrics* (Blackman, Levine, Markowitz, & Aufseeser, 1983). The first three of the four authors of this article are the same individuals as those who prepared the Examiner's Manual.

The Blackman et al. (1983) article provides background information as well as reliability and validity data for an earlier form of the PEET that was administered to a more or less "normal" community sample of 201 children and to a clinic sample of 59 subjects. These two samples of children represented participants in the Brookline Early Education Project (BEEP), a diagnostic and educational program aimed toward ascertaining the effects of providing school-based services to community families with young children.

In the two samples studied, a classification system of identifying children as manifesting behaviors of either "possible concern" or "no concern" was established. For 62 subjects, the percentage of agreement between examiners and observers on groups of items from the PEET ranged from 93.5 to 100 with corresponding kappa coefficients falling between .77 and 1.00, although caution needs to be exercised in interpreting these data in the light of the great imbalance in the proportions of individuals falling in the two categories of concern. Promising validity data were obtained in terms of significant differences in responses to key items between members of the community sample and those of the clinic sample. Correlations between the number of possible concerns within categories of the PEET and corresponding conceptually similar portions of the McCarthy Index Scales varied between .26 and .63 for the community sample of 201 subjects—all correlations being significant beyond the .001 level.

Empirically derived normative data appeared to be missing from the manual except to the extent that means and standard deviations provide limited information.

In summary, the PEET as a clinical procedure has considerable merit in that it can furnish useful information for diagnosis and possibly prescription. Far more data are needed, however, to establish both the reliability and validity of the many scales. The consumer must use great care, as the authors have recommended, in the interpretation and use of the scores derived from the scales. It is to be hoped that many additional investigations will be completed in the near future so that the results obtained can be incorporated within a revised manual that will permit both a reliable and valid assessment of the whole child.

REVIEWER'S REFERENCE

Blackman, J. A., Levine, M. D., Markowitz, M. T., & Aufseeser, C. L. (1983). The Pediatric Extended Examination at Three: A system for diagnostic clarification of problematic three-year-olds. *Developmental Behavioral Pediatrics*, *4*, 143.

Review of the Pediatric Extended Examination at Three by HOI K. SUEN, *Associate Professor of Educational Psychology, Pennsylvania State University, University Park, PA:*

The Pediatric Extended Examination at Three (PEET) is a relatively comprehensive assessment tool for the detection and clarification of problems with learning, attention, and behavior in children 3 to 4 years of age. As a result of the large variability in development and behavior of children at this age, results from PEET can best be regarded as descriptive and tentative. The authors quite correctly caution potential users that PEET should be used in conjunction with other evaluative input and vision and hearing tests, as well as data from repeated observations.

PEET is an individually administered evaluation procedure in which a child is asked to perform a series of 28 tasks. Some tasks contain several similar subitems (e.g., asking a child to repeat a series of words one at a time). The reported administration time along with physical examinations and visual screening ranges between 30 and 45 minutes. Because PEET requires a lengthy one-to-one evaluation, it is not suited for large-scaled screening purposes. It is suitable, however, for follow-up isolation of potential areas of concern after an initial screening test or referral.

The samples used for the norming, reliability estimation, and validity analyses of PEET consisted of a small (201 subjects) self-selected community sample from the Boston area and a clinic sample of 59 subjects from a hospital in Boston. Of the mothers of the community sample, 55% have a bachelor's degree or more. While 48% of the subjects were males, the ethnic composition of the community sample was not reported. Among the subjects in the clinic sample, 80% were males. It is clear that the sizes and characteristics of the samples employed in the development of PEET have severely limited the generalizability of the norms as well as evidence of reliability and validity. The use of PEET for subjects outside of the Boston area and/or with characteristics different from the norming sample will necessitate the establishment of local norms and the reassessment of reliability and validity.

The authors reported good interrater agreement indices (proportion agreements average .96, kappa coefficients range from .77 to 1.00) in classifying subjects as "possible concern" versus "no concern" in the five areas of developmental attainment assessment. In PEET, various information is also combined to yield scores in three "channels" of communication. The authors reported marginal Cronbach Alpha estimates, ranging from .695 to .731 for the three channel scores. No Cronbach Alpha was reported for the five areas of developmental attainment. Because some of these areas contain very few items (e.g., 3 items for memory and 4 items for language), had Cronbach Alphas been assessed, they could be expected to be low.

Interrater reliability estimates are generalizable only to raters with similar background and training as those used in an interrater reliability assessment study. As such, it is important to define the characteristics of the raters so that appropriate raters can be used in the future to ensure that the same level of interrater reliability can be expected. In this regard, the authors provided clear information. Specifically, interrater reliabilities were established based on data from the use of pediatricians as raters. However, the authors have gone beyond their data somewhat by suggesting that PEET may be administered by health care personnel in general or a team of physicians, nurses, and special educators. Although raters other than pediatricians may prove to be excellent ones, evidence of their interrater reliabilities has yet to be established.

It is important to note that PEET does not produce an overall score. Rather, a number of scores corresponding to various areas of development and communication are derived. evidence of concurrent validity was reported for the communication channel scores using the McCarthy Scales of Children's Abilities and known clinical identification as criteria in separate analyses. The strength of these pieces of statistical evidence is generally adequate to suggest that PEET channel scores can be used to differentiate between children with no concerns versus those with concerns in specific channel areas.

No data on predictive validity or construct validity were gathered; nor are they necessary given the relatively modest goal of the instrument. It should be emphasized that, because of this lack of evidence of predictive and/or construct validity, PEET should not be used alone as a diagnostic tool.

Scores on PEET are used to develop profiles. The authors suggest that an area in which a child's score is at least one standard deviation below the mean should be tentatively considered an area of "potential concern." The choice of one standard deviation appears to be arbitrary and implies that about 15% of the children can be expected to be of "potential concern" in each area. Evidence from the concurrent validity studies provided partial support for the appropriateness of the one-standard-deviation cutoff score.

Overall, PEET is a psychometrically sound evaluation tool for the specific purpose of *clarifying* potential developmental areas of concern, given both raters and subjects are similar in characteristics to those used in the Boston studies. It is inappropriate for screening or clinical diagnosis. It can be used, however, as one supplemental source of information in a comprehensive diagnostic system that includes multiple alternative sources of information. The major limitation of PEET is the lack of representativeness of the normative, reliability, and validity samples. Local norms as well as local evidence of reliability and validity are needed. Unless there are sufficient subjects for the establishment of local norms, applications of PEET may not be practical.

[282]
Perceptions of Parental Role Scales.
Purpose: "To measure perceived parental role responsibilities."
Population: Parents.
Publication Date: 1982.
Acronym: PPRS.
Scores: 13 areas in 3 domains: Teaching the Child (Cognitive Development, Social Skills, Handling of Emotions, Physical Health, Norms and Social Values, Personal Hygiene, Survival Skills), Meeting the Child's Basic Needs (Health Care, Food/Clothing/Shelter, Child's Emotional Needs, Child Care), Family as an Interface With Society (Social Institutions, the Family Unit Itself).
Administration: Group.
Price Data, 1988: $20 per 50 scales; $25 per kit including manual (41 pages) and 25 scales.
Time: (15) minutes.
Comments: Self-administered.
Authors: Lucia A. Gilbert and Gary R. Hanson.
Publisher: Marathon Consulting and Press.

Review of the Perceptions of Parental Role Scales by CINDY I. CARLSON, Associate Professor of Educational Psychology, University of Texas at Austin, Austin, TX:

The Perceptions of Parental Role Scales (PPRS) represents a departure from the numerous self-report tests developed to measure parenting style and rather provides a measure of parental role behaviors or responsibilities. The items of the PPRS are reponded to on a 5-point Likert scale ranging from "not at all important as a parental responsibility" to "very important as a parental responsibility." Thus the PPRS actually provides a measure of parental attitudes and beliefs regarding the importance of particular parental roles. The PPRS was developed as a research tool, primarily for dual-worker families. However, it has demonstrated utility in educational and counseling settings.

The PPRS directions for administration and scoring are clear and easy to follow. A manual for the measure is available and adequate. No response set problems in the items are observed. However, because questionnaires regarding parenting can be susceptible to social desirability, evaluation of this response bias is encouraged for researchers using the PPRS. Limitations of the PPRS include the requirement of an eighth grade reading level and English reading knowledge to complete the measure.

Regarding the psychometric quality of the PPRS, reliability studies have demonstrated both high internal consistency, with alpha coefficients in the .81 to .91 range, and high 1-month test-retest reliability, with coefficients ranging from .69 to .90 across subscales. Thus, the reliability of the PPRS is very good.

The high internal consistency reliability coefficients demonstrate that for each of the scales, the items reflect the same behavioral domain. The criterion-related validity of the PPRS has barely been examined. In the only available study of criterion validity, females were found to score significantly higher than males on a majority of the parenting responsibilities consistent with predictions based on previous research of marital roles. Regarding construct validity, the PPRS is clearly embedded within the theoretical frameworks of role theory and socialization theory. The 13 scales of the PPRS, however, are moderately to highly intercorrelated, suggesting that the scales are measuring aspects of the same construct rather than distinct constructs. Furthermore, an examination of the intercorrelations of the scales by domain suggests that scales are not more highly correlated within than across domains. Therefore, it would appear inappropriate for researchers to derive domain scores from the PPRS.

High intercorrelation of scales is generally considered an undesirable psychometric characteristic. The authors of the PPRS argue that the intercorrelation of scales is appropriate given the content of the measure. The high intercorrelation of scales does indicate that parental role is not a differentiated construct as measured by the PPRS. Moreover, the use of the highly correlated mean individual scale scores will be problematic for certain types of statistical analyses commonly used in research. The PPRS authors acknowledge that a factor analysis might produce a smaller number of scales that would account for the variance of the measure but argue against the desirability of this goal given the rational/intuitive development of the scales of the measure. Given the lack of empirical support for the existing scale differentiation researchers using the PPRS may consider factor scores as one possible solution to the scale intercorrelation dilemma.

To summarize the validity status of the PPRS, the rational derivation of scales has provided internally consistent scales, which all reflect to a greater or lesser extent the construct of parental role, but that do not empirically support a further differentiation of the parental role construct. The lack of criterion-related validity data currently limits possible evaluation of the usefulness and meaning of the scales of the PPRS.

As is common with measures developed for research purposes, the PPRS needs more normative data. Furthermore, descriptive data on the PPRS are extremely limited. The measure was developed with a white, middle-class, university-employed sample and was subsequently administered to a Midwestern rural and urban sample. Additional characteristics of these samples are not provided in the manual. The lack of adequate sample descriptions seriously limits the ability of users to meaningfully interpret scores on the PPRS or to evaluate the generalizability of the measure.

An additional concern regarding the PPRS is the lack of attention, both in development and psychometric evaluation, to child development. It has been established that parenting practices shift with the development of their children. Although the PPRS authors acknowledge in their directions to respondents that some of the questionnaire items are more appropriate for a younger child and others for an older child, there has been no systematic investigation of the impact of a respondent's varying experiences with children of different developmental stages. For example, do childless couples, parents with preschoolers, and parents with adolescents all respond similarly to this measure? The failure of the authors to either examine this question or to provide data regarding the ages and number of children of parents in their test development sample is another serious limitation of this measure.

In summary, the PPRS provides a reliable measure of the perceived importance of a variety of parenting activities. Given the dearth of measures with this particular focus, the PPRS provides a valuable contribution to the measurement of parental attitudes for research and educational use. The usefulness of the PPRS, however, is currently limited by a lack of descriptive and criterion-related validity studies. Parent perceptions of role responsibilities can be expected to vary by numerous mediating variables including ethnicity, socioeconomic status, family structure, and childrearing experience, which have not yet been examined in validation studies of the PPRS. In addition, the possibility of a social desirability response bias must be ruled out in the PPRS. Thus the PPRS demonstrates research and educational potential that can be ascertained only with additional empirical investigation.

Review of the Perceptions of Parental Role Scales by MARK W. ROBERTS, *Professor of Clinical Psychology, Idaho State University, Pocatello, ID:*

The Perceptions of Parental Role Scales (PPRS) was designed to measure adult perceptions of a comprehensive set of parenting responsibilities. Each of the 13 scales consists of 5 to 7 items, with 78 items in all. The response format is a 5-point rating (1 = not at all; 3 = moderately important; 5 = very important) of "how important you believe each item is as a parental responsibility during the various stages of rearing a child under normal circumstances." Testing time is reported at 15 minutes. Respondents require at least an eighth grade reading level.

The PPRS is designed for use by social scientists investigating group perceptions of parental roles and the many variables that might influence those perceptions (Gilbert & Hanson, 1983). An initial pool of 200 items was constructed following a literature review. Item analyses were performed to select items that most adults agreed were "major responsibilities" of parents for both male and female children; gender differences were further minimized by eliminating items that statistically covaried with adult gender. Items were also selected to maximize the internal consistency of each scale and to minimize item correlations with other scales. Consequently, normative data reflect strong endorsements of all scales, low scale variance, and relatively homogeneous item content within scales. Although the manual suggests clinical uses of the PPRS (e.g., comparing spouse perceptions during marital counseling), no published studies are available to support its clinical utility. Furthermore, test construction minimizes potential clinical usefulness by attenuating individual differences.

The internal consistency of the 13 scales appears to be strong. Coefficient alphas range from .81 to .91 (median .86). An unpublished report by Dail (1984) detected alpha coefficients all above .90. Using an earlier version of the PPRS Scales, Gilbert, Hanson, and Davis (1982) reported alpha levels between .80 and .87 for 7 of the eventual 13 scales. Farnill (1985) found alpha levels ranging from .51 to .81 (median = .76) for an abbreviated version of the PPRS. Because items were selected for scale homogeneity, it was not surprising to find high coefficient alphas across four different samples of subjects and three different versions of the PPRS.

Test-retest reliability coefficients range across the 13 scales from .69 to .90 (median .82). Standard errors of measurement are not available. For its intended use (group research), however, temporal reliability and internal consistency seem adequate.

Two samples of normative data are presented in the manual. Mean scale scores, scale standard deviations, and mean item scores for each scale are reported. The first sample (n = 202) (Gilbert & Hanson, 1983) is more heterogeneous, consisting of randomly selected fulltime university staff. Sex, age, marital status, parenthood, and employment orientation varied. Norms are presented across three nominal dimensions: gender, employment orientation (job vs. career), and married males' spouse employment status. A second more homogeneous sample (n = 249) (Dail, 1984) provides norms for married adults under 30 with at least one child. Data are reported by gender and residential categories. Farnill (1985), reporting norms for an Australian sample (n = 279) using an abbreviated PPRS Scale, found that Australian adults rank-ordered the PPRS scales quite similarly to Americans (rho = .92 for males and .79 for females). Finally, Gilbert et al. (1982) provided normative data for an earlier version of the PPRS using percent endorsement data. The published norms seem quite adequate for evaluating different subjects from different populations.

Validation of the PPRS is currently insufficient, but shows promise. Content validity is supported by the careful and comprehensive selection of items. Items appear representative of the domain of possible areas of parental responsibility. The need for 13 different scales, however, can be questioned. The median interscale correlation is reported at .56, indicating substantial shared variance. The authors reject the idea of producing more scale independence (e.g., using factor analysis) in order to protect the content validity of the PPRS. Criterion validity of the PPRS can be found in two published and three unpublished data sets. The overwhelming finding across all these sources is that parental gender is associated with a variety of PPRS scale scores. In contrast, most demographic variables (age, ethnicity, employment patterns, marital status, and ages and numbers of children) generally do not correlate with PPRS responding. Both Gilbert and Hanson (1983) and Dail (1984) found females endorsing higher levels of parental responsibility than males. Dail conceptualized different PPRS scales as representing traditional male roles ("instrumental scales") or female roles ("expressive scales"). Women, however, scored higher than men on both composite scores.

The response format of the PPRS items can be changed from rating parental responsibility to rating the preferred agent (self, spouse, or other) for discharging responsibilities or to rating parental satisfaction with current performance. Gilbert (1983), Gilbert, Gram, and Hanson (1983), and Farnill (1985) all reported that both spouses perceive that women assume more responsibility than men for discharging parental duties. Unfortunately, the later two projects reduced the number of PPRS items, rendering the data's association with the original test obscure. Gilbert et al. (1983) examined parental satisfaction with perceived role enactment and found that both sexes tended to rate the female spouse as more functional. Further, women who preferred low spouse and low other involvement with parenting were more satisfied with their own parenting than women who wanted higher levels of husband or other involvement. Intriguingly, neither spouse expected nonfamilial agents to assume much more than 10% to 20% of the responsibility for any parental role, with the exceptions of school-relevant cognitive and physical development.

Finally, the item format of the PPRS can be changed. Gilbert et al. (1982) created a male child and a female child version of the test. Parents generally agreed that most parental responsibilities were applicable regardless of child gender. When parents disagreed, it usually involved the fathers' belief that male children required more parental responsibility than female children.

The clear limitation of the PPRS is the possibility that it simply measures the cultural stereotype of parenting roles and the respondents' tendency to endorse socially desirable items. Low scale variance and gender effects are consistent with this interpretation. Criterion validation of each scale against independent measures of parenting behavior would add greatly to the current meaning of PPRS scores. Currently, an individual can be empirically identified as statistically deviant on a given scale. Such deviance, however, could reflect different beliefs, different parenting behaviors, and/or a different inclination to endorse socially desirable items. Therefore, the PPRS cannot be currently recommended as a test of valid individual differences. In contrast, the PPRS provides good normative data and serves as a good item pool for researchers interested in measuring adult perceptions of parenting responsibilities.

REVIEWER'S REFERENCES

Gilbert, L. A., Hanson, G. R., & Davis, B. (1982). Perceptions of parental role responsibilities: Differences between mothers and fathers. *Family Relations, 31*, 261-269.

Gilbert, L. A. (1983). *Working fathers: Parenting in contemporary society.* Paper presented at the annual meeting of the American Psychological Association, Anaheim, CA.

Gilbert, L. A., Gram, A., & Hanson, G. (1983). *Preferred parenting: Comparisons of working women and men.* Paper presented at the annual meeting of the American Psychological Association, Anaheim, CA.

Gilbert, L. A., & Hanson, G. R. (1983). Perceptions of parental role responsibilities among working people: Development of a comprehensive measure. *Journal of Marriage and the Family, 45*, 203-212.

Dail, P. W. (1984). Possible television influence on parental socialization: Implications for parent education (Doctoral dissertation, University of Wisconsin-Madison, 1983). *Dissertation Abstracts International, 44A*, 1712A.

Farnill, D. (1985). *Perceptions of parental responsibilities for children's career development: A neglected area.* Unpublished manuscript, Victoria College, Australia.

[283]

Personal Assessment of Intimacy in Relationships.

Purpose: "Measures the expected (ideal) versus the realized (perceived) degree of intimacy" in a relationship.
Population: Couples.
Publication Date: 1981.
Acronym: PAIR.
Scores, 6: Emotion, Social, Sexual, Intellectual, Recreational, Conventionality.
Administration: Group.
Price Data, 1987: $20 per complete test including item booklet, answer sheet, scoring template, couple feedback sheet, and procedure manual (14 pages).
Time: (20–30) minutes.
Comments: Self-report measure; forms may be photocopied after obtaining permission by submitting Abstract on Proposed Study.
Authors: David H. Olson and Mark T. Schaefer.
Publisher: Family Social Science.

Review of Personal Assessment of Intimacy in Relationships by RICHARD M. WOLF, Professor of Psychology and Education, Teachers College, Columbia University, New York, NY:

Personal Assessment of Intimacy in Relationships (PAIRS) is a 36-item self-report instrument that measures five dimensions of intimacy: Emotion, Social, Sexual, Intellectual, and Recreational. It also contains a Conventionality scale that is essentially a lie scale. An earlier version of the instrument also contained a scale for Spiritual Intimacy but this was dropped when there was insufficient data to support its use.

PAIRS was developed after a review of the theoretical and research literature on intimacy. Intimacy, as defined by the authors, is more than self-disclosure and involves a closeness and sharing. Each aspect of intimacy is uniquely defined. Items were generated to measure each aspect of intimacy and tried out several times with subjects before a final set of items was selected. Factor analysis was used to help in the grouping of items. The results suggest that each subset of items loads substantially on a particular factor. However, the absence of the full matrix of factor loadings makes it impossible to know how each item loads on other factors. Also, there is no correlation matrix showing the level of relationship among the scales.

Subjects respond twice to the items. First, each subject responds on the basis of how well the item describes his or her current marital situation. Second, each subject responds in terms of how he or she would like it to be. Two scores for each dimension are obtained for a husband and wife: a perceived score and an ideal score. These are then plotted on a profile sheet which is then used as a basis for counseling.

The test manual does not provide any normative information for interpreting the score although an article by the authors furnishes means and standard deviations obtained for a sample of "192 non-clinical couples before they began an enrichment weekend offered by a national enrichment program" (Schaefer & Olson, 1981, p. 52). The authors emphasize that normative information is not appropriate for this instrument because it is the discrepancy between the ideal and actual levels for each dimension for husband and wife that are important and should serve as a basis for counseling work. Little guidance is provided, however, on how to evaluate the discrepancies between real and ideal levels for husband and wife other than a statement that a discrepancy of less than 5 points between the husband and wife's perceptions is probably inconsequential. Otherwise, the counselor and clients are left to their own devices to interpret the results. This is clearly unsatisfactory. The literature on testing is full of caveats about the unreliability of discrepancy scores. The authors do not discuss these concerns.

The authors' article presents some validity information in terms of correlations with other instruments in the area, notably the Waring Intimacy Questionnaire, the Locke-Wallace Marital Adjustment Scale, an adapted version of one of Jourard's Self-disclosure scales, Truax and Carkhoff's Empathy Scale, and 6 of the 10 Moos' Family Environment Scales. The correlations are statistically significant, but highly variable. It is difficult to interpret these results because, outside of the Waring Intimacy Questionnaire, the other instruments appear to be measuring somewhat different constructs.

The reliability of the perceptions on the various dimensions is not very high, ranging from .70 to .77 with a mean of .726. This is, however, about as high as one can expect from scales that consist of six items. The reliability of the Conventionality (lie) scale is .80. In their 1981 article, the authors report that no test-retest information was available. This situation does not seem to have been corrected 9 years later.

The procedure manual for PAIRS contains fairly clear instructions for administering and scoring the instrument and some rather limited directions for using the results. The manual suffers from a number of defects. There is an unacceptable number of typographical errors, a reliability estimate for the abandoned Spiritual Intimacy scale is listed, and means and standard deviations are reported for only two scales (Social Intimacy and Conventionality). The burden of wise use of results is clearly on the counselor. It is questionable how wisely counselors will be able to use test results with so little guidance.

SUMMARY. PAIRS is an instrument that was developed as an aid in counseling married couples about issues of intimacy. Although the instrument seems to have been carefully planned on the basis of a review of both the theoretical and research literature, there is so little information on the resulting instrument that its use, even as a counseling tool, is questionable. It would seem that an instrument that was published in 1981 should have a much more extensive evidential base to justify its use. PAIRS, unfortunately, does not.

REVIEWER'S REFERENCE
Schaefer, M. T., & Olson, D. H. (1981). Assessing intimacy: The PAIR Inventory. *Journal of Marital and Family Therapy*, 7 (1), 47-60.

[284]

Personal Experience Inventory.

Purpose: "To identify problems associated with adolescent chemical involvement."
Population: Ages 12–18.
Publication Dates: 1988–89.
Acronym: PEI.
Scores: 45 scores/screens: Chemical Involvement Problem Severity Section: Basic Scales (Personal Involvement with Chemicals, Effects from Drug Use, Social Benefits of Drug Use, Personal Consequences of Drug Use, Polydrug Use), Clinical Scales (Social-Recreational Drug Use, Psychological Benefits of Drug Use, Transsituational Drug Use, Preoccupation with Drugs, Loss of Control), Validity Indicators (Infrequent Responses, Defensiveness, Pattern Misfit), Drug Use Frequency/Duration/Age of Onset (Alcohol, Marijuana, LSD, Psychedelics, Cocaine, Amphetamines, Quaaludes, Barbiturates, Tranquilizers, Heroin, Opiates, Inhalants); Psychosocial Section: Personal Risk Factor Scales (Negative Self-Image, Psychological Disturbance, Social Isolation, Uncontrolled, Rejecting Convention, Deviant Behavior, Absence of Goals, Spiritual Isolation), Environmental Risk Factor Scales (Peer Chemical Environment, Sibling Chemical Use, Family Pathology, Family Estrangement), Problem Screens (Psychiatric Referral, Eating Disorder, Sexual Abuse, Physical Abuse, Family Chemical Dependency, Suicide Potential), Validity Indicators (Infrequent Responses, Defensiveness).
Administration: Group.
Parts, 2: Chemical Involvement Problem Severity Section, Psychosocial Section.
Price Data, 1989: $170 per complete kit including 10 test/answer booklets and manual ('89, 103 pages); $17.50 per test/answer booklet (includes scoring service); $32.50 per manual; $270 per IBM microcomputer package including diskette (up to 25 uses) and user's guide.
Time: (45–55) minutes.
Authors: Ken C. Winters and George A. Henly.
Publisher: Western Psychological Services.

Review of the Personal Experience Inventory by TONY TONEATTO, Psychologist, Addiction Research Foundation, Toronto, Ontario, Canada:

The Personal Experience Inventory (PEI) was designed, according to the authors, to fill in the gaps in the assessment of drug use by adolescents by providing "clinicians with a comprehensive and standardized self-report inventory to assist in the identification, referral, and treatment of problems associated with teenage alcohol and drug abuse" (manual, p. 1). In doing so, the PEI goes beyond simply assessing the type and frequency of drug use but also describes the rewards, consequences, and social effects of drug use. In addition, the PEI also assesses "risk factors," both personal and environmental, that may be important in treating drug abuse (e.g., Negative Self-Image, Family Pathology, Sexual Abuse). These elements are organized into two parts, Chemical Involvement Problem Severity (CIPS; 153 questions) and Psychosocial (147 questions). Either part can also be administered on its own. Several types of validity indicators to assess response distortion tendencies are also built into the test, which further enhances the attractiveness of this instrument.

The authors describe precisely the content and purpose for each of the scales that comprise the PEI, the population to which the test can be appropriately administered (i.e., adolescents between the ages of 12 and 18 who are believed to be experiencing some drug problem), and limitations in its use. Two sets of norms are provided, drug clinic and school, to permit an evaluation of the subjects' standings relative to other drug users and to their own high school peers. The computerized scoring and interpretation service available to PEI users is presented in sufficient detail to allow prospective users to evaluate the kind of information the PEI is capable of providing.

The construction of the PEI was first preceded by an evaluation of existing assessment tools which defined the type of instrument that was most needed. Subjects (who were largely male, white, and between 15 and 17 years of age) were recruited from several treatment centers, with 40% of the sample originating outside of Minnesota, where the test was developed. The CIPS scales were developed on a sample of 398 subjects and replicated on a second sample of 247. Similarly, the Psychosocial scales were developed on a sample of 293 and replicated on a second sample of 165. In both replication samples reliability coefficients were quite favorable (range of .81 to .97 for CIPS scales and of .74 to .90 for the Psychosocial scales).

Reliability of the PEI was assessed for internal consistency (coefficient alpha) and temporal stability (test-retest) using subjects from a variety of settings (drug clinic, juvenile offenders, school). Internal consistency coefficients were good to excellent for all samples and subgroups ($N = 2,202$) averaging .89 for the 10 CIPS scales, .81 for the 12 Psychosocial scales, and .68 for the 4 Response Distortion scales. Test-retest data were reported for both 1-week and 1-month intervals and for both school ($N = 123$) and clinic samples ($N = 149$). As expected, reliability (1-month interval) for the school (median .79 for CIPS scales) and clinic waiting list samples (median .84 for CIPS scales, median .72 for Psychosocial scales) was very good; longer test-retest intervals, especially if subjects received treatment, yielded lower coefficients, as might be expected. The authors caution use of the PEI following interventions for drug abuse.

Content validity appears to be quite adequate. The authors used published research findings, experts in the field, and clinicians to develop their initial 600-item pool. One item of concern, however, is use of the response anchors for many questions which are not well defined (i.e., *sometimes, often, almost always*).

In order to establish construct validity, the authors demonstrate that the PEI possesses: (*a*) *convergent validity*: Correlations of several PEI scales were fairly high and significant with related measures such as the Alcohol Dependence Scale, the Drug Use Frequency Checklist, and the Minnesota Multiphasic Personality Inventory (MMPI); (*b*) *criterion validity*: The PEI scale scores, especially the CIPS scales, differentiated those with and without a prior treatment history (based on a sample of 348) and those who received more intensive treatment referrals ($N = 141$) from less intensive referrals (outpatient, $N = 72$; no treatment, $N = 47$); and (*c*) *discriminant validity*: PEI scores differentiated clinical (drug clinic; $N = 889$; juvenile offenders, $N = 160$) and nonclinical samples (school, $N = 567$). Unfortunately, predictive validity was not assessed although it was identified as a focus for future research. Analyses of the internal structure of the PEI show that one factor accounted for most of the variance (70%) of the CIPS scales, not unexpectedly, as the scales comprising this part of the PEI reflected a common content area. The factor analysis of the psychosocial scales yielded a four-factor solution (psychological maladjustment, deviance, alienation, and family problems) which correlated well with other PEI scales.

In summary, the PEI is a much needed addition to the battery of adolescent drug use and abuse assessment. It is comprehensive, well grounded theoretically, and possesses good psychometric properties.

Review of the Personal Experience Inventory by JALIE A. TUCKER, *Professor of Psychology and Co-Director of Clinical Training, Auburn University, Auburn, AL:*

The recent proliferation of adolescent substance abuse treatment programs has not been matched by comparable advances in the development of age-appropriate assessment (or treatment) procedures. Consequently, clinical assessment procedures developed with adult substance abusers often have been used uncritically with younger clients, or adolescent-specific measures designed for use in school-based survey research have been used clinically without evaluation of their adequacy for this purpose. The Personal Experiences Inventory (PEI) was developed in response to the need for a measure of adolescent substance abuse that is sufficiently comprehensive for use in clinical situations. Designed primarily for use by an experienced clinician as part of an initial clinical evaluation of 12- to 18-year-olds suspected of substance misuse, the PEI provides a multidimensional assessment of substance use patterns and problems for up to 12 classes of abused drugs. As the authors note, it is not intended for use as a survey research instrument or for arriving at a formal diagnostic statement, but is best suited for providing a broad-spectrum assessment of adolescent substance disorders that is essential for effective disposition decisions and treatment planning.

The 300-item questionnaire assesses multiple dimensions within two major domains of substance-related dysfunction (i.e., severity of chemical involvement and associated psychosocial dysfunction). This emphasis is consistent with current views of substance abuse as multidimensional disorders that are defined both by excessive substance use and by adverse psychosocial, health, and related consequences. The chemical involvement section comprises five "basic" and five "clinical" scales that evaluate primarily the severity of substance involvement; also included are questions about the quantity and frequency of use of different drugs. The psychosocial section assesses eight personal risk factors for substance misuse (e.g., Negative Self-Image, Social Isolation) and four environmental risk factors (e.g., Peer Chemical Environment, Family Pathology) and also screens for other serious problems, including Sexual and Physical Abuse, Eating Disorders, and Suicidal Potential, that have obvious referral implications. The two major sections were developed for use either independently or conjointly, and each contains several validity indicators to detect distorted or infrequent response patterns. The test is computer scored through services made available by Western Psychological Services, and a sixth grade reading level is required.

Test construction was meticulous, thorough, and attentive to research on adolescent substance abuse. Detailed description of the standardization procedures and reliability and validity studies are presented in the test manual and also are reported in journal articles (e.g., Henly & Winters, 1988; Winters & Henly, 1987). Initial item selection was derived from a review of relevant research and from several existing questionnaire measures of substance disorders. Separate standardization procedures were conducted for each of the two major test sections using 12- to 18-year-olds who were being evaluated for substance abuse treatment in Minnesota facilities (total combined $N = 1,120$). Although males and females with different backgrounds were included, most subjects were white males between the ages of 15 and 17. Additional normative data were collected from students in grades 7 through 12 ($N = 693$) and from juvenile offenders ($N = 389$) in different geographic areas in the U.S. and Canada.

Reliability studies showed good to excellent internal consistency as measured by alpha coefficients for the great majority of PEI scales, and these findings held across sample type, sex, age, and ethnic subgroups. Results pertaining to the temporal stability of scores across 1-week and 1-month intervals, although generally adequate, were somewhat less robust and varied by sample type. Of particular concern was the finding that subjects who underwent drug treatment during the 1-month test-retest interval showed increased reporting of substance use from the first to the second administration. The authors apparently attributed this to subjects' greater willingness to admit drug use after the treatment intervention, but the instability in responding cautions against the test's use as a measure of treatment outcome in evaluation research.

Validity studies conducted to date indicated that the PEI, and especially the chemical severity section, effectively discriminated among subjects who varied by prior treatment history, treatment referral decisions, sample type (e.g., drug clinic vs. school), and intake diagnosis. Modest associations were obtained between subject and parent reports of some PEI scales, but the lack of significant agreement for most scales is a worrisome limitation that warrants further investigation. Also, some convergence was observed between subjects' PEI scores and scores on other measures of substance-related dysfunction (e.g., the Alcohol Dependence Scale; Horn, Skinner, Wanberg, & Foster, 1984) and psychopathology (i.e., the Minnesota Multiphasic Personality Inventory [MMPI]), but the appropriateness of using these instruments developed with adults for comparison with the PEI is questionable. Moreover, the PEI was not compared with existing measures of alcohol expectancies that have a demonstrated predictive relationship with subsequent alcohol use in adolescents (reviewed by Leigh, 1989). This oversight is worth pursuing in future research.

The results of factor analytic studies were not particularly encouraging about the internal structure of the PEI, and this comprises its major limitation. Analysis of the five basic scales of the chemical severity section yielded a single factor that accounted for over 70% of the variance and that was highly correlated with a single scale (the Personal Involvement With Chemicals scale). Analysis of the psychosocial scales yielded a four-factor solution that bore little relationship to the organizational structure of the 12 scales included in this section of the PEI. Also, the scales and factors included in the chemical severity and psychosocial sections were intercorrelated to a considerable degree, which further attests to the need to reduce scale redundancies in revisions of the PEI. Finally, research evaluating the ability of pretreatment PEI scores to predict treatment outcome is lacking and is important for establishing the overall utility of the measure.

These unresolved validity issues notwithstanding, the PEI has much to recommend its use for the clinical purposes for which it was designed. The test fills an important gap in the assessment of adolescent substance disorders and, if used as intended as part of an overall clinical evaluation, it should assist clinicians in obtaining the comprehensive information required for effective disposition decisions and treatment development. Although modification of the complex scale structure to reduce redundancies seems indicated, the authors' careful attention to the relevant research and their focus on the multidimensional nature of substance misuse in developing the PEI are commendable. If revisions of the PEI are equally attentive to empirical and conceptual considerations, the instrument should come to enjoy widespread clinical usage.

REVIEWER'S REFERENCES

Horn, J. L., Skinner, H. A., Wanberg, K., & Foster, F. M. (1984). Alcohol Dependence Scale (ADS). Toronto: Addiction Research Foundation.

Winters, K. C., & Henly, G. A. (1987). Advances in the assessment of adolescent chemical dependency: Development of a Chemical Use Problem Severity Scale. Psychology of Addictive Behaviors, 1, 146-153.

Henly, G. A., & Winters, K. C. (1988). Development of Problem Severity Scales for the assessment of adolescent alcohol and drug abuse. International Journal of the Addictions, 23, 65-85.

Leigh, B. C. (1989). In search of the seven dwarves: Issues of measurement and meaning in alcohol expectancy research. Psychological Bulletin, 105, 361-373.

[285]
Personal History Checklist for Adults.

Purpose: To obtain historical information during routine intake procedures.
Population: Adult clients of mental health services.
Publication Date: 1989.
Scores: Item scores only.
Administration: Individual.
Manual: No Manual.
Price Data, 1990: $26.95 per 25 checklists.
Time: Administration time not reported.
Comments: Checklist can be completed by client or clinician.
Author: John A. Schinka.
Publisher: Psychological Assessment Resources, Inc.

Review of the Personal History Checklist for Adults by THOMAS A. WIDIGER, Professor of Psychology, University of Kentucky, Lexington, KY:

The Personal History Checklist for Adults (PHCA) was developed as an aid for the completion of a client's personal history. It consists of 119 items that cover the presenting problem (8 items), family background (13 items), childhood and adolescent history (37 items), educational and occupational history (21 items), medical history and current health (16 items), family history (8 items), and current situation (16 items). The clinician can either provide the checklist directly to the client, or use it as a guide when conducting an intake interview.

The PHCA has no manual, validation research, or scoring system. The author of the PHCA was simply trying to respond to an expressed need for a means by which clinicians could provide a systematic review and explicit documentation of the information that is routinely collected during an initial or an intake interview. The clinician would have on file whether the client has a history of poor grades, any current medical treatment, a (nuclear) family history of problems with alcohol, a recent change in appetite, a loss of a driver's license because of drinking, was ever sentenced to the stockade while in the service, and learned to walk and talk earlier or later than most children. Interpretation is at the item level. One hardly needs any research to test the validity of items assessing race, the client's country of origin, age when starting the ninth grade, the number of times the client has been married, whether the client was the youngest or oldest child in the family of origin, and the approximate age of the mother at the time of the client's birth. Clinicians may provide their own unique interpretation to some of the items, but no suggestions or recommendations regarding interpretations are made by the test's author. The PHCA is a fact-finding and documenting instrument, not an interpretative inventory.

In hindsight, it might have been useful to submit the PHCA to a sample of clinicians for a systematic review. The PHCA was constructed on the basis of suggestions by clinicians, and it was revised as a result of informal reviews. A subjective reading of the instrument suggests that it is likely to be useful and informative. Some of the items are perhaps of questionable use, such as asking whether an adult client has had a tonsillectomy or worked on the school yearbook during high school. One or two areas might be inadequately covered. Inquiry is made of specific medical illnesses in relatives (including arthritis, epilepsy, and "problems with digestive system"), but not of specific psychological disorders (such as depression) other than alcohol and drug abuse. However, these comments could be petty and idiosyncratic to this reviewer. The actual utility and credibility of the instrument would be addressed better by a systematic consumer satisfaction study.

Clinicians who do not conduct systematic intakes would be well advised to use the PHCA or any similar alternative. Some clinicians perhaps begin therapy as soon as the client enters the office, allowing most of the background information to unfold as therapy progresses. This is unnecessarily blind, wasteful, and at times even risky. Most clinicians will have the client complete a background questionnaire. The PHCA is likely to be more comprehensive than questionnaires currently in use, with the exception of inventories to assess clinical pathology. The PHCA contains items that concern clinical symptomatology (e.g., anxiety and drug use), but it is not a diagnostic instrument and there are obviously many detailed and comprehensive inventories to assess the presence, manner, and degree of clinical functioning. The most efficient use of the PHCA would be to have the client complete it and then conduct an interview to clarify or focus on areas of concern. Conducting the initial interview with the PHCA is likely to be somewhat stilted.

The PHCA should not be used in research. The PHCA may provide an excessive amount of irrelevant information and an inadequate coverage of the particular domain of interest. Any researcher is fully capable of constructing a comparable questionnaire that would be more specifically tailored to the needs of a particular study. However, this is not a criticism of the PHCA because it was not intended to be used in research.

The primary function of the PHCA is to provide the clinician with a means to document explicitly the assessment of background information. It will clearly serve this purpose. Any competent clinician could construct a questionnaire that would be more specific to his or her own needs, but those who wish to save time and to use an instrument with a professional appearance will be happy with the PHCA.

[286]
Personal Resource Questionnaire.

Purpose: Provides information about adults' social networks and perceived levels of social support.
Population: Ages 18–80.
Publication Dates: 1981–87.
Acronym: PRQ-85.
Scores: Part I, 3 scores: Size of Network, Number of Problems Experienced, Degree of Satisfaction with Help Received; Part II, total score only.
Administration: Group.
Parts, 2: I, II.
Manual: No manual.
Price Data, 1990: $3 per instructions and Questionnaire; additional copies may be photocopied locally.
Time: (10–15) minutes.
Comments: May be self-administered; Parts I and II can be administered independently of each other.
Authors: Patricia Brandt and Clarann Weinert.
Publisher: Patricia Brandt and Clarann Weinert.

Review of the Personal Resource Questionnaire by ESTHER E. DIAMOND, Educational and Psychological Consultant, Evanston, IL:

The Personal Resource Questionnaire (PRQ) is a self-report inventory that measures two types of adult social support. Part I measures the scope of the support network (i.e., the number of interpersonal resources of the social network the respondent can turn to across 10 life situations, and the level of satisfaction with each of these resources). Part II assesses the respondent's *perceived* level of social support.

Part I deals with 10 everyday personal and family situations or problems and asks the respondent to consider each statement in light of his or her own situation. The respondent then checks one or more of a list of 13 resources from which to seek help in the event of "urgent needs," indicates whether or not there have been urgent needs in the past 6 months, and if so, the level of satisfaction (on a 6-point Likert scale) with the help received. The list of resources seems comprehensive without becoming too specific—for example, parent, child or children, spouse or partner or significant other, relative, spiritual advisor, professional, agency, self-help group. The needs or problems include caring for a sick or handicapped family member; concerns about the relationship with a spouse, partner, or other intimate person; problems with a family member or friend; financial problems; loneliness; illness; conditions of life; and work-related problems. Part I yields three scores—Size of the Network, Number of Problems Experienced, and Degree of Satisfaction with the Help Received. It does not yield a total score.

Part II is a Likert scale of 25 self-report statements designed to measure the individual's perceived level of support. The statements represent internalized, subjective feelings rather than the more descriptive responses called for in Part I (e.g., "There is little opportunity in my life to be giving and caring to another person"; "There is no one to talk to about how I am feeling"; "I belong to a group in which I feel important.") Part II yields a total score. Although it was developed with five subscales in mind, factor analysis supported only three subscales, and until adequate evidence from replications of the factor analysis confirm or contradict these results, the authors have opted to encourage users, who are mostly researchers, to use the total score—the total of the 25 scale values. Development of a social desirability scale to detect response bias has been ruled out. There is no evidence of a gender-related response pattern.

The two parts of the PRQ can be self-administered and used independently of each other. There is no manual as yet, but use of the PRQ by the authors and other researchers has provided a body of data on which to establish a normative baseline. Studies so far have involved groups of "basically well" persons: 20-to-30-year-old young adults; middle adults 30 to 50 years old; and older adults to approximately 80 years of age. These data are now available to researchers for making comparisons between studies. Response data by educational level, income, race, and other demographic variables are still being collected.

The test-retest estimate of reliability for 100 adults ages 30 to 37 was .81 for interpersonal resources (Part I) and .72 for perceived social support (Part II), $p < .001$. Cronbach's alpha reliability coefficients for the Part II total score from several studies range from .85 to .93 for groups of young, middle, and older adults with the groups varying in size from 45 to 188.

For evidence of construct validity, correlations were obtained for each social support variable with four mental health and personality variables— Beck's Depression Inventory (BDI), Spielberger's Anxiety scale, and the Introversion and Extroversion scales of Eysenck's Personality Inventory (EPI). Significant negative correlations were obtained between Part II's perceived support total score and Spielberger's Anxiety ($r = -.37$), Beck's Depression ($r = -.42$), and Eysenck's Introversion (Neuroticism) scales ($r = -.28$), and a positive correlation ($r = .32$) with Eysenck's Extroversion scale. There were no significant correlations between the quantitatively defined Part I support measures and the four mental health indicators. The authors interpret these results as indicating that the PRQ measures a different construct from that measured by the four mental health and personality variables. There is no explanation, however, of the significant positive correlation with the Eysenck Extroversion scale, which indicates modest overlap between the two measures.

At present, the PRQ is being made available only for research purposes. The authors are wisely trying to establish a strong psychometric basis for this measure of social support, which they foresee as being applicable in multidisciplinary research. They are also interested in developing the PRQ for clinical application, and are seeking to have it administered to multiple samples with varied demographic profiles and to groups of persons experiencing physical, psychological, or social stress.

In summary, the PRQ is a two-part self-report instrument for measuring the social and interpersonal resource systems of adults. Both parts—the first dealing with the size of the social network, number of problems experienced, and degree of satisfaction with help received, and the second the perceived levels of social support—may be administered and used separately. A brief report on the data collected prior to 1991 indicates that the PRQ may be

measuring something not measured by other personality or problems-checklist instruments, but until more studies have been conducted, it should be used on an experimental basis only. Further research should also explore the relationship between Part I and Part II. Production of a manual for the experimental form is strongly recommended and should be extremely helpful to those interested in conducting research on the PRQ.

[287]
Personal Style Assessment.
Purpose: To assess an individual's personal style of communication.
Population: Adults.
Publication Dates: 1980–87.
Scores, 4: Thinker, Intuitor, Sensor, Feeler.
Administration: Group.
Manual: No manual.
Price Data, 1988: $40 per set of 20 including tests and answer sheets, information ('87, 4 pages), and instructor guidelines ('80, 2 pages).
Time: (15–25) minutes.
Comments: Self-administered, self-scored.
Author: Training House, Inc.
Publisher: Training House, Inc.

Review of the Personal Style Assessment by CATHY W. HALL, Assistant Professor of Psychology, East Carolina University, Greenville, NC:

The Personal Style Assessment is a measure of an individual's communication style and is designed to be used with adults. It is based on Carl Jung's theory of four psychological functions: thinking, feeling, intuiting, and sensing. Although a person is capable of using each of these functions, Jung's premise is that one function typically will dominate (superior function) and the second strongest function will usually be an auxiliary function to the first. The weaker functions may be repressed and not recognized at the conscious level. The preferable balance would be for all four functions to be equally developed. However, this is thought to occur only when the self has become actualized, and this is never fully achieved (Jung, 1971; Hall & Lindzey, 1978).

The purpose of the Personal Style Assessment is to provide a measure of each of these four functions. Four scores are computed: Thinker, Intuitor, Sensor, and Feeler. The scores are obtained by having the person respond to 10 groups of four words each. A 4 is assigned to the word that best characterizes the individual, 3 for the next best, then 2, and finally a 1 for the word that is least descriptive. The words have been assigned to one of the four scales, and a score for each scale is computed based on the person's ratings of these descriptors. The form is self-administered and self-scored.

No information was presented concerning how the descriptors were chosen or assigned to the four categories; nor were any data reported concerning the scores obtained through the self-administration. Standardization, reliability, and validity information is notably absent. Once an individual has obtained the four scores, no process is offered to judge whether significant differences exist among the scores. In fact, no treatment of the auxiliary functions and their purposes is delineated.

In addition to the above-mentioned problems in regard to standards for test development, several questions arise concerning the theoretical assumptions made by the Personal Style Assessment. Supposedly, the score is able to give the individual an understanding of his/her personal style of communicating. The authors state: "Our success in relating to others depends on the degree to which our communication style is 'in sync' with the other person's. By knowing the cues and clues that indicate a person's communication style, we are able to modify our own style to narrow the gap." Although the Personal Style Assessment *might* give an understanding to an individual about his/her own superior function, it is not at all clear how one would readily recognize another's style—let alone be able to quickly change one's style to "fit" the situation. This problem in adapting communication styles seems particularly acute because the theoretical presumption is the weaker functions may be repressed and unconscious. Is this assessment to be used by only those who have come close to being fully actualized? Jung postulated this was a prerequisite to acquiring a balance among all four functions. The authors do provide a brief four-page overview of "Your Four Communication Styles." Strengths and weaknesses of each primary style are presented as well as "typical telephone behavior," "typical office decor," and "typical style of dress." Is this how another's style is determined?

Jung's typology has been applied to various settings, and O'Brien (1985) provides a brief overview of some of the assessment devices that purport to measure typology. Other measures such as the Myers-Briggs Type Indicator (Myers & McCaulley, 1985; 10:206) provide far better validated instruments than the Personal Style Assessment. The Personal Style Assessment raises more questions than it answers and appears to be a hastily developed and superficial assessment device without any thought to proper standards for psychological test development or theoretical postulates. Jung's theory is highly complex. An individual does not gain a meaningful understanding of these theoretical assumptions by using a brief self-administered, self-scored form.

REVIEWER'S REFERENCES

Jung, C. (1971). A psychological theory of types. In *Psychological types: The collected works of C. G. Jung* (Vol. 6). Princeton, NJ: Princeton University Press.
Hall, C., & Lindzey, G. (1978). *Theories of Personality* (3rd ed.). New York: John Wiley & Sons.
Myers, I., & McCaulley, M. (1985). *Manual: A guide to the development an use of the Myers-Briggs Type Indicator.* Palo Alto, CA: Consulting Psychologists Press.
O'Brien, R. (1985). Using Jung more (and etching him in stone less). *Training, 22* (5), 53-66.

Review of the Personal Style Assessment by GERALD L. STONE, Professor of Counseling Psychology and Director, University Counseling Service, The University of Iowa, Iowa City, IA:

The Personal Style Assessment (PSA) is a paper-and-pencil self-assessment exercise. The instrument is designed to identify characteristics associated with four styles of communication—Intuitor, Thinker, Feeler, and Sensor. The PSA is linked to Jung's type theory as interpreted by John Bledsoe in an article in a 1976 issue of *Training*, a magazine concerned with human resources.

In the Self-Assessment exercise, participants are presented with two sheets. The first sheet contains the instructions, examples, and 10 groups of four words. Within each group of words, participants are asked to assign a 4 to the word that best characterizes them, a 3 to the next best, a 2 to the next best, and a 1 to the word that is least descriptive. The record sheet, a noncarbon reproducing scoring sheet with scoring directions, enables each participant to sum his or her scores for each of the four communication styles.

Although the two-page Self-Assessment exercise is reported to take 5 minutes to complete, the guidelines for the PSA embed the exercise in a training workshop situation. The guidelines recommend completion of the Self-Assessment followed by explanations based on Jung's work and a reprint of a four-page article titled "Your Four Communicating Styles." After hearing the explanations and reading the article, discussion questions and dyadic exercises (e.g., "guess the style of another") are recommended to the participants. Cautions are briefly mentioned about stereotyping and value-laden tendencies ("Which is the best type?"). It is suggested that each person makes use of all four styles, although the mixture differs from person to person.

There is no manual. The instrument, as well as the workshop format, are presented uncontaminated by evaluation and/or psychometric data. There is no attempt to link the instrument to other related instruments (e.g., Myers-Briggs Type Indicator, MBTI; 10:206), nor is there any evidence of behavioral validations for these communication styles.

In summary, the PSA can be categorized only as a "parlor game" until validity evidence for the instrument is presented. Although the MBTI is not without problems (e.g., type versus continuous dimensions), validation data have been presented, thus suggesting those interested in communication analyses from a Jungian perspective may be better served by the MBTI.

REVIEWER'S REFERENCE

Bledsoe, J. L. (1976). Why, when, and how to use each of your four communicating styles. *Training, 13*, 18-21.

[288]
Personnel Assessment Selection System.

Purpose: To "screen out potential problem employees" before hiring, by screening for trust risk, alienation, and emotional stability.
Population: Retail and business applicants, and applicants for police/fire/security positions.
Publication Dates: 1970–86.
Acronym: PASS.
Scores: Total score only.
Administration: Group.
Price Data: Available from publisher for test materials including validity/reliability information booklet ('86, 5 pages), information booklet (no date, 13 pages), and validity manual (no date, 95 pages).
Comments: The PASS series are various combinations of the T.A., A.I., E.S., and D.A. Surveys to serve the specific requirements of organizations (PASS includes T.A., A.I., and E.S. Surveys; PASS II includes T.A. and A.I. Surveys; PASS III includes condensation of T.A., A.I., and D.A. Surveys); 4 surveys may be administered separately or in combination.
Author: Alan L. Strand.
Publisher: Psychological Surveys Corporation.

a) ALIENATION INDEX.
Purpose: "A method of determining pre-employment alienated attitudes toward work, employees, work conditions, and fellow employees."
Publication Date: 1982.
Time: (15) minutes.
Comments: Test booklet title is A.I. Survey.

b) TRUSTWORTHINESS ATTITUDE.
Purpose: A trust prediction instrument based purely on attitudinal questions.
Publication Dates: 1970–83.
Time: (15) minutes.
Comments: Test booklet title is T.A. Survey.

c) EMOTIONAL STABILITY.
Purpose: Self-report questionnaire to indicate emotional status.
Population: Applicants for police and security positions.
Time: (5–10) minutes.
Comments: Test booklet title is E.S. Survey.

d) DRUG ATTITUDE.
Purpose: Evaluates an applicant's attitude toward illegal drug usage and abuse of alcohol.
Time: Administration time not reported.
Comments: Test booklet title is D.A. Survey.
Cross References: For reviews by John K. Butler, Jr., and Denise M. Rousseau of the T.A. Survey, see 9:1223.

Review of the Personnel Assessment Selection System by MICHAEL B. BUNCH, Vice President, Measurement Incorporated, Durham, NC:

There are at least five surveys available from Psychological Surveys Corporation. The ADT (Alcohol, Drugs, Trust) is a combination of parts of shorter tests. The other four surveys assess motivation/alienation, attitudes about alcohol and drugs, attitudes about leniency and theft, and supervisory attitudes. Each survey is presented in the same format, a series of statements to which the applicant is asked to respond "Yes," "?," or "No."

The purpose of the Personnel Assessment Selection System (PASS) is to screen out potential problem employees without resorting to polygraph tests or invasive personality or honesty tests. Such tests might ask the candidate, for example, to reveal past theft or drug use. Noninvasive measures instead ask about attitudes about such activities by presenting statements and asking applicants to tell whether they believe the statements are true. For example, applicants might be asked to respond as noted above to the statement, "Most people steal things every now and then." The theory is that people who have actually stolen at some time would be more likely to agree with such a statement than people who have not stolen.

The theoretical foundation for such assertions is alluded to in the five-page technical manual but never directly addressed. I requested additional information from the publisher and received a literature review. The annotated bibliography goes back to the 1939 Hawthorne studies and cites a variety of sources from social and industrial psychology. Some of the references are quite relevant; others are not. A few simply stretch the point. Yet, on the whole, there seems to be a reasonable argument for the relationship between attitude and behavior, if not in the specific terms of the PASS, then at least in general terms.

If one accepts the basic premise that attitude predicts behavior, the sole remaining criterion for acceptance of the PASS is that it accurately measure defined attitudes and predict specific behaviors. Evidence must include item analysis data and data from reliability and validity studies.

The attitudes measured by some items are unclear. For all but the ADT survey, 20–30% of items discriminate only modestly (i.e., 10% or less difference between "high" and "low" scorers). The LT (leniency-theft) scale contains five items that actually discriminate negatively. The AD scale (alcohol and drugs) has two items that do not discriminate at all, and the other scales have one to three negatively discriminating items. One item, for example, states that people steal for the thrill of it rather than because of need. Only about half of all applicants agree. Trustworthy applicants (i.e., those who score low on the total scale) disagree 12% more often than untrustworthy applicants. Perhaps untrustworthy applicants have actually stolen for a thrill, whereas the more trustworthy applicants believe (incorrectly, it would seem) that most people who steal do so because they are in need. Although this item represents the most extreme case, it appears in two of the surveys and there are eight others with similar problems (out of a total of 360 items across five surveys).

Reliability, measured as split-half coefficients, ranges from .85 to .94 for the various scales. The publisher reports one set of reliability coefficients for small samples (e.g., 132 retail clerk applicants) and then higher sets of coefficients for large samples (e.g., 12,000 applicants for all positions over a multi-year period). No test-retest coefficients are given.

The technical manual reports validity coefficients in terms of point biserial coefficients with polygraph results. At other points the manual describes relationships between PASS scores and evaluations by professional psychologists, again reported as point biserial correlation coefficients.

A separate document entitled "Validity" was also provided by the publisher. This document described additional validity studies. It is apparently an in-house document and is extremely difficult to use because it is devoid of table of contents, page numbers, or an index. Quality of the various studies is uneven. One study purports to show the relationship between scores and job seniority. Only the scores of 32 employees with 2 or more years' tenure are provided. Their mean score is lower than the national mean. The study fails to report the scores of other employees at the same establishment, even though those scores are available. Other studies are more thorough. For example, one study at Wal-Mart reports quite accurate prediction of retention 3 and 6 months after hiring. Other studies indicate results of the PASS accurately predict supervisor ratings 6 months after hiring.

The publisher has conducted a series of bias studies and found little difference between scores of white and black applicants or between those of male and female applicants when socioeconomic variables are controlled. Significant socioeconomic status differences were found, however. The fact that the surveys appear to be free of ethnic and gender bias is a distinct point in their favor.

The PASS surveys are a welcome alternative to polygraph tests and invasive or intrusive questionnaires. Although some of the items are fakable, they seem on the whole to be far less fakable than questions about past deviant behavior. Given the stated objective of ranking applicants for further interview (rather than labeling them as low or high risks), the reported reliability coefficients are adequate, particularly when the number of applicants far exceeds the number of positions. Similarly, validity information, particularly that reported in the supplemental document "Validity," would support use of the surveys.

To the publisher, I would recommend two things. First, take a close look at the discriminating power of the items in each survey. Eliminate or replace those

with weak or negative discriminating power. This step may actually help shorten the surveys without decreasing reliability. Second, organize the background literature and the sounder validity studies and include them in the next technical manual. To the potential user, I would recommend one thing: Ask for and read the literature review and "Validity" before you proceed further. This set of instruments is potentially worthwhile, so long as the user is aware of and understands its limitations.

[289]
Personnel Relations Survey.
Purpose: "To assess the understanding and behavior of managers in their interpersonal relationships."
Population: Managers.
Publication Date: 1967–87.
Scores 6: Exposure and Feedback scores for each of 3 relationships (with Colleagues, Employees, and Supervisors).
Administration: Group.
Price Data, 1990: $6.95 per booklet ('87, 18 pages).
Time: Administration time not reported.
Comments: Self-administered, self-scored; based on the Johari Window Model of interpersonal relationships.
Authors: Jay Hall and Martha S. Williams.
Publisher: Teleometrics International.

[290]
Phoenix Ability Survey System.
Purpose: To test vocationally related abilities and interests through the use of computer analysis to find specific jobs which fit clients' abilities, special needs, and interests.
Population: High school and junior college students, handicapped adults, educationally disadvantaged, unemployed adults, non-English-speaking.
Publication Dates: 1985–86.
Acronym: PASS.
Scores: 30 ability factors: Motor-Unilateral (Finger Dexterity, Wrist-Finger Speed, Arm-Hand Steadiness), Motor-Bilateral (Manual Dexterity, Two-Arm Coordination, Two-Hand Coordination, Hand-Tool Dexterity, Multi-Limb Coordination, Machine Feeding), Perceptual (Perceptual Accuracy, Perceptual Speed, Spatial Perception, Depth Perception), Perceptual-Motor Coordination (Aiming, Reaction Time, Fine Perceptual Motor Coordination, Visual Motor Reversal), Intelligence (Abstract Reasoning, Verbal Reasoning, Numerical Reasoning, Response Orientation), Achievement (Reading, Arithmetic), Strength (Hand Strength, Lifting Ability), People Relationships (Leadership-Consideration, Leadership-Structure, Sales, Following Directions).
Administration: Individual.
Price Data, 1989: $8,200 (includes software and required training available from publisher).
Special Edition: Non-English-speaking edition available.
Time: (240–360) minutes.
Author: Edward J. Hester.
Publisher: Hester Evaluation Systems, Inc.

[291]

Phonological Processes Assessment and Intervention.

Purpose: "Provides for assessment and intervention in 11 phonological processes that commonly occur in the speech of children who are developing speech normally as well as those who demonstrate phonological process disorders."

Population: Children with articulation disorders.

Publication Date: 1987.

Acronym: PPAIP.

Scores, 12: Initial Consonant Deletion, Deletion of Final Consonant, Prevocalic Voicing, Weak Syllable Deletion, Fronting, Stopping, Consonant Cluster Reduction, Postvocalic Devoicing, Stridency Deletion, Gliding of Liquids, Vocalization, Traditional Articulation.

Subtests: Available as separates.

Administration: Individual.

Levels, 2: Level 1, Level 2 (Deep Tests).

Price Data, 1989: $165 per complete kit including blackline masters (107 pages), 1,908 3 x 5 cards, and manual (15 pages).

Time: Administration time not reported.

Comments: Orally administered.

Authors: Allan K. Bird and Anne P. Higgins.

Publisher: DLM Teaching Resources.

Review of the Phonological Processes Assessment and Intervention by PENELOPE K. HALL, Associate Professor of Speech Pathology and Audiology, The University of Iowa, Iowa City, IA:

The authors of the Phonological Processes: Assessment and Intervention Program (PPAIP) state that the purpose of the instrument is to "assist speech-language therapists in planning assessment and intervention for children who have articulation disorders" (p. 2). This assistance comes in the form of two assessment processes (Level One and Level Two), and materials with which to implement an intervention program based on the results of the assessments. A specific rationale and information about the development of the PPAIP are not provided by the authors.

Level One Assessment consists of imposing the analysis of 11 phonological processes on the whole-word transcriptions of responses made to a standardized articulation test. Among the copious number of blackline masters included in the program are forms which facilitate this level of assessment for three commercially available articulation tests. Level Two Assessment involves administration of the Deep Tests developed for each of the 11 phonological processes. The Deep Tests materials provided consist of numerous picture-card stimuli and blackline masters for each of the tests. The Intervention Program consists of three sections: (*a*) introduction of the process, (*b*) drill and practice (which emphasizes use of minimal pairs), and (*c*) a home practice program. Materials and specific directions and suggestions are provided for each remedial section.

The authors of the PPAIP acknowledge that the developmental sequence of phonological processes is not agreed upon. Nonetheless, they state that the presumed developmental order presented in the PPAIP is that to which clinicians should adhere in both the assessment and intervention aspects. The authors provide no basis for this ordering. In fact, a comparison of the PPAIP sequence with that presented by other major phonological analysis instruments reveals major differences on this issue.

The program includes 1,908 black and white picture-card stimuli, which appear to be well drawn. These are used for the Level Two assessment Deep Tests and for the minimal pairs used in the second section of the Intervention Program. However, the vocabulary words may be too advanced and the drawings too abstract for an assessment and intervention program aimed at preschool and early elementary school-age clients. Examples of this concern include the use of *gable*, *sag*, and *gaze* as stimuli for the Fronting Deep Test. Including the written word on the face of the card may provide wanted or unwanted graphemic cues for clients with reading skills.

The physical packaging of the PPAIP presents a problem. The outer case is not large enough for all nine of the smaller file cases containing the Deep Test and minimal pairs picture stimuli. To fit, several must be tipped on end and, because the smaller file cases do not close securely, the potential of spilling them is very likely. In addition, the Deep Test and minimal pairs cards for two of the processes are divided among several of the picture cases. This increases the examiner's difficulty in selecting specific stimuli during administration. This reviewer also suggests that the authors edit the PPAIP manual to eliminate the repeated references to the professional as a *therapist*, a term the American Speech-Language-Hearing Association (ASHA) has officially discouraged for a number of years.

The PPAIP assesses 11 processes, which may limit its usefulness with many clients. By comparison, the Assessment of Phonological Processes—Revised (Hodson, 1986) addresses 30 error patterns, and the Khan-Lewis Phonological Analysis (Khan & Lewis, 1986; 10:164) addresses 15 processes. These are preferred assessment instruments because they are more comprehensive and are based on stronger rationales and supporting research.

REVIEWER'S REFERENCES

Hodson, B. W. (1986). The Assessment of Phonological Processes—Revised. Austin, TX: PRO-ED, Inc.

Khan, L. M. L., & Lewis, N. (1986). Khan-Lewis Phonological Analysis. Circle Pines, MN: American Guidance Service, Inc.

Review of the Phonological Processes Assessment and Intervention by MARY PANNBACKER, Professor and Program Director, Department of Communication Disorders, School of Allied Health Professions, Louisiana State University Medical Center, Shreveport, LA and GRACE MIDDLETON, Associate Professor, Speech-Language Pathology Program, College of Nursing, University of Texas, El Paso, TX:

The Phonological Processes: Assessment and Intervention Program (PPAIP) is based on phonological processes identified by Ingram, Shriberg, and Weiner. The program is appropriate if speech has multiple misarticulations and is somewhat intelligible or unintelligible. The PPAIP is also appropriate when there are few misarticulations and speech is intelligible. It takes about 30 minutes to administer according to the VHS demonstration tape. Included are: (*a*) forms and instructions for using popular standardized articulation tests (Goldman-Fristoe Test of Articulation, The Photo Articulation Test, and The Arizona Articulation Proficiency Scale) to complete a phonological process analysis; (*b*) criterion-referenced deep tests for each process with accompanying summary forms; (*c*) picture word cards and stuffed animals; (*d*) IEP forms; (*e*) traditional articulation therapy materials; and (*f*) a home practice program.

Eleven phonological processes that commonly occur in the speech of young children are considered in developmental order: Initial Consonant Deletion; Deletion of Final Consonant; Prevocalic Voicing; Weak Syllable Deletion; Fronting; Stopping; Consonant Cluster Reduction; Postvocalic Devoicing; Stridency Deletion; Gliding; and Vocalization. Guidelines for rating severity are based on performance on a standardized articulation test and a phonetic inventory, occurrence of phonological processes, syllable structure, intelligibility, and stimulability. Two assessment levels, standardized articulation testing to identify the presence and severity of an articulation disorder and deep testing for each process are offered, each containing from 40 to 210 words. The criterion for concluding the testing results in reduced time spent in completing the phonological analysis (about 10 minutes), and focuses on the performance at the developmental age level rather than on a complete analysis of the child's entire phonological system.

Intervention consists of first introducing the process performing drill and practice and instituting a home practice program. Practicing speech-language pathologists using the PPAIP describe it as "systematic" and "worth the money." They rate the IEP and Home Practice Program as being of particular value. They report that their young clients especially like the Tommy Turtle character in the program. The structured and completely packaged PPAIP is recommended by clinicians for speech-language pathologists who are beginning their careers as service providers.

The review of the background literature for the program is limited and dated. There is one reference to a scholarly journal, which is a state publication.

Although the American Speech-Language-Hearing Association adopted the term speech-language pathologist in 1976, Bird and Higgins use the term "speech-language therapist" or "therapist" (Cornett & Chabon, 1988). The term *widgets* for picture cards representing a nonsense word in a minimal pair may be more appreciated by the adult administrators of the program than young children for whom the program was designed. Some of the pictures targeting one of several items may be confusing for children until they memorize the vocabulary desired for each.

REVIEWER'S REFERENCE

Cornett, B., & Chabon, S. (1988). *The clinical practice of speech-language pathology*. Columbus, OH: Merrill Publishing Co.

[292]

The Pictorial Scale of Perceived Competence and Social Acceptance for Young Children.

Purpose: Measures "perceived competence and perceived social acceptance" in young children.
Population: Preschool through second grade.
Publication Dates: 1980–83.
Scores, 4: Cognitive Competence, Peer Acceptance, Physical Competence, Maternal Acceptance.
Administration: Individual.
Forms, 2: Preschool/Kindergarten, First/Second Grade.
Price Data, 1989: $15 per booklet of pictures (preschool/kindergarten for girls ['80, 54 pages], preschool/kindergarten for boys ['80, 54 pages], first/second grade for girls ['81, 54 pages], first/second grade for boys ['81, 54 pages]); $7 per manual ('83, 21 pages).
Time: Administration time not reported.
Comments: Downward extension of the Perceived Competence Scale for Children.
Authors: Susan Harter and Robin Pike in collaboration with Carole Efron, Christine Chao, and Beth Ann Bierer.
Publisher: Susan Harter.

TEST REFERENCES

1. Anderson, P. L., & Adams, P. J. (1985). The relationship of five-year-olds' academic readiness and perceptions of competence and acceptance. *The Journal of Educational Research, 79*, 114-118.
2. Simmons, C. H., & Zumpf, C. (1986). The gifted child: Perceived competence, prosocial moral reasoning, and charitable donations. *The Journal of Genetic Psychology, 147*, 97-105.
3. Gullo, D. F., & Ambrose, R. P. (1987). Perceived competence and social acceptance in kindergarten: Its relationship to academic performance. *The Journal of Educational Research, 81*, 28-32.
4. Lobato, D., Barbour, L., Hall, L. J., & Miller, C. T. (1987). Psychosocial characteristics of preschool siblings of handicapped and nonhandicapped children. *Journal of Abnormal Child Psychology, 15*, 329-338.
5. Ulrich, B. D. (1987). Perceptions of physical competence, motor competence, and participation in organized sport: Their interrelationships in young children. *Research Quarterly for Exercise and Sport, 58*, 57-67.
6. Pasnak, R., Denham, S., & Groff, R. (1988). Accelerated cognitive development of kindergarteners: One year later. *Child Study Journal, 18*, 249-263.
7. Knapp, P. A., & Deluty, R. H. (1989). Relative effectiveness of two behavioral parent training programs. *Journal of Clinical Child Psychology, 18*, 314-322.
8. Holguin, O., & Sherrill, C. (1990). Use of a pictorial scale of perceived competence and acceptance with learning disabled boys. *Perceptual and Motor Skills, 70*, 1235-1238.
9. Fantuzzo, J. W., DePaola, L. M., Lambert, L., & Martino, T. (1991). Effects of interparental violence on the psychological adjustment

and competencies of young children. *Journal of Consulting and Clinical Psychology, 59,* 258-265.

Review of The Pictorial Scale of Perceived Competence and Social Acceptance for Young Children by WILLIAM B. MICHAEL, *Professor of Education and Psychology, University of Southern California, Los Angeles, CA:*

In both the Preschool-Kindergarten and the First and Second Grade versions of The Pictorial Scale of Perceived Competence and Social Acceptance for Young Children, each of the four scales—Cognitive Competence, Physical Competence, Peer Acceptance, and Maternal Acceptance—consists of six items comprising two pictures placed side by side. Each pair of pictures portrays an activity having contrasting levels of perceived competence or social acceptance. The 12 items in the first two of the four scales represent what the authors have termed Perceived Competence; the other 12 items in the third and fourth scales, Social Acceptance. Each of the two versions of the instrument geared to different age levels has two forms with parallel items, one for boys and the other for girls, with the only appreciable difference being the placement of the individual of central interest (usually intended to be the examinee in a learning or social situation) in the picture having the same gender as the subject.

Within each of the two 6-item scales pertaining to perceived competence, for three of the items the picture in the left-hand position represents high competence, and for the remaining three items, the picture in the left-hand position reflects low competence. A comparable statement can be made for the placement of pictures in the two 6-item scales portraying social acceptance.

In this individually administered scale, the examiner shows the subject simultaneously the two pictures in an item and tells the subject what is taking place in the situation portrayed. Then the examinee is asked to pick the child in the picture most like him or her and to indicate by pointing to one of four appropriate circles (two circles below each picture) whether that child is "a lot like him or her (the big circle)" or "just a little like him or her (the smaller circle)." The examinee who points to the larger circle associated with the picture revealing the presence of perceived competence or of social acceptance receives 3 points; the child who points to the smaller circle corresponding to the picture reflecting perceived competence or social acceptance earns 3 points. If the picture revealing low perceived competence or social acceptance is chosen as being like the respondent, 2 points are assigned to the small circle and 1 point to the large circle. Thus for each of the four scales, the total number of points may range from 6 to 24. The use of four alternatives receiving differential weights probably serves to reduce the presence of response sets associated with

social desirability or acquiescence, as well as possible random selection of alternatives (guessing).

In the procedural manual that accompanies the test booklets, the authors have constructed what they term the "Teacher's Rating Scale of Child's Actual Competence and Social Acceptance." Its items parallel the intended content of each of the six items in the first three of the four 6-item scales administered to the children. The scale pertaining to maternal acceptance was not duplicated because the authors thought, quite appropriately, that the teacher would not be in a position in most instances to formulate accurate judgments. Also parallel to the items in the first three scales to which the children responded are four alternatives for each item description that the teacher selects, with the statements of "really true," "pretty true," "sort of true," or "not very true" carrying 4, 3, 2, or 1 points in the scoring procedure respectively. The rating scales completed by the teachers provide a basis for establishing the degree of congruence between the perceptions of teachers and those of the children in their classes. Obviously, substantial discrepancies point to the need for the teacher to increase her or his level of communication with the child and to try to determine the basis for the discrepancies noted.

Unfortunately, the publication of the very attractively prepared test forms was probably premature, as a technical manual affording information regarding validity, reliability, and normative data is not available. At the time of the preparation of this review, it was necessary for the potential consumer interested in psychometric data to consult a 1984 article, written by the two authors of the test, that appeared in *Child Development.* In this well-done article, the authors have employed subsamples of 90 preschool, 56 kindergarten, 65 first-grade, and 44 second-grade children primarily from middle-class families of Anglo ethnicity in the Denver, Colorado area to obtain means, standard deviations, internal-consistency estimates of reliability, and intercorrelations of subscales. In addition, oblique factor analyses were done of the intercorrelations among the items for two subsamples of preschool and kindergarten children and of first- and second-grade pupils to provide evidence of the factorial validity of the instrument.

For the Cognitive, Physical, Peer, and Maternal scales, reliability coefficients relative to various subgroups fell between .52 and .79, .50 and .66, .74 and .83, and .72 and .85, respectively. The two combined scales of 12 items in the competence and acceptance domains yielded corresponding reliability coefficients ranging between .66 and .80, and between .84 and .89, respectively. Both factor analyses revealed two correlated dimensions that were clearly identified as Perceived Competence and Social Acceptance. The 12 items in the Cognitive

Competence and Physical Competence scales and the 12 items in the Peer Acceptance and Maternal Acceptance scales, respectively, defined the two dimensions of competence and acceptance. Intercorrelations among subscales tended to range, for the most part, between .30 and .60, with the exception of the two acceptance scales that exhibited correlations between .62 and .80.

In summary, this instrument can be anticipated to provide important information to teachers and parents concerning the self-confidence children express in their perceived competencies and perceived levels of acceptance. The relative ease of administration and the seemingly intrinsic interest of the items in sustaining the motivation of the examinees are positive features. Very much needed are normative data and additional reliability and validity studies with numerous samples of children from families of diverse cultural backgrounds and socioeconomic levels, so that more adequate interpretations can be made of the scores obtained. At the moment, the use of these scales for research purposes is to be encouraged. Other indicators of perceived cognitive capabilities and of perceived relationships in interpersonal relations are needed to supplement any data obtained from the four scales. It is hoped the authors will continue to carry out the necessary additional research and developmental work to establish this instrument as one that can provide valid assessment of early childhood behaviors hypothesized within its structure.

Review of The Pictorial Scale of Perceived Competence and Social Acceptance for Young Children by SUSAN M. SHERIDAN, Assistant Professor of Educational Psychology, University of Utah, Salt Lake City, UT:

The Pictorial Scale of Perceived Competence and Social Acceptance for Young Children (PSPCSA) is a self-report instrument designed to assess perceptions of young children in four domains (i.e., Cognitive Competence, Physical Competence, Peer Acceptance, Maternal Acceptance). The test uses a unique item format ("structured response format"), which is sensitive to the developmental capacities of young children. This format is assumed to allow children to identify more readily to test items, and to make meaningful differentiations between possible responses. The PSPCSA has some characteristics that make it a potential addition to social-emotional assessment batteries. However, several conceptual and methodological limitations reduce its overall usefulness.

MANUAL. The manual accompanying the PSPCSA provides good administration guidelines and scoring criteria. Verbal and procedural instructions are clear and concise, and they assist in making the test easy to administer. Likewise, individual scoring and profile sheets (included in an appendix) allow for simple calculation and plotting of scores.

Although the PSPCSA is "user-friendly" in terms of administration and scoring, the manual is extremely incomplete and fails to meet the *Standards for Educational and Psychological Testing* (AERA, APA, & NCME; 1985). The authors refer test users to a related publication (Harter & Pike, 1984) that describes the underlying theory, rationale, scale construction efforts, and psychometric properties of the instrument. Given that these critical issues are not presented in the manual, there is great potential for general misuse and/or misinterpretation of test data.

STANDARDIZATION. A limited normative group was used in the standardization of the PSPCSA. Although 255 preschool through second grade subjects were included, preschoolers appeared to be overrepresented ($n = 90$), and second graders appeared to be underrepresented ($n = 44$). All subjects were from middle-class neighborhoods, and 96% were Caucasian. Thus, caution must be exercised when using the test with children from other socioeconomic, cultural, and educational groups.

RELIABILITY/VALIDITY. Psychometric support for the PSPCSA is equivocal. Alpha correlation coefficients for the total test are adequate (.88 for the preschool/kindergarten sample and .87 for the first/second- grade sample). Internal consistencies for the Acceptance factor is also good (alpha = .87 for the preschool/kindergarten sample and .86 for the first/second- grade sample; however, they are lower for the Competence factor (alpha = .76 and .77 for the preschool/kindergarten and first/second-grade samples, respectively). As expected, individual subscale reliabilities are the lowest, with an alpha range of .53 to .83 across samples.

According to the authors, factor analysis with the PSPCSA revealed a two-factor solution, with the competence subscales defining one factor and the acceptance subscales defining the second. However, even with the very liberal procedure that was used (oblique promax rotation), very low correlations were obtained, especially for the preschool/kindergarten sample (with individual item loadings ranging from .19 to .58 on Factor 1 and from .23 to .70 on Factor 2). Thus, the degree to which we can interpret separate factors as reflective of the constructs they are purported to measure is questioned.

Harter and Pike (1984) provide evidence of convergent, discriminant, and predictive validity for the PSPCSA. However, because only limited data are presented, the studies reported may be inadequate in estimating the accuracy of the test with larger and more diverse groups of children.

TEST CONSTRUCTION/ITEM SELECTION. The construction of the PSPCSA is not described by the authors. However, it appears items were selected based on subjective, rather than empirical (i.e., item analysis), methods. Some of the pictures used to depict various skills and behaviors appear inconsistent with their corresponding verbal descriptions, and may be misrepresentative of the intended content or purpose of the item. Relatedly, several of the stimulus pictures fail to differentiate adequately between the intended behavioral poles, and may be confusing to young children who rely on pictorial cues when making judgments. Thus, child responses may be dependent upon an individual's interpretation of test items, rather than the test stimuli.

Additional problems with test items are apparent. For example, some items appear developmentally and conceptually inconsistent, such as "Stays overnight at friends' house" and "Eats dinner at friends' house." These items appear on the Peer Acceptance subscale at the preschool/kindergarten level; however, the degree to which children at this age normatively engage in these activities is questioned. These same items appear on the Maternal Acceptance subscale at the first/second-grade level, yet they seem to be more dependent on peer-mediated characteristics than on maternal relationship factors. The conceptual ambiguity this presents is apparent.

INTERPRETATION. Related to problems with discrete items, the interpretive framework for this test is extremely vague. A high degree of intercorrelation between subscales exists. This presents confusion regarding what the "separate" subscales actually measure, and may increase interpretive errors for users who incorrectly perceive each as an independent domain. This, coupled with the fact that factor analysis does not support the maintenance of four separate subscales, suggests emphasis should be placed on factor scores rather than individual subtest scores. However, the authors explicitly encourage the use of separate subscale scores in interpreting individual profiles. Low, medium, and high ratings for each subtest are suggested; however, these appear to be based on arbitrary cutoff scores rather than empirical support.

SUPPLEMENTAL MATERIALS. In addition to the standard test materials, a Teacher Rating Scale is supplied which corresponds by item to the child self-report. As an additional index of external validity, correlations between child and teacher ratings were calculated by the authors. Although significant correlations were obtained for the competence ratings, they were negligible for peer acceptance. However, items on the Teacher Rating Scale are poorly defined and subjective, and no psychometric evidence is available to support its use. Thus, the use of the TRS is discouraged, awaiting empirical documentation.

SUMMARY. In sum, The Pictorial Scale of Perceived Competence and Social Acceptance for Young Children has some characteristics (i.e., appealing test format, ease in implementation and scoring, acceptable reliability) that increase its potential in social-emotional assessments. However, several limitations of the scale are evident, including its inadequate test manual, limited standardization sample, questionable factorial validity, insufficient data on test construction, and lack of an interpretive framework. The authors fail to provide sufficient guidelines to enhance the clinical utility of the test, and the potential for misinterpretation is great. Additional research is needed to support its use in research and practice.

REVIEWER'S REFERENCES

Harter, S., & Pike, R. (1984). The pictorial scale of perceived competence and social acceptance for young children. *Child Development*, 55, 1969-1982.

American Educational Research Association, American Psychological Association, & National Council on Measurement in Education. (1985). *Standards for educational and psychological testing*. Washington, DC: American Psychological Association, Inc.

[293]

The Pin Test.

Purpose: "Designed to provide an easily administered and objectively scored measure of manual dexterity."

Population: Ages 16 to 69 with normal or corrected vision.

Publication Date: 1989.

Scores, 3: Dominant Hand, Nondominant Hand, Advantage Index.

Administration: Individual.

Price Data, 1990: $79 per complete kit (includes test, manual, and materials for 50 administrations); $49 per test; $17 per replacement set (contains materials for 50 administrations); $14 per manual (53 pages).

Time: 2(7) minutes.

Authors: Paul Satz and Lou D'Elia.

Publisher: Psychological Assessment Resources, Inc.

TEST REFERENCES

1. De Moja, C. A., Reitano, M., & De Marco, P. (1987). Anxiety, perceptual and motor skills in an underwater environment. *Perceptual and Motor Skills*, 65, 359-365.

Review of the Pin Test by ANNETTE M. IVERSON, Assistant Professor of School Psychology, University of Missouri, Columbia, MO:

Traditionally, clinical neuropsychologists have used manual motor tests to make inferences regarding brain-behavior relations (i.e., lateralized brain dysfunction). Such tests include the Finger Tapping Test (Reitan & Davison, 1974), the Grip Strength Test (Reitan & Davison, 1974), and the Purdue Pegboard (Purdue Research Foundation, 1948; T3:1948).

The Pin Test, most similar to the Purdue Pegboard, provides a measure of distal visuomotor coordination and speed. The authors contend the instrument is not a neuropsychological screening test but is to be administered within the context of a comprehensive evaluation. However, a compelling rationale for the procedure is not provided. The authors suggest that the aforementioned traditional procedures have questionable "reliability" but provide support for this statement by discussing concurrent validity studies of the amount of agreement between these tests and self-reported handedness. The introduction suggests the authors' intent was to develop a procedure that would be a better predictor of self-reported dominance than the traditional measures.

The Pin Test is compact, attractively designed, and portable. The test can be given in an office or at bedside. Administration and scoring can be accomplished by people with minimal background in psychological testing, and the directions are well written and clear. The subject is presented a form board with two curvilinear sequences of holes and is then given a pin and instructed to punch as many holes through the board as possible in 30 seconds. Scores for both dominant and nondominant hands are obtained. Guidelines for interpretation are included, with an appropriate cautionary note that professional training is required. A strength of the Pin Test manual is the explanation of calculation of norms.

The process of preparing materials for administration is a disadvantage. At least 7 minutes are required to ready the cardboard sheet with 202 pinholes. This must be done for every 10th client. A straight pin is used to make the pinholes in the cardboard and the procedure may be uncomfortable or painful to the preparer's fingers. Some might be tempted to choose a pin with a rounded plastic head in order to improve grip and lessen discomfort. However, this deviation from standardization may affect subject's performance and lessen the validity of comparisons to the normative sample. An additional criticism of the material preparation is the lack of photographs or diagrams depicting the step-by-step process; no accuracy check is provided for the preparer. Finally, although the directions are to prepare a new cardboard sheet for every 10th subject, latter clients sticking pins in preformed holes may have an advantage over earlier clients simply because the holes have enlarged and less pressure is required.

The normative sample (598 subjects) is neither random or stratified; subjects are urban, solicited volunteers identified solely on the basis of sex, age, self-reported handedness, and preferred writing hand. Potential differences between manual laborers and white collar or professional workers, for example, are not controlled. It is conceivable that "soft" hands would feel discomfort and may be more adversely affected than "hardened" hands. Another characteristic of the normative sample is 51% were self-reported left-handers. This deviation from the base rate of left-handed individuals is also found in the validity research reported in the manual.

A limited amount of supporting research on the Pin Test was presented in the manual. The one reliability study evaluated the stability of the instrument by having 25 subjects take the test a second time following a variable interval ranging from 5–20 days. Test-retest correlations were .83 and .74 for Total Hits for the dominant and nondominant hands, respectively. The mean Total Hits scores were significantly greater for the second administration, indicating a positive practice effect. However, the reliability coefficients indicate that the subjects' positions in the score distribution remained relatively consistent.

The authors reported a validity study that examined the relationships among Pin Test performance, self-reported handedness, scores on a handedness questionnaire, and performance on a finger-tapping device. A subsample (555 subjects) of the normative sample completed all measures. Agreement between the Pin Test and self-reported handedness was very high for both handedness groups (98% for right-handers and 96% for left-handers). Agreement between the finger-tapping task and self-reported handedness was also high, but yielded lower concordances especially for left-handers (90% for right-handers and 81% for left-handers). Results pooled across handedness groups were: Pin Test = 97% and finger-tapping = 86%. Concordance rates on the handedness questionnaire were similar: Pin Test = 94% and finger-tapping = 85%. Although these figures appear compelling, no statistical confirmation for the significance of these differences was reported. In addition, the authors did not use the administration instructions for the Finger Tapping test which are most frequently employed by clinical neuropsychologists.

In summary, the Pin Test represents a good attempt by the authors to improve upon existing measures of distal visuomotor coordination and speed. If a fine motor procedure is more closely associated with true lateral dominance, then clinical inferences drawn from dominant-nondominant discrepancies may be more valid. Therefore, if the Pin Test is truly more sensitive to handedness than existing motor procedures and if it provides a valid measure of visuomotor speed, this procedure may be a valuable addition to the clinical neuropsychologist's armamentarium of tests. However, limited validity data for this procedure were reported and the validity data presented in the manual are flawed in ways that may have placed the finger-tapping procedure at a disadvantage for predicting dominance. Practical limitations for the examiner who has to prepare the materials, and for the subject who may find the procedure physically uncomfortable, further attenuate the suitability of this procedure for mainstream clinical practice. Further research is needed to establish the psychometric properties of the Pin Test before it can be recommended for widespread use.

REVIEWER'S REFERENCES

Purdue Research Foundation. (1948). *Examiner's manual for the Purdue Pegboard.* Chicago: Science Research Associates.

Reitan, R. M., & Davison, L. A. (1974). *Clinical neuropsychology: Current status and applications.* Washington, DC: Wiley.

Review of The Pin Test by RODERICK K. MAHURIN, Clinical Assistant Professor, Department of Psychiatry, University of Texas Health Science Center, San Antonio, TX:

PURPOSE. The Pin Test is described in its manual as a brief, portable, and nonthreatening test of manual dexterity. Suggested areas of use include research on handedness and lateralized brain function, neuropsychological testing for effects of neurological disorders, and measurement of functional change in rehabilitation settings. The manual suggests that persons with limited background in psychological assessment may administer the test, but appropriately cautions that an experienced clinician should interpret findings in relation to the results of a comprehensive neuropsychological evaluation.

MATERIALS AND ADMINISTRATION. Materials include a common straight pin, a metal plate and holder (approximately 4 by 5 inches in size), a reusable piece of resistance cardboard, paper trial sheets, and a Record Form. The metal plate is drilled with a sinusoidal pattern of 101 small holes, through which the subject must sequentially insert and withdraw the pin as rapidly as possible. The trial sheets, which are placed between the cardboard backing and the metal plate, contain numbered dots corresponding to the pattern of holes in the plate.

Supplied materials are sufficient for 50 administrations, after which replacement materials (e.g., cardboard and trial sheets) need to be ordered from the test publisher. Complete administration requires four 30-second trials, alternating between dominant and nondominant hands. After each trial the examiner lifts the metal plate, removes the paper, and inserts a fresh trial sheet.

Scores are determined by the number of holes punched in the four trial sheets, including Total Hits for dominant and nondominant hands (i.e., the sum of the two trials for each) and an Advantage Index (AI). The AI is the calculated ratio of Total Hits for the dominant hand divided by Total Hits for the nondominant hand. The entire test takes approximately 10 minutes to administer and score.

Administration of the test is well described in the manual. Manipulation of the pin itself, which is smaller in size than other commonly used test materials, may be difficult for some test takers. Long fingernails, perspiration on the hands, or arthritis of the fingers may adversely affect test performance. There also may be mild discomfort to the pad of the fingertip associated with repeatedly pressing down on the head of the pin, a problem frequently commented on by subjects tested by this reviewer. It should be noted that the pin itself holds a slight, but possibly significant, risk for certain patient groups. For this reason, caution should be used in testing psychiatric, geriatric, or young pediatric populations prior to gaining familiarity with the subject's physical and test-taking abilities.

In addition to demands on fine-motor coordination, the Pin Test has a substantial visual component. The manual states a subject should have vision "adequate to read newspaper text" in order to take the test. If a subject does have visual problems, an alternative measure of fine-motor ability requiring minimal visual feedback should be used, such as the Finger Tapping test (Reitan & Davison, 1974).

NORMATIVE DATA. The normative sample for the Pin Test consisted of 598 subjects (369 females and 229 males) recruited through university and community newspaper advertisements. Subjects were screened to exclude those with motor, sensory, or neurological disorders. No other relevant information regarding the composition of the normative sample is provided, such as socioeconomic status, occupation, education, or ethnic background. The manual thoroughly describes the technique of continuous norming used in generating the age-based normative tables (Zachary & Gorsuch, 1985).

The manual provides separate normative tables for right-handers and left-handers, including Total Hits/Right Hand, Total Hits/Left Hand, and AI. Norms are further subdivided into six age groups: 16–19 years, 20–29 years, 30–39 years, 40–49 years, 50–59 years, and 60–69 years. There is no breakdown by gender, and it is not stated whether gender differences were found in the normative sample. The normative tables are well organized, providing percentile and standard scores of sufficient range to encompass expected levels of performance. Separate normative data on the AI, which compares performance of the dominant and nondominant hands, should be especially useful in clinical settings. The manual also contains an Interpretation section that should prove helpful to clinicians with limited experience in motor testing.

RELIABILITY AND VALIDITY. Several development studies are reported in the manual. The first tested the relationship between the Pin Test and a self-report handedness questionnaire from a sample of 555 normal subjects. The concordance between handedness and the Pin Test was very high, ranging from 98% for right-handers to 96% for left-handers. This was a higher correlation than obtained between handedness and a concurrently administered test of finger-tapping speed.

Two studies examined possible practice effects of repeated testing. In the first ($n = 30$) a 10% intrasession improvement in performance was found from Trial 1 to Trial 3 with the nondominant hand, with no change in the AI. The second study examined test-retest reliability over an interval of from 5 to 20 days ($n = 25$). Test-retest correlations ranged from .83 for the dominant hand, to .74 for the nondominant hand. Although it was stated that both dominant and nondominant Total Hits increased significantly on the second administration, the actual magnitude of change was not provided. This information would be useful in longitudinal studies or rehabilitation settings when determining a subject's relative change independent of practice effects.

A further study examined Pin Test scores in a small group ($n = 14$) of patients with traumatic brain injury. These patients were described as having "moderate to severe" head injury (post-traumatic amnesia anywhere from 4 days to 3 months), and were tested between 3 weeks and 12 months post-injury. Of the 14 patients, 8 showed impaired performance on at least one measure of the Pin Test. No data were provided regarding lateralized test differences in relation to the focus of brain injury, or on the association between severity of injury and degree of deficit on the test. There are, as yet, few published studies validating the Pin Test in clinical populations. One recent paper found a strong association between performance on the test and the Wisconsin Card Sorting Test, an established measure of frontal lobe functioning (Green, Satz, Ganzell, & Vaclav, 1992). The authors suggest this high correlation may reflect sensitivity of the Pin Test to neuromotor sequencing deficits that underlie higher level cognitive processing. However, further validation studies, which use rigorously defined diagnostic groups and documented locus of cerebral involvement, are necessary before clinicians can confidently use the test as a behavioral marker for lateralized brain dysfunction.

A potential user of the Pin Test may question whether its primary purpose is, as stated, to document handedness (preference) or to test fine-motor ability (proficiency). The test was apparently developed as part of a study of familial handedness and cerebral organization (Orsini, Satz, Soper, & Light, 1985), and the supporting data emphasize its strong relationship to handedness. However, unlike handedness, visuomotor skills factor into a number of independent abilities (Fleishman, 1972). Additional studies of incremental validity that compare the Pin Test with established measures of visuomotor coordination, including Finger Tapping, Grooved Pegboard, and Purdue Pegboard tests (see Lezak, 1983), would help clarify this issue.

CONCLUSION. In summary, the Pin Test appears to measure reliably a specific fine visuomotor skill that correlates highly with hand preference. It has a well-developed normative base, is brief, and is relatively easy to administer. The manual states the Pin Test is designed for neuropsychological assessment, the primary focus of which is identifying and diagnosing neurobehavioral pathology. Although there is preliminary evidence the test is sensitive to brain dysfunction, its validity as a marker for lateralized cerebral injury has not yet been demonstrated. Further validation studies would be welcome to establish the clinical and diagnostic utility of this new test.

REVIEWER'S REFERENCES
Fleishman, E. A. (1972). On the relation between abilities, learning, and human performance. *American Psychologist, 27,* 1017-1032.
Reitan, R. M., & Davison, L. A. (1974). *Clinical neuropsychology: Current status and applications.* Washington, DC: V. H. Winston & Sons.
Lezak, M. D. (1983). *Neuropsychological assessment* (2nd ed.) (pp. 529-532). New York: Oxford University Press.
Orsini, D. L., Satz, P., Soper, H. V., & Light, R. K. (1985). The role of familial sinistrality in cerebral organization. *Neuropsychologia, 23,* 223-232.
Zachary, R. A., & Gorsuch, R. L. (1985). Continuous norming: Implications for the WAIS-R. *Journal of Clinical Psychology, 41,* 86-94.
Green, M. F., Satz, P., Ganzell, S., & Vaclav, J. F. (1992). Wisconsin Card Sorting Test in schizophrenia: Remediation of a stubborn deficit. *American Journal of Psychiatry, 149,* 62-67.

[294]
Pollack-Branden Inventory.

Purpose: "To identify students who are in need of remediation, that is not readily diagnosed by standardized tests, and may be manifested in certain language weaknesses symptomatic of dyslexia."
Population: Grades 1–12.
Publication Date: 1986.
Acronym: P.B.I.
Scores: Item scores only.
Administration: Individual in part.
Price Data: Available from publisher.
Authors: Cecelia Pollack and Ann Branden.
Publisher: Book-Lab.

a) SPELLING INVENTORY.
Time: (8-10) minutes.
b) DICTATED SENTENCES AND HANDWRITING.
Levels, 2: Grades 3-5, 6-12.
Time: (9-12) minutes.
c) SOUND/SYMBOL INVENTORY.
Administration: Individual.
Time: (6-8) minutes.
d) INVENTORY OF ORAL READING SKILLS.
Administration: Individual.
Time: (7-10) minutes.
e) MATHEMATICS INVENTORY.
Time: (15-20) minutes.
f) WRITTEN COMPOSITION.
Population: Grades 3 and over.
Time: Administration time not reported.

Review of the Pollack-Branden Inventory by ANNE ANASTASI, Professor Emeritus of Psychology, Fordham University, Bronx, NY:

Although the authors do not specify the type of user for whom this inventory was designed, it is apparent from statements in the User's Guide that it is intended for teachers. Its object is twofold: first, as an informal screening instrument for identifying potential dyslexics, who will then be more fully assessed by psychologists or learning disability specialists (p. 28); second, as a guide for the teacher in correcting deficiencies through an Individualized Educational Plan (IEP) prepared for each student (p. 20).

COVERAGE. Four of the six parts of the Pollack-Branden Inventory (P.B.I.) are directed primarily to problems in the use of written symbols, considered to be symptomatic of dyslexia. These include phonics, spelling, dictation, handwriting, decoding, and the handling of written grammar, syntax, and punctuation. It should be noted that on the Sound/Symbol Inventory, an adult or child who has not been taught reading by the phonics method would need considerable preliminary explanation and pretest practice to produce the sound of visually presented letters and letter combinations, such as c, x, scr, and nk, occurring outside of normal word contexts.

Although the P.B.I. was designed principally to detect errors in the structural aspects of symbolic language, it also touches on difficulties in conceptualization, in both oral reading and written expression. The latter is assessed in the optional Written Composition. A short Mathematics Inventory is also included, consisting of 28 simple computational problems, which are worked out in the Student Booklet, so that the teacher can identify the nature of the errors.

ADMINISTRATION AND SCORING. Any one of the inventories may be used singly or in combination with one or more of the others. Results from the different inventories are not aggregated into an overall measure. All instructions for administering the P.B.I. are given in the User's Guide. For the four group-administered inventories, students record all responses in the single Student Booklet. Items are arranged in increasing order of difficulty; broad guidelines are provided for entry and exit cutoffs for different grade levels, from Grade 2 (or 3) to Grade 6 (or 7) and up. For the two individually administered inventories, the student reads the items aloud from the Student Booklet and the teacher records the responses on "Error Recording Copies" and "Comprehension Questions" copies (for the Inventory of Oral Reading Skills), for which ditto masters are included in the Appendix to the User's Guide.

The Appendix also provides Error Analysis Sheets for each of the six inventories, on which the errors are classified and the number of errors in each category is recorded. On the basis of the information on these Error Analysis Sheets, the teacher rates the student's performance on each inventory by checking one of three levels: mastered, partially mastered, or not yet mastered. No guidelines are provided for this threefold evaluation; presumably the teacher judges mastery level in terms of his/her expectation for the appropriate grade level. On some inventories, several aspects of performance are evaluated. For example, in Dictated Sentences and Handwriting, there is a summary evaluation for errors (covering punctuation, capitalization, and spelling) and another for handwriting deficiencies. For the Inventory of Oral Reading Skills, there are separate mastery evaluations for rate, accuracy, fluency, and comprehension.

The User's Guide includes a case study, which is actually a demonstration of the recording and scoring procedures, rather than a case study in the usual, clinical sense. There is also an Individual Record Form and a Class Record Form for summarizing mastery levels on each inventory in the whole battery.

The organization and format of the User's Guide could be substantially improved. It is now necessary to keep turning pages back and forth from text to Appendix in order to locate the relevant forms. Moreover, the headings introducing each separate inventory are inconspicuous in type and position on the page. It would have been helpful for the user to have the ditto masters of different record sheets (now in the Appendix) as a separate packet. It would have been still better to have all the necessary record sheets available for use in the required quantities.

INDIVIDUALIZED EDUCATIONAL PLAN (IEP). Insofar as can be determined from the User's Guide, the IEP for each student (p. 20, pp. 27–28) is essentially a translation of the entries on the Error Analysis Sheets for the six inventories into a set of educational objectives. These objectives call for teaching the specific items where errors occurred, such as particular misspelled words.

CONSTRUCTION OF THE P.B.I. The User's Guide contains one paragraph explaining the basis for selecting both the variables to be assessed in the six parts of the inventory and the specific items within each. Essentially, the instrument was developed through the authors' personal clinical experience. The short section labeled "Test Development" opens and closes as follows: "The authors have had the experience of diagnosing and remediating dyslexic students over a period of sixteen years with over 1,000 subjects of all ages ranging from first grade through adulthood . . . . The present P.B.I. represents a distillation of their experience" (p. 4). No data (quantitative or qualitative) are reported regarding norms, reliability, or validity, nor are any other published sources cited.

OVERVIEW. The P.B.I. is not a test in the usual psychometric sense. In its present form, it consists of a set of carefully chosen materials that can be used by experienced teachers who have some knowledge of dyslexia and of the phonics method of teaching reading. The authors do not call the P.B.I. a test, but use the term "inventory," both for the entire battery and for the separate parts. Nevertheless, even when all qualifications and limitations are taken into account, it would be desirable to make available some empirical data, in whatever form, about such questions as how well teachers are able to use the materials, what difficulties they encounter in administering and scoring the inventories, how children screened by the P.B.I. as potential dyslexics fare when examined comprehensively by professional specialists and when judged by classroom performance, what level of achievement actually corresponds to mastery at different grade levels, how effective the Individualized Educational Plan is, and to what extent it leads to improvement beyond the specific items covered by the P.B.I.

Review of the Pollack-Branden Inventory by VERNA HART, Professor of Special Education, University of Pittsburgh, Pittsburgh, PA:

The Pollack-Branden Inventory (P.B.I.) is a criterion-referenced test designed to generate a profile of characteristics of students with dyslexia as well as generate a plan for remediation of their difficulties. Its title states it is "For Identification of Learning Disabilities, Dyslexia and Classroom Dysfunction."

The P.B.I. is based on the authors' experience diagnosing and remediating students with dyslexia and presents what they call a "dyslexic pattern." With the current professional interest in differentiating students with learning disabilities, dyslexia, and reading disabilities, the title of the test makes it seem particularly relevant. However, careful examination of the contents of the inventory results in questioning its ability to diagnose the targeted audiences. The main problems center on the lack of information regarding the test construction, its reliability, and its validity. The User's Guide offers little information regarding any of these.

Because a criterion-referenced test is to generalize from a few items to the broader domain from which those items were sampled, a well-defined domain seems necessary. This appears to be missing in the inventory. Although some broad considerations for identifying dyslexia are noted, they are undocumented and lack specificity. There is a heavy emphasis on phonics and a statement that a knowledge of specific phonic rules must be the basis for reteaching. Auditory and cognitive processing abilities are not assessed. Knowledge of spelling, writing, and computation rules receive great emphasis in the items and error analysis, but there is no documentation that a lack of such knowledge can be used to identify those with dyslexia or learning disabilities.

Further weaknesses are the lack of rationale for the types of items included, documentation of the representativeness of the test items, and the extent to which they measure the traits of learning disabilities, dyslexia, and classroom dysfunction. Information is

not provided that would show that the dyslexic or the person with learning disability can be described by using the test scores.

In addition, there are too few items to cover the content tested. For example, 36 spelling words, the total administered to those in grade 6 and up, are analyzed for 26 different types of errors. Although a few of the errors can be found in more than one word, most of the errors examined can be found in only one. With words like *obsequious* and the commonly misspelled *accommodate* among them, one questions whether the score obtained is representative of a person with learning disabilities or dyslexia, or even whether the score represents an individual's ability to use specific spelling rules.

This lack of sufficient numbers of items, as well as lack of item statistics, is seen throughout all of the subinventories. The error analysis to be used for each inventory has a larger number of analyses than the item pool would warrant. There are also cutoff points and timed responses in several of the inventories, but no rationale for them. They are offered as absolutes in one of the subinventories and as "broad guidelines" in another. There are no data regarding the consistency of responses of the students, nor of the scoring, particularly of the Written Composition which has subjective components.

Although the authors state that error analysis rather than numerical scores will identify dyslexia and provide for remediation, scores of all the subinventories are converted to numbers; 1 = mastered, 2 = partially mastered, and 3 = not yet mastered, again with no rationale. These numbers are then transferred to an Individual Record Form. Thus, when looking at the Individual Record Form, it is impossible to determine where the individual difficulties exist for any particular child.

Nearly a third of the text of the brief User's Guide is devoted to writing the Individualized Educational Plan (IEP) and completing the Class Record Form from the results of the inventory. Although the idea is a very good one, the sequence is confusing. After the IEP is written, the guide states "there is a probable indication of dyslexia which should be affirmed by more complete assessment procedures." If the IEP is that mandated by P.L. 94–142, the child would have to be assessed by using more than one appropriately normed instrument and determined to have a learning disability *before* the writing of the IEP, which by law must have certain components and participants. Equally confusing is the Class Record Form with the names of several students and level of mastery noted for each of the subinventories. Instructions are given for the teacher to determine which skills have Level 3s and to teach them to the entire class because all students lack mastery. Does this mean that all of the students in the class have been assessed with the instrument? No additional information is provided, but even assuming such a fact, the Class Record Form could not be used as recommended, for there is no information offered as to the areas within the inventories where the children are experiencing difficulties.

Given the three levels of achievement, criterion-oriented validity is also missing. There is no evidence provided that relates to the question of whether assignment for particular intervention on the basis of scores will result in greater achievement than random assignment, regardless of test scores, to various treatments.

In addition to the problems with test construction, reliability, and validity, the test has several typing, spelling, and other errors. Two of these could affect the test scores: poor sentence structure in the Inventory of Oral Reading Skills, and a dollar-sign ($) requirement for a correct answer in one of the mathematics answers when none is shown in the problem in the student booklet.

Although the idea of a very short, easy-to-administer test to identify learning disabilities, dyslexia, and classroom dysfunction is a good one, this instrument was not constructed with the rigorousness needed to accomplish this goal. Until much more work is completed on the inventory, it should not be used for the purpose designated.

[295]
Portable Tactual Performance Test.
Purpose: To assess tactual performance.
Population: Ages 5 to adult.
Publication Date: 1984.
Acronym: P-TPT.
Scores, 3: Dominant Hand, Non-dominant Hand, Both Hands.
Administration: Individual.
Price Data, 1987: $265 per test kit including 25 record forms, form boards in case, and manual (8 pages); $5 per 50 record forms.
Time: (10–15) minutes per trial.
Comments: A portable alternative to the original Tactual Performance Test for use with the Halstead-Reitan Neuropsychological Test Battery.
Author: Michael David.
Publisher: Psychological Assessment Resources, Inc.

Review of the Portable Tactual Performance Test by CALVIN P. GARBIN, Associate Professor of Psychology, University of Nebraska-Lincoln, Lincoln, NE:

The materials, instructions, procedures, and scoring of adult and child versions of the Portable Tactual Performance Test (P-TPT) are exactly the same as those for the original Tactile Performance Test (TPT) of the Halstead-Reitan Neuropsychological Test Battery (9:463) which has been reviewed in *The Mental Measurements Yearbook*. The portable version comes in a sturdy wooden carrying case, which can be set up to position either form of

the board at the appropriate angle for task completion.

An Instruction Manual is included that describes the basics of administering and scoring the test, and provides a very brief discussion of the clinical relevance of a few patterns of response data. Additional information about the interpretation and clinical relevance of test results, as well as a discussion of how this test comprises a functional part of the full Halstead-Reitan Neuropsychological Test Battery, can be found in either the manual for the Halstead-Reitan (9:463) or a related text by Reitan and Wolfson (1985).

REVIEWER'S REFERENCE
Reitan, R. M., & Wolfson, D. (1985). The Halstead-Reitan Neuropsychological Test Battery: Theory and clinical interpretation. Tucson: Neuropsychology Press.

[296]
PRE-LAS English.
Purpose: "To measure young children's expressive and receptive abilities in three linguistic components of oral language: morphology, syntax, and semantics."
Population: Ages 4–6.
Publication Date: 1985–87.
Acronym: PRE-LAS.
Scores, 8: Simon Says, Choose A Picture, What's in the House, Say What You Hear, Finishing Stories, Let's Tell Stories, Total, Level.
Administration: Individual.
Price Data, 1988: $69 per complete kit including 50 test booklets ('85, 4 pages), Cue Picture Booklet and House, audio cassette, scoring and interpretation manual ('87, 28 pages), and administration manual ('86, 16 pages); $8.95 per Technical Report ('85, 47 pages).
Foreign Language Edition: Spanish edition available.
Time: (10–20) minutes.
Comments: 2 forms: A, B; downward extension of the Language Assessment Scales (LAS) (9:584).
Authors: Sharon E. Duncan and Edward A. De Avila.
Publisher: CTB Macmillan/McGraw-Hill.
Cross References: For a review by Lyn Haber of the Language Assessment Scales, see 9:584 (1 reference); see also T3:1281 (4 references).

Review of the PRE-LAS English by PATSY ARNETT JAYNES, Second Language Program Evaluation Specialist, Jefferson County Public Schools, Golden, CO:

De Avila and Duncan developed the PRE-LAS to measure the general oral English language ability of young children from ages 4 to 6. The prototype of this assessment is their Language Assessment Scales (LAS; 9:584), designed to be used with children aged 6 to 12. Like the LAS, the PRE-LAS measures expressive and receptive language abilities in the areas of morphology, syntax, and semantics. The test purports to measure a spectrum of language performance rather than a single aspect of language.

The PRE-LAS will be of special interest to kindergarten and pre-kindergarten programs where knowledge of language ability in English is necessary for program placement, entry and exit level criteria, and for diagnostic pre-post data. The PRE-LAS is available in Spanish to assist in the assessment of language dominance for bilingual children. Two parallel forms of the PRE-LAS are available (Form A and Form B), making it possible to pre- and posttest with different items and different stories. There is, however, only one form published in Spanish. This limits the test's usefulness in program planning.

The test package contains student response booklets, a cue picture book, an administrator's manual, and a scoring and interpretation manual. These materials are bound in a three-ring notebook thus improving ease of administration. An audiocassette tape of the test and an audiocassette tape of the mini-stories are available as optional material. With young children, however, these tapes are not necessary as the test flows quite smoothly with the examiner and child in a one-on-one relationship. The PRE-LAS is individually administered and takes approximately 10 minutes to complete. Raw scores are converted to weighted scores by using a variety of different tables. Both the Finishing Stories and the Let's Tell Stories subtests are compared to transcriptions of sample responses at each PRE-LAS level. These sample responses are presented in age-related groupings. This allows the examiner to compare each child's language production to an appropriate comparison sample.

A "Simon-Says" format is used to structure some of the children's responses. They are asked to identify vocabulary items by pointing to pictures according to the instructor's oral cue. They are asked to repeat sentences with the instructor listening for the accuracy of a portion of the sentence that has imbedded key morphological and syntactical items. This format constitutes 55% of the total PRE-LAS score. The remaining 45% of the test is in the format of open-ended responses that elicit more productive and creative language from the child. There is an oral cloze exercise where the child is asked to supply the missing word or words to finish a story. To finish the test the child listens to a short story and is asked to repeat the story immediately after hearing it. Stimulus pictures are provided to help the child remember the story sequence. The PRE-LAS stories are shorter and of a greater variety than the LAS stories. The child must retell two stories to employ the scoring system.

The statistical data concerning the PRE-LAS are not included in the administrator's materials. They must be purchased separately in the PRE-LAS Technical Report, available from Linguametrics. Reliabilities from the separate subtests show the listening sections are less reliable than the speaking sections. Coefficients among the subtests range from .69 to .93. The norming information was based on a group of 850 students from nine different locations in the United States. Statistical data are provided, but no accompanying interpretative discussion is available. The PRE-LAS seems appropriate for young children in terms of its visual stimuli: large colored and cartoon-like pictures. The language tasks are appropriate for the age of children to be tested; however, the language models for story-retelling comparison give more weight to academic language competence than communicative competence. The PRE-LAS would appear to be a more valid measure of language proficiency than for language screening done for special program needs. Often tests such as the Boehm Test of Basic Concepts (46 and 10:32) are used inappropriately for similar purposes.

The PRE-LAS is an improvement over the LAS for language testing of very young children. The length of the test matches the young child's short attention span. The optional use of the tape cassette is commendable as the personalization of the testing ambience increases the opportunities to elicit real language from the children.

A thorough knowledge of the test and scoring system must be acquired before administering the PRE-LAS. Score computation is simpler with the PRE-LAS than the LAS, but the examiner must still be alert in changing the raw score to the converted score. The PRE-LAS, like the LAS, is open to the criticism that scoring the two oral subsections is too subjective and thus does not provide an accurate measure. The authors have given considerable attention to the interpretation of the language samples dictated by the children and have provided numerous models of comparison. For those children who fall between levels, additional language sampling is suggested before a final score is given. Such additional sampling may make the difference in deciding if a child is English proficient or limited-English proficient, very often a cutoff point for special program participation.

By relying on a convergent assessment of semantics, syntax, and morphology that is the foundation of the LAS, the PRE-LAS will provide a measure of the English language proficiency of young children (the Spanish version was not reviewed). The PRE-LAS is short, succinct, and enjoyable for both the child and adult. Preschool and kindergarten programs will profit from using this test to help identify participants by their English language proficiency levels. The PRE-LAS will also provide pre-post program data for English language proficiency achievement along with diagnostic information for individual children.

Review of the PRE-LAS English by KIKUMI TATSUOKA, Associate Professor, Computer-Based

Education Research Laboratory, University of Illinois at Urbana-Champaign, Urbana, IL:

PRE-LAS materials include two manuals, a four-page response sheet, a cue picture booklet (21 pages), a 16-inch x 11-inch picture of a house, and an audiocassette. The administration manual (How to Administer PRE-LAS English) is divided into five sections. Section 1 highlights the need for examiners to be quite conversant with all aspects of the test before attempting an administration.

This 10-minute, individually administered test has six subscales. Scales I–IV are composed of 10 items each. Scale I, Simon Says, is a test of a child's ability to follow instructions. For example, children are asked to "put the paper on the floor" and "put the pencil on the floor." A small but important standardization concern is that examiners are not told in what initial positions the paper and pencil should be placed. Scale II, Choose a Picture, is intended to test the child's understanding of language. Scale III is a test of expressive language. The content of the probes are common household objects. Scale IV, Say What You Hear, tests a child's morphological and syntactical ability.

Scale V, Finishing Stories, is the most difficult of the scales and measures the child's ability to supply an appropriate clause to complete a compound or complex sentence. The final scale, Let's Tell Stories, requires the child to retell stories. These scales are scored with ratings of 0–3 and 0–5 respectively. Helpful descriptions are listed to assist in uniform scoring. Many examples of responses are provided in Appendices A and B. Scale VI examples are grouped by age so that differential stages of maturity can be taken into account when scoring.

In general the items are carefully constructed and appropriate for measuring language skills in 4–6-year-olds whose primary language is not English. Although a method to establish interrater reliability is presented, I would suggest the authors replace their rather idiosyncratic approach with a more useful method such as Kendall's tau.

Following raw score transformations, a child's language proficiency is given a 1–5 (5 equals most proficient) rating. Standard error of measurement (*SEM*) is discussed and confidence intervals are presented. There is some discrepancy between the example given on page 10 of the scoring manual and the cutoff scores given on Table 5. This and other typographical errors should be corrected.

Although the PRE-LAS is a promising test, the technical development of the instrument requires continued attention. Data on reliability and validity are missing. Although *SEM* is presented, more information is needed to assess the reliability of the proposed intervals. Means and standard deviations of raw and composite scores should be provided in the manual to allow for inspection and evaluation.

[297]
Preliminary Diagnostic Questionnaire.

Purpose: To assess the functional capacities of persons with disabilities in relation to employability.

Population: Persons involved with vocational rehabilitation agencies or facilities and workers' compensation claimants.

Publication Date: 1981.

Acronym: PDQ.

Scores: 8 subscales: Work Information, Preliminary Estimate of Learning, Psychomotor Skills, Reading Retention, Work Importance, Personal Independence, Internality, Emotional Functioning.

Administration: Individual.

Restricted Distribution: Restricted to persons who have completed the publisher's training course and are certified; group training by arrangement.

Price Data, 1990: $100 per person per complete self-paced training kit; $50 per 100 client booklets.

Time: (60) minutes.

Comments: Orally administered.

Author: Joseph B. Moriarty.

Publisher: West Virginia Research and Training Center.

TEST REFERENCES

1. Minskoff, E. H., Hawks, R., Steidle, E. F., & Hoffmann, F. J. (1989). A homogeneous group of persons with learning disabilities: Adults with severe learning disabilities in vocational rehabilitation. *Journal of Learning Disabilities, 22,* 521-528.

Review of the Preliminary Diagnostic Questionnaire by STEVE GRAHAM, Associate Professor, and DEBRA NEUBERT, Assistant Professor of Special Education, University of Maryland, College Park, MD:

The Preliminary Diagnostic Questionnaire (PDQ) is a screening instrument designed to provide vocational rehabilitation counselors with a quick assessment of clients' cognitive, physical, and emotional functioning as well as their disposition to work. The instrument is described as a casework tool, or an assistive device for gathering information on a client's functional assets and limitations, developing tentative hypotheses concerning employability, formulating additional questions and client assessment needs, and determining eligibility for rehabilitation services. The authors of the PDQ indicate that an additional advantage of the instrument is that it helps to structure the diagnostic process by providing counselors with a framework for gathering, analyzing, synthesizing, and sharing information with their clients.

The PDQ is given individually and reportedly takes only 1 hour to administer. Much of the information collected from the client is obtained through a structured interview format. The developers of the instrument claim that adequate administration requires the diagnostic interviewing skills of a trained and experienced vocational rehabilitation counselor. As a result, the instrument is available only to persons who have received training and certification through the West Virginia Research and Training Center (WVRC), the developer of the PDQ. In order to obtain certification, counselors must complete seven training modules, administer the PDQ to five clients, and submit their work to the WVRC for evaluation and feedback.

The instrument includes nine sections: demographic data and eight scales. Demographic data include questions concerning the client's employment history, social environment, medication, and so forth. Six of the demographic items (sex, marital status, work status, disability, education, and age) are used to calculate a client's probability of competitive employment. The utility of this estimate is questionable, because important factors such as severity of disability, motivation to work, physical capabilities, and so forth are not considered. Furthermore, it is not clear how this scale was devised or if clients' scores on this measure are adequate predictors of their employability.

The first four scales of the PDQ are performance-based. The Work Information subtest includes questions designed to tap the client's knowledge of the world of work. The questions are generally oriented to knowledge of blue collar jobs and unions. The relevance of some of the items (for example, "What is George Meany famous for?") is questionable. The Preliminary Estimate of Learning (PEL) subtest reportedly measures intellectual functioning. The PEL consists primarily of general information questions. Although the authors of the PDQ indicated correlations between the PEL and the Wechsler Adult Intelligence Scale ranged from .70 to .78, they also found that the word recognition (reading) subtest from the Wide Range Achievement Test had a similar association (.79) with the PEL, thus raising questions as to what the subtest actually measures. The Psychomotor Skills subtest involves copying geometric figures from the Beery Developmental Test of Visual-Motor Integration and filling and addressing an envelope. Although such measures are economical, they tap a very limited range of the variety of motor behaviors necessary across a wide range of occupations. The Reading subtest involves reading a passage with paragraphs ranging from 4th to 11th grade level. In addition to this rather unusual format, the accompanying comprehension questions deal almost exclusively with retention; inference and other reading skills that may be important to job success are not emphasized.

The last four scales of the PDQ employ a self-report format. Work Importance is measured by having clients note their degree of agreement/disagreement with statements regarding attitudes, perceptions, and values concerning employment. The Estimate of Personal Independence assesses the client's physical limitations in terms of self-care, mobility, and range of motion. The subtest Internality measures the client's locus of control with regard to work-related situations. It must be noted that concurrent validity for this scale has not been adequately established, as the authors of the PDQ have not examined the association between this measure and more traditional measures of locus of control. Finally, Emotional Functioning is assessed by asking clients to indicate how often they exhibit behavior representative of anxiety, depression, aggression, withdrawal, and bizarreness.

One significant drawback to the PDQ is that the authors do not provide a technical manual. Information concerning normative data, reliability, and validity are included in several published and unpublished reports. This arrangement makes it difficult for users to judge the technical adequacy of the instrument. Moreover, these reports do not contain important information such as a detailed description of how the scales were constructed.

The PDQ was standardized on a sample of 2,972 vocational rehabilitation clients from 30 states. Unfortunately, data on the normative sample are incompletely reported. Procedures for selecting persons for inclusion in the normative sample are vague; it does not appear that a systematic plan was used to select a representative sample. Although the normative sample was reasonably similar in terms of sex, race, age, education, marital status, work status, and area of disability to a randomly selected sample of all clients served in Vocational Rehabilitation agencies nationwide, additional information detailing the specific characteristics of the standardization sample, such as severity of disability or more detailed information on ethnicity (more than White, Black, or Other), are needed.

In the available published and unpublished reports, the authors of the PDQ review a variety of studies they claim provide support for the reliability and validity of the instrument. Until both further and independent investigations are undertaken, the results from these studies must be interpreted cautiously. A particular concern relates to the reliability of specific subtests, especially because the PDQ is used to make decisions about individual clients. Test-retest reliability coefficients were unavailable for two scales and were less than .80 on four others. Similarly, on a measure of internal consistency, the reliability coefficients for three scales were less than .80. It also does not appear that the majority of the scales are predictive of employment, as measured by presence or absence of earnings or earnings above or below the minimum wage. Moreover, it is not clear if the instrument or the individual scales discriminate between the disabled who have difficulty obtaining employment and nondisabled groups.

The authors of the PDQ should be commended for providing appropriate cautions for the administration and interpretation of the instrument. For instance, the PDQ is not recommended for persons with severe visual, hearing, or communicative handicapping conditions. Furthermore, the instrument, in our estimation, is not appropriate for clients with severe handicapping conditions.

In summary, the PDQ appears to be best suited for experimental work. Additional evidence on the normative sample, reliability, and validity is needed before the PDQ can be recommended as an instrument for making individual assessments on vocational rehabilitation clients.

Review of the Preliminary Diagnostic Questionnaire by THOMAS G. HARING, Associate Professor in Special Education, University of California, Santa Barbara, CA:

The expressed purpose of the Preliminary Diagnostic Questionnaire (PDQ) is to provide an initial assessment of the functional capabilities of vocational rehabilitation clients through a combination of structured interview questions and test items that assess specific abilities presumed to predict employability. This instrument allows a quick screening (approximately 1 hour) of vocational abilities, attitudes, and degree of physical independence through the use of eight subscales relevant to vocational rehabilitation: Work Information, Preliminary Estimate of Learning, Psychomotor Skills, Reading Ability and Comprehension, Work Importance, Estimate of Personal Independence, Internality, and Emotional Functioning. Results are recorded on a convenient profile that allows analysis across the eight sections in stanines. The PDQ was developed to be more than an initial diagnostic assessment. It attempts to provide a structure for organizing casework, conducting counseling sessions, and treating motivational and emotional barriers to successful vocational placement and planning rehabilitation goals. The PDQ is available only in conjunction with training from the West Virginia Research and Training Center. In order to use the PDQ, a counselor must be certified.

REVIEW OF TRAINING MODULES. The training for certification is composed of seven modules: introduction to the PDQ; philosophic basis of functional assessment; administration of the PDQ; interpretation of case studies; techniques of diagnostic interviews; interpretation of locus of control; and casework implications of the PDQ including guidelines for conducting therapeutic interviews.

An analysis of the written materials in the training package suggested the content of the training modules goes beyond the information needed to use the PDQ. The modules provide fairly detailed descriptions of counseling methods that can be used to probe beyond the test items themselves to determine motivational, emotional, and family factors that might impede or facilitate the vocational rehabilitation process. The training modules do a nice job of giving guidelines for interpreting the

profiles of scores across the eight subscales. Patterns of scores are identified that might suggest a need for further exploration through interviews with the client or more comprehensive testing in specific areas. The strengths of the training modules are: (*a*) The manuals are written in a style easily understandable to counselors who may not be formally trained in assessment, (*b*) the modules include a broad range of suggestions for interpretation and problem solving with clients, and (*c*) the information provided is more than adequate to use the PDQ effectively.

There are, in my view, some shortcomings with the training modules as well: (*a*) The focus of the training and interpretation examples are generally with clients who are fairly verbal and capable of responding to more traditional question-and-answer formats. The PDQ training modules are not set up to allow training and interpretation of clients with more moderate and severe developmental disabilities, a population the field of vocational rehabilitation is coming under increasing congressional pressure to serve. (*b*) In several places the manuals (e.g., the manuals on motivation, interviewing, and management implications) go beyond data collection and interpretation of interview results into therapeutic procedures. This may pose a potential problem if the theoretical orientation of the user does not correspond to that promoted within the modules. This material, which is basically extraneous to use of the PDQ, makes the amount of training seem unnecessarily great. (*c*) The training and interpretation guidelines given relate to a concept of vocational rehabilitation that is rooted in the assessment of underlying traits and abilities (e.g., general intelligence and internal vs. external locus of control) that deals with vocational development as a predictive process and an interpersonal counseling process, rather than as a job of matching the specific service needs of a client with the specific demands of a range of work environments. Curiously, the training manuals discuss the characteristics of jobs and work environments in relation to subscale scores and client characteristics quite infrequently. Thus, the PDQ may be of somewhat limited use in guiding directly the selection of jobs or in direct planning of vocational options.

Content Analysis of the PDQ.

DEMOGRAPHIC DATA. In addition to the eight subscales, the PDQ includes a form for the collection of routine demographic information. This form may be useful to vocational rehabilitation counselors in organizing data from external sources relevant to case management and planning. Using the demographic section, the user can estimate the probability of future competitive employment based on six variables: sex, marital status, current work status, type of disability, education level, and age. To do this analysis, the data from the cover sheet are categorized by using a simple numerical code. The coded number is then transferred to a table that gives the likelihood of competitive employment for a person with that specific set of demographic variables. While most of the decisions needed to use this probability table and formulate the code are relatively straightforward, there are two areas of ambiguity. First, in classifying the primary disability of a client, six choices are offered: Visual, Hearing, Orthopedic, Amputation, Mental, and Other. The descriptions in the manual are not clear as to what types of disabilities should be classified as "Mental." For example, would this include adventitious brain injury and all levels of mental retardation, as well as psychiatric disorders? In addition, it is unclear what disabilities were lumped together to create the "other" category. The breadth of the types and severities of disabilities that are lumped together makes the use of these tables a rough estimate at best, and at worst, misleading as to the employment potential of an individual.

Whether or not a person is currently employed is by far the strongest predictor of future employment. For example, a woman who is married, currently employed, orthopedically disabled, has 15 years of education, and is 41 to 60 years old, has a probability of successful employment of .97. If she were not currently employed, this probability would drop to .26. It is impossible to estimate the effects of factors, such as just being laid off, on these probabilities. The authors point out these data should be used only as a rough estimation of future employability. The use of these data in the allocation of services, however, is another issue that requires closer ethical scrutiny and stronger discussion in the manual. In my view, these data are far too cursory for such use.

WORK INFORMATION. The authors state the purpose of the Work Information subscale is to determine if "the individual has assimilated enough work information to function effectively on the job." An analysis of the items on this subscale raises questions at the face-validity level as to the scale's ability to perform this task. Seventeen items on the scale are scored as right or wrong. The items range from being able to define the difference between being laid off and being fired, knowing what a part-time job is, and knowing what a time clock is, to knowing who George Meany is and defining the acronyms AFL-CIO and OSHA. Five of the 17 items on the scale relate to knowledge of unions; thus, workers with experience in nonunion settings may have a more difficult time with this test. The authors acknowledge the test is similar to a verbal section on an ability test in content and construction. Given the brevity of the test and the fact the test apparently was not constructed based on a content

analysis by experts in analysis of characteristics of work settings (as would be a typical procedure from which to claim content validity in tests of this type), the claim that this test assesses work information needed to function on the job is not well justified.

There is a high likelihood this section of the PDQ taps heavily into a more general ability factor than it does the specific skills needed to function effectively in a workplace. The correlation between the Work Information subscale and the WAIS Information subtest ($n = 43$) was .63. In addition, in a factor analytic study the Work Information section loaded significantly on Factor 1, which was interpreted as indicating general intellectual ability.

The internal consistency coefficient (KR-20) on a sample of 151 clients from West Virginia was .85. In addition, the internal consistency of the Work Information section was assessed by correlating the individual items from the subscale with the total score on a sample of 292 clients from 16 states achieving correlations "at the level of .38 or higher" (p. 41). Mean correlations and the entire range of correlations are not reported. A test-retest correlation of .81 ($n = 28$) was reported. As with other technical descriptions within the manual, much information that would be important in making informed decisions about the use of the PDQ is missing or poorly stated. The samples used in the validity and reliability studies are too small, unsystematic, and inadequately described.

PRELIMINARY ESTIMATE OF LEARNING (PEL). The PEL was designed to give a quick estimate of intelligence. It contains 30 items scored as correct or incorrect that reflect general knowledge rather than reasoning or problem solving. The items range from knowing in what month Christmas is celebrated, how many days are in a week, and who is the president, to who wrote *Paradise Lost*, what is a definition of entomology, and who wrote "Night on Bald Mountain." In analyzing the content of this subscale, the items measure knowledge most likely acquired through participation in education and strongly favor the recall of learned facts. As such, persons who have limited participation in formal academic instruction would have a more difficult time with this subscale. For example, such fact-based instruction is rarely employed in special education. The PEL was validated on a sample of 151 clients from the West Virginia Rehabilitation Institute. The population is not adequately described. The manual states the sample contains "a higher percentage of mentally retarded than would the average field caseload." With this sample, the internal consistency (KR-20) of .97 indicates high internal consistency. Using a national sample of 292 clients from 16 states (again with only cursory descriptions of the sampling of disabilities), item-to-total correlation ranged from .26 to .66, indicating a moderate level of internal consistency. Using the West Virginia sample, the PEL correlated .79 with the WAIS Information score ($n = 43$), .71 with the WAIS full scale score ($n = 100$), .74 with the Peabody General Information score ($n = 50$), and .78 with the Peabody Reading Comprehension Score ($n = 15$). These moderate correlations are typical for a short form test such as this.

A study comparing PEL scores of mentally retarded and nonretarded clients indicated scores in the mentally retarded group were significantly lower. To assess test-retest reliability, 28 clients from the West Virginia sample were retested after 30 days. The test-retest coefficient was .97.

The sample sizes employed in the reliability and validation studies for the PEL are much smaller than generally acceptable in more comprehensive tests of general intelligence. In addition, the samples are poorly described in terms of degrees and types of disabilities and other relevant characteristics of the populations used in the studies. The national sample was predominantly white; the only minority group represented was black (12%). The logic for selection of the 16 states in the national sample and the method of sampling clients within those states are not given.

PSYCHOMOTOR SKILLS. The section on psycho-motor skills consists of two tasks. The first task is to fold a piece of paper for insertion into an envelope and address the envelope. Four criteria are given to score the correctness of the paper-folding task. The second task consists of a reprint of five items from the Developmental Test of Visual-Motor Integration (VMI) by Beery and Buktenica (1967). The VMI consists of copying figures (e.g., circles and three-dimensional stars) from samples. The scoring protocol for these five items is taken directly from the VMI and calls for judgments concerning the accuracy of copying the figures. Referring to the VMI manual, the five items selected correspond to developmental norms of 5 years, 6 months; 7 years, 11 months; 11 years, 2 months; 12 years, 8 months; and 13 years, 8 months.

The use of the VMI reflects the PDQ's underlying approach to measurement based on the assessment of underlying abilities in contrast to a more direct assessment of vocationally relevant skills. While the paper-folding task does show face validity for vocational placement, the VMI does not.

The method of determining the norms for this subsection is bewildering. A sample of 58 students from West Virginia University were administered five drawing items *not* on the VMI. The mean from this test was 3.1 correct drawings. The authors then assume these college students would have obtained a perfect score on the 4 envelope tasks from the VMI. Thus, an estimated score of 7.1 was derived. This was compared to the mean score on the Psychomotor Section (that is, drawings plus paper folding) of 6.82 from the national sample of 292 vocational rehabilitation clients. Apparently, these data were used to determine that a score of 7 ought to determine the middle score for norming purposes. However, the relevance of the study with college students using a different series of test items is difficult to determine. An item-to-total correlation was "above .37." The mean and range are not given. An ANOVA was conducted that compared the performance of clients diagnosed as mentally retarded to other clients. The report claims the group with mental retardation was significantly lower; however, the p value is not given.

Overall, the Psychomotor section is not well validated. It does not include measures with the necessary predictive relationship to vocational placement.

READING. The Reading section appears to be useful in that the ability to read and comprehend written material and to recall written facts may have important implications in planning a program of vocational rehabilitation. The PDQ offers a quick assessment of reading skills. The Reading section is administered orally and consists of reading a story that is approximately one page in length. Errors of refusal, omission, reversal, insertion, and mispronunciation are scored. In addition, the client is given an 18-item reading comprehension test after reading the passage twice, once orally and once silently.

One hundred thirteen vocational rehabilitation clients from West Virginia were administered this section to determine the norms. This sample produced a mean of 10.6. The national sample of 292 clients achieved a mean of 11.39. The mean from the norm table is given at 12 to 14. The reason for this discrepancy is not given. A group of 26 West Virginia clients was retested after 1 month. The test-retest coefficient was .78. The internal consistency of the reading section was tested with 113 West Virginia clients and yielded a coefficient (KR-20) of .85, indicating a reasonably high level of internal consistency.

WORK IMPORTANCE. The Work Importance section consists of a 10-item, 4-point, Likert scale. This section is designed to assess the client's attitude toward work. Clients are asked to indicate the extent of their agreement with statements such as "I am satisfied with most aspects of my life" and "My chances of getting a job are excellent." A good feature of this subscale is the inclusion of items that assess the degree of support the client feels from friends and family in obtaining employment. It also provides an assessment of the client's own perspective of the importance of employment in his or her own life. This information could be critical in developing a vocational rehabilitation plan.

The norms for this section were developed with a sample of students from West Virginia University and the 292 clients from the national sample. In the college sample, the coefficient alpha was .85, indicating a high degree of internal consistency. In addition, the range of item-to-total correlations was from .44 to .61, which is an acceptable level for Likert-type scales.

PERSONAL INDEPENDENCE. This section is designed to assess a client's physical abilities. The personal independence section consists of 29 items. On 20 items, the client verbally indicates if he or she can do a response without assistance, with an assistive device, with the assistance of another person, or cannot do the response. The responses include eating, drinking, dressing, and walking up and down steps. The remaining nine items are of a demonstration type in which the client is asked to raise his or her right arm above the head, stand on his or her left foot, and kneel on the floor. The information from this section may be very important in matching a client's current physical capabilities to the demands of various jobs and employment settings. The scale was designed so a perfect score (indicating no functional physical limitations) would yield a score in the middle stanine. A comparison of scores from orthopedically disabled clients with nonorthopedically disabled clients indicated this scale can discriminate physically disabled clients from nondisabled clients.

INTERNALITY. This section is composed of a 15-item, 4-point, Likert-type scale that assesses a client's degree of internal versus external locus of control. The scale has good face validity for use in vocational rehabilitation settings because generally the items reflect attitudes toward supervisors, and reasons for work-related events such as getting fired or getting promoted.

The production of the norms for this subscale is described inadequately in the manual. Scores of 0 (strongly external) through 60 (strongly internal) were possible. The sample of West Virginia clients had a mean of 29.17. A sample of 58 college students had a mean of 35.41, and the national sample of clients had a mean of 32.31. However, the authors designated 41 to 42 as the midpoint of the scale. In interpreting these data, it is typical that a college population will have mean scores that are somewhat strongly indicative of internal locus of control, yet the midpoint of this scale is set *above* the mean for the college sample. Many users will look at the profile and expect that scores above the midpoint indicate an internal locus of control and scores below that point indicate an external locus of control. In fact, the presentation of data in stanine scores means the fifth stanine correponds to the mean. The manual states, "Scores below the fifth stanine on the PDQ Internality section suggest persons who feel unable to control the events that shape their lives." An external locus of control is presumably a negative predictor of vocational success. Based on the PDQ profile, to score at the mean or into the internal range, a vocational rehabilitation client would have to score well above the mean from the validation study and above the mean of a college sample. Based on a standard deviation of 5.44 for the national sample, the midpoint of the profile is set almost 2 standard deviations above the mean. The discrepancy between the field test data and the construction of the norms is not explained or justified. Without further explanation and justification, I would not recommend the use of the profile in assessing the locus of control of vocational rehabilitation clients. Problems of this type call into question the adequacy of the construction of the PDQ.

EMOTIONAL FUNCTIONING. This section is designed to provide a preliminary assessment of the emotional functioning and psychological well-being of a client. The section consists of 20 items such as "I get nervous" and "I get mad." The client indicates the frequency of that characteristic on a 4-point scale: *never, sometimes, often, always.* The inclusion of this section is a valuable addition to the PDQ because it has been well accepted for some time that social emotional factors are powerful predictors of future successful employment (Goldstein, 1964).

On this subscale the mean for the national sample was used to set the midpoint of the scale. The test-retest reliability was assessed after 30 days with 28 clients yielding a coefficient of .89. An internal consistency coefficient of .87 indicates strong internal consistency. A statistical comparison comparing the scores of clients classified as having a mental illness with those not classified suggested significant differences between the groups. However, the mean for the mentally ill group (61.18) was less than 1 standard deviation (8.21) from the midpoint of the scale (64), indicating that although the scale will pick up significant differences in group averages, there is considerable overlap in the distribution of scores between individuals with mental illness and those not classified.

SUMMARY EVALUATION. The PDQ was designed to fill a substantial need in the diagnosis, planning, and management of vocational rehabilitation casework. An adequately developed scale that allowed the rapid collection of data across the areas sampled by the PDQ would be of great use if viewed, as the authors advocate, as a screening instrument to determine which more comprehensive tests and assessments are needed to get a clear picture of the vocational rehabilitation of a client. The Reading section, Work Importance section, and Personal Independence section show the highest degrees of usefulness and technical adequacy. Unfortunately, the overall development of the PDQ contains numerous psychometric shortcomings that should preclude its use until further and more rigorous scaling, reliability studies, and validity studies are undertaken.

REVIEWER'S REFERENCE

Goldstein, H. (1964). Social and occupational adjustment. In H. A. Stevens & R. Heber (Eds.), *Mental retardation: A review of research* (pp. 214-258). Chicago: University of Chicago Press.

[298]
Preliminary Test of English as a Foreign Language.

Purpose: Measures "the English proficiency of nonnative speakers."
Population: College and other institutional applicants, grade 11 and over, from non-English-language countries.
Publication Dates: 1983–89.
Acronym: Pre-TOEFL®.
Scores, 4: Listening Comprehension, Structure and Written Expression, Reading Comprehension and Vocabulary, Total.
Administration: Group.
Price Data, 1990: $12 examination fee with minimum charge of $120 per institution per administration; fee includes machine scoring by publisher, test results, and use of booklets and administrative materials which must be returned to publisher.
Time: 70 minutes.
Comments: A shorter test measuring the same components of language proficiency as the regular TOEFL; 2 forms per year; offered only through the TOEFL Institutional Testing Program.
Authors: Jointly sponsored by College Entrance Examination Board, Graduate Record Examination Board, and Educational Testing Service.
Publisher: Educational Testing Service.
Cross References: For reviews by Brenda H. Loyd and Kikumi K. Tatsuoka of the Test of English as a Foreign Language, see 9:1257 (1 reference); see also T3:2441 (9 references), 8:110 (15 references), and T2:238 (4 references); for reviews by Clinton I. Chase and George Domino of the TOEFL, see 7:266 (10 references).

Review of the Preliminary Test of English as a Foreign Language by ROGER A. RICHARDS, Dean of Academic Affairs, Bunker Hill Community College, Boston, MA;

The concept of the Preliminary Test of English as a Foreign Language (Pre-TOEFL) is a welcome addition to the well-established, highly useful TOEFL program. An adaptation of the original test, the Pre-TOEFL provides a shorter version that is designed specifically for use with "nonnative speakers at the beginning and intermediate levels of proficiency in English." The maximum score on the Pre-TOEFL is 500, in contrast to the highest TOEFL score of 677 on the same scale.

The obvious advantages of the Pre-TOEFL are that it is more efficient to use than the parent test and that it spares the less able students the frustration of trying to cope with materials that are beyond their ability.

Section 1, Listening Comprehension, presents three kinds of items. Part A requires students to select from four printed sentences the one that is closest in meaning to a sentence on the tape that is played to administer this section. Part B presents very brief dialogues, each of which is followed by a question based upon what is said in the dialogue. Part C consists of two passages (a conversation between two students and an expository paragraph) of several sentences in length, each of which is followed by four questions based on information presented in the passage.

This section is excellent. The content is at an appropriate level of difficulty and should be of general interest to test takers. Both the quality of the tape and the pacing are very good.

Section 2, Structure and Written Expression, begins with a multiple-choice cloze exercise of 10 sentences. The items seem quite easy, primarily because many distractors appear rather far-fetched. One wonders if nonnative speakers really use such wrong constructions as "Both are hardwoods and softwoods are used for sculpture."

Following the cloze exercise are 15 sentences in which the test taker is required to indicate which underlined portion of a sentence "must be changed in order for the sentence to be correct." The errors involve case of pronouns, verb tense, word order, subject-verb agreement, idiomatic expressions, confusion of adjective and adverb, comparison of adjectives, and confusion of noun and verb.

This portion of the test does not seem to tap really crucial matters of English usage. Some sentences seem to be measuring specific academic content as much as English usage. A couple of items border on gibberish and others seem contrived for the purposes of constructing a test rather than to reflect a common error in English usage.

Section 3, Vocabulary and Reading Comprehension, opens with 20 sentences in which the student must select the word or phrase that " *best keeps the meaning* of the original sentence." The words tested are appropriate and represent the language of everyday discourse. One can, of course, quibble about a few of the right answers: Does "moved" really capture the essence of " *drifted* from one job to another"? Does "understanding of" mean the same as " *knowledge of* "? (We know many things that we cannot understand.) And doesn't "obey" go beyond the sense of " *heed* their commanders"?

The second half of Section 3 follows the familiar format of a paragraph followed by three to five questions about the passage. A few questions require the students to make inferences but most are straightforward measures of comprehension. A few require nothing more than the ability to pick out the exact words of the passage without demonstrating any awareness of what the words mean.

A fundamental question raised by an analysis of the test's items is how they are constructed. Are they based on actual usage by nonnative speakers? Or are they manufactured by the item writers? One hopes that the former is the case. It would seem easy enough to base a multiple-choice exercise, for example, on free-response administrations of the items to develop a stock of real-world errors from which to select the distractors. Similarly, it ought to be easy enough to consult the actual writing of nonnative students to find sentences that contain real errors.

These practices may, in fact, have been followed. Many of the items suggest, however, that they were not, and the only information given concerning the construction of the tests makes the reader uneasy: "All TOEFL and Pre-TOEFL questions are written by English-as-a-foreign-language specialists, who are given rigorous training in writing questions for the test before they undertake actual writing assignments." Would it not be more reassuring to read that all questions are adapted from instances of actual English language usage by nonnative students? Given the vast resources of the Educational Testing Service, such an approach should be feasible.

We are told that "all questions are pretested on representative groups of foreign students," so perhaps this reviewer's apprehensions are unfounded. But there is no information on how many students actually selected each of the four responses to each question.

The Pre-TOEFL appears to be riding on the coattails of the TOEFL. The only publication specifically about the Pre-TOEFL consists of four pages of typewritten information—two pages are devoted to descriptions of the test and the other two pages contain three tables related to scores.

A request to the publisher for further information brought the response that "There are no additional publications that provide information exclusively about the Pre-TOEFL." The same letter explains that the Pre-TOEFL is "constructed by selecting the less difficult TOEFL test items." It further states that no validity study of the Pre-TOEFL has been conducted. The writer offers the "opinion that the validity of TOEFL transfers to the Pre-TOEFL" (Letter from Stella R. Cowell, October 19, 1990).

It is possible that such faith is justified, but it does not follow automatically that because the TOEFL has been shown to be valid, this adaptation of the TOEFL is also valid. If, for example, the items selected for the Pre-TOEFL happen to be the weakest (we know that they are the easiest) of the TOEFL, it is possible that the Pre-TOEFL could be far less valid than the original. But why must we be forced to speculate? We hope that the validity of the Pre-TOEFL will be independently studied.

Beyond the issue of validity, additional information of other kinds is also needed by the potential user of the Pre-TOEFL. Because of the lack of a manual for the Pre-TOEFL, we must rely on the 1990–91 TOEFL Test and Score Manual. That document provides assurance that the TOEFL has been extensively researched. In fact, it lists 31 reports of TOEFL research, one of which contains summaries of 80 other studies. This reviewer hopes that ETS will choose to make summaries of the results of such rich research more accessible in future manuals.

The kinds of questions that need to be answered include the following: Upon what rationale is the test based? How does English as a Foreign Language differ from English as a domestic language? (One research report concluded that the TOEFL is not psychometrically appropriate for native speakers of English. What makes it inappropriate?) What test blueprint is followed in the construction of the many TOEFL forms? (It would be difficult to develop a blueprint if there were no rationale.) What is the scope and source of the vocabulary sampled by the test? What major grammatical concepts are covered? Are any grammatical issues deliberately not addressed? How are the reading selections chosen? What content areas are used? At what grade levels are the passages written?

SUMMARY. Considering the lack of specific validity studies on the Pre-TOEFL and the dearth of information about how the test is constructed, this reviewer cannot offer a definitive evaluation of it. Those who have been satisfied with the TOEFL will probably want to try the Pre-TOEFL because of the economies it offers.

Review of the Preliminary Test of English as a Foreign Language by CHARLENE RIVERA, Director, The Evaluation Assistant Center East, The George Washington University, Arlington, VA:

The Preliminary Test of English as a Foreign Language (Pre-TOEFL) is a lower level version of the Test of English as a Foreign Language (TOEFL; 9:1257). The TOEFL was developed cooperatively by a number of organizations in 1963 and has since been operated by Educational Testing Service (ETS). The TOEFL was designed to assess the English language proficiency of nonnative English speakers applying for admission to American colleges and universities. Subsequent use of the test for placement purposes by English language schools suggested that it was too difficult for low and intermediate level students. Thus, in 1985, ETS developed the Pre-TOEFL.

Two forms of the Pre-TOEFL are prepared each year. The form reviewed here is Pre-TOEFL, Level

2, Form 3MPET1. The test is administered only as part of the TOEFL Institutional Testing Program (ITP) by approved facilities and businesses throughout the world.

The Pre-TOEFL consists of 95 items drawn from the TOEFL item pool. Like the TOEFL, it has three sections: Listening Comprehension, Structure and Written Expression, and Vocabulary and Reading Comprehension. This three-part structure is the result of research on the TOEFL carried out over several years (Pike, 1979; Pitcher & Ra, 1967; Swineford, 1971).

Section 1, Listening Comprehension, consists of three parts and is intended to assess comprehension of spoken English. Part A involves listening to 12 sentences and selecting the response closest in meaning to the statement. Ten very short two-person conversations are presented in Part B. A single question is posed and examinees select one option from among four possible responses. Part C requires examinees to listen to one conversation and one monologue. After each, four questions are posed.

The next section, Structure and Written Expression, measures the use of standard English structure and grammar in formal written English. The first items in this two-part section assess basic grammar. From 10 single sentences, the examinee is required to select the correct response (from among four) that will complete each sentence. In part two, words and phrases in 15 single sentences are underlined. The task for the examinee is to identify the word or phrase not consistent with standard written English usage.

The final section, Vocabulary and Reading Comprehension, assesses recognition of vocabulary and the ability to read with understanding. The vocabulary section consists of 20 sentences where one word or phrase is underlined. The examinee chooses from four options the best meaning of the underlined word or phrase. For the Reading Comprehension section, examinees read five passages that are academic in nature; they then select correct responses for three to five questions related to each passage.

According to ETS, the Pre-TOEFL can be used: (*a*) to assess English language proficiency of students entering or completing English as a second language (ESL) or English as a foreign language (EFL) courses; (*b*) to assign students to English as a second language courses at the appropriate level of difficulty; (*c*) to determine if students have enough English to function in an all-English learning environment; (*d*) to determine if someone has an adequate command of English to pursue an occupation requiring English language proficiency.

The first two purposes listed above are appropriate uses of the Pre-TOEFL. Its validity for these uses is supported by research and by years of experience by admissions officers and the directors of English language schools that prepare students for college or university admission. However, the Pre-TOEFL's validity for the latter two uses warrants some qualification.

According to the TOEFL Test and Score Manual, approximately 75% of colleges and universities require a TOEFL score above 500 for admission. Thus, the Pre-TOEFL could not be used to determine if students can function in an all-English learning environment at most American or Canadian colleges and universities. Similarly, more than half the community colleges that require TOEFL scores for admissions purposes require a score of 500 or above. Thus, the Pre-TOEFL could not be used at these institutions either, because the maximum score one can attain on the Pre-TOEFL is 500.

The final purpose mentioned above may also be questioned. In occupational testing, the relationship between the content of the test and the job must be established. Because the TOEFL and the Pre-TOEFL are basically tests of academic English, they may not be suitable for evaluating applicants for jobs not requiring proficiency in academic English.

The examinee is given 70 minutes to complete the Pre-TOEFL. Scoring is based on an abridged TOEFL scale with a scaled score range between 200 and 500. This is in contrast to a scaled score range of 200–677 for the TOEFL. The test is scored by ETS. Three section scores and a total score are reported to students.

The reliability of the Pre-TOEFL is not as high as one normally finds in commercially published standardized tests. The reported reliabilities are: Section 1—.76, Section 2—.80, Section 3—.85, and total score—.91. Although these coefficients are lower than those derived from the TOEFL, this will be problematic only if the test is used to make important decisions, such as college admission. In the case of college admissions, use of the TOEFL would seem preferable.

There is no test manual for the Pre-TOEFL. As a result, one has to search through various publications and information sheets to gather information on the test. The publication of a short test manual, giving the history and rationale for the test and information on how it is being used and its relative efficiency of measurement in comparison with the TOEFL, would be helpful.

In summary, the Pre-TOEFL seems to be a valid and adequately reliable instrument for placing students into academically oriented English language instruction programs.

REVIEWER'S REFERENCES

Pitcher, B., & Ra, J. B. (1967). *The relationships between scores on the Test of English as a Foreign Language and the ratings of actual theme writing.* (Statistical Report No. 67-9). Princeton, NJ: Educational Testing Service.

Swineford, F. (1971). *Test analysis—Test of English as a Foreign Language.* (Statistical Report No. 71-112). Princeton, NJ: Educational Testing Service.

Pike, L. (1979). *An evaluation of alternative item formats for testing English as a Foreign Language.* (TOEFL Research Report No. 2). Princeton, NJ: Educational Testing Service.

[299]

Pre-School Behaviour Checklist.

Purpose: "To help identify children with emotional and behavioural problems by providing a tool for the systematic and objective description of behaviour."
Population: Ages 2–5.
Publication Date: 1988.
Acronym: PBCL.
Scores: Total score only.
Administration: Group.
Price Data, 1989: £17.20 per administration kit; £5.75 per checklist; £5.70 per manual; £3.40 per scoring overlay.
Time: (8–10) minutes.
Comments: Behavior checklist.
Authors: Jacqueline McGuire and Naomi Richman.
Publisher: NFER-Nelson Publishing Co., Ltd. [England].

Review of the Pre-School Behaviour Checklist by ROGER D. CARLSON, *Visiting Associate Professor of Psychology, Whitman College, Walla Walla, WA:*

The potential user of the Pre-School Behaviour Checklist (PBCL) must consider the use of this checklist with respect to two issues of paramount importance: the specific content of the items that are included and the criterion used for referring a child for further professional attention.

The authors' choice of the Checklist's items make the PBCL inherently value-laden. The choice must be carefully examined in light of the values of the user and the uses to be made of the checklist. Checklist items seem representative of ones that would be valued by preschool workers. The items are based partly on interviews with preschool workers as to their observations concerning what behaviors are considered problematic in this age group of children.

The potential user must understand that both the purposes of the Checklist's development, as well as the items and results of its use, are developed for the furtherance of institutional or group goals rather than those that are necessarily best for the individual child. The authors are to be commended on their recognition that the results of the Checklist can lead to administrative reform. However, in commenting on potential administrative uses of the scale, the authors fail to suggest questions that keep the focus of attention upon the best interests of the child. Examples are given that imply the thrust of administrative reform is not so much in the direction of criticizing institutional structure and practices as causative of a child's disruptive behavior (reform of institutional structure, aims, goals, and priorities), as it is to make changes that can result in the more effective control of children (staffing shortages, training deficits, comparisons to other institutions).

Furthering the best interests of the institution may not always further the best interests of the child.

With institutional goals and values in mind, however, the items seem to be good ones when held up against the validation procedures that were undertaken by the authors. Validity studies included agreements between psychiatric judgments and PBCL scores of 122 children, as well as staff member judgments and PBCL scores of 113 children. In the latter, overall agreement was 81 percent. The PBCL did well in identifying 23 children with behavior problems in a therapeutic day center compared with 123 children in nursery school classes and 67 in local authority day nurseries. The finding that the scores of day nursery children tended to be higher than those of nursery school children coincides with the fact that day nurseries tend to take children with families under stress— thus giving support for the validity of the PBCL.

A problem endemic to the use of checklists and psychometrics generally is the use of nominally scaled items answered in a binary fashion and then summated into a ratio-scaled score. In the case of the PBCL, the authors created a criterion point for referring children for further counsel. Fortunately, because of careful external validation procedures, the criterion seems to be a well-founded value. Children who had scores exceeding the criterion were those who by and large were judged to be either in need of referral or who were in treatment programs of various kinds.

Although no individual item analyses are reported by the authors, factor and cluster analyses were reported that reveal three groupings of items: conduct/restless (too active, not liked, poor concentration, difficult to manage, etc.), isolated/immature (unclear speech, reluctant to talk, withdrawn from peers, wanders), and emotional (miserable, demands attention, whines, sensitive). Seventy-three scores on the PBCL were correlated with those of a similar instrument, the Preschool Behaviour Questionnaire (Behar & Stringfield, 1974) for the same children, and yielded a Pearson product moment correlation coefficient of .89 ($p < .001$).

Interrater reliability studies revealed 83 percent agreement between raters of the same child (Pearson $r = .68$, $n = 108$, $p < .001$). Agreement between raters in terms of the criterion point selected for referral occurred only 38 percent of the time. The authors suggest that disagreement between raters is due to differences in familiarity with the child, as well as to the authors' deliberate selection of a criterion that would maximize the PBCL's sensitivity. Therefore, the authors report their selection of a criterion point for referral has a tendency to identify false positives rather than to reject false negatives. No statistically significant differences were found between professionals using the checklist with different levels of training (teachers or nursery nurses). Test-retest reliability was found to be respectably high over a 2-week period ($r = .88$, $p < .001$). Measures of internal consistency also were high (Cronbach's alpha $= .83$, and Spearman-Brown split-half method, $r = .83$).

Overall, for an instrument of its type that attempts to ascertain how well a child fits into a social context and meets social expectations, the PBCL appears to be a very well-researched and documented one. Although the items have been developed on the basis of professionals' judgments of face value, and perhaps are overly arbitrary given the goals, situations, and concerns of the authors, it is not a carelessly conceived checklist. Likewise, although over-reliance on quantification often can lead to overlooking the tangible goals, aims, and concerns of the developer and user of such a checklist, the authors are explicit in stating caveats in the PBCL's development and use, so as to dissuade the user from the inadvertent use of a "number magic."

REVIEWER'S REFERENCE

Behar, L., & Stringfield, S. (1974). A behavior rating scale for the pre-school child. *Developmental Psychology, 10,* 601-610.

Review of the Pre-School Behaviour Checklist by GARY STONER, *Assistant Professor, School Psychology Program, College of Education, University of Oregon, Eugene, OR:*

The Pre-School Behaviour Checklist (PBCL) manual contains the following statement: "The PBCL is designed to help identify children with emotional and behavioural problems by providing a tool for the systematic and objective description of behaviour. It is intended for use with 2- to 5-year-olds and, unlike most checklists, allows staff to look at the severity as well as the incidence of a particular behaviour." Whether the PBCL actually lives up to this description is questionable. In fact, all behavior rating scales provide subjective, indirect measures of behavior, with endorsed items or ratings reflecting a rater's impressions that are influenced by her or his environment, expectations, professional training, and other variables.

The PBCL consists of 22 items, each comprising three or four alternative descriptions of the behavior or characteristics of young children. Raters are asked to choose the alternative that best describes the child's current behavior. Item selection was based on a combination of the authors' research and experience with preschool children, as well as discussions with staff working in nurseries and preschools in and around London, England.

Apparently as a function of face validity, the authors consider items to be members of five different categories: (*a*) emotional difficulties (5 items); (*b*) conduct problems (5 items); (*c*) capacity to concentrate and play constructively (3 items); (*d*)

social relations (3 items); and (*e*) a catch-all category (5 items) focusing on speech and language, habits, wetting, and soiling. A few items are unclear as to whether the descriptions are of the target child, or of other children and caregivers (e.g., "Seems to be liked by other children" and "Easy to manage and control"). Additionally, several items are composed of alternatives that are potentially confusing to raters in that more than one behavior, adjective, or adverb is used in the description (e.g., the choices for one item are "Rarely demands a great deal of attention," "Sometimes asks for a lot of attention, but can work or play independently," "Frequently demands attention"). An alternative, and perhaps more clear approach, would have items consist of a description (e.g., demands attention) and numerically coded choices indicating frequency (e.g., $0 = rarely$, $1 = sometimes$, and $2 = often$).

Clearly stated administration directions are printed at the beginning of each PBCL; however, the rater is referred to the manual for further details on completing the checklist. The one-paragraph explanation to raters in the manual could be integrated readily with those directions on the checklist to eliminate the need for two sources of directions.

Each item rating is scored either 0, 1, or 2, and these scores are summed to yield a total score. A cutoff score of 12 is suggested for use to screen for children who have "definite problems" and thus are in need of follow-up services.

Empirical support for this cutoff score is minimal. For example, test-retest reliability estimates based on ratings 2 weeks apart by the same raters yielded a .88 correlation, and 91% agreement regarding a child's falling above or below the cutoff score of 12. Another report suggested, however, that with ratings of 108 children by one observer resulting in 29 children above the cutoff score, an independent rating identified 11 of those 29 children (or 38%) in the same category.

In discussing score interpretation, the authors discuss the clinical usefulness of high scores, low scores, and scores above the cutoff point, thus accurately indicating that any given score could be cause for concern for any given child. If any score is important, however, it follows that what is crucial is *how* a child obtains a score, and not the score itself. Also, if *any* score yielded by the instrument is potentially educationally or clinically significant, then these scores may add nothing meaningful about child behaviors beyond information gathered via staff observations and anecdotal reports.

Another criticism of the PBCL is that normative data are not even mentioned in the PBCL Handbook. Within the 2–5-year-old age range one should expect a great deal of variability in behaviors such as social initiation, toileting skills, interfering with others, crying, ability to concentrate, and required amount of attention from staff. In addition, staff expectations for these children would be expected to vary widely, and thus influence their ratings of items such as "too active," "some reluctance to play with other children," and "rarely fearful, mild fears only." Differing expectations also will influence one's interpretation about whether a particular item endorsement is indicative of a problem.

The authors of the PBCL manual suggest the instrument is useful for making a variety of important decisions about children. These are:

1. Screening for children in need of further services, based on a nonempirically derived cutoff score of 12. This is the only use of the instrument supported by any data.

2. Intervention planning, based on a "pattern of scores" that "can readily be used . . . as a basis for discussion and to encourage development of ideas on intervention" (p. 4). It would be premature either to conclude that an intervention is warranted based on a PBCL score, or to plan an intervention based on a pattern of scores. For example, an intervention may be unwarranted, given circumstances such as unrealistic expectations on the part of a rater or the developmental appropriateness of the behavior of interest.

3. Program evaluation or "how sucessful programmes of intervention are proving" (p.4). Unfortunately, no evidence is presented to suggest the PBCL is sensitive to changes in children's behavior in preschool settings due to intervention or education.

4. Program planning, which suggests administration with respect to all children in a given setting to contribute to decisions regarding, for example, inservice training and resource development and allocation. Here again, data are needed to validate the usefulness of the PBCL in making these types of decisions.

In summary, the content of the PBCL appears to be reasonably thorough and complete for a brief rating scale intended to screen for problems in need of attention with target preschool children. Unfortunately, the manner in which some items assess a content area may contribute to a lack of clarity as to what is being measured. Finally, despite the authors' broader claims, only minimal empirical support for the PBCL as a screening tool is provided. For this purpose, practitioners also should consider alternative, well-developed instruments such as the Social Skills Rating System (Gresham & Elliott, 1990).

REVIEWER'S REFERENCE

Gresham, F. M., & Elliott, S. N. (1990). Social Skills Rating System. Circle Pines, MN: American Guidance Service.

[300]
Prescriptive Teaching Series.

Purpose: "To give the educator a concrete tool with which to work and to enable him to more effectively plan educational experiences."

Population: Grades 1–8.
Publication Date: 1971.
Acronym: PTS.
Scores: 6 skill areas: Math Skills, Reading and Language Skills, Auditory Skills, Motor Skills, Visual-Motor Skills, Visual Skills.
Administration: Individual.
Price Data, 1987: $15 per 20 Visual Skills booklets; $15 per 20 Visual-Motor Skills booklets; $20 per 25 Motor Skills booklets; $20 per 25 Auditory Skills booklets; $20 per 25 Reading and Language Skills booklets; $35 per 25 Math Skills booklets; $5 per manual (8 pages); $63 per specimen set including 1 copy of all booklets and manual.
Time: (10–20) minutes per test.
Comments: Skills checklist; can accumulate data for 4 rating periods; booklets available as separates.
Author: Sue Martin.
Publisher: Psychologists and Educators, Inc.

Review of the Prescriptive Teaching Series by RANDY W. KAMPHAUS, Associate Professor of Educational Psychology, The University of Georgia, Athens, GA:

According to the author the Prescriptive Teaching Series (PTS) is intended to aid the individualization of instruction by identifying appropriate instructional goals for pupils at the elementary school level. The scales of the PTS include Visual, Visual-Motor, Motor, Auditory, Reading and Language, and Math. These, however, are not scales that are directly administered to students. The rating scales are used by teachers to rate the skill level of individual students. Each skill is rated on a 4-point scale where "0 = *not introduced; no opportunity*, 1 = *introduced, but not achieved*, 2 = *partially achieved*, 3 = *satisfactorily achieved*." The number of items in each curricular domain is large. Even shorter scales such as the Auditory Skills scale includes 31 items. These 31 items also have items with "sub-items" that require rating.

One of the more interesting comments made in the manual is that the PTS scales are not tests. Consequently, the author eschews the need for evidence of concurrent or predictive validity studies or reliability investigations. There are no psychometric data whatsoever included in the manual. Less than half a page is devoted to the topics of reliability and validity.

The individual scales are presented on $8^1/2$ x 11 inch sheets and are color coded. The layout of the scales seems reasonable and readily understandable by classroom teachers. The typesetting of the scales is rather crude. In fact, it looks as if some of the graphics were done by hand with a pencil and ruler. From a practical standpoint some of the domains seem so lengthy that I suspect that teachers may be resistant to using them. The Math Skills scale, for example, includes 315 items for the teacher to rate, but this does not include ratings of "sub-items" that can be rather lengthy in and of themselves. For example, on Item 62 having to do with multiplication, the teacher has to rate the child's overall competence in multiplication as well as knowledge of the multiplication tables for every number combination from 1 through 9.

In terms of psychometric evidence, the author makes a case for the quality of the item pool selected. The author maintains that the item pool was selected after considerable review of the elementary school curriculum and related research. It would be helpful if the manual were to give more detail as to the specific sources used for item development and whether or not the opinions of other content experts besides the author were used in the process of item selection. The author concludes that the item pools possess "high face validity" and, as such, the demands of content validity are satisfied. Face validity, of course, is something of a controversial topic in psychometric circles. It should, however, never be considered as a substitute for establishing the content validity of a scale as was apparently done in the case of the PTS.

With regard to conducting statistical investigations of the psychometric properties of the various checklists the author concludes, "No subscale scores or total scores are obtained in the booklets. With such a format comparative statistics are difficult at the very least. Since the series is not a test, it does not lend itself to the traditional parametric statistical analyses common to tests per se." I do not agree with the author's agreement that the validity and reliability of the PTS checklist should not be investigated. This can be done without the computation of total scores. This lack of psychometric information results in the PTS being an unknown entity. It would be difficult to make the case to educators that the PTS checklists assess all or some degree of the core skills necessary for elementary school achievement. It also should not be argued that the PTS is "an instrument to indicate pupil progress and achievement," without having some evidence of the reliability with which pupil progress and achievement is assessed by these scales.

My conclusion regarding the PTS is that this is an informal group of checklists for the assessment of academic skills that has a paltry amount of evidence to support its use for the purposes given in the manual. Based on the data currently available on the PTS, it should be considered as an experimental measure that will require local norming, reliability, and validation studies if it is going to be used for making important curricular decisions.

Review of the Prescriptive Teaching Series by DEBORAH KING KUNDERT, Assistant Professor of Educational Psychology and Statistics, University at Albany, State University of New York, Albany, NY:

The Prescriptive Teaching Series (PTS) is a criterion-referenced checklist of learning concepts and skills to use in diagnosing students' strengths and weaknesses and plotting students' progress. Six booklets included in the series are intended to serve as a tangible list of teaching goals in the areas of Visual Skills, Visual-Motor Skills, Motor Skills, Auditory Skills, Reading and Language Skills, and Math Skills. An eight-page manual is included with the series, though the author states that it is "not the purpose of this *manual* to become a *test* manual by indicating exactly how each item should be observed or tested." The age range for which the PTS is appropriate is not indicated, but a review of the skills would seem to indicate that it might address skills taught in elementary school.

According to the manual, items were selected based on research of elementary curricula. Furthermore, it is stated that items were sequenced on the checklists based on "repeated research." In examining the checklists, this reviewer questioned the sequential and developmental order of some of the items. For example, in the reading and language booklet under the word knowledges skill, "understands the meaning of proverbs" is rated as the first item and "has an adequate sight vocabulary" is rated as the seventh item. Logically and developmentally, this does not appear to be correct. In addition to inappropriate item orderings, this reviewer also questioned the classification of some of the skills on the checklists (e.g., syllabication was listed as an alphabetizing skill). Finally, some of the items on the PTS were vague, and therefore it would seem that they would be difficult to rate (e.g., "does not demonstrate significant difficulties in oral reading").

Educators using the PTS rate a student based on their knowledge of student performance or based on planned observations. The rating scale used across all of the booklets is as follows: 0 = *not introduced/no opportunity*; 1 = *introduced, but not achieved*; 2 = *partially achieved*; 3 = *satisfactorily (functionally) achieved*. The manual does not include any directions or criteria on which to distinguish between the different levels (e.g., how would one differentiate between partial and satisfactory achievement?).

Evidence of the psychometric properties of the PTS is lacking and/or inappropriate. According to the manual, the reliability of the scale is inherent and "lies in its item validity." Raters are cautioned that consistency is important, though no estimates of interrater reliability are reported. The PTS is based on "established developmental skills and learned concepts." As such, it is stated that the checklist has high face validity which incorporates content validity. It is unclear to this reviewer what this statement means. The author goes on to state that "concurrent or predictive validity studies would provide little more information" because the PTS is not a test. This is a serious omission; what inferences can be drawn from the ratings, and how might the ratings be used in instructional planning?

The author of the PTS claims that the checklist is not a test. It seems to this reviewer that this scale is a criterion-referenced measure, or it might be classified as an informal measure. Criterion-referenced and informal measures may serve a purpose in the assessment process, but certain, specific information is necessary for examiners to use the instrument appropriately. Specific criteria have been outlined by Popham (1978) for developing and selecting criterion-referenced measures (e.g., adequate number of items, focus, validity).

In summary, the PTS was designed to identify areas of dysfunction among children and adolescents. The absence of specific item selection procedures, detailed administration and scoring guidelines, interpretation details, as well as the lack of important reliability and validity data, preclude the use of the PTS at this time. It is unclear how the use of this checklist would aid in determining student strengths and weaknesses and in planning educational remediation programs.

REVIEWER'S REFERENCE

Popham, W. J. (1978). *Criterion-referenced measurement*. Englewood Cliffs, NJ: Prentice-Hall, Inc.

[301]
The Preverbal Assessment-Intervention Profile.

Purpose: "To ascertain information relative to the child's ability to communicate awareness, attending, and orienting."
Population: Severely, profoundly, and multihandicapped individuals.
Publication Date: 1984.
Acronym: PAIP.
Administration: Individual.
Levels: 3.
Price Data, 1990: $44 per complete kit including 5 assessment record booklets and manual (49 pages); $17 per 5 assessment record booklets; $29 per manual.
Time: Administration time not reported.
Comments: Ratings by practitioners acquainted with the individual.
Author: Patricia Connard.
Publisher: PRO-ED, Inc.
 a) STAGE ONE.
Scores, 7: Preliminary Scores (Communication, Motor), Diagnostic Scores (Visual Awareness of Objects, Auditory Awareness of Sounds, Earliest Interaction Record, Reflex/Motor, Tactile Acceptance/Defensiveness).
 b) STAGE TWO.
Scores, 6: Preliminary Scores (Communication, Motor), Diagnostic Scores (Visual Attending, Auditory Attending, Social Bond Attending, Reflex/Motor).
 c) STAGE THREE.

Scores, 5: Preliminary Scores (Communication, Motor), Diagnostic Scores (Orienting to Objects, Orienting to Persons, Reflex/Motor).

Review of the Preverbal Assessment-Intervention Profile by KAREN T. CAREY, Assistant Professor of Psychology, California State University, Fresno, Fresno, CA:

Instruments that rely on structured observations have been neglected by test developers. However, the Preverbal Assessment-Intervention Profile (PAIP) was designed to make use of naturalistic and contrived observational situations in order to assess severely/profoundly and multihandicapped children's preverbal communication and motor skills.

Three stages of development are included: ages 0 to 1 month, 1 to 4 months, and 4 to 8 months. The professional completes a Preliminary Placement Evaluation for each stage and, depending upon the results, in-depth observational assessments are conducted. Protocols for these assessments are provided in the materials. In addition, the manual includes a listing of possible goals and objectives for each developmental stage. Finally, as many specialized terms are used throughout the manual, a glossary is furnished.

Although the observational format is intriguing and may provide the professional with information that would not otherwise be obtained, this test has numerous limitations. First, the directions and protocols are very complex and require several readings. An enormous amount of time would need to be devoted to training as well as to the learning of methods for completion of the forms. Furthermore, there are no time limits placed on length of the observations. Although it is recommended that the child be observed in a variety of situations, the settings in which the observations are to occur are left to the discretion of the observer.

Second, there are difficulties with the technical adequacy of the profile. The PAIP was developed from an initial pool of 785 sensorimotor behaviors and field tested with 20 teachers of severely handicapped persons. However, no further information is provided as to the means by which the items were selected.

There are also significant weaknesses with the reliability and validity studies presented in the manual. Interobserver reliability was based on a sample of 50 severely/profoundly or multihandicapped persons ranging in age from 8 to 37 years. The observers were 25 pairs of graduate students who had received 12 hours of "lecture, recitation, and simulation practices." Each pair of students observed two handicapped persons. The average interobserver reliability agreement as reported in the manual was 92%. However, this result must be viewed with skepticism; it is not known whether the calculation is an artifact of the training or whether the instrument is indeed reliable.

Test-retest reliability was completed with 15 handicapped persons. Two examiners completed the observations at intervals varying from 14 to 40 days (average of 26 days). Connard (the test author) states that "All received the same communication and reflex/motor stage placement during both testing situations." With the small sample size and the limited number of stages (i.e., three), individual profiles could be widely disparate but result in assignment to the same stage. In addition, no information is given relative to the ages of these individuals. However, in the manual Connard repeatedly states that the PAIP is designed for severely/profoundly and multihandicapped *children*.

Validity was assessed by comparing five domains of the Early Learning Accomplishment Profile (ELAP) with the "low stage placement score" of the PAIP. Unfortunately, this reference is made only in this section; it is not known to what PAIP score the author was referring. The sample consisted of 35 handicapped students; again, ages are not provided. The age range for the ELAP is 0 to 3 years. In addition, no validity or reliability information on the ELAP is available (Bailey & Wolery, 1984). Thus, the correlations provided for the PAIP (ranging from .84 to .94) are meaningless.

The goals and objectives section of the manual is also limited. Although such information might assist a teacher in writing Individualized Education Plans (IEPs), no guidelines for the teaching of functional skills are provided. Furthermore, professionals who have worked with severely handicapped children know that teaching such a child to sit with limited support or attempting to eliminate tactile defensive behavior require intensive intervention efforts. No suggestions or recommended readings are presented to assist with these difficult tasks.

In conclusion, the PAIP should not be used in practice. Minimal information is provided on how the profile was constructed and reliability and validity data are lacking. The PAIP may, however, be useful for teaching graduate students to carefully observe behaviors of handicapped individuals.

REVIEWER'S REFERENCE

Bailey, D. B., Jr., & Wolery, M. (1984). *Teaching infants and preschoolers with handicaps.* Columbus, OH; Merrill.

Review of the Preverbal Assessment-Intervention Profile by JOE OLMI, School Psychology Predoctoral Intern, Department of Educational Psychology, Mississippi State University, Mississippi State, MS:

The Preverbal Assessment-Intervention Profile (PAIP) is an observational system designed to aid in the assessment and program design of severely, profoundly, and multihandicapped preintentional learners. Having as its basis the Piagetian sensorimotor Stages I–III (Reflexes, Primary Circular Reac-

tions, and Secondary Circular Reactions), the PAIP was developed in an attempt to contribute to the growing need for criterion-referenced comprehensive assessment instruments standardized on handicapped populations. It is for use with prelinguistic individuals (i.e., primarily infants and developmentally delayed children).

Rather than select items for inclusion based on cognitive, motor, language, social, and self-help domains so commonly used in infant developmental inventories, the items of the PAIP are classified according to the four domains of the sensorimotor areas of development (auditory, visual, vocal/oral, and motor). The PAIP is intended to provide information related to information-processing abilities (interaction with things), communication abilities (interaction with people), and motor abilities. Limited theoretical rationale was provided for this approach.

Reliability and validity studies were conducted with a sample of 50 individuals selected from residential and day school facilities who had diagnoses of severe, profound, and/or multiple handicaps. Chronological ages ranged from 8 to 37 years of age and developmental functioning ranged from 0 to 9 months. The sample consisted of 2 severely retarded, 17 profoundly retarded, and 31 multihandicapped individuals. The Assessment Manual provided no information as to the nature of the multihandicapping conditions nor the demographic composition of the sample other than chronological and developmental ages.

Twenty-five pairs of graduate level preservice teachers of the hearing impaired, orthopedically handicapped, and moderately-severely-profoundly retarded were trained in the observational procedure in order to provide interobserver reliability information. Interobserver reliability agreement percentages ranged from 88% for Stage II to 96% for Stage I to a total agreement percentage of 92%. Test-retest reliability procedures resulted in identical stage placement for each testing situation. Again, no information was provided in the manual regarding the demographic composition of the observers or previous years of experience in the field.

Concurrent validity was established using the Early Learning Accomplishment Profile (ELAP). Spearman rank correlation coefficients for the Communication area of the PAIP and the areas of the ELAP ranged from .86 for language to .94 for social. Coefficients for the Reflex/Motor area of the PAIP and the motor areas of the ELAP ranged from .84 for fine motor to .94 for gross motor. A major flaw in the technical support data is the lack of information related to content validity.

The manual indicates that the "results of standardization studies strongly suggest that the PAIP can be used reliably and validly with severely, profoundly, and multihandicapped individuals." Given the limitations of the sample size and composition and the lack of information pertaining to content validity, this statement can be made tenuously at best.

The brief Assessment Manual provides the examiner with an introduction to the instrument, instructions for administration and scoring of each of the three stages, and goals and personalized objectives. It is accompanied by the Record Booklet which contains the Preliminary Placement Evaluation Profile, Diagnostic Profiles (Communication and Motor), plus Preliminary Placement Evaluations and Assessment Records for each stage. The Assessment Manual also contains Narrative Plans for each stage which can be developed depending on the assessment results of the observed child. No user qualifications were noted in the manual.

The instructions for administration and scoring of the PAIP were difficult to follow and confusing. The manual instructions seemed inadequate in terms of procedural specification. The labeling of the forms also proved inadequate. For example, the instructions referred to Information Processing Forms A and B and Communicative Abilities Form C, whereas the forms were simply labeled Form A, Form B, and so on. The reader was left to assume that Forms A and B were the Information Processing portion of the instrument. The same held true for the Communicative Abilities subtest.

Completing some of the various forms provided in the Record Booklet proved intricate at times. Understanding of the instructions and Record Booklet forms would have been enhanced had specific terms been defined and examples provided. The examples that were provided in the manual were helpful but inadequate.

Correct entry on certain forms requires the practitioner to have mastered a specified coding system in order to record accurately any observed data. Use of the instrument demands that the practitioner possess a very well-trained eye and valuable experience to be able to observe minute behaviors and judge the intentionality of such behaviors as related to preintentional or presymbolic communication.

On the positive side, the PAIP provides an excellent checklist assessment of reflex/motor functioning. This segment of the instrument is most user friendly. Another strength of the instrument is its attempt to assess interactional patterns between the child and caregiver given the importance of such interaction in child development. The instrument is a good attempt at bridging the gap between assessment and intervention. A strength of the instrument, which may be viewed as a weakness by some, is its lack of cutoffs to indicate deficit functioning. It is designed to assess where the child is currently functioning and proceed from that point, rather than emphasize labels or performance designations.

In summary, the PAIP is a Piagetian-based stage-to-stage observational system designed to provide criterion-based diagnostic information that can be used to develop appropriate intervention strategies specific to the needs of the child observed. To be used effectively and efficiently, it would require a measure of training on the part of the practitioner and even more training on the part of others who may be asked to use the procedure, for example, paraprofessionals and parents. Without training in observational skills and sufficient experience with the instrument, the beginning practitioner as well as other service providers may find its format and content confusing, thus shying away from its use. In short, given the weaknesses described, the PAIP falls short in its attempt to provide a comprehensive assessment procedure that would result in effective and efficient design of appropriate intervention strategies for severely and profoundly handicapped children.

[302]
Pre-Verbal Communication Schedule.

Purpose: "The Schedule is aimed mainly at assessing existing non-verbal and vocal communication skills and other abilities which may be relevant in programme development."
Population: Children and adolescents and adults.
Publication Date: 1987.
Acronym: PVCS.
Administration: Individual.
Forms, 2: Full Form, Short Form.
Price Data, 1988: £26.45 per complete set including 10 scoring sheets and manual (20 pages); £14.95 per 10 checklists.
Time: (120–150) minutes.
Comments: Behavior checklist.
Authors: Chris Kiernan and Barbara Reid.
Publisher: NFER-Nelson Publishing Co., Ltd. [England].
a) SCORE SHEET 1.
Scores: 27 sections: Needs and Preferences, Vision and Looking, Use of Visual Cues, Control of Hands and Arms, Social Interaction Without Communication, Hearing and Listening, Development of Sounds, Control of Speech Musculature, Consistent Use of Noise, Expression of Emotion (Non-Communicative), Music and Singing, Motor Imitation, Vocal Imitation, Giving, Communication Through Pictures or Objects, Communication Through Whole Body Action, Communication Through Gestures, Communication Through Manipulation, Communication Through Pointing, Communication Through Looking, Communicative Use of Sounds, Expression of Emotion (Communicative), Manipulation of Emotion, Understanding of Non-Vocal Communication, Understanding of Vocalization and Speech, Understanding of Emotion, Use of Communication Through Symbols/Signs or Speech.

b) SCORE SHEET 2 (SHORT FORM PVCS).
Scores: 6 category scores: Attention Seeking, Need Satisfaction, Simple Negation, Positive Interaction, Negative Interaction, Shared Attention.

Review of the Pre-Verbal Communication Schedule by E. W. TESTUT, Associate Professor of Audiology, Department of Speech Pathology/Audiology, Ithaca College, Ithaca, NY:

The Pre-Verbal Communication Schedule (PVCS) provides a means for assessing nonverbal individuals of all ages who possess severe mental handicaps and who are being considered for placement in initial speech or nonspeech communication programs. The PVCS emphasizes communication rather than language and assesses communication by providing checklists of behaviors thought to reflect an individual's readiness for various communication development strategies. Scoring is accomplished by pooling information gathered from one or more caregivers (e.g., teachers, parents, and others with whom the individual has contact). Two types of scores can be obtained from this instrument: (*a*) a full PVCS score, which is based on information gathered about communicative behaviors and related, but noncommunicative, behaviors; and (*b*) a short PVCS score, which is based on information gathered about only communicative behaviors. The authors also provide suggestions for appropriate communication treatment strategies based on schedule results.

The PVCS has many strengths. It offers a concise, practical way to relate easily observable milestone behaviors to the potential for developing communication skills. The suggested educational strategies based on PVCS performance offers health professionals a starting point in determining the most appropriate intervention strategies. The PVCS does not use labels, categorizations, and normative data for comparisons. Instead, it focuses on the implied relationship between certain behaviors and potentially appropriate rehabilitation strategies. Furthermore, the PVCS is constructed in such a manner that input from nonprofessionals (e.g., parents) is possible and, indeed, encouraged. In this way it provides a more complete picture of the individual's communication profile than might be possible if only professional input were obtained.

The PVCS uses an informal, practical format which, while offering many advantages, also yields limitations. Because the PVCS is intended for use with individuals of all ages, some information about developmental norms for communication behaviors, where appropriate, would be helpful to those administering and interpreting the PVCS. Also, this reviewer's impression is that many of the behavioral categories and some of the individual behaviors within the categories seem arbitrary. These might be more effectively combined into more inclusive,

larger categories, or omitted altogether. For example, categories exist that are evaluated on the basis of a very limited number of behaviors, some behaviors described within the manual as having low interrater reliability are still included in the schedule, and a flow chart presumably intended to express the relationship among developmental communication behaviors (Score Sheet 1) instead reflects a chaotic, arbitrary relationship among many of the categories. Finally, the PVCS contains idioms not common to American-English usage. Examples include, "to hoover" (i.e., to vacuum), "sellotape" (i.e., cellophane tape), and "fussed" (i.e., teased). Fortunately, the idioms are few in number, are provided to clarify targeted behaviors for raters, and should present little difficulty to American-English users.

The technical information provided about development of the PVCS is difficult to evaluate. The manual discusses the validity and reliability of the PVCS, but little is provided with respect to how the test was put together and how individual items were found to merit inclusion. Interrater reliability of items was explored in one study of 48 students. Percentage of agreement among raters for each item are provided in the manual. The number of raters for this study was not provided. All items rated were kept in the PVCS Full Form regardless of the interrater agreement. The authors state that the Short Form (Score Sheet 2) contains only items of high reliability and validity, although six of these have percentages of agreement among raters from 64.10 to 69.77. No other indication of the statistics used or the levels of significance observed is provided within the test booklet, its manual, or was made available to this reviewer.

In summary, the PVCS attempts to determine the readiness of nonverbal individuals possessing severe mental handicaps for initial speech or nonspeech communication programs. Checklists of communication and related behaviors thought to reflect the readiness of individuals for various communication development strategies are provided and a clinician or team of individuals familiar with the client simply identifies whether the client evidences the behaviors. Scoring of the results is straightforward, and suggestions for interpreting the final results of either the Full or Short Forms are provided. Although the appropriateness of the suggestions for communication treatment strategies may not reflect agreement among professionals, in general, the items making up the PVCS do. In fact, if nothing else, the PVCS provides a single means for assessing the presence of behaviors thought to signal readiness for the development of communication skills.

Review of the Pre-Verbal Communication Schedule by SUSAN ELLIS WEISMER, Assistant Professor of Communicative Disorders, University of Wisconsin, Madison, WI:

The Pre-Verbal Communication Schedule (PVCS) is intended to be used with individuals (from children to adults) who have severe mental handicaps. It is designed to assess precommunicative and communicative behaviors in persons who are being considered for entry into a speech or nonverbal communication program.

The PVCS has two forms, the Full Form, Score Sheet 1, and the Short Form, Score Sheet 2. The Full PVCS consists of 195 items divided into 27 sections that tap precommunicative behaviors, informal communicative behaviors, and formal communicative skills. Each section contains from 2 to 14 items. The majority are checklist items on which the examiner must judge whether the individual demonstrates the particular abilities or behaviors. These items are scored as *Usually/Rarely/Never*. Other items are directly testable through observation of the individual and are scored as *Yes/No* or given a numerical value corresponding to the number of times the person responds correctly. Score Sheet 1 contains a lattice of boxes representing each of the 27 sections of the PVCS. By using contrasting colors of ink to mark sections on which the student performs differentially, it is possible to obtain a visual display of areas of strengths and limitations.

The Short Form consists of four sections from the Full Form (Motor Imitation, Vocal Imitation, Understanding of Non-Vocal Communication, and Understanding of Vocalization and Speech) plus 35 items drawn from different sections of the PVCS that reflect six categories of functional communication use (Attention Seeking, Need Satisfaction, Simple Negation, Positive Interaction, Negative Interaction, and Shared Attention). The authors suggest that items rated as *Usually, Yes, 3/3*, or *2/3* be summed to obtain a score for the four sections and the six categories of use. Score Sheet 2 provides a numerical summary of the individual's scoring profile for the Short Form of the PVCS. The PVCS manual also includes a Programme Planning Sheet, which provides a means of summarizing information, such as the overall goal of programming, the target behavior to be taught, and the conditions surrounding remediation.

The authors present no theoretical framework or discussion of the conceptual basis for this measure. The manual does not include a section that reviews pertinent research or theoretical issues germane to this assessment tool (cf. Siegel-Causey & Guess, 1989), though a brief list of references is provided. The decision not to include sections on the PVCS that assess cognitive abilities was apparently guided by practical considerations rather than conceptual concerns relating to the notion of prerequisite skills. The authors state that other tests (such as the Behavior Assessment Battery by Kiernan & Jones, 1982) are available to evaluate cognitive functioning that may be viewed as important for the development of communicative skills.

This measure appears to have undergone limited test development procedures that are inadequately described in the manual. With regard to development of the PVCS, field testing began in 1979 at the Thomas Coram Research Unit in England. According to the authors, a content validity study was conducted in 1985 on 80 items from the PVCS that had been shown to have high interrater reliabilities. However, specific findings from this study are not reported and no reference is cited.

A drawback of the PVCS that impacts upon content validity is that no specific directions are provided regarding administration of items on the scales that are designed to elicit particular behaviors. The categories of communicative function represented on Score Sheet 2 are presumably based on the results of the factor analyses completed in the two investigations that are mentioned on page 3 of the manual. The sketchy summary of the results of these studies does not allow the test user to interpret the findings without referring to the original sources. There is no description of how the 27 sections or the individual items on the PVCS were selected. Further, no information regarding concurrent validity is provided to indicate how this scale compares to other measures such as The Preverbal Assessment-Intervention Profile (Connard, 1984). The authors state that several studies have demonstrated that behavior assessed by the PVCS cannot be predicted from other measures of language development and general cognitive development; they therefore contend that this finding supports the need for the PVCS. In fact, this finding may suggest a lack of criterion-related validity for this measure, at least for those specific areas.

Limited information is provided regarding the reliability of the PVCS. One study involving 48 students is reported in which the percentage of interrater agreement was determined for each item on the scale. According to the data listed in the Appendix, the percentage of agreement between raters fell below 70% for 32 items (i.e., 16% of the items on the Full Form of the PVCS). These items have been retained in the current version of the PVCS. It is unclear how interrater agreement on the PVCS was determined given that the authors recommend using pooled responses based on input from various individuals who are familiar with the person being tested. No indication is given as to the amount of training required to reliably administer the PVCS. There are no reported studies examining test-retest reliability or internal consistency of the PVCS. For the reliability and validity studies that are reported, no information is provided concerning subject characteristics such as age, sex, race, ethnicity, socioeconomic status, developmental level, or linguistic background.

In summary, the PVCS is not recommended for research or clinical purposes in its current form. It lacks a clearly articulated conceptual framework and there is insufficient evidence that it meets basic psychometric standards of reliability and validity. Practitioners who are currently relying on informal procedures to undertake the difficult task of evaluating potential communicative abilities of nonverbal individuals may find aspects of the PVCS useful as a means of organizing observations. There is definitely a need for this type of assessment measure and further development is encouraged.

REVIEWER'S REFERENCES

Kiernan, C., & Jones, M. C. (1982). Behaviour Assessment Battery, Second Edition. Windsor, England: NFER-Nelson Publishing Co., Ltd.
Connard, P. (1984). The Preverbal Assessment-Intervention Profile. Austin, TX: PRO-ED, Inc.
Siegel-Causey, E., & Guess, D. (1989). Enhancing nonsymbolic communication interactions among learners with severe disabilities. Baltimore: Paul H. Brookes.

[303]
The Problem Solving Inventory.

Purpose: "To assess an individual's perceptions of his or her own problem-solving behaviors and attitudes."
Population: Age 16 and above.
Publication Date: 1988.
Acronym: PSI.
Scores, 4: Problem-Solving Confidence, Approach-Avoidance Style, Personal Control, Total.
Administration: Group and individual.
Price Data, 1989: $14.50 per 25 test booklets; $3 per scoring key; $12 per manual (27 pages); $13 per specimen set (includes manual, test booklet, scoring key).
Time: (10–15) minutes.
Comments: Self-ratings scale.
Author: P. Paul Heppner.
Publisher: Consulting Psychologists Press, Inc.

TEST REFERENCES

1. Rich, A. R., & Bonner, R. L. (1987). Interpersonal moderators of depression among college students. Journal of College Student Personnel, 28, 337-342.
2. Nezu, A. M., & Ronan, G. F. (1988). Social problem solving as a moderator of stress-related depressive symptoms: A prospective analysis. Journal of Counseling Psychology, 35, 134-138.
3. Baker, S. B., & Roberts, D. M. (1989). The factor structure of the Problem-Solving Inventory: Measuring perceptions of personal problem solving. Measurement and Evaluation in Counseling and Development, 21, 157-164.
4. Larson, L. M. (1989). Problem-solving appraisal in an alcoholic population. Journal of Counseling Psychology, 36, 73-78.
5. Nezer, A. M., & Perri, M. G. (1989). Social problem-solving therapy for unipolar depression: An initial dismantling investigation. Journal of Consulting and Clinical Psychology, 57, 408-413.
6. Bourgeois, L., Sabourin, S., & Wright, J. (1990). Predictive validity of therapeutic alliance in group marital therapy. Journal of Consulting and Clinical Psychology, 58, 608-613.
7. Elliott, T. R., Godshall, F., Shrout, J. R., & Witty, T. E. (1990). Problem-solving appraisal, self-reported study habits, and performance of academically at-risk college students. Journal of Counseling Psychology, 37, 203-207.
8. Larson, L. M., Piersel, W. C., Iamo, R. A. K., & Allen, S. J. (1990). Significant predictors of problem-solving appraisal. Journal of Counseling Psychology, 37, 482-490.
9. Dixon, W. A., Heppner, P. P., & Anderson, W. P. (1991). Problem-solving appraisal, stress, hopelessness, and suicide ideation in a college population. Journal of Counseling Psychology, 38, 51-56.
10. Heppner, P. P., Cook, S. W., Strozier, A. L., & Heppner, M. J. (1991). An investigation of coping styles and gender differences with farmers in career transition. Journal of Counseling Psychology, 38, 167-174.
11. Wright, D. M., & Heppner, P. P. (1991). Coping among nonclinical college-age children of alcoholics. Journal of Counseling Psychology, 38, 465-472.

Review of The Problem Solving Inventory by CAMERON J. CAMP, *Professor of Psychology, University of New Orleans, New Orleans, LA:*

The Problem Solving Inventory (PSI) is an instrument used to "assess an individual's perceptions of his or her own problem-solving behaviors and attitudes." Problem solving is "considered synonymous with coping" by the author of the PSI manual. The PSI is designed to measure an individual's perception of problem-solving capabilities, and not actual problem-solving skills.

The PSI consists of 35 statements. Three of the statements are "research items" and are not scored, leaving 32 items from which measures are derived. For each statement, respondents use a 6-point scale to rate the extent to which they agree or disagree with the statement (1 = *strongly agree*; 6 = *strongly disagree*). Low scores represent positive appraisals of problem-solving ability. Fifteen items are negatively worded and require reverse scoring.

A total score is achieved by adding the scores of all responses. This score is a measure of the respondent's perception of general problem-solving abilities. In addition, three scales are derived from these items: Problem-Solving Confidence (defined as self-assurance while engaged in problem-solving activities), Approach-Avoidance Style (a general tendency to approach or avoid problem-solving activities), and Personal Control (being in control of one's emotions and behaviors while solving problems). There are 11, 16, and 5 items on these three scales, respectively. Because there are so few items per scale, omissions should be avoided. The manual states that if two or more items are omitted from one scale, or if three or more total items are omitted, the respondent should be retested if possible.

The PSI has been used primarily as a research instrument to determine relationships between cognitive, affective, and behavioral measures related to coping as they in turn relate to perceived problem-solving skill. Additional suggested uses included evaluation of training outcomes for problem-solving workshops or seminars and contrasting problem-solving appraisals with more objective measures of actual abilities. In this latter case, observed discrepancies between measures of perceived and actual abilities might have some clinical utility.

The manual is clearly written and easy to use. The manual states that the PSI should be administered by "professionals who have expertise in tests and measurement and are familiar with the literature on coping and problem solving." However, the test is self-administered, and can be given in a group format. The directions to the respondents on the actual instrument are relatively clear. The print on the test instrument is small, and could present problems for individuals with impaired vision. The reading level of the instrument might also pose a problem for individuals with cognitive impairments and/or low levels of education. The test items cover the front and back of a single 8 x 11 inch page, and respondents circle a number (1–6) next to each statement. A scoring key for hand scoring of the PSI is provided.

The three factors of the scale were derived through factor analytic techniques. Subsequent research cited in the manual showed that the Personal Control factor did not replicate well in a confirmatory factor analysis. Interscale correlations range from $r = .38$ to .49, indicating that the scales are to some extent measuring similar constructs.

Test-retest reliability measures for the three scales and the Total PSI score range from .83 to .89 across 2 weeks, from .77 to .81 for a new sample tested over 3 weeks, and from .44 to .65 for a third sample tested after a 2-year period. Alpha coefficients for the three scales and the total score range from .72 to .91 across three independent samples. Most data on test-retest reliabilities and other psychometric properties of the instrument were collected from university students. Concurrent validity was assessed by correlating students' PSI scores with ratings of their problem-solving skills and with ratings of perceived level of satisfaction with such skills. These correlations ranged from -.24 to -.46. PSI scores do not correlate strongly with measures of aptitude or academic achievement, social desirability, or an objective measure of problem-solving ability (the first three stories of the Means-End Problem-Solving Procedure). PSI scores are not strongly related to measures of creativity or personality type. Correlations with the Rotter Internal-External Locus of Control Scale for all PSI scores were significant, with individuals who appraise their problem-solving skills positively tending to report having an internal locus of control. The manual describes research in which PSI scores were related to measures of psychological health, marital adjustment, parenting behavior, career indecision, and attributions.

It must be noted that 18 of the original items of the PSI "were reworded to make them easier to understand," and that these reworded items are those which are included in the current form of the test. A cursory examination of the original items and the current items indicated that the content of the new items matched that of the originals, and that the new wording did make items more readable and clear. However, it appears that most or all of the psychometric data gathered thus far on the PSI involve the originally worded items. This must be kept in mind when using the current version of the test.

The strengths of the PSI are its ease of administration, its connection with a research base, and its manual. A clear description of the construction of the test and its scales, relevant research, tables, etc., are easy to access within the manual. The weaknesses of the PSI include the need for a sounder psychometric base (e.g., with regard to utilizing larger and more disparate samples with the newest version of the test), the lack of machine-scoring capabilities for the test forms, the small print size of the test forms, and a reading level of items that may be too high for some adults.

SUMMARY. The PSI is designed to measure perceived problem-solving abilities. It is a self-administered, paper-and-pencil test which can be completed within 15 minutes. Its primary use is in research dealing with affective, cognitive, and behavioral correlates of coping with real world problems. Some preliminary research has shown a relationship between the PSI and more "clinical" phenomena such as psychological health and marital adjustment. Although the test has demonstrated generally adequate psychometric properties with previous versions, its psychometric soundness should be demonstrated using larger and more diverse (nonstudent) samples with the latest version of the instrument.

Review of The Problem Solving Inventory by STEVEN G. LoBELLO, *Assistant Professor of Psychology, Auburn University at Montgomery, Montgomery, AL:*

The Problem Solving Inventory (PSI) is a 35-item instrument for assessing self-perceived problem-solving skills. The test comprises three scales which measure an individual's confidence in problem-solving abilities, tendency to approach or avoid problem situations, and degree of personal control of emotions and behavior. A total score is also obtained by summing the scores on the three scales. Each item statement is rated by the client on a Likert scale that ranges from 1 (*Strongly Agree*) to 6 (*Strongly Disagree*). There are approximately equal numbers of positively and negatively worded items in the inventory to prevent overrater or underrater response bias. Low scores are associated with a positive self-appraisal of problem-solving skills.

The test manual is concise, yet contains a substantial amount of validity and reliability data. The individual scales were derived through factor analysis, and factor structure of the Problem Solving Inventory has generally been confirmed in a variety of samples. The individual scales and total score have adequate internal consistency coefficients ranging from .72 to .91. The test-retest reliability is in the .80s with a 2-week interval and drops to the .60s with a 2-year interval. The only exception is the Personal Control Scale which has a test-retest reliability coefficient of .44 after 2 years. Thus, caution should be exercised in interpreting this scale.

Concurrent validity is demonstrated by significant correlations between PSI scale scores and self-rated evaluation of problem-solving skills and satisfaction with those skills. Discriminant validity is supported by negligible correlations between PSI scores and various measures of academic achievement and aptitude. The relationships between the PSI and selected other personality measures are generally weak, with the exception of the Rotter Internal-External Locus of Control Scale. This supports the expected relationship between positive appraisal of problem-solving skills and internal locus of control. Other construct validation studies have highlighted the differences between high and low scorers on the PSI. Individuals with high PSI scores tend to have more pathological Minnesota Multiphasic Personality Inventory (MMPI) profiles, and evidence greater maladjustment on the SCL-90 and the Cornell Medical Index. Moreover, high scores are associated with marital distress and lower confidence in occupational potential.

There are several weaknesses of the Problem Solving Inventory which bear mentioning. Interpretation of scale scores is made difficult by a lack of specificity regarding what constitutes a "high" or a "low" score. Also, it is reported that the three scales of the inventory are moderately intercorrelated with coefficients ranging from .38 to .49. Therefore, interpretation of the three scales as measuring independent aspects of problem-solving behavior is questionable. The weak evidence for the long-term stability of the Personal Control Scale is also a related concern which is not helped by the brevity of this scale (five items). The more serious problem, however, is the inadequacy of the normative data. The manual reports normative data for a large sample of introductory psychology students, although data from smaller samples of other groups (e.g., elderly adults, inpatient alcoholics) are also provided. However, some of these normative data are taken from published research reports and the manual does not adequately describe how these subjects were selected or provide complete information about subject characteristics. The author wisely cautions against reliance on these data, but this does not compensate for the lack of a representative normative sample drawn from the general population.

In summary, the Problem Solving Inventory appears to have great promise as an assessment tool in research, counseling, and other applied settings. However, lack of normative data for the general population limits its current use to those individuals for whom adequate normative data are available.

Production and Maintenance Technician Test.

Purpose: "To evaluate the knowledge and skill of industrial production and maintenance workers in specific subject areas."

Population: Applicants or incumbents for jobs where production and maintenance knowledge is a necessary part of training or job activities.

Publication Date: 1985.

Scores: 9 areas: Pneumatics/Hydraulics, Piping/Pumps, Lubrication/Bearings/Power Transmission, Print Reading, Mechanical Maintenance/Tools/Shop Mechanics, Rigging, Welding, Chemical Processes/Instrumentation & Control, yielding 1 Total Score.

Administration: Group.

Price Data, 1988: $10 per reusable test booklet; $40 per 500 answer sheets; manual (18 pages) and hand-scoring keys also available from publisher.

Time: 120(130) minutes.

Author: Roland T. Ramsay.

Publisher: Ramsay Corporation.

Review of the Production and Maintenance Technician Test by BRUCE K. ALCORN, Director of Certification, Teachers College, Ball State University, Muncie, IN:

The Production and Maintenance Technician Test (P&MTT) is one in a series of three tests of knowledge and skill in industrial production and maintenance. The other two are the Process Technician Test (10:296) and the Electronic and Instrumentation Technician Test (10:106). All three are intended to be used in making employment and/or job placement decisions.

The tests were apparently developed together for a specific industrial situation, a proposed electrogalvanizing facility. The technical data provided in the manual and in a separate one-page "Executive Summary, Electrogalvanizing Technicians Test Validation Report" generally do support its use in that one specific situation, assuming the author was involved in the training of those who administer the test and use the results in decision making.

In its present form, the use of the P&MTT is questionable without the assistance of a testing professional who can complete the work necessitated by the missing elements: adequate treatment of validity and score interpretation.

VALIDITY. For a test of this type which measures knowledge and skill, content validity is of utmost importance and it was evidently demonstrated to the satisfaction of the corporation wishing to use it. However, even in that single instance, it should be pointed out that the content validity decision was based upon the judgement of only three "experts," a general manager, a production manager, and a mechanical engineer. All other potential users must go through the process of determining the content validity for their situations, that is, determining if the knowledge and skills measured by this instrument match the knowledge and skills required in their industrial production and maintenance situations. Before this test can be used elsewhere, the manual should be improved to provide one or both of the following: specific instructions and further aids on how to conduct a local validity study and/or data demonstrating its validity in more than one very specific industrial setting.

To assist with the former (local content validity study), Tables 1 and 3 need improving and/or combining. The items are grouped in the test booklet into 15 labeled groups. Table 1 classifies the groups by knowledge and skill and gives the item numbers involved in each. Table 3 also presents 15 groups or categories (knowledge areas) with subareas, but they are not quite the same, adding to the confusion. For example, in Table 1 and in the test booklet, "Bearings" is a separate category, but in Table 3 it is a subcategory under "Power Transmissions." In addition, Table 3 has a category of "Safety" which is not mentioned in Table 1 nor in the test booklet. A note in Table 3 does state that there is a "safety item in each area," but they are not readily apparent when examining the items themselves. These two tables could be combined and expanded to provide the percentage of items (weight) devoted to each category or knowledge area. Also, the subcategories should be revised or eliminated because as they now exist they suggest a more diverse list of knowledge areas than are actually measured. For example, the "Rigging" category lists five subcategories, two of which are "wire rope and chains" and "fiber rope and knots." The seven items devoted to "Rigging" (Items 149–155) make no mention or use of ropes of any kind. There also ought to be instructions, for the nonprofessional, on how to determine whether or not the P&MTT has enough content validity for their use.

To accomplish the second suggestion for improving the manual (demonstrating content validity in other settings) the author will need to conduct and adequately report validity studies in numerous industrial facilities involving many more than three "experts."

SCORE INTERPRETATION. The manual (p. 5) instructs the test administrator to "Count the number of incorrect and blank items and subtract that number from 200." This produces a total raw score, indicating the number of items the examinee answered correctly out of a total of 200. The only hint of instructions about what to do with the total raw score to bring meaning to it is contained in a section at the very end of the manual titled "Normative Data." That section starts out by saying, "Normative data on tests facilitate the comparisons of persons scoring at a given level with a reference group; e.g., employed workers, skilled craft workers,

etc." That statement is followed by Table 5 which presents the percentile equivalents of raw scores derived by administering the test to 66 *former* processing workers. No further description of the sample is provided, nor is the use of *former* workers explained. Why not provide norms based upon *current* production and maintenance technicians and using a much larger sample? Further, no instructions are provided for using the table. The separately provided one-page "Executive Summary, Electrogalvanizing Technicians Test Validity Report" does provide both a "Cutoff" and a "Marginal" score which were derived using Angoff's method "requiring subject experts to estimate the proportion of borderline candidates who could pass each item of each test." There is nothing wrong with the method used here, just with the small number of experts, reported in the manual to be three! There is also no information on how to use the raw scores in relation to the "Marginal" score. Once again, the data presented in the "Executive Summary" may have been acceptable to the specific industrial situation, but no evidence is presented as to its applicability in other situations, nor are there instructions for other users who wish to develop their own cut scores.

MISCELLANEOUS COMMENTS. The instructions for the administration of the P&MTT seem to have been written for the examinees used during the test development rather than for operational examinees as seen when the purpose of the test is explained. The test administrator is also encouraged to look, after the test has started, for "behavior which might indicate that the test results may not represent accurate measurement of ability." One example given of such behavior is someone who reads English slowly due to being educated elsewhere. Why wait to do this after the test has started?

The test items themselves can use some editing. For example, Items 197 and 198 could be more consistent. They both measure ability to read pressure gages, but in one case the numerical answers are followed by "psi" and in the other they are not (the three items dealing with reading temperature gages are consistent).

Although the Production and Maintenance Technician Test may be acceptable for the specific industrial plant for which it was developed, it is not ready in its present state of development for use at other industrial sites.

[305]

Productive Practices Survey.

Purpose: "To assess, describe, and pinpoint specific practices of the manager which support—or fail to support—organizational productivity."
Population: Managers.
Publication Date: 1987.
Acronym: PPS.

Scores, 12: Dimension I (Management Values, Support Structure, Managerial Credibility, Total), Dimension II (Impact, Relevance, Community, Total), Dimension III (Task Environment, Social Context, Problem Solving, Total).
Administration: Group.
Price Data, 1990: $6.95 per Test Manual (25 pages); $15 per Leader's Guide (18 pages).
Time: (30–35) minutes.
Comments: Based on model of organizational functioning called Competence Theory; self-ratings; self-scored.
Author: Jay Hall.
Publisher: Teleometrics International.

[306]
Productivity Environmental Preference Survey.

Purpose: "An inventory for the identification of adult preferences of conditions in a working and/or learning environment."
Population: Adults.
Publication Dates: 1979–82.
Acronym: PEPS.
Scores, 20: Sound, Light, Warmth, Formal Design, Motivated/Unmotivated, Persistent, Responsible, Structure, Learning Alone/Peer-Oriented Learner, Authority-Oriented Learner, Several Ways, Auditory Preferences, Visual Preferences, Tactile Preferences, Kinesthetic Preferences, Requires Intake, Evening/Morning, Late Morning, Afternoon, Needs Mobility.
Administration: Group.
Price Data, 1988: $6 per 60 answer sheets with questions; $4 or less per individual profile (produced when sent in for computer scoring); $.40 per individual interpretative booklet; $9 per manual ('82, 61 pages); $11 per specimen set including answer sheet, interpretative booklet, and manual.
Time: (20–30) minutes.
Comments: Computer scored.
Authors: Gary E. Price, Rita Dunn, and Kenneth Dunn.
Publisher: Price Systems, Inc.

TEST REFERENCES

1. Dunn, R., Sklar, R. I., & Beaudry, J. S. (1990). Effects of matching and mismatching minority developmental college students' hemispheric preferences on mathematics scores. *Journal of Educational Research, 83,* 283-288.

Review of the Productivity Environmental Preference Survey by CRAIG N. MILLS, Executive Director, GRE Testing and Services, Educational Testing Service, Princeton, NJ:

The Productivity Environmental Preference Survey (PEPS) is a 100-item survey designed to diagnose adults' productivity and learning styles. According to the manual, the results can be used to structure the workplace to maximize output and the instrument can also be used for recruiting, screening, selecting, and promoting individuals. Unfortunately, evidence to support these claims is not provided.

CONTENT AND INSTRUMENT DEVELOPMENT. The PEPS instrument was developed by "identifying the research variables that appeared to describe the ways individuals prefer to learn or work." The manual does not contain a reference list of the research, nor does it specifically identify the variables identified in the research. Thus, it is not possible for the prospective user to evaluate the appropriateness of the content of the items. The instrument was refined through two pilot administrations. The first administration sample is not described. The second sample is described as "nonrandom" and consisted of 589 adults.

In a factor analysis, 31 factors with eigenvalues greater than 1.00 were identified. This resulted in 21 scores. Exactly how 21 scores resulted from 31 factors is unclear.

No information is reported to indicate that data related to observed productivity or work/learning environment were collected during instrument development. There is also no explanation provided of how the lists of suggested environmental modifications were developed.

The technical information provided is difficult to interpret. For example, the following are reported for one measure: Standard Deviation = 1.85; Reliability = .83; Standard Error of Measurement = .68. Calculating the standard error of measurement by multiplying the standard deviation by the square root of 1.0 minus reliability does not yield the same result.

Average scores are also difficult to interpret. For example, in one area there are three items and the mean is reported as 2.95. It appears that means were developed for items in a true/false format. If so, it seems unlikely that this scale is meaningful. An alternative explanation is that this mean is based on administration of the items in a Likert format (the current format of the measure). However, other areas in the same table have means of less than 1.0, an unlikely occurrence.

SCORES AND INTERPRETATION. Scores are reported as standard scores with a mean of 50 and a standard deviation of 10. For each of the 21 scores, desirable features of the work or learning environment are suggested for individuals with scores of 60 and above or 40 and below. Given the low reliabilities of the scales and the size of the standard error of measurement, there appears to be a limited psychometric basis for making the distinctions between individuals with scaled scores that are 10 points from the mean. No justification is provided for the use of these scores as cutoff points, nor is there evidence that the suggested actions are supported empirically.

RELIABILITY. "Hoyt" reliabilities are reported, but information related specifically to the manner in which they were calculated is not provided. The reliabilities are low. None exceed .90 and five are under .50. This is not surprising, given the limited number of questions that can be related to a given score. Nonetheless, the reliabilities suggest that the results are not likely to be particularly useful for decision-making purposes.

It appears the reliabilities were obtained through administration of the survey in a True-False format. The manual states the format of the survey has been changed to a Likert scale, partly to address the reliability issue. Data from the survey in its revised form are not provided.

VALIDITY. The lack of validity evidence is particularly troubling, given the drawbacks pointed out previously with regard to instrument development, score interpretation, and reliability. Several research studies are reported in the manual, but they suffer, in general, from small sample sizes. More importantly, they do not address the construct or predictive validity of the instrument; they only provide descriptive information.

To determine the construct validity of the instrument, data would need to be gathered not only on people's environmental preferences, but also on their current environment and their current productivity. Without data on current environment, the user has data only on preferences and no data on how important the preferences might be. With respect to predictive validity, information would need to be available demonstrating that changing a work or learning environment to more or less closely match the respondent's stated preferences increases or decreases productivity in the expected direction. No such data are provided.

The manual indicates the survey can be useful in structuring environments to increase productivity in learning or working situations. However, none of the studies summarized in the manual are related to a work environment. To the extent the samples are described, the research appears to have been conducted exclusively with undergraduate and graduate students.

SUMMARY. The Productivity Environmental Preference Survey collects information about individuals' preferences related to 21 environmental factors. It provides recommendations for structuring an environment to maximize productivity. Technical information is sparse, but indicates that the instrument is not likely to be sufficiently reliable for decision making. The research summarized in support of the measure does not adequately address the construct validity of the measure, its predictive power, or the recommendations for environmental changes made on the basis of the scores.

Review of the Productivity Environmental Preference Survey by BERTRAM C. SIPPOLA, Associate Professor of Psychology, University of New Orleans, New Orleans, LA:

The Productivity Environmental Preference Survey (PEPS) is the adult version of the Learning Style Inventory (LSI; 203), which exists in versions for students in grades 3 and 4 and in grades 5–12. Both tests are authored by Rita and Kenneth Dunn and Gary E. Price. The PEPS consists of 100 items (5-point Likert scale) that yield scores on 20 factors. It is designed for easy administration, with all of the items and instructions appearing on an Opscan answer sheet. Scoring may be done by the publisher or the test may be taken and scored on a microcomputer.

The LSI is one of many somewhat similar instruments (some with almost identical names) (e.g., Canfield, 1976–80, 9:609; Renzulli & Smith, 1978, 9:608). These test instruments assume that students differ in terms of their preferred "style" in the learning process and that matching the educational environment to preferred style will maximize learning. The LSI shares with those tests noted above an apparent insularity from other measures, with each test reflecting its own authors' beliefs.

Some learning-style scales are based on theoretical work, such as that of Murray (1938, 1951) ("environmental press": the phenomenological experience of one's interaction with the environment) or Weber (1946) (the common-denominator characteristics of organizational settings). Murray's work provides the basis for at least two well-known sets of measures, the Stern Environment Indexes (Stern, Walker, Pace, Winters, Archer, Meyer, & Steinhoff, 1957–72) and the Social Climate Scales (Moos & Associates, 1974–87). Each of these, as well as the PEPS, includes forms that deal with adult preferences in "work" or other settings (Organizational Climate Index and Work Environment Scale, respectively).

The authors of the LSI (and others) argue that such theoretical bases are inappropriate. They emphasize the importance of the empirical development of their instruments using content and item analysis and factor analytic studies. They note that such continuing studies (G. E. Price, personal communication, to Buros Institute of Mental Measurements, July 19, 1988) have led to the recent reduction of PEPS factors from 21 to 20. The authors stress that the "scale does not measure underlying psychological motivation . . . Rather, it yields information concerned with . . . patterns through which the highest levels of productivity tend to occur. . . . *how* an employee prefers to produce or learn best, not why" (1982, p. 2). Thus, the major interpretive portion of their manual is devoted to "suggestions" for adapting the working or learning environment, based on an individual's or a group's scores on the profile (raw scores are reported and standard scores are listed and graphed as plus or minus one standard deviation). There is little justification presented for all of these prescriptions, and very few other data are presented to indicate criterial validity. Thus, there is no evidence that carrying out the prescriptions would have a demonstrable effect on improved productivity, or even on job performance in general.

Currently, the PEPS Manual is undergoing revision; a revised version was not available at the time of review. Most of the data presented in the 1982 Manual deal with the PEPS' reliability and internal structure. These data illustrate the continuing process of clarifying factor structure and revising the instrument. As a result, the current PEPS factor structure represents a mixed bag of constructs: physical environmental variables, personality or motivational characteristics of the individual, social preferences, and even task-structuring behaviors. The physical variables have face validity; temperature, noise/sound levels, lighting levels, and amount of formal structure (possibly even time of day) are all standard variables discussed in the environment and behavior literature. However, it must be noted that instruments such as the PEPS do not assess an environment, or even a perceived environment, but simply ask raters to indicate what they believe they prefer (cf. James Richards' review of the Moos Social Climate Scales in the *Eighth Mental Measurements Yearbook*, 1978). The environmental literature is rife with examples of environmental effects of which the subject was not aware. Reported are some studies correlating productivity style and GPA (undergraduate and graduate) that suggest one direction for further validation studies, but they do not extend the PEPS outside of "learning environments."

The reliabilities reported seem to be in the acceptable ranges. However, it is worth noting that they report only 68% of the reliabilities are equal to or greater than .60; seven factors have reliabilities greater than .80, but none reaches .90. The standardization sample is rather ill-defined (589 adults "from several states and from various academic and industrial settings"). In general, insufficient data are presented to allow the reader to assess independently the applicability of the PEPS to different groups of workers in regard to "real" environments. Data are reported for right- versus left-handers, and for field-dependent versus field-independent.

Would I use this survey? It is, as claimed, easy to use; sample raters finished in 12 to 28 minutes. These raters felt it was a "simplistic" test; its apparent superficiality may stem from the lack of theoretical basis, which means individual items are tied directly to the factors or scales. We would not use it for individual personnel decisions, in that it seems to lack the validity to withstand employee challenges. The authors seem to suggest that its best

use is as a "counseling measure," by a supervisor or a placement advisor. The PEPS provides quickly and systematically the kind of information that could be developed in an interview. It could thus be used as a preliminary stage to the "interview." It could also be an interesting component of a research program that included both environmental assessment and performance/productivity measures as outcome criteria.

REVIEWER'S REFERENCES

Murray, H. A. (1938). *Explorations in personality.* New York: Oxford University Press.

Weber, M. (1946). *Essay in sociology* (H. H. Garth & C. W. Mills, Trans.). New York: Oxford University Press.

Murray, H. A. (1951). Toward a classification of interaction. In T. Parsons & E. A. Shils (Eds.), *Toward a general theory of action* (pp. 434-464). Cambridge, MA: Harvard University Press.

Stern, G. G., Walker, W. J., Pace, C. R., Winters, C. L., Jr., Archer, N. S., Meyer, D. L., & Steinhoff, C. R. (1957-72). Stern Environment Indexes. Syracuse, NY: Evaluation Research Associates.

Moos, R. H., & Associates. (1974-87). The Social Climate Scales. Palo Alto, CA: Consulting Psychologists Press.

Canfield, A. A. (1976-80). Learning Styles Inventory. Rochester, MI: Humanics Media.

Renzulli, J. S., & Smith, L. H. (1978). Learning Styles Inventory. Mansfield Center, CT: Creative Learning Press.

Richards, J. M., Jr. (1978). [Review of The Social Climate Scales.] In O. K. Buros (Ed.), *The eighth mental measurements yearbook* (Vol. I, pp. 1085-1087). Highland Park, NJ: The Gryphon Press.

[307]
Program for the Acquisition of Language with the Severely Impaired.

Purpose: "Provides assessment tools, training strategies, and training activities which target essential presymbolic and early symbolic skills in language-delayed clients of all ages."

Population: Severely impaired children and adults.

Publication Date: 1982.

Acronym: PALS.

Scores: 3 subtests: Caregiver Interview and Environmental Observation, Developmental Assessment Tool (DAT), Diagnostic Interactional Survey (DIS).

Administration: Individual.

Price Data, 1989: $89 per complete kit including 12 DIS/DAT and 12 Caregiver Interview and Environmental Observation forms, Training Level Activities Guide (214 pages), and manual (111 pages); $15 per 12 DIS/DAT forms; $15 per 12 Caregiver Interview and Environmental Observation forms; $39 per Training Level Activities Guide; $30 per manual.

Time: Administration time varies by component and client.

Comments: Behavior checklist; subtests available as separates.

Author: Robert E. Owens, Jr.

Publisher: The Psychological Corporation.

Review of the Program for the Acquisition of Language with the Severely Impaired by LAURIE FORD, Assistant Professor, Department of Educational Psychology, Texas A&M University, College Station, TX:

The Program for the Acquisition of Language with the Severely Impaired (PALS) program is a systematic, individualized developmental approach to language development that incorporates cognitive, psycholinguistic, and sociolinguistic literatures into its programming for individuals with severe language impairments. The program provides assessment tools, training strategies, and training activities that target presymbolic and early symbolic skills in individuals with severe language delays. The program was developed for use with individuals with severe and profound disabilities ages infancy through adulthood. The complete PALS kit includes: (*a*) a training activities guide, (*b*) a program manual, (*c*) 12 Developmental Assessment Tool (DAS) forms, and (*d*) 12 Caregiver and Environmental Observation forms.

The PALS intervention model, according to the authors, is a communication-centered approach to early language training with a goal of functional communication for the individual. Three training models, incidental teaching, stimulation, and formal training are designed for use in the communication environments of the client (home, classroom, clinic, or living unit). According to the authors, incidental teaching provides a strategy for reinforcing and stabilizing formal training through the use of the client's own content. With young children this vehicle is often play. The stimulation component is operationalized by teaching caregivers the most effective communication strategies and methods through introducing new materials. Formal training, typically the hallmark of other training programs, is given less focus in the PALS. The PALS training program is designed for use by speech-language therapists who in turn incorporate caregivers into the training process when possible. The caregiver is viewed not as a "cotherapist" but rather, according to the author, as a "communication partner." The environmental approach, used in contrast to traditional behavioral approaches, enhances the generalization of training content. However, highly structured educational situations are needed to facilitate maximum communication. The program allows the individual's own unique experiences to serve as the basis of training to increase generalization and maximize what the individual brings to the learning situation.

The model on which the PALS was developed, according to the authors, is designed to evaluate and train presymbolic and early symbolic communication skills. The presymbolic training levels are ordered in a training progression: Auditory Recognition, Attention, Responding/Turn-Taking, Motor Imitation, Object Permanence, Turn-Taking, Functional Use of Objects, Means, Communicative Gestures, Receptive Language, and Sound Imitation. Symbolic training levels are organized by semantic function: word imitation, nomination, negation, possession, attribution, recurrence, notice, location, and action. The goal is to maximize

communication and the development of symbolic code.

The PALS is well conceptualized and based on current, progressive models of language development for individuals with severe disabilities. A more cognitive-based (rather than behavioral) ecological psycholinguistic approach is used. The behavioral model has been the model of choice for working with persons with severe disabilities. The manual and training level activities guide are well written and carefully explain program philosophy and implementation. Specific teaching strategies are explained clearly with suggested adaptation for individualization and strategies to increase generalization.

The PALS program uses three assessment tools to assist in understanding the client's communication abilities and interactions. These tools utilize a developmental approach which can be interpreted in light of the PALS training program. The assessment begins with a caregiver interview and environmental observation followed by an informal didactic observation and a developmental assessment. During the caregiver interview, the therapist gathers information about clients' developmental levels of functioning and commonly used communication strategies. A five-item screening is utilized to facilitate a more efficient evaluation. The authors report that the Primary Caregiver interview takes approximately 20 minutes to complete.

As a part of the evaluation, the therapist/evaluator completes an Environmental Observation in "as many different settings as possible" to gain a sample of communicative behaviors. Although this open-ended assessment approach may have many benefits, it may also lead to inaccuracies because of nonstandardized administrations. Anyone who administers the PALS should be trained in clinical interviewing and observational strategies.

The two-step client evaluation process consists of both an informal observation and a more formal developmental assessment. The evaluation may be carried out in the natural environment and/or a clinical setting. Flexibility in scoring and administration facilitate the identification of maximum levels of communication. The Diagnostic Interaction Survey (DIS) rates caregiver-client interactions on 10 behaviors. Caregiver behaviors include use of: Natural Reinforcement, Physical Space, Imitation, Expansion, Reply/Extension, and Content/Client Lexicon. Client behaviors rated include: Attending, Referencing, Physical Space, and Naming/Verbalization. According to the manual, the DIS behaviors correlate highly with professional subjective evaluations on quality of interaction. However, technical information to support this claim is not reported in the manual. Appendices give detailed descriptions of behaviors to be observed with details for scoring.

The Diagnostic Assessment Tool (DAT) is administered as the most formal component of the PALS assessment. It includes a speech sample gathered via audiotape and with follow-up coding procedures corresponding to each level in the training program. The DAT is a "content-free" evaluation. The authors suggest the purpose of the DAT is to describe the client's presymbolic and symbolic skills relative to the individual's communicative context and content rather than make norm-referenced comparisons against a standard criteria. As a result, the client's favorite items can be used and the caregiver is invited to participate in the evaluation. Once again, scoring is challenging and the examiner/therapist must have a good working understanding of both the training activities and the assessment instrument. The results of this evaluation yield a full description of the individual's communication abilities and interactions.

SUMMARY. The PALS program is a systematic, individualized developmental approach to language instruction for individuals with severe language impairments. The program provides a comprehensive training system that targets presymbolic and early symbolic language skills. The training program is well developed and based on a theory with strong empirical support. The ecological approach to training facilitates greater generalizability of learned communication skills. Although technical support for the instrument is somewhat limited, the PALS represents a promising language curriculum that can serve as a starting point for a therapist wanting to become more familiar with this approach to language instruction. However, it may be necessary to supplement activities over time. The assessment tools developed for use with the PALS use a combination of formal and informal ratings and observation systems. The assessment tools are directly linked to the PALS curriculum. As a result, they provide excellent clinical utility for program planning with the PALS system. However, these tools have less utility for use with other language curricula.

Review of the Program for the Acquisition of Language with the Severely Impaired by JOE OLMI, School Psychology Predoctoral Intern, Department of Educational Psychology, Mississippi State University, Mississippi State, MS:

The Program for the Acquisition of Language with the Severely Impaired (PALS) is a comprehensive assessment, instructional, and training program designed to aid in the development of communication skills (i.e., presymbolic and symbolic language) with severely language-impaired individuals of all ages. It is to be used primarily by speech/language pathologists, but may provide important clinical

information to teachers of the severely disabled, psychologists, educational specialists, and other service providers. Its usefulness as a language development program is based on its strong developmental and programming rationale and its emphasis on the functional communication skills needed by an individual in everyday experiences and interactions. The diagnostic prescriptive program has as its aim the development of "functional language that generalizes to the client's natural communication environment" (pp. 1–2).

Two phases comprise the program: formal and informal assessment and communication training. These phases combine in an individualized communication intervention program developed to use and maximize communicative capacities.

The assessment phase, lasting approximately 2 hours, begins with the Caregiver Interview and Environmental Observation. The author recommends interviewing parents, caregivers, teachers, and others important to the client's progress. He also recommends anecdotal and interval observations of nonteaching interactions between the caregiver and client in various settings including the home and classroom.

During a 10-minute observation of client-caregiver interactions, client vocalizations/verbalizations are tape recorded and later analyzed for semantic and illocutionary functions and mean length of utterances using the Developmental Assessment Tool (DAT). No taped language sample would be available for the presymbolic or nonspeaking individual. An approximate developmental level can be obtained from the results of the DAT.

Communicative behaviors of the caregiver and client during these interactions are entered on the Diagnostic Interactional Survey (DIS). To respond properly on the DIS the observer is required to tally the number of interactions by type observed in 1-minute intervals during the 10-minute period for both the client and caregiver. Information entered on the DIS is translated into a score by simply summing the interval tally marks of caregiver behaviors and client behaviors. A total of 20 or fewer interactions, according to information contained in the manual, is indicative of "poor interaction." "Good interaction" would be indicated by 80 or more interactions. The score is of limited diagnostic value, but may be valuable for programming purposes.

The client's approximate developmental level, the last successful item of the DAT, determines the beginning or entry level of the second phase of the PALS, the training phase. For example, if the last achieved item of the DAT was Visible Physical Imitation, the service provider would begin the intervention or training plan with that corresponding section of the Training Level Activities Guide.

The training aspect of the program stresses the importance of the caregiver in the potential success or failure of therapy. The author emphasizes that the caregiver should attend weekly therapy sessions with the client in order to receive training in the PALS modes of teaching—incidental teaching, language stimulation, and formal training.

Incidental teaching involves seizing potential teaching moments that may arise in the everyday activities of the client (e.g., cuing the client to imitate splashing water during bathing). Language stimulation procedures are those general and training level procedures employed by the caregiver and/or teacher to stimulate or reinforce communication growth such as speaking in short, clear sentences or repeating sentences to the client. Formal training is characterized by graphically represented structured teaching procedures designed to be employed in rather strict fashion. The author of the PALS stresses the formal training should be deemphasized because it is felt to retard spontaneous communication. Spontaneous communication is the basis of the program.

Mean intrajudge reliability for the DIS was 87.1% and interjudge agreement was 77.3%. Interjudge and intrajudge agreement for the illocutionary act taxonomy of the DAT was 91.3%. Considering the observational nature and purpose of the system, these figures are adequate.

In summary, the Program for the Acquisition of Language with the Severely Impaired (PALS) has several strengths, including emphasis on functional communication skills, involvement of caregiver in assessment and program design, ecological approach to assessment, ease of understanding of written materials, and organization. Its sound developmental and programming basis make it a worthy program that could serve both service providers and program recipients.

[308]

Programmer Analyst Aptitude Test (Basic Version).

Purpose: "To evaluate the candidate's aptitude and potential for programming and analyzing business problems."
Population: Applicants for programmer/analyst positions.
Publication Dates: 1984–88.
Acronym: PAAT.
Scores, 3: Programming, Analytical, Total.
Administration: Group.
Price Data, 1989: $20 per basic battery including test booklet ('84, 14 pages) and manual ('88, 8 pages).
Time: 120(125) minutes.
Comments: Tests scored by publisher only.
Author: Wolfe Personnel Testing & Training Systems, Inc.
Publisher: Wolfe Personnel Testing & Training Systems, Inc. [Canada].

Review of the Programmer Analyst Aptitude Test (Basic Version) by FREDERICK BESSAI, Professor of Education, University of Regina, Regina, Saskatchewan, Canada:

The Programmer Analyst Aptitude Test (Basic Version) (PAAT) appears to be a fairly valid measure of an individual's ability to comprehend and follow complex instructions in dealing with symbolic material. It is intended to be used by employers to screen and select applicants for positions in programming and in the general application of computers in business. There is a time limit of 2 hours for the six test problems, each of which has a series of subproblems. The test is strictly timed and, therefore, evaluates examinees on their speed and accuracy as well as on their ability. The instructions for some of the problems are as long as 450 words, so reading comprehension and short-term memory components can be assumed. The ability to code and the ability to translate codes from symbolic to numeric and graphic form appear to be the main variables measured.

The instructions for taking the test are clearly given in the test booklet. Time guidelines for each of the six problems are given at the top of each page. The candidate is not required to adhere to these, but can move back and forth among the six problems during the 2 hours allotted for the test. The test booklet also contains a biographical information page, which asks for details about the candidate's educational background and work history. This reviewer questions whether this information needs to be included because most employers usually collect it on employment application forms. One explanation for its inclusion is that the publisher provides the exclusive scoring service and may use some of this information in reporting results to clients. However, there is no evidence of this in the manual or in the sample report included.

No information is provided about the validity of the PAAT. The manual states only that a validation study is in progress. There is no mention whatsoever of reliability. A precaution is noted in the administration instructions that if a candidate has taken the test previously, there should be a 3-month waiting period before retesting.

Norming information is virtually nonexistent. The manual states that percentiles were obtained from a norming group of 500 applicants. There is no information about how these applicants were selected, and no biographical characteristics are given. A norms table is provided with percentiles for the raw score range (0–100), but there is no title to the table and no accompanying text. A small table below it, entitled Sample Statistics, contains descriptive statistics for a population of 212. The reader can only guess whether these are a subset of the 500 mentioned earlier in the manual or a different group entirely. The sample report to clients reports the raw scores on each of the problems in each subtest (i.e., programming skill [Problems 1–4] and analytical skill [Problems 5–6]), and a possible range for each score is given. The candidate's performance on each subtest is then described as "above average," "average," or "below average." The test user has no way to evaluate whether 12 out of 16 for a given problem is indeed average, and if it is, in what group is it an average?

In its present state of development, there is little to recommend the PAAT for general use. Much research is still needed to establish its specific validity and to determine its reliability. In the absence of this information, the test may well screen out desirable candidates. The PAAT appears to have good face validity and is a test that merits further study and research. It would be very helpful to know how the two subscores of the PAAT correlate with other cognitive tests, particularly tests of reasoning ability and reading comprehension. Another necessary detail is its reliability in comparison to other tests of its kind. Finally, the test should be carefully normed with various types of applicants who have different levels of formal education and differing amounts of computer training and experience. Norms for each of these subgroups would be essential if the authors intend to fully realize their stated purpose.

Review of the Programmer Analyst Aptitude Test (Basic Version) by RALPH F. DARR, JR., Professor of Education, Department of Educational Foundations, The University of Akron, Akron, OH:

The Programmer Analyst Aptitude Test (PAAT) kit contains a test manual and one test booklet. The manual (Basic Version) notes that this instrument is designed "to evaluate the candidate's aptitude and potential for programming and analyzing business problems." A general description of the instrument then follows.

The manual notes that the first four questions are designed to measure the respondent's logical and general programming skills. The last two problems assess the respondent's ability to follow complex business procedures and to analyze and correct errors in these procedures. Although this manual is intended for the PAAT Basic Version, the Screening Version and the Comprehensive Version are briefly reviewed. The other two versions include personality measures with the Basic Version.

A sample question is provided. This sample is later used as part of Problem 5. The constructors suggest the PAAT is a valid screening device for: (a) entry level analyst positions (no prior experience or education); (b) computer trainees; (c) computer science graduates; and (d) applicants who are experienced in the field. The mental operations measured by the test are: (a) logical ability; (b)

interpretation of intricate specifications; (c) ability to follow directions precisely; (d) attention to detail; (e) accuracy; (f) problem solving with symbols; (g) ability to interpret complex business procedures; and (h) ability to translate business solutions into symbolic logic. The manual reviews each of the six problems in terms of item content and tasks (mental operation) required.

The test is administered over a strictly timed 2-hour period, and examinees are instructed to make all calculations in the test booklet. The instrument may be administered to any number of persons at one time, but it can be scored only by Wolfe Personnel Testing and Training Systems. Three procedures for handling results are provided, including a 2-hour-turnaround telephone option. A sample of a scored report is provided. The manual concludes with a table for converting weighted raw scores to percentile ranks and a description of what is described as "sample statistics" from a group of 212.

The client is provided a weighted raw score and written narrative for each problem and an overall total score and recommendation for each candidate. Only the total weighted score can be converted to a percentile rank using the table provided.

The PAAT is composed of six independent problems of increasing difficulty. Although all items have correct answers, none can be answered by memory alone. All problems require mental operations that exceed the knowledge level. The cognitive complexity of the problems increases as examinees progress through the test. Time guidelines for problems also increase as the test progresses. Problem 1 requires the respondent to follow directions in plotting a flow chart (10 minutes). In Problem 2, the candidate uses a set of rules to create new words. This item requires both comprehension and application (10 minutes). Problem 3 is a three-part alphabetizing task. Task difficulty increases across the three parts (15 minutes). Problem 4 is another flow chart task with a variety of interrelated rules (20 minutes). Problem 5 deals with analysis, synthesis, and evaluation in solving typical business problems (25 minutes). Problem 6 has two parts. Part 1 requires the examinee to create a numeric code to solve information storage and retrieval problems. In Part 2, the respondent is given a numeric code problem in which the code is faulted. The candidate is required to correct the code so the problem can be solved (35 minutes).

The PAAT is strong in content validity. If one assumes that a successful programmer must be able to think symbolically in order to generate codes to store and retrieve information, this instrument would appear to demonstrate high content validity. Although the context of the six problems varies, all appear to have some degree of application to business.

No evidence of predictive or concurrent validity is provided by the test producer. The test manual notes that a validation study is in progress but gives no indication of what procedures are being used or when results will be available. It would be interesting to investigate the relationship between the Basic Version and the additional items in the Screening and Comprehensive versions.

The PAAT test manual notes that test-retest is possible, but a waiting period of at least 3 months is recommended. No test-retest data are presented. Internal reliability would be difficult to calculate meaningfully because of the limited number of responses per problem, the unknown weight assigned each item in scoring, and the increasing complexity of each problem. Because the weighted scoring system is not explained (i.e., 28 responses can result in a maximum score of 100 points), interpreting the results is difficult. Finally, because all tests are scored by Wolfe, it is impossible to determine exactly how respondents performed on each problem beyond their raw scores.

SUMMARY. The PAAT is a six-problem 2-hour test of the applicant's aptitude to learn the skills required of a program analyst and to analyze complex business problems. As the text progresses, problems appear to require increasingly more complex cognitive skills. After analyzing the individual problems, this reviewer concluded that the instrument has high content validity. However, the test developers offer no evidence of the instrument's reliability or other types of validity. There is little question in this reviewer's mind that the PAAT assesses the test taker's higher order cognitive skills. An unanswered question is how consistently does it measure these skills?

[309]
Progressive Achievement Tests in Mathematics.
Purpose: "To determine the levels of achievement reached by students in . . . mathematics."
Population: Australian students in years 3–8.
Publication Dates: 1983–84.
Acronym: PATMATHS.
Scores: Total score only.
Administration: Group.
Price Data, 1989: A$2.50 per 10 answer sheets; $3 per scoring stencil; $12.70 per manual, all levels in one ('84, 38 pages); $29.60 per specimen set; scoring service: $20 per test.
Time: 45(60) minutes.
Comments: 2 forms: A, B; Australian adaptation of the New Zealand Progressive Achievement Tests: Mathematics.
Authors: Manual prepared by Graham Ward and Stephen Farish from material developed by Neil A. Reid and David C. Hughes (New Zealand manual).
Publisher: Australian Council for Educational Research Ltd. [Australia].
a) LEVEL 1.

Population: Years 3–5.
Price Data: $1.60 per test booklet, Form A or B (11 pages).
b) LEVEL 2.
Population: Years 5–8.
Price Data: $1.60 per test booklet, Form A or B (12 pages).
c) LEVEL 3.
Population: Years 6–8.
Price Data: $1.60 per test booklet, Form A or B (10 pages).
Cross References: For information on the New Zealand edition, see T3:1911 (1 reference); for additional information and a review by Harold C. Trimble, see 8:288.

TEST REFERENCES

1. Share, D. L., Moffitt, T. E., & Silva, P. A. (1988). Factors associated with arithmetic-and-reading disability and specific arithmetic disability. *Journal of Learning Disabilities, 21*, 313-320.
2. Williams, S., McGee, R., Anderson, J., & Silva, P. A. (1989). The structure and correlates of self-reported symptoms in 11-year-old children. *Journal of Abnormal Child Psychology, 17*, 55-71.

Review of the Progressive Achievement Tests in Mathematics by JAMES C. IMPARA, Associate Professor of Research, Evaluation, and Policy Studies, Virginia Polytechnic Institute and State University, Blacksburg, VA:

The Teacher's Handbook for the Progressive Achievement Tests in Mathematics describes five functions for the three levels of this test: estimating broadly student mathematical achievement (to provide information for such things as grouping students who are on similar levels); setting goals and planning programs for students; identifying students who may need special diagnostic and remedial attention; indicating students who may qualify for enrichment; and locating within a class areas of weakness and strength related to the mathematics objectives and curriculum.

This test is adapted from tests developed originally by the New Zealand Council for Educational Research (8:288). It is designed for and normed on Australian students. The precise changes from the original are not described fully. Some of the item revisions are not likely to be of concern in terms of what is being measured (e.g., changing from New Zealand to Australian currency). Other modifications may have altered the original intent of the item (e.g., rewriting items that originally depended on understanding set notation to items not dependent on set notation). Additionally, a new optional section on sets and logic was added. As a result of these modifications it is difficult to know just how much of the original tests remain. That question, however, does not detract from the fact that items are interesting and well presented and they provide what appear to be excellent illustrations of items measuring higher taxonomic levels.

Some items contain country-specific content (e.g., Australian coins and language idioms). It seems to this reviewer that most English-speaking students, whether inside or outside Australia, would have little difficulty adjusting to such content. The mathematical content is universal and whether a coin is valued at $.25 or $.20 or $.02 can be accommodated.

The test manual is generally complete and well presented. As in the test forms, some of the language is country specific and the administration instructions may require adaptation for use in other locales. Students in the United States may be confused by the word "working" for example, as it is used in the directions read to the student in the Teacher's Guide (p. 6) which indicates: "For a few questions you may need to do some working. Working paper has been given to you for this." Making language accommodations would not have a negative impact on validity or standardization.

It is not likely that the use of standardization norms would be useful outside Australia, perhaps even in Australia. The test was normed in 1983. Although the sample described in the manual appears to be broadly representative of Australia, the age of the norms raises questions about their current utility.

Each of the three levels of the test has two forms. Forms were constructed using Rasch scaling of trial test items. The final test forms were assembled such that within each form, items were grouped by topic in order of increasing difficulty. Each level is more difficult than the lower numbered one. Although the levels overlap in terms of appropriate year/grade, the manual cautions against using higher levels at the low end of the year range except for advanced students. Examination of the test forms confirms that each higher level is progressively more difficult. Examination of the manual confirms that items progress in difficulty within forms. Data are presented that suggest Forms A and B may not be of equal difficulty at Levels 2 and 3. At each level, it appears that Form B is the more difficult. Level 1 has 47 items, Level 2 has 57 items, and Level 3 has 55 items. In the norming sample Level 3 was, as designed, more difficult. The highest mean number correct reported for any year or form for Level 3 was 22.3 (Form A, year 8) and the lowest mean was 13.9 for Form B, year 6 (the expected chance score, i.e., the score expected if students just guessed at every item, for Form B is 11.5).

The reliability coefficients reported (KR20) ranged from .80 (for Level 3B administered to year 6 students) to .94. All reliability estimates for Level 3 were less than .90, and all estimates for Levels 1 and 2 exceeded .90.

The principal validity concern is content validity. Although some evidence of content validity is reported in the Teacher's Guide, and the topical content coverage is listed, it is recommended that any potential user compare a sample copy of the test to the curriculum of potential examinees.

Three major concerns about the test and the claims made for it relate to timing, use of the scores diagnostically, and directions for administration when computer scoring is used. First, the timing of the test administration is 60 minutes. The inclusion of the section on Sets and Logic is optional, yet the norms and the timing information provided are with the inclusion of that section. No separate timing instructions or norms information are provided for when the short version of the test is administered. There is a raw score to scale score conversion table for the shortened versions, but no adjusted percentile ranks based on actual student data are presented. (This applies only to Levels 2 and 3.)

The second concern rests with using the test diagnostically. Two diagnostic uses were suggested: placing students in groups with other students at the same level and determining strengths and weaknesses of classes. It is assumed, implicitly, that students on the same level may have similar difficulties and strengths. This assumption is not necessarily valid; thus, while students may be placed into levels with some degree of accuracy, such placement represents only a portion of the kind of help teachers may need. In assessing class strengths or weaknesses (and by implication assessing the same for individual students given the suggested use of goal setting and planning programs of work for individual students) only norm-referenced suggestions are made. The manual correctly cautions users that inferences about individual strengths and weaknesses on few items are not appropriate, but the Teacher's Handbook indicates that such a use is intended. No information is provided in the manual to assist teachers in determining how this might be done properly, if at all.

A third, and minor, concern occurs if the tests are to be computer scored. The directions for administration may need modification for administration to large groups of students (e.g., administration in a large lecture hall or similarly large room).

In summary, the tests are constructed using items that appear to measure higher level taxonomic skills in mathematics across several years of schooling. The tests may be useful in placing students in groups with others with equal skill levels, but who may not all need instruction on the same topics. Levels 1 and 2 of the test have high levels of reliability; Level 3 has lower but acceptable reliability. Some evidence for validity is presented, but potential users should conduct their own content validity study. (Potential users outside Australia may also need to verify that certain content and language in both the test and the directions for administration would be understandable to their students.) Norming data are not recent and are restricted to Australia; such data should be used cautiously.

Review of the Progressive Achievement Tests in Mathematics by A. HARRY PASSOW, Schiff Professor of Education, Teachers College, Columbia University, New York, NY:

The Progressive Achievement Tests in Mathematics (PATMATHS) aim at helping teachers determine the level of achievement in the basic skills and understandings of mathematics of Australian students in grades 3–8. Prepared by the Measurement and Evaluation Division of the Australian Council for Educational Research, the tests represent an adaptation of the Progressive Achievement Tests: Mathematics prepared about a decade earlier by the New Zealand Council for Educational Research (NZCER). The Teacher's Handbook, for example, was based on the 1974 handbook developed by the NZCER.

The three tests, each with two forms, cover years 3 through 8 with some overlap. Test 1, with 47 items, is designed for years 3–5; Test 2, with 57 items, covers the broadest spread of years 5–8; and Test 3, with 55 items, covers years 6–8.

In adapting the tests, the original New Zealand tests were examined by panels of Australian curriculum specialists to determine the conformity or congruence with current Australian curricula, while not adhering to the syllabus of any of the state education departments. Items were examined for applicability to the Australian context, resulting in changing such things as names, currency, and prices. Items that reflected a notation based on set theory were revised to eliminate dependence on set theory and a special section was introduced to test sets and logic. New items were added to fill content area gaps. The tests were then tried in schools in four separate state education systems and revised.

The PATMATHS tests are designed to be administered early in the school year so that they can be used by teachers in planning their instruction and in making decisions about suitable instructional programs for students of different ability and achievement levels. They provide considerable diagnostic information.

The Teacher's Handbook contains very clear and specific instructions for both administering the test and interpreting the results. The interpretation section begins with a number of caveats regarding the test scores—cautions which apply to all such achievement testing but which always need to be called to the attention of teachers. Because raw scores have limits regarding the information they provide about student achievement, two kinds of scaled scores are provided: (*a*) The Rasch-scaled PATMATHS scale scores relate student attainment and item difficulty to a single scale of achievement and (*b*) the norm-referenced percentile rank and stanine scores relate student attainment to the attainment of a national reference student group. The clear and concise presentation of the procedures by which these two scales are developed and their meaning represents a good in-service experience for teachers who take the time to read them.

In the opening section of the Teacher's Handbook, five possible functions of the PATMATHS tests are listed and each of these is discussed and illustrated in a section on using the test results. Teachers are reminded that standardized tests provide only one facet of information needed to make decisions about a student's instructional program. This is followed by an effective section with cautions about the use of test results and the need to guard against misuse and misinterpretation of tests.

The technical information about the construction, calibration, and standardization procedures used in adapting the NZCER tests is well described. All of the reliability coefficients are reported as being relatively high so that the tests can be considered satisfactorily stable. The content validity is established by the usual methods of a thorough and detailed examination of the test content to ascertain structure and emphases, congruence with accepted curricula and widely used textbooks, and the appropriateness and representativeness of the items selected for inclusion on the test. This process is highly subjective so that teachers are urged "to work systematically through the items of each test, to evaluate the appropriateness of the content for a class, and to test the extent to which it matches the teacher's set of objectives." It is observed that an indirect indication of the tests' content validity is found by the fact that there is regular and marked achievement increase from one year to the next.

The tests consist of the usual multiple-choice type items, with the items arranged in content groups and ordered from easiest to most difficult. It is suggested that where there is overlap in the years for which the test can be used (e.g., year 5 between Levels 1 and 2 and years 6–8 between Levels 2 and 3, prior experience should determine whether the easier or more difficult test should be administered). The answer sheets can be scored manually or by computer. For the former, a set of score key overlays are provided. The ACER Test Scoring Service can be used for machine scoring.

The PATMATHS tests constitute a useful measure of student achievement in the basic skills and understandings of mathematics, with an emphasis on basic skills. Because they represent an adaptation of a set of tests which were technically well developed and used over a period of time, PATMATHS builds on the experience of the New Zealand Council with the result that, for Australian schools, teachers have a set of tests that can be used appropriately in designing their instruction.

[310]
Progressive Achievement Tests in Reading: Reading Comprehension and Reading Vocabulary Tests.

Purpose: "To assist teachers in determining the level of development attained by their students in the basic skills of reading comprehension and word knowledge."

Population: Years 3–9 in Australian school system.

Publication Dates: 1973–86.

Acronym: PAT.

Scores, 2: Reading Comprehension, Reading Vocabulary.

Administration: Group.

Levels: 2 parallel forms for both Comprehension and Vocabulary: A, B; 6 parts: Part 2 (Year 3), Part 3 (Year 4), Part 4 (Year 5), Part 5 (Year 6), Part 6 (Year 7), Part 7 (Year 8), Part 8 (Year 9).

Price Data: Available from publisher.

Time: 40(50) minutes Reading Comprehension, 30(40) minutes Reading Vocabulary.

Author: Australian Council for Educational Research Ltd.

Publisher: Australian Council for Educational Research Ltd. [Australia].

Cross References: For information on an earlier edition, see T3:1912 (4 references); for a review of an earlier edition by Douglas A. Pidgeon, see 8:738 (1 reference); see also T2:1579 (1 reference); for excerpted reviews by Milton L. Clark and J. Elkins, see 7:699.

TEST REFERENCES

1. Share, D. L., & Silva, P. A. (1986). The stability and classification of specific reading retardation: A longitudinal study from age 7 to 11. *British Journal of Educational Psychology, 56*, 32-39.

2. Moffitt, T. E., & Silva, P. A. (1987). WISC-R verbal and performance IQ discrepancy in an unselected cohort: Clinical significance and longitudinal stability. *Journal of Consulting and Clinical Psychology, 55*, 768-774.

3. Share, D. L., Moffitt, T. E., & Silva, P. A. (1988). Factors associated with arithmetic-and-reading disability and specific arithmetic disability. *Journal of Learning Disabilities, 21*, 313-320.

4. Williams, S., McGee, R., Anderson, J., & Silva, P. A. (1989). The structure and correlates of self-reported symptoms in 11-year-old children. *Journal of Abnormal Child Psychology, 17*, 55-71.

Review of the Progressive Achievement Tests in Reading: Reading Comprehension and Reading Vocabulary Tests by PAUL C. BURNETT, Lecturer in Psychology, Queensland University of Technology—Kelvin Grove Campus, Brisbane, Australia:

This is the second edition of the Progressive Achievement Tests in Reading (PATR). The first edition produced in 1973 (see 8:735) was an Australian adaption of the New Zealand Council of Educational Research's 1969 edition (see 7:699). The PATR is a group-administered test of Reading Comprehension and Reading Vocabulary for students in years (i.e., grades) 3–9 (ages 8–4). Two alternative forms of the tests are available in reusable booklets. The Reading Comprehension tests each have 97 items, whereas the Reading Vocabulary tests have 125. The starting points for the year level are staggered with examinees completing an average of 44 Reading Comprehension items (range 40–47) and an average of 57 Reading Vocabulary items (range 45–65). This overlapping format is effective, in that it allows for the assessment of seven year levels with the minimum amount of questions and materials.

The PATR materials are well developed and produced with all resources clearly labelled for easy identification. The 54-page manual is excellent in terms of format and thoroughness. It includes a description of the tests, an outline of the uses of the test, a section that delineates the administration and scoring directions, information regarding the interpretation and use of the test scores, and a description of the tests' technical information. The following are specifically addressed in the latter section: test construction, standardization, test and item statistics, reliability, validity, and norming.

The Reading Comprehension tests measure factual and inferential comprehension of prose material and the Reading Vocabulary tests assess word knowledge. The rationale for assessing these skills centers on Bloom's conceptualization of comprehension and knowledge. The purpose of the test is presented as being to assist teachers in determining the level of skill development attained by their students in reading comprehension and vocabulary. A major use of the tests is as screening devices to identify children who are in need of special assistance in the remedial or extension areas. However, further diagnostic assessment would be needed to devise remedial programs for students whose results indicated developmental delays in reading skills or reading difficulties.

The administration instructions are comprehensive and easy to follow. Specific instructions are highlighted and easy to read to students. The tests' answer sheets can be hand or machine scored. Raw scores are translated into percentile ranks, percentile ranges at the 68% confidence interval, and stanine scores. Norms for each year level are presented but no age norms are given.

An extensive renorming of the PATR was completed in November 1984. The norming samples were large, ranging from 726 to 986 for each year level, and were selected using a complex sampling design. Government, Catholic, and Independent schools were represented. The reliability for each scale was evaluated using the KR-20 formula. Consistently high reliability coefficients are reported (range .84 to .94). These figures are similar to those obtained with the previous Australian and New Zealand samples. A weakness of the current norming was the failure to collect new validity data. A small amount of outdated validity data collected during previous standardization are reported. It would have been useful to present meaningful, updated concurrent validity data.

In summary, the second edition of the PATR is the renorming of a well-developed and well-constructed test. The updated manual is extensive and thorough with the exception of the validity section. Some of the criticisms forwarded by previous reviewers have been rectified. For example, the previous manual had separate norms for each of the states and the Australian Capital Territory whereas the new manual presents Australia-wide norms. Additionally, the many meaningless concurrent validity correlations reported in the previous manual are not in the updated manual.

REVIEWER'S REFERENCE

Bloom, B. S. (1956). *Taxonomy of educational objectives: The classification of educational goals, handbook I: Cognitive domain.* New York: McKay.

Review of the Progressive Achievement Tests in Reading: Reading Comprehension and Reading Vocabulary Tests by RICHARD LEHRER, Associate Professor of Educational Psychology, University of Wisconsin-Madison, Madison, WI:

The Progressive Achievement Tests in Reading consist of multiple-choice measures of Reading Comprehension and Vocabulary. The Reading Comprehension test includes a commendable variety of genres (narrative, descriptive, and expository), cultural themes, and content areas. Comprehension questions tap both explicit and inferential knowledge of the test passages. The Reading Vocabulary test presents a word in the context of a sentence and requires students to select the best synonym from a list of five alternatives.

Both tests appear easy to administer and score. The directions provided in the accompanying teacher's handbook are well written. Indeed the entire manual is exemplary, providing information about the intentions and theoretical predilections of the test constructors, clear directions, and substantial guidance in the interpretation of students' scores. Other strengths of the measures include high reliability (KR-20) and two alternate forms for both Reading Comprehension and Vocabulary Knowledge.

The standardization sample is Australian. The standardization sample was extensive, and the manual reports a stratified random sampling procedure based upon school enrollments and geographical location. It appears that one could use the associated norms with confidence. Unfortunately, there is no international standardization sample reported. Hence, these measures could not be used as intended in other English-speaking countries.

The only other caveat is that the validation of the measures is not reported nearly as well as other aspects of these tests. For example, the manual reports high correlations of the comprehension tests with two other measures of "reading" without specifying clearly the nature of these other measures. It is not clear if the correlations between the vocabulary and comprehension tests are higher than those between each test and other measures of vocabulary and reading comprehension. Thus the

extent to which the Vocabulary and Reading Comprehension tests measure separate but related abilities is unknown. Nevertheless, the tests should provide teachers with useful, normative information about their students' reading abilities.

In summary, the Progressive Achievement Tests in Reading Comprehension and Vocabulary are easy to administer and score, and appear valid for the purposes for which they were designed. The Reading Comprehension test in particular samples a commendable number of genres, cultural themes, and content areas. The accompanying teachers' manual is clearly written and provides useful information about the interpretation of students' scores. When used with Australian students, these tests should help teachers make informed decisions about suitable instructional materials for their students.

[311]

Prout-Strohmer Personality Inventory.
Purpose: "Designed to identify maladaptive personality patterns" among mentally retarded adolescents and adults.
Population: Mildly mentally retarded and borderline intelligence individuals ages 14 and over.
Publication Date: 1989.
Acronym: PSPI.
Scores, 7: Thought and Behavior Disorder, Impulse Control, Anxiety, Depression, Low Self-Esteem, Total Pathology, Lie Scale.
Administration: Group.
Price Data, 1989: $77.50 per 25 kits including manual (103 pages); $202.50 per kit with scoring software.
Time: (25–30) minutes.
Comments: Part of Prout-Strohmer Assessment System; intended for use with Strohmer-Prout Behavior-Rating Scale; instrument is to be renamed Self-Report Inventory and will be part of the Emotional Problems Scales (EPS).
Authors: H. Thompson Prout and Douglas C. Strohmer.
Publisher: Psychological Assessment Resources, Inc.
[The following reviews are based on an initial version of this instrument by these test authors. The renamed and revised instrument available from this publisher will be reviewed at a future time.—Ed.]

Review of the Prout-Strohmer Personality Inventory by RICHARD BROZOVICH, Director, Psychology and Learning Clinic, and ERNEST A. BAUER, Testing Consultant, Oakland Schools, Waterford, MI:

The Prout-Strohmer Personality Inventory (PSPI) is a self-report procedure in which respondents mark a yes/no dichotomy to indicate whether a statement describes their feelings, thoughts, or actions. The authors' intent was to provide a method "to identify maladaptive personality patterns among mildly mentally retarded and borderline intelligence adolescents and adults." To achieve their purpose the authors carefully selected self-report items at a low reading level. Respondents complete the items while having them read aloud to them and reading along if possible. These innovations were useful in developing what to these reviewers is a unique instrument to assess personality patterns among people with borderline and mentally retarded development.

The manual for the PSPI is poorly edited. For example, on page 8 the word "obviates" is used when its antonym appears to fit the context. Several instances of faulty reasoning raise more serious questions about the instrument. For example, the authors cite data from studies of children and adolescents and feel the data have relevance for their population "because mildly mentally retarded and borderline intelligence individuals are at lower levels of cognitive and social development." The apparent implication that mildly mentally retarded adults have patterns of personality characteristics similar to those of children is not consistent with personality theory or clinical experience.

The technical data in the manual are inadequate. The conceptual framework for much of the validity data is weak. The clarity and thoroughness of data presentation have glaring inadequacies. In presenting validity studies, for example, the authors divide their norm group into two populations based on presumably dichotomous variables such as, on medication/not on medication, or involved with a behavior plan/not involved with a behavior plan. The authors then present subscale mean scores for these groups and use differences between the group means to support validity claims. No attempt was made to control for other possibly related factors. No variance data, numbers in each group, or other relevant summary statistics are presented for the groups. No tests of significance between means are reported.

A most surprising omission in the data presentation was the lack of information (except for a range) regarding IQ distribution in the norm group. Because a major assertion of the authors is that maladaptive personality patterns occur more frequently among low IQ groups, their failure to report detailed statistics regarding IQ distribution in the norm group is puzzling. This failure to report important statistical parameters in detail is characteristic of the manual.

A table in Appendix C shows the correlations among the 6 scales from the PSPI and 14 scales from the Strohmer-Prout Behavior Rating Scale. The magnitude of these 84 correlations ranges from .01 to .25. These findings make it clear that results from the PSPI are virtually useless as predictors of an individual's scores on the Behavior Rating Scale. However, in the interpretation section of the manual, the authors suggest that PSPI scores can be used to predict scores on the Behavior Rating Scale and actual behavior of individuals. For example, with individuals having an elevated score on the Impulse Control Scale the authors say: "Arguing with peers, talking back, and verbal provocation of others may be observed." The apparent support for this statement was a correlation of .23 between two scale scores. More alarming is the authors' description of individuals with high scores on the Low Self-Esteem scale. "It is possible that they have gotten in trouble because of sexual behavior and seem preoccupied with sexual issues and may engage in inappropriate sexual contacts." This is based on a correlational relationship of .13. The difference between statistically significant relationships among aggregated data and clinically meaningful relationships to predict individual behavior is not acknowledged by the authors.

The authors do "strongly advocate" the use of the PSPI as part of a multitrait, multimethod approach. Considering the size of the relationships between the self-reported scales and other data sources, results of the PSPI on individual respondents should be treated as extremely tentative and not used as a basis to predict behavior.

Review of the Prout-Strohmer Personality Inventory by PETER F. MERENDA, Professor Emeritus of Psychology and Statistics, University of Rhode Island, Kingston, RI:

The Prout-Strohmer Personality Inventory (PSPI) is, according to its developers and authors, "a self-report assessment instrument specifically designed to identify maladaptive personality patterns among mildly mentally retarded and borderline intelligence adolescents and adults." The PSPI is accompanied, as it should be, by a comprehensive test manual consisting of 55 pages of text and 43 pages of appendices. However, the strong points of this inventory begin and end at this point, at least from a psychometric point of view. Although the manual appears to be well written, it is fraught with errors of both commission and omission.

A major omission involves the failure of the authors to include the description, results, and empirical data of the confirmatory factor analysis they claim to have performed on the inventory that is alleged to support the hypothesized scale structure. The reader of the manual has only the authors' word for this—and without the benefit of any reference to published assertion in refereed professional journals. This is not enough for verification of such a claim. This omission is of primary importance because (*a*) a personality factor structure of six specific dimensions is claimed, and (*b*) such a structure is alleged to be measured by and to fit a model emanating from dichotomous responses to stimulus items.

It is noted that in the standardization sample (which admittedly is not representative of a cross section of persons in the mild mental retardation and borderline intelligence ranges in the United States and Canada) a total of 746 subjects in the age range of 14 years to 73 years were administered the PSPI. This total number of subjects is important to keep in mind when reviewing the results of the so-called "validity" studies presented in the manual.

Before discussing the alleged validity findings with the inventory, attention must be focused on issues relating to the psychometric properties of internal consistency and reliability. In Section IV of the manual, the authors confuse internal consistency with reliability. The former is a measure of the homogeneity of the items that comprise the Pathology scales, whereas the latter refers to the stability of the scores, over time, yielded by the individual personality dimensions of the PSPI. Standard 2.6 of the current APA *Standards for Educational and Psychological Testing* (AERA, APA, & NCME, 1985) admonishes authors and users of psychological instruments not to substitute measures of internal consistency for measures of reliability.

In this same section coefficients of stability (i.e., test-retest *reliability* coefficients) are also reported. These are based on only 41 of the 746 cases available in the standardization sample and involve only 4- to 6-week intervals. When it is claimed that the six subscales of the PSPI represent *pathological* scales, these must be viewed as traits, not states or moods. Therefore, reliabilities are required to be established on large test-retest samples with time intervals extending over relatively long periods of time (i.e., several months or years). An additional test-retest study is reported, but unfortunately this was based on even fewer subjects ($N = 36$) and a shorter time interval (2 weeks). The statement by the authors to the effect that all the clinical scales have demonstrated acceptable test-retest reliabilities is open to serious question and challenge.

Regarding claims of validity of the clinical scales and the inventory as a whole (Total Pathology score), none is deemed justified on the basis of the data that are presented in the manual. The number of cases on which the data were based is, in each instance, pitifully small with *N*s ranging from 15 to 26 for retarded samples when they are even reported. Still more serious is the fact that in no study were these so-called validity data treated to any statistical analyses! Merely statements appear such as, "As can be seen, there are higher scores on each scale for subjects in a treatment program." It is likely for this reason that there are no published reports on the PSPI to be found in high quality refereed professional journals.

In light of the foregoing, it is the considered judgment of this reviewer that the authors of the Prout-Strohmer Personality Inventory (PSPI) have failed to meet the professionally recognized criteria required of sound psychological assessment instruments. The test cannot be recommended for any use. In summary, the PSPI may possess the potential

for accomplishing the purpose for which it has been designed, namely, to identify maladaptive personality structure among mildly mentally retarded young and mature persons. However, its ability to do so has not yet been demonstrated either by its authors or users. Still lacking are sound empirical evidences of the scale structure of the inventory, item homogeneity of the scales, stability over sufficiently long time periods of the scale scores, and their validities against reasonable and meaningful criterion measures. The authors and publishers are therefore advised to withdraw the inventory from distribution until these deficiencies are rectified. Barring such action, users are cautioned by the usual Caveat Emptor.

REVIEWER'S REFERENCE

American Educational Research Association, American Psychological Association, & National Council on Measurement in Education. (1985). *Standards for educational and psychological testing*. Washington, DC: American Psychological Association, Inc.

[312]

PSB-Health Occupations Aptitude Examination.

Purpose: Measures "abilities, skills, knowledge, and attitudes important for successful performance of students in the allied health education programs."

Population: Candidates for admission to programs of study for the allied health occupations.

Publication Dates: 1978–87.

Scores, 7: Academic Aptitude (Verbal, Numerical, Nonverbal), Spelling, Reading Comprehension, Information in the Natural Sciences, Vocational Adjustment Index.

Administration: Group.

Price Data, 1988: $5 per test booklet; $5 per answer sheet including scoring and reporting service; $10 per technical manual ('87, 65 pages); $10 per specimen set including test booklet, answer sheet, and administrator's manual ('78, 4 pages).

Time: 120(145) minutes.

Author: Staff of the Psychological Services Bureau with consultant contributions.

Publisher: Psychological Services Bureau, Inc.

Review of the PSB-Health Occupations Aptitude Examination by STEPHEN B. DUNBAR, Associate Professor of Measurement and Statistics, The University of Iowa, Iowa City, IA:

The PSB-Health Occupations Aptitude Examination (HOAE) is a multifaceted test battery that provides its users with a student profile of general academic ability and vocational attitudes to be used by educators in the allied health professions. The stated purposes of the examination relate primarily to admissions and placement in postsecondary job training programs in health-related fields. According to the test manual, ancillary purposes involve student guidance, curriculum planning, and evaluation.

DESCRIPTION OF THE BATTERY. This is an exam that is clearly designed to yield high correlations with overall performance in a variety of educational programs. It is thus not surprising that a major part of the exam is reminiscent of tests of general cognitive ability. Test I in this battery is called Academic Aptitude and contains Verbal, Numerical, and Nonverbal item types. The Verbal items present five moderately difficult words and require the examinee to choose the word that is different from the others. The Numerical items are word problems that require general arithmetic skills and perhaps some rudimentary algebra. The Nonverbal items are figural analogies in which the examinee is asked to choose the geometric shape that completes the analogy based on the first three shapes presented. Although the three item types are discussed in the manual as if they formed distinct subtests (scores in each area *are* reported), the item types are actually spiralled in the test booklet. Cycles of one Verbal item, followed by one Numerical item, and then one Nonverbal item are repeated until 30 items of each type have been presented. The 30-minute time limit for this portion of the battery introduces a factor of speededness into the scores that is acknowledged in the manual and argued to be relevant to the prediction of success in the allied health professions.

Tests II and III in the battery measure Spelling and Reading Comprehension skills. The Spelling items present words drawn from health-related vocabulary spelled three different ways, one of which is correct. The Reading subtest consists of three reading passages of one-paragraph length, each followed by either 10 or 15 comprehension questions. Speed is an acknowledged component of the Spelling and Reading Comprehension subtests as well.

Text IV, Information in the Natural Sciences, is the portion of this battery most specifically tailored to the health professions. The content of this test was derived from analyses of coursework and textbooks used in the schools for which this exam was designed. Examinees must answer the 90 items in this subtest in 30 minutes.

Test V, the Vocational Adjustment Index, is a series of attitude statements with which the examinee is asked to agree or disagree. There is a considerable range of content in the 105 items making up this scale. For example, there are items about physical ailments ("I am often troubled by constipation"), daily habits ("I keep a diary"), self-assessments ("I can always be relied upon"), attitudes toward people ("Most people mean well"), and work ("Any job I start, I finish"). The manual describes the aggregate score based on these items as "a composite estimate of the selected traits . . . felt to be important to the satisfactory adjustment of the allied health professional as a student and as a practitioner" (p. 10).

STANDARDIZATION AND NORMS. The normative data for the PSB-HOAE are based on a sample of 2,881 examinees from nine geographic regions of the U.S. and 20 different health professions. The actual procedures used to select participants are not discussed in the manual nor is there a clear indication of the primary sampling unit. It appears from the manual that multiple training programs from the same allied health school were sampled. There is also no indication of any nonresponse rate associated with requests by the publisher for participation in the standardization, nor an indication of when the standardization data were collected. Because the manual states that the examinees used in the standardization sample were restricted to those who were applying for admission, it appears that all normative data are based on users of the exam. The description of the sampling procedures makes it difficult to determine the representativeness of the norms for this test. In addition, the publisher provides no norms tables in the technical manual.

OTHER TECHNICAL CONSIDERATIONS. The technical manual presents substantial evidence regarding the reliability and criterion-related validity of the battery. The test-retest reliability estimates for the five parts of the battery range from .94 to .98. Reliability estimates of difference scores are presented for all pairs of subtests and range from .80 to .95.

Criterion-related validity evidence is presented in the form of correlations between subtest scores and various measures of success in health-related educational programs. Average validity coefficients for predicting grade-point averages in such programs are quite high for a selection test and samples that were selected on the basis of that test, ranging from .64 to .93. No indication is given in this manual as to whether these values were adjusted for reliability or range restriction, but considering the fact that the reported predictive validity coefficients are higher than most of the correlations among subtests, it is likely that some adjustments were made.

The manual is unclear about the recency of reliability and validity data and the form of the test to which they apply. A number of supplementary validity studies authored by users of the exam are appended to the technical manual. The correlations reported in these studies are markedly lower than those provided in the manual itself.

EVALUATIVE COMMENTS. On balance, this battery of tests appears to make a useful contribution to admissions decisions in the allied health professions. However, there are several issues, principally related to test construction, that potentially complicate the interpretation of scores from this exam. Three such issues deserve comment.

First, the figural analogies items, which form the Nonverbal scale of the Academic Aptitude subtest, are identical to items used in other tests from the same publisher (i.e., PSB-Aptitude for Practical Nursing Examination [T3:1920] and PSB-Nursing

School Aptitude Examination [313]) and have not changed, aside from ordering, over the several revisions of these other exams. There is also considerable item overlap among this publisher's tests of verbal and numerical aptitude. No indication is given in any accompanying manuals that they overlap to the extent that they do, nor is any justification provided for the overlap in light of the different audiences the tests appear intended to serve.

A second issue about which the manual is vague pertains to the degree of speededness of the battery. No completion rates are reported, so one can only speculate about the degree to which speed contributes to total scores and is relevant to the criteria this test is intended to predict. Fifteen comprehension questions for a one-paragraph reading passage also seems excessive, and tends to yield a high proportion of items that measure only literal meaning, and given the time limits, speed of locating information.

A third point of concern regards interpretation of the Vocational Adjustment Scale. This scale pools responses of a fairly heterogeneous set of attitude items into a single score. Although the scale is suggested to be useful in counseling, it is also intended to rank order examinees for selection purposes. It is not clear from the manual exactly how this scale can be justified for a multitude of interpretations, especially given the acknowledged bipolar nature of many of its items.

CONCLUDING REMARKS. The PSB-HOAE offers users supplementary information about applicants' abilities and attitudes for further study in allied health professions. Although it is likely that individual users can develop clear guidelines for valid interpretations of scores given enough experience with the instrument, it is difficult to judge the utility of this test battery solely on the basis of the documentation provided in the technical manual. The quality and recency of normative data are a particular concern in this regard, as is the publisher's commitment to periodic updates of test content.

Review of the PSB-Health Occupations Aptitude Examination by LAWRENCE M. RUDNER, Director of the Educational Resources Information Center Clearinghouse on Tests, Measurement and Evaluation (ERIC/TME), American Institutes for Research, Washington, DC, and Director of Research, LMP Associates, Chevy Chase, MD:

The Psychological Services Bureau cites the PSB-Health Occupations Aptitude Examination as useful in selecting prospective students in a wide range of allied health fields as well as in counseling students once they have been admitted. Norms are provided for 20 different types of allied health programs.

The five tests in the examination—Academic Aptitude, Spelling, Reading Comprehension, Information in the Natural Sciences, and Vocational Adjustment Index—take a total of 2 hours plus management time to administer. There is a speed component to some of these tests.

Documentation provided with this examination addresses the major issues raised in the APA guidelines for technical manuals within the *Standards for Educational and Psychological Testing* (AERA, APA, & NCME, 1985). These include outlining the purpose of the tests, the test development process, the characteristics of the test norms, evidence of validity, and information on reliability. As a result, they could serve as a model for other test publishers. Test characteristics that may be troublesome, such as speededness and the test items being presented in order of difficulty, are fully discussed. The manual, however, was written for a technical audience. More contextual and descriptive information would benefit less technically sophisticated users.

The technical qualities of the test appear to be quite impressive. The carefully conceived development process led to what may be a reliable set of tests that predict subsequent performance in allied health education. The tests were standardized on a sample of 2,881 applicants covering a wide range of allied health programs. The reported test-retest reliabilities are all at or above .94. KR-21 reliabilities computed by this reviewer are all above .93. Validity is supported with content, concurrent, and predictive evidence. Correlations with instructor ratings, GPA, and related instruments are quite high, typically above .80.

However, the reliability and validity information is based on relatively small samples. Only 127 applicants were used to compute reliability estimates. Sample sizes in the validity studies ranged from 32 to 133 students. Additional evidence using more representative samples should be provided.

It is recommended that potential users of the test obtain a specimen set and examine the instrument in light of their own program, applicant pool, and information needs. The print used in the test booklet is small and may be intimidating. The speeded nature of some sections may unduly penalize certain groups of students. The time requirements may be exorbitant.

In summary, this examination was developed using well-regarded procedures. Although the evidence is scant, it appears to be appropriate for use as an aid in screening applicants to allied health education programs. Because it was developed and normed specifically for this population, the examination has intrinsic appeal. However, there is no evidence supporting the second claimed use of the examination, namely, counseling students already admitted to allied health programs.

REVIEWER'S REFERENCE

American Educational Research Association, American Psychological Association, & National Council on Measurement in Education. (1985).

Standards for educational and psychological testing. Washington, DC: American Psychological Association, Inc.

[313]
PSB-Nursing School Aptitude Examination (R.N.).

Purpose: Predicts "readiness or suitability for specialized instruction in a school/program of professional nursing."
Population: Prospective nursing students.
Publication Dates: 1978–84.
Scores, 8: Academic Aptitude (Verbal, Arithmetic, Nonverbal, Total), Spelling, Reading Comprehension, Information in the Natural Sciences, Vocational Adjustment Index.
Administration: Group.
Price Data, 1988: $5 per test booklet; $5 per answer sheet including scoring and reporting service; $10 per technical manual ('84, 61 pages); $10 per specimen set including test booklet, answer sheet, and administrator's manual ('78, 5 pages).
Time: 168(185) minutes.
Authors: Anna S. Evans, Phyllis G. Roumm, and George A. W. Stouffer, Jr.
Publisher: Psychological Services Bureau, Inc.

Review of the PSB-Nursing School Aptitude Examination (R.N.) by KURT F. GEISINGER, Professor of Psychology, Fordham University, Bronx, NY:

This battery was developed for use in making admissions decisions at diploma schools of nursing and associate degree (in nursing) granting institutions. The manual implies that it could be used for placement and guidance purposes, although no data bearing upon this use are presented.

The battery is composed of five tests, four assessing cognitive/educational skills (Academic Aptitude, Spelling, Reading Comprehension, and Information in the Natural Sciences) and the fifth, called the Vocational Adjustment Index (VAI), representing the noncognitive realm. The cognitive tests employ multiple-choice format questions with varying numbers of options; the VAI contains traditional agree-disagree personality inventory items. The Academic Aptitude Test is composed of equal groupings of items from Verbal (vocabulary only), Numerical (verbally presented arithmetic computation and knowledge questions), and Nonverbal (Spatial Relations/Visualization-type questions) domains. Academic Aptitude provides scores for each of these subareas as well as total score, although analyses presented employ only the total scores. The Spelling Test contains three versions each for 60 words; test takers must select the correct spelling. Many of these words would not normally be used by nurses, nursing students, or any other readily identifiable group. Certainly, one must question the relevance of a spelling test on a test of academic readiness to learn to become a nurse. The Reading Comprehension Test contains three brief passages followed by questions assessing a varied degree of comprehension/inference. The passages

are quite dated and their printing is too small (8-point type) and runs across the entire test page, making them difficult to read. Information in the Natural Sciences is generally restricted to knowledge of science facts; little conceptual understanding or application of principles is required. All of the above sections of the test would appear to be heavily weighted by speed, given the relatively large number of test questions per time allotted. However, the test manual suggests that speededness is only a factor for a small minority of examinees.

The fifth component of this battery, the VAI, yields a single score in purporting to provide a composite estimate of selected traits (i.e., is the individual usually cheerful, objective, dependable, self-reliant, helpful, conscientious, insightful, mature in his or her approach to adult problems, not overly anxious, and free from psychosomatic complaints?) felt to be important to the satisfactory adjustment of the prospective nurse as a student and as a practitioner. Apparently the test authors feel the findings from the Vocational Adjustment Index might best be used to provide "an estimate of the individual's potential for successful adjustment to the environment in which the professional nurse will live, study, and work" (manual, p. 12). The appropriateness of such claims must be strongly questioned as is discussed below.

TEST DEVELOPMENT AND STANDARDIZATION. The test authors performed a number of appropriate steps to select and refine questions for their examination. Many questions which were retained were unusually difficult, some well below the chance level.

The standardization sampling included 2,170 applicants from 64 educational programs—representing 6% of appropriate programs nationally during the 1978–79 period, a potentially accurate sampling with care given to geographic representation. Factors such as type of educational program (associate or diploma), age, educational level, and sex of test takers are described.

Raw scores are provided along with percentile ranks. The distributions are markedly positively skewed, further evidence of test difficulty. Tables of test scores and percentile rank equivalents are provided in the manual and are acceptable. Stanines may also be used.

Suggestions regarding cutoff scores for the acceptance of applicants are made. These suggestions appear based on speculation rather than validated evidence or other structured procedures.

RELIABILITY AND INTRATEST RELATIONSHIPS. Test-retest reliability coefficients are provided for the five scales. Periods between testing examinees apparently range from 10–30 days and all are too short; memory causes such estimates to overrepresent test reliability for tests of this type. The reliability sample is quite small (119) and undefined, and it also exhibited a most unusual profile of average test scores, with some well above the standardization mean and others well below it. The test-retest coefficients are high—higher than would be expected for tests of this length and quality and range from .92 (VAI) to .98 (Academic Aptitude and Reading Comprehension).

Based upon correlations with this small sample of 119, the tests exhibit higher intratest correlations than would be desired. Among the cognitive tests, the range is from .63 (between Academic Aptitude and Spelling) to .86 (between Academic Aptitude and Information in the Natural Sciences). The manual incorrectly refers to these intercorrelations as "independent of the others to a substantial degree" (p. 34). These correlations should be provided for the entire standardization sample.

VALIDATION. The test authors attempt to justify test use in terms of content, construct, and, primarily, predictive validation. No evidence of either of the former two techniques of validation is presented. Summaries of predictive validity coefficients are presented for several criteria. In each case, the coefficients are presented for the five tests. Throughout these studies, no information is provided as to the number of schools involved, numbers of minority students, test conditions, or the nature of the criteria. Other relevant factors are similarly elusive. Errors were apparently made in calculating the average validity coefficients that are presented (Table 17, p. 37) at least with regard to correlations with cumulative grade-point average in nursing school in that a number are outside the range of validity coefficients found. From the limited available data presented in the manual, this reviewer recomputed average validity coefficients as ranging from .49 to .58 for the five tests composing this battery. Validity coefficients are also provided with graduating rank in class; these validity coefficients range from .66 (Spelling) to .88 (Academic Aptitude). Validity coefficients with licensing examination scores based on an undefined sample of 103 range from .72 (Spelling) to .93 (Academic Aptitude). Validity coefficients with instructor ratings of 132 undescribed students range from .83 (VAI) to .95 (Information in the Natural Sciences). Finally, 52 students' Academic Aptitude test scores were correlated with Full Scale Wechsler Adult Intelligence Scale scores with a .92 validity coefficient resulting. Significant questions regarding the validity coefficients must be raised because the validity coefficients presented above are so unusually high for a test of academic aptitude, the conditions from which the coefficients are determined are so poorly described, and quantitative errors are apparent.

OVERVIEW. The content of this examination must be questioned. Why was a spelling test included?

The Information in the Natural Sciences test measures only rudimentary factual information. This is somehow almost demeaning to potential nurses and potentially irrelevant to their ability to apply information.

The number of options varies among tests. Questions on the VAI have two options; three for Spelling, four for Reading Comprehension, and five for the other two tests help make this examination unnecessarily difficult for test takers who may not have substantial test sophistication. Other factors—substantial test speededness; small print of reading passages; outdated, poorly written, and boring reading passages; the spelling of antiquated and unused words—make taking this test punishing.

The VAI suffers from a great number of problems. The test authors have attempted with 105 true-false personality test items to develop an index of academic and vocational adjustment. Whether such a measure should be a part of an entrance battery must be questioned, especially when these scores are not applied by trained psychologists. Clearly, the potential for misuse is abundant. Just as troubling is the lack of construct validation of this scale. A measure of a hypothetical variable such as vocational adjustment requires proof that the instrument indeed assesses this quality. None has been provided. Finally, although the test authors refer to the VAI as a test, the *Standards for Educational and Psychological Testing* (AERA, APA, & NCME, 1985, pp. 4–5) suggest against such use.

Problems exist in both reliability and validity analyses. The values presented in the manual are simply too high. Other forms of test reliability (e.g., coefficient alpha) should be estimated and provided. Apparently, the validity coefficients have been adjusted in some manner, but no mention of this statistical or experimental adjustment is cited. Given that the validity analyses are based on the five test scores, cross-validated multiple regression analyses should also have been performed. Similarly, validations of combinations of the test scores in the actual manner in which they are used in making admissions decisions would be helpful. Substantial clarification and elaboration of the studies that have been performed are needed. Information on the use of this examination with minority group members must be provided.

This test should not be used unless local validation has shown that it is indeed effective at the institution in question. Another examination such as the Registered Nursing Admissions Test or a high quality, more general measure such as the ACT Assessment Program (9:43) should be used in the interim.

REVIEWER'S REFERENCE

American Educational Research Association, American Psychological Association, & National Council on Measurement in Education. (1985).

Standards for educational and psychological testing. Washington, DC: American Psychological Association, Inc.

Review of the PSB-Nursing School Aptitude Examination (R.N.) by JAMES C. IMPARA, Associate Professor of Research, Evaluation, and Policy Studies, Virginia Polytechnic Institute and State University, Blacksburg, VA:

The technical manual for the PSB-Nursing School Aptitude Examination (R.N.) contains several errors, omissions, and inconsistencies that detracted from a high degree of confidence in the utility of the test to assist in selecting successful candidates for admission to Associate Degree or Diploma nursing programs. The manual indicates the test battery is intended for use in such programs. The publication date on the manual indicates it was revised in 1983–84. Each of the five subtests is described and a rationale for each is provided.

The battery is quite long—administration time is approximately 3 hours. The authors recommend providing examinees with a break at some time during the administration; however, no indication of when the break should be given is offered, resulting in administrations that differ from the standardization sample and potentially modifying the norms.

The rationale for each subtest and the length of the total battery is logically sound. The authors advocate that Academic Aptitude, Spelling, Reading Comprehension, and Information in the Natural Sciences represent content related either directly to nursing or to learning skills in general. They do not advocate that the Vocational Adjustment Index be used in the selection process (p. 8). All statistics provided, however, include data (including validity coefficients) for using the Vocational Adjustment Index for selection.

Each subtest is timed. The directions for administration, which are clearly written, advise examinees that not everyone is expected to finish every subtest. The only information on completion rates is the statement that over 90% of the examinees in a tryout sample completed the tests, and that time is not a factor for competent examinees: "The small percentage of examinees who do not complete all items within the allowed time perform at a substantially lower level of accuracy than those who do complete all items" (technical manual, p. 9). However, in estimating reliability, test-retest is used exclusively because of the timing factor.

The academic aptitude subtest consists of three dimensions: verbal, numerical, and nonverbal. The items are spiraled (i.e., appear in the order indicated in triads), and a total score is provided. The nonverbal items are principally measures of spatial relations (how things look if rotated). The nonverbal portion is relatively easy compared to the other two components, thus it contributes less to the total score. The chance score is eight correct for each of these components (the score expected of an examinee who just guessed randomly at every item). This score corresponds to the 12th, 25th, and first percentile rank, respectively, for these three dimensions. There are 120 items used to compute the total score for this subscale. A table showing conversions of raw scores to percentile ranks has conversion data for up to 125 items. (The publisher indicates this was an error not caught in the proofreading.)

The other subtests also vary in their level of difficulty, as indicated by the variability of the percentile rank associated with the chance score. The chance score for the Academic Aptitude total score is 24, which corresponds to the third percentile, whereas the chance score for the spelling subtest is 20 which corresponds to the 21st percentile rank. The Reading Comprehension and Information in the Natural Sciences subtests have chance scores corresponding to the seventh and fifth percentile ranks, respectively.

The percentile rank conversions are based on performance by a norming sample that initially had 2,632 applicants from 64 programs (39 associate degree and 25 diploma) from across the United States. It is noted that this sample represents an unknown percentage of the applicants to programs, but that between August, 1978, and June, 1979, there were approximately 76,000 students admitted to such programs. These are the only dates provided relative to the norming sample. (A call to the publisher indicated the data from the norming sample were collected in 1983–84 and that norms are updated periodically.)

The data in the tables used to convert from raw scores to percentile ranks and data describing the characteristics of the norming sample are actually on a reduced sample of 2,170 examinees. The lower figure was due to attrition of some schools. There is no indication of where or what type of schools were dropped from the original sample, thus no indication of the extent of potential bias in the sample.

Information on the standard error of measurement and standard error of the mean for each subtest is presented for each of the five subtests separately. These statistics are presented in such a way as to imply that they are based on the entire norm sample. The standard error of measurement is, in fact, based on a sample of 119 examinees described later in the manual in the section on test reliability. The representativeness of these 119 examinees to the norming sample is doubtful. The standard error of the mean is explained as a statistic to help the user evaluate the quality of the sample of schools. Almost the entire discussion of the standard error of the mean is specious and misleading, in part because the statistic is computed using number of examinees (based on information given this reviewer in a telephone conversation with the publisher) as a base instead of number of schools (as is implied in the manual).

There is discussion about the comparability of norm group performance for special populations and the need for special norms for subpopulations. No separate norms are provided for men, or for racial or ethnic minorities. The manual reports that such norms were developed but they did not differ significantly from the "heterogeneous applicant population" (p. 29). No information about sample sizes or statistical methodology for comparing the two sets of norms is provided.

In addition to percentile ranks a table for converting raw scores to stanines is also provided. It is implied in the manual that stanines can be interpreted as a ratio scale. It is not clear how stanines are useful in prediction, but it is notable that the chance score on spelling is at the fourth stanine.

Reliability, as noted above, was assessed by administering a retest to 119 examinees using a time interval between 10 and 30 days. There is no indication of where the examinees came from nor if their initial testing was done in conjunction with the standardization study. The manual indicates the sample of 119 examinees is representative of the population of applicants, yet their average academic aptitude score on the initial administration is at the 70th percentile rank. No data are provided on the second testing (i.e., means and standard deviations are from the initial testing only). The manual indicates there was no significant mean gain as a result of practice effect. The data shown suggest that an error might have been made in reporting the results for several subtests. Given the intercorrelations among subtests, the high Aptitude score would seem to indicate that the mean score on Reading Comprehension should be above the reported value of the 26th percentile rank. Average scores on the other two academically oriented subtests (Spelling and Information on Natural Sciences) were at the 56th and 60th percentile ranks, respectively. (The publisher, in a telephone call, indicated that an error may have been made in the table, but to discover it would require reanalyzing the original data.)

Reliabilities are extremely high—ranging from .92 to .98. Given the nature of the sample (higher than average academic ability) and the existence of admitted errors in descriptive statistics, the generalizability of the reported coefficients is doubtful.

The discussion of reliability includes a table showing reliability of difference scores across subtests and the intercorrelations among subtests. The authors suggest the intercorrelations among subtests are low, thus demonstrating that each subtest is providing unique information. Of the four academically oriented subtests, the intercorrelations range from a low of .63 (Academic Aptitude with Spelling) to a high of .86 (Academic Aptitude with Information in the Natural Sciences). Shared variances ranging from 40% to nearly 74% do not seem to this reviewer to deem any of these measures unique.

The crux of the information about utility of this test is related to its validity; particularly its predictive validity. There is discussion of the content- and construct-related validity of the test, but because the principal use of scores is to predict success in associate degree or diploma programs for registered nurses, the predictive validity is of utmost importance. Additional problems arise in this section of the technical manual, too. The predictive validity data are based on data from schools that participated in the standardization sample (reminding one of the lesson taught in Cureton's classic article "Reliability, Validity, Baloney" not to use the same sample for estimating both reliability and validity). One criterion used for estimating validity coefficients was cumulative grade-point average (CGPA). The manual indicates that CGPA was collected by the schools (not all schools used the same method of grade assignment, thus many grade reports had to be "translated uniformly into a numerical value" [technical manual, p. 36]). The CGPA was collected at 6-month, 1-year, and 2-year time intervals. The subtest scores were correlated with CGPA to provide validity estimates. It is implied that several estimates were computed, perhaps one for each school. It is not clear how many estimates were based on each of the time periods for which CGPA were collected. (The publisher indicated, by phone, that the criterion was CGPA, but gave no specific answer to the question related to the exact time frame for collection of the criterion. This is important because as the time frame extends the sample of students tends to get smaller due to attrition, and the correlations will be influenced by the change in sample.) A table of average correlations is given, as is the interval plus and minus one standard deviation around that average correlation. There are errors in that table. It is reported that the average correlation between academic aptitude and CGPA is .89, but the range of correlations around that average is .23 to .76. In response to a telephone inquiry, the publisher indicated that all correlations were corrected for attenuation. It is possible that only the average was corrected, thus creating the totally unbelievable data shown in Table 17 of the technical manual. The average validity coefficients reported range from .69 to .89. These values are extraordinarily high. The authors correctly caution the reader that there is variation across various schools and programs.

Similarly, rank in graduating class data were available for 120 of the 2,100+ examinees in the standardization sample. Each subtest score was correlated with the rank in class for these examinees; the correlations ranged from .66 to .88. (These correlations were apparently corrected for attenuation also—as per telephone conversation with the publisher—although there is no indication of such a correction discussed in the manual.) As noted above, these correlations are remarkably high. Validity coefficients were also computed between the subtests and scores on licensure examinations. These correlations (also apparently corrected for attenuation) ranged from .72 to .93 for a sample of 103 examinees.

The predictive validity evidence is impressive, but almost too good to be true. The omissions (e.g., failing to report that correlations are corrected for attenuation) and errors in the manual suggest extreme caution be used in applying the results reported to any school.

In an undated memorandum addressed to "Fellow Professional" from Anna S. Evans, the principal author, cut scores for admission are recommended for each subtest. No empirical data justifying the cut scores are provided. Of the cut scores recommended, the one for Spelling is at the chance level. All recommended cut scores are between the 20th and 25th percentile rank based on the standardization sample. It is correctly recommended that the "best" cut scores are those developed based on local experience.

In summary, there are numerous errors, omissions, and inconsistencies included in the technical manual that raise questions about the accuracy of the data reported relative the reliability and validity of this test battery. However, the nature of the test and the data reported suggest that it may have utility for predicting success for nursing students. The nature of the intercorrelations among subtests suggests that administration of the entire battery may be excessive; sufficient information about an applicant's potential for success may be obtained by administering only the Academic Aptitude subtest or the Information in the Natural Sciences subtest.

[314]
PSB-Reading Comprehension Examination.

Purpose: "To reveal the student's comprehension or understanding of what he or she reads."
Population: Secondary and postsecondary students applying to or enrolled in terminal vocational or occupational programs.
Publication Dates: 1978–87.
Scores: Total score only.
Administration: Group.
Price Data, 1988: $5 per test booklet; $3 per student for answer sheet and scoring and reporting service; $10 per technical manual ('80, 50 pages); $8 per specimen set including test booklet, answer sheet, and administrator's manual ('78, 5 pages).
Time: 30(40) minutes.

Author: Psychological Services Bureau, Inc.
Publisher: Psychological Services Bureau, Inc.

Review of the PSB-Reading Comprehension Examination by JOSEPH C. CIECHALSKI, Assistant Professor of Counselor Education, East Carolina University, Greenville, NC:

The PSB-Reading Comprehension Examination is a Level A test (i.e., a test that can be administered and interpreted with the materials provided by the publisher) designed to measure understanding of what is read. It was constructed for students interested in enrolling in an occupational or paraprofessional career program.

The test consists of four reading passages of between 325 and 450 words. Each reading passage is followed by either 10 or 15 multiple-choice items (with four options) for a total of 50 items. In examining the items, this reviewer found that 90% of them appeared to be dependent on the reading passages. Therefore, the test appears to measure reading comprehension rather than general knowledge.

ADMINISTRATION AND SCORING. Directions for administering the test are presented in the Administrator's Manual and test booklet. The directions in the Administrator's Manual are detailed, yet easy to follow.

The time limit of 30 minutes was designed to allow most of the students time to complete. Examinees are informed in the general directions of the test booklet that they are not expected to answer all of the items.

The examinees use a separate answer sheet to record their responses. These answer sheets are scored by the publisher, and the results are returned using a "Class Record and Report Sheet" and the "Student Test Record and Profile Chart."

STANDARDIZATION AND NORMS. The general standardization population contained 3,654 students. In terms of grade level, the norming population represented persons who attained between 8th and 16th grade levels. Population ages ranged from 16 to 60 years. In addition, 52.6% of the population were males and 47.7% were females.

Special norms were provided for practical/vocational nursing programs. These norms were based on a sample of 3,213 individuals drawn from nine regions in the United States. Out of 1,316 schools contacted, 265 were represented. These included adult schools, colleges, community and junior colleges, vocational-technical schools, hospitals, and public and private schools.

According to the technical manual, minority groups comprised 16% of the general norms and 13% of the special norms. The authors state that, before actual publication, the test "was reviewed by members of different ethnic groups for possible offensive, stereotyped, culturally restricted, or racialist material."

Local norms may be prepared by the publisher. However, the publisher believes the general national norms give more useful information than local norms.

RELIABILITY. Test-retest reliability was reported for 324 cases as .95 over a 15-to-30-day time interval. A standard error of measurement of 3.5 was also reported in this category.

Split-half reliability was not reported. The authors address this issue by claiming that split-half reliability results in an "overestimate of reliability." The authors explain their reasoning further in the technical manual. Additional evidence of reliability is needed.

VALIDITY. Evidence of concurrent validity was demonstrated by correlating the test with the Preliminary Scholastic Aptitude Test ($n = 203$) which resulted in a coefficient of .89. A coefficient of .93 was reported using both the PSB-Aptitude for Practical Nursing Examination ($n = 78$) and the School and College Ability Test ($n = 213$). Using the Reading Comprehension subtest of the Nelson-Denny Reading Test ($n = 123$), a coefficient of .73 was reported. A coefficient of .71 was reported using the Otis Quick Scoring Mental Ability Test ($n = 152$).

Predictive validity was established using data provided by a vocational technical school. Using overall GPA and State Board scores as the criteria, the correlations of .87 and .85 were reported respectively ($n = 124$). For three cosmetology programs, a correlation coefficient of .91 was reported using the scores obtained from a state licensing examination ($n = 127$).

Construct validity was not specifically reported. The authors view construct validity as a "generalized concept" that is included in other types of validity. They also state this examination has "some" content validity.

INTERPRETATION AND SCORING. The scores are reported as raw scores and percentiles using the "Class Record and Report Sheet" and the "Student Test Record and Profile Chart." These forms are very easy to use and understand. For example, using the "Student Test Record and Profile Chart," examinees who scored below the 25th percentile or above the 75th percentile can be readily identified. In addition, the technical manual adequately describes the use of percentiles.

Stanines can be found for individuals in terminal vocational and practical nursing programs using the tables provided in the technical manual.

SUMMARY. Test items depend upon the information obtained from the passages, thus the test appears to be a valid measure of reading comprehension. However, additional research regarding the reliability of this instrument is needed. An alternate form would have been useful in establishing reliability. Therefore, until additional reliability data are provided, I would recommend this test be used for its intended purpose but with some caution.

Review of the PSB-Reading Comprehension Examination by BRANDON DAVIS, Research Fellow, Ball State Neuropsychology Laboratory, and JOHN A. GLOVER, Director of Research, Teachers College, Ball State University, Muncie, IN:

The PSB-Reading Comprehension Examination is suggested by its authors to be a Level A assessment device. It is designed specifically for students who are enrolled, or who have intentions of being enrolled, in terminal occupational postsecondary education programs (e.g., landscape technologists, legal secretaries, dental laboratory technicians, etc.). As such, this test has the very singular purpose of assessing levels of reading comprehension with such students and, as stated in the manual, users of the test are advised against using the test with other population groups for other assessment purposes. The test has a 30-minute time limit and consists of four passages with 50 accompanying questions. One assessment score is obtained that is translatable into accompanying percentiles. Computer scoring also is available from the publisher.

The publishers present a modest, yet well-defined, rationale of their intentions for this measure. They suggest the measure will be useful in the selection process of students interested in vocationally oriented courses. The measure also is offered as a potential screening device for possible interventions with those students who score below the 40th percentile. However, the measure was not designed as a diagnostic reading test. The publisher has indicated that the test measures the examinee's ability: (*a*) to understand direct statements; (*b*) to interpret passages; (*c*) to see the intent of those writing passages; (*d*) to observe the organization of ideas; and (*e*) to extract information from passages with respect to ideas and purposes. Although the test does have a 30-minute time limit and technically may be referred to as a "speed test," the publishers intend the measure to be used as a "power test." Previous administrations have determined 90% of the norm-group examinees completed the test in the allowed time.

The strength of any norm-referenced measure is its technical sophistication. In this regard, the material presented in the PSB-Reading Comprehension Examination manual provides a more than adequate basis for psychometric review. The test is based on 3 years of study and research, having been subjected to a series of tryouts, analyses, and revisions. The end result is a test that has a 4-passage/50-question format. The passages range from 325 to 450 words in length and were, according to the manual, based on textbooks used by students in vocational programs. Unfortunately, the manual does not provide a referenced list of examined textbooks, nor some indication of the "readability" (if, in fact, this was determined) of the textbooks upon which the passages were based. Further, the manual reveals that all passage material was reviewed by "authorities" in the field of reading; however, there are no accompanying citations, nor an indication of the criticisms and suggestions made by these authorities.

Actual standardization procedures were undertaken with a fairly large group of examinees for whom the test was intended. Sampling was carried out in nine broadly defined areas of the United States with four distinct community population sizes: Rural, Suburban, Urban I, and Urban II (i.e., more than 100,000). Also taken into consideration were varieties of schools, programs, ages, types of course instruction, and socioeconomic status. Students' grade levels ranged from grade 8 to grade 16, with approximately 83% of the students having 11 to 13 years of education. Ages in the sample ranged from 16 to 60 years, with approximately 60% of the sample in the 16–20-year bracket. Of the total sample, 52.6% were males and 47.4% were females. Minority representation was not specifically included in the sample; however, a post-hoc analysis by the publishers suggested approximately 16% of the sample were minorities. The manual also provides a section on norms for special populations and mentions the publisher's offer to assist those interested in developing local norms.

Test-retest reliability ($N = 324$), the only reliability function quoted in the manual, was .95 with a mean raw score of 26.95, an SD of 15.65, and an SEM of 3.50. Formal selection procedures were not undertaken to establish content validity. The publishers justify this anomaly because the materials are representative of textbooks judged to be appropriate by a group of "experts."

Concurrent validity, however, was given a more appropriate evaluation by the authors. The PSB-Reading Comprehension Examination was compared to the verbal subtests of the Preliminary Scholastic Aptitude Test (PSAT) and the PSB-Aptitude for Practical Nursing Examination, and with the comprehension subtest of the Nelson-Denny Reading Test. Pearson product-moment correlations were .89 and .73 respectively for first and last mentioned comparisons.

Based on the previous and other samples, predictive validities are offered, which range between .91 and .85, between the measure and both grade-point averages and state examinations. Unfortunately, these latter mentioned tests are poorly referenced.

In sum, this test is a viable assessment device for those persons involved in selection procedures at vocational schools. The norming procedures, although not necessarily complete, offer good evidence of the measure's reliability and validity. From a technical standpoint the book is poorly referenced. However, the publishers of the PSB-Reading Comprehension Examination have succeeded in developing a test for a very select population, and quite appropriately portray its limitations for populations other than those for whom it is intended. Taken in this vein, the test represents an appropriate choice for reviewing the reading comprehension abilities of students applying for vocational programs.

REVIEWER'S REFERENCES

Educational Testing Service. (1970). Preliminary Scholastic Aptitude Test. Princeton, NJ: Educational Testing Service.
Evans, A. S., Yanuzzi, J. R., & Stouffer, G. A. (1972). Aptitude Test for Practical Nursing Examination. St. Thomas, PA: Psychological Services Bureau.
Educational Testing Service. (1973). School and College Ability Test. Princeton, NJ: Educational Testing Service.
Brown, J. I., Nelson, M. J., & Denny, E. C. (1976). Nelson-Denny Reading Test. Boston, MA: Houghton Mifflin.

[315]

The Psychap Inventory.

Purpose: Measures how happy an individual is as a person in order to help one understand how to "get more happiness and satisfaction from life."
Population: Adolescents and adults.
Publication Dates: 1971–85.
Acronym: PHI.
Scores, 5: Achieved Happiness, Happy Personality, Happy Attitudes and Values, Happiness Life-Style, Total.
Administration: Group.
Forms: 2 sets of equivalent forms: Set 1 (Forms A and B), Set 2 (Forms C and D).
Price Data, 1988: Available from publisher for 4 color-coded testing booklets, answer sheets, scoring stencils, general interpretation sheet, administration and scoring directions sheets, copy of the article "Psychap Inventory" which serves as a manual, and complete computer program including diskette and information for administration, scoring, and interpretive reporting.
Time: (10–15) minutes per form.
Comments: IBM or compatible with 64K and 1 single-sided drive required for administration of microdiskette version.
Author: Michael W. Fordyce.
Publisher: Cypress Lake Media.

Review of The Psychap Inventory by GEORGE ENGELHARD, JR., Associate Professor of Educational Studies, Emory University, Atlanta, GA:

The Psychap Inventory (PHI) is a self-report instrument developed by Michael W. Fordyce to measure personal happiness. There are two sets of alternate forms available; Set 1 (Forms A and B) is the original and most researched set, and Set 2 (Forms C and D) was added later in order to produce a wider range of response by including more extreme response alternatives.

There are 80 items in each form, and items consist of two paired statements that describe a characteristic believed to distinguish between a happy and unhappy person; for example, "I am content" is paired with "I am not content." In addition to a total score on the PHI, scores from four subscales are also provided: Achieved Personal Happiness Scale (16 items), Happy Personality Scale (24 items), Happiness Attitudes and Values Scale (19 items), and Happiness Life-Style Scale (21 items).

The PHI was previously called the Self Description Inventory. A technical manual is not available; however, an article by Fordyce (1985) and a Supplement (Fordyce, 1987) with numerous summary tables are provided. The items in the PHI were developed on the basis of earlier reviews of the literature that led to the identification of the characteristics of "happy individuals." Responses to a pool of items were correlated with a two-item measure of happiness (Fordyce, 1977) and the Depression Adjective Checklist (Lubin, 1967) in order to select the final set of items. According to the author, the PHI is designed for use in research, counseling, and clinical assessment. The author also recommends its use as a diagnostic instrument to identify "strengths and weaknesses" related to happiness which are directly associated with Fordyce's "fourteen fundamentals to increase personal happiness" program (Fordyce, 1981).

The PHI has been used primarily with community college students in Florida. The normative data, as well as most of the technical evidence for the PHI, are based almost exclusively on this population. This is not necessarily a major weakness, but does need to be kept in mind by the potential user. The potential user also needs to be warned about problems with the Supplement; a great deal of data are presented (over 400 pages of tables) and the tables are poorly organized. For example, the correlations over time between Forms A and B are reported in the chronological order in which the studies were conducted, rather than by length of time between testings. A major improvement would be to add summaries to the tables which might include the median correlations and ranges over the data reported. A technical manual that summarizes the relevant information and integrates the validity studies would be even more helpful to the user. The Supplement, as currently presented, tends to be more of a hindrance than a help in evaluating the PHI.

Preliminary norms are based on samples of 1,437 community college students for Forms A and B, and 527 students for Forms C and D. Means and standard deviations are also presented in the Supplement for other selected populations, such as married individuals, retired businessmen, lesbians in professional careers, and college professors. Although most of the examinees are from Florida, Fordyce (1985) indicates that he has presented a "somewhat representative cross-section of adult Americans" (p. 24). This claim for national representativeness is not adequately documented.

No estimates of the internal consistency of the PHI are presented. The test-retest correlations for each form and subscales are also not reported. These are serious weaknesses making it impossible to judge the reliability of the PHI and the appropriate standard errors to use with the scores. It is somewhat surprising this evidence is not provided, given the extensive data which are presented for the correlations between forms. Short-term and long-term equivalent forms reliabilities are fairly high. Short-term equivalent forms correlations average around .92 (same testing session to a week interval); the correlations between forms over longer time periods are typical for instruments of this type with average correlations of about .86 (2- to 3-week interval) and .74 (3-month interval).

Fordyce (1985, 1987) reports on an extensive set of validity studies. In terms of convergent validity, the PHI correlates positively with other measures of happiness and negatively with a variety of indices of depression. The concurrent validity also appears to be adequate, with the PHI correlating with other personality characteristics that the literature on subjective well-being (Diener, 1984) suggests as being associated with happiness. Overall, the evidence for the validity of the PHI is fairly strong in terms of its correlations with other self-report inventories of various personality characteristics, such as the Minnesota Multiphasic Personality Inventory (Hathaway & McKinley, 1951), Edwards Personal Preference Schedule (Edwards, 1959), and the Myers-Briggs Type Indicator (Myers, 1962).

An important question that is not addressed is whether or not the classification of the items into subscales of the PHI makes any sense. Either a content validity study or an item factor analysis (Bock, Gibbons, & Muraki, 1988) would contribute to our knowledge regarding the internal structure of the PHI. Without this type of information, it is not clear that the classification of the items into subscales is based on anything other than the whim of the author.

In the section on the comparability of forms, Fordyce (1985) claims that the forms can be considered as being "identical," and he later suggests the forms be used in "tandem (since no two are identical), especially in time series and repeated measures designs" (p. 9), and in the "monitoring or follow-up assessment of programs" (p. 26). Given the differences in the means and standard deviations between the forms, they are clearly *not* comparable. If different forms were used in a time series study, it would not be possible to separate form effects from individual changes in happiness over time. Further, an unscrupulous evaluator could use Form D ($M =$ 45.39 for the normative sample) for the pretest where scores tend to be lower on the average, and then use Form A ($M = 55.16$ for the normative sample) for the posttest on which the examinees are likely to have higher scores regardless of any program effects. This can be resolved by using standard scores and equating the four forms onto an equal interval scale.

In summary, much of the early work on subjective well-being arose from survey research conducted with various indicators of the quality of life. Some of the earlier measures of "happiness" were single items included in larger surveys (Diener, 1984). The PHI represents significant progress over this work and represents a step towards the development of an instrument to measure important aspects of individual happiness. Although the PHI appears to offer a promising measure of self-reported levels of well-being, the lack of evidence regarding reliability (internal consistency estimates and test-retest correlations) is a serious weakness. The validity coefficients are comparable to those found for similar self-report inventories of personality characteristics. In spite of the strong buy-this-instrument and enroll-in-my-program tone that permeates the material, the PHI should be considered by researchers interested in the assessment of subjective well-being. The evidence presented does not support the usefulness of the PHI for counseling or clinical assessment.

REVIEWER'S REFERENCES

Hathaway, S. R., & McKinley, J. C. (1951). Minnesota Multiphasic Personality Inventory. San Antonio, TX: The Psychological Corporation.
Edwards, A. L. (1959). Edwards Personal Preference Schedule. San Antonio, TX: The Psychological Corporation.
Myers, I. (1962). Myers-Briggs Type Indicator. Palo Alto, CA: Consulting Psychologists Press, Inc.
Lubin, B. (1967). Depression Adjective Check List. San Diego, CA: EdITS/Educational and Industrial Testing Service.
Fordyce, M. W. (1977). Development of a program to increase personal happiness. Journal of Counseling Psychology, 24, 511-521.
Fordyce, M. W. (1981). The psychology of happiness: A brief version of the fourteen fundamentals. Fort Myers, FL: Cypress Lake Media.
Diener, E. (1984). Subjective well-being. Psychological Bulletin, 95, 542-575.
Fordyce, M. W. (1985). The Psychap Inventory: A multi-scale test to measure happiness and its concomitants. Social Indicators Research, 18, 1-33.
Fordyce, M. W. (1987). Research and tabular supplement for the Psychap Inventory. Fort Myers, FL: Cypress Lake Media.
Bock, R. D., Gibbons, R., & Muraki, E. (1988). Full-information item factor analysis. Applied Psychological Measurement, 12, 261-280.

Review of The Psychap Inventory by ALFRED L. SMITH, JR., Personnel Psychologist, Federal Aviation Administration, U.S. Department of Transportation, Washington, DC:

The Psychap Inventory purports to be a multidimensional measure of the full range of happiness characteristics and its major concomitants. At first glance, a measure of "happiness" seems overly simplistic and lacking sufficient merit to warrant much attention. This idea was reinforced by the test materials which have spelling, typographical, and grammatical errors, and seemingly naive or obvious

comments on the profiles and reports that are to be given to the test taker. For example, test takers are told how their scores compare to those who "score happily," and that those who get a high score are "probably a pretty happy person because of" their similarity to the "happiest people." It is likely that people who might be given this inventory can as easily tell their therapist about their happiness or unhappiness as they can complete the inventory. Voluntary clients are likely to be fairly willing to do so and involuntary clients probably can fake the answers either way.

On second glance and careful review of Fordyce (1985), the journal article which serves as the only manual for the instrument, there does appear to be considerable value to using The Psychap in some circumstances. Most notable of these is for the situation for which it was developed—as a diagnostic tool for use in conjunction with a prescriptive program for increased happiness. The author, of course, hopes users of the inventory will also use his program for building happiness. Inventory items were designed to mesh with this program, and so to identify specific areas where a person can take steps to become more satisfied (e.g., developing relationships with people, self-knowledge and self-acceptance, or a more optimistic outlook).

It is likely that this inventory can be more helpful than interview techniques in helping people to pinpoint strengths and weaknesses contributing to their own sense of happiness, well-being, or self-satisfaction, and to set goals and objectives for positive change. Development of The Psychap is based on a firm empirical base. Clearly, considerable time and effort have gone into the identification of what constitutes and is concomitant to happiness and how to measure it. The instrument contains conceptually developed subscales covering four aspects: Achieved Personal Happiness, Happy Personality, Happiness Attitudes and Values, and Happiness Life-Style.

Extensive research reported in the journal article/manual provides information about the instrument's reliability and validity. Two sets of alternate forms exist (A–B and C–D). Within each set, alternate forms reliability (called test-retest by the author) is high. No attempt has been made to identify the two sets as equivalent, because C and D were specifically designed to eliminate response bias by creating more extreme items. Means obtained on C and D are consistently lower across studies. Review of the items clearly shows that some are so extreme that almost no one could pick the "happy" alternative. Perhaps a better approach to understanding response bias would be to examine results obtained under instructions to "fake happy" or "fake unhappy."

The author has gone to considerable length to examine the construct validity of the inventory by looking at convergent and divergent validity using concurrent administration of a lengthy number of personality instruments. Evidence is provided of positive relationships between scores on The Psychap and such things as extroversion, emotional stability, and vitality. There are strong negative relationships between happiness scores and negative emotions such as hostility, depression, and anxiety. Reliability and validity data reported in Fordyce (1985) are easily comprehended, but the cumbersome and unwieldy tables provided with the test materials are of little help to instrument evaluation for clinical use (although one might appreciate them for research use). Although norms are available, both Fordyce and this reviewer agree more work on norms is needed.

Fordyce has concluded, based on the research with The Psychap and other research, that happiness is so basic a personality factor that attempts to measure it by almost any means will be successful (even, as suggested early in this review, just by asking people). This is probably true. One could probably use almost any of the personality instruments against which The Psychap was evaluated. The latter has the advantage, however, of being less threatening as the issue is "happiness," not "self-concept" or "personality" or negative-toned concepts such as "depression," and wording and content of the items reflect this. As stated earlier, it also has the advantage of items and subscales of items geared toward specific focuses for change.

In summary, The Psychap Inventory has been well-researched and considerable effort has been expended to ensure it covers the full domain of that which goes along with and/or characterizes happiness. Thus, it appears to have acceptable psychometric properties. It provides a fairly nonthreatening way to identify such things as values, attitudes, characteristics, and behaviors that directly contribute to a person's happiness and/or satisfaction (or lack thereof), and is likely to be of use in counseling normal populations. Test materials need to be brought up to professional standards, however, including a concise manual to replace the lengthy journal article currently serving as a manual.

REVIEWER'S REFERENCE

Fordyce, M. W. (1985). The Psychap Inventory: A multi-scale test to measure happiness and its concomitants. *Social Indicators Research*, 18, 1-33.

[316]
Psychiatric Diagnostic Interview—Revised.

Purpose: "Designed to determine if an individual is suffering, or has ever suffered, from a major psychiatric disorder."
Population: Ages 18 and older.
Publication Date: 1989.
Acronym: PDI-R.

Scores, 21: 17 basic syndromes: Organic Brain Syndrome (OB), Alcoholism (Al), Drug Abuse (Dr), Depression (De), Mania (Ma), Schizophrenia (Sc), Antisocial Personality (As), Somatization Disorder (So), Anorexia Nervosa (AN), Bulimia (Bu), Post-Traumatic Stress Disorder (PS), Obsessive-Compulsive Disorder (OC), Phobic Disorder (Ph), Panic Disorder (Pa), Generalized Anxiety (GA), Mental Retardation (MR), Adjustment Disorder (Ad), and 4 derived syndromes: Polydrug Abuse (Poly), Schizoaffective Disorder (Sc-Af), Manic-Depressive Disorder (Ma-De), Bulimarexia (Bu-AN).
Administration: Individual.
Price Data, 1991: $110 per complete kit including reusable administration booklet, 25 recording booklets, and manual (174 pages); $55 per administration booklet; $17.50 per 25 recording booklets; $42.50 per manual; $215 per microcomputer disk (IBM).
Time: (15–30) minutes for normals; (60) minutes for those with 2 or more syndromes.
Comments: Computer-assisted interview is available along with scoring and recording instructions.
Authors: Ekkehard Othmer, Elizabeth C. Penick, Barbara J. Powell, Marsha R. Read, and Sieglinde C. Othmer.
Publisher: Western Psychological Services.

TEST REFERENCES

1. Powell, B. J., Penick, E. C., Liskow, B. I., Rice, A. S., & McKnelly, W. (1986). Lithium compliance in alcoholic males: A six month followup study. *Addictive Behaviors, 11*, 135-140.
2. Larson, L. M. (1989). Problem-solving appraisal in an alcoholic population. *Journal of Counseling Psychology, 36*, 73-78.
3. Streiner, D. L., & Miller, H. R. (1990). Maximum likelihood estimates of the accuracy of four diagnostic techniques. *Educational and Psychological Measurement, 50*, 653-662.

Review of the Psychiatric Diagnostic Interview—Revised by BRIAN BOLTON, Professor, Arkansas Research and Training Center in Vocational Rehabilitation, University of Arkansas, Fayetteville, AR:

The revised Psychiatric Diagnostic Interview (PDI-R) is a structured interview that evaluates 17 basic syndromes and four derived syndromes. Its purpose is to determine whether an examinee is suffering or has ever suffered from a major psychiatric disorder. The questions that compose each of the 17 basic syndromes are organized into four sections that are administered sequentially. If the critical symptoms in any section are not present, the remaining sections are omitted. Because the PDI-R is a criterion-referenced instrument, there are no norms. However, base rates for the syndromes and diagnoses are given for various populations.

The administrative format of the PDI-R parallels the strategy used by skilled clinicians, beginning with very general questions and moving to increasingly specific questions, but only if earlier questions suggest the presence of a disorder. The four levels of assessment in the PDI-R are: Cardinal questions, Social Significance questions, Auxiliary questions, and Time Profile questions. The Time Profile questions identify the age of onset and the duration of the symptoms. After all 17 basic syndromes are reviewed, a current diagnosis and a lifetime diagnosis are established.

The PDI-R is based on the traditional assumption that psychiatric disorders are discrete categories. It follows that diagnosis is a classification problem, rather than a measurement task. The hierarchical ordering of the 21 basic and derived syndromes, which assumes that certain syndromes take precedence over others, and the time profile information provide the foundation for differential diagnosis with the PDI-R. Comparative studies support the validity of the PDI-R diagnostic strategy.

The median number of questions in each of the four sections forming the 17 basic syndromes are: Cardinal (2), Social Significance (7), Auxiliary (20), and Time Profile (4). Clearly, a substantial reduction in administration time may result if the questioning for any syndrome is terminated after the Cardinal section or the Social Significance section. Considering the small number of positive syndromes that actually occur in samples of hospitalized medical patients ($M = .26$), psychiatric outpatients ($M = 1.85$), and hospitalized psychiatric patients ($M = 2.51$), it is apparent that the PDI-R's process of contingent questioning provides a comprehensive evaluation with great economy of effort.

The original PDI was constructed to operationalize the Feighner diagnostic criteria developed by a team of researchers at the Washington University School of Medicine in the late 1960s. Publication of the third edition of the *Diagnostic and Statistical Manual of Mental Disorders* (*DSM-III*) in 1980 necessitated a revision of the PDI. Two of the original syndromes were deleted (Homosexuality and Transsexualism) and four syndromes were added (Bulimia, Post-Traumatic Stress Disorder, Generalized Anxiety, and Adjustment Disorder). To further increase the correspondence between the PDI-R and *DSM-III* diagnostic categories, the criteria used to define PDI-R syndromes were modified and interview questions were added. Because the validity of the PDI-R depends in good part on studies conducted with the original PDI, all changes should be specified in the manual.

The PDI-R was designed to be administered by a carefully trained and supervised graduate student or psychiatric technician. Using either the paper-and-pencil version or the computer-assisted version, the PDI-R can be readily administered to most examinees. Like all structured interviews, the PDI-R is essentially a self-report assessment, thus requiring considerable judgment by the examiner. Thorough training including supervised practice is especially critical with an interview that uses a "skip out" or contingent procedure, because evaluation of syndromes may be prematurely terminated if the decision is wrong. The manual properly advises continuation to the next section when in doubt.

With the paper-and-pencil version of the PDI-R, scoring is accomplished simultaneously with the administration of the syndromes. The manual provides detailed guidelines with examples for scoring each of the 17 syndromes. A series of tables may be used to translate PDI-R results into *DSM-III* and Revised *DSM-III* diagnoses. The computer-assisted interview, which includes automatic branching, scores all syndromes, generates current and lifetime diagnoses, and converts PDI-R responses to *DSM-III* and *DSM-III-R* diagnoses.

Because the reliability and validity of the PDI-R could be inferred from relevant studies of the original PDI-R, if the two instruments were determined to be measuring the same constructs, it was important to establish the diagnostic concordance of the two editions. The median agreement for the 13 basic syndromes common to both interviews was 96% and identical diagnoses were obtained in 80% of cases. In another study, seven expert judges rated the PDI-R's implementation of the *DSM-III*'s diagnostic criteria for comparable disorders to be uniformly good for all syndromes except Organic Brain Syndrome.

Reliability studies of the original PDI produced the following results: (*a*) six judges agreed perfectly on the current and lifetime diagnoses and syndrome scoring for four patients; (*b*) four of the judges were in perfect agreement 3 months later with their earlier diagnoses and scoring and with each other; (*c*) test/retest agreement for syndrome identification with a 6-week interval between interviews was 93%; diagnostic agreement ranged from 67% to 93%, depending on whether categories were combined; and (*d*) syndrome identification agreement of between 66% to 92% and diagnostic agreement ranging from 70% to 100% against an extended or complete administration (i.e., all questions were asked) supported the reliability of the PDI "skip out" or branching format.

Because the PDI-R was developed to implement previously established diagnostic guidelines in a standardized format, the validity of the instrument is a function of the correspondence between the symptomatic criteria and the interview questions constituting the PDI-R syndromes. In other words, validity depends upon how accurately the clinical standards were translated into PDI-R questions. Research indicates substantial diagnostic agreement between the PDI-R and psychiatrists using conventional examination procedures.

Four validity investigations of the original PDI produced these findings: (*a*) the PDI diagnoses for psychiatric inpatients agreed (78% to 82%) with the diagnoses given by a psychiatrist, (*b*) the PDI diagnoses for outpatients agreed (63% to 84%) with those rendered by psychiatric residents, (*c*) the PDI correctly identified 90% of the cases in eight diagnostic reference groups, and (*d*) the PDI and the Diagnostic Interview Schedule agreed on syndrome identification (91%) and current diagnosis (79%). Because of the demonstrated similarity between the PDI and the PDI-R, these data by extension strongly support the diagnostic validity of the PDI-R.

SUMMARY. The PDI-R is a carefully developed structured interview for evaluating psychiatric patients. Its goal is to establish the presence or absence of 17 major psychiatric disorders. The PDI-R provides a comprehensive, standardized assessment that may be converted to *DSM-III* and *DSM-III-R* diagnostic categories. The manual is exemplary, with thorough explanations of the rationale, construction, and technical studies conducted, as well as detailed directions for administration and scoring. The reliability and validity evidence support the clinical utility of the instrument. It can be concluded that the PDI-R is a highly efficient screening procedure that generates diagnostic information potentially useful in treatment planning.

Review of the Psychiatric Diagnostic Interview— Revised by PETER F. MERENDA, Professor Emeritus of Psychology and Statistics, University of Rhode Island, Kingston, RI:

The Psychiatric Diagnostic Interview—Revised (PDI-R) was originally published in 1981 and revised in 1989. The accompanying revised manual, which is both comprehensive and extensive (155 pages) was prepared by only one of the three original coauthors, Elizabeth C. Penick. The PDI-R is a structured diagnostic interview technique designed to complement a clinician's use of the *Diagnostic and Statistical Manual of Mental Disorders, 3rd Edition (DSM-III)*. The current revised form includes several modifications in the number and kinds of syndromes reviewed by the instrument as compared to the original PDI. There have also been changes in the criteria used to define the various syndromes as well as the addition of specific items or questions. However, the basic underlying theoretical rationale and format of the instrument remain unchanged. The modifications and the theoretical foundations appear to have a sound basis, and for these the authors are to be complimented. It is also heartening to realize that the major work, original and revisional, was accomplished twice within a decade.

Because the instrument has been designed to determine whether an individual is suffering or has ever suffered from a major psychiatric disorder, its use is limited to highly sophisticated and well-trained (generally speaking) clinicians as well as those who have also been trained specifically in its application and limitations. Although the manual does explain the steps that should be taken for the reliable and ethical applications of the PDI-R, there

is no indication that either the authors or the publisher are making any significant effort to restrict sales only to those persons who have demonstrated competence in its use. In fact, in the publisher's order form, the only pertinent information regarding a purchaser's qualifications is "highest academic degree." Furthermore, so much information is given in the manual regarding scoring and interpretation of the instrument, and case studies as well, that unqualified buyers could use the manual as a "cook book." A computer-assisted version, complete with a microcomputer test report, is available to anyone, presumably, who states on the order form that he or she possesses a master's or docotal degree *in any field*!

Regarding standardization procedures and the psychometric properties possessed by the PDI-R, it is difficult to evaluate these from the information and data given and not given in the manual. For instance, were the items and questions tried out on representative samples of adults, 18 years or older? If so, who were these persons; how many were there; how representative were the samples?

Reliability is claimed through results reported from several studies conducted over a 10-year period. These measures of reliability include interrater, intrarater, and test-retest reliabilities. However, they are all based on inadequately small samples, overwhelmingly males, (4–6 judges; 4–67 patients). Retest intervals were relatively short ranging from 11 days to 3 months, with an average interval of approximately 6 weeks. More importantly, however, these studies were all conducted with the PDI and none with the PDI-R. The distinction between the PDI and PDI-R is significant because the revised version includes substantial modifications and additions. It is therefore not possible to evaluate the reliability of the PDI-R.

The demonstration of validity is claimed through the reporting of several validation studies with the PDI and two with the PDI-R. All were conducted on samples that are considered quite small for validation purposes. One study conducted with the PDI was based on a rather large sample ($N = 485$). However, it was a "naturalistic" study, not an empirical one. Hence, it does not support evidence of validity as required by the *Standards for Educational and Psychological Testing* (AERA, APA, & NCME, 1985). There is also the question as to whether there has been proper statistical treatment of the data in these studies. For example, inspection of the data in Tables 5 and 6, without further explanation in the text on pages 102–103, suggests that a 3 x 2 analysis of variance was performed on percentages. If so, this would have been highly irregular and incorrect. And the statistical results reported in Table 6 would be uninterpretable. In any event, the paucity of validity studies with positive results, reported by the authors or others over the 10-year period of the operational use of the PDI and PDI-R, fails even to approach the APA standard of validity as a "unitary concept." This standard, which has become widely accepted by psychometricians, states that validity is demonstrated only through substantial supportive evidence over long periods of time of the inferences made by scores yielded by psychometric instruments.

In addition to the ethical concerns expressed by the authors in the manual (pp. 3–4) there are two additional ones that arise to this reviewer: (*a*) the introduction of computer administration, scoring, and reporting of the PDI-R without apparent or evident compliance with APA Guidelines (APA, 1986); and (*b*) unwarranted claims by the publisher regarding the usefulness of the instrument to clinicians. It is stated in a promotional piece that "clinicians find the PDI-R useful because: It provides a reliable record . . . . It reduces the chance of diagnostic error . . . . It provides a systematic and efficient approach to diagnosis." Such claims require substantiated unequivocal evidences of reliability and validity of the PDI-R. In this reviewer's judgment, these important psychometric properties have yet to be convincingly demonstrated for this instrument.

In summary, the authors and their collaborators are to be commended for their 10-year effort in producing both an instrument and manual that could prove to be useful to well-qualified and trained clinicians in making effective psychiatric diagnoses. However, before the PDI-R is deemed ready for operational use, considerably more and better evidence of its reliability and validity than exists at present must be demonstrated. The authors and publisher are also admonished to heed the standards made explicit in the references to this review; to monitor more carefully who can gain access to the instrument; and to be more restrained in the claims made of the PDI-R until such time that they can support these with the necessary documentation.

REVIEWER'S REFERENCES

American Educational Research Association, American Psychological Association, & National Council on Measurement in Education. (1985). *Standards for educational and psychological testing.* Washington, DC: American Psychological Association, Inc.

American Psychological Association. (1986). *Guidelines for computer-based tests and interpretations.* Washington, DC: American Psychological Association.

[317]
Psychoeducational Profile.

Purpose: "To identify uneven and idiosyncratic learning patterns."
Population: Autistic, psychotic, and developmentally disabled children functioning at preschool age levels.
Publication Date: 1979.
Acronym: PEP.
Scores, 13: Pathology (Affect, Relating, Use of Materials, Sensory Modes, Language), Developmental Functions (Imitation, Perception, Fine Motor, Gross Motor, Eye-Hand Integration, Cognitive Performance, Cognitive Verbal, Developmental Score).
Administration: Individual.
Parts, 2: Pathology, Developmental Functions.
Price Data, 1989: $29 per manual (234 pages); $12 per pad of profile sheets.
Time: (45–75) minutes.
Comments: Volume 1 in the Individualized Assessment and Treatment for Autistic and Developmentally Disabled Children series; other test materials (e.g., jar of bubbles, tactile blocks) must be supplied by examiner.
Authors: Eric Schopler and Robert Jay Reichler.
Publisher: PRO-ED, Inc.

Review of the Psychoeducational Profile by GERALD S. HANNA, Professor of Educational Psychology and Measurement, Kansas State University, Manhattan, KS:

The Psychoeducational Profile (PEP) was developed to enable direct translation of assessment results into individualized teaching programs and to pinpoint each examinee's emerging skills (Volume I, p. xi). This diagnosis theme recurs repeatedly throughout the manual. Moreover, a profile enables graphic comparison of relative strengths and weaknesses by means of estimated age equivalents, and a companion volume "explains how the diagnostic information from the PEP is translated into individualized teaching programs" (Volume I, p. 3).

Clearly, profile analysis is used in interpreting PEP results. Therefore, issues of central importance to the informed professional use of the instrument concern reliability and validity of differences among scores in the profile.

RELIABILITY. The manual provides no data regarding the reliability of the (*a*) total scores, (*b*) subscores, or (*c*) differences among the subscores that are used for programming.

VALIDITY. Although validity is argued on several bases, the only case this reviewer found at all persuasive was the case made for content validity. However, as the authors recognized, the key validity question is, "'Can the PEP be used for effective educational and home programming?' There are no formal data, but there is empirical clinical evidence, because the PEP has been used successfully as the main programming instrument for 10 years in our program and within a statewide program in North Carolina. These programs have received considerable recognition for their effectiveness by both professionals and parents" (Volume I, pp. 91–92). Overall, then, users are provided with no meaningful validity research, only with authorial testimony that the instrument has been considered effective by those who have used it.

NORMATIVE DATA. A sample of 276 normal children between ages 1 and 7 were chosen from the Chapel Hill-Carrboro area, apparently mainly on the basis of availability. The demographic data provided leave the impression that (*a*) the sample did not closely parallel the population of the country; and (*b*) the subsamples were not well matched from age to age.

The only kind of derived score provided is estimated age equivalents. Yet age-equivalent scores are well-known to be unsuitable for profile analysis, owing to (*a*) the likelihood of unequal variability among the subscales and (*b*) unequal units of measure. This inadequacy alone would compromise the suitability of the PEP for pinpointing examinee weaknesses.

SUMMARY. Interpretation of PEP scores is seriously handicapped by the inadequacy of the sample and the inappropriateness of the kind of derived score provided. The absence of meaningful validity studies for the recommended purpose of the instrument is also a concern. Perhaps most damaging is the total lack of evidence that scores and profiles are reliable enough to warrant use in educational programming. Collectively, these limitations lead this reviewer to view the release of the PEP as quite premature and to be unable to recommend it for applied use.

Review of the Psychoeducational Profile by MARTIN J. WIESE, School Psychologist, Wilkes County Schools, Wilkesboro, NC:

The Psychoeducational Profile (PEP) is designed to offer a developmental approach to the assessment of autistic and psychotic children. It is an inventory of behaviors and skills used to identify idiosyncratic learning patterns. The PEP provides information on developmental functioning in seven areas: Imitation, Perception, Fine Motor, Gross Motor, Eye-Hand Integration, Cognitive Performance, and Cognitive Verbal Skills. In addition to the seven developmental areas, the PEP also provides a Pathology Scale that indicates the severity of the child's behaviors. The Pathology Scale is divided into five subunits: Affect, Relating/Cooperating/Human Interest, Play/Interest, Sensory Modes, and Language. In total, the test scores yield a profile depicting relative strengths and weaknesses in several different areas.

The PEP consists of a set of toys and play activities presented to the child by an examiner who also observes, evaluates, and records the child's responses. The test materials for the PEP can be constructed according to the instructions found in the Appendices or an assembled kit may be purchased directly. The test items are developmentally arrayed from ages 1 to 7 and minimize the amount of language needed to understand the directions. Standardized verbal directions have been avoided and nonverbal gestures and demonstrations are acceptable administration techniques.

The child is scored on each developmental item as passing, failing, or emerging according to criteria established in the manual. All developmental items are scored during administration and the pathology items are scored immediately following the testing situation. Scoring criteria for the pathology items are based on clinical judgment (e.g., appropriate, age-appropriate, or within normal limits). After the examiner has scored all items, the scores are transferred to the Test Profile. The profile provides a graphical representation of the test scores for easier interpretation.

Interpretation of the PEP scores and the profile provides information on the nature of the child's difficulties. The profile is used to determine the best approximation of the educational expectations for the subject. Uneven profiles are thought to be characteristic of psychotic or retarded children. Planning for the child includes working on the individual child's strengths and weaknesses. It is recommended that a written summary or report complement the subject's scores, and a sample outline for the report is provided in the manual.

It is important to note the PEP is not a test in the traditional framework of a norm-referenced test, nor is it a criterion-referenced test. As a result, normative data on the PEP are limited. A normal comparison group was used, not as a standardization group, but to assist in the construction of the scales. A sample of 276 normal children, all from North Carolina, were tested with the PEP to arrange the items developmentally and to construct the scales. One limitation is that the majority of the children in the initial sample were white and from high socioeconomic groups. Again, the normal comparison sample was not intended to be used as a standardization group because the PEP is not designed to yield an overall standard score. The main purpose of the test is to provide information on the child's idiosyncratic learning patterns.

There are a number of other limitations and difficulties with the PEP. First, there are no reliability or validity studies reported in the manual. The authors defend the lack of measurement data by stating the test should not be used to construct a standard score that allows comparisons with other children. Therefore, each administration is individualized to the child and reliability should not be an issue.

Similarly, no validity studies are reported. Even so, the authors suggest the PEP has good content validity and construct validity but do not cite any empirical evidence. No established procedure was used to identify the seven developmental function areas, even though the manual states the activities were empirically established as suitable for the target population. It is not clear how the content domains were specified, and it appears the items and procedures evolved through a series of trial and error modifications.

Finally, even though it was designed to guide programming and planning for autistic children, there has been no formal evaluation of the PEP's effectiveness for this purpose. The authors close, stating the PEP has been used many years and has received considerable recognition for its effectiveness by other professionals.

Overall, the PEP does provide a method of gaining information about children considered untestable by standard means. Unfortunately, its lack of reported validity and reliability undermines its effectiveness as an assessment instrument. At a minimum, the authors should determine test-retest reliability if the PEP is to be used to measure educational progress with autistic and communication-disordered children.

[318]
Quality of Life Questionnaire.
Purpose: "Developed to assess the quality of an individual's life across a broad range of specific areas."
Population: Ages 18 and over.
Publication Date: 1989.
Acronym: QLQ.
Scores, 17: Material Well-Being, Physical Well-Being, Personal Growth, Marital Relations, Parent-Child Relations, Extended Family Relations, Extramarital Relations, Altruistic Behavior, Political Behavior, Job Characteristics, Occupational Relations, Job Satisfiers, Creative/Aesthetic Behavior, Sports Activity, Vacation Behavior, Social Desirability, Total Quality of Life.
Administration: Group.
Price Data, 1989: $32 per complete kit including 25 QuikScore forms and manual (43 pages); $16 per 25 QuikScore forms; $18 per manual.
Time: (30) minutes.
Authors: David R. Evans and Wendy E. Cope.
Publisher: Multi-Health Systems, Inc.

Review of the Quality of Life Questionnaire by GARY B. SELTZER, Associate Professor of Social Work, University of Wisconsin-Madison, Madison, WI:

The Quality of Life Questionnaire (QLQ) is a 192-item, self-report instrument that includes 15 subscales, a Social Desirability scale, and a summative scale score. The construct, life quality, is often beset by theoretical and methodological ambiguity. In contrast, the authors of the QLQ have specified the QLQ's theoretical underpinnings and developed subscale items that tend to empirically support their theoretical approach. The QLQ posits that life quality is related to the adaptive behavioral responses that occur within specific types of environmental domains. Life quality, as assessed by the QLQ, yields information about how individuals behave in response to environmental contingencies. This ecological approach to life quality differs from approaches that have focused upon a person's

perception of life satisfactions (e.g., Campbell, Converse, & Rodgers, 1976; Handal, Barling, & Morrissy, 1981; Michalos, 1979) or approaches that aggregate social indicators such as access to community services, quality of social institutions, and other community characteristics (e.g., Andrews, 1976). Because this test provides information about multidimensional and behaviorally specific approaches to psychological assessment, it may be useful to clinicians and researchers who are interested in measuring the effect of systematic treatment on clients.

The QLQ can be administered in a group or individually. It can also be computer administered and scored. The advantages of computer-based assessments are many and have been addressed elsewhere by Butcher (1987). The QLQ manual addresses the advantages of computerized administration, scoring, and interpretation. In addition, the paper-and-pencil administration, scoring, and interpretation have been carefully thought through. A respondent is given a six-page test booklet that has clear instructions about how to respond. A carbonized answer sheet is used to organize the true or false answers on the top sheet and to organize the subscales on the carbonized sheet. On the back of the carbonized sheet, there is a profile form that helps the test administrator easily convert raw subscale scores into T-scores. The purpose and computational significance of T-scores are explained in the manual.

Throughout the manual, the authors provide helpful, general information about psychometric principles; however, not all of it applies to the psychometric investigations that are conducted on the QLQ. Scoring standards and cautions are presented in enough detail so that the intended test interpreter, a person qualified in the standards of test and measurement, should be able to develop useful clinical or research protocols about respondents.

Although the researchers used a sophisticated two-stage area probability sampling strategy to recruit respondents for both their initial normative sample and the cross-validation sample, these samples were limited to persons living in London, Ontario. Because the authors failed to provide standard sociodemographic characteristics of the sample such as race, ethnicity, age, and occupational level, clinicians, researchers, and other users might have difficulty comparing the people they test to this sample. In addition, the authors do not report the number or characteristics of the respondents who were selected but did not complete the QLQ.

Sufficient studies of the QLQ's reliability have been conducted. Both test-retest and internal consistency data are provided; however, the former was conducted with a small number of subjects and is available only on six subscales and the total Quality of Life score. The authors are to be commended for conducting a cross-validation study on the scale-item-related statistics and the KR-20 estimates of internal consistency estimates. On the cross-validation sample, the alpha reliabilities ranged between .55 and .97.

Information about content, construct, concurrent, and predictive validity is also presented. The authors used a number of previously published works to select items, subscales, and their five quality of life domains. The rigorous item selection process used supports the content validity of the QLQ. A table depicting the intercorrelations among the QLQ scales is presented. Almost all of the subscales are significantly intercorrelated and the pattern of intercorrelations fits together in support of the subscales' content. For example, Material Well-Being is correlated highly with job-related scales. Several factor analyses are conducted in order to explore the QLQ's construct validity. These analyses result in the following factors (*a*) occupational/material well-being, (*b*) social well-being, and (*c*) personal/family well-being. These factors differ from the postulated quality of life domains that the authors used when developing the 15 subscales of the QLQ. No mention of this discrepancy is made. The authors do note, however, that after the various factor analytic strategies are completed, it may be appropriate to consider only one general quality of life factor because much of the covariation among scales in the QLQ can be explained by a single general factor. This finding has serious implications when one considers using the subscales of the QLQ in research and clinical endeavors. Lastly, concurrent validity is supported in the manual by the report of studies in the areas of physical health, community alcohol use, life satisfaction, and personality measures such as self-esteem and sense of humor. The authors report on a predictive validity study that tested the impact of a liver transplant on patients' life quality as measured by using selected scales of the QLQ and the Campbell, Converse, and Rodgers (1976) indices of quality of life. Although the number of subjects in this study is small (i.e., $n = 31$), the authors miss an opportunity here to examine the criterion-related validity between the Campbell et al. measure and the QLQ.

In summary, there are many positive reasons for using the QLQ as a measure of life quality. The manual is very well written, comprehensive, and provides a clear and readable presentation of psychometric information. Both the pencil-and-paper and the computer-administered and scored versions are "user friendly." The thoughtful and careful design of the QLQ's test materials greatly facilitates the process of test taking, data collection, and report writing. Further psychometric work should explore

the interrelationships among subscales and factors underlying the QLQ. Until this work is completed and reported, caution should be exercised in providing interpretations about the specific content of the subscales. Nevertheless, the QLQ can be used with confidence when an ecological approach to overall life quality is the target of inquiry.

REVIEWER'S REFERENCES

Andrews, F. M., & Withey, S. B. (1976). *Social indicators of well-being*. New York: Plenum.

Campbell, A., Converse, P. E., & Rodgers, W. L. (1976). *The quality of American life*. New York: Russell Sage Foundation.

Michalos, A. C. (1979). Life changes, illness and personal life satisfaction in a rural population. *Social Science and Medicine, 13A*, 175-181.

Handal, P. J., Barling, P. W., & Morrissy, E. (1981). Development of perceived and preferred measures of physical and social characteristics of the residential environment and their relationship to satisfaction. *Journal of Community Psychology, 9*, 118-124.

Butcher, J. N. (1987). *Computerized psychological assessment: A practitioner's guide*. New York: Basic Books.

Review of the Quality of Life Questionnaire by RICHARD B. STUART, *Clinical Professor of Psychiatry, University of Washington School of Medicine, Seattle, WA:*

The Quality of Life Questionnaire (QLQ) was developed by David R. Evans and Wendy E. Cope for use "in helping to identify community needs for improving mental health services, obtaining funding for needed programs, and promoting quality of life in general." In addition, the authors suggest that the instrument can be used in the evaluation of individual, family, or group treatments.

The authors began by identifying five areas that other researchers had targeted as contributing major sources of the variance in quality of life: general well-being, interpersonal relations, organizational activity, occupational activity, and leisure and recreational activity. These five areas were further analyzed, yielding a total of 15 subdomains. A second review of the literature resulted in the selection of 15 items to measure each of these subdomains. The advantage of this approach is that it reflects concerns expressed in the contemporary literature; its disadvantage, however, is it is essentially atheoretical (Dierner, 1984) and may not tie directly to any intervention approaches.

Two naive item writers rewrote the selected items in true/false form that would be endorsed by persons high and low in each dimension, creating a pool of 452 items. These items were submitted to 298 subjects randomly selected in London, Ontario, Canada. Of this sample, 61% were female, 70% were married, and 39% had a college diploma or university degree. Items were chosen for inclusion in the QLQ if they: were selected by more than 15%, but fewer than 85% of the sample; were not too highly correlated with social desirability; had acceptable infrequency scores; were not too highly correlated with items selected for other scales; and had an efficiency index greater than zero. Additional samples of 163 and 274 subjects, respectively, were used as the basis of cross-validation studies and the development of norms.

The QLQ consists of 192 true/false items addressing respondents' evaluations of the quality of their lives from varied perspectives. The majority of the items are self-assessments of the frequency of various actions (e.g., "I rarely attend a sports event" or "I have never done any writing [i.e., book, poetry, short stories]") or reactions (e.g., "I can usually laugh at myself" or "I seldom lose my temper"). Other items are self-descriptions (e.g., "I have trouble living up to my own expectations" or "I put myself down too much"). And the remaining items assess personal relationships (e.g., "My partner and I have a good sexual relationship" or "Most of the time I can depend upon my relatives to help me when I need it"), employment settings (e.g., "My work is meaningful to me" or "Where I work people rarely quit their job"), and respondents' physical environments ("Where I live the streets are well kept" or "Friends have commented on how nice my home is"). Six true and six false items are included for each of the 15 subscales in addition to a 12-item Social Desirability scale. Answers are recorded on a quick-scoring blank that includes instructions for conversion to T-scores and the generation of a profile.

Considerable care has gone into controlling for potential sources of bias in responses. For example, equal numbers of positive and negative items have been selected to control for any tendency for "yeasaying" or "naysaying." Also, a Social-Desirability scale was constructed by selecting the 12 items that correlated most closely with the Personality Research Form, Version E (PRF-E) Social Desirability Scale (Jackson, 1974).

Normative means of the 12-item subscales range from 5.8 (for Political Behavior) to 9.6 (for Material Well-Being) with standard deviations ranging from 1.9 (for Material Well-Being) to 3.3 (for Sports Activity). Mean item p values range from .46 (for Sports Activity) to .76 (for Marital and Parent-Child Relations), with Kuder-Richardson internal consistency coefficients of .61 (for Physical Well-Being) to .98 (for Parent-Child Relations). Comparable results have been obtained in the authors' 163-subject cross-validation sample).

Test-retest reliabilities of .77 to .89 have been reported for only six of the content scales and the total Quality of Life score. Varimax factor analysis yielded three components for which the authors do not supply names, in part because of the heterodox grouping of subscales loading on each factor. In addition, the subscales intercorrelated rather highly with the Quality of Life score, ranging from a low of .41 (for Extended Family Relations) to a high of .64 (for Job Characteristics).

The authors correctly caution users to consider the overall picture of respondents' lives when interpreting the QLQ to allow for adjustments in interpretations for mood, stage in life cycle, ethnic differences, and those whose cognitive abilities are not within the normal range.

Potential users of the QLQ should also recall that the normative data are drawn from a relatively homogeneous group that may not generalize throughout Canada much less to North Americans in general. In addition, users may wish to resist the authors' attempt to adjust responses in instances in which one or more of the subscales may not apply (e.g., to those who are unmarried, childless, and/or unemployed). The adjustment is made by discarding scales on which respondents did not answer at least four items and by computing a composite Quality of Life score for anyone answering four or more scales. This is accomplished simply by multiplying the average raw score on the subscales answered by 15. Regrettably, no weights are provided for the various subscales, a troubling omission in light of the probability that the subscales contribute unequal proportions of the variance in respondents' satisfaction with the quality of their lives. It is therefore likely that either the recommended procedures would undermine the validity of responses, that the QLQ is much longer than necessary, or that it is unsuitable for use with certain groups (e.g., those who are unmarried, unemployed, etc.).

Data are presented to show that various subscales of the QLQ correlate at moderate levels with varied aspects of physical health, general behavior, alcohol use, life satisfaction, and so forth. The instrument can be used to explore such associations as one of several assessment protocols. Unfortunately, no data are presented to show the convergence between QLQ subscales and more broadly used measures of satisfaction with marital, family, and employment situations. Moreover, because responses to subscales are shown to overlap somewhat, the QLQ may be essentially a unifactorial measure. If so, its role in needs assessment may be more efficiently served by the 25-item General Well-Being Schedule (National Center for Health Statistics, 1977) for which considerable normative, reliability, and validity data are available and which is in the public domain.

REVIEWER'S REFERENCES

Jackson, D. N. (1974). Personality Research Form. Goshen, NY: Research Psychologists Press.

National Center for Health Statistics. (1977). *A concurrent validational study of the NCHS General Well-Being Schedule.* Hyattsville, MD: U.S. Department of Health, Education, and Welfare, Public Health Service, Health Resources Administration.

Diener, E. (1984). Subjective well-being. *Psychological Bulletin, 95,* 542-575.

[319]

Questionnaire on Resources and Stress.

Purpose: "Measures stress in families who are caring for ill or disabled relatives."

Population: Families with children who have developmental disabilities, psychiatric problems, renal disease, cystic fibrosis, neuromuscular disease, or cerebral palsy.
Publication Date: 1987.
Acronym: QRS.
Scores, 15: Personal Problems Scales (Health/Mood, Time Demands, Attitudes, Overprotection/Dependency, Social Support, Overcommitment, Pessimism), Family Problems Scales (Family Integration, Family Opportunity, Financial Problems), Problems of Index Case Scales (Physical Problems, Limited Activities, Limited Occupation, Obtrusiveness, Difficult Personality); SHORT FORM, 11 scores: Dependency and Management, Cognitive Impairment, Limits on Family Opportunities, Life Span Care, Family Disharmony, Lack of Personal Reward, Terminal Illness Stress, Physical Limitations, Financial Stress, Preference for Institutional Care, Personal Burden for Respondent.
Administration: Individual.
Forms, 2: Short form, long form.
Price Data, 1989: $70 per complete set including manual (146 pages), 5 test booklets, 25 answer sheets, 25 profile sheets, and set of scoring templates; $15 per 5 reusable test booklets; $10 per 5 short form test booklets; $18.50 per 25 answer sheets; $11.50 per 25 short form answer sheets; $14.50 per set of scoring stencils; $14.50 per set of short form scoring stencils; $5 per 25 profile sheets; $24.95 per manual; $30 per specimen set.
Time: (60) minutes.
Comments: Completed by any family member other than the "identified patient."
Author: Jean Holroyd.
Publisher: Clinical Psychology Publishing Co., Inc.

TEST REFERENCES

1. Kazak, A. E. (1988). Stress and social networks in families with older institutionalized retarded children. *Journal of Social and Clinical Psychology, 6*, 448-461.
2. Adams, J. W., & Tidwell, R. (1989). An instructional guide for reducing the stress of hearing parents of hearing-impaired children. *American Annals of the Deaf, 134*, 323-328.
3. Scott, R. L., Thompson, B., & Sexton, D. (1989). Structure of a short form of the Questionnaire on Resources and Stress: A bootstrap factor analysis. *Educational and Psychological Measurement, 49*, 409-419.

Review of the Questionnaire on Resources and Stress by DEBORAH ERICKSON, Associate Professor of Education, Niagara University, Niagara University, NY:

The Questionnaire on Resources and Stress for Families with Chronically Ill or Handicapped Members (QRS) is designed to measure stress in families caring for ill or disabled relatives by examining the impact the illness or handicap has on the family members. It also examines the resources the family has to assist them in the care of the ill or handicapped member. The instrument claims to allow the clinician working with the family to determine problems in need of priority treatment and to be helpful for comparisons among families for the purpose of selecting families to be the recipients of care if resources are limited.

The questionnaire has 285 self-administered True/False items that require approximately 1 hour for completion. The test is designed to be taken by any member of the family having at least a sixth grade reading level ability. The short form of 66 items is designed for screening purposes.

The test layout is easy to read. However, scoring the test with the templates provided with the manual is a visual discrimination challenge. Counting the marks seen through geometric designs and recording the raw scores on the QRS profile yields *T*-scores. A score below 60 indicates the respondent answered in a way similar to respondents from the control groups having no chronically ill or handicapped individuals in their family. A score above 70 is considered significant and interpretation from the manual is appropriate. Percentiles are also available.

The clinical interpretation of significant scores is discussed in detail in the manual. A user of the test must be committed to spending the time necessary to become familiar with the 137-page manual before accurate interpretation of the profile is possible. Numerous research studies evaluating a variety of populations are cited intermittently throughout the manual. Summaries addressing the test application for specific populations would be a valuable addition to the manual.

The manual is elaborate and the author appears to have made substantial effort to research this test instrument before publishing. The manual follows recommendations found in the *Standards for Educational and Psychological Testing* (AERA, APA, & NCME, 1985) for thorough discussion of test construction, reliability, validity, and limitations for use.

The test construction section begins with a description of the item development and the factor analysis used to create the various scales. The normative data are limited to 107 cases from California, Georgia, and New Zealand. Random sampling methods were not used and 42 of these cases did not complete the short form.

The manual demonstrates reliability through studies using the Kuder-Richardson-20 method for measuring internal consistency. The overall Kuder-Richardson internal consistency is reported to be .96 for the long form and .79 or .85 for the short form, depending on the study. Individual scale Kuder-Richardson reliability estimates ranged from .24 to .88 on the long form and from .31 to .82 on the short form. Test-retest or alternate test form reliability coefficients are not yet available.

Content, criterion, and construct validity are discussed in depth. Content validity is established through item rating by 12 judges. Although this method of achieving content validity is common, it is a qualitative rather than a quantitative measure. Criterion validity is difficult to establish by comparing other measures to the QRS because there are no commercially available instruments that have achieved general acceptance in this topical area.

Therefore, the author chose to give brief summaries of 24 research studies related to the use of this instrument as a manner of establishing a "quasicriterion" for indicating validity. Some of these studies lacked adequate control groups or failed to use the complete instrument in the research design and, therefore, this approach supports the premise of validity in the anecdotal sense only. Construct validation remains to be established.

In summary, the "quasicriterion" validity studies do demonstrate the QRS is capable of differentiating groups with differing levels of stress. This is useful in a clinical setting as a qualitative tool in the evaluation process. However, the limited normative data, the lack of test-retest or alternate form reliability information, and the lack of rigor in the validity studies minimizes the general use of this instrument as a standardized diagnostic assessment tool for indicating stress in families of chronically ill or handicapped individuals.

REVIEWER'S REFERENCE

American Educational Research Association, American Psychological Association, & National Council on Measurement in Education. (1985). *Standards for educational and psychological testing.* Washington, DC: American Psychological Association, Inc.

[320]
QUIC Tests.

Purpose: Designed "to establish or verify the functional level of proficiency in the areas of either mathematics or the communicative arts."
Population: Grades 2–12.
Publication Dates: 1989–90.
Scores, 8: Mathematics (Computation, Concepts, Problem Solving, Total), Communicative Arts (Reading, Reference Skills, Language Arts, Total).
Administration: Individual or group.
Price Data, 1991: $36.95 per starter set including 20 tests (specify content area Mathematics or Communicative Arts and Form A or B), 20 response forms, and examiner's manual; $16.25 per 20 response forms; $9.50 per examiner's manual; $15 per specimen set (including 1 test and response form for each of content areas and examiner's manual).
Time: (30) minutes.
Comments: Self-administered; competency-based interpretation.
Author: Scholastic Testing Service, Inc.
Publisher: Scholastic Testing Service, Inc.

Review of the QUIC Tests by DELWYN L. HARNISCH, Associate Professor of Educational Psychology, University of Illinois at Champaign-Urbana, Champaign, IL:

INTRODUCTION. In its literature, the QUIC Tests promise to provide convenient measures of student functioning levels in the areas of mathematics and communicative arts at the second through twelfth grade levels. As its mnemonic title implies, the QUIC tests offer Quick Uncomplicated Immediate results leading to Competency-based interpretation. These measures seem particularly useful in

that they may be given in 30 minutes or less to establish or verify student functional levels of proficiency. Scholastic Testing Service, Inc. (STS) claims that these measures are accurate measures of whole class and individual student performance.

The STS identifies the specific strengths of the QUIC as: (*a*) easy administration with scoring and interpretation possible within minutes; (*b*) uncomplicated forms with color coding of all related materials to allow for rapid access to materials; (*c*) little or no preparation on the part of the examiner; (*d*) use of a self-scoring response form; (*e*) immediate access to results allowing for quick application of findings; (*f*) inclusion of a student response form for filing; and (*g*) a unique reporting measure of functional ability based on the student's competency-based grade-equivalent score (reported as Q-GE Scores—to represent QUIC-Grade Equivalents).

All items used in the QUIC Tests were taken from the 6,000+ item bank developed for the STS Educational Development Series. This testing battery consists of 13 level-forms designed for use at the kindergarten through twelfth grade levels. Items were analyzed initially using a Rasch one-parameter item response theory (IRT) procedure with common items for adjacent levels included to allow for calibration of all levels on a single scale. Items were selected for use in the QUIC on the basis of relevance of content to specific grade level and appropriate item difficulty.

It is important to look at the construction of the QUIC rather carefully to better understand how these items were utilized in the development of the QUIC. Each of the QUIC tests consists of blocks of items with each block of items focusing on specific content. This content was selected by STS as being uniquely representative of a specific grade level. Blocks of items were then selected from the content areas of communicative arts and mathematics. These blocks were viewed as representing unique content topics from within each grade level. These blocks of items were then balanced throughout the range of the test to ensure adequacy of coverage.

It is not a student's total score or ability on a specific block of content that alone determines the Q-GE, but rather the pattern of item responses. The blocks of content/grade-matched items just described are used as the basis for the comparison of an individual student's patterns of responses against those of a representative group of students at the various grade levels on the same items. The results of that comparison are expressed in terms of a performance index that indicates whether or not the student matches the achievement of the normative group. By using IRT, comparisons of student patterns of achievement as indicated by these successively achieved performance indices are said to determine the highest grade level at which the examinee was able to function successfully.

PRACTICAL APPLICATIONS/USES. The QUIC has been designed to verify and/or provide a quick establishment of functional grade level ability. As such, it is not intended to replace the use of more extensive achievement batteries. This is a critical point to consider for education professionals planning to use the QUIC. As STS puts it the QUIC "was not designed to assess the full range of subject area objectives and domains that exist at any single grade level. Hence, if one were seeking a full-spectrum assessment of a student's strengths and weaknesses, one's purposes would be better served by using a more elaborate instrument intended for this purpose" (Development and Standardization Manual, p. 2). The QUIC should be viewed as a special purpose tool, not a panacea.

This is not to downplay the potentially powerful applications for which the QUIC is uniquely suited. As it is very easy to administer and score, the QUIC is particularly useful for administration to individuals about whom little information is available regarding functional level, such as new students entering a school system whose records are delayed. In a like fashion, the QUIC can be very helpful in estimating the accuracy of existing student information when the current student record is of questionable value. These screening and verifying applications of the QUIC alone would make the QUIC worth considering as part of a more encompassing evaluation program.

In addition to QUIC's ease of use, the QUIC's construction lends itself nicely for use in both educational research and remediation programs. As the QUIC exists in two parallel forms (A and B) pre/post comparisons of student functional level may be easily obtained via the QUIC. A caveat must be mentioned, however, in that the test user should remember to view QUIC results as being an overall indication of student functional level and not to overgeneralize findings relying solely on the QUIC.

The QUIC examiner's manual contains careful suggestions for standard administration procedures and offers helpful suggestions to use in the event that variations from normal testing procedures are necessary. In a typical administration, the student will need a QUIC test booklet, an appropriate response sheet, and a soft-leaded pencil. Scratch paper must also be available for the mathematics section.

Administration of the QUIC is simple. The examiner instructs the student to open the testing booklet, read the directions, and notify the examiner when ready to begin. For students with insufficient reading ability, the examiner may read and clarify the directions to the student. Following clarification of any student questions the student is instructed to turn to the appropriate page of the test booklet and to begin. Although briefly mentioned in the documentation, it is critical that the examiner should verify that the student is beginning at the correct block of items and give alternative instructions if necessary to supersede those provided in the student instructions. The examiner times the test. The student is instructed to stop working after 30 minutes and close the test booklet. It is important that the examiner remain physically present during administration as the student is instructed to stop working any time there are four to five items in a row that he knows nothing about.

For cases in which the transfer of answers to the response sheets may prove problematic (e.g., a student with a physical disability in marking an answer sheet), it is suggested by STS that answers be recorded directly in the testing booklet itself. If this option is exercised, however, the examiner is advised to transfer the student response to a response sheet to allow for easier scoring and record keeping.

To score the QUIC, the examiner opens the response form, discards the carbon, and follows the easy-to-use instructions contained on the inner page. The inclusion of scoring directions on the response form itself is a positive feature which lends to the overall ease-of-use associated with the QUIC. These directions are repeated in an illustrative section of the examiner's manual which minimizes potential misscoring concerns.

Scoring itself is done by looking for the student's "X" appearing in a box. This indicates a correct response unless the box was circled by the student in which case it indicates a change of answer by the student. The examiner circles the number right in the appropriate column to the right of the student responses. This number is associated with either a "-" or a "?" or a "+" which serves as the performance index for that block of items. The total number correct is entered at the bottom of the form as are the performance indices for each block of seven items constituting a competency-based grade equivalent. When either a "-" or the second "?" is recorded, the series is finished and the functional level is determined. Total score analyses are included without regard to the item-blocks, which allows for comparison against normative groups.

TECHNICAL ASPECTS. As has been earlier mentioned, all items used in the QUIC were taken from the 6,000+ item bank developed for the 13-level kindergarten–twelfth grade STS Educational Development Series (EdSeries). Following an initial item analysis, using the Rasch one-parameter IRT procedure in which items for adjacent levels were included to allow for calibration of all levels on a single scale, items were selected for inclusion on the basis of relevance of content to specific grade level and appropriate item difficulty. Item statistics were computed for selected items using a constructed data base derived from the EdSeries studies. All students who had been tested at midyear were selected from the master library file of 1985–1986. Additional selections were made based on the forms used, the national normative data, and midyear item statistics based on both traditional and IRT approaches. This selection process yielded 1,000 students who were representative of the national performance for their grade.

This student data base had the following demographic characteristics: (a) the boy/girl ratio was 51% to 49%, (b) 4% of the students were classified as having English as their second language, and (c) approximately 2% of the students were classified as having some type of handicap or learning disability. Care was taken to insure a representative national sample with 19% being drawn from the West, 26% from the North Central, 33% from the South, and 22% from the Northeast.

The initial screening of items for face validity and adequate item-test discrimination values was accomplished during the EdSeries item bank construction. Because of this, decisions regarding which items to include for use in the QUIC were determined by content to unique grade level match and item difficulty. An average item difficulty range of 50–55% was selected for items at each grade level block. Within each block, preference was given to items that fell in the 45–65% range of difficulty. To minimize success due to chance, a minimum of five items was included for those items with five foils and seven items for those items with a four-foil response.

CRITIQUE. The QUIC's basic design is to identify and select blocks of items with each block focusing on content that is uniquely representative of a specific grade level. The content within grade level is then proportionately balanced across the entire range of the test with scores obtained for each item-block being administered. Implicit in this design is the assumption that specific content is unique to certain grade levels and that this content can then be partitioned out with mastery of such content indicating grade level proficiency. This assumption, although perhaps valid at some levels, is problematic in many cases. First, in a spiral curriculum in which conceptual areas reappear over time it becomes difficult to identify specific grade level skills. By taking the position that these areas are presented only at a certain time and in a predetermined sequence, the QUIC reinforces many outmoded ideas of curriculum and instruction that have been replaced by modern cognitive and developmentally based approaches. This is not a trivial concern. Secondly, issue may be taken with STS's claim that a student with a Q-GE of 5.5 in mathematics has not only demonstrated an equal footing with the average fifth grade student on representative content, but has also demonstrated this competency.

The developers of the QUIC should be applauded for their use of item response analysis as an attempt to remedy these potential difficulties. The use of extensive item response analysis in the development of the QUIC instruments insures that it is not just the students' overall score which is the basis of comparison in determining competency-based grade equivalents but, rather, it is the entire pattern of item responses exhibited by the student.

As the QUIC is very easy to administer, it is very important that potential users do not skimp on their own preparation for testing. Many of the same factors that lead to the QUIC's ease of use can also be problematic if a cavalier attitude is taken toward administration. For example, the QUIC includes blocks of items ranging in ability from kindergarten through twelfth grade. This has the potential of being traumatic for younger students as they come across increasingly more difficult items. This is carefully discussed in the examiner's manual. A cursory examiner may miss this very important point. Care should be taken by the examiner to prepare the students for this eventuality. As this is a different form of testing than that with which the students may be familiar, it is important the examiner practice greater sensitivity to any frustrations or anxieties expressed by the students.

SUMMARY. The QUIC lives up to its name delivering Quick Uncomplicated Immediate results leading to Competency-based interpretation. Although not intended to replace the use of more extensive achievement batteries, the QUIC provides a convenient instrument to supplement a traditional testing program. Due to its ease of administration and scoring, the QUIC is particularly useful for administration to individuals about whom little information is available regarding functional level. The QUIC can be very helpful when new students enter an existing school system and their records are delayed. In a like fashion, the QUIC can assist in verifying existing student information when the current student record is of questionable value. The screening and verifying application of the QUIC alone would make it worth considering for inclusion into a more comprehensive evaluation program. Two primary concerns in using this instrument are (a) failure to respect the developmental nature of mathematics learning and (b) the possibility that users may not attend to the test instructions because the tests seem so easy to administer. The information provided by the QUIC must be interpreted carefully, lest overgeneralization take place.

[321]
Quick Cognitive Inventory.
Purpose: To observe school-related skills in students who do not speak English or have language delays or deficits.

Population: Grades 1–3.
Publication Date: 1990.
Acronym: QCI.
Scores, 5: Drawing, Copying, Analogies, Math, Total.
Administration: Individual or group.
Price Data, 1991: $30 per complete kit including 10 test booklets/record forms and manual (39 pages); $15 per 10 test booklets/record forms; $12 per specimen set.
Time: [45] minutes.
Comments: "Criterion-referenced."
Author: Annabelle M. Markoff.
Publisher: Academic Therapy Publications.

Review of the Quick Cognitive Inventory by AL-BERT C. OOSTERHOF, Professor of Education, Florida State University, Tallahassee, FL:

The Quick Cognitive Inventory (QCI) is "given to find those students whose success or failure in school depends on providing a balance between increased stimulation and increased direct instruction" (manual, p. 5). The manual as a whole provides virtually no further insight into what it is this instrument measures. No evidence of validity or reliability is presented. No instruction is given as to how results from the inventory are to be used. Basically, from a psychometric perspective, the QCI has little going for it.

The QCI is divided into four subtests: Spontaneous Drawing, Copying, Figural Analogies, and Visual Arithmetic (sometimes referred to in the test materials as Visual Math). For the Spontaneous Drawing subtest, the child is asked to draw a picture of herself or himself. When scoring the drawing, one point is awarded for each characteristic contained in the drawing that matches a checklist. The checklist includes items as diverse as head, nostrils, skirt, fetus, speech, and insignia. Twelve of the maximum 100 points are simply blanks in which the examiner can write in and give points for any unlisted elements that may have appeared in the drawing. In the Copying subtest, the child is asked to create a verbatim copy of a short sentence. One point is awarded for each of 20 characteristics as varied as letter formation, consistent spacing between words, consistent slant of letters, fluency, and lack of various qualities such as omission of a word or transposition. The scoring criteria are vague for many of these 20 characteristics. In the Analogies subtest (also referred to as Figural Analogies), a series of three geometric drawings is presented and the child is asked to identify the one drawing from a list of four options that completes the analogy implicit in the series. The correct response is straightforward within each of the 20 analogies, although the author's assertion that items within the QCI are easy for the majority of children in early elementary grades seems optimistic for this subtest. The Visual Arithmetic subtest consists of 25 items that require the child to solve problems involving addition, subtraction, multiplication, or division.

Some problems require the child to work with objects, such as counting dots, whereas others require working with numerals such as adding three 4-digit numbers.

The manual provides two sets of directions for administering the QCI. The first set is for use with children who can understand oral English directions. These directions are often wordy and confusing. The other set of directions is for students with "limited English language competence." Here, the examiner is directed to use pantomimes to convey tasks to the child. One must assume a child's performance is largely governed by the examiner's actions.

The manual contains a section entitled Instructional Implications in which global statements are made about numerous topics such as the need to provide students a good education, and problems caused by the alleged prevalent belief that IQ is fixed. The manual provides no normative information. No information is provided that would allow for a criterion-referenced interpretation. Educators would be well advised to take the copyright of this instrument seriously and not reproduce its contents in any form.

Review of the Quick Cognitive Inventory by GREGORY A. SHANNON, Supervisor of Testing, Virginia State Assessment Program, Virginia Department of Education, Richmond, VA:

PURPOSE OF TEST. The stated purposes of the Quick Cognitive Inventory (QCI) are to "allow teachers to observe a sample of school related skills in students who arrive in their classes either speaking a foreign language, or exhibiting language delays, or deficits" and to identify students "for whom the combination of stimulation and direct teaching will be critical to" academic success. The instrument was designed for first grade children, but may be used with second and third graders. The manual suggests that the inventory can serve as a screening test.

TEST DESCRIPTION. The test booklets are consumable and consist of 2 pages of record-keeping forms and 12 pages of test content and evaluator checklists in four test sections: (*a*) Spontaneous Drawing, a measure of concept development; (*b*) Copying, a measure of eye-hand coordination; (*c*) Figural Analogies, a measure of the understanding of sets of relationships between concepts and the patterns in relationships; and (*d*) Visual Math, a measure of simple math concepts and operations. The last two sections are in a multiple-choice format, except for 10 free-response numeric problems in the Visual Math section.

The manual advises users that the test covers "a few school-related skills." In my view, the sample is too small and unrepresentative of the cognitive and motor domains that many teachers perceive as school skills. This insufficient sample limits the usefulness of QCI scores for teachers who must accommodate children for whom any combination of developmental skills might be relevant to their instructional program.

RELIABILITY AND VALIDITY. No empirical evidence of reliability or validity of the QCI is reported in the manual. However, the inventory's author, A. M. Markoff (personal communication, November 9, 1990), indicated that some reliability data should be available within a year. The manual includes a table of raw score means and ranges based on QCI scores earned by six classes of students: two classes each from grades 1, 2, and 3. Any interpretations may be dubious due to the absence of descriptive information about the data, such as sampling procedures, class sizes, instructional programs, and academic and demographic characteristics of the students.

CONTENT. The stimuli-response symbols (pictures, geometric figures, or numbers) in the Visual Math and Figural Analogies sections may pose a problem for first grade students. These figures are too small, and too many are presented on each page, usually smaller than one-half inch square and averaging about 50 symbols per page. For some primary grade students, especially those with learning or language difficulties, these figures may be too difficult to recognize, distinguish, and process, introducing a source of test score unreliability.

Because a stated purpose of the QCI is to focus on identifying students who lack entry-level skills, the author claims most first graders should complete the test "easily and well." My visual examination of Figural Analogies and Visual Math items suggests that these sections may be more difficult than intended.

The QCI test booklets require improved editing. For example, the directions for the Visual Math section instruct students to proceed to Item 7 after completing the sample items, yet, the sample items are followed immediately by Item 4.

SCORING/PASSING SCORE. No norms are reported for the QCI; the author indicates that the instrument should not be used to rank students. Section scores are obtained by summing the number of acceptable student responses or evaluator entries. The author suggests that students who earn scores lower than 50% of the maximum section score may require additional instruction or assessment. Unfortunately, no rationale was stated for cut score selection or modification, or any evidence of the standard errors at the cut scores. The use of the same cutoff for all test sections is questionable because they are described in the manual as measures of distinguishable constructs.

Lack of clarity about the precision of the cut scores and their interpretability seems most troublesome because the QCI was designed for testing students with language, speech, or learning difficulties. For such students, true levels of proficiency may be expected to differ widely depending on their disabilities, psychological or physical development, perceptions of testing tasks, and sociocultural experiences. Without the availability of meaningful, reliable cut scores or appropriate population norms, QCI scores may be misleading, especially for inexperienced teachers.

ADMINISTRATION/STUDENT PREPARATION. The author indicated that the QCI may be administered to students either individually or in groups. Separate directions are provided for students proficient or nonproficient in the English language. The QCI requires about 45 minutes of administration time and is not to be considered a power test.

The test administration instructions consist of little more than test directions and a list of required materials. Insufficient detail is provided regarding the testing environment, qualifications of the administrator, guidelines for judging whether students should be tested, and student preparation. The administration of tests to young children in a group setting can be a complicated operation, especially if test administrators are not advised about steps to minimize sources of unreliability. Particularly disturbing is the lack of guidance regarding the preparation of students with limited English proficiency; these children may require special instruction such as practice with vocabulary they should know to adequately complete the testing tasks.

TEST INTERPRETATION/INSTRUCTIONAL IMPLICATIONS. No data are provided that show comparative test or item performance of student subgroups defined as gender, race, socioeconomic status, or other demographic factors that may confound interpretation of academic measures. In addition, no descriptions of test development procedures or field testing are provided.

I found the discussion of score interpretation to be overly simplistic, with little discussion of possible misinterpretations or misuses. For example, a child's low score on the copying task may be symptomatic of perceptual difficulties rather than eye-hand coordination.

It is not clear from the manual how QCI scores are to be used to improve student learning. The author indicates that the QCI may be used to identify students for whom success in school would be dependent on providing a balance between increased stimulation and increased direct instruction. However, the manual provides no examples or specific explanation for teachers to help them understand how to achieve such a balance, why such a balance would be important to student learning, or how QCI scores might be used to improve student learning.

SUMMARY. Whereas the Quick Cognitive Inventory offers advantages such as easy scoring and brief test administration time, this instrument has serious shortcomings. There is no evidence of reliability or validity. The absence of normative data, and the insufficiency of information about score interpretation and instructional utility may present serious disadvantages for teachers, especially inexperienced teachers. For the purpose of assessing developmental and school-related skills of primary grade students who may or may not be experiencing speech, language, or learning deficiencies, users are advised to seek a psychometrically sound, minimally nonverbal, comprehensive developmental inventory with clear instructional implications. The Slingerland Screening Tests for Identifying Children with Specific Language Disability, Form A (9:1141), appears to be useful for this general purpose; however, users would have to overcome the limitation of lack of norms (see reviews by Fujiki [1985] and Wiig [1985] in *The Ninth Mental Measurements Yearbook*).

REVIEWER'S REFERENCES

Fujiki, M. (1985). [Review of the Slingerland Screening Tests for Identifying Children with Specific Language Disability.] In J. V. Mitchell, Jr. (Ed.), *The ninth mental measurements yearbook* (pp. 1398-1399). Lincoln, NE: Buros Institute of Mental Measurements.
Wiig, E. H. (1985). [Review of the Slingerland Screening Tests for Identifying Children with Specific Language Disability.] In J. V. Mitchell, Jr. (Ed.), *The ninth mental measurements yearbook* (pp. 1399-1400). Lincoln, NE: Buros Institute of Mental Measurements.

[322]
Quick Spelling Inventory.

Purpose: To "identify the grade level at which a student can function in spelling."
Population: Grades 1–6.
Publication Date: 1988.
Acronym: QSI.
Scores: Total score only.
Administration: Group or individual.
Manual: No manual.
Price Data, 1991: $10 per 50 recording forms and plasticized word list with directions.
Time: Administration time not reported.
Author: Bob Wright.
Publisher: Academic Therapy Publications (High Noon Division).

Review of the Quick Spelling Inventory by KEVIN D. CREHAN, Associate Professor of Educational Psychology, University of Nevada, Las Vegas, Las Vegas, NV:

The Quick Spelling Inventory (QSI) is designed to determine grade level functioning in spelling for grades 2 through 6. The test consists of 45 words reportedly arranged in order of increasing spelling difficulty. The test is administered orally and can be used with a group or individual. Words are pronounced by the examiner, used in a phrase, and pronounced again (e.g., "Number 1, dog . . . the dog barks . . . dog"). Scoring is either number correct preceding five consecutive incorrect spellings or simply number correct if there is not a sequence of five incorrect spellings. A table is provided to convert raw scores to grade level (e.g., a raw score between 21 and 25 has a grade level equivalent of "Grade 4 beginning").

Because the QSI does not have a manual, the publisher was asked to provide information and documentation underlying test development and interpretation. The publisher's response indicated that the QSI's author was deceased and no information on word selection or score interpretation was available.

It is difficult to provide a critical review of this instrument based on the testing materials alone. The plasticized card on which the test words, directions, and grade conversion chart are printed is attractively prepared and seems durable. The words appear to get more difficult and the grade equivalent conversion seems reasonable. However, without evidence to support anything other than its attractiveness and durability, there is little to recommend the QSI over competing spelling tests (e.g., Test of Written Spelling [Revised Edition]; 10:374), or more general tests of written language (e.g., Test of Written Language—2; 444).

Review of the Quick Spelling Inventory by DALE P. SCANNELL, Professor and Dean, College of Education, University of Maryland at College Park, College Park, MD:

The Quick Spelling Inventory (QSI) consists of a cover sheet, a packet of record forms, and a laminated page with the spelling inventory on one side and instructions on the other side. The instructions include a short, one-paragraph introduction, a section titled Administration, a section labeled Scoring, and a table for converting raw scores into spelling grade levels. No manual is available.

The test comprises 45 words, which the author reports are presented in "increasing spelling difficulty." Teachers are directed to read a word, read a phrase that includes the word, and repeat the word. For example, line one on the test is: dog . . . the dog barks . . . dog. The test is untimed but the author indicates that "students should need no longer than 15 seconds per word." Teachers are advised to watch the examinees to ensure that they are keeping up with the presentation.

The conversion table indicates that 1–5 words correct corresponds to grade 2 beginning or below, 6–10 corresponds to grade 2 end, etc. Each succeeding group of five words converts to a grade beginning or a grade end.

If a teacher is seeking an instrument unencumbered by a complex manual, technical data, a rationale or theory, or suggestions for how the test results might be useful, this may be the one to buy. The task of reviewing a test with these characteristics is relatively easy. The main task is to identify a few questions a prospective user is not able to answer. For example:

1. On what basis was this sample of words identified: Are they among some list of most frequently misspelled words? Are they on some list of most frequently used words at grades 1–6?

2. How did the author determine that the sequence of words is in increasing spelling difficulty?

3. What item selection technique was used to determine, for example, that scores of 21–25 would mean that the student's "spelling skills are equivalent to those of students in the first semester of fourth grade"?

4. What is the evidence of validity—rational, curricular, empirical?

5. What is the reliability of the scores on this test? What is the standard error of measurement?

When a test lacks a manual, these and other questions of general interest to prospective users cannot be answered. Of course, these are types of information necessary for a test publication to be in conformity with accepted standards.

As shown in the descriptive entry preceding this review, $10 will get a user a packet of recording forms and a plasticized word list. A user could make such a purchase, use the 50 forms, and then use the plasticized list with students writing on plain, lined paper. An investment of $10 for a lifetime supply of what is needed may be about right for a test that lacks everything testing standards suggest should be available.

[323]
Racial Attitude Test.

Purpose: Measures attitudes toward an examiner-selected group of people using a generic semantic differential method.
Population: Adults.
Publication Date: 1989.
Scores, 8: Physical, Ego Strength (Dominance, Control, Anxiety, Ethics, General Social, On the Job), You Would Object.
Administration: Group.
Manual: No manual.
Price Data, 1989: $19.95 per test booklet which may be photocopied for local use.
Time: Administration time not reported.
Comments: No reliability or validity; no norms.
Author: Thomas J. Rundquist.
Publisher: Nova Media, Inc.

Review of the Racial Attitude Test by RICHARD I. LANYON, Professor of Psychology, Arizona State University, Tempe, AZ:

There is no stretch of the imagination by which the Racial Attitude Test could be considered a test in the accepted sense of the term for psychology. The entirety of the material available from the publisher and the author consists of four sheets of thick paper, stapled in the corner, for which a price

of $9.95 is stated on the front page. Also given on the front page is the address of the publisher and ISBN number. The second and third sheets list 46 bipolar items preceded by the following instructions: "The selected group to what degree have these traits 1 to 5. Circle your choice of 1, 2, 3, 4, or 5. For example, for the trait Dirty to Clean, one would pick a number from 1 to 5 to show what degree from Dirty to Clean he felt the selected group had." The 46 items are grouped into eight categories, the names of which are given below. The number of items in each category ranges from 2 through 13. Following the 46 items is the statement, "When you complete the survey, please bring the test up to the administrators."

The fourth sheet gives instructions for interpretation. I quote it in full. (Heading) "Evaluating Results." (Paragraph) "If testing more than one person, Xeroxing of the question sheet is allowed. This is figured in your initial price. We allow you to Xerox up to 25 copies. After that a new test booklet should be purchased. Generally, a high score for each question or each section (Physical, Ego Strength, Control, Anxiety, Ethics, General Special, On the Job, You Would Object) means a more positive attitude by the test taker toward the group. However, the reality of the general population's attitude for a selected group as shown in each question would need to be based on extensive testing. For some of the traits there may be a difference of opinion as to whether it is positive or negative."

A telephone call to the author revealed that nothing further was available, but that data were currently being collected "from a couple of colleges." No mention was made of test development procedures, item analyses, reliability, validity, norms, or a manual.

Clearly the Racial Attitude Test is not usable as an assessment instrument in its present form, and it should be withdrawn from the market until further development work is done. Guidelines for such test development can be found in the 1985 *Standards for Educational and Psychological Testing* published jointly by the American Psychological Association and other organizations.

A general comment on the study and assessment of racism is in order. Two aspects are usually addressed: (*a*) the *content* of stereotypes, as to what attitudes are salient in judging different races; and (*b*) *social distance*, as to how willing people are to engage with the race in a variety of activities of differing social distance. The two sections of the Racial Attitude Test do conform to this structure, suggesting that there might be a foundation for the ultimate development of a useful instrument. Readers wishing to advance their own knowledge of this area are referred to Brewer and Kramer (1985) and McConahay, Hardee, and Batts (1981).

REVIEWER'S REFERENCES

McConahay, J. B., Hardee, B. B., & Batts, V. (1981). Has racism declined in America? *Journal of Conflict Resolution, 25*, 563-579.
American Educational Research Association, American Psychological Association, & National Council on Measurement in Education. (1985). *Standards for educational and psychological testing.* Washington, DC: American Psychological Association, Inc.
Brewer, M. B., & Kramer, R. M. (1985). The psychology of intergroup attitudes and behavior. *Annual Review of Psychology, 36*, 219-243.

Review of the Racial Attitude Test by STEVEN G. LoBELLO, Assistant Professor of Psychology, Auburn University at Montgomery, Montgomery, AL:

The Racial Attitude Test is a 46-item scale which may be administered individually or in groups. The test is designed to measure attitudes toward any ethnic, religious, or racial group specified by the examiner. The test has three scales that are ambiguously entitled You Would Object/Accept, Physical, and Ego Strength (Dominance, Control, Anxiety, Ethics, General Social, and On the Job are subscales). The You Would Object/Accept scale asks the test taker to rate level of acceptance of the specified group in various social situations. The format is a bipolar Likert-type scale with adjectival opposites to which the test taker responds by circling a number 1 (negative) through 5 (positive). High scores on each scale or item are presumed to reflect more positive attitudes toward the specified group.

The only test instructions provided are three very awkwardly worded lines at the top of the first page of the test. There is no test manual and, consequently, there are no norms, reliability, or validity data. There is no information provided about internal consistency of the individual scales, some of which consist of fewer than four items. There is a brief, one-paragraph information sheet attached to the back of the test which provides no information about test construction, for whom the test was designed, or how the scores should be used. The purpose of the test is patently transparent with no provision for measuring social desirability, or overrater or underrater response sets.

In summary, the Racial Attitude Test reflects a naive and irresponsible approach to test construction with no attention given to even the minimum psychometric standards as outlined in the *Standards for Educational and Psychological Testing* (1985, APA, AERA, & NCME). Anyone choosing to use this test could not have the slightest confidence that it is actually measuring racial attitudes toward a specified group. The Racial Attitude Test is actually a nontest and it should not be used until the author provides adequate supporting data.

REVIEWER'S REFERENCE

American Educational Research Association, American Psychological Association, & National Council on Measurement in Education. (1985). *Standards for educational and psychological testing.* Washington, DC: American Psychological Association, Inc.

Reading Ability Series.

Purpose: To provide an assessment of reading skills children need at school and at home as well as diagnostic information concerning reading difficulties.
Population: Ages 7-0 to 8-11, 8-0 to 9-11, 9-0 to 10-11, 10-0 to 11-11, 11-0 to 12-11, 12-0 to 13-11.
Publication Date: 1989.
Scores, 6: Narrative, Expository, Total, Percentile, Standardised Score, Scale Score.
Administration: Group.
Price Data, 1990: £20.65 per specimen set including Teacher's Handbook ('89, 76 pages), reading booklets, Levels A–C and F ('89, 8 pages), Level D ('89, 12 pages), Level E ('87, 11 pages), work booklets, Levels A–D ('88, 12 pages), Levels E and F ('88, 16 pages).
Authors: Anne Kispal, Tom Gorman, and Chris Whetton.
Publisher: NFER-Nelson Publishing Co., Ltd. [England].
a) LEVEL A.
Population: Ages 7-0 to 8-11.
Price Data: £5.70 per pack of 5 reading booklets; £5.20 per pack of 10 work booklets; £2.90 per answer key.
Time: 60(70) minutes.
b) LEVEL B.
Population: Ages 8-0 to 9-11.
Parts, 2: Narrative, Expository.
Price Data: Same as Level A.
Time: 45(55) minutes per part.
Comments: Parts 1 and 2 need to be administered at least 1 day and not more than 7 days apart.
c) LEVEL C.
Population: Ages 9-0 to 10-11.
Comments: Parts, Price Data, and Time same as Level B.
d) LEVEL D.
Population: Ages 10-0 to 11-11.
Comments: Parts, Price Data, and Time same as Level B.
e) LEVEL E.
Population: Ages 11-0 to 12-11.
Comments: Parts, Price Data, and Time same as Level B.
f) LEVEL F.
Population: Ages 12-0 to 13-11.
Comments: Parts, Price Data, and Time same as Level B.

Review of the Reading Ability Series by CLEBORNE D. MADDUX, Chairman, Department of Curriculum and Instruction, University of Nevada, Reno, NV:

The Reading Ability Series is a group-administered, norm-referenced reading test consisting of a series of six reusable reading booklets and six consumable work booklets. The manual states the purpose of the test is to measure the "interpretation, appreciation and/or use of whole pieces of text" (p. 4). Subjects take the test at one of six levels corresponding to their year in school. The reading booklet for each level includes one narrative and one expository passage. After reading each passage silently, subjects respond in writing to both multiple-choice (cloze format) and open-ended questions presented in the work booklets. The narrative and expository passages and related test items are completed in two sessions with an interval of at least 1 day, but not more than 7 days between (only Level A is to be completed in one session). All children respond to all questions, and the responses are scored 1 or 0 by the examiner after administration is completed. Scoring is accomplished by referring to a series of marking keys. These keys are priced separately and are not supplied as part of the basic test package.

Raw scores can be converted to various standard scores for "quantitative" analysis, and to quintiles for "qualitative" analysis. This latter analysis is to be accomplished by referring to pages 19–64 in the manual. This section of the manual contains typical reading skills and difficulties of students who fall into each quintile on each level of the test.

NORMATIVE DATA. The test manual states that The Reading Ability Series is based on the work of the Assessment and Performance Unit (APU) in its language surveys in England and Wales. Although no further information about this work is given, the manual goes on to state that the reading passages were taken from published material and are those that children are likely to encounter both inside and outside the classroom. No evidence is presented in support of this contention. The test authors merely state that they initially selected a number of passages after conducting a search of children's literature, reference works, and new articles, and that several schools were visited to obtain reactions to these proposed texts. Further, the authors assert that multicultural and gender issues were considered. Again, no evidence is presented concerning these claims. Twenty-one passages were then selected and piloted in 90 schools, with at least 300 students exposed to each passage. No further information on the piloting process or on passage selection is given.

Even a cursory examination of the passages reveals a major problem in cultural specificity. The readings are heavily sprinkled with British slang and other cultural idiosyncracies. This, in itself, would not be a weakness. However, some test questions are so structured that lack of understanding of these cultural specificities could cause subjects to respond incorrectly, thus artificially depressing scores. One of countless examples occurs in Level A, in which subjects must first read a restaurant menu in which prices are given in pounds, then report the price of a meal.

The final version of the test was standardized in 1987 using a stratified random sample of schools in England and Wales. The sample consisted of 12,255 students from 375 schools stratified on the basis of region, Local Education Agency type, school type, and school size. No information is provided on gender, socioeconomic status, or numbers or types of handicapped students in the normative sample. Mean and maximum raw scores for the expository and narrative sections and for the test as a whole were calculated. Tables are provided for conversion of level raw scores to standard scores (mean = 100, $sd = 15$), percentiles, series scale scores, and quintiles. The work booklets include a summary sheet on the back for recording scores, as well as a scale to facilitate graphing confidence intervals of standardized scores.

RELIABILITY. Internal consistency was investigated by calculating KR20 coefficients for each of the six levels of the series and separately for narrative and expository sections at each level. All coefficients are .90 or greater for complete subtests and .83 or greater for individual narrative or expository sections except for Level D narrative, which was .65. It is unclear whether these coefficients were calculated using the scores of all pupils in the normative sample, or whether some subset of that sample was used.

Test-retest reliability was calculated for subsets of the original standardization sample who were given the same level of the test approximately 1 week after original testing. No information is given on how that subset was selected. Sample sizes for each of the six levels varied from 220 to 371, whereas correlation coefficients varied from .83 to .93. All but the latter coefficient (Level A) were below .90.

Interlevel consistency was investigated by administering the two adjacent levels of the test to a subset of the normative sample. Again, no data were given on how the subset was selected. Sample sizes varied from 147 to 376. Raw score correlations varied from .71 to .83.

VALIDITY. The only validity information presented is information on content of the test, discussed above under the heading of Normative Data.

SUMMARY. The Reading Ability Series is a norm-referenced, group reading test based apparently on the unstated assumption that reading ability can be measured by examining the written responses of subjects to test items after silent reading. Although the use of written, rather than oral responses to questions would be considered controversial by some educators, the issue is never addressed in the test manual. An unfortunate lack in the analysis of the test is the authors' failure to address concurrent validity by studying the relationship of Reading Ability Series scores to scores on more conventional reading tests. No such studies were reported. It is unclear, therefore, whether the Reading Ability Series measures reading ability, writing ability, or some combination of these or other skills.

The manual suggests the Series can be used for qualitative analysis of children's reading abilities. However, the authors suggest that such an analysis be carried out by determining a subject's membership in one of five quintiles and by then consulting pages 19 to 64 in the test manual. These pages contain exhaustive descriptions of "typical" students who score within specific quintiles, as well as typical characteristics of those students who make specific correct and incorrect responses to individual test items. These descriptions constitute little more than stereotypes, and it is unclear why the authors chose to include them in lieu of analyses of specific, individual behaviors of the students being tested.

British language usage is so pervasive the test would be virtually useless for administration outside the United Kingdom, perhaps even for use outside England and Wales. In addition, reliability studies of the Series are incompletely reported. Validity has not been investigated.

In light of the problems described above, the Reading Ability Series does not represent progress, and adds little, if anything, to the primitive state of the art in reading assessment.

Review of the Reading Ability Series by HOWARD STOKER, Research Professor, Bureau of Educational Research and Service, University of Tennessee, Knoxville, TN:

The Reading Ability Series (RAS) represents a type of assessment of reading comprehension that differs from what one finds in most standardized tests published in the United States. The stimulus materials "involve the use of texts such as children are likely to encounter inside and outside the classroom." Although this claim would not be unique, what distinguishes the tests is that all students respond in Work Booklets, calling for hand scoring, and use a modified cloze technique for measuring comprehension. Where standardized tests in the U.S. typically report the appropriate grade level, these tests are leveled by ages, ranging from 7 to 13.

There are two booklets for each of the six levels of tests. One booklet is entitled "Read About" and contains the stimulus material. These booklets are bound with heavy covers, printed in several colors, and designed to last and to be attractive to the students. The Work Booklet is designed for one-time use. Color coding helps distinguish the Levels A–F. Students read the stimulus material and then complete the exercises in the Work Booklet. They do not answer questions, in the usual sense of that phrase, because most of the "questions" are embedded in what amounts to another reading passage. Where questions do appear, they call for constructed responses, at all levels of testing.

Directions for test administration are less restrictive in these tests than are those found in the typical standardized test published in the U.S. The directions for administering the Stanford Achievement Test, for example, contain specific statements that are to be read to the pupils. Time limits are exact, in most cases. These specific instructions and the time limits are what leads to a "standardized" test (i.e., the *standard administration* of a test). For the RAS, one finds the statement in the Teacher's Handbook "Except where otherwise indicated, the teacher is free to convey the instructions in words that seem most appropriate to the particular age and experience of the children." Obviously, emphasis on standard administration is not considered critical for this test.

Scoring is done by hand, following protocols for each level. Two types of scores are derived—quantitative, based on the number of correct answers to the objective items, and qualitative, derived by comparing the pupil's constructed responses with sample answers, contained in the separate marking keys. The marking keys were not available to the reviewer.

According to the Teacher's Handbook, "The marking keys allow for a variety of acceptable answers, with a sample of answers presented to reflect those most commonly given by pupils as indicated by the extensive pre-publication trials of the materials. Nevertheless, other acceptable answers to such questions may occur and the person marking the booklets will, in these cases, need to give an answer careful thought before awarding a mark of 1 or 0, in much the same way as s/he would when marking a pupil's normal classwork or assessing an oral response to a question about a piece of reading."

Hence, the qualitative scores would be subject to unreliability, depending, perhaps, on the marker's familiarity with the relevant text in the Reading Booklet, years of teaching experience, and familiarity with the children being tested. If one were marking booklets for pupils in his or her own class, the scores would probably be inflated by some form of halo effect.

The answer keys are said to include information on what to look for when the difference between an "acceptable" and an "unacceptable" answer appears to be a fine-line decison. Marking keys also contain "frequently occurring wrong answers, again taken from the pre-publication trials."

Instructions for finding standardized scores appear in the Teacher's Handbook. A child's age in years and "completed months" is calculated and combined with the Total Raw Score to produce a Standard Score and a Percentile. For each level, the Total Raw Score can be converted to a Series Scale Score. Raw scores from the Narrative and Expository parts of each level can be converted to Quintile scores for those parts, within each level. Hence, when scoring and recording is completed, each child will have: raw scores and Quintiles for Narrative and Expository, a Total Raw Score and Standard Score, Percentile Rank, and Series Scale Score. Where students are retested, after one or more years, a level-to-level progress score may be determined. Finally, a 90% confidence interval for the Standard Score can be obtained easily from the chart printed on the record sheet, which is the back cover of the answer document.

Technical information provided in the Teacher's Handbook appears to be adequate. The section begins with a description of how the text material was selected, and how the material was pilot tested prior to the compilation of the final test versions. This section, and later information, emphasize the content validity of the tests. For measures of current reading ability, content validity is judged most appropriate.

The standardization sample appears to be appropriate for the schools in England and Wales. Region, Local Education Agency type, school type, and school size were used as stratification variables. Approximately 2,000 pupils were tested at each level of the RAS. "Selected pupils in each school" completed the Test of Initial Literacy, but information on how they were selected and the correlations between the two tests does not appear in the Teacher's Handbook.

Reliability estimates, KR-20s, and test-retest correlations, based on a 1-week time lapse, are provided. All are judged adequate for a test of this type. Given that the scores on the Narrative and Expository sections of each test are, to some extent, judgmental, the reliabilities may be higher than one would anticipate.

Information is provided on the correlations between Raw Scores on adjacent levels of the series, which were obtained from samples of pupils who participated in this phase of the standardization exercise. These data were used to compute the Series Scale Scores and will permit comparisons to be made of a pupil's progress over time.

EVALUATION. The Reading Ability Series appears to be well designed for use by classroom teachers in *England and Wales* for reading assessment. The tests are not designed for use, nor would they work well, in the schools in the United States. It is interesting to conjecture what an Americanized version would look like, and how well it would be accepted.

An interesting, and valuable, part of the Teacher's Handbook is Section 7, Interpretation of Responses. The authors/publishers provide many pages of diagnostic information pertaining to pupils' responses to the Narrative and Expository parts of the tests. This reviewer is of the opinion that such information will be of considerable value to the teacher in determining why raw scores are higher, or lower, than anticipated for a pupil. Interpretation of

test scores is a common problem for classroom teachers—these pages should make that task much easier.

[325]
Reading Comprehension Inventory.

Purpose: To assess a student's strengths and weaknesses in reading and to determine a student's capacity to extract meaningful information from narrative passages.
Population: Grades K–6.
Publication Date: 1988.
Acronym: RCI.
Scores: 3 sets of structural features: Narrative Elements, Response Level, Information Sequencing.
Administration: Group.
Price Data, 1988: $24.95 per starter set including 20 workbooks with student profiles and manual (33 pages); $18 per 20 workbooks with student profiles; $8.50 per manual; $13 per specimen set.
Time: Administration time not reported.
Author: Gerard Giordano.
Publisher: Scholastic Testing Service, Inc.

Review of the Reading Comprehension Inventory by ALICE J. CORKILL, Assistant Professor of Psychology, University of Western Ontario, London, Ontario, Canada:

The Reading Comprehension Inventory attempts to assess the functional and operational skills of elementary school age readers. The test consists of six narrative passages beginning with a simple five-sentence story and progressing to a more complex four-paragraph story. Each passage is followed by five questions which are designed to assess the following five Narrative elements of the passage: character(s), location(s), time(s), plot, and rationale. Each question also provides information concerning the Response Level: factual, critical, or extrapolative and Information Sequencing: presituational, situational, or postsituational.

The first passage, "Snake," is the least complex on all features requiring only simple, factual, situational responses to the five questions. The passages gradually become more complex with the last passage, "Fire," requiring complex information in all areas.

The passages may be read orally or silently during administration. Test administrators are encouraged to have the examinee continue with the test until comprehension falls below 60 percent. How this is to be determined, however, is not discussed. These procedures suggest the inventory is individually administered, although this is not clearly stated in the administrator's manual.

An "Analysis of Questions" is provided for each of the six passages. The analysis provides answers to each question, a point value for each correct response, and a description of the Narrative Element, the Response Level, and the Information Sequencing as assessed by each question. Each of the five questions that accompany a passage is differentially weighted. Simple, factual information may receive a small number of points while more complex, interpretive questions garner a larger number of points. The weights were devised by a group of "20 experienced teachers" (no other information about the teachers or their experience is provided), who read each passage and distributed a total of 100 points to five questions that they created which assessed each of the five narrative elements. As a result, the point values assigned to each narrative element vary from passage to passage.

In four of the six passages the answers provided for the question assessing the location narrative element are incomplete or incorrect. For example, in the passage titled "Creature" the examinee is questioned about the location of a trap set to capture the creature. The answer provided is "backyard," however, the passage states, "They decided to set a trap in their yard." As a result, "yard" or "outside" might be better answers and although "backyard" could be considered appropriate, it is not necessarily the best or most correct response. In the other passages the responses seem somewhat incomplete. The examinee has access to the passage while responding to the questions. As a consequence, detailed or specific answers are readily available and could be expected. Other passages with problems with this narrative element include "Alone," "Crash," and "Fire."

For two passages, "Cave" and "Creature," additional correct responses could be provided for the question assessing rationale (often more than one correct response is provided). For the passage "Crash" the character question may be asking for too much to be inferred from the passage. If administrators of the test are inclined to employ a literal use of the responses provided in the test manual, the results of the test may incorrectly identify an examinees' strengths and/or weaknesses.

In each instance an examinee receives all the points assigned to a question or none of the points. A brief perusal of the responses provided in the administrator's manual, however, clearly shows that some responses are more complete or precise. Because more than one correct response is provided, in many instances, a possibility worth considering would be to assign more correct responses, in terms of detail or specificity, with higher point values and less correct or complete responses with lower point values.

Each test booklet includes the six test passages and a strength and weakness worksheet. This worksheet is to be used by the administrator in an effort to identify an examinee's pattern of strengths and weaknesses. The administrator is instructed to assign and total an examinee's points. These point totals are not used for anything, at least not according to the manual. Careful examination of the sample strength and weakness worksheet, however, suggests that the point total indicates percentage of comprehension. Further use of the strength and weakness worksheet is in identifying areas in which an examinee excels or fails. Insufficient information is provided for this use of the strength and weakness worksheet. A more complete example or more than one example of using the worksheet would be beneficial.

Half of the administrator's manual is devoted to 23 instructional activities designed to address the identified deficiencies of an examinee. This is a potentially valuable portion of the manual; however, use of these activities may be restricted by the nature of the problems associated with use of the strength and weakness worksheet.

No reliability or validity information is provided in the administrator's manual. The lack of information in this area is a critical deficiency in the Reading Comprehension Inventory. Some attempt should be made to determine the reliability of the instrument, perhaps via test-retest if no other option seems suitable. The validity of the inventory also needs to be established, if only the content validity. The value of this instrument cannot be completely determined without evidence of reliability and validity.

If the problems associated with scoring procedures are rectified, the Reading Comprehension Inventory could be a valuable instrument for use by classroom teachers. Its value lies in ease of administration, teacher scoring, and suggested instructional activities developed to assist in strengthening identified deficiencies. Its shortcomings center on incomplete or incorrect responses, lack of directions for completing the strength and weakness worksheet, and undocumented reliability and validity information.

Review of the Reading Comprehension Inventory by BRANDON DAVIS, *Research Fellow, Ball State Neuropsychology Laboratory, and* JOHN A. GLOVER, *Director of Research, Teachers College, Ball State University, Muncie, IN:*

The Reading Comprehension Inventory (RCI) was designed to evaluate reading comprehension in school-aged children from a criterion-referenced standpoint; age ranges are not included in the manual. The test consists of six reading passages, each accompanied by five differentially weighted questions. This weighting process is intended to correspond both to different items within each passage and also across the six passages; with the first passage being the simplest with respect to comprehension issues and the sixth passage being the most complicated. Accordingly, item values are given weights ranging from 5 to 60 points. There is no total score, but rather individual scores for each story with the diagnostician circling weaknesses in each story based on the three possible categories of assessment for each question and the three to five subcategories for each category. The manual includes a series of exercises that purport to offer guidance in the remediation of the identified comprehension deficits.

In a poorly delineated introduction, the author suggests that the test "is an actual test of reading comprehension rather than a test of skills that correlate with reading." One is left with the impression that the author has presumed comprehension is easily bifurcated from the myriad of other cognitive skills in reading. Indeed, this perception appears confirmed as the author has offered nothing in the way of approximate readability levels for any of the six passages. Further, the manual suggests that students can be assessed in either an oral or silent diagnostic mode; and while the author suggests the test is intended as a classroom evaluation tool, the manual does not specify whether such assessment is to be carried out in an individual or group fashion.

The author offers a gratuitous figure (Figure 1, p. 1) in the introduction of the manual enjoining the reader in an appreciation of the fact that the processes of reading bring to bear on the reader a variety of physical, linguistic, cognitive, academic, social, and emotional factors. Apparently, the RCI is designed to respond to this blending of intellective factors in the six passages making up the test.

The six passages are arranged in order of increasing complexity based on the matrix of three sets of features (i.e., Narrative Elements, Response Level issues, and Information Sequencing concerns) with corresponding levels of structure within each set (i.e., character, location, time, plot, and rationale for the Narrative Elements; factual, critical, and extrapolative issues for the Response Level set; and, presituational, situational, and postsituational concerns for the Sequencing of Information set). The last story represents the most complex interaction of these variables, whereas the first story represents the simplest interaction.

Such an assessment outline would seem to suggest a sophisticated attempt directed toward the assessment of the comprehension processes in the student. Unfortunately, the technical information in the manual does little to substantiate this impression. In fact, it is not apparent that any criteria, as delineated in *Standards for Educational and Psychological Testing* (AERA, APA, & NCME, 1985), have been applied in the test's construction. There is no information available as to the test's reliability or validity. The author does not make mention of the differential issues of criterion-referencing versus norm-referencing. However, it appears from its construction that it would best fit into the norm-referenced category. Even allowing for the fact that this test is criterion-referenced, one might expect some reference to

minimal issues of psychometric test construction (Carver, 1974; Salvia & Ysseldyke, 1981; Womer, 1974). One singular reference to test construction suggests the process of assigning values to each of the five questions in the six stories was carried out with the collaboration of 20 experienced teachers.

Also notable by its absence is support for those concepts on which the construction of the test is based. Indeed, there is no theoretical or empirical support offered lending credence to the author's perspective on issues of reading comprehension. In the introduction of the manual the author suggests that his test attempts to measure the reading process (i.e., comprehension) in tandem with all the other mechanical skills of reading (i.e., syllabification, phonics, spelling, word derivation, etc.) rather than separate from them. However, appropriate test construction would have better dealt with this issue. In fact, without the necessary psychometric concerns that would control for the age and grade levels of words chosen in his passage, it would be impossible to assume that the test (*a*) is assessing comprehension; or (*b*) is appropriate for a given segment of the school population. In fact, such inappropriate test construction would allow word recognition to confound issues of comprehension to the degree that word recognition, not comprehension, is actually being assessed.

In sum, the RCI attempts to represent a defined theoretical perspective on the assessment of reading comprehension. Unfortunately, the author has neglected to support this perspective by applying basic test construction principles to his measure and has offered only a minimum of technical data. For instance, even criterion-referenced measures should include the targeted school population. Essentially, the RCI represents an extremely arbitrary and subjective attempt at test construction. There are significant problems with every aspect of this measure.

REVIEWER'S REFERENCES

Carver, R. P. (1974). Two dimensions of tests: Psychometric and edumetric. *American Psychologist, 29* (7), 512-518.
Womer, F. B. (1974). What is criterion-referenced measurement? In W. E. Blanton, R. Farr, & J. J. Tuinman (Eds.), *Measuring reading performance* (pp. 34-43). Newark, DE: International Reading Association.
Salvia, J., & Ysseldyke, J. E. (1981). *Assessment in special and remedial education.* Boston: Houghton-Mifflin.
American Educational Research Association, American Psychological Association, & National Council on Measurement in Education. (1985). *Standards for educational and psychological testing.* Washington, DC: American Psychological Association, Inc.

[326]
Reading Evaluation Adult Diagnosis (Revised).

Purpose: Assess existing reading competencies.
Population: Illiterate adult students.
Publication Dates: 1972–82.
Acronym: READ.
Scores: 4 parts, 26 scores: Sight Words (List A, List B, List C, List D), Word Analysis Skills (Letter Sounds Not

Identified, Letter Names Not Identified, Reversal Problems, Consonant-Vowel-Consonant Not Known, CV-CC, Initial Blends Not Known, Final Blends Not Known, Initial Digraphs Not Known, Final Digraphs Not Known, Variant Vowel Problems (R-Controlled, L-Controlled, W-Controlled, Y-Controlled, Vowel Digraphs, and Vowel Plus E), Suffixes Not Known, Soft C and G Problems, Silent Letter Problems, Multi-Syllabic Word Problems), Reading/Listening Inventory (Word Recognition, Reading Comprehension, Listening Comprehension), Group Screening Test.

Administration: Individual in part; student responds orally in part.

Price Data, 1989: $7.25 per test booklet/manual('82, 55 pages); $1.50 per tester's recording pad; $20 per test trainer's kit including trainer's guide and cassette tape.

Time: Administration time not reported.

Comments: Examiner must be trained to administer test.

Authors: Ruth J. Colvin and Jane H. Root.

Publisher: Literacy Volunteers of America, Inc.

TEST REFERENCES

1. Fox, B. J., & Fingeret, A. (1984). Test review: Reading Evaluation Adult Diagnosis (Revised). *Journal of Reading, 28,* 258-261.

Review of the Reading Evaluation Adult Diagnosis (Revised) by MARY E. HUBA, Professor of Research and Evaluation, Iowa State University, Ames, IA:

The Reading Evaluation Adult Diagnosis (Revised) is an evaluation instrument to be used as part of an instructional program designed for adults and teens by the Literacy Volunteers of America, Inc. The intended administrators of the test are instructors (tutors) in adult basic reading, and references are continually made in the test manual to *Tutor,* the basic text designed by the same authors for training tutors to teach. The tutors (and thus testers) are assumed to be those who have had no experience in teaching.

The primary evaluation instrument is an individually administered diagnostic test to assist tutors in assessing both student reading needs and student reading progress. The test is organized into three parts that are standard elements in many reading tests (Sight Words, Word Analysis Skills, Reading/Listening Inventory). The manual is well organized and the paragraphs to be used in the Reading/Listening portion of the test are appropriate in content for an adult audience. Testers are trained in an 18-hour workshop in which instructions are provided from an audio-cassette tape and a leader is present to facilitate understanding. In addition to training in the administration and scoring of right/wrong items, instruction in evaluating oral reading ability (i.e., recording omissions, substitutions, self-corrections, etc.) is also included.

The authors recommend that the test be given both before and after the tutoring experience, although according to the manual, the test can be readministered at any time to assess student status. The approach appears to be criterion-referenced in

the Sight Word and Word Analysis sections. In the former, words are sampled from successive quarters of "the list of the 300 words most commonly used in print." No citation for this reference is provided. This list apparently forms the corpus of sight words taught in the instructional program. In the latter, skills commonly included in reading inventories and presumed to be essential for mastering the reading task are presented. In contrast, in the Reading/Listening section, the authors purport that paragraphs evaluated with a readability formula correspond in difficulty to those typically found in elementary textbooks from grades 1 to 5.5.

Another evaluation instrument described in the manual is a Group Screening Test for use with a large number of students in order to "help determine which students should be tested further." The test is a word-matching exercise assessing speed and accuracy of visual perception. Twenty-five target words (primarily two- and three-syllable words) are presented vertically on a page. Next to each are four alternatives, one of which is the target word. The student must underline the word that is the same as the target word. Responses are not scored for accuracy; rather, the only score consists of the number of seconds to complete the test. According to the authors, "experience has shown that students who require more than seventy-five seconds to complete this test will probably have many reading problems," and "further diagnosis is advised."

The chief concern with these instruments is that absolutely no information whatsoever is provided in the manual regarding their psychometric properties. According to the publisher, two in-house studies have been conducted, but summaries were not available at the time of this review. The purpose of the tests is to make inferences regarding reading skill in an instructional setting in which learning is presumed to take place. However, no evidence that scores can effectively address this purpose (validity) is presented. Further, without data supporting reliability, confidence in the consistency of scores is not possible. The limitation this creates is particularly evident for the Group Screening Test in which neither the content nor the score is directly related to the reading task. Empirical evidence that scores are related to those from a more detailed test or assessment process is needed.

The need for psychometric information is also critical with regard to several of the authors' recommendations for use of the diagnostic test. First, minimal information about scoring procedures for the subtests is provided by the authors. For most subtests, the guideline is simply that three or more errors signal a need for instruction in the area. No data are presented to verify the usefulness of this cutoff, and further, no norms are presented. For subtests that must be mastered in order to read (like letter sounds) and in which the items represent the entire universe of items in the domain, a purely criterion-referenced approach may not be inappropriate. However, for these sections, as well as for other areas of the test in which items are samples from a universe, normative data for various groups of adults would be instructive. Because several critical aspects of the testing situation are rather atypical (i.e., type of instructor—volunteers usually having no formal training in reading education, learners—illiterate or low-achieving adults, and instructional setting—informally arranged meetings either individually or in groups), data on the ability of the instrument to detect learning effects under these conditions are needed.

Second, on the Sight Word and Reading/Listening portions of the diagnostic test, the paragraphs to be read either by the student or by the tutor change from pretest to posttest. Evidence of their equivalence is needed. Third, for the Word Analysis portions of the diagnostic test, the items do not change from pretest to posttest. There appears to be no recognition on the authors' part that, for some subtests (such as decoding CVCs, CVCCs, digraphs, and blends), administering the tests as often as desired during instruction may weaken the ability to infer that posttest scores are the result of increased reading ability.

In sum, the use of this test, either in the specific setting for which it is intended or in other settings, is not recommended until information supporting the reliability and validity of test scores is available. Also needed is information supporting the effectiveness of the training program in producing reliable test administrators. The issue of using volunteers without formal academic training in the assessment and remediation of reading difficulties is also relevant; however, it is considered to be outside the scope of this review.

Review of the Reading Evaluation Adult Diagnosis (Revised) by DIANE J. SAWYER, Director, Consultation Center for Reading, Syracuse University, Syracuse, NY:
Reading Evaluation Adult Diagnosis (Revised) (READ) is a carefully constructed tool that permits a systematic approach to describing the word- and passage-reading skills of an adult who reads below a fifth grade level (approximately). It was designed to provide diagnostic information in word recognition and analysis with the hope that specific weaknesses might be addressed through tutoring. Further, READ provides an estimate of the difficulty level of text material that might be used in tutoring or offered for independent reading between tutoring sessions. Comprehension questions following passages require primarily literal recall, although some questions do encourage linkages between text and personal experience.

READ is an informal reading inventory. Normative data for interpreting test performance are not available. Instead, analysis of reader behavior is dependent upon examiner skill. Because this test is intended for use by volunteer tutors from various walks of life, the quality of the test booklet/manual and possible instructional interpretations is critical. In addition, the volunteer examiner/tutor is referred to *TUTOR*, a separate handbook also published by Literacy Volunteers of America, Inc. (LVA). Preparation or training to administer READ is offered through LVA chapter offices or a test trainers kit (a trainer's guide and audio cassette) offered for purchase through LVA. In this reviewer's opinion, it would be very difficult for anyone lacking previous background in teaching reading to learn to administer and interpret the test without guidance beyond that which is provided in the test trainers kit.

No specific information is offered regarding the reliability or validity of READ. However, both construct and content validity are apparent and consistent with the purposes for which this test was designed. Within the "discrete skills" view of reading, proficiency in reading is presumed dependent upon mastery of a hierarchy of specific content such as that contained in the word lists and word analysis subtests of READ. Meaning is presumed to be in the text and the reader's task is to accurately decode words so that the author's meaning may become apparent. Difficulties in decoding words must, therefore, be addressed through direct instruction in specific phonic elements or in the use of context clues to aid recognition. Clearly the "discrete skills" approach is the view of reading upon which development of READ is predicated. The tasks, as well as interpretations of failure on the tasks, are consistent with this approach and with the typical content and sequence of instruction that would be provided to someone after completion of READ.

The absence of information regarding reliability is a more serious concern. Tutors are urged to administer READ as soon after the first "get acquainted" meeting as possible. Most adults who are poor readers are embarrassed by their reading performance. It may be that adults would do worse than usual if required to read aloud before a virtual stranger who is carefully writing down all errors. This would seem to pose a serious threat to the accuracy of the profile of skill needs obtained. Test-retest reliability data appear essential to support the stability of scores before recommendations based on these scores are to be carried out by tutors.

Another problem is related to the manner in which reading materials are selected for instruction and recreation based on the reading level score obtained using READ. Though many cautions are provided in the manual concerning the selection of material that is appropriate for adults both in terms of difficulty and content, no specific sources or examples are offered. The passages used to estimate reading level are taken from adult experience stories and thus reflect adult experiences, vocabulary, and syntax. Although a readability formula was used to rank a given passage at beginning second grade, for example, it will be inherently more adult than a trade book written for beginning second graders to read. Further, adults reading that trade book are likely to make more errors because of the constrained vocabulary and syntax which seems unnatural to them. It would seem critical that more specific suggestions be offered to tutors regarding selection of reading materials if READ is to serve adequately the objective of identifying the appropriate level of material through which instruction should be offered.

Overall, READ is a well-constructed informal reading inventory (IRI) with good potential to serve the identification of specific instructional needs within the traditional discrete skills approach to reading acquisition. However, as with most IRIs, the potential usefulness of READ is commensurate with the training and experience of its user.

[327]
Reading-Free Vocational Interest Inventory, Revised.

Purpose: "To provide systematic information on the range of [vocational] interest patterns of the exceptional male and female who is diagnosed as mentally retarded, learning disabled, or disadvantaged."
Population: Ages 13 and over.
Publication Dates: 1975–88.
Acronym: R-FVII.
Scores, 11: Automotive, Building Trades, Clerical, Animal Care, Food Service, Patient Care, Horticulture, Housekeeping, Personal Service, Laundry Service, Materials Handling.
Administration: Individual or group.
Price Data, 1989: $25.50 per 20 test booklets; $13.50 per Occupational Title list; $10.50 per manual ('88, 60 pages); $22.75 per sample set including 10 test booklets and manual.
Time: (10) minutes.
Comments: Earlier edition listed as AAMD-Becker Reading-Free Vocational Interest Inventory; self-administered.
Author: Ralph L. Becker.
Publisher: Elbern Publications.
Cross References: See T3:1996 (2 references); for reviews by Esther E. Diamond and George Domino of an earlier edition, see 8:988 (6 references).

Review of the Reading-Free Vocational Interest Inventory, Revised by ROBERT J. MILLER, Assistant Professor of Special Education, Mankato State University, Mankato, MN:

The Reading-Free Vocational Interest Inventory (R-FVII) is a vocational interest inventory that requires no reading comprehension or written language skills of the subject completing the inventory. It was devised to gather vocational preference information on "the exceptional male and female who is diagnosed as mentally retarded, learning disabled, or disadvantaged." The instrument consists of a total of 165 illustrations arranged in 55 sets of three pictures each (triads). These pictures are simple black and white line drawings of men and women participating in work activities. These work activities are clearly represented. The inventory may be easily distributed, administered, and collected within a 45-minute class period. The average time for completion of the inventory is 20 minutes or less. The test booklet is consumable and all information is hand scored.

Directions for administration are to be given orally and the subject is directed to compare the three pictures and circle the one picture that "you like best." This leads to some confusion. Is the subject to circle the picture "you like best" as described on the test booklet, or is the subject to "find which job you like the best and put a circle on that picture" as suggested in the test manual. The picture one likes is not necessarily the job one would most choose to do.

Prior to the 1981 edition, this instrument used separate formats for males and females. This limitation in sex equity was addressed by the authors in the 1981 edition. The inventory now provides scores in 11 areas of interest for both males and females.

The major changes between the current manual and the previous 1981 edition are the addition of norms for public day school males and females in different age groups with moderate mental retardation (TMR), and norms for adult males and females categorized as disadvantaged. No changes were made in the test booklet from the 1981 publication date.

Although the work activities pictured in the inventory are clearly represented, the choice of work activities included in the inventory must be questioned. The kinds of employment activities included in the inventory seem far too narrow. Far too many of the activities pictured are low functioning jobs that seem quite limited and stereotypical of the kinds of activities perceived to be appropriate for special needs populations. The manual is of little help in this matter suggesting that "all items in the *Inventory* represent the kind and type of occupations in which mentally retarded, learning disabled, or disadvantaged individuals are productive and proficient." Although the manual suggests the instrument provides information on a wide range of occupations and job tasks at the unskilled, semi-skilled, and skilled levels, a review of the test booklet reveals the vast majority of activities presented are in the unskilled range of labor. One should question the appropriateness of the work activities presented as representative of jobs appropriate for persons with learning disabilities or for adults categorized as disadvantaged.

With this concern registered, a companion material, the Occupational Title Lists, does provide the teacher or counselor with additional information regarding unskilled, semiskilled, and skilled jobs within the 11 areas. These job lists include reference to *Dictionary of Occupational Title* numbers and do address a portion of the stated concern.

During 1980–81, normative data were developed for the R-FVII on a nationwide basis for males and females grades 7 through 12 with mild mental retardation (EMR) and learning disabilities (LD). In addition, normative data were developed for persons with mental retardation working in sheltered workshops and vocational training centers. Norms for adults with environmental and economic disadvantages were developed during 1986–87. Public norms consist of 2,132 EMR and 2,034 LD males, and 2,163 EMR and 1,967 LD females from the public school systems of 30 states. Norms for adults with mental retardation consist of 1,121 males and 1,106 females from 17 states. Norms for adults with economic and environmental disadvantages include 897 males and 781 females.

A comparison study of normative data by sex and age group of subjects with moderate mental retardation (TMR) grades 7 through 12 is referenced in the test manual. However, the results of the 867 males and 814 females of school age are not included in a norming table. Instead, the manual suggests that tables applicable for the male EMR school-aged population are also applicable for male subjects with moderate retardation. Norms for school-aged females with EMR are suggested to be applicable for school-aged females with moderate retardation. Norm tables for subjects with moderate mental retardation should be included for maximum benefit to persons gathering information on this population. I hope this limitation will be addressed in future revisions of the inventory.

Norm tables are used to convert raw scores to percentile and *T* scores. The Individual Profile Sheet is charted based on percentiles with scores above the 75th percentile apparently considered to reflect high interest and percentiles below the 25th percentile considered low interest areas.

The reliability of the R-FVII is adequate when presented. Test-retest reliabilities are based on a 2-week interval between testings, and are reported on EMR, LD, Adult Sheltered Workshop populations, and adult disadvantaged populations. In each case, the reliability is predominantly in the .70s and .80s. No reliability information is included regarding the males or females with moderate mental disabilities (TMR). Again, this limitation should be addressed.

Validity of the test instrument is assessed by three methods: content validity, concurrent validity, and construct validity. The discussion of content validity seems limited. To substantiate content validity, a "complete search was made of jobs known to be appropriate and realistic for mentally retarded and learning disabled individuals." The discussion of content validity is brief and unclear. The impression that the items must be valid because they were reviewed by a study team was not very convincing. This reviewer's perceptions of the limited and stereotypical nature of the work activities presented in the inventory has already been discussed. Concurrent validity is the extent to which R-FVII scores compare with scores of the 1964 edition of the Geist Picture Interest Inventory (GPII). A random sample of subjects who were involved in the collection of test-retest data on reliability were also administered the GPII. Product-moment correlations are adequate and generally support the concurrent validity of the R-FVII. Construct validity was studied using 619 public day school (EMR) and sheltered workshop males with mental retardation and 640 public day school (EMR) and sheltered workshop females with mental retardation in the 11 occupational areas. Scoring of the R-FVII demonstrated that groups of workers with mild mental retardation and adult workshop participants scored highest in their own occupation as opposed to any of the other occupational areas. No information is included as to how membership in an occupational group was defined. The empirical validation study was limited to that segment of the population with mild mental retardation and the adult workshop population.

In conclusion, the R-FVII appears to be an adequate instrument for gathering vocational preference information on persons with mild mental retardation. The integration of the revised instrument to include both males and females in the same test booklet in 1981 should be applauded and does addresses sex equity issues. Concern regarding the R-FVII center on two issues. First, the work activities pictured in the inventory are stereotypical of the kinds of activities perceived to be appropriate for special needs populations. To this end, greater information concerning content validity is needed. Second, the test manual does not include any reliability information or norm tables for persons with moderate mental retardation (TMR). Persons using the R-FVII should carefully weigh these concerns when choosing to use this instrument.

[328]
Reading Style Inventory.
Purpose: "To identify the individual reading style preferences and strengths of youngsters when they read."
Population: Grades 1–12.
Publication Dates: 1980–87.

Acronym: RSI.

Scores: 30 elements: Environmental Stimuli (Sound-Quiet, Sound-Music/Talking, Light, Temperature, Design-Formal/Informal, Design-Organization), Emotional Profile (Peer-Motivated, Adult-Motivated, Self-Motivated, Persistence, Responsibility, Structure-Choices, Structure-Directions, Structure-Work Checked When, Structure-Work Checked by Whom), Sociological Preferences (Prefers Reading to a Teacher, With Peers, Alone, With Peers and the Teacher, With One Peer, Intake, Prefers Reading in the Morning, Prefers Reading in Early Afternoon, Prefers Reading in Late Afternoon, Prefers Reading in the Evening, Mobility), Perceptual Strengths/Preferences (Auditory Strengths, Visual Strengths, Tactual Preferences, Kinesthetic Preferences).

Administration: Group; individual for first grade. ·

Price Data, 1990: $10 per 25 test booklets; $8 per 30 answer sheets; $12 per manual ('84, 76 pages); $20 per specimen set including test booklet, sample profiles, Research Supplement ('83, 39 pages), manual, and free processing of 1 RSI.

Foreign Language Edition: Spanish edition available.

Time: (20–40) minutes.

Comments: Based upon learning style model; scoring service offered by publisher.

Author: Marie Carbo.

Publisher: National Reading Styles Institute, Inc.

TEST REFERENCES

1. Carbo, M. (1984). Research in learning style and reading: Implications for instruction. *Theory Into Practice, 23* (1), 72-76.

Review of the Reading Style Inventory by JERI BENSON, Associate Professor of Measurement, Statistics and Evaluation, University of Maryland, College Park, MD:

The Reading Style Inventory (RSI) consists of 52 items to which a student responds using either a three-choice or two-choice format to indicate their reading preferences. The scale is thought to measure 30 elements of reading style grouped into four stimuli: Environmental, Emotional, Sociological, and Physical. The items were developed based upon student comments and observations of students while reading. However, the author provides no information as to how many initial items were generated nor whether item analyses were used to produce the final set of 52 items.

From a rough categorization of items, there appear to be 28 items covering the three areas of Environmental, Emotional, and Sociological stimuli with the remaining 24 items representing Physical stimuli. Given the purpose of the RSI is primarily diagnostic, there appears to be an overrepresentation of items in the Physical area and too few in the remaining three areas. It would be helpful if the author would provide a table of specifications indicating which item measures which stimulus and the rationale for the breakdown. In addition, a rationale should be given as to why 14 of the items have a 3-point response scale and 38 items have a 2-point response scale. Finally, a Spanish version of the RSI is available, but no psychometric data are provided nor information as to the quality of the item translation or equivalence to the English version.

The author is to be commended for the emphasis she places on setting a good testing environment for the student (especially younger students). Carefully worded warm-up exercises are provided so the students understand what is meant by indicating a "preference." Another strength of the RSI is that no special administrator training is necessary other than familiarization with the items and item format.

Many helpful illustrations to aid the classroom teacher in developing and providing appropriate reading instruction and supporting material are given in the printouts and Chapters VI and VII of the manual. However, some rationale as to how the suggestions were developed would be useful. Are the recommendations based upon the research in the field of reading? If so, the authors should cite the research.

A glaring omission in the technical manual is the scoring protocol for the RSI. The answer sheets must be sent to the author for scoring. This procedure represents an additional expense. Although very detailed diagnostics per student and for the class as a whole are provided, it would be helpful psychometrically to know what combination of items went into developing the diagnostic profile. Additionally, no normative data are provided in terms of score profiles for different grades (ages), gender, reading ability, or other relevant background factors.

The only reliability data presented are from a study involving students in grades 2, 4, 6, and 8. There were approximately 70 students per grade for the total sample of 293 drawn from inner-city and suburban areas of New York. Test-retest reliabilities of .63 to .77 were reported, over a 1-month interval. Although these data are acceptable, evidence for the stability of the RSI across all grades in more than one geographical area is needed.

With regard to the reported content validation of the scale, the author indicates that practitioners stated the RSI items "accurately measured the elements of reading style." A more precise description of the practitioners is required for content validation; in fact, the persons chosen for the content validation are often described as *experts* in the field. Thus, while the items "appear" to reflect reading style, a more controlled study describing the procedures used to obtain the item evaluations by acknowledged experts in the field of reading/learning is warranted.

The author should provide the concurrent validity correlations between the RSI and the other "instruments that measure similar variables" in the technical manual itself and not just refer to the studies (p. 12). Furthermore, the two comments on pages 12–

13 of the Research Supplement that (*a*) the RSI was selected in a nationwide survey as "one of fourteen learning style instruments that qualified for inclusion in the *Learning Styles Network's Instruments Assessment Analysis*," and (*b*) the respondents to the nationwide survey indicated that the "RSI printouts were accurate" are not validity data and should be removed from the validity section of the manual.

In terms of establishing the construct validity of the RSI, the known-group procedure of reporting mean level differences from the samples used in the reliability study cited above are presented. The data are impressive, but a few statistical questions remain. Given that data were available on grade, gender, and reading ability, why were one-way ANOVA results presented instead of factorial ANOVA results? Table 8 is titled two-way ANOVAS, yet only one variable (reading level) is described for the results. With so many subtests (elements), was the probability of a Type I error controlled either by a multivariate analysis or a Bonferonni adjustment for the ANOVAs reported? Generally, the communication of information in the Research Supplement and Research Update could be improved by having a psychometrician edit these documents.

In sum, the RSI appears to be a promising diagnostic tool to enable teachers to provide specific reading instruction and materials for their students. If the author can provide additional data on the consistency of the RSI over all grades, specific content and concurrent validity data, information as to how the RSI is scored, and data for the Spanish version, I could recommend the RSI for general use. Given the present data, however, I can recommend the RSI only for use in research settings.

Review of the Reading Style Inventory by ALICE J. CORKILL, Assistant Professor of Psychology, University of Western Ontario, London, Ontario, Canada:

The Reading Style Inventory (RSI) is designed to identify individual differences in reading preferences and strengths as differentiated by a set of 52 questions that assess 30 separate elements. The 30 elements are based on learning styles (see elements listed in test entry). The Inventory is not a reading skills test and should not be considered as such. Rather it is designed to provide information about how a student learns best. The purpose in using the Inventory is not only to discover an individual's reading preferences, but to provide information that will assist in designing reading instruction with the best fit to an individual's personal reading style.

Students who cannot read at a beginning fourth grade reading level must have the Inventory read to them. As a result, students in the lower elementary grades will need considerable assistance when taking the Inventory. In addition, a computer scan sheet is used as the answer sheet. Some students may not be able to use the sheet. In these instances it is

suggested the students be allowed to mark in the test booklet, then requiring the teacher to mark the answer sheet at a later time.

The Inventory is scored by the publisher with no other option available. Each student who takes the Inventory is provided with an "Individual Reading Style Profile" which includes a diagnosis in perceptual strengths and preferences, the preferred reading environment, an emotional profile, the sociological preferences, and the physical preferences of each child. It also includes recommended strategies for teaching reading based on that child's preferences with references to suggestions listed in the RSI manual.

In addition each profile includes recommendations of reading methods and reading materials. The reading methods listed include the phonic method, the linguistic method, the Orton-Gillingham Method, the whole-word method, individualized methods, the Carbo recorded-book method, the language-experience method, and the Fernald word-tracing method (for more complete descriptions see the administrator's manual). The reading materials listed include Basal reader programs, language-experience programs, individualized programs, and supplementary reading materials (which include games, activity cards, reading kits, skill development books and duplicating masters, and audio-visual materials). Each method or type of material is listed as either highly recommended, recommended, acceptable, or not recommended for an individual based on his/her responses to the Inventory.

A "Reading Style Group Profile" is also available. The group profile compiles the information from individual profiles to reveal group patterns. Two different methods of reporting group profiles are currently in use (only one is listed in the manual). The two group profiles differ in the format of data presentation. In the method described in the manual, the data are presented in the following format: name of examinee on the left margin and preferences or reading method recommendations across the top of the page. In the second method, the data are presented such that individuals are grouped by response strength on preferences and by the degree of recommendation (highly recommended, recommended, acceptable, or not recommended) on the reading method recommendations. The group profiles provide the same information as the individual profiles. This component of the RSI may be particularly useful for classroom teachers who may choose to use the profile information when selecting activities, reading materials, or reading methods for an entire class.

The questions in the Inventory are simple and easy to understand. For example, students are asked to choose between statements similar to the following: "A) I read best where it's quiet with no music playing, B) I read best where there is music playing, C) I read about the same where it's quiet or where there is music playing." Suggestions for preparing younger students to take the Inventory are included in the RSI manual.

As with any self-report inventory, it is possible students will not provide accurate information. This may be especially true when considering older students. Students beyond grades 7 or 8 may find the statements too simplistic. The questions are obviously geared toward younger students. Most students beyond elementary school who read regularly already know what their preferences are in terms of reading style. In addition, the recommended reading methods and materials are geared toward younger readers. As a result, the information provided by the Inventory may be of little value with regard to older students.

The reliability of the instrument was established via a test-retest method using 293 second-, fourth-, sixth-, and eighth-grade students. The sample was taken from inner-city and suburban schools in New York City and Nassau County, New York, and considered the reading ability (high, average, or below average) of the student as a critical variable. The test-retest reliability coefficients range from .55 to .81, with most coefficients falling between .67 and .72. Because of the nature of this self-report inventory, the reported reliability is acceptable. Assessing other types of reliability (i.e., coefficient alpha) might provide information that would assist in improving the Inventory. In addition, a more representative sample, including older students (the Inventory is listed for use with grades 1 through 12) and/or other geographic locations, might enhance the usefulness of the Inventory.

The validity of the instrument has been addressed in several ways. The content validity was assessed by 87 educators representing 23 states, 93% of whom stated that the RSI measured the elements of reading style in an accurate, appropriate, and representative fashion. In addition, the Inventory has been submitted to experts in the field for review and was selected by the National Center for the Study of Learning/Teaching Styles for inclusion in the *Learning Styles Network's Instruments Assessment Analysis*, one of only 14 instruments that qualified.

The RSI manual devotes considerable attention to suggestions for matching reading styles with reading programs. Several studies (reported in a research update booklet provided with the Inventory) have suggested that educators, specifically elementary teachers, who match students' reading preferences with appropriate reading materials and methods, observed considerable improvement in reading skill. This is especially evident for students with learning disabilities. As a consequence, if the results of this inventory are viewed in a prescriptive fashion a considerable increase in reading skill may be the final product.

The incremental value of the Reading Style Inventory is unclear. It may provide assistance to teachers of beginning reading or special education by suggesting the best method and materials for teaching reading on an individual or small group basis. The results of the Inventory match closely with teacher observations of students, so much so that teacher observation may provide ample information for making reading method and material decisions, thus rendering the information from an inventory like the RSI redundant. In contrast, the reported research suggests significant gains in reading skill by matching reading style with teaching methods. If the RSI is the only method for acquiring this information, it may be well worth the time required to administer and score it.

[329]

Receptive One-Word Picture Vocabulary Test: Upper Extension.

Purpose: Constructed to measure "hearing vocabulary."

Population: Ages 12-0 to 15-11.

Publication Date: 1987.

Acronym: ROWPVT.

Scores: Total score only.

Administration: Individual.

Price Data, 1991: $60 per complete kit including test plates, 25 record forms (English), and manual (39 pages); $23 per set of test plates; $20 per 50 English record forms; $10 per 25 Spanish record forms; $14 per manual; $14 per specimen set.

Time: (10–15) minutes.

Comments: Upward extension of the Receptive One-Word Picture Vocabulary Test (329); Spanish form available.

Author: Rick Brownell.

Publisher: Academic Therapy Publications.

Cross References: For reviews by Janice A. Dole and Janice Santogrossi of the lower extension, see 10:312.

Review of the Receptive One-Word Picture Vocabulary Test: Upper Extension by LAURIE FORD, Assistant Professor of Educational Psychology, Texas A&M University, College Station, TX:

OVERVIEW. The Receptive One-Word Picture Vocabulary Test: Upper Extension (ROWPVT) is an individually administered, norm-referenced measure of receptive language, designed for use with adolescents ages 12 years through 15 years 11 months of age. It is an extension of the original ROWPVT (10:312), which was developed for use with children 2 years through 11 years 11 months of age. The purpose of the ROWPVT is to estimate the adolescent's single-word receptive or hearing vocabulary learned from home and school education. The test was designed to accompany the Expressive One-Word Picture Vocabulary Test (EOWPVT; 9:403). The ROWPVT and the EOWPVT yield similar scores (median $r = .83$) making direct comparisons between the two instruments possible. According to the author, when the ROWPVT is used along with the EOWPVT, it yields a measure of receptive vocabulary that can be accurately compared to the EOWPVT to determine whether a discrepancy exists between the individual's ability to understand language and the ability to speak language.

ADMINISTRATION. The ROWPVT contains 70 item plates arranged in order of increasing difficulty. Each plate has four black-and-white hand-drawn pictures, sequenced from right to left in a wire-bound format. Although the drawings are adequate, the poor quality and unengaging nature of the drawings may be a drawback of the instrument. The individual is asked to identify the picture that matches the word presented orally by the examiner. The complete kit includes test plates, 25 record forms (English), and a manual. Spanish record forms are also available. The author states that administration takes approximately 10 to 15 minutes. Scoring takes less than 5 minutes. It is a power rather than timed test. Examinees should be allowed ample time to review illustrations and respond to items. Administration and scoring procedures for the Spanish version parallel the English form with directions for monolingual children. The authors note the Spanish version should be used only by individuals fluent in Spanish. It is important to note that no standardization of the Spanish version was undertaken and norms are based solely on English-speaking children. The manual states appropriate caution regarding score interpretation, yet inappropriately recommends the use of the test in developing English language programs for Spanish-speaking adolescents.

SCORING. Scoring is based on the notion of a "critical range" of items with an eight consecutive item basal and a six to eight item ceiling. Raw scores are calculated that are converted easily to a language age, standard score, percentile, and stanine through the use of easy-to-read tables provided in the manual. The term "language-age" may be somewhat misleading, however, because the test measures only one component of language, "receptive vocabulary." Procedures are outlined for comparing performance using standard scores on the EOWPVT and the ROWPVT.

STANDARDIZATION. The authors report a series of standardization procedures that were followed to ensure the content of the test would be appropriate with a sufficient range of difficulty for children ages 12 years through 15 years 11 months of age. Efforts were made to ensure equivalence with the EOWPVT. Items were administered to 283 students ages 12 through 15 years 11 months of age along with the EOWPVT. Although the authors go into great detail regarding the standardization procedures, the sample is inadequate because it represents a relatively homogeneous sample from San Francisco, California. Little information is provided concerning the sample. In addition, users should note that administration procedures were used to develop individual norms.

RELIABILITY AND VALIDITY. Reliability was determined for each age group using Cronbach's alpha. These are reported along with standard errors of measurement (SEM) for raw and standard scores. The reliability coefficients range from .88 to .94 with a median of .90. The SEMs for raw scores range from 2.43 to 2.59 with a median of 2.50. For the standard scores, the SEMs range from 3.64 to 5.15 (median 4.68). These figures are acceptable; however, test-retest information is lacking. The content and criterion-related validity are discussed briefly in the manual. The information provided is very limited, however. Only correlations with the EOWPVT are reported. No comparisons with the widely used Peabody Picture Vocabulary Test—Revised (PPVT-R; 9:926) (which purports to measure similar constructs) are reported. As a result of the similarity between these two instruments, comparisons with the PPVT-R are inevitable. The PPVT-R is clearly the superior instrument based on technical properties and standardization sample.

SUMMARY. The ROWPVT is an individually administered test of receptive vocabulary of single words, designed to accompany the EOWPVT. The ease of administration and scoring, as well as the ROWPVT's equivalency with the EOWPVT make it an attractive measure at first review. However, technical information on the instrument is limited. Although reliability data are adequate, validity information is lacking and standardization procedures are limited. More extensive normative studies are needed to support its wide-scale use. As a result, the PPVT-R appears to be still the superior measure of receptive language abilities.

Review of the Receptive One-Word Picture Vocabulary Test: Upper Extension by WILLIAM D. SCHAFER, Associate Professor of Educational Measurement, Statistics, and Evaluation, University of Maryland, College Park, MD:

The Upper Extension of the Receptive One-Word Picture Vocabulary Test (ROWPVT) consists of 70 four-choice items. For each item, the examinee is presented with a horizontal arrangement of four numbered pictures and a word spoken by the examiner. The examinee is asked to point to or give the number of the picture that corresponds to the word. Responses are recorded on a separate scoring sheet. Two examples are given prior to the scored items. The ROWPVT was designed specifically to be used in conjunction with the Expressive One-Word Picture Vocabulary Test: Upper Extension (EOWPVT; 9:403) and the scores compared. Although a Spanish version is available, it was developed through translation of the English version into Spanish, not by a test development effort in Spanish parallel to that which was done for the English version, and no norms are given for Spanish-speaking examinees. The manual contains some psychometric misconceptions (e.g., reliability is incorrectly described as including validity), typographical errors, and the use of gender-specific pronouns that do not conform to current practice.

The manual devotes six pages to administration and scoring of the test. The bulk of the information is related to administration. Although the material in the manual is fairly easy to understand more step-by-step directions would be helpful. It is unclear whether the examiner may repeat the stimulus word without the child asking for it to be repeated (that it can be repeated on the child's request is included in the directions) or whether the examiner may spell the word on request. It is important that the words be pronounced correctly and a guide to pronunciation is included in the manual. It would have been helpful to have that guide included on the scoring sheet, which the examiner is using at the time of administration. The effects of a mismatch between the accents of the examiner and the child are not considered. The directions make the point that the recording of responses should be done with the same number of strokes for right and wrong answers so that no information about correctness is communicated to the child. A modification of the scoring sheet (e.g., with Rs and Ws that are circled instead of a blank line) would make sense. An attractive feature of the scoring sheet is that it provides spaces for recording information about the child and about the testing session, particularly as it might affect the validity of the results for that child. The latter section is prominently placed on the form.

The stimulus words are ordered in difficulty and the test begins with either Item 20 or Item 30 depending on the child's age. Testing concludes once a basal level (defined by eight consecutive correct responses) and a ceiling (six incorrect responses in a sequence of eight items) are found, so it is unlikely that all 70 items will be administered. There is no justification given for requiring eight consecutive items to be answered correctly for the basal level or six incorrects out of eight for the ceiling. The procedure for establishing a raw score is clear.

Based on the raw score, a language age is determined in years and months. The language age is converted to a language standard score (mean of 100, standard deviation of 15) by entering a table using the child's chronological age.

The norms for the ROWPVT were based on a local sample of 283 public junior or senior high school students who had taken the EOWPVT; a special form was used in a group administration of the 100 items in the initial pool. The norms were developed on the 70 final items by making raw scores on the ROWPVT equivalent to raw scores on the EOWPVT using simple equipercentile equating. This procedure entails assigning to each ROWPVT raw score the language standard score for the EOWPVT raw score found equivalent to it. Equipercentile equating requires estimation of percentiles on each test for these examinees. Unfortunately, the estimation of percentiles using such a small sample size is not sufficiently precise (particularly at the extremes). In addition, the nature of the norming sample is not appropriately representative and the context of the examination is not sufficiently similar to that described in the directions to allow confidence in the norms that appear in the manual. Percentile ranks and stanines are given for the various language standard scores as aids in interpretation. It is stated that the use of stanines avoids problems associated with the standard error of measurement. This assertion is arguable at best. The manual does not discuss how the language age, percentile ranks, or stanines were determined. Circumstances are described for which stanine and percentile rank interpretations might be considered but there are no norms given for differences between the ROWPVT and the EOWPVT on these scales.

The stated intent of the ROWPVT is for concurrent use with the EOWPVT. To facilitate this comparison, the standard error of the difference in standard scores is provided for each 1-year age span. The half-length of an 85% confidence interval for the difference is provided and it is recommended that differences exceeding this amount be judged meaningful. The authors fail to warn users that this procedure will result in 15% of examinees who have identical language ages being found meaningfully different. No discussion or references are given to guide the user about the interpretation of reaction to the finding of a meaningful difference for a child and thus such an outcome seems to be a diagnosis without a prescription.

Alpha coefficients for 1-year age spans are reported as reliability estimates without a discussion of evidence supporting that interpretation. The alphas ranged from .88 to .94 with a median of .90. These internal consistency coefficients are likely to be overestimates because they were calculated using the same data (a subsample of 200 from the equating sample) that were used to select the final 70 items based on an item analysis of the initial pool of 100 words.

Correlations of the ROWPVT with the EOWPVT on the item-selection sample of 200 students broken down into four 1-year age groups are the only empirical validity evidence reported. These correlations ranged from .78 to .86 with a median of .83. There are no comparisons of the ROWPVT with other tests of similar content, with any subsequent criterion measure, or with success as a result of any intervention. The manual states the final test form contains no words that are peculiar to any specific ethnic group, region, or gender and only words that can be translated into Spanish. The process by which these guarantees were generated is not specified.

The ROWPVT should be viewed as an untested diagnostic tool for which the value has not been established. More extensive norming data, documentation of validity and lack of bias, more careful description of administration procedures, and information about the value for practitioners of the trait it measures would enhance its utility.

[330]
Reiss-Epstein-Gursky Anxiety Sensitivity Index.

Purpose: To measure the fear of anxiety in order to "identify patients with high anxiety sensitivity" and "to obtain information relevant to the diagnosis of agoraphobia, panic disorder, or posttraumatic stress disorder."
Population: Adults.
Publication Date: 1987.
Acronym: ASI.
Scores: Total Anxiety Sensitivity.
Administration: Individual or group.
Price Data, 1988: Annual rental/licensing fee of $19 (private practitioners) or $40 (clinics, mental health centers, school districts) allows photocopying and use of test; $10 per 50 additional printed copies of test (licensed users only); $15 per manual (20 pages).
Time: [5] minutes.
Authors: Rolf A. Peterson and Steven Reiss.
Publisher: International Diagnostic Systems, Inc.

Review of the Reiss-Epstein-Gursky Anxiety Sensitivity Index by HARRISON G. GOUGH, Professor of Psychology Emeritus, University of California, Berkeley, CA:

Considering the many self-report scales for anxiety already published, a first question about any new measure must concern its relationship to its predecessors. Specifically, a potential user of the new scale will want to know how it resembles, or differs from, prior measures, and whether it lags behind, equals, or exceeds these other measures in practical utility. It would also be helpful to know how the new scale fits into the historical scheme of things for assessing anxiety, for instance, as this story has been told by Cattell and Scheier (1961), McReynolds (1968), and Spielberger (1972).

The 16-item Anxiety Sensitivity Index (ASI) was first published in 1987, although it was antedated by several research reports in the 1980s. Among its most important competitors as single tests are the IPAT Anxiety Scale Questionnaire (Cattell & Scheier, 1961; 9:537) for covert and overt anxiety,

and the State-Trait Anxiety Inventory (STAI; Spielberger, Gorsuch, Lushene, Vagg, & Jacobs, 1983; 9:1186).

Anxiety is also assessed by scales embedded in more general personality inventories, such as the Rosen Anxiety Reaction (Ar), Taylor Manifest Anxiety (MAS), and Welsh Anxiety (A) scales for the Minnesota Multiphasic Personality Inventory (MMPI; 244), Wiggins' Phobic Reactions content scale for the MMPI, the anxiety scale for the Multiple Affect Adjective Check List (Zuckerman & Lubin, 1985; 10:205), the anxiety (A) scale for the Millon Clinical Multiaxial Inventory (Millon, 1987; 239), the Leventhal (1966) anxiety scale for the California Psychological Inventory (54), and the QII second order factor scale for anxiety on the Sixteen Personality Factor Questionnaire (16PF; 9:1136) (see Karson & O'Dell, 1976). Just recently, Friedman, Webb, and Lewak (1989) have introduced new 22-item content scales for anxiety and fear, scorable on the MMPI-2.

In addition to all of these measures, there are various special purpose anxiety scales, including test-taking anxiety (Sarason & Mandler, 1952), death anxiety (Templer, 1971), and medical illness (Robbins, 1962).

The authors seek to differentiate their instrument from others in two ways. The first is the emphasis of the ASI on fear of or sensitivity to anxiety, rather than on a direct reporting of the symptoms of anxiety. For example, instead of items stating "I feel faint," "my heart beats rapidly," or "I am unable to keep my mind on a task," the ASI introduces each of these symptoms with the phrase "It scares me when . . ." In fact, 8 of the 16 items in the ASI contain the word "scare" or "scares" as a response to a self-detected reaction. Whether or not these linguistic variants make a difference in the implications of scores on the ASI versus those on other scales is, of course, something that must be determined empirically. Because of the frequent reference to being scared or frightened, differentiation between the ASI and measures of fear also should be examined.

In regard to other anxiety scales, the manual reports correlations of .55, .23, and .07 with the state anxiety scale of the STAI, and of .46 with the MAS. The samples on which these coefficients were computed are either small ($N = 48$), specialized (medical students), or unusually selected (one-sigma deviates up or down on the ASI). Until more of the anxiety scales mentioned above have been compared with the ASI, on samples more representative of the groups with which clinicians and counselors work, the question of similarity between the ASI and its competitors must remain open.

With several experimental self-report measures of fear, correlations with the ASI were on the order of

.64. However, factor analysis of the items from both the ASI and a Fear Survey Schedule found that the former subset defined its own distinct factor. Nevertheless, more inquiry is needed relating the ASI to other general and specific measures of fear, such as the Friedman, Webb, and Lewak scale for fears on the MMPI-2.

Validational information in the manual includes contrasts of ASI scores for persons admitting to agoraphobia, panic reactions, post-traumatic stress, anxiety states, and heroin dependency, versus both adult and college student norms. Within a college student sample, ASI scores for those admitting to panic attacks were significantly related to the effectiveness with which respondents said that they coped with the experiences.

Data such as those just summarized represent useful steps towards establishing the utility of the ASI as a diagnostic tool, but so far nothing has been reported on the essential question of comparative validity. For instance, in each of the above evaluations, how well would other widely used measures such as Welsh's "A" scale on the MMPI, the "A" scale on the Millon Clinical Multiaxial Inventory, and the state and trait scales on the STAI make the same discriminations, or contribute to the magnitude of a multiple regression of scales against a criterion? Unless evidence of this kind can be presented, there is no reason for users of the MMPI, the STAI, or the other inventories cited above to turn to the ASI as an alternative or additional measure.

REVIEWER'S REFERENCES

Sarason, S. B., & Mandler, G. (1952). Some correlates of test anxiety. *Journal of Abnormal and Social Psychology*, 47, 810-817.
Cattell, R. B., & Scheier, I. H. (1961). *The meaning and measurement of neuroticism and anxiety.* New York: Ronald Press.
Robbins, P. R. (1962). Some explorations into the nature of anxieties relating to illness. *Genetic Psychology Monographs*, 66, 91-141.
Leventhal, A. M. (1966). An anxiety scale for the CPI. *Journal of Clinical Psychology*, 22, 459-461.
McReynolds, P. (1968). The assessment of anxiety: A survey of available techniques. In P. McReynolds (Ed.), *Advances in psychological assessment* (Vol. 1, pp. 244-264). Palo Alto, CA: Science and Behavior Books.
Templer, D. I. (1971). The relationship between verbalized and nonverbalized death anxiety. *Journal of Genetic Psychology*, 119, 211-214.
Spielberger, C. D. (Ed.). (1972). *Anxiety: Current trends in theory and research* (Vol. 2). New York: Academic Press.
Karson, S., & O'Dell, J. W. (1976). *A guide to the clinical use of the 16PF.* Champaign, IL: Institute for Personality and Ability Testing.
Spielberger, C. D., Gorsuch, R. L., Lushene, R., Vagg, P. R., & Jacobs, G. A. (1983). *Manual for the State-Trait Anxiety Inventory STAI (Form Y).* Palo Alto, CA: Consulting Psychologists Press.
Zuckerman, M., & Lubin, B. (1985). *Manual for the Multiple Affect Adjective Check List.* San Diego: EdITS.
Millon, T. (1987). *Millon Clinical Multiaxial Inventory II manual.* Minneapolis: National Computer Systems.
Friedman, A. F., Webb, J. T., & Lewak, R. (1989). *Psychological assessment with the MMPI.* Hillsdale, NJ: Lawrence Erlbaum Associates.

[331]

The Reversals Frequency Test.

Purpose: "To assess objectively number and letter reversals frequency."
Population: Ages 5-0 to 15-11.
Publication Date: 1978.
Scores, 3: Execution, Recognition, Matching.

Administration: Individual.
Price Data, 1988: $12 per complete kit including 3 subtests and manual (21 pages).
Time: [10–15] minutes.
Author: Richard A. Gardner.
Publisher: Creative Therapeutics.

TEST REFERENCES

1. Bow, J N. (1988). A comparison of intellectually superior male reading achievers and underachievers from a neuropsychological perspective. *Journal of Learning Disabilities, 21*, 118-123.

Review of The Reversals Frequency Test by FRANK M. GRESHAM, Professor of Psychology, Hofstra University, Hempstead, NY:

The Reversals Frequency Test (RFT) is designed to measure the frequency of letter and number reversals made by children. The RFT has three subtests: Execution, which requires the child to write numbers and letters presented orally by the examiner; Recognition, which requires the child to determine which numbers and letters are pointing in the wrong direction; and Matching, which requires the child to match numbers and letters.

Oscar Buros once stated that most tests probably should never have been published. The RFT represents the embodiment of Dr. Buros' wisdom. The manual describing the RFT is a 22-page, poorly written document that: (*a*) never provides a clear rationale for the test; (*b*) is vague and ambiguous; (*c*) provides absolutely no reliability and validity data; (*d*) inadequately describes standardization, administration, and scoring; and (*e*) provides only one reference (to the test author) to document statements made about the test. The RFT violates virtually every accepted standard for test construction and omits even the most rudimentary information in the test manual.

According to the RFT manual, the test was standardized on "500 normal children (249 girls and 251 boys) ages 5-0–15-11, who were in regular classes in the public schools of Bergen County, New Jersey (a suburb of New York City)" (pp. 1–2). The author states that only children whose IQs ranged between 90–110 were included in the standardization sample. No information is provided on how IQ was assessed, what tests were used, who administered the tests, or the mean and standard deviation of intelligence test scores in the sample. Moreover, the author states that children who repeated grades, needed special tutoring, or who were placed in classes for the learning disabled were excluded from the sample. No information is provided in the manual on what percent of the school population was excluded for these reasons. In short, the RFT was standardized on an unrepresentative sample of 500 children from New Jersey.

The RFT manual reports raw score means and standard deviations for boys and girls ages 5-0-14-11, although the author specifically states the test is for children up to age 15-11. Also, the author inaccurately presents what is referred to as percentiles for numbers of errors when in fact what is presented are deciles. A major blow to the validity of the RFT is the fact that 8-year-olds made more reversal errors on the Matching subtest than 7-year-olds and 11-year-olds made more reversal errors on the Execution subtest than either 8-, 9-, or 10-year-olds. This could mean one of three things: (*a*) the sample is unrepresentative, (*b*) the test does not measure what it is intended to measure, or (*c*) both of the above are true.

The author reports comparisons of "normal and MBD children" on the RFT (pp. 11–18). One assumes that MBD refers to minimal brain dysfunction; however, no information is presented with respect to how these children were diagnosed, by whom, or geographically, where these children resided. The author's report of comparisons between MBD and normal children was based on "statistical analysis." Comparisons, by some unknown "statistical analysis," between normals and MBD children on all three RFT subtests revealed no consistent pattern of differences at various ages. For example, normals and MBD children in the 5- to 7-year-old range could not be differentiated on the Execution subtest nor could 7- and 15-year-olds. Fundamentally, the RFT does not reliably differentiate what the author considers to be an MBD child from a normal child.

SUMMARY. The RFT is a poor test. The manual, besides providing little information, contains several instances of incomplete sentences and poor grammar (e.g., "And the statistical analysis of the data verifies this," p. 13). In teaching undergraduate tests and measurement courses, I require students to construct a test according to the *Standards for Educational and Psychological Testing* (AERA, APA, & NCME, 1985). If a student turned in a manual such as the RFT, he or she would not receive a passing grade on the project.

REVIEWER'S REFERENCE

American Educational Research Association, American Psychological Association, & National Council on Measurement in Education. (1985). *Standards for educational and psychological testing.* Washington, DC: American Psychological Association, Inc.

Review of The Reversals Frequency Test by DAVID J. MEALOR, Chair of Educational Services Department, College of Education, University of Central Florida, Orlando, FL:

The Reversals Frequency Test (RFT) is a simple, easy-to-administer test devised to determine whether a child exhibits an abnormal number of letter or number reversals. The author notes that most children will reverse letters when they first learn to write, particularly those letters that are mirror images of each other. Although children may reverse letters, there may be a number of different operations contributing to reversal errors. The author divides reversals into four categories: mirror image,

inversions, inverted reversals, and rotation. If a child reverses letters, it may be beneficial to note the type of reversal problem manifested.

The Reversals Frequency Test is divided into three parts. The Execution subtest evaluates for the presence of reversals when the child is asked to write numbers and letters. The child is provided an examination sheet with no written instructions. He or she is instructed to determine "how well you can write numbers or letters." The numbers 0, 1, and 8 are omitted as are the letters i, l, m, n, o, u, v, w, and x because they can be written in mirror image forms. There is no time limit for this first test.

The second test, the Recognition subtest, evaluates the child's ability to differentiate between correctly oriented letters and numbers and their mirror images. The child "must retrieve from storage that information that will enable him to form an internal visual display that will serve as a model for writing the requested letter." The author notes that this particular test is a modification of a test designed in the 1930s by Dr. Samuel T. Orton. The subtest has four sections and is arranged from easiest (number pairs) to the more difficult (letters in isolation). The child is directed to draw a cross or an "X" over the number or letter that is pointing in the wrong direction.

The third test, the Matching subtest, assesses the child's capacity to match a normally oriented letter or number with one of four samples that is correctly oriented. This is a test of visual discrimination and is the easiest of the three.

Although the RFT comprises three subtests, 249 girls and 251 boys comprised the standardization group for the Execution subtest and the Recognition subtest. These children ranged in ages from 5-0 to either 14-11 or 15-11 (there is a discrepancy in the manual) and were enrolled in regular classes in the Bergen County, New Jersey, Public Schools. All were reported to be in the average range of intelligence. None had repeated a grade or were in need of remedial tutoring. The Matching subtest normative data were collected on 139 boys and 115 girls with age ranges 5-0 to 8-11 who were enrolled in regular classes. It was noted that 7- and 8-year-olds seldom made any errors on this particular subtest.

The author notes that by third grade children rarely exhibit reversals, yet the standardization group contains high school students. Minimal errors were noted after age 9-0 for the Execution and Recognition subtests.

Although there are some grammatical errors, the RFT manual is organized adequately and gives clear directions to the user for both administration and scoring. An Errata sheet accompanies the manual and includes two graphs that were omitted from the manual although respective captions appear on pages 14–15.

Although the manual provides means, standard deviation, and error ranges by age group for each of the respective subtests, basic psychometric information is missing. No reliability or validity studies are reported. Assumptions are made, yet recent research findings related to the prevalence and meaning of letter and number reversals in children are not incorporated. It is very difficult to determine if the RFT does what it purports to do. Technical aspects appear to have been overlooked.

In order to compare performance of a child's reversals with that of a child "known to have a neurologically based learning disability," the author administered the Execution and Recognition subtests to 343 minimally brain-damaged children enrolled in special classes or schools, "specifically devoted to the education of children with neurologically based learning disabilities." No other data are provided about these children. Without detailed information about the two groups, comparative analysis may be questionable. The author indicates that the RFT is "not designed to be a simple screening instrument for dyslexia", however, it is noted that the instrument has proven to be a valuable screening battery for dyslexia. It would have been desirable to have included support for the instrument being used as a screening measure.

To summarize, the RFT may prove to be an excellent screening instrument, yet much technical work is needed. Reliability and validity studies must be conducted and the standardization group expanded. Until then the value of the RFT will be limited.

[332]
Revised Behavior Problem Checklist.
Purpose: Screening for behavior problems.
Population: Grades K–12.
Publication Dates: 1979–87.
Acronym: RBPC.
Scores, 6: Conduct Disorder, Socialized Aggression, Attention Problems—Immaturity, Anxiety-Withdrawal, Psychotic Behavior, Motor Tension-Excess.
Administration: Individual.
Price Data, 1991: $30 per complete kit including 50 checklists, scoring templates, and manual ('87, 45 pages); $25 per 100 checklists; $7 per set of scoring templates; $12 per manual.
Time: Administration time varies.
Comments: Ratings by teachers and parents.
Authors: Herbert C. Quay and Donald R. Peterson.
Publisher: Herbert C. Quay, Ph.D.
Cross References: For a review by Anthony A. Cancelli, see 9:1043 (31 references); see also T3:2012 (6 references).

TEST REFERENCES

1. Quay, H. C. (1983). A dimensional approach to behavior disorder: The Revised Behavior Problem Checklist. *School Psychology Review, 12,* 244-249.

2. Aman, M. G., & Werry, J. S. (1984). The Revised Behavior Problem Checklist in clinic attenders and non-attenders: Age and sex effects. *Journal of Clinical Child Psychology, 13,* 237-242.

3. Cullinan, D., Matson, J. L., Epstein, M. H., & Rosemier, R. A. (1984). Behavior problems of mentally retarded and nonretarded adolescent pupils. *School Psychology Review, 13,* 381-384.

4. Emery, R. E., & O'Leary, K. D. (1984). Marital discord and child behavior problems in a nonclinic sample. *Journal of Abnormal Child Psychology, 12,* 411-420.

5. Kazdin, A. E., & Heidish, I. E. (1984). Convergence of clinically derived diagnoses and parent checklists among inpatient children. *Journal of Abnormal Child Psychology, 12,* 421-436.

6. Lessin, S., & Jacob, T. (1984). Multichannel communication in normal and delinquent families. *Journal of Abnormal Child Psychology, 12,* 369-384.

7. Ludwig, G., & Cullinan, D. (1984). Behavior problems of gifted and non-gifted elementary school girls and boys. *Gifted Child Quarterly, 28,* 37-39.

8. Lueger, R. J., & Hoover, L. (1984). Use of the MMPI to identify subtypes of delinquent adolescents. *Journal of Clinical Psychology, 40,* 1493-1495.

9. Stone, W. L., & LaGreca, A. M. (1984). Comprehension of nonverbal communication: A reexamination of the social competencies of learning-disabled children. *Journal of Abnormal Child Psychology, 12,* 505-518.

10. Strauss, C. C., Forehand, R., Frame, C., & Smith, K. (1984). Characteristics of children with extreme scores on the Children's Depression Inventory. *Journal of Clinical Child Psychology, 13,* 227-231.

11. Villeneuve, C., & Roy, L. (1984). Psychological distance in "clinic" and control families. *Canadian Journal of Behavioural Science, 16,* 216-223.

12. Blechman, E. A., Tinsley, B., Carella, E. T., & McEnroe, M. J. (1985). Childhood competence and behavior problems. *Journal of Abnormal Psychology, 94,* 70-77.

13. Cullinan, D., Epstein, M. H., Cole, K., & Dembinski, R. (1985). School behavior problems of behaviorally disordered and nonhandicapped girls. *Journal of Clinical Child Psychology, 14,* 162-164.

14. Henggeler, S. W., Hanson, C. L., Borduin, C. M., Watson, S. M., & Brunk, M. A. (1985). Mother-son relationships of juvenile felons. *Journal of Consulting and Clinical Psychology, 53,* 942-943.

15. Hershorn, M., & Rosenbaum, A. (1985). Children of marital violence: A closer look at the unintended victims. *American Journal of Orthopsychiatry, 55,* 260-266.

16. Kilpatrick, D., & Duncan, P. (1985). The effect of sex of rater and sex of child on adult ratings of child behavior. *Child Study Journal, 15,* 237-249.

17. Marks, M., & Barling, J. (1985). Does understanding of social learning principles influence children's behavior? *The Journal of Genetic Psychology, 146,* 501-505.

18. Phelps, R. E., & Slater, M. A. (1985). Sequential interactions that discriminate high- and low-problem single mother-son dyads. *Journal of Consulting and Clinical Psychology, 53,* 684-692.

19. Stringer, S. A., & LaGreca, A. M. (1985). Correlates of child abuse potential. *Journal of Abnormal Child Psychology, 13,* 217-226.

20. Aman, M. G., & Turbott, S. H. (1986). Incidental learning, distraction, and sustained attention in hyperactive and control subjects. *Journal of Abnormal Child Psychology, 14,* 441-455.

21. Borduin, C. M., Pruitt, J. A., & Henggeler, S. W. (1986). Family interactions in black, lower-class families with delinquent and nondelinquent adolescent boys. *The Journal of Genetic Psychology, 147,* 333-342.

22. Firestone, P., Crowe, D., Goodman, J. T., & McGrath, P. (1986). Vicissitudes of follow-up studies: Differential effects of parent training and stimulant medication with hyperactives. *American Journal of Orthopsychiatry, 56,* 184-194.

23. Henggeler, S. W., Rodick, J. D., Borduin, C. M., Hanson, C. L., Watson, S. M., & Urey, J. R. (1986). Multisystematic treatment of juvenile offenders: Effects on adolescent behavior and family interaction. *Developmental Psychology, 22,* 132-141.

24. Houts, A. C., Peterson, J. K., & Whelan, J. P. (1986). Prevention of relapse in full-spectrum home training for primary enuresis: A components analysis. *Behavior Therapy, 17,* 462-469.

25. Hunter, N., & Kelley, C. K. (1986). Examination of the validity of the Adolescent Problems Inventory among incarcerated juvenile delinquents. *Journal of Consulting and Clinical Psychology, 54,* 301-302.

26. Kotsopoulos, S., & Mellor, C. (1986). Extralinguistic speech characteristics of children with conduct and anxiety disorders. *Journal of Child Psychology and Psychiatry and Allied Disciplines, 27,* 99-108.

27. LaFiosca, T., & Loyd, B. H. (1986). Defensiveness and the assessment of parental stress and anxiety. *Journal of Clinical Child Psychology, 15,* 254-259.

28. Lahey, B. B., & Piacentini, J. C. (1986). An evaluation of the Quay-Peterson Revised Behavior Problem Checklist. *Journal of School Psychology, 23,* 285-289.

29. Norvell, N., & Towle, P. O. (1986). Self-reported depression and observable conduct problems in children. *Journal of Clinical Child Psychology, 15,* 228-232.

30. Panella, D., & Henggeler, S. W. (1986). Peer interactions of conduct-disordered, anxious-withdrawn, and well-adjusted black adolescents. *Journal of Abnormal Child Psychology, 14,* 1-12.

31. Wagner, W. G., & Geffken, G. (1986). Enuretic children: How they view their wetting behavior. *Child Study Journal, 16,* 13-18.

32. Aman, M. G., Mitchell, E. A., & Turbott, S. H. (1987). The effects of essential fatty acid supplementation by Efamol in hyperactive children. *Journal of Abnormal Child Psychology, 15,* 75-90.

33. Brunk, M., Henggeler, S. W., & Whelan, J. P. (1987). Comparison of multisystemic therapy and parent training in the brief treatment of child abuse and neglect. *Journal of Consulting and Clinical Psychology, 55,* 171-178.

34. Carlson, C. L., Lahey, B. B., Frame, C. L., Walker, J., & Hynd, G. W. (1987). Sociometric status of clinic-referred children with attention deficit disorders with and without hyperactivity. *Journal of Abnormal Child Psychology, 15,* 537-547.

35. Grace, W. C. (1987). Strength of handedness as an indicant of delinquents' behavior. *Journal of Clinical Psychology, 43,* 151-155.

36. Hinshaw, S. P., Morrison, D. C., Carte, E. T., & Cornsweet, C. (1987). Factorial dimensions of the Revised Behavior Problem Checklist: Replication and validation within a kindergarten sample. *Journal of Abnormal Child Psychology, 15,* 309-327.

37. Houts, A. C., Whelan, J. P., & Peterson, J. K. (1987). Filmed versus live delivery of full-spectrum home training for primary enuresis: Presenting the information is not enough. *Journal of Consulting and Clinical Psychology, 55,* 902-906.

38. Johnson, P. L., & O'Leary, D. (1987). Parental behavior patterns and conduct disorders in girls. *Journal of Abnormal Child Psychology, 15,* 573-581.

39. Jouriles, E. N., Barling, J., & O'Leary, K. D. (1987). Predicting child behavior problems in maritally violent families. *Journal of Abnormal Child Psychology, 15,* 165-173.

40. Long, N., Forehand, R., Fauber, R., & Brody, G. H. (1987). Self-perceived and independently observed competence of young adolescents as a function of parental marital conflict and recent divorce. *Journal of Abnormal Child Psychology, 15,* 15-27.

41. Matson, J. L., & Nieminen, G. S. (1987). Validity of measures of conduct disorder, depression, and anxiety. *Journal of Clinical Child Psychology, 16,* 151-157.

42. Mattison, R. E., Bagnato, S. J., & Strickler, E. (1987). Diagnostic importance of combined parent and teacher ratings on the Revised Behavior Problem Checklist. *Journal of Abnormal Child Psychology, 15,* 617-628.

43. McCombs, A., Forehand, R., & Brody, G. H. (1987). Early adolescent functioning following divorce: The relationship to parenting and non-parenting ex-spousal interactions. *Child Study Journal, 17,* 301-310.

44. Raine, A., & Jones, F. (1987). Attention, autonomic arousal, and personality in behaviorally disordered children. *Journal of Abnormal Child Psychology, 15,* 583-599.

45. Roberts, P. M. (1987). Coping responses and adaptational outcomes of children undergoing orthopedic surgery. *Journal of Clinical Child Psychology, 16,* 251-259.

46. Schaughency, E., Frame, C. Y., & Strauss, C. C. (1987). Self-concept and aggression in elementary school students. *Journal of Clinical Child Psychology, 16,* 116-121.

47. Strauss, C. C., Frame, C. L., & Forehand, R. (1987). Psychosocial impairment associated with anxiety in children. *Journal of Clinical Child Psychology, 16,* 235-239.

48. Walker, J. L., Lahey, B. B., Hynd, G. W., & Frame, C. L. (1987). Comparison of specific patterns of antisocial behavior in children with conduct disorder with or without coexisting hyperactivity. *Journal of Consulting and Clinical Psychology, 55,* 910-913.

49. Abrams, B. J. (1988). The values and value stability of emotionally handicapped and normal adolescents. *Adolescence, 23,* 721-739.

50. Archer, R. P., Gordon, R. A., Giannetti, R. A., & Singles, J. M. (1988). MMPI scale clinical correlates for adolescent inpatients. *Journal of Personality Assessment, 52,* 707-721.

51. Cohen, M. (1988). The Revised Conners Parent Rating Scale: Factor structure replication with a diversified clinical sample. *Journal of Abnormal Child Psychology, 16,* 187-196.

52. Green, S. B., & Kelley, C. K. (1988). Racial bias in prediction with the MMPI for a juvenile delinquent population. *Journal of Personality Assessment, 52,* 263-275.

53. Hagborg, W. J. (1988). A study of the intensity and frequency of crisis intervention for students enrolled in a school for the severely emotionally disturbed. *Adolescence, 23,* 825-836.

54. Lee, M., & Prentice, N. M. (1988). Interrelations of empathy, cognition, and moral reasoning with dimensions of juvenile delinquency. *Journal of Abnormal Child Psychology, 16,* 127-139.

55. Moffitt, T. E., & Silva, P. A. (1988). Self-reported delinquency, neuropsychological deficit, and history of attention deficit disorder. *Journal of Abnormal Child Psychology, 16,* 553-569.

56. Slotkin, J., Forehand, R., Fauber, R., McCombs, A., & Long, N. (1988). Parent-completed and adolescent-completed CDIS: Relationship to adolescent social and cognitive functioning. *Journal of Abnormal Child Psychology, 16,* 207-217.

57. Wagner, W. G., & Johnson, J. T. (1988). Childhood nocturnal enuresis: The prediction of premature withdrawal from behavioral conditioning. *Journal of Abnormal Child Psychology, 16,* 687-692.

58. Wierson, M., Forehand, R., & McCombs, A. (1988). The relationship of early adolescent functioning to parent-reported and adolescent-perceived interparental conflict. *Journal of Abnormal Child Psychology, 16,* 707-718.

59. Blaske, D. M., Borduin, C. M., Henggeler, S. W., & Mann, B. J. (1989). Individual, family, and peer characteristics of adolescent sex offenders and assaultive offenders. *Developmental Psychology, 25,* 846-855.

60. Bursuck, W. (1989). A comparison of students with learning disabilities to low achieving and higher achieving students on three dimensions of social competence. *Journal of Learning Disabilities, 22,* 188-194.

61. Duncan, P., & Kilpatrick, D. (1989). Use of extreme rating categories in ratings of child behavior. *Child Study Journal, 19,* 51-64.

62. Fuchs, D., & Fuchs, L. S. (1989). Exploring effective and efficient prereferral interventions: A component analysis of behavioral consultation. *School Psychology Review, 18,* 260-283.

63. Hogan, A. E., Quay, H. C., Vaughn, S., & Shapiro, S. K. (1989). Revised Behavior Problem Checklist: Stability, prevalence, and incidence of behavior problems in kindergarten and first-grade children. *Psychological Assessment, 1,* 103-111.

64. Jouriles, E. N., Murphy, C. M., & O'Leary, D. (1989). Interspousal aggression, marital discord, and child problems. *Journal of Consulting and Clinical Psychology, 57,* 453-455.

65. Lahey, B. B., Hynd, G. W., Stone, P. A., Piacentini, J. C., & Frick, P. J. (1989). Neuropsychological test performance and the attention deficit disorders: Clinical utility of the Luria-Nebraska Neuropsychological Battery—Children's Revision. *Journal of Consulting and Clinical Psychology, 57,* 112-116.

66. Lahey, B. B., Russo, M. F., Walker, J. L., & Piacentini, J. C. (1989). Personality characteristics of the mothers of children with disruptive behavior disorders. *Journal of Consulting and Clinical Psychology, 57,* 512-515.

67. McGee, R., Williams, S., Moffitt, T., & Anderson, J. (1989). A comparison of 13-year-old boys with attention deficit and/or reading disorder on neuropsychological measures. *Journal of Abnormal Child Psychology, 17,* 37-53.

68. Nieminen, G. S., & Matson, J. L. (1989). Depressive problems in conduct-disordered adolescents. *Journal of School Psychology, 27,* 175-188.

69. Sanders, M. R., Rebgetz, M., Morrison, M., Bor, W., Gordon, A., Dadds, M., & Shepard, R. (1989). Cognitive-behavioral treatment of recurrent nonspecific abdominal pain in children: An analysis of generalization, maintenance, and side effects. *Journal of Consulting and Clinical Psychology, 57,* 294-300.

70. Wierson, M., Forehand, R., Fauber, R., & McCombs, A. (1989). Buffering young male adolescents against negative parental divorce influences: The role of good parent-adolescent relations. *Child Study Journal, 19,* 101-115.

71. Cohen, M., Becker, M. G., & Campbell, R. (1990). Relationships among four methods of assessment of children with Attention Deficit-Hyperactivity Disorder. *Journal of School Psychology, 28,* 189-202.

72. Fondacaro, M. R., & Heller, K. (1990). Attributional style in aggressive adolescent boys. *Journal of Abnormal Child Psychology, 18,* 75-89.

73. Hagborg, W. J. (1990). The Revised Behavior Problem Checklist and severely emotionally disturbed adolescents: Relationship to intelligence, academic achievement, and sociometric ratings. *Journal of Abnormal Child Psychology, 18,* 47-53.

74. Ollendick, T. H., Greene, R. W., Weist, M. D., & Oswald, D. P. (1990). The predictive validity of teacher nominations: A five-year followup of at-risk youth. *Journal of Abnormal Child Psychology, 18,* 699-713.

75. Scerbo, A., Raine, A., O'Brien, M., Chan, C., Rhee, C., & Smiley, N. (1990). Reward dominance and passive avoidance learning in adolescent psychopaths. *Journal of Abnormal Child Psychology, 18,* 451-463.

76. Watson, S. M., Henggeler, S. W., & Whelan, J. P. (1990). Family functioning and the social adaptation of hearing-impaired youths. *Journal of Abnormal Child Psychology, 18,* 143-163.

77. Duncan, P., & Kilpatrick, D. L. (1991). Parent ratings of the behaviors of normal male and female children with one child per family versus cross-sex siblings. *Child Study Journal, 21,* 95-115.

78. Frentz, C., Gresham, F. M., & Elliott, S. N. (1991). Popular, controversial, neglected, and rejected adolescents: Contrasts of social competence and achievement differences. *Journal of School Psychology, 29,* 109-120.

79. Short, R. J. (1991). Interpreting scale score differences on the Revised Behavior Problem Checklist. *Educational and Psychological Measurement, 51*, 385-392.

80. Williamson, J. M., Borduin, C. M., & Howe, B. (1991). The ecology of adolescent maltreatment: A multilevel examination of adolescent physical abuse, sexual abuse, and neglect. *Journal of Consulting and Clinical Psychology, 59*, 449-457.

Review of the Revised Behavior Problem Checklist by DENISE M. DEZOLT, *Instructor in School Psychology, Illinois State University, Normal, IL:*

The Revised Behavior Problem Checklist (RBPC) is an individually administered measure that can be completed by parents or teachers to screen for behavior problems of children in grades K–12. The authors describe a multitude of purposes for which this instrument has been used such as a screening measure as part of a diagnostic battery, as a measurement of behavior change, and for a range of research purposes. Administration and interpretation should be conducted by professionals with a masters degree or greater and appropriate psychometric training.

The behavior problems included in the RBPC were derived primarily from a review of more than 40 published studies that reported factors related to clinical child problems (e.g., conduct disorder, anxiety, withdrawal). The authors attempted to eliminate the following types of items: (*a*) those that overlap into multiple domains (e.g., failing grades); (*b*) global descriptors of pathology such as "obsessions"; (*c*) high frequency behaviors likely to be found in a random sample of children (e.g., nailbiting); (*d*) items requiring the rater to infer a particular behavior, such as preoccupied with certain thoughts; (*e*) somatic complaints; and (*f*) sexual behavior items. Four separate factor analytic studies were conducted from clinical samples (age range 5–23). Four major scales (i.e., Conduct Disorder [CD], Socialized Aggression [SA], Attention Problems—Immaturity [AP], Anxiety-Withdrawal [AW]) and two additional scales (i.e., Psychotic Behavior [PB] and Motor Tension-Excess [ME]) emerged from these studies.

The RBPC uses weighted scoring (2 = severe problem; 1 = mild problem; 0 = not a problem, no opportunity to observe, don't know) of the 89 items wherein respondents are instructed to indicate the degree to which the listed problems describe the child. Only 77 of the 89 items are scored and the manual offers no explanation about the remaining 12 items. Scoring templates are included in the test kit.

This instrument lacks national norms and the authors recommend developing local norms, especially when considering for large scale local use. The manual provides means and standard deviations for scale scores from diverse samples, both clinical and nonclinical, and from parent and teacher ratings. It is difficult to know how representative these samples are due to the limited descriptions provided within the manual. Based on setting and reason for referral, the examiner must select from the appropriate comparison group to ascertain the normalized *T* score. Given the poor layout of the manual, locating the appropriate group and determining the correct score is somewhat time consuming. The manual states that this instrument has been translated into eight foreign languages but fails to indicate if appropriate norms have been developed for its use in these languages.

The psychometric properties of the RBPC have been extensively evaluated and there is brief discussion of these studies in the manual. An examination of the discussion of these requires frequent reference to tables located at the end of the manual. Whereas some subscales are relatively independent, others demonstrate intercorrelations and expected shared variance. Results of interrater reliability studies demonstrate some inconsistency. Generally, interparent ratings and interteacher ratings demonstrated acceptable levels of agreement. Correlations between parents and teachers, however, were highly variable in one study cited. The authors question these results on the basis of possible rater (parent) limitations. Clearly, this area warrants further evaluation. Results of test-retest reliability indicate moderate to high stability on the scales.

According to the authors, concurrent validity of the RBPC was examined in a study with clinical versus normal children in which significant differences were found between the means on all six scales. Results of comparisons between this instrument and specific classifications from the *Diagnostic and Statistical Manual of Mental Disorders* (DSM-III, American Psychological Association, 1980) were generally in the expected direction. The authors reported several construct validation studies. Correlational studies conducted with the scales and behavioral observations and peer nominations found the relationships to be consistent with expectations. Studies of the relationship between the scales and intelligence and academic achievement support the differential validity of the AP scale and that the ME scale is negatively related to task attention. Other research examining the relationship between the RBPC scales and behavior checklists, affective inventories, self-concept scales, and other measures offer additional support for the differentiating capabilities of this instrument.

Hagborg (1990), in a study of emotionally disturbed adolescents, examined the relationship of the RBPC scales and intelligence, academic achievement, and sociometric ratings. The AP scale was found to be related to intelligence scores and mathematics achievement. Sociometric ratings of social acceptance were related to four of the scales, whereas peer acceptance was related to one.

In summary, the RBPC would serve as a useful screening instrument for potential behavior problems. More extensive analysis of behavioral status soliciting data from direct observations, parents, teachers, peers, and youth self-reports will be necessary for appropriate determination of status and recommendations for intervention. Development of local norms is strongly urged if this instrument is to be used to any great extent.

REVIEWER'S REFERENCES

American Diagnostic Association. (1980). *Diagnostic and statistical manual of mental disorders* (3rd ed.) DSM-III. Washington, DC: The Author.

Haborg, W. (1990). The Revised Behavior Problem Checklist and severely emotionally disturbed adolescents: Relationships to intelligence, academic achievement, and sociometric ratings. *Journal of Abnormal Child Psychology, 18,* 47-53.

Review of the Revised Behavior Problem Checklist by EDWARD S. SHAPIRO, Professor and Director, School Psychology Program, and STEWART M. SHEAR, Graduate Student in School Psychology, Lehigh University, Bethlehem, PA:

The Revised Behavior Problem Checklist (RBPC) is a behavioral rating scale designed to be completed by adults familiar with the child or adolescent of interest. The original version of this scale was published in 1967 and was called the Behavior Problem Checklist (BPC). A subsequent interim manual was published in 1980 after attempts were made to strengthen the psychometric properties of the checklist. The current manual, containing updated information and psychometric data, was published in 1987.

The RBPC contains 89 items. Unlike the original BPC (1967), a weighted number of 0 (indicating no problem, no opportunity to observe, or no knowledge about the item), 1 (indicating a mild problem), or 2 (indicating a severe problem) is now used for scoring items. Informants are instructed to complete every item. One problem evident with the scoring criteria is the failure to discriminate between the three possible responses represented by a zero score. Thus, an RBPC completed by a parent showing zero scores across items may only reflect lack of knowledge of the child's problem and not the absence of behavioral difficulties.

The RBPC manual reports the results of several subsamples upon which the scale validation appears to have been based. Four of the samples were used for deriving the factor structure of the scale. These samples included children in private psychiatric facilities, in outpatient and inpatient facilities, in a private school for children with learning disabilities, and in a community-sponsored school for children with learning disabilities. The other two subsamples included a group of children with diabetes attending a summer camp and children in grades 1 through 8 in two public schools. Very little additional information about these samples is provided. Their geographic location, mode of selection, representative-ness to overall populations of children in the United States, and so forth, are largely unreported.

Several factor analyses of the RBPC using multiple and very diverse samples were conducted to develop the factor structure of the scale. These analyses have resulted in six subscales found across studies: (*a*) Conduct Disordered (CD), (*b*) Socialized Aggression (SA), (*c*) Attention Problems—Immaturity (AP), (*d*) Anxiety-Withdrawal (AW), (*e*) Psychotic Behavior (PB), and (*f*) Motor Tension-Excess (ME). The authors consider the first four factors entitled CD, SA, AP, and AW as the major scales, whereas PB and ME are identified as minor scales. There are 12 additional items on the protocol that apparently do not contribute to any of the six subscales. One particular problem with the factor analyses reported for the scale is the failure to provide separate analyses for different age and/or gender groupings. Given that normative scores are reported separately for males and females in grades K–3, 4–6, and 7–8 for children without identified handicaps, and in grades K–6 and 7–12 for children with serious emotional disturbances, factor structures across these groups may not be identical.

No subscales were reported to show intercorrelations greater than .80. However, considerable overlap in variance appears to be shared when examining the six different samples where scale interrelationships were tested. In particular, variance overlap was noted between CD and SA (9%–42%), CD and AP (20%–31%), and CD and ME (9%–49%). The authors indicated that CD, SA, AP, and ME were felt to reflect the "externalizing" dimension of behavior disorders, whereas AW and AP reflect "internalizing" dimensions. When using the RBPC, it is clear that one must use more than one subscale when interpreting outcomes due to the substantial amount of shared variance across subscales.

RELIABILITY. Quay and Peterson report the results of several studies in which various types of reliability were assessed. Internal consistency within subscales across each of the six subsamples noted above appears good, ranging from .70 to .95. Interrater reliability (teachers) from one of the samples was listed as ranging from .85 (CD) to .52 (AW). Test-retest (2 months) reliability by teachers was reported as .63 for CD, .49 for SA, .83 for AP, .79 for AW, .61 for PB, and .68 for ME. One of the problems with the test-retest calculations was the apparent use of students without handicaps in the evaluation. Given that a large proportion of these students were scored at zero levels on multiple subscales, a truncated range was clearly evident in the calculation of test-retest reliability. No test-retest reliability was reported for populations involving children with serious emotional disturbance.

VALIDITY. The RBPC manual reported primarily concurrent validity. In addition, some attempt to provide discriminant validity was offered. Moderate to high correlations with the original BPC were reported, ranging from .97 (SA) to .63 (PB). In addition, correlations with the Child Behavior Profile (CBP) (Achenbach & Edelbrock, 1983) were examined. For boys, the CD scale of the RPBC was found to correlate .84 with the Externalizing scale of the Child Behavior Profile (CBP), .43 with SA, and .43 with AP. For girls, correlations between the Externalizing scale and the RBPC were .77 with CD, .75 with SA, .88 with AP, and .92 with ME. The Internalizing scale of the CBP correlated .65 and .84 with AW, and .51 and .45 with PB for boys and girls, respectively. The manual reports several studies in which the RBPC subscales were correlated to measures of depression, inattention, and self-concept.

Some attempt to show discriminant validity of the measure was reported in comparisons using the RBPC to contrast clinical and nonclinical samples. Substantial and statistically significant differences were noted among these samples on the RBPC. Additionally, similar findings were noted in comparing results of the RBPC with *Diagnostic and Statistical Manual of Mental Disorders* (DSM-III) categories. One shortcoming of these findings was the failure to use the current DSM-III-R psychiatric classification systems.

One final report of validity studies was included in the manual in which the RBPC results were contrasted to direct observations and peer nominations. A small sample ($N = 34$) with data collapsed between boys and girls produced correlations ranging from .00 (ME with motor activity) to .72 (CD with aggression). In general, the interrelationships among direct observations and RBPC subscales were small and nonsignificant. These findings are consistent with most literature that contrasts direct observation with informant report measures.

NORMS. The RBPC does not contain representative, national normative data. This is clearly a disadvantage of the scale. The authors alternatively suggest that if a large scale use of the RBPC is undertaken, local norms should be developed for interpretation. Such a suggestion is unrealistic and may severely limit the potential interpretation of the scale. Indeed, one must wonder and question the inclusion of two sets of tables that are designed to convert raw scores to normalized T scores. It is unclear in the manual exactly from where these tables are generated. The authors tend to report multiple samples from which they draw conclusions about the scale's factor structure, reliability, and validity characteristics. In fact, the authors state, "By reference to Tables 10 to 22 it is possible to interpret a given score with respect to its distance from the means of varying normal and clinical samples" (p. 15). Unfortunately, how a score is placed into a distribution is not clear. Using these tables for interpretation is not advised because students with similar characteristics (e.g., gifted fourth graders, Table 12) were scored differently by their homeroom teacher and special teacher on similar subscales.

The failure to provide a national, normative sample is very problematic given the diversity of populations on which the RBPC might be used. Reported samples appear not to be based on any systematic attempt to collect representative norms but more on the basis of availability of samples. The authors would be wise to try to provide a more systematic and representative sampling plan for future revisions of the scale.

SUMMARY. In general, the RBPC appears to be an attempt to update and revise a scale that has been present in the clinical literature for many years. Although the authors certainly have attempted to provide significant and helpful information in their manual and the collective information of the scale suggests that it is psychometrically sound, the failure of the authors to conduct a systematic and planned evaluation of the scale's characteristics and normative base raises serious questions about its potential use. The scale most likely can be used for individual clinical cases, with very cautious interpretation of results using the data reported in the manual. Despite the psychometric and potential normative problems inherent in the scale, the RBPC does offer another measure for potential use in child and adolescent assessment. Given its history, it is likely to see continued use in the clinical literature.

REVIEWER'S REFERENCE

Achenbach, T. M., & Edelbrock, C. (1983). *Manual for the Child Behavior Checklist and Revised Child Behavior Profile.* Burlington, VT: Queen City Printers.

[333]
Reynolds Adolescent Depression Scale.
Purpose: "To assess depressive symptomatology in adolescents."
Population: Ages 13–18.
Publication Dates: 1986–87.
Acronym: RADS.
Scores: Total score only.
Forms, 3: HS, I, G.
Comments: Self-report measure.
Author: William M. Reynolds.
Publisher: Psychological Assessment Resources, Inc.
  a) FORM HS.
  Administration: Individual and small group.
  Price Data: $25 per complete kit including scoring key, HS answer sheets, and manual ('87, 47 pages).
  Time: [5–10] minutes.
  Comments: Hand-scored.
  b) FORM I.
  Administration: Individual in part.
  Price Data: $47.50 or less per 10 prepaid answer sheets including scoring and reporting by publisher; $12 per manual.

Time: [5–10] minutes.
Comments: Machine-scored.

c) FORM G.
Administration: For large groups.
Price Data: $100 or less per 50 prepaid answer sheets including scoring and reporting by publisher; $12 per manual.
Time: [5–10] minutes.
Comments: Machine-scored; for screening programs and research projects.

TEST REFERENCES

1. Reynolds, W. M., & Coats, K. I. (1986). A comparison of cognitive-behavioral therapy and relaxation training for the treatment of depression in adolescents. *Journal of Consulting and Clinical Psychology, 54*, 653-660.
2. Matson, J. L., & Nieminen, G. S. (1987). Validity of measures of conduct disorder, depression, and anxiety. *Journal of Clinical Child Psychology, 16*, 151-157.
3. Nieminen, G. S., & Matson, J. L. (1989). Depressive problems in conduct-disordered adolescents. *Journal of School Psychology, 27*, 175-188.
4. Davis, N. L. F. (1990). The Reynolds Adolescent Depression Scale. *Measurement and Evaluation in Counseling and Development, 23*, 88-91.
5. Kahn, J. S., Kehle, T. J., Jenson, W. R., & Clark, E. (1990). Comparison of cognitive-behavioral, relaxation, and self-modeling interventions for depression among middle-school students. *School Psychology Review, 19*, 196-211.
6. Carey, T. C., Finch, A. J., & Carey, M. P. (1991). Relation between differential emotions and depression in emotionally disturbed children and adolescents. *Journal of Consulting and Clinical Psychology, 59*, 594-597.

Review of the Reynolds Adolescent Depression Scale by BARBARA J. KAPLAN, Associate Professor of Psychology, State University of New York College at Fredonia, Fredonia, NY:

The Reynolds Adolescent Depression Scale (RADS) is described by its authors as being a measure of depressive symptomatology rather than being a diagnostic measure of depression. As such, it appears that the RADS may be most effectively used for research purposes and not as a clinical screening measure or an aid to diagnosis. This type of quickly administered self-rating scale should not be considered as a substitute for more extensive diagnostic interviewing, a point the authors of the RADS make in several places.

The standardization sample for the RADS consisted of 2,460 adolescents drawn from grades 7 through 12 at two junior high schools and one high school in a midwestern community. Information regarding heterogeneity of the sample is reported and suggests that racial mix and the range of socioeconomic status are reflected in the norming of the test. Though the standardization sample was drawn from only one geographic location, the authors report that subsequent data do not indicate that additional locations would change the norms. In the process of its construction and revision, the test was administered to over 10,000 adolescents.

Multiple measures of the internal consistency of the RADS demonstrate high internal consistency. A brief discussion of the difficulties of evaluating test-retest reliability in assessing mood accompanies and clarifies data presented for retests of different samples at intervals of 6 weeks, 3 months, and 1 year. Concurrent validity for the RADS is demonstrated through joint administration of the RADS and the Hamilton Rating Scale (Hamilton, 1960).

The data and analyses demonstrating the RADS's psychometric qualities are impressive, and the authors have taken pains to compare their test results with other measures of depression and to provide some evaluation of the clinical significance of high and low scores. A useful feature of the RADS is the opportunity to convert raw scores to percentile ranks for sex, grade, and sex x grade. Analyses are available by age, race, and sex. Test means reflect the higher scores for females that are reported in numerous studies of depression.

The question still remains, does the RADS add anything to already existing measures of depression? I believe the answer is no. There is neither a theory of adolescence nor of adolescent depression that illuminates or justifies the construction of the test. The items on the RADS are significantly and highly correlated with other measures of depression, even though those measures were not specifically designed for adolescents. In addition, other individual characteristics such as anxiety and general self-esteem are highly correlated with the RADS. These correlations have absolute values ranging from .65 to .80. Although a number of studies of depression show low self-esteem and high anxiety as elements in the clinical picture of depression, the RADS offers little in the way of increased discriminability of these several factors.

Although weak on theory, the RADS appears to be equal to many of the other, more commonly used self-report measures of depression. In assessing the outcome of various therapeutic or educational interventions or in research where some measure of adolescent depressive symptoms might be needed, the RADS would be a reasonable choice. However, if comparisons with other studies of depression are indicated, one of the more popular measures of depression such as the Beck Depression Inventory (BDI; Beck, Ward, Mendelson, Mock, & Erbaugh, 1969), the Hamilton (1960), or the Zung (1965) rating scales would be a better choice.

REVIEWER'S REFERENCES

Hamilton, M. (1960). A rating scale for depression. *Journal of Neurology, Neurosurgery, and Psychiatry, 23*, 56-62.
Beck, A. T., Ward, C., Mendelson, M., Mock, J., & Erbaugh, J. (1961). An inventory for measuring depression. *Archives of General Psychiatry, 4*, 561-571.
Zung, W. W. K. (1965). A self-rating depression scale. *Archives of General Psychiatry, 12*, 63-70.

Review of the Reynolds Adolescent Depression Scale by DEBORAH KING KUNDERT, Assistant Professor of Educational Psychology and Statistics, University at Albany, State University of New York, Albany, NY:

The Reynolds Adolescent Depression Scale (RADS) is a questionnaire designed to assess the severity of depression in adolescents. Examinees respond to 30 sentences that describe feelings using a 4-point Likert-type format indicating how they usually feel (*almost never, hardly ever, sometimes,* or *most of the time*). The scale may be used for adolescents 13-18 years of age, it is appropriate for group or individual administration, and it may be machine or hand scored. Three different forms are available, depending on scoring and administration preference.

The primary use of the RADS is to assess symptoms associated with depression. The author indicates that this questionnaire was not designed to provide a diagnosis of specific depressive disorder; specific diagnosis would require a more extensive evaluation. As outlined in the manual, the RADS may be used as part of a screening procedure for identifying the extent of depressive symptomatology among adolescents (e.g., in schools or institutions). The author provides a multiple-stage screening method for assessment of depression in schools in the manual. Another application of the RADS is in the evaluation of prevention and treatment programs for depression.

Responses on the RADS are based on frequency of occurrence and are weighted from 1 to 4 points, with a total score range of 30 to 120. The author uses a cutoff score approach (at or above 77) to identify those who need further evaluation. According to the author, this cutoff score indicates a "level of symptom endorsement associated with clinical depression."

Standardization of the RADS is based on a sample of 2,460 students from a suburban/rural midwestern high school. Since completion of the initial field testing, additional data from a variety of sources have been collected (over 10,000 subjects). These data have not been found to differ significantly from the original sample. Significant differences were found for sex and grade, but not for race. As a result, separate norm tables for converting raw scores to percentile ranks are provided for sex and grade. Limited information (one study) is provided on using this questionnaire with special populations.

To estimate the reliability of the RADS, internal consistency and test-retest procedures were used. Coefficient alphas ranged from .90 to .94 and the split-half estimate was .91. Test-retest evaluations were conducted at 6 weeks (.80), 3 months (.79), and 1 year (.63).

Several types of validity data are presented for the RADS. The content validity of the scale was assessed by examining the congruence of questionnaire items with clinically specified symptomatology and item-total scale correlations. The RADS items were developed to reflect descriptive components of depression; items were not developed based on a specific theory of depression. Following this orientation, items on the RADS reflect the symptomatology outlined in *DSM-III* for major depression and dysthymic disorder, as well as symptoms of depression specified by the Research Diagnostic Criteria (RDC). Items assess cognitive, somatic, psychomotor, and interpersonal areas. The author indicates that not all symptoms associated with depression are assessed by the RADS. The item-total correlations are presented as additional evidence of the content validity of the questionnaire. The majority of these correlations ranged from the .50s to the .60s, with a median correlation of .53.

Criterion-related validity of the RADS was examined using the Hamilton Rating Scale clinical interview. These measures were administered to a sample of 111 adolescents. The correlation between the RADS and the rating scale was .83.

Evidence offered for construct validity is in the form of significant correlations of the RADS with other self-report measures of depression (e.g., Beck Depression Inventory, Children's Depression Inventory). In addition, significant correlations between the RADS and related constructs (e.g., self-esteem, anxiety, loneliness) are reported to support the construct validity of the scale. Lower correlations between the RADS and variables unrelated to depression (e.g., social desirability, academic achievement) suggest minimal relationship between these variables and RADS scores. Results of factor analytic studies are presented as descriptive information, and not as validity investigations, because the scale was developed based on symptomatology and not on a theory.

The clinical validity of the RADS was evaluated by examining treatment sensitivity and diagnostic efficacy. Results from two studies indicate a high level of classificatory agreement between RADS scores and clinical severity ratings (using the Hamilton Rating Scale; 89% agreement) and between the RADS and clinical interviews (using the Schedule for Affective Disorders and Schizophrenia-SADS; 82% agreement). Further evidence for the clinical utility of the RADS was obtained from the results of a study comparing treatment approaches for depression (cognitive-behavioral vs. relaxation training vs. waiting list controls).

A technical analysis of the RADS indicates that it is a moderately well-developed instrument that clinicians should find useful as a screening measure of depressive symptoms in adolescents. The manual is clearly and concisely written, which meets the author's expectation that it should serve as both a technical guide and a clinical guide for evaluating depression in adolescents. The ease of administration and scoring are additional assets. As indicated by the author, only initial investigations supporting the psychometric properties of the RADS are presented; further research will contribute to a better understanding of the relationship between the RADS and depression in adolescents.

Reynolds Child Depression Scale.
Purpose: Provides screening for and a measure of depressive symptomatology.
Population: Grades 3–6.
Publication Dates: 1981–89.
Scores: Total score only.
Administration: Group or individual.
Forms, 2: HS (hand-scored), G (machine-scored).
Price Data, 1990: $35 per complete kit including 25 test booklet/answer sheets (Form HS), scoring key, and manual ('89, 60 pages); $15 per 25 test booklet/answer sheets (Form HS); $100 per 50 test booklet/answer sheets (Form G) (scoring and reporting included in price); $7 per scoring key; $15 per manual.
Time: (10–15) minutes.
Comments: Test booklet title is *About Me*; self-ratings.
Author: William M. Reynolds.
Publisher: Psychological Assessment Resources, Inc.

TEST REFERENCES

1. Reynolds, W. M., & Graves, A. (1989). Reliability of children's reports of depressive symptomatology. *Journal of Abnormal Child Psychology, 17*, 647-655.

Review of the Reynolds Child Depression Scale by JANET F. CARLSON, Assistant Professor of Education, Graduate School of Education, Fairfield University, Fairfield, CT:

The Reynolds Child Depression Scale (RCDS) is a self-report, paper-and-pencil measure, intended to assess the severity of depressive symptomatology in 8- to 12-year-old children. Although it is not intended for diagnostic purposes, it was developed in accordance with widely accepted diagnostic systems, such as the *Diagnostic and Statistical Manual of Mental Disorders—Third Edition, Revised (DSM III-R; American Psychiatric Association, 1987) and the Research Diagnostic Criteria (RDC; Spitzer, Endicott, & Robins, 1978). The development of test specifications also made use of other diagnostic approaches such as the Weinberg criteria (Weinberg, Rutman, Sullivan, Penick, & Dietz, 1973) and Poznanski's clinical interview approach (Poznanski, Cook, & Carroll, 1979). The test author utilized these models of depressive symptomatology in order to develop a clinically meaningful measure of depression in this age group. Overall, he appears to have accomplished this goal, as the remainder of this review indicates.

Throughout the test manual, the test author issues many caveats for potential test users, in an effort to assure proper test use and interpretation. Although doing so might be construed as merely complying with the responsibilities set forth by the *Standards for Educational and Psychological Testing* (American Educational Research Association, American Psychological Association, & National Council on Measurement in Education, 1985), the author's extensive coverage, relating especially to possible misuses or misinterpretations, is laudable. Many times, for example, the RCDS is distinguished as a measure of "clinically relevant" depressive symptoms and not as a diagnostic indicator.

The test manual also presents a solid base of studies pertaining to standardization procedures and psychometric properties of the RCDS. Respectable sample sizes were used in the normative procedures, as the total standardization sample contained 1,620 students and grade level samples ranged from 263 to 460. Percentages regarding ethnicity of the sample are presented; however, comparison figures, such as data from the U.S. Census Bureau, are not provided. Although the normative sample was drawn solely from the west and midwest, I concur with the test author's logic that geographic representativeness is not necessary, because location does not appear to influence the incidence of depression.

Information regarding reliability and validity is quite impressive, overall, especially considering the recent publication date of the RCDS. Internal consistency coefficients (coefficient alpha), and split-half coefficients, corrected for length by the Spearman-Brown formula, were in the upper .80s and lower .90s within and across grades, gender, and ethnic groups, as well as for a subset of learning disabled children. Findings by seven other investigators are presented in the manual with similar results. Test-retest reliability was surprisingly good (.82 and .85), given that depression is probably a state construct to some degree.

To establish validity, the test author addresses content, criterion-related, and construct validities. The author presents his perception that content validation has occurred, based on the fact that the items are congruent with several diagnostic systems and were selected according to item-total scale correlations. A stronger statement could be made if experts were asked to judge blindly the degree of congruence between individual items and the various diagnostic formulations. Criterion-related validity was supported by comparing RCDS performance with scores on two other measures of depression in children. There were seven such studies conducted by other researchers, and in all instances, significant correlations in the mid-.70s were obtained. Construct validity was investigated by attempts to establish convergent and divergent validity. Moderately high convergence was found in five studies using measures of self-esteem and three studies of anxiety. Low convergence (i.e., divergence) was found in six studies using measures of academic achievement.

Several pragmatic concerns make the RCDS appealing for those test users who wish to screen a large number of students for possibly meaningful levels of depression. First, the measure readily lends itself to group administration procedures. The reading level required is well below that of the youngest child for whom the measure is appropriate.

Further, the format of the measure is easy to comprehend and is one with which most students will already be familiar. Lastly, the brief administration time makes wide range applications feasible, and the availability of machine scoring through a mail-in service makes such screenings convenient.

If one chooses the hand-scoring route, the procedures are quite simple, and the test kit includes the scoring template for this purpose. The advantage to hand scoring is that the scorer can visually evaluate the validity of the protocol, as suggested by the test author. That is, patterns of unlikely responses (i.e., a pattern of sequentially ascending or descending responses), or the endorsement of the same response for all items, would be obvious to the manual scorer. The test author also notes that three item pairs are composed of statements that are inverses of each other, and hence provide a validity check because they should yield equivalent scores. Unfortunately, it appears that the machine-scoring process does not include any of these types of data screening. Therefore, some invalid profiles may be present, but not detected, when the RCDS is scored by optical scanning.

In summary, the RCDS provides reliable, valid information regarding the severity of depressive symptoms in children in grades 3 through 6. When administered on a large scale basis, it serves as a screening instrument for such symptoms. When used on an individual or small scale basis, it yields clinically meaningful information concerning the extent of depressive symptomatology. Its ease of administration, familiar format, sound psychometric properties, and detailed user information make it a good candidate for inclusion in a comprehensive assessment battery.

REVIEWER'S REFERENCES

Weinberg, W. A., Rutman, J., Sullivan, L., Penick, E. C., & Dietz, S. G. (1973). Depression in children referred to an educational diagnostic center: Diagnosis and treatment. *Journal of Pediatrics, 83,* 1065-1072.

Spitzer, R. L., Endicott, J., & Robins, E. (1978). Research diagnostic criteria: Rationale and reliability. *Archives of General Psychiatry, 35,* 773-782.

Poznanski, E. O., Cook, S. C., & Carroll, B. J. (1979). A depression rating scale for children. *Pediatrics, 64,* 442-450.

American Educational Research Association, American Psychological Association, & National Council on Measurement in Education. (1985). *Standards for educational and psychological testing.* Washington, DC: American Psychological Association, Inc.

American Psychiatric Association. (1987). *Diagnostic and statistical manual of mental disorders* (3rd ed., rev.). Washington, DC: Author.

Review of the Reynolds Child Depression Scale by CYNTHIA A. ROHRBECK, *Associate Professor of Psychology, The George Washington University, Washington, DC:*

Although childhood depression has been receiving increased attention in child psychology, the lack of well-developed assessment instruments has hindered systematic research in this area. Self-report ratings make up many of the newer assessment measures, despite earlier research questioning children's ability to report depressive affects and cognitions. Self-reports may be especially important, however, when assessing depression, given that many depressive symptoms reflect subjective feelings. The Reynolds Child Depression Scale (RCDS) is a self-report rating scale designed to measure symptoms of depression in children in grades 3–6 (ages 8–12). It can serve as a screener (group administered in classrooms) and as an assessment and evaluation instrument in clinical and research settings.

The RCDS test booklet is entitled "About Me." Children are told to choose responses that tell how they have been feeling for the last 2 weeks. The author recommends that items be read out loud for children in grades 3 and 4. The scale includes 30 items (at a second grade reading level) that tap cognitive, motoric-vegetative, somatic, and interpersonal symptoms of depression—29 use a 4-point (Likert-type) response format, with choices of *almost never, sometimes, a lot of the time,* and *all the time.* The last item consists of five faces with expressions that range from happy to sad; the child is asked to choose the circle that shows how he or she feels (scale of 1–5). Several items on the scale ($n = 7$) are reverse scored. This is a strength of the measure; response sets and inconsistent responding (for the three items which are duplicated) can be checked.

It should be noted (and is stated several places in the manual) that the RCDS assesses depressive symptomatology, but does not provide a diagnosis of depression. Items were based on symptomatology in the *Diagnostic and Statistical Manual* (*DSM III-R;* American Psychiatric Association, 1987) and the Research Diagnostic Criteria (RDC; Spitzer, Endicott, & Robins, 1978). The RCDS contains an empirically derived cutoff score to indicate a clinical or pathological level of depressive symptoms. It is recommended that children scoring above this cutoff be assessed further.

The RCDS is a practical test to use. A clear and thorough manual accompanies the test and includes a history of the development of the measure, along with psychometric information. It concludes with normative tables for the total normative sample, and by grade and gender. The manual also includes discussions of RCDS cutoff scores, validity checks, and information on individual items. There are six items designated as "critical items" based on their ability (on another scale) to discriminate between clinically depressed and nondepressed adolescents. Both hand-scored (with an easy-to-use answer key) and OCR versions of the RCDS are available; the OCR form can be scored by a mail-in service, particularly useful for large-scale administrations. The manual notes that potential users of the RCDS include mental health professionals with training in psychological test use and interpretation. The manual clearly explains measurement concepts necessary for appropriate test use and interpretation.

RCDS norms were based on a standardization sample of 1,620 elementary school children in the midwest and western areas of the U.S. The sample seems representative of those regions; the normative sample included approximately 30% ethnic minority children from urban, suburban, and rural areas. Subgroup norms are available by grade and gender. Internal consistency is strong (.90 for the total sample, ranging from .79 to .91 for specific ethnic, gender, and grade subsamples). Two test-retest studies have yielded reliability coefficients of .82 ($N = 24$) and .85 ($N = 220$). Thus, the RCDS seems to be a stable (for periods of less than 4 weeks) measure of depression.

The manual also provides thorough information on RCDS validity studies. Evidence for content validity is that items were developed to reflect the *DSM III-R* and RDC symptoms of depression. As evidence of construct validity, there have been several studies of convergent validity (the RCDS correlates with the Children's Depression Inventory [CDI; Kovacs, 1979] and with measures of self-esteem and anxiety). The RCDS correlates (.76) with the Children's Depression Scale—Revised, a semistructured interview for depression (Poznanski, Grossman, Buchsbaum, Banegas, Freeman, & Gibbons, 1984). Some evidence of discriminant validity is available; the RCDS did not correlate significantly with students' achievement test scores or teachers' ratings of academic ability. Finally, there is also evidence of the scale's clinical utility; the scale's specificity of 97% and sensitivity of 73% are adequate.

In summary, the RCDS was designed to measure self-reported depression in children in grades 3–6. Eight years of research attest to its reliability and validity. Given that it is a self-report measure, however, it should not be used as the sole means of identifying depressed children. It would be important to include ratings by others (e.g., parents) because they may identify different symptoms (e.g., more behavioral signs of depression). Also, child and parent ratings have shown little correlation (this relationship is not provided for the RCDS). Despite this caveat, self-report measures like the RCDS may provide information that is not provided by other types of assessment measures. The RCDS manual also notes the scale should not be used to assess potential suicidality; children who are suicidal might be missed by use of only self-report measures like the RCDS.

An alternate, and probably the most widely used, child self-report measure of depression is the Children's Depression Inventory (CDI; Kovacs, 1979; 66). The CDI is a 27-item severity measure of depression; each item consists of three sentences that range from normal, to slight symptoms of depression, to severe and clinically significant symptoms of depression. Compared to the CDI, the brief one-line items on the RCDS may be more easily understood by younger children, especially those to whom the scale is read.

REVIEWER'S REFERENCES

Spitzer, R. L., Endicott, J., & Robins, E. (1978). Research diagnostic criteria: Rationale and reliability. *Archives of General Psychiatry, 35,* 773-782.

Kovacs, M. (1979). *Children's depression inventory.* Unpublished manuscript, University of Pittsburgh School of Medicine.

Poznanski, E. O., Grossman, J. A., Buchsbaum, Y., Banegas, M., Freeman, L., & Gibbons, R. (1984). Preliminary studies of the reliability and validity of the Children's Depression Rating Scale. *Journal of the American Academy of Child Psychiatry, 23,* 191-197.

American Psychiatric Association. (1987). *Diagnostic and statistical manual of mental disorders* (3rd ed., rev.). Washington, DC: Author.

[335]
Richmond Tests of Basic Skills: Edition 2.

Purpose: "Comprehensive and continuous measurement of the growth of an individual child in the fundamental skills."
Population: Ages 8-0 to 13-11.
Publication Dates: 1975–88.
Acronym: RTBS: Edition 2.
Scores: 11 tests: Vocabulary, Reading Comprehension, Language Skills (Spelling, Use of Capital Letters, Punctuation, Usage), Work-Study Skills (Map Reading, Reading Graphs and Tables, Knowledge and Use of Reference Materials), Mathematics Skills (Mathematics Concepts, Mathematics Problem Solving).
Administration: Group.
Levels: 6 overlapping levels (ages 8-0 to 8-11, 9-0 to 9-11, 10-0 to 10-11, 11-0 to 11-11, 12-0 to 12-11, 13-0 to 13-11) in a single reusable booklet.
Price Data, 1990: £4.90 per pupil's book; £6.05 per 25 answer sheets (specify level); £7.80 per scoring overlay (specify level); £6.05 per 25 pupil profile charts; £6.05 per 25 circular profiles; £14.90 per administration manual ('88, 96 pages); £20.65 per specimen set; scoring service offered by publisher.
Time: (60) minutes per test.
Comments: British adaptation of Iowa Tests of Basic Skills (184).
Authors: A. N. Hieronymus, E. F. Lindquist, and Norman France.
Publisher: NFER-Nelson Publishing Co., Ltd. [England].
Cross References: For additional information and reviews by Michael Berger and Thomas Kellaghan of an earlier edition, see 8:25.

TEST REFERENCES

1. Bynner, J. M., & Romney, D. M. (1986). Intelligence, fact or artefact: Alternative structures for cognitive abilities. *British Journal of Educational Psychology, 56,* 13-23.
2. Webley, P. (1987). The relationship between physical and social reasoning in adolescents. *Journal of Genetic Psychology, 148,* 375-384.
3. Annett, M., & Manning, M. (1989). The disadvantages of dextrality for intelligence. *British Journal of Psychology, 80,* 213-226.

Review of the Richmond Tests of Basic Skills: Edition 2 by CARMEN J. FINLEY, Research Psychologist, retired, Santa Rosa, CA:

The Richmond Tests of Basic Skills (RTBS), originally developed in 1974, is a British adaptation of the Iowa Tests of Basic Skills (ITBS; 184). Other than content modifications necessary to reflect the

British environment and current curriculum practices, and standardization on a sample of U.K. school children, it is a faithful representation of the ITBS. As such, it would be considered, by American standards, a psychometrically sound achievement test battery. Reviewers of the first edition, both British, point out legitimate concerns in trying to make such an adaptation, some of which will be addressed here. Readers of this review, however, should read in full the previous reviewers' comments found in the earlier edition of *The Mental Measurements Yearbook* (8:25).

The 1988 revision of the Richmond Tests of Basic Skills has retained much of the content of the first edition. According to the test publisher there was minor editing, some reordering of items, and prices in money questions "were altered as appropriate to bring them in line with present-day costs."

Improvements have been made in the Administration Manual, both in format and in content. Format changes are designed to highlight requirements of standard administration. Spacing and type size have improved readability. Content changes include a new section on the reliability of score differences, thus attending to one of the criticisms of an earlier reviewer. Another new section, Examining the Test Scores, addresses ways to develop and use pupil profile charts and class scattergrams, emphasizing the unreliability of low scores. In addition, the new Administration Manual contains both the Teacher's Guide and the Tables of Norms book from the first edition.

The section on technical data has been expanded and improved. The standardization design included 500 pupils at each of six test levels and eight school levels randomly selected in England, Wales, and Northern Ireland. Independent schools in England and Wales were included, thus addressing a criticism of a previous reviewer. The design allowed for nonparticipation, but not to the extent that actually occurred. Nonparticipating schools cited such reasons as "pressure of work," "short of staff," "involved in other research," "dates clashed with other examinations." An additional 7% of schools that agreed to cooperate failed to complete the test. The actual number of children on whom norms are based, per level, thus varied from 959 to 1,435. (The targeted number of pupils per test level was 1,500 including 500 at each of three consecutive levels.) It is impossible to evaluate the real effect of selective participation of schools in the standardization sample in this case. However, in general, selective participation generally leads to somewhat inflated results (i.e., the norms may be a bit higher than if all schools had agreed to participate).

Kuder-Richardson reliability coefficients are quite good ranging from .781 (Punctuation) to .947 (Reading Comprehension). A number of validation studies on both the first and second editions are reported. The first edition Reading Comprehension test correlated .58 to .65 with four other tests of reading, showing only a moderate overlap in skills being measured. Predictive validities and test-retest reliabilities of the first edition are also reported, with no particular surprises. Factor analytic studies of the second edition as well as an alternative technique, LISREL (Linear Structural Equation Relationships), offer support to the construct validity of the tests.

PRACTICAL CONSIDERATIONS. According to reviewers of the first edition, some practical concerns were expressed regarding the teachers' use of this test considered complex by comparison with the simpler formats that were in use in Great Britain. The RTBS like the ITBS requires the handling of test booklets containing 11 subtests covering six different levels. The handling of separate answer sheets also represented a change over more familiar procedures. In addition, the question was raised as to whether teachers used to shorter tests would feel the time requirement of four sessions ranging from 65 to 85 minutes each would be worth the investment. In other words, would the RTBS be used properly and would it be used to any great extent?

Because it is difficult for an American reviewer to address these concerns, correspondence was initiated with the previous reviewers and the publisher. According to the publisher, RTBS is "the most popular basic skills test used in UK schools . . . Sales would indicate that both first and second editions are used widely with a gradual but steady move to the new edition from schools who have used the first edition for some years." The skill with which teachers administer and interpret test results was not addressed by any of the correspondents.

The most serious concern, however, has to do with basic philosophical differences between the British and the American approach to testing. Thomas Kellaghan, a reviewer of the first edition, states:

In Britain at the moment there is a strong emphasis on the development of tests in the context of the new national curriculum. The new tests (or more accurately testing situations) will employ tasks that ask students, often in tasks that are longer and more complex than those involved in traditional multiple-choice tests, to supply answers, produce products and perform experiments. Assessments may be based on observations of students while they are engaged in the normal activities of their programmes of study. Since these developments have official government backing and are being developed in the context of a nationally prescribed curriculum and assessment procedures for schools, I would predict that tests such as the Richmond Tests will find the British educational scene to be an inhospitable environment. How long that remains the case will depend on how successful efforts to develop the new generation of assessment procedures will be.

In summary, the second edition of the RTBS, by American standards should be considered as sound as its parent, ITBS. However, because there are considerable differences between Great Britain and America in their basic philosophical approaches to testing, the days of an American model in Great Britain may be numbered.

[336]

Rivermead Perceptual Assessment Battery.

Purpose: "To assess deficits in visual perception following a stroke or head injury."
Population: Adult stroke and head injury patients.
Publication Date: 1985.
Acronym: RPAB.
Scores, 16: Picture Matching, Object Matching, Colour Matching, Size Recognition, Series, Animal Halves, Missing Article, Figure Ground Discrimination, Sequencing/Pictures, Body Image, R/L Copying Shapes, R/L Copying Words, 3D Copying, Cube Copying, Cancellation, Body Image/Self Identification.
Administration: Individual.
Price Data, 1987: £235 per complete set containing all items for each subtest, layout guide, 25 record forms, and manual (83 pages) in a carrying case; £6.50 per 25 record forms; £16.95 per manual.
Time: (49–59) minutes.
Authors: S. Whiting, N. Lincoln, G. Bhavnani, and J. Cockburn.
Publisher: NFER-Nelson Publishing Co., Ltd. [England].

Review of the Rivermead Perceptual Assessment Battery by JEFFERY P. BRADEN, Associate Professor of Psychology, San Jose State University, San Jose, CA:

The Rivermead Perceptual Assessment Battery (RPAB) is intended to provide occupational therapists in the United Kingdom with the means to identify severe perceptual deficits in brain-injured patients, and to monitor their progress in response to therapy intended to ameliorate perceptual deficits. Most other neuropsychological batteries require that the examiner hold advanced training in psychology or neurology in order to conduct assessments using the battery. Thus, the RPAB is distinguished from most other neuropsychological batteries in that it is intended for independent use by supporting professionals, such as occupational therapists, rather than psychologists or neurologists. However, the RPAB shares the purpose of most other neuropsychological batteries, which is to infer neuropsychological normality or abnormality based on test responses.

DEVELOPMENT, RELIABILITY, AND VALIDITY. The RPAB is a collection of 16 tests selected from an initial pool of 27 tests. The final selection of 16 tests from the initial pool was made on the basis of psychometric considerations (e.g., reliability, correlations with other tests). Although psychometric characteristics provide valid reason to exclude tests, neuropsychological theory was not explicitly considered in the selection process. Some neuropsychological characteristics may be important to assess, and yet may be relatively unrelated to other tasks.

The reliability (actually, the stability) data reported in the RPAB manual are based on 19 patients (15 men, 4 women), assessed 4 weeks apart. The rank-order correlation coefficients derived from this sample are positive and statistically significant for the most part (median $r_s = .74$), but they vary widely across tests (r_s range from -.56 to 1.00, and two tests had no calculable r_s). A second test-retest study is included in the manual to further investigate three tests with low reliabilities. The second study uses 20 subjects, who were not described, and reports values for two of the three subtests that are also inadequate. It should be noted that the test-retest procedures were not "blind," in that the same person assessed all 19 patients on both occasions and presumably might anticipate scores on the second administration. No internal consistency coefficients are provided. Interrater reliability using three raters of six sets of patient data showed good to excellent agreement among raters (coefficients of concordance range from .72 to 1.00, median = .96) for each subtest. No mention of "blind" procedures was made in the interrater agreement study, leaving open the possibility that expectancy effects may inflate interrater agreement.

Construct validity data are presented in the form of RPAB correlations with other tests. Correlations with other tests are based on 57 patients, 41 of whom suffered strokes and 16 of whom received head injuries. The 16 RPAB subtests showed a pattern of modest correlations with other psychological tests believed to assess perception, and showed smaller correlations with most psychological tests not believed to assess perception. These data suggest adequate convergent and divergent validity (i.e., the 16 subtests correlate with related tests, and do not correlate with unrelated tests). A second validity study linking the RPAB to the Rivermead ADL Self Care Scale (RADL) was inexplicably placed in the Interpretation section of the manual (pp. 61–62). This study of 54 patients, who were not described, suggests low scores on the RPAB are associated with low scores on the RADL, again providing modest evidence of construct validity.

Discriminant validity was established by comparing the mean scores of the 57 patients used in the correlational study to 69 adults, 16–69 years of age, who were recruited primarily from hospital staff. The differences between group means on most tests were unusual (i.e., statistically significant). The magnitude of differences between groups was often larger than one standard deviation of the normal group, which is a substantial difference. A secondary analysis showed the RPAB cannot discriminate between right- and left-hemisphere-damaged patients (i.e., the means of the two patient groups were similar for most of the 16 subtests).

The 69 normal subjects, who were subdivided into above average, average, and below average intelligence groups, were described as the normative sample for the RPAB. Although the sample is small and cannot be construed as representative of any typical population, it could be adequate if the construct being sampled has little variability. For example, a sample of 25 or 30 people is adequate to show that the "normative" value for number of fingers is 10; expanding the normative sample to better represent the population does not affect this conclusion. Unfortunately, only four of the tests in the RPAB appear to meet the criterion of little variability across the three ranges of intelligence. The other 12 subtests show meaningful variability across levels of intelligence. Consequently, the "normative" sample of the RPAB is inadequate, because it is limited in its representation of the underlying population (in number and in type of person represented), and because there is reason to believe that the traits measured by the test would vary within the general population to a substantial degree.

ADMINISTRATION, SCORING, AND MATERIALS. The manual provides sufficient information for relatively untrained professionals to reliably administer and score the battery. The instructions and directions are clear, and are presented in an easy-to-follow format. Those unfamiliar with psychological testing may need more coaching on how to provide supportive but nonspecific responses—the examples provided (i.e., "That's fine," "All right") are ambiguous, in that they could easily imply "You did it correctly." The layout of materials is also clear. The manual does a fine job of providing sufficient directions without getting bogged down in unnecessary details.

Scoring is straightforward and uncomplicated for most tasks. My only concerns are (a) there is no scoring key for the Cancellation test, (b) the scoring rules for the Cancellation test fail to penalize subjects who simply cross out all letters rather than only the target letter, and (c) there are no scoring examples for the Copy Shapes test. The lack of guidance may be a particular problem for those who have little formal training in psychological testing (i.e., the occupational therapists for whom the battery is intended).

The materials are generally bright, attractive, and well made. I noticed nothing about the materials which was specific to the United Kingdom. My only complaints about the materials are: (a) the bags that hold the cards are a tight fit, meaning the cards are likely to become bent at the corners; (b) nothing was provided to hold the pieces from the two puzzles together; (c) the cards arrived in incorrect order, meaning they must be resorted before administration; and (d) some of the cube models were broken when I received them, and had to be reglued before use (a photo of the model would help). These complaints are minor and are not intended to detract from the generally high quality of the materials. There is good news and bad news with respect to "consumable" copying tests. The good news is that masters are provided, and test users are free to reproduce sheets for consumption as often as needed. The bad news is that the 11.75 x 8.25 inch masters are a nonstandard size (by North American standards), and so examiners must be creative in how they reproduce these masters.

INTERPRETATION. The manual delineates three steps for determining perceptual deficits. The first step is establishing or estimating the subject's premorbid intellectual level. The second step establishes critical values on the 16 tests for each premorbid intellectual level (i.e., above average, average, below average). The third step is deciding whether a subject has a perceptual deficit (i.e., three or more RPAB subtest scores below the critical level). Two case histories are provided to illustrate scoring and interpretation. Within the case histories, and on the record form, it is suggested that the 16 RPAB tests be grouped into eight classes, purportedly measuring constructs such as "form constancy" and "sequencing."

Unfortunately, there are no data to support the interpretation practices in the manual. The most important sin of omission in this regard is the failure to justify the three-or-more rule for defining perceptual deficits. A simple 2 x 2 table, showing the frequencies of those with three-or-more versus those with less than three critical values by patients versus normals, would help users anticipate the accuracy of the RPAB for discriminating normal from abnormal persons. Simply knowing that the means of normals and patients differ does not tell users the clinical accuracy of diagnoses provided by the RPAB.

This failure is compounded by the fallacy which underlies many neuropsychological batteries (viz., that because brain-damaged persons have extreme scores, others who have extreme scores are brain damaged). This is logically equivalent to assuming that because squirrels eat nuts, anybody who eats nuts is a squirrel. The only way to circumvent the fallacy is to show that *only* brain-damaged persons obtain unusual scores. The RPAB fails to provide such a demonstration.

There are two other problems with the interpretation section of the manual. The first is that the manual recommends estimating premorbid IQ on the basis of a postmorbid test. Because there is substantial covariance between scores on intelligence tests and the RPAB, postmorbid intelligence tests are confounded with perceptual deficit. Thus, the recommendation to use postmorbid IQs as estimates of premorbid intelligence is poor clinical practice. The recommendation to assume average intelligence, and modify this assumption based on premorbid educational or career attainment, is a better strategy. The second problem is the grouping of RPAB subtests into eight classes. No evidence is provided to support this practice, although a factor analysis would certainly be possible and recommended. Again, the information needed for these analyses is apparently available, but not provided.

SUMMARY. The RPAB attempts to provide a tool that will allow occupational therapists to identify and monitor perceptual deficits in clients. The tasks, materials, and directions included in the RPAB clearly meet the pragmatic need for high quality materials that are easily administered and, with few exceptions, accurately scored. The technical data offered in the manual provide modest support for the potential of the RPAB. Unfortunately, the limited norms and complete lack of interpretive data render the clinical utility of the RPAB unknown. Consequently, its use in clinical settings, particularly by those with limited training in neuropsychological assessment, cannot be recommended.

[337]
Ross Information Processing Assessment.

Purpose: Constructed to assess "communication disorders" in patients with closed head injuries.
Population: Adolescent and adult patients with closed head injuries.
Publication Date: 1986.
Acronym: RIPA.
Scores, 20: Immediate Memory, Recent Memory, Temporal Orientation (Recent Memory, Remote Memory), Spatial Orientation, Orientation to Environment, Recall of General Information, Problem Solving and Abstract Reasoning, Organization, Auditory Processing and Retention, Diacritical Scores (Error, Perseveration, Repeat Instructions/Stimulus, Denials, Delayed Response, Confabulation, Partially Correct, Irrelevant, Tangential, Self-Corrected).
Administration: Individual.
Price Data, 1991: $64 per complete kit including 25 response record sheets, 25 test record sheets, and manual (43 pages); $39 per set of test forms including 25 response record sheets and 25 test record sheets; $27 per manual.
Time: (40–45) minutes.
Author: Deborah G. Ross.
Publisher: PRO-ED, Inc.

Review of the Ross Information Processing Assessment by JONATHAN EHRLICH, Speech-Language Pathologist, Somerset, NJ:

As both linguistic and cognitive breakdown can contribute to the communication deficits observed in adults with closed head injury (CHI), accurate assessment and classification of these communication disturbances often prove challenging. The Ross Information Processing Assessment (RIPA) was designed to assist in the assessment of communication functioning in subjects with CHI. The stated goals of this tool are to identify and measure information-processing deficits, assist in establishing treatment goals, and measure progress in CHI individuals.

The RIPA is organized into 10 separate subtests, each one consisting of 10 verbally presented questions or requests. The subject responds verbally to each item and is scored on a 0 to 3 scale for correctness. Responses are scored as follows: *unintelligible/no response* (0), *error/denial* (1), *partial correct* (2), and *correct* (3). The RIPA also provides a diacritical scoring system to code for more qualitative information about responses such as delays, perseverations, and confabulation. The test manual offers some helpful guidelines and examples to aid scoring of these response behaviors; however, these categories were not mutually exclusive and were presented with some overlap. Similarly, the distinction between the *error* (1) and *partial correct* (2) responses is not always clear.

The RIPA's subtests are intended to relate to different components of the author's view of information processing. The first subtest, Immediate Memory, tests subjects' ability to repeat verbal material that increases in length and complexity. The middle subtests of Recent Memory, Temporal Orientation (Recent Memory), Temporal Orientation (Remote Memory), Spatial Orientation, and Orientation to Environment, offer a thorough examination of orientation to person, place, and time. No explanation for the redundant content in several of these subtests is given. For example, questions about the current day, subject's location, and the first thing done in the morning, were repeated in Subtest 2 and Subtests 3, 5, and 6 respectively.

The seventh subtest, Recall of General Information, which is similar to the Information subtest on the Wechsler Adult Intelligence Scale, appears to tap long-term memory and retrieval. In the next subtest, Problem Solving and Abstract Reasoning, the subject is expected to generate solutions and explanations to hypothetical situations and more complex verbal expressions such as proverbs. The ninth unit, Organization, presents both semantic categorization tasks (e.g., "What are chairs, tables, and sofas?") and word fluency or generation tasks (e.g., "Name as many fruits as you can in one minute"). In the final subtest, Auditory Processing, subjects are presented with yes/no questions that contain temporal, spatial, and comparative markers.

Notwithstanding the lack of distinction between some of the error categories, the RIPA scoring system is a useful addition to most available tests of orientation and mental status. It attempts a closer examination of many response behaviors that typically occur in middle to late stages of CHI and yields a severity rating.

The major weakness of the RIPA stems from inadequate construct validity. The premise of this test is that impairment to information processing or "cognitive disorganization" is largely responsible for the communication deficits of CHI subjects in the middle to later stages of recovery. The author, however, does not adequately define what is meant by information processing or cite any specific model. Without a conceptual framework defining the scope of the construct it purports to test, the basis for how the test content areas were selected is questionable. Moreover, two of the subtests were justified based on the "author's experience." Even if this test content proves to be clinically relevant to CHI subjects, the RIPA fails to demonstrate validity for what it claims to be testing.

Content validity is similarly compromised. The subtests included in the RIPA certainly relate to auditory processing but neglect other modalities of information processing such as vision. The RIPA also fails to control for the potential influence of the verbal mode on other capabilities. As both stimulus questions and responses are verbal, a subject's linguistic functioning and general fund of knowledge may confound or bias the evaluation of memory and orientation abilities. For example, an item purporting to tap spatial orientation abilities, such as "Where is Mexico?" may be compromised by limited comprehension or paraphasic distortion. Also, failure to comply with the request to follow a three-step command may represent poor comprehension, an immediate memory deficit, or some combination. Numerous other items fail to adequately differentiate between information processing and primary linguistic impairments. Thus, the stated aim of the RIPA, to determine the breakdown of information processing, is not achieved as the test lacks both control and comprehensiveness.

In addition, the RIPA manual contains insufficient standardization information. The 100 normal control subjects who were administered the RIPA performed correctly; only two items, involving proverb interpretation, yielded errors for 7% of the normal group. A mixed group of 102 CHI and right-brain-damaged patients were also tested. Although percentile rankings are provided, there is no evidence showing how well this test differentiates brain-damaged patients from normals, as well as CHI from other neuropathologies. Intratest comparison of subtests found relatively better scores for immediate memory, spatial orientation, and auditory processing. Test-retest data are also provided for 38 patients and high correlations between trials were demonstrated with the higher scores at the second

administration. Unfortunately, the RIPA reports no research to support inter- and intrascorer reliability and validity.

In summary, the RIPA measures selected verbally mediated aspects of information processing such as orientation, memory, and problem solving. This test might be useful as a clinical tool for examining these functions, rating their severity, and suggesting treatment areas. However, the RIPA is not recommended as a clinical test because it lacks construct validity, shows a verbal bias, contains repetitive content, and fails to meet the minimum standards of test design.

[338]
Sales Motivation Inventory, Revised.

Purpose: Designed for "assessment of interest in, and motivation for, sales work."
Population: Prospective and employed salespeople.
Publication Dates: 1953–88.
Acronym: SMI.
Scores: Total score only.
Administration: Group.
Price Data: Available from publisher.
Time: (20–30) minutes.
Author: Martin M. Bruce.
Publisher: Martin M. Bruce, Ph.D., Publishers.
Cross References: For reviews by Robert M. Guion and Stephan J. Motowidlo of an earlier edition, see 9:1067; see also T2:2408 (5 references); for a review by S. Rains Wallace, see 5:948 (2 references).

Review of the Sales Motivation Inventory, Revised by LEO M. HARVILL, Professor and Assistant Dean for Medical Education, James H. Quillen College of Medicine, East Tennessee State University, Johnson City, TN:

This inventory was originally published in 1953; the 1985 edition represents the same set of 75 items in the original inventory with a few sexist language changes. The inventory is labeled Form A but there is only one form available. The current manual is dated 1988; two previous editions were published in 1953 and 1965. The publisher also has a 1984 Manuals Supplement that contains two paragraphs of information about the Sales Motivation Inventory, Revised, and two other brief references to the inventory in two reported studies. The information provided about this particular inventory does not warrant the purchase of the supplement.

Administration and scoring of the inventory seem straightforward. It appears the inventory is somewhat "transparent" but that is true of many self-report instruments. The author does discuss the issue of faking the test in the manual.

There are many deficiencies in the manual. The deficiencies are of two basic types: Errors are presented and pertinent information is omitted. Examples of errors are: (a) A value is given as 14% in a table (p. 4) and as 11% in the text and another value is given as 21% in the table and as 20% in the text; (b) a nonsales cross-validation group is called a sales group (p. 5); (c) a median value is called a mean (p. 6); (d) an F value and a related t value (p. 7) are inconsistent; the t value is appropriate given the data presented whereas the F value appears to be too low; (e) the manual states (p. 10) that there is an accompanying table which provides correlations between the inventory and other test scores; no such table or correlations are provided; (f) the manual states (p. 13) that "Three quarters of this group were tested by one brokerage firm as applicants for positions as *customers men and women*" [italics added].

Omissions include: (a) No description or values for the reliability and the standard deviation used in calculating the stated standard error are reported (p. 4); (b) no dates are given for the original inventory construction, the revisions, or the cross validation study; (c) no dates are given for four validation studies (p. 6); (d) no details are given in describing a potentially interesting predictive study (p. 7); (e) no dates are given for any of the reliability studies (p. 8); (f) dates are given for only 6 of the 25 normative groups; the dates given for those 6 groups range from 1956 to 1959.

Some positive things can be said for the manual. The author suggests the use of broader inventories may be more appropriate in some circumstances and recommends the development of local norms. Excellent split-half and test-retest reliabilities are reported for the inventory. Many different norm groups are presented for the examiner's use but the lack of dates for many of these groups and the age of the other norms negate their value to some extent.

In summary, it is difficult to follow the history of this inventory in the manual. It is unclear from reading the manual when the inventory was constructed and revised and what those revisions were. It is also unclear when the reliability, validity, and normative studies were completed and, therefore, it is difficult to know which version of the inventory was used for each study. Because of the errors and omissions in the manual, it is difficult to recommend the use of this inventory. The only study presented in the manual which presents specific data concerning the difference between "successful" and "unsuccessful" salespersons is marred by apparent errors in reporting the statistical analysis of the data. Little evidence has been accumulated over the 35-year history of the inventory that people who obtain high scores on this inventory will be happier in sales, will be more "successful" in sales, or will remain in sales longer than people who obtain low scores. Such evidence would be very useful in deciding whether to use this inventory.

[339]

The Salience Inventory.

Purpose: Assesses an individual's "participation in, commitment to, and value expectations of five major life roles."

Population: Upper elementary through adult.
Publication Date: 1986.
Acronym: SI.
Scores, 15: 5 roles (Study, Work, Home and Family, Leisure, Community Service) on 3 scales (Commitment, Participation, Value Expectations).
Administration: Group.
Price Data, 1988: $16.50 per 25 reusable test booklets; $14.50 per 50 answer sheets; price data per 50 profiles available from publisher; $10 per manual (47 pages); $11 per specimen set; price data for scoring service available from publisher.
Time: (30–45) minutes.
Comments: Developed as part of the international Work Importance Study; the Work Importance Study has inventories in 7 different languages.
Authors: Dorothy D. Nevill and Donald E. Super.
Publisher: Consulting Psychologists Press, Inc.

TEST REFERENCES

1. Ellermann, N. C., & Johnston, J. (1988). Perceived life roles and locus of control differences of women pursuing nontraditional and traditional academic majors. *Journal of College Student Development, 29,* 142-146.

Review of The Salience Inventory by ROSA A. HAGIN, Professor of Psychological and Educational Services, Graduate School of Education, Fordham University-Lincoln Center, New York, NY:

Set in the context of the Life-Career Rainbow conceptualized by Super (1973), the Salience Inventory (SI) assesses the relative importance an individual assigns to the major life roles in Study, Work, Community Service, Home and Family, and Leisure activities. The relative importance of each of these roles (i.e., their salience) is assessed by means of three types of measures: (a) behavioral participation ("What you actually do or have done recently"), (b) affective commitment ("How you feel about it"), and (c) value expectations ("What opportunity do you see now or in the future to . . ."). The authors propose that the SI be used for study of changing life roles in research on salience and as a counseling aid. Their preliminary research suggests its usefulness in individual counseling, career development workshops, and needs surveys (Nevill & Super, 1984).

A particular strength of the SI is its potential for use in cross-cultural research. It was developed by an international consortium of vocational psychologists in 12 European, American, and Asian countries, as part of the Work Importance Study, a collaborative effort to understand the role of work and the values individuals seek or hope to find in various life roles. Transnational teams collaborated on reviewing their respective literatures, developing a rationale for the test, defining terms, developing and refining items, and pilot testing of the measure. The scale is available in seven languages. The appendix of the manual presents descriptive statistics for samples of high school students, college students, and adults from the U.S., Canada, and Yugoslavia, and for high school students in Portugal.

The administration of the SI is generally straightforward, well within the 30- to 45-minute time requirement, even allowing time for hand scoring, although machine scoring is available. As a self-report inventory, the reading level is appropriate for the educational levels indicated. Some items appeared to be redundant (e.g., Participation Item G: I am active in . . .; Participation Item I: As often as I can, I take part in . . .), although the test authors have used an interesting reversed item design to investigate what they call "fatigue" factors (Super & Nevill, 1983).

The test manual provides clear-cut instructions for administration and scoring. A section on interpretation shows the use of the SI in career development and in research on occupational, cultural, social, and life stage differences. The test authors recommend (very wisely) caution in the use of the SI in counseling. Ipsative interpretation (i.e., in relation to the counselee's own scores) permits intrapersonal, intrarole, and interrole comparisons. The manual provides a single case study to illustrate this use of the SI as part of a battery of interest, career development, and values scales.

The most significant shortcoming of the SI is the lack of representative normative data. The inventory has been administered to 2,000 subjects, but these samples have been chosen for their convenience rather than their representativeness. The U.S. sample, for instance, consists of approximately 600 high school students from three counties in central New Jersey, 800 college students from Florida and Maryland, and 400 adults from an adult education program and an industrial management sample. Although the authors state data are being collected to develop norms that reflect demographic diversity, such information is not provided in the current manual.

The inventory does not reach desirable standards of reliability and validity for use as an independent measure in counseling. In a study of a college sample ($N = 85$), test-retest reliabilities below .70 were found for 10 of the 15 scales. Alpha coefficients show that internal consistency is acceptable. Although the collaborative process by which this test was developed provides some evidence of content validity, the authors do not present convincing evidence of construct or concurrent validity. For the former, they depend upon some isolated studies that yielded low order correlations, which may reach statistical significance but could not serve as a basis for decision making in counseling with individual clients. For the latter, the authors provide only intercorrelations of the three scales of the SI. Especially needed is evidence of the relationship of the SI to some of the measures conventionally used in career development counseling.

To summarize, although the unique transnational collaboration and the conceptual framework that produced the Salience Inventory must be recognized, further work is needed if it is to fulfill its purposes in either research or service delivery. The test authors themselves have recognized the need for a more representative normative sample and, according to the manual, are in the process of collecting data designed to reflect diversity in regional origin, age, sex, education, and socioeconomic levels. It is to be hoped that analysis of these data will produce more systematic studies of the instrument's reliability, clearer understanding of its relationship to other measures used in career counseling, and additional evidence of its validity.

REVIEWER'S REFERENCES

Super, D. E. (1976). *Career education and the meaning of work.* Washington, DC: U.S. Government Printing Office.
Super, D. E., & Nevill, D. D. (1983). *The values scale and the Salience Inventory of the Work Importance Study.* Gainesville, FL: University of Florida, Work Importance Study.
Nevill, D. D., & Super, D. E. (1984). *Career maturity and commitment to work and home in college students.* Unpublished manuscript.

Review of The Salience Inventory by TIMOTHY M. OSBERG, Professor of Psychology, Niagara University, Niagara University, NY:

The Salience Inventory (SI) was developed to correct for a gap in available published tests. No measure had been available to assess the relative importance placed upon one's work role in relation to other life roles. Such information is critical to vocational psychologists engaged in research or career counseling. Consequently, the SI was developed by an international team of psychologists to assess the relative importance ascribed by the individual to five major life roles including student, worker, homemaker (including spouse and parent), leisurite, and citizen (manual, p. 1).

The SI is a cleverly designed measure. The physical design of the reusable question booklet and accompanying computer answer sheet achieves an economy of space. The SI consists of three parts that assess Participation, Commitment, and Value Expectations concerning each of the five life roles. The Participation scale measures amount of activity devoted to each role and is thus more of a behavioral measure of role importance. The Commitment scale taps how the person feels about each role and is thus more affective in content. Finally, the Value Expectations scale is also affective in nature and assesses "the degree to which major life satisfactions or values are expected to be found" in each role (manual, p. 11).

Interestingly, the authors themselves note their data suggest a response set develops across the first two scales of the SI. Findings suggest respondents use the same set in responding to the first two scales of the SI. Consequently, the second scale, Commitment, may not assess much that is different from the data obtained on the Participation scale. The user is advised that, if time is an issue, the Commitment scale may be omitted. Thus, for most research purposes wherein subject response time needs to be minimized, administering only the first and third scales may be advisable. However, for counseling purposes, the Commitment scale may yield additional useful data. Perhaps any plan for revision of the SI will take this problem into account.

Another awkward aspect of the SI is that a common rating scale is used across its 170 items (a 4-point scale ranging from *never* to *always*). However, what may be confusing for some respondents is that some questions require a judgment of time spent and others require a judgment of amount or quality. Although the first page of the test booklet gives a clear example of how the respondent should adapt the scale for either type of judgment (e.g., a "1" can be used to denote *never* or *little or none*), the answer sheet repeats only the *never-to-always* scale. A revision of the answer sheet listing both response scales throughout would be helpful.

Other than these awkward aspects, the SI appears to be a sound measure. The manual provided is a model after which other test manuals should be patterned. It is one of the most useful and complete test manuals this reviewer has ever seen. It provides a detailed literature review and theoretical rationale behind the development of the SI as well as thorough descriptions of each scale and procedures for scoring (SI answer sheets may be either sent away for computer scoring or hand scored). The authors also provide a very extensive section outlining the variety of potential uses of the SI. One very important use specified was the potential to consider scores on the SI in interpreting scores on widely used interest inventories like the Strong-Campbell Interest Inventory or the Kuder Occupational Interest Survey. Scores on these interest measures take on different meanings depending on the relative importance placed upon one's work role in relation to other life roles. The seeds for numerous other research ideas, such as a more in-depth investigation of role conflict or new investigations of leisure or citizen roles, were planted.

Extensive normative data also are presented in the test manual. Reflecting its truly international character, high school through adult norms are reported for U.S., Canadian (both English and French), Yugoslavian, and Portuguese samples. Reliability data are presented for each of the five roles within each of the three scales. Alpha coefficients for samples of high school, college, and adult subjects (the latter being relatively small, $n = 20$) were all in the .80s and .90s. Test-retest reliability coefficients were generally lower, ranging from .59 to .83 for roles within the Participation scale, .60 to

.77 for roles within the Commitment scale, and .37 to .67 for roles within the Value Expectations scale. The authors report that a follow-up investigation did not suggest the decline in reliability coefficients across the three scales is due to a fatigue effect. The lowest reliability coefficient was found for Value Expectations judgments of leisure ($r = .37$), a role for which Value Expectations might be expected to be less stable.

The extensive procedures followed during scale construction (detailed in the SI's manual) give this reviewer reasonable confidence in its content validity. However, construct validity data reported in the manual are more modest. The authors rightfully contend that the expected patterns of change in role importance observed across several samples of high school, college, and adult subjects appear to support the construct validity of the SI. However, the size of many of the validity correlations, although statistically significant, are often modest. The authors themselves acknowledge the need for larger adult samples and more data to support the SI's predictive validity. Nevertheless, at this early stage there is adequate evidence to support the validity of the SI and reason to expect more supportive data will accumulate. For example, one more recent study found significant relationships between some SI scales and attitudinal and cognitive indices of career maturity (Nevill & Super, 1988).

In summary, the SI appears to be a sound psychometric device. It provides an efficient method of assessing the relative importance the individual places on five major life roles. The procedures used in development, the layout of the test, and the content of the test manual provide a model for other potential test developers to follow.

REVIEWER'S REFERENCE

Nevill, D. D., & Super, D. E. (1988). Career maturity and commitment to work in university students. *Journal of Vocational Behavior, 32,* 139-151.

[340]

Scale of Social Development.
Purpose: "Measures social skill development."
Population: Birth to age 6.
Publication Date: 1987.
Acronym: SSD.
Scores, 4: Identifies/Investigates, Compiles/Prefers, Participates/Socializes, Total.
Administration: Individual.
Levels, 2: Screening, Comprehensive.
Price Data, 1989: $39 per complete kit including examiner's manual (12 pages), administration manual (38 pages), and 20 recording forms; $19 per 20 recording forms; $9 per examiner's manual; $14 per administration manual.
Time: (45–50) minutes.
Comments: Also called Scale of Social Development for the Deaf and Multihandicapped.
Authors: John J. Venn, Thomas S. Serwatka, and Robert A. Anthony.
Publisher: PRO-ED, Inc.

Review of the Scale of Social Development by SCOTT R. McCONNELL, Associate Professor of Educational Psychology, Institute on Community Integration, University of Minnesota, Minneapolis, MN:

The Scale of Social Development for the Deaf and Multihandicapped (SSD) is an observation-based instrument for assessing the social skill development of children between birth and 6 years of age. The authors note the SSD was developed for use with children developing normally and those with hearing impairments or multiple disabilities, and can be used for either screening or comprehensive assessment. The SSD is intended to identify an individual child's strengths, weaknesses, and gaps in social development, especially for the purposes of identifying programming needs and establishing IEP goals and objectives.

The SSD is made up of 120 items at eight different age levels; 48 items, identified as "developmental milestones," make up the screening instrument, and all 120 items are completed for comprehensive assessment. Specific items were selected following a review of 17 existing scales of social development and adaptive behavior, and were generated using four criteria: (*a*) Items had to require little or no verbal performance, to avoid biasing assessment of children with hearing or language deficits; (*b*) items had to be observable by the examiner, rather than reported by caregivers or teachers; (*c*) items had to be appropriate for subsequent intervention; that is, each item was intended to reference a skill that was functional and teachable; and (*d*) each item had to relate directly to social development.

ADMINISTRATION PROCEDURES. The SSD is designed to be completed during direct observations of the target child in one or more environments where social interaction may take place. Individual items are scored two different ways. For the screening test, each item is scored pass or fail. For comprehensive assessment, the examiner is encouraged to employ a five-level system, scoring each item from *task resistive* (i.e., "individual refuses to perform the task even with complete assistance") to *independence* (i.e., "individual has mastered the task and is responsible for 100% of the performance"); this latter level of performance is described by the authors as equivalent to "pass" on other developmental scales.

Although these five levels of evaluation are described in the manual and passing criteria are provided for most individual items, specific scoring procedures are extremely confusing and open to administrator interpretation. For instance, Item E9 ("[Child] attempts to help complete a chore or clean-up task") is scored a pass if, after the evaluator encourages the child to help pick up objects, "the child complies on a consistent basis" (Scale, p. 20).

Scoring individual items on a pass/fail basis often depends on an examiner's idiosyncratic interpretation of vague criteria (e.g., what constitutes *consistent compliance?*), and appears likely to introduce error to scoring. Further, the assessment of different levels of performance for individual items is similarly complex. In this latter instance, the examiner must judge the percent of performance completed by the child and the extent of prompting and assistance required. Again, scoring on these dimensions appears to rely substantially on idiosyncratic or subjective evaluations, and as a result may significantly attenuate the reliability of resulting evaluations.

INTERPRETATION. An individual child's performance is evaluated by computing a Social Development Age score, assigning months of credit for each item passed. These scores can then be interpreted in a profile of performance by scale categories (i.e., Identifies/Investigates, Complies/Prefers, Participates/Socializes). No normative data are provided, nor do the authors specifically describe how items were assigned to age levels for scoring. As a result, the SSD should not be used typically for screening or eligibility classification.

Additionally, interpretation of SSD age scores is quite problematic. First, the use of age equivalents or Social Development Age scores may lead many practitioners and parents to make faulty conclusions (e.g., judging that a 4-year-old child is "functioning" at 2 years of age). Second, without much clearer explanation and evaluation of the normative level of individual items, there is no empirical support for computing these age scores. As a result, use of summary age scores from this scale cannot be recommended.

Use of the SSD as a criterion-referenced instrument appears to possess more face validity, but this practice also must be viewed with caution. The authors provide no specific guidelines for selecting individual skills for intervention, nor do they provide evidence that individual SSD items are functionally related to social development and competence or will contribute to more successful interaction and adaptation in classroom or home environments.

PSYCHOMETRIC PROPERTIES. Psychometric evaluations of the SSD are based on two small-sample studies completed by the authors. One sample included 14 preschool children (mean age of 3 years, 5 months) attending a summer camp with their families, and the second included 15 toddlers and preschool children (mean age 2 years, 10 months) identified by the authors as multihandicapped. Other than age, no demographic information is provided for these two groups.

The authors report generally high reliability and validity coefficients for the SSD in these two groups. Split-half reliability for the combined sample ($N =$

29) was .99, and concordance between screening test and full scale scores is reported at .98. Comprehensive SSD scores were also found to correlate with chronological age ($r = .72$), individuals' scores on the Doll Preschool Attainment Record ($r = .91$), and unidentified measures of language ability ($r = .64$ to .91). No data are reported for evaluations of interrater agreement, temporal stability, or discrimination between children with known differences in social development. The authors do include, however, anecdotal reports of the functional utility of this scale from practitioners in diagnostic centers and intervention programs.

To date, substantial evidence for psychometric characteristics of the SSD is not available. Given the design of this instrument, it is imperative that evidence be gathered for interrater reliability and stability of children's scores across time and settings. Further evaluation of the validity of age-level assignments for individual items and computation of Social Development Age scores, both for children who are developing normally and those with handicaps, is essential. Although initial evaluations reported in the SSD manual are encouraging, the authors correctly assert that "more research needs to be conducted to support the conclusion of these pilot studies" (manual, p. 4).

CONCLUSIONS. The Scale of Social Development for the Deaf and Multihandicapped has several promising features. First, the scale provides one means of assessing the development of social interaction and related skills among children from birth to age 6, thus addressing a critical need in the area of early intervention. Second, the SSD provides for direct assessment of social skills and development via observations conducted in one or more settings. This represents a substantial gain over more global, indirect evaluations elicited by informant ratings or interviews. Third, individual SSD items appear to cover many important aspects of social development. Although the validity of individual items and categories still requires external validation, this breadth of assessment is noteworthy among existing measures of social development.

At present, however, the SSD has several significant limitations. To date, there is extremely little evidence supporting the psychometric quality of this instrument. All evaluations are based on two studies, both conducted by the authors with extremely small samples in one particular region. No information is available regarding interrater agreement, test-retest reliability, or the effects of different environments on individual children's scores. It is essential that the reliability of this instrument be evaluated more fully, both across different samples and on different dimensions than those reported by the authors. Further, additional validity studies are needed to support the use of this instrument. At a minimum,

evidence is needed regarding the discriminant validity of this instrument (especially with respect to the assessment of language and adaptive behavior) and its ability to distinguish between children at different levels of social development.

In conclusion, the SSD has promise for researchers in the area of social development. In particular, the scale warrants additional evaluations of its psychometric properties. At this time, however, there is little evidence to support the use of this scale for individual or group assessment and decision making in applied intervention programs. Until further evaluation of the psychometric quality of this instrument is completed, use of the SSD in applied settings should be limited.

Review of the Scale of Social Development by JAYNE E. STAKE, *Professor of Psychology, University of Missouri-St. Louis, St. Louis, MO:*

The Scale of Social Development (SSD) has the alternate title, the Scale of Social Development for the Deaf and Multihandicapped. The authors describe the SSD as a measure of social skill development for normal and disabled children. The Comprehensive Form of the SSD consists of 60 items for the birth-to-2-year age range and 60 items for the 3-to-6-year age range; the Screening Form of the SSD consists of a total of 48 of these items. The Comprehensive Form requires several hours to administer; the Screening Form can be completed in approximately 45 minutes.

Items were selected for the SSD from 17 previously developed instruments for young children. It was the authors' intention to select items that represent aspects of social development, require little or no verbal ability, are directly observable, and are relevant for determining treatment goals. No original items were developed for this test.

Despite these criteria for item selection, the content of some of the test items does not appear to be relevant to social development. The authors state that separate scores can be obtained for three categories of test items: Identifies/Investigates, Complies/Prefers, and Participates/Socializes. Only the third category of items appears to relate directly to social development. The authors fail to provide any psychometric evidence to justify either the inclusion of individual items on the SSD or the clustering of items into the three categories of behavior.

All items are grouped by age levels from Level A (0–5 months) to Level H (5 years and above). Items were grouped apparently on the basis of what is expected in normal development, but the authors do not indicate how they determined age norms for the SSD items. No normal children were tested as a means of developing norms and scoring procedures for the SSD. References are provided for all items in the test booklet. It seems that the authors relied on these references for information concerning the age appropriateness of the tested behaviors.

The authors administered the SSD to a small group of deaf (n = 14) and multihandicapped (n = 15) children, aged 11 months to 5 years, 11 months. No children under 11 months were tested, although the SSD includes the age categories, 0–5 months and 6–11 months. Results from this sample indicate that the scale is internally consistent. The split-half reliability coefficient was .99 and the correlation between the Screening and Comprehensive Forms was .98. No information on the stability of test results was provided.

The authors also reported the correlation between the SSD and the nonverbal items of the social development section of the Preschool Attainment Record was .95 and the correlation between the SSD and age was .72 (.85 in the deaf sample and .26 in the multihandicapped sample). These findings constituted the only convergent validity information provided in the SSD manual.

The authors report correlations between the SSD and what they refer to as "measures of language ability," but fail to identify these measures. The coefficients are .64 for the deaf sample and .91 for the multihandicapped sample. These high correlations suggest that SSD performance is strongly influenced by verbal ability. Therefore, test users should note that the authors have not substantiated their claim that the SSD does not penalize individuals who have language deficits.

In summary, psychometric data for the SSD are quite limited. Although the internal consistency of the SSD was found to be high, no measures of stability are available. Validation data are meager, and the authors have not demonstrated that all items are relevant to social development nor that the SSD measures social development independent of language ability. Further, test data are available from only 29 children, so normative data are clearly needed. In the absence of more extensive validation research, the SSD social development age index cannot be assumed to be an accurate reflection of social development, particularly for children with language deficits.

[341]
SCAN: A Screening Test for Auditory Processing Disorders.

Purpose: "To identify children who have auditory processing problems which may complicate or compound language or learning problems."
Population: Ages 3–11.
Publication Date: 1986.
Acronym: SCAN.
Scores, 4: Filtered Words, Auditory Figure Ground, Competing Words, Composite.
Administration: Individual.
Price Data, 1988: $59 per complete program including 25 record forms, test audiocassette, and manual (107 pages); $15 per 25 record forms; $30 per test audiocassette; $25 per examiner's manual.
Time: (20) minutes.
Comments: Stereo cassette player necessary for administration.
Author: Robert W. Keith.
Publisher: The Psychological Corporation.

TEST REFERENCES
1. Brugha, T. S., Wing, J. K., Brewin, C. R., MacCarthy, B., Mangen, S., Lesage, A., & Mumford, J. (1988). The problems of people in long-term psychiatric day care: An introduction to the Camberwell High Contact Survey. *Psychological Medicine, 18*, 443-456.
2. Feagans, L. V., Merriwether, A. M., & Haldane, D. (1991). Goodness of fit in the home: Its relationship to school behavior and achievement in children with learning disabilities. *Journal of Learning Disabilities, 24*, 413-420.

Review of the SCAN: A Screening Test for Auditory Processing Disorders by SAMI GULGOZ, Assistant Professor of Psychology, Auburn University at Montgomery, Montgomery, AL:

The SCAN is a screening test of speech perception problems. It is designed for individual administration to children between the ages of 3–11. However, the author warns that testing 3- and 4-year-olds may be especially difficult and unreliable. In addition, this test is not suitable for children with articulation problems.

The SCAN is composed of three subtests: Filtered Words, Auditory Figure-Ground, and Competing Words. The Filtered Words subtest consists of repeating the two separate lists of 20 filtered monosyllable words presented to each ear. The filtering process muffles the speech, thus preventing easy identification of the words. The auditory Figure-Ground test is similar to Filtered Words but this time, words are not filtered, rather, they are presented on a background of multitalker speech babble noise. The Competing Words subtest consists of presenting a pair of words simultaneously. One word of each pair is presented to each ear and the listener is expected to repeat both. There are two lists of 25 monosyllable word pairs. For the first list, the word presented to the right ear is repeated first and for the second list the word presented to the left ear is repeated first. These subtests provide individual test scores to allow detailed problem identification and are combined to create a composite score.

Administration of the SCAN test is relatively simple. The equipment needed to administer the SCAN is a regular cassette player with headphones. Each side of the SCAN tape contains the instructions to the test taker and the test items, alleviating the need to reverse the tape during testing or rewinding afterwards. The only task of the examiner is to indicate across each item on the scoring sheet whether it is repeated correctly. All the scoring is done on the scoring sheet and a summary is generated by referring to the norms in the booklet. The examiner should use a calculator in the scoring procedure. The summary could be prepared in approximately 15 minutes.

There are two potential problems related to equipment. One is the variations in the quality of the sound between different cassette players. In order to avoid such a problem one might consider using the same equipment that was used in the standardization procedure. The second problem is the decline in the sound quality as a result of the wear of the tape. Periodic replacements may be necessary to avoid such a problem.

The test booklet includes a wealth of information that would be useful in test administration and interpretation of test scores as well as remediation. Implications of subtests are well explained and three case studies that provide insight to the meaning of the test scores are included.

The norms are presented in terms of percentiles and standard scores with a mean of 100 and standard deviation of 15. The standardization sample consisted of 1,034 children, ages 3–11. A comparison of the sample to the U.S. Census figures according to region, sex, race, and Spanish origin demonstrated representativeness. Percentiles and standard scores are presented only for the overall group but separate means for males and females, for Blacks and Whites, and for Hispanics and non-Hispanics are provided. Some differences exist between the groups. Separate group norms may be necessary.

Both internal consistency and test-retest types of reliability estimates are provided. Cronbach's coefficient alpha was calculated for each age group separately for the complete test and the subtests, using the standardization sample. The sample size for age groups ranged from 40 to 169. The coefficients ranged between .82 and .97 for the complete test and between .57 and .97 for the subtests. The Competing Words subtest showed the highest correlations overall. Despite a careful item selection procedure some alpha coefficients were rather low.

Test-retest reliability was obtained by retesting a subsample ($N = 68$) of the standardization sample. The two testings took place approximately 6 months apart and the subjects were students in grades 1 and 3 at the time of the initial testing. For grade 1 students the correlations were .42, .40, and .73 for Filtered Words, Auditory Figure-Ground, and Competing Words subtests, respectively. The test-retest reliability coefficient for the composite score was .65. For grade 3, the Filtered Words subtest did not yield a significant test-retest reliability coefficient whereas Auditory Figure-Ground (.41), Competing Words (.44), and the composite score (.42) did. The calculation of test-retest reliabilities is compromised by developmental patterns in young children. The SCAN's variable stability estimates deserve further attention.

The content validity of the SCAN is given appropriate attention in the booklet through research on auditory processing disorders. Construct validity is well documented in three different manners: (*a*) increase in the test scores with age, (*b*) intercorrelations among subtests, and (*c*) factor analysis. In the criterion-related validity study, 31 students in grades 1 through 3 who were suspected of having auditory processing problems were tested with the SCAN and four other measures of language and auditory development. These criterion measures included the Clinical Evaluation of Language Functions (CELF), the Goldman-Fristoe Woodcock (GFW) Auditory Skills Battery, the GFW Test of Auditory Discrimination, and the Staggered-Spondaic Word Test (SSW). Few of the correlations were significant, ranging between .37 and .60. Considering the low alpha consistency coefficients of some subtests, it is reasonable to consider that the validity of the test will be limited. However, there was a tendency to observe significant correlations between the SCAN and subtests of other tests that had similar purposes.

Overall, the SCAN test is a good test of auditory processing difficulties designed for quick screening of children between the ages 3–11. It is a meritorious test that is easy to administer and interpret. The test booklet is a strength. The information provided on the validity of the test is convincing. The test-retest reliability coefficients are smaller than would be desired. As a screening test, the SCAN is adequate but further validity and reliability studies seem to be necessary.

[342]
The Schedule of Growing Skills.

Purpose: "Screening for and recording developmental progress."
Population: Ages 0–5 years.
Publication Date: 1987.
Scores, 9: Passive Postural Skills, Active Postural Skills, Locomotor Skills, Manipulative Skills, Visual Skills, Hearing and Language Skills, Speech and Language Skills, Interactive Social Skills, Self-Care Social Skills.
Administration: Individual.
Price Data, 1990: £73.60 per starter set including set of materials, 10 Child Records, and 50 Profiles; £47.15 per set of materials including stimulus materials, Colour Matching Cards, Picture Book, and User's Handbook (14 pages); £50.60 per 50 Child Record Forms; £27.60 per 50 Profiles; £6.85 per User's Handbook; £12.40 per *Schedule of Growing Skills in Practice* (108 pages); £51.75 per Introductory Training Video including *Schedule of Growing Skills in Practice*.
Time: (10–20) minutes.
Comments: Based on the STYCAR Developmental Sequences; some test materials (rattle, large ball, small box, small book) must be supplied by examiner.
Authors: Martin Bellman and John Cash.
Publisher: NFER-Nelson Publishing Co., Ltd. [England].

Review of The Schedule of Growing Skills by MICHELLE M. CREIGHTON, Doctoral Student in School Psychology, and SCOTT R. McCONNELL, Associate Professor of Educational Psychology, Institute on Community Integration, University of Minnesota, Minneapolis, MN:

The Schedule of Growing Skills is a screening procedure for monitoring the development of children between birth and 5 years of age and identifying children who should be referred for more comprehensive assessment. The Schedule was developed in Britain to enable health visitors, general practitioners, pediatricians, and other professionals involved in the care of young children to obtain a snapshot of a child's developmental skills across a range of areas.

The Schedule includes 180 items in nine skill areas: Passive Postural Skills, Active Postural Skills, Locomotor Skills, Manipulative Skills, Visual Skills, Hearing and Language Skills, Interactive Social Skills, and Self-Care Social Skills. The nine skill areas are further subdivided into 23 skill sets. For example, passive postural skill items are divided into the skill sets of supine position, ventral suspension, pull to sit, and sitting position. Specific items were selected from the STYCAR sequences, a set of developmental sequences tests developed by Mary Sheridan.

MATERIALS AND ADMINISTRATION. The Schedule is packaged in a small plastic briefcase. The test kit includes the User's Handbook, Child Records, Profiles, several toys, and *The Schedule of Growing Skills in Practice*, an abbreviated technical manual.

The Schedule is designed to be administered in a 15-minute session with the child and a parent. The authors note that it is not necessary to follow either the order of skill areas as they appear on the Child Record form or the order of items within each skill area. The practitioner is encouraged to use clinical judgment regarding basal and ceiling rules, as well.

Most responses are observed by the examiner, but some items are scored on parent report. Each item is scored on the Child Record form if the child can perform the task. However, if the child's performance is of poor quality, as determined by the examiner's clinical judgment, a "Q" is marked in the response column, and the item is still scored as a pass.

Although passing criteria are provided for most individual items, specific scoring procedures are open to administrator interpretation. Examiners may interpret this vague scoring criteria idiosyncratically, which is likely to introduce error to scoring.

INTERPRETATION. Scores are computed for each of the nine skill areas and recorded on a profile. The profile visually depicts the child's developmental age for each skill area. A horizontal line drawn at the child's chronological age is intended to aid interpretation. The authors recommend that children who fall one or more age ranges below the horizontal line in a particular skill area should be referred for further assessment. However, the age ranges are at uneven intervals, making it easier for younger children to meet this criterion. Because of this inconsistency, the authors recommend that interpretation remain flexible enough to allow for clinical judgment. Thus, interpretation is highly dependent upon the examiner's experience. Further, it is not clear how the items were assigned to age levels for scoring. The authors state that the Schedule is firmly based on Mary Sheridan's STYCAR sequences, which was normed on a sample of British children, but no information is provided on the development of that instrument. There is no apparent empirical support for computing these developmental age scores. Additionally, interpretation of the Schedule's developmental age scores may lead practitioners and parents to reach faulty conclusions (e.g., judging that a 4-year old child is functioning at the level of a 2-year-old).

PSYCHOMETRIC PROPERTIES. Many of the Schedule's items were adapted from the STYCAR sequences, which the authors describe as a well-known and well-respected set of tests of developmental sequence. However, the technical adequacies of the Schedule cannot be evaluated in the absence of information about the STYCAR's psychometric properties.

The original version of the Schedule, the National Childhood Encephalopathy Study (NCES), was used as a research instrument with children from birth to 3 years of age. After the NCES was field tested and items from the STYCAR for ages 4–5 were added, it was modified and renamed to become The Schedule of Growing Skills. Psychometric evaluations of the Schedule are based on two small-sample studies of children 3 to 5 years of age. One interobserver reliability study obtained correlations that range from .47 to .97. However, the method of evaluating interrater reliability was highly questionable. One examiner would observe the other examiner administer the Schedule, and then they would reverse roles. These results should not be taken as an indication of how reliable two independent examiners would be.

Concurrent validity was evaluated with the Griffiths Mental Development Scales for Testing Babies and Young Children from Birth to Eight Years of Age. Correlations ranged from .52 to .96; however, the Griffiths scales could not be split into the same skill areas as the Schedule, so several of the Schedule's skill areas were collapsed to better correspond. It is not clear how the combined skill areas were summarized. Also, these validity data are dubious because of the lack of psychometric data available on the Griffiths.

Since the validity and reliability studies were completed, the Schedule has been further refined, and items that were not clinically useful have been omitted. Psychometric evaluations have not been conducted on this current form. To date, adequate evidence for the psychometric characteristics of The Schedule of Growing Skills is not available.

CONCLUSIONS. The Schedule of Growing Skills may be a clinically useful instrument in experienced hands. At present, however, it has several significant limitations. There is very little evidence supporting the Schedule's psychometric qualities. Both the concurrent validity and the interobserver reliability studies were methodologically flawed. Similarly, no information is available about test-retest reliability, predictive validity, and most importantly, discriminant validity. Given the lack of evidence for the Schedule's ability to distinguish between children with developmental delays and children without developmental delays, this instrument should not be used for screening individual children.

Review of The Schedule of Growing Skills by DONNA SPIKER, Clinical Assistant Professor of Pediatrics, Stanford University School of Medicine, and Stanford Center for the Study of Families, Children, and Youth, Stanford, CA:

The Schedule of Growing Skills is a developmental screening test for children from birth to 5 years of age. It was developed over a period of over 10 years in Great Britain as an outgrowth of the National Childhood Encephalopathy Study (NCES) in that country. It is based on the STYCAR sequences (Sheridan, 1976; Bellman, Rawson, Wadsworth, Ross, Cameron, & Miller, 1985). The test comes in a briefcase-size, lightweight kit containing a spiral-bound 14-page User's Guide with administration and scoring instructions and notes about a small subset of items; a 108-page paperback book, *The Schedule of Growing Skills in Practice,* which serves as a technical manual for the test; and a collection of toys, picture cards, and other items for administering the test items. Two forms are provided for use with the test: the Child Record, which is a permanent record containing the list of all 180 items for the entire age range, and the Profile, which is a one-page form for summarizing performance for each individual administration of the screening test.

The instrument contains 180 items that cover nine developmental areas across the 0–60 month age range (unless otherwise noted). The nine areas are: Passive Postural Skills (0–6 months), Active Postural Skills (0–12 months), Locomotor Skills (9–60 months), Manipulative Skills, Visual Skills, Hearing and Language Skills, Speech and Language Skills, Interactive Social Skills, and Self-Care Social Skills (6–60 months), each area arranged in developmental sequences. Items are scored as pass or fail, and a

notation of "Q" is used to note a poor quality response (which is nevertheless scored as passing). The raw scores are recorded by shading in a box on the Profile for each area, the boxes show the raw scores corresponding to age equivalents. By drawing a solid line at a particular chronological age across the Profile, the pattern of age equivalents across areas relative to the chronological age is displayed. According to the manual, the test takes about 15 minutes to administer and requires minimal examiner training.

The authors explain that the purpose of the test is "to provide an accurate and reliable method of developmental screening, to be used as part of any child surveillance programme" (manual, p. 22), and "to facilitate referral" (p. 16). They also provide a good deal of discussion about the definition of developmental delay, acknowledging that consensus is lacking. The authors base their own definition of delay on Drillien (1977) who suggests that developmental delay is functioning that is four-fifths or less of the chronological age level. The Profile form has been constructed based on this definition so that scores that are more than one age interval below the chronological age are suspect, and referral for further detailed assessment should be considered.

The User's Handbook contains detailed administration instructions for only a limited number of the 180 items. This raises questions about standardization of administration across examiners. Clinical practices for eliciting specific infant behaviors and the resultant performances are likely to vary across examiners unless procedures are clearly described.

Information presented in the manual about the standardization procedures and sample is sketchy, and the data about reliability and validity are weak. Preliminary development of the instrument took place with the NCES sample of "over 1000 cases" (p. 80) of children from birth to age 3. The children were from all parts of Great Britain, but no other background data are reported. A subset of these cases, "approximately 500," were administered other assessments, including the Griffiths Mental Development Scales (Griffiths, 1967), a British standardized developmental test. To assess validity, data comparing the mean age differences for passing for the 97 items common to both tests are presented; they show discrepancies of 2 months or less for 85% of the items. These comparisons represent only slightly over half of the Schedule's items, however. Additionally, for 100 cases, the modified STYCAR schedule and the Griffiths scales were administered "by different observers within a few days of each other" (p. 85). Correlations for each of four comparable developmental areas are reported to be between .92 and .95 for 25 cases. Not enough information is given about the ages of the children in the validity studies to determine the validity of the test at different ages.

To assess reliability, the authors report that 20 cases were examined with the Schedule by two different examiners. These results are reported in the same way that the validity data are reported, and correlations for the four developmental areas are reported to be between .93 and .96. Again, the ages of the 20 subjects in the reliability study are not given, raising questions about the reliability of the test at different ages.

To summarize, there are several problems with the reported validity and reliability data. First, the number of subjects used is too small. Second, the ages of the children need to be reported because the validity or reliability of a test may vary at different ages. And finally, the reported reliability and validity data refer to subsets of items from the final published instrument, making it impossible to evaluate the psychometric adequacy of the existing instrument. This latter issue is important because the instrument is based on the STYCAR Sequences, for which there is also limited reliability and validity information available.

SUMMARY. The Schedule of Growing Skills is a developmental screening test for use with children from birth to 5 years of age. Data presented about the reliability and validity of the instrument are inadequate because they apply to an unidentified subset of items and not to the final published instrument. As a clinical tool to be used in health care settings as part of a screening process for referral for more complete assessments, this instrument might be helpful. Its standardization with a British sample may limit its generalizability to other populations, however. For North American users, without further psychometric work with other populations, it is not clear whether this test is an improvement over existing developmental screening instruments, flawed as they may be, such as the Denver Developmental Screening Test—Revised (Frankenberg & Dodds, 1981; 9:311).

REVIEWER'S REFERENCES

Griffiths, R. (1967). Griffiths Mental Development Scales. High Wycombe, England: The Test Agency.

Sheridan, M. D. (1976). Children's developmental progress from birth to five years. The STYCAR sequences, 4th edition. Windsor, England: The NFER-Nelson Publishing Company, Ltd.

Drillien, C. M. (1977). Developmental assessment and development screening. In C. M. Drillien & M. B. Drummond (Eds.), Neurodevelopmental problems in early childhood (pp. 44-92). Oxford, England: Blackwell.

Frankenberg, W. K., & Dodds, J. B. (1981). Denver Developmental Screening Test, Revised 1981 Edition. Denver: LADOCA Publishing Foundation.

Bellman, M. H., Rawson, N. S. B., Wadsworth, J., Ross, E. M., Cameron, S., & Miller, D. L. (1985). A developmental test based on the STYCAR sequences used in the National Childhood Encephalopathy Study. Child: Care, Health, and Development, 11, 309-323.

[343]

Scholastic Aptitude Scale.

Purpose: "Provides a general index of overall cognitive functioning and predicts . . . performance on achievement measures."

Population: Ages 6-0 to 17-11.
Publication Date: 1991.
Acronym: SAS.
Scores, 4: Quantitative Reasoning, Verbal Reasoning, Nonverbal Reasoning, General Aptitude Quotient.
Administration: Individual.
Price Data, 1991: $74 per complete kit; $36 per picture book; $14 per 25 profile/examiner record forms; $27 per manual ('91, 50 pages); $79 per computer software scoring system (specify IBM or Apple).
Time: (60–70) minutes.
Authors: Brian R. Bryant and Phyllis L. Newcomer.
Publisher: PRO-ED, Inc.

Review of the Scholastic Aptitude Scale by J. DOUGLAS AYERS, Professor Emeritus, University of Victoria, Victoria, B.C., Canada:

The Scholastic Aptitude Scale (SAS) was designed as "an aptitude test that provides a general index of overall cognitive functioning and predicts, to a reasonable extent, performance on achievement measures." It has three scales: (a) Quantitative reasoning, based on various types of number series, (b) Verbal Reasoning, based on verbal analogies, and (c) Nonverbal Reasoning, based on a variation of the progressive matrices, with 40, 35, and 40 items respectively. The scales are usually individually administered, and standard score norms are provided for each half-year age group from 6-0 through 17-11 for each scale. A General Aptitude Quotient can be obtained by summing and averaging the standard scores of any two of the scales or of all three.

Administration and scoring procedures are clear and concise and generally well written except for the directions for use with small groups. The test materials are clear and sufficiently large for individual administration, but probably not for small groups.

Test development and standardization descriptions are sketchy. Apparently, the subtests and the types of items for each subtest were chosen on the basis of some sort of author consensus of what other individual and group tests have included. There were 225 cases in the tryout, apparently spread over ages from 6 to 17 years. Items selected for standardization had minimum point biserials of .30 but these were for the complete age range. What difficulties were actually used is not stated.

The SAS was standardized on 1,448 examinees in 18 states between April 1989 and February 1990. Six of the age groups had fewer than 110 cases. This means that the norms for half-year groups were based on as few as 50 cases. The sample was based on cases, supplied by professionals who used the publisher's diagnostic tests, that would be representative of students in their areas. Additional cases were obtained from four major census districts that had similar demographic characteristics to the nation as a whole. The authors conclude the sample is representative apparently because their sample has some gross demographic characteristics that are similar to that of the population, (e.g., urban-rural). It would seem that in view of the fact that the standardization is based primarily on a convenience sample, more detailed information on demographic characteristics as well as socioeconomic characteristics would be required.

The purpose for developing the scale is not stated directly, but rather by indicating that there is no satisfactory alternative available. The authors claim that despite the plethora of aptitude scales made available since 1957, "many of the tests were poorly constructed, inadequately standardized, and unduly suited for predicting general scholastic aptitude . . . and biased against minority students" (p. 1). The biasing is attributed to the scales being "laden with verbal stimuli" underestimating the ability of students with language or general deficiencies. No evidence is presented to support their position. Also, there is no recognition that most of the problems may not be with the instruments being too verbal, because most have nonverbal components, but rather with the interpretation of results. Thus, there is no clear rationale for another general aptitude measure. In fact, the authors are quite presumptuous in stating that "weaknesses identified by other cognitive tests (e.g., . . . Wechsler Intelligence Scale for Children—Revised . . .) can be quickly verified by administering the SAS."

Technical data are sparse. The data reported are generally inadequate; for example, the only discrimination and difficulty values reported are averages by age group. There are no data on functional ranges of the SAS for each of the age groups, and it is obvious that two of the subtests do not have sufficient ceilings. As raw score means and standard deviations are not reported for each age group it is not possible to check on reported reliabilities. There are reported reliabilities in the .90s at age levels and for subtests that did not have sufficient ceilings. At the same time, retest reliabilities for a group of 90 students, ages ranging from 73 months to 213 months, over a 1-week period, ranged from .77 to .82 for the three subtests.

There is no evidence that the SAS is generally preferable to a group cognitive skills test such as the Test of Cognitive Skills (9:1248), which has number series, nonverbal analogies, and memory and verbal reasoning subtests with correlations in the .50s, .60s, and .70s between these subtests and the California Achievement Tests (10:41) subtests. The SAS correlations are mostly much lower with similar subtests even after inappropriate corrections for attenuation had been made.

Finally the authors criticize earlier tests for not meeting "American Psychological Association set standards for test authors," and although they include all of the topics in the standards, the data supplied are inadequate. Also, their understanding of certain concepts, in particular construct validity, is superficial. For example, they assume that increase in performance by age proves that scales are developmental.

Overall, the test materials and directions are clear and well presented. There is nothing else to recommend this test for use.

Review of the Scholastic Aptitude Scale by KEN-NETH D. HOPKINS, Professor of Education, University of Colorado, Boulder, CO:

The Scholastic Aptitude Scale (SAS) is designed for ages 6-0 through 17-11 as a quick, easily administered individual test of overall cognitive functioning, general scholastic aptitude, global aptitude, and intellectual ability. The authors claim that the SAS also can be given to small groups. Compared to its formidable competitors, the Stanford-Binet or the Wechsler tests (hereafter designated as "the competition"), its primary appeal is its practicability. The SAS Examiner's Manual indicates that each of the three subtests of 35–40 items (Quantitative, Verbal, and Nonverbal Reasoning) can ordinarily be completed in 20 minutes, resulting in 1 hour testing time; but 1 hour is not greatly different from the competition. The SAS uses basals and ceilings (five consecutive correct and incorrect answers, respectively) in scoring, thus the typical examinee responds to perhaps only half the items (the administration time of older examinees probably averages considerably less than 1 hour). The principal advantages of the SAS over the competition are in the ease and the cost of administration (the amount of training for good test administration is much less).

The SAS Examiner's Manual abounds with psychometric naivete (e.g., an inaccurate history of "scholastic aptitude"; normalizing is misunderstood and applied; the final item analysis was done on only 50 examinees per age group, instead of using the entire norming sample of 102–167 per age group; and criterion-related validity coefficients are given only after correction for attenuation, etc.)—the test suffers greatly from lack of psychometric expertise. On the other hand, the SAS does *not* make grandiose and deliberately misleading claims—there are many appropriate cautions about proper test use and interpretation.

STANDARDIZATION AND NORMS. The norms are based on a convenience sample gathered by a network of acquaintances of the authors. Demographic characteristics are given only for the entire norming sample, not separately for each age level. Consequently the norms must be judged as very crude, and cannot be used with any confidence without further substantiation. The plateau in age differential between ages 10–13 probably results more from noncomparability in the samples than in any genuine temporary deceleration in growth rate.

Performance on each subtest is described using a standard score with mean of 100 and standard deviation of 15; the three standard scores are aggregated to generate a "General Aptitude Quotient—GAQ," also having the same mean and standard deviation. No information is given regarding the shapes of the distributions of the scores, no indices of skewness, etc. The percentile ranks associated with the scores are correct *only* if the distributions are normal (converting standard scores to percentiles is misconstrued as normalizing, rather than the converse). The manual designates 2.34% of the scores will fall above 130, in the "Very Superior" range, yet the highest possible subtest score at several age ranges is " > 129." Inexplicably, the SAS truncates the conversion to quotient standard scores on the three subtests at approximately 130 (e.g., raw scores of 30–35 at ages 8-6 through 10-5 each becomes " > 130"); a table for converting to GAQ suggests that quotients of 35–165 are possible, yet scores above 140 (and below 54) are mathematically impossible at any age. The age groupings are too crude at the younger age levels (children from ages 6-0 through 6-5 with the same raw score receive identical IQ scores).

VALIDITY. Apart from the validity consequences of the questionable norms, the construct validity of the SAS appears to be satisfactory, but could be improved substantially. Each of the three SAS subtests has a restricted scope of cognitive processes that are sampled; this enhances reliability, but decreases the domain sampling and construct validity: All Quantitative Reasoning items are numerical series; all Verbal Reasoning items are semantic analogies; all Nonverbal items employ matrices. In addition, construct validity of some Verbal Reasoning items is attenuated by some "bookish" items that measure achievement more than aptitude—a bright, but unschooled person might not be familiar with such terms as "heribivore," "proton," "Quixote," and "graphology." The need for fine-tuning is evident throughout.

Concurrent validity coefficients between SAS scores and certain achievement tests are given only after correcting for attenuation! Unfortunately, many test users/purchasers are not familiar with disattenuated correlation coefficients and, consequently, are likely to exaggerate the degree of concurrent relationship between the SAS and the achievement measures.

RELIABILITY. The tests appear to have high reliability (although the authors appear unaware that the standard scores are not a linear transformation of the raw scores), hence the reliability of the raw scores (KR 20) is different from the reliability of the SAS standard scores because at the younger ages the groupings are coarse and GAQ scores are truncated.

SUMMARY. The SAS is in an embryonic stage of development. It clearly is not currently on a par with the best individual (and group) measures of scholastic aptitude. From a perspective of technical adequacy, it was marketed prematurely. With refinement and a proper standardization it could become a good measure. A better alternative to the hopelessly inadequate norming/standardization, calibrated norms would have been less expensive and far superior.

[344]
School Attitude Measure, Second Edition.
Purpose: "To evaluate students' views of their academic environment and of themselves as competent students."
Population: Grades 1–2, 3–4, 5–6, 7–8, 9–12.
Publication Dates: 1980–90.
Acronym: SAM.
Scores: 5 scales: Motivation for Schooling, Academic Self-Concept—Performance Based, Academic Self-Concept—Reference Based, Student's Sense of Control over Performance, Student's Instructional Mastery.
Administration: Group.
Levels, 6: C/D, E, E/F, G/H, I/J, K/L.
Price Data, 1990: $38.95 per 25 machine-scorable booklets; $30.20 per 25 reusable booklets; $13 per 35 answer sheets; $4.10 per directions for administration; $17.50 per Technical/Norms manual ('90, 55 pages); $26.25 per grades 1–8 test review kit; $5.25 per high school level test review kit.
Foreign Language Edition: Spanish edition available.
Time: (30–40) minutes.
Comments: Level E is a machine-scorable version of Level E/F.
Authors: Lawrence J. Dolan and Marci Morrow Enos.
Publisher: American Testronics.

TEST REFERENCES
1. Greene, J. C. (1985). Relationships among learning and attribution theory motivational variables. *American Educational Research Journal, 22,* 65-78.
2. Karnes, F. A., & Whorton, J. E. (1987). Comparison of school attitudes for students intellectually gifted and outstanding in fine and performance arts in grades 4 to 6. *Psychological Reports, 61,* 587-590.

Review of the School Attitude Measure by DAN WRIGHT, School Psychologist, Ralston Public Schools, Ralston, NE:

The School Attitude Measure (SAM) is an ambitious attempt to provide an assessment tool for a student characteristic that is not often quantified—attitude toward school. It is part of a larger assessment package, the Comprehensive Assessment Program, which includes measures of academic achievement (National Achievement Test; NAT; 254) and cognitive ability (Developing Cognitive Abilities Test; DCAT; 110). This review deals primarily with the SAM, although certain issues involve the entire program.

The SAM is presented in five forms which cover grade levels 1 through 12. The number of items ranges from 40 at grades 1–2 to 100 at grades 9–12. There is a four-choice response format for grades 3 and above and a "yes–no" format for younger students, who are to have the items read aloud to them. All responses are on forms designed for machine scoring; except for the response booklet for younger students, these are part of a larger form that presents sections for the NAT and DCAT, as well. Forms must be returned to the publisher for scoring. In addition to yielding a total score, the SAM offers scores on five subscales at all age levels: Motivation for Schooling, Academic Self-Concept—Performance Based, Academic Self-Concept—Reference Based, Student's Sense of Control Over Performance, and Student's Instructional Mastery. These tap five presumably distinct variables the authors believe contribute toward school attitude based upon their survey of research. All scores are presented in terms of both national percentiles and weighted raw scores, using the Rasch model for transformation.

According to the prepublication technical material, the SAM apparently underwent an extensive process of development and norming. Nearly 90,000 students composed a sample that was stratified according to geographic region, school district size, and socioeconomic status. Students were assessed in both the fall and spring in order to gain information about attitude change during the course of the school year. Although the process of item writing and tryout is not presented in detail, the reader is assured that final items have been demonstrated to be free of ethnic, gender, or regional bias.

Reliability of the SAM is mildly disappointing. As one might expect, reliability is poorer with the shorter subscales presented at the lower age levels. Presented in the Teacher's Manual, KR-20 coefficients for the five subscales range from .69 to .88 across grade levels 4–6 to 9–12, with a median value of .78. These values are broken down in more detail in the technical and normative manual. In this document, subscale coefficients are not presented at all for Level C/D, the lowest grade level, but it is acknowledged that they dipped "below .65." Coefficients for the SAM Total range from .90 to .96 across the five levels. The implication of this variability is that profile interpretation might be ill-advised depending on the level and subscales under consideration.

Validity of the SAM is a topic that leaves much to be established. The authors appeal to face validity for the content of the five subscales, and it is evident that the items in each were crafted with a coherent purpose. Beyond that, there is little support. A single 1983 study found by the reviewer in the research literature, and apparently alluded to in the Teacher's Manual, establishes a degree of concurrent validity of the SAM with measures of achievement, self-esteem, and parent and teacher ratings on similar scales. However, because the five subscales pertain to meaningfully different constructs, a study of discriminant validity is very much needed. Intercorrelations of the SAM subscales with the DCAT and the subtests of the NAT are not promising. The median correlation of the SAM Total with subtests of achievement ranges from a low of .02 at grade 1 to a high of .33 at grades 9–10, and the correlations are generally uniform across subtests within grade levels. Below grade 4 these values are essentially zero. Because the authors discuss the interrelationship of attitude and achievement, and refer to correlation values of about .50 in previous studies, one must wonder if the SAM has missed the mark. By contrast, the DCAT shows much stronger correlations with achievement, with coefficients of consistently moderate to high magnitude.

Beyond these considerations, there is a feeling of ambiguity of purpose about the SAM. A single theory is not offered as having guided its development. For example, the Student's Sense of Control Over Performance scale, a locus of control scale, is drawn from learning theories of motivation, whereas the two scales dealing with Academic Self-Concept appear to be drawn from attribution theory. This may not diminish the utility of results, but the origin of these constructs and a better sense of their meaning should be provided. The reviewer is only marginally familiar with the complex literature on achievement motivation, but feels reasonably certain that most teachers and administrators have even less background in this area. In addition, no coherent model or theory is articulated to tie the SAM together with the NAT and the DCAT. The authors consider attitude and achievement to have reciprocal influences; each is both a cause and a result of the other. But how does one intervene? The authors suggest directing attention toward individuals who display dramatic differences across the five subscales of the SAM, but low subscale reliabilities will make that an imprecise endeavor. They suggest looking for individual discrepancies between attitude and achievement, but one can see that the relationship of the SAM with the NAT is very modest, which renders discrepancies meaningless. Suggestions are offered for examining the attitudinal features of groups or whole classes, but it is acknowledged that few schools offer programs designed to affect student attitude.

It is also acknowledged that information from the SAM, NAT, and DCAT must be interpreted along with information on students' social and behavioral histories, teacher observations, school grades, age, and any other special situations or conditions. Again, a framework within which to attempt this must be provided by the user. It is difficult to imagine that a typical classroom teacher will have the time and enthusiasm to do this for an entire class. The SAM might make an interesting and useful tool for guidance counselors and school psychologists who want a mass screening instrument, but in its present form it does not offer one the flexibility to select particular subscales at given age levels, or to use it on an individual basis at all. This is unfortunate because the instrument addresses some important constructs and has a wealth of background information yet to be developed. For example, the prepublication technical manual offers some really interesting information on fall-spring changes and trends across grade levels for the five subscales. The SAM holds promise for further development, but is not yet ready for practical use.

In summary, the SAM must be commended in its attempt to assess students' attitudes toward school and to make that information available to teachers and administrators who wish to make positive interventions. At the present time, however, it does not appear to possess adequate reliability at all age levels, and the actual relationship of its results with school achievement appears quite low. Much work remains to establish the validity of the scales, especially studies of discriminant validity with the five subscales, which purport to assess different constructs. Most importantly, the SAM requires an overarching model or framework to integrate it with the other components of the Comprehensive Assessment Program. A model is necessary before one can address questions such as how or where to intervene, or even what outcomes are desired. Until these issues are resolved, the SAM should still be regarded as in a research and development stage.

[345]
SCREEN [Senf-Comrey Ratings of Extra Educational Need].

Purpose: Designed "to identify children with a high risk for . . . academic and adjustment problems in school."
Population: Grades K–3.
Publication Date: 1988.
Acronym: SCREEN.
Scores, 9: Child Tests (Self Concept and School Adjustment, Visual Skills, Auditory Skills, Basic Knowledge, General Readiness), Teacher Ratings (TR-I Cognitive-Perceptual Skills, TR-II Behavioral Adjustment, TR-III Social Adjustment, TR-IV Immaturity).
Administration: Group.
Price Data, 1991: $50 per 10 student booklets; $15 per administrator's manual (49 pages); $15 per technical manual (161 pages); $15 per specimen set.
Time: [60] minutes over 4 sessions.
Comments: "Norm-referenced."
Authors: Gerald M. Senf and Andrew L. Comrey.
Publisher: Academic Therapy Publications.

Review of the SCREEN [Senf-Comrey Ratings of Extra Educational Need] by JOHN W. FLEENOR, Research Associate, Center for Creative Leadership, Greensboro, NC:

The Senf-Comrey Ratings of Extra Educational Need (SCREEN) was developed to alleviate shortcomings found in procedures used to identify children having a high risk for educational problems. The test contains four modules that provide scores on five subtests (listed above). The Figure Copying subtest is omitted from the 1988 edition. Each subtest consists of 24 to 45 items, with a total of 135 items. The teacher reads each item aloud, and students mark happy or sad faces to indicate a positive or negative response to the item (e.g., "Do you hate school work?"). The Teacher Rating Scale consists of 40 items (e.g., "Is uncooperative"), which provide scores on four factors (listed above). These items are rated by the teacher on a 5-point scale (1 = *Always or Almost Always*, 5 = *Almost Never or Never*).

Previous editions were published in 1974 and 1975. Although the item domain of the 1988 version is conceptually the same as the first edition, there has been a substantial reduction in length of the test.

ADMINISTRATION AND SCORING. The instrument is administered in the classroom; no special training is required. The answer booklets are mailed to the test publisher for scoring; however, they are not returned. The normal turnaround time for scoring is 2 weeks.

An individual report is prepared for each student. The report averages three pages in length, and provides the following: (*a*) identifying information; (*b*) educational history; (*c*) a profile of the subtest scores with a statement indicating the degree of risk that each score represents; (*d*) a narrative section describing areas of significant weakness; (*e*) the pattern of scores in narrative form; and (*f*) a summary indicating the behaviors to which the teacher should be attentive, and a recommendation for follow-up testing, if necessary.

Because the test is scored by the publisher, only limited information about the scoring procedure is described in the manual. Some of the subtests yield subscores, resulting in a total of 17 scores. All scores are derived so that lower scores indicate better performance (i.e., raw scores equal number of errors).

NORMS. The SCREEN is normed solely by grade (K through 3); however, normative data are also broken down by sex and population density (i.e., urban, rural, etc.). Norms were developed from a stratified sample of elementary school children who were administered the 1975 version. Sample sizes range from 1,526 to 2,021. Tables reporting the means and standard deviations for the 10 subtest scores are provided; however, grade equivalents for raw scores are not furnished.

RELIABILITY. The manual reports split-half and internal consistency (KR 20) reliabilities for scores of the sample described above. Estimates of reliability are reported for each grade separately. For the 10 subtests, split-half reliabilities range from .55 to .96, with a median of .87. Reliabilities of the Visual Skill scores are lower for second and third graders (.67 and .55, respectively). Estimates of internal consistency for the four subtests containing dichotomous items range from .72 to .90, with a median of .82. These reliabilities are consistent across grades.

Test-retest reliabilities with a 2-week interval are reported for a sample of 252 students. These reliabilities range from .51 to .99, with a median of .85. Test-retest reliabilities of the Self Concept and School Adjustment Index (SC & SAI) and the Visual Skills subtest are generally lower than the other subtests; several are below .70.

VALIDITY. The Self Concept (SC) and School Adjustment Index (SAI) and the Teacher Rating Scale are factorially defined; however, the other subtests are rationally defined. The authors give secondary importance to construct considerations; they chose test items to maximize prediction and relevant information. A factor analysis of the 17 subscores indicates that the ability subtests load heavily on the first factor, and the teacher ratings load heavily on the second factor. This provides some evidence of factorial validity for the test.

The authors report results of multiple correlation analyses with SCREEN subtests as predictors, and scales from several readiness and achievement tests as criteria (e.g., the Gates-MacGinitie Reading Tests). Sample sizes range from 25 to 1,088. The resulting concurrent validity coefficients (average multiple correlations) range from .71 to .73. Additional correlational analyses demonstrating similarly positive results are presented in the manual.

The ability of the SCREEN to predict two achievement criteria (individual vs. group administration) is compared to a battery of three diagnostic tests (e.g., WISC-Verbal). The predictive power of the SCREEN compares favorably with the individually administered diagnostic instruments. However, the SCREEN appears to be a better predictor of group achievement test performance than a predictor of individually administered achievement tests. The SCREEN also demonstrates predictive validity using various other tests as criteria, including the SRA Assessment Survey, the Iowa Test of Educational Development, and the Stanford Achievement Test.

CONCLUSION. Overall, the SCREEN demonstrates acceptable levels of reliability; however, the reported reliabilities of the Visual Skills and the SC and SAI subtests are somewhat low. The authors attribute the low reliability of the Visual Skills subtest to a restriction of range in scores, because this subtest is extremely easy for older children. The lower test-retest reliabilities of the SC and SAI are attributed to true variability in the children's emotional reaction after the 2-week interval. These explanations may account, in part, for the relatively low reliabilities of these subscales. An impressive amount of validity evidence for the SCREEN is presented in the manual. The test appears to be a good predictor of academic achievement and readiness.

The technical manual is in need of revision. Much of the information in the manual pertains to the 1975 version of the SCREEN. This earlier version contains more items and subtests than the 1988 edition.

The SCREEN was developed to provide teachers with usable results and to serve as a focus for diagnostic follow-up, in a cost-effective manner. The authors seem to have succeeded in their purpose. The SCREEN appears to be an effective screening device for classroom teachers to use in the identification of students with potential academic and adjustment problems. Because the instrument is theoretically neutral, it can be administered in conjunction with any pupil assessment program.

Review of the SCREEN [Senf-Comrey Ratings of Extra Educational Need] by RODNEY W. ROTH, Professor of Educational Research and Dean, College of Education, The University of Alabama, Tuscaloosa, AL:

The primary purposes of the Senf-Comrey Ratings of Extra Educational Need (SCREEN) test are to identify children with a high risk for encountering academic and adjustment problems in school, to provide teachers with a broad basis for making educational decisions about each pupil, and to provide a focus for diagnostic follow-up.

The 1988 edition of the SCREEN is really the 1975 version, minus the Figure Copying subtest. The Figure Copying section was omitted in order to reduce scoring cost. The SCREEN requires four 15-minute pupil test sessions. Each test session covers a subtest. The four subtests are: (*a*) Self Concept and School Adjustment Index. It is assessed with 24 YES or NO type items. For example, "Do you hate school work?"; (*b*) Visual Skills. This subtest assesses letter knowledge, incidental memory, and integration of designs; (*c*) Auditory Skills. This subtest assesses auditory discrimination, listening comprehension, and digit memory; and (*d*) Basic Knowledge. This subtest assesses vocabulary, basic concepts, general information, reasoning, and quantitative knowledge. The Basic Knowledge is combined with Visual Skills and Auditory Skills to produce an overall General Readiness Score. Each test booklet contains 40 items to which the teacher responds for each pupil tested. These 40 items produce four scores. They are Cognitive-Perceptual Skills, Behavioral Adjustment, Social Adjustment, and Immaturity. In addition, each booklet has 17 pupil information items. These include previous special testing and demographic information.

The SCREEN Technical Manual presents various reliability and validity studies. These studies are well done and appropriate for this type of test. The split-half and K-R 20 reliabilities average over .85 when combined for kindergarten and first grade students. They are slightly lower for second and third grade students. The test authors indicate the test was developed primarily for K–1 students and that grade 2–3 reliabilities suffer from range restriction. A test-retest validity study was also completed. Students and teachers completed the test and 2 weeks later the same students and teachers completed the test. The test-retest reliability results tended to compare favorably with the split-half and K-R 20 values. The various reliability studies indicate the test has appropriate reliability given the purposes of the test.

The content validity of the test is addressed in the technical manual by describing the procedures for test construction. Most of the items are rationally defined sets to measure the various skills. The authors also used techniques developed by Wepman, Dolch, Wechsler, and Binet to develop items. The content validity of the test is greatly enhanced by factor analyses techniques. Concurrent validity studies were conducted by correlating SCREEN scores with various achievement tests and diagnostic tests. The various concurrent validity studies indicated significant amounts of shared variance among the measures. The predictive validity studies for the SCREEN test are very impressive. The SCREEN test results were correlated with various diagnostic and achievement tests after time intervals of several months to almost 3 years. In all of these studies, the results indicated strong predictive validity for the SCREEN.

The test was normed in 1975 by testing almost 10,000 K–3 pupils from 70 different school districts in the state of Illinois. These districts represented rural, small town, suburban, and city-urban school districts. Most of the validity and reliability studies were conducted with this sample or subsets of this sample.

The SCREEN student test booklet is attractive, colorful, and well designed for testing younger students. The items are designated with various colors and common animals. The student responses are marked in the booklet. The Administrator's Manual is also well designed. It enables a teacher to administer the test easily in a group setting. The test cannot be locally scored. The test booklets must be sent to the publisher. The publisher prepares a SCREEN individualized report for each tested student. This report contains student background information, a performance index reported as a T score for each subtest, a percentile rank for each subtest, and a short interpretation of each subtest (e.g., serious problem, average, or above). In addition, the individual report presents a helpful narrative explanation of each subtest. The report also contains a total test summary and recommendations. The individual reports are written to be very helpful for teachers. This reviewer would like to point out, however, that the sample individual report sent to me by the publisher had two incorrect percentile rank scores on the summary chart. I hope the publisher is more careful with real individual reports.

In conclusion, the SCREEN is a very reliable and valid instrument to identify younger students who might currently need special attention in order to improve their future academic achievement.

[346]
Screening Children for Related Early Educational Needs.

Purpose: "To focus on early academic related behaviors in the areas of oral language, reading, writing, and mathematics."
Population: Ages 3–7.
Publication Dates: 1981–88.
Acronym: SCREEN.
Scores, 5: Achievement Quotient, Language, Reading, Writing, Math.
Administration: Individual.
Price Data, 1988: $69 per complete kit including 25 Profile/Record forms, 25 student workbooks, Picture Book, and examiner's manual ('88, 100 pages).
Time: (25–50) minutes.
Authors: Wayne P. Hresko, D. Kim Reid, Donald D. Hammill, Herbert P. Ginsburg, and Arthur J. Baroody.
Publisher: PRO-ED, Inc.

Review of Screening Children for Related Early Educational Needs by DAVID W. BARNETT, Professor, School Psychology and Counseling, University of Cincinnati, Cincinnati, OH:

Screening Children for Related Early Educational Needs (SCREEN) is considered by the authors to be an achievement measure, or alternatively, a measure of academically related behaviors pertinent to identifying children with mild to moderate learning difficulties. The stated purposes of SCREEN are identifying young children with possible delays in "early academic areas" (p. 6), determining strengths and weaknesses, and monitoring progress of children in intervention programs through retesting. The administration time is reported to be between 15 to 40 minutes, depending on the child's age and ability.

SCREEN comprises the following components: Oral Language, Reading, Writing, and Mathematics. However, as examples, early "writing" tasks include pointing to pictures of a stamp or pencil, while an early "reading" item involves identifying the top of a book. In addition, a global SCREEN Early Achievement Quotient (SEAQ) is provided, based on the child's performance on the four components. Items for inclusion were selected from other measures available from the same publisher: The Test of Early Language Development (TELD; 9:1250) (Hresko, Reid, & Hammill, 1981); The Test of Early Reading Ability (TERA; 9:1253) (Reid, Hresko, & Hammill, 1981); Test of Early Written Language (TEWL; 430) (Hresko, 1988); and Test of Early Mathematics Ability (TEMA; 9:1252) (Ginsburg & Baroody, 1983).

The administration and scoring of the SCREEN are relatively straightforward. Some common materials must be supplied by the examiner (i.e., blocks, coins, chips, or other items for counting). The provided test materials include a Picture Book, a Student Workbook, and a Profile/Record Form. Scoring is unambiguous for the most part. Correct items are given 1 point and incorrect responses receive 0 points. Suggested entry items based on chronological age are used to reduce testing time by indicating places to begin. In addition, basal and ceiling levels are used for the SEAQ. Testing is continued from the entry level until six consecutive items are missed. If the child is unsuccessful on the first item, the examiner proceeds backwards until six consecutive items are passed. After the basal is established, the examiner proceeds from the original starting point and discontinues testing following six consecutive failed items. Computer scoring is available.

To aid in test interpretation, standard scores, percentiles, and descriptive phrases are included (i.e., *very superior* and *superior* at one extreme, to *poor* and *very poor* at the other). The standard scores, including the SCREEN Early Achievement Quotient and the four component quotients, have a mean of 100 and standard deviation of 15.

The technical characteristics of the SCREEN include a reasonably large standardization sample ($N = 1,355$ children in 20 states). However, no information is given concerning SES. Children of poverty are typically underrepresented in standardization efforts but are disproportionately referred. The number of cases at half-year age levels from age 3 to age 7-11 ranged from 105 to 174. The older children in the sample (from age 6 upward) are better represented than younger children.

Reliability was analyzed through the use of coefficient alpha, Rasch, and test-retest procedures. By half-year age intervals, overall alphas were .95 or higher for all intervals except children from 3.6 to 3.11 (alpha = .85). Coefficient alphas for individual subtests were typically lower; only 17.5% were above .90. Thus, the components should be interpreted with caution. The test-retest results (2-week

interval, no sample size given, ages 6 to 7.3) were quite high, ranging from .87 to .98 with a median of .93 for components.

Validity evidence is presented in several overlapping ways. Content validity was closely related to test construction as mentioned. Construct validity was supported by significant correlations between the SCREEN performance, chronological age, school experience, other developmental measures, and discrimination of identified groups of children with or without learning problems. Criterion-related validity was supported by the correlations between the original measures from which the items were selected and a range of various criterion measures. The correlations ranged from .40 to .75 with a median of .55. Criterion-related validity is also suggested by the correlations between the SCREEN and several alternative criterion measures. The resulting validity coefficients range from .46 to .68 with a median of .54. The SCREEN Overall Score was moderately related to various measures of intelligence (i.e., ranged from .44 to .66, with a median of .57).

Several cautions to potential users should be mentioned. First, one of the stated purposes of the SCREEN is to enable practitioners to develop profiles of specific strengths and weaknesses. In fact, the authors encourage the use of profile interpretations of the SCREEN. Given the high degree of intercorrelations found between SCREEN subtests, actual profiles may be quite tenuous, if not impossible, to interpret. For example, the correlation between Language and Reading was .95, and the correlation between Reading and Math was .96. The intercorrelations frequently exceed scale reliabilities at various age levels. Thus, it is quite likely that a general factor underlies the scale. Furthermore, given the many examples of moderate relationships with alternative screening measures, the reliability of *decisions* (e.g., whether or not a child is "at risk") is likely to be quite low.

Second, because the SCREEN is purported to be a screening measure, the test user should be cognizant of important issues related to screening (Adelman, 1982; Barnes, 1982). If used for wide-scale screening efforts, such measures can be error-prone and are not likely to be cost-effective, especially in situations in which the base rates of children with educational needs are either very high or low. Because many preschool programs include well-developed curriculum and opportunities for ongoing teacher/parent observation and consultation, curriculum-based alternatives to screening merit primary consideration.

Third, the SCREEN has an inadequate floor and ceiling for the ages that encompass the intended use of the scale. As examples of the former problem, children who receive a raw score of 1 at ages 3.0 to

3.5 receive a scaled score of 86 on the SCREEN LQ. At the same age level, a raw score of 1 is equivalent to a scaled score of 100 on the SCREEN MQ. At the other extreme, children at age level 7.6 to 7.11 with raw scores of 17 (out of a possible 18) receive standard scores of 100 on three out of four subtests.

Fourth, the item gradients are quite uneven throughout the test, which may result in interpretive difficulties. As an example, a child between the ages of 5.6 to 5.11 who achieves a raw score of 9 on the SCREEN WQ (writing component) receives a scaled score of 100. A child of the same age who receives credit for one more correct item (a raw score of 10) receives a scaled score of 113. At the other extreme, a child aged 3.6 with a raw score of 21 receives a SCREEN SEAQ equal to 119, whereas a child receiving a raw score of 31 has a SCREEN SEAQ of 123.

In sum, despite the fact that overall reliabilities and evidence for validity are similar to many other screening devices, the goal of developing "academic profiles" for young children cannot be met by this device. Although the only potential use of this scale would be to help identify young children based on downward extensions of PL 94-142 to meet state regulations that are developing with respect to PL 99-457, based on the technical properties of the scales, such decisions are likely to be associated with high error rates. Numerous screening alternatives are available, founded on practices related to organizational/systems approaches to screening, parent and teacher consultation, and curriculum-based methods.

REVIEWER'S REFERENCES

Hresko, W. P., Reid, D. K., & Hammill, D. D. (1981). The Test of Early Language Development. Austin, TX: PRO-ED, Inc.
Reid, D. K., Hresko, W. P., & Hammill, D. D. (1981). The Test of Early Reading Ability. Austin, TX: PRO-ED, Inc.
Adelman, H. S. (1982). Identifying learning problems at an early age: A critical appraisal. Journal of Clinical Child Psychology, 11, 255-261.
Barnes, K. E. (1982). Preschool screening: The measurement and prediction of children at-risk. Springfield, IL: Thomas.
Ginsburg, H. P., & Baroody, A. J. (1983). Test of Early Mathematics Ability. Austin, TX: PRO-ED, Inc.
Hresko, W. P. (1988). Test of Early Written Language. Austin, TX: PRO-ED, Inc.

Review of Screening Children for Related Early Educational Needs by LIZANNE DeSTEFANO, Assistant Professor of Educational Psychology, University of Illinois at Urbana-Champaign, Champaign, IL:

Screening Children for Related Early Educational Needs (SCREEN) measures the early development of academic abilities in children 3 through 7 years of age. Item analysis was used to identify for inclusion on the SCREEN the most discriminating items on four well-known tests of early development: The Test of Early Language Development (TELD; 9:1250); (Hresko, Reid, & Hammill, 1981)—18 items; The Test of Early Reading Ability (TERA; 9:1253) (Reid, Hresko, & Ham-

mill, 1981)—18 items; the Test of Early Written Language (TOWL; 430) (Hresko, 1988)—16 items; and the Test of Early Mathematics Ability (TEMA; 9:1252) (Ginsburg & Baroody, 1983)—18 items.

In an excellent historical review of research and practice, the authors describe the test as a direct assessment of academic achievement for young children, clearly differentiating it from traditional indirect or predictive measures, such as developmental inventories or readiness measures. The stated purposes of the test include: to identify students who are below their peers in certain academic areas and who may be candidates for early intervention; to identify strengths and weaknesses in individual students; to document students' progress as a consequence of early intervention programs; and to serve as a measure of early academic achievement in research. The authors stress the use of the test as a screening device, offering suggestions for further assessment if weaknesses are noted in the SCREEN. Given the recent growth in early intervention programs as a result of the implementation of PL 99-457, the appearance of this test is timely.

The SCREEN is divided into four components: Oral Language, Reading, Writing, and Mathematics. The SCREEN Early Achievement Quotient (SEAQ) is based on the child's total score on all components, representing a global measure of early academic achievement. Similar quotients, with means equal to 100 and standard deviations of 15, are available for each of the four components. Percentile scores are also available. No grade or age equivalents are used, which may be seen as a disadvantage by teachers and others who are used to using these metrics, but because of problems with interpretation and the quality of these scores, the authors should be commended for not promoting their use.

Because of the variety in the types of skills measured, the test demands a broad repertoire of responses from the child. He/she must read, copy, write, manipulate small objects, analyze small black and white line drawings presented in a Picture Book, respond verbally with words and sentences, and attend to rather long oral instructions. Although all of these responses are among those most often called upon in school learning, the wide response demand may confound the content being measured for some items, and may place students with certain disabilities at a disadvantage. For example, a mathematics item asks the child to count out 19 pennies (or other small item) from a larger group. If a child has problems with a pincer grasp or other fine motor skills, failure on this task may not reflect lack of the number concept 19, but rather inability to perform the motor demands of the task. To offset this problem, alternative explanations for weakness on a particular item or subset of items should be considered in the manual.

The manual is well written, providing detailed instructions for administration of the SCREEN along with some general guidelines for testing young children and suggestions for modifying the test to make it more valid for certain geographic locations and types of children. A script is provided for the examiner. Examples of correct responses are provided as an aid to scoring. Unfortunately, the script and the scoring examples are in the Examiner's Manual and not the Picture Book, making it rather cumbersome for the examiner to juggle the manual, Picture Book, and other materials. An adaptive testing format uses the child's age to determine the starting point for the test. Basal and ceiling rules are used to minimize the number of items administered and the resulting testing time. A computerized scoring package is available (Hresko & Schlieve, 1988).

The manual provides a clear description of the procedures for scoring and using the test, including suggestions and cautions for interpreting each type of score, guidelines for sharing results, extraneous influences on test performance to consider in test interpretation, and a discussion of the distinction among legal, statistical, and clinical discrepancies between scores. The authors should be commended for the cautious approach they have taken in the interpretation and use of test scores, as well as their effort made to educate users of the test with regard to basic test theory.

The standardization sample consisted of 1,355 children ages 3 years to 7 years 11 months, in 20 states. Over 100 children are included in each 6-month age cohort. Characteristics of the sample relative to sex, place of residence, race, geographic region, ethnicity, and age are presented and compare favorably with national figures for the *Statistical Abstract of the United States* (1985). Information on the procedure for obtaining subjects, ability levels, and the socioeconomic information for the sample is not reported, making it difficult to judge the overall quality of the sample. Users of the test should be encouraged to develop local norms in order to better understand the performance of children in their school in relation to the standardization sample.

Internal consistency of the test was measured using both coefficient alpha and Rasch analysis. Both techniques provided evidence that the SCREEN has sufficient internal consistency to be used to make educational decisions about children. As is the case for reliable tests, the standard error of measurement for each component and for the overall test was small. Test-retest reliability studies, conducted with two groups of unreported size and age, produced stability coefficients from .87 to .98. Given the instability of some constructs such as intelligence at lower age levels, it seems further analysis of the stability of SCREEN scores over short intervals of time by age is warranted.

Evidence of construct, criterion, and content validity is presented in the manual. Content validity is attributed to the validity of the parent instruments and the process used to select items for the SCREEN. As evidence of criterion validity, component scores were correlated with each of the tests from which they were taken. These correlations exceeded .90. In addition, a table showing the correlation of SCREEN scores with scores on several selected criterion tests was presented. Although significant, these correlations were moderate, indicating the SCREEN measures something different from traditional tests for this age.

As evidence of construct validity, students' mean scores on the SCREEN were shown to increase as they became older and as they progressed from grade to grade. Correlations of SCREEN scores with a variety of intelligence measures were moderate to moderately high (.44 for the Math Quotient to .66 for SEAQ), indicating the abilities measured on the SCREEN and those measured on intelligence tests are highly related. The component scores in each content area (Reading, Oral Language, Writing, and Mathematics) were highly intercorrelated (.84 to .98), supporting the premise that they all contribute to the measurement of a unitary construct, early academic achievement, but calling into question whether each component measures a unique set of skills. Although one of the stated purposes of the test was to identify strengths and weaknesses by comparing performance across components, the high intercorrelation indicates this comparison may not be a valid one. It may be that interpretation should be limited to only the SEAQ. In a test of the SCREEN's ability to distinguish between children with normal learning capacity and children who are learning disabled, the test was administered to 22 six-year-old children. Differences between the handicapped and nonhandicapped groups averaged between 21 and 28 points in favor of the nonhandicapped group. Unfortunately, as for many of the reliability and validity studies, the sample was not well described, limiting the use of this information.

In summary, the SCREEN is a well-constructed direct assessment of early academic skills. It is probably best used as a measure of global academic achievement, to identify students for more intensive evaluation and perhaps remediation, thus meeting a great need in the growing field of early intervention. Unfortunately, many of the reliability and validity studies for the SCREEN used small or poorly described samples. Additional work in this area is warranted, along with research examining the relationship of performance on the SCREEN to school performance in later years.

REVIEWER'S REFERENCES

Hresko, W. P., Reid, D. K., & Hammill, D. D. (1981). The Test of Early Language Development. Austin, TX: PRO-ED, Inc.

Reid, D. K., Hresko, W. P., & Hammill, D. D. (1981). The Test of Early Reading Ability. Austin, TX: PRO-ED, Inc.

Ginsburg, H. P., & Baroody, A. J. (1983). Test of Early Mathematics Ability. Austin, TX: PRO-ED, Inc.

Statistical abstract of the United States. (1985). Washington, DC: U.S. Bureau of the Census.

Hresko, W. P. (1988). Test of Early Written Language. Austin, TX: PRO-ED, Inc.

Hresko, W. P., & Schlieve, P. L. (1988). PRO-SCORE System for the SCREEN (Apple and IBM versions). Austin, TX: PRO-ED, Inc.

[347]
Screening Test for Developmental Apraxia of Speech.

Purpose: "To assist in the differential diagnosis of developmental apraxia of speech."
Population: Ages 4–12.
Publication Date: 1980.
Scores, 9: Expressive Language Discrepancy, Vowels and Diphthongs, Oral-Motor Movement, Verbal Sequencing, Articulation, Motorically Complex Words, Transpositions, Prosody, Total.
Administration: Individual.
Price Data, 1988: $49 per complete test including 50 test forms and manual (42 pages); $24 per 50 test forms.
Time: (10) minutes.
Author: Robert W. Blakeley.
Publisher: PRO-ED, Inc.

Review of the Screening Test for Developmental Apraxia of Speech by RONALD K. SOMMERS, Professor of Speech Pathology and Audiology, Kent State University, Kent, OH:

It is difficult to review this test. One cannot easily comment on the validity of this screening test, because there is no valid criterion measure in existence. As aptly pointed out by Guyette and Diedrich (1983), the Screening Test for Developmental Apraxia of Speech is premature. The absence of any criterion measure obviates the value of a screening test designed to locate children who might have the disorder. Furthermore, in the absence of definitive knowledge of the symptomatology of children having developmental apraxias, development of a criterion test appears to have a very low probability of success.

To make the case that this screening test has validity, the author used discriminative analysis "as a score weighting approach to the measurement of probability." The sample used consisted of 169 children ages 4–12 who had some articulation errors and were waiting for speech therapy in schools or clinics. All subjects were reported as having normal IQs, essentially normal hearing, and were Caucasian. Presumably, none had been diagnosed on a criterion measure of developmental apraxia (none known to exist) which, based upon their scores on the screening test, then could have been used to place them into this category. All the discriminative analysis appeared to do was show that 149 of 150 cases had patterns of performance that differed

substantially enough to show that subjects belonged in one of two groups, one suspect for developmental apraxia and one of children having general articulation disorders. This appears to be a circular form of reasoning, because the author merely asserted that subjects in the sample were "known" to have developmental apraxia. Thus, the criteria for labeling them as having this disorder prior to the discriminative analysis may have been the same ones used in the screening test.

The clinical entity "developmental apraxia" has been challenged by some authorities who maintain that it represents an attempt to apply a diagnostic classification upon an extreme form of a more general condition, that is, children's articulation disorders (Guyette & Diedrich, 1981). On the other hand, it is common to find that experienced practitioners believe in the existence of a special type of articulation disorder. This disorder is often highly resistant to correction when traditional approaches are used, usually not accompanied by significant language impairments, and unique in the difficulties that children show in performing and remembering motor speech patterns. If one is willing to assume that the term "developmental apraxia" is a non sequitur but that some children having the above symptoms exist, it would be important first to develop and test the criterion measure thoroughly and then attempt to validate a screening test. Obviously, if one is convinced that this disorder does not exist, any attempt to develop a criterion test and screening tests for it is contraindicated.

Substantial criticisms have focused also on the lack of agreement in the literature about the symptomatology of developmental apraxia and the inclusion of subtests that presume to measure them in this screening test. Among these criticisms are errors of interpretation of some research findings, influences of symptomatology thought to characterize adult apraxics that are subsequently considered as symptoms of developmental apraxia, and overgeneralizations of some research evidence. Thus, even at the content level of validity assessment, this test is very controversial. This reviewer's analysis of the makeup of this test and the research evidence to support it is in strong agreement with these past criticisms.

The selection of subtests used in this screening test was heavily influenced by reports of the symptomatology of adults having acquired apraxias. This fact is alluded to by the screening test author who stated in the test manual that "The developmental disorder analogue to its more *authenticated* acquired counterpart, acquires validity by its likeness to this prototype even though there are significant differences." Thus, the author acknowledges the strong possibility of "significant differences" but essentially follows the model for assessment of the adult apraxic. To the author's credit, some items and subtests on the screening test reflect a familiarity with appropriate research literature. The possibility that much of the available literature is flawed by an unexamined overlay of adult symptoms on a developmental disorder cannot be dismissed, however.

This reviewer compared the subtests and items on a popular diagnostic test for adults having acquired apraxia, the Apraxia Battery for Adults (9:77; Dabul, 1979), and identified many subtests similar to those found on this screening test for developmental apraxia. Although a small number of subtests were uniquely different between these two tests, many were highly similar. Only a few examples will be provided. Measures of oral motor control are largely the same on both tests, articulation assessment to determine if speech accuracy deteriorates in longer words (e.g., "aluminum") and related measures of whether transpositions of sounds and syllables occur in words are found on both tests and assessment of the prosodic aspects of speech production also occur on both tests. These are major areas of overlap between a diagnostic test for adult apraxia and one for children.

Finally, it should be mentioned that no reliability data of any type were reported for this test. Without data concerning the reliability of this test (of special importance with screening devices), validity concerns are also apparent.

REVIEWER'S REFERENCES

Dabul, B. (1979). Apraxia Battery for Adults. Tigard, OR: C. C. Publications, Inc.

Guyette, T., & Diedrich, W. (1981). A critical review of developmental apraxia of speech. In N. Lass (Ed.), Speech and language: Advances in basic research and practice (Vol. 5, pp. 1-49). New York: Academic Press.

Guyette, T., & Diedrich, W. (1983). A review of the screening test for developmental apraxia of speech. Language, Speech and Hearing Services in the Schools, 14, 202-209.

[348]
Screening Test for the Luria-Nebraska Neuropsychological Battery: Adult and Children's Forms.

Purpose: Screening tests for "predicting which individuals would probably show 'normal' or 'clinical' patterns if they were administered the appropriate form of the full Luria-Nebraska Neuropsychological Battery."
Population: Ages 8–12, 13 and older.
Publication Date: 1987.
Acronym: ST-LNNB-C, ST-LNNB-A.
Scores: Running total score.
Administration: Individual.
Forms, 2: Children's Form, Adult Form.
Price Data, 1988: $80 per complete set including 25 administration and scoring booklets for children, 25 administration and scoring booklets for adults, set of stimulus cards, and manual; $67.50 per adult kit or children's kit each containing 25 administration and scoring booklets, set of stimulus cards, and manual; $13.50 per 25 administration and scoring booklets (specify adult or children's form); $28.50 per set of stimulus cards; $27.50 per manual.
Time: (20) minutes.

Comments: For screening purposes only.
Author: Charles J. Golden.
Publisher: Western Psychological Services.

Review of the Screening Test for the Luria-Nebraska Neuropsychological Battery: Adult and Children's Forms by ARLENE COOPERSMITH ROSENTHAL, Educational Psychologist and Consultant, Olney, MD:

The Screening Test for the Luria-Nebraska Neuropsychological Battery: Adult and Children's Forms (ST-LNNB) comprises 15 items taken exactly from the Full Scale Luria-Nebraska Neuropsychological Battery (LNNB; 212). The stated purpose of the screening instrument is to predict which individuals will show significant levels of clinical difficulty on the full-length battery. The time of administration is approximately 20 minutes as compared with the 2–3 hour administration of the full battery. The test manual is 26 pages: seven pages are devoted to administration of the test items; three pages are devoted to a description of various facets of the full length battery. The only four tables in the manual refer to the LNNB. An entire three pages are devoted to the development of the ST-LNNB; this includes: a rationale for selecting the total LNNB score as the parameter of overall LNNB performance to be compared with the ST-LNNB; item selection procedures; development of scoring procedures for the ST-LNNB and a validation study to demonstrate criterion-related validity. The author gives a brief, and not thoroughly convincing, rationale for the development of the screening test. The following sections summarize the test manual (although the brevity of the manual suggests it is a summary itself).

ITEM SELECTION. In an adult and child sample, stepwise multiple regression analyses were used to determine the final subset of 15 items comprising the final screening test. This has been recommended as the best of the variable selection procedures although it is not without disadvantages. Specific statistical analyses are not provided in the manual. It would appear that several hundred variables were thrown helter-skelter into a regression equation and the best 15 were selected? Stepwise procedures rely solely on mathematical models with no concommitant theoretical rationale for variable selection. The complexities of stepwise analyses are described in most basic regression texts. This reviewer would find it heartening if technical data for item selection were included!

The final 15-item subset was correlated with the overall total score from the LNNB for both an adult and child sample and cross validated in a second similar sample. These correlations ranged from .89 to .96, which the author defines as "well within the bounds of statistical and clinical needs for the study" (p. 5).

SCORING. Development of scoring procedures for the ST-LNNB is briefly described. Basically, the screening test was scored two ways (simple total score vs. weighted regression formula score) and correlations with the full-length battery overall score were compared. The correlations were slightly reduced using the simple total score. The reduction was "negligible" and the author felt it satisfactory to use a simple total score as the final measure of the screening test.

VALIDITY. The final technical (actually quasi-technical) aspect of the test was to evaluate the effectiveness of the screening test in predicting clinical performance on the full-length battery. The manual states an examination of the total raw score distribution suggested that a cutoff total ST-LNNB score of 7 and 3 (adult and child forms, respectively) be used in the prediction of a normal LNNB profile. A higher total score would result in the prediction of an abnormal profile. Neither raw score distributions, nor any other technical data, are available for examination in the manual. Essentially, this study describes the percentage of correct and incorrect classifications, based on the ST-LNNB cutoff scores for samples of patients whose LNNB performance was classified as normal, borderline, and abnormal. Correct classification rates were around 90%.

To summarize, the author must provide a more convincing rationale for the utility of such a screening test in the first place. For example, how much more effective is the ST-LNNB than clinical judgment in predicting performance on the LNNB? A screening test is probably not justified for individuals with no history of neuropsychological difficulty nor for those with clear neuropsychological difficulty. What are the specific characteristics of the population for which the ST-LNNB would be most useful? It should also be noted that the LNNB itself has been controversial and subject to criticism for its theoretical, statistical, and methodological limitations (it should be noted that the author of the ST-LNNB is also the author of the full-length battery). The author purports that one goal of the ST-LNNB (p. 3) is to predict the degree of severity of overall LNNB performance. No studies supporting the ability of the screening test to do this are cited. This statement seems inappropriate given the lack of technical data provided in the manual.

The ST-LNNB was apparently developed for use despite maintaining considerably less than the highest standards of psychometric excellence. It is inconceivable to this reviewer how such a test can be published with no accompanying psychometric data. It appears the author felt a screening test would be a time saver, threw some variables into a computer, derived the best subset, and formulated a so-called "screening instrument." The test author seems to have ignored the basic tenets of the standards for psychological tests (i.e., an examination of norms, reliability, validity, item analysis, etc.). Aiding clinicians with an easy-to-administer and time-efficient instrument may be admirable but this test needs major work before it can be recommended for clinical use. Examination of the references does not reveal a single published or unpublished study to support its use. The majority of references deal with forensic/legal issues in clinical psychology. In this reviewer's opinion the test, as it is currently, more accurately represents a preliminary phase of a progression towards publication of a screening instrument, not a finished product.

Review of the Screening Test for the Luria-Nebraska Neuropsychological Battery: Adult and Children's Forms by W. GRANT WILLIS, Associate Professor of Psychology, University of Rhode Island, Kingston, RI:

The adult and children's forms of the Screening Test for the Luria-Nebraska Neuropsychological Battery were developed to predict overall performance on the Luria-Nebraska Neuropsychological Battery: Forms I and II (Golden, Purisch, & Hammeke, 1985; 212) and the Luria-Nebraska Neuropsychological Battery: Children's Revision (Golden, 1987; 211), respectively. The adult form was designed for individuals aged 13 years and older, and the children's form for individuals aged 8 to 12 years. Each form comprises 15 items selected from the respective full-length battery and, according to the test manual, can be completed in less than 20 minutes. This represents substantial reductions from the full-length batteries, which comprise between 149 and 279 items each (depending on the particular battery) and require between $1^1/_2$ and 5 hours to administer. Materials include separate Administration and Scoring Booklets for each version and a single Stimulus Cards Booklet. Administration procedures are clear and scoring criteria are objective. The manual emphasizes that results are only intended to predict whether administration of the particular full-length battery is likely to yield useful information, rather than to predict organic-nonorganic classifications. Thus, only those patients who score over a particular cut score on the screening test are administered the full-length battery. Whether or not the full-length battery actually can yield useful information lies in an independent evaluation of that test, which is beyond the scope of this review (see reviews in this volume for the Luria-Nebraska Neuropsychological Battery: Forms I and II [212] and the Luria-Nebraska Neuropsychological Battery: Children's Revision [211]).

The total score on each full-length battery was selected as the criterion of severity of a patient's performance, and separate stepwise multiple regression analyses were conducted to select the subset of

15 items that best predicted this criterion for each battery. The adult and child samples comprised heterogeneous groups of 526 and 360 patients, respectively, who were referred for neuropsychological assessment. Age, gender, and racial distributions within these samples are not specified in the test manual, no data on demographic characteristics are presented, and, although diagnostic categories are identified, the nature of the clinical setting is unspecified. It is well known that performance on neuropsychological tests (including the Luria-Nebraska batteries) can vary in relation to such subject characteristics as age, education, and minority-group status. It is not possible, therefore, to evaluate the generalizability of these samples, and this significantly undermines the utility of the tests.

Regression formulas were cross-validated with similar but nonoverlapping samples of 526 adult and 359 child patients referred for neuropsychological assessment. Finally, weighted and unweighted regression formulas were compared, and the latter were found to result in negligible drops in correlations for both the adult (multiple R reduced from .943 to .937) and the child (multiple R reduced from .893 to .890) samples. Thus, a simple total (i.e., summed) score was adopted for both screening tests in lieu of a more complicated regression formula.

Perhaps the most serious criticism of these screening tests is that reliability data are omitted from the test manual. The manual does report a stability coefficient of .96 for total scores ($n = 30$) on a full-length battery, but the test-retest interval and nature of the sample on which this coefficient is based are not specified. No data on internal consistency over the entire full-length batteries are reported (even in the manuals for the full-length batteries). Given that the full-length batteries range from 149 to 279 items, the length of the screening tests (i.e., 15 items) are reduced by a factor of between .05 and .10. Even assuming relatively high internal consistencies for the full-length batteries, therefore, the estimated reliability of the screening test scores (according to the Spearman-Brown Prophecy Formula) would be quite low, despite their intended use for screening purposes. This suggests that a substantial proportion of the variability in these screening-test scores likely reflects error.

Evidence presented for the validity of the screening tests includes four classification accuracy analyses, one each for the initial and cross-validation samples for the adult and child groups. Here, separate cut scores for the adult and child versions of the screening tests were established to predict the presence of an abnormal profile on the respective full-length battery. All of these analyses showed that classification accuracy improved on base rates, but this is not surprising given that these are the same data upon which the development of the screening tests was based.

Two other classification accuracy analyses are reported, however, that comprised independent samples of 30 adults and 30 children each. These studies supported the validity of the screening tests by showing substantial improvements in classification accuracy over chance (i.e., base rates) in these particular samples. Unfortunately, the nature of these samples is inadequately described, the procedure is unclear, and the reliability of these results is not addressed. Thus, potential test users neither are able to generalize these results to other circumstances nor to estimate the proportion of test takers who would be classified in a similar way on different occasions.

In summary, the Screening Test for the Luria-Nebraska Neuropsychological Battery: Adult and Children's Forms cannot be recommended for clinical use because information presented in the test manual is inadequate to assess its psychometric soundness. The information that is presented on the sample is incomplete, there are no reliability data provided, and data that are presented to address validity are inadequate. Thus, at this time, clinicians who choose to use these screening instruments do so with no information about the generalizability of the information to their particular circumstances, no information about the stability of the measures, and only limited information that the intended purpose truly is being addressed.

REVIEWER'S REFERENCES

Golden, C. J., Purisch, A. D., & Hammeke, T. A. (1985). Luria-Nebraska Neuropsychological Battery: Forms I and II. Los Angeles: Western Psychological Services.

Golden, C. J. (1987). Luria-Nebraska Neuropsychological Battery: Children's Revision. Los Angeles: Western Psychological Services.

[349]

S-D Proneness Checklist.

Purpose: "Intended to be used for the measurement of depression and suicide-proneness."

Population: Depressed or suicidal clients.

Publication Dates: 1970–72.

Scores, 3: Suicide, Depression, Total.

Administration: Individual.

Price Data, 1989: $8.25 per 25 rating forms; $5 per specimen set.

Time: (5) minutes.

Comments: Checklist completed by interviewer.

Author: William T. Martin.

Publisher: Psychologists and Educators, Inc.

Cross References: For a review by Charles Neuringer, see 8:664.

[350]

Search Institute Profiles of Student Life.

Purpose: Designed to "assist . . . school officials . . . in monitoring a series of indicators related to student well-being."

Population: Grades 6–12.

Publication Date: 1988–90.

Scores: 3 Group Summary Areas: Social and Personal Resources, Behavior Patterns, Opportunities for Helping Your Youth.
Administration: Group.
Editions, 3: Alcohol and Other Drugs, Sexuality, Attitudes and Behaviors.
Price Data, 1991: $1,400 per survey service for the first 800 participating students, $1.25 per student thereafter.
Time: (30–40) minutes.
Authors: Search Institute.
Publisher: Search Institute.

Review of the Search Institute Profiles of Student Life by ERNEST A. BAUER, Research, Evaluation, and Testing Consultant, Oakland Schools, Waterford, MI:

The Search Institute Profiles of Student Life includes three separate surveys: Attitudes and Behaviors, Alcohol and Other Drugs, and Sexuality. They were developed as the result of several studies the Search Institute conducted for various clients in business, education, social service agencies, and religious organizations. The authors claim the surveys are useful as needs assessment devices or evaluation instruments. Respondents are anonymous, so only summary data are available.

The four-page Administration Manual consists of directions for administering and returning the surveys. The manual contains no information about content or concurrent validity, internal consistency, readability, test development procedures, or norming. There are no references of any kind. Personal correspondence from the Search Institute assured this reviewer that, "items stem from research projects we have conducted in the past; again, validity and reliability have been established through the field testing and extensive analyses associated with these in-depth projects." Unfortunately, information about those analyses is unavailable.

A brochure for each of the surveys contains broad claims with no references to any research or other literature. This reviewer sought additional information about the surveys and was provided with the computerized "Sample Report" available for the Alcohol and Other Drugs survey (described below) and the book-sized report based on 46,799 6th through 12th grade students who took the Behavior Patterns survey as a component of the RespecTeen project of the Lutheran Brotherhood.

This reviewer, then, had two computer-generated sample reports that the company provides users and the surveys themselves to examine. (He was informed that a similar report for the Sexuality survey was not available.) Each report shows the distributions of grade level, gender, and race/ethnicity. Some items have national norms because they are taken from the national Monitoring the Future Project. The Sample Report for the Alcohol and Other Drugs survey contains Wisconsin norms for

nine items about substance usage rates. Each report uses an inadequately described process to eliminate respondents who made inconsistent responses, reported unrealistically high use of drugs, or had high levels of nonresponse.

The Behavior Patterns report is organized into three major parts: Social and Personal Resources (11 subareas with 1–10 items each), Behavior Patterns (10 subareas with 3–13 items each), and Opportunities for Helping Your Youth (9 items). The survey attempts to cover a very broad range of student experiences and, consequently, the coverage is skimpy in several of the areas (e.g., "sexuality" is measured with three items). The other surveys go into greater detail in these areas, but many of the items are redundant if more than one of the surveys were to be used in a single school.

Generally, all of the items relating to a subarea are reported on the top of one page with "Key Findings" for the area reported at the bottom of the page. For example, "Frequent TV watching is highest in grade 6." This message (and others like it) appears to be triggered by some statistical analysis which is not described. A footnote refers to "a technical appendix with scale composition and confidence intervals" but this reviewer was unable to acquire it. Most Key Findings appear to be percentages from the item data put into prose; some appear to be based on more than one item.

In one case, "Values as Behavior Determinants," a one-item subarea, a whole page is devoted to reporting how students respond to: "It is against my values to have sex while I am a teenager." The Key Findings area cites their own research which showed that, "Values, therefore, are more powerful than even peer pressure in determining intentions concerning intercourse." No references are provided. If responses to this item are so predictive of behavior, perhaps the area deserves a few more items.

The definitions used sometimes seem idiosyncratic. For example, in the 20-factor "at-risk index," "Gang Fights: twice or more in last 12 months" and "Used knife, gun, or club to get something from someone, twice or more in last 12 months" are treated as equivalent to "Cigarettes: 1 or more cigarettes per day" and "School Absence: skipped school 2 or more days in last month." It is not surprising that 85% of seniors report they experienced at least one of the indicators and 58% report three or more.

The very readable reports present percentages of respondents who used the top two choices (or bottom two on negatively worded items) by grade, gender (not simultaneously), and total group. Users are cautioned that self-reported alcohol and drug use data are "consistent with other methods of collecting chemical use data" (no reference), but that, "The validity of other kinds of self-reported data (e.g., sexual activity, physical abuse, sexual abuse) is less clearly understood."

Each survey is printed in its own eight-page, scannable, professionally designed booklet. The surveys have a reasonable amount of eye appeal. They seem to provide broad coverage of the areas for which they are intended. They are reported to be the result of in-depth work in a variety of areas. The computerized scoring program generates reports that are readable. Unfortunately, none of the technical characteristics of the surveys are documented. They are relatively expensive. They may be useful as needs assessment devices for some organizations or as evaluation devices for some programs if local survey design capabilities are limited or if program goals and definitions of terms happen to match those of the authors.

Review of the Search Institute Profiles of Student Life by SHARON JOHNSON-LEWIS, Director of Research, Evaluation, and Testing, Detroit Public Schools, Detroit, MI:

The Search Institute Profiles of Student Life consists of three instruments designed to provide information about students' (*a*) attitudes and behaviors in general, as well as their attitudes and behaviors related to (*b*) alcohol and other drugs, and (*c*) sexuality.

Each instrument is priced separately at $2,500 per survey service ($1,000 if only computer output is required) plus $1.25 per student.

At first glance, the price appears high. However, after conducting a thorough examination of the materials and the scoring package, one can certainly conclude that the money is well spent. The Profiles are extremely comprehensive and very well developed. However, for use with small groups of students, the cost may still be prohibitive, in spite of the quality. For example, to administer one of the three instruments to a group of 400 students, and receive full service, would cost $3,000 or $7.50 per pupil, for 300 students a total of $2,875 or $9.58 per pupil. Of course, these prices would multiply if more than one profile is administered.

A small number of core questions appear in each of the three instruments. For example, each has a few questions related to drug use and non-use, peer and parent relationship, and sexuality. In addition, the demographic probes for each are similar. However, each instrument contains specialty items.

ALCOHOL AND OTHER DRUGS. This survey specializes in questions designed to assess the degree to which students participate in alcohol and drug use. The survey asks questions about student attitudes and frequency of use related to drinking alcohol, cigarette and marijuana smoking, and use of LSD, PCP, and smokeless tobacco.

The instrument also asks questions concerned with how students think their parents would react to their alcohol and drug use, student's knowledge of school rules, behaviors of friends, and knowledge of community or school support groups, religious beliefs, and school expectations.

ATTITUDES AND BEHAVIORS. The Attitudes and Behaviors Profile asks students questions related to recreation, being popular, having money, religious preference, helping people, school likes and dislikes, skipping school and classes, self-concept, sex, love, decision making, and relationships with people, parents, and friends. Items also assess the degree in which students are involved in extracurricular activities, and use of alcohol, cigarettes, and drugs. In addition, the survey attempts to assess the quality of parent/child interaction, how much, if any, physical and sexual abuse exists, and how much students worry about the future.

SEXUALITY. The Sexuality Profile is designed to ascertain where students learned about sex, if they are interested in learning more about sex-related issues, concerns about sexism, and sexually transmitted diseases. Students indicate to whom they would talk about sex, how often they have engaged in sexual intercourse, and their knowledge of body changes during puberty.

Students also rate the quality of conversations they have had with their parents about sex, and indicate if statements such as "Males have stronger sex drives than females" or "Using birth control makes having sex less romantic" are facts or myths.

Because of the explicit nature of these questions, it is strongly recommended that a thorough review of the survey items be conducted prior to use.

SURVEY ADMINISTRATION. Survey administration times range from 30 to 40 minutes. The questions are multiple choice and students can respond quite rapidly to the fixed answer choices. The test format and layout allows for easy reading.

The user can administer the survey to the total student population or a sample of students. The scoring service includes consultation on how to select an appropriate sample.

The survey directions are clear and concise and are quite explicit. For instance, on the Sexuality Profile the directions state, "The words 'having sex' or 'had sex' mean the act of having sexual intercourse, that is, a male's penis going into a female's vagina."

The manual also contains suggestions for testing students arriving late to do the survey.

SUMMARY. The Search Institute Profiles of Student Life is a battery of three instruments— Alcohol and Other Drugs, Sexuality, and Attitudes and Behaviors. Although the surveys contain a common core of items they also have "speciality" items.

The surveys are well constructed and are comprehensive. Because of the explicit nature of the questions, the potential user should review the Sexuality Profile prior to purchase.

The reports are also well designed and comprehensive, providing the user with a thorough understanding of the results through the use of tables and graphics. National norms are seldom used for comparison purposes.

The major weakness is the cost, which is extremely high especially for small groups of students.

REPORTING. Report forms for the Attitude and Behavior Profile were provided for review. Survey results are reported in the percents of students responding positively or negatively to each item. Data are disaggregated by grade and gender. Data are combined for groups of students smaller than 30.

The results are divided into three parts: Social and Personal Resources, Behavior Patterns, and Opportunities For Helping Your Youth. Each part comprises tables and graphs which profile the given subheading. The subheadings are composed of several characteristics:

Part I: Social and Personal Resources —Family Characteristics, Attitudes Toward School, Parent Involvement in Schooling, Use of Time, Involvement in Youth Activities, Access to Positive Adult Influence, Peer Influence, Student Values, Values as Behavior Determinants, Self-Concept, and View of the Future.

Part II: Behavior Patterns —Prosocial Behavior, Alcohol Use, Other Alcohol Issues, Tobacco Use, Other Drug Use, Alcohol and Drug Use Patterns, Comparisons to National Norms (seniors—alcohol and drug use), Sexuality, Anti-social Behavior, Days School Skipped, Physical and Sexual Abuse, At-risk Indicators and Stress, Depression and Suicide.

Part III: Opportunities for Helping Youth —Interests, Factors related to at-risk behaviors and a comprehensive discussion of how, based on research and data, the school, family, and community might help students. The commentary also provides data sources that can be used to develop strategies for helping students prosper. This section encourages a multilevel approach to helping students involving families, schools, churches, government, businesses, and community organizations.

The Sexuality brochure indicates that the items were normed on a sample of 1,800 students in four major cities. A major flaw in the reporting is that national norms for comparison purposes are seldom used.

[351]
Second Language Oral Test of English.

Purpose: "To assess the ability of non-native English speakers to produce standard English grammatical structures."
Population: Child and adult nonnative English speakers.

Publication Date: 1983.
Acronym: SLOTE.
Scores, 21: Affirmative Declarative, Articles, Present Participle, Possessive, Present Tense (third person-regular), Comparative, Superlative, Present Tense (third person-irregular), Preposition, Past Participle (regular), Negative, Past Participle (irregular), Subject Pronoun, Object Pronoun, Possessive Pronoun, Plural (irregular), Imperative, Yes/No Question, Wh-Question, Plural (regular), Total.
Administration: Individual.
Price Data, 1987: $16.95 per manual (136 pages) including 2 preliminary pictures, 5 practice pictures, and 60 test items with pictures.
Time: (15) minutes.
Author: Ann K. Fathman.
Publisher: The Alemany Press.

Review of the Second Language Oral Test of English by ALEX VOOGEL, *Assistant Professor, TESOL/MATFL Program, Monterey Institute of International Studies, Monterey, CA:*

The Second Language Oral Test of English (SLOTE) is an individually given oral test. It is interesting in that test tasks are pragmatic (rather than grammatical), but scoring is for correctness of discrete structural items. For the most part the tasks work well and keep the examinee's attention on communicating rather than grammar. It is in the scoring and interpretation of discrete items that some difficulty arises.

The manual suggests the SLOTE may be used for proficiency and placement purposes. However, other than raw score cutoffs for three levels (beginning, intermediate, advanced) no interpretive data are provided. The cutoffs were established with 502 subjects between 6 and 18 years of age. A study validated that the SLOTE distinguishes between three levels in this group. But without more descriptive information of the subject group, a definition of the levels, and some normative data, users will have to develop their own criteria for interpreting SLOTE scores.

Another suggested use for the SLOTE is to measure gain between a course pretest and posttest. Test-retest reliability (.98) provides some confidence in the test for this purpose. However, the user should bear in mind that this coefficient was obtained with a 40-subject sample over a 1-week period.

The manual suggests the test can be used in both oral and written form. A written test has the advantage that several students can be tested at the same time. But, no comments are made regarding possible differences in what is measured by oral and written tasks. It also would be appropriate to have data on the equivalent forms reliability of the spoken and written forms of the SLOTE. No data are provided.

It takes about 15 minutes to administer the SLOTE to one subject. Scoring is done by the examiner during testing. In scoring it is not the subject's overall response, but some structural aspect (in morphology or word order) of the subject's response that is marked right or wrong. The structural aspect of an item varies, depending on the subtest. The examiner has to be knowledgeable about the focus of each item in order to score the test. Administration of the SLOTE requires, therefore, both trained personnel and time.

Although linguistic and pictorial contexts are used to limit the response possibilities, items are still open-ended. This means that sometimes an unpredicted correct response can occur. For example, for Item 32 the manual indicates that the subject should "use correct word order and negative element." The subject sees a picture of a boy reading a book and a second picture of a boy *not* reading a book. The examiner describes the first picture "This boy is reading a book," then points to the second picture and prompts with "But this boy . . ." The expected answer is "isn't reading a book." In testing the SLOTE with a 6-year-old the following response occurred: "Is finished." For this same item an 8-year-old answered "read the book." These children did not perform as expected because their responses did not use the negative marker, but the responses are not wrong. Items 46, 47, and 48, which are intended to measure knowledge of irregular plurals, can just as well be answered with "others" instead of the expected irregular plurals. Several other items show the possibility of a variety of responses. How should the examiner interpret these responses? No guidance is given in the manual. This means that rater judgement is involved and different raters may come up with different total scores for the same responses. Using two raters and a sample of 20 students, an interrater reliability of .97 was obtained. It is encouraging that such a high reliability is possible, but what degree of rater training and experience is required to get such stable results? More complete information, and studies with different raters and students would be appropriate.

The reported internal consistency of the overall SLOTE is a high .95, based on a sample of 1,100 students. The overall test results should be stable. However, if the SLOTE is used for diagnosis the user should remember that the subtests contain only three items each. These brief subtests may not provide stable results. If a subject scores poorly on a subtest this information is preliminary rather than conclusive.

A survey of the items shows that they do not deal with complex English structure. Some users may feel the advanced level may not fit their definition of advanced. Most of the test items work well, but a few do not. Item 17 pictures a small and a large

apple. According to the manual, the examiner must point to the small apple and say "This apple is big," then point to the large apple and say "But this apple is even . . ." (and elicit "bigger"). Item 35 shows a woman in the doorway, but the subject is supposed to say "she has left." The visual and verbal messages conflict. This is confusing.

The test and manual are conveniently packaged as one booklet. A student and class score sheet are also included. These may be freely copied and should serve as convenient summaries of individual and group performance on the SLOTE. It would have been helpful if score sheets (or the test questions in the booklet) included the structural focus of items. The examiner needs this information to evaluate and score each response. Instead, the examiner (or at least the less experienced examiner) must frequently flip back to another section for this crucial information.

If you wish to measure ability to use grammatical structures in pragmatic contexts and do not need a measure that takes into account communicative competence as a whole, the SLOTE is appropriate. However, the user should consider the following limitations. The SLOTE does not test complex structures so it will not distinguish between different levels of superior students. It requires trained examiners and time. Although the written form would save time, its validity and reliability is an open question. Large scale testing may not be practical. Finally, users will have to develop their own guidelines for score interpretation.

[352]
Secondary School Admission Test.

Purpose: "Measures developed verbal and mathematical reasoning abilities and reading comprehension" for students who are applying for admission to grades 6–11.
Population: Grades 5–7, 8–11.
Publication Dates: 1957–88.
Acronym: SSAT.
Scores, 4: Verbal, Quantitative, Total, Reading Comprehension.
Administration: Group.
Levels, 2: Lower, Upper.
Price Data, 1989: $40 per examinee; no charge for student information bulletin, registration information, supervisor's manual ('87, 35 pages), interpretive guide for school personnel, explanation of scores; $5 per study guide (specify level); additional price data available from publisher.
Time: 65(90) minutes.
Comments: Tests administered 7 times annually (January, February, March, April, June, October, December) at centers established by publisher.
Author: Secondary School Admission Test Board.
Publisher: Program administered for the Secondary School Admission Test Board by Educational Testing Service.
Cross References: See T3:2118; for additional information, see 8:478; see also 7:24 (1 reference); for

reviews by Charles O. Neidt and David V. Tiedeman of earlier forms, see 6:24 (1 reference).

Review of the Secondary School Admission Test by JAMES B. ERDMANN, Associate Dean, Jefferson Medical College, Thomas Jefferson University, Philadelphia, PA:

The Secondary School Admission Test (SSAT) is a test developed and administered in the best classical tradition. Therein, perhaps, lie both its major strength and weakness. Technically, it meets most of the usual requirements and satisfies the standards of the profession. The SSAT is professionally prepared and offered and if certain updating is performed, the test and its supporting materials should withstand the critical review of the test professional as well as meet the needs of the independent school admission process.

On the other hand, the test specifications address a relatively narrow range of skills pertinent to the kind of instruction that has become more common in the independent school system. More of the schools in this system have modified curricula to emphasize the development of a broader range of cognitive skills and have explicitly identified competencies which become the guideposts for instructional development and student evaluation. These programs have been characterized as emphasizing traits such as self-directed learning, self-assessment skills, critical thinking and judgment, and the like. These innovations are seen in contrast to more traditional programs that focus on the accumulation of knowledge and an increased refinement of the understanding of the elements of such a body of information and their interrelationships. Such nuances and distinctions in meaning are amenable to relatively straightforward assessment in the traditional sense of the standardized "objective" examination and thus a whole generation of tests leaned heavily on sophistication in vocabulary (i.e., synonyms, antonyms, and verbal analogies). Fortunately for the industry, this sophistication in language or verbal fluency was highly correlated with a general competency factor and was thus an effective predictor because of that general relationship and because many programs of instruction stopped short of offering experiences beyond that point. However, given an apparent trend toward curricular goals that are more diversified, cover a broader range of competencies, and are evaluated in increasingly nontraditional ways, it seems appropriate for the test sponsors to take several steps. First, the validity studies that served as the general basis justifying use of the test should be repeated. These data are already over 10 years old and if the kind of changes discussed previously are real, some real differences in validity coefficients would likely emerge with significant implications for the test's specifications. A revised validity study should obviously look at

curricular differences and attempt to define major curricular models for which it is practical to develop validity data and at least determine whether different regression weights should be associated with the different models. This may not be such a major undertaking if a sufficient number of independent schools have utilized the SSAT Validity Studies Service offered by the contractor.

The preceding comments focused on the verbal section of the test but comparable criticisms pertain to the reading comprehension and quantitative sections of the test. Both of these focus heavily on a basic vocabulary and similarly rely on relatively passive manipulation of information rather than require a rather active organization, structuring, evaluation, and judgment concerning presented information. These comments are most decidedly not meant to lead to the abandonment of the traditional test of scholastic aptitude but rather to emphasize the importance of broadening the definition of those skills which are important for continuing learning and later life.

TECHNICAL CHARACTERISTICS. The reported measures of reliability and validity (assuming resolution of the preceding issue) are certainly at acceptable levels if not at the upper bounds for admissions tests. However, aside from a comment that test questions are reviewed for possible content bias, no information is provided bearing on the presence of subgroup bias using data derived from examinee performance. Based on the sizeable number of minority examinees (reported to be about 15%) and given the direction that standards for acceptable practice are moving, data of this kind should be developed and reported. Related to this issue is the absence of norms for racial/ethnic subgroups. Such an absence is very difficult to defend given the evidence which suggests that different criteria should be weighed in the admission of different categories of applicants.

The Interpretive Guide provides some very valuable information and should be of considerable interest to the test user; however, it is not at all clear why the topic of "Comparisons of Individual Performance" is relegated to the Appendix. It is not that supporting data are presented in the Appendix, but rather that the topic is addressed only there. If the test is to serve its primary purpose, namely, a common standard of comparison for all applicants, comparisons of scores of different candidates is of paramount importance. Accordingly, the limitations and cautions in that use of scores should be a major topic of the Guide and could benefit from greater elaboration and specificity. For example, to communicate the risk associated with concluding that small differences in scores are meaningful and to demonstrate how misleading reported differences might be, it could be pointed out that even if one is prepared to make a mistake one out of every five times, one has to require a difference of at least 12 points for grade 11 students before making a judgment that two scores are different. Such a difference at the middle of the distribution (e.g., between 310 and 322) represents a percentile rank difference of some 26 percentage points (i.e., between a percentile rank of about 41 and 67). Acknowledgement of such fallibility of test score comparisons and the corresponding precautions in their interpretation is the responsibility of the test sponsor and/or contractor to foster.

It would also be important to include in the Guide some rationale for the Total Score as presently calculated. For example, test users should be told the reasons that a single index does not include reading comprehension, the implications of using the Total Score as the sole index, and the conceptual justification for the Verbal component being given more weight in the Total Score.

The Bulletin of Information is very comprehensive, well presented, and well indexed. The sequence of topics seems more suited to the interests of test administration than to the examinee; however, this is a small matter. The description of the test is a little sparse and the implications of the scoring system for guessing behavior would seem to deserve to be highlighted. Some reference to the sources for specific reliability and validity data would also be an improvement.

The Supervisor Manual is extremely well done. The experience of the test contractor is evident in the presentation of the instructions to the chief proctors.

Finally, the practice test materials seem to be a worthwhile offering, especially the helpful suggestions regarding test-taking strategies for each of the testing formats.

SUMMARY. The SSAT is obviously a professional program with very strong psychometric credentials, especially from the perspective of the historically proven approach to admissions testing. Some suggested program improvements include an updating of the validity studies, attention to potential bias in subgroup performance, the preparation of special norms for pertinent subgroups, and more emphasis on the precautions that need to be taken in interpreting differences in scores among candidates. Because the scoring system contributes to the hazards of overinterpreting small differences, consideration may be given to developing a new scale involving fewer distinctions among examinees and thus reducing the risk of judging meaningless differences to be meaningful. In general, therefore, a high degree of confidence can be placed in the results of this test by test score recipients but more can and should be done to assist the user in the proper interpretation of scores and their appropriate weighting in the full range of variables relevant to the admissions process.

Review of the Secondary School Admission Test by ANTHONY J. NITKO, *Professor of Education, University of Pittsburgh, Pittsburgh, PA:*

The primary purpose of the Secondary School Admission Test (SSAT) is to facilitate the selection of children for admission to grades 6 through 11 in selective independent schools. The SSAT appears to be a children's version of the Scholastic Aptitude Test (SAT; 343). One is struck by the similarity of the two, not only in the format of their items, but also in the ways in which the programs are described to parents and children, in the registration and score-reporting procedures, and in the practice and interpretive materials.

The publisher is to be commended for pointing out to school officials early in the Interpretive Guide that the SSAT should not be the sole criterion for admission: "The student's curriculum, grades, teachers' recommendations and personal recommendations, standardized test results, writing sample, and interview should all be considered during decision making" (p. 2). Like the SAT, the SSAT items represent an excessively narrow sample of the kinds of knowledge, skills, and abilities that children ought to be developing in school. Given the ready availability in a child's admission dossier of the seven types of relevant educational development information described in the preceding quotation, and given the child's young age, one wonders whether the SSAT has outlived its usefulness. The Secondary School Admission Test Board (SSATB) may wish to undertake studies on how to obtain for each youngster an admissions portfolio that includes broader-band indicators for "determining the appropriateness of a particular school" (p. 2) for the child.

The Interpretive Guide summarizes a 1978–79 correlational study of 21 SSATB schools. SSAT scores in eighth grade were correlated with ninth grade English and Mathematics grades and with the GPA for academic subjects. Data are reported for the six largest schools ($N = 63$ through 115) and for a pooled group of 1,182 children. For the school official wanting to use the SSAT, the six schools' correlations, although not representative of the 21 schools' correlations, are more informative than the pooled data for the 1,182 children. The data for these six schools illustrate how widely the predictive validities of the SSAT vary from one school to the next. For example, correlations of Reading scores with English/Literature grades range from .14 to .63 and of Quantitative scores with mathematics grades from .07 to .56. Thus, one cannot assume that in their school the SSAT will correlate even moderately with grades.

The publisher wisely recommends that each school conduct its own predictive validity study. In my view, such validity studies are necessary, rather than optional. Further, such studies should include data from each of the previously mentioned seven types of relevant information. A school's validity studies should be oriented toward ascertaining the incremental contribution of the SSAT scores to predicting school success criteria (see below). The publisher sells such validity services; also, there may be staff members in a school capable of conducting such studies on a microcomputer. A school now using the SSAT should not continue to use it (or other admission data for that matter) without supporting the use with validation studies.

The multiple correlation data reported in the Interpretive Guide may be misunderstood by school officials. The data reported are the multiple-regression weights of the SSAT Reading, Verbal, and Quantitative scores and the multiple correlation coefficients for predicting English grades, mathematics grades, and academic subject GPA. The analyses include SSAT subscores, but include none of the other types of admission data recommended in the Guide for decision making. As a result, the incremental contribution of the SSAT to the predictive validity of other available admission data such as previous GPA, standardized achievement test scores, ratings on a writing sample, ratings by former teachers, and ratings by an interviewer cannot be determined. It may be that the SSAT adds very little to predicting success in school once other variables have been considered.

The SSAT percentile ranks help to interpret the scores, but they are not meant to be national norms. The comparison group consists of everyone who took the SSAT during the largest administrations from 1984–1987. Separate percentile ranks are provided for boys and for girls within each grade level. Local norms are more useful than these, and an appendix of the Interpretive Guide tells how they can be constructed.

Depending on the grade level and subtest, boys score from 1 to 5 scaled score points higher than girls at the elementary level, except for Reading where they are within 1 point of each other. At the high school level, boys and girls are within about 5 points of each other in Reading, Verbal, and Quantitative subtests. Data are not provided on the performance of minority children, who constitute about 15% of the test takers.

Internal consistency reliabilities are in the .80s and .90s; the standard errors of measurement (SEMs) are between 6 and 7 scaled score points for the subscores and 4 to 5 points for the Total. The standard errors of difference scores are approximately 1.4 times larger than the SEMs. Thus, counselors and admissions officers should exercise extra caution when interpreting profiles (e.g., Verbal vs. Quantitative) or differences between students (e.g., Sally's

score vs. Billy's score). An appendix in the Interpretive Guide gives clear and easy-to-follow explanations for how to interpret difference scores.

SUMMARY. The SSAT is a technically well-developed test measuring a very narrow range of the knowledge, skills, and abilities children must learn in school. The SSAT must not be used as the primary criterion for admission to selective independent schools. Schools using the SSAT have a serious obligation to conduct local validity studies showing the extent to which the SSAT improves predictive validity over combinations of several other types of data available in a child's admission dossier.

[353]
Self-Awareness Profile.
Purpose: "This self-assessment provides insight into the basic personality attributes that influence the way we behave."
Population: Industry.
Publication Dates: 1980–87.
Scores, 4: Dominance, Influence, Conformity, Evenness.
Administration: Individual or group.
Price Data, 1988: $80 per 20 complete sets including 16-item inventory ('80, 4 pages), interpretation sheet ('86, 4 pages), planning sheet ('87, 4 pages), and 10 profiles for each set.
Time: (80–100) minutes.
Author: Scott B. Parry.
Publisher: Training House, Inc.

Review of the Self-Awareness Profile by TIMOTHY M. OSBERG, Professor of Psychology, Niagara University, Niagara University, NY:

The Self-Awareness Profile (SAP) is designed to assist individuals to better understand "how they respond to situations and people, and how this relates to their effectiveness at work." It consists of four parts (some of which are optional) and may be administered individually or in groups. The first part of the SAP involves having the respondent choose, from among 10 descriptions of prototypic employees, the one or two that are most self-descriptive. These descriptions vary in the combination of four trait dimensions assessed by the SAP: Dominance, Influence, Conformity, and Evenness. Although the first three are relatively familiar trait dimensions, Evenness is defined as the "desire to perform at a steady pace and maintain harmony."

In the second part of the SAP, respondents are presented with 16 sets of four trait terms. Respondents then rank order the four traits within each set in terms of their self-descriptiveness using a 1–4 rating scale. Unknown to the subject, each of the four trait terms corresponds to one of the four trait dimensions. After self-scoring their responses, the last two parts of the SAP involve having respondents: (a) judge which trait dimensions are best suited for several occupations and (b) respond to several open-ended questions that assess their reactions to the feedback they received from scoring the earlier parts of the SAP.

As a whole, the four parts of the SAP are probably better considered an exercise rather than a psychological test. The single sheet of instructor guidelines that accompanies the test (there is no manual) refers to the SAP as an exercise, although the second part involving ranking of sets of trait terms is parenthetically labelled as the "test." Employers and others may mistakenly believe it to be a standardized test, however.

A closer assessment of the SAP suggests that the publisher avoids calling it a test for good reason. The SAP appears to resemble more a game than a standardized psychological test. In many ways it is reminiscent of the type of "rate yourself" tests that are commonly published in newspapers and magazines. The second part of the SAP most closely resembles the structure of a test. It is set up in a very clever manner so that it allows the respondents to record their ratings for the 16 sets of trait terms and then score them in an efficient manner. I believe many respondents would be engaged by the process. However, the lack of a manual leaves many questions concerning the technical aspects of the SAP. No norms, reliability, or validity data are presented.

The self-scoring for the four trait dimensions is particularly primitive. Respondents are asked simply to total their ratings in the four columns of the response sheet to obtain their four trait scores. The respondent then forms a self-assessment of whether he or she is high or low on each dimension by determining how much each score deviates from a score of 40 (which would be a rough estimate of an "average" score if the test's total possible 160 points were equally distributed across the four dimensions). No actual norms are presented, however. In addition, the theoretical basis for choosing to focus on the trait dimensions of Dominance, Influence, Conformity, and Evenness as they relate to adjustment to the work setting (other than that they form the acronym, DICE), and not some other combination of trait dimensions, is unclear. The theoretical basis for selecting the 64 traits to tap these dimensions is similarly left unspecified.

Other aspects of the SAP are problematic. When respondents compute their scores for the four traits, they are then presented lengthy descriptions of each dimension. However, these descriptions are stated so generally that they read like horoscopes. The descriptions of the last two dimensions (Conformity and Evenness), in particular, are hard to differentiate.

In summary, the limitations of the SAP far outweigh its strengths. Its derivation appears not to have been based on any explicitly presented theory. In addition, there is no information available to evaluate its psychometric properties. If the SAP's technical merits could be demonstrated, it might provide a useful workshop device to be presented in work settings. However, at present it would be unwise for employers or others to assume it is a valid indicator of the dimensions it purports to assess. For those interested in assessing personality dimensions such as those tapped by the SAP, I would recommend such standards in the field as Jackson's Personality Research Form (10:282) or Gough's California Psychological Inventory (54).

[354]

Self-Esteem Index.

Purpose: "Designed to elicit children's perceptions of their personal traits and characteristics."
Population: Ages 7-0 to 18-11.
Publication Dates: 1990–91.
Acronym: SEI.
Scores, 5: Familial Acceptance, Academic Competence, Peer Popularity, Personal Security, Self-Esteem Quotient.
Administration: Group.
Price Data, 1991: $69 per complete kit including 50 student response booklets, 50 profile/record forms, and manual ('91, 51 pages); $24 per 50 student response booklets; $24 per 50 profile/record forms; $24 per manual.
Time: (30–35) minutes.
Authors: Linda Brown and Jacquelyn Alexander.
Publisher: PRO-ED, Inc.

Review of the Self-Esteem Index by E. SCOTT HUEBNER, Assistant Professor of Psychology, University of South Carolina, Columbia, SC:

The Self-Esteem Index (SEI) is an 80-item, self-report instrument designed to provide a "reliable, valid, and theoretically sound norm-referenced measure of self-esteem in school-aged children and adolescents" (manual, p. 1). Based on a multidimensional model of self-esteem, the SEI consists of four 20-item scales: Perception of Familial Acceptance, Perception of Academic Competence, Perception of Peer Popularity, and Perception of Personal Security. An estimate of global or general self-esteem, the Self-Esteem Quotient (SEQ), is also provided. This score is derived by summing the responses to all SEI test items.

The test is user friendly. The test manual is clearly written. Administration and scoring procedures are simple and described adequately. Scale raw scores can be converted to percentile ranks and standard scores with a mean of 10 and a standard deviation of 3. The SEQ can be expressed as a percentile rank or standard score with a mean of 100 and a standard deviation of 15. The author provides a nice section describing the strengths and weaknesses of the various derived scores. This section could go a long way toward preventing common misinterpretations of test scores.

Extensive item analysis and standardization information are provided in the manual. Standardization was conducted in 1988 and 1989 on 2,455 students from between 8-0 years and 18-11 years from 19 states. The sample size exceeded 100 students in each of the 11 age groups. The demographic characteristics of the sample compare favorably to comparative statistics for the United States population with respect to gender, race, domicile, geographic region, ethnicity, and parental educational attainment. The only unfavorable comparison involved students who came from families in which English was the primary language in the home versus students who came from families in which English was not the primary language (2.5% in SEI sample versus 11.4% in U.S. population). Overall, the standardization data are excellent, surpassing those of other commonly used children's self-esteem instruments.

Reliability data include only internal consistency estimates, along with the standard error of measurement. Alpha coefficients are reported for the scale scores and SEQ for each of the 11 age levels. The alphas are acceptable, mostly falling in the .80s and .90s throughout the age range. At age 8, the scale alphas range from .73 on Peer Popularity to .78 on Personal Security (and .87 for the SEQ), suggesting that the user should interpret scores at this age level with increased caution.

Much to this reviewer's disappointment, test-retest data are not available for scale or SEQ scores. Such information could provide the user with crucial additional information about the meaningfulness of children's responses to SEI items.

Validity data are promising but far too sparse to support the clinical or research usefulness of the SEI. Several problems with the validation data bear highlighting. First, although there is an extensive discussion of the problems of dissemblance (e.g., socially desirable responses) on self-report scales, no empirical data are provided with regard to this matter. For example, demonstrating a nonsignificant relationship between SEI scores and a children's social desirability scale would increase support for the construct validity of the instrument. Second, concurrent validation studies demonstrate promising correlations with other self-esteem measures (i.e., Piers-Harris Children's Self-Concept Scale—Revised, Coopersmith Self-Esteem Inventory—School Form [SEI-SF]), and another theorically related measure (i.e., Index of Personality Characteristics); however, all of the studies included less than 30 students from severely restricted age ranges. Similarly, the data presented on the ability of the SEI to discriminate between emotionally disturbed, learning disabled, gifted, and nonhandicapped behavior-disordered children were based on unacceptable sample sizes (e.g., 16 emotionally disturbed students). Third, much additional validation work is needed to support the use of scale level scores.

Although preliminary factor analytic data support the multidimensionality of the scale, the correlations between SEI scales and criterion measures are unacceptable in several instances (e.g., .04 between SEI Academic Competence and SEI-SF School-Academics; .29 between SEI Peer Popularity and Piers-Harris Popularity) thereby reducing the interpretability of the separate scales.

In sum, the SEI shows substantial potential, but the potential remains to be demonstrated. Much additional work needs to be done before it can be considered reliable, valid, or theoretically sound. Because of the outstanding standardization work, I hope that such research will be conducted. Until then, I recommend the Piers-Harris (9:960) or the Coopersmith SEI-SF (9:267), both of which have received far more empirical support through numerous research studies.

Review of the Self-Esteem Index by RALPH O. MUELLER, Assistant Professor of Educational Research and Management, and PAULA J. DUPUY, Assistant Professor of Counselor and Human Services Education, University of Toledo, Toledo, OH:

The Self-Esteem Index (SEI) is a norm-referenced, self-report instrument designed to measure children's (8-0 years through 18-11 years) perceptions of their personal traits and characteristics (self-esteem). The instrument's intended uses include: (*a*) identification of students with self-esteem, behavior, emotional, or adjustment problems; (*b*) verification of referrals; and (*c*) generation of specific goals for further evaluation and/or interventions. Specifically, the SEI consists of 80 items, each scored on a 4-point Likert-type scale, that are combined into an overall standardized Self-Esteem Quotient and four subscales: Perception of Familial Acceptance, Academic Competence, Peer Popularity, and Personal Security. SEI evaluations are reported on a well-organized profile form that includes personal information, raw and normative SEI results, results from other test evaluations, a graphic display of normative SEI and other test scores, and specific administration conditions.

The test user will appreciate the complete and well-written manual that contains all pertinent information regarding the rationale, construction, administration, scoring, interpretation, and psychometric characteristics of the SEI. Most notably, the authors give operational definitions of all important terms and provide justifications and detailed descriptions of procedures that were used to investigate the psychometric properties of the instrument.

For normative purposes, data from 2,455 students in 19 states were collected between October 1988 and October 1989. The authors give a complete demographic description of the sample (gender, domicile, race, geographic area, ethnicity, principal language, parents' education, age) and show its representativeness of the U.S. population by providing comparative national statistics. Suitable tables to convert SEI raw scores into overall deviation quotients (Self-Esteem Quotient, $M = 100$, $SD = 15$), standard scores ($M = 10$, $SD = 3$), and percentile ranks are provided in the manual. Due to the absence of any significant gender or age differences on SEI scales, multiple tables were not required. It should be noted, however, that possible race differences were not investigated.

We concur with the authors' statement that the test user should interpret results in the validity and reliability section of the manual as initial and preliminary evidence of strong psychometric properties of the SEI. Insufficiently described, small validation samples lead to uncertainties about the population(s) from which the samples were drawn and make it difficult to generalize reported results.

Content validity was established by a careful item selection process, including consulting relevant literature and knowledgeable professionals and reviewing related appraisal tools. Appropriate item discrimination coefficients (between .30 and .80) and factor analysis results (varimax rotation), both based on $N = 550$ students, provide evidence of the construct validity of the instrument. The authors report various correlational studies (N between 23 and 105) relating the SEI to other measures of self-esteem/self-concept and personality as evidence of concurrent validity. Mostly moderate correlations were found between the SEI scales and (a) teacher evaluations of self-esteem (r between .21 and .44); (b) the Piers-Harris Children's Self-Concept Scale—Revised (r between .29 and .77); (c) the Self-Esteem Inventories—School Form (r between .01 and .93); and (d) the Index of Personality Characteristics (r between .10 and .96). Initial indications that the SEI can distinguish between groups of handicapped (emotionally disturbed [$N = 16$], behavior disordered [$N = 18$], learning disabled [$N = 64$]), and intellectually gifted students [$N = 19$] provided additional validity evidence. Finally, alpha coefficients, generally above .80 at each of 11 one-year age intervals ($N = 550$), indicate adequate internal consistency reliability of the SEI. Stability coefficients are not reported.

SUMMARY. In our opinion, the SEI is a useful addition to the existing array of self-esteem measures in most areas of intended use (identification of children with self-esteem problems, verification of referrals, and generation of intervention goals). The norming data, collected from a representative sample of the general U.S. population, give the test user a solid foundation for interpreting most SEI results. Overall, the authors' goal to develop a psychometrically sound instrument appears to have been accomplished.

Our two concerns with the SEI are similar to those usually found with newly published instruments. First, the appropriate use of the SEI with special populations has not been well established. Specifically, the authors' suggestion that the SEI can identify/differentiate between groups of handicapped children should be taken with caution due to small samples. Second, although initial evidence of the validity and reliability is strong, additional studies based on larger and more representative samples are needed to substantiate the test's psychometric properties.

[355]
Self-Motivated Career Planning.
Purpose: To help the individual develop vocational objectives through self-administered exercises.
Population: High school and college and adults.
Publication Dates: 1949–84.
Acronym: S-MCP.
Scores: 7 pencil/paper exercises (Personal Orientation Survey, Education Summary, Career Experience Summary, Personal Career Life Summary, Career Strengths and Interests, Next Career Steps, Personal Development Summary) plus a 16PF personality assessment and interpretive report (Personal/Career Development Profile).
Administration: Group.
Price Data, 1988: $32.25 per complete kit including manual ('84, 126 pages), Personal Career Development Profile manual, and scoring service of the Personal Career Development Profile by the publisher.
Time: (50–120) minutes per exercise.
Authors: Verne Walter and Melvin Wallace.
Publisher: Institute for Personality and Ability Testing, Inc.
Cross References: For reviews by Robert H. Dolliver and Kevin W. Mossholder of an earlier edition, see 9:1099.

Review of Self-Motivated Career Planning by LARRY COCHRAN, Professor of Counselling Psychology, The University of British Columbia, Vancouver, BC, Canada:

Self-Motivated Career Planning (SMCP) is a workbook that is intended to guide a person through four major steps: developing an understanding of oneself in relation to occupations, making a career plan, putting a plan into action, and reviewing career progress. Through completing these steps well, the aim is to help people to achieve what they want most in a career. The workbook includes paper-and-pencil exercises, the Sixteen Personality Factor Questionnaire (16PF) (which is machine scored and returned with a personality description and a list of occupational possibilities), recommendations (such as consulting a career counselor), and detailed instructions.

Self-understanding is cultivated through a sentence completion test called the Personal Orientation Survey, short-answer questions (such as in what areas of school did one perform best and worst), and summaries of educational and occupational accomplishments. Career planning is forwarded by first reviewing the strengths and options provided by the 16PF, summarizing possible directions and one's eligibility for pursuing these directions. Next, by reviewing the results of self-understanding exercises and the 16PF, the person attempts to translate and integrate previous work into concise statements of growth needs, career goals, and action plans. Last, it is recommended that the person consult a counselor or someone who could act in that capacity to check the realism and accuracy of self-assessment and planning. Putting one's plan into action is really a chapter of instructions and exercises on how to organize and conduct a successful job search. The final chapter on reviewing career progress simply advocates periodic review and provides reasons for doing so.

The workbook is reasonably clear and upbeat. It provides opportunities not only to enhance self-awareness, but also to integrate or at least compare the results of various exercises. The exercises show purposeful movement and meaningful connections, beginning with self-understanding and moving toward an occupational specification and search. There is stress upon different sources of evidence and information, and upon convergence to support conclusions, much like triangulation is used in case study research. Although these strong points of the workbook seem promising, there are also a number of weak points or at least areas that seem questionable.

It is unclear for whom the workbook is intended. There are many indirect indications that it is to be used by employed adults in organizational settings, but this should be specified clearly.

There are numerous unsupported claims. Within the workbook, for example, there is the exceedingly optimistic statement that "you now have accurate information about how well your skills match the job market" (p. 41). Rewards for doing the program tend to be glowing, unqualified, and unsupported: "Many people achieve greater control over their futures . . . Confusion about which career path to follow disappears" (p. iv). The order form for the workbook claims that the program takes people through a "tested step-by-step examination of career-relevant experiences, goals, and ambitions." These claims imply that empirical studies have been conducted in developing the workbook and to test its effects, yet, I am not aware of any studies and none were cited.

The philosophy advocated throughout the program is self-realization. Although this view is certainly legitimate and desirable in many ways, it is worth questioning whether it applies very well to current forms of work, which are often trivial,

fragmented, repetitious, and compromising. Several researchers have demonstrated the alienating character of many job situations, suggesting that self-realization is apt to be a misguided expectation in work for a large number of people.

The authors state that the SMCP "is not a self-counseling tool" (p. iv) and that most everything one does "takes place with the help of a professional" (p. iv), but the workbook specifies only one 60-minute interview with a career counselor at the end of making a career plan. It seems unlikely that a trained career counselor would accept such a short involvement—such a reduced role. In a one-shot session, would a counselor really be able to check the accuracy of a person's self-image and plans? And if a counselor were involved early, would he or she want to be bound to the SMCP in place of the wide array of other career counseling possibilities?

What the SMCP most needs is evidence of effectiveness. Does the workbook produce the benefits claimed such as enhanced control over one's future? Are people willing to complete the work or to complete it thoroughly and thoughtfully? Are people capable of interpreting their own responses to sentence completions? Is the 16PF a reliable and valid instrument for the intended use of career guidance or how does it compare with more standard instruments such as the Strong Interest Inventory? At the present time, the most basic kinds of evidence that would allow one to recommend the SMCP are lacking, leaving a host of questions and no answers at all.

Review of Self-Motivated Career Planning by SAMUEL JUNI, Professor of Applied Psychology, New York University, New York, NY:

As described in the earlier reviews (9:1099) the Self-Motivated Career Planning (SMCP) provides an individual with a series of exercises that are then to be interpreted with the help of a counselor. The Sixteen Personality Factor Questionnaire (16PF) is used to generate a narrative about career planning, but the details of this process are not given in the manual. The actual interpretation of the exercises is quite subjective, with no hint of reliability or interpretative validity. Norms are not even salient to the procedure.

There is also no evidence of any theory upon which this procedure is based. Indeed, much of the procedure may well be a systematic elucidation of common-sense guidelines. The manual wanders off eventually into giving resumé writing guidelines, advice about seeking employment, pep talks about interview behavior, and lectures about the employment field.

The SMCP is neither a mental measurement nor a test, and does not belong in the *Mental Measurements Yearbook*.

Self-Perception Inventory: Nursing Forms.

Purpose: "The primary purpose of the SPI is research."
Population: Student nurses and professional staff.
Publication Dates: 1967–85.
Acronym: SPI.
Scores: 7 scales: Self-Concept, Self-Concept/Nurse, Ideal Concept/Nurse, Reflected Self/Supervisors, Nurse-Rating Scale/Students, Nurse-Rating Scale/Professionals, Nurse-Rating Scale/Patient.
Administration: Group.
Price Data, 1989: $.40 per scale sheet; $.25 per answer sheet; $10 per test manual ('85, 41 pages).
Time: (5–20) minutes per scale.
Authors: Anthony T. Soares and Louise M. Soares.
Publisher: SOARES Associates.
Cross References: For additional information on other forms and a review by Janet Morgan Riggs of other forms, see 9:1101 (2 references); see also T3:2139 (1 reference); for a review by Lorrie Shepard of other forms, see 8:673 (2 references).

Review of the Self-Perception Inventory: Nursing Forms by GERALD E. DEMAURO, Senior Examiner, Educational Testing Service, Princeton, NJ:

The Self-Perception Inventory (SPI): Nursing Forms are extensions of earlier self-perception inventories designed by Anthony and Louise Soares. The instruments are designed primarily as research tools, with possible other uses. Each form takes from 5–20 minutes to administer, taking up to 80 minutes to complete the four forms required of a respondent. All forms are designed to assess the respondent's perception of self, including self as reflected in the perceptions and behaviors of others. Specifically, the SPI Nursing Forms require each respondent to rate himself or herself as a person (SC), as a nurse (SC/N), as reflected in supervisors' views (RS/sup), and as the kind of nurse the respondent would ideally like to be (IC). Forms are also available to enable two significant others (e.g., supervisors, patients, or professional colleagues) to rate the respondent.

Three of the four forms include 38 pairs of bipolar adjectives. The Self-Concept as a person (SC) Form contains 37 adjective pairs. Respondents are to describe themselves as being like one or the other adjective on a 4-point continuum. Response choices include two extreme values (e.g., "very" like) and two intermediate values (e.g., more like). Two or three blanks are left on each form for respondents to evaluate themselves on up to a total of 40 dimensions they think are important for effective nurses. The SPI Self-Concept as Nurse (SC/N), Ideal Concept (IC), reflected supervisors' views of self (RS/sup), and ratings of significant others present the same 38 adjective pairs, or dimensions. The Self-Concept as a person (SC) shares 10 of these dimensions and a number of other dimensions in which at least one adjective is the same, or one or both are synonymous with adjectives that describe dimensions of the other forms.

DEVELOPMENT. The Nursing Forms were developed using earlier work on Teacher Forms. The Teacher Forms used expert judgment and a literature review to develop traits related to teacher effectiveness. Experts in nursing, including nurses, nursing teachers, nurse and hospital supervisors, and student nurses, were asked to contribute traits related to nursing or to review the Teacher Forms. Two additional pairs, not found on the Teacher Forms, were added. The manual provides no further detail about the number of experts used, the methods employed to gather their judgments, or the criteria used to decide which adjective pairs would be included on the Nursing Forms and which would be rejected.

NORMS AND STANDARDS. Each item can be scored in a range from +2 for very positive to -2 for very negative. There is no 0 or middle point. Means and standard deviations are provided on the Self-Concept (SC), Self-Concept as Nurse (SC/N), Reflected Self/supervisor (RS/sup), and Ideal Concept as Nurse (IC) for undergraduate nursing students ($n = 106$), students in a hospital R.N. program ($n = 55$), and nurses in urban hospitals ($n = 249$). Other statistics labeled "S.E." are provided that do not appear to be either standard errors of measurement or standard errors of the mean given the reported sample sizes and reliabilities. More information in the manual about how these three groups were sampled and how well they represent potential inventory respondents would help users evaluate the utility of the descriptive information derived from these groups. Based on the total group of 410, stanines are presented for raw scores on each form.

Suggestions are made for interpreting responses including discrepancies between total form scores for individuals, means of absolute difference values on comparable dimensions across forms, and comparisons of single dimensions from form to form. Instructions are also given for plotting stanines for each form. A consideration should be given to providing distributions of total form discrepancy scores, dimension differences, and profiles, and to providing information about the psychometric characteristics of these in the manual to assist inventory users in interpreting observed scoring patterns.

RELIABILITY AND VALIDITY. Test-retest data for 6-week intervals for the four forms ranged from .89 to .94. Sample sizes are not cited in the manual. An internal consistency coefficient of .83 is cited, but it is not clear how this is estimated.

The manual presents validity information in the form of correlations with various criterion measures. The correlation of the SC/N form with on-the-job success (.43) is quite respectable. Other reported correlations for the SC/N are .56 with program effectiveness, .52 with internship competence, and .49 with supervisors' ratings. Other correlations with program effectiveness are .54, .48, and .49 with the SC, RS/sup, and IC forms, respectively. A description in the manual of how the criterion variables were measured would greatly assist potential users in their evaluations of these data. The SC form has a reported correlation of -.72 with the MMPI Introversion-Extroversion scale. Intercorrelations among forms (.54 to .77) suggest modest discriminant properties of the forms. Criterion-related validity is given as .63 and construct validity as .61 in the manual without further explanation.

CONCERNS. The major concern is about the interpretation of scores. Data to help interpret discrepancies in total scores among the forms, differences in single dimension scores, or respondent profiles would be most useful in the manual. Also, differences from form to form in the ratings given to the same dimension may be difficult to interpret because dimensions have no middle ratings, leaving a gap in possible difference scores. The authors present possible meanings of moderate, high, and low levels of Self-Concept (SC), Ideal Concept (IC), and Reflected Self (RS/sup); however, these same observed levels may have different interpretations. The different possible meanings of extreme scores on the forms can obscure the interpretation of mean differences and correlation coefficients.

These considerations would diminish the value of the forms for such uses as clinical identification. The research potential of the forms is greater. Other measures could help define the characteristics of respondents in different score ranges or with different profiles.

Review of the Self-Perception Inventory: Nursing Forms by MICHAEL R. HARWELL, Assistant Professor of Psychology and Education, University of Pittsburgh, Pittsburgh, PA:

The Self-Perception Inventory (SPI): Nursing Forms purports to assess self-concept and a respondent's perception of how others view the respondent. It is the fourth form of the SPI, the others involving students, adults, and teachers. The manual states that "The scales are particularly helpful in nurses' training programs and seem to have good predictability." There are several scales within a form: how the individual sees self as a person (Self-Concept), how the individual sees self as a nurse (Self-Concept/Nurse), what kind of nurse the individual would like to be (Ideal Concept/Nurse), how the nurse believes the supervisor sees the respondent as a nurse (Reflected Self/Supervisor), how the supervisor views the student nurse (Nurse-Rating/Students), and how others view the trained nurse in practice (Nurse-Rating/Professionals). The scale items are of the semantic-differential variety,

requiring respondents to indicate their feeling about paired traits using a 4-point forced-choice format. The adjective pairs are identical for all scales except Self-Concept. An especially appealing feature of the SPI is that actual and idealized responses can be compared.

USABILITY. This is the strongest feature of the SPI Nursing Forms. First-time users can expect little difficulty in learning to administer the inventory. Respondents likewise should have little trouble following directions. The instructions state that the person administering the inventory can respond to questions about particular items, but no guidelines are provided for how administrators should respond. Perhaps the experience of the authors of the test is that structured guidelines are not needed; if so, it would be helpful if this was stated in the manual. Another strength of this inventory is the theoretical rationale and guidelines for interpreting patterns of scale scores provided by the authors. Users are cautioned against overinterpreting the results or ascribing too much weight to scale scores.

SCORING. The scoring system for the SPI Nursing Form is easy to use and understand. Each item is scored "+2," "+1," "-1," or "-2," with the maximum range for a summative score being -76 to +76. The authors provide a conversion table that makes it easy to convert SPI scale scores to stanines and to develop a profile for each respondent or group of respondents. The authors suggest three ways of using the scores. One is to create discrepancy or difference scores in which, for example, a respondent's score on the Self-Concept/Nurse scale might be subtracted from their score on the Ideal Concept/Nurse scale. As pointed out in an earlier review of the SPI (Shepard, 1978), this strategy may mask important differences in response patterns. For example, suppose that a respondent received a +2 for each item on the Self-Concept/Nurse scale and a -2 for each item on the Ideal Concept/Nurse scale. The mean discrepancy score would be zero, suggesting no difference between actual and ideal self-concept and ignoring varying and potentially important patterns of responses. The authors also suggest calculating the average of the absolute value of the difference between paired items across scales. This method is less likely to mask key trends in the responses. Finally, the authors suggest calculating discrepancy scores for paired items across scales. This method has little merit because of the likely instability of information provided by one pair of items.

NORMS. Normative information is reported for three groups: undergraduate nursing students ($N = 106$), student nurses enrolled in a hospital R.N. program ($N = 55$), and trained nurses in urban hospitals ($N = 249$). Little information about the samples is reported, leaving several important questions unanswered. Are these respondents from the same geographic area? Are all respondents from an urban setting? Are all respondents female? Are the respondents volunteers? At the top of the answer sheet for several of the scales is a place for the respondents to place their age, but no normative information about age is provided. Does this mean that age of respondent and self-concept scores as measured by the SPI are uncorrelated? Also, it is not clear whether the three groups should differ from one another in key ways (e.g., in Self-Concept scores) or whether this has been investigated empirically. Finally, it is not clear whether all three of the normative groups or some subset were used to generate the table for converting raw scores to stanines. The absence of documentation that addresses questions of this nature suggests that the normative data are of limited usefulness.

RELIABILITY. The test-retest (6 weeks) reliability coefficients for the four reported scales are high (Self-Concept, Self-Concept/Nurse, Ideal Concept/Nurse, Reflected Self/Supervisor), ranging from .89 to .94. A single internal consistency value of .83 is reported, but it is not clear to which scale this applies or what sample size was used in calculating internal consistency. The absence of information about the reliability of discrepancy scores is a serious omission because such scores are typically unreliable.

VALIDITY. The manual reports criterion (.63) and construct (.61) validity coefficients, but it is not clear which scales these coefficients apply to, what the criterion was, or how construct validity was assessed. Other reported evidence of validity is based on the correlation of the Self-Concept scale with the Social Introversion-Extroversion scale of the Minnesota Multiphasic Inventory (-.72), Self-Concept/Nurse Scale with ratings of internship competence (.52), Self-Concept/Nurse Scale with on-the-job success (.43, although it is not clear how on-the-job success is measured), Self-Concept/Nurse Scale with supervisor ratings (.49), and SPI scale scores with an unexplained, mysterious variable called "perceptions of program effectiveness." The sample size used in calculating these correlations is not reported, but it is likely that each correlation is statistically significant. A more useful statistic is the square of each correlation, indicating the variance shared by the two measures. The squared correlations indicate quite modest predictive relationships. Oddly, the authors report intercorrelations among the SPI scales in the validity section of the manual. This is unusual because high intercorrelations among the scales do not, by themselves, provide evidence of validity (except perhaps face validity).

ADDITIONAL ISSUES. The authors state that the Self-Concept scale should be given first, but from then on the order in which scales are administered is unimportant. Because in many settings the order in which multiple test forms are administered does matter, the authors should provide some rationale for their comment. Is there empirical evidence indicating that order of administration does not matter? A final quibble: Perhaps all users will realize that in the normative data section M stands for mean, SD for standard deviation, and SE for standard error of measurement, but it would be advisable to define these letters in future editions and provide an example of how to interpret these statistics.

SUMMARY. The measurement of traits like self-concept is a formidable undertaking, likely to be fraught with many difficulties. Although the difficulty of the undertaking should be kept in mind in evaluating the SPI Nursing Forms, this difficulty also suggests that the authors need to go to great lengths to provide empirical evidence to support their claims. Many of the concerns expressed earlier would likely disappear if the authors invested the same thoroughness and attention to detail in empirically documenting the statistical and measurement properties of the SPI Nursing Forms that is evident in their theoretical rationale. The impression that is made is that three relatively small convenience samples were used to generate normative data of questionable value to produce yet another variation of the SPI. Still, it is probably true that using the SPI Nursing Forms is somewhat better than users attempting to develop a similar instrument from scratch.

REVIEWER'S REFERENCE

Shepard, L. (1978). [Review of the Self-Perception Inventory.] In O.K. Buros (Ed.), *The eighth mental measurements yearbook*, (pp. 1056-1057). Highland Park, NJ: Gryphon Press.

[357]
Self-Perception Profile for College Students.

Purpose: To measure college students' self-concept.
Population: College students.
Publication Date: 1986.
Scores: 13 domains: Creativity, Intellectual Ability, Scholastic Competence, Job Competence, Athletic Competence, Appearance, Romantic Relationships, Social Acceptance, Close Friendships, Parent Relationships, Finding Humor in One's Life, Morality, Global Self-Worth.
Administration: Group.
Price Data, 1989: $9 per manual (84 pages).
Time: 30(40) minutes.
Authors: Jennifer Neemann and Susan Harter.
Publisher: University of Denver.

TEST REFERENCES

1. Masciuch, S. W. (1990). The Harter Self-Perception Profile: Some normative and psychometric data. *Psychological Reports, 67,* 1299-1303.

Review of the Self-Perception Profile for College Students by ROBERT D. BROWN, Carl A. Happold

Distinguished Professor of Educational Psychology, University of Nebraska-Lincoln, Lincoln, NE:

Three inventories are included in this package of self-perception instruments: "What I Am Like," "Importance Ratings," and a "Social Support" scale. The instruments can be used separately or as part of a package. The "What I Am Like" inventory is designed to assess college students' self-rating of their global self-worth and in 12 specific domains: Creativity, Intellectual Ability, Scholastic Competence, Job Competence, Athletic Competence, Appearance, Romantic Relationships, Social Acceptance, Close Friendships, Parent Relationships, Humor, Morality, and a Global Self-Worth rating. Each of the content domain subscales has four items and the Global Self-Worth subscale has six items. Estimated completion time is 30 minutes. The "Importance Ratings" inventory parallels the Self-Worth inventory with two items for each of the 12 content domain scales. Finally, the "Social Support" scale has four items each for subscales labelled: Close Friends, Mother, Father, People in Campus Organizations, and Instructors.

The scales and scoring information are provided in the manual and the authors inform readers that they should feel free to copy the instruments directly from the manual.

The "What I Am Like" inventory items ask students to select which one of two self-descriptions (e.g., "Some students are not satisfied with their social skill," and "Other students think their social skills are just fine") are *Really true for me* or *Sort of true for me.* The self-descriptions are on the same lines with the word "But" between them. There is no middle response of "undecided" or "neither." Responses are recorded either on the left margin or on the right margin, depending upon which statement the student believes describes them. Items are scored on a 1 to 4 scale where 4 represents the most competent or adequate self-judgment. Half the items have the high competency phrasing on the left and the other half have the high competency phrasing on the right. Response formats for the "Importance Ratings" and "Social Support" scales are similar and the items are also similar in general content.

The "What I Am Like" inventory parallels similar instruments designed by Harter and associates for use with children, adolescents, and adults. The college student form was developed to fill the developmental gap between the adolescent and adult populations.

The current form of the instruments was developed using data obtained from 300 students, mostly single and Caucasian. Internal consistency assessed by coefficient alphas for the "What I Am Like" inventory were reasonably high for the Self-Worth scales with only one scale below .80. Factor analysis with an oblique rotation and using a scree test resulted in 12 scales perfectly matching the designed scales. (The Global Self-Worth scale was not included.) Intercorrelations among the scales range from low (e.g., Athletic to Scholastic Competence, $r = .02$), to modest (Social Acceptance to Morality, $r = .24$), to moderate (Intellectual Ability to Scholastic Competence, $r = .65$). Reliabilities were less strong for the "Importance Ratings" scales ranging from .53 to .84 but reasonably high for the "Social Support" scale with the range from .76 to .90.

A variety of preliminary validity data are reported which provide interesting as well as supportive information. Gender differences are noted with males having higher self-worth ratings on Appearance and Athletic Competence, but lower importance ratings on Intellectual Ability, Scholastic Competence, and Close Friendships. Unexpectedly, the authors found no gender differences on the social support scales. Overall, Appearance, Social Acceptance, Job Competence, Scholastic Competence, and Intellectual Ability correlated most strongly with the Global Self-Worth scale on the "What I Am Like" inventory and the same general pattern held for the "Importance Ratings."

The authors suggest ways the instruments can be used for research purposes such as examining the relationship of resilience to stress and self-esteem and for individual therapy. In the latter use, they provide examples of how profiles of the self-worth and importance ratings can provide useful insights as well as how to use discrepancy scores. Such information can be useful for helping students determine what aspects of their self they wish to develop.

Personality measures designed specifically for use with a college population are too rare. Too many instruments were developed using clinical populations or focus extensively on problems. One of the most prominent instruments available for use with a normal college population for developmental purposes is the Student Developmental Task and Lifestyle Inventory (384), which has proven useful for research purposes and for working with individual students. Researchers, counselors, and trained mentors will find it appropriate to consider use of these self-perception scales as well. Indeed, a worthwhile research topic would be to explore the relationship among the scales on these instruments and how receptive they are to intervention strategies.

If the self-perception inventories are deficient, beyond the fact that only preliminary validity data are available, it is because of what is omitted rather than what is present. It is unfortunate that the designers did not go further beyond the domains they already had covered in the adolescent and adult version than they did. Several domains immediately come to mind such as leisure-recreational skills, self-management (e.g., stress management) skills, aesthetic/artistic competency, multicultural awareness, and basic living skills (e.g., budgeting, car maintenance). Two important domains are also missing from the social support domains: other students and religious/church affiliation. As I read the Campus Organization subscale items I suspect that most students will respond by thinking about their peers in general rather than solely campus organizations, but it would have been cleaner to have such a peer scale titled as such.

As noted earlier, the authors tell readers to feel free to copy the scales. This fact, plus the fine preliminary work performed on these scales, should make them useful to researchers and others interested in trying to understand and assist college students during their college years.

Review of the Self-Perception Profile for College Students by STEPHEN F. DAVIS, *Professor of Psychology, Emporia State University, Emporia, KS:*

Although self-concept scales have been developed for children, adolescents, and adults, such an instrument has been lacking for the college-age population. The rather extensive and thorough manual for the Self-Perception Profile for College Students indicates that while some scales/domains from the adolescent and adult instruments developed previously by one of the authors are appropriate for college students, others are not. Therefore, several of the domains tested by this new instrument were contributed by each of these previous tests. A total of 13 domains, including Global Self-Worth, comprises the present test.

The full scale consists of 54 items—four items each for Domains 1–12 and six items for the Global Self-Worth domain. Each question asks the examinee "to indicate which of two types of students they are most like." This is accomplished by checking one of two boxes (*Really True, Sort of True*) for one of the two student types described by each item. One description is positive whereas the second is negative. Within each domain the items are balanced with regard to the number of positive and negative statements that appear first. As the pairs of answer boxes are located at opposite ends of each item, there may well be a tendency to check one box in each pair. Although such an admonition is built into the instructions to the examiner, it will need to be emphasized to the students and the first few answers monitored to avoid more than one response per item. The full scale may be individually or group administered within approximately 30 minutes. A set of clear instructions to be read to the students is included.

The response to each item is assigned a score of 1, 2, 3, or 4 depending upon the degree of competence or self-judgement reflected by the answer. These scores are then summed on a domain-by-domain basis to yield a separate score for each subscale.

It is noteworthy that the students ($N = 300$; 70 males, 230 females) employed for the development of this instrument were predominantly freshmen (47.33%) from the University of Denver and Colorado State University. Very few juniors (13.66%) and seniors (7.66%) were represented in the sample. Additionally, a majority (84%) were commuters. The mean age of this predominantly Caucasian (93%), predominantly single (94%) sample was 19.8 years. Such demographics suggest potential areas of concern for the representativeness of the sample. As "the target population of this measure is the traditional full-time college student, ages 17–23," the potential usefulness of the instrument may be limited somewhat.

The reliabilities of the four-item subscales, as measured by coefficient alpha, ranged from .76 to .92 with only one domain (Job Competence) falling below .80. Suggesting the absence of ceiling and floor effects, subscale means clustered around 3.00 (sd = approximately .80). Three reliable gender effects were reported. Females scored higher on Close Friendship, whereas males scored higher on Athletic Competence and Appearance. The results of Cattell's scree test "indicated that twelve factors should be extracted, and these corresponded perfectly to the intended twelve subscales." A subsequent principle components factor analysis yielded high factor loadings (average = .78, range = .52–.92) with no cross-loadings.

In an attempt to place this scale within the theoretical model of William James who proposed that global self-esteem resulted from an "evaluation of the ratio of one's *successes* to one's *pretensions*," an Importance Scale also was developed. By determining the discrepancy between the competence score for a domain and the importance score of that domain, the authors suggest that they have operationalized James' theory. The Importance Scale consists of 24 questions (2 from each domain).

The items for the Importance Rating Scale are balanced and scored in the same manner as are those for the Self-Perception Profile. The internal reliabilities (coefficient alpha) range from .53 to .84 with only three subscales falling below .72. For two-item subscales such figures are quite acceptable. Other descriptive measures show that the importance means are rather high (range = 2.68–3.75) with one-half of the measures falling above 3.50. The standard deviations fall within an acceptable range of .45 to .83.

The most sensitive use of the importance scores appears to be in conjunction with the global measure of self-worth. When importance *and* competency scores are plotted for each domain for high, medium, and low self-worth subjects, it is clear that although the importance ratings did not vary, the competence scores decreased dramatically from high to low self-worth. Although this is an excellent and informative use of these scores, the rationale behind the formation of the three self-worth categories is not explained or substantiated. They were formed "For demonstration purposes only." Hence, other configurations and results are possible.

Finally, recognizing that self-worth may be related to the process of socialization, the authors have included a Social Support Scale evaluating the importance of Close Friends, Mother, Campus Organizations, Father, and Instructors. This scale, which has a total of 20 items (4 per subscale), is administered and scored in the same manner as the Self-Perception Profile. The subscale reliabilities (coefficient alpha) range from .76 to .90. Although the subscale means are rather high (3.10–3.64) there is sufficient variability (*sd* range = .53–.70).

Reflecting some lack of organization in preparing the manual, it is not until page 45 that one finds information concerning validity and the target population for the Self-Perception Profile. (Such information is not given for the Importance Ratings and Social Support scales.) As these sections are rather short, they should have been incorporated directly into an earlier section. As validity information is presented for only three subscales (Social Acceptance, Close Friendships, and Parent Relationships), it is clear that additional work is needed in this area. The fact, however, that all three reported measures are quite reliable ($p = .001$) is encouraging. Similarly, the authors occasionally refer to appendices that may have been planned but which are not to be found in the completed manual.

The descriptive portion of the manual concludes with a section on applications. The authors suggest the Self-Perception Profile can be used in research, as a predictor of the resilience to stress, and as a therapeutic adjunct. The remainder of the manual is devoted to complete versions of each of the three scales, scoring keys, and an Individual Profile Form.

As the user is given permission to reproduce the scales and the profile form, all of the necessary elements for administering, scoring, and interpreting this scale are contained in this manual. Based upon the information provided here, the Self-Perception Profile and its two related scales should prove to be quite informative and helpful to those interested in evaluation of the self-concept of college-age subjects.

[358]
Sentence Comprehension Test, Revised Edition.
Purpose: "To assess children's comprehension of English and/or Panjabi."
Population: Ages 3–5.
Publication Dates: 1979–87.
Acronym: SCT.
Scores: 10 subtests: Simple Intransitive, Simple Transitive, Intransitive with Adjective, Plural, Past,

Future, Negative, Prepositions, Embedded Phrase, Passive.
Administration: Individual.
Price Data, 1988: £30.55 per complete set including 25 record forms (English version), 25 record forms (Panjabi bilingual version), picture book ('87, 45 pages), and manual ('87, 43 pages); £5.20 per 25 record forms (English version); £6.90 per 25 record forms (Panjabi bilingual version); £16.70 per picture book; £12.65 per manual.
Foreign Language Edition: Panjabi bilingual version available.
Time: (10–20) minutes.
Authors: Kevin Wheldall, Peter Mittler, Angela Hobsbaum, Dorothy Gibbs (Panjabi bilingual version), Deirdre Duncan (Panjabi bilingual version), and Surinder Saund (Panjabi bilingual version).
Publisher: NFER-Nelson Publishing Co., Ltd. [England].
Cross References: For reviews by Francis X. Archambault and Mavis Donahue of the experimental edition, see 9:1107.

TEST REFERENCES
1. Gregory, H. M., & Beveridge, M. C. (1984). The social and educational adjustment of abused children. *Child Abuse & Neglect, 8*, 525-531.

Review of the Sentence Comprehension Test, Revised Edition by GABRIEL DELLA-PIANA, Professor of Educational Psychology, University of Utah, Salt Lake City, UT:

The Sentence Comprehension Test (SCT), Revised Edition, has the same purpose and structure as the earlier experimental edition. The test is designed "to measure a child's ability to comprehend sentences of varying length and grammatical complexity by requiring him to select appropriately from sets [of four] pictures" the one representing an orally presented stimulus sentence. The major changes introduced in the revised version are reduced testing time (due to fewer subtests) and redrawing of all pictures (for clarity, elimination of sex stereotyping, and including multicultural representation of persons illustrated). In addition, new studies of reliability and validity and some normative data support the revised edition.

The intended use of this measure of comprehension of orally presented sentences is primarily diagnostic, "[to] help . . . pinpoint the sentence constructions" that are causing the child some difficulty and to "lead to more systematic and specific approaches to remediation." It is also intended as a "quick screening device" to identify children whose performance deviates markedly from other children. Thus, the key questions to be addressed are: adequacy of reliability, validity, and norms for these purposes; ease of administration and scoring by testers; and usefulness of the manual to support the intended interpretations and uses of test results.

The administration procedure is simple and the record form is easy to use. An example illustrates the procedure. The tester presents a set of four black and white drawings (e.g., a black ladder, a white ladder, a black chair, and a white chair). The tester then asks the child to look at the pictures and says, "Show me the black chair." Although feedback and help are given on practice items, during the actual test only noncontingent social reinforcement is given. A record form has a matrix of four squares corresponding to the four drawings coded as T (for target or correct response) or for type of error (e.g., S for subject error, V for verb error, etc.). The procedure allows the tester to attend to the child rather than to written instructions. Scoring is also simple, allowing a quick tally.

There are no statements concerning the qualifications needed to properly administer, score, or interpret the test, and there is little help in the manual to support interpretations and uses recommended. For example, the manual advises that "although one can say that the child scored 30/40 on the Test, it is more useful to examine the profile of subtests." But no examples of profiles are given, nor is there any information about how one might interpret and use a profile. The fact that "failure on specific test items or on the Test as a whole may result from . . . boredom . . . failure to scan pictures, listen to the message or relate what is heard to what is seen; or being too interested in the picture" suggests the need for training and for examples or guides to such analyses. However, none are to be found.

The test-retest reliability of .79 for total score and .77 for number of subtests passed on an N of 50 is only fair. The Spearman-Brown coefficient was .77 on the first test and .83 on the second testing. Because the age range tested sampled 3-, $3^1/_2$-, 4-, $4^1/_2$-, and 5-year-olds, one might expect higher reliabilities. Yet, at lower age levels, high reliabilities are often difficult to obtain. At any rate, it would be worth exploring what contributes to the only moderately high reliabilities obtained. Reliability data are not reported for separate age levels, even though normative data were gathered on a sample of 30 3-year-olds and 50 each of $3^1/_2$-, 4-, $4^1/_2$-, and 5-year-olds.

Data are presented showing approximate ages by which 50% and 75% of children tested have passed each subtest. Also, graphs show the mean total score and subtest pass rates for each age level. These data are appropriate to "screening" decisions, as suggested earlier in the manual. However, one would also want to recommend local testing for normative data because the normative sample in the study is small, and one might expect local variations in spite of the sample being selected to represent the general population in the "Registrar General's categories."

Validity is supported by SCT mean scores developing linearly over ages for the test as a whole but not for all subtests. Also, for the test as a whole, subtests passed and mean vocabulary age of the sample increase linearly for age groups along with SCT scores. However, because the manual suggests that it is more useful to examine the profile of subtests than the total score, validity relevant to interpreting the profiles would be very helpful.

Finally, this reviewer is not an expert on bilingual assessment and did not refer to the Panjabi bilingual version of the test in the above review. A quick overview suggests that the test has promise. However, this reviewer will have to leave it to others to assess whether or not the test has possibilities for assessing whether language problems of this population are problems with English or with language in general.

In summary, the SCT does appear to sample oral sentence comprehension in a way that identifies specific grammatical structures that require further diagnosis or remedial attention. Many of the earlier difficulties in the test have been corrected in the current version. However, the diagnostic possibilities of the test continue to warrant further development. In the hands of an experienced clinical educational diagnostician, the test has its most immediate current use.

[359]
Sequential Assessment of Mathematics Inventories: Standardized Inventory.

Purpose: "To differentiate among students in terms of their overall performance in mathematics and to measure an individual student's particular strengths and weaknesses in learning the mathematics curriculum."

Population: Grades K–8.

Publication Date: 1985.

Acronym: SAMI.

Scores, 9: Mathematical Language (Grades K–3 only), Ordinality (Grades K–3 only), Number/Notation, Computation, Measurement, Geometric Concepts, Mathematical Applications (Grades 4–8 only), Word Problems, Total.

Administration: Individual.

Price Data, 1991: $80.50 per complete program including easel, 12 student response booklets, 12 record forms, examiner's manual (95 pages), and case; $26 per 12 each of student response booklets and record forms; $48.50 per easel; $20.50 per manual.

Time: (20–60) minutes.

Comments: May be used in conjunction with the SAMI Informal Inventory.

Authors: Fredricka K. Reisman and Thomas A. Hutchinson (manual).

Publisher: The Psychological Corporation.

Review of the Sequential Assessment of Mathematics Inventories: Standardized Inventory by JOHN W. FLEENOR, Research Associate, Center for Creative Leadership, Greensboro, NC:

The Sequential Assessment of Mathematics Inventories (SAMI) is intended for use by educators who normally assess or teach students with difficulties in mathematics. It has two purposes: (a) to compare student performance to national norms, and (b) to measure the achievement of specific content objectives. Each of the eight subtests measures a curriculum "strand," that is "a set of mathematics content and operations that spans several grade levels."

ADMINISTRATION AND SCORING. The SAMI can be administered by school psychologists, educational diagnosticians, or teachers familiar with individual testing. It is based on free-response items rather than multiple choice. The items are presented to the student using the easel (a booklet of flip charts). The examiner reads each item aloud to minimize the effects of reading ability. The student answers using one of the three response modes (pointing, telling, or writing), and the examiner records correct responses on a form. A booklet is provided for written responses. Start points are provided for the Number/Notation and Computation subtests. A subtest is discontinued after three consecutive incorrect responses are given.

Each subtest consists of from 8 to 77 items, with a total of 243 items. Raw scores equal the number of correct responses for each subtest. Subtest scores are added to calculate a total score. Confidence intervals are provided for these scores.

NORMS. Norms were constructed using Item Response Theory (IRT). Scale values were determined for the Number/Notation and Computation subscales using the Rasch model, which estimates item difficulty. The other subtests were scaled onto this metric. The scale values represent the relative difficulty of each item based on a national sampling of students in grades K–8 (n = about 1,400). A proficiency measure was estimated for each possible raw score. Using these estimates, norm tables were constructed for each subtest and grade level.

Two types of norms are presented: within-group percentile ranks, and across-group scores expressed as grade equivalents. Standard scores for subtests (M = 10, SD = 3) were determined from the percentile ranks at each grade interval. Grade equivalents were calculated using the median raw score for each grade interval.

RELIABILITY. The manual reports test-retest reliabilities with a 6-week interval for samples of third, fifth, and eighth graders (n = 25 to 32). The reliabilities range from .43 to .89, with a median of .65. For five of the subtests, reliabilities are below .50 (e.g., for grade 3, .46 for the Computation subtest and .43 for the Word Problem subtest).

Internal consistency (KR-20) reliabilities are reported for the Number/Notation and Computation subtests for each grade separately. They range from .72 to .97, with a median of .93, and are fairly stable across grades. For the other subtests, reliabilities are reported by grade groupings (i.e., K–3, 4–6, and 7–8). These estimates of internal consistency range from .37 to .98, with a median of .88. They are somewhat consistent across grade groups; however, the reliability of the Mathematical Language subtest for grades K–3 is .37.

VALIDITY. The SAMI samples six domains generally accepted as essential for elementary school mathematics curricula. The other two domains (Mathematical Language and Ordinality) appear to be important for early learning of mathematics. To ensure correspondence between the item content and what is actually taught in classrooms, mathematics curricula around the nation were sampled. Over 1,000 items were developed before the final 243 were selected.

As evidence of construct validity, the authors report intercorrelations of the subtests by grade groups. Sample sizes range from 146 to 200. For students in grades K–3, intercorrelations range from .26 to .74, with a median of .62. The correlation of the Number/Notation subtest with the Geometric Concepts subtest is .31, and .26 with the Computation subtest. For students in grades 4–8, the intercorrelations range from .49 to .74, with a median of .66. The lowest correlation is between the Computation subtest and the Geometric Concepts subtest.

These intercorrelations appear to be theoretically consistent. They are positive and, for the most part, moderately high. Because each subtest measures a different domain, extremely high correlations are not expected. The low correlation of the Geometric Concepts subtest with other subtests is attributed to the particular domain of that subtest. It measures a student's ability to identify and name basic shapes, which may be learned outside the classroom and not highly correlated with early mathematics achievement.

As evidence of criterion-related validity, the authors report correlations between a composite score on the Number/Notation and Computation subtests, and Reading and Math scores from the California Achievement Test (CAT). Correlations are reported separately for each grade (1–7), and sample sizes range from 21 to 26. The correlations with CAT Reading scores range from .32 to .59, with a median of .49. The correlations with CAT Math scores range from .50 to .82, with a median of .72. Overall, the SAMI scores are more highly correlated with the CAT Math scores than with the CAT Reading scores. This provides some evidence of construct validity for the SAMI.

A similar analysis was conducted using the Metropolitan Readiness Test with kindergarten children. No differences are reported between the correlations of the SAMI composite score with the Metropolitan prereading and quantitative scores, which indicates a failure of the SAMI to demonstrate construct validity. This lack of discriminant validity is an indication that the SAMI may not be accurately measuring the math achievement of kindergarten children, because the scores are correlated with the verbal scores from the Metropolitan Readiness Test to the same extent they are related to the quantitative scores.

CONCLUSION. The strengths of the SAMI are: (a) the development of its items, (b) the standardization and norming methodology, and (c) the technical manual. The manual is well written and clearly explains the test development, administration, and interpretation procedures. Appendices containing confidence intervals, percentile ranks, standard scores, and grade equivalents greatly assist in the interpretation of the results.

The SAMI suffers, however, from the dearth of reliability and validity data reported in the manual. The evidence of reliability is based on a few studies with small sample sizes. Validity evidence is limited to reporting the intercorrelations of subtests, and one study of the relationship between two SAMI subtests and two standardized achievement tests. The SAMI appears to have promise as a measure of mathematics performance; however, it cannot be recommended without qualification until considerably more data supporting the reliability and validity of the test are made available to the user.

Review of the Sequential Assessment of Mathematics Inventories: Standardized Inventory by SYLVIA T. JOHNSON, Professor, Research Methodology and Statistics and Acting Editor-In-Chief, Journal of Negro Education, Howard University, Washington, DC:

The Sequential Assessment of Mathematics Inventories: Standardized Inventory (SAMI) is designed to measure the performance of students in a K–8 mathematics curriculum. Each of the eight subtests measures a curriculum strand. The first two, Mathematical Language and Ordinality, are to be used to diagnose early math difficulties that may influence readiness for the regular mathematics curriculum. The remaining items are organized in subtests designed to span several grades: Number and Notation, Computation, Measurement, Geometric Concepts, Mathematical Applications, and Word Problems. Scores are intended to permit norm-referenced comparison of students in overall mathematics performance, and to allow within-subject appraisal of the individual's strengths and weaknesses. All items are free-response rather than multiple-choice format.

TEST DEVELOPMENT AND STANDARDIZATION. The manual describes a test development process involving a careful attempt to tie test items to curriculum objectives in use over a range of school districts. As a part of another project, the publisher had developed nearly a thousand objectives and

detailed item specifications for creating objective-referenced mastery tests using Basal texts and curriculum guides from a broad range of school systems. All SAMI objectives and item specifications were adjusted to meet this compendium of materials. In the initial tryout, 448 items were administered in group settings to 757 subjects across grades K–8 in one school district. All subjects took two forms including items at above and below grade level. The process involved the use of both "screening" forms, which sampled a few key instructional targets from a wide range of curriculum areas, and "diagnosis" forms, which sampled a larger number of more specific instructional targets from a narrower range of the curriculum. This distinction was not maintained in the finished test, but was a device to gain maximum information on item performance across the tryout group.

A second tryout used 520 items administered in group settings with 10 items per strand provided to subjects in grades 1, 3, 5, and 7. These subjects also were administered reading and spelling items and items from a norm bank used in validating the items. Item difficulty and discrimination statistics were computed at this step.

Nine forms for grades K–8 were constructed and group administered to a representative national sample of 5,727.

The standardization sample ($n = 1,456$) was drawn from 88 school districts in six states in four regions of the country. Within each district, a representative class was sampled at each K–8 grade level. The manual states that an effort was made to select districts that would produce an oversampling of minorities, especially of Black and Spanish origin. However, only two large urban districts are included in the norm group: Philadelphia, Pennsylvania, and Little Rock, Arkansas. Others are included in the item tryout group. The sample contains 18.8% Black and 5.5% Hispanic students. The author indicates a belief that the latter figure reflects underreporting of the school-aged Hispanic population.

Item response theory, through the one-parameter Rasch model, was used to estimate scale values for all items. One scale was established for the Number/Notation computation items, and the six remaining subtests were scaled onto this metric. This resulted in a single common scale containing all SAMI items.

The fact that all test development was done on a group administration basis and the instrument itself is individually administered should be considered. Item selection, assignment of items to strands and subjects, and all item and subtest tryouts were done under group administration conditions. Because this item information is then used in the scaling, the scales constructed may be in part influenced by this test administration factor.

Norm tables provide percentile ranks and standard scores within grade levels for all grades for the subtests and for the total score. NCEs and stanine conversions from percentile ranks are also provided, as well as grade equivalents constructed from the median raw score for each observed grade interval. The grade equivalent scores are adequate for interpretation of the Total score and the 77-item Computation score, but grade equivalent scores for the other subscales are useful only at the specific grade levels where most items on the subscales are directed. Small score differences may yield an erroneous picture on the other grade levels. This point is alluded to in the section, "Cautions for Interpreting Grade Equivalents," in the manual.

VALIDITY. An achievement test such as the SAMI requires content, criterion-related, and construct validation studies, all of which are reported in the manual.

In general, the instrument construction procedures support the content validity of the test. Some items were constructed to meet specific objectives common across many school systems. Other items were rejected if they were related to objectives that were not common to many curriculum guides. Some SAMI items were constructed to be similar to, and tied to the same objectives of, items in an item bank that had been tried out on large national samples. However, the performance on similar-appearing items does not always fit as well as we think it should. It would have been better to have either included some of the SAMI items in these tryouts to obtain correlations with item bank items, or to have done subsequent empirical work to more firmly support the relationships.

Construct validity is supported by moderate correlations between most subtests, with low correlations between dissimilar subtests (e.g., for Computation and Number/Notation, $r = .74$; for Geometric Concepts and Computation, $r = .26$). Construct validity is further supported by the similarity of correlation coefficients between the same subtests among different parts of the sample. This finding is a by-product of the item sampling design employed to obtain information for scaling the items. The design was used to obtain test information from a large number of children, but only a sample of the items was administered to any one child. Thus, sets of correlation coefficients cutting across subscales were produced, rather than a single correlation matrix. In this case, the sets of coefficients when computed on the same subscales yielded similar values within the different subsamples.

Criterion-related validity is obtained for the SAMI by using the California Achievement Test (CAT), Form C, as a criterion. The findings show correlations for the SAMI and the CAT Mathematics that are uniformly higher than those for the SAMI and the CAT Reading over the grade 1–7 range, with values from .72 to .82 for grades 3–6, and from .50 to .59 for grades 1, 2, and 7. This also suggests a stronger criterion relationship for the SAMI in the middle grades.

At the kindergarten level, the Metropolitan Readiness Test was used as a criterion. The SAMI Number/Notation subtest correlated equally well with both the Metropolitan Pre-Reading and the Metropolitan Quantitative subscales ($r = .72, r = .73$), whereas the SAMI Computation scale also correlated at about the same level with these Metropolitan scales ($r = .51, r = .46$). The similarities in these pairs of coefficients, together with the smaller coefficients at the upper and lower grade levels for the CAT criterion, suggest that the SAMI may have stronger criterion-related validity at the middle grade levels. Lower reliability in the performance of younger children on tests generally is an alternate interpretation.

RELIABILITY. A positive feature is the reporting of test-retest reliabilities at grades 3, 5, and 8, measured over a 6-week interval. Total score reliability coefficients were .89, .84, and .78 for those grade levels, respectively. Test-retest reliability is infrequently reported, and is especially useful in an instrument such as the SAMI that is intended to be used diagnostically as well as to differentiate among students in overall mathematics performance.

Test-retest coefficients for subtests are varied, ranging from .43 and .46 for grade 3, Word Problems and Computation, respectively, to .81 and .89 for grade 5 Computation and grade 3 Math Language, respectively. Internal consistency coefficients are quite high for the total test score for all grade levels (.93–.98) and for the two longest subscales, Number/Notation and Computation (.96) for grades 7–8. However, the KR-20 internal consistency reliability coefficient for grades K–3 for the Mathematical Language subtest is .37. Because this test is indicated only for those lowest grade levels, this is a concern. However, the other subscales for the K–3 level are in the upper ranges, nearly as high as for the middle and upper grades. The standard error of measurement is reported for the Number/Notation and Computation subtests for each grade level, along with confidence bands for score interpretation.

TEST ADMINISTRATION. This individually administered test is intended for use by school psychologists, educational diagnosticians, or math teachers trained in individual testing. Test administration directions are clear and brief. A few bold headings would be useful additions to indicate special instructions for certain subtests, but the trained examiner would likely highlight these points in the initial reading of the manual. Scoring information is also well presented. The testing materials themselves are clearly drawn, unambiguous, and attractive.

SUMMARY AND CONCLUSION. The entire manual, which is well written with a tone of concern about the teaching and testing of mathematics, provides useful interpretive information. The brief interpretation chapter summarizes this information, raises questions, and provides a few examples. A listing of the objectives for each of the items is included in an appendix. They are clearly stated so that additional items or exercises could be generated, if desired. Comprehensive information on the instrument is presented which supports the use of the SAMI in measuring the mathematics performance of individual children relative to a normative group, and in comparing the levels of performance on major dimensions or "strands" of mathematics learning within the individual. The low reliabilities on some subtests should be considered when interpreting within-individual scores. The data suggest the instrument is somewhat stronger for these purposes in the middle grades. However, the performance of younger children is less reliable in general, and the lower item and scale statistics for younger children may reflect this developmental issue.

[360]
Shipley Institute of Living Scale.

Purpose: "Designed to assess general intellectual functioning in adults and adolescents and to aid in detecting cognitive impairment in individuals with normal original intelligence."

Population: Ages 14 and over.

Publication Dates: 1939–86.

Acronym: SILS.

Scores, 6: Vocabulary, Abstraction, Combined Total, Conceptual Quotient, Abstraction Quotient, Estimated WAIS or WAIS-R IQ.

Administration: Group.

Price Data, 1988: $70 per complete kit including 100 tests, scoring key, and manual ('86, 100 pages); $9.50 per scoring key; $32.50 per manual.

Microcomputer Edition: [WPS Test Report: Microcomputer Edition]. 1984; administers, scores, and prints a complete interpretation; IBM PC or IBM XT with 128K memory, two-sided disk drive, and printer required; $119.50 per 25-use diskette and user's guide ('84, 23 pages).

Time: 20 minutes.

Comments: Formerly called Shipley-Hartford Retreat Scale for Measuring Intellectual Impairment and Shipley-Institute of Living Scale for Measuring Intellectual Impairment.

Authors: Walter C. Shipley (test and original manual) and Robert A. Zachary (revised manual).

Publisher: Western Psychological Services.

Cross References: See 9:1122 (13 references), T3:2179 (64 references), 8:677 (39 references), and T2:1380 (34 references); for a review by Aubrey J. Yates, see 7:138 (21 references); see also P:244 (38 references), 6:173 (13 references), and 5:111 (23 references); for reviews by E. J. G. Bradford, William A. Hunt, and Margaret Ives, see 3:95 (25 references).

TEST REFERENCES

1. Alfano, A. M., Thurstin, A. N., Bancroft, W., Jr., Haygood, J. M., & Sherer, T. M. (1984). Development and validation of an automatic treatment referral system. *Journal of Clinical Psychology, 40*, 842-850.

2. Armour, M. T., & Savitsky, J. C. (1984). The legal decision making of well-informed subjects: The effect of Miranda warnings. *Criminal Justice and Behavior, 11*, 341-347.

3. Caine, E. D., Yerevanian, B. I., & Bamford, K. A. (1984). Cognitive function and the dexamethasone suppression test in depression. *American Journal of Psychiatry, 141*, 116-118.

4. Gilbertson, A. D. (1984). Perceptual differentiation among drug addicts: Correlations with intelligence and MMPI scores. *Journal of Clinical Psychology, 40*, 334-339.

5. Kreutzer, J. S., Schneider, H. G., & Myatt, C. R. (1984). Alcohol, aggression and assertiveness in men: Dosage and expectancy effects. *Journal of Studies on Alcohol, 45*, 275-278.

6. Merritt, R. D., & Balogh, D. W. (1984). The use of backward masking paradigm to assess information-processing deficits among schizotypics. *The Journal of Nervous and Mental Disease, 172*, 216-224.

7. Savitsky, J. C., & Karras, D. (1984). Competency to stand trial among adolescents. *Adolescence, 19*, 349-358.

8. Watson, G. M. W., & Dyck, D. G. (1984). Depressive attributional style in psychiatric inpatients: Effects of reinforcement level and assessment procedure. *Journal of Abnormal Psychology, 93*, 312-320.

9. Woody, G. E., McLellan, T., Luborsky, L., O'Brien, C. P., Blaine, J., Fox, S., Herman, I., & Beck, A. T. (1984). Severity of psychiatric symptoms as a predictor of benefits from psychotherapy: The Veterans Administration-Penn study. *American Journal of Psychiatry, 141*, 1172-1177.

10. Bauer, W. D., & Twentyman, C. T. (1985). Abusing, neglecting, and comparison mothers' responses to child-related and non-child-related stressors. *Journal of Consulting and Clinical Psychology, 53*, 335-343.

11. Bell, A. H., Walsh, D., & Barnes, T. (1985). Replication of alcoholism acceptance scores as a function of treatment. *Psychological Reports, 56*, 31-36.

12. Beutler, L. E., Storm, A., Kirkish, P., Scogin, F., & Gaines, J. A. (1985). Parameters in the prediction of police officer performance. *Professional Psychology: Research and Practice, 16*, 324-335.

13. Clark, D. C., Clayton, P. J., Andreasen, N. C., Lewis, C., Fawcett, J., & Scheftner, W. A. (1985). Intellectual functioning and abstraction ability in major affective disorders. *Comprehensive Psychiatry, 26*, 313-325.

14. Donovan, D. M., Kivlahan, D. R., Walker, R. D., & Umlauf, R. (1985). Derivation and validation of neuropsychological clusters among men alcoholics. *Journal of Studies on Alcohol, 46*, 205-211.

15. Haley, W. E. (1985). Social skills deficits and self-evaluation among depressed and nondepressed psychiatric inpatients. *Journal of Clinical Psychology, 41*, 162-168.

16. Hyer, L. A., Jacobsen, R., & Harrison, W. R. (1985). Irrational ideas: Older vs. younger inpatients. *The Journal of Nervous and Mental Disease, 173*, 232-235.

17. Ingram, J. C., Marchioni, P., Hill, G., Caraveo-Ramos, E., & McNeil, B. (1985). Recidivism, perceived problem-solving abilities, MMPI characteristics, and violence: A study of black and white incarcerated male adult offenders. *Journal of Clinical Psychology, 41*, 425-432.

18. Leber, W. R., Parsons, O. A., & Nichols, N. (1985). Neuropsychological test results are related to ratings of men alcoholics' therapeutic progress: A replicated study. *Journal of Studies on Alcohol, 46*, 116-121.

19. Moore, R. H. (1985). Construct validity of the MacAndrew Scale: Secondary psychopathic and dysthymic-neurotic character orientations among adolescent male misdemeanor offenders. *Journal of Studies on Alcohol, 46*, 128-131.

20. Scaturo, D. J., & LeSure, K. B. (1985). Symptomatic correlates of alcohol abuse as a presenting problem. *Journal of Clinical Psychology, 41*, 118-123.

21. Sengel, R. A., Lovallo, W. R., & Pishkin, V. (1985). Verbal recall in schizophrenia: Differential effect of retroactive interference in nonparanoid patients. *Comprehensive Psychiatry, 26*, 164-174.

22. Webster-Stratton, C. (1985). Comparison of abusive and nonabusive families with conduct-disordered children. *American Journal of Orthopsychiatry, 55*, 59-69.

23. Zachary, R. A., Crumpton, E., & Spiegel, D. E. (1985). Estimating WAIS-R IQ from the Shipley Institute of Living Scale. *Journal of Clinical Psychology, 41*, 532-540.

24. Zachary, R. A., Paulson, M. J., & Gorsuch, R. L. (1985). Estimating WAIS IQ from the Shipley Institute of Living Scale using

continuously adjusted age norms. *Journal of Clinical Psychology*, *41*, 820-831.

25. Adamakos, H., Ryan, K., Ullman, D. G., Pascoe, J., Diaz, R., & Chessare, J. (1986). Maternal social support as a predictor of mother-child stress and stimulation. *Child Abuse and Neglect*, *10*, 463-470.

26. Alberts-Corush, J., Firestone, P., & Goodman, J. T. (1986). Attention and impulsivity characteristics of the biological and adoptive parents of hyperactive and normal control children. *American Journal of Orthopsychiatry*, *56*, 413-423.

27. Crandell, C. J., & Chambless, D. L. (1986). The validation of an inventory for measuring depressive thoughts: The Crandell cognitions inventory. *Behaviour Research and Therapy*, *24*, 403-411.

28. Fowles, G. P., & Tunick, R. H. (1986). WAIS-R and Shipley estimated IQ correlations. *Journal of Clinical Psychology*, *42*, 647-649.

29. Hyer, L., Harkey, B., & Harrison, W. R. (1986). MMPI scales and subscales: Patterns of older, middle-aged, and younger inpatients. *Journal of Clinical Psychology*, *42*, 596-601.

30. Keltner, N. L., McIntyre, C. W., & Gee, R. (1986). Birth order effects in second-generation alcoholics. *Journal of Studies on Alcohol*, *47*, 495-497.

31. Miller, I. W., III, & Norman, W. H. (1986). Persistence of depressive cognitions within a subgroup of depressed inpatients. *Cognitive Therapy and Research*, *10*, 211-224.

32. Morgan, S. F., & Hatsukami, D. K. (1986). Use of the Shipley Institute of Living Scale for neuropsychological screening of the elderly: Is it an appropriate measure for this population? *Journal of Clinical Psychology*, *42*, 796-798.

33. Retzlaff, P., Slicner, N., & Gibertini, M. (1986). Predicting WAIS-R scores from the Shipley Institute of Living Scale in a homogeneous sample. *Journal of Clinical Psychology*, *42*, 357-359.

34. Rohrbeck, C. A., & Twentyman, C. T. (1986). Multimodal assessment of impulsiveness in abusing, neglecting, and nonmaltreating mothers and their preschool children. *Journal of Consulting and Clinical Psychology*, *54*, 231-236.

35. Schear, J. M., Harrison, W. R., & Sherman, C. J. (1986). Estimating WAIS IQ of neuropsychiatric patients at three educational levels. *Psychological Reports*, *58*, 947-950.

36. Tamkin, A. S., Hyer, L. A., & Carson, M. F. (1986). Comparison among four measures of depression in younger and older alcoholics. *Psychological Reports*, *59*, 287-293.

37. Thurstin, A. H., Alfano, A. M., & Sherer, M. (1986). Pretreatment MMPI profiles of A.A. members and nonmembers. *Journal of Studies on Alcohol*, *47*, 468-471.

38. Dalton, J. E., Pederson, S. L., & McEntyre, W. L. (1987). A comparison of the Shipley vs. WAIS-R subtests in predicting WAIS-R Full Scale IQ. *Journal of Clinical Psychology*, *43*, 278-280.

39. Fawcett, J., Clark, D. C., Aagesen, C. A., Pisani, V. D., Tilkin, J. M., Sellers, D., McGuire, M., & Gibbons, R. D. (1987). A double-blind, placebo-controlled trial of lithium carbonate therapy for alcoholism. *Archives of General Psychiatry*, *44*, 248-256.

40. Heimberg, R. G., Nyman, D., & O'Brien, G. T. (1987). Assessing variations of the thought-listing technique: Effects of instructions, stimulus intensity, stimulus modality, and scoring procedures. *Cognitive Therapy and Research*, *11*, 13-24.

41. O'Connor, M. J., Sigman, M., & Brill, N. (1987). Disorganization of attachment in relation to maternal alcohol consumption. *Journal of Consulting and Clinical Psychology*, *55*, 831-836.

42. Tamkin, A. S., & Jacobsen, R. H. (1987). Age-corrected norms for Shipley Institute of Living Scale scores derived from psychiatric inpatients. *Journal of Clinical Psychology*, *43*, 138-142.

43. Woody, G. E., McLellan, T., Luborsky, L., & O'Brien, C. P. (1987). Twelve-month follow-up of psychotherapy for opiate dependence. *The American Journal of Psychiatry*, *144*, 590-596.

44. Calvert, S. H., Beutler, L. E., & Crago, M. (1988). Psychotherapy outcome as a function of therapist-patient matching on selected variables. *Journal of Social and Clinical Psychology*, *6*, 104-117.

45. Jacobsen, R. H., Tomkin, A. S., & Hyer, L. A. (1988). Factor analytic study of irrational beliefs. *Psychological Reports*, *63*, 803-809.

46. Penn, N. E., Jacob, T. C., & Brown, M. (1988). Comparison between Gorham's Proverbs Test and the revised Shipley Institute of Living Scale for a black population. *Perceptual and Motor Skills*, *66*, 839-845.

47. Ammerman, R. T., Van Hasselt, V. B., & Hersen, M. (1989). Psychometric properties and social correlates of assertion measures in chronic alcoholics. *Addictive Behaviors*, *14*, 11-21.

48. Epstein, S., & Meier, P. (1989). Constructive thinking: A broad coping variable with specific components. *Journal of Personality and Social Psychology*, *57*, 332-350.

49. Frisch, M. B., & Jessop, N. S. (1989). Improving WAIS-R estimates with the Shipley-Harford and Wonderlic Personnel Tests: Need to control for reading ability. *Psychological Reports*, *65*, 923-928.

50. Klassen, D., & O'Connor, W. A. (1989). Assessing the risk of violence in released mental patients: A cross-validation study. *Psychological Assessment*, *1*, 75-81.

51. Larson, L. M. (1989). Problem-solving appraisal in an alcoholic population. *Journal of Counseling Psychology*, *36*, 73-78.

52. Newlin, D. B., Hotchkiss, B., Cox, W. M., Rauscher, F., & Li, T. K. (1989). Autonomic and subjective responses to alcohol stimuli with appropriate control stimuli. *Addictive Behaviors*, *14*, 625-630.

53. Parks, R. W., Cassens, G., Crockett, D. J., Herrera, J. A., Latterner, R., Lorenzo, G., Carner, R., & Dodrill, K. L. (1990). Correlation of the Shipley Institute of Living Scale with regional cerebral glucose metabolism as measured by positron emission tomography in dementia. *The International Journal of Clinical Neuropsychology*, *12*, 14-19.

54. Parsons, O. A., Schaeffer, K. W., & Glenn, S. W. (1990). Does neuropsychological test performance predict resumption of drinking in posttreatment alcoholics? *Addictive Behaviors*, *15*, 297-307.

55. Salthouse, T. A., & Mitchell, D. R. O. (1990). Effects of age and naturally occurring experience on spatial visualization performance. *Developmental Psychology*, *26*, 845-854.

56. Mason, C. F., Lemmon, D., Wayne, K. S., & Schmidt, R. (1991). Shipley Institute of Living Scale: Formulas for abstraction quotients from a normative sample of 580. Sex and socioeconomic status considered as additional moderating variables. *Psychological Assessment*, *3*, 412-417.

Review of the Shipley Institute of Living Scale by **WILLIAM L. DEATON,** *Professor and Associate Dean, College of Education, Auburn University, Auburn University, AL:*

INTRODUCTION. The Shipley Institute of Living Scale (SILS) has not been revised since it was developed in 1940, although modifications have been made in the instructions, answer sheets, scoring keys, and standard scores. The manual was revised in 1986.

The SILS was designed as a measure of intellectual impairment. The authors assume vocabulary does not decline as much as abstract thinking under conditions of intellectual deterioration. The difference between vocabulary scores and abstraction scores is postulated to indicate the extent of impairment. The SILS is claimed to be useful in obtaining a quick, accurate estimate of intellectual functioning. Scores on the SILS may be used to estimate full scale IQ scores on the Wechsler Adult Intelligence Scale (WAIS) or the Wechsler Adult Intelligence Scale—Revised (WAIS-R).

ADMINISTRATION AND SCORING. The SILS can be administered to individuals or groups. It consists of a 40-item Vocabulary test and a 20-item Abstraction test. Each of the tests has a 10-minute time limit and each test has items arranged in increasing order of difficulty. The instructions for the Vocabulary test state that respondents should guess if they do not know the answer. No statements about guessing are made in the instructions for the Abstraction test.

Six scores result from the SILS: Vocabulary, Abstraction, and Total scores are obtained from actual responses to the test, whereas the Conceptual Quotient, Abstraction Quotient, and estimated WAIS or WAIS-R scores are derived from the three obtained scores. The Vocabulary items are presented in a four-alternative multiple-choice format and are scored with the key supplied. Vocabulary items not attempted or left blank are worth one-fourth point each. Items on the Abstraction test require respondents to complete a series by supplying the numerals or letters that best complete the stimulus sequence. The number of Abstraction items answered correctly is multiplied by 2 to obtain the raw score. The Total score is found by summing the raw scores on the Vocabulary and Abstraction tests. The minimum Total score is 10 and the maximum is 80.

Tables are included in the manual to convert raw scores to T-scores. The tables are based upon age ranges of respondents. The manual states that raw scores are converted to "normalized T-scores and percentile rank equivalents," yet a simple linear transformation is applied to raw scores rather than an area transformation that would produce normalized scores. Either the explanations of the transformation given on page 48 of the manual are incorrect or the T-scores provided by the manual do not have the characteristics described and the percentile ranks and subsequent interpretations of the scores based on the normal distribution are incorrect. In either case, score interpretations given in the manual are potentially incorrect and misleading.

Conversion tables are provided for estimating WAIS and WAIS-R full scale scores and IQ. Equations and examples are also given to provide more accurate estimates of full scale IQ scores on the WAIS and WAIS-R. However, the example in Table 11 in the manual refers to Equation 2, yet no equation is so identified. There are two equations for this procedure given in an article published by Zachary, Crumpton, and Spiegel (1985, p. 536).

The SILS is available for administration or scoring on an IBM microcomputer. Scores provided in the manual for six case studies were used as input into the program. The results from the computer administrations were then compared to the results provided in the manual. Estimated WAIS-R IQ scores and Vocabulary, Abstraction, and Total SILS T-scores produced by the computer administration were different from the same scores given in the manual for each of the six case studies. The greatest discrepancy occurred with Case Study F. Apparently, the scoring procedure for items not completed on the Vocabulary test was not applied in the manual but was applied in the computer version for Case Study F.

TEST DEVELOPMENT AND STANDARDIZATION. The SILS was developed in the 1930s with a sample of 462 students: high school freshmen, high school juniors and seniors, and college upperclassmen. No information was provided on the number of students per grade level, age, socioeconomic level, geographic location, ethnicity, or gender of the students. Items for the Abstraction test were chosen based on discrimination among the three groups. Vocabulary items were chosen by matching the difficulty indices of Abstraction items.

The original standardization sample consisted of 542 grammar school children (grades 4 to 8), 257 high school students, and 217 college students. No data were presented concerning age, number of students per category, gender, socioeconomic level, geographic location, or ethnic background. A "revised normative sample" of 290 psychiatric patients was used to create the stratified age norms for ages 16 to 45 and over. This group is described as "distributed widely across the adult age span, but had a mean age of 34.9 years. The ratio of males to females was very evenly divided, and included individuals from lower, middle, and upper socioeconomic backgrounds."

RELIABILITY. Estimates of test-retest reliabilities were based on studies published from 1966 through 1977 of six groups of all female student nurses and one group of undergraduates (gender not given). Testing intervals varied from 2 to 16 weeks across samples and reliability estimates ranged from .31 to .77 (median = .60) for the Vocabulary scores, .47 to .88 for Abstraction scores (median = .66), and .62 to .82 (median = .78) for Total scores.

Split-half reliability estimates were based on 322 army recruits "heterogeneous in terms of their assessed verbal capacities." Item responses were split into odd and even items and values corrected for attenuation of .87, .89, and .92 were obtained for the Vocabulary, Abstraction, and Total scores, respectively. The manual notes that "since this speeded test is graduated in difficulty, split-half reliabilities are more appropriate than a more general measure of internal consistency such as Cronbach's coefficient alpha." However, the *Standards for Educational and Psychological Testing* (AERA, APA, & NCME, 1985, p. 21) states that "split-half coefficients that are obtained from scoring odd and even numbered test items separately yield an inflated estimate for a highly speeded test and are thus inappropriate."

VALIDITY. Correlation coefficients reported of SILS scores with other measures of intelligence and academic achievement ranged from .49 to .78. The correlation of SILS scores and WAIS and WAIS-R scores contained in the manual tended to range from the mid .70s to mid .80s. These studies were based mainly on samples of hospital patients and psychiatric patients.

One table summarizes the results of six studies published from 1964 to 1985 reporting correlation coefficients between SILS Vocabulary and Abstraction tests. With one exception, the values reflect decreasing correlations between the two scores as the extent of mental deterioration increases. The exception to this trend occurred with a sample of 485 normal adolescents. It should be noted that the other five studies had sample sizes ranging from 36 to 290.

Evidence of the validity of the Conceptual Quotient (CQ), derived as a ratio of Vocabulary and Abstraction mental age, as an index of cognitive impairment, is very well stated in the manual: "In conclusion, most of the available research does not support use of the CQ as a screening measure to assess intellectual impairment or deterioration."

EVALUATION. If the value of an instrument is reflected in its popularity, the SILS may be of value. It has been used since the 1930s as a clinical tool to estimate general levels of intellectual functioning and to screen for possible intellectual impairment. As noted above, its use for detecting intellectual deterioration has not been heavily supported by research results. The SILS manual has been revised but the instrument itself remains essentially the same as it was over 50 years ago. Normative data are very limited and restricted to groups with unique characteristics. Only one form of the test is available restricting its potential use to situations that do not require parallel forms.

The SILS manual is unusual in that it presents results of studies that do not support all recommended uses of the test. On the other hand, the presentations are weakened by a lack of direct evidence to support many assertions made. From a psychometric point of view, the SILS is woefully inadequate. Practitioners and clinicians will have to judge whether the use of the SILS will improve the diagnoses and services offered to clients.

REVIEWER'S REFERENCES

American Educational Research Association, American Psychological Association, & National Council on Measurement in Education. (1985). *Standards for educational and psychological testing.* Washington, DC: American Psychological Association, Inc.

Zachary, R. A., Crumpton, E., & Spiegel, D. (1985). Estimating WAIS-R IQ from the Shipley Institute of Living Scale. *Journal of Clinical Psychology, 41* (4), 532-540.

[361]
Short Category Test, Booklet Format.

Purpose: A sensitive indicator of brain damage measuring an individual's ability to solve problems requiring careful observation, development of organizing principles, and responsiveness to feedback.
Population: Ages 15 and over.
Publication Dates: 1986–87.
Acronym: SCT.
Scores: Total score only.
Subtests, 5: 1, 2, 3, 4, 5.
Administration: Individual.
Price Data, 1989: $105 per complete kit; $79.50 per set of stimulus cards, 5 booklets ('86, 20 cards per booklet); $13.50 per 100 answer sheets ('87); $17.50 per manual ('87, 40 pages).
Time: (15–30) minutes.
Comments: Revision of the Halstead-Reitan Category Test (9:463).
Authors: Linda Wetzel and Thomas J. Boll.
Publisher: Western Psychological Services.

Review of the Short Category Test, Booklet Format by SCOTT W. BROWN, *Associate Professor of Educational Psychology, University of Connecticut, Storrs, CT:*

The Short Category Test (SCT) is designed to assess an individual's ability to solve problems requiring abstract concept formation, based on the presentation of geometric shapes and configurations. The SCT does this without the equipment requirements and in less time than the longer Category Test. It transforms Halstead's nine subtests containing 360 items, presented using a semiautomated slide format with a rear projection screen, into five subtests of 20 items each, presented using a booklet format. The purpose of the SCT is to serve as a screening tool for individuals between the ages of 15 years through adulthood in a variety of medical and educational settings. The scores obtained from this instrument are purported to assess an individual's use of abstract principles, adaptive skills, and cognitive flexibility.

During administration of the SCT, the individual views figures or designs and responds with a number between 1 and 4, based on what rule the picture suggests to him or her. The response format may be either manual (pointing) or oral. The examiner provides feedback to each response by stating "right" or "wrong." All 100 items are administered to all subjects.

The SCT retains many of the original principles of the Category Test, with each SCT subtest containing various geometric shapes, lines, colors, and/or figures focusing on one of the following organizing principles: (*a*) the number of figures in a linear array; (*b*) the ordinal position of the atypical figure in a linear display; (*c*) the identification of the atypical quadrant; and (*d*) the number of quadrants joined by solid lines. The individual being assessed must view the cards, generate a hypothesis about the rule for the correct response, and check that rule against the feedback provided by the examiner.

The manual reports reliability and validity data for both the SCT and the Category Test. A reliability coefficient of .81 was obtained for the SCT using the split-half procedure with a Spearman-Brown correction formula. However, as the manual notes, the reliability coefficient must be interpreted with some caution because the items are linked together within subtests (because of feedback), resulting in some artifacts.

Test-retest reliability coefficients were not reported for the SCT, failing to provide an indication of the potential practice effects resulting from multiple testings. This is an extremely important, unfortunate deficit because the manual states the SCT may be used to assess changes that could result from various treatments.

Criterion-related and discriminative validity procedures are reported in the manual. The results of a study correlating the scores obtained by a group of 50 undergraduates on the Category Test and the SCT indicates that the two tests are highly related (.93 and .80, depending on the order of administration), suggesting the two tests are measuring similar abilities. Further analyses revealed a statistically significant practice effect when the Category Test was administered first, but not when the SCT was administered first. Unfortunately, the authors misinterpret this as evidence indicating a lack of a practice effect for the SCT.

Discriminative validity was assessed using a group of individuals with psychiatric and neurological diagnoses and a group of volunteers with no neurological damage. Analyses between the error scores of the "brain-damaged" and "non-brain-damaged" subjects indicated a high degree of predictability for group membership after controlling for age and education level ($p < .001$). When cutoff scores were used based on the creation of two age groups, those 45 years and younger and those 46 years and older, 83% of the total group were correctly classified. Additional analyses examining the correlation coefficients of a group of neurological patients for the SCT and the Category Test with several other neuropsychological measures yielded similar correlation coefficients. The validity data reported in the manual suggest that the SCT may be an effective screening tool for detecting neurological impairments affecting problem-solving abilities and that the results will be similar to those obtained on the Category Test.

The normative sample consisted of 120 volunteers and an independent clinical sample of 70 psychiatric and neurological patients. The manual reports the breakdown of the normal sample for sex, age, education, occupational level, and race with all stratifying variables within the appropriate range, except for age. No individuals in the normal sample were under the age of 20, yet the SCT manual reports that the test can be used for individuals 15 years of age and older. Without the age group of 15 to 19 included as part of the normative sample, the use of the SCT with this age group is inappropriate.

Analyses of the scores of the 190 subjects in the normative group controlled for the age and educational level of the individual. Subsequent analyses yielded two different cutoff scores, a cutoff score of 41 errors for subjects 45 and under and a cutoff score of 46 for subjects 46 and over, correctly classifying 83% of the total group as either brain-damaged or non-brain-damaged. Normative tables are provided for both age groups indicating percentiles and T-scores.

The SCT manual is well written and organized containing the pertinent psychometric and administration information. The inclusion of case studies using the SCT enables the examiner to interpret the scores and response patterns of different types of patients.

In summary, the SCT provides an alternative to the Category Test to assess impairments in the problem-solving abilities of individuals suspected of psychiatric or neurological dysfunctions. Two problems that need to be addressed when considering the use of the SCT are the age of the individual and practice effects. Using the SCT with individuals under the age of 20 should be done with extreme caution because there are no normative data available for this age group. Further, without test-retest reliability estimates, the practice effects from multiple administrations of the SCT are unknown. The SCT should provide, however, very similar results to the Category Test in a shorter amount of time and with less equipment.

Review of the Short Category Test, Booklet Format by HOPE J. HARTMAN, *Associate Professor of Social & Psychological Foundations, School of Education, The City College, City University of New York, New York, NY:*

The Halstead-Reitan Category Test (HRCT; 9:463) was revised because this sensitive screening device indicating brain damage had several limitations resulting in its frequent exclusion from clinical assessments. Administration was very time consuming, the equipment was expensive and broke down frequently, and it was difficult to use at bedside. Additionally, research has demonstrated that it is subject to practice effects, making improved retesting results difficult to interpret.

Several prior attempts to shorten the HRCT and simplify its administration included slides, cards, and booklet formats. These efforts were of limited value due to item sequencing problems and lack of, or unsuccessful, cross-validation results. Additional weaknesses were in reliability data, norms, and other psychometric information.

The Short Category Test, Booklet Format (SCT) was developed to: cut administration time by at least half, simplify the equipment needed, ensure the test's comparability to the original test in relation to standard neurological batteries, and discriminate between brain-damaged and non-brain-damaged individuals.

A spiral-bound booklet contains the 20 items (cards) which result in 5 subtests. In each subtest, items selected in sequence from the HRCT are organized according to a single principle, either number of objects, ordinal position of figures on the card, number of quadrants, or missing quadrant. The task is to formulate an organizing concept for each card sequence. The subject responds to each card by orally answering "one," "two," "three," or "four," or by pointing to the answer on the card shown. The test administrator marks the response and says "right" or "wrong." Item selection had an empirical base, but because no gender or race data were provided for the sample, generalizability of item appropriateness is unclear.

One source of confusion in the manual is an inconsistency between the narrative description of the test and Table 1. The narrative implies the second subtest has the organizing principle of "ordinal position," whereas Table 1 identifies the organizing principle of Subtest 2 as "original position." Some careful editing of the manual is in order.

Administration and scoring procedures appear relatively simple. In fact, the manual states administration and scoring can be done by a trained paraprofessional.

The rationale underlying the scoring procedure seems questionable. Instructions provide the subject with more cues for obtaining the correct answer on Subtest 2 than on Subtest 1, yet weigh these subtest errors the same. Although the manual mentions that Subtest 1 often is considered a warm-up exercise, all nine figures illustrating the answer sheet and scoring show the "Total Raw Error Scores" as the sum of *all* subtests. The Appendix contains a table providing Normalized *T*-Scores and Percentile Rank Equivalents corresponding to the Total Raw Error Score. The table provides separate data for Older and Younger Adults; age 45 is the cutoff.

The Percentile Rank Equivalents provided in the manual are potentially confusing. Why are they used instead of percentile ranks? The manual states that a person with a percentile rank equivalent score of 58 had *more errors* than approximately 58% of the normative sample in the appropriate age group. Therefore, the higher the "percentile rank equivalent score," the *worse* the level of performance. Conventionally, a "percentile rank" score means the higher the percentile rank, the *better* the level of performance. Representation of percentile rank equivalent data on the table in the Appendix by "%," the *percentage* symbol, could engender misinterpretation. Use of "%ileE" or "PRE" would be clearer.

The manual provides some reliability and validity data. Estimation procedures produced corrected split-half reliability coefficients of .81 for the SCT and .89 for the HRCT. The manual states both are probably artificially high because of item interdependence. There were no significant differences between the HRCT and SCT for even-odd item means. Test-retest reliability data were provided for the HRCT, but not for the SCT. No standard error of measurement data were reported.

In demonstrating equivalence between the two versions, the authors controlled for practice effects between the SCT and the HRCT by counterbalancing order of presentation and correlated percent of error scores. Subjects were primarily women undergraduates (only 14 males); race was unspecified. Pearson product-moment correlations were .93 for HRCT-SCT and .80 for SCT-HRCT. With HRCT-SCT presentation order, reliability was .84; with SCT-HRCT order, reliability was .42 (Summers & Boll, 1987), suggesting a significant lack of practice effects for the SCT. This implies better SCT scores upon retesting are more likely to reflect improved mental functioning than improvement on the HRCT. SCT items and the test overall were demonstrated to correlate with other neuropsychological measures. Correlation patterns were similar to comparisons of those tests to the HRCT.

The manual reports discriminative validity of the SCT for distinguishing brain-damaged from non-brain-damaged individuals. After controlling for age and education, ANCOVA results showed highly significant discriminability for these groups. Using age-corrected cutoff scores ("41" $\leq$ age 45; "46" $\geq$ age 46), 83% of normative and impaired subjects combined were classified correctly. This is an impressive hit rate for a single test and comparable to the classification rate of the HRCT. The manual states interpretations should be made by professionals with advanced clinical training and experience, and within the context of other measures. It also notes the test taker must have adequate motivation, vision, and attention span.

Standardization data appear to be primarily from white, middle-class males. The clinical sample was fairly homogeneous: primarily middle class, with high school education; the ratio of males to females was approximately 3:1 (15 females). Race was unspecified. The nonimpaired sample was somewhat more heterogeneous: a wider range of socioeconomic status and educational levels, and relatively balanced for gender. However, most individuals had at least a high school education and 87.5% were White. Research showed both age and educational level to affect significantly SCT performance. When comparing clinical and normal samples, the developers controlled for age and education. Norms are provided for different age groups but not different educational levels. The manual notes interpretations should take this into account. Race and gender were *not considered*. Research on nonverbal material demonstrates males and females, as well as Blacks and Whites, may differ significantly in their performance.

Overall, the SCT is appealing in format, short, and easy to use. Its apparent lack of practice effects is noteworthy. It may contribute to clinical diagnostic practice and treatment by serving as an improved alternative to the HRCT. However, before an unqualified recommendation can be given, several improvements are necessary. First, components of the manual and scoring statistics should be improved. Second, additional research is needed to test its reliability further, and to generate norms based on educational level. Finally, research is needed to determine whether the SCT's validity and norms can be generalized across race and gender.

REVIEWER'S REFERENCE

Summers, M., & Boll, T. (1987). Comparability of a short booklet version and the traditional form of the Category Test. *International Journal of Clinical Neuropsychology, 9* (4), 158-161.

[362]
Silver Drawing Test of Cognitive Skills and Adjustment.

Purpose: Designed to assess levels of ability in three areas of cognition: sequential concepts, spatial concepts, and association and formation of concepts; and to screen for depression.
Population: Ages 6 and over.
Publication Dates: 1983–90.
Acronym: SDT.
Scores, 5: Predictive Drawing, Drawing from Observation, Drawing from Imagination, Total, Emotional Content (Projection).
Administration: Group.
Price Data, 1990: $39.95 per complete battery including manual ('90, 100 pages), 10 test booklets, 10 scoring forms, and layout sheet; $15.95 per additional 10 test booklets, 10 scoring forms, and layout sheet; $27.95 per manual.
Time: (15–20) minutes.
Comments: Revision of Silver Drawing Test of Cognitive and Creative Skills.
Author: Rawley Silver.
Publisher: Ablin Press Distributors.
Cross References: For reviews by Clinton I. Chase and David J. Mealor of an earlier edition, see 10:333.

Review of the Silver Drawing Test of Cognitive Skills and Adjustment by KEVIN D. CREHAN, Associate Professor of Educational Psychology, University of Nevada Las Vegas, Las Vegas, NV:

The Silver Drawing Test of Cognitive Skills and Adjustment (SDT) is a revision of the Silver Drawing Test of Cognitive and Creative Skills previously reviewed in *The Mental Measurements Yearbook* (10:333). The stated purpose for development of the SDT was the need for an instrument to assess cognitive abilities of language-impaired children with a special concern for identifying latent abilities not recognized by other techniques. More specifically, the manual states four goals for the SDT: "to bypass language in evaluating the ability to solve conceptual problems, to provide greater precision in evaluating cognitive strengths or weaknesses that may escape detection on verbal measures, to facilitate the early identification of children or adolescents who may be depressed, and to provide a pre-post instrument for assessing individual progress or the effectiveness of educational or therapeutic programs."

The theoretical rationale for using drawing products to assess cognitive ability is related to the basic mathematical structures of class, space, and order reported by Piaget. The author suggests that although these concepts are usually developed through language, they can be assessed through visual representations. The concepts of class, space, and order are further related to Bannatyne's recategorization of the Wechsler Intelligence Scale for Children (WISC) subscales into groupings of spatial, conceptual, and sequential abilities for improved diagnosis of learning disabilities.

The SDT consists of three subtests: Predictive Drawing, Drawing from Observation, and Drawing from Imagination. The Predictive Drawing subtest consists of three tasks: drawing lines on six empty soda glasses to show what happens as one drinks the soda, drawing lines on an upright and "titled" [*sic*] bottle to show each half filled, and drawing a house on a steep slope. Each task is scored 0 to 5, respectively, based on the accuracy of showing a gradual decline in level of soda in the glasses, degree of horizontality of the liquid in the tilted bottle, and degree of verticality and support of the house. The drawing from observation subtest entails reproducing a display of three cylindrical shapes and a small stone differing in height, circumference, and distance from the observer. The drawing is scored 0 to 5 on three aspects: horizontal ordering, vertical ordering, and depth representation. The drawing from imagination subtest allows the examinee to select one picture from each of two displays of six sketches depicting persons, animals, and objects. The direction is to draw a picture using the two selected picture ideas in relation and "imagine something happening between them." A title or description of the product is requested. Again, the picture is scored 0 to 5 on three dimensions: the degree to which the representation shows interaction between the two selected sketches; the degree of coordination through depth space utilization, or showing more than one relational picture; and creativity. An additional 0 to 5 rating, not included in the score, is suggested for emotional content based on the judged degree of negativism-positivism of the picture's theme. This additional rating is new to the SDT revision. Adequate scoring guidelines with interpretations of sample drawings are provided.

Grade norms (first to eighth, tenth, twelfth, and adult) based on modest sample sizes (16 to 127) permit raw score conversion to T scores and percentile ranks. The norms show SDT scores generally increasing with age.

The author does not provide direct guidance in score or subtest score pattern interpretation but suggests the test user should consider subtest score differences in his/her diagnosis and intervention plan.

The manual presents reliability and scoring objectivity evidence based on two small sample 1-month test-retest and seven interscorer reliability studies. Test-retest reliabilities for total score ranged from .39 to .87 across five scorers and .08 to .70 for subtest scores based on 10 subjects. Interscorer reliability was generally acceptable for a performance measure with several correlations in the .70 to .90 range. Reported exceptions to acceptable interscorer reliability are adequately explained by the author.

Several studies of concurrent evidence of validity are reported in the manual. The criterion measures include commonly used achievement measures, WISC, Wechsler Adult Intelligence Scale (WAIS), Draw-A-Man, and the Bender Gestalt. Correlations with achievement measures are generally quite low which suggests discriminant evidence of validity between nominal achievement measures and the SDT. However, correlations with other nominal aptitude measures are too low to offer support of convergence. For 22 correlations between SDT subscale scores and the various achievement measures the range was -.15 to .95 with a median of .45. SDT total score correlation with the achievement measures ranged from .17 to .76. Correlations of the three SDT subtests and total score with WISC and WAIS performance scores were .33, .16, .37, .29, and .59, .37, .50, .60, respectively. SDT with WISC verbal correlations were near zero. Correlations with the Bender were negative and with the Draw-A-Man were .75, .31, .62, and .72.

The author presents a compelling introductory case study which convincingly develops the need for an instrument like the SDT but the measure and its documentation falter on important concerns. The theoretical basis is inadequately developed and construct evidence of validity is, at best, weak. Although the relationship of the SDT conceptualization to Bannatyne's WISC categories is cited, no empirical evidence is provided to support such a relationship. Concurrent evidence of validity with "accepted measures" of cognitive ability is mixed and so low in some instances to suggest that the SDT may be measuring a different construct. The norms appear to be based on (small) convenience samples and the conditions under which the data were collected are not described. One of the most notable weaknesses is the absence of sufficient guidelines for interpretation. Although the responsibility for appropriate interpretation of test scores lies with the user, the test manual should provide adequate examples of appropriate interpretations and cautions concerning potential over interpretation or misinterpretation.

Although the author has given considerable thought and effort toward the development of the SDT, the job remains unfinished and the current product leaves little to recommend it over other measures of cognitive abilities for the language-impaired (e.g., the WISC Performance scale, the Test of Nonverbal Intelligence, or the Arthur Adaption of the Leiter International Performance Scale).

Review of the Silver Drawing Test of Cognitive Skills and Adjustment by ANNIE W. WARD, President of Ward Educational Consulting, Inc. and of the Techne Group, Inc., Daytona Beach, FL:

The Silver Drawing Test of Cognitive Skills and Adjustment (SDT) is designed to assess levels of ability in three areas of cognition: sequential concepts, spatial concepts, and association and formation of concepts; and to screen for depression and emotional needs.

When this test was reviewed in 1989 (10:333) it was called the Silver Drawing Test of Cognitive and Creative Skills. The change in title mirrors a dropping of claims for measuring creativity and the adding of a claim to assess depressive and emotional needs. The theoretical base and scoring instructions for the *creativity* score were judged to be inadequate; however, the same thing is true of the *depression* score, which is also referred to as the "projection" score.

This test grew out of the author's work with deaf and language-impaired children and her observation that some of these children exhibited better cognitive skills than they were able to demonstrate on the usual type of intelligence test.

Although previous reviewers (Chase, 1989; Mealor, 1989) commended the intent of the test and supported the need for such an instrument, neither of them felt the technical documentation was sufficient to recommend the test for anything but exploratory use. Sadly, this reviewer finds nothing in the documentation in this manual to change this recommendation. Specifically, there is no real evidence of *validity*, that is, whether the test does what it is intended to do; reliability evidence is very scanty and insufficient; real norms are nonexistent; and there is little support for the scoring criteria. An attempt has been made to improve scoring by providing examples and the rationale for the scores. Also, a few additional correlations between the SDT and nationally normed achievement tests and between the SDT and some other tests have been run.

However, the manual provides no evidence of any hypothesized relationship between these measures, the sample sizes are for the most part very small, and the correlations provide little evidence of any expected relationships. In fact some of them are so bizarre as to raise questions as to the accuracy of the computation. In addition, the tables in which these data are reported do not indicate the makeup of the samples and some of the tables contain misleading information about sample size. Finally, some unfortunate typographical and formatting errors make the entire manual suspect.

VALIDITY: COGNITIVE. The manual presents a theoretical background that reviews the work of Piaget, et al.; Bannatyne, Bruner, and Torrance; and others. The literature review is used to raise a question about the common assumption that *thinking* is dependent on *language*; instead, it may be that the inverse is true, that is, that *language* is dependent on *thinking*. Also, the literature review leads the author to conclude that learning-disabled children as a group are high in visual-spatial skills, moderate in conceptual skills, and low in sequencing skills.

The three subtests of the SDT are described as assessing these three types of skills. Drawing What You Predict is designed to require sequencing; Drawing What You See, concepts of space; and Drawing What You Imagine, the ability to form concepts. One would predict, then, that the language-impaired would tend to score highest on Drawing What You See, and lowest on Drawing What You Predict. Unfortunately, there are no data to investigate this expectation. Furthermore, what little normative data there are, based presumedly on normal students and adults, also follow this pattern. Furthermore, these data do not support strongly an expectation, usually held for tests on cognitive ability, that mean scores should increase with age.

Correlations are reported between subtests on the SDT and several achievement and intelligence tests. For most of these reports, the groups are very small, the subjects are not described, and there is no rationale for selection of the tests. The correlations range from an unbelievable $+.945$ for SDT Imagination and the SRA Reading Achievement Test Reading for first grade students ($n = 25$) to $-.59$ for SDT Imagination and the Bender Visual Motor Gestalt Test ($N = 38$). Many of these data seem to be the same as those reviewed and found wanting in the previous reviews. Also, many of the table legends are erroneous or misleading. Some of the test titles are listed incorrectly and, in several tables, the N value provided is the sum of all cases, although the data are actually based on several groups.

VALIDITY: ADJUSTMENT (DEPRESSION AND EMOTIONAL NEEDS). The theoretical background for the use of this instrument to screen for emotional illness is very skimpy. It is largely based on the author's observation that "children perceive the same stimulus drawings differently" and a belief that "responses to the Drawing from Imagination task can provide a source of information about a child's problems." Evidence is anecdotal and based only on the author's experience.

NORMS. The normative data are totally inadequate. Apparently they are based on a "convenient sample" and provide little guidance for interpreting scores. Because the scoring standards are based largely on intuitive rather than empirical standards,

much more work needs to be done before the scores can be interpreted meaningfully.

SUMMARY AND RECOMMENDATIONS. This reviewer concurs with previous reviewers in concluding that this test is a creative attempt to address an important aspect in assessment of cognitive skills for a special population. However, even though some additional material has been added to the literature review and a few additional studies have been done, there is no basis for deciding what the test measures or how well it measures it. Much additional work needs to be done. Examples of needed studies follow.

1. Conduct a thorough construct validity study. This will involve (*a*) preparation of a careful specification of the construct of the test, that is the definition of the construct and some hypotheses as to how measures of the construct should relate to other variables; and (*b*) collection of data to check the accuracy of predictions made from the hypotheses. Suggestions of hypotheses which might be tested: (*a*) Measures of cognition should increase with age; (*b*) language/hearing-impaired children should score as high as normal children on *Observation* but not so high on *Prediction*; (*c*) for children with normal language and hearing, correlations between the SDT and other measures of intelligence and achievement should be as high as the reliability of each test; and (*d*) for language/hearing-impaired children, correlations between *Observation* and other measures of intelligence and achievement should be equal to those for children with normal language and hearing; correlations between *Prediction* and those measures should be lower than for children with normal language and hearing.

2. Collect reliability data of two types: (*a*) Intrajudge: Correspondence between ratings of the *same* judge for different examinees and at different times; and (*b*) Interjudge: Correspondence between *different* judges for the same examinees.

3. Collect normative data based on carefully selected samples of both language/hearing-impaired and normal language/hearing students and adults.

4. If the test is to be offered as a measure of depressive/emotional needs, the relationship between scores on it and other measures of these variables must be established.

Until these or similar studies are completed, users must be very cautious in making any decisions based on this instrument. The only defensible usage at this time is for exploratory or experimental studies.

REVIEWER'S REFERENCES

Chase, C. I. (1989). [Review of the Silver Drawing Test of Cognitive and Creative Skills.] In J. C. Conoley & J. J. Kramer (Eds.), *The tenth mental measurements yearbook* (pp. 745-746). Lincoln, NE: Buros Institute of Mental Measurements.

Mealor, D. J. (1989). [Review of the Silver Drawing Test of Cognitive and Creative Skills.] In J. C. Conoley & J. J. Kramer (Eds.), *The tenth mental measurements yearbook* (pp. 747-748). Lincoln, NE: Buros Institute of Mental Measurements.

[Re Sixteen Personality Factor Questionnaire.] Vocational Personality Report for the 16PF—Form E.

Purpose: Designed as "a computer-generated report that provides information on VR clients' vocationally-relevant personality characteristics for use in employability counseling and service planning."

Publication Date: 1987.

Acronym: VPR.

Scores, 16: Personality Scales (Extraversion, Adjustment, Tough-mindedness, Independence, Discipline), Psychopathology Scales (Anxiety and Depression, Sociopathic Tendency), General Interest Scales (Humanitarian/Interpersonal, Productive/Creative, Managerial/Leadership), Occupational Scales (Realistic Orientation, Investigative Orientation, Artistic Orientation, Social Orientation, Enterprising Orientation, Conventional Orientation).

Price Data, 1989: $12.50 per complete set including manual ('87, 36 pages) and floppy disk; $10 per 5¹/₄-inch floppy disk (IBM compatible); $4 per manual.

Author: Brian Bolton.

Publisher: Arkansas Research & Training Center in Vocational Rehabilitation.

Review of the Vocational Personality Report for the 16PF—Form E by THOMAS H. HARRELL, Professor and Associate Dean, School of Psychology, Florida Institute of Technology, Melbourne, FL:

INTRODUCTION. The purpose of the Vocational Personality Report (VPR) is to provide personality information useful for vocational rehabilitation counseling and service planning. Based on scores derived from the Sixteen Personality Factor Questionnaire (16PF; 9:1136), the report is intended for use with a wide range of individuals seeking vocational rehabilitation, and as the report utilizes the simplified E form of the 16PF (16PF-E) it may be used with individuals who read at grade 3 level. The VPR accepts 16PF-E raw scores for input and produces a report which numerically and graphically presents the 16 VPR scale scores on a sten scale. These scores are transformations of the primary personality dimension scores of the 16PF-E. VPR score presentations are followed by standard interpretive statements describing personality and vocational correlates of high scores on each VPR scale in actuarial terms. The VPR does not administer the 16PF-E, and the report is not designed for use as an integrated narrative report. The VPR was developed under Federal grant and is in the public domain. The program and manual are available from the publisher at cost.

HARDWARE REQUIREMENTS. The VPR is available for use with MS-DOS compatible computers with at least 128K RAM, one disk drive, and a printer. The program may be placed on a hard disk. There is no capability for writing the report to a text file. The report must be printed following input of scores.

VPR SCALE DEVELOPMENT. As described in the manual, the VPR incorporates 16 scales representing four conceptual areas of vocational personality functioning: (*a*) five personality scales, (*b*) two psychopathology scales, (*c*) three general interest scales, and (*d*) six occupational orientation scales. The personality scales (Extraversion, Adjustment, Tough-mindedness, Independence, Discipline) are the second-order personality dimensions derived from the 16PF by Krug and John, and adapted to the 16PF-E by the author. The psychopathology scales (Anxiety/Depression, Sociopathic Tendency) were developed by Bolton and Dana (1988) via canonical redundancy analysis of the relationships between the 16PF-E and the Psychiatric Status Schedule in a sample of rehabilitation clients. The general interest scales (Humanitarian Commitment, Productive Creativity, Managerial Attitude for males, Interpersonal Interaction, Creative Pursuits, Leadership Preference for females) were derived from an investigation of relationships between vocational interests as measured by the California Occupational Preference Survey and the 16PF-E personality dimensions (Bolton, 1986). The occupational orientation scales (Realistic, Investigative, Artistic, Social, Enterprising, Conventional), developed from a discriminant analysis of the 16PF profiles of 69 occupational groups, and allocated to Holland's vocational topology (Bolton, 1985), are reported in the 16PF handbook. Similarity coefficients from this study are used to calculate the VPR occupational orientation scale scores. All other scale scores are calculated from linear transformations of the 16PF-E raw scores.

VALIDITY. The validity of the VPR is a function of the validity of the 16PF and its E form, the derivative VPR scales, and the specific interpretive statements made in the report. The factorial validity of the 16PF is supported by a large body of research, and reviews of studies utilizing the 16PF-E in rehabilitation samples have supported its utility and factor structure in persons with disabilities. The normative sample for the 16PF-E and the VPR scales consisted of 519 male and 473 female rehabilitation clients. The sample was heterogeneous with respect to basic demographic characteristics and included conditions reflecting medical (61%), emotional (27%), and intellectual (11%) disabilities. Thus, the normative sample appears to be appropriate and representative. However, no evidence is provided for either the concurrent or predictive validity of the 16PF-E or the VPR scales. Criterion-related and discriminative validity data for the VPR scales are clearly needed.

The interpretive statements in the VPR are limited to statements descriptive of the personality and vocational correlates of high scores. Although not stated in the manual or the report itself, sten scores greater than 7.0 are typically denoted as high. No correlates are reported for average or low scores. Each report prints all 45 interpretive statements, with one to three statements following each associated scale. For each VPR scale, the user must decide if the statements are in any way applicable based upon the reported scale score. No probability data are given for correct predictions of the personality characteristics or occupational categories associated with high scores. The specific interpretive statements associated with high scores are based on the relationships between VPR scales and measures of personality, psychopathology, vocational interest, and occupational orientation. As noted in the previous section, these relationships were derived by the author in several research investigations. On the whole these studies are well planned and executed, and are limited primarily by the absence of independent replications. However, the limited number of interpretive statements, the lack of correlates associated with low or average scores, and the lack of classification rates significantly attenuates the sensitivity and specificity of the interpretations. The importance of evaluating all statements in light of other determinants of vocational interest, aptitude, and opportunity is not clearly stated in the manual, but cannot be overemphasized.

RELIABILITY. The VPR manual reports reliability coefficients for all VPR scales with the exception of the occupational orientation scales, along with 6-year stability coefficients for all scales. With the exception of the general interest scales, the reported reliabilities, ranging from .60 to .85 are minimally adequate for the purposes of the VPR. The stability coefficients average .50, with eight of the scales yielding stability coefficients of .60 or greater. The overall reliability of the VPR scales is not high, but is typical of vocational and personality inventories.

PROGRAM INTERFACE. The user-computer interface of the VPR is relatively elementary and straightforward, but leaves much to be desired. Although data entry prompts, input editing, and verification are adequate, the program does not evaluate entries for accuracy. Error checking routines are essential in programs where inappropriate data entry directly results in inaccurate score calculations. In the case of the VPR, sex (a necessary variable for accurate calculations) is not evaluated for correct content and raw scores are not evaluated for out-of-range score entry. Thus, it is possible to generate a report where sex has been entered as "None" and raw scores above 10 have been entered, without the program or the report advising the user that incorrect data have been entered. Additionally, user-computer dialogue should never be allowed to reach a dead end with no apparent corrective action available to the user. In the VPR, this condition occurs when all data have been entered, but the

printer is off-line. Any action other than placing the printer on-line will result in loss of entered data and return the user to the operating system. A needed feature is the option to interrupt the program at any point, saving the entered data to disk for later completion or report generation. In summary, although the interface is uncomplicated and easy to follow, it allows inappropriate data input and is rather unforgiving of human or equipment error.

SUMMARY. The VPR represents a significant initial step in the development of an instrument and interpretive program useful for vocational rehabilitation clients, a population in which below average language skills and cultural disadvantages limit the use of instruments such as the Strong Vocational Interest Blank. Additionally, the VPR provides basic personality information and a measure of psychopathology. Replication of those studies which form the basis of VPR scale development and research establishing the criterion-related validity of the VPR scales is needed. Research in this area is warranted by the potential of the VPR. Human factor shortcomings in the operation of the VPR need to be addressed directly by upgraded programming of data entry routines. Nevertheless, the VPR provides useful supplementary information for service planning and decision making in an area where assessment resources of this nature are very limited. Given the very low cost of the program, the cost/benefit ratio of the VPR merits its consideration by vocational rehabilitation agencies and clinicians who work extensively with vocational rehabilitation clients.

REVIEWER'S REFERENCES

Bolton, B. (1985). Discriminant analysis of Holland's occupational types using the Sixteen Personality Factor Questionnaire. *Journal of Vocational Behavior, 27,* 210-217.

Bolton, B. (1986). Canonical relationships between vocational interests and personality of adult handicapped persons. *Rehabilitation Psychology, 31,* 169-182.

Bolton, B., & Dana, R. (1988). Multivariate relationships between normal personality functioning and objectively measured psychopathology. *Journal of Social and Clinical Psychology, 6,* 11-19.

[364]
Skills Assessment Module.

Purpose: To assess a student's affective, cognitive, and manipulative strengths and weaknesses in relation to vocational skills required in various training programs within a school system.

Population: Average, handicapped, and disadvantaged vocational training school students ages 14–18.

Publication Date: 1985.

Acronym: SAM.

Scores, 13: Digital Discrimination, Clerical Verbal, Motor Coordination, Clerical Numerical, Following Written Directions, Finger Dexterity, Aiming, Reading a Ruler (Measurement), Manual Dexterity, Form Perception, Spatial Perception, Color Discrimination, Following Diagrammed Instructions.

Administration: Individual in part.

Price Data: Available from publisher.

Time: (90–150) minutes.

Comments: Module also includes Revised Beta Examination (2nd ed.) (The Psychological Corporation), Learning Styles Inventory, and Personnel Test for Industry (The Psychological Corporation); other test materials (e.g., mail sorter, file box, etc.) must be supplied by examiner.

Author: Michele Rosinek.

Publisher: Piney Mountain Press, Inc.

Review of the Skills Assessment Module by JEAN POWELL KIRNAN, Assistant Professor of Psychology, Trenton State College, Trenton, NJ:

The Skills Assessment Module (SAM) is a diagnostic tool for use in vocational school settings with students aged 14 through 18. The authors specifically state the instrument is not intended for selection, but rather results should be used for placement and/or remediation within the vocational school curriculum. Ideally, it is administered prior to entering a vocational program. Test results should indicate strengths and weaknesses.

Slight discrepancies exist between the user's manual and the technical guide. These will be highlighted when relevant. The SAM purports to measure affective, cognitive, and manipulative abilities for average, handicapped, and disadvantaged clients. This initial description, however, is misleading. One learns through subsequent analysis that the measures of interest, general intelligence, ability to follow oral instructions, and work behaviors are determined from other tests, school records, or ratings by instructors. The SAM itself provides 12 skills modules and a learning styles inventory.

Although the test package is supposed to include the Revised Beta Examination (general intelligence) and the Personnel Test For Industry (ability to follow oral directions), the sample sent for review lacked these instruments nor is there any recommendation for an interest inventory. I have a concern about the accuracy of measuring the affective behaviors (work behaviors such as appearance, endurance, etc.), which are to be rated by the evaluator, an instructor, or through school records on a scale of 1 (Superior) to 5 (Needs Improvement). Although training the evaluators would not seem time or cost effective, the use of behavioral anchors in the rating scales would introduce some degree of standardization and comparability.

It is beyond the scope of this review to evaluate all the instruments cited above despite the fact they are necessary for the SAM to be successful. The remainder of the review will concentrate on the Skills Modules and the Learning Styles Inventory provided in the SAM.

The Skills Modules are excellent in content and realism. The 12 tasks are quite diverse and include Mail Sort, Alphabetizing, Etch-a-Sketch, Payroll, Patient Information, Small Parts, Ruler Reading, Pipe Assembly, O-Rings, Block Design, Color Sort, and Circuit Board. As promised by the authors, they are nonthreatening and present the student with real-life tasks.

Most of the scoring is clear and easy to accomplish. In particular, the scoring for the Mail Sort and Alphabetizing is nothing short of ingenious. Because of slight markings on the cards, one can score the entire exercise by stacking the cards and turning them sideways to view the markings. All modules except the Color Sort are timed.

Scores from the Skills Modules, Work Behaviors Ratings, intelligence test, and Personnel Test for Industry are combined in the Vocational Performance Matrix. Twenty-four traits are listed and instructors of specific vocational courses (e.g., agriculture, business, and office) are instructed to rate the significance of each trait for their classes. Next, the student's performance is entered and thus a comparison of relative strengths and weaknesses can be made. Having instructors at the school rate the traits for relevancy allows the SAM to be specifically geared for each institution. The entering of student performance data could be facilitated by indicating which modules/ratings/tests measure each of the 24 traits. The Interest Inventory and the Learning Styles Inventory are not used in the matrix and it is unclear how these results are best integrated.

Although the test purports to have norms for average, handicapped, and disadvantaged students and separate norms for industry, only two normative tables are provided in the user's manual. One table is clearly industry-related. However, it is unclear upon which group the student norms are based. (Clearly marked norm tables are provided for each of the three student groups in the technical guide.) The normative data table for students is easy to read and converts the raw scores for the 12 skills modules to percentiles. The industry norms are not based on actual trials with employees but rather time values were derived using a Methods-Time-Measurement technique that studies the body movements required to perform each task. Because of this, no percentiles or consideration to deviation are given and it is unclear how one would interpret a student who scores slightly below the industry time.

Test-retest reliability with a time interval of 3–5 days was reported for 11 of the skills (Color Sort was not included) using time scores. The reliability coefficients were quite good ranging from .80 to .95.

Three types of validity are discussed. Content validity is claimed by participating instructors' determination of the relationship of the 24 traits to their specific courses. The claim to content validity would seem stronger if there was general agreement across a number of instructors in specified subject areas about the utility of the 24 traits. More importantly, the instructors should have evaluated not only whether the traits were relevant to the courses, but if any traits deserving of measurement were *missing*. Also, it is unclear if the instructors were allowed to view all 12 modules and the other measures. In other words, the *traits* may be content valid but there is no information to support the construct validity of the tests and modules.

Criterion-related validity is claimed because grades and prevocational skills correlate with test scores. No statistical evidence is provided, however, to support this claim. Industry norms are described as supporting predictive validity. Because the instrument is not intended to predict industry performance, but only success in vocational school, this seems to be a questionable strategy. The technical guide offers a chart of the 12 modules and corresponding psychological traits to support claims for the SAM's construct validity. There is no information, however, as to how or by whom the chart was constructed.

The brief test description states that test materials such as the mail sorter and file box must be supplied by the examiner. A separate parts list is included at the end of the user's manual. Necessary equipment for the skills modules may be ordered. This writer is unclear as to the standardization of these supplies. Variations in testing equipment may reduce the reliability of these measures. Additionally, some parts are not listed and it is unclear how one is to attain them. For example, the screw, nut, and handle for the Pipe Assembly, and more critically, the cards with color stickers for the Color Sort are not listed as available for order.

The Learning Styles Inventory is a self-report instrument containing 45 statements. Each statement is ranked on a scale of 1 (Least Like Me) to 4 (Most Like Me). The inventory is designed to measure learning style across three parameters: learning (auditory language, visual language, auditory numerical, visual numerical, and auditory-visual-kinesthetic), working (group learner or individual learner), and expression (oral or written). A worksheet facilitates the scoring of these nine styles. Scores are interpreted as a major learning style (raw score of 32–40) or a minor style (raw score of 20–32).

No information is given as to how the learning style cutoff scores were derived. Additionally, there are no reliability or validity data provided concerning the Learning Style Inventory.

A personal computer program to aid in scoring and interpretation is also available for Apple users. Interestingly, this version provides predetermined ratings as to the significance of each of the 24 traits in the various vocational programs (Vocational Performance Matrix). These ratings of importance may be a useful comparison base for test users and so should appear in the user's manual, not just in the computer-supported scoring package.

The authors deserve commendation for recognizing the need to consider more than just simple abilities in determining the best vocational curriculum. The strengths of the SAM include its consideration of the entire individual (e.g., interests, learning styles, work behaviors) and the Vocational Performance Matrix that attempts to tailor results to each institution. However, a number of weaknesses exist, for example, the lack of solid evidence for validity of the modules and the total lack of reliability or validity for the Learning Styles Inventory. The test could be further improved by refining the rating system used to describe work behaviors, providing a method that fully integrates all the test components, and editing the manual to clarify administration details.

REVIEWER'S REFERENCE

Bower, E. (1969). *Early identification of emotionally handicapped children in the school* (2nd ed.). Springfield, IL: Charles Thomas.

Review of the Skills Assessment Module by WILBUR L. LAYTON, Professor of Psychology, Iowa State University, Ames, IA:

The Skills Assessment Module (SAM) was designed to assess a student's affective, cognitive, and manipulative strengths and weaknesses in relation to vocational performances required in the various training programs within a school system. It was developed to accommodate secondary and adult educators in the dual role of instructor and evaluator. The SAM consists of 3 paper and pencil tests and 12 "hand-on modules." The tests, published by other publishers, are the Learning Styles Inventory, Revised Beta Examination, and Personnel Test for Industry. According to the manual, the SAM may also be used to rate certain affective work behaviors such as: appearance, communication skills, endurance, follows rules and regulations, initiative, interpersonal traits, reactions to assigned tasks, and safety consciousness. A Student Data Form is also a part of the SAM and is used to record medical, social, educational, and other data. The target population is mildly handicapped and disadvantaged youth between 14 and 18 years of age; mildly handicapped refers to students classified as mildly learning disabled, mildly retarded, or mildly emotionally disturbed. Disadvantaged refers to students who are economically or educationally deprived and are functioning at least one grade below grade level.

Normative data for the hands-on modules are presented for 112 average students, 121 handicapped students, and 61 disadvantaged students. Demographic characteristics of the samples are given. An important omission is the race of the subjects, particularly because race seems to be related to the need for special education, and all students presumably were enrolled in Georgia schools. Interestingly, socioeconomic data are presented as Urban, Suburban, and Rural. No rationale for this breakdown is given.

Data demonstrating the reliability and validity of the SAM are meager. The technical manual reports test-retest data (3–5 day interval) for the hands-on modules for a sample of 50 "average" students. No reliability data are given for the targeted population. The manual stresses the use of the standard error of measurement to evaluate a person's scores and urges practice and retesting until the scores reach certain criteria. The manual discusses content and curricular validity, criterion-related validity, and construct validity. The latter section gives a table outlining a "non-technical factor analysis" of the hands-on modules. This reviewer assumes this tabular analysis was someone's judgment of what the modules reflect. The table indicates that 7 out of the 12 modules get at perceptual skills, 3 reflect motor skills, and 2, cognitive skills. Ruler Reading is one of the skills listed as cognitive! No data are presented for the validity of the use of the three paper and pencil tests in the SAM context. The evidence presented for reliability and validity is totally inadequate for substantiating the claims of the author and publisher. There are no research data evaluating and supporting the use of the SAM.

The Skills Assessment Module appears to be intended as a guidance tool to be used by educators to assess special needs of special education students. The reliability and validity and hence, worth, of the SAM is not yet demonstrated. This reviewer cannot recommend the use of the SAM until more research data are available.

[365]
Smoker Complaint Scale.
Purpose: Designed to measure changes in physiological/emotional/craving states as a function of smoking cessation.
Population: Persons quitting smoking.
Publication Date: 1984.
Acronym: SCS.
Scores: Total score and item scores only.
Administration: Group.
Manual: No manual.
Price Data, 1989: Instrument available without charge from publisher.
Time: (1–5) minutes.
Comments: Self-administered.
Author: Nina G. Schneider.
Publisher: Nina G. Schneider.

[366]
Snijders-Oomen Non-Verbal Intelligence Test.
Purpose: Developed as an untimed, nonverbal test of intelligence.
Publication Dates: 1939–88.
Administration: Individual.
Price Data: Available from publisher.

Foreign Language Edition: Dutch and German editions available.
Comments: Administered in pantomime (for hearing impaired) or orally.
Publisher: Swets Test Services [The Netherlands].
a) SNIJDERS-OOMEN NON-VERBAL INTELLIGENCE SCALE FOR YOUNG CHILDREN.
Population: Dutch children ages 2-6 to 7-0.
Acronym: SON $2^1/_2$–7.
Scores, 6: Sorting, Mosaic, Combination, Memory, Copying, Total.
Time: (45–50) minutes.
Comments: Also called Non-Verbal Intelligence Scale S.O.N. $2^1/_2$–7.
Authors: J. T. Snijders and N. Snijders-Oomen.
b) SON-R.
Population: Dutch children ages 5-6 to 17-0.
Acronym: SON-R $5^1/_2$–17.
Scores, 8: Categories, Mosaics, Hidden Pictures, Patterns, Situations, Analogies, Stories, Total.
Time: (60–120) minutes.
Comments: Revised version of the SON-'58 and SSON; older versions out-of-print.
Authors: J. T. Snijders, P. J. Tellegen, J. A. Laros, N. Snijders-Oomen (test), and M. A. H. Huijnen (test).
Cross References: For reviews by Douglas K. Detterman and Timothy Z. Keith of an earlier edition, see 9:1146; see also T3:2221 (1 reference) and T2:512 (5 references); for a review by J. S. Lawes of the 1958 edition, see 6:529 (2 references).

[367]
Social and Prevocational Information Battery—Revised.
Purpose: "To assess knowledge of certain skills and competencies regarded as important for the community adjustment of students with mild mental retardation."
Population: Mildly mentally retarded students in grades 7–12.
Publication Dates: 1975–86.
Acronym: SPIB-R.
Scores, 10: Purchasing Habits, Budgeting, Banking, Job Related Behavior, Job Search Skills, Home Management, Health Care, Hygiene and Grooming, Functional Signs, Total.
Administration: Group.
Price Data, 1987: $34.25 per 20 hand-scorable test books ('86, 16 pages) and class record sheet; $8.50 per examiner's manual ('86, 107 pages); $10.80 per specimen set including hand-scorable test booklet, class record sheet, and examiner's manual.
Time: (20–30) minutes per test.
Comments: Orally administered.
Authors: Andrew S. Halpern, Larry K. Irvin, and Arden W. Munkres (design).
Publisher: CTB Macmillan/McGraw-Hill.
Cross References: For reviews by M. Harry Daniels and Carol Kehr Tittle of an earlier edition, see 9:1147; see also T3:2224 (7 references); for a review by C. Edward Meyers of the original edition, see 8:984 (2 references).

Review of the Social and Prevocational Information Battery—Revised by TERRY OVERTON, Assistant

Professor of Special Education, Longwood College, Farmville, VA:

DESCRIPTION AND PURPOSE. The Social and Prevocational Information Battery—Revised (SPIB-R) is designed to assess knowledge of employability, economic self-sufficiency, family living, personal habits, and communication in persons with mild mental retardation. A total of 277 items are included in each of the nine tests. Each test contains from 26 to 36 items and requires approximately 20 minutes to administer. The test authors recommend testing in about three sessions within a time period of 1 week. This revised edition of the SPIB, like the original version, is administered orally to small groups of students, or proctored larger groups, who respond by marking answers in the student test book. The test battery assesses a variety of concepts useful for community adjustments such as comparative shopping, buying on time, banking, interest rates, appropriate communication with supervisors and coworkers, job assistance agencies, completing job application forms, food preparation procedures, proper use of medication, good health practices, and functional sign reading. Most of the items are presented in a true/false format; however, there are several items that present pictures from which the student must select the correct answer(s). Sample items are given to the students before test administration in an effort to determine that students understand the tasks of the test. Students who are unable to respond correctly are given additional instruction before they are allowed to proceed with the test.

The authors report the major changes of the revised SPIB are the replacement or revision of 34 test items and updating and revising the administration manual. The focus of the new manual appears to be the integration of the assessment instrument and teacher planning for instruction. The manual provides coverage of instructional planning based on the results of student performance. Information is given for obtaining the additional curriculum, Skills for Independent Living Teacher Resource Files, which is available from the same source.

SCORES. Responses are scored as 1 for correct and 0 for incorrect. Norms are provided for determining the percent correct and percentile ranks by junior or senior high group levels. Derived scores are based on the original SPIB norm group performance.

STANDARDIZATION. The revised edition of the SPIB is based on the normative data of the original instrument. The original version of the SPIB included a normative sample of approximately 900 students from Oregon who were primarily Caucasian. An equal number of students were included in the junior high (grades 7, 8, 9) and senior high (grades 10, 11, 12) groups. Student ages ranged from 14 to 20 years and the mean IQ of the

reference group was 68. No effort was made to include additional ethnic or geographic representation in the normative sample. Although no new normative data are presented in the manual of the SPIB-R, the test authors report they will continue to collect data on the revised edition for several years.

Statistics reported for the original SPIB include the median, mean, and standard deviation of the nine tests and for the total test by junior and senior high groups. The standard deviation ranges from 3.9 to 5.6 on individual tests and 31.1 to 34.3 on the total test for the senior and junior high groups, respectively.

RELIABILITY. Reliability information presented in the test manual for the original SPIB includes internal reliability studies using the KR 20, which yielded coefficients ranging from .65 to .82 for tests and .93 to .94 for the total battery. Test-retest reliability coefficients ranged from .62 to .79 for tests and .91 to .94 for the total battery. Internal reliability tended to vary more in the junior high group whereas test-retest reliability tended to vary more at the senior high level.

Standard error of measurement for individual tests ranged from 1.79 to 2.74. For the total test battery, 8.40 was reported for the junior high group and 9.33 was reported for the senior high group. All data are from the original SPIB.

VALIDITY. Predictive validity of the original SPIB was studied through the use of a rating instrument designed by the test authors to measure student performance of 130 students who were receiving vocational rehabilitation a year after high school graduation. A moderate relationship was reported by the test authors. Additional criterion-related validity studies (by the authors of the original SPIB) that included students from eight other states are given in the manual. These studies included representation of black and other ethnic populations. Concurrent validity coefficients ranged from .56 to .86.

EVALUATION. The ease of administration, test content, and provision of methods for instructional planning through the additional curriculum (Skills for Independent Living) available from the publishers make this instrument attractive to the special education teacher. Group administration, easy scoring, and attention to planning for student Individual Educational Programs (IEPs) and unit or program planning provide needed assistance for busy classroom teachers.

The variability of item and test difficulty, complex vocabulary, multiple-step instructions, forced-choice answer format, and lack of evidence to support test content and the relationship to applied knowledge continue to plague this instrument. Although the authors warn against using this instrument for program or placement decisions (and encourage the use of multiple instruments), in practice the inclusion of percentile ranks may result in the use of this instrument for inappropriate educational decisions. The reliability of the nine tests seems insufficient for the basis of individual educational decisions.

The test content of Home Management, Health Care, and Hygiene and Grooming may not be representative of these domains. The number and type of items included seems scant and indeed entire test batteries could be written to measure ability and knowledge of any of these tests.

The largest areas of concern are the lack of new normative data on the revised SPIB and the small nonrepresentative samples used to develop the original normative data. Once again the consumer must be cautioned about using this instrument for any purpose other than monitoring educational programs or class instructional planning. New normative data using representative samples and additional research from independent sources would add to the credibility of this instrument.

Review of the Social and Prevocational Information Battery—Revised by TERRY A. STINNETT, Assistant Professor of Psychology, Eastern Illinois University, Charleston, IL:

The Social and Prevocational Information Battery—Revised (SPIB-R) is a forced-choice self-report inventory designed for mild mentally retarded adolescents and young adults. Its purpose is to assess knowledge needed for successful post-school community adjustment.

This criterion-referenced test can identify the student's strengths and weaknesses and links the assessment data to treatment using a "program-related assessment model" (PRA). Five important areas for potential intervention are reflected by the test content: employability, economic self-sufficiency, family living, personal habits, and communication. The areas can be used as long-range educational goals and are measured by nine separate tests.

Each test consists of 26 to 36 orally presented items. The examinee simply marks an "X" on the word "True" or "False" as a choice for each item. A few items require the student to choose between pictures instead of the true or false choices. Each test can be administered in 20 to 30 minutes individually or in groups of 10 or less. The authors recommend the battery be completed in at least three separate sessions to ensure the examinee's optimum performance is obtained. The oral administration and simple response format minimizes the reading requirements for the examinee. Administration suggestions and procedures are clearly written and the test could be administered easily by paraprofessionals.

The SPIB-R yields three types of scores for the separate tests and for the total battery: raw scores, percentage of items correct, and percentile rank scores. Scoring is straightforward; the examinee's raw score is calculated by summing the number of items correct and the corresponding percentage correct and percentile rank scores are derived by using the appropriate reference group norm table (junior high or senior high).

The most useful score for linking assessment to treatment yielded by the SPIB-R is the percentage correct score. The authors suggest two methods for using the percentage correct scores. First, an examinee who scores ± one Standard Error of Measurement (*SEM*) (7 percentage points) from the reference group mean could be considered to have high or low knowledge in the particular area. Second, the authors suggest that percentage correct scores can be compared to predetermined local mastery standards for instruction, for example performance standards that are stated on Individual Education Plans (IEPs).

This latter use of the score assumes there is a direct match between instruction and the SPIB-R test content. Because the test merely samples knowledge of various social and prevocational information domains and does not define them, it is possible that actual instruction in the curriculum will not perfectly match the test results. Additionally, the test measures *knowledge* of social and prevocational information and does not directly measure the behaviors needed for success. An examinee might have adequate knowledge in a specific area but still fail to perform the actual behaviors needed for mastery at the appropriate time and at the appropriate level. The test could identify knowledge/skill deficits and not identify these performance deficits.

Another problematic characteristic of the test is that the scores for ninth grade students can be derived from either the junior or senior high school norm tables. The authors make no suggestions to guide the norm group choice and state the decision is arbitrary. Different percentile ranks can be obtained for the same raw score depending on which reference group is used. The high school norms yield lower percentile rank scores than do the junior high norms. Fortunately, the percentile rank scores are the least critical for linking SPIB-R data to treatment.

The most substantive change between the SPIB-R and its predecessor, the Social and Prevocational Information Battery (SPIB), is the updated administration manual. Scrutiny of the manual reveals there is a detailed emphasis on the PRA model and how to use SPIB-R data to interface with the Skills for Independent Living Teacher Resource Files (SIL). The SIL is a curriculum based on the content of the SPIB and can be used to guide intervention and to design IEPs. Use of the SIL with the SPIB-R will provide an integrated package for the user and might circumvent some of the treatment validity problems previously noted.

The original SPIB technical data are reported in the SPIB-R manual. The authors suggest these data be used to evaluate the SPIB-R psychometric characteristics. The authors contend that because only 34 of the original 277 SPIB test items (12%) have been revised and/or replaced, the SPIB data should be appropriate. However, it is likely that the *SEM*s will be different for the SPIB-R and thus use of the ± one *SEM* criterion to determine level of knowledge with the percentage correct scores becomes inappropriate. Prudent test users might also agree that the lack of SPIB-R data prohibits the use of percentile rank scores for the SPIB-R, because the scores are based on the original sample and do not reflect the item revisions.

The description of the original SPIB student sample reported in the SPIB-R manual is inadequate. The original sample is based on 453 junior high and 453 senior high mild mentally retarded students enrolled in the Oregon schools (total $N = 906$). Chronological ages of the students are reported to range from 14 to 20 years; IQ ($M = 68$, $SD = 8$). Demographics for sex, race, grade, and socioeconomic status, and detailed classification data about IQ and adaptive behavior, are not reported. The authors do report most subjects were Caucasian, that the number of males and females were about equal, and that no significant performance differences were found among the 7th through 9th graders. Also no significant differences were found among the 10th through 12th graders. As a result, the data were collapsed into two groups: junior and senior high. Data for the 9th graders were included in the junior high group except when the 9th grade was located at a senior high, then the data were included in the senior high group. They also report no sex differences on the separate tests or total score. Information about the number of schools sampled and whether the battery was individually or group administered is omitted.

Validity and reliability data are now included in the manual; however, they are the original SPIB normative data, because SPIB-R data are not yet available. Kuder-Richardson formula 20 (KR 20) internal consistency reliability estimates for the nine SPIB tests are somewhat lower than is desirable for reliability coefficients and ranged from .65 to .79 (mdn = .75) for the junior high group and from .72 to .82 (mdn = .75) for the high school group. Total battery KR 20s are acceptable (.94 and .93 for junior and senior high groups respectively). Test-retest reliabilities were calculated based on a 2-week interval (.70 to .79, mdn = .75 for junior high students, and .62 to .78 mdn = .73 for the high school sample). Total battery test-retest estimates are

adequate (.94 and .91 for junior and senior high samples respectively). It should be noted that the students were apparently all participating in a work experience program during this time. Effects associated with this educational experience might have lowered the test-retest reliabilities.

A review of curriculum guides and research studies pertaining to mild mentally retarded students was done to establish content validity of the SPIB. Various long and short range objectives were defined through this effort and 26 secondary teachers of mild mentally retarded students rated these objectives in terms of importance. No information is reported to describe the demographic characteristics of the teacher raters. Typically, content validity is developed with the assistance of subject-matter experts; however, without specific teacher information it is impossible for SPIB or SPIB-R users to estimate the level of the teachers' expertise. New SPIB-R items were developed after SPIB users were identified from CTB/McGraw-Hill records and surveyed about the SPIB. A total of 285 SPIB users responded to the survey (42% response rate). Items that were identified as ambiguous, as having vocabulary or syntax problems, or having outdated concepts and/or content were revised.

Halpern, Raffeld, Irvin, and Link (1975) examined SPIB predictive validity using a 1972–73 experimental version of the test. Vocational rehabilitation counselors rated 220 mild mentally retarded students 1 year after graduation from high school with a scale that reflected general adaptation in community integration, economic self-sufficiency, communication, family living, and personal habits. A canonical correlation of .58 was obtained between the SPIB tests and the five criterion subscales. Thus, the experimental SPIB and the five-scale criterion measure shared about 34% of the variance. Predictive validity estimates for the SPIB-R are not available.

Concurrent validity of the final version of the SPIB was examined by the test authors. Mild mentally retarded clients of the Department of Vocational Rehabilitation aged 18–21 ($N = 103$) were administered the SPIB and were rated by their counselors with the five-scale criterion measure used in the original predictive validity study. A canonical correlation of .60 was obtained between the SPIB tests and the five criterion scales. Thus, the final-version SPIB and the five-scale criterion measure shared about 36% of the variance. Information about the concurrent validity of the SPIB-R is not available.

Some additional reliability and validity studies have been conducted with the SPIB. Irvin and Halpern (1977) obtained four new samples of mildly retarded junior and senior high students from Alaska and Kentucky, and a sample of mild mentally retarded Oregon high school graduates to reexamine the SPIB reliability. The Oregon sample was also used to reexamine the validity of the test. Coefficient alpha reliability estimates across the four samples and the nine SPIB scales ranged from .58 to .80 and are lower than desirable for test reliabilities. A canonical correlation of .61 was obtained between the SPIB tests and a five-scale rating measure that was completed by the Oregon subjects' vocational rehabilitation counselors. It is not clear if the rating scale was the same one that had been used in the previous studies. The SPIB and the five-scale criterion measure shared about 37% ($.61^2$) of the variance. These results are consistent with the earlier reliability and validity studies that were conducted with the original standardization sample.

Halpern, Irvin, and Landman (1979) further investigated the SPIB's criterion-related validity. Mildly retarded high school students from Oregon, Washington, California, Texas, Arizona, Minnesota, and Ohio were assessed with the SPIB and four separate criterion measures. A two-option multiple-choice and a three-option multiple-choice test were developed based on SPIB items to assess social and prevocational information. A parent-completed Behavior Rating Form (BRF) and behavior performance tests were also used as criterion measures. Intercorrelations between the SPIB and the multiple-choice measures ranged from .82 to .86, whereas the relationship between the SPIB and the BRF was lower ($r = .40$). The relationship of the SPIB and the behavior performance tests was .78. Multiple regression analyses were conducted using the SPIB and the parent ratings (BRF) to predict the behavior performance scores. Results indicated the SPIB is a good predictor ($R = .72$, $R^2 = .52$). The addition of the BRF also helped account for slightly more of the variance than was accounted for by the SPIB in isolation (SPIB in isolation; $R = .69$, $R^2 = .48$). These results suggest the SPIB is valid for predicting actual behavior for young mildly retarded adults.

EVALUATION. The SPIB-R should be titled "SPIB—Revision in progress." The test has an admirable purpose, to link assessment to treatment, but at present it is technically inadequate for the stated purpose. The absence of revised normative data is problematic. The original norms are too regional and outdated. The SPIB norms underrepresent minority students and necessary demographic information about the standardization sample is too vague. Reliability estimates of the original SPIB are lower than are desirable. The SPIB shows promise as a valid test, but additional validity information on the SPIB-R is required. Although there is a great need for this type of device, and there are no comparable tests, the SPIB-R cannot be recommended until updated data are collected, and reliability and validity are further investigated.

REVIEWER'S REFERENCES
Halpern, A., Raffeld, P., Irvin, L., & Link, R. (1975). Measuring social and prevocational awareness in mildly retarded adolescents. *American Journal of Mental Deficiency, 80*, 81-89.
Irvin, L. K., & Halpern, A. S. (1977). Reliability and validity of the Social and Prevocational Information Battery for mildly retarded individuals. *American Journal of Mental Deficiency, 81*, 603-605.
Halpern, A. S., Irvin, L. K., & Landman, J. T. (1979). Alternative approaches to the measurement of adaptive behavior. *American Journal of Mental Deficiency, 84*, 304-310.

[368]

Social-Emotional Dimension Scale.

Purpose: Provides a means for rating nonacademic student behaviors "which may be judged by teachers as problems in the classroom setting."
Population: Ages 5.5–18.5.
Publication Date: 1986.
Acronym: SEDS.
Scores: 6 scores (Avoidance of Peer Interaction, Aggressive Interaction, Avoidance of Teacher Interaction, Inappropriate Behavior, Depressive Reaction, Physical/Fear Reaction) plus a Behavior Quotient and a Behavior Observation Web.
Administration: Group.
Price Data, 1987: $34 per complete kit including 50 profile/examiner record forms and examiner's manual (54 pages); $19 per 50 profile/examiner record forms; $17 per examiner's manual.
Time: Administration time not reported.
Comments: Behavior checklist for ratings by school personnel.
Authors: Jerry B. Hutton and Timothy G. Roberts.
Publisher: PRO-ED, Inc.

Review of the Social-Emotional Dimension Scale by JEAN POWELL KIRNAN, Assistant Professor of Psychology, Trenton State College, Trenton, NJ:

The Social-Emotional Dimension Scale (SEDS) assesses a student's nonacademic behaviors that may interfere with learning in the classroom setting (either their own learning or that of classmates). Designed for use in kindergarten through the senior year of high school, the rating scale identifies individuals who are "at risk" for problematic behaviors. SEDS is not designed as a stand-alone instrument but should be used in conjunction with other tests and observations. It should serve as a screening tool and areas of high risk are to be interpreted as requiring further assessment rather than demanding immediate action.

The scale consists of 32 items on which the student's behavior is rated on a 3-point scale (*never or rarely*, *occasionally*, and *frequently*). Ratings are conducted independently by the teacher primarily responsible for the student as well as by other knowledgeable school personnel. A minimum of 3 weeks of observation is recommended prior to rating the behaviors. The SEDS provides six behavioral subscores (Avoidance of Peer Interaction, Aggressive Interaction, Avoidance of Teacher Interaction, Inappropriate Behavior, Depressive Reaction, and

Physical/Fear Reaction) as well as a total score, corresponding percentiles, and a behavior quotient (BQ).

The manual is quite comprehensive including sample SEDS rating forms and sample cases. The scoring requires simple computations and a detailed example is provided. A table of normative data provides for easy translation of raw scores into percentiles. A wealth of demographic information is provided for the normative sample of 1,097 students and their corresponding 198 raters. There appears to be a good representation of geographical area, sex, ethnic, and educational levels. However, a date should be provided for this study. No separate norms are reported for sex or age groups.

Percentiles for the six behaviors are graphed on a Behavior Observation Web (BOW)-Individual. This provides a visual representation of the high and low risk areas. Users are cautioned not to rely heavily on the six separate behavior scores. It is suggested that an "at risk" score in any category be confirmed through instruments specifically designed to measure that behavior.

A summary record form is used to combine and compare scores across the various raters. The BOW graph on this form, referred to as a BOW-Setting as opposed to the BOW-Individual, reflects the summary measure of behavior quotients for each rater and not the six individual behavior percentiles. Although this allows for an interesting comparison of the student's overall behavior across settings and raters, more guidance could be provided as to how to interpret discrepancies among raters. A consultation with all raters present may lead to understanding differences and may provide an opportunity to share special techniques/approaches that are successful with a particular student.

The scale is based on Bower's (1969) definition of emotional disturbance and behavioral disorders in emotionally disturbed children. Items were constructed that represented observable behaviors of these dimensions. Items were pilot tested in a school setting using teachers as raters. These data were then used in an item analysis and factor analysis, which revealed six major problematic behaviors.

A number of different techniques were used to establish reliability. Due to the small number of items in the separate behavioral measures, all reliability was measured for total score. Test-retest was conducted for five different groups of students (two normal, one in a Title I Program, one group of emotionally disturbed, and the last learning disabled). All coefficients were acceptable for this type of measure (ratings) and ranged from .67 to .96. Acceptable internal consistency was demonstrated for each of 13 age levels in both a normal and mildly handicapped sample and ranged from .78 to .94, and .81 to .93, respectively. Interrater reliabili-

ty was demonstrated in a series of studies comparing ratings of homeroom teachers, physical education teachers, art teachers, language therapists, and special education and regular education instructors. The student sample included learning disabled, mentally retarded, mildly handicapped, and unclassified. The resulting correlations ranged from .48 to .71. This range is acceptable given the variation in teacher interaction and educational settings.

Content validity was established in the construction of the instrument through reliance on Bower's dimensions of school-related behaviors. It appears, however, the content was evaluated by the authors only. The use of outside experts would add more strength to this claim. Concurrent criterion-related validity is claimed through the correlation of SEDS scores with scores on a similar instrument, the Walker Problem Behavior Identification Checklist. Correlations were reported in the range of .77 to .88. Support for construct validity is reported in a factor analysis of contrasting groups—handicapped and normal students. Additionally, a comparison of teacher ratings on the SEDS and peer ratings on a sociometric measure of students you would most like/least like to sit next to provided further support for the instrument. Most importantly, the SEDS was able to differentiate between students identified as normal versus those identified as handicapped.

All reliability and validity information refers to total test scores. The usefulness of the six separate scores is questionable because the small number of items precludes separate reliability and validity investigations. Because separate scores are supposedly indicative of problem areas and require further assessment, it would be informative if the authors reported how often these indicators were confirmed by subsequent assessment.

Four comprehensive case studies facilitate the user's understanding of SEDS and how it might fit into a comprehensive evaluation. In addition, suggestions for intervention are provided for each of the six factors. These suggestions are generally based on learning principles and stress the need to provide opportunities for appropriate behaviors, decrease opportunities for inappropriate behavior, and administer the proper rewards for both the "at risk" students and their peers.

Development and psychometric evaluations of the SEDS are extremely comprehensive and professionally accomplished. The manual provides detailed instructions, examples, and case studies which are of tremendous benefit to the user. The instrument provides a unique perspective on the student's behaviors by involving a variety of school personnel who view the student in different settings. Its limitations lie in the conclusions one can draw from the individual percentiles and the total scores. However, this is the authors' intention—that it be used as a screening process or in conjunction with other measures of student behavior.

REVIEWER'S REFERENCE

Bower, E. (1969). *Early identification of emotionally disturbed children in the school* (2nd ed.). Springfield, IL: Charles Thomas.

[369]
Social Intelligence Test: George Washington University Series [SPECIAL EDITION].

Purpose: To measure certain factors of judgment, information, and memory related to ability to get along with people and function in interpersonal relationship situations.
Population: Grades 9–16 and adults.
Publication Dates: 1947–78.
Acronym: SIT.
Scores, 3: Judgment in Social Situations, Observation of Human Behavior, Total.
Administration: Group.
Price Data, 1990: $12 per 25 test booklets including manual ('55, 5 pages) and key.
Time: 30(35) minutes.
Authors: F. A. Moss, T. Hunt, and K. T. Omwake.
Publisher: The Center for Psychological Service.
Cross References: See T3:2228 (3 references); see also T2:1386 (15 references), P:250 (3 references), 6:176 (14 references), and 4:89 (7 references); for reviews by Glen U. Cleeton and Howard R. Taylor, see 3:96 (9 references); for a review by Robert L. Thorndike, see 2:1253 (20 references).

[370]
Social Reticence Scale.

Purpose: To assess an individual's shyness.
Population: High school and college and adults.
Publication Date: 1986.
Acronym: SRS.
Scores: Total score only.
Administration: Individual or group.
Price Data, 1987: $4 per 25 test booklets; $1.50 per scoring key; $10 per manual (30 pages); $11 per specimen set including test booklet, scoring key, and manual.
Time: (5–10) minutes.
Author: Warren H. Jones.
Publisher: Consulting Psychologists Press, Inc.

TEST REFERENCES

1. Briggs, S. R. (1988). Shyness: Introversion or neuroticism? *Journal of Research in Personality, 22,* 290-307.

Review of the Social Reticence Scale by OWEN SCOTT, III, Clinical Psychologist, The Psychology Clinic, Baton Rouge, LA:

The Social Reticence Scale (SRS) is a brief (20-item), self-administered instrument designed to measure shyness. The authors conceptualize shyness as a form of social anxiety that inhibits effective performance in social situations. The word shyness does not appear in the title or items in order to avoid communicating the exact construct being measured to respondents. Each of the items is rated on a 5-point, Likert-type scale with half of the items scored in the reverse direction. Information on the reading level of the test is not provided; similarly, no recommendations are given as to the age range for whom the test is intended. Inspection of the items suggests that it is probably appropriate for persons of high school age and educational level and above. The potential range of scores is 20 to 100. The test can be quickly and easily administered and scored using the scoring key provided with the test. The test score may be computed by hand or with the aid of a calculator.

The stated purpose of the test is to provide an index of shyness for basic research on personality variables and for applied uses, which include assessing the relative degree of individuals' shyness, providing feedback to persons on their shyness, and assessing treatment effects in interventions aimed at reducing shyness. The authors recommend against using the SRS at the present time for diagnostic purposes, such as determining whether an individual needs treatment for shyness or other problems, due to the lack of empirical data on these issues.

The manual provides a very satisfactory summary of the rationale, development, and validation of the SRS in a clear and succinct style. Substantial evidence is presented for the reliability and validity of the instrument. Internal consistency and test-retest reliability of the SRS, as determined in a sample of 252 college students and replicated in a heterogeneous sample of over 1,100 high school and college students and adults, are impressive. For example, test-retest correlations for a sample of 101 college students over an 8-week interval were .81, .89, and .87 for men, women, and the combined sample, respectively. Similarly, a great deal of data are presented to show the SRS is a valid measure of shyness as intended by the authors. Typical of the construct validity findings are correlations between the SRS and the first order factors of the Sixteen Personality Factor Questionnaire (16PF). As expected, the SRS correlated significantly with all components of the second-order factor Introversion-Extraversion in the expected directions, with the greatest correlation (-.82) occurring for Factor H (shy, threat-sensitive vs. bold, adventurous). Smaller, but significant, correlations were also found with two anxiety factors, guilt-proneness (Factor 0), and ergic tension (Factor Q4). In addition to showing good convergent and discriminant validity, a particularly impressive finding was the correlation between SRS scores and judges' ratings of brief, videotaped self-descriptions by the 30 respondents ($r = .50$ for ratings of shyness, $p < .002$). The SRS has also been found in several studies to predict self-reported indices of social activity and support. Other evidence is presented to show the SRS does measure shyness rather than related constructs (e.g., sociability and fear of negative evaluation) and that it does not appear excessively influenced by social desirability.

Replicated factor analyses of the SRS revealed that it has two correlated factors, isolation from others and ease of social communication. The authors provide directions for computing subscale scores, should the test user wish to do so.

For the applied user, tables presenting means and standard deviations for several normative groups, most notably college students, high school students, and nonclinical adults, are provided. Data on the distribution of SRS scores in terms of percentages of 2,645 respondents scoring within 9-point ranges (e.g., 20–28, 29–37, etc.) are presented in an Appendix.

The manual of the SRS concludes with recommendations for future research on shyness as related to the use of the test.

The authors are to be commended for providing a conservative and incisive analysis of promising directions for research that illuminates the present and potential utility of the SRS. In general, the SRS is a reliable, valid, and solidly constructed instrument for the measurement of shyness. It is short and easy to administer, yet it possesses very satisfactory psychometric properties. Researchers in the area of shyness would be advised to consider this instrument strongly when selecting a self-report measure of the construct. The SRS also has much promise for clinical applications, although, as the authors point out, additional research is needed to determine the full extent of clinical implications of shyness and to identify cutoff scores for classifying subjects in relation to criteria of interest (e.g., impaired ability to form important relationships). For the applied user, the systematic collection of normative data on various populations of interest (e.g., persons of different ages, ethnic groups, and geographic regions) would add to the utility of the test. Overall, the SRS compares very favorably to other specific self-report measures of shyness and warrants the consideration of researchers and clinicians interested in this variable.

Review of the Social Reticence Scale by WILLIAM K. WILKINSON, Assistant Professor of Counseling and Educational Psychology, New Mexico State University, Las Cruces, NM:

The Social Reticence Scale (SRS) is a 20-item, self-report instrument designed to measure shyness. Respondents rate SRS items on a 5-point Likert-type scale (1 = *not at all characteristic*, 5 = *extremely characteristic*) yielding a total score used to evaluate interpersonal reticence. The normative sample consists primarily of college students ($N = 2,250$), but also includes separate samples of high school students, adults, convicted felons, hospital workers, and parents of adolescents in counseling.

One of the strongest features of the SRS is its evidence of reliability and validity. Regarding reliability, the stability of self-reported ratings across an 8-week administration period is reported as .87 for a sample of 101 college students. This stability coefficient meets appropriate standards as an estimate of reliability.

Further, evidence regarding the three major components of validity are all discussed in the test manual. In terms of content validity, the test manual clearly distinguishes the steps in the derivation of SRS items. For instance, items were derived from Zimbardo's (1981) analysis of shyness as defining seven interpersonal areas (e.g., problems in meeting strangers, excessive self-consciousness, etc.), with three items then written for each of the seven domains. Subsequently, items were statistically analyzed, and only those items demonstrating appropriate statistical standards were retained. Thus, the SRS appears content valid with respect to the shyness construct.

Evidence of validity is presented in three forms. Concurrent validity was investigated by correlating the SRS with four other measures of shyness. The correlations varied from .72 to .81, revealing that SRS scores are highly related to scores on other measures of the shyness construct. In addition, SRS scores obtained for 128 freshmen during the first week of college were related to the number of new friends, social network and its density, and social supports established 2 months later, thus testing predictive validity. The correlations were significantly negative, thus revealing that low scores on the SRS (low shyness) predicted the presence of more new friends, denser social network, and more social support than those with high SRS scores. As further evidence of predictive validity, SRS scores predicted judges' ratings of shyness for 30 college students observed individually during a 2-minute period of self-disclosure.

The SRS also appears construct valid. That the instrument predicts scores on other measures of shyness lends support to this statement. In addition, the SRS does not appear to measure constructs antithetical to shyness. For example, SRS scores are negatively related to the Sixteen Personality Factor Questionnaire (16PF; 9:1136) scales pertaining to social boldness ($r = .-61$) and outgoing ($r = -.82$), and also are inversely correlated with extraversion ($r = -.73$) and assertiveness ($r = -.63$).

In sum, although there is little doubt the SRS provides sufficient evidence of reliability and validity, there are troublesome aspects to the SRS. Of particular concern is the interpretation of individual scores. Interpretation is problematic for the following reasons.

First, determining a respondent's degree of shyness relative to the normative group is limited, because the only normative data presented are means, standard deviations, and percentages within raw score intervals (20–28, 29–37, etc.). Using just this descriptive information, the test interpreter is limited to comparing a respondent's score with the mean score of the normative sample. Interpretation of the SRS would be significantly improved if each raw score in the normative sample was converted to a derived score, such as percentiles or T-scores. Derived scores would help determine the magnitude of a respondent's shyness relative to the normative sample, and enable more precise statements to be made regarding what raw score constitutes a "significant" degree of shyness.

Even if derived scores were included for the SRS, a more pervasive issue is the fact that the distribution of raw scores for the normative sample looks positively skewed. Positive skewness may exist in that about 88% of the scores fall below the raw score point of 64, although the theoretical median value of the raw scores should be 60 (multiplying the midpoint value of three for each item by the number of items). In other words, a rough interpolation suggests that around 80% of the normative sample averaged an endorsement of three or less per item. Yet, is it safe to conclude that a respondent with a raw score of 60 (the theoretical median) is "significantly" shy? Probably not, although this raw score would surpass approximately 80% of the normative sample. Thus, test interpreters need to guard against the possibility of interpreting SRS scores as indicative of shyness when, in fact, they are not.

Because SRS interpretation is severely limited, the instrument is clearly not appropriate for diagnostic purposes. To the test developer's credit, the test manual warns potential test consumers not to use the SRS for diagnostic reasons. This does not mean the SRS cannot be used in applied settings. Rather, its applied use is restricted to individual feedback in cases where shyness is clearly an interpersonal weakness.

The exact degree of a respondent's shyness (e.g., relative magnitude) will have to be determined by the test interpreter through conversion of the raw score to a derived score. Further, what constitutes a "significant" degree of shyness must be carefully considered in light of the potentially skewed distribution of raw scores observed for the normative sample. To guard against the possibility of overinterpreting SRS results, it may be advisable to adopt a relatively high raw score value (e.g., 80 or above) as suggestive of "significant" shyness.

The SRS might be useful in research efforts. Before adopting the SRS, however, as an investigative tool, its relative strengths and weaknesses should be compared to other instruments of shyness, such as the measures developed by Morris (1984), and Cheek and Buss (1981), as well as other well-

known instruments that seem to measure constructs similar to shyness (e.g., 16PF).

REVIEWER'S REFERENCES

Cheek, J. M., & Buss, A. N. (1981). Shyness and sociability. *Journal of Personality, 41*, 330-339.
Zimbardo, P. G., & Radl, S. L. (1981). *The shy child.* New York: McGraw-Hill.
Morris, T. L. (1984). *A longitudinal study of personality influences on social support.* Unpublished master's thesis, University of Tulsa, Tulsa, OK.

[371]

Social Skills Inventory, Research Edition.

Purpose: "To assess basic social communication skills."
Population: Ages 14 and over reading at or above the eighth grade level.
Publication Date: 1989.
Acronym: SSI.
Scores, 7: Emotional Expressivity, Emotional Sensitivity, Emotional Control, Social Expressivity, Social Sensitivity, Social Control, Total.
Administration: Group and individual.
Price Data, 1990: $20 per 25 test booklets; $3 per scoring key; $25 per 50 answer sheets; $14 per manual (24 pages); $17 per specimen set (includes manual, test booklet, scoring key); scoring service offered by publisher.
Time: (30–45) minutes.
Comments: Test booklet title is Self-Description Inventory; self-administered.
Authors: Ronald E. Riggio.
Publisher: Consulting Psychologists Press, Inc.

TEST REFERENCES

1. Riggio, R. E., Tucker, J., & Throckmorton, B. (1987). Social skills and deception ability. *Personality and Social Psychology Bulletin, 13*, 568-577.
2. Riggio, R. E., & Sotoodeh, Y. (1989). Social skills and birth order. *Psychological Reports, 64*, 211-217.
3. Riggio, R. E., Lippa, R., & Salinas, C. (1990). The display of personality in expressive movement. *Journal of Research in Personality, 24*, 16-31.

Review of the Social Skills Inventory, Research Edition by JUDITH C. CONGER, Director of Clinical Training, Purdue University, West Lafayette, IN:

RATIONALE. The Social Skills Inventory (SSI) is a 90-item self-report inventory designed to measure social communication skills. The six scales tap three major areas—Expressivity, Sensitivity, and Control. These are each measured on two levels, Emotional and Social, thus yielding six domains. The author indicates the total SSI score reflects "a global level of social skill development indicative of overall social competence or social intelligence" (p. 2). Although most researchers would agree the social competence construct is multidimensional in nature, they might not agree that social communication skills, social skills, social competence, and social intelligence are equivalent or interchangeable terms owing to the fact their meanings are tied to the social, behavioral, or individual difference traditions that spawned them. Further, although the author discusses "social intelligence" in terms of general intelligence in an effort to discriminate between them, the "apparent" similarity stops there. That is, it should be noted that traditional intellectual measures are based on performance or samples of behavior; this measure is not. It is designed to measure the *self-report* of social behavior and not the behavior itself.

The development of the SSI is tied to previous work in nonverbal communication (e.g., Rosenthal, 1979; Friedman, 1979) and is reported to be an extension of the Affective Communication Test (ACT; Friedman, Prince, Riggio, & DiMatteo, 1980). The ACT is a measure of nonverbal expressiveness. The measure was developed originally for social psychological research. The exact nature of the item pool from which the measure is derived or the construction of the items in the SSI is not reported in detail, although the author reports several years of pretesting and refinement in the selection of the items. Further, the measure is embedded in a theoretical context and is part of an active, ongoing research program by the author.

RELIABILITY. Internal consistency estimates for the individual scales and the total scale are reported. Most appear to be adequate, although the internal consistency of the Emotional Expressivity and Emotional Sensitivity scales for males is only .62 and .67, respectively (total range = .62–.87). Although two samples of both men and women were tested, complete descriptive data are reported only on Sample 1.

Test-retest reliability is based on a 2-week interval ($N = 40$) and ranges from .81 to .96 for the individual scales, with the reliability of the total SSI being .94. These are strong test-retest estimates; however, evidence for the stability of the SSI over longer time intervals is needed.

VALIDITY CONSIDERATIONS. Evidence for the validity of the SSI is derived from several sources. With regard to the internal structure, the author states the relationship among the component social skills should be positive, given that the possession of one skill should predispose one to possess other skills. The intercorrelations among the scales, although indicating a preponderance of positive relationships, also indicate some variability. That is, roughly one third of the correlations are negative and some scales show no relationship or a weak relationship to other scales. Most notably, Social Sensitivity shows no meaningful relationship to Emotional Expressivity in the total sample matrix or in the matrices for each sex. Further, although most of the scales correlate positively with the total SSI score, Social Sensitivity correlates extremely weakly or not at all (r s = .06, -.03, or .00).

Inspection of the intercorrelations among the scales does not suggest six different factors; however, the author reports a factor analysis using a confirmatory factor analytic approach that indicates the presence of six different factors. This approach allows the investigator to specify a model, a priori, that is then tested. Although this particular model was not rejected, it is also possible that a simpler model using fewer factors would not be rejected either. This approach requires the testing of different models against one another, which if done, was not reported. Thus, the argument for six factors based just on this analysis is not compelling and needs replication.

The SSI shows a range of correlations with other measures, most strongly with the ACT and more weakly with the Profile of Nonverbal Sensitivity (PONS). The correlational results suggest the SSI is tapping some of the same constructs measured by these other inventories (16 Personality Factor Questionnaire [16PF], Personality Research Form [PRF], Eysenck Personality Inventory [EPI], etc.). However, some of these correlations raise questions about the nature of what is being measured in terms of the subscales. For example, the Social Sensitivity scale (SS) correlates most highly with Public Self-Consciousness (.58) and Social Anxiety (.37), whereas relationships with the ACT and PONS were minimal. The SS scale also had virtually no relationship to the total SSI score. This scale may be measuring something other than that which was intended and probably needs further examination. One of the strongest scales in the SSI is Social Expressivity (SE). The test-retest reliability (.96) is as good as that of the total SSI (.94). Often its relationship to other measures is similar in patterning to the total SSI and the strength of those relationships was often as good, if not better, than the total SSI. Future researchers may want to examine how well this scale performs in comparison to the total SSI, as it may do just as well in some situations.

Other validity work appears to be ongoing in terms of relating the SSI to performance measure of social competence, as well as indirect measures such as social networks. Although the manual indicates this research is favorable, specific data are not always reported. All studies are, however, referenced. Further, there appears to be an ongoing research program by Riggio and his colleagues which is a credit to the author and should shed additional light on the SSI.

Although the test is designed for use with adults at an eighth-grade reading level, the primary population used in the development and investigation of the SSI was made up of college students at the undergraduate and graduate levels. To the author's and publisher's credit, this is clearly spelled out in the manual.

In summary, the SSI appears to be a serious attempt to design a self-report measure of social competence. This is a worthy goal. The SSI definitely has some strengths and some weaknesses.

More specifically, clearer evidence regarding validity is needed. Further research guided by additional clarification of the theory should shed light on these issues.

Review of the Social Skills Inventory, Research Edition by SUSAN M. SHERIDAN, Assistant Professor of Educational Psychology, University of Utah, Salt Lake City, UT:

The Social Skills Inventory (SSI) is a self-report measure for adults based on an information-processing model of social skills. It consists of six scales that measure social communication skills on two levels: Emotional and Social. Expressivity, Sensitivity, and Control are evaluated in each. The SSI appears to be theoretically and psychometrically sound, and has several positive characteristics that contribute to its utility. When used in conjunction with behavioral measures of social skills, the SSI may be a helpful instrument in research and applied settings.

MANUAL. The manual for the SSI is clear and complete. Sections on theory and background, procedural details, psychometric qualities, and research applications are included. The procedures for administration, scoring, and interpretation are well documented, and appear to be especially helpful to test users.

ADMINISTRATION AND SCORING. The SSI is very user-friendly in terms of its administration and scoring procedures. The instrument is self-administered, and is appropriate for individuals with an eighth-grade reading level. Items are written clearly, and the SSI could be adapted easily to group administrations.

Scoring of the SSI is clear and simple. Items are scored on a 5-point Likert scale, with scores on the six scales ranging from 15–75. A total score is provided that is described as a global level of social skill or competence. Scoring is aided by the use of a scoring template. Descriptive data and cutoff scores for each scale and for the Total SSI are reported, with separate norms for males and females.

One potential scoring problem with the SSI is the way it handles unanswered items. The author, Riggio, notes that a protocol containing more than 15 unanswered items is invalid; however, the necessary number of completed items within each scale is not reported. He further recommends that unanswered items be given a score of 3 (the midway point on the 5-point scale), implying that this will not greatly affect a protocol that contains few unanswered items across scales. However, if a test contains several unanswered items within the same scale, and the respondent rated the majority of items within that scale consistently high or low, it may significantly alter the scale score and test profile for that individual. It may be more appropriate to compute the mean for completed items, and impose this mean rating onto unanswered items. This procedure appears to be more sensitive to individual responses in the profile analysis.

STANDARDIZATION. A limited normative group was used in the standardization of the SSI. Descriptive statistics and cutoff scores from two undergraduate college samples are reported ($n = 453$ and 199, respectively). Although the author recommends cautious interpretation when using the scale with other populations, he discusses other applications of the instrument in detail (e.g., counseling, couples research, and leadership training). Further research in these areas is needed before the instrument can be put to widespread use.

TEST DEVELOPMENT. Riggio (1989) reports that early pretesting of the SSI was done on hundreds of items. Two versions of the test were constructed, tested, and refined; however, specific procedures of item development and evaluation are not provided. A 105-item scale was used in the validity studies; however, one social skill scale (Social Manipulation) was subsequently eliminated with no rationale, yielding the final version with 90 items.

RELIABILITY/VALIDITY. The SSI has good psychometric properties. Test-retest reliabilities of the separate scales range from .81 to .96 (2-week interval), and alpha coefficients range from .62 to .87. Across male and female samples, the three emotional scales revealed the lowest alpha coefficients, suggesting lower consistency within these subtests.

Riggio reported the results of several validity studies using a variety of instruments (including the Affective Communication Test, Bem Sex-Role Inventory, 16 Personality Factor Questionnaire, Personality Research Form, and Eysenck Personality Inventory). A great deal of data are provided that generally support the convergent and discriminant validity of the scale. Although several predicted relationships emerged, some unexpected relationships were also found. Unfortunately, many of the instruments used in the studies may be unfamiliar to test users, and the overwhelming presentation of the data makes this information difficult to interpret. It should also be noted that college student samples were used in all of the validity studies, limiting the scale's use pending future research.

Evidence of factorial validity is also provided for the SSI. Factor analysis was conducted by grouping items for each of the scales into sets of five items each, resulting in 18 total item sets. The purpose for this grouping procedure is unclear; however, the author reported it was due to the large number of items on the test. A six-factor solution with varimax rotation was used, and all six of the predicted factors emerged with strong factor loadings. One possible exception is with a subset of items purported to load on the Social Expressivity scale. A relatively low factor loading (.28), along with a high intercorrelation with the Social Control scale (.66) suggests that interpretation of this factor may be difficult.

INTERPRETATION. Factor analysis of the SSI generally allows test users to interpret subscales as reflective of the underlying constructs they are purported to measure. Descriptive statistics, cutoff scores by sex, and sample profiles are provided to aid in the interpretation of individual profiles.

Riggio argues the basic social skill components are assumed to be additive (i.e., contributing to a total score), but also recognizes appropriately that the relation between any single skill area and "social effectiveness" is not always linear. According to the author, "It is not only the extent to which individuals have developed particular social skills . . . that is important, but it is the balance among them that is related to overall social competence" (p. 7). Thus, he recommends the use of an "imbalance score" using the standard deviation of the six social skill scales for each individual. A formula to compute standard deviation is provided, but is very cumbersome and impractical for clinicians in its current form.

One fundamental assumption of the test is that individuals can, in fact, be accurate raters of their own social skills; however, this assumption has no empirical support. Test users must recognize that the SSI is primarily a self-*perception* instrument, and this distinction should be clarified when interpreting individual profiles.

SUMMARY. The SSI has several characteristics that make it an appealing instrument, including its ease in administration and scoring, and its sound psychometric qualities. It shows potential as a meaningful component in the assessment of social skills. However, continued research with broader samples is needed before the scale can be used clinically with confidence.

[372]
Social Styles Analysis.

Purpose: Constructed to identify a person's social style of presentation and interaction.
Population: Adults.
Publication Date: 1989.
Scores: 4 categories: Analytical, Driver, Amiable, Expressive.
Administration: Group.
Editions, 2: Self, Other.
Manual: No manual.
Price Data, 1991: $25 per package for self analysis (5¼-inch or 3½-inch diskette); $50 per package for other analyses (5¼-inch or 3½-inch diskette).
Time: Administration time not reported.
Comments: IBM microcomputer necessary for scoring.
Authors: Wilson Learning Corporation.
Publisher: Pfeiffer & Company International Publishers.

Review of the Social Styles Analysis by C. DALE CARPENTER, Professor of Special Education, Western Carolina University, Cullowhee, NC:

The Social Styles Analysis consists of two editions. One is called Social Styles Analysis/Self; the other is called Social Styles Analysis/Other. Each consists of a one-page survey form. Answers to items are entered on an IBM PC-compatible diskette provided for scoring perceptions. A computer printout gives an interpretation of results. In concert, Social Styles Analysis purports to measure the assertiveness, responsiveness, and versatility of an individual based on perceptions of the person's communication behaviors as seen by others.

Social Styles Analysis/Self requires the subject to rate 15 items on a scale of 1–7. Examples of items include: Desires to control; is warm; is adaptable. No explanation is provided. Social Styles Analysis/Other requires those who know the subject to rate the subject on 30 items on a similar scale. Samples of items are: Is sociable; is a risk taker; is dependable; makes people feel comfortable.

The materials for administering and scoring consist of the survey forms, diskette, and a four-page Guide to Using Social Styles Materials, which is a brief description of the eight product components. The guide provides little actual help in using the materials.

In the sampler provided this reviewer, a four-page Social Style Profile printout describes the subject as Driver, Analytical, Amiable, or Expressive. Combinations are possible. Additionally, the subject's versatility is described. Suggestions for interacting with those with different styles is also provided.

Research support for the Social Styles Analysis is contained in a publication titled *The Statistical Adequacy of the Social Style Profile* (Lashbrook, Lashbrook, & Wiley, 1986), which was provided only upon request and is not part of materials normally available. This publication does not meet acceptable standards for empirical research. Summaries of studies are given. Cited publications are not all listed in references. Fourteen of 33 references are unpublished. It is difficult to evaluate the norms, reliability, and validity of the Social Styles Analysis. Although information regarding norms, reliability, and validity is reported, the information lacks credibility because of the problems cited.

This instrument has serious deficiencies. No appropriate evidence is presented to support the four social styles used. The items to be rated are so short and nonspecific that respondents cannot avoid diverse interpretations. No comprehensible judgment can be made from a variety of respondent ratings. Furthermore, the technical adequacy of the instrument is unknown.

CRITIQUE. The Social Styles Analysis lacks construct validity related to any theory. If a cogent theory exists utilizing the four social styles, it is not presented. The assessment approach used is woefully flawed due in part to the items on each of the surveys. Attempting to gather information from a variety of respondents is desirable. However, no criteria are used to select respondents and the items are so poor they are unlikely to elicit useful impressions. The Social Styles Analysis cannot be recommended for the purposes described. The materials are inadequate and validity and reliability data are lacking.

REVIEWER'S REFERENCE

Lashbrook, W. B., Lashbrook, V. J., & Wiley, R. J. (1986). *The statistical adequacy of the Social Style Profile.* San Diego: Wilson Learning Corporation.

[373]
Spanish Structured Photographic Expressive Language Test.

Purpose: Assessment of "the monolingual or bilingual child's generation of specific morphological and syntactical structures."
Population: Ages 3-0 to 5-11, 4-0 to 9-5.
Publication Date: 1989.
Acronym: SPELT.
Scores: Item scores only.
Administration: Individual.
Time: Administration time not reported.
Comments: The design of the Spanish SPELT tests is patterned after the original SPELT-II and SPELT-P (9:1198), however, it is not a direct translation of them. Many of the grammatical structures in the English edition were able to be translated into Spanish. When necessary, to allow for differences in the two languages, grammatical structures were either deleted or added.
Authors: Ellen O'Hara Werner and Janet Dawson Kresheck.
Publisher: Janelle Publications, Inc.
a) SPANISH STRUCTURED PHOTOGRAPHIC EXPRESSIVE LANGUAGE TEST-II.
Population: Ages 4-0 to 9-5.
Acronym: SPELT-II.
Price Data, 1990: $49 per 10 response forms, 50 color photographs, and manual ('89, 39 pages); $12 per 50 response forms.
b) SPANISH STRUCTURED PHOTOGRAPHIC EXPRESSIVE LANGUAGE TEST-PRESCHOOL.
Population: Ages 3-0 to 5-11.
Acronym: SPELT-P.
Price Data: $39 per 10 response forms, 37 color photographs, and manual ('89, 34 pages); $10 per 50 response forms.
Cross References: For a review by Joan D. Berryman of the original SPELT, see 9:1198 (2 references).

Review of the Spanish Structured Photographic Expressive Language Test by RONALD B. GILLAM, Assistant Professor of Communicative Disorders, University of Missouri-Columbia, Columbia, MO and LINDA S. DAY, Director of Clinical Services, Program in Communication Disorders, University of Missouri-Columbia, Columbia, MO:

Like the original Structured Photographic Expressive Language Test-II (SPELT-II; 9:1198) and the Structured Photographic Expressive Language Test-Preschool (SPELT-P; 9:1198), the Spanish versions of these tests use examiner comments and questions about color photographs to elicit various morphological and syntactic structures from the child. The Spanish SPELT was designed to be used by professionals concerned with bilingual education. All stimuli and responses are spoken in Spanish, so examiners must either be bilingual themselves or utilize bilingual assistants. The preschool version (Spanish SPELT-P) consists of 25 items; 50 items are included on the SPELT-II.

Despite the authors' claims to the contrary, the majority of the items on the Spanish SPELT are translations of English SPELT items with minor vocabulary changes. Item order has been altered in some cases. Elliptical answers to examiner questions are likely and can be scored as correct as long as critical aspects of the targets are preserved in the child's response. The photographs used for some stimulus items have been reshot to include Hispanic children. As with the original versions, the stimulus photographs are engaging.

Unlike the English SPELT, age norms are not provided for the Spanish SPELT versions. The authors refer to the linguistic and cultural heterogeneity of the Spanish-speaking population in explaining why a national standardization was not feasible, and recommend that school districts establish their own local norms. A brief procedural outline for calculating standard deviations, deviation boundaries, and standard scores is provided. Unfortunately, considerations such as dialectal variation, amount of exposure to English, loss of language ability, level of acculturation, and amount of education will be just as critical in the establishment of local norms as they would have been in establishing national norms. The difficult decisions involved in norming this test have not been alleviated by the authors' decision to forgo a large-scale standardization effort.

The authors have not established the concurrent validity of this test. Test-retest reliability studies by a single examiner were completed for both the Spanish SPELT-P and Spanish SPELT-II using Pearson product moment correlations. SPELT-P test-retest reliability for 30 subjects was .92; SPELT-II reliability for 30 subjects was .91.

Two primary purposes for using the Spanish SPELT are presented. The authors claim that this test may be used to identify Spanish-speaking children who are in need of language intervention. Yet, the test has not been normed and no predictive validity studies are reported. A critical consideration in purchasing the Spanish SPELT as an identification tool is the time and resources that are available for establishing local norms. Clinicians choosing to undertake such projects must have access to a large Spanish-speaking population. Examiners are advised to include a minimum of 30 regular classroom children at each age level in their normative samples. No time limits are given, but a conservative estimate of Spanish SPELT-II test administration time is 20 minutes per child. If a clinician were to establish Spanish SPELT-II norms for the five age groups for whom the test is intended, a minimum of 50 hours of child contact time would be required. Additional time would need to be set aside for finding and selecting subjects, making arrangements for testing children, and analyzing data. A local clinician would need approximately one month, working full time on this project alone, to norm the Spanish SPELT on the minimum number of subjects recommended in the manual.

Second, the authors suggest that examiners can use the Spanish SPELT to systematically inventory language strengths and weaknesses. One question related to using the SPELT as a criterion-referenced measure concerns whether the test targets forms that are critical for assessing Spanish language development. As noted above, creation of the Spanish SPELT-II involved translating the majority of the English SPELT-II items into Spanish. One consequence of this approach to test construction is that some Spanish structures are underrepresented. Only one of many obligatory uses of present subjunctive is required in any response. On the other hand, plural morphemes and possessive targets are overrepresented. Finally, some important aspects are not represented at all. For example, gender agreement, which could reasonably be elicited on some of the six possessive items, is not targeted, nor is number agreement. True passive voice, although targeted in the English SPELT, is omitted in the Spanish version. When planning criterion-referenced testing, clinicians should consider creating their own informal probes for eliciting target forms that are not represented on the Spanish SPELT.

Examiners are advised to compare the child's SPELT performance to developmental guidelines for Spanish-speaking children that are available in the manual. A table of expected ages for the development of verbs, syntax, and linguistic markers is provided. The reader is not informed whether age ranges represent first appearance or mastery. No explanations are given for those items that appear in more than one age category. Further explanation is needed for the inclusion of imperative forms as examples of present subjunctive.

In summary, the Spanish SPELT is nearly a parallel translation of the English SPELT, so it assesses Spanish equivalents of the structures targeted in the English version. The Spanish versions of the SPELT have not been normed. Therefore, the test is experimental in nature. Neither predictive nor concurrent validity has been established. Test users should realize that they are expected to undertake local norming efforts.

[374]
Spatial Orientation Memory Test.

Purpose: "Assesses the development of a child's ability to retain and recall the orientation of visually presented forms."
Population: Ages 5–10.
Publication Dates: 1971–85.
Scores: Total score only.
Administration: Individual.
Forms, 2: Form 1, Form 2.
Price Data, 1989: $60 per complete kit including stimulus cards ('71, 44 cards), 25 score sheets ('85, 2 pages), and manual ('75, 4 pages); $52 per set of stimulus cards; $13.50 per pad of 100 score sheets; $7.90 per manual.
Time: (10) minutes.
Comments: Orally administered.
Authors: Joseph M. Wepman and Dainis Turaids.
Publisher: Western Psychological Services.
Cross References: See T3:2251 (2 references).

TEST REFERENCES

1. Boller, F., Passafiume, D., Keefe, N. C., Rogers, K., Morrow, L., & Kim, Y. (1984). Visuospatial impairment in Parkinson's Disease: Role of perceptual and motor factors. *Archives of Neurology, 41*, 485-490.

Review of the Spatial Orientation Memory Test by DEBORAH ERICKSON, Associate Professor of Education, Niagara University, Niagara University, NY:

The Spatial Orientation Memory Test is designed to assess the developmental level of a 5–10-year-old child's visual orientation ability. Average to high performance on the test indicates successful recall of the orientation of visually presented forms. The authors suggest that this ability is related to successful letter discrimination, sequential ordering of letters in words, and establishment of basic right-left dominance. Poor test performance suggests difficulty for the child in mastering these reading readiness skills. According to the authors, difficulty with the test may indicate a need for training in visual orientation and organization and a further evaluation for visual perception deficits.

The test requires little motor or verbal involvement aside from pointing or simple identification of the correct choice. Two alternate test forms are available. Directions for administering and scoring the 20 items are on the answer sheet and in the manual. They are written in a clear, concise manner. The test takes 10 minutes to complete.

The manual has a short section on interpretation, reliability, and validity of the test. There is no discussion on general test construction such as item selection and analysis.

The reliability data presented in the manual are limited to one 1971 study of 292 children between the ages of 5 and 8 with correlations for the alternate forms ranging from .60 to .74.

Supporting evidence for test validity is not extensive. Two studies are cited as evidence for the developmental nature of the test. These consisted of test performance results for 292 6- and 7-year-old children from three states correlated with age. The manual also cited two 1971 studies comparing the Metropolitan Reading Readiness Test and The Metropolitan Achievement Test with the total score on the Spatial Orientation Memory Test. The results indicated a marginally acceptable correlation of .42 and .50, respectively. Another 1981 study examined the relationship between perceptual abilities, intelligence, and reading achievement. Without providing supporting information, the authors suggest that spatial orientation ability is the single best predictor of reading ability.

In summary, The Spatial Orientation Memory Test is an acceptable instrument for screening visual orientation and organization ability. However, it has not been acceptably validated as a diagnostic test for general visual perception ability or for predicting success in reading. As the authors of the test suggest, further evaluation by a more complete instrument or battery of tests is necessary to determine the extent of a child's visual perception ability and the relationship of a visual perception problem to reading ability.

Review of the Spatial Orientation Memory Test by NORA M. THOMPSON, Clinical Assistant Professor, Southwest Neuropsychiatric Institute and Department of Psychiatry, The University of Texas Health Science Center at San Antonio, San Antonio, TX:

PURPOSE. The Spatial Orientation Memory Test (SOMT) was designed to measure the child's "ability to retain and recall the orientation of visually presented forms." The SOMT is intended to identify "children who are slower than their peers in developing spatial orientation ability" and to diagnose "a perceptual deficit in underachieving children." The authors developed the test in order to assess the ability to perceive and retain visual percepts without the need for a complex fine motor response, such as is required for the Frostig Developmental Test of Visual Perception (Frostig, 1966; 9:650), the Beery Developmental Test of Visual-Motor Integration (Beery, 1989; 9:329), and a number of other visual-perceptual tests. The intended population is children 5 to 10 years of age with known or suspected reading or perceptual problems. The construct of spatial orientation memory is proposed to underlie the visual-perceptual aspects of reading, including letter and word discrimination.

CONTENTS. The test contains 20 items, each of which consists of a stimulus design and either a 4- or 5-choice array of the same stimulus design in various planar orientations. The SOMT is individually administered by showing the child a design for 5 seconds and then asking the child to choose the design that is "pointing exactly the same direction" from the array presented on the subsequent card. Two sample items precede administration of the test items, which requires no specialized training. The total correct is summed and a Rating Scale Range, based on cumulative frequencies, is obtained. The ratings range from -2 (below level of threshold of adequacy) to +2 (very good development). The cutting score for intervention is set at the 15th percentile, although the rationale for this determination is not provided.

NORMATIVE DATA. There is no information presented in the manual that describes the size or other important characteristics of the normative sample such as IQ, socioeconomic status, gender, and reading level. A note accompanying the normative table states that Rating Scale Ranges for three of the six grade levels were interpolated, suggesting that the normative data are insufficient. Despite these shortcomings, the manual encourages the test user to consult the normative table to evaluate individual change over time as well as to recommend psychoeducational intervention. Cutting scores are identified, yet the standard error of measurement is not available. Individuals intent on using the test clinically would be well advised to collect local normative data.

RELIABILITY. A study of alternate-form reliability is described, although again, important technical data are lacking, including order of administration and interval between administrations. The alternate-form reliability coefficients generated are low (.60 to .74). There is no report of test-retest reliability, although the manual encourages the test user to evaluate individual change.

VALIDITY. The authors support the validity of the test with two lines of investigation. The first supports "the developmental nature of the test" by showing that older children obtain higher scores than younger children. The second line of investigation consists of two correlational studies of the SOMT and various reading tests. Insufficient information is presented in the manual to evaluate the studies. One study is not referenced and the results of the second (obtained from the primary reference, Miller & McKenna, 1981) show nearly equivalent correlations for a picture vocabulary test with reading ($r = .34$) as for the SOMT with reading ($r = .36$). There are no studies comparing the SOMT with other spatial or memory measures nor is there evidence that the SOMT discriminates good from poor readers. In general, construct and criterion-related validity are lacking for this test.

CONCLUSION. At this time, the SOMT cannot be used with confidence for its intended purposes. There is insufficient evidence supporting its use as a screening instrument for reading delay, which is not surprising in the light of the multiple complex and dynamic factors underlying the development of reading skills. There is no evidence presented to validate its use against other measures of visual-spatial ability. In short, without expanded validation studies, the SOMT offers limited practical information to the clinician, school psychologist, or teacher. It may have research applications.

REVIEWER'S REFERENCES

Frostig, M. (1966). Developmental Test of Visual Perception, Revised. Palo Alto, CA: Consulting Psychologists Press.

Miller, J. W., & McKenna, M. C. (1981). Disabled readers: Their intellectual and perceptual capacities at differing ages. *Perceptual and Motor Skills, 52,* 467-472.

Beery, K. E. (1989). The Developmental Test of Visual-Motor Integration. Cleveland: Modern Curriculum Press.

[375]

Spellmaster.
Purpose: "A method of analyzing spelling errors for sequential prescriptive instruction."
Population: Elementary and junior high school students.
Publication Dates: 1974–87.
Scores: Total score only on each test.
Administration: Group.
Levels: 8 overlapping levels.
Price Data, 1987: $59 per complete kit; $9 per 50 student answer sheets; $5 per 25 scoring forms (specify level 1–8); $24 per examiner's manual ('87, 107 pages).
Time: Administration time not reported.
Comments: "Criterion-referenced"; 27 tests.
Author: Claire R. Greenbaum.
Publisher: PRO-ED, Inc.
Cross References: For reviews by C. Dale Carpenter and Steve Graham of an earlier edition, see 9:1162.

Review of the Spellmaster by PATTI L. HARRISON, Associate Professor of Behavioral Studies, College of Education, The University of Alabama, Tuscaloosa, AL:

Spellmaster is designed to yield prescriptive, criterion-referenced information for planning spelling instruction. Its use is limited, however, due to absence of technical data. The system consists of several levels and types of spelling tests, as well as supplementary word lists, guidelines for teaching spelling, and examples of spelling activities. The manual does not describe any similarities or differences between the current and 1974 editions.

Spellmaster, which may be group or individually administered, includes three entry level tests and eight levels each of comprehensive regular word, irregular word, and homophone tests. Each entry test requires about 10 minutes for administration and each comprehensive test requires about 20 minutes. Examiners administer items by saying the words and using them in sentences; students write the words on an answer sheet.

Administration begins with an entry test (regular word, irregular word, or homophones). Each entry test has eight levels which correspond to levels on the comprehensive tests. Entry tests provide quick estimates of students' mastery, instructional, and frustration spelling levels. Students' instructional level on an entry test indicates the level of the comprehensive test to be administered.

Regular word tests are emphasized for diagnostic testing and error analyses. Regular word tests contain phonetically regular words that can be spelled according to dependable generalizations. The tests measure phonetic and structural *elements* such as consonants, beginning blends, endings, and open and closed syllables. An average grade range is indicated for each level. Levels 1 and 2 measure auditory elements; Levels 3 through 6, auditory and visual elements; and Levels 6 through 8, conceptual elements.

Irregular word tests measure spelling of words that violate phonic rules. Homophone tests measure spelling of words that have the same pronunciations as other words, but different meanings. Error analyses are not provided and use of these tests is not clearly described. The author indicates only that the tests are usually administered after regular phonic patterns are learned and may be used with students designated as top spellers on the regular word tests.

For the level of regular word, irregular word, and homophone tests administered to the student, the number of correctly spelled words is calculated. Error analyses for regular word levels are accomplished on scoring forms that list parts of words and their corresponding elements. Only a few elements are measured at each level; scorers may indicate that students made errors corresponding to an element not measured, but lower levels must be administered to conduct error analyses for these elements. Therefore, administration of any level provides only a partial analysis of spelling errors. In addition, many elements occur infrequently, with the majority of elements occurring only 2 or 3 times, resulting in a limited sampling for elements.

Guidelines for interpretation focus on the total number of correctly spelled words. The manual indicates the number of correct words that identify top, middle, and bottom spellers. Top spellers may be given the next highest regular word level or the irregular words or homophones tests, or may be excused from systematic spelling instruction. Middle spellers may be given instruction at their level and bottom spellers may be retested at a lower level. No guidelines are given for interpreting the error analyses of regular words, a notable omission given the purpose of the system.

With the exception of a brief statement concerning field testing, *no information about test development or psychometric properties is reported in the Spellmaster manual.* Many types of technical data are required for appropriate use of Spellmaster and absence of technical data greatly limits the confidence that can be placed in test results. The fact that Spellmaster is criterion-referenced, and not norm-referenced, does not excuse the author from supplying evidence of appropriate developmental procedures, reliability, and validity.

There is no evidence that any part of Spellmaster represents spelling skills necessary in today's schools. The author simply states that words on Spellmaster are likely to be seen in classroom materials and the regular word elements are frequently applied. Detailed information concerning selection of words and elements for the tests is necessary to judge the relationship between test content and school curriculum at each grade level.

Data must support the author's assumptions that regular word levels measure cumulative elements, that item difficulty corresponds to the grade ranges specified for levels, and that homophone items are sequenced according to difficulty. Entry level tests should be equated to their corresponding comprehensive tests. Criteria for identifying top, middle, and bottom spellers should be based on accepted standards for mastery and take into account normative data for students at different grade levels. Without information about the relationship between test content and school curriculum, item data, and data supporting criteria for mastery, school personnel have no way of determining the relationship between Spellmaster results and expected performance on actual classroom materials at each grade level.

Standard data are needed to support reliability of decisions using total scores and error analyses. Correlations between Spellmaster and other measures, analysis of Spellmaster scores for previously identified good and poor spellers, and data concerning effectiveness of remediating weaknesses identified by Spellmaster represent just three of many investigations needed to support construct and criterion-related validity.

In conclusion, the organization of Spellmaster is attractive and supplementary spelling lists and teaching activities may be useful in some classrooms. However, the tests are not recommended for use. Content validity is of primary importance for criterion-referenced tests, yet the Spellmaster manual provides no evidence that the tests represent an adequate sample of spelling skills needed in schools. There are no item, normative, reliability, and construct and criterion-related validity data to support decisions resulting from scores. Without this necessary technical information, teachers should not identify poor spellers or plan instruction using Spellmaster tests.

Review of the Spellmaster by MARGARET ROGERS WIESE, Assistant Professor of School Psychology, Appalachian State University, Boone, NC:

The Spellmaster Assessment and Teaching System (Spellmaster), revised in 1987 after initial publication in 1974, is a criterion-referenced test and instructional system designed to measure and teach spelling skills. The test is group or individually administered and purports to identify spelling strengths and weaknesses of children in primary grades and junior high. Teaching techniques and multimodal activities are provided to help remediate skill weaknesses.

The major changes in Spellmaster since the initial publication seem to be in test packaging and introduction of the entry level tests. Currently, the assessment system comprises four categories of tests including entry level, regular word, irregular word, and homophone. Each of the four categories of tests is broken down into eight test levels. Although no empirical evidence is provided, the author suggests these eight test levels contain spelling skills typically learned between grades K–10.

Between grades K–10? The manual initially states the tests and teaching materials are appropriate for primary grade children and junior high youngsters, then goes on to suggest that high schoolers, adults, and children who speak English as a second language would benefit as well. This is confusing information. The manual needs to state specifically for which age ranges the materials were developed. In addition, if the materials were designed for a broader population, then appropriate forms should be provided.

The second problem with test administration concerns the regular word entry level tests that serve as the beginning point in the assessment sequence. Cutoff scores are provided for these tests and they yield information concerning the mastery, frustration, and instructional levels of test takers. The problem is that no explanation is provided for how cutoff scores were determined. Also, do these cutoffs have any relation to an outside standard? This is important information that is missing from the manual.

The third administrative problem concerns the discontinue rule during group administration. The manual recommends that examiners discontinue group testing when it is clear that students have met their respective frustration levels (i.e., when four items in one level have been missed). However, in a classroom of 25 students, how is the examiner supposed to simultaneously review everyone's response sheet to insure that premature termination does not occur? It is unrealistic to require the examiner to perform this feat.

Once the regular word entry level test has been administered, the examiner proceeds with further testing using the other entry level tests and the regular word test, irregular word test, and homophone test. These latter tests provide information concerning knowledge of phonic and structural spelling elements, knowledge of irregular spelling rules, and ability to spell homophones. The tests are all administered via dictation whereby words are dictated in isolation, then within a sentence, then repeated in isolation. Students are provided with separate answer sheets to record responses.

Scoring the irregular word and homophone tests is easily achieved by matching the response to the stimulus word and calculating raw scores based on the total number of correct responses. Scoring the regular word tests requires additional procedures because each response is scored several times. First, the whole word is scored for overall accuracy and second, the word is scored for the accuracy of the phonic and structural elements that make it up. Omissions, additions, and sequencing errors are also noted. Special scoring forms are provided for scoring each of the eight levels of the regular word test.

The manual supplies cutoff scores that allow for instructional groupings into "top spellers," "middle spellers," and "bottom spellers" but again, does not specify how these cutoffs were determined. The groupings are intended to help teachers identify students who need additional instruction or further testing.

All testing and teaching materials, with the exception of the student answer sheets and scoring forms, are provided in an attractive soft-cover ring binder. Two methods for organizing test results are available in the binder and can be duplicated: class data sheets and individual progress records. Both general and specific test administration directions are given in the front of the binder with actual test items contained in the appendices. This results in the examiner having to flip back and forth in the manual during test administration. Supplementary regular word tests are also provided in the back of the binder along with an array of instructional activities for helping to remediate spelling difficulties. However, these instructional activities do not specify the objective of the task or what demonstrates mastery of a skill.

Although reviews of the previous edition of the Spellmaster clearly highlighted weaknesses in reliability and validity as well as test development, no substantive improvements within these areas over the last 13 years seem to have occurred. In this reviewer's opinion, the most important limitation of the Spellmaster continues to be the lack of test development, reliability, and validity data. A test manual typically contains technical psychometric information. The Spellmaster manual does not. A review of the test manual yields no specific information concerning test item development and selection. The authors suggest that classroom teachers and specialists provided input in helping to shape

the materials but do not specify the nature of this input.

A field test in New England using over 2,500 children is described but no information regarding when field testing occurred, or the age ranges, socioeconomic levels, and racial and ethnic composition of the participants is provided. These are crucial data which need to be documented adequately.

In summary, the absence of reliability and validity data and test development information significantly limits the applicability of these materials. In order to make this program more meaningful, test-retest reliability data, standard errors of measurement, content validity data, and criterion validity data must be collected and documented. Also, the manual should contain information concerning examiner qualifications. Although the Spellmaster is attractively designed and packaged and contains a variety of interesting teaching strategies, psychometric weaknesses must be addressed before the system can be recommended for use.

[376]

SRA Achievement Series, Forms 1 and 2, and Survey of Basic Skills, Forms P and Q.
Population: Grades K.5 to 12.9.
Publication Dates: 1978–1987.
Administration: Group.
Comments: Full Scoring and Custom Scoring services available from publisher.
Author: Science Research Associates, Inc.
Publisher: CTB Macmillan/McGraw-Hill.
a) SRA ACHIEVEMENT SERIES, FORMS 1 AND 2.
Purpose: Designed to assess "broad areas of knowledge, general skills and their application."
Publication Dates: 1978–1987.
Acronym: ACH.
Forms, 2: 1, 2.
Price Data, 1991: $1.55 per coordinator's handbook; $1.80 per user's guide; $10.65 per complete set of technical reports (1–3); $24.20 per answer keys, norms and conversion tables booklet (all levels included) ('86, 150 pages); $17.95 per 100 student profile sheets (specify Level A–D or Level E–H); $19 per 100 student growth scale charts and one wall chart; $17.10 per 10 wall charts.
1) Level A.
Population: Grades K.5–1.5.
Scores, 11: 8 achievement scores: Reading (Visual Discrimination, Auditory Discrimination, Letters and Sounds, Listening Comprehension, Total), Mathematics (Concepts, Total), Composite, plus 3 Educational Ability Scales (EAS) scores: Verbal, Nonverbal, Total.
Price Data: $52.50 per 25 ACH with EAS test booklets including 1 examiner's manual ('78, 23 pages); $41.75 per 25 ACH without EAS test booklets plus 1 examiner's manual; $3.25 per 25 practice sheets; $1.50 per extra examiner's manual; $5.35 per review kit including test booklet with EAS, practice sheet, and examiner's manual.

Time: (135) minutes total achievement testing time; (30) minutes EAS testing time.

2) Level B.

Population: Grades 1.5–2.5.

Scores, 13: 10 achievement scores: Reading (Auditory Discrimination, Letters and Sounds, Listening Comprehension, Vocabulary, Reading Comprehension, Total), Mathematics (Concepts, Computation, Total), Composite, plus same 3 EAS scores as for Level A.

Price Data: $58.50 per 25 ACH with EAS test booklets including one examiner's manual ('78, 24 pages); $47.50 per 25 achievement without EAS test booklets; practice sheets, extra examiner's manual and review kit prices same as for Level A.

Time: (180) minutes total achievement testing time; EAS time same as for Level A.

3) Level C.

Population: Grades 2.5–3.5.

Scores, 16: 13 achievement scores: Reading (Letters and Sounds, Listening Comprehension, Vocabulary, Reading Comprehension, Total), Mathematics (Concepts, Computation, Total), Language Arts (Mechanics, Usage, Spelling, Total), Composite, plus same 3 EAS scores as for Level A.

Price Data: $58.50 per 25 achievement with EAS test booklets including 1 examiner's manual ('78, 25 pages); other prices same as for Level A.

Time: (205) minutes total achievement testing time; EAS time same as for Level A.

4) Level D.

Population: Grades 3.5–4.5.

Scores, 14: 11 achievement scores: Reading (Vocabulary, Reading Comprehension, Total), Mathematics (Concepts, Computation, Total), Language Arts (Mechanics, Usage, Spelling, Total), Composite, plus same 3 EAS scores as for Level A.

Price Data: $43.75 per 25 reusable ACH test booklets; $15.50 per 25 EAS test booklets; $55 per 100 SRA edition answer sheets including 3 examiner's manuals ('78, 17 pages); $76 per 100 NCS edition answer sheets plus 3 examiner's manuals; $9.20 per set of scoring stencils (for use with SRA answer sheets only); remaining prices same as for Level A.

Time: (167) minutes total achievement testing time; EAS time same as for Level A.

5) Level E.

Population: Grades 4.5–6.5.

Scores, 18: 15 achievement scores: Reading (Vocabulary, Reading Comprehension, Total), Mathematics (Concepts, Computation, Problem Solving, Total), Language Arts (Mechanics, Usage, Spelling, Total), Reference Materials, Social Studies, Science, Composite, plus same 3 EAS scores as for Level A.

Price Data: $1.50 per extra examiner's manual ('78, 21 pages); remaining prices same as for Level D.

Time: (275–330) minutes total achievement testing time; EAS time same as for Level A.

6) Level F.

Population: Grades 6.0–8.5.

Scores, 18: Same as for Level E.

Price Data: Same as for Level E.

Time: Same as for Level E.

7) Level G.

Population: Grades 8.0–10.5.

Scores, 18: Same as for Level E.

Price Data: Same as for Level E.

Time: Same as for Level E.

8) Level H.

Population: Grades 9.0–12.9.

Scores, 17: 14 achievement scores: Reading (Vocabulary, Reading Comprehension, Total), Mathematics (Problem Solving, Concepts/Computation, Total), Language Arts (Spelling, Mechanics/Usage, Total), Reference Materials, Social Studies, Science, Survey of Applied Skills, Composite, plus same 3 EAS scores as for Level A.

Price Data: Same as for Level E.

Time: (285–330) minutes total achievement testing time; EAS time same as for Level A.

b) SURVEY OF BASIC SKILLS, FORMS P AND Q.

Purpose: Designed to assess general academic achievement "based on the learner objectives most commonly taught in the United States."

Publication Dates: 1985–1987.

Acronym: SBS.

Forms, 2: P, Q.

Price Data: $1.75 per user's guide ('85, 95 pages); $1.50 per coordinator's handbook; $18 per 100 student profile sheets (specify Level 20–22 or Level 23, 34–37); $19 per 100 student growth scale charts and one wall chart; $16.90 per 10 wall charts; $20.05 per Level 20–23, 34 sample set including test book with EAS, practice sheet, and examiner's manual; $24.70 per Level 23, 34–37 sample set including test book with EAS, answer sheet, and examiner's manual.

1) Level 20.

Population: Grades K.5–1.5.

Scores, 8: Reading (Auditory Discrimination, Letters and Sounds, Decoding, Listening Comprehension), Mathematics Concepts and Problem Solving, plus 3 EAS scores: Verbal, Nonverbal, Total.

Forms: Available in Form P only.

Price Data: $41 per 25 consumable, machine-scorable SBS test booklets and one examiner's manual; $51.75 per 25 consumable, machine-scorable SBS and EAS test booklets and one examiner's manual; $3.25 per 25 practice sheets; $6.70 per answer keys, norms, and conversion tables; $1.50 per additional examiner's manual.

Time: (103) minutes.

2) Level 21.

Population: Grades 1.5–2.5.

Scores, 10: Reading (Letters and Sounds, Listening Comprehension, Vocabulary, Reading Comprehension), Language Arts (Mechanics), Mathematics (Mathematics Concepts and Problem Solving, Mathematics Computation), plus same 3 EAS scores as Level 20.

Forms: Available in Form P only.

Price Data: $46.75 per 25 consumable, machine-scorable SBS test booklets and one examiner's manual; $57.50 per 25 consumable, machine-scorable SBS and EAS test booklets and one examiner's manual; remaining prices same as for Level 20.

Time: (166) minutes.

3) *Level 22.*

Population: Grades 2.5–3.5.

Scores, 11: Reading (Letters and Sounds, Vocabulary, Reading Comprehension), Language Arts (Mechanics, Usage, Spelling), Mathematics (Mathematics Concepts and Problem Solving, Mathematics Computation), plus same 3 EAS scores as Level 20.

Forms: Available in Form P only.

Price Data: Prices same as for Level 21.

Time: (168) minutes.

4) *Level 23.*

Population: Grades 3.5–4.5.

Scores, 11: Reading (Vocabulary, Reading Comprehension), Language Arts (Mechanics, Usage, Spelling), Mathematics (Mathematics Concepts and Problem Solving, Mathematics Computation), Reference Materials, plus same 3 EAS scores as Level 20.

Forms, 2: P, Q.

Price Data: $46.75 per 25 consumable, machine-scorable SBS test booklets (Form P only) and one examiner's manual; $57.50 per 25 consumable, machine-scorable SBS with EAS test booklets (Form P only) and one examiner's manual; $19 per 100 practice sheets (optional for this level) and 4 administration manuals; $1.50 per extra examiner's manual; $13.35 per answer keys, norms, and conversion tables (including data and scoring stencil for Forms P and Q); $39.75 per 25 reusable SBS test booklets (specify Form P or Q); $15.25 per 25 EAS test booklets (for local scoring only); $54 per 100 SRA edition answer sheets for local scoring and 3 examiner's manuals; $75 per 100 NCS edition answer sheets for local scoring and 3 examiner's manuals.

Time: (213) minutes.

5) *Level 34.*

Population: Grades 4.5–6.5.

Scores, 14: Reading (Vocabulary, Reading Comprehension), Language Arts (Mechanics, Usage, Spelling), Mathematics (Mathematics Computation, Mathematics Concepts, Mathematics Problem Solving), Reference Materials, Social Studies, Science, plus same 3 EAS scores as Level 20.

Forms, 2: P, Q.

Price Data: $43 per 25 reusable SBS test booklets (specify Form P or Q); $15.25 per 25 EAS test booklets (for local scoring only); $19 per 100 (optional) Level 34–36 practice sheets including 4 administration manuals; $1.50 per additional examiner's manual; $13.35 per answer keys, norms, and conversion tables; $54 per 100 SRA edition answer sheets for local scoring and 3 examiner's manuals; $75 per 100 NCS edition answer sheets for local scoring and 3 examiner's manuals.

Time: (278) minutes.

6) *Level 35.*

Population: 6.5–8.5.

Scores, 14: Same as for Level 34.

Forms, 2: P, Q.

Price Data: Same as for Level 34.

Time: Same as for Level 34.

7) *Level 36.*

Population: 8.5–10.5.

Scores, 14: Same as for Level 34.

Forms, 2: P, Q.

Price Data: Same as for Level 34.

Time: Same as for Level 34.

8) *Level 37.*

Population: 9.0–12.9.

Scores, 15: Reading (Vocabulary, Reading Comprehension), Language Arts (Mechanics, Usage, Spelling), Mathematics (Mathematics Computation, Mathematics Concepts, Mathematics Problem Solving), Reference Materials, Social Studies, Science, Survey of Applied Skills, plus same 3 EAS as for Level 20.

Price Data: Same as for Level 34 except no practice sheets are available.

Time: Same as for Level 34.

Cross References: For reviews by Samuel T. Mayo and Gary J. Robertson of an earlier edition of the ACH, see 9:1164 (10 references); see also T3:2260 (25 references); for reviews by Robert H. Bauernfeind and Frederick G. Brown of earlier forms, see 8:1 (11 references); see also T2:29 (3 references); for reviews by Miriam M. Bryan and Fred M. Smith, see 7:18 (9 references); for a review by Jacob S. Orleans, see 6:21 (3 references); for reviews by Warren G. Findley and Worth R. Jones, see 5:21.

TEST REFERENCES

1. Rudisill, E. M., Yarborough, B. H., & Johnson, R. A. (1982). Nongraded instruction, mathematics ability, and mathematics achievement in elementary schools. *Journal for Research in Mathematics Education, 13*, 61-66.

2. Wilkinson, L. C., & Spinelli, F. (1983). Using requests effectively in peer-directed instructional groups. *American Educational Research Journal, 20*, 479-501.

3. Booth, J. (1984). A comparison of SLEP scores with SRA and LAS scores. *TESOL Quarterly, 18*, 738-740.

4. Bradley, R. H., & Caldwell, B. M. (1984). The relation of infants' home environments to achievement test performance in first grade: A follow-up study. *Child Development, 55*, 803-809.

5. Chandler, H. N. (1984). The American public school: Yes, we have no standards. *Journal of Learning Disabilities, 17*, 186-187.

6. Cox, J., & Wiebe, J. H. (1984). Measuring reading vocabulary and concepts in mathematics in the primary grades. *The Reading Teacher, 37*, 402-410.

7. Durkin, D. (1984). Poor black children who are successful readers: An investigation. *Urban Education, 19*, 53-76.

8. Gerler, E. R., Jr., & Danielson, H. A. (1984). The quieting reflex and success imagery. *Elementary School Guidance & Counseling, 19*, 152-155.

9. Mangano, N. G., Smith, N. J., & Flahaven, E. L. (1984). A study of teacher-pupil interaction following the reading of basal stories. *National Reading Conference Yearbook, 33*, 207-213.

10. Mengano, N. G., & Benton, S. L. (1984). Comparison of question-response-feedback interactions during basal reader instruction. *Journal of Educational Research, 78*, 119-126.

11. Phillips, D. (1984). The illusion of incompetence among academically competent children. *Child Development, 55*, 2000-2016.

12. Piersel, W. C., & Kinsey, J. H. (1984). Predictive validity of the First Grade Screening Test. *Educational and Psychological Measurement, 44*, 921-924.

13. Prout, H. T., & Celmer, D. S. (1984). A validity study of the Kinetic School Drawing technique. *Psychology in the Schools, 21*, 176-180.

14. Schunk, D. H., & Rice, J. M. (1984). Strategy self-verbalization during remedial listening comprehension instruction. *Journal of Experimental Education, 53*, 49-54.

15. Holmes, B. C., & Allison, R. W. (1985). The effect of four modes of reading on children's comprehension. *Reading Research and Instruction, 25*, 9-20.

16. Lindow, J. A., Wilkinson, L. C., & Peterson, P. L. (1985). Antecedents and consequences of verbal disagreements during small-group learning. *Journal of Educational Psychology, 77*, 658-667.

17. Olson, M. W. (1985). Text type and reader ability: The effects on paraphrase and text-based inference questions. *Journal of Reading Behavior, 17*, 199-214.

18. Peterson, P. L., & Swing, S. R. (1985). Students' cognitions as mediators of the effectiveness of small-group learning. *Journal of Educational Psychology, 77*, 299-312.

19. Rothlisberg, B. A., & Dean, R. S. (1985). Reading comprehension and lateral preference in normal readers. *Psychology in the Schools, 22*, 337-342.

20. Tindal, G., Fuchs, L. S., Fuchs, D., Shinn, M. R., Deno, S. L., & German, G. (1985). Empirical validation of criterion-referenced tests. *Journal of Educational Research, 78*, 203-209.

21. Tolfa, D., Scruggs, T. E., & Bennion, K. (1985). Format changes in reading achievement tests: Implications for learning disabled students. *Psychology in the Schools, 22*, 387-391.

22. Fuchs, L. S., Fuchs, D., & Tindal, G. (1986). Effects of mastery learning procedures on student achievement. *The Journal of Educational Research, 79*, 286-291.

23. Gildemeister, J., & Friedman, P. (1986). Sequence memory and organization in recall of black third and fifth graders. *Journal of Negro Education, 55*, 142-154.

24. MacDonald, J. D. (1986). Self-generated questions and reading recall: Does training help? *Contemporary Educational Psychology, 11*, 290-304.

25. Spraggins, C. C., & Rowsey, R. E. (1986). The effect of simulation games and worksheets on learning of varying ability groups in a high school biology classroom. *Journal of Research in Science Teaching, 23*, 219-229.

26. Curcio, F. R. (1987). Comprehension of mathematical relationships expressed in graphs. *Journal for Research in Mathematics Education, 18*, 382-393.

27. Henderson, J. G., Jr. (1987). Effects of depression upon reading: A case study for distinguishing effortful from automatic processes. *Perceptual and Motor Skills, 64* (1), 191-200.

28. Johnson, D. M., & Smith, B. (1987). An evaluation of Saxon's algebra text. *The Journal of Educational Research, 81*, 97-102.

29. Johnson, E. S., & Meade, A. C. (1987). Developmental patterns of spatial ability: An early sex difference. *Child Development, 58*, 725-740.

30. Nagy, W. E., Anderson, R. C., & Herman, P. A. (1987). Learning word meanings from context during normal reading. *American Educational Research Journal, 24*, 237-270.

31. Richards, H. C., & Bear, G. W. (1987). Stability and criterion-related validity of the Estes Attitude Scales. *Educational and Psychological Measurement, 47* (2), 493-498.

32. Swanson, H. L. (1987). Verbal-coding deficits in the recall of pictorial information by learning disabled readers: The influence of a lexical system. *American Educational Research Journal, 24*, 143-170.

33. Thompson, R. A. (1987). Creating instructional and counseling partnerships to improve the academic performance of underachievers. *The School Counselor, 34*, 289-296.

34. Wright, D., & Piersel, W. C. (1987). Usefulness of a group-administered ability test for decision making. *Journal of School Psychology, 25*, 63-71.

35. Hannafin, M. J. (1988). The effects of instructional explicitness on learning and error persistence. *Contemporary Educational Psychology, 13*, 126-132.

36. Miller, R. B., Kelly, G. N., & Kelly, J. T. (1988). Effects of logo computer programming experience on problem solving and spatial relations ability. *Contemporary Educational Psychology, 13*, 348-357.

37. Pilkington, C. L., Piersel, W. C., & Ponterotto, J. G. (1988). Home language as a predictor of first-grade achievement for Anglo- and Mexican-American children. *Contemporary Educational Psychology, 13*, 1-14.

38. Ryder, R. J., & Slater, W. H. (1988). The relationship between word knowledge frequency and word knowledge. *The Journal of Educational Research, 81*, 312-317.

39. Wright, D., & Wiese, M. J. (1988). Teacher judgment in student evaluation: A comparison of grading methods. *The Journal of Educational Research, 82*, 10-14.

40. Zimmerman, S. O. (1988). Problem-solving tasks on the microcomputer: A look at the performance of students with learning disabilities. *Journal of Learning Disabilities, 21*, 637-641.

41. Berger, R. S., & Reid, D. K. (1989). Differences that make a difference: Comparisons of metacomponential functioning and knowledge base among groups of high and low IQ learning disabled, mildly mentally retarded, and normally achieving adults. *Journal of Learning Disabilities, 22*, 422-429.

42. Denner, P. R., McGinley, W. J., & Brown, E. (1989). Effects of story impressions as a prereading/writing activity on story comprehension. *The Journal of Educational Research, 82*, 320-326.

43. Houck, C. K., & Billingsley, B. S. (1989). Written expression of students with and without learning disabilities: Differences across the grades. *Journal of Learning Disabilities, 22*, 561-567, 572.

44. Mantzicopoulos, P. (1990). Coping with school failure: Characteristics of students employing successful and unsuccessful coping strategies. *Psychology in the Schools, 27*, 138-143.

45. Taylor, B. M., Frye, B. J., & Maruyama, G. M. (1990). Time spent reading and reading growth. *American Educational Research Journal, 27*, 351-362.

46. Ferguson, P. C. (1991). Longitudinal outcome differences among promoted and transitional at-risk kindergarten students. *Psychology in the Schools, 28*, 139-146.

Review of the SRA Achievement Series, Forms 1 and 2, and Survey of Basic Skills, Forms P and Q by GERALD S. HANNA, *Professor of Educational Psychology and Measurement, Kansas State University, Manhattan, KS:*

The SRA Survey of Basic Skills (SBS) is apparently an in-house revision of the SRA Achievement Series. The SBS materials are spaciously and attractively formatted in easy-to-read test booklets, but essential supportive technical information is not available. The achievement battery is accompanied by the short optional Educational Ability Series (EAS).

VALIDITY. The developmental research seems to have conformed to commonly accepted practices. A feature this reviewer especially appreciates is the generous use of interpretive exercises in Science, Social Studies, Reference Materials, and Reading. This relating of many test questions to novel stimulus materials presented in the test tends to reduce the amount of purely factual information assessed and helps the test to emphasize students' higher mental processes. In general, the test questions seem to be at least as good as those typically found in survey batteries. The extent to which the content of the SBS assesses those curricular outcomes stressed by local school districts must, of course, be judged at the district level.

The manuals provide no criterion-related validity data comparing SBS scores with those of other achievement tests or with school grades.

Tables of subtest score intercorrelations reveal substantial overlap. Yet the SBS probably should not be faulted for this because such overlap is common among achievement batteries. Nonetheless, the redundance among subtests does limit the degree to which profile interpretation can be fruitful. The manuals fail to supply corresponding tables of correlations among the short measures of specific skills for which data are supplied for individual students.

A feature that compares favorably with most achievement tests is the SBS's candid, useful, and ethical directions concerning guessing. In the context of number right scoring, students should not be—and in SBS directions are not—encouraged to omit items. In this respect, SBS directions help to prevent test wiseness regarding guessing from contaminating validity.

RELIABILITY. Alternate form reliability data are reported. This information is not useful, however, because no descriptive data are provided for the sample. Nor is mention made of the time interval, if any, between the administration of the two forms.

KR20s ranging from adequate to impressive, are reported for SBS subtests, subtotals, and composites. Data on speededness of the SBS seem adequate to justify the conclusion that the tests are not too speeded for appropriate use of KR20 estimates of internal consistency. KR20s are also reported for the EAS, but because no speededness data are supplied for the tests, the legitimacy of using KR20 cannot be judged.

The KR20s appear to have been computed for subsets of the standardization samples, and it is not clear how the variability of the KR20 samples compare with those of the standardization samples. Users are therefore unable to judge whether or not the KR20 estimates are realistic.

Many of the KR20s reported are inappropriate for one or both of two reasons. First, KR20 is suitable only for independent items; yet the items within interpretative exercises may not be wholly independent. This issue tends to cause reliability to be slightly overestimated.

The second reason is more worrisome. KR20s are suited for homogeneous materials, such as subtests. They are not appropriate for the types of heterogeneous composite scores for which they are reported. Moreover, when KR20s are used on heterogeneous composites, they tend to yield lower estimates than some of the homogeneous subtests upon which they are based. Yet no such trend is evident in the data reported. The interpretation of this discrepancy raises some doubt concerning what procedures were used to derive the reported coefficients.

It is entirely possible (even likely) the battery would, if adequate research were conducted and reported, meet prevailing standards concerning reliability; but this is speculative. What is certain is the publisher has failed to describe sufficient research to meet minimum professional standards concerning the provision data.

NORMATIVE DATA. SRA also failed to describe adequately the standardization process and sample. Without this information, prospective users cannot judge the adequacy of the normative data.

The SBS standardization design was based on eight district enrollment strata, nine geographic regions, and five socioeconomic levels. The resulting 360 cells (8 x 9 x 5) were collapsed into 49 by an undescribed process. Because no three integers greater than 1 have a product of 49, it appears that the 360 cells were grouped by some method other than making straight "slices" through the sampling matrix. The peculiarity of such a sampling design merits explanation, yet none is provided.

Districts were randomly sampled within cells and schools were randomly sampled within selected districts. No data are provided concerning nonresponse rate, nor are readers told whether same-cell replacements were sought for districts or schools that declined to participate.

The standardization sample was weighted for school and district population factors. Yet readers are not informed what factors were used for weighting or what the range of weighting values were.

Comparisons are needed between the population of school-aged children and the final weighted and unweighted samples with respect to the stratification variables (or other correlates of achievement). No such comparisons are provided. The adequacy of the match therefore cannot be judged.

In summary, the description of the normative sample raises more questions than it answers. Without a means of judging the adequacy of the norms, the battery should not, in this reviewer's judgment, be recommended.

OTHER CONSIDERATIONS. A scoring service provides a record of individual student's performance in each of several specific skills per subtest and compares this performance with the national norms. "It also provides a record of the student's mastery of the skill-categories objectives measured in the test and helps assess strengths and weaknesses in the student's performance in each skill area, so that appropriate grouping and instruction can be planned" (User's Manual, p. 19). This raises two problems. First, it encourages profile interpretation among "subskills" that have not been shown to exist. For example, reading comprehension is subdivided into "subskills" that research has repeatedly failed to verify and for which no SBS intercorrelations are reported. Second, the number of items used to assess the various subskills range down to 3. How reliable could the information based on so few items be? Not very! Moreover, no reliability data are provided at the subskill level. Encouraging interpretation of data based on so few items in the absence of reliability data (or even caveats) is a serious oversight.

A variety of other issues are puzzling. An example will illustrate the seriousness of the problems. Why are the confidence bands for group data at least as wide as those provided for pupils? Surely group data are more reliable than data for individuals.

The accompanying EAS continues to suffer from several worrisome problems detailed for an earlier edition by Robertson (1985). For example, it has a standard score scale (mislabeled a quotient) having a standard deviation of 16 and a mean of 100 at kindergarten that drifts up to 108 by grade 12. Neither explanation nor rationale is provided for these strangely ascending means.

SUMMARY. Most of the problems concerning the SBS raised in this review concern missing or incomplete information rather than information that signals definite inadequacies. However, the apparent lack of concern for conventions of scholarly reporting leave this reviewer unfavorably impressed. It is suggested that districts considering the SBS take a very hard look at its competitors.

REVIEWER'S REFERENCE

Robertson, G. J. (1985). [Review of the SRA Achievement Series.] In J. V. Mitchell, Jr. (Ed.), *The ninth mental measurements yearbook* (pp. 1428-1430). Lincoln, NE: Buros Institute of Mental Measurements.

Review of the SRA Achievement Series, Forms 1 and 2, and Survey of Basic Skills, Forms P and Q by KEVIN L. MORELAND, Associate Professor of Psychology, Fordham University, Bronx, NY:

The 1985 SRA Survey of Basic Skills, Levels 20–37 (SBS) is the successor to the venerable SRA Achievement Series (ACH), which went through four editions between 1954 and 1978. The SBS and its companion scholastic aptitude measure, the Educational Ability Series (EAS), constitute a new comprehensive testing program for the assessment of pupils in grades kindergarten through 12. This review will, for the most part, follow the same format as Robertson's (1985) excellent review of the fourth edition of the SRA Achievement Series. Readers are invited to consult Robertson's review and Mayo's (1985) review to judge for themselves the degree to which the SBS improves upon its predecessor.

MATERIALS AND FORMAT. The materials and format of the SBS differ, in several ways, from those of the ACH. The general appearance, typography, and graphic design of the SBS materials are, with very minor exceptions, good, whereas Robertson (1985) found those for the ACH "uneven." In particular, the directions for test administration at the lower grade levels are improved. The use of bold type of a larger size makes it easy for administrators to distinguish instructions they need to read aloud from instructions meant only for them. This is especially critical because many of the test items for younger pupils are read to them by the test administrator. The only apparent fault of the SBS materials lies in the handful of items that use photographs. The photographs are very dark and hard to make out.

Most levels of the SBS are available in two parallel forms: P and Q. However, unlike the ACH, only one form (P) is available for Levels 20–22, which span the grades from kindergarten to the first semester of the third grade.

The SBS was designed with computer scoring in mind. In particular, it was designed to be scored by the publisher. The publisher has developed four new reporting formats that, together with the seven that were available for the ACH, provide an impressive array of data that will be helpful to many users (cf. Mayo, 1985). Scoring keys and norm tables are made available for local scoring if users prefer.

The Individual Item Analysis provides individual student's responses to items in a curriculum area, as well as relevant normative data. The District/School Alpha Report provides an alphabetical listing of schools' average scores within a district. A Numeric Research Grid is provided on each answer sheet so that students can be grouped in any manner the user deems relevant. The most impressive new report, the Narrative Report, provides an individualized interpretation of the student's scores, in addition to the scores themselves. The Narrative Report is stilted and, at times, overly technical (e.g., "An 87 percentile means that your student scored better than 87 percent of the students . . . who took the test *during standardization*" [italics added]). Nevertheless, it should improve upon the generic interpretive leaflet of yesteryear when it comes to communicating the meaning of test scores to pupils and their parents. As with the ACH, SRA deserves special commendation for the excellent User's Manual for the SBS. One might quibble that some of the information in the User's Manual (e.g., description of the item selection procedures) should have been included in the technical report instead, but that is truly a small quibble.

CONTENT AND ITEM DEVELOPMENT. Good craftsmanship is perhaps most evident in the development of the item content of the SBS. In addition to the SRA's editorial staff, 37 curriculum experts helped SRA ensure the accuracy, curricular relevance, and currency of the battery's contents. Fourteen representatives of minority and women's groups reviewed all proposed items for obvious race or gender bias. In addition, tallies were made of the numbers of ethnic references, males and females, and representation of males and females in traditional and nontraditional roles in passage and item content and illustrations. These tallies resulted in adjustments to make sure that all forms and levels of the SBS complied with SRA's bias-free publishing guidelines. SRA pretested over three times as many items as were eventually retained in the final forms of the battery. Over 100,000 students from 485 schools located in 40 states participated in the pretesting. Unfortunately, the statistical procedures used to select items are not described in detail:

> Item analysis data was [sic] used to eliminate or occasionally revise items . . . Items that survived the initial selection process were checked for distracter efficiency. . . . [A Rasch model analysis] was run on each item. Every attempt was made, within the restrictions of content balance, to eliminate nonfitting items. All items were statistically . . . analyzed for cultural, social, rural/urban, and sex-role fairness. (User's Manual, p. 5)

Which item analysis data? How did the data fit the Rasch Model? Were any biased items retained in the name of content balance? It's too bad these questions go unanswered because, judging from Robertson's (1985) review, clear and complete description of these kinds of technical details was one of the ACH's major strengths.

These procedures yielded items that are, almost invariably, clearly written, carefully edited, and devoid of obvious bias. The item-level problems in the ACH carefully detailed by Robertson (1985) appear to have been resolved in the SBS. The SBS developers apparently heeded Robertson's (1985) compliments too. The positive features of the ACH item pool remain evident in the SBS item pool even though the SBS comprises an entirely new item pool.

STANDARDIZATION PROCEDURES. The standardization sample consisted of 89,549 pupils who were tested during the first week of October, 1983, over 88% of whom were tested again during the second week of April, 1984. The standardization sample was developed by stratified random sampling with school district size, geographic region, and socioeconomic level as the stratifying variables. Both the sampling plan itself and the detailed description of it respond to most of Robertson's (1985) questions about, and criticisms of, the ACH sampling plan. A couple of his questions linger. What was the participation rate among the school districts sampled? How were nonparticipants replaced, if at all, in the final sample? The developers' laudable use of socioeconomic level as a stratification variable raises a new question. Why did the developers use an obscure measure of socioeconomic level like the Orshansky Poverty Indicator? More importantly, use of the Orshansky measure leaves one to wonder how the socioeconomic level of the standardization sample compares with census data. Although available, no post hoc analyses of median family income and median family education level were provided.

NORM-REFERENCED INTERPRETATION. A variety of norm-referenced derived scores are provided: within-grade percentile ranks and stanines, grade equivalents, normal curve equivalents, and Growth Scale Values (GSVs). The utility of the GSVs for "tracing students' educational growth from year to year and for predicting future growth" (User's Manual, p. 14) seems doubtful in view of the fact this purportedly longitudinal measure was developed using cross-sectional data. However, the GSVs are useful because they were developed using the Rasch Model to provide a single scale applicable across both forms and all levels of the SBS. Furthermore, this scale was equated to the ACH GSVs using the equipercentile method. Both these equating procedures improve on those used with the ACH (cf. Robertson, 1985).

CRITERION-REFERENCED INTERPRETATION. To paraphrase Robertson (1985), school personnel seeking well-developed criterion-referenced test instruments will not find the SBS well suited to their needs. However, one of the publisher's computer-generated reports makes it possible to use the SBS as a quasi criterion-referenced measure. The Group Item Analysis Report makes it possible to compare students' performance on homogeneous skill clusters within each subtest with performance in the local school district (or school, or classroom). (For example, the Mechanics subtest of the Level 22 Language Arts measure comprises three homogeneous skill clusters: alphabetization [four items], capitalization [eight items], and punctuation [12 items].) This approach makes provision for local curricular emphases, but it is still norm-referenced—only the norm group has changed. Unfortunately, this approach is cumbersome, involving the use of two reports (one for the student and one for the comparison group) and requires psychometric sophistication not usually found among school personnel.

RELIABILITY. Reliability data for the SBS norm-referenced scores are quite complete. Internal consistency (KR 20), alternate-forms reliability, and stability data are available. Within-grade internal consistency reliabilities for the total reading, total mathematics, and total language scores typically fall in the mid .90s and the "3R" composite of those three scores usually falls in the upper .90s. Most of the subtest internal consistencies are also acceptable, centered in the mid to high .80s. Not surprisingly, exceptions to this generalization occur most often with subtests developed for younger pupils. Exceptions include Auditory Discrimination, for which KR 20 values are .72 and .74 for Level 20, and Listening Comprehension, for which internal consistencies range from .67 to .73 for Levels 20 and 21. The Letters and Sounds subtest is questionable at Level 22, with KR 20 values of .76 and .80. Math Concepts has low internal reliabilities (.75–.83) at Level 34 and at Level 35 when that form is used with sixth graders and first semester seventh graders. The KR 20 values for Reference Materials typically fall in the mid to upper .80s. However, the internal consistencies for Social Studies and Science are not consistently in the .80s until Level 35 is used with spring semester sixth graders; those values are not consistently in the mid .80s for another year. The internal consistency of the Applied Skills score, which is available only in Level 37, is consistently in the upper .80s and low .90s.

Alternate forms coefficients are, as one would expect, somewhat lower than the KR 20 values. These values, which are not available for Levels 20, 21, and 22, range from .70 to .94. Those for the three "total" scores cluster in the high .80s, whereas the "3R" composite score is consistently in the .90s. The content-saturated tests (Reference Materials, Social Studies, and Science) had the lowest alternate forms reliability, with coefficients consistently in the .70s.

No true test-retest stability data are available for the SBS. However, 6-month stability coefficients are available for pupils tested with adjacent levels of the SBS and for pupils tested with alternate forms of the battery. The adjacent levels coefficients range from .53 for second graders administered the Level 21 and Level 22 Computation subtest to .94 for the "3R" composite for eighth graders who took Levels 35 and 36. Most of the adjacent levels correlations for the subtests are in the .70s, those for the three total scores are in the .80s, and those for the "3R" composite in the low .90s. The alternate forms stabilities are in the same range as the adjacent levels correlations.

In all, these reliability figures are as impressive as any you are likely to see for a multiscale achievement battery. One need only be cautious in interpreting a few subtest scores for younger pupils. Unfortunately, as was the case with the ACH, no reliability data are reported for the "criterion-referenced" homogeneous skill clusters. Because the skill clusters are shorter than any of the subtests, they are, no doubt, less reliable. In view of the available reliability data, it is reasonable to suppose that their reliability is low enough to preclude confident interpretation.

VALIDITY. Content, concurrent, and criterion-related validity data are available for the SBS. Intercorrelations among the SBS scores are also available, making inferences about construct validity possible. Extensive documentation is provided for content coverage of the battery in the User's Manual. Criterion-related validity was established by correlating the SBS with the ACH. The correlations among like tests and subtests ranged from .29 for Letters and Sounds among first graders to .92 for the "3R" composite among fifth, sixth, seventh, and eighth graders. As with the various reliability figures, correlation between the two batteries is lowest for the youngest pupils. Moreover, the correlations tend to be low among scales Robertson (1985) and I found unreliable. Letters and Sounds, for example, was found to be among the least reliable of the ACH and SBS scales, the intercorrelation of which yielded the lowest concurrent validity coefficient. In general, the three "total" scores and the "3R" composite yield correlations that span the mid .80s to the low .90s, although the subtests intercorrelate in the .70s for the most part. All these data are comparable to the alternate forms reliability of the SBS, suggesting that the two batteries are essentially parallel forms. This is important for two reasons. First, only one form of the SBS is available at Levels 20, 21, and 22. If you want to make a second assessment of pupils at those levels (using one of SRA's achievement measures), uncontaminated by identical content, you must turn to the ACH. Second, the criterion-related validation of the ACH was more extensive than that of the SBS (e.g., correlations with course grades, correlations with

other achievement batteries). The close empirical linkage between the ACH and the SBS should make users more confident in their interpretations of the achievement scores on the SBS. On the other hand, it should be noted that, as with the ACH, no appropriate criterion-related validity data are available for the SBS Applied Skills test.

Mayo's (1985) summary of the construct validity of the ACH applies to the SBS too:

> Data on intercorrelations of various test scores within the [SBS] battery were less encouraging [than the data on criterion-related validity]. Coefficients were predominantly on the high side [more than 75% > .69 for Level 37] in comparison to similar tests and also in relation to the reviewer's expectations for tests which purport to measure different subject-matter contents and skills. (p. 1429)

EDUCATIONAL ABILITY SERIES. My opinion of this feature of the battery is much the same as Robertson's (1985):

> The EAS is offered as an optional test for those users who want to compare scholastic aptitude with achievement. While achievement-ability comparisons are generally justifiable given suitable measures, the EAS is not well suited for making such comparisons . . . In fact, this reviewer feels EAS is the weakest part of the SRA assessment program. No data are reported to justify the type of content selected for EAS . . . . These concerns are reflected in correlations reported for EAS vs. the [the SBS] battery composite scores, grades [2]–12, that range from [.69 to .84, with a median of .82]. . . Especially troublesome is the derivation of the "quotient scores" . . . . the mean standard score is arbitrarily increased by .5 of a unit in each successive grade . . . . The publisher gives no rationale for selecting these particular mean scores, which vary between 100 in grade K and 108 in grade 12. . . . There is no . . . justification provided to support the derivation of the percent of items answered correctly on the verbal and nonverbal components of EAS . . . (p. 1434)

In short, look elsewhere for a measure of academic aptitude.

CONCLUSION. Robertson (1985) and Mayo (1985) recommended the ACH in spite of the criticisms they leveled and this reviewer will do the same for the SBS. For the most part, the SBS provides a well-developed, norm-referenced measure of academic achievement. This is especially so for Levels 23–37 spanning the second semester of the third grade through high school. The one SBS measure I cannot recommend is the Applied Skills test. That measure is face valid, but lacks appropriate external criterion data. I cannot recommend the EAS either. Very high intercorrelations with the SBS "3R" composite makes it likely that the EAS is a good omnibus measure of academic achievement rather than academic aptitude.

At this writing the fate of the SBS is unclear. SRA is no more and CTB Macmillan/McGraw-Hill now owns the SBS. If CTB elects to discontinue the Survey of Basic Skills in favor of their own excellent California Achievement Tests (CAT; 10:41), I hope they incorporate the desirable features of the former into the latter. Judging from Wardrop's (1989) review of the CAT, the SBS is superior when it comes to the provision of test-retest reliability data, and the quality of the User's Manual and the computer-based reporting services.

REVIEWER'S REFERENCES

Mayo, S. T. (1985). [Review of the SRA Achievement Series.] In J. V. Mitchell, Jr. (Ed.), *The ninth mental measurements yearbook* (pp. 1428-1430). Lincoln, NE: Buros Institute of Mental Measurements.

Robertson, G. J. (1985). [Review of the SRA Achievement Series.] In J. V. Mitchell, Jr. (Ed.), *The ninth mental measurements yearbook* (pp. 1430-1434). Lincoln, NE: Buros Institute of Mental Measurements.

Wardrop, J. L. (1989). [Review of the California Achievement Tests, Forms E and F.] In J. C. Conoley & J. J. Kramer (Eds.), *The tenth mental measurements yearbook* (pp. 128-133). Lincoln, NE: Buros Institute of Mental Measurements.

[377]
Stanford Achievement Test, Eighth Edition.

Purpose: "To measure the important learning outcomes of the school curriculum."
Population: Grades 1.5 to 9.9.
Publication Dates: 1923–90.
Administration: Group.
Levels, 8: Primary (1, 2, 3), Intermediate (1, 2, 3), Advanced (1, 2); Forms, 2: J, K; Editions, 2: hand scored, machine scored.
Price Data, 1989: $12 per 25 individual record forms (select level); $9 per 25 preview for parents; $7 per 25 practice tests (select level); $17 per test coordinator's handbook (multilevel); $18 per guide for organizational planning (multilevel; '89, 92 pages); $9 per guide for classroom planning (select level); $9 per index of instructional objectives (select level); $8 per 25 understanding test results (select level); $25 per handbook of instructional strategies; $15 per norms booklet (select level); $30 per multilevel norms booklet; $33 per Technical Data Report ('90, 232 pages).
Special Editions: Large type and braille editions for Form J, grades 2.5–12 available from American Printing House for the Blind, Inc.
Comments: Seventh edition still available; subtests in Reading and Mathematics available as separates.
Author: The Psychological Corporation; earlier edition authors: Eric F. Gardner, Herbert C. Rudman, Bjorn Karlsen, and Jack Merwin.
Publisher: The Psychological Corporation.
a) PRIMARY 1.
Population: Grades 1.5 to 2.5.
Scores, 14: Reading (Word Study Skills, Word Reading, Reading Comprehension, Total), Mathematics (Concepts of Number, Mathematics Computation, Mathematics Applications, Total), Language, Spelling, Environment, Listening, Basic Battery, Complete Battery.
Price Data: $62 per 25 machine-scorable (by publisher) test booklets; $72 per 25 machine-scorable (local) test booklets; $42 per 25 hand-scorable test booklets; $54 per set of scoring stencils.
Time: (280–330) minutes in 10 sessions.
b) PRIMARY 2.

Population: Grades 2.5 to 3.5.
Scores, 14: Reading (Word Study Skills, Reading Vocabulary, Reading Comprehension, Total), Mathematics (Concepts of Number, Mathematics Computation, Mathematics Applications, Total), Language, Spelling, Environment, Listening, Basic Battery, Complete Battery.
Price Data: Same as level *a* above.
Time: (285–335) minutes in 10 sessions.
c) PRIMARY 3.
Population: Grades 3.5 to 4.5.
Scores, 20: Reading (Word Study Skills, Reading Vocabulary, Reading Comprehension, Total), Mathematics (Concepts of Number, Mathematics Computation, Mathematics Applications, Total), Language (Mechanics, Expression, Total), Spelling, Study Skills, Science, Social Science, Listening, Using Information, Thinking Skills, Basic Battery, Complete Battery.
Price Data: $79 per 25 machine-scorable (by publisher) test booklets (complete battery); $89 per 25 machine-scorable (local) test booklets (complete battery); $46 per 25 hand-scorable test booklets; $62 per 25 machine-scorable (by publisher) test booklets (basic battery); $72 per 25 machine-scorable (local) test booklets (basic battery); $28 per 25 machine-scorable (by publisher) Science/Social Science test booklets; $38 per 25 machine-scorable (local) Science/Social Science test booklets; $46 per 25 reusable test booklets (complete battery); $44 per 25 reusable test booklets (basic battery); $32 per 25 Reading test booklets; $30 per 25 Mathematics test booklets; $37 per 100 machine-scorable (by publisher) answer sheets; $44 per 100 machine-scorable (local) answer sheets; $10 per 25 hand-scorable answer sheets; $69 per set of scoring stencils for test booklets; $15 per set of scoring stencils for answer sheets.
Time: 360(430) minutes in 13 sessions.
d) INTERMEDIATE 1.
Population: Grades 4.5 to 5.5.
Scores, 19: Reading (Vocabulary, Comprehension, Total), Mathematics (Concepts of Number, Computation, Applications, Total), Language (Mechanics, Expression, Total), Spelling, Study Skills, Science, Social Science, Listening, Using Information, Thinking Skills, Basic Battery, Complete Battery.
Price Data: $48 per 25 reusable test booklets (complete battery); $46 per 25 reusable test booklets (basic battery); $32 per 25 reading test booklets; $30 per 25 mathematics test booklets; $37 per 100 machine-scorable (by publisher) answer sheets; $44 per 100 machine-scorable (local) answer sheets; $10 per 25 hand-scorable answer sheets; $15 per set of scoring stencils.
Time: (345–405) minutes in 12 sessions.
e) INTERMEDIATE 2.
Population: Grades 5.5 to 6.5.
Scores, 19: Same as *d* above.
Price Data: Same as *d* above.
Time: Same as *d* above.
f) INTERMEDIATE 2.
Population: Grades 6.5 to 7.5.
Scores, 19: Same as *d* above.
Price Data: Same as *d* above.
Time: Same as *d* above.

g) ADVANCED 1.
Population: Grades 7.5 to 8.5.
Scores, 19: Same as *d* above.
Price Data: Same as *d* above.
Time: Same as *d* above.
h) ADVANCED 2.
Population: Grades 8.5 to 9.9.
Scores, 19: Same as *d* above.
Price Data: Same as *d* above.
Time: Same as *d* above.
Cross References: For reviews by Mark L. Davison and Michael J. Subkoviak and Frank H. Farley of the 1982 Edition, see 9:1172 (19 references); see also T3:2286 (80 references); for reviews by Robert L. Ebel and A. Harry Passow and an excerpted review by Irvin J. Lehmann of the 1973 edition, see 8:29 (51 references); see also T2:36 (87 references); for an excerpted review by Peter F. Merenda of the 1964 edition, see 7:25 (44 references); for a review by Mirian M. Bryan and an excerpted review by Robert E. Stake (with J. Thomas Hastings), see 6:26 (13 references); for a review by N. L. Gage of an earlier edition, see 5:25 (19 references); for reviews by Paul R. Hanna (with Claude E. Norcross) and Virgil E. Herrick, see 4:25 (20 references); for reviews by Walter W. Cook and Ralph C. Preston, see 3:18 (33 references). For reviews of subtests, see 9:1173 (1 review) 9:1174 (1 review), 9:1175 (1 review), 8:291 (2 reviews), 8:745 (2 reviews), 7:209 (2 reviews), 7:527 (1 review), 7:708 (1 review), 7:802 (1 review), 7:895 (1 review), 6:637 (1 review), 5:656 (2 reviews), 5:698 (2 reviews), 5:799 (1 review), 4:419 (1 review), 4:555 (1 review), 4:593 (2 reviews), 3:503 (1 review), and 3:595 (1 review).

TEST REFERENCES

1. Ysseldyke, J. E., & Marston, D. (1982). A critical analysis of standardized reading tests. *School Psychology Review, 11,* 257-266.
2. Baroody, A. J., Ginsburg, H. P., & Waxman, B. (1983). Children's use of mathematical structure. *Journal for Research in Mathematics Education, 14,* 156-168.
3. Carbonell, J. L. (1983). Inmate classification systems: A cross-tabulation of two methods. *Criminal Justice and Behavior, 10,* 285-292.
4. Llabre, M. M., & Cuevas, G. (1983). The effects of test language and mathematical skills assessed on the scores of bilingual Hispanic students. *Journal for Research in Mathematics Education, 14,* 318-324.
5. Nugent, G. C. (1983). Deaf students' learning from captioned instruction: The relationship between the visual and caption display. *The Journal of Special Education, 17,* 227-234.
6. Allen, T. E. (1984). Test-response variations between hearing-impaired and hearing students. *The Journal of Special Education, 18,* 119-129.
7. Badian, N. A. (1984). Can the WPPSI be of aid in identifying young children at risk for reading disability. *Journal of Learning Disability, 17,* 583-587.
8. Cabello, B. (1984). Eenie, meenie, miny, mo. *Thrust For Educational Leadership, 14* (3), 16-18.
9. Fagan, W. T. (1984). Word identification strategies in context of a gain and no-gain remedial reading group. *Reading World, 24* (1), 54-64.
10. Hansen, L. (1984). Field dependence-independence and language testing: Evidence from six Pacific island cultures. *TESOL Quarterly, 18,* 311-324.
11. Martin, D. S. (1984). Cognitive modification for the hearing impaired adolescent: The promise. *Exceptional Children, 51,* 235-242.
12. May, D. C., & Welch, E. L. (1984). The effects of developmental placement and early retention on children's later scores on standardized tests. *Psychology in the Schools, 21,* 381-385.
13. Morgenstern, C. F., & Renner, J. W. (1984). Measuring thinking with standardized science tests. *Journal of Research in Science Teaching, 21,* 639-648.
14. Watkins, E. O., & Wiebe, M. J. (1984). Factorial validity of the Stanford Achievement Test for first-grade children. *Educational and Psychological Measurement, 44,* 951-954.

15. Wolk, S. (1984). The moderating influence of student characteristics on the stability of reading and mathematics assessment over a five-year period. *The Journal of Experimental Education, 52,* 234-239.
16. Wolk, S., & Allen, T. E. (1984). A 5-year followup of reading-comprehension achievement of hearing-impaired students in special education programs. *The Journal of Special Education, 18,* 161-176.
17. Airasian, P. W. (1985). [Review of the Stanford Achievement Test.] *Journal of Educational Measurement, 22,* 163-167.
18. Gibson-Harman, K., & Austin, G. F. (1985). A revised form of the Tennessee Self-Concept Scale for use with deaf and hard of hearing persons. *American Annals of the Deaf, 130,* 218-225.
19. Kickbusch, K. (1985). Minority students in mathematics: The reading skills connection. *Sociological Inquiry, 55,* 402-416.
20. Nolen, S. B., & Wilbur, R. B. (1985). The effects of context on deaf students' comprehension of difficult sentences. *American Annals of the Deaf, 130,* 231-235.
21. Scruggs, T. E., & Tolfa, D. (1985). Improving the test-taking skills of learning-disabled students. *Perceptual and Motor Skills, 60,* 847-850.
22. Scruggs, T. E., Bennion, K., & Lifson, S. (1985). An analysis of children's strategy use on reading achievement tests. *Elementary School Journal, 85,* 479-484.
23. Stockard, J., Lang, D., & Wood, J. W. (1985). Academic merit, status variables, and students' grades. *Journal of Research and Development in Education, 18* (2), 12-20.
24. Tolfa, D., Scruggs, T. E., & Bennion, K. (1985). Format changes in reading achievement tests: Implications for learning disabled students. *Psychology in the Schools, 22,* 387-391.
25. Valenzuela de la Garza, J., & Medina, M., Jr. (1985). Academic achievement as influenced by bilingual instruction for Spanish-dominant Mexican American children. *Hispanic Journal of Behavioral Sciences, 7,* 247-259.
26. Waldron, K. A. (1985). The effects of an intermediary placement on learning disabled and low-achieving adolescents. *Journal of Learning Disabilities, 18,* 154-159.
27. Wolk, S., & Zieziula, F. R. (1985). Reliability of the 1973 edition of the SAT-HI over time: Implications for assessing minority students. *American Annals of the Deaf, 130,* 285-290.
28. Badian, N. A. (1986). Improving the prediction of reading for the individual child: A four-year follow-up. *Journal of Learning Disabilities, 19,* 262-269.
29. Bjorklund, D. F., & Bernholtz, J. E. (1986). The role of knowledge base in the memory performance of good and poor readers. *Journal of Experimental Child Psychology, 41,* 367-393.
30. Collis, B., Ollila, L. O., & Yore, L. D. (1986). Predictive validity of the Canadian Readiness Test and selected measures of cognitive development for grade one reading and mathematics achievement. *The Alberta Journal of Educational Research, 32,* 2-11.
31. Dirgi, D. R. (1986). Does the Rasch model really work for multiple choice items? Not if you look closely. *Journal of Educational Measurement, 23,* 283-298.
32. Felson, R. B., & Reed, M. (1986). The effect of parents on the self-appraisals of children. *Social Psychology Quarterly, 49,* 302-308.
33. Hofmann, R., & Zippco, D. (1986). Effects of divorce upon school self-esteem and achievement of 10-, 11-, and 12-year-old children. *Perceptual and Motor Skills, 62,* 397-398.
34. Leu, D. J., Jr., DeGroff, L. C., & Simons, H. D. (1986). Predictable texts and interactive-compensatory hypotheses: Evaluating individual differences in reading ability, context, use, and comprehension. *Journal of Educational Psychology, 78,* 347-352.
35. May, D. (1986). Relationships between the Gesell School Readiness Test and standardized achievement and intelligence measures. *Educational and Psychological Measurement, 46,* 1051-1059.
36. Swanson, H. L., & Rathgeber, A. J. (1986). The effects of organizational dimension on memory for words in learning-disabled and nondisabled readers. *Journal of Educational Research, 79,* 155-162.
37. Young, T. W., & Shorr, D. N. (1986). Factors affecting locus of control in school children. *Genetic, Social, and General Psychology Monographs, 112,* 407-417.
38. Akanatsu, C. T., & Armour, V. A. (1987). Developing written literacy in deaf children through analyzing sign language. *American Annals of the Deaf, 132,* 46-51.
39. Brandon, P. R., Newton, B. J., & Hammond, O. W. (1987). Children's mathematics achievement in Hawaii: Sex differences favoring girls. *American Educational Research Journal, 24,* 437-461.
40. Connell, J. P., & Ilardi, B. C. (1987). Self-system concomitants of discrepancies between children's and teachers' evaluations of academic competence. *Child Development, 58,* 1297-1307.
41. Davey, B. (1987). Relations between word knowledge and comprehension: Generalization across tasks and readers. *The Journal of Educational Research, 80,* 179-183.
42. Griswold, P. C., Gelzheiser, L. M., & Shepherd, M. J. (1987). Does a production deficiency hypothesis account for vocabulary learning among adolescents with learning disabilities? *Journal of Learning Disabilities, 20,* 620-626.

43. Grunau, R. V. E., & Low, M. D. (1987). Cognitive and task-related EEG correlates of arithmetic performance in adolescents. *Journal of Clinical and Experimental Neuropsychology, 9,* 563-574.

44. Harper, L. V., & Huie, K. S. (1987). Relations among preschool children's adult and peer contacts and later academic achievement. *Child Development, 58,* 1051-1065.

45. Pudlas, K. A. (1987). Sentence reception abilities of hearing impaired students across five communication modes. *American Annals of the Deaf, 132,* 232-236.

46. Swanson, H. L. (1987). Verbal-coding deficits in the recall of pictorial information by learning disabled readers: The influence of a lexical system. *American Educational Research Journal, 24,* 143-170.

47. Widaman, K. F., & Kagan, S. (1987). Cooperativeness and achievement: Interaction of student cooperativeness with cooperative versus competitive classroom organization. *Journal of School Psychology, 25,* 355-365.

48. Abikoff, H., Ganeles, D., Reiter, G., Blum, C., Foley, C., & Klein, R. G. (1988). Cognitive training in academically deficient ADDH boys receiving stimulant medication. *Journal of Abnormal Child Psychology, 16,* 411-432.

49. Badian, N. A. (1988). The prediction of good and poor reading before kindergarten entry: A nine-year follow-up. *Journal of Learning Disabilities, 21,* 98-103, 123.

50. Craig, H. B., & Gordon, H. W. (1988). Specialized cognitive function and reading achievement in hearing-impaired adolescents. *Journal of Speech and Hearing Disorders, 53,* 30-41.

51. Davey, B. (1988). The nature of response errors for good and poor readers when permitted to reinspect text during question-answering. *American Educational Research Journal, 25,* 399-414.

52. Diebold, T. J., & Waldron, M. B. (1988). Designing instructional formats: The effects of verbal and pictorial components on hearing-impaired students' comprehension of science concepts. *American Annals of the Deaf, 133,* 30-35.

53. Gordon, R. A. (1988). Increasing efficiency and effectiveness in predicting second-grade achievement using a kindergarten screening battery. *The Journal of Educational Research, 81,* 238-244.

54. Hooper, S. R. (1988). Relationship between the clinical components of the Boder Test of Reading-Spelling Patterns and the Stanford Achievement Test: Validity of the Boder. *Journal of School Psychology, 26,* 91-96.

55. Johnson, H. A., & Barton, L. E. (1988). TDD conversations: A context for language sampling and analysis. *American Annals of the Deaf, 133,* 19-25.

56. MacGregor, S. K., & Thomas, L. B. (1988). A computer-mediated text system to develop communication skills for hearing-impaired students. *American Annals of the Deaf, 133,* 280-284.

57. Martin, R. P., Drew, K. D., Gaddis, L. R., & Moseley, M. (1988). Prediction of elementary school achievement from preschool temperament: Three studies. *School Psychology Review, 17,* 125-137.

58. McCord, J. S., & Haynes, W. O. (1988). Discourse errors in students with learning disabilities and their normally achieving peers: Molar versus molecular views. *Journal of Learning Disabilities, 21,* 237-243.

59. Oliva, A. H., & La Greca, A. M. (1988). Children with learning disabilities: Social goals and strategies. *Journal of Learning Disabilities, 21,* 301-306.

60. Phillips, S. E., & Mehrens, W. A. (1988). Effects of curricular differences on achievement test data at item and objective levels. *Applied Measurement in Education, 1,* 33-51.

61. Scruggs, T. E., & Mastropieri, M. A. (1988). Acquisition and transfer of learning strategies by gifted and nongifted students. *The Journal of Special Education, 22,* 153-166.

62. Sheard, C., & Readence, J. E. (1988). An investigation of the inference and mapping processes of the componential theory of analogical reasoning. *The Journal of Educational Research, 81,* 347-353.

63. Suinn, R. M., Taylor, S., & Edwards, R. W. (1988). Suinn Mathematics Anxiety Rating Scale for Elementary School Students (MARS-E): Psychometric and normative data. *Educational and Psychological Measurement, 48,* 979-986.

64. Watson, B. V., & Goldgar, D. E. (1988). Evaluation of a typology of reading disability. *Journal of Clinical and Experimental Neuropsychology, 10,* 432-450.

65. Braden, J. P. (1989). The criterion-related validity of the WISC-R Performance Scale and other nonverbal IQ tests for deaf children. *American Annals of the Deaf, 134,* 329-332.

66. Chew, A. L., & Morris, J. D. (1989). Predicting later academic achievement from kindergarten scores on the Metropolitan Readiness Tests and the Lollipop Test. *Educational and Psychological Measurement, 49,* 461-465.

67. Moore, R. L., & Rust, J. O. (1989). Printing errors in the prediction of academic performance. *Journal of School Psychology, 27,* 297-300.

68. Spencer, P., & Delk, L. (1989). Hearing-impaired students' performance on tests of visual processing: Relationships with reading performance. *American Annals of the Deaf, 134,* 333-337.

69. Ulissi, S. M., Brice, P. J., & Gibbins, S. (1989). Use of the Kaufman-Assessment Battery for Children with the hearing impaired. *American Annals of the Deaf, 134,* 283-287.

70. Davey, B., & Macready, G. B. (1990). Applications of latent class modeling to investigate the structure underlying reading comprehension items. *Applied Measurement in Education, 3,* 209-229.

71. Diamond, K. E. (1990). Effectiveness of the Revised Denver Developmental Screening Test in identifying children at risk for learning problems. *Journal of Educational Research, 83,* 152-157.

72. Finn, J. D., & Achilles, C. M. (1990). Answers and questions about class size: A statewide experiment. *American Educational Research Journal, 27,* 557-577.

73. Hagborg, W. J. (1990). The Revised Behavior Problem Checklist and severely emotionally disturbed adolescents: Relationship to intelligence, academic achievement, and sociometric ratings. *Journal of Abnormal Child Psychology, 18,* 47-53.

74. Kelly, M. D., & Braden, J. P. (1990). Criterion-related validity of the WISC-R Performance Scale with the Stanford Achievement Test—Hearing-Impaired Edition. *Journal of School Psychology, 28,* 147-151.

75. Marks, D. (1990). Cautions in interpreting district-wide standardized mathematics achievement test results. *Journal of Educational Research, 83,* 349-354.

76. Zagar, R., Arbit, J., Sylvies, R., Busch, K. G., & Hughes, J. R. (1990). Homicidal adolescents: A replication. *Psychological Reports, 67,* 1235-1242.

77. Bryan, T., & Bryan, J. (1991). Positive mood and math performance. *Journal of Learning Disabilities, 24,* 490-494.

78. Freberg, L. (1991). Relationships between chronological age, developmental age, and standardized achievement tests in kindergarten. *Psychology in the Schools, 28,* 77-81.

Review of the Stanford Achievement Test, Eighth Edition by FREDERICK G. BROWN, Professor of Psychology, Department of Psychology, Iowa State University, Ames, IA:

Any test battery that has survived to an eighth edition, as has the Stanford Achievement Test Series (SAT), obviously has many satisfied users. With the SAT it is not difficult to see why. It is a professionally crafted product that provides a variety of useful and understandable information to educational administrators, teachers, and students and their parents.

The SAT clearly, and unashamedly, continues in the tradition of norm-referenced, survey achievement test batteries. The content of each subtest was selected to provide "representative and balanced coverage of [a] national consensus curriculum" (National Norms Booklet-Primary 1, p. 9), that is, to cover those concepts and skills most commonly taught in U.S. schools. To ensure this coverage, test specifications were developed after a review of state guidelines for education, state and district curricula, and the most widely used textbook series. The content areas covered are typical for this genus of achievement test batteries, as is the item format (multiple choice). An optional writing exercise, which was included in the seventh (1982) edition, is not included in the Eighth Edition.

The publisher provides a large variety of useful materials that facilitate preparation for testing, administration and scoring, and interpretation and use of the scores. Unfortunately, when this review was written (October 1990), no technical manual was available, only a *Preliminary Technical Data Report.* As this report, and other available publications, contain only limited information and data on the test construction procedures and on the psychometric properties of the battery, definitive judgments about the quality of the SAT are not possible.

CONTENT. All items on the Eighth Edition are new; none have appeared in previous editions. The item tryout sample ($n = 215,000$) was representative of the nation in terms of school district size, geographic area, and socioeconomic status. Over 1,000 schools participated, and data from at least 700 students were collected for each prospective item. In addition to editorial and content reviews, no item was included unless its item-subtest correlation was .35 or higher. Although items were said to be of "appropriate difficulty," what constitutes appropriate difficulty was not specified nor were any statistics on item difficulties reported.

The instructional objectives measured by each item are given in two publications. The *Compendium of Test Objectives* is organized by subtests and lists the objective assessed by each item at each level. The *Indices of Instructional Objectives* (not available to the reviewer) describes the behavior measured and the cognitive level of each item. Together these publications should help educators ascertain how well the test coverage reflects their local instructional objectives.

A panel of educators from various minority groups reviewed all items for possible ethnic, gender, socioeconomic, cultural, or regional bias. The test authors also attempted to balance the frequency and nature of gender and ethnic references within the test. Rasch model and Angoff delta estimates of item difficulty were computed for two gender and three ethnic groups (African American, Hispanic, White), and items exhibiting large differences were flagged for possible exclusion. No information on the criterion used to flag items, nor on the numbers of items flagged and excluded, was presented in the preliminary technical report.

The quality of the individual items appears to be very good. Numerous items incorporate graphs, tables, maps, diagrams, or drawings; many items attempt to assess the ability to apply knowledge and skills; and there is widespread use of "real life" stimuli such as menus, TV schedules, and the phone book. Items are clearly and legibly presented. One can, of course, find an occasional weak item; for example, the Intermediate 1 Science subtest includes an item ("Which animal belongs with those above?") that can be answered on any of a number of bases.

The inclusion of a Listening test is a desirable feature of the battery, as much instruction requires active listening skills. But the format of the subtest—having the classroom teacher read the items—raises some possible concerns. An advantage of this approach is that students will be listening to a familiar voice. Disadvantages include the lack of standardization across administrators and the possibil-

ity that some teachers may inadvertently give students clues to the correct answer. I would have liked to have seen data on the consistency of scores on this test across administrators. (Similar questions could be raised about the teacher-dictated sections of the Primary level batteries.)

SCORES AND NORMS. Performance is described by percentile ranks, stanines, scaled scores, normal curve equivalents, grade equivalents, and ability/achievement comparisons. Scores are reported for tests (e.g., Reading), subtests (e.g., Vocabulary and Comprehension), and content clusters (e.g., synonyms, context, and multiple meanings). A variety of reporting formats are available, both for individual students and for groups. These are clear and well designed, but some users may be overwhelmed by the amount of information presented in each report.

Normative data are available by grade level, fall or spring administration, and test form. Although the specific samples used are not described, the norms are based on large samples (total $n = 300,000$) that are representative of U.S. schools in terms of geographic region, socioeconomic status, urban/rural location, and ethnicity. No subgroup norms (e.g., by gender or ethnicity) are reported.

The major types of scores are clearly explained in the wide variety of clearly written and useful interpretive aids available. Three aspects of the score reporting, however, bothered me. The inclusion of ability/achievement comparisons is problematic, because such scores are easily misinterpreted, often misused, and have well-known statistical deficiencies. If these scores are to be reported on the group summary forms, it would be useful to know the percent of students in each ability range (high/average/low) who were achieving above, at, and below expectation. Second, I could not find any explanation of the "skills groupings" in any of the manuals and materials accompanying the test. And, like the ability/achievement comparisons, skills grouping data often are misinterpreted and misused. Third, there was insufficient warning that all scores contain some measurement error, and thus should not be considered to be precise indicators.

RELIABILITY. Kuder-Richardson 20 reliability coefficients are presented for each test and subtest for each form and level. The large majority of these coefficients are high enough to justify interpretation of scores of individuals on the tests and subtests (most are at least .85 and many are over .90). The lowest coefficients are for the Listening test, and even these are all .80 or higher. In a rare misleading statement, the *Preliminary Technical Data Report* (p. 41) describes internal consistency reliability coefficients as indicating consistency across test forms.

Alternative form reliability coefficients tend to be slightly lower than the corresponding KR20 coefficients, but almost all are .80 or higher. The

Listening, Study Skills, and Science tests have the lowest alternative forms coefficients. Limited data are presented on the consistency of scores from the seventh (1982) to Eighth Edition. Interestingly, these data are used as evidence of criterion-related validity.

A significant omission is the lack of reliability data for the content clusters. As scores on these clusters are reported, and educators may use them to make instructional decisions, evidence of the reliability of these scores should be available (see the AERA/APA/NCME *Standards for Educational and Psychological Testing*, 1985).

VALIDITY. A major shortcoming of the series is the lack of convincing arguments and data in support of the validity of the battery. The *Preliminary Technical Data Report* gives only cursory consideration—less than one page—to the topic of validity. Although this report suggests that users should obtain evidence of content validity by comparing the test items to their local instructional objectives, and points out that the manuals listing the instructional objectives underlying the test items will be useful in making this determination, it gives no further suggestions as to how such a study should be conducted. Furthermore, no evidence is presented to demonstrate the subtests have content validity in terms of their stated goal of representing the national consensus curriculum.

As noted previously, correlations between scores on the seventh (1982) and Eighth Edition are presented as evidence of criterion-related validity. No data relating scores on the SAT to grades or other indicators of academic achievement are presented.

Intercorrelations among the SAT subtests and correlations between the SAT subtest and the Otis-Lennon School Ability Test are presented as evidence of construct validity, with minimal discussion. As the large majority of these correlations are .60 or higher, it appears that the subtests on the Stanford Achievement Test, like those on other achievement test batteries, have a low degree of discriminative validity.

CONCLUSION. Anyone needing a norm-referenced, survey achievement test battery would be well advised to give the Stanford Achievement Test Series strong consideration. It is a well-reasoned, professionally crafted battery accompanied by a wide variety of clearly written and useful materials that help ensure correct interpretation and use of the scores. My criticisms of the battery, for the most part, result from the absence of specific and essential data about the construction of the battery and the evaluation of its psychometric properties; deficiencies that can be alleviated by further studies and publication of a technical manual. With its many strengths, the Eighth Edition retains the SAT's position as one of the best achievement batteries of its type.

REVIEWER'S REFERENCE

American Educational Research Association, American Psychological Association, & National Council on Measurement in Education. (1985). *Standards for educational and psychological testing*. Washington, DC: American Psychological Association, Inc.

Review of the Stanford Achievement Tests, Eighth Edition by HOWARD STOKER, Research Professor, Bureau of Educational Research and Service, University of Tennessee, Knoxville, TN:

Reviewing the Stanford Achievement Test Series, Eighth Edition (SAT), is not a task to be taken lightly, nor is it an easy task. Subkoviak and Farley (1985), in reviewing the 1982 Edition said, "The origin of the Stanford Achievement Test can be traced to the early 1920s, and the test has had a long history of excellence. Its development has traditionally been guided by highly qualified test authors, and it is published by a well-respected publisher; for these reasons it is widely used in schools." They conclude their review, in part, by saying, "In summary, the 7th Edition of the SAT continues a long tradition of excellence."

In his review of the 1973 Edition of the SAT, Ebel (1978) stated the test "offers even a critical reviewer more to commend than to question." Although Ebel questioned the lack of detail with respect to the question of content validity, he finished his review with the statement, "Let us conclude with a summary judgment that this is an excellent test, reflecting the competence of its authors and the conscientiousness of its publisher."

How, then, does one critique a series that has provided interpretative test data to schools for 70 years without resorting to nit-picking? The Stanford tryout sample of students was selected so as to represent school children in the national school population. Would it be fair to ask if the sample fairly represented students in Tennessee, Florida, or Wyoming? This reviewer believes such questions would not be fair.

Perhaps a better way to review the SAT is to examine the multitude of documents—tests, answer sheets, manuals, etc.—alongside the *Code of Fair Testing Practices in Education* (1988), a document "that has as its aim the advancement, in the public interest, of the quality of testing practices."

The *Code* was developed by a Joint Committee on Testing Practices, composed of members of the American Educational Research Association, the American Psychological Association and the National Council on Measurement in Education.

The Code . . . states the major obligations to test takers of professionals who develop or use educational tests . . . . Although the Code has relevance to many types of educational tests, it is directed primarily at professionally developed tests such as those sold by commercial test publishers or used in formally administered testing programs . . . . The Code addresses the roles of test developers and test users separately . . . . Test developers are people who actually construct tests as well as those who set policies for particular testing programs. (p. 1)

It seems appropriate, then, to use the *Code* as a standard against which to compare the development of the Stanford Achievement Test Series. The activities specified for developers are highlighted, followed by relevant information from the materials supplied by the publishers. There are many guides, reports, and booklets accompanying the test. These are referred to throughout the subsequent sections.

DEVELOPING/SELECTING APPROPRIATE TESTS.

Test developers should: Define what each test measures and what the test should be used for. Describe the population(s) for which the test is appropriate.

The publishers are careful to define what the tests measure, what they should be used for, and the populations for which the tests are appropriate. They say, for example, "The Stanford Achievement Test Series is designed to provide information upon which decisions for improving curriculum and instruction can be made." As in past editions, the tests were designed to reflect what the authors believe is being taught in schools in the United States, at several grade levels. The populations would, of course, be the students in those schools, at the appropriate grade levels.

Test developers should: Accurately represent the characteristics, usefulness, and limitations of tests for their intended purposes.

The characteristics, usefulness, and limitations of the tests—really the test results—can be found in several documents. The *Guide for Organizational Planning* contains information that describes the series, lists ways in which the results can be used, and identifies the limitations of the tests (and standardized tests in general). The facts that tests simply provide data and that such data are only part of a total program evaluation in a school cannot be repeated too often (though these facts are frequently ignored). Issues related to the use of results are presented, along with cautions about the misuse of results.

Test developers should: Explain relevant measurement concepts as necessary for clarity at the level of detail that is appropriate for the intended audience(s).

The *Guide for Organizational Planning* contains a 13-page section on Basic Measurement Concepts. The definitions are short, easily read, and while they might not satisfy a psychometrician, are adequate for the intended audience—the school or district level test director. Definitions in the *Preliminary Technical Data Report* are a little more lengthy and the appropriate tables of correlation coefficients, standard errors, etc., are included. As often happens when one "writes down" to explain complex

concepts, mistakes occur. The formula for KR-21, in the *Guide for Organizational Planning* may be "more commonly used (by teachers)" but it is transcribed incorrectly in the manual.

Test developers should: Describe the process of test development. Explain how the content and skills to be tested were selected.

The process of test development is described in more than one of the booklets and appears to be a fairly typical process, starting with the all-important test blueprint. A *Compendium of Instructional Objectives* is available, as is an *Index of Instructional Objectives*.

Test developers should: Provide evidence that the test meets its intended purpose(s).

Evidence for this part of the *Code* is difficult to identify. Perhaps the evidence lies in the acceptance of the SAT series, as represented by sales and use—what one might call "cash validity." Such evidence would not, normally, be published.

Test developers should: Provide either representative samples or complete copies of test questions, directions, answer sheets, manuals, and score reports to qualified users.

All of the items referred to in this section of the *Code* are available. The *Preview for Parents* contains sample items; the *Guide for Classroom Planning* contains sample reports. Other materials would be available when the tests are ordered, or as part of a specimen set of materials.

Test developers should: Indicate the nature of the evidence obtained concerning the appropriateness of each test for groups of different racial, ethnic, or linguistic backgrounds who are likely to be tested.

Rasch model analyses were used to compare performance in the two gender groups, and in three racial groups—African Americans, Whites, and Hispanics. Items failing to meet established criteria were "flagged for possible exclusion from the pool of tryout items." Item p-values were compared using the Angoff delta statistic. Again, items showing large between-group differences were identified for further review. The *Preliminary Technical Data Report* does not provide actual data from these analyses, nor does it report what was actually done with the flagged items.

Test developers should: Identify and publish any specialized skills needed to administer each test and to interpret scores correctly.

The *Directions for Administration* and the *Guide for Classroom Planning* contain the information needed for test administration and score interpretation. If there was some way to insure that teachers would read these booklets, measurement professionals would be happier in their work.

INTERPRETING SCORES.

Test developers should: Provide timely and easily understood score reports that describe test performance clearly and accurately. Also explain the meaning and limitations of reported scores.

As with any standardized test, the SAT can be hand scored or machine scored. How timely the reporting is will depend on the number of students tested, the number of different tests used, the time of testing, and the method selected for scoring. For scoring services, one trades the immediacy of hand scoring for a wide range of computer generated score reports which are considered, by many, worth the wait. Delivery of these reports within a 3–4 week "turn-around" time appears to be within the capability of the developer.

Help in score interpretation appears in many places and forms. The *Guide for Organizational Planning* contains samples of reports for boards of education, the community, and the media. Reference is made to the Stanford Ready Graphs Plus (RGP) program which "can produce graphs to answer six commonly asked assessment questions." The program takes local school data as input and provides custom designed graphs for schools, grades within or across schools, content areas, etc.

The *Guide for Classroom Planning* provides information about what the tests measure, and the kinds of scores reported and what they do and do not mean. In general, it tells teachers how to get the most out of the scores they receive. Also available is a Posttest Workshop Kit, a highly recommended aid for explaining test results to teachers. The Kit comes with material for organizing and adapting the workshop for local needs, a script—with notes to the presenter inserted at critical points—and a set of very well designed transparencies.

Test developers should: Describe the population(s) represented by any norms or comparison group(s), the dates the data were gathered, and the process used to select the samples of test takers.

Two kinds of data were collected, the first being a national item tryout sample, the second being the norming sample. Both samples are well described in the *Preliminary Technical Data Report* and the National Norms Booklets describe the norming sample. Samples used for equating forms and equating levels are also described. Rasch model procedures were used for both equating tasks.

Test developers should: Warn users to avoid specific, reasonably anticipated misuses of test scores.

Warnings appear in more than one Stanford booklet.

Test developers should: Provide information that will help users follow reasonable procedures for setting passing scores when it is appropriate to use such scores with the test.

Passing scores are inappropriate for a test of this type. The *Understanding Test Results* booklets say, "Students cannot pass or fail a test such as the Stanford. Nor are results used to assign marks." One can only hope that teachers heed these remarks.

Test developers should: Provide information that will help users gather evidence to show that the test is meeting its intended purpose(s).

Whether the Stanford meets its intended purpose will depend on the use of the test results by school and system personnel. Sufficient information is provided by the developers to facilitate such use and direct users toward the intended purposes of the tests.

STRIVING FOR FAIRNESS.

Test developers should: Review and revise test questions and related materials to avoid potentially insensitive content or language.

The *Preliminary Technical Data Report* contains a discussion of the procedures that were used to control for bias. An advisory panel was assembled to review items on the tryout edition of the Stanford Series. Statistical methods were used to identify and eliminate items that did not meet predetermined specifications for differential item functioning. The magnitude of this task can be understood only when one realizes that the tryout for the Series included some 27,500 items.

Test developers should: Investigate the performance of test takers of different races, gender, and ethnic backgrounds when samples of sufficient size are available. Enact procedures that help to ensure that differences in performance are related primarily to the skills under assessment rather than to irrelevant factors.

No evidence is provided to indicate that this type of research has been done. One would anticipate that as data are generated through the use of the Eighth Edition of the Stanford such studies would be done, either by the developer or with the support of the developer.

Test developers should: When feasible, make appropriately modified forms of tests or administration procedures available for test takers with handicapping conditions.

Braille and Large Type editions of the Stanford are available.

INFORMING TEST TAKERS.

The guidelines in this section are judged to be responsibilities that do not apply to the developers of the Stanford Achievement Test Series.

In summary, it appears the developers of the Stanford Series have met the criteria established in the *Code of Fair Testing Practices in Education*. One would expect nothing less.

REVIEWER'S REFERENCES

Ebel, R. L. (1978). [Review of the Stanford Achievement Test, 1973 Edition.] In O. K. Buros (Ed.), *The eighth mental measurements yearbook* (pp. 98-102). Highland Park, NJ: The Gryphon Press.

Subkoviak, M. J., & Farley, F. H. (1985). [Review of the Stanford Achievement Test, 1982 Edition.] In J. V. Mitchell, Jr. (Ed.), *The ninth mental measurements yearbook* (pp. 1450-1452). Lincoln, NE: Buros Institute of Mental Measurements.

Code of Fair Testing Practices in Education. (1988). Washington, DC: Joint Committee on Testing Practices.

[378]
Stanford Early School Achievement Test, Third Edition.

Purpose: Measures school achievement.
Population: Grades K.0–K.5, K.5–1.5.
Publication Dates: 1969–89.
Acronym: SESAT.
Administration: Group.
Price Data, 1991: $70 per 25 machine-scorable tests (scored by publisher) (select level); $9 per 25 practice tests (select level); $14.50 per individual record forms; $3.50 per class record form; $10.50 per 25 previews for parents; $7 per administration directions (select level); $3.50 per administration directions for practice test (select level); $25 per norms booklet (select level); $17 per coordinator's handbook; $18 per examination kit including test booklet, administration directions, and practice test with directions (select level).
Comments: Downward extension of the Stanford Achievement Test Series.
Author: The Psychological Corporation.
Publisher: The Psychological Corporation.
a) LEVEL 1.
Population: Grades K.0–K.5.
Scores, 8: Sounds and Letters, Word Reading, Total, Mathematics, Listening to Words and Stories, Total for Basic Battery, Environment, Total for Complete Battery.
Price Data: $80 per 25 machine-scorable test booklets (scored locally on NCS scanners); $45 per 25 hand-scorable test booklets; $62.50 per set of scoring keys.
Time: (190) minutes over 9 sessions.
b) LEVEL 2.
Population: Grades K.5–1.5.
Scores, 9: Sounds and Letters, Word Reading, Sentence Reading, Total, Mathematics, Listening to Words and Stories, Basic Battery Total, Environment, Complete Battery Total.
Price Data: $82 per 25 machine-scorable test booklets (scored locally on NCS scanners); $47 per 25 hand-scorable test booklets; $65.50 per set of scoring keys.
Time: (225) minutes over 9 sessions.
Cross References: For a review of an earlier edition by Mary J. Allen, see 9:1179 (1 reference); see also T3:2293 (9 references); for a review by Courtney B. Cazden of an earlier edition, see 8:30 (6 references); see also T2:38 (1 reference); for reviews by Elizabeth Hagen and William A. Mehrens of Level 1, see 7:28.

TEST REFERENCES

1. Lewis, C. D., & Houtz, J. C. (1986). Sex-role stereotyping and young children's divergent thinking. *Psychological Reports, 59*, 1027-1033.
2. Hinshaw, S. P., Morrison, D. C., Carte, E. T., & Cornsweet, C. (1987). Factorial dimensions of the Revised Behavior Problem Checklist: Replication and validation within a kindergarten sample. *Journal of Abnormal Child Psychology, 15*, 309-327.
3. Samson, G. E., Strykowski, B., Weinstein, T., & Walberg, H. J. (1987). The effects of teacher questioning levels on student achievement: A quantitative synthesis. *The Journal of Educational Research, 80*, 290-295.
4. Sprafkin, J., & Gadow, K. (1987). An observational study of emotionally disturbed and learning-disabled children in school settings. *Journal of Abnormal Child Psychology, 15*, 393-408.
5. Wade, J., & Kass, C. E. (1987). Component deficit and academic remediation of learning disabilities. *Journal of Learning Disabilities, 20*, 441-447.
6. Sprafkin, J., Gadow, K. D., & Grayson, P. (1988). Effects of cartoons on emotionally disturbed children's social behavior in school settings. *Journal of Child Psychology and Psychiatry and Allied Disciplines, 29*, 91-99.
7. Sinatra, R. (1989). Verbal/visual processing for males disabled in print acquisition. *Journal of Learning Disabilities, 22*, 69-71.
8. Mantzicopoulos, P., & Morrison, D. (1990). Characteristics of at-risk children in transitional and regular kindergarten programs. *Psychology in the Schools, 27*, 325-332.

Review of the Stanford Early School Achievement Test, Third Edition by PHILLIP L. ACKERMAN, Associate Professor of Psychology, University of Minnesota, Minneapolis, MN:

Level 1 of the Stanford Early School Achievement Test, Third Edition (SESAT) is described by the publisher as measuring "children's cognitive abilities from the time of entrance into Kindergarten to the middle of Kindergarten." Level 2 is described as "intended for use from the middle of Kindergarten to the middle of Grade 1."

RELIABILITY/VALIDITY. The SESAT was first published in 1969–1970. Reviews of the First Edition of the SESAT in the *Seventh Mental Measurements Yearbook* (Hagen, 1972; Mehrens, 1972) and in the *Eighth Mental Measurements Yearbook* (Cazden, 1978); and reviews of the Second Edition in the *Ninth Mental Measurements Yearbook* (Allen, 1985) all either stressed or noted the serious lack of validity information presented by the test publisher. The only validity coefficients presented in these previous editions, and indeed, in the current, Third Edition, are between the SESAT tests and the Otis-Lennon School Ability Test (OLSAT). With the Third Edition, the intercorrelation between the SESAT 2 Complete Battery and the OLSAT Total was .81 ($N = 5,967$). The SESAT Total Reading composite correlates .62 and .61 with OLSAT Verbal and Nonverbal components, respectively, and the SESAT Mathematics composite correlates .72 and .71 with OLSAT Verbal and Nonverbal components. Even with the meager data that are provided from the SESAT-OLSAT comparisons, it is clear that there is a lack of differentiable abilities in these respective batteries.

One study has emerged that discussed validity/reliability of the SESAT (albeit the earlier edition of the battery). Ames, Becker, and Dalton (1977) found that, with a relatively small sample of students, correlations between the SESAT 2 and the Stanford Achievement Test Primary 1 were modest over a 9-month period. Average correlations between the respective verbal and mathematics subscales were .52 and .45. Although other sources of data would be more diagnostic for validity (such as teacher ratings or correlations with other achievement tests), these data seem to indicate the test does not provide much information that is meaningful for individual students. At a level of aggregation that considers intact classes as a whole in comparison to state and national norms, the test may provide useful information, but again validity data of this sort are not reported by the publishers.

As noted by earlier *Mental Measurements Yearbook* reviewers, there is too much attention given to "Content Clusters," which are again prepared without any documentation of reliability and validity issues. Given the high intercorrelations across the five subtests (average $r = .63$ for the SESAT 2), it seems doubtful that all but the most discrepant scores would be meaningful, when as few as *three* items comprise the various content clusters. A factor analysis of the subtest intercorrelations suggests that at most two highly correlated factors likely underlie the battery, one defined by Word Reading and Sounds & Letters, the other containing all of the tests except for Word Reading. As such, it makes little sense to present 8 test scores (each of the 5 tests and 3 composites), along with 12 more separate content clusters, as are shown in sample score reports. If anything, such presentation of data to teachers and parents probably leads to overinterpretation of meaningless differences between various scores.

NORMS. The publishers present a substantial narrative regarding the procedures followed for elimination or attenuation of bias or adverse impact. The procedures, which include panels of subject-matter experts, interested minority group representatives, and use of item-level analyses of group differences, seem reasonable; however, no specific data are presented regarding sex, race, ethnic group, socio-economic status, or regional differences. Without reporting of such quantitative data, it simply is not possible to provide an overall evaluation of test bias on the basis of face validity.

ADMINISTRATION/NORMS. A wealth of materials have been compiled by the publisher, ranging from guides for interpretation of scores by parents and teachers, extensive directions for administration, and discussion of statistical concepts of norms, percentiles, stanines, and the like. Overall, these materials are extensive and are written at a level understandable by layperson and expert alike. However, some inconsistencies in the materials for both parents and teachers should be noted. For example, regarding the meaningfulness of differences between subtest scores (and confidence bands), parents are correctly told that "If the bands *do* overlap, there is probably too little difference between the two scores to have any meaning." However, on the preceding page, the parents are told that, for a fictitious student, "her performance was considerably better" on one test compared to another, even though according to the provided profile, the two test bands were indeed *overlapping*. Also, in the Directions for Administering, the teacher is told that "SESAT is not a 'readiness' test." Yet, in the *Special Report* series, "Readiness" is one of the ways in which the publisher describes the test "might be used."

SUMMARY. The SESAT continues to be a major test that is predicated, almost solely, on the basis of content validity. Although the content validation appears thorough, the SESAT, even in its third edition (after 21 years), still does not meet the minimum standards for information regarding test-retest reliability, construct validity, and criterion-related validity. Given these persistent limitations, and in concordance with previous *Mental Measurements Yearbook* reviews (e.g., Cazden, 1978), until such time as adequate reliability and validity data are reported, the test cannot be recommended by the reviewer for use.

REVIEWER'S REFERENCES

Hagen, E. (1972). [Review of the Stanford Early School Achievement Test.] In O. K. Buros (Ed.), *The seventh mental measurements yearbook* (pp. 52-54). Highland Park, NJ: The Gryphon Press.

Mehrens, W. A. (1972). [Review of the Stanford Early School Achievement Test.] In O. K. Buros (Ed.), *The seventh mental measurements yearbook* (pp. 54-56). Highland Park, NJ: The Gryphon Press.

Ames, S. G., Becker, L. D., & Dalton, S. (1977). The predictive validity of the Stanford Early School Achievement Test. *Educational and Psychological Measurement, 37,* 505-507.

Cazden, C. B. (1978). [Review of the Stanford Early School Achievement Test.] In O. K. Buros (Ed.), *The eighth mental measurements yearbook* (pp. 107-108). Highland Park, NJ: The Gryphon Press.

Allen, M. J. (1985). [Review of the Stanford Early School Achievement Test (1982 Edition).] In J. V. Mitchell, Jr. (Ed.), *The ninth mental measurements yearbook* (pp. 1465-1466). Lincoln, NE: The Buros Institute of Mental Measurements.

Review of the Stanford Early School Achievement Test, Third Edition by C. DALE CARPENTER, Professor of Special Education, Western Carolina University, Cullowhee, NC:

The Stanford Early School Achievement Test (SESAT) measures in a general way "what children learn before they enter school and what they learn during their first years there" (Gardner, Rudman, Karlsen, & Merwin, 1987, p. 2). Two levels, SESAT 1 and SESAT 2 are available as in earlier editions. In a review of the 1982 edition, Allen (1985) stated the most serious problem was the lack of information on interpreting the profile of scores. This problem seems to be less serious now with more printed information available for parents to interpret tests results. One would always like clear meaningful information to assist parents in interpreting test results and criticism is easily generated on this point. Although there is room for improvement, information available with the SESAT is a good attempt to provide such information.

The norm sample included more than 700 subjects at each level. Although specific demographic information for the SESAT is not reported, the representations for the Stanford Achievement Series closely match proportions in the 1980 Census for total U.S. school enrollment in terms of regions, SES status, urbanicity, and ethnicity. Students with handicaps are underrepresented although they are notably represented. Students from private schools constituted approximately 11% of the sample. Separate norms are available for students attending private schools, students attending Catholic schools, and students residing in high socioeconomic communities. No other information is available on group differences such as gender or ethnic group. One clue to another difference pertinent to the SESAT is that SESAT Level 1 assumes no prescribed kindergarten program and SESAT Level 2 assumes that some formal instruction has taken place (Directions for Administering).

Internal consistency reliability is the only type of reliability reported. Overall coefficients for Level 1 and 2 are .95 and .96 respectively. Subtests are above .80 except for Environment at both levels and Word Reading at Level 1. Reliability coefficients for those subtests are .77, .77, and .78. No other reliability information is available.

Validity information is not abundant. Item difficulty values and scale scores provide support for developmental progression. Student scores in the spring exceed fall scores. Further construct validity is supported through intercorrelations between subtests at each level and between both levels.

Directions are carefully clear. Teacher and student instructions are adequate and developmentally appropriate. Tasks within subtests are not always arranged well. For example, in the same sitting students are asked to find pictures that begin with the same sound and then a few items later to find pictures that rhyme. Young children who are able to perform either task sometimes become confused. On the Practice Tests tasks switch more often and more quickly. Upon scrutiny, items appear to be reasonably free of gender and handicap bias.

CRITIQUE. The SESAT appears to be an adequate measure in most respects. It is constructed well and the norm sample includes a large representative group. Validity and reliability information are meager in detail, but information reported supports the technical adequacy of the test. Information to interpret scores has been improved since previous editions. On at least one subtest, the sequence of tasks should be altered. Overall, more specific technical information is needed. Otherwise, the SESAT appears to be a comprehensive measure of early school knowledge.

REVIEWER'S REFERENCES

Allen, M. J. (1985). [Review of the Stanford Early School Achievement Test (1982 Edition).] In J. V. Mitchell, Jr. (Ed.), *The ninth mental measurements yearbook* (pp. 1465-1466). Lincoln, NE: The Buros Institute of Mental Measurements.
Gardner, E. F., Rudman, H. C., Karlsen, B., & Merwin, J. C. (1987). *Understanding test results: A guide for parents.* San Antonio: The Psychological Corporation.

[379]

State-Trait Anger Expression Inventory, Research Edition.

Purpose: To provide "concise measures of the experience and expression of anger."
Population: Ages 13 and over.
Publication Dates: 1979–88.

Acronym: STAXI.
Scores, 8: State Anger, Trait Anger, Angry Temperament, Angry Reaction, Anger-in, Anger-out, Anger Control, Anger Expression.
Administration: Group.
Forms, 2: HS, G.
Price Data, 1989: $39 per complete kit including manual ('88, 27 pages), 50 test booklets, and 50 rating forms; $18 per 50 test booklets; $14 per 50 rating forms; $9 per manual; scoring service offered by publisher.
Time: (15–17) minutes.
Comments: Test booklet title is Self-Rating Questionnaire.
Author: Charles D. Spielberger.
Publisher: Psychological Assessment Resources, Inc.

TEST REFERENCES

1. Stoner, S. B., & Spencer, W. B. (1987). Age and gender differences with the Anger Expression Scale. *Educational and Psychological Measurement, 47* (2), 487-492.
2. Hoogduin, C. A. L., & Duivenvoorden, H. J. (1988). A decision model in the treatment of obsessive-compulsive neuroses. *British Journal of Psychiatry, 152,* 516-521.
3. Brom, D., Kleber, R. J., & Defares, P. B. (1989). Brief psychotherapy for posttraumatic stress disorders. *Journal of Consulting and Clinical Psychology, 57,* 607-612.
4. Jorgensen, R. S., & Richards, C. S. (1989). Negative affect and the reporting of physical symptoms among college students. *Journal of Counseling Psychology, 36,* 501-504.
5. Deffenbacher, J. L., McNamara, K., Stark, R. S., & Sabadell, P. M. (1990). A comparison of cognitive-behavioral and process-oriented group counseling for general anger reduction. *Journal of Counseling and Development, 69,* 167-172.
6. Schill, T., & Wang, S. (1990). Correlates of the MMPI-2 anger content scale. *Psychological Reports, 67,* 800-802.
7. Fuqua, D. R., Leonard, E., Masters, M. A., Smith, R. J., Campbell, J. L., & Fischer, P. C. (1991). A structural analysis of the State-Trait Anger Expression Inventory. *Educational and Psychological Measurement, 51,* 439-446.
8. Sharkin, B. S., & Gelso, C. J. (1991). The Anger Discomfort Scale: Beginning reliability and validity data. *Measurement and Evaluation in Counseling and Development, 24,* 61-68.

Review of the State-Trait Anger Expression Inventory, Research Edition by BRUCE H. BISKIN, Senior Psychometrician, American Institute of Certified Public Accountants, New York, NY:

The State-Trait Anger Expression Inventory (STAXI) is the product of several decades of research by Charles D. Spielberger and his associates. As noted in the manual, the STAXI was developed as part of long-term study of anxiety, anger, and curiosity. This research program also spawned the often-used State-Trait Anxiety Inventory (STAI; 9:1186).

The STAXI attempts to measure several facets of anger. The Inventory comprises 44 items, which may be conceptualized as representing two domains: anger experience and anger expression. Anger experience is represented by two 10-item scales: State Anger (S-Anger) and Trait Anger (T-Anger). T-Anger includes two four-item subscales: Angry Temperament and Angry Reaction. Anger expression is represented by three eight-item scales: Anger-in (AX/In), Anger-out (AX/Out), and Anger Control (AX/Con). A total Anger Expression (AX/EX) score may be computed from the latter three scales, though the manual notes, "The psychometric properties of the AX/EX scale have not been thoroughly investigated" (p. 11).

The test booklet for the self-scoring version (Form HS) is printed clearly in a larger-than-average typeface and is accompanied by a self-scoring answer form. The computer-scorable form (Form G) is printed in a smaller, but bolder, typeface. This version contains the items directly on the answer form.

The STAXI items are grouped into three parts: Part I comprises the S-Anger items; Part II comprises the T-Anger items; and Part III comprises AX/In, AX/Out, and AX/Con. The instructions for each part are clear and seem appropriate for the constructs they measure. The self-scoring form booklet contains a profile chart that can be completed by the administrator. This chart requires the administrator to enter percentile scores instead of raw scores, which some may find confusing at first.

The STAXI manual is impressive. I found it to be well written and complete. It reports six sets of norms: adolescents, college students, and adults, each reported for men and women separately. The norms are reported as both percentiles and *T*-scores in Appendix A. The manual also reports several special interest norms in Appendix B. As Spielberger appropriately points out, STAXI users should apply these norms with care and, where feasible, develop local norms whenever those reported in the manual are inappropriate for the user's purpose.

There are some apparent inconsistencies in the normative data, however. Tables 1 and 2 of the manual (p. 4) report means, standard deviations, and sample size for each of the six norm groups. The sample sizes do not correspond to those reported in the text on page 3. Also, the tabled means do not correspond to *T*-scores of 50 as reported in Appendix A. These apparent discrepancies should be clarified in future editions of the manual. In addition, I suggest including sample sizes in the norm tables in Appendix A for clarity.

I appreciated the amount of detail included in the chapter on "Conceptual Issues and Scale Development." Though this chapter may be too technical for some users, it conveys clearly the major issues that Spielberger and his associates confronted in developing the STAXI. It also describes how their concept of anger expression changed to include Anger/Control. Psychometric information is extensive, if not complete (see below). Median reliability (coefficients alpha) reported in the manual for all the STAXI scales is about .82. The scales measuring angry feelings (S-Anger and T-Anger) are somewhat more internally consistent (median = .85) than those for anger expression (AX/In, AX/Out, and AX/Con; median = .78).

The manual also reports item-remainder correlations within and across scales. These provide evidence for both convergent and discriminant validity of the STAXI items. For example, each item on the T-Anger scale correlates more highly with its own scale than it does with the T-Anxiety or T-Curiosity scales. Spielberger also reports the results of factor analyses of the various scales, which support further the STAXI's construct-related validity. These analyses seem to have been carefully carried out. Curiously, none of the correlations among the STAXI scales are reported. These should be included in the next revision of the manual. This would provide further evidence regarding the STAXI's construct-related validity.

Test-retest correlations are not included in the manual. Besides providing additional reliability estimates, such correlations could serve as further validity indicators. For example, presumably T-Anger should have larger test-retest correlations than S-Anger does, even for short time intervals between administrations.

In contrast with the high quality of the inventory forms, the manual's layout is less than optimal. The typeface is small, and there is little space between words and lines. As a result, I found it somewhat difficult to read. I expect many readers with even minor visual impairments would find it even more difficult to read than I did. With so much care put into the content of the STAXI manual and the formats of the Inventory forms, I was surprised and disappointed by the manual's presentation. Perhaps when PAR reprints the manual, it could improve the layout.

SUMMARY. The STAXI is a welcome addition to those few instruments now available to measure various aspects of anger. It has an excellent conceptual foundation and very good measurement characteristics. However, until the STAXI's research and clinical bases grow, its scores should be interpreted cautiously by users.

Review of the State-Trait Anger Expression Inventory, Research Edition by PAUL RETZLAFF, Assistant Professor of Psychology, University of Northern Colorado, Greeley, CO:

The State-Trait Anger Expression Inventory (STAXI) assesses two major types of anger, State Anger and Trait Anger. Trait Anger is additionally subdivided into Angry Temperament and Angry Reaction. The STAXI additionally measures three primary modes of anger expression: Anger-in, Anger-out, and Anger Control. Finally, an overall Anger Expression score is derived from the three primary anger expression scales.

There are two forms of the test for administration. The first is a hand-scored form. The questions are on a two-page booklet and a separate answer sheet is used for endorsement. The separate answer sheet is a multipart form that allows for immediate scoring by examining the carbon copy. The scoring is a little difficult, as only item numbers are listed for keying and no arrows or color coding are on the sheet for visual aid. The second form of the test is a single computer form that can be given to subjects for research and then mailed to the publisher for group scoring. Computer-scoring access may assist future research efforts with the STAXI.

The test has a total of 44 items endorsed on a 4-point scale. State and Trait Anger have 10 items each. The two Trait subscales of Temperament and Reaction have only four items apiece. This small number of items appears minimal for a scale. Each of the three primary anger expression scales has eight items, with Anger Expression a composite of the three primary scores.

Different test development approaches were used in the construction of the STAXI. The State and Trait scales were developed via a domain construction technique. The Anger Expression scales were developed by factor analytic methods. As such, item level statistics, item inclusion/exclusion, and potential overlap were not well managed across the test as a whole.

Internal consistencies are generally good for the main scales: State Anger (.93), Trait Anger (.87), Anger-in (.82), Anger-out (.74), and Anger Control (.84). The four-item Temperament subscale holds up well with around .86, but the other four-item Reaction scale suffers with .70s. The composite Anger Expression scale would have a reliability that is a function of the underlying 24 items, but this coefficent is not reported in the manual. Information of test validity is, perhaps, the most problematic aspect of the test. Due to its recent release, there are relatively few validity estimates presented in the manual. There is no reported evidence that the State Anger scale is sensitive to experimental manipulations. Although anger manipulation would be difficult, some study of frustrating driver's license applicant procedures or questionable football replay videos may be indicated. Trait Anger is correlated with hostility scales, but in the introduction to the test, the author points out the need to separate the domains of anger, hostility, and aggression. Convergent and divergent validity for the anger expression scales involve intercorrelation with state-trait anxiety and curiosity. Why these variables were chosen is not explained and perhaps others (e.g., hostility, depression) would be more appropriate. Finally, perhaps too much of the research is in the form of unpublished theses and dissertations.

Additionally, a complete intercorrelation matrix of all the STAXI scales is not made available. With the parallel construction of the scales, it is particularly important to prove scale specificity. The correlations reported are high between Anger-out and Anger Control, as well as between Anger-out and Trait Anger.

In summary, the STAXI is designed to tap an important domain, is easy to administer and score, and will probably be as popular as the State-Trait Anxiety Inventory (9:1186). Its face validity is good. Although suggesting a piecemeal construction, its scales are rigorously developed. Reliabilities are generally good, but additional validity estimates are necessary.

[380]

STIM/CON: Prognostic Inventory for Misarticulating Kindergarten and First Grade Children.

Purpose: "Measures stimulability for defective sounds and the consistency of error of defective sounds."
Population: Grades K–3.
Publication Date: 1987.
Scores, 4: Stimulability Percentage (for phonemes tested), Inconsistency Percentage (for phonemes tested), Stimulability/Inconsistency Average, Overall Prognostic Score.
Administration: Individual.
Price Data: Price data for test including manual ('87, 32 pages) available from publisher.
Time: (5–20) minutes.
Comments: 3 forms: Form for Stimulability Assessment, Predictive Summary for Kindergarten Children, Predictive Summary for First Grade Children; orally administered.
Author: Ronald K. Sommers.
Publisher: United Educational Services, Inc.

Review of the STIM/CON: Prognostic Inventory for Misarticulating Kindergarten and First Grade Children by NICHOLAS W. BANKSON, Professor and Chair, Department of Communication Disorders, Boston University, Boston, MA:

STIM/CON is a test of phonology for kindergarten and first grade children that is designed to provide a prognostic indicator regarding whether or not a child will need treatment to correct phonological misarticulation. The test is designed to assess phonemes already produced in error on a more comprehensive assessment of a child's phonology (i.e., inventory; conversational sample). Thus, this instrument could be considered a part of a phonological assessment battery.

The test consists of two parts: Part 1 measures the child's ability to imitate the correct forms of misarticulated sounds in nonsense syllable contexts (i.e., stimulability), and Part 2 measures the consistency with which the child misarticulates sounds in the repetition of sentences containing target sounds (i.e., consistency). The underlying concept is that a child's stimulability and consistency in articulation can be used to calculate measures of an index of the probability that the child will learn to master the misarticulated sounds without treatment.

On the stimulability portion of the test, stimulus pictures are included for 13 frequently misarticulated consonant sounds. These form the target phonemes for this part of the test. Stimulus materials consist of a spiral-bound picture book, with each page containing nine pictures designed to test one of the 13 target sounds. Each of the nine pictures can be described by a word that contains the target sound in one of three positions: initial, medial, or final. For example, Santa, seal, and sun, test /s/ in the initial position; ice cream, bicycle, and grasshopper test /s/ in the medial position; and house, horse, and bus test /s/ in final position. In addition to the nine pictured word items for each phoneme, nine nonsense syllables are included for imitative testing of each phoneme. These syllables are similar to the ones originally described by Carter and Buck (1958).

Stimulus items for the consistency portion of the test consist of 10 target sentences for each targeted sound, each sentence of which tests the phoneme in a different phonetic context (e.g., for testing /s/, I made some cakes; I can see you). Subjects repeat after the examiner the 10 sentences containing the correct form of the sound being tested.

The testing protocol first requires the child to name each of the stimulus pictures. The child is then asked to imitate the nonsense syllables that contain the target sounds in those positions that the child misarticulated on the picture naming. Finally, the child is tested for consistency on the sentence repetitions for any sounds that were assessed on the stimulability portion of the test. The percentage of correction in stimulability testing (based on the quantitative difference in correctly produced sounds between the picture naming and the imitative task) is combined with the percentage of consistency of phoneme production. Together, these percentages result in a combined percentage score to which the authors ascribe a prognostic statement.

Two types of scoring forms are provided with this instrument. (There are three actual forms, but Form 3 is the first-grade version of Form 2, which is for kindergartners.) The first type of form lists the nine words that correctly describe the pictures used to illustrate each target phoneme and the nine nonsense syllables used in the stimulability test of the same phoneme. The examiner records the number of correct sound productions on each measure and then records the percentage of change from picture-naming productions to syllable-imitation productions. The second type of form provides a table for recording stimulability and inconsistency percentages for each phoneme. A third column for the average of these two percentages is also provided; however, this reviewer was uncertain as to how this figure was to be used. To calculate the index, the examiner averages the stimulability and consistency percentages for each phoneme across all phonemes. The average stimulability and inconsistency are then

added and divided by two to produce an "overall prognostic score."

The STIM/CON reflects a concept that has some face validity to clinicians. Although there are data to support stimulability as a prognostic indicator, the data that support consistency for this use are much weaker, and most are not published. The author presents these data in a rather cursory review of the literature, in addition to a set of tables reflecting data from studies of his own (Sommers et al., 1967; Sommers, 1968) plus some other nonreferenced tables. The author implies that these data are sufficient to support the validity of the STIM/CON. This is a leap of faith or logic and is the critical flaw of this instrument. The suggestion that children with scores below 25% will require intervention, those with a score above 60% may with time and maturity improve their speech without intervention, and those in-between may need intervention, is based on the author's opinion. No data that relate directly to the validity and reliability of this instrument are given.

The information about test administration and scoring is sketchy and poorly organized. Examiners who are unfamiliar with stimulability and consistency testing will find it somewhat difficult to discern what is to be done. For example, the procedures for the consistency testing portion are presented in part under the section about stimulability testing and in part under "Examiner Requirements." Step-by-step administration procedures would help this instrument. The procedures for scoring should be presented more systematically, including the example that is provided.

In summary, the STIM/CON represents a good idea, but it appears to have been hastily developed and presented. The lack of a data base for this instrument might have been acceptable for the field three decades ago, but test users today expect more sophisticated and carefully developed tests. The author would do well to take this concept back to the drawing board for further development.

REVIEWER'S REFERENCES

Carter, E., & Buck, M. (1958). Prognostic testing for functional articulation disorders among children in the first grade. *Journal of Speech and Hearing Disorders, 23,* 124-133.

Sommers, R., Leiss, R., Delp, M., Gerber, A., Fundrella, D., Smith, R., Revuckny, M., Ellis, D., & Haley, V. (1967). Factors related to the effectiveness of articulation therapy for kindergarten, first, and second grade children. *Journal of Speech and Hearing Research, 10,* 428-437.

Sommers, R. (1968). *Research report: A guide to case selection. Articulation errors responding to speech therapy, their relationship to total defectiveness and stimulability assessment.* Norristown, PA: The Montgomery County Pennsylvania Schools.

Review of the STIM/CON: Prognostic Inventory for Misarticulating Kindergarten and First Grade Children by ALLAN O. DIEFENDORF, *Associate Professor, and KATHY S. KESSLER, Speech/Language Pathologist, Indiana University School of Medicine, Indianapolis, IN:*

The STIM/CON is a prognostic inventory given subsequent to traditional articulation testing or screening to predict a child's chance for articulation improvement of defective sounds without therapy. The STIM/CON attempts to provide clinicians with a systematic means for deciding which misarticulations should be included in corrective therapy and what priority each should have when follow-up therapy is recommended. Stimulability (assessed through spontaneous production of words and imitation of nonsense syllables) and consistency (determined through sentence imitation) are tested for only those phonemes found to be misarticulated on traditional tests of articulation. Outcome scores are averaged to determine an overall prognostic score.

The test design and development are based on scientific studies that provide a strong foundation for the author's rationale for why the STIM/CON was developed and for whom it is appropriate. The purpose of providing separate predictive summaries for children in kindergarten and in first grade is based on a solid data base with a well-developed rationale. The author's decision to use spontaneous words and nonsense syllables as stimuli for determining predictability is also well supported. The manual is informative about studies that investigated the predictive validity of stimulability and consistency in speech disorders; however, some important details are slightly confusing due to explanations that assume the reader knows more about the cited studies than may be true. Moreover, although the well-cited rationale supports the validity of stimulability and consistency measures to predict changes in the articulatory performance of children, no direct evidence supporting the validity of the STIM/CON for this purpose is provided.

The test materials consist of an informative administration manual, a professional-looking picture manual, and three organized forms for scoring. However, no test form is provided for the second portion of the test (consistency testing) and the manual does not make it clear that this portion, Test 2, consists of the "Imitated Sentences for Consistency Agreement." The use of terminology (consistency vs. inconsistency) is not consistent, which could cause serious confusion in scoring. The stimulability assessment test form does not provide the test administrator with information about how to calculate or define what is called % *change*.

The test manual does not discuss how the overall prognostic score was developed or its accuracy. Further, without any evidence of the predictive validity of the STIM/CON, it is impossible to establish the accuracy of the predictions. It is not clear how the standards for identifying those in need of direct intervention (scores 25% and below) and those who are likely to improve without intervention

(60% and above) were derived. Although the author cites references to high inter- and intrajudge reliabilities among clinicians and researchers for evaluating the accuracy of speech-sound productions, the reliability of the STIM/CON specifically is not addressed.

Requirements for test administration are provided and some procedural cautions are suggested (i.e., seating arrangements, one opportunity only for sound production, trial experiences, reinforcement). The author emphasizes that sound productions must be all or nothing; that is, clinicians must recognize "correct" sound productions from "errors" and score them as either correct or incorrect. Giving the child the opportunity to produce the phoneme in the given context more than once alters the test's prognostic value and should not be done. The author notes the potential for biased scoring on the basis of regional and social variations and reminds examiners that "phoneme productions should be considered within the bounds of normalcy." However, new and/or inexperienced clinicians who are unfamiliar with dialectal differences could obtain highly variable scores when administering this test. The contamination of this variable must be emphasized in the context of accurate scoring. Potential problems from this source of error impact over- and under-referral rates, and can reduce the predictive value of this test. Therefore, the author's view that reliability "should be good to excellent" with this test must be viewed with skepticism.

For the most part, the drawings that depict the pictures are clear, although more than a few of them would not be obvious to many children and prompting would be required. In these situations, the examiner is encouraged to use leading questions to elicit responses. Because such examiner intervention could have great impact on the reliability of the test, a discussion about specific types of prompts to use would be appropriate; however, no such information is given. Specific prompting tools that should be used if the child fails to understand the task or generate the target appropriately are also not suggested. There is no indication why the words or pictures used were selected, so it is not clear if they are appropriate for the age groups in the potential testing population. Similarly, no information is provided to establish that the sentences consist of vocabulary that is age-appropriate to the test population.

In summary, the rationale behind the development of the STIM/CON is effectively substantiated. The clinical usefulness of a prognostic tool like the STIM/CON is well founded. However, several issues related to the development of this particular measure prevent these reviewers from recommending this test as it presently exists. If the weaknesses described were corrected, the STIM/CON would likely find a welcome place within the core battery of assessment tools used by communication disorder specialists.

[381]
Stress Response Scale.

Purpose: A measure of children's emotional status "designed for children referred for possible emotional adjustment problems."
Population: Grades 1–8.
Publication Dates: 1979–86.
Acronym: SRS.
Scores, 6: Impulsive (Acting Out), Passive-Aggressive, Impulsive (Overactive), Repressed, Dependent, Total.
Administration: Group.
Price Data, 1988: $8 per 25 rating scales; $8 per 25 profile sheets (specify male or female); $18.50 per sample set including manual ('86, 26 pages).
Special Edition: *The Stress Response Scale for Children: A Profile Analysis Program.* 1985; "a program for the interactive entry of SRS data"; 2 modes: clinical applications, research applications; Apple II/II+/ IIe/IIc (64K RAM) or IBM-PC/XT/AT (or 100% compatibles) required; printer is recommended, but not required; $79 per program and manual; Mark D. Shermis and Louis A. Chandler; Mark D. Shermis.
Time: Administration time not reported.
Comments: Ratings by parents or teachers; manual title is *The Stress Response Scale for Children, 1986 Revision.*
Author: Louis A. Chandler.
Publisher: Louis A. Chandler.

TEST REFERENCES

1. Chandler, L. A. (1983). The Stress Response Scale: An instrument for use in assessing emotional adjustment reactions. *School Psychology Review, 12,* 260-265.
2. Johnson, G. S. (1989). Emotional indicators in the human figure drawings of hearing-impaired children: A small sample validation study. *American Annals of the Deaf, 134,* 205-208.

Review of the Stress Response Scale by MARY LOU KELLEY, Associate Professor of Psychology, Louisiana State University, Baton Rouge, LA:

The Stress Response Scale is a 40-item rating scale designed to measure children's emotional status. Items are short descriptors of children's behavioral or emotional responses rated on a 6-point scale (0 = *never* to 5 = *always*). The scale is intended to be completed either by parents or teachers, depending on who is making the referral for evaluation.

Scale content is based heavily upon the author's theoretical beliefs. The scale was developed on the assumption that children's reactions to stress represent behavioral responses to specific stimuli characterized as stressors. Maladaptive behaviors are considered extreme examples of normal coping responses. Based upon the author's "stress response" model, which utilizes two dimensions of personality (introversion-extraversion and passive-active), four patterns of behavior emerge. The items of the Stress Response Scale are grouped according to the four symptom patterns labelled: Dependent, Impulsive, Passive-Aggressive, and Repressed.

Factor analytic studies generally supported the item groupings. Factor analysis yielded five factors that accounted for 64% of the variance. The symptom clusters noted remained consistent with the conceptual underpinnings of the test. However, the "Impulsive" symptom grouping was represented by two factors. Illustrative items included in each factor are: (*a*) *Impulsive-Acting Out*: demanding, selfish, impulsive; (*b*) *Impulsive-Overactive*: easily excited, not quiet or withdrawn, talkative; (*c*) *Dependent*: lack of participation, lacks self-confidence, lacks independence; (*d*) *Passive-Aggressive*: daydreams, underachiever, doesn't care about schoolwork; and (*e*) *Repressed*: worries, sensitive, easily upset, afraid of new situations.

The author provides a well-written, well-organized, and informative manual. The manual describes the intended uses of the test, the conceptual basis behind the test, and the target population with whom the test is used. The procedures for administering and scoring the test are unambiguous and simple. The manual details the reliability and validity of the test in a very clear, user-friendly manner.

The test has been standardized with a relatively large sample, and norms are available for boys and girls at varying ages. Thus, the test takes into account developmental and gender differences often seen in children. Standard scores and percentile rankings are easily derived from tables provided in the manual. Profile charts are available for both males and females at different ages, making the test easy to score by trained personnel. It is unclear, however, whether the standardization data are based on parent or teacher ratings.

The reliability of the test is well documented, based on information detailed in the manual and other publications. The test has been shown to be internally consistent and to possess good test-retest reliability, both in terms of total scores and factor scores. However, it appears the author has not examined interrater reliability, which could potentially be quite low, given the lack of behavioral specificity of the items. For example, agreement between mothers and fathers or teachers and parents apparently has not been evaluated.

The author is to be commended for the extent of measurement validation that has been conducted on the SRS. The author and others have examined the construct, content, factorial, discriminant, and criterion-related validity of the instrument. For example, factor-analytic studies suggested that 64% of the variance was accounted for with the five-factor solution described earlier. This factor analysis included 34 of the 40 items contained in the test. With regard to criterion-related validity, Chandler, Shermis, and March (1985) evaluated the ability of the scale to predict psychiatric group membership.

The authors compared the SRS subscale scores with psychiatric diagnoses given to the children by clinicians. This study and other work by Chandler indicated that scores obtained from the measure predicted group membership.

It should be clear the SRS appears to have a number of positive features and the instrument may be a useful screening measure in clinical settings. The test is very brief and probably takes only a few minutes to complete because many of the items are just one or two words. A clear, succinct manual describing the test and scoring criteria makes the measure easy to use.

In spite of the positive features of the test, I have some reservations about the reliability of the test. The items generally are very global descriptors of children's emotions and behavior, and therefore are particularly subject to rater bias.

Although the author purports that the SRS measures responses to stress and that this construct is supported in the literature, it is not clear how this test differs from other available instruments not based on the same conceptual underpinnings. For example, other instruments measure children's maladaptive behavioral and emotional responses. Whereas the author's conceptualization of stress may or may not be accurate, I fail to understand how the conceptualization is reflected in the SRS in ways that make the test unique.

Thus, in spite of the positive features of the SRS, it is not clear how this instrument is better than other more behaviorally anchored instruments such as the Child Behavior Checklist (CBCL; 64). The CBCL, for example, contains more items and several additional factors (Achenbach & Edelbrock, 1979). The CBCL also has more comprehensive reliability and validity data supporting the instrument. However, should the reader be interested in a brief instrument that assesses global characteristics in children as perceived by an adult caretaker, the SRS is one test to consider.

REVIEWER'S REFERENCES

Achenbach, T., & Edelbrock, C. (1979). The Child Behavior Profile: II. Boys aged 12–16 and girls aged 6–11 and 12–16. *Journal of Consulting and Clinical Psychology, 47,* 223-233.

Chandler, L. A., Shermis, M. D., & Marsh, J. (1985). The use of the Stress Response Scale in diagnostic assessment. *Journal of Psychoeducational Assessment, 3,* 16-29.

Review of the Stress Response Scale by WILLIAM K. WILKINSON, Assistant Professor of Counseling and Educational Psychology, New Mexico State University, Las Cruces, NM:

The Stress Response Scale (SRS) is a rating scale appropriate for use with children aged 5 to 14. The 40-item instrument is completed by an adult familiar with the target child's behavior, with each statement rated from 0 (*never*) to 5 (*always*). The scale is constructed to yield one global score, and six separate profile types—Acting Out, Passive-Aggressive, Overactive, Dependent, Repressed, and Mixed—which purportedly reflect a child's "emotional status." The global SRS raw score is convertible to both *T*-scores and percentile ranks. The normative sample for the SRS consists of 947 schoolchildren in western Pennsylvania who were rated by their respective teachers.

The SRS test materials include a technical manual that provides information concerning the intended use and application of the scale, a conceptual model on which the test was based, reliability, validity, normative information, and guidelines for scoring and interpretation. The 40 statements comprising the SRS are contained on one response sheet. A particularly nice feature of the instrument is the inclusion of computer software designed to aid in scoring and interpretation. This material is presented in a binder containing clear, step-by-step instructions for computer use. Finally, separate profile sheets are included for those test users opting to hand score and interpret SRS data. Overall, the SRS is professionally marketed, with test materials nicely organized and clearly identifiable.

In reviewing the SRS technical manual and several published articles concerning the scale, several concerns are noteworthy. Perhaps the most pervasive difficulty involves the nature of the stress construct and its measurement.

For example, the construct of stress is not directly measured by the SRS, but rather, is an explanatory variable that may account for maladaptive levels of those personality characteristics purportedly measured by the instrument. The SRS is not designed to measure stress response per se; rather, it provides data in the form of adult ratings of children on traits such as shy, defiant, and cooperative. An interpretation regarding why an adult rates a child at any particular level of a measured trait, whether stress response or some other reason, goes beyond the scope of the SRS and would require careful analysis and interpretation across a wide array of assessment procedures. Unfortunately, because the instrument was named the Stress Response Scale, it may mislead test users to purchase the scale as a direct measure of stress response, or to interpret a child's score as a result of stress. Clearly, caution is needed in these respects.

Given the SRS is not a measure of stress response, then what does it measure? Although the technical manual contains terms such as "emotional status," "emotional adjustment," "coping strategies," "personality," "stress response," "behavior," and "response style," the items and factor descriptions appear consistent with other trait measures (e.g., Eysenck, Cattell, Conners, Achenbach). In fact, the technical manual notes the similarities between SRS factors and other personality descriptions, although no empirical data regarding these relationships are presented. The lack of these data undermines a test user's confidence in the instrument's construct validity.

There is evidence of factorial validity—the profile factors are stable in unique samples (nonreferred vs. clinic referred), but these data do not address the issue of similarities or differences between the SRS factors and those measured by other scales. Further, establishing the stability of the factors across different samples does not entirely support the statement in the manual that "emotional adjustment reactions may be seen as extreme patterns of normal coping behavior." This statement could be verified through the inclusion of the separate profile scores (means and standard deviations) for the nonreferred versus clinic-referred groups. Ideally, both the total score and each profile factor score should be significantly greater for the clinic-referred children than their nonreferred peers. However, the only information in the technical manual is that clinic-referred children receive higher total score ratings than the nonreferred children.

Regarding separate profile scores, instead of presenting descriptive statistics concerning group differences across the five profile factors, data regarding the frequencies of SRS profile types for the entire normative sample ($N = 857$) and a group of clinic-referred children ($N = 84$) are given. The evidence presented hardly supports the SRS as a diagnostic tool, because only one (Acting Out) of the five SRS factors (excluding the mixed profile) reached acceptable levels of statistical significance in differentiating the proportions of each sample within diagnostic categories.

Further, although two studies are cited as support for the scale's ability to predict diagnostic group membership, these data are either difficult to evaluate or inherently limited. For instance, the statement that the SRS reduces error in predicting psychiatric group membership is hard to interpret without further explanation (e.g., what type of error, what was the procedure for initial classification, what were the diagnostic categories, was the reduction statistically significant, how tested, etc.). Also, that SRS scores predict a diagnostic criterion with two outcomes—special education or a specific type of special education—is troublesome because the criterion suffers from such a restricted range. Thus, further support of predictive validity is clearly needed if the instrument is to gain a reputation as being diagnostically useful.

As for reliability data, this information is presented in terms of stability of ratings across a test-retest period of one month. The correlations for separate scale scores range from .72 to .90, demonstrating the SRS meets technically adequate levels of stability reliability. However, it should be noted that these reliability correlations were obtained with teachers only, so that the reliability of ratings for different groups (parents) is presently unknown.

In general, it seems the conclusions reached in the SRS manual are far overstated, given the instrument's format and technical qualities. Test users should know the limitations of rating formats in general (e.g., items emphasize problem behavior, bias in rater perception) and keep these weaknesses in mind when judging the appropriateness of the SRS for assessment and treatment planning.

Further, the conclusion that the SRS provides data about the impact of stress on a child's behavioral adjustment clearly goes beyond the scope of the instrument. If a measure of stress response was desired, stress, and response to it, would be operationally defined, directly measured, and ultimately validated. None of these steps is found in the SRS, emphasizing the point that the instrument is not intended to measure either stress response or the effects of stress on personality.

Rather, the only legitimate conclusion is the instrument appears to measure selected personality traits. Thus, the SRS may be appropriate as a measure of certain personality dimensions, pending the collection of necessary validation data regarding the traits it purportedly measures. Until then, the use of this scale is not recommended.

[382]
Stroop Neuropsychological Screening Test.

Purpose: Provides "an efficient and sensitive neuropsychological screening measure based on the Stroop procedure."
Population: Ages 18 and over.
Publication Date: 1989.
Acronym: SNST.
Scores, 2: Color, Color-Word.
Administration: Individual.
Price Data, 1990: $39.95 per complete kit; $27 per 50 stimulus sheets (25 of each form); $9.95 per 25 record forms; $8 per manual (14 pages).
Time: 4(9) minutes.
Authors: Max R. Trenerry, Bruce Crosson, James DeBoe, and William R. Leber.
Publisher: Psychological Assessment Resources, Inc.

TEST REFERENCES

1. Miller, B. L., Lesser, I. M., Boone, K., Goldberg, M., Hill, E., Miller, M. H., Benson, D. F., & Mehringer, M. (1989). Brain white-matter lesions and psychosis. *British Journal of Psychiatry, 155*, 73-78.

Review of the Stroop Neuropsychological Screening Test by MANFRED J. MEIER, Professor of Neurosurgery, Psychiatry, and Psychology and Diplomate in Clinical Neuropsychology, University of Minnesota, Twin Cities, Minneapolis, MN:

The Stroop Neuropsychological Screening Test (SNST) is designed to measure the experimentally established interference effect that occurs during color naming when the colors to be named are printed in names that do not match the colors

(Stroop effect). This procedure addresses the purpose of differentiating individuals with known organic cerebral involvement from normals, based on early reports of increasing order of the Stroop interference effect across normal, nonaphasic with left-hemisphere lesion, right-hemisphere lesion, and aphasic with left-hemisphere lesion groups. Evidence cited in the manual relates to a stronger effect in patients with left frontal cerebral involvement as compared to other focal lesion groups and successful discrimination of a combined psychiatric and normal control sample from a group classified as brain damaged. The SNST was developed to extend applications in neuropsychology by addressing methodological and practical issues that were not adequately controlled in previous versions and to introduce reliability and validity data based on a normative sample and representative groups with known neurological involvements.

The procedure consists of two components, a Color Task that is administered first and requires the reading of color names (with self-correction) without regard for the (always) discrepant color shown. Although this procedure may introduce a priming effect for the primary Color-Word Task, it does not appear to add to the discriminative validity of the instrument and is not used in interpretation. The Color-Word Task is then administered and requires the naming of the color of the word rather than the word itself when, again, the actual color shown is discrepant from the word in all instances. Time and error scores are then computed after a response time of 120 seconds per task. An age effect has consistently been demonstrated in this literature so that percentile and probability values are provided separately for adults in the 18–49 and the 50+ age ranges. Definitive gender or level-of-education effects have not been demonstrated. Interpretation assumes control of peripheral and color-vision disturbances, and strict adherence to the procedure as described in the manual.

Normative data for a sizeable group that is free of neurological or psychiatric illness are reported along with scores derived from the Color and Color-Word Tasks for small groups of left- and right-hemisphere cerebral vascular accident patients, a larger group of closed head injury (CHI) patients, and a small group of mixed neurological patients. Discriminant function analysis of the presence or absence of brain damage as inferred from these classifications as a dependent variable and a Color-Word score as a predictor revealed statistically significant percentages of predictive accuracy. The most efficient cutoff scores for the younger and older samples suggested a higher canonical correlation and greater predictive efficiency in the older groups. False negatives were characteristically low though false positive rates in the younger group were substantial (40%). The use

of a different score between the Color and Color-Word Tasks did not add to predictive efficiency. A first attempt at cross validation, achieved by assigning subjects in each group randomly to one of two comparison groups without regard to age, yielded comparable canonical correlation and correct classification rates when the initially derived discriminant function was applied to the homologous group. Considering the low numbers in the patient groups with definitive cerebral vascular lesions and the relatively minor effects suggested for the closed head injury group, these analyses would appear to reflect a somewhat lower level of predictive validity than is implied in the manual for this instrument. Thus, the failure to analyze the effectiveness of the Color-Word score for differentiating closed head injury from the combined normal sample is noteworthy, particularly when the younger CHI sample appeared to score better than the combined normal sample, which included a sizable group of individuals in the 50+ age group.

Although promising, at least for identifying individuals with major cortical involvement such as represented in the smaller cerebral vascular accident subgroups, the sensitivity of this instrument may not be sufficient to differentiate less conspicuous types of cerebral and subcortical involvement such as represented in the closed head injury sample. Further validation work is obviously necessary before this instrument is used for more than the screening of major neurological involvement. Studies cited in the manual relating to apparent sensitivity to left prefrontal involvement should also be replicated with comparisons to tests of known sensitivity to prefrontal lesions such as the Oral Controlled Word Association Test (Borkowski, Benton, & Spreen, 1967), the Wisconsin Card Sorting Test (Milner, 1964), and the Halstead Category Test (Reitan, 1964). Neuropsychological screening with this test in a psychiatric setting would depend on a more extensive normative base, comparative data among selected psychiatric groups, and an expansion in the number and kinds of patients with known neurological involvement, focal and diffuse. Identification of maximal effect for left-prefrontal lesions would also be essential before applying this procedure to the differentiation of diffuse from focal lesions, a goal that is not addressed in the manual. In the meantime, the test would appear to have some limited applicability to help confirm or disconfirm the presence of organic cerebral dysfunction within the context of a more comprehensive assessment of higher cortical functions in individuals with suspected cerebral involvement.

REVIEWER'S REFERENCES

Milner, B. (1964). Some effects of frontal lobectomy in man. In J. M. Warren & K. Akert (Eds.), *The frontal granular cortex and behavior*. New York: McGraw-Hill.

Reitan, R. M. (1964). Psychological deficits resulting from cerebral lesions in man. In J. M. Warren & K. Akert (Eds.), *The frontal granular cortex and behavior.* New York: McGraw-Hill.

Borkowski, J. G., Benton, A. L., & Spreen, O. (1967). Word fluency and brain damage. *Neuropsychologia, 5,* 135-140.

Review of the Stroop Neuropsychological Screening Test by CECIL R. REYNOLDS, Professor of Educational Psychology, Texas A&M University, College Station, TX:

The Stroop Neuropsychological Screening Test (SNST) is another test in the continuing, seemingly inevitable, hasty publication of an interesting, clever clinical or experimental technique gone sorely awry through bad psychometric practice. The SNST is apparently intended as a measure for helping to screen organic from functional psychiatric patients that claims to have been "standardized and validated for ages 18 and older" (manual, p. 3). The administration has been standardized, the technique is simple (a simplification and standardization of many variants of the Stroop procedure that have emerged over the years), and the idea well presented. Here the positive features of the SNST cease.

The Stroop procedure requires a patient to read color names printed in discrepant colors (e.g., read the word blue printed in green ink) and to announce the color of words in which the words are discrepant from the color. The number of correct and incorrect responses may be scored as well as the discrepancy between the two conditions. The SNST manual provides a brief (1.5 pages) review of older literature on this procedure and it does appear to discriminate well between functional and organic patients.

The goals of improving the procedure and providing reliable scores and norms have not been accomplished in this new variant of the Stroop. Data in the manual are minimal and psychometrically naive at best.

The SNST is reportedly standardized for ages 18–79 with normative data split into two groups for reporting and scaling purposes, ages 18–49 ($N = 106$) and ages "50+" ($N = 50$). Why 50+ and not 50–79? Apparently, this would limit the market for the test for no data are available to suggest its use above 79 is appropriate. The sample appears to have been one entirely of convenience and limited demographic data are provided (age, years of education, and gender) that show severe discrepancies from population proportionate sampling. Restriction of range is also evident on each of the first two variables and that causes one to discount the correlational data presented and to dismiss the importance of such data. The stability of the scaling parameters with Ns of such small size is quite poor. Additionally, the manual argues this sample of unknown origin was screened to rule out individuals with problematic neurological histories, yet, we are not told how or with what.

Cut scores were established for designating "brain-damaged" patients and were developed in a single study reported in one paragraph with no description of the brain-damaged sample (see pp. 5–6 of manual). We are told only that a study was done and that discriminant analysis was used to set cutoffs to maximize hit rates. Without full reporting, the reader cannot begin to judge the merits of the approach. Clearly, no estimates of cross-validation shrinkage are presented (e.g., see Willson & Reynolds, 1982) and no argument for the generalizability of those scores is made—it is just accepted.

A single reliability study is reported. A test-retest study was conducted with $N = 30$ over a widely disparate time span ($M = 59.4$ days, $SD = 37.8$ days). The $r_{1,2}$ was .90. This is high for a stability estimate but the findings were not controlled for age effects. This is potentially a serious omission because raw scores were used and age and raw scores are correlated on the SNST. A significant practice effect was observed but cannot guide interpretation due to the disparate time to retest across subjects. Regrettably, no indications of internal consistency of the Color-Word scores, which could and should have been calculated are reported.

Nearly one full page of the manual is devoted to reporting on a validity study that uses subsamples of individuals with various forms of brain damage. No journal citation is given and the meager data presented in the manual on subject selection and qualification, data analyses, and derivation of cutoffs are not adequate to assess the utility of the study. Moderate correlations (.44, .49, and .46) are reported between the SNST Color-Word score and WAIS-R Verbal, Performance, and Full Scale IQ, respectively. The Halstead Category Test correlated -.57 with the SNST Color-Word score for this same sample of 25 brain-damaged individuals (no other data are provided on this sample).

The SNST is a useful idea that begs for adequate execution. The present version is unsuitable and indefensible for clinical use and should have been released as a clearly labeled "experimental edition" or not at all. The SNST is not appropriately normed and its use with the elderly must be considered especially suspect. Appropriate cautions are absent from the manual. A great deal of work remains before the SNST acquires clinical utility.

REVIEWER'S REFERENCES

Willson, V. L., & Reynolds, C. R. (1982). Methodological and statistical problems in determining membership in clinical populations. *Clinical Neuropsychology, 4,* 134-138.

[383]

Student Adaptation to College Questionnaire.

Purpose: "Designed to assess how well a student is adapting to the demands of the college experience."
Population: College freshmen.
Publication Date: 1989.

Acronym: SACQ.
Scores, 5: Academic Adjustment, Social Adjustment, Personal Emotional Adjustment, Attachment, Full Scale.
Administration: Group or individual.
Price Data, 1991: $82 per complete kit including 25 hand-scorable questionnaires and manual (76 pages) plus 2 prepaid computer-scored answer sheets; $32.50 per 25 hand-scorable questionnaires; $32.50 per manual; $6.95–$9.50 (depending on quantity purchased) per computer-scored answer sheet; $185 per IBM computer disk.
Time: (20) minutes.
Authors: Robert W. Baker and Bohdan Siryk.
Publisher: Western Psychological Services.

TEST REFERENCES

1. Smith, M. A., & Baker, R. W. (1987). Freshman decidedness regarding academic major and adjustment to college. *Psychological Reports*, *61*, 847-853.
2. Lopez, F. G., Campbell, V. L., & Watkins, C. E., Jr. (1989). Effects of marital conflict and family coalition patterns on college student adjustment. *Journal of College Student Development*, *30*, 46-52.
3. Saracoglu, B., Minden, H., & Wilchesky, M. (1989). The adjustment of students with learning disabilities to university and its relationship to self-esteem and self-efficacy. *Journal of Learning Disabilities*, *22*, 590-592.
4. Haemmerlie, F. M., Robinson, D. A. G., & Carmen, R. C. (1991). "Type A" personality traits and adjustment to college. *Journal of College Student Development*, *32*, 81-82.

Review of the Student Adaptation to College Questionnaire by E. JACK ASHER, JR., Professor Emeritus of Psychology, Western Michigan University, Kalamazoo, MI:

The Student Adaptation to College Questionnaire (SACQ) by Baker and Siryk is a 67-item self-report for college freshmen. The questionnaire was designed to assess student adjustment to college. The goal of the assessment is to provide counselors information they may use in assisting students to adjust to the college environment. The questionnaire is designed only to seek information about the students' adjustment to the college; it does not supply feedback to the college about its adaptation to the needs of students. This limitation may account for the shortage of norms for public universities.

The SACQ is divided into four subscales: Academic Adjustment (24 items), Social Adjustment (20 items), Personal-Emotional Adjustment (15 items), and Goal Commitment/Institutional Adjustment (15 items). It is obvious from the item count that several items appear on more than one scale. The SACQ is published in a hand AutoScored form and a computer-scannable answer sheet form. It is also available for microcomputer administration and scoring. The student response is marked and scored on a 9-point scale from (1) *applies very closely to me* to (9) *doesn't apply to me at all*. High scores represent good adjustment to college. The scale contains a number of negatively stated and scored items. The administration of the questionnaire is said to take about 20 minutes.

The SACQ raw scores are converted to a *T* score (mean = 50, sd = 10) and a percentile rank. The scoring conversion for the hand AutoScore is rather tedious. The norm group for the *T* score and percentile consisted of 1,424 freshmen at Clark University who were administered the questionnaire in 1980–81, 1981–82, 1982–83, and 1983–84. Norms are reported by sex and freshmen semester of testing. There is no report of the number of men and women in the norm sample nor is there any other demographic description of the group. The manual does present a study to show that mean scores on the subscales differ by sex and freshmen semester. No norms are available for other institutions, type of institution, or for any ethnic groups. The manual suggests that the scores from other institutions indicate that institutional differences may be small. These data are far from conclusive. In fact, the manual states "suitability of the normative or other psychometric data for other populations should not be taken for granted." Thus, it seems clear that the provided *T* scores and percentiles are of little value to institutions outside the norm group.

Validity evidence of the SACQ is presented in a variety of ways. First, intercorrelations between the subscales and the Full Scale are presented for the norm group. These data show that each subscale correlates with the Full Scale; the correlations are in the .7 to .8 range. Similar intercorrelations are presented from studies at other institutions. However, the manual does not report a full intercorrelation matrix for the current 67-item scale. Second, a one factor principle component analysis was performed on data from a broad range of institutions. This analysis showed a relatively large loading for each variable, thus justifying the use of the subscales say the authors. Finally, a series of studies are reported to show the relation between the Full Scale, the subscales, and a variety of external criteria. The first study showed that the Academic Adjustment scale correlated slightly with first year GPA at Clark University. The correlations ranged from .17 to .48 with the median being .34. The Social Adjustment scale was found to correlate .47 with a measure of social activity used at Clark University. The Attachment scale was found to correlate -.27 to -.41 with first year attrition at Clark. A number of other studies are reported from other universities. The most compelling of these show that the Social Adjustment scale correlates -.66 to -.79 with the U.C.L.A. Loneliness scale and that the Personal-Emotional Adjustment scale correlates .40 to .54 with a Self-Esteem Inventory. These studies along with the relatively strong face and content validity suggest that the questionnaire is probably measuring some of the elements that relate to a student's adjustment to college. However, the validity as reported does not suggest that use at other institutions is justified without further study at that institution.

The total score and subscores reliability of the SACQ are estimated by coefficient alpha. The Full

Scale reliability is reported to range from .92 to .95. The subscale reliabilities range from .77 for Personal-Emotional Adjustment to .91 for Attachment and Social Adjustment. Additional reliability studies are reported for item clusters of 3 to 9 items each under the assumption that counselors may find meaning in them. The reliability of these clusters, although reported in the .56 to .91 range, should be suspect for two reasons. First, internal consistency measures on small item groups may be unstable. Second, the reliance on a sample of 3 to 9 item responses to represent such things as Motivation or Psychological Adjustment is of highly questionable value.

The manual for the SACQ is full of useful test information and contains a number of cautions about the use of self-report data. The purpose of the questionnaire is clearly stated, as are a number of comments to potential users and counselors. The information necessary for administration and scoring is easy to read. A number of ethical issues are raised and a strong recommendation is made that this is a research instrument. However, the fact that norms are provided may lead potential users to disregard this caution.

The SACQ appears to have high potential as an aid to college counselors and some possible research applications. However, it should be used with caution outside of its norm population area (i.e., small private colleges in the northeast). If an instrument of this type is to be used, it probably should be administered during the first freshmen semester. This is the time during which the new student begins to recognize his or her adjustment difficulties. Information gathered by counselors at this time should enable them to help students with small problems that could become larger in a short time. However, in many instances a complex questionnaire is usually not necessary to identify individual student problems. A more significant problem at many institutions is to differentiate students with personal adjustment problems from those with institutionally caused problems. This questionnaire is not designed to assist in this effort. Thus, this instrument is likely to have limited usefulness at institutions with large populations of beginning freshmen.

[384]
Student Developmental Task and Lifestyle Inventory.
Purpose: "Assisting students in understanding their own development and establishing goals and plans to shape their own futures."
Population: College students ages 17–24.
Publication Date: 1987.
Acronym: SDTLI.
Scores, 12: Establishing and Clarifying Purpose Task (Educational Involvement Subtask, Career Planning Subtask, Life Management Subtask, Lifestyle Planning Subtask, Cultural Participation Subtask), Developing

Mature Interpersonal Relationships Task (Peer Relationships Subtask, Tolerance Subtask, Emotional Autonomy Subtask), Academic Autonomy Task, Salubrious Lifestyle Scale, Intimacy Scale, Response Bias Scale.
Administration: Group.
Price Data, 1987: $45 per 50 reusable test booklets; $20 per 50 answer sheets; $12.50 per 50 Understanding and Using the SDTLI: A Guide for Students (6 pages); $9 per manual (50 pages).
Time: (30–40) minutes.
Comments: Revision of the Student Developmental Task Inventory, Revised, Second Edition.
Authors: Roger B. Winston, Jr., Theodore K. Miller, and Judith S. Prince.
Publisher: Student Development Associates, Inc.
Cross References: For reviews by Fred H. Borgen and Steven D. Brown of the Second Edition, see 9:1199 (5 references).

TEST REFERENCES

1. Furr, J. D., Staik, I. M., & Bagby, S. A. (1984). The assessment of developmental tasks in college women. *College Student Journal, 18*, 253-256.
2. Blann, F. W. (1985). Intercollegiate athletic competition and students' educational and career plans. *Journal of College Student Personnel, 26*, 115-118.
3. Williams, M., & Winston, R. B., Jr. (1985). Participation in organized student activities and work: Differences in developmental task achievement of traditional aged college students. *NASPA Journal, 22* (3), 52-59.
4. Itzkowitz, S. G., & Petrie, R. D. (1986). The Student Developmental Task Inventory: Scores of northern versus southern students. *Journal of College Student Personnel, 27*, 406-413.
5. Stonewater, J., Daniels, M. H., & Heischmidt, K. (1986). The reliability and validity of the Student Developmental Task Inventory–2: Pilot studies. *Journal of College Student Personnel, 27*, 70-74.
6. Straub, C. A., & Rodgers, R. F. (1986). An exploration of Chickering's theory and women's development. *Journal of College Student Personnel, 27*, 216-224.
7. Winston, R. B., Jr., & Polkosnik, M. C. (1986). Student Developmental Task Inventory (2nd Edition): Summary of selected findings. *Journal of College Student Personnel, 27*, 548-559.
8. Jordan-Cox, C. A. (1987). Psychosocial development of students in traditionally Black institutions. *Journal of College Student Personnel, 28*, 504-512.
9. Greeley, A. T., & Tinsley, H. E. A. (1988). Autonomy and intimacy development in college students: Sex differences and predictors. *Journal of College Student Development, 29*, 512-520.
10. Cheatham, H. E., & Slaney, R. B. (1990). Institutional effects on the psychosocial development of African-American college students. *Journal of Counseling Psychology, 37*, 453-458.
11. Tinsley, D. J., Hinson, J. A., Holt, M. S., & Tinsley, H. E. A. (1990). Level of psychosocial development, perceived level of psychological difficulty, counseling readiness, and expectations about counseling: Examination of group differences. *Journal of Counseling Psychology, 37*, 143-148.
12. Winston, R. B., Jr. (1990). The Student Developmental Task and Lifestyle Inventory: An approach to measuring students' psychosocial development. *Journal of College Student Development, 31*, 108-120.
13. Tinsley, D. J., Holt, M. S., Hinson, J. A., & Tinsley, H. E. A. (1991). A construct validation study on the Expectations About Counseling-Brief Form: Factorial validity. *Measurement and Evaluation in Counseling and Development, 24*, 101-110.

Review of the Student Developmental Task and Lifestyle Inventory by MARY HENNING-STOUT, Assistant Professor of Counseling Psychology, Lewis and Clark College, Portland, OR:

The purpose of the Student Developmental Task and Lifestyle Inventory (SDTLI) is to gauge the social-emotional development of college students. The SDTLI and its earlier versions have been most commonly applied in the articulation of developmental tasks that face individual students. The authors suggest that the successful completion of these tasks is necessary for continued progress both in the prevailing culture and within one's historical cohort. According to the authors who ground their inventory in the theory of Chickering (1969), these tasks lead to development and clarification of life purpose, mature interpersonal relationships, academic autonomy, mature intimacy, and healthy lifestyles.

This version of the SDTLI, published in 1987, represents a second revision of the Student Developmental Task Inventory first published in 1974 (Prince, Miller, & Winston, 1974). The current version differs from the others in its response to psychometric questions of scale structure, to consumer objections to the exclusive focus on heterosexual relationships, and to the need for addressing lifestyle issues such as cultural activity and health maintenance. In addition, a response bias scale is built into the most recent version of this inventory.

ADMINISTRATION. The SDTLI may be administered individually or to groups provided the groups complete the inventory under supervision. Accompanying the test materials is a guide for students that provides step-by-step instructions to examinees for completing, scoring, and interpreting the instrument. Given the complexity of the notion of developmental tasks and the likelihood of students being unfamiliar with it, facilitation of response interpretation by a qualified examiner seems advisable.

Students respond to 140 questions by indicating whether the stem is representative (true) or not representative (false) of their current experience. Their responses are made on a form with a carbon and scoring guide attached.

Scores are obtained for three "developmental tasks" (Establishing and Clarifying Purpose, Developing Mature Interpersonal Relationships, and Academic Autonomy) and three scales (Salubrious Lifestyle, Intimacy, and Response Bias). Based on factor analytic findings reported in the manual, these seem to be six distinct constructs. The first two tasks break into subtasks which are also scored.

Once recorded, the raw scores can be converted to T scores using the tables provided in the manual. The authors suggest that normative interpretation of inventory results be confined to use in program evaluation and research studies. When the scale is used with an individual for counseling or advising, ideopathic interpretation of scale scores and individual items is advised. This interpretation can then be applied in consultation with the individual to plan for personal change.

PSYCHOMETRIC PROPERTIES. The descriptions of research presented in the manual indicate that the reliability and validity of this instrument are well established. Reliability was gauged using test-retest and internal consistency procedures. In both instances, reliability was sufficient to warrant acceptance of the consistency of this inventory's results. Validity was also measured in two ways. Construct validity was given initial support with reports of the factor analyses conducted to develop the test (and reported in the test development section of the manual). Additional research on the constructs of this measure were not reported. The potential user of the SDTLI is encouraged to seek information on more recent construct validation as it may be presented in the professional literature. The presentation of evidence of the scale's concurrent validity is more thorough. The SDTLI shows appropriate correlation with the Mines-Jensen Interpersonal Relationship Inventory, the Iowa Developing Autonomy Inventory Scales, and selected scales from the Omnibus Personality Inventory.

One potential weakness of the scale is evident in the standardization sample ($n = 1,200$). The authors admit the middle-class bias of the items in the scale suggesting that, "The primary reason for this is that colleges in North America are basically middle-class social institutions." Information on the socioeconomic status of the standardization sample is not provided and is, therefore, assumed consistent with the above statement. In general, the information provided on the standardization process is minimal. There is no indication of how selection was made and whether the distributions reported are stratified categories. Most of the subjects are from the southeastern United States ($n = 394$) and the fewest are from the western United States ($n = 62$).

Descriptive statistics on the standardization sample reveal that women's and men's scores were significantly different on the Intimacy and Salubrious Lifestyle Scales. Standardized scores for these two scales are provided by gender. Additional reported statistical data indicate other discrepancies that are not accounted for in standardized scoring. For example, Blacks scored significantly lower on the Intimacy Scale and Southeasterners scored significantly lower than Westerners and Northeasterners on the three developmental tasks. No explanation or caution accompanies these statistics.

PRACTICAL AND RESEARCH UTILITY. Along with the problems mentioned above regarding the potential bias in standardization and item content of the SDTLI, there is an additional bias that emerges as a result of the fact that this instrument is based on Chickering's (1969) work. That work and his subsequent research efforts with Havighurst (Chickering & Havighurst, 1981) focused primarily on the experiences of men in the typical college age group. The designation and selection of scales based on this research and theory may preclude consideration of some of the developmental tasks faced by minority and women college students. It is likely that both men and women experience the developmental challenges represented in this inventory, a likelihood partially supported by the factor analytic data emerging from the standardization sample in which women outnumbered men by approximately 7:4. The question of what may be overlooked given a theoretical perspective emerging from research focusing on the experience of White men remains an important one for the authors of this instrument. Research in this area by the authors is encouraged.

The suggestions for application of this measure offered in the manual are useful and clear. The primary consumers of this scale would be counselors, advisors, and student life staff for undergraduate programs. The individualized use of the scale seems most appropriate as an ideopathically interpreted vehicle for therapeutic interchange between a student and service provider.

The suggestions made by the authors for application of this instrument as a program evaluation or research tool are excellent. As a part of needs assessment for program development and subsequent evaluation, the SDTLI seems well suited. The suggestions for use with advising and training students in peer support also seem appropriate for this measure. For the purposes of research, the authors provide useful cautions and direction, especially regarding the vulnerability of this instrument to social desirability response sets and the importance of examiner-examinee rapport.

In summary, the SDTLI is a psychometrically sound inventory that can prove useful in program development and has potential research applications. Its utility for individual assessment seems best if the results are interpreted ideopathically and used to enhance the psychotherapeutic communication process. The possible limitations of this scale as described above stem from its basis in theory which has emerged from research focused primarily on White men. This focus does not render the scale irrelevant for women and minorities, but does perhaps overlook developmental tasks that are important for the excluded groups.

REVIEWER'S REFERENCES

Chickering, A. W. (1969). *Education and identity*. San Francisco: Jossey-Bass.

Chickering, A. W., & Havighurst, R. J. (1981). The life cycle. In A. W. Chickering (Ed.), *The modern American college: Responding to the new realities of diverse students and a changing society*. San Francisco: Jossey-Bass.

Review of the Student Developmental Task and Lifestyle Inventory by WILLIAM D. PORTERFIELD, Academic Coordinator and Adjunct Assistant Professor of Educational Administration, Commission on Interprofessional Education and Practice, The Ohio State University, Columbus, OH:

The Student Developmental Task and Lifestyle Inventory (SDTLI) is a revision of the Student Developmental Task Inventory—2 published by Winston, Miller, and Prince in 1979. The SDTLI (1987) is intended for use with traditional college age students (17–24 years old) to provide a snapshot of their developmental accomplishments in areas of Establishing and Clarifying Purpose, Developing Mature Interpersonal Relationships, and Developing Academic Autonomy. Scores are also obtained for a Salubrious Lifestyle Scale, a Response Bias Scale, and an experimental Intimacy Scale. The authors note a number of uses for the instrument in the college setting including individual counseling, student development research, and programming.

The theoretical base for the SDTLI is derived from A. W. Chickering's study of college students (1969) and Chickering and Havighurst's (1981) revision of the earlier research. Chickering outlines seven vectors of student development. The vectors of development consist of patterns of attitudes and behaviors that seem to be consistent among college students. The SDTLI, thus, has a solid and identifiable theoretical base, and represents a major accomplishment in translating some of Chickering's (1969) ideas into educational practice.

The authors note that the instrument is contextually based in middle class values, and attempt to note the basic values that are inherent in the instrument. This, in the reviewer's opinion, is a valuable statement of limitations of the instrument, as well as an excellent statement for researchers and educators considering using the instrument with various populations and campuses.

The instrument consists of 140 items to which respondents mark whether the item is true or false within the context of their personal experiences. The instrument is self-scoring through use of a carbon sheet between the answer sheet and the score sheet. The instrument takes approximately 25 to 30 minutes to complete. Thus, in terms of administration and scoring, the instrument should receive high marks for efficiency and cost effectiveness to the user.

The package of materials includes an extensive manual with descriptions of the developmental tasks and scales. Additionally, the manual includes extensive normative data for use in interpreting scores. Current normative data are based on respondents from 20 colleges and universities in the United States and Canada. An extensive treatment of reliability and validity estimates is also included in the manual. The manual is professionally presented, and achieves a balance in content between the interests of the potential researcher and the practitioner. The manual is easily read and interpreted.

The manual also discusses the significance of data on racial ethnic backgrounds, age, and gender. This is a strength of the research on the SDTLI as well as the manual. Clearly, continued research on the differences in student development across these groups is needed, and the SDTLI authors are sensitive to this need in their own research, and in the presentation of their results. Appropriate cautions about the generalizability of test results are noted throughout the manual.

The package of materials on the SDTLI also includes a Guide for Students. This six-page worksheet assists students in understanding their tests, the results of their tests, and offers concrete suggestions for facilitating their own growth. This makes the instrument and the packet of materials very attractive for programmers and counselors in higher education.

In summary, the SDTLI represents a solid research effort geared toward college students aged 17–24. Additionally, the research effort has a definitive theoretical base. The instrument is effective and efficient in terms of administration and scoring. The manual is detailed in terms of interpretation of results, and as a general guide for higher education practitioners. Limitations and potential uses of the instrument are stated with clarity. A reviewer of the instrument manual could, based on the data presented, make judgments about the relative utility of the materials in research and programming. The instruments and materials are reasonably priced.

The SDTLI is a useful and efficient instrument for higher education practitioners involved in working with traditional college-aged students. It is also a useful tool for further research with college students. This instrument could be valuable to graduate programs as a teaching tool, and to graduate students as one of the more valid and reliable measures of Chickering's vectors of college student development.

REVIEWER'S REFERENCES

Chickering, A. W. (1969). *Education and identity*. San Francisco: Jossey-Bass.
Chickering, A. W., & Havighurst, R. J. (1981). The life cycle. In A. W. Chickering and Associates (Eds.), *The modern American college: Responding to the new realities of diverse students and a changing society*. San Francisco: Jossey-Bass.

[385]
Student Opinion Inventory, Revised Edition.

Purpose: To assess students' opinions concerning many facets of the school and to "solicit students' recommendations for improvement."
Population: Secondary school students.
Publication Dates: 1974–88.
Scores: 6 subscales: Student Involvement, Student/Teacher Relations, Student/Counselor Relations, Student/Administration Relations, Curriculum/Instruction, School Image.
Administration: Group.
Parts, 2: A (Likert-scale items), B (open-ended items regarding recommendations).
Price Data, 1991: $6.50 per 50 inventories (Part A); $4.50 per 50 inventories (Part B); $5 per 50 machine-scored answer sheets; $3 per manual ('88, 12 pages).

Time: (35–40) minutes.
Author: National Study of School Evaluation.
Publisher: National Study of School Evaluation.
Cross References: See T3:2335 (1 reference).

[386]
Student Referral Checklist.

Purpose: Assesses behavioral and emotional signs of developmental or emotional problems.
Population: Grades K–6, 7–12.
Publication Date: 1988.
Scores: Unscored.
Administration: Individual.
Levels, 2: Grades K–6, Jr.–Sr. High.
Manual: No manual.
Price Data, 1989: $17.95 per 50 checklists (specify level).
Time: Administration time not reported.
Comments: Reliability and validity data not reported; problems checklist.
Author: John A. Schinka.
Publisher: Psychological Assessment Resources, Inc.

Review of the Student Referral Checklist by AYRES G. D'COSTA, Associate Professor of Education, The Ohio State University, Columbus, OH:

This is a set of two problem Checklists (one for children in grades K–6, and the other for adolescents in junior and senior high), which the author indicated were based on his own clinical practice. Each Checklist provides "a list of behavioral and emotional signs which may be important indicators of developmental or emotional problems" (See DIRECTIONS box on cover page of the Checklists).

The Checklist for Grades K–6 has 184 items organized under the following nine categories: Emotions, Self-Concept/Self-Esteem, Peer Relations, General School Attitude, Motor Skills/Activity Level, Language and Cognition, Behavioral Style, Moral Development, and Health and Habits. Space is also provided to write in Additional Problems. The Checklist for Jr-Sr High has 179 items with identical categories, but with slight variations in the items (behavioral signs) listed in each category. The directions suggest that the Checklists are completed by a referring school teacher and forwarded to another school professional. Items are checkmarked if relevant, and circled if most significant.

In a personal communication with the author, this reviewer understood that the Student Referral Checklist is not intended to be used as a test. There is no manual, no scoring system, no scale scores, nor any theoretical/psychometric basis for thinking of the nine categories as scales. Indeed the author questioned that his Checklists should even be reviewed in the *Mental Measurements Yearbook* as a test. A cover sheet to the Checklists cautions the user of this fact, but there is no such caution on the Checklist itself. This reviewer received the Checklists without the cover sheet. Users should be aware that some other checklists are indeed viewed as tests and reviewed in the *Mental Measurements Yearbook* as such.

The author does not claim any theoretical basis for his Checklists, nor is any psychometric or practice-relevant guide available to users from the author/publisher. Users are accordingly advised that they use these Checklists at their own risk. The fact that these Checklists are published suggests that they may have some clinical utility, although there is no evidence of this forthcoming from the author/publisher, nor is assistance available to new users from existing or old users.

Having seen other problem checklists of this type at various levels of psychometric development, this reviewer reiterates the author's caution that his Checklists not be viewed as tests. Even their use in clinical practice needs extreme caution given the lack of theoretical basis. Authors and publishers of this and similar checklists should consider the wisdom of publishing such instruments prior to assessing appropriate psychometric information. At the very least, publishers should place an appropriate caution on the instrument to inform users of the intended use of the checklist.

[387]
Study Habits Evaluation and Instruction Kit.

Purpose: "To identify the areas of weakness in study habits that individual students have, and to provide students with a means of improving their study habits."
Population: New Zealand secondary school students (Forms 4–6).
Publication Date: 1979.
Acronym: SHEIK.
Scores, 7: The Place of Study, Study Times, Organization for Study, Textbook Reading Skills, Taking Notes, Studying for Examinations, Examination Technique.
Administration: Group.
Price Data: Available from publisher.
Time: (30–40) minutes.
Comments: Self-administered; self-scored.
Authors: Peter F. Jackson, Neil A. Reid, and A. Cedric Croft.
Publisher: New Zealand Council for Educational Research [New Zealand].

Review of the Study Habits Evaluation and Instruction Kit by SANDRA L. CHRISTENSON, Associate Professor of Educational Psychology, University of Minnesota, Minneapolis, MN:

The Study Habits Evaluation and Instruction Kit (SHEIK) is self-administered and self-scored by secondary school students for the purposes of identifying areas of weakness in study habits and suggesting ways to improve study habits. The SHEIK comprises the Inventory Study Habits and seven instructional lessons. The kit is an inventory, not a test; therefore, it is commendable that information is provided related to construction, standardization, norming procedures, reliability, and validity. However, limited information is provided on specific characteristics of the standardization sample, resulting in questions about the usefulness of the norms. Normative data are restricted to New Zealand secondary school students.

The seven areas examined by the inventory, Place of Study, Study Times, Organization for Study, Textbook Reading Skills, Taking Notes, Studying for Examinations, and Examination Techniques, have good face validity. In addition, internal consistency estimates of reliability for each scale are adequate, and obtained intercorrelations for the seven scales of the inventory suggest the scales are sufficiently independent dimensions. Reported criterion-validity data indicate that the relationship between achievement and the behaviors sampled by the Inventory of Study Habits is explained by more than mental ability.

The reliability and validity of the inventory are adequate. Although group use of the SHEIK is possible, users should note that the inventory is designed to be self-administered and interpreted by the student. Student motivation and well-developed reading skills may be prerequisites for successful student use of the inventory. For many students, direction from and interaction with teachers may be essential in order to accurately complete and interpret the inventory. The inventory may not be informative or helpful for students who are most in need of study skills instruction.

A global strength of the kit is its focus on an assessment-intervention link. Seven instructional units, corresponding to each area examined, are provided in the kit. Students are provided with information to improve study habits in each of seven areas by reading a three- to four-page lesson, completing a review exercise that highlights salient points, and engaging in a class discussion. Users should be aware that the information provided in each instructional unit is very general. The empirical basis for the content of the instructional unit is not provided. In addition, there is no application of the skills to course content materials nor a discussion of metacognitive approaches to study skills. The instructional material, if not supplemented by teachers, may at most inform students of what areas are important in developing good study skills. Without supplemental materials, it is unclear whether students would apply the information to completion of school assignments.

The SHEIK is adequate for introducing students to the basics of study skills; however, it is very limited as a study skills instructional program. The Study Habits Evaluation and Instruction Kit was published one decade ago, which may explain its lack of inclusion of more recent research on approaches to study skills, application of skills to existing course content, and use of learning strategies.

Review of the Study Habits Evaluation and Instruction Kit by KENNETH A. KIEWRA, Associate Professor of Educational Psychology, University of Nebraska-Lincoln, Lincoln, NE:

Study skill training is being implemented in increasing numbers of secondary schools. A problem is that few secondary school personnel are trained in evaluating students' current skills or in developing and implementing a program to increase study skill proficiency. Fortunately, there are several evaluation and instruction programs marketed for these purposes. This review describes and critiques one such secondary school program called the Study Habits Evaluation and Instruction Kit (SHEIK).

The SHEIK has two objectives—the identification of weaknesses in study habits and improvement in study habits. The kit includes an Inventory of Study Habits to meet the first objective, and Instructional Units to meet the second objective. The materials are intended for group or individual use. I will discuss the Inventory and Instructional Units, in turn, before making concluding comments.

INVENTORY OF STUDY HABITS. The Inventory consists of a reusable Item Booklet and a consumable booklet that combines a Response Sheet, Marking Key, and Profile Sheet. The Item Booklet contains seven, 25-item, self-report scales, each assessing a different aspect of studying. The seven scales are as follows:

1. The Place of Study: The physical conditions under which studying is done.

2. Study Times: The time of day and amount of time associated with studying.

3. Organization of Study: The efficient organization of study time.

4. Textbook Reading Skills: The use of skills involved in effective reading.

5. Taking Notes: The practice of taking notes from text or lectures.

6. Studying for Examinations: The methods used and time spent studying for exams.

7. Examination Technique: The techniques used during examinations.

Students mark their responses on the Response Sheet. The response mode for all items consists of five choices ranging from "never or almost never" to "always or almost always." As students mark the Response Sheet, their responses show through onto the Marking Key on the opposite side of the page indicating a score of 0, 1, or 2 for each item. Students are instructed to total these numbers within each scale and arrive at a raw score ranging from 0–50. Students then enter the seven raw scores onto the Profile Sheet. This enables them to compare

their performance with the performance of other students at that grade level by using percentile ranks. The norms used in these comparisons are based on results from a total of about 1,500 randomly selected students in grades 10, 11, and 12 from 30 secondary schools in New Zealand. The schools were selected to represent schools differing with respect to location, size, and type. Students can also use provided *t*-scores from the Profile Sheet to compare their relative performance on the various scales. This helps them to see their area(s) of greatest need. The authors state that students can self-administer the Inventory within a 40-minute period. It is unclear, however, whether that time estimate includes the activities of marking answers and interpreting results.

RELIABILITY AND VALIDITY OF THE INVENTORY. The internal consistency of the Inventory was calculated using both split-half and Kuder-Richardson Formula 8 (KR-8) estimates. Both estimates showed that the Inventory was reliable with coefficients ranging from .75 to .88 for the split-half estimates, and from .77 to .90 for the KR-8 estimates.

The authors did not calculate test-retest reliability. Therefore, nothing is known about the stability of scores. Without this information, it would be unwise to administer the Inventory prior to and following instruction, and to then assume that performance changes on the Inventory were the result of instruction.

The validity of each scale of the Inventory was calculated against a composite score of four subtests on the School Certificate exam for 11th and 12th grade students. All correlations between the scales and the criteria were significant at the .01 level. When both Inventory scale scores and a standardized measure of intelligence were used to predict performance on the composite subtests of the School Certificate Exam, results indicated that the Inventory scale scores measured behaviors related to the composite score beyond that measured by general intelligence.

Subscale correlations were also calculated to determine the degree of interdependence among the subscales. Ideally, test constructors want specific scales to measure relatively independent behaviors. Results, however, indicated that scores from each scale correlated significantly ($p < .01$) with each of the other scale scores. Intercorrelations between individual scale scores and total score were not reported. These data suggest that individual scales might not measure the particular study habit(s) they purport to measure.

DEVELOPMENT OF THE INVENTORY. The original Inventory was modeled after and adapted from existing inventories. How it is different is not addressed. It was field tested using approximately

1,500 secondary students throughout New Zealand. At each administration, the students' teachers provided information on the overall academic achievement of each student. This information was used to select items that discriminated between high and low achievers. The final items were then reviewed by guidance counselors or counseling trainers and final revisions (that are unspecified) were made.

There are several problems associated with development. First, initial item construction was not apparently tied to any theoretically or empirically based model of studying. For example, the Inventory does not tap whether students process information at a surface level or more generative level (Wittrock, 1974), whether students make internal and external connections while studying (Mayer, 1984), or whether they are motivated (Nolan & Haladyna, in press) or behave metacognitively (Flavell, 1981).

A second problem concerns the faulty logic used to select items. Items that discriminated between high and low achievers were retained. However, it was never established to what degree high achievers were successful because of their study habits. It is possible that high achievement occurred not because of effective study habits, but in spite of them. High achievement was perhaps more the result of high intelligence, knowledge, or motivation. Some studies, in fact, show that high achievers are not at all strategic (Thomas & Rowher, 1986).

A third problem is that Inventory items were reviewed solely by people affiliated with guidance counseling. My hunch is that training for these people in learning theory, in general, and study skills, in particular, is quite limited. The Inventory should also be validated by experts in Psychology and Educational Psychology who are focused on learning and cognition as they apply to studying.

INSTRUCTIONAL UNITS. The Instructional Units, which can also be used in groups or individually, consist of seven reusable booklets with the same names as the comparable scales of the Inventory. Each is three or four pages long and provides topical advice, in a didactic manner, under a series of convenient headings and subheadings. The booklets seem well written, age appropriate, organized, and interesting. Often, they contain illustrations and graphics that facilitate learning.

Accompanying each instructional booklet is a one-page (front and back) Review Section intended to summarize the lesson and to help the students to evaluate their learning. Part I of each Review Section contains a paragraph about the topic containing approximately 25 blank spaces for the student to complete. One limitation of this exercise is that many of the blanks can be completed without ever having studied the material. For example, "Homework and revision *should* be done when you are

alert." Therefore, this exercise is more for the purpose of review than self-testing.

Part II presents a problem for students to solve such as "Develop a personal study time plan for a normal school week." Suggested responses for both Parts I and II are provided on the back of each Review Sheet.

My general impression of the instructional materials is that they are superficially presented and the content is outdated. With respect to the breadth of the materials, techniques and strategies are presented in almost a laundry list fashion. Students are given little conditional knowledge for understanding how and why the strategies are effective, nor about potential applications. Research has shown that conditional knowledge is an important component of strategy instruction (e.g., Paris & Jacobs, 1984).

Several important and contemporary ideas are absent from the instructional materials. Students using these materials would not be trained to do the following: orchestrate strategies such as note taking and review; identify knowledge patterns and text structures; represent information in spatial forms such as hierarchies, sequences, and matrices; relate new information to prior knowledge; study differentially for various types of learning tasks (i.e., declarative knowledge, procedural knowledge); increase self-motivation; self-monitor performance; conduct error analysis.

CONCLUSION. The materials are sleek, easy to use, and might even be somewhat helpful to those who can pick up a helpful study hint or two in a short time with little effort. For the most part though, they are hollow. They offer minimal knowledge about the learning system, few effective strategies, and virtually no opportunity to practice skills. Procedural skills such as reading, note taking, and reviewing require considerable practice. Furthermore, The SHEIK is neither empirically founded nor empirically tested. There is no evidence demonstrating that students achieve higher in school because of this program.

REVIEWER'S REFERENCES

Wittrock, M. C. (1974). Learning as a generative process. *Educational Psychologist, 11*, 87-95.

Flavell, J. H. (1981). Cognitive monitoring. In W. P. Dickson (Ed.), *Children's oral communication skills*. New York: Academic Press.

Mayer, R. E. (1984). Aids to text comprehension. *Educational Psychologist, 19*, 30-42.

Paris, S. G., & Jacobs, J. E. (1984). The benefits of informed instruction for children's reading awareness and comprehension skills. *Child Development, 55*, 2083-2093.

Thomas, J. W., & Rohwer, W. D. (1986). Academic studying: The role of learning strategies. *Educational Psychologist, 21*, 19-41.

Nolan, S. B., & Haladyna, T. M. (in press). Motivation and studying in high school science. *Journal of Research in Science Teaching*.

[388]

Study of Children's Learning Behaviors, Research Edition.

Purpose: Identifies dysfunctional learning behaviors for an early assessment of how a child will perform academically.

Population: Prekindergarten to grade 4.
Publication Dates: 1981–88.
Acronym: SCLB.
Comments: Adaptation of the Preliminary Guide to the Child's Learning Skills; manual title is Learning Behaviors Scale and Study of Children's Learning Behaviors; ratings by teachers; manual also used with the Learning Behaviors Scale (LBS) (199).
Scores, 4: Inattentive, Avoidant, Overly Independent, Total.
Administration: Individual.
Price Data, 1990: $36 per complete kit including 5 SCLB and 5 LBS Ready-Score™ questionnaires and manual ('88, 113 pages); $29 per 25 Ready-Score™ questionnaires; $24 per manual.
Time: (1–2) minutes per child.
Authors: Denis H. Stott, Paul A. McDermott, Leonard F. Green, and Jean M. Francis.
Publisher: The Psychological Corporation.

TEST REFERENCES

1. Glutting, J. J., Kelly, M. S., Boehm, A. E., & Burnett, T. R. (1989). Stability and predictive validity of the Boehm Test of Basic Concepts—Revised among black kindergarteners. *Journal of School Psychology, 27,* 365-371.

Review of the Study of Children's Learning Behaviors, Research Edition by DALE P. SCANNELL, Professor and Dean, College of Education, University of Maryland at College Park, College Park, MD:

The Study of Children's Learning Behaviors, Research Edition (SCLB) is an inventory of 16 statements descriptive of possible children's behaviors in learning situations. The inventory can be completed by any adult who knows a child well but normally would be used by a child's teacher. The rater judges whether each of the statements usually applies, sometimes applies, or does not apply to the child being rated and circles the dot corresponding to the appropriate descriptor. The form has features of a self-scoring answer sheet with the key preprinted on the back of the rating form. The authors recommend that scoring be done by a school psychologist or someone with training in assessment.

Although not specified in the manual, it would seem the rating would be done usually with the subject not present and at the convenience of the rater. The authors recommend the teacher be given an opportunity to become familiar with the items on the rating scale and then have ample opportunity to observe the child before doing the ratings. A minimum of 50 days is recommended. The teacher is to rate the child on the basis of typical behaviors, not the behaviors during a specific learning task.

The manual for this instrument is well done. The organization is appropriate, with early chapters presenting discussions of how the inventory is to be administered and scored and how the results can be interpreted and used. The following chapters discuss development and standardization, reliability and factor structure, and information related to validity. The manual is easily read, and the information presented is relevant and comprehensive.

The derived scores for the test are linear standard scores with a mean of 50 and standard deviation of 10, called *T*-scores by the authors. Four separate conversion tables are provided for prekindergarten, kindergarten, grades 1–2, and grades 3–4. The authors indicate that raw score distributions are skewed, with the heavy concentration at the "good" end of the scale, and with 5% at the highest end classified as serious risk, and 10% classified as at-risk. The authors assert they wished to preserve the shape of the raw score distribution. This seems to be defensible because the diagnostic focus of the test is limited to those children with dysfunctional learning behaviors.

Two criteria were used to select items. First, both positive and negative statements had to be included. Second, the items had to describe actual behaviors. The authors met the first criterion by having eight positive and eight negative statements; score values are reversed for these groups of items so as to have a unidimensional, additive scale. Relative to the second criterion, most of the statements are descriptions of behavior. However, two items use the term, "is willing," thus requiring some inference based on what is observable. The tryout items were developed initially from a review of literature on behavior rating instruments and final selection was based on factor analyses.

The standardization sample included 2,036 children, about half and half boys and girls, ranging from 158 at the prekindergarten level to 1,513 in kindergarten. The sample represented 93 different classrooms. From data presented in the manual, one would infer that the number of teacher-raters was 9 for prekindergarten, 67 in kindergarten, 9 in grades 1 and 2, and 8 in grades 3 and 4. The child is the unit of analysis for technical studies even though the ratings were made by a markedly smaller number of teachers. Although the total sample represents geographic diversity, the samples for the various groups are geographically homogeneous.

As noted in the descriptive entry above, four scores are reported, for three dysfunctional learning dimensions and the total. Most of the technical data were presented for the four different scores, with an emphasis at the kindergarten level where the test may be most often used.

Internal consistency reliabilities average .91 for the three scales across grade levels and .94 for the total score. Test-retest reliabilities with a 2-week interval range from .70 to .88. Correlations between the ratings of two teachers for 76 children were about .80 except for the overly independent score which was .60. Factor analyses of all standardization samples produced similar results, with three factors present in all analyses. The rotated three-factor solution for the kindergarten sample accounted for 66% of item variance, and similar results were obtained in the other samples. Items loaded differently across samples and some items loaded on more than one factor. Scoring reflects the latter finding.

The chapter on validity presents comprehensive evidence. Initial empirical studies were done with the Preliminary Guide to the Child's Learning Skills, the precursor of this test. The information reported for the SCLB includes studies of relationships with measures of general intelligence and social adjustment, indicating a variance overlap of 14.3% for intelligence and 25.3% for social adjustment. These correlations, then, would be .38 and .50, respectively. The chapter also cites studies on the predictive power of the SCLB with achievement test scores and teacher grades used as criterion measures. Similar information on concurrent validity is presented. The final section describes evidence of discriminate validity. The data reported support the observation that the SCLB is a useful test providing unique information that should be helpful to teachers and school counselors.

The SCLB is an instrument that is easy to use, relatively easy to score, based on a strong rationale, and presented with a very good and useful manual. This test clearly meets commonly accepted standards for psychometric instruments.

[389]

Study Process Questionnaire.
Purpose: "To assess the extent to which a tertiary student at college or university endorses different approaches to learning and the more important motives and strategies comprising those approaches."
Population: College students.
Publication Dates: 1985–87.
Acronym: SPQ.
Scores, 10: Surface Motive, Surface Strategy, Deep Motive, Deep Strategy, Achieving Motive, Achieving Strategy, Surface Approach, Deep Approach, Achieving Approach, Deep-Achieving Approach.
Administration: Individual or group.
Price Data, 1989: A$4.85 per 10 questionnaires, $2.50 per 10 answer sheets; $3 per score key; $29.95 per monograph entitled *Student Approaches to Learning and Studying* ('87, 151 pages); $13.20 per manual ('87, 44 pages).
Time: 20(40) minutes.
Comments: Secondary counterpart of the Learning Process Questionnaire (202).
Author: John Biggs.
Publisher: Australian Council for Educational Research Ltd. [Australia].
Cross References: For a review by Robert D. Brown of both the Learning Process Questionnaire and the Study Process Questionnaire and a review by Cathy W. Hall of the Learning Process Questionnaire, see 202.

TEST REFERENCES

1. Watkins, D., Hattie, J., & Astilla, E. (1986). Approaches to studying by Filipino students: A longitudinal investigation. *British Journal of Educational Psychology, 56*, 357-362.
2. Miller, C. D., Finley, J., & McKinley, D. L. (1990). Learning approaches and motives: Male and female differences and implications for learning assistance programs. *Journal of College Student Development, 31*, 147-154.

Review of the Study Process Questionnaire by CATHY W. HALL, Assistant Professor of Psychology, East Carolina University, Greenville, NC:

The Study Process Questionnaire (SPQ) is a 42-item, self-report questionnaire that measures process factors involved in learning strategies and learning motives with tertiary students. (There is an accompanying questionnaire, Learning Process Questionnaire [LPQ], for use with secondary students.) Biggs (1987) points out that the three motives and strategies are likely to lead to different levels of learning. The surface approach is likely to lead to the accurate but unintegrated recall of information for a brief period of time in order to meet minimal requirements. The deep approach leads to the greatest structural complexity and is motivated by need to pursue personal interests in a particular area. Finally, the achieving approach is seen when a student is motivated to do well and employs a strategy that is likely to lead to whatever goals are necessary to achieve high grades. Problems may arise when there is a discrepancy between a student's motive and strategy regarding a particular subject, or when a student's approach is not in line with the requirements of a course of study. The SPQ provides a way of assessing these areas in order to make an instructional decision and/or a decision to refer the student for academic counseling.

Three primary learning approaches are measured (surface, deep, and achieving) with each factor having two subscales consisting of motives and strategies. Nine scores are possible given the three motives, three strategies, and three approaches. In addition to these nine scores, an additional score is possible for a Deep-Achieving Approach which combines the salient aspects of the deep *and* achieving processes. Biggs (1987) also discusses a Surface-Achieving Approach, but norming data are not provided for this approach. The range of scores is 7 to 35 for each of the motive and strategy subscales. Scoring for the SPQ may be done by hand, machine, computer, or by sending the protocols to the Australian Council for Educational Research.

The SPQ was standardized on an Australian population of 2,402 subjects at five universities and ten colleges (Centers for Advanced Education—CAEs). Subjects were not chosen on a random basis, as with the LPQ, and the author notes this limitation. Norm tables are provided in the manual for males and females scores, universities and CAEs, and further broken down into Arts, Education, and Science disciplines. Subject representation in each of these groups is limited and variable and represents a significant problem of this assessment device.

Reliability and validity data are presented for the SPQ. Test-retest information was not available due to the sampling restrictions. Internal consistency data demonstrated satisfactory results as reported in the manual with a range of .51 to .85. Construct validity specific to the SPQ was assessed by utilizing students' self-rated performance, satisfaction with performance, and future education goals. Correlations with actual performance (grade-point average—GPA) were obtained in a study conducted by Watkins and Hattie (1981) and were supportive of the SPQ.

The manual does not provide information on minority representation, subject age, demographic variables, or socioeconomic variables. However, a detailed account of these variables can be found in *Student Approaches to Learning and Studying* (Biggs, 1987). In addition to the above, Biggs' text offers detailed information concerning theoretical development, relevant research, and implications of the SPQ.

Use of the SPQ outside Australia should be done with the understanding that the norms are limited and more information is needed on the utilization of these learning approaches in an educational setting. Research has indicated that other factors, such as ability to understand and use language effectively, may also need to be taken into consideration when interpreting the SPQ (Wilson, 1987).

The SPQ provides a promising research tool for the assessment of learning approaches and studying the development of metacognition. If administered outside Australia, additional factor analyses and normative data would be helpful and informative. The author addresses the limitations and the need for future research with this instrument in his text. The manual is far from comprehensive, however, and it is strongly recommended that anyone choosing to adopt the SPQ also acquire the text— *Student Approaches to Learning and Studying* (Biggs, 1987).

REVIEWER'S REFERENCES

Watkins, D., & Hattie, J. (1981). The learning processes of Australian university students: Investigations of contextual and personological factors. *British Journal of Educational Psychology, 51*, 384-393.
Biggs, J. (1987). *Student Approaches to Learning and Studying.* Melbourne: Australian Council for Educational Research Ltd.
Wilson, A. (1987). Approaches to learning among third world tertiary science students: Papua New Guinea. *Research in Science & Technological Education, 5* (1), 59-67.

[390]

Style of Learning and Thinking.

Purpose: To indicate a student's learning strategy and brain hemisphere preference in problem solving.
Population: Grades K–5, 6–12.
Publication Date: 1988.
Acronym: SOLAT.
Scores, 3: Whole Brain, Left Brain, Right Brain.
Administration: Group.
Forms, 2: Elementary, Youth.
Price Data, 1988: $28 per 35 tests (specify Elementary or Youth Form); $10 per Administrator's manual (46 pages); $15 per specimen set including manual and 1 each Elementary and Youth Form questionnaires.
Time: [30–40] minutes.
Comments: Self-scored.
Author: E. Paul Torrance.
Publisher: Scholastic Testing Service, Inc.

TEST REFERENCES

1. Torrance, E. P. (1987). Some evidence regarding development of cerebral lateralization. *Perceptual and Motor Skills, 64* (1), 261-262.
2. Beer, J. (1988). Hemispheric dominance inferred from Your Style of Learning and Thinking on reports of Necker cube reversals and maze learning. *Perceptual and Motor Skills, 66*, 887-890.

Review of the Style of Learning and Thinking by KENNETH A. KIEWRA, Associate Professor of Educational Psychology, University of Nebraska-Lincoln, Lincoln, NE, and DAMIAN McSHANE, Associate Professor of Psychology, Utah State University, Logan, UT:

The Style of Learning and Thinking (SOLAT) is an inventory for determining a student's brain hemisphere preference (left, right, or integrative) and associated learning style in problem solving. Its purpose, although not stated, is probably to help educators assist students in identifying their brain hemisphere/learning style profile and in planning solutions for strengthening their profile. Below, the materials are briefly described and three basic assumptions are presented that must be met in order to support the use of the SOLAT.

DESCRIPTION OF MATERIALS. There are two SOLAT forms: the Elementary Form intended for first through fifth grade students, and the Youth Form intended for students in grades 6 through 12. Both forms can be administered in classroom-size groups, although it is suggested that first graders be tested in smaller groups. The Elementary Form contains 25 items and the Youth Form contains 28 items. In both forms, items present a pair of statements and the student is directed to place a check mark next to one of them, both of them, or neither of them based on how the statements "fit" the responder. For each item, one statement purportedly describes a behavior representative of left-brain dominance (e.g., "I like to get to work and not be silly," or "I think well when I sit straight up"), whereas the other statement supposedly describes a behavior representative of right-brain dominance (e.g., "I like to be silly and play around" or "I think well lying down on my back"). The student who marks both statements from a pair is said to be integrative and functioning from a whole-brain perspective. People who are left-brain dominant purportedly display learning styles associated with conformity, organization, logic, detail, and verbal processing. People who are right-brain dominant are supposedly more nonconforming, explorative, intuitive, global, and spatially oriented.

As students mark the test sheet their responses are recorded onto an answer key through carbon paper. The answer key has designated each statement as indicative of left- (L) or right-brain (R) dominance. A student simply totals the number of Ls, the number of Rs, and the number where both statements were checked—whole-brained (W). (The number of items for which neither statement was checked is not totalled.) These three scores are entered respectively onto three raw score scales. A vertical line is then drawn through each point so that it crosses a standard score scale above these scales and a percentile scale below. Students then estimate their standard and percentile scores. Finally, the raw, standard, and percentile scores for left, right, and whole are entered onto a chart to aid interpretation.

BASIC ASSUMPTIONS GOVERNING THE USE OF THE SOLAT. We think that there are three assumptions that govern the use of the SOLAT. These are that (*a*) the left and right hemispheres of the brain are uniformly responsible for different thoughts and behaviors; (*b*) SOLAT is a reliable and valid instrument; and (*c*) learning styles instruction should be developed to support, compensate for, or facilitate individual learning styles.

The assumption that the left and right hemispheres of the brain are uniformly responsible for certain types of thoughts and behaviors is not well supported (e.g., Bradshaw & Nettlton, 1983). Most neuroscientists dismiss the popularized idea of simple left- and right-brain lateralization, and favor a view suggesting a more complex functional model that includes neural networks spanning multiple regions of the brain. PET scan studies, for example, show major involvement by multiple regions of the brain, spanning the left and right regions, in both simple and complex tasks. Furthermore, even if one attempted to categorize thoughts and behaviors by regions of the brain in a gross fashion, then a left-right distinction is still too simplistic. The posterior and anterior regions of the brain are generally associated with certain thoughts and behaviors such as initial processing of visual stimuli and complex thinking, respectively.

The second assumption deals with the reliability and validity of the SOLAT. *Reliability* data are surprisingly limited (or unreported). The manual reports a single estimate of reliability for the Elementary Form based on 129 sets of responses (Cronbach alpha was .77 for the Left Scale, and .73 for the Right Scale) and a single estimate for the Youth Form based on the responses of 441 eighth graders (Cronbach alpha was .77 for the Left Scale, and .74 for the Right Scale). Also limited are data on test-retest reliability. Data on the Elementary Form are based on 41 elementary students, (grade level[s] unspecified), whereas the Youth Form is based on the scores from 106 high school students (grade level[s] unspecified). Product-moment reliability coefficients were .74 (L), .61 (R), and .67

(W) for the elementary students, and .73 (L), .57 (R), and .47 (W) for the high school students. All reliability data are unpublished. Overall, these data generally support the SOLAT's reliability. Additional tests by grade level, however, are warranted particularly at the elementary school level.

With respect to *content validity* there is very little clinical or research support (Bradshaw & Nettlton, 1983; Bryden, 1982; Geschwind & Galaburda, 1987) for the proposition that SOLAT items are related to and/or differentiate particular hemisphere-specific, lateralized functions. In addition, a multiple-choice, self-report, paper-and-pencil format cannot control for "attentional," pre-existing "set," and "activation" variables that affect hemisphere lateralized response tendencies.

With respect to *construct validity*, the author reports roughly 40 studies showing that performance on the SOLAT is related to certain characteristics such as visual and verbal learning styles, and to group affiliation such as artists, musicians, and the gifted. One limitation of these studies is that the bulk of them are in relation to the right subscale only. Groups as varying as the gifted, psychologists, coaches, underachievers, elementary students, and students with behavior problems all scored high on the right subscale. It is difficult to integrate findings showing that measurement students scored high on the left subscale, whereas educational psychology students (who are very similar) scored high on the right subscale; or why public administrators scored high on the right subscale, whereas business students scored high on the left subscale; or why both gifted/honors students and underachievers scored high on the right subscale.

Serious questions arise concerning the *concurrent validity* of the SOLAT when the few studies using widely accepted techniques and measures are examined. The only study using dichotic listening found no significant relationships with SOLAT scores. Another study using conjugate lateral eye movements (CLEM) found no significant relationships, and a second study using CLEM found no relationship to right or whole-brain subscales and only a small correlation with the left subscale.

Much more troubling are results of the study with the Differential Aptitude Test (DAT) which showed Verbal Reasoning, Abstract Reasoning, and Spelling subtest scores significantly correlated with the right subscale and not the left as would be expected given the nature of these subtests. Conversely, Numerical and Mechanical Reasoning subtest scores correlated with the left subscale, not the right. Similar confusion results from the finding that the Armed Services Vocational Aptitude Clerical Composite score is negatively correlated with the left subscale, contrary to expectations based on the constructs involved.

The author does not try to resolve the contradiction inherent in the finding that while three visual-spatial tests were found to correlate positively with the right subscale, the Bender-Gestalt was negatively correlated with the right subscale. Finally, whereas right-hemisphere-specific contributions to reading and math performance have been widely published, the SOLAT right subscale is negatively correlated with Stanford Achievement Tests in reading and math.

In summary, while the author emphasizes the left-brain orientation of educational systems, the most robust findings are that an incredibly diverse set of populations score higher on the right subscale, and that most of the relationships with subtest scores on other instruments and measures are in relation to the right subscale. In fact, some of the language-based, left-hemisphere-oriented subscales on other measures are correlated positively with the right subscale, raising serious questions about content and construct validity, regardless of the SOLAT's internal consistency.

Even had the SOLAT met the previous two assumptions we doubt that it has much of a place in school learning. We agree with the author that students should use a range of thinking in solving academic problems as well as personal and social ones. However, it is suggested that the link between these thinking styles and brain hemisphere preference is weak, misleading, and unnecessary.

Given that the ultimate objective of the SOLAT is to facilitate a range of thinking, it is on this ground that the materials are most inadequate. Surprisingly, little is said in the Administrator's Manual about interpretation or implications. With respect to interpretation, readers are told that "a standard score of 120 [the 84th percentile] may be regarded as identifying a dominant pattern," and that "some children may not have any dominant pattern." The manual suggests that teachers should help students to clarify fuzzy profiles by "wondering" along with them. The implications of the survey are not clear. Teachers are encouraged to help students to "select . . . the greatest weakness" from their profile, and have "time set aside for discussing improvement." How profiles can be improved is not addressed in the manual other than to say that students should "capitalize on their strengths, and to work towards a whole-brained kind of functioning."

For those still interested in using some instrument to measure brain hemisphere preference, we recommend Gordon's (1983) Cognitive Laterality Battery (CLB). It is a group-administered test that takes about an hour to administer. Although the use of a self-report instrument is still problematic, Horner and Freider (1989) found a significant relationship between the CLB and *extreme* responses on a cognitive style questionnaire.

REVIEWER'S REFERENCES

Bryden, M. P. (1982). *Laterality: Functional asymmetry in the intact brain.* New York: Academic Press.

Bradshaw, J. L., & Nettlton, N. C. (1983). *Human cerebral asymmetry.* Englewood Cliffs, NJ: Prentice Hall.

Gordon, H. W. (1983). Cognitive Laterality Battery. Pittsburgh, PA: University of Pittsburgh Western Psychiatric Institute and Clinic.

Geschwind, N., & Galaburda, A. M. (1987). *Cerebral lateralization.* Cambridge, MA: M.I.T. Press.

Horner, M. D., & Freider, D. (1989, February). The relationship between cognitive style and cognitive competency. Paper presented at the Seventeenth Annual Conference of the International Neuropsychological Society, Vancouver, BC.

Review of the Style of Learning and Thinking by DONALD U. ROBERTSON, *Professor of Psychology, and* VIRGINIA L. BROWN, *Director, Institute for Research and Community Service, Indiana University of Pennsylvania, Indiana, PA:*

According to the author, E. Paul Torrance, the Style of Learning and Thinking (SOLAT) was developed in response to the need to assist educators to utilize the rapidly expanding knowledge and new information related to specialized functioning of brain hemispheres. Specifically, Torrance asserts that recent research indicates the left and right cerebral hemispheres each have the following independent and specialized functions: The left hemisphere "seems to be the locus of logical, analytical, propositional thought" and is the center of most language, information ordering, and time sense; "the right hemisphere seems to be the locus of visuospatial and appositional thought and imagination," is nonverbal, and "makes itself known through dreams and fantasy." With respect to information processing, the left hemisphere is considered to be linear and sequential whereas the right hemisphere is nonlinear and capable of relating and associating information simultaneously. Early versions of the SOLAT were designed to tap these two cerebral functions in adults.

Unspecified "item analyses" of the adult SOLAT produced a 25-item Elementary Form for children in grades K to 5 (norms are provided for grades 1 to 5) and a 28-item Youth Form for grades 6 to 12. The adult version is now called the Human Information Processing Survey (10:144), and the SOLAT refers to the two versions for children and youth. Test items consist of a pair of statements; one statement is considered to reflect right cerebral hemispheric functioning, the other left hemisphere. Children are instructed to check the statement that is true of them and are permitted to check both or neither statement of each pair. Raw scores for the Right Brain scale are computed by adding the number of items for which only the right hemisphere statement was checked, the Left Brain score by summing the left only statements, and the Whole Brain score by summing the items for which both statements were checked. Although the test giver is cautioned to note the number of items for which no statements were checked, test scores are not affected by it. Because of this feature, the test in effect has a variable length. However, the transformation of raw scores to standard scores and percentiles does not take this into account. A child who completed only the first five items on the test and left the remainder blank could receive the same score on two of the three scales as a child who omitted no items.

Test-retest reliability (stability) coefficients and coefficient alpha are reported for both forms. Test-retest coefficients (10-week delay) for the Left, Right, and Whole Brain scales were .71, .61, and .67 for the Elementary Form and .73, .57, and .47 for the Youth Form (12-week delay). The test authors assert that "the reliabilities are satisfactory for this type of test." Although they may be satisfactory for the test, they are not satisfactory for use of the test with individual children in an attempt to identify learning style. Coefficient alphas were also relatively low: .77 and .73 for the Left and Right scales on the Elementary Form and .77 and .74 for the Youth Form.

Norms for the test are based on a large sample (4,315) of students in grades 1 through 12. The composition of the sample is not, however, well described. We are told the states from which the students came and the overall racial composition of the sample, but the distribution of these variables across grades is not given. No information about the gender composition of the sample, socioeconomic status, characteristics of the schools (e.g., urban or rural, large or small), or inclusion/exclusion criteria (were learning disabled children included?) was given. There are no norms for kindergarten children; the sample size of the first graders is small; and separate norms for males and females are not provided.

The test manual contains nearly seven pages of validity information, all of which was based on previous forms of the test and much of which is with adults. Four types of validity evidence were presented: content, construct, concurrent, and predictive. Torrance argues that these studies are relevant because the Youth and Elementary Form items came from the same item pool. In other words, the contention is that if we can demonstrate valid measurement of a construct in an adult population, then it is possible to use similar measurement procedures to assess the construct in children. Despite the assertion of a kind of validity generalization that probably should be demonstrated, the argument hinges on the construct validity of the original measures.

Although there are many ways of providing evidence that bears on the construct validity of a measurement, at a minimum one must clearly identify properties of the construct and rudimentary elements of the empirical relationships into which the construct should and should not enter. The construct validity evidence that is provided in the test manual consists of brief descriptions of about 30 studies that either compare groups such as gifted adolescents with norms or correlate the previous forms of the SOLAT with other paper-and-pencil tests (such as the What Kind of Person are You? test). This sort of cataloging of studies, although it may seem impressive to some, is not evidence of construct validity. Critical issues such as response sets, method variance, and discriminant validity are not mentioned.

The basic issue is what construct(s) is being measured and what are the empirical relationships entailed. Is this a measure of hemispheric dominance, hemispheric preference (and if so, what is that?), learning style, or personality traits? At times the author seems to suggest all of the above, creating the illusion that because there is some basic research which indicates hemispheric specialization that the SOLAT is measuring (a) a biologically based construct, that (b) results in individual differences in information processing, that (c) are related to the way children best learn, and (d) is reflected in behavioral preferences for activities such as lying on one's back or sitting up straight. The rather lengthy chain of hypotheses is not supported by data that consist of correlations between paper-and-pencil tests and group differences. Finally, as Messick (1981) and others have pointed out, without some evidence of construct validity one cannot determine what a test score means.

Direct evidence for validity of the Youth and Elementary Forms of the SOLAT is almost nonexistent. One study with the Youth Form was discussed in much detail, but was based on a sample of six second-graders. Three unpublished studies were cited as initial evidence for the Youth Form; two were conducted by eighth grade students and one by a high school sophomore. There is no way to evaluate the adequacy of these studies.

In summary, the reliability of the SOLAT is relatively poor and does not qualify it for individual use. The direct validity information about the Youth and Elementary Forms is inadequate. The major shortcoming of this test is the conceptual looseness associated with the nature of the construct being measured and the direction of validation research.

REVIEWER'S REFERENCE

Messick, S. (1981). Constructs and their vicissitudes in educational and psychological measurement. *Psychological Bulletin, 89,* 575-588.

[391]

Styles of Teamwork Inventory.

Purpose: Assess individual feelings about working in teams and the behaviors one typically employs in work-team situations.

Population: Individuals whose work responsibilities require work-team cooperation.
Publication Dates: 1963–87.
Acronym: STI.
Scores, 5: Synergistic, Compromise, Win-Lose, Yield-Lose, Lose-Leave.
Administration: Group.
Price Data, 1990: $6.95 per manual ('87, 28 pages).
Time: Administration time not reported.
Comments: Based on Team Behaviors Model of analysis of individual behaviors in a team setting; self ratings; self scored; formerly called Group Encounter Survey (T3:1014).
Authors: Jay Hall.
Publisher: Teleometrics International.
Cross References: See 8:1048 (2 references).

[392]
Suffolk Reading Scale.

Purpose: "To provide a standardized measure of reading attainment and to monitor the progress of individuals and groups."
Population: Ages 6–12.
Publication Dates: 1986–87.
Scores: Total score only.
Administration: Group.
Levels: 3 overlapping levels: Level 1 (ages 6–7), Level 2 (ages 8–10), Level 3 (ages 10–12); 2 parallel forms: A, B.
Price Data, 1987: £5.20 per set of 10 Level 1A booklets or Level 1B booklets or Level 2A booklets or Level 2B booklets; £6.35 per set of 10 Level 3A booklets or Level 3B booklets; £5.75 per set of 25 Level 3 answer sheets; £6.90 per Teacher's Guide ('87, 48 pages); scoring service for Level 3 offered by publisher.
Time: (35–45) minutes.
Author: Fred Hagley.
Publisher: NFER-Nelson Publishing Co., Ltd. [England].

Review of the Suffolk Reading Scale by ROBERT B. COOTER, JR., Associate Professor of Elementary Education, Brigham Young University, Provo, UT:

DESCRIPTION. The Suffolk Reading Scale is a group-administered norm-referenced test of reading ability intended for children from 6 to 12+ years of age. Three levels of the Suffolk Reading Scales are available (1, 2, 3) with two alternate forms (Forms A and B).

Each level of the test presents the child with sentences arranged in increasing difficulty with a single word missing (e.g., *The milkman drove down the _____*). The task is to supply the missing word from multiple choices shown below the sentence (e.g., *robe road door milk read*). Children simply circle the word in the test booklet for Levels 1 and 2. They may do likewise on Level 3 or use a machine-scored answer sheet. This modified cloze format provides the sole basis for reading assessment with the Suffolk.

TEST DEVELOPMENT AND TECHNICAL FEATURES. The genesis of the Suffolk Reading Scale is very interesting and admirable. Educators in Suffolk County, England saw a need "to update and improve upon the tests currently being used . . . and to avoid disjointed results from the use of different tests with different age groups." Thus, educators in the County of Suffolk set out to create a new test matching their curricular standards and to establish local norms for the new test.

Teachers in 42 schools in Suffolk were selected to work on the project with teachers selected from all levels and across a variety of subject specializations. They were asked to suggest material relating to the reading experiences in their classes. This process yielded some 500 potential items. Finally, a panel of "Advisory Teachers" and "Educational Psychologists" edited the items using preestablished criteria.

Two provisional forms of the test were constructed for further development within Suffolk. During the Autumn term of 1982, the Suffolk Reading Scale was administered to some 300 children in the county at each age level (6+, 8+, 10+, and 12+). These results were then subjected to item analysis by the National Foundation for Educational Research (NFER) using both classical item analysis and Rasch scaling methods.

Following the initial construction and field use of the Suffolk Reading Scale, it was decided to establish national norms prior to publication. The NFER assisted in this effort and developed a standardization sample of children across the 6+ to 13+ age range attending schools in England, Wales, and Northern Ireland. Socioeconomic considerations were taken into account in the development of the sample. Some 38,625 students participated in the standardization process conducted in March of 1986.

Scores on the Suffolk Reading Scale may be interpreted in several ways from the norm tables. A student's raw score may be converted into a Standard Score (SS), Percentile Rank (PR), and/or a Grade Equivalent (GE). Section III of the manual provides useful directions for interpretation and use of derived scores.

Reliability estimates for the Suffolk are satisfactory. Several estimates of the test's reliability were made including checks for internal consistency and test-retest reliability. Test-retest results indicate reliability coefficient scores ranging from a low of .89 for Level 3, Form B to a high of .96 for Level 1, Form B. Internal consistency estimates (KR-20) range from .92 (Level 3, Form A) to .95 (Level 1). The author points out that these data are based on a "first occasion of testing only"; that is, the children had never taken either form of the test before. Thus, one might expect scores to be slightly higher on subsequent testings.

Validity was primarily determined by comparing students' test performance with teachers' estimates of their reading ability. In addition, readability levels of children's current school reading books were considered. Correlations were computed using the Rasch Ability Score, which forms the basis of age equivalent scores for the Suffolk Reading Scale. When comparing teacher estimates of pupils' reading ability with performance on the Scale, correlation coefficients ranged from .76 to .83. Readability level of pupils' current reading books compared to reading ability estimates derived from the Suffolk Reading Scale yielded correlations ranging from .61 to .74. These figures indicate that the Suffolk Reading Scale is associated with both teacher estimates of reading level and with the readability level of their school reading books.

Finally, the Suffolk Reading Scale has at least a degree of curricular validity by virtue of the method of test construction used. As mentioned above, teachers from all grade levels and content specialties were involved in the construction of the test items. Although this would not seem to represent a rigorous application of curricular validity standards, some recognition of the process seems warranted.

EVALUATION AND CONCLUSIONS. The Suffolk Reading Scale represents a significant contribution to the reading assessment field, not so much because of its content, but for the process it represents. Many reading assessment theorists recognize that standardized tests are significant indicators of educational progress when used as part of an overall evaluation (Calfee, 1987). This being the case, then one may likely conclude that a test of reading ability constructed by local professionals and normed using local populations would be preferable to other commercial tests. If a similar process were adopted by all school systems then validity of measurement would be greatly improved. However, as a commercial test of reading ability for general application, the Suffolk Reading Scale has a number of serious problems.

One major difficulty with the Scale is that it does not reflect recent advances in our understanding of the reading process (Valencia & Pearson, 1987). Important factors such as affect, concepts about print, reading/study skills, and even basic word identification/recognition strategies are not addressed. In essence the Scale is a series of modified cloze sentences of progressive difficulty, a task generally considered to measure inferential comprehension and context clues. Thus, one can in no way consider this test to be a comprehensive test of reading skill.

A second related problem is the failure of the Scale's author either to articulate or adhere to any known construct or understanding of the reading process. Nowhere in the Teacher's Guide is a rationale offered indicating reasoning behind the format of the test, or exclusion of important aspects of the reading process. Our only insight into test construction is the knowledge that teachers were asked to generate items for inclusion in the scales. Failure to explain the philosophical underpinnings of any assessment instrument creates a great deal of suspicion regarding overall validity.

It is difficult to determine how the Suffolk Reading Scale has any great benefit to classroom instruction beyond determining gross reading levels. Because no specific reading abilities have been identified or correlated to test scores it would appear that the Scales could only be used for school or district reporting. Possibly the Scale could be used for initial screenings of reading ability for children in Great Britain.

Finally, the test makers should consider inclusion of a section in the Teacher's Guide explaining how these test results may be used as part of an overall assessment package. Limitations of the test should be pointed out and suggestions for building a complete assessment program offered. The 1990s are likely to call not only for the integration of more holistic teaching methods in the classroom, but also for the inclusion of process-oriented measures of reading ability.

REVIEWER'S REFERENCES
Calfee, R. C. (1987). The school as a context for assessment of literacy. *The Reading Teacher, 40*, 738-743.
Valencia, S., & Pearson, P. D. (1987). Reading assessment: Time for change. *The Reading Teacher, 40*, 726-732.

Review of the Suffolk Reading Scale by RICHARD LEHRER, Associate Professor of Educational Psychology, University of Wisconsin-Madison, Madison, WI:

The Suffolk Reading Scale consists of multiple-choice, sentence-completion items that may be administered either individually or to a group. The items sample a commendable range of content areas. Other strengths include easy administration, simple scoring, and high reliability. The national standardization sample also appears adequate, so the accompanying standard scores are meaningful.

Despite these strengths, the Scale suffers from an essentially theory-free approach toward the assessment of reading. It seems as if the Scale measures vocabulary and neglects other aspects of reading, such as comprehension. The validation of the Scale offers little assistance in resolving this dilemma. The only validity data presented in the manual consist of correlations between teachers' estimates of students' reading ability and the scores obtained from administration of the Scale. It is not clear how teachers' estimates were scaled, nor is it clear if the teachers who provided the estimates were also those who were involved in the original test construction. Moreover, because many test items were created from materials the children were reading, it is not surprising that teachers' estimates of children's reading ability and children's performance on the Scale were associated highly.

No other forms of concurrent validity are provided nor is any attempt made at discriminating between the Scale and other forms of mental assessment, including other measures of reading skill. Hence, very little can be concluded at this time about the validity of the Suffolk Reading Scale.

An additional problem is that the Scale may not be valid across cultures, due to the inclusion of terms such as "petrol" and "lorry" that are apt to be unfamiliar to children in the United States. The directions for administration are also vague, leaving it to individual teachers to translate into practice phrases such as, "Explain that they have to choose one word which best fits into the sentence."

In summary, the Suffolk Reading Scale provides an easy and quick assessment of some aspects of children's reading skills, perhaps primarily vocabulary. Although the Scales are reliable, they suffer from a vaguely defined theory of reading and an inadequate attempt at validation. At the present time, more established measures of reading skills may be a better choice for the assessment of children's reading.

[393]
Suicidal Ideation Questionnaire.
Purpose: To measure suicidal ideation.
Population: Grades 7–9, 10–12.
Publication Dates: 1987–88.
Acronym: SIQ.
Scores: Total Suicidal Ideation.
Administration: Group.
Levels, 2: SIQ (senior high school), SIQ-JR (junior high school).
Forms, 2: G (machine-scored), HS (hand-scored).
Price Data, 1988: $12 per 25 hand-scorable answer sheets; $3 per scoring key; $15 per manual ('88, 47 pages); $100 or less per 50 prepaid mail-in answer sheets including scoring and reporting by publisher.
Time: (5–10) minutes.
Author: William M. Reynolds.
Publisher: Psychological Assessment Resources, Inc.

TEST REFERENCES
1. Ranieri, W. F., Steer, R. A., Laurence, T. I., Rissmiller, D. J., Piper, G. E., & Beck, A. T. (1987). Relationships of depression, hopelessness, and dysfunctional attitudes to suicide ideation in psychiatric patients. *Psychological Reports, 61*, 967-975.
2. Ritter, D. R. (1990). Adolescent suicide: Social competence and problem behavior of youth at high risk and low risk for suicide. *School Psychology Review, 19*, 83-95.

Review of the Suicidal Ideation Questionnaire by JAMES C. CARMER, *Clinical Psychologist, Immanuel Medical Center, Omaha, NE:*

The Suicidal Ideation Questionnaire (SIQ) is an instrument designed to assess the presence of suicidal ideation in adolescents. Two versions of the SIQ have been developed; the 30-item SIQ targets adolescents in grades 10–12, and the 15-item SIQ-JR targets adolescents in grades 7–9. Administration takes 5–10 minutes. If the students have reading difficulties, the items can be read aloud by the examiner.

The author builds a clear and careful rationale for the distinction of the concept of suicidal ideation from the general concept of depression. The SIQ is not a subtle scale; it is a direct, simple self-report. The subject is asked to rate the frequency the items have occurred as thoughts over the past month. A 7-point scale ranging from *almost every day* to *I never had this thought* yields a score reflecting the overall frequency of suicidal ideations.

The author suggests a cutoff score to help determine who should be referred for further evaluation of potentially significant psychopathology and suicide risk. A proposed fall-back cutoff score for mass screening is proposed at approximately the 84th percentile and above based on the standardization samples.

Eight "critical items" provide an immediate screen as to suicidal intention. These items include indications of having a specific suicide plan. Guidelines are given for using these critical items in assessing the possibility of self-destructive behavior. The author cautions the proposed guidelines are based on a subjective rationale rather than empirical findings.

The standardization sample consisted of 890 adolescents for the SIQ and 1,290 adolescents for the SIQ-JR. Additional profiles of 4,000 adolescents have also been collected by the author.

Reported reliability coefficients range from .93 to .97 by grade and .97 for the total sample reliability for the SIQ. Further indications of the homogeneity of item content are shown by item-total scale correlations ranging from .70 to .90. Test-retest reliability based on a 4-week period between testings yielded a coefficient of .72. Because the objective of the SIQ is to measure the state of suicidal ideation, this moderate test-retest reliability would be expected.

The SIQ statements themselves have face validity, as all represent some kind of morbid or suicidal thought. As expected, scores on the SIQ correlate significantly with other measures of depression. Measures of hopelessness, self-esteem, and anxiety all correlated moderately with SIQ scores. A multiple regression analysis resulted in significant correlation coefficients associated with measures of depression, anxiety, and hopelessness and the SIQ, suggesting these variables share significant variance with the SIQ. Significant correlations between SIQ scores and negative life events, hassles, and social support were also obtained. The SIQ was demonstrated to be independent from academic achievement. An exploratory factor analysis is reported.

Clinical validity is argued by a retrospective assessment of recent adolescent suicide attempters. Interestingly, only two thirds of the suicide attempters endorsed levels of suicidal ideation above the cutoff score although the SIQ was administered within 36 hours of hospital admission. Significant SIQ score differences between attempters and nonattempters of suicide have been reported.

The author is careful to define the purpose of the SIQ as solely a screening device of self-reported levels of suicidal ideation. Conceptually, the opportunity to take a pencil-and-paper test, either individually or in a group setting, offers the adolescent the means to "cry for help." As such, the SIQ would be a helpful part of a school crisis response team or overall prevention program, using the SIQ to identify adolescents to be evaluated further by clinicians.

The derivation of the cutoff score is unclear. Given the previous finding that one third of suicide attempters scored below the cutoff, users of the SIQ should not rely solely on the cutoff score to identify those in need of further clinical evaluation. Until a more discriminating cutoff is developed, each SIQ protocol should be individually screened. Subjects endorsing *any* critical item should be referred for further clinical evaluation.

The author includes many caveats about the use of the SIQ and cautions against the use of the SIQ as a predictor of suicidal behavior. Ultimately we are all vitally interested in understanding more clearly the relationship between suicidal ideation and suicidal behavior. The development of an extensive database utilizing the SIQ could contribute to this understanding. The potential gains in knowledge would be well worth the sizeable effort required.

In summary, the SIQ may serve as a useful group screening device for school settings and as an individually administered screening device for school and other clinical settings. It is most important the SIQ be administered in situations where there can be timely, thorough follow-up and evaluation of those identifying themselves as having suicidal ideation.

Review of the Suicidal Ideation Questionnaire by COLLIE W. CONOLEY, *Associate Professor of Educational Psychology, University of Nebraska-Lincoln, Lincoln, NE:*

The Suicidal Ideation Questionnaire (SIQ) is a self-report assessment for identifying adolescents who have high frequency of suicidal ideation. The SIQ requires the adolescent to report how often thoughts occur that have some suicidal or morbid content. The strength of the SIQ is that it can be used on a large scale for identifying adolescents who will reveal they are thinking a great deal about killing themselves. The problem is the scale relies on the adolescents' desire to be identified and may have a high probability of false positives.

These problems should be understood in the context of currently available approaches. For example, it is currently impossible to use a brief self-report instrument to discover suicidal potential when the person does not wish to reveal the threat. For instance, the MMPI (Minnesota Multiphasic Personality Inventory—2; 244) requires more than an hour. The problem of a large number of false positives seems defensible also. With life and death issues at stake, it is obviously safer to err on the side of including more rather than fewer adolescents in a follow-up program. The SIQ appears to be a strong test for screening large numbers of adolescents.

There are two forms of the Suicidal Ideation Questionnaire. The standard SIQ is a 30-item form for use with older adolescents in grades 10 to 12. The SIQ-JR is a 15-item form for use with adolescents in grades 7 to 9. The author reports the purpose of developing the SIQ-JR was to accommodate the slower reading rate of the younger adolescents. There is no reference to the reading level of the questionnaire. The SIQ is reported to require 5–10 minutes to complete and can be administered in groups or individually.

The manual presents important information about the integration of the SIQ into a prevention program. The ethical issues related to responding to possible or probable suicide attempts are important and are presented effectively.

The SIQ has a normative sample of 890 adolescents; the SIQ-JR has 1,290 adolescents. The sample appears to be drawn from one high school and two junior high schools from an urban/suburban community in the midwestern United States. The normative groups are almost equal in gender representation. The ethnicity makeup of the SIQ is 78% White, 19% Black, 1.5% Asian, 0.4% Hispanic, and 1% other. The SIQ-JR group contains 74% White, 22% Black, 1.7% Asian, 0.8% Hispanic, and 1.6% other. There were consistent differences between gender with females scoring 7.36 points higher than males on the SIQ and 2.76 points higher on the SIQ-JR. There were differences between grades for the SIQ but a small omega squared revealed small practical differences. No significant differences between ethnic groups were apparent.

Internal consistency reliability was computed using Cronbach's coefficient alpha. The standardization sample was used by grade. The SIQ alpha ranged from .969 to .974; the SIQ-JR alpha ranged from .932 to .938. A test-retest reliability coefficient was computed for only the SIQ and not for the SIQ-JR. A sample of 801 adolescents over a 4-week period had a reliability coefficient of .72. The author believes .72 is justifiable because of the state nature of the SIQ. An important issue that was not addressed is whether the test-retest reliability decreases substantially with a suicidal population. Knowing the volatility of the scores would affect the

SIQ's effectiveness if the SIQ is used for screening purposes. For example, how often should the screening be repeated?

Validity estimation is difficult for a low probability behavior that is lethal. Traditional controlled experimental designs are out of the question. However, several correlational studies have suggested that the SIQ has a very strong probability of identifying the post-suicide-attempter (Reynolds, 1991; King, Raskin, Gdowski, Butkus, & Opipari, 1990; Spirito, Stark, Fristad, Hart, & Owens-Stively, 1987). For these findings to be useful in judging the adequacy of the SIQ one must hope there is not a significant difference between the post- and pre-suicide attempter.

Content validity was addressed by presenting a hierarchical continuum of suicidal thoughts that are believed by the author to cover the domain of important suicidal ideation. Unfortunately, there is no substantiation of the importance of the suicidal thoughts presented as the model.

Eight items are specified as critical on the SIQ. The items appear to be the standard questions in lethality scales (e.g., thought about killing myself, how I would kill myself, when I would kill myself). There appear to be no data substantiating these items as critical in the context of the SIQ. One wonders about the omission of one question that is typically asked, "Do you have the means of killing yourself available to you?" Also, lethality is often determined by the manner in which someone thinks of dying, the more active and violent the more lethal.

Construct validity is presented as how well the SIQ correlates with the theoretically related variables of depression, hopelessness, self-esteem, anxiety, and academic achievement. The SIQ was correlated with the depression measures of the Beck Depression Inventory (r = .69 and .70), the Reynolds Adolescent Depression Scale (r = .58, .61, and .63), and a learned helplessness scale (r = .36). The SIQ-JR was correlated with the Reynolds Adolescent Depression Scale (r = .55 and .59) and the Children's Depression Inventory (r = .65 and .66). The SIQ was correlated with the Rosenberg Self-Esteem Scale (r = -.52 and -.56) and the Academic Self-Concept Scale—High School Version (= -.39 and -.42). The SIQ-JR was correlated with the Rosenberg Self-Esteem Scale (r = -.54) and the Academic Self-Concept Scale—High School Version (r = -.42). The Children's Manifest Anxiety Scale—Revised was correlated with the SIQ (r = .56 and .58) and the SIQ-JR (r = .54 and .56).

In summary, the SIQ may be a useful screening measure. Continued refinement is necessary to ascertain how it can be most helpful in identifying and intervening with adolescents at risk for suicide attempts.

REVIEWER'S REFERENCES

Spirito, A., Stark, L., Fristad, M., Hart, K., & Owens-Stively, J. (1987). Adolescent suicide attempters hospitalized on a pediatric unit. *Journal of Pediatric Psychology, 12*, 171-189.

King, C. A., Raskin, A., Gdowski, C. L., Butkus, M., & Opipari, L. (1990). Psychosocial factors associated with urban adolescent female suicide attempts. *Journal American Academy of Child and Adolescent Psychiatry, 29*, 289-294.

Reynolds, W. M. (1991, August). *Efficacy of the SIQ for the identification of suicidal youth.* Paper presented at the annual meeting of the American Psychological Association, San Francisco.

[394]

Supervisory Change Relations.

Purpose: "To measure knowledge about change relations."
Population: Supervisors and prospective supervisors.
Publication Dates: 1970–78.
Scores: Total score only.
Administration: Group.
Price Data: Available from publisher.
Time: (20–25) minutes.
Comments: Self-administered.
Authors: W. J. Reddin and E. Keith Stewart.
Publisher: Organizational Tests Ltd. [Canada].

[395]

Supervisory Coaching Relations.

Purpose: Measures "knowledge of sound methods of coaching subordinates."
Population: Supervisors and potential supervisors.
Publication Dates: 1970–78.
Acronym: SCORE.
Scores: Total score only.
Administration: Group.
Manual: No manual; fact sheet available.
Price Data, 1989: $30 per complete kit including 10 test booklets, fact sheet, and user's guide.
Time: (15–20) minutes.
Comments: Self-administered.
Authors: W. J. Reddin and E. Keith Stewart.
Publisher: Organizational Tests Ltd. [Canada].

[396]

Supervisory Communication Relations.

Purpose: "To measure knowledge about communications relations."
Population: Supervisors and potential supervisors.
Publication Dates: 1970–81.
Acronym: SCOM.
Scores: Total score only.
Administration: Group.
Manual: No manual; fact sheet available.
Price Data, 1990: $30 per complete kit including 10 test booklets, fact sheet, and user's guide.
Time: (15–20) minutes.
Comments: Self-administered.
Authors: E. Keith Stewart, W. J. Reddin, and K. J. Rowell.
Publisher: Organizational Tests Ltd. [Canada].

Review of Supervisory Communication Relations by NIELS G. WALLER, Assistant Professor of Psychology, University of California, Davis, CA:

The Supervisory Communication Relations test (SCOM) is an 80-question, true-false measure of knowledge of communication skills important in the workplace. The test, which is recommended for both supervisors or potential supervisors, is based on the premise that one must have a sound knowledge of communication skills before one can put those skills into practice. Several areas of communication skills are tapped by the SCOM, including knowledge of effective verbal and nonverbal communication with subordinates, coworkers, and superiors; communication when giving orders; and the art of introducing change. Recommended uses of the SCOM are: (*a*) group discussion of items as a training activity, (*b*) training needs identification, (*c*) selection, and (*d*) manpower inventory and planning. According to the test authors, the SCOM is appropriate with both blue- and white-collar workers, and the items are both jargon free and written at a moderate reading level.

In many respects, the SCOM is similar to another measure of supervisory effectiveness, the Supervisory Human Relations test (SHR; 397). This is not an accident, as both tests were developed by the same authors. Consider the following similarities: (*a*) both tests are moderately short instruments designed to measure aspects of supervisory effectiveness, (*b*) both tests can be either individually or group administered, (*c*) both tests utilize a clever booklet design which enables them to be hand scored in less than 2 minutes, (*d*) both tests were normed on an international sample of 1,895 supervisors, and most importantly, (*e*) both tests lack a manual. This latter point means that, unfortunately, it is also impossible to evaluate the psychometric worth of both tests. Indeed, the two instruments are so similar that the comments I made in my review of the SHR in this volume are equally applicable to the SCOM. Instead of repeating those comments here, I refer the reader to the aforementioned review (397).

It is worthy of note that the authors of the SCOM remark that the test "emphasizes principles and common sense rather than theory." Frankly, I find it disturbing that while academic psychology approaches its centennial anniversary, an assemblage of items grouped together on the basis of nothing more than "common sense" can be marketed, without proper validation work, as a psychological test that can be used for such an important task as the selection of individuals for supervisory positions. If I have not made my point clear, let me do so now. The use of the SCOM for selection purposes is irresponsible, as well as unethical. I do not mean to say the SCOM has no utility. In general, the items *do* have good face validity, and I suspect the test could be profitably used as a vehicle for generating interesting discussions on effective supervisory communications. However, until data are available demonstrating the utility of the SCOM for its intended purposes, common sense dictates that the

SCOM be considered nothing more than a collection of interesting statements.

[397]

Supervisory Human Relations.
Purpose: Measures "attitudes toward others."
Population: Supervisors and potential supervisors.
Publication Dates: 1970–81.
Acronym: SHR.
Scores: Total score only.
Administration: Group.
Manual: No manual; fact sheet available.
Price Data, 1990: $30 per complete kit including 10 test booklets, fact sheet, and user's guide.
Time: (15–20) minutes.
Comments: Self-administered.
Authors: W. J. Reddin and E. Keith Stewart.
Publisher: Organizational Tests Ltd. [Canada].

Review of Supervisory Human Relations by NIELS G. WALLER, Assistant Professor of Psychology, University of California, Davis, CA:

The supervisory Human Relations test (SHR) is an 80-question, true-false measure of attitudes toward superiors, coworkers, and subordinates in the workplace. The test is designed for "supervisors, those who supervise them, and potential supervisors." Overall, the SHR has many attractive qualities. The test is moderately short. It takes approximately 15 to 20 minutes to complete. It has good face validity and it is designed to provide test scores that are minimally influenced by acquiescence response set. The SHR can be individually or group administered, and an imaginative booklet format enables the instrument to be scored in less than 2 minutes. Suggested uses of the SHR include (*a*) group discussion of items as a training activity, (*b*) training needs identification, (*c*) selection, and (*d*) manpower inventory and planning.

It is important to note that the SHR is a measure of *knowledge* of human relations, not a measure of supervisory effectiveness. The authors caution, for example, that, "a high score . . . indicates only a very positive attitude toward others. It does not necessarily follow that this is the best approach for the supervisor in the situation in which he finds himself" (SHR Fact Sheet). Additional information on the appropriate uses and limitations of the SHR is, unfortunately, hard to come by as the test currently has no manual. Consequently, potential users of the SHR will be frustrated if they desire knowledge of the theoretical rationale, or the psychometric properties of the test. An Instrument Administration Guide (IAG) and an SHR Fact Sheet are distributed with the SHR test booklets; however, these supplements do not provide adequate information needed to make a reasoned evaluation of the instrument.

The IAG contains sound advice on test administration and interpretation guidelines. The Fact Sheet provides information more pertinent to the SHR. For persons with little knowledge of psychometric theory the Guide provides answers to frequently posed questions about test reliability and test validity. I found these statements, however, overly general and consequently of little value. For example, the Guide notes that "All of the tests were constructed by skilled trainers and all tests were inspected by from ten to over a hundred judges," and "The face validity (what reading the statements appears to indicate) appears to be high" (Guide, p. 4). Such global statements, I suspect, will not satisfy the more intellectually inquisitive test users who will wonder: How can I be confident that this test *reliably* measures what it purports to measure? Do variables such as gender, race, age, or socioeconomic status influence test performance? How was the test constructed, and on what basis were the final items retained?

The SHR Fact Sheet provides norms from an impressively large sample of supervisors ($n = 1,895$). Unfortunately, the sample was not broken down with respect to any potentially meaningful variables (e.g., gender, race, or age). A table displays percentile equivalents for several raw score ranges. Inspection of this table indicates that the score distribution is highly skewed to the left. For example, answering 41 of 80 items in the keyed direction places an individual in the 15th percentile of the score distribution, but answering 61 of 80 items in the keyed direction places an individual in the 95th percentile. Consequently, the instrument is unable to discriminate effectively in the high end of the scale distribution.

The available information regarding the psychometric properties of the SHR falls far short of meeting the requirements set forth by the *Standards for Educational and Psychological Testing* (AERA, APA, & NCME, 1985). Does this mean that I do not recommend use of the SHR? No. On the contrary, the items of the SHR appear to have good face validity, and thus they should help generate useful discussions on effective supervisory behavior. But this is very different from recommending use of the instrument for *testing* purposes, where one goal is the placement of individuals on a meaningful psychological continuum. Until more adequate norms and other pertinent psychometric information are available for the SHR, the SHR should not be used for selection or other testing purposes.

REVIEWER'S REFERENCE

American Educational Research Association, American Psychological Association, & National Council on Measurement in Education. (1985). *Standards for educational and psychological testing.* Washington, DC: American Psychological Association, Inc.

[398]
Supervisory Job Discipline.
Purpose: Measures knowledge of disciplinary techniques.

Population: Supervisors and potential supervisors.
Publication Dates: 1970–78.
Acronym: SJD.
Scores: Total score only.
Administration: Group.
Manual: No manual; fact sheet available.
Price Data, 1989: $30 per complete kit including 10 test booklets, fact sheet, and user's guide.
Time: (15–20) minutes.
Comments: Self-administered.
Author: E. Keith Stewart.
Publisher: Organizational Tests Ltd. [Canada].

[399]
Supervisory Job Instruction.
Purpose: Measures "knowledge of sound job instruction techniques."
Population: Supervisors and potential supervisors.
Publication Dates: 1970–81.
Acronym: SJI.
Scores: Total score only.
Administration: Group.
Manual: No manual; fact sheet available.
Price Data, 1990: $30 per complete kit including 10 test booklets, fact sheet, and user's guide.
Time: (15–20) minutes.
Comments: Self-administered.
Authors: W. J. Reddin and E. Keith Stewart.
Publisher: Organizational Tests Ltd. [Canada].

[400]
Supervisory Job Safety.
Purpose: Measures "knowledge of and attitudes toward safety practices."
Population: "Blue-collar" supervisors and potential supervisors.
Publication Dates: 1970–81.
Acronym: SJS.
Scores: Total score only.
Administration: Group.
Manual: No manual; fact sheet available.
Price Data, 1990: $30 per complete kit including 10 test booklets, fact sheet, and user's guide.
Time: (15–20) minutes.
Comments: Self-administered.
Author: E. Keith Stewart.
Publisher: Organizational Tests Ltd. [Canada].

[401]
Supervisory Potential Test.
Purpose: "To measure supervisory potential."
Population: Supervisors or potential supervisors.
Publication Dates: 1970–81.
Acronym: SPT.
Scores, 9: New Role Clarity, Productivity, Superior Relationship, Change Introduction, Subordinate Motivation, Subordinate Development, Subordinate Evaluation, Discipline, Total.
Administration: Group.
Manual: No manual; fact sheet available.
Price Data, 1990: $30 per complete kit including 10 test booklets, fact sheet, and user's guide.
Time: (15–20) minutes.
Comments: Self-administered.
Authors: W. J. Reddin and J. Brian Sullivan.

Publisher: Organizational Tests Ltd. [Canada].

[402]
Supervisory Profile Record.

Purpose: "To identify candidates with a high potential for success in first-line supervisory classifications."
Population: Prospective supervisors.
Publication Dates: 1981–85.
Acronym: SPR.
Scores, 10: Judgment Record (Employee Communication-Motivation, Employee Training-Evaluation, Problem-Resolution, Disciplinary Practices, General Style-Practices, Total), Background Record (Present Self Concept-Evaluation, Present Work Values-Orientation, Total), Total.
Administration: Individual or group.
Price Data, 1989: $8 per reusable test booklet; $20 per answer sheet (includes scoring by publisher); $5 per administrator's guide (21 pages); $40 per specimen set including test booklet, answer sheet, technical reports (195 pages), and administrator's guide.
Time: (180) minutes.
Author: Richardson, Bellows, Henry & Co., Inc.
Publisher: Richardson, Bellows, Henry & Co., Inc.

Review of the Supervisory Profile Record by SHELDON ZEDECK, Professor of Psychology and Director, University of California, Berkeley, CA:

The Supervisory Profile Record (SPR) is a very good instrument to be used as one device in the process of determining who should be advanced or hired into a first-line supervisory position. The current version (1985) of the SPR is composed of two parts: Part I contains 80 statements and descriptions of situations about which the candidate needs to make judgments or decisions; the response mode is generally a choice from five alternatives. Part II contains 100 multiple-choice type questions that pertain to a candidate's interests and experiences. A total score for the SPR as well as for each part and categories within parts is available. Only the total score is used to aid an employer in the decision to hire or advance.

A positive aspect of the SPR is that the items are empirically keyed such that only items that yield response patterns that are significantly related to performance ratings have been retained for use. Although the surviving items were grouped into the category scores based on a rational clustering procedure, it would be informative if the "Technical Reports" presented more background on the rationale for the choice of the items and their alternatives.

The strategy and data base for the development of the SPR are impressive. The "Technical Reports" contains three technical reports that describe the validation process that has resulted in the present form. In general, about 25,000 supervisory incumbents, representing over 100 companies, have participated in the research; the general data collection process has been conducted through eight consortia studies. Comprehensive tables with regard to the demographics of the participants are provided. As part of the development and validation of the SPR, there is a "Job Requirements Questionnaire" that is used to conduct the job analysis for the supervisory position in the participating organization and a "Supervisory Performance Evaluation Record" that is used to obtain criterion measures on job duties and requisite abilities. The empirical validities, obtained via concurrent and predictive validation strategies, generally range in the .20s (unrestricted rs); across all participants (N = over 17,000 incumbents), the validity is .31. Although the "Executive Summary" that accompanies the package of SPR materials concludes that the "data also show that SPR scores are valid for and can be equally applied to all ethnic groups and males and females," caution must be taken in accepting this conclusion because the only ethnic group on which there is a reasonable sample size is the Black group; there are analyses for Hispanics, but the sample size for this group is relatively low.

Future research with the SPR should address a number of issues. First, although there are discussions of utility and expectancies, there is no formal utility analysis in terms of economics or "dollars and cents" savings. Second, more data need to be collected and presented with regard to the reliability of the SPR and its scale scores. No information is provided with respect to the internal consistency of the SPR. Test-retest results are reported for a portion of the samples involved in the research, but there is ambiguity with respect to the interval between testings, or the reasons for the retestings. Third, there is a need to compare the SPR to alternative tests used to select first-line supervisors; it is hard to imagine that among the 100 companies participating in the research no other selection tests were available that could have been used as points of comparison with the SPR.

A positive outcome of the SPR research program is a considerable contribution to an understanding of supervisory behavior. For example, the research shows that supervisory jobs have a common core of duty and ability requirements across organizations, job groups, and industries. Another finding—that no matter what the organization type, geography, or job group, the SPR total score is a valid predictor—contributes to the body of knowledge pertaining to validity generalization for selection devices.

Overall, the SPR, its supporting documents, and its program of research are sufficiently described and developed to allow a user to make a choice in determining the appropriateness of the SPR for the user's organization. There are good descriptions of the administrative requirements for the test, job analysis data collection, and supervisory evaluations. In addition, the examples provided for test score interpretation are clear. The evidence suggests that the test can be used to select first-line supervisors; more research is needed to determine whether the SPR is better than other test devices or whether it can provide incremental validity to other test devices.

[403]
Supervisory Union Relations.

Purpose: "To measure attitude about union relations."
Population: Supervisors and potential supervisors.
Publication Dates: 1970–81.
Acronym: SUR.
Scores: Total score only.
Administration: Group.
Manual: No manual; fact sheet available.
Price Data, 1990: $30 per complete kit including 10 test booklets, fact sheet, and user's guide.
Time: (15–20) minutes.
Comments: Self-administered; may be self-scored.
Authors: W. J. Reddin and E. Keith Stewart.
Publisher: Organizational Tests Ltd. [Canada].

[404]
Survey of Functional Adaptive Behaviors.

Purpose: To assess an individual's skill level of adaptive behavior.
Population: Ages 16 and over.
Publication Date: 1986.
Acronym: SFAB.
Scores, 5: Residential Living Skills, Daily Living Skills, Academic Skills, Vocational Skills, SFAB Total Score.
Administration: Individual.
Manual: No manual.
Price Data, 1988: $24.50 per 25 surveys.
Authors: Jack G. Dial, Carolyn Mezger, Theresa Massey, Steve Carter, and Lawrence T. McCarron.
Publisher: McCarron-Dial Systems.

Review of the Survey of Functional Adaptive Behaviors by STEVEN W. LEE, Assistant Professor of Educational Psychology and Research, University of Kansas, Lawrence, KS:

The Survey of Functional Adaptive Behaviors (SFAB) was designed as a comprehensive rating of adaptive behavior for individuals 16 years of age or older. A 12-page protocol is provided to those administering the test. Data on the standardization sample, including reliability and validity of the instrument, are provided in a four-page handout.

The SFAB is an untimed test that can be completed by (*a*) case history information, (*b*) interview, or (*c*) behavioral observation. No empirical data are provided indicating these three rating methods provide equivalent adaptive behavior ratings. Regardless of the method used to obtain the information, a rating of 2 (Task performed independently), 1 (Task performed inadequately or requires assistance, prompting, or cueing), or 0 (Task not performed) is used by the evaluator to rate each of 135 behavioral items.

These items are divided into four skill areas. The four skill areas include: Residential Living, Daily Living, Academic, and Vocational Skills areas. Standard scores for each skill area can be obtained as well as a Total Adaptive Behavior score. A secondary rating system is mentioned that seems to be designed to identify the training needs (i.e., none, remedial, or adaptive devices needed) for the client being evaluated for each of the 135 behavioral items. The scoring and uses for this secondary system are, however, not elucidated.

No manual is provided for the SFAB. The psychological reasoning or theory underlying the test is not provided, nor is any description of item selection, item analysis, or other research leading to the development of the test. Furthermore, no information regarding how the test should be interpreted is included, nor are there any warnings against possible misuses of the instrument. The educational qualifications for the test users are not mentioned. Specific instructions related to each of the three methods of administration of the SFAB are not provided, so the user cannot determine how to use case histories, behavioral observations, or interviews to complete the SFAB in a manner consistent with that of the normative sample. For example, in using the interview method, who should be the respondent? Are the behavioral observations to be structured or unstructured, and over what period of time should the behavioral observations be done? Scoring of the SFAB protocol is done in a clear and straightforward manner; however, converting the raw scores into standard scores is more difficult. No continuous norm tables are provided with the SFAB. As a result, interpolation or rounding will often be necessary to obtain standardized *T*-scores for SFAB raw scores. Neither the SFAB protocol nor the associated handout provides a method for obtaining standard scores not listed in the table. This problem introduces additional and unnecessary error into estimates of adaptive behavior skills.

The normative sample of the SFAB included 567 adults with ages ranging from 15 to 62. These adults had a mean IQ of 85 (*SD* = 17). The sample was appropriately stratified for both race and sex according to the U.S. population; however, the sampling procedure was not clearly specified and did not appear to be randomized. Forty percent of the sample (*n* = 245) had neurological damage, while 57 percent (*n* = 322) were intellectually in the average range and competitively employed. However, of this latter group, 195 were visually impaired, 92 were nondisabled, and information on the remaining 35 was not provided. The U.S. region of residence of the sample was noted only for the neurologically impaired group. No measures of central tendency or variability are provided for the normative sample. This is particularly unfortunate, given the unique nature of the sample (i.e., visually and neurologically impaired), as psychological and educational measures with large normative samples are difficult to obtain for these specialized groups. Given the unique characteristics of large groups within the sample, accurate estimates of adaptive behavior from the obtained scores would be quite difficult to make.

The reliability of the SFAB was reportedly assessed by interrater and test-retest methods. Test-retest reliability over a 7-to-14-day period, using 100 neurologically and visually disabled persons, was quite good and ranged in the high .80s to low .90s for the skill areas, and was $r = .92$ for the Total Adaptive Behavior score. No true interrater reliability was reported as no simultaneous ratings of behaviors were made. The rating method (i.e., case history, interview, or behavioral observation) used in the above mentioned study was not specified; therefore, the consumer would not know which method yielded the above mentioned results. No other data on the reliability of the SFAB were provided.

The validity of the SFAB was assessed through a comparison with other McCarron-Dial measures of adaptive behavior (Behavior Rating Scale [BRS] and Street Survival Skills Questionnaire [SSSQ]). These criterion measures were not described except through abbreviations, so the consumer could not evaluate their adequacy as criterion instruments. A concurrent validity study was reported with 52 mentally retarded adults. In this study, the SFAB correlated at $r = .90$ with Part I and $r = .65$ with Part II of the AAMD Adaptive Behavior Scale. Although these results are encouraging, the AAMD-ABS is viewed as having questionable psychometric viability (Sattler, 1988).

Finally, the authors report a "concurrent validity" study comparing SFAB scores for 372 sighted adults in eight different levels on the vocational continuum from daycare to professional competitive employment. The correlations of the SFAB with these vocational levels would potentially provide criterion-related validity. For this comparison, however, the Pearson Product Moment correlation coefficient was inappropriately used. The correct correlational statistic for comparing interval (SFAB) with nominal data (vocational level) is Eta.

In summary, the SFAB is deficient as a normative measure of adaptive behavior. The instrument has no clearly designated manual. No descriptive statistics of the normative sample are provided. Information on the development of the test, qualifications of users, administration methods, and scoring procedure are either unclear, confusing, or nonexistent. As noted above, the psychometric properties of the tool are weak. The main value of the SFAB may be as an informal tool used to evaluate adaptive behavior of adults without making comparisons to the normative sample.

REVIEWER'S REFERENCE
Sattler, J. M. (1988). *Assessment of children* (3rd ed.). San Diego: Jerome M. Sattler.

Review of the Survey of Functional Adaptive Behaviors by STEVEN I. PFEIFFER, Director, Institute of Clinical Training and Research, The Devereux Foundation, Devon, PA:

The Survey of Functional Adaptive Behaviors (SFAB) is described as a comprehensive rating scale of adaptive behavior. The scale consists of 135 items clustered within four skill areas. "Residential Living Skills" consists of self-care and home management (30 items). "Daily Living Skills" is made up of money management; community, social, and recreational resources; and travel (40 items). "Academic Skills" includes numerical reasoning, functional language, and literacy and writing (20 items). "Vocational Skills" incorporates physical ability and vocational attributes (45 items).

The scale is one of a set of tests developed and published by the McCarron-Dial Systems, with the support of the Texas Commission for the Blind.

The scale is appropriate for clients 16 years of age and older, and the authors state the instrument may be rated from case history information, interview, and/or behavioral observation. Clients are rated on a 3-point scale of skill level: Task performed independently (accommodations permitted); Task performed inadequately or requires assistance, prompting, or cueing; and Task not performed. When a client obtains a skill-level rating on any item indicating either inadequate performance or task not performed, a secondary rating is provided that allows the examiner to record whether intervention or adaptive accommodation may be needed.

Test results are expressed on the record form in standard scores, based on a normative sample of 567 adults (aged 15–62). Reliability and validity studies were based on this same normative group. Reliability indices appear adequate—test/retest scores of .92 for the SFAB Total Score and .85 to .94 for the four factor scores. However, validity data are rather meager; the authors report only one concurrent validity study, with the SFAB correlating .80 with the AAMD Adaptive Behavior Scale ($n = 52$). A second validity study indicated that the SFAB correlated .88 with one of eight assigned vocational program levels of independence ($n = 372$).

The scale is a promising instrument, with a great majority of the 135 items tapping relevant adaptive behaviors and critical normative developmental skills. The SFAB does not omit any significant domains and is quite easy to rate and score. However, the scale has its weaknesses, some rather critical. First and foremost, there is no technical manual. Information on technical adequacy was provided in a four-page letter summarizing the research sent by the publisher, McCarron-Dial Systems. No information was available on the underlying theoretical model, rationale for the four scales, or how the items were selected and evaluated. It is unclear how ratings based on review of a case history, clinical interview, or behavioral observation can yield sufficiently similar and valid scores.

Instructions are sketchy and consist of only one paragraph on the record form. Although the secondary rating procedure is a unique and valuable feature, the record form provides no information on how to determine whether remediative intervention for the particular skill is indicated. Many of the academic skill items are too difficult for developmentally disabled individuals, which raises the question of the specific proposed use for the scale. The normative sample was primarily drawn from the southwestern United States, and 42% of the subjects were visually impaired (legally or totally blind).

The SFAB seems to cover adequately the domain of skills and competencies considered important in programming for developmentally disabled adults. However, the scale does not meet minimal technical standards and will need restandardization and more extensive norms, rigorous reliability and validity studies, and a technical manual before it can be endorsed as anything but a research tool.

[405]
Survey of Management Practices.
Purpose: To assess a manager's organizational practices, and whether they enhance employee productivity.
Population: Subordinates of managers.
Publication Date: 1987.
Acronym: SMP.
Scores, 12: Dimension I (Management Values, Support Structure, Managerial Credibility, Total), Dimension II (Impact, Relevance, Community, Total), Dimension III (Task Environment, Social Context, Problem Solving, Total).
Administration: Group.
Price Data, 1990: $6.95 per manual (21 pages); $15 per Leader's Guide (18 pages).
Time: Administration time not reported.
Comments: Manager behavior rated by subordinates.
Authors: Jay Hall.
Publisher: Teleometrics International.

[406]
Survey of Organizational Climate.
Purpose: To assess an individual's opinion of his/her organizational climate.
Population: Employees.
Publication Dates: 1977–85.
Scores, 12: Clarity of Goals, Job Interest and Challenge, Rewards and Satisfactions, Standards of Excellence, Degree of Responsibility, Personal Development, Working Relationships, Advancement/Mobility, Job Security, Management's Credibility, Personnel Policies and Procedures, Self-Confidence.

Administration: Group.
Manual: No manual.
Price Data, 1988: $5 per person for initial composite only; $10 per person for individual profiles and initial composite; $20 per extra composite; scoring service offered by publisher.
Time: Administration time not reported.
Author: Training House, Inc.
Publisher: Training House, Inc.

Review of the Survey of Organizational Climate by CHARLES K. PARSONS, *Professor of Management, Georgia Institute of Technology, Atlanta, GA:*

The Survey of Organizational Climate is a 60-item survey with responses on an agree-disagree format. When scored, the survey yields 12 scales; thus there are approximately five items per scale. Because the scoring routine is not provided, the precise number cannot be determined. The respondent answers on a separate answer sheet and this sheet is mailed to the survey publisher who does all scoring and provides all feedback reports.

The response format is somewhat unconventional in that it asks the respondent to respond to a scale that is anchored by ++, +, -, --, where ++ represents definitely agree and -- represents definitely disagree. The definitions of the response scale are given to the respondent in the instructions, but do not appear on the answer sheet itself. This could cause some confusion.

One of the 12 scales is titled Self-Confidence. Its inclusion is justified by the author(s) in that it may help explain negative attitudes derived from the previous 11 scales regarding the work environment. However, this reviewer feels that an instrument focusing on perceptions of work environment should not confuse what is being assessed by including a measure of self-confidence.

The intended use of the survey is to have it completed by work group members, their leader, and other work group leaders in the same organizational unit. This allows the interpretation of an individual's scores, the work group's scores, and the leader's score. Areas of disagreement can then be discussed.

The feedback form gives each individual his or her own scores, the average scores of his or her work group peers, and the average scores of the management group to which the leader belongs. If the respondent is a leader, the feedback report also reports the distribution of responses by his or her subordinates. One potential problem with the feedback of subordinate responses is that in small work groups, leaders may be able to identify how their subordinates responded.

On the other hand, the comprehensiveness of the feedback report should be quite useful when combined with the 10 diagnostic questions provided. There is also a recommendation that the respondent further explore answers to the diagnostic questions by discussing them with subordinates, peers, and supervisors.

There is also an instruction sheet for how a group leader should distribute and discuss the feedback reports. Because each subordinate receives a separate report and there is quite a bit of information contained in it, the recommendation is to distribute them (with the confidential seal intact), give them some time to absorb the information, then perhaps set up a time of 10–15 minutes to discuss the results with each one individually. I think that the instructions for conducting the feedback sessions are quite clear and should be very useful.

There are two deficiencies in the package I received. First, in discussing the concept of climate, the terms organizational climate and psychological climate were used interchangeably. The terms have more precise definitions in the academic literature on climate and the authors should update their usage of the terms.

Second, there was no report of any psychometric studies of the instrument. The user has no idea of the internal consistency of scales, intercorrelation of scales, test-retest reliability, or the criterion-related or construct validity. References are made to an assumed relationship between climate and productivity, but no data are provided to substantiate that such a finding has been produced for this instrument. I would strongly encourage the publisher to conduct such studies and provide future users with the information. This would provide a much better foundation for an otherwise comprehensive package.

[407]
Survey of Organizational Culture.

Purpose: Identification of organizational purpose and mission, perception of customers, and interrelationships of organization members.
Population: Employees of organizations.
Publication Dates: 1987–89.
Acronym: SOC.
Scores: 15 scales: Culture (Orientation to Customers, Orientation to Employees, Orientation to Stakeholders, Impact of Mission, Managerial Depth, Decision Level/Autonomy, Communication/Openness, Human Scale, Incentive/Motivation, Cooperation/Competition, Organizational Congruence, Behavior Under Pressure, Theory-S/Theory-T, 13 Scales Aggregated), Job Characteristics (Job Satisfaction, Organizational Commitment).
Administration: Group.
Editions, 2: Select Items, Professional.
Manual: No manual.
Price Data: Available from publisher.
Time: (20–25) minutes.
Authors: Robert W. Tucker and Walt J. McCoy.
Publisher: Human Services Resource Group.

Review of the Survey of Organizational Culture by
BERTRAM C. SIPPOLA, *Associate Professor of*
Psychology, University of New Orleans, New Orleans, LA:

The Survey of Organizational Culture (SOC) by Robert W. Tucker and Walt J. McCoy is an instrument still in development; it does not yet have a manual. A set of papers by the authors (Tucker & McCoy, 1988a, 1988b, 1989) presents an excellent starting point for a manual. The first paper lays out some developmental background, and the latter two report 10 validation studies, some of which were still ongoing at the time of publication. The authors' goal has been to develop an instrument to measure "organizational culture" across a variety of organizational settings; they summarize its use in eight different settings.

A consensual definition of organizational culture (OC) has not yet been achieved, with each researcher developing his/her own. "OC is a concept recently applied in the social systems area of organizational psychology, and is differentiated from 'organizational climate,' which is often seen as referring to individual psychological perceptions of the characteristics of an organization's practices and procedures" (Muchinsky, 1990, p. 284). As an emergent property of group interactions, an organization's culture is broadly defined as the language, values, beliefs, attitudes, customs, and expectations shared by its members; "what a group learns over a period of time as that group solves its problems of survival in an external environment and its problems of internal integration" (Schein, 1990). Tucker and McCoy believe "that values will emerge as one of several indispensable elements in a mature conception of organizational life" (1988a, p. 13). Others (Wiener, 1988) suggest a consensus that "shared values" are a core element of organizational culture. Thus, the focus in the SOC is not to report in summary form the reactions of individual employees to their organizational environment, but to gain an understanding of a particular organizational unit as a culture, including its patterns of acculturation (or socialization) of new members, using "values" as the central measurable concept.

The SOC consists of 55 Likert-type items, on which respondents rate characteristics of both the "actual" and the "desired" organization. (The published forms of the SOC have also included 12 to 20 additional items designed to assess job satisfaction and organizational commitment.) The 55 items of the basic SOC are scored on 13 dimensions developed as noted below. Thus, the SOC generates three sets of data: those summarizing the perceived situation, those summarizing the "desired" situation, and the difference scores between the these two. The difference scores might then provide a measure of the acculturation of the members of the organization. By using different groups of respondents (such as management vs.

"workers"), one could compare "relative acculturation" or perceptions of the organization's culture. One could compare the difference scores of new employees before and after initial training and orientation to check the level of acculturation. One could also conclude that there was little consensus on the values making up an organization's culture if the scale scores were to show a great deal of variance.

Who interprets these results? The forms are apparently scored by the test's publisher, although their "license agreement" does not specify what is to be provided in either scoring services or interpretation. A manual would answer these questions and tell us what items are included in each of the 13 dimensions. Because Tucker and McCoy believe the literature has not yet established what the dimensions of OC should be, they adopted an empirical, bootstrapping developmental process, working directly and interactively with leaders and managers of both private and public organizations to develop from qualitative bases the set of dimensions for which the items making up the quantitative SOC were developed. An unanswerable question is whether the process went deep enough to measure "learned culture," or whether the SOC really deals only with "social climate," a surface manifestation of culture. The authors' primary criterion seems to be face validity: managers are impressed by the relevance of the "factors." The question remains whether the initial set of items was broad enough or relevant enough to support the factor analytic validation. There may be no way to know whether the dimensions used in any survey are the same ones actually functioning at the deeper levels of culture.

Over the series of studies reported by Tucker and McCoy (1988b), the SOC shows generally good psychometric properties. Split-half reliabilities are reported as over .90, whereas test-retest measures which were included in two studies show correlations of .73 and .84 over 3- to 4-week periods. Internal consistencies of the 13 dimensions are supported by alpha coefficients that are within acceptable ranges, although somewhat variable. The authors suggest that some of this variability may be due to the different educational backgrounds of respondents, with further work needed to fit the SOC language to appropriate respondents. It may be that within a given organization, shared meaning is reduced by language differences among individuals at different status levels.

The authors note that "there are no formal instruments or other standardized bases of observation against which the SOC can be assessed" (1988b). Thus, construct validity is supported by a number of converging data, some of which are quantitative, but is not documented against any external instruments. One of their measures of validity is the correlation of some of the dimensions with the attitudinal measures of job satisfaction and organizational commitment, or with the behavioral measures of turnover, absenteeism, and productivity. At the same time, they present data to suggest that there is enough independence, as shown by low- to medium-level correlations, with these other constructs. They report that "participating managers and leaders rated ten of the thirteen SOC scales [dimensions] from above average to superior in realism, salience, significance, and usefulness" (1989, p. 13). They also present analysis of variance data that suggest that the SOC is sensitive to between-organization cultural differences and within-organization similarities.

It would have been interesting and potentially valuable to see a study in which the Survey of Organizations (Taylor & Bowers, 1967–74; T3:2369), the embodiment of Likert theory of organizations, and the SOC were given to the same set of organizational members. Not only might this provide cross-validation regarding correctness of respondent perceptions, but it could provide a direct comparison between these two approaches to studying the nature of organizations.

Despite the use of management persons in the developmental stages, the results of the SOC may well not be self-evident to many managers. Therefore, the primary users of the SOC will most likely be researchers who may be studying either organizational cultures or more specific organizational questions (especially in the near-term), or consultants who will integrate these results into their overall evaluations and recommendations. The authors note that "more lies ahead than behind in the development of the SOC" (1988b, p. 33). The SOC shows interesting promise in terms of giving both managers and researchers information on the nature of OC, especially in terms of the uniqueness of any specific organization; on the pressures for organizational change; and for measuring the communication within an organization. It appears that the SOC provides an opportunity to widen the range of the literature on OC, rather than moving it toward a consensual definition that could provide a single, widely accepted instrument measuring OC.

REVIEWER'S REFERENCES

Taylor, J. C. & Bowers, D. G. (1967–80). Survey of Organizations. Ann Arbor, MI: Organizational Development Research Program of the Center for Research on Utilization of Scientific Knowledge, Institute for Social Research, University of Michigan.

Tucker, R. W., & McCoy, W. J. (1988a, August). Toward the rigorous assessment of values in studying organizational culture. Paper presented at the Annual Meeting of the American Psychological Association, Atlanta, GA.

Tucker, R. W., & McCoy, W. J. (1988b, August). Can questionnaires measure culture: Eight extended field studies. Paper presented at the Annual Meeting of Division 14 of the American Psychological Association: Society for Industrial and Organizational Psychology, Atlanta, GA. (ERIC Document Reproduction Service No. TM 012 665).

Wiener, Y. (1988). Forms of value systems: A focus on organizational effectiveness and cultural change and maintenance. Academy of Management Review, 13, 534-545.

Tucker, R. W., & McCoy, W. J. (1989, August). *Objective assessment of organizational culture: Generalizations from 10 validation studies.* Paper presented at the Annual Meeting of the Academy of Management, Washington, DC.

Muchinsky, P. M. (1990). *Psychology applied to work: An introduction to industrial and organizational psychology* (3rd ed.). Pacific Grove, CA: Brooks/Cole.

Schein, E. H. (1990). Organizational culture. *American Psychologist, 45* (2), 109-119.

[408]
Survey of Organizational Stress.

Purpose: To "provide a comprehensive anonymous analysis and feedback for both individuals and management as they jointly pursue a program of Health Maintenance to reduce stress-related illness."

Population: High school and college, government and private enterprise.

Publication Dates: 1981–86.

Acronym: SOS.

Scores, 5: 4 Life Style Needs (Security, Achievement, Recognition, Belonging) and Total Stress.

Administration: Group.

Forms, 2: Quality of Life Survey in Your Educational Setting, Quality of Life Survey in Your Organizational Setting.

Price Data, 1988: $36 per comprehensive manual ('85, 80 pages); price data for workshop training available from publisher; computer analysis for individual and organizational scores available from publisher.

Time: Administration time not reported.

Comments: Not available without special preparation including workshop training.

Author: Charles W. Nelson.

Publisher: Management Research Associates.

a) QUALITY OF LIFE SURVEY IN YOUR EDUCATIONAL SETTING.

Population: High school and college.

Publication Date: 1985.

b) QUALITY OF LIFE SURVEY IN YOUR ORGANIZATIONAL SETTING.

Population: Government and private enterprise.

Publication Date: 1981.

Review of the Survey of Organizational Stress by PHILIP G. BENSON, Associate Professor of Management, New Mexico State University, Las Cruces, NM:

The Survey of Organizational Stress is actually two very similar tests. These include the Quality of Life Survey in Your Educational Setting and the Quality of Life Survey in Your Organizational Setting. The forms differ in their primary application. The first is for use in educational settings, especially at the university level, and the second is for use primarily in private- and public-sector organizations. Both forms of the Survey of Organizational Stress include 100 items, divided into six major sections: Appraisal of Organizational Climate, Sources of Role Conflict, Available Coping Resources, Stress Reaction Awareness, Overall Evaluation of Situation, and a final section that essentially covers demographic information and a brief survey of personal health habits.

The survey is part of a consulting practice, which has as its focus the reduction of stress and stress-related illness in various organizational settings. The essential purpose of this approach is to reduce stress-related illness by teaching individuals to cope with frustration of needs, which in turn can reduce the experienced stress that leads, in turn, to various illnesses. The Survey of Organizational Stress is used as a diagnostic tool within the context of this overall approach.

The primary source of documentation for the survey is a technical report which outlines the general theoretical justification for the tests and a number of analyses related to the use of the surveys in overall stress reduction programs. This document is 80 pages in length, but is less than a comprehensive description of the necessary technical details for evaluation of the quality of the measures. In addition, the documentation for the survey refers to other measures of life styles that relate to stress; although these measures are related to the use of the Survey of Organizational Stress, they were not included with the materials provided and will not be reviewed here.

Reliabilities for the Stress Areas were calculated as "Spearman-Brown Odd-Even and Split Half coefficients of reliability," although a single value is reported for each. Reliabilities are reported to be .80 for Organizational Climate, .77 for Role Conflict, .76 for Coping Resources, and .54 for Stress Reaction Awareness. In addition, the Overall Stress measure has a reported reliability of .93. These reliabilities are best viewed as no better than adequate, and for scales of 20 items in length (for the first four scales) these may be a bit low. The highest reliability for the overall measure is based on a set of only seven items; however, the other scales have a number of subscales included, and an examination of the tests themselves suggests the possibility that the items are measuring constructs that are too heterogeneous to meet the assumptions of internal consistency reliability. No reliabilities are reported for subsets of the Stress Area scales. Item-level statistics are not provided to allow consideration of this possibility.

Normative data presented for the scales are based on a sample of 1,245 college students. These norms are presented as normal curve percentile equivalents. For each scale, the tables highlight those scores that are presented as low, average, and high. To determine the percentiles to be highlighted, the standard error of measurement was used to determine the .05 level confidence bands around the means, suggesting that these scores are statistically higher or lower than average. The average score is set at the 50th percentile, whereas the high and low scores vary with scale reliability, but range from the 33rd and 67th percentiles to the 13th and 88th percentiles.

Validity of the surveys is presented in several ways. First, all four of the area scales were found to be correlated with the Overall Stress measure, with correlations of .64, .81, .75, and .72 for the measures of Organizational Climate, Role Conflict, Coping Resources, and Stress Reaction Awareness, respectively. It is interesting to note that these correlations are very high, considering the reliabilities reported for each scale. Indeed, the discriminant validity of the scale could be questioned on the basis of these findings.

Content validity was addressed in the development of the items included in the surveys. Professionals in industrial sociology, social psychology, clinical psychology, and the health professions were utilized in developing the various scales. In addition, one question in the demographic section asks respondents to assess the degree to which the questions in the survey are reasonable measures; the manual reports that 85% gave favorable responses, thus supporting content validity. It would be possible to argue that respondent assessments are a better measure of face validity than of content validity, but the data are useful nonetheless.

To assess criterion-related validity, analyses were done to correlate the scale scores with the self-reported measures of alienation, health habits, and morale. In addition, correlations were performed with the demographic variables, but fewer significant correlations were found, and it is not clear that these should relate as strongly. The strongest of these correlations was with alienation from the organization, with a value of .56. Other correlations were found with burnout (.30), aspiration (.19), and control (.18). Overall, the correlations found do tend to suggest a relationship of scale scores to experienced stress.

The correlations are further interpreted in support of construct validity, and the theoretical justification for the relationships is expanded. In addition, much of the supporting manual covers the nature of stress and the findings of stress research. In a very real sense, much of the documentation seems to be a research report on the reduction of occupational stress, rather than a traditional test manual.

Overall, the surveys seem to have some promise, and do have face validity. However, the documentation is simply not sufficient as supporting the surveys from a measurement perspective. More details are needed, especially regarding technical issues.

In addition, the production of the manual does not build one's confidence in the surveys. For example, the word "criterion" is consistently used as a plural form. In giving the formula for the standard error, a number 6 is used instead of a small sigma. The manual consistently uses "he" and "his," in spite of the clear admonition in the APA *Publication Manual* (APA, 1983) (and in technical writing generally) to avoid gender bias in language. The manual refers to "related criterion" validity at several points. Although all of this does *not* prove the inadequacy of the tests themselves, this does cause the reviewer to be uneasy in evaluating the work performed.

Overall, the measures may have promise. However, they are only available through the publisher, in combination with a program of training and stress reduction in organizations. Within such a context, the measures may work quite well. As measures, however, they should be viewed as experimental in nature based on the data available to date.

REVIEWER'S REFERENCE

American Psychological Association. (1983). *Publication manual of the American Psychological Association* (3rd ed.). Washington, DC: Author.

Review of the Survey of Organizational Stress by DAVID M. SAUNDERS, Assistant Professor, Faculty of Management, McGill University, Montreal, CANADA:

The Survey of Organizational Stress is presented as two forms of the Quality of Life Stress Survey (QLSS): one for educational settings and one for organizational settings. The items on each form appear comparable, although the forms are not identical. The test publisher recommends a 3-day workshop before using the QLSS. The QLSS is part of a larger organizational development program for managing stress throughout organizations. The QLSS produces group and individual scores for Total Stress, four individual Life Style Needs (Security, Achievement, Recognition, Belonging), and four Sources of Stress (Organization Climate, Role Conflict, Coping Resources, Stress Reaction).

The manual contains an accessible review of historic and modern literature on stress, a discussion of how to manage stress at the organizational level, and some information about scale reliability and validity. There is very little information in the manual about which items belong to which scale, and how they were selected. No definition of the Total Stress scale is given in the manual, although the reader can infer that it is a composite of the four Life Style Needs scores. In addition, each of the first 80 items in the QLSS appears to be used in two scales: once as a Life Style Need item, and once as a Source of Stress item.

The QLSS was normed on a sample of 1,245 full-time college undergraduates, presumably with the Educational Setting Form. Spearman-Brown reliability coefficients are in the .70s for the four Life Style scales, over .90 for Total Stress, over .70 for Organizational Climate, Role Conflict, and Coping Resources, and .54 for Stress Reaction. Given that there are 20 items on each subscale, some of these reliability coefficients are somewhat low.

The four Life Style Needs scales correlate in the .90s with the Total Stress scale, not surprising if the latter is a composite of the former scales. No discussion of the correlations among the Life Style Needs scales is presented within the manual. The scales are discussed as if they were completely independent, but documentation to support this claim is needed. Similarly, no discussion of the correlations among the four Sources of Stress scales is presented. Although these scales are discussed as if they were independent, evidence supporting this claim is also necessary.

Evidence of the validity of the QLSS is very weak. Discriminant and convergent validity are not discussed directly, although correlations of .37 between the Total Stress scale and two subscales of the College and University Educational Survey (level of morale, faculty-student relationships) does suggest some convergent validity. No comparison with alternative stress scales is made. Evidence of criterion-related validity is extremely weak. Four single-item criteria are arbitrarily labelled with one of the scale anchors and presented as criteria. Although the correlation of the "combined criterion" is .45, this is difficult to interpret because each of the items on this criteria scale is on different metrics. Correlations of the Total Stress scale with Personal Health Habits ($r = .25$) and the Public Health Life Style Profile ($r = .26$) suggest that the scale might have some predictive validity.

In summary, the QLSS does not currently achieve generally accepted standards of test construction. The manual does not present any information about the independence of the subscales of the QLSS, and the information about scale validity and reliability is unimpressive. More extensive validation of the QLSS is required. Validation of the Organizational Setting form needs to be done with a sample of employees. Claims of criterion-related validity and discussions suggesting that the subscales are independent should be treated with caution until further psychometric evidence is presented. I suggest that potential users of the QLSS give serious consideration to alternative instruments.

[409]
Surveys of Problem-Solving and Educational Skills.

Purpose: To "provide a profile of a student's strengths and weaknesses in problem-solving processes, educational skills, and learning strategies."
Population: Ages 9-0 to 14-11.
Publication Date: 1987.
Acronym: SPES.
Administration: Individual.
Parts: 2 tests: Survey of Problem-Solving Skills, Survey of Educational Skills.
Price Data, 1988: $35 per videotape; $8.50 per examiner's manual (90 pages).
Time: (60–90) minutes for the battery.

Comments: "Criterion-referenced"; training videotape available.
Author: Lynn J. Meltzer.
Publisher: Educators Publishing Service, Inc.
  a) SURVEY OF PROBLEM-SOLVING SKILLS.
Acronym: SPRS.
Scores: 6 tasks: Nonlinguistic (Series Completion, Categorization, Matrix Completion), Linguistic/Verbal (Category Shift, Sequential Reasoning, Classification).
Price Data: $8 per stimulus book; $16 per 24 record forms.
  b) SURVEY OF EDUCATIONAL SKILLS.
Acronym: SEDS.
Scores: 4 skills: Reading, Writing, Spelling, Mathematics.
Price Data: $6 per stimulus booklet; $18.50 per 12 record forms; $17.50 per 12 workbooks.

Review of the Surveys of Problem-Solving and Educational Skills by RON EDWARDS, Professor of Psychology, University of Southern Mississippi, Hattiesburg, MS:

The Surveys of Problem-Solving and Educational Skills (SPES) is described as providing a "profile of a student's strengths and weaknesses in problem-solving processes, educational skills, and learning strategies." A major objective is the construction of functional profiles that can be "matched with remedial and teaching techniques." The manual suggests that the SPES can be used by "diagnosticians, teachers, and educational specialists to enhance their understanding of a student's learning style." It is a "diagnostic *approach* to the assessment and treatment of subtle learning difficulties and should *not* be considered a comprehensive *test* to be used in isolation."

The technical data provided for the SPES are woefully inadequate. Although the scales are described as criterion referenced, except for a theoretical model, initial development procedures are unspecified. The items were pilot tested with a sample of 200 normally achieving students randomly selected from three New England school districts. The pilot subjects were of average intelligence, from middle-class communities, and ranged in age from 9-0 to 14-11. No other subject characteristic data are provided. For most SPES subtests, scores are designated as "concerns," "age appropriate," or "strengths." Concerns and strengths represent scores one *SD* below or above the mean obtained by the 200 pilot subjects.

The Survey of Problem-Solving Skills (SPRS) consists of six reasoning subtests with only six items per subtest. A number correct score is yielded by all subtests along with a highly subjective rating of the "problem-solving processes" used. Instructions and scoring criteria are minimal and raise many questions. The only reliability information provided is a statement that "interrater reliability was checked across six different raters and studies revealed median reliability values greater than 90 percent across all six subtests." Although the SPRS is *not* a cognitive measure according to the author, validity is supported by data regarding its relationship to Wechsler Intelligence Scale for Children—Revised (WISC-R) scores. Two SPRS subtests (Classification and Category Shift) account for most of the shared variance with the WISC-R. The Classification and Category Shift subtests involve similar tasks and the Classification subtest was designed to be highly similar to the WISC-R Similarities subtest.

The Survey of Educational Skills (SEDS) is described as focusing on the identification of each "child's specific learning style and . . . characteristic error patterns in reading, writing, spelling, and mathematics." The SEDS contains a number of tasks assessing performance in each academic area with exceedingly complex and confusing administration instructions and scoring procedures. Administration involves juggling four flimsily constructed booklets with frequent flipping back and forth across booklets. No reliability information is provided for the SEDS. The complexity of its administration and scoring procedures suggests that examiners would need extensive training to produce reliable results. Validity is supported by a statement that the results of comparisons with the Metropolitan Achievement Test "indicated a significant proportion of common variance in each achievement area."

The primary source of support for the validity of both the SPRS and the SEDS is a comparison study involving 342 normal achievers (NA) and 284 students with learning difficulties (LD). Although the SPES is said to be designed to assess subtle learning difficulties, the LD group seems likely to have had rather serious learning problems. Children were included in the LD group if they were enrolled in a "substantial special education program outside the regular classroom" or met two or more other criteria reflecting relatively serious academic difficulties. Other than a 2:1 ratio of males over females, no further information regarding these subjects is provided. For the SPRS, tables are provided showing the percentage of LD and NA students by age group (9–10, 11–12, and 13–14) "experiencing difficulty" on each SPRS subtest. "Experiencing difficulty" means achieving a score in the "concern" range. In general, the percentage of LD students experiencing difficulty is higher than the percentage of NA students. However, in some cases the percentage difference is quite small and in other cases only a very small percentage of either group experienced difficulty. Bar graphs displaying the table data are also provided, but in a number of cases the graphs are not in agreement with the tabular data. Results of discriminant analysis are also included indicating that the SPRS was able to discriminate the NA and LD groups fairly well.

Similar information is provided for the SEDS although not all SEDS subtests are represented.

Throughout the SPES manual, the inventories are described as yielding information which can be used to develop effective instructional strategies suited to a student's specific learning style. No data are provided supporting this contention. Frequent reference is made to supporting literature but most of the references cited are from local paper presentations, submitted articles, or publications in very weak journals. A case study is included illustrating use of the SPES that concludes with 13 somewhat specific instructional recommendations. However, virtually all of the recommendations could have been generated based on the child's background and school history information without reference to the SPES results.

SUMMARY. According to the author, the SPES is not a test. Given the absence of appropriate technical data, it is easy to agree with this statement. There is little doubt that the SPES yields information regarding a student's reasoning abilities and academic skills which may be useful in a clinical evaluation. However, use of the quantitative scores cannot be justified based on accepted psychometric criteria. The manual repeatedly stresses that the SPES should be used only in conjunction with other neurodevelopmental and educational testing. If the results of a battery of adequate psychoeducational instruments are available, the probability that the SPES would add significantly to this information is doubtful. The contention that the SPES can yield valuable information linking a student's learning style to instructional strategies must be considered in light of the absence of support for such contentions in the research literature. If the primary assessment objective is the development of specific instructional strategies, the use of curriculum-based assessment procedures is likely to be more fruitful.

Review of the Surveys of Problem-Solving and Educational Skills by RONALD K. HAMBLETON, Professor of Education and Psychology, University of Massachusetts at Amherst, Amherst, MA:

The Surveys of Problem-Solving and Educational Skills (SPES) is an individually administered diagnostic instrument for assessing problem-solving skills, educational skills, and learning strategies of children between the ages of 9 and 15. The SPES is an untimed instrument intended for children who are having difficulties in school. According to the author, the typical student usually needs between 60 and 90 minutes to complete the SPES. The tasks included in the test were chosen to permit the evaluation of connections among problem-solving strategies, learning processes, and educational outcomes. By drawing these connections, the author's expectation is that more valid recommendations for planning interventions for students in need of help will result.

On the surface, the SPES probably appears to be one of several instruments that purport to accomplish much the same purposes, that is, provide clinicians and teachers with information that can help them understand the reasons for a student's learning difficulties in school, and provide them with useful information for designing individualized programs to enhance school achievement. In fact, however, the SPES, which is divided into two parts, the Survey of Problem-Solving Skills (SPRS) and the Survey of Educational Skills (SEDS), is a complex, theory-driven, comprehensive instrument that appears to require a considerable amount of sophistication in testing to administer, to score, and to interpret. Administration of the test generates a large amount of data on each student.

The SPES consists of six documents: the test (stimulus) booklets for the SPRS and SEDS (which are reusable); student workbook for the SEDS (not reusable); student record forms for the SPRS and SEDS (not reusable); and the examiner's manual (which contains descriptions of the surveys; relevant psychological theory; descriptions of the subtests; administration, scoring, and technical information; and interpretation guides).

The SPRS is based upon a theoretical model developed by the author that links five problem-solving strategies (each with associate components) to the learning difficulties of students. In order to measure these problem-solving strategies which are (a) efficiency of selecting strategies, (b) flexibility of selecting strategies, (c) methods of applying strategies, (d) styles of applying strategies, and (e) explanations of strategies, six problem-solving tasks or scales (each with six questions) were prepared. Through student efforts to solve the tasks and interrogations of students after they complete each question, test administrators are able to assess their problem-solving strategies and related component skills. The problem-solving tasks are organized into two categories, Nonlinguistic and Linguistic/Verbal. The tasks are Series Completion, Categorization, Matrix Completion, Category Shift, Sequential Reasoning, and Classification.

The SEDS looks like a fairly typical achievement test to measure basic skills, in this case, basic skills in the areas of Reading, Writing, Spelling, and Mathematics. But there is one main difference. Of special interest in the scoring of the SEDS are the processes and strategies that students use to answer the questions as well as their error patterns in responding to the questions.

The student test (stimulus) booklets and the workbook are clearly printed and appear to contain appropriate questions. Certainly there is evidence in the examiner's manual (such as the description of

the test development activities and the item analysis results) that the two tryouts (and perhaps others) were instrumental in improving the directions, scoring keys, and test questions.

The directions for the administration of the Surveys are complex, perhaps not surprising given the diverse nature of the subtests and the very large amount of information that must be compiled by test administrators. But contributing to the complexity is the difficulty of finding necessary information in the examiner's manual and using it. More use of main headings and bold-face type, highlighting directions to be read to students, and scoring methods, etc. would have been helpful. I suffered a major headache each time I tried to work through the administration and scoring section of the examiner's manual and I had to study this material several times to be sure I understood it. Also contributing to the complexity is the inclusion of material on test score uses and interpretations in the same part of the manual as the directions for administration and scoring. The utility of the manual would be enhanced with the inclusion of a *separate* section on test score interpretations.

The interpretative material too would be enhanced if supporting documentation for more of the recommended test score interpretations was provided. For example, on page 14 this interpretative statement appears, "Performance on the Matrix Completion task has relevance for the organization and efficient production of writing and mathematics. Students who cannot identify the correct choice on the matrix items may struggle with the spacing of letters and words, with organization and planning skills, and with their ability to orient information appropriately on a page." Where is the evidence to support the validity of this interpretation of a student's performance on the Matrix Completion task? A similar criticism could be made of many of the other recommended score interpretations.

There is another main problem with the interpretative material in the examiner's manual. There are pages and pages of summary scores and evaluative comments (37 pages to be exact) that are collected during the testing process. How is the full set of available data to be integrated by the clinician and used to produce an educational program for the student? One case study is offered in the manual but *many* more are needed if valid interpretations and uses of the complex data are to result.

The reliability of information (i.e., scores or ratings and descriptions) obtained from a psychological instrument is always of interest. When an instrument is short (in the SPRS, for example, each scale contains *only* six questions) and much of the test information is judgementally determined by test administrators, questions about instrument reliability seem critical. Unfortunately, the amount of reliability information in the examiner's manual is particularly sparse. The full extent of the information on the SPRS is as follows: "Inter-rater reliability was checked across six different raters and studies revealed median reliability values greater than 90% across all six subtests" (p. 67). No details were provided about (a) the amount of training of test administrators, (b) the specific design features of the reliability studies, or (c) the method of calculating the reliability statistics (for example, were reliability statistics corrected for chance agreement?). No evidence is offered concerning the stability of test information over short periods of time. All in all the reporting of reliability information comes up very short of the guidelines for reporting reliability described in the *Standards for Educational and Psychological Testing* (AERA, APA, & NCME, 1985).

In contrast to the reliability information, the validity information is extensive and comprehensive, and the reporting of the information is well done. The results of factor analyses were fully reported and used in the organization of subtests and score results. Impressively sized differences between normal achieving students and students with learning difficulties were obtained at the three main age groups (9–10, 11–12, 13–14) on just about every variable that is measured in the SPES. And too, results from discriminant analyses and regression analyses showed the reasonable predictive power of the SPES. Convergent validity studies showed substantial overlap between subtests of the SPRS and the Wechsler Intelligence Scale for Children—Revised (WISC-R). All of these analyses and many others were conducted on reasonable sized samples (about 200 during pilot testing and 625 during the validation phase).

In summary, there are many features of the SPES that are noteworthy: (a) A definite need is met by the presence of this instrument; (b) the scales appear to evolve from a carefully conducted and systematic research project and a well-documented theory about problem-solving strategies and school achievement; and (c) ample evidence is reported that normal children and children having learning difficulties differ substantially on nearly all of the scales. On the other hand, there appear to be four serious shortcomings associated with the SPES: (a) There is an absence of detailed reliability information—both interrater and stability; (b) directions for administration and scoring in the examiner's manual are not presented in a clear, convenient or readable format; (c) many of the recommended score interpretations do *not* seem to be supported by validity evidence (or, at least, the evidence is not reported in the examiner's manual); and (d) an insufficient number of guidelines are provided for effective uses of the complicated score report forms. Overall, the SPES

appears to have considerable merit, but attention to the criticisms above should strengthen the validity and the utility of future editions. In the meantime, users must be cautioned that considerable training appears to be necessary for test administrators, and test score interpretations should be done only by persons with a clear understanding of the theoretical underpinnings of the SPES and how the available information relates to classroom learning and remediation. Users can hope that a casebook to support proper score interpretations of the complex information that the SPES provides will be available with the next edition.

REVIEWER'S REFERENCE

American Educational Research Association, American Psychological Association, & National Council on Measurement in Education. (1985). *Standards for educational and psychological testing.* Washington, DC: American Psychological Association, Inc.

[410]

Sutter-Eyberg Student Behavior Inventory.
Purpose: "Constructed to provide a comprehensive, narrow-band measure of conduct problem behaviors."
Population: Ages 2–17.
Publication Date: [1984].
Acronym: SESBI.
Scores, 2: Intensity, Problem.
Administration: Individual.
Manual: No manual.
Price Data: No charge for one copy; may be photocopied for research or clinical use.
Time: [5] minutes.
Comments: Ratings by teachers.
Author: Joseph Sutter and Sheila M. Eyberg.
Publisher: Sheila M. Eyberg, Ph.D.

TEST REFERENCES

1. Funderburk, B. W., & Eyberg, S. M. (1989). Psychometric characteristics of the Sutter-Eyberg Student Behavior Inventory: A school behavior rating scale for use with preschool children. *Behavioral Assessment, 11*, 297-313.

2. Burns, G. L., & Owen, S. M. (1990). Disruptive behaviors in the classroom: Initial standardization data on a new teacher rating scale. *Journal of Abnormal Child Psychology, 18*, 515-525.

Review of the Sutter-Eyberg Student Behavior Inventory by T. STEUART WATSON, Assistant Professor of Educational Psychology, Mississippi State University, Starkville, MS:

The Sutter-Eyberg Student Behavior Inventory (SESBI), a teacher-report measure, is a companion instrument to the Eyberg Child Behavior Inventory (ECBI; 9:404). The SESBI contains 11 items from the ECBI and 36 items overall. Two scores, an Intensity Score and a Problem Score, are derived from the SESBI. The Intensity Score is a reflection of how often a behavior occurs, ranging from *never* (1) to *always* (7). The total Intensity Score may range from 36–252. The Problem Score is a sum of the number of times the respondent answered affirmatively that a behavior is problematic. This score can range from 0–36.

The stated uses of the SESBI are as a brief screening instrument to differentiate normal and conduct problem behavior children and adolescents in the classroom. Another is to measure change in the classroom during the course of treatment for conduct problem behaviors. The primary purpose of this instrument is to measure conduct problem behaviors as a unidimensional construct in children aged 2 to 17.

Five types of reliability have been reported across studies: internal consistency, split-half, item to total, test-retest, and interrater. Internal consistency coefficients (Cronbach's alpha) across studies ranged from .95–.98 for the Intensity Scores and from .93–.96 for the Problem Scores. These internal consistency coefficients lend support that the SESBI is measuring a single, homogeneous construct.

Split-half correlations ranged from .89–.92 for the Intensity Scores to .86–.88 for the Problem Scores. Item to total coefficients ranged from .30 to .89 for the Intensity Scale and from .06–.84 for the Problem Scale. Test-retest coefficients ranged from .90–.94 and .89–.98 for the Intensity and Problem Scales, respectively. SESBI scores did not decrease on second administration, a problem noted with other behavior rating scales. This is especially important as a decrease in scores from the first to second administrations could mistakenly be interpreted as a result of beneficial treatment effects.

Interrater reliability ranged from .85–.95 for the Intensity Scores and from .84–.87 for the Problem Scores. This is a strength of the SESBI in that it is one of the few behavior rating inventories that presents interrater reliability.

Moderate correlations ranging from .57–.65 have been observed between the Intensity and Problem Scores. This finding suggests that the two scales of the SESBI are measuring a closely related, but not identical, construct.

Convergent and discriminant validity have been assessed by correlating the SESBI with the Internalizing and Externalizing Factors of other behavior rating instruments. Correlations between the Intensity and Problem Scores and the Externalizing Score of the Achenbach Teacher Rating Form yielded coefficients of .87 and .71, respectively. The Internalizing Score of the Achenbach was marginally related to the Intensity Score ($r = .25$). The Problem Score was said to be unrelated to the Internalizing Score.

Mean SESBI scores of children diagnosed with disruptive behavior disorders were significantly higher than children diagnosed with internalizing disorders and no emotional or behavioral diagnosis. Further analyses revealed that, when the disruptive behavior disorders were divided into conduct or attention problems, only the conduct problem group differed from the other groups on the Problem score. However, both groups differed from the internalizing disorders and no disorders groups on the Intensity score. The SESBI is able to distinguish between children with severe conduct behavior problems and children with none to few, based on significant differences between mean rating scores. The discriminant ability of the SESBI ratings in differentiating conduct problem children from non-conduct problem children and control children is well supported.

The SESBI Intensity Score correlated highly (.94) with the Conners Total Score, giving evidence of concurrent validity. Correlations of the SESBI with the Preschool Behavior Questionnaire (PBQ) yield further evidence of concurrent validity. Both scores of the SESBI correlated highly with the Externalizing Factor and Total Score of the PBQ. The Internalizing Factor of the PBQ also correlated significantly with the Intensity ($r = .40$ to $.57$) and Problem Scores ($r = .27$ to $.42$).

Sensitivity of the SESBI to treatment effects has been suggested due to the reduction in pre- to post-treatment scores of a group of children ages 2–7 when compared to no treatment groups. For this same group of subjects, the pre- and post-treatment ECBI and SESBI ratings were not significantly correlated. However, the difference scores (pre treatment minus post treatment) were correlated for the two groups ($r = .78$).

Principal components factor analysis has shown consistently that one primary factor emerges for both scales, accounting for 38–53% of the variance. Although as many as six factors have been identified for the Intensity Scale and eight for the Problem Scale, none (other than the first factor) accounted for as much as 10% of the variance.

Significant effects for age or gender generally have not been observed for either scale. One study did show that males' mean Intensity Scores were higher than those for females. Preliminary findings suggest that teachers rate Asian children as having fewer problems than Whites, who are rated as having fewer than Blacks. These results are based on very limited numbers of Black and Asian subjects.

The SESBI has a number of advantages over other behavior rating instruments intended for school use. The first is that it identifies those behaviors that are typically most troublesome for classroom teachers. It can be completed and scored in a short amount of time. Third, it assesses the problem status of a particular behavior. Although a behavior may occur frequently, it may not be problematic for the respondent. And fourth, it helps to identify behaviors that merit intervention.

Despite its ease of administration and scoring, it would be helpful to have a short reference manual that summarizes the psychometric properties, intended uses, and clinical data collected on the SESBI. A number of studies have been conducted regarding reliability and validity. These results have not been consolidated into one source, however, and would be especially helpful to the clinician or researcher wishing to evaluate and use the instrument.

Psychometrically, the SESBI could be substantially strengthened by obtaining data on children ages 8 to 17, a group not included in previous studies. Use of the SESBI with children in this range should proceed with caution. The 2–7-year age group has adequate reliability and validity data, although larger and more varied samples are needed. The utility of extending the SESBI to the 2–3-year age range is questionable, given that most children are not attending school at these ages. It seems that the ECBI would be more appropriate for children of this age.

The SESBI has accomplished what it was intended to do. It appears to have utility as a brief screening instrument that can be used in schools to detect a wide range of conduct problem behaviors. It can be used to determine if treatment is necessary and if further assessment is warranted. If more in-depth information is required, for conduct problems as well as other behavior patterns, then an instrument such as the Achenbach Child Behavior Checklist—Teacher Report Form (64) would be more appropriate. The Achenbach has well-established reliability and validity and stratified norms with broad age ranges.

[411]

The TARC Assessment System.

Purpose: "Provides a short-form behavioral assessment of the capabilities of retarded or otherwise severely handicapped children on a number of skills related to education."

Population: Ages 3–16.

Publication Date: 1975.

Acronym: TARC.

Scores, 17: Self-Help Skills (Toileting, Washing, Eating, Clothing Management, Total), Motor Skills (Small Muscle Coordination, Large Muscle Coordination, Pre-Academic Skills, Total), Communication Skills (Receptive, Expressive, Pre-Academic, Total), Social Skills (Observed Behavior, Pre-Academic Skills, Total), Total.

Administration: Individual.

Price Data, 1989: $16 per complete kit including 10 assessment sheets and manual (7 pages); $13 per 10 assessment sheets; $5 per manual.

Time: Administration time not reported.

Comments: Behavior checklist.

Authors: Wayne Sailor and Bonnie Jean Mix.

Publisher: PRO-ED, Inc.

Review of the TARC Assessment System by STEVEN W. LEE, Assistant Professor of Educational Psychology and Research, University of Kansas, Lawrence, KS:

The TARC (Topeka [Kansas] Association for Retarded Citizens) Assessment System was devel-

oped as a "quick assessment" which provides a "snapshot" of the current functioning level of mentally retarded and severely handicapped children. The TARC "kit" provides a seven-page manual, with 10 eight-page assessment sheets. The manual provides some psychometric information as well as instructions on scoring and interpreting the TARC. The assessment sheet is well laid out and easy to use. Instructions for scoring are also provided on the assessment sheet, including a page for charting the examinee's profile. The assessment is untimed and should be done by an examiner after at least 3 weeks of observation of the child. No other special qualifications of the examiner are mentioned. If a skill to be rated has not been observed, it is recommended that the examiner "test" these directly, although the procedure for doing this is not elucidated.

The TARC was developed using a "narrow sampling" of behaviors in representative skill areas presumably to provide an estimate of the examinee's current skills in various domains. Items on the TARC are grouped into subsections (e.g., Toileting, Washing, Eating, Clothing Management, etc.) that are subsumed under the Self-Help, Motor, Communication, and Social Skill areas. The sum of section scores provides a Total Score. There are two types of items on the TARC, scaled and categorical items. On the scaled items, the rater circles a numbered statement from a graduated, behaviorally anchored list of skills that have been observed by the examiner in a specific skill area (e.g., eating or dressing). The categorical items are a nongraduated list of behaviors within a skill area. The examiner must endorse all the behaviors within the skill area that can be successfully completed by the examinee. For example, in the Large Muscle Coordination area some skills are: walks, runs, hops on one foot, skips, climbs, swings, etc.

The manual reports that standardization was completed on 283 "severely handicapped" children between the ages of 3 and 16. Severely handicapped is defined as those children who were moderately mentally retarded or below (AAMD classification), as well as autistic, cerebral palsied, perceptually handicapped, or learning disabled. The rationale or method for selecting the sample was not provided, nor were the norms subdivided by age, sex, handicap, or IQ. Also omitted is the geographic location from which the sample was drawn, although presumably it was drawn from the Kansas area. The omission of the sample characteristics limits accurate interpretation of the TARC results. For example, might we expect a 3-year-old diagnosed as TMR to have fewer basic skills than TMR children who are 10 years older? Yet, if the 3-year-old is lower in skills with reference to the 3- to 16-year-old normative sample, his or her TARC scores may be interpreted as low, even though the child may have average skills when compared with other TMR preschool children. This is a serious deficit if the test is to be used in a normative way.

Subsection, section, and the total raw scores are plotted on a profile sheet (located on page 2 of the assessment sheet). In this way, raw scores can be converted to standard scores with a mean of 50 and a standard deviation of 20. The average range may then be construed as 30 to 70. Given the large age range and varying handicapping conditions in the standardization sample, a high degree of variability or error exists within the ratings which serves to limit the discriminative power of the test. In addition, the TARC has a limited ceiling in the Toileting, Washing, Eating, Clothing Management, Receptive, and Expressive Language subskill areas, further reducing the ability of the test to discriminate among functionally retarded children in these areas.

No psychometric information is provided on how the test was developed. Reliability data are provided in the form of an interrater reliability study using 66 severely handicapped children (50 of whom were institutionalized and 16 who were in day care). Interrater correlations were poor for the Self-Help ($r = .59$) and Motor ($r = .63$) scales, average for the Communication ($r = .77$) and Social ($r = .78$) scales, and good for the Total ($r = .85$) scale. A test-retest reliability study is mentioned, with reliability coefficients for the above mentioned scales exceeding the .80s over a 6-month time span. Unfortunately, no sample, examiners, or setting characteristics are provided for this study. No standard errors of measurement or validity data are provided in the TARC manual.

Instructions for interpreting the TARC are included in the manual. These instructions seem to confuse the differences between normative and relative strengths and weaknesses. According to the TARC authors, relative strengths or weaknesses are defined as scores that fall above or below a standard score of 50, respectively. Two problems are noted here. First from a normative perspective, scores falling within ±1 standard deviation of the mean would be considered average range scores and therefore could not be considered strengths or weaknesses. Second, *relative* strengths or weaknesses can be defined as those skill areas that are significantly higher or lower than the other skill areas in a specific child's profile. For example, a child with standard scores of around 20 in the Self-Help, Motor, and Communication skill areas may have a *relative* strength in Social Skills with a standard score of 40 (but still below the mean). Due to these problems, the instructions for interpretation of the TARC are quite problematic.

In sum, the TARC is quite limited as a normative measure of adaptive behavior. Accurate interpretation of TARC scores would be quite difficult given the lack of norms divided by age, sex, or handicapping condition. In addition, the limited ceiling in a number of the subskill areas, and the misleading instructions for interpretation serve to minimize the normative usefulness of the instrument. Add to these problems the equivocal reliability data and no published validity information, and the TARC cannot be considered a psychometrically viable, normative measure of adaptive behavior. However, as is mentioned in the manual, the TARC may be valuable as an informal assessment or screening tool leading to a more comprehensive assessment of adaptive behavior. The TARC may also be helpful in the development of instructional objectives for severely handicapped children.

Review of The TARC Assessment System by PAT MIRENDA, Associate Professor of Special Education and Communication Disorders, University of Nebraska-Lincoln, Lincoln, NE:

The TARC Assessment System, so named because it was developed with the cooperation of the Topeka (Kansas) Association for Retarded Citizens, is intended to be used as an alternative to more complex omnibus assessment inventories used with children with mental retardation or other severe handicaps. It is not intended to replace comprehensive assessment instruments, but rather to provide a general picture of a child's functioning in a number of areas. In order to do so the TARC provides an inventory to be completed by someone who "knows" the target child—"knowing" being defined as having spent a minimum of 3 weeks observing the child in a group or class setting. The inventory is completed by circling the option under each subsection that most closely describes the child's ability. These responses are then totaled to arrive at a raw score and plotted on a profile sheet that allows a comparison with standard scores (mean = 50, standard deviation = 20). Thus, the final scores are not stated in terms of either developmental or mental age and are not necessarily related to IQ or other common indices of this type.

The manual provides standardization information based on a population of 283 male and female children labelled moderately, severely, or profoundly handicapped and ranging in age from 3–16. No socioeconomic or racial/ethnic information about the subjects is provided, nor are the male/female ratio, the mean age of subjects, or information about the age range distribution made available. Information about the subjects' residence is not stated although at least subgroups of the sample are identified as living in an institution and a day-care situation. According to the manual, the sample included children with mental retardation, autism, cerebral palsy, perceptual handicaps, and learning disabilities; however, neither the proportions nor mean IQs of these subgroups are stated in the manual. Salvia and Ysseldyke (1988) recommend that the minimum number of subjects for which a full range of percentiles can be computed is 100; and that, therefore, a norm sample should contain at least 100 subjects per age. Based on this criterion, a sample that spans 13 years (ages 3–16) should have at least 1,300 subjects. Using this standard, the sample of 283 subjects for the TARC is inadequate. Furthermore, the lack of information about the sample group along the parameters mentioned previously seriously detracts from the utility of the instrument, as the specific population for whom its use would be appropriate is not at all clear.

The manual provides an intercorrelation matrix in which each subsection is correlated with each other subsection based on this sample. The matrix indicates that all correlations are significant at the p < .05 level (range = .54–.98) and that the Motor Skills section is the most predictive of the total inventory score. Interrater reliability was calculated on a subsample of 66 severely handicapped children, 50 of whom lived in an institution. The raters were two staff or teachers who were familiar with the children. The resulting "coefficients of correlation" (the exact procedure used is not named) on the subsections were found to be between .59 (Self-Help) and .78 (Social), with an overall correlation of .85; all were significant at p < .01. Test-retest reliabilities were conducted with the same subsample 6 months after the first administration and are reported as all being .80 or greater. Neither concurrent or construct validity information is provided, nor are any references available that indicate the source or sources of the items appearing on the inventory. Thus, within the limits of the standardization sample size, the TARC appears to be at least moderately reliable both across raters and over time, and is internally consistent in most areas. However, the sample size used for standardization is seriously deficient, the sample is inadequately described, and there is no information provided about the validity of the test items or their derivation.

The manual provides no guidelines concerning the use of the TARC assessment information to plan educational programs, aside from general statements that "the low points on the profile can be used to formulate educational goals and instructional objectives for the child" and that "many individual categorical items can also be translated into instructional objectives," with an example provided of how this might occur. Further, the test is quite out of date in terms of the type of educational program currently considered to be state-of-the-art for students with severe handicaps. Indeed, it is an irony that the first author of this now-outdated 1975 test is today one of the leading innovators in the area of integration and functional curricula for persons with severe handicaps. While the TARC measures functional skill ability more than many other assessments of its kind, it fails to provide a wide range of functional, chronological-age-appropriate items intended to measure educational needs in both school and community settings. Alternative assessment instruments that do provide such information include: the *Teaching Research Curriculum for Handicapped Adolescents and Adults: Assessment Procedures* (Peterson, Trecker, Egan, Fredericks, & Bunse, 1983); and the *Individual Student Community Life Skill Profile System for Severely Handicapped Students* (Freagon, Wheeler, McDaniel, Brankin, & Costello, 1983).

Overall, the TARC is an example of the type of assessment that was developed in the mid-1970s as an alternative to the standard, developmentally normed instruments often used with children who experience severe handicaps. It is seriously deficient in the size and description of the standardization sample used but otherwise appears to be moderately reliable. The validity of the TARC as an assessment instrument is questionable, and it should not be used (nor was it intended to be used) as a substitute for a comprehensive educational assessment in a variety of functional, relevant life skill domains. It may be used to pinpoint general areas of educational concern when used along with other measures.

REVIEWER'S REFERENCES

Freagon, S., Wheeler, J., McDaniel, K., Brankin, G., & Costello, D. (1983). *Individual student community life skill profile system for severely handicapped students.* DeKalb, IL: DeKalb County Special Education Association.
Peterson, J., Trecker, N., Egan, I., Fredericks, B., & Bunse, C. (1983). *Teaching research curriculum for handicapped adolescents and adults: Assessment procedures.* Monmouth, OR: Teaching Research.
Salvia, J., & Ysseldyke, J. E. (1988). *Assessment in special and remedial education* (4th ed.). Boston: Houghton Mifflin.

[412]
TAT Analysis Sheet.
Purpose: "Tool to facilitate interpretation and analysis of the TAT protocol."
Population: Ages 4 and over.
Publication Date: 1974.
Scores, 19: Section I (Hero or Heroine, General Theme, Dependency Needs, Specific Drives, Views of Special Figures, Trends and Similarities), Section II (Depression, Mania, Paranoid Ideation, Antisocial Reaction, Schizoid Personality, Paranoid Personality, Anxiety, Conversion Reactions, Obsessive-Compulsive, Schizophrenia, Simple Schizophrenia, Paranoid Schizophrenia, Summary).
Administration: Individual.
Manual: No manual.
Price Data, 1989: $15 per 25 analysis forms; $4.50 per specimen set.
Time: (10–20) minutes.
Author: John A. Blazer.
Publisher: Psychologists and Educators, Inc.

Teacher Evaluation Rating Scales.

Purpose: To evaluate teacher performance.
Population: Teachers.
Publication Date: 1988.
Acronym: TeachERS.
Scores: Item scores only.
Administration: Individual.
Price Data, 1989: $54 per complete kit including supervisor's manual ('88, 57 pages), 5 teacher's manuals ('88, 15 pages), 25 supervisor's scales, 25 teacher's self-assessment scales, and 25 instructional improvement plan forms; $9 per 25 supervisor's scales; $9 per 25 teacher's self-assessment scales; $9 per 25 instructional improvement plans; $23 per supervisor's manual; $9 per teacher's manual.
Time: Administration time not reported.
Comments: Scale for ratings by supervisors and for self-ratings.
Authors: James E. Ysseldyke, S. Jay Samuels, and Sandra L. Christenson.
Publisher: PRO-ED, Inc.

Review of the Teacher Evaluation Rating Scales by FRANK M. GRESHAM, *Professor of Psychology, Hofstra University, Hempstead, NY:*

The Teacher Evaluation Rating Scales (TeachERS) is described by its authors as "a comprehensive system for instructional improvement." Unlike traditional approaches to teacher evaluation, the TeachERS is designed to improve teachers' instructional approaches based on the wealth of data regarding effective teaching. The TeachERS comprises two separate scales: Teacher's Self-Assessment Scale and Supervisor's Scale. Each of these scales taps six broad domains of effective teaching: (*a*) Instructional Planning (4 items), (*b*) Instructional Management (3 items), (*c*) Teaching Procedures (5 items), (*d*) Monitoring Procedures (2 items), (*e*) Personal Qualities (3 items), and (*f*) Professionalism (3 items). Each of these items is rated on a 5-point scale ranging from Outstanding to Unsatisfactory.

The manual describes explicitly how the scales are to be administered, scored, and used to evaluate teachers. Particular attention is devoted to scale-of-measurement considerations in using TeachERS. The authors point out the 20 components (items) of effective teaching are *not* mutually exclusive or discrete categories of effective teaching. In addition, the 5-point scale used is described as an ordinal rather than an equal-interval scale and each of the components is not equally weighted. According to the authors, "The 20 components of the TeachERS are not equally weighted; they have no known value or weighting" (p. 8). Given that the definition of measurement is the assignment of numbers to individuals or objects according to specified rules such that further information is provided about individuals or objects, the TeachERS may not represent *measurement*. In other words, it is difficult to see how the TeachERS measures something when what it is supposed to be measuring has no known value or weighting.

TECHNICAL CHARACTERISTICS. Items for the TeachERS were selected from over 600 teaching behaviors/practices contained in the effective teaching literature. Chapter 4 of the manual provides numerous references from the effective teaching literature documenting the importance of each of the 20 components contained in the scales. The manual states that the authors rated items independently within categories as essential, important, or unnecessary to reduce the item pool. No information is provided with respect to interrater reliability of the items selected for the final item pool. The manual describes three studies conducted to verify the importance and necessity of each component on the TeachERS. These studies involved graduate students (Study 1), experienced teachers (Study 2), and administrators (Study 3). No information is provided regarding the interrater agreement among these three groups on each component of the scale. Also, Study 2 had an extremely low return rate (28%) which may compromise the meaning of the results.

The manual states that the TeachERS is an "individually referenced system" and, as such, "traditional concepts of reliability do not apply." It is difficult to understand the authors' rationale for this statement. For example, it would be required at a minimum that two supervisors observing the same teacher at the same time would agree at a relatively high level if the scale components are clearly and objectively operationalized. Moreover, it seems reasonable to expect that supervisors' ratings would be relatively stable over short time periods in the absence of feedback on teacher performance if the scale is to measure anything consistently. Finally, one might reasonably expect a significant correlation between the teacher self-assessment scale and the supervisor scale if these scales are measuring the same thing (i.e., convergent validity). Traditional concepts of interrater and test-retest reliability as well as convergent validity do apply to the TeachERS. No discussion of why these concepts do not apply to the scale is presented in the manual.

SUMMARY. The TeachERS represents an improvement over traditional systems of teacher evaluation and holds promise for improving instruction. The most redeeming feature of the scale is its content validity based on a huge body of empirical literature on effective teaching. In spite of the many admirable qualities of the TeachERS, it appears the scale requires additional empirical work before it is used to evaluate teachers. There are no data supporting the interrater reliability of the scale, the stability of the scale, or the sensitivity of the scale to feedback regarding teaching behavior/practices. The scale should be subjected to empirical scrutiny to evaluate its psychometric qualities. Users of the TeachERS should exercise caution in evaluating teachers given the unknown qualities of the scale.

Review of the Teacher Evaluation Rating Scales by PATRICIA WHEELER, *Senior Research Associate, The Evaluation Center, Western Michigan University, Kalamazoo, MI and Independent Consultant, Livermore, CA:*

The Teacher Evaluation Rating Scales (TeachERS) is described by its authors as "a comprehensive system for instructional improvement." It covers six areas: Instructional Planning, Instructional Management, Teaching Procedures, Monitoring Procedures, Personal Qualities, and Professionalism. Each area has from two to five components, or statements of teacher behaviors or practices. There is a total of 20 components across the six areas.

The development of TeachERS followed a standard approach for performance assessments: literature review, identification of key areas and components, formatting, and a content validation study. However, there was no input in the early phases, concurrent with the literature review, by experienced teachers and their supervisors. Identification of key areas and components was done by the authors, who independently reviewed the 600-plus statements generated from the literature review. They identified those that had empirical evidence to support their importance and that were congruent with their model of teacher evaluation. Much teacher-effectiveness research is based on teacher-centered classrooms, or on specific styles or models of teaching; thus TeachERS may not be appropriate for use in other types of teaching situations (e.g., student-centered classes such as labs, repeated practice such as band, or independent study centers). Also, the authors did not define their model of teacher evaluation, a criterion that all components had to meet. If TeachERS is to be used for teacher evaluation or instructional improvement in a variety of teaching situations, the authors should clearly specify both the teaching model and the evaluation model they used.

Rationale statements are provided for most, but not all, areas and components. In all cases, such rationales should be provided to both teachers and supervisors. The component statements in the two manuals (i.e., teacher and supervisor manuals) generally match. However, there are some differences in wording (see number 4 under "Adapting Instruction," where teacher knowledge and ability are assumed to equal teacher practice). Also, there are differences between the supervisor's and teacher's manuals in the matching of question numbers under a component (see "Establishing Rules of Conduct"). Such differences could result in different ratings and interfere with communication between the teacher and supervisor when they interpret the results.

The manuals mention the importance of in-service training in the use of TeachERS and of a teacher interview as part of the evaluation process. However, the manuals do not contain information on how or when to conduct the training or the interview. Training materials in interviewing, observing, rating, interpreting, and developing an instructional improvement plan should be provided. Interview questions are provided in the supervisor's manual for one area only, "Monitoring Procedures." Interview questions are particularly important for those components that cannot be easily evaluated by classroom observation (e.g., "Selection and Establishment of Goals," "Working with Parents").

Three validation studies by educators questioned the "importance" and "necessity" for teacher evaluation. The distinction between importance and necessity is not made clear. Also, the importance of the behaviors or practices described by the component statements for teaching is not addressed. This is a serious deficit. Minimal information is provided on the experience of the educators who reviewed the component statements. Information about subjects and grade levels taught, types of students with whom they have worked, types of school settings, etc., should be provided to aid the users in assessing the appropriateness of the results of these reviews for their local situations.

The authors do not address reliability and state that, "Traditional concepts of reliability do not apply to the TeachERS." This statement may be true, but reliability should be addressed in ways other than those traditionally used with multiple-choice tests. Examples include carefully selecting and training evaluators, and using evaluators who are knowledgeable in the subject area being taught and with the types of students in the classroom of the teacher being evaluated. Other methods of assessing reliability are interrater reliability measures and multiple administrations of TeachERS with the same teacher and supervisor.

The current format of TeachERS consists of ratings on a 5-point Likert scale for each of the 20 components. The teacher's self-rating is subtracted from the supervisor's rating, providing a discrepancy. This discrepancy figure is not the best place to start the development of an improvement plan. Instead, the teacher and supervisor should first identify those components that have an unsatisfactory rating from one or both of them, decide which of these components warrant immediate attention, and then develop the improvement plan. Additionally, the format should provide not only the recording of ratings, but the collection of actual evidence that can be used to interpret the ratings better and to develop the improvement plan.

In summary, the involvement of the teacher and the effort to have teachers reflect on their own behavior are strengths of TeachERS. This system could be useful in both the professional development and formative evaluation of student teachers as well as in-service teachers, if the teaching model reflected by TeachERS is applicable. The system should have a training component for both the teacher and evaluator, a series of interview questions, a means of collecting evidence, and a revised interpretation procedure that focuses initially on the components with low ratings. In addition, there should be a plan to use the materials on multiple occasions during the school year so that it becomes a process for professional development. TeachERS could be used for teacher self-assessment and for professional development, working with a mentor teacher. It does not appear to be a good tool for formal teacher evaluation and personnel decisions.

[414]
Teacher Opinion Inventory, Revised Edition.

Purpose: To assess teachers' opinions concerning many facets of the school, to "compile teachers' recommendations for improvement," and to provide "data to guide the school's professional staff in decision making relative to program development."
Population: Elementary and secondary school teachers.
Publication Dates: 1981–88.
Scores: 7 subscales: Organization/Administration, Instruction, Student Support Climate, School/Community Relations, Job Satisfaction, Program, Student Activities.
Administration: Group.
Parts, 2: A (Likert-scale items), B (open-ended items regarding recommendations).
Price Data, 1991: $4 per 25 inventories (Part A); $3 per 25 inventories (Part B); $3 per 25 machine-scored answer sheets; $3 per Administrator's Manual ('88, 12 pages).
Time: Untimed.
Author: National Study of School Evaluation.
Publisher: National Study of School Evaluation.

[415]
Teacher Stress Inventory.

Purpose: Assesses the degree of occupational stress experienced by teachers.
Population: American public school teachers.
Publication Date: 1988.
Acronym: TSI.
Scores, 11: Time Management, Work-Related Stressors, Professional Distress, Discipline and Motivation, Professional Investment, Emotional Manifestations, Fatigue Manifestations, Cardiovascular Manifestations, Gastronomic Manifestations, Behavioral Manifestations, Total.
Administration: Group.
Price Data, 1989: $8.75 per 10 test forms; $15 per manual (97 pages); $16 per sampler set.
Time: (15–20) minutes.
Comments: Test booklet title is Teacher Concerns Inventory; self-ratings scale.

Author: Michael J. Fimian.
Publisher: Clinical Psychology Publishing Co., Inc.

TEST REFERENCES

1. Fimian, M. J., & Krupicka, W. M. (1987). Occupational stress and receipt of professional counseling in special education. *Perceptual and Motor Skills, 65,* 995-999.
2. Fimian, M. J. (1988). The alpha and split-half reliability of the Teacher Stress Inventory. *Psychology in the Schools, 25,* 110-118.
3. Schutz, R. W., & Long, B. C. (1988). Confirmatory factor analysis, validation and revision of a teacher stress inventory. *Educational and Psychological Measurement, 48,* 497-511.
4. Cecil, M. A., & Forman, S. G. (1990). Effects of stress inoculation training and coworker support groups on teachers' stress. *Journal of School Psychology, 28,* 105-118.

Review of the Teacher Stress Inventory by G. MICHAEL POTEAT, Associate Professor of Psychology, East Carolina University, Greenville, NC:

The Teacher Stress Inventory (TSI) consists of 49 self-report items designed to measure the occupational stress experienced or exhibited by public school teachers. The 49 items have been grouped into 10 factors or subscales. Five factors (Time Management, Work-Related Stressors, Professional Distress, Discipline and Motivation, and Professional Investment) are sources of stress. The other five factors (Emotional, Fatigue, Cardiovascular, Gastronomic, and Behavioral) are labeled as manifestations of occupational stress. The self-report items are completed by the teacher using a 1 to 5 rating format. A rating of 1 indicates that the item is not noticeable or that the item is not a strength for the respondent. A rating of 5 indicates that the item represents a major strength or is extremely noticeable. The 49 items are included on a 4-page protocol labeled the "Teacher Concerns Inventory." A separate score for each of the 10 factors is obtained by averaging the ratings for the items contained on each factor. A total score is then obtained by adding the average scores for each of the 10 factors. Total scale and subscale decile cutoff points are provided and are based on samples of both regular and special education faculty.

The TSI is intended to be used in (*a*) research on teacher stress, (*b*) as a method for teachers to assess their own stress levels, and (*c*) as a survey instrument to assess the amount of stress present within an educational system. The TSI is not intended for use by administrators to identify teachers who need counseling or other interventions. The author strongly recommends that the instrument be completed anonymously.

The 88-page manual provides a great deal of information about the development of the TSI and also contains a review of research on occupational stress in public school faculty. The TSI is the primary instrument for assessing occupational stress in this population and has no specific competitor. Considerable effort has been expended in developing the TSI and the author presents reasonable psychometric data. First, the TSI was originally developed based on the literature concerning occupational stress and potential items were evaluated by university faculty and public school teachers. The content validity of the TSI was further assessed using expert opinion ($n = 226$) sampled over a 5-year period. Second, the evidence for the internal consistency of the TSI is adequate for both the total scale and the 10 subscales. Most of the coefficient alphas were above .80 and are above .90 for the total scale. Third, the construct validity of the TSI was assessed using factor analysis and the results used to identify the 10 subscales. The division of items is intuitively reasonable and is supported by the factor analysis. Finally, support for the criterion-related validity of the TSI is provide by a variety of data demonstrating its correlation with variables including seeking counseling for work-related problems and scores on the Maslach Burnout Inventory. The TSI has also been demonstrated to correlate with stress ratings of the respondents provided by a "significant other."

Given the intended purpose of the TSI, the psychometric properties of the instrument appear to be adequate. However, two weaknesses stand out. First, the norms—although based on 3,401 respondents—are obviously not representative of the population of public school teachers. The vast majority of respondents were special education teachers ($n = 2,352$) and 87% had advanced degrees. Much of the normative data were collected during workshops on stress and the overall sample is limited geographically. More information concerning the development of norms and a more representative sample are needed. The author acknowledges the norms are limited and tables are provided for different groups making up the normative sample (e.g., regular education faculty, males, etc.). A second concern is the need for more data on the stability of the TSI. Test-retest reliability has been assessed but the data are limited both in sample size and the length of time between administrations. Despite these weaknesses, the TSI can be recommended for the uses intended by the author.

Review of the Teacher Stress Inventory by MARTIN J. WIESE, School Psychologist, Wilkes County Schools, Wilkesboro, NC:

The Teacher Stress Inventory (TSI) is described by its author as "a 49-item, 10-factor instrument that assesses the degree of strength of occupational stress experienced by American teachers in the public schools." The TSI assesses numerous stressful teaching events experienced on the job and in the schools. The structure of the TSI is such that five factors represent sources of stress and five factors represent manifestations of stress. The inventory can be completed and scored in about 15 minutes.

The five stress source factors are Time Management, Work-Related Stressors, Professional Distress, Discipline and Motivation, and Professional Invest-

ment. The five stress manifestations factors are Emotional Manifestations, Fatigue Manifestations, Cardiovascular Manifestations, Gastronomic Manifestations, and Behavioral Manifestations. The five stress source and five stress manifestations subscale scores can be summed and divided by 10 to obtain a Total Stress Score.

The author states that the TSI construct is different from other models of stress and burnout such as the Maslach Burnout Inventory (MBI) or the Social Readjustment Rating Scale (SRRS). Unlike the MBI, which measures burnout (the result of long-term stress), and the SRRS (which measures the stress of everyday life events), the TSI assesses much more teacher-specific factors.

It is suggested that the TSI be administered for three purposes. First, it can be used by teachers to assess their stress levels in comparison to the TSI norm group. Individual TSI respondents' subscale and scale scores can be compared to the norms established for regular education teachers, special education teachers, and a combined sample (both regular and special education teachers). Gender (male vs. female) and grade level comparisons (elementary, middle school, and secondary) are also possible. Second, the TSI can be useful in group settings, such as teacher workshops. Both of these uses are intended to provide data to individual teachers about their relative level of stress compared to the norm group. A third use suggested by the author includes school-wide or system-wide surveys of teacher stress to identify and assess stress problems at a systems level.

The development of the scale began with an initial pool of 135 sources and manifestations of teacher stress. These were categorized by the author into 13 a priori factors. Sixty-three items were then selected and used in the first round of factor validation studies. This scale was distributed to 365 special education teachers from Connecticut and the resulting data were submitted to principal components factor analysis. Thirty of the original items were retained and acted as the core of the new Teacher Stress Inventory.

To improve the psychometric properties of the scale, 12 conceptually similar items were added to the factors with the lowest reliability. This resulted in a 42-item scale which was then distributed to regular and special education teachers in Vermont. Following factor analytic procedures, one item was eliminated from the item pool. The factor patterns and reliability estimates from the Vermont data were nearly identical to those found in the Connecticut study. After a content appraisal by 226 stress experts, one additional factor of eight items related to time management was added to the TSI. Based on analysis conducted on the data aggregated from 21 different teacher samples from eight states ($n =$

3,401), the five stress source and five stress manifestation factors were identified.

Internal consistency reliability estimates for the TSI subscales and total scale were examined using Cronbach's coefficient alpha. The whole scale alpha reliability for the combined sample was .93. Subscale reliability estimates ranged from a low of .75 (Professional Investment) to a high of .88 (Gastronomic Manifestations). All reliabilities were judged adequate for inclusion in the TSI. The manual does not include a table of the standard errors of measurement. These must be calculated by the user if a confidence interval is to be established around the obtained scores.

To establish test-retest reliability, the TSI was completed twice by a sample of 60 North Carolina special education teachers. The time span between administrations ranged from 2 hours to 2 weeks. Paired sample *t*-tests were used to determine the correlations between initial and retest samples. Test-retest reliabilities ranged from .67 (1-week interval) to .99 (2-week interval) for the whole scale. Limited split-half and alternate forms reliability are also reported in the manual.

Evidence for the content, convergent, and factorial validity of the TSI has also been collected. Five samples of "experts" provided data to establish the content validity of the TSI. Each expert had authored an article on stress, conducted stress research, or conducted stress management seminars. Overall, there was slightly more agreement among the experts about the causes of teacher stress than the manifestations of stress. Convergent validity was demonstrated by correlating teachers' TSI scores with independent ratings. Teachers who scored highly on the TSI were observed by their significant other as being subject to very strong stress.

Construct validity is also evidenced through examination of the TSI factor structure. In order to identify stress factors, principal components factor analyses were conducted followed by varimax and oblique rotations. Ten factors emerged that accounted for 58% of the stress variance. Final acceptance or deletion of the TSI items was based on the factor validity. Component loadings, item means, and standard deviations for the 10-factor solution are provided in the manual.

Individual TSI respondents' scores can be compared to the norms established for the combined sample, the regular education sample ($n = 962$), or the special education sample ($n = 2,352$). Cutoff points for significance levels were set at one standard deviation above and below the mean for each subsample. One standard deviation above the mean means significantly strong stress; one standard deviation below the mean indicates significantly weaker stress.

The manual also includes a graphic representation of high-low cutoff points for the TSI scales; however, it is not recommended for use. The mean scores and standard deviations reported elsewhere in the manual (p. 57) do not correspond to the graphical representation of these scores. Therefore, the personalized profile of stress ratings (p. 18–19) will not provide an accurate assessment of the respondents' responses.

In sum, the TSI is a potentially valuable instrument for use in public school settings to assess teacher stress. The manual provides extensive support for its reliability and validity as well as a fair description of the norm group. The TSI is simple to complete, score, and interpret. Even so, the user should avoid use of the graphical representation when making comparisons to the norm group and rely solely on the norm tables. The lack of a table with the standard errors of measurement is also a drawback. One recommendation would be for users to develop their own system-wide norms. School systems and teacher demands are so different that it is unrealistic for the norms to be useful to all districts.

[416]
Team Process Diagnostic.
Purpose: To analyze and classify group processes according to their implications for member and team effectiveness.
Population: Individuals whose work responsibilities require work-team cooperation.
Publication Date: 1974–1989.
Scores: 9 clusters in 3 modes: Problem Solving (Integrative, Content-Bound, Process-Bound), Fight (Perceptual Difference, Status-Striving, Frustration), Flight (Fear, Indifference, Powerlessness).
Administration: Group.
Price Data, 1990: $6.95 per manual ('89, 21 pages).
Time: Administration time not reported.
Comments: Team associate ratings, self ratings, self scored.
Authors: Jay Hall.
Publisher: Teleometrics International.

Review of the Team Process Diagnostic by LAWRENCE M. ALEAMONI, Associate Head and Professor of Educational Psychology, University of Arizona, Tucson, AZ:

The Team Process Diagnostic manual begins with an excellent argument about the need for "process analysis." The stated rationale for the design of the Team Process Diagnostic is to allow individuals and their teams to analyze current and past practices into discrete components and then use these in a constructive way to improve both individual and team effectiveness.

The Team Process Diagnostic instrument consists of "32 descriptive statements covering most of the behaviors which team members are likely to use in the course of their work with one another." These statements are to be used by each team member to characterize each of the other team members as well as themselves. Unfortunately, no empirical evidence is provided to support the rationale for the selection or development of these 32 statements nor why most of them describe several behaviors rather than focusing on a single behavioral dimension.

The section "Preliminary Instructions: Organizing Your Data for Analysis" contains a summary form to record each team member's selected descriptive statements and their self-assessment. This form also contains nine Clusters of six items each. An inspection of the nine Clusters of six items each indicates that the individual items appear in more than one Cluster creating some dependence between Clusters. Because no mention is made about how these Clusters were determined, it was assumed that they were purely subjective groupings. No rationale or evidence is provided as to why only six statements should appear in each Cluster. The nine Clusters are grouped into three Modes: Problem-Solving, Fight, and Flight, again with no evidence provided to support the grouping.

The section "Instructions for Converting and Plotting Personal Scores" clearly indicates how raw scores should be transformed into weighted scores, but no rationale is provided as to why this is needed. The instructions for plotting average Cluster Scores on the Bar Graph of Personal Impact are very clear, but the vertical axis of the graph should be labelled "Weighted Average Cluster Scores" instead of "Weighted Cluster Scores." The table for plotting Member Average Ratings incorporated "self" in the averaging, but no rationale is provided for that inclusion. Also, the subsequent Bar Graph of Team Goals and Work Mode should have its vertical axis labelled "Weighted Team Average Cluster Scores" instead of "Weighted Cluster Scores."

In the section "How to Interpret Your Scores on the Team Process Diagnostic," Douglas McGregor is mentioned with no formal reference citation. In the subsection, Some Basic Considerations, the author claims that "it has become apparent over time that certain practices, various member contributions, and certain patterns of communication may lead to superior team performance" without providing any substantiating evidence. Later in this section the author claims that team performance has been the subject of extensive basic research but offers no evidence or citations. Continuing, the author claims that the Team Process Diagnostic is based on the findings of this unidentified research and then proceeds to state six facts, some of which are linked to the working model of group decision making abstracted from B. E. Collins and H. Guetzkow's (the only cited, dated reference in the manual) 1964 book. Although Collins and Guetzkow's model provides an interesting framework for some of the

"facts" stated in the manual, there is no evidence that the paths indicated by the directional arrows in their model have been empirically verified (for example, no discussion or reference is made to the use of Path Analysis).

The section "The Team Process Diagnostic: Focus and Use" contains many claims about effectiveness, internal consistency of Clusters, motivational significance of Clusters, additive effect among Clusters, etc., without any formal evidence being cited. In fact, references are frequently made to the existence of research with no substantive citations provided. When citations are given, they are incomplete (for example, two citations are provided but no dates are given).

The section on "Cluster Descriptions" is very well done but seems entirely logically based rather than empirically based. This is problematic in that when one attempts to interpret differences in the "Sample Mode Graphs and Interpretations" section there is no statistical rationale provided to determine if the differences observed are "real."

In summary, the idea of providing an instrument and system to analyze and classify group processes in order to improve member and team effectiveness is excellent. The manual presents a very attractive, well-organized, and compelling format for accomplishing such a task. However, the lack of supporting evidence and empirical research for the many claims and materials presented raise serious doubts about such claims as well as the utility of the Team Process Diagnostic.

[417]

Teamness Index.

Purpose: To "survey . . . conditions of work and the array of feelings that might exist among two or more people as they seek to work together."

Population: Individuals whose work responsibilities require work-team cooperation.

Publication Date: 1988.

Scores: Item scores only.

Administration: Group.

Price Data, 1990: $6.95 per manual (12 pages).

Time: Administration time not reported.

Comments: Self-ratings; self-scored.

Authors: Jay Hall.

Publisher: Teleometrics International.

Review of the Teamness Index by BARBARA LACHAR, Vice President, Psychological Assessment Services, Inc., Sugar Land, TX:

The Teamness Index is a self-administered, self-scored inventory designed to measure the degree to which an individual and his or her co-workers meet criteria for defining themselves as a team. All available material is contained within the test booklet, which includes directions for administration, scoring, and interpretation. There is no manual. It is apparent that the value of this survey is

NOT as a psychometric instrument that provides a measure of the construct of "teamness" with documented reliability and validity. Instead, this survey is for the purpose of promoting understanding, dynamic interaction, and corrective action among team members. Whether or not the Teamness Index achieves its intended objectives needs to be determined, as empirical studies of reliability and validity are not currently in evidence.

The Teamness Index consists of 24 items, each stated in two parts. The first part states the condition positively and the second part expresses the negative pole of the same condition (e.g., "I feel that my contribution plays an essential role in team performance. *As opposed to feeling the team could get along just as well without me* "). Items were written to measure four minimum conditions necessary for team functioning as defined by Sherif and Sherif (no reference provided): (*a*) team goals and objectives; (*b*) team structure; (*c*) team standards, values, and norms of performance; and (*d*) positive identification with the team, its members, and its work.

There is no time limit and instructions direct the respondent to rate the accuracy of the item for the team on a 9-point scale ranging from *true all the time* to *never true*. The reliability of these ratings needs to be assessed, as it is questionable whether respondents can make reliable judgements on a scale in which verbal anchors appear ambiguous and not clearly discriminable.

Individual team members respond to the items and then meet as a group to score and interpret the index. The author states that approximately 15 minutes are required for scoring and 45 minutes for discussion of results. Average item ratings for the entire team are plotted by each individual with his or her own individual item ratings on a continuum of teamness. These points may be connected to form a profile. According to the author, values of 1–3 indicate a state of "separateness," values of 4–6 indicate a state of "transition," and values of 7–9 indicate "teamness." The team reviews the results together and decides whether the group has the properties of a team. If not, the author provides some suggestions for team development.

The author presents no information concerning procedures for the development or selection of items, and no description of attempts to determine measurement error. If the Teamness Index is to be regarded as a psychometric instrument, reliability studies are required. Evaluations of internal consistency, profile stability over time, and interrater reliability are needed to determine whether "teamness" as a construct may be assessed with some degree of precision. Without determining the reliability of the instrument and the degree of measurement error, the user does not know if score discrepancies, whether between team members or

from the ideal, are due to perceptual differences or measurement error.

The interpretation of scores appears to have a theoretical basis. However, norms obtained from various organizations, departments, and functional teams would allow users an opportunity to interpret their results within a reality-based frame of reference. These data could also form the basis for validity studies. In fact, the combination of appropriate norm groups and a specific theoretical model makes for the strongest basis in studying validity.

Suggestions for validity studies include correlations of total index scores with global assessments of team members of the four basic components of teamness in the Index Model: goals and objectives, structure, norms, and identification or attraction. Index scores could also be related to behavioral assessments of team functioning including conflict among members and time spent dealing with crisis situations. Utility of scores could also be determined by correlating index results and change scores with objective criteria such as absences, grievances, percent goal attainment, and profitability where appropriate.

This survey is completed independently by all members of an intended team, but is scored and interpreted jointly for the purpose of promoting communication and positive change. While no information concerning item development, reliability, validity, or normative data is provided, the Teamness Index can probably be useful as a developmental tool. There are few, if any, similar instruments available to assess team functioning and promote problem solving in a structured setting. While the psychometric properties of this instrument remain unknown, it seems to fill a need and may, by stimulating communication between team members, fulfill its basic purpose.

Review of the Teamness Index by FREDERICK T. L. LEONG, Assistant Professor of Psychology, The Ohio State University, Columbus, OH:

The Teamness Index is presented in a 12-page booklet that serves as both the test and the manual. The 24 questions that make up the Index are presented in the first two pages, while the manual portion of the booklet (pp. 3–12) is sealed with instructions not to open until instructed to do so.

The items of the Index appear to have good face validity and have been developed to assess several dimensions of the "teamness" construct which have been identified by others as important to effective teamwork. The work of William Dyer is cited in the manual portion of the booklet as having been very influential in the development of the Index. Participants are asked to refer to the references for the Dyer citation, but no such references are provided. The following dimensions of teamness are assessed by the Index: (a) clear and shared goals, (b) clear and shared structure, (c) clear and shared performance standards, and (d) mutual attraction. Each dimension is measured by six items representing different manifestations of that dimension. Each item is bipolar in that the positive aspect is presented first followed by the opposite condition. For example, the first item begins with the statement, "I have a clear understanding of team goals and objectives," followed by a sentence printed in a different print style, stating "as opposed to being unsure or confused about what the team is responsible for accomplishing." Participants are asked to indicate their level of agreement with the item on a 9-point Likert scale (1 = *never true*, 9 = *true all the time*).

The manual is not a test manual in the traditional sense but, instead, is a guidebook to help participants understand their scores and the dimensions underlying these scores. The manual recommends using the scores as both individual and group ratings in order to provide both personal and team profiles. The team profile is computed by adding all participants' responses for each item and then obtaining the group average. This averaging of scores is repeated for all items and then plotted on the Teamness Profile provided in the manual. Participants are then instructed to plot their personal profile by recording their scores on the same Teamness profile, each in a different color pen. Besides scoring and profile instructions, the manual also provides brief descriptions of the teamness dimensions assessed by the Index (e.g., shared goals and objectives, team structure), three sample Teamness profiles to illustrate different levels of teamness, and some suggestions for team development activities presented in a table format.

Using computerized bibliographic searches, this reviewer could find no research concerning the reliability, validity, and utility of the Teamness Index. The author of the Index was finally contacted and the reviewer was informed by the author that the Index was not really designed as a test or assessment instrument but rather as a group exercise to facilitate discussion about teamness in groups. While the line between "test" and "group exercise" can be ambiguous within the areas of organizational consulting and development, I have taken the position that, because the Teamness Index provides instructions for scoring individual and group profiles that have implications for psychological interventions, it is an assessment device and should be subject to all the standards pertaining to tests outlined in the *Standards for Educational and Psychological Testing* (AERA, APA, & NCME, 1985). As such, the Teamness Index is very inadequate because no reliability or validity data have been collected to justify its use in any setting. There is no technical manual for users to evaluate the psycho-

metric qualities of the Index. According to the test author, there are no plans to collect any psychometric data. Furthermore, while the items possess good face validity, they are all written in a single direction, positive statement first and negative statement second, which may make the Index scores vulnerable to an acquiescent response set. That is, how a person responds to the items may be influenced by the fact that the positive statement is always first. In addition, given the recommended group format for the use and scoring of the Index, it would not be unreasonable to suspect that a person may be so influenced by the setting in which the Index is scored and discussed that he or she provides responses that are more socially acceptable than purely honest.

There are viable alternatives to the Teamness Index which would serve as better assessment devices for the construct of "teamness." These alternative measures, with varying levels of reliability and validity, include: (a) the Workgroup Esprit de Corp scale within the Psychological Climate Questionnaire (Jones & James, 1979); (b) the Work Group Functioning module within the Michigan Organizational Assessment Questionnaire with subscales measuring group homogeneity, group goal clarity, group cohesiveness, open group process, and internal fragmentation (Seashore, Lawler, Mirvis, & Cammann, 1983); (c) the Perceived Team Collaboration measure (Aram, Morgan, & Esbeck, 1971); and (d) the Team Cohesiveness measure (Dailey, 1979).

In summary, the Teamness Index is an assessment device developed to provide feedback to groups and to provide individual members of the groups information on their levels of teamness across several dimensions. That team building and team work is central to organizational performance and productivity is generally well accepted (see Galagan, 1986; Kanter, 1982; and Vogt & Griffith, 1988). However, the Teamness Index, in the absence of normative data and of any supporting research on its reliability and validity, is of questionable value in this area of organizational theory development and intervention. While it is intuitively appealing, use of the Index in any applied settings is not warranted given that lack of basic psychometric data. This negative recommendation is further supported by the fact that there are viable alternative measures to the Teamness Index.

What remains unresolved is the extent to which unresearched and unvalidated assessment devices such as the Teamness Index will continue to be used in organizational development given the ambiguous policies and standards about the appropriate use of such devices. The use of an "aspirational" set of standards for test development also ensures that this pattern of test use (i.e., using unvalidated tests) will not change quickly.

REVIEWER'S REFERENCES

Aram, J. D., Morgan, C. P., & Esbeck, E. S. (1971). Relation of collaborative interpersonal relationships to individual satisfaction and organizational performance. *Administrative Science Quarterly, 16*, 289-296.

Dailey, R. C. (1979). Group, task, and personality correlates of boundary spanning activities. *Human Relations, 32*, 273-285.

Jones, A. P., & James, L. R. (1979). Psychological climate: Dimensions and relationships of individual and aggregated work environment perceptions. *Organizational Behavior and Human Performance, 23*, 201-250.

Kanter, R. M. (1982). Dilemmas of managing participation. *Organizational Dynamics, 11*, 5-27.

Seashore, S. E., Lawler, E. E., Mirvis, P., & Cammann, C. (Eds.). (1983). *Assessing organizational change: A guide to methods, measures, and practices.* New York: Wiley.

American Educational Research Association, American Psychological Association, & National Council on Measurement in Education. (1985). *Standards for educational and psychological testing.* Washington, DC: American Psychological Association, Inc.

Galagan, P. (1986). Work teams that work. *Training and Development Journal, 40*, 32-35.

Vogt, J. F., & Griffith, S. J. (1988). Team development and proactive change: Theory and training implications. *Organizational Development Journal, 6*, 81-87.

[418]

Teamwork Appraisal Survey.

Purpose: To assess "an associate's feelings about working in teams and the behaviors he or she employs in work-team situations."

Population: Individuals whose work responsibilities require work-team cooperation.

Publication Date: 1987.

Acronym: TAS.

Scores, 5: Synergistic, Compromise, Win-Lose, Yield-Lose, Lose-Leave.

Administration: Group.

Price Data, 1990: $6.95 per manual (24 pages).

Time: Administration time not reported.

Comments: Based on Team Behaviors Model of analysis of individual behaviors in a team setting; work associates rate each other's behavior.

Authors: Jay Hall.

Publisher: Teleometrics International.

[419]

Technical Test Battery.

Purpose: "Designed for occupational selection and placement."

Population: Technical job applicants and incumbents entry level to professional.

Publication Date: 1990.

Acronym: TTB.

Scores: Total score only for each of 9 tests.

Administration: Individual or group.

Price Data, 1991: $250 per administration set; $19 per reusable test booklet; $20 per hand-scoring key (specify test); $5 per answer sheet; $6.50 per bureau-scored answer sheet; $6 per administration cards (specify test); $5 per 25 test logs; $8.50 per 10 practice leaflets; $30 per manual ('90, 87 pages); $50 per optic-scan capability file per test; $50 per specimen set; scoring service offered by publisher.

Comments: Subtests available as separates.

Author: Saville & Holdsworth Ltd.

Publisher: Saville & Holdsworth Ltd.

a) FOLLOWING INSTRUCTIONS (VTS1).

Time: 20(25) minutes.

b) NUMERICAL COMPUTATION (NT2).

Time: 10(15) minutes.

c) MECHANICAL COMPREHENSION (MT4).

Time: 15(20) minutes.

d) NUMERICAL ESTIMATION (NTS2).

Time: 10(15) minutes.

e) MECHANICAL COMPREHENSION (MTS3).

Time: 15(20) minutes.

f) FAULT FINDING (FTS4).

Time: 20(25) minutes.

g) DIAGRAMMATIC THINKING (DTS6).

Time: 20(25) minutes.

h) SPATIAL REASONING (ST7).

Time: 20(25) minutes.

i) DIAGRAMMATIC REASONING (DT8).

Time: 15(20) minutes.

Review of the Technical Test Battery by SAMI GULGOZ, Assistant Professor of Psychology, Auburn University at Montgomery, Montgomery, AL:

The Technical Test Battery (TTB) is a set of nine tests developed for occupational selection and placement. The battery is designed for group testing of applicants for technical jobs. Each test of the battery is administered and scored separately. Therefore, any number of tests from the battery can be used to match the needs of the user. The Technical Test Battery aims to assess skills that are primarily pertinent to jobs such as engineering, building, textiles, electronics, and scientific laboratories. It includes tests of four general aptitudes: Following Instructions, Numerical Computation, Numerical Estimation, and two Mechanical Comprehension tests. Also, there are four tests of skills related to areas of recent technology: Fault Finding, Diagrammatic Thinking, Spatial Reasoning, and Diagrammatic Reasoning.

Following Instructions is a specialized test of verbal skills assessing one's comprehension of instructions in a technical context. Although the test claims to make no assumption of prior knowledge, benefits of familiarity with the topics are obvious. Numerical Computation is a quantitative skills test with questions that require basic arithmetic skills. Numerical Estimation, although similar to Numerical Computation, increases the number of steps and the magnitude of the numbers used in the problems. This test assesses the ability to estimate results of calculations within a margin of error. The publisher may want to modify instructions so that the strategy of estimation is emphasized to prevent test takers from calculating the actual results. In addition, the Battery includes two tests of Mechanical Comprehension. Both assess understanding of basic mechanical principles but at varying degrees of difficulty.

Four tests in the TTB evaluate aptitudes for more recent technology. Fault Finding involves discovering the dysfunctional unit within a rule-governed system. Diagrammatic Thinking tests the ability to follow a symbol through a flow chart and make decisions and changes according to the instructions.

Both Fault Finding and Diagrammatic Thinking are complex tests that require substantial skill for even minimum performance.

Spatial Reasoning is a test of matching two-dimensional drawings to their three-dimensional counterparts. All items are based on the same concept of matching three-dimensional pictures of boxes with unfolded boxes. Finally, the Diagrammatic Reasoning test involves discovering the logical rules in sequences. Despite similar names, this test is quite different from the Diagrammatic Thinking test in nature and difficulty.

Each TTB test is a separate booklet with individual answer sheets. The high-quality booklets are easy to use. In rare cases, wording of some questions may be problematic for readers with average to low reading skills. Scoring is simple. Hand scoring keys are provided. The publisher also offers a computer-scoring service. The instructions for both the examiners and test takers are clear and easy to follow. The battery includes clear profile charts with percentiles, t-scores, and stens both with and without norms so the user can enter updated or company norms. One caution about the use of the TTB is the fatigue effect. Administering all the tests in the battery would take at least 3 hours. Difficulty of some tests would lead to fatigue that would prevent obtaining the true scores and create a floor effect.

The Technical Test Battery includes norm tables for six different groups: mechanics, field service engineers, technician apprentices in electrical and mechanical engineering industries, engineering technical staff, technician apprentices in automotive industry, and applicants for ship building industry. Norms for mechanics and field service engineers are from the U.S. and the other four groups are from the U.K. Each norm group took three to five out of the nine tests of the battery. The data from all the groups are combined to create the composite group norms for all the nine tests. The norm tables provide both percentiles and stens.

There are problems with the U.S. norm groups that should be noted. First, the norms are based on a relatively small number of subjects ($N = 31$–84). Second, each group is recruited from only one company. These two problems reduce the representativeness of these norms. The publisher mentions probable gender differences in many tasks but separate norms are not presented.

The reliability of the tests is measured by Cronbach's coefficient alpha and Kuder-Richardson (KR-20) reliability coefficients. The nature of the samples is not indicated but the size varies between 173 and 672. The reliability coefficients are within an acceptable range (.72–.89). Because no test-retest reliability is mentioned, there is no indication of the stability of the battery.

The Technical Test is validated by criterion-related procedures. Four different validation studies are reported, each involving a different occupational group. The first study employed 84 mechanics in a U.S. company taking five of the tests. The criteria were nine performance dimensions measured concurrently. Only significant correlations are reported and they vary between .23 and .34. The scores from the Diagrammatic Reasoning test did not produce any significant correlations. Following Instructions, Numerical Computation, and Mechanical Comprehension produced a multiple correlation of .33. These correlations are quite low; however, the criterion may not be reliable and the employees with 9 years of experience when tested, create a restricted range.

The second study was also a concurrent study using 31 field service engineers of a U.S. company. The criterion was an overall performance rating jointly decided by four supervisors. Out of five tests, only Following Instructions and Mechanical Comprehension led to significant correlations (both .33).

The third study was a predictive validation procedure where 590 applicants to a craft apprenticeship program in the U.K. were given two tests and later evaluated on workshop performance and performance on academic examinations. The tests correlated with some of the 11 dimensions used to evaluate workshop performance with a range of coefficients between .10 to .26. The overall performance rating had a significant correlation of .20 with the Mechanical Comprehension test. The significant correlations with the examination scores were within a range of .21–.37.

The final validation study included 78 applicants to technician and craft apprenticeships in a predictive procedure. Four tests of the TTB were given to the subjects and two criteria were used (workshop evaluation and examination scores). With the workshop performance ratings, the coefficients varied between .22 and .34 with only the significant correlations reported. The correlations were somewhat higher with the examinations scores (.24–.50).

The publisher of the TTB reports the validation studies are ongoing and the registered users will be provided with the updates. The correlations obtained in these validation studies are not, however, very impressive. Under the current circumstances, using the TTB as a predictive device for personnel selection may not provide a much better tool than random selection. Correlations with academic test performance are somewhat higher, but the job-performance-based validity of these tests is not known. The publisher has included in the manual a description of different decision-making procedures to be used by the employers in hiring. At this point, when there is a lack of alternatives, the TTB is best used in conjunction with the decision-making theory with a rather low selection ratio. This procedure is one outlined in the manual.

In conclusion, the TTB is a well-prepared and reliable test. It is easy to administer with clear and straightforward instructions. The major weaknesses of the TTB are the low correlations in the criterion-related validity studies and the lack of test-retest reliability measures. Still, employers may find it a useful tool when used with other personnel selection strategies and in concert with a local norm and validity development program.

[420]
Technician Electrical Test.
Purpose: "To measure the knowledge and skills required for electrical jobs."
Population: Electrical workers and applicants.
Publication Date: 1987.
Scores: Total score only.
Administration: Group.
Price Data, 1989: $498 per 10 reusable booklets, 1 administration manual (12 pages), 1 scoring key, and 100 blank answer sheets.
Time: (120) minutes.
Author: Ramsay Corporation.
Publisher: Ramsay Corporation.

[421]
Technician Mechanical Test.
Purpose: Measures "knowledge and skill in the mechanical area."
Population: Mechanical workers and applicants.
Publication Dates: 1987–88.
Scores: Total score only.
Administration: Group.
Price Data, 1989: $498 per 10 reusable booklets, 1 administration manual ('88, 15 pages), 1 scoring key, and 100 blank answer sheets.
Time: (120) minutes.
Author: Ramsay Corporation.
Publisher: Ramsay Corporation.

[422]
TEMAS (Tell-Me-A-Story).
Purpose: Identifies "both strengths and deficits in cognitive, affective, and intrapersonal and interpersonal functioning."
Population: Ages 5–13.
Publication Dates: 1986–88.
Acronym: TEMAS.
Scores, 34: Quantitative Scales (Cognitive Functions [Reaction Time, Total Time, Fluency, Total Omissions], Personality Functions [Interpersonal Relations, Aggression, Anxiety/Depression, Achievement Motivation, Delay of Gratification, Self-Concept, Sexual Identity, Moral Judgment, Reality Testing], Affective Functions [Happy, Sad, Angry, Fearful]), Qualitative Indicators (Affective Functions [Neutral, Ambivalent, Inappropriate Affect], Cognitive Functions [Conflict, Sequencing, Imagination, Relationships, Total Transformations, Inquiries, Omissions and Transformations scores for each of the following: Main Character, Secondary Character, Event, Setting]).
Administration: Individual.

Forms, 2: Short, Long.
Versions, 2: Minority, Nonminority.
Price Data, 1989: $175 per complete kit including nonminority stimulus cards ('86, 36 cards), minority stimulus cards ('86, 36 cards), 25 record booklets, administration instruction card, and manual ('88, 166 pages); $65 per set of stimulus cards; $8.70 per 25 record booklets; $6.50 per administration instruction card; $55 per manual.
Time: (45–60) minutes (short form); (120) minutes (long form).
Authors: Giuseppe Costantino, Robert G. Malgady (manual and record booklet), and Lloyd H. Rogler (manual).
Publisher: Western Psychological Services.

TEST REFERENCES

1. Costantino, G., Malgady, R. G., Rogler, L. H., & Tsui, E. C. (1988). Discriminant analysis of clinical outpatients and public school children by TEMAS: A thematic apperception test for Hispanics and Blacks. *Journal of Personality Assessment, 52*, 670-678.

Review of the TEMAS (Tell-Me-A-Story) by WILLIAM STEVE LANG, Assistant Professor of Educational Leadership, Technology and Research, Georgia Southern University, Statesboro, GA:

The TEMAS (Tell-Me-A-Story) is a new projective instrument designed to assess personality characteristics of children and adolescents. Additionally, the TEMAS instrument purports to be designed as culture-free and useful when testing minority clients, especially Hispanic and Black youth. The TEMAS claims to address weaknesses found in traditional projective testing, such as the well-known Thematic Apperception Test (TAT; 9:1287). Specifically, the TEMAS makes use of chromatic (color) stimulus cards and "depicts minority characters interacting in urban settings." These deviations from the TAT are meant "to enhance the realism of situations, and . . . to 'pull' for specific ego functions" (Rogler, 1982, p. 3). Essentially, the authors consider current thematic apperception testing culture-bound and unusable with Black and Hispanic children who have been evaluated as "less verbally fluent." The TEMAS was developed to challenge the limitations of the TAT as it is commonly used in personality measurement.

The TEMAS comes in parallel forms for minority (Black and Hispanic) children and nonminority (White) children. Both forms contain 23 stimulus cards, some of which are sex-specific. The cards can be scored for 18 Cognitive functions, 9 Personality (ego) functions, and 7 Affective functions. The TEMAS can be administered in 45 minutes (short form) to 2 hours (long form) and comes with an extensive manual with complete scoring instructions and illustrations of responses. The test's directions and scoring are understandable for professionals familiar with projectives. Case studies for interpretation of the results are also included, which is helpful in learning the use of a new projective where clinical training is unlikely. The manual contains descriptive statistics and norms for children ages 5 through 13. The test can be used with children clinically to age 18, but normative data are available only to age 13.

Construct validity concerns are described in depth in the test manual. Even though some researchers might disagree with test construction decisions made in the TEMAS, the authors document their rationale for the use of color, the importance of social-learning theory, the cognitive framework of children, and the bipolar nature of ego functioning. The authors do not define the theoretical reasons for their affective functions as well as other areas, but in general the literature supporting the framework of the TEMAS is appropriate. The authors of the test also describe one illustration of face validity where 14 practicing psychologists could usually indicate the personality function illustrated by the stimulus cards. The manual has mislabeled this as "content validity." They have not performed an organized study of a set of items that represent a defined domain. Instead, they simply obtained agreement that test items appear to be measuring what they purport to measure.

Internal consistency reliability estimates were reported by the manual for the 34 functions (Cognitive, Personality, and Affective) suggested by the authors. The Cronbach's alpha ranged from .31 to .98 with half below an acceptable level (.70), even for projective tests. Test-retest reliabilities were alarmingly low where the highest function correlation was $r = .53$ and 26 of the 34 functions showed correlations near zero. Because the interrater reliabilities were typically moderate to high, the test-retest correlations suggest an extremely situational nature to this instrument. The functions proposed by the authors might vary with time, but should be more stable within individuals than illustrated by the test-retest data reported. The most likely conclusion at this time is that the TEMAS simply does not measure the constructs it proposes to measure, or does so with a large proportion of each score attributable to error.

It is important to note that establishing reliability and subsequent validity has been a common problem for projective testing in general (Nunnally, 1978). Innovative, standardized scoring systems have been used to demonstrate reasonable psychometric properties for such tests. John Exner's (1978) chapter entitled "The Issue of Reliability: Temporal Consistency of the Structural Data" from his text *The Rorschach: A Comprehensive System* discusses similar issues, and he illustrates what can be done to support these tests.

The TEMAS manual implies criterion-related validity using a rather complex regression analysis that concludes 6 to 22% of the variance of therapeutic outcomes is predicted using four stand-ardized measures and four ratings of graduate students as criteria. Unfortunately, the TEMAS does not compare itself in the manual to the TAT it is designed to replace (concurrent validity), nor does it argue better predictive validity with regard to minority students. The analysis reported is not sufficient evidence to conclude that correlational validity has been established.

In independent research, the authors of the TEMAS do illustrate more verbal responsiveness of Hispanic children to the instrument than to the TAT, except that the children were more responsive to both the minority and nonminority versions of the instrument (Rogler, 1982). This demonstrates a lack of differential effectiveness attributed to minority cards. Additionally, greater verbal response does not necessarily indicate that the scores for Black or Hispanic students were more valid measures of personality than the scores that might have been obtained on the TAT.

The norm sample is mixed Black and Hispanic students from urban areas. It seems simplistic to assume that Black and Hispanic culture, even if restricted to urban areas, is similar. If the authors' premise is accurate that cultural differences in projective testing need differential instruments, then Black and Hispanic children would probably constitute different groups, to say nothing about the vast difference between urban and rural subcultures.

In conclusion, although the TEMAS is based on a reasonable premise (i.e., existing projective techniques may be culturally insensitive) and the measure ρ has promising construct related validity, it has not yet established criterion-related validity and has yet to show that it is better than the TAT or similar measures at assessing the personality characteristics of minority children. The well-established TAT is still the suggested standard for thematic projective investigations. The reliability of the TEMAS is not acceptable when estimated with both internal consistency and test-retest methods. The TEMAS is not an improvement over other projective tests and may have poorer psychometric properties than existing measures. The TEMAS cards may be useful for research purposes so direct comparisons to the TAT and other personality instruments are encouraged. Clinical or predictive uses of the TEMAS are still questionable and caution is recommended, even when minority children are the clients.

REVIEWER'S REFERENCES

Exner, J. E. (1978). *The Rorschach: A comprehensive system, volume 2: Current research and advanced interpretations.* New York: John Wiley & Sons.

Nunnally, J. C. (1978). *Psychometric theory* (2nd ed.). New York: McGraw-Hill.

Rogler, L. H. (1982). *Research bulletin, Hispanic Research Center, volume 5, number 4.* Bronx, NY: Hispanic Research Center. (ERIC Document Reproduction Service No. ED 226 078).

Temperament Assessment Battery for Children.

Purpose: "Designed to measure basic personality-behavioral dimensions (temperaments) of children."
Population: Ages 3–7.
Publication Date: 1988.
Acronym: TABC.
Scores, 6: Activity, Adaptability, Approach/Withdrawal, Intensity, Distractibility, Persistence.
Administration: Individual.
Forms, 3: Clinician, Parent, Teacher.
Price Data, 1989: $19.20 per 10 tests (specify form); $24.95 per manual (107 pages); $30 per sampler set.
Time: (10–20) minutes.
Comments: Scale for ratings of children; forms available as separates.
Author: Roy P. Martin.
Publisher: Clinical Psychology Publishing Co., Inc.

TEST REFERENCES

1. Cardell, C. D., & Parmar, R. S. (1988). Teacher perceptions of temperament characteristics of children classified as learning disabled. *Journal of Learning Disabilities, 21*, 497-502.
2. Martin, R. P., Drew, K. D., Gaddis, L. R., & Moseley, M. (1988). Prediction of elementary school achievement from preschool temperament: Three studies. *School Psychology Review, 17*, 125-137.

Review of the Temperament Assessment Battery for Children by DAVID MacPHEE, Associate Professor of Human Development and Family Studies, Colorado State University, Fort Collins, CO:

Efforts to assess children's temperament have been hampered by a lack of well-articulated theories and sound instruments. Among the many deficiencies from which temperament scales typically suffer (Hubert, Wachs, Peters-Martin, & Gandour, 1982), this review will focus on two: lack of clarity regarding the temperament construct and lack of transsituational stability manifest as poor interrater reliability.

INADEQUATE CONCEPTUAL FRAMEWORK. The Temperament Assessment Battery for Children (TABC), as with Carey's scales (e.g., McDevitt & Carey, 1978), is based on the work of Thomas and Chess (1977). As a result, the author makes assumptions about which behavior dimensions constitute temperament that are neither supported in the literature (Hubert et al., 1982) nor by his own data. The TABC retains six of the nine Thomas and Chess dimensions, although factor analyses of it (and other temperament scales) support three: emotionality, persistence, and sociability. I concur with the author's reasoning in an earlier paper: "Since these factors appear to be measuring constructs similar to those described by [others], and because their internal consistency is higher than that of the constituent scales, it is suggested that these factor scales should be the primary data in the clinical and research applications of the instrument" (Martin, 1983, p. 268). However, the TABC *manual* argues against using aggregated scales because of somewhat different loadings for the three

forms, even though the item content varies across forms.

Although the manual acknowledges that existing theories do not provide much guidance for identifying a core set of temperaments, the author does not describe his own theoretical framework beyond a conceptual definition of temperament. As a consequence, no guidance is given for the construct validity of six scales as opposed to three. Further, although the TABC is related to child behavior problems, there is neither a discussion of what this relation means nor of how temperament is a construct distinct from "psychopathology." Given the uncertainties about the construct and the proliferation of other scales, the absence of data on convergent and discriminant validity is perplexing. Finally, the theoretical rationale for the TABC's use of educational criterion variables is murky: The empirical articles provide some background but the manual does not. For instance, why should one expect correlations with IQ, achievement, or teacher attitudes?

The TABC's criterion validity must be questioned for other reasons as well. First, all of the studies finding consistent relations with IQ are unpublished, and the manual does not describe which correlations were *non*significant. Second, descriptions of the criterion variables are missing in some cases, or nonstandardized measures (e.g., grades) were used to assess achievement. Third, criterion contamination or halo effects may have resulted from having the same teacher who assigned grades or administered achievement tests also rate the child's temperament (Martin, Drew, Gaddis, & Moseley, 1988). To the author's credit, some of these problems were resolved in later studies that did long-term follow-ups with different teachers and standardized criterion variables. Still, one must scrutinize the empirical articles for this information.

SITUATIONAL AND TEMPORAL STABILITY. Temperament is defined often in terms of transsituational and temporal stability. However, when individual differences are not consistently observed across raters and contexts, is it due to deficiencies in the scale's interrater reliability or to valid variations in behavior across contexts? The manual provides a cogent discussion of such sources of variance in ratings of child behavior and then establishes a rationale for developing forms for different observers. The actual interrater reliabilities are typical for temperament scales: modest values for mother-father agreement (r s = -.21 to .70, median of .43; median = .51 excluding the referred sample) and lower correlations if different forms are used (r s = -.04 to .50 for Parent vs. Teacher; median = .35). Regarding temporal stability, test-retest reliabilities are adequate for both teachers (median = .79 after

6 months) and parents (rs = .31-.75; median = .58 after 1-2 years).

There may be several explanations for the low interrater reliabilities. First, the author acknowledges the variation in item content across raters. But if transsituational stability is a central feature of temperament, why was agreement across sources not used as one criterion for item selection? Second, Hubert et al. (1982) emphasized that differential experience with the child may account for lack of agreement among raters, yet it appears that parental involvement in child care has not been examined as a covariate of TABC ratings. On a related note, the author recommends that teachers not complete the TABC if they have known the child for less than 2 months, yet clinicians are permitted to rate the child after only a single assessment session. Raters must be familiar with the child across time and settings in order to make judgements about *enduring* traits (Cairns & Green, 1979; Carey, 1983). It is instructive that the lowest internal reliabilities (below) are generated by clinicians who are least familiar with the child.

UTILITY. The TABC is suggested for several uses: in descriptive research; as a potential screening device for identifying psychopathological symptoms; and to provide information to parents about the socioemotional characteristics of their children. However, the alpha coefficients are too low (parents: .65-.86; teachers: .69-.86; clinicians: .54-.81) to warrant use of the TABC for individual diagnosis. In addition, cut scores have not been developed for screening purposes.

Whether the TABC is appropriate for use with various ethnic and social class groups is not entirely clear. A convenience sample of 1,381 children (84% between 4 and 5 years of age) from three regions of the country was used to norm the Parent Form. Information on the representation of ethnic groups and especially SES is inadequate, both in the manual and published articles. The Teacher Form was normed on 577 children but it is not clear how many *raters* contributed these data. Across samples, it appears that fewer than 35 teachers participated, which raises serious concerns about the disproportionate effect of rater biases in a small sample and this form's actual reliability if based on the appropriate unit of analysis.

In light of Hubert et al.'s (1982) critique of the field, the TABC is not a significant improvement over the most viable alternative, the Behavioral Styles Questionnaire (McDevitt & Carey, 1978). Although the TABC is shorter by 52 items and was normed on a more representative population, it also omits the one scale (Mood) with the greatest construct validity in samples of parents. The two measures' drawbacks are prevalent in other temperament scales: lack of clarity about which dimensions to include, atheoretical selection of criterion variables, failure to demark the construct's boundaries through convergent and discriminant validation, and an absence of data on why ratings are inconsistent across sources. These deficiencies lend support to Hubert et al.'s (1982) call for a moratorium on constructing temperament scales until there are breakthroughs in theory.

REVIEWER'S REFERENCES

Thomas, A., & Chess, S. (1977). *Temperament and development*. New York: Brunner/Mazel.

McDevitt, S. C., & Carey, W. B. (1978). The measurement of temperament in 3-7 year old children. *Journal of Child Psychology and Psychiatry, 19,* 245-253.

Cairns, R. B., & Green, J. A. (1979). How to assess personality and social patterns: Observations or ratings? In R. B. Cairns (Ed.), *The analysis of social interactions: Methods, issues, and illustrations* (pp. 209-226). Hillsdale, NJ: Erlbaum.

Hubert, N. C., Wachs, T. D., Peters-Martin, P., & Gandour, M. J. (1982). The study of early temperament: Measurement and conceptual issues. *Child Development, 53,* 571-600.

Carey, W. B. (1983). Some pitfalls in infant temperament research. *Infant Behavior and Development, 6,* 247-254.

Martin, R. P. (1983). Temperament: A review of research with implications for the school psychologist. *School Psychology Review, 12,* 266-273.

Martin, R. P., Drew, K. D., Gaddis, L. R., & Moseley, M. (1988). Prediction of elementary school achievement from preschool temperament: Three studies. *School Psychology Review, 17,* 125-137.

Review of the Temperament Assessment Battery for Children by LOGAN WRIGHT, Professor of Psychology, and KENNETH V. WHITE, Research Associate, University of Oklahoma, Norman, OK:

The Temperament Assessment Battery for Children (TABC) provides a means for rating six different personality ("temperament") dimensions of children ages 3 through 7. These dimensions include Activity, Adaptability, Approach/Withdrawal, Emotional Intensity, Distractibility, and Persistence. Each dimension is assessed by three different scales designed for completion by teachers, parents, and clinicians, respectively. The Teacher and Parent Forms consist of 48 questions each; the Clinician Form has 24. Each item is rated on a 1-7 Likert-type scale for frequency of the behavior from 1 (*hardly ever*) to 7 (*almost always*).

The TABC battery had its beginnings in Eysenck's (1953) dimensions of Introversion/Extraversion and Neuroticism. Using factor analysis of Eysenck's EPI Scale, Buss and Plomin (1975) developed four new personality constructs. These were emotionality, sociability, impulsivity, and activity. Items from the Buss and Plomin categories as well as the New York Longitudinal Study (Meili, 1959) were then used in developing the Thomas, Chess, and Korn Parent/Teacher Questionnaires (Thomas & Chess, 1977). The Thomas, Chess, and Korn scale consisted of nine temperament dimensions which could be rated on two forms, one for parents and one for teachers.

The items from the Thomas, Chess, and Korn scale were eventually used by Martin to created the TABC. This was done by eliminating those items which failed to contribute to the internal consistency of the various subscales. This process also served to reduce the number of temperament dimensions from nine to six. Martin then added a third form for clinicians. Thus, the TABC is simply a shorter version of the scale already published by Thomas and Chess but reshaped into six subscales, which are assessed by clinicians as well as parents and teachers.

Normative data for the TABC are very limited. In addition, the children Martin reports using in the development of the Clinician Form are exclusively white, middle- and upper-class residents of northern Georgia. The mean IQ of all child subjects used in construction of the Clinical Form was 116.

The interrater reliability coefficients reported by Martin also involve test-retest intervals. These coefficients are quite low, ranging from -.21 to .70. However, in light of the fact that relatively high test-retest reliabilities are reported on this battery, one must assume that the TABC possesses significant problems in the area of interrater reliability (objectivity).

Internal consistency studies of the various TABC temperament subscales yield alpha coefficients varying from .54 to .87. The 1-year test-retest reliabilities based on the ratings of 224 children ages 30 to 80 months ranged from .37 to .70 on the Parent Form. Six-month test-retest reliabilities for the Teacher Form ranged from .69 to .87. No data are reported by the author for test-retest reliabilities for the Clinician Form. The rather low test-retest reliabilities reported for some of the subscales up to 1 year are possibly due to the fact that the measured behavior itself (temperament) is not particularly reliable in developing children under 7 years of age.

Validity data reported for the TABC are probably best described as "concurrent" rather than "construct" because the manual provides no rationale for the latter. Validity data were obtained by correlating the TABC with instruments designed to measure psychopathology and achievement. Where psychopathology is concerned, the Parent Form has been shown to differentiate between children who are, and those who are not, referred for a psychological evaluation. The Teacher Form has also been shown to correlate with teacher ratings on the Quay-Peterson Behavior Problem Checklist. Finally, five of the Parent Form temperament scales, as rated by mothers, have been significantly correlated with the Bristol Social Adjustment scale, as completed by teachers.

With respect to achievement, using a sample of 80 first grade children, multiple correlations between the entire temperament set on one hand, and reading and mathematics grades on the other, were .76 and .65, respectively. All of the TABC temperament subscales, with the exception of emotional intensity, have been found to correlate significantly

with the American School Achievement Test. Finally, TABC Teacher Form ratings have been shown to add significantly (above that provided by IQ data alone) to the prediction of student achievement.

In summary, the TABC is deficient in the areas of standardization and objectivity (interrater reliability). No reliability or validity data are reported for the Clinician Form. Although a usually acceptable array of validity studies is provided for the Parent and Teacher Forms of the TABC, potential users should remember that a close similarity exists between the items on these Forms and the already existing Thomas, Chess, and Korn Parent/Teacher Questionnaires (1977). Because the unrefined (psychometrically) Clinician Form constitutes the only unique feature of the TABC, it is difficult to see what advantages are gained in using it over the Thomas, Chess, and Korn Questionnaires. Making the TABC available at this time, for the purpose of further research, may be justified, but commercial publication and marketing seem premature.

REVIEWERS' REFERENCES

Eysenck, H. (1953). *The structure of human personality.* London: Methuen.

Meili, R. (1959). A longitudinal study of personality development. In L. Jessner & E. Pavenstedt (Eds.), *Dynamic psychopathology in childhood* (pp. 106-123). New York: Grune and Stratton.

Buss, A. H., & Plomin, R. (1975). *A temperament theory of personality development.* New York: Wiley.

Thomas, A., & Chess, S. (1977). *Temperament and development.* New York: Brunner/Mazel.

[424]
Tennessee Self-Concept Scale [Revised].

Purpose: Measures self-concept.

Population: Ages 12 and over.

Publication Dates: 1964–88.

Acronym: TSCS.

Administration: Individual or group.

Price Data, 1989: $75 per complete kit including 10 test booklets (5 of Form C and 5 of Form C & R), 10 hand-scored answer-profile sheets, and manual ('88, 92 pages); $21 per 10 test booklets; $14.50 per set of scoring keys (Form C & R only); $12.50 per 25 hand-scored answer-profile sheets; $27.50 per manual; $8.50 per supplemental monograph; scoring service: $8.90 per examinee (price includes test booklet and answer sheet).

Time: (10–20) minutes.

Comments: Self-administered.

Authors: William H. Fitts (test and manual) and Gale H. Roid (manual).

Publisher: Western Psychological Services.

a) COUNSELING FORM (FORM C).

Scores, 14: Self-Criticism, 9 self-esteem scores (Identity, Self-Satisfaction, Behavior, Physical Self, Moral-Ethical Self, Personal Self, Family Self, Social Self, Total), 3 variability of response scores (variation across the first 3 self-esteem scores, variation across the last 5 self-esteem scores, total), Distribution Score.

b) CLINICAL AND RESEARCH FORM (FORM C & R).

Scores, 42: the 14 scores in *a* above plus the following 28 scores: True-False Ratio, Net Conflict, Total Conflict, 6 empirical scales (Defensive Positive, General Maladjustment, Psychosis, Personality

Disorder, Neurosis, Personality Integration), Deviant Signs, 5 scores consisting of counts of each type of response made, 13 supplementary scores (Stanwyck-Garrison Faking Good, Seeman Personality Integration Index, Number of Integrative Signs, Self-Actualization, 9 Psychological Harmony scores [Identity, Self-Satisfaction, Behavior, Physical Self, Moral-Ethical Self, Personal Self, Family Self, Social Self, Total]).

c) COMPUTER-SCORABLE FORMAT.

Scores: Same as b above.

Cross References: See 9:1236 (60 references), T3:2413 (120 references), 8:693 (384 references), and T2:1415 (80 references); for reviews by Peter M. Bentler and Richard M. Suinn and an excerpted review by John O. Crites of an earlier edition, see 7:151 (88 references); see also P:266 (30 references).

TEST REFERENCES

1. Aitken, M. J. (1982). Self-concept and functional independence in the hospitalized elderly. *The American Journal of Occupational Therapy, 36,* 243-256.
2. Cupie, S. H., & Kaplan, K. (1982). A case analysis method for the model of human occupation. *The American Journal of Occupational Therapy, 36,* 645-656.
3. Brown, D., Fulkerson, K. F., Vedder, M., & Ware, W. B. (1983). Self-estimate ability in black and white 8th-, 10th-, and 12th-grade males and females. *The Vocational Guidance Quarterly, 32,* 21-28.
4. Chodzinski, R. T. (1983). Validity concerns for counsellors using the 1978 edition of the Career Maturity Inventory. *Canadian Counsellor, 18,* 5-12.
5. Garrison, D. R. (1983). Psychosocial correlates of dropout and achievement in an adult high school completion program. *The Alberta Journal of Educational Research, 29,* 131-139.
6. Gunter, N. C., & Bedell, J. R. (1983). The peer-managed small group versus the rehabilitation model of treatment of chronic patients. *Hospital and Community Psychiatry, 34,* 724-728.
7. Heppner, P. P., Reeder, B. L., & Larson, L. M. (1983). Cognitive variables associated with personal problem-solving appraisal: Implications for counseling. *Journal of Counseling Psychology, 30,* 537-545.
8. Hill, C. E., Carter, J. A., & O'Farrell, M. K. (1983). A case study of the process and outcome of time-limited counseling. *Journal of Counseling Psychology, 30,* 3-18.
9. McNair, D., & Brown, D. (1983). Predicting the occupational aspirations, occupational expectations, and career maturity of black and white male and female 10th graders. *The Vocational Guidance Quarterly, 32,* 29-36.
10. Wolf, E. M., & Crowther, J. H. (1983). Personality and eating habit variables as predictors of severity of binge eating and weight. *Addictive Behaviors, 8,* 335-344.
11. Angle, S. S., & Goodyear, R. K. (1984). Perceptions of counselor qualities: Impact of subjects' self-concepts, counselor gender, and counselor introductions. *Journal of Counseling Psychology, 31,* 576-579.
12. Byrne, B. M. (1984). The general/academic self-concept nomological network: A review of construct validation research. *Review of Educational Research, 54,* 427-456.
13. Colosimo, M. L. (1984). Attitude changes with initial teaching experience. *College Student Journal, 18,* 119-125.
14. Connors, M. E., Johnson, C. L., & Stuckey, M. K. (1984). Treatment of bulimia with brief psychoeducational group therapy. *American Journal of Psychiatry, 141,* 1512-1516.
15. Crook, R. H., Healy, C. C., & O'Shea, D. W. (1984). The linkage of work achievement to self-esteem, career maturity, and college achievement. *Journal of Vocational Behavior, 25,* 70-79.
16. Dembo, M. H., Sweitzer, M., & Lauritzen, P. (1984). An evaluation of group parent education: Behavioral, PET, and Adlerian programs. *Review of Educational Research, 55,* 155-200.
17. Erdwins, C. J., & Mellinger, J. C. (1984). Mid-life women: Relation of age and role to personality. *Journal of Personality and Social Psychology, 47,* 390-395.
18. Gadzella, B. M., & Williamson, J. D. (1984). Differences between men and women on selected Tennessee Self Concept scales. *Psychological Reports, 55,* 939-942.
19. Gadzella, B. M., & Williamson, J. D. (1984). Study skills, self-concept, and academic achievement. *Psychological Reports, 54,* 923-929.
20. Gellen, M. I., & Hoffman, R. A. (1984). Analysis of the subscales of the Tennessee Self-Concept Scale. *Measurement and Evaluation in Counseling and Development, 17,* 51-55.
21. Hoffman, R. A., & Gellen, M. I. (1984). Generalizability of the Tennessee Self-Concept Scale norms. *Perceptual and Motor Skills, 58,* 140-142.
22. Jacobs, S. B., & Wagner, M. K. (1984). Obese and nonobese individuals: Behavioral and personality characteristics. *Addictive Behaviors, 9,* 223-226.
23. Kelly, K. R., & Colangelo, N. (1984). Academic and social self-concepts of gifted, general, and special students. *Exceptional Children, 50,* 551-554.
24. Knapp, S., & Mierzwa, J. A. (1984). Effects of systematic desensitization and self-control treatments in test-anxiety reduction programs. *Journal of College Student Personnel, 25,* 228-233.
25. Lee, C. C. (1984). An investigation of the psychosocial variables in the occupational aspirations and expectations of rural black and white adolescents: Implications for vocational education. *Journal of Research and Development in Education, 17* (3), 28-34.
26. Lee, C. C. (1984). Predicting the career choice attitudes of rural Black, White, and Native American high school students. *The Vocational Guidance Quarterly, 32,* 177-184.
27. Lutz, D. J., Roback, H. B., & Hart, M. (1984). Feminine gender identity and psychological adjustment of male transsexuals and male homosexuals. *The Journal of Sex Research, 20,* 350-362.
28. Martin, J. D., & Coley, L. A. (1984). Intercorrelations of some measures of self-concept. *Educational and Psychological Measurement, 44,* 517-521.
29. Niebuhr, R. E., & Davis, K. R., Jr. (1984). Self-esteem: Relationship with leader behavior perceptions as moderated by the duration of the superior-subordinate dyad association. *Personality and Social Psychology Bulletin, 10,* 51-59.
30. Schmitt, J. P., & Kurdek, L. A. (1984). Correlates of social anxiety in college students and homosexuals. *Journal of Personality Assessment, 48,* 403-409.
31. Seagull, E. A. W., & Weinshank, A. B. (1984). Childhood depression in a selected group of low-achieving seventh-graders. *Journal of Clinical Child Psychology, 13,* 134-140.
32. Serok, S., & Bar, R. (1984). Looking at Gestalt group impact: An experiment. *Small Group Behavior, 15,* 270-277.
33. Slater, E. J., & Haber, J. D. (1984). Adolescent adjustment following divorce as a function of familial conflict. *Journal of Consulting and Clinical Psychology, 52,* 920-921.
34. Tharenou, P., & Harker, P. (1984). Moderating influence of self-esteem or relationships between job complexity, performance, and satisfaction. *Journal of Applied Psychology, 69,* 623-632.
35. Thompson, R. A. (1984). The critical needs of the adolescent unwed mother. *The School Counselor, 31,* 460-466.
36. Tucker, L. A. (1984). Physical attractiveness, somatotype, and the male personality: A dynamic interactional perspective. *Journal of Clinical Psychology, 40,* 1226-1234.
37. Mellinger, J. C., & Erdwins, C. J. (1985). Personality correlates of age and life roles in adult women. *Psychology of Women Quarterly, 9,* 503-514.
38. Anooshian, L. J., Ashbrook, P., & Hertel, P. T. (1985). Self-esteem and beliefs about memory in environmentally stable and relocated students. *Journal of Research in Personality, 19,* 457-471.
39. Beatrice, J. (1985). A psychological comparison of heterosexuals, transvestites, preoperative transsexuals, and postoperative transsexuals. *The Journal of Nervous and Mental Disease, 173,* 358-365.
40. Blodgett, C. (1985). Renal failure adjustment and coping style. *Journal of Personality Assessment, 49,* 271-272.
41. Bredehoft, D. J., & Hey, R. N. (1985). An evaluation study of self-esteem: A family affair. *Family Relations, 34,* 411-417.
42. Carver, D. S., & Smart, D. W. (1985). The effects of a career and self-exploration course for undecided freshmen. *Journal of College Student Personnel, 26,* 37-43.
43. Crump, B. R. R., Hickson, J. H., & Laman, A. (1985). Relationship of locus of control to achievement and self-concept in education majors. *Psychological Reports, 57,* 1055-1060.
44. Farber, S. S., Felner, R. D., & Primavera, J. (1985). Parental separation/divorce and adolescents: An examination of factors mediating adaptation. *American Journal of Community Psychology, 13,* 171-185.
45. Gadzella, B. M., Williamson, J. D., & Ginther, D. W. (1985). *Perceptual and Motor Skills, 61,* 639-645.
46. Gibson-Harman, K., & Austin, G. F. (1985). A revised form of the Tennessee Self-Concept Scale for use with deaf and hard of hearing persons. *American Annals of the Deaf, 130,* 218-225.
47. Lynch, A. D., & Clark, P. (1985). Relationship of self-esteem, IQ, and task performance for a sample of USA undergraduates. *Psychological Reports, 56,* 955-962.
48. Ortiz, N. S. C., & Campbell, N. J. (1985). Self-concept and anxiety: A comparison of students from Puerto Rico and the United States. *College Student Journal, 19,* 416-423.
49. Pavlak, M. F., & Kammer, P. P. (1985). The effects of a career guidance program on the career maturity and self-concept of delinquent youth. *Journal of Vocational Behavior, 26,* 41-54.

50. Rainey, D., & Wigtil, J. (1985). Aerobic running as a counseling technique for undergraduates with low self-esteem. *Journal of College Student Personnel, 26,* 53-57.

51. Sohlberg, S. C. (1985). Personality and neuropsychological performance of high-risk children. *Schizophrenia Bulletin, 11,* 48-60.

52. Solomon, R. (1985). Creativity and normal narcissism. *The Journal of Creative Behavior, 19,* 47-55.

53. Sultan, F. E., & Johnson, P. J. (1985). Characteristics of dropouts, remainers, and refusers at a psychosocial rehabilitation program for the chronically mentally disabled. *The Journal of Psychology, 119,* 175-183.

54. Tzeng, O. C. S., Maxey, W. A., Fortier, R., & Landis, D. (1985). Construct evaluation of the Tennessee Self Concept Scale. *Educational and Psychological Measurement, 45,* 63-78.

55. Walsh, R. W. (1985). Changes in college freshmen after participation in a student development program. *Journal of College Student Personnel, 26,* 310-314.

56. Balogun, J. A. (1986). Muscular strength as a predictor of personality in adult females. *The Journal of Sports Medicine and Physical Fitness, 26,* 377-383.

57. Balogun, J. A. (1986). Reliability and construct validity of the Body Cathexis Scale. *Perceptual and Motor Skills, 62,* 927-935.

58. Brown, R. D., & Harrison, J. M. (1986). The effects of a strength training program on the strength and self-concept of two female age groups. *Research Quarterly for Exercise and Sport, 57,* 315-320.

59. Cofe, J. E., Harris, D. P., & Vipond, E. (1986). A psychometric evaluation of a residential treatment facility: An illustration of an interpretable research design without a control group. *Adolescence, 21,* 67-79.

60. Cochrane, G., & Friesen, J. (1986). Hypnotherapy in weight loss treatment. *Journal of Consulting and Clinical Psychology, 54,* 489-492.

61. Dykens, E. M., & Gerrard, M. (1986). Psychological profiles of purging bulimics, repeat dieters, and controls. *Journal of Consulting and Clinical Psychology, 54,* 283-288.

62. Gadzella, B. M., Ginther, D. W., & Williamson, J. D. (1986). Differences in self-concept between deep and shallow processors. *Psychological Reports, 59,* 544-546.

63. Kerr, B. A. (1986). Career counseling for the gifted: Assessments and interventions. *Journal of Counseling and Development, 64,* 602-604.

64. Parker, J. C., Smarr, K. L., Granberg, B. W., Nichols, W. K., & Hewett, J. E. (1986). Neuropsychological parameters of carotid endarterectomy: A two-year prospective analysis. *Journal of Consulting and Clinical Psychology, 54,* 676-681.

65. Schumaker, J. F., Small, L., & Wood, J. (1986). Self-concept, academic achievement, and athletic participation. *Perceptual and Motor Skills, 62,* 387-390.

66. Shiller, V. M. (1986). Joint versus maternal custody for families with latency age boys: Parent characteristics and child adjustment. *American Journal of Orthopsychiatry, 56,* 486-489.

67. Thompson, R. A. (1986). Developing a peer group facilitation program on the secondary school level: An investment with multiple returns. *Small Group Behavior, 17,* 105-112.

68. Ward, D. A. (1986). Self-esteem and dishonest behavior revisited. *The Journal of Social Psychology, 126,* 709-713.

69. Brockner, J., O'Malley, M. N., Hite, T., & Davies, D. K. (1987). Reward allocation and self-esteem: The roles of modeling and equity restoration. *Journal of Personality and Social Psychology, 52,* 844-850.

70. Plummer, O. K., & Koh, Y. O. (1987). Effect of "aerobics" on self-concepts of college women. *Perceptual and Motor Skills, 65,* 271-275.

71. Thompson, R. A. (1987). Creating instructional and counseling partnerships to improve the academic performance of underachievers. *The School Counselor, 34,* 289-296.

72. Weinmann, C. A., & Sifft, J. M. (1987). Effects of cognitive information on college students' self-concept. *Perceptual and Motor Skills, 64,* 1159-1162.

73. Wierzbicki, M., & Bartlett, T. S. (1987). The efficacy of group and individual cognitive therapy for mild depression. *Cognitive Therapy and Research, 11,* 337-342.

74. Wyatt, R. C., & Meyers, L. S. (1987). Psychometric properties of four 5-point Likert-type response scales. *Educational and Psychological Measurement, 47* (1), 27-35.

75. Bergin, A. E., Stinchfield, R. D., Gaskin, T. A., Masters, K. S., & Sullivan, C. E. (1988). Religious life-styles and mental health: An exploratory study. *Journal of Counseling Psychology, 35,* 91-98.

76. Forest, J. J. (1988). Exploring more on the effects of psychological self-help paperbacks. *Psychological Reports, 63,* 891-894.

77. Gutierres, S. E., & Reich, J. W. (1988). Attributional analysis of drug abuse and gender: Effects of treatment and relationship to rehabilitation. *Journal of Social and Clinical Psychology, 7,* 176-191.

78. Hill, C. E., Helms, J. E., Spiegel, S. B., & Tichenor, V. (1988). Development of a system for categorizing client reactions to therapist interventions. *Journal of Counseling Psychology, 35,* 27-36.

79. Lobel, T. E. (1988). Personality correlates of Type A coronary-prone behavior. *Journal of Personality Assessment, 52,* 434-440.

80. Marsh, H. W., & Richards, G. E. (1988). Tennessee Self Concept Scale: Reliability, internal structure, and construct validity. *Journal of Personality and Social Psychology, 55,* 612-624.

81. Netz, Y., Tenenbaum, G., & Sagiv, M. (1988). Pattern of psychological fitness as related to pattern of physical fitness among older adults. *Perceptual and Motor Skills, 67,* 647-655.

82. Cavaiola, A. A., & Schiff, M. (1989). Self-esteem in abused chemically dependent adolescents. *Child Abuse & Neglect, 13,* 327-334.

83. Coursey, R. D., Lees, R. W., & Siever, L. J. (1989). The relationship between smooth pursuit eye movement impairment and psychological measures of psychopathology. *Psychological Medicine, 19,* 343-358.

84. Kalliopuska, M. (1989). Empathy, self-esteem and creativity among junior ballet dancers. *Perceptual and Motor Skills, 69,* 1227-1234.

85. Nadler, A., & Ben-Shushan, D. (1989). Forty years later: Long-term consequences of massive traumatization as manifested by Holocaust survivors from the city and the Kibbutz. (1989). *Journal of Consulting and Clinical Psychology, 57,* 287-293.

86. Snyder, D. K., & Wills, R. M. (1989). Behavioral versus insight-oriented marital therapy: Effects on individual and interspousal functioning. *Journal of Consulting and Clinical Psychology, 57,* 39-46.

87. Salokun, S. O. (1990). Comparison of Nigerian high school male athletes and nonathletes on self-concept. *Perceptual and Motor Skills, 70,* 865-866.

88. Levy-Shiff, R., Goldshmidt, I., & Har-Even, D. (1991). Transition to parenthood in adoptive families. *Developmental Psychology, 27,* 131-140.

89. Tymchuk, A. J. (1991). Self-concepts of mothers who show mental retardation. *Psychological Reports, 68,* 503-510.

Review of the Tennessee Self-Concept Scale [Revised] by FRANCIS X. ARCHAMBAULT, JR., Professor of Educational Psychology and Department Head, University of Connecticut, Storrs, CT:

The Tennessee Self-Concept Scale (TSCS) is easy to complete, multidimensional in its description of self-concept, and suitable for use with anyone 12 years of age or older who can read on at least a fourth-grade level. It can also be used across the full range of psychological adjustment, from healthy, well-adjusted individuals to psychotic patients. Given these features, it is not surprising that the TSCS is one of the most popular measures of self-concept available today. Despite its broad appeal and widespread use, however, some questions remain about the psychometric properties of the scale, particularly its dimensionality.

The TSCS contains 90 Likert-Scale items designed to measure three internal dimensions (i.e., Identity, Self-Satisfaction, and Behavior) and five external dimensions (i.e., Physical Self, Moral-Ethical Self, Personal Self, Family Self, and Social Self) of self-concept. An additional 10 items measure self-criticism, a lie scale patterned after a similar Minnesota Multiphasic Personality Inventory (MMPI) Scale. Two forms of the instrument are available: (*a*) a Counseling Form (Form C) which provides scores for the three internal and five external dimensions, a self-criticism score, four variability scores, and a time score; and (*b*) a Clinical and Research Form (Form C & R) which provides all of the above scores as well as more detailed variability scores, additional lie and faking scores, and a number of empirically derived scores found to separate various clinical groups from nonpatients and from each other.

Form C is easy to administer and complete, somewhat more difficult to score, but still suitable for use in schools and other counseling settings. Form C & R is also easy to administer (the same items are used in both forms), but scoring and interpretation are more difficult, particularly for the empirically derived scales. As suggested by the authors, these scores should be interpreted only by someone with clinical training and experience, and even then the interpretations should be considered tentative hypotheses to be supported or disconfirmed by findings from other sources.

The 1988 revision of the TSCS is different from the earlier edition in a number of ways. First, the new publisher, Western Psychological Services, provides improved hand-scoring answer sheets and a new computerized scoring and interpretation service. Although the hand-scoring improvements are largely cosmetic, scoring Form C is a little easier. But hand scoring Form C & R remains a tedious and time-consuming job. Potential users should note, however, that the computerized reports available for this form provide a large amount of easy-to-read and useful information, that the processing typically takes only one day, and that the service is reasonably priced.

The revised TSCS also provides adolescent normative data not available with earlier editions. However, the new normative sample includes no 12- or 13-year-olds and only one 14-year-old, and it is not representative of adolescents in the population in terms of either SES or ethnicity. Further, adolescent normative data are available only for Form C & R. This means that the *T*-scores and percentiles provided on the hand-scored answer sheets are derived from an adult sample and that no separate answer sheets are available for adolescents. Adding even more confusion, the adult norm group overrepresents college students, persons under 30 years of age, and whites. Because research has shown ethnicity, socioeconomic status, and age to be related to TSCS scores, and because cross-cultural differences in self-concept have been found, caution should be exercised in interpreting TSCS scores for groups not represented in the norming sample.

The revised test manual also provides information on the internal consistency of the TSCS, including previously unreported data on the scale scores, results of a new study of the stability of TSCS scores, a large amount of information on the relationship between TSCS scores and scores derived from both other self-concept measures and measures of related constructs, and results of factor analyses investigating the instrument's dimensionality. Concerning reliability, studies of the internal consistency and stability of the TSCS total score have typically reported coefficients around .90, thereby suggesting that the total score remains stable over time and that the 90 scale items provide a good measure of a single construct. The one study addressing the internal consistency of the subscales reported alpha coefficients that were typically .70 or better for an adolescent sample typically .70 or better for an adolescent sample and .80 or better for an adult sample. Test-retest reliabilities for the subscale scores are reported to be between .80 and .91 for the three internal and five external dimensions, around .90 for the empirically derived scales, and generally around .70 or better for the remaining scales. However, these results are based on a sample of 60 college students tested in 1965. A more recent study provides some information on the amount of change that might be expected across two test administrations, but these results are based on a mixed sample (i.e., archived data aggregated across age groups, varying intervals between tests, etc.), and they are spotty. More information on the stability and internal consistency of subscale scores should be provided.

Concerning validity, correlations between the TSCS total score and the Piers-Harris Children's Self-Concept Scale have been found to range between .51 and .80. Correlations with the Coopersmith Self-Esteem Inventory were found to be .64 in one study and .75 in another. Because the Piers-Harris and Coopersmith scales tap academic and peer domains not measured by the TSCS, these correlations provide strong support for the validity of the TSCS total score. Additional support comes from generally predictable correlations of TSCS scores with Rokeach's Dogmatism Scale, the State-Trait Anxiety Scale, the IPAT Anxiety Scale, Rotter's Internal-External Locus of Control, the High School Personality Questionnaire, and various other measures. Correlations of TSCS scale scores with MMPI Scales, the Taylor Manifest Anxiety Scale, The Cornell Medical Index, and several other personality measures also provide some support for the various TSCS scales, as do the results of studies with various clinical groups. But factor analytic studies, including recent confirmatory factor analyses, fail to support the multidimensional structure of the TSCS. Even the authors are willing to concede this point: "The question of the dimensionality of the TSCS has been widely examined and debated from many viewpoints, and yet, a definitive answer awaits the application of more sophisticated item-factoring methods" (p. 84). Without such additional evidence, the value of the many TSCS scale scores is somewhat suspect.

In summary, the Tennessee Self-Concept Scale is a popular measure of self-concept that is easy to administer, widely applicable, and quite carefully researched. Strong support exists for the validity and reliability of the total score; some but less convincing evidence exists in support of the scale's dimensionality. Hand scoring is somewhat cumbersome, making the new computerized scoring and interpretive service an attractive alternative for users of Form C & R. Given its many appealing features, the TSCS should be given careful consideration by anyone interested in assessing self-concept.

Review of the Tennessee Self-Concept Scale [Revised] by E. THOMAS DOWD, Professor and Director of Counseling Psychology, Kent State University, Kent, OH:

The Tennessee Self-Concept Scale (TSCS) is a 100-item self-descriptive scale, organized into two forms, a counseling form, Form C, and a clinical and research form, Form C & R. Each form has a variety of subscales in a 3 x 5 matrix. The very complete manual was recently revised to incorporate the latest research on the scale, as well as new adolescent norms. The scale, so far as can be ascertained, has not been revised since its last review in the *Seventh Mental Measurements Yearbook* (7:151). In addition, there are five supplementary scales which were apparently developed since the last reviews because no mention of these scales was made by the previous reviewers.

The revised manual contains separate chapters for standard administration, scoring, and interpretation, and for computerized scoring and interpretation. As noted in the previous review, the hand scoring is laborious and complex, so that the computerized method would be a welcome relief. Interpretation instructions and a case study, both frustratingly sketchy and incomplete, are included in the manual. Indeed, the TSCS, like the Minnesota Multiphasic Personality Inventory (MMPI), is complex enough so that a separate interpretation manual is probably necessary to use the instrument fully.

A major lack noted in the previous review was the absence of internal consistency reliability data. This has now been rectified. The manual refers to several reliability studies, with coefficients ranging from .66 to .94. Test-retest reliabilities are reported from .60 to .92. In general, these are adequate to excellent, and speak well for the reliabilities of the separate scales.

The validity information is extensive, including construct, criterion, content, and validity derived from intervention studies. In general, the data are impressive, although some of the validity criteria appear to be only tangentially related to self-concept. In contrast, the information on the normative sample is disappointingly sparse.

A previous review (Bentler, 1972) noted that no factor analytic studies were reported and that the scale likely contained only a few dimensions or was possibly unidimensional. This manual, in an apparent attempt to remedy this defect, presents a number of factor analytic studies. The authors argue that the earlier simple orthogonal-varimax methods failed to uncover the inherent multidimensionality of the TSCS. Perhaps not, but the factor analytic

evidence offered in this manual is decidedly mixed. Some studies found evidence for some TSCS dimensions, whereas others found evidence for other dimensions. But no study seems to have found evidence for all the dimensions. Thus, the factor structure of the TSCS appears to be still in doubt.

Perhaps the original method of scale construction is the reason for the confusing factorial findings. Most of the scales were developed by the intuitive procedure. After the items were generated, seven clinical psychologists classified them in the rows and columns, with perfect agreement being necessary for acceptance. Other scales, however, were developed by the empirical method, where items that discriminated one group from another were included in that scale. One would not necessarily expect that a scale derived in such a fashion would decompose factorially into the original dimensions. Thus, one is left with the disquieting feeling that the scale dimensions may not really measure discrete entities nor even measure what they are purported to measure.

Despite these defects, the Tennessee Self-Concept Scale is a comprehensive instrument that may provide a multifaceted look at an individual's self-concept. However, it might be questioned whether it provides enough additional information to warrant its use rather than a shorter, tighter instrument. Each potential user will have to make that decision based on the need.

REVIEWER'S REFERENCE

Bentler, P. M. (1972). [Review of the Tennessee Self Concept Scale.] In O. K. Buros (Ed.), *The seventh mental measurements yearbook* (pp. 366-367). Highland Park, NJ: Gryphon Press.

[425]

Test of Attitude Toward School.

Purpose: To assess a student's attitude toward school.
Population: Boys in grades 1, 3, 5.
Publication Dates: 1973–84.
Acronym: TAS.
Scores, 2: Scholastic Attitude Score, Evaluation by the Teacher.
Administration: Individual.
Price Data, 1988: $12 per set of 16 drawings; $18 per 25 teacher questionnaires ('84, 3 pages); $15 per manual ('84, 116 pages).
Time: Administration time not reported.
Comments: Projective test.
Authors: Guy Thibaudeau, Cathy Ingram-LeBlanc (translation from French), and Michael Dewson (verification of technical terms).
Publisher: Institute of Psychological Research, Inc. [Canada].

Review of the Test of Attitude Toward School by BERT A. GOLDMAN, Professor of Education, University of North Carolina, Greensboro, NC:

Guy Thibaudeau has done a painstakingly thorough job of preparing a document that is not like a test manual or technical report, but more like a monograph or thesis on the measurement of scholastic attitude.

He begins with definitions and explanations of key terms and concepts. Then he surveys the literature to analyze existing methods of measuring scholastic attitude. In presenting each method Thibaudeau points out its value and then explains its shortcomings. Each detailed, descriptive analysis ends with the identification of a major weakness. As a result of this systematic process of elimination, the author leads up to the need for the creation of a new test of scholastic attitude, the Test of Attitude Toward School, abbreviated T.A.S.

Next, the author presents each test item and its rationale for being included. From this point on, the monograph takes the form of an experiment to test the validity of the T.A.S. Thibaudeau describes the sample used, the procedure employed, the collection of data, and the analysis of the data followed by a discussion and conclusion.

The author presents a rather compelling case for the validity of the T.A.S. by showing very close agreement between scores generated by the instrument and the teachers' evaluations of their students' scholastic attitude.

The author claims the T.A.S. is proved valid because the evaluation of the sample subjects' attitude toward school measured by their teachers using a brief questionnaire which employs a 7-point scale similar to that of the T.A.S. came within 1 score point of the T.A.S. score for 60% of the sample. A major weakness of the validity study centers upon the sample.

Although the sample was chosen using stratified random sampling taking account of the underprivileged, middle class, and privileged, the sample included only males within Montreal, Canada. The youngsters were selected from only grades 1, 3, and 5 with no indication of their racial makeup. Further, the sample was selected by the experiment office of Montreal's Catholic School Board and is claimed to represent the primary school population of the Montreal Catholic School Board. Given no explanation concerning the matter, it appears that the sample is part of a parochial school system.

The manual provides no information concerning test reliability.

Each of the 14 drawings making up the T.A.S. was carefully composed in an effort to prevent them from being ambiguous to the subjects (i.e., 100 subjects were questioned to determine whether they could easily and correctly identify the situation depicted by each drawing). There was anywhere from 88% to 99% agreement on 10 of the 14 drawings. The remaining four items (Numbers 6, 8, 10, and 14) produced 54% to 82% agreement among the subjects concerning item content. Given this amount of item content ambiguity for four items, one wonders why the author retained these four items instead of either eliminating or revising them.

Directions for administering the T.A.S. are relatively easy to follow; however, the scoring procedure appears to be cumbersome, difficult to follow, and at times indecisive. First, a numerical or raw score is obtained by determining the frequency of positive and negative responses. However, in this process, the test administrator must determine whether each "happy" response is indeed indicative of a positive school attitude. The manual provides a few examples to illustrate how a positive response may actually be a negative one, but executing such a revision of responses appears tenuous. Next, a constant of 1.5 is subtracted from positive and negative raw scores. The rationale for this correction is based upon the difference between average teachers' evaluations and T.A.S. results. Actually the difference was 1.67 but the author indicated that it would be more practical and adequate to use 1.5. Now the terminology becomes confusing because the manual indicates that cumulative frequencies are placed on a measurement scale to obtain the raw score. Earlier the manual indicated that we were already working with raw scores. In any case, the last phase in scoring requires that both positive and negative results together be placed on a 7-point scale ranging from .5 (very positive) to 7.5 (very negative) to determine scholastic attitude. There is a problem in determining the single raw score when the positive and negative values are located in adjacent categories on their respective scales. When this occurs the converted scholastic attitude score can be either of two. For example, if the positive value is 7 and the negative value is 6, the single raw score can be either 3.5 or 4. The score of 4 is interpreted as an indifferent scholastic attitude, but the 3.5 cannot be clearly interpreted because it falls between a slightly positive scholastic attitude and an indifferent one.

The manual, although attractively printed and bound, has well over a dozen errors including an incomplete sentence.

The test author has attempted to present a convincing rationale for accepting the T.A.S. as the ultimate solution to the dilemma of choosing an appropriate instrument for measuring scholastic attitude. He may well have created the best approach yet for handling this task. However, this reviewer feels that the test author needs to replicate his validity study using a representative sample of youngsters selected by sex, race, age, and geographic location, especially if he expects to market the instrument in the United States. Four of the items should be revised to reduce ambiguity. Reliability should be determined. The scaling system needs to be made more decisive. The directions for scoring lack clarity. Finally, the errors in the manual need to be removed. Until these suggestions are addressed, this reviewer urges caution in the use of the T.A.S.

[426]
Test of Auditory Analysis Skills.
Purpose: Constructed to assess "a child's auditory perceptual skills."
Population: Children.
Publication Date: 1975.
Acronym: TAAS.
Scores: Total score only.
Administration: Individual.
Manual: No manual (Directions on each form).
Price Data, 1991: $10 per 50 test forms.
Time: Administration time not reported.
Comments: "Criterion-referenced"; may be used in conjunction with the Test of Visual Analysis Skills (442).
Author: Jerome Rosner.
Publisher: Academic Therapy Publications.

Review of the Test of Auditory Analysis Skills by ALLAN O. DIEFENDORF, Associate Professor, and KATHY S. KESSLER, Speech/Language Pathologist, Indiana University School of Medicine, Indianapolis, IN:

The Test of Auditory Analysis Skills (TAAS) was designed to evaluate a child's auditory perceptual skill. Specifically, this test is intended to examine how children analyze spoken language into separate parts and recognize the sequence of those parts. Mastery of the test itself, with or without additional "training methods," is purported to enhance reading and spelling skills in children. Additional "training methods" are available from the author of the TAAS.

For many children with learning disabilities the classification "auditory perceptual dysfunction" has been adopted and used to explain their speech, language-learning, reading, and/or spelling disability. Unfortunately, the complexity of ideas represented by the term "auditory perception" are vague, lack accepted definitions, and are lacking in research evidence that suggests that remedial programs based on auditory- and listening-improvement strategies produce useful results for children so classified. Nevertheless, many clinicians hold to the view that auditory processing skills underlie language, reading, and spelling disorders, and learning failures.

The TAAS appears to be based on a model consistent with an "auditory processing view." This view makes the following assumptions: (*a*) auditory perception and auditory processing are fundamental to learning language, reading, and spelling; (*b*) auditory perceptual deficits cause language-learning, reading, and spelling disorders; (*c*) auditory processing and auditory perception can be broken down into specific components (e.g., awareness, attention, memory, integration, discrimination, and sequenc-ing); and (*d*) these auditory subcomponents to language learning, reading, and spelling are improved by training. These assumptions, in addition to auditory processing skills as fundamental to reading and spelling, are highly controversial because there is widespread uncertainty regarding the specific "auditory" skills that are fundamental. At the heart of the issue is a disagreement among professionals aimed at whether disorders in auditory processing skills cause reading and spelling deficiencies or whether they are just highly correlated. Therefore, the basic premise underlying the construction of this test must be questioned.

The TAAS has no manual, therefore there is no explanation of how this test was developed or on whom the test was normed. There is no explanation as to how the stimuli were selected or how the author developed his scoring criteria. It does appear that the author has attempted to develop test items in a developmental hierarchy where words, syllables, phonemes, and consonant blends are eliminated from compound words, polysyllabic words, monosyllabic words with initial and final phonemes, and monosyllabic words beginning with consonant blends, respectively. However, it is unclear as to how the stimuli chosen and a child's receptive vocabulary could interact to contaminate test result outcomes. The lack of normative data raises many questions, specifically, interpretation alternatives and responsible recommendations. With only 13 total test items, sample size renders any ability to differentiate on the basis of clustering errors or developmental trend impossible. Although the TAAS scores suggest a grade performance level, there is no information presented on age equivalent or grade equivalent scores. An administration protocol is suggested, but the potential for false positive and false negative outcomes could be high on the basis of how individual examiners deal with instructions, rate and volume of verbal presentations, and reinforcement. Finally, there is no information on reliability or validity; without this information a clinician is unable to determine the amount of confidence to be placed in the observations or outcome score.

If a child falls below his or her grade level, it is uncertain what the recommended follow-up would be or should be for that matter. The author suggests that clinicians use the training methods outlined in his book, although the rationale for this recommendation is rather broad and assumptive. A supportive data base is missing such that documentation of the author's claim (reading and spelling enhancement) cannot be substantiated.

Three significant concerns disallow recommending this test: (*a*) The theoretic foundation from which this test was developed is controversial; (*b*) the lack of a test manual does not permit critical evaluation of the test's construct; and (c) the assumption that remedial procedures can be derived from 13 test items is an oversimplification of a complex problem.

Review of the Test of Auditory Analysis Skills by RICK LINDSKOG, Associate Professor of Psychology and Counseling, Pittsburg State University, Pittsburg, KS:

The Test of Auditory Analysis Skills (TAAS) is designed to evaluate auditory perceptual skills for children in kindergarten to the third grade. The total instrument consists of 15 items. In each case, the task consists of the child repeating a stimulus word pronounced by the examiner, then repeating the word again, but with a syllable omitted. For example, sample Item 1 instructs the examiner to say, "Say 'cowboy'. . . .Now say it again, but don't say 'boy.' " There are two sample items followed by 13 items which comprise the test. The child's score is determined by the ordinal number of the final item administered prior to the second successive error. The raw score is converted to a grade level equivalency by using a chart on the front of the test protocol. The equivalencies are expressed in 1-year increments (K–3).

The materials provided to this reviewer did not cite validity or reliability figures, and explanatory comments indicated the instrument is "criterion referenced," yet the raw scores are converted into grade levels. In addition, it would be unusual for analysis beyond a basic screening to occur with a 13-item instrument. Yet the protocol states that "the child can be taught to pass the test and the effects of the teaching will be apparent elsewhere—most importantly in his reading and spelling."

Despite the ungrounded claims, the instrument does sample an area that currently enjoys significant research interest relating to learning disabilities, that is, phonological awareness. At present, the instrument is limited in use due to lack of supportive psychometric data. It shows some potential for use in screening or research but is insufficient in scope to yield comprehensive data.

In summary, the TAAS is a "criterion-referenced" 15-item instrument that tests auditory analysis skills. The publisher's claim that test items can be taught to the child to improve reading and spelling is dubious. Although the area of phonological awareness is currently being researched, there were no data presented that related to test reliability or validity. The TAAS may be of limited use as a criterion-referenced screening device for research or local norm purposes. This reviewer would recommend Wepman's Auditory Discrimination Test (ADT; 9:100) or the Lindamood Auditory Conceptualization Test (9:623) also be considered as alternatives when auditory skills are evaluated.

[427]
Test of Awareness of Language Segments.

Purpose: "Assesses a child's ability to segment the stream of spoken language into words, syllables, and phonemes (sounds)."
Population: Ages 4-6 and over.
Publication Date: 1987.
Acronym: TALS.
Scores, 4: Sentence-to-Words, Words-to-Syllables, Words-to-Sounds, Total.
Administration: Individual.
Levels: 2 overlapping levels (ages 4-6 to 5-6 and 5-7 and over) in a single booklet.
Price Data: Price data for test including manual ('87, 47 pages) available from publisher.
Time: Administration time not reported.
Comments: Orally administered.
Author: Diane J. Sawyer.
Publisher: Aspen Publishers, Inc.

Review of the Test of Awareness of Language Segments by CAROLYN CHANEY, Associate Professor, Speech and Communication Studies, School of Humanities, San Francisco State University, San Francisco, CA:

The Test of Awareness of Language Segments (TALS) is an individually administered screening test for one type of metalinguistic knowledge—the ability to segment spoken language into words, syllables, and sounds (phonemes). Research studies conducted since the early 1970s have consistently demonstrated a strong relationship between performance on tasks of language segmentation and early reading achievement; children who can segment sentences into words and words into component syllables and sounds perform better on concurrent and subsequent tests of reading achievement than those who cannot. This strong (and probably causal) link between metalinguistic segmentation skill and early reading acquisition manifests the need for a standardized test of segmentation such as the TALS. Such a test can be used as a screening device to identify those children whose lack of awareness of language segments makes them at risk for reading failure and who may profit from supplemental instruction in linguistic segmentation as a precursor to "phonics" instruction. A standardized test of segmentation will also be a useful element in a diagnostic reading and/or language development battery when specific aspects of a reading or language deficit need to be described. The Test of Language Segments does not attempt to assess all or even many of the variety of metalinguistic skills that are related to reading achievement and, therefore, should not be used as an indicator of overall metalinguistic awareness, language development, or cognitive-linguistic maturity, as suggested in the test manual. Instead, use of the TALS should be reserved for evaluating the ability to segment speech into its component parts.

The three subtests of the TALS: Sentences-to-Words, Words-to-Syllables, and Words-to-Sounds (phonemes) are straightforward in their administration, and clear instructions are provided in the test manual. The test is fairly quick to administer and it may be given by any skilled examiner who has the ability to segment words at the sound, not letter, level. In each subtest the child listens to a stimulus sentence or word and represents the number of segments with colored blocks. The TALS has several features that enhance the examinee's success and enjoyment: The tasks are preceded by sufficient demonstration and practice, a failed item is followed by additional demonstration and a second opportunity, the three subtests and the items within the first subtest are arranged in order of increasing difficulty, and provisions are made to stop testing after a number of failures. Because the examinee responds dually to each item by placing a block and simultaneously naming the segment that it represents, the examiner receives a double check on the correctness of the segmentation, and accurate recording is enhanced. The recording form is clearly organized and contains the test items for ease in administration and scoring and later reference.

Coding and scoring procedures and criteria are clearly described in the test manual, and numerous examples are provided. One positive feature of the coding-scoring system is that all errors are to be described by type as well as scored for correctness, thereby facilitating error analysis and educational planning. The coding-scoring system has two potential drawbacks. First, oversegmentation errors (e.g., "Fa / ther / works / hard") are scored as correct, whereas undersegmentation errors (e.g., "Father / workshard") are marked incorrect. This practice may obscure the fact that oversegmentation is less developmentally mature than correct segmentation, as well as more developmentally mature than undersegmentation (Chaney, 1989). The second drawback is that the omission of a required segment results in a whole item being scored incorrect, even if the child segmented the remaining parts correctly. As a result, short-term memory deficits may be confounded with segmentation difficulties, especially on the Sentences-to-Words subtest.

Interpretation of scores is somewhat complex and may limit the usefulness of the TALS. One problem is that TALS raw scores are not converted to standard scores, language age scores, or grade level equivalents, and thus the normative data are confusing to interpret. Instead, two tables are provided (one for beginning kindergartners and one for all first grade and older children) that describe probable "Performance Behaviors" for High Performance, Average Performance, and Low Performance on the TALS. To interpret a TALS score, the examiner locates the performance group in which the score falls, considers the probable behaviors described for that performance group, and determines whether the actual test behavior of the child is consistent with them. If not, the examiner finds described performance behaviors that appear to fit those of the examinee, and from these behaviors makes educational recommendations. This method of interpretation may result in examiner unreliability. Furthermore, the method of establishing cutoff scores for the performance groups does not inspire confidence that TALS scores and performance behaviors reliably predict appropriate reading group placement. Data reported in the manual indicated that at least 8% of pupils were misclassified for assignment to reading groups, based on TALS scores. Fortunately, mean scores and standard deviations for kindergartners and first graders tested at varying times of the year are tucked away in the test manual section "Development of the TALS." This normative information seems more useful than the performance group cutoff scores.

Although cutoff scores should be used with caution, two excellent sections of the test manual illustrate how the descriptive test results can be applied to instructional planning. "Examples of Scored Protocols with Instructional Recommendations" provides sample test results for an average kindergartner and first grader, a low-performance kindergartner, and for older poor readers. In this section, aspects of test behavior are highlighted and linked to recommended instructional strategies. "Planning Instruction Based on Responses on the TALS" presents the results of field studies in which children received instructional activities based on their performance behaviors on the TALS. This chapter provides a wealth of educational suggestions for facilitating the growth of metalinguistic segmentation and integrating this skill within an early reading program.

Standardization information is described in the manual under "Development of the TALS." Although some background information was provided about the population of the school district where data were collected, the description of the standardization sample was somewhat sketchy, and even the sample size was unclear. A number of statistical analyses were performed to establish reliability, validity, and predictive power of the TALS. Cronbach alpha coefficients, test-retest reliability coefficients, and means, standard deviations, standard errors of the mean, and 95% confidence interval limits for administration of the TALS at different times indicated that TALS scores were reliable. Validity was determined in several ways. Content validity, including validity of the tasks, the items, and the ordering of subtests was based on substantive theoretical framework; one of the strengths of the TALS is in its application of recent metalinguistic research. Statistical estimates of concurrent validity used TALS correlations with measures of language processing, reading readiness, and reading achievement (i.e., auditory discrimination: $r = .55-.75$, auditory blending: $r = .40-.48$, receptive vocabulary: $r = .40-.45$, reading readiness: $r = .40-.70$, word recognition: $r = .55-.78$, reading comprehension: $r = .50-.70$). It should be remembered that only the TALS and none of these other tests actually measure language segmentation. The capability of the TALS to predict reading achievement was established with a series of regression analyses, multiple regression analyses, and analyses of covariance. The TALS was found to predict reading achievement through second grade, particularly if administered toward the end of kindergarten or early in first grade, and to contribute significantly to the prediction over and above other traditional reading readiness measures. This is doubtless because the TALS measures metalinguistic segmentation, a recognized predictor of reading achievement, whereas the traditional readiness tests do not.

In summary, the TALS was developed from recent research and a solid theoretical framework. It measures linguistic segmentation, an aspect of metalinguistic knowledge that is highly related to reading achievement but not included in traditional language development or reading readiness tests. Administration and scoring are straightforward and clearly described in the test manual, but test results should be interpreted with caution due to procedures used in establishing cutoff scores in the standardization process. With this limitation in mind, the TALS may be a welcome addition to the reading and/or language development test battery. The classroom teacher will appreciate the helpful sections on application of test results to classroom instruction.

REVIEWER'S REFERENCE

Chaney, C. F. (1989). I pledge a legiance tothe flag: Three studies in word segmentation. *Applied Psycholinguistics, 10*, 261-281.

Review of the Test of Awareness of Language Segments by MARY E. HUBA, Professor of Research and Evaluation, Iowa State University, Ames, IA:

The rationale for the Test of Awareness of Language Segments (TALS) derives from many studies in which auditory segmentation ability has been found to be related to reading achievement. Performance is interpreted primarily in terms of the type of reading instruction most appropriate based on score analysis, as well as on an informal analysis of errors made.

The manual addresses all important topics and is useful for educators considering using the TALS, as well as for those wishing to increase their understanding of reading as a language-based activity. The information provided clearly warrants consideration of the test by users. Despite this reviewer's generally favorable view of the test, some points of potential concern are included in the following discussion.

ADMINISTRATION AND SCORING. Administration takes place in three parts: the segmentation of spoken sentences to words (Part A), words to syllables (Part B), and words to sounds (Part C). Each part is preceded by a training phase in which the examiner models correct performance and then engages the child in the task. Modifications in number of items administered are made based on several factors (e.g., age). A flowchart in the manual and directions on the response sheet guide the administrator in making appropriate administration decisions.

In each part the examiner presents the stimulus orally and the child speaks each component part of the stimulus while moving a block from a box to the table. Right/wrong scoring is easily accomplished and the child's actual response is also easily indicated. A number of acceptable and unacceptable response variations are illustrated and scoring directions are provided.

Some concerns related to administration and scoring are as follows. First, in Part C the examiner is directed to pronounce each word "in a natural way" (manual, p. 8) without exaggerating the sounds. Presumably, the author wishes stimuli from Parts A and B to be presented in this way also, but such directions are not included.

Second, children are not required to repeat the sentences in Part A before attempting to segment them. This precludes detection of possible difficulties with auditory acuity, attention to the task, or limitations in short-term memory. Because some stimuli intended for older children are quite long (e.g., Mary didn't go to school today because she was sick), and because a single omission can render an otherwise correct response incorrect, the issue of short-term memory limitations may be important in score interpretation.

Third, there is no mention that children who can correctly detect the number of syllables in a word sometimes do not syllabicate at conventional syllable boundaries. Although two examples of this are provided on sample protocols (and scored as correct), inexperienced examiners may consider such responses as incorrect, especially because the stimuli are preprinted on the record sheet with conventional boundaries indicated.

Finally, two features of the test may be confusing or distracting to some children. First, the blocks which children move are of five colors. This may impair the performance of some (younger) children who may attend to color (an irrelevant feature) in their selection of blocks. Second, the examiner uses terms like *sentence* and *word* when providing directions to children. Some children capable of auditory segmentation may not understand the concepts to which these words refer (Ehri, 1979; Francis, 1973).

PSYCHOMETRIC PROPERTIES. Considerable attention has been paid to establishing the reliability and validity of scores with children from a socioeconomically varied school district adjacent to Syracuse, NY. In this district formal reading instruction is apparently included in the kindergarten curriculum.

RELIABILITY. Internal consistency reliability coefficients of total scores ranging from .82 to .94 are presented from administrations at four different times. It is unclear whether these are from the same sample of children or independent samples (more desirable). Additional reliability information is provided in the form of test-retest coefficients from prekindergarten (.92), kindergarten (.89), and first grade (.83). Although coefficients are acceptable, sample sizes from these analyses are quite small ($n = 20, 35, 41$, respectively).

VALIDITY. Content-related evidence includes an adequate description of the construct and the tasks designed to measure it, with reference to the literature. Construct-related evidence is addressed in a brief narrative which adds little to information previously provided. At a minimum, correlations of TALS scores with those from other segmentation tasks would have been helpful. (See Yopp [1988] for a comprehensive discussion of measures of simple and compound phonemic awareness.) Because subtests are intended to be hierarchical and items within subtests are to increase in difficulty, data regarding item difficulty would have been informative.

Criterion-related evidence abounds in the form of correlations of scores from the TALS and other predictors (e.g., prereading tests, a group IQ test) with various measures of reading readiness and reading achievement. Correlations are generally low to moderate and the author makes inferences in favor of the TALS by visual inspection of the matrices. Such inferences are suspect without taking into account the covariance among the predictors. Indeed, the most convincing evidence for the TALS as a predictor derives from regression analyses in which TALS scores added significantly to the prediction of reading achievement after other more traditional predictors were entered into the equation. Finally, the topic of differential predictive validity is addressed, although the discussion is too abbreviated to understand completely the intent and results of the study. In fact, one stated conclusion ("Children of mothers who have not completed high school may be expected to obtain lower scores on the TALS," p. 44) does not logically follow from the results that are summarized.

Those wishing to use test scores in planning individualized instruction will find Parts III and IV of the manual to be as relevant to validity as the section on psychometric properties. In these sections norms are presented for grouping kindergartners and first graders in terms of their readiness for instruction or their need for additional prereading experiences. The procedure for establishing cutoff scores for three groupings at each age is explained and validation data are provided. Further, an analysis of the pattern of segmentation errors is encouraged. Suggestions are offered for a variety of instructional interventions. Data illustrating the effectiveness of this approach are presented from a longitudinal study with three cohorts of kindergartners and first graders. Unfortunately, it is unclear whether all children in the district or just those in certain schools participated in the project, and this creates some confusion in terms of some of the author's inferences.

SUMMARY. The TALS appears useful as a predictor of reading achievement for beginning elementary children and as an aid in planning instruction for children at this level. Some cautions have been pointed out which derive from the nature of the task and from lack of precision in summarizing what appears to be a considerable amount of data gathered by the author. Users may wish to keep these concerns in mind as they attempt to ascertain the usefulness of the test for achieving their particular purposes.

REVIEWER'S REFERENCES

Francis, H. (1973). Children's experience of reading and notions of units in language. *British Journal of Educational Psychology, 43,* 17–23.
Ehri, L. (1979). Linguistic insight: Threshold of reading acquisition. In T. G. Waller & G. E. MacKinnon (Eds.), *Reading research: Advances in theory and practice* (Vol. 1, pp. 66-114). New York: Academic Press.
Yopp, H. K. (1988). The validity and reliability of phonemic awareness tests. *Reading Research Quarterly, 23* (2), 159-177.

[428]

Test of Early Mathematics Ability, Second Edition.

Purpose: To "identify those children who are significantly behind or ahead of their peers in the development of mathematical thinking."
Population: Ages 3-0 to 8-11.
Publication Dates: 1983–90.
Acronym: TEMA-2.
Scores: Total score only.
Administration: Individual.
Price Data, 1991: $109 per complete kit; $34 per picture book; $24 per 50 profile/record forms; $28 per Assessment Probes and Instructional Activities manual; $27 per examiner's manual ('90, 48 pages).
Time: (20–30) minutes.
Authors: Herbert P. Ginsburg and Arthur J. Baroody.
Publisher: PRO-ED, Inc.
Cross References: For a review by David P. Lindeman, see 9:1252.

TEST REFERENCES

1. Song, M., & Ginsburg, H. P. (1987). The development of informal and formal mathematical thinking in Korean and U.S. children. *Child Development, 58,* 1286-1296.

Review of the Test of Early Mathematics Ability, Second Edition by JERRY JOHNSON, Professor of Mathematics, Western Washington University, Bellingham, WA:

Introduced in 1983, the Test of Early Mathematics Ability (TEMA) was designed to fill a specific need—to identify young children either with learning problems in mathematics or expected to develop such problems. The TEMA provided valuable information regarding the strengths and weaknesses in the mathematical thinking of young children, while also suggesting appropriate instructional activities for specific situations. The new edition (TEMA-2) is more of an enhancement than a revision. First, new items are included at the lower age levels so that the test can be used with preschoolers as young as 3 years of age. Second, the technical adequacy of the TEMA was to be improved by the inclusion of additional normative data.

The TEMA-2 attempts to measure both the informal and the formal components of mathematical thinking, based on the pedagogical conceptualizations found in Ginsburg (1989). Designed to reflect the mathematical thinking that begins prior to school experiences, the informal components include concepts of relative magnitude, counting skills, and calculation skills. In contrast, the formal components measure competence in mathematics taught in school, including the knowledge of convention (reading and writing of numerals and symbols), number facts, calculation, and base-ten concepts.

Designed to be administered to students individually in approximately 20 minutes, the TEMA-2 uses entry points keyed to the age of the child. The test continues until both a ceiling (five consecutive incorrect items) and a basal (five consecutive correct items) are established for each child. The 65 questions are read by the examiner and require either oral responses or written calculations, with some questions involving the use of Picture Cards (provided), a Student Worksheet (provided), and materials such as pennies (not provided).

The manual is excellent in its guidance of the examiner in both the proper administration of the TEMA-2 and the scoring of the student responses. Additional information includes a helpful discussion of the nature of mathematical thinking in young children, the construction of a profile of the child's mathematical thinking, and the interpretation of results. If areas needing further evaluation are identified, each item on the TEMA-2 is keyed to probes that explore the child's strategies and concepts in greater depth. Described in the accompanying manual, *Assessment Probes and Instructional Activities*, the key ingredients are an explanation of what was being measured in the associated TEMA-2 item, specific probes that focus on the child's comprehension and learning potential for the given task, and suggestions of appropriate instructional activities.

All 50 items in the TEMA are included in the TEMA-2, but are now preceded by 15 "easier items." The new items were selected from an experimental version of the TEMA-2 that involved the TEMA and 20 additional questions. This experimental version was administered to 35 preschool children in Austin, Texas. Using item difficulty and item discrimination, the final set of 15 new questions was determined and added to the TEMA to produce the TEMA-2. The normative sample for the TEMA-2 involved 896 children (only 75 at age 3) from 27 states, which includes 426 of the original 617 children used to standardize the TEMA and an additional new set of 470 children. The normative sample was nationally representative, using sex, residence, race, ethnicity, and geographic area. The normed scores include a percentile rank and a mathematical quotient (MQ). Based on a distribution (mean of 100 and *SD* of 15), the MQ is a proposed index or ranking of the child's overall performance relative to peers of the same chronological age. Some cautions are raised in the use of either the percentiles or the MQs.

Estimates of test reliability of the TEMA-2 was determined by measures of internal consistency and standard error of measurement. Coefficient alphas for each age level are in the acceptable range of .92–.96. Unfortunately, no measure of test-retest reliability for the TEMA-2 was reported nor was an explanation given to support this lapse. In its place, the authors repeat their description of the measure of test-retest reliability coefficient (.94) of the TEMA using 71 4- and 5-year-olds. This lapse is unfortunate for two reasons. First, the authors have not responded to Lindeman's (1985) review of the TEMA, where he questioned the assumption that the test-retest reliability of the TEMA was stable across all age groups. Second, the authors can be faulted for the absence of any discussion of their apparent assumption that the test-retest reliability statistics of the TEMA are maintained or duplicated for the TEMA-2, despite its additional 15 test items and expansion to lower grade levels. The standard errors of measurement provided for the TEMA-2 range from 3–4.

Validity evidence of the TEMA-2 results was provided in the three standard areas: content, criterion-related, and construct. Content validity was established supposedly through the "systematic and controlled item selection and analysis" used in building the TEMA-2. Criterion-related validity was determined by two attempts to measure its concurrent validity, with no attempt made to measure its predictive validity. First, scores on the TEMA portion of the TEMA-2 were correlated against scores for the TEMA-2, with the resulting coefficient of .93. The authors suggest that this value allows the extension of the TEMA's concurrent validity coefficient of .40 and .59 with the Diagnostic Achievement Battery to also represent the validity of the TEMA-2. This extension is questionable because the new questions in the TEMA-2 were considered easier than those on the TEMA and were clearly designed for a lower age level not measured previously. Second, using 35 6-year-olds, scores on a short form of the TEMA-2 were correlated with scores on the Math subtest of the Quick Score Achievement Test, with a resulting coefficient of .46. As no information is provided regarding the composition of the short form and due to the absence of lower-age children in this comparison, the value of this measure of concurrent validity also is suspect in its transfer to the TEMA-2. Construct validity was determined using several traits—age differentiation, relationship to tests of school achievement and tests of aptitude, and group differentiation. The authors produce "solid evidence" of construct validity, though again there is an unjustified reliance on previous TEMA results and comparisons using students in the upper age ranges.

In summary, like its predecessor, the TEMA-2 does meet an important need in its identification of strengths and weaknesses of a child's mathematical thinking. However, no arguments or documentation are given for the necessity of extending the testing to the lower grades. Also, the suggested addition of "extensive normative data" is positive, though the resulting measures of reliability and validity raise numerous concerns. Additional research needs to be done in these areas. In a comparison of the TEMA-2 and the TEMA, the most welcome change is the addition of the new manual, *Assessment Probes and Instructional Activities*, which can be of great benefit to elementary teachers who want further insight into how their students think mathematically.

REVIEWER'S REFERENCES

Lindeman, D. P. (1985). [Review of the Test of Early Mathematics Ability.] In J. V. Mitchell, Jr. (Ed.), *The ninth mental measurements yearbook* (pp. 1560-1561). Lincoln, NE: Buros Institute of Mental Measurements.

Ginsburg, H. P. (1989). *Children's arithmetic: How they learn it and how you teach it* (2nd ed.). Austin, TX: PRO-ED, Inc.

Review of the Test of Early Mathematics Ability, Second Edition by JOYCE R. McLARTY, Director, Work Keys Development, Center for Education and Work, American College Testing Program, Iowa City, IA:

The Test of Early Mathematics Ability, Second Edition (TEMA-2) is the 1990 revision of a test introduced in 1983 and reviewed in 1985 in *The Mental Measurements Yearbook* (9:1252). The new edition retains all of the original items, adds 15 easier items, and offers more extensive technical

data. Like its predecessor, the TEMA-2 is designed to measure informal and formal mathematical thinking in order to (*a*) identify those children who are significantly behind or ahead of their peers in the development of mathematical thinking; (*b*) identify specific strengths and weaknesses in mathematical thinking; (*c*) suggest instructional practices appropriate for individual children; (*d*) document children's progress in learning arithmetic; and (*e*) serve as a measure in research projects.

The 65 items are arranged in ascending difficulty order. Testing begins at a point determined by the child's age and continues upward until the child misses five items consecutively (ceiling). If the child has not yet responded to five consecutive items correctly, testing resumes at the starting point and proceeds downward until the child does so (basal). For scoring purposes, items below the basal are assumed correct; those above the ceiling, incorrect. Item content ranges from simple counting ("Show me two fingers") to mental subtraction of two-digit numbers. Picture cards (supplied) and small countable objects (not supplied) are required. Questions have multiple parts and no partial credit is given. Testing is untimed but expected to average 20 minutes; breaks are to be offered as needed.

Detailed administration and scoring instructions and a manual of *Assessment Probes and Instructional Activities* are provided. The probes are used with children who perform poorly on the TEMA-2 to determine: (*a*) whether the child understands the question, (*b*) what strategies the child is using to solve the problem, and (*c*) how capable the child is of learning the material when provided with hints or focused teaching. They can be used separately or, if norm information based on TEMA-2 scores is not required, interspersed with the test administration.

The primary TEMA-2 score is the Math Quotient (MQ) which is calculated based on the child's age using a table supplied. The authors caution that the MQ provides only a ranking of the child relative to peers and is not intended to imply that the child possesses or lacks a mental trait. The authors also provide directions for converting scores on other tests to the MQ scale so that they may be compared with the MQ score, and suggest consideration of the child's profile of informal (35 items) and formal (30 items) mathematical thinking.

Evaluation of the statistical characteristics of the TEMA-2 items, norms, and scales is seriously hampered by a lack of detail in the Examiner's Manual. Standardization data were from 426 of the 617 cases in the original normative study and an additional 470 current cases using the new form for a total of 896 cases in 27 states. No criteria for dropping cases from the original data are offered. New cases were solicited from current test users to make the sample as representative as possible of the national population.

Item data are presented as medians by student integer age (3–8). It is unclear whether data represented by these medians included all items or some subset of them deemed appropriate to the age level. Difficulties (*p*-values) ranged from .42 to .58; internal consistency reliability estimates from .92 to .96; and standard errors of measurement from 3 to 4 points on the MQ scale. Median point biserial correlations with total test scores were .09, .27, .57, .72, .64, and .79 for ages 3–8, respectively. It is unclear how a median point-biserial correlation of .09, which is unacceptably low, can be associated with an internal consistency reliability of .95. It is also unclear how these statistics were computed or should be interpreted. Because individual students actually took varying numbers of items, it would be inappropriate to assume the same reliability or error of measurement for their scores. Within-age comparisons to the national population were not presented, but it is unlikely that data from 75 (age 3) to 209 (age 6) cases can provide a stable age or national norm base. In addition, it is technically unsound to convert scores on tests with other content and technical characteristics and normed on other populations to the MQ number system for comparison purposes.

Content validity evidence is attributed to systematic and controlled item selection and analysis, and a fairly complete rationale for the choice of item content is offered. Criterion-related validity evidence is provided as a correlation of .93 between the original TEMA items and the TEMA-2 score (a part-whole correlation which would be expected to be high), of .40 and .59 with the Math Calculation subtest of the Diagnostic Achievement Battery, and of .46 for a subset of the TEMA-2 items with the Math subtest of the Quick Score Achievement Battery. Construct validity evidence is based on TEMA-2 scores increasing with the child's chronological age, correlating with scores on tests of school achievement, correlating with scores on aptitude tests, and differentiating between groups of "high risk" or learning disabled and "normal" or norm group students.

The TEMA-2 delivers both less and more than it promises. Unfortunately, technical support for the test remains weak and poorly documented. There is no statistical basis for this test as a measure of mathematical ability; the validity evidence would be equally persuasive for its interpretation as a test of mathematical achievement. Both statistical and construct validity evidence supporting the separate interpretation scores on formal and informal mathematical items are also lacking.

The item discrimination data strongly recommend that this measure be used only as a qualitative indicator for 3- and 4-year-old children, and be interpreted with great caution for 5-year-olds. Comparisons between TEMA-2 scores and those on other tests should be avoided. In fact, avoiding the MQ scale altogether is recommended. Although the percentile information provided is not based on a truly nationally representative sample, it should provide a useful starting place for interpreting TEMA-2 scores. Once a sufficient number of tests has been administered, local percentile tables can be constructed to aid in score interpretation.

Fortunately, none of the purposes cited for the TEMA-2 requires an MQ, the comparison of TEMA-2 scores with those on other tests, or national norms. The greatest strengths of the TEMA-2 lie in its appropriateness for identifying and exploring the mathematical skills and reasoning processes of younger children. The assessment probes are particularly impressive. In the hands of a skilled examiner, the TEMA-2 should yield invaluable insights into the nature and extent of a child's mathematical difficulties and promising directions for addressing them. Users who can avoid the temptation to overinterpret TEMA-2 scores should find the test a useful adjunct to their efforts to assess and assist the development of children's mathematical thinking.

[429]

Test of Early Reading Ability—2.

Purpose: "Measures children's ability to attribute meaning to printed symbols, their knowledge of the alphabet and its function, and their understanding of the conventions of print."

Population: Ages 3-0 to 9-11.

Publication Date: 1981–89.

Acronym: TERA-2.

Scores, 1: Total score with the capability for individual item analysis in the areas of Alphabet Knowledge, Word Meaning, and Reading Conventions.

Administration: Individual.

Forms, 2: A, B.

Price Data, 1990: $89 per complete kit; $38 per administration/picture book; $17 per 50 profile/record forms (specify form A or B); $21 per manual ('89, 50 pages).

Time: (15–30) minutes.

Authors: D. Kim Reid, Wayne P. Hresko, and Donald D. Hammill.

Publisher: PRO-ED, Inc.

Cross References: For reviews by Isabel L. Beck and Janet A. Norris of the original edition, see 9:1253.

TEST REFERENCES

1. Wixson, S. E. (1985). The Test of Early Reading Ability. *The Reading Teacher, 38*, 544-547.

Review of the Test of Early Reading Ability—2 by MICHAEL D. BECK, President, BETA, Inc., Pleasantville, NY:

The Test of Early Reading Ability—2 (TERA-2) is an individually administered test of the ability to construct meaning from print, to know the alphabet and its functions, and to discover the conventions of print. Composed of 46 items, it is intended to assess the early reading skills of children from ages 3 through 9.

CONTENT. Test items are grouped into three clusters—16 testing Meaning, 15 Alphabet, and 15 Conventions. The two forms, described as "equivalent," have similar normative distributions, but differ markedly in content. For example, Form A tests four logos, Form B only one; Form A tests one word concept grouping, Form B tests four; Form A tests four homophones, B tests none; A has two "finger following" dictated items, B has none; etc. Item difficulty considerations apparently took precedence over a content outline in forms assignment. This poses interpretive problems in understanding the three purported constructs.

More disconcerting are the significant numbers of items that are curiously classified. For example, reading a sentence aloud, matching a picture to a word, pointing to a numeral, and identifying the dictated word among four printed words are all called Alphabet items. On the other hand, matching an upper-case letter with its corresponding lower-case representation and choosing the letter from among three numerals and a letter are called Conventions or Meaning items. Some homophone items are classified as Conventions, others as Alphabet. The manual describes the item classifications as being based on an 85% agreement of 11 expert judges. It is improbable that the TERA-2 item classifications would be replicable. Further, it seems most unlikely that any statistical clustering technique would yield such item groupings. These questionable categorizations are critical in that non-normative interpretations of TERA-2, as well as its purported theoretical underpinnings, are based on this three-component structure. Further work in defining and distinguishing these components is indicated.

In general, test items are of acceptable quality, though improved item editing would be beneficial. The use of examiner-constructed logo identification items is troubling on a norm-referenced test. The Conventions items are sound and creative; Meaning items suffer from apparent lack of clarity in construct definition; Alphabet items are generally weak, often seemingly misclassified, and irregular in coverage.

FORMAT AND ADMINISTRATION. TERA-2 is attractively formatted and packaged. The manual, curiously unlabeled as such, contains a sample printout from a software scoring system that this reviewer would not recommend. It yields data/information that appear to be of no use at best and, more likely, are very misleading. The software package is fortunately mentioned only in passing in the manual.

The comb-bound Picture Book contains the individually presented items, separately on each sheet. Forms A and B are contained in the same book—on opposite sides of the pages. Directions to the administrator are boxed at the top of each page. Items are generally well presented although some, mostly minor, formatting problems occur (crowded type or drawings, poor type choices, superfluous words or drawings, awkward or incomplete directions, etc.).

Scores and related information are recorded on a Profile/Examiner Record Form. This form is complete, though it is curious that only about $1/8$ of the sheet is devoted to the response record for the test. Space for noting individual responses or irregularities would be advisable, especially because many items involve multipart scoring. The Administration Conditions section is a positive feature, giving appropriate attention to the relevance of such factors in test performance.

The back of each Profile Form contains an "Instructional Target Zone" for the three TERA-2 constructs. Items assessing each construct are arranged from easy to hard and matched to a targeted age. The manual properly cautions that this profile provides only a "probing device . . . a starting point." However, little rationale for this system is provided. What is stated depends heavily on concepts of mental age and the long-maligned MA/CA quotient concept of intelligence. Some individual item placements are very curious. For example, recognizing that two lines are transposed in a simple three-line text is targeted for age 9-0, naming four lower-case letters is age 7-9, noting that an isolated primary-level word is upside down is age 7-0, saying the ABCs is age 6-3, etc. Extreme professional caution in interpreting this information is urged.

The basic test directions in the manual are sound and helpful. Scoring guidelines are generally acceptable, though the claim that "few qualitative judgments are required" seems questionable. Base and ceiling rules are clear. The rule for ending administration after five consecutive item failures is problematic due to irregular grading of content by difficulty. For example, naming four lower-case letters appears as item 37 of 46—after several items that require children to read words or even sentences. Item difficulty data are not contained in the manual and a publisher representative stated that none were available. Such data should be presented, as the hierarchical difficulty of the items is a fundamental component of the test. The TERA-2 interpretive scheme implies that the items form a Guttman-type scale; this can be supported empirically most easily with item difficulty data.

Interpretive information in the manual is generally sound and appropriate. Recommendations sharing results with children and the cautions in interpreting the results are especially good.

TECHNICAL INFORMATION. Developmental activities for TERA-2 appear to have been well conceived and conducted. Norms are based on a sample of roughly 100–150 students for each 6-month age range. According to the publisher, all students took both Forms A and B during the norming program. If so, details concerning counterbalancing procedures and interform time periods should be reported. For tests such as TERA-2, administered to such young test-naive subjects, some practice effect on a second form would be anticipated.

The normative sample appears to have been as nationally representative as possible for such a small group in terms of typical demographic data. One-half of the participating schools were in Texas, however. Another disparity in representativeness was the 55–45% mix of females to males.

Percentile ranks and NCEs are provided by form by 6-month age intervals (full years at ages 3 and 9). Both metrics are inexplicably reported in tenths of a unit. The discussion of NCEs is poor; however, users forced to report this metric will undoubtedly be no more confused by the TERA-2 explanations than by those offered by assorted governmental agencies.

Given the manual's sound arguments against grade and age equivalents, it is unfortunate that the publisher chose to provide "reading quotients" for TERA-2. These scores are obviously intended to resemble deviation IQs (mean of 100, SD of 15). However, they are totally inappropriate to this test—likely only to cause confusion or misinterpretation. Because the quotient is described as being "not an aptitude score," provision of the metric is regrettable.

Coefficient alpha reliability data and corresponding standard errors of measurement are presented by age and form. The coefficients are acceptably high enough to permit interpretation of individual scores. The manual contains a confusing mention of the use of Rasch analytic techniques as an additional reliability indicator. Finally, test-retest alternate-form reliability data are reported for a small group of heterogeneous-aged subjects. If TERA-2 was normed by administering both forms of the test to all students, such a small ancillary study should have been unnecessary.

Validity evidence presented in the manual is sketchy. Criterion-related validity was assessed by two small-scale correlational studies that yielded encouraging results. Construct validity indicators are less complete. TERA-2 is reported as correlating highly with age (as do height, weight, and many other nonreading variables at these ages), as yielding below-average means for 22 previously identified learning-disabled students, and as correlating with a writing readiness test (the same study referenced under criterion-related validity). Support for construct validity is also incorrectly claimed from high item-total point-biserial data.

SUMMARY. TERA-2 is portrayed as being appropriate for ages 3 through 9. It is actually functional only for students in the average ranges from ages 4-6 through 7 (at age 4-5, the median score is only 8 of 46 items; by age 7-11, the 25th percentile is 37 correct). This narrower effective age coverage is unsurprising given the content assessed, but the advertised age range is misleading to potential users.

To assess the early reading behavior of kindergarten through grade 2 pupils, would I recommend this instrument? If an individually administered test is desired, TERA-2 seems acceptable, although I find the Basic Achievement Skills Individual Screener (BASIS; 9:112) superior in content and technical quality for ages 6 and above. For those whose primary interest is in the "Print Conventions" dimension, TERA-2 is very appealing. For the other two purported constructs, the reading portions of most group achievement tests are far more efficient, comprehensive, and technically superior. The effort to build a test consistent with modern early-reading theory is to be encouraged. Further study and development are indicated.

Review of the Test of Early Reading Ability—2 by ROBERT W. HILTONSMITH, *Associate Professor of Psychology, Radford University, Radford, VA:*

The Test of Early Reading Ability—2 (TERA-2) is an expansion and revision of the Test of Early Reading Ability (TERA). Among its notable features are new norms with a larger norm sample, an extension of the upper age range of the test from 7 to 9 years, and the provision of two equivalent forms (A and B). However, both the theoretical underpinnings and the stated purposes of the test remain the same. In terms of theory, the TERA-2 is built on research into the nature of early reading that points to at least three different (though highly interrelated) components that are "discovered" by children in the preschool years. These relate to children's efforts to (*a*) construct meaning from print, (*b*) learn and use the alphabet, and (*c*) elicit the arbitrary conventions used in reading and writing English. Consonant with this research base are the stated purposes of the TERA-2 that include (*a*) identifying those children who are significantly different from their peers in the early development of reading, (*b*) documenting children's progress in learning to read, (*c*) serving as a measure in research projects, and (*d*) suggesting instructional practices.

The 46 test items reflect the three components (referred to as "constructs" by the authors) of early reading noted above. Sixteen items relate to constructing meaning from print, 15 to learning and using the alphabet, and 15 to the ability to respond to the conventions of print. Unlike the original edition, items are used only in one category. Items were assigned to constructs by a "sample of nationally-known experts in language and reading." No confirmatory evidence from task analyses of items, factor analyses, or other techniques is presented. Finally, users can create an "Instructional Target Zone" by examining the child's performance across the three construct areas.

TEST MATERIALS AND PROCEDURES. The test materials consist of 46 double-sided cards that are conveniently organized in a spiral-bound book. This is a major improvement over the stack of loose cards included in the first version. Test users must complete approximately a half-dozen of the cards by pasting actual stimulus items such as coupons and familiar product logos directly on the card. This was done so that "examiners are able to tailor items to the local children's knowledge and, thereby, provide the most favorable test conditions for assessing those children's awareness of environmental print." A single paragraph in the test manual provides suggestions for creating these items. This is a very clever concept, but the user should note that the suggestions are very general and it would appear that some degree of error variance will be introduced through examiner differences in the selection and presentation of these user-generated items.

Administration is straightforward. Basal and ceiling levels as well as age-specified entry points are used to shorten testing time. The test authors feel that "because the responses to the TERA-2 are scored as either 'correct' or 'incorrect,' scoring is relatively simple." There is no reason why test items scored as "correct" or "incorrect" should necessarily be simple to score, and unfortunately the test manual includes no scoring guidelines should any questions arise. Though most items are indeed easy to score, some are not. For instance, Item 10 on Form A shows the child three lines of sentences in a script-like font. The child is asked, "What is this? Tell me about it." It is not clear what answers the child may give that can be counted as correct. There is little room on the record form to note questionable responses, nor can notations be made easily if the child answers some but not all of the components within a single item (e.g., recognizes two of the three letters presented).

The child's raw score can be converted to a percentile score, Reading Quotient (RQ), and NCE. Wisely, the authors do not provide age- and grade-equivalent scores or mental ages, and provide a nice rationale for not using them. Yet in the section of the manual devoted to describing the child's Instructional Target Zone, the authors instruct the test user to use the child's "mental age" as a demarcation for identifying concepts that can later be taught. They even include a formula for converting standard scores into mental ages, in case the test user is so unlucky as to have information on the child's general mental abilities expressed only in standard scores.

Finally, the authors encourage test users to compare the child's standard score on the TERA-2 with other tests that "use quotients that correspond to those used on the TERA-2." Although general comparisons may be made, the authors should remind the user that interpretation of the absolute differences between TERA-2 scores and scores on other measures with the same mean and standard deviation cannot be done, because any difference could actually be an artifact of the differences in the standardization samples of the two measures.

TEST NORMS AND STANDARDIZATION. The TERA-2 was standardized on a sample of 1,454 children residing in 15 states. Major demographic characteristics appear generally consistent with the population as a whole, although there appears to be a slight overrepresentation of rural versus urban residence. When the sample was stratified into seven age groups, 7-year-olds comprised the biggest group, accounting for nearly one-quarter of the subjects. This is surprising given the fact that the test probably has limited utility with children of this age and older. Additional concerns with the TERA-2 norms include insufficient floor and steep item gradients for ages 3-0 to 4-5, particularly on Form B. This makes it difficult to identify children who are significantly delayed in the acquisition of early reading abilities, which is touted by the authors as one of the major advantages of the test.

RELIABILITY. Two types of reliability are reported, internal consistency and stability. Both coefficient alphas and Rasch analytic techniques were used to determine internal consistency. Results point to coefficients of .89 and above for 3- to 7-year-olds on both forms. The internal consistency coefficient was .78 for 9-year-olds on Form A, and .80 for both 8- and 9-year-olds on Form B. These lower estimates for older children are still acceptable given the purposes of the test, and probably are inconsequential because the TERA-2 has limited utility for older children, who can be administered more comprehensive measures of reading ability.

Test-retest (stability) data were gathered using the alternate forms in a study with 49 children ages 7 to 9 years residing in Dallas, Texas. Raw scores for Form A were correlated with those for Form B, and the influence of age was partialled out. The resulting coefficient was .79. The authors then separated the influence of time sampling error, using statistical techniques developed by Anastasi, and the resulting coefficient was found to be .89. Although these coefficients are satisfactory given the nature of the

TERA-2, additional reliability data using younger children would be most desirable.

VALIDITY. The authors devote several pages of the TERA-2 manual to the discussion of test validity. Evidence is presented for content, criterion-related, and construct validity. The TERA-2 appears to correlate well with performance on the Reading subtest of the Basic School Skills Inventory-Diagnostic, and moderately well with scores on the Paragraph Reading subtests of the Test of Reading Comprehension. Construct validity data show relationships between TERA-2 scores and both age and school experience, as well as significant differences in mean scores between typical and learning-disabled children on the TERA-2. The authors rightfully acknowledge that establishing validity is a cumulative process, and encourage users of their test to conduct investigations regarding the validity of the TERA-2 and share the results.

SUMMARY. The TERA-2 is a thoughtful and generally well-constructed measure of skills related to early reading in children. It seems best suited to identifying children who have learned to read without formal instruction, and perhaps for identifying those who are delayed in their acquisition of early reading concepts. It is less useful as a diagnostic tool, or as a device for documenting children's progress in reading. Even with the addition of the Instructional Target Zone, the authors caution that TERA-2 test profiles should be used "only as a probing device" and "as a starting point for instructional design." This test represents a nice effort at translating current research in emergent literacy into educational practice. Its practical usefulness will ultimately depend on the experience of its users and the accumulation of evidence regarding its validity.

[430]
Test of Early Written Language.

Purpose: "(a) To identify those students who are significantly below their peers in the academic area of writing; (b) to identify writing strengths and weaknesses of individual students; (c) to document students' progress in written language as a consequence of special intervention programs; and (d) to serve as a measurement device in research studies pertaining to the academic achievement of young children."
Population: Ages 3–7.
Publication Date: 1988.
Acronym: TEWL.
Scores: Total score only.
Administration: Individual.
Price Data, 1989: $66 per complete kit including 25 record forms, 25 workbooks, 7 picture cards, and manual (68 pages); $9 per 25 record forms; $32 per 25 workbooks; $6 per 7 picture cards; $23 per manual.
Time: (10–30) minutes.
Author: Wayne P. Hresko.
Publisher: PRO-ED, Inc.

Review of the Test of Early Written Language by PATRICIA WHEELER, *Senior Research Associate, The Evaluation Center, Western Michigan University, Kalamazoo, MI and Independent Consultant, Livermore, CA:*

The Test of Early Written Language (TEWL) was developed to assess the early writing abilities of children, ages 3 to 7 years. The items on the TEWL cover five areas of writing: transcription, conventions of print, communication, creative expression, and record keeping. These areas were identified through a review of the literature on writing and of writing assessments designed for use with older children.

The TEWL has a total of 42 items. The starting item varies by age level. An item is graded as 1 if correct or 0 if incorrect. Each item counts equally, although some require more responses or information from the child than others. The examiner continues with the test administration until the child is unable to respond correctly to five items in a row. If a child is unable to do the starting item for his/her age level, the examiner works backwards until a basal level of five correct responses has been reached.

The test is individually administered. Training requirements for examiners are described in the Examiner's Manual as follows: "(a) basic understanding of test and testing statistics; (b) knowledge of general procedures governing test administration, scoring, and interpretation; and (c) specific information about academic achievement evaluation." The manual contains several rules for administering tests to young children in order to standardize the administration and to obtain more accurate results. Specific directions for administering and scoring each item are clearly provided. The materials include a set of cards to which the child points to indicate responses for several items. With continued use, each card will become soiled and the answer will be indicated by the area on the card with the most smudges. The cards should be laminated by the publisher and the examiner should be instructed to wipe them off so they stay clean.

The TEWL was normed on a sample of 1,355 children, ages 3 to 7 years, in 20 states. Demographic characteristics of this sample are provided in the manual. The sample is very similar to national data for the U.S. population. However, no demographic data are provided for each of the 10 age groups between ages 3-0 and 7-11, which vary in size from 105 to 174, nor are there comparisons to national data for children ages 3 to 7 years.

Although the sample contains a wide range of children based on their background characteristics, there is no indication in the manual that item data were analyzed by these background characteristics. Some items have regional objects in them (e.g., raincoat, snowman, cowboy). Other items might be more difficult for migrant or homeless children, or for children in rural areas as compared to those in urban areas. Some objects, such as the telephone booth, are not seen as frequently as they used to be and have rarely been seen in some areas (rural, isolated). Such analyses by the background characteristics of the children should be done and the results presented in the manual.

The results of the TEWL are reported as a Written Language Quotient (WLQ). The definition and scale look very similar to "IQ." This can lead to misinterpretation of results. The term "quotient" should not be used, and a scale that looks less similar to the "IQ" scale should be used to report results.

The author reported reliability data in two ways: coefficient alphas as measures of internal consistency and test-retest correlations as measures of stability. The coefficient alphas are reported for each of the 10 age groups and range from .74 (for 4-0 to 4-5 years) to .95 (for 3-0 to 3-5 years). The test-retest reliability coefficients are based on two groups of children, ages 6-0 to 7-3 years, tested 2 weeks apart. These correlations are .97 and .94. No test-retest correlations were reported for younger age groups.

Evidence of content, criterion-related, and construct validity is provided in the manual. Content validity is based on the review of the literature, the item analysis results which looked at item difficulty level and item discriminating power (point-biserials) across the 10 age groups, and the use of a variety of response formats to more closely reflect real-life writing activities. The TEWL was correlated with three other measures of writing ability as evidence of criterion-related reliability. These were based on groups of 7-year-olds, ranging in number from 35 to 41. No criterion-related validity data are provided for other age groups. The construct validity is based on correlations of TEWL quotients with chronological age (and, implied in that, school experience), correlations with measures of academic ability, and a study of group differentiation, comparing normal children with a group of 22 learning-disabled 6-year-olds.

Additional validity data should be provided, especially for the younger age groups. Comparing children with and without preschool experience would be a more appropriate way to study the relationship of performance on the TEWL to school experience. The TEWL should be compared to other writing measures and to academic ability and developmental measures for younger children.

The TEWL provides three types of scores: raw score, written language quotient, and percentile. The percentiles are shown for the total group only, not for the 10 chronological age groups. However, because the quotients are computed for each age group, based on the distribution of scores for each age group, the percentiles do, in essence, represent age-level norms. The author says he does not provide age norms (or grade norms) because they are the same as age equivalents (or grade equivalents), both of which have serious limitations. Norms are not the same as age or grade equivalents. If the TEWL is to be used to assess educational programs for young children, percentile ranks and normal curve equivalents, based on larger samples, should be shown for raw scores for each of the 10 age groups. These data would be useful for interpreting individual and group results and for program evaluation.

With increasing emphasis on educational programs for young children and early preparation for schooling, procedures to assess the developmental skills and academic abilities of young children are needed. The TEWL is one of several recent efforts to provide such assessments. Although it has some technical limitations as described above, with further instrument development and review of the content, the TEWL could be useful in assessing and planning educational activities for individual children as well as for evaluating educational programs designed to promote writing skills of young children.

[431]

Test of Economic Knowledge.
Purpose: Measures knowledge of economic concepts.
Population: Grades 8–9.
Publication Date: 1987.
Acronym: TEK.
Scores: Total score only.
Administration: Group.
Forms, 2: A, B.
Price Data: Available from publisher.
Time: (40–45) minutes.
Comments: "Designed to replace the Junior High School Test of Economics."
Authors: William B. Walstad and John C. Soper.
Publisher: Joint Council on Economic Education.

Review of the Test of Economic Knowledge by WILLIAM A. MEHRENS, Professor of Educational Measurement, Michigan State University, East Lansing, MI:

The Test of Economic Knowledge and the accompanying Examiner's Manual are described as a "standardized nationally-normed test and discussion guide for the junior high school level." The test replaces the Junior High School Test of Economics (a review by Ehman [1978] of that test appeared in the *8th MMY*). Each of the two forms of the test contains 39 items, of which 20 are common items to each form.

The test developers apparently took very seriously the criticisms made by Ehman of the previous test. He was critical of item development as well as the poor content validity and lack of construct validity of the Junior High School Test of Economics. The current test is a vast improvement over its predecessor.

The content of the test is based on the 1984 publication of the Joint Council on Economic Education: *A Framework for Teaching the Basic Concepts*. The test was developed by "a national committee of test experts, economists, and classroom teachers." These individuals, and their affiliations, are listed in the Examiner's Manual. This committee developed the test specifications, selected and revised old items that fit the specifications, and wrote new items. Two 50-item versions were tried out in an initial field test, the data were used for revisions, the revised drafts (each with 44 items) were tried out, there were more revisions, and finally two 40-item versions were developed. One item from each form was dropped based on data from the national norm group. Thus, the final versions each have 39 items with, as mentioned, 20 items in common.

The Examiner's Manual presents a two-way table of specifications for the content: concepts by cognitive levels. There are four broad content categories: fundamental economic concepts (25.6%), microeconomic concepts (33.3%), macroeconomic concepts (28.2%), and international economic concepts (12.8%). Each broad category is divided into several subcategories. The cognitive levels are knowledge (33.3%), comprehension (30.8%), and application (35.9%). Each item in each form is keyed to the table of specifications, although the authors admit the classifications may be somewhat arbitrary. This reviewer thought the classifications were about on target. At any rate, the table of specifications and the item classifications are explicit and are published as part of the available materials. Individuals considering the use of this test can determine whether the content validity of the test is adequate for their particular purposes. The authors state they followed "guidelines suggested by the National Advisory Committee regarding the economic content that *ought* to be tested."

The items appear to be well written. The manual presents a rationale for each item, the percentage of the norm group that got the item correct (for two samples—those with and without economic training), and the corrected item-total correlation. In addition, tables showing the percentage of all students responding to each of the four options and the percentage of omitted responses are presented. For all but two items, the percentage correct was greater for the group that had economic training. For one of the two exceptions, the percentages were equal and for the other item, the percentage was actually greater for the group that had not had economic training. This was a supply-demand model item. One of the foils was too attractive—perhaps

correct (46% marked one foil and only 26% marked the keyed answer).

The norms were obtained from a nationwide sample of 6,887 students (3,230 for Form A and 3,657 for Form B). Separate norms tables are given for each form, and a conversion table is given equating Form A scores to Form B scores. The equating was accomplished through the equipercentile approach, but the manual also presents the linear converting equation for those who would prefer to use it. The forms are comparable. The norms sample comes from 91 different schools (listed in the appendix of the manual), and is diverse with respect to geographical regions, type of area (urban, etc.), and school size. Although "no claim is made that the group tested is exactly representative of the student population enrolled in the 8th and 9th grades nationwide . . . A case can be made that the norm sample contains a representative distribution of students by general ability, socio-economic status, ethnic-racial mix, and other characteristics." This quoted statement from the manual seems exactly right to me. A table in the manual presents the means and standard deviations for various subgroups that have and have not been exposed to economics instruction. The groups are by sex, grade level, scholastic aptitude (3 levels), race/origin, type of community, region, course type, and income level.

Cronbach's alpha is .82 on Form A and .85 on Form B. Standard errors are about 2.8. These are adequate for the "low stakes" uses suggested for the test. Content validity evidence is presented *via* the table of specifications, as mentioned earlier, and users can draw their own conclusions about the appropriateness of the content for the domain to which they wish to infer. Construct validity evidence is meager, but students with economics instruction do perform about 3.3 points higher on the tests than those without instruction.

The manual suggests that the test(s) can be used as a pretest, a posttest, or midway into the course (for formative evaluations). Generally the suggested uses of the test are appropriate.

In summary, the Test of Economic Knowledge is a carefully developed test with fairly complete evidence concerning the technical qualities of the items and the test as a whole. Educators interested in obtaining evidence on the knowledge seventh and eighth grade students have of the economic content covered should give serious consideration to this test. It is certainly far better constructed than the average teacher-constructed test would be over this content.

REVIEWER'S REFERENCE

Ehman, L. H. (1978). [Review of Junior High School Test of Economics.] In O. K. Buros (Ed.), *The eighth mental measurements yearbook* (pp. 1429-1430). Highland Park, NJ: The Gryphon Press.

Review of the Test of Economic Knowledge by
ANTHONY J. NITKO, *Professor of Education,*
University of Pittsburgh, Pittsburgh, PA:

This test measures knowledge in four areas: fundamental economic ideas, microeconomics, macroeconomics, and international economics. There are two forms, each containing 39 four-option, multiple-choice items. The authors suggest the forms be used as pretest and posttest.

The test samples the domain of economic concepts defined by the Joint Council on Economic Education's (JCEE) revised Master Curriculum Guide in Economics. The test's development relied heavily on a committee composed of three economists, two social studies teachers, and a foundation vice president. The final version was reviewed by a panel of five economists.

The authors correctly caution teachers who disagree with the learning objectives implied by the test to use it judiciously or not at all. As Ochoa (1985) stated when reviewing the high school version of this test, most American students are taught economics in social studies courses with broad, integrative objectives, and therefore, an economist's definition of economic education may be too narrow "to determine what is taught or tested in the context of preparing citizens who need to be able to understand, analyze, and decide whether economic practices are desirable or not" (p. 1567).

According to the manual, the primary value of the test is "to assess understanding of the basic economic concepts [*sic*] that students should know to fulfill present and future roles as consumers, workers, and voters" (p. 2). The test's narrow domain and limited item designs attenuate the attainment of this broad interpretation of the test scores, however. For example, the stem of item 5 reads, "Specialization allows more goods and services to be produced with a given quantity of resources because it results in . . ." Items written in such abstract academic language, instead of in concrete common language, do not seem capable of testing a student's deeper understanding of economic explanations of everyday events. The great majority of items are of the incomplete sentence variety, which further increases their complexity for average eighth and ninth grade readers. More sophisticated item types (e.g., those involving tabular material, scenarios, and interpretive materials) are not used, so the full range of "understanding" performances are not represented in the test.

Factors other than understanding basic economic concepts appear to influence the test scores inordinately. A student's general vocabulary and reading abilities play a heavier than necessary role. This view is supported by the (*a*) correlation (.54 and .56) of the test scores with a vocabulary test (Quick Word Test), (*b*) relatively low mean scores of the norm groups, (*c*) relatively small differences (mean of 3 to 4 points) between students trained and untrained in economics, and (*d*) mean test score differences favoring white students over blacks and students from high-income families over those from low-income families.

Coefficient alphas are .82 for Form A and .85 for Form B, and the standard error of measurement for each form is approximately 2.8. The latter seems rather large. The manual does not report test-retest or alternate forms reliabilities. These are especially important to someone planning to use the test to measure gain from instruction. Although the two forms of the test have 20 items in common, it should not be assumed that the form's raw scores are interchangeable. Form B is slightly easier and slightly more variable than Form A. A table for equating scores is provided, however. Teachers and program evaluators should use the equated scores, rather than the raw scores, when both forms are being administered.

The manual encourages interpreting a class's results at the item level. A unique and especially useful feature is that a "rationale" for why the keyed answer is considered the best choice is printed in the manual beside the text of the item. Also reported for each item are the percent of the norm group choosing each alternative and the percent of the economics-instructed and noninstructed groups choosing the correct alternative. The rationales and percentages are helpful when a teacher "goes over the test" with students who took it.

Percentile ranks norms are provided for various eighth and ninth grade subgroups and aggregations of subgroups, some as small as 210 students. More important than norm group size, however, is that the schools selected for the standardization sample do not seem to be representative of their states.

The manual suggests using any variety of answer sheet that permits students to mark 39 items with four options each. This suggestion is too cavalier because sometimes the use of different answer-sheet formats will alter a test's norms. This point should be subjected to further research.

Because of the test's narrow focus, it cannot be used as a valid basis for grading students. The manual provides insufficient data to estimate the reliability of individual students' pretest-to-posttest gain scores, but it is likely this reliability is low. Caution should be exercised, too, when measuring group growth. The average difference between students with and without exposure to economics training is only about 3 or 4 points, and Form B is about 1 point easier than Form A. One wonders whether a difference of a few points after a term or two of economics represents a practical gain in students' understanding of economic principles, especially because such a gain can be obtained by memorizing the basic terminology.

SUMMARY. The Test of Economic Knowledge is a useful tool for assessing a rather narrow view of what should constitute a junior high school student's understanding of economic concepts and principles. The test does not seem to sample a wide range of economic applications, nor does it test an ability to explain phenomena typically experienced by eighth and ninth grade students as they go about their daily routine. Even if one adopts the narrow definition of economics education implied by the test items, one should exercise caution when interpreting students' test scores. The scores appear to be influenced unduly by a student's general vocabulary reserve and reading ability.

REVIEWER'S REFERENCE

Ochoa, A. S. (1985). [Review of Test of Economic Literacy.] In J. V. Mitchell, Jr. (Ed.), *The ninth mental measurements yearbook* (pp. 1567-1568). Lincoln, NE: Buros Institute of Mental Measurements.

[432]
Test of English for International Communication (TOEIC).

Purpose: To evaluate in real-world, business-related situations the English reading and speaking skills of those whose native language is not English.
Population: Nonnative speakers of English engaged in international business, commerce, and industry.
Publication Dates: 1980–86.
Acronym: TOEIC.
Scores, 3: Listening, Reading, Total.
Administration: Group.
Price Data, 1989: $5 per test administration package including an audiocassette and test administration manual ('84, 9 pages); $4 per extra audiocassette; $8 per inspection copy package including a test booklet for retired form of test, script, answer sheet, Bulletin of Information ('85, 27 pages), Guide for TOEIC Users ('86, 7 pages), and validity study.
Time: (120) minutes.
Comments: Test administered by the client on-site; one-half of test (100 questions) administered by audiocassette tape recording; separate answer sheet.
Authors: Educational Testing Service, A. G. Angell ('83 test analysis), E. C. Callahan ('83 test analysis), and D. S. Robinson ('83 test analysis).
Publisher: Educational Testing Service.
   a) SELF-SCORE.
   Forms, 2: 1, 2.
   Price Data: $110 per 10 test booklets and self-correcting answer sheets with self-contained scoring and score conversion.
   Comments: Scored by client.
   b) SCAN.
   Forms, 4: 1, 2, 3, 4.
   Price Data: $100 per 5 test booklets and answer sheets (volume discounts available).
   Comments: Higher security version scored by the TOEIC program office using optical scanner; individual score reports issued and certificate service available.

Review of the Test of English for International Communication by DAN DOUGLAS, Associate Professor of English, Iowa State University, Ames, IA:

The Test of English for International Communication (TOEIC) was introduced in 1979 by the Educational Testing Service (ETS) in response to a request from Japanese government and industrial representatives for a test that could be administered worldwide to assess the ability of people in commerce and industry to communicate in English. This specialized population presented a unique challenge for test developers, because most tests of English as a Second Language (ESL) are aimed at assessing ability to communicate with native speakers of English, whereas in this case, the aim was to assess ability to use English as a medium of communication among nonnative speakers from widely diverse backgrounds. Furthermore, although most major ESL tests are designed to address academic needs, the TOEIC was designed to measure English skills outside the traditional academic context. The test comprises direct measures of listening and reading skills, and has been shown to be an indirect indicator of speaking and writing skills as well. Suggested uses for the test include establishing the level of English skills of employment applicants, selecting employees for special training programs to be conducted in English, assigning employees to field offices in countries where English is a medium of communication, and encouraging employees to upgrade existing English skills. Beginning with 5,000 candidates in Japan in 1979, the TOEIC was given to 264,500 candidates in 10 countries in 1987–88.

The TOEIC Program has offices in a number of countries where three new versions of the test are given each year: Japan, Korea, Taiwan, Hong Kong, People's Republic of China, Thailand, Indonesia, Spain, France, and Switzerland. The test can be arranged to be given, under the Institutional Program, at the request of international corporations or government bodies that have a number of people they want tested at their own institution, and there is a U.S. based Corporate Program to serve the needs of U.S. companies. The TOEIC is accompanied by ample documentation, including a "Guide for TOEIC Users," published in English, French, Spanish, and German, a "Bulletin of Information," containing sample items, validation and reliability information, and interpretive data, and a semiannual newsletter, *The Reporter*, containing information on who uses the TOEIC and for what purposes, program developments, and score interpretation. The first of what promises to be a series of technical TOEIC Research Reports was published in September 1989, and is a study of criterion-referenced score interpretation.

FORMAT. The test contains 100 listening comprehension items and 100 reading comprehension items. The 45-minute listening comprehension section is tape-recorded and comprises four parts: picture descriptions, question/response, short conversations, and short talks. The reading section contains three parts: sentence completion, error recognition, and comprehension of short texts. Candidates are given 75 minutes to complete the reading comprehension items.

CONTENT AND TEST METHOD. Overall, the situational and semantic content of the items in the test is related to commerce and industry. An exception is the section containing the single pictures, only about a third of which are directly business related. Most of the sentence completions are business oriented in content, although at times the register is a bit unnatural (e.g., "Mr. Franklin accused Jack of procrastination when he handed in his report a week late" seems more like a boys' novel than a business text). The content of the other reading tasks (error-recognition and short texts) is also predominantly business related.

Regarding the "method effect," or the influence of test format on candidates' performance, it should first be borne in mind that the tasks required on the test are all receptive (i.e., listening and reading) and not productive (i.e., writing or speaking). Further, it must be said that few of the tasks offer candidates opportunities to demonstrate their English skills in any sort of realistic, business-related activity; that is, employees seldom if ever have to choose the best description of a picture, the best response to a question, or the best answer to a question about an overheard conversation. Neither do they often have to select completions to single sentences. Listening to short talks and announcements and answering questions about them, spotting errors in written texts, and reading memos, advertisements, and announcements, and answering questions about them do seem to be more realistic tasks. However, only about 40% of the 200 items on the test can be said to be *direct* measures of the English language skills required in international commerce and industry. This is not to say that the test is badly designed, or that the indirect tasks are invalid; it does suggest that caution is needed in interpreting results for candidates who may perform poorly on unrealistic tasks while demonstrating a higher level of skill on more life-like sections of the test.

RELIABILITY. The reliability of the TOEIC was estimated using the Kuder-Richardson Formula 20 on the performance of Japanese candidates who took the test in 1979. The results indicate that the TOEIC is acceptably reliable: Listening Comprehension .92, Reading Comprehension .93, Test Total .96 (Woodford, 1982).

CONSTRUCT VALIDITY. The type of knowledge required to do well on the TOEIC is predominantly grammatical (phonological, syntactic, and semantic) in nature. The error-recognition section is the most overtly grammatical, requiring knowledge of such elements as subject-verb agreement, tense, aspect, number, and gender. Other types of language knowledge are also tested, though not with the thoroughness of grammatical knowledge. For example, some of the longer reading passages require a sensitivity to rhetorical organization, some language functions are tested in the longer listening and reading passages, and knowledge of appropriate register and cultural references is required in some items. Overall, users should be aware that the TOEIC requires primarily a knowledge of English grammar and vocabulary, with an overlay of commerce-oriented subject matter. Very little else of language knowledge—textual, illocutionary, or sociolinguistic knowledge—is being tested.

CONCURRENT VALIDITY. When the TOEIC was introduced in 1979, a validity study was carried out in Japan. Some 500 subjects were presented with a variety of direct English listening, reading, writing, and speaking tasks. Comprehension questions were asked in Japanese by live interviewers and answered in Japanese by the subjects. Results showed strong correlations, ranging from .79 to .90, between the TOEIC and the direct measures. The same subjects were also given the Test of English as a Foreign Language (TOEFL; 9:1257), and correlations between their TOEIC and TOEFL performances ranged from .74 to .87. This analysis also suggested that the TOEIC is better than the TOEFL at discriminating subjects at lower proficiency levels (Woodford, 1982). Finally, in a 1989 study in Japan, France, Mexico, and Saudi Arabia, performance on the TOEIC was compared with that on the Language Proficiency Interview (LPI), a form of the Interagency Language Roundtable Oral Interview (Wilson, 1989). Correlation coefficients between the LPI and TOEIC were high. All this evidence suggests the TOEIC is a reasonably valid indicator of listening and reading skills in English, and is also a reasonable predictor of English speaking and writing skills.

CONCLUSION. The TOEIC is the only large scale, standardized test of English for international business related purposes. Its authors have taken pains to produce a reliable and valid test and to provide statistical evidence of this. Though the content of the test is overwhelmingly commerce oriented, the test tasks themselves are not as closely related as they might be to what business people actually have to do.

REVIEWER'S REFERENCES

Woodford, P. E. (1982). The Test of English for International Communication (TOEIC). In C. Brumfit (Ed.), *English for international communication* (pp. 61-72). Oxford: Pergamon Press.

Wilson, K. M. (1989). *Enhancing the interpretation of a norm-referenced second-language test through criterion-referencing: A research assessment of experience in the TOEIC testing context* (TOEIC Research Report No. 1). Princeton, NJ: Educational Testing Service.

Review of the Test of English for International Communication by ROGER A. RICHARDS, Dean of Academic Affairs, Bunker Hill Community College, Boston, MA:

The Test of English for International Communication (TOEIC) promises to do for the international business community what the Test of English as a Foreign Language (TOEFL; 9:1257) has done for the education profession. In the words of the publisher, "TOEIC measures English language proficiency in the work environment of international trade, unlike other tests that focus on English as it is used in an academic environment."

To date the TOEIC has been used primarily in Japan; the test analysis for the form under review, as a matter of fact, was based on an administration to 3,370 examinees in Japan. That the publishers plan expansion to other parts of the world is indicated by the establishment of TOEIC offices in Korea, Taiwan, Hong Kong, Thailand, Indonesia, Mexico (serving Central America), and The Netherlands (serving Europe).

The test seems long, and although its length undoubtedly contributes to its high reliability, one wonders if it might not be possible to gain an estimate of language proficiency in somewhat less than 2 hours. The test's 200 items are evenly divided between Listening and Reading, but 50 minutes are allowed for Listening and 75 minutes for Reading.

The Listening section, administered by audiotape, consists of four parts. The tape is of good quality for an individual listener, but the reviewer did not have the opportunity to test it in a large room with many subjects. It is straightforward, using the same voices throughout and avoiding any kinds of gimmicks that are so often used on foreign language materials to try to make them seem more true-to-life but end up sounding artificial. The language appears to be suitable for the intended audience. The pace seems brisk. At one point this reviewer had to "cheat" by pressing the pause button to think about an answer. The test taker, of course, does not have that option.

For Part I, the test booklet presents a series of 20 pictures and the tape presents a question and four possible answers for each. The questions are quite easy, as evidenced by the reported mean score of 14.21, or 71.05%—the highest mean percentage of any of the seven sections. This part of the test is not well done. The pictures are of very poor quality in terms of both composition and the quality of the reproduction. Many would not be acceptable for a high school yearbook. They are grainy, lack sharpness, and sometimes obscure the very detail the question deals with. Several of them struck this reviewer as depressing. At least one picture seems culture-bound: In a circle of children and two adults, a woman is holding a ball in the air. The test taker is supposed to know that this means that the game is about to begin.

One wonders why greater economy was not achieved by using two or three questions about each picture, rather than only one question per picture. There is generally enough content in each picture to support additional items.

In Part II, 30 taped questions are presented, each followed by three possible answers from which the subject is to select the most appropriate answer. As in Part I, no portion of the material is printed in the test booklet. But the instruction to "Mark your answer on your answer sheet" is given 30 times, once for each item; only the item number changes. One wonders why the direction to mark the answer could not have been incorporated into the tape, as in Part I. The dedication of almost three entire pages to a single sentence repeated 30 times seems both foolish and wasteful.

Part III consists of 30 short conversations, for each of which a question and four responses are printed in the test booklet. Many of the questions require the ability to draw inferences based on synonyms of words and expressions used in the conversations. On the whole, the items are well written, the distractors being more plausible than for most of the rest of the test.

Part IV extends the format of Part III from brief conversations to "short talks," offering two or three questions for each talk. The fact that the questions are printed enables those taking the test to guide their listening by glancing at the questions. This feature is probably helpful, because the listener would otherwise have to almost memorize the entire passage to be sure to have focused on the specific detail referred to by the question. The overall quality of this section is high.

The Reading section uses the familiar formats of the TOEFL. First there is a multiple-choice cloze exercise of 40 items in Part V, followed by 20 sentences with underlined segments one of which contains an error in Part VI, followed by 14 short passages with two to five questions about each (total of 40 items) in Part VII.

The Reading part of the test needs a good editing. Considering that many of those taking the test may have learned a conservative version of English grammar, questions should not contain usages that will appear to many to be errors. Regardless of whether or not one happens to agree with more relaxed standards of English usage, the use of controversial expressions and structures cannot be justified because it introduces unnecessary distractions. Item 103 states that "The corporate headquarters *are* located . . ." There are those who still consider "headquarters" to be singular.

Item 148 will confuse many traditionally schooled learners of English: "[A] *Due to* the popularity of the stars, theater patrons [B] *are advised* to [C] *contact* the box office as soon as [D] *possibly*." A good student might never get to [D], having already marked "A" in recognition that "Due to" ought to be "Because of." In Item 150, the publisher states in an unmarked part of the sentence that "the data is presented." Many students have been taught that the word *data* is plural. A missing comma will surely make Item 136 more difficult than it is intended to be. A cloze item, it reads "For the new museum visitor_____for the veteran museum goer, the Museum Highlights Tour offers an excellent opportunity to see the most popular exhibits." The correct answer, "as well as," will be missed by those whose English is good enough to enable them to recognize that "as well as" is a parenthetical expression and needs to be set off by commas.

These lapses, like the inferior quality of the photographs and the clumsiness of the format of Part II, give the TOEIC the appearance of a rough draft that needs to be worked on further before it is released to the world. Such shortcomings do not seriously invalidate the test, but they prevent it from inspiring confidence, and they are regrettable in the work of a publisher as reputable as the Educational Testing Service.

This reviewer's reservations about the Preliminary Test of English as a Foreign Language (see 298) are generally applicable to the TOEIC. The TOEIC is better documented, with convincing validity data being presented. (As the test gains greater use outside Japan, its validity for populations from different cultures will need to be addressed.) But the rationale undergirding the test and the specifications which guided the test constructors are no clearer. Despite the needed improvements, the test should be helpful to those who must assess the English language skills of nonnative speakers in the business world.

[433]
Test of English Proficiency Level.

Purpose: "To determine a student's instructional level for placement in an English as a Second Language Program."
Population: Limited-English-proficient students in secondary and adult programs.
Publication Date: 1985.
Acronym: TEPL.
Scores: 4 skill area scores: Oral, Structure, Reading, Writing.
Administration: Individual in part.
Price Data, 1987: $49.95 per complete set including test booklet blackline masters, student answer sheet blackline masters, Scantron scoring key, hand-scored scoring key, and manual (89 pages); $7.50 per 50 Scantron answer forms.
Time: Oral Section, (5–20) minutes; Written Section, 60(70) minutes.
Author: George Rathmell.
Publisher: The Alemany Press.

Review of the Test of English Proficiency Level by ALAN GARFINKEL, Associate Professor of Spanish and Foreign Language Education, Purdue University, West Lafayette, IN:

The Test of English Proficiency Level (TEPL) offers the prospective purchaser a clearly defined purpose, along with convincing evidence of success in fulfilling that purpose. For these reasons, it can be recommended as a useful classroom tool despite its lack of complete quantitative data on reliability and validity.

One of the problems facing some tests is an overly ambitious statement of purpose that can be interpreted as an attempt to make a test look useful for all purposes. Because a test is more likely to successfully fulfill a specific purpose than a broad range of purposes, the author and publisher of this test are to be congratulated for staking out the arena of placement in measurement without being excessively ambitious in setting goals.

Placement, as defined in the TEPL manual, involves more than a simple decision on whether or not a given student needs English as a Second Language instruction. Placement measures must be able to assist in selecting an appropriate point for each student on a range from zero proficiency to native proficiency, keeping in mind that an English as a Second Language student can achieve "peer-appropriate second language conversational skills" in about 2 years, while needing 5 to 7 years to achieve parity with peers in second language academic skills. Because these chronological estimates cannot be applied to all students in all English as a Second Language classes, the TEPL authors wisely state its results in levels named with letters rather than numbers. This avoids confusion with chronologically determined levels of instruction.

Further, the TEPL does measure knowledge "about the language," and the measured concept of placement also includes a "dynamic continuum of different but interacting skills." This careful thinking about purpose makes an important contribution to the usefulness of the TEPL.

Content validity of the instrument is self-evident to the experienced instructor. That determination is supported by the use of well-known measures of readability in preparing the TEPL and by comparisons with other tests. Similarly, additional confidence in the TEPL is provided by association with well-known English as a Second Language practitioners and by publication by a firm known for excellence in the ESL field.

The TEPL is not norm referenced. It is intended to estimate placement level for one student, not to measure the achievement of large groups. However, the test's structure and reading sections have been used in an attempt to estimate reliability. Further efforts to establish validity are now under way. Their results would certainly be valuable additions to future editions of the manual. It would also be well to determine interscorer reliability on a reasonably large sample of scorers and students. Showing such reliability could be demonstrated would further enhance the confidence of prospective users.

The manual is made all the more complete by including recommendations of a range of useful teaching materials and resources. It is not useful to compare this test to others, because none of the other well-known tests for English as a Second Language specifically measure placement level as defined by the TEPL manual.

The TEPL was published in 1985 after years of experimentation. This reviewer applauds the ongoing efforts to provide new information on reliability and validity while recommending the test for widespread use in making English as a Second Language placement decisions.

Review of the Test of English Proficiency Level by MAURICE TATSUOKA, Professor Emeritus of Psychology, University of Illinois at Urbana-Champaign, Champaign, IL:

This test purports to measure what the author characterizes as a full range of language skills, consisting of oral proficiency, the ability to identify correct structures in sentences, reading comprehension, and the ability to communicate in written English. The oral part, which must be administered on a one-on-one basis, is said to take between 5 and 20 minutes (depending on how far the examinee can progress), while the three written subtests, which may be administered to a group, take 60 minutes. The test is intended for limited-English-proficient students in secondary and adult programs designed to teach English as a second language. Its results are given not in numerical scores but by classifying examinees in one of seven instructional levels in each of the four skill areas, for the purpose of placing each student in what is judged to be the appropriate level in the program.

The oral section consists of five sets of six questions each, arranged in increasing order of difficulty. Nineteen of the questions refer to a series of pictures labeled A through S, and the remaining 11 are general ones, such as "Do you like to go to the movies?" and "Is it raining today?" In order to earn credit for their answers, examinees must answer in complete sentences that contain certain key clauses specified in the manual.

The written section contains five open-ended questions that require writing sentences or paragraphs about specified topics, interspersed among 88 multiple-choice questions embedded in 11 passages that alternately test for structure-identification and reading comprehension. (Actually, the passages in which the questions dealing with structure-identification occur are not single-theme narratives but sets of six sentences each.)

Besides the tests, the manual includes a list of "suggested materials for each of the four skills and at each of the seven levels," and a separate list of teacher resources intended to help teachers both in testing and instruction in English as a Second Language programs at the secondary or adult level.

At the end of the manual there is a set of answer and scoring sheets, including ruled boxes for the examinee to write answers to four of the five open-ended writing questions. (The fifth and last writing question is, for some reason, to be answered on a separate sheet.) The answer sheets for all but the oral and written questions include both hand-scorable and machine-scorable types.

For overall clarity of instructions, completeness, and "face validity" of the questions, this reviewer gives the Test of English Proficiency Level (TEPL) fairly high scores. As for "completeness," the manual even has a two-page section entitled "Questions and Answers About T.E.P.L.," presumably to allay some doubts a potential user of the test might entertain about it. However, some of the answers given are themselves questionable, as I shall indicate below. But first, to dwell a little longer on the positive aspects of the test: I believe, for one thing, that the gradation in difficulty of the questions—from easy to hard—is done quite effectively and smoothly. Also, even the easiest questions do not seem to insult the intelligence of the adolescent/adult examinees. The pictures for 19 of the oral questions are drawn quite expertly and attractively. In the written test, the reading-comprehension questions, in particular, are carefully constructed to be nontrivial, attention-holding, and informative of things and ways American for the immigrant examinee. Another positive—even remarkable—aspect of the test is that each page of the written test and of the answer sheets carries the statement, "Permission granted to reproduce for classroom use," alongside the copyright statement. One somehow wonders whether the publisher does not regret the overly generous stance of the author (who is the copyright holder) and the fact the manual and test booklet were not published separately—with permission "to reproduce for classroom use" granted for neither. (However, I do *not* suggest that this be done in future editions!)

Coming now to the negative aspects, by far the worst, in this reviewer's opinion, is the paucity of technical information given about the test. The $2^1/_3$ pages (pp. 30–32) devoted to this matter give the mean, median, standard deviation, standard error of measurement, and *a* reliability coefficient of the set of 88 items constituting the structure-identification and reading-comprehension parts of the written test, but *no* validity coefficient. (Even for the reliability coefficient—which, incidentally, is mis-typeset as "reliability factor"—it is not stated what *type* of coefficient it is: split-half, test-retest, KR-20, or what?) The table on page 32 giving "comparisons with [seven] other tests" is not accompanied by a description of just how these comparisons were derived. Data on means and percentile ranks are compared with TEPL classifications for three of the tests. For the other four tests (for which only the "corresponding levels" are given), one wonders whether they might not have been made by "intuitive Procrustes fitting."

In the two-page "Questions and Answers" section referred to above (pp. 34–35), it is claimed that "The structure and reading parts of T.E.P.L. have undergone a standardization process as a check on validity," but the meager data given on page 30 hardly constitute a standardization, much less a validation, of the test. It is stated several times in the manual that further data are "now being gathered" to provide more accurate statistical analyses, but it seems the 3 or 4 years that have elapsed since the test first appeared should have been sufficient to permit at least the addition of an appendix giving some validation data. Another self-serving answer is given to the question, "Is T.E.P.L. less reliable than norm-referenced tests?" (viz., "In terms of comparing scores with large-scale averages, yes; but that is not its function"). This sounds like gobbledygook to me.

A minor but nevertheless non-negligible irritation the manual caused me was that, at two places in the instructions for the oral test (pp. 50 and 52), "i.e." is used when "e.g." is clearly intended. This is a fairly common error even among sophisticated writers, but its commission in a manual of an English test sets a poor example, to say the least.

[434]
Test of Initial Literacy.
Purpose: To provide teachers with diagnostic information about children who have difficulty with reading and writing.
Population: Ages 7–12.
Publication Date: 1989.
Acronym: TOIL.
Scores, 9: Letter Matching, Word Matching, Copying, Grammatical Punctuation, Orthographic Punctuation, Spelling of Homophones, Spelling, Style, Free Writing.
Administration: Group.
Price Data, 1990: £6.70 per 10 test booklets; £8 per teacher's set, including test booklet and manual ('89, 39 pages).
Time: Untimed.
Comments: Complements Reading Ability Series.

Authors: Anne Kispal, Alison Tate, Tom Gorman, and Chris Whetton.
Publisher: NFER-Nelson Publishing Co., Ltd. [England].

Review of the Test of Initial Literacy by JERRI-LYN V. ANDREWS, Coordinator Research/Statistics, Department of Educational Accountability, Montgomery County Public Schools, Rockville, MD:

The Test of Initial Literacy (TOIL) was designed as a diagnostic instrument to help teachers determine whether pupils who are experiencing difficulty learning reading and writing skills may have specific language difficulties and, if so, to identify them. This test suffers from a variety of problems that make it impossible for this reviewer to recommend it. The technical information about the test falls well below the acceptable level.

The manual is very clear that the test was designed strictly as a diagnostic instrument. The nine exercises are separate, results are never summed, and no norms or standard scores are provided. However, the TOIL does include a level of adequacy cut score for each of the exercises and provides the percentage of the trial sample scoring below that level. Unfortunately, the manual does not adequately explain how these cut scores were set.

The tryout of the TOIL was conducted in conjunction with the standardization of the Reading Ability Series (RAS). While the sample of schools appears to have been selected to be broadly representative of Great Britain, the instructions to teachers for identifying the students for the TOIL sample were to select the students the teacher judged to be having more difficulty with reading and writing than the majority of students. The manual does not include any demographic information about the 1,512 students in the TOIL sample beyond the number of students by age, grade, and level of the RAS they also took.

With the exception of the Spelling of Homophones exercise, all the exercises have simple, easy-to-follow directions. The manual does suggest repeating or explaining the instructions if students do not understand. The TOIL, which was developed in Great Britain, includes several items whose language would probably confound students outside Britain and Wales (e.g., "Put in capital letters, full stops and anything else you think is missing").

Scoring of four exercises, Letter Matching, Word Matching, Grammatical Punctuation, and Spelling of Homophones, is straightforward. While scoring the Orthographic Punctuation and Spelling exercises is also simple, a student could get a perfect score by inserting or correcting as required even if the student also added several additional mistakes.

The other three exercises, Copying, Style, and Free Writing, require teachers to compare what their pupils produce to the samples provided and to assign points accordingly. The manual includes interrater reliability only for the Copying exercise, which is clearly the simplest to score. Based on a sample of 150 tests, that correlation was only .75, so it is possible that the scoring for the other two more subjective exercises could be lower.

The reliability of each exercise except Copying was assessed using Cronbach's alpha. The alphas ranged from a very low .43 on the five-item Orthographic Punctuation test to a high of .91 on the five-item Letter Matching test.

Only content validity is mentioned in the technical manual. Potential users are told that they must judge whether the content is appropriate for their intended use. The domains for some of the nine exercises are not clearly defined, and no rationale is offered for the inclusion of skills. For example, the Orthographic Punctuation exercise asks students to insert missing elements, such as periods, capital letters, and apostrophes. Why those three elements were selected is never explained.

The steps in developing the TOIL are explained in general terms. However, the user does not learn why the initial list of tasks was selected, how many items were tried for each exercise, what the criteria were for selecting specific items, or how the number of items to include in each exercise was determined.

It certainly can be valuable to identify the skills that students do have and the errors that they are making. However, the small number of items on the TOIL coupled with the weak technical information give little reason to recommend using this test. A simple teacher-made screening test should do the job as well.

Review of the Test of Initial Literacy by CLE-BORNE D. MADDUX, Professor and Chairman, Department of Curriculum and Instruction, University of Nevada—Reno, Reno, NV:

The Test of Initial Literacy (TOIL) is a group-administered, non-norm-referenced diagnostic test. The manual states that the purpose of the test is to "provide detailed information about the individual capabilities and problems of children who are having more difficulty with reading and writing than the majority of pupils in the same age-group" (p. 1).

Thus, the purpose of the test seems to be similar to that of more traditional informal reading inventories, although, unlike most such inventories, the TOIL does attempt to provide some information concerning writing. The format of the test, however, varies markedly from that of informal reading inventories. The test consists of nine "exercises," which yield nine separate scores. Total scores are not recommended because the results of the exercises are meant for diagnostic use. The exercises include Letter Matching, Word Matching, Copying, Grammatical Punctuation, Orthographic Punctuation, Spelling of Homophones, Spelling, Style, and Free Writing. Markedly absent from this list are exercises in which reading is the primary focus.

The manual includes a detailed section on scoring, including the number of errors to be deemed "acceptable." The user is advised to consult the interpretation section of the manual for interpreting the scores of children whose scores do not reach the acceptable level. This section presents stereotypic information regarding the errors made on each section of the test by students included in the "field trials." For example, under Letter Matching, the manual advises that reversal of symbols may be an indication of specific reading problems and that if these errors also take place in the child's daily work, the teacher should "use specific diagnostic tests designed to obtain more detailed information about patterns of reversal."

TECHNICAL CONSIDERATIONS. The TOIL is not a norm-referenced instrument. However, the manual does provide some information on test construction, reliability, and validity. The manual suggests that the validity of this non-norm-referenced test lies in its content. While some description of the sample used to test the pilot and final versions of the test is given, no information is presented regarding the rationale for initial selection or eventual refinement of subtests.

Correlations are presented between total scores on the TOIL and raw scores on five levels (A through E) of the Reading Ability Series (RAS), a standardized instrument developed by the same authors. These five correlation coefficients are based on sample sizes from 114 to 530, and are .64, .54, .71, .46, and .54. Four of these are very low showing that there is some relationship between the two tests, though it is not very strong. The authors state that they have calculated TOIL total scores for the sole purpose of establishing the scores on the RAS tests below which it would be appropriate for TOIL to be administered.

Internal reliability is discussed and Cronbach's alpha was calculated. Most exceed .70 and over half exceed .80. The alpha for Exercise 5 (Orthographic Punctuation) is only .43, which, the authors acknowledge, suggests that the items in that section are not measuring the same skill. They included the exercise nonetheless, but caution against overinterpretation of results. An intercorrelation matrix for all subtests is presented, and the manual concludes that because the coefficients are low, the exercises are measuring distinct skills. However, no factor analysis was performed to lend support to this claim, and the matrix is not so clear-cut as to obviate such an analysis.

The manual states that "levels of adequacy" (allowable number of errors) for each subtest were set after taking into consideration (*a*) frequency of each score on each exercise, (*b*) marking key, and (*c*) difficulty of the exercise. However, no information is given on how these variables were taken into consideration.

SUMMARY. The usefulness of the TOIL as a diagnostic instrument lies in the relevance of skills included in the subtests. The manual fails to establish this relevance. On its face, the test appears to emphasize a collection of random discrete skills and de-emphasize reading comprehension. If skills such as matching letters or words or punctuating sentences are highly correlated with reading comprehension, then the evidence for these relationships should be set forward in the manual. Such evidence is not presented, nor is representativeness of test items to the tested skill even mentioned. The latter is a suspect area for Letter Matching, for example, because this subtest contains only five items.

The test may lack even face validity, because the authors have provided no evidence that the skills tested are central to literacy. Correlations with the Reading Ability Series cannot be judged as evidence for concurrent validity, because the RAS itself is of unknown reliability and validity.

In addition, the test was constructed in England and Wales, and contains so many cultural specificities that it would be virtually unusable outside these countries. Examples include use of the symbol for the monetary pound as well as liberal use of slang that would be without meaning for most children outside Britain.

In conclusion, the test appears to be of little value to teachers interested in diagnostic information about literacy. Such teachers would probably be better advised to engage in diagnostic teaching than to employ the Test of Initial Literacy.

[435]
Test of Language Competence—Expanded Edition.

Purpose: "To evaluate delays in the emergence of linguistic competence and in the use of semantic, syntactic, and pragmatic strategies."
Publication Dates: 1985–89.
Acronym: TLC-E.
Scores: 5 subtest scores: Ambiguous Sentences, Listening Comprehension: Making Inferences, Oral Expression: Recreating Speech Acts, Figurative Language, Remembering Word Pairs (supplemental subtest for Level 2 only), plus 4 composite scores: Expressing Intents, Interpreting Intents, Screening Composite, TLC-Expanded Composite.
Administration: Individual.
Price Data, 1991: $235 per complete kit including 25 Level 1 & 2 record forms, Level 1 & 2 stimulus manuals, administration manual ('89, 311 pages), technical manual ('89, 98 pages), and portfolio; $200 per complete kit without portfolio; $107 per Extension kit including 25 Level 1 record forms, 1 Level 2 record form, Level 1 stimulus manual, and administration manual; $49.50 per administration manual; $36.50 per technical manual.
Time: (60–70) minutes per level.

Authors: Elisabeth H. Wiig and Wayne Secord.
Publisher: The Psychological Corporation.
a) LEVEL 1.
Population: Ages 5-0 to 9-11.
Price Data: $24 per 25 record forms; $37 per stimulus manual.
b) LEVEL 2.
Population: Ages 9-0 to 18-11.
Price Data, 1991: $24 per 25 record forms; $37 per stimulus manual.

TEST REFERENCES

1. Santos, O. B. (1989). Language skills and cognitive processes related to poor reading comprehension performance. *Journal of Learning Disabilities, 22,* 131-133.

Review of the Test of Language Competence—Expanded Edition by DOLORES KLUPPEL VETTER, Professor and Associate Dean, University of Wisconsin-Madison, Madison, WI:

The Test of Language Competence—Expanded Edition (TLC-E) provides a combination of the original Test of Language Competence, which was appropriate for ages 9-0 to 18-11 years (Level 2), with a downward extension for ages 5-0 to 9-11 years (Level 1). Theoretical models and research literature are presented to support the choice of subtest content and context. Reasonable evidence is presented for content, criterion, and construct validity. Internal consistency, test-retest reliability (three-week interval), and interrater reliability are also reported.

Normative samples were large and selected to approximate the U.S. population with regard to geographic region, gender, race, and Spanish origin. Normalized standard scores and percentile ranks are provided for the subtests at half-year intervals below 11 years of age, at yearly intervals from 12 to 14 years, and at 2-year intervals thereafter. Composite standard scores are available for combinations of two, or all four, subtests. In addition to the normalized standard scores and the composite standard scores, age equivalent scores are also found in tables in the Administration Manual. However, given the caution that accompanies age-equivalent scores, it is unclear why they were provided. Separate norms for gender are not provided because no significant differences between genders were found. Although the administration manual of the test stresses the importance of taking dialectical variations into account, the authors suggest that caution should be exercised in interpreting scores of minority students.

The overlap in ages in the standardization samples was deliberate to allow clinical judgment about the student's abilities (e.g., reading) to influence the choice of level to administer to children between 9-0 and 9-11 years.

The TLC-E provides extensive technical information about its development and standardization. The authors repeatedly state that they were attempting to assess an array of language content in several communicative contexts. Evidence supporting criterion validity is presented for groups of learning disabled and nondisabled children and adolescents. Correlations with the Wechsler Intelligence Scale for Children—Revised (WISC-R), the Test of Adolescent Language (TOAL), the Test of Language Development-2 (TOLD-2), the Clinical Evaluation of Language Fundamentals—Revised (CELF-R), the Peabody Picture Vocabulary Test—Revised (PPVT-R), and the Educational Abilities Series are reported separately for the two levels of the TLC-E, although all groups did not take all tests. The correlations are moderate for the composite scores of the TLC-E and verbal subtests, and lower with performance/motor subtests.

The TLC-E is a well-constructed test from a psychometric perspective, and the authors have taken care to provide a basis for the test in theory and research. No other test currently available provides such a broadly based estimate of language competence in children and adolescents. The TLC-E, however, is not a criterion-referenced test. Therefore, subtest performance should not be used prescriptively in planning intervention for those children or adolescents scoring poorly on individual subtests. The composite standard scores for the four subtests are more global indicators of language competence and are preferable for clinical interpretation.

Review of the Test of Language Competence—Expanded Edition by CAROL E. WESTBY, Senior Research Associate, University Affiliated Program, University of New Mexico, Albuquerque, NM:

The Test of Language Competence—Expanded Edition (TLC-E) is one of very few tests designed to assess oral language of children from 5 to 18 years and one of very few standardized tests that attempt to go beyond discrete point testing. The purposes of the test are to identify students who do not exhibit adequate metalinguistic language competence and to provide a strategy approach to the assessment of language. It is unlikely that any standardized test can adequately evaluate language competence, a fact Wiig and Secord readily acknowledge, but the TLC-E is closer to evaluating language competence, particularly for older students, than most other language tests. Unlike the majority of language tests, the TLC-E goes beyond the usual assessment of vocabulary and syntactic knowledge, focusing on semantic-syntactic interactions and pragmatics. The TLC-E evaluates language competence, defined by the authors as appropriate understanding and/or expression of language content to the communicative demands of specific contexts.

The TLC-E subtests were constructed to sample literal and figurative language content in restrictive or narrow contexts and in interactive or broad, communicative-like contexts. The authors provide an excellent review of the research literature on understanding ambiguous sentences and metaphors, schema and script theory, and grammatical theory that supports their choices of subtests and test items. Two test levels are available, one for students from ages 5 to 9 years old and one for students from ages 9 to 19 years old. Students in the 5 to 9 year age range are just becoming aware of figurative and ambiguous elements in language. Consequently, Level 1 would probably not be appropriate for students in this age range who have severe language problems. The authors suggest that Level 1 is best for students with mild language problems or (as a downward extension of Level 2) for older students who have deficits in this area.

Other language tests have included comprehension of literal and figurative or metaphoric expressions; however, in addition, the TLC-E permits the examiner to distinguish students' comprehension and use of language in context-reduced tasks from language in context-embedded tasks. Subtest 1 (interpreting ambiguous sentences) and Subtest 2 (making inferences from short scripts) are context-reduced tasks for which students are provided with only minimal situational information upon which to base their judgements. Subtest 3 (formulating speech acts or sentences about a scene using specific words) and Subtest 4 (interpreting metaphoric language) provide students with more contextual or situational information upon which to base their judgements.

Although both Level 1 and Level 2 have the same subtests, the structure of the subtests differs. All of the subtests in Level 1 include visual stimuli support, whereas only Subtest 3 in Level 2 includes pictures. On Subtests 1 and 4 of Level 1 students are asked to give two interpretations of an ambiguous sentence or interpret a metaphor; they are then shown four pictures and asked to point to the pictures that depict the meaning. In corresponding Level 2 subtests students do this without visual support. On Subtest 2 of Level 1 students are asked to select two pictures that show events that could have occurred between the beginning and end of the story read by the examiner. Again, the comparable Level 2 subtests do not provide picture options.

Although reading is not required, students may follow the printed questions and options in the stimulus manual. Students who cannot read the items on Level 2 may have heavier memory loads placed on them, a factor that is not addressed by the authors. Because of the differences in degree of visual support and verbal memory requirements between the two levels, context-reduced subtests of Level 1 may provide more contextual information support to students than those of Level 2. Consequently, one cannot assume that children who perform adequately on Level 1 when they are 8 years old will perform adequately on Level 2 when they are 9 years old.

Although the degree of contextual support is an important distinction in this test, no composite scores for context-reduced and context-embedded materials are provided. The authors do provide composite scores for expressing intents (Subtests 1 and 3) and interpreting intents (Subtests 2 and 4). The authors provide little explanation or rationale for these composite scores. Because all four tasks require oral expression, these scores are not equivalent to expressive and receptive scores on many traditional language tests.

The TLC-E administration guidelines are detailed. The authors include scripts to use during the test administration, specify time limits for student responses, illustrate marking for record forms, provide practice protocols for subtests that require subjectivity, and discuss interpretation of typical case patterns. Some of the time limits are quite long (45 to 60 seconds), and it is not clear if the examiner should allow the full amount even when students indicate they have nothing more to say. Although the scored protocols are helpful, particularly in understanding the holistic scoring used on Subtest 3, some discussion about the scores given for protocol items would have made them more useful. The examiner is left to infer why an item may not have received full credit.

The authors emphasize that the responses of racial and ethnic minority students should be scored against their dialect backgrounds. To assist in this, the authors provide a section on common nonstandard dialects (Black English, Southern White, and Appalachian) and a brief list of Spanish influences on English syntax. No clear guidance is given, however, about how students' responses should be scored if their constructions are influenced by dialect or language interference (i.e., are the students given full credit?). It should be noted that distinctions between dialect difference and delays in syntactic development are not easy to make without additional information from other members in the child's linguistic environment.

The guidelines for observing behavior during the testing and the supplemental and extension testing that are used when students perform more than one standard deviation below the mean on the four subtests are a novel and valuable addition to a testing repertoire. At the end of each of the subtests the authors list common behavioral patterns exhibited by normal and learning-disabled students taking the tests. The examiner checks characteristics of the students' behaviors, such a responding impulsively or after reflection, or responding fluently or dysfluently with revisions. Extension testing on the

subtests enables the examiner to explore the strategies the students have used in arriving at their answers. For each subtest the authors provide a systematic series of tasks to determine how the student has approached and interpreted the test items. For example, the Remembering Word Pairs supplementary test in Level 2 enables the examiner to explore students' memory strategies.

The technical manual is explicit and thorough. The authors provide detailed discussion of the technical characteristics of the TLC-E. They describe the field testing and the standardization sample—a total of 2,188 students for Level 1 and 1,796 students for Level 2 from the northern, southern, and western regions of the United States. The Level 1 sample contained approximately 30% Black and Spanish-origin students. Level 2 contained approximately 14% Black and Spanish-origin students. A problem with norms based on diverse populations is that they may represent no one. The authors are aware of this problem. They note that in one regional sample, Blacks scored significantly lower than Whites and they discuss the issues in the development of local norms.

The authors carefully explain content, criterion-related, predictive, and construct validity. Few other tests of adolescent language are available to establish criterion-related validity. The TLC-E correlates highly with the Wechsler Intelligence Scale for Children—Revised (WISC-R) verbal scale, the Clinical Evaluation of Language Functions—Revised (CELF-R), and the Test of Adolescent Language (TOAL). It also correlates moderately with the Educational Abilities Series (EAS). The TLC-E content is more variable than the TOAL content, as would be expected given the authors' goal to evaluate two types of language usage in two different contexts. Factor analysis confirms the four separate subtests, as well as a general overall language factor. The TLC-E evidences good predictive validity. Ninety-six percent of students classified as language learning disabled (LLD) by the schools were classified as LLD by the TLC-E; and 93% not classified as LLD by the schools were also not so classified by the TLC-E. Detailed data is also provided on the internal consistency, standard error of measurement, test-retest reliability, and interrater reliability on the subtests that require examiner judgements.

Wiig and Secord have done much more than most authors of language tests in providing a theoretical basis for the subtests and test items. They have gone beyond traditional discrete point testing by selecting items that require integration of semantic, syntactic, and pragmatic language skills and they have attended to the strategies that students use in responding. Based on current literature, the TLC-E appears to have good construct validity. The extension testing and supplemental tests may be more valuable than the test itself because they provide insight into the variables that contribute to students' errors and guidelines for remediation.

[436]

Test of Language Development-2 Intermediate.

Purpose: "To identify children who are significantly below their peers in language proficiency, to determine children's specific strengths and weaknesses in language skills, to document children's progress in language as a consequence of special intervention programs, and to measure language in research studies."

Population: Ages 8-6 to 12-11.

Publication Dates: 1982–88.

Acronym: TOLD-2 Intermediate.

Scores, 11: Subtests (Sentence Combining, Vocabulary, Word Ordering, Generals, Grammatic Comprehension, Malapropisms), Composites (Spoken Language, Listening, Speaking, Semantics, Syntax).

Administration: Individual.

Parts, 2: Subtests, Composites.

Price Data, 1989: $53 per complete kit including examiner's manual ('88, 60 pages) and 50 record forms ('88, 6 pages); $32 per 50 record forms; $23 per examiner's manual; $69 per computer scoring system (Apple or IBM).

Time: (30–60) minutes.

Comments: Revision of Test of Language Development Intermediate (9:1261); primary edition also available; orally administered; examiners need some formal training in assessment.

Authors: Donald D. Hammill and Phyllis L. Newcomer.

Publisher: PRO-ED, Inc.

Cross References: For a review by Doris V. Allen of an earlier edition of the entire Test of Language Development, see 9:1261 (5 references).

TEST REFERENCES

1. Camarata, S. M., Hughes, C. A., & Ruhl, K. L. (1988). Mild/moderate behaviorally disordered students: A population at risk for language disorders. *Language, Speech, and Hearing Services in Schools, 19,* 191-200.
2. Gibbs, D. P., & Cooper, E. B. (1989). Prevalence of communication disorders in students with learning disabilities. *Journal of Learning Disabilities, 22,* 60-63.
3. McGregor, K. K., & Leonard, L. B. (1989). Facilitating word-finding skills of language-impaired children. *Journal of Speech and Hearing Disorders, 54,* 141-147.
4. Merritt, D. D., & Liles, B. Z. (1989). Narrative analysis: Clinical applications of story generation and story retelling. *Journal of Speech and Hearing Disorders, 54,* 438-447.
5. Fodness, R. W., McNeilly, J., & Bradley-Johnson, S. (1991). Test-retest reliability of the Test of Language Development—2: Primary and Test of Language Development—2: Intermediate. *Journal of School Psychology, 29,* 161-165.

Review of the Test of Language Development-2 Intermediate by REBECCA J. McCAULEY, Assistant Professor of Communication Science and Disorders, University of Vermont, Burlington, VT:

TEST STRUCTURE. The Test of Language Development-2 Intermediate (TOLD-2 Intermediate) is a revision of the 1982 TOLD-Intermediate and a companion to the TOLD-2 Primary (which is intended for younger test takers). The TOLD-2 Intermediate is designed to assess comprehension and production of spoken language in children from ages 8-6 to 12-11. It was constructed using a two-dimensional model of language structure comprising two linguistic systems (listening and speaking) and two linguistic features (semantics and syntax). The test includes six subtests: Sentence Combining, Vocabulary, Word Ordering, Generals, Grammatic Comprehension, and Malapropisms. Of the six subtests, three are identical to subtests in the 1982 version of the test, one (Word Ordering) is a revision of an earlier subtest, and two (Vocabulary and Malapropisms) are entirely new. A short form of the test consists of the Sentence Combining and Generals subtests.

TEST ADMINISTRATION AND INTERPRETATION. The entire test is designed to be administered in 30 to 60 minutes. With few exceptions, test manual descriptions of tester qualifications, administration, and scoring procedures are quite clear. Considerable attention is paid to cautioning users about likely errors. The authors also provide specific and appropriately conservative suggestions regarding the collection and use of local norms and regarding adaptive testing procedures to be used *after* standardized administration to help in test interpretation and intervention planning.

In addition to raw scores, three types of scores are provided to summarize test performance: composite scores for five selected groups of subtests, as well as standard scores and percentiles for individual subtests. One of the composite scores (the Spoken Language Quotient) summarizes performance across the entire six subtests comprising the test. The remaining four composite scores represent summaries across varying groups of subtests corresponding to language systems and features: receptive language (the Listening Quotient), expressive language (the Speaking Quotient), semantics (the Semantic Quotient), and syntax (the Syntax Quotient). The test authors recommend that test users interpret within-individual differences using composite, rather than subtest, scores because of the greater reliability of the composite scores. Nonetheless, additional clarification of the relative importance of subtest versus composite scores and of their joint interpretation would have been helpful. The authors prudently caution test users against the use of age-equivalent scores and provide no tables to support their use, but do supply a formula to accommodate test users who are required to report age-equivalent scores because of local regulations.

NORMS. Norms for the TOLD-2 Intermediate are based on a sample of 1,214 children—471 of whom were given the new version of the test. The remainder of the sample consisted of children who had been given the TOLD-Intermediate in 1982. Thus the norms for the two new subtests and the

TOLD-2 Intermediate in its entirety are in fact based on the smaller 1987 sample, rather than the pooled sample. The composition of the pooled sample approximates comparable national percentages in terms of sex, race, place of residence (rural versus urban), geographic distribution, and parental occupation. Pooled sample sizes for the normative subgroups used to interpret test performances appear to exceed the generally accepted minimum of 100 (Sattler, 1988; Salvia & Ysseldyke, 1987).

RELIABILITY. Reliability data include reliability coefficients obtained through test-retest and internal consistency procedures and standard errors of measurement based on internal consistency coefficients. The authors report high internal consistency reliability coefficients and, consequently, relatively low standard errors of measurement. Test-retest reliability evidence is confined to two studies and is generally less satisfactory because of small sample sizes over few age groups. One of these studies was an unpublished master's thesis in which test performances obtained with a 2-week hiatus were examined for a group of 56 children whose ages are not reported in the test manual. The second study examined test performances obtained with a 1-week hiatus using a group of 30 fifth and sixth graders. With the exception of the Vocabulary subtest, the results of these studies yielded correlations suggestive of acceptable stability for the limited age ranges considered. No information regarding interexaminer reliability is reported.

VALIDITY. Evidence of validity provided by the authors falls within the traditional categories of content, criterion-related, and construct validity. Overall, this evidence suggests the test's validity for many potential test takers for three of its four stated purposes: (a) the identification of children who are significantly below their peers in language proficiency (clinical identification), (b) the measurement of language in young research subjects (research measurement), and, to a lesser extent, (c) the identification of strengths and weaknesses. Evidence is lacking for the use of the TOLD-2 Intermediate in the documentation of progress resulting from intervention.

Content validity for the three purposes of clinical identification, research measurement, and identification of strengths and weaknesses was suggested by the authors' thorough description of the item writing and selection processes, as well as by an empirical study of professionals with expertise in language and language disabilities. These individuals favorably compared subtest descriptions to the theoretical model of language structure guiding test 'construction. However, the content of the test has also been criticized for the predominance of tasks involving metalinguistic skills rather than spoken language proficiency (Westby, 1988).

Concurrent criterion-related evidence was limited to significant, moderate correlations between scores on the TOLD-2 Intermediate with comparable oral language scores on the Test of Adolescent Language (the TOAL; Hammill, Brown, Larsen, & Wiederholt, 1980) reported for a group of 56 children in grades 5 and 6, the only age groups covered by both tests. Use of an existing test as a sole criterion measure has been strongly criticized (e.g., Anastasi, 1982) and is especially suspect here because of limited support for the validity of the TOAL.

Construct validity is addressed extensively through the testing of hypotheses regarding age differentiation, subtest interrelationships, the relationship of the TOLD-2 Intermediate subtest to those of the TOAL, the differentiation from the normative sample of 14 students receiving language therapy in school using the TOLD-2 Intermediate, a factor analysis, and the discriminating power of test items. The available data are generally suggestive of the instrument's validity for the purposes described above. However, there are some weaknesses in the evidence. Of greatest concern is the small ($n = 14$) and largely undefined sample used to examine the test's ability to correctly identify language-impaired subjects. The factor analytic study is not discussed in sufficient detail, particularly as its results relate to subtest interpretation. In addition, no studies are reported addressing the interpretation of strengths and weaknesses in terms of composite scores, although the test authors encourage users to use those scores in intraindividual comparisons.

SUMMARY. The TOLD-2 Intermediate is a well-designed and generally well-documented test for use in the assessment of language abilities in children from ages 8-6 to 12-11. Although additional evidence is still needed, substantial support is offered suggesting the test's validity for use in the identification of impairment and as a research measure. However, there is almost no support for its use in the assessment of progress in treatment and weak support for its use in the assessment of strengths and weaknesses. The test appears to be appropriate for a large number of test takers, but local norms will be required for children who differ appreciably from the normative sample in native language and dialect, socioeconomic status, and so on. This is a promising test that (when used with the caution appropriate to its limitations) seems a valuable addition to the small number of "comprehensive" language tests available for children from ages 8-6 to 12-11.

REVIEWER'S REFERENCES

Hammill, D. D., Brown, V. L., Larsen, S. C., & Wiederholt, J. L. (1980). Test of Adolescent Language. Austin, TX: PRO-ED, Inc.
Anastasi, A. (1982). *Psychological testing* (5th ed.). New York: Macmillan Publishing.
Salvia, J., & Ysseldyke, J. E. (1987). *Assessment in special and remedial education* (4th ed.). Boston: Houghton Mifflin.

Sattler, J. M. (1988). *Assessment of children* (3rd ed.). San Diego: Jerome M. Sattler, Publisher.

Westby, C. (1988). Test review: Test of Language Development-2 Primary and Test of Language Development-2 Intermediate. *The Reading Teacher, 42*, 236-237.

Review of the Test of Language Development-2 Intermediate by KENNETH G. SHIPLEY, Professor of Speech-Language Pathology, California State University-Fresno, Fresno, CA:

The Test of Language Development-2 Intermediate (TOLD-2 Intermediate) is a very commonly used test of language development and is intended for children between 8-6 and 12-11 years of age. Its six subtests consist of the following:

1. Sentence Combining in which children combine two sentences into one (e.g., combining two sentences about finding a nickel and a dime into a sentence such as "We found a nickel and a dime").

2. Vocabulary where two words are judged as being *similar* (stern-firm), *opposite* (thin-thick), or *neither* similar nor opposite (tribute-rummage).

3. Word Ordering in which children put between three and seven words into one correctly ordered sentence. For example, the words *Bobby, who, his, walk, dog,* and *saw* are ordered into the sentence "Who saw Bobby walk his dog?" for a correct response.

4. Generals where children identify the common properties of three different words. For example, a pencil, pen, and typewriter are all *writing tools.*

5. Grammatic Comprehension in which the child identifies whether a sentence like "He drinked the cola" is correct or incorrect.

6. Malapropisms where a child identifies an incorrect word used within a stimulus sentence. For example, the word *poultry* is incorrect in the sentence "Shakespeare wrote beautiful poultry."

Each subtest ranges from 25 to 40 items that increase sequentially in difficulty. There are suggested starting points within each subtest. A ceiling is established with five consecutive failures (except Grammatic Comprehension, in which the ceiling is 3 errors in 5 items).

The manual reports that administering the entire test will take 30–60 minutes. The TOLD-2 is not timed, and individual subtests may be administered on different occasions. The test is only to be used with children within the intended age range and not with "students who are deaf or who do not speak English" (p. 7).

The authors caution that some formal training in test administration is advisable. Knowledge of statistical concepts; general test administration, scoring, and interpretation; and evaluation of mental abilities are suggested within the manual. This reviewer would note that a working knowledge of statistics; validity, reliability, and standardization; as well as test interpretation will be necessary to understand the test manual.

Some very attractive aspects to the TOLD-2 include the following:

1. It is relatively easy to administer and score.

2. Generally, children within the age level tested seem to enjoy the tasks, which simplifies the testing process.

3. It is not timed and individual subtests can be administered on separate occasions, which is very helpful with certain children.

4. There are individual subtest scores, as well as several overall language quotients. Although care is needed when making such interpretations, certain patterns of language deficiency can be seen with some children.

5. There is a relative paucity of language tests for this age group, so its use can be helpful within these ages.

Additional very positive aspects of the test and its manual include its discussion of the language model employed, examples of scoring, percentile rank data, "rules" for test administration, arguments against presenting language-age conversions, and the use of (and reference for) local norming.

It is also helpful to know that, if older or younger children are seen, there are somewhat similar tests that can be used for those age levels (Hammill, Brown, Larsen, & Wiederholt, 1987; Newcomer & Hammill, 1988). This effectively extends the range of children who can be tested with the same type of model.

Although there are these several attractive aspects of the test, certain cautions are also needed. These relate primarily to the language model used for testing and to the treatment of various standardization and statistical analyses of the test.

Although somewhat oversimplified here, the authors see their test as sampling two types of linguistic features (semantics and syntax) within two linguistic systems (listening and speaking). Individual subtests are then categorized by feature and system. For example, the Vocabulary subtest samples the listening system within the semantic area. These categorizations become the basis for content validity with the test. As the authors state (p. 36), the items within the subtests do relate to the underlying language constructs they have presumed within test construction. However, the careful examiner will want to exercise care in overinferring significance or generality of the results to these general language areas. For example, knowledge of vocabulary is only one aspect of semantics. Extended conclusions about a child's listening semantic abilities from this subtest might be unwarranted. From a practical standpoint, this underscores the authors' cautions that test results do not necessarily translate directly into daily educational (or treatment) goals or programs.

The TOLD-2 manual contains extensive discussions of the validity, reliability, and standardization results that underpin this test and its use. While certain discussions of the bases and actual findings within these matters are among the most thorough and well written found within this type of test, there are also some real inadequacies apparent with careful reading. The following are only four examples.

The standardization is based on data from 1,214 children from 21 states. By counting the acknowledgments, one can guess that there may have been about 190 testers. However, all the reader can really infer from the manual is that the testers were customers of or somehow affiliated with the test's publisher. The actual number of testers, as well as their professions and levels of training/experience, are not described.

Similar problems are encountered within the validity section. There are six aspects of construct validity described, two of which include age differentiation and group differentiation. There is a positive but rather weak series of correlations (ranging from .15 to .38 with a median of .205) between age and scores on the subtests. The authors' conclusion that age and test scores are related and, therefore, reinforce the construct validity of the TOLD-2 is accurate, but should be interpreted carefully.

A second type of construct validity is group differentiation (i.e., does performance on the test differ with children known or presumed to have language deficiencies?). To test this construct, the following information was reported. Fourteen children receiving language therapy in a rural Texas public school were tested and their standard scores were considerably below the standardization sample. This was viewed as further evidence of the test's construct validity. Given the imprecise and ambiguous level of subject description, this evidence would appear to be somewhat cursory.

Parts of the reliability information are also a little difficult to interpret. For example, stability (test-retest in this case) reliability is based on Fodness' (1987) study of 56 normal children in Michigan and on Hammill and Newcomer's (1982) report of reliability using a previous edition of the TOLD-2 with 30 normal fifth- and sixth-grade children in Texas. Although there is little reason to doubt the basic reliability of the TOLD-2, more precise information about the studies with the current edition would have been helpful.

In conclusion, the TOLD-2 can be a useful test for evaluating children within the targeted age population. It can be helpful in identifying overall language functioning and providing some preliminary insights into areas of relative strength and weakness, particularly when used in conjunction with other measures. However, the examiner is cautioned to analyze the test carefully prior to administration and when interpreting any results obtained. It is recommended that the test manual be carefully evaluated. A large amount of good data are presented; however, care is needed to interpret what some of the information really means and how strong a faith one should actually place in this information.

REVIEWER'S REFERENCES

Fodness, R. (1987). *Test-retest reliability of the Test of Language Development-Intermediate.* Unpublished master's thesis, Central Michigan University, Mt. Pleasant, MI.
Hammill, D. D., Brown, V. L., Larsen, S. C., & Wiederholt, J. L. (1987). Test of Adolescent Language—2. Austin, TX: PRO-ED, Inc.
Newcomer, P. L., & Hammill, D. D. (1988). Test of Language Development-2 Primary. Austin, TX: PRO-ED, Inc.

[437]

Test of Language Development-2 Primary.

Purpose: "To identify children who are significantly below their peers in language proficiency, to determine children's specific strengths and weaknesses in language skills, to document children's progress in language as a consequence of special intervention programs, and to measure language in research studies."
Population: Ages 4-0 to 8-11.
Publication Dates: 1977–88.
Acronym: TOLD-2 Primary.
Scores, 13: Subtests (Picture Vocabulary, Oral Vocabulary, Grammatic Understanding, Sentence Imitation, Grammatic Completion, Word Discrimination, Word Articulation), Composites (Spoken Language, Listening, Speaking, Semantics, Syntax, Phonology).
Administration: Individual.
Parts, 2: Subtests, Composites.
Price Data, 1989: $94 per complete kit including examiner's manual ('88, 84 pages), picture plates ('88, 87 pages), and 50 record forms; $32 per 50 record forms; $41 per picture plates; $24 per examiner's manual; $69 per computer scoring system (Apple or IBM).
Time: (30–60) minutes.
Comments: Revision of Test of Language Development Primary; intermediate edition also available; orally administered; examiners need some formal training in assessment.
Authors: Phyllis L. Newcomer and Donald D. Hammill.
Publisher: PRO-ED, Inc.

TEST REFERENCES

1. Reynolds, C. R. (1983). Some new and some unusual psychological and educational measures: Description and evaluation. *School Psychology Review, 12,* 481-488.
2. Hess, C. W., Ritchie, K. P., & Landry, R. G. (1984). The type-token ratio and vocabulary performance. *Psychological Reports, 55,* 51-57.
3. Perozzi, J. A. (1985). A pilot study of language facilitation for bilingual, language-handicapped children: Theoretical and intervention implications. *Journal of Speech and Hearing Disorders, 50,* 403-406.
4. Beitchman, J. H., Nair, R., Clegg, M., & Patel, P. G. (1986). Prevalence of speech and language disorders in 5-year-old kindergarten children in the Ottawa-Carleton region. *Journal of Speech and Hearing Disorders, 51,* 98-110.
5. Brinton, B., Fujiki, M., Winkler, E., & Loeb, D. F. (1986). Responses to requests for clarification in linguistically normal and language-impaired children. *Journal of Speech and Hearing Disorders, 51,* 370-378.
6. Davis, J. M., Elfenbein, J., Schum, R., & Bentler, R. A. (1986). Effects of mild and moderate hearing impairments on language, educational, and psychosocial behavior of children. *Journal of Speech and Hearing Disorders, 51,* 53-62.

7. Grossman, F. M. (1986). Statistical interpretation of intraindividual variability on the Test of Language Development—Primary. *Perceptual and Motor Skills, 63,* 329-330.

8. Kamhi, A. G., & Catts, H. W. (1986). Toward an understanding of developmental language and reading disorders. *Journal of Speech and Hearing Disorders, 51,* 337-347.

9. Lieberman, R. J., & Michael, A. (1986). Content relevance and content coverage in tests of grammatical ability. *Journal of Speech and Hearing Disorders, 51,* 71-81.

10. Roth, F. P., & Spekman, N. J. (1986). Narrative discourse: Spontaneously generated stories of learning-disabled and normally achieving students. *Journal of Speech and Hearing Disorders, 51,* 8-23.

11. Friend, T. J., & Channell, R. W. (1987). A comparison of two measures of receptive vocabulary. *Language, Speech, and Hearing Services in Schools, 18,* 231-237.

12. Nelson, L. K., Kamhi, A. G., & Apel, K. (1987). Cognitive strengths and weaknesses in language-impaired children: One more look. *Journal of Speech and Hearing Disorders, 52,* 36-43.

13. Rather, N. B., & Sih, C. C. (1987). Effects of gradual increases in sentence length and complexity on children's dysfluency. *Journal of Speech and Hearing Disorders, 52,* 278-287.

14. Brinton, B., Fujiki, M., & Sonnenberg, E. A. (1988). Responses to requests for clarification by linguistically normal and language-impaired children in conversation. *Journal of Speech and Hearing Disorders, 53,* 383-391.

15. Mallard, A. R., & Westbrook, J. B. (1988). Variables affecting stuttering therapy in school settings. *Language, Speech, and Hearing Services in Schools, 19,* 362-370.

16. Weismer, S. E., & Murray-Branch, J. (1989). Modeling versus modeling plus evoked production training: A comparison of two language intervention methods. *Journal of Speech and Hearing Disorders, 54,* 269-281.

17. Howell, K. K., Harrison, T. E., Stanford, L. D., Zahn, B. H., & Bracken, B. A. (1990). An empirical evaluation of three preschool language curricula. *Psychology in the Schools, 27,* 296-302.

18. Slavin, R. E., Madden, N. A., Karweit, N. L., Livermon, B. J., & Dolan, L. (1990). Success for all: First-year outcomes of a comprehensive plan for reforming urban education. *American Educational Research Journal, 27,* 255-278.

19. Stern, L. M., Walker, M. K., Sawyer, M. G., Oades, R. D., Badcock, N. R., & Spence, J. G. (1990). A controlled crossover trial of fenfluramine in autism. *Journal of Child Psychology and Psychiatry, 31,* 569-585.

20. Fodness, R. W., McNeilly, J., & Bradley-Johnson, S. (1991). Test-retest reliability of the Test of Language Development—2: Primary and Test of Language Development—2: Intermediate. *Journal of School Psychology, 29,* 161-165.

Review of the Test of Language Development-2 Primary by LINDA CROCKER, Professor in Foundations of Education, University of Florida, Gainesville, FL:

The Test of Language Development-2 Primary (TOLD-2) was developed for use in identifying English-speaking children who may be deficient in language proficiency and for diagnosing specific strengths and weaknesses in language development. The test is not intended for use with the hearing impaired or nonnative English speakers. The subscales measure various elements of phonology, syntax, and semantics; additional composite scores are created by adding across several subscale scores that involve receptive and expressive language skills respectively.

The time required to administer the Primary test may vary from 30 to 60 minutes. Some formal training in individual assessment techniques is recommended for test administrators. There is no need to establish a basal level; the ceiling on all subtests is reached when the examinee misses five items contiguously. The scoring instructions in the manual are clear, but in some cases (i.e., Oral Vocabulary), there is a rather fine distinction between acceptable and unacceptable responses. It is

not clear whether these distinctions were based on arbitrary judgements or upon empirical responses of more proficient and less proficient examinees.

Subtest raw scores may be converted to percentile ranks and standard scores. Quotients are available for composite scores. Normative scores for some of the subtests were based on data from examinees tested in 1976, 1981, and 1987. This pooling of data from earlier normings is questionable, even though the authors report that the means from the separate samples were nearly identical.

Internal consistency estimates, based on Cronbach's alpha, were calculated for 50 students at each age level from 4 to 8 years of age. These estimates ranged in the .80s and .90s for the separate subtests and were all in the .90s for the composites. Test-retest reliability coefficients, ranging from .74 to .99, were obtained from two separate studies with 2-week and 5-day intervals.

Content validity evidence was garnered by having a panel of 50 experts read descriptions of the five TOLD-2 subtests according to the degree to which they measure semantics or syntax and listening or speaking skills. Although these experts indicated that subtests were consistent with the test developer's conceptualization, it is important to recognize that these experts were not reviewing the actual items and scoring instructions.

Evidence of criterion-related validity is offered in the form of subtest correlations with a variety of criteria (e.g., the Wechsler Intelligence Scale for Children [WISC] Vocabulary, the Peabody Picture Vocabulary Test, and the Auditory Discrimination Test). The reported correlations ranged from .54 to .86, but these values were corrected for attenuation for unreliability in the tests. These data, however, seem more relevant to the construct validity of the test scores than to criterion-related validity per se.

Multiple approaches to establishing construct validity are described in the test manual. First, means on all subtests increased progressively for children in the standardization sample from age 4 to 8. In addition, positive correlations of subtest scores with age were reported for several other samples. Second, subtest intercorrelations ranged from .26 to .66, with most values in the .40s and .50s. (Note that these were not corrected for attenuation due to unreliability.) Third, correlations with several criteria were determined for various samples as well as correlations with scores on measures of reading, writing, school readiness, and overall achievement. Finally, when factor analysis was applied to the TOLD-2 subtests alone, they loaded on one general factor. In combination with criterion tests, however, results from both a two-factor and seven-factor solution were presented. The authors argued in favor of the seven-factor solution; but the two-factor solution was more consistent with conventional psychometric standards, although less supportive of the test authors' position.

In summary, from this evidence it appears that the TOLD-2 shares some commonality with verbal intelligence tests, auditory discrimination tests, articulation tests, and vocabulary tests as well as with achievement in school subjects requiring verbal aptitude. Its subtests and composite scores have adequate reliability. It is, however, less clear whether the specific construct of language development measured by the TOLD-2 is distinct from verbal aptitude measured by intelligence tests. In addition, at this point, the body of empirical evidence is relatively weak for interpreting the separate subtest scores for diagnostic purposes.

Review of the Test of Language Development-2 Primary by CAROL E. WESTBY, Senior Research Associate, Developmental Disabilities, University of New Mexico, Albuquerque, NM:

According to the authors, the Test of Language Development-2 (TOLD-2) uses a 2-dimensional linguistic model involving linguistic systems (Listening and Speaking) and linguistic features (Phonology, Syntax, and Semantics). The seven subtests of the TOLD-2 sample each component of the model. The TOLD-2 Primary assesses semantic abilities by having the child define words and point to pictures that best represent words spoken by the examiner. Syntactic abilities are assessed by having the child repeat verbatim sentences of increasing complexity, complete sentences begun by the examiner, and select one of three pictures that best represents a sentence spoken by the examiner. Phonology is assessed by the child's production when labeling pictures and the child's judgement of whether two words spoken by the examiner are the same or different. The content of each subtest is controlled so as to assess isolated elements of syntactic, semantic, and phonological knowledge, uninfluenced as much as possible by the other elements. Language is not, however, sequences of independent elements. Consequently, the ecological validity of such discrete point testing is questionable.

The construct validity (theoretical basis) of the TOLD-2 Primary is also weak. The authors state that they have incorporated contributions of a number of linguists and psycholinguists. Although they cite names, they do not discuss the specific ideas they have used and how they have used them. They have provided only minimal support from the literature to justify their choice of subtests and subtest items. Their rationale for the majority of subtests is that these types of subtests have been used on other language tests.

The examiner's manual provides useful information relevant to all standardized testing—suggestions for when and how to "test the limits," how to share the test results with others, guidelines for establishing local norms, and cautions when interpreting tests. Specific scripts to use in the administration of each subtest are given. The length and the sentence complexity of many of these scripts may make understanding the test instructions more difficult than the actual test items for some students. A number of items in the phonological and syntactic subtests may be affected by nonstandard dialect, but the authors do not address how such responses should be scored. Thorough explanations on how to calculate and interpret the various scores (raw scores, percentiles, subtest standard scores, and composite quotients) are given. Much to the authors' credit, they do not give language-age-equivalent scores and they explain why use of age equivalencies is inappropriate.

The standardization sample of 2,436 students reflects an excellent representation of geographic area, sex, race, and occupation of parents. The test user should be cautious, however. A broad population sample does not guarantee the valid use of a test with diverse groups. Vaughn-Cooke (1983) noted that when all possible population subgroups are included in test samples, the resulting norms reflect the true performance of no one. Consequently, the norms may be too high for students in one area and too low for students in another area.

Newcomer and Hammill are thorough in their discussion of the TOLD-2's standard error of measurement, internal consistency, and stability reliability, and they give more attention to the issue of validity than do most test authors. Content validity was evaluated by having professionals rate the degree to which each of the subtests measures the test dimensions—Listening and Speaking, and Phonology, Syntax, and Semantics. Criterion-related validity was determined by correlating it with a number of traditional discrete-point language tests used to assess articulation, syntax, and semantics. According to Newcomer and Hammill, construct validity includes the concepts that the subtests should be related to chronological age, should be highly correlated because they all measure aspects of spoken language, should correlate well with the scores of other tests of academic achievement, and should differentiate between groups of children known to be normal in spoken language and those known to be poor in spoken language. These components are part of construct validity, but more importantly, construct validity should refer to the theoretical relevance of a test. It is unfortunate that Hammill and Newcomer do not address the issue of ecological validity—do the test items represent anything that the child actually does with language in the real world?

The TOLD-2 Primary is well designed in terms of meeting established psychometric criteria for reliability and criterion-related validity, but in the light of current knowledge on language development and assessment, it does not have good construct and ecological validity. The TOLD-2 does not assess language as it is used in the real world. A paradigm shift has occurred in recent years in language assessment—from discrete-point to integrative testing; the TOLD represents the old paradigm. Its usefulness for diagnosing and understanding the nature of children's language disabilities is limited.

REVIEWER'S REFERENCE

Vaughn-Cooke, F. (1983). Improving language assessment in minority children. *ASHA, 25*, 29-34.

[438]

Test of Legible Handwriting.
Purpose: Assesses handwriting legibility.
Population: Ages 7.6–17.11.
Publication Date: 1989.
Acronym: TOLH.
Scores: 6 writing sample scores: Creative Essay, Biographical Sketch, Correspondence, Report, Previous Work Sample, Legibility Quotient.
Administration: Group.
Price Data, 1989: $39 per complete kit including examiner's manual (62 pages) and 50 profile/scoring forms; $21 per 50 profile/scoring forms; $20 per examiner's manual.
Time: 15(20) minutes per writing sample.
Authors: Stephen C. Larsen and Donald D. Hammill.
Publisher: PRO-ED, Inc.

Review of the Test of Legible Handwriting by GREGORY J. CIZEK, *Assistant Professor of Educational Research and Measurement, University of Toledo, Toledo, OH:*

The authors of the Test of Legible Handwriting (TOLH) build a strong case for the need for handwriting assessment. They note that "of all school subjects, handwriting typically receives the least attention and generally is the most poorly taught." They also comment that "an individual's failure to learn to write legibly may adversely affect academic success and have implications for later occupational and social success."

However, despite the perceived importance of the skill, handwriting assessment apparently occurs infrequently. Further, the authors note that "at present, no norm-referenced, nationally standardized tests of handwriting are available that permit the valid and reliable assessment of a person's [handwriting] ability." It is suggested that one reason handwriting assessment and research into handwriting may be lagging is that instruments with demonstrated reliability and validity have been unavailable. The TOLH was put forth to address these critical needs in the area of handwriting assessment.

ADMINISTRATION AND SCORING. The TOLH is easily administered to students in grades 2 through 12. The authors recommend that examiners who administer the test have "formal training in assessment," a "basic understanding of testing statistics," and "specific information about educational evaluation." It is doubtful that such expertise is truly necessary to administer the TOLH, although it may be helpful. Those characteristics certainly should be required of anyone interpreting the test results, as the authors note.

Administration of the TOLH is accomplished by obtaining a sample (or samples) of the student's handwriting. The sample can be an extant piece of writing or can be elicited through use of one of the two picture prompts provided. Clear directions are provided for use with the picture prompts. It should be noted that students are *not* informed they are being evaluated for handwriting legibility. Therefore, a "usual" handwriting sample is obtained, rather than one that reflects maximum performance. TOLH test results should be interpreted in this light.

Scoring of the TOLH is accomplished by matching the student's writing sample to one of three basic scoring protocols—one for right-slant or perpendicular cursive, one for left-slant cursive, and one for manuscript or modified manuscript handwriting. Within each of the three protocols are four graded writing guides. A raw score from 1 to 9 results from matching the student's writing sample as closely as possible to one of the guides. When matching writing samples to the guides, scorers are instructed to "rate the sample as holistically as possible" and to "disregard specific deficits such as spacing, letter formation, inconsistent slant, and so forth."

INTERPRETATION. Several scores can be obtained from the TOLH. The authors warn that "raw scores have no clinical, instructional, or diagnostic value." However, percentile ranks, standard scores, grade-equivalent scores, and a "legibility quotient" are provided, along with a list of descriptors from "very poor" to "very superior" corresponding to the range of standard scores. Appropriate guidelines for interpreting these scores are also given. Admirably, a section of the TOLH is also devoted to "Cautions in Interpreting Test Scores" and information regarding sources of measurement error is provided.

NORMS. The TOLH was normed in 1987 using 1,723 students, ages 7 to 17, from 19 states. Information regarding how the sample was obtained is provided, as are demographic characteristics of the standardization sample. Overall, the sample appears to be highly appropriate and nationally representative.

RELIABILITY. The authors report several indices to describe the reliability of scores on the TOLH. The average index of internal consistency (coefficient Alpha) across four age ranges is reported to be .86. An average test-retest correlation of .90 is also reported. An adjusted test-retest correlation to isolate the temporal stability of the TOLH is reported as .97.

Perhaps the most important aspect of reliability is the extent to which a student's writing sample receives consistent scores across raters. To investigate this, two trained raters each scored 70 writing samples and obtained an interrater reliability coefficient of .95.

All of the reliability evidence presented regarding the TOLH appears impressive. Users of the TOLH should be cautioned, however, about being overly impressed by the high reliability indices. The manual for the TOLH errs in not providing the detailed training procedures required for a user to actually obtain the reported degree of reliability. For example, it is recommended that users of the TOLH "become thoroughly familiar with the contents of [the] test manual" and "practice scoring the sample stories." These instructions seem inadequate.

Also conspicuously absent is strong advice to the user to gather multiple writing samples and to consider having multiple raters assign scores to a writing sample. It has long been known that implementing these procedures can greatly reduce error variance associated with ratings of handwriting (Feldt, 1962). Such an omission is surprising in light of the fact that the TOLH allows for the various scores reported to be based on the combination of scores from as many as five writing samples.

VALIDITY. The manual for the TOLH includes a somewhat weak attempt to define the construct of "legible handwriting." However, the rather circular definition provided may be about as good as construct definition gets in the area of handwriting; it has often been noted by researchers in the area that "the term [legibility] resists precise definition" (Graham, 1986, p. 64).

Several kinds of validity evidence are provided for the TOLH. The authors' claims regarding the content validity of the TOLH are moderately supported. It is noted that factors affecting legibility were incorporated into the scoring guides. However, the use of nonstructured responses to picture prompts means that critical elements of legibility (e.g., letter formation) may not be sampled.

Some evidence for construct validity is also reported. It is reported that mean scores on the TOLH across grade levels differed significantly, supporting the notion that handwriting skill generally increases with age. Comparison of TOLH scores with scores on the Test of Written Language—2 (TOWL-2; 444) by Hammill and Larsen (1988) showed small correlations with other written language skills such as spelling and style. Finally, a group of 30 students with poor handwriting as judged by their teachers were administered the TOLH. Their mean score on the TOLH was significantly below average. Similar analyses for samples with average and superior handwriting are not reported.

Moderate evidence is offered to substantiate a claim of high criterion-related validity. The coefficient of .92 was obtained by correlating the ratings (1 to 5) of experienced teachers for 30 student handwriting samples with TOLH scores (1 to 9) for the same samples. It is somewhat unsurprising that the two similar measures correlated highly. Perhaps, for subsequent versions of the TOLH, expanded research into its criterion-related validity will be reported.

OTHER FEATURES. The TOLH contains several very helpful features. As previously mentioned, an Appendix to the TOLH manual contains several writing samples for test administrators' practice use. Another excellent characteristic is an entire chapter of the manual devoted to assessing and remediating handwriting problems. The authors are to be commended for recognizing the important link between assessment and instruction.

Finally, although the TOLH is touted as "an ecological approach to holistic [handwriting] assessment," the authors recognize the importance of identifying specific handwriting deficiencies. A diagnostic scoring form is provided for use with student writing samples elicited using the TOLH picture prompts. The diagnostic form allows the user to assess the formation of individual letters, alignment, spacing, slant, letter size, rate, and other characteristics. Results from this checklist can be translated into specific remediation strategies.

SUMMARY. The TOLH is used to obtain and evaluate student handwriting samples for legibility. The test does not attempt to provide criterion-referenced information, that is, the level of handwriting considered to be perfect, worst, or acceptable. Instead, the TOLH provides norm-referenced information about a student's handwriting legibility. The instrument is extremely easy to administer, the scoring guides are straightforward, and the tables used to obtain derived scores are reasonably easy to use with some practice.

Norms for the TOLH appear to have been recently and rigorously developed. The reliability data provided indicate that the instrument is quite reliable, although the user should be cautioned that such high reliability indices will probably not be realized in less controlled situations. The manual for the TOLH fails to provide users with detailed training procedures necessary to obtain reliable scores.

The TOLH manual presents evidence for several aspects of validity. Although the validity evidence and research presented are only weak to moderate, the authors commendably inform the user about proper interpretations and uses of TOLH scores.

The TOLH should fill the need for a reliable, standardized, norm-referenced assessment of handwriting legibility. In addition to filling this need, it also provides a means of identifying specific handwriting deficiencies and, admirably, provides users with guidance for remediation.

REVIEWER'S REFERENCES

Feldt, L. S. (1962). The reliability of measures of handwriting quality. *Journal of Educational Psychology, 53,* 288-292.

Graham, S. (1986). A review of handwriting scales and factors that contribute to variability in handwriting scores. *Journal of School Psychology, 24,* 63-71.

Hammill, D. D., & Larsen, S. C. (1988). Test of Written Language—2. Austin, TX: PRO-ED, Inc.

Review of the Test of Legible Handwriting by STEVE GRAHAM, *Associate Professor of Special Education, University of Maryland, College Park, MD:*

The Test of Legible Handwriting (TOLH) was developed to measure the readability of children's and adolescents' handwriting, grades 2 through 12. According to the authors, this norm-referenced test can be used to identify students who have handwriting problems, to pinpoint students' specific strengths and weaknesses in penmanship, and to document students' progress in developing handwriting skills. The authors of the test also indicate that it is a suitable tool for use in research involving penmanship.

The TOLH is administered individually by collecting between one and five handwriting samples from the target student. One sample is collected by asking the student to write a story in response to a picture (either a prehistoric or a futuristic space picture) contained in the accompanying test protocol. The other samples include a previous specimen of the student's handwriting taken from actual schoolwork, as well as a biographical sketch, a correspondence (e.g., personal or business letter), and a report taken under more controlled conditions.

Each of the obtained handwriting samples is scored by matching the student's specimen as closely as possible to a set of graded samples with scores ranging from 1 to 9. Three different sets of graded samples are available: one for manuscript writing, another for cursive writing that is either perpendicular or slanted to the right, and a final scale for cursive writing that slants left. Although the test developers do not provide a rationale for devising two separate scales for cursive writing, there is some evidence to suggest that reliability in handwriting assessment can be increased when the slant of students' handwriting is taken into consideration (Herrick & Erlebacher, 1963).

The raw scores obtained for each of the handwriting specimens are converted to standard scores and percentile ranks. If more than one handwriting specimen is collected, a legibility quotient ($M = 100$, $SD = 15$) is also computed. The authors should be commended for not including tables for grade- or age-equivalent scores as part of the test. They do, however, provide examiners with a formula for computing grade-equivalent scores, but they appropriately caution against their use.

In addition to the general measure of legibility obtained for the student's handwriting sample(s), the test protocol includes a section for completing an informal analysis of handwriting errors. Two checklists are provided, one for manuscript and one for cursive. Both checklists contain three sections: errors in the formation of individual letters, difficulties in spatial relationships (e.g., alignment, uniformity of slant, spacing, and so forth), and rate of writing. The inclusion of the "rate of writing" section is questionable, because the method used to collect student specimens is influenced not only by handwriting speed but by factors involved in planning the written product. A more appropriate assessment would involve measuring the speed at which a familiar selection is copied.

The TOLH was standardized on 1,723 students ranging in age from 7 to 17 years of age. Although the sample is similar to national norms on a number of variables such as sex, race, ethnicity, and residence, data on the normative sample are incompletely reported. For example, no information on the SES or handedness of the students in the normative sample is provided. The description of procedures for selecting students is also vague. One means of selecting students, for instance, involved asking previous purchasers of PRO-ED tests (PRO-ED, Inc. publishes the TOLH) to administer the TOLH to 20 or 30 children in their area.

The developers of the TOLH do not present a strong or convincing case regarding the reliability and validity of the instrument. Interscorer reliability of the test was established by having two members of the "PRO-ED research department" independently score the same 70 handwriting specimens. The obtained reliability coefficient was high (.95), but it is unlikely that normal users of the scale would obtain an equivalent level of reliability (see Graham, 1986; and Graham, Boyer-Schick, & Tippets, 1989 for evidence regarding this point). Similarly, the data the authors present to support the validity of the instrument are quite meager; only a few studies were reported and they typically involved small numbers of subjects or handwriting samples. The data that are presented provide little insight into what the test actually measures; for example, does it measure general legibility or does a single element such as letter formation or neatness primarily account for the variability in students' scores on the test?

It should also be noted the TOLH does not include samples of the least able and best possible handwriting. Moreover, a scale that measures only nine gross levels is probably not sufficiently precise to monitor gradual improvement; it is probably best used as a general gauge of handwriting competence. The authors, however, do provide valuable suggestions in the test manual concerning additional handwriting assessment and instruction. They further include eight practice samples for examiners to score. Surprisingly, a suggested legibility score for each individual sample is not provided.

In summary, two noteworthy aspects of the TOLH include the inclusion of separate scoring scales for different types of writing and the emphasis on the collection of multiple samples of students' penmanship. Nonetheless, the TOLH appears to be best suited as a screening device for identifying students in need of instructional assistance. Even this recommendation must be tempered, though, because the reliability and validity of the instrument have yet to be adequately established.

REVIEWER'S REFERENCES

Herrick, V., & Erlebacher, A. (1963). The evaluation of legibility in handwriting. In V. Herrick (Ed.), *New horizons for research in handwriting* (pp. 207-236). Madison: University of Wisconsin Press.
Graham, S. (1986). A review of handwriting scales and factors that contribute to variability in handwriting scores. *Journal of School Psychology, 24*, 63-71.
Graham, S., Boyer-Shick, K., & Tippets, E. (1989). The validity of the handwriting scale from the Test of Written Language. *Journal of Educational Research, 82*, 166-171.

[439]
Test of Nonverbal Intelligence, Second Edition.

Purpose: "A language-free measure of abstract/figural problem solving."
Population: Ages 5-0 to 85-11.
Publication Dates: 1982–90.
Acronym: TONI-2.
Scores: Total score only.
Administration: Individual.
Forms, 2: A, B.
Price Data, 1991: $119 per complete kit; $43 per picture book; $26 per 50 answer booklets (specify form); $28 per manual ('90, 65 pages).
Time: (15–30) minutes.
Comments: May be administered to small groups by an experienced examiner.
Authors: Linda Brown, Rita J. Sherbenou, and Susan K. Johnsen.
Publisher: PRO-ED, Inc.
Cross References: For reviews by Philip M. Clark and Samuel T. Mayo, see 9:1266.

TEST REFERENCES

1. Shelly, M. H. (1985). Test of Nonverbal Intelligence. *Journal of Reading, 28*, 422-425.
2. Kamhi, A. G., & Catts, H. W. (1986). Toward an understanding of developmental language and reading disorders. *Journal of Speech and Hearing Disorders, 51*, 337-347.
3. Vance, B. (1988). Concurrent validity of The Quick Test, the Test of Nonverbal Intelligence, and the WISC-R for a sample of special education students. *Psychological Reports, 62*, 443-446.
4. Parmar, R. S. (1989). Cross-cultural transfer of non-verbal intelligence tests: An (in)validation study. *British Journal of Educational Psychology, 59*, 379-388.
5. McGhee, R. L., & Lieberman, L. R. (1990). Test-retest reliability of the Test of Nonverbal Intelligence (TONI). *Journal of School Psychology, 28*, 351-353.
6. Whorton, J. E., & Morgan, R. L. (1990). Comparison of the Test of Nonverbal Intelligence and Wechsler Intelligence Scale for Children—Revised in rural Native American and white children. *Perceptual and Motor Skills, 70*, 12-14.
7. Frederick, R. I., & Foster, H. G. (1991). Multiple measures of malingering on a forced-choice test of cognitive ability. *Psychological Assessment, 3*, 596-602.
8. Miller, S. A., Manhal, M., & Mee, L. L. (1991). Parental beliefs, parental accuracy, and children's cognitive performance: A search for causal relations. *Developmental Psychology, 27*, 267-276.
9. Valliant, P. M., & Antonowicz, D. H. (1991). Cognitive behaviour therapy and social skills training improves personality and cognition in incarcerated offenders. *Psychological Reports, 68*, 27-33.

Review of the Test of Nonverbal Intelligence, Second Edition by KEVIN R. MURPHY, Professor of Psychology, Colorado State University, Fort Collins, CO:

The Test of Nonverbal Intelligence, Second Edition (TONI-2) is designed to provide a language-free method of assessing general intelligence. This test consists of a series of abstract/figural problem-solving items similar to those found on tests such as the Ravens Progressive Matrices (9:1007), and is designed for nonverbal administration. The test administrator delivers instructions by gesture and pantomime, and the examinee responds by pointing to or otherwise indicating the correct response alternative. This culture-reduced test is appropriate for both children and adults, and is optimal for assessing individuals with poor or impaired linguistic skills, different linguistic backgrounds, or impaired motor skills. For example, the manual suggests this test is useful for assessing aphasics, non-English speakers, individuals who are hearing impaired, or individuals who have suffered a variety of severe neurological traumas. This test is not designed to replace broad-based intelligence tests, but rather to provide an alternative method of assessment when language or motor difficulties make it difficult to reliably administer standard tests.

There is no time limit for the TONI-2, although it usually can be administered in 15 minutes. Like many other intelligence tests, the TONI-2 is partially adaptive, in the sense that individuals respond to a subset of items that are appropriately difficult. The test manual gives a clear description of the procedures for determining basal and ceiling levels. Test items range widely in difficulty, and it is unlikely that most examinees will respond to all test items.

This test has several appealing features. For example, the test manual strongly encourages comparing scores on the TONI-2 with scores on other ability and achievement tests. The test form has a place for recording the results of up to five additional tests, and for constructing a profile of scores. The test form also requires the examiner to consider explicitly both environmental conditions (e.g., noise) and respondent conditions (e.g., energy level, understanding of the test) that might be relevant in interpreting test scores.

The scoring of this test is simple and quick, and

test scores are presented in terms of both percentile ranks and deviation quotients (the test manual avoids the term IQ), with a mean of 100 and a standard deviation of 15. Test norms are based on a large and apparently representative sample that is described clearly in the manual.

The test manual presents evidence of both reliability and validity. Item-total correlations are generally large, and coefficient alpha exceeds .90 for most ages. Alternative-form reliabilities are somewhat smaller, but they exceed .80 for all ages. There is some evidence of temporal stability, although this is based on small samples. Moderate to high correlations with other measures of ability (e.g., the Wechsler Intelligence Scale for Children—Revised [WISC-R]) and achievement are presented as evidence of criterion-related validity, and additional evidence of construct validity (e.g., correlations between age and scores, score differences in groups known to differ in general intelligence, factor analyses) is presented. Because this test is designed for use with special populations, it is critical to demonstrate reliability and validity in these populations, and the test manual does just that. Evidence from several studies of learning disabled, retarded, non-English-speaking, and neurologically impaired populations document the reliability and validity of the TONI-2 as a tool for assessing members of these groups.

An earlier version of this test was reviewed by Clark (1985) and Mayo (1985). These reviews were generally positive, but called for more empirical evidence of criterion-related validity, better description of the normative samples, and better evidence of the appropriateness of this test for special populations. The TONI-2 has, in my opinion, addressed all of these criticisms well. The test manual is a model of clarity and completeness. I was especially glad to see clear statements, repeated several times in the manual, of the purpose of the test, and its relationship to other tests. There are several populations that are difficult to assess with most tests of general intelligence, and the TONI-2 fills this niche nicely. It is not designed to replace tests such as the WISC-R or the Kaufman Assessment Battery for Children (K-ABC), but rather provides a well-validated method for assessing special populations whose language or motor difficulties make it difficult for them to respond adequately to this type of test. I recommend the TONI-2 as a potentially useful test, especially for psychologists and educators who deal with these populations.

My only real criticism of the test is that the manual suggests that it can be administered to small groups. Although this might be possible in a few cases, the difficulties in accurately assessing individuals with linguistic or motor impairments (or individuals who speak little or no English) suggest to me that individual administration is almost always preferable, and that group administration would run the risk of faulty assessments.

REVIEWER'S REFERENCES

Clark, P. M. (1985). [Review of the Test of Nonverbal Intelligence.] In J. V. Mitchell, Jr. (Ed.), *The ninth mental measurements yearbook* (pp. 1580-1581). Lincoln, NE: Buros Institute of Mental Measurements.
Mayo, S. T. (1985). [Review of the Test of Nonverbal Intelligence.] In J. V. Mitchell, Jr. (Ed.), *The ninth mental measurements yearbook* (pp. 1581-1583). Lincoln, NE: Buros Institute of Mental Measurements.

Review of the Test of Nonverbal Intelligence, Second Edition by T. STEUART WATSON, Assistant Professor of Educational Psychology, Mississippi State University, Starkville, MS:

The Test of Nonverbal Intelligence, Second Edition (TONI-2) is a revised version of the original 1982 TONI. The purpose of the instrument, its basic format, and theoretical underpinnings have not changed since development of the TONI.

Briefly, the TONI-2 is intended to provide a "culture-reduced," language-free, and motor-reduced measure of cognitive functioning. The test consists of abstract items that require nonverbal reasoning and problem solving. Hence, perhaps a more appropriate and accurate name for this test would be the Test of Nonverbal Problem Solving.

A basic assumption of this and other similar tests is that cognitive ability can be easily partitioned into verbal and nonverbal tasks. Furthermore, within each category (i.e., verbal and nonverbal) there are specific abilities that are within the exclusive domain of that category. To claim that a test is language-free because it can be administered in a nonverbal format and the response is nonverbal is erroneous. Although such a test may have face validity, does the examiner know that the examinee did not rely on internal or silent language to solve a problem?

ADMINISTRATION AND SCORING. General administration, basal and ceiling rules, and scoring are essentially the same as the TONI. The administration and scoring section of the examiner's manual contains no noticeable improvements from the original. Many of the criticisms from the TONI relative to this section remain. The clarity of the standardization procedures could be enhanced, particularly on establishing rapport, explaining the purpose and use of the test to the examinee, and the pantomime instructions.

Because this test is nonverbal, the authors should have given greater attention to the section on using pantomime instructions. For example, how would the examiner know when the examinee did not understand the task? If failure of all six training items was an indication, was it because the subject did not know the answer or because the task was unclear? This dilemma may be especially problematic for children who do not understand the abstract concepts of "same" and "different." It would be extremely helpful if the authors presented some alternative strategies to use for examinees who have considerable difficulty comprehending the nature of the task.

Although the authors claim the test may be administered to groups of no more than five subjects, it seems that group administration may compound some of the problems noted in the administration procedures. In all likelihood, an experienced examiner would probably not attempt to test more than one person at a time using this instrument.

The scoring protocol of the TONI-2 is simple and easy to follow. Starting points for each age range are listed beside the appropriate item. However, the correct answer is already circled on the scoring form, which may be somewhat confusing. The examiner is supposed to make an X over the examinee's response and then count the number of Xs that are on the circles. A scoring template to place over the scoring form could make scoring a little easier.

ITEM CONTENT. Ten items, five for each form, were added to the upper end of the TONI. Thus, the new items were tested only on those examinees 14.6–85.0 years of age. The revision of the TONI is only applicable for subjects in this age range. For younger subjects, there has been no change in item content. Addition of items to these age ranges (14.6–85.0) addresses the criticism of the TONI that gifted examinees may never reach a true ceiling.

The 10 additional items were derived from a potential pool of 23 that were considered for addition. Items that were included on the TONI-2 were selected based on item discrimination and item difficulty analyses. Items were retained if their discrimination coefficients ranged from .30 to .80 across nine age intervals. These coefficients indicate that the TONI-2 is internally consistent and that the items are measuring a similar construct.

Another barometer used to retain items was item difficulty, or the percentage of examinees who pass a given item. The authors used a range of 15% to 85% with an average of 50%. Item difficulty is closely related to item discrimination in that an item that is too easy or too hard will not successfully discriminate between those who score high or low on the overall test. All of the additional items fell within the 15–85% range of item difficulty across the nine age intervals.

Appropriately, the authors explain how items for the TONI were developed. In the text and accompanying tables, however, statistical information is presented for the combined original 100 items plus the 10 new items. This is extremely confusing for the reader who is attempting to determine the coefficients and percentages for each item at the nine age intervals. The tables are poorly labeled and it is not immediately clear, unless one reads the text,

which age ranges were affected by additional items. Even the text is confusing by presenting information for both versions of the TONI within the same paragraph.

STANDARDIZATION. Overall, the sample for the TONI-2 appears adequate. The total N has increased from 1,929 to 2,764. The degree of specificity provided for stratification of the normative sample has not improved since the original TONI. A table is provided that lists the percentage of subjects along eight demographic dimensions. One cannot determine, however, how many of the 7-year-olds were white females living in the rural South with parents who have completed high school. It would also be helpful to know how many aphasic, deaf, severely mentally retarded, language disordered, and non-English-speaking persons were included in the normative sample. This type of information is crucial for a test that purports to be designed for these special populations.

A minor point of contention is the authors' use of outdated terms to describe race (e.g., Caucasoid, Negroid, Mongoloid). The information provided in the Predominant Race category overlaps with Ethnicity, which should be used instead of race classifications. The authors also state that the primary language spoken in the home is indicated in the table of demographic information. Unless they are equating primary language and ethnicity, there is no such information listed.

RELIABILITY. Reliability for the TONI-2 is based on split-half Alpha, immediate test-retest with alternate forms, and delayed test-retest with alternate forms coefficients. Data are also presented on reliability studies with special populations.

Adequate split-half and immediate test-retest reliability was demonstrated for each of the age ranges. Average split-half coefficients were .95 for Form A and .96 for Form B. The mean coefficient for immediate test-retest was .86. Delayed test-retest reliability was estimated at .85, but only 39 pairs of data were used to compute this coefficient.

Data for reliability on 12 special populations were derived from six studies. Although some populations have excellent sample sizes (e.g., Spanish speaking [Mexico], $n = 1,652$), others are quite poor (e.g., Mentally Retarded, $n = 10$; Non English Proficient, $n = 11$, Deaf, $n = 46$). For populations without proper representation, the best that can be said is that reliability has not yet been demonstrated.

VALIDITY. The TONI-2 attempts to establish evidence for content, criterion, and construct validity. As stated previously, empirical evidence for item content is strong.

Data for criterion validity are presented in Table 4.7. This table is difficult to read and extends across two pages. The headings are poorly labeled, which makes initial viewing of the table confusing. An alternative method would have been to present the information in several tables to allow for clear comparisons between measures.

In examining the correlation coefficients between the TONI-2 and various achievement measures, a number of findings emerge that warrant closer scrutiny. For example, the TONI-2 had a .74 and .78 correlation for Forms A and B, respectively, with the Language Arts subtest of the SRA Achievement Series. Does this mean that, despite its nonverbal format, the TONI-2 measures language development in some way? Also, the low to moderate correlations with most measures of academic achievement were explained by the authors as being due to the novel nature of this test. One of the primary purposes of intelligence tests is to predict academic achievement, and this test is not very good at it.

Correlations with various intelligence tests are presented in Table 4.8. Again, the TONI-2 has substantial correlation coefficients with various language-based, as well as non-language-based measures, most noticeably the Verbal Scale of the Wechsler Intelligence Scale for Children—Revised (WISC-R). The recurrent inability of the TONI-2 to correlate reliably or highly with nonverbal measures while showing low correlations with verbal measures furthers the notion that intelligence is neither verbal nor nonverbal, but rather an interaction between the two types of skills.

One of the criticisms regarding the original TONI was the lack of factor analytic research. In the research manual, the authors present the results of one study ($n = 91$) that failed to show any strong subfactors. Clearly, more factor analytic research needs to be done to define the different skills measured by the TONI-2.

SUMMARY. Revision of a test usually indicates that major improvements have been made over previous versions. Unfortunately, that is not the case with the TONI-2. Most of the criticisms leveled at the TONI remain as valid criticisms of the TONI-2. From the outset, the TONI-2 is on shaky theoretical ground in assuming that a cognitive task is either entirely verbal or entirely nonverbal. The most noticeable deficiency lies in the psychometric data which fail to support both its theoretical basis and its use with the intended populations. The questions that continue to arise in reviewing this test are why do we need another intelligence test and what does this test provide, in terms of diagnostic or treatment information, that others do not? After careful review of this test and its materials, neither question has been answered.

[440]
Test of Relational Concepts.
Purpose: "To identify deficits in the comprehension of relational concepts."

Population: Ages 3-0 to 7-11.
Publication Date: 1988.
Acronym: TRC.
Scores, 1: Concept Score.
Administration: Individual.
Price Data, 1989: $64 per complete kit including examiner's manual (31 pages), picture book (118 pages), and 50 record forms; $37 per picture book; $9 per 50 record forms; $21 per examiner's manual.
Time: (10–15) minutes.
Comments: Orally administered; examiner must have previous training in the administration and interpretation of individual measures.
Authors: Nellie K. Edmonston and Nancy Litchfield Thane.
Publisher: PRO-ED, Inc.

Review of the Test of Relational Concepts by ROGER D. CARLSON, Visiting Associate Professor of Psychology, Whitman College, Walla Walla, WA:

The Test of Relational Concepts (TRC) is based upon an unusually carefully developed research and theoretical base. The authors have documented the cognitive, developmental, and psycholinguistic bases for their decisions to include the domains tested by the items. An extensive bibliography of substantive research is included in the manual. The artistic work in the test book is quite well done, and characterizations are without ambiguity.

One thousand children from 3 to almost 8 years of age were used in the norming. Considerable effort was made to assure that the sample was demographically representative of various aspects of the U.S. population, namely regional, urban versus rural, occupational, racial, and sexual representativeness. The sample used for norming appears to represent quite closely those demographic characteristics of the U.S. In the norming study, the test was administered by volunteer professionals or supervised student clinicians. The examiner qualifications for the test call for any professional trained in the administration and interpretation of individual evaluation instruments. Given the quite specific nature of administration and the clearly discrete and unambiguous response choices available, it appears that restricting administration to only persons who have such training may be overly stringent.

Measures of test-retest reliability and internal consistency yielded quite respectable correlation coefficients. Breakdowns by ages also yield satisfactorily high coefficients with the lowest occurring at the higher age levels.

Empirical validity measures were used by relating results of the TRC to those obtained by the Peabody Picture Vocabulary Test—Revised, the Boehm Test of Basic Concepts (Form B), and teachers' ratings. Correlations of TRC results with each of those measures were .619, .866, and .450 respectively. (All correlations were significant at the .0001 level.)

It is interesting that the authors note significant correlations with teacher judgments. One wonders whether more economical results might be gotten by teacher judgments; the test may be of most value where such judgments are not available or where the test is used in a corroborative fashion.

Perhaps the weakest aspect of the TRC is that it uses only one item to sample each domain of interest (although a case could be made that if the child "has" the relational concept, then he/she would get all items of its type correct all of the time). Thus a single sampling from a domain represents the child's knowledge of the concept. Such argumentation does not take into account contextual and cultural familiarity and developmental progression of a given concept. A child may only gradually come to acquire a thoroughgoing knowledge of a given concept. Further, children may know the difference between their right and left hands, but not which of two objects placed before them is on their left. Likewise, a child may know that a hat is *on* one's head, but not that the book is *on* the table. By using only a sampling of one item from each domain, the authors seem to imply that cognition is an all-or-nothing logical phenomenon that takes place in a cultural vacuum. For these reasons, it would be of interest to see whether a longer form may have yielded different results in the pilot testing of the TRC.

Overall, the TRC has been developed in a way consistent with the highest standards of test development. Unusually painstaking work was undertaken in the theoretical and research literature reviews, and the results of that work were used in developing the test. A norming sample was used that would assure representativeness of the major demographic characteristics of the U.S. The only reservation about the TRC is item selection, which was not thoroughly discussed. Research comparing results of the TRC with more, and with more varied items measuring the specific relational concepts, is recommended.

Review of the Test of Relational Concepts by LENA R. GADDIS, Assistant Professor of Educational Psychology, Northern Arizona University, Flagstaff, AZ:

The Test of Relational Concepts (TRC) is intended for use as a screening measure of the comprehension of concepts whose mastery is often considered imperative to the academic success of young children. It consists of 56 items, all of which are administered to every child. The stimulus book presents simple line drawings from which the child must select the alternative (via a pointing response) that matches the statement made by the examiner. Also contained in the stimulus book are the examiner's verbal directions, which make administration of the TRC quite simple. Likewise, scoring is accomplished easily.

NORMS. The standardization sample consisted of 1,000 children, 100 at each of 10 six-month age groups between the ages of 3-0 and 7-11. The sample closely resembles the U.S. population in the 1980 census report with regard to gender, geographic region, urban/rural residence, occupational categories, and ethnicity.

SCORES. The test yields both percentile ranks and standard scores ($m = 50$, $sd = 10$), which are not interchangeable because they were derived separately from the raw scores. The authors recommend that users consider a standard score of 40 or below be used to identify children in need of special assistance.

As is the case with many tests of a developmental nature, the TRC does not have adequate floor and ceiling at the extreme age levels (i.e., it is not possible to obtain scores 3 standard deviations above and below the mean, which would accommodate in excess of 99% of the population). For example, at the age level of 7.6–7.11, the range of possible standard scores is 1 to 62, meaning that an obtained *perfect* raw score would correspond to a standard score only slightly more than 1 standard deviation above the mean. This is not necessarily a weakness of the test in that it would be expected that many children over the age of 6 years may have indeed mastered the "basic" concepts covered by the test, but it is certainly worthy of discussion in the manual in order to guard against any possible misuse of the test. Frequently users will adopt the use of any test designated as a "screening" instrument to identify children for further assessment for possible services of either gifted programs or services appropriate for "at risk" children. The TRC would not be appropriate for either of these purposes, in that it would certainly fail to identify either young low-functioning or older high-functioning youngsters.

RELIABILITY. Test-retest reliability (1- to 4-week interval; $n = 196$) across the 10 age levels is good ($r = .95$). Adequate test-retest reliability was noted for each of the age levels of 3-0 to 6-11 (range = .80 to .96). However, the reliability coefficients for the two upper age levels are inadequate (range = .48 to .70). Internal consistency reliability estimates were adequate, with a reported KR-20 coefficient of .97 for the entire sample and coefficients ranging from .79 to .93 for the individual age levels.

VALIDITY. The authors went to great lengths to ensure the construction and design of the TRC were based on a thorough review of the relevant literature, which speaks to its content validity. Also, care was taken to control for extraneous factors (e.g., visual-perception, test and response format) so that the user can have confidence the TRC measures what it claims. Evidence provided to support the criterion validity of the TRC included significant correlations with the Peabody Picture Vocabulary

Test—Revised ($n = 203$, $r = .62$) and the Boehm Test of Basic Concepts ($n = 144$, $r = .87$). Additionally, it was found to relate significantly with teachers' ratings of subjects' ($n = 489$) knowledge of the concepts encompassed by the TRC ($r = .45$). As acquisition of language comprehension, and hence concepts, is theorized to be developmental in nature, the finding that the mean scores get progressively higher with each successive age level is offered as support for construct validity of the TRC.

Although there is considerable evidence for validity of the TRC, many validation domains have not been sufficiently tapped or have gone untapped. For example, no studies regarding the predictive validity of the TRC are reported. This is of particular concern, considering the test is intended as a screening instrument. Related questions that remain unanswered include: (*a*) How adequately does it identify children who are truly deficient in the comprehension of concepts?; and (*b*) to what extent does it overidentify or underidentify such children? Also, once a child is identified as deficient by the test, where does the user proceed—should the examiner conduct a more extensive evaluation or are we to assume the items that comprise the scale can then be used to prepare an instructional plan for each individual child or to aid a teacher in planning his/her instruction for the entire class?

SUMMARY. The TRC is a screening measure of the comprehension of concepts. It possesses fair to good psychometric qualities. It has good content validity, an excellent standardization sample, and adequate reliability at all but the two upper age levels. There is evidence to support the concurrent validity of the TRC, but there is no evidence provided for predictive validity. The test is easily administered and scored and the manual is quite readable. Limitations of the manual include failure on the part of the authors to caution the consumer more strongly regarding the questionable reliability evident for the upper age groups and failure to discuss the inherent ceiling and floor effects, and possible related misuses of the TRC.

With the recent emphasis on early identification and intervention, it is not surprising there has been a deluge of preschool instrumentation emerging, a number of which tap the construct of basic concepts. Among all other similar measures, is the TRC the instrument of choice? Although the authors note the TRC includes items representative of a number of concepts (e.g., temporal, quantitative, dimensional, spatial), there is no evidence that these domains are sufficiently tapped and the TRC yields only a single score. In contrast, the Bracken Basic Concept Scale (BBCS; Bracken, 1984; 10:33) yields scores for seven categories in addition to the total score. Thus, the BBCS allows the user to better determine the pattern of individual strengths and weaknesses. Additionally, Bracken (1984) provides the user with guidelines for criterion-referenced interpretation, remediation, and developing Individualized Educational Plans. In conclusion, many consumers will find the BBCS more useful in planning remediation and performing program evaluation. However, with additional documentation of the predictive validity of the TRC, it should serve the user well (at the lower age ranges) as a screening device.

REVIEWER'S REFERENCE
Bracken, B. A. (1984). Bracken Basic Concept Scale. The Psychological Corporation: San Antonio, TX.

[441]
Test of Sensory Functions in Infants.

Purpose: Developed to measure "sensory processing and reactivity in infants."

Population: Infants ages 4–18 months with regulatory disorders or developmental delays.

Publication Date: 1989.

Acronym: TSFI.

Scores, 6: Reactivity to Tactile Deep Pressure, Adaptive Motor Functions, Visual-Tactile Integration, Ocular-Motor Control, Reactivity to Vestibular Stimulation, Total.

Administration: Individual.

Price Data, 1991: $110 per complete kit including set of test materials, 100 administration and scoring forms, and manual (45 pages); $49 per set of test materials; $22.50 per 100 administration and scoring forms; $27.50 per manual.

Time: (20) minutes.

Authors: Georgia A. DeGangi and Stanley I. Greenspan.

Publisher: Western Psychological Services.

Review of the Test of Sensory Functions in Infants by MARK ALBANESE, Adjunct Associate Professor of Biostatistics and Educational Statistics and Director, Office of Consultation and Research in Medical Education, The University of Iowa College of Medicine, Iowa City, IA:

OVERVIEW. The Test of Sensory Functions in Infants (TSFI) provides an overall measure of sensory processing and reactivity in infants, ages 4–18 months. The test has five subtests which the authors selected on the basis of their clinical significance in the identification of children with sensory integrative dysfunction, with an emphasis on children at risk for learning disabilities. The authors argue that although there are numerous developmental scales that can be used in screening motor and neurological functions in infants, until recently there were no instruments available to screen infants for sensory dysfunction. The TSFI was designed as both a research and clinical tool with recommended use in the assessment of infants with regulatory disorders, developmental delays, and those at risk for learning and sensory processing disorders.

The authors state that the identification of preschool children who evidence sensory integrative dysfunction can play a major role in facilitating early intervention and prevention approaches, which may circumvent later problems in emotional development as well as balance, postural mechanisms, spatial perception, and in learning to read, write and do mathematics.

The TSFI is recommended for use as a diagnostic tool in conjunction with the Bayley Scales of Infant Development: Motor and Mental Scale and other standardized comprehensive developmental scales in order to make decisions regarding the infant's developmental status. It is further recommended that the TSFI be administered by pediatricians, psychologists, infant educators, and occupational and physical therapists with training and background in interpretation of test results in the domain of sensory functions.

DESCRIPTION OF TSFI. The TSFI is a 24-item assessment measuring five subdomains of sensory processing and reactivity:

1. Reactivity to tactile deep pressure applied to various parts of the body.

2. Adaptive motor functions in the ability to motor plan and initiate exploratory movements in handling textured toys.

3. Visual-tactile integration in the toleration of contact with various visually interesting textured toys.

4. Ocular-motor control in the lateralization of the eyes and visual tracking.

5. Reactivity to vestibular stimulation in vertical, circular, and inverted prone and supine body positions.

The 24 items used in the scale were chosen from among a larger group of 44 based upon their sensitivity to developmental changes occurring in normal infants between ages 4 and 18 months and/or discriminated between groups of normal, developmentally delayed or regulatory disorder infants. Each of the items is rated using scales with from two to four options.

CRITIQUE OF STRENGTHS. The various strengths of the TSFI include its ease of use and clear directions. Case studies provided in the test manual are likely to be helpful to users in providing guidance in how to use the test. The authors have used the instrument successfully in a number of research studies and compellingly argue the merits of its use for diagnosis and prevention. The items contained on the TSFI have been submitted to review by a panel of eight experts who favorably evaluated each item for its relevance to the domain it is intended to measure and the extent to which the collection of domains assessed is representative of the entire domain contained in the area of sensory functioning for the infant population. The authors

report good interobserver reliabilities ranging from .88 to .99 for the five subscores and .95 for the total test. Test-retest reliabilities for a 1- to 5-day lag period ranged from .64 to .96 for the various subscores with the exception of Reactivity to Vestibular Stimulation (.26). The authors note that the children involved in the test-retest assessment were a very homogeneous group (20 to 26 were from 4–6 months old) and that superior results would be expected with a more heterogeneous sample.

CRITIQUE OF WEAKNESSES. The weaknesses of the TSFI are focused, for the most part, on the sampling done in the selection of the items included in the scale and the generation of the cutoff scores distinguishing normal from delayed classifications. The vast majority of the infants (92%) upon which these decisions were based were white and from middle-class home environments. Without additional information to support generalizability to other populations, use of the instrument with these groups would not be recommended.

To facilitate clinical interpretation of the test results, the authors present cutting scores for each subscale according to the age of the child. These cutting scores were developed to maximize discrimination between infants in the normal and delayed groups. Data on the resulting accurate and inaccurate classifications of the sample are then provided to describe the effectiveness of the cutting scores. These cutting scores and data have several problems. Perhaps the most serious problem is that they are based upon too few data to yield sufficient confidence in their stability. The worst case is for the 4–6 month age group for which there are only four infants in the delayed group. Even in the largest age group there are only 18 infants in the combined delayed and regulatory disorder groups. With such small numbers upon which to derive the cutting scores, it is not surprising that the percentage of false normal and false delayed classifications on subscores were as high as 100% and ranged from 7% to 75% on the overall score. Further, because the cutting scores were derived such that they maximize differences in this sample, the error rates on any other sample are likely to be even larger.

Another problem relates to the derivation and interpretation of the subscores. There are few data to support the integrity of the subscores. The authors interpret low intercorrelations among the subscores (maximum .47) as confirming that the subscores are measuring different sensory functions and low correlations with four other types of tests as supporting the criterion-related validity of the TSFI. It could just as easily have been concluded that the items comprising the subtests and the total score do not represent a homogeneous set of items. The strongest data come from correlations between each of the subscores and the total score which range from .30 to .74. However, because each subscore contributes to the total score, the interpretation is confused. It is highly likely that the size of the correlations is more related to the size of the variance of the subscores than to the relationship underlying the scales.

The authors preclude the use of factor analytic procedures to support the construct validity of subscores because two of the sets of items represent two different ratings of infant behavior resulting from the same stimulus. This dependency would distort the relationship between the items. This problem could be addressed by computing two separate factor analyses in which only one of the sets of dependent items were entered into each. The issue of subscore integrity could also be addressed by computing an internal consistency reliability estimate (such as coefficient alpha) for each subscore. Alternately, the authors could report subscore correlations with the total test if the item set contained in the subscore were not included in the total test score.

Data that are not reported in the manual, but that would be very useful, are the means and standard deviations of the subscores and total test for the normal and delayed samples and each age group. Three of the subscores appear to suffer from ceiling effects having only a 1-point range in the cutoff scores across the age groups. Reporting the means and standard deviations would enable a better understanding of the nature of the data.

One final observation is that during the testing of infants using the TSFI, they are picked up, held close, and held in at-risk positions. Under these testing conditions, any child who has experienced physical abuse may react in ways that would lead them to be classified as delayed. No mention is made in the manual of the potential impact of administering the TSFI to child abuse victims. Given the fact that children who are developmentally delayed may be at higher risk of child abuse, this seems like a serious omission.

SUMMARY. In summary, the TSFI fills a useful niche in developmental diagnostic testing. Expert review yielded positive assessments of the content validity of the instrument. The directions for administering the TSFI are quite complete, including photographs of each part of the examination in addition to written descriptions. High interobserver reliabilities were obtained. The arguments and documentation used to support the importance of assessing sensory functions in infants are compelling.

The major weaknesses of the TSFI are that the psychometric data are based on a narrow population of infants and the numbers of infants in the delayed groups used to develop cutoff scores are insufficient to yield precise values. Additional data should be collected to support the integrity of the subscores and additional statistics reported on the subscores in

the test manual. Finally, the test manual needs to address the complications in assessing infants who have been abused.

Given these weaknesses, it would be difficult to recommend that the TSFI be used for anything other than research purposes at the present time.

ACKNOWLEDGEMENT. The reviewer wishes to acknowledge S. Clair Selzer, Ph.D., Clinical Psychologist in the Division of Developmental Disabilities within the Department of Pediatrics at the University of Iowa, for reviewing an earlier draft of this document.

[442]
Test of Visual Analysis Skills.
Purpose: Constructed to assess "a child's ability to understand the relationship of parts to wholes."
Population: Children.
Publication Date: 1975.
Acronym: TVAS.
Scores: Total score only.
Administration: Group.
Manual: No manual.
Price Data, 1991: $15 per 10 test booklets; $2 per direction card.
Time: Administration time not reported.
Comments: "Criterion-referenced"; may be used in conjunction with the Test of Auditory Analysis Skills.
Author: Jerome Rosner.
Publisher: Academic Therapy Publications.

[443]
Test of Word Finding.
Purpose: Designed to assess word-finding disorders.
Population: Grades 1–6.
Publication Dates: 1986–89.
Acronym: TWF.
Scores: 5 sections (Picture Naming: Nouns, Sentence Completion Naming, Description Naming, Picture Naming: Verbs, Picture Naming: Categories) yielding 4 scores: Accuracy, Item Response Time, Word Finding Profile, Comprehension Summary.
Administration: Individual.
Levels, 2: Primary, Intermediate (on 1 overlapping form).
Price Data, 1991: $125 per complete kit including easel-binder test book, 25 response booklets, administration manual ('89, 173 pages), and technical manual ('86, 127 pages); $24 per 25 response booklets.
Time: (20–30) minutes.
Comments: Prorated accuracy rescoring summary allows for interpretation when comprehension is low; speed can be measured in actual or estimated item response time; estimated response time can be done during testing and eliminates need for stopwatch or tape recorder; if actual response time is desired, a tape recorder and stopwatch are needed.
Author: Diane J. German.
Publisher: DLM Teaching Resources.
Cross References: For reviews by Mavis Donahue and Priscilla A. Drum, see 10:373.

TEST REFERENCES

1. Guilford, A. M., & Nawojczyk, D. C. (1988). Standardization of the Boston Naming Test at the kindergarten and elementary school levels. *Language, Speech, and Hearing Services in Schools, 19*, 395-400.

Review of the Test of Word Finding by SHARON L. WEINBERG, Professor of Quantitative Studies, New York University, New York, NY:

The Test of Word Finding (TWF) is designed to assess word-finding skills in children aged 6 years 6 months to 12 years 11 months in grades 1 through 6. Although the manual indicates there is no evidence at the present time of a link between word-finding skills and academic achievement, word-finding deficits have been found in various groups of elementary school children as well as adults.

According to the manual, word-finding problems have been identified as a correlate of aphasia in adults, and as a correlate of learning disabilities, reading problems or dyslexia, language impairment, and fluency disorders in children. Although the source of this language disorder is not clear, research has linked it to the following characteristics in the connected speech of children: (*a*) prolonged pauses and circumlocutions; (*b*) use of empty place holders and stereotyped meaningless phrases; (*c*) excessive use of starters, indefinites, and words lacking specificity; and (*d*) redundant and perserverative repetitions and substitutions of prefixes and suffixes. From another perspective, children with word-finding problems have been shown to have "difficulties in recalling and retrieving specific words accurately and speedily when they are asked to name pictures or objects, find proper names, describe past experiences or events, or speak in spontaneous conversation" (Wiig & Semel, 1984, p. 110).

Based on an extensive program of research aimed at determining the stimulus contexts and items most appropriate for assessing word-finding skills in children, the TWF was developed over a period of 8 years. In its thoroughness and technical soundness, the test development approach used by its author, Diane J. German, offers an exemplary model for other prospective test developers. The test manual, consisting of two volumes, also is highly detailed and complete, covering such topics as purpose and theoretical perspective, test development and standardization, reliability, validity, administration, scoring, and interpretation.

The TWF is an individually administered test consisting of a primary form (80 items) for grades 1 and 2, and an intermediate form (90 items) for grades 3 through 6 organized into five naming sections and a sixth section on comprehension. Example and starter items are provided in all sections. According to the manual, the test takes approximately 20 to 30 minutes to administer.

Section 1, Picture Naming: Nouns, assesses a student's speed and accuracy when naming picture referents of noun target words. The target words are of one to four syllables and represent semantic categories. Some examples are pictures of a chin, barrel, lighthouse, and microphone. Section 2, Sentence Completion Naming, assesses a student's accuracy when naming target words in an intrasensory, auditory, cloze-procedure format. The student is asked to complete a declarative present-tense sentence stated by the examiner by naming the most suitable target word. Two examples are "On a cake you blow out your birthday _____" (answer: candles); "The yellow part of an egg is a _____" (answer: yolk). Section 3, Description Naming, assesses a student's accuracy when naming words in an intrasensory auditory task where the student is required to name a target word implied by a description given by the examiner. An example is "What is something used to sweep the floor, has a long handle and bristles at the bottom?" (answer: broom). Section 4, Picture Naming: Verbs, assesses a student's accuracy when naming picture referents of action words. All pictures represent verbs in the present participle form. Some examples are pictures of a person climbing, skiing, spraying, and weighing. Section 5, Picture Naming: Categories, assesses a student's accuracy when naming category words represented by pictures of three subordinate or basic-level words. In one example, a student is shown a picture of an apple, a banana, and grapes and is asked for that word which would name all three (answer: fruit). Examples of other category words are vegetables, jewelry, planets, and shapes. The final section, Section 6, Comprehension Assessment, assesses the student's comprehension of those target words that he or she had difficulty naming on the five word-finding sections. The underlying rationale for this section is that, by definition, a word-finding problem exists only when there is difficulty recalling or retrieving a word in the presence of good comprehension of that word.

As indicated, the TWF measures either accuracy, speed, or both depending on a particular test section. Accuracy is defined as the raw number of correct first responses given within a 15-second time limit, converted to a derived score (a standard score or percentile rank) published in the test manual, that is based on both grade and age norms. Speed is defined as total response time, either estimated or actual. In the former case, the examiner estimates for each item whether the child takes greater than or less than 4 seconds to respond. The total estimated item response time is obtained by tallying the number of responses given after 4 seconds. Actual response time is measured after the testing session and relies on the use of a stopwatch and an audio tape recording of that session. In addition to accuracy and speed, the presence of secondary characteristics of word-finding difficulty, gestures, or extra verbalizations, may also be scored on the test form.

As indicated earlier in this review, the TWF comes with a detailed psychometric profile that supports its technical soundness. Age and grade norms are based on a national stratified sample of 1,200 normal children in grades 1 through 6. In addition, norms based on 40 children with linguistic handicaps are also provided. Using item response theory (IRT), the author was able to calibrate both the primary and intermediate forms on a single, common scale for purposes of direct comparison between the two forms. Reliability indices, using both IRT and traditional measures of assessment, are high; the content, concurrent, and construct validity measures provided offer strong support for the overall validity of this instrument.

In sum, the Test of Word Finding is a well-conceived and psychometrically sound measure of word-finding problems in children. If, as the manual states, the development of this test responds to "a need and demand expressed by professionals" in the area, then this area is now better served. Professionals may now turn their attention to what appears to be the next pressing issue in this area: the development of appropriate intervention strategies for the treatment of such children.

REVIEWER'S REFERENCE

Wiig, E. H., & Semel, E. M. (1984). *Language assessment and intervention for the learning disabled* (rev. ed.). Columbus, Toronto, London, Sydney: Merrill.

Review of the Test of Word Finding by SUSAN ELLIS WEISMER, Assistant Professor of Communicative Disorders, University of Wisconsin, Madison, WI:

The Test of Word Finding (TWF) is a diagnostic measure designed to assess word-finding skills in elementary school-aged children in grades 1 through 6. According to the author, the TWF can be used clinically to identify children with word-finding problems, provide information relevant to programming, and evaluate remedial progress. It is also intended to be used as a research tool for investigating children's word-finding abilities.

The TWF comprises a primary form (grades 1 and 2) and an intermediate form (grades 3 through 6). The test consists of five naming sections— Picture Naming: Nouns, Sentence Completion Naming, Description Naming, Picture Naming: Verbs, and Picture Naming: Categories. Section 6, Comprehension Assessment, evaluates knowledge of erred words from the naming sections.

Item formats for the first five sections include confrontation naming of pictured objects or actions, response to wh-questions that incorporate three attributes of the target word (e.g., What floats in the sky, may be full of rain, and is gray or white?), and completion of the last word of definitional and associative sentences (i.e., cloze procedures). For the comprehension assessment, a recognition procedure is employed in which the child points to one of four pictures named by the examiner. Accuracy scores are obtained on each section, as well as response times on the picture naming of nouns. Raw scores can be interpreted in terms of standard scores and percentiles for the child's age or grade level. Based on the accuracy and time scores, a word-finding profile is determined that has implications for remediation. Children are categorized with regard to their word-finding skills as fast and inaccurate, slow and inaccurate, fast and accurate, or slow and accurate. Additionally, the TWF includes informal assessment of secondary characteristics (gestures and extra verbalizations) and a substitution analysis.

The TWF was nationally standardized on 1,200 normally developing children (200 at each year for grades 1–6) residing in 18 states. Data from the 1980 U.S. Census were used as a basis for determining adequate representation for the stratification variables, which included sex, geographic region, parents' educational level, and race or ethnicity. The author followed the recommendation of Salvia and Ysseldyke (1981) that the standardization population used with assessment tools designed to identify individuals with particular problems should include subjects who manifest those problems. Thus, subjects with linguistic handicaps (defined in terms of word-finding problems) represented 3% (40 children) of the standardization population. A strength of the TWF is that a child's score can be compared to either the normative sample or to the group with linguistic handicaps.

The administration, scoring, and interpretation manual is comprehensive and well written. It provides both general and specific instructions that are illustrated by a number of helpful examples. Adequate numbers of sample items are provided on the test and the stimulus pictures clearly depict the target word. For the most part, administration and scoring of the TWF are straightforward and can be accomplished with ease. The exception to this is the response time measurements for the first naming section. The five trial administrations recommended in the manual seem insufficient to prepare the test user to smoothly and efficiently manage all aspects of the task for this section (turning pages of the picture booklet, monitoring the stopwatch, and recording responses). Scoring and interpretation of the TWF are aided by case studies and appendices, which contrast acceptable synonyms with error responses and provide classifications of typical target-word substitutions.

The conceptual framework for the TWF is well developed. The technical manual includes a comprehensive review of research examining word-finding difficulties in adult aphasics and in children with learning disabilities, reading disorders, language disorders, and fluency problems. The author provides an extensive discussion of the diagnostic model of word-finding assessment underlying the TWF that is drawn from this literature on word-finding disorders. This model takes into account indices used to define word-finding problems in children and adults (accuracy, response time, and substitution types) and variables affecting word-finding behavior (situational and stimulus contexts, nature and frequency of occurrence of the target word, and facilitating cues).

The extensive test development and standardization procedures are described in depth in the technical manual, including reports of numerous investigations focused on item selection and on establishing reliability and validity.

The content validity of the TWF is supported by the results of the literature on word-finding disorders. Additionally, the author has made attempts to ensure that the TWF is a measure of children's ability to retrieve words from their lexicon rather than an assessment of word knowledge. This has been done by including only items that the normative sample comprehended with 95% accuracy on the final version of the test and by testing comprehension of target words on which naming errors occur.

With respect to criterion-related validity, studies have demonstrated significant, but moderate, correlations between scores on the TWF and other standardized confrontation naming tasks, rapid automatic naming tasks, and association naming tasks. In addition, concurrent validity has been established based on speech-language pathologists' ratings on a word-finding survey. No studies of predictive validity are reported for the TWF.

Construct validity has been demonstrated on the basis that scores on the TWF discriminate groups of children according to chronological age and expressive language skills, as well as through factor analytic techniques and intercorrelations between accuracy and response time indices. Reliability of the TWF was investigated using the Rasch Latent Trait model. Data are provided that indicate the test meets the goodness-of-fit criterion for this model. Traditional reliability assessments demonstrated high test-retest reliability and acceptable internal consistency for both accuracy and time indices.

In summary, the TWF is a reliable and valid assessment instrument for evaluating children's word-finding abilities. It can be employed clinically or for research purposes. One caution should be noted, however, in the interpretation of the findings from the TWF. This test cannot distinguish between word-finding problems that are due to deficits in retrieval strategies and those stemming from inadequate lexical storage (Kail & Leonard, 1986).

Because these two sources of naming problems have different implications for programming (McGregor & Leonard, 1989), further investigation of this issue is warranted.

REVIEWER'S REFERENCES

Salvia, J., & Ysseldyke, J. (1981). *Assessment in special and remedial education.* Boston: Houghton-Mifflin.
Kail, R., & Leonard, L. (1986). Word-finding abilities in language-impaired children. *ASHA Monographs, 25,* 1-39.
McGregor, K., & Leonard, L. (1989). Facilitating word-finding skills of language-impaired children. *Journal of Speech and Hearing Disorders, 54,* 141-147.

[444]
Test of Written Language-2.

Purpose: "(a) To identify students who perform significantly more poorly than their peers in written expression and who as a result need special help; (b) to determine a student's particular strengths and weaknesses in various writing abilities; (c) to document a student's progress in a special writing program; and (d) to conduct research in writing."

Population: Ages 7-0 to 17-11.
Publication Dates: 1978–88.
Acronym: TOWL-2.
Scores: 10 subtest scores (Vocabulary, Spelling, Style, Logical Sentences, Sentence Combining, Thematic Maturity, Contextual Vocabulary, Syntactic Maturity, Contextual Spelling, Contextual Style) plus 3 composite scores (Contrived Writing, Spontaneous Writing, Overall Written Language).
Administration: Individual or group.
Forms, 2: A, B.
Price Data, 1989: $97 per complete kit including 25 response booklets A, 25 response booklets B, 50 scoring forms, and manual ('88, 158 pages); $27 per 25 A or B response booklets; $23 per 50 scoring forms; $24 per manual; $69 per Apple or IBM Pro-Score System.
Time: (90–120) minutes.
Authors: Donald D. Hammill and Stephen C. Larsen.
Publisher: PRO-ED, Inc.
Cross References: For reviews by Edward A. Polloway and Robert T. Williams of an earlier edition, see 9:1278.

TEST REFERENCES

1. Hess, C. W., Ritchie, K. P., & Landry, R. G. (1984). The type-token ratio and vocabulary performance. *Psychological Reports, 55,* 51-57.
2. Zentall, S. S., Falkenberg, S. D., & Smith, L. B. (1985). Effects of color stimulation and information on the copying performance of attention-problem adolescents. *Journal of Abnormal Child Psychology, 13,* 501-511.
3. MacArthur, C. A., & Graham, S. (1987). Learning disabled students' composing under three methods of text production: Handwriting, word processing, and dictation. *The Journal of Special Education, 21* (3), 22-42.
4. Graham, S., Boyer-Shick, K., & Tippets, E. (1989). The validity of the handwriting scale from the Test of Written Language. *The Journal of Educational Research, 82,* 166-171.
5. Morton, L. L., Lindsay, P. H., & Roche, W. M. (1989). A report on learning disabled children's use of lab-based word processing versus pencil-and-paper for creative writing. *The Alberta Journal of Educational Research, 35,* 283-291.
6. Morton, L. L., Lindsay, P. H., & Roche, W. M. (1989). Word processing effects on writing productivity and revision at elementary and junior high school levels. *The Alberta Journal of Educational Research, 35,* 145-163.

Review of the Test of Written Language-2 by STEPHEN L. BENTON, *Associate Professor of Educational Psychology, Kansas State University, Manhattan, KS:*

Tests of writing ability are typically classified as being one of two types: direct assessments, which require that students actually generate text; and indirect assessments, which appear in the form of multiple-choice tests that measure such knowledge as conventional English usage, linguistics, punctuation, and grammar. The clear advantage of the Test of Written Language-2 (TOWL-2) is that it combines these two seemingly disparate methods into one test instrument that provides an Overall Written Language quotient that has sound reliability and validity.

The TOWL-2 was published in 1988 in response to criticisms about an earlier version. Among the changes made are the construction of two forms of the test, Forms A and B; the elimination of the Handwriting and Word Usage subtests; and the addition of five new subtests (Syntactic Maturity, Contextual Spelling, Contextual Style, Logical Sentences, and Sentence Combining). The 10 subtests that now comprise the TOWL-2 can be categorized along two dimensions: *components* of writing and testing *formats*. Each subtest presumably assesses one of three writing components: (*a*) *conventional* standards pertaining to punctuation, capitalization, and spelling; (*b*) *linguistic* elements pertaining to syntax, morphology, and semantics; or (*c*) *conceptual* aspects of writing pertaining to expression of ideas. Subtests are of either contrived (indirect) or spontaneous (direct) formats. The five contrived subtests form a Contrived Writing quotient and the five spontaneous subtests derived from a direct writing sample form a Spontaneous Writing quotient. All 10 subtests are used to produce an Overall Written Language quotient.

Although the subtests and resulting quotients appear to have adequate content validity, it is important to note that they do not tap all aspects of the writing process. An examination of the subtests within the context of the Hayes and Flower (1980) model of writing reveals, for example, that several key components are neglected in the TOWL-2. For example, Graham (1989) has noted that *revising* is not tapped in any significant way on any of the subtests. The Logical Sentences and Sentence Combining subtests do require that students reorganize sentences to improve local coherence, but the 15-minute writing sample limits students to *planning* and *generating*, and not revising, prose. In addition, the brief time limit does not allow for assessment of students' abilities to *set goals* and *organize* text in a meaningful fashion.

In addition, very little assessment is made of students' knowledge of discourse or text structure. Most of the subtests focus on what can be described as *microstructures* (e.g., sentence combining, spelling, punctuation) with very little assessment of *macrostructures* (e.g., organizing sentences within paragraphs, planning the overall structure of text). Finally, there is no assessment of audience awareness, a metacognitive component of writing that is critical for generating prose meaningful to a specific audience. In fact, the directions for writing the story do not even specify the nature of the intended audience.

The validity of the spontaneous writing format rests upon a 15-minute writing assignment within a narrative genre. One must question whether this single sampling of students' writing is a valid assessment of their ability. Criterion-related validity was assessed with a sample of 68 students (inadequately described) who took both the SRA Achievement Series and the TOWL-2. None of the spontaneous subtests nor the Spontaneous Writing quotient correlated beyond .49 with the SRA Language Arts test. The Contrived Writing quotient fared better with a correlation of .70. In addition, a different group of 51 students wrote essays, holistically scored, and took the TOWL-2. Again, no correlations between holistic impressions and the TOWL-2 scores correlated beyond .47. The Overall Written Language quotient, however, correlated .61 which should encourage users to rely most heavily on this score. It should be noted that these correlations were corrected for attenuation but that the correlations prior to attenuation were not reported.

Construct validity was measured in several ways. Correlations between the ages of the 2,216 students in the standardization sample and their subtest scores ranged from .36 to .74. Correlations ranging from .39 to .77 were also observed between subtest scores and grade level. These results suggest abilities measured by the TOWL-2 are developmental in nature, as would be expected. The highest correlations were observed on Vocabulary, Spelling, and Contextual Vocabulary.

A second indicant of construct validity is that all subtests were significantly intercorrelated, which suggests they each measure some aspect of writing. The authors also attempted to support construct validity by differentiating less skilled from skilled writers. Their method of doing so, however, was unconventional because they simply averaged the subtest scores of 32 "learning disabled" students and made no attempt to identify skilled writers.

Moderate significant correlations between the TOWL-2 and scores on the SRA Achievement Series were considered evidence that writing ability is related to the construct of intelligence. The moderate correlations are consistent with similar findings by Percival (1966). One might question, however, whether the SRA scores are good measures of intelligence.

As additional evidence of construct validity, a factor analysis was performed on scores from the entire standardization sample. Results revealed all subtests loaded on a principal component considered to be Overall Written Language and, with varimax rotation, two factors emerged that were considered to be Spontaneous and Contrived Writing.

Reliability was also supported in several ways. Two individuals independently scored 20 TOWL-2 protocols. Their subtest interrater correlations ranged from .91 to .99. It should be noted, however, that one of the raters was a test author. It might have been preferable to train naive raters to establish that the scoring methods are easily learned and consistent across less sophisticated raters.

A test-retest with alternate forms study was conducted with 77 students in grades 1-7. No other information was provided regarding the demographics of the sample. The time between testing using Forms A and B varied from 1 day to 3 weeks, which most likely contributed some error variance to the analysis. Corrected (for restricted range) coefficients were reported along with obtained coefficients. Test-retest correlations ranged from .61 to .77, with the Overall Written Language quotient being .85. Finally, an examination of the TOWL-2's reliability relative to Anastasi's (1982) formula for calculating stability on the basis of interscorer, content sampling, and time sampling reliabilities revealed r values ranging from .59 to .99 with the Overall Written Language quotient equal to .90.

In general, the authors should be commended for their efforts. They have established basals and ceilings for each contrived subtest; provided detailed information about administration, scoring, and interpretation; cautioned prospective users about the kinds of interpretations that are appropriate; provided particularly useful guidelines on teaching spelling; and discouraged the use of grade and age equivalents. If an individual has the $1\frac{1}{2}$ to 2 hours available to administer the test, the Overall Written Language quotient provides a valid and reliable measure of writing ability.

REVIEWER'S REFERENCES

Percival, E. (1966). The dimension of ability in English composition. *Educational Review, 18,* 205-212.

Hayes, J. R., & Flower, L. S. (1980). Identifying the organization of writing processes. In L. W. Gregg & E. R. Steinberg (Eds.), *Cognitive processes in writing* (pp. 3-30). Hillsdale, NJ: Lawrence Erlbaum Associates.

Anastasi, A. (1982). *Psychological testing* (5th ed.). New York: Macmillan.

Graham, S. (1989). Is new necessarily better? A review of the TOWL-2. *Learning Disabilities Focus, 5,* 47-49.

Review of the Test of Written Language-2 by JOSEPH M. RYAN, *Associate Professor of Education, University of South Carolina, Columbia, SC:*

The authors of the Test of Written Language-2 (TOWL-2) propose a model for writing that contains three components and a model for writing assessment that requires two formats. The writing components are conventional, linguistic, and conceptual; the assessment formats are "contrived" methods that "focus on the isolated evaluation of the smallest units of written discourse" and "spontaneous" methods that are based on samples of students' writing. The three components are assessed with each of two formats yielding six categories with one or two subtests within each category. There are a total of 10 subtests. The conventional-contrived category includes Style and Spelling subtests. The conventional-spontaneous category includes Contextual Style and Spontaneous Spelling. The linguistic-contrived category includes Sentence Combining and Vocabulary subtests and the linguistic-spontaneous includes Syntactic Maturity and Contextual Vocabulary. The conceptual-contrived category includes Logical Sentences and the conceptual-spontaneous category includes Thematic Maturity.

The TOWL-2 manual provides detailed information about the instrument's development, administration, and the interpretation of data collected. However, potential users must carefully examine three issues before deciding whether the TOWL-2 will be helpful for a particular application. These issues are (*a*) the content validity of the conceptual model and subtests and the use of two assessment formats; (*b*) the value of the norm-referenced approach to assessment; and (*c*) the relevance and appropriateness of information about reliability and validity.

The first issue deals with conceptualizing writing into three components with further subdivisions. This approach views writing as an amalgam of discrete skills that can be meaningfully examined separately as subtests and then quantitatively combined into composite scores. In contrast, many writing educators argue that writing is a wholistic, unified process in which the synergistic integration of identifiable components is greater than the sum of the discrete parts. These two different views of writing lead to assessment approaches that are also different from each other (e.g., analytic and wholistic assessment). Although the "contrived" and "spontaneous" formats on the TOWL-2 may seem to reflect the analytic and wholistic assessment approaches, a closer look at the "spontaneous" format reveals that students' writing samples are scored in terms of discrete, separate skills. For example, in the Spontaneous Format, Syntactic Maturity is defined as "the number of words in the composition that is used to form grammatically acceptable sentences," and Contextual Style as "the number of instances in which different punctuation and capitalization rules are used correctly."

The second major set of issues relates to the fact that the TOWL-2 was developed and the results are analyzed using classical test theory's norm-referenced approach. With this approach, students' scores are interpreted in terms of their position relative to other students' scores (e.g., the scores of the norm group, not relative to some criterion or curricula expectation). The norming sample and norming procedures of the TOWL-2 have several shortcomings. The norm sample includes 2,216 nonrandomly selected students, ranging in age from 7 to 17, an age range that includes roughly grades 2 to 11. The population of students in grades 2 to 11 is rarely treated as a single group in school settings and, thus, the norming sample seems to represent a school population for whom curriculum and instruction is rarely organized and delivered.

This norming sample is said to be representative "of the national population" based on percentages of students in various demographic categories such as sex, geographic region, etc. The percentages are, in fact, quite close but this does not warrant the conclusion. The appropriate "national population" should be restricted only to people between ages 7 and 17, the age range of the target population. In addition, it is far more critical to show that the norming sample resembles some target population with respect to writing because the purpose of the TOWL-2 is to provide norms for assessing writing ability. The norm group might be unusually proficient or deficient in writing ability and thus provide abnormally high or low norms. Demographic percentages are not central to this issue and the problem cannot be resolved because there is no information on the basis of which to evaluate the representativeness of the norm sample's writing ability.

The most serious difficulty with the norming procedures is that the norm tables (Appendices 1 and 2) are presented for groups of students combined into narrow-ranged age clusters (e.g., 7 years, 6 months to 8 years, 5 months). Percentile and standard scores tables are presented for 16 and 17 age groups respectively for Forms A and B. These age group clusters are the actual samples on whom the norms are calculated and no data about the representativeness or even the number of subjects within these groups are presented.

The third major set of issues relates to information provided about the reliability and validity of the TOWL-2. There are three problems in this regard. First, virtually all of the statistical measures of reliability and validity are inflated by the fact that the samples used are extremely heterogeneous. For example, the very high interscorer reliability coefficients in Table 6-5 are based on samples of students' work from grades 3, 7, and 10. It is easier for scorers to agree when rating papers from such a wide range of grades and, more importantly, the magnitude of statistical correlations increases as the variability or heterogeneity of the sample increases. The second problem with TOWL-2 reliability and validity information is that the groups to which this information applies are not clear. For example, the interscor-

er reliability coefficients are based on a sample with students from grades 3, 7, and 10, and thus would not necessarily apply to a sample from grades 4 and 5 or a sample from grades 8 and 9. Most critically, it is unlikely that the reliability and validity statistics calculated on samples that are quite heterogeneous would be accurate estimates of reliability and validity for the narrow-ranged age (homogeneous) clusters used to actually calculate the TOWL-2 norms. Lastly, the construct validity of the TOWL-2 is not supported by the evidence presented. The basic TOWL-2 construct for writing includes three components with subtests within these components. This construct or model can be examined with subtests' intercorrelations (Table 6-12) and the principal components analysis (Table 6-13). The subtests do not "hang together" or correlate within the components but correlate more highly with subtests in other components. The principal components analysis reveals one major component to which all the subtests are highly related rather than the three components that would confirm the hypothesized three components used to construct the TOWL-2. The principal components analysis suggests that a single, global aptitude is being measured.

In summary, educators must determine whether they agree with the way "writing ability" is conceptually and operationally defined in the TOWL-2. In addition, the norms and information about reliability and validity must be interpreted with caution. The TOWL-2 may be useful in some situations as a very broad, general screening device and the authors provide some useful practical suggestions for such applications. Potential users should evaluate the TOWL-2 relative to their testing needs and bear in mind the limitations described in this review.

[445]
Tests of Achievement and Proficiency, Form J.

Purpose: Constructed to appraise student progress in basic skills and curricular areas.
Population: Grades 9–12.
Publication Dates: 1978–90.
Acronym: TAP.
Administration: Group.
Levels, 4: 15, 16, 17, 18.
Price Data, 1991: $62.55 per 35 separate level test books (specify level) including directions for administering; $3 per scoring key booklet ('90, 6 pages); $21.30 per 35 MRC answer sheets (specify level) including 35 pupil report folders, teacher's guide ('90, 93 pages), and materials needed for machine scoring; $129 per 250 NCS answer sheets (for local scoring); $16.35 per set of MRC scoring masks for complete battery (specify level); $9 per 35 student profile charts; $7.95 per 35 pupil report folders; $9 per 35 profile charts for averages; $9 per 35 class record folders; $8.40 per teacher's guide; $4.05 per Directions for Administering Separate Level Books ('90, 18 pages); $18 per school administrator's manual ('90, 108 pages); $6 per school administrator's

supplement ('90, 36 pages); $7.50 per skill objectives booklet ('90, 44 pages); $1.98 per administrator's summary ('90, 22 pages); $8.10 per special norms booklet (select large city, Catholic, high socioeconomic, or low socioeconomic); $21 per specimen set; extensive scoring services available from publisher.

Comments: Form G Listening Supplement and Writing Supplement may be used with Form J; Forms G, H, and T are still available from publisher; Forms G, H, and J are parallel forms.

Authors: Dale P. Scannell, Oscar M. Haugh, Alvin H. Schild, and Gilbert Ulmer.

Publisher: The Riverside Publishing Co.

a) BASIC BATTERY.

Scores, 7: Reading Comprehension, Mathematics, Written Expression, Using Sources of Information, Basic Composite, plus Minimum Competency and Applied Proficiency Skills scores.

Price Data: $3.90 per multilevel test booklet.

Time: 160(200) minutes.

b) COMPLETE BATTERY.

Scores, 9: Reading Comprehension, Mathematics, Written Expression, Using Sources of Information, Social Studies, Science, Complete Composite, plus Minimum Competency and Applied Proficiency Skills scores.

Price Data: $4.95 per multilevel test booklet.

Time: 240(280) minutes.

Cross References: For a review by Elaine Clark of Forms G and H, see 10:375 (2 references); for reviews by John M. Keene, Jr. and James L. Wardrop of an earlier edition, see 9:1282.

TEST REFERENCES

1. Donovan, J. F., Sousa, D. A., & Walberg, H. J. (1987). The impact of staff development on implementation and student achievement. *The Journal of Educational Research, 80,* 348-351.

2. Alvermann, D. E. (1988). Effects of spontaneous and induced lookbacks on self-perceived high- and low-ability comprehenders. *The Journal of Educational Research, 81,* 325-331.

3. Reynolds, A. J., Oberman, G. L., & Perlman, C. (1988). An analysis of a PSAT coaching program for urban gifted students. *The Journal of Educational Research, 81,* 155-164.

4. Sosniak, L. A., & Ethington, C. A. (1988). School quality and high school seniors' attitudes toward academic coursework. *The Journal of Educational Research, 82,* 113-119.

[446]

Tests of Adult Basic Education, Forms 5 and 6, and Survey Form.

Purpose: "Designed to measure achievement in reading, mathematics, language, and spelling."

Population: Adults in basic education programs.

Publication Dates: 1957–87.

Acronym: TABE.

Administration: Group.

Levels: 4 overlapping levels: E (Easy) (grades 2.6–4.9), M (Medium) (grades 4.6–6.9), D (Difficult) (grades 6.6–8.9), A (Advanced) (grades 8.6–12.9).

Forms, 3: Survey Form, Complete Battery (Form 5), Complete Battery (Form 6).

Price Data, 1988: $18.75 per 25 Practice Exercise and Locator Test test books; $9.35 per 25 Practice Exercise and Locator Test SCOREZE answer sheets; $9.50 per 50 Practice Exercise and Locator Test hand-scorable answer sheets; $9.50 per 50 Practice Exercise and Locator Test answer sheets for SCANTRON stand-alone scanner; $9.50 per 50 Practice Exercise and Locator Test answer

sheets for SCANTRON computer-linked scanner; $7.75 per Practice Exercise and Locator Test hand-scoring stencil; $6 per Norms Book ('87, 146 pages); $8.50 per Test Coordinator's Handbook ('87, 59 pages); $8.50 per Technical Report ('87, 60 pages); $12 per Multi-Level Test Review Kit (specimen set) including Test Reviewer's Guide, descriptive brochure, Examination Materials booklet, Practice Exercise and Locator Test, Practice Exercise and Locator Test answer sheets, 1 test book of the Survey Form and for each level of the Complete Battery (Form 5), Complete Battery Examiner's Manual with answer key (for all levels), Survey Form Examiner's Manual with answer key (for all levels), Complete Battery hand-scorable answer sheet, SCANTRON answer sheets, Norms Book, and Group Record Sheet.

Time: 20(25) minutes for the Practice Exercise and Locator Test.

Comments: Locator tests included to determine appropriate level of either test form to be administered; optional practice test also included; Apple and IBM software available to aid scoring.

Author: CTB/McGraw-Hill.

Publisher: CTB Macmillan/McGraw-Hill.

a) SURVEY FORM.

Purpose: Shortened version of Form 5 to be used for screening purposes.

Publication Date: 1987.

Scores, 3: Total Reading, Total Mathematics, Total Language.

Price Data: $34 per 25 test books including Examiner's Manual with answer key (specify Level E, M, D, or A); $12 per 25 SCOREZE answer sheets (specify level); $9.50 per 50 hand-scorable answer sheets; $9.50 per 50 SCANTRON answer sheets (for computer-linked scanners); $9.50 per 50 SCANTRON answer sheets (for stand-alone scanners) (specify Reading and Mathematics or Language); $9.50 per 50 NCS answer sheets; $7.75 per hand-scoring stencil for use with hand-scorable answer sheet (specify level); $6 per Examiner's Manual with answer key (for use with Practice Exercise and Locator Test).

Time: 108(128) minutes.

b) COMPLETE BATTERY, FORMS 5 AND 6.

Publication Dates: 1957–87.

Scores, 11: Reading (Vocabulary, Comprehension, Total), Mathematics (Computation, Concepts and Applications, Total), Language (Mechanics, Expression, Total), Total Battery, Spelling.

Forms, 2: 5, 6 (parallel forms).

Price Data: $34 per 25 test books including Examiner's Manual with answer key (specify Level E, M, D, or A and Form 5 or 6); $12 per 25 SCOREZE answer sheets (specify Reading, Mathematics, or Language and Spelling and Level E, M, D, or A); $18 per 50 hand-scorable answer sheets; $9.50 per 50 SCANTRON answer sheets for use with computer-linked scanners (specify Reading, Mathematics, or Language and Spelling); $9.50 per 50 SCANTRON answer sheets for use with stand-alone scanners (specify Reading, Mathematics, or Language and Spelling); $9.50 per 50 NCS answer sheets (specify Reading, Mathematics, or Language and Spelling); $23.25 per 3 hand-scoring stencils (specify Level E, M, D, or A); $5.30 per 25 Individual Diagnostic Profile/Analysis of Learning Difficulties (specify Level E, M, D, or A);

$.80 per Complete Battery Group Record Sheet; $6 per Examiner's Manual with answer key; $9.50 per Large-Print Edition Locator Test test book; $20 per Large-Print Edition test book (specify Level E, M, D, or A); $5.60 per 10 Large-Print Edition hand-scorable answer sheets; $5.60 per 10 Large-Print Edition Locator Test answer sheets.

Special Edition: Large-Print Edition available for Form 5.

Time: 203 (223) minutes.

Cross References: For reviews by Thomas F. Donlon and Norman E. Gronlund of an earlier edition, see 8:33 (1 reference); for a review by A. N. Hieronymus and an excerpted review by S. Alan Cohen of an earlier edition, see 7:32.

TEST REFERENCES

1. Stewart, W. W., Davis, P. D., Wilson, R. C., & Porter, T. (1981). Expressed versus tested vocational interests of incarcerated and non-incarcerated adolescents. *Journal of Applied Rehabilitation Counseling, 12,* 126-129.
2. Kender, J. P., Greenwood, S., & Conard, E. (1985). WAIS-R performance patterns of 565 incarcerated adults characterized as underachieving readers and adequate readers. *Journal of Learning Disabilities, 18,* 379-383.

Review of the Tests of Adult Basic Education, Forms 5 and 6, and Survey Form by ROBERT W. LISSITZ, Professor of Education and Psychology and Chairperson, Department of Measurement, Statistics, and Evaluation, University of Maryland, College Park, MD:

The Tests of Adult Basic Education (TABE) examination is designed to assess achievement in Reading, Mathematics, Language, and Spelling. Equivalent Forms 5 and 6 are intended to provide norm-referenced scores as well as criterion-referenced scores for basic skills. The test is organized in four separate levels—Easy, Medium, Difficult, and Advanced. The level of the test to be administered is determined by a Locator Test consisting of 25 mathematics items and 25 vocabulary items. There is also a Survey Form that is a shortened version of the TABE 5 and has items from all areas except Spelling. Its purpose is to provide, with less time investment, benchmark scores for Reading, Mathematics, and Language. It also uses the Locator Test, which takes 37 minutes. Combined with Reading (22 minutes), Mathematics (28 minutes), and Language (21 minutes), the Survey Form still takes 1 hour and 48 minutes, plus time for whatever practice exercises or orientation is allocated to the assessment. If a school is looking for a quick test to use for students to get a general evaluation, this is probably not going to be satisfactory.

There are numerous booklets available, including one for norms, a technical manual, a coordinator's manual, an examiner's manual for the Survey Form, and another for Forms 5 and 6. Along with sample copies of the tests, there are inches of material to read. Fortunately, the material is well written and attractively presented. The test and supporting documents were professionally done and clearly will be a competitive product in the marketplace.

The test was developed by examining current curriculum guides, textbooks, and instructional programs obtained from adult education programs throughout the country (Technical Manual, p. 5). The material was used to identify a common set of basic skills, and items were written by professionals, many of whom were experienced teachers. A "Tryout Edition" was reviewed for content, instructions, and time limits. The process for development also included extensive review for potential bias against Blacks, Hispanics, and Asians. No information is given about the Hispanic and Asian samples.

The development process is the sole basis for validity of the tests. Content validity is the only type of validity justification. Because the user is encouraged to test for diagnostic purposes and the test is likely to be used for admissions and classification decisions as well, some criterion-validity evidence should supplement the curriculum analysis as supporting evidence. The test also emphasizes its potential usage with a wide variety of educational environments (adult offenders, juvenile offenders, and vocational/technical school enrollees), but no justification, even content validity, is included for these.

The TABE subtests were correlated with the subtests of the Tests of General Educational Development (GED) and the set of coefficients is interesting to examine. They provide a multimethod, multitrait matrix, but unfortunately no discussion of differential validity is provided. Further, the GED is either passed or not passed, and the predictability of this overall decision, using the TABE, would be a nice addition to the manual.

All test analyses utilized the 3-parameter IRT model and LOGIST-5 computer program (from Educational Testing Service). The information function is calculated and the conditional Standard Error of Measurement (*SEM*) is presented as a function of the scale score. This is quite important, particularly because the *SEM* curves are presented for each of the four levels of test difficulty. In many of the cases the Advanced and Difficult forms do not differ in their *SEM* curves as much as we might expect or might hope. In these cases, they are interchangeable test forms, as far as accuracy of estimation is considered. Another concern with the reliability of the test is that only internal consistency is estimated (using KR20). Additional evidence, such as test-retest and parallel form reliabilities, would be helpful to users of the test. In fact, no discussion of the equivalence of Forms 5 and 6 was found in the material submitted for review.

There is some useful information from an equating study of Form 5 and Form 3 (from 1976). Scale score to scale score conversion tables are available, according to the technical manual. The California Achievement Tests (CAT E) provided a set of anchor items for use in the equating study, and these permit an additional conversion table for the TABE 5 and 6 to the CAT E and F. These test conversion tables, and the work relating the TABE to the GED, are potentially very helpful. For a technical manual, however, there is not much detail on any of these additions.

One of the more interesting tables in the Technical Manual (p. 35, also in the section on equating and norming) shows that 49% of the norming sample were in the 15-to-24-year age group and an additional 31% were in the 25-to-34-year age range. This is a very young adult group and it is not clear to the reviewer why there were any persons under age 18 in the norms sample at all, given the name of the test (Tests of *Adult* Basic Education). It was also surprising that almost 71% of the norming sample were males (5,731 out of 8,125). One of the nice features of the test is the availability of norms for adult offenders, juvenile offenders, and vocational/technical school enrollees.

Another strong feature of the TABE is the use of the Locator Test, although it would be more defensible if additional information was provided. For example, this reviewer would like to see a description of the process used in deciding to have only mathematics and vocabulary items in the Locator, and to see how the cutoffs are justified for referral to each of the four levels. Evidence of the effect of the referral test upon the efficiency of the testing process would also be useful. Additional validation work is needed to justify the Locator process as well.

The material on test reports for the teacher and/or student is also not as convincing as I would have liked. For example, the design of the reports would be more user friendly with pictorial representations of the *SEM* as a band on the latent ability rather than a numerical presentation.

In summary, the TABE, Forms 5 and 6, and the Survey Form are well-done instruments with considerable justification for their use. The supporting material is nicely done, although the technical manual would benefit from considerable expansion, particularly with additional work on reliability and validity.

Review of the Tests of Adult Basic Education, Forms 5 and 6, and Survey Form by STEVEN J. OSTERLIND, Associate Professor and Director, Center for Educational Assessment, University of Missouri-Columbia, Columbia, MO:

The Tests of Adult Basic Education (TABE) examination, Forms 5 and 6, is a completely rewritten version of the popularly used earlier TABE forms. Virtually every aspect of test construction was done anew for the TABE, Forms 5 and 6: The content was reorganized after a thorough review of relevant curricular materials, all of the test's items

were freshly prepared, an entirely new standardization process was undertaken, a Locator test was added, the test's reports were redesigned, and most of the ancillary materials were rewritten. Also, a microcomputer software package for scoring answer sheets, looking up norms, and calculating objectives mastery information is available for the first time.

The publisher's claims for the information yielded by this new assessment instrument are manifold. According to CTB Macmillan/McGraw-Hill, the TABE, Forms 5 and 6, can (*a*) predict the probability of passing the Tests of General Educational Development (GED); (*b*) provide objective-referenced curriculum scores; (*c*) produce norm-referenced scores (to four specific adult populations); and (*d*) can be equated to earlier TABE Forms 3 and 4. Further, throughout the promotional brochures and administration materials, the publisher boasts of technical rigor, citing claims of "reliability" again and again. We shall examine the merit of these claims later in this review.

Several features are added to the TABE, Forms 5 and 6, that make it attractive to users. In particular, the Practice Exercise, the various scoring options, the microcomputer-based system for interpreting results, and the reports are all appealing features of this instrument. The Practice Exercise is a brief and useful activity intended to acquaint examinees with the format for test items they will confront on the test. The score reports—of which there are two, an individual report (that may be obtained with or without objectives performance) and a summary report—are pleasing and will likely prove easily read by test users. The scoring options are especially alluring. Either a convenient SCOREZE answer sheet or a scannable form may be used. The administrator must then access the TABE Norms System through a microcomputer, or the same information can be gotten through a series of lookup tables. The Locator Test will probably be useful to test administrators, despite the shortcoming of having only vocabulary and mathematics items included.

Two ancillary publications, the Test Coordinator's Handbook and the Examiner's Manual, are especially helpful. CTB/McGraw-Hill's success in using parallel materials in other achievement tests has proven to the TABE's benefit. They are easily read, attractively formatted, and very informative to workaday practitioners.

All of these features are clear pluses for a testing system that is obviously trying to be "user friendly."

When one looks beyond these superficial aspects of the test, however, and into the merits for valid interpretations of the numbers yielded by this instrument, serious concerns arise. For example, little technical information is offered about such important aspects of test construction as scaling, norming, score comparability, and equating. Yet, claims to each of these aspects are made in the promotional literature. For example, the Technical Report provides scant data about the validity of the score interpretations recommended. This is too serious an omission to call it an oversight. Weak Pearson correlation coefficients to GED scores are about all that is presented for external-related validity evidence. Nothing at all is mentioned about data gathered for supporting diagnostic uses of the test.

Only cursory information about the norming sample is provided, but this is obviously one of the areas of greatest interest to test users. A table cites their numbers but no information is provided about the relevant characteristics of this sample. The same criticism is true for the equating study cited. The reader is left to wonder what happened. The materials say a study was conducted, but it is not described and the results are not presented for inspection.

As another example, information about standard errors of the various subtests is not provided in any meaningful way. Beyond printing in the Technical Report IRT standard error curves (without accompanying explanation and without mentioning their relevance to score interpretation for test users), one is left uninformed about this important aspect of mental measurements.

The issue of test bias is important, both in fact and in perception about a test. Here, the test's developers seem to have invested more energy in explaining the procedures used than in some other equally important areas.

In summary, while there are appealing aspects of the ease of use of the TABE, Forms 5 and 6, it appears CTB/McGraw-Hill did not follow the precepts put forth in the *Standards for Educational and Psychological Testing* (AERA, APA, & NCME, 1985) to a disturbing degree, especially as it concerns that most-important-of-all-test-development concerns: valid interpretations of the scores. This leads one to recommend that if the TABE, Forms 5 and 6, is adopted for use, it should be done so by users who are aware that much about the psychometric underpinnings of this test is unexplained.

REVIEWER'S REFERENCE

American Educational Research Association, American Psychological Association, & National Council on Measurement in Education. (1985). *Standards for educational and psychological testing.* Washington, DC: American Psychological Association, Inc.

[447]
Tests of General Educational Development [the GED Tests].

Purpose: To "assess skills representative of the typical outcomes of a traditional high school education" for the purpose of awarding a secondary school level (GED) diploma.

Population: Candidates for high school equivalency diplomas.
Publication Dates: 1944–91.
Acronym: GED Tests.
Scores, 6: Writing Skills, Social Studies, Science, Interpreting Literature and the Arts, Mathematics, Total.
Administration: Group.
Forms: 12 U.S. English Operational (secure) full-length forms available; 4 U.S. English forms available of Official GED Practice test (nonsecure half-length test).
Price Data, 1991: Operational (secure) forms not available for purchase and are available only to and administered at Official GED Testing Centers; Official GED Practice Tests: $18 per 10 test batteries; $10.95 per 50 universal machine-scorable answer sheets; $9.96 per 10 self-scorable answer sheets (for use with U.S. English Form CC only); $19.95 per Administrator's set including Teacher's Manual ('89, 203 pages) and required scoring materials (stencils, conversion tables); C$27 per 10 Canadian English batteries (or C$4.98 each); C$13.68 per 50 Canadian English universal answer sheets; C$24.99 per Canadian English Administrator's set; $24 per 10 Spanish Edition batteries (or $3.99 each); $9 per English Large Print edition; $44.95 per English Audio Cassette edition.
Foreign Language and Special Editions: Operational (secure) full length GED batteries: Canadian English (6 forms), Spanish (3 forms), French (2 forms), Spanish audio cassette, and U.S. English large print, audio cassette, and Braille editions available; Official GED Practice Tests: Canadian English (2 forms), Spanish, French, Spanish audio cassette, and U.S. English large print and audio cassette editions available.
Time: 120(125) minutes for Writing Skills, 85(90) minutes for Social Studies, 95(100) minutes for Science, 65(70) minutes for Interpreting Literature and the Arts, 90(95) minutes for Mathematics [all times are for Operational (secure forms) tests].
Comments: Tests administered throughout the year at official GED centers; tests originated in 1942 for granting high school/college credit for veterans, in mid-1950s GED program extended to all non-high school graduates; extensive 1988 revisions include addition of essay component to Writing Skills test and increased emphasis on higher order cognitive skills (e.g., application, analysis/evaluation, and math problem solving) throughout the battery.
Author: General Educational Development Testing Service of the American Council on Education.
Publisher: General Educational Development Testing Service of the American Council on Education.
Cross References: For reviews by J. Stanley Ahmann and A. Harry Passow, see 9:1284 (1 reference); see also T3:2485 (2 references), 8:35 (20 references), and 7:34 (21 references); for a review by Robert J. Solomon of earlier forms, see 5:29 (39 references); for a review by Gustav J. Froehlich, see 4:26 (27 references); for reviews by Herbert S. Conrad and Warren G. Findley, see 3:20 (11 references). For reviews by Charlotte W. Croon of an earlier form of the expression subtest, see 3:122; for reviews by W. E. Hall and C. Robert Pace of an earlier form of the social studies reading subtest, see 3:528.

TEST REFERENCES

1. Carbol, B. C., & Maguire, T. O. (1986). Benefits and disappointments from participation in the Alberta High School Equivalency Program. *The Alberta Journal of Educational Research, 32,* 66-76.

2. Whitney, D. R., Malizio, A. G., & Patience, W. M. (1986). Reliability and validity of the GED tests. *Educational and Psychological Measurement, 46,* 689-698.

Review of the Tests of General Educational Development by BRUCE G. ROGERS, Professor of Educational Psychology and Foundations, University of Northern Iowa, Cedar Falls, IA:

The Tests of General Educational Development (GED test) was developed in 1942 to aid veterans of World War II who had not yet completed high school. Its intent was to provide a means for the assessment and recognition of a level of educational development comparable to that of a traditional high school graduate. The test became so well accepted that, during the next two decades, the client population served by the program shifted from one consisting largely of military veterans to one that was largely civilian. In 1988, over 700,000 individuals took the tests, and more than 70% of these examinees qualified for the high school equivalency diploma.

The GED test has benefitted from the influence of many experienced psychometricians. Ralph Tyler, who had directed the Eight Year Study of the Progressive Education Association, supervised the United States Air Force Institute Examinations staff at the University of Chicago. He strongly emphasized the need to measure the major and lasting outcomes generally thought to be the result of a high school education. E. F. Lindquist, who had recently developed the Iowa Tests of Educational Development (ITED), emphasized the appraisal of what he called "general educational development." In fact, the first GED examination was an adaptation of the newly published ITED. Down through the years, the GED test has continued to reflect structural similarities to the ITED battery and a similar point of view.

The GED test uses a hierarchal approach to describe the critical thinking skills that are assessed. An adaptation of the *Taxonomy of Educational Objectives* (developed under the direction of Benjamin S. Bloom in 1956) is now used to classify the items. None of the tests have items that measure recall of information alone; but all of them have items that require the skills of comprehension, application, and analysis. Synthesis is required in the Writing Skills test, evaluation is required in the Social Studies and Science tests, and application is entailed in the Mathematics section. The importance of the use of knowledge in higher skills is repeatedly emphasized in all of the supporting literature that accompanies the tests.

Originally, the GED program consisted of a high school battery leading to the equivalency diploma and a college battery focusing on general education coursework for purposes of college placement. During the 1950s, the college battery became the forerunner of the College Level Examination Program (CLEP) tests, which is now the current credit-by-examination program. Since then, the GED program has focused exclusively on the high school equivalency test.

The five achievement tests were extensively reviewed during the 1970s and revised in 1978 in an attempt to adapt them to contemporary secondary school emphases. During the 1980s, a 5-year review process was conducted to make further revisions for the 1988 edition (which is currently in use). These revisions included the addition of a writing sample, the strengthening of the emphasis on critical thinking, the inclusion of items related to computer technology, and the assessment of consumer skills in common adult settings. It is in the context of this historical development that the current edition of the GED test must be viewed in order to evaluate its strengths and weaknesses as they pertain to contemporary society.

During the 1980s, several survey studies were conducted which confirmed the centrality of the historical GED goal to enable individuals to earn a high school credential; these studies also pointed out the need for the test to be job oriented. Toward this end, the tests were revised to include items that simulate work-setting skills, such a writing a work report, interpreting graphs, and recognizing the logical ordering of steps in a simple computer program. Because individuals use the GED test scores for a wide variety of purposes including university admissions and job advancement, the authors of the test have attempted to continue to develop items that reflect these goals.

When the GED test was first developed, examinees were allowed some flexibility in time constraints, but, as the test began to be used by large civilian populations, practical considerations necessitated the use of strict time limits. The test currently requires five sessions, ranging from 1 to 2 hours in length. Because it is purported to be a power test, an extensive work-rate study was conducted to establish appropriate lengths and time limits for the various subtests. It was found that, on the average, older students required more time to complete the test. Therefore, they may need practice to develop the requisite proficiencies and speed prior to taking the test.

In the past few years, considerable discussion has centered on the use of minimal competency tests as a requirement for high school graduation, and some critics have suggested the GED test be limited to the assessment of minimal competency skills. The authors of the GED test decided not to make such a drastic change because, first, high school graduates generally are assumed to have progressed beyond minimal level skills, and second, there currently is little agreement on which minimal skills should be included. Accordingly, the Official Teacher's Guide emphasizes that all of the items in the test are above the knowledge level. And there is considerable support for the position that those who can demonstrate higher level skills also possess the lower level skills. It would be useful to test that assumption with suitable groups and to report the results as one type of evidence relevant to the content validity of the test.

Since the beginning of the program, GED test results have been expressed as "standard scores" (T scores in particular) with the intent that they would be interpreted as reflecting normative standing in the population of high school seniors. In the 1980s consideration was given to establishing performance standards for a criterion-referenced interpretation. These two approaches do not necessarily require separate instruments, as evidenced by the fact that most of the nationally normed standardized tests given in schools provide both types of interpretations. The survey of users in the 1980s suggested that there was widespread agreement that passing scores should be set in terms of norms, so the authors have continued to use that interpretation of the scores. It might, however, be useful to classify the items by skill, provide criterion-referenced interpretations, and compare the results with normative interpretations. Such studies would constitute further evidence of content validity and might provide useful information for those who help prepare candidates to take the test.

Evidence of reliability and validity was not provided in the first editions of the GED test, an omission that was pointedly emphasized in previous *Mental Measurements Yearbook* reviews. Admittedly, gathering such data is difficult, and particularly so for this test, due to the nature of the population. The authors currently provide KR20 reliability estimates, based on the 1987–1988 standardization administration. Most of the internal consistency reliabilites are above .90, with only a few as low as .87. These values certainly compare favorably with other standardized test results. The authors did not provide alternate form reliability coefficients, but the gathering of such data for this test would be a worthwhile project for future studies.

As far as this reviewer knows, no formal technical manual exists that addresses norms, reliability, and validity for the test. However, some of this type of information is available from other sources. For example, evidence of content validity is found in the detailed test outlines printed in the Official Teacher's Guide and in the published practice tests which show examples of the types of items used to measure the outline topics. An examination of these materials confirms that the authors have attempted to select those topics that are most likely to be covered in

high school texts and that they have constructed items requiring the examinee to understand and apply verbal concepts in reasonably realistic settings. Additionally, there is some evidence in the Research Reports related to the empirical validity of the test. When mean scores from a large sample of 1980 high school graduating seniors were compared with those of GED examinees, strong agreement was found in each of the test areas. Another type of evidence that might be appropriate would be correlational studies based on test scores and grade point averages among graduating seniors.

A holistically scored writing sample is now included in the GED test. In the mid-1980s, studies were conducted to assess the reliability and validity of these measures. When two readers read each paper, the interrater reliability was found to lie between .6 and .7. On about one-third of the papers, the readers agreed exactly, and on about one-half, they differed by a single point. To assess concurrent validity, essay scores were compared with scores on the multiple-choice section of the Writing Skills test; the resulting correlation coefficients ranged between .5 and .7. This type of evidence was used to justify the combining of essay scores and multiple-choice scores into a single Writing Skills score.

Although the GED test originally was designed for veterans, the composition of the client population has changed over the years. Of those examined during the 1980s, about 58% were female, half were age 21 or less, half had ninth grade educations or less, and half reported that they generally received school grades of "C" or below. About one-third of the examinees took the test as a requirement for employment and another third took it to gain admission to postsecondary education programs. In preparation for the test, about half had taken at least one course, and about half had spent more than 30 hours studying. There are wide variations from these median and modal values, and the description of the test-taking population has enabled the test authors to better address the needs of that population.

Over the past 40 years, the *Mental Measurements Yearbook* reviewers of the GED test have made suggestions for improvements, many of which have been incorporated in subsequent revisions of the test. For example, the reading level of the tests has been reduced, a stronger emphasis has been put on higher order thinkings skills, the number of discrete items (as opposed to passage related items) has been increased, and a writing sample has been included. An Official Teacher's Guide has been prepared, which gives content outlines for the tests, sample items with commentaries, suggestions for teaching, and guidelines for score interpretation. The manual is well written but, because it does not contain suggested schedules for presenting the material, teachers will need to create their own.

Since its inception, reviewers of the GED test have questioned whether a paper-and-pencil instrument can adequately measure ethical values, or skills attained in the laboratory, or those intangibles such as a favorable emotional orientation toward a subject, all of which good high school courses are envisioned to provide. There is probably as much, or more, difference of opinion with respect to these questions today as in the past, but a sampling of the GED Research Reports indicates the test authors have attempted to address those issues. Continued interest in these issues would be laudable.

Two practice tests are now provided, each about half as long as the GED test. A teacher's manual is provided for the practice tests, which gives suggestions for helping students and discusses, in great detail, the logic for solving sample items. The practice items reflect considerable sophistication, and the manual, which is written in very understandable prose, reflects careful thought.

Five subtests comprise the 1988 edition of the GED test, all of which are revisions of those in the previous edition, and all of which contain five-option multiple-choice items. In order of presentation, they are: (a) Writing Skills, Part 1, 55 items covering sentence structure, usage, and mechanics, most of which require the correction or revision of sentences, and Part 2, the Writing Sample, which presents a single topic in two or three sentences and requires the examinee to write a 200-word composition to explain their response; (b) Social Studies, 64 items covering history, economics, political science, geography, and behavioral science, giving approximately equal emphasis to each of the cognitive levels of comprehension, application, analysis, and evaluation; (c) Science, 66 items divided equally between life science and physical science with approximately equal emphasis on the same four cognitive levels as in Social Studies; (d) Interpreting Literature and the Arts (formerly entitled Reading), 45 items, half on popular literature and the other half on classical literature (of the 19th and 20th Centuries) and the arts, most of which are at the comprehension level; and (e) Mathematics, 56 items, half on arithmetic and half on algebra and geometry, most of which require the solutions to problems, with a strong emphasis on proportions. The student is informed that none of the items are "trick" items and that the time limits have been adjusted so that the tests can function as power tests if the student works efficiently.

The Writing Skills test focuses upon the ability of the student to recognize errors in mechanics, usage, and structure of sentences. Some previous reviewers have criticized the test for emphasizing the recognition of editorial material at the expense of actual writing skills, so the 1988 revision included a writing sample. To score the writing sample, an elaborate system was devised to select persons with adequate professional background in writing and to train them to implement holistic scoring principles. Each paper is read two or three times to help ensure interrater reliability. The correlation between scores on the multiple-choice and essay sections is high. The presence of the writing sample enhances the content validity of the Writing Skills test.

Traditionally, social studies tests are notorious for emphasizing names and dates for which it is difficult to get agreement among experts as to their importance. An examination of the practice items for the Social Studies test, however, shows no items requiring only factual knowledge but, rather, an ability to use knowledge in higher level activities such as the reading of a diagram of a globe to make inferences. The emphasis on current information in some of the items will require that the tests be revised about every decade, as they have in the past.

An early criticism of the Science test was that it had too few diagrams. In the 1988 version, diagrams are used extensively. For example, each one of the practice tests has four diagrams which require the student to carefully study structures. Some reviewers have questioned the relative emphases of the topics because half of the items pertain to biology. This, however, probably is justified. Many high school students take 1 year each of general science (which usually is an introduction to some basic principles in earth science, chemistry, and physics) and biology. The authors have stated their intention to include topics of current interest. Although laudable, this will necessitate a continuous comparison of the test table of specifications with the content of widely used textbooks to ensure that the test continues to measure the important outcomes of a high school education.

In earlier editions, the social science and natural science tests heavily emphasized the interpretation of reading materials in those areas. Over the years, there has been concern that the subject matter measures were confounded by the required reading levels. As a result, for the 1988 edition, instructions were given to the item writers to prepare their items using readability levels typical of texts used in high school. An examination of the items in the practice tests suggests that the item writers adhered to these instructions reasonably well. The examinee is required to have more background knowledge in order to answer the questions correctly because fewer of the items are passage dependent. Originally, the GED test included a test entitled Interpretation of Literary Materials that presented both prose and poetry passages. In the 1978 edition, this test was replaced by the Reading Skills test, but it still contained items covering prose and poetry. In the 1988 revision, the test title was again changed, this time to Interpreting Literature and the Arts. A strong emphasis is placed upon the understanding of current and classical literature and the arts. To illustrate this to the candidates, the practice tests include one passage from *Pride and Prejudice* and another from a newspaper review of a 1985 popular opera.

Although the Mathematics test is half arithmetic, there are no lengthy computations. Rather, the focus is on practical problems that require thinking and a small amount of computation. Some items on basic manipulation of algebraic and geometric concepts are used, including some on scientific notation. None of the test questions actually requires material beyond first-year algebra, but most students will not achieve the understanding required until they have had further experiences requiring applications of these skills. This view is consistent with the data showing that when the test was administered to students from all four grades in high school, the scores increased in each successive grade.

SUMMARY. Just as the 1978 revision of the GED battery was widely perceived as being an improvement over previous editions, the 1988 revision is likely to be perceived as being a further polishing of that instrument. With the continued emphasis upon the need for higher education, it is expected that the test will continue to be widely used both among immigrants and among native born who, for various reasons, do not complete a high school education.

Previous reviewers have struggled with the content validity of a paper-and-pencil test to measure all of the outcomes expected from a high school education, particularly those of a noncognitive nature. No solution has been found that is satisfactory to all concerned, but the variety of studies in the GED program attests to the continued interest of both authors and other scholars relative to this question. As the curriculum of high schools changes over time, there is a need for the test to be revised; yet frequent revisions are very expensive, and detecting curriculum changes, that are both consistent across schools at any one time and stable across several years, is a challenging task. The GED test has remained stable in one respect, however, namely, the attempt to measure the attainment of some of the major objectives of the general education program in American high schools.

Review of the Tests of General Educational Development by MICHAEL S. TREVISAN, Research Associate, RMC Research Corporation, Portland, OR:

The addition of an essay examination makes this revision of the Tests of General Educational Development (GED) the most profound to date. The items have also been revised to reflect the context of working adults. The topics of computers and computer technology have been added to the content of the items wherever possible. In short, this

revision of the GED was done with an attempt to project its use into the 1990s.

A connection to the previous edition has been maintained by the continuation of five tests. These tests are: Writing Skills, Social Studies, Science, Interpreting Literature and the Arts, and Mathematics. The Writing Skills test is composed of a multiple-choice component and an essay component. "Interpreting Literature and the Arts" is the new name for the "Reading Skills" test of the previous edition. Also, to address previous criticism of the Mathematics test, the number of computation problems has been decreased, and more algebra problems added.

Bloom's thinking skills taxonomy (Bloom, Englehart, Furst, Hill, & Krathwohl, 1956) was used to classify the cognitive level of the items. All items require the comprehension or manipulation of concepts in order to solve. None of the items were designed to test the mere recall of facts.

ADMINISTRATION AND SCORING. All items with the exception of the essay component of the Writing Skills test are in multiple-choice format and contain five options. Seven hours and 35 minutes of testing time is required to complete the battery. This is an increase of approximately 1 hour over the previous edition and, in large part, is due to the addition of the essay component of the Writing Skills test.

The raw scores on each test are converted to *standard scores*; these are normalized standard scores transformed to a *T*-scale, with a mean of 50 and a standard deviation of 10, and range from 20 to 80. The standard scores are used by each state or territory to determine the minimum score for passing. Percentiles are also reported.

NORMS. A norming study was conducted in 1987 using a stratified random sampling plan with the following variables: geographic region, public versus private schools, and socioeconomic status for public schools. More than 20,000 U.S. 12th grade students near graduation participated in the norming. No GED examinees were included in the norming sample, as was done in the 1980 norming study.

RELIABILITY. Internal consistency reliability coefficients (KR-20) for the 1987 standardization are acceptably high, ranging in magnitude from .90 to .94.

VALIDITY. No validity data are available at this time. However, validity studies are in progress.

THE ESSAY. The Tests Specification Committee, which was convened for purposes of this revision, recommended that no one be given high school equivalency without demonstrating the ability to write. Consequently, an essay was added to the battery as a component to the Writing Skills test. This addition is unusual among achievement test batteries, and poses technical problems that multiple-choice tests do not. Therefore, considerable space in this review will be used to address this aspect of the revision.

The essay topic is expository in nature and requires the production of ideas, unlike the other parts of the GED battery that require analyzing or understanding particular concepts. The essay is holistically scored. This method of scoring rank orders the papers. This process is, therefore, consistent with the norm-referenced nature of the GED. Scores are defined in a "scoring guide," range from a low of 1 to a high of 6, and reflect the reader's general impression of the essay. Each paper is scored by two readers and the sum of these scores is subsequently given to the essay. Therefore, a candidate's score on the essay will range from 2 to 12. If the scores from the two readers differ by more than one point, a third reader will read the paper. The score for the paper will then be the average of the three ratings multiplied by 2.

TRAINING. A chief reader from each scoring site was sent to Washington DC for extensive training in the use of the scoring method. These readers were certified and, in turn, trained staff at their respective sites. The sites were then certified and periodically monitored.

The subjective nature of the scoring process begs the reliability question. To this end, the work of the GED Testing Service (GEDTS) is applauded. Two different reliabilities were established. First, the consistency of readers within a site was examined. This type of reliability the GEDTS refers to as *reading reliability*. Specifically, it is a measure of the consistency of different readers rating the same papers in a particular reading session. The second type of reliability investigated is referred to as *scale stability*. It is a measure of the agreement between the site readers and the GEDTS Writing Committee readers. Because scores may be awarded consistently within site but not across sites (referred to as scale drift), a measure of scale stability is warranted.

There is considerable confusion among practitioners regarding the appropriate statistic to use when establishing different measures of reliability of data obtained from observation and judgment (Suen & Ary, 1989). Despite wanting a measure of agreement between the site and the Writing Committee (scale stability), obtaining the percent agreement, as is often done with writing and other performance assessments, is not a true measure of reliability in the classical sense (Tinsley & Weiss, 1975). One can have high agreement and low reliability, and vice versa. Also, the Pearson product moment correlation, although often used, is not sensitive to scale drift because the scale is standardized in this statistic. The appropriate statistic to use in this case is the intraclass correlation coefficient (ICC). The GEDTS used this statistic for both reliability measures. For the measure of scale stability, the

GEDTS also used the particular ICC that treats differences between raters (in this case, differences between the site and the Writing Committee) as error variance. This variance detracts from the consistency between the site and the Writing Committee.

The magnitude of the reading reliability coefficients range from .44 to 1.00, with most in the .80s. The scale stability was reported for only one site. The value is .72. Percent agreement was also calculated between each site and the Writing Committee and appropriately used to determine any problems in the application of the scoring guide if the magnitude of scale stability was low for a particular site.

The scores on the essay were weighted and combined with the multiple-choice component which make up the Writing Skills test. The net result is a respectable reliability coefficient of approximately .87 for the Writing Skills test.

CONCERNS. Despite the sound approach used for test development, the lack of validity information for the GED is a major weakness of the battery. Especially with the addition of an essay, validity evidence is crucial. It is incumbent upon the test developer to provide this information before the battery is marketed. Validity studies from the previous version (which were sent to this reviewer) are no substitute. This lack of technical data renders the task of a complete evaluation of the GED impossible at this time.

SUMMARY. The extensive review and revision process and the addition of an essay component to the battery are indicative of the solid approach to test construction employed by the GEDTS for over 40 years. This approach also lays the foundation for a sound test battery. The reliability study for the essay is a blueprint which other test developers should read before conducting one of their own. Without adequate validity information, however, it is still an open question as to whether or not the scores can be used for the stated purpose.

REVIEWER'S REFERENCES

Bloom, B. S., Englehart, M. D., Furst, E. J., Hill, W. H., & Krathwohl, D. R. (1956). *Taxonomy of educational objectives: The classification of educational goals handbook I: Cognitive domain.* New York: David McKay.

Tinsley, H. E. A., & Weiss, D. J. (1975). Interrater reliability and agreement of subjective judgments. *Journal of Counseling Psychology, 22,* 358-376.

Suen, H. K., & Ary, D. (1989). *Analyzing quantitative behavioral observation data.* Hillsdale, NJ: Lawrence Erlbaum Associates.

[448]

Tests of Reading Comprehension.

Purpose: "They aim at assessing the extent to which readers are able to obtain meaning from text."

Population: Grades 3–7, 6–10.

Publication Date: 1987.

Acronym: TORCH.

Scores, 14: Grasshoppers; The Bear Who Liked Hugging People; Lizards Love Eggs; Getting Better;

Feeding Puff; Shocking Things, Earthquakes!; The Swamp-creature; The Cats; A Horse of Her Own; Iceberg Towing; The Accident; The Killer Smog of London; I Want to be Andy; The Red Ace of Spades.
Administration: Individual or group.
Levels: 2 overlapping test booklets: A, B.
Price Data, 1988: A$50 per complete kit including test booklet A, test booklet B, 16 answer sheets, set of photocopy master sheets, and manual (84 pages).
Time: Untimed.
Comments: "Content-referenced" and/or "norm-referenced."
Authors: Leila Mossenson, Peter Hill, and Geoffrey Masters.
Publisher: Australian Council for Educational Research, Ltd. [Australia].

Review of the Tests of Reading Comprehension by
ROBERT B. COOTER, JR., Associate Professor of
Elementary Education, Brigham Young University,
Provo, UT:

The Tests of Reading Comprehension (TORCH) are a set of 14 group-administered reading tests for use with students in Years (grades) 3 to 10. The TORCH is untimed and provides both norm-referenced and "content-referenced" information for classroom use. Each testing package contains an Examiner's Manual, Test Booklets A and B, consumable TORCH Answer Sheets, and a very helpful set of Photocopy Masters of the TORCH Answer Sheets.

The TORCH passages were selected from published materials and reflect a wide variety of fiction and nonfiction literature. Test Booklet A is intended for Years (grades) 3 to 7, and Test Booklet B is for Years 6 to 10. Students are instructed to read each passage of text, then complete a retelling of the passage. The retelling is very much like a cloze passage with key words or ideas missing. Students fill in the gaps with one or more of their own words. The TORCH authors feel that this process allows readers to produce their own reconstruction of the author's intended meaning, and acts as a probe causing them to consider particular details in the text.

Scoring on the TORCH is done much more holistically than with most reading assessment instruments. Score keys are presented in the examiner's manual that suggest several appropriate responses for each blank in the retelling, as well as responses judged to be unacceptable. If the student offers a response not included in the key, examiners are instructed to judge the semantic similarity of the student's answer to responses on the list. Although this scoring process may take considerably longer, the results should be much more valid and offer useful classroom implications.

Another appealing aspect of the TORCH is the availability of what the authors refer to as "content-referenced" interpretations. By analyzing the 302

items from all 14 subtests the authors were able to identify 11 distinct kinds of comprehension tasks (e.g., Provide subject of story, Infer emotion, Reconstruct the writer's general message). By applying student responses to a "TORCH Scale" included at the bottom of each answer sheet the examiner is able to easily deduce which comprehension tasks need attention.

The examiner's manual is very well written and offers many useful suggestions for administering and scoring the TORCH. Particularly helpful are the numerous figures and tables detailing such information as comparisons between student ability levels and test difficulty, sources for reading passages, case study examples illustrating how to use the scoring keys, and reading comprehension tasks rated according to a scale of increasing difficulty. Examiners should find it relatively easy to familiarize themselves with the materials and procedures after a careful reading of the Manual.

TECHNICAL CONSIDERATIONS. The TORCH was developed in 1982 by staff of the Western Australian Education Department. As mentioned above, all passages were selected from published materials. The authors especially wanted to avoid what they termed "stilted prose," that which has limited content and carefully controlled vocabulary. A balance was maintained between questions of a literal and inferential nature.

Standardization of the TORCH was carried out in 1982 and 1984 in Western Australian Government schools. The TORCH performance scale, which runs from near zero to about 100, was developed through a calibration and equation process using Rasch measurement methods. This allows for the direct comparison of ability estimates of children who have taken different tests and allows for the selection of tests that are appropriate to the reading levels of individual children. Full details of the calibration and equating of the TORCH tests in Western Australia are offered in the Manual.

Reliability estimates for the TORCH, indicating the extent to which the test offers consistent results, seem to be quite satisfactory. The Kuder-Richardson (KR-20) procedure was employed and provides some indication of the internal consistency of the test items. Reliability coefficients range from .90 to .93 for the various passages. Generally a subtest reliability coefficient of .75 is considered acceptable, so the TORCH figures are very adequate.

Validity is generally considered to be an estimate of how well a test measures the skill or ability it is intended to measure. Two types of validity often considered by test makers are content (or curricular) validity and construct validity. The TORCH authors have failed to provide any direct evidence of either. However, they have not left the issue entirely unattended. Care has been taken in the construction of the TORCH to identify 11 specific comprehension abilities assessed on the 14 passages through a kind of factor analysis procedure. Thus, educators can review the list and compare these abilities to the school curriculum. To the extent that the test has identified abilities of interest to local personnel, it may be considered either valid or invalid. No evidence concerning construct validity is provided in the TORCH manual. In summary, one must conclude that very little evidence of validity has been offered by the authors.

Finally, the authors have included a very thorough appendix that provides other technical benefits. Perhaps the most notable is a listing of the 11 comprehension tasks identified through factor analysis and a key that matches each ability to test item examples. The difficulty level for each ability has been computed along with text and exercise sample items. This allows examiners not only to review a definition of the ability, but also to see a concrete example of each. Correlation of comprehension skills on the test to the school curriculum is made much easier with this very functional appendix.

SUMMARY AND CONCLUSIONS. The Tests of Reading Comprehension (TORCH) represent a step forward in the literacy assessment field. It appears that the primary advantages of the TORCH have to do with reliability, holistic scoring, and classroom applicability. First, there is little question that the TORCH is a reliable instrument when used with students in Western Australia. The normative work was completed with a reasonable degree of rigor and should provide data of some use to school administrators. In addition, the manual indicates that educators in other school systems may develop their own local norms by following a procedure described by Chew and others (1984). Development of local norms is an important step in the overall improvement of literacy assessment. Second, and probably the most important aspect of the TORCH, is its use of more holistic scoring procedures. Allowing examiners to evaluate each response qualitatively moves comprehension assessment closer to the source, namely students' thought processes. Understanding what they do and do not understand has direct implications for classroom intervention. Third, performance on the TORCH may be applied to classroom instruction in at least two ways: (a) through the qualitative analysis of test item responses (as mentioned above), and (b) through the correlation of test performance to specific reading comprehension tasks using the TORCH Scale. This second procedure permits the identification of specific strengths and deficits in reading comprehension that may be most helpful in curricular decision making.

As with all assessment instruments, the TORCH has several limitations. One concern has to do with

the identification of the 11 comprehension tasks assessed by the TORCH. It seems that the test was developed first and that identification of the comprehension abilities assessed followed. This would appear to be backwards. For an assessment instrument to be truly valid one should first identify the belief system or philosophy of reading subscribed to by the school system, generate a list of competencies to be measured that are consistent with that belief system, and finally, develop test items keyed to each competency. In that way the test is driven by the curriculum and not the other way around. The TORCH is not driven by a well-defined belief system, but seems to be driven by itself. A common classroom result in this scenario is teachers teaching to the test rather than having the test serve as an independent measure of student growth.

Another problem with the TORCH is that the format of the test (modified cloze) assumes that the child is capable of working independently, is capable of writing well enough to be understood, and possesses sufficient inferential comprehension skills to guess missing words in mutilated sentences. Certainly the cloze format works well with many students, but not with all. Thus, if a student fails to perform well on the TORCH, one should not conclude that s/he has poor comprehension ability without further investigation using other assessment techniques.

The Tests of Reading Comprehension (TORCH) are an interesting new addition to the arsenal of commercial reading measures presently available. Perhaps as school systems, reading specialists, and researchers experiment with potential uses of the TORCH we will learn of its true significance as part of a comprehensive assessment program. At present it appears that its greatest contribution is the insight it offers into more qualitative forms of cognitive-process assessment.

REVIEWER'S REFERENCE

Chew, A. L., Kesler, E. B., & Sudduth, D. H. (1984). A practical example of how to establish local norms. *The Reading Teacher, 38,* 160-163.

Review of the Tests of Reading Comprehension by DIANE J. SAWYER, Director, Consultation Center for Reading, Syracuse University, Syracuse, NY:

The Tests of Reading Comprehension (TORCH) was developed to assess comprehension competence by engaging students in completing a printed retelling of a passage read. Students fill in blanks (similar to the Cloze procedure). Eleven different kinds of tasks tap comprehension processes. Blanks associated with each of these tasks are presented for each passage. These tasks include: provide story subject given multiple references, verbatim recall of parts of sentences, completion of simple rewordings of text, completion of paraphrases, connecting pronouns with referent, connecting ideas separated in text, giving details in the presence of distracting ideas, giving details in the presence of competing answers, giving evidence of understanding motive underlying actions, reconstructing the writer's general message from specific statements, inferring emotion from scattered clues, and writer's tone.

A student is asked to read just one passage and to complete the retelling of that passage in one untimed sitting. Passages in each booklet are ordered according to difficulty and range in length from 200 to 900 words. Each is an excerpt from a longer passage but can stand alone as a short story or descriptive article in its own right. For each student, the teacher/administrator is to select a passage whose difficulty is closely aligned with the student's reading competence. All children in a given class or at a given grade level need not read the same passage. Analysis of the items missed on the retelling allows the teacher to identify the kinds of comprehension tasks the student can accomplish and provides direction for focusing instruction on those tasks next in need of development. Adequate guidance for interpreting responses into a list of instructional needs is provided in the manual.

In addition to diagnostic information, some normative data are also available. The norming population was drawn from schools in Western Australia. Eight passages were used with the norming sample (over 6,000 students in grades 3–10). Norms for the remaining six passages appear to have been estimated based upon scores obtained from an earlier administration in Western Australia. National Australian norms were derived statistically through a procedure (Rasch calibration and common item-linking procedures) that linked student scores on a TORCH passage to the same student's score on the Progressive Achievement Tests in Reading. Raw scores on any passage are converted to a standard score (TORCH score) that may be compared to the normal curve. For example, a TORCH score of 45 is associated with the 85th percentile rank among third graders, the 47th percentile for fifth graders, and the 15th percentile for seventh graders. The authors do caution users that differences in the student population served, as well as in the time of the year when testing takes place, makes it advisable for schools to establish their own norms. This reviewer would add the caution that differences in the reading curricula between Australia and the United States/Canada is an equally strong reason for developing local norms to assist in interpreting TORCH performance, if comparisons are deemed important.

Reliability of the TORCH is reported in terms of Kuder-Richardson reliability coefficients calculated for only the eight passage retellings used in the norming study. These range between .90 and .93 and suggest a strong degree of internal consistency for those passages. No comment regarding reliability

for the remaining six passages is offered. These reliability coefficients were also used to compute the standard error of measurement (SEM) for each of the 14 retellings. These range from 3 raw-score points at the mid-range of scores to 7 raw-score points at the two extremes. The authors caution that very high or very low scores are probably not valid indicators of a child's reading competence. In cases of extreme scores teachers are urged to discuss the retelling with the child and to consider another administration of an easier or harder passage.

The authors state that since content validity must be established largely on the basis of subjective examination of the test's content in relation to accepted curricula, "the best approach is for the teacher to work systematically through the items of each test, to evaluate the appropriateness of the content for a class, and to test the extent to which the test and the objectives match the teacher's set of objectives."

TORCH appears to be an excellent attempt to shift the focus of comprehension assessment from product to process; from a concern for discrete skills to a concern for strategies engaged. However, in its current form TORCH is best thought of as an informal assessment, dependent upon significant levels of teacher expertise to select an appropriate passage for a given child and to interpret performance. For example, in a figure comparing student ability with test difficulty (Figure 1, p. 3, TORCH manual) it appears that a given third grader might be assigned any one of the first four passages in Booklet A since item difficulty for each ranges well below third grade level. However, some passage 1 items appear to be challenging for most fourth graders, but difficult passage 2 items might not be sufficiently challenging for very able third graders. Further, passage 3 appears to have many more easy items than either of the first two passages, yet some items would be challenging for most fifth graders. It seems reasonable to expect that teachers might have to use these passages several times in order to gain sufficient insight into their unique demands before efficient assignment of students to passages might be achieved.

Further, reliability appears to be only partially specified for the test passages and the question of validity has been left to the judgement of the user. Under these circumstances, potential users are cautioned to consider TORCH an instrument still in the process of becoming a useful tool. How useful it may one day be is essentially dependent upon the skills and energies of the user.

Finally, the normative data reflect only the performance of the children of Western Australia on Australian reading curricula. It would seem imprudent to compare the TORCH performance of children in the United States or Canada to that of the norming group.

[449]

Time Perception Inventory.

Purpose: Measures perceptions of time use including degree of personal concern about time usage and frame of reference (past, present, future) used.
Population: Students in time management courses.
Publication Dates: 1976–87.
Scores, 4: Time Effectiveness, Orientation (Past, Present, Future).
Administration: Group.
Price Data, 1989: $25 per complete kit; $17.50 per 10 inventories including profile; $8.25 per manual ('87, 8 pages).
Time: Administration time not reported.
Comments: Manual has been revised; self-administered.
Author: Albert A. Canfield.
Publisher: Western Psychological Services.

Review of the Time Perception Inventory by DOUGLAS J. McRAE, Vice President for Publishing, CTB Macmillan/McGraw-Hill, Monterey, CA:

PURPOSE. The Time Perception Inventory (TPI) is designed to provide data on (*a*) the way in which individuals view their use of time and (*b*) the general time frame of reference (past, present, future) individuals use in thinking about the world.

DESCRIPTION. The TPI consists of two parts. Part 1 (Time Effectiveness) consists of 10 "How often do you . . ." questions, to which the examinee responds on a 4-point scale (*Rarely, Occasionally, Frequently, A Great Deal*). Each response for each question is weighted, and a total score is obtained by adding the weights assigned for each of the 10 responses. This total score may then be converted to a percentile score for interpretation. Part 2 (Orientation) consists of eight items designed to elicit an individual's tendency to think in the past, the present, or the future. Again, each response is weighted, and separate total scores are obtained for Past, Present, and Future scales by adding the weights assigned to each of the eight responses. The total scores may then be converted to percentiles for interpretation. The TPI is self-administered without time limits. It typically takes 10 minutes or less to complete.

RATIONALE. The TPI is most typically used in courses on time management. Scores on the Time Effectiveness component (Part 1) are designed to determine whether a person feels he/she has a problem managing time. Low scores on the Time Effectivenss component may be used to identify people who are susceptible to effective learning of time management skills. Scores on the Orientation component (Part 2) may be used as a self-analysis that may be related back to specific job assignments. The suggestion is made that a balanced orientation profile (roughly equal emphasis on Past, Present,

and Future) may be the most productive profile for business people.

TECHNICAL INFORMATION. The revised manual available to the reviewer contained a minimum of technical information. The manual indicated the percentile scores for all four scales were based on a sample of more than 2,000 primarily white, male, middle-class, middle-aged, middle-management students taking classes at a midwestern university's business school or attending time use seminars conducted by the author. No information was provided on the derivation of weights used to produce scores for the four scales, nor was reliability or validity information provided.

EVALUATION. The Time Perception Inventory is potentially useful as an instrument to elicit a self-examination about effective use of time, and one's orientation regarding time. It may be used as a discussion starter in courses or seminars on effective time management. It does not have a thorough enough rationale or a sufficiently strong technical base to support inferences of potential effectiveness in job assignments or inferences for diverse populations of individuals. Therefore, its appeal as a guidance instrument is extremely limited. However, as a lead-in for discussion of time management, it may be an effective instrument.

[450]

Time Problems Inventory.

Purpose: Identifies reasons people waste time.
Population: Management and administrative personnel.
Publication Dates: 1980–87.
Scores, 4: Priorities, Planning, Delegation, Discipline.
Administration: Group.
Price Data, 1989: $25 per complete kit; $17.50 per 10 inventories ('87); $8.25 per manual ('87, 8 pages).
Time: (20–25) minutes.
Comments: Manual has been revised; self-administered.
Author: Albert A. Canfield.
Publisher: Western Psychological Services.

[451]

Transit Operator Selection Inventory.

Purpose: "To identify those applicants who . . . have a high probability of success as bus drivers."
Population: Applicants for municipal and urban transit bus operators.
Publication Dates: 1979–84.
Acronym: TOSI.
Scores, 1: Probability of Successful Performance.
Administration: Group.
Price Data, 1988: $11 or less per booklet (minimum order 25) for mail-in scoring method (price includes booklets, scoring, and reports); $12 or less per booklet (minimum order 25) for telephone-scoring method (price includes booklets, scoring, and reports); $6.50 or less per booklet (minimum order 250) for PC-based scoring systems (available with or without data collection for analysis, price includes booklets and software diskettes for IBM-PCs and compatibles); $7.50 per booklet (1,000 minimum) for PC-based scoring system including

booklets, software diskettes, and leased IBM-compatible PC.

Time: (60) minutes.

Comments: All first-time users must submit a job analysis questionnaire entitled Skills and Attributes Inventory (SAI) to demonstrate their bus operator job is similar to those for which the test battery was validated.

Author: Melany E. Baehr.

Publisher: London House, Inc.

Review of the Transit Operator Selection Inventory by LAWRENCE M. RUDNER, Director of the Educational Resources Information Center Clearinghouse on Tests, Measurement and Evaluation (ERIC/TME), American Institutes for Research, Washington, DC and Director of Research, LMP Associates, Chevy Chase, MD:

Virtually every urban area is faced with the problem of selecting transit operators. Poor selection can result in hiring individuals prone to having accidents, using sick leave, being absent, abusing drugs, and receiving traffic violations. This, in turn, can lead to a poor public image, increased liability, increased administrative problems, and increased costs. A test that can improve hiring and thus reduce the problems associated with poor selection decisions should be welcomed by any transit authority.

Developing a test that can be used with multiple population groups and that can withstand the test of time, however, is not an easy task. Based on extensive federally funded research, the Transit Operator Selection Inventory (TOSI) comes close to meeting this standard. But, the TOSI is not without its problems. Three areas warranting careful consideration are local validity, the age of the test, and its reliance on self-report data.

The TOSI consists of three subtests that quantify the applicant's background, skills, and emotional health. The Background subtest uses 35 biodata items and emphasizes job history. The Skills subtest is a self-report instrument in which applicants rate themselves on 96 skills related to bus driving. In the Emotional Health subtest, applicants are asked to rate themselves on 108 psychological characteristics related to working with the public. Several scale scores are available in addition to a composite "Probability of Successful Performance" (PSP) index. Consistent with good practice, the publisher advocates that this PSP score be used with other selection procedures, such as interviews, driving record checks, and driving tests.

The TOSI was developed over a 9-year period with funding from the U.S. Department of Transportation. An extensive job analysis was conducted, a test instrument was piloted, and the final instrument was validated using a variety of concurrent and predictive validation procedures. Special attention was paid to racial and gender differences. The original validation study, conducted in 1975, included over 1,000 bus drivers.

A more recent validation study (circa 1985) involving 210 bus drivers showed an adjusted multiple correlation of .45 between PSP scores, on one hand, and long-term quarterly rates of chargeable accidents, sick days, traffic citations, absenteeism, and supervisory suspensions. Mean PSP scores for Blacks, Whites, and Hispanics were extremely close (all approximately equal to .54) and the different groups had similar validity coefficients. These results were quite similar to the original validation studies.

Despite its impressive history, the TOSI is not necessarily appropriate for all transit authorities. Three possible threats are the congruence between the skills measured on the TOSI and those needed by a particular transit authority, aging of the test, and dependence on self-report data. The publisher has long recognized the first threat and requires a local job analysis. An instrument is available to assist with that task.

Aging of the TOSI is of concern. As the job of bus driver changes with new technology and new demands, the validity of the TOSI can be expected to decline. Relying on demographic characteristics, the predictive validity of biodata questions are particularly time-bound. For example, an annual income of $10,000 may have been highly associated with success as a bus driver in 1975. Such a response would probably detract from predictive validity in 1991. The biodata portion of the TOSI contains numerous items that appear to be time-sensitive.

Another concern is dependence on self-report data. This format allows the test to cover a wide range of skills and attributes related to success as a bus driver. Rather than asking a person to answer 10 questions on depth perception, for example, the TOSI asks one question—How good is your depth perception? The trade-off is that there is no information regarding the accuracy of the individual's response. Because the answer is easy to fake and there is an incentive for applicants to exaggerate their situation or ability, an individual's scores will not necessarily reflect his or her history, skills, or attributes. This trade-off underscores the need stated by the publisher to go beyond the TOSI in evaluating bus driver applicants.

[452]

Typing Skill Test.

Purpose: Measures "speed and accuracy in copying from printed or typed material."

Population: Applicants for clerical positions.

Publication Date: 1988.

Scores, 2: Typing Speed (Gross Words per Minute, Net Words per Minute).

Administration: Group.

Forms, 4: C (Manuscript), D (Manuscript), K (Random Letters), 2 (Random Numbers).

Price Data, 1991: $50 per complete kit including manual (no date, 4 pages).

Time: 5(10) minutes.
Author: E. F. Wonderlic Personnel Test, Inc.
Publisher: E. F. Wonderlic Personnel Test, Inc.

Review of the Typing Skill Test by DIANE BILLINGS FINDLEY, Doctoral Candidate, Louisiana State University, Baton Rouge, LA:

The Typing Skill Test is an instrument designed to measure a job applicant's speed and accuracy of typing when copying from printed or typed material. Directions for test administration, which are provided in the four-page manual, are concise and easy to understand. No special training in test administration or scoring is required.

The applicant is given a practice exercise (included in the test kit) for warming up before being given the Typing Skill Test. The time allotted for the practice exercise is not to exceed 5 minutes. Directions for testing, which include a brief script to be read by the test administrator, are provided in the manual. The applicant is given one of the four forms provided in the test kit and has exactly 5 minutes to copy as accurately as possible from the form. Directions for scoring the test are provided in the manual and are clear and easy to understand. Both a Net Words Per Minute Score and a Gross Words Per Minute Score are obtained. Guidelines for interpreting the results are provided in the manual, with an emphasis on the requirements of the job being filled. No reliability data are provided. However, the manual does include results of one validation study which demonstrated that scores on the Typing Skill Test were related to job performance, with job performance being defined as salary level. Those who had higher salary levels also had higher scores on the Typing Skill Test.

The test involves copying material of "standard" difficulty, such as would be found in "articles in typical digest magazines," rather than complex material, such as that which involves arranging tables, copying from a rough draft, or blocking out a business letter. The rationale given by the test developers for utilizing this simpler format rather than one that is more difficult is that typists who can copy printed material quickly and accurately can learn easily to perform more complex tasks within a short period of time. Empirical support for this assumption would provide a stronger rationale for using this typing test over one that measures more advanced (and perhaps more frequently required) typing skills.

In conclusion, the Typing Skill Test appears to be a simple, easy-to-use screening measure of typing skill, useful for identifying applicants who are skilled in speed and accuracy of copying material from printed material. Reliability data are not available but the test has demonstrated validity in one study. It does not identify applicants for more complex typing skills, such as arranging tabular material and copying from a rough draft. However, for companies requiring only a simple screening of typing speed and accuracy, the Typing Skill Test appears to be an adequate measure.

Review of the Typing Skill Test by SHERRI K. MILLER, Assistant Director, American College Testing Program, Iowa City, IA:

The Typing Skill Test is a 5-minute timed typing test that measures speed and accuracy of copying from typed material. The publisher states that "most typists who can copy printed material quickly and accurately can easily develop, in a few weeks, the skills to successfully handle typing tasks with special or complex requirements." No evidence is given, however, to substantiate this statement. The publisher also states that the test is designed for use in selecting typists, particularly beginning typists, for office work. Given the task required of the applicant it appears that the test would be *best* for selecting beginning typists and may not measure well the skills of a more advanced typist such as setting up tables and letters. The user must also be aware the test requires the applicant to type only from typed material and therefore, may not measure the applicant's ability to type from nontyped material.

The validity data given in the manual are not much help in determining the population for which the test is valid. The one reported validity study employed 101 subjects (51 who were currently employed and 50 who were terminated). The subjects were loan office cashiers. *When* the study was done and in *what* geographical region it was conducted are not reported. Because the publisher markets this test as a selection test, the validity data reported are insufficient.

No reliability data are reported in the manual. Given the length of the test and the purpose of the test, reliability data must be published. It might be wise to give each applicant both forms of the Manuscript Test. The average score could then be used. Such a procedure is suggested because the test-retest reliability of the test is unknown.

The instructions given for test administration are well done. Scoring instructions are also given and explained clearly. However, once scores are obtained the user may have difficulty interpreting them. The interpretation is left open for the user to decide depending on the specific requirements of the company. Some guidelines are suggested. It is not clear, however, whether the guidelines are for the Manuscript Test, the Random Letters Test, or the Random Numbers Test. Some suggestions on how to interpret and use the different test forms would be helpful to users.

In summary, as part of the selection process for a beginning typist, the Typing Skill Test seems to be a practical measure. However, the user must be aware of its limitations. Its use as a sole criterion for job selection is very suspect.

[453]
USES Basic Occupational Literacy Test.

Purpose: "Provides measures of literacy achievement in the areas of reading and arithmetic expressed in terms of occupational requirements for reading and arithmetic" in order to facilitate "vocational counseling and placement by providing direct comparison of a person's literacy skills with literacy skills required for satisfactory performance in various occupations."
Population: Educationally disadvantaged adults.
Publication Dates: 1971–83.
Acronym: BOLT.
Administration: Group.
Parts: 5 tests: Wide-Range Scale, Reading Vocabulary, Reading Comprehension, Arithmetic Computation, Arithmetic Reasoning.
Price Data: Price data and ordering information for tests, answer sheets, scoring stencils, record card, information brochure, manual and manual revisions, DOT supplements, pretesting orientation booklet and other materials for use by individuals and organizations must be cleared through appropriate State Employment Security Agencies.
Comments: Each subject matter area test and screening test may be administered and interpreted independently; developed and published for use primarily by State Employment Security Agencies.
Author: U.S. Department of Labor.
Publisher: U.S. Department of Labor.
   a) WIDE-RANGE SCALE.
   Purpose: Screening test to determine appropriate level of BOLT to administer.
   Scores, 2: Vocabulary, Arithmetic.
   Time: (15–25) minutes.
   b) READING VOCABULARY.
   Acronym: RV.
   Levels, 4: Advanced, High Intermediate, Basic Intermediate, Fundamental.
   Time: Same as for *a* above.
   c) READING COMPREHENSION.
   Acronym: RC.
   Levels, 4: Same as for *b* above.
   Time: Same as for *a* above.
   d) ARITHMETIC COMPUTATION.
   Acronym: AC.
   Levels, 4: Same as for *b* above.
   Time: (30–40) minutes.
   e) ARITHMETIC REASONING.
   Acronym: AR.
   Levels, 3: Advanced, Intermediate, Fundamental.
   Time: Same as for *d* above.
Cross References: For reviews by Lee J. Cronbach and Bruce W. Tuckman, see 8:489.

Review of the USES Basic Occupational Literacy Test by GARY L. MARCO, Executive Director, Statistical Analysis, College Board Programs Division, Educational Testing Service, Princeton, NJ:

The USES Basic Occupational Literacy Test (BOLT) tests basic reading and arithmetic skills, and its content is especially selected to appeal to the experiences of disadvantaged adults. The BOLT provides test results that are related to occupational requirements for reading and arithmetic, and is intended for use in vocational counseling and placement. Among the test materials are workbooks for use in training test administrators. Training materials like these—though often not provided by testing agencies—help ensure the standardization of test administrations. The test directions to test takers and test administrators are clear, and the items in the test were pretested and carefully selected. The test booklets and answer sheets are printed in such a way that the responses in the test booklet line up with the circles on the answer sheet, thus eliminating the confusion that might arise if the test taker had to use a conventional answer sheet.

The BOLT subtests in Reading Vocabulary, Reading Comprehension, and Arithmetic Computation are offered at four levels ranging from Fundamental to Advanced; the Arithmetic Reasoning is offered at three levels. The test battery includes a broad range of tasks, from those that would be appropriate in difficulty for 2nd graders to those that would be appropriate for 12th graders. For a given skill area three alternate forms of the BOLT are available for use at each level except for the Advanced Level, which is represented by two forms.

The test administrator first gives the Wide-Range Scale to route the test taker to the appropriate levels of the reading or arithmetic subtests, and then administers forms at the appropriate reading or arithmetic levels. The tests are scored by counting the number or items answered correctly, and the raw score is transformed into a standard score. The standard score is linked to both General Educational Development Levels and grade equivalents. The results are used in vocational counseling and placement.

Grade equivalents and corresponding GED levels were established in the early 1970s by equating BOLT scores on the two reading and two arithmetic tests to scores on appropriate subtests from the Stanford Achievement Test (SAT). GED levels and grade equivalents were not reestablished in 1983 but continued to be based on the previous associations. I question whether the GED levels and grade equivalents are still accurate, and recommend that the Department of Labor reexamine the relationship of BOLT scores to General Educational Development norms and grade equivalents.

These possibly outdated linkages of BOLT scores to GED levels and grade equivalents seem to me to be the weakest part of the BOLT testing program. Knowing the GED levels is critical to providing appropriate guidance to the adult who is trying to decide on an appropriate occupation.

The technical material provided for the tests has improved over time but is still lacking in some regards. In February 1983, revised score conversion tables and reliability information were announced to users (United States Department of Labor, Employment and Training Administration, 1983). This information resulted from a special study designed to measure test-retest reliability and to equate scores from the various test forms on a new standardization sample (Western Test Development Field Center, Utah Department of Employment Security, 1981). In addition to the revised score conversions, the alternate form reliability coefficients and standard errors of measurement yielded by this study are useful additions to the development section of the test manual (manual, 1973), which originally provided only KR-20 reliability coefficients and no standard errors of measurement.

Given the importance of this and other information announced to users since the development of the original test manual, I recommend that the test publisher produce an updated version of the test manual that incorporates the supplementary information, so that all of the important information about the BOLT appears in one place.

Because the BOLT battery is intended to be used with disadvantaged adults who may have had little schooling, it is important to take account of reading ability in assessing what the nonreading tests measure. A low score on Arithmetic Reasoning, for example, could be due to deficiency in reading rather than to a deficiency in numerical reasoning per se. Thus, the test publisher should establish the discriminant validity of the four subtests at each of the different levels (Fundamental, Intermediate, etc.). The test manual reports no information that allows the prospective user to judge the relationships among the skills and abilities measured by the BOLT subtests. At least correlations among scores on the four subtests at each level should be reported.

Data regarding the effectiveness of the Wide-Range Scale in routing test takers to the appropriate level of the test battery are also lacking. Use of the routing test should theoretically help reduce the number of test takers who take an inappropriate level of the BOLT. The 1983 study did give mean raw scores for test takers who took a particular form of the BOLT but had different Wide-Range Scale reading and arithmetic scores. These data show the mean score generally increases as the Wide-Range Scale score increases. The data also suggest, however, that determining the test level according to years of education results in routing some test takers to forms that are too easy for them. I recommend that years of education not be considered in selecting the test level unless the validity of this practice can be demonstrated empirically. More information is needed on the effectiveness of the Wide-Range Scale in routing test takers to the appropriate test level.

In summary, the BOLT battery is an impressive set of instruments that have been carefully developed with the disadvantaged adult in mind. The battery comes with clear and detailed instructions for administering and scoring the tests. Empirical data are still needed in a number of regards, however. Empirical data linking scores on the battery to grade equivalents (and thus to GED levels) are seriously out of date. Data are also lacking regarding the discriminant validity of the different subtests, the effectiveness of the Wide-Range Scale in routing test takers, and the overall effectiveness of the BOLT instruments in counseling and placing test takers. Moreover, it is time for the publisher to issue a new test manual that incorporates supplemental data that have been collected since the introduction of the BOLT. Despite these deficiencies, the BOLT battery serves a special need that justifies its continued use and development. The test publisher should undertake research that provides additional interpretive and validity information about the battery.

REVIEWER'S REFERENCES

Western Test Development Field Center, Utah Department of Employment Security. (1981, May). *Summary report of BOLT forms comparability and reliability study* (USES Special Technical Report No. 42). Salt Lake City: Author.
United States Department of Labor, Employment and Training Administration. (1983, September). *Revised USES Basic Occupational Literacy Test (BOLT)*. (Employment Service Program Letter No. 9-83). Washington, DC: Author.

Review of the USES Basic Occupational Literacy Test by DEAN H. NAFZIGER, Executive Director, and AMY H. SHIVELY, Research Associate, Far West Laboratory, San Francisco, CA:

PURPOSE. The United States Employment Service USES Basic Occupational Literacy Test or BOLT was developed by the United States Department of Labor in 1972, and released for public use in 1973. The administration manual states that the BOLT was designed to assess the literacy skills of "disadvantaged" or "low education" adults.

The content, format, instructions, timing, norms, and difficulty level were designed to specifically meet the needs of this diverse, "disadvantaged" population. (No description is included in any of the provided test manual materials to define the "disadvantaged" adult.) The BOLT was developed to measure basic skills in four content areas. These areas are Reading Comprehension, Reading Vocabulary, Arithmetic Computation, and Arithmetic Reasoning.

A myriad of reasons are listed in the manual to explain the purpose and development of the USES Basic Occupational Literacy tests. These tests were originally authored in the early 1970s. The goals of the BOLT included filling the need for a test geared to interests and experiences of disadvantaged adults; setting occupational norms, norms that set the minimum literacy necessary for satisfactory job performance; helping employers set more realistic hiring standards; offering a short, diagnostic test suitable to disadvantaged adults who have minimal test-taking skills; and finally, offering a test with alternate forms so that retesting could be possible. All these reasons seemed appropriate in the early 1970s. However, before using this instrument a counselor or administrator must ask an important question. The questions is, "How does literacy ability, based on four subtests of vocabulary, comprehension, and arithmetic, influence what and how well an adult can perform a job?" The predictive validity of this instrument for disadvantaged adults appears limited. This assessment is not complex enough to report on skills needed in the job environment. Instead it provides measurement of very low level skills—those at the bottom of Bloom's taxonomy, such as memorizing or identifying facts or concepts.

TEST OVERVIEW. The Wide Range Scale, a screening test to determine the appropriate level of BOLT to administer, involves 15 to 20 minutes of time. The Wide Range Scale is made up of eight vocabulary items and eight arithmetic items. It may be administered in groups or individually. The manual advises the test administrator to use a combination of the Wide Range Scale and the individual's reported years of education to determine which level of the BOLT to administer.

BOLT Reading Vocabulary, Reading Comprehension, and Arithmetic Computation test forms are available at four levels of difficulty: Advance, High Intermediate, Basic Intermediate, and Fundamental. BOLT Arithmetic Reasoning test forms are available at three levels of difficulty: Advanced, Intermediate, and Fundamental. Alternate forms of each subgroup are also available. Two forms are available at the advanced level for each subgroup and three forms are available at the High Intermediate, Basic Intermediate, and Fundamental. All directions to examinees are identical across levels and forms of a subtest. This allows for testing several examinees at different levels within a subgroup. A Fundamental level Reading Comprehension test may be administered at the same time as an Advanced level Reading Comprehension test.

The BOLT is a timed test. Each reading subtest is to be administered in 15 minutes. The arithmetic tests are 30 minutes each. A 10 to 15 minute break is suggested between two administered subtests. An estimated total testing time, including the 16-item Wide Scale Range, is about 2 hours. The manual does caution that if the test taker is showing fatigue, a break may be allowed as needed. Timed tests add a dimension of stress. Adults who are unfamiliar with multiple-choice tests will not benefit from speeded tests.

The Reading Vocabulary subtest consists of 14 items for each form while the Reading Comprehension subtest consists of 12 items for each form. In the Arithmetic subtests, the Computation form has 14 items at the Advanced level and 20 items at the Fundamental level. The Reasoning subtest has 12 items at the Advanced level and 14 items at the Fundamental level. For an assessment of this nature, to determine language and arithmetic literacy skills, 12 or 14 items is not a representative number of concepts to measure (Nitko, 1983).

TEST POPULATION. The BOLT is used with disadvantaged adults who are seeking employment. The BOLT manual states the test may also be used to determine if a non-English-speaking adult, with or without education, can be placed in work training or a work environment that primarily uses English. The BOLT administrator's manual points out that examinees should be reassured that the test is being given "to help them find suitable employment or training." They are told to try all answers even if they must guess at some. As noted in the introduction, this test is not suitable to determine the abilities an adult might have in order to perform well at a given occupation. Encouraging the examinee to guess is a questionable practice in any assessment situation.

SCORING. The BOLT may be scored by hand with a grid or by machine. It is recommended that if a test is handscored, a second person should rescore the test. If a second person is not available, the first person should rescore the test.

Raw scores on each subtest are transformed into Standard Scores and a matching General Educational Development (GED) level. For raw scores of 0, 1, or 2 there are no corresponding Standard Scores or GED levels. A raw score this low is below the chance level of guessing. In this situation the examinee must be retested. How often an adult should be retested or how long an adult should wait before being retested is not addressed in the manual.

RELIABILITY. Test developers decided the appreciable benefits to disadvantaged examinees that would result from shorter administration time justified the reduction in reliability of some BOLT forms as indicated by the KR20 coefficients. This compromise, to have a short, quick, test that is less reliable and less able to predict ability, does not seem justified. If the test results incorrectly match an adult to an occupation, neither the employer nor the employee has profited.

The BOLT reports KR20 reliability coefficients at .85 to .61 for reading and at .82 to .68 for arithmetic, dropping much lower when 50% time was used. Alternate forms might have produced more reliable coefficients. No means or standard deviations were reported. The KR20 and alpha coefficients are influenced by speed in the same manner as split-half coefficients and are not recommended for use with speeded tests. The KR20 is also affected by the length of the test as well as its homogeneity (Nitko, 1983). Therefore, choosing the KR20 statistic may not have been the best choice in light of the fact that the BOLT is short (12–14 items), homogeneous, and speeded.

When the BOLT was originally released in 1972, promises of further research were made. Some research has been accomplished in the last 18 years but the test remains as originally printed in 1972. Changes include new conversion tables and expanded interpretation instructions for the administrator to attach to the original manuals. The new conversion tables increase the accuracy of comparisons of scores across test Forms A, B, and C. The Reading subtests and the Arithmetic subtests were equated.

Research accomplished includes a BOLT Forms Comparability and Reliability Study prepared by Western Test Development Field Center, Utah Department of Employment Security (1981). Standard errors of measurement (SEM) were produced. The advanced tests for both Reading and Arithmetic report small SEMs; Reading Vocabulary 4A reports an SEM of 4. The lower difficulty tests reflect greater standard errors; for example, Reading Vocabulary 1A reports an SEM of 6. This pattern repeats itself throughout the SEM table; the low difficulty tests seem to have some problems with reliability.

In 1983, the U.S. Department of Labor, Employment and Training Administration, produced a report suggesting that Grade Equivalent Scores with the corresponding GED levels be provided as revised materials for the BOLT. The report recommended that Grade Equivalent Scores be approved and published for operational use (U.S. Department of Labor, 1983).

VALIDITY. Validity research has not been reported. As Cronbach states in his 1978 review, "No proper judgment can be made when the validation research does not find out how many unqualified workers the [BOLT] standards certify as qualified" (Cronbach, 1978).

NORMS. Interim occupational norms were developed with the promise for further research. This research was to develop new norms, based on determining the minimum BOLT scores obtained by persons who have the literacy skills needed to perform adequately in jobs or in occupational training. The research has yet to be accomplished. The interim occupational norms that were derived consisted of about 22% of each of the reading and arithmetic samples tested for the BOLT item analyses. Stanford Achievement Test (SAT) Intermediate II reading and arithmetic tests as well as the BOLT sample scores were used to derive the interim norms. Total numbers of subjects tested were 1,890

for reading and 1,743 for the arithmetic sample. The following states participated: Alabama, California, Florida, Illinois, Michigan, Mississippi, Missouri, New Jersey, North Carolina, Ohio, Pennsylvania, Tennessee, and Texas. Approximately equal numbers of males and females were included as well as minority groups. The age of participants ranged from 16 years to 65 years. Approximately 800 participants reported zero to eight years of education while approximately 1,000 reported nine or more years.

Originally BOLT scores were equated to GED levels by the following process:

1. SAT scores were converted to Standard Scores with a mean of 100 and a standard deviation of 20 by means of a linear transformation.

2. Equipercentile method was used to equate the BOLT content areas to the scaled SAT scores.

3. SAT scores were converted to grade equivalents.

4. SAT grade equivalents were grouped according to the ranges of academic grade level that correspond to GED levels 1, 2, 3, and 4.

SUMMARY. The present reviewers have serious questions and reservations about the BOLT. Research points to the fact that until assessments mirror the needs of industry they are flawed (Levine, 1990). Is it enough to know of how much vocabulary an adult has command when the question is: What kind of work can an adult do? Application of skills assessments are a more valid and authentic way to assess what an adult can and cannot do. If adults are language reluctant, what they are capable of doing will not be obvious by asking them to define 14 vocabulary words or to add two-digit numbers.

In 1972 the reporting of comprehension and knowledge skills may have seemed relevant. In 1991, however, it is acknowledged that higher order skills are necessary to perform successfully on the job. Only careful study can ascertain if these skills are measured accurately by the BOLT's multiple-choice items. Although research on the relationship between job performance and basic skills is not definitive, it is clear that it is more important for workers to be able to apply basic skills in a job performance situation than to demonstrate these skills on a literacy test (Marshall & Osterman, 1989).

The assessment materials claim that the BOLT can be used as an element in adult career choice. The BOLT claims to be a test to use with hard-to-test populations, but it is difficult for the present reviewers to envision an appropriate use for it. The BOLT sheds little light on the question industry is asking: What can this adult do?

REVIEWER'S REFERENCES

Cronbach, L. J. (1978). [Review of the USES Basic Occupational Literacy Test.] In O. K. Buros (Ed.), *The eighth mental measurements yearbook* (pp. 673-74). Highland Park, NJ: The Gryphon Press.

Western Test Development Field Center, Utah Department of Employment Security. (1981). *Summary report of BOLT forms comparability and reliability study* (USES Special Technical Report No. 42). Salt Lake City: The Author.

Nitko, A. J. (1983). *Educational tests and measurement, an introduction.* New York: Harcourt Brace Jovanovich, Inc.

United States Department of Labor. (1983). *Revised USES Basic Occupational Literacy Test (BOLT)* (Employment Service Program Letter No. 9-83). Washington, DC: The Author.

Marshall, R., & Osterman, P. (1988, April). *Workforce policies for the 1990s. A new labor market agenda. The possibilities of employment policy.* Papers presented at the Economic Policy Institute Seminar on Labor Market Policy, Washington, DC.

Levine, K. (1990). *The future of literacy and literacies of the future* (Literacy Lessons). Geneva, Switzerland: International Bureau of Education.

[454]
Utah Test of Language Development—3.

Purpose: To assess listening (comprehension) and speaking (expression).
Population: Ages 3-0 to 9-11.
Publication Date: 1958–89.
Acronym: UTLD-3.
Scores, 3: Language Comprehension, Language Expression, Language Quotient.
Administration: Individual.
Price Data, 1990: $59 per complete kit including picture book, 50 profile/examiner record forms, and manual ('89, 36 pages); $22 per picture book; $17 per 50 profile/examiner record forms; $23 per manual.
Time: Administration time not reported.
Comments: Revised edition of Utah Test of Language Development; earlier edition called Utah Verbal Language Development Scale.
Author: Merlin J. Mecham.
Publisher: PRO-ED, Inc.
Cross References: For reviews of an earlier edition by Joan I. Lynch and Michelle Quinn, see 9:1306 (3 references); see also T3:2541 (5 references) and T2:2097 (4 references); for reviews of an earlier edition by Katharine G. Butler and William H. Perkins, see 7:973.

TEST REFERENCES

1. Brinton, B., Fujiki, M., & Sonnenberg, E. A. (1988). Responses to requests for clarification by linguistically normal and language-impaired children in conversation. *Journal of Speech and Hearing Disorders, 53,* 383-391.
2. Keenan, P. A., & Lachar, D. (1988). Screening preschoolers with special problems: Use of the Personality Inventory for Children (PIC). *Journal of School Psychology, 26,* 1-11.

Review of the Utah Test of Language Development—3 by LYNN S. BLISS, Professor of Communication Disorders and Sciences, Wayne State University, Detroit, MI:

The Utah Test of Language Development—3 (UTLD-3) is a revision of two earlier forms (1967, 1978). The rationale for the latest edition and a description of how this version differs from the previous ones are not presented in materials accompanying the test.

The UTLD-3 is a norm-referenced competency test which was designed to "determine whether a given child falls outside the 'normal' limits, the degree of severity of a problem, and if special classification or placement is warranted" (p. 3). It is geared for children between the ages of 3 to 9 years.

CONTENT. The UTLD-3 is composed of two sections, Language Comprehension and Language Expression. The Language Comprehension section is further divided into items which assess semantic content and grammatical form as well as the processing levels of recognition, short-term memory, and representational comprehension. The items require the child to point to pictures, answer questions, follow commands, present analogies and/or opposites, and make metalinguistic judgments regarding grammaticality. The language production items involve naming, sentence repetition, word association, rhyming, sentence construction, and giving synonyms and opposites.

ADMINISTRATION. Administration requires 15 to 30 minutes. A basal score consists of five consecutive correct items and a ceiling is reached when five consecutive items are missed. The manual presents clear guidelines for general testing procedures and specific instructions for each item. There is a picture book and a response form.

SCORING. Four types of scores are obtained. The raw scores equal the total number of correct items for each subtest. Each subtest yields a standard score. This score is placed into one of seven interpretive categories ranging from Very Poor to Very Superior. Percentile ranks for both sections are obtained by referring to conversion tables of raw scores. A Language Quotient reflects an overall index of a child's language functioning. This score is interpreted with the same scale used for the standard scores.

STANDARDIZATION. Test standardization involved 1,708 children from 29 states. The children were divided into yearly age levels with over 100 children in each level. The demographics of the sample approximated national distributions for sex, residence (urban-rural), race, geographic region, and ethnicity. There is no description of how the children were selected or how they were identified as normal.

RELIABILITY AND VALIDITY. Internal consistency was estimated through the use of a correlation coefficient alpha. This measure, reflecting homogeneity of test items, is not really an index of reliability. In the manual coefficient alphas are presented which exceed .71 for each age level in both comprehension and expression sections. The standard error of measurement (again not directly a reliability measure but rather a measure of consistency) is presented as 1 for each age level in both test sections. There are no data pertaining to interscorer, intrascorer, and test-retest reliability.

Content validity is addressed in an item analysis evaluating discriminatory power and percentage of difficulty. Values for these measures are presented in the manual and appear to be relatively high. Criterion-related validity was described in terms of the correlations between the Language Quotient and the Peabody Picture Vocabulary Test—Revised and the Preschool Language Scale. The number of children upon which these determinations were made and their demographic characteristics were not presented. The correlations, ranging from .41 to .73, were all significant. Construct validity was addressed through the assertion that the test items are developmental in nature and that correlations between age and each subtest score were significant. Data are presented to demonstrate group differences obtained in scores on the UTLD-3 by language-impaired and nonimpaired children. Forty-one children enrolled in language remediation programs were administered the test and all scored in the poor or below average range. Subject description and testing conditions were not presented.

CONCLUSIONS. The strengths of the UTLD-3 are in the relatively brief administration time; ease of administration, scoring, and interpretation; and clarity of the visual stimuli and instructions. The weaknesses lie in several areas. First, the reliability and validity information are too general to inform potential users. Interpretation must be done very cautiously given these limitations. Second, the items pose many cross modality interferences. For example, vision, expressive language behavior, and memory will affect many of the auditory comprehension items. Third, the test does not delve into the area of pragmatics or morphology and syntax. Without an index of natural communicative functioning, the test is not very useful. At best, the UTLD-3 would need to be supplemented with a more sensitive language measure as well as a language sample analysis which would permit the analysis of functional communication. In summary, the UTLD-3 does not appear to provide an examiner with a useful clinical tool to assess language functioning.

[455]
Vincent Mechanical Diagrams Test, 1979 Revision.
Purpose: "Assesses the individual's ability to understand the concepts of cog, pulley and lever systems and general mechanical reasoning ability."
Population: Ages 15–adult.
Publication Dates: 1936–79.
Acronym: VMD.
Scores: Total score only.
Administration: Group.
Price Data, 1987: £10.35 per 10 test booklets ('79, 13 pages); £2.25 per 10 answer sheets; £3.25 per marking key; £1.50 per instruction card (no date, 2 pages).
Time: 12(15) minutes.
Comments: Subtest of NIIP Engineering Selection Test Battery.
Author: National Institute of Industrial Psychology.

Publisher: NFER-Nelson Publishing Co., Ltd. [England].

[456]
Visual Skills Appraisal.
Purpose: "Developed to assist teachers and other educators, who may not have specialized training in visual skills assessment, to identify visual inefficiencies that affect school performance."
Population: Grades K–4.
Publication Date: 1984.
Acronym: VSA.
Scores: 6 subtests: Pursuits, Scanning, Aligning, Locating, Eye-Hand Coordination, Fixation Unity.
Administration: Individual.
Price Data, 1989: $44 per complete kit including manual (112 pages), stimulus cards, 25 design completion forms, 25 red/green trail forms, 25 score sheets, and red/green glasses; $4 per stimulus cards; $6 per 25 design completion forms, 25 red/green trail forms, or 25 score sheets; $7 per red/green glasses; $12 per manual; $10 per Classroom Visual Activities manual.
Time: (10–15) minutes.
Authors: Regina G. Richards and Gary S. Oppenheim in consultation with G. N. Getman.
Publisher: Academic Therapy Publications.

TEST REFERENCES

1. Richards, R. G. (1985). Wasting teacher time. *Academic Therapy, 20,* 411-418.

[457]
VITAL Checklist and Curriculum Guide.
Purpose: Evaluates "essential problem solving and adaptability skills."
Population: Elementary and secondary students.
Publication Date: 1987.
Acronym: VCCG.
Comments: "Criterion-referenced"; ratings by professionals/paraprofessionals familiar with the student.
Scores, 8: 2 parts (Student, Program Emphasis) with 4 adaptability scores (Decision Making, Independence, Self-Evaluation, Adjustment) for each part.
Administration: Individual.
Price Data: Available from publisher.
Time: Administration time not reported.
Authors: Dennis E. Mithaug, James E. Martin, and Donald L. Burger.
Publisher: Exceptional Education.

Review of the VITAL Checklist and Curriculum Guide by GREGORY J. CIZEK, Assistant Professor of Educational Research and Measurement, University of Toledo, Toledo, OH:

The VITAL Checklist and Curriculum Guide (VCCG) is a two-part instrument for assessing problem-solving and adaptability skills. The first component, the VITAL Checklist, was designed to be "a criterion referenced assessment that evaluates the essential problem solving and adaptability skills all students need to become independent at school, at home, and at work." A companion instrument, the VITAL Curriculum Guide, is intended to help users "specify goals and objectives that will reduce identified needs."

The Checklist consists of 43 questions (skill statements) designed to elicit information in four areas—Decision Making ability, Independence, Self-Evaluation skills, and Adjustment skills. No special training is required to administer the checklist; the only requirement stated by the authors is that it be completed by "professionals or paraprofessionals familiar with the student's patterns of responding in different instructional settings." The authors also indicate that "there is no need to set up situations for observations"; instead, the Checklist can be completed at any convenient time. Although no estimate of administration or scoring time is provided, it appears that the Checklist can be quickly and easily completed. No information about the cost of VCCG materials is provided.

To complete the Checklist, a qualified observer simply checks "Yes," "No," or "Don't Know" to record the presence or absence of the listed skills. These responses can then be rerecorded on the Curriculum Guide to identify programmatic strengths and weaknesses. VCCG users can also translate Checklist results for an individual student into profile format on a form provided.

Although the VCCG may be useful as a record-keeping device for educational programs, it would not qualify as a psychometric instrument. The authors' claim that the VCCG "evaluates the essential problem solving and adaptability skills all students need to become independent" is overstated. The scales seem more appropriately targeted to students with learning disabilities, although even for that population, no theoretical or practical basis for including or excluding specific skills is provided.

The Teacher's Manual provided with the VCCG also serves as a technical manual. Two pages of the Manual are used to describe the validity and reliability of the Checklist. As previously mentioned, evidence of construct validity is absent; similarly, criterion-related or concurrent validity concerns are not mentioned. The Manual founders in its attempt to identify any reason why the 43 chosen skills are assessed or what interpretations can or should be made from test results.

In terms of validity research, the authors do report that the Checklist was administered to 428 elementary and secondary school students in Colorado ($n = 35$ "nonhandicapped lower elementary students"; $n = 73$ "students with behavior problems"; $n = 191$ "students with learning disabilities"; and $n = 129$ "students with mental retardation"). The authors provide no information about important demographic characteristics of the group, or how or why these groups were selected. The authors report that the groups showed similar profiles across the four subtests and that the groups' mean scores were consistently ordered from "Elementary" (high) to "Mental Retardation" (low) on the subtests. However, it is unclear what these results mean, or what light they shed on the more substantive validity concerns.

Reliability information provided in the Manual is also inadequate. A test-retest reliability index (using $n = 241$ Colorado elementary, secondary, and adult students tested at 4-week intervals) is reported to have a mean of 74%, although it is not stated whether this index refers to diagnoses based on composite scores, an average of the four subtest scores, or ratings of the 43 skill statements. The evidence for interrater agreement is similarly ambiguous and poorly constituted. The Manual indicates that three teachers and their aides rated 22 secondary students with a mean interrater agreement of 92%.

In summary, the VCCG is critically deficient in many essential areas of psychometric propriety. The supporting documentation contains scanty evidence of theoretical grounding and no relevant critical research related to use of the instrument. Little, if any, clear evidence regarding the Checklist's reliability or validity for any purpose is given. A test purchaser or user could not make an informed judgment about the value of the instrument based on the information provided by the authors.

The Checklist could possibly be best used as a subjective check-off list of some needed adaptability skills. It is easily completed by anyone familiar with the abilities of the student being assessed, and the directions for displaying the results in profile format are clear and easy to follow. But under no circumstances should the results be used to diagnose learning disabilities or make or support placement in special programs.

[458]

Vocational Research Interest Inventory.

Purpose: To provide accurate and meaningful information about the occupational interests of students and clients in vocational counseling, and rehabilitation and job training program participants.
Population: High school and adults.
Publication Date: 1985.
Acronym: VRII.
Scores, 12: Artistic, Scientific, Plants/Animals, Protective, Mechanical, Industrial, Business Detail, Selling, Accommodating, Humanitarian, Lead/Influence, Physical Performing.
Administration: Group.
Price Data, 1989: $17.25 or less per package including 25 test forms; $12.50 per specimen kit including 5 test forms and manual (36 pages); $295 per Apple or IBM software package.
Foreign Language Edition: Spanish edition (entitled Inventario Investigativo de Interes Vocacional) available.
Time: (15–20) minutes.
Comments: Uses idiographic Individual Profile Analysis to determine relatively high interest areas.
Authors: Howard Dansky, Jeffrey A. Harris, and Thomas W. Gannaway.

Publisher: Vocational Research Institute.

Review of the Vocational Research Interest Inventory by JOSEPH G. LAW, JR., Associate Professor of Behavioral Studies, University of South Alabama, Mobile, AL:

The authors of the Vocational Research Interest Inventory (VRII) have succeeded in linking their 162-item inventory to the powerful data base of the U.S. Department of Labor's Guide to Occupational Exploration (GOE). The VRII is a refinement of the computerized inventory (APTICOM) with some rewritten items and a reading level adjusted downwards to fourth grade level. Items for APTICOM and the VRII were written in an attempt to capture the activities characteristic of the 12 occupational interest areas which are central to the GOE system. The U.S. Employment Service uses an in-house inventory (USES 1.1) to assess interest areas compatible with the GOE system. APTICOM (and later the VRII) was designed to provide easier access to the GOE data base. An awareness of the VRII's origins through APTICOM is important to potential test users because much of the reliability and validity data in the manual is on the relationship of APTICOM to USES 1.1.

The manual reports on internal consistency and test-retest reliability for APTICOM, but not for the VRII. The authors evidently think that the high internal consistency and test-retest reliability of the parent inventory will extend to the VRII, which is highly correlated with APTICOM scales. The mean alpha coefficient for the 12 APTICOM areas is .86 in comparison with .85 for USES 1.1. Test-retest correlations average .83 for the 12 APTICOM areas versus .84 for USES 1.1.

The authors of the VRII are to be commended for attempts to include representative numbers of Black and Hispanic subjects in the normative groups. The addition of a Spanish-language version of the test and manual is also a plus. Using the GOE system as a basis for occupational exploration allows counselors and clients to utilize much already available data. This should prove especially useful in vocational rehabilitation settings where the GOE approach lends itself to a search for transferable skills and abilities. The manual contains a worksheet for individual profile analysis. It can be duplicated and used by counselors. The foldover answer sheet contains profiles and tables allowing the client and counselor to use the results immediately.

The manual has much to commend it. It is written with an emphasis on practical use, with the sections on administration, scoring, and interpretation preceding the portion that discusses item selection and norming. An appendix contains a discussion of the VRII's compliance with standards on sex fairness in interest inventories which is thorough and enlightening. Most of the tables are clear and readable.

Unfortunately, there are limited data available in the manual on the reliability and validity of the VRII. The authors administered the VRII and USES 1.1 to a subsample of 554 in the norm sample and found that all but five interest areas correlated at least .75 with the USES inventory. The authors cite this as evidence of the construct validity of the VRII. The Spanish version (IIIV) was administered at a 1-week interval to 139 subjects. Eleven of the 12 interest areas correlated above .75 with each other. Although these data suggest acceptable validity and reliability, there is still a paucity of reported data in the manual on the test-retest reliability and internal consistency of the English version. Many questions remain unanswered. For example, what is the relationship between VRII scores and occupations clients eventually choose? Is there any correlation between high scores on particular VRII interest areas and occupational scales or basic occupational themes of the Strong Campbell Interest Inventory? How do VRII scores relate to the Kuder or Vocational Preference Inventory? These questions are not addressed in the manual, other than mention of a study relating the GOE interest areas to Holland's six basic occupational themes.

A review of *Psychological Abstracts* and ERIC from 1985 to September 1990 found no references to the VRII. I hope research is underway into the predictive and concurrent validity of this promising new inventory. Its brevity, fourth grade reading level, sex fairness, inclusion of significant numbers of Blacks and Hispanics in the norm groups, and bilingual manual should make it a worthwhile instrument for use with minorities and clients with limited education. The availability of separate norms for vocational and student populations is also a plus. Further studies of its relationship to more widely used interest inventories such as the Strong and the Kuder is warranted, as well as the addition to the manual of more data on reliability and validity.

[459]

A Voice Assessment Protocol for Children and Adults.

Purpose: "Assesses five parameters of the voice: pitch, loudness, quality, breath features, and rate/rhythm."
Population: Children and adults.
Publication Date: 1987.
Scores: 5 assessments: Pitch, Loudness, Quality, Breath Features, Rate/Rhythm.
Administration: Individual.
Price Data, 1989: $34 per complete kit including 25 protocols, audiocassette, and manual (24 pages); $16 per 25 protocols; $9 per audiocassette; $12 per manual.
Time: Administration time not reported.
Author: Rebekah H. Pindzola.
Publisher: PRO-ED, Inc.

Review of A Voice Assessment Protocol for Children and Adults by MAYNARD D. FILTER, *Head, Speech Pathology and Audiology, James Madison University, Harrisonburg, VA:*

A Voice Assessment Protocol for Children and Adults (VAP) was devised to better organize and guide the decision-making process related to voice assessment. It guides the examiner through an evaluation program in which selected auditory parameters of the voice are described perceptually. A unique feature of this protocol is the use of a "grid-marking" system that forces the examiner to make choices between variable descriptions that are dichotomous (yes-no) or on a continuum such as severe, moderate, and slight. The author defined this grid-marking system as a Likert scale; however, choices on the grid-marking system are not assigned numerical values. With some creative ingenuity an examiner could assign values to the choices on the scale; if this were done, the values would represent ordinal data or nominal data where the only choice is that a variable is present or not present.

Administration instructions indicate that a tape recording of the voice should be saved for reliability ratings, but fail to indicate how reliability should be measured. There are no instructions related to training of the listener on perceptually rating/judging samples of voice/speech. These instructions also claim the VAP, because it is a prelisted form, ensures that particular deviations are not overlooked; this statement suggests that the VAP's list of choices for describing variables is exhaustive. In fact, some well-accepted characteristics of the voice, such as vocal fry and falsetto, are not included on the protocol.

The manual instructions on pitch assessment do not provide specific directions of how to measure pitch nor do the instructions include any reference or directions on how to use the accompanying audiotape of "Pitch Level Samples." No data on the reliability of pitch-matching tasks are provided.

For loudness assessment, the clinician is instructed to judge whether tension or strain are evident in loudness. it is not clear how this is measured. Is the tension judged auditorily or visually?

Under quality assessment "hoarseness" is defined as breathiness and harshness; can harshness be defined reliably? Can listeners reliably differentiate between hoarseness and harshness, or between hoarseness and breathiness? It is suggested that assimilation nasality is a "mild case"; could assimilation nasality fall within the moderate range of hypernasality? Under the category of glottal attacks, the category "soft attack" could be confused with breathiness or with glottal fry.

Breathiness is defined as an audible escape of air; this definition seems to exclude inefficient use of the airstream for voiced phonemes especially when an "audible escape of air" cannot be heard. Region of breathing is identified when describing breath features; is the region of breathing always readily observable? The clinician should be aware of the difficulty of obtaining reliable samples of prolonged /s/ and /z/ phonemes; this is a difficult task for many children.

The manual indicates that rate can affect other variables of speech and voice. Does rate affect these variables, or do these variables such as breathing, phrasing, pause-time, and fluency affect rate? Are rate/rhythm parameters of the voice or parameters of prosody that are related more to fluency than to voice?

The manual summary does not provide suggestions on how to prepare a concise report with the information obtained from the use of the VAP. Perhaps a one-page protocol summary sheet would assist the clinician in summarizing information for an evaluation report. Also, the summary does not mention the importance of acoustic measures of the voice. Occasionally, gender-specific language is used. No data on reliability of clinician judgments are provided.

One advantage of using the VAP is that it does provide a one-page form listing some of the important features for each of five parameters of speech/voice. The VAP does not provide any information on any unique features; virtually all of the features listed on the VAP forms are also included in other voice evaluation forms such as the Voice Profile rating scales developed by D. Kenneth Wilson (1987). If the clinician prefers an abbreviated "grid-marking" voice protocol system rather than an equal-interval rating system already available in the literature, then the VAP might be a good choice.

REVIEWER'S REFERENCE

Wilson, D. K. (1987). *Voice problems of children* (3rd ed.). Baltimore: Williams & Wilkins.

[460]
Walker-McConnell Scale of Social Competence and School Adjustment.

Purpose: "For use in the screening and identification of social skills deficits."
Population: Grades K–6.
Publication Date: 1988.
Scores, 4: Teacher-Preferred Social Behavior, Peer-Preferred Social Behavior, School Adjustment Behavior, Total.
Administration: Individual.
Price Data, 1989: $44 per complete kit including examiner's manual (55 pages) and 50 profile/rating forms; $23 per 50 profile/rating forms; $23 per examiner's manual.
Time: (5–10) minutes.
Comments: Ratings by teachers.
Authors: Hill M. Walker and Scott R. McConnell.
Publisher: PRO-ED, Inc.

TEST REFERENCES

1. Merrell, K. W. (1989). Concurrent relationships between two behavioral rating scales for teachers: An examination of self-control, social competence, and school behavioral adjustment. *Psychology in the Schools, 26,* 267-271.
2. Merrell, K. W., & Shinn, M. R. (1990). Critical variables in the learning disabilities identification process. *School Psychology Review, 19,* 74-82.
3. Jenkins, J. R., Jewell, M., Leicester, N., Jenkins, L., & Troutner, N. M. (1991). Development of a school building model for educating students with handicaps and at-risk students in general education classrooms. *Journal of Learning Disabilities, 24,* 311-320.
4. Merrell, K. W. (1991). Teacher ratings of social competence and behavioral adjustment: Differences between learning-disabled, low-achieving, and typical students. *Journal of School Psychology, 29,* 207-217.

Review of the Walker-McConnell Scale of Social Competence and School Adjustment by NORMAN A. CONSTANTINE, Director of Assessment Services, Far West Laboratory for Educational Research and Development, San Francisco, CA, and Lecturer in Pediatrics, Stanford University School of Medicine, Stanford, CA:

The Walker-McConnell Scale of Social Competence and School Adjustment (WMS) "was designed primarily for use in the screening and identification of social skills deficits among elementary aged children in school" and "was not designed as either a diagnostic or classification instrument" (manual, pages 1 and 3). The WMS is quickly administered and scored, and focuses on important domains of child functioning. Refreshingly divergent from most other rating scales of child behavior, the WMS is positively focused (i.e., it centers around skills rather than problems in both the item wording and the resulting scales). The manual is well written and includes an excellent section describing additional resources and information on social skills.

CONSTRUCT VALIDITY. A major potential strength of the WMS is its close conceptual link to recent theoretical work in the area. One limitation, however, is that the authors do not present a persuasive integration of the available validation evidence in support of the purportedly measured theoretical constructs, particularly for the three separate subscales. The presentation in the manual neither effectively integrates the diversity of evidence, nor adequately recognizes its limitations and the work remaining to be done.

The interscale correlations reported for the national norm sample of .67, .74, and .67 are too large to support the case for separate subscales. At the same time, the factor analyses presented reveal one dominant factor rather than three. This is true even for those studies reported where, for some unexplained reason, only the 19 factorially purest items were included in the analyses. These findings do not in themselves negate the value of separate subscales, but the burden of evidence is clearly with the authors to justify the subscale distinctions.

A large section of the validity material is presented under the heading of Discriminant Validity. Most of this actually consists of group difference studies as opposed to what is traditionally meant by discriminant validity (i.e., in the multitrait/multimethod context where similar methods used to measure different constructs are expected to show low correlations). These studies demonstrate the instrument's sensitivity to a variety of expected group differences, and therefore provide some support for the construct validity of the test as a whole. What is missing, however, is convincing discriminant validity evidence (of the traditional type) among the three subscales. Other results reported in the manual might be enlisted in support of the arguments that the authors need to make, but small and unrepresentative samples and nonstandard administration conditions limit much of the potentially most supportive evidence. After attempting to assemble the best possible case myself, I concluded that the available evidence does offer some promise, and that future research should be further enlightening.

RELIABILITY. The interrater reliabilities reported are low to moderate, ranging from .11 to .74 (median = .49) for the subscales. Interrater reliabilities for the total score are .53 and .62 for two samples of 13 and 17 severely disturbed children of elementary and middle school age, and .63 to .83 for a sample of 19 Head Start children ages 4 and 5 years. As the authors indicate, these relatively low agreement levels are not uncommon for this type of instrument. At the same time, interrater inconsistency does raise important questions about the constancy of the traits measured as well as the influence of rater characteristics on the ratings. Many of the item ratings require subtle judgements or interpretations as opposed to simple behavioral observations, and therefore are especially susceptible to rater influences. This area requires further investigation with larger and more representative samples.

The manual reports test-retest reliabilities from five studies. These are moderate to high, ranging from .90 to .97 for a 2-week interval, and from .61 to .70 for a 6-month interval. High coefficient alphas are reported that exceed .90 for all grade levels for all scales, including the total score. Raw-score standard errors of measurement based on the coefficient alphas also are provided. More useful, and better reflecting the actual level of measurement error to be expected, would be standard errors reported in standard-score rather than raw-score units and based on interrater reliabilities from representative sample groups.

No evidence of individual item reliability is reported. Given that interpretation at the individual item level is recommended, at least I would like to see interrater and test-retest reliabilities for all items. It also would be helpful to have the inter-item correlation matrix, which, judging from the high alphas, can be expected to contain some very high correlations.

INTERPRETATION. The norms group is large, geographically diverse, and provides good coverage of all intended grade levels (K–6) and both sexes. The authors do not adequately justify the decision to collapse norms across sexes and grades, however. Other child behavior rating instruments typically provide separate sex and/or grade level (or age) norms. Non-zero (and presumably significant) score-by-sex correlations are reported in the manual. These demonstrate at least some relationship between skills ratings and sex for all three scales as well as the total score.

Explicit cut scores for social skills deficits are not provided, but a general recommendation is made to obtain further evaluation for children scoring 1 to 1.5 standard deviations below the mean of the norms sample on any scale. The scale means and standard deviations provided for selected abnormal and handicapped groups are based on small, single site samples. Minimal discussion or direction for interpreting profile patterns is provided. The authors strongly recommend remediation of any social skill receiving an item rating of 1 or 2. This type of application is questionable in the absence of individual item reliability information.

SUMMARY. The WMS is a quick and compact scale focused on two important domains of child behavior. It appears to be based conceptually in solid theory. Its major weakness is that a convincing argument for the construct validity of its three separate subscales has not been made. Better evidence of interrater consistency would strengthen both the validity arguments and one's confidence in the reliabilities of the measurements themselves. The absence of individual item reliability information detracts from the strongly recommended use of individual items. The WMS has good potential for use as a quick screening device, one of its primary intended applications. For more extensive applications, such as determining student remediation needs or evaluating programs, results must be interpreted cautiously while further evidence of construct validity and interrater consistency is amassed. An alternative to consider is a new instrument published by American Guidance Service, the Social Skills Rating System (Gresham & Elliott, 1990).

REVIEWER'S REFERENCE

Gresham, F. M., & Elliott, S. N. (1990). Social Skills Rating System. Circle Pines, MN: American Guidance Service.

Review of the Walker-McConnell Scale of Social Competence and School Adjustment by J. JEFFREY GRILL, Associate Professor of Special Education, Carroll College, Helena, MT:

The Walker-McConnell Scale of Social Competence and School Adjustment is intended for "the screening and identification of social skills deficits among elementary aged children in school." The scale consists of 43 items distributed among three subscales: (a) Teacher-Preferred Social Behavior (16 items), (b) Peer-Preferred Social Behavior (17 items), and (c) School Adjustment Behavior (10 items). The 43 items are randomly ordered throughout the scale's two-page protocol, but each item is coded (1, 2, or 3, as listed above) for identification with one of the subscales.

Each item is presented as a statement of a positive behavior, and each may be used as a social skills objective in the Individualized Education Plans for children identified as handicapped. Items are rated individually on frequency-of-occurrence scales of 1 (Never) to 5 (Frequently); for ratings between these extremes, raters are instructed to check 2, 3, or 4 to indicate their best estimates of the rates of occurrence. Raw scores are sums of ratings for items on each subscale and the total scale. Norm tables, derived from a sample of 1,812 children, allow for conversion of raw scores for each subscale and the total scale to standard scores, each with a mean of 100 and standard deviation of 15, and/or to percentile ranks. The single sheet, folded protocol includes: space for pupil demographic information, the rating instructions, all items and rating scales, space for recording raw scores, standard scores and/or percentile ranks, and ample space for narrative comments. The authors state that the entire scale may be completed and scored in about 5 minutes, but only by teachers who have had, at a minimum, 2 months' experience with the child being rated.

The manual evidences the authors' impressive efforts to provide, with clarity and brevity, a sound rationale for the scale; unusually extensive technical data to support the scale's development, validity, reliability, and normative data; and discussion of the use, scoring, and interpretation of the scale. Indeed, the first section of the manual, "An Overview and Description of the Scale," is at once a lucid, succinct, and thorough apologia for the scale and for the significance of the social competence and social skills of children in the overall scheme of education in the United States.

The extensive discussion of technical characteristics (27 pages of narrative and tables—more than half the manual) of the scale provides welcomed documentation. The authors offer unusually large numbers of studies, not all of which are fully supportive, to document the scale's development, validity, and reliability. In fact, the quantity and nature of these studies is likely to be daunting to users of the scale who are not sophisticated in the statistical procedures of factor analysis and discriminant function analysis. Nonetheless, the evidence offered clearly supports the careful development and selection of items included in the scale.

Six subtypes of validity are discussed, but discussions of both content and item validity essentially extend and reiterate (albeit briefly) the discussion of item selection. A study of factorial validity, using an undescribed subset ($n = 762$) of the norm sample, revealed that the total scale is dominated by items from Subscale 1, Teacher-Preferred Social Behavior.

The authors report at least 13 studies dealing with discriminant validity (i.e., the effectiveness of the scale to discriminate among groups of children "known to differ on dimensions to which social skills . . . may be related"). This dazzling and sometimes bewildering (because of overlapping samples of children) display of data includes studies of children labelled normal, antisocial, seriously emotionally disturbed, and those of varying sociometric status. Overall, these studies provide moderate to strong support for the scale's ability to discriminate among the various groups of children. However, the reporting of all these studies is less than adequate, with inconsistent amounts of detail and description offered. The authors would have made a more credible case had they provided full details for the most germane of the studies (or at least those with nonoverlapping pupil samples). As it stands, the discussion of discriminant validity amounts to obfuscation by overkill.

The more traditional criterion-related validity is supported by reports of eight studies of correlations of Walker-McConnell Scale scores with an array of parent and teacher ratings, or with results of other measures of social skills. Results of these studies clearly provide strong support for the validity of the Walker-McConnell Scale.

The discussion of construct validity (i.e., the extent to which the scale measures the constructs—one presumes these to be the three subscales—it purports to measure) provides mixed evidence to support this aspect of validity. The particular problem here is that the authors do not consistently identify the specific constructs they intend to validate.

Compared to the massive amount of information on the various aspects of validity, the discussion of the scale's reliability is incredibly brief. Test-retest, internal consistency, and interrater reliabilities are discussed, with five studies reported to support test-retest reliability, four of which provide generally strong support for the scale, although with varying numbers (13 to 323) of children as subjects, and with varying amounts of time (2 weeks to several months) between test and retest. Unusually strong support for the scale's internal consistency is provided by no coefficient alpha lower than .95 being calculated for the total norm sample.

Despite this strong evidence to support two types of reliability, interrater reliability may well be most important for this type of instrument. Results of a few relatively small studies suggest low interrater reliability coefficients. Because this scale relies on teacher judgement and perception, and because these can be highly variable from one teacher to another, interrater reliability is of primary importance. Unfortunately, the Walker-McConnell Scale misses the mark here. To their credit, the authors acknowledge this problem.

The norm sample of 1,812 children, although certainly sufficient in number, seriously misrepresents the nation's population distribution, at least geographically. Not only is the Northeast section of the United States grossly underrepresented, Alaska, which contributed 331 children (18% of the sample) to the norm group, is extraordinarily overrepresented. Sex and ethnic/racial distributions in the norm group more closely approximate national distributions of these variables.

In summary, the Walker-McConnell Scale is an entirely appropriate instrument for *screening* children on social competence and school adjustment skills. It is easy and quick to use, is well developed, valid, and generally reliable. The principal shortcomings are the lack of geographic representativeness of the norm sample and the unavoidable reliance on observers' perceptions for completing the ratings. The latter seems intrinsic to rating scales. To rectify this significant problem would entail substantial revision of the scale, and would render it undesirable, at best, and unused at worst, by those who are most likely to use it well. The Walker-McConnell Scale should be used; despite its few flaws, it is a valuable addition to the extant array of behavior assessment instruments.

[461]
Watson-Barker Listening Test—High School Version.

Purpose: "Designed to assess overall listening ability."
Population: Grades 7–12.
Publication Dates: 1985–89.
Acronym: HS-WBLT.
Scores, 6: Evaluating Message Content, Understanding Meaning in Conversations, Understanding and Remembering Information in Lectures, Evaluating Emotional Meanings in Messages, Following Instructions and Directions, Total.
Administration: Group.
Forms, 2: A (pre-test) and B (post-test).
Price Data, 1989: $229.95 per Form A and B package (including video tape, facilitator's guide ('89, 42 pages), and 100 answer sheets); $149.95 per test package including all above listed material (specify form).
Time: 35 minutes.
Comments: May be self-scored for awareness training; VHS video tape player and 17-inch (minimum size) color TV monitor needed; high school version of Watson-Barker Listening Test (10:384).

Authors: Kittie W. Watson, Larry L. Barker, and Charles V. Roberts.
Publisher: SPECTRA Incorporated, Publishers.
Cross References: For reviews by James R. Clopton and Joseph P. Stokes of the adult version, see 10:384.

Review of the Watson-Barker Listening Test—High School Version by MICHAEL R. HARWELL, Assistant Professor of Psychology and Education, University of Pittsburgh, Pittsburgh, PA:

The Watson-Barker Listening Test—High School Version (HS-WBLT) is an extension of the WBLT for adults and is designed to assess overall listening ability for grades 7 through 12. The authors suggest several potential uses of this test, including identifying listening skills that need improvement, assessing the effectiveness of differing instructional strategies, and diagnosing listening differences among unique student populations. The HS-WBLT is a paper-and-pencil test administered in a group setting. All instructions, examples, and test items appear on a videotape that requires a videotape playback unit for test administration. There are two forms of the test (A and B) which, according to the authors, can be used as alternate forms. Test items take the form of videotaped vignettes in which two or more students or adults speak to one another. Respondents are then asked to choose the most logical of four possible answers for that item. A total of 50 test items are used, 10 in each of five subsections (Evaluating Message Content, Understanding Meaning in Conversations, Understanding and Remembering Lectures, Evaluating Emotional Meanings in Messages, and Following Instructions and Directions). Test administration directions are clear and to the point, and respondents and users administering this test for the first time should have little trouble following instructions.

SCORING. Subsection and total scores are generated by summing the relevant item scores. The highest possible score for any subsection is reported to be 20, which presumably means that each correct answer has a score value of 2; incorrect answers are apparently scored 0, although this is not specifically stated in the manual. All subsections are equally weighted. Answer keys are provided in the test packet; the correct responses also appear in the test manual.

NORMS. The manual states that normative data for the HS-WBLT were generated over a 3-year period using a sample from a variety of socioeconomic groups and geographical areas across the United States. Unfortunately, none of the socioeconomic groups or geographic areas are identified. A total of 397 junior and senior high school students (218 female, 179 male) were used in the normative sample. How many of the 397 were junior high students and how many were senior high students is not reported. Both forms of the test were administered to 259 of the 397 students. Average scores for the normative sample are reported by subsection and by gender for each form and for the total sample. Standard deviations are reported by subsection and total scores only. The authors report that there were significant differences between males and females on total scores for both forms and, apparently, on some subsections within forms. They contend that such differences are consistent with the literature in this area. Some guidance is provided for interpreting scores on the HS-WBLT. The authors indicate that interpretations of test results should emphasize positive listening behaviors and that helpful suggestions should be made where appropriate.

Several aspects of the normative data reported for the HS-WBLT are troubling. The use of averages as a guide to rank-ordering respondents with respect to listening ability scores is less useful than a scale that reflects performance over a range of scores (e.g., stanines). Total scores are reported by deciles for the adult version of this test. It is hoped that the authors plan to follow a similar strategy for HS-WBLT scores in the near future. Another problem with the normative data is the failure to report standard deviations and standard errors of measurement by gender for each subsection of each form. These shortcomings also apply to the normative data reported for the 12 through 14 year and 15 through 18 year age groups. On the positive side, the authors state that they will send the latest available normative information to users upon request. Considering the inadequacy of the normative information in the manual, this is a much needed service.

RELIABILITY. The only reliabilities reported for the HS-WBLT are correlations between corresponding subsections for Forms A and B and between total scores for the two forms. The correlations for corresponding subsections range from .11 to .38, and the correlation between total scores on the two forms is given as .53. Each of these correlations is reported to be statistically significant. This is a serious problem. The size of the correlations suggests that some of the corresponding subsections on the two forms have little in common. In effect, particular subsections for Forms A and B can be viewed as supplying nonredundant information and, thus, the authors' contention that Forms A and B can be used interchangeably or in a pretest/posttest format is highly suspect. Curiously, classical item analysis results are not reported even though items are apparently scored dichotomously.

The authors do report the results of a multiple regression analysis in which the total score for Form A was regressed upon the five subsection scores (i.e., predictors) of Form B. Unfortunately, the authors' reversal of this statement in the manual: "the five parts of Form B regressed on the total score for

Form A" is incorrect and may confuse some users. The resulting squared multiple correlation between the dependent variable total score on Form A and the five predictors is reported to be .29, meaning that approximately 29% of the variance in Form A total scores can be predicted from the set of subsection predictor variables from Form B. Considering that Forms A and B are treated as interchangeable by the authors, this value is not impressive. Further, the multiple regression analysis fails to take gender into account, which the authors make clear is correlated with student performance. Thus, the regression results are likely to be biased.

VALIDITY. Astonishingly, no empirical validity evidence is reported for the HS-WBLT. Validity evidence for the adult WBLT version is mentioned. This is far and away the most serious shortcoming of the HS-WBLT. At a minimum, the authors need to obtain evidence that the HS-WBLT correlates satisfactorily with similar tests and to perform analyses that might shed light on what Forms A and B are measuring.

SUMMARY. The authors of the HS-WBLT have not provided sufficient empirical documentation to suggest that the test measures what it purports to measure and that it does so reliably. The incomplete nature of the reported normative data and reliability information, along with the absence of any empirical validity evidence other than face validity, give little credibility to the claims of the authors about this test. The fact that the authors are continuing to obtain normative data presents them with the opportunity to correct these deficiencies in future editions.

Review of the Watson-Barker Listening Test—High School Version by CAROL KEHR TITTLE, Professor of Educational Psychology, Graduate School, City University of New York, and DEBORAH HECHT, Associate Project Director, Center for Advanced Study in Education, Graduate Center, City University of New York, New York, NY:

The high school version of the Watson-Barker Listening Test is intended to assess listening skills and is similar to the adult version of the Watson-Barker Listening Test. The test administration is controlled by using a videotape, which runs for 40 minutes; the tape includes all directions, listening situations, and questions. Students mark answers to multiple-choice questions on an answer sheet. Questions and answer choices are read by the narrator, and the answer choices are also listed on the screen.

The test has five sections of 10 items each. Section I, titled Evaluating Message Content, contains short statements of one or two sentences, with one question for each sentence. Section II, Understanding Meaning in Conversations, contains five brief interactions with one to three questions after each. Section III, Understanding and Remem-

bering Lectures, contains two short talks with five questions after each. Section IV, Evaluating Emotional Meaning, contains brief, one-sentence interactions, with one question after each sentence, and Section V, Following Instructions and Directions, contains three short talks with three or four questions after each talk. The listening situations are intended to be similar to those students might encounter in educational, work, or home settings. The test is available in two forms, A and B. This reviewer found the sound and visual presentations of the videotape for Form B clear and the general instructions clearly presented.

The Facilitator's Guide is inadequate in many areas, including the information provided for scoring. Based upon the data in the guide, the user must assume that each item in the 50-item test is given a value of 2, because the score range is 0 to 100 (p. 5). The authors suggest comparing a student's individual scores on the various subsections with the means given separately for junior high school and senior high school students. These means are difficult to interpret. They are not the same for the two forms, and the differences are not consistent between forms. The males in this sample (179 males and 218 females) scored consistently lower than the females, and it is not clear how many students formed the basis of the junior high school and high school means. Page 5 of the guide contains a set of score ranges with seven evaluation categories from *Very Poor* to *Excellent*. There is no information on how these categories were established.

The classroom instructional uses suggested include encouraging student awareness of listening skills and pre/post instructional unit evaluation. As a "listening measurement tool," the uses suggested are diagnosis, research, and evaluation. Unfortunately, these reviewers must restate for this version the negative evaluation that the adult version of the test received in earlier reviews. The data presented in the manual are inadequate and discouraging for the uses suggested. Reliability estimates are given based on alternate form correlations, and these are very low for individual use (.53 for the total score and from .11 for Part IV to .38 for Part V). Decision making for individual students is not warranted with the present instrument except in the most cautious manner and then using only the total score.

The most serious concern, however, is the discussion of the validity of the test. No theoretical rationale and no model of the listening process are provided as a basis for the items and parts of the test. Current models and some of the assessments in reading comprehension take into account the structure of discourse (passage mapping to ensure that test items focus on important ideas); the reader's knowledge about reading, text factors, and strategy uses; the reader's self-report of performance, effort, and interest; and the reader's familiarity with the topic (Michigan Educational Assessment Program, 1989). Current models of speech perception include similar factors (Boothroyd, in press): the analysis of the speaker—intent, message, language patterns, movement patterns, and immediate context (linguistic, physical, social); and the "perceiver"—knowledge and contextual evidence (linguistic, physical, social). If the test is intended for classroom use, a model, a well-defined rationale, and the implications for instruction are needed. What is known about the meaning of the scores to teachers? What uses, if any, do teachers make of the test information?

Absent the theory or supporting research literature to argue for the test structure, empirical evidence on item-part correlations and factor analyses of the items/parts are needed. The manual makes reference to earlier factor analyses of the adult version, but no data are presented for the high school version. Inspection of the speech situations and the items suggest that Parts III and V require similar skills in remembering details for lists. In Part IV, Interpreting the Emotional Context to Establish Meaning, Items 2 and 5 might have alternative keys. In Part V, knowledge of the perceiver's goals, context, and familiarity with the topic are likely to influence score interpretations.

The low reliability and lack of validity-related information for the high school version of the Watson-Barker Listening Test argue against its use except in carefully limited situations. Teachers might use the test in class discussions to raise awareness of listening skills, but comparisons of scores with the data from the manual are likely to be of limited value. Even this use should be undertaken only after teachers' reviews of the items suggest that there is meaning for both teacher and students for this instructional purpose. Users should also review the videotape listening situations and items for their appropriateness and meaningfulness for urban, ethnically diverse student populations.

REVIEWER'S REFERENCES

Michigan Educational Assessment Program. (1989, July). *Essential skills reading test blueprint* (5th ed.). Lansing, MI: Michigan Department of Education.
Boothroyd, A. (1991, in press). Speech perception, sensorineural hearing loss and hearing aids. In G. Studebaker & I. Hochberg (Eds.), *Accoustical factors affecting hearing aid performance* (pp. 59, mimeo). Austin, TX: PRO-ED, Inc.

[462]
Ways of Coping Questionnaire, Research Edition.

Purpose: "To identify the thoughts and actions an individual has used to cope with a specific stressful encounter."
Population: Adults.
Publication Date: 1988.
Scores, 8: Confrontive Coping, Distancing, Self-Controlling, Seeking Social Support, Accepting

Responsibility, Escape-Avoidance, Planful Problem-Solving, Positive Reappraisal.
Administration: Group.
Price Data, 1990: $42 per 10 prepaid test booklet/answer sheets; $12 per 25 handscorable test booklet/answer sheets; $12 per manual (37 pages); $13 per specimen set (includes manual and 1 prepaid test booklet); computer scoring available with prepaid answer sheets.
Time: (10–15) minutes.
Comments: Self-administered.
Authors: Susan Folkman and Richard S. Lazarus.
Publisher: Consulting Psychologists Press, Inc.

TEST REFERENCES

1. Foley, F. W., Bedell, J. R., LaRocca, N. G., Scheinberg, L. C., & Reznikoff, M. (1987). Efficacy of stress-inoculation training in coping with multiple sclerosis. *Journal of Consulting and Clinical Psychology, 55,* 919-922.
2. Frank, R. G., Umlauf, R. L., Wonderlich, S. A., Askanazi, G. S., Buckelew, S. P., & Elliott, T. R. (1987). Differences in coping styles among persons with spinal cord injury: A cluster-analytic approach. *Journal of Consulting and Clinical Psychology, 55,* 727-731.
3. Martelli, M. F., Auerbach, S. M., Alexander, J., & Mercuri, L. G. (1987). Stress management in the health care setting: Matching interventions with patient coping styles. *Journal of Consulting and Clinical Psychology, 55,* 201-207.
4. Blanchard-Fields, F., & Irion, J. C. (1988). Coping strategies from the perspective of two developmental markers: Age and social reasoning. *Journal of Genetic Psychology, 149,* 141-151.
5. Folkman, S., & Lazarus, R. S. (1988). Coping as a mediator of emotion. *Journal of Personality and Social Psychology, 54,* 466-475.
6. McIntosh, E. G. (1988). Development of a scale to assess jealous behaviors. *Perceptual and Motor Skills, 67,* 554.
7. MacCarthy, B., & Brown, R. (1989). Psychosocial factors in Parkinson's disease. *British Journal of Clinical Psychology, 28,* 41-52.
8. Revenson, T. A., & Felton, B. J. (1989). Disability and coping as predictors of psychological adjustment to rheumatoid arthritis. *Journal of Consulting and Clinical Psychology, 57,* 344-348.
9. Solomon, Z., Avitzur, E., & Mikulincer, M. (1989). Coping resources and social functioning following combat stress reaction: A longitudinal study. *Journal of Social and Clinical Psychology, 8,* 87-96.
10. Vitaliano, P. P., Katon, W., Maiuro, R. D., & Russo, J. (1989). Coping in chest pain patients with and without psychiatric disorder. *Journal of Consulting and Clinical Psychology, 57,* 338-343.
11. Nicholson, W. D., & Long, B. C. (1990). Self-esteem, social support, internalized homophobia, and coping strategies of HIV+ gay men. *Journal of Consulting and Clinical Psychology, 58,* 873-876.
12. Sloper, P., Cunningham, C., Turner, S., & Knussen, C. (1990). Factors related to the academic attainments of children with Down's Syndrome. *The British Journal of Educational Psychology, 60,* 284-298.
13. Wright, T. A. (1990). The ways of coping instrument: Reliability and temporal stability for a sample of employees. *Psychological Reports, 67,* 155-162.
14. Fairbank, J. A., Hansen, D. J., & Fitterling, J. M. (1991). Patterns of appraisal and coping across different stressor conditions among former prisoners of war with and without posttraumatic stress disorder. *Journal of Consulting and Clinical Psychology, 59,* 274-281.
15. Heppner, P. P., Cook, S. W., Strozier, A. L., & Heppner, M. J. (1991). An investigation of coping styles and gender differences with farmers in career transition. *Journal of Counseling Psychology, 38,* 167-174.
16. Levy-Shiff, R., Goldshmidt, I., & Har-Even, D. (1991). Transition to parenthood in adoptive families. *Developmental Psychology, 27,* 131-140.

Review of the Ways of Coping Questionnaire, Research Edition by JUDITH C. CONGER, Director of Clinical Training, Purdue University, West Lafayette, IN:

RATIONALE. The Ways of Coping Questionnaire is a 66-item instrument designed to investigate the coping style used by individuals when dealing with stress. The basic rationale underlying the instrument is that it is the *way* people cope with stress, rather than the stress per se, that is related to physical, social, and psychological well-being. The authors eschew the notion that the instrument is a test, but rather prefer to conceive of it as "an evolving strategy for measurement" to be used primarily as a research instrument in studies of the coping process. Further, coping is viewed as a dynamic interaction between the individual and the environment for which traditional trait approaches do not apply because they are dispositional and underestimate the multidimensional and dynamic nature of the coping process. Additionally, traditional approaches equate adequate coping with mastery which this approach does not. Rather, quality of coping is viewed within the context in which it occurs and allows for the fact that the same coping strategy may be maladaptive in one situation, but adaptive in another. The theoretical context is important. Because of their position, the authors disavow traditional measures of reliability such as test-retest estimates. They do, however, examine some estimates of stability (see below).

DEVELOPMENT. This instrument was an outgrowth of an earlier, similar instrument (Ways of Coping Checklist) developed in 1976–1977. Various strategies and revisions over the period that followed were employed in the development of this questionnaire and the second author, Richard Lazarus, has a long and distinguished research career in the stress area.

The normative sample on which the coping scales were developed was composed of 75 middle and upper-middle class married couples, having at least one child at home. Thus, the sample tends to be restricted in terms of marital status, SES, race, and age or at least "stage of life." Both members of the couples were interviewed individually, five times over a 5-month period, and asked to describe their most stressful encounter during the previous week and to fill out the questionnaire.

Observations from the five observations were pooled and data are presented for individual items in terms of means, standard deviations, skewness, and factor loadings. Although there is variable skewness among the scales, the confrontive Coping Scale seems quite skewed in the positive direction indicating infrequent use of that particular coping strategy. Nevertheless, the authors chose to include this.

The authors report that three separate factor analyses were done using differing person-occasion combinations. It is reported that these three analyses yielded similar factor structures and led to the exclusion of some items that, although retained in the questionnaire, are not used. That is, the authors report that after the preliminary factor studies, a final principal factor analysis was performed on the final 50 items using the 750 observations. (Apparently only 50 items are used, although the form contains 66.) This final analysis resulted in eight factors represented by eight scales reflecting differ-

ent coping strategies. Although much of the research reported confirms the factor structure, there are subsequent analyses, albeit done with other populations, that are not completely consistent with the initial findings, raising some concern over factor stability.

RELIABILITY AND VALIDITY CONSIDERATIONS. Because the questionnaire measures "coping processes" and is not a "test" in the conventional sense, the authors feel that traditional test-retest estimates are inappropriate and chose to focus on internal consistency estimates such as the Cronbach's alpha. These, as the authors note, fall at the low end of the acceptable range. Some of the estimates are quite low. For example, the alpha for Distancing is .61 and the estimate for Accepting Responsibility is .66 (range = .61 to .79 for all scales). Despite the stated disavowal of traditional test-retest estimates, stability was measured using the mean autocorrelation across the five occasions investigating stressful encounters. Those that were reported were generally quite low (<.25), with the highest estimate being Positive Reappraisal (r = .47).

The internal consistency estimates are not very strong, no doubt due in part to the small number of items in each scale. Additionally, the stability estimates are quite weak. Although the authors may have theoretical reasons for rejecting traditional conceptions of reliability, the estimates that were used do not provide compelling evidence for the dependability of the measure. This is especially true if one considers that reliability tends to place limits on the upper value of a validity coefficient in that, in general, validity cannot exceed the square root of the reliability coefficient. The authors discuss several studies they feel provide evidence for the validity of their measure. The discussion, however, provides no direct data so the reader cannot easily evaluate validity claims. References are provided.

Additionally, a selective review of research using the measure is presented in terms of situational and personality correlates, gender differences, psychological adjustment, and age differences in coping. Presumably, this speaks to the construct validity as well as concurrent, convergent, and divergent validity issues, although this was not always clearly spelled out in the above terms. Again, studies in this section were described with little or no "hard data" reported, although, again, all were referenced.

Although the authors want this measure construed as an "evolving strategy" rather than a test and further, feel that traditional reliability notions are not applicable, so much of the data are presented in "traditional" terms (correlates, stability, etc.) that it is impossible *not* to apply "old fashioned" test theory principles. On those grounds, the measure appears questionable. Further, one cannot help but ask, "Do certain individuals tend to share common coping mechanisms (a trait-like conjecture, to be sure)?" or "Are similar strategies used in similar situations?" especially when these strategies are linked to personality variables in the manual. If the "coping process" is so variable and not subject to traditional test theory considerations, then I am not sure how one would evaluate this measure. How is one to know that "coping processes" are being captured? Even radical behaviorists who feel that behavior is quite situationally determined employ traditional psychometric considerations in evaluating the measurement of a behavior.

Thus, although it is clear that a great deal of work has been done in conjunction with this measure, it is a "research measure" that should be used with caution, given the current limitations discussed in the review.

Review of the Ways of Coping Questionnaire, Research Edition by KATHRYN D. HESS, Consultant, Montgomery, AL:

The Ways of Coping Questionnaire (WCQ) was "designed to identify the thoughts and actions an individual has used to cope with a specific stressful encounter" in everyday living (manual, p. 1). The authors, Folkman and Lazarus, see the WCQ as an evolving strategy for measuring the coping *process* rather than coping *dispositions* or styles. Although the WCQ is used primarily as a research tool, the authors note its potential "as a stimulus for discussion in clinical, training, and workshop settings" or "as a research tool in clinical settings" for measuring intervention effects.

THEORETICAL BACKGROUND. In describing the conceptual background of the WCQ the authors define coping as "the cognitive and behavioral efforts to manage specific external and/or internal demands appraised as taxing or exceeding the resources of the individual" (manual, p. 2). They write "This definition has four key features: (1) it is process-oriented; (2) it speaks of management rather than mastery; (3) it makes no a priori judgement about the quality of coping processes; and (4) it implies a stress-based distinction between coping and automatic adaptive behaviors" (manual, p. 2).

DEVELOPMENT OF SCALES. A historical overview of the WCQ and the earlier version, Ways of Coping Checklist (WCC), is provided in the manual. The questionnaire consists currently of 66 items in a 4-point Likert scale format that allows individuals to indicate the frequency with which they use each strategy.

The sample for the derivation of the WCQ coping scales consists of 750 observations from 75 middle and upper-middle class, white, married couples with at least one child living at home. The husbands and wives in each couple were interviewed individually in five monthly interviews (150 individuals, five interviews each). At each interview they were asked to describe the most stressful encounter experienced in the previous week and to complete the WCQ. The authors report that the observations from the five interviews were pooled. Means, standard deviations, skewness, and factor loadings for each of the 50 items that were included in the final eight scales are found in the manual's Appendix.

Three factor analyses yielding similar factor patterns were performed on: (*a*) the entire set of 750 observations; (*b*) a subset of 150 stressful encounters, one per subject equally representing the five time periods; and (*c*) a second set of 150 observations selected from the remaining 600 items—again one observation per person equally representing the five time periods. When those items that did not load consistently on the same factor were eliminated a final principle factor analysis was performed on the remaining 50 items resulting in eight factors. (Apparently 16 of the 66 items do not contribute to the scales.)

The eight scales, their descriptions, and the items found in each scale are found in the WCQ manual (pp. 8, 31–33). Confrontive Coping describes aggressive efforts to alter the situation and is evidenced in items such as "I expressed anger to the person(s) who caused the problem." Distancing describes cognitive efforts to detach oneself and to minimize the significance of the event such as "Went on as if nothing had happened." Self-Controlling deals with efforts to regulate one's feelings and actions, for example, "I tried to keep my feelings to myself." Seeking Social Support describes efforts to obtain informational, tangible, and emotional support using items such as "Talked to someone to find out more about the situation." Accepting Responsibility acknowledges one's role in the problem and attempts to rectify the situation (e.g., "Criticized or lectured myself"). Escape-Avoidance describes wishful thinking or escape behaviors such as "Hoped a miracle would happen," or "Slept more than usual." Planful Problem-Solving describes deliberate, analytic problem-focused efforts to remedy the situation such as "I made a plan of action and followed it." Positive Reappraisal, the eighth scale, describes efforts to create positive meaning through personal growth (e.g., "Changed or grew as a person in a good way").

The instructions on the answer sheet ask the respondent to think of the most stressful event ("difficult or troubling for you") they experienced in the past week, and to ponder the details of this stressful situation before responding to the items. Raw scores and relative scores (a derived score controlling for unequal numbers of items on each scale and differences in subject's response rates) for each scale are provided by the publisher through prepaid answer sheets. Although the manual notes that permission from the publisher is required for researchers wishing to perform their own on-site scoring, hand-scored test booklets and answer sheets are available from the publisher.

RELIABILITY. Folkman and Lazarus deem test-retest measures not to be appropriate to their measure. The internal consistency of the measure, however, using Cronbach's coefficient alpha is presented. The authors also present references to current research supporting the reliability and stability of the factor structure across various populations. They do not, however, present the research so the reader can evaluate the findings without locating the original sources. Means, standard deviations, levels of significance, sample parameters, or factor loadings from the research are not presented in the manual.

VALIDITY. The authors report the items have face validity because they "are those that individuals have reported using to cope with the demands of stressful situations" (manual, p. 14). They note the face validity of the five foreign language translations has not been determined. Nor was evidence presented to show face validity across different cultural or ethnic groups other than the white, middle-class one on which the scales were developed.

Although the authors report that "Evidence of construct validity is found in the fact that the results of our studies are consistent with our theoretical predictions" they failed to provide evidence to support this claim. The interested reader can use the references provided to survey the literature; however, the manual itself provides general findings of the studies, not specific results and levels of significance.

CONCLUSIONS. The WCQ is a measure that appears to have potential for examining how an individual copes with stress. The instrument may be adaptable to a wide variety of situations and settings. Although the WCQ manual describes clearly the theoretical basis for the measure and summarizes the historical development of the scales, it has several limitations. These relate to the manual's vagueness in meeting the technical standards described in the *Standards for Educational and Psychological Testing* (AERA, APA, & NCME, 1985). It is apparent from the manual that much research has been completed on the WCQ and WCC, but not enough evaluative information is presented. As a result, both the manual and the original sources must be obtained to determine if this test is appropriate to a given situation. Computer scoring provides the researcher with raw scores for each scale and a "relative" or proportional score for each scale. Although the manual notes that a study "indicated that the relative scores revealed relations among ways of coping that can be blurred with the raw score technique" (manual, p. 12) it did not indicate what those relationships were or what populations were used in the study. Perhaps the authors were attempting to be succinct and not create a large cumbersome manual. However, it would seem that a "Research Edition" would err in the direction of more specific rather than general findings.

Folkman and Lazarus, in the opening page of the manual, write that they view the WCQ as an evolving measurement strategy rather than a test. In fact, using a critical incident methodology, they developed a set of scaled items that do not have the normative data to be used as a measure in the technical sense but can serve researchers and clinicians as a bountiful resource. The WCQ can be used to stimulate discussion, prompt recall of stressful events, and help inventory peoples' responses to stress in their life experiences, which, after all, is what the authors intended.

REVIEWER'S REFERENCE

American Educational Research Association, American Psychological Association, & National Council on Measurement in Education. (1985). *Standards for educational and psychological testing.* Washington, DC: American Psychological Association, Inc.

[463]

[Re Wechsler Intelligence Scale for Children—Revised.] WISC-R Microcomputer-Assisted Interpretive Report.

Purpose: "A computer program designed to summarize the results of a WISC-R administration and to aid psychologists and other qualified professionals in the interpretation of those results."

Publication Dates: 1986–90.

Acronym: WISC-R Micro.

Price Data, 1992: $175 per complete package including user's manual ('86, 52 pages) and 1 computer disk (specify IBM Version 5¼-inch disk or 3½-inch disk or Apple Version 5¼-inch disk).

Author: The Psychological Corporation.

Publisher: The Psychological Corporation.

Review of the WISC-R Microcomputer-Assisted Interpretive Report by JOHN C. BRANTLEY, Professor and Chair, School Psychology Program, University of North Carolina, Chapel Hill, NC and WAYDE JOHNSON, School Psychology Program, University of North Carolina, Chapel Hill, NC;

SYSTEM DESCRIPTION. The WISC-R Microcomputer-Assisted Interpretive Report is available in IBM and Apple versions. These reviewers used the Apple II Version 1.2. The Run Time speed is 7–10 minutes.

In December 1989 The Psychological Corporation recalled an earlier pay-for-use version of this program and replaced it with an unprotected, unlimited-use version for both the Apple and IBM. The 1990 cost of this program was $167. Users may divide the program cost by their average or expected usage per year to arrive at an average "run-cost." For example, if two cases per week were anticipated for a year, each run would average $1.67 ($167 divided by 100 runs).

According to the publisher (J. Sugerman, Psychological Corporation, personal communication, February 7, 1990) memory required for the Apple IIe version is approximately 36K, which is well within the Apple memory available. The Apple version requires an Apple II+, IIe, or IIc with at least 64K RAM, one disk drive, and a compatible printer. The IBM version requires an IBM PC with at least 128K RAM, IBM PC DOS 2.0 (or above) or compatible, one disk drive, and compatible printer. At present there are no provisions for software interface options. The Apple version saves current case data onto the program disk but not in a form that is easily accessible for processing with other programs. The publisher is considering an enhancement to save text files onto a separate disk (a feature already available on the IBM version) for further word processing. The Apple version saves the current file onto the program disk. The program will not run if the disk is write protected, which leaves the disk potentially vulnerable to overwriting or erasure.

PROGRAM CLAIMS. Using subtest raw scores provided by the user, the WISC-R Microcomputer-Assisted Interpretive Report analyzes and reports most of the necessary scores used for interpreting the WISC-R. A 2–6-page interpretive report is provided in a technical record format that is unlike the typical "psychological report." If and when text editing is available, part or all of the record could be included in a final psychological report.

Among WISC-R software available on the market at this time, this program appears to be the only one that derives scores directly from raw score input. (Others require scales scores as input. Two other companies, HAPP and Precision People, no longer distribute raw score conversion programs, which they previously made available.)

The statements provided by this program are descriptive in nature and will be familiar to anyone with professional knowledge of the WISC-R. They are of the following types: (a) statistically significant discrepancies, confidence intervals, and internal consistency; (b) explanatory interpretations describing the content/abilities represented by test components; (c) descriptive interpretations of the client's strengths and weaknesses in abilities; and (d) inferential interpretations of personal, experiential, and environmental factors which may have influenced the client's pattern of strengths and weaknesses.

VALIDITY ISSUES. Most of the basic decision rules employed in WISC-R profile analysis are declared in the User's Manual (pp. 15–19). These include: criteria for subtest discrepancies, integrity limits for subtest scatter, and statistical significance levels. These rules are consistent with recommendations by acknowledged authorities such as Sattler, Kaufman, Glasser and Zimmerman, Kellerman and Burry, and Matarazzo, who are referenced in the manual (pp. 45–46). The sequence of analysis proceeds from the global level to shared abilities to unique subtest strengths and weaknesses.

Actual programming statements are considered by the publisher to be proprietary. Samples of decision outcomes are provided in the manual (pp. 15–19). The publisher states, for purposes of this review, that approximately 50 decision statements constitute the program's library, and that as many as 24 logical branching alternatives may be invoked (J. Sugerman, Psychological Corporation, personal communication, February 2, 1990).

The interpretive statements are "descriptive" (rather than inferential), and are based upon research (rather than on opinion or assertion). The manual (p. 17) states that the program's interpretations are derived from a "clinical" rather than a "factor analytic" system. Six patterns of "shared abilities" are included in this program. A much larger number, 46, are identified in the research literature by Kaufman (1979). The publisher's justification for selecting these six patterns is that they are best supported by empirical evidence. The publisher's "expert opinion" is employed in making this distinction.

Error trapping is satisfactory but not complete. The program checks for logical inconsistencies between date of birth, test date, and age appropriateness for test norms, and recognizes errors and requests corrections. Subtest raw scores are rejected if above or below logical values. However, decimal values are accepted and read as whole numbers (e.g., .2 = 2). The degree of risk created by this oversight is not known; however, error trapping could be further tightened to eliminate this possibility.

MAINTENANCE OF SOFTWARE AND HARDWARE. Prior to publication, the publisher engaged a series of independent consultants and beta reviewers (manual, p. 21) who verified accuracy of the program's interpretations using a series of case studies with known outcomes. A responsive "technical support" service is maintained by the publisher. The only instance known of program malfunction involves printer incompatibility. Print commands may not be executed consistently on some printers, which can result in overprinting and/or page length discrepancies. During the current review, the printing problems described above occurred consistently on three different Imagewriter II printers. The publisher is revising the program to eliminate this problem and expects to recall and replace this program version in the near future.

CLARITY OF THE MANUAL AND OPERATING FEATURES. The program manual is clearly written and understandable by the novice user. Essential issues are addressed and references are complete.

The manual describes the model of analysis used, explains the decision rules that are applied, and cautions the user about overinterpretation.

A helpful feature is the option to expand the "Additional Information" section of the report to accommodate additional text.

Cursor movement within screens is optimal. However, there is a major limitation in movement between data screens. There is no way to back up to earlier data screens in the event of an error in raw data entry. Data entered in a screen cannot be recovered once the next data screen is displayed. If a mistake in data entry is discovered past the "point of no return," the user is obliged to restart the program and reenter all data. The manual warns about this feature, but users could find it a major annoyance at times.

SECURITY ISSUES. The Psychological Corporation's review of user's qualifications is the standard for the industry and this software is assigned the highest level of requirements for purchase. Buyers must have appropriate training and experience in assessment and belong to appropriate professional associations, hold licensure, or document the equivalence of their credentials.

In the Apple version of this program, current case data are saved onto the program disk during the run. Previous data are simultaneously erased. Because the case file is not accessible using common word processing programs, confidentiality is not a concern.

GENERAL SUMMARY. The WISC-R Microcomputer-Assisted Interpretive Report provides important advantages, some of them unique to this program, that enhance psychologists' accuracy and consistency in professional decision making, and save professional time. So long as raw scores are entered accurately, the program eliminates potential clerical errors which commonly occur in transforming raw scores into derived scores. This is a major advantage, currently available only with this program. A second advantage lies in the precise calculation of discrepancy scores and their comparison with critical values which eliminates a second major source of clerical errors. In addition, the printout displays the actual discrepancy scores and comparison values so that the user can verify findings directly. The descriptive and explanatory interpretations generated by the program are those commonly expected and used in both clinical and school applications. Printed output does not resemble a typical psychological report. Thus users are appropriately discouraged from distributing the printout as if it were a final report. The manual is clear and helpful. Appropriate cautions about overinterpretation appear in the manual and on the printout. The major disadvantage of this program, its cost-per-use feature, has been eliminated, thus

making it affordable for frequent use. In addition to these features, the program reduces the time typically required for WISC-R analysis from 30-60 minutes to 10 minutes or less.

One limitation of the program is a lack of case storage either to facilitate multiple case processing, or to accommodate text editing into a final report. Another limitation, depending upon persuasion of the user, is the program's capacity to produce only six of Kaufman's 46 shared abilities. The publisher argues that, in their opinion, the six hypotheses available are those best established by research. But it could also be argued that all of the available research-based hypotheses should be presented for the user to consider. A final problem involves the lack of access to data for correction or revision once data analysis has begun. Users should be provided with an additional opportunity to revise data when the initial analysis appears on screen.

REVIEWER'S REFERENCES

Kaufman, A. S. (1979). *Intelligent testing with the WISC-R.* New York: John Wiley & Sons.

[464]

[Re Wechsler Intelligence Scale for Children—Revised.] WISC-Riter "Complete."

Purpose: "Provides the psychologist, teacher, counselor, and other educational and mental health personnel with a printed psychological report based on the client's performance on the WISC-R."
Publication Date: 1986.
Price Data, 1990: $495 per complete program including disk, manual (31 pages), and resource book of educational recommendations; $99 per additional disks with the purchase of a program.
Comments: Free preview available; licensing available; requires Apple II series (dual drive) or IBM computer and printer.
Author: Charles L. Nicholson.
Publisher: Southern MicroSystems.
Cross Reference: For a review by Sylvia Sibley, see 10:386.

Review of the WISC-Riter "Complete" by RONALD H. ROZENSKY, Associate Chairman, Department of Psychiatry, Evanston Hospital/Northwestern University Medical School, Evanston, IL:

The WISC-Riter "Complete" software (IBM compatible version) is described by its author as designed to provide "the psychologist, teacher, counselor, and other educational and mental health personnel with a printed psychological report based upon the client's performance on the WISC-R." The software utilizes IQ scores, scaled scores, and grade equivalent and standard scores from any achievement test as input. The author states the program will "facilitate report writing and provide the psychologist with information to make better interpretations and recommendations." The author clearly and appropriately states that the output of this program is not designed to be the final report, is designed (only) to assist in report writing, and (in the author's own capital letters) "THE PSYCHOLOGIST MUST INTERJECT HIS/HER OBSERVATIONS AND IMPRESSIONS INTO THE FINAL REPORT." The author's caveats conclude with the warning that the software does not use internal subtest scatter, quality of answers, interaction between child and psychologist, or any other factors that can be important in evaluating the child. The author again reminds the psychologist that he or she MUST interject these and other relevant factors into the final report.

The output of the WISC-Riter is a seven-page narrative report that is presented in a logical order with succinct interpretive statements and clearly written remediation suggestions. The manual presents a page-by-page, brief explanation of, and justification for, the various statements in the report. Specific references are offered for various formulae as well as for the primary sources of interpretative statements used by the program in generating the narrative. Initial statements of intellectual strengths and weakness come from standard sources such as Kaufman (1979) and are based upon comparison to the general population.

The program then determines the patient's own level of ability by comparing scores on a standardized achievement test with the student's expected level of achievement given the IQ scores and mental age. "Learning disability levels" are presented next. Formulae and guidelines for these levels are offered in the manual. The manual briefly introduces the use of factors based upon factor analytic studies of the WISC in describing a student's strengths and weaknesses. Three sets of factor scores are presented based upon Performance and Verbal, Performance only, and Verbal only subtest scores. Tabled data printed in the report briefly define the factor titles and level of score on each factor. As many of the factors utilize all subtest scores, the program author suggests administration of all subtest of the WISC-R (Wechsler Intelligence Scale for Children—Revised) in order to assure a full range of factors available for interpretation. Although factor titles appear face valid and are described briefly in an appendix, the psychologist should become familiar with the source material (references are offered). Only then can one fully understand the import of a given factor and accurately (and ethically) utilize the individual factor scores in a meaningful interpretative fashion along with other objective and clinical data. Only the "major factors" by Kaufman (1979) of Verbal Comprehension, Freedom from Anxiety, and Perceptual Organization are presented for discussion in narrative form, and then only if these scores are at a significant level.

The manual next presents a brief discussion of the WISC, WISC-R and WAIS (Wechsler Adult Intelligence Scale) "hav[ing] not been successful and the results hav[ing] not been encouraging" for their use in diagnosing "emotional problems." In italics and in bold, the manual presents cautions about using the test for discussing emotional problems while encouraging the psychologist to seek other testing and clinical interview sources to substantiate emotional diagnoses. Even so, the program narrative then prints out a series of "possible reasons for significant elevated or depressed subtest scaled scores" pertaining to either emotional issues or possible learning disabilities. Source material references for these statements are offered.

The final page of the printout offers recommendations for educational remedial instructions based upon those subtest scores below expected levels. The recommendations are based on the program authors' own work (Nicholson & Alcorn, 1983) and that of others (Banas & Wills, 1978). Final narrative recommendations for learning are based upon those factors that are significantly below expectations. Source materials for those statements are not offered.

Program output can go directly to the printer or be stored as a text file. This reviewer was able to access the files with the word processing program *Wordperfect 5.0* in order to customize the final report. This customization is encouraged by the program author. In fact, users should customize as the actual product of the program reads as a "cookbooky" list of brief interpretative statements, factor scores, and some sentences based solely on numbers (e.g., "The 50% discrepancy level based on the Verbal Scale is 2.4"). Although many of the output statements are clinically relevant, few, if any of the statements on the seven pages of output can or should stand alone without integrating the material with descriptive or clinical observations, interpretation of data, or one's own clinical skills as an integrating theme. The printout includes a table summarizing the individual subtest scale scores, percentiles, and IQs. This output can serve as a convenient shorthand for those who routinely incorporate such information into their reports. The educational remediation suggestions from the original Nicholson and Alcorn (1983) work are helpful and again serve as a shorthand for the clinician who uses this source material or writes such recommendations in his or her own words. The "psychological" or emotional diagnostic conclusions and therapeutic recommendations in the narrative should be reviewed by the clinician as hypotheses (as suggested by the manual) and other test or clinical sources should be included that support those conclusions.

Patient confidentiality issues are minimal with this software in that input and data storage remain in the clinician's own PC. Routine use of clerical staff to input data can occur with minimal and appropriate training and with appropriate confidentiality strictures.

The manual is clearly written in general. A completed first report took less than half an hour from mail box to final keystroke. An addendum to the manual facilitated adding the program to the hard disk. Some knowledge of the PC was necessary in that a specific boot-up command was not included in the manual instructions thus relying on the user to understand what a command file looks like in the directory. Cursor-control keys are learnable, but not intuitively obvious. For example, HOME moves the cursor to the beginning of the current data item rather than to the top left hand corner of the screen. Similarly (re)learning of other cursor controls would occur with routine use of the program. After scoring, the manual says that you can scroll through the report in order to review its content prior to printing or storage. This occurs at a rate much too fast to read on screen and the CTRL-S command on this user's COMPAQ 286e did not stop the scrolling as per the manual. A letter to the manufacturer regarding this scrolling problem and a small printing problem was not answered. A follow-up phone call to the manufacturer a month later was handled in a polite fashion and with some recognition of the caller's letter. Only a "your hardware" problem answer was received with an assurance that there were no other complaints of a similar nature. The voice on the phone said that the majority of the software users used a dot matrix printer. I can only assume that the computer to laser printer link was the problem as the printing errors occurred on a second COMPAQ-laser system as well.

In general, the WISC-Riter "Complete" offers an easy data entry system for WISC-R subscale scores, IQs, and achievement test data. A sample data input form is offered to ease data entry. The documentation of scoring analogues and interpretive statements appears brief, but clear, with specific reference to most source materials. Appropriate caveats are offered regarding the use of computer-generated materials for final test report preparation. The report output is accessible with word processing programs and must be customized to provide a meaningful and clinically accurate product. Given the price of the program ($495), it is up to each user to determine the "cost/benefit" for the generation of the skeletal report the software provides. For this reviewer, the source materials would appear cheaper, look good on the book shelf, and be needed in your library anyway to ethically support this software. In terms of the time for scoring the factor scores and looking up interpretive statements, the experienced clinician should have a useful knowledge of these and a facility for their use already. The novice, for educational purposes, should be encouraged to look

them up to understand the source material and supporting research documentation to appreciate and understand their basis rather than rely on the computer as a shortcut. There is no doubt, however, that time is saved in organizing the report and providing a basis from which to customize. For the cost, the clinician should determine time saved with this program over having the shell of a report already formatted in storage in his or her word processor. The publisher offers preview disks to try out the software and the clinician should closely monitor time saved versus quality of output and time necessary to customize the report. Finally, neither the manual nor publisher's catalog provided any requirements as to professional qualifications of the purchaser of this software.

REVIEWER'S REFERENCES

Banas, N., & Wills, I. H. (1978). *WISC-R prescriptions: How to work creatively with individual learning styles.* Novato, CA: Academic Therapy Publications.
Kaufman, A. (1979). *Intelligent testing with the WISC-R.* New York: John Wiley & Sons.
Nicholson, C. L., & Alcorn, C. L. (1980). *Educational applications of the teacher's guide.* Los Angeles: Western Psychological Services.

[465]
Wechsler Memory Scale—Revised.

Purpose: Constructed to assess "memory for verbal and figural stimuli, meaningful and abstract material, and delayed as well as immediate recall."
Population: Ages 16–74.
Publication Dates: 1945–87.
Acronym: WMS-R.
Scores, 18: Verbal Memory (Logical Memory I, Verbal Paired Associates I, Total), Visual Memory (Figural Memory, Visual Paired Associates I, Visual Reproduction I, Total), Total General Memory, Attention/Concentration (Mental Control, Digit Span, Visual Memory Span, Total), Delayed Recall (Logical Memory II, Visual Paired Associates II, Verbal Paired Associates II, Visual Reproduction II, Total), Information and Orientation.
Administration: Individual.
Price Data, 1991: $220 per complete kit including 25 record forms and manual ('87, 158 pages); $32.50 per figural memory stimulus booklet; $66.50 per visual paired associates stimulus booklet; $17 per set of visual paired associates cards; $17 per set of visual memory span cards; $17 per set of visual reproduction cards; $23 per 25 record forms; $50.50 per manual; $36.50 per case.
Time: [50] minutes.
Author: David Wechsler.
Publisher: The Psychological Corporation.
Cross References: See 9:1355 (49 references); see also T3:2607 (96 references); 8:250 (36 references), T2:592 (70 references), and 6:561 (9 references); for reviews by Ivan Norman Mensh and Joseph Newman of an earlier edition, see 4:364 (6 references); for a review by Kate Levine Kogan, see 3:302 (3 references).

TEST REFERENCES

1. Baker, L.A., Cheng, L. Y., & Amara, I. B. (1983). The withdrawal of benztropine mesylate in chronic schizophrenic patients. *British Journal of Psychiatry, 143,* 584-590.

2. Bolter, J. F., Stanczak, D. E., & Long, C. J. (1983). Neuropsychological consequences of acute, high-level gasoline inhalation. *Clinical Neuropsychology*, 5, 4-7.

3. Braunstein, W. B., Powell, B. J., McGowan, J. F., & Thoreson, R. W. (1983). Employment factors in outpatient recovery of alcoholics: A multivariate study. *Addictive Behaviors*, 8, 345-351.

4. Gudjonsson, G. H. (1983). Suggestibility, intelligence, memory recall and personality: An experimental study. *British Journal of Psychiatry*, 142, 35-37.

5. McKay, S., & Ramsey, R. (1983). Correlation of the Weschler Memory Scale and the Luria-Nebraska Memory Scale. *Clinical Neuropsychology*, 5, 168-170.

6. Crosson, B., Hughes, C. W., Roth, D. L., & Monkowski, P. G. (1984). Review of Russell's (1975) norms for the Logical Memory and Visual Reproduction subtests of the Wechsler Memory Scale. *Journal of Consulting and Clinical Psychology*, 52, 635-641.

7. Gerver, D., Longley, P., Long, J., & Lambert, S. (1984). Selecting trainee conference interpreters: A preliminary study. *Journal of Occupational Psychology*, 57, 17-31.

8. Hamblin, D. K., Hyer, L. A., Harrison, W. R., & Carson, M. F. (1984). Older alcoholics: Profile of decline. *Journal of Clinical Psychology*, 40, 1510-1516.

9. Klesges, R. C., Fisher, L., Pheley, A., Boschee, P., & Vasey, M. (1984). A major validational study of the Halstead-Reitan in the prediction of CAT-scan assessed brain damage in adults. *Clinical Neuropsychology*, 6, 29-34.

10. Knight, R. G., & Godfrey, H. P. D. (1984). Reliability and validity of a scale for rating memory impairment in hospitalized amnesiacs. *Journal of Consulting and Clinical Psychology*, 52, 769-773.

11. Larcombe, N. A., & Wilson, P. H. (1984). An evaluation of cognitive-behaviour therapy for depression in patients with multiple sclerosis. *British Journal of Psychiatry*, 145, 366-371.

12. Lawson, J. S., Williamserdahl, D. L., Monga, T. N., Bird, C. E., Donald, M. W., Surridge, D. H. C., & Letemendia, F. J. J. (1984). Neuropsychological function in diabetic patients with neuropathy. *British Journal of Psychiatry*, 145, 263-268.

13. Lothstein, L. M., & Roback, H. (1984). Black female transsexuals and schizophrenia: A serendipitous finding? *Archives of Sexual Behavior*, 13, 371-386.

14. Margolis, R. B., & Scialfa, C. T. (1984). Age differences in Wechsler Memory Scale performance. *Journal of Clinical Psychology*, 40, 1442-1449.

15. Mattes, J. A., Boswell, L., & Oliver, H. (1984). Methylphenidate effects on symptoms of attention deficit disorder in adults. *Archives of General Psychiatry*, 41, 1059-1063.

16. McDowd, J., & Botwinick, J. (1984). Role and gist memory in relation to type of information, sensory mode, and age. *The Journal of Genetic Psychology*, 145, 167-178.

17. Novack, T. A., Daniel, M. S., & Long, C. J. (1984). Factors related to emotional adjustment following head injury. *Clinical Neuropsychology*, 6, 139-142.

18. Rosenberg, S. J., Ryan, J. J., & Prifitera, A. (1984). Rey Auditory-Verbal Learning Test performance of patients with and without memory impairment. *Journal of Clinical Psychology*, 40, 785-787.

19. Ryan, J. J., Rosenberg, S. J., & Mittenberg, W. (1984). Factor analysis of the Rey Auditory-Verbal Learning Test. *Clinical Neuropsychology*, 6, 239-241.

20. Sher, K. J., Mann, B., & Frost, R. O. (1984). Cognitive dysfunction in compulsive checkers: Further exploration. *Behaviour Research and Therapy*, 22, 493-502.

21. Skenazy, J. A., & Bigler, E. D. (1984). Neuropsychological findings in diabetes mellitus. *Journal of Clinical Psychology*, 40, 246-258.

22. Stanton, B. A., Jenkins, C. D., Savageau, J. A., Zyzanski, S. J., & Aucoin, R. (1984). Age and educational differences on the Trail Making Test and Wechsler Memory Scales. *Perceptual and Motor Skills*, 58, 311-318.

23. Vargo, M. E., & Black, F. W. (1984). Normative data for the Spreen-Benton sentence Repetition Test: Its relationship to age, intelligence, and memory. *Cortex*, 20, 585-590.

24. Varney, N. R., Alexander, B., & MacIndoe. (1984). Reversible steroid dementia in patients without steroid psychosis. *American Journal of Psychiatry*, 141, 369-372.

25. Warren, E. W., & Groome, D. H. (1984). Memory test performance under three different waveforms of ECT for depression. *British Journal of Psychiatry*, 144, 370-375.

26. Whelihan, W. M., Lesher, E. L., Kleban, M. H., & Granick, S. (1984). Mental status and memory assessment as predictors of dementia. *Journal of Gerontology*, 39, 572-576.

27. Zagar, R., Arbit, J., Stuckey, M., & Wengel, W. W. (1984). Developmental analysis of the Wechsler Memory Scale. *Journal of Clinical Psychology*, 40, 1466-1473.

28. Aguirre, M., Broughton, R., & Stuss, D. (1985). Does memory impairment exist in narcolepsy-cataplexy? *Journal of Clinical and Experimental Neuropsychology*, 7, 14-24.

29. Baker, E. L., White, R. F., & Murawski, B. J. (1985). Clinical evaluation of neurobehavioral effects of occupational exposure to organic solvents and lead. *International Journal of Mental Health*, 14 (3), 135-158.

30. Berry, D. T. R., & Webb, W. B. (1985). Sleep and cognitive functions in normal older adults. *Journal of Gerontology*, 40, 331-335.

31. Bigler, E. D., Hubler, D. W., Cullum, C. M., & Turkheimer, E. (1985). Intellectual and memory impairment in dementia. Computerized axial tomography volume correlations. *The Journal of Nervous and Mental Disease*, 173, 347-352.

32. Bilder, R. M., Sukdeb, M., Rieder, R. O., & Pandurangi, A. K. (1985). Symptomatic and neuropsychological components of defect states. *Schizophrenia Bulletin*, 11, 409-419.

33. Butters, N., Wolfe, J., Martone, M., Granholm, E., & Cermark, L. S. (1985). Memory disorders associated with Huntington's Disease: Verbal recall, verbal recognition, and procedural memory. *Neuropsychologia*, 23, 729-743.

34. Daniel, M., Haban, G. F., Hutcherson, W. L., Bolter, J., & Long, C. (1985). Neuropsychological and emotional consequences of accidental, high-voltage electrical shock. *Clinical Neuropsychology*, 7, 102-106.

35. Graff-Radford, N. R., Damasio, H., Yamada, T., Eslinger, P. J., & Damasio, A. R. (1985). Nonhaemorrhagic thalamic infarction. *Brain*, 108, 485-516.

36. Heaton, R. K., Nelson, L. M., Thompson, D. S., Burks, J. S., & Franklin, G. M. (1985). Neuropsychological findings in relapsing-remitting and chronic-progressive multiple sclerosis. *Journal of Consulting and Clinical Psychology*, 53, 103-110.

37. Horne, R. L., Pettinati, H. M., Sugerman, A., & Varga, E. (1985). Comparing bilateral to unilateral electroconvulsive therapy in a randomized study with EEG monitoring. *Archives of General Psychiatry*, 42, 1087-1092.

38. Kermani, E. J., Borod, J. C., Brown, P. H., & Tunnell, G. (1985). New psychopathologic findings in AIDS: Case report. *Journal of Clinical Psychiatry*, 46, 240-241.

39. Larrabee, G. J., Kane, R. L., Schuck, J. R., & Francis, D. J. (1985). Construct validity of various memory testing procedures. *Journal of Clinical and Experimental Neuropsychology*, 7, 239-250.

40. Larson, E. B., Reifler, B. V., Sumi, S. M., Canfield, C. G., & Chinn, N. M. (1985). Diagnostic evaluation of 200 elderly outpatients with suspected dementia. *Journal of Gerontology*, 40, 536-543.

41. Margolis, R. B., Dunn, E. J., & Taylor, J. M. (1985). Parallel-form reliability of the Wechsler Memory Scale in a geriatric population with suspected dementia. *The Journal of Psychology*, 119, 81-86.

42. Mattes, J. A. (1985). Methylphenidate in mild depression: A double-blind controlled trial. *Journal of Clinical Psychiatry*, 46, 525-527.

43. McGlone, J. (1985). Can spatial deficits in Turner's Syndrome be explained by focal CNS dysfunction or atypical speech lateralization? *Journal of Clinical and Experimental Neuropsychology*, 7, 375-394.

44. McSweeny, A. J., Grant, I., Heaton, R. K., Prigatano, G. P., & Adams, K. M. (1985). Relationship of neuropsychological status to everyday functioning in healthy and chronically ill persons. *Journal of Clinical and Experimental Neuropsychology*, 7, 281-291.

45. Naugle, R. I., Cullum, C. M., Bigler, E. D., & Massman, P. J. (1985). Neuropsychological and computerized axial tomography volume characteristics of empirically derived dementia subgroups. *The Journal of Nervous and Mental Disease*, 173, 596-604.

46. Newton, N. A., & Brown, G. G. (1985). Construction of matched verbal and design continuous paired associate tests. *Journal of Clinical and Experimental Neuropsychology*, 7, 97-110.

47. Oscar-Berman, M., & Bonner, R. T. (1985). Matching- and delayed matching-to-sample performance as measures of visual processing, selective attention, and memory in aging and alcoholic individuals. *Neuropsychologia*, 23, 639-651.

48. Pomara, N., Stanley, B., Block, R., Berchou, R. C., Stanley, M., Greenblatt, D. J., Newton, R. E., & Gershon, S. (1985). Increased sensitivity of the elderly to the depressant effects of diazepam. *Journal of Clinical Psychiatry*, 46, 185-187.

49. Prifitera, A., & Barley, W. D. (1985). Cautions in interpretation of comparisons between the WAIS-R and the Wechsler Memory Scale. *Journal of Consulting and Clinical Psychology*, 53, 564-565.

50. Seidenberg, M., Parker, J. C., Nichols, W. K., Davenport, J., & Hewett, J. E. (1985). Carotid stenosis and atherosclerotic heart disease: Interactive effects on cognitive status. *Clinical Neuropsychology*, 7, 45-48.

51. Skenazy, J. A., & Bigler, E. D. (1985). Psychological adjustment and neuropsychological performance in diabetic patients. *Journal of Clinical Psychology*, 41, 391-396.

52. Snow, W. G., & Sheese, S. (1985). Lateralized brain damage, intelligence, and memory: A failure to find sex differences. *Journal of Consulting and Clinical Psychology*, 53, 940-941.

53. Townes, B. D., Martin, D. C., Nelson, D., Prosser, R., Pepping, M., Maxwell, J., Peel, J., & Preston, M. (1985). Neurobehavioral approach to classification of psychiatric patients using a competency model. *Journal of Consulting and Clinical Psychology*, 53, 33-42.

54. Wysocki, J. J., & Sweet, J. J. (1985). Identification of brain-damaged, schizophrenic, and normal medical patients using a brief neuropsychological screening battery. *Clinical Neuropsychology*, 7, 40-44.

55. Taylor, A. E., Saint-Cyr, J. A., Lang, A. E., & Kenny,, F. T. (1986). Parkinson's disease and depression: A critical re-evaluation. *Brain*, 109, 279-292.

56. Andreasen, N., Nasrallah, H. A., Dunn, V., Olson, S. C., Grove, W. M., Ehrhardt, J. C., Coffman, J. A., & Crossett, J. H. W. (1986). Structural abnormalities in the frontal system in schizophrenia. *Archives of General Psychiatry*, 43, 136-144.

57. Baron, J. C., D'Antona, R., Pantano, P., Serdaru, M., Samson, Y., & Bousser, M. G. (1986). Effects of thalamic stroke on energy metabolism of the cerebral cortex: A positron tomography study in man. *Brain*, 109, 1243-1259.

58. Berry, D. T. R., Webb, W. B., Block, A. J., Bauer, R. M., & Switzer, D. A. (1986). Nocturnal hypoxia and neuropsychological variables. *Journal of Clinical and Experimental Neuropsychology*, 8, 229-238.

59. Bolter, J. F., & Hannon, R. (1986). Lateralized cerebral dysfunction in early and late stage alcoholics. *Journal of Studies on Alcohol*, 47, 213-218.

60. Carbotte, R. M., Denburg, S. D., & Denburg, J. A. (1986). Prevalence of cognitive impairment in Systemic Lupus Erythematosus. *The Journal of Nervous and Mental Disease*, 174, 357-364.

61. Cullum, C. M., & Bigler, E. D. (1986). Ventricle size, cortical atrophy and the relationship with neuropsychological status in closed head injury: A quantitative analysis. *Journal of Clinical and Experimental Neuropsychology*, 8, 437-452.

62. Curry, J. F., Logue, P. E., & Butler, B. (1986). Child and adolescent norms for Russell's revision of the Wechsler Memory Scale. *Journal of Clinical Child Psychology*, 15, 214-220.

63. Dalby, J. T., & Williams, R. (1986). Preserved reading and spelling ability in psychotic disorders. *Psychological Medicine*, 16, 171-175.

64. Dalton, J. E., Dizzonne, M. F., Wallace, B. S., Blom, B. E., & Holmes, N. R. (1986). Scoring criteria and illustrations for visual reproduction of the Wechsler Memory Scale. *Clinical Neuropsychology*, 8, 104-109.

65. Eskelinen, L., Luisto, M., Tenkanen, L., & Mattei, O. (1986). Neuropsychological methods in the differentiation of organic solvent intoxication from certain neurological conditions. *Journal of Clinical and Experimental Neuropsychology*, 8, 239-256.

66. Fecteau, G. W., & Duffy, M. (1986). Social and conversational skills training with long-term psychiatric inpatients. *Psychological Reports*, 59, 1327-1331.

67. Gass, C. S., & Russell, E. W. (1986). Differential impact of brain damage and depression on memory test performance. *Journal of Consulting and Clinical Psychology*, 54, 261-263.

68. Hallett, S., Quinn, D., & Hewitt, J. (1986). Defective interhemispheric integration and anomalous language lateralization in children at risk for schizophrenia. *The Journal of Nervous and Mental Disease*, 174, 418-427.

69. Klonoff, P. S., Costa, L. D., & Snow, W. G. (1986). Predictors and indicators of quality of life in patients with closed-head injury. *Journal of Clinical and Experimental Neuropsychology*, 8, 469-485.

70. Madison, L. S., George, C., & Moeschler, J. B. (1986). Cognitive functioning in the fragile-x syndrome: A study of intellectual, memory and communication skills. *Journal of Mental Deficiency Research*, 30, 129-148.

71. Magner, J. R., Kirzinger, S. S., & Spector, J. (1986). Viral encephalitis: Neuropsychological assessment in differential diagnosis and evaluation of sequelae. *Clinical Neuropsychology*, 8, 127-132.

72. Manton, K. G., Siegler, I. C., & Woodbury, M. A. (1986). Patterns of intellectual development in later life. *Journal of Gerontology*, 41, 486-499.

73. Martin, A., Brouwers, P., Lalonde, F., Cox, C., Teleska, P., & Fedio, P. (1986). Towards a behavioral typology of Alzheimer's patients. *Journal of Clinical and Experimental Neuropsychology*, 8, 594-610.

74. Parker, J. C., Smarr, K. L., Granberg, B. W., Nichols, W. K., & Hewett, J. E. (1986). Neuropsychological parameters of carotid endarterectomy: A two-year prospective analysis. *Journal of Consulting and Clinical Psychology*, 54, 676-681.

75. Perlick, D., Stastny, P., Katz, I., Mayer, M., & Mattis, S. (1986). Memory deficits and anticholinergic levels in chronic schizophrenia. *American Journal of Psychiatry*, 143, 230-232.

76. Piersma, H. L. (1986). Wechsler Memory Scale performance in geropsychiatric patients. *Journal of Clinical Psychology*, 42, 323-327.

77. Schear, J. M. (1986). Utility of half-credit scoring of Russell's revision of the Wechsler Memory Scale. *Journal of Clinical Psychology*, 42, 783-787.

78. Simpson, N., Black, F. W., & Strub, R. L. (1986). Memory assessment using the Strub-Black Mental Status Examination and the Wechsler Memory Scale. *Journal of Clinical Psychology*, 42, 147-155.

79. Solomon, G. S., Greene, R. L., Farr, S. P., & Kelly, M. P. (1986). Relationships among Wechsler intelligence and Memory Scale quotients in adult closed head injured patients. *Journal of Clinical Psychology*, 42, 318-323.

80. Steinman, D. R., & Bigler, E. D. (1986). Neuropsychological sequelae of ruptured anterior communicating artery aneurysm. *Clinical Neuropsychology*, 8, 135-140.

81. Svanum, S., & Schladenhauffen, J. (1986). Lifetime and recent alcohol consumption among male alcoholics. Neuropsychological implications. *The Journal of Nervous and Mental Disease*, 174, 214-220.

82. Sweet, J. J., & Kolden, G. G. (1986). Effectiveness of Wechsler Memory Scale scoring guidelines for improving scorer reliability: A followup study. *Clinical Neuropsychology*, 8, 38-40.

83. Tarbox, A. R., Connors, G. J., & McLaughlin, E. J. (1986). Effects of drinking pattern on neuropsychological performance among alcohol misusers. *Journal of Studies on Alcohol*, 47, 176-179.

84. Taylor, A. E., Saint-Cyr, J. A., & Lang, A. E. (1986). Frontal lobe dysfunction in Parkinson's disease: The cortical focus of neostriatal outflow. *Brain*, 109, 845-883.

85. Abikoff, H., Alvir, J., & Hong, G. (1987). Logical memory subtest of the Wechsler Memory Scale: Age and education norms and alternate-form reliability of two scoring systems. *Journal of Clinical and Experimental Neuropsychology*, 9, 435-448.

86. Albert, M., Duffy, F. H., & Naeser, M. (1987). Nonlinear changes in cognition with age and their neuropsychologic correlates. *Canadian Journal of Psychology*, 41 (2), 141-157.

87. Alekoumbides, A., Charter, R. A., Adkins, T. G., & Seacat, G. F. (1987). The diagnosis of brain damage by the WAIS, WMS, and Reitan Battery utilizing standardized scores corrected for age and education. *The International Journal of Clinical Neuropsychology*, 9, 11-27.

88. Baird, A. D., Brown, G. G., Adams, K. M., Shatz, M. W., McSweeny, A. J., Ausman, J. I., & Diaz, F. G. (1987). Neuropsychological deficits and real-world dysfunction in cerebral revascularization candidates. *Journal of Clinical and Experimental Neuropsychology*, 9, 407-422.

89. Brown, G. G., Sawyer, J. D., Nathan, A., & Shatz, M. W. (1987). Effects of lateralized cerebral dysfunction on the continuous paired-associate test. *Journal of Clinical and Experimental Neuropsychology*, 9, 680-698.

90. Butters, N., Granholm, E., Salmon, D. P., Grant, I., & Wolfe, J. (1987). Episodic and semantic memory: A comparison of amnesic and demented patients. *Journal of Clinical and Experimental Neuropsychology*, 9, 479-497.

91. Charter, R. A., Adkins, T. G., Alekoumbides, A., & Seacat, G. F. (1987). Reliability of the WAIS, WMS, and Reitan Battery: Raw scores and standardized scores corrected for age and education. *The International Journal of Clinical Neuropsychology*, 9, 28-32.

92. DeHaan, E. H. F., Young, A., & Newcombe, F. (1987). Faces interfere with name classification in a prosopagnosic patient. *Cortex*, 23, 309-316.

93. Denburg, S. D., Carbotte, R. M., & Denburg, J. A. (1987). Cognitive impairment in systemic lupus erythematosus: A neuropsychological study of individual and group deficits. *Journal of Clinical and Experimental Neuropsychology*, 9, 323-339.

94. Gabrys, J. B., Schumph, D., & Utendale, K. A. (1987). Short-term memory for two meaningful stories and self-report on the adult Eysenck Personality Questionnaire. *Psychological Reports*, 61, 51-59.

95. Habib, M., & Sirigu, A. (1987). Pure topographical disorientation: A definition and anatomical basis. *Cortex*, 23, 73-85.

96. Hadar, U., Jones, C., & Mate-Kole, C. (1987). The disconnection in anomic aphasia between semantic and phonological lexicons. *Cortex*, 23, 505-517.

97. Hart, R. P., Kwentus, J. A., Taylor, J. R., & Harkins, S. W. (1987). Rate of forgetting in dementia and depression. *Journal of Consulting and Clinical Psychology*, 55, 101-105.

98. Horton, A. M., Jr., Slone, D. G., & Shapiro, S. (1987). Neuropsychometric correlates of the Mini-Mental State Examination: Preliminary data. *Perceptual and Motor Skills*, 65, 64-66.

99. Ivnik, R. J., Sharbrough, F. W., & Laws, E. R., Jr. (1987). Effects of anterior temporal lobectomy on cognitive function. *Journal of Clinical Psychology*, 43, 128-137.

100. Jacobson, R. R., & Lishman, W. A. (1987). Selective memory loss and global intellectual deficits in alcoholic Korsakoff's syndrome. *Psychological Medicine*, 17, 649-655.

101. Larrabee, G. J. (1987). Further cautions in interpretation of comparisons between the WAIS-R and the Wechsler Memory Scale. *Journal of Clinical and Experimental Neuropsychology*, 9, 456-460.

102. Loring, D. W., & Papanicolaou, A. C. (1987). Memory assessment in neuropsychology: Theoretical considerations and practical utility. *Journal of Clinical and Experimental Neuropsychology*, 9, 340-358.

103. Martin, A. (1987). Representation of semantic and spatial knowledge in Alzheimer's patients: Implications for models of preserved learning in amnesia. *Journal of Clinical and Experimental Neuropsychology*, 9, 191-224.

104. Mitchell, M. (1987). Scoring discrepancies on two subtests of the Wechsler Memory Scale. *Journal of Consulting and Clinical Psychology*, 55, 914-915.

105. Naugle, R. I., Cullum, C. M., Bigler, E. D., & Massman, P. J. (1987). Handedness and dementia. *Perceptual and Motor Skills*, 65, 207-210.

106. Nixon, S. J., Kujawski, A., Parsons, O. A., & Yohman, J. R. (1987). Semantic (verbal) and figural memory impairment in alcoholics. *Journal of Clinical and Experimental Neuropsychology*, 9, 311-322.

107. Rothke, S., Bleiberg, J., & Freedland, K. (1987). Neuropsychological test correlates of anticipatory behavior deficit in closed head injury. *The International Journal of Clinical Neuropsychology*, 9, 81-83.

108. Ryan, C. M., Morrow, L. A., Bromet, E. J., & Parkinson, D. K. (1987). Assessment of neuropsychological dysfunction in the workplace: Normative data from the Pittsburgh occupational exposures test battery. *Journal of Clinical and Experimental Neuropsychology*, 9, 665-679.

109. Sohlberg, M. M., & Mateer, C. A. (1987). Effectiveness of an attention-training program. *Journal of Clinical and Experimental Neuropsychology*, 9, 117-130.

110. Tsushima, W. T., & Pang, D. B. (1987). Neuropsychological test performance in Alzheimer's Disease: An 11-year case study. *The International Journal of Clinical Neuropsychology*, 9, 120-124.

111. Warner, M. H., Ernst, J., Townes, B. D., Peel, J., & Preston, M. (1987). Relationships between IQ and neuropsychological measures in neuropsychiatric populations: Within-laboratory and cross-cultural replications using WAIS and WAIS-R. *Journal of Clinical and Experimental Neuropsychology*, 9, 545-562.

112. Williams, J. M., Little, M. M., Scates, S., & Blockman, N. (1987). Memory complaints and abilities among depressed older adults. *Journal of Consulting and Clinical Psychology*, 55, 595-598.

113. Wilson, R. S., Como, P. G., Garron, D. C., Klawans, H. L., Barr, A., & Klawans, D. (1987). Memory failure in Huntington's disease. *Journal of Clinical and Experimental Neuropsychology*, 9, 147-154.

114. Yoder, C. Y., & Elias, J. W. (1987). Age, affect, and memory for pictorial story sequences. *British Journal of Psychology*, 78, 545-549.

115. Charter, R. A., & Alekoumbides, A. (1988). An abbreviated version of a psychometric battery for the diagnosis of brain damage utilizing for standardized scores corrected for age and education. *The International Journal of Clinical Neuropsychology*, 10, 123-129.

116. Corrigan, J. D., & Hinkeldey, N. S. (1988). Patterns of performance within the Halstead-Reitan Neuropsychological Test Battery. *The International Journal of Clinical Neuropsychology*, 10, 25-34.

117. Goldstein, L. H., Canavan, A. G. M., & Polkey, C. E. (1988). Verbal and abstract designs paired associate learning after unilateral temporal lobectomy. *Cortex*, 24, 41-52.

118. Grady, C. L., Haxby, J. V., Horwitz, B., Sundaram, M., Berg, G., Schapiro, M., Friedland, R. P., & Rapoport, S. I. (1988). Longitudinal study of the early neuropsychological and cerebral metabolic changes in dementia of the Alzheimer type. *Journal of Clinical and Experimental Neuropsychology*, 10, 576-596.

119. Heilbronner, R. L., Buck, P., & Adams, R. L. (1988). Factor analysis of the Wechsler Memory Scale (WMS) with the WAIS and WAIS-R. *The International Journal of Clinical Neuropsychology*, 10, 20-22.

120. Kelly, D., Greene, R. L., & Farr, S. P. (1988). Sensitivity of two visual reproduction tests to alcoholic brain impairment. *Psychological Reports*, 62, 435-441.

121. Moses, J. A., & Maruish, M. E. (1988). A critical review of the Luria-Nebraska Neuropsychological Battery literature: II. Construct validity. *The International Journal of Clinical Neuropsychology*, 10, 5-11.

122. Moses, J. A., & Maruish, M. E. (1988). A critical review of the Luria-Nebraska Neuropsychological Battery literature: III. Concurrent validity. *The International Journal of Clinical Neuropsychology*, 10, 12-19.

123. Ponsford, J. L., & Kinsella, G. (1988). Evaluation of a remedial programme for attentional deficits following closed-head injury. *Journal of Clinical and Experimental Neuropsychology*, 10, 693-708.

124. Quart, E. J., Buchtel, H. A., & Sarnaik, A. P. (1988). Long-lasting memory deficits in children recovered from Reye's syndrome. *Journal of Clinical and Experimental Neuropsychology*, 10, 409-420.

125. Saykin, A. J., Janssen, R. S., Sprehn, G. C., Kaplan, J. E., Spira, T. J., & Weller, P. (1988). Neuropsychological dysfunction in HIV-infection characterization in a lymphadenopathy cohort. *The International Journal of Clinical Neuropsychology*, 10, 81-95.

126. Sewell, K. W., Downey, R. G., & Sinnett, E. R. (1988). Convergence and divergence of clinical memory tests. *Psychological Reports*, 62, 291-297.

127. Squire, L. R., & Zouzoums, J. A. (1988). Self-ratings of memory dysfunction: Different findings in depression and amnesia. *Journal of Clinical and Experimental Neuropsychology*, 10, 727-738.

128. Tweedy, J. R., & Vakil, E. (1988). Evaluating evidence for automaticity in frequency of occurrence judgments: A bias for bias? *Journal of Clinical and Experimental Neuropsychology*, 10, 664-674.

129. Wilson, J. T. L., Wiedmann, K. D., Phillips, W. A., & Brooks, D. N. (1988). Visual event perception in alcoholics. *Journal of Clinical and Experimental Neuropsychology*, 10, 222-234.

130. Aysto, S. (1989). Cross-validation of Das's simultaneous and successive cognitive processes with neurological patients. *The International Journal of Clinical Neuropsychology*, 11, 111-120.

131. Berry, D. T. R., McConnell, J. W., Phillips, B. A., Carswell, C. M., Lamb, D. G., & Prine, B. C. (1989). Isocapnic hypoxemia and neuropsychological functioning. *Journal of Clinical and Experimental Neuropsychology*, 11, 241-251.

132. Bieliauskas, L. A., & Glantz, R. H. (1989). Depression type in Parkinson disease. *Journal of Clinical and Experimental Neuropsychology*, 11, 597-604.

133. Bornstein, R. A., Chelune, G. J., & Prifitera, A. (1989). IQ-memory discrepancies in normal and clinical samples. *Psychological Assessment*, 1, 203-206.

134. Brown, G. G., Kieran, S., & Patel, S. (1989). Memory functioning following a left medial thalamic hematoma. *Journal of Clinical and Experimental Neuropsychology*, 11, 206-218.

135. Casey, J. E., Ferguson, G. G., Kimura, D., & Hachinski, V. C. (1989). Neuropsychological improvement versus practice effect following unilateral cartotid endarterectomy in patients without stroke. *Journal of Clinical and Experimental Neuropsychology*, 11, 461-470.

136. D'Elia, L., Satz, P., & Schretlen, D. (1989). Wechsler Memory Scale: A critical appraisal of the normative studies. *Journal of Clinical and Experimental Neuropsychology*, 11, 551-568.

137. Glosser, G., Goodglass, H., & Biber, C. (1989). Assessing visual memory disorders. *Psychological Assessment*, 1, 82-91.

138. Halperin, J. M., Healey, J. M., Zeitchik, E., Ludman, W. L., & Weinstein, L. (1989). Developmental aspects of linguistic and mnestic abilities in normal children. *Journal of Clinical and Experimental Neuropsychology*, 11, 518-528.

139. Isaacs-Glaberman, K., Medalia, A., & Scheinberg, I. H. (1989). Verbal recall and recognition abilities in patients with Wilson's disease. *Cortex*, 25, 353-361.

140. Larrabee, G. J., & Crook, T. H. (1989). Dimensions of everyday memory in age-associated memory impairment. *Psychological Assessment*, 1, 92-97.

141. Lawson, M. J., & Rice, D. N. (1989). Effects of training in use of executive strategies on a verbal memory problem resulting from close head injury. *Journal of Clinical and Experimental Neuropsychology*, 11, 842-854.

142. Loring, D. W., Lee, G. P., Martin, R. C., & Meador, K. J. (1989). Verbal and visual memory index discrepancies from the Wechsler Memory Scale—Revised: Cautions in interpretation. *Psychological Assessment*, 1, 198-202.

143. Meyers, J. E., & McMordie, W. R. (1989). The LNNB memory scale and WMS as memory screening instruments. *The International Journal of Clinical Neuropsychology*, 11, 137-142.

144. Milberg, W., & Albert, M. (1989). Cognitive differences between patients with progressive supranuclear palsy and Alzheimer's disease. *Journal of Clinical and Experimental Neuropsychology*, 11, 605-614.

145. Miller, B. L., Lesser, I. M., Boone, K., Goldberg, M., Hill, E., Miller, M. H., Benson, D. F., & Mehringer, M. (1989). Brain white-matter lesions and psychosis. *British Journal of Psychiatry*, 155, 73-78.

146. O'Connor, N., & Hermelin, B. (1989). The memory structure of autistic idiot-savant mnemonists. *British Journal of Psychology*, 80, 97-111.

147. Richards, P. M., & Ruff, R. M. (1989). Motivational effects on neuropsychological functioning: Comparison of depressed versus nondepressed individuals. *Journal of Consulting and Clinical Psychology*, 57, 396-402.

148. Rothke, S. (1989). The relationship between neuropsychological test scores and performance on a driving evaluation. *The International Journal of Clinical Neuropsychology*, 11, 134-136.

149. Schlosser, D., & Ovison, D. (1989). Assessing memory deterioration with the Wechsler Memory Scale, the National Adult Reading Test, and the Schonell Graded Word Reading Test. *Journal of Clinical and Experimental Neuropsychology*, 11, 785-792.

150. Sullivan, E. V., Sagar, H. J., Gabrieli, J. D. E., Corkin, S., & Growdon, J. H. (1989). Different cognitive profiles on standard behavioral tests in Parkinson's disease and Alzheimer's disease. *Journal of Clinical and Experimental Neuropsychology*, 11, 799-820.

151. VanGorp, W. S., Miller, E. N., Satz, P., & Visscher, B. (1989). Neuropsychological performance in HIV-1 Immunocompromised patients: A preliminary report. *Journal of Clinical and Experimental Neuropsychology*, 11, 763-773.

152. Altman, E., Hedeker, D., Davis, J. M., Comaty, J. E., Jobe, T. H., & Levy, D. L. (1990). Neuropsychological test deficits are associated with smooth pursuit eye movement impairment in affective disorders but not in schizophrenia. *The International Journal of Clinical Neuropsychology*, 12, 49-59.

153. Besson, J. A. O., Crawford, J. R., Parker, D. M., Ebmeier, K. P., Best, P. V., Gimmel, H. G., Sharp, P. F., & Smith, F. W. (1990). Multimodal imaging in Alzheimer's Disease: The relationship between MRI, SPECT, cognitive and pathological changes. *British Journal of Psychiatry*, 157, 216-220.

154. Chlopan, B. E., Hagen, R. L., & Russell, E. W. (1990). Lateralized anterior and posterior lesions and performance on digit span and Russell's revision of the Wechsler Memory Scale. *Journal of Consulting and Clinical Psychology*, 58, 855-861.

155. Heilbronner, R. L., Buck, P., & Adams, R. L. (1990). Discrepancies between Wechsler's FSIQ's and MQ's in brain damaged and

nonbrain damaged adults. *The International Journal of Clinical Neuropsychology, 12*, 24-28.

156. Parsons, O. A., Schaeffer, K. W., & Glenn, S. W. (1990). Does neuropsychological test performance predict resumption of drinking in posttreatment alcoholics? *Addictive Behaviors, 15*, 297-307.

157. Partridge, F. M., Knight, R. G., & Feehan, M. (1990). Direct and indirect memory performance in patients with senile dementia. *Psychological Medicine, 20*, 111-118.

158. Sutker, P. B., Galina, Z. H., West, J. A., & Allain, A. N. (1990). Trauma-induced weight loss and cognitive deficits among former prisoners of war. *Journal of Consulting and Clinical Psychology, 58*, 323-328.

159. Williams, K. M., Iacono, W. G., Remick, R. A., & Greenwood, P. (1990). Dichotic perception and memory following electroconvulsive treatment for depression. *British Journal of Psychiatry, 157*, 366-372.

160. Atkinson, L. (1991). Three standard errors of measurement and the Wechsler Memory Scale. *Psychological Assessment, 3*, 136-138.

161. Christensen, H., Hadzi-Pavlovic, D., & Jacomb, P. (1991). The psychometric differentiation of dementia from normal aging: A meta analysis. *Psychological Assessment, 3*, 147-155.

162. Christensen, K. J., Multhaup, K. S., Nordstrom, S., & Voss, K. (1991). A cognitive battery for dementia: Development and measurement characteristics. *Psychological Assessment, 3*, 168-174.

163. Malec, J. F., Ivnik, R. J., & Hinkeldey, N. S. (1991). Visual spatial learning test. *Psychological Assessment, 3*, 82-88.

164. Mittenberg, W., Thompson, G. B., & Schwartz, J. A. (1991). Abnormal and reliable differences among Wechsler Memory Scale—Revised subtests. *Psychological Assessment, 3*, 492-495.

165. Tangalos, E. G., Petersen, R. C., Kokmen, E., & Kurland, L. T. (1991). Wechsler Memory Scale: IQ-dependent norms for persons ages 65 to 97 years. *Psychological Assessment, 3*, 156-161.

166. Waldstein, S. R., Ryan, C. M., Manuck, S. B., Parkinson, D. K., & Bromet, E. J. (1991). Learning and memory function in men with untreated blood pressure elevation. *Journal of Consulting and Clinical Psychology, 59*, 513-517.

Review of the Wechsler Memory Scale—Revised by E. SCOTT HUEBNER, *Assistant Professor of Psychology, University of South Carolina, Columbia, SC:*

The Wechsler Memory Scale—Revised (WMS-R) is an individually administered clinical instrument designed to serve "as a diagnostic and screening device for use as part of a general neuropsychological examination, or any other clinical examination requiring the assessment of memory functions." It should be noted that the WMS-R is aimed primarily at assessing memory deficits; thus, most of its subtests have limited ceilings precluding the assessment of superior memory abilities.

The WMS-R, which represents a major revision of the 1949 Wechsler Memory Scale (WMS; 9:1355), is intended for use with adolescents and adults ranging in age from 16 to 74. Major changes included the provision of stratified norms, replacement of the single global summary score with five composite scores, addition of measures of delayed recall as well as measures of figural and spatial memory, and modification of scoring criteria for two subtests.

The complete WMS-R consists of eight short-term memory subtests, four delayed-recall subtests, and a brief screening measure of mental status (i.e., Information and Orientation questions). Scores on the latter subtest, which contains simple questions (e.g., name, age, date) that are typically answered correctly by nonimpaired examinees, are not included in the calculation of the General Memory Index or other subscores. The eight tests of short-term memory can be combined to yield four composite scores: Verbal Memory, Visual Memory, General Memory (Verbal + Visual Memory), and Attention/Concentration. The delayed-recall measures, which involve delayed-recall (after a 30-minute interval) trials for four of the short-term memory subtests, can be combined to derive a fifth composite score. When time is limited, the manual recommends administering a short form of the instrument that excludes the delayed-recall measures.

The test manual is well written. Instructions and scoring criteria are described in detail and useful tables (e.g., standard error of measurement) are provided to aid interpretation. The manual is particularly impressive with regard to the extensive validity data presented.

Inspection of the standardization data reveals some concerns, however. Although the standardization sample appears representative with respect to gender, race, geographic region, and education, the size of the total sample ($n = 316$) was small, with only about 50 cases in each of six age groups (ages 16–17, 20–24, 35–44, 55–65, 65–69, 70–74). Thus, norms had to be estimated for ages 18–19, 25–34, and 45–54.

Reliability and stability data also reveal serious concerns. According to the manual, "the average reliability coefficients across age groups for subtests and composites ranges [sic] from .41 to .90 with a median value of .74." None of the subtests or composites achieved an average reliability coefficient of .90 or above, except Attention/Concentration. Similar stability data are reported. Thus, the user must be cautioned that the poor reliabilities of individual subtests preclude interpretation of subtest differences. Profile analysis of composite scores is also limited by their low reliabilities, except for the Attention/Concentration composite and possibly the General Memory composite (average $r = .81$). Overall, these reliability data reflect the most serious shortcoming of the WMS-R.

As mentioned previously, the manual provides extensive validity information including studies of the WMS-R as well as its predecessor, the WMS. Support for the construct validity of the WMS-R is provided in numerous ways. For example, data are presented regarding the relationship between the WMS-R and gender, age, and educational level. The analyses yielded the predicted relationships. Data are also presented regarding the ability of the WMS-R to differentiate between clinical samples of individuals known or expected to have memory deficits and the nonimpaired standardization sample. The clinical samples included individuals with diagnoses of depression, alcoholism, dementia, Huntington's Disease, alcohol-related Korsakoff's Syndrome, closed head injury, strokes, brain cancer, seizure disorders, multiple sclerosis, and worksite neurotoxin impairment. For each of the groups, the

WMS-R demonstrated satisfactory discrimination power.

The results of several factor analyses are also presented. These data temper the support for the construct validity of the WMS-R as the findings generally indicate support for a two-factor model in contrast to the hypothesized five-factor model that guided the construction of the WMS-R. In other words, the data only support the interpretation of two composite indexes, the General Memory Index and the Attention/Concentration Index. The evidence does not support the interpretation of the other three indexes.

In summary, the WMS-R represents a major improvement over the original WMS. It also should represent the instrument of choice for many purposes with regard to research involving the detection of memory deficits in adults. However, it must be used very cautiously in making clinical decisions about *individuals*. The lack of reliability of the subtests and most of the index scores, as well as the lack of support for the construct validity of three of the indexes (Verbal Memory, Visual Memory, Delayed Recall), restrict interpretation of the WMS-R to that of a measure of global memory and attention/concentration ability. Interpretation of the individual subtests scores and the other three index scores is indefensible.

Review of the Wechsler Memory Scale—Revised by ROBERT C. REINEHR, *Associate Professor of Psychology, Southwestern University, Georgetown, TX:*

The Wechsler Memory Scale—Revised (WMS-R) is an individually administered instrument for appraising major dimensions of memory functions in adults. It is intended as a diagnostic and screening device for use as a part of any clinical examination requiring the assessment of memory functions.

The WMS-R, published in 1987, is an extensive revision of the earlier Wechsler Memory Scale (WMS) and includes new norms for nine different age levels, replacement of the Memory Quotient with a set of five composite scores, addition of several new subtests, and revision of the scoring procedures for several of the subtests.

In addition to a set of 14 information and orientation questions, there are eight subtests intended to measure short-term memory. Four of these subtests are repeated later in the testing session to yield a measure of delayed-recall ability. The administration of subtests is sequenced so that about 30 minutes separate the presentations of those subtests that are administered twice. The total testing time required is between 45 minutes and 1 hour.

Raw scores are converted to the five composite index scores by applying a weighting procedure and converting each weighted score with the use of a table provided in the manual. Each of the five composite index scores has been adjusted to yield a mean of 100 and a standard deviation of 15. Norms are available for nine different age groups, ranging from ages 16–74. A separate table presents cumulative frequencies for the number of Information and Orientation questions answered correctly by each age group in the standardization sample.

The standardization sample was stratified by age, sex, race, and geographic region. The standardization sample was very small: There were only 50–55 subjects in each age group. Each person included in the sample was administered both the WMS-R and the Wechsler Adult Intelligence Scale—Revised (WAIS-R). In some age groups, a short form of the WAIS-R was substituted for the full-length version. WAIS-R scores were used as a selection criterion for inclusion in the sample, but the relationship of WAIS-R scores to the five WMS-R Composite Scores is not reported. The average Full Scale IQ of the various age groups ranged from 100.0 to 106.7.

Educational level was not specified for individual members of the sample, but three levels of education (0–11 years, 12 years, or 13 or more years) were included in the same proportion in which they appeared in the 1980 U.S. Census. Only nonimpaired individuals were included in the sample, although the methods of screening for impairment are not described in the manual.

Split-half reliability coefficients were calculated for six age groups across all subtests. Averaged across age groups, obtained coefficients ranged from .41 to .88, with a mean value of .65. Similar coefficients for the five composite scores ranged from .59 to .90, with a mean of .79. Test-retest stability coefficients for the composite scores were calculated for three age groups (20–24, 55–64, and 70–74), based on administrations 4 to 6 weeks apart. Coefficients ranged from .80 to .93, with a mean of .85.

Validity information in the manual is of three basic types: the results of factor analyses of the WMS-R, the relationships of demographic variables to WMS-R scores, and the performance of clinical groups on the WMS-R.

Factor analysis yielded a two-factor solution in which Factor I was a general memory and learning factor and Factor II was an attention-concentration factor.

No relationship was found between gender and WMS-R scores. The relationship between age and the five composite scores was much like that between WAIS-R scores and age: Older subjects performed somewhat more poorly and a scaled score of 100 for a 74-year-old subject indicates a lower level of absolute function than a similar scaled score for a 25-year-old subject. For all age groups, scatter between Composite Index scores was large: Differences of less than 15 points were not significant for any pairing of indexes.

Education was significantly correlated with all five Composite Indexes, correlation coefficients ranging from .42 to .49, with a mean of .46. The average scores of subjects with less than 12 years of education and those with more than 12 years of education differed significantly, sometimes by nearly an entire standard deviation.

A considerable portion of the validity information presented in the manual refers to the ability of the WMS-R to differentiate between clinical groups and normals. Dementia, alcoholism, Huntington's Disease, Korsakoff's Syndrome, stroke, brain cancer, seizure disorder, and multiple sclerosis are all addressed. The ability to differentiate between these clinical groups and normals relates only indirectly to the validity of the WMS-R, however. There is no suggestion that any score or pattern of scores is diagnostic of any specific disorder.

Although the reported reliability information is encouraging, the WMS-R has little else to recommend it as a psychometric instrument. The standardization sample was very small, the relationship between WMS-R scores and education is very substantial, large differences between Composite Index scores are typical, the correlation with intelligence is not addressed adequately in the manual, and validation against external criteria amounts to the demonstration that some clinical groups do less well on the WMS-R than do groups of normal subjects. Diagnostic decisions based on the WMS-R are essentially clinical rather than psychometric. For screening purposes, the WAIS-R seems likely to provide information for drawing many of the same sorts of clinical inferences.

[466]
Wechsler Preschool and Primary Scale of Intelligence—Revised.
Purpose: Developed "for assessing the intelligence of children."
Population: Ages 2-11 to 7-3.
Publication Dates: 1949–89.
Acronym: WPPSI-R.
Scores, 13 to 15: Verbal (Information, Comprehension, Arithmetic, Vocabulary, Similarities, Sentences [optional], Total), Performance (Object Assembly, Geometric Design, Block Design, Mazes, Picture Completion, Animal Pegs [optional], Total), Total.
Administration: Individual.
Price Data, 1991: $389 per complete kit including 25 maze tests, 50 geometric design sheets, 25 record forms, manual ('89, 239 pages), and attache case; $354 per basic kit without case; $32 per 25 maze test books; $10 per 50 geometric design sheets; $49.50 per set of 14 blocks; $27.50 per set of 28 animal house cylinders; $65 per animal house board; $36.50 per information, arithmetic, vocabulary, and similarities stimulus booklet; $33 per geometric design, block design, and picture completion stimulus booklet; $29 per 25 record forms; $49.50 per manual.
Time: [75] minutes.

Author: David Wechsler.
Publisher: The Psychological Corporation.
Cross References: For a review by B. J. Freeman of an earlier edition, see 9:1356 (33 references); see also T3:2608 (280 references), 8:234 (84 references), and T2:538 (30 references); for reviews by Dorothy H. Eichorn and A. B. Silverstein, and excerpted reviews by C. H. Ammons and O. A. Oldridge (with E. E. Allison), see 7:434 (56 references).

TEST REFERENCES

1. Berg, R. A., Ch'ien, L. T., Bownan, W. P., Ochs, J., Lancaster, W., Goff, J. R., & Anderson, H. R., Jr. (1983). The neuropsychological effects of acute lymphocytic leukemia and its treatment—a three year report: Intellectual functioning and academic achievement. *Clinical Neuropsychology*, 5, 9-13.
2. Money, J., Lehne, G. K., & Norman, B. F. (1983). Psychology of syndromes: IQ and micropenis. *American Journal of Diseases of Children*, 137, 1083-1086.
3. Teglasi, H., & Freeman, R. W. (1983). Rapport pitfalls of beginning testers. *Journal of School Psychology*, 21, 229-240.
4. Walden, T. A., & Ramey, C. T. (1983). Locus of control and academic achievement: Results from a preschool intervention program. *Journal of Educational Psychology*, 75, 347-358.
5. Wilson, R. S., & Matheny, A. P., Jr. (1983). Mental development: Family environment and genetic influences. *Intelligence*, 7, 195-215.
6. Anastasi, A. (1984). The K-ABC in historical and contemporary perspective. *The Journal of Special Education*, 18, 357-366.
7. Badian, N. A. (1984). Can the WPPSI be of aid in identifying young children at risk for reading disability? *Journal of Learning Disability*, 17, 583-587.
8. Burdg, N. B., & Graham, S. (1984). Effects of sex and label on performance ratings, children's test scores, and examiners' verbal behavior. *American Journal of Mental Deficiency*, 88, 422-427.
9. Chatman, S. P., Reynolds, C. R., & Willson, V. L. (1984). Multiple indexes of test scatter on the Kaufman Assessment Battery for Children. *Journal of Learning Disabilities*, 17, 523-531.
10. Flynn, J. R. (1984). The mean IQ of Americans: Massive gains 1932 to 1978. *Psychological Bulletin*, 95, 29-51.
11. Guzman, A. M., & Johnson, D. L. (1984). The responses of Mexican American children to cognitive demands in a testing situation. *Hispanic Journal of Behavioral Sciences*, 6, 261-275.
12. Haynes, J. P., & Atkinson, D. (1984). Factor structure of the WPPSI in mental health clinic settings. *Journal of Clinical Psychology*, 40, 805-808.
13. Hopkins, K. D., & Hodge, S. E. (1984). Review of the Kaufman Assessment Battery (K-ABC) for Children. *Journal of Counseling and Development*, 63, 105-107.
14. Kagan, J., Reznick, J. S., Clarke, C., Snidman, N., & Garcia-Coll, C. (1984). Behavioral inhibition to the unfamiliar. *Child Development*, 55, 2212-2225.
15. Kaufman, A. S. (1984). K-ABC and controversy. *The Journal of Special Education*, 18, 409-444.
16. Marston, D., & Ysseldyke, J. (1984). Concerns in interpreting subtest scatter on the tests of cognitive ability from the Woodcock-Johnson Psycho-Educational Battery. *Journal of Learning Disabilities*, 17, 588-591.
17. McGowan, R. J., & Johnson, D. L. (1984). The mother-child relationship and other antecedents of childhood intelligence: A causal analysis. *Child Development*, 55, 810-820.
18. Niklason, L. B. (1984). Nonpromotion: A pseudoscientific solution. *Psychology in the Schools*, 21, 485-499.
19. Quereshi, M. Y., & McIntire, D. H. (1984). The comparability of the WISC, WISC-R, and WPPSI. *Journal of Clinical Psychology*, 40, 1036-1043.
20. Ritvo, E. R., Freeman, B. J., Yuwiler, A., Geller, E., Yokota, A., Schroth, P., & Novak, P. (1984). Study of fenfluramine in outpatients with the syndrome of autism. *The Journal of Pediatrics*, 105, 823-828.
21. Shaheen, S. J. (1984). Neuromaturation and behavior development: The case of childhood lead poisoning. *Developmental Psychology*, 20, 542-550.
22. Silverstein, A. B. (1984). Pattern analysis: The question of abnormality. *Journal of Consulting and Clinical Psychology*, 52, 936-939.
23. Simner, M. L. (1984). Predicting school readiness from stroke directions in children's printing. *Journal of Learning Disabilities*, 17, 397-399.
24. Taylor, R. L., & Partenio, I. (1984). Ethnic differences on the Bender-Gestalt: Relative effects of measured intelligence. *Journal of Counseling and Clinical Psychology*, 52, 784-788.
25. Telzrow, C. F. (1984). Practical applications of the K-ABC in the identification of handicapped preschoolers. *The Journal of Special Education*, 18, 311-324.

26. Valencia, R. R. (1984). Concurrent validity of the Kaufman Assessment Battery for Children in a sample of Mexican-American children. *Educational and Psychological Measurement, 44*, 365-372.

27. Valencia, R. R., & Rothwell, J. G. (1984). Concurrent validity of the WPPSI with Mexican-American preschool children. *Educational and Psychological Measurement, 44*, 955-961.

28. Aram, D. M., Ekelman, B. L., Rose, D. F., & Whitaker, H. A. (1985). Verbal and cognitive sequelae following unilateral lesions acquired in early childhood. *Journal of Clinical and Experimental Neuropsychology, 7*, 55-78.

29. Arboleda, C., & Holzman, P. S. (1985). Thought disorder in children at risk for psychosis. *Archives of General Psychiatry, 42*, 1004-1013.

30. Barocas, R., Seifer, R., & Sameroff, A. J. (1985). Defining environmental risk: Multiple dimensions of psychological vulnerability. *American Journal of Community Psychology, 13*, 433-447.

31. Evans, E. D. (1985). Longitudinal follow-up assessment of differential preschool experience for low income minority group children. *Journal of Educational Research, 78*, 197-202.

32. Feingold, A. (1985). Reliability of score differences on the Wechsler Preschool and Primary Scale of Intelligence. *Psychological Reports, 57*, 663-664.

33. Haskins, R. (1985). Public school aggression among children with varying day-care experience. *Child Development, 56*, 689-703.

34. Jordan, T. E. (1985). Prospective longitudinal study of superior cognitive readiness for school, from 1 year to 7 years. *Contemporary Educational Psychology, 10*, 203-219.

35. Kaplan, H. B. (1985). A comparison of the Vane Kindergarten Test with the WPPSI and a measure of self-control. *Psychology in the Schools, 22*, 277-282.

36. Kashani, J. H., Carlson, G. A., Horwitz, E., & Reid, J. C. (1985). Dysphoric mood in young children referred to a child development unit. *Child Psychiatry and Human Development, 15*, 234-242.

37. Kops, C., & Belmont, I. (1985). Planning and organizing skills of poor school achievers. *Journal of Learning Disabilities, 18*, 8-14.

38. Partenio, I., & Taylor, R. L. (1985). The relationship of teacher ratings and IQ: A question of bias? *School Psychology Review, 14*, 79-83.

39. Pellegrini, A. D., Brody, G. H., & Sigel, I. E. (1985). Parents' book-reading habits with their children. *Journal of Educational Psychology, 77*, 332-340.

40. Silverstein, A. B. (1985). A formula for the standard error of estimate of deviation quotients on short forms of Wechsler's scales. *Journal of Clinical Psychology, 41*, 408-409.

41. Tephly, J. (1985). Young children's recall in every-day and alternate-day school schedules. *Child Study Journal, 15*, 283-292.

42. Wilson, R. S. (1985). Risk and resilience in early mental development. *Developmental Psychology, 21*, 795-805.

43. Aylward, E. H., & Schmidt, S. (1986). An examination of three tests of visual-motor integration. *Journal of Learning Disabilities, 19*, 328-330.

44. Badian, N. A. (1986). Improving the prediction of reading for the individual child: A four-year follow-up. *Journal of Learning Disabilities, 19*, 262-269.

45. Block, J. H., Block, J., & Gjerde, P. F. (1986). The personality of children prior to divorce: A prospective study. *Child Development, 57*, 827-840.

46. Block, J., & Funder, D. C. (1986). Social roles and social perception: Individual differences in attribution and error. *Journal of Personality and Social Psychology, 51*, 1200-1207.

47. Block, J., Gjerde, P. F., & Block, J. H. (1986). More misgivings about the Matching Familiar Figures Test as a measure of reflection-impulsivity: Absence of construct validity in preadolescence. *Developmental Psychology, 22*, 820-831.

48. Borduin, C. M., Henggeler, S. W., Sanders-Walls, M., & Harbin, F. (1986). An evaluation of social class differences in verbal and nonverbal maternal controls, maternal sensitivity and child compliance. *Child Study Journal, 16*, 95-112.

49. Campbell, S. B., Ewing, L. J., Breaux, A. M., & Szumowski, E. K. (1986). Parent-referred problem three-year-olds: Follow-up at school entry. *Journal of Child Psychology and Psychiatry and Allied Disciplines, 27*, 473-488.

50. Feitelson, D., Kita, B., & Goldstein, Z. (1986). Effects of listening to series stories on first graders' comprehension and use of language. *Research in the Teaching of English, 20*, 339-356.

51. Gjerde, P. F., Block, J., & Block, J. H. (1986). Egocentrism and ego resiliency: Personality characteristics associated with perspective-taking from early childhood to adolescence. *Journal of Personality and Social Psychology, 51*, 423-434.

52. Green, R., Mandel, J. B., Hotvedt, M. E., Gray, J., & Smith, L. (1986). Lesbian mothers and their children: A comparison with solo parent heterosexual mothers and their children. *Archives of Sexual Behavior, 15*, 167-184.

53. Henderson, R. W., & Rankin, R. J. (1986). Preschoolers viewing of instructional television. *Journal of Educational Psychology, 78*, 44-51.

54. Kashani, J. H., Horwitz, E., Ray, J. S., & Reid, J. C. (1986). DSM-III diagnostic classification of 100 preschoolers in a child development unit. *Child Psychiatry and Human Development, 16*, 137-147.

55. Kroft, S. B. W., Ratzlaff, H. C., & Perks, B. A. (1986). Intelligence and early academic underachievement. *British Journal of Clinical Psychology, 25*, 147-148.

56. Neils, J., & Aram, D. M. (1986). Family history of children with developmental language disorders. *Perceptual and Motor Skills, 63*, 655-658.

57. Nicholson, M. W., & Moran, J. D., III. (1986). Teachers' judgments of preschoolers' creativity. *Perceptual and Motor Skills, 63*, 1211-1216.

58. Raviv, A., Rahmani, L., & Ber, H. (1986). Cognitive characteristics of learning-disabled and immature children as determined by the Wechsler Preschool and Primary Scale of Intelligence test. *Journal of Clinical Child Psychology, 15*, 241-247.

59. Rice, T., Corley, R., Fulker, D. W., & Plomin, R. (1986). The development and validation of a test battery measuring specific cognitive abilities in four-year-old children. *Educational and Psychological Measurement, 46*, 699-708.

60. Riva, D., & Cazzaniga, L. (1986). Late effects of unilateral brain lesions sustained before and after age one. *Neuropsychologia, 24*, 423-428.

61. Rose, D. H., Slater, A., & Perry, H. (1986). Prediction of childhood intelligence from habituation in early infancy. *Intelligence, 10*, 251-263.

62. Simmons, C. H., & Zumpf, C. (1986). The gifted child: Perceived competence, prosocial moral reasoning, and charitable donations. *The Journal of Genetic Psychology, 147*, 97-105.

63. Tsushima, W. T., & Stoddard, V. M. (1986). Predictive validity of a short-form WPPSI with prekindergarten children: A 3-year follow-up study. *Journal of Clinical Psychology, 42*, 526-527.

64. Voeller, K. K. S. (1986). Right-hemisphere deficit syndrome in children. *American Journal of Psychiatry, 143*, 1004-1009.

65. Watkins, C. E., Jr. (1986). Validity and usefulness of WAIS-R, WISC-R, and WPPSI short forms: A critical review. *Professional Psychology: Research and Practice, 17* (1), 36-43.

66. Ben-Yochanan, A., & Katz, Y. (1987). Validation and use of a school readiness battery in an Israeli elementary school integration program. *Perceptual and Motor Skills, 64*, 1083-1087.

67. Cooper, C. S., Peterson, N., & Meier, J. H. (1987). Variables associated with disrupted placement in a select sample of abused and neglected children. *Child Abuse & Neglect, 11*, 75-86.

68. Dollaghan, C. A. (1987). Fast mapping in normal and language-impaired children. *Journal of Speech and Hearing Disorders, 52*, 218-222.

69. Drabman, R. S., Tarnowski, K. J., & Kelly, P. A. (1987). Are younger classroom children disproportionately referred for childhood academic and behavior problems? *Journal of Consulting and Clinical Psychology, 55*, 907-909.

70. Field, M. (1987). Relation of language-delayed preschoolers' Leiter scores to later IQ. *Journal of Clinical Child Psychology, 16*, 111-115.

71. Gouze, K. R. (1987). Attention and social problem solving as correlates of aggression in preschool males. *Journal of Abnormal Child Psychology, 15*, 181-197.

72. Lovaas, O. I. (1987). Behavioral treatment and normal educational and intellectual functioning in young autistic children. *Journal of Consulting and Clinical Psychology, 55*, 3-9.

73. Massoth, N. A., Kalmar, K., Gallagher, D., Westerveld, M., Lanzi, A., D'Amico-Novaky, D., & Riley, E. (1987). Torque as an indicator of reduced cerebral laterality. *The International Journal of Clinical Neuropsychology, 9*, 62-67.

74. Maziade, M., Coté, R., Boutin, P., Bernier, H., & Thivierge, J. (1987). Temperament and intellectual development: A longitudinal study from infancy to four years. *American Journal of Psychiatry, 144*, 144-150.

75. Ozer, D. J. (1987). Personality, intelligence, and spatial visualization: Correlates of mental rotations test performance. *Journal of Personality and Social Psychology, 53*, 129-134.

76. Silverstein, A. B. (1987). Multidimensional scaling vs. factor analysis of Wechsler's intelligence scales. *Journal of Clinical Psychology, 43*, 381-386.

77. Tanaka, J. S. (1987). "How big is big enough?": Sample size and goodness of fit in structural equation models with latent variables. *Child Development, 58*, 134-146.

78. Whitworth, R. H., & Chrisman, S. M. (1987). Validation of the Kaufman Assessment Battery for Children comparing Anglo and Mexican-American preschoolers. *Educational and Psychological Measurement, 47* (3), 695-702.

79. Azmitia, M. (1988). Peer interaction and problem solving: When are two heads better than one? *Child Development, 59*, 87-96.

80. Badian, N. A. (1988). The prediction of good and poor reading before kindergarten entry: A nine-year follow-up. *Journal of Learning Disabilities, 21*, 98-103, 123.

81. Brodsky, P. (1988). Follow-up on the youngest REHABIT client: Importance of caution. *Perceptual and Motor Skills, 66* (2), 383-386.

82. Carvajal, H., Hardy, K., Smith, K. L., & Weaver, K. A. (1988). Relationships between scores on Stanford-Binet IV and Wechsler Preschool and Primary Scales of Intelligence. *Psychology in the Schools, 25*, 129-131.

83. Humphreys, L. G., & Davey, T. C. (1988). Continuity in intellectual growth from 12 months to 9 years. *Intelligence, 12*, 183-197.

84. Kutsick, K. A., & Wynn, E. E. (1988). Comparison of the K-ABC Achievement Scale and WPPSI IQs of preschool children. *Psychological Reports, 63*, 143-146.

85. Kutsick, K., Vance, B., Schwarting, F. G., & West, R. (1988). A comparison of three different measures of intelligence with preschool children identified at-risk. *Psychology in the Schools, 25*, 270-275.

86. Lloyd, M. E., & Zylla, T. M. (1988). Effect of incentives delivered for correctly answered items on the measured IQs of children of low and high IQ. *Psychological Reports, 63*, 555-561.

87. Matilainen, R., Heinonen, K., & Siren-Tiusanen, H. (1988). Effect of intrauterine growth retardation (IUGR) on the psychological performance of preterm children at preschool age. *Journal of Child Psychology and Psychiatry and Allied Disciplines, 29*, 601-609.

88. Rizzo, T. A. (1988). The relationship between friendship and sociometric judgments of peer acceptance and rejection. *Child Study Journal, 18*, 161-191.

89. Sprafkin, J., Gadow, K. D., & Grayson, P. (1988). Effects of cartoons on emotionally disturbed children's social behavior in school settings. *Journal of Child Psychology and Psychiatry and Allied Disciplines, 29*, 91-99.

90. Stroebel, S. S., & Evans, J. R. (1988). Neuropsychological and environmental characteristics of early readers. *Journal of School Psychology, 26*, 243-252.

91. Walker, T., & Johnson, D. L. (1988). A follow-up evaluation of the Houston Parent-Child Development Center: Intelligence test results. *Journal of Genetic Psychology, 149*, 377-381.

92. Braden, J. P. (1989). Fact or artifact? An empirical test of Spearman's Hypothesis. *Intelligence, 13*, 149-155.

93. Enright, K. M., & Ruzicka, M. F. (1989). Relationship between perceived parental behaviors and the self-esteem of gifted children. *Psychological Reports, 65*, 931-937.

94. Ferguson, J., & Fletcher, C. (1989). An investigation of some cognitive factors involved in person-perception during selection interviews. *Psychological Reports, 64*, 735-745.

95. Glutting, J. J. (1989). Introduction to the structure and application of the Stanford-Binet Intelligence Scale—Fourth Edition. *Journal of School Psychology, 27*, 69-80.

96. Glutting, J. J., & McDermott, P. A. (1989). Using "teaching items" on ability tests: A nice idea, but does it work? *Educational and Psychological Measurement, 49*, 257-268.

97. Maziade, M., Coté, R. Bernier, H., Boutin, P., & Thivierge, J. (1989). Significance of extreme temperament in infancy for clinical status in pre-school years. I. Value of extreme temperament at 4–8 months for predicting diagnosis at 4.7 years. *British Journal of Psychiatry, 154*, 535-543.

98. Peterson, C. C., & Peterson, J. L. (1989). Positive justice reasoning in deaf and hearing children before and after exposure to cognitive conflict. *American Annals of the Deaf, 134*, 277-282.

99. Rose, S. A., Feldman, J. F., Wallace, I. F., & McCarton, C. (1989). Infant visual attention: Relation to birth status and developmental outcome during the first 5 years. *Developmental Psychology, 25*, 560-576.

100. Said, J. A., Waters, B. G. H., Cousens, P., & Stevens, M. M. (1989). Neuropsychological sequelae of central nervous system prophylaxis in survivors of childhood acute lymphoblastic leukemia. *Journal of Consulting and Clinical Psychology, 57*, 251-256.

101. Streissguth, A. P., Barr, H. M., Sampson, P. D., Darby, B. L., & Martin, D. C. (1989). IQ at age 4 in relation to maternal alcohol use and smoking during pregnancy. *Developmental Psychology, 25*, 3-11.

102. Tuber, S., & Coates, S. (1989). Indices of psychopathology in Rorschachs of boys with severe gender identity disorder: A comparison with normal control subjects. *Journal of Personality Assessments, 53*, 100-112.

103. Glutting, J. J., & McDermott, P. A. (1990). Patterns and prevalence of core profile types in the WPPSI standardization sample. *School Psychology Review, 19*, 471-491.

104. Godwin, L. J., & Moran, J. D., III. (1990). Psychometric characteristics of an instrument for measuring creative potential in preschool children. *Psychology in the Schools, 27*, 204-210.

105. James, A., & Taylor, E. (1990). Sex differences in the hyperkinetic syndrome of childhood. *Journal of Child Psychology and Psychiatry, 31*, 437-446.

106. Katz, Y., & Ben-Yochanan, A. (1990). Reading and cognitive abilities: Research note on a longitudinal study in Israel. *Perceptual and Motor Skills, 70*, 47-50.

107. Kaufman, A. S. (1990). The WPPSI-R: You can't judge a test by its colors. *Journal of School Psychology, 28*, 387-394.

108. Longstreth, L. E., & Alcorn, M. B. (1990). Susceptibility of Wechsler spatial ability to experience with related games. *Educational and Psychological Measurement, 50*, 1-6.

109. Pianta, R. C., Erickson, M. F., Wagner, N., Kruetzer, T., & Egeland, B. (1990). Early predictors of referral for special services: Child-based measures versus mother-child interaction. *School Psychology Review, 19*, 240-250.

110. Razavieh, A., & Shahim, S. (1990). Retest reliability of the Wechsler Preschool and Primary Scale of Intelligence restandardized in Iran. *Psychological Reports, 66*, 865-866.

111. Blaha, J., & Wallbrown, F. H. (1991). Hierarchical factor structure of the Wechsler Preschool and Primary Scale of Intelligence—Revised. *Psychological Assessment, 3*, 455-463.

112. LoBello, S. G. (1991). A short form of the Wechsler Preschool and Primary Scale of Intelligence—Revised. *Journal of School Psychology, 29*, 229-236.

113. Lobello, S. G. (1991). A table for determining probability of obtaining verbal and performance scale discrepancies on the Wechsler Preschool and Primary Scale of Intelligence—Revised. *Psychology in the Schools, 28*, 93-94.

114. Lobello, S. G. (1991). Significant differences between individual subtest scaled scores and average scaled scores on the Wechsler Preschool and Primary Scale of Intelligence—Revised. *Psychology in the Schools, 28*, 15-18.

115. LoBello, S. G., & Gulgoz, S. (1991). Factor analysis of the Wechsler Preschool and Primary Scale of Intelligence-Revised. *Psychological Assessment, 3*, 130-132.

116. Rose, S. A., Feldman, J. F., Wallace, I. F., & Cohen, P. (1991). Language: A partial link between infant attention and later intelligence. *Developmental Psychology, 27*, 798-805.

117. Rose, S. A., Feldman, J. F., Wallace, I. F., & McCarton, C. (1991). Information processing at 1 year: Relation to birth status and developmental outcome during the first 5 years. *Developmental Psychology, 27*, 723-757.

118. Sattler, J. M. (1991). Normative changes on the Wechsler Preschool and Primary Scale of Intelligence—Revised Animal Pegs subtest. *Psychological Assessment, 3*, 691-692.

Review of the Wechsler Preschool and Primary Scale of Intelligence—Revised by BRUCE A. BRACKEN, Professor of Psychology, Memphis State University, Memphis, TN:

The revision of the Wechsler Preschool and Primary Scale of Intelligence (WPPSI; Wechsler, 1967) was the result of The Psychological Corporation's effort to update one more instrument in the popular series of Wechsler intelligence scales. The Wechsler scales have long been the psychologist's "work-horse" (Chattin & Bracken, 1989), and the revision of the WPPSI will likely extend the popularity of the Wechsler scales downward even further.

The original WPPSI had been criticized because of its drab color; lack of materials and activities appropriate for preschool children; inordinate administration time requirements; few opportunities for examinee second chances on items where the first attempt was failed; limited number of sample items; and so on. Ironically, despite these many criticisms, the WPPSI was among the most technically adequate preschool instruments (Bracken, 1987) and it has long been the criterion against which newly developed preschool intelligence scales have been compared. Put in perspective, the WPPSI was a psychometrically sound measure of intelligence that was in need of revision and restandardization; the WPPSI-R was an admirable attempt to meet that need.

The revised Wechsler Preschool and Primary Scale of Intelligence—Revised (WPPSI-R) is designed for use with children between the ages of 2 years, 11 months, and 16 days through 7 years, 3 months, and 15 days. As such, the instrument dips further into the preschool years by 1 year than its predecessor and advances 6 months further into childhood. A principal complaint about the WPPSI had been that its $2^1/_2$-year age range (i.e., 4 to $6^1/_2$ years) was too narrow. The WPPSI-R now serves a full 4-year age span, and overlaps with the Wechsler Intelligence Scale for Children—III (WISC-III; Wechsler, 1991) by slightly more than 1 year. The overlap between the WPPSI-R and WISC-III allows examiners to choose whichever instrument is more appropriate for clients within this age range (e.g., WPPSI-R predictably might be better for low-functioning 6-year-olds and the WISC-III better for gifted 6-year-olds). The extended age range and overlap with the WISC-III allows for early preschool assessment, flexibility in choice of instrument at the upper preschool ages, and continuity in longitudinal assessment from ages 3 to 75 years.

Although the original WPPSI had been criticized as being little more than a downward extension of an adult scale, the WPPSI-R is much more appropriate for young children and includes new colorful materials, larger sized stimuli, more child-like activities, simplified directions, increased number of sample items, inclusion of a puzzle completion task (i.e., Object Assembly), and increased opportunities for second chance responses on test items—all of which have made the instrument especially attractive to preschool children.

Not only is the WPPSI-R more suitable for young children, but it will likely be perceived as considerably more attractive than its predecessor to the psychologists who will use the scale. The improved characteristics that will facilitate examiner WPPSI-R administration, scoring, and interpretation include: a new "crack-back" examiner's manual that stands alone, a new self-supporting Object Assembly and Block Design shield, improved scoring materials and criteria for the Geometric Design subtest, and simplified directions and more comprehensive scoring examples for all subtests. In some instances these changes have resulted in significantly improved technical adequacy of the instrument, as in the improved rater-rater reliability of the Geometric Design subtest.

In terms of technical adequacy, the WPPSI was among the very best preschool measures of intelligence; the WPPSI-R in most cases is just as good an instrument, or better. Most preschool instruments have weak floors for low-functioning children below age 4, and although the WPPSI-R is no exception, its subtest and scale floors are generally stronger than most similar instruments. The validity of the WPPSI-R has been shown in part by the manual's comparison of the original WPPSI with other instruments. By extension one can reason that the newly revised scale would also be a valid measure of intelligence. In addition, several concurrent validity studies are presented in the WPPSI-R examiner's manual that attest to the comparability of the instrument with other current preschool intelligence tests. Finally, factor analyses of the instrument are reported in the examiner's manual, as well as other sources (Stone, Gridley, & Gyurke, in press). These construct validation studies consistently provide strong support for the Verbal-Performance scale dichotomy.

The WPPSI and WPPSI-R are among the most reliable (internally consistent and stable) of all comprehensive preschool intelligence scales. For example, the average internal consistency coefficient for the Verbal IQ (VIQ) is reported in the examiner's manual as .95; Performance IQ (PIQ) = .91; and the average Full Scale IQ internal consistency coefficient is .96. Test-retest reliability over a 3- to 7-week interval is similarly high, with the VIQ stability coefficient equal to .90, PIQ = .88, and Full Scale IQ = .91 (manual, p. 131). In an apparent oversight, the WPPSI-R manual failed to provide practitioners with confidence intervals for the subtests or scales; however, standard errors of measurement are provided and examiners can compute confidence intervals given the *SEMs* reported in the examiner's manual.

The WPPSI-R is a well-normed instrument, with the standardization sample very closely matching the 1986 U.S. Census demographics. The sample included 1,700 children, with 100 boys and girls sampled from each $^1/_2$-year level between the ages of 3 and 7; from age 7 to 7 years, 3 months an additional 50 boys and 50 girls were included. The WPPSI-R standardization sample was stratified on the basis of age, gender, geographic region, ethnic heritage, and parental education and occupation.

Although the WPPSI revision is commendable for the many reasons cited above, as with all instruments there are still some aspects of the instrument that could be improved. However, many of the difficulties that beset the WPPSI-R are minor and are related to the population for whom the instrument was designed, and not the instrument per se. For example, the WPPSI-R requires approximately $1^1/_4$ hours for administration. Although adults and older children can easily attend and participate for that length of time, it is difficult for preschool children to attend that long. An obvious solution to this problem would have been to shorten the instrument; however, to do so would also reduce the test's reliability, ceiling, floor, item gradient, and so on. It is my opinion that quality assessment should not be sacrificed for the sake of brevity. Examiners should accommodate young clients by administering the scale in more than one sitting when necessary. The Block Design and Geometric Design subtests are additional examples of where lengthy administration and/or scoring time requirements make the instrument more technically adequate, but require more time, effort, and psychological expertise than examiners might be used to expending. Given the plethora of "self-administering," carousel-type instruments available, the WPPSI-R's interactive materials and activities are a welcome change—especially for preschool children.

In an effort to render the test more useful for low-functioning young children and high-functioning older students, many of the WPPSI-R subtests have been extended by mixing item types and requirements. Rather than presenting a unified collection of items within a subtest, many subtests assess more than one foundational skill. For example, the Vocabulary subtest includes a collection of picture vocabulary items that require no verbal response, as well as oral vocabulary items that require verbal expression and definition. As such, the Vocabulary subtest is not particularly sensitive to children with receptive versus expressive language difficulties. This sort of confounding item combination has infiltrated most of the WPPSI-R Verbal and Performance subtests, and will likely frustrate the examiner's effort to differentially diagnose clients' specific receptive or expressive communication difficulties.

Although the WPPSI-R examiner's manual is refreshingly brief, it fails to provide detailed information about the instrument's theoretical orientation or the manner in which the instrument should be interpreted. The manual devotes less than 10 pages to both of these topics combined; approximately 6 pages are related to the instrument's theoretical orientation and 2 pages are allotted to WPPSI-R interpretation. Given the current trend toward the development of more comprehensive test manuals, the WPPSI-R manual leaves a good bit to be desired.

In summary, the revised WPPSI is a welcome addition to the collection of available preschool intellectual instrumentation. The revision has improved an already technically superior test, and provides psychologists with one more good (and current) instrument from which to choose. Given the foibles of other preschool intelligence tests, the WPPSI-R will likely be the test of choice for psychologists who are willing to expend the time and energy to conduct comprehensive, interactive assessments to obtain thorough understandings of their preschool clients.

REVIEWER'S REFERENCES

Wechsler, D. (1967). Wechsler Preschool and Primary Scale of Intelligence. San Antonio, TX: The Psychological Corporation.

Wechsler, D. (1974). Wechsler Intelligence Scale for Children—Revised. San Antonio, TX: The Psychological Corporation.

Bracken, B. A. (1987). Limitations of preschool instruments and standards for minimal levels of technical adequacy. Journal of Psychoeducational Assessment, 4, 313-326.

Chattin, S. H., & Bracken, B. A. (1989). School psychologists' evaluation of the K-ABC, McCarthy Scales, Stanford-Binet IV, and WISC-R. Journal of Psychoeducational Assessment, 7, 112-130.

Stone, B. J., Gridley, B. E., & Gyurke, J. S. (1991). Confirmatory factor analysis of the WPPSI-R at the extreme end of the age range. Journal of Psychoeducational Assessment, 9, 263-270.

Review of the Wechsler Preschool and Primary Scale of Intelligence—Revised by JEFFERY P. BRADEN, Associate Professor of Psychology, San Jose State University, San Jose, CA:

The Wechsler Preschool and Primary Scale of Intelligence—Revised (WPPSI-R) is the second generation of the WPPSI. The WPPSI-R promises psychologists a new and improved instrument for assessing intelligence in preschool children. This review will address the degree to which to WPPSI-R fulfills its promise to improve on the WPPSI.

DESCRIPTION. The WPPSI-R is a collection of 12 distinct subtests (see description), organized into two scales—a Verbal Scale, and a Performance Scale. The six Verbal Scale tests use language-based items, whereas the six Performance Scale tests use visual-motor items that are less dependent on language. Five of the six subtests in each scale are used to derive scale-specific IQs (i.e., Verbal IQ [VIQ] and Performance IQ [PIQ]), and these two IQs are then used to derive a Full Scale IQ. This organization of tests is popular for many reasons, including: (a) its consistency with child and adult versions of the Wechsler tests (providing a "womb-to-tomb" test sequence with the WPPSI-R, Wechsler Intelligence Scale for Children—Revised and Wechsler Intelligence Scale for Children—III [WISC-R/WISC-III], and Wechsler Adult Intelligence Scale—Revised [WAIS-R]), (b) the ability to independently estimate intelligence on language-loaded versus language-reduced tasks, and (c) the varied format holds the interest of the client in long test sessions.

NORMS AND RELIABILITY. The normative data describe a large sample ($N = 1,700$) representing the 1986 U.S. Census data in most respects (children from urban areas are over-sampled). Subtest consistencies across all ages are moderate to excellent (.54 to .93 for subtests, median .81), and the consistency of IQs is very good to excellent (.85 to .97, median .93). Subtest stability coefficients, based on 175 children divided into older and younger groups, are adequate to very good (.52 to .82, median .74) and IQ stability is very good to excellent (.88 to .91), over a 3–7-week period. The manual provides a wealth of technical data that consistently attest to the adequacy of the instrument.

VALIDITY. The WPPSI-R factor structure is congruent with the proposed hierarchical model (i.e., Full Scale IQs [FSIQs] estimate broad intelligence, with subfactors created by the Verbal and Performance Scales). The congruence of factor structure is a pleasant contrast to other Wechsler scales, which often yield three, rather than the desired two, factors. Thus, the construct validity of the test is supported by factor analyses of the test battery. These analyses are described in the manual and elsewhere (e.g., Gyurke, Stone, & Beyer, 1990).

The scores derived from the WPPSI-R correlate well with the WPPSI, WISC-R, Stanford Binet (4th ed.), and McCarthy Scales (*rs* between WPPSI-R FSIQs and other test composites range from .74 to .90). The correlation between the WPPSI-R FSIQ and the Kaufman-Assessment Battery for Children (K-ABC) Mental Processing Composite is low (.49), but the K-ABC has consistently yielded lower correlations with other intelligence tests as well. These results imply good criterion validity for the WPPSI-R. There are also studies showing the discriminant validity of the WPPSI-R with gifted, mentally deficient, learning disabled, and speech/language impaired children. Although the numbers of subjects in these groups were small, the results were consistent with expected values except for speech/language impaired children. There was no difference between PIQ and VIQ for this group, although both were in the low average range. Thus, examiners should be cautious in using PIQ/VIQ comparisons for differential diagnosis of speech/language impairments until other, independent studies are available to support its use with this population.

Unfortunately, there are no data in the manual, nor in the literature at large, that describe the treatment validity of the WPPSI-R. I use the term "treatment validity" to refer to data that demonstrate the relationship between test results and differential response to treatments or interventions. Given the popularity of ipsative profile analysis (e.g., inferring psychological deficits and suggesting psychoeducational programs on the basis of differences between scores), the lack of treatment validity data is disappointing. On the positive side, the manual presents tables reporting the reliability (i.e., the degree to which a difference is due to chance) and the prevalence (i.e., how frequently a difference occurs in the normative sample) of differences between IQs, subtest scaled scores, and other metrics of psychometric deviance. The lack of accompanying treatment validity data is disappointing; the publisher clearly encourages ipsative profile analyses by providing tables, but does not provide data which allow users to evaluate the validity of such practices.

DIFFERENCES BETWEEN THE WPPSI AND THE WPPSI-R. The WPPSI has been criticized for the following characteristics: (*a*) long administration time, (*b*) limited floor and ceiling (i.e., insensitive for older gifted and younger retarded children), (*c*) insufficient interpretive guidelines, (*d*) subjective (and possibly unreliable) scoring criteria, and (*e*) the lack of a sixth distinct Performance subtest.

The WPPSI-R addresses some of these issues effectively, and adds some unsolicited improvements. There are expanded scoring criteria, and more scoring examples. The interrater reliability coefficients reported in the manual are very good to excellent (.88 to .96), indicating these scoring changes were successful in improving interrater agreement for scoring. The revised WPPSI also adds a sixth Performance Scale subtest (Object Assembly). The addition of Object Assembly to the WPPSI-R is likely to improve its attractiveness to young children, and provides examiners with a more varied menu of subtests. The WPPSI-R's extended age ranges should appeal to those who assess preschoolers. The new "crack-back" manual binding allows examiners to prop up the manual and have both hands free for handling materials. The manual provides comprehensive technical information regarding the test (much more so than any other Wechsler scale to date). I also found the materials more durable, colorful, and likely to interest children. Perhaps the best improvement, from the child's perspective, is increased opportunities to demonstrate and teach items to children. The additional sample items, teaching items, and provision of second chances when children fail items increase the probability that the test measures the child's ability to perform, rather than the child's ability to guess what the examiner wants. The fact that the WPPSI-R yields lower scores (about 8 FSIQ points) than the WPPSI is a good thing, because the population generally improves in IQ over time (i.e., more recent tests *should* yield lower IQs than older tests).

Some problems are partially addressed in the WPPSI-R. Floor and ceiling problems are improved on the WPPSI-R, but they are not eliminated. Those wishing to differentially diagnose children beyond 2 standard deviations from the mean will be disappointed with this test. In such situations, examiners might want to use instruments developed for older children (e.g., the WISC-III) or infants (e.g., the Bayley Scales of Infant Development [10:26]). The WPPSI-R manual provides limited guidelines for interpretation of test results and no evidence of treatment validity. In view of the fact the WPPSI-R will be frequently used for differential diagnosis and psychoeducational programming decisions, the absence of these data is disappointing.

The WPPSI-R fails to resolve other problems. The first unresolved problem is long administration time. The manual states that it takes 1 hour and 15 minutes to administer the test (my experience is that $1\frac{1}{2}$ hours is a better estimate), but either estimate exceeds the sustained attention span of most young children. I think the publisher's decision to improve reliability by sacrificing short administration is a wise trade-off. The manual recommends that examiners minimize children's boredom by taking breaks between subtests, although no data are provided regarding the effects of breaks on scores. A problem that may be introduced by the WPPSI-R is the shift in task demand between certain items in the same subtest. This problem was created in the effort to solve the floor/ceiling problem (i.e., to make beginning items sufficiently easy, and ending items sufficiently difficult, the publisher changed task demands within the subtest). Although children in the normative sample were not confused by this procedure, it may be a problem for atypical or clinically unusual children (Bracken & Delugach, 1990; cf. Gyurke, 1990). Test users should be cautious, because most children who are referred for assessment are clinically unusual, and therefore may be susceptible to confusion when task demands change within subtests. Finally, the WPPSI-R is expensive, particularly in view of the limited range of ages and domains included in the battery (e.g., gross motor, fine motor, adaptive behavior, and readiness/achievement domains are not included in the WPPSI-R).

SUMMARY. The WPPSI-R is certainly a new and improved version of its predecessor, the WPPSI, and is a technically sound complement to the Wechsler family (stable?) of tests. Its changes are nearly all for the better from the perspective of the practitioner and the psychometrician. Although the publisher fails to provide data in a few areas (most notably the omission of treatment validity data), the manual provides substantially more information than any other in the Wechsler series—and most other tests as well. I suspect the WPPSI-R will be the test of choice for those who wish to assess the intelligence of young children, although the Differential Ability Scales (111) and the Woodcock-Johnson Psycho-Educational Battery—Revised are worthy (and more economical) contenders to the preschool throne. Given the popularity of the Wechsler series among practitioners and researchers, the WPPSI-R is likely to provide the standard. As Dr. Eichorn (1972) said in her review of the WPPSI, "some of a generally good thing is better than none" (p. 807). The WPPSI-R is definitely more of a generally good thing.

REVIEWER'S REFERENCES

Eichorn, D. H. (1972). [Review of the Wechsler Preschool and Primary Scale of Intelligence.] In O. K. Buros (Ed.), *The seventh mental measurements yearbook* (pp. 806-807). Highland Park, NJ: Gryphon Press.
Bracken, B. A., & Delugach, R. R. (1990). Changes improve test. *Communique, 19* (2), 21-22.
Gyurke, J. (1990). Response. *Communique, 19* (2), 22.
Gyurke, J. S., Stone, B. J., & Beyer, M. (1990). A confirmatory factor analysis of the WPPSI-R. *Journal of Psychoeducational Assessment, 8,* 15-21.

[467]
Wepman's Auditory Discrimination Test, Second Edition.

Purpose: Measures children's ability to hear spoken English accurately, specifically to "discriminate between commonly used phonemes in the English language."
Population: Ages 4-0 to 8-11.
Publication Dates: 1958–87.

Acronym: ADT.
Scores: Total score yielding Qualitative score, Standard score, Percentile rank.
Administration: Individual.
Forms, 2: 1A, 2A.
Price Data, 1991: $70 per complete kit; $25 per 100 tests (specify form); $27.50 per manual ('87, 58 pages).
Time: (15–20) minutes.
Authors: Joseph M. Wepman (test) and William M. Reynolds (manual).
Publisher: Western Psychological Services.
Cross References: For information regarding an earlier edition, see T3:226 (31 references), 8:932 (74 references), and T2:2028 (82 references); for a review by Louis M. DiCarlo of the original edition, see 6:940 (2 references).

TEST REFERENCES

1. Perlmutter, B. F., & Bryan, J. H. (1984). First impressions, ingratiation, and the learning disabled child. *Journal of Learning Disabilities, 17,* 157-161.
2. Simpson, R. G., Haynes, M. D., & Haynes, W. O. (1984). The relationship between performance on the Wepman Auditory Discrimination Test and reading achievement among adolescents. *Educational and Psychological Measurement, 44,* 353-358.
3. Shinn-Strieker, T. (1986). Patterns of cognitive style in normal and handicapped children. *Journal of Learning Disabilities, 19,* 572-576.
4. Arffa, S., Fitzhugh-Bell, K., & Black, F. W. (1989). Neuropsychological profiles of children with learning disabilities and children with documented brain damage. *Journal of Learning Disabilities, 22,* 635-640.
5. Harrison, K. A., & Romanczyk, R. G. (1991). Response patterns of children with learning disabilities: Is impulsivity a stable response style? *Journal of Learning Disabilities, 24,* 252-255.

Review of Wepman's Auditory Discrimination Test, Second Edition by MARY PANNBACKER, Professor and Program Director, Department of Communication Disorders, School of Allied Health Professions, Louisiana State University Medical Center, Shreveport, LA and GRACE MIDDLETON, Associate Professor, College of Nursing, University of Texas, El Paso, TX:

The Auditory Discrimination Test (ADT) was originally published in 1958, and revised by Wepman in 1973. The test is "for the assessment of children's ability to discriminate between commonly used phonemes in the English language." It "measures the ability to hear spoken language accurately." The test format, test items (word pairs), and mode of presentation are the same for all editions of the test. The test consists of 40 word pair of similar sounding words or contrasts and similars.

Administered individually, the test involves instructing the child to indicate if the word pairs read aloud by the examiner are the "same" or "different." If the child passes two (or if necessary five) practice items, the examiner proceeds with the test items without repeating the word pairs or providing visual cues. The final score is computed and can be compared to that of children in "the same age group from a stratified national sample." Other scores, including a qualitative score, standard score, and percentile rank, can be used to describe performance.

The revised test was standardized on a sample of 1,885 children, ages 4 through 8 years, living in 30 states, and representing different ethnic and socioeconomic backgrounds. The ADT contains little information about the examiners or listening conditions. Irwin, Moore, and Rampp (1972, p. 285) indicated "variation is possible in test-word preservation of an individual examiner and between different examiners. Variation may occur because of rate of presentation and emphasis of word pairs may affect the results." There was no reported attempt to assess inter- and intraexaminer reliability. Differences in listening conditions (quiet vs. background noise) may also cause variation. Furthermore, sound discrimination may vary with the context of the words selected (Spriestersbach & Curtis, 1951).

Winitz (1989) describes the ADT as a general auditory discrimination test because it does not specifically examine the phonemes that a child misarticulates. In fact, no standardized specific auditory discrimination test has been published. Weiner (1967) theorized that test items on the ADT will contain sounds more severely involved individuals misarticulate making the test items particularly relevant to them and creating a positive relationship between articulation and general discrimination in individuals with multiple articulation errors.

The empirical basis for testing auditory discrimination "is not strong" (Newman & Creaghead, 1989, p. 86). As Locke (1979, p. 125) pointed out when reviewing the 1973 edition of the ADT, the relevance of auditory discrimination to articulation and reading was "an interesting claim." Schwartz (1983, p. 139) believes "the relationship between phonological perception and production abilities is still unclear."

The ADT is an easily administered test—to score and interpret. It might be used with caution as a screening test. However, major management decisions should not be based on this test. Before using the ADT, two major concerns should be considered. First, it is not clear that poor auditory discrimination is a significant contributing factor to articulation problems. Second, considerable information about examiner reliability and listening conditions for this test remains lacking.

REVIEWER'S REFERENCES

Spriestersbach, D., & Curtis, J. (1951). Misarticulation and discrimination of speech sounds. *Quarterly Journal of Speech, 37*, 483-491.
Weiner, P. (1967). Auditory discrimination and articulation. *Journal of Speech and Hearing Disorders, 32*, 19-28.
Irwin, J., Moore, J., & Rampp, D. (1972). Nonmedical diagnosis and evaluation. In M. Marge & J. Irwin (Eds.), *Principles of childhood language disabilities* (pp. 237-286). New York: Appleton-Century-Crofts.
Locke, J. (1979). Auditory Discrimination Test (ADT). In F. Darley (Ed.), *Evaluation of appraisal techniques in speech and language pathology* (pp. 124-127). Reading, MA: Addison-Wesley Publishing Company.
Schwartz, R. (1983). Diagnosis of speech sound disorders in children. In I. Meitus & B. Weinberg (Eds.), *Diagnosis in speech-language pathology* (pp. 113-150). Baltimore: University Park Press.
Newman, P., & Creaghead, N. (1989). Assessment of Articulatory and Phonological Disorders. In N. Creaghead, P. Newman, & W. Secord (Eds.), *Assessment and remediation of articulation and phonological disorders* (pp. 69-126). Columbus, OH: Merrill Publishing Company.
Winitz, H. (1989). Auditory considerations in treatment. In N. Creaghead, P. Newman, & W. Secord (Eds.), *Assessment and remediation of*

articulation and phonological disorders (pp. 243-264). Columbus, OH: Merrill Publishing Company.

[468]

The Western Personality Inventory.
Purpose: Identifies alcoholics and potential alcoholics and measures extent of alcohol addiction.
Population: Adults.
Publication Dates: 1963–88.
Acronym: WPI.
Scores, 14: Anxiety, Depressive Fluctuations, Emotional Sensitivity, Resentfulness, Incompleteness, Aloneness, Interpersonal Relations, Total, Regularity of Drinking, Preference for Drinking over Other Activities, Lack of Controlled Drinking, Rationalization of Drinking, Excessive Emotionality, Total.
Administration: Individual or group.
Manual: No manual; use manuals for The Manson Evaluation and The Alcadd Test.
Price Data, 1989: $60 per complete kit; $36.50 per 25 test booklets including profile ('88, 10 pages); $250 per IBM microcomputer package including diskette (tests up to 25) and user's guide; scoring service: $11.50 per test (price includes answer sheet).
Time: Administration time not reported.
Comments: Combination of The Manson Evaluation and The Alcadd Test.
Author: Morse P. Manson.
Publisher: Western Psychological Services.

[469]

Whitaker Index of Schizophrenic Thinking.
Purpose: Measures degrees of schizophrenic thinking.
Population: Mental patients.
Publication Dates: 1973–80.
Acronym: WIST.
Scores, 4: Similarities, Word Pairs, New Inventions, Total.
Administration: Individual.
Forms, 2: A, B.
Price Data, 1987: $29.50 per complete kit; $7.90 or less per 25 tests (specify Form A or B); $4.40 per scoring key; $14.20 per manual ('80, 92 pages).
Time: (20) minutes.
Comments: Manual title is *Objective Measurement of Schizophrenic Thinking: A Practical and Theoretical Guide to the Whitaker Index of Schizophrenic Thinking.*
Author: Leighton C. Whitaker.
Publisher: Western Psychological Services.
Cross References: See T3:2620 (20 references); for reviews by Bertram D. Cohen and Robert W. Payne, see 8:710 (4 references).

TEST REFERENCES

1. Peake, T. H., & Albott, W. L. (1981). WIST predictions of brain damage: A follow-up to Albott and Gilbert. *Journal of Clinical Psychology, 37*, 180-182.
2. Phillips, W. M. (1981). The minimax problem of personal construct organization and schizophrenic thought disorder. *Journal of Clinical Psychology, 37*, 692-698.
3. Puente, A. E., & Sanders, C. H. (1981). Differentiation of schizophrenics with and without brain damage using the Whitaker Index of Schizophrenic Thinking. *Journal of Clinical Psychology, 37*, 465-466.
4. Bilett, J. L., Jones, N. F., & Whitaker, L. C. (1982). Exploring schizophrenic thinking in older adolescents with the WAIS, Rorschach and WIST. *Journal of Clinical Psychology, 38*, 232-243.
5. Puente, A. E., Heidelberg-Sanders, C., & Lund, N. (1982). Detection of brain damage in schizophrenics as measured by the Whitaker

Index of Schizophrenic Thinking and the Luria-Nebraska Neuropsychological Battery. *Perceptual and Motor Skills, 54*, 495-499.

6. Yaroush, R. A. (1982). Application of the Whitaker Index of Schizophrenic Thinking to a non-English-speaking population. *Journal of Clinical Psychology, 38*, 244-252.

7. Leslie, B. A., Landmark, J., & Whitaker, L. C. (1984). The Whitaker Index of Schizophrenic Thinking (WIST) and thirteen symptoms for diagnosing schizophrenia. *Journal of Clinical Psychology, 40*, 636-648.

8. Sengel, R. A., Lovallo, W. R., & Pishkin, V. (1984). Associative response bias and severity of thought disorder in schizophrenia and mania. *Journal of Clinical Psychology, 40*, 889-892.

9. Noriega, N. A., Gonzales, M. A., Puente, A. E., & Whitaker, L. C. (1985). The measurement of schizophrenic conceptualization using a Spanish translation of the Whitaker Index of Schizophrenic Thinking. *Journal of Clinical Psychology, 41*, 157-161.

10. Pishkin, V., Lovallo, W., & Bourne, L. E., Jr. (1986). Thought disorder and schizophrenia: Isolating and timing a mental event. *Journal of Clinical Psychology, 42*, 417-424.

11. Puente, A. E., & Anderson, C. (1987). Schizophrenic thinking and neuroleptic dosage. *Journal of Clinical Psychology, 43*, 189-196.

12. DiFrancesca, K. R., & Meloy, J. R. (1989). A comparative clinical investigation of the "How" and "Charlie" MMPI subtypes. *Journal of Personality Assessment, 53*, 396-403.

Review of the Whitaker Index of Schizophrenic Thinking by STEPHEN G. FLANAGAN, Clinical Associate Professor of Psychology, The University of North Carolina at Chapel Hill, Chapel Hill, NC:

The Whitaker Index of Schizophrenic Thinking (WIST) is offered as a measure of schizophrenic thinking, defined as thinking that is "illogical," "impaired," and "unwitting." The WIST has two main uses: to differentiate persons with schizophrenia from those without schizophrenia, and to serve as an objective measure of degree of thinking impairment. It is for use with people from age 16 and up who have at least an eighth grade education and an IQ of 80.

There are two nonequivalent alternate forms for the test: Form A includes item content selected for its potential to arouse emotion or anxiety and Form B has more neutral item content (persons with acute schizophrenia were hypothesized to be more susceptible to anxiety arousal and associated thinking impairment, relative to chronic patients). Twenty-five multiple-choice items comprise each form of the test, nine "similarities" items that require selecting the answer that is most similar to a given word, nine "word pair" items requiring selection of an answer that is most similar in meaning to a given pair of words, and seven "new inventions" items requiring selection of the most likely consequence of a new invention. The test is individually administered and timed, yielding a "Time" score in minutes. In an inquiry following completion of all items, each incorrect item is readministered until the correct response is achieved, and any additional errors are recorded. Response alternatives are weighted to reflect degree of impairment as follows (e.g., "kill" as word): Correct, 0 ("cause to die"); Loose association, 1 ("stab"); reference, 2 ("bloody me"); clang association, 3 ("mill"); nonsense, 4 ("bapple"). Each item has one of each of these types of choices. The sum of weights across all items selected, including multiple incorrect answers during inquiry,

constitutes the "Score." Three scores are recorded on the WIST: Score, Time, and Index. The "Index" is the sum of Score and Time, and serves as the primary value in interpreting the WIST.

The manual contains evidence for reliability including internal consistency measures on an "early version of Form A" (not further specified) yielding a Kuder-Richardson Formula 20 reliability coefficient of .77 on unweighted scores. Hoyt reliability coefficients on Forms A and B were approximately .80 using unweighted scores. Forms A and B differ as described above, and are noted to be noncomparable for the purpose of reliability estimation. Test-retest reliability is considered impractical because the subject learns the correct answer during the inquiry. The manual refers to one published report including test-retest reliability estimation, but findings are not cited. Additional evidence of WIST reliability would be desirable.

The WIST standardization sample included 38 hospitalized acute and 44 chronic schizophrenic patients, 55 hospitalized nonschizophrenics, and a "normal" group of 50 including 26 maintenance workers and 24 college students. Careful patient selection is described. Evidence for differentiation of persons with schizophrenia from nonschizophrenics starts with a statistically significant trend for schizophrenics, chronic and acute, to have higher Score, Time, and Index values than nonschizophrenics, patient and nonpatient. Further analysis showed that maximum differentiation of diagnosed schizophrenics and nonschizophrenics, at approximately 80% efficiency, was achieved using the Index (Score plus Time) value and a cutoff of 20 on Form A, 17 on Form B.

Such accuracy clearly makes the WIST useful for research applications, but presents difficulty if the WIST is used for clinical assessment and individual decision making. At the recommended Index cutoffs, nearly one-third of those diagnosed schizophrenic are missed (false negatives) and about 10% of nonschizophrenics are misclassified (false positives). Whitaker defends this level of discriminative efficiency by citing the inadequacy of psychiatric diagnosis to provide a serviceable criterion. He suggests that future research with objective measurement of thought disorder will ultimately yield better criteria. In fact, schizophrenic symptoms, including thought disorder as measured by the WIST, and bizarre delusions not directly measured by the WIST, are but one of a number of criteria relevant to various diagnostic systems. For example, Mezzich and Slayton (1984) considered seven frequently cited diagnostic systems for schizophrenia, and described five dimensions including schizophrenic symptoms (used in all 7 systems), exclusion criteria such as affective (manic or depressive) symptoms (5 of 7), duration of illness (4 of 7), social disability or impairment (3 of 7), and age at onset (2 of 7). It is probably unwise to expect any single measure to provide a definitive diagnosis of schizophrenia, given the complexity and multidimensional nature of schizophrenia as a clinical entity.

A second application of the WIST is to document objectively degree of thinking disorder. The manual cites several studies that have supported the use of the WIST Form A Index to classify degree of thinking deficit in a sample of clinically diagnosed schizophrenics, finding expected relationships to conceptual rule transfer performance and errors on a concept identification task. Although Whitaker argues the WIST measures a particular type of thinking disorder specific to schizophrenia, others argue that the WIST reflects generalized cognitive deficit. For example, Lovallo, Sengel, Leber, Shaffer, and Pishkin (1983) assessed 20 schizophrenics (10 paranoid, 10 nonparanoid) and 10 nonschizophrenic patients, finding the WIST Index did not differentiate well between schizophrenic and nonschizophrenic patients, but the WIST Index had a significant negative correlation with the Shipley Institute of Living Scale, which measures general cognitive functioning.

Additional clinical uses for the WIST discussed in the manual include discriminating acute versus chronic schizophrenia, differentiating paranoid and nonparanoid subtypes, identifying patterns of episodic dyscontrol, and using Form A to identify specific areas of conflict such as orality, hostility, or sexual themes. Empirical support for these applications is weak or is left to future research.

In sum, the WIST may best serve as an economically obtained, objective measure of thinking impairment. Although it may be useful in differentiating schizophrenics from nonschizophrenics, such use may involve unacceptable error rates for individual decision-making purposes. Clinically, the measure may be used most effectively as part of a more extensive assessment employing clinical interview and multiple measures.

REVIEWER'S REFERENCES

Lovallo, W. R., Sengel, R. A., Leber, W. R., Shaffer, B., & Pishkin, V. (1983). Convergent and discriminant validity of the WIST. *Journal of Clinical Psychology, 39* (3), 321-325.
Mezzich, J. E., & Slayton, R. I. (1984). Assessment and diagnosis. In A. S. Bellack (Ed.), *Schizophrenia: Treatment, management, and rehabilitation.* New York: Grune and Stratton.

[470]
Wide Range Assessment of Memory and Learning.

Purpose: "Psychometric instrument which allows the user to evaluate a child's ability to actively learn and memorize a variety of information."
Population: Ages 5 through 17.
Publication Date: 1990.
Acronym: WRAML.
Scores, 4: Verbal Memory Index, Visual Memory Index, Learning Index, General Memory Index.

Administration: Individual.
Price Data, 1991: $245 per complete kit including 25 sets of forms, supplies, and manual (160 pages); $25 per 25 examiner forms; $25 per 25 response forms; $30 per manual.
Time: (45–60) minutes.
Comments: Screening section available on Examiner Form.
Authors: David Sheslow and Wayne Adams.
Publisher: Jastak Associates, Inc.

Review of the Wide Range Assessment of Memory and Learning by RICHARD M. CLARK, Chair, Department of Educational Psychology and Statistics, State University of New York at Albany, Albany, NY:

The Wide Range Assessment of Memory and Learning (WRAML) is designed as a clinical instrument to assess memory and learning functions across the school years. The battery consists of nine subtests, and each subtest yields a norm-referenced score. In turn, scores on three subtests are combined to give a Verbal Memory Index, a Visual Memory Index, and a Learning Index. The scaled scores for these three indexes are then summed to yield a General Memory Index. Four of the nine subtests (Verbal Learning, Story Memory, Sound Symbol, and Visual Learning) ask for both immediate and delayed recall. Interpretations are provided, based on the age of the child tested, of the difference between the immediate and delayed score. Based on this score, children are classed as "atypical," "borderline," "low average," "average," or "bright average." A similar procedure may be used with the story memory task, which is given first as a free recall measure. If performance is poor, the child may be asked to respond to a recognition version. Thus, the nine subtests of the WRAML yield a total of 18 scores.

The test was normed and standardized based on samples of children from 5 years to 16 years of age. Children up to age 14 were divided into 6-month intervals, with approximately 112 children in each subgroup. The total norming group consisted of 2,363 individuals. A great amount of detail is included in the Administration manual concerning the representativeness of the norming samples. The Administration Manual also includes a commendable amount of detail on the psychometric aspects of the test, including coefficient alpha measures of internal consistency for each subtest for each age. For the nine subtests, these reliability coefficients are usually between .80 and .85. When subtests are combined, reliabilities range from approximately .90 to .96. Test reliability is as high for younger as for older children. Information is also included concerning the standard error of measurement for each subtest and index for each age group, along with correlations between scores on the WRAML and other standardized instruments such as the McCarthy Memory Index, Stanford Binet Short-Term Memory, and the Wechsler Memory Scale.

The authors also display correlations between subtests for children age 8 and younger ($N = 903$) and age 9 and older ($N = 1,406$), as well as a principal components factor analysis. The simple correlations were all statistically significant, but the majority were less than .30. The authors had theorized that each of the subtests could be classified as assessing either verbal, visual, or learning processes. If this conceptualization was correct, the three subtests designated as verbal, for example, should correlate more highly with each other than with other subtest scores. Also, these subtests should cluster when factor analysis was performed. As the authors point out, these expectations were not completely fulfilled. For example, the Story Memory subtest was placed by the authors as a verbal measure, but it loaded more on the learning factor. Users of the test should be aware that more research is needed concerning the construct validity of the instrument.

The major use for the WRAML, as illustrated in the Administration Manual, is clinical in terms of providing incremental information in making an individual diagnosis. The instrument is designed to be given by a well-trained individual such as a school or clinical psychologist. Administration time is 45 minutes to 1 hour. In the clinical examples given, an individual is referred because of a specific problem, and information from an extensive battery of assessments is provided. Then a profile from the WRAML is presented and comments are made concerning how these data augment the diagnosis and affect the recommendations for future action. The authors are appropriately conservative in these examples, using many qualifying terms such as "there appears to be" and "may be related." The instrument is too new to have been subjected to necessary research. We do not yet know the degree to which a skilled clinician, given a considerable body of information, would make a different diagnosis or different recommendations if WRAML data were added, and certainly we do not know if the recommendations would lead to better programming for an individual.

Little is said by the authors concerning the possible use of the instrument by researchers studying processes of memory and learning, but this use seems promising. Many of the subtests developed here are similar to tasks used in studies of memory. However, interpreting performance on such tasks is difficult because they have not been normed and relatively little is known about the sample used in a particular study. Sheslow and Adams provide clear instructions concerning how their battery of tests should be administered along with extensive infor-mation concerning the relationships of subtests to each other and to other measures.

As a new instrument that is designed to tap a complex domain of behavior, adaptation by the research community would be of great value in clearing up some of the inconsistencies related to constructs the test is actually measuring. Those studying processes of memory and learning can benefit from a kit of attractive materials and the extensive standardization provided by the authors, Sheslow and Adams.

Review of the Wide Range Assessment of Memory and Learning by FREDERIC J. MEDWAY, Professor of Psychology, University of South Carolina, Columbia, SC:

The Wide Range Assessment of Memory and Learning (WRAML) was designed to evaluate the ability of school-age children (ages 5–17) to both memorize and actively learn verbal and visual information. The WRAML consists of nine subtests varying verbal versus visual information, meaningfulness of information, and immediate recall versus acquisition over trials. Optional procedures for assessing delayed recall also are available.

The WRAML consists of three major scales: Verbal Memory, Visual Memory, and Learning. Each scale is derived from three subtests. Separate "index" scores are available for each major scale and the test also yields a General Memory Index (GMI) based on all nine subtests. The GMI and Verbal, Visual, and Learning Indexes can be computed in percentiles and standard scores. Individual subtests yield scaled scores.

Administration time ranges from about 45 minutes to 1 hour if optional subtests are given. A screening form, made up of four subtests, correlates well with the total scale and can be given in 10 to 15 minutes.

SUBTEST DESCRIPTION. The three verbal subtests measure the ability to recall auditorily presented information on tasks increasing in semantic complexity. The child is asked to repeat series of mixed numbers and letters (Number/Letter Memory), to repeat meaningful sentences (Sentence Memory), and to recall information contained in two stories varying in interest level and linguistic complexity (Story Memory). The three visual subtests measure recall of visual stimuli and increase in meaningfulness from recall of patterns (Finger Windows), to designs (Design Memory), to parts of pictures (Picture Memory). The three learning subtests measure the ability to retain information presented over trials. One subtest assesses the ability to learn a word list (Verbal Learning), another the ability to memorize locations of designs (Visual Learning), and a third to recall sounds associated with abstract figures (Sound Symbol). All three learning subtests and one Verbal scale subtest (Story Memory) have delayed recall procedures.

ADMINISTRATION AND MATERIALS. The complete WRAML kit includes the administration and scoring manual, test materials, and scoring protocols. The basic technical data are presented in the manual, and administration and scoring procedures are easy to follow. The protocols are multicolored to facilitate administration and scoring. A nylon carrying case can be purchased separately but is necessary to transport the test material conveniently.

Test materials are attractive and the use of colored pictures holds the interest of examinees. However, some test materials are not well constructed and may not withstand frequent handling and extended use. The plastic lamination on Picture Memory cards is thin and the plastic foam used in the Visual Learning Board is flimsy. In addition, the symbol size on Sound Symbol cards is rather small and the examiner must ensure that the examinee is free from visual problems.

TEST CHARACTERISTICS. The WRAML was normed on 2,363 children representative of national population statistics based on the 1980 U.S. Census and the *1988 Rand McNally Commercial Atlas and Marketing Guide*. The standardization sample is approximately 78% White, 12% Black, 7% Hispanic, and 3% other groups. No racial or gender differences are reported; however, only about 20 nonwhite children were tested at each age group.

Person and item separation statistics (construct validity) used in Rasch measurement indicate excellent item definitions of variables measured and internal consistency. Various techniques were used to calculate reliability. Subtest coefficients range from .78 to .90 and median coefficients for the three scales meet or exceed .90. The GMI coefficient alpha is .96. The lowest level of reliability reported is test-retest for Sound Symbol (.61). Thus, reliability for all subtests, except Sound Symbol, is satisfactory to excellent. Standard errors of measurement for the nine subtests also are satisfactory.

The WRAML was correlated with the Wechsler Intelligence Scale for Children—Revised (WISC-R), subtests of the McCarthy Scales, subtests of the Stanford-Binet Intelligence Scale, 4th Edition, and the Wechsler Memory Scale—Revised (WMS-R) for different age groups. Correlations of the WRAML and WISC-R are moderate and indicate that the WRAML is not simply measuring general cognitive ability. Correlations of the WRAML GMI with the other scales vary from .54 to .80. Correlations generally are strongest among the WRAML and measures of short-term verbal memory and attention/concentration. Compared to the WRML Verbal Scale, the WRAML Visual and Learning Scales appear to represent more unusual assessment instruments in relation to other available scales.

COMPARISON WITH THE WMS-R. Besides the WRAML, the only comprehensive memory scale available is the WMS-R. However, the WMS-R was designed for adults and the WMS-R and WRAML only overlap in the 16- to 17-year age range. The WRAML appears superior to the WMS-R for use with adolescents. The WMS-R was standardized on only 50 adolescents and has a lower reliability coefficient than the WRAML. The WMS-R also is difficult to use and not reliable for individual diagnosis (Kaufman, 1990).

WRAML LIMITATIONS. Although the WRAML manual reviews models of memory, the test, like others available, has not been derived from any unified theoretical framework. Subtest selection was based on mixing a variety of tasks reflecting different types of memory functioning. As it stands, the test appears to be a better measure of immediate recall and concentration than of evaluation of memory strategies. The battery was designed, at least in part, to assist clinicians working with developmentally disabled children. Although the manual presents some case studies using the test with these populations, disabled children were not part of the standardization sample. Future studies are needed in which the WRAML is given to clinical samples with known deficient memories such as children with diffuse brain damage, Turner's Syndrome, mental retardation, and autism.

SUMMARY. The WRAML is a new instrument with a great deal of promise. Much care went into test development and standardization. The WRAML is relatively easy to administer and score, and will hold the attention even of young children. Compared to existing measures, the test assesses unique memory aspects; however, it appears primarily to be measuring short-term concentration and attention. Although further research is necessary, the WRAML does fill the need for a comprehensive battery assessing children's memory functioning. Used in conjunction with standard intelligence and achievement measures, the WRAML has the potential to allow for a more thorough understanding of children's learning problems.

REVIEWER'S REFERENCE

Kaufman, A. S. (1990). *Assessing adolescent and adult intelligence*. Boston: Allyn and Bacon.

[471]

The Wilson Battery of Multi-Level Management & Organization Surveys.

Purpose: Designed to identify group or individual training needs, to assess the effects of training, to use in organizational/management studies, and to support participatory management or "quality circle" programs.
Population: Managers and employees.
Publication Dates: 1977–89.
Administration: Group.
Price Data: Available from publisher.
Time: Administration time not reported.

Author: Clark L. Wilson.

Publisher: Clark Wilson Publishing Company.

a) SURVEY OF MANAGEMENT PRACTICES.

Purpose: Assesses interactions and attitudes between managers and their subordinates.

Population: Subordinates, managers, and supervisors.

Publication Dates: 1981-84.

Acronym: SMP.

Scores, 15: Clarification of Goals and Objectives, Upward Communications and Participation, Orderly Work and Planning, Expertise, Work Facilitation, Feedback, Time Emphasis, Control of Details, Goal Pressure, Delegation, Recognizing and Reinforcing Performance, Approachability, Teambuilding, Interest in Subordinate Growth, Building Trust.

b) THE SURVEY OF GROUP MOTIVATION AND MORALE.

Purpose: Assesses "climate" among work group members.

Population: Subordinates, managers, and supervisors.

Publication Dates: 1981–84.

Acronym: SGMM.

Scores, 8: Work Involvement, Co-Worker Competence, Team Atmosphere, Opportunity for Growth, Tension Level, Organization Climate, General Morale, Commitment.

c) SURVEY OF PEER RELATIONS.

Purpose: To assess relationships between equals.

Population: Managers and subordinates.

Publication Dates: 1981–84.

Acronym: PEER.

Scores, 14: Clarifying Goals, Clarity of Communications, Encouraging Peer Participation, Orderly Work Planning, Problem Solving, Expertise, Teamwork, Peer Feedback, Time Emphasis, Attention to Detail, Pressure on Peers, Recognizing Peer Performance, Approachability, Dependability.

d) SURVEY OF SALES RELATIONS.

Purpose: Assesses relations between a sales representative and customers and prospects.

Population: Prospective and actual customers, sales representatives and their superiors.

Publication Date: 1984.

Acronym: SSR.

Scores, 10: Account Service, Professionalism, Analyzing Needs, Presenting Benefits, Technical Competence, Asking for the Order, Answering Objections, Selling Pressure, Compatibility, Trust/Rapport.

e) THE SURVEY OF LEADERSHIP PRACTICES.

Purpose: Assesses qualities inherent in leadership positions.

Population: Managers and supervisors.

Acronym: SLP.

Scores, 23: Vision/Imagination, Risk-Taking/Venturesomeness, Organizational Sensitivity, Personal Awareness, Persuasiveness, Teaming, Standards of Performance, Perseverence, Push/Pressure, Recognition, Effectiveness/Outcomes, Personal Standards, Consistency, Charisma, Coping with Stress, Giving/Withholding Rewards, Influential Connections, Position or Title, Pressuring Subordinates, Technical Competence, Managerial Competence, Teaming with Others, Compatible Personal Values.

Authors: Clark L. Wilson and Donal O'Hare.

f) THE SURVEY OF SALES MANAGEMENT PRACTICES.

Purpose: To assess activities and attitudes of managers in the sales profession.

Population: Managers who work in sales.

Acronym: SSMP.

Comments: SSMP represents SMP for sales managers.

g) SURVEY OF AGENT RELATIONS.

Purpose: Assesses the manner in which insurance agents relate to clients and customers.

Population: Clients and customers of insurance agents.

h) SURVEY OF CUSTOMER RELATIONS.

Purpose: To assess the manner in which a customer service/sales force relates with clients and customers.

Population: Clients and customers who deal with a customer service or sales force.

i) THE SURVEY OF EXECUTIVE LEADERSHIP.

Purpose: "Assesses the skills and attributes needed to develop and communicate mission, long range visions and strategic plans; handle the complexities and uncertainties that go with top level responsibilities; sense the organization's environment, develop the culture and top staff to implement their strategic plans."

Population: Top level management.

Acronmy: EXEC.

Scores, 20: Strategic Vision, Risk-Taking/Venturesomeness, Organization Savvy (Perceptiveness), Managing Complexities, Developing Organization Culture, Developing Managers, Drive, Push/Pressure, Stress Management, Sharing Credit, Effectiveness/Outcomes, Personal Standards, Connections, Job Title, Pressure, Rewarding Others, Technical Expertise, Managerial Competence, Teamwork, Compatible Values.

Authors: Donal O'Hare and Clark L. Wilson.

j) OUR TEAM.

Purpose: Assesses the manner in which a group of individuals works together (perspective of the team).

Population: Supervisors, managers, and employees.

Scores, 13: Clarity of Goals/Priorities, Co-Worker Competence, Newcomer Support, Team Atmosphere, Consensus Development, Tension/Stress Level, Domination, Conflict Resolution, Management Support, Management Feedback, Recognition/Satisfaction, Effectiveness/Outcomes, Satisficing.

Authors: Clark L. Wilson and Donal O'Hare.

k) MY TEAM-MATES.

Purpose: Assesses the manner in which a group of individuals works together (perspective of the team members).

Population: Supervisors, managers, and employees.

Scores, 12: Clarity of Perosonal Goals, Imagination, Technical Competence, Teamwork, Negotiating Skills, Contribution to Consensus, Persuasiveness, Coping withStress/Ambiguity, Attention to Details, Pressure on Team-mates, Standards of Performance, Acknowledgement of Peer Contributions.

Authors: Clark L. Wilson and Donal O'Hare.

[472]

Wisconsin Behavior Rating Scale.

Purpose: "A least biased adaptive behavior scale" to "provide adequate assessment, intervention, and evaluation" of severely and profoundly retarded individuals and of persons functioning below the developmental level of 3 years.

Population: Persons functioning below the developmental level of 3 years.

Publication Dates: 1979–83.

Acronym: WBRS.

Scores, 12: Gross Motor, Fine Motor, Expressive Language, Receptive Language, Play Skills, Socialization, Domestic Activity, Eating, Toileting, Dressing, Grooming, Total.

Administration: Group.

Price Data, 1987: $9 per 25 scales; $33.50 per 100 scales ('79, 8 pages); $1.25 per specimen set including scale and manual ('83, 30 pages).

Time: (10–15) minutes.

Comments: "The assessment is performed by interviewing informants who are most familiar with the behavior of the person being evaluated."

Authors: Agnes Song, Stephen Jones, Janet Lippert, Karin Metzgen, Jacqueline Miller, and Christopher Borreca.

Publisher: Central Wisconsin Center for the Developmentally Disabled.

TEST REFERENCES

1. McGrew, K., & Bruininks, R. (1989). The factor structure of adaptive behavior. *School Psychology Review, 18*, 64-81.

Review of the Wisconsin Behavior Rating Scale by PAT MIRENDA, Associate Professor of Special Education and Communication Disorders, University of Nebraska-Lincoln, Lincoln, NE:

The Wisconsin Behavior Rating Scale (WBRS) is both a criterion- and norm-referenced assessment instrument used to assess individuals functioning at a developmental level under approximately 3 years. Specifically, it is considered to be applicable to infants and preschool children, persons with severe/profound mental retardation, and persons with multiple handicaps such as cerebral palsy and dual sensory impairments (i.e., both deafness and blindness). It consists of 176 items and can be completed through an interview with an informant familiar with the target individual in 10–15 minutes. The informant is asked to rate each item on a 0–2 scale, in which 0 = requires complete assistance, 1 = independent < 50% of the time, and 2 = independent > 50% of the time. Thus, the WBRS is intended to be a gross measure of developmental age (referred to as "behavioral age" in the manual), and as an instrument that identifies general areas of strengths and weaknesses for evaluation, programming, and monitoring. It does not provide detailed information concerning specific areas for instructional emphasis and remediation. A unique feature of the test is that it provides alternative items in some cases for persons with dual sensory impairments and visual impairments, and allows the scorer to accept alternative forms of communication (e.g., manual signs, symbols, etc.) as correct responses.

The WBRS was normed on a stratified random sample of 175 male and 150 female residents of a state institution for persons with mental retardation ranging in age from 1–72 years of age. The sample was composed primarily of persons with profound mental retardation, though it also included persons in the mild, moderate, and severe categories as well as 35 persons with dual sensory impairments. No racial or socioeconomic data are provided for these subjects, and all resided in Wisconsin. In addition, the instrument was administered to a "community group" of 184 normal infants and children from a small rural-urban area in Wisconsin. These subjects ranged in age from birth to 4 years and included approximately 10 males and 10 females in each of the eight half-year groups in this range. The mean occupational levels of the community sample are compared in the manual with both U.S. and Wisconsin census figures, and a related study which accompanied the review materials provides the same information concerning the community sample's racial distribution (Song, Jones, Lippert, Metzgen, Miller, & Borreca, 1984). The comparison data were from the 1970 census and were thus outdated at the time the test was published; however, the comparison indicates that the community sample was generally representative of the population as a whole within ± 6 percentage points. A more important issue is related to the size of the two standardization samples. Salvia and Ysseldyke (1988) recommended that the minimum number of subjects for which a full range of percentiles can be computed is 100. A norm sample, therefore, should contain at least 100 subjects per age. Based on this criterion, the institutional sample, which spans 72 years (ages 1–72), should have at least 7,200 subjects; and the community sample, which spans 4 years (ages 0–4), should have at least 400. Using these standards, both the institutional and community samples of 325 and 184 subjects respectively are inadequate in size. Therefore, though the standardization subjects are generally well described and appear to be fairly representative of the WBRS target populations, the reliability and validity data provided in the manual must be interpreted with caution.

The manual provides tables that display age-equivalent means and ranges for each of the items on the WBRS, "behavioral ages" for total raw scores, and age equivalents for the subscale raw scores; it is not clear from the manual whether data from the community sample were included with data from the institutional sample to construct these tables. The test booklet provides a table of percentile ranks for both subscale and total scores; these were derived using only an institutional sample of 286 residents. The specific test items in the WBRS are based on "numerous" rating scales published since 1960, including those from a longitudinal research project conducted at the institution housing the standardization sample. Given the ambiguity concerning the samples used in establishing the norms, the norm values should be applied only to persons with severe-profound mental retardation who live in institutional settings; and, even for those individuals, results should be interpreted with caution given the small size of the samples used to construct the tables.

A number of reliability measures are reported in the manual and in the accompanying published article. Interrater reliability coefficients for the entire institutional sample were calculated based on the independent scores of 109 professional staff who were paired as raters and who completed the scale within 2–21 days of each other after a 1-hour workshop. All coefficients were .87 or above, with an overall interrater reliability coefficient of .95. The median interrater percentages of agreement for each of the subscale items are also reported and compared to the median chance agreement and the median weighted kappa statistic; all comparisons were significant at $p < .01$. For the community sample, interrater reliabilities were calculated for the independent scores of a single pair of trained, independent raters who interviewed the parents of a subsample of 30 infants and children from birth to 4 years of age. The coefficients between the two raters were .97 and .98. In addition, an intercorrelation matrix was computed for the institutional sample for the relationship between all of the subscale and total scores on the WBRS. These scores ranged from .4446 between the Gross Motor and Expressive Language subscales to .8938 between the Toileting and Grooming subscales. In general, these data indicate the interrater reliability and internal consistency of the WBRS are quite acceptable. However, no reliability indices of stability are provided, nor are standard error of measurement tables provided for any of the data. Thus, the overall reliability evidence for the WBRS is incomplete.

For the entire institutional sample ($n = 325$), concurrent validity scores were calculated between the WBRS and two similar instruments: the Fairview Self-Help Scale (Ross, 1970) and a level of responsiveness index which rates the developmental level of a subject on a 1 to 9 scale. Pearson r values of .93 between the WBRS and the Fairview and .84 between the WBRS and the level of responsiveness scale were obtained. The scores indicate high concurrent validity with these measures; however, neither of the comparison measures is in widespread distribution, and their own validities and reliabilities are questionable. Scores on the Vineland Social Maturity Scale (Doll, 1965) and the WBRS were compared for the community sample ($n = 142$);

the resulting correlation was .97, indicating that, for the community sample, the WBRS compares well to a widely used and well-respected measure of adaptive behavior. In terms of construct validity, correlations between the subscale scores obtained for the institutional sample on the WBRS, the AAMD Adaptive Behavior Scale (ABS; Nihira, Foster, Shellhaas, & Leland, 1975), and the Fairview were examined to determine if the WBRS measures the same general areas of behavior as these tests. The correlation coefficients between the WBRS and the ABS ranged from .2785 to .5492. When the WBRS and the Fairview were compared, the coefficients were from a .5547 to .9313. These scores indicate the ABS does not measure the same behaviors as the WBRS, while the Fairview does. For the community sample, the subscales of the WBRS were compared to those on the Vineland, with a resulting coefficient of .97, indicating high construct validity between these two measures. Principal component factor analysis with a varimax rotation was also performed in order to identify the principal categories of adaptive behavior represented in the WBRS. The results of that analysis indicate that, for both the community and institutional samples, the subscales can be collapsed into two factors related to cognition and psychomotor ability, although there are differences in the specific subscales comprising these factors for the two subject groups. These results suggest the original 11 subscales are highly correlated and should not be interpreted singly or in a profile analysis.

Overall, the WBRS is a simple-to-administer test that appears to yield similar scores across trained raters. However, there are no indicators that the test produces stable results over time, nor that it is valid when compared to similar types of tests with high validity and reliability that are used with persons with severe handicaps. It could be used as a general measure of overall functioning for this population, but only with appropriate cautions given these concerns and the small institutional sample size. Although it compares well with the Vineland when used with normal infants and children from birth to 4 years of age, it has no clear advantage in use for this population over other widely accepted measures of this type.

REVIEWER'S REFERENCES

Doll, E. (1965). Vineland Social Maturity Scale. Circle Pines, MN: American Guidance Service.

Ross, R. (1970). Fairview Self-Help Scale. Costa Mesa, CA: Fairview State Hospital.

Nihira, K., Foster, R., Shellhaas, M., & Leland, H. (1975). AAMD Adaptive Behavior Scale (rev. ed.). Washington, DC: American Association on Mental Deficiency.

Song, A., Jones, S., Lippert, J., Metzgen, K., Miller, J., & Borreca, C. (1984). Wisconsin Behavior Rating Scale: Measure of adaptive behavior for the developmental levels of 0 to 3 years. American Journal of Mental Deficiency, 88, 401-410.

Salvia, J., & Ysseldyke, J. E. (1988). Assessment in special and remedial education (4th ed.). Boston: Houghton Mifflin.

Review of the Wisconsin Behavior Rating Scale by HARVEY N. SWITZKY, Professor of Educational Psychology, Counseling, and Special Education, Northern Illinois University, DeKalb, IL:

The Wisconsin Behavior Rating Scale (WBRS) was developed to aid practitioners in obtaining psychometrically adequate, in-depth assessment and evaluation of the adaptive behavior of individuals with multiple handicaps and/or severe and profound mental retardation as well as persons functioning developmentally below the 3-year level. Specifically the WBRS is applicable to: (*a*) infants and preschool children; (*b*) severely/profoundly retarded; and (*c*) multiply handicapped (deaf/blind, cerebral palsied, nonambulatory, and/or nonverbal) persons.

Items on 11 domains of adaptive behavior are arranged in an empirically derived normal developmental sequence and include: Gross Motor (28 items); Fine Motor (14 items); Expressive Language (27 items); Expressive Language for Deaf/Blind (19 items); Receptive Language (20 items); Receptive Language for Deaf/Blind (14 items); Play Skills (18 items); Socialization (12 items); Socialization for Deaf/Blind (9 items); Domestic Activities (9 items); Eating (15 items); Toileting (10 items); Dressing (6 items); Grooming/Tooth Brushing (3 items); Grooming/Hand/Face Washing (6 items); Grooming/Bathing (5 items); and Grooming/Hair Combing/Brushing (3 items). The assessment may be performed by interviewing informants who are most familiar with the behavior of the person being evaluated. The informants' responses may be double-checked by either direct observation of the individual or from interviewing other informants. A first-person assessment procedure may be used if the rater is sufficiently familiar with the individual's behavior.

Each scale item is evaluated according to the following scoring criteria: 0 = The individual does not perform or respond; requires complete assistance; 1 = The behavior is emergent; the individual performs independently *less* than 50% of the time or requires assistance/supervision; 2 = The individual performs skillfully or performs independently *more* than 50% of the time; and, (No Opportunity) to observe behavior. The subscale domain scores are obtained by summing all the scores in that section. A total scale score can be obtained by adding all 11 subscale scores. Raw scores can be converted to percentile ranks (based on a standardization sample of 325 institutionalized, severely/profoundly retarded, multiply handicapped individuals of all chronological ages who function below the developmental level of 3 years). A score called Behavioral Age can be computed from the total raw score. This score is meant to suggest the average performance expected from a nonhandicapped child at different ages. Age Equivalent Scores can be obtained from raw domain subscores which indicate the approximate age level at which an average child can perform the respective subscale items. The community standardization sample on which the Behavioral Age and Age Equivalent Scores were obtained consisted of 184 nonhandicapped children ranging in age from birth to 4 years.

The WBRS is designed to be used for the following purposes: (*a*) for assessing an overall level of functioning; (*b*) for ascertaining a quick profile of development in basic behavioral areas in order to identify areas of strengths and weaknesses for evaluation and programming; (*c*) for follow-up of individual development or monitoring progress following training and/or improved opportunity; and (*d*) for programming and remediation.

The WBRS is probably among the best functional developmental assessment screening instruments that can be completed quickly and present an overview of the individual's current level of skill over various adaptive behavioral skill domains currently available for individuals with severe/profound mental retardation and/or multiple handicaps. (See Switzky, 1979, for reviews of other screening instruments.) The major innovations of the WBRS are the inclusion of expressive and receptive language scales for deaf/blind populations, detailed item scale content arranged in empirically derived developmental sequences of adaptive behavioral skill domains, and attempts to use more sophisticated psychometric techniques (i.e., reliability, age differentiation, correlation with other tests, factorial analysis, to attempt construct validation) in the construction of the instrument. (See Crocker & Algina, 1986; Switzky & Heal, 1990, for discussions of construct validation in special education research.)

Construct validation strategies used on the WBRS were flawed, however, in my opinion because all the data obtained from the various standardization samples were obtained from a *single* informant (an institutional aid for the institutional samples, or a parent for the community sample of nonhandicapped children). Therefore, there is no way to assess the *validity* of the informants' responses. Thus the elaborate attempts to obtain independent reliability of measurements of the scales on the WBRS and the attempts to obtain concurrent and construct validation of the WBRS are based on potentially biased informants because no cross-checks were obtained with other knowledgeable informants, or any direct observation of the individuals being evaluated. It is difficult to understand why the authors did not take their own advice as suggested in the manual and cross-check their assessments.

The authors defend their test construction strategy as it relates to reliability by suggesting their interest was in scale reliability—especially item reliability. They did not investigate interrater reliabilities, test-retest reliability, or attempt a type of predictive validity study by comparing scores on the instrument from informants to scores generated by direct observation (Song, Jones, Lippert, Metzgen, Miller, & Borreca, 1984).

I cannot accept the authors' decisions regarding research methodology because I regard the scoring criteria as rather vague and difficult to use. Further, the input of more than one knowledgeable informant and direct observation of the individuals assessed seems to be absolutely essential to demonstrate simple reliability of measurements. This is vital before one can demonstrate construct validity. The behavioral functioning of individuals with severe and profound mental retardation has been found to be extremely variable over time (Switzky & Haywood, 1985)—yet another reason to use more than one informant and attempt cross-checking by direct observation.

The WBRS is based on a functional developmental model of adaptive behavior. I doubt if it matters very much if raw scores, percentile rank scores, or Age Equivalent Scores are used to assess levels of functioning. The authors provide sufficient caution in interpreting the age norms derived from the normative sample of community children and the percentile ranks derived from the institutionalized sample. If, however, practitioners desire models of adaptive behavior based on criterion-referenced assessment of domain-specific practical skills, the WBRS is not for them.

In summary, the WBRS is a good attempt to carefully construct a functional developmental screening instrument to assess the adaptive behavioral functioning of individuals with severe and profound mental retardation and/or multiple handicaps whose developmental level is below 3 years of age. The WBRS will be useful to many practitioners. Technical data are lacking, however, so publishers should continue refinement of the measure.

REVIEWER'S REFERENCES

Switzky, H. N. (1979). Assessment of the severely and profoundly handicapped. In D. A. Sabatino & T. L. Miller (Eds.), *Describing learner characteristics of handicapped children and youth* (pp. 415-478). New York: Grune & Stratton.

Song, A., Jones, S., Lippert, J., Metzgen, K., Miller, J., & Borreca, C. (1984). Wisconsin Behavior Rating Scale: Measurement of adaptive behavior for the developmental levels of 0 to 3 years. *American Journal of Mental Deficiency, 88,* 401-410.

Switzky, H. N., & Haywood, H. C. (1985). Perspectives on methodological and research issues concerning severely retarded persons. In D. Bricker & J. Filler (Eds.), *Severe mental retardation* (pp. 264-284). Reston, VA: Council for Exceptional Children.

Crocker, L., & Algina, J. (1986). *Introduction to classical and modern test theory.* New York: Holt, Rinehart & Winston.

Switzky, H. N., & Heal, L. (1990). Research methods in special education. In R. Gaylord-Ross (Ed.), *Issues and research in special education* (Vol. 1, pp. 1-81). New York: Teachers College Press.

Wolfe Microcomputer User Aptitude Test.

Purpose: To evaluate the practical and analytical skills required for the effective use of microcomputers.
Population: Applicants for positions involving the use of microcomputers.
Publication Dates: 1986–88.
Scores: Item scores and total score only.
Administration: Group.
Price Data, 1989: $55 per test (scored by publisher) including test manual ('86, 5 pages); additional $35 per candidate for 2-hour scoring service available from publisher by phone.
Foreign Language Edition: French edition available.
Time: 75(80) minutes.
Author: Richard Label.
Publisher: Wolfe Personnel Testing & Training Systems, Inc.

Review of the Wolfe Microcomputer User Aptitude Test by ROBERT FITZPATRICK, Consulting Industrial Psychologist, Pittsburgh, PA:

This is intended to be a test of aptitude for those who will use microcomputers in their work. It is not aimed at selecting computer programmers.

The test consists of four problems, each of which was designed to evaluate an ability thought to be important in typical work with microcomputers. Problem 1 simulates the operation of a spreadsheet. Problem 2 is a complex clerical checking task. Problem 3 includes three reasoning items, using some concepts found in computer programming. Problem 4 requires the examinee to follow complex instructions in another context similar to a computer program.

The problems seem ingeniously designed and are fun to work. However, there is no rationale given for their design, and there seems no reason to suppose these problems would do a better job in selecting computer users than would conventional tests of comprehension, following instructions, and reasoning. No evidence is provided that these are the most important abilities for computer users.

The Manual is skimpy and vague. It is not clear whether the test is to be timed. A time is stated for each problem, but apparently this is done merely to help the examinee stay within a total time of "approximately" 75 minutes. The examiner is not explicitly instructed to enforce a time limit. The Manual says the test may be administered with "only clerical supervision," and that "Once begun, it is self-instructive." However, the instructions are somewhat complex and not entirely clear. Some substantial reading comprehension is needed to deal with the instructions.

No reliability data are presented. It seems likely that the reliability is low, because the number of separate items is small and some of these are interdependent. For example, in Problem 1, there are only five items; to get the correct answer to Item

2 (except by accident), one must have answered Item 1 correctly; and the same relationship holds between Items 3 and 2.

No scoring procedures or norms are provided in the Manual. The publisher offers a scoring service, which includes recommendations for hiring or training. However, the user is in the dark as to the bases for these recommendations. There is no apparent reason for the scoring to be complex or esoteric. The publisher owes the potential user either (*a*) instructions for scoring and norms or (*b*) an explanation of the reason for scoring secrecy.

The publisher has provided a report of one criterion-related validity study. Only part of the study is relevant to the intended application of the test. That part is based on a sample of only 35 college students, and the resulting correlation is low. The publisher's summary of the overall study is misleading and, in part, inaccurate.

The Wolfe Microcomputer User Aptitude Test could possibly be used in some specialized research. However, in view of the lack of evidence for validity or reliability, the secrecy of scoring, and the lack of normative information, it is decidedly not recommended for use in personnel selection.

[474]
Wolfe-Winrow Structured Analysis and Design Concepts Proficiency Test.

Purpose: "Evaluates candidate's knowledge of structured analysis and design methodology, as well as commonly used tools and techniques."
Population: Candidates for EDP systems analysts/designers.
Publication Date: 1983.
Scores: Total score only.
Administration: Group.
Price Data, 1987: $35 ($50 if scored by publisher) per test including manual (no date, 8 pages).
Time: 35(45) minutes.
Author: Wolfe Personnel Testing & Training Systems, Inc.
Publisher: Wolfe Personnel Testing & Training Systems, Inc.

Review of the Wolfe-Winrow Structured Analysis and Design Concepts Proficiency Test by DAVID O. ANDERSON, Senior Measurement Statistician, Educational Testing Service, Princeton, NJ:

The Wolfe-Winrow Structured Analysis and Design Concepts Proficiency Test (WWSAD) was designed "to evaluate candidate knowledge of structured analysis and design methodology, as well as commonly used tools and techniques." Proposed uses of the test include: hire and promotion decisions, training needs analysis, skills inventory analysis, and training program evaluation. The topics covered in the test include systems development methodology, the structured analysis and design process, data flow diagramming, structure charts, and the concepts of data dictionary, coupling,

cohesion, packaging, and system testing. The WWSAD is one of a series of tests in the Wolfe-Winrow Dial-A-Skill Series dealing with the testing of data processing personnel for purposes of hiring and training. Other subjects in the series include TSO/SPF, OS/JCL (MVS, OS VSI), Structured COBOL, and so forth.

There are four sections of the WWSAD test (labeled Questions 1–4), three of which contain another eight to nine individual items (also called questions). Section 1 requires the candidate to complete a data flow diagram based on a paragraph of requirements (7 minutes). Section 2 contains eight multiple-choice and one matching question related to stages in the systems development life cycle (13 minutes). Section 3 has eight matching items about a structure chart requiring filling in the blanks (5 minutes). Miscellaneous topics are covered by eight multiple-choice items in Section 4 (10 minutes). The section times are advisory only; the 35-minute time limit for the test is enforced. All items were typed in upper-case font, making them more difficult than necessary to read.

There apparently is only one form of the test. This can be inferred by the fact that candidates are not allowed to retest within any 6-month period. Should a candidate want scores sent to another company, that company would have to subscribed to the Wolfe-Winrow Dial-A-Skill test series. Scores are sent to client companies, not individuals.

TEST DEVELOPMENT. The seven-page test manual contains a general description of the test and one sample question (which, in fact, is an actual item on the test!). The several quotations in this review are from this test manual. Although the manual indicates several intended uses of the test, there is no job analysis information, no validity information, and no reliability data with which to evaluate these claims. No details are provided as to the test development process leading to the current test. Criterion validity is vitally important for a test of this nature. It is not clear to what criteria (work sample, performance ratings, low error rates, etc.) the test items are linked. The sections and items appear to have some face validity, but without a detailed job analysis, it remains unclear how relevant and complete the skills being tested are. A validation study is mentioned as being in progress as of April 1983, but no details were provided.

GRADING AND SCORE REPORTS. The final score is "a total raw score . . . obtained as a percentage out of 100." Most items are scored "right" or "wrong"; however, partial-credit scoring is done for items requiring the candidates to create answers. The discussion about partial-credit scoring is overly general, in that candidates are advised that "specific point deductions are made for pre-defined errors with the most severe being for logic misinterpretations and the least severe being for clerical-type errors." More details about the severity of certain errors would be welcome.

This raw score leads to a summary performance rating (i.e., 97–100 Excellent, 93–96 Very High . . . , 0–29 Very Low) but no documentation is provided to substantiate the meaning of this categorization; it does not appear to be based on normative data. Worse, the score report includes a "recommendation as to whether or not the candidate should be assigned duties in the tested topic area" with no documentation as to a standard setting study to establish the appropriateness of the decision.

The client is also provided a one-page narrative report, describing each candidate's performance on each section, along with an overall summary outlining apparent strengths and weaknesses in the tested topic. Performance ratings are provided for each section, but again, there is no documentation supporting the section rating system. Actual responses to all items are also reported to the client. The candidates do not receive any written reports.

Scoring can be done by the client using a secure scoring key provided by the test publisher. Test booklets must be sent to a central scoring service in order for the client to receive the narrative reports.

The test manual does include some tabled data based on 183 "experienced candidates," containing statistics such as median, mode, mean, variance, and a score distribution with percentile ranks (labeled percentile ratings). The mean, median, mode, and sample variance were 68, 73, 80, and 358, respectively. No breakdowns relative to gender, ethnicity, or experience level of this sample were provided; consequently, it is difficult to determine how comparable this sample is to actual candidates. It is likewise unclear whether or not the summative performance ratings are related in any way to this data set. Almost half of the percentile ranks are marked with an asterisk, referring to a footnote that reads: "Differences due to time factor." This reviewer could not interpret that footnote.

SUMMARY. Because of the lack of detailed information about test development, validity, norming, scoring, and reliability, this reviewer doubts that the test is useful as a hiring, promotion, training, or evaluation device as claimed. The publisher must first conduct thorough job analysis, validity, reliability, and norming studies, and the test manual should then be rewritten with detailed information about test development, validity, scoring, reliability, norming, and reporting in conformity with the AERA/APA/NCME *Standards* (1985).

REVIEWER'S REFERENCE

American Educational Research Association, American Psychological Association, & National Council on Measurement in Education. (1985). *Standards for educational and psychological testing.* Washington, DC: American Psychological Association, Inc.

Review of the Wolfe-Winrow Structured Analysis and Design Concepts Proficiency Test by CYNTHIA ANN DRUVA-ROUSH, Assistant Director, Evaluation and Examination Service, The University of Iowa, Iowa City, IA:

The manual for the Wolfe-Winrow Structured Analysis and Design Concepts Proficiency Test (WWSAD) states that this test is designed to measure a candidate's knowledge of system development methodology, the structured analysis and design process, as well as detailed knowledge of such topics as the data flow diagram and structure chart. It consists of three sections with 15 questions tapping the ability to construct a flow diagram at an interpretation behavioral level, 15 questions concerning system development at a knowledge behavioral level, 8 questions concerning interpretation of a design, again at a knowledge level, and 8 questions concerning definitions of terms used in structured design theory. Although over 60% of the test is in a multiple-choice format, the test is hand scored.

The directions for administration lack standardization procedures. The four problem situations are to be administered in a 35-minute time period. No specific instructions are provided to the test administrator. The only suggestion is that the test participant be seated in a room that is relatively quiet, "preferably without a telephone that might ring during the test." Although the manual suggests that the results from this test may be used to select candidates for programming and systems analysis positions, no evidence is provided to support either the content validity or the construct validity of the test. The *Standards for Educational and Psychological Testing* (AERA, APA, & NCME, 1985) suggest that when tests are used in an employment setting, "content validation should be based on a thorough and explicit definition of the content domain of interest" and that "the domain should be based on a job analysis . . . . If construct-related evidence is to be a major support of validity for personnel selection, there should be evidence for the validity of the test as a measure of a construct, and then evidence for the validity of the construct as a determinant of major factors of job performance." Although programming type skills tap various higher order thinking skills, questions are at a relatively low behavioral objective level. Although the test was first published in 1983, no results from validation studies are reported. The test manual provides an interpretation of various score ranges (e.g., 97%–100% correct = Excellent). The test manual provides a table to convert test scores to percentile rank. No reference is given to the source of this norm group. Each candidate is asked to provide demographic information as to their level of schooling, work experience, and whether they have taken the Structured Analysis and Design test before. The test manual makes no reference to any research linking scores with any of this demographic information. No criterion-related validity is provided. For completion-type items, no interrater reliability is provided. In fact, no reliability figures for any part of the test are provided.

The WWSAD should not be taken seriously as a selection or guidance tool. It fails to meet even the minimum standards needed for reliable and valid measurement. If non-multiple-choice type items are desired, items tapping design and structure analysis problems should be solicited from experts in the field. A procedure should be developed to guarantee reliable scoring of these items. Multiple-choice items should be constructed to tap higher order thinking skills. Item analyses should be performed to help in selecting items of moderate difficulty providing for maximal discrimination between able and less able candidates. Some interpretation beyond reference to a percentile rank based upon an inadequate norm group is needed. As this is to be used as a selection tool, evidence to support criterion-related validity is essential. A criterion essential to adequate performance as a systems analyst, structural designer, should be discerned.

REVIEWER'S REFERENCE

American Educational Research Association, American Psychological Association, & National Council on Measurement in Education. (1985). *Standards for educational and psychological testing.* Washington, DC: American Psychological Association, Inc.

[475]
Wonderlic Personnel Test.

Purpose: "For testing adults in business and industrial situations. It is useful as a selection instrument in hiring and placing applicants and also as an indicator of future promotion and reassignment possibilities."
Population: Adults.
Publication Dates: 1939–89.
Acronym: WPT.
Scores: Total score only.
Administration: Group.
Forms: Available in 16 comparable and similar forms; forms for business, industry, and government: A, B, I, II, IV, V; forms available on restricted basis to business, industry, and government: T-11, T-21, T-31, T-14; forms for those involved in job counseling other than ultimate employers: EM, APT, BPT, CPT; forms restricted to use of educational institutions evaluating the academic potential of students: Scholastic Level Exam (SLE), created in 1982 by reformatting of Forms T-51 and T-71 (4 equivalent forms of SLE now available: IV, V, T-51, T-71); WPT Interpretive Software available for use on IBM-PC/XT/ST/PS-2 and compatibles.
Price Data, 1990: $45 per 25 tests (any form), scoring key, and manual ('83, 28 pages); $65 per 25 large-print version tests, scoring key, and manual; $225 per Interpretive Software (specify 5¹/₄ -inch or 3¹/₂ -inch disk).
Foreign Language and Special Editions: French, Spanish, Cuban, Mexican, Puerto Rican, and large-print editions available.
Time: 12(20) minutes.

Author: E. F. Wonderlic.
Publisher: E. F. Wonderlic Personnel Test, Inc.
Cross References: For reviews by Frank L. Schmidt and Lyle F. Schoenfeldt, see 9:1385 (8 references); see also T3:2638 (24 references) and T2:482 (10 references); for reviews by Robert C. Droege and John P. Foley, Jr., see 7:401 (28 references); for reviews by N. M. Downie and Marvin D. Dunnette, see 6:513 (17 references); see also 5:400 (59 references); for reviews by H. E. Brogden, Charles D. Flory, and Irving Lorge, see 3:269 (7 references); see also 2:1415 (2 references).

TEST REFERENCES

1. Davou, D., & McKelvie, S. J. (1984). Relationship between study habits and performance on an intelligence test with limited and unlimited time. *Psychological Reports, 54,* 367-371.
2. Hines, M., & Shipley, C. (1984). Prenatal exposure to diethylstilbestrol (DES) and the development of sexually dimorphic cognitive abilities and cerebral lateralization. *Developmental Psychology, 20,* 81-94.
3. Deffenbacher, J. L., & Hazaleus, S. L. (1985). Cognitive, emotional, and physiological components of test anxiety. *Cognitive Therapy and Research, 9,* 169-180.
4. Edinger, J. D., Shipley, R. H., Watkins, C. E., Jr., & Hammet, E. B. (1985). Validity of the Wonderlic Personnel Test as a brief IQ measure in psychiatric patients. *Journal of Consulting and Clinical Psychology, 53,* 937-939.
5. Adams, N. A., & Holcomb, W. R. (1986). Analysis of the relationship between anxiety about mathematics and performance. *Psychological Reports, 59,* 943-948.
6. Arnkoff, D. B. (1986). A comparison of the coping and restructuring components of cognitive restructuring. *Cognitive Therapy and Research, 10,* 147-158.
7. Crowley, C., Crowley, D., & Clodfelter, C. (1986). Effects of a self-coping cognitive treatment for test anxiety. *Journal of Counseling Psychology, 33,* 84-86.
8. Hakstian, A. R., Wooley, L. K., & Schroeder, M. L. (1987). Validity of a large-scale assessment battery in an industrial setting. *Educational and Psychological Measurment, 47* (1), 165-178.
9. Raphall, D. (1988). High school conceptual level as an indicator of young adult adjustment. *Journal of Personality Assessment, 52,* 679-690.
10. Frisch, M. B., & Jessop, N. S. (1989). Improving WAIS-R estimates with the Shipley-Harford and Wonderlic Personnel Tests: Need to control for reading ability. *Psychological Reports, 65,* 923-928.

Review of the Wonderlic Personnel Test by MAR-CIA J. BELCHER, Senior Research Associate, Miami-Dade Community College, Office of Institutional Research, Miami, FL:

Since its adaptation in 1938 from the Otis Self-Administering Tests of Mental Ability, The Wonderlic Personnel Test has become a well-known tool in the selection of individuals for a wide variety of jobs throughout business and industry. More recently, the Wonderlic also entered the academic realm, creating the Scholastic Level Exam (SLE) in 1982. The SLE version of the Wonderlic with its two forms (T-51 and T-71) is limited to educational institutions evaluating the academic potential of students.

The Wonderlic Personnel Test has been reviewed many times in the *Mental Measurements Yearbook.* The last reviews by Schmidt (1985) and Schoenfeldt (1985) covered the most recent norms and test manual. This review, therefore, will emphasize the academic uses of the Wonderlic, an area mentioned very little in previous reviews.

All 16 versions of the Wonderlic are designed to measure general mental ability through an omnibus spiraled format of 50 items with a 12-minute time limit. The author states that although the test was designed for business and industry, "because the test score is highly predictive of success in learning situations, it is frequently used as a selection and counseling tool in both industrial training and post secondary education." The manual reports that the Personnel Test correlates .56–.80 with the Aptitude G of the General Aptitude Test Battery and .91–.93 with the Weschler Adult Intelligence Scale—Full Scale IQ.

Test takers encounter a variety of item types, including vocabulary, sentence rearrangement, logic, arithmetic problem solving, and interpretation of proverbs. Some of the items appear to be designed to see how quickly information can be processed (i.e., finding the number of pairs of items that are exact duplicates from a list of names or numbers). Foreign-born test-takers—even those who understand English well—may have particular difficulty with the number of proverbs included (e.g., a rolling stone gathers no moss).

It is unclear how the SLE differs from other versions of the Wonderlic. The test manual simply states that it was created from other versions, and the Wonderlic Technical Report on the SLE provides no other enlightenment. Comparison of Form I and T-51 seems to indicate that the SLE versions are more highly verbal and at a higher level of difficulty than those developed for business and industry. The conversion table at the back of the manual does not include the SLE in the forms listed so level of difficulty cannot be assessed.

The Wonderlic norms are extensive. The 1983 norms are based on over 126,000 individuals. The norms for minimum occupational scores reported for a variety of jobs are less extensive. This set of norms is based on results published in 1966 from 703 companies; in a number of instances the minimum scores are based on data from as few as five companies.

The norms for the SLE version of the Wonderlic are less easy to judge, both because of lack of information and method of presentation. Although the total numbers of scores included for student and job applicants appear satisfactory, numbers for specific job categories appear inadequate in a number of cases. There is also little information on when the data were gathered and who participated. Norms information is particularly critical in this area because the Wonderlic is being used in post-secondary education to decide who has the "ability to benefit" and thus receive federal financial aid. The back of the SLE manual includes tables relating student loan defaults and Wonderlic scores.

The reliability of the Wonderlic is well documented. Test-retest reliabilities range from .82 to .94, even after a period of some years. Alternate form reliabilities range from .73 to .95. No separate information is presented for the SLE.

The validity of the Wonderlic as a predictor of training success and job performance is well-researched and documented, especially by Hunter (1989). There is less evidence that the Wonderlic is equally valid in academic settings where the learning situation may be somewhat different, both in terms of presentation mode and pace of instruction. The SLE Admissions Testing manual notes that the selection decision is different for schools than for employers, because schools are more likely than businesses to be interested in including everyone who has an opportunity for success. The manual urges schools to conduct their own validity studies and develop their own norms in addition to using the student applicant and job applicant scores provided by training program title.

Special mention must be made of the interpretation of scores for those whose native language is not English, especially because increasing numbers of both potential students and employees fit this category. One of the greatest stumbling blocks for this group is that the Wonderlic relies heavily on speed of response in calculating general ability. Toward this end, points are added to compensate for age for any test taker who is 30 or older. Yet no accommodation is made for non-native English speakers who will also process information more slowly.

In this area, then, the Wonderlic fails to meet the *Standards for Educational and Psychological Testing* (AERA, APA, & NCME, 1985). Instances of noncompliance include failure to provide a testing situation designed to minimize threats to test reliability and validity arising from language differences (Standard 13.1) and lack of information necessary for appropriate test use and interpretation with linguistically diverse test takers (Standard 13.3). In addition, recommendations of minimum scores by occupation may not account for language proficiency requirements (Standard 13.5).

Allowing test takers an unlimited amount of time for completing the test would help to alleviate this problem. However, after over 50 years, the manual has yet to provide norms to correspond to this testing situation.

In general, the Wonderlic is a well-established and researched instrument suitable for personnel selection in business situations. Its validity, however, is less grounded in academic settings and for test takers whose first language is not English. In these areas, users should proceed with caution in score use and interpretation.

REVIEWER'S REFERENCES

American Educational Research Association, American Psychological Association, & National Council on Measurement in Education. (1985). *Standards for educational and psychological testing.* Washington, DC: American Psychological Association, Inc.

Schmidt, F. L. (1985). [Review of the Wonderlic Personnel Test.] In J. V. Mitchell, Jr. (Ed.), *The ninth mental measurements yearbook* (pp. 1755-1757). Lincoln, NE: Buros Institute of Mental Measurements.

Schoenfeldt, L. F. (1985). [Review of the Wonderlic Personnel Test.] In J. V. Mitchell, Jr. (Ed.), *The ninth mental measurements yearbook* (pp. 1757-1758). Lincoln, NE: Buros Institute of Mental Measurements.

Hunter, J. E. (1989). *The Wonderlic Personnel Test as a predictor of training success and job performance.* Northfield, IL: E. F. Wonderlic Personnel Test, Inc.

[476]
Work Personality Profile.

Purpose: Designed to "assess fundamental work role requirements that are essential to achievement and maintenance of suitable employment."
Population: Vocational rehabilitation clients.
Publication Date: 1986.
Acronym: WPP.
Scores, 16: Acceptance of Work Role, Ability to Profit from Instruction or Correction, Work Persistence, Work Tolerance, Amount of Supervision Required, Extent Trainee Seeks Assistance from Supervisor, Degree of Comfort or Anxiety with Supervisor, Appropriateness of Personal Relations with Supervisor, Teamwork, Ability to Socialize with Co-Workers, Social Communication Skills, Task Orientation, Social Skills, Work Motivation, Work Conformance, Personal Presentation.
Administration: Individual.
Price Data, 1986: $5 per manual (40 pages); $10 per floppy disk; $5 per 50 tests; $17 per specimen set (including manual, diskette, and 50 tests).
Time: (5–10) minutes.
Comments: Observational ratings by vocational evaluators; to be administered after one week (20–30 hours) in evaluation setting; available on diskette.
Authors: Brian Bolton and Richard Roessler.
Publisher: Arkansas Research & Training Center in Vocational Rehabilitation.

Review of the Work Personality Profile by RALPH O. MUELLER, Assistant Professor of Educational Research and Measurement, and PAULA J. DUPUY, Assistant Professor of Counselor and Human Services Education, University of Toledo, Toledo, OH:

The Work Personality Profile (WPP) was designed as a comprehensive observational test to assess strengths and weaknesses of the work personality of disabled clients at vocational rehabilitation centers. Results from the WPP are meant to serve as a basis for (*a*) the assignment of clients to remedial programs, (*b*) the measurement of improvement in specific behaviors, and (*c*) the matching of individual clients with specific jobs. Evaluators rate an individual on 58 items (4-point Likert-type scales) after the client's completion of 1 week (20–30 hours) in the vocational evaluation setting. Raters score and summarize the client's results on a well-organized report form that provides space for (*a*) personal information, (*b*) a graphical representation of raw scores for criterion-referenced diagnostic purposes, (*c*) approximate percentile equivalents for norm-referenced applications, and (*d*) the identification of specific employability problem areas. A floppy disk can be purchased that allows the evaluator to rate clients and produce report forms on an IBM-compatible personal computer. No informa-

tion regarding the parallelism of the two forms is provided as dictated by the *Standards for Educational and Psychological Testing*, Standard 4.6 (American Educational Research Association, American Psychological Association, & National Council on Measurement in Education, 1985, p. 34).

SCALE DEVELOPMENT. The development of the WPP is largely based on the authors' previously published work (Roessler & Bolton, 1983). The instrument was revised twice before the current version was published. Averaged results on various items form 11 rationally derived scales (Acceptance of Work Role, Ability to Profit from Instruction or Correction, Work Persistence, Work Tolerance, Amount of Supervision Required, Extent Trainee Seeks Assistance from Supervisor, Degree of Comfort or Anxiety with Supervisor, Appropriateness of Personal Relations with Supervisor, Teamwork, Ability to Socialize with Co-Workers, and Social Communication Skills).

Five additional scales (Task Orientation, Social Skills, Work Motivation, Work Conformance, and Personal Presentation) were developed from a factor analysis of the 58 items using data from the normative sample. Evaluation of these scales is difficult, because a thorough justification for, and specific results from, the analysis are missing in the manual. In addition, the descriptions of the factors (p. 9) are often overlapping (contrary to the *Standards*, Standard 1.8, AERA, APA, & NCME, 1985, p. 15), leading to possible misinterpretations. For example, how well a client works in group situations is given as a characteristic of both Social Skills and Work Motivation.

NORMS. The authors describe the normative sample (*n* = 243) as "large" and "excellent." This is hard to judge because the year of the data collection is not given and the description of the sample does not include participants' race or socio-economic background (see the *Standards*, Standard 4.4, p. 33). Specific disabilities and their severities are not reported (contrary to the *Standards*, Standard 14.2, p. 79). Instead, the authors classify members of the normative sample by three broad disabling conditions (i.e., physical, intellectual, emotional).

RELIABILITY. Estimates of internal consistency and intra- and interrater reliability (without standard errors of measurement) are presented. Acceptable alpha coefficients (between .71 and .92) are based on the normative sample. Adequate intrarater reliability estimates after 2 (*n* = 79), 4 (*n* = 61), and 6 weeks (*n* = 25) of observation are generally in the .75 to .95 range. Estimates of interrater reliability are consistently low. For example, coefficients for the 11 rationally derived scales range from .17 to .60 (median of .48) for ratings completed after 2 weeks of observation. Although the authors recommend the averaging of WPP results across two or more independent evaluators (p. 15, 22), this caution should have been stated up front rather than given in the reliability and summary sections only.

VALIDITY. Evidence of content-related validity is provided in the development section of the manual. The authors' decision to include empirically based (in addition to the rationally derived) scales implies limited construct validity of the rational scales. Judgements regarding the criterion-related validity (concurrent and predictive) are based on data from a sample of 181 clients in a comprehensive residential rehabilitation center. No demographic description of this sample is given (contrary to the *Standards*, Standard 1.5, p. 14) and only 8 of the 16 scales were used in the analyses. Relatively weak evidence of concurrent validity is provided by reporting low to moderate correlations of WPP scales with the General Aptitude Test Battery (GATB), United States Employment Service Interest Inventory (USES-II), and the Sixteen Personality Factor Questionnaire (16PF). Although interpretations of these correlations concentrate on differences between male and female clients, only an overall correlation matrix is provided, making it difficult to ascertain if/how gender affects validity.

The authors' claim of "impressive" predictive validity is questionable. Significantly higher mean scores were found on only three WPP scales for a group of clients ($n = 61$) who completed vocational training programs versus a combined group of 112 clients who did not complete such programs for various reasons. In addition, vocational instructors rated program completers on (*a*) general vocational competencies and (*b*) competencies that were specific to a particular training area (e.g., custodial, clerk responsibilities). Only four scales moderately correlated with ratings of general competencies. In support of predictive validity, however, none of the WPP scales correlated significantly with the ratings of specific competencies.

MANUAL CONTENT. Overall, the manual contains adequate coverage of the development and psychometric properties of the first published version of the WPP. However, a separate section specifically for test users that includes directions for administration, scoring, and interpretation is missing. Such a section might help to reduce some of the inconsistencies between evaluators' ratings. The overall tone of the manual implies the WPP is a comprehensive and sufficient instrument for diagnosing clients and reaching intervention decisions based on a client's work personality. This can be a dangerous presumption of any diagnostic tool. Specifically, the manual does not refer to the involvement of the client in intervention decisions, the need for multifaceted assessment, and the possible situational dependence of WPP results.

SUMMARY. The WPP is an easy-to-use, short, economical observational instrument designed to assess work personalities of disabled clients in rehabilitation centers. Its major purpose is to identify employability weaknesses that are to be used to generate and evaluate intervention strategies. Although the instrument might serve as a helpful criterion-referenced diagnostic tool, its usefulness for norm-referenced applications is limited due to a weak description of the normative sample. The evaluator should be aware of other shortcomings (lack of justification for item selection and scale composition, low interrater reliability, inadequate description of the validation sample, and insufficient validity evidence) and should use the WPP only with caution.

REVIEWERS' REFERENCES

Roessler, R., & Bolton, B. (1983). Assessment and enhancement of functional vocational capabilities: A five year research strategy. Richard J. Baker Memorial Monograph Series. *Vocational Evaluation and Work Adjustment Association*, 1.

American Educational Research Association, American Psychological Association, & National Council on Measurement in Education. (1985). *Standards for educational and psychological testing*. Washington, DC: American Psychological Association, Inc.

[477]
Written Language Assessment.
Purpose: Assesses writing ability.
Population: Grades 3–12.
Publication Date: 1989.
Acronym: WLA.
Scores, 5: General Writing Ability, Productivity, Word Complexity, Readability, Written Language Quotient.
Administration: Group.
Price Data, 1989: $58 per complete kit including 25 each of 3 writing record forms, 25 scoring/profile forms, manual ('89, 111 pages), and hand counter; $15 per 25 each of 3 writing record forms; $8 per 25 scoring/profile forms; $20 per manual; $12 per hand counter; $20 per specimen set.
Time: (45–60) minutes.
Authors: J. Jeffrey Grill and Margaret M. Kirwin.
Publisher: Academic Therapy Publications.

Review of the Written Language Assessment by STEPHEN JURS, *Professor of Educational Psychology, Research, and Social Foundations, College of Education and Allied Professions, University of Toledo, Toledo, OH:*

The Written Language Assessment (WLA) is a measure of writing ability that consists of three writing tasks. The tasks include expressive writing, instructive writing, and creative writing. Including writing for different purposes is intended to provide a broad assessment of writing ability. A strength of this instrument is that it is a direct, realistic assessment of written discourse.

The WLA is intended primarily for ages 8 to 18 but it can be used effectively with older examinees. Normative data, however, do not extend beyond age 19 years 11 months. The writing forms present interesting tasks. The expressive and creative writing tasks provide intriguing pictures as prompts. Each form is one page long. Students are to write on the front and back, and additional pages can be attached if needed.

Teachers can give the test to groups or to individuals in about 15 to 20 minutes. Scoring takes approximately 15 minutes per examinee. This speed of scoring can be achieved with minimal practice. The scoring consists of counting the number of words, sentences, and syllables and rating the written response on rhetoric, legibility, and overall quality.

Several scores are derived from this information. The General Writing Ability score represents such things as style, fluency, eloquence, legibility, and overall quality. The Productivity score is the total number of words from all three writing samples. The Word Complexity score is the total number of syllables minus the total number of words. The Readability score is based on the commonly used Fry graph for estimating readability.

Raw scores are transformed to scaled scores that have a mean of 10 and standard deviation of 3, and then to percentile ranks. There are conversion tables in the manual for ages 8 years to 19 years, 11 months. The sum of the scaled scores is then converted to a Written Language Quotient which has a mean of 100 and a standard deviation of 15. Percentile ranks are also available for the Written Language Quotient.

The authors recommend that placement decisions be based on the composite score (the Written Language Quotient) rather than on the subtest scores. They also caution against comparing the composite score to other normed tests, such as intelligence tests, that use the same mean and standard deviation. This warning would not be necessary if the composite score was not called a quotient and if different values were used for the mean and standard deviation.

The test forms and the manual are well designed and easy to use. Technical information is presented in clear language that is understandable to those with limited background in statistics. The development of the WLA and its rationale are well described.

Concerns about the WLA are recognized by the authors and are addressed to some extent in the manual. For example, the rating of general writing ability includes ratings for rhetoric, legibility, and overall quality. Some may argue that the legibility of handwriting and the judgment of overall quality should not be weighted equally.

Ratings for rhetoric on a scale of illiterate, poor, good, excellent, and superb cause some difficulty because raters find many examinees to be somewhere between good and excellent, but the answer form does not encourage score values between the

numbers on the 0 to 4 rating scale. Fortunately, the manual does provide five examples of scored tests which should enhance the consistency of the ratings.

It should be noted that examinee responses containing dialogue also contain shorter sentences and substantially more punctuation and one-syllable words. While these responses may be very effective, they will still receive lower scores because of the WLA's emphasis on word complexity and readability in scoring.

Normative data are based on 1,025 students in grades 3 through 12 who were tested in 1987–88. The students were from upstate New York, 46% of them from rural areas, and 94% of them white. The norms for different ages were based on as few as 30 (8-year-olds) to as many as 124 (13-year-olds). These norms may not be relevant for many schools.

Internal consistency reliability coefficients are presented for each age level. Median coefficients are General Writing Ability, .86; Productivity, .81; Word Complexity, .81; Readability, .61; and Written Language Quotient, .90. Three studies of interrater reliability indicate that over 95% of the judgments of two ratings of General Writing Ability are within one point of each other.

What the authors call criterion-related validity evidence, which many will recognize more readily as evidence of concurrent validity, is based on correlations with the Picture Story Language Test ($n = 158$). All subtests of the WLA were significantly correlated with the Words and Abstract-Concrete Scale scores of the Picture Story Language Test but were not correlated with the Syntax Quotient score. Construct validity data consists of moderate intercorrelations among the WLA subtests and moderate correlations with age of examinee.

Students in regular classes ($n = 18$) had significantly higher means on the WLA subtests than did students ($n = 18$) in special education resource rooms. This reviewer believes that, unfortunately, an inappropriate statistical analysis was used in this study. Multivariate analysis of variance should have been used instead of the univariate repeated measures analysis of variance that was reported.

The Written Language Assessment is a new test that is limited by inadequate normative data and a lack of studies supporting its usefulness in a variety of applications. The WLA requires an actual written product, can be used comfortably in a classroom setting, and has straightforward scoring procedures. It has the potential to be an important component of a school testing program.

Review of the Written Language Assessment by MARY ROSS MORAN, Professor of Special Education, University of Kansas, Lawrence, KS:

OVERVIEW. In its direct, untimed, spaced, multiple sampling in natural settings, and in its attempt to combine holistic (overall impression) and analytic (separate rating categories) scoring, the Written Language Assessment (WLA) incorporates some current views of writing assessment. The test is forward-looking in using "structured behavior sample tests" (American Educational Research Association, American Psychological Association, & National Council on Measurement in Education, 1985; p. 4). Nevertheless, the WLA scoring system—founded on no model of writing components and dependent on judgments unsupported by criteria—raises serious validity and reliability questions. In the hands of the untrained raters the authors address, the instrument could not provide useful information about student writing competencies. The ways in which scoring categories were derived and the directions for assigning scores depart so extensively from standard practices that the instrument cannot be recommended for the purposes stated in the manual.

Normed on 1,025 New Yorkers, excluding special education students and underrepresenting minorities, the WLA is introduced as "appropriate for use in making decisions about students' instruction and their instructional placements" (p. 19). However, this statement is contradicted later in the manual. The interpretation section states that "these scores do not . . . provide information that can be used directly for instructional planning" (p. 39). Furthermore, as reliabilities are reported, the manual recommends that "only the WLQ [Written Language Quotient] be used for making placement decisions" (p. 57).

Neither instructional nor placement decisions should be based on an instrument that purports to measure the complex competencies involved in composition yet is to be "scored and interpreted by . . . classroom teachers, reading or speech and language specialists, school psychologists or psychometrists, school administrators, and others familiar with the characteristics of standardized tests" (p. 21) without training for the task. Reasons for differing with the notion that untrained professional persons could reliably score writing samples can be found in any account of large-scale holistic reading sessions. Standard practice calls for intensive training for the rating task (National Assessment of Educational Progress, 1985).

Furthermore, commonly used procedures require two raters for each paper, three in cases of disagreement. The WLA is scored by a single judge, a practice associated with low reliabilities (Cooper, 1984).

ADMINISTRATION. Tasks consist of three separate untimed writing sessions in which students are given two combined verbal and visual prompts and one that is verbal alone. Students work unassisted by dictionaries or other sources; examiners are instructed to offer no suggestions and to respond to questions by saying that decisions must be made by writers. Students write on lined paper on which the prompts appear.

Prompts consist of black and white photographs with captions read aloud by examiners as students follow along. Sample 1 reads: "Here is a picture of [two intertwined] hands. Look at it, and look at your own hands. Write about hands." The Sample 3 photograph shows a young woman reclining on a sofa covered by a heavy quilt on which a cat is partially in view, facing the camera. The direction reads: "Look at this picture. Make up a story about *the cat* in it." Sample 2, on lined paper without a photograph, instructs examinees to: "Write how you would tell a little kid about the danger of fire." Prompt 2 could introduce invalid sources of variance if some writers reduce their language complexity when they address younger children.

SCORING. In accord with APA recommendations, the WLA prompts were field tested before norming. However, in standard practice, the field-test essays should then become the source of an empirical scoring rubric to be applied to future testing with those prompts. For example, one anchor paper is selected from field trials to represent each assigned value (from 0 to 4 for the WLA) to show how a typical paper at that value would look; raters then combine anchor papers with a set of criteria to assign values. The WLA did not follow this practice; instead of anchor papers representing each score value, five varied scoring samples are provided in an appendix.

The WLA further departs from standard practice for analytic scoring, which calls for repeated passes through each essay. Typically, raters read a paper once for each separate scoring category so that a rating can be given without contamination by other categories. Thus, "an analytic reading can take 4, 5, 6 times longer than holistic" (Cooper, 1984, p. 36). In contrast, the WLA manual states: "The GWA ratings require one or two fast but careful readings of each writing sample, followed by your assigning ratings to each sample for each of the three categories" (p. 25).

VALIDITY. Although APA standards recommend that the content domain be empirically derived by examining responses to field trials or that measurement categories be subjected to expert consensus, neither practice is reported for the WLA. Nor do scoring categories represent clear definitions of the universe represents; the Rhetoric category is defined several ways, including "style . . . literary qualities and eloquence" without accompanying criteria. In contrast, a state manual for assessing writing devotes four pages to empirically derived criteria for rhetoric, and instructive writing alone is evaluated on voice, information, organization, and controlling idea (California Department of Education, 1986, pp. VI-14-17).

In the WLA, both instructive information (p. 40) and organization (p. 42) are to be evaluated informally rather than as part of the test. If such substantive components of the instructive writing task are omitted from the scoring rubric, content validity is compromised. Experts would not be expected to agree that rating legibility and counting syllables, words, and sentences (nonoperationally defined as *a complete thought*) are more important to instructive writing than informative content and organization.

The manual claims that content validity is "evident because . . . the content . . . consists only of writing" (p. 60), but "the validity of direct assessment cannot simply be presumed because it requires writing" (Cooper, 1984, p. 16). The categories the developers chose to score are not satisfactorily justified. In particular, the novel scoring category of readability, according to the *APA Standards* (AERA, APA, & NCME, 1985), should have been documented by research.

Construct validity is discussed in terms of assumptions that "the four WLA scores represent measures of different aspects of writing" and that performance is "better among older students than among younger students" (p. 61). Both points are addressed statistically without reference to conceptual models of writing components or developmental data from writing research.

RELIABILITY. Internal consistency and interrater reliability are reported; neither test-retest nor intrarater reliabilities are mentioned. The National Assessment of Educational Progress (1980) obtains inter-rater reliability on 10% of essays to be scored, and approaches 80% agreement across raters. WLA exact reliabilities are reported for 150 of some 3,000 norm-group papers as .44 to .65 for raters identified as "trained in scoring the WLA and . . . experienced at the time of the studies" (p. 57). Because the WLA manual presents no training requirements, a more legitimate test of interrater reliability would have been accomplished with randomly selected teachers, school psychologists, and speech-language pathologists. Without training in the WLA or detailed scoring criteria, test users cannot be expected to provide more than unsupported judgment calls.

In conclusion, the WLA represents a welcome effort to move writing evaluation in the direction of direct assessment of product, if not process. However, the attempt fails to yield a useful instrument because what is measured is not agreed by experts as representing important writing competencies, and the lack of specific criteria or anchor papers renders the scoring inappropriate even for experienced holistic raters, much less the untrained professional persons said to be the target users of the WLA.

REVIEWER'S REFERENCES

National Assessment of Educational Progress. (1980). *Writing achievement 1969–79*. Supt. of Documents No. ED 1.118: 10-W-010203. Denver: NAEP.

Cooper, P. L. (1984). *The assessment of writing ability: A review of research*. Educational Testing Service, Princeton, NJ. (ERIC Document Reproduction Service No. ED 250332).

California Assessment Program. (1986). *Writing assessment handbook*. Sacramento: California Department of Education.

American Educational Research Association, American Psychological Association, & National Council on Measurement in Education. (1985). *Standards for educational and psychological testing*. Washington, DC: American Psychological Association, Inc.

CONTRIBUTING TEST REVIEWERS

PHILLIP L. ACKERMAN, Associate Professor of Psychology, University of Minnesota, Minneapolis, MN

MARK ALBANESE, Adjunct Associate Professor of Biostatistics and Educational Statistics and Director, Office of Consultation and Research in Medical Education, The University of Iowa College of Medicine, Iowa City, IA

BRUCE K. ALCORN, Director of Certification, Teachers College, Ball State University, Muncie, IN

LAWRENCE M. ALEAMONI, Associate Head and Professor of Educational Psychology, University of Arizona, Tucson, AZ

NANCY L. ALLEN, Research Scientist, Educational Testing Service, Princeton, NJ

SARAH J. ALLEN, Assistant Professor of Psychology, The University of Rhode Island, Kingston, RI

ANNE ANASTASI, Professor Emeritus of Psychology, Fordham University, Bronx, NY

DAVID O. ANDERSON, Senior Measurement Statistician, Educational Testing Service, Princeton, NJ

JOHN O. ANDERSON, Faculty of Education, University of Victoria, Victoria, B.C., Canada

JERRILYN. V. ANDREWS, Coordinator Research/Statistics, Department of Educational Accountability, Montgomery County Public Schools, Rockville, MD

FRANCIS X. ARCHAMBAULT, JR., Professor of Educational Psychology, and Department Head, The University of Connecticut, Storrs, CT

ROBERT P. ARCHER, Professor of Psychiatry and Behavioral Sciences, Eastern Virginia Medical School, Norfolk, VA

PHILIP ASH, Director, Ash, Blackstone and Cates, Blacksburg, VA

E. JACK ASHER, JR., Professor Emeritus of Psychology, Western Michigan University, Kalamazoo, MI

JEFFREY A. ATLAS, Deputy Chief Psychologist and Assistant Clinical Professor, Bronx Children's Hospital, Albert Einstein College of Medicine, Bronx, NY

JAMES T. AUSTIN, Assistant Professor, University of Illinois, Urbana, IL

STEPHEN N. AXFORD, Faculty Member, University of Phoenix, Colorado Campus, Aurora, CO, and School Psychologist, Academy District Twenty, Colorado Springs, CO

J. DOUGLAS AYERS, Professor Emeritus, University of Victoria, Victoria, B.C., Canada

GLEN P. AYLWARD, Associate Professor of Pediatrics and Psychiatry, Southern Illinois University School of Medicine, Springfield, IL

PATRICIA A. BACHELOR, Associate Professor of Psychology, California State University, Long Beach, CA

LYLE F. BACHMAN, Professor of Applied Linguistics, University of California at Los Angeles, Los Angeles, CA

ELLEN H. BACON, Assistant Professor of Human Services, Western Carolina University, Cullowhee, NC

K. DENISE BANE, Graduate Student, North Carolina State University, Raleigh, NC

NICHOLAS W. BANKSON, Professor and Chair, Department of Communication Disorders, Boston University, Boston, MA

LAURA L. B. BARNES, Assistant Professor Applied Behavioral Studies, Oklahoma State University, Stillwater, OK

DAVID W. BARNETT, Professor of School Psychology and Counseling, University of Cincinnati, Cincinnati, OH

ANDRÉS BARONA, Associate Professor of Psychology in Education, Arizona State University, Tempe, AZ

WILLIAM M. BART, Professor of Educational Psychology, University of Minnesota, Minneapolis, MN

ERNEST A. BAUER, Research, Evaluation, and Testing Consultant, Oakland Schools, Waterford, MI

MICHAEL D. BECK, President, BETA, Inc., Pleasantville, NY

MARCIA J. BELCHER, Senior Research Associate, Miami-Dade Community College, Office of Institutional Research, Miami, FL

CAMILLA PERSSON BENBOW, Professor of Psychology, Iowa State University, Ames, IA

KATHRYN M. BENES, Assistant Professor of Psychology, Iowa State University, Ames, IA

JERI BENSON, Associate Professor of Measurement, Statistics and Evaluation, University of Maryland, College Park, MD

PHILIP G. BENSON, Associate Professor of Management, New Mexico State University, Las Cruces, NM

STEPHEN L. BENTON, Associate Professor of Educational Psychology, Kansas State University, Manhattan, KS

H. JOHN BERNARDIN, University Professor of Research, Florida Atlantic University, Boca Raton, FL

JEAN-JACQUES BERNIER, Professor, Department of Measurement and Evaluation, University of Laval, Quebec, Canada

FREDERICK BESSAI, Professor of Education, University of Regina, Regina, Saskatchewan, Canada

LISA G. BISCHOFF, Assistant Professor of Educational Psychology, University of Nebraska-Lincoln, Lincoln, NE

BRUCE H. BISKIN, Senior Psychometrician, American Institute of Certified Public Accountants, New York, NY

MARTHA W. BLACKWELL, Associate Professor of Psychology, Auburn University at Montgomery, Montgomery, AL

LYNN S. BLISS, Professor of Communication Disorders and Sciences, Wayne State University, Detroit, MI

CAROL A. BOLIEK, Assistant Research Scientist, Speech and Hearing Sciences, University of Arizona, Tucson, AZ

BRIAN BOLTON, Professor, Arkansas Research and Training Center in Vocational Rehabilitation, University of Arkansas, Fayetteville, AR

R. A. BORNSTEIN, Associate Professor of Psychiatry, Neurosurgery and Neurology, The Ohio State University, Columbus, OH

GREGORY J. BOYLE, Senior Lecturer in Psychology, University of Queensland, St. Lucia, Queensland, Australia

BRUCE A. BRACKEN, Professor of Psychology, Memphis State University, Memphis, TN

JEFFREY P. BRADEN, Associate Professor of Psychology, San Jose State University, San Jose, CA

JOHN C. BRANTLEY, Professor and Chair, School Psychology Program, University of North Carolina, Chapel Hill, NC

FREDERICK G. BROWN, Professor of Psychology, Iowa State University, Ames, IA

JAMES D. BROWN, Director, Enlish Language Institute, Honolulu, HI

ROBERT D. BROWN, Carl A. Happold Distinguished Professor of Educational Psychology, University of Nebraska-Lincoln, Lincoln, NE

SCOTT W. BROWN, Associate Professor of Educational Psychology, University of Connecticut, Storrs, CT

VIRGINIA L. BROWN, Director, Institute for Research and Community Service, University of Pennsylvania, Indiana, PA

RICHARD BROZOVICH, Director, Psychology and Learning Clinic, Oakland Schools, Waterford, MI

KAREN S. BUDD, Associate Professor of Psychology, Illinois Institute of Technology, Chicago, IL

MICHAEL B. BUNCH, Vice President, Measurement Incorporated, Durham, NC

MARY ANNE BUNDA, Director, University Assessment, Western Michigan University, Kalamazoo, MI

LINDA K. BUNKER, Professor of Education and Associate Dean for Academic and Student Affairs, Curry School of Education, University of Virginia, Charlottesville, VA

PAUL C. BURNETT, Lecturer in Psychology, Queensland University of Technology—Kelvin Grove Campus, Brisbane, Australia

BRENDA R. BUSH, Psychologist, Beatrice State Developmental Center, Beatrice, NE

R. T. BUSSE, Graduate Student, Department of Educational Psychology, University of Wisconsin-Madison, Madison, WI

KATHARINE G. BUTLER, Professor and Chair, Communication Sciences and Disorders, Division of Special Education & Rehabilitation, Syracuse University, Syracuse, NY

CAMERON J. CAMP, Professor of Psychology, University of New Orleans, New Orleans, LA

KAREN T. CAREY, Assistant Professor of Psychology, California State University, Fresno, Fresno, CA

CINDY I. CARLSON, Associate Professor of Educational Psychology, University of Texas at Austin, Austin, TX

JANET F. CARLSON, Assistant Professor of Education, Graduate School of Education, Fairfield University, Fairfield, CT

JOELLEN V. CARLSON, Director of Testing Standards, New York Stock Exchange, New York, NY

ROGER D. CARLSON, Visiting Associate Professor of Psychology, Whitman College, Walla Walla, WA

JAMES C. CARMER, Clinical Psychologist, Immanuel Medical Center, Omaha, NE

C. DALE CARPENTER, Professor of Special Education, Western Carolina University, Cullowhee, NC

CAROLYN CHANEY, Associate Professor, Speech and Communication Studies, School of Humanities, San Francisco State University, San Francisco, CA

SANDRA L. CHRISTENSON, Associate Professor of Educational Psychology, University of Minnesota, Minneapolis, MN

JOSEPH C. CIECHALSKI, Assistant Professor of Counselor Education, East Carolina University, Greenville, NC

GREGORY J. CIZEK, Assistant Professor of Educational Research and Measurement, University of Toledo, Toledo, OH

RICHARD M. CLARK, Chair, Department of Educational Psychology and Statistics, State University of New York at Albany, Albany, NY

LARRY COCHRAN, Professor of Counselling Psychology, The University of British Columbia, Vancouver, B.C., Canada

WILLIAM E. COFFMAN, E. F. Lindquist Professor Emeritus, University of Iowa, Iowa City, IA

JUDITH C. CONGER, Director of Clinical Training, Purdue University, West Lafayette, IN

COLLIE W. CONOLEY, Associate Professor of Educational Psychology, University of Nebraska-Lincoln, Lincoln, NE

NORMAN A. CONSTANTINE, Director of Assessment Services, Far West Laboratory for Educational Research and Development, San Francisco, CA, and Lecturer in Pediatrics, Stanford University School of Medicine, Stanford, CA

ALICIA SKINNER COOK, Professor of Human Development and Family Studies, Colorado State University, Fort Collins, CO

ROBERT B. COOTER, JR., Associate Professor of Elementary Education, Brigham Young University, Provo, UT

ALICE J. CORKILL, Assistant Professor of Psychology, University of Western Ontario, London, Ontario, Canada

MERITH COSDEN, Associate Professor of Education, University of California, Santa Barbara, CA

KEVIN D. CREHAN, Associate Professor of Educational Psychology, University of Nevada, Las Vegas, Las Vegas, NV

MICHELLE M. CREIGHTON, Doctoral Student in School Psychology, University of Minnesota, Minneapolis, MN

LINDA CROCKER, Professor in Foundations of Education, University of Florida, Gainesville, FL

WILLIAM L. CURLETTE, Professor of Educational Foundations, Georgia State University, Atlanta, GA

RIK CARL D'AMATO, Associate Professor of School Psychology and Director of the School Psychology Programs in the Division of Professional Psychology, University of Northern Colorado, Greeley, CO

RALPH F. DARR, JR., Professor of Education, Department of Educational Foundations, The University of Akron, Akron, OH

BRANDON DAVIS, Research Fellow, Ball State Neuropsychology Laboratory, Ball State University, Muncie, IN

STEVEN F. DAVIS, Professor of Psychology, Emporia State University, Emporia, KS

LINDA S. DAY, Director of Clinical Services, Program in Communication Disorders, University of Missouri-Columbia, Columbia, MO

AYRES G. D'COSTA, Associate Professor of Education, The Ohio State University, Columbus, OH

WILLIAM L. DEATON, Professor and Associate

Dean, College of Education, Auburn University, Auburn University, AL

GABRIEL DELLA-PIANA, Professor of Educational Psychology, University of Utah, Salt Lake City, UT

GERALD E. DEMAURO, Senior Examiner, Educational Testing Service, Princeton, NJ

LIZANNE DESTEFANO, Assistant Professor of Educational Psychology, University of Illinois at Urbana-Champaign, Champaign, IL

DENISE M. DEZOLT, Instructor in School Psychology, Illinois State University, Normal, IL

ESTHER E. DIAMOND, Educational and Psychological Consultant, Evanston, IL

ALLAN O. DIEFENDORF, Associate Professor, Indiana School of Medicine, Indianapolis, IN

DAVID N. DIXON, Professor and Department Chair, Department of Counseling Psychology and Guidance Services, Ball State University, Muncie, IN

DAN DOUGLAS, Associate Professor of English, Iowa State University, Ames, IA

E. THOMAS DOWD, Professor and Director of Counseling Psychology, Kent State University, Kent, OH

ROBERT J. DRUMMOND, Professor of Education and Program Director, Counselor Education, University of North Florida, Jacksonville, FL

CYNTHIA ANN DRUVA-ROUSH, Assistant Director, Evaluation and Examination Service, The University of Iowa, Iowa City, IA

STEPHEN B. DUNBAR, Associate Professor of Measurement and Statistics, The University of Iowa, Iowa City, IA

PAULA J. DUPUY, Assistant Professor of Counselor and Human Services Education, University of Toledo, Toledo, OH

RON EDWARDS, Professor of Psychology, University of Southern Mississippi, Hattiesburg, MS

JONATHAN EHRLICH, Speech-Language Pathologist, Somerset, NJ

ARTHUR S. ELLEN, Assistant Professor of Psychology, Pace University, New York, NY

STEPHEN N. ELLIOTT, Professor of Educational Psychology, University of Wisconsin-Madison, Madison, WI

GEORGE ENGELHARD, JR., Associate Professor of Educational Studies, Emory University, Atlanta, GA

JOHN M. ENGER, Professor of Education, Arkansas State University, State University, AR

WILLIAM P. ERCHUL, Associate Professor of Psychology and Director of the School Psychology Program, North Carolina State University, Raleigh, NC

JAMES B. ERDMANN, Associate Dean, Jefferson Medical College, Thomas Jefferson University, Philadelphia, PA

DEBORAH ERICKSON, Associate Professor of Education, Niagara University, Niagara University, NY

JOAN ERSHLER, Postdoctoral Student, School Psychology Program, University of Wisconsin-Madison, Madison, WI

JULIAN FABRY, Clinical Supervisor, Department of Rehabilitation Psychology, Immanuel Medical Center, Omaha, NE

R. W. FAUNCE, Consulting Psychologist, Minneapolis, MN

STEVEN FERRARA, Chief, Measurement, Statistics, and Evaluation Section, Maryland State Department of Education, Division of Instruction, Baltimore, MD

MAYNARD D. FILTER, Head, Speech Pathology and Audiology, James Madison University, Harrisonburg, VA

DIANE BILLINGS FINDLEY, Doctoral Candidate, Louisiana State University, Baton Rouge, LA

CARMEN J. FINLEY, Research Psychologist, Retired, Santa Rosa, CA

ANNE R. FITZPATRICK, Manager of Applied Research, CTB Macmillan/McGraw-Hill, Monterey, CA

ROBERT FITZPATRICK, Consulting Industrial Psychologist, Pittsburgh, PA

STEPHEN G. FLANAGAN, Clinical Associate Professor of Psychology, The University of North Carolina at Chapel Hill, Chapel Hill, NC

JOHN W. FLEENOR, Research Associate, Center for Creative Leadership, Greensboro, NC

LAURIE FORD, Assistant Professor of Educational Psychology, Texas A&M University, College Station, TX

JIM C. FORTUNE, Professor of Educational Research and Evaluation, College of Education, Virginia Tech, Blacksburg, VA

ROBERT K. GABLE, Professor of Educational Psychology, and Associate Director, Bureau of Educational Research and Service, University of Connecticut, Storrs, CT

LENA R. GADDIS, Assistant Professor of Educational Psychology, Northern Arizona University, Flagstaff, AZ

GLORIA A. GALVIN, School Psychologist, Dodgeville School District, Dodgeville, WI

CALVIN P. GARBIN, Associate Professor of Psychology, University of Nebraska-Lincoln, Lincoln, NE

ALAN GARFINKEL, Associate Professor of Spanish and Foreign Language Education, Purdue University, West Lafayette, IN

KURT F. GEISINGER, Professor of Psychology, Fordham University, Bronx, NY

RONALD B. GILLAM, Assistant Professor of Communicative Disorders, University of Missouri-Columbia, Columbia, MO

JOHN A. GLOVER, Director of Research, Teachers College, Ball State University, Muncie, IN

BERT A. GOLDMAN, Professor of Education, University of North Carolina, Greensboro, NC

RONALD H. GOOD, III, Assistant Professor of Counseling and Educational Psychology, College of Education, University of Oregon, Eugene, OR

ELLIOT L. GORY, Psychologist, Getz School for the Developmentally Disabled, Tempe, AZ

HARRISON G. GOUGH, Professor of Psychology, Emeritus, University of California, Berkeley, CA

JOHN R. GRAHAM, Professor of Psychology, Kent State University, Kent, OH

STEVE GRAHAM, Associate Professor of Special Education, University of Maryland, College Park, MD

FRANK M. GRESHAM, Professor of Psychology, Hofstra University, Hempstead, NY

J. JEFFREY GRILL, Associate Professor of Special Education, Carroll College, Helena, MT

RICHARD E. GUEST, Assistant Professor of Human Development and Family Studies, Colorado State University, Fort Collins, CO

SAMI GULGOZ, Assistant Professor of Psychology, Auburn University at Montgomery, Montgomery, AL

ROSA A. HAGIN, Professor of Psychological and Educational Services, Graduate School of Education, Fordham University-Lincoln Center, New York, NY

THOMAS M. HALADYNA, Professor of Educational Psychology, Arizona State University West, Phoenix, AZ

BRUCE W. HALL, Chair, Department of Educational Measurement and Research, University of South Florida, Tampa, FL

CATHY W. HALL, Assistant Professor of Psychology, East Carolina University, Greenville, NC

PENELOPE K. HALL, Associate Professor of Speech Pathology and Audiology, The University of Iowa, Iowa City, IA

RONALD K. HAMBLETON, Professor of Education and Psychology, University of Massachusetts at Amherst, Amherst, NY

WADE L. HAMIL, Research Assistant, University of Oklahoma, Norman, OK

GERALD S. HANNA, Professor of Educational Psychology and Measurement, Kansas State University, Manhattan, KS

THOMAS G. HARING, Associate Professor in Special Education, University of California, Santa Barbara, CA

DELWYN L. HARNISCH, Associate Professor of Educational Psychology, University of Illinois at Urbana-Champaign, Champaign, IL

THOMAS H. HARRELL, Professor and Associate Dean, School of Psychology, Florida Institute of Technology, Melbourne, FL

PATTI L. HARRISON, Associate Professor of Behavioral Studies, College of Education, The University of Alabama, Tuscaloosa, AL

VERNA HART, Professor of Special Education, University of Pittsburgh, Pittsburgh, PA

HOPE J. HARTMAN, Associate Professor of Social & Psychological Foundations, School of Education, The City College, City University of New York, New York, NY

ANNE L. HARVEY, Measurement Statistician, Educational Testing Service, Princeton, NJ

LEO M. HARVILL, Professor and Assistant Dean for Medical Education, James H. Quillen College of Medicine, East Tennessee State University, Johnson City, TN

MICHAEL R. HARWELL, Assistant Professor of Psychology and Education, University of Pittsburgh, Pittsburgh, PA

STEVEN C. HAYES, Professor of Psychology and Director of Clinical Training, University of Nevada, Reno, NV

DEBORAH HECHT, Associate Project Director, Center for Advanced Study in Education,

Graduate Center, City University of New York, New York, NY

MARTINE HÉBERT, Assistant Professor, Department of Measurement and Evaluation, University Laval, Quebec, Canada

NATALIE L. HEDBERG, Professor of Communication Disorders and Speech Science, University of Colorado, Boulder, CO

NANCY HEILMAN, Graduate Student in Psychology, Illinois Institute of Technology, Chicago, IL

MARY HENNING-STOUT, Assistant Professor of Counseling Psychology, Lewis and Clark College, Portland, OR

DAVID O. HERMAN, President, Measurement Research Services, Inc., Jackson Heights, NY

ALLEN K. HESS, Professor and Department Head, Auburn University at Montgomery, Montgomery, AL

KATHRYN D. HESS, Consultant, Montgomery, AL

JOHN R. HESTER, Associate Professor of Psychology, Francis Marion College, Florence, SC

ROBERT W. HILTONSMITH, Associate Professor of Psychology, Radford University, Radford, VA

J. SCOTT HINKLE, Assistant Professor, Department of Counselor Education, University of North Carolina, Greensboro, NC

L. MICHAEL HONAKER, Adjunct Professor, Florida Institute of Technology, Melbourne, FL

STEPHEN R. HOOPER, Assistant Professor of Psychiatry, Psychology Section Head, The Clinical Center for the Study of Development and Learning, University of North Carolina School of Medicine, Chapel Hill, NC

KENNETH D. HOPKINS, Professor of Education, University of Colorado, Boulder, CO

MARY E. HUBA, Professor of Research and Evaluation, Iowa State University, Ames, IA

E. SCOTT HUEBNER, Assistant Professor of Psychology, University of South Carolina, Columbia, SC

JAN N. HUGHES, Associate Professor of Educational Psychology, Texas A&M University, College Station, TX

SELMA HUGHES, Professor of Psychology and Special Education, East Texas State University, Commerce, TX

JAMES C. IMPARA, Associate Professor of Research, Evaluation, and Policy Studies, Virginia Polytechnic Institute and State University, Blacksburg, VA

ANNETTE M. IVERSON, Assistant Professor of School Psychology, University of Missouri, Columbia, MO

PATSY ARNETT JAYNES, Second Language Program Evaluation Specialist, Jefferson County Public Schools, Golden, CO

JEFFREY JENKINS, Attorney, KeLeher & McLeod, P.A., Albuquerque, NM

JERRY JOHNSON, Professor of Mathematics, Western Washington University, Bellingham, WA

SYLVIA T. JOHNSON, Professor, Research Methodology and Statistics and Acting Editor-In-Chief, Journal of Negro Education, Howard University, Washington, DC

WAYDE JOHNSON, School Psychology Program, University of North Carolina, Chapel Hill, NC

SHARON JOHNSON-LEWIS, Director of Research, Evaluation and Testing, Detroit Public Schools, Detroit, MI

SAMUEL JUNI, Professor of Applied Psychology, New York University, New York, NY

STEPHEN JURS, Professor of Educational Psychology, Research, and Social Foundations, College of Education and Allied Professions, University of Toledo, Toledo, OH

JAVAID KAISER, Associate Professor of Educational Research and Evaluation, College of Education, Virginia Tech, Blacksburg, VA

RANDY W. KAMPHAUS, Associate Professor of Educational Psychology, The University of Georgia, Athens, GA

DAVID E. KAPEL, Dean, School of Education and Related Professional Studies, Glassboro State College, Glassboro, NJ

BARBARA J. KAPLAN, Associate Professor of Psychology, State University of New York College at Fredonia, Fredonia, NY

WALTER KATKOVSKY, Professor of Psychology, Northern Illinois University, DeKalb, IL

MICHAEL G. KAVAN, Director of Behavioral Sciences and Assistant Professor of Family Practice, Creighton University School of Medicine, Omaha, NE

JERARD F. KEHOE, District Manager, Selection and Testing, American Telephone & Telegraph Co., Morristown, NJ

MARY LOU KELLEY, Associate Professor of

Psychology, Louisiana State University, Baton Rouge, LA

KATHY S. KESSLER, Speech/Language Pathologist, Indiana University School of Medicine, Indianapolis, IN

KENNETH A. KIEWRA, Associate Professor of Educational Psychology, University of Nebraska-Lincoln, Lincoln, NE

ERNEST W. KIMMEL, Executive Director, Test Development, Educational Testing Service, Princeton, NJ

JEAN POWELL KIRNAN, Assistant Professor of Psychology, Trenton State College, Trenton, NJ

HOWARD M. KNOFF, Associate Professor of School Psychology and Director of the School Psychology Program, University of South Florida, Tampa, FL

WILLIAM R. KOCH, Associate Professor of Educational Psychology, The University of Texas, Austin, TX

ERNEST J. KOZMA, Professor of Education, Clemson University, Clemson, SC

JAY KUDER, Associate Professor and Chairperson, Department of Special Educational Services/Instruction, Glassboro State College, Glassboro, NJ

DEBORAH KING KUNDERT, Assistant Professor of Educational Psychology and Statistics, University at Albany, State University of New York, Albany, NY

BARBARA LACHAR, Vice-President, Psychological Assessment Services, Inc., Sugar Land, TX

DAVID LACHAR, Associate Professor of Psychiatry and Behavioral Sciences, University of Texas Medical School at Houston, Houston, TX

MATTHEW E. LAMBERT, Assistant Professor of Psychology, Texas Tech University, Lubbock, TX

SUZANNE LANE, Associate Professor of Education, University of Pittsburgh, Pittsburgh, PA

WILLIAM STEVE LANG, Assistant Professor of Educational Leadership, Technology and Research, Georgia Southern University, Statesboro, GA

RICHARD I. LANYON, Professor of Psychology, Arizona State University, Tempe, AZ

JOSEPH G. LAW, JR., Associate Professor of Behavioral Studies, University of South Alabama, Mobile, AL

WILBUR L. LAYTON, Professor of Psychology, Iowa State University, Ames, IA

STEVEN W. LEE, Assistant Professor of Educational Psychology and Research, University of Kansas, Lawrence, KS

IRVIN J. LEHMANN, Professor of Measurement, Michigan State University, East Lansing, MI

RICHARD LEHRER, Associate Professor of Educational Psychology, University of Wisconsin-Madison, Madison, WI

FREDERICK T. L. LEONG, Assistant Professor of Psychology, The Ohio State University, Columbus, OH

S. ALVIN LEUNG, Assistant Professor of Educational Psychology, University of Houston, Houston, TX

MARY A. LEWIS, Director, Organizational and Employment Technology, PPQ Industries, Inc., Pittsburgh, PA

RICK LINDSKOG, Associate Professor of Psychology and Counseling, Pittsburg State University, Pittsburg, KS

ROBERT W. LISSITZ, Professor of Education and Psychology and Chairperson, Department of Measurement, Statistics, and Evaluation, University of Maryland, College Park, MD

STEVEN G. LOBELLO, Assistant Professor of Psychology, Auburn University at Montgomery, Montgomery, AL

STEVEN H. LONG, Assistant Professor of Speech Pathology and Audiology, Ithaca College, Ithaca, NY

DAVID MACPHEE, Associate Professor of Human Development and Family Studies, Colorado State University, Fort Collins, CO

CLEBORNE D. MADDUX, Professor and Chairman, Department of Curriculum and Instruction, University of Nevada-Reno, Reno, NV

RODERICK K. MAHURIN, Clinical Assistant Professor, Department of Psychiatry, University of Texas Health Science Center, San Antonio, TX

KORESSA KUTSICK MALCOLM, School Psychologist, Augusta County School System, Fishersville, VA

GARY L. MARCO, Executive Director, Statistical Analysis, College Board Programs Division, Educational Testing Service, Princeton, NJ

BRIAN K. MARTENS, Associate Professor of

Psychology and Education, Syracuse University, Syracuse, NY

CHARLES WM. MARTIN, Assistant Dean, University College, Ball State University, Muncie, IN

REBECCA J. MCCAULEY, Assistant Professor of Communication Science and Disorders, University of Vermont, Burlington, VT

SCOTT R. MCCONNELL, Associate Professor of Educational Psychology, Institute on Community Integration, University of Minnesota, Minneapolis, MN

JOYCE R. MCLARTY, Director, Work Keys Development, Center for Education and Work, American College Testing Program, Iowa City, IA

ROBERT F. MCMORRIS, Professor of Educational Psychology and Statistics, State University of New York at Albany, Albany, NY

MALCOLM R. MCNEIL, Professor of Communicative Disorders, University of Wisconsin-Madison, Madison, WI

DOUGLAS J. MCRAE, Vice-President for Publishing, CTB Macmillan/McGraw-Hill, Monterey, CA

DAMIAN MCSHANE, Associate Professor of Psychology, Utah State University, Logan, UT

DAVID J. MEALOR, Chair of Educational Services Department, College of Education, University of Central Florida, Orlando, FL

FREDERIC J. MEDWAY, Professor of Psychology, University of South Carolina, Columbia, SC

WILLIAM A. MEHRENS, Professor of Educational Measurement, Michigan State University, East Lansing, MI

MANFRED J. MEIER, Professor of Neurosurgery, Psychiatry, and Psychology, and Diplomate in Clinical Neuropsychology, University of Minnesota, Twin Cities, Minneapolis, MN

KEVIN MENEFEE, Certified School Psychologist, Barkley Center, University of Nebraska-Lincoln, Lincoln, NE

PETER F. MERENDA, Professor Emeritus of Psychology and Statistics, University of Rhode Island, Kingston, RI

WILLIAM R. MERZ, SR., Professor and Coordinator, School Psychology Training Program, California State University, Sacramento, Sacramento, CA

WILLIAM B. MICHAEL, Professor of Education

and Psychology, University of Southern California, Los Angeles, CA

GRACE MIDDLETON, Associate Professor, Speech-Language Pathology Program, College of Nursing, University of Texas, El Paso, TX

M. DAVID MILLER, Associate Professor of Foundations of Education, University of Florida, Gainesville, FL

ROBERT J. MILLER, Assistant Professor of Special Education, Mankato State University, Mankato, MN

SHERRI K. MILLER, Assistant Director, American College Testing Program, Iowa City, IA

CRAIG N. MILLS, Executive Director, GRE Testing and Services, Educational Testing Service, Princeton, NJ

PAT MIRENDA, Associate Professor of Special Education and Communication Disorders, University of Nebraska-Lincoln, Lincoln, NE

MARY ROSS MORAN, Professor of Special Education, University of Kansas, Lawrence, KS

KEVIN L. MORELAND, Associate Professor of Psychology, Fordham University, Bronx, NY

PAMELA A. MOSS, Assistant Professor, University of Michigan, Ann Arbor, MI

RALPH O. MUELLER, Assistant Professor of Educational Research and Measurement, University of Toledo, Toledo, OH

ANN M. MUENCH, Research Associate, Far West Laboratory for Educational Research and Development, San Francisco, CA

KEVIN R. MURPHY, Professor of Psychology, Colorado State University, Fort Collins, CO

DEAN H. NAFZIGER, Executive Director, Far West Laboratory for Educational Research and Development, San Francisco, CA

JACK A. NAGLIERI, Professor of School Psychology, Ohio State University, Columbus, OH

ROSEMERY O. NELSON-GRAY, Professor of Psychology and Director of Clinical Training, University of North Carolina at Greensboro, Greensboro, NC

DEBRA NEUBERT, Assistant Professor of Special Education, University of Maryland, College Park, MD

DIANNA L. NEWMAN, Associate Professor of Educational Theory and Practice, University at Albany/SUNY, Albany, NY

DAVID S. NICHOLS, Supervising Clinical Psychologist, Department of Psychology, Dammasch State Hospital, Wilsonville, OR

ANTHONY J. NITKO, Professor of Education, University of Pittsburgh, Pittsburgh, PA

JANET NORRIS, Associate Professor of Communication Disorders, Louisiana State University, Baton Rouge, LA

JOHN E. OBRZUT, Professor of Educational Psychology, University of Arizona, Tucson, AZ

JUDY OEHLER-STINNETT, Assistant Professor of Psychology, Eastern Illinois University, Charleston, IL

STEPHEN OLEJNIK, Professor of Educational Psychology, University of Georgia, Athens, GA

JOE OLMI, School Psychology Predoctoral Intern, Department of Educational Psychology, Mississippi State University, Mississippi State, MS

ALBERT C. OOSTERHOF, Professor of Education, Florida State University, Tallahassee, FL

TIMOTHY M. OSBERG, Professor of Psychology, Niagara University, Niagara University, NY

STEVEN J. OSTERLIND, Associate Professor and Director, Center for Educational Assessment, University of Missouri-Columbia, Columbia, MO

TERRY OVERTON, Assistant Professor of Special Education, Longwood College, Farmville, VA

STEVEN V. OWEN, Professor of Educational Psychology, University of Connecticut, Storrs, CT

MARY PANNBACKER, Professor and Program Director, Department of Communication Disorders, School of Allied Health Professions, Louisiana State University Medical Center, Shreveport, LA

CHARLES K. PARSONS, Professor of Management, Georgia Institute of Technology, Atlanta, GA

A. HARRY PASSOW, Schiff Professor of Education, Teachers College, Columbia University, New York, NY

MARY ELLEN PEARSON, Professor of Special Education, Mankato State University, Mankato, MN

STEVEN I. PFEIFFER, Director, Institute of Clinical Training and Research, The Devereux Foundation, Devon, PA

JOSEPH G. PONTEROTTO, Associate Professor

of Education, Division of Psychological and Educational Services, Graduate School of Education, Fordham University—Lincoln Center, New York, NY

MARK POPE, President, Career Decisions, San Francisco, CA

WILLIAM D. PORTERFIELD, Academic Coordinator and Adjunct Assistant Professor of Educational Administration, Commission of Interprofessional Education and Practice, The Ohio University, Columbus, OH

G. MICHAEL POTEAT, Associate Professor of Psychology, East Carolina University, Greenville, NC

THOMAS E. POWELL, Doctoral Candidate, Department of Psychology, North Carolina State University, Raleigh, NC

ELIZABETH M. PRATHER, Professor of Speech and Hearing Science, Arizona State University, Tempe, AZ

BARRY M. PRIZANT, Professor, Division of Communication Disorders, Emerson College, Boston, MA

NAMBURY S. RAJU, Professor of Psychology, Illinois Institute of Technology, Chicago, IL

BIKKAR S. RANDHAWA, Professor of Educational Psychology, University of Saskatchewan, Saskatoon, Canada

BARBARA A. REILLY, Assistant Professor of Psychology, Clemson University, Clemson, SC

ROBERT C. REINEHR, Associate Professor of Psychology, Southwestern University, Georgetown, TX

ROBERT A. REINEKE, Evaluation Specialist, Lincoln Public Schools, Lincoln, NE

PAUL RETZLAFF, Assistant Professor of Psychology, University of Northern Colorado, Greeley, CO

CECIL R. REYNOLDS, Professor of Educational Psychology, Texas A&M University, College Station, TX

ROGER A. RICHARDS, Dean of Academic Affairs, Bunker Hill Community College, Boston, MA

CHARLENE RIVERA, Director, The Evaluation Assistance Center East, The George Washington University, Arlington, VA

MARK W. ROBERTS, Professor of Clinical Psychology, Idaho State University, Pocatello, ID

DONALD U. ROBERTSON, Professor of Psychology, Indiana University of Pennsylvania, Indiana, PA

BRUCE G. ROGERS, Professor of Educational Psychology and Foundations, University of Northern Iowa, Cedar Falls, IA

CYNTHIA A. ROHRBECK, Associate Professor of Psychology, The George Washington University, Washington, DC

ARLENE COOPERSMITH ROSENTHAL, Educational Psychologist and Consultant, Olney, MD

RODNEY W. ROTH, Professor of Educational Research and Dean, College of Education, The University of Alabama, Tuscaloosa, AL

BARBARA A. ROTHLISBERG, Associate Professor of Educational Psychology and School Psychology 1 Program Director, Ball State University, Muncie, IN

RONALD H. ROZENSKY, Associate Chairman, Department of Psychiatry, Evanston Hospital/Northwestern University Medical School, Evanston, IL

DONALD L. RUBIN, Professor of Language Education, The University of Georgia, Athens, GA

LAWRENCE M. RUDNER, Director of the Educational Resources Information Center Clearinghouse on Tests, Measurement and Evaluation (ERIC/TME), American Institutes for Research, Washington, DC, and Director of Research, LMP Associates, Chevy Chase, MD

JOSEPH M. RYAN, Associate Professor of Education, University of South Carolina, Columbia, SC

DARRELL SABERS, Professor of Educational Psychology, University of Arizona, Tucson, AZ

VINCENT J. SAMAR, Associate Professor of Communication Research, National Technical Institute for the Deaf, Rochester Institute of Technology, Rochester, NY

ELEANOR E. SANFORD, Research Consultant, Division of Accountability Services/Research, North Carolina Department of Public Instruction, Raleigh, NC

DAVID M. SAUNDERS, Assistant Professor, Faculty of Management, McGill University, Montreal, Canada

WILLIAM I. SAUSER, JR., Associate Vice President and Professor, Office of the Vice President for Extension, Auburn University, Auburn, AL

DIANE J. SAWYER, Director, Consultation Center for Reading, Syracuse University, Syracuse, NY

DALE P. SCANNELL, Professor and Dean, College of Education, University of Maryland at College Park, College Park, MD

WILLIAM D. SCHAFER, Associate Professor of Educational Measurement, Statistics, and Evaluation, University of Maryland, College Park, MD

GEOFFREY F. SCHULTZ, Associate Professor of Educational Psychology and Special Education, Indiana University-Northwest, Gary, IN

OWEN SCOTT, III, Clinical Psychologist, The Psychology Clinic, Baton Rouge, LA

GARY B. SELTZER, Associate Professor of Social Work, University of Wisconsin-Madison, Madison, WI

MARCIA B. SHAFFER, School Psychologist, Lancaster, NY

GREGORY A. SHANNON, Supervisor of Testing, Virginia State Assessment Program, Virginia Department of Education, Richmond, VA

DAVID A. SHAPIRO, Associate Professor of Communication Disorders, School of Education and Psychology, Western Carolina University, Cullowhee, NC

EDWARD S. SHAPIRO, Professor and Director, School Psychology Program, Lehigh University, Bethlehem, PA

STEWARD M. SHEAR, Graduate Student in School Psychology, Lehigh University, Bethlehem, PA

JUNE ELLEN SHEPHERD, Postdoctoral Pediatric Psychology Fellow in the Pediatric Comprehensive Neurorehabilitation Unit at the Kennedy Institute of Johns Hopkins University School of Medicine, Baltimore, MD

SUSAN M. SHERIDAN, Assistant Professor of Educational Psychology, University of Utah, Salt Lake City, UT

KENNETH G. SHIPLEY, Professor of Speech-Language Pathology, California State University-Fresno, Fresno, CA

AMY H. SHIVELY, Research Associate, Far West Laboratory for Educational Research and Development, San Francisco, CA

ARTHUR B. SILVERSTEIN, Professor of Psychiatry, University of California, Los Angeles, CA

BERTRAM C. SIPPOLA, Associate Professor of Psychology, University of New Orleans, New Orleans, LA

ALFRED L. SMITH, JR., Personnel Psychologist, Federal Aviation Administration, U.S. Department of Transportation, Washington, DC

JEFFREY H. SNOW, Neuropsychologist, Capital Rehabilitation Hospital, Tallahassee, FL

GARGI ROYSIRCAR SODOWSKY, Assistant Professor of Educational Psychology, University of Nebraska-Lincoln, Lincoln, NE

DAVID C. SOLLY, Associate Professor and Chairperson, Department of Psychology & Counseling, Pittsburg State University, Pittsburg, KS

RONALD K. SOMMERS, Professor of Speech Pathology and Audiology, Kent State University, Kent, OH

DONNA SPIKER, Senior Research Associate, Department of Psychiatry and Behavioral Sciences, Stanford University School of Medicine and Stanford Center for the Study of Families, Children, and Youth, Stanford, CA

JACLYN B. SPITZER, Chief, Audiology and Speech Pathology, Veterans Administration Medical Center, West Haven, CT, and Associate Clinical Professor, Department of Surgery (Otolaryngology), Yale University School of Medicine, New Haven, CT

STEVEN A. STAHL, Associate Professor of Reading Education, The University of Georgia, Athens, GA

GARY J. STAINBACK, Senior Psychologist, Department of Pediatrics, East Carolina University School of Medicine, Greenville, NC

JAYNE E. STAKE, Professor of Psychology, University of Missouri-St. Louis, St. Louis, MO

STEPHANIE STEIN, Assistant Professor of Psychology, Central Washington University, Ellensburg, WA

HARLAN J. STIENTJES, School Psychologist, Heartland Educational Agency II, Johnston, IA

TERRY A. STINNETT, Assistant Professor of Psychology, Eastern Illinois University, Charleston, IL

WILLIAM A. STOCK, Professor of Exercise Science, Arizona State University, Tempe, AZ

HOWARD STOKER, Research Professor, Bureau of Educational Research and Service, University of Tennessee, Knoxville, TN

GERALD L. STONE, Professor of Counseling Psychology and Director, University Counseling Service, The University of Iowa, Iowa City, IA

GARY STONER, Assistant Professor, School Psychology Program, College of Education, University of Oregon, Eugene, OR

LOIS T. STRAUSS, Associate Professor of Psychology, Glassboro State College, Glassboro, NJ

RICHARD B. STUART, Clinical Professor of Psychiatry, University of Washington School of Medicine, Seattle, WA

MICHAEL J. SUBKOVIAK, Professor of Educational Psychology, University of Wisconsin-Madison, Madison, WI

HOI K. SUEN, Associate Professor of Educational Psychology, Pennsylvania State University, University Park, PA

GAIL M. SULLIVAN, Chief, Geriatric Medicine, and Associate Chief of Staff for Education, Veterans Administration Medical Center, Newington, CT, and Assistant Professor of Medicine, University of Connecticut, Farmington, CT

NORMAN D. SUNDBERG, Professor Emeritus of Psychology, University of Oregon, Eugene, OR

ROSEMARY E. SUTTON, Associate Professor of Education, Cleveland State University, Cleveland, OH

MARK E. SWERDLIK, Professor of Psychology, Illinois State University, Normal, IL

HARVEY N. SWITZKY, Professor of Educational Psychology, Counseling, and Special Education, Northern Illinois University, DeKalb, IL

KIKUMI TATSUOKA, Associate Professor, Computer-Based Education Research Laboratory, University of Illinois at Urbana-Champaign, Urbana, IL

MAURICE TATSUOKA, Professor Emeritus of Psychology, University of Illinois at Urbana-Champaign, Champaign, IL

JAMES TERWILLIGER, Professor of Educational Psychology, University of Minnesota, Minneapolis, MN

E. W. TESTUT, Associate Professor of Audiology, Department of Speech Pathology/Audiology, Ithaca College, Ithaca, NY

NORA M. THOMPSON, Clinical Assistant Professor, Southwest Neuropsychiatric Institute and Department of Psychiatry, The University of Texas Health Science Center at San Antonio, San Antonio, TX

GERALD TINDAL, Assistant Professor of Special Education, University of Oregon, Eugene, OR

CAROL KEHR TITTLE, Professor of Educational Psychology, Graduate School, City University of New York, New York, NY

RUTH E. TOMES, Assistant Professor of Family Relations and Child Development, Oklahoma State University, Stillwater, OK

KATHLEEN T. TOMS, Assistant Professor of Education, College of St. Rose, Albany, NY

TONY TONEATTO, Psychologist, Addiction Research Foundation, Toronto, Ontario, Canada

ROGER L. TOWNE, Assistant Professor of Speech Pathology and Audiology, Illinois State University, Normal, IL

MICHAEL S. TREVISAN, Research Associate, RMC Corporation, Portland, OR

CAROLYN TRIAY, Department of Psychology, University of New Orleans, New Orleans, LA

JALIE A. TUCKER, Professor of Psychology and Co-Director of Clinical Training, Auburn University, Auburn, AL

NICHOLAS A. VACC, Professor and Chairperson, Department of Counselor Education, University of North Carolina, Greensboro, NC

WILFRED G. VAN GORP, Assistant Professor in Residence, Department of Psychiatry and Behavioral Sciences, UCLA School of Medicine, and Chief, Neuropsychology Assessment Laboratory, Department of Veterans Affairs Medical Center West Los Angeles, Los Angeles, CA

DOLORES KLUPPEL VETTER, Professor and Associate Dean, University of Wisconsin-Madison, Madison, WI

PETER VILLANOVA, Assistant Professor of Psychology, Northern Illinois University, De-Kalb, IL

ALEX VOOGEL, Assistant Professor, TESOL/MATFL Program, Monterey Institute of International Studies, Monterey, CA

JOHN F. WAKEFIELD, Associate Professor of Education, University of North Alabama, Florence, AL

NIELS G. WALLER, Assistant Professor of Psychology, University of California, Davis, Davis, CA

ANNIE W. WARD, President of Ward Educational Consulting, Inc. and of The Techne Group, Inc., Daytona Beach, FL

T. STEUART WATSON, Assistant Professor of Educational Psychology, Mississippi State University, Starkville, MS

SHARON L. WEINBERG, Professor of Quantitative Studies, New York University, New York, NY

SUSAN ELLIS WEISMER, Assistant Professor of Communicative Disorders, University of Wisconsin, Madison, WI

J. STEVEN WELSH, Assistant Professor, Nichols State University, Thibodaux, LA

BERT W. WESTBROOK, Professor of Psychology, North Carolina State University, Raleigh, NC

CAROL E. WESTBY, Senior Research Associate, University Affiliated Program, University of New Mexico, Albuquerque, NM

ALIDA S. WESTMAN, Professor of Psychology, Eastern Michigan University, Ypsilanti, MI

PATRICIA WHEELER, Senior Research Associate, The Evaluation Center, Western Michigan University, Kalamazoo, MI

KENNETH V. WHITE, Research Associate, University of Oklahoma, Norman, OK

THOMAS A. WIDIGER, Professor of Psychology, University of Kentucky, Lexington, KY

MARGARET ROGERS WIESE, Assistant Professor of School Psychology, Appalachian State University, Boone, NC

MARTIN J. WIESE, School Psychologist, Wilkes County Schools, Wilkesboro, NC

LINDA F. WIGHTMAN, Vice President—Test Development and Research, Law School Admission Services, Newton, PA

WILLIAM K. WILKINSON, Assistant Professor of Counseling and Educational Psychology, New Mexico State University, Las Cruces, NM

JANICE G. WILLIAMS, Assistant Professor of Psychology, Clemson University, Clemson, SC

JOHN M. WILLIAMS, Graduate Assistant, Coordinator of Educational Research Computing Laboratory, College of Education, Virginia Tech, Blacksburg, VA

ROBERT T. WILLIAMS, Professor, School of Occupational and Educational Studies, Colorado State University, Fort Collins, CO

W. GRANT WILLIS, Associate Professor of Psychology, University of Rhode Island, Kingston, RI

HILDA WING, Personnel Psychologist, Federal Aviation Administration, Washington, DC

L. ALAN WITT, Personnel Research Psychologist, Civil Aeromedical Institute, Federal

Aviation Administration, Oklahoma City, OK

RICHARD M. WOLF, Professor of Psychology and Education, Teachers College, Columbia University, New York, NY

CLAUDIA R. WRIGHT, Assistant Professor of Educational Psychology, California State University, Long Beach, CA

DAN WRIGHT, School Psychologist, Ralston Public Schools, Ralston, NE

LOGAN WRIGHT, Professor of Psychology, University of Oklahoma, Norman, OK

THOMAS A. WROBEL, Assistant Professor of Psychology, University of Michigan-Flint, Flint, MI

JAMES E. YSSELDYKE, Professor of Educational Psychology, University of Minnesota, Minneapolis, MN

SHELDON ZEDECK, Professor of Psychology and Director, University of California, Berkeley, CA

LELAND C. ZLOMKE, Clinical Coordinator of Intensive Treatment Services, Beatrice State Developmental Center, Beatrice, NE

INDEX OF TITLES

INDEX OF ACRONYMS

This Index of Acronyms refers the reader to the appropriate test in The Eleventh Mental Measurements Yearbook. In some cases tests are better known by their acronyms than by their full titles, and this index can be of substantial help to the person who knows the former but not the latter. Acronyms are only listed if the author or publisher has made substantial use of the acronym in referring to the test, or if the test is widely known by the acronym. A few acronyms are also registered trademarks (e.g., SAT); where this is known to us, only the test with the registered trademark is referenced. There is some danger in the overuse of acronyms, but this index, like all other indexes in this work, is provided to make the task of identifying a test as easy as possible. All numbers refer to test numbers, not page numbers.

CLASSIFIED SUBJECT INDEX

The Classified Subject Index classifies all tests included in The Eleventh Mental Measurements Yearbook *into 18 major categories: Achievement, Behavior Assessment, Developmental, Education, English, Fine Arts, Intelligence and Scholastic Aptitude, Mathematics, Miscellaneous, Multi-Aptitude Batteries, Neuropsychological, Personality, Reading, Science, Sensory-Motor, Social Studies, Speech and Hearing, and Vocations. Each category appears in alphabetical order and tests are ordered alphabetically within each category. Each test entry includes test title (first letter capitalized), population for which the test is intended (lower case), and the test entry number in* The Eleventh Mental Measurements Yearbook. *All numbers refer to test entry numbers, not to page numbers. Brief suggestions for the use of this index are presented in the introduction.*

ACHIEVEMENT

Adult Basic Learning Examination, Second Edition, adults with less than 12 years of formal schooling, see 9

Assessment and Placement Services for Community Colleges, entering community college students, see 19

Canadian Tests of Basic Skills, Forms 7 and 8, grades K.1–1.5, K.8–1.9, 1.7–2.6, 2.7–3.5, 3, 4, 5, 6, 7, 8–9, 9, 10, 11, 12, see 55

College Basic Academic Subjects Examination, college students having completed the general education component of a college curriculum (i.e., late sophomores or early juniors), see 76

Comprehensive Tests of Basic Skills, Fourth Edition, grades K.0–K.9, K.6–1.6, 1.0–2.2, 1.6–3.2, 2.6–4.2, 3.6–5.2, 4.6–6.2, 5.6–7.2, 6.6–9.2, 8.6–11.2, 10.6–12.9, see 81

Differential Ability Scales, ages 2-6 to 7-11, 5-0 to 17-11, see 111

End-of-Course Tests, secondary school students, see 135

Guidance Centre Classroom Achievement Tests, grades 3–8, 9–12, see 152

High-School Subject Tests, grades 9–12, see 160

Iowa Tests of Basic Skills, Form J, grades K.1–1.5, K.8–1.9, 1.7–2.6, 2.5–3.5, 3, 4, 5, 6, 7, 8–9, see 184

National Achievement Test [Second Edition], grades K, 1, 2, 3, 4, 5, 6, 7, 8, 9/10, 11/12, see 254

National Educational Development Tests, grades 9–10, see 255

National Proficiency Survey Series, high school students completing specific courses, see 256

Peabody Individual Achievement Test—Revised, grades K–12, see 280

QUIC Tests, grades 2–12, see 320

Richmond Tests of Basic Skills: Edition 2, ages 8-0 to 13-11, see 335

Scholastic Aptitude Scale, ages 6-0 to 17-11, see 343

SRA Achievement Series, Forms 1 and 2, and Survey of Basic Skills, Forms P and Q, grades K.5–12.9, see 376

Stanford Achievement Test, Eighth Edition, grades 1.5 to 9.9, see 377

Stanford Early School Achievement Test, Third Edition, grades K.0–K.5, K.5–1.5, see 378

Tests of Achievement and Proficiency, Form J, grades 9–12, see 445

Tests of General Educational Development [the GED Tests], candidates for high school eqivalency diplomas, see 447

BEHAVIOR ASSESSMENT

DEVELOPMENTAL

EDUCATION

ENGLISH

FINE ARTS

INTELLIGENCE AND SCHOLASTIC APTITUDE

MATHEMATICS

MISCELLANEOUS

MULTI-APTITUDE BATTERIES

NEUROPSYCHOLOGICAL

PERSONALITY

READING

Reading Style Inventory, grades 1–12, see 328
The Reversals Frequency Test, ages 5-0 to 15-11, see 331
Suffolk Reading Scale, ages 6–12, see 392
Test of Awareness of Language Segments, ages 4-6 and over, see 427

Test of Early Reading Ability—2, ages 3-0 to 9-11, see 429
Test of Initial Literacy, ages 7–12, see 434
Tests of Reading Comprehension, grades 3–7, 6–10, see 448

SCIENCE

ACT Proficiency Examination in Microbiology, college and adults, see 4

Australian Biology Test Item Bank, Australian years 11–12, see 23

SENSORY-MOTOR

[Bender-Gestalt Test], ages 4 and over, see 40
Lateral Preference Schedule, ages 7 and over without physical disabilities, see 196
The Modified Version of the Bender-Gestalt Test for Preschool and Primary School Children, ages 4-6 to 8-5, see 247

Motor Skills Inventory, 6–84 months and older handicapped children, see 249
The Pin Test, ages 16 to 69 with normal or corrected vision, see 293
Visual Skills Appraisal, grades K–4, see 456

SOCIAL STUDIES

Basic Economics Test, grades 4–6, see 27
Test of Economic Knowledge, grades 8–9, see 431

SPEECH AND HEARING

Arizona Articulation Proficiency Scale, Second Edition, ages 1-6 to 13-11, see 17
Assessing Linguistic Behaviors: Assessing Prelinguistic and Early Linguistic Behaviors in Developmentally Young Children, children functioning below 2 years of age, see 18
Behavior Analysis Language Instrument, individuals with severe and profound handicaps, see 35
CID Phonetic Inventory, hearing-impaired children, see 67
CID Picture SPINE, hearing-impaired children ages 6–13, see 68
Clinical Evaluation of Language Fundamentals—Revised, ages 5-0 to 16-11, see 72
Computer Managed Articulation Diagnosis, students with articulation disorders, see 83
Computer Managed Screening Test, ages 3–8, see 84
Dysarthria Profile, dysarthric adults, see 118
Elicited Articulatory System Evaluation, ages 3 and over, see 129

Frenchay Aphasia Screening Test, normals and aphasics, see 145
Living Language, language-impaired children, see 209
Oral Speech Mechanism Screening Examination—Revised, ages 5 through adults, see 272
PACS Pictures: Language Elicitation Materials, ages 3–6, see 275
Phonological Processes Assessment and Intervention, children with articulation disorders, see 291
SCAN: A Screening Test for Auditory Processing Disorders, ages 3–11, see 341
Screening Test for Developmental Apraxia of Speech, ages 4–12, see 347
STIM/CON: Prognostic Inventory for Misarticulating Kindergarten and First Grade Children, grades K–3, see 380
A Voice Assessment Protocol for Children and Adults, children and adults, see 459
Wepman's Auditory Discrimination Test, Second Edition, ages 4-0 to 8-11, see 467

VOCATIONS

PUBLISHERS DIRECTORY AND INDEX

CFKR Career Materials, Inc., P.O. Box 437, Meadow Vista, CA 95722-0437: 60

Louis A. Chandler, The Psychoeducational Clinic, University of Pittsburgh, 5D Forbes Quadrangle, Pittsburgh, PA 15260: 381

Clinical Psychology Publishing Co., Inc. (CPPC), 4 Conant Square, Brandon, VT 05733: 36, 247, 319, 415, 423

The College Board, 45 Columbus Avenue, New York, NY 10023-6992: 19, 108, 109

Communication Skill Builders, 3830 East Bellevue, P.O. Box 42050, Tucson, AZ 85733: 25, 70, 83, 84, 118

COMPUSCORE, Box 7035, Ann Arbor, MI 48107: 92

Consulting Psychologists Press, Inc., 3803 East Bayshore Road, P.O. Box 10096, Palo Alto, CA 94303: 1, 54, 155, 237, 303, 339, 370, 371, 462

Creative Learning Press, Inc., P.O. Box 320, Mansfield Center, CT 06250: 93

Creative Therapeutics, P.O. Box R, Cresskill, NJ 07626-0317: 331

CTB Macmillan/McGraw-Hill, Del Monte Research Park, 2500 Garden Road, Monterey, CA 93940-5380: 51, 52, 53, 81, 135, 255, 296, 367, 376, 446

Curriculum Associates, Inc., 5 Esquire Road, North Billerica, MA 01862-2589: 49, 252

Cypress Lake Media, ATTN: Michael W. Fordyce, Cypress Lake Professional Center, 9371-19 Cypress Lake Drive, Fort Myers, FL 33919-4938: 154, 315

Dallas Educational Services, P.O. Box 831254, Richardson, TX 75083-1254: 102

Department of Research Assessment and Training, New York State Psychiatric Institute, 722 West 168th Street, New York, NY 10032: 147

DLM Teaching Resources, One DLM Park, P.O. Box 4000, Allen, TX 75002: 30, 37, 45, 291, 443

EdITS/Educational and Industrial Testing Service, P.O. Box 7234, San Diego, CA 92167: 113

Edmark Corporation, 14350 NE 21st St., P.O. Box 3218, Redmond, WA 98073-3218: 35

Educational Activities, Inc., P.O. Box 392, Freeport, NY 11520: 178

Educational Assessment Service, Inc., Apple Publishing Company, W6050 Apple Road, Watertown, WI 53094: 3, 150

Educational Records Bureau, Inc., Bardwell Hall, 37 Cameron Street, Wellesley, MA 02181: 174

Educational Research Centre, Test Department, St. Patrick's College, 66 Richmond Road, Dublin 3, Ireland: 116

Educational Teaching Aids, 199 Carpenter Avenue, Wheeling, IL 60090: 63

Educational Testing Service, Publication Order Services, P.O. Box 6736, Princeton, NJ 08541-6736: 103, 298, 352, 432

Educators'/Employers' Tests & Services Associates, 341 Garfield Street, Chambersburg, PA 17201: 139

Educators Publishing Service, Inc., 75 Moulton Street, Cambridge, MA 02138-1104: 281, 409

Elbern Publications, P.O. Box 09497, Columbus, OH 43209: 33, 327

Exceptional Education, 18518 Kenlake Pl. N.E., Seattle, WA 98155: 457

Sheila M. Eyberg, Department of Clinical and Health Psychology, Box J-165, Health Sciences Center, University of Florida, Gainesville, FL 32610: 410

Family Social Science, 290 McNeal Hall, 1985 Buford Avenue, University of Minnesota, St. Paul, MN 55108: 140, 283

General Educational Development Testing Service of the American Council on Education (GED), One Dupont Circle, NW–Suite 20, Washington, DC 20036-1163: 447

G.I.A. Publications, Inc., 7404 South Mason Avenue, Chicago, IL 60638: 180

Grune & Stratton, Inc., 465 South Lincoln Drive, Troy, MO 63379: 40

Guidance Centre, Faculty of Education, University of Toronto, 10 Alcorn Avenue, Toronto, Ontario M4V 2Z8, Canada: 152

H & H Publishing Co., Inc., 1231 Kapp Drive, Clearwater, FL 34625: 198

Hanson Silver Strong & Associates, Inc., 10 West Main Street, Moorestown, NJ 08057: 201, 204

Susan Harter, Psychology Department, HD 09613, University of Denver, 2040 South York Street, Denver, CO 80208: 292, 357

Hester Evaluation Systems, Inc., 2410 Granthurst, Topeka, KS 66611-1274: 290

Hilson Research, Inc., P.O. Box 239, 82-28 Abingdon Road, Kew Gardens, NY 11415: 161, 162, 183

Human Sciences Research Council, P.O. Box 32410, Braamfontein 2017, South Africa: 181

Human Services Resource Group, College of Business Administration, University of Nebraska-Omaha, Omaha, NE 68182-0048: 407

Humanics Publishing Group, 1482 Mecaslin Street, N.W., P.O. Box 7400, Atlanta, GA 30357-0400: 170, 210

Industrial Psychology International Ltd., 11 North Market Street, Champaign, IL 61820: 86, 185

Institute for Behavioral Research in Creativity, 1570 South 1100th East, Salt Lake City, UT 84105: 125

Institute for Personality and Ability Testing, Inc., Test Services Division, P.O. Box 188, Champaign, IL 61824-0188: 156, 169, 188, 355

Institute for the Advancement of Philosophy for Children, Montclair State College, Upper Montclair, NJ 07043: 259

Institute of Psychological Research, Inc., 34 Fleury Street West, Montreal, Quebec H3L 1S9, Canada: 425

International Diagnostic Systems, Inc., 15127 So. 73rd Ave., Suite H-2, Orland Park, IL 60462: 330

International Training Consultants, Inc., P.O. Box 35613, Richmond, VA 23235-0613: 205

Janelle Publications, Inc., 625 W. Church Street, New York, NY 10128: 373

Jastak Associates, Inc., P.O. Box 3410, Wilmington, DE 19804-0250: 470

Joint Council on Economic Education, 432 Park Avenue, South, New York, NY 10016: 27, 431

Keystone Publications, 1657 Broadway, 4th Floor, New York, NY 10019-6707: 89

John D. King, 4209 Avenue C, Austin, TX 78751: 207

INDEX OF NAMES

Carlson, C. L.: ref, 87(10), 332(34)
Carlson, E.: ref, 244(396)
Carlson, G. A.: ref, 66r, 466(36)
Carlson, J. E. V.: rev, 262, 277
Carlson, J. F.: rev, 112, 334
Carlson, K. A.: test, 238
Carlson, L.: test, 195
Carlson, M.: ref, 40(27), 191(6)
Carlson, R. D.: rev, 299, 440
Carlson, V.: ref, 64(215)
Carmelli, D.: ref, 54(83), 155(4)
Carmen, R. C.: ref, 383(4)
Carmer, J. C.: rev, 233, 393
Carner, R.: ref, 360(53)
Carnine, D.: ref, 81(42)
Caroff, S.: ref, 212(79)
Carpenter, C. D.: rev, 372, 375, 378
Carpenter, R.: ref, 18r
Carpenter, R. L.: test, 18
Carper, L. B.: ref, 31(92)
Carr, E. G.: ref, 212(12)
Carr, J.: ref, 257(31)
Carr, M. A.: ref, 212(60)
Carr, R. P.: ref, 87(65)
Carr, S.: ref, 31(189)
Carr, T.: ref, 64(172)
Carrier, C. A.: ref, 81(60), 274(30)
Carrigan, S.: ref, 239(21)
Carrillo, R.: ref, 244(571,636)
Carroll, B. J.: ref, 334r
Carroll, L.: ref, 64(179)
Carroll, S.: ref, 31(158)
Carson, M. F.: ref, 239(31), 244(390), 360(36), 465(8)
Carswell, C. M.: ref, 465(131)
Carte, E. T.: ref, 146(41), 332(36), 378(2)
Carter, C.: ref, 188(4), 244(239)
Carter, C. W., Jr.: ref, 17r
Carter, E.: ref, 380r
Carter, J. A.: test, 90; ref, 244(20), 424(8)
Carter, J. D.: ref, 244(422)
Carter, J. E.: ref, 244(46)
Carter, S.: test, 404
Carvajal, H.: ref, 466(82)
Carver, C. S.: ref, 31(2,79)
Carver, D.: ref, 31(209), 66(46)
Carver, D. S.: ref, 424(42)
Carver, R. P.: ref, 325r
Casey, J. E.: ref, 465(135)
Casey, W.: ref, 257(32)
Cash, J.: test, 342
Cash, T. F.: ref, 239(57)
Caskey, W. E., Jr.: ref, 280(51)
Cassel, C. A.: ref, 244(69)
Cassens, G.: ref, 360(53)
Castelli-Sawicki, D.: ref, 188(2)
Casualty Actuarial Society: test, 13, 14, 15
Catalano, R. F.: ref, 64(207)
Catchlove, R. F. H.: ref, 244(185)
Cates, J.: ref, 276r
Cattell, M. D.: test, 188; ref, 188r
Cattell, R. B.: test, 185, 188; ref, 2r, 95r, 169r, 186r, 188(7,8), 188r, 193r, 330r
Catterson, J. H.: ref, 149r
Catts, H. W.: ref, 437(8), 439(2)
Cautela, J.: test, 144

Cautela, J. R.: test, 144
Cavaiola, A. A.: ref, 424(82)
Cavanaugh, J. L., Jr.: ref, 244(518)
Cayton, T. G.: ref, 244r
Cazden, C. B.: rev, 378; ref, 378r
Cazzaniga, L.: ref, 466(60)
Ceci, S.: ref, 64(19)
Cecil, M. A.: ref, 415(4)
Cecil, N. L.: ref, 146(6)
Celmer, D. S.: ref, 376(13)
Celmer, V.: ref, 244(580)
Ceniti, J.: ref, 244(47)
Center for Applied Linguistics: test, 28; ref, 136r
Center for the Study of Ethical Development: ref, 104r
Cermak, L. S.: ref, 465(33)
Cermak, S. A.: ref, 280(9)
Cernovsky, Z.: ref, 244(48,302,303,304)
Cernovsky, Z. Z.: ref, 244(186,187,305,306,419)
Cerullo, F. M.: test, 126; ref, 126(1), 184(24)
Cesarelli, M.: ref, 212(45)
Chabon, S.: ref, 291r
Chacko, T. I.: ref, 241r
Chadwick, O.: ref, 257(3,5,39)
Chadwick, P. D. J.: ref, 31(215)
Chaiyasit, W.: ref, 64(104,176)
Chajczyk, D.: ref, 87(35,65)
Chamberlain, K.: ref, 54(80), 244(472)
Chambers, J.: ref, 212(62)
Chambless, D. L.: ref, 244(188), 360(27)
Champion, L.: ref, 40(4), 280(10)
Chan, C.: ref, 332(75)
Chan, D. W.: ref, 31(263)
Chan, F.: ref, 40(26), 231r
Chan, M.: ref, 31(167)
Chandler, H. N.: ref, 376(5)
Chandler, L. A.: test, 381; ref, 381(1), 381r
Chaney, C.: rev, 427
Chaney, C. F.: ref, 427r
Chaney, E. F.: ref, 244(245)
Channell, R. W.: ref, 437(11)
Chao, C.: test, 292
Charision, J.: ref, 31(141)
Charles, D.: test, 90
Charles, L.: ref, 87r
Charles, R. I.: ref, 81(11)
Charney, N.: ref, 146(57)
Charter, R. A.: ref, 465(87,91,115)
Chartrand, J. M.: ref, 31(216)
Chase, C. I.: rev, 298, 362; ref, 362r
Chatman, S. P.: ref, 191(14), 466(9)
Chattin, S. H.: ref, 466r
Chauvin, S.: ref, 125r
Chavoya, G. A.: ref, 244(228)
Chawluk, J. B.: ref, 212(79)
Cheatham, H. E.: ref, 384(10)
Checkley, K. L.: ref, 244(447)
Chee, P.: ref, 87(44)
Cheek, J. M.: ref, 370r
Chelune, G. J.: ref, 465(133)
Chemers, M. M.: ref, 244(512)
Cheng, L. Y.: ref, 465(1)
Chenggue, W.: ref, 31r
Chernyk, B.: ref, 31(1)
Cherry, R. D.: ref, 179r
Chertkoff, J. M.: ref, 54(47)

Dattore, P. J.: ref, 244(18)
Datwyler, M. L.: ref, 244(5), 274(1)
Daugherty, S. R.: ref, 31(60)
Daughton, D. M.: test, 168
Dauterive, R.: ref, 17(6)
Davenport, J.: ref, 465(50)
Davenport, L.: ref, 146(37)
Davey, B.: ref, 146(55), 377(41,51,70)
Davey, T. C.: ref, 466(83)
David, A. S.: ref, 147(6)
David, E.: ref, 147(2)
David, M.: test, 295
Davidson, G. V.: ref, 274(30)
Davidson, R. S.: ref, 239(14,15,16,26,27)
Davidson, W. B.: ref, 54(4)
Davies, A.: ref, 244(423)
Davies, D. K.: ref, 424(69)
Davies, M.: ref, 31(208)
Davis, A. K.: ref, 244(432)
Davis, B.: rev, 314, 325; ref, 282r
Davis, B. M.: ref, 54(91)
Davis, C.: ref, 31(8)
Davis, C. J.: ref, 244(283)
Davis, D. D.: ref, 40(71), 50(7)
Davis, H. G.: ref, 244r
Davis, J.: ref, 147(5)
Davis, J. M.: ref, 64(44), 212(102), 280(52,112), 437(6), 465(152)
Davis, K. R., Jr.: ref, 424(29)
Davis, L. J., Jr.: ref, 244(561)
Davis, N. L. F.: ref, 333(4)
Davis, P. D.: ref, 446(1)
Davis, S. F.: rev, 20, 357
Davis, T. W.: ref, 31r
Davis, Z. T.: ref, 81(51)
Davison, L. A.: ref, 293r
Davison, M.: test, 104
Davison, M. L.: rev, 377
Davou, D.: ref, 475(1)
Dawis, R. V.: test, 243; ref, 243r
Dawson, G.: ref, 65(3)
Dawson, J.: ref, 212(86)
Dawson, J. E.: ref, 212(78)
Dawson, M. E.: ref, 244(255)
Day, A.: ref, 31(27)
Day, A. M. L.: ref, 87(46)
Day, L. E.: ref, 64(207)
Day, L. S.: rev, 373
Day, R. D.: ref, 140(7)
Deahl, M.: ref, 31(72)
Deal, S. L.: ref, 31(82)
Dean, R. S.: test, 196; ref, 159r, 196(1,2,3), 196r, 274(24), 376(19)
Deaton, A. V.: ref, 244(453)
Deaton, J.: ref, 54(2)
Deaton, W. L.: rev, 200, 360
De Avila, E. A.: test, 296
DeBoe, J.: test, 382
De Boeck, P.: ref, 147(20)
Decker, S. N.: ref, 280(12,35,85)
DeCoff, C.: test, 190
D'Costa, A. G.: rev, 7, 386
D'Elia, L.: test, 293; ref, 465(136)
Defares, P. B.: ref, 379(3)

Defense Activity for Non-Traditional Education Support: test, 103
Deffenbacher, J. L.: ref, 244(335), 379(5), 475(3)
DeFrancesco, J. J.: ref, 54(45)
DeFries, J. C.: ref, 280(36,76,87,113)
DeGangi, G. A.: test, 441
DeGroff, L. C.: ref, 377(34)
DeHaan, E. H. F.: ref, 465(92)
deHirsch, K.: ref, 247r
Dehne, P.: test, 236
Deimling, G.: ref, 244(80)
DeJarnette, G.: ref, 17(4,10)
Deklyen, M.: ref, 117(11)
Delancy, M.: ref, 244(348)
Delaney, D.: ref, 31(94)
Delatte, G. M.: ref, 244(203)
Delatte, J. G., Jr.: ref, 244(45,203)
DeL'Aune, W. R.: ref, 244(361)
Delclos, V. R.: ref, 191(8), 280(20)
de Lemos, M. M.: test, 2; ref, 2r
Delis, D. C.: ref, 212r
Delk, L.: ref, 377(68)
Della Valle, J.: ref, 203(5)
Della-Piana, G.: rev, 179, 358
Dellinger, J.: ref, 30r
DeLong, R. S.: test, 105
DeLongis, A.: ref, 155(3)
Delp, M.: ref, 380r
Delugach, R. R.: ref, 466r
Deluty, B. M.: ref, 31(2)
Deluty, R. H.: ref, 31(2), 292(7)
deMan, A. F.: ref, 244(424)
De Marco, P.: ref, 293(1)
DeMauro, G. E.: rev, 193, 356
Dembinski, R.: ref, 332(13)
Dembo, M. H.: ref, 424(16)
DeMeis, D. K.: ref, 31(229)
deMendonca, M.: ref, 244(60)
DeMeo, P. W.: ref, 117(9)
Demers-Desrosiers, L. A.: ref, 244(185)
De Moja, C. A.: ref, 393(1)
DeMotts, J.: ref, 244(267)
Denburg, J. A.: ref, 244(300,425), 465(60,93)
Denburg, S. D.: ref, 244(300,425), 465(60,93)
Denham, S.: ref, 274(42), 292(6)
Denk, C. E.: ref, 155(4)
Denmark, R. M.: test, 89
Denne, T. C.: ref, 274(10)
Denner, P. R.: ref, 376(42)
Dennis, M.: ref, 31(230)
Denny, B.: ref, 113(3)
Denny, E. C.: ref, 314r
Deno, S. L.: ref, 376(20)
Densem, J. F.: ref, 26(4)
DePaola, L.M.: ref, 64(20), 292(9)
Der, G. J.: ref, 31(76)
Derins, G. M.: ref, 244(480)
Derr, A. M.: ref, 280(32)
Derrick, A.: ref, 239(21)
DeRubeis, R. J.: ref, 31(219), 32(7)
Desch, L. W.: ref, 40(83,84)
DeStefano, L.: rev, 199, 346
Detterman, D. K.: rev, 366; ref, 186r
de Villiers, P. A.: ref, 148r
DeVore, J.: ref, 244r

Engle, D.: ref, 31(240,260)
Englehart, M.: ref, 110r
Englehart, M. D.: ref, 447r
Ennis, J.: ref, 31(152)
Ennis, R. H.: test, 88
Eno, L.: ref, 280(14)
Enos, M. M.: test, 344
Enright, K. M.: ref, 466(93)
Entwistle, N.: ref, 202r
Entwistle, N. J.: ref, 202r
Enyart, P.: ref, 66(2)
Epperson, D. L.: ref, 244(5), 274(1)
Epps, S.: ref, 280(6)
Epstein, L. H.: ref, 31(119)
Epstein, M. H.: ref, 87(1,11), 280(3), 332(3,13)
Epstein, N.: test, 131
Epstein, S.: test, 250; ref, 250r, 360(48)
Erbaugh, J.: ref, 265r, 333r
Erchul, W. P.: rev, 3, 112
Erdmann, J. B.: rev, 19, 352
Erdwins, C. J.: ref, 54(6,33), 424(17,37)
Erickson, D.: rev, 319, 374
Erickson, L. G.: ref, 146(26,46,48)
Erickson, M. F.: ref, 64(195), 280(114), 466(109)
Erickson, M. T.: ref, 64(69)
Erickson, R. C.: rev, 264
Erickson, W. D.: ref, 244(429)
Erlebacher, A.: ref, 438r
Ernst, J.: ref, 465(111)
Eron, L. D.: ref, 244(96,97,438)
Errera, J.: ref, 40(36)
Ershler, J.: rev, 30
Esbeck, E. S.: ref, 417r
Eshbaugh, D. M.: ref, 244(392)
Eskelinen, L.: ref, 465(65)
Eslinger, P. J.: ref, 465(35)
Esonis, S.: test, 144
Espey, L.: test, 213
Estes, R.: ref, 193(7)
Estes, R. E.: ref, 191(13), 193(2), 280(33)
Estrada, P.: ref, 184(6)
Esveldt-Dawson, K.: ref, 64(12,89)
Ethington, C. A.: ref, 445(4)
Evans, A.: ref, 257(16)
Evans, A. S.: test, 313; ref, 314r
Evans, C. S.: ref, 55(3)
Evans, D. A.: ref, 64(17)
Evans, D. R.: test, 318
Evans, E. D.: ref, 466(31)
Evans, H. E.: ref, 66r, 265r
Evans, I. M.: ref, 39r
Evans, J. R.: ref, 280(97), 466(90)
Evans, M. D.: ref, 31(219), 32(7)
Evans, R.: ref, 108(2), 280(61)
Evans, R. G.: ref, 239(66), 244(67,364)
Evans, R. M.: ref, 244(68)
Evans, R. W.: ref, 87(30), 244(317)
Evenson, R. C.: ref, 64(114)
Everitt, B.: ref, 87(17)
Ewing, L. J.: ref, 64(42,43), 466(49)
Ewing-Cobbs, L.: ref, 64(185)
Exner, J. E.: ref, 422r
Eyberg, S. M.: test, 410; ref, 410(1)
Eyde, L. D.: ref, 245r
Eysenck, H.: ref, 423r

Eysenck, H. J.: rev, 54, 244

Fabry, J.: rev, 107, 234
Faculty of The University of the State of New York: test, 4
Fagan, W. T.: ref, 377(9)
Fagg, J. R.: ref, 31(234)
Fagin, H. T.: test, 165, 166
Faigley, L.: ref, 179r
Fairbank, J. A.: ref, 244(100,201,228,623), 244r, 462(14)
Fairbanks, L.: ref, 244(38)
Fairburn, C. G.: ref, 31(242)
Fairchok, G. E.: ref, 250r
Falk, J. R.: ref, 244(202)
Falkenberg, S. D.: ref, 444(2)
Fallon, J. H., Jr.: ref, 244(439)
Fantuzzo, J. W.: ref, 64(206), 292(9)
Farage, C.: ref, 212(51)
Farage, C. M.: ref, 212r
Faravelli, C.: ref, 244(318)
Farber, S. S.: ref, 424(44)
Farish, S.: test, 309
Farley, F. H.: rev, 377; ref, 377r
Farmer, F. F.: ref, 140(24)
Farnill, D.: ref, 282r
Farr, S. P.: ref, 465(79,120)
Farrell, A. D.: ref, 244(430)
Fathman, A. K.: test, 351
Fauber, R.: ref, 66(25), 332(40,56,70)
Faulkner, L. M.: test, 160
Faull, K. F.: ref, 212(71)
Faulstich, M. E.: ref, 66(2), 244(45,203)
Faunce, R. W.: rev, 213
Faurie, W. C.: ref, 244(583)
Faust, D.: ref, 244(511)
Fawcett, J.: ref, 360(13,39)
Feagans, L.: ref, 280(15,53)
Feagans, L. V.: ref, 280(120), 341(2)
Feather, N. T.: ref, 31(73), 32(3)
Fecteau, G. W.: ref, 465(66)
Fedde, N. M.: ref, 117(5)
Federico, P. A.: ref, 196r
Fedio, P.: ref, 465(73)
Feehan, M.: ref, 465(157)
Feeman, D. J.: ref, 146(21)
Fefer, A.: ref, 244(432)
Fein, G.: ref, 146(37)
Feingold, A.: ref, 466(32)
Feinstein, C.: ref, 64(6)
Feitelson, D.: ref, 466(50)
Fekken, G. C.: ref, 244(431,544)
Feldesman, A. B.: ref, 54(23)
Feldman, J. F.: ref, 466(99,116,117)
Feldman, M.: ref, 40(51)
Feldman, R. A.: ref, 64(17,70)
Feldman, R. S.: ref, 64(139)
Feldstein, M.: ref, 64(106,174)
Feldt, L. S.: ref, 438r
Feldt, R. C.: ref, 146(56,63)
Felner, R. D.: ref, 66(24), 424(44)
Felson, R. B.: ref, 377(32)
Felton, B. J.: ref, 462(8)
Felton, R. H.: ref, 87(47)
Fennell, M.: ref, 31(262)

Harder, R.: ref, 54(41)
Hardesty, R. A.: ref, 81(55), 280(74)
Hardesty, V. A.: ref, 64(30)
Harding, C. M.: ref, 147(16)
Harding, K.: ref, 31(177)
Harding, L. M.: ref, 257(14)
Harding, T.: ref, 244(542)
Hardy, K.: ref, 466(82)
Hare, R. D.: ref, 54(25), 244(213)
Har-Even, D.: ref, 117(17), 244(626), 424(88), 462(16)
Hargrave, G. E.: ref, 54(94), 244(488)
Haring, T. G.: rev, 6, 297
Harker, P.: ref, 424(34)
Harkey, B.: ref, 244(342), 360(29)
Harkins, S. W.: ref, 40(65), 465(97)
Harmon, L. R.: ref, 244r
Harmon, T. M.: ref, 244(588)
Harms, T.: test, 141
Harnisch, D. L.: rev, 76, 320; ref, 81r
Harper, D. C.: ref, 244(350)
Harper, J.: ref, 274(44)
Harper, L. V.: ref, 377(44)
Harrell, T. H.: rev, 363
Harrington, D. M.: ref, 95r
Harris, A. J.: ref, 146r
Harris, B.: ref, 31(165)
Harris, D.: ref, 95r, 114r
Harris, D. J.: ref, 184(16)
Harris, D. P.: ref, 424(59)
Harris, G. E.: ref, 64(76)
Harris, J.: ref, 64(162)
Harris, J. A.: test, 458
Harris, J. C.: ref, 64(15,123)
Harris, J. W.: ref, 54(52)
Harris, L.: test, 18
Harris, L. A.: rev, 184
Harris, M. D.: ref, 212(46)
Harris, R. F.: ref, 244(274)
Harris, R. N.: ref, 31(118), 54(50)
Harris, T.: ref, 78r
Harrison, J. M.: ref, 424(58)
Harrison, K. A.: ref, 40(91), 467(5)
Harrison, P. L.: rev, 196, 208, 255, 375
Harrison, R. H.: ref, 244(328)
Harrison, S. D.: ref, 244(432)
Harrison, T. E.: ref, 437(17)
Harrison, W. R.: ref, 244(342,343,439,490,499), 360(16,29,35), 465(8)
Harris-Stefanakis, E.: ref, 191(3)
Harsh, C. M.: rev, 41
Hart, K.: ref, 66(54), 393r
Hart, K. J.: ref, 66(26)
Hart, M.: ref, 424(27)
Hart, R. P.: ref, 40(65), 465(97)
Hart, R. R.: ref, 244(79,330)
Hart, V.: rev, 177, 294
Hartdagen, S.: ref, 244(537)
Harter, S.: test, 292, 357; ref, 31(132), 292r
Hartlage, L. C.: test, 36
Hartlage, S.: ref, 31(151)
Hartman, H. J.: rev, 75, 361
Hartmann, E.: ref, 244(436)
Hartsoe, K.: ref, 274(44)
Hartup, W. W.: ref, 64(124), 140(15)
Harvey, A. L.: rev, 138, 262

Harvey, P. D.: ref, 31(5,26)
Harvey, R. J.: ref, 31(63)
Harvill, L. M.: rev, 25, 338
Harwell, M. R.: rev, 356, 461
Haskell, A.: ref, 244(566)
Haskett, M.: ref, 81(31)
Haskins, R.: ref, 466(33)
Hassanyeh, F.: ref, 31(66), 32(4)
Hasselt, V. B. V.: ref, 64(29)
Hastings, J. T.: rev, 377
Hastrup, J. L.: ref, 31(93)
Hathaway, S. R.: test, 244; ref, 54r, 244r, 315r
Hatsukami, D.: ref, 244(6)
Hatsukami, D. K.: ref, 360(32)
Hatten, J. T.: ref, 164r
Hattie, J.: ref, 389(1), 389r
Hauck, W. E.: ref, 274(10)
Haugh, O. M.: test, 445
Hause, E. S.: ref, 1r
Havel, Z.: ref, 244(80)
Havighurst, R. J.: ref, 384r
Hawkins, D.: ref, 64(207)
Hawkins, J. A.: ref, 184(15)
Hawks, R.: ref, 9(1), 244(554), 297(1)
Hawley, D. E.: ref, 55(8), 82(1)
Hawley, G. A.: test, 233
Haws, D.: ref, 66(36)
Hawthorne, D.: ref, 87r
Hawton, K.: ref, 31(27,230)
Haxby, J. V.: ref, 465(118)
Hayden, R. M.: ref, 31(6)
Hayes, J. R.: ref, 444r
Hayes, S. C.: rev, 101, 198; ref, 31(61), 244(116,471)
Haygood, J. M.: ref, 244(33), 360(1)
Hayne, C.: ref, 31r
Haynes, J. E.: ref, 146(9)
Haynes, J. P.: ref, 188(11), 274(32), 466(12)
Haynes, M.: ref, 280(101)
Haynes, M. D.: ref, 467(2)
Haynes, N. M.: ref, 198(1,2)
Haynes, W. O.: test, 129; ref, 377(58), 467(2)
Haywood, H. C.: ref, 191(8), 280(20), 472r
Haywood, T. W.: ref, 244(518)
Hazaleus, S. L.: ref, 475(3)
Heal, L.: ref, 472r
Healey, J. M.: ref, 87(72), 465(138)
Healy, B.: ref, 31(223)
Healy, C. C.: ref, 424(15)
Heath, G. A.: ref, 64(30)
Heaton, R. K.: ref, 196r, 244(240), 280(41), 465(36,44)
Hebert, M.: rev, 55
Hecht, D.: rev, 461
Hedayat, M. M.: ref, 244(619)
Hedberg, N. L.: rev, 238
Hedeker, D.: ref, 212(102), 465(152)
Hedlund, B. L.: ref, 54(8)
Heiby, E. M.: ref, 244(331)
Heidelberg-Sanders, C.: ref, 469(5)
Heidish, I. E.: ref, 64(11), 332(5)
Heilbronn, M.: ref, 244(288)
Heilbronner, R. L.: ref, 465(119,155)
Heilbrun, A. B., Jr.: rev, 113; ref, 54(26), 244(81,82,214,215)
Heilbrun, M. R.: ref, 54(26), 244(214)
Heilman, N.: rev, 117, 155

Logue, P. E.: ref, 244(4), 465(62)
Loher, B.: test, 80
Lohnes, P. R.: rev, 59
Lomax, R. G.: ref, 81(17), 146(47)
London House: ref, 24r
Lonergan, W. G.: test, 222
Loney, J.: ref, 87r
Long, B. C.: ref, 415(3), 462(11)
Long, C.: ref, 244(194), 465(34)
Long, C. A.: test, 276
Long, C. J.: ref, 244(14,126), 465(2,17)
Long, J.: ref, 465(7)
Long, N.: ref, 66(25), 332(40,56)
Long, S. H.: rev, 83, 129; ref, 238(1)
Longley, K. F.: ref, 40(73)
Longley, P.: ref, 465(7)
Longstreth, L. E.: ref, 466(108)
Long-Suter, E.: ref, 54(81)
Loosen, P. T.: ref, 31(270)
Lopez, F. G.: ref, 31(183), 383(2)
Lorandos, D. A.: ref, 40(87), 244(593)
Lord, C.: ref, 65(1)
Lorenzo, G.: ref, 360(53)
Lorge, I.: rev, 475
Loriaux, D. L.: ref, 64(103), 244(445)
Loring, D. W.: ref, 465(102,142)
Lorr, M.: ref, 244(235)
Lorys, A. R.: ref, 64(209), 87(51)
Lotaif, F.: ref, 40(39)
Lothstein, L. M.: ref, 40(12), 244(112), 465(13)
Louks, J.: ref, 31r
Loup, K.: ref, 125r
Louscher, P. K.: ref, 244(26)
Louttit, C. M.: ref, 244r
Lovaas, O. I.: ref, 466(72)
Lovallo, W.: ref, 469(10)
Lovallo, W. R.: ref, 360(21), 469(8), 469r
Love, A. W.: ref, 31(33), 244(449)
Lovegrove, W.: ref, 257(6)
Lovejoy, M. C.: ref, 64(191), 87(75)
Lovell, V. R.: test, 182
Lovett, M. W.: ref, 280(77)
Low, M. D.: ref, 40(64), 377(43)
Lowe, C. F.: ref, 31(215)
Lowman, R. L.: ref, 41(1)
Lownsdale, W. S.: ref, 40(82), 244(552)
Lowy, M. T.: ref, 31(114), 244(503)
Loyd, B. H.: rev, 298; ref, 332(27)
Lubin, B.: ref, 31r, 244r, 315r, 330r
Luborsky, L.: ref, 360(9,43)
Lucas, A. R.: ref, 244(232)
Lucas, M. J.: ref, 244(319)
Ludenia, K.: ref, 244(135)
Ludman, W. L.: ref, 465(138)
Ludwig, G.: ref, 332(7)
Lueger, R. J.: ref, 244(113), 332(8)
Luisto, M.: ref, 465(65)
Luk, S. L.: ref, 87(32,58)
Lukács, D.: ref, 244(286)
Lumb, D.: test, 121
Lumb, M.: test, 121
Lumry, A. E.: ref, 244(284)
Lumsden, E. A.: ref, 239(54)
Lund, N.: ref, 469(5)
Lundeen, D. J.: ref, 118r

Lundholm, J. K.: ref, 239(58,59)
Luria, A. R.: ref, 211r
Lushene, R.: ref, 330r
Lustman, P. J.: ref, 244(124)
Lutwak, N.: ref, 104(6)
Lutz, D. J.: ref, 244(330), 424(27)
Lutz, R. W.: ref, 244(108)
Luxenberg, M. G.: ref, 244(429)
Lyman, H. B.: rev, 280
Lynch, A. D.: ref, 274(19), 424(47)
Lynch, D.: test, 47, 91, 232, 240; ref, 240r
Lynch, G.: ref, 87r
Lynch, J. I.: rev, 454
Lynch, S.: test, 91
Lynn, E. J.: ref, 244(59)
Lynn, R.: ref, 54(107)
Lynn, S. J.: ref, 244(458)
Lyons, T. M.: test, 100
Lytton, H.: ref, 280(78,79)
Lyytinen, H.: ref, 64(209)

Ma, H. K.: ref, 104(17)
Maag, J. W.: ref, 31(184)
Maas, J. W.: ref, 147(5)
Mabe, P. A., III: ref, 64(172), 66(10)
Mabey, B.: test, 24
MacAndrew, C.: ref, 244(7), 244r
MacArthur, C. A.: ref, 444(3)
MacAvoy, J.: ref, 81(58)
MacCarthy, B.: ref, 31(76,185), 341(1), 462(7)
Macciocchi, S. N.: ref, 212(61), 280(7)
MacDermid, S. M.: ref, 87(70)
MacDonald, J. D.: ref, 376(24)
MacDonald, M. R.: ref, 31(108)
Maceyko, S. J.: ref, 54(31)
MacGinitie, R. K.: test, 146
MacGinitie, W. H.: test, 146
MacGregor, S. K.: ref, 377(56)
MacIndoe: ref, 465(24)
MacIntyre, R. B.: ref, 64(140)
Maclean, R.: ref, 257(11,13,22,23)
Mac Millan, J. S.: ref, 244(450)
MacPhee, D.: rev, 170, 423; ref, 170r
Macready, G. B.: ref, 377(70)
Madden, N. A.: ref, 81(21,22), 437(18)
Maddux, C. D.: rev, 257, 324, 434; ref, 229(13)
Madigan, M. J.: ref, 201(1)
Madison, C. L.: ref, 17(7)
Madison, L. S.: ref, 17(5), 465(70)
Maggio, M.: ref, 274(45)
Magner, J. R.: ref, 212(64), 465(71)
Maguire, T. O.: ref, 447(1)
Mahan, J. M.: ref, 244(23)
Maheady, L.: ref, 274(9)
Maher, C.: ref, 7r
Mahurin, R. K.: rev, 85, 293
Maitland, G.: ref, 274(9)
Maiuro, R. D.: ref, 244(329), 462(10)
Maj, M.: ref, 212(45)
Makarec, K.: ref, 244(236)
Malamuth, N. M.: ref, 244(47)
Malatesha, R. N.: ref, 40(53), 146(43)
Malcolm, K. K.: rev, 88, 157
Malec, J. F.: ref, 465(163)
Malek, V. F.: test, 160

The Psychological Corporation: test, 71, 377, 378, 463; ref, 24r
Psychological Services Bureau, Inc.: test, 314
Psychological Services, Inc.: test, 143
Puccio, G. J.: ref, 193(3)
Pudlas, K. A.: ref, 377(45)
Puente, A. E.: ref, 212(16), 244(502), 469(3,5,9,11)
Pugh, G.: ref, 244(447)
Pullis, M.: ref, 274(34)
Purcell, K.: ref, 100(1)
Purdue Research Foundation: ref, 293r
Purisch, A. D.: test, 212; ref, 212(81), 212r, 348r
Putnam, J.: ref, 146(39)
Pyant, C. T.: ref, 31(279)
Pyle, R.: ref, 244(6)
Pyrczak, F.: rev, 184
Pyszczynski, T.: ref, 31(111,194)

Quart, E. J.: ref, 465(124)
Quay, H.: ref, 39r
Quay, H. C.: test, 332; ref, 37r, 64(131), 64r, 332(1,63)
Quellmalz, E.: ref, 179r
Quereshi, M. Y.: ref, 466(19)
Query, W. T.: ref, 244(134,373)
Quigley, R.: ref, 64(197)
Quinn, B.: ref, 146(72)
Quinn, D.: ref, 465(68)
Quinn, D. W.: ref, 146(62)
Quinn, E. P.: ref, 87(62)
Quinn, M.: rev, 454
Quinn, P. J.: ref, 146(25), 203(3)
Quinn, S. O.: ref, 87(62)

Ra, J. B.: ref, 298r
Rabianski-Carriuolo, N.: ref, 56r
Rabin, A. S.: ref, 31(44), 244(457)
Rabins, P.: ref, 244(319)
Rachlin, V. C.: ref, 117(8)
Rack, J.: ref, 280(104)
Radenhausen, R. A.: ref, 31(113,239)
Radke-Yarrow, M.: ref, 147(7)
Radl, S. L.: ref, 370r
Radloff, L. S.: ref, 31r
Raeburn, S. O.: ref, 31(130)
Raffeld, P.: ref, 367r
Raggio, D. J.: ref, 40(90), 87(81), 280(116)
Ragsdale, J. D.: ref, 17(6)
Rahe, A.: ref, 244(396)
Rahe, D. F.: ref, 54(23)
Rahe, R. H.: ref, 155r
Rahmani, L.: ref, 466(58)
Raine, A.: ref, 332(44,75)
Raines, M. G.: ref, 244(392)
Rainey, D.: ref, 424(50)
Rainwater, G.: ref, 244(17)
Raju, N. S.: rev, 182, 184
Ralph, N.: ref, 64(213)
Ramanan, J.: ref, 280(124)
Ramey, C. T.: ref, 170r, 280(4), 466(4)
Ramirez, C.: ref, 54(2)
Ramirez, L. F.: ref, 31(114), 244(503)
Rampaul, W. E.: ref, 55(4)
Rampp, D.: ref, 467r
Ramsay Corporation: test, 420, 421
Ramsay, R. T.: test, 128, 304

Ramsay, S. A.: ref, 12r
Ramsden, P.: ref, 202(1), 202r
Ramsey, E.: ref, 64(163)
Ramsey, R.: ref, 212(6,22), 465(5)
Ramsey-Klee, D. M.: ref, 244(332)
Randhawa, B. S.: rev, 71, 135; ref, 274(46)
Range, L. M.: ref, 244(468)
Ranieri, W. F.: ref, 31(42), 393(1)
Rankin, R. J.: ref, 81(63), 466(53)
Ranseen, J.: ref, 212(61), 280(7)
Ranseen, J. D.: ref, 31(245)
Rantakallio, P.: ref, 40(54)
Rao, A. V.: ref, 40(40)
Rao, D. C.: ref, 188(7)
Rapaport, K.: ref, 54(14)
Rape, R. N.: ref, 31(43)
Raphall, D.: ref, 475(9)
Rapkin, B. D.: ref, 81(54)
Rapoport, J. L.: ref, 87(23)
Rapoport, S. I.: ref, 465(118)
Rappaport, N. B.: ref, 244(237)
Rapport, M. D.: ref, 87(62,66), 87r, 280(60)
Rasinski, T.: ref, 146(53)
Raskin, A.: ref, 393r
Raskin, D. C.: ref, 54(27)
Raskin, R.: ref, 54(82), 244(559)
Rasmussen, N. H.: ref, 64(191), 87(75)
Rastatter, M.: ref, 17(4,8)
Rather, N. B.: ref, 437(13)
Rathgeber, A. J.: ref, 377(36)
Rathmell, G.: test, 433; ref, 28r
Rattan, G.: ref, 196(2)
Ratzlaff, H. C.: ref, 466(55)
Rauscher, F.: ref, 360(52)
Raviv, A.: ref, 466(58)
Rawl, R. K.: ref, 81(4), 274(4)
Rawson, N. S. B.: ref, 342r
Ray, G. E.: ref, 64(208)
Ray, J. B.: ref, 244(149)
Ray, J. S.: ref, 466(54)
Ray, S.: test, 5
Raymond, K. L.: ref, 64(164)
Razavieh, A.: ref, 466(110)
Read, M. R.: test, 316
Readence, J. E.: ref, 377(62)
Reader, M. J.: ref, 54(3)
Reams, R.: ref, 31(83)
Rebal, R.: ref, 244(249)
Rebgetz, M.: ref, 87(63), 332(69)
Redd, C.: ref, 244(12)
Reddin, W. J.: test, 77, 214, 215, 394, 395, 396, 397, 399, 401, 403
Redfering, D.: ref, 244(13)
Redlich, F.: ref, 65r
Reed, C.: ref, 231r
Reed, K. G.: test, 90
Reed, M.: ref, 377(32)
Reed, R.: ref, 7r
Reeder, B. L.: ref, 424(7)
Reeve, R. E.: ref, 280(19)
Regan, D. T.: ref, 270r
Regan, N. J.: ref, 244(301)
Rehm, L.: ref, 207r
Rehm, L. P.: ref, 31(44,91), 66(20), 244(262,374,457)
Reich, J.: ref, 239(18,41,42,43), 244(263)

Reich, J. W.: ref, 424(77)
Reich, W.: ref, 64(96)
Reichers, A. E.: ref, 80r
Reichler, R. J.: test, 65, 317
Reid, B.: test, 302
Reid, D. K.: test, 346, 429; ref, 26r, 100r, 149r, 346r, 376(41)
Reid, J. B.: ref, 64(97)
Reid, J. C.: ref, 466(36,54)
Reid, N. A.: test, 309, 387
Reifler, B. V.: ref, 465(40)
Reifler, J. P.: ref, 64(123)
Reilly, B. A.: rev, 155
Reinehr, R. C.: rev, 111, 465
Reineke, R. A.: rev, 36, 160
Reisman, F. K.: test, 359
Reiss, S.: test, 330
Reitan, R. M.: ref, 293r, 295r, 382r
Reitano, M.: ref, 293(1)
Reiter, G.: ref, 87(21), 377(48)
Reivich, M.: ref, 212(79)
Rembert, W. I.: ref, 81(46)
Remick, R. A.: ref, 465(159)
Remmers, H. H.: rev, 184
Renner, B. R.: test, 65
Renner, J. W.: ref, 274(23,27), 377(13)
Renshaw, P. D.: ref, 81(8)
Rentsch, J. R.: ref, 80r
Renwick, S.: ref, 104(10)
Renzulli, J. S.: ref, 306r
Repto, G. R.: ref, 239(19), 244(264)
Reschly, D.: ref, 39r
Reschly, D. J.: ref, 120r
Resnick, G.: ref, 64(36)
Resnick, M. D.: ref, 140(11)
Resnick, S. M.: ref, 212(79)
Rest, J. R.: test, 104; ref, 104(22), 104r
Retzlaff, P.: rev, 12, 379; ref, 360(33)
Retzlaff, P. D.: ref, 239(25,44,45)
Reuterfors, D.: ref, 244(4)
Reutzel, D. R.: ref, 146(18,74)
Revenson, T. A.: ref, 462(8)
Revis, E. S.: ref, 244(444)
Revuckny, M.: ref, 380r
Rey, J. M.: ref, 64(98,165)
Reynolds, A. J.: ref, 184(20), 445(3)
Reynolds, C. R.: rev, 239, 382; ref, 64(157), 81(18), 191(14), 212(32), 239r, 382r, 437(1), 466(9)
Reynolds, H.: test, 35
Reynolds, S.: ref, 31(226,280)
Reynolds, S. K.: ref, 244(606)
Reynolds, W. M.: test, 17, 333, 334, 393, 467; ref, 64(102), 66(9), 87r, 115r, 333(1), 334(1), 393r
Reznick, J. S.: ref, 466(14)
Reznikoff, M.: ref, 31(22), 462(1)
Rhee, C.: ref, 332(75)
Rhodewalt, F.: ref, 31(195)
Rhue, J. W.: ref, 244(458)
Ribich, F. D.: ref, 202r
Ricca, J.: ref, 201(2)
Rice, A. S.: ref, 316(1)
Rice, D. N.: ref, 465(141)
Rice, J. M.: ref, 376(14)
Rice, T.: ref, 466(59)
Rich, A. R.: ref, 303(1)

Richards, A.: ref, 31(246)
Richards, C. S.: ref, 31(171), 379(4)
Richards, G. E.: ref, 424(80)
Richards, H. C.: ref, 376(31)
Richards, I.: ref, 64(98)
Richards, J. M., Jr.: ref, 306r
Richards, P. M.: ref, 465(147)
Richards, R. A.: rev, 298, 432
Richards, R. G.: test, 456; ref, 456(1)
Richardson, Bellows, Henry & Co., Inc.: test, 221, 402
Richman, C. L.: ref, 146(13), 188(12)
Richman, L. C.: ref, 40(63), 244(350)
Richman, N.: test, 299
Richman, R. A.: ref, 40(5), 64(10), 280(18)
Ricks, D.: ref, 54(12), 244(106)
Riding, R. J.: ref, 257(25)
Rieder, R. O.: ref, 465(32)
Riggio, R. E.: test, 371; ref, 371(1,2,3)
Riggs, D. S.: ref, 31(267)
Riggs, J. M.: rev, 356
Riley, E.: ref, 466(73)
Riley, N. J.: ref, 280(105)
Riley, W.: ref, 64(172)
Rimm, S.: ref, 150r
Rimm, S. B.: test, 3, 150; ref, 3r
Rinehart, S. D.: ref, 146(26,46,48,69)
Ringle-Bartels, J.: test, 18
Rintelmann, J. W.: ref, 280(109)
Rio, A.: ref, 64(170)
Riordan, J.: ref, 46(1), 46r
Risko, V. J.: ref, 81(47)
Rissmiller, D. J.: ref, 31(42), 393(1)
Ritchie, K. P.: ref, 437(2), 444(1)
Rittenhouse, J. A.: ref, 50(1)
Ritter, D. R.: ref, 64(35,61,166,196), 393(2)
Ritvo, E.: ref, 40(2), 191(5)
Ritvo, E. R.: ref, 466(20)
Ritz, G.: ref, 54(68), 244(461)
Riva, D.: ref, 466(60)
Rivas-Vazquez, A.: ref, 64(170)
Rivera, C.: rev, 136, 298
Rivers, D.: ref, 191(21), 280(95)
The Riverside Publishing Co.: test, 256
Rizzo, T. A.: ref, 466(88)
Roback, H.: ref, 40(12), 244(112), 465(13)
Roback, H. B.: ref, 424(27)
Robbins, F.: ref, 81(31)
Robbins, F. R.: ref, 87(5)
Robbins, P. R.: ref, 31(45), 330r
Robbins, S.: test, 104
Robbins, S. B.: ref, 239(63)
Roberge, J. J.: ref, 259r
Roberson, M. K.: ref, 244(402), 280(65)
Robert, J. A.: ref, 239(20), 244(29)
Roberts, A. O. H.: rev, 41
Roberts, C. V.: test, 461
Roberts, D. M.: ref, 303(3)
Roberts, G.: ref, 244(594)
Roberts, J. S.: ref, 54(11)
Roberts, M. A.: ref, 87(77), 87r
Roberts, M. W.: rev, 227, 282
Roberts, N. L.: ref, 31(162)
Roberts, P. M.: ref, 332(45)
Roberts, R. S.: ref, 31(249)
Roberts, T. G.: test, 368

Smith, E. R.: ref, 146(33)
Smith, F. M.: rev, 376
Smith, F. W.: ref, 465(153)
Smith, G.: ref, 50(1)
Smith, G. R.: rev, 11
Smith, J.: test, 254; ref, 31r
Smith, K.: ref, 332(10)
Smith, K. L.: ref, 466(82)
Smith, L.: ref, 466(52)
Smith, L. B.: ref, 244(510), 444(2)
Smith, L. H.: ref, 306r
Smith, L. S.: ref, 196r
Smith, M. A.: ref, 383(1)
Smith, M. E.: ref, 244(337)
Smith, N. J.: ref, 376(9)
Smith, N. L.: rev, 85
Smith, P.: test, 270
Smith, P. E.: ref, 244(145)
Smith, R.: ref, 146(60), 380r
Smith, R. A.: test, 113
Smith, R. E.: ref, 244(265)
Smith, R. J.: ref, 379(7)
Smith, R. L.: ref, 244(327)
Smith, S.: ref, 107(1)
Smith, T. C.: ref, 40(75)
Smith, T. E. C.: ref, 191(21), 280(95)
Smith, T. W.: ref, 31(264), 244(275,385,386)
Smithies, C.: ref, 40(24)
Snarey, J.: ref, 54(12), 244(106)
Sneddon, W.: ref, 257(14)
Snider, R. L.: ref, 280(109)
Snidman, N.: ref, 466(14)
Snijders, J. T.: test, 366
Snijders-Oomen, N.: test, 366
Snow, J.: ref, 211r, 212(35)
Snow, J. H.: rev, 212, 247; ref, 40(83,84)
Snow, W. G.: ref, 244(346), 465(52,69)
Snowden, L. R.: ref, 244(146,147,387,388)
Snyder, C. R.: ref, 31(118), 54(50)
Snyder, D. K.: ref, 244(229,276,565), 424(86)
Snyder, S.: ref, 244(257)
Snyder, S. H.: ref, 87r
Snyter, C. M.: ref, 244(148)
Soares, A. T.: test, 11, 356
Soares, L. M.: test, 11, 356
Sobol, M. P.: ref, 87(64)
Society of Actuaries: test, 13, 14, 15
Sodowsky, G. R.: rev, 78, 192
Sohlberg, M. M.: ref, 465(109)
Sohlberg, S.: ref, 147(19)
Sohlberg, S. C.: ref, 40(42), 424(51)
Solan, H. A.: ref, 146(58)
Soldatos, C. R.: ref, 244(153)
Sollee, N. D.: ref, 64(101)
Solly, D. C.: rev, 231
Solodow, W.: ref, 31(179)
Solomon, G. S.: ref, 244(149), 465(79)
Solomon, R.: ref, 244(277), 424(52)
Solomon, R. J.: rev, 447
Solomon, Z.: ref, 237(1), 462(9)
Solotar, L. C.: ref, 64(80)
Solovay, M. R.: ref, 244(465)
Solovitz, B. L.: ref, 64(76)
Sommers, R.: ref, 380r
Sommers, R. K.: test, 380; rev, 17, 84, 347

Song, A.: test, 472; ref, 472r
Song, M.: ref, 428(1)
Song, W.: ref, 244(609)
Sonnenberg, E. A.: ref, 437(14), 454(1)
Sonnenschein, P.: ref, 280(106)
Soper, H. V.: ref, 293r
Soper, J.: ref, 31(227)
Soper, J. C.: test, 431
Sorbom, D.: ref, 77r, 193r
Sorell, G. T.: ref, 140(14)
Sorenson, C.: test, 80
Sorenson, S. B.: ref, 66r, 265r
Sorri, A.: ref, 147(9), 244(466,570)
Sosniak, L. A.: ref, 445(4)
Sothmann, M. S.: ref, 244(150)
Soto, L. D.: ref, 184(13)
Sotoodeh, Y.: ref, 371(2)
Sotsky, S. M.: ref, 31(231)
Sousa, D. A.: ref, 184(5), 445(1)
Spanier, G. B.: test, 117; ref, 92r, 117r
Sparks, C. P.: ref, 221r
Sparnacki, R. L.: ref, 37(1)
Sparrow, S. S.: ref, 6r
Speck, N. B.: ref, 188(14)
Spector, J.: ref, 212(64), 465(71)
Speece, D. L.: ref, 280(63)
Speer, T. K.: ref, 244(231)
Spekman, N. J.: ref, 274(35), 437(10)
Spence, J. G.: ref, 87(80), 437(19)
Spence, S. H.: ref, 66(39)
Spencer, A.: ref, 65(3)
Spencer, P.: ref, 377(68)
Spencer, W. B.: ref, 379(1)
Speth, C.: test, 80; ref, 202r
Spiegel, D.: ref, 360r
Spiegel, D. E.: ref, 360(23)
Spiegel, S. B.: ref, 244(489), 424(78)
Spieker, S. J.: ref, 31(136)
Spielberger, C. D.: test, 379; ref, 330r
Spiers, P. A.: ref, 212(36), 212r
Spiker, D.: rev, 45, 342
Spinelli, F.: ref, 376(2)
Spinelli, J.: ref, 31(201)
Spira, T. J.: ref, 465(125)
Spirito, A.: ref, 66(26,54), 66r, 244(511), 393r
Spitzer, J. B.: rev, 10
Spitzer, R. L.: test, 147; ref, 147r, 239(22,33), 334r
Spokane, A. R.: test, 269
Sprafkin, J.: ref, 87(15,16,36,37), 274(41), 378(4,6), 466(89)
Spraggins, C. C.: ref, 376(25)
Sprague, R. L.: test, 7; ref, 87r
Spreen, O.: ref, 382r
Sprehn, G. C.: ref, 465(125)
Spriestersbach, D.: ref, 467r
Spring, B.: ref, 244(566)
Spring, C.: ref, 280(112)
Sprinthall, N. A.: ref, 104(32)
Sprock, J.: ref, 244(138)
Spurling, S.: ref, 137(1)
Squire, L. R.: ref, 107(2), 465(127)
SRA/London House: ref, 24r
Staff of the Psychological Services Bureau: test, 312
Stafford, M.: ref, 70r
Stagner, B.: ref, 244(189)

Wan, C. K.: ref, 31(205), 244(567)
Wanberg, K.: ref, 284r
Wanberg, K. W.: ref, 12r
Wang, S.: ref, 244(359,596), 379(6)
Ward, A. W.: rev, 105, 362
Ward, C.: ref, 333r
Ward, C. H.: ref, 265r
Ward, D. A.: ref, 424(68)
Ward, E. M.: ref, 87r
Ward, G.: test, 69, 309
Ward, L. C.: ref, 244(160,399,400,535)
Ward, M.: ref, 81(4), 274(4)
Wardrop, J. L.: rev, 445; ref, 81(64), 376r
Ware, W. B.: ref, 229(7), 424(3)
Warlow, C.: ref, 31(230)
Warner, L.: ref, 244(403)
Warner, M. H.: ref, 465(111)
Warren, E. W.: ref, 465(25)
Warren-Leubecker, A.: ref, 146(5,59)
Washburn, S. E.: ref, 40(47)
Wasinger, K.: ref, 66(61)
Wasyliw, O. E.: ref, 244(487,518)
Waters, B.: ref, 66(21), 104(24)
Waters, B. G. H.: ref, 257(37), 466(100)
Watkins, B.: ref, 257(32)
Watkins, C. E., Jr.: ref, 31(183), 60r, 244(572), 383(2), 466(65), 475(4)
Watkins, D.: ref, 389(1), 389r
Watkins, E. O.: test, 40; ref, 377(14)
Watkins, J. B.: ref, 64(179)
Watkins, J. M.: ref, 64(127)
Watkins, J. T.: ref, 31(231)
Watson, B. V.: ref, 64(128), 377(64)
Watson, C. G.: ref, 244(161,267)
Watson, D.: ref, 31(124,274), 154r
Watson, G. M. W.: ref, 360(8)
Watson, J. A.: ref, 81(46), 184(2)
Watson, K. W.: test, 461
Watson, L.: ref, 65(3)
Watson, R. E. L.: ref, 117(9)
Watson, S. M.: ref, 64(199), 140(26), 332(14,23,76)
Watson, T. E.: ref, 229(5)
Watson, T. S.: rev, 53, 410, 439
Watts, D.: ref, 280(78,79)
Waugh, M. H.: ref, 244(247)
Waxman, B.: ref, 377(2)
Waxman, H. C.: ref, 81(24)
Wayne, K. S.: ref, 360(56)
Weaver, K. A.: ref, 466(82)
Weaver, R.: ref, 244(376)
Webb, J. T.: ref, 244r, 330r
Webb, N. M.: ref, 81(6)
Webb, W. B.: ref, 465(30,58)
Webber, J. E.: ref, 31(172)
Webber, T.: test, 151
Weber, M.: ref, 193r, 306r
Webley, P.: ref, 335(2)
Webster, I.: ref, 87(61)
Webster, J.: ref, 146(2)
Webster, J. S.: ref, 212(10,40,41,48)
Webster, R. E.: ref, 280(50,98,125)
Webster-Stratton, C.: ref, 31(125), 64(20,21,38,39,129, 200), 360(22)
Wechsler, D.: test, 465, 466; ref, 72r, 85r, 466r
Wechsler, F. S.: ref, 40(35), 212(50)

Wedding, D.: ref, 212(12)
Weed, K.: ref, 146(3)
Weeks, M. O.: rev, 172
Wegner, D. M.: ref, 31(126)
Wehr, S. H.: ref, 184(9)
Wehrspann, W.: ref, 64(23)
Wei, L.: ref, 31r
Weibe, M. J.: ref, 65r
Weidemann, C.: ref, 146(27)
Weigel, C.: ref, 64(106,174)
Weinberg, S. L.: rev, 229, 443
Weinberg, W. A.: ref, 280(99,109), 334r
Weiner, D. N.: ref, 244r
Weiner, P.: ref, 244(395), 467r
Weinert, C.: test, 286
Weingartner, H.: ref, 87(23)
Weinmann, C. A.: ref, 424(72)
Weinshank, A. B.: ref, 64(16), 424(31)
Weinstein, B.: ref, 10r
Weinstein, C.: ref, 117r
Weinstein, C. E.: test, 198
Weinstein, L.: ref, 244(566), 465(138)
Weinstein, T.: ref, 378(3)
Weintraub, S.: ref, 7r, 34r, 244(284)
Weismer, S. E.: rev, 302, 443; ref, 437(16)
Weiss, B.: ref, 64(105,175,176,216), 66(12,63)
Weiss, D. J.: test, 243; ref, 447r
Weiss, D. S.: ref, 64(48), 244(573,623)
Weiss, J.: ref, 81(35)
Weiss, L.: ref, 274(38)
Weissberg, R. P.: ref, 184(15)
Weissman, A.: ref, 207r
Weist, M. D.: ref, 332(74)
Weisz, J. R.: ref, 64(74,104,105,155,156,175,176,216), 66(12,63)
Welch, D. L. H.: test, 167
Welch, E. L.: ref, 377(12)
Welfel, E. R.: ref, 104(2)
Welge, P.: ref, 30r
Welkowitz, J.: ref, 31(180)
Weller, C.: ref, 280(47)
Weller, P.: ref, 465(125)
Wells, L. E.: ref, 146(51)
Welsh, G. S.: ref, 95r, 244r
Welsh, J. D.: ref, 147(7)
Welsh, J. S.: rev, 65
Welsh, M. C.: ref, 31(94)
Wenck, L. S.: ref, 280(103)
Wendel, F. C.: ref, 208(1)
Wender, P. H.: ref, 87r
Wendler, C. L. W.: ref, 40(22)
Wengel, W. W.: ref, 40(23), 465(27)
Wenzlaff, R. M.: ref, 31(126)
Wepman, J. M.: test, 374, 467
Werder, J. K.: ref, 249(1)
Werner, E. E.: ref, 40(60), 54(57)
Werner, E. O. H.: test, 373
Werner, P. D.: ref, 54(58), 244(401)
Werry, J. S.: ref, 87r, 332(2)
Wertlieb, D.: ref, 64(106,174)
Wesselman, R.: ref, 146(39)
Wessely, S.: ref, 147(12)
West, J. A.: ref, 31(255), 244(597), 465(158)
West, J. D.: ref, 155(1)
West, R.: ref, 466(85)

SCORE INDEX